Oxford Collocations Dictionary

for students of English

OXFORD WITHDRAWN

UNIVERSITY PRESS

OXFORD
UNIVERSITY PRESS

Great Clarendon Street, Oxford OX2 6DP

Oxford University Press is a department of the University of Oxford.
It furthers the University's objective of excellence in research, scholarship,
and education by publishing worldwide in

Oxford New York

Auckland Cape Town Dar es Salaam Hong Kong Karachi
Kuala Lumpur Madrid Melbourne Mexico City Nairobi
New Delhi Shanghai Taipei Toronto

With offices in

Argentina Austria Brazil Chile Czech Republic France Greece
Guatemala Hungary Italy Japan Poland Portugal Singapore
South Korea Switzerland Thailand Turkey Ukraine Vietnam

OXFORD and OXFORD ENGLISH are registered trade marks of
Oxford University Press in the UK and in certain other countries

The British National Corpus is a collaborative project involving Oxford
University Press, Longman, Chambers, the Universities of Oxford and
Lancaster and the British Library

ISBN-13: 978 0 19 431243 1

Text capture and typesetting by Oxford University Press

Printed in China

CONTENTS

List of usage notes

List of special pages

Preface

In recent years, teachers and students have become increasingly aware of the importance of collocation in English language learning. However, no matter how convinced learners are in principle of the importance of collocation, it is difficult for them to put these principles into practice without the benefit of an up-to-date, corpus-based dictionary of collocations. We at Oxford University Press were determined to provide such a dictionary but it has taken us many years to produce the dictionary that we feel best meets the needs of students and teachers.

Over the years, a large number of lexicographers and editors have been involved in this project and I wish to take this opportunity to thank them all for the contributions they have made. In particular, I wish to thank the three Managing Editors, Sheila Dignen, Jonathan Crowther and Diana Lea. The Managing Editors worked on the policy for this dictionary, striving to ensure that it was in its design as helpful and accessible to users as possible. In the introduction that follows, Diana Lea explains the principles that were established through consultation and experiment to determine which collocates to include and where they should be listed.

It is our hope that this dictionary will provide you with invaluable assistance in expressing your ideas cogently in idiomatic English. If you wish to explore the dictionary's potential as a learning tool, you will find the Guide to the Entries (page xii-xiii) and the Study Pages (between pages 446 and 447) very helpful.

Moira Runcie
January 2002

Advisory Board

Dr Keith Brown   Professor Gabriele Stein
Professor Guy Cook   Dr Norman Whitney
Dr Alan Cruse   Professor Henry Widdowson
Ms Moira Runcie

Managing Editors

Jonathan Crowther   Sheila Dignen   Diana Lea

Editors

Margaret Deuter   James Greenan   Joseph Noble   Janet Phillips

Lexicographers

Colin Hope   Carole Owen
Gillian Lazar   Valerie Smith
Fiona McIntosh

Project administration

Julie Darbyshire
Julia Hiley

Publishing Systems Manager

Frank Keenan

Data capture and typesetting

Bill Coumbe
Tim Teasdale

Keyboarders

Anna Cotgreave
Kay Pepler
Ben Pritchett

Design

Page design: Peter Burgess and Holdsworth Associates, Isle of Wight
Study pages: Sarah Nicholson
Cover design: Richard Morris, Stonesfield Design

Illustrations

Harry Venning

Thanks are also due to those who helped with administration and keyboarding for shorter periods during the course of the project:
Anne-Marie Amphlett, Elizabeth Aracic, Stephanie Donaghy, Abigail Pringle, Katrina Ransom

Introduction

Imagine a student writing an essay on the environment. She knows the themes she wishes to cover and the ideas and arguments to get across. She already has a stock of useful vocabulary, especially high-content nouns like *environment, pollution, ozone layer*. What is missing are the words that can link these high-content vocabulary items together into a coherent whole – a narrative or an argument. Pollution is a problem, but what needs to be done about it? Looking up the entry for **pollution** in the *Oxford Collocations Dictionary* and skimming down to the verbs section offers the choice of *avoid/prevent, combat/control/fight/tackle, cut/limit/minimize/reduce* or *monitor*. With the back-up help of a good monolingual learner's dictionary (such as the *Oxford Advanced Learner's Dictionary*) if need be, the student can choose the most appropriate verb, the one that expresses most exactly what she wants to say.

What is collocation?

Collocation is the way words combine in a language to produce natural-sounding speech and writing. For example, in English you say *strong wind* but *heavy rain*. It would not be normal to say **heavy wind* or **strong rain*. And whilst all four of these words would be recognized by a learner at pre-intermediate or even elementary level, it takes a greater degree of competence with the language to combine them correctly in productive use. To a native-speaker these combinations are highly predictable; to a learner they are anything but.

Combinations of words in a language can be ranged on a cline from the totally free – *see a man/car/book* – to the totally fixed and idiomatic – *not see the wood for the trees*. This idiom is not only fixed in form, it also has nothing whatever to do with wood or trees. Between these two extremes, there is a whole range of nouns that take the verb *see* in a way that is neither totally predictable nor totally opaque as to meaning. These run from the fairly 'weak' collocation *see a film* (which elementary students learn as a 'chunk' without pausing to reflect that this is not quite the literal meaning of *see*) through the 'medium strength' *see a doctor* to the 'stronger' collocations of *see danger/reason/the point*. All these combinations, apart from those at the very extremes of the cline, can be called collocation. And it is combinations such as these – particularly in the 'medium-strength' area – that are vital to communicative competence in English.

Why is collocation important?

Collocation runs through the whole of the English language. No piece of natural spoken or written English is totally free of collocation. For the student, choosing the right collocation will make his speech and writing sound much more natural, more native-speaker-like, even when basic intelligibility does not seem to be at issue. A student who talks about **strong rain* may make himself understood, but possibly not without provoking a smile or a correction, which may or may not matter. He will certainly be marked down for it in an exam.

But, perhaps even more importantly than this, language that is collocationally rich is also more precise. This is because most single words in the English language – especially the more common words – embrace a whole range of meanings, some quite distinct, and some that shade into each other by degrees. The precise meaning in any context is determined by that context: by the words that surround and combine with the core word – by collocation. A student who chooses the best collocation will express himself much more clearly and be able to convey not just a general meaning, but something quite precise. Compare, for example, the following two sentences:

This is a good book and contains a lot of interesting details.
This is a fascinating book and contains a wealth of historical detail.

Both sentences are perfectly 'correct' in terms of grammar and vocabulary, but which communicates more (both about the book under discussion *and* the person discussing it)?

Why use a Collocations Dictionary?

A normal dictionary, whether monolingual or bilingual, splits up meaning into individual words; it has a lot of power in dissecting the meaning of a text. Its power is more limited when it comes to constructing texts. Good learner's dictionaries give as much help as they can with usage, with grammar patterns clearly explained, register labels and example sentences showing words in context. Modern dictionaries are increasingly giving attention to collocation. But they are still hampered by trying to provide a whole range of information about any word besides its collocations. A grammar provides an analysis of the general patterns that exist in a language. But its productive power is limited by the degree to which it generalizes in order to come up with 'grammatical rules'. A collocational dictionary doesn't have to generalize to the same extent: it covers the entire language (or a large part of it!) on a word by word, collocation by collocation basis. It manages this by not attempting to account for every possible utterance, only for what is most typical.

By focusing on the specific rather than the general, a collocations dictionary is also able to 'pre-digest' a lot of the grammar involved, presenting collocates in their most typical form in context, even if this is not the usual dictionary citation form. For example at the entry for **baby**, you will find the collocation *be teething*, reflecting the fact that this verb is always used in the progressive tenses. Use the collocations dictionary systematically and you become much more aware of the extent to which English makes use of the passive, an aspect of grammar that even advanced students may be reluctant to put to full productive use.

By covering the language systematically from A-Z, a collocations dictionary allows students to build up their own collocational competence on a 'need-to-know' basis, starting from the words they already know – or know in part. Occasional, or even regular, collocations exercises in coursebooks cannot fulfil this role, although they do a useful job of raising the profile of collocation as an essential feature of the language, and teach some useful collocations in the process.

Which collocations are included in this dictionary?

The approach taken to this question was pragmatic, rather than theoretical. The questions asked were: is this a typical use of language? Might a student of English want to express this idea? Would they look up this entry to find out how? The aim was to give the full range of collocation – from the fairly weak (*see a film, an enjoyable holiday, extremely complicated*), through the medium-strength (*see a doctor, direct equivalent, highly intelligent*) to the strongest and most restricted (*see reason, burning ambition, blindingly obvious*) – for around 9,000 headwords. Totally free combinations are excluded and so, for the most part, are idioms. Exceptions to this rule are idioms that are only partly idiomatic: *not see the wood for the trees* may have nothing to do with wood or trees, but *drive a hard bargain* is very much about bargaining even if the expression as a whole can be considered an idiom.

The first question (Is this a typical use of language?) required that all the collocations be drawn from reliable data. The main source used was the 100 million word British National Corpus. From this, compilers of the dictionary were able to check how frequently any given combination occurred, in how many (and what kind of) sources, and in what particular contexts. The corpus also supplied many of the example sentences, most of which were either taken directly from the authentic texts included in the corpus, or with minor modifications to make them more accessible (but without, of course, altering any collocations). For fast-changing areas of language, such as computing – particularly rich in collocation – corpus information was supplemented by using the Internet as a resource.

The second question asked (Might a student of English want to express this idea?) led to a focus on current English: language that students not only need to understand but can be expected to reproduce. It was felt that, for productive use, students were better concentrating on one variety of English, and British English was chosen. Consideration was also given to the kind of texts that students might wish to write. Primary attention was given to what might be called 'moderately formal language' – the language of essay and report writing, and formal letters – treating all subjects – business, science, history, sport, etc. (this list could go on for half a page) at the level of the educated non-specialist. In addition, the dictionary includes some of the most important collocations from some specialist areas, particularly law and medicine; collocations from popular fiction, particularly useful in treating more personal subjects such as feelings and relationships; informal collocations and those very frequent in spoken language; and a few of the most frequent collocations from British journalism. Technical, informal and journalistic uses are labelled as such.

The third question asked (Would a student look up this entry to find this expression?) led to the exclusion of noun collocates from verb and adjective entries. When framing their ideas, people generally start from a noun. You might think of *rain* and want to know which adjective best describes rain when a lot falls in a short time. You would be unlikely to start with the adjective *heavy* and wonder what you could describe with it (*rain, breathing, damage, gunfire?*) Similarly, you might be looking for the verb to use when you do what you need to do in response to a *challenge*. But you would not choose meet and then choose what to meet (*a challenge, an acquaintance, your death, the expense*).

'The full range of collocation', as well as implying collocations of different strengths, also covers all the following types of combination:

adjective + noun: *bright/harsh/intense/strong* **light**
quantifier + noun: *a beam/ray of* **light**
verb + noun: *cast/emit/give/provide/shed* **light**
noun + verb: **light** *gleams/glows/shines*
noun + noun: *a* **light** *source*
preposition + noun: *by the* **light** *of the moon*
noun + preposition: *the* **light** *from the window*

adverb + verb: **choose** *carefully*
verb + verb: *be free to* **choose**
verb + preposition: **choose** *between two things*
verb + adjective: *make/keep/declare sth* **safe**
adverb + adjective: *perfectly/not entirely/environmentally* **safe**
adjective + preposition: **safe** *from attack*

plus short phrases including the headword: *the speed of* **light**, *pick and* **choose**, **safe** *and sound*

Most of the collocations in the dictionary can be called 'word collocations', that is, these are the precise words that combine with each other: *small fortune* cannot be changed to *little fortune*, even though *small* and *little* would seem to be synonymous. There is another area of collocation that might be called 'category collocation', where a word can combine with any word from a readily definable set. This set may be quite large, but its members are predictable, because they are all words for nationalities, or measurements of time, for example. At the entry for *walk*, one of the groups of collocates is given as 'three-minute, five minutes', etc.': the 'etc.' is to indicate that any figure may be substituted for 'three' or 'five' in these expressions.

It also happens that certain sets of words share all or most of their collocations. This is particularly true of very strictly defined sets such as days of the week, months and points of the compass, but it also applies to slightly less rigid, but still limited sets such as currencies, weights and measures and meals. In order to show how these collocations are shared by a number of headwords, the dictionary includes 25 usage notes, each treating the collocations of a particular set. The entries for the individual members of the set include a cross-reference to the usage note. In cases where all the collocations are shared (months, for example) the cross-reference replaces all other information in the entry. In cases where some of the collocations are shared, but others apply only to an individual member of the set (for example, seasons), the individual collocations are given at the entry, and a cross-reference directs the user to the shared collocations in the usage note. A full list of the usage notes and where they may be found is given on page iv. The 9,000 headwords include most of the commonest words in the language that upper-intermediate students will already know, plus some words that they will start to encounter as they move to a more advanced level of English. Some very common words – such as the verbs *make* and *do* – do not merit entries of their own. This is because these verbs have no real collocations of their own. They themselves *are* the collocations of lots of nouns, and appear in the entries for those nouns. There are also two pages of exercises in the central study section addressing this notorious area of difficulty.

How to use this dictionary

This dictionary is intended for productive use, most typically for help with writing. The collocations in each entry are divided according to part of speech; within each part of speech section they are grouped according to meaning or category. (In the example above from **pollution**, *avoid* and *prevent* are roughly synonymous, as are *combat, control, fight* and *tackle*, and so on). The groups are arranged in an order that tries to be as intuitive as possible: in this case from the 'strongest' form of action (*avoid/prevent*) to the 'mildest' (*monitor*). Many collocate groups have illustrative examples showing one or more of the collocations in context.

Because this is a type of dictionary that may be totally new to many students it is recommended that users familiarize themselves with how the dictionary works by working through some of the exercises in the photocopiable study section in the centre of the dictionary. The first of these aims to show the overall concept of the dictionary by looking at a single entry (**idea**) in some detail. The next few exercises take users systematically through the different sections of the entries for nouns, verbs and adjectives. Two pages of exercises get students thinking about the common verbs *make, do, have, give* and *take*; and the remaining exercises range across the whole dictionary, testing collocations linked to various themes, including politics, jobs and money.

Other information in this dictionary

The focus of this dictionary is very much on collocation. In order to make the collocational information as comprehensive and accessible as possible, non-collocational information has largely been excluded. Definitions of headwords are given only insofar as they are necessary to distinguish different senses of the same word, when they have different collocations and need to be treated separately. These are not full definitions, but rather 'sense discriminators', just detailed enough to allow the senses to be distinguished. Register information is given when any pair of words in *combination* take on a different register from the two words separately. Examples would be *do drugs* (*informal*) – though neither *do* nor *drugs* are informal in themselves – or *hear a lecture* (*formal*). (Exceptions to this rule are collocates labelled *taboo* where the label applies to the single word and to any combination it occurs in.) Collocations are also labelled if they belong to a particular field of language such as *law* or *medical*. For a full list of the usage labels used in this dictionary, see inside the front cover. In addition to these labels, more specific usage restrictions such as 'in football' or 'used in journalism' are given in brackets.

The most frequent usage label used in the dictionary is *figurative*. It is a feature of English that when the meaning of a word is extended and used in a non-literal sense, the collocations of the literal sense are often carried over: that is, both literal and figurative meanings of a word may share collocations. The dictionary indicates where this is so: for example, at **way**, the collocation *lose* is given, followed by the examples: *She lost her way in the fog.* and (*figurative*) *The project seems to have lost its way*. With strong collocations that are slightly idiomatic, a short explanation of the meaning may be given. For example, at **bargain**, the phrase *drive a hard bargain* has the gloss (= force sb to agree to the arrangement that is best for you).

The dictionary also includes ten special pages on different topics such as business, meetings and sport. These pull together collocations from the different topics and can be used as the basis for topic work in class, or for brainstorming vocabulary for an essay, for example. A full list of special topic pages and where to find them is given on page iv.

It is hoped that this dictionary will be of use not only to students of English of upper-intermediate level and above, but also to teachers (both non-native speaker and native-speaker teachers, looking for ways to present collocations to their students), translators, academics, business people, and all who wish to write fluent and idiomatic English. The Guide to the Entries (pages xii-xiii) is there as a quick reference, to give help as needed, but the whole dictionary has been designed to be accessible, and (we hope) enjoyable to use.

Guide to the entries

nouns

Sense numbers and short definitions distinguish between the different senses of **mountain**.

adjectives that collocate with **mountain** or nouns that function like adjectives

quantifiers: words that mean 'an amount/ number of something'

verbs that come before **mountain**, and verbs that follow **mountain**

nouns that follow **mountain**

Collocates are grouped according to meaning or category.

prepositions that combine with **mountain**

common phrases that include **mountain**

---

mountain *noun*

1 very high hill

● ADJ. **big, great, high, huge, large, lofty, massive, tall, towering | small | steep | low | beautiful, dramatic, fine, majestic, spectacular | surrounding** *The surrounding mountains make the city difficult to evacuate.* | **distant | isolated, remote | inland | jagged, rocky, rugged, | snow-capped, snow-covered, snowy | holy** *the holy mountain of the Lapp community*

● QUANT. **chain, range** *a chain/range of mountains*

● VERB + MOUNTAIN **ascend, climb, come/go up, scale | come/go down, descend, walk down | walk in** *We enjoy walking in the mountains.* | **cross (over)**

● MOUNTAIN + VERB **rise, soar, tower** *The mountains here rise to well over 2 000m.* | **fall** *The mountains fall to the east to the flat expanse of the plateau.* | **surround sth** *Towering mountains surrounded the village.* | **shake** *The earth tremor made the mountains shake.*

● MOUNTAIN + NOUN **chain, range | area, country, environment, region** *Between the two towns was 50 miles of mountain country.* | **height** *We crossed the rugged mountain heights.* | **pass, path, road, route, track | landscape, scenery | crag, face, flank, peak, ridge, side, slope, top, valley, wall | cave | lake, stream | air** *Many people come to the resort simply to enjoy the fresh mountain air.* | **pasture | barrier** *The invading army could only penetrate the mountain barrier at one point.* | **village | fastness, fortress, stronghold | hut, lodge, resort | folk, men, people | climber, climbing, walking, walks | guide | rescue, rescue team | bike, biker, biking | sickness | boot | goat, gorilla, hare, sheep**

● PREP. **across/over/through the ~** *a pass through the mountains* **down/up a/the ~** *She arranged to meet the others halfway up the mountain.* **in the ~s** *This type of goat lives high up in the mountains.*

● PHRASES **the flank/side/slope of a mountain, the foot/bottom/top of a mountain**

2 large amount/number of sth

● ADJ. **great | debt | paper | butter, food, etc.** *They revealed a solution to reduce Europe's butter mountain.*

● VERB + MOUNTAIN **generate | reduce**

● PHRASES **a mountain of paper/paperwork** *The enquiry generated a mountain of paperwork.*

---

adjectives

verbs that come before **famous**

adverbs that collocate with **famous**

prepositions that follow **famous**

common phrases that include **famous**

---

famous *adj.*

● VERBS **be | become | make sb/sth** *The school was made famous by its association with Charles Dickens.*

● ADV. **really, very | quite | internationally, locally** *internationally famous rock stars* | **justly, rightly** *The city is justly famous for its nightclubs.*

● PREP. **as** *He was famous as both a teacher and a scientist.* **for** *The town became famous for its lace.*

● PHRASES **rich and famous** *One day I'll be rich and famous, you'll see!* **world famous** *He became a world famous conductor.*

verbs

	remind *verb*
adverbs that collocate with **remind**	• ADV. **constantly, frequently, repeatedly** | **gently** *She gently reminded him that the baby was getting cold and should be taken indoors.*
verbs that come before **remind**	• VERB + REMIND **not have to, not need to** *I'm sure I don't need to remind you that we have lost our last ten matches.* | **serve to** *An event like this serves to remind us that we do not have control over nature.*
prepositions that follow **remind**	• PREP. **about** *I rang to remind him about the party.* **of** *She looked at her watch to remind him of the time.*
common phrases that include **remind**	• PHRASES **keep reminding sb**
Phrasal verbs are treated separately at the end of the entry.	PHRASAL VERB **remind sb of sb/sth** • ADV. **forcefully, forcibly, sharply, strongly, vividly** *The building reminded me strongly of my old school.* | **irresistibly** | **suddenly** *I was suddenly reminded of a tiger defending its cubs.* | **always** *Mrs Nolan always reminded Marie of her own mother.*

other features of the entries

	black *adj.*
A short use note shows a restriction on the use of the collocation *pitch black*.	• ADV. **very** *The sky looks very black.* | **all** *His hands were all black from messing about with the car.*
a cross-reference to the special page at **colour**, which has further collocations of **black** and other colours	• ADJ. **jet, pitch** (used about the night) *She had beautiful jet-black hair.* ◊ *It was pitch black outside.* ⇨ Special page at COLOUR

	abode *noun*
Register labels show that **abode** may be formal, humorous or a technical term in law, depending on its context and collocations.	• ADJ. **humble** (*humorous*) *Welcome to my humble abode.* • VERB + ABODE **take up your** (*formal or humorous*) *I had been invited to take up my abode at Government House.* • PHRASES **of no fixed abode** (*law*) (= without a permanent address) *An 18-year-old man of no fixed abode appeared at Teesside magistrates court yesterday.* **the right of abode** (*law*) (= the right to live in a place)
short explanations of the meaning of particular phrases	

	wilderness *noun*
In particular collocations **wilderness** takes on a figurative meaning.	• ADJ. **last** | **great** | **barren, desert, desolate** | **frozen** | **uncharted** | **unspoilt** | **political** (*figurative*) *the man who brought the party back from the political wilderness* • VERB + WILDERNESS **transform** *They transformed the wilderness into a garden.* | **explore** *They set out to explore the earth's last great wilderness, Antarctica.* • WILDERNESS + NOUN **years** (*figurative*) *His wilderness years* (= when he was out of politics and the public eye) *in the 1990s were spent in North America.* • PREP. **in the~** *We were hopelessly lost in the wilderness.*

	aristocracy *noun*
'etc.' shows that words for other nationalities also collocate with **aristocracy**.	• ADJ. **British, French, etc.** | **landed, landowning** | **local** • PHRASES **a member of the aristocracy**

For more help with noun, verb and adjective entries, see study pages S3-9 in the central section of the dictionary.

Aa

abandon verb

1 leave sb/sth
- ADV. **hastily** *The village had been hastily abandoned.*
- PHRASES **be found/left abandoned** *The car was found abandoned in a nearby town.*

2 stop doing/supporting sth
- ADV. **altogether, completely, entirely, totally** *The government does not propose to abandon the project altogether.* | **effectively, largely, virtually** *This principle has now been effectively abandoned.* | **simply** *Traditional policies were simply abandoned.* | **formally** | **quickly** | **quietly** *The plans for reform were quietly abandoned.* | **temporarily** | **voluntarily**
- VERB + ABANDON **be forced to** | **decide to**
- PREP. **for** *He abandoned the army for politics.* **in favour of** *She abandoned her teaching career in favour of sport.*

abashed adj.

- VERBS **be, look**
- ADV. **a little, slightly** | **suitably** *He glanced at Juliet accusingly and she looked suitably abashed.*

abbreviation noun

- ADJ. **common, standard**
- ABBREVIATION + VERB **stand for** *The abbreviation PC stands for 'personal computer'.*
- PREP. **~ for** *A/C is the standard abbreviation for 'account'.* **~ of** *Ad lib is an abbreviation of the Latin phrase 'ad libitum'.*

abhorrent adj.

- VERBS **be** | **become** | **find sth**
- ADV. **totally, utterly** *I find the idea totally abhorrent.*
- PREP. **to** *Such a savage punishment is abhorrent to a civilized society.*

ability noun

1 skill/power to do sth
- ADJ. **exceptional, extraordinary, great, outstanding, remarkable, uncanny** | **inherent, innate, natural** *discovering the natural abilities of each child* | **proven** | **academic, acting, artistic, athletic, creative, intellectual, linguistic, mathematical, musical, reading, technical** | **mental, physical**
- VERB + ABILITY **have** | **demonstrate, show** *Both players demonstrated their ability to hit the ball hard.* | **acquire, develop** | **lack** | **lose** *I seem to have lost my ability to attract clients.* | **appreciate, recognize** *Fox's abilities were soon recognized.*
- PHRASES **to the best of your ability** *We will keep you informed to the best of our ability.*

2 speed with which sb learns
- ADJ. **high** *The school does nothing for children of high ability.* | **limited, low** | **average, mixed** *It is much more difficult to teach a mixed-ability class.*
- VERB + ABILITY **assess, test**
- PHRASES **a level of ability** *There was a high level of ability among the school leavers.* **a range of ability/abilities** *I taught a wide range of abilities.*

ablaze adj.

- VERBS **be** | **set sth** *Truck after truck was set ablaze as the fire spread.*
- ADV. **well** *By the time firefighters were called the house was well ablaze.*

able adj.

1 able to do sth having the ability to do sth
- VERBS **be, feel, prove, seem**
- ADV. **perfectly, quite, well** *He is well able to take care of himself.* | **better, more** *Once you've had some sleep you'll feel better able to cope.* | **just** *I was just able to make out a dark figure in the distance.* | **barely, hardly, only just, scarcely** | **less**

2 clever; doing your job well
- VERBS **be, seem** *She seems very able.*
- ADV. **extremely, very** | **fairly, reasonably**

abode noun

- ADJ. **humble** *(humorous) Welcome to my humble abode.*
- VERB + ABODE **take up your** *(formal or humorous) I had been invited to take up my abode at Government House.*
- PHRASES **of no fixed abode** *(law)* (= without a permanent address) *An 18-year-old man of no fixed abode appeared at Teesside magistrates court yesterday.* **the right of abode** *(law)* (= the right to live in a place)

abolish verb

- ADV. **altogether, completely, totally** *Some MPs want to abolish the tax altogether.* | **virtually** | **largely** *Foreign exchange controls were largely abolished.*
- VERB + ABOLISH **seek to** | **decide to, vote to**

abortion noun

- ADJ. **back-street, illegal** | **legal** | **induced, spontaneous, therapeutic**
- VERB + ABORTION **have** *When she got pregnant at 16 she decided to have an abortion.* | **carry out, do** *(informal)*, **perform** *Some nurses wanted the right to refuse to perform abortions.*
- ABORTION + NOUN **law, legislation** *the country's strict abortion laws* | **clinic, counselling**
- PREP. **~on** *He carried out an abortion on a fifteen-year-old girl.*
- PHRASES **abortion on demand** (= the right to have an abortion if you want one) *Women's groups are calling for free contraception and abortion on demand.*

abscess noun

- VERB + ABSCESS **develop, get** *I developed an abscess on my neck.* | **burst, drain, lance** | **treat**
- ABSCESS + VERB **burst** *Once an abscess has burst it should be bathed with antiseptic liquid.*

absence noun

1 fact of not being present
- ADJ. **lengthy, long, prolonged** | **brief, temporary** | **unauthorized**
- QUANT. **period, spell** *You will not be paid for the full period of absence.*
- PREP. **during/in sb's ~** (= while sb is not there) *My father did all the cooking in my mother's absence.* | **~from** *absence from work*
- PHRASES **conspicuous/notable by your absence** (= very obviously absent when you ought to be present)

When it came to clearing up afterwards, Anne was conspicuous by her absence. **leave of absence** (= permission to be absent) *He asked for leave of absence from the army.*

2 lack
- ADJ. **complete, total | virtual | conspicuous, notable** *a conspicuous absence of evidence*
- PREP. **in the ~ of** *In the absence of stone, most houses in the area are built of wood.*

absent *adj.*

- VERBS **be | remain**
- ADV. **completely, entirely, quite, totally, wholly | virtually | largely | temporarily | conspicuously, markedly, notably, noticeably, strikingly** *Local people were conspicuously absent from the meeting.* | **strangely** *He played with an abandon that was strangely absent from his performance last week.*
- PREP. **from** *He was absent from work for two weeks.*

absorb *verb*

1 liquid/gas/energy, etc.
- ADV. **quickly, rapidly | directly, easily, readily**
- PREP. **into** *Nutrients are absorbed into the bloodstream.*

2 make part of sth larger
- ADV. **gradually | increasingly**
- PHRASES **be absorbed into sth** *These committees were gradually absorbed into the local government machine.*

3 information/atmosphere
- ADV. **easily, readily** *The information is presented so that it can be readily absorbed.* | **passively**

4 interest
- ADV. **completely, totally, utterly** *His work absorbed him completely.* | **deeply**

absorbed *adj.*

- VERBS **appear, be, look, seem | become, get | keep sb** *A jigsaw puzzle can keep me absorbed for hours.*
- ADV. **extremely, very | completely, fully, totally, utterly** *He was totally absorbed in his book.*
- PREP. **in**

abstract *adj.*

- VERBS **be**
- ADV. **highly, very | entirely, purely** *purely abstract drawing* | **increasingly | fairly, rather, somewhat**

absurd *adj.*

- VERBS **be, look, seem, sound | become | find sth** *She found the whole concept faintly absurd.*
- ADV. **absolutely, completely, quite, utterly | clearly, manifestly, patently | faintly, rather, slightly, somewhat | wonderfully**
- PHRASES **a sense of the absurd** *His sense of the absurd kept him from becoming too solemn.*

abundance *noun*

- ADJ. **great, sheer** *We were amazed by the sheer abundance of food.* | **relative**
- VERB + ABUNDANCE **have** *The country has an abundance of natural resources* | **produce, provide**
- PREP. **in ~** *Exotic plants grew there in great abundance.*

abuse *noun*

1 wrong/bad use of sth
- ADJ. **alcohol, drug, solvent, substance** (= drugs or solvents)
- VERB + ABUSE **be open to** *The legal system is open to abuse.*
- PHRASES **the abuse of power**

2 bad, usually violent treatment of sb
- ADJ. **emotional, physical, sex/sexual | child, elder** *victims of child abuse* | **human rights ~s** *allegations of human rights abuses* | **alleged, suspected**
- QUANT. **case** *six cases of suspected child abuse*
- VERB + ABUSE **carry out, subject sb to** *She was subjected to regular sexual abuse.* | **suffer, take** *The child had taken a lot of emotional abuse.* | **suspect sb of**
- ABUSE + VERB **happen, occur, take place**
- PHRASES **an allegation of abuse, a perpetrator of abuse, a victim of abuse**

3 insulting words
- ADJ. **verbal | personal, racial**
- QUANT. **stream, torrent** *He was subjected to a torrent of abuse.*
- VERB + ABUSE **hurl, scream, shout, shower sb with, subject sb to, yell | endure** *They had to endure continual racial abuse.*
- PHRASES **heap abuse on sb/sth** *Abuse and scorn were heaped on the proposals.* **a target for/of abuse** *The team who lost became a target of abuse for angry fans.* **a term of abuse** *Calling someone stupid is definitely a term of abuse.*

abuse *verb*

- ADV. **emotionally, mentally, physically, sexually, verbally** *All the children had been physically and emotionally abused.*

abusive *adj.*

- VERBS **be | become, get**
- ADV. **very | quite | openly** *He became openly abusive.*

academic *adj.*

- VERBS **be | become**
- ADV. **merely, purely, strictly** *The distinction being made is purely academic.* | **largely, rather, somewhat**

academy *noun*

- ADJ. **military, naval, police, riding**
- VERB + ACADEMY **attend, go to**
- PREP. **at an/the ~** *He later studied at the Royal Academy.*

accelerate *verb*

1 go faster
- ADV. **hard, quickly | smoothly** *The runners accelerated smoothly round the bend.* | **suddenly | away** *The car purred into life and accelerated away.*

2 develop quickly
- ADV. **dramatically, greatly, rapidly, sharply** *The Aids epidemic is accelerating dramatically.*

acceleration *noun*

1 increase in speed
- ADJ. **rapid**
- PREP. **~ in** *There has been a rapid acceleration in the growth of industry.*

2 ability of a car to accelerate
- ADJ. **fast, good** *This model has the best acceleration of any available sports car.* | **poor, slow**

accelerator *noun*

- VERB + ACCELERATOR **depress, hit, press, put your foot (down) on, step on** *She put her foot on the accelerator and we sped through the traffic lights.* | **take your foot off**
- ACCELERATOR + NOUN **pedal**

accent *noun*

- ADJ. **broad, marked, pronounced, strong, thick** *She had a pronounced Scottish accent.* | **slight | country, for-**

eign, local, regional | plummy, posh, public school | cockney | American, middle-class, northern, etc.
- QUANT. hint, trace *Her French was excellent, without a trace of an accent.*
- VERB + ACCENT have, speak in/with | acquire | affect, assume, imitate, put on *She put on a posh accent when she answered the phone.* | cultivate | lose *He lost his northern accent after moving south.*
- PREP. in an ~ *She spoke in a broad Midlands accent.* with/without an ~ *a tall man with an American accent*

accept *verb*

1 take/receive
- ADV. gladly, graciously, gratefully, willingly *She graciously accepted my apology.* | reluctantly
- VERB + ACCEPT be glad to, be happy to | be reluctant to, be unwilling to | be unable to *I am unfortunately unable to accept your kind invitation.*
- PREP. from *I accepted the gift from my sister.*

2 agree/admit
- ADV. readily *Some people readily accept that they may have to pay for medical treatment.* | fully
- VERB + ACCEPT be happy to, be prepared to, be ready to, be willing to | be reluctant to, be unwilling to | be unable to, refuse to | can/cannot, could (not), will/won't, would (not) *The university cannot accept responsibility for items lost or stolen on its premises.* | be forced to
- PHRASES be commonly/generally/universally/widely accepted *It is generally accepted that people are motivated by success.*

acceptable *adj.*

- VERBS be, prove, seem | become | make sth *an attempt to make the reforms acceptable to both sides* | consider sth, deem sth, find sth *We must come up with a solution that our shareholders will find acceptable.*
- ADV. eminently, highly, very *Her breeding and background made her eminently acceptable in royal circles.* | completely, entirely, fully, perfectly, quite, totally *Yogurt is a perfectly acceptable substitute for cream in cooking.* | fairly, reasonably | (not) remotely *the only national newspaper even remotely acceptable to the left wing* | generally, mutually, universally, widely | easily, readily | equally *Are all political and religious groups equally acceptable?* | publicly | commercially, culturally, environmentally, ethically, grammatically, morally, politically, socially *a grammatically acceptable sentence* ◊ *socially acceptable behaviour*
- PREP. to *a compromise that is acceptable to both sides*

acceptance *noun*

- ADJ. complete, full, total, unconditional, wholehearted | conditional, grudging, reluctant | gradual | greater, growing, increasing *Alternative medicines are now winning greater acceptance among doctors.* | general, popular, public, universal, wide, widespread | blind, easy, immediate, ready, uncritical, unquestioning, voluntary *Their attitude was condemned as blind acceptance of authority.* | implicit, passive, tacit | formal, official | social
- VERB + ACCEPTANCE find, gain, win *The idea was slow to gain general acceptance.* | seek *The group is now seeking formal acceptance.*
- ACCEPTANCE + NOUN speech

access *noun*

- ADJ. direct, easy, free, good, ready, unlimited, unrestricted *I lived deep in the country, without easy access to shops.* | limited, poor, restricted *Access to this information is severely restricted.* | improved | immediate, instant, quick, rapid | equal *Men and women should have equal access to education and employment.* | public | vehicular, wheelchair | random (*computing*) *random access memory*
- VERB + ACCESS have | gain, get | give (sb), offer (sb), provide (sb with) *The new computer provides access to all the files.* | demand | seek | allow (sb), grant (sb) | deny sb, prevent, refuse (sb), restrict *Some people are being denied access to proper medical care.*
- ACCESS + NOUN road, route
- PREP. ~for *improved access for disabled visitors* ~to *He was finally granted access to the medical records.*

accessible *adj.*

1 able to be reached
- VERBS be | become | remain | make sth
- ADV. directly, easily, freely, readily | fully | reasonably, relatively | publicly
- PREP. by *The museum is easily accessible by public transport.* for *All the buildings are accessible for people in wheelchairs.* from *The garden is accessible from the lane.* to *The beach should be accessible to everyone.*

2 easy to understand
- VERBS be | become | make sth
- ADV. easily, highly, immediately, readily, very *It is written in simple language, immediately accessible to the reader.* | widely
- PREP. to *The cartoon strips are designed to make Shakespeare accessible to children.*

accessory *noun*

1 extra item
- ADJ. essential, perfect, useful *This silk scarf is the perfect accessory for stylish summer evenings.* | bathroom, car, fashion

2 person who helps in crime
- PREP. ~to *an accessory to murder*
- PHRASES an accessory before/after the fact (= a person who knows about a crime before/after it was committed and protects the criminal) (*law*) *If you were lying to the police, then you have been an accessory after the fact for all these years.*

accident *noun*

1 unexpected event that causes damage/injury
- ADJ. dreadful, horrific, major, nasty, serious, terrible, tragic, unfortunate | fatal *a fatal road accident* | minor, slight | freak *Their boat sank in a freak accident.* | near (= that nearly happens, but does not) | hit-and-run | aircraft, canoeing, car, climbing, flying, industrial, motor, nuclear, road, traffic, etc.
- VERB + ACCIDENT be involved in, have, meet with *She met with an accident while on holiday in Spain.* | cause | prevent | survive
- ACCIDENT + VERB happen, occur, take place
- ACCIDENT + NOUN prevention | rates, statistics
- PREP. in an/the ~
- PHRASES an accident involving *He was badly hurt in an accident involving two cars and a lorry.* the scene of the accident *The ambulance took only six minutes to reach the scene of the accident.*

2 sth not planned in advance
- ADJ. pure, sheer *By pure accident he had come across the very man who could solve the mystery.*
- PREP. by ~ *We met by accident at the airport.*
- PHRASES be no accident that … *It is no accident that men fill most of the top jobs.* by accident or design *It happened, whether by accident or design, that Steve and I were the last two people to leave.*

accidental adj.

- VERBS be
- ADV. completely, purely, quite | almost

acclaim noun

- ADJ. great | general, public, universal, wide, widespread | popular | critical *Her latest novel has won great critical acclaim.* | international, national, worldwide
- VERB + ACCLAIM earn (sb), gain (sb), meet with, receive, win *His discoveries earned him wide acclaim.*
- PREP. to ... ~ *The play opened last week to universal acclaim.* | ~ for *She received international acclaim for her interpretation of Chopin.* ~ from *acclaim from the critics*

acclaim verb

- PHRASES be critically acclaimed, be highly/internationally/widely acclaimed *This book has been widely acclaimed as a modern classic.*

accolade noun

- ADJ. greatest, highest, supreme, ultimate *Four restaurants have been awarded the highest accolade of a three-star rating.*
- VERB + ACCOLADE earn, receive, win | award (sb), bestow, grant (sb) | deserve

accommodate verb

- ADV. comfortably, easily *It was a large hall, where a lot of people could be comfortably accommodated.*
- VERB + ACCOMMODATE can/could *The car park can accommodate about 200 cars.*

accommodation noun

1 place for sb to live/stay
- ADJ. comfortable, decent, good, suitable | inadequate, poor, substandard | excellent, luxurious | overnight, temporary | permanent | free | private, rented | holiday, hotel | living, residential | sleeping | bed-and-breakfast | furnished | sheltered *Many old people choose to live in sheltered accommodation.* | secure *We need more secure accommodation for young prisoners.* | student
- VERB + ACCOMMODATION have *The council should be able to help families who have no accommodation.* | look for, seek | find, get, secure | offer (sb), provide (sb with) *It is the duty of the local community to provide accommodation for the homeless.*
- ACCOMMODATION + NOUN costs
- PREP. in ~

2 satisfactory arrangement
- VERB + ACCOMMODATION come to, make, reach, work out | seek
- PREP. ~ between *Some accommodation between conservation and tourism is essential.* ~ to *accommodation to the harsh circumstances of rural life* ~ with *They were forced to reach an accommodation with the rebels.*

accompaniment noun

1 sth eaten/drunk with food
- ADJ. delicious, good, ideal
- VERB + ACCOMPANIMENT be, make
- PREP. ~ for/to *These wines also make a good accompaniment for vegetarian dishes.*

2 music played to go with singing, etc.
- ADJ. instrumental, musical, orchestral | piano, string, etc.
- VERB + ACCOMPANIMENT provide | compose, write
- PREP. to the ~ of *She sang to the accompaniment of guitars.* with an ~ *I prefer to sing with an accompaniment.*

3 sth that happens at the same time
- ADJ. essential, inevitable, necessary
- PREP. to the ~ of *The women's medical school opened in 1874, to the accompaniment of much ridicule of 'lady doctors'.* with the ~ of *the market, with its inevitable accompaniment of bustle and noise*

accomplice noun

- ADJ. willing | unwilling | unwitting | alleged
- PREP. ~ in *She became his unwitting accomplice in the robbery.* ~ to *an accomplice to murder*

accomplish verb

- ADV. safely, successfully *A rather difficult task had been successfully accomplished.* | easily

accomplished adj.

- VERBS be | become
- ADV. extremely, highly, very | technically *a technically accomplished musician*
- PREP. at *Sarah had become accomplished at running the house.* in *He came to London in 1976, already accomplished in the English language.*

accomplishment noun

- ADJ. considerable, great, real, significant | technical *Her technical accomplishment on the piano is startling.*
- PREP. of ... ~ *a work of real accomplishment* in *It is a great accomplishment in singing to take the melodic line up to a position of energy and hold it there.*

accord noun

- ADJ. draft | peace, trade
- VERB + ACCORD draw up, negotiate, reach *A peace accord was reached on 26 March.* | endorse, ratify, sign
- PREP. ~ between *a trade accord between Europe and the United States* ~ on *an accord on environmental protection* ~ with *They signed a trade accord with the Americans.*

accord verb

- ADV. fully
- PREP. with *His version of events does not accord fully with the facts.*

account noun

1 description
- ADJ. brief, short | blow-by-blow, comprehensive, detailed, full, graphic, vivid *He gave us a blow-by-blow account of the incident.* | accurate, clear, eyewitness, factual, first-hand, true, verbatim | glowing, good *She received a glowing account of her son's progress.* | newspaper *the newspaper account of the trial*
- VERB + ACCOUNT give (sb), provide (sb with), write (sb) *Can you give us an account of what happened?*
- PREP. in an/the ~ *Dr Richards describes this very well in his account of the events.*
- PHRASES by all accounts (= according to what people say) *I've never been there, but it's a lovely place by all accounts.* by sb's own account *By his own account he had an unhappy childhood.*

2 arrangement with a bank
- ADJ. bank, building society | current | deposit, investment, savings | personal | business | joint, separate *My husband and I have separate accounts.* | numbered *They have a numbered account in Switzerland.*
- VERB + ACCOUNT have, hold *Go and see the manager of the bank where your account is held.* | open *She opened a savings account at the building society.* | close | credit sth to, pay/put sth into *The money will be credited to your account tomorrow.* | debit (sth from), draw sth out (of),

pay sth from, take sth out (of), withdraw sth (from) *She had taken all her money out of her account.* | **overdraw** *Your account is overdrawn.*
- PREP. **~at** *He opened an account at a bank in Germany.* **~with** *an account with Barclays Bank*

3 accounts record of money a business earns/spends
- VERB + ACCOUNTS **do, keep** *Try to keep accurate accounts.* | **audit, check, look at** | **submit** *Your accounts will need to be submitted to the tax office.*
- ACCOUNTS + VERB **be in order** *The accounts are all in order.*
- ⇨ Special page at BUSINESS

4 arrangement with a shop/business
- ADJ. **expense** (= an arrangement to charge expenses to your own employers) *taking clients for expense account lunches*
- VERB + ACCOUNT **have** | **open** *I'd like to open an account, please.* | **close** | **pay off, settle** *It is best to settle the account each month.* | **charge sth to, debit (sth from), put sth on** *Charge this to my account, please.* | **credit sth to**
- PREP. **on~** *Ring for a cab on account.* | **~at/with** *an account with a large store*

account *verb*

PHRASAL VERB
account for sth
- ADV. **fully** *The increase can be fully accounted for.* | **partly** *The differences in achievement between the pupils are partly accounted for by differences in age.*

accountability *noun*

- ADJ. **greater, increased** | **local, public** *demands for greater public accountability in the police service* | **democratic, financial, managerial, moral, parliamentary, political, professional** | **government, police**
- VERB + ACCOUNTABILITY **enhance, improve, increase, strengthen** | **reduce, weaken** *This process of centralization further weakens accountability.* | **ensure**
- PREP. **~for** *to ensure accountability for decisions made* **~to** *police accountability to the public*
- PHRASES **a demand for accountability, a lack of accountability** *the apparent lack of accountability of the security forces* **a need for accountability** *There is a need for increased professional accountability.*

accountable *adj.*

- VERBS **be** | **become** | **make sb** | **hold sb** *The directors are held accountable by the shareholders.*
- ADV. **fully, properly** | **directly** *Senior managers are directly accountable to the Board of Directors.* | **publicly** *Local authorities should be publicly accountable to the communities they serve.* | **democratically** *a democratically accountable parliament* | **financially, politically**
- PREP. **for** *In the end, we are all accountable for our actions.* **to** *Politicians are accountable to Parliament.*

accountancy *noun*

- ADJ. **chartered** | **creative** *It had taken considerable 'creative accountancy' on my part to produce a set of figures that showed us making any profit at all.*
- ACCOUNTANCY + NOUN **firm, practice** | **body** *the members of the different professional accountancy bodies* | **profession**
- ⇨ Note at SUBJECT (for more verbs and nouns)

accountant *noun*

- ADJ. **certified, chartered** | **professional, qualified** | **trainee** | **retired** | **independent, self-employed** | **company** | **chief** *We talked to the company's chief accountant.*

| **management** | **investigating, reporting** *the investigating accountant's report*
⇨ Note at PROFESSIONAL (for verbs)

accumulate *verb*

- ADV. **gradually, slowly** | **steadily** | **rapidly**
- VERB + ACCUMULATE **begin to** | **be allowed to** *Dirt must not be allowed to accumulate.* | **tend to** *Toxic chemicals tend to accumulate in the body.*

accumulation *noun*

- ADJ. **rapid** | **steady** *the steady accumulation of evidence by the police* | **slow** | **great, impressive, large, massive** *a massive accumulation of facts about the motor industry* | **capital** (*finance*)
- VERB + ACCUMULATION **lead to** | **prevent**

accuracy *noun*

- ADJ. **absolute, complete, deadly, perfect, pinpoint, total, unerring** *The needle has to be positioned with pinpoint accuracy.* | **amazing, considerable, great, high** (*technical*), **remarkable, uncanny** | **reasonable, sufficient** | **factual, historical, technical**
- QUANT. **degree, level** *The missiles are capable of a very high degree of accuracy.*
- VERB + ACCURACY **improve, increase** *We are hoping to improve the accuracy of our forecasts.* | **check, confirm, test** | **ensure** *Great care is taken to ensure the accuracy of research data.* | **doubt, question** *Many people began to question the accuracy of his statement.*
- PREP. **with~** *It is possible to predict the outcome with reasonable accuracy.*

accurate *adj.*

- VERBS **be, prove** *His predictions proved accurate.*
- ADV. **deadly, extremely, highly, very** | **amazingly, remarkably, surprisingly, uncannily** | **completely, perfectly, totally** | **not completely, not entirely, not quite, not strictly, not wholly** *The figures he gave were not strictly accurate.* | **partially** | **broadly, fairly, generally, largely, pretty, quite, reasonably, sufficiently** | **historically, statistically**
- PHRASES **full and accurate** *He gave a full and accurate account of his movements.*

accusation *noun*

- ADJ. **serious** | **false, groundless, unfounded, unjust, wild** | **bitter** | **mutual** *They sank into mutual accusation and incrimination.* | **public** | **veiled** *She made a lot of thinly veiled accusations.* | **renewed, repeated**
- VERB + ACCUSATION **level at, make** *an accusation frequently levelled at junior doctors* | **face** *Their father now faces an accusation of murder.* | **deny, dismiss, refute, reject** | **prove, support** *New evidence has emerged which supports the accusation against her.*
- ACCUSATION + VERB **fly about/around** *There seem to be a lot of wild accusations flying around.*
- PREP. **amid ~s** *He fled the country amid accusations of fraud.* | **~ against** *You made a public accusation of misconduct against Nigel.*
- PHRASES **bring an accusation against sb** *She rejected all the accusations brought against her.*

accuse *verb*

- ADV. **practically, virtually** *She practically accused me of starting the fire!* | **falsely, unjustly, wrongly** | **angrily** | **openly, publicly** *They openly accused her of dishonesty.*
- VERB + ACCUSE **cannot/could not** *You can't accuse me of being selfish.*
- PREP. **of** *No one could ever accuse this government of not caring about the poor.*

● PHRASES   **stand accused of** *He stands accused of murdering his wife and children.*

accustomed *adj.* accustomed to sth

● VERBS   **be | become, get, grow** *She had grown accustomed to his long absences.*
● ADV.   **quite, well** *He was well accustomed to hard work.*

ace *noun*

1 playing card
⇨ Note at CARD

2 winning first hit in tennis
● VERB + ACE   **serve** *Rafter has served fifteen aces in the match so far.*

3 person who is very good at sth
● ADJ.   **fighter, flying, goal, motorcycle, soccer, tennis**

ache *noun*

1 physical pain
● ADJ.   **dull, nagging, throbbing | familiar | muscular, stomach, tummy**
● VERB + ACHE   **be aware of, feel** *I felt the familiar ache in my lower back.* | **ease** *He changed his position once again to ease the ache in his back.*
● ACHE + VERB   **throb** *A dull ache throbbed at the back of David's head.*
● PREP.   **~ in** *a nagging ache in her knee*
● PHRASES   **aches and pains** *He was always complaining about his various aches and pains.*

2 great sorrow
● ADJ.   **deep, dull, nagging**
● VERB + ACHE   **feel, have** *She kept feeling the nagging ache in her heart.*
● PREP.   **~ in** *She could hardly speak for the ache in her heart.* **~ inside, ~ of** *the ache of loneliness inside him*

ache *verb*

● ADV.   **badly, really** *My feet ached badly.* | **a bit** *My left foot ached a bit.*
● PREP.   **from** *I still really ache from all that cycling yesterday.*
● PHRASES   **ache all over** *Her head felt hot and she was aching all over.*

achieve *verb*

● VERB + ACHIEVE   **fail to** *The present law has failed to achieve its objectives.* | **be designed to | be difficult to, be easy to, be impossible to, be possible to**

achievement *noun*

1 thing done successfully
● ADJ.   **considerable, extraordinary, fine, great, important, impressive, major, no mean, notable, outstanding, real, remarkable, significant, tremendous** *This was no mean achievement for the government.* | **rare | unique | concrete, solid | crowning, main, proudest, supreme | lasting | modest | personal | architectural, artistic, cultural, economic, educational, engineering, literary, scientific, sporting, technical, technological**
● VERB + ACHIEVEMENT   **be, constitute, represent** *This conference in itself constitutes a solid achievement.*
● PREP.   **~ in** *She was given a prize for her achievements in textile design.*
● PHRASES   **quite an achievement** *To be offered a place at such a good university is quite an achievement.*

2 act of achieving sth
● ADJ.   **high** *two years of consistently high achievement* | **positive | individual, personal | human** *He believes European civilization was the high point of human achievement.* | **academic, educational, intellectual** *Suc-*

cess should not be measured solely by educational achievement.
● PHRASES   **a feeling/sense of achievement** *Climbing the mountain gave him a tremendous sense of achievement.* **a lack of achievement, a level/standard of achievement, a record of achievement** *an impressive record of achievement*

acid *noun*

1 chemical compound
● ADJ.   **concentrated, strong | dilute, weak | acetic, amino, carbolic, citric, folic, hydrochloric, lactic, nitric, nucleic, prussic, sulphuric, etc.**
● VERB + ACID   **produce | neutralize** *You will need a special chemical to neutralize the acid.*
● ACID + VERB   **burn sth** *The acid burned a hole in her overalls*

2 illegal drug
● VERB + ACID   **drop** *smoking joints and dropping acid*
⇨ Note at DRUG

acknowledge *verb*

1 admit/recognize
● ADV.   **fully | freely, readily | clearly, explicitly | effectively, implicitly, tacitly** *The peace settlement effectively acknowledged the country's independence.* | **formally, officially | openly, publicly** *He acknowledged publicly that he might have made a mistake.* | **privately | reluctantly, ruefully**
● VERB + ACKNOWLEDGE   **fail to, refuse to | be forced to** *Mental illness can exist for years before families are forced to acknowledge the truth.*
● PHRASES   **be generally/universally/widely acknowledged** *a truth that is universally acknowledged*

2 reply to letter
● ADV.   **duly** *The company duly acknowledged receipt of the letter.* | **hereby** *I hereby acknowledge receipt of your letter of 25 July.*

acknowledgement *noun*

● ADJ.   **brief | explicit | tacit | open,   public | formal, official | belated | welcome**
● VERB + ACKNOWLEDGEMENT   **amount to, be** *This amounted to an acknowledgement that she had been wrong.* | **get, receive** *I wrote to them but never got any acknowledgement.* | **grunt, nod, wave** *She merely nodded acknowledgement of his statement.*
● PREP.   **in ~ (of)** *He raised his hand to her in acknowledgement.* | **~ from** *She is still waiting for some acknowledgement from her fellow academics.*
● PHRASES   **with due acknowledgement** *He borrowed from a number of sources, with due acknowledgement.*

acne *noun*

● ADJ.   **bad, terrible**
● VERB + ACNE   **have, suffer from** *He had terrible acne when he was younger.* | **develop, get** *A lot of teenagers develop acne.* | **treat** *Doctors can treat acne with pills or creams.*
● ACNE + VERB   **clear (up)** *Acne often clears up with a change in diet.*

acquaintance *noun*

1 person you know
● ADJ.   **casual** *I bumped into a casual acquaintance in town.* | **new | close, old | business, mutual, personal, social**
● VERB + ACQUAINTANCE   **bump into, meet | greet (sb as)** *He was greeted as an old acquaintance.*
● PHRASES   **friends and acquaintances**

2 knowledge of sb/sth
- ADJ. **nodding, passing, slight** *a man with whom I had a passing acquaintance* | **brief, short** | **close, intimate**
- VERB + ACQUAINTANCE **make sb/sth's** (= become acquainted with sb/sth) *I first made his acquaintance in 1992.* | **strike up** *I first met Simon in 1998 and struck up an acquaintance with him.* | **renew**
- PREP. **of sb's ~** *He introduced me to a lady of his acquaintance.* | **~ with** *her acquaintance with modern French philosophy*
- PHRASES **have an acquaintance with** *They have little acquaintance with colloquial English.* **on close/closer acquaintance, on first acquaintance** *On first acquaintance she seemed a little odd.*

acquainted *adj.*

1 familiar with sth
- VERBS **be** | **become**
- ADV. **well** | **fully**
- PREP. **with** *Are you fully acquainted with the facts?*

2 knowing sb personally
- VERBS **be** | **become, get** *I would like to get acquainted with her.* | **get sb** *Playing a game with the children is a good way of getting them acquainted.*
- ADV. **closely, intimately, well** | **personally**
- PREP. **with** *I am not personally acquainted with her.*

acquisition *noun*

1 thing you have obtained
- ADJ. **latest, new, recent**

2 act of obtaining sth
- ADJ. **data, language, property** *Language acquisition begins in the first months of a baby's life.*
- VERB + ACQUISITION **complete, make** *The company has just made another acquisition.*

acquittal *noun*

- VERB + ACQUITTAL **return** *The jury returned an acquittal after only seventeen minutes.* | **direct, order** *The trial judge had directed an acquittal.* | **gain (sb), obtain, secure** | **lead to, result in** *The trial resulted in an acquittal.* | **uphold** *The judge upheld their acquittal.*

acre *noun*

⇨ Note at MEASURE

act *noun*

1 thing that sb does
- ADJ. **charitable, kind** | **heroic** *a heroic act of bravery* | **aggressive, barbaric, hostile, provocative, terrorist, violent** | **appalling, despicable, outrageous, terrible** | **criminal, illegal, unlawful, wrongful** | **careless, foolish, impulsive** | **conscious, deliberate, positive, voluntary, wilful** | **private** *a private act of revenge* | **public** | **creative, dramatic, physical, political, symbolic** | **homosexual, sex/sexual** | **balancing, disappearing, juggling, vanishing** *The UN must perform a difficult balancing act between the two sides in the conflict.*
- VERB + ACT **commit** (*law*), **perform** *charged with committing an act of gross indecency*
- PREP. **in the ~ of** (= doing something) | **~ of** *For Jane, the act of writing was always difficult.*
- PHRASES **an act of faith, love, violence, will, worship, etc., catch sb in the act (of doing sth)** *He was caught in the act of stealing.* **the simple/very act of doing sth** *The very act of writing out your plan clarifies what you need to do.*

2 (also **Act**) law made by a government
- VERB + ACT **bring in, introduce, pass** *The Act was passed by a majority of 175 votes to 143.* | **amend** | **repeal** *The old Act has now been repealed.* | **breach, contravene** *The company had breached the 1994 Companies Act.*
- ACT + VERB **become law, come into force** *The new Children's Act will come into force next year.* | **contain sth, say sth, state sth** *The Act contains regulations for banks and building societies.*
- PREP. **under an/the ~** *He was charged under the Firearms Act of 1977.*

3 entertainment; entertainers
- ADJ. **class** (*informal*) (used for sb who does sth well) *Their new striker looks a class act.* | **double** *comedy double act French and Saunders* | **live** *their reputation as one of rock's most impressive live acts* | **main, support** *The main act will come on at about ten o'clock.* | **cabaret, circus, comedy, song-and-dance, stage, variety**
- VERB + ACT **do, perform** *He does a little song-and-dance act.* | **rehearse, work on**

4 division of a play
- ADJ. **opening** | **final, last** | **first, second, etc.**
- PREP. **in (the) ~** *The king is killed in the opening act.*

5 insincere behaviour
- VERB + ACT **put on** *Don't take any notice—she's just putting on an act!*

act *verb*

1 do sth/behave
- ADV. **at once, immediately, promptly, quickly, swiftly** *The government must act promptly to change this law.* | **correctly, legally, properly** | **illegally, improperly, unconstitutionally, unlawfully, wrongly** | **reasonably, responsibly, sensibly, wisely** | **dishonestly, dishonourably, unreasonably** | **oddly, strangely, suspiciously** *Jenny has been acting rather strangely recently.* | **bravely** | **decisively** | **effectively** | **in good faith** *His defence was that he had acted in good faith.* | **in self defence** *The jury accepted that he had acted in self defence.* | **accordingly** *George knew about the letter and acted accordingly.*
- PREP. **against** *The government needs to act against the sale of these dangerous toys.* **for/on behalf of sb** *His solicitors are continuing to act for him.* **like** *Stop acting like a spoilt child.* ◇ *hormones in the brain that act like natural painkillers* **on** *Alcohol acts quickly on the brain.* **out of** *I suspected that he was acting out of malice.*
- PHRASES **act in sb's best interests** *We are all acting in the best interests of the children.*

2 perform in play/film
- ADV. **brilliantly, well** | **badly**

acting *noun*

- ADJ. **brilliant, excellent, good** | **bad, poor, wooden** *The film is spoiled by some very wooden acting.*
- VERB + ACTING **do** *I did quite a lot of acting when I was at college.*
- ACTING + NOUN **career, profession**

action *noun*

1 process of doing sth
- ADJ. **decisive, effective, firm, strong, vigorous** | **immediate, prompt, swift, urgent** | **drastic, emergency** *The situation calls for drastic action.* | **collective, concerted, joint, united** | **direct, positive** | **evasive** | **corrective, remedial** | **disciplinary, legal, military, political, strike** *Disciplinary action will be taken against students who cheat.* (see also **industrial action**)
- VERB + ACTION **take** | **call for** | **agree on** *The leaders have agreed on joint action to combat terrorism.* | **leap/spring/swing into** *The emergency services swung into action as soon as the disaster was reported.* | **carry out, perform, take** *Only the priest can perform these actions.* ◇ *We shall take whatever actions are necessary.* |

galvanize/prod/spur sb into *We have to galvanize people into action.* | **bring/put sth into** *We need to put these ideas into action.* | **keep/put sb/sth out of** *A fire has put the factory out of action.*
- PREP. **in~** *I have not yet seen the machines in action.* **out of~** *He is out of action following an ankle injury.* | **~against** *against drug dealers* **~on** *The government is taking strong action on refugees.*
- PHRASES **a course of action** *Is this the best course of action to follow?*

2 legal case
- ADJ. **court** | **civil, criminal, libel**
- VERB + ACTION **bring, take out** *Her husband brought a civil action against her after their divorce.*
- PREP. **~against**

3 fighting
- ADJ. **enemy** *He was killed during enemy action.*
- VERB + ACTION **see** *I never saw action during the war.*
- PHRASES **killed/missing/wounded in action** *He was reported missing in action.*

active *adj.*

- VERBS **be** | **become** | **keep** (*informal*), **remain** *Try to keep active in the cold weather.*
- ADV. **extremely, highly, very** *a highly active volcano* | **increasingly** | **fairly, quite, reasonably** | **equally** *a businessman who is equally active in politics* | **mentally, physically** *It's important to remain mentally active after retirement.* | **sexually** *A minority of children are sexually active before they are in their teens.* | **economically, politically** *When did you first become politically active?*
- PREP. **against** *drugs that are active against cancers* **in** *She has been active in local politics for some years.*

activity *noun*

- ADJ. **frantic, frenetic, heightened, increased, intense** | **criminal, illegal, subversive, terrorist** | **classroom, group** | **extra-curricular, leisure, leisure-time, outdoor, recreational, social** | **mental, physical, sexual** | **business, commercial, cultural, economic, industrial, intellectual, political, scientific** | **government, military, police, union** | **human** | **electrical, geological, volcanic**
- QUANT. **burst, flurry** *There was a flurry of activity as the film star appeared on the balcony.* | **level** *Newspapers report a higher level of activity in the foreign exchange markets.*
- VERB + ACTIVITY **do** *Here's an activity you can do with mixed ability classes.* | **be involved in, engage in, participate in, take part in, undertake** *We suspect he may be involved in illegal activities.* ◊ *Teachers here are not allowed to engage in any political activity.* | **stop, suspend, terminate** *The party's activities have been suspended.* | **stimulate** *It will only be possible to stimulate business activity with an injection of public funds.* | **curb** | **resume** | **buzz with** (only used when the **activity** is uncountable) *The room was buzzing with activity.*
- PHRASES **a hive of activity** (= a very busy place) *The classroom was a hive of activity as the children prepared for the concert.* **a sign of activity** *Police watched the house all day, but there was no sign of activity.*

actor, actress *noun*

- ADJ. **accomplished, born, brilliant, consummate, experienced, fine, good, great, talented, wonderful** *You're a born actor!* | **celebrated, famous, leading, principal, sought-after, star, veteran, well-known** | **successful** | **bit-part, struggling, unknown** | **out-of-work, unemployed** | **aspiring, would-be** | **frustrated** *Lecturers are often frustrated actors who enjoy performing before a live audience.* | **amateur** | **professional** | **character, classical, comedy/comic, Shakespearean, straight** |

film, Hollywood, screen, stage, television | **child** | **supporting** *the award for best supporting actor*
- VERB + ACTOR, ACTRESS **audition, cast**
- ACTOR, ACTRESS + VERB **act (sth), perform (sth), play (sth)** *The same actor plays three different parts in the film.* | **rehearse (sth)** | **audition** *He was one of many actors who auditioned for the part of Hamlet.*
⇨ Note at JOB

acumen *noun*

- ADJ. **considerable, great** | **business, commercial, critical, financial, political**
- VERB + ACUMEN **demonstrate, show** *He had demonstrated considerable business acumen.*

acupuncture *noun*

- QUANT. **course** *My doctor recommended a course of acupuncture.*
- VERB + ACUPUNCTURE **have** *I'm having acupuncture for a bad back.* | **give sb, practise, use** *Acupuncture has been practised in China for thousands of years.*
- ACUPUNCTURE + NOUN **point** *Needles are inserted into specific acupuncture points in the body.* | **needle**

ad *noun*

- ADJ. **classified, full-page, small** *You can put your own small ads in local papers.* | **magazine, newspaper, radio, television/TV** | **detergent, job, tobacco, etc.**
- VERB + AD **place, put, take out** *She took out a full-page ad in a women's magazine.* | **publish, run, show** | **answer, reply to, respond to**
- AD + VERB **appear** *The ad appeared on all major channels.* | **say sth, show sth, state sth** | **feature sb/sth**
- AD + NOUN **campaign** | **agency**
- PREP. **in an/the~** *A lot of claims are made in the ad.* | **~for** *TV ads for cars*

adapt *verb*

1 change your behaviour
- ADV. **successfully, well** *The children have adapted well to the heat.* | **quickly** | **easily, readily** *The company can easily adapt to changing demand.* | **accordingly** *We need to assess the new situation and adapt accordingly.*
- VERB + ADAPT **be able/unable to, can/cannot** | **have to, must** | **need to**
- PREP. **to**
- PHRASES **the ability to adapt** *Some animals have a remarkable ability to adapt to changing environments.* **find it difficult/hard to adapt** *A lot of companies have found it hard to adapt to the new system.*

2 change a thing
- PREP. **for** *to adapt a book for television.* **from** *The radio play had been adapted from a novel.*
- PHRASES **specially adapted** *The classroom has been specially adapted to take wheelchairs.*

adaptable *adj.*

- VERBS **be, prove** | **become** | **make sb/sth**
- ADV. **highly, very** *Many old market buildings have proved highly adaptable.* | **fairly, quite** | **easily, readily**
- PREP. **to** *The vehicles are large and not easily adaptable to new uses.*

adaptation *noun*

1 a change/the process of changing
- ADJ. **successful** | **special**
- VERB + ADAPTATION **make** *making adaptations to your home*
- ADAPTATION + VERB **occur** *Adaptations in plants occur over thousands of years.*

- PREP. **~for** *The Antarctic species have few special adaptations for polar life.* **~to** *adaptation to the workplace*
- PHRASES **a process of adaptation** *The process of adaptation to a new school is difficult for some children.*

2 film, TV programme
- ADJ. **film, screen, television/TV** *He specializes in screen adaptations of classic novels.*
- VERB + ADAPTATION **film, make, produce**

add *verb*

- ADV. **quickly, softly** *He added softly, 'I missed you.'*
- VERB + ADD **hasten to** *I hasten to add that I knew nothing of the fraud at the time.*

addict *noun*

- ADJ. **cocaine, drug, heroin, etc. | computer, television, etc.** *Many young boys become computer addicts.*

addicted *adj.*

- VERBS **be | become, get**
- ADV. **totally | hopelessly**
- PREP. **to** *She had become addicted to tranquillizers.*

addiction *noun*

- ADJ. **alcohol, cocaine, drug, etc.**
- VERB + ADDICTION **become, turn into** *A habit can easily become an addiction.* **| have | cause, lead to | feed** *He stole money from his parents to feed his addiction.* **| treat | beat, cure, overcome** *struggling to beat his heroin addiction*
- PREP. **~to** *She had an addiction to heroin.*

addictive *adj.*

- VERBS **be | become**
- ADV. **extremely, highly, very** *Cocaine is a highly addictive drug.*

addition *noun*

1 sth that is added
- ADJ. **useful, valuable, welcome, worthy | important, major, notable, significant | latest, new, recent**
- VERB + ADDITION **make** *We have made several additions to the collection recently.*
- PREP. **~ to** *the latest addition to the family* (= a new baby)

2 process of adding numbers/amounts
- ADJ. **simple** *He worked it out through simple addition.*
- VERB + ADDITION **do** *She can do addition, but she hasn't learned subtraction yet.*

address *noun*

1 where you live/work
- ADJ. **home, private | business | contact** *Please leave a contact address.* **| forwarding, return** *There was no return address on the back of the envelope.* **| postal | full** *Please write your full postal address.* **| false, wrong** *He gave a false address to the police.* **| correct, right | useful | secret | fashionable** *Cheyne Walk was a very fashionable address.*
- VERB + ADDRESS **give, leave, write**
- ADDRESS + NOUN **book**
- PREP. **at a/the ~** *I'm afraid there's nobody called Williams at this address.*
- PHRASES **a change of address** *Please inform us of any change of address.* **name and address, no fixed address** *a man of no fixed address*

2 speech
- ADJ. **short | inaugural, keynote, opening | public** *a*

public **address system | radio, televised/television | election | presidential**
- VERB + ADDRESS **deliver, give** *The prime minister delivered the keynote address at the conference.*
- PREP. **in a/the ~** *He gave details of the policy in an address to party members.* **| ~by** *an address by the Chancellor of the University* **~to** *a radio address to the nation*

address *verb*

1 write name and address
- ADV. **correctly, properly | personally** *The minister did not reply to my letter although I addressed it to him personally.*
- PREP. **to**
- PHRASES **a stamped addressed envelope** *Please send a stamped addressed envelope and we will send you a copy of our brochure.*

2 say sth to sb
- ADV. **by name, directly** *She did not address him by name.* ◇ *He never addressed her directly.*
- PREP. **to** *He addressed his comments to the chairman.*

3 deal with problem
- ADV. **directly, explicitly, specifically | fully | adequately** *These concerns were not adequately addressed in the report.* **| successfully**
- VERB + ADDRESS **seek to** *the problems we are seeking to address* **| fail to**
- PHRASES **address yourself to sth** *The authors of the book address themselves to the question of unemployment.*

adept *adj.*

- VERBS **be, seem | become**
- ADV. **extremely, highly, very | quite**
- PREP. **at** *He was highly adept at avoiding trouble.*

adequate *adj.*

- VERBS **be, prove, seem | remain | consider sth, think sth** *The trains were not considered adequate for use on the modern railways.*
- ADV. **really, very | perfectly, quite, totally | more than** *The system is more than adequate to deal with any problems.* **| barely, hardly, less than, not entirely, not wholly** *The grants given to students are less than adequate.* **| more or less** *The amount of money we have been given is more or less adequate.* **| still | no longer**
- PREP. **for** *The old computer is still perfectly adequate for most tasks.*

adhere *verb*

- ADV. **properly** *The tiles may not adhere properly if you do not use the correct glue.*
- PREP. **to** *The glue would not adhere to the metal surface.*

PHRASAL VERB

adhere to
- ADV. **closely, firmly, rigidly, rigorously, scrupulously, strictly** *This principle must be strictly adhered to.* **| fully, properly** *The guidelines were not always fully adhered to.*

adherence *noun*

- ADJ. **blind, close, faithful, firm, rigid, slavish, strict**
- PREP. **~to** *strict adherence to a diet*

adjacent *adj.*

- VERBS **be, be situated, lie, stand** *The vineyards of Verzy lie adjacent to those of Verzenay.*
- ADJ. **directly, immediately** *There is a row of houses immediately adjacent to the factory.*
- PREP. **to** *The miller's house stands adjacent to the mill.*

adjective noun

- ADJ. **attributive, predicative** *Attributive adjectives precede the noun.* | **possessive** *'My' is a possessive adjective.*
- VERB + ADJECTIVE **apply** *'Enterprising' is not an adjective you would apply to him!*
- ADJECTIVE + VERB **describe** *adjectives describing texture* | **modify, qualify** *Adjectives qualify nouns.* | **follow** *Predicative adjectives follow the noun.* | **precede**

adjourn verb

- ADV. **indefinitely** *The trial was adjourned indefinitely.*
- PREP. **for** *At midday the meeting was adjourned for lunch.* **pending** *The inquest was adjourned pending further investigations.* **to** *Shall we adjourn to your office?*

adjust verb

1 change sth slightly
- ADV. **slightly** | **finely** *It is important to have equipment that can be finely adjusted.* | **automatically** | **carefully** | **accordingly** *Children are sensitive to disapproval and adjust their behaviour accordingly.* | **downwards, upwards** *This estimate may have to be adjusted downwards.*
- PREP. **for** *Salaries are adjusted for inflation.*

2 get used to new situation
- ADV. **quickly, rapidly** | **gradually, slowly**
- VERB + ADJUST **be difficult/hard to**
- VERB + ADJUST **need/take time to** *It may take a little time to adjust to the climate here.*
- VERB + ADJUST **try to**
- PREP. **to** *She will gradually adjust to her new role.*

adjustable adj.

- VERBS **be**
- ADV. **fully** *The straps are fully adjustable to fit any size.*

adjustment noun

1 small change made
- ADJ. **delicate, fine, minor, slight, small** | **important, major, significant** | **appropriate, necessary** | **automatic** | **financial**
- VERB + ADJUSTMENT **make** *The mechanic made the necessary adjustments to the engine.* | **need, require**
- PREP. **~for** *a cut of 1.5% in real terms (after adjustment for inflation)* **~in** *adjustments in the exchange rates* **~to** *a few minor adjustments to the timetable*

2 process of changing
- ADJ. **successful** | **emotional, personal, social**
- PREP. **~to** *The company's adjustment to the new markets has been successful.*
- PHRASES **a period of adjustment** *There was a long period of adjustment under the new boss.* **the process of adjustment** *The process of adjustment to life in another country can be very difficult.*

administer verb

- ADV. **effectively, efficiently** | **centrally, locally** *The legislation was to be centrally administered by the Board of Education.* | **jointly**
- VERB + ADMINISTER **be difficult/easy/simple to, be cheap/expensive to**

administration noun

1 organizing how sth is done
- ADJ. **effective, efficient, good** | **poor** *The college loses a lot of money through poor administration.* | **day-to-day, routine** | **general** | **office** | **bureaucratic** | **central** | **arts, business, educational, financial, justice, social** | **government, public**
- VERB + ADMINISTRATION **be in charge of, be responsible for**

- ADMINISTRATION + NOUN **costs**

2 people who manage an organization
- ADJ. **college, hospital, prison, etc.**

3 government
- ADJ. **colonial, federal, local, municipal, provincial, regional, state** | **civil, imperial, royal** | **Conservative, Labour, etc.** | **caretaker, interim, temporary** | **coalition, joint** | **minority** | **civilian, military**
- VERB + ADMINISTRATION **form** *On September 27 a new coalition administration was formed.*

4 giving a drug
- ADJ. **intravenous, oral** | **drug**

admirable adj.

- VERBS **be** | **find sb/sth**
- ADV. **very** | **wholly** *She had acted in ways that he found wholly admirable.* | **truly**

admiral noun

- ADJ. **rear, vice**
⇨ Note at RANK

admiration noun

- ADJ. **deep, genuine, great, sincere, tremendous** | **frank, open** | **sneaking** *Inwardly, I had a sneaking admiration for them.* | **grudging, reluctant** | **mutual**
- VERB + ADMIRATION **be filled with, be full of, feel, have** *I'm full of admiration for him.* ◊ *I have the greatest admiration for the nurses.* | **express, show** *She wrote to him expressing her admiration.* | **compel, draw, fill sb with, gain, win** *a dignity that compels admiration* ◊ *The way he dealt with the crisis filled me with admiration.* ◊ *He gained the admiration of thousands of people.* | **be worthy of** *As a writer she is certainly worthy of admiration.* | **lose** *He never lost the admiration of his students.*
- PREP. **in~** *She stared at him in open admiration.* **with~** *gazing at her with admiration* | **~for** *admiration for his work*
- PHRASES **a gasp of admiration** *The picture was greeted with gasps of admiration.* **have nothing but admiration for sb/sth** *I have nothing but admiration for the way she tackled those bullies.*

admire verb

1 have high opinion of sb/sth
- ADV. **deeply, enormously, greatly, hugely, particularly, really** *He admires you enormously.* | **rather** | **clearly, openly** | **secretly** *She secretly admired and envied him.*
- VERB + ADMIRE **have to** *You have to admire their dedication and commitment.*
- PREP. **about** *What do you most admire about her?* **for** *I rather admire him for his determination.*
- PHRASES **be generally/widely admired** *He is widely admired as a journalist.* **can't/couldn't help admiring/but admire** *I couldn't help but admire his determination.* **you can only admire sb/sth** *You can only admire her courage and determination.*

2 look at sth attractive
- VERB + ADMIRE **pause to, stop to** | **stand/step back to** *He stood back to admire his handiwork.*

admirer noun

- ADJ. **ardent, devoted, fervent, great, keen** | **secret** *Perhaps the flowers were sent by a secret admirer!*
- QUANT. **band, circle, host** *She was always surrounded by a circle of admirers.*
- VERB + ADMIRER **have** | **gain, win** *She soon gained admirers in England and France.*
- PHRASES **friends and admirers** *The funeral was attended by the singer's friends and admirers.*

admission *noun*

1 entrance
- ADJ. **free, half-price** | **emergency** *emergency admissions to hospital* | **cinema, hospital, school, university**
- VERB + ADMISSION **apply for, seek** *He's applied for admission to the local college.* | **gain** *to gain admission to university* | **grant sb** | **refuse sb**
- ADMISSION + NOUN **charge, fee, price** | **criteria, policy** | **procedure** | **rate** *hospital admission rates*
- PREP. **on~** *On admission to hospital, you will be examined by a doctor.* | **~to**

2 statement admitting sth
- ADJ. **clear, frank, full** *This is a clear admission that you were wrong.* | **tacit** | **grudging**
- VERB + ADMISSION **make**
- PREP. **~of** *She has made no admission of any involvement in the plot.*
- PHRASES **an admission of defeat/failure/guilt/liability** *She saw his leaving the company as an admission of failure.* **by sb's own admission** *By his own admission he should never have driven so fast.*

admit *verb*

- ADV. **freely, readily** *He freely admitted that he had taken bribes.* | **frankly, honestly** | **openly** | **privately** *Some ministers admit privately that unemployment could continue to rise.* | **grudgingly, reluctantly** *In the end he'd done a good job, Caroline admitted grudgingly.*
- VERB + ADMIT **be forced to, have to, must** *I must admit that the results were disappointing.* | **refuse to** | **be honest enough to, be prepared to, be the first to, be willing to, dare (to), have the courage to** *He was honest enough to admit his mistake.* ◊ *She would be the first to admit that she is very difficult to work with.* ◊ *She dared not admit her fear.* | **be ashamed to, be embarrassed to, be loath to, be reluctant to, be unwilling to, hate to, not care to** *I hate to admit it, but I think he is right.* ◊ *He had caused her more pain than she cared to admit.*
- PREP. **to** *He admitted to feeling a bit tired.*
- PHRASES **I don't mind admitting** *I was scared and I don't mind admitting it.*

admittance *noun*

- VERB + ADMITTANCE **gain** *They were unable to gain admittance to the hall.* | **allow sb** | **deny sb, refuse sb**
- PREP. **~to** *The ticket will allow you admittance to the theatre.*

adolescence *noun*

- ADJ. **early, late**
- VERB + ADOLESCENCE **reach**
- PREP. **during/in~** *She developed the problem in early adolescence.*

adolescent *noun*

- ADJ. **young** | **spotty** | **awkward, disturbed**

adopt *verb*

1 child
- ADV. **legally** *The child has now been legally adopted.*
- PHRASES **have sb adopted** *She was forced to have her baby adopted.*

2 take and use sth
- ADV. **formally, officially** *The policy has not yet been formally adopted.*
- VERB + ADOPT **tend to** | **decide to** | **be forced to**
- PREP. **towards** *the policies employers adopt towards the labour force*

adoption *noun*

1 of child
- VERB + ADOPTION **offer sb for, place sb for, put sb up for** *She has decided to put the child up for adoption.* | **be available for** *When will the child be available for adoption?*
- ADOPTION + VERB **go through** *They were so happy when the adoption went through successfully.*
- ADOPTION + NOUN **agency**

2 taking/using sth
- ADJ. **general, widespread** | **formal** *The party announced the formal adoption of George Smith as their election candidate.*
- VERB + ADOPTION **recommend, urge** *The committee recommended the adoption of new safety procedures.*

adore *verb*

- ADV. **absolutely, simply** *She absolutely adores her grandchildren.* | **clearly, obviously**

adrenalin *noun*

- ADJ. **pure**
- QUANT. **burst, flow, rush, surge** *He felt a surge of pure adrenalin as he won the race.*
- VERB + ADRENALIN **feel**
- ADRENALIN + VERB **course, flow, pump, surge** *The adrenalin was coursing through his system.*
- ADRENALIN + NOUN **rush**
- PHRASES **get the adrenalin flowing/going** *We'll start with a bit of dancing to get the adrenalin going.*

adrift *adj.*

- VERBS **be** | **come** *I nearly suffocated when the pipe of my breathing apparatus came adrift.* | **cast sb/sth, cut sb/sth, set sb/sth** *Their boat had been set adrift.*
- PREP. **from** *(figurative) She had been cut adrift from everything she had known.* **in** *(figurative) cast adrift in a vulgar, materialistic society*

adult *noun*

- ADJ. **young** *This book will definitely appeal to teenagers and young adults.* | **single** *The number of single adult households has doubled in the past 30 years.* | **consenting** *What consenting adults do in private is their own business.* | **responsible** *I simply can't believe that responsible adults allowed a child to wander the streets.*
- ADULT + NOUN **life** *She spent her entire adult life caring for others.* | **education, literacy** | **population**

adultery *noun*

- VERB + ADULTERY **be guilty of, commit** | **accuse sb of** | **admit**
- PREP. **~with** *He admitted adultery with several women.*

adulthood *noun*

- ADJ. **early, young**
- VERB + ADULTHOOD **attain, reach** *children who lose their parents before reaching adulthood* | **make it to, survive into/to**
- PREP. **during/in~** *His problems began in early adulthood.* **into~** *Her childhood problems persisted into adulthood.* **towards~** *a step towards adulthood*

advance *noun*

1 forward movement
- ADJ. **rapid** | **Allied, British, German, etc.**
- VERB + ADVANCE **make** *The regiment made an advance on the enemy lines.* | **order** *The general ordered an advance to the front line.* | **halt, resist, stop**

● PREP. **on** ~ *the advance on Leningrad* **to** ~, **towards** ~ *the Russian advance towards Berlin*

2 development
● ADJ. **big, considerable, dramatic, enormous, great, spectacular, substantial, tremendous | important, major, notable, remarkable, significant | rapid, steady** *rapid advances in science and technology* **| recent |** **economic, educational, medical, political, scientific, social, technical, technological | theoretical**
● VERB + ADVANCE **make** *We need more money if we are to make any further advances in this area of science.*
● PREP. **in** ~ *two major advances in orthopaedic medicine* **on** ~ *an advance on the existing techniques* **towards** ~ *an advance towards a better understanding of God*

3 money
● ADJ. **large | cash**
● VERB + ADVANCES **give, pay** *The publishers have paid me an advance.* **| get, receive**
● PREP. ~**of** *an advance of £10 000* ~**on** *He was paid £5 000 as an advance on royalties.*

4 advances sexual
● ADJ. **amorous, sexual**
● VERB + ADVANCES **make** *He made amorous advances to one of his students.*
● PREP. ~**to**

advance *verb*

1 move forward
● ADV. **quickly, rapidly | cautiously, slowly**
● PREP. **from** *advancing from the south* **into** *The troops advanced into central Europe.* **on/upon** *The army advanced on the capital.* **towards** *He advanced towards me in aggressive style.*

2 develop
● ADV. **considerably, greatly, significantly | rapidly**
● PREP. **beyond** *Society needs to advance beyond prejudice and superstition.*

advanced *adj.*

1 modern and highly developed
● VERBS **be**
● ADV. **extremely, highly, very** *a highly advanced economy* **| fairly, quite, relatively | industrially, technically, technologically**

2 at a late stage of development
● VERBS **be**
● ADV. **far, greatly, well** *The disease was too far advanced for doctors to operate.* **| fairly, quite | further**

advancement *noun*

● ADJ. **individual, personal | collective | career | social | material** *society's need for material advancement* **| economic, scientific, technical, technological**
● PREP. ~ **in** *advancements in science* ◊ *advancement in the profession* ~ **to** *her advancement to the position of Supervisor*
● PHRASES **an opportunity for advancement** *There are good opportunities for advancement within the company.*

advantage *noun*

1 thing that helps
● ADJ. **big, considerable, enormous, great, huge, overwhelming | clear, decided/decisive, definite, distinct, material, obvious, positive, real** *Breastfeeding offers a clear advantage to your baby.* **| key, main, major, important, significant | dubious | unfair** *The company has an unfair advantage over its competitors.* **| added, additional** *These computers have the added advantage of being cheap.* **| special | potential | comparative, relative | mutual** *The plan would be to our mutual advantage.* **|**

natural *the natural advantages of countries with low labour costs* **| commercial, competitive, economic, educational, electoral, financial, military, personal, political, practical, psychological, social, strategic, tactical, technical, technological | cost, price, speed, tax**
● VERB + ADVANTAGE **have | gain, get** *He would gain considerable advantage from staying in that job.* **| bring (sb), give sb, offer (sb)** *Another qualification would give me a big advantage at job interviews.* **| press home** *The commanders were keen to press home their advantage with a further offensive in the north.* **| outweigh** *They argue that the possible risks attached to such vaccines vastly outweigh any advantages.*
● PREP. **to sb's** ~ *It is to your advantage to delay things for as long as possible.* **| ~ in** *There may be some advantage in laying down a clearer procedure.* ~ **over** *East coast resorts have the advantage over west coast ones.* ~ **to** *the advantage to both countries of closer economic ties*
● PHRASES **to good advantage, to sb/sth's best advantage** *The bright lighting showed the jewels to their best advantage.*

2 take advantage of make use of
● ADJ. **full, maximum** *We took full advantage of the hotel facilities.*

advantageous *adj.*

● VERBS **be, prove** *Membership of the union could prove advantageous.* **| become | make sth** *Lower fares make it advantageous to travel in winter.* **| find sth** *You may find it advantageous to wait a few weeks before replying.*
● ADV. **extremely, highly, very | fairly, quite | mutually** *This trade arrangement could be mutually advantageous* **| economically, financially | politically**
● PREP. **for** *This scheme could be advantageous for people on low incomes.* **to** *The new tax system is advantageous to higher-rate taxpayers.*

adventure *noun*

● ADJ. **big, exciting, great, wonderful | little** *We had a little adventure yesterday.* **| dangerous, perilous | hair-raising** *hair-raising adventure films* **| romantic | fantasy, foreign, historical, military, sexual**
● VERB + ADVENTURE **embark on, have | be looking for, want** *Those of you looking for adventure can shoot the rapids.* **| offer** *Perhaps the war offered adventure, travel, a use for his gifts.*
● ADVENTURE + NOUN **film, novel, story | holiday | playground**
● PHRASES **quite an adventure** (= very exciting) *Our trip to London was quite an adventure for the children.* **a sense/spirit of adventure** *The journey began cheerfully with a sense of adventure.*

adverb *noun*

● ADJ. **interrogative, sentence**
● ADVERB + VERB **modify sth, qualify sth** *Adverbs qualify verbs.*
● PHRASES **an adverb of degree/manner/place/time**

adversary *noun*

● ADJ. **fearsome, formidable | worthy** *The British considered him a worthy adversary.* **| old** *The two of them were old adversaries.*

adversity *noun*

● VERB + ADVERSITY **be faced with, meet with** *When faced with adversity she was never tempted to give up.* **| overcome, triumph over**
● PREP. **in** ~ *patience in adversity*
● PHRASES **in the face of adversity** *courage in the face of adversity*

advert noun

• ADJ. **classified, front-page, full-page | magazine, newspaper, television/TV | chocolate, job,** etc.
• VERB + ADVERT **place, put, take out** *I put an advert in the local newspaper.* ◇ *She took out a full-page advert in a magazine.* | **carry, publish, run, show** *The paper ran our advert last week.* | **find, see, spot** *I saw the advert in 'The Times'.* | **answer, reply to, respond to**
• ADVERT + VERB **appear** *The advert appeared in 'The Guardian'.* | **say sth, show sth, state sth | feature sb/sth** *The advert featured a dolphin swimming around a goldfish bowl.*
• PREP. **in a/the~** *A lot of claims are made in the advert.* | **~for** *an advert for jeans*

advertise verb

• ADV. **heavily** *These products have been advertised very heavily.* | **widely** *There are plans to advertise the job more widely.* | **locally, nationally**
• PREP. **for** *We are advertising for a babysitter.*

advertisement noun

• ADJ. **good | discreet | misleading | classified, front-page, full-page** *The classified advertisements are on page 25.* | **magazine, newspaper, press, television/TV | cigarette, job,** etc.
• VERB + ADVERTISEMENT **place, put, take out** *We placed advertisements in a number of national newspapers.* | **carry, display, publish, run, show** *Television and radio refused to carry advertisements for the record.* | **find, see, spot | answer, reply to, respond to**
• ADVERTISEMENT + VERB **appear | say sth, show sth, state sth | feature sb/sth**
• PREP. **in a/the~** *A lot of claims are made in the advertisement.* | **~for**

advice noun

• ADJ. **constructive, excellent, good, helpful, practical, sensible, sound, useful, valuable** *That's very sound advice.* | **bad, wrong** *I think my solicitor gave me the wrong advice.* | **clear | general | detailed | conflicting | confidential | impartial, independent | free | expert, professional, specialist | financial, legal, medical**
• QUANT. **bit, piece, word** *Can I give you a friendly word of advice?*
• VERB + ADVICE **give (sb), offer (sb), pass on, provide (sb with)** *I hope I can pass on some useful advice.* | **get, obtain, receive, take** *I think you need to take legal advice.* | **ask (for), go to sb for, seek, turn to sb for** *Go to your doctor and ask for advice.* ◇ *She asked her mother's advice.* | **accept, act on, follow, heed, listen to, take** *I wished that I had followed her advice.* | **ignore, reject**
• ADVICE + NOUN **centre** *The Local Authority runs an advice centre in the town.*
• PREP. **against sb's~** *Permission was given against the advice of the planning officers.* **on sb's~** *On the advice of his experts he bought another company.* | **~about** *advice about bringing up children* **~for** *Here is some advice for pregnant women.* **~ on** *Can you give me some advice on where to buy good maps?* **~to** *My advice to you would be to wait a few months.*

advisable adj.

• VERBS **be, seem | consider sth, deem sth, think sth** *We thought it advisable to seek police assistance.*
• ADV. **always** *It is always advisable to make a will.*

advise verb

1 tell sb what you think they should do
• ADV. **strenuously, strongly** *I strongly advise you not to do this.* | **badly, wrongly** *We were badly advised by our solicitor.* | **properly | legally**
• PREP. **about** *We can advise parents about education.* **against** *They advised me against sending cash by post.* **on** *We will be happy to advise on any financial matters.*
• PHRASES **be ill/well advised to do sth** *John would be ill advised to rely on their support.* ◇ *You would be better advised to consult an accountant.*

2 inform sb of sth
• VERB + ADVISE **be pleased to** *I am pleased to advise you that your application has been accepted.* | **regret to**
• PREP. **of**
• PHRASES **keep sb advised** *Please keep me advised of new developments in this case.*

adviser noun

• ADJ. **chief, lead, principal, senior, special** *the government's chief medical adviser* | **close, trusted** *The duke was the king's most trusted adviser.* | **personal | expert, professional | independent | government, presidential | business, careers, economic, environmental, financial, legal, medical, military, policy/political, public relations, scientific, security, technical**
• VERB + ADVISER **act as | appoint, appoint sb (as) | have** *Do you have a financial adviser?* | **consult (with), go to, see, speak to, talk to** *You ought to consult an independent legal adviser.*
• ADVISER + VERB **advise sb/sth**
• PREP. **~on** *an adviser on environmental issues* **~to** *She acts as an adviser to the president.*

advocate noun

1 sb who supports sth
• ADJ. **ardent, enthusiastic, firm, great, outspoken, powerful, staunch, strong** *She's a staunch advocate of free trade.* | **chief, leading, main, principal**
• PREP. **~for** *He is one of the leading advocates for a more modern style of worship.* **~ of** *an advocate of pacifism*

2 lawyer
• ADJ. **defence**
⇨ Note at PROFESSIONAL (for verbs)

advocate verb

• ADV. **seriously, strongly** *Heart specialists strongly advocate low-cholesterol diets.*
• PHRASES **be widely advocated** *These policies have been widely advocated.*

aerial noun

• ADJ. **radio, television/TV**
• AERIAL + VERB **transmit sth | pick sth up, receive sth** *The aerial receives signals from the ground.*

aeroplane noun

• ADJ. **private | vintage | model, paper**
• VERB + AEROPLANE **fly in, go in, travel in** *I've never flown in an aeroplane.* | **fly, pilot**
• AEROPLANE + VERB **fly** *aeroplanes flying overhead* | **take off | come down, land | crash | carry sb/sth** *The aeroplane was carrying 350 people.*
• PREP. **in a/the~** *flying in an aeroplane* **on a/the~** *The president was never on the aeroplane at all.*
⇨ See PLANE

affair noun

1 event/situation
• ADJ. **whole** *She saw the whole affair as a great joke.* | **glittering, grand** *I knew that the wedding would be a grand affair.* | **sordid, sorry, squalid**
• VERB + AFFAIR **deal with, handle** *Many people have*

criticized the way the government handled the affair. | **be involved in** | **investigate**
● PHRASES **sb's involvement in the affair** *He has tried to play down his involvement in the affair.* **a state of affairs** *How did this state of affairs come about?* **wash your hands of the affair** (= to refuse to be responsible for sth or involved in sth)

2 sexual relationship
● ADJ. **brief, casual** | **clandestine, secret** | **adulterous, extramarital** | **passionate, torrid** | **unhappy** | **love** *a torrid love affair*
● VERB + AFFAIR **carry on, conduct, have** *He's having an affair with a colleague.*
● AFFAIR + VERB **go on** *How long has the affair been going on?*
● PREP. **~between** *It's the story of a secret affair between a married teacher and her teenage student.* **~with** *an affair with a married man*

3 sth that concerns one person/small group
● ADJ. **family, personal, sb's own** *It's a family affair.*
● PHRASES **sb's affair** *What I do at the weekend is my affair.* **no affair of sb's** *That's no affair of yours.*

4 affairs important matters
● ADJ. **current** *a current affairs programme on television* | **private, public** | **domestic, home, internal, national** | **community, local** | **European, foreign, external, international, world** *the minister for foreign affairs* | **business, financial, legal** | **commercial, consumer, cultural, economic, environmental, military, political, religious, social**
● VERB + AFFAIRS **administer, arrange, attend to, conduct, manage, run** *I am trying to arrange my father's financial affairs.* | **settle, wind up** | **interfere in, meddle in**
● PHRASES **affairs of state** *The Cabinet will be discussing certain affairs of state.* **put/set your affairs in order** *I want to put my affairs in order before I die.* **a state of affairs** *the current state of affairs in schools*

affect *verb*

1 influence
● ADV. **greatly, materially, radically, significantly, very much** | **barely, hardly, not unduly** *Sales did not seem unduly affected.* | **slightly** | **clearly** | **directly** | **indirectly** | **adversely, badly, seriously, severely**
● VERB + AFFECT **be likely to** *developments that are likely to affect the environment*

2 make sb sad/angry
● ADV. **deeply, profoundly** *Her death affected him deeply.*

affection *noun*

● ADJ. **deep, genuine, great, real, special, strong, warm** | **mutual**
● VERB + AFFECTION **feel, have, hold sb in, retain** *He was held in great affection by hundreds of students.* | **display, express, give sb, show (sb)** | **get, receive** | **crave, need, want** *He just wants a bit of affection.* | **gain, win** *She had tried hard to win his affection.* | **alienate**
● PREP. **with ~** *He'll be remembered with genuine affection.* | **~for** *I have a deep affection for his mother.* **~to/towards** *The teacher showed affection towards all her pupils.*
● PHRASES **a display of affection** *I don't go in for public displays of affection.* **a feeling of affection** *a strong feeling of affection,* **love and affection** *I yearn for the love and affection I once had.* **the object of sb's affections** *The object of his affections was a young opera singer.* **a sign of affection, a show of affection**

affinity *noun*

1 strong feeling that you like/understand sb/sth
● ADJ. **close, great, natural, real, special, strong** *I felt a great affinity with the people of the Highlands.* | **natural** *He has a natural affinity with numbers.*
● VERB + AFFINITY **feel, have, share** *It's important that you share an affinity with your husband.* | **display, show**
● PREP. **~between** *an affinity between the two women* **~for** *Many girls do show an affinity for craft skills.* **~towards** *Jo feels a great affinity towards Pamela.* **~with** *an affinity with animals*

2 similar quality in two or more people/things
● ADJ. **close, great**
● QUANT. **degree, level**
● VERB + AFFINITY **have** *A house design should have some affinity with the surrounding architecture.* | **show** *In his poems he showed some affinity with Coleridge.*
● PREP. **~between** *There is a close affinity between these two species.* **~with** *an affinity with earlier poets*

afflict *verb*

● ADV. **badly, severely**
● PHRASES **be afflicted with** *He's badly afflicted with a skin disorder.*

afford *verb*

● ADV. **easily, well** *She can well afford to pay for herself.* | **barely, hardly, ill, (only) just, not really** *an amount which we could ill afford to pay*
● VERB + AFFORD **be able/unable to, can/can't, could (not)** *I can't afford to eat in restaurants.*

affront *noun*

● ADJ. **personal**
● VERB + AFFRONT **cause** | **regard/see/take sth as** *He took his son's desertion as a personal affront.*
● PREP. **~to** *This remark caused affront to many people.*

afloat *adj.*

1 floating on water
● VERBS **be** | **remain, stay** | **set sth** *The children set their new boat afloat on the lake.* | **keep sth** *struggling to keep the vessel afloat*

2 able to survive financially
● VERBS **keep, stay** *He is struggling to keep afloat after a series of emotional and health problems.* | **keep sth** *They had to sell their assets to keep the business afloat.*

afraid *adj.*

● VERBS **be, feel, look, seem** | **become, grow** | **make sb** *What has made you so deeply afraid of your boss?*
● ADV. **deeply, desperately, extremely, horribly, mortally, really, terribly, very** | **almost** *She was tense, almost afraid to open the letter.* | **a bit, half, a little, rather, slightly** *He was half afraid to look at her.* | **just, simply** *You do know, don't you? You are just afraid to tell me.* | **genuinely** | **suddenly** *He stopped abruptly, suddenly afraid to say the words out loud.* | **physically**
● PREP. **for** *Roger was very afraid for her.* **of** *Charlie is afraid of marriage.*
● PHRASES **nothing to be afraid of** *Don't worry. There's nothing to be afraid of.*

aftermath *noun*

● ADJ. **immediate** *The president visited the region in the immediate aftermath of the disaster.*
● VERB + AFTERMATH **cope with, deal with** *How does a country cope with the aftermath of war?*

● PREP. **in the ~ of** *He first took office in the aftermath of the civil war.*

afternoon *noun*

● ADJ. **this, tomorrow, yesterday | Friday, Saturday,** etc. **| early, late | April, May,** etc. **| spring, summer,** etc. **| long** *the long sunny afternoons* **| golden, hot, sunny, warm | grey, rainy, wet**
● VERB + AFTERNOON **spend** *We spent the afternoon sitting by the pool.*
● AFTERNOON + VERB **progress, wear on** *As the afternoon wore on he began to look unhappy.*
● AFTERNOON + NOUN **tea** *Afternoon tea is served on the terrace.* **| light, sun** *The afternoon sun shone full on her.*
● PREP. **by~, during the~, in the~, on Monday,** etc. **~**
● PHRASES **an/the afternoon off** *You deserve an afternoon off.*

age *noun*

1 how old sb/sth is
● ADJ. **early, young** *He was sent away to school at an early age.* **| advanced, great, old** *He was still active even at the advanced age of 87.* ◇ *White hair is a sign of great age.* ◇ *She dreaded old age.* **| middle** *a pleasant woman in early middle age* **| childbearing, pensionable, retirement, school, school-leaving, voting, working** *children of school age*
● VERB + AGE **attain, get to, live to, reach** *When you get to my age you get a different perspective on life.* ◇ *She lived to the age of 75.* **| feel, look** *She was beginning to feel her age* (= feel that she was getting old). **| lower, raise** *The voting age was lowered from 21 to 18 years.*
● AGE + NOUN **group, range | limit**
● PREP. **at a/the~** *At your age, I had already started work.* **between the~s** *children between the ages of five and eleven* **by the~** *He could read by the age of four.* **for sb's~** *He's quite a big boy for his age.* **over the~** *Twelve million people in Great Britain are over retirement age.* **under~** *It is illegal to sell alcohol to children who are under age* (= not legally old enough). **under the~** *It is illegal to sell alcohol to children under the age of 18.* **with~** *A lot of wines improve with age.* **| ~of** *He left school at the age of 18.*
● PHRASES **the age of consent** *The general age of consent for sexual activity is 16.* **sb's own age** *She needs a friend of her own age to play with.* **years of age** *He's 20 years of age.*
⇨ See OLD AGE

2 period of history
● ADJ. **another, different** *This exquisite little hotel seemed to belong to a different age.* **| Elizabethan, Victorian,** etc. **| Bronze, Ice, Stone | computer, modern, nuclear,** etc. **| golden** *the golden age of cinema*
● PREP. **during the~** *He lived during the Elizabethan age.* **in a/the~** *In an age when few women became politicians, her career was unusual.* **through the~s** *an exhibition of spinning through the ages* **| ~of** *the age of wireless communication*
● PHRASES **in this day and age** (= in the period we now live in) *Why dress so formally in this day and age?*

3 ages/an age a very long time
● VERB + AGE **spend, take** *It took an age for us all to get on the boat.*
● PHRASES **absolutely ages** *I've been sitting here for absolutely ages.* **ages ago** *Carlos left ages ago.* **for ages** *We had to wait for ages!*

age *verb*

● ADV. **considerably, greatly, a lot, really** *The shock has aged her considerably.* ◇ *My mother has really aged since she became ill.* **| a little** *He had put on weight and aged a* little. **| rapidly, suddenly** *a rapidly ageing population* **| prematurely | well** *This wine has not aged well.*

agency *noun*

● ADJ. **official | federal, government, public, state | UN | external, independent, outside | commercial, private | voluntary | international, local | multilateral | adoption, advertising, aid, dating, employment, estate, intelligence, marketing, news, press, recruitment, relief, research, travel,** etc. **| appropriate** *Details of the problem will be logged by the Help Desk staff who will then contact the appropriate agency.*
● PREP. **through an/the ~** *He managed to find a job through an agency.*
⇨ Note at ORGANIZATION (for verbs)

agenda *noun*

● ADJ. **agreed | clear** *A clear agenda will win votes in the next election.* **| five-point,** etc. *An 18-point agenda was drawn up for the meeting.* **| hidden, secret** *He accused the government of having a hidden agenda.* **| real | full | narrow** *The party has a rather narrow political agenda.* **| radical | public | domestic, international | economic, legislative, policy/political, research**
● VERB + AGENDA **have | agree on, draw up, establish, set** *The college needs to draw up an agenda for change.* **| follow** *We were following an agenda set by the students themselves.* **| add sth to, put sth on** *I will put this on the agenda for the next meeting.* **| leave sth off, remove sth from, take sth off** *The question of pay had been left off the agenda.* **| circulate** *A copy of the agenda is circulated to delegates a month before the conference.*
● AGENDA + NOUN **item**
● PREP. **on a/the~** *Safety at work is on the agenda for next month's meeting.* **off the~** (figurative) *An expensive holiday is definitely off the agenda this year* (= not sth we can consider). **| ~for** *We have an agreed agenda for action.*
● PHRASES **firmly/high on the agenda** *In our company, quality is high on the agenda.* **an item/a point on the agenda, next on the agenda** *Next on the agenda is deciding where we're going to live.* **top of the agenda** *Improving trade between the two countries will be top of the agenda at the talks.*
⇨ Special page at MEETING

agent *noun*

1 works in an agency
● ADJ. **advertising, election, estate, insurance, land, letting, literary, managing, parliamentary, patent, press, publicity, travel | local** *The company has developed sales through local agents in key markets.*
● VERB + AGENT **employ, have, use** *I have an agent who deals with all my contracts.* **| appoint, engage, get (sb), hire** *If you want to get published, get yourself an agent!* **| act as | sack**
● PREP. **through an~** *She got the work through an agent.* **| ~for** *an agent for a shipping company*
⇨ Note at JOB

2 spy
● ADJ. **intelligence | enemy, foreign | federal, government | secret, undercover | double** *As a double agent, he worked for the Americans and the Russians.*
● VERB + AGENT **work as**

3 person/thing that has an effect
● ADJ. **chief, main, primary, prime, principal | effective | human | moral, rational | free** *I told him I couldn't stop him, he was a free agent.*
● PREP. **~for** *The charity is an agent for social change.*
● PHRASES **an agent for/of change**

aggravate verb

- ADV. **greatly, seriously, severely** *Their negative reactions have greatly aggravated the situation.* | **further**

aggression noun

- ADJ. **extreme, intense** | **controlled, mild** | **naked, open** *a display of naked aggression* | **pent-up** *ways of releasing pent-up aggression* | **unprovoked** | **physical, verbal** | **human** | **external, foreign** *The president announced that the country would not tolerate foreign aggression.* | **American, British, etc.** | **military, police**
- QUANT. **act** *Acts of aggression against local shop owners should be reported to the police.*
- VERB + AGGRESSION **display, express, show** *the brutality and aggression displayed by the soldiers* | **channel, direct** *He managed to channel his aggression into sport.* | **control** | **release** | **encourage** *Do toy guns encourage aggression?*
- PREP. **~ against, ~ by** *Aggression by one nationality against another often leads to war.* **towards** *It showed no aggression towards other dogs.*

aggressive adj.

1 likely to fight/argue with other people
- VERBS **be, feel, look, seem, sound** | **become, get** | **make sb** *Watching violence on TV makes some children more aggressive.*
- ADV. **extremely, particularly, really, very** | **increasingly** | **quite, rather** | **openly** *Her mood became openly aggressive when his name was mentioned.*
- PREP. **towards** *He warned that his dog was aggressive towards strangers.*

2 behaving in a determined way
- VERBS **be**
- ADV. **extremely, highly, very** *the company's highly aggressive marketing techniques* | **fairly, somewhat**

aggrieved adj.

- VERBS **be, feel, look, sound**
- ADV. **deeply, much, very** | **rather, slightly, somewhat**
- PREP. **at** *James was rather aggrieved at Cameron.* **by** *The villagers felt deeply aggrieved by the closing of the railway station.*

agility noun

- ADJ. **considerable, great, surprising** | **mental, physical** *I admired his considerable mental agility.*
- VERB + AGILITY **have** | **show** *She shows great agility on the tennis court.*
- PREP. **with ~** *He jumped over the wall with surprising agility.*

agitated adj.

- VERBS **be, feel, look, seem, sound** *He sounded very agitated on the phone.* | **become, get, grow** | **make sb**
- ADV. **deeply, extremely, highly, very** | **increasingly** | **a little, quite, rather, slightly** | **visibly**
- PREP. **about** *She's agitated about getting there on time.* **at** *She started to grow agitated at the sight of the spider.*
- PHRASES **in an agitated state** *By now he was in a very agitated state.*

agitation noun

1 worry/excitement
- ADJ. **acute, considerable, extreme, great**
- VERB + AGITATION **show** *trying not to show her agitation* | **conceal, hide** *He could not hide his agitation.*
- PREP. **in sb's ~** *He knocked his glass over in his agitation.* **with ~** *She was wriggling on the seat with agitation.*
- PHRASES **a feeling/state of agitation**

2 public protest
- ADJ. **growing** | **mass, popular, public** | **political**
- VERB + AGITATION **engage in, turn to** *The organization is turning to political agitation in order to achieve its aims.*
- PREP. **~ against** *There has been mass agitation against the president.* **~ for** *There is growing agitation for reform of local government.*

agony noun

- ADJ. **extreme, intense** | **absolute, pure, sheer** | **exquisite** | **mental, physical** | **death** *The little creature squirmed in its death agonies.*
- VERB + AGONY **endure, go through, suffer** *He endured agonies of loneliness and misery.* ◇ *They went through agony in the search for their missing relatives..* | **cause, inflict** *She was causing David a great deal of agony.* | **prolong** *Don't prolong the agony—just tell me the result!* | **groan in, scream in** | **be contorted in, writhe in** *His face was contorted in agony as he tried to lift himself out of the chair.*
- PREP. **in ~** *The soldier died in agony.* **in an ~ of** *She mumbled an apology in an agony of embarrassment.*
- PHRASES **a groan/scream of agony**

agree verb

1 share opinion
- ADV. **heartily, strongly, very much** *I very much agree with the prime minister.* | **absolutely, completely, entirely, fully, wholeheartedly** *I agree entirely with what you have said.* | **broadly, generally** *It is generally agreed that more funding is needed for education.* | **unanimously** | **gravely, lamely, meekly, soberly, tartly** *'That's true,' she agreed gravely.*
- VERB + AGREE **cannot** | **be inclined to** *I'm inclined to agree there's nothing we can do.*
- PREP. **about** *We don't always agree about everything.* **on/upon** *Are we all agreed on this?* **with** *Do you agree with me that the scheme won't work?*
- PHRASES **I couldn't agree more** *I couldn't agree more with what has just been said.* **I quite agree, I'm sure you will agree** *I'm sure you'll agree that this issue is vitally important to the success of the company.*

2 say yes
- ADV. **voluntarily** | **readily** *She suggested a walk in the open air and he readily agreed.* | **grudgingly, reluctantly** | **kindly** *Edith Harlow has kindly agreed to help.* | **tacitly** | **provisionally**
- PREP. **to** *He agreed to our proposals.*

3 decide
- ADV. **expressly** | **tacitly** | **verbally** | **provisionally** *It was provisionally agreed that 12 August was to be the date.*
- VERB + AGREE **be unable to, fail to** *The two countries were unable to agree on a common strategy.*
- PHRASES **agree to differ/disagree** *We must just agree to disagree on this point.* **(be) mutually agreed** *working towards mutually agreed goals* **internationally/nationally agreed** *nationally agreed guidelines*

agreeable adj.

1 pleasant
- VERBS **be, look, sound** *It all sounds very agreeable.* | **find sb/sth** *He finds her very agreeable.* | **make yourself** *She did her best to make herself agreeable.* **highly, most, particularly, very** *It was a most agreeable evening.* | **quite**
- ADV. **mutually** *We tried to negotiate a mutually agreeable solution.*

2 willing to accept/do sth
- VERBS **be**
- ADV. **perfectly, quite**
- PREP. **to** *He was perfectly agreeable to the idea.*

agreement *noun*

1 contract/decision
- ADJ. **draft** *The draft agreement will be available two weeks before the meeting.* | **formal, written** | **legal, (legally) binding** *The agreement will be legally binding.* | **informal, tacit, verbal** | **voluntary** | **definitive** | **bilateral, international, multilateral, national** | **ceasefire, credit, hire-purchase, peace, trade**
- VERB + AGREEMENT **negotiate, work towards** *We are working towards a formal ceasefire agreement.* | **conclude, enter into, reach, sign** *After hours of talks the government and the union have reached an agreement.* | **have** *We have an agreement to always tell each other the truth about everything.* | **be bound by** *We signed the agreement so we are now bound by it.* | **adhere to, honour, keep to, stick to** *You have not kept to our agreement.* | **break, go back on, renege on, violate** *Some employers reneged on agreements once the recession set in.*
- PREP. **in an/the ~** *a clause in the agreement* **under an/the ~** *Under the agreement, the farmer is not allowed to use this field.* | **~ between** *an agreement between the company and the unions* **~ on** *They signed two agreements on improving economic co-operation.* **~ with** *a trade agreement with China*
- PHRASES **breach of agreement** *He sued the company for breach of agreement.* **the terms of the agreement** *The terms of the agreement do not allow such exports.*

2 state of agreeing
- ADJ. **absolute, complete, full, total** | **broad, general, widespread** | **mutual**
- VERB + AGREEMENT **arrive at, come to, reach** *I am hopeful that we can come to an agreement.* ◊ *The two sides failed to reach agreement.* | **nod** *He nodded his agreement.* | **get** *We will need to get the agreement of the local council.*
- PREP. **by ~** *The separation is by mutual agreement.* **in ~** *I think we are all in agreement that prices should be kept low.* **in ~ with** *I am in agreement with you that she should be given more responsibilities.* **with ~** *With the agreement of all members of the club, we decided to organize a trip.* | **~ among** *There is agreement among teachers that changes need to be made.* **~ between** *As yet there is no agreement between the two sides.* **~ on** *As yet there is no agreement on policies.*
- ⇨ Special page at MEETING

agriculture *noun*
- ADJ. **modern** | **efficient** | **intensive** | **organic** | **sustainable** | **traditional** | **peasant** | **subsistence**
- VERB + AGRICULTURE **be employed in, be engaged in, work in** | **depend on** *50 % of the country's population depend on agriculture.*

aid *noun*

1 money, food, etc.
- ADJ. **emergency** | **humanitarian** | **cash, development, economic, financial, food, legal, medical, military, relief** *Legal aid* (= government money for legal advice) *is a fundamental part of our system of justice.* | **federal, government, state** | **bilateral, external, foreign, international, overseas** *The country relies on foreign aid*
- VERB + AID **appeal for, call for** *The country's president has appealed for international aid in the wake of the disaster.* | **extend, give (sb), grant (sb), provide (sb with), send (sb)** | **get, receive** | **depend on, rely on** | **promise** | **cut (off), suspend, withdraw, withhold** *The British government has now suspended humanitarian aid to the area.*
- AID + NOUN **agency, worker** | **budget, package, programme** *a $14 million aid package*

2 help
- VERB + AID **ask for, enlist** *We enlisted the aid of John and his family.* | **come/go to sb's** (= to help someone) *She screamed loudly and two people came to her aid.*
- PREP. **in ~ of** *collecting money in aid of charity* **with/without the ~ of** *She is now able to walk with the aid of a stick.*

3 person/thing that helps
- ADJ. **effective, essential, excellent, important, useful, valuable** | **classroom, teaching, training** | **audio-visual, computer, visual** | **hearing, walking** | **memory** | **buoyancy**
- PREP. **~ to** *essential aids to learning*
- ⇨ See FIRST AID

aide *noun*
- ADJ. **close, trusted** *one of the prime minister's closest aides* | **senior, top** | **junior** | **personal, presidential, royal**
- VERB + AIDE **act as, serve as, work as**
- PREP. **~ to** *He served as an aide to the former president.*

Aids *noun*
- ADJ. **full-blown** *Once you are infected you will—sooner or later—develop full-blown Aids.*
- QUANT. **case** *Six cases of Aids have been reported.*
- VERB + AIDS **have, suffer from** | **be/become infected with, contract, develop, get** | **die of** | **diagnose**
- AIDS + NOUN **patient, sufferer, victim** | **virus**
- PHRASES **the spread of Aids** *a worldwide campaign to prevent the spread of Aids*
- ⇨ Special page at ILLNESS

ailment *noun*
- ADJ. **common, minor, trivial** | **chronic, serious** | **childhood** | **physical** | **chest, heart, stomach**
- VERB + AILMENT **be afflicted with, get, have, suffer from** *I got all the usual childhood ailments.* | **cure, treat** | **cause**

aim *noun*

1 purpose/goal
- ADJ. **broad, general, overall** | **basic, central, essential, fundamental** | **chief, first, key, main, major, primary, prime, principal, overriding** | **sole** *His sole aim in life is to enjoy himself.* | **clear, explicit** *It is important to have a clear aim in view.* | **ambitious, high, worthy** *Simple truth must be the highest aim of any real enquiry.* | **limited, modest** | **legitimate** | **common** *I want to see a strong and united country in which people work together with common aims.* | **underlying** *Although the report covers many areas, its underlying aim is to ensure that another accident never happens.* | **immediate, initial** | **original** | **eventual, ultimate** *His ultimate aim was to force the prime minister to resign.* | **long-term, short-term** | **avowed, declared, express/expressed, stated** *The express aim of the treaty is to keep the whole region free from nuclear weapons.* | **war** | **policy/political, strategic**
- VERB + AIM **have** | **set yourself** | **achieve, fulfil** *You will have to work hard to achieve your aim.* | **further, pursue** *They were intent on furthering their aims.* ◊ *The country is still pursuing its aim of joining the EU.*
- PREP. **with the ~ of** *She started the organization with the aim of helping local people.*
- PHRASES **aims and objectives** *What are the aims and objectives of this visit?*

2 pointing weapon, etc.
- ADJ. **careful** *I'll take more careful aim next time.* | **poor** *His aim was poor and he missed the target.*
- VERB + AIM **take**
- PREP. **~ at** *He took aim at the target and fired.*

aim verb

1 try/plan to achieve sth
- ADV. **directly**
- PREP. **at** *She's aiming at a scholarship this year.* ◇ *The initiative is aimed at helping young people.* **for** *He is aiming for a win in this race.*
- PHRASES **aim high** (= to attempt to achieve a lot) *a young man who is prepared to aim high*

2 intend sth for sb
- ADV. **clearly, directly, squarely | largely, mainly, mostly, primarily, principally | particularly, specifically**
- PHRASES **be aimed at** *educational courses aimed particularly at older people*

3 point/direct sth at sb
- ADV. **directly, straight | deliberately**
- PREP. **at** *She aimed the gun straight at the intruder.* **for** *Aim for his legs, not his body.*

air noun

1 gas/space
- ADJ. **hot, warm | chill, cold, cool, crisp | clean, clear, fresh, pure** *We need some fresh air in this stuffy room!* | **sweet** *The air was sweet with incense.* | **foul/foul-smelling, polluted, stale** *the polluted air of our cities* ◇ *the musty smell of stale air* | **damp, humid | dry | still** *Nothing moved in the still air.* | **thin** *It's difficult carrying such heavy loads in the thin air of the mountains.* | **thick** *The air was thick with cigarette smoke.* | **country, mountain, sea | evening, morning, night** *Music filled the night air.*
- QUANT. **blast, gust** *We felt a blast of cold air as she opened the door.* | **current** *warm currents of air* | **breath** *He drew in another breath of air.*
- VERB + AIR **breathe (in), gulp in, suck in** *Land crabs breathe air and cannot swim.* ◇ *She gulped in the fresh mountain air.* | **fight for, gasp for** *She was gasping for air as she ran out of the burning house.* | **smell, sniff** *The dog stretched and sniffed the air.* | **fill, hang in** *The tang of some wild herb hung in the air.*
- AIR + VERB **blow, rise, waft** *The cool night air wafted in the open windows.*
- AIR + NOUN **pollution | quality** *equipment to monitor air quality* | **pressure | current**
- PREP. **in/into the ~** *I kicked the ball high into the air.* **through the ~** *Spicy smells wafted through the air.*
- PHRASES **in the open air** (= outside) *The market is held in the open air.*

2 for planes
- AIR + NOUN **travel | fare | traffic** *We are cleared by Air Traffic Control to taxi and take off.* | **crash, disaster | attack, strike** *Three buildings were bombed last night in an air strike on the city.*
- PREP. **by ~** (= by plane) *It only takes three hours by air.* **from the ~** *The hideout is clearly visible from the air.*
- PHRASES **in mid-air** *The two planes collided in mid-air.*

3 impression
- VERB + AIR **have, retain** *You have an air of authority.* | **add, bring, give (sth)** *A stone balcony gives the building an air of elegance.*
- PREP. **with an/the ~** *He leaned towards Melissa with an air of great confidentiality.* | **~ of**

air verb

- ADV. **in public, openly, publicly** *The issues were openly aired and discussed by the group.*

aircraft noun

- ADJ. **fixed-wing, jet, light, low-flying, microlight, supersonic** *attacks by helicopters and fixed-wing aircraft* | **cargo, civil/civilian, commercial, passenger, private | combat, fighter, military, reconnaissance, surveillance,**

transport | enemy | burning, crashed, damaged, stricken | model *His passion is making model aircraft.*
- VERB + AIRCRAFT **fly, pilot** *The aircraft was flown by a young American pilot.* | **land | crash** *The pilot overshot the runway and crashed his aircraft.* | **shoot down** *To be an ace you had to shoot down five enemy aircraft.*
- AIRCRAFT + VERB **fly | take off** *The aircraft is due to take off at midnight.* | **land | taxi** *The aircraft taxied along the runway.* | **crash | carry sth | attack sth, bomb sth**
- AIRCRAFT + NOUN **industry | production | manufacturer | engine, parts | engineer | hangar | noise** *He claimed that aircraft noise was the worst form of air pollution in London.* | **wreckage**

airline noun

- ADJ. **big, large, major | domestic, international, national | commercial, private, state/state-owned** *He operates a private airline.* | **charter, scheduled** *Prices on charter airlines are usually lower.*
- VERB + AIRLINE **operate, run**
- AIRLINE + VERB **fly, operate** *The airline operates mainly between Florida and Puerto Rico.*
- AIRLINE + NOUN **business, company, industry | flight, service** *All scheduled airline services will be affected by the strike.* | **employee, operator, pilot | passenger | reservation, ticket**

airport noun

- ADJ. **big, large, major | small | busy | domestic, international, local, regional | civilian, military**
- VERB + AIRPORT **depart from, fly from, take off from** *We will fly from Chicago's O'Hare airport.* | **arrive at, land at, touch down at** *The plane touched down at Glasgow airport just before midday.* | **pass through, use**
- AIRPORT + NOUN **building, terminal | lounge | security | hotel**
- PREP. **at an/the ~** *waiting at the airport*

airspace noun

- ADJ. **controlled, restricted | British, French, etc.**
- VERB + AIRSPACE **cross (into), drift into, enter, fly into, stray into, violate** *The jet had crossed into Russian airspace.* | **fly out of, pass out of | open** *They have decided to open their airspace to commercial aircraft.* | **close**
- PREP. **in ~** *The glider was in Dutch airspace.* **out of ~** *They were now out of controlled airspace.*
- PHRASES **a violation of airspace** *The president said that all future violations of our airspace would result in serious consequences.*

ajar adj.

- VERBS **be, stand** *The office door stood ajar.* | **leave sth** *She had left the kitchen door slightly ajar.*
- ADV. **slightly**

akin adj. akin to sth

- VERBS **be**
- ADV. **closely** *This game is closely akin to rugby.* | **somewhat** *A balalaika is an instrument somewhat akin to a guitar.*
- PHRASES **something akin to sth** *She was wearing something akin to a pineapple on her head.*

alarm noun

1 fear/worry
- ADJ. **considerable, great | growing | sudden | public** *There is growing public alarm at this increase in crime.* | **unnecessary**

• VERB + ALARM **cause, create, provoke** *The head teacher's policies have provoked alarm among parents.* | **express, register** *Many people have expressed alarm at the plans.* ◊ *His face registered no alarm at all when I told him the news.*
• PREP. **in~** *He shouted out in alarm.* **to sb's~** *To her parents' alarm, she announced that she intended to travel the world.* **with ~** *The news has been greeted with alarm.* | **~ about/at/over** *There has been considerable alarm about the new proposals.*
• PHRASES **alarm and despondency** (*often humorous*) *He loves spreading alarm and despondency.* **cause for alarm** *I see no cause for alarm, as she often arrives late.*

2 warning of danger
• ADJ. **false** *The fire service was called out, but it was a false alarm.*
• VERB + ALARM **give, raise, sound** *The guard raised the alarm when he discovered that six prisoners had escaped.*
• ALARM + NOUN **call** *Many birds give alarm calls to warn of danger.*

3 device
• ADJ. **fire, smoke | burglar, intruder, security | car | personal, rape** *Lizzie was carrying a rape alarm but it was out of reach in her handbag.* | **radio**
• VERB + ALARM **set** *I set my alarm for 6.30.* | **activate, set off, trigger** *Unfortunately any little noise can set off the alarm.* | **switch off, turn off | be fitted with** *The fire brigade recommends that every house is fitted with a smoke alarm.* | **fit, install | test**
• ALARM + VERB **go off, ring, sound** *The alarm went off at 7 o'clock.* ◊ *Suddenly the alarm sounded and they all had to leave the building.*
• ALARM + NOUN **bell, clock, signal, system | call** *Book an alarm call if you need to make an early start.*

alarmed *adj.*
• VERBS **be, feel, look, seem, sound | become, get, grow** *She began to grow alarmed when she realized how late it was.*
• ADV. **extremely, greatly, seriously, thoroughly, very | increasingly | faintly, a little, quite, rather, slightly | (not) unduly** *The government is not unduly alarmed by these figures.*
• PREP. **at** *She was alarmed at the prospect of travelling alone.* **by** *I was slightly alarmed by what Susan told me.*
• PHRASES **nothing to be alarmed about** *The doctors have decided to keep him in hospital overnight but there is nothing to be alarmed about.*

alarming *adj.*
• VERBS **be, seem | find sth** *I find the prospect of being without work extremely alarming.*
• ADV. **extremely, particularly, very | faintly, a little, quite, rather, slightly**

album *noun*
1 book
• ADJ. **family, wedding | photo/photograph, stamp**
• PREP. **in an/the~** *I keep the photographs in an album.*

2 CD/cassette/record
• ADJ. **best-selling, good, great** *Their best-selling album has won three awards.* | **debut, first | double | live | solo** *It's the singer's first solo album.* | **compilation**
• VERB + ALBUM **make, produce, record** *The singer recorded her second album in Los Angeles.* | **put out, release** *She has not put out a new album this year.*
• ALBUM + VERB **come out** *His latest album comes out in the spring.*
• ALBUM + NOUN **chart**

alcohol *noun*
• ADJ. **excess/excessive** *the dangers of excessive alcohol* | **pure** *Is it possible for cars to run on pure alcohol?*
• QUANT. **drop, unit** *You need to be careful how many units of alcohol you drink in a week.* | **level** *The driver had more than the permitted level of alcohol in his blood.*
• VERB + ALCOHOL **consume, drink | avoid, keep off, not touch, stay off** *I haven't touched a drop of alcohol for three weeks.* | **abuse** (*formal*) *Most drinkers do not abuse alcohol at all.*
• ALCOHOL + NOUN **content, level** *It can take a long time for blood alcohol levels to fall.* | **consumption, intake, use | abuse, addiction, misuse | problem** *People can find it hard to admit they have an alcohol problem.*
• PHRASES **low alcohol** (= containing very little alcohol) *a low alcohol beer*

alcoholic *noun*
• ADJ. **chronic | reformed**
• VERB + ALCOHOLIC **become, turn into** *Howe was turning into an alcoholic because of the stress of his job.*
• ALCOHOLIC + VERB **dry out, recover** *I don't think an alcoholic can dry out without proper medical help.*

alcoholism *noun*
• ADJ. **chronic**
• VERB + ALCOHOLISM **suffer from** *Three people in the family suffer from alcoholism.* | **combat, treat**
➪ Special page at ILLNESS

ale *noun*
• ADJ. **fine, good** *This pub specializes in fine ales.* | **real** (= made and stored in the traditional way), **traditional** *the growth in demand for real ale* | **brown, light, pale | strong**
• QUANT. **pint | barrel, bottle, can, glass, tankard** *Fresh barrels of ale were brought up from the cellar.*
• VERB + ALE **down** (*informal*), **drink, sip** *He drank several pints of ale.* | **brew, make**
• ALE + NOUN **house**

alert *noun*
• ADJ. **red** *His sudden disappearance triggered a red alert among his friends.* | **nationwide | bomb, fire, flood, pollution, security** *A security alert was issued after four men escaped from the prison.*
• VERB + ALERT **issue, put out, raise, sound** *They rang the church bells to sound the alert and the villagers then fled.* | **spark, trigger | call off** *The alert was called off when it was found that the bomb was not live.*
• ALERT + VERB **go out** *A nationwide alert went out for three escaped prisoners.*
• PREP. **on the~ | ~for** *You should always be on the alert for anyone who looks suspicious.*
• PHRASES **be on full alert** *The security forces are now on full alert.* **keep/place/put sb on full alert** *Thousands of police were put on full alert at all main roads leading to the city.* **a state of alert** *The army was yesterday placed on a state of alert in case of more riots.*

alert *adj.*
• VERBS **be, look, seem | become | remain, stay | keep sb** *The machine should help to keep the pilot alert.*
• ADV. **very | fully | immediately, instantly, suddenly** *There was a noise outside and he was suddenly alert.* | **always, constantly | mentally** *He was as mentally alert as a man half his age.*
• PREP. **to** *Climbers need to be alert to possible dangers.*

A level noun

● ADJ. **mock** *I did all right in my mock A levels and then failed the real exams.*
● VERB + A LEVEL **do, sit, take** *She's doing her A levels this year.* | **retake** | **do well in, pass** | **do badly in, fail, flunk** | **have** *She has four A levels.* | **prepare for, revise for** *He can't come out—he's revising for his A levels.*
● A LEVEL + NOUN **course** | **exam** | **preparation, revision** | **paper, questions** | **grades, results**
● PREP. **in your ~s** *What grades did you get in your A levels?* | **~ in** *He's got A levels in maths and history.*

alias noun

● VERB + ALIAS **adopt, use** *After her escape from prison, Claire Potter adopted the alias Margaret Smith.*
● PREP. **under an/the ~** (= using another name) *Five years ago he had lived in France under an alias.*

alibi noun

● ADJ. **cast-iron, good, perfect, solid** *She was in the office all of Wednesday and so has a cast-iron alibi.* | **false**
● VERB + ALIBI **have** | **establish, provide, supply** *The videotape would have been useful to establish alibis for the defendants.*
● PREP. **~ for** *The accused was not able to provide an alibi for the evening.*

alien noun

● ADJ. **enemy** *During the war, he was imprisoned as an enemy alien.* | **illegal** *Illegal aliens are usually deported to their country of origin.* | **undesirable** | **resident**

alien adj.

● VERBS **be, feel, seem** | **become** | **find sth** *It was an act of violence that she found alien and shocking.*
● ADV. **very** | **completely, entirely, totally, utterly** | **quite, somewhat** | **essentially** *living in an essentially alien culture*
● PREP. **to** *They spoke a language totally alien to him.*

alienation noun

● ADJ. **growing**
● PREP. **~ from** *his growing alienation from his family*
● PHRASES **a feeling/sense of alienation** *There is a growing feeling of alienation among young unemployed people.*

alight adj.

1 burning
● VERBS **be** | **catch** *His clothing caught alight.* | **remain, stay** *hoping that the fire would remain alight overnight* | **set sth** *The building had been set alight by the killer.* | **keep sth** *The fires had to be kept alight each night.*
● ADV. **well** *The fire should be well alight by now.*

2 excited
● VERBS **be**
● PHRASES **alight with excitement/laughter/pleasure** *The children's eyes were alight with excitement.*

align verb

● ADV. **accurately, correctly, properly** | **fully** | **roughly** | **horizontally, vertically**
● PREP. **along** *He argued that important historical sites were aligned along straight lines of mystic energy.* **with** *This pillar is roughly aligned with the others.*

PHRASAL VERB
align yourself with sb/sth
● ADV. **closely, firmly** *The group does not want to align itself too closely with the government.*

alignment noun

1 arrangement in correct position
● ADJ. **correct**
● VERB + ALIGNMENT **bring sth into**
● PREP. **in ~ (with sth)** *The door needs to be in alignment with the frame before you start work on it.* **out of ~** *A few of the tiles were clearly out of alignment.*

2 political support
● ADJ. **close** | **military, political**
● VERB + ALIGNMENT **establish, form** | **maintain**
● PREP. **~ between** *It is very difficult to maintain the alignment between the two countries since the trade dispute.* **~ with** *Britain formed a close alignment with Egypt in the last century.*

alike adj.

● VERBS **be, look, seem**
● ADV. **remarkably, very (much)** | **exactly** *Though John and Andrew look exactly alike, they act quite differently.*
● PREP. **in** *The two towns are very much alike in size and population.*

alive adj.

1 living
● VERBS **be, seem** | **remain, stay** *Lost and so far from other human life, he faced a desperate struggle to stay alive.* | **keep sb** *Doctors fought to keep her alive.* | **be buried, be burnt**
● ADV. **very much** *The old rascal is still very much alive.* | **barely, only half** *For four days he seemed barely alive.* | **still** *I wasn't sure if he was still alive.*
● PHRASES **alive and kicking** *My mother is still alive and kicking.* **alive and well** *At any moment he may turn up alive and well.* **dead or alive** *The police are desperate to catch this man dead or alive.* **lucky to be alive** *It was a very narrow escape and we are lucky to be alive.* **more dead than alive** *Poor child, she looks more dead than alive.*

2 full of life
● VERBS **be, feel, seem** *I feel really alive in the country!* | **come** *The city comes alive at night.* | **bring sb/sth** *The wealth of detail in his book really brings it alive.*
● ADV. **really, truly, very** | **fully** | **intensely** | **only half** *She realized that she had only been half alive for the last four years.* | **suddenly** *His eyes were suddenly alive with excitement.*
● PREP. **with** *The hall was alive with the sound of voices.*

3 continuing to exist
● VERBS **be** | **remain** | **keep sth** *The people try to keep the old traditions alive.*
● ADV. **very much** *The old customs are still very much alive in this region.*
● PHRASES **alive and well** *The art of debate is alive and well in our schools.*

4 aware of sth
● VERBS **be** | **become** | **remain**
● ADV. **very much** | **keenly**
● PREP. **to** *He remained keenly alive to the dangers.*

allegation noun

● ADJ. **damaging, serious** | **false, unfounded, unproven, unsubstantiated, untrue, wild** | **true** *The defendants in the libel case maintain that their allegations are true.* | **fresh, further, new** *There have been fresh allegations of atrocities.* | **widespread** | **corruption**
● VERB + ALLEGATION **make, publish** | **retract, withdraw** *I advise you to withdraw your allegation before I contact my lawyer.* | **be at the centre of, be confronted with, face** *the school at the centre of these allegations* | **deny, dismiss, dispute, reject** | **answer, counter, refute** *The minister has the right to answer specific allegations.* ◇ *He*

will need to counter allegations that he accepted money from criminals. | **prove, support** *The committee found no evidence to support allegations of smuggling.* | **disprove** *It took over two months to disprove the allegation.* | **give rise to, lead to, prompt, provoke** *The sudden collapse of the business led to allegations of corrupt deals.* | **examine, investigate, look into, probe** (used in journalism) *The governor of the prison is investigating allegations that a prisoner was attacked and beaten by a prison warder.*
• PREP. **amid/amidst ~** *He has resigned amid corruption allegations.* | **~ about/concerning** *allegations about the president's private life* **~ against** *He has made certain allegations against the company.*

allegiance noun

• ADJ. **full, strong** *We will give our full allegiance to the party and everything it believes in.* | **traditional** | **changing, shifting** *It is hard to keep up with the changing allegiances between the various political parties.* | **political, religious** | **class, party**
• VERB + ALLEGIANCE **give, owe** *He owed his allegiance to the organization that had given him all his opportunities.* | **pledge, swear** *The rebels now have to swear allegiance to the queen they hate.* | **abandon** *Many people have abandoned their traditional party allegiances.* | **change, shift, switch, transfer** | **claim** *The various splinter groups all claim allegiance to the true spirit of the movement.* | **claim, command** *Catholicism claims allegiance from more than 80% of the population.* | **retain** *The union needs to retain the allegiance of all its members for the strike to succeed.*
• PREP. **to ~** *He is now very rich but his allegiance to his working-class origins is still strong.*
• PHRASES **an oath of allegiance** *Every day the schoolchildren pledge an oath of allegiance to their country.*

allergy noun

• ADJ. **food**
• VERB + ALLERGY **have, suffer from** | **develop** | **cause** *Hair and feathers can cause allergies.*
• ALLERGY + NOUN **sufferer**
• PREP. **~ to** *He developed an allergy to pollen.*
⇨ Special page at ILLNESS

alleviate verb

• ADV. **considerably, greatly** *These problems have been greatly alleviated by the passing of the new Act.* | **partly, somewhat**
• VERB + ALLEVIATE **be designed to, help (to)** *These measures are designed to alleviate the situation.* | **do little/nothing to** *Her words did little to alleviate his fears.*

alley noun

• ADJ. **dark** | **little, narrow** *a maze of narrow alleys* | **stinking** *I don't want to be left for dead in some stinking alley.* | **cobbled** | **back, side**
• ALLEY + VERB **lead onto sth, lead to sth** *The alley leads to the village square.*
• ALLEY + NOUN **cat**
• PREP. **along an/the ~** *I walked back along a side alley.* **down an/the ~** *a bookshop down a little alley* **in an/the ~** *They had cornered him in an alley.* **through an/the ~** *She wandered through the back alleys.* **up an/the ~**

alliance noun

• ADJ. **broad** *The organization is a broad alliance of many different groups.* | **grand** | **close** | **powerful, strong** | **fragile, loose, uneasy** *a loose alliance of opposition groups* ◇ *The uneasy alliance between such different people just cannot last.* | **shifting** *the shifting alliances among the various political groups* | **formal, informal** |

strategic, working | **unholy** *an unholy alliance between the Fascists and the Communists* | **unlikely** | **temporary** | **global** | **defensive, military, electoral, political, class** | **marriage**
• VERB + ALLIANCE **have** *They have alliances with other companies.* | **build (up), create, enter into, forge, form, make, strike up** *The government has tried to forge alliances with environmentalists.* | **cement** *To cement the alliance with England, Charles married Margaret, sister of the English king.* | **break off** *They broke off the alliance with Sparta.* | **seek**
• PREP. **in ~ with** *The government, in alliance with the army, has decided to ban all public meetings for a month.* | **~ against** *old alliances against enemies that no longer exist* **~ between** *an alliance between Britain and France* **~ with** *an alliance with Germany*

allied adj.

• VERBS **be**
• ADV. **closely** | **loosely** *an offensive by seven loosely allied guerrilla groups*
• PREP. **to** *His decision to move to London is closely allied to his ambition to become manager of the company.* **with** *The party is allied with the Communists.*

allocate verb

• ADV. **efficiently** *Local authorities have to learn to allocate resources efficiently.* | **randomly**
• PREP. **for** *More money should be allocated for famine relief.* **to** *More funds will now be allocated to charitable organizations.*

allocation noun

1 process of giving sth out
• ADJ. **efficient, inefficient** | **random** | **budget, grant, housing, land, resource, time**
• VERB + ALLOCATION **make** *The allocation must be made according to a strict set of criteria.*
2 amount given to sb
• ADJ. **big, generous, large** | **modest** | **total**
• VERB + ALLOCATION **give** *The school gave them a generous allocation of money with which to purchase books.* | **get, receive** | **increase, up** *The charity is trying to get its allocation upped for next year.* | **cut, reduce**

allowance noun

1 amount of sth that you are allowed
• ADJ. **baggage, holiday**
• VERB + ALLOWANCE **be entitled to, get, have** *I get four weeks' holiday allowance a year.*
2 amount of money sb receives regularly
• ADJ. **generous, large** | **meagre, small** | **annual, daily, monthly, weekly** | **child, disability, family, housing, living, travel**
• VERB + ALLOWANCE **be entitled to** *You may be entitled to a housing allowance if you are in a low-paid job.* | **get, receive** | **give sb, grant** *The company gives me a travel allowance.*
• PREP. **~ for** *The weekly allowance for each child is £15.*

allusion noun

• ADJ. **clear, direct** | **indirect, veiled** *She was made uncomfortable by his veiled allusion to the previous night.* | **classical, cultural, literary**
• VERB + ALLUSION **make** *He makes several allusions to these events in his latest book.*
• PREP. **~ to**

ally noun

• ADJ. **great, important, powerful, strong** | **close**

Charles remained a close ally of the French king. | **loyal, reliable, staunch, trusted** | **natural, useful, valuable** | **old, traditional** *Portugal is a traditional ally of England.* | **erstwhile, former** | **wartime** | **potential** | **European, NATO, Western,** etc. | **political**
• VERB + ALLY **have** *Jane felt that she had an ally.* | **find, gain, get** | **lose**
• PREP. **~against** *He now had an ally against his boss.*
• PHRASES **find/have an ally in sb** *She had found an ally in her old teacher.* **a friend and ally** *a friend and ally of the president*

almond *noun*

• ADJ. **whole** | **blanched, flaked, ground** *biscuits made with ground almonds* | **sugared, toasted** | **bitter**
• ALMOND + NOUN **essence, oil, paste** | **blossom, tree**

alone *adj.*

• VERBS **be, feel, sit, stand** *These islands are too small to stand alone as independent states.* | **leave sb, let sb** *Don't touch me! Leave me alone!*
• ADV. **very much** *I felt vulnerable and very much alone.* | **all, completely, entirely, quite** *Carol felt all alone in the world.* ◇ *He felt lost and completely alone.* | **together** *Finally the two of us were alone together.*
• PREP. **with** *She did not want to be alone with him.*

aloof *adj.*

1 not friendly
• VERBS **be, look, seem** | **find sb** *Some people find her aloof and unfriendly.*
• ADV. **a bit, a little, somewhat**
2 not involved in sth
• VERBS **hold (yourself), keep (yourself), remain, stand** *Some thought that Britain was standing aloof from Europe.* | **keep sb** *There were many things that had kept her aloof and apart from the crowd.*
• ADV. **largely**
• PREP. **from** *He has remained largely aloof from the hurly-burly of parliamentary politics.*

alphabet *noun*

• ADJ. **Arabic, Cyrillic, Greek, Hebrew, Latin, Roman** | **phonetic, runic**
• VERB + ALPHABET **know, learn**
• PREP. **in the~** *How many letters are there in the Greek alphabet?*
• PHRASES **the letters of the alphabet**

altar *noun*

• ADJ. **high, main** | **makeshift, portable** | **sacrificial**
• VERB + ALTAR **approach, go up to** *The bride approached the altar.*
• ALTAR + NOUN **boy** | **cloth, frontal** | **rail** | **table**
• PREP. **at an/the~** *Helen and Tony knelt at the altar.* **before an/the~** *He lay prostrate before the high altar.* **on an/the~** *He placed the candles on the altar.*

alter *verb*

• ADV. **considerably, dramatically, drastically, fundamentally, greatly, radically, significantly, substantially** *He had not altered greatly in the last ten years.* | **slightly**
• PHRASES **not alter the fact that** *Unemployment has come down slightly but this does not alter the fact that it is still a major problem.*

alteration *noun*

• ADJ. **dramatic, extensive, fundamental, major, material, radical, significant, substantial** | **minor, slight, small, subtle**
• VERB + ALTERATION **make** | **need, require** *The leaflets require no alteration from year to year.*
• PREP. **~in** *There will be no alteration in corporation tax.* **~to** *We will have to make a slight alteration to the plans.*

alternative *noun*

• ADJ. **attractive, constructive, effective, good, radical, useful** | **acceptable, available, credible, possible, practical, real, realistic, reasonable, satisfactory, serious, suitable, viable** *Is there a viable alternative to prison?* | **clear, obvious** | **cheap, healthy, interesting, safe** *a healthier alternative to fizzy drinks*
• VERB + ALTERNATIVE **have** *We have two alternatives.* | **offer, provide** *His idea seemed to offer a possible alternative.* | **seek** *seeking alternatives to nuclear power* | **find** *We'll have to find an alternative.*
• PREP. **~for** *There is no alternative for those with no car of their own.* **~to** *Is there an alternative to surgery for this complaint?*
• PHRASES **have little/no alternative (but to)** *She had no alternative but to do as he said.* **leave sb with no alternative (but to)** *He was left with no alternative but to hobble to the nearest telephone box.*

altitude *noun*

• ADJ. **great, high** | **low** | **cruising** *The plane took off and climbed to cruising altitude.*
• VERB + ALTITUDE **cruise at, fly at, maintain** *The aircraft maintained an altitude of 28 000 feet.* | **reach, rise to** *The aviators reported the columns of smoke rising to an altitude of 2 000 feet.* | **gain** | **lose** *The plane suddenly started to lose altitude.*
• ALTITUDE + NOUN **sickness**
• PREP. **at an/the~** *No trees will grow at that altitude.*

amateur *noun*

1 sb who does sport, etc. for pleasure, not money
• ADJ. **competent, gifted, talented, top** | **enthusiastic, keen** | **gentleman** *International affairs today are no longer for gentleman amateurs.*
2 sb who is not very good at sth
• ADJ. **rank, real** *The others had been skiing since they could walk and made her look a rank amateur.*

amaze *verb*

• ADV. **really** *His skill as a dancer really amazed me.*
• VERB + AMAZE **never cease to** *It never ceases to amaze me what some people will do for money.*

amazed *adj.*

• VERBS **be, look, seem, sound, stand**
• ADV. **absolutely, quite, totally, utterly** | **mildly** | **genuinely** | **always, constantly, continually** | **still** *I am still amazed that she won first prize.*
• PREP. **at** *Frances was amazed at her sudden strength.* **by** *I was totally amazed by the brilliance of her paintings.*
• PHRASES **never cease to be amazed** *I never cease to be amazed at the way people hurt one another.*

amazement *noun*

• ADJ. **complete, sheer, utter** | **mock** *She raised her eyebrows in mock amazement.*
• VERB + AMAZEMENT **express**
• PREP. **in ~** *He stared at the animal in amazement.* **to sb's ~** *To her amazement she got the job.* **with ~** *Laura looked around her with amazement.* | **~ at** *He expressed amazement at being left out of the match.*

amazing adj.

- VERBS **be, look, sound, taste** | **find sb/sth**
- ADV. **just, pretty, really, truly** *He remembered our names from ten years ago— isn't that just amazing?* ◇ *a truly amazing achievement* | **absolutely, most, quite** *I saw the most amazing film yesterday!*

ambassador noun

- ADJ. **former** | **British, French, etc.**
- VERB + AMBASSADOR **serve as** | **appoint, appoint sb (as), make sb** *She's been appointed British ambassador to the UN.* | **send** *The King sent an ambassador to Paris.* | **recall, withdraw** *The US ambassador was recalled to Washington in protest.* | **expel**
- PREP. **~ in** *the Israeli ambassador in London* **~ to** *He served as ambassador to Syria.*

ambiguity noun

- ADJ. **possible, potential** | **moral, sexual**
- QUANT. **degree, element** *There is a degree of ambiguity in this statement.*
- VERB + AMBIGUITY **lead to** *Incorrect choice of words leads to ambiguity for the reader.* | **avoid** *The document has been carefully written to avoid ambiguity.* | **reduce** | **remove, resolve** *They had to change some of the wording in the document to resolve the ambiguity.*
- AMBIGUITY + VERB **arise, occur** *Ambiguity arises when students' spoken English is very limited.*
- PREP. **~ about** *There will always be some ambiguity about what actually happened.* **~ in** *There was some ambiguity in what he said.*
- PHRASES **a source of ambiguity**

ambiguous adj.

- VERBS **be** | **remain** | **make sth, render sth** *The paragraph is rendered ambiguous by the writer's careless use of pronouns.*
- ADV. **highly, very** | **rather, slightly, somewhat** | **deliberately, intentionally** *I suspected that he was being deliberately ambiguous.*

ambition noun

1 strong desire to be successful
- ADJ. **driving, great, naked** *She's a woman of driving ambition.* | **personal**
- VERB + AMBITION **have** *He's got little ambition.* | **lack**
- AMBITION + VERB **burn** *Ambition burned within her.*

2 sth you very much want to have/do
- ADJ. **big, burning, driving, great, high, main, overriding, ultimate** *Her biggest ambition was to climb Everest.* | **lifelong, life's, longstanding** *At last he had realized his life's ambition.* | **modest** | **personal** | **secret** | **youthful** | **frustrated, thwarted, unfulfilled** *This is a tale of jealousy and thwarted ambitions.* | **career, imperial/imperialist, literary, political, presidential, social, sporting, territorial**
- VERB + AMBITION **cherish, harbour, have, nurture** *He had only one ambition in life.* | **abandon, give up** | **achieve, fulfil, realize** | **limit, restrain** | **frustrate, thwart** *He felt great resentment at having his ambition frustrated.*

ambitious adj.

1 determined to be successful
- VERBS **be, seem**
- ADV. **extremely, highly, very** *He is a highly ambitious politician.* | **socially**
- PREP. **for** *She is very ambitious for her four children.*

2 difficult to achieve
- VERBS **be, seem**

- ADV. **extremely, hugely, very** | **rather** | **overly** *Phases 2 and 3 seem overly ambitious.*

ambivalence noun

- VERB + AMBIVALENCE **feel** | **express, show** *The document expressed some ambivalence over the doctrine of predestination.*
- PREP. **with ~** *She viewed her daughter's education with ambivalence.* | **~ about** *their ambivalence about supporting the government* **~ over** *his ambivalence over money* **~ towards** *She felt a certain ambivalence towards him.*

ambivalent adj.

- VERBS **be, feel, sound** | **remain**
- ADV. **deeply, highly, very** *The party's position on nuclear weapons is deeply ambivalent.* | **fairly, rather, somewhat**
- PREP. **about** *He feels rather ambivalent about his role as teacher.*

ambulance noun

- ADJ. **air**
- VERB + AMBULANCE **call (for), get, phone/ring/telephone for, send for** *Quick, call an ambulance!* | **drive**
- AMBULANCE + VERB **be on its way** *Don't worry—the ambulance is on its way.* | **arrive, come** *When the ambulance came, I carried her out.*
- AMBULANCE + NOUN **service** | **crew, staff** | **driver, man, worker** | **station**
- PREP. **by ~** *She was rushed to hospital by air ambulance.* **in an/the~** *He went in the ambulance with Lizzy.*

ambush noun

- VERB + AMBUSH **lay, prepare, set up** *The soldiers set up an ambush on the road.* | **lie in, wait in** *The soldiers lay in ambush for the enemy troops.* | **carry out, stage** *They staged an ambush on an army patrol.* | **be caught in, run into, walk into** *We ran into an ambush in the valley.*
- AMBUSH + VERB **take place**
- PREP. **in an/the ~** *Twelve men were killed in the ambush.* | **~ on** *an ambush on an army patrol*

amenable adj.

- VERBS **be, seem** | **find sb/sth**
- ADV. **highly, most, very** *The manager was most amenable: nothing was too much trouble.*
- PREP. **to** *You should find him amenable to reasonable arguments.*

amendment noun

- ADJ. **important, major, significant** *A major amendment was introduced into the legislation.* | **minor, slight, small** | **draft, proposed** | **detailed** | **constitutional**
- VERB + AMENDMENT **introduce, make** | **draft** *The committee does not adequately consult others when drafting amendments.* | **move, propose, put forward, suggest, table** *He moved an amendment limiting capital punishment to certain very serious crimes.* | **withdraw** *She withdrew her amendment and left the meeting.* | **accept, adopt, approve, carry, pass, ratify, support, vote for** *Parliament accepted the amendment and the bill was passed.* ◇ *On a free vote, the amendment was carried by 292 votes to 246.* | **oppose, reject** | **be subject to** *The programme is subject to amendment.*
- PREP. **without ~** *The new clause was accepted without amendment.* | **~ to** *an amendment to the Clean Water Act*

amenity noun

- ADJ. **excellent** | **basic** | **local** *The campsite is close to all local amenities.* | **modern** *a hotel with all modern*

amenities | **public** *The building will be developed as a public amenity.* | **recreational, social**
● VERB + AMENITY **have** *The hotel has excellent amenities.* | **offer, provide** *They will provide an amenity for local residents.* | **lack** *The flats lacked basic amenities.*

amiable *adj.*

● VERBS **be, look, seem, sound**
● ADV. **very** | **perfectly** *a perfectly amiable young man* | **enough, quite** *I've only met Jane once but she seems amiable enough.*

ammunition *noun*

● ADJ. **live** | **blank**
● QUANT. **round**
● VERB + AMMUNITION **carry, have** | **issue** *They issued live ammunition to the troops.* | **fire, use** | **run out of** *A few of the jeeps had run out of ammunition.*
● AMMUNITION + NOUN **dump, store**

amnesty *noun*

● ADJ. **general, political**
● VERB + AMNESTY **give sb, grant, offer** *The government granted an amnesty to all political prisoners.* | **announce, declare**
● PREP. **under an/the ~** *He was released from prison under an amnesty.* | **~ for** *They announced a general amnesty for crimes committed during the war.*

amount *noun*

● ADJ. **considerable, copious ~s, enormous, huge, large, massive, significant, substantial, tremendous, vast** *a considerable amount of money* ◇ *He drank copious amounts of beer.* | **disproportionate, excessive, inordinate** | **increasing** | **fair** *There was a fair amount of traffic on the roads.* | **limited, minute, moderate, negligible, small, tiny** | **full, total** *You must pay back the full amount of money that you owe.* | **maximum, minimum** *He aimed to cause the maximum amount of embarrassment.* | **exact** | **equal, equivalent** *Mix the colours in equal amounts.* ◇ *an amount equivalent to 0.3% per annum* | **varying** *Tap water also contains varying amounts of rust and grit.*
● VERB + AMOUNT **double, increase** | **decrease, limit, reduce** *They want to limit the amount of cash available.*
● AMOUNT + VERB **double, increase** *The amount of reclaimed glass used in industry has doubled in the last five years.* | **decrease, fall** *The average amount of pocket money received by teenagers fell to £4 a week this year.*
● PREP. **~ of**

amuse *verb*

● ADV. **greatly** *Her discomfort amused him greatly.*
● VERB + AMUSE **seem to** *The thought of me on the stage seemed to amuse him.* | **try to**
● PREP. **with** *He amused us with his stories.*

amused *adj.*

● VERBS **be, look, seem, sound** *She looked faintly amused.* | **keep sb** *He kept the children amused for hours.*
● ADV. **greatly, highly, much, vastly, very** *He was much amused by all this talk.* | **not at all** *I was not at all amused to find they had eaten all the cake.* | **faintly, a little, mildly, quite, rather, slightly** | **clearly** *Mr Stopes was clearly amused by the confusion.* | **genuinely** | **wryly** | **quietly**
● PREP. **at** *Tony was very amused at the story.* **by** *She seemed greatly amused by his jokes.*

amusement *noun*

1 feeling of wanting to laugh
● ADJ. **great, much** | **faint, mild** | **quiet** | **ironic, sardonic, wry** | **genuine, real**
● QUANT. **gleam, glimmer** | **hint, note, trace** *There was a note of amusement in her voice.*
● VERB + AMUSEMENT **afford sb, cause, provide** *I am happy to have afforded you amusement.* | **derive, find, get** *He seemed to be deriving amusement from her discomfort.* | **show** | **conceal, hide**
● AMUSEMENT + VERB **show** *A glimmer of amusement showed in her eyes.*
● PREP. **for (sb's) ~** *What do you do for amusement round here?* ◇ *The play was written for the amusement of the other students.* **in ~** *Her wide mouth twitched in amusement.* **to sb's ~** *Much to their amusement, I couldn't get the door open.* **with ~** *She chuckled with amusement.*
● PHRASES **a source of amusement** *His son was a constant source of amusement to him.*

2 sth that makes time pass pleasantly
● ADJ. **popular** *She disapproved of popular amusements such as fairs.*
● AMUSEMENT + NOUN **arcade, park** | **machine**

amusing *adj.*

● VERBS **be, sound** | **find sth**
● ADV. **extremely, highly, most, really, very** | **mildly, quite, rather, vaguely** | **not remotely** *There is nothing even remotely amusing about the situation.*

anaesthetic *noun*

● ADJ. **general, local**
● VERB + ANAESTHETIC **administer, give sb** *He was given a general anaesthetic.* | **use** *The operation was completed in ten minutes using only local anaesthetic.* | **have** *She had a local anaesthetic to stop the pain.* | **come round from, recover from**
● ANAESTHETIC + VERB **take effect, work** *The anaesthetic began to take effect.* | **wear off**
● PREP. **under (an/the) ~** *It would have to be done under anaesthetic.* **without (an/the) ~** *They had to operate without anaesthetic.*

analogous *adj.*

● VERBS **be**
● ADV. **closely** | **directly, exactly** | **broadly, roughly** *The two situations are roughly analogous.*
● PREP. **to** *The company is in a position closely analogous to that of its main rival.* **with** *The national debt is analogous with private debt.*

analogy *noun*

● ADJ. **appropriate, apt, useful** | **close, obvious** *A close analogy with the art of singing can be made.*
● VERB + ANALOGY **draw, make, suggest, use** *She drew an analogy between running the economy and a housewife's weekly budget.*
● ANALOGY + VERB **fit, hold** *The Wild West analogy does not fit here.*
● PREP. **by ~ (to/with)** *We can understand this theory by analogy with human beings.* | **~ between** *She suggested an analogy between the human heart and a pump.* **~ for** *The computer is a useful analogy for the brain.* **~ with** *There is an analogy here with the way an engine works.*
● PHRASES **argument by/from analogy** *Argument from analogy is not always valid.*

analyse *verb*

● ADV. **carefully, critically, fully, in depth/detail, pains-**

takingly, scientifically, **systematically** *The results must be analysed in detail.*
● VERB + ANALYSE **attempt to, try to** | **be difficult to, be impossible to** *The precise reasons for the disaster are difficult to analyse.* | **be possible to**

analysis *noun*

● ADJ. **careful, close, comprehensive, detailed, in-depth, systematic, thorough** | **brief** | **objective, subjective** | **comparative, critical, qualitative, quantitative, statistical, theoretical** | **cost-benefit, discourse, economic, financial, historical, linguistic, strategic, structural, stylistic**
● VERB + ANALYSIS **carry out, do, make, perform** *They carried out an in-depth analysis of the results.* | **give** *He gave a brief analysis of the present economic situation.*
● ANALYSIS + VERB **indicate sth, show sth** *Analysis of the wine showed that it contained dangerous additives.*
● PREP. **in an/the ~** *In his analysis of the novel he discusses various aspects of the author's own life.*
● PHRASES **in the final/last analysis** *In the final analysis, the king's power was greater than the bishop's.*

analyst *noun*

● ADJ. **leading** *a leading business analyst* | **business, computer, data, financial, industry, investment, market, military, policy, political, retail, systems**
● PREP. **~of** *He was a shrewd analyst of players' strengths and weaknesses.*
⇨ Note at JOB

anarchy *noun*

● ADJ. **complete, total** | **near, virtual** *The high number of strikes resulted in near anarchy.*
● VERB + ANARCHY **cause, create, lead to, result in** *The defeat of the government would lead to anarchy.* | **collapse into, descend into, slide into** *If prices rise the country could slide into anarchy.* | **prevent, save sth from** *The parties joined forces to save the country from anarchy.*

anatomy *noun*

● ADJ. **animal, human** | **female, male** | **comparative**
● VERB + ANATOMY **study** *studying human anatomy*
● PHRASES **part of your anatomy** *(often humorous) He was hit in a rather sensitive part of his anatomy.*

ancestor *noun*

● ADJ. **direct** *The builder of the manor house is a direct ancestor of the present owner.* | **immediate** | **distant, early, remote** *a distant ancestor of mine* ◊ *Our earliest ancestors lived in a world fraught with danger.* | **common** *The two species share a common ancestor.* | **illustrious** *The Romans built these monuments to glorify their illustrious ancestors.*
● VERB + ANCESTOR **be descended from, have, share** *A lot of the people there are descended from a common ancestor.* | **trace** *He can trace his ancestors back to the reign of James the First.*

ancestry *noun*

● ADJ. **common** *The two species have developed from a common ancestry.* | **Celtic, French, etc.**
● VERB + ANCESTRY **claim, have, share** *She shares a common ancestry with the Queen.* | **trace** *We can trace our ancestry back to the 16th century.*
● ANCESTRY + VERB **date/go/reach/stretch back to** *The firm claims an ancestry dating back to 1727.*
● PHRASES **be of French, German, etc. ancestry** *He is of Chinese ancestry.*

anchor *noun*

● VERB + ANCHOR **cast, drop** *The ship cast anchor in the bay.* ◊ *We dropped anchor off a small island.* | **raise, weigh** *We raised the anchor and set sail.* ◊ *We weighed anchor next morning and sailed south.* | **lie at, ride at** *The ship lay at anchor in the bay.*
● PREP. **at~** *the ships at anchor in the harbour*

anchor *verb*

● ADV. **firmly, securely** *The crane is securely anchored at two points.*
● PREP. **to** *The ropes were anchored to the rocks.*

ancient *adj.*

● VERBS **be, look**
● ADV. **extremely, incredibly, very** | **quite** | **positively** *The man looked positively ancient.*

anecdote *noun*

● ADJ. **amusing, entertaining, humorous** | **personal**
● VERB + ANECDOTE **relate, tell** *She is good at telling anecdotes.* | **exchange, swap**
● PREP. **~about** *We swapped anecdotes about old friends.*

angel *noun*

1 heavenly being
● ADJ. **guardian** | **avenging** *He liked to think of himself as an avenging angel fighting for justice.* | **fallen** *a book about anti-heroes and fallen angels*
● QUANT. **choir, host** *a whole host of angels*

2 good/kind person
● ADJ. **absolute, little** *Deborah's children are little angels.* | **ministering** *I could hardly see Lisa in the role of ministering angel.*
● PHRASES **be an angel** *Be an angel and make the tea, will you?* **be no angel** *I'm no angel, but I wouldn't dream of doing a thing like that.*

anger *noun*

● ADJ. **bitter, black, cold, deep, fierce, great, savage, terrible** | **genuine, real** | **growing, mounting, rising** *mounting anger among teachers and parents* | **sudden** | **righteous** *Catherine appeared in the doorway, shaking with righteous anger.* | **controlled, pent-up, suppressed** | **popular, public** | **widespread**
● QUANT. **burst, fit, outburst** *He slammed the door in a fit of anger.*
● VERB + ANGER **be filled with, feel, shake with, tremble with** *His eyes were filled with anger.* ◊ *She was trembling with anger.* | **express, give vent to, show, vent, voice** *Children give vent to their anger in various ways.* | **control, hide, suppress** *It is not healthy to suppress your anger.* | **arouse, cause, fill sb with, fuel, provoke, stir up** *His words fuelled her anger.* | **change to, give way to, turn to** *His joy soon turned to anger when he heard the full story.*
● ANGER + VERB **boil over/up, bubble up, build up, flare (up), grow, mount, rise, well up** *Henry stood up, his anger rising.* | **abate, drain, evaporate, fade, subside** *The anger drained from his face.* ◊ *Her anger subsided as quickly as it had flared up.*
● PREP. **in ~** *He raised his voice in anger.* **with ~** *His face was flushed with anger.* | **~against** *her feelings of anger against the murderer* **~at** *I felt a sudden anger at his suggestion.* **~over** *There is much anger over plans to close the hospital.* **~towards** *her anger towards her parents*
● PHRASES **a feeling of anger, in a moment of anger** *He had walked out in a moment of anger.*

anger verb

- ADV. **deeply, greatly** *I was deeply angered by their lack of concern.*

angle noun

1 space between lines/surfaces that meet
- ADJ. **acute, oblique, obtuse, right** | **external, internal** | **narrow, sharp, steep** *The plane started descending at a steep angle.* | **shallow, slight, wide** *The instrument has a wide angle of view.* | **awkward, crazy, odd** *The calf's legs were splayed out at awkward angles.*
- VERB + ANGLE **form, make** *The vertical line makes an angle with the horizontal line.* | **draw** *Draw a 130° angle in your exercise books.* | **adjust, alter, change** *She adjusted the angle of the legs to make the table stand more firmly.* | **increase, reduce** | **measure** | **move through, rotate through** *Each joint can move through an angle of 90°.*
- PREP. **at an~** *The tower of Pisa leans at an angle.* | **~between** *the angle between these two lines*

2 position
- ADJ. **unusual** *The subject is considered from an unusual angle.* | **camera** *The variety of camera angles gives her photographs interest.* | **viewing**
- VERB + ANGLE **consider/look at/see/view sth from** *We've looked at the problem from every possible angle but still haven't found a solution.* ◇ *Seeing herself from this angle, she realized how like her mother she looked.*
- PHRASES **angle of vision** *How you see the building depends on your angle of vision.* **from all angles** *You need to consider the question from all angles.*

angry adj.

- VERBS **appear, be, feel, look, seem, sound** | **become, get, grow** | **remain, stay** *She couldn't stay angry with him for long.* | **make sb** *That man makes me angry every time I see him.*
- ADV. **bitterly, extremely, furiously, really, terribly, very, wildly** | **a bit, pretty, quite, rather** | **increasingly** | **coldly** | **suddenly**
- PREP. **about** *Local people are very angry about the plans to close another hospital.* **at** *The members of the group are frustrated and angry at their lack of power.* **with** *I got terribly angry with him.*

anguish noun

- ADJ. **bitter, deep, great, real** | **inner, personal, private** | **mental, physical, spiritual**
- VERB + ANGUISH **cause** *The loss of a pet can cause some people real anguish.* | **experience, feel, suffer** *He suffered the anguish of watching his son go to prison.*
- PREP. **in (sb's)~** *to cry out/groan/scream in anguish* ◇ *In her anguish, she turned to her father for help.* **with~** *His mouth felt dry with anguish.* | **~at/over** *his anguish at the death of his son*
- PHRASES **a cry/groan/scream of anguish, pain and anguish** *All the pain and anguish inside her rose like a tidal wave.*

animal noun

- ADJ. **dead, live, living** *the export of live animals for slaughter* | **cold-blooded, warm-blooded** | **higher, lower** | **dumb** | **stuffed** *glass cases of stuffed animals* | **dangerous** | **endangered, rare** | **extinct** | **social, solitary** | **tame** | **feral, stray, wild** | **exotic** | **caged, trapped, wounded** *(often figurative)* *He was pacing the room like a caged animal.* | **domestic, farm, laboratory, zoo** | **forest, land, marine** | **draught, pack** *pack animals such as mules*
- VERB + ANIMAL **have, keep** *In court he was banned from keeping animals.* | **breed, raise, rear** *animals bred*

in captivity | **tame, train** *This animal can be trained to follow simple orders.* | **hunt, trap** | **butcher, slaughter**
- ANIMAL + NOUN **life, species** | **behaviour, instinct** | **lover** | **husbandry** | **experiments, testing/tests** *protesting against animal experiments* | **rights, welfare** | **fat, products**
- PHRASES **the animal kingdom/world** *the wonders of the animal kingdom*

animosity noun

- ADJ. **personal**
- VERB + ANIMOSITY **bear** *Despite everything, she bore her former boss no animosity.* | **arouse, stir up**
- PREP. **without~** *They managed to discuss their past disagreements without animosity.* | **~between** *The two rivals for party leadership insist that there is no animosity between them.* **~towards** *the animosity of some locals towards asylum seekers*

ankle noun

- ADJ. **bad, broken, injured, sprained, swollen, twisted** | **slender, slim, well-turned** *She has long legs and slender ankles.*
- VERB + ANKLE **break, hurt, injure, sprain, turn, twist**
- ANKLE + NOUN **boots, socks** | **injury** | **bone, joint, ligament**
- PHRASES **ankle deep in sth** *We waded through the river, ankle deep in mud.*

annex verb

- ADV. **formally** *The region was formally annexed in 1892.* | **illegally**
- PREP. **to** *The territory had been annexed to Poland.*

annihilation noun

- ADJ. **total** | **nuclear**
- VERB + ANNIHILATION **face** *They were to surrender immediately or face total annihilation.* | **threaten**

anniversary noun

1 of an important event
- ADJ. **first, second, etc.**
- VERB + ANNIVERSARY **celebrate, commemorate, mark** *They held celebrations to mark the anniversary of Mozart's death.*
- ANNIVERSARY + VERB **be, fall** *The anniversary of the founding of the charity falls on 12th November.*
- PREP. **on an/the~** *on the 20th anniversary of his death*

2 of a wedding
- ADJ. **first, second, etc.** | **wedding**
- VERB + ANNIVERSARY **celebrate**
- PREP. **on sb's~** *He bought her a diamond ring on their tenth wedding anniversary.*
- PHRASES **a diamond, golden, silver, etc. wedding anniversary**

announce verb

- ADV. **formally, officially, publicly** | **proudly** *The company proudly announced the launch of its new range of cars.*
- VERB + ANNOUNCE **be expected to, expect to** *We expect to announce details of the scheme later this week.* | **be delighted to, be pleased to, be proud to** *Mr and Mrs James are pleased to announce the engagement of their daughter, Henrietta.* | **regret to** *We regret to announce the death of our chairman, Alfred Sidebottom.*

announcement noun

- ADJ. **formal, official** | **public** | **government** | **dra-**

matic, **surprise** *Baker issued his surprise announcement in Paris after two hours of talks.*
- VERB + ANNOUNCEMENT **issue, make** *We will make a formal announcement tomorrow.* | **greet, welcome** *The announcement of the ceasefire was greeted with relief.*
- ANNOUNCEMENT + VERB **come** *The announcement of further job losses comes at a bad time.*
- PREP. **in a/the~** *In an announcement to Parliament, the minister said that the peace negotiations would continue.* | **~ about** *an official announcement about the disaster* **~by/from** *an announcement from the prime minister*

announcer *noun*

- ADJ. **continuity, radio, sports, station, television/TV** *The station announcer warned us that the train was running late.*
- ⇨ Note at JOB

annoy *verb*

- ADV. **intensely, really** *His air of calm superiority annoyed her intensely.* ◊ *It really annoys me when people forget to say thank you.* | **slightly**
- VERB + ANNOY **be beginning to** *The wasps were beginning to annoy me.*
- PHRASES **do sth just/only to annoy sb** *I only stay out late to annoy my parents.*

annoyance *noun*

1 feeling of being annoyed
- ADJ. **deep, great, intense** *A look of deep annoyance crossed his face.* | **obvious** *She tapped the table with her pen in obvious annoyance.*
- QUANT. **flicker** *A flicker of annoyance crossed his face.* | **surge** *He felt a violent surge of annoyance.*
- VERB + ANNOYANCE **cause** *He had been causing annoyance to the other guests.* | **feel** *I felt some annoyance when he told me his plans.* | **express, show** *She tried not to show her annoyance.* | **conceal, hide**
- PREP. **in ~** *He shook his head in annoyance.* **with ~** *Her cheeks flushed with annoyance.* | **~ at/over, ~ with** *her annoyance with him over his failure to cooperate*
- PHRASES **a look of annoyance** *There was a look of annoyance on his face.* **a source of annoyance** *A dog that barks constantly can be a source of annoyance to the neighbours.* **(much) to the annoyance of sb, (much) to sb's annoyance** *I dropped out of university, much to the annoyance of my parents.*

2 thing that annoys you
- ADJ. **minor, petty** *A leaking roof is just one of life's petty annoyances!*

annoyed *adj.*

- VERBS **be, feel, look, seem, sound** | **become, get** | **make sb** *His attitude made me extremely annoyed.*
- ADV. **extremely, really, very** | **thoroughly** | **increasingly** | **faintly, a little, quite, rather, slightly, somewhat** | **clearly, obviously**
- PREP. **about** *I was a little annoyed about the whole thing.* **at** *We enjoyed the game but were rather annoyed at being beaten.* **by** *I was quite annoyed by her remarks.* **with** *Susan felt slightly annoyed with herself.*

annoying *adj.*

- VERBS **be, prove** | **become, get** *Please stop making that noise—it's getting annoying.* | **make sth** | **find sth** *I found it really annoying not to be able to communicate.*
- ADV. **extremely, really, very** | **a bit, mildly, rather**
- PREP. **to** *The proposal will probably prove annoying to opposition MPs.*

anonymity *noun*

- ADJ. **complete, total** | **relative** *This British author has chosen to live in relative anonymity on a Pacific island.*
- VERB + ANONYMITY **ensure, guarantee, preserve, protect** *Our company promises to preserve the anonymity of all its clients.* | **demand, insist on, prefer, request, seek** *Some people prefer the anonymity of life in a big city.*

anonymous *adj.*

- VERBS **be** | **become** | **remain**
- ADV. **completely, entirely**
- PHRASES **prefer/wish to remain anonymous** *My client wishes to remain anonymous.*

answer *noun*

1 sth that you say/write/do as a reply
- ADJ. **brief, quick, short** *The short answer to your query is that he has acted completely illegally.* | **blunt, direct, straight** *I expect a straight answer to a straight question.* | **detailed, full, precise** | **immediate** | **final** | **affirmative, positive** | **negative** | **honest, reasonable, sensible** | **dusty** (= unsatisfactory) *I complained to the water company and received a very dusty answer.*
- VERB + ANSWER **get, have, receive** *Did you ever get an answer to your letter?* | **demand** | **wait for** | **give sb, offer** *Please give her your answer, so she can make the necessary arrangements.* ◊ *She repeated her question, but he offered no answer.* | **guess, know** *I think you can guess the answer—they won't lend us the money.*
- ANSWER + VERB **come** *The answer came in a postcard she sent from Devon.*
- PREP. **in ~ to** *In answer to your enquiries, I can only say that we did not find her work of a satisfactory standard.* | **~ to** *her answer to his question*

2 solution to a problem
- ADJ. **easy, instant, ready, simple** | **clear, clear-cut, obvious** *The obvious answer would be to cancel the party.* | **logical, reasonable, sensible** | **adequate, real, satisfactory** | **complete, convincing, definitive, effective, good, long-term, perfect** | **partial**
- VERB + ANSWER **have, know** *We are aware of this problem, but we do not have the answer.* | **look for, seek** | **arrive at, come up with, find** *We have arrived at an answer which we hope will satisfy everyone.* | **give sb, offer, provide** *If you want to save time, this machine will provide the answer.*
- PREP. **~ to** *There is no easy answer to the problem.*
- PHRASES **have/know all the answers** *He's so arrogant, he thinks he knows all the answers.*

3 to questions in a test
- ADJ. **acceptable, appropriate, correct, right** | **incorrect, wrong** | **written** *This part of the exam requires a written answer.*
- VERB + ANSWER **give** | **guess** *It's not worth guessing the answer, as you may lose marks.* | **know** | **print, write** *Please print the answers to questions 1 to 9.*
- PREP. **~ to** *Do you know the answer to the question?*

answer *verb*

- ADV. **affirmatively, in the affirmative** *She answered in the affirmative.* | **in the negative, negatively** | **honestly, truthfully** *He tried to answer as honestly as he could.* | **correctly** | **fully** *What he told me does not fully answer the question of what his motives were.* | **satisfactorily** | **evasively** | **coldly, curtly** | **calmly** | **quietly, softly**

antagonism *noun*

- ADJ. **great, strong** | **mutual** | **class, personal, racial**
- VERB + ANTAGONISM **feel, have** *She felt nothing but antagonism towards her boss.* ◊ *He seems to have an antagonism to the local people.* | **express, show** | **arouse,**

cause, create, lead to, provoke *The new rules will create a lot of antagonism.*
● PREP. **~ between** *the antagonism between the two brothers* **~ to/towards** *her antagonism towards her mother*

anthology *noun*

● VERB + ANTHOLOGY **compile, edit, publish, put together** *We have put together an anthology of children's poetry.*
● PREP. **in an/the ~** *The essay first appeared in an anthology of feminist criticism.* **| ~ of**

anthropology *noun*

● ADJ. **cultural, social** *Social anthropology examines family relationships in detail.*
⇨ Note at SUBJECT (for verbs and nouns)

antibiotic *noun*

● ADJ. **effective**
● QUANT. **course, dose** *The doctor put her on a course of antibiotics.*
● VERB + ANTIBIOTIC **be on, take** *Did you remember to take your antibiotics?* **| give sb, prescribe, put sb on, treat sth with** *The doctor prescribed antibiotics.*

anticipate *verb*

● PHRASES **be eagerly/keenly anticipated** *one of the most eagerly anticipated arts events of the year* **be widely anticipated** *It is widely anticipated that she will resign.*

anticipation *noun*

● ADJ. **great, keen | eager, excited, happy, pleasurable** *We look forward to your lecture with eager anticipation.* ◇ *a feeling of pleasurable anticipation* **| growing** *There is growing anticipation that the prime minister will have to resign.*
● VERB + ANTICIPATION **be full of** *We are full of anticipation, and can't wait to visit you.*
● PREP. **in ~ of** *People are buying extra groceries in anticipation of heavy snowstorms.*
● PHRASES **a feeling/sense of anticipation, a shiver/thrill of anticipation** *The unexpected news sent a thrill of anticipation through the group.*

antics *noun*

● ADJ. **amusing, crazy, playful**
● VERB + ANTICS **get up to, perform** *The youngsters got up to all sorts of amusing antics.* **| enjoy, laugh at, smile at** *She was laughing at his antics.*

antidote *noun*

1 against poison/disease
● ADJ. **effective | natural**
● VERB + ANTIDOTE **administer, give** *The doctor administered an antidote.*
● PREP. **~ for** *Quinine is a natural antidote for this fever.* **~ to** *We do not have an effective antidote to this poison.*
2 thing that takes away the effects of sth unpleasant
● ADJ. **effective, good, perfect, powerful**
● VERB + ANTIDOTE **act as, serve as | offer, provide** *The resort offers the perfect antidote to the pressures of modern life.*
● PREP. **~ for** *I think that stricter punishment is the best antidote for crime.* **~ to** *Creative activity serves as an effective antidote to depression.*

antipathy *noun*

● ADJ. **deep, profound, strong, violent | growing, in-**

creasing **| mutual** *They have a mutual antipathy to each other.* **| personal** *Despite his personal antipathy to me he was still able to be polite.* **| natural** *a natural antipathy towards people in authority*
● VERB + ANTIPATHY **feel, have | express, show**
● PREP. **~ between** *There was a lot of antipathy between the two doctors.* **~ for** *his antipathy for his boss* **~ to/towards** *I feel a profound antipathy to using any weapon.*

antique *noun*

● ADJ. **fine | genuine | priceless, valuable**
● VERB + ANTIQUE **collect**
● ANTIQUE + NOUN **dealer | antiques fair/shop**

antiquity *noun*

1 ancient times
● ADJ. **classical, Greek, Roman, etc.** *legends from Greek antiquity* **| late | immemorial, remote**
● VERB + ANTIQUITY **date from, survive from | be lost in** *The origins of this ancient structure are lost in antiquity.*
● PREP. **from ~** *a study of urban life from antiquity to the present day* **in ~** *vases that were manufactured in late classical antiquity*
2 a work of art, etc. from ancient times
● ADJ. **classical, Egyptian, Greek, Roman, etc.**
● VERB + ANTIQUITY **collect** *He collects Egyptian and Roman antiquities.*
3 great age
● ADJ. **considerable, great** *the considerable antiquity of the rocks in this region*

antiseptic *noun*

● ADJ. **powerful | mild** *Mint is a mild antiseptic.*
● VERB + ANTISEPTIC **apply, put on** *You should put some antiseptic on that cut.*

antithesis *noun*

● ADJ. **complete, exact, very | sharp**
● VERB + ANTITHESIS **be, represent**
● PREP. **~ between** *the sharp antithesis between their views* **~ of** *The company represented the antithesis of everything he admired.*

anxiety *noun*

● ADJ. **acute, considerable, deep, great | chronic, constant, nagging | growing, increasing, mounting | natural, understandable | needless, unnecessary | public**
● QUANT. **level** *the high level of anxiety created by entering a new environment*
● VERB + ANXIETY **arouse, bring, cause, create, provoke | lead to | experience, feel, suffer from** *She felt a nagging anxiety that could not be relieved.* **| express, share** *The mothers were able to share their anxieties with each other.* **| cope with, deal with** *skills to cope with anxiety* **| allay, alleviate, dispel, reduce, relieve** *The aim is to reduce anxiety and help the patients relax.* **| aggravate, increase**
● ANXIETY + VERB **grow** *The more reports I study the more my anxiety grows.* **| arise (from/out of sth), surface** *A few anxieties surfaced during the meeting.*
● ANXIETY + NOUN **attack | level**
● PREP. **~ about** *her growing anxiety about her health* **~ at** *anxiety at the deterioration of relations between the powers* **~ for** *deep anxiety for the whole family* **~ over** *There are anxieties over the effects of unemployment.*
● PHRASES **fear and anxiety** *They were encouraged to express their fears and anxieties.*

anxious adj.

- VERBS **appear, be, feel, look, seem, sound** | **become, get, grow** *The bus was late and Sue began to get anxious.* | **make sb** *The delays only made him more anxious.*
- ADV. **desperately, extremely, very** | **increasingly** *She was watching the clock and becoming increasingly anxious.* | **a bit, a little, quite, rather, slightly, somewhat** | **genuinely** | **naturally, understandably** *Final-year students are naturally anxious about getting work after graduation.* | **unduly** *There's no need to get unduly anxious on my account.* | **suddenly**
- PREP. **about** *I'm becoming very anxious about my son.* **for** *We are extremely anxious for her safety.*

apartment noun

1 a flat
- ADJ. **large, spacious** | **small** | **comfortable, luxury** | **modern** | **one-bedroomed, two-bedroomed, etc.** | **studio** | **first-floor, second-floor, etc.** | **basement, penthouse** | **holiday, self-catering**
- VERB + APARTMENT **buy** | **lease, rent** *We will be renting the apartment for a year.* | **live in, share, stay in** *I share an apartment with two friends.* | **look for** *I'm looking for an apartment on the east side of the city.* | **find** | **move into/out of**
- APARTMENT + NOUN **block, building, complex, house** *high-rise apartment blocks*

2 apartments set of rooms
- ADJ. **private, royal, state** *the private apartments of the imperial family*

apathy noun

- ADJ. **general, widespread** | **political, public**
- VERB + APATHY **suffer from** | **fall into, sink into** *Once defeated, he sank into apathy.* | **lead to** *Such attitudes can only lead to apathy.*
- PREP. **~ among** *widespread apathy among students* **~towards** *a general apathy towards politics*

apologetic adj.

- VERBS **be, feel, look, sound**
- ADV. **profusely, very** | **almost** *Barney sounded almost apologetic.* | **faintly, slightly, vaguely** | **suitably** *I hope she was suitably apologetic afterwards.*
- PREP. **about** *He was profusely apologetic about the mistake.* **for** *She was apologetic for taking so long.*

apologize verb

- ADV. **sincerely** | **profusely** *He apologized profusely for the damage he had caused.* | **humbly** *I do apologize most humbly.* | **publicly**
- VERB + APOLOGIZE **ought to, should** | **want to, wish to, would like to** *I would like to apologize most sincerely for any embarrassment caused.*
- PREP. **for** *She apologized for being late.* | **to** *He apologized to his colleagues.*
- PHRASES **I do/must apologize** *I must apologize for cancelling our meeting at such short notice.*

apology noun

- ADJ. **abject, humble, profuse** *It was a mistake. My profuse apologies.* | **heartfelt, profound, sincere** | **full** | **formal** | **public** | **written**
- VERB + APOLOGY **convey, give sb, issue, make, offer (sb), publish, send (sb)** *The newspaper has issued an apology to the minister.* | **get, receive** | **demand, deserve, expect** *We expect a full written apology.* | **owe sb** *She certainly owes you an apology.* | **mumble, murmur, mutter** *John muttered an apology then went back to his book.* | **accept** *Please accept my sincere apologies.* | **reject** *She rejected my apology, saying it was not enough.*
- PREP. **without~** *He backed out arrogantly and without apology.* | **~for** *an apology for arriving late* **~from** *Apologies have been received from the Browns.* **~to** *my apologies to your wife*
- PHRASES **a letter of apology, make no apology/apologies for** *I make no apologies for bringing this issue to your attention once again.*

appalling adj.

- VERBS **be, look, sound**
- ADV. **really, truly** | **absolutely, the most, quite, utterly** *They had to wait for hours in the most appalling weather.*

apparatus noun

- ADJ. **breathing, chemical, electrical, experimental, laboratory, scientific** | **administrative, bureaucratic, legal, party, security, state** *the state's powerful security apparatus*
- QUANT. **piece** *a very sophisticated piece of laboratory apparatus*
- PHRASES **the apparatus of government/(the) state**

apparent adj.

- VERBS **be, seem** | **become** *It soon became apparent that the company was losing money.* | **make sth** *He made it apparent that he was very annoyed.*
- ADV. **glaringly, strongly, very** | **fully, quite** | **increasingly** | **all too** *His unhappiness was all too apparent.* | **quickly, soon** | **immediately, instantly** *The extent of their injuries was not immediately apparent.* | **easily, readily** | **clearly** | **painfully** *Local suspicion of the incomers was painfully apparent.*
- PREP. **to** *His lack of experience was quite apparent to everyone.*

appeal noun

1 serious request for sth you need/want very much
- ADJ. **desperate, emergency, emotional, urgent** | **direct** | **fresh, further** *a fresh appeal for witnesses to come forward* | **mute** *She gazed at him in mute appeal.*
- VERB + APPEAL **issue, make** *They made a direct appeal to the government for funding.*
- PREP. **~for** *an appeal for help* **~to** *an appeal to reason*

2 formal request to sb in authority
- ADJ. **formal, personal**
- VERB + APPEAL **bring, file, lodge, make** *He's lodged an appeal against the size of the fine.* | **win** | **lose** | **allow** (*formal*), **consider, hear** *The judge has agreed to allow his appeal.* ◇ *The court will hear the appeal on 10 June.* | **uphold** *His appeal was upheld and he was released immediately.* | **deny, dismiss, reject, throw out, turn down**
- APPEAL + VERB **fail** | **succeed**
- APPEAL + NOUN **court, tribunal** | **hearing** | **judge** | **procedure, process, system**
- PREP. **on~** *On appeal, it was held that the judge was correct.* **under~** *a case currently under appeal* | **~against** *an appeal against his conviction of fraud* **~for** *an appeal for leniency* **~to** *an appeal to the High Court*
- PHRASES **a court of appeal, give/grant sb leave to appeal, grounds of appeal, pending appeal** *The players have been suspended pending appeal.* **a right of appeal** *You have the right of appeal to the Constitutional Court.*

3 event for raising money
- ADJ. **charity, fund-raising** | **radio, television**
- VERB + APPEAL **hold, launch** *An appeal is to be launched on behalf of the refugees.* | **back, support**
- APPEAL + VERB **raise sth** *The radio appeal raised over three million pounds.*
- APPEAL + NOUN **fund**

4 attraction/interest

- ADJ. **considerable, great, growing, obvious, powerful, special, strong | immediate, instant** *the book's immediate appeal to young children* **| limited, little | broad, mass, popular, universal, wide** *a publication designed for mass appeal* **| aesthetic, commercial, electoral, intellectual, sex, visual** *Unfortunately, the film lacks commercial appeal.*
- VERB + APPEAL **have, hold** *His views hold no appeal for me.* **| broaden, extend, widen** *We are trying to broaden the appeal of classical music.* **| lose**
- APPEAL + VERB **lie in sth** *His considerable appeal lies in his quiet, gentle manner.*
- PREP. **~ for** *School lost its appeal for her in the second year.*

appeal *verb*

1 make serious request for sth

- ADV. **directly** *He went over the heads of union officials, appealing directly to the workforce.*
- PREP. **for, to** *Police have appealed to the public for information about the crime.*

2 to sb in authority

- ADV. **successfully, unsuccessfully | directly**
- PREP. **against** *She appealed unsuccessfully against her conviction for murder.* **to** *He has decided to appeal to the European Court.*

3 be attractive/interesting to sb

- ADV. **enormously, really, strongly** *The prospect of teaching such bright children appealed enormously.* ◊ *The idea of retiring early really appeals to me.* **| directly**
- PREP. **to** *These characters will appeal directly to children's imaginations.*

appealing *adj.*

- VERBS **be, look, seem, sound | make sth** *The large salary made their offer even more appealing to him.* **| find sth** *I find his manner very appealing.*
- ADV. **enormously, extremely, very | quite, rather | immediately**
- PREP. **to** *These toys are not immediately appealing to children.*

appear *verb*

1 come into sight

- ADV. **suddenly** *A man suddenly appeared in the doorway.* **| from nowhere** *A police officer appeared as if from nowhere and ordered us to halt.*

2 perform in public

- ADV. **currently**
- PREP. **at** *She is currently appearing at the Liverpool Playhouse.*
- PHRASES **appear on television** *She regularly appears on television.*

3 in court

- PREP. **at** *He will appear at Manchester Crown Court next week.*
- PHRASES **appear before a court/judge/magistrate** *The man will appear before magistrates in Birmingham later today.* **appear in court** *A man has appeared in court charged with the murder of seven women.*

appearance *noun*

1 way that sb/sth looks

- ADJ. **attractive, handsome, youthful | distinctive, odd, strange, striking | dishevelled, scruffy, unkempt, unprepossessing | external, general, outward, overall, personal, physical, visual** *attempts to improve the general appearance of the town centre* ◊ *attention to personal appearance and hygiene*
- VERB + APPEARANCE **have** *Inside, the house had the appearance of a temple.* **| take on** *Towns merged to take on the appearance of a city.* **| give** *The report gives an appearance of scientific credibility.* **| alter, change** *Shaving off his beard changed his appearance dramatically.* **| enhance, improve | keep up** *When she lost all her money, she was determined to keep up appearances* (= hide the true situation and pretend that everything was going well). **| judge (sb/sth) by** *To judge by appearances, Roger was rather embarrassed.*
- PREP. **contrary to ~s, despite ~s** *The American president, despite appearances, has only limited power.* **in ~** *rather bird-like in appearance*

2 arrival of sb/sth

- ADJ. **dramatic, sudden, surprise, unexpected | brief**
- VERB + APPEARANCE **make, put in** *She made a sudden appearance just as we were about to leave.* ◊ *I feel I must put in at least a brief appearance at the party.*

3 act of appearing in public

- ADJ. **first, second, etc.** *her first appearance on the stage* **| final, last | frequent, occasional, rare, regular | live, personal | public | cameo, guest | court, radio, stage, television/TV** *one of the actor's rare television appearances*
- VERB + APPEARANCE **make** *She made a cameo appearance in the film.*
- APPEARANCE + NOUN **money** *(sport)*

appendicitis *noun*

- ADJ. **acute | suspected**
- QUANT. **case**
- VERB + APPENDICITIS **have | get | diagnose**
- ⇨ Special page at ILLNESS

appendix *noun*

- ADJ. **burst, grumbling** (= painful from time to time), **inflamed, perforated, ruptured** *He was taken to hospital with a burst appendix.*
- VERB + APPENDIX **remove, take out** *Doctors had to take out his appendix.* **| have out** *She might have to have her appendix out.*
- APPENDIX + VERB **burst, rupture** *If the condition is not treated, the appendix can rupture.*

appetite *noun*

1 desire for food

- ADJ. **big, enormous, gargantuan, good, healthy, hearty, huge, insatiable, large, ravenous** *special double-decker sandwiches for big appetites* **| poor, small** *The symptoms of depression can include poor appetite and weight loss.* ◊ *I have always had a small appetite.* **| jaded** *magnificent meals to tempt the most jaded appetites*
- VERB + APPETITE **have** *She had no appetite and began to lose weight.* **| lose | build up, develop, work up** *I went for a walk to work up an appetite for breakfast.* **| get back, regain** *After a week she had regained her appetite.* **| give sb** *All that digging has given me an appetite.* **| give an edge to, increase** *The cold air had given an edge to my appetite.* **| control, curb, suppress** *(technical)*, **take away, take the edge off** *Some drugs can suppress the appetite.* **| ruin, spoil** *This is something you can eat between meals without ruining your appetite.* **| satisfy** *This meal will satisfy even the healthiest appetite.*
- APPETITE + VERB **grow, increase | come back, return** *His appetite has returned to normal.*
- PHRASES **a lack of appetite, a loss of appetite** *The symptoms include aching limbs and loss of appetite.*

2 strong desire for sth

- ADJ. **enormous, great, huge, insatiable, voracious** *an insatiable appetite for books* **| public** *The BBC recognizes the public appetite for serious information.* **| sexual**

• VERB + APPETITE **have | lose | give sb | increase, revive, whet** *Reading the first story whetted my appetite for more.* | **dull | satisfy**
• APPETITE + VERB **grow, increase**
• PREP. **~for** *His appetite for power had grown.*

applaud verb

1 clap your hands
• ADV. **loudly** *The audience applauded loudly.*

2 praise sb/sth
• ADV. **strongly, warmly** *The decision to save the company has been warmly applauded.*
• PHRASES **is to be applauded, should be applauded** *His efforts to help people should be applauded.*

applause noun

• ADJ. **deafening, loud, thunderous, tumultuous | enthusiastic, rapturous, warm, wild | prolonged, sustained | spontaneous** *a little burst of spontaneous applause* | **gentle, muted, polite** *To muted applause a small flag was raised over the building.*
• QUANT. **burst, ripple, roar, round** *The crowd gave them a round of applause.*
• VERB + APPLAUSE **be greeted with, draw, earn, get, receive, win** *The speech drew loud applause.* | **break into, burst into** *The audience broke into applause.* | **acknowledge** *She stood back and acknowledged the applause of the crowd.* | **deserve** *He deserves the respect and applause of his colleagues.*
• APPLAUSE + VERB **break out, greet sb/sth** *A great roar of applause broke out.* ◇ *Wild applause greeted this remark.* | **grow | die away/down, subside** *The applause died down as the curtain closed.*
• PREP. **to ~** *He left the stage to thunderous applause.* | **~for** *There was a ripple of applause for the speaker.*

apple noun

• ADJ. **sweet | sharp, sour, tart** *Add some sugar to the stewed apple—it's still a bit tart.* | **juicy | cider, cooking, dessert, eating | windfall | baked | bruised** *The apples were all bruised after being dropped on the floor.*
• VERB + APPLE **bite into, eat, munch (on)** *He just sat there munching on an apple.* | **core, grate, peel**
• APPLE + NOUN **crumble, pie | core, pip | tree**
⇨ Special page at FRUIT

appliance noun

• ADJ. **modern | faulty | electrical, gas | cooking, heating | domestic, household, kitchen | surgical**
• VERB + APPLIANCE **switch on, turn on | switch off, turn off** *Always switch off appliances that are not in use.* | **run, use** *Many household appliances are expensive to run.* | **maintain, service**

applicable adj.

• VERBS **be, prove, seem** *new developments in research that could prove directly applicable to the treatment of some cancers* | **become | make sth**
• ADJ. **broadly, generally, widely | universally | directly | immediately | equally** *The rules have now been made equally applicable to all members.* | **easily, readily** *The theory does not seem easily applicable in this case.*
• PREP. **for** *The offer is only applicable for journeys made during the week.* **to** *The law is applicable to everyone.*

applicant noun

• ADJ. **potential, prospective | suitable, suitably qualified** *Grant payments will be made to suitable applicants.* | **unsuitable | lucky, successful | disappointed, unsuc-** cessful *Unsuccessful applicants may appeal against the decision.* | **job | asylum, refugee**
• VERB + APPLICANT **attract** *The advertisement attracted a number of applicants.* | **shortlist** *Eighteen applicants were shortlisted.* | **interview | appoint, select | reject, turn away/down**
• APPLICANT + VERB **apply** *All applicants should apply in writing.*
• PREP. **~for** *There were over fifty applicants for the job.*

application noun

1 written request
• ADJ. **formal, written | successful** *I am pleased to tell you that your application for the post of Assistant Editor has been successful.* | **unsuccessful | job, membership, patent, planning, etc.** *All planning applications should be submitted to the local council.*
• VERB + APPLICATION **file, lodge, make, send in, submit** *The applicant must file a written application to the court.* | **withdraw | consider, examine, process, screen** *It takes time to process each application.* | **invite** *Applications are invited for the post of Lecturer in French.* | **grant** *(law) His application for bail was granted.* | **refuse** *(law)*, **reject, turn down**
• APPLICATION + NOUN **form**
• PREP. **by ~** *(formal) Admission is obtained by written application.* **on ~** *A permit is available on application to the company.* | **~for** *an application for a new licence* **~to** *an application to the local authority*

2 practical use
• ADJ. **practical** *What are the practical applications of this work?* | **general** *The program is designed for general application.* | **wide | agricultural, industrial**

3 computing
• ADJ. **client-server, database, multimedia, software**
• VERB + APPLICATION **run** *You can run several applications at the same time.* | **develop**
• APPLICATION + VERB **run**
⇨ Special page at COMPUTER

apply verb

1 be relevant
• ADV. **equally** *These principles apply equally in all cases.*
• PREP. **to** *These restrictions do not apply to us.*
• PHRASES **the same applies** *British companies are subject to international laws and the same applies to companies in Europe.*

2 put/spread on a surface
• ADV. **directly | evenly | freely | sparingly** *Apply the insecticide sparingly.*
• PREP. **over** *Apply the glue evenly over both surfaces.* **to** *Never apply the cleaning liquid directly to the surface.*

appointment noun

1 agreement to meet sb
• ADJ. **important, pressing, urgent | first, initial | follow-up | business | dental, hair | hospital, outpatient** *The hospital needs to allow more time for outpatient appointments.*
• VERB + APPOINTMENT **have | arrange, book, fix, make** *I'd like to make an appointment to see the doctor, please.* | **get** *I didn't know if I would get an appointment at such short notice.* | **give sb** *Tom has been given an appointment at the local hospital.* | **keep** *He failed to keep his appointment.* | **break, miss** *She has already broken three appointments.* | **cancel**
• PREP. **by ~** *Viewing is only allowed by appointment.* **with/without an ~** *He called without an appointment.* | **~with** *an appointment with a doctor*

2 job/position

• ADJ. **permanent, temporary | senior | academic, cabinet, court, diplomatic, ecclesiastical, executive, government, judicial, military, ministerial, political, public, university**
• VERB + APPOINTMENT **hold** *Employees may not hold any other appointments.* | **give sb, offer sb** *He was offered an appointment in the Education Department.* | **accept | obtain | take up** *He takes up his appointment in January.* | **resign** *Miss Green resigned her appointment as our regional representative.* | **secure** *By reorganizing the church hierarchy, the king was able to secure the appointment of men whom he personally favoured.*

3 choosing sb for job
• ADJ. **key** *The company has announced five key appointments at its Teesside plant.* | **formal, official | staff**
• VERB + APPOINTMENT **make | announce | confirm** *The board has confirmed the appointment of Howard Kendall as Sales Manager.*
• PREP. **to** *the first appointments to the new government*

appraisal *noun*

• ADJ. **detailed, full, thorough** *A detailed appraisal of the scheme will now be carried out.* | **frank, honest, realistic | independent | critical | economic, financial | project | performance, staff, teacher** *a formal system of performance appraisal*
• VERB + APPRAISAL **carry out, give, make** *He was asked to give an independent appraisal.* ◇ *She made a quick appraisal of the other guests.*
• APPRAISAL + NOUN **interview** *We are holding staff appraisal interviews.*

appreciate *verb*

1 recognize good qualities
• ADV. **really | fully, properly** *The sound quality was poor so we couldn't fully appreciate the music.*

2 be grateful
• ADV. **deeply, greatly, really, very much** *We do really appreciate your help.*

3 understand
• ADV. **fully, properly** *I fully appreciate your concern. We will do all in our power to help.* | **easily, readily** *The problems should be easily appreciated.*
• VERB + APPRECIATE **fail to** *The government failed to appreciate the fact that voters were angry.*
• PHRASES **be generally/widely appreciated** *It is generally appreciated that the rail network needs a complete overhaul.*

appreciation *noun*

1 understanding and enjoyment of sth
• ADJ. **deep, fine, great, real | aesthetic**
• VERB + APPRECIATION **have** *They have little appreciation of the arts.* | **show | cultivate, develop, gain** *I have now developed an appreciation of poetry.*
• PREP. **in~** *She gazed in appreciation at the scene.*

2 feeling of being grateful for sth
• ADJ. **deep, genuine, heartfelt**
• VERB + APPRECIATION **express, show** *I would like to express my appreciation and thanks to you all.*
• PREP. **in~(of)** *I'll be sending them a donation in appreciation of their help.* **with~** *'Thank you,' she murmured, with heartfelt appreciation.* | **~for** *his appreciation for all the work she had done*
• PHRASES **a lack of appreciation, (as) a token of your appreciation** *As a token of our appreciation we would like to offer you this small gift.*

3 understanding of what sth involves
• ADJ. **better, clear, deep, full, great, keen, real, wider | growing** *There is a growing appreciation of the need for change.*

• VERB + APPRECIATION **have | gain** *The course helped me to gain a deeper appreciation of what scientific research involves.*
• PREP. **~of** *She had no appreciation of the difficulties we were facing.*

apprehension *noun*

• ADJ. **considerable, great, growing | sudden**
• VERB + APPREHENSION **be filled with, be full of, feel** *They were filled with apprehension as they approached the building.* | **express, show | overcome | cause** *The change in the law has caused apprehension among many people.* | **allay** *How can I allay your apprehensions?*
• APPREHENSION + VERB **grow** *There were still areas of doubt and her apprehension grew.*
• PREP. **with ~** *School reports are always received with some apprehension.* | **~ about/over** *her apprehension about being in hospital* **~ at** *She felt some apprehension at the thought of seeing him again.* **~ for** *There is great apprehension for the future.*
• PHRASES **a feeling/look of apprehension**

apprehensive *adj.*

• VERBS **be, feel, look, seem, sound | become, get, grow | remain | make sb** *The long delay had made me quite apprehensive.*
• ADV. **deeply, extremely, very | a bit, a little, quite, rather, slightly**
• PREP. **about** *She was deeply apprehensive about her future.* **of** *He was rather apprehensive of failure.*

approach *noun*

1 way of dealing with sb/sth
• ADJ. **conventional, orthodox, traditional | alternative, different, fresh, new, novel** *We need to try alternative approaches to the problem.* | **cautious, conservative | creative, innovative | flexible | direct, no-nonsense, positive, practical, pragmatic, problem-solving, rational, useful | indirect | formal | informal | right | wrong | analytical, scientific, structured, systematic theoretical, | holistic, integrated | basic, general | objective | simplistic**
• VERB + APPROACH **have** *Some teachers have a more formal approach to teaching.* | **adopt, develop, take, try, use** *We need to adopt a more pragmatic approach.* | **favour, prefer** *She favoured the direct approach.*
• PREP. **~to** *I liked her approach to the problem*

2 act of coming nearer
• VERB + APPROACH **make** *The aircraft had to make a steep approach to the landing strip.*
• PREP. **at the~ of** *The children fell silent at the approach of their teacher.* **with the ~ of** *The weather turned colder with the approach of autumn.* | **~ to** *The plane crashed during its approach to the runway.*

3 discussion with sb in order to ask them for sth
• VERB + APPROACH **make | have, receive**
• PREP. **~ from** *We've received an approach from the director of a rival firm.* **~ to** *We'll have to make an approach to the managing director.*

approach *verb*

1 come nearer
• ADV. **slowly | cautiously, warily, with caution**
• PREP. **from** *The army approached from the south.*

2 come nearer in time
• ADV. **fast, rapidly** *The time is fast approaching when we will have to replace these old machines.*

3 speak to sb, usually to ask for sth
• ADV. **directly** *It's best to approach her directly.*
• VERB + APPROACH **be easy to | be difficult to** *She found her father difficult to approach.*

● PREP. **about** *Have you approached John about doing a concert?* **for** *I approached the bank for a loan.*

4 come close in amount/quality/style
● ADV. **closely** *Here Wordsworth's verse movement closely approaches that of Gray.* | **not nearly, not remotely** *There is no other player even remotely approaching her calibre.*

appropriate *adj.*

● VERBS **be, seem** | **consider sth, deem sth, think sth** *It was thought appropriate to award her the prize.*
● ADV. **extremely, very** | **entirely, quite**
● PREP. **for** *It might be appropriate for him to attend the course.* **to** *Tutors can construct tests appropriate to individual students' needs.*

approval *noun*

● ADJ. **full, total, unqualified, warm, wholehearted** *The scheme did not meet unqualified approval.* | **grudging, qualified** | **general, overwhelming, popular, public, unanimous, universal, widespread** | **final, initial, preliminary, prior** *All development requires the prior approval of the planning authority.* | **tacit** | **written** | **formal, official** | **government, parliamentary, royal**
● VERB + APPROVAL **need, require** | **seek, submit sth for** *We have submitted a design for approval.* | **gain, get, meet with, obtain, receive, win** *You are not allowed to build anything without first obtaining the approval of the local authority.* | **give, grant** *The government has now given its approval for the new examinations.* | **refuse, withhold** | **express, nod, show** *The people listening nodded approval.*
● PREP. **on~** *The goods were supplied on approval* (= they could be sent back if they were not satisfactory). **with ~** *Jane's father regards her fiancé with approval.* **with/without sb's ~** *You may not decorate the flat without the landlord's approval.* | **~ for** *He won approval for his project.* **~ from** *We're waiting for approval from the authorities.*
● PHRASES **a nod of approval** *She gave him a nod of approval.* **a roar of approval** *There was a roar of approval from the crowd.* **a seal/stamp of approval** *The government has given its seal of approval to the project.* **subject to approval** *The offer is subject to approval at the Annual General Meeting.*

approve *verb*

1 like sb/sth
● ADV. **heartily, strongly, thoroughly, very much, wholeheartedly** *I wholeheartedly approve of his actions.*
● PREP. **of** *I very much approve of these new tests.*

2 agree to sth
● ADV. **formally, officially** *His appointment has not been formally approved yet.* | **overwhelmingly, unanimously**

approximation *noun*

● ADJ. **close, good, nearest, reasonable** *This is the nearest approximation of cost that they can give us.* | **crude, rough** *This is only a crude approximation of the actual conditions in the area.*
● VERB + APPROXIMATION **make** *We do not have the true figures so we will have to make some approximations.* | **give (sb), provide (sb with)**

April *noun*
⇨ Note at MONTH

aptitude *noun*

● ADJ. **great, natural, special** *He has a natural aptitude for this work.*

● VERB + APTITUDE **have** | **display, show** *children who show an aptitude for sport*
● APTITUDE + NOUN **test**
● PREP. **~ for** *an aptitude for mathematics*

Arabic *noun*

● ADJ. **classical, modern**
● ARABIC + NOUN **script**
⇨ Note at LANGUAGE

arbitrary *adj.*

● VERBS **be, seem**
● ADV. **completely, entirely, purely, quite, wholly** | **fairly, rather, somewhat, to some extent** *The decision is to some extent arbitrary.* | **essentially** | **apparently**

arbitration *noun*

● ADJ. **binding** *Both sides have agreed that the arbitration will be binding.* | **independent, international**
● VERB + ARBITRATION **agree to, go to, refer sth to, submit (sth) to, take sth to** *Both parties agreed to independent arbitration.* ◇ *The matter will go to arbitration.* | **determine sth by, settle sth by** *The matter will be settled by arbitration.*
● ARBITRATION + NOUN **procedure, scheme, service, system**

arc *noun*

● ADJ. **great, high, long, sweeping, wide** *firing shells in a high arc over our heads* | **perfect**
● VERB + ARC **describe** (technical), **form, make** *forming a perfect arc in the sky*
● PREP. **in an ~** *The islands lie in a wide arc just off the mainland.*

arch *noun*

● ADJ. **pointed, round, semi-circular** | **brick, iron, masonry, stone** | **monumental, triumphal** | **Gothic, Romanesque, etc.** | **proscenium, railway** *an old theatre with a proscenium arch* ◇ *Mean little houses clustered under the railway arches.*
● VERB + ARCH **build, erect** *This huge triumphal arch was erected at the beginning of this century.* | **form, make** *The branches of the trees formed an arch over the bench.*
● PREP. **beneath an/the ~, through an/the ~, under an/the ~** *We rode under the arch.*

archaeologist *noun*

● ADJ. **amateur, professional**
● ARCHAEOLOGIST + VERB **excavate sth** | **dig sth up, discover sth, find sth, uncover sth, unearth sth** *examples of life thousands of years ago, unearthed by archaeologists*
⇨ Note at JOB

archaeology *noun*

● ADJ. **Anglo-Saxon, classical, medieval, etc.** | **environmental, industrial, marine, underwater**
⇨ Note at SUBJECT (for verbs and nouns)

archbishop *noun*

● ADJ. **Anglican, Roman Catholic**
● VERB + ARCHBISHOP **be appointed (as), become, be consecrated, be enthroned (as), be made, succeed sb as** *He was enthroned as archbishop in Canterbury Cathedral in 1980.*
● PREP. **~ of** *He was made Archbishop of Milan.*

architect noun

• ADJ. **famous, great, leading, talented** | **church, city, landscape, naval, railway**
• ARCHITECT + VERB **design sth, draw up plans (for sth)** *The house was designed by architect Louis Kahn.*
⇨ Note at PROFESSIONAL (for more verbs)

architecture noun

1 style/design of a building
• ADJ. **classical, medieval, modern | vernacular | Gothic, Romanesque, etc.** | **church, domestic, ecclesiastical, landscape, naval, railway**
• PHRASES **a school/style of architecture**
⇨ Note at SUBJECT (for verbs and nouns)

2 design and structure of a computer system
• ADJ. **client-server, hardware, network, processing, processor, software, system**

archive noun

• ADJ. **extensive** | **electronic, film, photo/photographic, sound** *The programme is preserved in the BBC sound archives.* | **company, corporate, county, family, local, national, official, personal, private, state**
• VERB + ARCHIVE **build up, create, set up** *collecting documents to build up an archive* | **house, keep, maintain** *the person responsible for keeping the archives* ◇ *the building which houses the state archives* | **hold sth in, keep sth in, preserve sth in** *The data is now held in the company archives.* | **consult, examine, look through**
• ARCHIVE + VERB **contain sth, hold sth**
• ARCHIVE + NOUN **collection** | **film, footage** *archive footage of the victory celebrations* | **material**
• PREP. **among/amongst the ~s** *There are many clues hidden amongst the archives of the local museum.* **from an/the ~** *some photographs from the library's archives* **in an/the ~** *No record of this letter exists in the archives.*

area noun

1 part of place
• ADJ. **huge, large, vast, wide** | **small** | **local** *She knows the local area very well.* | **surrounding** *The storms hit Edinburgh and the surrounding area.* | **central** | **geographical** | **isolated, outlying, remote** | **rural** | **built up, inner-city, metropolitan, urban** | **industrial** | **residential** | **coastal, mountain** | **conservation** | **deprived** *people living in socially deprived areas*
• VERB + AREA **live in** | **move into/to** *A lot of new people have moved into the area recently.* | **leave, move away from** | **cover** | **be scattered over, be spread over** *Wreckage from the plane was scattered over a large area.*
• AREA + NOUN **manager, office**
• PREP. **in an/the ~** *Few homes in the area had electricity.* **outside an/the ~** *I live outside the London area.* **within an/the ~** | **~around/round** *the area around London*

2 space
• ADJ. **dining, lounge, reception** | **picnic, play** | **no smoking, smoking** | **penalty**
• PREP. **in an/the ~** *I'll meet you in the reception area.*

3 subject/activity
• ADJ. **important, key, main** | **complex, difficult, problem, sensitive** *Taxation is a very complex area.* | **growth** *The big growth area of recent years has been in health clubs.* | **subject** | **grey** *The proposals contain too many grey areas (= aspects that are not clear).*
• VERB + AREA **cover** *The course covers two main subject areas.* | **identify** *The primary need is to identify problem areas.*
• PREP. **in an/the ~** *There have been some exciting new developments in this area.*
• PHRASES **an area of activity/life** *People with this disability can cope well in most areas of life.* **an area of con-**

cern/difficulty *We are generally pleased with how the scheme is operating but there are one or two areas of concern.* **an area of interest/research/study**

4 measurement
• ADJ. **large** | **small** | **total** | **floor, surface** *A large building with a floor area of 100m².*
• VERB + AREA **cover, have** *The estate covers an area of 106 acres.*

arena noun

1 for sports/entertainment
• ADJ. **Olympic** | **showjumping, sports** | **indoor**
• VERB + ARENA **enter** | **leave** *He left the arena to loud applause.*
• PREP. **in/into an/the ~** *The rider has to halt the horse in the arena.*

2 area of activity
• ADJ. **international, world** | **wider** *Trades unions are active both in individual workplaces and in the wider arena of the state.* | **public** | **commercial, political** | **competitive**
• VERB + ARENA **provide** *The conference should provide an arena for marketing our new products.* | **emerge into, enter, move into** *Some documents have now emerged into the public arena.* ◇ *He had no desire to enter the political arena.*
• PREP. **in/within an/the ~** *The company has been very successful in the commercial arena.* **outside an/the ~** *I want to work outside the arena of competition.*

argue verb

1 disagree
• ADV. **fiercely, furiously, heatedly** | **endlessly**
• PREP. **about** *arguing endlessly about money* **over** *They were arguing over who should have the car that day.* **with** *She's always arguing with her mother.*

2 give reasons to support opinion
• ADV. **forcefully, passionately, strongly** | **convincingly, persuasively, plausibly, successfully** *The report argues convincingly that economic help should be given to these countries.* | **sensibly**
• VERB + ARGUE **be disposed to, wish to** *I would wish to argue that appreciation of the arts should be encouraged for its own sake.* | **be prepared to** *Are you prepared to argue that killing is sometimes justified?* | **attempt to, try to** | **go on to** *In her paper she goes on to argue that scientists do not yet know enough about the nature of the disease.* | **be possible to** *It is possible to argue that the rules are too strict.* | **be difficult to**
• PREP. **against** *She argued against a rise in interest rates.* **for** *The general argued for extending the ceasefire.* **in favour of** *They argued in favour of stricter punishments.*

argument noun

1 angry discussion
• ADJ. **angry, bitter, heated, violent** | **big** *I had a big argument with my mother this morning.* | **little, silly, stupid**
• VERB + ARGUMENT **become/get involved in, get into, have** *I don't want to get into an argument with her.* | **cause, provoke, start** | **lose, win** *I was determined to win the argument.*
• ARGUMENT + VERB **arise, break out, develop, erupt** *Minutes later a violent argument erupted.*
• PREP. **~ about** *We had an argument about what we should buy.* **~ between** *an argument between her parents* **~ over** *The argument over decentralization will probably continue for ever.* **~ with** *an argument with his wife*

2 reason supporting opinion
• ADJ. **basic, general** | **main** | **good, major, powerful, sound, strong, valid** | **compelling, conclusive, convincing, persuasive** | **plausible** *Their argument sounds*

plausible but is it really valid? | **spurious, tenuous, weak** | **balanced** | **logical, rational, reasoned** | **economic, moral, political, theoretical**
- VERB + ARGUMENT **advance, deploy, offer, present, put forward** *He put forward some very convincing arguments.* | **develop** *This argument is developed further in the next chapter.* | **illustrate, support, underline** *Do you have any evidence to support your argument?* | **consider, hear, listen to** | **accept, agree with** | **dismiss, reject** *The company dismissed his arguments as alarmist.* | **counter, refute** *She tried to think how to refute the argument on moral grounds.*
- ARGUMENT + VERB **be based on sth** *The government's argument is always based on how much such a scheme would cost.* | **go, run** *Centralized government, so the argument goes, is too far removed from the problems of ordinary citizens.* | **apply (for sth)** *The same argument applies to fox-hunting.* | **justify sth** | **suggest sth** *These arguments suggest that the medical establishment had an interest in suppressing the research.*
- PREP. **~ against** *the arguments against increasing taxes* **~ concerning** *arguments concerning the nature of morality* **~ for** *There is a very good argument for increasing spending on education.* **~ in favour of** *What are the arguments in favour of change?*
- PHRASES **all/both sides of an argument** *He was able to see both sides of the argument.* **a flaw in the argument** *I can see no flaw in the argument as she has just explained it.* **a line of argument** *I can see a few problems with this line of argument.*

arise verb

- ADV. **naturally, spontaneously** | **directly**
- VERB + ARISE **may, might** | **be likely/unlikely to**
- PREP. **from** *Some learning difficulties arise from the way children are taught at school.* **out of** *The current debate arose out of the concerns of parents.*

aristocracy noun

- ADJ. **British, French, etc.** | **landed, landowning** | **local**
- PHRASES **a member of the aristocracy**

arithmetic noun

- ADJ. **basic, simple** | **mental** *a test of mental arithmetic*
- VERB + ARITHMETIC **do** *By the age of ten, the children can do simple arithmetic.* | **check** *I've worked out the price, but I need to check the arithmetic.*

arm noun

- ADJ. **left, right** | **upper** *the muscles of the upper arm* | **strong** | **good** *He used his good arm to support his weight.* | **bad, broken, weak, withered** *I've got a bad arm so I'm afraid I can't help you.* | **open** *(often figurative),* **outstretched** *They're sure to welcome you with open arms.* | **bare**
- VERB + ARM **bend, move** | **lower, raise** *The figure in the boat raised an arm.* | **break, dislocate, hurt, twist** | **hold out, open, stretch out** *He held out his arms with a broad smile.* | **cross, fold** *She folded her arms and stared at him.* | **link** *The couple linked arms and set off along the beach.* | **wave** *He was running towards them, waving his arms.* | **catch (at), catch hold of, grab, take** *A hand reached out and caught hold of her arm.* ◇ *She moved towards her father and took his arm.* | **grip, hold, squeeze, touch** | **fall into** *They fell into each other's arms.* | **draw/gather/pull sb into, take sb in** *He pulled her into his arms and kissed her.* | **hold sb in**
- ARM + VERB **drop** | **hang** *His arm hung awkwardly against his side.* | **tighten** *Her arms tightened convulsively round the child.*

- PREP. **by the ~** *The officer grabbed him by the arm* (= grabbed his arm). **in sb's ~** *The child lay in its mother's arms.* **on the ~** *She touched him gently on the arm.* **on your ~** *Lucy felt the warm sun on her bare arms.* ◇ *He walked in with a tall blonde on his arm* (= next to him and holding his arm). **under an/your ~** *She carried the dog under one arm.*
- PHRASES **arm in arm** *They walked along arm in arm* (= with the arm of one person linked with the arm of the other), **at arm's length** *He held the dirty rag at arm's length* (= as far away from his body as possible). **the crook of an/sb's arm** *She lay curled up in the crook of his arm.* **fling/put/throw, etc. your arms around/round sb/sth** *He ran towards her and flung his arms around her.* ◇ *He put an arm around her shoulders.* **in each other's arms** *They fell asleep in each other's arms* (= holding each other). **with arms akimbo** (= with your arms bent and your hands on your hips) *She stood looking at him with arms akimbo.*

armaments noun

- ADJ. **conventional, nuclear**
- VERB + ARMAMENTS **manufacture, produce**
- ARMAMENTS + NOUN **factory, industry, production**

armchair noun

- ADJ. **big, deep, large** | **comfortable, comfy** | **battered, old, worn** | **leather, upholstered, wicker, wooden**
- VERB + ARMCHAIR **be seated in, be slumped in, be sprawled in, sit in** | **collapse into, flop into, throw yourself into** | **curl up in, ease yourself into, settle into** *He eased himself into the big armchair.*

armed adj.

- VERBS **be**
- ADV. **heavily, well** | **lightly** | **fully**
- PREP. **with** *The soldiers were all armed with automatic rifles.*

armistice noun

- VERB + ARMISTICE **ask for, call for, seek** | **negotiate, work out** | **agree to, sign**
- PREP. **~ with** *to sign an armistice with the Americans*

armour noun

- ADJ. **full, heavy** | **light** | **body** *the police should be protected by body armour.* | **protective**
- VERB + ARMOUR **have on, wear** | **put on, take off** | **penetrate, pierce** *An arrow had pierced his armour.*
- PREP. **in ~** *warriors in full armour*
- PHRASES **a suit of armour** *He wore a suit of heavy armour and carried a sword.*

armoured adj.

- VERBS **be**
- ADV. **heavily** *a convoy of heavily armoured vehicles* | **lightly** | **fully** *a horse capable of carrying a fully armoured knight*

arms noun

- ADJ. **nuclear** | **small** *fighters using small arms and home-made grenades*
- VERB + ARMS **bear, carry** *The right to bear arms is enshrined in the constitution.* | **call sb to** *(formal) He called his comrades to arms* (= urged them to fight). | **take up** *(formal) The people took up arms to defend their country.* | **lay down** *(formal) The government called on them to lay down their arms and surrender.* | **supply** *He was accused of supplying arms to terrorists*

● ARMS + NOUN **race** | **control, embargo** | **deal, industry, sales, trade**
● PREP. **under ~** (*formal*) *There were more than a million men under arms during the American Civil War.*

army noun

1 group of soldiers
● ADJ. **great, huge, large, mighty, powerful** | **small** | **professional, regular, standing** | **reserve** | **conscript** | **volunteer** | **disciplined** | **modern** | **allied** | **enemy** | **opposing** | **foreign** | **national** | **private** | **guerrilla** | **rebel** | **advancing, invading, occupying, victorious** | **defeated, retreating**
● VERB + ARMY **have** | **go into, join** *After leaving school Mike went into the army.* | **leave** | **be in command of, command, lead** *He was in command of the British Army in Egypt.* ◊ *He led the army into battle.* | **drill, train** | **amass, build up, raise, recruit** *The king was unable to raise an army.* | **equip, supply** | **mobilize, deploy, field** *The French army was deployed in the Western Desert.* | **concentrate** | **crush, decimate, defeat, put to flight, rout** *The army was finally defeated in the autumn.* | **demobilize, disband** *The emperor was deposed and his army disbanded.*
● ARMY + VERB **gather** | **advance, march** *A huge army marched on London.* | **camp** | **go into action, invade** | **attack, clash, fight** *The two opposing armies clashed in battle.* | **occupy** | **flee, pull back, retreat, withdraw**
● ARMY + NOUN **captain, chief, commander, general, officer** | **corps, personnel, unit** | **barracks, base, camp, headquarters** | **career** | **patrol** | **greatcoat, uniform** | **wife**
● PREP. **in the ~** *Her husband is in the army.*

2 large group
● ADJ. **vast** *a vast army of personnel* | **small** *a small army of volunteers* | **growing, increasing** | **reserve**
● PREP. **of** *He argued that unemployment created a useful reserve army of labour.*

aroma noun

● ADJ. **pungent, rich, strong** | **distinctive** | **lingering** | **faint, subtle** | **pleasant, sweet, wonderful** | **appetizing, mouth-watering**
● VERB + AROMA **savour, smell** *As soon as I opened the front door I smelled the distinctive aroma of fresh coffee.* | **be filled with, have** *The room was filled with a strong aroma of woodsmoke.*
● AROMA + VERB **linger, waft** *The aroma of fresh baking wafted towards her.*

arrange verb

1 plan/organize sth
● ADV. **easily** | **with difficulty** *These things can be arranged with difficulty.* | **hastily, hurriedly, quickly** | **secretly** | **specially**
● VERB + ARRANGE **try to** | **be able to, can/could** *Todd will be able to arrange matters.* | **be difficult/easy/possible to** *These matters are easy to arrange.*
● PREP. **for** *I'd be very grateful if you could arrange for this work to be carried out.*

2 put in order; make neat/attractive
● ADV. **carefully, neatly** *Her red hair was carefully arranged and her face made up.* | **alphabetically, chronologically, symmetrically, systematically** *The books are arranged alphabetically by author.*
● PREP. **in** *She arranged the chairs in neat rows.* **into** *She took the list of visitors' names and arranged them into groups of four.*
● PHRASES **arrange sth in alphabetical/chronological order** *The names are arranged in alphabetical order.*

arrangement noun

1 plans/organization
● ADJ. **alternative, better, different, new, other** *It may be necessary to make alternative arrangements.* | **final** | **practical** | **satisfactory, sensible, suitable** | **careful, detailed** | **flexible** | **conventional** | **unconventional, unusual** | **special** *There are special arrangements for people working overseas.* | **formal** | **necessary, proper** | **administrative, organizational** | **domestic, funeral, holiday, living, pension, seating, security, sleeping, travel, working** *Their domestic arrangements were considered unconventional at the time.*
● VERB + ARRANGEMENT **make** | **complete, confirm, finalize** *Arrangements for the trip have now been completed.* | **discuss** *We are just discussing the final arrangements for the concert.* | **upset** *All her careful arrangements had been upset!*
● ARRANGEMENT + VERB **stand** *As far as I know the arrangement still stands.* | **fall through** *The catering arrangements for the conference have fallen through.*
● PREP. **~ for** *Arrangements for the funeral are complete.* **~ with** *I have made arrangements with the shop for the goods to be delivered here.*

2 agreement
● ADJ. **business, financial** *It's purely a business arrangement—there's no need to get emotionally involved.* | **convenient** | **special** | **formal** | **informal** | **voluntary** | **private** | **reciprocal** | **long-standing, long-term, permanent** | **interim, temporary**
● VERB + ARRANGEMENT **have** *The company has a special arrangement with the bank.* | **agree, come to, make** *She made an arrangement with her employer whereby she worked a reduced number of hours.*
● PREP. **by (an/the) ~** *Viewing of the property is only possible by arrangement with the owner.* ◊ *The couple have an arrangement by which they each contribute equally to the cost of the house.* **under an/the ~** *Under this arrangement you can pay for the goods over a longer period.* | **~ between** *an arrangement between the two men* **~ with** *He finally came to an arrangement with his landlord.*
● PHRASES **by prior arrangement** *A tour of the theatre is available by prior arrangement.*

3 group of things placed together
● ADJ. **complex, complicated** *a complex arrangement of rods and cogs* | **physical** *Even the physical arrangement of the classroom can influence the way children learn.* | **floral, flower**
● VERB + ARRANGEMENT **design, do** *Who did this beautiful flower arrangement?*

array noun

● ADJ. **broad, diverse, extensive, huge, vast, wide** | **bewildering, colourful, confusing, dazzling, fascinating, fine, formidable, glittering, impressive, remarkable, rich, splendid, staggering, stunning, wonderful** *a dazzling array of talent*
● VERB + ARRAY **have, offer, provide** *The store offers a bewildering array of garden tools.* | **be faced with** *The customer is faced with a formidable array of products.* | **choose from, select from** *It is difficult to choose from the vast array of wines on offer.*

arrears noun

● ADJ. **debt, mortgage, rent, tax**
● VERB + ARREARS **fall into, get into, owe** *They fell into arrears with their rent.* ◊ *The government has agreed to pay all arrears owed to members of the armed forces.* | **accumulate** *The country had accumulated arrears of $80 million on loans of $400 million.* | **pay (off)** *struggling to pay off her mortgage arrears* | **recover** *The local authority must try to recover arrears of rent.*

● ARREARS + VERB **amount to sth, total sth** *By this time the arrears amounted to £12 000.*
● PREP. **in~** *She was six months in arrears with the mortgage.* ◇ *You will be paid monthly in arrears.* | **~on** *There have been sharp increases in arrears on interest payments.*

arrest *noun*

● ADJ. **illegal, unlawful, wrongful | arbitrary | mass, widespread | citizen's** *He grabbed the intruder by the arm and said, 'I am making a citizen's arrest.'* | **house** *Following the coup, parliamentary leaders were put under house arrest.*
● VERB + ARREST **make | place sb under, put sb under | lead to** *A reward has been offered for information that leads to the arrest of the murderer.* | **avoid, escape, evade | resist** *He was charged with violent behaviour and resisting arrest.*
● ARREST + NOUN **warrant**
● PREP. **under~** *The man is now under arrest in London.* | **~for** *They made 11 arrests for possession of drugs.*
● PHRASES **the power of arrest** *The government may remove the power of arrest from military police.* **under close arrest** *Woolley was placed under close arrest for mutiny.* **a warrant for sb's arrest**

arrival *noun*

1 act of arriving
● ADJ. **early | late | timely** *The timely arrival of the cheque took away the need to borrow money.* | **eventual | dramatic, sudden, surprise, unexpected | expected, imminent, impending** *I told her of my brother's expected arrival.*
● VERB + ARRIVAL **announce, herald, signal** *A fanfare of trumpets heralded the arrival of the King.* | **expect | await** *a crowd awaiting the arrival of the film star* | **greet** *The staff greeted the arrival of the new head teacher with excitement.* | **celebrate, welcome | delay | hasten**
● ARRIVAL + NOUN **time**
● PREP. **on/upon (sb's)~** *Guests receive dinner upon arrival at the hotel.* **with the ~** *With the arrival of John's friends, the party became really enjoyable.* | **~ at** *his arrival at the theatre* | **in** *their arrival in Paris*
● PHRASES **arrival on the scene** *They were saved by the arrival on the scene of another boat.* **arrivals and departures** *There are 120 arrivals and departures every day.* **time of arrival** *your expected time of arrival is 7.15.*

2 sb/sth that arrives
● ADJ. **early, first | late** *Someone should stay here to meet the late arrivals.* | **latest, new, recent** *The club has a dinner to welcome new arrivals to the town.* ◇ *We're expecting a new arrival (= a baby) in the family soon.*
● VERB + ARRIVAL **expect | meet | welcome**

arrive *verb*

● ADV. **early, late | shortly, soon** *We should arrive shortly.* | **finally** *We finally arrived at our destination late that evening.* | **on time, punctually | safe and sound, safely | unannounced** *My uncle arrived unannounced yesterday evening.*
● VERB + ARRIVE **be due to** *We are due to arrive in Rome at ten o'clock.* | **fail to** *The package failed to arrive.*
● PREP. **at** *We arrived at the hotel late.* **in** *I should arrive in London tomorrow morning.*
● PHRASES **the first/last to arrive**

arrogance *noun*

● ADJ. **breathtaking, supreme | unconscious**
● VERB + ARROGANCE **have** *She had the arrogance to believe the law did not apply to her.* | **display, show**

arrow *noun*

1 weapon
● ADJ. **poison/poisoned**
● QUANT. **hail, volley** *A hail of arrows descended from the tower.*
● VERB + ARROW **fire, shoot**
● ARROW + VERB **hit sb/sth** *The arrow hit its target.* | **miss (sb/sth)** *She aimed carefully at the tree but the arrow missed.*
● ARROW + NOUN **head** (also **arrowhead**) | **slit** *the arrow slits in the castle's battlements*
● PHRASES **a bow and arrow** *The people used bows and arrows for hunting.*

2 symbol
● ADJ. **left, right | down, up** *The down arrow indicates rain.* | **broken, curved** *The old road is shown on the map by broken arrows.*
● VERB + ARROW **follow** *Follow the red arrows to get to the camp reception.*
● ARROW + VERB **denote sth, indicate sth, mark sth, point, show sth** *You will see an arrow pointing to the left.*
● ARROW + NOUN **key** *You can scroll through the text using the up and down arrow keys.*

arson *noun*

● ADJ. **attempted**
● ARSON + NOUN **attack**
⇨ Note at CRIME (for verbs)

NOTES
Works of art

a piece/work of art
 Michelangelo's Pietà is a magnificent work of art.
collect~
 She collects Jacobean portraits.
display, exhibit, show~
 The works will be displayed in the new wing of the museum.
~be (put) on display/exhibition/show
~go on display/exhibition/show
 paintings put on show for the first time
 The photographs are on exhibition until the end of September.
house~
 An annexe was built to house the sculptures.
a series of~
 a series of paintings by Van Gogh
a collection/exhibition of~
 an exhibition of early 20th century French masterpieces
an art/photographic/photography exhibition
 The open art exhibition will allow new artists to exhibit their work.
by~
 a sculpture by Barbara Hepworth

---

art *noun*

1 paintings, drawings, etc.
● ADJ. **great, high | abstract, avant-garde, commercial, conceptual, figurative, fine, graphic, performance, pop/popular, sacred, visual | contemporary, modern**
● VERB + ART **create, produce** *one of the greatest works of art ever produced*
● ART + NOUN **gallery | collector, critic, dealer, historian, lover | treasure, work** (also **artwork**) | **college, school | form** *Cinema became accepted as an art form.* | **history | market | world** *Many people from the art world attended the painter's funeral.*

2 the arts art, music, theatre, literature, etc.

● ADJ. **creative, decorative, dramatic, performing, plastic, visual**
● PHRASES **arts and crafts** *an exhibition of Peruvian arts and crafts* **funding for the arts, a patron of the arts, sponsorship of the arts**

3 arts not sciences
● ARTS + NOUN **subject | degree**
● PHRASES **arts and sciences**

4 ability/skill
● VERB + ART **master, perfect** *I've never mastered the art of making bread.*
● PREP. **~ of** *Television has ruined the art of conversation.*
● PHRASES **get sth down to a fine art** (= learn to do it very well) *She's got the business of buying Christmas presents down to a fine art.*

artery *noun*

● ADJ. **main, major | blocked, clogged | severed | carotid, coronary, pulmonary, etc.**
● VERB + ARTERY **block | widen** *The surgeon will widen her arteries.* **| rupture, sever**
● ARTERY + VERB **clog up** *Too much fatty food will make your arteries more likely to clog up.*
● PHRASES **hardening of the arteries** (= a disease of the arteries) *She suffers from hardening of the arteries.* **veins and arteries** *blood flowing through veins and arteries*

arthritis *noun*

● ADJ. **severe | chronic | rheumatoid**
● VERB + ARTHRITIS **have, suffer (from) | develop, get** *It is unclear why some people develop arthritis.* **| treat**
● ARTHRITIS + NOUN **sufferer**
● PHRASES **crippled with arthritis**
⇨ Special page at ILLNESS

article *noun*

1 piece of writing
● ADJ. **brilliant, excellent, good, informative, interesting | influential, major, seminal | controversial, critical, provocative | in-depth | feature, lead/leading, review** *A leading article in 'The Times' accused the minister of lying.* **| occasional** (= not part of a series) *It was her job to commission occasional articles.* **| offending** *An advertisement will now replace the offending article.* **| academic, learned, scholarly | journal, magazine, newspaper, periodical, press**
● QUANT. **series**
● VERB + ARTICLE **commission | do** *I'm doing an article about ways of preventing pollution.* **| contribute, submit | read, see** *Did you see the article on Europe in today's paper?* **| carry, feature, print, publish, run** *The magazine refused to print his article.*
● ARTICLE + VERB **appear** *The article appears in this week's edition of 'The Spectator'.* **| describe sth, detail sth, explain sth, point sth out, say sth, state sth | discuss sth, examine sth, explore sth, focus on sth, look at sth** *The article looks at two questions.* **| allege sth, argue sth, claim sth, imply sth, suggest sth | attack sb/sth, criticize sb/sth | cite sb/sth, quote sb/sth | continue, go on** *The article goes on to quote from Darwin's 'Origin of Species'.* **| conclude sth**
● PREP. **in an/the ~** *She admitted she was wrong in an article in the newspaper.* **| ~ about, ~ by** *an article about atomic clocks by Professor Keith Runcorn* **~ on** *an article on the dangers of sunbathing*
● PHRASES **an article called/entitled/headed sth** *an article entitled 'Think Yourself Thin'*

2 part of law
● ADJ. **key** *The key articles of the constitution can only be changed by referendum.*
● VERB + ARTICLE **be in breach of, breach, contra-**

vene, flout, infringe, violate *The actions of the organization are in breach of Article 12 of the treaty.*
● ARTICLE + VERB **provide sth, specify sth, state sth** *Article 10 provides that all businesses must be registered correctly.*
● PREP. **under an/the ~** *The judge ordered the child's return home under Article 12 of the Convention.*
● PHRASES **the terms of an article** *The terms of Article 3 will be changed by the new government.*

3 thing
● ADJ. **finished** *The finished article takes two months to manufacture.* **| the genuine** *Fake designer watches are sold at a fraction of the price of the genuine article.* **| offending | household, toilet**
● VERB + ARTICLE **make, manufacture, produce**
● PHRASES **an article of clothing**

4 grammar
● ADJ. **definite, indefinite**
● VERB + ARTICLE **take** *Names of countries in English do not usually take an article.*

articulate *verb*

1 pronounce sth carefully
● ADV. **carefully, clearly, well** *She spoke slowly, articulating each word clearly.* **| poorly**

2 express sth
● ADV. **clearly, well** *She cannot articulate her feelings very well.* **| fully | poorly**

articulate *adj.*

● VERBS **be | become**
● ADV. **highly, very** *a highly articulate woman*
● PREP. **about** *The teachers help the children to be more articulate about their strengths and weaknesses.*

artificial *adj.*

● VERBS **be, look, seem**
● ADV. **highly, very | completely, entirely, totally | increasingly | a little, quite, rather, slightly, somewhat | patently** *a patently artificial contrivance*

artillery *noun*

● ADJ. **field | heavy** *The enemy has enough heavy artillery to win the war.*
● ARTILLERY + NOUN **attack, barrage, bombardment, fire | piece, shell | train, unit** *The soldiers of the artillery train had panicked and cut the traces of their horses.* ◇ *nuclear artillery units*

artist *noun*

1 person who creates works of art
● ADJ. **gifted, great, talented | distinguished, established, famous, leading, major, successful, well-known | aspiring, budding, up-and-coming | struggling, unknown | amateur, professional | self-taught | serious** *He is a serious artist, and totally committed to his work.* **| local | female, woman | male | creative | real, true** *(figurative) My husband is a real artist in the kitchen.* **| abstract, avant-garde, commercial, conceptual, figurative, fine, graffiti, graphic, landscape, make-up, pavement, performance, pop/popular, scenic, visual, war, watercolour, wildlife | contemporary, living, modern, nineteenth-century, etc.**
● VERB + ARTIST **commission** *In 1942 the city commissioned war artist John Piper to paint its bombed cathedral.* **| feature** *an exhibition featuring wildlife artist Emma Gray*
● ARTIST + VERB **create sth, draw (sth), paint (sth), produce sth** *an artist who paints in oils* **| work** *artists who work in different media* **| exhibit sth, show sth** *Local*

watercolour artists are currently exhibiting their work in the town hall.
• PHRASES **an artist in residence** *the new artist in residence at the Tate Gallery*
2 (*also* **artiste**) a professional entertainer
• ADJ. **guest** *The Blue Note Quartet will be the guest artists tomorrow night.* | **solo** | **recording** | **cabaret, escape, mime, music hall, rap, reggae, trapeze, variety**
• VERB + ARTIST **feature** *The festival featured artists such John Mclaughlin and Russell Malone.*
• ARTIST + VERB **perform (sth)** | **work**
⇨ Note at JOB

ascend *verb*

• ADV. **gently** | **steeply**
• PREP. **from** *The road ascends steeply from the harbour.*

ascent *noun*

1 act of climbing/moving up
• ADJ. **gradual, slow**
• VERB + ASCENT **make** *The climbers made their ascent of the mountain without oxygen.*
• PREP. **~from** *the ascent from the valley* **~ to** *their ascent to the summit*
2 upward path/slope
• ADJ. **steep** | **long**
• VERB + ASCENT **climb** *climbing the steep ascent on to the plateau* | **to** *a steep ascent to the village*
3 becoming more important or powerful
• ADJ. **rapid** | **gradual** | **~to** *her rapid ascent to power*

ash *noun*

1 powder that is left after sth has burnt
• ADJ. **glowing, hot, red-hot, smouldering** *the glowing ashes of the dying fire* | **cold, dead** *The fire had died to cold ashes.* | **fine** *Fine ash covered the hill near the volcano.* | **bonfire, cigarette, coal, volcanic, wood**
• QUANT. **cloud** *A cloud of ash rose from the volcano.*
• VERB + ASH **flick, tap** (used about cigarette ash) *He flicked ash into the ashtray.* | **reduce sth to, turn to ~es** *a village reduced to ashes by war* ◇ (*figurative*) *All her dreams had turned to ashes.*
• ASH + VERB **fall** *Ash from the volcano fall over a wide area.*
• PHRASES **rise from the ashes** (*figurative*) *The party had risen, like a phoenix, from the ashes of electoral disaster.*
2 **ashes** remains of a dead body
• VERB + ASHES **scatter** *His ashes were scattered on his beloved farm.*

ashamed *adj.*

• VERBS **be, feel, look, seem, sound** | **make sb** *His foul-mouthed way of speaking made me ashamed of him.*
• ADV. **deeply, really, terribly, very** | **thoroughly** | **a little, rather, slightly, somewhat** | **bitterly** | **instantly, suddenly** *Then she smiled and Rose was instantly ashamed of her jealous feelings.*
• PREP. **about** *I've done nothing to be ashamed about.* **at** *He was slightly ashamed at having run away.* **of** *She was ashamed of what she had done.*

ask *verb*

1 put a question to sb
• ADV. **gently, quietly, softly** *'How do you feel?' she asked softly.* | **amiably, conversationally, politely** *'Did you sleep well?' he asked politely.* | **belligerently, crossly, icily, nastily, querulously, sarcastically, slyly, testily** | **casually, dryly, innocently** *'Oh, Sue went too, did she?' I asked innocently* (= pretending I did not know that this was important). | **curiously, incredulously, pointedly, suspiciously** | **anxiously, apprehensively, fearfully, so-**

licitously *'Will he be all right?' Sabrina asked anxiously.* | **legitimately** *We can legitimately ask what competence an official based in Whitehall has to solve the problems of rural Scotland.* | **rhetorically**
• VERB + ASK **long to, want to** *She longed to ask Mary if she knew what was wrong.* ◇ *I wanted to ask him a question.* | **dare (to)** *I wondered how old she was but I didn't dare ask.* | **forget to** *I completely forgot to ask his name.*
• PREP. **about** *He asked about her family.*
• PHRASES **get asked sth** *I often get asked that.* **if you don't mind me/my asking** *How old are you—if you don't mind my asking?*
2 request sth
• ADV. **nicely** *If you ask her nicely, she'll give you a sweet.*
• PREP. **for** *asking for money*

asleep *adj.*

• VERBS **be, lie, seem** *The baby lay peacefully asleep in its pram.* ◇ *All the houses seemed asleep.* | **drop, fall** *I fell asleep almost immediately.* | **remain, stay**
• ADV. **deeply, fast, heavily, sound** *The children were all sound asleep in bed.* | **almost, half, nearly** *At the end of the afternoon they were exhausted and half asleep.* | **peacefully** | **still**

aspect *noun*

• ADJ. **central, crucial, essential, fundamental, important, key, main, major, principal, significant** | **basic, broad, general** *Questions also cover much broader aspects of general health and fitness.* | **appealing, attractive, beneficial, encouraging, exciting, fascinating, interesting, pleasing, positive** | **alarming, controversial, difficult, disappointing, disturbing, negative, sinister, terrible, worst** *the worst aspects of tourism* | **bizarre, curious, intriguing, puzzling** | **remarkable, striking** | **subtle** | **mundane** | **neglected** | **formal, functional, practical, theoretical** *the formal aspects of the language system* | **business, commercial, cultural, economic, environmental, ethical, financial, historical, human, legal, military, moral, physical, political, psychological, religious, scientific, social, technical**
• VERB + ASPECT **have** *The project has two main aspects.* | **take on** *Events began to take on a more sinister aspect.* | **consider, cover, deal with, discuss, emphasize, examine, explore, focus on, look at, study** *We will be looking at many different aspects of pollution.* | **demonstrate, illuminate, illustrate** *a unique collection illustrating aspects of Irish transport history* | **ignore, neglect**
• PREP. **from the … ~** *This scheme is very good from the social aspect.* | **~to** *the positive aspects to retirement*
• PHRASES **all aspects of sth, (in) every aspect (of sth)** *The service was excellent in every aspect.*

aspiration *noun*

• ADJ. **high, lofty** *He has high aspirations and wants to improve his qualifications.* | **failed** | **career, national, personal, political, social**
• ADJ. **have** | **achieve, fulfil, meet, realize, satisfy** *a political party that fulfils the aspirations of the British people*
• PREP. **~ for** *an aspiration for personal power* **~ to** *the country's aspirations to independence* **~ towards** *aspirations towards starting his own business*
• PHRASES **dreams/hopes/needs/values and aspirations** *She talked about her hopes and aspirations.*

aspirin *noun*

• ADJ. **soluble**
• QUANT. **dose**
• VERB + ASPIRIN **take** *She took an aspirin and went to bed.* | **dissolve** *Dissolve two aspirin in water.*
• ASPIRIN + VERB **dissolve** *Aspirin dissolves quickly.*

assassin *noun*

- ADJ. **attempted, would-be | hired, professional** *He was killed by a hired assassin.* | **trained**

assassinate *verb*

- VERB + ASSASSINATE **attempt to, try to | plan to, plot to** *He was executed in 1887 for plotting to assassinate the tsar.*
- PHRASES **an attempt/a plot to assassinate sb**

assassination *noun*

- ADJ. **attempted | failed | political** *Three local leaders have been killed in political assassinations.* | **character** *a vicious campaign of character assassination*
- VERB + ASSASSINATION **carry out | plan, plot** *It is believed that they plotted the assassination of the king.* | **escape, survive** *The judge escaped assassination by drug dealers.*
- ASSASSINATION + NOUN **attempt, plot** *He has survived several assassination attempts.* | **squad**

assault *noun*

1 crime of attacking sb
- ADJ. **brutal, savage, vicious, violent | common** (*law*) | **aggravated** (*law*), **serious | alleged | attempted | indecent, physical, racial, sexual | police**
- QUANT. **series, wave**
- VERB + ASSAULT **carry out, commit** *assaults committed by teenagers* | **be the victim of, suffer**
- ASSAULT + VERB **happen, take place**
- PREP. **~against** *Better street lighting has helped reduce the number of assaults against women.* **~on/upon**
- PHRASES **allegations of assault** *allegations of police assault on the boy* **assault and battery** (*law*)
  ⇨ Note at CRIME (for more verbs)

2 military/verbal attack
- ADJ. **all-out, direct, frontal, full-scale, major, massive** *After an all-out assault the village was captured by the enemy.* | **fresh, further | sustained** *She used the article to make a sustained assault on her former political allies.* | **successful | air, amphibious, ground** *air assaults by fighter planes* | **military | verbal**
- QUANT. **series**
- VERB + ASSAULT **carry out, launch (into), lead, make, mount** *Enemy troops launched an assault on the town.* ◊ *He launched into a verbal assault on tabloid journalism.* | **come under** *The factory came under assault from soldiers in the mountains* | **withstand** *The garrison was built to withstand assaults.*
- ASSAULT + NOUN **course** *They took part in a vigorous army assault course.* | **rifle | force**
- PREP. **under~** *Today these values are under assault.* **~on** *a series of assaults on enemy targets*

assault *verb*

- ADV. **badly, brutally, savagely, seriously, violently | indecently, physically, sexually, verbally**

assemble *verb*

- ADV. **carefully | badly | hastily, quickly** *a hastily assembled force of warriors* | **easily | together**
- VERB + ASSEMBLE **begin to** *The French began to assemble an army* | **manage to | be easy to, be possible to | be difficult to**
- PREP. **for** *We had assembled for the first rehearsal.* **into** *the force that permits atoms to assemble into molecules*
- PHRASES **fully/partially assembled** *The shelves are available in kit form or fully assembled.*

assembly *noun*

1 elected group
- ADJ. **elected, representative | consultative, general, legislative | local, national, provincial, regional, state**
- VERB + ASSEMBLY **create, form, set up | elect, vote for | dissolve**
- ASSEMBLY + VERB **meet** *Provincial assemblies meet once a year.* | **vote** *The assembly voted to delay the legislation to allow further consultation to take place.*
- ASSEMBLY + NOUN **member | seat**
- PREP. **in an/the~** *These issues have been discussed in the regional assemblies.*
- PHRASES **a meeting/session of the assembly**
  ⇨ Note at ORGANIZATION

2 group gathered together
- ADJ. **public | peaceful | unlawful**
- VERB + ASSEMBLY **hold** *They demanded the right to hold peaceful assemblies.*
- ASSEMBLY + NOUN **point** *When the fire alarm sounds, leave the building and proceed to your assembly point.*
- PHRASES **freedom of assembly, the right of assembly** (= the right to gather freely)

3 at school
- ADJ. **school | morning**
- VERB + ASSEMBLY **conduct, have, hold** *We hold an assembly every morning.* | **attend, go to**
- ASSEMBLY + NOUN **hall**
- PREP. **at/during/in~** *The announcement was made during morning assembly.*

4 putting parts together
- ADJ. **easy | home** *furniture designed for home assembly* | **correct | final** *This factory deals with final assembly and testing.*
- ASSEMBLY + NOUN **line** *workers on the assembly line* | **plant** *The company has twenty assembly plants in Europe.* | **work**

assent *noun*

- ADJ. **common, general, universal** *Medicine is, by common assent, a good profession.* ◊ *There was general assent about his achievements.* | **royal** *The Education Act received the royal assent in 1944.*
- VERB + ASSENT **give sth, grant** *The government gave their assent to the project.* | **withhold | meet with, obtain, receive | express, grunt, indicate, nod** *He nodded his assent when I asked if I could leave.*
- PREP. **in~** *She smiled in assent.* **with/without sb's~** *The raising of taxes without the assent of Parliament was declared illegal.*
- PHRASES **a murmur/nod of assent** *The suggestion was greeted with a murmur of assent.*

assert *verb*

1 say sth clearly and firmly
- ADV. **boldly, confidently, emphatically, forcefully, strongly** *The report asserts confidently that the industry will grow.* | **directly, explicitly | simply** *He had no real evidence—he simply asserted that what he said was true.* | **repeatedly | rightly**

2 make other people recognize your rights/authority
- ADV. **successfully** *They successfully asserted their right to protect their homes.*
- VERB + ASSERT **need to | be determined to, wish to** *She wished to assert her independence from her parents.* | **seek to, try to | be able to, manage to** *He managed to assert his power over the media.* | **be unable to, fail to**

assertion *noun*

- ADJ. **bold, confident, proud | categorical, dogmatic, general, sweeping** *sweeping assertions about the role of women in society* | **simple** *The argument needs to pro-*

gress beyond the simple assertion that criminals are made not born. | **unfounded, unsubstantiated, unsupported**
● VERB + ASSERTION **make** *How can you make such an assertion?* | **justify, prove, support** *Your assertion is not supported by the facts.* | **accept, agree with** | **challenge, question** *Researchers have recently challenged these assertions.* | **reject** | **refute**
● PREP. **~about** *assertions about human nature*

assess *verb*

1 form an opinion
● ADV. **fully** | **accurately, correctly, properly**
● VERB + ASSESS **attempt to, try to** | **help to** | **be difficult to** *It is difficult to fully assess the damage.*
2 amount/value
● ADV. **accurately, correctly, properly**
● VERB + ASSESS **attempt to, try to** | **be difficult to** *It is difficult to assess the building's value properly without seeing it.*
● PREP. **at** *The legal costs have been assessed at £75 000.*

assessment *noun*

● ADJ. **broad, general, overall** | **individual** | **continuous, regular** *Examination is by continuous assessment.* | **quick, rapid** | **external, internal** | **initial** | **final** | **accurate, balanced, fair, good, proper, realistic** | **careful, comprehensive, detailed, formal, systematic, thorough** | **independent, objective** | **personal, subjective** *He was shrewd in his personal assessments.* | **adequate** | **critical** | **optimistic, pessimistic** | **course** | **tax** | **needs, performance, quality, risk** *Needs assessment is crucial if the hospital is to deliver effective health care.* | **environmental, financial, medical, psychiatric, scientific**
● VERB + ASSESSMENT **carry out, do, give, make, undertake** *The new manager carried out an assessment of the sales department.*
● ASSESSMENT + NOUN **methods, procedures, technique** | **criteria** | **process, system**
● PHRASES **a form/method of assessment**

asset *noun*

1 useful person/thing
● ADJ. **big, considerable, great, important, invaluable, precious, priceless, real, tremendous, useful, valuable** *The teachers are the school's biggest asset.* | **best, main, major, principal, prize** | **cultural** *The tourist industry requires that the country's cultural assets be made more accessible.* | **natural** *Bow windows are a natural asset to any room and should be highlighted.*
● PREP. **~to** *She will be an asset to any school she attends.*
2 what a company owns
● ADJ. **combined, total** | **gross** | **net** *The company's net assets are worth millions.* | **business, company, corporate** | **commercial, financial** | **current, disposable, liquid** *Liquid assets can be sold more quickly.* | **capital, fixed, non-cash, non-monetary, physical, property** | **tangible** | **intangible** | **depreciable, wasting** | **hidden** *They have hidden assets in banks around the world.* | **foreign, overseas** | **personal** | **national, public, state**
● VERB + ASSET **have, hold, own, possess** *assets held by the company in Asia* | **transfer** *He transferred all his assets into his wife's name.* | **accumulate, acquire, buy** | **dispose of, realize, sell** *The business disposed of all its capital assets.* | **increase, reduce** *The company has increased its UK assets.* | **freeze** *The courts can order a company's assets to be frozen.* | **release, unfreeze**
● ASSET + VERB **appreciate, grow** *Net assets have grown to $169 million.* | **decline, depreciate, dwindle**
● ASSET + NOUN **value** | **management** | **sale** | **stripping** *measures to prevent asset stripping*
● PHRASES **assets and liabilities**

assignment *noun*

1 task
● ADJ. **special** | **important** | **dangerous, difficult, tough** | **business, work** | **modelling, photographic**
● VERB + ASSIGNMENT **accept, take on** *Why did you take on this assignment if you're so busy?* | **carry out** | **refuse** *If you refuse this assignment you risk losing your job.* | **complete, finish** | **give sb**
● PREP. **on~** *The photographer is on assignment in China at the moment.*
2 piece of school/college work
● ADJ. **practical, reading, written**
● VERB + ASSIGNMENT **give, hand out, set** *The teacher set an assignment on pollution.* | **do** | **complete, finish** | **hand in** *The students handed in their assignments.*
● PREP. **~on** *an assignment on Roman history*

assimilate *verb*

1 learn/understand
● ADV. **easily, quickly, readily** *Children assimilate new information very quickly.*
2 become/make sb part of sth
● ADV. **fully** *Many new immigrants have not yet assimilated fully into the new culture.*
● PREP. **into**

assist *verb*

● ADV. **greatly, materially** *We have been greatly assisted by individuals and organizations.* | **actively**
● VERB + ASSIST **be designed to** *measures designed to assist people with disabilities*
● PREP. **in** *He had to assist her in opening the gates.* **with** *She offered to assist with the marketing of the product.*

assistance *noun*

● ADJ. **considerable, great, real, substantial** | **limited** | **invaluable, valuable** | **practical** | **special** | **direct, emergency, immediate** *People in the flooded areas are in need of direct assistance.* | **mutual** *The treaty pledged mutual assistance in the event of an attack on either country.* | **expert, professional** | **external, outside** | **foreign, international** | **government, national** *They argued the case for extra government assistance for the poorest regions.* | **public, social, welfare** *the stigma attached to receiving social assistance* | **personal** *disabled people who need personal assistance to enable them to live in their own homes* | **humanitarian** | **economic, financial, legal, material, medical, military, technical**
● VERB + ASSISTANCE **give sb, offer (sb), provide, render** *We provide assistance if your car breaks down.* | **get, receive** *Did you receive any assistance from the authorities?* | **pledge, promise (sb)** *The World Bank promised assistance to the value of $5 million.* | **be in need of, need, require** | **expect** | **ask for, call for, seek** *I advise you to seek assistance from the police.* | **turn to sb for** *She had no one to turn to for assistance.* | **be of, come to sb's** *Do let us know if we can be of any assistance to you.* ◇ *A sympathetic neighbour came to his assistance.* | **welcome**
● PREP. **with/without~** *The work was completed with the assistance of local carpenters.* | **~for** *humanitarian assistance for refugees* **~from** *assistance from friends and family* **~in** *assistance in finding suitable accommodation* **~with** *assistance with rent for people on a low income*

assistant *noun*

● ADJ. **chief, senior** | **personal** *I'll ask my personal assistant to deal with this.* | **administrative, care, catering, checkout, clerical, laboratory, library, production, research, sales, shop, technical** *She took up a post as research assistant in the Department of Pharmacology.*

42

associate

- VERB + ASSISTANT **employ (sb as)**, **have** *She had a clerical assistant to do her paperwork.* | **get**, **hire (sb as)**, **recruit (sb as)** *I'm getting a new assistant next month.* | **sack**
- PREP. **~to** *assistant to the Production Manager*
⇒ Note at JOB

associate *noun*

- ADJ. **close** *a close associate with whom he started a business* | **former**, **old** *Her former associates refused to see her.* | **business**, **political**

association *noun*

1 an organization
- ADJ. **international**, **local**, **national**, **regional** | **private**, **public**, **voluntary** | **arts**, **business**, **community**, **constituency**, **consumer**, **football**, **housing**, **industry**, **library**, **neighbourhood**, **parent-teacher**, **professional**, **student**, **trade**, etc.
- ASSOCIATION + VERB **meet** *The association meets four times a year.*
⇒ Note at ORGANIZATION (for more verbs)
2 relationship between people/organizations
- ADJ. **close** | **free** *It was to be a free association of equal partners.* | **loose** *a loose association of sovereign states* | **long**, **long-standing** | **personal**
- VERB + ASSOCIATION **form** | **maintain** *They have maintained a close association with a college in the US.*
- PREP. **in ~ with** (= together with) *The book was published in association with British Heritage.* | **~ between** *the association between the two countries* **~ with** *His association with such criminals can only destroy him.*
- PHRASES **freedom of association** *One of the most important political freedoms is freedom of association.*
3 connection between things
- ADJ. **clear**, **close**, **direct**, **intimate**, **strong** *a close association between the two nations* | **loose** | **early**, **long**, **traditional** | **formal** | **free** *the technique of free association in which the patient is encouraged to say the first thing that comes to mind*
- VERB + ASSOCIATION **have** *The city has had a long association with the mining industry.* | **form** *You want the child to form an association between good behaviour and rewards.* | **demonstrate**, **find**, **prove**, **show** *The research showed an association between diet and various diseases.*
- PREP. **by ~** *Dogs learn mainly by association.* **in ~ with** (= together with) *We are working in association with several charities.* | **~ between** *a clear association between good health and regular exercise* **~ with** *the traditional association of the Democrats with minority interests*
- PHRASES **guilty/tainted by association** *He was considered tainted by association with the corrupt regime.*
4 associations feelings/memories
- ADJ. **strong** | **happy**, **positive**, **pleasant** | **negative**, **unhappy**, **unpleasant** | **cultural**, **historical**, **literary** *Tourists visit the city for its historical associations.*
- VERB + ASSOCIATIONS **have**, **hold** *Does the name 'Baxter' have any associations for you?* | **call up**, **evoke**, **spark off**, **trigger** *The smell of fresh bread triggers all kinds of associations for me.*
- PREP. **~for**

assortment *noun*

- ADJ. **large**, **rich**, **wide** | **mixed**, **varied** | **odd**, **strange** *She was wearing an odd assortment of clothes.*
- PREP. **~of** *a mixed assortment of sweets*

assume *verb*

- ADV. **automatically**, **naturally** *I automatically assumed that you knew about this.* | **reasonably**, **safely** *I think we can safely assume that this situation will continue.*
- VERB + ASSUME **can**, **might** | **tend to** | **be fair to**, **be reasonable to**, **be safe to** *It is reasonable to assume that the economy will continue to improve.* | **be a mistake to**, **be wrong to** | **be easy to** *It's all too easy to assume that people know what they are doing.*
- PHRASES **let us assume** *Let us assume for a moment that the plan succeeds.*

assumption *noun*

- ADJ. **basic**, **fundamental**, **hidden**, **implicit**, **tacit**, **underlying**, **unspoken** | **common**, **conventional**, **general**, **shared**, **widespread** *shared assumptions between teachers and parents* | **correct**, **reasonable**, **valid** | **erroneous**, **false**, **flawed**, **incorrect**, **mistaken**, **questionable**, **wrong**
- QUANT. **number**, **series**, **set** *Your argument is based on a set of questionable assumptions.*
- VERB + ASSUMPTION **make** *She's always making assumptions about how much money people have.* | **base sth on**, **start from**, **work on** *We are working on the assumption that the techniques are safe.* | **accept** | **challenge**, **disprove**, **question**, **test**
- ASSUMPTION + VERB **underlie sth**, **underpin sth** *the assumptions underlying their beliefs*
- PREP. **on the ~ that** *I set the table for eight people, on the assumption that Jo would come.* | **~ about** *assumptions about how women should behave*

assurance *noun*

1 promise
- ADJ. **absolute**, **categorical**, **clear**, **firm**, **full** | **further**, **repeated** | **formal**, **official**, **personal**, **verbal**, **written** *He gave me his personal assurance that the vehicle was safe.*
- VERB + ASSURANCE **have** *We now have a firm assurance of support from the government.* | **give sb**, **offer sb**, **provide** | **gain**, **get**, **obtain**, **receive** | **ask for**, **demand**, **seek**, **want** | **accept**, **be satisfied with** *They accepted his assurance that patients would be treated as soon as possible.* | **go back on**, **renege on** *He accused the minister of reneging on assurances given earlier.*
- PREP. **~ about** *an assurance about the safety of this equipment* **~ by/from** *assurances from the head teacher*
- PHRASES **despite/in spite of assurances** *Despite assurances from the government, the chemicals are known to be dangerous.*
2 feeling of calm and confidence
- ADJ. **calm**, **quiet** *She spoke with calm assurance.*
- VERB + ASSURANCE **have** | **show** *Even at a very young age she showed a great deal of assurance.*

assure *verb*

- VERB + ASSURE **can** | **hasten to** *He hastened to assure us that the press would not be informed.*
- PREP. **of** *We can assure you of our full support.*
- PHRASES **let me assure you**

assured *adj.*

1 confident
- VERBS **be**, **feel**, **look**, **rest**, **seem** *You can rest assured that your children are in good hands.*
- ADV. **very** *Although the situation was tense, her voice was calm and very assured.* | **totally**
2 certain to happen
- VERBS **be**, **look**, **seem**
- ADV. **absolutely** | **virtually**

asthma *noun*

- ADJ. **severe** | **acute**, **chronic** | **bronchial**
- VERB + ASTHMA **have**, **suffer from** | **treat**
- ASTHMA + NOUN **attack** | **sufferer**
⇒ Special page at ILLNESS

astonished adj.

- VERBS **be, look, seem, sound**
- ADV. **absolutely, quite**
- PREP. **at** *She was quite astonished at his rudeness.* **by** *He was astonished by the amount of junk in the house.*

astonishing adj.

- VERBS **be, seem | find sth** *I find his attitude absolutely astonishing.*
- ADV. **really, truly | absolutely, quite**

astonishment noun

- ADJ. **great | absolute, utter | mild** *an air of mild astonishment* **| blank** *a look of blank astonishment*
- VERB + ASTONISHMENT **express | hide** *She could not hide her astonishment.*
- PREP. **in ~** *She gazed at him in astonishment.* **to sb's ~** *Then, to my great astonishment, he started to cry.* **with ~** *Everyone gasped with astonishment.* **| ~ at** *He expressed astonishment at the results.*
- PHRASES **a cry/gasp/look of astonishment**

astute adj.

- VERBS **be**
- ADV. **very | financially, politically**

asylum noun

1 protection given by a government
- ADJ. **temporary | political**
- VERB + ASYLUM **apply for, claim, request, seek** *She fled the country, and is now seeking asylum in Sweden.* **| give sb, grant sb, offer sb, provide (sb with) | get, receive | deny sb, refuse sb** *Over 400 people have been refused asylum.*
- ASYLUM + NOUN **seeker** *bogus/genuine asylum seekers* **| application, claim**
- PHRASES **an application for asylum, the right to asylum** *Those fleeing from the war have the right to asylum.*

2 mental hospital
- ADJ. **lunatic, mental**
- PREP. **in ~** *He spent three years in an asylum.*

atheist noun

- ADJ. **committed, confirmed, dedicated**

athlete noun

- ADJ. **fine, good, great, Olympic, outstanding, talented, top, world-class** *one of the greatest athletes of all time* **| natural** *She has the build and strength of a natural athlete.* **| all-round, field, track | amateur, professional**
- ATHLETE + VERB **train** *The athletes are training hard for the Olympics.* **| compete, perform** *Our field athletes have performed well.*

athletics noun

- ADJ. **indoor, outdoor | junior, senior | amateur, schools | international, world**
- VERB + ATHLETICS **compete in, do, take part in** *My daughter wants to compete in athletics.* **| take up** *She didn't take up athletics until she was 20.* **| quit**
- ATHLETICS + NOUN **championships, competition, event, meet, meeting | club, federation | stadium, track | star | coach | club, team | official | career** *the hardest event of her athletics career* **| circuit, scene, world** *competing on the international athletics circuit*
⇨ Special page at SPORT

atmosphere noun

1 general feeling in a place
- ADJ. **calm, congenial, convivial, cosy, family, friendly, happy, homely, informal, pleasant, relaxed, warm, welcoming | (highly) charged, emotional, heavy, hostile, oppressive, stifling, strained, tense | carnival, electric, heady, lively** *Before the parade, the atmosphere was electric.* **| intimate, romantic | gloomy | rarefied, unique** *the rarefied atmosphere of academic life*
- VERB + ATMOSPHERE **create** *She tries to create an atmosphere of calm and security for her children.* **| poison, ruin, sour, spoil** *His blunt comments really soured the atmosphere.* **| clear, improve, lighten** *His funny remarks lightened the atmosphere.* **| be aware of, be sensitive to, sense** *She could sense the hostile atmosphere in the room.*
- ATMOSPHERE + VERB **be charged (with sth)** *The atmosphere was charged with excitement.* **| pervade sth, prevail** *A relaxed atmosphere prevails in the club.*
- PREP. **~ between** *Since their argument there had been a strained atmosphere between them.*

2 the air
- ADJ. **heavy, humid, oppressive, polluted, smoky, stale, stifling, stuffy**
- VERB + ATMOSPHERE **poison, pollute** *Pesticides can kill wildlife and pollute the atmosphere.* **| clear** *Last night's storm had cleared the atmosphere.*

3 gases around the earth
- ADJ. **lower, upper**
- VERB + ATMOSPHERE **enter, leave, re-enter** *The spaceship should re-enter the earth's atmosphere later today.* **| be emitted/released into, escape into** *Dangerous gases have escaped into the upper atmosphere.*
- PREP. **in the ~** *levels of radiation in the atmosphere*

atom noun

- ADJ. **charged, unstable** *positively charged atoms* **| carbon, nitrogen, etc.**
- VERB + ATOM **split** *The scientist Ernest Rutherford was the first person to split the atom.*
- ATOM + NOUN **bomb**

atrocity noun

- ADJ. **appalling, dreadful, terrible, worst** *one of the worst atrocities of the war* **| alleged | terrorist**
- VERB + ATROCITY **be responsible for, carry out, commit, perpetrate** *In the war, both sides committed atrocities.* **| suffer**
- ATROCITY + VERB **occur, take place**
- ATROCITY + NOUN **stories**
- PREP. **~ against** *atrocities against the civilian population* **~ by** *reports of atrocities by gunmen*
- PHRASES **accounts/allegations/reports of atrocities**

attach verb

- ADV. **firmly, securely | loosely**
- PREP. **to** *He attached the rope securely to a tree.*

attached adj.

1 full of affection
- VERBS **be | become, grow** *We've grown very attached to this village and wouldn't want to move.* **| remain**
- ADV. **deeply, strongly, very | increasingly | quite | emotionally, personally**
- PREP. **to** *Mr Wells is obviously quite attached to you.*

2 joined to sth
- VERBS **be | remain, stay**
- ADV. **firmly, securely** *Make sure all the wires remain firmly attached.* **| loosely | directly | permanently | physically**
- PREP. **to** *The ball was attached to a length of thin chain.*

attachment *noun*

- ADJ. **close, deep, passionate, special, strong | enduring, lasting | emotional, romantic, sentimental**
- VERB + ATTACHMENT **feel, have** *I feel no attachment to the countryside.* | **develop, form** *Prisoners can develop attachments to their warders.*
- PREP. **to** *her strong attachment to her mother*

attack *noun*

1 violence against sb
- ADJ. **brutal, frenzied, horrific, savage, serious, vicious, violent | unprovoked | racist, sexual | arson, gun, knife** *an increase in knife attacks on police officers*
- QUANT. **series, spate, wave**
- VERB + ATTACK **carry out** *Two teenagers carried out a frenzied attack on a local shopkeeper.* | **be subjected to** *He was subjected to a violent attack.*
- ATTACK + VERB **happen, occur, take place** *Where did the attack happen?*
- PREP. **~against** *vicious attacks against pensioners* **~by** *an attack by an armed gang* **~on** *an attack on a bus driver*
- PHRASES **a victim of an attack**

2 act of violence in war
- ADJ. **all-out, full-scale, major | sustained | surprise | retaliatory | mock | flank, frontal | enemy, guerrilla, terrorist | air, bomb, missile, mortar, nuclear**
- QUANT. **series** *The southern border towns have suffered a series of attacks.*
- VERB + ATTACK **carry out, launch, lead, make, mount, spearhead** *The soldiers mounted an all-out attack on the village.* | **come under, suffer** *They came under sustained attack from the air.* | **repel, repulse, resist | survive, withstand** *Most of the population would stand little chance of surviving a nuclear attack.* | **press home, renew** *Bombers pressed home their attack, causing severe damage to harbour installations.*
- ATTACK + VERB **happen, occur, take place** *The attack took place under cover of darkness.* | **fail, succeed**
- PREP. **under~** *The province has been under attack from the rebels.* | **~against** *attacks against civilians* **~by** *an attack by rebel forces* **~on** *an attack on enemy positions*

3 criticism
- ADJ. **bitter, blistering, fierce, outspoken, savage, scathing, scurrilous, stinging, vigorous | personal** *Is this a personal attack on the president, or a criticism of the government?* | **concerted | verbal**
- VERB + ATTACK **deliver, go on the, launch, make, mount, unleash** *Doctors have gone on the attack, accusing the government of incompetence.* | **come under, provoke** *All politicians come under attack for their views.* ◇ *The government's decision has provoked an attack from leaders of the health service.*
- PREP. **~on/upon** *an attack on my integrity*
- PHRASES **a/the line of attack** *The first line of attack is often name-calling.* **open to attack** *He has laid himself wide open to attack.*

4 sudden illness
- ADJ. **acute, sudden | bad, nasty, severe | fatal | mild, slight | recurrent | asthma, heart, panic** *a fatal heart attack*
- VERB + ATTACK **experience, have, suffer (from)** *He suffers from attacks of anxiety.* | **bring on, cause, trigger** *a heart attack brought on by stress*
- ATTACK + VERB **happen, occur, take place**
- PREP. **~of** *a sudden attack of nerves*

attack *verb*

1 use violence
- ADV. **brutally, savagely, viciously, violently** *She was brutally attacked by two men.* | **physically**
- PREP. **with** *He attacked her with a knife.*

2 criticize
- ADV. **fiercely, savagely, sharply, strongly, vigorously**
- PREP. **for** *The police have been strongly attacked for not taking immediate action.*

attainable *adj.*

- VERBS **be, seem | become**
- ADV. **fully, perfectly** *We believe that this level of performance is fully attainable.* | **easily, readily**
- PREP. **by** *This standard of English should be easily attainable by every child in the class.*

attempt *noun*

- ADJ. **successful | abortive, botched, failed, fruitless, futile, ill-fated, unsuccessful, vain** *her vain attempt to save her son's life* | **conscious, deliberate | brave, bold, concerted, determined, serious, valiant | blatant | feeble, half-hearted, weak | clumsy, crude | desperate, frantic, last-ditch** *a desperate attempt to find survivors of the accident* | **repeated** *repeated attempts to break through enemy lines* | **assassination, coup, rescue, suicide** *Rescue attempts were stopped because of bad weather.*
- VERB + ATTEMPT **make** *She has made no attempt to contact her mother.* | **succeed in** *He succeeded in his attempt to break the world record.* | **abandon, fail in, give up** *He abandoned his attempt to reach the summit.* | **foil, thwart** *Their attempt to break out of prison was foiled.*
- ATTEMPT + VERB **succeed | fail**
- PREP. **in an/the~** *In an attempt to ward off criticism, the government has made education a priority.* | **~at** *He made a feeble attempt at a smile.* **~by** *an attempt by workers to prevent redundancies*
- PHRASES **an attempt on sb's life** (= to kill sb)

attend *verb*

- ADV. **regularly** *to attend church regularly.*
- VERB + ATTEND **be able/unable to | be asked to, be invited to** *He was invited to attend a seminar in Paris.*
- PHRASES **well attended** *The event was well attended.*

attendance *noun*

- ADJ. **good, large, record** *It was a record attendance for a midweek game.* | **low, poor | falling** *Despite falling attendances, the zoo will stay open.* | **average, daily** *The average attendance at matches increased last year.* | **total | constant, regular** *Regular attendance at lectures is important.* | **compulsory | church, cinema, school, etc.**
- VERB + ATTENDANCE **boost, improve, increase** *Building a new stadium has boosted attendances by 40%.*
- ATTENDANCE + VERB **drop, fall, go down** *Attendances at the pool always fall in winter.* | **go up, increase**
- ATTENDANCE + NOUN **figures, rate, record**
- PREP. **in~** *The emergency services were in attendance within 22 minutes.* | **~at** *attendance at the meetings*

attendant *noun*

- ADJ. **car park, cloakroom, garage, lavatory, museum, petrol pump, pool** *Pool attendants kept a constant watch on the swimmers.*
⇨ Note at JOB

attention *noun*

1 act of watching/listening/showing interest
- ADJ. **full, rapt, undivided** *They listened with rapt attention.* | **assiduous, careful, close, meticulous, scrupulous | scant** *Policy-makers paid scant attention to the wider issues.* | **urgent | special | unwanted, unwelcome | international, media, public**
- VERB + ATTENTION **devote, direct, give (sb/sth), pay, turn** *How many times do I have to ask you to pay attention?* ◇ *He had a cup of tea and then turned his attention*

to the report. | **get**, **have**, **receive** *Can I have your attention, please?* ◇ *These poems have received a lot of critical attention.* | **attract**, **call**, **capture**, **catch**, **command**, **compel**, **draw**, **excite**, **grab** *I tried to attract the waiter's attention.* ◇ *Wherever he goes, he commands attention.* ◇ *She doesn't like to draw attention to her illness.* | **deflect**, **distract**, **divert**, **draw** *The government is trying to divert attention away from the economy.* | **hold**, **keep**, **rivet** *There was something in the way he spoke that riveted her attention.* | **concentrate**, **confine**, **focus** *In this chapter we shall confine our attention to non-renewable energy sources.* | **refocus**, **transfer** *The firm decided to refocus its attention back onto its traditional strengths and expertise.* | **deserve**, **need**, **require** *a matter requiring urgent attention* | **jostle for**, **vie for** *dozens of concerns jostling for your attention* ◇ *She was surrounded by men all vying for her attention.* | **repay** *an interesting essay that repays close attention* | **bring sth to** *My boss was grateful that I had brought the matter to his attention.* | **come to** | **avoid**, **escape** *Her primary aim was to avoid the attentions of the newspapers.*
• ATTENTION + VERB **focus** *Media attention focused today on the prince's business affairs.* | **wander** *I felt my attention wandering during the lecture.*
• ATTENTION + NOUN **span**
• PREP. **for sb's ~**, **for the ~ of** *a letter for the attention of your doctor*
• PHRASES **attention to detail** *He is a designer known for his meticulous attention to detail.* **care and attention** *He was convicted of driving without due care and attention.* **the centre of attention** *Some children love being the centre of attention.* **the focus of attention** *The focus of attention must now be how to improve the economy.* **force your attentions on sb** *A man like Luke had no need to force his attentions on unwilling women.* **not pay much attention to sth**, **pay little/no attention to sth** (= not take something very seriously) *Pay no attention to what Bill said—he's a complete liar!*

2 care
• ADJ. **constant** | **individual**, **personal**, **special** *The child needs special attention.* | **medical**
• VERB + ATTENTION **devote**, **give**, **lavish** *He devoted all his attention to his mother.* ◇ *She lavishes attention on those silly little dogs.* | **be in need of**, **need**, **require**, **want** *a patient requiring attention*

attic *noun*

• ADJ. **cramped**, **little**, **small**, **tiny** | **converted** *Her photography studio was a converted attic.* | **dark**, **dusty**
• ATTIC + NOUN **bedroom**, **flat**, **room** | **stairs**, **steps** | **skylight**, **window**

attitude *noun*

• ADJ. **conciliatory**, **favourable**, **friendly**, **positive**, **responsible**, **right**, **sympathetic** *She seems to have the right attitude for the job.* | **aggressive**, **bad**, **belligerent**, **cavalier**, **critical**, **hostile**, **irreverent**, **negative**, **patronizing**, **wrong** | **carefree**, **casual**, **flexible**, **laid-back**, **liberal**, **relaxed** *The teachers seem to have a very relaxed attitude towards discipline.* | **conservative**, **inflexible**, **rigid**, **uncompromising** | **ambivalent** | **general**, **prevailing**, **public** *The general attitude of the public is sympathetic.* | **changing** | **mental**, **moral**, **sexual**
• VERB + ATTITUDE **adopt**, **have**, **take** *The government has taken a positive attitude to this problem.* | **change** *The experience changed his attitude to religion.*
• ATTITUDE + VERB **exist**, **persist**, **prevail** *This sort of attitude exists among certain groups of people.* | **change**
• ATTITUDE + NOUN **problem** *At school he was thought to have an attitude problem.*
• PREP. **~ about** *changing attitudes about death* **~ of** an *attitude of confidence and trust* ◇ *Youth is simply an atti-*

tude of mind. **~ to/towards** *There has been a marked change in attitude towards the European single currency.*
• PHRASES **a change in/of attitude**, **with attitude** (*informal*) (= having a confident, aggressive attitude that challenges what people think) *a rock band with attitude*

attraction *noun*

1 fact of attracting/being attracted
• ADJ. **fatal**, **irresistible**, **obvious**, **powerful**, **strong** | **mutual** *They shared a powerful mutual attraction.* | **gravitational**, **magnetic**, **physical**, **sexual**
• VERB + ATTRACTION **feel** *the strong attraction that she felt for him* | **see** *I could now see the attraction of a steady job and regular income.* | **have**, **hold** *Long holidays hold no attraction for him.* | **exert** *All matter exerts a gravitational attraction.*
• PREP. **~ between** *the attraction between two people* **~ to/towards** *His attraction to you is obvious.*
• PHRASES **the centre of attraction** *Sophie was plainly the centre of attraction in the room.*

2 sth that attracts people
• ADJ. **added**, **big**, **chief**, **great**, **main**, **major**, **obvious**, **special**, **star** *The main attraction of the place is the nightlife.* | **popular**, **tourist**
• VERB + ATTRACTION **have** *A freelance career has the attraction of flexibility.* | **be**, **prove** *Feeding the animals proved a popular attraction for visitors to the farm.*
• PREP. **for** *The lack of heat was an attraction for cyclists.*

attractive *adj.*

• VERBS **be**, **look** *She looked attractive and beautifully dressed.* | **become**, **grow** *She had grown more attractive with age.* | **make sb/sth** | **find sb/sth** *This is an idea that I find very attractive.*
• ADV. **extremely**, **very** | **stunningly** *a stunningly attractive woman* | **quite** | **physically**, **sexually**, **visually** *He no longer found her physically attractive.* ◇ *a visually attractive display*
• PREP. **to** *Schools must try to make science more attractive to youngsters.*

attribute *noun*

• ADJ. **chief**, **great**, **key**, **main** | **desirable**, **essential**, **important**, **necessary**, **positive**, **useful** *Patience is an essential attribute for a teacher.* | **common** | **divine**, **human** | **cultural**, **personal**, **physical**, **social** *Her physical attributes were much admired.*
• VERB + ATTRIBUTE **have**, **possess**

attribute *verb*

• ADV. **directly** | **solely** | **in large measure**, **largely**, **mainly** | **in part**, **partly**
• PREP. **to** *They claim that one in twenty deaths can be directly attributed to air pollution.*
• PHRASES **be commonly/generally/usually/widely attributed to** *The goals commonly attributed to management are status, power, salary and security.*

auction *noun*

• ADJ. **public** | **charity** | **art**, **cattle**, **furniture**, **etc.**
• VERB + AUCTION **hold** *The estate is holding an auction to raise money.* | **conduct** *My father will be conducting the auction tomorrow.* | **attend**, **go to** *He regularly attended auctions.* | **put sth up for** *The horse will be put up for public auction.* | **be/come/go up for** *The paintings will come up for auction next month.* | **pick sth up at** *a bargain that she had picked up at auction*
• AUCTION + VERB **take place**
• AUCTION + NOUN **house**, **room** | **price** | **market**, **mart**, **sale**
• PREP. **at ~** *I try to buy furniture at auctions because it is*

cheaper that way. ◊ *The house was sold at auction for half a million pounds.* **by~** *a jumble sale by auction*

audible *adj.*

- VERBS **be | become, grow**
- ADV. **clearly, perfectly** *The shot was clearly audible in the silence.* | **barely, hardly, scarcely | faintly, just** *The singer's voice was just audible.* | **almost**
- PREP. **above** *The noise was audible even above the roar of the engines.* **to** *The sounds made by bats are not audible to the human ear.*

audience *noun*

1 group of people watching/listening to sth
- ADJ. **big, capacity, large, mass, packed, vast, wide** *The museum is trying to attract a wider audience.* | **select, small | appreciative, enthusiastic, receptive, sympathetic | hostile | captive | potential,   target | cinema, live, radio, studio, television**
- VERB + AUDIENCE **address, perform to, play to** *He prefers playing to live audiences.* | **attract, draw, pull in** *Such a well-known politician should draw a big audience.* | **reach** *We want to reach a target audience that's younger in age.* | **captivate, grip, thrill** *The film has thrilled audiences throughout the country.* | **move** *The audience was visibly moved.*
- AUDIENCE + VERB **applaud, cheer** *The audience cheered loudly.* | **boo, jeer | laugh**
- AUDIENCE + NOUN **participation**
- PREP. **before/in front of an/the~** *He felt nervous standing up in front of the large audience.*

2 formal meeting with a very important person
- ADJ. **private**
- VERB + AUDIENCE **have | ask for, request, seek | give sb, grant sb** *The Pope granted him an audience.*
- PREP. **~with** *He sought a private audience with the Queen.*

audition *noun*

- VERB + AUDITION **do, go for/to, have** *I did an audition for the part of the queen.* | **give sb, hold** *holding auditions for new actors* | **pass | fail**
- PREP. **~for** *an audition for a place at drama school* **~with** *an audition with the Royal Ballet*

auditor *noun*

- ADJ. **company/company's | appointed | internal | independent | statutory | district** *The council and district auditors have agreed that the deals were unlawful.*
- PREP. **~to** *His firm has been appointed the auditors to the company.*
- PHRASES **the Auditor General, an auditors' report** ⇨ Note at PROFESSIONAL (for verbs)

auditorium *noun*

- ADJ. **huge, vast | 200-seat, 250-seater, etc. | empty, packed | darkened**
- VERB + AUDITORIUM **fill**
- AUDITORIUM + VERB **hold sb, seat sb** *The auditorium seats over a thousand people.* | **be filled with sth** *The darkened auditorium was filled with muttering.*

August *noun*

⇨ Note at MONTH

aunt *noun*

- ADJ. **aged, elderly | maiden, unmarried | maternal, paternal | great** (= the sister of one of your grandparents) *Great Aunt Emily*

aura *noun*

- ADJ. **magical | faint**
- VERB + AURA **be surrounded by, exude, have, retain** *He exuded an aura of wealth and power.* | **take on** *The picture seemed to take on the aura of an ancient work of art.* | **create, give sb/sth** *The sunlight created an aura of beauty around her.* | **lose**
- PREP. **~about, ~of** *There was always a faint aura of mystery about him.*

austerity *noun*

- ADJ. **post-war, wartime**
- AUSTERITY + NOUN **measures, package, plan, policies, programme**

authenticity *noun*

- VERB + AUTHENTICITY **cast doubt on, doubt** *Some journalists have cast doubt on the authenticity of the official version of events.* | **check, test | confirm, establish, prove, verify**
- PHRASES **a certificate of authenticity** *Despite its certificate of authenticity, the painting was found to be a fake.* **a debate over the authenticity of sth** *There has been some debate over the authenticity of his will.* **of doubtful authenticity** *a document of doubtful authenticity*

author *noun*

- ADJ. **best-selling | prolific | famous,   well-known | anonymous** *the anonymous author of this pamphlet* | **children's** *Primarily a children's author, she has also written books for adults.*
- VERB + AUTHOR **read** *Stephen King is an author I've never read.*
- AUTHOR + VERB **write (sth)** *The author was writing in the seventeenth century.*

authoritarian *adj.*

- VERBS **be | become**
- ADV. **highly, very | increasingly | rather**

authority *noun*

1 sth with the power to give orders
- ADJ. **district, local, regional | government, public | education, health, military, planning, tax** *The government is urging education authorities to spend less money.* | **competent, lawful, relevant, statutory**
- AUTHORITY + VERB **agree sth, claim sth, decide sth, deny sth, promise sth** *The local health authority denied negligence.* | **allow (sb) sth, give (sb) sth, grant (sb) sth** *The local authority has not granted planning permission.*

2 power/right to give orders
- ADJ. **absolute, complete, full, supreme | governmental, judicial, legal, ministerial, parental, presidential**
- VERB + AUTHORITY **have** *Parents have the authority to discipline their children.* | **assume** *He assumed full authority as tsar in 1689.* | **give sb | assert, demonstrate, establish, exercise, exert, show, use, wield** *The new manager obviously felt the need to demonstrate her authority.* | **delegate | give up, relinquish | abuse | challenge, defy, deny, rebel against, reject, undermine** *She had challenged my authority once too often.* | **usurp**
- AUTHORITY + NOUN **figure** *adult authority figures such as parents and teachers*
- PREP. **in~** *I need to talk to someone in authority.* **under the ~ of** *This can only be done under the authority of the government minister.* **without~** *He took the car without authority.* | **~ over** *Central government has extensive authority over teachers.*
- PHRASES **an air of authority** *He bore an air of author-*

ity. **position of authority** *She holds a position of authority in the local church.*

3 person with special knowledge
- ADJ. **leading, respected, world | unimpeachable, unquestioned**
- VERB + AUTHORITY **cite, invoke** *Copernicus justified his innovation by citing respected authorities.*
- PREP. **~on** *She's a leading authority on genetics.*

authorization *noun*

- ADJ. **formal, official, written | prior** *You will need prior authorization from your bank.*
- VERB + AUTHORIZATION **need, require | ask for, seek** *He asked for authorization to proceed with the plan.* | **get, have, obtain | give sb, grant (sb) | refuse (sb)** *The government will probably refuse authorization under these conditions.* | **revoke**
- PREP. **with/without~** *You cannot take a day off without authorization.* | **~for** *Formal authorization for the trip was given last week.* **~from** *The change of plan would require authorization from the minister.*

autistic *adj.*

- VERBS **be**
- ADV. **severely** *a school for severely autistic children* | **mildly**

autobiography *noun*

- VERB + AUTOBIOGRAPHY **write | publish | read**
- PREP. **in an/the ~** *In his autobiography, he recalls the poverty he grew up in.*

autograph *noun*

- VERB + AUTOGRAPH **give sb, sign** *He signed his autograph for the little girl.* | **ask for | get, have** *Can I have your autograph, please?*
- AUTOGRAPH + NOUN **album, book | hunter**

automatic *adj.*

1 working by itself
- VERBS **be** *The machine is fully automatic.*
- ADV. **completely, fully, totally**

2 certain to happen
- VERBS **be**
- ADV. **almost, virtually** *Promotion was almost automatic after two or three years.*

autonomous *adj.*

- VERBS **be | become**
- ADV. **completely, fully, totally | largely | relatively | effectively** *Although officially a dependent territory the island is effectively autonomous.* | **politically**
- PREP. **from** *Higher education is relatively autonomous from the state.*

autonomy *noun*

- ADJ. **considerable, greater, more | complete, full | relative | individual, personal | local, national, regional | administrative, cultural, economic, financial, managerial, political, professional, etc. | pupil, teacher, worker, etc.**
- QUANT. **degree, measure** *a high degree of autonomy*
- VERB + AUTONOMY **enjoy, have** *The subsidiary companies will now have more autonomy.* | **gain | seek, struggle for, want | give sb, grant (sb)** *Head office is giving the regional offices more autonomy.* | **increase** *the need to increase worker autonomy* | **reduce**
- PREP. **~from** *Schools have gained greater autonomy from government control.*

- PHRASES **a demand for autonomy** *demands for cultural autonomy*

autopsy *noun*

- VERB + AUTOPSY **carry out, conduct, do, perform**
- AUTOPSY + VERB **find sth, reveal sth, show sth** *The autopsy revealed that he had been poisoned.*
- AUTOPSY + NOUN **report, result**
- PREP. **~on** *They carried out an autopsy on the victim.*

autumn *noun*

- ADJ. **last, next, this (coming) | early, late, mid- | wet**
- AUTUMN + NOUN **weather | sun, sunlight, sunshine | frost/frosts, rain/rains | gale, wind | landscape, sky | colours** *The trees were beginning to turn orange and yellow with autumn colours.* | **leaf** *the sound of autumn leaves rustling* | **equinox | term** *classes to be held for schoolchildren during the autumn term* | **collection, exhibition** *their autumn collection of dresses*
⇨ Note at SEASON (for more collocates)

availability *noun*

- ADJ. **easy, ready** *the easy availability of many illegal drugs* | **general, wide, widespread | greater, increased | limited | land, staff, ticket, etc.**
- VERB + AVAILABILITY **check, ensure** *Before travelling we must ensure the availability of petrol and oil.* | **increase | reduce, restrict** *They want to restrict the availability of abortion.*
- PHRASES **subject to availability** *All holiday bookings are subject to availability.*

available *adj.*

1 that you can get, buy, use, etc.
- VERBS **be | become | make sth** *The product will now be made available throughout the market.*
- ADV. **easily, freely, readily | widely**
- PREP. **for** *Grants should be available for all students.* **from** *Details are available from the above address.* **to** *This information is freely available to anyone wishing to see it.*
- PHRASES **available for hire/sale**

2 free to be seen, talked to, etc.
- VERBS **be | become** *She is in a meeting at present, but I will let you know as soon as she becomes available.*
- PHRASES **not available for comment** *The chairman was not available for comment.*

avalanche *noun*

1 large amount of snow falling
- AVALANCHE + VERB **happen, strike sth** *The avalanche struck the ski resort in the late afternoon.* | **engulf sb/sth | kill sb** *They were killed by an avalanche in the Swiss Alps.*
- PREP. **in an/the~** *They died in an avalanche.*

2 large number/amount of sth
- VERB + AVALANCHE **be buried under**
- AVALANCHE + VERB **engulf sth** *the avalanche of lawlessness threatening to engulf our civilization*
- PREP. **~ of** *We've been almost buried under the avalanche of mail.*

avenue *noun*

1 wide street
- ADJ. **broad, wide | leafy, tree-lined**
- AVENUE + VERB **be lined with sth** *an avenue lined with elms*
- PREP. **along, down, in, through, up an/the~** *strolling down a tree-lined avenue*

2 way of doing/getting sth
- ADJ. **possible, promising | fruitful**

● VERB + AVENUE **explore, pursue, try** *We need to explore every possible avenue.* | **exhaust** *After two months of negotiations we had exhausted all avenues.* | **open (up), provide**
● AVENUE + VERB **be open to sb** *There was only one avenue open to him.*
● PREP. **~for** *to provide a new avenue for research* **~of** *the two main avenues of enquiry* **~to** *an avenue to success*

average noun

● ADJ. **annual** | **national** *The national average is just over two children per family.* | **overall** | **weighted** | **batting, bowling** (both in cricket)
● VERB + AVERAGE **arrive at, calculate, find, work out** *You'll have to calculate the average.*
● PREP. **above ~** *His test results are well above average.* **below~, on~** *On average, prices have risen 6%.*

average adj.

● ADV. **very** *Peter was a very average golfer.* | **fairly** | **above, below** *an above average climb in prices*

aversion noun

● ADJ. **strong** *He has a strong aversion to dogs.* | **natural**
● VERB + AVERSION **have** | **develop** | **overcome**
● AVERSION + NOUN **therapy** *I underwent aversion therapy for my addiction to smoking.*
● PREP. **~to** *Have you developed an aversion to babies?*

avert verb

1 prevent sth
● ADV. **narrowly** *A tragedy was narrowly averted when a lorry crashed into a crowded restaurant.*
● VERB + AVERT **attempt to, try to** | **manage to** *He managed to avert the closure of the factory.* | **fail to**
● PHRASES **an attempt/effort to avert sth**

2 turn sth away
● ADV. **hastily, quickly** *They hastily averted their faces to hide their giggles.*
● VERB + AVERT **try to**
● PREP. **from** *averting his eyes from the dead child*

avocado (also avocado pear) noun

● ADJ. **ripe**
● VERB + AVOCADO **eat, have** | **halve, peel, stone**
● AVOCADO + NOUN **dip, mousse**
⇨ Special page at FRUIT

avoid verb

1 prevent sth
● ADV. **altogether** *It is sometimes impossible to avoid conflict altogether.* | **narrowly** *They narrowly avoided defeat in the semi-final.* | **at all costs** *Getting involved in a court case is something to be avoided at all costs.*
● VERB + AVOID **be anxious to, want to, wish to** *They are anxious to avoid any further misunderstandings.* | **attempt to, try to** | **be careful to, take care to** *He was careful to avoid any sentimentality in his speech.* | **help (to)** | **be able to, manage to** | **be possible to** | **be difficult to, be impossible to**
● PHRASES **an attempt/effort to avoid sth** *He failed in his attempt to avoid having to pay.*

2 keep away from sb
● ADV. **carefully, deliberately, studiously** *The two men carefully avoided one another.*
● VERB + AVOID **try to**

3 not hit sb/sth when driving
● ADV. **narrowly** *He braked hard and narrowly avoided a parked van.*

● VERB + AVOID **brake to** | **swerve to** *She swerved to avoid a cyclist.*

avoidable adj.

● VERBS **be** *Most accidents are easily avoidable.*
● ADV. **entirely, wholly** | **easily**

await verb

● ADV. **anxiously** *She is anxiously awaiting a decision on her future.* | **eagerly, keenly, with interest** *The outcome of the appeal is awaited with interest.* | **patiently**
● PHRASES **long awaited** *her long awaited return to professional tennis*

awake verb

● ADV. **early, late** *She awoke early the next morning.*
● PREP. **from** *I awoke from a deep sleep at six o'clock.*

awake adj.

● VERBS **be, lie** *At night, he lay awake beside her.* | **come, jerk** *Claudia came awake slowly.* ◇ *Stephen jerked awake from a nightmare.* | **keep, remain, stay** *He was struggling to stay awake.* | **jerk sb, jolt sb, nudge sb, shake sb** *A few hours later Benjamin shook me awake.* | **keep sb** *The noise had kept her awake.*
● ADV. **fully, wide** *By now, the baby was wide awake.* | **hardly, only half** *It was very early and I was only half awake.* | **still** *The children were still awake when we went out.*

awaken verb

● ADV. **early, late**
● PREP. **from** *She was just awakening from sleep.*
● PHRASES **be rudely awakened** *He was rudely awakened by the sound of drilling.*

awakening noun

● ADJ. **rude, sudden** *If they expected a warm welcome, they were in for a rude awakening.* | **slow** | **political, sexual, spiritual** *the political awakening that followed the Second World War*
● PREP. **~from, ~to** *an awakening from a terrible vision to cheerful realities*

award noun

1 prize that sb gets for doing sth well
● ADJ. **annual** | **national** | **coveted, highest, major, prestigious, special, top** | **bravery, design, literary, man of the match, etc.** *His goalkeeping won him the man of the match award.*
● VERB + AWARD **give sb, hand out, make (sb), present (sb with)** *The award was made for his work in cancer research.* | **carry off, earn (sb), get, receive, win** *Stephen's quick thinking has earned him a bravery award.* | **accept**
● AWARD + VERB **go to sb** *The best director award went to Sam Mendes for 'American Beauty'.*
● AWARD + NOUN **ceremony, scheme**
● PREP. **~for** *the award for best actor* **~from** *to receive an award from the Queen*

2 money given to sb
● ADJ. **compensatory, discretionary, mandatory** | **pay** *The union is unhappy with this year's pay award.* | **damages, libel**
● VERB + AWARD **get, receive** | **grant, make** *The judge has the power to make discretionary awards.*

award verb

● ADV. **automatically** | **jointly** *He was jointly awarded*

the Nobel Prize with Alex Mueller. | **mentally** *She mentally awarded herself top marks for staying cool under pressure.* | **posthumously**
• PREP. **to** *Honours were automatically awarded to senior officials just because they were senior.*

aware *adj.*

1 conscious
• VERBS **be, seem | become | make sb** *We need to make people more aware of these problems.*
• ADV. **acutely, keenly, very, well | fully, perfectly** *Mr Bush did not appear fully aware of the importance of this act.* | **dimly, vaguely | hardly, not really** *He was not really aware of what he was doing.* | **horribly, painfully** *Moran was painfully aware of Luke's absence.*
• PREP. **of** *The police are well aware of the dangers.*

2 informed
• VERBS **be | become**
• ADV. **very | environmentally, politically, socially**

awareness *noun*

• ADJ. **full | greater, heightened, increased | dawning, growing, increasing** *a growing awareness of healthy living* | **acute, deep, intense, keen, strong | conscious, direct | intuitive | sudden | general, public | cultural, environmental, moral, political, religious, sexual, social, spatial, spiritual**
• VERB + AWARENESS **have** *Politicians now have much greater awareness of these problems.* | **build, develop, encourage, foster, heighten, increase, raise** *The group is trying to raise public awareness about homelessness.*
• AWARENESS + VERB **increase, spread** *Environmental awareness has increased over the years.*
• PREP. **~ among/amongst** *building awareness among the target audience* **~ of** *an increased awareness of the risks*
• PHRASES **a lack of awareness**

awe *noun*

• ADJ. **great**
• VERB + AWE **be/stand in, hold sb in** *Most people hold him in some awe.* | **feel | inspire** *Everest has always inspired awe and respect among climbers.*
• PREP. **in/with ~** *We gazed in awe at the massive building.* | **~ at** *What I mostly felt was awe at her achievement.*
• PHRASES **a sense of awe** *They experienced a tremendous sense of awe in the cathedral.*

awesome *adj.*

• VERBS **be, seem**

• ADV. **really, simply, truly** *The Niagara Falls are a truly awesome sight.* | **fairly, pretty, quite, somewhat**

awful *adj.*

• VERBS **be, feel, look, smell, sound, taste** *I felt awful when I realized what I'd done.* ◇ *The fish tasted awful.*
• ADV. **bloody** *(taboo),* **fucking** *(taboo),* **just, quite, really, simply, truly** *a truly awful book* | **absolutely, the most** *She's the most awful snob.* | **pretty, rather**

awkward *adj.*

1 difficult
• VERBS **be, look, seem | make sth**
• ADV. **extremely, very | a bit, rather, slightly, somewhat** *She asked some rather awkward questions.*
• PHRASES **make things awkward** *He could make things very awkward for me if he wanted to.*

2 not relaxed
• VERBS **be, feel, look | become | make sb** *He was embarrassed, which made him awkward.*
• ADV. **extremely, very | a bit, rather | painfully** *As a teenager he was painfully awkward in company.*
• PREP. **about** *They felt awkward about having to leave so soon.* **with** *She is awkward with people she doesn't know.*

axe *noun*

1 tool
• VERB + AXE **brandish, carry, hold, wield** *A man used to wielding an axe fought best on foot.* | **chop sth down/up with, use | swing | sharpen**
• AXE + VERB **fall** *The executioner's axe fell.*
• PREP. **with an/the ~** *to chop a tree down with an axe*
• PHRASES **a blow from/of an axe** *With a few swift blows of the axe, she severed the cable.*

2 the axe complete loss of sth/big reduction in sth
• VERB + AXE **swing, wield** *Wielding the axe on the prison plan would be one way of saving money.* | **face** *Up to 300 workers are facing the axe at a struggling Merseyside firm.* | **save sb/sth from** *Patients are delighted their local hospital has been saved from the axe.*
• AXE + VERB **fall** *We were expecting bad news but had no idea where the axe would fall* (= where the loss/reduction would be).

axis *noun*

• ADJ. **horizontal, vertical | x, y, z**
• PREP. **along an/the ~** *the wage is measured along the horizontal axis* **on an/the ~** *The earth spins on its axis.*
• PHRASES **an axis of rotation** *the earth's axis of rotation* **an axis of symmetry**

Bb

baby noun

● ADJ. **new, newborn, tiny | low birthweight, small, tiny** *Smoking in pregnancy increases the risk of producing a low birthweight baby.* | **big | full-term | pre-term, premature | stillborn | unborn | little, young | three-day-old, six-week-old, ten-month-old, etc.** | **beautiful, bonny, lovely | bouncing** (*informal*), **healthy, normal** *A bonny, bouncing baby, Freddie was her heart's desire and joy.* | **contented, good, perfect | colicky, crying, screaming | sleeping | growing** *He took an interest in the growing baby even before it was born.* | **bottle-fed, breast-fed | illegitimate | test-tube | abandoned, unwanted | war** (= born during the war)
● VERB + BABY **have** *I want to have a baby.* | **conceive, make babies** (*informal*) *Darling, I just want to stay with you and make babies!* | **carry, expect** *She's not sure yet how many babies she's carrying.* ◇ *She's expecting a baby in July.* | **give birth to, produce | deliver** *The baby was delivered by a midwife.* | **lose** *She lost her baby* (= had a miscarriage) *three months into her pregnancy.* | **care for, look after | feed | bottle-feed | breastfeed, nurse | burp** *The baby needed burping after every bottle.* | **wean** *You can start weaning your baby when it's four months old.* | **change** *You should change your baby about six times a day.* | **bath | comfort, cradle, cuddle, hold, pick up, rock, take** *She rocked the baby to sleep in her arms.* ◇ *Could you take the baby? I need to bring in the washing.* | **swaddle | play with | adopt** *They would like to adopt a newborn baby.* | **have adopted, put up for adoption** *She decided to put her baby up for adoption.* | **abandon | sleep like** *He was so tired after all his exertions, he slept like a baby.*
● BABY + VERB **be due** *The baby is due in October.* | **arrive, be born** *Their first baby arrived exactly nine months after the wedding.* | **bawl, cry, scream | babble, coo** *The baby cooed happily on the rug.* | **be sick, dribble, drool** *Babies drool a lot when they are teething.* | **be teething | crawl, sit up, take his/her first steps, toddle, walk | kick, move** *I could feel the baby moving inside me.* | **sleep**
● BABY + NOUN **boy, girl | brother, daughter, sister, son | bird, rabbit, etc. | clothes | food | buggy, carrier | alarm, monitor | bath | talk** *I didn't use baby talk with my children, but used proper words right from the start.* | **unit** *the hospital's special care baby unit* | **boom** (= a period when many more babies are born than usual)

bachelor noun

● ADJ. **confirmed** *He was 38, and a confirmed bachelor.* | **eligible** *one of the country's most eligible bachelors*
● BACHELOR + NOUN **days, life | flat, pad | status**

back noun

1 part of the body
● ADJ. **broad | lean, slender | muscled, muscular, powerful, strong | bent | erect, straight | lower, upper | bad, stiff** *He's off work with a bad back.*
● VERB + BACK **bend, stiffen, straighten | stretch** *He yawned and stretched his back as he got out of bed.* | **break, hurt, injure | arch** *The cat arched its back and hissed at the dog.* | **support | knead, massage | scratch**
● BACK + VERB **arch | stiffen** *His back stiffened as he saw the photographers waiting.* | **ache**
● BACK + NOUN **injury, pain, trouble | muscles | support** *a seat with good back support*
● PREP. **behind your~** *They blindfolded him and tied his hands behind his back.* ◇ (*figurative*) *People say bad things about him behind his back, but never to his face.* **flat on your~** *I was flat on my back for six weeks when I broke my leg.* **on your~** *He was carrying a small child on his back.* ◇ *She was lying on her back on the sofa.* **in the/your~** *I've got a nagging pain in my lower back.* | **~to** *He was standing with his back to the fire.*
● PHRASES **sb's back is turned** (*figurative*) *The boss was certain that the staff would stop working as soon as his back was turned.* **back to back** *The children sat back to back so they couldn't see each others' drawings.* **a pat/slap on the back** *He smiled and gave me a hearty slap on the back.* ◇ (*figurative*) *She deserves a pat on the back for her efforts.* **the small of your back** *She felt a sharp pain in the small* (= the lowest part of) *her back.* **turn your back (on sb/sth)** *Actors should never turn their backs on the audience.* ◇ (*figurative*) *She decided to turn her back on Paris and return to her home town.*

2 part furthest from the front
● PREP. **around/round the~** *If you'd like to come round the back* (= to the area behind the house), *I'll show you the garden.* **at the~** *We could only get seats at the back.* **down the~** *My money's all fallen down the back of the cushion.* **in the~** *Two passengers sat in the back of the car.* **to the~** *The man was refusing to go to the back of the queue.* **towards the~** *The arts page is usually towards the back of the newspaper.*
● PHRASES **back to front** *I had my pullover on back to front* (= with the back where the front should be).

back verb

1 move backwards
● ADV. **hastily, hurriedly** *She backed away hurriedly.* | **away, in, off, up** *If you can't drive in forwards, try backing it in.* ◇ *Back off! There's no need to yell at me.* ◇ *Can you back your car up so that I can get through?*
● VERB + BACK **try to** *He tried to back away.*
● PREP. **across** *She backed across the room.* **away from** *The children backed away from him in fear.* **into** *She backed into the garage.* **out of** *He backed out of the drive.*

2 support sb/sth
● ADV. **firmly, strongly** *Teachers are strongly backing the new educational policies.* | **fully | overwhelmingly | unanimously | openly, publicly | financially** *his election bid was financially backed by a soft drinks company.* | **up** *I'll back you up if they don't believe you.*

PHRASAL VERB
back down
● VERB + BACK DOWN **refuse to | be forced to, be obliged to**
● PREP. **from** *The government was forced to back down from implementing these proposals.* **on** *She refused to back down on a point of principle.* **over** *The committee finally backed down over the issue of spending cuts.*

backdrop noun

● ADJ. **dramatic, magnificent, perfect, picturesque, romantic | economic, historical, political**
● VERB + BACKDROP **have | provide**
● PREP. **against a/the~ of** *The conference begins this week against a backdrop of unmitigated gloom.* | **~for** *The Alps provided the perfect backdrop for a romantic holiday.* **~of** *The large bay has a superb backdrop of*

mountains. ~ **to** *War is more than just a dramatic backdrop to the novel.*

backfire *verb*

- ADV. **badly, disastrously**
- PREP. **on** *The surprise I had planned backfired on me.*

background *noun*

1 type of family/social class sb comes from
- ADJ. **broad, narrow** *It is important to have a broad educational background.* | **mixed** | **privileged, wealthy** | **deprived, disadvantaged, poor** | **middle class, upper class, working class** | **academic, class, cultural, educational, ethnic, family, military, professional, religious, social, socio-economic**
- VERB + BACKGROUND **come from, have** *He came from a very privileged background.* | **be drawn from** *The students are drawn from very mixed social backgrounds.*
- BACKGROUND + VERB **be in sth** *Her background was in biology and medicine.*
- PREP. **from a** ~ *children from deprived backgrounds* **with a** ~ *an economist with a background in business* | ~**in**
- PHRASES **a range/variety of backgrounds**

2 facts connected with a situation/event
- ADJ. **general** | **factual** | **cultural, economic, historical, political, technical**
- VERB + BACKGROUND **describe, give (sb), outline, provide (sb with)** *The book provides the background to the revolution.* | **form** *Those discussions formed the background to the decision.*
- BACKGROUND + NOUN **information, knowledge, reading** *background information on the country*
- PREP. **against the** ~ *Against that general background I shall give you a more detailed view of current medical practice.* | ~**to** *the technical background to the report*

3 part of a view/picture behind the main parts
- PREP. **against a/the** ~ *The areas of water stood out against the dark background.* **in the** ~ *The mountains in the background were capped with snow.* **on a/the** ~ *bright blue on a red background*

4 position in which sb/sth is not important/noticed
- VERB + BACKGROUND **blend into, fade into, melt/merge into, recede/retreat into, slip into** *The dispute over the new contract allowed her other problems to fade into the background.* ◇ *He had learnt how to melt invisibly into the background.* | **keep/remain/stay in** *He prefers to remain in the background and let his assistant deal with the press.* | **hover in** *I could see my secretary hovering in the background.*
- BACKGROUND + NOUN **music, noise, radiation**
- PREP. **in the** ~ *There was a radio on in the background.*

backing *noun*

- ADJ. **strong** | **full, unanimous, whole-hearted** *The teachers have the full backing of the school governors.* | **financial, legal** | **government, official, popular**
- VERB + BACKING **have** | **gain, get, receive, secure, win** *They have won financial backing from the EU.* | **need, seek** | **give sb, provide (sb with)** *Who's going to provide the backing?*
- BACKING + VERB **come from sb/sth** *The backing will come from the government.*
- PREP. **with/without the** ~ *They brought the legal action with the backing of their MP.* | ~**for** *They want backing for more research.* ~**from** *backing from management*

backlash *noun*

- ADJ. **conservative** *a conservative backlash against the feminism of the 80s* | **political** | **public**
- VERB + BACKLASH **cause, produce, provoke** *Such a*

decision may provoke a backlash from their supporters. | **expect, fear** | **face**
- PREP. ~**against** *a backlash against any future reforms* ~**from** *They face a backlash from shareholders.*

backlog *noun*

- ADJ. **big, considerable, enormous, huge, large**
- VERB + BACKLOG **be faced with, have** *We are faced with a backlog of orders we can't deal with.* | **catch up on, clear, deal with, reduce**
- BACKLOG + VERB **accumulate, build up** *A huge backlog of work had built up.*

backpack *noun*

⇨ See RUCKSACK

backstroke *noun*

⇨ Note at STROKE

backward *adj.*

- VERBS **be, seem**
- ADV. **very** | **rather, somewhat** *a rather backward child* | **economically, educationally**

bacon *noun*

- ADJ. **lean** | **streaky** | **back** | **crisp/crispy** *Fry the bacon until crisp.* | **smoked, unsmoked**
- QUANT. **bit, piece, rasher, slice** *I'll have two rashers of bacon and a fried egg.* | **side** *A whole side of bacon was hanging from a hook on the ceiling.*
- VERB + BACON **eat, have** | **cook, fry, grill** | **cure**
- BACON + NOUN **fat, rind** | **butty, sandwich**
⇨ Special page at FOOD

bacteria *noun*

- ADJ. **harmful** | **beneficial**
- VERB + BACTERIA **attack, destroy, fight, kill** *Neither chilling nor freezing kills all bacteria.*
- PHRASES **a strain of bacteria**

bad *adj.*

1 not good; serious
- VERBS **be, look, sound** | **become, get** *The weather got very bad later in the day.*
- ADV. **extremely, really, very** | **enough** *Things are bad enough without our own guns shelling us.* | **fairly, pretty, quite, rather** *John's in a pretty bad mood this morning.*
- PREP. **at** *He's really bad at maths.* **for** *Smoking is very bad for you.*

2 not safe to eat
- VERBS **be, look, smell, taste** *The sausages tasted bad.* | **go, turn** *This meat has gone bad.*

3 guilty/sorry
- VERBS **feel**
- ADV. **really, very** | **enough** *I feel bad enough without you constantly telling me how it was all my fault!* | **fairly, pretty, quite, rather**
- PREP. **about** *She felt pretty bad about leaving him.*

badge *noun*

- ADJ. **blazer, cap, lapel** | **club** | **name** | **button**
- VERB + BADGE **wear**
- BADGE + NOUN **holder**
- PHRASES **a badge of office** *His badge of office, a large gold key, hung round his neck.*

bad-tempered *adj.*

- VERBS **be, look, seem, sound** | **become, grow** | **make sb** *It is his illness that makes him bad-tempered.*

● ADV. **extremely, very | increasingly, more and more** *He grew more and more bad-tempered as the afternoon wore on.* | **rather**

baffled *adj.*

● VERBS **be, feel, look, sound | remain**
● ADV. **completely, totally, utterly | rather | clearly | frankly**
● PREP. **about** *Officials say they're baffled about the cause of the gas explosion.* **as to** *The referee remains baffled as to why his decision caused so much anger.* **by** *The doctors are completely baffled by her illness.*

bag *noun*

● ADJ. **strong | heavy | canvas, leather, paper, plastic, polythene, string | carrier, shopping | bin, dustbin, rubbish | clutch, shoulder** *Her crocodile skin clutch bag matched her shoes.* | **drawstring, duffel | evening | overnight, weekend, travel/travelling | sponge, toilet, wash | changing** *a baby changing bag* | **school | beach, camera, golf, sports | kit** (also **kitbag**) | **medical | crisp | sandwich | body** *The dead soldiers were put on the plane in body bags.* | **sick** (= a paper bag for a person to be sick into on a plane, boat, etc.) | **doggie** (= for taking uneaten food home from a restaurant) | **goody** (= a bag given as a gift with a variety of things in) *We're giving away a free goody bag with every children's meal.* | **sleeping | pannier, saddle** (also **saddlebag**) | **money** *(figurative) He could not convince those who held the money bags that his idea was viable.* | **diplomatic** (= an official government container that may not be opened by customs officials) | **mail** (also **mailbag**), **post** (also **postbag**)
● VERB + BAG **open, unfasten, unzip | close, zip up | pack | empty, unpack | seal sth in** *The mushrooms are sealed in a bag for freshness.* | **cram/push sth in/into, put sth in/into, shove sth in/into, slip sth in/into, stuff/thrust sth in/into** *The camera caught him slipping a CD into his bag.* | **draw sth out of, produce sth from, pull/take sth from/out of | delve in/into, dive into, ferret (around) in, fumble in, reach into, rummage in, scrabble in** *I rummaged in my bag for a pen.* | **clutch, hold | carry, drag, haul, lug** *There was no lift so I had to lug my bags up the stairs.* | **heave, lift | shoulder** *He shouldered his bag and left.* | **drop, dump, put down | deposit, drop off, leave** *We dropped our bags off at the hotel and went straight out.* | **grab, snatch** *She grabbed her bag and ran out of the door.* ◊ *Two youths snatched her bag as she was walking home.* | **swing** *He was walking along swinging his school bag.* | **look in, search | gather** *They were gathering their bags, preparing to leave.*
● BAG + VERB **bulge (with sth)** *The bag bulged with papers and letters.* | **contain sth, hold sth | be crammed with sth, be (stuffed) full of sth**
● PREP. **in a/the~, inside a/the~ | ~of** *a bag of groceries*
● PHRASES **the contents of a bag** *The customs officer asked him to empty out the contents of his bag.* **sling your bag over your shoulder** *She stepped down off the bus with her bag slung over her shoulder.*

baggage *noun*

● ADJ. **carry-on, hand | excess** *At the airport I found that I had 100kg of excess baggage.* | **emotional, spiritual** *(figurative) She's still carrying all that emotional baggage from her first marriage.*
● QUANT. **item, piece**
● VERB + BAGGAGE **carry | go through, search | check in** *Where do we check in our baggage?* | **claim, reclaim** *Let's claim our baggage first.*
● BAGGAGE + NOUN **allowance | trolley | handler | claim, reclaim** *the baggage reclaim hall* | **train** *Extensive baggage trains followed the troops.*

bail *noun*

● ADJ. **conditional, unconditional | police**
● VERB + BAIL **apply for | allow sb, give sb, grant (sb)** *She has been granted conditional bail.* | **set** *The judge set bail at £50 000.* | **get** *She couldn't get bail and now she's lost those 20 months she spent on remand.* | **oppose** *The police were successful in opposing bail.* | **refuse (sb) | post, put up, stand** *A wealthy businessman has stood bail for him.* | **free sb on, release sb on, remand sb on** *They were released on police bail pending further enquiries.* | **jump, skip** (= not return for your trial after bail has been granted)
● BAIL + NOUN **application | conditions | hostel** *He was sent to a bail hostel until the case came to court.*
● PREP. **(out) on~** *He committed another robbery while out on bail.* **without~** *The accused were held without bail.*
● PHRASES **an application for bail**

bailiff *noun*

● ADJ. **court | private**
● VERB + BAILIFF **send in** *Their landlord has threatened to send in the bailiffs if they don't pay their rent.*
● BAILIFF + VERB **seize sth** *The bailiffs seized the car and house.*

bait *noun*

● ADJ. **fresh, live** *He used maggots as live bait.*
● VERB + BAIT **put out, set out** *We'll put out the bait and see what happens.* | **use sth as | nibble (at), rise to, take** *(all often figurative) We hope that potential investors will take the bait.*

bake *verb*

● PHRASES **freshly/newly baked** *The house was filled with the scent of freshly baked bread.*

balance *noun*

1 even combination/distribution
● ADJ. **correct, equal, even, exact, ideal, necessary, optimum, perfect, proper, right** *With children, it is important to achieve the right balance between love and discipline.* | **comfortable, equitable, excellent, good, happy, harmonious, healthy** *a healthy balance of foods* | **acceptable, adequate, appropriate, fair, reasonable, sensible** *How do you find an acceptable balance between closeness and distance in a relationship?* | **careful, delicate, fine, subtle** *Being a good boss requires a fine balance between kindness and authority.* | **fragile, precarious, uneasy | overall** *It is the overall balance of the diet that is important.* | **ecological, natural** *Pulling up all the plants will disturb the natural balance of the pond.* | **hormonal, nutritional | ethnic, gender, social** *There is an even gender balance amongst staff and students* (= equal numbers of men and women).
● VERB + BALANCE **require | seek | achieve, create, find, strike** *We need to strike a balance between these conflicting interests.* | **keep, maintain, sustain** *You have to maintain a balance in your life or else you'll go crazy.* | **disturb, upset** *Tourists often disturb the delicate balance of nature on the island.* | **redress, restore | affect | alter, change, shift**
● BALANCE + VERB **change, shift**
● PREP. **on~** (= after considering all the information) *On balance, the company has had a successful year.* **in~** *It is important to keep the different aspects of your life in balance.* | **~between** *the balance between academic and practical work* **~of** *the balance of animals and plants in the environment*
● PHRASES **the balance of nature**

2 division of power/influence
● ADJ. **changing, shifting | military, political**

• VERB + BALANCE **hold** *to hold the balance of power* (= to be in a position where your support would be just enough to give overall power to one group or another) | **affect** | **change, shift** | **swing, tilt, tip** (= to influence a result/decision) *In an interview, smart presentation can tip the balance in your favour.*

• BALANCE + VERB **change, shift**

• PHRASES **the balance of advantage** *The balance of advantage has shifted from the unions to employers.* **the balance of forces/power** *the changing balance of power between the working and middle class* **checks and balances** *Democracy depends on a system of checks and balances.*

3 of the body

• ADJ. **excellent, good** | **poor**

• VERB + BALANCE **have** *Gymnasts have excellent balance.* | **affect** *Tightness in one set of muscles will affect your whole balance.* | **keep** *I struggled to keep my balance on my new skates.* | **lose** *She lost her balance and fell.* | **recover, regain** | **knock sb off, throw sb off** *The sudden movement threw him off balance.*

• PREP. **off~**

• PHRASES **a sense of balance** *Cats have a very good sense of balance.*

4 money

• ADJ. **account, bank** | **cash, money** | **credit, favourable, healthy, positive** | **debit, negative** | **cleared, net** *Interest is calculated on the daily cleared balance and paid direct to your account.* | **opening** | **final, outstanding** | **trade**

• VERB + BALANCE **have** *Everyone likes to have a healthy bank balance.* | **ask for, request** *He asked the cashier for the balance of his current account.* | **check** *I'll need to check my bank balance before I spend so much money.* | **show** | **achieve** | **be due** *The final balance is due six weeks before departure.* | **pay** *I'll pay the balance later.* | **use** *The balance of the proceeds will be used for new equipment.* | **bring forward, carry forward** *the balance brought forward from the previous year*

• BALANCE + NOUN **sheet** *the company's balance sheet*

• PHRASES **the balance of payments** (= the difference between the amount of money coming into and going out of a country), **the balance of trade** (= the difference in value between imports and exports)

balance *verb*

1 keep steady

• ADV. **carefully, precariously**

• PREP. **on** *He balanced the glasses carefully on the tray.*

2 compare two things; give them equal value

• VERB + BALANCE **have to, need to** | **seek to, try to** *The plan seeks to balance two important objectives.* | **manage to**

• PREP. **against** *We have to balance the risks of the new strategy against the possible benefits.* **with** *She tries to balance the needs of her children with those of her employer.*

balanced *adj.*

• VERBS **be** | **remain**

• ADV. **properly, well** *The report was accurate and well balanced.* ◇ *a properly balanced diet* | **completely, perfectly** *a perfectly balanced design* | **equally, evenly** | **fairly, reasonably, sufficiently** | **carefully, closely, delicately, finely, nicely** *The issues are finely balanced and there is no simple answer to the question.* | **beautifully** *a beautifully balanced orchestra* | **precariously**

• PREP. **between** *The parliament was evenly balanced between the two parties.*

bald *adj.*

• VERBS **be** | **go** *He started to go bald in his twenties.*

• ADV. **completely, quite, totally** | **almost, nearly** | **prematurely** *young men who go prematurely bald*

balding *adj.*

• VERBS **be** *He's in his twenties but already balding.*

• ADV. **already, prematurely**

ball *noun*

1 round object in games

• ADJ. **billiard, cricket, golf, rugby, tennis, etc.** | **beach** | **match, practice**

• VERB + BALL **play with** | **bat, blast, bounce, bowl, chip, dribble, head, hit, kick, roll, strike, throw** *The kids love to kick a ball against my wall.* | **clear, cross, pass** | **catch, stop** *He caught the ball.* | **control, trap** | **chase** *She chased the ball all over the pitch.* | **retrieve, run down** | **return** *The fielders try to retrieve the ball quickly and return it to the bowler.* | **miss** *The goalkeeper missed the ball.* | **drop, let go of** *Oh no! He's dropped the ball.* | **handle** | **give away, lose** | **win** | **retain**

• BALL + VERB **fly, go, roll, sail** *The ball flew over the bar into the sea of Middlesbrough fans.* ◇ *The ball's gone over the fence.* | **hit, land** *The ball hit the wall and rolled along the road.* | **bounce, rebound**

• BALL + NOUN **game** | **control, skills** *His ball control was excellent.*

⇨ Special page at SPORT

2 kick/hit of a ball

• ADJ. **good, great, superb** | **bad, loose** | **high, low** *He sent over a high ball.* | **long, short** | **quick, slow** | **cross, through** *a superb through ball from John Scott* | **hand** *He was penalized for hand ball.*

• VERB + BALL **play, send** | **pick up, pounce on, punish** *He pounced on a loose ball and scored.*

• PREP. **~from** *a great ball from Beckham*

3 round object like a ball

• ADJ. **tight** | **fiery** *The sun was a fiery ball, low on the hills.* | **crystal** (= used for telling fortunes) *Without a crystal ball it's impossible to say where we'll be next year.* | **cannon, musket**

• VERB + BALL **curl/roll (up) into** *The little girl curled up into a ball in her mother's arms.* | **form/make sth into, roll/screw sth (up) into, shape sth into** *He screwed the letter up into a tight ball.*

• PHRASES **a ball of fire/flame, a ball of string/wool**

• PHRASES **a ball and chain** (*figurative*) *The responsibility was a ball and chain around my ankle.*

4 party

• ADJ. **college, charity, hunt** | **costume, fancy dress, masked** *We're going to a masked ball.*

• VERB + BALL **have, hold, organize** *We're organizing a charity ball.* | **attend, go to**

• BALL + NOUN **gown**

• ADJ. **at a/the~** *She met him at the college ball.*

ballet *noun*

1 style of dance

• ADJ. **classical, modern**

• VERB + BALLET **study** *He's studying classical ballet.*

• BALLET + NOUN **music** | **dancer** | **company** | **shoe** | **class, lesson, school** | **teacher**

2 performance of a ballet

• ADJ. **classical, modern, romantic**

• VERB + BALLET **compose, write** | **choreograph**

⇨ Note at PERFORMANCE (for more verbs)

balloon *noun*

1 toy

• ADJ. **helium** *helium balloons for the children's party*

• VERB + BALLOON **blow up, inflate** | **burst, pop**

● BALLOON + VERB **burst, pop**

2 in the sky

● ADJ. **barrage, hot-air**

● VERB + BALLOON **go up in** *We went up in a balloon.*

● BALLOON + NOUN **flight | race**

● PREP. **by~** *She crossed the Atlantic by hot-air balloon.*

ballot *noun*

● ADJ. **secret | open | postal | national | first, second | leadership | strike**

● VERB + BALLOT **carry out, hold | organize | cast** *Only 40% of eligible voters cast their ballots.*

● BALLOT + NOUN **box | paper | rigging**

● PREP. **at a/the~** *They voted against him at the second ballot.* **by ~** *The jury cast their vote by secret ballot.* **in a/the~** *The club members decided in a ballot to suspend the captain.* **on a/the~** *I voted for her on the first ballot.* **| ~for** *a ballot for the Conservative leadership* **~on** *a ballot on the new contracts* **~over** *a ballot over strike action*

ban *noun*

● ADJ. **blanket, complete, total | partial | temporary | overtime | advertising** *a blanket advertising ban on tobacco* **| driving | test** *a nuclear test ban treaty*

● VERB + BAN **impose, introduce, place, put** *The EU has imposed a ban on the import of seal skins.* **| lift, overturn, remove | tighten | ease** *The ban on exports has now been eased.* **| call for, demand | oppose, reject | comply with | defy** *The students took to the streets, defying a ban on political gatherings.*

● BAN + VERB **come into force, start | apply to sth, cover sth** *The ban only covers tropical hardwood.*

● PREP. **~on** *a ban on traffic in the town centre*

ban *verb*

● ADV. **effectively | formally, officially**

● VERB + BAN **attempt to, seek to, try to | vote to** *MPs voted to ban hunting with dogs.*

● PREP. **from** *He has been banned from driving for a year.*

● PHRASES **an attempt/a move to ban sth** *a move to ban cigarette adverts* **a decision to ban sth**

banana *noun*

● ADJ. **ripe | green | mashed**

● QUANT. **bunch** *I bought a small bunch of bananas.*

● VERB + BANANA **eat, have | pick | peel**

● BANANA + NOUN **skin** *(figurative) The company has acquired an unhappy knack of slipping on banana skins* (= being led into making mistakes that make it look stupid). **| plant, tree | leaf | grove, plantation**

⇨ Special page at FRUIT

band *noun*

1 group of musicians

● ADJ. **big | brass, string, wind | blues, dance, jazz, rock | marching, military, regimental | school | live** *the excitement of seeing a live band* **| one-man** *(often figurative) He runs the business as a one-man band* (= does everything himself).

● VERB + BAND **form | join, play in, sing in** *She plays in a rock band.* **| conduct, lead**

● BAND + VERB **perform, play | strike up** *We heard a band strike up in the park.*

● BAND + NOUN **leader, member**

● PREP. **in a/the ~** *a singer in a rock band* **with a/the ~** *a drummer with a jazz band*

● PHRASES **a member of the band**

2 group of people

● ADJ. **select, small** *He is one of a select band of top class players.* **| dwindling | growing**

● VERB + BAND **join**

● PREP. **~of** *a band of rebels*

3 range

● ADJ. **age, price, tax** *the 25–35 age band*

● VERB + BAND **be in, fall into** *Which tax band do you fall into?*

bandage *noun*

● ADJ. **tight | loose | crepe**

● VERB + BANDAGE **put on, wind around/round, wrap around/round** *Wrap the bandage firmly around the injured limb.* **| have on, wear | change, remove, take off**

● PREP. **~ around/round, ~on** *She had a bandage on her arm.*

● PHRASES **be in bandages, be swathed/wrapped in bandages** *He'll be in bandages for a few weeks.*

bandwagon *noun*

● VERB + BANDWAGON **climb on, join, jump on** *Competitors have jumped on the bandwagon and started building similar machines.*

● BANDWAGON + VERB **be rolling, gather momentum/pace, sweep along** *The Scottish Nationalist bandwagon is gathering pace.* **| slow down**

● BANDWAGON + NOUN **effect** *There is now a bandwagon effect with more and more firms joining the scheme.*

● PHRASES **get/start a bandwagon rolling** *They seem to have got an anti-government bandwagon rolling.*

bang *noun*

1 sudden loud noise

● ADJ. **almighty, big, enormous, huge, loud, massive, terrific, tremendous**

● VERB + BANG **let out, make** *The engine let out a bang.* ◇ *Will the firework make a loud enough bang?* **| hear** *We suddenly heard an almighty bang from the kitchen.*

● BANG + VERB **echo**

● PREP. **with a~** *She slammed the door with a loud bang.*

2 sudden hard hit

● ADJ. **nasty** *He got a nasty bang on the head.*

● VERB + BANG **get, have**

bang *verb*

1 hit noisily

● ADV. **hard, loudly**

● PREP. **against** *He kept banging his chair against the wall.* **on** *She banged loudly on the table.*

● PHRASES **bang sth about, bang (sth) down, bang (sth) open/shut** *The bedroom door banged shut.* ◇ *She banged the door shut.*

2 part of the body/person

● ADV. **badly, hard** *I had banged my head badly.*

● PREP. **into** *He banged into me in the corridor.* **on** *I banged my leg on the table.*

bank *noun*

1 for money

● ADJ. **big, large, major | small | central, clearing, commercial, investment, issuing, reserve, savings** *The central bank has put up interest rates.* ◇ *The bond will be priced by the issuing bank.* ◇ *She has her money in one of the largest savings banks.* **| private | foreign, international, overseas**

● VERB + BANK **go to | borrow (sth) from**

● BANK + VERB **lend sb sth** *The bank lent her money to buy a car.* **| underwrite sth** *A group of ten international banks is to underwrite and sell the bonds.* **| collapse, crash** *Investors lost millions when the bank crashed.*

● BANK + NOUN **account, balance, charges, deposit, loan, statement | manager | robber**

● PREP. **from a/the~** *He got a large loan from the bank.* **in a/the~** *I'll put half the money in the bank and spend the rest.* **out of a/the~** *I need to get some money out of the bank.*

2 by a river/canal
● ADJ. **far, opposite, other** *We could see them waving on the opposite bank.* | **canal, river**
● VERB + BANK **burst, overflow** *The River Frome had burst its banks after torrential rain.*
● PREP. **along a/the~** *We strolled along the river bank.* **on a/the~** *a picnic on the banks of the Thames*

3 area of sloping ground
● ADJ. **steep** | **grassy**
● PREP. **down a/the~** *The children rolled down the grassy bank.* **up a/the~**

4 mass of cloud, etc./row of machines, etc.
● ADJ. **huge, vast** *a huge bank of switches and buttons*
● PREP. **~of** *a vast bank of cloud*

banking *noun*

● ADJ. **business, commercial, corporate** | **investment, merchant** | **retail, wholesale** | **domestic, national** | **global, international** | **e-, electronic, Internet, online** *At first consumers were wary of e-banking.*
● BANKING + NOUN **system** | **market** | **group** | **business, industry, sector** | **community** *the international banking community*
● PREP. **in~** *This software is used in banking.*

bankrupt *adj.*

● VERBS **be** | **become, go** *Hundreds of firms went bankrupt during the recession.* | **adjudge sb, adjudicate sb, declare sb, make sb** *She had to pay the mortgage after her husband was declared bankrupt.*
● ADV. **almost, nearly, virtually** | **economically, ideologically, morally** *(figurative)*
● PREP. **of** *(figurative) a government bankrupt of new ideas*

bankruptcy *noun*

● ADJ. **personal**
● VERB + BANKRUPTCY **face** *Small travel operators are facing bankruptcy.* | **be close to, be on the brink/verge of** | **be driven/forced/thrown into, go into** | **file for, petition for** *The company has been forced to file for bankruptcy.* | **declare** *It is the only country to have declared bankruptcy.* | **be saved from, escape (from)**
● BANKRUPTCY + NOUN **order, proceedings** *The defendant has a bankruptcy order against him.*
● PHRASES **the threat of bankruptcy**

banner *noun*

● VERB + BANNER **drape, hang (out)** | **carry** | **wave** | **unfurl**
● BANNER + VERB **hang** | **flutter, fly, wave** *banners waving in the wind* | **bear sth** *The demonstrators carried banners bearing various slogans.* | **demand sth, proclaim sth, read sth, say sth** *Banners demanded the president's resignation.* | **be strung across sth** *A banner strung across the road read, 'Welcome home, boys!'*

banquet *noun*

● ADJ. **grand, great, lavish, sumptuous** | **veritable** *(humorous) The meal that followed was a veritable banquet.* | **five-course, six-course, etc.** | **formal, official** | **royal, state** | **celebration/celebratory, farewell, wedding** | **medieval** *Visitors to the castle can enjoy a medieval banquet with entertainment, in an authentic setting.*
● VERB + BANQUET **give, hold** | **arrange, prepare (for)** *The kitchens are preparing for a lavish banquet.* | **attend** *The Lord Mayor attended a state banquet last night.*

● PREP. **at a/the~** *He was suddenly taken ill at a banquet given in his honour.* | **~for** *a banquet for the president*

banter *noun*

● ADJ. **easy, friendly, good-natured, lively, pleasant** | **idle** | **bawdy, ribald**
● VERB + BANTER **swap** | **be engaged in, engage in** *She engages in friendly banter with her customers.*

bar *noun*

1 for drinks/food
● ADJ. **licensed** | **crowded** | **lounge, public, saloon** | **gay, singles** | **cocktail, wine** | **breakfast, coffee, salad, sandwich, snack**
● VERB + BAR **drop into, go to, stop at** *He often drops into a bar on the way home from work.* | **manage, run**
● BAR + NOUN **food, menu, snacks** | **stool**
● PREP. **in a/the~** *There were not many people in the bar.*

2 counter
● VERB + BAR **be propping up** *(humorous)*, **drink at, lean on, sit at, stand at** *You can usually find him propping up the bar of the Red Lion.* | **serve behind** *I didn't recognize the man who was serving behind the bar.*
● PREP. **at the~** *They were chatting at the bar.* **behind the~** *The barmaid stood behind the bar.*

3 in music
● VERB + BAR **hum, play, sing** *She played a few bars on the piano.*
● PREP. **in a/the~** *the notes in the first bar*
● PHRASES **two, four, etc. beats to the bar**

bar *verb*

● ADV. **effectively**
● PREP. **from** *The curfew has effectively barred migrant workers from their jobs.*

bare *adj.*

1 not covered by clothing
● VERBS **be** *He was standing there, completely bare!*
● ADV. **completely**

2 not containing/covered by anything
● VERBS **be, look** | **remain** | **leave sth** *You shouldn't have left the wires bare.* | **lay sth, strip sth** *The earth had been laid bare.* ◊ *The walls have been stripped bare.*
● ADV. **very** | **completely, quite** *The room was completely bare.* | **almost, rather** | **strangely** *The room looked strangely bare without the furniture.*
● PREP. **of** *The house was almost bare of furniture.*

barefoot *adj., adv.*

● VERBS **be, go, pad, stand, walk** *The children had to go barefoot because there was no money for shoes.* ◊ *He padded barefoot across the carpet.*

bargain *noun*

1 sth sold at a lower price
● ADJ. **absolute, amazing, good, real**
● VERB + BARGAIN **find, get, pick up** *I picked up a really good bargain in the market.*
● BARGAIN + NOUN **buy, price** | **hunter, hunting** | **holiday** | **basement**

2 agreement
● ADJ. **excellent, good**
● VERB + BARGAIN **make, strike**
● PREP. **into the~** *(= as well) He's very strong and completely fearless into the bargain.* | **~between** *A bargain was struck between the employers and the unions.* **~with** *I'll make a bargain with you.*
● PHRASES **drive a hard bargain** *(= force sb to agree to the arrangement that is best for you),* **keep (to) your**

half/part/side of the bargain *You haven't kept your side of the bargain.* **sb's side/part/half of the bargain** *Her part of the bargain was to look after the car.*

bargain *verb*

- ADV. **hard** *He bargained hard and was stubborn.* | **collectively** *the right of workers to bargain collectively*
- PREP. **about** *He was prepared to bargain about money.* **for** *to bargain for a decent wage* **over** *crowds of men bargaining over horses* **with** *He tried to bargain with her.*

bargaining *noun*

- ADJ. **hard** *There will be some hard bargaining before an agreement is reached.* | **collective** *Unions were insistent on the right to collective bargaining.* | **plea** (= where a defendant pleads guilty to a lesser charge in return for having a more serious charge dropped)
- BARGAINING + NOUN **position, power** *We are now in a strong bargaining position.*

barge *noun*

- ADJ. **brightly painted** | **canal, river** | **sailing** | **cargo, coal, etc.**
- VERB + BARGE **tow** | **load (sth into), unload (sth from)** | **moor, tie up**
- BARGE + VERB **be laden/loaded with sth, carry sth**
- PREP. **by ~** *I travelled by barge.* **in/on a/the ~** *cruising the canals of France in a barge*

baritone *noun*

- ADJ. **lusty, melodious, pleasant, rich**
- BARITONE + NOUN **voice** | **solo**
- PREP. **in a … ~** *He sang in his rich baritone*

bark *noun*

1 on a tree
- ADJ. **rough** | **tree** | **birch, cinnamon, willow, etc.**
- VERB + BARK **peel off, strip** *The people strip the bark and use it in medicines.*
- BARK + VERB **peel off** *The bark peels off in summer.*
- BARK + NOUN **chippings**

2 of a dog
- ADJ. **loud, noisy**
- VERB + BARK **give** *The dog gave a loud bark.*

3 loud sound/voice
- ADJ. **short** | **harsh**
- VERB + BARK **give** *He gave a harsh bark of laughter.*
- PHRASES **a bark of laughter**

bark *verb*

- ADV. **excitedly, frantically, furiously, loudly**
- PREP. **at** *The dog was barking furiously at a cat.*

barley *noun*

- ADJ. **malted/malting** *Malt whisky is made from malted barley.* | **roast/roasted** | **pearl** | **spring, winter**
- QUANT. **ear** | **field**
- VERB + BARLEY **grow** | **sow** | **cut, harvest, thresh** | **grind**
- BARLEY + VERB **grow** | **ripen**
- BARLEY + NOUN **harvest** | **field**

barometer *noun*

1 instrument that measures air pressure
- ADJ. **aneroid, digital** | **high, low** | **steady** *The barometer has been steady for three days now.*
- VERB + BAROMETER **check, read** | **tap** *He tapped the barometer and noted where the needle was pointing.*
- BAROMETER + VERB **rise** | **drop, fall**

2 sth that shows the state of sth
- ADJ. **accurate, good, reliable, sensitive, useful** *Infant mortality is a highly sensitive barometer of socio-economic conditions.* | **political**
- PREP. **~ of**

baron *noun*

1 noble
⇨ Note at PEER

2 powerful businessman
- ADJ. **media, newspaper, press** | **cocaine, drug, oil** *the oil barons of Texas* | **robber**

baroness, baronet *noun*

⇨ Note at PEER

barracks *noun*

- ADJ. **army, military, police** | **fortified**
- VERB + BARRACKS **live in** | **be confined to** *He was confined to barracks for three weeks as a punishment.* | **besiege** | **go back to, return to, withdraw to**

barrage *noun*

1 firing of guns
- ADJ. **heavy, intense** | **artillery**
- VERB + BARRAGE **launch, unleash**
- BARRAGE + NOUN **balloon**
- PREP. **~ of** *Troops unleashed a barrage of grenades.*

2 large number of questions, etc.
- ADJ. **constant, continuous, endless**
- VERB + BARRAGE **be faced with, endure, face** | **keep up** *The reporters kept up a constant barrage of questions.*
- PHRASES **a barrage of abuse/complaints/criticism/questions** *The president is facing a barrage of criticism over his handling of the crisis.*

3 wall of earth
- ADJ. **tidal**
- VERB + BARRAGE **build, construct**
- PREP. **~ across** *They built a barrage across the bay.*

barrel *noun*

1 container
- ADJ. **beer, wine**
- VERB + BARREL **fill** *They filled the barrels with cider*
- BARREL + VERB **contain sth**
- PREP. **a/per ~** *The price of oil had fallen to $16 per barrel.* **by the ~** *Beer is sold by the barrel.* | **~ of** *a barrel of beer/oil*

2 of a gun
- ADJ. **gun, rifle** *I felt the gun barrel at my head*
- VERB + BARREL **look down, peer/squint along** *She found herself looking down the barrel of a gun.* ◊ *Pulling his rifle to his shoulder he squinted along the barrel.*
- BARREL + VERB **point**
- PHRASES **the barrel of a gun**

barren *adj.*

- VERBS **appear, be** | **become** | **make sth** *The years of growing cotton had made the land completely barren.*
- ADV. **completely, entirely, utterly** | **almost** | **largely**

barricade *noun*

- ADJ. **human**
- VERB + BARRICADE **build, construct, erect, put up, set up** | **form** *The protesters formed a human barricade.* | **dismantle, remove, take down** | **smash, storm** *The army used tanks to storm the barricades.* | **man** *There were six miners manning the barricades.*
- PREP. **behind a/the ~** *fighting from behind their barri-*

cades **over a/the~** *The two sides watched each other over the barricades.* | **~across** *a barricade across the main road* **~against** *Students built a barricade against the police.* **~of** *a barricade of wooden benches*

barrier *noun*

1 fence/gate
- ADJ. **physical | crash, crush, flood, police, protective, security, ticket | sound** *(figurative) the first plane to break the sound barrier*
- VERB + BARRIER **build, erect, install | break through** *The crowd managed to break through the barriers and get onto the pitch.*
- PREP. **at a/the ~** *Please show your ticket at the barrier.* **behind a/the ~** *The police waited behind the barriers.* **through a/the~** *There was a slow trickle of people through the barriers.*

2 thing that causes problems
- ADJ. **effective, formidable, major | class, cultural, language, racial, trade**
- VERB + BARRIER **build, create, erect, put up, set up** *The old laws created barriers to free trade.* | **break down, lift, lower, reduce, remove | cross** *They believe that sport can cross any barriers.* | **be faced with, encounter, face | overcome, transcend**
- PREP. **~against** *The country has set up barriers against imports.* **~between** *a class barrier between the two families* **~to** *a formidable barrier to communication*

3 physical object that prevents sb/sth passing
- ADJ. **impassable, impenetrable | natural**
- VERB + BARRIER **form**
- PREP. **~between** *The mountains form a natural barrier between the two countries.*

barrister *noun*

- ADJ. **brilliant, good, leading, successful, top | practising, qualified | junior, trainee | defence/defending, prosecuting/prosecution**
- PREP. **~for** *the barrister for the ferry company* ◊
⇨ Note at PROFESSIONAL (for verbs)

base *noun*

1 lowest part
- ADJ. **firm, solid, strong**
- VERB + BASE **have** *The statue has a solid concrete base.*

2 original idea/situation
- ADJ. **firm, secure, solid, sound, strong | economic, ideological** *His arguments have a sound economic base.*
- VERB + BASE **have | establish, give sb, provide (sb with)** *These policies give us a solid base for winning the next election.* | **use sth as**
- PREP. **~for** *He used the notes as a base for his lecture.*

3 of support/income/power
- ADJ. **solid, sound | broad, narrow** *These policies have a broad base of support.* | **power** *a politician with a rural power base* | **commercial, economic, financial, industrial, manufacturing, tax** *The country has a sound commercial base.* | **client, customer**
- VERB + BASE **have | develop, expand, improve, increase** *The company is trying to expand its customer base.*
- BASE + VERB **grow | shrink**

4 main place
- ADJ. **excellent, ideal, perfect**
- VERB + BASE **have** *The company has its base in New York.* | **establish, set up** *The company has set up its new base in the north.*
- BASE + NOUN **camp**
- PREP. **~for** *an ideal base for mountain expeditions*

5 military centre

- ADJ. **foreign** *Demonstrators demanded the removal of foreign bases.* | **air, air force, military, missile, NATO, naval, RAF**
- VERB + BASE **have | build, establish** *The Americans established a naval base on the island in the 1960s.*
- PREP. **at a/the~** *equipment kept at the base* **on a/the ~** *people living on the air force base* **to (the) ~** *The planes have all returned to base.*

base *verb*

PHRASAL VERB
base sth on/upon sth
- ADV. **closely, firmly | broadly, loosely** *The novels are all loosely based on the author's life.* | **largely** *Their research was based largely on anecdotal evidence.*

basement *noun*

- ADJ. **dark, unlit, windowless | bargain** *(often figurative) bargain basement prices*
- BASEMENT + NOUN **apartment, bar, flat, kitchen, room, studio | door, stairs, steps, window | car park**
- PREP. **in a/the~** *The canteen is down in the basement.*

bash *noun*

1 strong hit
- VERB + BASH **give sb/sth | get**
- PREP. **on** *She got a bash on the head.*

2 party
- ADJ. **big | birthday, charity, farewell**
- VERB + BASH **give, throw** *They're throwing a big bash to celebrate their anniversary.*

bash *verb*

- ADV. **hard** *She bashed him so hard she broke his nose.*
- PREP. **on** *Someone bashed him on the nose.* **with** *She bashed him with her book.*
- PHRASES **bash sb about/up** *He had been attacked and bashed about a bit.*

basics *noun*

- VERB + BASICS **grasp, know, learn, master, pick up, understand | cover** *The book covers the basics of massage.* | **concentrate on, stick to** *It's best to stick to basics when planning such a large party.* | **get/go back to, get down to** *It's time our education system got back to basics.*
- PHRASES **get the basics right** *The important thing is to get the basics right.*

basis *noun*

1 starting point
- ADJ. **firm, solid, sound**
- VERB + BASIS **form, provide**
- PREP. **~for** *The proposal provides a sound basis for a book.*
- PHRASES **have no basis in sth** *These allegations have no basis in fact.*

2 principle/reason
- ADJ. **whole**
- PREP. **on the ~ of** *We made our decision on the basis of the information we had.* | **~for** *The whole basis for your argument is false.*

3 way sth is done/organized
- ADJ. **regular | daily, monthly, weekly, etc.** *Staff are employed on a monthly basis.* | **permanent, temporary | casual, part-time, voluntary | commercial**
- PREP. **on a ... ~**

basket noun

1 container
- ADJ. **cane, straw, wicker/wickerwork, wire, woven | laundry, sewing | bread, food, fruit, shopping | waste/waste-paper | cat, dog | bicycle** *She was cycling along with her bicycle basket full of shopping.* **| picnic | flower, hanging** *hanging baskets full of summer flowers*
- VERB + BASKET **make, weave | fill, load (sth into), pack (sth into), put sth in | take sth from/out of, unpack | carry, heave, pick up** *She heaved the huge basket onto the table.* **| swing | put down, set down**
- BASKET + VERB **be filled with sth, be full of sth, contain sth** *a basket filled with delicious fruit*
- PHRASES **in/into a/the~** *The cat lay curled in its basket.* **| ~of** *a basket of flowers/fruit*

2 in basketball
- VERB + BASKET **shoot | make, score, sink**

basketball noun

- ADJ. **college, professional**
- QUANT. **game**
- VERB + BASKETBALL **play | watch**
- BASKETBALL + NOUN **championship, match | court | coach, player, star, team | referee, umpire**
- ⇨ Special page at SPORT

bass noun

1 lowest part in music
- ADJ. **boomy, loud, pounding | solid** *The bass clarinet forms a solid bass for the woodwind group.* **| ground** *The church organist may improvise on a ground bass.* **| figured** (= a bass line in which the chords are represented by figures, not written out in full) *the abandonment in the late 18th century of figured bass in favour of completely written out orchestral scores*
- VERB + BASS **sing** *He sings bass in our local choir.* **| turn down/up** *He always plays his stereo with the bass turned right up.*
- BASS + NOUN **note, sound | line** *a pounding bass line* **| clef**

2 lowest male singing voice
- ADJ. **deep, low**
- VERB + BASS **sing** *Don has agreed to sing bass* (= sing the bass part).
- BASS + NOUN **voice | part**
- PREP. **in a ... ~** *He answered my question in a surprisingly deep bass.*

3 bass guitar
- ADJ. **electric | fretless**
- VERB + BASS **tune (up)**
- BASS + NOUN **guitar**
- ⇨ Special page at MUSIC

bassoon noun

- ⇨ Special page at MUSIC

bat noun

1 in games
- ADJ. **baseball, cricket, table tennis**
- VERB + BAT **grip, hold | carry | swing**

2 small flying animal
- ADJ. **fruit, pipistrelle, vampire**
- BAT + VERB **flutter, fly | roost | squeak**
- PHRASES **a species of bat**

bat verb

- VERB + BAT **go in to** *Hick went in to bat after Hussain.* **put sb in to** *India won the toss and put England in to bat.*
- PREP. **for** *Smith was first to bat for Warwickshire.*

batch noun

1 number of people/things
- ADJ. **large, small | whole** *A whole batch of original drawings will be on sale.* **| fresh, new** *He baked a fresh batch of rolls.* ◊ *Each summer a new batch of students tries to find work.* **| latest** *the latest batch of opinion polls*
- PREP. **in the~** *How many books are there in each batch?* ◊ *We deliver the goods in batches.* **| ~of** *a batch of letters*

2 in computing
- BATCH + NOUN **job** *to process a batch job* **| file, program | processing | mode** *to run in batch mode* **| queue**

bath noun

- ADJ. **hot, warm | cold | long | quick | bubble** *lying in a hot bubble bath* **| baby, bird**
- VERB + BATH **fill, run** *Could you run the bath for me?* **| have, take | lie in, soak in | need**
- BATH + NOUN **tap, water** (also **bathwater**) **| mat, towel | time** *It's the children's bath time.*
- PREP. **in the~** *Please answer the phone. I'm in the bath!*

bathroom noun

- ADJ. **steamy | large, spacious | tiny | luxurious, luxury | fitted | tiled | adjoining, en suite | communal, shared | private | downstairs, upstairs**
- VERB + BATHROOM **go to, use** (= go to the toilet)
- BATHROOM + NOUN **cabinet, cupboard | accessories, equipment, fittings, suite | mirror | scales** *I weigh myself on the bathroom scales every day.* **| facilities**

baton noun

1 used by police/soldiers
- ADJ. **electric | wooden | police**
- VERB + BATON **carry, hold | draw, use** *The police were ordered to draw their batons and disperse the crowd.*
- BATON + NOUN **charge** *Five people were injured in the baton charge.*

2 used by a conductor
- VERB + BATON **raise, wave**
- PREP. **under the~ of** *The orchestra made the recording under the baton of a young German conductor.*

3 used in a relay race
- ADJ. **hand, pass** *Each runner passes the baton to the next.* **| take (up) | drop**

4 used by a drum majorette
- VERB + BATON **swing, twirl**

battered adj.

- VERBS **be, feel, look | become, get**
- ADV. **badly, very | a bit, a little, rather, slightly | emotionally** *She felt emotionally battered.*
- PHRASES **battered old** *She wore a battered old robe.*

battery noun

1 for electricity
- ADJ. **dead, flat** *The car won't start—the battery's flat.* **| rechargeable | car, torch | alkaline, lithium**
- VERB + BATTERY **charge, recharge | change, replace | connect** *Is the battery connected correctly?* **| be powered by, run on, use, work on** *The machine can also run on batteries.*
- BATTERY + VERB **give out, go dead, run down, run out** *After about six hours, the battery will run down.*
- BATTERY + NOUN **power | life** *With our product you get longer battery life.* **| failure | charger**
- PHRASES **battery-operated, battery-powered** *a small battery-powered car*

2 large group of similar things

- ADJ. **full, whole**
- PREP. **~of** *I had to answer a whole battery of questions.*
- PHRASES **a battery of tests**

battle *noun*

1 between armies
- ADJ. **bloody, fierce | pitched** *The two armies fought a pitched battle on the plain.* **| decisive | great, important, major | famous, historic | land, naval, sea**
- VERB + BATTLE **fight (in) | win | lose | do, give, go into, join** *Charles V refused to give battle.* ◊ *The two armies joined battle.* **| send sb into** *Many young men were sent into battle without proper training.*
- BATTLE + VERB **begin, take place | rage | continue | be over, end**
- PREP. **at a/the ~** *Napoleon was defeated at the Battle of Waterloo.* **in (a/the)~** *He died in battle.*

2 violent fight between two groups
- ADJ. **fierce | pitched | running | gun**
- VERB + BATTLE **fight**
- PREP. **~against** *Police fought a pitched battle against demonstrators.* **~between** *a gun battle between police and drug smugglers* **~with** *Scores of people have been hurt in running battles with police.*

3 struggle
- ADJ. **bitter, fierce | real** *There's now a real battle at the top of the First Division.* **| constant, continuing, long, long-running, ongoing, prolonged | losing, uphill** *We seem to be fighting a losing battle.* **| successful | court, legal**
- VERB + BATTLE **be engaged in, do, fight** *Are you prepared to do battle with your insurance company over the claim?* **| face | win | lose**
- BATTLE + VERB **begin | be over, end**
- PREP. **~against** *his long battle against cancer* **~between** *a fierce battle between developers and the local community* **~for** *The battle for human rights* **~over** *The government now faces a new battle over tax increases.* **~with** *They are engaged in a long-running legal battle with their neighbours.*
- PHRASES **a battle of ideas/words, a battle of wills/wits, a battle royal** (= a major battle in which all available forces take part), **fight your own battles** *My parents believed in leaving me to fight my own battles.*

battle *verb*

- ADV. **hard | bravely** *The child battled bravely for her life.* **| in vain** *Doctors battled in vain to save his life.* **| constantly | away** *We'll keep battling away and hope that the goals start to come.*
- PREP. **against** *Rescuers battled against torrential rain and high winds.* **for** *battling for control of the party* **over** *Residents are battling over plans for a new supermarket.* **through** *We battled through the snowstorm.* **with** *Riot police battled with 4 000 students.* ◊ *battling with leukaemia*
- PHRASES **battle it out** *Competitors battled it out against the clock.* **battle your way** *He battled his way to the bar.*

bay *noun*

1 part of a coast
- ADJ. **sheltered | wide | sandy**
- VERB + BAY **overlook** *holiday flats overlooking the bay*
- PREP. **across the~** *Lights twinkled across the bay.*

2 area used for a particular purpose
- ADJ. **docking, landing, loading**

bayonet *noun*

- ADJ. **fixed** *troops with fixed bayonets*

- VERB + BAYONET **fix | thrust** *A bayonet had been thrust through his belly.*

beach *noun*

- ADJ. **beautiful, fine, lovely, magnificent, palm-fringed, sun-drenched | golden, sandy, white | pebble, shingle | bathing, pleasure | deserted, empty, private, secluded**
- BEACH + VERB **stretch** *a beautiful golden beach stretching for miles*
- PREP. **along a/the ~** *He walked along the beach.* **at a/the ~** *They met at the beach.* **on a/the ~** *She lay on the beach and read her book.*

bead *noun*

1 small piece of glass, wood, etc.
- ADJ. **amber, glass, wooden, etc. | prayer, rosary**
- QUANT. **strand, string** *a string of wooden beads*
- VERB + BEAD **wear | fasten, put on | take off, undo, unfasten | thread** *She threaded the beads carefully.*
- BEAD + VERB **hang** *A strand of coral beads hung round her neck.*
- BEAD + NOUN **curtain**

2 small drop of liquid
- PHRASES **a bead of moisture/perspiration/sweat**

beak *noun*

- ADJ. **short, small | large, long | curved, hooked, pointed, sharp | powerful | black, yellow**
- VERB + BEAK **open | close**

beaker *noun*

- ADJ. **glass, plastic** *a glass beaker containing copper sulphate solution* ◊ *She drank from a plastic beaker.*
- VERB + BEAKER **fill, refill | drain, empty | lift, pick up, raise | place, put down, replace, set down | drink from/out of**
- BEAKER + VERB **contain sth**

beam *noun*

1 ray of light
- ADJ. **bright, intense, piercing, powerful | narrow, thin | electron, laser, searchlight, torch**
- VERB + BEAM **direct, point, send, shine | play** *He played the beam of his torch over the wall of the cave.* **| catch sb/sth in** *He was suddenly caught in the full beam of a searchlight.*
- BEAM + VERB **shine | illuminate sth, light sth up**
- PREP. **~from** *the beam from the lighthouse* **~of** *A beam of sunlight shone in through the window.*
- PHRASES **on full beam** *car headlights on full beam*

2 long piece of wood/metal
- ADJ. **timber, wooden | oak | iron, metal, steel | old, original** *a cottage with original beams and a thatched roof* **| exposed** *a cosy pub with exposed oak beams* **| horizontal, vertical**
- BEAM + VERB **support sth**

beam *verb*

- ADV. **broadly** *He beamed broadly at them, clearly very pleased to see them.* **| positively** *She positively beamed with satisfaction.* **| cheerfully, happily, proudly**
- PREP. **at** *She beamed happily at Maxim.* **with** *His face beamed with pleasure.*

bean *noun*

1 vegetable
- ADJ. **black-eyed, broad, butter, chilli, French, green, haricot, kidney, runner, soya, string | canned, dried, refried | baked** *baked beans on toast*

● VERB + BEAN **eat**, **have** | **plant** | **grow** *She grows her own broad beans.* | **cook** | **drain, strain** | **soak** *If using dried beans, soak them overnight first.*
● BEAN + NOUN **curd** | **sprout**
⇨ Special page at FOOD

2 seed of other plants
● ADJ. **cocoa, coffee**
● VERB + BEAN **roast** | **grind**

bear *verb*

1 accept/deal with sth
● VERB + BEAR **be able/unable to, can/could** (**hardly/scarcely**) *Don't leave me alone. I wouldn't be able to bear it.* ◇ *How can you bear this awful noise?* ◇ *We could hardly bear to be outdoors in the blinding sunlight.*

2 be responsible for sth
● VERB + BEAR **have to, must** *Do parents have to bear the whole cost of tuition fees?* ◇ *You must bear at least some responsibility for what has happened.*

PHRASAL VERB
bear on/upon sb/sth
● ADV. **heavily** *The burden of the tax bore most heavily on the poor.*

bearable *adj.*

● VERBS **be** | **become** | **make sth** *The camaraderie among fellow employees made the tedious work just bearable.* | **find sth** *He found the dullness of his work scarcely bearable.*
● ADV. **almost** | **hardly, scarcely** | **just**
● PREP. **for** *The money made life more bearable for her.*

beard *noun*

● ADJ. **bristling, bushy, full, shaggy** | **neat, neatly-clipped** | **patchy, straggly, wispy** | **goatee** | **pointed** | **ginger/gingery, greying, reddish, white,** etc. | **fake, false**
● VERB + BEARD **grow** | **have, sport, wear** *He sported a neat goatee beard.* | **clip, cut, trim** | **shave (off)** | **pull (at), stroke, tug (at)** *Jim stroked his beard reflectively.*
● BEARD + VERB **grow** *My beard's grown a lot.* | **be streaked with sth** *His beard is streaked with grey.*
● BEARD + NOUN **growth, stubble** *He had two days' beard growth across his jowls and chin.*
● PREP. **with a/the ~** *She's scared of men with beards.*
● PHRASES **a three-day/seven-day,** etc. **growth of beard, a three-day-old,** etc. **beard**

bearing *noun*

1 way in which sth is related
● ADJ. **direct, important, significant** *The rise in interest rates had a direct bearing on the company's profits.*
● VERB + BEARING **have**
● PREP. **~on**

2 direction/position
● ADJ. **compass**
● VERB + BEARING **check** *He checked his bearings on the map in the car.* | **find, get** *Everything was in darkness and it was difficult to get my bearings.* | **keep** *To keep your bearings in a desert sandstorm is impossible.* | **lose** *She lost her bearings in the thick forest.*
● PHRASES **take a (compass) bearing on sth** *Take a compass bearing on that mountain.*

beast *noun*

1 animal
● ADJ. **ferocious, savage, snarling, wild** *Savage beasts once roamed these forests.* | **exotic, fabled, fantastic, legendary, mythical, rare, strange** *paintings of mythical beasts* | **great, huge, magnificent, mighty**

● PHRASES **a beast of burden, a beast of prey**

2 unpleasant/cruel person
● ADJ. **filthy** *You filthy beast!* | **sex** *Local people live in fear of this unknown sex beast.*
● PHRASES **the beast in sb** (= the violent or sexual part of sb's character) *The beast in her wanted to destroy his house.* **bring out the beast in sb** *Somehow she brought out the beast in him.*

beat *noun*

1 rhythm
● ADJ. **regular, rhythmic, steady** | **pounding**
● VERB + BEAT **clap to, dance to, sway to** *They danced to the rhythmic beat of the music.*
● PHRASES **two, three, four,** etc. **beats to the bar** *The piece has four beats to the bar.* **sb's heart misses/skips a beat** (= sb feels very nervous) *As I opened the letter, my heart missed a beat.*

2 of a police officer
● VERB + BEAT **pound, walk** *We have two officers walking the beat after midnight.*
● PREP. **on the ~** *officers on the beat*

beat *verb*

1 in a game
● ADV. **comfortably, comprehensively, convincingly, easily, hands down, soundly** *He beat her hands down.* | **narrowly** *He was narrowly beaten by his opponent.*
● PREP. **at** *She beat him at chess.* **by** *beating her by just three points*
● PHRASES **beat sb into second, third,** etc. **place** *He was beaten into second place by the American.*

2 hit sb
● ADV. **badly, brutally, savagely, severely, violently**
● PREP. **with** *She was beaten with a metal bar.*
● PHRASES **beat sb about/over the head** *He had been beaten about the head with a rock.* **beat sb to death, beat sb unconscious**

3 of heart/wings
● ADV. **fast, frantically, painfully, rapidly, wildly** *I could feel my heart beating wildly.*

4 mix
● ADV. **thoroughly, well** *Beat the mixture well, until it is light and creamy.* | **lightly** *Add three eggs, lightly beaten.*

PHRASAL VERB
beat down
● ADV. **mercilessly, relentlessly**
● PREP. **on/upon** *The African sun beat relentlessly down on his aching head.*

beating *noun*

● ADJ. **brutal, savage, severe, terrible, violent**
● VERB + BEATING **get, receive, suffer, take** *The team took a terrible beating.* | **give sb/sth** *They caught him and gave him a violent beating.*

beautiful *adj.*

● VERBS **be, feel, look, seem** | **become, grow** | **make sb/sth** *We did all we could to make the room beautiful.* | **find sb/sth** *He found her exquisitely beautiful.*
● ADV. **exceptionally, extraordinarily, extremely, outstandingly, really, remarkably, supremely, truly, very** | **absolutely, perfectly, quite, utterly** | **just, simply** (*informal*) *'They're just beautiful,' breathed Jo, when she saw the earrings.* | **almost** *I remember her as pretty, almost beautiful.* | **rather** | **astonishingly, breathtakingly, dazzlingly, incredibly, staggeringly, startlingly, strikingly, stunningly, unbelievably, wonderfully** | **uniquely** | **exquisitely** | **serenely** | **classically** *Her features were classically beautiful, with perfectly structured high cheek-*

bones. | **coldly** *The designs were pure, austere and coldly beautiful.* | **achingly, eerily, hauntingly, painfully** *a hauntingly beautiful melody*

beauty *noun*

1 quality of being beautiful
- ADJ. **breathtaking, extraordinary, great, outstanding, sheer** *an area of breathtaking beauty* | **classical** *the classical beauty of her face* | **natural** | **physical** | **scenic**
- BEAUTY + VERB **last** | **fade** *Her beauty faded as she got older.*
- BEAUTY + NOUN **competition, contest** | **queen** | **parlour, salon** | **treatment** | **spot**
- PHRASES **beauty is in the eye of the beholder, beauty is only skin-deep**

2 beautiful person or thing
- ADJ. **great** *She was known as a great beauty in her time.* | **absolute, real** *My new car's a real beauty!* | **little** *Isn't she a little beauty?*

bed *noun*

1 piece of furniture for sleeping on
- ADJ. **double, king-size, single, twin** | **bunk, camp, feather, folding, four-poster, hospital, sofa** | **warm** | **unmade** *a messy room, with an unmade bed and clothes on the floor* | **marriage**
- VERB + BED **do** (*informal*), **make, make up** | **strip** *Please strip the beds and put the sheets in the washing machine.* | **climb into, crawl into, get into, go to, tumble into** *She crawled into bed exhausted.* | **climb out of, get out of, leap out of** | **lie (down) on, lie in, sit on** *He lay in bed, reading his book.* ◇ *Elizabeth was sitting on her bed writing a letter.* | **put sb to, tuck sb up in** *It's your turn to put the children to bed.* | **wet** *Don't punish a child who wets the bed.*
- BED + NOUN **clothes, linen**
- PREP. **in~** *I like to be in bed before 11 o'clock.* **out of~** *Are you out of bed yet?*
- PHRASES **bed and breakfast, the edge/side of the bed, the foot/head of the bed, get sb into bed** (= have sex with sb), **go to bed with sb** (= have sex with sb), **take to your bed** (= go to bed because you are ill), **time for bed** *Come on, children, it's time for bed.*

2 piece of ground for growing flowers, vegetables, etc.
- ADJ. **flower, rose, strawberry** | **ornamental** | **raised**
- PREP. **~of** *ornamental beds of roses*

bedroom *noun*

- ADJ. **attractive, elegant, pleasant, pretty** | **comfortable, cosy** | **big, enormous, large, spacious** | **cell-like, little, modest, small, tiny** | **double, single, twin** | **en suite** | **main, master, principal** | **nursery** | **study** | **attic, back, downstairs, first-floor, front, upstairs** | **guest, spare** | **hotel**
- VERB + BEDROOM **share** *I used to share a bedroom with my brother.* | **convert** *They converted the spare bedroom into an office.* | **decorate, redecorate**
- BEDROOM + NOUN **furniture, suite** | **window** | **slippers** | **scene** *The actress refused to appear naked in the bedroom scenes.*
- PREP. **around a/the ~** *There were dirty clothes strewn around the bedroom.* **in a/the~**
- PHRASES **a 3-bedroom, etc. house** *The larger houses are four-bedroom houses.*

bedside *noun*

- VERB + BEDSIDE **be called to, be summoned to** *The doctor was summoned to his bedside.* | **stay at/by** | **leave** *His wife never left his bedside.*
- BEDSIDE + NOUN **cabinet, lamp, light, table**

- PREP. **at sb's/the~, by sb's/the~** *I like to keep a glass of water by my bedside.*

bedtime *noun*

- ADJ. **normal, usual**
- BEDTIME + NOUN **reading, story** | **drink**
- PREP. **at~, before sb's~, past sb's~** *It's well past my normal bedtime.*

bee *noun*

- ADJ. **bumble** (also **bumblebee**), **honey, killer** | **queen, worker** | **angry** *He was stung by thousands of angry bees.*
- QUANT. **swarm**
- BEE + VERB **buzz, hum** *A bee buzzed in my ear.* | **sting (sb)** | **fly, swarm** *The bees swarmed round the hive.*
- BEE + NOUN **hive** (also **beehive**) | **sting** | **keeper** (also **bee-keeper**)

beef *noun*

- ADJ. **fresh** | **lean** | **fatty** | **tender** | **tough** | **prime** | **organic** | **medium, rare, well done** *'How would you like your beef?' 'Rare, please.'* | **roast** | **corned, minced, salted** *a kilo of very lean minced beef*
- QUANT. **bit, piece, slice** | **fillet, joint, rib, side**
- VERB + BEEF **eat** | **boil, braise, cook, fry, roast, stew** | **carve, cut** *carving a joint of beef*
- BEEF + NOUN **stew, stock** | **cattle** | **farmer** | **industry, production**

beer *noun*

- ADJ. **excellent, good, great, quality** | **strong** | **alcohol-free, light, low-alcohol, no-alcohol** | **cold, ice-cold** | **warm** | **foaming** *a glass of foaming ice-cold beer* | **black, blonde, dark** | **bottled, cask, draught, keg** | **flat** (= that the gas has gone out of) | **stale** *The pub smelled of stale beer.* | **home-brewed** | **designer** *The shop specializes in designer beers.*
- QUANT. **litre, pint** *I ordered half a pint of beer with my sandwich.* | **barrel, bottle, can, glass, keg, tankard** | **crate**
- VERB + BEER **drink** *Do you drink beer?* | **have** *Will you have a beer?* | **down** *He downed his beer in one go.* | **gulp (at), sip (at), swig, take a gulp/sip/swig of** | **draw, pour (sb)** *This beer should be drawn slowly.* ◇ *He poured us all a beer.* | **order** *I saw him at the bar ordering a beer.* | **go for** *I'm going for a beer with Carl tonight.* | **brew** | **chill**
- BEER + VERB **chill** *Put the beer in the fridge to chill.* | **foam** | **go flat** | **flow** (*figurative*) *The beer flowed freely after the match.* | **slop** *He slammed his glass down and the beer slopped over the sides.*
- BEER + NOUN **drinker, lover** | **maker** | **barrel, bottle, can, crate, glass, keg, mug, tankard** | **mat** | **festival** | **consumption, production, sales** | **cellar, garden** *The pub has a beer garden round the back.* | **belly** *He's only twenty but he's already got a beer belly* (= a fat stomach from drinking too much beer). | **money** *Playing non-league football keeps him in beer money* (= earns him enough money to buy beer, but he has to do another job to earn a living).

beg *verb*

1 ask sb for food, money, etc.
- VERB + BEG **be forced to, have to**
- PREP. **for** *begging for food* **from** *He had to beg food from passers-by.*

2 ask for sth with great emotion
- ADV. **almost, practically** *In the end they almost begged him to take the job.* | **humbly** *We humbly beg Your Majesty to show mercy.* | **silently** *Don't leave me, he begged her silently.*

• VERB + BEG **be forced to, have to**
• PREP. **for** *We went to him to beg for forgiveness.* **of** (*formal*) *Do not do that, I beg of you.*

begin *verb*

• ADV. **(all over) again** *Once it has finished, the video automatically begins again.* ◇ *We had to begin all over again.*
• VERB + BEGIN **be due to, be expected to, be scheduled to** *The entertainment was due to begin at 8.30.* | **be ready to** | **be about to, be going to** *A new life was about to begin for him.*
• PREP. **by** *Let's begin by writing down a few ideas.* **with** *We will begin with a brief discussion of the problems.* ◇ *Can you think of a word beginning with V?*
• PHRASES **begin at the beginning** *Begin your story at the beginning, and carry on to the end.*

beginner *noun*

• ADJ. **absolute, complete, real**

beginning *noun*

• ADJ. **new** *She spoke of a new beginning for the nation.*
• VERB + BEGINNING **herald, mark** *This invention marked the beginning of the modern age.* | **see** *2001 saw the beginning of a period of rapid growth.*
• PREP. **at the ~ (of sth)** *I'm paid at the beginning of each month.* **from the ~** *Tell me the whole story, right from the beginning.* **in the ~** *In the beginning I found the course very difficult.*
• PHRASES **the beginning of the end** *That holiday together was the beginning of the end of our friendship.* **early/first beginnings** *The society had its early beginnings in discussion groups.* **from beginning to end** *The play was rubbish from beginning to end.* **from humble/modest/small beginnings** *From these small beginnings it grew into the vast company we know today.* **the very beginning** *I disliked her from the very beginning.*

behave *verb*

• ADV. **impeccably, perfectly, well** | **aggressively, badly, disgracefully, outrageously** *Children who behave badly are rejecting adult values.* | **appropriately, correctly, properly, responsibly** *The enquiry investigated whether officers had behaved correctly.* | **improperly, irresponsibly** | **rationally, reasonably** | **stupidly, unreasonably** | **normally** | **oddly, out of character, strangely, suspiciously** | **accordingly** *Children, if they are used to being treated with respect, will behave accordingly.* | **naturally** *the freedom to behave naturally*
• PREP. **as if/though** *He behaved as if nothing out of the ordinary was happening.* **like** *Stop behaving like a three-year-old!* **towards** *He had always behaved in a friendly manner towards us.*

behaviour *noun*

• ADJ. **exemplary, good** *He had his jail term cut for good behaviour.* | **acceptable** | **antisocial, bad, unacceptable, undesirable** | **deviant, problem** *Teachers can't always respond effectively to problem behaviour.* | **normal** | **strange** | **aggressive, criminal, disruptive, violent** | **animal, human, sexual, social**
• VERB + BEHAVIOUR **control, influence** *Parents can influence the behaviour of their children.* | **alter, change, modify** | **display, exhibit, show** *Animals in zoos often display disturbed behaviour.*
• BEHAVIOUR + NOUN **pattern**
• PREP. **~ towards** *his behaviour towards his parents*
• PHRASES **behaviour and attitudes, be on your best behaviour** (= to behave very well in order to impress sb), **a code of behaviour, a pattern of behaviour, standards**

of behaviour *a new study looking at the behaviour and attitudes of young men*

being *noun*

1 living creature
• ADJ. **human, living** *the rights of all human beings* | **intelligent, rational** *I work on the assumption that people are rational beings.* | **strange, supernatural**

2 state of existing
• VERB + BEING **be brought into, come into** (= to start to exist) *How do you think the world came into being?*

belief *noun*

• ADJ. **absolute, deep-seated, deeply held, fervent, firm, passionate, profound, strong, strongly held, unshakeable** | **genuine, honest, sincere** *She was strict with her children in the genuine belief that it was the right thing to do.* | **entrenched, fanatical** | **common, commonly held, general, popular, widely held, widespread** | **growing** | **long-held, long-standing** | **basic, central, core, fundamental** *the basic beliefs of Christianity* | **personal, private** *I think the rights and wrongs of eating meat are a matter of personal belief.* | **rational, reasonable** | **irrational, superstitious** | **instinctive** | **naive** | **strange** | **conflicting, contradictory** | **erroneous, false, misguided, mistaken** *I took the job in the mistaken belief that I would be able to stay in London.* | **ancient, traditional** *The people still follow their traditional beliefs.* | **orthodox** | **cultural, moral, political, religious, spiritual** *They were persecuted for their religious beliefs.* | **Catholic, Christian, pagan, etc.**
• QUANT. **set, system** *Each religion has its set of beliefs.*
• VERB + BELIEF **have, hold** *I have very firm beliefs about moral issues.* | **share** *He shared his father's belief that people should work hard for their living.* | **adhere to, cling to, follow, hold on to, stick to** *She clung to the belief that he would come back to her.* ◇ *The Labour Party must stick to its beliefs.* | **abandon, give up, renounce** | **lose** *She has lost her belief in God.* | **affirm, assert, declare, express, state** *Here the apostle Peter affirms his belief that the scriptures are 'inspired'.* | **emphasize, stress** | **encourage, foster, fuel** *The exam results encouraged the belief that he was a good teacher.* | **confirm, reinforce, strengthen, support** *This latest evidence strengthens our belief that the government is doing the right thing.* | **question, shake, shatter, undermine, weaken** *The child's death shook her belief in God.* | **respect** *You must respect other people's beliefs.* | **beggar, defy** (= to be impossible to believe) *It beggars belief how things could have got this bad.*
• BELIEF + VERB **persist** *Belief in the magical properties of this herb persisted down the centuries.*
• BELIEF + NOUN **system**
• PREP. **beyond ~** (= too great, difficult, etc. to be believed) *Dissatisfaction with the government has grown beyond belief.* ◇ *icy air that was cold beyond belief* **in the ~ that** *She did it in the belief that it would help her career.* | **~ about** *beliefs about the origin of the universe* **~ among** *There is a belief among young people that education is a waste of time.* **~ in** *a belief in God*
• PHRASES **contrary to popular belief** (= in spite of what people think) *Contrary to popular belief, rainforests are not jungles through which you have to slash a path.*

believable *adj.*

• VERBS **be, sound** | **find sth**
• ADV. **very** *All the characters were very believable.* | **hardly** *I find her story hardly believable.*

believe *verb*

• ADV. **firmly, really, seriously** (only used with nega-

tives), **sincerely** *He firmly believed that he was right.* ◇ *No one seriously believes that this war will happen.* | **mistakenly**
• VERB + BELIEVE **can't/cannot, could not** *I couldn't believe what I was hearing.* | **be hard to** *It's hard to believe that this campaign has been going on for ten years.* | **give sb to** *The boss gave me to believe that we would all get a pay rise.* | **have reason to** *We have reason to believe that the escaped prisoner may be hiding in this house.* | **be inclined to** *I'm inclined to believe you.* | **lead sb to** *The advertisement led us to believe that all prices had been cut.*
• PHRASES **can/could hardly/scarcely believe sth, not believe a word of sth** *I didn't believe a word of what he said.*

believer *noun*

1 sb who has religious faith
• ADJ. **devout, genuine, true | religious**

2 sb who believes that sth is good
• ADJ. **fervent, firm, great, passionate, staunch, strong**
• PREP. **~in** *I'm a firm believer in the benefits of exercise.*

bell *noun*

1 hollow metal object that rings
• ADJ. **church, temple | wedding** (*often figurative*) *The two of them went everywhere together and their friends could already hear wedding bells* (= were sure they would get married). | **cow | distant**
• VERB + BELL **ring | hear**
• BELL + VERB **chime, clang, jangle, peal, ring (out), sound, tinkle, toll** *The bells on the harness tinkled softly.* ◇ *The church bells tolled for Evensong.*
• BELL + NOUN **tower | pull, rope**
• PHRASES **a chime of bells** *the faint chime of bells* **a peal of bells** *She heard a peal of church bells.* **a sound of bells** *The sound of bells echoed across the valley.*

2 other object that rings
• ADJ. **bicycle, door** (also **doorbell**) | **dinner, school | electric | alarm, warning** (*often figurative*) *Alarm bells were ringing inside Stuart's head.*
• VERB + BELL **press, ring, sound | answer** *She hurried to answer the doorbell.*
• BELL + VERB **go, ring, sound** *The school bell goes at three every afternoon.*
• BELL + NOUN **push**

bellow *noun*

• ADJ. **great, loud | angry**
• VERB + BELLOW **give, let out** *She gave a great bellow of laughter.* | **hear**
• PREP. **with a~** *He woke with a bellow of rage.* | **~of**
• PHRASES **a bellow of laughter, a bellow of rage**
⇨ Note at SOUND

belly *noun*

• ADJ. **empty, full | flat | fat, pot** *Since he turned 30 he's started to develop a pot belly.* | **distended, swollen | beer** (= a fat stomach from drinking too much beer)
• BELLY + VERB **bulge | hang** *He's so fat, his belly hangs over his trousers.* | **swell**
• PREP. **in your~** *She felt the child in her belly kick.*

belongings *noun*

• ADJ. **personal**
• VERB + BELONGINGS **collect/gather (together/up), pack (up)** *She collected up her personal belongings and left.* | **go through, look through, rifle through, search** *In her absence, someone had gone through her belongings.* | **sort through** *He was trying to sort through his belongings and bring them to some sort of order.*

beloved *adj.*

• VERBS **be**
• ADV. **dearly, much** *the death of his much beloved wife*
• PREP. **by** *an area beloved by artists* **of** *She ran one of the little tea rooms so beloved of Londoners at the turn of the century.*

belt *noun*

1 narrow piece of leather, etc. worn round the waist
• ADJ. **broad, wide | narrow | thick | studded | cartridge, money, sword | trouser**
• VERB + BELT **buckle, do up, fasten | unbuckle, undo, unfasten | tighten | loosen**
• BELT + NOUN **buckle, loop**
⇨ Special page at CLOTHES

2 in a machine
• ADJ. **conveyor, drive, fan**

3 area of land
• ADJ. **wide | narrow, thin | coastal, mountain | corn, cotton, wheat | green, industrial** *New roads are cutting into the green belt* (= open land round a city where building is strictly controlled). | **commuter, stockbroker**
• PREP. **~of** *a narrow belt of trees*

bemused *adj.*

• VERBS **be, look, seem, sound | become**
• ADV. **totally** *Sarah looked totally bemused.* | **a bit, faintly, a little, quite, rather, slightly, somewhat** *I was beginning to feel slightly bemused.*
• PREP. **by** *Connie was rather bemused by all the attention she was getting.*

bench *noun*

1 long seat
• ADJ. **long | narrow | hard | padded | wooden | garden, park | replacements', subs', substitutes'** (*sport*) *They have several top players on the subs' bench.*
• VERB + BENCH **sit (down) on**
• BENCH + NOUN **seat**
• PREP. **on a/the~** *He often sleeps on park benches.*

2 in Parliament
• ADJ. **government, Opposition | Conservative, Labour, etc. | back, front** (Government ministers and the most important members of the Opposition sit on the **front benches. Back-bench** MPs have no official position besides that of MP.)
• VERB + BENCH **be on, sit on**
• PREP. **from the ... ~s** *There were cheers from the Labour benches.* **on the ... ~s** *Some MPs on the government back benches are starting to question the government's handling of the war.*

3 long narrow table that people work at
• ADJ. **work** (also **workbench**) | **carpenter's, laboratory**
• PREP. **at a/the~** *He was working at his bench.*

bend *noun*

• ADJ. **gentle, slight, wide | hairpin, sharp, tight** *Some of the hairpin bends had Ruth clinging to her seat.* | **dangerous | blind** *mountain roads with steep gradients and blind bends* | **left-hand, right-hand | final** (= in a race) *He had a winning lead off the final bend.*
• QUANT. **series** *a series of dangerous bends*
• VERB + BEND **come round, negotiate, round, take, turn** *He slowed down to negotiate the bend.*
• PREP. **around/round a/the~** *The car vanished round a bend.* **into a/the~** *I inched the car into the bend.* **off a/the~** *He came off the bend in the lead.* **on a/the~** *Slow down on the tight bends.* | **~in** *a wide bend in the river*

bend *verb*

● ADV. **slightly | quickly, swiftly | backwards, forwards | down, over** *I bent down and tied my shoelace.* | **close, nearer** *Sarah bent close to him.* | **double** *I had to bend double to get under the table.*
● PREP. **at** *Avoid bending at the waist when lifting heavy objects.* **towards** *He came closer and bent towards her.*

benefactor *noun*

● ADJ. **generous, kind | wealthy | great | anonymous, mysterious, unknown | private | public** *He was a great public benefactor and gave land for building the sea wall.*
● BENEFACTOR + VERB **donate sth, give sth** *A private benefactor donated £20 000.*
● PREP. **~ to** *She was a generous benefactor to the library.*

beneficial *adj.*

● VERBS **be, prove** *Some alternative treatments may prove highly beneficial.* | **consider sth**
● ADV. **extremely, highly, very | entirely, wholly | clearly | mutually** *The arrangement was mutually beneficial.* | **medically, socially**
● PREP. **for** *I think it would be beneficial for each committee member to have a copy of the report.* **to** *Exercise is extremely beneficial to health.*

benefit *noun*

1 advantage
● ADJ. **considerable, enormous, great, major, real, substantial** *This could bring real benefits for teachers.* | **maximum | additional** *The scheme has many additional benefits.* | **fringe** (= extra things that an employer gives as well as wages) *The fringe benefits include free health insurance.* | **mutual** *The different environmental groups could work together to their mutual benefit.* | **potential | long-term, short-term | economic, environmental, financial, health, social | tax**
● VERB + BENEFIT **enjoy, have** *The motor industry will be one of the first to enjoy the benefits of the recovery.* ◇ *children who have the benefit of a stable home background* | **derive, gain, get, obtain, reap, receive** *The company derived substantial benefit from the deal.* ◇ *I reaped the benefits of all my early training.* | **bring, offer, provide** *The new factory will bring considerable benefits to the area.* ◇ *This deal will offer major benefits to industrialists and investors.*
● BENEFIT + VERB **accrue** *the benefits that accrue from a good education*
● PREP. **for sb's ~** *We shall do this for the benefit of the patients.* **of ~ to** *This arrangement will be of great benefit to you both.* **to sb's ~** *It will be to everyone's benefit.* **with/without the ~ of** *managing to work without the benefit of modern technology* | **~ for** *the benefits for companies* **~ from** *the benefits from tourism* **~ of** *the benefit of a steady income* **~ to** *What are the benefits to investors?*

2 money
● ADJ. **welfare | state | means-tested, universal** *One way to cut spending is to move from universal benefits—those paid to everyone regardless of need—to means-tested ones.* | **cash | child, housing, sickness, social security, unemployment**
● QUANT. **amount, level**
● VERB + BENEFIT **be eligible for, be entitled to, qualify for | claim** *You may be able to claim housing benefit.* | **draw, get, receive** *He receives unemployment benefit.* | **be dependent on | lose** *She is worried that if she takes on a job she will lose her benefits.* | **cut** *The government has cut unemployment benefit.* | **increase**
● BENEFIT + VERB **be paid** *Benefit is paid monthly.*

● BENEFIT + NOUN **benefits agency | office | payment | system**
● PREP. **on ~** *He's on social security benefit.*

benefit *verb*

● ADV. **considerably, enormously, greatly, substantially | fully | clearly, obviously, undoubtedly** *The new law clearly benefits those earning the most money.* | **equally | disproportionately | directly** *We benefited directly from the reorganization.* | **indirectly | financially** *We both benefited financially from the arrangement.*
● PREP. **from**

benign *adj.*

● VERBS **be, look, seem**
● ADV. **fairly, rather, relatively** *The effects of this chemical are fairly benign.* | **environmentally** *We are looking for an environmentally benign alternative to bleach.*

bent *noun*

● ADJ. **natural | artistic, intellectual, literary, philosophical, scientific**
● VERB + BENT **have** *She has an artistic bent.* | **show** *He showed a literary bent from a young age.*
● PREP. **with ~** *a child with a scientific bent* | **~ for** *a natural bent for languages*

bent *adj.*

● VERBS **be, look | become, get** *The lamp post got bent in the crash.*
● ADV. **slightly** *He stood with knees slightly bent.*
● PHRASES **bent double** *The man shuffled back a few paces, bent almost double.*

bequest *noun*

● ADJ. **generous, large, substantial** *The library has received a generous bequest from a local businessman.* | **small | charitable**
● VERB + BEQUEST **leave (sb), make (sb)** *In his will he made a substantial bequest to his wife.* | **receive**
● PREP. **by ~** *The picture was acquired by bequest in 1921.* | **~ from** *a bequest from the late Jack Dawkins* **~ to** *a bequest to his son*

bereaved *adj.*

● VERBS **be**
● ADJ. **newly, recently** *a recently bereaved family*

bereavement *noun*

● ADJ. **recent | family, personal**
● VERB + BEREAVEMENT **suffer** *He has suffered a bereavement.* | **come to terms with, cope with, get over**
● BEREAVEMENT + NOUN **counselling, counsellor**
● PHRASES **the pain/shock of bereavement**

berry *noun*

● ADJ. **ripe | wild | poisonous | holly, juniper, etc.**
● VERB + BERRY **have, produce** *Does this bush have berries?* | **pick** *We picked a few of the berries.* | **eat**
● BERRY + VERB **ripen | drop off**
⇨ Special page at FRUIT

berth *noun*

● ADJ. **empty | upper | lower**
● VERB + BERTH **have | book, get, take** *I've managed to get berths on the overnight ferry.*
● PHRASES **a two-berth, three berth, etc. cabin**

best *adj.*

- VERBS **be | consider sth, deem sth, judge sth, think sth** *Owen judged it best to make no reply.*
- ADV. **very** *We aim to give our guests the very best attention.* **| by far, easily** *This is by far the best restaurant in the town.*
- PREP. **at** *Who in the class is best at maths?* **for** *I'm only trying to do what's best for you.*

bet *noun*

- ADJ. **good, safe, sure | fair | outside** (= with a very small chance of winning)
- VERB + BET **have, make, place, put** *I'm going to place a bet on that white horse.* **| accept, take** *We are now taking bets on the election result.* **| win | lose**
- PREP. **~ on** *I had a bet on the three o'clock race.* **~ with** *I made a bet with a friend.*
- PHRASES **do sth for a bet, my bet is/it is my bet (that)**... *My bet is that Liverpool will win.*

betrayal *noun*

- ADJ. **personal | final, ultimate** *His defection to the other side was the ultimate betrayal.*
- VERB + BETRAYAL **regard sth as, see sth as, view sth as** *The business community regarded the measures as a betrayal of election promises.*
- PREP. **~ of** *a betrayal of his friends* ◇ *The decisions were a betrayal of everything my father stood for.*
- PHRASES **an act of betrayal, a betrayal of (sb's) trust, a feeling/sense of betrayal**

better *adj.*

1 comparative of 'good'

- VERBS **be, feel, look, seem | get** *Cars are getting better all the time.* **| make sth** *We must make our inner cities better to live and work in.* **| consider sth, deem sth, judge sth, think sth** *I thought it better to tackle him outside of business hours.*
- ADV. **a damned/darned sight, even, far, a lot, markedly, (very) much, still, substantially, ten/a hundred/a thousand times** *His latest book is a darned sight better than the one before.* **| a bit, a good/great deal, a little, marginally, slightly**
- PHRASES **no better** *Charles VII was a bad king, and Charles VIII was no better.* **nothing better than** *There's nothing better than a nice juicy peach!*

2 recovered from an illness

- VERBS **be, feel, look, seem | get** *I hope you get better soon.* **| get sb, make sb** *Don't worry. The doctor will soon make you better.* **| kiss sth** *Did you hurt yourself? Poor thing—come here and let me kiss it better.*
- ADV. **a lot, (very) much | a bit, a good/great deal, a little, slightly**

bewildered *adj.*

- VERBS **be, feel, look, seem, sound | become | leave sb** *She packed her bags and left—leaving Matthew bewildered and confused.*
- ADV. **very | completely, quite, thoroughly, totally, utterly | a little, rather, slightly, somewhat**
- PREP. **at** *He was rather bewildered at seeing her there.* **by** *She was totally bewildered by his message.*

bewildering *adj.*

- VERBS **be, seem | find sth** *I found the experience quite bewildering.*
- ADV. **very** *It was all very bewildering.* **| completely, quite, totally** *a totally bewildering array of different wines* **| a bit, rather**

bias *noun*

- ADJ. **clear, definite, marked, obvious, strong | left-wing, right-wing | cultural, political**
- VERB + BIAS **have** *The newspaper has a clear bias towards the Conservative Party.* **| display, show | avoid, eliminate, reduce | correct** *We have now tried to correct the bias in our original report.* **| be free from** *The newspaper was free from political bias.*
- BIAS + VERB **creep in, exist** *Bias often creeps in through the wording of questions.*
- PREP. **with/without ~** *All material must be selected and presented without bias.* **with a ~** *a newspaper with a strong left-wing bias* **| ~ against** *a bias against women* **~ in favour of/towards** *a bias in favour of small firms*

biased *adj.*

- VERBS **be**
- ADV. **extremely, heavily, hopelessly, strongly, very | a little, slightly | naturally | inherently | ideologically, politically | racially**
- PREP. **against** *Fate was strongly biased against him.* **in favour of** *The methods they employed were heavily biased in the gentry's favour.* **towards** *Managers are naturally biased towards projects showing a quick return.*

Bible *noun*

- ADJ. **Holy**
- VERB + BIBLE **read, study**
- BIBLE + VERB **say sth, tell sb sth, teach sth** *The Bible teaches that all people are equal before God.*
- BIBLE + NOUN **reading, story | study**
- PREP. **in the ~** *You can read the story of Noah in the Bible.*

bibliography *noun*

- ADJ. **brief, select, selective | comprehensive, extensive** *an extensive bibliography of books and articles*
- VERB + BIBLIOGRAPHY **compile, put together | contain, include | publish | consult** *Consult the bibliography for further reading on the subject.*
- PREP. **in a/the ~** *You'll find the professor's book in the bibliography.* **| ~ of** *The book includes a selective bibliography of works on French art.*

bicycle *noun*

- VERB + BICYCLE **ride | get on, mount** *He mounted his bicycle and rode off.* **| get off | come off, fall off** *She came off her bicycle when it skidded on some wet leaves.* **| knock sb off | pedal** *She pedalled her bicycle up the track.* **| push, wheel** *I dismounted and began to push my bicycle up the hill.* **| park | hire**
- BICYCLE + VERB **get/have a puncture**
- BICYCLE + NOUN **ride | chain, frame, wheel | rack, shed | hire**
- PREP. **by ~** *Did you come by bicycle?* **on a/the ~** *watching the boys on their bicycles*
- PHRASES **lean/prop a bicycle against sth**

bid *noun*

1 attempt

- ADJ. **successful | failed, unsuccessful | desperate | takeover**
- VERB + BID **launch, make, mount** *A German firm launched a takeover bid for the company.* **| succeed in | fail in** *They failed in their bid to buy the holiday company.*
- BID + VERB **succeed | fail**
- PREP. **in a/the ~** *He attacked his guards in a desperate bid for freedom.* **| ~ by** *a bid by the president to boost his popularity* **~ for** *This play was her last bid for recognition.*
- PHRASES **a bid for freedom/power, a bid to escape**

2 offer of a sum of money to buy sth
- ADJ. **high | low | opening | cash**
- VERB + BID **make, put in, submit** *He made a cash bid for the company.* | **retract | call for, invite** *They have invited bids for the property.* | **increase, raise | accept**
- PREP. **~ by/from** *a £24-million bid by a rival football club* **~ for** *a bid for the chair* **~ of** *a bid of £100*

bid *verb*

1 offer money for sth
- PREP. **against** *Two dealers bid against each other for the antique table.* **for** *She bid £10 000 for the painting.*

2 offer to do work
- ADV. **successfully**
- PREP. **for** *We have successfully bid for the contract.*

big *adj.*

1 large
- VERBS **be, look, seem | become, get, grow**
- ADV. **extremely, incredibly, really, very | fairly, pretty, quite, rather** *This house is rather big for us. We need something smaller.*
- PHRASES **big fat** *He was a big fat chap with a beard.*

2 important
- VERBS **be**
- ADV. **extremely, really, very** *hoping the show would be a really big success* | **fairly, pretty** *This is a fairly big decision to make.*

bike *noun*

- ADJ. **mountain, racing, touring, trail | exercise**
- VERB + BIKE **ride | get on** *He got on his bike and rode off.* | **get off | come off, fall off** *She came off her bike when it skidded on some wet leaves.* | **knock sb off | pedal** *She pedalled her bike up the track.* | **push, wheel** *We had to push our bikes up the hill.* | **park | hire**
- BIKE + VERB **get/have a puncture**
- BIKE + NOUN **ride | shed**
- PREP. **by ~** *Did you come by bike?* **on a/the ~** *watching the boys on their bikes*
- PHRASES **lean/prop a bike against sth**

bikini *noun*

- ADJ. **brief, minuscule, skimpy**
- BIKINI + NOUN **bottoms, top | line**
⇨ Special page at CLOTHES

bilingual *adj.*

- VERBS **be | become**
- ADV. **fully | virtually**
- PREP. **in** *He is virtually bilingual in Spanish and Portuguese.*

bill *noun*

1 showing money owed for goods/services
- ADJ. **big, high, huge, large | outstanding, unpaid | itemized | electricity, fuel, gas, hospital, hotel, phone/telephone, etc. | tax**
- VERB + BILL **get, have** *Could I have the bill please?* ◇ *I've just got a huge tax bill.* | **be landed with, face** *The company could now face higher fuel bills.* | **run up** *We ran up a very large hotel bill.* | **foot, pay, pick up, settle** *Don't worry—the company will pick up the bill.* | **present sb with, send sb, submit** *They presented us with a very large bill.* | **cut, reduce** *We need to cut our electricity bills.*
- PREP. **on a/the ~** *Are the coffees on the bill?* | **~ for** *the bill for the meal*

2 proposal for a new law
- ADJ. **controversial | emergency | private member's**
- VERB + BILL **bring before Parliament, bring for-** ward/in, introduce, propose, put forward, submit *The bill will be brought before Parliament next year.* ◇ *The government has put forward an emergency bill to limit the powers of the police.* | **force through, push through, railroad through, rush through** *The opposition will try to force the bill through Parliament.* | **draft, prepare | amend | debate | adopt, approve, pass | support, vote for | defeat, reject, throw out, veto | oppose, vote against | shelve, withdraw**

3 programme of entertainment
- ADJ. **double**
- VERB + BILL **head, top** *Tom Jones is topping the bill.*
- PREP. **on a/the ~** *Mozart is on the bill this evening.*

bin *noun*

- ADJ. **litter, rubbish, waste, wastepaper** *She threw the letter in the wastepaper bin.* | **storage | pedal, wheelie**
- VERB + BIN **chuck sth in/into, put sth in, throw sth in/into**
- BIN + NOUN **bag, liner | man**
- PREP. **in a/the ~** *Put the wrapper in the bin.*

bind *noun*

- ADJ. **awful, dreadful, real, terrible | double**
- PREP. **in a ~** *He's in a double bind: he needs experience to get a job but he can't get experience without working.*

bind *verb*

1 tie with rope/fabric
- ADV. **tightly** *They bound his hands together tightly.*
- ADV. **together**
- PREP. **to, with** *The sails are bound to the mast with cord.*
- PHRASES **bind and gag sb, bind sb hand and foot** *She found herself bound hand and foot.*

2 make sb do sth
- ADV. **contractually, legally, morally**

3 book
- PHRASES **be beautifully/handsomely/richly bound, be bound in sth** *two volumes bound in leather*

binding *adj.*

- VERBS **be | become**
- ADV. **absolutely | legally, morally**
- PREP. **on/upon** *The decisions of the European Court are binding on the United Kingdom.*

binge *noun*

- ADJ. **drinking, drunken | eating**
- VERB + BINGE **go on, have** *He went on a drunken binge when he heard the bad news.*

binoculars *noun*

- ADJ. **high-powered, powerful**
- QUANT. **pair**
- VERB + BINOCULARS **look through | focus, train** *He focused his binoculars on the building in the distance.* | **adjust | lift, raise** *She raised her binoculars to the distant road across the valley.* | **lower**
- PREP. **through ~** *watching the race through binoculars*

biography *noun*

- ADJ. **authorized, official | unauthorized, unofficial | brief, potted** *The book gives potted biographies of all the major painters.*
- VERB + BIOGRAPHY **work on, write | publish | read**
- PREP. **~ by** *a biography by Antonia Fraser* **~ of** *a biography of the prime minister*

biologist noun

- ADJ. **distinguished, senior | field, research** *She's a research biologist for a pharmaceutical company.* | **evolutionary, forensic, marine, molecular | plant, wildlife**
⇨ Note at JOB

biology noun

- ADJ. **cell, developmental, environmental, evolutionary, human, marine, molecular, population, reproductive | applied | modern**
⇨ Note at SUBJECT (for verbs and nouns)

bird noun

- ADJ. **wild | exotic, rare | game | predatory | migratory | land, sea** (also **seabird**), **tropical, wading, woodland** *Seabirds flocked above our heads.*
- QUANT. **flock**
- BIRD + VERB **flit, fly, glide, soar, swoop (down)** *We watched a bird of prey swoop down on a mouse.* | **flap its wings | flock | migrate** *The birds migrate in September.* | **chirp, sing, twitter, warble | peck** *birds pecking at the corn* | **build a nest, nest** *birds nesting on the roof of the church* | **breed, lay eggs | moult**
- BIRD + NOUN **call | sanctuary | life** *an area with a very varied bird life* | **watcher, watching**
- PHRASES **a bird of passage** (= a migratory bird), **a bird of prey** (= a predatory bird), **a breed/species/type of bird**

birth noun

- ADJ. **live** *Better living conditions mean more live births and fewer stillbirths.* | **normal | breech, Caesarean, premature | multiple | legitimate | illegitimate | home**
- VERB + BIRTH **give** *She gave birth to a baby boy.* | **register**
- BIRTH + NOUN **certificate | rate | weight**
- PREP. **at~** *The baby weighed 7 pounds at birth.* **at/during a/the~** *The child's father was present at the birth.* **by~** *He was American by birth, but lived in France.*
- PHRASES **births, marriages and deaths** *a registry of births, marriages and deaths,* **your date/place of birth, of low/noble birth** (= born to a poor/aristocratic family), **the moment of birth**

birth control noun

- ADJ. **effective**
- VERB + BIRTH CONTROL **practise, use**
- PHRASES **a form/method of birth control**

birthday noun

- ADJ. **last, next** *I'll be 28 next birthday.*
- VERB + BIRTHDAY **have** *I hope you have a nice birthday.* | **spend** *She spent her 50th birthday in Paris.* | **celebrate | mark** *an exhibition to mark the artist's 70th birthday* | **forget, remember | approach** *He is approaching his 40th birthday, and thinking of retiring from sport.*
- BIRTHDAY + NOUN **gift, present | card | cake | party | surprise** *He had a portrait painted as a birthday surprise for his daughter.* | **treat** *We're taking him to see the new film for his birthday treat.*
- PREP. **for your~** *What do you want for your birthday?* **on your~** *She'll be 34 on her next birthday.*
- PHRASES **Happy birthday!, wish sb a happy birthday** *Wish John a happy birthday from me.*

birthmark noun

- ADJ. **large, small | disfiguring, unsightly | faint | purple, red**
- VERB + BIRTHMARK **have**
- BIRTHMARK + VERB **fade**

biscuit noun

- ADJ. **dry | soggy, stale | chocolate, ginger, etc. | digestive, shortbread, wafer | cat, dog**
- QUANT. **box, packet, tin** *a packet of coconut biscuits*
- VERB + BISCUIT **eat, have | nibble | bake, make | cut out** *He was cutting biscuits out and putting them on a baking tray.*
- BISCUIT + NOUN **barrel, tin | crumbs** *He brushed the biscuit crumbs from his jacket.*
- PHRASES **cheese and biscuits**
⇨ Special page at FOOD

bishop noun

- ADJ. **Anglican, Episcopal/Episcopalian, (Greek/Russian) Orthodox, Roman Catholic | diocesan** *He's the diocesan bishop and he has three suffragan bishops to help him.* | **assistant, suffragan**
- VERB + BISHOP **appoint, appoint sb (as), make sb | succeed sb as**
- PREP. **~of** *He was appointed Bishop of Ely.*

bit noun

1 a bit small amount
- ADJ. **little, teensy** (*informal*), **wee** *He helped me a little bit in the afternoon.*
- PHRASES **just a bit** *I'm still just a bit confused.*

2 a bit large amount
- ADJ. **fair, good** *It rained a fair bit during the night.* ◇ *We made a good bit of progress.*
- VERB + BIT **take** *The new system will take quite a bit of getting used to* (= it will take a long time to get used to).
- PHRASES **quite a bit** *It rained quite a bit during the night.* **just a bit** (*ironic*) *'Has it been difficult for you at work?' 'Just a bit* (= it has been very difficult).*'

3 part/piece of sth
- ADJ. **little, small, tiny | big, large** *A big bit of stone had fallen off the wall.* | **good, nice** *The best bit of the holiday was seeing the Grand Canyon.* ◇ *I've got us a nice bit of fish for dinner.* | **boring** *I read it, but I missed out the boring bits.* | **odd** *He managed to get odd bits of work, but no regular bits.*
- VERB + BIT **pick out, pick up** *Listen to the interview again and pick out the bits you want to use in the article.* ◇ *She tore the letter up and threw it on the floor. Marion stooped to pick up the bits.* ◇ *I picked up a bit of information that might interest you.*
- BIT + VERB **fall off** *I'm worried because bits keep falling off my car.*
- PREP. **~of**
- PHRASES **bits and bobs/pieces** (= small items of various kinds) *My mother has some bits and pieces to give you.* **blow/pull/smash sth to bits** *All the crockery had been smashed to bits.* **do your bit** (= do your share of a task) *We can finish this job on time if everyone does their bit.* **fall to bits** *My briefcase eventually fell to bits.*

bite noun

1 act of biting/amount of food
- VERB + BITE **have, take**
- PREP. **between ~s** *She tried to talk between bites.* | **~from** *I took a bite from the apple.* **~of** *Can I have a bite of your sandwich?* **~out of** *She took a bite out of the slab of cake.*

2 of an insect/animal
- ADJ. **insect, mosquito, snake, etc.**
- VERB + BITE **get** *I got a lot of mosquito bites last night.*
- BITE + NOUN **mark**
- PREP. **~from** *a bite from a poisonous snake*

3 small amount to eat
- ADJ. **quick**

- VERB + BITE **grab, have** *We managed to grab a bite at the theatre before the show started.*
- PREP. **~of** *a quick bite of lunch*
- PHRASES **a bite to eat** *We'll have a bite to eat in town.*

bite verb

1 use your teeth
- ADV. **badly** *Their cat was badly bitten by a dog.* | **off** *He bit off a chunk of bread.*
- PREP. **at** *He bit at his lower lip.* **into** *She bit into the apple.* **through** *The dog had bitten right through its rope.*
- PHRASES **bite sth in half/two**

2 have an effect
- ADV. **deep, hard** *As the recession bites harder, many small companies are going bankrupt.*
- VERB + BITE **begin to, start to** *After two cold months, the coal shortage was beginning to bite.*

bitter adj.

1 angry/unhappy
- VERBS **be, feel, seem | become, grow, turn** *He had grown bitter as the years passed.* ◇ *Loving relationships can turn bitter.* | **remain | leave sb, make sb** *The divorce had left her bitter.*
- ADV. **extremely, very | quite, rather, slightly**
- PREP. **about** *She still seems quite bitter about it.* **towards** *I felt very bitter towards them.*

2 very cold
- VERBS **be | become, turn** *The weather turned bitter.* | **remain**
- ADV. **extremely, really, very | quite, rather**

3 having a sharp taste
- VERBS **be, taste** *The drink tasted bitter.*
- ADV. **extremely, very | rather, slightly, somewhat**

bitterness noun

- ADJ. **considerable, great, real**
- QUANT. **edge, hint, touch, trace**
- VERB + BITTERNESS **feel** *She feels no bitterness towards him.* | **show** *He's never shown any bitterness.*
- PREP. **with/without ~** *She spoke slowly and with some bitterness.* | **~about/over** *their bitterness over the strike* **~against/towards** *his bitterness towards his own father* **~among** *the bitterness among nurses about this pay deal* **~between** *There is no bitterness between them.*

bizarre adj.

- VERBS **be, seem, sound | become | find sth** *I found the whole situation very bizarre.*
- ADV. **most, truly, very** *He walked off in a most bizarre fashion.* | **quite, totally** *He made some totally bizarre comments.* | **increasingly | a little, pretty, rather, slightly, somewhat** *It's a pretty bizarre film.*

black adj.

- ADV. **very** *The sky looks very black.* | **all** *His hands were all black from messing about with the car.*
- ADJ. **jet, pitch** (used about the night) *She had beautiful jet-black hair.* ◇ *It was pitch black outside.*
⇨ Special page at COLOUR

blackboard noun

- VERB + BLACKBOARD **write on | copy from** *Please copy the homework from the blackboard.* | **clean**
- BLACKBOARD + NOUN **work**
- PREP. **at a/the ~** *You can't just stand at the blackboard and talk.* **on a/the ~** *The homework is on the blackboard.*

blacklist noun

- VERB + BLACKLIST **place sb on, put sb on | draw up**
- PREP. **on a/the ~** *She was on the company's blacklist.*

blackmail noun

- ADJ. **emotional, moral**
- BLACKMAIL + NOUN **threat**
⇨ Note at CRIME (for verbs)

blackmail verb

- ADV. **virtually**
- VERB + BLACKMAIL **attempt to, try to**
- PREP. **into** *She says she was virtually blackmailed into giving up her claim to the property.*

black market noun

- ADJ. **thriving**
- PREP. **on the ~** *You could buy anything you needed on the black market.* | **~in** *During the war, there was a thriving black market in food.*

bladder noun

- ADJ. **full | irritable, weak**
- VERB + BLADDER **empty**
- BLADDER + NOUN **control | cancer, infection, problem** *He died of bladder cancer.*

blade noun

- ADJ. **sharp | blunt | pointed, serrated | knife, razor, saw, sword | rotary**
- VERB + BLADE **sharpen**

blame noun

- VERB + BLAME **get** *My brother broke the window, but I got the blame.* | **accept, bear, shoulder, take** *The company refused to accept any blame for the damage.* | **apportion, attach, attribute, lay, pin, place, put** *They placed the blame squarely on the doctor.* | **share** *The government must share the blame for this confusion.* | **escape, shift** *trying to shift the blame onto someone else* | **absolve sb from/of** *He was absolved of all blame.*
- BLAME + VERB **fall on sb, lie with sb, rest with sb** *The blame lies with the police, who failed to act quickly enough.*
- PREP. **~for** *He tried to escape blame for what he did.*
- PHRASES **lay the blame at sb's door, part of the blame, a share of the blame** *The government tried to lay the blame at the door of the unions.*

blame verb

- ADV. **unfairly, unjustly**
- VERB + BLAME **can't/cannot, couldn't, don't** *'I just slammed the phone down when he said that.' 'I don't blame you!'* | **can/could hardly** *You can hardly blame Peter for being angry with her.*
- PREP. **for** *I don't blame Jack for the mistake.* **on** *Whenever something goes wrong, everyone blames it on me.*
- PHRASES **be (partly) to blame (for sth)** *A spokesman said that bad weather was to blame for the delay.* **be widely blamed for sth** *The government has been widely blamed for the crisis.*

blameless adj.

- VERBS **be**
- ADV. **quite** (= totally) *She herself was quite blameless.* | **far from, not entirely** *Johnson himself was far from blameless.*

blank *noun*

1 empty space on paper
- VERB + BLANK **fill in** *In the test, we had to fill in the blanks.* | **leave** *If you don't know the answer, just leave a blank.*

2 cartridge for a gun
- VERB + BLANK **fire** *Soldiers fired blanks into the sky.*

blank *adj.*

1 with nothing written, recorded, etc. on
- VERBS **be** | **go** *The screen's gone blank.* | **remain** | **leave sth** *I left the third column blank.*
- ADV. **completely, entirely**

2 without emotion/interest/understanding
- VERBS **be, look** *Gina looked blank; then understanding dawned.* | **go** *What if my mind goes completely blank with panic?* | **remain**
- ADV. **completely** | **studiously** *His expression remained studiously blank.*

blanket *noun*

- ADJ. **heavy, thick** | **thin** | **warm** | **electric**
- VERB + BLANKET **cover sb with, wrap sb in** | **draw up, pull up** *She pulled the blanket up and went to sleep.* | **kick off, push off, throw off**
- PREP. **beneath/under a/the~** *They shivered under their thin blankets.*

blasphemous *adj.*

- VERBS **be, seem** | **consider sth** | **declare sth, deem sth** *The book was declared blasphemous and all copies ordered to be burnt.*
- ADV. **almost**

blasphemy *noun*

- VERB + BLASPHEMY **commit**
- BLASPHEMY + NOUN **law**
- PREP. **~against** *His writings were branded as obscene and a blasphemy against God.*
- PHRASES **a charge of blasphemy**

blast *noun*

1 explosion
- ADJ. **huge, powerful** | **bomb, nuclear, shotgun**
- BLAST + VERB **hit sth, rip through sth, rock sth** *A huge bomb blast rocked central London last night.*
- PREP. **in a/the~** *Twenty people were killed in the blast.*

2 sudden rush of air/wind
- ADJ. **hot, icy** *She felt an icy blast of air.*
- PREP. **~of** *a blast of cold air*

3 sudden loud sound
- ADJ. **long** | **short** | **shrill**
- VERB + BLAST **give**
- PREP. **~on** *He gave a short blast on his trumpet.*

blaze *noun*

- ADJ. **fierce, intense, massive**
- VERB + BLAZE **attend, fight, tackle** *The fire brigade attended the blaze.* | **control, bring/get under control** | **extinguish, put out** | **fan** *Strong winds fanned the blaze.*
- BLAZE + VERB **spread, sweep through sth** *The blaze swept through the whole building.*
- PREP. **in a/the~** *The antiques were destroyed in a blaze last year.*

bleak *adj.*

1 without hope
- VERBS **appear, be, look, seem** | **become** | **remain**

- ADV. **extremely, very** *Prospects for the industry are extremely bleak.* | **increasingly** | **unnecessarily** *The report paints an unnecessarily bleak picture of the town.*

2 bare/empty/without pleasant features
- VERBS **be, look, seem** *The moors looked bleak and desolate in the rain.* | **become**
- ADV. **very** | **a bit, rather** *It was a rather bleak and dismal place.*

bleed *verb*

- ADV. **badly, heavily, profusely** | **easily** *The small blood vessels in the nose bleed easily.*
- PREP. **from** *She was bleeding heavily from a head wound.*
- PHRASES **bleed to death**

bleeding *noun*

- ADJ. **heavy, massive** | **uncontrollable** | **internal**
- VERB + BLEEDING **have, suffer from** | **cause** | **control, staunch, stem, stop**
- PREP. **~from** *Some drugs can cause bleeding from the small intestine.*

blemish *noun*

- ADJ. **minor, slight**
- VERB + BLEMISH **have** *The police say the suspect has a slight blemish on his left cheek.*
- PREP. **without (a)~** *(figurative)* *He was pilloried, but she escaped without blemish.*

blend *noun*

- ADJ. **delightful, good, perfect, right** *just the right blend of work and relaxation* | **curious, special, strange, subtle, unique** *a scarf with a subtle blend of colours*

blend *verb*

1 mix
- ADV. **together** *Blend all the ingredients together.*
- PREP. **into** *Blend the cocoa into the eggs.* **with** *Blend a little milk with two tablespoons of treacle.*

2 combine well
- ADV. **happily, harmoniously, perfectly, well** | **in** *The colour of the carpet doesn't blend in.*
- PREP. **with** *The ornamental pool blends perfectly with its surroundings.*

blessing *noun*

1 thing that brings happiness/improves your life
- ADJ. **great, real** | **mixed** (= a thing that has advantages and disadvantages)
- PREP. **~for** *A TV can be a real blessing for old people.*
- PHRASES **a blessing in disguise** (= a thing that seems unfortunate, but is later seen to be fortunate), **count your blessings** (= to be grateful for the good things you have)

2 approval/support
- ADJ. **full** | **official**
- VERB + BLESSING **have** | **give sb/sth** *The government has given its official blessing to the project.* | **get, receive** *She received the full blessing of her employers.*
- PREP. **with/without sb's~** *He went off to Latin America with his mother's blessing.*

3 prayer
- ADJ. **traditional**
- VERB + BLESSING **give, make, pronounce, say** *The blessing was said in Hebrew.* | **ask (for)**
- PREP. **~on** *ask God's blessing on their pastoral work*

blind *noun*

- ADJ. **roller, venetian**

● VERB + BLIND **open, pull up, raise | close, draw, lower, pull down**
● PREP. **through** a/the ~ *She saw a shadowy figure through the blind.*

blind *verb*

● ADV. **almost, nearly** *The strong light almost blinded him.* | **momentarily, temporarily**

blind *adj.*

1 unable to see
● VERBS **be, be born | be registered (as) | go** *She went blind at the age of ten.* | **make sb**
● ADV. **totally | almost, virtually | partially**
● PHRASES **as blind as a bat, be blind in one eye/in both eyes** *He is almost blind in one eye.*
2 blind to sth not willing to notice/admit sth
● VERBS **be, seem | become | make sb**
● ADV. **completely, totally** *His own problems have made him completely blind to the sufferings of others.*

blink *verb*

● ADV. **hard** *He blinked hard and forced a smile.* | **rapidly**
● PREP. **at** *She blinked at him, astonished.* **in/with** *He blinked in surprise.*
● PHRASES **blink away a tear, blink back tears** *She had to blink back her tears before she continued her story.* **blink your eyes/your eyes blink**

bliss *noun*

● ADJ. **sheer** *The first six months of marriage were sheer bliss.* | **domestic | marital, married, wedded** *They're celebrating 25 years of wedded bliss.*
● PHRASES **sb's idea of bliss** *My idea of bliss is a hot day and an ice-cold beer.*

blister *verb*

● ADV. **badly** *Her feet were badly blistered.*

blitz *noun*

1 sudden military attack, often by air
● ADJ. **bombing | wartime**
● VERB + BLITZ **carry out**
● PREP. **during/in** a/the ~ *Many people died in the London blitz.* | ~ **on** *Enemy bombers carried out a blitz on the city.*
2 campaign; sudden, great effort
● ADJ. **marketing, media, sales**
● VERB + BLITZ **have, launch, mount** *We decided to have a blitz on the kitchen* (= to clean the kitchen thoroughly).
● PREP. ~ **on** *a blitz on illegal parking*

blizzard *noun*

● ADJ. **fierce, howling**
● VERB + BLIZZARD **blow** *After a short while it began to blow a blizzard.*
● BLIZZARD + VERB **hit (sth), strike (sth)** *The blizzard struck while we were still on the mountain.* | **blow, rage**
● BLIZZARD + NOUN **conditions**
● PREP. **in/into** ~ *We got stuck in a howling blizzard.* **through** ~ *He fought his way through the blizzard.*

bloc *noun*

● ADJ. **large, solid, substantial** *A solid bloc of union members support the decision.* | **economic, military, trading | Communist, Eastern, Soviet** *Eastern bloc countries*
● PREP. **in/within** a/the ~ *There have been growing tensions within the trading bloc.*
● PHRASES **en bloc** (= all together; all at the same time)

block *noun*

1 solid piece of sth
● ADJ. **big, huge, large, massive | small | solid | concrete, stone, wooden | building | starting** (for a runner) *aiming to be first out of the starting blocks* | **breeze**
2 large building divided into offices/flats
● ADJ. **high-rise, tower | administration, apartment, cell, office** *The prisoners had been transferred to a different cell block.*
● PREP. **in** a/the ~ *She lives in a modern apartment block.* | ~ **of** *a block of flats*
3 temporary loss of abilities
● ADJ. **mental, writer's** *The author denies that she is experiencing writer's block.*
● VERB + BLOCK **experience, have, suffer from** *I suddenly had a mental block and couldn't remember his name.*

block *verb*

1 make it difficult to pass
● ADV. **completely | almost | partially, partly | off, up** *The old route is completely blocked off.* ◇ *Don't block up the corridor with all these boxes.*
● VERB + BLOCK **try to | move to** *One of the men moved to block their path.*
● PREP. **with** *The exit was blocked with beer crates.*
2 prevent sth being done
● ADV. **successfully | effectively** *The new rules would effectively block protesters' attempts to assert their rights.*
● VERB + BLOCK **attempt to, seek to, try to | move to** *The group has moved to block the government's proposals.*

PHRASAL VERB
block sth out
● ADV. **completely** *Black clouds had completely blocked out the sun.* | **almost**

blockade *noun*

● ADJ. **complete, total | tight | partial | virtual | economic, military, naval**
● VERB + BLOCKADE **impose | end, lift, remove | enforce, maintain | tighten | ease, relax | break, get through, run** *They attempted to break the blockade by using submarines.*
● PREP. ~ **against** *the need to enforce a naval blockade against the country* ~ **around/round** *a blockade around the city* ~ **by** *the blockade by Western nations* ~ **of**, ~ **on** *The president imposed a complete blockade on the island's harbours.*

blockage *noun*

● ADJ. **complete, total | partial**
● VERB + BLOCKAGE **cause, create | prevent | clear, remove** *They used chemicals to clear the blockage.*

bloke *noun*

● ADJ. **decent, good, great, lovely, nice | average, ordinary** *He's an ordinary bloke, despite being famous.* | **funny** *He's a funny bloke—you never really know what he's thinking.* | **poor** *He's got so many problems, poor bloke!*
● PHRASES **the kind/sort/type of bloke** *He's the sort of bloke who will never let you down.*

blonde *noun*

● ADJ. **attractive, beautiful, gorgeous, pretty, sexy, stunning | blue-eyed | dumb** *She's not just a dumb blonde.* | **natural** *She was slender and a natural blonde.* | **bottle | ash, platinum, strawberry** *a tall, strawberry blonde with stunning legs*

blonde (*also* blond) *adj.*

- VERBS **be, look | go, turn | dye sth**
- ADV. **very | quite**
- ADJ. **ash, dirty, platinum, strawberry** *ash blond hair*

blood *noun*

- ADJ. **cold, warm** *animals with warm blood* | **clotted, congealed, dried | arterial, venous | menstrual | contaminated | aristocratic, noble, royal** *I doubt if I have a single drop of aristocratic blood in my veins.* | **Mediterranean, Spanish, etc.**
- QUANT. **drop, pool, trickle** *The body lay in a pool of blood.* ◇ *A thin trickle of blood ran down from a cut above her eye.* | **spots, traces** *He worked to remove all traces of blood.*
- VERB + BLOOD **lose** *She'd lost a lot of blood and doctors decided to do a transfusion.* | **shed, spill** (*literary*) *He was a hot-headed warrior, always too quick to shed blood.* ⊣ **donate, give** *The hospital appealed for more people to give blood* (= for blood transfusions). | **pump** *The heart pumps blood around the body.* | **choke on** *He choked on his own blood after being shot in the throat.* | **smear** *There was blood smeared down his shirt.*
- BLOOD + VERB **dribble, drip, flow, gush, ooze, run, seep, splash, spurt, stream, trickle, well (up)** *Blood oozed slowly from the corner of his mouth.* | **spread** *The blood spread rapidly from where he lay.* | **spatter, splatter** *Blood spattered the seats of the vehicle.* | **soak (into) sth | cake sth, stain sth** *Dried blood caked his hands.* | **clot, coagulate, congeal | circulate** *He rubbed his limbs vigorously to get the blood circulating.* | **course, rush, surge** *I felt the blood coursing in my veins as I ran.* ◇ *The blood rushed to her face as she realized her error.* | **drum, hammer, pound, pulse, thud, thunder** *The blood drummed in her ears.* | **drain** *The blood drained from his face when I told him the news.* | **freeze, run/turn cold, turn to ice** (*figurative*) *Our blood ran cold at the thought of how easily we could have been killed.*
- BLOOD + NOUN **cell | group, type** *What blood group are you?* | **sample, test | loss | donation, donor | bank | circulation, flow, supply | pressure | clot, coagulation | cancer, disease, disorder, poisoning | cholesterol, fats, glucose, sugar**
- PREP. **in ~** *His shirt was soaked in blood.* **in sb's/the ~** *Traces of an illegal substance were found in his blood.* | **~ from** *My handkerchief was soaked in blood from my nose.*
- PHRASES **caked in/with blood** *The dog's fur was caked in blood when we found him.* **covered in/with blood** *He was lying on the floor, covered in blood.* **in cold blood** *He shot them in cold blood* (= in a way that was planned and deliberately cruel).

blood pressure *noun*

- ADJ. **high, low, normal**
- VERB + BLOOD PRESSURE **check, measure**

bloodshed *noun*

- ADJ. **further | massive, widespread**
- VERB + BLOODSHED **cause, end in, lead to** *This election result could well lead to further bloodshed.* | **end, halt, stop | avoid, prevent**

bloodstream *noun*

- VERB + BLOODSTREAM **enter | absorb sth into** *The drug is quickly absorbed into the bloodstream.*
- PREP. **in sb's/the ~** *Traces of banned substances were detected in his bloodstream.* **into sb's/the ~** *Bacteria was introduced into his bloodstream through an unsterile needle.* **through sb's/the ~** *Red blood cells transport oxygen through the bloodstream.*

blood transfusion *noun*

- ADJ. **emergency**
- VERB + BLOOD TRANSFUSION **have, receive | give sb | need, require**

blood vessel *noun*

- ADJ. **major | broken, burst**
- VERB + BLOOD VESSEL **block, constrict | dilate, enlarge | burst** *He burst a blood vessel in a fit of coughing.*
- BLOOD VESSEL + VERB **carry sth, supply sth** *blood vessels supplying nutrition to the skin* | **burst | dilate, enlarge | contract**

bloom *noun*

- ADJ. **beautiful, exquisite, perfect** *a tree with exquisite blooms* | **fragrant | exotic**
- VERB + BLOOM **bear, have, produce | burst into, come into** *The spring flowers have come into bloom.*
- BLOOM + VERB **appear** *The small white blooms appear in May.* | **fade** *The blooms have started to fade now.*
- PREP. **in ~** *banks of rhododendrons in bloom*
- PHRASES **in full bloom** *The roses are now in full bloom.*

blossom *noun*

- ADJ. **beautiful, lovely | pale, pink, white** *a tree with pale pink blossoms* | **apple, peach, etc.**
- VERB + BLOSSOM **bear, have, produce** *Hopefully the tree will produce some blossom next year.*
- BLOSSOM + VERB **be out** *It's lovely in the spring when the cherry blossom is out.* | **come out**
- PREP. **in ~** *He loves it when the apple trees are in blossom.*
- PHRASES **in full blossom** *The plum tree is now in full blossom.*

blouse *noun*

- ADJ. **long-sleeved, short-sleeved, sleeveless | high-necked | cotton, silk, etc. | embroidered, frilled, frilly | see-through | school**
- VERB + BLOUSE **have on, wear | put on | button up, unbutton | take off**

blow *noun*

1 act of blowing
- VERB + BLOW **give sth** *Give your nose a blow.*

2 hard knock that hits sb/sth
- ADJ. **hard, heavy, nasty, painful, powerful, severe, sharp, stinging, violent | fatal, final, mortal | glancing, light** *Jack caught him a glancing blow on the jaw.* | **single** *He killed the man with a single blow of his cricket bat.*
- QUANT. **flurry, hail** *The man went down in a hail of blows.*
- VERB + BLOW **get, receive, suffer, take** *He suffered a severe blow to the head.* | **catch sb, deal sb, deliver, give sb, land, rain (down), strike sb** *It was the gardener who delivered the fatal blow.* ◇ *She landed a nasty blow on his nose.* ◇ *He rained heavy blows on the old woman.* | **exchange** *The boys exchanged blows with the police.* | **come to** *The children came to blows over the new toy.* | **aim** *She aimed a blow at Lucy.* | **avoid, deflect, dodge, parry, ward off**
- BLOW + VERB **fall, land** *The blow landed on my right shoulder.*
- PREP. **~ of** *two blows of the axe* **~ on** *a nasty blow on the head* **~ to** *a blow to the victim's chest*

3 sudden shock/disappointment
- ADJ. **big, great, major, serious, severe, terrible | bitter, crippling, cruel, crushing, devastating, knock-out | double | decisive, mortal** *a mortal blow to British industry* | **body**

• VERB + BLOW **deal (sb/sth)**, **deliver**, **strike** *His defeat dealt a crushing blow to the party.* | **receive**, **suffer** | **cushion**, **soften** *to soften the blow of tax increases* | **come as** *The news came as a bitter blow to the staff.*
• BLOW + VERB **come**, **fall** *The blow came at a meeting on Saturday.*
• PREP. **~for** *A tax on books would be a body blow for education.* **~to** *Her decision to live abroad was a terrible blow to her parents.*
• PHRASES **a bit of a blow**

blow *verb*

1 of wind/air, etc.
• ADV. **hard**, **strongly** | **gently**
• PREP. **from** *a gale blowing from the west* **off** *The wind blew the papers off the table.*
• PHRASES **be blowing a gale** *It's blowing a gale out there!* **blow sth off course** *The ship was blown off course in the storm.*
2 send air out of your mouth
• ADV. **hard**
• PREP. **on** *He blew on his soup to cool it.*

blue *adj.*

• ADV. **very** | **quite**, **slightly**
• ADJ. **dark**, **deep**, **rich** | **light**, **pale** | **bright**, **brilliant**, **vivid** *a brilliant blue sky* ◊ *her vivid blue eyes* | **cobalt**, **navy**, **royal**, **slate** *a navy blue jumper*
⇨ Special page at COLOUR

blueprint *noun*

• ADJ. **new** | **final** | **economic**, **personal**
• VERB + BLUEPRINT **have** *The government does not have a blueprint for reform.* | **create**, **develop**, **draw up** | **act as**, **form**, **provide**, **serve as** *The charter should serve as a blueprint for cooperation.*
• PREP. **for** *a blueprint for change*

blues *noun*

1 type of slow sad music
• VERB + BLUES **play**, **sing** *He plays blues on the accordion.* ◊ *She was in the back of a smoky bar singing the blues.*
• BLUES + NOUN **band**, **musician**, **singer** | **song**
2 the blues state of feeling sad/depressed
• QUANT. **attack**, **fit** *a bad attack of the blues*
• VERB + BLUES **have** | **get**, **suffer from** | **banish**, **beat** *I plan a holiday as a way to beat the blues.*

blunder *noun*

• ADJ. **big**, **major** | **stupid** | **fatal**, **terrible**, **tragic** | **tactical** | **administrative**, **bureaucratic**, **economic**, **political**
• QUANT. **series**
• VERB + BLUNDER **commit**, **make** *The minister has made a series of political blunders.*

blur *noun*

• ADJ. **dim**, **faint**, **pale** *The object was a dim blur in the moonlight.*
• PREP. **~of** *a blur of colours and patterns*
• PHRASES **be all a (bit of a) blur/just a blur** *I can't remember that day very well. It's all a bit of a blur.*

blush *noun*

• ADJ. **deep**, **fiery**, **hot**, **warm** | **faint**
• VERB + BLUSH **produce** *His jokes produced blushes from the ladies.* | **hide** *She tried to hide her fiery blush.*
• BLUSH + VERB **deepen** | **creep**, **rise**, **spread** *A deep blush spread from her head to her neck.*
• PREP. **with/without a~** *She lowered her eyes with a deep blush.* | **~of** *a hot blush of embarrassment*
• PHRASES **a blush comes to sb's cheeks/face**, **bring a blush to sb's cheeks/face**, **save/spare sb's blushes** (= to save sb from an embarrassing situation)

blush *verb*

• ADV. **deeply**, **furiously**, **hotly** | **faintly**, **a little**, **slightly** | **readily** *She blushed more readily when she was a teenager.* | **angrily**, **guiltily**
• VERB + BLUSH **make sb** *Stop teasing him—you're making him blush.*
• PREP. **at** *He blushed at the mention of her name.* **with** *She blushed crimson with embarrassment.*
• PHRASES **blush crimson/scarlet**

board *noun*

1 flat piece of wood, plastic, etc.
• ADJ. **chess**, **dart**, **drawing**, **emery**, **ironing**, **notice**, **running**, **skirting**, **sounding**
• PREP. **on a/the~** *There's a notice on the board.*
2 group of people who control an organization
• ADJ. **advisory**, **editorial**, **executive**, **management** | **health**, **school**, etc.
• VERB + BOARD **be on**, **serve on**, **sit on** *He sits on the company's management board.* | **join** | **appoint sb to** | **resign from** | **go to** *The project will go to the board for consideration.* | **put sth to**, **submit sth to**, **take sth to** *She put her ideas to the board.*
• BOARD + NOUN **member** | **meeting**
• PREP. **~of** *the company's board of directors*
• PHRASES **at board level** *The issue has been discussed at board level.* **chairman of the board**, **a member of the board**, **a seat on the board** *She was promoted and offered a seat on the board.*
3 meals that are provided when you stay in a hotel
• ADJ. **full** | **half**
• PHRASES **board and lodging**

boardroom *noun*

• ADJ. **company**, **corporate**
• BOARDROOM + NOUN **battle**, **coup**, **row**, **shake-up** | **table** | **pay**, **salary** *The massive boardroom pay awards were criticized by the workers.*
• PHRASES **in a/the ~** *The directors were working overtime in the boardroom.*

boast *noun*

• ADJ. **proud** | **empty**, **idle**, **vain**
• VERB + BOAST **make**
• PREP. **~about** *a boast he made about his achievements* **~of** *her boast of having seen all the countries of Africa*

boast *verb*

1 talk with too much pride
• ADV. **openly**
• PREP. **about/of** *He openly boasted of his talents.*
2 have sth good/impressive
• ADV. **proudly** *This is a region which proudly boasts its own distinct culture.*

boat *noun*

• ADJ. **little**, **small** | **open** *He was adrift in an open boat for three days.* | **flat-bottomed** | **glass-bottomed** | **inflatable**, **plastic**, **rubber** | **wooden** | **motor**, **paddle**, **pedal**, **power**, **rowing**, **sailing**, **speed**, **steam** | **canal**, **narrow**, **river** *We spent our holiday going up a canal on a narrow boat.* ◊ *a Mississippi river boat* | **banana**, **cargo**, **charter**, **ferry**, **fishing**, **flying**, **passenger**, **patrol**, **pilot**, **pleasure**, **racing**, **rescue**, **torpedo**, **touring** | **model**,

paper, toy | **stricken** *The lifeboat was preparing to go to the aid of the stricken boat.* | **upturned**
- QUANT. **fleet, flotilla** *a flotilla of small boats*
- VERB + BOAT **take out** *You couldn't take a boat out in that wild sea.* | **take sb out in** *My brother took us all out in his new boat.* | **get into/on/onto** | **get off/out of** | **launch, lower** *A new type of patrol boat was launched from the Essex coast yesterday.* | **push out** *I pushed the boat out into the middle of the river.* | **propel, row, sail** *The boat is propelled by a powerful outboard motor.* | **handle** *Where did you learn to handle a boat?* | **guide, steer, turn** | **pilot, skipper** | **crew** *Normally the boat is crewed by five people.* | **beach** *He beached the boat and the children leapt out to explore.* | **moor, tie up** | **untie** | **anchor, berth** *The harbour was crowded, with boats berthed two and three abreast.* | **load, unload** | **rock** *Sit down, you're rocking the boat.* ◇ *(figurative) She was told to keep her mouth shut and not rock the boat* (= take unnecessary action that would cause problems). | **capsize, overturn, upset** | **swamp** *The boat was swamped by a huge wave.* | **build, design** | **catch, take** *They crossed the island to catch a boat for islands south of Skye.* | **miss** *(often figurative) If you don't buy now, you may find that you've missed the boat* (= cannot take advantage of this offer because it is too late). | **meet** *Beth had gone down to Bombay to meet the boat on which her sister was arriving.*
- BOAT + VERB **chug, go, sail** *The boat chugged out to sea.* | **head, pass** *The boat headed upriver.* | **arrive, come in, dock** | **return** | **bob** *boats bobbing up and down in the estuary* | **float, glide** | **drift, heave, lunge, lurch, pitch, rock, roll** *The boat pitched violently from side to side.* | **list** | **leak** | **fill** *The boat slowly filled with icy water.* | **capsize, overturn** | **founder, sink** | **operate, ply** *Ferry boats ply regularly between all the resorts on the lake.* | **carry sth, ferry sth, hold sth, take sth**
- BOAT + NOUN **cruise, excursion, ride, trip** | **race** | **club** | **house** (also **boathouse**) | **train** (= the train scheduled to connect with a particular sailing) *the 7.30 p.m. boat train to Harwich* | **building** | **builder, crew, owner** | **people** (= refugees who arrive by boat)
- PREP. **by ~** *The cave can only be reached by boat.* **in a/the ~** *I took them in my boat.* **on a/the ~** *They ate on the boat.* | **~ from, ~ to** *a boat from Jamaica to Trinidad*

bob *verb*

- ADV. **gently** | **about, along** *an old cigarette packet bobbing along in the current*
- PHRASES **bob up and down** *the small boats bobbing gently up and down in the harbour*

body *noun*

1 whole physical form of a person/an animal
- ADJ. **whole** *Her whole body trembled.* | **upper** | **lower** | **healthy** | **human**
- BODY + NOUN **heat, temperature** | **shape, size, weight** *to maintain your ideal body weight* | **fat** | **odour** | **language**
- PREP. **in the/your ~** *Extreme heat may cause changes in the body.* **on the/your ~** *She still had the marks from the ropes on her body.*
- PHRASES **part of the body, sell your body** (= to work as a prostitute)

2 dead human body
- ADJ. **dead** | **decomposed, decomposing** | **bloated**
- VERB + BODY **examine** | **bury, cremate, embalm** | **exhume**
- PREP. **on a/the ~** *A diary was found on the body.*

3 amount of sth
- ADJ. **large, substantial, vast** *a large body of evidence*
- PHRASES **a body of water** *The two islands are separated by a large body of water.*

4 main part of sth

- ADJ. **main** *The bar is in the main body of the hotel.*

5 group of people who work/act together
- ADJ. **advisory, corporate, executive, governing, legislative, professional, statutory** | **national, public** | **government, student** | **independent** | **voluntary** | **elected** | **politic** (always after **body**) *Freedom of speech is necessary for the health of the body politic.*
- VERB + BODY **create, establish, form, set up** | **elect**
- PREP. **in a ~** *The students marched in a body to the government offices.*
- ⇨ Note at ORGANIZATION

6 object
- ADJ. **foreign** *They removed a foreign body from her eye.* | **celestial, heavenly** *Stars are celestial bodies.*

bodyguard *noun*

- ADJ. **armed** | **personal** *He never goes anywhere without his personal bodyguards.*
- VERB + BODYGUARD **have, keep** *She has to have an armed bodyguard wherever she goes.*
- BODYGUARD + VERB **protect sb**
- PREP. **~ of** *He keeps a bodyguard of ten men.* **~ to** *a former bodyguard to the prince*
- ⇨ Note at JOB

bog *noun*

- ADJ. **vast** | **stagnant, swampy** | **peat**
- VERB + BOG **sink into** *The more she struggled the deeper she sank into the bog.*
- PREP. **in a/the ~** *He found himself in a vast stagnant bog.* **through a/the ~** *walking through a bog*

bogged down *adj.*

- VERBS **be** | **become, get**
- ADV. **badly, hopelessly, very** *The lorry had become hopelessly bogged down in the sand.* | **thoroughly, totally** | **rather** *I've been rather bogged down with work.*
- PREP. **by** *bogged down by small details* **in** *We mustn't get bogged down in all the detail.* **with**

bogus *adj.*

- VERBS **be, look, seem** | **dismiss sth as** *75 paintings which art experts dismiss as bogus*
- ADV. **completely, entirely** | **largely**

boil *noun*

1 the boil state of boiling
- VERB + BOIL **come to** *Just before the milk comes to the boil, turn down the heat.* | **bring sth to** *Bring the soup to the boil, then simmer for five minutes.* | **go off** (*usually figurative) He played brilliantly for the first set but then went rather off the boil.*

2 infected spot
- VERB + BOIL **burst, lance** *The doctor lanced the boil.*
- BOIL + VERB **erupt** *A boil had erupted on his neck.* | **burst**

boil *verb*

- ADV. **rapidly** *Boil the beans rapidly for ten minutes.*
- VERB + BOIL **put sth on to** *I'll put the kettle on to boil.*

boiler *noun*

- ADJ. **coal-fired, coke, electric, gas, gas-fired, oil-fired, solid-fuel, steam, water** | **central-heating**
- VERB + BOILER **install, put in** | **service**
- BOILER + VERB **come on** *I've just heard the hot water boiler come on.* | **go off** | **burst, explode**
- BOILER + NOUN **system** | **suit**

boiling point *noun*

- VERB + BOILING POINT **reach** | **bring sth to, heat sth to** *Bring the sauce to boiling point.*
- PREP. **at ~** *Add the powder when the water is at boiling point.*

bold *adj.*

- VERBS **be, feel** | **become, grow** | **make sb** *The exciting news had made him bold.* | **consider sth**
- ADV. **extremely, really, very** | **quite, rather**

bolt *noun*

1 for fastening things together
- VERB + BOLT **tighten (up)** | **loosen** | **undo, unscrew**
- PHRASES **nuts and bolts**

2 for fastening a door
- VERB + BOLT **draw back, pull back, slide back** | **push home, slide home** *She closed the door quickly and pushed the bolts home.*

bolt *verb*

- ADV. **firmly, securely** *Make sure that the rails are securely bolted in place.* | **together** *The two parts are bolted together.*
- PREP. **to** *The yacht's keel is bolted to the hull.*

bomb *noun*

- ADJ. **big, huge, large, massive** | **small** | **cluster, fire, high explosive, incendiary, mortar, nail, petrol, smoke** | **atom/atomic, hydrogen, neutron, nuclear** | **bouncing, flying** | **terrorist** | **home-made** | **unexploded** | **stray** *Their truck was hit by a stray bomb.* | **dummy, fake** *a practice flight with dummy bombs* | **car** | **letter, parcel** | **time** *(figurative) He described global warming as 'an environmental time bomb ticking away'.*
- VERB + BOMB **place, plant, put** *Police suspect terrorists planted the bomb.* | **carry** *The plane had been adapted to carry bombs.* | **drop, release** *Enemy planes dropped bombs along the railway line.* | **defuse** | **detonate, explode, set off** | **build, construct, develop** (These verbs are only used about countries.) *India started to build a nuclear bomb.* | **make** *He used a clock to make a home-made bomb.*
- BOMB + VERB **fall, rain (down)** *Eighty people died when bombs rained down on the city's crowded streets.* | **hit sth** | **detonate, explode, go off** | **blow sb/sth to pieces, blow sth up, destroy sth, kill sb, rip through sth** *Fifteen people were blown to pieces by the car bomb.* ◇ *A terrorist bomb ripped through the town's packed shopping centre.* | **be ticking away**
- BOMB + NOUN **attack, blast, explosion** | **alert, scare, threat, warning** | **hoax** | **disposal, squad** | **shelter** | **crater** *The land was scarred with bomb craters.* | **damage** | **site** | **victim** | **suspect** | **test** *the fallout from atomic bomb tests*

bomb *verb*

- ADV. **heavily** *The city had been very heavily bombed.*

bombard *verb*

1 attack with bombs
- ADV. **heavily** *The city has been heavily bombarded for the last three days.*

2 direct a lot of things at sb
- ADV. **constantly, continually**
- PREP. **with** *We're all constantly bombarded with television advertisements.*

bombardment *noun*

- ADJ. **constant, continuous** | **heavy, intense** | **aerial, artillery, naval**
- VERB + BOMBARDMENT **conduct, launch, mount** | **stop** | **be subjected to, be under, come under, suffer** | **survive, withstand** *They have withstood heavy bombardment for many months.*
- BOMBARDMENT + VERB **begin, start** | **continue, resume** | **(come to an) end, cease, stop**
- PREP. **during/in a/the ~** *Many people were killed in the bombardment.* **under ~** *The city has been under constant bombardment for three days.* | **~ against** *The army launched artillery bombardments against enemy positions.* **~ from** *bombardments from the sea* **~ with** *a three-hour bombardment with rockets and mortars*

bombing *noun*

- ADJ. **aerial** *the aerial bombing of ports* | **precision** | **wartime** | **area, carpet, indiscriminate, saturation** | **strategic** | **enemy** *The neighbourhood was badly damaged by enemy bombing.* | **terrorist** | **suicide**
- BOMBING + NOUN **attack** | **blitz, campaign** | **mission, raid, sortie** *He was shot down during a bombing raid over London.* | **target** | **victim**

bombshell *noun*

- VERB + BOMBSHELL **be, come as** *The news came as a bombshell.* | **drop** *Then she dropped the bombshell—she was pregnant.*
- BOMBSHELL + VERB **come, drop**

bond *noun*

1 feeling of friendship
- ADJ. **close, strong** | **common** | **natural** | **emotional, spiritual** *A strong spiritual bond exists between them.*
- VERB + BOND **be linked by, feel, have** *She felt a bond of affection for the other girls.* | **create, develop, forge, form** | **strengthen** | **break, destroy**
- BOND + VERB **exist** | **link sb** *the bond that links us*
- PREP. **~ between** *trying to forge bonds between the different communities* **~ of** *bonds of friendship*

2 certificate for money you have lent
- ADJ. **long-term** | **government, savings, treasury** | **junk** *the high yield on junk bonds*
- VERB + BOND **buy, invest in, purchase, put money into** *I decided to invest in some government bonds.* | **cash in, redeem** *The bonds were redeemed in 2002.* | **issue, sell**
- BOND + NOUN **market**

bone *noun*

- ADJ. **delicate, fine** *the delicate bones of her face* | **healthy** | **brittle, fragile** *She was diagnosed as having brittle bones.* | **broken, cracked, splintered** | **weary** | **bleached, dry** *Her eyes were black in a face the colour of bleached bones.* | **ankle, breast, cheek, collar, hip, leg, shin, thigh** | **animal, chicken, dinosaur, human**
- VERB + BONE **break, chip, crack, fracture** | **rest** *He longed to get home to bed and rest his weary bones.*
- BONE + NOUN **structure** *The black and white photographs emphasized her fine bone structure.* | **marrow** *a bone marrow transplant* | **cancer, disease, disorders** | **graft, surgery**
- PHRASES **(break/jar) every bone in sb's body** *The shock jarred every bone in his body.* **skin and bone** *He's all skin and bone after his illness.*

bonfire *noun*

- ADJ. **blazing, roaring**
- VERB + BONFIRE **build, have, make** | **light** | **put out** | **put sth on, throw sth on** | **gather/sit around/round**

● BONFIRE + VERB **blaze, burn**
● BONFIRE + NOUN **Night** *It was 5 November—Bonfire Night—and the children were excited.*

bonkers *adj.*

● VERBS **be** | **go** *I went a bit bonkers when he told me the news.* | **drive sb** *The noise nearly drove me bonkers.*
● ADV. **absolutely, completely, plain, stark raving, totally** *I think he's absolutely stark raving bonkers!* ◇ *The whole idea is just plain bonkers.* | **a bit**

bonus *noun*

1 money added to wages, etc.
● ADJ. **big, huge, large | extra, special | cash | annual, Christmas** *All employees get an annual bonus before the summer holidays.* | **loyalty, performance, productivity | no claim(s)** (= a bonus for not claiming on your car insurance)
● VERB + BONUS **award (sb), give sb, pay sb | earn, get, receive** *You will receive a bonus for high levels of productivity.* | **lose** *If you don't meet our targets, you'll lose your bonus.*
● BONUS + NOUN **payment, scheme** *All workers participate in the bonus scheme.*
● PREP. **~of** *He was awarded a cash bonus of £200.*

2 sth extra that is good
● ADJ. **great, huge, major, real | added, extra** *The house is very comfortable, and as an added bonus, it's near to buses and trains.* | **unexpected | welcome**
● PREP. **~for** *The sunshine on the final day was a welcome bonus for the spectators.*

boo *noun*

● ADJ. **loud**
● VERB + BOO **be greeted/met with** *His speech was met with boos.*
● PREP. **~from** *There were loud boos from the audience.*

book *noun*

1 for reading
● ADJ. **latest, new, recent | forthcoming | hardback, paperback, printed** *one of the earliest printed books* | **rare | second-hand | delightful, excellent, fascinating, fine, good, great, interesting, remarkable, useful** *There's nothing like curling up with a mug of tea and a good book.* | **famous, important, influential | controversial** *a controversial book about the royal family* | **favourite** *a survey to find the nation's favourite children's book* | **library | set** *'Emma' was one of our set books for A level.* | **children's, comic, cookery, guide, hymn, phrase, picture, prayer, reference, school, story, text** (also **textbook**) | **travel | address, autograph, cheque, exercise, log, order, phone/telephone, sketch**
● QUANT. **copy** *How many copies of the book did you order?*
● VERB + BOOK **be deep/engrossed/immersed in, flick/skim through, look at, read | look up from** *She looked up from her book and smiled at him.* | **co-author, write | bring out, publish, put out | reprint | edit, proofread, revise | translate | illustrate | bind | ban, censor | dedicate, inscribe** *The book is dedicated to his mother.* ◇ *Her name was inscribed in the book.* ◇ *The collector had many books inscribed to him by famous authors.* | **review | borrow, have out, take out** (= from a library) *How many books have you got out?* | **return, take back** (= to a library) | **renew** *Do you want to renew any of your library books?* | **stock | plagiarize**
● BOOK + VERB **appear, come out** *His latest book will appear in December.* | **be/go out of print**
● BOOK + NOUN **title | shop** (also **bookshop**) | **review, reviewer | club**

● PREP. **in a/the~** *These issues are discussed in his latest book.* | **~about/on** *She's busy writing a book on astrology.* **~by** *a book by Robert Grout* **~for** *a book for new parents* **~from** *a new book from the publishing company, Bookworm* **~of** *a book of walks in London*

2 books company records
● ADJ. **account**
● VERB + BOOKS **audit, do, keep** *She does the books for us.*

book *verb*

● ADV. **early, in advance** *There are few places on the course, so it is essential to book in advance.*
● PREP. **with** *Book with Suntours and kids go free!*
● PHRASES **be booked solid** (= be fully booked), **be booked up, be fully booked**

bookcase *noun*

● ADJ. **glass-fronted**
● PREP. **from a/the~** *I chose a book from the bookcase.* **in a/the~** *I found this book in your bookcase.*

booking *noun*

● ADJ. **advance, early | late | priority | double** (= two bookings for the same time) | **block** (= a large number of seats booked together) | **postal, telephone**
● VERB + BOOKING **make** *I made the booking through a travel agent.* | **cancel | confirm | change | accept, take** *We accept both telephone and postal bookings.*
● BOOKING + NOUN **fee, form, system | office | clerk**
● PREP. **~for** *a booking for the Saturday performance*

bookkeeping *noun*

● ADJ. **double-entry | routine, simple**
● VERB + BOOKKEEPING **do** *I run the shop and my wife does the bookkeeping.*
● BOOKKEEPING + NOUN **entry | system**

boom *noun*

1 period of sudden increase
● ADJ. **great | post-war | consumer, credit, economic, investment, spending | building, housing, property | oil | baby**
● VERB + BOOM **cause, create, fuel, lead to** *The boom was fuelled by accelerated demand for consumer products.*
● BOOM + NOUN **period, time, year | town**
● PREP. **during/in a/the~** *He was born during the post-war baby boom.* | **~in** *a boom in house prices*
● PHRASES **boom and bust/slump** *the ordinary business cycle of boom and bust*

2 deep hollow sound
● ADJ. **big | deep | distant | sonic** (= the explosive sound made when an aircraft flies faster than the speed of sound) *We heard the sonic boom of a jet overhead.*
● VERB + BOOM **hear**
● BOOM + VERB **echo** *The deep boom of a foghorn echoed across the bay.*
● PREP. **with a~**

boon *noun*

● ADJ. **enormous, great, real, tremendous**
● VERB + BOON **be, come as, prove**
● PREP. **~ for** *The building scheme comes as an enormous boon for the building industry.* **~ to** *These machines have proved a real boon to disabled people.*

boost *noun*

● ADJ. **big, great, major, tremendous | much-needed, welcome | unexpected | confidence, financial, morale, psychological**

● VERB + BOOST **give sb, provide (sb with)** | **need** | **get, receive**
● PREP. **~for** *a boost for British products* **~ in** *a big boost in exports* **~ to** *a boost to the economy*

boost *verb*

● ADV. **considerably, greatly, substantially**
● VERB + BOOST **help (to)** *The new service helped boost pre-tax profits by 10%.*
● PREP. **to** *The total was boosted to nearly £200 by donations from parents.*

boot *noun*

● ADJ. **heavy** | **lightweight** | **high** | **ankle, calf-length, knee-length, thigh-length** | **muddy** | **polished** | **fabric, kid, leather, plastic, suede** | **gum, rubber, Wellington** | **high-heeled, hob-nailed, lace-up, nailed, steel-capped, studded, thick-soled** | **army, baseball, climbing, cowboy, desert, football, hiking, riding, rugby, ski, walking**
● QUANT. **pair** *a pair of heavy walking boots*
● VERB + BOOT **have on, wear** | **put on, take off** | **lace up, unlace** | **polish**
● BOOT + NOUN **polish**
● PHRASES **as tough as old boots** *The meat was as tough as old boots.* **the toe of sb's boot** *She kicked at the snow with the toe of her boot.*
⇨ Special page at CLOTHES.

booth *noun*

● ADJ. **phone, photo, polling, ticket, voting**
● PREP. **in a/the~** *She waited in the phone booth.*

booty *noun*

● ADJ. **war**
● VERB + BOOTY **capture, carry off, seize, take** | **divide, share, split** *They divided the booty among the troops.*

booze *noun*

● ADJ. **cheap** | **free** *There was free booze at the party.*
● VERB + BOOZE **smell** *I could smell booze on his breath.* | **bring, take** *We need to take some booze to the party.* | **turn to** *He turned to booze* (= started drinking a lot of alcohol) *when his wife died.* | **kick** *She's still trying to kick the booze* (= stop drinking so much alcohol).
● BOOZE + NOUN **problem**
● PREP. **off the~** (= not drinking alcohol) *She's been off the booze for a month now.* **on the~** (= drinking alcohol) *He was dry for years but now he's back on the booze.*

border *noun*

1 line that divides two countries
● ADJ. **open** | **closed** | **common** *Poland has a common border with Germany.* | **disputed**
● VERB + BORDER **arrive at, reach, stop at** | **cross, drive across/over, slip across/over** *They slipped across the border at nightfall.* | **escape across/over, flee across/over** | **form, mark** *A river forms the border.* | **draw (up), establish, fix** | **guard, patrol** | **open** | **close, seal**
● BORDER + NOUN **crossing, post** | **region, town** | **control, guard, troops** | **clash, dispute, war** | **raid** | **clash, incident, skirmish**
● PREP. **across/over a/the~** *to smuggle goods across the border* **along a/the ~** *There has been fighting along the border.* **at/on a/the ~** *We were stopped on the border.* **on the~of** *a farm on the border of Oxfordshire and Buckinghamshire* **up to the~** *He drove us right up to the Russian border.* | **~ between/of** *the border between Austria and Switzerland* **~with** *the border with Mexico*
● PHRASES **north/south of the border, one side/both**

sides of the border *There has been fighting on both sides of the border.*

2 decorative band/strip round the edge of sth
● ADJ. **wide** | **narrow** | **decorative**
● VERB + BORDER **have** *The tablecloth has a narrow lace border.* | **draw**
● PREP. **with a/the~** *a white handkerchief with a blue border* | **~ around/round** *She drew a decorative border around the picture.*

borderline *noun*

● BORDERLINE + NOUN **case** | **applicant, candidate**
● PREP. **on the ~** *She's on the borderline between a first- and second-class honours degree.* | **~between** *the borderline between myth and philosophy*

bore *noun*

1 person
● ADJ. **awful, crashing, dreadful, real, terrible, utter** *Her husband is a crashing bore.*
● PHRASES **a bit of a bore**
2 a bore sth that you have to do
● ADJ. **awful, great, real, terrible** *It's an awful bore having to meet my aunt for lunch.*

bore *verb*

● ADV. **easily** *I'm very easily bored.*
● PREP. **with** *I won't bore you with too many details.*
● PHRASES **bore sb out of their (tiny) mind, bore sb rigid/silly/stiff, bore sb to death/distraction/tears** *That lecture bored me to tears!*

bored *adj.*

● VERBS **be, feel, look, seem, sound** | **become, get, grow** *Some children get bored very quickly.* | **remain**
● ADV. **really, terribly, very** | **thoroughly** | **a bit, faintly, a little, pretty, rather, slightly**
● PREP. **at** *bored at the prospect of going shopping* **by** *He seemed faintly bored by the whole process.* **with** *He was bored with their conversation.*
● PHRASES **bored out of your (tiny) mind** *He walked along, bored out of his mind.* **bored rigid/silly/stiff** *I remember being bored stiff during my entire time at school.* **bored to death/distraction/tears** *She was alone all day and bored to death.*

boredom *noun*

● ADJ. **sheer, utter** | **terminal**
● VERB + BOREDOM **prevent** | **alleviate, combat, relieve** *A walkman can relieve the boredom of running.* | **die from/of, go mad with** *I'd die of boredom if I lived in the country.* | **drive sb mad with** *Unemployment can drive you mad with boredom.*
● PHRASES **a high/low boredom threshold** *Sorting mail is not a job for people with a low boredom threshold.*

boring *adj.*

● VERBS **be, look, seem, sound** | **become, get** | **make sth** *Try not to make the diet boring.* | **consider sb/sth, find sb/sth, think sb/sth** *She found her job boring.*
● ADV. **awfully, dead, extremely, incredibly, really, terribly, very** *That film was dead boring.* | **completely, downright, utterly** | **a bit, fairly, pretty, quite, rather, slightly**
● PREP. **for** *The game was boring for the spectators.*
● PHRASES **boring old** *Green is much better than boring old white.*

born *verb* be born

- ADV. **prematurely**
- PREP. **into** *She was born into a wealthy family.* **of** *(formal) to be born of noble parents* **to** *babies who are born to very young mothers* **with** *Their child was born with a serious medical problem.*
- PHRASES **American, British, etc. born** *The part is played by an American-born actress.* **be born alive/dead, be born and bred/brought up/raised** *I was born and bred in Liverpool.* **be born blind, deaf, etc., be born out of wedlock/outside marriage**

borough *noun*

- ADJ. **county, metropolitan, municipal**
- BOROUGH + NOUN **council, councillor**
- PREP. **in/within a/the ~** *to establish unemployment committees in all metropolitan boroughs* **throughout a/the ~** *There are factories scattered throughout the borough.* | **~ of** *the London borough of Lambeth*

borrow *verb*

1 money/things
- ADV. **heavily** *He borrowed heavily to set the company up.*
- PREP. **from** *She borrowed £50 from her mother.* **off** *(informal) I'll borrow some coffee off the neighbours.*

2 ideas, etc.
- ADV. **freely**
- PREP. **from** *His designs borrow freely from the architecture of ancient Egypt.*

bosom *noun*

- ADJ. **ample, enormous, large, full**
- BOSOM + VERB **heave, rise and fall** *Her bosom rose and fell; she was out of breath from keeping up with him.*
- PHRASES **clutch sb/sth to your bosom** *(literary) She clutched her son tightly to her bosom.*

boss *noun*

- ADJ. **big** | **company, party, union**

bother *noun*

- VERB + BOTHER **have** *I had a little bother finding your house.* | **cause, give sb** *Your little boy didn't give me any bother.* | **go to** *I wouldn't go to the bother of making the cakes myself.* | **put sb to** *I'd love to come and stay with you, but I don't want to put you to any bother.* | **save sb** *Getting a taxi will save you the bother of picking me up from the station.*
- PHRASES **a bit/a little/a lot/a spot of bother** *He's in a spot of bother with the police.* **no bother** *The children were no bother.*
- PREP. **without any ~** *We found the hotel without any bother.* | **~ to** *I don't mind looking after your dog—it's no bother to me.* **~ with** *He's got a spot of bother with his eyes.*

bothered *adj.*

- VERBS **be, look, seem, sound** | **get** *He never got too bothered about the mess.*
- ADV. **not at all, not in the least** *I'm not in the least bothered about the price.* | **not particularly, not really, not (all) that, not too** *They're not really bothered about what you do.* ◊ *He is not that bothered about his appearance.*
- PREP. **about** *He wasn't too bothered about the slight leak.* **by** *He was still bothered by a persistent leg injury.* **with** *They did not want to be bothered with her problems.*
- PHRASES **can't/couldn't be bothered** *He couldn't even be bothered to turn round.* **(get all) hot and bothered** *She had got herself all hot and bothered about the test.*

bottle *noun*

- ADJ. **full** | **empty** | **recyclable, returnable** | **beer, medicine, milk, etc.** | **hot-water** | **feeding**
- VERB + BOTTLE **fill** *She filled the bottle with water.* | **empty** | **break/crack open** *(only used about alcoholic drinks),* **open, uncork** *Let's crack open a bottle of champagne to celebrate.* | **drink, have, wash sth down with** *We washed the stew down with a bottle of cheap red wine.* | **share** | **bring** (= to bring a bottle of drink to a party)
- BOTTLE + NOUN **top** | **opener** | **bank** | **feeding**
- PREP. **over a/the ~** *We discussed the problem over a bottle of wine.* | **~ of**
- PHRASES **be on the bottle** (= to be an alcoholic), **hit the bottle/take to the bottle** (= to start drinking alcohol heavily)

bottom *noun*

1 lowest part of sth
- ADJ. **false** *a case with a false bottom*
- VERB + BOTTOM **arrive at, fall to, get to, reach, sink to** *He reached the bottom of the steps in no time.* ◊ *The boat sank to the bottom of the sea.* | **touch** *She could only just touch the bottom* (= of a swimming pool, etc.).
- BOTTOM + NOUN **end, half**
- PREP. **along the ~** *We rode along the bottom of the valley.* **at the ~** *at the bottom of the hill* **from the ~** *strange sounds from the bottom of the well* **in the ~** *in the bottom of my bag* **on the ~** *on the bottom of the box* **near/towards the ~** *near the bottom of the page*

2 least important position
- VERB + BOTTOM **start at, work up from** *He started at the bottom and worked his way up through the company.*
- PREP. **at the ~, near/towards the ~** *He's near the bottom of the class.*

3 part of the body
- ADJ. **bare**
- VERB + BOTTOM **smack**

4 basic cause of sth/truth about sth
- VERB + BOTTOM **be at, lie at** *I'd love to know what lies at the bottom of all this.* | **get to** *The only way to get to the bottom of it is to confront the chairman.*

boulevard *noun*

- ADJ. **broad, wide** | **tree-lined**
- BOULEVARD + VERB **be lined with sth** *a boulevard lined with pavement cafes*
- PREP. **along, down, up, etc. a/the ~** *They sauntered along the tree-lined boulevard.*

bounce *verb*

- ADV. **high** *The ball bounced high and she missed it.* | **back, off** *The stone hit the window but bounced off.*
- PREP. **against, down, into, off, on, towards** *Short sound waves bounce off even small objects.*

bound *adj.*

1 bound to do sth certain to do sth
- VERBS **be, seem**
- ADV. **almost** *These problems were almost bound to arise.*

2 bound (to do sth) obliged to do sth
- VERBS **be, feel** | **become** | **remain** | **hold sb** *The president said the country could not be held bound by a treaty signed by the previous regime.*
- ADJ. **absolutely** | **irrevocably** | **by law, contractually, legally** *Officials are bound by law to investigate any possible fraud.* ◊ *He was legally bound to report them to the authorities.* | **(in) honour, in duty** (also **duty-bound**), **morally** *I felt in duty bound to report the incident.*
- PREP. **by** *We are legally bound by this decision.*

3 travelling in a particular direction
- VERBS **be**
- ADV. **homeward, outward**
- PREP. **for** *tourists who are bound for Europe*

4 bound up closely connected
- VERBS **be | become**
- ADV. **closely, intimately | inevitably, inextricably | intrinsically | together** *A person's name and their sense of their own identity are often closely bound up together.*
- PREP. **with** *From that moment my life became inextricably bound up with hers.*

boundary *noun*

1 line that marks the limits of a place
- ADJ. **common | northern, southern, etc. | national, state | district, parish**
- VERB + BOUNDARY **have | form, mark** *The river forms the boundary.* **| share | draw, establish, fix, set** *The boundary was fixed just south of the farm.* **| redraw | cross** *We've just crossed the boundary into Sussex.* **| extend**
- BOUNDARY + NOUN **fence, hedge, line, wall | dispute** *a boundary dispute with their neighbours*
- PREP. **across/over the ~** *They drove across the boundary.* **along the ~** *We continued along the southern boundary of the county.* **at/on the ~** *We had to stop at the boundary.* ◇ *on the boundary of the two countries* **beyond the ~** *She had never strayed beyond the city boundaries.* **within the ~s** *within the boundaries of the old city walls* **| ~ between** *the boundary between Sussex and Surrey* **~with** *The state has a boundary with Ontario.*

2 limit
- ADJ. **traditional**
- VERB + BOUNDARY **cross** *This job crosses the traditional boundary between social work and health care.* **| extend, push back** *research which extends the boundaries of human knowledge* **| overstep**
- PREP. **across ~s** *His policies appeal across party political boundaries.* **beyond the ~s** *going beyond the boundaries of accepted behaviour* **on the ~** *on the boundary of physics and chemistry* **within the ~s** *keeping within the boundaries of the law* **| ~ between** *the boundary between sanity and insanity*
- PHRASES **the boundaries of taste** *In her performance she had clearly overstepped the boundaries of good taste.*

bouquet *noun*
- ADJ. **huge, large | small | bridal, wedding**
- VERB + BOUQUET **carry | send (sb)**
- PREP. **in a/the ~** *Are there any roses in your bouquet?* **| ~ of** *He sent her a large bouquet of wild flowers.*

bout *noun*
- ADJ. **bad, nasty, prolonged, serious, severe** *I got a bad bout of flu last winter.* **| mild | drinking**
- VERB + BOUT **get, have, suffer from**
- PREP. **during a/the ~ | ~ of** *a bout of depression*

boutique *noun*
- ADJ. **chic, elegant, exclusive, smart | fashion**
- VERB + BOUTIQUE **open | run**

bow¹ /baʊ/ *noun*

1 act of bowing
- ADJ. **deep, low | little, slight | formal, stiff**
- VERB + BOW **give, make** *He gave a formal bow and left the room.* **| take** (= used about a performer) *The song ended and Albert took a bow.* ◇ *(figurative) The team's chairman takes his final bow at this match* (= is retiring after this match).
- PREP. **~ to** *He made a deep bow to the king.*

2 front part of a ship
- ADJ. **port, starboard** *There's a small boat on the port bow.*
- VERB + BOW **cross** *A huge whale crossed our bows.*
- PREP. **across the ~** *They fired a shot across our bows.* **in the ~** *We left two men in the bows to receive the cargo.* **off the ~** *100 yards off our bows* **on the ~** *The ship's name was printed on her bow.* **over the ~** *There were huge waves breaking over the bows.*

bow² /baʊ/ *verb*
- ADV. **deeply, low** *He swept off his hat and bowed deeply to the Queen.* **| slightly | politely, respectfully | down**
- PREP. **before** *The Emperor's subjects bowed down before him.* **to** *The pianist stood up and bowed to the audience.*

bow³ /bəʊ/ *noun*

1 knot with two loops
- ADJ. **neat | double**
- VERB + BOW **tie (sth into)** *Can you tie a bow?* ◇ *She tied the ribbon into a neat bow.*

2 weapon for shooting arrows
- VERB + BOW **be armed with, carry, have | aim, draw, raise** *She drew and aimed her bow.* **| lower**
- PHRASES **a bow and arrow**

3 for playing a violin, etc.
- VERB + BOW **draw** *She drew the bow across the strings.*

bowel *noun*
- ADJ. **large, small**
- VERB + BOWEL **empty, evacuate, move, open**
- BOWEL + NOUN **action, function, habit, movement** *Patients are asked to report any change in bowel habit.* ◇ *He's been having painful bowel movements.* **| frequency | wall | cancer, disease, disorder, obstruction, problems, tumour | biopsy, surgery**
- PREP. **in the ~**
- PHRASES **irritable bowel syndrome**

bowl *noun*
- ADJ. **deep, shallow | empty, full | ceramic, china, crystal, cut-glass, earthenware, enamel, glass | food, fruit, porridge, pudding, punch** (also **punchbowl**)**, salad, soup, sugar, water** *I refilled the dog's water bowl.* **| mixing, serving | washing-up | finger** *I put down the chicken bone and rinsed my fingers in the finger bowl.* **| begging** *(figurative) The school is always having to get out the begging bowl for books and basic equipment.* **| goldfish | lavatory, toilet**
- VERB + BOWL **fill, pour (sb), pour sth into** *He poured himself a bowl of soup.* **| empty | drink from/out of, eat from/out of**
- BOWL + VERB **contain sth, hold sth** *a bowl containing flour* ◇ *This bowl holds about four pints.* **| overflow** *The washing-up bowl was overflowing.*
- PREP. **from a/the ~** *I helped myself to an apple from the bowl.* **out of a/the ~** *The boy was drinking milk out of a bowl.* **in/into a/the ~** *Mix the ingredients in a deep bowl.* ◇ *Sieve the flour into a bowl.* **| ~ of** *a bowl of cherries*

bowling *noun*

1 indoor game
- ADJ. **tenpin**
- VERB + BOWLING **go** *Let's go bowling on Saturday.*
- BOWLING + NOUN **ball | alley | green**
- ⇨ Special page at SPORT

2 in the game of cricket

● ADJ. **fast, pace, quick | slow | seam, spin, swing | short-pitched | intimidatory**
● VERB + BOWLING **open** *McArthur opened the bowling on the first day of the match.*
● BOWLING + NOUN **attack** *England were no match for the Indian bowling attack.* | **average | crease**

box noun

1 container
● ADJ. **oblong, rectangular, square | upturned** *They were sitting round the fire on upturned boxes.* | **cardboard | storage | chocolate, cigar, egg | jewel/jewellery, shoe, tool** (also **toolbox**) **| cassette, CD, video | gift | lunch, sandwich | first-aid | (safe/safety) deposit, security** *There is a safety deposit box in every room of the hotel.* | **cash, money** *The cash box was kept in the safe at the back of the shop.* ◇ *She opened her money box to see if she had saved enough for a tennis racket.* | **collection, donation** *The exhibition is free, but there is a collection box for donations.*
● QUANT. **pile, stack**
● VERB + BOX **fill, pack** *She filled the box with old clothes.* | **pack sth in/into, put sth in/into, put sth away in, store sth in** *We packed all the books into boxes.* | **remove sth from, take sth out of | empty, unpack | open | close, shut | lock**
● BOX + VERB **contain sth, be filled with/full of sth, hold sth** *This box holds ten candles and costs £21.* | **be labelled sth, be marked sth** *a box marked 'fragile'* | **be covered in/with sth, be lined with sth** *The dog sleeps in a box lined with an old blanket.*
● PREP. **in/into a/the ~, inside a/the ~, out of a/the ~ | ~ of** *a box of chocolates*
● PHRASES **the lid of a box**

2 enclosed area
● ADJ. **soundproof | call, phone, telephone | jury, witness | commentary, press** *There was a babble of languages in the commentary box when the race began.* | **director's, executive, hospitality** *They drank champagne as they watched the match from the executive box.* | **private, Royal** *a private box at the theatre* | **signal | horse** (also **horsebox**) *The car in front was pulling a horsebox.*
● PREP. **in/into a/the ~**

3 square on a form/screen
● ADJ. **appropriate, relevant** *Tick the relevant box below.* | **dialog/dialogue** *Click on 'open file' in the dialogue box.* | **question**
● VERB + BOX **fill in, put sth in, tick, write (sth) in** *Put a cross in the box if you agree with the comments.*
● PREP. **in/into a/the ~**

boxing noun

● ADJ. **heavyweight, lightweight, middleweight, etc. | amateur, professional, unlicensed** *Unlicensed boxing can be very dangerous.* | **world** *the most respected coach in world boxing* | **kick, Thai | shadow** (also **shadow-boxing**) (= boxing with an imaginary opponent) *(figurative) The two candidates engaged in shadow-boxing before the election.*
● VERB + BOXING **do** *He does boxing in his spare time.*
● BOXING + NOUN **boot, glove | competition, match, tournament | title | champion | ring | skill, technique | coach, promoter | career | enthusiast, fan | writer | circles** *He is highly respected in boxing circles.*
⇨ Special page at SPORT

box office noun

● BOX OFFICE + NOUN **hit, success | receipts, takings** *Box office receipts for the film have hit $50 million.*
● PREP. **at a/the ~** *Tickets are available at the box office.*
● PHRASES **do well/badly at the box office** *The musical has done very well at the box office* (= a lot of tickets have been sold).

boy noun

● ADJ. **big** *Your boy is quite big for his age.* ◇ *Don't cry— you're a big boy now.* | **little, small** *A little boy rode by on a tricycle.* ◇ *Their boy is small for his age.* | **young** *Our youngest boy is just starting school.* | **elder, eldest, older** *How old is your eldest boy?* | **baby | adolescent, teenage | good** *Eat up your greens—there's a good boy.* | **naughty | bright, clever**
● VERB + BOY **have** *They've had a baby boy.* ◇ *I've got three boys.*

boycott noun

● ADJ. **mass, total, worldwide | consumer, economic, trade** *a consumer boycott of GM foods*
● VERB + BOYCOTT **declare, impose, introduce** *Opposition groups declared a boycott of the elections.* | **call for, threaten** *Lawyers threatened a boycott of the courts.* | **end, lift** *Politicians want to end their boycott of the talks.* | **join** *There is pressure on the biggest union to join the boycott.*
● BOYCOTT + NOUN **campaign**
● PREP. **~ by** *a boycott by international singers* **~ of** *The group is calling for a mass consumer boycott of these products.* **~ on** *The US has imposed a boycott on some European goods.*

boycott verb

● ADV. **officially**
● VERB + BOYCOTT **threaten to | call on sb to, urge sb to** *They have urged people to boycott foreign products.*

boyfriend noun

● ADJ. **current, latest, new | ex-, former, old | long-standing, long-term, serious, steady | live-in | jealous | jilted** *She was stalked by a jilted ex-boyfriend.*
● QUANT. **string, succession** *She had a string of wealthy boyfriends before she finally married.*
● VERB + BOYFRIEND **have** *Have you got a boyfriend?* | **meet | live with | sleep with | marry**
● BOYFRIEND + NOUN **trouble** *She's unhappy because she's been having boyfriend trouble.*

bra noun

● ADJ. **padded, strapless, underwired, uplift | maternity, nursing | sports**
● VERB + BRA **put on | take off | do up | undo, unhook**
● BRA + NOUN **strap**
⇨ Special page at CLOTHES

brace noun

1 for supporting a part of the body
● ADJ. **leg, neck, shoulder**
● VERB + BRACE **have, wear** *I used to wear a brace.*
● PREP. **~ on** *a brace on his teeth*

2 braces for holding trousers up
● BRACES + VERB **hold sth up , support sth** *The braces held up his trousers.*
⇨ Special page at CLOTHES

bracket noun

1 brackets marks round extra information in writing
● ADJ. **angle, curly, round, square**
● VERB + BRACKETS **enclose sth in, give sth in, put sth in** *The prices are given in square brackets.*
● PREP. **in** *The words in brackets should be deleted.* **in-**

side, **outside**, **within** *The numbers outside the curly brackets are the sales figures.*

2 range

- ADJ. **age, income, price, tax | higher, top, upper | middle | lower**
- PREP. **in/within** *These machines are in the higher price bracket.* **outside** *people outside this age bracket*

brain *noun*

1 part of the body

- ADJ. **human | left, right** *The left brain controls the right-hand side of the body.*
- BRAIN + NOUN **cell, tissue | region | function, process | activity | damage, disease, disorder, failure, haemorrhage, illness, injury, tumour | scan | surgeon, surgery**
- PREP. **in the/your ~** *Doctors tried to reduce the swelling in his brain.* **on the/your ~** *He was found to have a blood clot on his brain.* ◇ *(figurative) He's got football on the brain* (= thinks about nothing but football).
- PHRASES **blow your brains out** *While cleaning his shotgun he had accidentally blown his own brains out.*

2 ability to think/intelligence

- ADJ. **fertile, fine, good, great, quick | muddled, tired** *My tired brain couldn't cope with such a complex problem.* **| analytical**
- VERB + BRAIN **rack** *We racked our brains but we couldn't come up with a solution.* **| pick sb's** (= ask sb for information because they know more about a subject than you) *I need to pick your brains: what can you tell me about credit unions?* **| take** *It doesn't take much brain to work out that both stories can't be true.*
- BRAIN + VERB **function, tick over, work** *It's important to keep your brain ticking over.* **| reel** *His brain reeled as he realized the implication of his dismissal.* **| register sth** *The stopping distance includes the time taken for the brain to register the need to stop.*
- BRAIN + NOUN **power** (also **brainpower**)
- PREP. **~ behind** *the brains behind the robberies*
- PHRASES **brains and brawn/brains and not brawn**, etc. *They relied on brains rather than brawn* (= intelligence, not strength). **have a brain for sth** *She has a good brain for mathematics.*

brake *noun*

- ADJ. **defective, faulty | front, rear | foot, hand | air, anti-lock, disc, drum, vacuum**
- VERB + BRAKE **apply, hit, jam on, put/slam your foot on, put on, slam on** *She slammed on the brakes to try to avoid the dog.* **| keep your foot on | let off, release, take your foot off** *He released the brake and sped off.*
- BRAKE + VERB **work** *My brakes are not working properly.* **| fail** *The car crashed after its brakes failed.* **| screech, squeal | be on/off** *Is the brake on?*
- BRAKE + NOUN **failure | cable, fluid, lights, pads, pedal, pipes**
- PHRASES **act/serve as a brake on sth** *(figurative)*, **put a brake/the brakes on sth** *(figurative) The need to earn some money put the brakes on my wilder ambitions.* **a screech/squeal of brakes** *We heard the screech of brakes, followed by a loud crash.*

brake *verb*

- ADV. **hard, heavily, sharply, suddenly, violently**
- PHRASES **brake to a halt** *The train braked to a shuddering halt.* **brake to avoid sth** *She braked suddenly to avoid a cat.*

branch *noun*

1 part of a tree

- ADJ. **top/topmost | low, overhanging** *Be careful of*

overhanging branches. **| bare, dead** *the bare branches of a tree in winter*

2 part of a larger organization

- ADJ. **central, high street, local, overseas, regional**
- VERB + BRANCH **establish, open, set up** *The store is opening more local branches.* **| close (down)**
- BRANCH + NOUN **chairman, manager, member, office, representative, secretary**
- ⇒ Special page at BUSINESS

brand *noun*

1 type of product made by a particular manufacturer

- ADJ. **leading, major, principal, top** *the world's leading brand of whisky* **| famous, favourite, popular, well-known | own** (= goods marked with the name of a particular shop instead of that of the manufacturer) *Supermarkets make a lot of profit on their own brand products.*
- BRAND + NOUN **identity, image, name** *The company owes its success to brand image.* **| leader | loyalty**
- PREP. **~ of** *a well-known brand of toothpaste*

2 particular type of sth

- ADJ. **particular, special, unique** *His designs have a unique brand of stylishness.* **| ~ of** *his particular brand of humour*

brandy *noun*

- ADJ. **double, large | single, small | stiff** *a stiff brandy and soda* (= containing a lot of brandy and not much soda) **| straight | cherry, plum, etc.**
- QUANT. **dash, drop, nip** *He added a dash of brandy to his coffee.* **| measure, shot, tot** *She poured herself a large measure of brandy.* **| bottle, flask, glass, hip-flask**
- VERB + BRANDY **drink** *Do you drink brandy?* **| have** *I'll have some brandy, please.* **| pour (sb) | sip | gulp, swig | down, finish | distil, produce**
- BRANDY + NOUN **bottle | balloon** (= a kind of glass), **glass** *He sat cradling his brandy glass.*

brass *noun*

1 metal

- ADJ. **gleaming, glittering, polished, shiny | solid**
- VERB + BRASS **be made from/in/(out) of** *candlesticks made of solid brass*
- PREP. **in ~** *The door knocker was a female figure in brass.*

2 musical instruments made of brass

- BRASS + NOUN **band | instrument | section** *the brass section of the orchestra*
- ⇒ Special page at MUSIC

bravado *noun*

- ADJ. **sheer | mere | false, forced**
- PREP. **out of ~** *He behaved aggressively out of bravado.* **with ~** *'I'll be fine on my own,' she said with bravado.*
- PHRASES **a display/show of bravado**

brave *adj.*

- VERBS **be, feel, seem, sound | make sb** *The whisky had made me brave.*
- ADV. **exceptionally, extremely, really, terribly, very | quite | amazingly, incredibly**

bravery *noun*

- ADJ. **great, outstanding**
- VERB + BRAVERY **demonstrate, display, show**
- BRAVERY + NOUN **award, medal**
- PREP. **with ~** *The men fought with great bravery.*
- PHRASES **an act of bravery**

brawl noun

- ADJ. drunken | bar-room, pub, street | mass
- VERB + BRAWL provoke, spark, start | be/become/get involved in, be/get caught up in, get into
- PREP. in a/the~ *They got caught up in a street brawl.* | ~between *a brawl between different gangs of football supporters.* ~over *a brawl over a woman*

breach noun

1 breaking of a law/an agreement/a rule
- ADJ. clear, fundamental, grave, serious | deliberate, flagrant *He refused to bow to the Queen, in deliberate breach of etiquette.* | minor | security
- VERB + BREACH constitute *Such behaviour constitutes a breach of confidentiality.* | commit
- PREP. in ~ of *The court's decision is in breach of the European Convention on human rights.* | ~ of *a minor breach of discipline*
- PHRASES a breach of confidence/trust, a breach of confidentiality/contract *He was sued for breach of contract.* a breach of security/the peace, a breach of the peace

2 break in friendly relations
- VERB + BREACH cause, lead to | heal, repair
- PREP. ~ between *What caused the breach between the two brothers?* ~ with *She left home following the breach with her family.*

bread noun

- ADJ. fresh | hard, mouldy, soggy, stale *This bread is going stale.* | crusty *some nice crusty white bread* | sliced | unleavened | home-baked, home-made | fried | garlic | black, brown, granary, naan, pitta, rye, soda, white, wholemeal | French, Italian, etc.
- QUANT. loaf | chunk, crumb, crust, hunk, morsel, piece, slice *She tore off a large hunk of bread.*
- VERB + BREAD bake, make *the smell of freshly-baked bread* | cut, slice | butter, put sth on, spread *bread thickly spread with plum jam* | toast
- BREAD + NOUN dough | pudding, roll, sauce | bin, knife
- PREP. on the~ *What would you like on your bread?*
- PHRASES bread and butter/margarine *a plate of bread and butter* bread and cheese/jam, bread and water *He had to live on bread and water for two weeks.* bread and wine (= the food given to Christians during the Communion service) *People started going up to receive the bread and wine.*
- ⇨ Special page at FOOD

breadth noun

1 distance between two sides of sth
- PREP. in~ *The pool is 5 metres in breadth.*
- PHRASES the length and breadth of sth *He travels the length and breadth of* (= all over) *the country.*

2 great extent or variety
- ADJ. full, great, sheer
- PHRASES breadth of experience *I need a greater breadth of experience.* breadth of interest/knowledge/understanding, breadth of mind, breadth of vision

break noun

1 short rest/holiday
- ADJ. short | coffee, lunch, tea | Christmas, Easter *Are you going away for the Easter break?*
- VERB + BREAK have, take *We'll take a break now and resume in half an hour.* | need
- BREAK + NOUN time
- PREP. at~ *I'll see you at break.* during (a/the)~ *I had a word with John during the break.* without a~ *We worked all day without a break.* | ~for *a break for lunch* ~from *a break from looking after the children*

2 change/interruption in sth
- ADJ. clean, complete | career | commercial
- VERB + BREAK make *His new work makes a break with the past.* ◇ *I wanted to leave but was nervous about making the break.*
- PREP. ~from *a break from tradition* ~in *a break in the weather* ~with*

3 opportunity
- ADJ. big, lucky
- VERB + BREAK get *I always knew I would get my lucky break one day.* | give sb *He's the director who gave her her first big break.*

break verb

- ADV. easily | in half, in two *She broke the chocolate bar in two and gave a piece to me.* | up *She broke the chocolate up into small pieces.*
- PREP. into *The glass broke into hundreds of pieces.*

PHRASAL VERBS

break down
1 fail
- ADV. completely, irretrievably *They were divorced on the grounds that their marriage had broken down irretrievably.*

2 start crying
- PHRASES break down and cry/weep, break down in tears *She broke down in tears as she spoke to reporters.*

break off
- ADV. abruptly *He broke off abruptly when Jo walked in.*
- PREP. from *She broke off from the conversation to answer the telephone.*

breakdown noun

1 mechanical failure
- ADJ. electrical, mechanical
- BREAKDOWN + VERB occur
- BREAKDOWN + NOUN organization, service *The national breakdown organizations are on hand to help motorists 24 hours a day.* | crane, lorry, vehicle

2 failure/end of sth
- ADJ. serious | complete, irretrievable *The only ground for divorce is the irretrievable breakdown of the marriage.* | communication, family, marital, marriage, relationship
- VERB + BREAKDOWN cause, lead to
- PREP. ~in/of *a breakdown in negotiations*

3 collapse of mental health
- ADJ. emotional, mental, nervous, psychological
- VERB + BREAKDOWN have, suffer

4 list of the details of sth
- ADJ. detailed, full | cost
- VERB + BREAKDOWN prepare *I have prepared a detailed cost breakdown for the project.* | give sb, provide (sb with)
- PREP. ~by, ~of *Please provide us with a breakdown of expenditure by department.*

breakfast noun

- ADJ. big, full, good, hearty, large, proper, solid, substantial | light, modest | cooked, fried | continental, English, American-style *a full English breakfast of cereal, bacon and eggs and toast* | buffet/buffet-style | hasty, hurried, quick | leisurely, long | early, late | working | champagne
- BREAKFAST + NOUN cereal | dishes, things *Would you clear away the breakfast things?* | room | meeting | show, television

● PHRASES **bed and breakfast** *Bed and breakfast accommodation is available near the museum.* **breakfast in bed** *He treated his wife to breakfast in bed on her birthday.*
⇨ Note at MEAL (for verbs)

break-in noun

● ADJ. **attempted | factory, house, etc.**
● BREAK-IN + NOUN **happen, take place**
● PREP. **~at** *a break-in at the factory*

breakthrough noun

● ADJ. **big, crucial, great, historic, important, major, real, significant | diplomatic, medical, political, scientific, technological**
● VERB + BREAKTHROUGH **be, represent | achieve, make** *We have achieved a real breakthrough in the search for peace.*
● BREAKTHROUGH + VERB **come, happen** *The crucial breakthrough came almost by accident.*
● PREP. **~ for** *The new deal represents a major breakthrough for the company.* **~ in** *a significant breakthrough in computer design*

breakup noun

● ADJ. **family, marital, marriage**
● VERB + BREAKUP **lead to**

breast noun

1 part of a woman's body
● ADJ. **ample, big, full, heavy, large | little, small | bare, naked | firm, pert, pointed | round, shapely | sagging**
● BREAST + NOUN **cancer | screening | milk**
● PHRASES **put a baby to the breast** (= to feed a baby from the breast), **take the breast** (= to feed from the breast)

2 your chest
● PHRASES **beat your breast, hold/clutch sb/sth to your breast** *He held the letter to his breast.*

breaststroke noun

⇨ Note at STROKE

breath noun

● ADJ. **big, deep, long, slow | quick, shallow, short | bad** *Smoking gives you bad breath.*
● VERB + BREATH **draw (in), suck in, take** *He spoke solidly for twenty minutes, barely pausing to draw breath.* ◊ *Take a deep breath and try to relax.* **| let out** *He let out a long breath.* **| hold** *How long can you hold your breath for?* **| get back** *I needed a few minutes to get my breath back after the run.* **| catch** *When he said he had resigned, I caught my breath in surprise.* **| gasp for** *He came up out of the water gasping for breath.* **| pause for** *She poured out her story, hardly pausing for breath.* **| save** (*figurative*) *It's useless talking to him—you may as well save your breath.* **| waste** (*figurative*) *Don't waste your breath. He never listens to advice.*
● BREATH + VERB **come in gasps/pants/puffs** *His breath came in short gasps.*
● PREP. **on sb's~** *I could smell gin on her breath.* **out of~** *I'm a bit out of breath after my run.* **under your~** *He was whispering rude remarks about her under his breath.* **| ~of** *It was a still day, without a breath of wind.*
● PHRASES **a breath of fresh air** *I'm going outside for a breath of fresh air.* **an intake of breath** *When the news was announced, there was a sharp intake of breath.* **in the same breath** *How can we trust a government that mentions community care and cutbacks in the same breath?* **short of breath** *I felt a bit short of breath and had to sit*

down. **take sb's breath away** (*figurative*) *The sheer audacity of the man took my breath away.*

breathe verb

1 air/breath
● ADV. **fast, quickly, rapidly | slowly | deeply | shallowly | hard, heavily** *They were both breathing hard from the steep climb.* **| gently | easily, steadily** *She was beginning to breathe more easily.* **| normally, properly** *I can't breathe properly—I'm gasping for air!* **| raggedly** *He was breathing raggedly, mouth open.* **| in, out** *She breathed slowly in and out.*
● VERB + BREATHE **can/can't, could/couldn't, could barely/hardly/scarcely | not dare** *He hardly dared breathe in case they heard him.*
● PREP. **through** *Always breathe through your nose.*

2 say quietly
● ADV. **huskily, softly** *'I love you,' she breathed softly.*

breather noun

● ADJ. **quick, short, slight**
● VERB + BREATHER **have, stop for, take | enjoy | give sb** *The weekend will give me a slight breather to finish this work in.*

breathing noun

● ADJ. **deep | shallow | controlled, even, regular, steady | hoarse, laboured, uneven** *His breathing was laboured, and he could hardly speak.* **| heavy** *She picked up the phone and heard sounds of heavy breathing.*
● BREATHING + NOUN **apparatus | difficulties | exercise** *Try breathing exercises to calm your nerves.*

breathless adj.

● VERBS **be, feel, seem, sound | become | leave sb, make sb** *The unaccustomed exercise left him breathless.*
● ADV. **very | a little, quite, rather, slightly, somewhat** *He felt quite breathless.* **| suddenly**
● PREP. **with** *By the end of the walk, she was breathless with exertion.* ◊ *The children peered through the open door, breathless with excitement.*

breathtaking adj.

● VERBS **be**
● ADV. **absolutely, quite, truly**

breed noun

1 type of animal
● ADJ. **new | rare | hardy**
● VERB + BREED **keep** *a farm that keeps rare breeds*
● PREP. **~of** *a new breed of dairy cattle*

2 particular type of person
● ADJ. **new | dying, rare** *Entertainers of this sort are now a dying breed.*
● PREP. **~of** *a new breed of international criminals*
● PHRASES **a breed apart** *Health workers are a breed apart in their commitment and dedication to duty.*

breed verb

● ADV. **in captivity | successfully | commercially | selectively** *fish that have been selectively bred for their appearance*
● PREP. **for** *dogs that are bred for their fighting ability* **from** *She's a lovely cat. Will you breed from her?*

breeding noun

1 activity of producing plants/animals
● ADJ. **animal, fish, plant | selective** *Certain character-*

istics can be developed through selective breeding. | **captive** *a campaign to save the condor by captive breeding*
- BREEDING + NOUN **season | stock | programme**

2 good manners/behaviour
- ADJ. **good** *Her good breeding shows in her exquisite manners.*
- VERB + BREEDING **have** *The young man clearly has breeding.*

breeze *noun*
- ADJ. **faint, gentle, light, little, slight, soft | stiff, strong | sudden | cold, cool, fresh | warm | pleasant** *pleasant sea breezes* **| evening, morning, night | sea, summer | northerly, westerly, etc.**
- BREEZE + VERB **blow, come, drift** *A light breeze came off the sea.* **| ruffle sth, rustle sth, stir sth** *A sudden breeze rustled the long dry grass.* **| come up** *A breeze came up in the late afternoon.* **| drop**
- PREP. **in a/the ~** *The curtains fluttered in the night breeze.*

breezy *adj.*
1 windy
- VERBS **be**
- ADV. **very | a little, slightly** *It's a little breezy up here.*
- PHRASES **bright and breezy** *The weather at the seaside was ideal—bright and breezy.*

2 cheerful and relaxed
- VERBS **be, seem, sound** *She tried to sound breezy on the phone.*
- PHRASES **bright and breezy** *His bright and breezy manner sometimes irritated people.*

bribe *noun*
- VERB + BRIBE **give sb, offer (sb), pay sb** *He admitted paying bribes to police officers.* **| accept, take**
- PREP. **in ~s** *He paid out millions of dollars in bribes.* **| ~ of** *a bribe of £200*

bribery *noun*
- ADJ. **political**
- VERB + BRIBERY **resort to**
- BRIBERY + NOUN **scandal**
- PHRASES **bribery and corruption** *The charge in the present case is one of bribery and corruption.*
⇨ Note at CRIME (for more verbs)

brick *noun*
- ADJ. **red** *a house of red brick*
- VERB + BRICK **lay** *learning to lay bricks properly*
- BRICK + NOUN **wall | building | works** *He got a job at the local brick works.*
- PREP. **in/of ~** *houses of brick*
- PHRASES **brick by brick** *They moved the whole house, brick by brick.* **bricks and mortar** *investing in bricks and mortar* **a course of bricks** *They put an extra course of bricks round the pool.*

bride *noun*
- ADJ. **beautiful, lovely, radiant | blushing | child, teenage, young | new | future, intended, prospective** (also **bride-to-be**) **| jilted**
- VERB + BRIDE **give away** *The bride's father traditionally walks with her to the altar to give her away.* **| toast** *Everyone raised their glasses to toast the bride.*
- BRIDE + VERB **wear sth | receive the guests**
- PHRASES **the bride and groom**

bridegroom *noun*
- ADJ. **future, prospective**
- BRIDEGROOM + VERB **receive the guests** *The bride and bridegroom received their guests in the great hall.*
- PHRASES **the bride and bridegroom**

bridesmaid *noun*
- ADJ. **chief**
- VERB + BRIDESMAID **toast** *The bridegroom asked the guests to stand and then toasted the bridesmaids.*

bridge *noun*
1 structure across a river, road, etc.
- ADJ. **high, humpback, narrow | railway, road | Bailey, cantilever, pontoon, suspension | toll**
- VERB + BRIDGE **build, erect | destroy | wash away** *Floods washed away several bridges.* **| cross** *Cross the bridge and turn right into the town.*
- BRIDGE + VERB **cross sth, span sth** *The new bridge will cross the Thames at this point.* **| link sth**
- PREP. **across over a/the ~** *driving over a humpback bridge* **under a/the ~** *The road goes under the old railway bridge.* **| ~ across, over** *a bridge over the river*

2 card game
- QUANT. **game, rubber** *I enjoy a game of bridge occasionally.*
- VERB + BRIDGE **play**
- BRIDGE + NOUN **tournament | partner, player**

brief *noun*
- ADJ. **clear, detailed, written | legal, technical**
- VERB + BRIEF **prepare, produce, write**
- PREP. **in a/the ~** *She makes all these points in her brief.* **outside sb's ~** *How the new policy is to be implemented is outside his brief.* **| ~ on** *a technical brief on food hygiene*
- PHRASES **be part of sb's brief** *It's not part of my brief to advise on financial matters.*

brief *verb*
- ADV. **fully, properly, well**
- PREP. **about** *The men have been fully briefed about the intended mission.* **on** *Each member of my crew took it in turn to brief me on his particular duties.*

brief *adj.*
- VERBS **be** *I promised to be brief.* **| keep sth, make sth** *Could you make it brief? I've got a meeting in ten minutes.*
- ADV. **extremely, very | fairly, quite, rather | comparatively, relatively | necessarily** *This necessarily brief account concentrates on two main areas.* **| mercifully** *The wait was mercifully brief, little more than an hour.* **| tantalizingly** *The diary entries were tantalizingly brief.*

briefcase *noun*
- ADJ. **battered** *He wore a torn suit and carried a battered briefcase.* **| bulging | executive | leather, plastic**
- VERB + BRIEFCASE **open, snap open, unlock | close, lock, shut, snap shut | carry, hold, pick up | drop, put down**
- BRIEFCASE + VERB **be bulging with sth, be full of sth, be stuffed with sth, contain sth**

briefing *noun*
- ADJ. **detailed, full, thorough | formal, informal | final** *She returned to Washington for a final briefing.* **| press**
- VERB + BRIEFING **give sb** *All staff will be given a full briefing tomorrow.* **| get, receive | arrange, hold** *I asked him to arrange a formal briefing.* **| attend**

- BRIEFING + NOUN **session | document, paper**
- PREP. **at a/the~** *Details of the scheme will be announced at a press briefing later today.* | **~ by/from** *a briefing by the commanding officer* **~ on** *a briefing on security issues*

brigade *noun*

- ADJ. **armoured, fire, infantry**
- VERB + BRIGADE **command, lead | form** *A special army brigade is to be formed.* | **join**
- BRIGADE + NOUN **commander | headquarters**
- PREP. **in a/the~** *units in 1st Commando Brigade* | **~ of** *a brigade of infantry*

brigadier *noun*

⇨ Note at RANK

bright *adj.*

- VERBS **be, look, seem** *The factory's future now looks quite bright.* | **become**
- ADV. **exceptionally, extremely, incredibly, intensely, really, surprisingly, unusually, very** *a really bright child* | **fairly, pretty, quite, reasonably** *The morning was quite bright, but it clouded over in the afternoon.* | **unnaturally** *Her eyes were unnaturally bright.*

brighten *verb*

- ADV. **considerably | a bit, a little | visibly** *Their rather heavy faces brightened visibly.* | **suddenly | up** *She brightened up a bit at the thought of the holiday.*

brilliance *noun*

- ADJ. **great, sheer | academic, intellectual, technical**
- QUANT. **flash** *There were flashes of brilliance from several of the players.*
- PREP. **with~** *He played with great brilliance.*

brilliant *adj.*

- VERBS **be, look**
- ADV. **bloody** (*taboo*), **just, really** *Winning that race was just brilliant.* | **absolutely, quite, totally, utterly** *an absolutely brilliant idea* | **technically** *Her performance was technically brilliant but lacked feeling.*
- PREP. **at** *He's brilliant at football.*

brim *noun*

1 top edge of a cup, bowl, etc.
- PHRASES **be filled/full to the brim, fill sth to the brim** *She filled the bowl to the brim.*

2 flat edge around the bottom of a hat
- ADJ. **broad, deep, wide** *a straw hat with a wide brim*
- PREP. **beneath/under a/the ~** *She watched the crowd from beneath the brim of her hat.*

bring *verb*

PHRASAL VERB
bring sb up
- ADV. **badly, well** *children who have been well brought up*

brink *noun*

- ADJ. **very**
- VERB + BRINK **be (poised) on, hover on, stand on, teeter on** *Scientists are on the brink of making a major new discovery.* ◇ *animals hovering on the very brink of extinction* | **bring sb to | fight/pull back from | bring/pull sb/sth back from** *He pulled the company back from the brink* (= saved it from disaster).
- PREP. **~ of** *the brink of bankruptcy/death/war*

broad *adj.*

- VERBS **be**
- ADV. **extremely, very | fairly, pretty, quite, rather, reasonably, relatively | enough, sufficiently** *He questioned whether the school curriculum was broad enough in scope.* | **unusually** *His job gave him an acquaintance with an unusually broad spectrum of society.*

broadcast *noun*

- ADJ. **radio, satellite, television | live | outside | election, news, party political, religious**
- VERB + BROADCAST **give, make** *The president gave a radio broadcast to mark the end of the war.* | **hear, see**
- PREP. **in a/the ~** *More details will be given in our news broadcast.* | **~ by** *a broadcast by the prime minister* **~ on** *a radio broadcast on the problems of unemployment*

broadcast *verb*

- ADV. **live**
- PREP. **from** *We will broadcast live from the ship.* **to** *a Christmas message broadcast to the nation*

broadcaster *noun*

- ADJ. **commercial** *Existing commercial broadcasters claim the new stations are illegal.* | **independent | public service** *The country needs a national public service broadcaster like the BBC.* | **local, national | satellite**

brochure *noun*

- ADJ. **(full) colour, glossy | illustrated** *Send for our illustrated brochure.* | **holiday, hotel, travel**
- QUANT. **copy**
- VERB + BROCHURE **browse/leaf/look through** *I leafed through the travel brochure.* | **produce, publish**

broke *adj.*

- VERBS **be | go** (= go bankrupt) *The company went broke last year.*
- ADV. **completely, flat** (*informal*), **stony** (*informal*) *I'm stony broke at the moment.* | **nearly**

broken *adj.*

- VERBS **be | get** *How did the jug get broken?*
- ADV. **badly** *One of his legs was badly broken.*

broker *noun*

- ADJ. **credit, insurance, mortgage** *Ask advice from an insurance broker.* | **honest** (= an independent person or country that acts between two sides in a dispute)
- VERB + BROKER **be, act as**
- PREP. **~ between** *acting as broker between the two opposing sides* **~ for** *a broker for the company*
⇨ Note at JOB

bronchitis *noun*

⇨ Special page at ILLNESS

bronze *noun*

1 metal
- VERB + BRONZE **be cast in, be made from/in/(out) of** *The figure was cast in bronze.*
- BRONZE + NOUN **ingot**
- PREP. **in~** *She works mainly in bronze.*

2 (*also* **bronze medal**) in sports
- ADJ. **Olympic**
- VERB + BRONZE **get, take, win** *She got a bronze in the long jump.*

brooch noun

- ADJ. **cameo** | **diamond, pearl, etc.**
- VERB + BROOCH **have on, wear** | **pin** *She pinned a large amethyst brooch to her lapel.*

broom noun

- ADJ. **witch's** | **stiff**
- VERB + BROOM **sweep sth with, use**
- BROOM + NOUN **cupboard** | **handle**

brothel noun

- VERB + BROTHEL **go to, visit** *He used to visit a brothel in Paris.* | **run** *She ran a brothel in Soho.*
- BROTHEL + NOUN **keeper**
- PREP. **in a/the~** *She works in a brothel in Brighton.*

brother noun

- ADJ. **big, elder, older** *Bill idolizes his big brother, who is a professional footballer.* | **baby, kid, little, small, wee, younger** | **twin** | **full** (= sharing both parents) | **half-** (= sharing one parent), **step-** (also **stepbrother**) (= the son from an earlier marriage of your stepfather or stepmother) | **beloved, much-loved** *She wrote daily to her beloved brother, Leo.* | **long-lost** *His old teacher greeted him like a long-lost brother.* | **dead, deceased, late** *He married the wife of his late brother.* | **bachelor, unmarried**
- PHRASES **blood brothers** (= close friends who have sworn to remain friends for life), **brother and sister** *Have you got any brothers and sisters?* **like brothers** *The boys are so close, they're like brothers.*

brow noun

1 eyebrow
- ADJ. **dark, heavy** | **bushy, shaggy** | **winged** | **delicate** | **sardonic** *She raised a sardonic brow.*
- VERB + BROW **arch, raise** *She arched a brow when she saw the bill.* | **draw together, knit** *He knitted his brows in concentration.*
- BROW + VERB **lift, rise** | **twitch** | **draw together, snap together** *His brows snapped together ferociously when he heard the remark.*

2 forehead
- ADJ. **broad, wide** | **furrowed** *He stared at the visitors beneath a furrowed brow.* | **stern** | **weary** | **damp, perspiring, sweating** | **fevered**
- VERB + BROW **mop, wipe** | **furrow, pucker, wrinkle** *She wrinkled her brow thoughtfully.*
- BROW + VERB **crease, furrow, pucker, wrinkle** *His brow furrowed as he racked his brains over the question.* | **clear** *For a while she looked puzzled; then her brow cleared.* | **darken** *His brow darkened in anger.*
- PREP. **across your ~** *His shaggy grey hair fell loosely across his brow.* **from your~** *She brushed back a stray lock of hair from her brow.* **over your ~** *His hair fell over his brow as he turned his head.*

brown adj.

- ADV. **very** *He looked very brown after his holiday.* | **quite, rather, slightly** | **uniformly** *The once-green fields were now uniformly brown.*
- ADJ. **dark, deep** *her dark brown eyes* | **light, pale, soft** | **rich, warm** *a lovely warm brown colour* | **bright** *monkeys with bright brown fur* | **drab, dull, muddy** | **chestnut, chocolate, golden, reddish, rusty**
⇨ Special page at COLOUR

browser noun

- ADJ. **web** | **default** *What do you use as your default browser?* | **frames-capable, frames-enabled**
- VERB + BROWSER **update, upgrade**
- BROWSER + VERB **support frames**
- BROWSER + NOUN **toolbar, window**
- PREP. **on a/the ~** *Click the 'back' button on your browser.*
⇨ Special page at COMPUTER

bruise noun

- ADJ. **black, dark, livid, purple** | **swollen**
- VERB + BRUISE **suffer** *She suffered only minor cuts and bruises.*
- BRUISE + VERB **form** *A bruise had formed below his left eye.* | **fade**

bruise verb

- ADV. **badly** *His face was quite badly bruised.* | **easily** *She has delicate skin and bruises easily.*

brunt noun

- ADJ. **full, main**
- VERB + BRUNT **bear, take** *The prime minister has taken the brunt of the criticism.*
- PREP. **the~of**

brush noun

- ADJ. **fine, soft, stiff** *Scrub the wood thoroughly with water and a stiff brush.* | **nylon, wire** | **clothes, lavatory, nail, pastry, scrubbing, shaving, toilet**
- VERB + BRUSH **apply sth with** *Apply the paint with a clean brush.* | **use, wield**
- BRUSH + NOUN **stroke** *The artist has used tiny brush strokes.*
- PREP. **with a/the ~** *Remove all the rust with a wire brush.*
- PHRASES **a brush and comb, a dustpan and brush**

brush verb

1 clean with a brush
- ADV. **down** *She hummed happily as she brushed down her coat.*
- PREP. **at** *Lucille brushed at the blood on his jacket.*
- PHRASES **brush sth clean**

2 touch lightly
- ADV. **gently, lightly** | **accidentally**
- PREP. **against** *She carefully avoided brushing against the man sitting beside her at the table.* **by** *She brushed by him and dashed up the stairs.* **past** *I hardly noticed the man who brushed past me in the corridor.* **with** *He brushed her lips with his.*

brutality noun

- ADJ. **extreme, great** | **police** *There have been many complaints of police brutality.*
- QUANT. **act** *This was an act of extreme brutality.*
- PREP. **~against** *brutality against prisoners* **~by** *brutality by the security forces* **~to/towards** *brutality to others*

bubble noun

- ADJ. **air, soap**
- VERB + BUBBLE **blow** *children blowing bubbles* | **burst** *They jumped about, bursting the bubbles.*
- BUBBLE + VERB **form** *Soap bubbles formed on the surface.* | **burst**

bubble verb

1 form bubbles
- ADV. **furiously** *The water in the saucepan was bubbling furiously.* | **away, up** *The soup was bubbling away on the stove.*

2 feeling

● ADV. **to the surface** *Emotions quickly bubble to the surface.* | **over, up** *He was bubbling over with excitement.*
● PREP. **inside** *She could feel the anger bubbling up inside her.* **with** *The business was still small but I was bubbling with ideas.*

bucket *noun*

● ADJ. **empty, full** | **galvanized, metal, plastic** | **leaky** | **champagne, ice** | **water** | **slop, waste** *a slop bucket full of scraps of food* | **mop** | **coal** | **fire** *The sand had spilt from the fire bucket.*
● VERB + BUCKET **fill** *She filled the bucket with fresh water.* | **carry** | **empty, pour, throw** *She poured the bucket of dirty water down the drain.*
● BUCKET + VERB **be filled with/full of sth, contain sth, hold sth** | **overflow**
● PREP. **in a/the~** | **~of** *a bucket of oats for the horses*
● PHRASES **a bucket and spade** *The children ran down to the beach with their buckets and spades.* **mop and bucket** *The cleaner put down his mop and bucket and sat down.*

buckle *noun*

● ADJ. **belt, shoe**
● VERB + BUCKLE **do up, fasten** | **undo, unfasten**
⇨ Special page at CLOTHES

bud *noun*

● ADJ. **flower, leaf**
● VERB + BUD **be in, come into** *The roses are in bud.*
● BUD + VERB **burst, open**

Buddhism *noun*

● ADJ. **Zen** *She became interested in Zen Buddhism.*
⇨ Note at RELIGION (for verbs and phrases)

Buddhist *noun*

● ADJ. **devout**
● BUDDHIST + NOUN **beliefs, philosophy, teaching** | **monk**

budge *verb*

● VERB + BUDGE **refuse to, will/would not**
● PREP. **from** *He refuses to budge from his principles.* **on** *The union won't budge on its demand.*
● PHRASES **not budge an inch** *He threw all his weight against the door, but it wouldn't budge an inch.*

budget *noun*

● ADJ. **fixed, limited, low, shoestring, small, tight** | **generous, large** | **annual, monthly, weekly, yearly** | **family, personal** | **federal, government, municipal, national, state** | **defence, education, health, housing, military, social security, (social) welfare** | **advertising, marketing, training** | **draft**
● VERB + BUDGET **get, have** *The organization has a large annual budget.* | **allocate, draw up, plan, set** *The council has to draw up its budget for next year.* | **present, propose, submit** | **approve** | **balance** *The school has a struggle to balance its budget.* | **adhere to, keep to, stick to** *Work out a weekly budget and stick to it.* | **exceed, go over, overspend** | **cut, reduce, slash** | **increase**
● BUDGET + NOUN **expenditure** | **deficit,   surplus** | **constraint, limit** | **cuts** | **plans, proposals, allocation** | **Budget Day** (= when the government announces its budget)
● PREP. **in the ~** *Is there any money left in the budget?* **below/under~** *Costs have been held below budget.* **on (a)~** *All his projects are on time and on budget.* ◇ *This hotel caters for people travelling on a tight budget.* **over~** *The*

project is now well over budget. **within ~** *to keep within budget* | **~for** *The budget for next year has not yet been set.* **~of** *a budget of $5 000*

budget *verb*

● ADV. **carefully, sensibly** *If we budget carefully we should be able to afford a holiday this year.*
● PREP. **for** *We have budgeted £10 000 for advertising.*

buffer *noun*

● VERB + BUFFER **act as** | **provide** | **use sth as**
● BUFFER + NOUN **state, zone**
● PREP. **~against** *A family can provide a buffer against stress at work.* **~between** *The organization acts as a buffer between the management and the union.*

buffet *noun*

1 on a train/in a station
● ADJ. **station**
● BUFFET + NOUN **bar, car, service**
2 meal
● ADJ. **delicious, excellent** | **extensive, generous** | **cold, salad** | **running** *The running buffet is available from 6 p.m. to 2 a.m.* | **finger, fork** | **lunchtime**
● VERB + BUFFET **serve** *A finger buffet will be served.* | **lay out** *A buffet was laid out for the conference delegates.*
● BUFFET + NOUN **breakfast, dinner, lunch, meal, supper** | **table** | **reception** | **style** *Breakfast is served buffet style.*

bug *noun*

1 infectious illness
● ADJ. **nasty** | **flu, stomach, tummy**
● VERB + BUG **have** | **catch, come/go down with, get, pick up**
● BUG + VERB **go around/round** *A stomach bug has been going round at school.* | **strike sb down**
● PREP. **with a/the~** *off work with a flu bug*
⇨ Special page at ILLNESS
2 sudden interest in sth
● VERB + BUG **be bitten by, catch, get** *She's been bitten by the travel bug.*
● BUG + VERB **bite (sb)**
3 sth wrong in a system/machine
● ADJ. **minor, slight** | **computer, software**

buggy *noun*

● ADJ. **baby** | **beach, golf**
● VERB + BUGGY **push** *parents pushing baby buggies*

build *noun*

● ADJ. **average, medium** | **slight, slim, thin** | **heavy, muscular, powerful, stocky, strong, thickset** | **athletic**
● PREP. **in ~** *He's heavier in build than his brother.* **of ~** *She is slight of build and very agile.* **with a ~** *a small woman with a slim build*

builder *noun*

● ADJ. **good, reputable** | **jobbing, self-employed** | **local** *We got a local builder to do the work for us.*
● VERB + BUILDER **be apprenticed to**
● BUILDER + VERB **build sth**
● PHRASES **builder's merchant, builder's yard** *The house looked like a builder's yard, with stacks of bricks and piles of sand in the garden.*
⇨ Note at JOB

building *noun*

1 house, church, school, etc.
- ADJ. **big, high-rise, large, tall** | **low, single-storey, small** | **attractive, beautiful, fine, imposing, impressive, magnificent** | **crumbling, derelict, dilapidated, ramshackle, tumbledown** | **ancient, historic, old** | **seventeenth-century, etc.** | **listed** *They were refused planning permission for a modern extension because it was a Grade II listed building.* | **brick, concrete, stone, timber, wooden** | **industrial, public, residential** | **airport, apartment, church, factory, farm, headquarters, hospital, office, prison, school**
- VERB + BUILDING **build, erect, put up** *Several new buildings are now being put up.* | **demolish, destroy, flatten, gut, knock down, pull down, raze, tear down** *The building was gutted by fire.* | **damage** | **renovate, restore** *They're renovating the old farm buildings.*
- BUILDING + VERB **collapse**

2 process/business of building sth
- ADJ. **nest, road** | **empire, team**
- BUILDING + NOUN **business, company, contractor, firm, industry, sector, trade** | **programme, project, scheme** | **activity, development, work** *We're having some building work done.* | **controls, regulations** | **land, site** | **materials** | **boom** | **costs** | **worker**

build-up *noun*

1 gradual increase
- ADJ. **gradual, slow** | **steady** | **rapid** | **massive**
- VERB + BUILD-UP **cause, lead to** *The leak led to a slow build-up of carbon dioxide.* | **avoid, prevent**
- PREP. **during/in the ~** | **~ of**

2 period of time before an event
- ADJ. **pre-match, pre-trial, etc.**
- PREP. **~ to** *Tension is mounting in the build-up to the elections.*

bulb *noun*

1 (*also* **light bulb**) part of an electric lamp
- ADJ. **electric** | **bare, naked, unshaded** | **100-watt, 60-watt, etc.** | **bright, dim** | **bayonet-cap, ES** | **energy-efficient, energy-saving, long-life, low-energy** | **fluorescent** | **halogen** | **clear, coloured, pearl** | **flash** *My camera needs a new flash bulb.*
- VERB + BULB **change, replace** *Switch the light off before you change the bulb.* | **put in** | **remove, take out** *Can you take out the clear bulb and put a pearl one in?* | **switch on** | **take** *The fitting in the kitchen takes a fluorescent bulb.*
- BULB + VERB **light sth** *The room was lit only by a single 40-watt light bulb.* | **fail, go** *I think the bulb over the sink is going to go. It's been flickering all evening.* | **flicker** | **flash, go off** *Coloured bulbs flashed on and off around the sign.* ◊ *There was a startled look on his face when the flash bulb went off.* | **dangle, hang** *A single electric light bulb dangled from the ceiling.* | **last** *These low-energy bulbs last much longer than the ordinary ones.*
- PHRASES **by the light of a … bulb** *They sat reading by the light of a 40-watt bulb.* **the glow of a light bulb**

2 round plant root
- ADJ. **autumn, spring, spring-flowering, summer, summer-flowering** | **daffodil, hyacinth, tulip, etc.** | **garden, indoor** | **dwarf**
- VERB + BULB **place, plant, put in** *I'm putting in some bulbs for next year.* ◊ *Place the bulbs close together.* | **dig up, take up, uproot** | **grow** | **water** *She usually waters the indoor bulbs once a week.* | **force, treat** *These daffodils flower so early because the bulbs have been forced.*
- BULB + VERB **grow** | **flower** | **be over, go over** *The bulbs were over. All that remained of them were clumps of brown leaves.* | **increase** *Over the years the bulbs grad-*

ually increase. | **sprout** | **shrivel** *Get the bulbs into the ground, or they will begin to shrivel.*

bulk *noun*

1 large size
- ADJ. **considerable, formidable, huge, massive, sheer** *I was amazed by the sheer bulk of the creature.* | **dark, looming, solid**
- VERB + BULK **ease, heave, shift** (used about people) *He heaved his considerable bulk into the chair.*

2 large amount
- ADJ. **great, large, overwhelming, vast**
- BULK + NOUN **buying, order, purchasing**
- PREP. **in ~** *Sugar is imported in bulk from the mainland.*
- PHRASES **the bulk of** (= most of) *The great bulk of the work has now been done.* **buy in bulk** *It's usually cheaper to buy in bulk.*

bullet *noun*

- ADJ. **live** | **stray** | **explosive** | **plastic, rubber** | **.45 calibre, etc.** | **machine-gun, rifle, tracer**
- VERB + BULLET **fire, spray sth with** *The embassy was sprayed with bullets.* | **shoot** (used of a gun) *faster than a machine-gun can shoot bullets* | **be riddled with** *The body was riddled with bullets.* | **put** *They had put a bullet through his brain.*
- BULLET + VERB **hit sb/sth, shoot sb, strike sb/sth** *The second bullet hit her in the back.* | **miss sb/sth** *The bullet missed his heart by less than an inch.* | **enter sb/sth** | **kill sb** | **be lodged, lodge** *Surgeons are trying to remove a bullet lodged near his spine.* | **go, pass** | **fly across, around, etc. sb/sth, rip through sb/sth, smash/thud into sb/sth, whistle past sb/sth** *A stray bullet whistled past his ear.* | **bounce, ricochet** *The bullets ricocheted off the stones.*
- BULLET + NOUN **hole** | **wound** | **scar**
- PREP. **~ from** *It is a bullet from the same gun that killed the Italian.* **~ in/through** *The second bullet hit her in the back.*
- PHRASES **a hail/volley of bullets** *They died in a hail of bullets.* **a sniper's bullet** *She was shot through the head by a sniper's bullet.*

bulletin *noun*

1 short news report/official statement
- ADJ. **official** | **news, weather**
- VERB + BULLETIN **issue, put out, release** *The government will issue an official bulletin later this week.*
- PREP. **in a/the ~** *More details will be given in our next news bulletin.* | **~ on** *a bulletin on the president's health*

2 short newspaper
- ADJ. **annual, monthly, quarterly, weekly**
- VERB + BULLETIN **produce, publish** | **read**
- PREP. **in a/the ~** *The details are in the June bulletin.*

bully *noun*

- ADJ. **big, real** *Leave him alone, you big bully!* ◊ *He's a real bully!* | **class, playground, school**

bum *noun*

1 person's bottom
- VERB + BUM **feel, pinch** *A man pinched her bum on the train so she hit him.* | **sit on** *They've been sitting on their bums all day, doing nothing.*

2 lazy/useless person
- ADJ. **low-down, no-good** | **lazy** | **beach** *He dropped out of college and became a beach bum.*

bump noun

1 sudden strong blow
- ADJ. **loud** | **slight**
- PREP. **with a~** *We landed with a loud bump.*

2 lump on the body
- ADJ. **big** | **little, small**
- VERB + BUMP **have** | **get**
- PREP. **~on** *He got a nasty bump on his head.*

3 lump in a flat surface
- VERB + BUMP **hit** *We hit a bump and the car swerved.*
- PREP. **~in** *a bump in the road*

bump verb

- ADV. **accidentally**
- PREP. **against** *I ran after her, bumping against people in my rush.* **into** *I bumped into the corner of a table as I left.* **on** *I bumped my head on the door frame.*

bumper noun

- ADJ. **front** | **back, rear**
- PHRASES **bumper to bumper** *The cars crawled along bumper to bumper* (= very close to each other).

bun noun

1 small round cake
- ADJ. **fresh** | **stale** | **cinnamon, cream, currant, hot cross, iced, sticky** | **hamburger**
- VERB + BUN **eat, have** | **bake, make**
- ⇨ Special page at FOOD

2 hair fastened in a round shape
- ADJ. **neat, severe, tight** | **loose**
- PREP. **in a~** *a woman with her hair in a loose bun*
- PHRASES **pull/draw your hair back in(to) a bun** *Her black hair was drawn back into a neat bun.* **tie your hair (back) in a bun, wear your hair in a bun**

bunch noun

1 things fastened/growing together
- ADJ. **big, huge, large** | **small**
- PREP. **in a~** *She put all the flowers together in one big bunch.* | **~of** *He gave me a huge bunch of red roses.*

2 group of people
- ADJ. **mixed, motley**
- PREP. **~of** *They are a bunch of amateurs.*

bundle noun

- ADJ. **big, large, thick** *carrying a thick bundle of clothes*
- VERB + BUNDLE **tie sth (up) in, wrap sth (up) in** *He tied his belongings up in a bundle and left.*
- PREP. **in a/the~** *The papers are in a bundle on my desk.* | **~of** *a bundle of newspapers*

bungalow noun

- ADJ. **two-bedroom/two-bedroomed, etc.** | **detached, semi-detached** | **suburban** | **ranch-type** | **modern** | **holiday, retirement**

burden noun

1 responsibility/worry
- ADJ. **great, heavy, onerous** | **crippling, intolerable** | **administrative, economic, financial, tax**
- VERB + BURDEN **bear, carry** *The manager carries the greatest burden of responsibility.* | **assume, shoulder, take on** *She had to shoulder the burden of childcare.* | **impose, place** *His illness placed an intolerable burden on his family.* | **increase** | **ease, lighten, reduce, relieve** | **lift, remove** *The administrative burden must be lifted from local government.* | **shift** *plans to shift the burden of tax-*

ation onto larger companies | **share** *I need to share my burden with someone.*
- BURDEN + VERB **fall on sb/sth** *The economic burden falls mainly on businesses.*
- PREP. **~for** *a burden for the whole family* **~of** *the burden of high taxation* **~on/upon** *easing the financial burden on families* **~to** *She felt she was a burden to her parents.*
- PHRASES **the burden of proof** (*law*) (= the responsibility of proving that sth is true) *The burden of proof falls on the prosecution: the accused is presumed innocent until proved guilty.* **have a burden on your shoulders** *He has the burden of a large family on his shoulders.* **lift a burden from sb's shoulders**

2 heavy load
- VERB + BURDEN **carry** *The women carried their burdens on their backs.* | **pick up** | **lay down, put down**
- PHRASES **a beast of burden** (= an animal used to do heavy work such as pulling or carrying things)

bureau noun

- ADJ. **citizen's advice, employment, information, missing persons** | **government, press**
- VERB + BUREAU **contact, go to**
- BUREAU + VERB **deal with sth, handle sth** *The information bureau handles millions of enquiries each year.*
- BUREAU + NOUN **staff**
- PREP. **at a/the~** *You can get more information at your local citizen's advice bureau.* **in a/the~** *She had a friend in the press bureau.*

bureaucracy noun

1 administrative system
- ADJ. **vast** | **government, state**

2 official rules and procedures
- ADJ. **cumbersome, excessive, unnecessary**
- VERB + BUREAUCRACY **cut out, eliminate, reduce** *The organization has promised to eliminate cumbersome and unnecessary bureaucracy.* | **increase**

bureaucrat noun

- ADJ. **faceless** *He was just another faceless bureaucrat.* | **unelected** | **high-ranking, senior** | **career** *battles between political appointees and career bureaucrats* | **state** | **party**

bureaucratic adj.

- VERBS **be** | **become**
- ADV. **extremely, highly, very** *The organization is highly bureaucratic.* | **rather, somewhat** | **unnecessarily**

burglar noun

- ADJ. **professional** | **cat** (= a burglar who climbs up the outside of buildings) | **suspected**
- VERB + BURGLAR **hunt** (*informal*) *Police are hunting burglars who stole property worth £3 500.* | **catch**
- BURGLAR + VERB **break in** *The burglar had broken in through a window.* | **steal sth** | **strike** *Burglars had already struck twice that week in their road.*
- BURGLAR + NOUN **alarm**

burglary noun

- ADJ. **attempted** | **aggravated** (*law*) (= burglary involving further violence or unpleasant behaviour) | **house**
- BURGLARY + VERB **happen, take place**
- PREP. **~at** *Audio equipment was stolen in a burglary at a house in Main Road.*
- ⇨ Note at CRIME (for more verbs)

burial *noun*

- ADJ. **decent, proper** | **Christian**, etc.
- VERB + BURIAL **give sb** *We want to give him a decent Christian burial.* | **attend, be present at, go to**
- BURIAL + VERB **take place**
- BURIAL + NOUN **chamber, ground/grounds, mound, place, plot, site, vault** *disturbing an ancient burial site* | **ceremony, rites, service**
- PREP. **for ~** *His body was returned home for burial.* | **~ in** *preventing the body's burial in consecrated ground*

burn *noun*

- ADJ. **horrific, nasty, serious, severe, terrible** | **minor, slight** | **first-/second-/third-degree** | **cigarette**
- VERB + BURN **suffer** | **die from/of** | **treat, treat sb for**
- BURN + NOUN **mark**
- PHRASES **20, 50, etc. per cent burns** *He was treated in hospital for 60 per cent burns.*

burn *verb*

1 damage/injure by fire/heat
- ADV. **badly, seriously, severely** | **completely** *The car was found abandoned in a wood, completely burnt out.* | **partially, partly** | **easily** *fair skin that burns easily* | **ceremonially** *Bishop Tunstall preached a sermon against the book, after which copies were ceremonially burnt.* | **down, out** *The factory burned down last year.*
- PHRASES **be burnt alive, be burnt to ashes/a cinder/a crisp** *I like my steak burnt to a cinder on the outside and blood red and juicy inside.* **burn/be burnt to death** *Several people were burnt to death.* **be burnt to the ground** *The building was burnt to the ground.*

2 be on fire
- ADV. **fiercely** *The fire was still burning fiercely.* | **steadily** | **slowly** *Fresh leaves will burn slowly with billows of smoke.*

3 produce light
- ADV. **brightly** *Their torches burnt brightly in the dark.*

4 be filled with strong feeling
- ADV. **fiercely** *Her eyes burned fiercely.* | **slowly** *She could sense the anger burning slowly inside him.*
- PREP. **with** *He was burning with indignation.*

burrow *verb*

- ADV. **deep** | **away, down** *He switched off the bedside lamp and burrowed down beneath the bedclothes.*
- PREP. **beneath/under** *Rabbits had burrowed under the fence.* **into** *Earthworms burrow deep into the subsoil.* **through** *worms that burrow through dead wood*
- PHRASES **burrow your way** *Ivy had burrowed its way through the walls.*

bursary *noun*

- ADJ. **sports, travel**
- VERB + BURSARY **award sb, offer sb, provide sb with**

burst *noun*

- ADJ. **short** *a short burst of energy* | **sudden** *a sudden burst of enthusiasm* | **rapid** *a rapid burst of gunfire* | **intense** *an intense burst of anger*
- PREP. **in ~s** *He works in short bursts.* | **~ of**

burst *verb*

- ADV. **suddenly** | **apart** *The ship was burst apart and its crew blasted to pieces.*
- VERB + BURST **be about to, be going to, be ready to** *My whole head felt like a ripe tomato, ready to burst.*

- PREP. **with** *(figurative)* *He felt he would burst with anger.*

PHRASAL VERB
burst into sth
- ADV. **suddenly** | **immediately, instantly, promptly** *She took one look at the mess and promptly burst into tears.*
- VERB + BURST INTO STH **be about to, be going to, be ready to** *He was just about to burst into song.*

bury *verb*

1 dead person
- PHRASES **be dead and buried** *Those people are now all dead and buried.* ◇ *(figurative)* *Their ambitions were finally dead and buried.* **bury sb alive**

2 hide in the ground
- ADV. **deep** | **underground** *The waste is buried deep underground.*

3 cover
- ADV. **completely** *a fallen tree trunk almost completely buried in the long grass*
- PHRASES **be buried alive** *The miners were buried alive when the tunnel collapsed.* **be/get buried beneath/under sth** *The building was now buried under three metres of soil.* ◇ *Your letter got buried under a pile of papers.*

4 put sth deeply into sth
- ADV. **deep/deeply** *He slumped forward, the knife buried deep in his chest.* ◇ *(figurative)* *her deeply buried pain*
- PHRASES **lie/remain buried** *(often figurative)* *The king is dead and lies buried at Jedburgh Abbey.* ◇ *What secrets lie buried in the past?*

bus *noun*

- ADJ. **regular** *There are regular buses to the city centre.* | **double-decker, open-topped** | **last** *I missed the last bus and had to walk.* | **airport, local, school, sightseeing, tourist**
- VERB + BUS **go by, go on, take, travel by, use** | **wait for** *I waited 40 minutes for a bus.* | **run for** *I left work a bit late and had to run for my bus.* | **catch, get** | **miss** | **board, get on/onto** | **get off** | **drive**
- BUS + VERB **go, run** *Local buses run regularly to and from the nearest town.* | **arrive, come** | **pull up, stop** *The bus pulled up and we got on.* ◇ *The buses stop outside the post office.* | **pick sb up** *The double-decker bus stopped to pick up some more passengers.* | **go from, leave (from)** *Buses leave from here every hour or so.* | **carry sb** *a bus carrying 56 passengers*
- BUS + NOUN **times, timetable** *Look up the bus times in the local timetable.* | **route** | **lane** | **depot, shelter, station, stop** | **queue** | **journey** *a short bus journey to work* | **conductor, driver, passenger** | **fare** | **pass, ticket** | **company, service**
- PREP. **by ~** *It's about 15 minutes away by bus.* **on a/the ~** *people travelling on buses* | **~ for** *Is this the bus for Oxford?* **~ from, ~ to** *We took the bus from Reading to Bristol.*

bush *noun*

1 plant
- ADJ. **gorse, rose, thorn**, etc. | **prickly, scrubby**
- QUANT. **clump** *a large clump of rose bushes*
- VERB + BUSH **plant** | **prune** *to prune the rose bushes*
- BUSH + VERB **grow**
- PREP. **among/in the ~es** *She was hiding in the bushes at the side of the lane.*

2 wild land in Africa/Australia
- ADJ. **dense, thick** | **native** *hills that have become a wasteland after the removal of native bush*
- BUSH + NOUN **fire**
- PREP. **in/into the ~** *going out into the bush*

business noun

1 buying and selling of goods
- ADJ. **big | profitable | private | core** *It's time to focus on the company's core business.* | **retail, wholesale | catering, computer, investment,** etc.
- VERB + BUSINESS **carry on** (*often law*)**, conduct, do, transact** *a company that has ceased to carry on business* ◇ *He's someone I can do business with* (= that I find it easy/pleasant to do business with). | **work in** *She works in the computer business.* | **go into, set up in | go out of** *The firm went out of business during the recession.* | **put sb/sth out of** *The new regulations will put many small firms out of business.*
- BUSINESS + NOUN **deal, transaction | meeting | lunch | trip | community | executive, manager, partner | contact | affairs, interests, matters | investment | secret** *protecting business secrets* | **plan | acumen | card | hours** *You can call the helpline during normal business hours.* | **school | studies | park** *The company's offices are located in the new business park out of town.*
- PREP. **in~** *He's in business.* ◇ *What business are you in?* ◇ (*figurative*) *All we need is a car and we'll be in business* (= we'll have everything we need to start what we want to do). **on~** *going to Paris on business*
- PHRASES **business as usual** (= things will continue as normal in spite of a difficult situation) *It's business as usual at the factory, even while investigators sift through the bomb wreckage.* **business or pleasure** *Is the trip to Rome business or pleasure?* **mix business with pleasure** *When I travel abroad I like to mix business with pleasure.* **a place of business**

2 amount of trade done
- ADJ. **brisk, good** *Business was brisk and they had sold out by midday.* | **bad, slack, slow**
- VERB + BUSINESS **drum up, generate** *She's in Europe drumming up business for her new company.* | **tout for** *insurance salesmen touting for business* | **lose** *We're losing business to our main rivals.*
- BUSINESS + VERB **boom** *Business is booming for estate agents in the south as the property market hots up.* | **pick up** *After a slack period business is now picking up.*

3 firm/shop
- ADJ. **large, medium-sized, small | family | international, local | private | state-owned | profitable, successful | mail order, retail, wholesale**
- VERB + BUSINESS **have, own | manage, run** *It was always my dream to run my own business.* | **set up, start** *They decided to start their own business.* | **build up** *We built up the business from nothing.* | **work in** *He works in the family business.* | **take over | expand, grow** *We are looking to grow the business over the next couple of years.* | **join, leave**
- BUSINESS + VERB **do/go well, take off** *After six months the business really took off.* | **expand, grow** *The business is expanding fast.* | **collapse, fail**
- BUSINESS + NOUN **assets, premises | failure**
- ⇨ Note at ORGANIZATION

4 work/responsibility
- ADJ. **daily**
- VERB + BUSINESS **go about** *market traders going about their daily business* | **make sth** *I shall make it my business to find out who is responsible.*
- PHRASES **have no business doing sth/to do sth** *You have no business* (= no right) *being here.* **mind your own business** (= think about your own affairs and not try to get involved in other people's) '*What are you reading?*' '*Mind your own business!*' ◇ *I was just sitting there, minding my own business, when a man started shouting at me.* **none of your business/no business of yours** *My private life is none of your business* (= does not concern you).

5 important matters
- ADJ. **private | important, pressing, urgent | unfinished** *We've got some unfinished business to discuss.*
- VERB + BUSINESS **get down to** *OK, let's get down to business.* | **deal with, discuss, talk** *I'm not going to talk business tonight.*
- PHRASES **any other business** (= items discussed at the end of a meeting) *I think we've finished item four. Now, is there any other business?*

6 situation/event
- ADJ. **whole** *I'll be glad when the whole business is over and done with.* | **awful, bad, dreadful, terrible** *It was an awful business—he couldn't work for months.* | **funny, strange**

businesslike adj.

- VERBS **be, sound | become | remain | keep sth** *I'd rather keep the relationship strictly businesslike.*
- ADV. **very** *a very businesslike manner* | **strictly | quite**

businessman, businesswoman noun

- ADJ. **leading, prominent, successful | astute, clever, good, shrewd | millionaire, wealthy | small** *an association of small businessmen* (= who run small businesses) | **local** *charities supported by local businessmen* | **retired**

busy adj.

- VERBS **be, look, seem | become, get | keep, remain** *She needed to keep busy.* | **keep sb** *I've got enough work to keep you busy.*
- ADV. **awfully, extremely, really, terribly, very | exceptionally, particularly | desperately, frantically | a bit, fairly, pretty, quite, rather | constantly**
- PREP. **with** *She was busy with her make-up.*

butcher noun

- ADJ. **local | halal, kosher | master**
- ⇨ Note at JOB

butter noun

- ADJ. **fresh | rancid | melted** *Brush the pastry with a little melted butter.* | **clarified | salted, unsalted | brandy, cocoa, garlic, herb, peanut**
- QUANT. **knob, pat, slab** *He put a large knob of butter on the potatoes.*
- VERB + BUTTER **put on, spread (sth with)** *Put some butter on the crackers, please.* ◇ *He spread butter on the roll.* | **heat, melt, soften | beat (in), cream, mix, rub in** *Cream the butter and icing sugar together until light and fluffy.* ◇ *Rub the butter into the flour.* | **make**
- BUTTER + VERB **spread** *This butter doesn't spread very well.* | **melt** *The butter melted in the heat.*
- BUTTER + NOUN **sauce | dish, knife**
- PREP. **in~** *courgettes sautéed in butter*
- PHRASES **bread and butter**
- ⇨ Special page at FOOD

butter verb

- ADV. **generously, thickly | lightly** *lightly buttered toast*

butterfly noun

1 insect
- VERB + BUTTERFLY **collect**
- BUTTERFLY + VERB **flit, flutter, fly | emerge** *The butterfly emerged from the pupa.*
- BUTTERFLY + NOUN **wing**

2 swimming stroke
- ⇨ Note at STROKE

BUSINESS

Starting out …

set up	launch
an agency	an advertising campaign
a branch	an initiative
a company	an operation
a firm	a product
in business	a programme
an organization	a project
a project	a scheme
a venture	a takeover bid

operating at full capacity

Now we're in business …

do	make	manage	operate	run
the accounts	an appointment	a business	at full capacity	an airline
business	a bargain	a company	an airline	a bar
the catering	cutbacks	demand	a company	a business
a deal	a deal	the economy	a flight	a campaign
the marketing	an investment	a factory	the railways	a company
the paperwork	a killing	the finances		the economy
some research	a loan	a firm		a factory
the stocktaking	money	the funds		the finances
	a profit	a restaurant		a restaurant
	a transaction	a team		

Doing well …

boost		generate	
demand	spending	capital	profit
the economy	takings	cash	publicity
employment	tourism	demand	revenue
production	trade	employment	
profits	turnover	income	

making a fat profit

… and not so well …

a company goes under/goes to the wall
a deal falls apart/falls through
the euro falls to a new low
growth slows
negotiations break down
profits plummet/plunge
recession looms
sales are down
shares plummet/plunge

buttock *noun*

- ADJ. **firm | plump, rounded | scrawny**

button *noun*

1 for fastening clothes

- ADJ. **bottom, top** *The top button of his shirt was undone.* | **coat, shirt, etc.**
- VERB + BUTTON **do up, fasten | undo, unfasten | fumble with | lose** *My coat has lost a button.* | **rip off | sew on**
- BUTTON + VERB **be missing, come off, pop (off)** *There was a button missing from his shirt.*
- ⇨ Special page at CLOTHES

2 small switch

- ADJ. **on, start/starter | off, stop | control | fast forward, pause, play, rewind | alarm, panic** *She hit the alarm button as fast as she could.* | **mouse | self-destruct** *(often figurative)*
- VERB + BUTTON **click (on)** *(computing)*, **depress, hit, hold down, press, push** *Click the left mouse button twice.* | **keep your finger on | release, take your finger off**
- PHRASES **at the touch of a button** *The remote control allows you to change channel at the touch of a button.*
- ⇨ Special page at COMPUTER

buy *verb*

- ADV. **cheaply** *Old bikes can be bought quite cheaply.*
- VERB + BUY **can/can't afford to**
- PREP. **for** *He bought a car for his daughter.* ◇ *I bought it for £25.* **from** *I bought some books from a friend.*
- PHRASES **buy and sell** *She makes her living buying and selling antiques.* **money can/can't buy** *It's the best that money can buy.* ◇ *There are some things money can't buy.*

buyer *noun*

- ADJ. **potential, prospective | first-time** *The houses are small and inexpensive, ideal for first-time buyers.*
- VERB + BUYER **have | find, get** *They quickly found a buyer for their house.* | **sell sth to**
- PREP. **~ for** *Have you got a buyer for your house yet?*
- PHRASES **buyer beware** *In matters of second-hand cars, your motto should be 'buyer beware'* (= the buyer is responsible for checking the quality of the goods). **a buyer's market** *In a buyer's market, the commodity is plentiful and so its price is not high.*

buzz *noun*

- ADJ. **a high/high-pitched | low | loud | angry** *the angry buzz of a wasp* | **background** *the background buzz of conversation*
- VERB + BUZZ **hear**
- PREP. **~ of** *(figurative) I love the buzz* (= excitement) *of a big city.*
- PHRASES **a buzz of conversation, a buzz of excitement** *There was a buzz of excitement all round the room.*

buzzer *noun*

- VERB + BUZZER **press, sound** *Press the buzzer when you want to talk.*
- BUZZER + VERB **go (off), sound** *The buzzer went off at eight o'clock.*

bypass *noun*

- QUANT. **stretch** *That stretch of bypass will be finished by January.*
- VERB + BYPASS **build**
- PREP. **along a/the ~** *speeding along the bypass* **on a/the ~** *the traffic on the bypass* **round a/the ~** *We drove round the bypass to the airport.* | **~ around/round** *building a new bypass around the town*

Cc

cab noun

- ADJ. **black, yellow** *London black cab drivers* | **taxi** | **hackney, hansom** | **horse-drawn**
- VERB + CAB **go by, take** *Let's take a cab.* | **call (sb), get (sb), order (sb), phone for** *I'll call you a cab.* | **find** *We couldn't find a cab anywhere near.* | **catch, hail** *I tried to hail a cab but none of them would stop.* | **get into/out of** | **drive** | **pay for/off** | **share** *We decided to share a cab.*
- CAB + VERB **draw up, pull up** *The cab pulled up and they got out.* | **pick sb up, take sb** *I ordered a cab to take him home.*
- CAB + NOUN **driver** | **rank** | **fare** | **ride**
- PREP. **by ~** *I came by cab.* **in a/the ~** *The driver was sitting in his cab.*
- PHRASES **the back of a cab** *I left my umbrella in the back of the cab.*

cabbage noun

- ADJ. **green, red, white** | **savoy, spring** | **boiled, pickled, raw**
- VERB + CABBAGE **eat, have** | **boil, cook, prepare** | **chop, shred**
- CABBAGE + NOUN **leaf** | **patch**
⇨ Special page at FOOD

cabinet noun

1 (usually **Cabinet**) in government
- ADJ. **full** *There was a meeting of the full Cabinet this afternoon.* | **inner** *The inner Cabinet is to meet again today.* | **shadow** (= the most important members of the opposition party) | **war**
- VERB + CABINET **appoint, choose, form** | **enlarge, expand** | **reshuffle** *The prime minister reshuffled (= changed) his Cabinet yesterday.* | **enter, join** | **leave, quit** | **consult** | **force** *The defeat in the vote forced the Cabinet to change its policy on immigration.* | **persuade, urge**
- CABINET + VERB **meet** | **discuss sth**
- CABINET + NOUN **member, minister** | **meeting** | **reshuffle** *The affair led to a mid-term Cabinet reshuffle (= when the prime minister/president changes some of the people in the Cabinet).*

2 cupboard
- ADJ. **glass/glass-fronted** | **bathroom, bedside, kitchen** | **medicine** | **china, display, trophy** *a glass-fronted china cabinet* | **cocktail, drinks** | **filing** | **storage**
- PREP. **in a/the ~** *Past reports are kept in the filing cabinet in my office.*

cable noun

- ADJ. **electric, telephone** | **overhead, underground** | **fibre-optic**
- QUANT. **length** *a length of electric cable*
- VERB + CABLE **lay, run** *Roads have to be dug up to lay underground cables.* ◇ *Engineers plan to run the telephone cables under the river.* | **connect** *Connect the cable to the correct terminal.*
- CABLE + VERB **go, run** *a cable running under the road* | **connect sth** *new cables connecting major cities in Europe* | **carry sth** *These fibre-optic cables can carry telephone calls and computer data.*

cackle noun

- VERB + CACKLE **give, let out** *The old woman gave a cackle of laughter.* | **hear**
- PHRASES **a cackle of laughter**

cackle verb

- ADV. **loudly, wildly** *He cackled wildly at the thought.*
- PREP. **with** *to cackle with delight/glee/laughter/mirth/pleasure*

cadet noun

- ADJ. **army, military, naval, police** | **officer** *The military academy trains up to 2 000 officer cadets each year.*
- VERB + CADET **train**
- CADET + NOUN **corps**

cafe noun

- ADJ. **pavement, transport**
- VERB + CAFE **go to** | **manage, run** | **own**
- CAFE + VERB **serve sth** *a pavement cafe serving drinks and light meals*
- PREP. **in a/the ~**

cake noun

- ADJ. **home-made** | **moist, rich, sticky** *a rich, moist fruit cake* | **apple, carrot, chocolate, cream, fruit, seed, sponge** | **layer, sandwich** | **birthday, Christmas, wedding** *I blew out the candles on my birthday cake.*
- QUANT. **bit, piece, slice** *He cut her a slice of cake.*
- VERB + CAKE **eat, have** | **bake, make** | **decorate, ice, spread with sth** *Spread the cake with the butter cream.* | **cut** *Everyone cheered as the bride and groom cut the wedding cake.*
- CAKE + NOUN **crumbs** *She brushed some cake crumbs off her lap.* | **recipe** | **mix, mixture** *a packet of cake mix* ◇ *Pour the cake mixture into a greased and lined tin.* | **board, tin** | **shop, stall, stand**
⇨ Special page at FOOD

calculate verb

1 work out a number, etc.
- ADV. **accurately, exactly**
- PREP. **according to** *The amount is calculated according to the number of years you have paid into the scheme.* **at** *The sum involved was calculated at $82 million.*

2 guess
- ADV. **carefully, shrewdly** | **correctly** *He correctly calculated that the others would not dare fight back.*

calculating adj.

- VERBS **be**
- ADV. **coldly, coolly** *She caught a coolly calculating glint in the other woman's eye.*
- PHRASES **cold and calculating** *He has a cold and calculating mind.*

calculation noun

1 act of calculating/sum calculated
- ADJ. **accurate, correct, exact, precise** *an exact calculation of the amount spent so far* ◇ *If your calculations are correct, then we will make a large profit.* | **incorrect, wrong** *It turned out that our calculations were incorrect.* |

approximate, rough *Even a rough calculation shows that you have spent too much.* | complex, detailed | simple | quick, rapid | arithmetical, mathematical | economic, financial
● VERB + CALCULATION **do, make** *She did a rapid calculation in her head.* ◇ *We cannot make a precise calculation of the price until we have all the costs.*
● PHRASES **a method of calculation**
2 careful planning to get what you want
● ADJ. **cold, cool**
● QUANT. **act** *an act of cold calculation*

calculator *noun*

● ADJ. **desk, hand-held, pocket** | **electronic, programmable** | **advanced** *Exam candidates are not allowed to use advanced calculators with database capability.*
● CALCULATOR + NOUN **display**

calendar *noun*

● ADJ. **busy, full** *The group has a busy sporting calendar.* | **golfing, racing, social, sporting, etc.**
● PREP. **in/on a/the ~** *the most important event in the year's golfing calendar*

calf *noun*

● ADJ. **bull, heifer** | **beef, dairy, veal** | **weaned**
● VERB + CALF **produce** *A dairy cow needs to produce a calf each year.* | **rear** *These calves are reared for beef.* | **graze** *The calves are grazed intensively during their first season.*
● CALF + VERB **graze, suckle**
● PREP. **in/with ~** *Their prize cow is in calf* (= pregnant).

call *noun*

1 on the telephone
● ADJ. **phone/telephone** | **long** | **quick, short** *I'll just make a quick phone call.* | **local** | **international, long-distance, trunk** | **direct-dialled** | **incoming** | **outgoing** | **emergency** | **anonymous, hoax, nuisance, obscene, unsolicited** | **wake-up** *I ordered a wake-up call for 6.30 the next morning.* ◇ (figurative) *Last night's defeat should be a wake-up call for the team.*
● VERB + CALL **give sb, make, place** *Give us a call to say when you have arrived.* ◇ *She asked her secretary to place a call through to England.* | **get, have, receive** | **answer, take** *I'll take the call upstairs.* | **return** *I left a message but he didn't return my call.* | **put through, transfer** *Ask the receptionist to put your call through to my room.*
● CALL + NOUN **box**
● PREP. **~ for** *Were there any calls for me while I was out?* **~ from** *You had a call from Fred.* **~ to** *I made a call to a friend in London.*
2 sound to attract attention
● ADJ. **loud** | **distinctive** *the distinctive call of the cuckoo* | **plaintive** *the bird's plaintive call* | **distress** | **bird** | **clarion, rallying** (both figurative) *This election is a clarion call for our country to face the challenges of the new era.*
● VERB + CALL **let out** | **hear**
● PREP. **~ for** *a call for help*
3 short visit
● ADJ. **business, courtesy, social**
● VERB + CALL **make, pay (sb)** *The doctor has several calls to make this morning.*
● PREP. **on a ~** *She's out on a call.* | **~ on** *Her first call was on the local library.*
● PHRASES **first/last/next port of call** *Our first port of call* (= the first place we went to) *was the chemist's.*
4 request/demand
● ADJ. **renewed, repeated** | **last** *This is the last call for*

passengers travelling on British Airways flight 199 to Rome.* | **strike**
● VERB + CALL **issue** | **renew** *Drink-drive campaigners have renewed their call for the introduction of random breath tests.* | **answer, heed, respond to** *Around 10 000 workers heeded the union's strike call.* | **reject**
● PREP. **~ for** *The charity issued a call for donations to assist victims of the earthquake.*
● PHRASES **a call to arms** (= a strong request for people to fight in the army) (figurative) *The president's speech was a call to arms to restore the vitality of the American dream.*

call *verb*

● ADV. **commonly** | **originally** | **collectively** *a range of very small organisms, collectively called nanoplankton* | **variously** *a plant variously called 'cow parsley' and 'Queen Anne's lace'* | **aptly** | **quaintly** | **euphemistically** *The prison is euphemistically called a 'rehabilitation centre'.*
● PREP. **by** *We usually call him by his nickname.*

calm *noun*

1 peaceful situation/manner/feeling
● ADJ. **apparent** *Under his apparent calm lay real anxiety.* | **inner** *the pursuit of inner calm* | **uneasy** | **forced, studied** *With a forced calm she said, 'How do you know?'* | **dead** *She felt not fear, but a kind of dead calm.* | **deadly, icy** *'I'm calling the police,' he stated with deadly calm.*
● VERB + CALM **appeal for, call for** *The government appealed for calm after the riots broke out.*
● CALM + VERB **descend, settle** *After the bomb, an uneasy calm settled on the city.*
● PHRASES **a period of calm**
2 at sea
● ADJ. **dead, flat** *Seals basked on boulders in a flat calm.*

calm *adj.*

1 not worried or angry
● VERBS **appear, be, feel, look, seem, sound** *I may have appeared calm, but I certainly did not feel it!* | **become** | **keep, remain, stay** *Sit down and keep calm!* ◇ *The pilot urged the passengers to remain calm.* | **keep sb** *Keep the patient calm.*
● ADV. **extremely, remarkably, very** *You seem remarkably calm.* | **completely, perfectly, utterly** *Her voice was firm and perfectly calm.* | **fairly, pretty, quite** | **apparently, outwardly** | **curiously, strangely** *The pain had receded and he felt curiously calm.* | **reassuringly** *The voice sounded reassuringly calm.*
● PREP. **about** *She seemed pretty calm about it.*
● PHRASES **cool, calm and collected** *He remained at all times cool, calm and collected.*
2 not rough or stormy
● VERBS **be, look** | **become**
● ADV. **absolutely, dead, flat, perfectly** *The sea was dead calm.* ◇ *flat calm conditions* | **fairly, quite, relatively**

calorie *noun*

● ADJ. **empty** *Sweets and biscuits have a lot of empty calories in them.*
● VERB + CALORIE **contain, have** | **consume, eat** | **burn (off)** *You need to exercise more to burn off the calories.* | **count, watch** *Some people count calories all their lives.* ◇ *I'm trying to watch my calories at the moment.*
● CALORIE + NOUN **content, intake** *foods with a high calorie content*
● PHRASES **high/low calorie** *a low calorie drink* **high/low in calories** *Fruit is relatively low in calories.*

camera *noun*

- ADJ. **3D, automatic, box, cine, closed-circuit, digital, electronic, infra-red, microfilm, movie, pinhole, polaroid, SLR, television/TV, underwater, video** | **compact** | **security, surveillance** | **hand-held, mobile** | **candid**
- VERB + CAMERA **focus, point** *Simply point your camera at the subject and press the button.* | **pose for** *The royal couple posed for the cameras.* | **brave, face** *He couldn't bring himself to face the cameras and left by a back exit.* | **mount** *The film was taken by a camera mounted on a hang-glider.* | **install** *Closed-circuit cameras have been installed throughout the building.* | **set up** *The crews have been setting up their cameras.* | **load**
- CAMERA + VERB **film sth** | **catch sth** *The camera has caught the expression on the Queen's face beautifully.* | **focus on** | **roll** *The director gave the signal and the cameras rolled.* | **click** *She stepped onto the balcony and a thousand cameras clicked.*
- CAMERA + NOUN **crew, team** | **assistant** | **bag, equipment, lens, tripod** | **angle, position** | **work**
- PREP. **in front of the ~s** *He played his first match at Everton in front of the TV cameras.* **off ~** *The incident occurred off camera* (= was not filmed). **on ~** *The moment was caught on camera.*

camouflage *noun*

- ADJ. **effective, excellent, good, perfect** | **protective** | **army** *He was wearing army camouflage.*
- VERB + CAMOUFLAGE **act as, provide** *The animal's markings provide effective camouflage.* | **wear**

camouflage *verb*

- PREP. **with** *They camouflaged their truck with fallen pine branches.*
- PHRASES **be carefully/heavily/well camouflaged** *The vehicles were all well camouflaged.*

camp *noun*

1 in tents/huts
- ADJ. **makeshift, temporary** | **holiday, summer** | **base** *The mountaineers set up their base camp at the foot of the mountain.* | **transit** | **gypsy, travellers'** | **army, military** | **training**
- VERB + CAMP **make, pitch, set up** *We pitched camp just outside the woods.* | **break, strike** *We broke camp early the next morning.* | **leave**
- CAMP + NOUN **fire** (also **campfire**) *sitting round the campfire* **site** (also **campsite**)
- PREP. **at a/the ~** *The children are spending a week at a summer camp.*

2 prison, etc.
- ADJ. **concentration, detention, internment, labour, prison, prisoner-of-war** | **death, extermination** | **refugee** *the appalling conditions in the refugee camps*
- PREP. **in a/the ~** *She spent five years in a labour camp.*

3 group with shared beliefs
- ADJ. **hostile, opposing, rebel, rival** | **ideological, political** | **armed** *The region split into two armed camps.*
- VERB + CAMP **switch** *a politician who switches camp when it suits him* | **divide into, split into**
- PREP. **in a/the ~** *people in both main political camps*
- PHRASES **have a foot in both camps** (= show loyalty to two different groups) *He can unite the party because he has a foot in both camps.*

campaign *noun*

- ADJ. **big, huge, major, massive** | **lengthy, long, long-running, sustained** | **brief** | **effective, successful** | **unsuccessful** | **determined, intensive, strong, vigorous** | **bitter, fierce, vicious** | **concerted, orchestrated** *a care-*

---

fully orchestrated campaign against striking workers | **joint** | **official, public** | **local, international, national, nationwide, worldwide** | **one-man/one-woman, personal** *She has fought a one-woman campaign for ten years about the lack of childcare provision in the town.* | **election, electoral, leadership, political, presidential, re-election, referendum** | **advertising, marketing, promotional, sales** | **propaganda, publicity, public relations** | **media, poster, press, television/TV** | **anti-corruption, anti-drug, anti-smoking, etc.** | **protest** | **awareness** *a health awareness campaign to promote a healthy lifestyle* | **lobbying** | **fund-raising** | **literacy** | **recruitment** | **air, bombing, guerrilla, military** *the terrorists' bombing campaign* | **hate, terror/terrorist, dirty tricks, smear, whispering** *Her political opponents ran a whispering campaign against her.*
- VERB + CAMPAIGN **launch, mount, start** *The company launched a huge advertising campaign.* | **conduct, fight, organize, run, wage** *People have criticized the way in which she conducted her election campaign.* | **lead, manage, spearhead** *She led a successful campaign against the closure of the library.* | **take part in** | **intensify, step up** *The government has intensified the military campaign against the rebels.*
- CAMPAIGN + VERB **begin, get underway, start** *The general election campaign gets underway today.* | **be aimed at sb/sth** *a concerted campaign aimed at educating young people about the dangers of drugs* | **aim to** *The campaign aims to inform the public of the dangers of this disease.* | **call for sth, demand sth** | **fail to** *The campaign failed to achieve its objectives.*
- CAMPAIGN + NOUN **manager, team** | **strategy** | **issue** *Education has become an important campaign issue.* | **trail** *election candidates on the campaign trail* (= travelling around the country campaigning)
- PREP. **during a/the ~** *They met regularly during the campaign.* | **~ against** *a fierce campaign against hunting* **~ by** *the political campaign by the Labour Party* **~ for** *the campaign for racial equality*
- PHRASES **a plan of campaign** *After sliding in the opinion polls, the party had to rethink its plan of campaign.*

campaign *verb*

- ADV. **actively, hard, strongly, tirelessly, vigorously** *We will campaign hard for an end to the ivory trade.* | **effectively, successfully** *Local people have successfully campaigned against the building.* | **openly, publicly**
- PREP. **against** *Local communities are campaigning against the dumping of toxic waste.* **for** *We have campaigned for better rural transport.* **on** *The group campaigns on a range of environmental issues.* **on behalf of** *campaigning on behalf of the British consumer*

campaigner *noun*

- ADJ. **effective, good, great, successful** | **active, tireless, vigorous** | **experienced, seasoned, veteran** | **leading, prominent**
- PREP. **~ against** *a prominent campaigner against drugs* **~ for** *an active campaigner for animal rights* **~ on behalf of** *a veteran campaigner on behalf of the disabled*

campus *noun*

- ADJ. **large** | **small** | **college, university**
- VERB + CAMPUS **have** *De Montfort University has campuses in Milton Keynes and Leicester.*
- CAMPUS + NOUN **novel**
- PREP. **at a/the ~** *Students at the Belfast campus have access to excellent sports facilities.* **off ~** *They moved off campus to share a flat in the town.* **on ~** *She lives on campus.*

can *noun*

- ADJ. **metal, tin** | **rusty** | **food** *The floor was littered*

with rusty food cans. | 300g, 250ml, 11oz, etc. *a 200g can of tuna* | beer, coke | jerry, petrol | oil | paint | watering | aerosol, spray
• VERB + CAN **come in** *This special type of milk comes in a can.* | **open** *We opened a can of sardines for lunch.* | **drain, empty** *She drained her can of beer and threw it away.* ◊ *He emptied a can of beans into the pan.* | **drink, sip at** | **fill** *He was filling a jerry can with petrol from the pump.* | **recycle**
• CAN + NOUN **opener** (also **can-opener**)
• PREP. **in a/the~** | **~of** *cans of oil*

canal *noun*

• ADJ. **irrigation** | **ship**
• VERB + CANAL **build, dig**
• CANAL + NOUN **barge, boat** | **bank** | **towpath**
• PREP. **along a/the~** *The barge moved slowly along the canal.* **on a/the~** *sailing on the canal*

cancellation *noun*

• ADJ. **last-minute** | **sudden** | **outright** *They opted for rescheduling rather than outright cancellation.*
• VERB + CANCELLATION **have** *We may be able to offer you some tickets if we have any cancellations.* | **make** *Cancellations must be made in writing.* | **cause** *Heavy seas can cause cancellation of ferry services.*
• CANCELLATION + NOUN **charge, fee**

cancer *noun*

• ADJ. **breast, cervical, lung, prostate, skin, etc.**
• VERB + CANCER **have, suffer from** | **contract, get, develop** | **cause** | **screen sb for** *Most of the women employees have now been screened for breast cancer.* | **diagnose** | **die from/of**
• CANCER + VERB **spread** *The cancer has spread to his stomach.*
• CANCER + NOUN **cell** | **patient, sufferer, victim** | **risk** *The cancer risk among smokers was found to be higher.* | **research** | **drug, treatment**
• PHRASES **a battle/struggle against cancer** *He died after an 18-month battle against cancer.*
⇨ Special page at ILLNESS

candid *adj.*

• VERBS **be**
• ADV. **very** | **extraordinarily, remarkably** | **perfectly, quite** | **less than**
• PREP. **about** *He was quite candid about the way the case had been handled.* **with** *I felt she was being less than candid with me.*

candidate *noun*

• ADJ. **potential, prospective** *Prospective parliamentary candidates met party leaders last week.* | **likely, possible** *She's a likely candidate for promotion.* | **good, ideal, suitable** *There were no suitable candidates for the position.* | **unsuitable** | **successful** *The successful candidate will be fluent in French and German.* | **congressional, ministerial, parliamentary, presidential** | **Conservative, Democratic, etc.**
• VERB + CANDIDATE **put yourself forward as, stand as** *She decided to stand as a candidate in the union elections.* | **field, nominate, put up, run** *Our organization is putting up five candidates in the elections.* | **back, support, vote for** | **choose, select** *The committee will select the best candidate for the job.* | **reject** *We rejected most of the candidates as unsuitable.*
• PREP. **~for** *She was the only candidate for the post.*

candle *noun*

• ADJ. **lighted** | **flickering**
• VERB + CANDLE **light** | **blow out, snuff (out)**
• CANDLE + VERB **burn** | **flicker** | **go out**
• CANDLE + NOUN **flame**

cannabis *noun*

• QUANT. **trace** *Traces of cannabis were found in the pilot's blood.*
• VERB + CANNABIS **smoke** | **grow**
• CANNABIS + NOUN **leaf, plant, resin**
⇨ Note at DRUG (for more verbs and nouns)

cannon *noun*

• ADJ. **water** *Riot police used water cannon and tear gas to disperse the crowd.*
• VERB + CANNON **load** | **aim** | **fire, shoot**
• CANNON + VERB **boom, roar, thunder** *Cannons thundered to their right.* | **fire (sth)** *As the king stepped ashore the cannons fired a salute.*
• CANNON + NOUN **ball, shell** | **fire, shot** | **crew** | **fodder** (figurative) *The foot soldiers were just used as cannon fodder* (= considered not as people but as material to be used up in war).

canoe *noun*

• ADJ. **dugout, open**
• VERB + CANOE **paddle**
• PREP. **by~** *We crossed the lake by canoe.*

canopy *noun*

• ADJ. **dense, thick** *a thick canopy of branches* | **forest, leafy, tree**
• VERB + CANOPY **form** *The trees formed a leafy canopy above their heads.*
• PREP. **beneath/under a/the~** | **~of** *sitting beneath a canopy of branches*

cap *noun*

1 soft flat hat
• ADJ. **flat, peaked** | **cloth** | **baseball, bathing, cricket, forage, school, shower, skull, swimming**
• CAP + NOUN **badge**
⇨ Special page at CLOTHES
2 covering for the end/top of sth
• ADJ. **filler, hub, lens** | **screw** *The bottle has a screw cap.*
• VERB + CAP **put on, screw on** *Put the cap back on the pen.* | **remove, take off, unscrew**

capability *noun*

• ADJ. **enormous** | **limited** *The company's manufacturing capability is quite limited.* | **potential** | **proven** *the proven capability of this technology* | **human** *beyond the scope of human capability* | **intellectual, mental** | **technical, technological** | **manufacturing, production** | **research** | **computing, design, graphics, multimedia, networking, printing, processing, sound, video** | **defence, fighting, military, missile, nuclear, offensive, weapons**
• VERB + CAPABILITY **have** *She has the capability to become a very fine actress.* | **increase** *The government wants to increase its military capability.* | **lose**
• PREP. **beyond your~** *Organizing a whole department is beyond his capability.* **within your~** *I'm sure that your new job is well within your capabilities.* | **~for** *her capability for making sensible decisions*

capable adj.

1 having a lot of skill
- VERBS **be, seem** *She seems very capable.*
- ADV. **extremely, highly, quite, very** *He has proved himself an extremely capable manager.*

2 capable of able to do sth
- VERBS **appear, be, feel, look, prove, seem | become | believe sb, consider sb** *She could hardly believe him capable of such kindness.*
- ADV. **fully, more than, perfectly, quite, well** *She is more than capable of looking after herself.* | **barely, hardly, scarcely** *He was barely capable of writing his own name.* | **reasonably | clearly, obviously | potentially, theoretically | physically** *He was not physically capable of climbing out of the window.*

capacity noun

1 amount held/produced
- ADJ. **high, large** *a high capacity electric pump* ◇ *large capacity disk drives* | **limited, small | maximum, total** *a total capacity of 50 litres* | **excess, spare** *spare capacity in the health service* | **economic, productive | earning** *The qualification should increase my earning capacity.* | **carrying, nuclear, seating, storage | engine, lung**
- VERB + CAPACITY **have | be filled/packed to** *The theatre was filled to capacity* (= was full) *for every performance.* | **expand, increase | reduce**
- CAPACITY + NOUN **audience, crowd**
- PHRASES **operate/work at full capacity** (= to produce the maximum amount possible)

2 ability
- ADJ. **amazing, enormous, great, remarkable | limited | innate, natural** *Children have an innate capacity to understand language.* | **intellectual, mental | human** *the human capacity for compassion*
- VERB + CAPACITY **have | lose** *She seems to have lost the capacity to enjoy herself.* | **increase | reduce, restrict**
- PREP. **beyond your~** *This maths is beyond the capacity of most school children.* **within your~** *The mountain walk is well within the capacity of most fit people.* | **~ for** *her amazing capacity for organization*

3 official position
- ADJ. **official | personal, private, unofficial, voluntary | professional | acting, caretaker | advisory | judicial**
- VERB + CAPACITY **act in, work in** *I have worked in an advisory capacity with many hospitals.*
- PREP. **in your~** *In my capacity as president, I would like to thank Jack for his hard work.*

capital noun

1 money used to start a business, etc.
- ADJ. **fixed, starting | working | foreign, private | equity, investment, share | risk, venture**
- VERB + CAPITAL **have** *We don't have enough capital to buy new premises.* | **accumulate, attract, borrow, generate, raise** *He had various ideas on how to raise capital for the project.* | **invest, provide, put (up), sink** *The company has put a lot of capital into the project.* ◇ *We can't expect the government to put up the capital.* ◇ *He sank vast amounts of capital in the venture.* | **free up, release, unlock | tie up** *Our capital is all tied up in property.*
- CAPITAL + NOUN **assets, goods, resources, stock | costs, expenditure, investment, outlay, repayment, spending | accumulation, growth | account | grant | project** *investment in major capital projects* | **gain, loss | flows, inflow, movement, outflow, receipt | value** *the capital value of the property* | **market**
- PHRASES **capital intensive** *capital intensive industries* **an injection of capital** *Inner city areas require a large injection of capital.* **a return on your capital** *Investors want an immediate return on their capital.*

⇨ Special page at BUSINESS

2 city
- ADJ. **great, major** *The department store has branches in all major capitals.* | **British, Japanese, etc. | foreign | provincial, regional, state | cultural, financial, etc.**
- PREP. **in a/the~** *the fast pace of life in the capital* | **~ of**
- PHRASES **... capital of the world** *Las Vegas is the gambling capital of the world.*

capitalism noun

- ADJ. **advanced, contemporary, late, modern | global, world | competitive, consumer, entrepreneurial, free market, industrial, laissez-faire, liberal, monopoly, popular, state, welfare**
- VERB + CAPITALISM **fight (against), protest against, struggle against | abolish, overthrow, replace**
- PREP. **under~** *a study of the development of agriculture under capitalism*
- PHRASES **the advance/rise of capitalism, the fall of capitalism** *predicting the fall of world capitalism*

capsule noun

- VERB + CAPSULE **swallow, take** *To avoid capture by the enemy, he swallowed a cyanide capsule.*
- CAPSULE + VERB **contain sth** *capsules containing a poisonous drug*

captain noun

⇨ Note at RANK

captive noun

- VERB + CAPTIVE **free, release** *The terrorists will only release their captives if they get what they want.*

captive adj.

- VERBS **be | take sb** *He was taken captive on the border.* | **hold sb, keep sb** *She was held captive in a castle.*

captivity noun

- VERB + CAPTIVITY **hold/keep sb in** *The children were held in captivity until British soldiers entered the village.* | **bring/take sb into | free/release sb from** *The prisoners were released from captivity after three months.* | **escape from**
- PREP. **during (sb's)~** *She was tortured many times during her captivity.* **in~** *trout bred in captivity*

capture noun

- VERB + CAPTURE **avoid, escape, evade** *The refugees evaded capture by hiding in the forest.* | **lead to** *This information led to the capture of the murderer.*

capture verb

- ADV. **perfectly** *That description captures perfectly the feeling of being invisible.* | **brilliantly, neatly**
- VERB + CAPTURE **attempt to, try to | manage to | fail to** *The exhibition on India fails to capture the great diversity of this fascinating country.*

car noun

- ADJ. **fast | new | second-hand, used** *a used car salesman* | **veteran, vintage | private** *The government wants more people to use public transport instead of private cars.* | **diesel, electric, motor, petrol | estate, hatchback, saloon, sports | armoured, Panda, patrol, police, squad, unmarked** *Police in an unmarked car had been following the stolen vehicle for several minutes.* | **racing, rally, stock | company, hire | getaway** *The robbers aban-*

doned their getaway car in Sealand Road. | **parked** *There was a line of parked cars in front of the building.*
- VERB + CAR **go/travel by** | **drive** | **have, own, run** *It's very expensive to run a car these days.* | **take** *It's too far to walk. I'll take the car.* | **get in/into, pile into** *He got in the car and they drove off.* ◇ *The kids all piled into the car.* | **get out of** | **get out** *You lock up the house and I'll get the car out.* | **stop** | **back, reverse** | **overtake, pass** | **lose control of** *I lost control of the car and it spun off the road.* | **leave, park** | **abandon, dump** | **build, make, manufacture, produce** | **repair, service, work on** | **take in** *I've got to take the car in for service.* | **wash** | **hire** | **break into, steal**
- CAR + VERB **start** *Despite the cold, the car started first time.* | **run on sth** *cars that run on diesel* | **do sth** *The car does 55 miles per gallon.* ◇ *The car was doing over 100 miles an hour.* | **pull out, turn out** *What cheek! That car pulled out right in front of me!* | **drive off, pull away** | **overtake sb/sth, pass sb/sth** | **accelerate** | **slow down** | **come to a halt, draw up, pull up, stop** | **skid, spin** *Her car skidded on a patch of ice.* | **break down, stall** | **collide with sth, crash, hit sth, leave the road** *His car hit a van coming in the opposite direction.*
- CAR + NOUN **boot, door, engine, horn, key, phone, tyre, window** *a car boot sale* (= an outdoor sale where people sell things from the backs of their cars) | **park, parking** *There's not enough car parking in the town centre.* | **driver** | **dealer, salesman, showroom** | **accident, crash** | **wash** | **tax** | **ferry**
- PREP. **by ~** *They take the children to school by car.* **in a/the ~** *I'll wait for you in the car.*
- PHRASES **cars on the roads** *The number of cars on the roads is increasing all the time.* **a make/model of car**

caravan *noun*

- ADJ. **horse-drawn, motor** | **gypsy** | **holiday, touring**
- VERB + CARAVAN **pull, tow** | **live in, stay in**
- CARAVAN + VERB **park** *The local farmer lets holiday caravans park on his land.*
- CARAVAN + NOUN **holiday** | **park, site** | **rally**

carbohydrate *noun*

1 substance in food
- VERB + CARBOHYDRATE **be rich/high in, contain** *Cashew nuts are rich in carbohydrate.*
- CARBOHYDRATE + NOUN **content** | **diet** *a high carbohydrate diet*
- PHRASES **a source of carbohydrate**

2 food
- ADJ. **simple** | **complex** *complex carbohydrates such as pasta* | **refined** | **unrefined**

carbon *noun*

- ADJ. **pure** *Diamonds are crystals of pure carbon.* | **organic** | **radioactive** | **activated**
- CARBON + NOUN **content** *iron with a high carbon content* | **atom, isotope** | **fibre**
- PHRASES **a form of carbon**

carbon dioxide *noun*

- VERB + CARBON DIOXIDE **absorb, take in** *Trees absorb carbon dioxide and produce oxygen.* | **emit, give out, produce, release** | **form, give** *How is carbon dioxide formed?* ◇ *Coke burns with oxygen to give carbon dioxide.*
- CARBON DIOXIDE + NOUN **emissions**
- PHRASES **a build-up of carbon dioxide, emissions of carbon dioxide**

card *noun*

1 giving information
- ADJ. **business, calling, visiting** | **appointment, invi-**

tation | **identity, membership** | **index, record, report** | **flash** (also **flashcard**) | **swipe** | **smart**
- PREP. **on a/the ~** *She wrote the main points of her speech on index cards.*

2 used to pay/get money
- ADJ. **plastic** *He had a wallet full of plastic cards.* | **cash, charge, cheque** (**guarantee**)**, credit, debit** | **phone** | **ration**
- VERB + CARD **pay by, put sth on, use** *She paid for her holiday by credit card.* ◇ *I'll put the meal on my card.* | **accept, take** *The restaurant accepts all major credit cards.* | **issue** (**sb with**) *The bank hasn't issued me with a cheque card yet.*
- CARD + NOUN **number** | **holder** | **fraud**

3 greetings card
- ADJ. **greeting/greetings** | **birthday, Christmas, get-well, sympathy**
- VERB + CARD **give sb, send sb** | **sign, write** *Everyone at work signed a card for her.* | **get, receive**

4 used for a game
- ADJ. **playing** | **winning** | **court, picture, trump** (*figurative*) *This defender's ability to score vital goals has often proved a trump card.* | **wild**
- QUANT. **deck, pack**
- VERB + CARD **cut, deal, shuffle** | **pick** '*Pick a card,*' *said the conjurer.* | **hold** (*often figurative*) *The kidnappers hold all the cards* (= are in control of the situation).
- CARD + NOUN **game, player, table**

5 cards game
- QUANT. **game**
- VERB + CARDS **play** *We play cards every Friday night.* | **lose/win at** *He always wins at cards.*
- CARD + NOUN **game**

NOTE
Playing cards

two, three, etc. of ~s
   the four of hearts
jack, queen, king, ace of ~s
   the ace of spades
high, low ~
   a low club
black, red ~
   You can't put a red five on a red six.
pick up, take ~
   Why didn't you pick up the king?
have, hold ~
   He knew his opponents held only spades and diamonds.
lay/put down, play ~
   She put down a joker.
lead ~
   You should have led a high spade.
draw ~
   Use your ace and king to draw the trumps.
trump ~
   He trumped my ace!
~ be trumps/wild/high
   Spades are trumps.
   Let's play again. This time twos are wild, aces high.
~ trick (in games like bridge and whist)
   We needed to take three more spade tricks.
on a/the ~
   You can play either a nine or a jack on a ten.

---

cardboard *noun*

- ADJ. **thick** | **thin** | **stiff** | **corrugated**
- QUANT. **piece, sheet** *a sheet of stiff black cardboard*

● VERB + CARDBOARD **be made from/(out) of, make sth from/out of** | **cut**
● CARDBOARD + NOUN **box, carton, tube** | **cut-out** *There was a life-size cardboard cut-out of Elvis Presley in the shop window.*

cardigan *noun*

● ADJ. **wool/woollen/woolly** | **hand-knitted**
● VERB + CARDIGAN **knit**
⇨ Special page at CLOTHES

care *noun*

1 looking after sb/sth
● ADJ. **good, great** *He loved his books and took great care of them.* | **loving, tender** *She's still very frail and will need lots of tender loving care.* | **private** | **voluntary** | **constant, full-time, round-the-clock** | **continuing, long-term** | **short-term, temporary** | **daily, day-to-day, routine** | **intensive** *Last night she was critically ill in intensive care.* ◊ *an intensive care unit* | **clinical, emergency, health, medical, nursing, patient** | **hospital, inpatient, institutional, residential** | **day, non-hospital, outpatient** | **community** | **domestic, domiciliary, home, home-based** | **primary, secondary, tertiary** | **antenatal, dental, psychiatric** | **palliative** | **formal, informal** *The couple relied on informal care from relatives.* | **foster** | **public** *children in public care* | **pastoral, spiritual** | **client, customer** | **hair, skin**
● VERB + CARE **take** *He left his job to take care of his sick wife.* ◊ *I'll take care of hiring the car.* | **provide (sb with)** | **need, require** | **receive** | **take sb into** *The boys were taken into care when their parents died.*
● CARE + NOUN **services** | **centre, home, unit** | **manager, worker** | **management** | **plan, policy, programme** | **allowance** | **needs, order**
● PREP. **in ~** *He had been in foster care since he was five.* **in sb's ~** *You won't come to any harm while you're in their care.* ◊ *Many historic sites are in the care of the National Trust.* **under the ~ of** *He's under the care of Dr Parks.* | **~of**
● PHRASES **the quality/standard of care**

2 attention/thought given to sth
● ADJ. **extreme, good, great** *Great care should be taken to ensure that the equipment is clean.* | **extra, special** | **infinite, the utmost** | **exquisite, meticulous, painstaking, scrupulous** *The little girl was writing her name with painstaking care.* | **exaggerated, excessive** *He takes excessive care of his appearance.* | **due** (*formal*), **proper, reasonable** *The householder has a duty to take reasonable care for the visitor's safety.*
● VERB + CARE **exercise, take**
● PREP. **with ~** *A label on the box read: 'Glass—handle with care'.* **without ~** *He was found guilty of driving without due care and attention.*

care *verb*

● ADV. **deeply, genuinely, a lot, passionately, really, truly** | **hardly, not greatly, not much, not particularly** *He hardly cares what he does any more.* ◊ *I don't know which she chose, nor do I greatly care.*
● PREP. **about** *He really cares about the environment.* **for** *You genuinely care for him, don't you?*
● PHRASES **be past caring** *I'm past caring what he does* (= I don't care any more).

career *noun*

1 series of jobs that a person has
● ADJ. **long** | **brief, short** | **brilliant, distinguished, glittering, good, great, successful** *He had a distinguished career as a diplomat.* | **promising** | **flagging** *He did a film for Hollywood to boost his flagging career.* |

chosen *She achieved a lot in her chosen career.* | **academic, acting, diplomatic, literary, medical, military, musical, political, sporting, teaching** | **playing, professional, recording, stage** *the album that launched his recording career*
● VERB + CAREER **build, carve out, have, make, pursue** *He made a good career for himself in football.* ◊ *She pursued a successful career in medicine.* | **begin, embark on, launch, start (out on)** *young actors just starting out on their careers* | **boost** | **abandon, give up** | **cut short, end, ruin, wreck** *a car crash which wrecked his career* | **resume** | **change**
● CAREER + VERB **last sth, span sth** *Her stage career spans sixty years.* | **start, take off** | **be over, end**
● CAREER + NOUN **careers advice/guidance/information, careers adviser/officer, careers service** | **break** *a career break to have children* | **advancement, development, ladder, path, progression** *a move higher up the career ladder* | **choice, move** *a smart career move* | **opportunities, prospects, structure** *The profession has no clear career structure.* | **civil servant, diplomat, soldier** | **girl, woman**
● PREP. **during/throughout your ~** *She won many awards during her acting career.* | **~ in** *a career in computers* **~ with** *a brilliant career with the Royal Ballet*
● PHRASES **the peak/height of your career** *She was at the peak of her playing career when she injured herself.* **a change of career**

2 period of your life spent working/doing sth
● ADJ. **chequered, colourful, turbulent, varied** *He has had a somewhat chequered career.* | **school, working** *She started her working career as a waitress.*
● VERB + CAREER **have** | **start**

career *verb*

● ADV. **wildly** *A sudden gust caught her hat and sent it careering wildly down the road.* | **around** *children careering around the playground*
● PREP. **down, into, off, through** *The lorry careered off the road and hit a tree.*

careful *adj.*

● VERBS **be** | **make sb** *Bitter past experience had made her careful of what she confided to Nadia.*
● ADV. **awfully, doubly, especially, extra, extremely, particularly, really, specially, very** *Be extra careful when walking along country roads.* | **a bit, a little, fairly, quite** | **scrupulously**
● PREP. **about** *She was quite careful about how she spoke to him.* **of** *He's very careful of his reputation.* **with** *She's extremely careful with money.*

careless *adj.*

● VERBS **be** | **become, get, grow** *She had begun to grow careless.* | **make sb** *Boredom made him careless.*
● ADV. **extremely, very** | **a bit, a little, rather** *a rather careless mistake* | **notoriously**
● PREP. **about** *She's careless about her spelling.* **of** *When performing his stunts he was notoriously careless of his own safety.* **with** *He's very careless with money.*

caress *noun*

● ADJ. **gentle, light** *the gentle caress of his fingers* | **warm**

caress *verb*

● ADV. **gently, lightly** *His fingers gently caressed her cheek.*

cargo noun

- ADJ. **big, bulk, heavy, large | small | precious, valuable** *a precious cargo of antiques* | **deadly** *The terrorists parked the van with its deadly cargo in a dark alleyway.* | **dry** *dry cargo, such as fruit* | **human** *The boats discharged their human cargo a little way from the shore.*
- VERB + CARGO **carry | load, take on** *The ship stopped to take on a cargo of fruit.* | **discharge, unload | handle** *The port handles cargo from all over Europe.*
- CARGO + NOUN **aircraft, boat, carrier, plane, ship, vessel | bay, hold | handler, handling**

caricature noun

1 funny drawing of sb
- VERB + CARICATURE **draw** *She draws caricatures of well-known politicians.*
- PREP. **~ of** *a caricature of Sherlock Holmes*

2 exaggerated description of sb/sth
- ADJ. **crude, grotesque**
- VERB + CARICATURE **give** *The film gives a crude caricature of African history.*
- PREP. **~ of**

carpet noun

1 material for covering floors
- ADJ. **deep-pile, soft, thick | threadbare, worn | patterned, plain | woven | oriental, Persian | fitted, wall-to-wall | flying, magic | red** *(figurative) I didn't expect to get the red carpet treatment* (= be treated like an important person).
- QUANT. **roll**
- VERB + CARPET **make, weave | fit, lay** *I'm having the carpets fitted today.* | **roll back/up, take up | beat**
- CARPET + NOUN **design | tile** *They grey vinyl floor gave way to carpet tiles.* | **fitter | cleaner, sweeper**
- PREP. **on a/the ~** *The cat curled up on the carpet.*

2 thick layer of sth that covers the ground
- ADJ. **deep, thick**
- VERB + CARPET **form** *The leaves formed a carpet under the trees.*
- PREP. **~ of** *a deep carpet of snow*

carpeted adj.

- VERBS **be**
- ADV. **richly, softly, thickly** *the quiet, thickly carpeted corridors* | **fully, throughout** *a comfortable, fully carpeted bedroom* ◇ *The house is carpeted throughout.*
- PREP. **with** *(figurative) The churchyard was thickly carpeted with snowdrops and primroses.*

carriage noun

1 vehicle pulled by horses
- ADJ. **horse-drawn, open**
- VERB + CARRIAGE **ride in | drive | climb into, get into | alight from, get out of, step out of**
- PREP. **in a/the ~**

2 part of a train
- ADJ. **railway | full | empty | first-class, second-class | no-smoking/non-smoking, smoking**
- VERB + CARRIAGE **get in/into | get out of | pull**
- CARRIAGE + NOUN **door, window**
- PREP. **in a/the ~** *There's a seat in the next carriage.*

carriageway noun

- ADJ. **dual, single | northbound, etc.**
- PREP. **on a/the ~** *The accident happened on the southbound carriageway of the M1.*

carrot noun

1 vegetable
- ADJ. **raw | baby | diced, grated**
- VERB + CARROT **eat, have | cook, prepare | peel, scrape | chop, dice, grate**
- CARROT + NOUN **top | cake | juice**
- ⇒ Special page at FOOD

2 sth attractive offered to sb
- VERB + CARROT **dangle, hold out, offer (sb)** *They dangled the carrot of a large salary in front of me.*
- PHRASES **a carrot and stick** *to adopt the carrot-and-stick approach* (= to persuade sb to try harder by offering them a reward if they do, or a punishment if they do not)

cart noun

1 vehicle pulled by animals
- ADJ. **heavy | bullock, donkey, horse-drawn, ox | farm**
- VERB + CART **drive | draw, pull | ride in | climb off/on/onto, get off/on/onto | load, unload**
- CART + VERB **roll | creak, lumber** *The cart creaked on up the street.* | **carry sth**
- CART + NOUN **track**
- PREP. **by ~** *In the old days coal supplies came by cart.* **in a/the ~** *She brought the vegetables in an ox cart.* **on/onto a/the ~** *piling their furniture onto a cart*
- PHRASES **the back of a cart** *Jump in the back of my cart.* **a horse/pony and cart**

2 small vehicle
- ADJ. **golf, hand, ice-cream**
- VERB + CART **push, trundle, wheel** *a man wheeling an ice-cream cart along* | **drive** *driving a golf cart*

carton noun

- ADJ. **cardboard, plastic | ice-cream, juice, milk, yogurt** *Why are these milk cartons so difficult to open?*
- VERB + CARTON **open**
- PREP. **in a/the ~** *The soup is sold in cartons.* | **~ of** *a carton of cream*

cartoon noun

- ADJ. **animated, strip**
- VERB + CARTOON **draw** *He draws strip cartoons for 'The Guardian'.*
- CARTOON + NOUN **character | strip | series**

carved adj.

- VERBS **be**
- ADV. **beautifully, delicately, elaborately, finely, intricately, ornately, richly** *a richly carved doorway* | **crudely, roughly** *a crudely carved wooden figure*

case noun

1 example
- ADJ. **classic, textbook, typical | clear, obvious, simple** *It was a simple case of mistaken identity.* | **borderline** *After the exams, the teacher gave all borderline cases a spoken test.* | **extreme | isolated, rare** *Except in a few rare cases, bee stings are not dangerous.* | **exceptional, special | striking**
- VERB + CASE **highlight, illustrate, show** *He highlighted the case of Harry Farr, 25, who was executed for cowardice in 1916.*
- CASE + VERB **arise, occur** *The committee has full powers to deal with any cases of malpractice that arise.*
- CASE + NOUN **study** *a case study of an Amazonian tribe* | **example**
- PREP. **in sb's/this ~** *In her case, she failed the exam because she wasn't well.* | **~ of** *a case of animal cruelty*
- PHRASES **case by case/on a case by case basis** *Com-*

plaints are dealt with on a case by case basis. **a case in point** *Many professions feel they deserve higher pay, and nurses are a case in point.*

2 true situation
- VERB + CASE **be, remain** *It remains the case that not enough graduates are going into teaching.* | **overstate, understate** *I agree with him, but don't you think he slightly overstates the case?*

3 of a disease
- ADJ. **acute, chronic | advanced, serious, severe | mild**
- CASE + NOUN **history** *Medical students study the case histories of many patients.* | **file, notes, records, report**
- PREP. **~of** *a severe case of food poisoning*

4 police investigation
- ADJ. **notorious | tragic | murder, robbery**
- VERB + CASE **investigate, work on** *Four police officers are investigating the case.* | **crack, solve** *They never solved the Jones murder case.*
- CASE + NOUN **officer** *Carter was the senior case officer on the investigation.*
- PREP. **on the~** *A detective is on the case at the moment.* | **~of** *a case of theft*

5 in a court of law
- ADJ. **court | criminal | civil | test** *This is a test case which will influence what other judges decide.* | **divorce**
- VERB + CASE **bring** *The victim decided to bring a case of rape against him.* | **handle** *This was the hardest case she had handled since becoming a lawyer.* | **consider, hear, try** *The court will consider the case soon.* ◇ *The case will be heard in the Court of Appeal.* | **adjourn | dismiss, throw out** *The case was thrown out for lack of evidence.* | **drop** *The prosecution decided to drop the case.* | **decide, settle** *The case was settled out of court.* | **win | lose | review**
- CASE + VERB **come before sb, come to court, go to court, go to trial** *The case came before Judge Hales in the Crown Court.* ◇ *He was so clearly innocent, the case should never have gone to court.* | **collapse** *The case against her collapsed when a key witness was proved to have lied.* | **centre on sth, hinge on sth, rest on sth, turn on sth** *The case hinged on the evidence of the only witness to the killing.* | **raise sth** *The case raises a number of issues.*
- PREP. **in a/the~** *the evidence in the case* | **~against** *The case against her was very weak.* **~ of**
- PHRASES **a/no case to answer** *The judge ruled that the defendant had no case to answer, as the evidence had been discredited.* **the circumstances/facts of a case**

6 arguments
- ADJ. **convincing, good, powerful, strong | open-and-shut, unanswerable** *With his current superb form, he presents an unanswerable case for selection in the team.* | **weak | defence, prosecution/prosecution's**
- VERB + CASE **have** *Our lawyer didn't think we had a case* (= had enough good arguments to win in a court of law). | **prepare** *The defendant requested more time to prepare his case.* | **outline, set out | deliver, make (out), present, put, state** *You can make out a case for changing our teaching methods.* | **argue, plead** *I thought she argued her case very well.* | **take up** *The local MP has taken up the case of the family of six who have been left homeless.* | **judge** *The teacher must judge each case according to its merits.* | **bolster, help, support** *What evidence do you have to support your case?* | **weaken**
- CASE + VERB **exist** *A strong case exists for adopting a similar system in this country.*
- PREP. **~against** *Is there a case against wearing school uniforms?* **~ for**
- PHRASES **the case for the defence/prosecution, the merits of a case** *The disciplinary committee considered the merits of his case before fining him.*

7 container

- ADJ. **display** *She kept all her trophies in a display case.* | **presentation** *a gold wristwatch in a presentation case* | **carrying** *He put the binoculars back in their carrying case.* | **packing | glass** *The room was full of stuffed animals in glass cases.* | **cigarette, glasses, jewellery, pencil, pillow | guitar, violin, etc.**
- PREP. **in/inside a/the~, out of a/the~**

8 suitcase
- ADJ. **attaché | overnight**
- ⇨ See SUITCASE (for other collocates with **case**)

9 grammar
- ADJ. **ablative, accusative, dative, genitive, instrumental, locative, nominative, vocative**
- VERB + CASE **take** *In Polish the verb 'to be' takes the instrumental case.*
- CASE + NOUN **ending**

cash *noun*

1 money in the form of coins or notes
- ADJ. **hard, ready** *The drugs are sold for hard cash.* | **petty**
- VERB + CASH **pay (in)** *We'll have to pay cash for the tickets.* | **hold** *The bank should hold enough cash to satisfy customer demand.* | **convert/turn sth into**
- CASH + NOUN **desk, register | dispenser, machine | balance | book**
- PREP. **in ~** *The thieves stole £200 in cash.* ◇ *You can pay by cheque or in cash.*
- PHRASES **cash in hand** (= if you pay for goods and services **cash in hand**, you pay in cash, especially so that the person being paid can avoid paying tax on the amount), **cash on delivery** (= a system of paying for goods when they are delivered)

2 money in any form
- ADJ. **ready, spare | hard-earned** *Imagine having to pay some of my hard-earned cash on a parking fine!*
- VERB + CASH **generate, raise** *They had a football match to raise cash for the hospital.* | **be short of, be strapped for, run out of**
- CASH + NOUN **holdings, reserves, resources | flow** *The company is having cash flow problems.* **inflow, injection | outflow | deposit, payment, settlement | benefits, offer, prize | management | limit | market | crisis | crop** *farmers who grow cash crops for export* **economy | cow** (= the part of a business that always makes a profit)
- ⇨ Special page at BUSINESS

casserole *noun*

1 dish of meat/vegetables
- ADJ. **beef, chicken, vegetable, etc.**
- VERB + CASSEROLE **eat, have | cook, make, prepare**
- CASSEROLE + NOUN **dish**

2 dish for cooking casseroles
- ADJ. **deep, large | shallow | flameproof, ovenproof**
- PREP. **in a/the~** *Put the chicken pieces in a casserole.*

cassette *noun*

- ADJ. **audio, video | tape | blank | bootleg, pirated | music | accompanying** *a set of four course books, each with an accompanying cassette*
- VERB + CASSETTE **insert** *He inserted a cassette into the machine.* | **play, put on** *She put on a U2 cassette.* | **pause, stop | eject | fast forward, rewind**
- CASSETTE + NOUN **deck, player, recorder | tape | box | format, version**
- PREP. **on ~** *I've got it on cassette.*

cast *noun*

- ADJ. **huge, large | small | strong | all-star, star-studded | supporting | all-female, all-male**

• VERB + CAST **have** *The play has a large cast of characters.* | **join** | **head** *Jane Simms heads the cast of this brilliant production.*
• CAST + VERB **perform sth**
• CAST + NOUN **list, member**
• PREP. **in a/the~** *Who is in the cast?*
• PHRASES **a cast of characters, a member of the cast**

caste *noun*

• ADJ. **high, low** *He belongs to one of the highest castes.*
• VERB + CASTE **belong to**
• CASTE + NOUN **system** *the Hindu caste system*
• PHRASES **a member of a caste, of high/low caste**

castle *noun*

• ADJ. **grand, great, magnificent, splendid | strong | turreted | historic | ancient, medieval | royal | ruined | fairy/fairy-tale, fantasy**
• VERB + CASTLE **approach** *They had to approach the castle through thick swamps.* | **build, fortify | attack, besiege, lay siege to | capture, seize, take | defend, hold** *Edinburgh castle was loyally held in the queen's name.*
• CASTLE + VERB **perch, stand** *The castle perches on a high rocky outcrop.* | **overlook sth** *The castle overlooks the town.*
• CASTLE + NOUN **gate, grounds, keep, tower, wall | ruins**
• PREP. **in a/the~**

casual *adj.*

• VERBS **appear, be, sound | become**
• ADV. **extremely, very | almost** *She sounded almost casual.* | **fairly, quite, rather | apparently, seemingly | carefully, elaborately, studiedly** *There was something a little too carefully casual in his tone.* | **deceptively**
• PREP. **about** *He was very casual about it all.*

casualty *noun*

1 person killed/injured in a war/an accident
• ADJ. **heavy, high, serious | light | pedestrian | road | civilian, military | human**
• VERB + CASUALTY **cause, inflict** *The guerrillas inflicted heavy casualties on the local population.* | **incur, suffer** *Our division suffered only light casualties.*
• CASUALTY + NOUN **figures, list, rate**
2 part of a hospital
• VERB + CASUALTY **be admitted to** *He was admitted to casualty with head injuries.* | **rush sb to, take sb to**
• CASUALTY + NOUN **department, unit, ward**
• PREP. **in~** *He works as a doctor in casualty.*

cat *noun*

• ADJ. **domestic, family, household, pet | big** *She went to Africa to photograph big cats.* | **feral, wild | alley, stray | pedigree | long-haired, short-haired | black, tabby, tortoiseshell, etc. | tom** (also **tomcat**) | **playful | sleek | Cheshire** *He was grinning like a Cheshire cat.* | **fat** *(figurative) the fat cats of big business*
• VERB + CAT **have, keep, own** *We have a pet cat called Archie.* | **feed | stroke | neuter, spay** *They didn't want kittens, so they had their cat spayed.* | **worm** *The stray cats are wormed and treated with flea powder.* | **put down** *The cat was in constant pain so they had it put down.*
• CAT + VERB **hiss, mew, miaow, purr, spit, yowl** *The cat miaowed pitifully.* ◇ *There was a cat yowling outside my window last night.* | **bite (sb), scratch (sb) | creep, pad, (be on the) prowl, slink** *A cat padded silently past.* ◇ *The cat slunk away into the darkness.* | **arch its back | cower, crouch | curl up | catch sth, hunt (sth), stalk sth | leap, pounce (on sth), spring | spray (sth)** *Cats mark their territory by spraying.*

• CAT + NOUN **door, flap | food | litter | lover, owner | phobia | nap** (also **catnap**) *A catnap at lunchtime can make you feel refreshed.*
• PHRASES **fight like cat and dog** *In our childhood Irina and I fought like cat and dog.* **play (a game of) cat and mouse** *Young car thieves enjoy playing cat and mouse with the police.*

catalogue *noun*

1 list of books/objects
• ADJ. **exhibition, library**
• VERB + CATALOGUE **produce, publish** *The gallery produced a catalogue of young artists.* | **look through** *Look through the catalogue and find this picture.*
• PREP. **in a/the~** *More details are given in our catalogue.*
2 book of goods for sale
• ADJ. **colour, illustrated | mail-order**
• VERB + CATALOGUE **produce, publish | browse through, look at/through | send (off) for** *Send off for our illustrated catalogue of garden plants.*
• PREP. **in a/the~**

cataract *noun*

• VERB + CATARACT **have | develop | remove** *A cataract can be removed under local anaesthetic.*
• CATARACT + NOUN **operation, surgery**

catastrophe *noun*

• ADJ. **absolute, big, complete, great, major, terrible, total | minor | national | global, international, world | ecological, economic, environmental, natural, nuclear**
• VERB + CATASTROPHE **cause, lead (sth) to** *These policies could lead the country to environmental catastrophe.* | **have** *We had a few catastrophes with the food for the party.* | **be faced with, be heading for, face** *The area is now facing economic catastrophe.* | **avert, avoid, head off, prevent** *moves to avert a national catastrophe*
• CATASTROPHE + VERB **happen, occur, take place**

catastrophic *adj.*

• VERBS **be, prove**
• ADV. **absolutely, quite | potentially**
• PREP. **for** *potentially catastrophic for the environment*

catch *noun*

1 act of catching sth
• ADJ. **brilliant, clean, easy, fine, good, nice**
• VERB + CATCH **take** *Roger took some brilliant catches at today's match.* | **drop, miss**
2 number of fish that sb has caught
• ADJ. **big, bumper, good, huge, large, record** *Fishermen have been landing record catches this season.* | **poor**
• VERB + CATCH **land, make**
• CATCH + VERB **decline, fall** *Catches fell because of the new dam.* | **go up, increase**
• PREP. **~of** *a bumper catch of tuna*
• PHRASES **the day's catch** *a restaurant where you can sample the day's catch*
3 device for fastening sth
• ADJ. **door, window | safety** *the safety catch on a gun*
• VERB + CATCH **slip (off), undo, unfasten, unlock** *Fran slipped the catch on the door, then turned to say goodbye.* | **close**

categorize *verb*

• ADV. **conveniently, easily** *These factors can be conveniently categorized under three headings.*
• VERB + CATEGORIZE **be difficult to, be hard to, be impossible to** *Her work is difficult to categorize.*
• PREP. **according to** *categorizing people according to*

their jobs **by** *We categorize voters by their choice of news-paper.* **into** *Categorize the plants into four groups.*

category *noun*

- ● ADJ. **broad, general | narrow | distinct, separate | special** *We have created a special category for part-time workers.* | **high** *(law) the highest category of sexual assault* | **high-risk** *Intravenous drug users are in a high-risk category for hepatitis C.* | **age, social**
- ● VERB + CATEGORY **be included in, belong to, come into, fall into, fit** (into) *The towns investigated fell into two broad categories.* | **assign sb/sth to, divide sb/sth into, group sb/sth under, put sb/sth in/into | create, define, establish**
- ● CATEGORY + VERB **comprise sth, include sth**
- ● PREP. **in/within a/the~** *He competed in the youngest age category.* | **~of** *a higher category of prison*
- ● PHRASES **be in a category (all) of its/your own** (= to be unique)

catering *noun*

- ● ADJ. **commercial, contract, industrial | hotel, in-flight, school**
- ● VERB + CATERING **do** *Who's doing the catering for the party?*
- ● CATERING + NOUN **business, industry, service | establishment, firm | equipment, facility | assistant, manager, staff, team | college, student | course | management**

cathedral *noun*

- ● ADJ. **great, magnificent | medieval, modern | baroque, Gothic, Romanesque | Anglican, Catholic**
- ● VERB + CATHEDRAL **build | see, visit**
- ● CATHEDRAL + VERB **dominate sth** *The great Gothic cathedral dominates the city.*
- ● CATHEDRAL + NOUN **city, town | church**
- ● PREP. **in a/the~** *We went to mass in the cathedral.*

Catholic *noun*

- ● ADJ. **Roman | devout | practising | lapsed**
- ● VERB + CATHOLIC **be brought up** (as)

Catholicism *noun*

- ● ADJ. **ardent, fervent | Roman**
- ● VERB + CATHOLICISM **convert to**

cattle *noun*

- ● ADJ. **beef, dairy | horned | highland, hill, upland | lowland | indigenous, native | wild**
- ● QUANT. **head** *5 000 head of cattle died of the disease in one month.* | **herd**
- ● VERB + CATTLE **keep, rear | breed | tend | graze** *Villagers traditionally have the right to graze their cattle on the common land.* | **drive, herd, round up** *Farmers drove cattle along major roads as a protest against high taxes.* | **slaughter | raid, rustle, steal | domesticate** *Cattle were first domesticated in Neolithic times.*
- ● CATTLE + VERB **browse, graze** *cattle grazing in the fields* | **low | stray, wander** *Cattle that stray onto the electric railway line are killed instantly.*
- ● CATTLE + NOUN **auction, market | breeding, ranching, rearing | breeder, dealer, farmer | farm, ranch | feed, food | grid** *There was a cattle grid across the road to stop the cows escaping.* | **prod** *Electric cattle prods were used against the demonstrators.* | **truck**
- ● PHRASES **a breed of cattle**

cause *noun*

1 sb/sth that makes sth happen
- ● ADJ. **real, root, true, underlying** *the root cause of the problem* | **deeper, greater** *A greater cause for resentment is the discrepancy in pay.* | **biggest, chief, clear, fundamental, important, main, major, primary, prime, principal, significant | common** *Smoking is a common cause of premature death.* | **likely, possible | known, unknown | direct, indirect | immediate, initial | long-term, short-term | reasonable** *There is no reasonable cause to suspect an unnatural death.* | **contributory | hidden | social** *the social causes of ill health*
- ● VERB + CAUSE **discover, find, identify** *attempts to identify the immediate cause of the breakdown*
- ● CAUSE + VERB **be, lie in sth** *The real cause of the problem lies in the poor construction of the bridge.*
- ● PHRASES **cause and effect, the cause of death, due to/from/of natural causes** *He died of natural causes.*

2 reason
- ● ADJ. **good, great, real, reasonable**
- ● VERB + CAUSE **have** *We have good cause to believe that he was involved in the crime.* | **find** *The experts may find cause to disagree with the school's decision.* | **give** (sb) *Her health is giving us great cause for concern.* | **show** *The onus is on government departments to show cause why information cannot be disclosed.*
- ● PREP. **~for** *There is no cause for alarm.*
- ● PHRASES **cause for concern, with/without good cause, without just cause**

3 aim that people believe in
- ● ADJ. **deserving, good, just, noble, worthwhile, worthy** *The money she left went to various worthy causes.* | **bad, unjust | common** *The different groups support a common cause.* | **hopeless, lost** (= one that has failed or that cannot succeed) | **humanitarian, social | communist, socialist, etc.**
- ● VERB + CAUSE **be committed/sympathetic to, champion, fight for, further, help, promote, serve, support** *young men willing to fight for the cause* ◇ *She was keen to do anything that would further the cause.* | **take up** *She has taken up the cause of animal rights.* | **plead** *He pleaded the cause of the local fishermen.*
- ● PREP. **in a/the~** *prominent figures in the socialist cause* **in the ~ of** *to disregard the strict letter of the law in the cause of true justice*
- ● PHRASES **a cause célèbre** (= a controversial issue that attracts a great deal of public attention), **(all) for/in a good cause** *The function took a lot of organizing, but was all in a good cause.*

caution *noun*

1 great care
- ● ADJ. **considerable, extreme, great, utmost** *The utmost caution must be exercised when handling explosives.* | **excessive | due** *We proceeded with due caution.*
- ● VERB + CAUTION **exercise | advise, counsel, urge** *We urge caution in the use of this medication.*
- ● PREP. **with ~** *The information should be treated with some caution.*
- ● PHRASES **err on the side of caution** (= to be too cautious), **the need for caution** *I must stress the need for caution.* **sound a note of caution** *The minister sounded a note of caution about the economy.* **cast/throw caution to the wind/winds** (= to start taking risks), **a word of caution** *I would just like to add a word of caution.*

2 spoken warning given by a judge/policeman
- ● ADJ. **formal** *He received a formal caution.*
- ● VERB + CAUTION **get off with, receive | give sb, issue, let sb off with** *They let her off with a caution.*

cautious adj.

● VERBS **be | become, get, grow | remain | make sb** *Her experiences have made her cautious.*
● ADV. **distinctly, extremely, highly, very | fairly, a little, quite, rather | sensibly, suitably, understandably** *Doctors are understandably cautious about this new treatment.* **| excessively, unduly** *He accused the government of being unduly cautious.* **| deliberately | suddenly** *What's made you so suddenly cautious?*
● PREP. **about** *cautious about spending money* **of** *He warned us to be cautious of accepting their statements as fact.*

cave noun

● ADJ. **deep, large | shallow, small | dark | damp, dank | rocky, mountain, underground** *We explored the rocky caves along the beach.* **| crystal, limestone**
● VERB + CAVE **explore**
● CAVE + VERB **collapse** *a collapsed limestone cave*
● CAVE + NOUN **ceiling, entrance, floor, mouth, roof, wall | system | art, drawing, painting | dweller**
● PREP. **in a/the ~** *We took shelter in a dark, dank cave.*
● PHRASES **the ceiling/floor/roof/wall of a cave, the entrance to/mouth of a cave**

CD noun

● ADJ. **budget, full-price, mid-price | double | audio, music, multimedia, photo**
● VERB + CD **insert** *She inserted a CD into the machine.* **| play, put on | record** *You can record your own CD if you have the right equipment.* **| burn, burn sth onto, copy, duplicate, record | listen to | release** *The band's new CD is released next week.*
● CD + NOUN **drive | player, sound system | burner, maker, recorder, rewriter, ripper, writer | burning, duplication, recording | cover, sleeve | format**
● PREP. **on ~** *That was the first album to come out on CD.* **on a/the ~** *How many tracks are on the CD?* **| ~ of**

CD-ROM noun

● ADJ. **multimedia | interactive | educational**
● VERB + CD-ROM **burn (sth onto), duplicate** *Now you can burn your photos onto a CD-ROM.* **| install**
● CD-ROM + VERB **contain sth**
● CD-ROM + NOUN **drive | driver | player | burner, burning | title | edition** *This is the CD-ROM edition of the encyclopedia.*
● PREP. **on ~** *This dictionary is also available on CD-ROM.*
⇨ Special page at COMPUTER

cease verb

● ADV. **altogether, completely, entirely** *The flow slowed, then ceased altogether.* **| all but, almost, virtually | largely | effectively** *My job had effectively ceased to exist.* **| forthwith, immediately** *These violations of the code must cease forthwith.* **| soon | abruptly, suddenly** *The bird's song ceased abruptly.* **| rapidly | gradually | momentarily | eventually, finally | long (since)** *The conversation had long ceased to interest me.* **| automatically**
● PREP. **with** *The matches ceased with the outbreak of war.*
● PHRASES **without ceasing** *Prayer was made without ceasing.*

ceasefire noun

● ADJ. **complete | immediate | unilateral**
● VERB + CEASEFIRE **call for, demand, order** *The UN has passed a resolution calling for an immediate ceasefire.* **| achieve, secure | agree (to), declare, sign | broker,**

negotiate | call *A 24-hour ceasefire was called to allow the distribution of aid.* **| observe | break, violate**
● CEASEFIRE + VERB **come/go into effect | hold, last** *There are concerns that the ceasefire might not hold.*
● CEASEFIRE + NOUN **agreement, terms**
● PREP. **~ between** *a ceasefire between the government and the rebels*
● PHRASES **a violation of a ceasefire**

ceiling noun

1 top surface inside a room

● ADJ. **high, low | domed, sloping, suspended, vaulted | painted** *The palace is famous for its 17th-century painted ceilings.*
● CEILING + VERB **collapse**
● PREP. **on the ~** *a fly on the ceiling*
● PHRASES **from ceiling to floor/from floor to ceiling** *The bathroom has mirrors from ceiling to floor.*

2 top limit on wages/prices, etc.

● ADJ. **expenditure, price**
● VERB + CEILING **impose, place, put, set** *They have put a ceiling on the price of petrol.* **| abolish | lift, raise** *The government has decided to lift price ceilings on bread, milk and other staples.* **| lower**
● PREP. **~ on** *a ceiling on imports*

celebrated adj.

● VERBS **be | become**
● ADV. **very | justly, rightly** *his justly celebrated portrait of Queen Juliana* **| internationally**
● PREP. **as** *He has become celebrated as an artist.* **for** *The area is celebrated for its food and wine.*

celebration noun

● ADJ. **big, great, noisy | little, quiet, small | family | joyous** *a joyous celebration of life* **| double** *a double birthday celebration* **| special | national, official, public, street** *There were wild street celebrations when England won the Cup.* **| anniversary, birthday, centenary, Christmas, New Year, victory, wedding** (usually with **celebrations**) *50th anniversary celebrations* **| religious**
● VERB + CELEBRATION **have, hold** *They held a special celebration in his honour.* **| join (in)** *I hope you'll join in the Christmas celebrations.*
● CELEBRATION + NOUN **dinner**
● PREP. **in ~ of** *They organized a dinner in celebration of the year's successes.*
● PHRASES **a cause for celebration** *The victory was a cause for great celebration.* **a celebration of (sb's) life, a celebration to mark sth** *They held a celebration to mark forty years of the lifeboat service.*

celebrity noun

● ADJ. **minor | local, international, national | overnight | guest, visiting | showbiz, sporting, television**
● QUANT. **host** *Tonight show features a host of celebrities.*
● VERB + CELEBRITY **make sb** *The show's success made her an overnight celebrity.*
● CELEBRITY + NOUN **status | chef**
● PHRASES **something of a celebrity** *He became something of a celebrity in his home town.*

celery noun

● QUANT. **stick**
● VERB + CELERY **eat, have | cook, prepare | chop, dice, slice** *Chop the celery and add it to the salad.*
● CELERY + NOUN **leaf, salt, stalk, stick**
⇨ Special page at FOOD

cell *noun*

1 smallest living part of an animal/a plant body
- ADJ. **dead, living | abnormal, normal | blood, brain, muscle, nerve, skin** *red and white blood cells* **| egg, sperm | cancer | animal, human, plant,** etc.
- VERB + CELL **form**
- CELL + VERB **divide** *Cells divide and form new cells.*
- CELL + NOUN **proliferation**
- PHRASES **the nucleus of a cell, the proliferation of cells** *the proliferation of cells in leukaemia*

2 small room
- ADJ. **monk's, nun's | police, prison | padded**
- PREP. **in a/the~**

cellar *noun*

- ADJ. **damp, dark | deep, underground | vaulted | coal, wine | pub | beer, jazz | disused**
- CELLAR + NOUN **steps | bar, bistro**
- PREP. **in/into the~** *I went down into the cellar for more wine.*

cello *noun*

⇨ Special page at MUSIC

cement *noun*

- ADJ. **wet | dental**
- VERB + CEMENT **mix**
- CEMENT + VERB **harden, set**
- CEMENT + NOUN **mixer | factory, works**

cemetery *noun*

- ADJ. **local | private, public** *He was buried in a private cemetery.* **| military | Catholic, Jewish,** etc.
- VERB + CEMETERY **be buried in | visit**
- PREP. **in a/the~**

censor *verb*

- ADV. **heavily** *The film has been heavily censored.*

censorship *noun*

- ADJ. **strict | government, military, state, wartime | film, media, political, press**
- VERB + CENSORSHIP **impose** *The government has imposed strict censorship on the press.* **| abolish, lift | tighten** *Political censorship has been tightened under the new regime.* **| relax | practise** *to take action against institutions practising censorship*

censure *noun*

- ADJ. **severe | public**
- VERB + CENSURE **come under, face** *He could face censure from his colleagues.* **| avoid, escape** *Costs will have to be kept down if severe public censure is to be avoided.*
- CENSURE + NOUN **motion**
- PHRASES **a motion/vote of censure** *Right-wing parties tabled a motion of censure against the government.*

censure *verb*

- ADV. **severely** *The manager was severely censured for negligence.*
- PREP. **for**

census *noun*

- ADJ. **complete, full | general, national, official | decennial | population**
- VERB + CENSUS **carry out, conduct, take** *A national census is taken every ten years.*

- CENSUS + NOUN **data, figures, records, results, return, statistics**
- PREP. **in a/the~** *the questions asked in the census*

centenary *noun*

- VERB + CENTENARY **celebrate, commemorate, mark** *The club will hold a party to celebrate its centenary.*
- CENTENARY + NOUN **celebrations, year**

centimetre *noun*

⇨ Note at MEASURE

central *adj.*

1 in the centre
- VERBS **be**
- ADV. **very** *Our house is very central, so we can easily get to theatres and cinemas.* **| quite**

2 most important
- VERBS **be**
- ADV. **absolutely** *This distinction is of absolutely central importance.*
- PREP. **to** *These facts are central to the case.*

centralized *adj.*

- VERBS **be**
- ADV. **highly** *a highly centralized bureaucracy* **| fully | increasingly**

centre *noun*

1 middle point/part of sth
- ADJ. **dead, very** *We've bought a flat in the very centre of Cambridge.* **| city, town | soft** *chocolates with soft centres*
- PREP. **at the ~ (of)** *at the centre of the universe* **in the~ (of)** *a museum in the centre of Birmingham*
- PHRASES **the centre of the city, the centre of (the) town**

2 important place for sth
- ADJ. **important, leading, main, major, nerve** (*figurative*) *the economic nerve centre of Germany* **| international, local, national, regional, world | commercial, cultural, economic, financial, industrial, trading, urban** *London is one of the main financial centres of the world.*
- PREP. **~for** *The university is a major centre for scientific research.*
- PHRASES **a centre of excellence** (= a place where a particular kind of work is done well), **a centre of government/population/power**

3 the centre moderate political position
- CENTRE + NOUN **party | ground** *a party that occupies the centre ground of British politics*
- PHRASES **left/right of centre** *Politically, she is slightly left of centre.*

century *noun*

- ADJ. **19th, 20th,** etc. *a 17th-century building* **| earlier, last, later, past, previous** *Later centuries saw the development of a complex transport system.* **| new, next** *a celebration to welcome the new century* **| present**
- PREP. **during the~** *The town's population doubled during the 19th century.* **for~s** *There have been orchards in this region for centuries.* **in the…~** *He lived in the 16th century.* **over the~s** *a marble floor worn smooth over the centuries* **through the~s** *a tradition passed down through the centuries* **throughout the~** *America's influence on culture grew throughout the 20th century.*
- PHRASES **centuries old** *a centuries old custom* **the turn of the century**

cereal noun

1 plant
- VERB + CEREAL **grow, produce | harvest**
- CEREAL + NOUN **crop, foods, products | farmer, grower, producer | production**

2 food
- ADJ. **fortified** *fortified breakfast cereals* | **breakfast | bran, wholegrain, wholewheat**
- QUANT. **bowl** *a big bowl of cereal* | **packet**
- VERB + CEREAL **eat, have** *having cereal for breakfast*
- CEREAL + VERB **be fortified** *a wholewheat cereal fortified with B group vitamins*
- CEREAL + NOUN **bowl, packet**

ceremonial adj.

- VERBS **be**
- ADV. **purely** *The monarch's role is purely ceremonial.* | **essentially, largely, primarily**

ceremony noun

1 formal public/religious event
- ADJ. **brief, short | quiet, simple | elaborate, glittering | moving, solemn | private, public | formal, important, official, special** *an official ceremony to welcome the new director* | **opening** *the opening ceremony of the Olympic games* | **closing | award/awards | civil | cake-cutting, dedication, degree, funeral, graduation, inauguration, initiation, marriage, naming, presentation, prize-giving, signing, swearing-in, tea, unveiling, wedding, wreath-laying** *the Japanese tea ceremony*
- VERB + CEREMONY **conduct, hold, perform** *The marriage ceremony was performed by the bishop.* | **attend, be present at, take part in**
- CEREMONY + VERB **take place | mark sth** *a special ceremony to mark the end of the war*
- PREP. **at a/the** ~ *the guest of honour at the ceremony* **during a/the** ~ *A lot of people wept during the funeral ceremony.* **in a/the** ~ *They were married in a simple ceremony.*

2 formal behaviour/traditional actions and words
- VERB + CEREMONY **stand on** *I won't stand on ceremony* (= be formal).
- PREP. **without** ~ *Without ceremony, the woman slammed the door shut in my face.*
- PHRASES **pomp and ceremony** *the pomp and ceremony of a royal wedding* **with due/great ceremony** *With due ceremony, he took the oath to become president.*

certain adj.

- VERBS **be, feel, look, seem** *Digby looked certain to be the next president.* | **become, grow** *I grew more and more certain that she was lying to me.* | **make** *Make certain that you lock the door if you go out.*
- ADV. **very | absolutely, quite | by no means** *It's by no means certain that she'll get the job.* | **almost | fairly, pretty**
- PREP. **about/of** *Are you quite certain about this?*
- PHRASES **can't/couldn't say for certain** *I think she's a teacher, but I couldn't say for certain.* **not know for certain** *I don't know for certain how many people are coming.*

certainty noun

- ADJ. **absolute, complete | reasonable, virtual** *It's a virtual certainty that petrol will go up in price.*
- QUANT. **degree** *It's difficult to predict with any degree of certainty how much it will cost.*
- PREP. **with** ~ *I couldn't say with absolute certainty that he's here.*
- PHRASES **a lack of certainty** *There seems to be a lack of certainty over what we should do.* **the one/only certainty** *The one certainty left in a changing world is death.*

certificate noun

- ADJ. **birth, death, marriage | medical | school, school-leaving**
- VERB + CERTIFICATE **award (sb), issue** *The police are waiting for the doctor to issue a death certificate.*
- PREP. ~ **of** *a certificate of motor insurance*

chain noun

1 line of rings joined together
- ADJ. **long** *She wore a long gold chain round her neck.* | **rusty | bicycle | daisy, paper**
- QUANT. **length**
- CHAIN + VERB **clank**
- CHAIN + NOUN **mail** (= armour made of chains)
- PREP. **in** ~**s** *The prisoner was led away in chains.* **off sb's/the** ~ *Let the dog off its chain.* **on a/the** ~ *They kept the dog on a chain all day long.*
- PHRASES **a chain of office** *The mayor was wearing his chain of office.* **a chain on the door** *Put the chain on the door before you go to bed.* **a link in the chain**

2 number of things in a line
- ADJ. **island, mountain | human**
- VERB + CHAIN **form** *The people formed a human chain to pass the supplies up the beach.*
- PREP. ~ **of** *a chain of volcanic islands*
- PHRASES **a chain of command** (= a system by which instructions are passed from one person to another)

3 group of shops, etc. owned by the same company
- ADJ. **big, large | small | hotel, supermarket, etc.**
- CHAIN + NOUN **store**
- PREP. ~ **of** *a chain of clothes shops*
- PHRASES **part of a chain** *This hotel is part of a large chain.*

4 number of connected events/situations
- ADJ. **complex** *the complex chain of events that led to the war* | **unbroken** *There has been an unbroken chain of great violinists in the family.* | **causal | food** *efforts to ensure that dioxins do not enter the food chain*
- CHAIN + NOUN **reaction**
- PHRASES **a chain of events**

chair noun

1 piece of furniture
- ADJ. **comfortable, comfy, cushioned, padded, plush, soft, upholstered | hard, uncomfortable | deep, low | high-backed, straight-backed, wing-backed, winged | rush-seated, tubular | rickety | reclining, swivel** *He lay back in the reclining chair and went to sleep.* ◇ *She returned to the swivel chair behind her desk.* | **folding | matching** *a dining table and four matching chairs* | **empty** *'Please, be my guest.' He gestured towards an empty chair.* | **antique | mahogany, plastic, steel, wooden | dining, fireside, kitchen**
- QUANT. **row | set** *a set of antique mahogany dining chairs*
- VERB + CHAIR **draw up, pull up** *'Can I join you?' 'Yes, pull up a chair.'* | **pull out** *He pulled out a chair for her.* | **have, take** *Come in and take a chair.* | **give sb** *He gave her his chair.* | **push back** *He pushed back his chair and got to his feet.* | **collapse into/onto, flop (back/down) in/into/on/onto, lower yourself into, settle (back) in/into/on, sink (back/down) into, slump (back/down) in/into, sit (down) in/on** *She dropped her bags and flopped down into the nearest chair.* | **lean back in, lie back in, lounge (back) in, recline (back) in, relax (back) in, sprawl/be sprawled in** *He put his feet up on the desk and lay back in his chair.* | **lean forward in | straighten (up) in** *They straightened in their chairs when the manager burst in.* | **get out of, get up from/off, jump (up) from/out of, leap out of/from, rise from** *He got up from his chair to address the meeting.* | **rock backwards and forwards**

in/on, shift (about) in, tip back *He was shifting about uneasily in his chair.* ◇ *She tipped her chair back and fixed her gaze full upon him.* | **swivel (on), swivel (round) in** *She swivelled round in her chair and picked up the phone.*
- CHAIR + VERB **be placed, stand** *A chair stood facing the window.* | **swivel** | **fall over, tip up, topple over** | **creak** *The chair creaked every time I moved.*
- CHAIR + NOUN **arm, back, leg, seat** | **cover, frame** | **lift** *A chair lift carried us to the top of the ski run.*
- PREP. **into a/the~** *He sank into his chair and opened the letter.* **in a/the~** *She leaned back in her chair and lit a cigarette.* **on a/the~** *A cat was asleep on the chair.*
- PHRASES **the arm/back/edge/leg of a chair** *She gripped the arm of her chair as she spoke.* ◇ *He sat nervously on the edge of his chair.*
⇒ See ARMCHAIR

2 person controlling a meeting
- ADJ. **acting, deputy**
- VERB + CHAIR **occupy, take** *Anne took the chair (= was chairperson) in Carol's absence.* | **address (sth to)** *Please address your questions to the chair.* | **appoint sb (as), elect sb (as)**
- PREP. **in the~** *Paul Ryan was in the chair (= was chairman) at today's meeting.*

3 position of university professor
- ADJ. **professorial**
- VERB + CHAIR **hold, occupy** *He held the Chair of Botany at Cambridge University for thirty years.* | **appoint sb to** | **relinquish, resign** | **endow, establish** *A private benefactor endowed the new Chair of Japanese Literature.*

chairman, chairwoman *noun*

- ADJ. **club, committee, company, party** *She is married to a company chairman.* | **acting, former, incoming, new, outgoing** *a report by the outgoing chairman*
- VERB + CHAIRMAN, CHAIRWOMAN **hold the post of** | **elect (sb)**
- CHAIRMAN, CHAIRWOMAN + VERB **resign, stand down** *The chairman resigned following the allegations.*
⇒ Note at JOB

chalk *noun*

1 white rock
- VERB + CHALK **quarry**
- CHALK + NOUN **cliff, downs, hill** | **pit, quarry**

2 small stick of chalk
- ADJ. **coloured** *a box of coloured chalks*
- QUANT. **piece, stick**
- CHALK + NOUN **drawing** | **dust**
- PREP. **in~** *She had scrawled a note in chalk across the blackboard.* **with~** *to write with chalk*

challenge *noun*

1 sth new and difficult
- ADJ. **big, considerable, enormous, great, huge, radical, real, serious, significant, strong** | **difficult, tough** | **major, main** | **fresh, new** | **exciting, interesting** | **economic, environmental, intellectual, political, technical, technological** *Liszt's piano music presents an enormous technical challenge.*
- VERB + CHALLENGE **be, pose, present** | **face, meet, respond to, rise to, take on/up** *The gallery has risen to the challenge of exhibiting the works of young artists.* ◇ *He has taken on some exciting new challenges with this job.*
- CHALLENGE + VERB **face sb** *the challenges facing nurses in casualty*

2 that shows that sb refuses to accept sth
- ADJ. **serious** | **direct** | **effective** | **legal**
- VERB + CHALLENGE **be, present, represent** *The demonstration represents a direct challenge to the new law.*
- PREP. **~to** *a legal challenge to the president's power*

3 invitation to compete
- ADJ. **leadership, title** *his title challenge to the heavyweight champion*
- VERB + CHALLENGE **issue, mount** *plans to mount a leadership challenge within the party* | **accept, take up** *I accepted his challenge to a game of chess.* | **beat off, fight off** *Our team will have to fight off the challenge from better trained teams.*
- PREP. **~from** *a challenge from the other political party*

challenge *verb*

1 question whether sth is right/true
- ADV. **directly** *The newspaper was directly challenging the government's legitimacy.* | **seriously** | **effectively** *She was effectively challenging the whole basis on which society was run.* | **successfully** *The story was completely untrue and was successfully challenged in court.*
- PREP. **on** *She challenged him on his old-fashioned views.*

2 invite sb to compete, argue, etc.
- ADV. **seriously** *No one has seriously challenged the champion.* | **successfully, unsuccessfully**
- PREP. **for** *She was poised to challenge for the party leadership.* **to** *The count challenged him to a duel.*

challenger *noun*

- ADJ. **closest, main, nearest, serious, strong** *Her nearest challenger is the vice-president.*
- VERB + CHALLENGER **take on** *He took on various challengers, but refused to fight Jackson.*
- PREP. **~for** *the main challengers for the European title* **~to** *a challenger to the prime minister*

challenging *adj.*

- VERBS **be, prove** | **make sth** *We have changed the course to make it more challenging.* | **find sth** *He found the course academically challenging.*
- ADV. **extremely, very** | **quite** | **enough, sufficiently** *The tasks were not challenging enough for me and I got bored.* | **academically, intellectually, politically**

chamber *noun*

1 room/enclosed space
- ADJ. **dark, dim** | **secret** | **inner, main, outer** | **underground, subterranean** | **burial, tomb** *a Bronze Age burial chamber* | **torture** | **gas** *Millions died in the gas chambers in the war.* | **decompression**
- CHAMBER + NOUN **door**

2 large room, especially used for formal meetings
- ADJ. **grand, great, large, vast** | **high-ceilinged, vaulted** | **conference, council, debating**
- PREP. **in a/the~**

3 part of a government
- ADJ. **first, lower, second, upper** | **elected** *She believes there should be an elected second chamber to replace the House of Lords.* | **legislative, parliamentary**
- PHRASES **the Chamber of Deputies**

champagne *noun*

- ADJ. **excellent, fine, good** | **French** | **expensive** | **cheap** | **vintage** | **non-vintage** | **fake** | **pink** | **chilled, iced**
- QUANT. **bottle, magnum** | **glass**
- VERB + CHAMPAGNE **have** *I'll have some champagne, please.* | **drink, quaff, sip** *Do you drink champagne?* ◇ *They sat sipping their champagne.* | **pour (sb)** | **celebrate (sth) with** | **chill**
- CHAMPAGNE + VERB **flow** *(figurative) The champagne flowed like water at the wedding reception.* | **be/go flat** *The champagne had been left open and had gone flat.*

• CHAMPAGNE + NOUN **bottle, flute** (= a kind of glass), **glass** | **cork** *We heard the sound of popping champagne corks next door.* | **breakfast, reception** *There was a champagne reception before the concert.* | **house** (= company)

champion *noun*

• ADJ. **great, supreme, undisputed** | **defending, reigning** *The reigning champion will defend her title tonight.* | **former** | **national, world** | **Olympic** *the Olympic skating champion* | **boxing, snooker, etc.**
• VERB + CHAMPION **become, be crowned** *He was crowned champion after his fight in Atlanta.*
• CHAMPION + VERB **defend her/his title**
• CHAMPION + NOUN **fighter, jockey, etc.**

championship *noun*

1 competition
• ADJ. **major** | **international, national, world** | **British, European, etc.** | **swimming, tennis, etc.**
• VERB + CHAMPIONSHIP **hold** *The championships are to be held in Rome.* | **compete in, take part in** *Over thirty children will compete in the swimming championships.* | **win** *She has won four major championships in the last five years.* | **lose**
• CHAMPIONSHIP + VERB **take place**
• CHAMPIONSHIP + NOUN **final, game, match, race** | **title, winner**
• PREP. **at a/the ~** *I saw him play at last year's tennis championship.* **in a/the ~** *the teams in the championship*

2 position/title of champion
• VERB + CHAMPIONSHIP **hold** *Who holds the championship at the moment?* | **take, win** *He's won the championship for the third time in a row.* | **lose** | **regain** | **retain** *She managed to retain the championship.*

chance *noun*

1 possibility
• ADJ. **excellent, good, high, strong** | **fair, fighting, sporting, realistic, reasonable** *There's a fair chance that nobody will come to the talk.* | **little, the merest, million-to-one, minimal, outside, slender, slim, slight** *There was only a million-to-one chance of it happening.* ◇ *As long as there is an outside chance, we will go for it.* | **fifty-fifty, one-in-three, -four, etc., 10, 20, etc. per cent** *They have a 90 per cent chance of success.* | **survival** *What are his survival chances?* | **election, electoral**
• VERB + CHANCE **give sb** *The doctors gave him (= said that he had) little chance of surviving the night.* | **be in with, have, stand** *After a poor start, they are now in with a chance of winning the league.* ◇ *He doesn't stand a chance of winning against such an experienced player.* | **assess, rate** *How do you rate our chances of finding her?* | **fancy** *I don't fancy our chances of getting there on time.* | **boost, enhance, improve, increase, maximize** | **compromise, jeopardize, lessen, minimize, prejudice, reduce, ruin, scupper, spoil**
• PREP. **by any ~** *Are you by any chance Mr Ludd?* | **~ of** *The missing climber's chances of survival are slim.*
• PHRASES **fat chance** *(informal)* **Fat chance** (= there is no chance) *of him helping you!* **have every chance** *She has every chance of passing the exam if she works hard.* **no chance!** *'Will he lend us his car?' 'No chance!'* **on the off chance** (= just in case) *I rang the firm just on the off chance that they might have a vacancy.*

2 opportunity
• ADJ. **fair, good, great, ideal, wonderful** *She played left-handed to give her opponent a fair chance.* ◇ *This is the ideal chance for him to show his ability.* | **big** *This is your big chance—grab it with both hands.* | **once-in-a-lifetime** | **last, second** *The teacher gave her one last chance to prove she could behave.* ◇ *There are no second chances in this business.* | **educational, life** *The new college is in-*

tended to improve the life chances of children in the inner city. | **clear, clear-cut, scoring** *(sport)*
• QUANT. **element** *There is always an element of chance in buying a used car.*
• VERB + CHANCE **get, have** *I finally had the chance to meet my hero.* | **deserve** *He deserves the chance to give his side of the story.* | **welcome** *I would welcome the chance to give my opinion.* | **give sb, offer (sb), provide (sb with)** | **deny sb** *No child should be denied the chance of growing up in a family.* | **wait for** | **create, make** *(sport)* *The team created several clear chances but failed to score.* | **spot** *She spotted her chance of making a quick profit.* | **grab, grasp, jump at, seize, take** *Travis had left the door open— she seized her chance and was through it like a shot.* ◇ *Take every chance that comes your way.* | **blow, miss, pass up, squander, throw away, turn down, waste** *They blew their chance to go second in the league.* ◇ *I wouldn't pass up the chance of working for them.*
• CHANCE + VERB **arise, come up, come your way** *When the chance came up to go to Paris, she jumped at it.*
• PHRASES **given the chance** *Given the chance, I'd stop work tomorrow.* **half a chance** *The dog always runs off when it gets half a chance.* **let a chance slip (by)** *If she let this chance slip, she would regret it for the rest of her life.*

3 risk
• VERB + CHANCE **take** *The guide book didn't mention the hotel, but we decided to take a chance.*
• PREP. **~ on** *The manager took a chance on the young goalkeeper.* | **~ with** *The police were taking no chances with the protesters.*

4 luck/fortune
• ADJ. **pure, sheer** | **happy, lucky** *By a happy chance he bumped into an old friend on the plane.* | **unlucky**
• VERB + CHANCE **leave sth to** *Leaving nothing to chance, he delivered the letter himself.*
• PREP. **by ~** *The police came upon the hideout purely by chance.* **due to ~** *The results could simply be due to chance.* **through ~** *I got most answers right through sheer chance.*
• PHRASES **a game of chance** *Chess is not a game of chance.* **take your chances** (= take a risk in the hope that things will turn out well) *He took his chances and jumped into the water.*

change *noun*

1 becoming/making sb/sth different
• ADJ. **big, considerable, dramatic, drastic, enormous, extensive, far-reaching, fundamental, important, major, marked, massive, momentous, profound, radical, revolutionary, sea, significant, substantial, sweeping, wholesale** *Television has undergone a sea change in the last two years.* | **complete** | **irreversible** | **systematic** | **cosmetic, marginal, minimal, minor, slight, small, subtle** | **long-term, short-term** | **abrupt, rapid, sudden** | **gradual** | **seasonal** | **net, overall** *net change in incomes* | **global** | **qualitative, quantitative** | **beneficial, desirable, effective, exciting, nice, pleasant, refreshing, welcome** | **unwelcome** | **unanticipated, unexpected, unforeseen** | **climate, constitutional, cultural, demographic, economic, environmental, legislative, organizational, political, population, social, structural, technological** | **culture, gear, name, policy, rule, sex** *the need for a culture change within the industry* ◇ *He made a rapid gear change as he approached the bend.*
• VERB + CHANGE **make** *I made a couple of minor changes to my opening paragraph.* ◇ *It made a pleasant change not having to work.* | **bring about, cause, effect, force, produce** *How far does war bring about social change?* | **introduce** *We are going to introduce a few changes to the system.* | **undergo** | **show** *He needs to show a change in attitude if he is to succeed.* | **reflect** *Courses offered in schools reflect changes in the job market.* | **adapt to** *Businesses have to adapt to change.* | **call for, demand** *He called for a change of mood in Scottish polit-*

ics. | **oppose, resist** *We resist change because of fear of the unknown.* | **prevent** | **be subject to** *Train times are subject to change without notice.*
• CHANGE + VERB **occur, take place** *Major economic changes have occurred recently.*
• PREP. **for a~** *I usually take the bus to town, but today I cycled for a change.* | **~ from, ~ in** *The last few years have seen a change in attitudes to single parents.* **~ of** *a change of government* **~ to** *the change from the old to the new system*
• PHRASES **a change for the better/worse** *I reckon we've all made a big change for the better.* **a change of clothes** (= an extra set of clothes to change into) *Take a change of clothes in case you get dirty.* **a change of heart/mind** *He said he's not coming, but he might have a change of heart.* **a change of scene** *I needed a change of scene after being in the job for so long.* **a climate of change** *In the current climate of change, adaptability is vital.* **the pace/rate of change** *A successful company must keep up with the pace of technological change.* **a period of change** *The eighties were a period of great change in publishing.* **the tide of change** *The president realized he could not hold back the tide of change, and resigned.*

2 coins/notes of low value
• ADJ. **loose, small** *He emptied his pockets of loose change.*
• PREP. **in ~** *I've got about 25 dollars in change.* | **~ for** *Ask the cashier if she has change for a £20 note.*

3 money you get back if you pay too much
• VERB + CHANGE **check, count** | **give** *This machine does not give change.* | **get** | **take** | **keep** *I told the taxi driver to keep the change.*
• PREP. **~ from/out of** *The meal left me with not much change from £100.*

change verb

• ADV. **considerably, dramatically, fundamentally, a lot, radically, significantly** *Our way of life has changed dramatically over the last ten years.* ◇ *Jane has changed a lot since she went to university.* | **completely** | **(very) little** *The village has actually changed very little in the last hundred years.* | **all the time, constantly, continually** *The language is changing all the time.* | **fast, rapidly, suddenly** *Attitudes to marriage are changing fast.* | **gradually, slowly**
• PREP. **from** *Leeds changed from a small market town into a busy city.* **into, to** *His anger changed to sadness.*
• PHRASES **change out of all recognition** *The town had changed out of all recognition.*

channel noun

1 television/radio station
• ADJ. **radio, television/TV, video** | **cable, satellite, terrestrial** | **commercial, independent** | **movie, sports,** etc.
• VERB + CHANNEL **change (to), switch (to/over to), tune (in) to** *I changed channels when the news came on.*
• CHANNEL + VERB **broadcast** *This channel broadcasts 24 hours a day.*
• PREP. **on a/the~** *There's an interesting documentary on Channel 4 tonight.*

2 route for sending information
• ADJ. **direct, indirect** *Journalists always have indirect channels for getting information.* | **formal, official** *She first tried to get a doctor's certificate through official channels.* | **informal** | **appropriate, conventional, normal, proper, right, usual** | **effective** *an effective channel for communication* | **diplomatic** | **communication, distribution** *worldwide distribution channels*
• VERB + CHANNEL **go through, use** *If you want a visa, you will have to go through the proper channels.* | **establish, open (up)** *attempts to open up new channels of communication*

• PREP. **through a/the ~** *The government hopes to settle the dispute through diplomatic channels.*
• PHRASES **a channel of communication, channels of distribution**

3 narrow area of water
• ADJ. **deep** | **narrow** | **drainage, irrigation** *Irrigation channels supply the crops with water.* | **river, water** *The estate has fountains and water channels.* | **shipping**

chant noun

• ADJ. **incessant** | **melodious** | **ritual, traditional** | **Gregorian** *a group of monks singing Gregorian chant* | **football** *You could hear the football chants a long way from the stadium.*
• VERB + CHANT **sing** | **keep up** *The crowd kept up an incessant chant of 'Out! Out! Out!'* | **hear**
• PREP. **amid~s, to~s** *The band left the stage to chants of 'We want more! We want more!'* | **~ of**

chaos noun

• ADJ. **absolute, complete, total, utter** | **general** | **administrative, domestic, economic, financial, political, social, traffic**
• VERB + CHAOS **bring, cause, create, lead to** *A serious road accident caused traffic chaos yesterday.* | **end in, result in** *The game ended in chaos.* | **be plunged/thrown into, descend/slide into** *The country is sliding into economic chaos.* | **face** | **avert, avoid**
• CHAOS + VERB **break out, ensue** *Chaos broke out when the fire started.* ◇ *I lost my bag in the ensuing chaos.* | **reign, rule** *The government collapsed and chaos reigned.*
• PREP. **in~** *The airport was in chaos during the strike.*
• PHRASES **on/to the brink of chaos** *The country was brought to the brink of chaos.* **order out of chaos** *His brave leadership has created order out of chaos.* **a route to chaos, a scene of chaos** *Doctors worked day and night amid scenes of utter chaos.* **a state of chaos**

chaotic adj.

• VERBS **appear, be, look, seem** *Things often appear chaotic to the outsider.* | **become, get** *Things have been getting chaotic in the office recently.*
• ADV. **really, very** *It was really chaotic just before the show started.* | **absolutely** *Heathrow airport is absolutely chaotic.* | **increasingly** | **a bit, fairly, pretty, quite, rather, somewhat** *Things can be fairly chaotic in our house.*

chap noun

• ADJ. **clever, decent, good, jolly, lucky, nice, pleasant** *He was a pleasant chap but didn't talk much.* | **good-looking, handsome** | **young** | **old** | **poor** *The poor old chap was very shaken by the experience.* | **ordinary**
• PHRASES **not (such) a bad chap** *He's not such a bad chap really.* **sort of chap** *He's a decent sort of chap.*

chapel noun

1 part of a church; room/building used as a church
• ADJ. **little, small** | **side** *The funeral was conducted in one of the smaller side chapels.* | **family, hospital, memorial, prison, private, royal, school, wedding** *They were married in a wedding chapel in Las Vegas.*
• CHAPEL + VERB **be dedicated to sb** *The chapel is dedicated to St Michael.*
• PREP. **in a/the~**

2 church for some Protestant groups
• ADJ. **Baptist, Methodist, Nonconformist,** etc.
• VERB + CHAPEL **attend, go to** *He goes to chapel every Sunday.*
• PREP. **at~** *They are still at chapel* (= at a service). **at a/the~** *They agreed to meet at the chapel after the service.*

chapter *noun*

1 part of a book
- ADJ. **introductory, opening**
- VERB + CHAPTER **read** *I read the first few chapters and then got bored.*
- PREP. **in a/the ~** *His influence on other writers will be discussed in the next chapter.* | **~about/on** *a chapter on the city's architecture*

2 particular period
- ADJ. **difficult, sad, unhappy** *Her return to France ended a particularly unhappy chapter in her life.*

character *noun*

1 person's nature/person with a particular nature
- ADJ. **good, excellent, exemplary, impeccable | generous, gentle, likeable, lovable, popular | colourful, larger-than-life, lively, real** *You must have come across some real characters, working in the circus.* | **reformed** *He used to go out every night, but now he's a reformed character.* | **complex, elusive, enigmatic, odd | forceful, formidable, strong | weak | volatile | prickly, unpleasant | bad, evil, ruthless, violent | dubious, shady, suspicious** *Who's that suspicious character hanging around outside?* | **true | local** *The pub was full of colourful local characters.* | **human | moral** *a woman of impeccable moral character*
- VERB + CHARACTER **be, have | form, make up | reveal** *She revealed her true character when anyone disagreed with her.* | **conceal, hide | reflect** *His scruffy appearance does not reflect his character.*
- CHARACTER + NOUN **trait | defect | change** *She's undergone a complete character change since her promotion.* | **reference** *Applicants were required to obtain character references before being considered for the work.* | **assassination** *The defence lawyer attempted a character assassination of the witness* (= tried to show the witness had a bad character). | **actor, actress**
- PREP. **in sb's ~** *It's not in his character to tell lies.* **out of ~** *The lawyer argued that his client's violent behaviour was out of character.*

2 nature of sth
- ADJ. **distinctive, individual, unique | essential, fundamental, intrinsic | original | traditional** *The renovated buildings retain their traditional character.* | **international, national, regional** *Food in Italy has a distinct regional character.* ◊ *the features that make up the national character* | **intimate | public** *the public character of material published on the Internet* | **serious** *offences of a serious character* | **military, political | rural, urban** *The development detracts from the rural character of the area.*
- VERB + CHARACTER **have** *Each house in the street has its own distinctive character.* | **assume, take on** *As you move north, the landscape takes on a different character.* | **form, make up** *factors that form the character of a nation* | **lose** *The town centre has lost much of its original character.* | **retain | preserve | give sth** *It's the basil that gives the sauce its essential character.*
- PREP. **in ~** *The houses are Mediterranean in character.*

3 interesting quality that sth has
- ADJ. **considerable, great**
- VERB + CHARACTER **have** *His face has character—I'll say that for it.* | **add, give sth** *the individual touches that give character to a house*
- PREP. **of ~** *buildings of considerable character*
- PHRASES **full of character** *The restaurant is cheap and full of character.* **have a character of its own/all (of) its own** *Your handwriting has a character of its own.*

4 person's inner strength
- ADJ. **great**
- VERB + CHARACTER **show** *The team showed great character in coming back to win.* | **build** *Adventure camps are considered to be character-building.*

- PHRASES **strength of character**

5 person in a story/film, etc.
- ADJ. **central, chief, leading, main, principal | minor, supporting | fictional, fictitious | believable | sympathetic, unsympathetic | comic, heroic, tragic | cartoon**
- VERB + CHARACTER **play, portray** *The main character is played by Nicole Kidman.* | **develop** *the artist who developed the Superman character* | **kill off** *The writers killed off her character when she wanted to leave the soap.*
- CHARACTER + NOUN **development**
- PREP. **in ~** *The actors remained in character to answer questions from the audience.*

6 letter/sign in writing/printing
- ADJ. **Chinese | ASCII, numeric**
- QUANT. **set, string**
- VERB + CHARACTER **insert | delete**
- CHARACTER + NOUN **set, string**

characteristic *noun*

- ADJ. **defining, distinctive, distinguishing, identifying, individual, marked, special, striking, unique | personal | common, family, inherited, national, shared | basic, general | chief, dominant, main, major, outstanding, principal | essential, fundamental, important, key, salient | desirable | behavioural, biological, cultural, demographic, economic, genetic, physical, psychological, racial, sexual, social | human**
- VERB + CHARACTERISTIC **have** *The two species have several characteristics in common.*

characteristic *adj.*

- VERBS **be | become**
- ADV. **deeply, extremely, highly, very** *his highly characteristic features* | **entirely, utterly | fairly, quite**
- PREP. **of** *a problem that was fairly characteristic of late eighteenth century society*

charade *noun*

- ADJ. **clever, elaborate | pathetic, ridiculous**
- VERB + CHARADE **continue, go along with, keep up, maintain, take part in** *I refused to go along with their pathetic charade.*
- PREP. **~of** *She struggled to maintain the charade of not being afraid.*

charcoal *noun*

- ADJ. **activated**
- QUANT. **lump, piece**
- VERB + CHARCOAL **make, produce | burn**
- CHARCOAL + NOUN **stick | drawing, sketch**

charge *noun*

1 price asked for sth
- ADJ. **heavy, high | reasonable, small | minimum | fixed, standard | total | annual, daily, etc. | standing** *There is a quarterly standing charge.* | **additional, extra, further | admission, bank, call, call-out, cancellation, commission, cover, handling, hire, interest, maintenance, prescription, service**
- VERB + CHARGE **impose, introduce, levy, make** *We make a small charge for wrapping your gift.* | **waive** *They agreed to waive the cancellation charges.* | **incur** *All cancellations incur a charge.* | **pay | increase | reduce | reverse the ~s** (= when telephoning)
- PREP. **at a ~** *This service is available at a nominal charge.* **for a ~** *The hotel operates a bus service to the village for a small charge.* | **~for** *There is no charge for cashing traveller's cheques.* **~on** *a charge on company profits*
- PHRASES **free of charge** (= without any charge) *The company will deliver free of charge.*

2 official statement accusing sb of a crime
- ADJ. **grave, serious | lesser, reduced** *He was found guilty on a reduced charge of assault.* | **baseless, false, trumped-up | civil, criminal, disciplinary | assault, corruption, drug/drugs, fraud, murder, etc.**
- VERB + CHARGE **bring, file, lay, level, make** *Police have brought a charge of dangerous driving against the man.* | **bring, prefer, press** (only used with **charges**) | **drop, withdraw | answer, face** *She is almost certain to face criminal charges.* | **admit** *He has admitted the murder charge.* | **deny, dismiss, refute, reject** *The prime minister dismissed the charge that he had misled Parliament.* | **fabricate, trump up** *He accused the government of fabricating the charges for political reasons.* | **investigate | prove, substantiate** *The charges will be difficult to prove.* | **dismiss, throw out** *The court dismissed the charge against him.*
- CHARGE + VERB **allege sth** *new charges alleging the misuse of funds*
- CHARGE + NOUN **sheet** *At the police station a charge sheet was made out.*
- PREP. **on a/the ~** *She appeared in court on charges of kidnapping and assault.* **without~** *to be detained/held/released without charge* | **~ against** *The charges against you have been dropped.* **~ of** *a charge of armed robbery* **~ relating to** *charges relating to the embezzlement of public funds*
- PHRASES **bring/prefer/press charges (against sb)** *Many victims of crime are reluctant to press charges against their attackers.*

3 control
- ADJ. **overall** *The conductor has overall charge of the train.* | **personal** *She took personal charge of the files.* | **sole** *Stephen will resume sole charge for the time being.* | **temporary**
- VERB + CHARGE **have | take** *We need somebody to take charge of the financial side.* | **resume | place/put sb in** *John has been put in charge of marketing.*
- PREP. **in ~ (of sb/sth)** *I need to feel more in charge of my life.* **in/under sb's ~** *The child is under my charge until the mother returns from abroad.*

4 sudden attack
- ADJ. **baton, cavalry** *They were driven back by a police baton charge.*
- VERB + CHARGE **lead** *Allen led the charge, but could they get a goal back?* | **sound** *The bugle sounded the charge.*
- CHARGE + VERB **drive sb back**

charge *verb*

1 ask sb to pay money
- ADV. **directly**
- VERB + CHARGE **be entitled to, be free to, have a right to** *Firms are free to charge whatever they like for their services.*
- PREP. **against** *Research and development expenditure is charged against profits in the year it is incurred.* **at** *Stamp Duty will be charged at one per cent.* **for** *We don't charge for delivery.* **on** *The bank charges a commission on all foreign currency transactions.* **to** *The cost is charged directly to the profit and loss account.*
- PHRASES **charge sth to sb's account** *£50 will be charged to your account.*

2 make an official accusation
- ADV. **formally | jointly** *The teenagers were jointly charged with attempted murder.*
- PREP. **in connection with** *A man has been charged in connection with the attack.* **with** *She has not yet been formally charged with the offence.*

3 rush/attack
- ADV. **headlong | around/round, in, out** *The children were all charging around outside.*

- PREP. **at** *I was worried that the animal might charge at us.* **down** *I heard the sound of feet charging down the stairs.* **into** *She charged into the room.* **out of, through, towards** *The rhino charged headlong towards us.* **up**

charged *adj.*

1 full of electricity
- VERBS **be**
- ADV. **fully** *It's wise to take a fully charged spare battery with you.* | **negatively, positively | oppositely | electrically** *electrically charged particles*
- PREP. **with**

2 full of strong feeling
- VERBS **be**
- ADV. **highly** *She had a highly charged emotional life.* | **emotionally, erotically, politically** *an emotionally charged atmosphere*
- PREP. **with** *The room was charged with hatred.*

charity *noun*

- ADJ. **local, national | registered | private | animal, cancer, conservation, educational, housing, medical**
- VERB + CHARITY **donate (money) to, give (money) to, support | go to** *All the proceeds from the sale will go to charity.* | **ask for | accept** *They are proud people who don't accept charity.* | **depend on, live on** *They have no money and are forced to live on charity.*
- CHARITY + NOUN **appeal, auction, ball, concert, event, match, show | school | shop | work | worker**
- PREP. **for~** *The school raised over a hundred pounds for charity.* | **~for** *a charity for sick children*
- PHRASES **an act of charity**

charm *noun*

- ADJ. **considerable, great, immense** *a woman of considerable charm* | **easy, natural, quiet, real, special** *His natural charm and wit made him very popular.* | **personal | boyish, feminine | old-fashioned, period, traditional | rural, rustic** *The farmhouse had a certain rustic charm about it.*
- VERB + CHARM **have, possess | keep, retain** *The village still retains a lot of its old-world charm.* | **use** *He can certainly turn on the charm when he wants to!* ◇ *I nagged him for a week and used all my feminine charm.* | **exude, ooze** *He oozes charm, but I wouldn't trust him.* | **be immune to, resist** *He was unable to resist her charms.* | **succumb to** *Many women had succumbed to his charms.* | **be lacking in, lack** *The dining room was dark and gloomy, and the food was similarly lacking in charm.* | **lose** *The idea of being a farmer had lost its charm for me by this time.*

charming *adj.*

- VERBS **be, look, seem | find sb/sth**
- ADV. **extremely, really, very | absolutely, altogether, perfectly, quite, thoroughly, utterly** *She looked small and gentle and altogether charming.* | **rather | exquisitely** *an exquisitely charming portrait*

charred *adj.*

- VERBS **be**
- ADV. **badly | slightly** *The meat was slightly charred.* | **hideously** *her hideously charred and blackened features*

chart *noun*

1 diagram showing information
- ADJ. **bar, flow, pie | flip, wall** *Each classroom has a flip chart to write on.* | **organization, progress, weather**
- CHART + VERB **give sth, show sth** *a bar chart showing how sales have increased*

• PREP. **in a/the ~** *the information given in the chart* **on a/the ~** *The percentage of school-leavers is shown on the chart.*

2 detailed map of the sea/sky
• ADJ. **aviation, nautical, navigation**
• PREP. **on a/the ~** *The islands were not marked on their chart.*

3 the charts list of pop music records
• ADJ. **album, pop, singles**
• VERB + CHART **enter, go into, hit** *Their single went straight into the charts at number one.* ◇ *His latest single hit the charts last week.* | **be top of, top** *The song topped the charts for three weeks.*
• CHART + NOUN **hit**
• PREP. **in the ~** *Is that song still in the charts?*

charter *noun*

1 official written statement of principles, rights, etc.
• ADJ. **draft | founding | environmental, social | national, UN/United Nations | citizens', patients', etc.**
• VERB + CHARTER **draw up | sign**
• CHARTER + VERB **set sth out** *The charter clearly sets out children's rights.*
• PREP. **~ for** *a national charter for the protection of animals* **~ of** *a charter of workers' rights*

2 document giving rights to a town/an organization
• ADJ. **royal**
• VERB + CHARTER **give sb/sth, grant sb/sth, issue | sign | apply for | receive | revoke**
• PREP. **by ~** *They were given this right by royal charter.*

chase *noun*

• ADJ. **long, short | high-speed | car** *The film ends with a long car chase.* | **police | wild goose** *He sent us on a wild goose chase* (= a search for sth that cannot be found).
• VERB + CHASE **give, take up** *The old lady shouted for help and then gave chase.* ◇ *A police officer arrived on the scene and took up the chase.* | **abandon, give up** *Exhausted and hungry, the hunters finally gave up the chase.* | **join (in)** *Several children joined in the chase.*
• PREP. **in ~ (of)** *She ran in chase of the pram.*
• PHRASES **the thrill of the chase** *What did he really want? Was it just the thrill of the chase?*

chasm *noun*

1 hole in the ground
• ADJ. **deep, gaping, great, huge, yawning**
• CHASM + VERB **open (up)** *Suddenly a huge chasm opened in the earth.*

2 great difference of feelings/interests
• ADJ. **great, huge, unbridgeable, wide, yawning**
• VERB + CHASM **bridge**
• CHASM + VERB **separate sth** *A chasm separates my generation from my parents'.*
• PREP. **~ between** *an attempt to bridge the unbridgeable chasm between the two cultures* **~ of** *a huge chasm of hate and prejudice*

chat *noun*

• ADJ. **brief, little, quick, short | long | cosy, fireside, friendly, good, nice | casual, informal | quiet | interesting | idle | confidential, private**
• VERB + CHAT **have** *We had a nice chat over a cup of tea.*
• CHAT + NOUN **show**
• PREP. **~ about** *a chat about his new job* **~ between** *a chat between Mr Blair and a journalist* **~ to/with** *I'll have a chat to John about it.* ◇ *a friendly chat with a neighbour*

chat *verb*

• ADV. **briefly | amicably, casually, easily, informally** *You will have a chance to circulate and chat informally.* | **politely | away** *They chatted away to each other.*
• PREP. **about** *We chatted briefly about the weather.* **to** *George was in the kitchen chatting to some friends.* **with** *I spent a happy half-hour chatting with a friend.*

chatter *noun*

• ADJ. **constant, endless, incessant** *Her constant chatter was starting to annoy me.* | **excited, nervous, noisy | idle** *I wish you'd stop wasting time in idle chatter.*
• PREP. **~ about** *She was full of chatter about her new friends.*

chatter *verb*

• ADV. **excitedly, happily | away, on** *He chattered on happily for about half an hour.*
• PREP. **about** *We chattered about work.* **to** *chattering excitedly to her friends*

chauffeur *noun*

• ADJ. **uniformed**
• CHAUFFEUR + VERB **drive (sb/sth)** *The chauffeur drove them straight to the theatre.*
• PHRASES **chauffeur-driven** *The newly-weds set off in a chauffeur-driven limousine.*
⇨ Note at JOB

chauvinism *noun*

• ADJ. **male | national | British, Russian, etc.**

chauvinist *noun*

• ADJ. **male**
• PHRASES **a male chauvinist pig**

cheap *adj., adv.*

1 low price
• VERBS **be, be going** *a brand new radio going cheap* | **buy sth, sell sth** *They're selling fabrics cheap this week.* | **not come** *Shoes like that don't come cheap.*
• ADV. **amazingly, extremely, incredibly, remarkably, ridiculously, very** *It's a good restaurant, and incredibly cheap.* | **comparatively, fairly, pretty, quite, reasonably, relatively | hardly, not exactly** *At £60 000 the car is not exactly cheap* (= it is very expensive). | **suspiciously** *The watch was suspiciously cheap; it was probably a fake.* | **buy/get sth on the cheap** *The school managed to get a couple of computers on the cheap.*

2 poor quality
• VERBS **be, look** *The glasses are plain without looking cheap.*
• PHRASES **cheap and nasty** *cheap and nasty products with brand names you've never heard of*

check *noun*

1 close look to make sure sth is safe/correct
• ADJ. **complete, full, thorough | careful, close, rigorous, tight | cursory, quick | periodic, regular, routine | annual, daily, etc. | constant, continuous | random, spot** *In a series of spot checks, police searched buses crossing the border.* | **cross (also cross-check), double (also double-check) | independent | visual** *I did a quick visual check of the engine.* | **dental, fitness, health, medical | police, safety, security | identity | customs, immigration, passport | stock | quality | spell/spelling** *I do a spell check on all my emails.* | **sound** *The band wants to do a sound check before the concert.*
• VERB + CHECK **carry out, conduct, do, give sth,**

have, make, run *I'll just have a quick check to see if the letter's arrived.* ◇ *A thorough check is made before the luggage is put on the plane.* ◇ *We're running a police check on all applicants for the job.* | keep, maintain *Police are keeping a close check on the house.* | go for *I have to go for a dental check.*
• PREP. ~on *a routine check on the factory*

2 control/restraint
• ADJ. natural *Leaving some fields fallow provided a natural check on insect populations.*
• VERB + CHECK act as, provide | hold sth in, keep sth in *You need to keep your temper in check!*
• PREP. ~on *The law acts as a check on people's behaviour.*

check verb

• ADV. always, daily, regularly *Always check that the electricity is switched off before you start.* ◇ *Check the engine oil level regularly.* | carefully, thoroughly
• VERB + CHECK had better, must, need to, should *We had better check that all the doors are locked.*
• PREP. against *I'll need to check these figures against last year's.* for *Check the roof for loose slates.* with *I checked with her to see if she needed any help.*
• PHRASES be worth checking *It's worth checking that there is no rust on the car.* check to see if/whether *He was just checking to see if I was in my room.*

checklist noun

• ADJ. useful | mental
• VERB + CHECKLIST have | use | draw up, produce *My boss is drawing up a checklist of my duties.* | go through, run through *We ran through the checklist of points to consider when buying a computer.*
• PREP. ~ for *a useful checklist for assessing different schools* ~of *a checklist of questions*

checkout noun

• ADJ. supermarket
• VERB + CHECKOUT go through, walk through *You can't just go through the checkout without paying!*
• CHECKOUT + NOUN assistant, girl, operator
• PREP. at the~ *He hates waiting at the checkout.*

checkpoint noun

• ADJ. border | army, military | vehicle
• VERB + CHECKPOINT set up *The army has set up checkpoints on all the major roads in the area.*
• PREP. at a/the ~ *We were stopped at the checkpoint.* through a/the~ *The police waved our car through the border checkpoint.*

check-up noun

• ADJ. thorough | regular | annual, monthly, etc. | routine | dental, health, medical
• VERB + CHECK-UP go for, have *At your age, you should have regular check-ups.* | do, give (sb) *The company doctor does check-ups on Wednesdays.*

cheek noun

1 part of the face
• ADJ. flushed, hot | cool | smooth, soft | ashen, pale, pallid, pasty | blushing, pink, rosy, scarlet | sunken *His red-rimmed eyes and sunken cheeks betrayed his lack of sleep.* | hamster/hamster-like, plump | unshaven | tear-stained, wet *Her cheeks were wet with tears.*
• VERB + CHEEK brush, dab (at), stroke, touch *She dabbed at her cheeks with a handkerchief.* | kiss, peck | give (sb), proffer *She proffered her cheek to kiss.*

• CHEEK + VERB blaze, burn, flame, grow hot, redden *He felt his cheeks burning with shame.*
• PREP. across sb's/the ~ *She gave him a sharp slap across his cheek.* against sb's~ *She laid her cheek against his.* down sb's~ *A tear slid down her cheek.* in sb's~s *She had a healthy bloom in her cheeks.* on sb's/the~ *He kissed his mother on both cheeks and got on the train.*
• PHRASES bring the colour (back) to your cheeks, the colour floods/rises/rushes to your cheeks *The colour flooded to his cheeks when he realized he was being watched.* a kiss/peck on the cheek *She gave him a peck on the cheek and said goodbye.*

2 lack of respect
• ADJ. awful, bare-faced, colossal *It's an awful cheek, the way he keeps asking you to lend him money.* | bleeding (taboo), bloody (taboo), damned
• VERB + CHEEK have *He's got a cheek, making you wait outside his office.*
• PHRASES Of all the cheek!/What (a) cheek! *He asked you for money? Of all the cheek!*

cheekbone noun

• ADJ. high, prominent | perfect, sculptured | broken, cracked, fractured
• PREP. beneath sb's ~s *The hollows beneath his cheekbones showed his stress.* on sb's ~s *A flush of anger appeared on her cheekbones.* over sb's ~s *The skin stretched taut over his cheekbones.*

cheer noun

• ADJ. big, deafening, great, hearty, huge, loud, rousing *The players were greeted by rousing cheers.*
• VERB + CHEER give (sb) *They gave a big cheer when I finally arrived.* | be greeted by/with, get, raise *She got a loud cheer when she finished speaking.*
• CHEER + VERB go up *A deafening cheer went up from the crowd.*
• CHEER + NOUN leader
• PREP. amid/amidst~ *He accepted the prize amid cheers.* to ~s *She went off the stage to loud cheers.* | ~for *a cheer for democracy* ~ from *There were loud cheers from the crowd.* ~of *cheers of welcome*
• PHRASES three cheers for sb/sth *Three cheers for Mr Jones, who has been such a wonderful teacher!*

cheer verb

1 shout to encourage sb
• ADV. loudly, wildly *The crowd cheered loudly as the goalkeeper made a brilliant save.*
• PREP. for *The fans cheered for their team.*

2 make sb happy/more hopeful
• ADV. greatly, a lot *I was greatly cheered by this news.* ◇ *Talking to Jane cheered me up a lot.* | a bit | up
• PREP. (up) with *I cheered her up with memories of our holidays together.*

cheerful adj.

• VERBS appear, be, feel, look, seem, sound | become | keep, remain, stay *I'm amazed that she keeps so cheerful.* | keep sb *We tried to keep him cheerful.*
• ADV. amazingly, extremely, incredibly, remarkably, very | almost | fairly, quite | falsely *'The doctor is on her way,' said Mrs Morris, sounding falsely cheerful.*

cheese noun

• ADJ. hard | soft | sharp, strong | mild | full-fat, low-fat | grated, melted, toasted | processed | blue, cottage, cream, curd, goat's, smoked | Cheddar, Parmesan, etc. | Dutch, Swiss, etc.
• QUANT. chunk, crumb, hunk, lump, piece, slice

• VERB + CHEESE **eat, have | make | cut, grate, slice** *Cut the cheese into cubes.* | **melt | sprinkle (sth with), top (sth with)** *Sprinkle the cheese over the beans.* ◊ *Sprinkle the potatoes with grated cheese and grill for a few minutes.*
• CHEESE + NOUN **fondue, omelette, roll, sandwich, sauce, soufflé | board** (= a board on which cheese is cut and served; a selection of cheeses served during a meal) | **factory**
• PHRASES **bread and cheese, cheese and biscuits, cheese on toast, a selection of cheeses**
⇨ Special page at FOOD

chef *noun*

• ADJ. **excellent, good | cordon bleu | head, maître, master | apprentice, second, sous, trainee** *He took a job as a sous chef in a London hotel.*
⇨ Note at JOB

chemical *noun*

• ADJ. **pure | organic | inorganic, synthetic | dangerous, harmful, hazardous, poisonous, toxic | agricultural, household, industrial**
• VERB + CHEMICAL **manufacture, produce | discharge, dump** *chemicals discharged by industry into our lakes and rivers* | **be exposed to** *Many workers are regularly exposed to dangerous chemicals.*
• CHEMICAL/CHEMICALS + NOUN **factory, plant, works** *pollution from a big chemicals plant* | **business, company | industry, manufacturing**

chemist *noun*

1 person who prepares and sells medicines
• ADJ. **local | dispensing**
• PHRASES **chemist's (shop), the chemist's** *I've just got to go to the chemist's.*
2 specialist in chemistry
• ADJ. **distinguished, leading | government, industrial | analytical, research | inorganic, organic**
⇨ Note at JOB

chemistry *noun*

1 subject of study
• ADJ. **analytical, applied, theoretical | environmental, physical | industrial | inorganic, organic**
• CHEMISTRY + NOUN **set** *For her twelfth birthday, she asked for a chemistry set.*
⇨ Note at SUBJECT (for verbs and nouns)
2 chemical structure of substance
• ADJ. **blood, soil, water, etc. | body** *natural changes in body chemistry*
3 personal feelings/attraction
• ADJ. **personal | sexual**
• PREP. **~ between** *The personal chemistry between the two stars of the film is obvious.*

cheque *noun*

• ADJ. **large | blank | bad, dud, forged | crossed, post-dated, signed | personal | giro, pay, traveller's**
• VERB + CHEQUE **issue, make out, sign, write (out), write sb** *Shall I make the cheque out to you?* ◊ *Can I write you a cheque?* | **draw** *He drew a large cheque on his company's account.* | **make payable** *Cheques should be made payable to Toyland plc.* | **give sb, hand sb, hand over | deposit, pay in** *She deposited the cheque in her husband's account.* ◊ *I've got to go to the bank to pay this cheque in.* | **pay by | cash** *I'll cash a traveller's cheque at the bank.* | **accept** *Does the restaurant accept cheques?* | **clear, honour, pass** *He was sacked for passing bad cheques.* | **bounce | cancel, stop | endorse**

• CHEQUE + VERB **bounce** *The cheque will bounce if your salary doesn't reach your account today.*
• CHEQUE + NOUN **account | (guarantee) card** *Cheques must be supported by a cheque guarantee card.* | **book, stub**
• PREP. **~ for** *a cheque for ten pounds*

cherry *noun*

• ADJ. **black, red | glacé, morello | juicy, sour, sweet**
• QUANT. **bunch**
• CHERRY + NOUN **stone**
⇨ Special page at FRUIT

chess *noun*

• ADJ. **computer, machine**
• QUANT. **game**
• VERB + CHESS **play**
• CHESS + NOUN **board, piece, set, table | move | position | grandmaster, master, player | buff | championship, match, tournament | club | computer | world** *a star of the chess world*

chest *noun*

• ADJ. **broad, manly, massive, muscular, muscled, powerful, strong | narrow, puny | flat** *She wears loose clothes to hide her flat chest.* | **bare, naked | hairy, hairless | bad, weak, wheezy | lower, upper**
• VERB + CHEST **clutch (at)** *Clutching his chest in agony, he fell to the ground.* | **thump** *'You've got to have courage,' he said, thumping his chest.*
• CHEST + VERB **expand, heave, rise and fall | puff (out/up), swell** *His chest puffed out with indignation at the suggestion.* ◊ *His chest swelled with pride as he accepted the award.* | **tighten** *Her chest tightened with fear.* | **ache** *She ran until her chest ached.*
• CHEST + NOUN **pain, tightness | injury | ailment, complaint, condition, disease, infection, problems, trouble | radiograph, X-ray | muscles | hair | cavity**
• PREP. **in the/your~** *She was hit in the chest by two of the bullets.* **on the/your~** *the hairs on his chest* **to the/your~** *He suffered burns to the chest and neck.* ◊ *She clutched her baby tightly to her chest.*

chestnut *noun*

• ADJ. **bright, glossy, rich | dark, deep**
⇨ Special page at COLOUR

chew *verb*

• ADV. **well, thoroughly | vigorously | thoughtfully | up** *Chew your food up thoroughly before you swallow it.*
• PREP. **at** *She was chewing at her lower lip.* **on** *The baby chewed on a rusk.*

chicken *noun*

1 bird
• ADJ. **battery, corn-fed, free-range** *Battery chickens have miserable lives.* | **plump | scrawny | live** *a crate of live chickens*
• VERB + CHICKEN **keep | kill | pluck | truss (up)** *Are we just going to sit here like trussed up chickens?*
• CHICKEN + VERB **peck | scratch** *A few scrawny chickens were scratching around the yard.* | **cluck | roost | wander**
• CHICKEN + NOUN **farmer | coop, run | wire | feed**
2 meat
• ADJ. **fresh, frozen | juicy, succulent, tender | cold**
• QUANT. **piece**
• VERB + CHICKEN **eat, have | cook | barbecue, fry, grill, roast, etc. | stuff**
• CHICKEN + NOUN **breast, drumsticks, giblets, joint,**

leg, liver, piece, thigh, wing | casserole, curry, pie, salad, sandwich, soup, stock
● PHRASES **(a) breast/leg of chicken, chicken and chips**
⇒ Special page at FOOD

chickenpox *noun*

⇒ Special page at ILLNESS

chief *noun*

● ADJ. **tribal | army, council, industry, intelligence, military, party, police, security, union | education, health, etc.**
● PHRASES **chief of police, chief of staff**

child *noun*

● ADJ. **little, small, young** *My father died while I was still a small child.* | **teenage** *We've got three teenage children.* | **good, obedient, well-behaved | delinquent, difficult, disobedient, fractious, mischievous, naughty, problem, sulky, unruly, wayward, wilful** *She works in a centre for delinquent children.* ◊ *He's always been a problem child.* ◊ *The children were quite unruly and ran around the house as if they owned it.* | **bright, gifted, intelligent, precocious** *a school for gifted children* ◊ *What a precocious child—reading Jane Austen at the age of ten!* | **dull, slow** *Teaching is particularly difficult when a class contains both slow and bright children.* | **well-cared for | abandoned, abused, neglected** *therapy for sexually abused children* | **sickly | loving | only** *It was a bit lonely being an only child.* | **fatherless, motherless | illegitimate | unborn** *an organization that campaigns for the rights of the unborn child* | **dependent** *tax concessions for families with dependent children* | **street** *There are a lot of street children in the poorer parts of the city.*
● VERB + CHILD **have** *How many children have you got?* | **give birth to, have** *She didn't have her first child until she was nearly forty.* | **conceive** *We had trouble conceiving our first child.* | **expect** *They are expecting a child in June.* | **adopt | bring up, raise, rear** *He had old-fashioned ideas on how to bring up children.* | **indulge, pamper, spoil** *You can't spoil a child by giving it all the affection it wants.* | **abduct | abandon**
● CHILD + VERB **be born** *Their first child was born with a rare heart condition.* | **develop, grow (up)** *Children grow up so quickly!* ◊ *good food for growing children* | **cry, scream, whimper, whine | misbehave**
● CHILD + NOUN **actor, bride | welfare**
● PREP. **with~** *(literary) big with child* (= pregnant)

childbirth *noun*

● ADJ. **natural**
● VERB + CHILDBIRTH **die in** *His wife died in childbirth in 1928.*
● PHRASES **the pain of childbirth** *She dreaded the pain of childbirth.*

childhood *noun*

● ADJ. **happy | deprived, difficult, lonely, traumatic, unhappy | normal | early** *From earliest childhood she'd had a love of dancing.* | **late** *His health remained poor into later childhood.*
● VERB + CHILDHOOD **have** *She had a very happy childhood.* | **spend** *He spent most of his childhood in Egypt.* | **survive** *Her second son didn't survive childhood.*
● CHILDHOOD + NOUN **days, years | dream, experience, fantasy, memories | friend, sweetheart | home | disease, illness, mortality**
● PREP. **during ~** *He became diabetic during childhood.* **from~** *She still retained many friends from childhood.* **in~**

She died in childhood. **throughout ~** *He travelled a lot throughout his childhood.*
● PHRASES **scenes from/of sb's childhood**

chill *noun*

1 coldness
● ADJ. **bitter, deep | cold, damp | slight | evening, morning, night | autumn/autumnal, winter**
● VERB + CHILL **feel** *I could feel the chill as soon as I went outside.* | **take off** *I'll add some hot water to the milk to take the chill off it* (= to make it slightly warmer).
● CHILL + NOUN **factor** *With the chill factor, it's nearly minus forty here.*
● PHRASES **a chill in the air** *There's a slight chill in the air.*

2 feeling of fear
● ADJ. **sudden | icy**
● VERB + CHILL **feel** *She felt a sudden chill at the thought of the dangers he faced.* | **strike** *Her words struck a chill in his heart.*
● CHILL + VERB **run down/up sb's spine, run through sb** *A chill ran through me at the thought.*
● PREP. **~ of** *a chill of fear*
● PHRASES **send a chill through sb/down sb's spine** *The news sent a chill down her spine.*

3 mild illness
● ADJ. **bad, nasty, severe | slight**
● VERB + CHILL **catch, get** *I caught a nasty chill after my swim last week.*
⇒ Special page at ILLNESS

chilled *adj.*

● VERBS **be, feel** *I suddenly felt chilled and had to go indoors.* | **serve sth** *The wine is best served chilled.*
● PHRASES **chilled to the bone/marrow** *You must be chilled to the bone sitting out here!*

chilli *noun*

● ADJ. **fresh | dried | hot | green, red**
● CHILLI + NOUN **pepper | oil, powder, sauce | beans**
⇒ Special page at FOOD

chilly *adj.*

● VERBS **be, feel** *She was beginning to feel chilly.* | **get** *We were starting to get a bit chilly.* | **turn** (only used about the weather) *It turned chilly in the afternoon.*
● ADV. **decidedly, distinctly, very | a bit, pretty, quite, rather, somewhat**

chimney *noun*

● ADJ. **high, tall | short | narrow, wide | tapering | smoking** *The air was black from smoking chimneys.* | **sooty | factory, industrial**
● VERB + CHIMNEY **clean, sweep**
● CHIMNEY + VERB **belch sth** *factory chimneys belching smoke over the town* | **draw** *This chimney doesn't draw very well.*
● CHIMNEY + NOUN **breast, flue, piece, pot, stack | sweep**

chin *noun*

● ADJ. **square | pointed/pointy | firm, jutting | non-existent, receding, weak | dimpled | determined, resolute | smooth | stubbled/stubbly, unshaven | double**
● VERB + CHIN **lift, raise, stick out, tilt** *She tilted her chin at him defiantly.* | **finger, rub, scratch, stroke** *He stroked his chin thoughtfully.* | **rest** *She sat with her elbows on the table, resting her chin on her cupped hands.*
● CHIN + VERB **rise** *His chin rose in a proud gesture.*

- CHIN + NOUN **strap** *Fasten the chin strap or the helmet will fall off.*
- PREP. **beneath/under sb's ~** *He put his hand under her chin and lifted her face to his.* **down sb's ~** *The juice dribbled down his chin.* **on sb's/the ~** *He had bits of food on his chin.* ◇ *She caught him with a hard blow on the chin.*

china *noun*

1 hard white substance
- ADJ. **fine | bone** *fine bone china tableware*
- VERB + CHINA **be made of**
- CHINA + NOUN **cup, dish, etc. | clay**

2 cups/plates, made of china
- ADJ. **best** *She got out the best china for the visitors.* | **broken, cracked**
- QUANT. **set**

Chinese *noun*

- ADJ. **Mandarin**
- CHINESE + NOUN **character**
- ⇨ Note at LANGUAGE

chip *noun*

1 (usually **chips**) long thin piece of fried potato
- ADJ. **greasy | frozen, oven-ready**
- QUANT. **bag, plate**
- VERB + CHIP **eat, have** *All he'll eat is chips.* | **live on** *I never cook anything grand—we live on chips and baked beans.* | **cook, fry**
- CHIP + NOUN **pan | shop**
- PHRASES **and/with chips** *fish and chips*
- ⇨ Special page at FOOD

2 microchip
- ADJ. **computer, silicon | graphics, memory, microprocessor**
- VERB + CHIP **make, manufacture, produce | design, develop | use** *This computer uses the DX chip.*
- CHIP + VERB **contain sth** *a chip containing the coding devices*
- CHIP + NOUN **design, technology | set** *a Pentium-compatible chip set*
- PREP. **on a/the ~** *Advances in chip technology have made it possible to pack even more circuits on a chip.*
- ⇨ Special page at COMPUTER

chip *verb*

- ADV. **badly** *She fell and chipped her tooth quite badly.* | **away** *He was chipping away at the stone.* ◇ *(figurative) They chipped away at the power of the government (= gradually made it weaker).*
- PREP. **off** *We chipped the paint off the wood.*

chocolate *noun*

1 sweet brown food
- ADJ. **dark, plain | milk | white | bitter | cooking**
- QUANT. **bar, slab | bit, piece, square** *He broke off a few squares of chocolate.* | **box** *I gave her a box of hand-made Belgian chocolates.*
- VERB + CHOCOLATE **eat | have | break (up) into pieces/squares** *She broke a bar of dark chocolate into four pieces.* | **grate | melt** *Melt 100g of cooking chocolate in a basin over hot water.* | **coat/cover sth in/with, dip sth in, spread/sprinkle (sth with)** *a box of brazil nuts coated in chocolate*
- CHOCOLATE + VERB **melt** *Stir until the chocolate has melted.*
- CHOCOLATE + NOUN **bar, chip | biscuit, cake, eclair, egg, gateau, ice cream, mousse, sauce | factory**
- ⇨ Special page at FOOD

2 small sweet made from chocolate
- ADJ. **soft-centred | hand-made**
- QUANT. **box**
- CHOCOLATE + NOUN **box**

3 drink made from powdered chocolate
- ADJ. **hot | drinking**
- QUANT. **cup, mug**

choice *noun*

1 act of choosing
- ADJ. **careful, good, informed, right, wise** *a careful choice of words* | **bad, wrong | difficult, hard, stark** *She faced the stark choice of backing the new scheme or losing her job.* | **natural | moral** *Doctors have to make moral choices every day of their lives.* | **career**
- VERB + CHOICE **make | be faced with, face**
- PREP. **by/from/out of ~** (= because you have chosen) *I wouldn't have come to this bar by choice!* **of ~** (= that is/should be chosen by a particular group of people for a particular purpose) *It's the software of choice for business use.* **of your ~** (= that you choose yourself) *First prize will be a meal for two at a restaurant of your choice.* | **~ about** *to make choices about their future*

2 chance/ability to choose
- ADJ. **clear | free** *Students have a free choice from a range of subjects.* | **first** *You can have first choice of all the rooms.* | **multiple** *a test with multiple choice questions* | **consumer, parental**
- VERB + CHOICE **have** *I now had a clear choice: either I accept their terms or I leave.* | **exercise** *Everyone in a democracy has the right to exercise choice.* | **give sb, present sb with** *We gave her the choice, and she decided she'd like a bike for her birthday.* | **extend**
- PREP. **~ about** *He had no choice about that.* **~ as to** *to extend parental choice as to which schools children should attend* **~ between** *She has a choice between three different universities.* **~ of** *a choice of wines*
- PHRASES **freedom of choice, have little/no choice but to do sth** *I had no choice but to cancel my holiday.* **have no choice in the matter** *The way he behaved meant that we had no choice in the matter.* **leave sb with little/no choice** *Your decision leaves me with no choice but to resign.*

3 things from which you can/must choose
- ADJ. **good, wide | limited | available** *a range of available choices*
- VERB + CHOICE **have, offer** *We offer a choice of ten different holiday destinations.*
- CHOICE + VERB **be available (to sb), be open to sb** *a range of choices available to buyers*
- PREP. **~ of** *The shop has a very limited choice of ties.*
- PHRASES **be spoilt for choice** (= to have a large number of things from which to choose)

4 sb/sth that is chosen
- ADJ. **excellent, good, happy** *It was a happy choice of venue* | **obvious** *Bill is the obvious choice for captain of the team.* | **popular | first, second** *Our first choice for a holiday is the north of Scotland.*
- PREP. **~ as** *Mary is a popular choice as chair of the committee.* **~ for** *I think she's a very good choice for captain.*

choir *noun*

- ADJ. **massed** *a massed choir of local schoolchildren* | **50-strong, etc. | ladies', male-voice, mixed, etc. | school | cathedral, church, etc.**
- VERB + CHOIR **be in, sing in** *She sings in the church choir.* | **conduct | accompany**
- CHOIR + NOUN **practice** *Choir practice is on Wednesday evenings.*
- PREP. **in a/the ~** *two of the girls in the choir*

choke *verb*

- ADV. **almost, nearly**
- VERB + CHOKE **threaten to** *The panic rising in his throat threatened to choke him.* | **make sb** *The fumes from the burning tyres made her choke.*
- PREP. **on** *My son nearly choked on one of those sweets.*
- PHRASES **choke (sb) to death** *He choked to death when a fish bone got stuck in his throat.*

cholera *noun*

- VERB + CHOLERA **have, suffer from** | **catch, contract** | **die from/of**
- QUANT. **outbreak**
- CHOLERA + NOUN **epidemic, outbreak** *A cholera epidemic swept the country.* | **toxin** | **case, victim**
⇨ Special page at ILLNESS

cholesterol *noun*

- ADJ. **high, raised** | **low** | **blood** *raised blood cholesterol levels*
- QUANT. **level** *a high/low level of cholesterol*
- VERB + CHOLESTEROL **have** (only used with *high* or *low*) *He has high cholesterol.* | **contain** *chips containing no cholesterol* | **reduce** *Eating garlic can significantly reduce cholesterol in the blood.*
- CHOLESTEROL + NOUN **level**
- PHRASES **be high/low in cholesterol** *foods that are low in cholesterol*

choose *verb*

- ADV. **carefully** *He chose his words carefully.* | **freely** *They can choose freely from a wide range of courses.*
- VERB + CHOOSE **be able to, be free to, can** *You are free to choose whichever courses you want to take.*
- PREP. **between** *She had to choose between giving up her job or hiring a nanny.* **from** *There are several different models to choose from.*
- PHRASES **pick and choose** *You have to take any job you can get—you can't pick and choose.*

chop *noun*

- ADJ. **lamb, mutton, pork** | **loin** *pork loin chops*
- VERB + CHOP **eat, have** | **braise, cook, fry, grill**
⇨ Special page at FOOD

chop *verb*

- ADV. **finely** *Add finely chopped parsley.* | **roughly** *Roughly chop the cabbage.* | **up** *I spent the day chopping up wood.* | **down** *There are concerns over how quickly the forests are being chopped down.* | **off** *He chopped off the small branches before cutting down the tree.*
- PREP. **into** *Chop the meat into small cubes.*
- PHRASES **chop sth to pieces** *The furniture had been chopped to pieces.*

chord *noun*

- ADJ. **major, minor** | **C, D, etc.** | **augmented, diminished** *a diminished 7th chord* | **dominant, tonic, etc.** | **7th, 9th, etc.** | **full** | **broken** | **jazz** | **guitar, piano**
- VERB + CHORD **play, strum**
- CHORD + NOUN **change, progression, sequence**

chore *noun*

- ADJ. **little, small** | **daily, day-to-day, routine** | **administrative, domestic, household**
- VERB + CHORE **carry out, do** *It'll take me an hour to do the household chores.*

chorus *noun*

1 part of a song that is repeated
- ADJ. **rousing** | **final**
- VERB + CHORUS **join in, sing**

2 sth that a lot of people say together
- ADJ. **general** | **growing** *There is a growing chorus of protest against the policy.*
- VERB + CHORUS **join** *Many teachers have joined the chorus of voices that disapprove of the new tests.* | **be met with, bring** *His suggestions were met with a chorus of jeers.*
- CHORUS + VERB **greet sb/sth**
- PREP. **in ~** (= all together) *'Hello,' they shouted in chorus.* | **~ of** *a chorus of boos*
- PHRASES **a chorus of voices**

3 large group of singers/dancers
- ADJ. **double** | **female, male** | **dawn** (= of birds before dawn)
- CHORUS + NOUN **girl, line**
- PREP. **in a/the ~** *She is singing in the chorus.*
- PHRASES **a member of the chorus**

christening *noun*

- VERB + CHRISTENING **attend, go to**
- CHRISTENING + VERB **take place**
- CHRISTENING + NOUN **gift, present** | **mug, spoon** | **robe/robes** | **party**
- PREP. **at a/the ~** *We all got together at the christening.*

Christian *noun*

- ADJ. **believing, committed, devout, good, practising** | **born-again, evangelical, fundamentalist**
- VERB + CHRISTIAN **be brought up (as)**

Christianity *noun*

- ADJ. **evangelical, fundamentalist, orthodox** | **muscular** *Victorian 'muscular Christianity' was all about achieving self-control through strict mental and physical discipline.* | **Catholic, Orthodox, Protestant**
⇨ Note at RELIGION (for verbs and phrases)

Christmas *noun*

- ADJ. **good, nice** | **traditional** | **white** *hoping for a white Christmas* (= with snow on the ground)
- VERB + CHRISTMAS **have, spend** *Did you have a good Christmas?* ◇ *We're going to spend Christmas at home this year.* | **celebrate** *to celebrate Christmas in the traditional way* | **get sth for** *What did you get for Christmas?*
- CHRISTMAS + VERB **come** *Christmas is coming and the food shops are full.*
- CHRISTMAS + NOUN **dinner** | **party** | **present, cake, pudding** | **lights, tree** *We're going up to town to see the Christmas lights.* | **carol** | **Day** | **holiday/holidays** | **celebrations**
- PREP. **at ~** *There are lots of parties at Christmas.* **for ~** *For Christmas he gave her a silk blouse.* **over ~** *The library is closed over Christmas.*
- PHRASES **Happy/Merry Christmas!, wish sb a happy/merry Christmas**

chronological *adj.*

- VERBS **be**
- ADV. **strictly** *a strictly chronological account of the events* | **broadly** *The anthology is broadly chronological.*

chuckle *noun*

- ADJ. **little, soft** | **deep/deep-throated, low**
- VERB + CHUCKLE **give, have, let out** *She gave a little chuckle.* | **suppress** | **hear**
- PREP. **with a ~** *'I was only kidding,' he said with a low*

chuckle. | **~ about/over** *We had a chuckle about it after-wards.*

chuckle *verb*

- ADV. **softly**
- PREP. **about/over** *She was still chuckling about the story the next day.* **at** *He chuckled at the thought of the two of them stuck in the snow.*
- PHRASES **chuckle to yourself** *She chuckled softly to herself as she remembered his astonished look.*

chug *verb*

- ADV. **slowly, steadily** *The train chugged steadily along the West Highland Line.*
- PREP. **along, down, in, out, past, etc.** *The boat chugged slowly down the river.*

chunk *noun*

- ADJ. **big, great, huge, large, sizeable, substantial** *He bit a great chunk out of the apple.* ◇ *This one project has taken a substantial chunk of our budget.* | **bite-size/bite-sized, manageable** *He cut the food up into bite-size chunks.* ◇ *(figurative) The listening texts consist of short, bite-sized chunks which are accessible to beginners.* | **pineapple** *a tin of pineapple chunks*
- VERB + CHUNK **cut sth (up) into**
- PREP. **in a/the ~** *I bought the cheese in one big chunk.* | **~ of** *a huge chunk of meat / rock / text*

church *noun*

1 building where Christians go to worship
- ADJ. **local, parish, village**
- VERB + CHURCH **build | consecrate, found** *The church was consecrated in 1250.* | **dedicate** *The church is dedicated to St Paul.*
- CHURCH + NOUN **bells, clock, steeple, tower | hall | fête**
- PREP. **at a/the ~** *a chamber concert at our local church* **in a/the ~** *There's an interesting organ in the village church.*

2 meeting for public worship in a church
- VERB + CHURCH **attend, go to** *Do you go to church?*
- CHURCH + NOUN **service | music**
- PREP. **after/before ~** *Come to our place for lunch after church.* **at/in ~** *Mrs Parsons wasn't at church this Sunday.*

3 the Church all Christians regarded as a group
- ADJ. **early** *The early Church believed miracles were proof of who Jesus was.*
- VERB + CHURCH **enter, go into** *He went into the Church (= became a priest) when he was 23.* | **leave** *He left the Church after a loss of faith.*
- CHURCH + NOUN **authorities, leaders, member**

4 particular group of Christians
- ADJ. **high, low** *He loves all the high church traditions—incense and processions and vestments.* | **evangelical, fundamentalist | established** (= official), **free** (= non-conformist) | **Christian, etc.**
- CHURCH + NOUN **authorities, elder, leader, member**
- PHRASES **a member of a church**

chute *noun*

- ADJ. **garbage, laundry, rubbish, water** *a swimming pool with a long water chute*
- PREP. **down a/the ~** *The rubbish goes down the chute into a large bin.*

cider *noun*

- ADJ. **dry | sweet | rough, strong** *The cider was very strong and went straight to our heads.* | **farmhouse**
- QUANT. **litre, pint | bottle, glass, jug**

- VERB + CIDER **have** *I'll have a glass of dry cider, please.* | **drink | sip, swig, take a sip/swig of**
- CIDER + NOUN **apples | vinegar**

cigar *noun*

- ADJ. **fat | expensive | cheap**
- QUANT. **box**
- VERB + CIGAR **smoke | draw on, pull on** *He paused and drew on his cigar.* | **light | extinguish, put out, stub out**
- CIGAR + VERB **burn** *Her thin cigar burned quite quickly.* | **glow** *His cigar glowed in the darkened room.*
- CIGAR + NOUN **ash, smoke | butt, end | case, holder | smoker**
- PHRASES **brandy/port and cigars** *They left the men to their port and cigars.*

cigarette *noun*

- ADJ. **lighted, lit** *carelessly throwing a lighted cigarette in the litter bin* | **half-smoked | illicit** *She slipped outside for an illicit cigarette.* | **filter tip, hand-rolled, king size, low-tar, menthol**
- QUANT. **pack, packet** *She smokes a packet of cigarettes a day.*
- VERB + CIGARETTE **smoke | draw on, pull on, suck on** *He pulled on his cigarette and waited for the train.* | **light | extinguish, put out, stub out** *Please extinguish all cigarettes now.* | **roll** *She rolls her own cigarettes.* | **flick (away)** *The old man flicked his cigarette onto the roadside.* | **advertise** *Posters advertising cigarettes have to carry government health warnings.*
- CIGARETTE + VERB **burn** *The cigarette burned slowly in the ashtray.* | **glow** *The cigarettes glowed in the dark.*
- CIGARETTE + NOUN **ash, smoke** *the smell of stale cigarette smoke* | **butt, end | case, packet | holder, lighter | smoker | burn | advertising**

cinder *noun*

- ADJ. **glowing, hot, red** *a fireplace full of glowing red cinders*
- CINDER + NOUN **path, track**
- PHRASES **burnt to a cinder** (= completely burnt) *By the time I got home, the cake was burnt to a cinder.*

cinema *noun*

1 place where you go to see a film
- ADJ. **packed** *The cinema was packed every night for 'Shrek'.* | **multiplex** *a new multiplex cinema on the edge of town*
- VERB + CINEMA **go to** *How often do you go to the cinema?* | **be on at** *What's on at the cinema tonight?*
- CINEMA + NOUN **screen | audience | advertising, commercial | chain**

2 films in general
- ADJ. **commercial, Hollywood, mainstream, popular | art, arthouse, independent | avant-garde, modernist, realist, social | silent** *She started making films in the last years of silent cinema.*

circle *noun*

1 shape
- ADJ. **complete, full** *The stones form a complete circle.* ◇ *How long does it take for the dial to rotate through a full circle?* | **concentric | widening** *The water rippled in widening circles round the fountain.* | **overlapping** *a design of overlapping circles* | **tight** *He turned the car in a tight circle.* | **half | Antarctic, Arctic, polar**
- VERB + CIRCLE **draw | describe** (*technical*), **go around/round in** *If you follow the road signs you will simply find yourself going round in a circle.* | **form, make | cut out**

• PREP. **in a/the ~** *The children stood in a circle.* ◇ *The planets move in circles round the sun.* | **~ of**
• PHRASES **the area/circumference/diameter/radius of a circle, the centre/middle of a circle**

2 group of people
• ADJ. **wide** *She has a wide circle of acquaintances.* | **narrow, small** | **charmed, close/closed, intimate, magic, select** *He invited only a select circle of friends to the wedding.* | **exalted, high** | **immediate** *They treat anyone outside their immediate circle with suspicion.* | **inner** *He's joined the inner circles of the court early in his career.* | **academic, aristocratic, artistic, business, court, diplomatic, government, intellectual, literary, official, political, royal, social, sporting, theatrical ~s** *She moves in the highest social circles.* | **family**
• VERB + CIRCLE **have** | **move in** *My brother and I move in completely different circles* (= we have very different friends). | **join** | **widen** *You need to widen your circle of friends.*
• PREP. **in a/the ~** *Talk of religion was forbidden in the family circle.* ◇ *friends in government circles*
• PHRASES **a circle of acquaintances/admirers/friends**

3 in a theatre
• ADJ. **dress, upper** *Our seats are in the front row of the dress circle.*

circle *verb*

1 move in a circle
• ADV. **slowly** *The helicopter was circling slowly, very low.* | **overhead** *A buzzard was circling overhead.*
• PREP. **above** *Several airliners were circling above the airport.* **around/round** *The vultures were already circling around the dead animal.*

2 draw a circle round sth
• PHRASES **circle sth in black, red, etc.** *She circled her birthday in red on the calendar.*

circuit *noun*

1 path for an electric current
• ADJ. **short** *The lights were not working because of a short circuit.* | **closed** | **integrated, printed** | **electrical, electronic**
• VERB + CIRCUIT **break**
• CIRCUIT + NOUN **diagram**

2 places visited by sb in a particular job/sport
• ADJ. **amateur, professional** *Talent scouts spotted him playing on the amateur circuit.* | **international, world** | **cabaret, festival, lecture, tennis, etc.**
• PREP. **on a/the ~** *She's a well-known figure on the international lecture circuit.*

3 circular journey around sth
• ADJ. **complete**
• VERB + CIRCUIT **do, make** *We did a complete circuit of the park in twenty minutes.*
• PREP. **~ of**

circular *adj.*

• VERBS **be, look** *From a front view the small birds can look almost circular.*
• ADV. **perfectly** *He had round unblinking eyes and a perfectly circular head.* | **almost, nearly, roughly, virtually** *The crater was two miles across and roughly circular.*

circulate *verb*

1 liquid/gas/air
• ADV. **freely** *Air can circulate freely through the tunnels.*
• PREP. **around/round** *The heart circulates blood around the body.* **through** *Blood circulates through the arteries and veins.*

2 story/idea/information
• ADV. **widely** *The book was circulated widely in Russia.* | **freely**
• PREP. **among/amongst** *newspapers circulating among minority communities* **around/round** *There's a story circulating around the office that you are about to leave the company.* **to** *The document will be circulated to all members.*

circulation *noun*

1 movement of blood round the body
• ADJ. **good** | **bad, poor** | **blood**
• VERB + CIRCULATION **have** *I've got poor circulation.* | **improve, stimulate** *to have a massage to stimulate your circulation*
• PHRASES **the circulation of the blood**

2 passing of sth between different people
• ADJ. **general** | **restricted** *Restricted circulation of the report will reduce the risk of leaks outside the ministry.*
• VERB + CIRCULATION **go into** *The new banknotes will go into general circulation next year.* | **put sth into** | **take sth out of, withdraw sth from** *Copies of the magazine were withdrawn from circulation.*
• PREP. **in/out of ~** *the amount of money in circulation* ◇ *(figurative) I was out of circulation for months after the baby was born.*

3 of a newspaper/magazine
• ADJ. **large, mass, wide** | **limited, small** | **daily, monthly** | **national, nationwide**
• VERB + CIRCULATION **enjoy, have** *The newspaper has a daily circulation of 20 000.* | **boost, increase**
• CIRCULATION + VERB **increase, rise** | **fall**
• CIRCULATION + NOUN **figures**
• PREP. **~ of**

circumference *noun*

• VERB + CIRCUMFERENCE **have** | **calculate, measure** *to measure the circumference of a circle*
• PREP. **in ~** *an area three miles in circumference*

circumstance *noun*

1 (usually **circumstances**) facts/events that affect sth
• ADJ. **favourable** *The scheme might work better with more favourable circumstances.* | **adverse, difficult, tragic, trying, unfavourable** *people facing adverse circumstances* ◇ *He died in tragic circumstances.* | **normal** *In normal circumstances I would let you use my car, but today I need it.* | **exceptional, special, unusual** *Only if the circumstances are exceptional will we accept late applications.* | **mysterious, suspicious** *She died in rather suspicious circumstances.* | **extenuating, mitigating** *His sentence was reduced because of the extenuating circumstances.* | **changed, changing, different** | **unavoidable, unforeseen** | **economic, financial, political, social** *life in the changing economic circumstances of China*
• QUANT. **set** *an unfortunate set of circumstances that made her life difficult*
• CIRCUMSTANCE + VERB **change** | **conspire, dictate sth** *I felt that circumstances were conspiring against me.* ◇ *Circumstances dictate that I should leave this town forever.*
• PREP. **according to ~** *The amount paid will vary according to circumstances.* **due to … ~s** *Due to unforeseen circumstances, we have had to reschedule the concert.* **in … ~s** *She died in suspicious circumstances.* **in/under the ~s** *In the circumstances, you'd better ring the police.* | **~ surrounding** *The bank will investigate the circumstances surrounding the robbery.*
• PHRASES **by/through force of circumstance** *The survivors ate plants and insects through force of circumstance.* **circumstances beyond our control** *The delays were due to circumstances beyond our control.* **a combination of circumstances** *We lost our position in the market*

due to a combination of circumstances. **in/under no circumstances** *Under no circumstances should you leave the door unlocked.* **a victim of circumstance** *He was simply a victim of circumstance.*

2 circumstances amount of money you have
- ADJ. **desperate, reduced, straitened | domestic, family, personal**
- CIRCUMSTANCES + VERB **improve | worsen**
- PREP. **in … ~** *He was a writer living in straitened circumstances.*

cite verb

- ADV. **above, already, earlier, previously** *This is similar to the example cited above.* | **commonly, frequently, often** *The most commonly cited reasons for stopping the treatment were lack of efficacy and side effects.* | **widely**
- PREP. **as** *He cited the fall in unemployment as one of the government's successes.*

citizen noun

- ADJ. **full** *a group of indigenous people fighting for acceptance as full citizens of the country* | **naturalized | Italian, Thai, etc.** | **decent, good, honest, law-abiding, respectable, responsible, upright** *This terrible crime has shocked all law-abiding citizens.* | **leading, prominent** *She is a prominent citizen of the town.* | **average, ordinary** *It's not clear how the new law will affect the ordinary citizen.* | **second-class** *minorities who felt they had been treated as second-class citizens* | **private** *The king was visiting France as a private citizen.* | **senior** *travel concessions for senior citizens*

citizenship noun

- ADJ. **full | dual | British, Chinese, etc.**
- VERB + CITIZENSHIP **have, hold** *He has German citizenship.* | **give sb, grant sb** *They were granted full French citizenship.* | **acquire, take** *Ten years later, she chose to take Australian citizenship.* | **refuse sb | be stripped of, lose** *He was stripped of his citizenship when he criticized the government.* | **give up, renounce** *You will have to renounce citizenship of this country if you apply for citizenship of another.* | **apply for**

city noun

- ADJ. **big, large, major | small | great** *Rome is one of the great cities of the world.* | **ancient, historic, old | beautiful | industrial | cosmopolitan | coastal | home, native** *Her native city is Tokyo.* | **capital | provincial | cathedral, university | walled** *the old walled city of York* | **twin** *Bonn is Oxford's twin city.*
- VERB + CITY **build, found**
- CITY + VERB **grow** *The city grew rapidly in the nineteenth century.* | **flourish**
- CITY + NOUN **dweller | centre, street** *Parking is difficult in the city centre.* | **council | life**
- PREP. **in a/the ~** *We live in a big city.* **outside a/the ~** *There's a park just outside the city.*
- PHRASES **the centre/middle/heart of a city, the edge/outskirts of a city**

civil adj.

- VERBS **be | become**
- ADV. **extremely, remarkably, very | perfectly, quite**
- PREP. **to** *The teachers were all quite civil to me.*

civilian noun

- ADJ. **innocent, unarmed** *We demand an end to the killing of innocent civilians.*

civilization noun

- ADJ. **ancient, early** *the early civilizations of the Middle East and China* | **modern** *the benefits of modern civilization* | **advanced | primitive | Greek, Roman, etc.** | **European, Western** *disaeses that are common in Western civilization* | **great** *the great civilizations of the past* | **industrial | human** *Art and music are among the great products of human civilization.*
- VERB + CIVILIZATION **bring** *to bring civilization to the outer reaches of the country* | **create** *a movement that aims to create a new civilization* | **destroy | save**
- PHRASES **the beginnings/dawn of civilization, civilization as we know it** *Could this be the end of civilization as we know it?* **the collapse/decline/end of a civilization, a level of civilization** *to reach a higher level of civilization*

clad adj.

- VERBS **be**
- ADV. **fully** *He returned fully clad.* | **lightly, partially, scantily** *a scantily clad young woman* | **appropriately, suitably** *She went home and returned more suitably clad.* | **decently**
- PREP. **in** *Ed, clad in his best suit, was waiting for her.*

claim noun

1 statement saying that sth is true
- ADJ. **false, unfounded, unsubstantiated | conflicting** *There are conflicting claims about the cause of the fire.* | **absurd, astonishing, extravagant, grandiose**
- VERB + CLAIM **make** *The company had made false claims about its products.* ◊ *I make no claim to understand modern art.* | **accept** *They accepted her claim that she had been ill-treated.* | **challenge | deny, dismiss, dispute, reject** *Claims of a cover-up were dismissed.* | **back up, substantiate, support** *They were able to produce witnesses to support their claim.* | **investigate**
- PREP. **~ about** *to investigate claims about appalling prison conditions* **~ of** *Claims of corruption within the police force were denied.*

2 demand for sth
- ADJ. **large, small | excessive** *excessive wage claims* | **legal, legitimate | bogus, fraudulent** *The police are investigating fraudulent claims for fire damage.* | **accident, compensation, damage/damages, insurance, pay, wage | civil** *to file a civil claim for damages*
- VERB + CLAIM **bring, file, lodge, make, put forward/in, submit** *She brought a claim for damages against the company.* | **drop, waive, withdraw | investigate | allow, uphold** *His claim for compensation was upheld in court.* | **dismiss | win | meet, pay, settle** *We will need extra funds to meet all the insurance claims.*
- CLAIM + VERB **arise** *claims arising out of accidents at work* | **fail** *The claim failed because the company had not been misled.*
- CLAIM + NOUN **form**
- PREP. **~ against** *claims against the company for breach of contract* **~ for** *a claim for compensation* **~ on** *to make a claim on your insurance policy* ◊ *I have many claims on my time.*

3 right to have sth
- ADJ. **good, strong | competing, rival** *competing claims for public money* | **prior** *She had a prior claim on his affections.* | **moral | territorial**
- VERB + CLAIM **have** *He has a good claim to the land.* | **assert, lay, press, stake** *Four men laid claim to leadership of the country.* ◊ *to stake a claim to some of the prize money* | **establish, prove** *You will have to prove your claim to the property in a court of law.* | **relinquish, renounce, withdraw**
- PREP. **~ on** *His children have a claim on his estate.* **~ to** *She renounced her claim to the property.*

claim *verb*

1 say that sth is true
- ● ADV. **justifiably, rightfully, rightly | falsely, wrongly** *The company had falsely claimed that its products were biodegradable.*
- ● VERB + CLAIM **attempt to, try to** *He tried to claim that he had acted in self-defence.*

2 ask for sth you think you have a right to have
- ● ADV. **back** *You can claim back some of the cost of your treatment.*
- ● VERB + CLAIM **be able to, be entitled to, can/could** *You might be entitled to claim compensation if you are injured at work.* **| attempt to, try to**
- ● PREP. **on** *Can't you claim on your insurance?*

clamour *noun*

- ● ADJ. **noisy, raucous | growing | public | sudden**
- ● VERB + CLAMOUR **still** *He raised a hand to still the clamour.*
- ● CLAMOUR + VERB **break out | grow | subside**
- ● PREP. **above/amid the ~** *She could barely make herself heard above the clamour of the rain.* **| ~ for** *The clamour for her resignation grew louder.*

clamp *verb*

- ● ADV. **firmly, tight/tightly | together** *Clamp the pieces of wood together while the glue sets.*
- ● PREP. **around/round** *She clamped her arms around him.* **on/onto** *He clamped his hand firmly onto Jack's shoulder.* **over** *A large hand clamped over her mouth.* **to** *The dog's jaws were clamped to his leg.*
- ● PHRASES **clamped between your teeth** *He had a large cigar clamped between his teeth.* **clamp shut** *His mouth clamped shut.*

PHRASAL VERB

clamp down
- ● ADV. **hard**
- ● PREP. **on** *to clamp down hard on bullying*

clang *noun*

- ● ADJ. **loud | metallic**
- ● VERB + CLANG **give, let out | hear**
- ● PREP. **with a ~** *The door shut with a loud clang.* **| ~ of**
- ● PHRASES **the clang of metal**
- ⇨ Note at SOUND

clank *noun*

- ● ADJ. **loud**
- ● PREP. **with a ~** *The door opened with a clank.* **| ~ of the** *clank and rattle of the trams*
- ● PHRASES **the clank of machinery**

clap *noun*

- ● ADJ. **big**
- ● VERB + CLAP **give sb**
- ● PREP. **~ for** *A big clap for our last contestant!*

clap *verb*

- ● ADV. **enthusiastically, loudly** *The audience clapped enthusiastically.*

clarification *noun*

- ● ADJ. **further**
- ● VERB + CLARIFICATION **ask for, call for, seek** *Employers are seeking further clarification of the proposals.* **| need, require | give sb, provide sb with**

clarify *verb*

- ● ADV. **fully | further** *Headings and sub-headings further clarify the structure of the article.*
- ● VERB + CLARIFY **attempt to, seek to, try to | need to | help (to), serve to | should | be delighted to, be happy to, be pleased to** *I am happy to clarify any points that are still unclear.*

clarinet *noun*

⇨ Special page at MUSIC

clarity *noun*

- ● ADJ. **absolute, complete | admirable, crystal, exceptional, great | increasing | sufficient | chilling, painful, startling, terrible** *With painful clarity she remembered the day he had died.* **| conceptual**
- ● VERB + CLARITY **have | lack**
- ● PREP. **with (…) ~** *She expressed herself with great clarity.* **| ~ of** *clarity of thought*
- ● PHRASES **for the sake of clarity** *For the sake of clarity she went back over the key points.*

clash *noun*

- ● ADJ. **angry, bitter, fierce, serious | armed, bloody, violent | head-on** *The leaders are preparing for a head-on clash at the summit.* **| culture, personality**
- ● VERB + CLASH **lead to**
- ● CLASH + VERB **break out**
- ● PREP. **in a/the ~** *Several people were injured in violent clashes with the police.* **| ~ between** *Clashes between the rebels and government forces have broken out in the north.* **~ of** *a clash of opinions* **~ over** *Differences in the aims of the two unions have led to serious clashes over policy.* **~ with**
- ● PHRASES **a clash of cultures/interests/wills**

clash *verb*

- ● ADV. **violently | repeatedly**
- ● PREP. **on/over** *He has clashed repeatedly with the team coach over training schedules.* **with** *They often clash violently with rival gangs.*

clasp *verb*

- ● ADV. **tightly** *She clasped her bag tightly as she walked through the crowd.* **| lightly, loosely | warmly** *He clasped my hand warmly in welcome.* **| together** *She faced Will, her hands clasped together.*

class *noun*

1 lesson/group of students
- ● ADJ. **big, large | small | advanced, beginners', elementary, intermediate | biology, history, etc. | evening**
- ● VERB + CLASS **attend, go to, take** *He's taking classes in pottery.* **| miss | hold** *The institute holds evening classes throughout the year.* **| conduct, give, take, teach** *Who's taking the class today?* **| dismiss** *Class dismissed!* **| observe, sit in on**
- ● CLASS + NOUN **member, teacher | size**
- ● PREP. **in (a/the) ~** *We'll start the exercise in class and you can finish it for homework.* ◇ *Which history class are you in?* **| ~ in** *She's going to evening classes in Italian.*
- ● PHRASES **the back/front of the class** *He sat at the back of the class.* **be/come top of the class** *She came top of the class in maths.*

2 social/economic group
- ● ADJ. **lower, lower-middle, middle, upper, upper-middle, working** *sections of the working class* **| chattering (informal), educated, landed, landowning, privileged, professional, ruling** *topics being discussed at the breakfast tables of the chattering classes* **| dominant |**

social *Membership of gardening clubs is drawn from all social classes.*
• CLASS + NOUN **structure, system | consciousness | interests | conflict, differences, divisions, struggle, war**

3 group of things
• ADJ. **large, small | distinct | rare**
• VERB + CLASS **form** *These writers form a distinct class in Russian literature.*
• PREP. **~of** *a rare class of butterflies*
• PHRASES **be in a class of your own/in a different class** (= to be much better than sb/sth)

4 high quality/style
• ADJ. **great, real** *a player of great class*
• VERB + CLASS **have** *She's got real class.*
• PHRASES **a touch of class** *The musical entertainment added a touch of class to the occasion.*

classic *noun*

1 famous book/play, etc.
• ADJ. **great | minor | contemporary, modern | all-time | pop/popular**
• PREP. **~of** *one of the great classics of English literature*

2 Classics study of Greek/Roman culture
⇨ Note at SUBJECT

classification *noun*

• ADJ. **broad | detailed | simple | higher, lower** *The rooms are of the standard expected from a hotel in a higher classification.* | **arbitrary | social | security** *a document with the security classification 'confidential'*
• VERB + CLASSIFICATION **defy** *a style of dancing that defies classification*
• CLASSIFICATION + NOUN **system**
• PREP. **~into** *the broad classification of music into classical and pop*
• PHRASES **a system of classification**

clatter *noun*

• ADJ. **loud, noisy, terrible | metallic | sudden**
• VERB + CLATTER **make** *The wheels of the cart made a terrible clatter on the cobblestones.* | **hear**
• PREP. **with a~** *She dropped her fork with a clatter.* | **~of** *There was a clatter of hooves and a party of riders drew up.*

clatter *verb*

• ADV. **noisily**
• PREP. **against** *The mug clattered against her teeth.* **down** *Something heavy came clattering down the stairs.* **on** *His boots clattered on the stairs.* **to** *The knife clattered noisily to the floor.*
• PHRASES **come clattering**

clause *noun*

1 in a legal document
• ADJ. **clawback** (= for retrieving money already paid out), **confidentiality, escalator** (= that allows for a rise in wages or prices under certain conditions), **force majeure, indemnity, liability, limitation, penalty** *The penalty clause specifies that late delivery will be fined.* | **escape, exclusion, exemption, get-out, let-out, opt-out**
• VERB + CLAUSE **contain, have** *The contract contains a confidentiality clause.* | **add, include, insert, put in** *We added an opt-out clause to the agreement.* | **delete, take out | amend**
• PREP. **in a/the~** *There is some ambiguity in this clause.* **under a/the~** *Under Clause 5.8, the company is responsible for the health of its employees.* | **~on** *a clause on pollution*

2 in grammar
• ADJ. **main, subordinate | conditional, coordinate,**

dependent, finite, independent, infinitive, non-finite, relative | non-restrictive, restrictive *a restrictive relative clause* | **adverbial, nominal, noun**
• PREP. **in a/the ~** *The completed action is in the main clause.*

claustrophobia *noun*

• VERB + CLAUSTROPHOBIA **get, suffer from | give sb** *I hate lifts—they give me claustrophobia.*
• PHRASES **a feeling of claustrophobia**

claustrophobic *adj.*

• VERBS **be, feel, seem** *I felt a bit claustrophobic in the tiny room.* | **become, get | make sb** *Crowds make me claustrophobic.* | **find sth** *I find that building intensely claustrophobic.*
• ADV. **intensely, very | a bit, rather, somewhat** *The atmosphere was somewhat claustrophobic.*

claw *noun*

• ADJ. **sharp** *a cat with sharp claws* | **powerful, strong**
• VERB + CLAW **sharpen | dig, sink** *The tiger dug its claws into his leg.* | **show** *The lion growled and showed its claws.* | **retract**
• CLAW + NOUN **mark**
• PREP. **in sb's~s** *The cat held a bird in its claws.*

clay *noun*

• ADJ. **heavy | fine | soft | damp, sticky, wet | china, modelling**
• QUANT. **lump**
• VERB + CLAY **mould, shape** *She moulded the clay into the shape of a head.* | **bake, fire | be made from/in/(out) of, make/mould sth from/in/out of** *a figure made of clay*
• CLAY + NOUN **modelling | mould**
• PREP. **in~** *plants that grow in damp clay*

clean *verb*

• ADV. **effectively, well** *This product cleans baths very effectively.* | **properly, thoroughly** *I clean the house thoroughly once a week.* | **carefully, gently** *He gently cleaned the wound and dressed it.* | **out, up** *I cleaned out all the cupboards.*
• PREP. **off** *I cleaned the mud off the kitchen floor.* **with** *Clean the glass with a soft cloth.*
• PHRASES **need cleaning** *Your shoes need cleaning!*

clean *adj.*

• VERBS **be, look, seem, smell** *The room smelled clean and fresh.* | **stay** *The bathroom doesn't stay clean for long.* | **brush sth, get sth, scrape sth, scrub sth, wipe sth** *scrubbing the floor to get it clean* ◊ *She wiped all the surfaces clean.* | **leave sth** *Please leave the kitchen clean.* | **keep sth** *You're supposed to keep your room clean.*
• ADV. **extremely, very | spotlessly** *The whole house was spotlessly clean.* | **almost, nearly** *It's almost clean. I've just got to wipe the table.* | **fairly, pretty, quite**
• PHRASES **clean and tidy** *Is your room clean and tidy now?* **lovely and clean** *The water was lovely and clean.*

cleaner *noun*

1 person who cleans
• ADJ. **hospital, office, school, street**
⇨ Note at JOB

2 substance/instrument used for cleaning
• ADJ. **bathroom, carpet, household, oven, toilet** *chemicals that are found in all household cleaners*

cleanliness *noun*

- ADJ. **excessive** | **personal** *His mother gave him a lecture about personal cleanliness.*
- PHRASES **a standard of cleanliness**, **a state of cleanliness** *The bathroom was in a good state of cleanliness.*

cleanse *verb*

- ADV. **thoroughly** | **gently**
- PREP. **of** *a treatment to cleanse the body of toxins*

clear *verb*

1 remove sth that is not wanted/needed
- ADV. **completely**, **totally** *The site must be completely cleared and made safe for children.* | **partially** | **hastily**, **quickly** *She hastily cleared a space for him to sit down.* | **away** *Can you clear away all your toys now?*
- PREP. **from** *They cleared the mud from the steps.* **of** *We cleared the path of leaves.* **off** *Clear those papers off the desk.*

2 your head/mind
- ADV. **suddenly** *His face suddenly cleared as understanding dawned.*
- VERB + CLEAR **try to** *I went for a walk to try to clear my head.* | **help (to)** *Correct breathing helps to clear the mind and reduce tension.*

3 prove sb innocent
- ADV. **formally** *The three defendants were formally cleared by the judge.*
- PREP. **of** *Four men accused of assault have been cleared of all charges.*

clear *adj.*

1 easy to understand
- VERBS **be**, **seem** | **become** | **make sth** | **find sth**
- ADV. **abundantly**, **extremely**, **very** | **crystal**, **perfectly**, **quite** *You've got to make your intentions crystal clear to them.* | **by no means**, **not entirely**, **not quite** *It wasn't entirely clear whether she wanted us to help.* | **fairly**, **pretty**, **reasonably**
- PREP. **to** *It was clear to us that there was a problem.*

2 sure/certain
- VERBS **be**
- ADV. **extremely**, **very** | **absolutely**, **quite**
- PREP. **about** *She was quite clear about her reasons for leaving.* **on** *Are you clear on that point?*

3 easy to see/hear
- VERBS **be**, **look** | **become**
- ADV. **extremely**, **very** *The photograph wasn't very clear.* | **fairly**, **pretty**, **reasonably**

4 easy to see through
- VERBS **be** | **become**
- ADV. **extremely**, **very** | **absolutely**, **completely** | **fairly**, **reasonably** *The water was fairly clear.*

5 free from things that are blocking the way
- VERBS **be**, **look**, **seem** | **remain**, **stay** | **keep sth** *Make sure you keep all gutters and drainpipes clear of leaves.*
- ADV. **completely** | **fairly**, **pretty**, **reasonably**
- PREP. **of** *The roads are reasonably clear of snow.*

clearance *noun*

1 removal of sth old/unwanted
- ADJ. **forest**, **land**, **site**, **slum**
- CLEARANCE + NOUN **work** | **sale** (= in a shop when goods are sold cheaply to get rid of them quickly)

2 official permission
- ADJ. **official** | **customs**, **diplomatic**, **entry**, **security**
- VERB + CLEARANCE **get**, **obtain**, **receive** *You'll need to get security clearance for this job.* | **apply for**, **seek** |

give sb, **grant sb** *The pilot was granted clearance to land.* | **refuse sb**

3 distance between sth and sth passing under/beside it
- ADJ. **ground** *We need to increase the vehicle's ground clearance.*
- VERB + CLEARANCE **allow (sb/sth)**, **give sb/sth**, **leave** *Make sure you allow enough clearance on each side.* ◇ *Always give cyclists plenty of clearance.*
- PREP. **~ above** *Always give clearance above the light to prevent overheating* **~ between** *There wasn't enough clearance between the bus and the top of the bridge.*

clench *verb*

- ADV. **tight/tightly** *His jaw was tightly clenched.* | **involuntarily** *Her hands clenched involuntarily.* | **together** *She sat with hands clenched together in her lap.*
- PHRASES **clenched between sb's teeth** *He had a pipe clenched between his teeth.*

clerk *noun*

- ADJ. **chief**, **senior** | **assistant**, **junior** | **articled** *an articled clerk working for a large law firm* | **bank**, **council**, **office**, **parish**, **railway**, **solicitor's** | **accounts**, **booking**, **filing**
- PREP. **~ to** *He held the post of Clerk to the Council.*
- PHRASES **the office/post of clerk**
- ⇨ Note at JOB

clever *adj.*

1 intelligent/skilful
- VERBS **be**, **seem**, **sound**
- ADV. **awfully**, **extraordinarily**, **extremely**, **incredibly**, **really**, **very** | **pretty**, **quite**, **rather**
- PREP. **at** *I'm not very clever at maths.* **with** *clever with his hands*
- PHRASES **too clever by half** *Bob irritates me—he's too clever by half!* **too clever for your own good**

2 (of a thing) ingenious
- VERBS **be**
- ADV. **extremely**, **fiendishly**, **really**, **very** *a simple yet fiendishly clever idea* | **quite**, **rather**

cliché *noun*

- ADJ. **old**, **tired**, **usual**, **well-worn**, **worn-out** | **popular** *a popular cliché about the English*
- VERB + CLICHÉ **use** *Try to avoid using clichés in your writing.*
- PREP. **~ about**

click *noun*

- ADJ. **loud**, **sharp** | **audible** | **faint**, **little**, **quiet**, **soft** | **metallic** | **double**, **single** (used about clicks on a computer mouse) *a double click on the filename* | **mouse**
- VERB + CLICK **give (out)** *The answerphone gave a sharp click.* | **hear**
- PREP. **with a ~** *He closed his briefcase with a click.* | **~ of** *She heard the click of shoes on the marble floor.*

client *noun*

- ADJ. **big** *The company needs to focus on its biggest clients.* | **new** | **potential**, **prospective** | **established**, **existing**, **regular** | **business**, **corporate** | **private**
- VERB + CLIENT **serve** *A new branch has been opened to serve clients in East London.* | **act for**, **represent** | **take on** *She's so busy that she's not taking on any new clients.* | **attract** *a campaign to attract new clients*
- PREP. **on behalf of ~** *On behalf of my client, I would like to remind you of your obligations in this matter.*

clientele noun

• ADJ. **large, small | broad, narrow | regular, usual | exclusive, fashionable, select | international**
• VERB + CLIENTELE **attract, have** *The restaurant has a large regular clientele.* | **cater for/to, serve** *The boutique caters for a rather select clientele.* | **build (up), establish** *It takes time to build up a clientele.*

cliff noun

• ADJ. **high, towering | low | dramatic, precipitous, sheer, steep | craggy, jagged, rocky, rugged | chalk, limestone, etc. | coastal, mountain, river, sea**
• QUANT. **line** *a long line of cliffs surrounding the bay*
• VERB + CLIFF **climb, scale**
• CLIFF + VERB **fall (away), rise (up)** *The cliffs fall away to the north.* ◇ *Rugged sandstone cliffs rose up from the beach.* | **overlook sth, tower** *Steep cliffs towered above the river.* | **crumble** *crumbling cliffs*
• CLIFF + NOUN **edge, face, ledge, top | path, walk**
• PHRASES **be perched (high) on a cliff** *The hotel was perched high on a cliff overlooking the sea.* **the base/bottom/edge/foot/top of the cliff**

climate noun

1 weather conditions of a particular region
• ADJ. **hot, warm | cold, cool | mild | extreme, harsh, inhospitable, severe** *the severe northern climate* | **damp, humid, wet | arid, dry | equatorial, Mediterranean, subtropical, temperate, tropical | northern, southern, etc. | global** *global climate change*
• VERB + CLIMATE **have** *The city has a warm climate.*
• CLIMATE + NOUN **change**
• PREP. **in a/the~** *Little grows in such a dry climate.*

2 opinions, etc. people have at a particular time
• ADJ. **favourable | hostile, unfavourable | current, present, prevailing | changed, changing | business, economic, emotional, financial, ideological, intellectual, moral, political, social**
• VERB + CLIMATE **create**
• PREP. **in a/the~** *His ideas on equality are viewed as utopian in the current political climate.* | **~for** *a climate for economic recovery* **~of** *The new policies have created a climate of fear.*
• PHRASES **a climate of opinion**

climax noun

1 exciting/important event, point in time, etc.
• ADJ. **big, dramatic, exciting, grand, great, powerful, thrilling | fitting**
• VERB + CLIMAX **come to, reach** *The crisis reached its climax in the 1970s.* | **approach, near, rise to, build up to, work up to** *The story gradually builds up to a powerful climax.* | **bring sth to** *The affair was brought to a climax when the chairman resigned.* | **mark** *Yesterday marked the climax of the celebrations.*
• CLIMAX + VERB **come** *The climax came at the end of the second act of the play.*
• PREP. **at the~** *The hero dies at the climax of the opera.* **in a/the~** *In a dramatic climax, our team lost the match by one goal.* | **~to** *His promotion was a fitting climax to a worthy career.*

2 highest point of sexual pleasure
• ADJ. **sexual**
• VERB + CLIMAX **achieve, reach** *She found it hard to achieve a/reach climax.*

climb noun

1 act of climbing
• ADJ. **long, slow | short | arduous, difficult, exhausting, hard, sharp, steep | easy | steady**

• VERB + CLIMB **do, make** *I was fitter the first time I did the climb.*
• PREP. **on a/the~** *I broke my ankle on a climb last week.* | **~from/to** *the short climb from the road to the summit* **~up** *They began the long climb up the hill.*

2 increase in value/amount/status
• ADJ. **long, slow | rapid | gradual, steady**
• PREP. **~against** *the dollar's climb against the euro* **~in** *a steady climb in the cost of travel* **~out of** *a long slow climb out of recession* **~to** *her rapid climb to stardom*

climb verb

1 move up towards the top of sth
• ADV. **high** *Don't climb too high.* | **slowly**
• PREP. **up** *He climbed slowly up the ladder.*
• PHRASES **climb to the top** *We climbed right to the top of the mountain.* **go climbing** (= climb up mountains for sport) *He goes climbing in Scotland every summer.*

2 move/lead upwards
• ADV. **gradually, slowly | steadily | steeply | up**
• VERB + CLIMB **begin to** *The path began to climb quite steeply.*
• PREP. **from** *The road gradually climbs up from the village.* **to** *The plane took off and climbed to 20 000 feet.*

3 increase
• ADV. **sharply, steeply** *Prices have climbed sharply in recent months.* | **steadily**
• PREP. **above** *The temperature had climbed above 90 degrees.* **from, to** *Unemployment has climbed from two million to three million.*

cling verb

1 hold tightly
• ADV. **firmly, tightly | desperately, precariously** *houses clinging precariously to sheer cliffs* | **together** *The children clung together in fear.*
• PREP. **onto** *She clung onto my arm.* **to** *He clung tightly to the raft to keep himself afloat.*

2 stay close
• ADV. **close/closely** *The ground mist clung closely to the hedgerows.*
• PREP. **to**

PHRASAL VERB
cling (on) to sth
• ADV. **still | rigidly, stubbornly, tenaciously** *He still clings stubbornly to his socialist ideas.* | **desperately, fiercely** *She was desperately clinging on to life.*

clinic noun

• ADJ. **hospital | health | special | private | outpatient | abortion, antenatal, birth control, family planning, fertility/infertility, maternity | breast, eye, etc. | diabetic, psychiatric, etc.**
• VERB + CLINIC **attend, go to | hold** *The surgery holds a baby clinic every Wednesday afternoon.* | **be treated at** *She is being treated at a special diabetic clinic.*
• PREP. **at a/the~** *He was treated at the hospital's eye clinic.* **in a/the~** *She works in a birth control clinic.* | **~for** *a clinic for asthma sufferers*

clinical adj.

• VERBS **be, seem**
• ADV. **purely** *She regarded her patients from a purely clinical standpoint.* | **almost** *He looked at the body with an almost clinical detachment.*
• PREP. **about** *How can you be so cold and clinical about your son's accident?*

clip noun

1 used for holding things together
- ADJ. **bulldog, crocodile, spring | bicycle, hair, nose, paper, suspender, tie**
- VERB + CLIP **fasten, put (in/on)** *She put a clip in her hair.* ◇ *He put his bicycle clips on and set off.* | **take off, undo, unfasten**
- CLIP + VERB **hold sth** *Paper clips held the picture in place.*

2 small section from a film
- ADJ. **brief, short | film, movie, video**
- VERB + CLIP **see | show**
- PREP. **in a/the ~** *You will see in this clip how well she acts.* | **~ from** *a clip from a Sherlock Holmes movie*

cloak noun

- ADJ. **heavy | hooded**
- VERB + CLOAK **be wrapped in | drape, throw** *She threw a heavy woollen cloak over her shoulders.* | **draw, pull, wrap** *He pulled his cloak tightly around himself.* | **throw off**
- CLOAK + VERB **flow, fly, sweep, swirl** *a flowing black cloak* ◇ *She stormed off, her cloak flying behind her.*
- ⇨ Special page at CLOTHES

clock noun

- ADJ. **12/24-hour | atomic, digital, electric | bedside, kitchen | alarm, carriage, cuckoo, grandfather, long-case, time, travelling, wall**
- VERB + CLOCK **set, wind** *I've set my alarm clock for six tomorrow.* | **put back/forward** *He forgot to put his clock forward and turned up an hour late.* | **stop** (for example in a game) *Pressing the 'Yes' or 'No' response button stops the clock.* | **glance at, look at | watch** *employees who are always watching the clock* (= wanting their day's work to end)
- CLOCK + VERB **chime (sth), strike sth, tick** *The clock struck the hour.* ◇ *I could hear a clock ticking somewhere in the house.* | **stop | be fast/slow, gain/keep/lose time** *This clock doesn't keep time.* | **go back/forward** *The clocks go back* (= for a return to standard time)/*forward* (= for summer time) *tonight.* | **say sth** *The clock on the mantelpiece said twelve o'clock.* | **go off** *My alarm clock didn't go off this morning.*
- CLOCK + NOUN **face, tower | radio**
- PREP. **against the ~** *to work against the clock* (= to work fast in order to finish before a particular time) **around/round the ~** (= all day and all night) *to work around the clock* **by the ~** *It's ten o'clock by the kitchen clock.*
- PHRASES **the dial/face/hands of a clock**

close noun

- VERB + CLOSE **bring sth to** *The chairperson brought the meeting to a close.* | **come to, draw to** *The decade drew to a close with the threat of war hanging over Europe.*
- PREP. **at/by/towards the ~ of** *At the close of trading, he had lost thousands of pounds on the stock market.*

close verb

1 door, book, eyes, etc.
- ADV. **firmly, tightly** *He closed the door firmly.*

2 shop, business, road, etc.
- ADV. **permanently, temporarily | down, off, up** *That factory's been closed down now.*
- PREP. **to** *The museum has been temporarily closed to the public.*

close adj.

1 near
- VERBS **be | draw, get** *She grew increasingly nervous as the date of the audition drew closer.* | **keep, stay** *Keep close to me.*
- ADV. **extremely, very | fairly, quite | together** *Their birthdays are very close together.*
- PREP. **to** *Get close to the microphone.*

2 friendly and loving
- VERBS **be, feel, seem** *The two sisters seemed very close.* | **become, grow** *After the death of their parents the two children grew very close.* | **remain**
- ADV. **very | quite**
- PREP. **to** *He was quite close to his older brother.*

closed adj.

- VERBS **be | remain** *The library will remain closed until next week.* | **keep sth** *Keep that door closed, will you?*
- ADV. **firmly, properly, tightly** *Are the windows firmly closed?* ◇ *Her mouth was tightly closed.* | **completely, fully** *Make sure the lid is completely closed.* ◇ *The valve can be adjusted from fully open to fully closed.* | **almost, nearly** *squinting through almost closed eyes* | **half, partially, partly** *Her eyes were half closed.* | **officially | permanently, temporarily**
- PREP. **for** *The building is closed for repairs.* **to** *Twenty-five miles of beaches were officially closed to the public.*

close-up noun

- ADJ. **extreme**
- CLOSE-UP + NOUN **detail** *The slide gave close-up detail of petal formation.* | **photograph, picture, shot, view**
- PREP. **in ~** *The wound was photographed in extreme close-up.*

closure noun

- ADJ. **complete, total** *The accident caused the complete closure of the road.* | **partial | immediate | eventual | permanent, temporary | indefinite | planned, possible, proposed, threatened | enforced | factory, hospital, pit, road, school, etc.**
- VERB + CLOSURE **be earmarked for, be threatened with, face** *Several schools face eventual closure.* | **cause, force** *Imposing higher taxes would force the closure of many bookshops.* | **prevent, save sth from, stop** *The mine has been saved from closure.*
- CLOSURE + NOUN **plan, programme | order**
- PHRASES **(be) under threat of closure**

clot noun

- ADJ. **blood** *a blood clot on her brain*
- VERB + CLOT **dissolve, remove**
- CLOT + VERB **form**

cloth noun

1 material used for making clothes, curtains, etc.
- ADJ. **coarse, fine | homespun | woven | cotton, damask, linen, woollen** *a jacket made from woollen cloth*
- QUANT. **bale, bolt, length | piece, scrap, strip**
- VERB + CLOTH **make, produce, weave | dye**
- CLOTH + NOUN **industry, manufacture, merchant, mill, trade**

2 piece of cloth used for a particular purpose
- ADJ. **damp, dry, soft** *Wipe the table with a damp cloth.* | **cleaning, floor, polishing | table** (also **tablecloth**) | **tea | loin** (also **loincloth**)

clothed adj.

- VERBS **be**

CLOTHES

You can **wear** clothes or jewellery or you can **have** clothes/jewellery **on**:

I'm going to wear my little black dress to the party.
He's got a very strange hat on.

You can **be dressed in** clothes, fabric or a colour:

She was dressed | *in jeans.*
| *all in black.*
| *in green velvet.*

You can **put on** and **take off** any sort of clothing. You can also:

I'll just slip into something more comfortable.

pull on	pull up	slip on	slip into	shrug into	throw on
boots	jeans	a dressing gown	something more	a coat	a coat
gloves	knickers	a jacket	comfortable	a jacket	a jacket
a jacket	pants	a pair of sth			
a pair of sth	a skirt	a robe			
socks	socks	shoes			
a sweater	trousers				
tights					
trousers					

She pulled on a pair of faded jeans and a sweater.
Wait while I slip into something more comfortable.
Throwing on his coat, he made for the door.

● ADV. **fully** *Jenny was fully clothed.* | **lightly, partially** *It was warm and she was lightly clothed.* ◇ *Her partially clothed body was found in woods nearby.*
● PREP. **in** *clothed in white*
● PHRASES **fed and clothed** *the problems of keeping the family fed and clothed*

clothes *noun*

● ADJ. **beautiful, elegant, fancy, fine, lovely, nice, pretty | cheap, expensive | clean, fresh | dirty, dishevelled, ragged, shabby, soiled | tight | baggy, ill-fitting, loose, sloppy | designer, fashionable, trendy | dowdy, nerdy, old-fashioned | second-hand | comfortable, sensible | best, evening, formal, smart** *He wore his best clothes to the interview.* | **casual, everyday, ordinary | outrageous, strange, wacky | warm | summer, winter | outdoor, outer | baby, maternity, mourning, night, riding, school, sports, work, working | civilian, plain** *an officer in plain clothes (= not in uniform)*
● QUANT. **set, suit** *I'm going to take a set of clean clothes with me.* ◇ *a new suit of clothes for the baby*
● VERB + CLOTHES **put (back) on | remove | change** *Aren't you going to change your clothes for the party?* | **make | dry, iron, mend, wash**
● CLOTHES + NOUN **shop | designer | basket | sense**

● PREP. **in** ~ *She didn't recognize him in his sloppy everyday clothes.*
● PHRASES **a change of clothes**

clothing *noun*

● ADJ. **light | heavy, warm | loose | tight | comfortable, sensible, suitable | casual | designer | cast-off, second-hand, used | summer, winter | outdoor | outer | protective, waterproof** *Workers at the factory wear protective clothing.* | **sports**
● QUANT. **article, item, piece | layer**
● CLOTHING + NOUN **business, company, factory, firm, industry, manufacturer, shop, store, trade**
● PHRASES **a change of clothing**

cloud *noun*

1 mass of very small drops of water in the sky
● ADJ. **dense, heavy, thick | light | fluffy | cirrus, cumulus | high, low | broken, scattered** *skies of broken cloud* | **fast-moving, scudding | black, dark, grey, white | rain, storm, threatening, thunder** *Rain clouds were looming on the horizon.*
● QUANT. **band, bank, layer, mass, wisp** *a layer of high cloud*
● VERB + CLOUD **seed** (= to place a substance in a cloud to make it produce rain)
● CLOUD + VERB **form, gather, mass** *Dark clouds were*

remove	pull off	pull down	drop	kick off	shrug off
clothes	a coat	knickers	pants	sandals	a coat
a coat	gloves	pants	trousers	shoes	a jacket
glasses	a hat	a skirt			
a hat	a jacket	trousers			
a jacket	a mask				
a mask	a shirt				
a shirt	shoes				
shoes	socks				

He removed his glasses and rubbed the bridge of his nose.
With a dramatic gesture she pulled off her mask.
I kicked off my sandals and felt the warm sand slipping between my toes.

fasteners

do up/undo	zip up/unzip	button up/ unbutton	lace up/unlace	fasten/ unfasten
a bra	an anorak	a blouse	boots	a belt
a buckle	a dress	a coat	shoes	a buckle
buttons	flies	flies	trainers	buttons
flies	a jacket	a jacket		
shoelaces	jeans	a shirt		
a zip	a skirt			

His fingers fumbled to do up the small buttons on his shirt.
My shoelaces came undone and I nearly tripped.
Tom buttoned his overcoat up to his neck and raised his collar.

---

gathering in the west. | **cover sth, envelop sth, obscure sth** | **break, clear, disperse, lift, part** *The clouds broke a little, and the sun came out.* | **drift, float, hang, hover, loom, move, pass, race, roll, scud, swirl** *Thick cloud hung over the moor.* ◇ *A cloud passed over the sun.* ◇ *White clouds scudded across the sky.*
● CLOUD + NOUN **bank, cover, formation** *The cloud cover is quite dense today.*
● PREP. **above/below the ~s** *flying above the clouds* | **through the ~s** *She could see the sun through the clouds.*
● PHRASES **a break in the cloud(s), a layer of cloud**

2 mass of smoke, dust, etc.
● ADJ. **great, huge** *a great cloud of grey smoke* | **dense, thick** | **billowing, swirling** | **mushroom** *the mushroom cloud from a nuclear bomb* | **dust, radioactive, smoke**
● PREP. **~of** *a thick cloud of steam*

cloudy *adj.*

1 full of clouds
● VERBS **be** | **start** *England and Wales will start cloudy.* | **become** *Later it will become cloudy with rain in places.* | **remain, stay** *It stayed cloudy for most of the day.*
● ADV. **very** | **rather, slightly** *a rather cloudy sky*

2 not clear
● VERBS **be, look** *The beer looked cloudy.* | **become** | **make sth** *The warm water is made cloudy by adding some milk.*

● ADV. **very** | **rather, slightly** *Sometimes the drinking water becomes rather cloudy.*

clout *noun*

● ADJ. **considerable, enormous** *a politician with enormous clout* | **economic, financial, political** *the growing political clout of the army*
● VERB + CLOUT **carry, have, wield** *He has a lot of clout within the party.* | **exercise, use** *The companies used their clout to influence the policy.*

club *noun*

1 group of people who meet to share an interest
● ADJ. **exclusive, private, top** *one of the top football clubs in the country* | **local** | **social** | **youth** | **fan, sports** | **football, golf, etc.** *She plays at the local tennis club.* | **book, record**
● VERB + CLUB **belong to** *She belongs to a book club.* | **become a member of, join** | **form, start** | **run** *Who runs the tennis club?*
● CLUB + NOUN **chairman, manager, member, official, player, secretary** | **cricket, football** | **bar**
● PREP. **in a/the~** *How many people are there in the club?*
⇨ Note at ORGANIZATION

2 where people go and listen to music, dance, etc.
● ADJ. **jazz, night** (also **nightclub**)

- CLUB + NOUN **scene** *a new style of music on the London club scene*

3 playing card
⇨ Note at CARD

clue *noun*

- ADJ. **good, important, useful, valuable | vital | telltale | obvious**
- VERB + CLUE **have, hold** *So far, the police haven't got any clues as to the motive for the crime.* ◇ *Diet may hold the clue to the causes of migraine.* | **give (sb), furnish/provide/supply (sb with), yield** *The hat gives a clue to the identity of the killer.* ◇ *The letter yielded no clues.* | **hunt for, look for, search for | discover, find, uncover | leave** *The burglar left no clues.* | **follow (up)**
- PREP. **~ about** *This research might provide an important clue about how cancer develops.* **~ (as) to** *a clue as to her whereabouts*

clump *noun*

- ADJ. **great, large | little, small | dense** *These plants quickly form dense clumps.* | **straggling, tangled**
- VERB + CLUMP **form**
- PREP. **in a/the ~** *situated in a clump of trees* | **~ of** *great clumps of rhododendrons*

cluster *noun*

- ADJ. **little, small | compact, dense**
- PREP. **in a/the ~** *The church stood in a small cluster of farmers' cottages.* | **~ of** *a dense cluster of buildings*

cluster *verb*

- ADV. **closely, tightly | together** *The group clustered together closely.*
- PREP. **about/around/round** *The children clustered around their teacher.*

clutch *noun*

1 sb/sth's **clutches** sb/sth's power/control
- VERB + CLUTCHES **fall into** *She fell into the clutches of the rebel forces.* | **escape (from)**
- PREP. **in sb's ~** *They had him in their clutches.* **out of sb's ~** *Once she was out of their clutches, she fled across the border.*

2 in a car
- VERB + CLUTCH **drop, engage, put your foot on | disengage, let in/out, release, take your foot off** *Put it into first gear and let the clutch out slowly.* | **ride** (= to keep in a state between full engagement and disengagement) *The driver at the traffic lights was riding his clutch.*
- CLUTCH + VERB **engage | disengage | slip**
- CLUTCH + NOUN **pedal**

clutch *verb*

- ADV. **firmly, tightly | desperately**
- PREP. **at** *He felt himself slipping and clutched at a branch.*
- PHRASES **clutch sth in your hand** *She clutched her handbag tightly in one hand.* **clutch sth to your chest** *She clutched the letter to her chest.*

clutter *noun*

- ADJ. **personal | screen** *to get rid of screen clutter* (= on a computer)
- VERB + CLUTTER **clear (up), get rid of**
- PREP. **amid/amidst/among/amongst the ~** *The cat managed to find a spot to sleep amidst all the clutter of my study.* **in a/the ~** *The garage is in such a clutter that we can't find anything.*

coach *noun*

1 bus for longer journeys
- ADJ. **express | private | luxury | air-conditioned**
- VERB + COACH **go by, travel by | board, get on | get off | drive | hire**
- COACH + NOUN **station | driver | holiday, journey, tour, trip | travel | party | company | service**
- PREP. **by ~** *They are planning to tour the United States by coach.* | **in/on a/the ~**

2 large carriage pulled by horses
- ADJ. **royal**
- VERB + COACH **drive | ride in**
- COACH + VERB **drive**
- COACH + NOUN **road** *This is the old coach road.* | **house**
- PHRASES **a coach and four/six** (= a coach and four/six horses) *a gateway wide enough for a coach and four to drive through* **a coach and horses**

3 person who trains people in sport, etc.
- ADJ. **good, successful, top** *a top football coach* | **professional | chief, head | assistant | national | club | athletics, basketball, football, tennis, etc. | sports | acting, drama, voice**
⇨ Note at JOB

coal *noun*

1 black mineral
- ADJ. **hard | soft | brown | bituminous, coking | opencast** *opencast coal mining*
- QUANT. **lump, piece**
- VERB + COAL **mine, produce | burn, use | shovel**
- COAL + VERB **burn**
- COAL + NOUN **fire | mine, pit | mining, production | merchant, miner | company | industry | field, seam | bucket, bunker, cellar, scuttle | dust, gas**

2 (usually **coals**) burning pieces of coal
- ADJ. **burning, glowing, hot, live, red-hot**
- VERB + COAL **glow** *Red-hot coals glowed in the fireplace.*

coalition *noun*

- ADJ. **strong | loose | broad, broad-based, rainbow, umbrella** *an umbrella coalition of human rights organizations* | **grand** *a grand coalition of various environmental groups* | **centre-left, centre-right, conservative, left-wing, liberal, radical, right-wing | two-party, three-party, etc. | cross-party | governing, government, ruling | opposition | wartime | political**
- VERB + COALITION **create, form** *The centre-right parties have formed a coalition.* | **join | lead** *a coalition led by the Socialist Party*
- COALITION + VERB **break up, collapse, fall (apart)**
- COALITION + NOUN **government | forces, member, partner, party**
- PREP. **in (a/the) ~** *The two parties governed in coalition for four years.* ◇ *the biggest party in the government coalition* | **~ between** *a coalition between the Socialists and Communists* **~ of** *a broad coalition of democratic and republican groups* **~ with** *They formed a coalition with the Greens.*

coast *noun*

- ADJ. **forbidding, rocky, rugged, wild | north, northern, etc. | indented | mainland | sea**
- QUANT. **stretch** *the long stretch of coast between Lowestoft and Felixstowe*
- VERB + COAST **follow, hug** *The path hugs the coast all the way to Tenby.*
- COAST + VERB **stretch** *The coast stretched far into the distance.*
- COAST + NOUN **road**

● PREP. **along the ~** *We travelled south along the coast.* **around/round the ~** *They sailed round the coast to Falmouth.* **at the ~** *We spent a day at the coast.* **off the ~** *an island two miles off the west coast of Scotland* **on the ~** *a village on the Mediterranean coast*

coastline *noun*

● ADJ. **long | beautiful, spectacular | rocky, rugged | wild | unspoilt | indented**
● QUANT. **stretch** *long stretches of unspoilt coastline*
● VERB + COASTLINE **follow** *The road follows the Pacific coastline.* **| erode**
● COASTLINE + VERB **stretch** *The coastline stretches for miles.*
● PREP. **along a/the ~** *They sailed along the rugged coastline.* **around/round a/the ~** *sailing around the Atlantic coastline of France* **off a/the ~** *the search for oil off the Welsh coastline*

coat *noun*

1 piece of clothing
● ADJ. **long | short | three-quarter-length | heavy | light | winter | waterproof | fur-trimmed | double-breasted, single-breasted | belted | duffle, frock, morning, tail, trench**
● VERB + COAT **pull on, shrug (yourself) into, shrug on, throw on | pull off, shrug off | button (up)** *The coat was buttoned up wrong.* **| unbutton | hang (up)**
● COAT + NOUN **collar, pocket, sleeve, tail | hook**
⇨ Special page at CLOTHES

2 fur/hair covering an animal's body
● ADJ. **long | short | thick | rough | smooth | curly, fluffy, furry, shaggy, silky, woolly** *a dog with a long shaggy coat* **| glossy | spotted, striped | winter**
● VERB + COAT **shed** *The dog sheds its winter coat once the weather becomes warmer.*

3 layer of sth covering a surface
● ADJ. **thick | thin | fresh, new** *The room needs a fresh coat of paint.* **| base | final, top**
● VERB + COAT **apply, put on** *Make sure the base coat has thoroughly dried before applying the top coat.*
● COAT + VERB **dry**
● PREP. **~of** *a coat of paint/varnish*

coat *verb*

● ADV. **completely | heavily, thickly | lightly | specially** *The fabric has been specially coated to improve its water resistance.*
● PREP. **in** *Coat the fish in the sauce.* **with** *The furniture was thickly coated with dust.*

coating *noun*

● ADJ. **thick | fine, thin | outer, surface | protective | magnetic | chocolate, metal, plastic**
● VERB + COATING **be covered in/with, have** *The fruit is covered in a thick coating of milk chocolate.* **| apply** *Apply a thin coating of glue to the surface.*

coax *verb*

● ADV. **gently**
● VERB + COAX **try to | manage to | fail to**
● PREP. **from** *He could coax tears and laughter from his audience.* **into** *He gently coaxed life back into my frozen toes.* **out of** *She never failed to coax good results out of her pupils.*

cocaine *noun*

● ADJ. **crack, freebase**
● QUANT. **line, packet**

● VERB + COCAINE **freebase, inject, shoot, smoke, sniff, snort**
● COCAINE + NOUN **possession | injection | export | baron | cartel**
⇨ Note at DRUG (for more verbs and nouns)

cock *noun*

● ADJ. **fighting | barnyard** *The market traders cried out like barnyard cocks.*
● COCK + VERB **crow** *The cock crowed at dawn.*
● COCK + NOUN **fight, fighting**

cocktail *noun*

1 mixed alcoholic drink
● ADJ. **pre-dinner | champagne**
● VERB + COCKTAIL **mix | have, drink | sip**
● COCKTAIL + NOUN **bar, cabinet | circuit** *a familiar face on the cocktail circuit* **| dress | hour | lounge | party | shaker | waiter, waitress**

2 dish of small pieces of food
● ADJ. **prawn, seafood | fruit**

3 mixture of different things
● ADJ. **deadly, lethal | heady, powerful** *The show was a heady cocktail of jazz, dance and political satire.*
● PREP. **~of** *a lethal cocktail of drink and drugs*

cock-up *noun*

● ADJ. **complete, real, total**
● VERB + COCK-UP **make** *He made a real cock-up of it.*
● PREP. **~over** *There's been a bit of a cock-up over the travel arrangements.*

coconut *noun*

● ADJ. **desiccated, fresh**
● QUANT. **bunch** *huge bunches of fresh coconuts*
● VERB + COCONUT **eat, have | grow | harvest, pick | break open, open** *She broke open the coconut and drank its sweet milk.*
● COCONUT + NOUN **milk, oil | palm, tree** *a bay fringed with swaying coconut palms* **| fibre, husk, matting, shell**

code *noun*

1 system of letters, numbers, etc. for secret information
● ADJ. **secret | Morse**
● VERB + CODE **break, crack, decipher** *The code was difficult to crack.* **| use, write in | invent, make up**
● CODE + NOUN **word**
● PREP. **in~** *All the messages were in code.*

2 numbers/letters for identifying sth
● ADJ. **area, dialling** *What's the area code for Bath?* **| post/postal | bar, charge | DNA, genetic | binary** (= a system of computer programming instructions) **| error** (= on a computer)
● CODE + NOUN **number**

3 set of rules for behaviour
● ADJ. **strict | ethical, moral | civil, criminal, disciplinary, penal | Highway** *the Highway Code* (= the official rules for users of public roads in Britain) **| dress**
● VERB + CODE **have | devise, draw up, establish, formulate, lay down** *The company has drawn up a new disciplinary code.* **| comply with, follow | break, infringe, violate** *He was thrown out for infringing the club's strict dress code.*
● PHRASES **a code of behaviour/conduct/ethics/honour/practice** *The profession has a strict code of practice.*

coexist *verb*

● ADV. **peacefully** *What makes it difficult for the communities to coexist peacefully?*

• PREP. **alongside/with** *Modern farming methods coexist with more traditional practices.*

coffee *noun*

• ADJ. **strong** | **weak** | **black, dark** *a mug of strong black coffee* | **milky, white** *She drinks very milky coffee with lots of sugar.* | **frothy** | **sugary, sweet** | **bitter** | **hot, steaming** *a pot of piping hot coffee* ◇ *He brought in two mugs of steaming coffee.* | **lukewarm, tepid** | **cold** | **iced** | **fresh** *The others will be back soon—I'll go and make some fresh coffee.* | **excellent, expensive, good** | **decaffeinated** | **ersatz** | **filter, percolated, real** | **instant** *Would you like real or instant coffee?* | **Irish** (= with whiskey added), **Turkish** (= very strong, black and sweet)
• QUANT. **cup, mug, pot**
• VERB + COFFEE **drink** *Do you drink coffee?* | **have** *I had two coffees while I waited.* | **take** *'How do you take your coffee?' 'Milk, no sugar, thanks.'* | **sip, take a mouthful/sip of** *He took a sip of his coffee.* | **drain, drink up, finish** | **stir** | **pour (sb)** | **go for** *Let's go for a coffee when you've finished your essay.* | **brew, make** *freshly-brewed coffee* ◇ *I'll make some coffee for breakfast.* | **grind** *a packet of freshly-ground coffee*
• COFFEE + VERB **get/go cold** | **be laced with sth** *coffee laced with cognac*
• COFFEE + NOUN **cup, mug** | **machine, percolator, pot** | **dregs** | **break**
• PREP. **in your~** *I have milk but no sugar in my coffee.*
• PHRASES **an aroma/a smell of coffee** *An inviting smell of coffee wafted into the room.* **coffee-making facilities** *Tea and coffee-making facilities are available in the kitchen.*

coffin *noun*

• VERB + COFFIN **carry, take** | **lower** *The coffin was lowered into the grave.*
• PREP. **in a/the~**

coherence *noun*

• ADJ. **internal** *Your essay lacks internal coherence.* | **ideological, intellectual, logical, theoretical** *theories which lack ideological coherence*
• VERB + COHERENCE **have, possess** | **achieve, create, give sth, maintain** *They have struggled to create coherence within the group.* | **lack**
• PREP. **~between** *a lack of coherence between the policy and the speech* **~in/within** *There's a strong sense of coherence in the school curriculum.*
• PHRASES **a degree/sense of coherence**

coherent *adj.*

• VERBS **be, seem** | **become**
• ADV. **remarkably, very** *You're not being very coherent.* | **perfectly** *a perfectly coherent remark* | **reasonably**

coil *noun*

• ADJ. **neat, tight** | **thick** *thick coils of blonde hair*
• COIL + VERB **unwind**
• PREP. **in a~** *She wore her hair in a neat coil.* | **~of** *a coil of rope*

coil *verb*

• ADV. **tightly** | **loosely** | **neatly** | **up** *He coiled the rope up tightly and put it away.*
• PREP. **around/round** *The snake coiled itself around a branch.* **into** *Her hair was neatly coiled into a bun.*

coin *noun* ·

• ADJ. **copper, gold, silver** | **antique, rare** | **commemorative** | **counterfeit, fake** | **penny, pound, etc.**

• VERB + COIN **issue** | **mint, strike** *The first English gold coin was struck in 1255.* | **flip, spin, toss** *They tossed a coin to see who should go first.* | **collect**
• COIN + VERB **be in circulation, circulate** *Very few old 5p coins are still in circulation.* | **clink, jingle** *coins jingling in his pockets*
• COIN + NOUN **collector**

coincide *verb*

1 happen at the same time
• ADV. **exactly** *Her visit coincided exactly with a visit by the American president.* | **roughly**
• VERB + COINCIDE **be planned to, be timed to**
• PREP. **with** *The singer's arrival was timed to coincide with the opening of the festival.*

2 be the same
• ADV. **closely** | **exactly**
• PREP. **with** *Our views on this issue coincide closely with yours.*

coincidence *noun*

• ADJ. **complete, pure, sheer** *It was pure coincidence that they were both in Paris on the same day.* | **mere** | **happy** *What a happy coincidence to meet you at the airport just when I wanted to see you.* | **unfortunate, unhappy** | **amazing, curious, extraordinary, funny, incredible, odd, remarkable, strange, wonderful**
• QUANT. **series, set, string** *They met through a series of strange coincidences.*
• COINCIDENCE + VERB **happen** *Remarkable coincidences do happen in real life.*
• PREP. **by (a)~** *By coincidence, we both went to the same school.* ◇ *By an unfortunate coincidence, their house was burgled on the day he lost his job.*

coincidental *adj.*

• VERBS **be**
• ADV. **entirely, merely, purely, quite** *These parallels cannot be merely coincidental.* | **largely**

coke *noun*

1 Coke drink
• ADJ. **diet**
• QUANT. **bottle, can, glass**
• VERB + COKE **have** *I'll have a Coke, please.* | **drink, sip**
• COKE + NOUN **bottle, can** | **machine**
• PHRASES **rum and Coke**

2 cocaine
• QUANT. **line**
• VERB + COKE **sniff, snort**
• COKE + NOUN **fiend, sniffer**
⇨ Note at DRUG

3 fuel
• QUANT. **lump, piece**
• VERB + COKE **manufacture, produce** | **burn, use**
• COKE + NOUN **works** | **boiler, fire**

cold *noun*

1 lack of heat; low temperature
• ADJ. **biting, bitter, extreme, freezing**
• VERB + COLD **feel** *I don't feel the cold as badly as many people.* | **keep out** *The house has double glazing to keep out the cold.* | **be blue with, be numb with** *My hands were blue with cold.*
• PREP. **against the~** *We were well wrapped up against the cold.* **out in the~** *He stood out in the cold and waited.* ◇ (*figurative*) *When the coalition was formed the Liberals were left out in the cold* (= were not invited to join it).

2 common illness

• ADJ. **bad, heavy, nasty** *She won her match despite suffering from a heavy cold.* | **slight** | **common** *When will they find a cure for the common cold?* | **chest, head**
• VERB + COLD **have, nurse, suffer from** *Jim stayed at home because he was nursing a cold.* | **catch, go down with, take** *I must have caught a cold on the bus.* ◇ *If you stay out in the rain you'll catch cold!* ◇ *He took cold, developed pneumonia, and that was the end of him.*
⇒ Special page at ILLNESS

cold *adj.*

1 not hot or warm
• VERBS **be, feel, look, seem** | **become, get, grow, turn** *As evening fell it got very cold.* ◇ *The room grew cold.* ◇ *In January it turned very cold.* | **make sb/sth** *The rain overnight had made the water cold.* | **keep sth** *Use ice to keep the drinks cold.*
• ADV. **bitterly, extremely, freezing, ice-, icy, terribly, very** *It's bitterly cold outside.* ◇ *There was a freezing cold wind.* ◇ *an ice-cold beer* | **fairly, quite, rather**

2 not cooked/having become cold after cooking
• VERBS **be** | **get, go** *Your dinner's getting cold.* ◇ *I'm afraid the coffee's gone cold.* | **eat sth, serve sth** *Bake in the oven for twenty minutes. Serve hot or cold.*
• ADV. **stone** *This soup is stone cold!*

coldness *noun*

1 state of being cold
• ADJ. **icy** *The icy coldness of the water revived her.*

2 unfriendliness
• ADJ. **marked** *There was a marked coldness in her voice.*
• VERB + COLDNESS **treat sb with**
• PREP. **~between** *the coldness between Jack and Martha* **~towards** *his coldness towards his parents*

colic *noun*

• ADJ. **violent** | **biliary** | **infantile**
• QUANT. **attack, bout**
• VERB + COLIC **have, suffer from** | **develop** | **treat**
⇒ Special page at ILLNESS

collaborate *verb*

• ADV. **actively, closely**
• PREP. **on, with** *We have collaborated closely with the university on this project.*

collaboration *noun*

• ADJ. **active, close** | **effective, fruitful, happy, successful** | **international**
• PREP. **in ~ with** *Rock musicians are working in collaboration with an orchestra to create a new opera.* | **~between** *a collaboration between two writers* **~with** *the results of a fruitful collaboration with the industry*
• PHRASES **a degree of collaboration**

collapse *noun*

1 building, etc. suddenly falling
• ADJ. **sudden** *the sudden collapse of the bridge*
• PHRASES **be in danger of collapse**

2 medical condition
• ADJ. **sudden** | **mental, nervous, physical**
• VERB + COLLAPSE **be close to, be on the point/verge of** *She was on the verge of nervous collapse.*
• PREP. **~from** *his collapse from exhaustion*
• PHRASES **a state of collapse** *He was in a state of mental and physical collapse.*

3 sudden/complete failure of sth
• ADJ. **complete, total** | **general** | **virtual** | **sudden** | **economic, financial** *the sudden economic collapse of 2001*

• VERB + COLLAPSE **bring about, contribute to, lead to, result in** *The war has led to the collapse of agriculture in the area.* | **face, be faced with** | **be on the brink/point/verge of** | **prevent**
• PREP. **~into** *a collapse into anarchy*

collapse *verb*

1 of a building
• ADV. **completely**
• PREP. **into** *Several buildings have collapsed into the sea.* **under** *The roof collapsed under the weight of snow.*

2 of a sick person
• ADV. **suddenly**
• PREP. **against** *The man collapsed against the wall and slid down it.* **from** *She collapsed suddenly from a heart attack.* **with** *He collapsed with shock.*

3 fail
• ADV. **eventually, finally** *In November the strike finally collapsed.* | **quickly, rapidly** | **suddenly** | **virtually**
• PHRASES **to collapse in the face of sth** *The scheme collapsed in the face of determined opposition.*

collar *noun*

1 on a shirt, coat, dress, etc.
• ADJ. **open, undone** *His tie was knotted below his open collar.* ◇ *His collar was undone.* | **button-down, turned-down** | **tight** | **starched, stiff** | **detachable** | **coat, shirt, etc.** | **high, stand-up, wing** | **clerical, dog** *The vicar had his dog collar on.*
• VERB + COLLAR **have** *The shirt had a button-down collar.* | **have on, wear** | **button, do up, fasten** | **unbutton, undo, unfasten** | **raise, turn up** *She turned up her coat collar for extra warmth.* | **turn down** | **loosen**
• COLLAR + NOUN **stud** | **size**
• PHRASES **collar and tie** *He wore a collar and tie for the occasion.*

2 round an animal's neck
• ADJ. **dog** | **flea**
• VERB + COLLAR **have on, wear** | **slip** *The dog slipped its collar and ran off.*

colleague *noun*

• ADJ. **close, trusted** | **junior, senior** | **female, male** | **professional, work** | **academic, business, medical** | **cabinet, parliamentary**

collection *noun*

1 group of objects
• ADJ. **big, extensive, huge, large, major, substantial, vast** | **small** | **growing** | **complete, comprehensive** | **core, permanent** *The permanent collection is displayed on the first floor, whilst the ground floor houses temporary exhibitions.* | **reserve** *The museum has a large reserve collection in storage, which members of the public rarely get to see.* | **amazing, extraordinary, fascinating, fine, good, great, important, impressive, interesting, magnificent, outstanding, remarkable, rich, stunning, superb, unique, useful, valuable** | **bizarre, disparate, diverse, heterogeneous, jumbled, miscellaneous, motley, odd, random, strange, varied** | **representative** *to assemble and analyse a representative collection of data* | **celebrated, distinguished, famous, prestigious, renowned** | **family, personal, private** *the largest private art collection in the world* | **public** | **international, local, national** | **historical** | **reference, research** *a research collection available for study by archaeologists* | **archive, library, museum** *a historical archive collection of 20 000 documents* | **antiques, art, book, CD, coin, manuscript, photographic, picture, plant, record, stamp**
• VERB + COLLECTION **boast, have** *The museum boasts a superb collection of medieval weapons.* | **ac-**

quire, amass, assemble, build up, compile, make *He built up his collection over a period of ten years.* ◊ *She made a collection of Roman coins and medals.* | start | add to *a new painting to add to their collection* | complete *She needed only one more stamp to complete her collection.* | hold, house *a new building to house the national collection of arms and armour* | display, exhibit, show *A glass-fronted cabinet displayed a collection of china figurines.* | view, visit, see *I was allowed to view his family collection of portrait miniatures.* | consult, study *Historians frequently ask to consult the collection.* | organize *She had the task of cataloguing the library and organizing the collection of rare manuscripts.*

● COLLECTION + VERB **consist of sth, contain sth, include sth** *The collection contains some 500 items.* | cover sth *The collection covers all phases of Picasso's career.* | come from ... | date from ... *major collections dating from the 11th to the 19th century* | grow *The museum's collection is growing all the time.* | be available, be/go on display/show/view *The collection is to go on public display for the first time next month.* ◊ *The collection is rarely on view to the public.*

● PREP. **~of** *a valuable collection of antique porcelain*
⇨ Note at ART

2 taking sth away/bringing sth together
● ADJ. **routine, systematic** *the systematic collection of data* | **efficient** | **free** *The council offers free collection of waste.* | **weekly** | **data** | **debt, rent, revenue, tax** *the need for more efficient tax collection* | **refuse, rubbish, waste**
● VERB + COLLECTION **await, be ready for** *Your car is awaiting collection at our garage.* | **arrange, organize** *They will arrange collection of the chairs.*
● COLLECTION + NOUN **point** *a lack of collection points for waste paper* | **service** *a refuse collection service*
● PREP. **~of** *There are some difficulties with the collection of reliable data.*
● PHRASES **a method of collection** *different methods of data collection*

3 poems/stories/music
● VERB + COLLECTION **compile, edit, publish** *to publish a collection of scholarly essays*
● PREP. **~of**

4 money
● ADJ. **house-to-house, street** | **charity, church**
● VERB + COLLECTION **have, make, organize, take** *We will have a collection for charity at the end of the concert.* ◊ *A collection will be taken at the end of the service.*
● COLLECTION + NOUN **box, plate** *the church collection plate*
● PREP. **~for** *a street collection for famine relief*

5 new clothes
● ADJ. **new** | **autumn, spring, etc.** | **ready-to-wear**
● VERB + COLLECTION **show, unveil** *the first designer to unveil his collection for the spring season*

collector *noun*

● ADJ. **great, major** *a major collector of Japanese art* | **ardent, assiduous, avid, enthusiastic, keen, serious** | **private** | **art, coin, plant, record, stamp**
● PHRASES **a collector's item** *This vase is quite rare and is almost a collector's item.*

college *noun*

● ADJ. **community, local** | **sixth form, tertiary** | **tutorial** | **university** | **agricultural, art, FE/further education, military, music, police, secretarial, teacher training, technical, theological, veterinary, etc.**
● VERB + COLLEGE **attend, go to** | **finish, graduate from**
● COLLEGE + NOUN **lecturer, principal, teacher** | **staff** | **student** | **course** | **chapel, library, room**

● PREP. **at~** *She's at college in Swindon.* **in~** *Not all the lecturers are in college at any one time.*
● PHRASES **a college of (further/higher) education**

collide *verb*

● ADV. **nearly** | **head-on** *Two trains collided head-on.*
● PREP. **with** *His car nearly collided with a bus.*

collision *noun*

● ADJ. **serious** | **near** | **multiple** | **head-on, mid-air**
● VERB + COLLISION **be involved in, have** *I had a near collision with a lorry.* | **avoid** | **cause**
● COLLISION + VERB **happen, occur** *The collision occurred near the hospital.*
● PREP. **in a/the~** *She was injured in a collision.* **in~with** *The car was in collision with a lorry.* | **~between** *a head-on collision between two cars* **~with** *a collision with a train*
● PHRASES **be on a collision course with sth** *An iceberg was on a collision course with the ship.*

colonel *noun*

⇨ Note at RANK

colony *noun*

1 country ruled by another country
● ADJ. **overseas** *Britain's overseas colonies* | **self-governing** | **penal, plantation**
● VERB + COLONY **establish** *Settlers established a new colony in the early 18th century.*
● PREP. **in a/the~**

2 group of animals/plants
● ADJ. **huge, large, thriving** | **small** | **breeding** | **ant, bird, seal, etc.** | **coral**
● VERB + COLONY **form** *Some of the insects will leave to form a new colony.*
● PREP. **in a/the~** *The birds nest in huge colonies.* | **~of** *a colony of ants*

colour *noun*

1 quality that makes sth red, etc.
● ADJ. **bold, bright, brilliant, vivid, vibrant** | **dark, deep** *Dark colours suit you best.* | **intense, rich, strong** *the intense colour of new leaves* | **light, muted, pale, pastel, soft, subdued, subtle** | **dull** | **garish, gaudy, loud, lurid** | **autumn/autumnal, earthy, warm** | **sombre** | **attractive, beautiful, lovely** | **complementary, contrasting** | **matching** | **basic** | **primary, secondary** | **indeterminate, neutral** | **natural** | **blue, red, etc.** *The curtains went a strange orange colour when we washed them.* | **eye, hair, skin** *What is her natural hair colour?*
● QUANT. **dash, flash, splash** | **mass, riot** *The garden is a riot of colour in spring.* | **spot, touch**
● VERB + COLOUR **change** *The chameleon changes colour to match its surroundings.* | **add** *The silk cushions add colour to an otherwise dull room.*
● COLOUR + VERB **match (sth)** | **clash** | **fade** | **run** *This colour runs, so wash the shirt separately.*
● COLOUR + NOUN **combination, range, scheme** *We have to choose a colour scheme for the dining room.* | **illustration, photograph, photography, printing, reproduction** | **monitor, television**
● PREP. **in~** *The flowers are pale blue in colour.* ◊ *Is the film in colour or black and white?* ◊ *The book is lavishly illustrated in full colour.* **in a~** *The scarf is available in six different colours.*
● PHRASES **a combination/range of colours**

2 redness in the face
● ADJ. **heightened, high** *You could tell she was excited by the heightened colour in her cheeks.* | **faint**

COLOURS

Things can **be**, **look**, **go** or **turn** a particular colour. Or you can **make sth** or **colour**, **dye**, **paint** or **stain sth** a colour.

The pages of the book have gone yellow.
I've dyed the curtains green.

pale	light	dark	deep	dull
blue	blue	blue	blue	brown
brown	brown	brown	brown	green
green	green	green	orange	red
grey	grey	grey	pink	
orange	pink	pink	purple	
pink	purple	purple	red	
purple	red	red	yellow	
red	yellow			
yellow				

She was wearing a dark green skirt.
They chose deep purple for the curtains.
light blue eyes
a pale yellow blouse
The bricks are a dull red.

Other expressions:

a shade of ~

a beautiful shade of red

in ~

She was dressed all in pink.
Have you got this shirt in blue?

wear ~

I can't wear yellow—it makes my eyes look strange.

~ suits sb

Orange suits you.

bright	brilliant	rich	vivid	warm
blue	blue	blue	blue	brown
green	green	brown	green	orange
orange	orange	green	orange	red
pink	pink	orange	pink	
purple	red	pink	red	
red		red	yellow	
yellow		yellow		

a bright red car
The water was a brilliant blue.
The room was decorated in rich browns and oranges.
His eyes were a vivid green.
warm brown eyes

• VERB + COLOUR **have** *You have a bit more colour in your cheeks now.* | **bring** *The walk brought colour to her face.* | **be drained of, drain of, lose** *His face drained of all colour.*
• COLOUR + VERB **flood sth, rise** *Colour flooded her cheeks.* ◇ *The colour rose in his face.* | **drain** *The colour drained from her face when she saw him.* | **come back, return** *Gradually the colour returned to his cheeks.*
• PREP. **off~** (= looking or feeling ill)

3 interesting or exciting details
• ADJ. **local** *a journalist in search of a bit of local colour*
• VERB + COLOUR **add, give sth, lend** *His asides lent colour to the story.*
• PHRASES **full of colour**

colour *verb*

• ADV. **heavily, strongly** *His opinions are heavily coloured by his own experiences.* | **naturally**

coloured adj.

- VERBS **be**
- ADV. **boldly, brilliantly, brightly, gaily, highly, richly, strikingly, strongly, vividly** *She wore a richly coloured silk dress.* | **beautifully** | **delicately** | **uniformly** | **variously** *variously coloured birds*
- ADJ. **dark, light** | **cream, gold, etc.**

colouring noun

- ADJ. **natural** | **dark, fair**
- VERB + COLOURING **have** *Her daughter has very fair colouring.*

column noun

1 tall stone post
- ADJ. **huge, tall** | **fluted** *colonnades of fluted Doric columns* | **classical** | **Corinthian, Doric, Ionic**
- COLUMN + VERB **support sth** *The roof is supported by four huge columns.*

2 piece of writing in a newspaper
- ADJ. **regular** *He has a regular column in a weekly newspaper.* | **daily, weekly, etc.** | **newspaper** | **agony, correspondence, death, editorial, financial, gossip, leader, letters, lonely hearts** (= with advertisements for a new lover or friend), **obituary, personal, travel**
- VERB + COLUMN **have, write** | **syndicate**
- COLUMN + NOUN **inches** *So many column inches are devoted to film stars.*
- PREP. **in a/the ~** *She saw his name in an obituary column.* | **~ about/on** *a weekly column on films showing in London*

3 long line of people, vehicles, etc.
- ADJ. **huge, long** | **armoured, tank** | **marching**
- PREP. **in ~s** *to march in columns* | **~ of** *a column of troops*
- PHRASES **the head of the column**

coma noun

- ADJ. **deep** | **irreversible**
- VERB + COMA **fall into, go into, sink into, slip into** *He sank into a coma after suffering a brain haemorrhage.* | **come out of**
- COMA + NOUN **victim**
- PREP. **in a/the ~** *He has been in a coma since his car accident three months ago.*

comb noun

1 used for making your hair tidy
- VERB + COMB **use**
- PHRASES **a brush and comb, drag/run a comb through sth** *She ran a comb through her tangled hair.*

2 act of combing
- VERB + COMB **could do with, need** *Your hair could do with a comb!* | **give sth** *She gave her hair a comb.*

combat noun

- ADJ. **fierce, mortal** | **armed, unarmed** | **close, hand-to-hand** | **open** | **single** | **aerial**
- VERB + COMBAT **be engaged in, be locked in, engage in** *The troops were locked in hand-to-hand combat.* | **send sb into**
- COMBAT + NOUN **mission** | **zone** | **force, troops, unit** | **aircraft, vehicle** | **boots, fatigues, gear, jacket, kit, suit, uniform**
- PREP. **in ~** *He was killed in combat.* **in ~ with** *The soldiers are in combat with rebel forces.* | **~ against** *in mortal combat against dragons* **~ between** *a fierce combat between two champions*

combat verb

- ADV. **effectively** *She argued that the only way to combat inflation effectively was to keep interest rates high.*
- VERB + COMBAT **help (to)** | **be designed to**
- PHRASES **action/efforts/measures/policies to combat sth** *proposing measures to combat crime*

combination noun

- ADJ. **perfect, right, unbeatable, winning** *The orchestra played with a winning combination of gusto and precision.* | **attractive, delicious, good, happy, powerful** | **curious, rare, strange, unique, unusual** | **colour** *an unusual colour combination*
- PREP. **in ~ (with)** *The materials can be used singly or in combination.* ◊ *Hepatitis D exists only in combination with the hepatitis B virus.* | **~ of** *a delicious combination of flavours*

combine verb

- ADV. **successfully** *She successfully combines her career with family life.*
- PREP. **against** *to combine against a common enemy* **with** *Combine the flour with the water to make a stiff paste.*

comeback noun

- ADJ. **big, dramatic, fighting, great, remarkable, successful** | **long-awaited** | **political**
- VERB + COMEBACK **make, stage** *He made one of the most remarkable comebacks in modern politics.* | **attempt**
- COMEBACK + NOUN **trail** *The player is on the comeback trail after a serious knee injury.*

comedian noun

- ADJ. **celebrated, great, popular** | **film, radio, stand-up, television/TV** *He started out as a stand-up comedian in Liverpool.* | **alternative**
⇨ Note at JOB

comedy noun

- ADJ. **high, low** | **alternative, black, light, musical, romantic, situation, slapstick, stand-up** *a popular romantic comedy* ◊ *The show contains some wonderful slapstick comedy.*
- VERB + COMEDY **do, play** *Does he play comedy?*
- COMEDY + NOUN **actor, actress, writer** | **film, series, show**
- PHRASES **a comedy of manners**
⇨ Note at PERFORMANCE (for more verbs)

comfort noun

1 having all your body needs/a pleasant life
- ADJ. **great, maximum, modest, reasonable** *They live in modest comfort.* | **comparative, relative** | **added** *a quilted cover for added comfort* | **domestic, personal, physical**
- PREP. **for ~** *I dress for comfort rather than glamour.* **in ~** *I like to travel in reasonable comfort.*
- PHRASES **a degree/standard of comfort, in the comfort of your own home, too close/hot for comfort** *The hotel offers a high standard of comfort.* ◊ *The sound of gunfire was too close for comfort.*

2 help/kindness to sb who is suffering
- ADJ. **great** | **cold** *A drop in the unemployment rate was cold comfort for those without a job* (= not much comfort at all).
- QUANT. **crumb, word**
- VERB + COMFORT **bring sb, give sb, offer sb, provide sb with** *His kind words brought some comfort to the grieving parents.* | **derive, draw, find, get, seek, take**

They sought comfort in each other. ◇ *We took great comfort from the fact that at least some of our savings were safe.*
- COMFORT + NOUN **food** *Chocolate is a great comfort food.*
- PREP. **~in** *She found comfort in music.*
- PHRASES **a source of comfort**

3 sb/sth that helps when you are suffering, etc.
- ADJ. **great**
- PREP. **~ to** *The children have been a great comfort to me through all of this.*

4 sth that makes life easier
- ADJ. **modern | creature, home, material** *I hate camping – I miss all my creature comforts.* **| spiritual**

comfort verb

- ADV. **greatly** *The idea that he was not alone comforted him greatly.*
- PHRASES **be comforted to know** *He was comforted to know that most people in the class knew even less than he.* **being comforted by family/friends/relatives** *The victim's widow was today being comforted by family and friends.* **feel comforted**

comfortable adj.

1 allowing you to feel relaxed
- VERBS **be, feel, look** *The bed felt comfortable.* **| make sth** *We must think how we can make the room more comfortable for you.*
- ADV. **extremely, incredibly, superbly, very, wonderfully** *an extremely comfortable chair* **| perfectly | enough, fairly, moderately, quite, reasonably** *The hotel was comfortable enough.* **| surprisingly**

2 not having any pain/worry
- VERBS **be, feel, look** *Did you feel comfortable and relaxed at the party?* **| become, get** *This bed is lumpy—I just can't seem to get comfortable.* **| make sb/yourself** *Make yourself comfortable!*
- ADV. **very | completely, entirely, quite, totally** *I was not entirely comfortable about the plans they had made.*
- PREP. **about** *They didn't feel comfortable about her travelling alone.* **with** *I don't feel comfortable with him.*

3 having/providing enough money for all your needs
- VERBS **be**
- ADV. **very | quite, relatively** *I had a relatively comfortable life in Brazil.*

comforting adj.

- VERBS **be, feel | find sth**
- ADV. **extremely, most, very, wonderfully | hardly, not particularly | strangely** *She found his voice strangely comforting.*

comic adj.

- VERBS **be**
- ADV. **richly, truly, wonderfully** *Many of the scenes in the book are richly comic.* **| almost | faintly, mildly, slightly | blackly, grotesquely** *a blackly comic futuristic fantasy*

comical adj.

- VERBS **be, look, sound | become | make sth** *What made it so comical was that their hats kept falling off.*
- ADV. **extremely, very | almost | faintly, quite, rather, slightly, somewhat** *He is a faintly comical figure who fears being made fun of.*

command noun

1 order
- ADJ. **peremptory**
- VERB + COMMAND **carry out, obey | bark, give,**

issue *an army officer barking commands at his men* ◇ *He issued the command to retreat.*
- PREP. **at sb's ~** *I am at your command* (= ready to obey you). ◇ *At her command all work stopped.*

2 control over sb/sth
- ADJ. **complete, full, total** *He was in complete command of the situation.* **| direct** *under the direct command of Lieutenant Sykes* **| sole** *She was in sole command of one million pounds.* **| personal | integrated, joint, unified** *NATO's integrated military command* **| overall | high, supreme** *the military high command* **| army, military**
- VERB + COMMAND **have** *He had command of 3 000 soldiers.* **| assume, take (over) | give sb, put sb in | relinquish | lose, be relieved of** *She has lost command of her senses.*
- PREP. **in ~** *Who is in command?* ◇ *She is second in command.* **in ~ of** *He was put in command of the navy.* **under sb's ~** *The division was under the command of General George.* **| ~ over** *his command over resources*
- PHRASES **the chain/line of command**

3 ability to do/use sth
- ADJ. **excellent, fluent, good, perfect | poor**
- VERB + COMMAND **have**
- PREP. **at your ~** *The vast knowledge of the country he has at his command will be invaluable in the job.* **| ~ of** *She has an excellent command of French.*

commander noun

- ADJ. **supreme | deputy | air force, army, military, naval, navy, police | company, flight, group, platoon, squadron, station | Allied** *General Eisenhower was Supreme Allied Commander in Western Europe.*
- PHRASES **Commander-in-Chief**
⇒ Note at RANK

commend verb

- PREP. **for** *He was commended for his brave actions.* **to** *She said she would commend the proposal to the Board.*
- PHRASES **be highly/widely commended** *His book was highly commended.* **sth has little/much to commend it** *The proposed site has much to commend it.*

commendable adj.

- VERBS **be, seem**
- ADV. **highly, very** *The government's action here is highly commendable.* **| entirely, wholly**

comment noun

- ADJ. **brief | fair, favourable** *What she said was (a) fair comment.* **| adverse, derogatory, disparaging, hostile, negative, sad, unfair, unfavourable** *The attack is a sad comment on the public's understanding of mental illness.* **| critical** *Highly critical comments have been made about the conduct of some ministers.* ◇ *a book with critical comment on the various strands of feminism* **| caustic, ironic, sarcastic, sardonic, scathing, wry | constructive, helpful | cryptic | incisive, interesting, perceptive, shrewd | uninformed | general | detailed | casual, off-the-cuff, passing, throwaway** *He made a few casual comments to her about her hair and now she's gone and chopped it all off!* ◇ *This idea deserves more than passing comment.* **| editorial, official, personal, press, public** *Editorial comment in 'The Guardian' tended to support the government in this matter.* **| written | political, social** *Her novels were a vehicle for shrewd social comment.*
- VERB + COMMENT **have, make, pass** *If you have any comments, please send them to the above address.* ◇ *She made a cryptic comment about how the film mirrored her life.* ◇ *I would prefer not to pass comment before I have more information on the case.* **| attract, cause, draw, elicit, excite** *The programme attracted much adverse com-*

ment. | **invite, welcome** *The school has invited comments from parents about the new curriculum.* | **receive** *We have received many helpful comments from fellow-sufferers.*
● PREP. **without** ~ *She accepted his diagnosis without comment.* | **~ about/on** *a general comment on the weather*
● PHRASES **be available/not available/unavailable for comment** *The minister was unavailable for comment last night.* **no comment** *When asked about the rumours, the chairman replied, 'no comment'.* **a source of comment** *His visits were the source of much comment.*

comment verb

● ADV. **favourably | adversely, critically, unfavourably | bitterly | drily, wryly | publicly**
● VERB + COMMENT **decline to, refuse to** *The minister refused to comment on the affair.*
● PREP. **about** *People were commenting about her gifts and abilities.* **on** *He commented favourably on the proposals.* **to** *She commented to me that she liked it.*

commentary noun

1 on the radio/television
● ADJ. **brief | live | running** (= continuous) *She kept up a running commentary on the festivities.* | **radio, television** *listening to the radio commentary on the match*
● VERB + COMMENTARY **give, keep up, provide | listen to**
● COMMENTARY + NOUN **box** *the reporters in the commentary box*
● PREP. **~ on** *BBC1 will give a live commentary on the election results.*

2 criticism/discussion of sth
● ADJ. **detailed | critical | political, social**
● VERB + COMMENTARY **provide** *The novel provides a powerful social commentary on post-war Germany.*
● PREP. **~ on**
● PHRASES **be a sad commentary (on sth)** (= to reflect badly on sth) *The petty quarrels were a sad commentary on the state of the government.*

commentator noun

1 person who commentates on sth
● ADJ. **cricket, football, rugby, sports, etc. | match, race | radio, television/TV**
⇨ Note at JOB

2 person who gives opinions on sth in the media
● ADJ. **influential | independent | foreign | media | cultural, economic, political, social** *Political commentators are predicting that the minister will have to resign.*
● PREP. **~ on** *a commentator on current affairs*

commerce noun

● ADJ. **domestic, international**
● VERB + COMMERCE **carry on, engage in** *The marketplace was where commerce was traditionally carried on.*
● PREP. **~ between** *commerce between Germany and Italy* **~ with** *the development of commerce with Asia*
● PHRASES **a chamber of commerce, the world of commerce** *She has little experience of the world of commerce.*

commercial noun

● ADJ. **cinema, radio, television/TV | 30-second, etc.**
● VERB + COMMERCIAL **do, make** *She ended up doing commercials, which ironically revived her acting career.* ◇ *The company has made commercials for leading sportswear manufacturers.*
● COMMERCIAL + VERB **appear | feature sb/sth** *The commercial features a teenage girl with spots.*

● COMMERCIAL + NOUN **break** *The film was so full of commercial breaks it was impossible to enjoy.*
● PREP. **in a/the** ~ *She's in a commercial for cars.* | **~ for**

commission noun

1 asking sb to do a piece of work for you
● ADJ. **private, public**
● VERB + COMMISSION **accept, get, receive** *I have received a private commission to paint the prince's family.* | **give sb**

2 official group asked to report on sth
● ADJ. **international, national | joint | independent | government, judicial, official, parliamentary, royal | permanent, standing | special | roving | working | economic, election, electoral, fact-finding, investigating, investigative, planning**
● VERB + COMMISSION **appoint, establish, set up** *The government has set up a joint commission to consider the problem.* | **chair, head, preside over**
● PREP. **~ for** *the commission for racial equality* **~ on** *a commission on domestic violence*
● PHRASES **a commission of enquiry**

3 money for selling sth/providing a service
● ADJ. **big, high | small | fixed**
● VERB + COMMISSION **earn, get, receive | pay | charge** *That bank charges a high commission for cashing traveller's cheques.* | **deduct**
● PREP. **in** ~ *She earned £2 000 in commission last month.* **on** ~ *Most of the salespeople are on commission.* | **~ for/on** *They get a 10% commission on every encyclopedia they sell.*
● PHRASES **on a commission basis** *to work on a commission basis*

commission verb

● ADV. **specially** *specially commissioned works*
● PREP. **from** *The report was commissioned from scientists in five countries.*

commissioner noun

● ADJ. **high | assistant, deputy | special | European Union/EU, police, United Nations/UN**
● VERB + COMMISSIONER **appoint, appoint sb (as)**
● PREP. **~ for** *He was appointed United Nations High Commissioner for refugees.*

commitment noun

1 willingness to give time/energy to sth
● ADJ. **absolute, complete, full, total | clear, deep, firm, genuine, great, passionate, real, serious, strong | continued, continuing, increased, increasing, lifelong, long-term, ongoing | general, open-ended | government, personal, professional, public | emotional, ideological, moral, political, religious**
● QUANT. **degree, level**
● VERB + COMMITMENT **give, make** *The prime minister made a firm commitment to increasing spending on health.* | **demonstrate, display, show** *to demonstrate a commitment to human rights* | **lack | affirm, reaffirm | require** *Learning to play the violin requires strong commitment.* | **gain** *The government has managed to gain the commitment of employers to the scheme.*
● PREP. **~ on** *The government avoided giving any commitments on pensions.* **~ to** *his lifelong commitment to the socialist cause*
● PHRASES **a lack of commitment**

2 a responsibility
● ADJ. **big, considerable, major | binding | prior | international, overseas | business, domestic, family, financial, military, social, teaching, work**
● VERB + COMMITMENT **have, take on** *I don't want to take on any more commitments.* | **fulfil, honour, meet** *She*

can't meet her financial commitments. | **get out of, wriggle out of** He is trying to wriggle out of his various domestic commitments.
• PREP. **~on** to honour commitments on reduction of air pollution
3 agreeing to use money/time/people for sth
• ADJ. **heavy** a heavy commitment of capital

committed adj.

• VERBS **be, feel | become | remain**
• ADV. **deeply, fiercely, firmly, heavily, highly, seriously, strongly, very | absolutely, completely, fully, totally, wholly | genuinely | irrevocably** The country was now irrevocably committed to war. | **actively | personally** The prime minister is personally committed to this legislation. | **emotionally, financially, ideologically, politically** She cared for Jem in her way but did not want to become emotionally committed.
• PREP. **to** We are committed to improving services.

committee noun

• ADJ. **central | joint | standing | ad hoc, special | select | executive, management, steering | advisory, consultative | disciplinary | appeal | audit, finance, planning, selection, strike**
• VERB + COMMITTEE **create, establish, form, set up | chair** Lord Stansfield will chair the committee. | **appoint (sb to), elect (sb to)** He was appointed to the advisory committee last month. | **be on, serve on, sit on** She serves on several committees. | **leave, stand down from | disband**
• COMMITTEE + VERB **meet** The committee meets every Thursday.
• COMMITTEE + NOUN **member | meeting**
• PREP. **on a/the ~** I talked to some of the people on the committee. | **~on** a committee on the safety of medicines
⇒ Note at ORGANIZATION

commodity noun

1 product/raw material
• ADJ. **basic, important, primary | cheap | expensive | rare, scarce** Coal is becoming a rare commodity. | **export, marketable, saleable | perishable | agricultural, industrial** basic agricultural commodities
• VERB + COMMODITY **produce**
• COMMODITY + NOUN **market | futures, prices | export, trade, trading | broker, trader**
• PHRASES **trade in commodities**
2 sth that is useful
• ADJ. **precious, valuable** Time is a very valuable commodity. | **rare, scarce**

common adj.

1 happening/found often
• VERBS **be, seem | become | remain**
• ADV. **extremely, very | increasingly | fairly, quite** These problems now seem fairly common.
2 shared
• VERBS **be**
• PREP. **to** This attitude is common to most young men in the armed services.
• PHRASES **have sth in common** Jane and I have nothing in common (= share no interests, ideas, etc.). ◊ I have nothing in common with Jane. ◊ The two cultures have a lot in common (= have the same features, characteristics, etc.). **hold sth in common** They hold the property as tenants in common (= they share it). **in common with** Britain, in common with (= like) many other industrialized countries, has experienced major changes over the last 100 years.
3 showing a lack of education

• VERBS **be, seem, sound** I wish you wouldn't use that word—it sounds so common.
• ADV. **very | a bit, rather, slightly** I don't like Sandra. She seems a bit common to me.

common ground noun

• VERB + COMMON GROUND **have, share** The people on the course all share a lot of common ground. | **establish, find | find yourself on**
• PREP. **on ~** We found ourselves on common ground on the question of education. | **~between** to find common ground between the two sides
• PHRASES **an area of common ground**

commonplace adj.

• VERBS **be, seem | become | regard sth as** Such actions were regarded as commonplace during the war.
• ADV. **very | almost | enough, fairly, quite, rather** Her situation sounded commonplace enough.
• PREP. **among/amongst** These ideas are commonplace among teenagers.

common sense noun

• ADJ. **good, sound | plain, pure, simple | practical**
• VERB + COMMON SENSE **have** That child has got no common sense! ◊ At least he had the common sense to turn the water off before he left. | **exercise, rely on/upon, show, use** Use a bit of common sense!
• COMMON SENSE + VERB **prevail** I hope that common sense will prevail. | **dictate sth, suggest sth, tell sb sth** Common sense should tell you that people will find out sooner or later.
• PHRASES **(not) an ounce of common sense** He hasn't an ounce of common sense.

commotion noun

• ADJ. **dreadful, great, terrible | sudden**
• VERB + COMMOTION **cause, make, set up** The people upstairs were making a great commotion. ◊ The dogs set up a terrible commotion as we came near the house. | **hear**
• COMMOTION + VERB **break out | die down**
• PREP. **in a/the ~** Lots of furniture had been knocked over in the commotion. | **~about/over** What's all the commotion about?

commune noun

• ADJ. **hippy**
• VERB + COMMUNE **join** He gave up his job in the city and joined a commune. | **belong to | form, set up**
• PREP. **in/on a/the ~** She lives in a commune.

communicate verb

• ADV. **clearly, effectively, successfully, well | directly | easily | verbally** By the age of two most children have begun to communicate verbally. | **electronically**
• PREP. **by** We usually communicate by letter. **through** We communicated through an interpreter. **to** She is unable to communicate her ideas to other people. **with** couples who communicate well with one another

communication noun

1 act of communicating
• ADJ. **effective, good** Good communication is important for business. | **poor | direct | open | two-way | interpersonal | regular | electronic, non-verbal, verbal, written | business**
• VERB + COMMUNICATIONS **have** I haven't had any communication with him for several years. | **establish | facilitate, improve | prevent** measures which prevented the prisoners' communication with the outside world

● COMMUNICATION + VERB **break down** *Communication between the two sides has broken down.*
● COMMUNICATIONS + NOUN **skills | breakdown**
● PREP. **in ~ with** *We are in regular communication with the kidnappers.* | **~ between** *to establish direct communication between the lookout towers* **~ by** *communication by letter* **~ with** *We need better communication with clients.*
● PHRASES **a breakdown in communication(s)**, **channels/lines of communication** *to keep open the channels of communication* **a lack of communication**, **a means/method/system of communication** *Letters are their only means of communication.*

2 communications systems for sending information
● ADJ. **good | online | global**, **international | mass |** **radio, rail, road, telephone**
● VERB + COMMUNICATIONS **have | cut off, disrupt**
● COMMUNICATIONS + NOUN **centre, links, network, satellite, system, technology**
● PREP. **~ between** *They tried to disrupt communications between the two headquarters.* **~ with** *Paris has good rail communications with other major cities.*

3 message
● ADJ. **formal, official**
● VERB + COMMUNICATION **receive | send**
● PREP. **~ about** *He received an official communication about the reorganization of the Ministry.* **~ from, ~ to** *a communication from the officer to the general*

communion *noun*

1 Communion in church
● ADJ. **Holy | First**
● VERB + COMMUNION **go to** *We went to Holy Communion in the cathedral.* | **administer, celebrate, give** *Communion was celebrated by the Reverend John Harris.* | **receive, take** *Most of the people present took Communion.*
● COMMUNION + NOUN **service**
● PREP. **at ~** *There were only half a dozen people at Communion.*

2 sharing thoughts/feelings
● ADJ. **close | personal**
● PREP. **in ~ with** *He lived in close communion with nature.* | **~ with** *her personal communion with God*

communiqué *noun*

● ADJ. **official, unofficial**
● VERB + COMMUNIQUÉ **issue**
● PREP. **in a/the ~** *The announcement was made in a communiqué issued by the Defence Minister.*

communism *noun*

● ADJ. **revolutionary | international**
● VERB + COMMUNISM **embrace | overthrow, reject**
● PREP. **under ~** *a book describing life under communism*
● PHRASES **the collapse/fall of communism**, **the fight/struggle against communism**, **the rise/spread of communism**

communist *noun* (also **Communist**)

● ADJ. **militant, revolutionary | hardline, old-style, orthodox | reform/reformed | former** *The president of the new democracy is actually a former Communist.*

community *noun*

● ADJ. **large, small | close, close-knit, tight-knit** *a close-knit fishing community* | **lively, thriving, vibrant | international, local | wider** *the concerns of the local and wider community* | **ethnic, immigrant, minority, religious | Asian, black, etc.** *the Asian community in Britain* | **Christian, Muslim, etc. | farming, mining, etc. | rural, village | academic, business, gay, scientific**

● COMMUNITY + NOUN **care, centre, college, service, work | action, relations | group, leader | spirit**
● PREP. **in/within a/the ~** *divisions within the scientific community*
● PHRASES **the community as a whole/at large** *a cultural programme that should benefit the community at large* **a member of the community, part of a community, a pillar of the community** (= a strong supporter of the community), **a sense of community** *There is a strong sense of community in this town.*

commute *verb*

● ADV. **daily, every day**
● PREP. **between** *He commuted daily between London and Surrey.* **from, to** *She commutes from Peterborough to London every day.*

companion *noun*

● ADJ. **agreeable, amusing, boon, charming, delightful, good, entertaining, pleasant, wonderful | close, constant, faithful, inseparable | life | female, male | canine, human | dinner, drinking, travelling, walking** *He was an entertaining travelling companion.*
● PREP. **~ for/to** *She lived in the house as a companion to our grandmother.*

companionship *noun*

● ADJ. **close | constant | female, male | human | intellectual**
● VERB + COMPANIONSHIP **need | provide (sb with)** *A dog provides some companionship.* | **seek | enjoy**
● PREP. **for ~** *She had only her cat for companionship.* | **~ with** *She had never had any close companionship with another woman.*

company *noun*

1 business organization
● ADJ. **big, large, major, medium-sized, small** *a major European company* | **start-up** *a small start-up software company* | **associated, commercial, joint-stock, limited, private, public** *a public limited company* | **international, multi-national, national | trading** *an international trading company* | **bus, record, etc.** *a small insurance company*
● QUANT. **group**
● VERB + COMPANY **create, establish, form, found, set up, start (up) | manage, operate, run | acquire, buy, take over | dissolve | work for** *She's been working for the same company for 15 years.* | **join | leave, resign from**
● COMPANY + VERB **make sth, produce sth** *The company produces cotton goods.* | **expand, grow | shrink | fail, go bankrupt, go bust, go into liquidation, go out of business, go to the wall** (*informal*), **go under** *During the recession many small companies went out of business.*
● COMPANY + NOUN **director, policy, profits | car**
● PREP. **in a/the ~** *He has shares in several companies.* **within a/the ~** *the division of power within a company*
● PHRASES **a director of a company**
⇨ Special page at BUSINESS

2 group of actors/dancers, etc.
● ADJ. **large, small | touring | ballet, theatre, etc.** *a small touring theatre company*
⇨ Note at ORGANIZATION (for verbs)

3 being with sb else
● ADJ. **good, pleasant** *He's very good company.* | **poor**
● VERB + COMPANY **have** *It's nice to have a bit of company for a change.* | **keep sb** *I'll stay and keep you company.* | **need, want | provide (sb with)** *A cat would provide her with some company.* | **seek | enjoy** *I always enjoy her company.*

- PREP. **for ~** *I took my mother with me for company.* **in sb's ~** *He's nervous in the company of his colleagues.*
- PHRASES **have/request the pleasure of sb's company** (*formal*), **like/prefer your own company** (= to like being alone)

4 group of people together
- ADJ. **mixed** (= men and women) | **assembled** *He glanced round the assembled company.*
- VERB + COMPANY **keep** (= to spend time with) *John's mother was worried about the company he kept.*
- PREP. **in ~** *Those children don't know how to behave in company.* ◊ *That's not something to say in mixed company.*
- PHRASES **get into/keep bad company** (= to be friends with people that others disapprove of), **present company excepted** (= used after being rude or critical about sb to say that the people you are talking to are not included in the criticism)

5 visitor or visitors
- VERB + COMPANY **expect**, **have** *We're expecting company this afternoon.*

comparable *adj.*

- VERBS **be** | **become**
- ADV. **closely** *Its brain is closely comparable to the brain of a chimpanzee.* | **directly**, **exactly** | **almost** | **broadly**, **roughly** | **not strictly** | **not remotely** *No other country at that time had an organized public opinion remotely comparable to Britain's.* | **easily**, **readily**
- PREP. **in** *The two machines are comparable in size.* **to** *a job comparable to mine* **with** *The earthquake was comparable with others in recent years.*

compare *verb*

- ADV. **favourably**, **well** *The city compares favourably with other parts of Brazil.* | **unfavourably**
- VERB + COMPARE **cannot**, **do not** *These mountains do not compare with* (= are not nearly as high, impressive, etc. as) *the Himalayas.*
- PREP. **with** *Few things compare with* (= are as good as) *the joy of cycling on a bright, sunny spring morning.*
- PHRASES **be nothing compared to sb/sth** *I've had some difficulties but they were nothing compared to yours* (= they were not nearly as bad as yours).

comparison *noun*

- ADJ. **favourable**, **unfavourable** | **broad**, **crude**, **simple** | **close**, **detailed**, **direct** | **fair**, **good**, **meaningful**, **useful**, **valid** | **unfair**
- VERB + COMPARISON **draw**, **make** *It's difficult to make a direct comparison—the two things are so different.* | **allow**, **enable**, **facilitate**, **invite** *The similarity between the two invites comparison.* | **bear**, **stand** *Our problems don't bear comparison with those elsewhere.*
- PREP. **by ~(with)** *Jane is still quite young, and Fiona seems old by comparison.* **for ~** *Let's put them side by side for comparison.* **in ~ to/with** *The glasses are small in comparison with the old ones.* | **~between** *a comparison between figures for last year and this year* **~with** *a comparison with other schools*
- PHRASES **a basis for comparison** *to provide a basis for comparison* **a point of comparison**

compartment *noun*

1 section of a railway carriage
- ADJ. **first-class**, **second-class** | **non-smoking**, **smoking** | **passenger**, **sleeping**, **luggage**
- PREP. **in a/the ~**

2 section of a container, etc.
- ADJ. **separate** | **secret** | **battery**, **freezer**, **glove**, **storage** *Your sunglasses are in the glove compartment.*

- VERB + COMPARTMENT **be divided into** *The case is divided into four separate compartments.*
- PREP. **in a/the ~**

compass *noun*

- ADJ. **magnetic**
- VERB + COMPASS **use** | **check**
- COMPASS + VERB **show sth** *A compass shows you which direction is north.*
- COMPASS + NOUN **needle** | **bearing**, **reading** | **direction**, **point** | **error**
- PHRASES **a map and compass**, **the points of the compass** *The railway fanned out from Moscow to all points of the compass.*

compassion *noun*

- ADJ. **deep**, **great** | **genuine**
- VERB + COMPASSION **be filled with**, **feel**, **have** *I survived. Someone or something had had compassion on me.* | **show (sb)** | **lack**
- PREP. **~for** *He was filled with overwhelming love and compassion for his wife.* **~towards** *I felt no compassion towards her.* | **with ~** *The old people are treated with great compassion.*
- PHRASES **love and compassion**

compassionate *adj.*

- VERBS **be**, **feel**, **sound**
- ADV. **deeply**, **very** *a deeply compassionate man*

compatible *adj.*

- VERBS **be**, **seem**
- ADV. **highly**, **very** | **entirely**, **fully**, **perfectly**, **quite**, **totally**, **wholly** *three different, yet entirely compatible programs* | **directly** | **hardly** | **logically**, **sexually**, **technologically**
- PREP. **with** *The theory does not seem compatible with his other ideas.*

compelling *adj.*

1 holding your attention
- VERBS **be** | **become** | **find sth**
- ADV. **very** | **utterly** | **oddly**, **strangely** *His eyes were strangely compelling.*

2 strong/convincing
- VERBS **be**
- ADV. **extremely**, **very** | **logically** *There is no logically compelling argument to support their claims.*

compensate *verb*

1 remove/reduce the bad effect of sth
- ADV. **amply**, **fully** | **more than** *The advantages of the scheme more than compensate for the risks associated with it.* | **partially**, **partly**
- PREP. **for**

2 pay money for a loss/injury
- ADV. **adequately**, **properly** | **fully**, **in full** *People whose health has suffered will be compensated in full.* | **financially** *I expect to be compensated financially.*
- PREP. **for** *The company will compensate you for the losses you have suffered.*

compensation *noun*

- ADJ. **full** | **partial**, **small** | **adequate**, **appropriate**, **sufficient** | **financial**, **monetary**
- QUANT. **amount**
- VERB + COMPENSATION **award (sb)**, **give (sb)**, **grant (sb)**, **offer (sb)**, **pay (sb)**, **provide (sb with)** | **accept**, **gain**, **get**, **obtain**, **receive** *She got some compensation for*

damages. | deny sb, refuse sb | claim, demand, fight for, seek | be eligible for, be entitled to
● COMPENSATION + VERB **be payable** *If the government is proved negligent, compensation will be payable.*
● COMPENSATION + NOUN **claim | fund | order | payment | scheme**
● PREP. **as ~ (for)** *She received £7 000 as compensation for her injuries.* **in ~ (for)** *They will have to pay £5 000 in compensation.* | **~ for** *The money was small compensation for unfair dismissal.* **~ from** *compensation from the government* **~ to** *compensation to Mrs Parker*
● PHRASES **compensation in money**

compete *verb*

● ADV. **effectively, successfully | directly** *Their products compete directly with ours.* | **internationally, nationally** *The price must be right in order to compete internationally.* | **fiercely** *The big firms are competing fiercely on price.*
● VERB + COMPETE **can't/cannot** *Small independent bookshops can't compete with the large stores.*
● PREP. **against** *He welcomed the chance to compete against professional athletes.* **for** *Animals in the wild have to compete for food.* **in** *He regularly competes in road races.* **with** *We have to compete with several larger companies.*

competence *noun*

1 ability to do sth well
● ADJ. **great | basic | administrative, managerial, professional, social, technical | communicative, language, linguistic, reading**
● VERB + COMPETENCE **have | demonstrate, display, prove, show** *She shows a high level of technical competence.* | **lack | achieve, acquire, develop, gain** *He gradually developed the competence to deal with the more difficult cases.* | **challenge, question**
● PREP. **beyond sb's ~** *I'm afraid the work is beyond his competence.* **within sb's ~** *This should be well within your competence.* | **~ as** *Students had questioned her competence as a teacher.* **~ for** *He displayed great competence for the job.* **~ in** *competence in English*
● PHRASES **a level/standard of competence**

2 power to deal with sth
● ADJ. **formal | exclusive**
● VERB + COMPETENCE **have** *The commission has no formal competence in cultural matters.*
● PREP. **outside sb/sth's ~** *matters that fall outside the court's competence* **within sb/sth's ~** *The decisions come within the competence of the council.*
● PHRASES **an area of competence**

competent *adj.*

● VERBS **be, feel, look, seem | become | make sb** *A year of college had made her more socially competent.* | **consider sb, regard sb as** *He was not considered competent to teach seven-year-olds.*
● ADV. **extremely, highly, very** *a small number of highly competent officials* | **fully, perfectly | fairly, moderately, quite, reasonably | mentally** *She was mentally competent and she had the capacity to decide for herself.* | **socially, technically**
● PREP. **in** *She is competent in five languages.*

competition *noun*

1 event in which people try to win sth
● ADJ. **international, national | knock-out | dancing, piano, sporting, etc.**
● VERB + COMPETITION **win** *She won an international dancing competition.* | **lose | have, hold, stage** *We're going to have a competition to see who can swim the furthest.* | **enter, take part in | withdraw from**

● COMPETITION + VERB **take place | be open to sb** *The competition is open to all readers of the magazine*
● PREP. **in a/the ~** *I won the car in a competition.* | **~ between** *a competition between the best teams in the country* **~ for** *a competition for the best chef*

2 trying to achieve the same thing/gain an advantage
● ADJ. **cut-throat, fierce, intense, keen, serious, severe, stiff, strong, tough** *intense competition for the contract* | **direct** *Public transport is run in direct competition with the private sector.* | **fair, free, healthy, open | domestic | foreign, global, international, overseas | economic**
● VERB + COMPETITION **be up against, face | go into** *to go into competition with British Telecom* | **beat off, fight off** *to fight off competition from foreign firms*
● PREP. **against ~** *They won the order against fierce international competition.* **in ~ with** *We are in competition with some very large companies.* **in the face of ~** *The gas companies are having to lay off staff in the face of stiff competition from oil.* | **~ among/between** *There is a lot of competition between rival airlines.* **~ for, ~ from** *We face strong competition from other countries.*

competitive *adj.*

● VERBS **be | become | remain, stay | make sth** *skills training to make our industries more competitive in world markets* | **keep sth**
● ADV. **extremely, fiercely, highly, intensely, very** *a fiercely competitive sport* ◇ *highly competitive prices* ◇ *a very competitive person* | **fairly, quite, rather**
● PREP. **with** *Investment in research is needed to keep Britain competitive with countries like Japan.*

competitor *noun*

1 in business
● ADJ. **biggest, chief, leading, main, major | fierce, serious, strong** *The company has no serious competitors in this area.* | **closest, direct, nearest | domestic, local | foreign, international, overseas**
● PREP. **~ for** *fierce competitors for the dominant position in the Asian market*

2 person who takes part in a competition
● ADJ. **strong, top** *She is one of the sport's top competitors.* | **successful**
● COMPETITOR + VERB **enter sth** *Ten competitors entered the race.*

complacent *adj.*

● VERBS **appear, be, seem, sound | become, get, grow**
● ADV. **extremely, remarkably, very | far from** *Teachers are far from complacent about this problem.* | **rather, somewhat | alarmingly, dangerously** *This view seems alarmingly complacent.*
● PREP. **about** *It is vital that we do not get complacent about this disease.*

complain *verb*

● ADV. **bitterly** *She complained bitterly about the lack of help she received.* | **loudly | constantly, repeatedly**
● VERB + COMPLAIN **can't/couldn't, can/could hardly** *It was entirely my own idea, so I can hardly complain.* | **have cause to, have reason to, have a right to** *He really has no right to complain.* | **begin to, start to**
● PREP. **about** *All the guests complained about the noise.* **at** *She complained at the unfairness of it all.* **to** *I'm going to complain to the council about this!*

complaint *noun*

1 act of complaining
● ADJ. **bitter, serious | common, familiar, frequent | formal, official | consumer, customer**

• VERB + COMPLAINT **have** *I have a complaint about the food.* | **bring, file, lodge, make, register, voice** *He brought a complaint against his former manager.* ◇ *They filed a complaint with the European Commission.* | **get, have, receive** *We have had some serious complaints from parents.* | **deal with, handle, hear, investigate, respond to** *The tribunal heard complaints against the director.* | **resolve** | **reject**
• COMPLAINT + VERB **arise** *complaints arising from late payment* | **concern sth, relate to sth**
• COMPLAINT + NOUN **complaints procedure**
• PREP. **~ about** *a complaint about working conditions* **~ against** *a complaint against the police* **~ from** *a complaint from the neighbours* **~ of** *a complaint of unfair dismissal* **~ to** *to make a complaint to the authorities*
• PHRASES **cause/grounds for complaint** *The way I was treated gave me no cause for complaint.* **a chorus of complaint, a letter of complaint, a matter of complaint**

2 illness
• ADJ. **mild, minor** | **chronic** | **common** *Not being able to sleep at night is a very common complaint.* | **back, chest, etc.** | **medical**
• VERB + COMPLAINT **have, suffer from** *He has a minor skin complaint.*

complement noun

1 sth that goes well with sth else
• ADJ. **ideal, natural, necessary, perfect**
• PREP. **~ to** *This wine is the perfect complement to fish.*

2 total number that makes a group complete
• ADJ. **full** | **large** | **normal**
• VERB + COMPLEMENT **take** *We've taken our full complement of trainees this year.*
• PREP. **~ of**

complement verb

• ADV. **well** | **perfectly** *The flavours in the dish complement each other perfectly.*

complementary adj.

• VERBS **be**
• ADV. **essentially** | **mutually** *These two aims are not always mutually complementary: at times they conflict.*
• PREP. **to** *We provide a service that is essentially complementary to that of the banks.*

complete verb

1 finish sth
• ADV. **on schedule, on time** | **successfully** *The project has now been successfully completed.*

2 write information
• ADV. **accurately, correctly** *Has the form been correctly completed?*

complete adj.

1 having/including all the parts
• VERBS **be, seem** | **survive** *The book survives complete only in the second edition of 1533.* | **make sth** *You've made my life complete.*
• ADV. **remarkably, unusually** *a remarkably complete account of the negotiations* | **far from, less than, not quite** | **almost, nearly, virtually** | **fairly, reasonably**

2 finished
• VERBS **be, seem**
• ADV. **almost, nearly, substantially, virtually** *The job is almost complete.* | **far from** | **not yet**

completion noun

• ADJ. **rapid, speedy** | **early** | **satisfactory, successful**
• VERB + COMPLETION **near, reach** *The renovation of the theatre is now nearing completion.* | **bring sth to** *to bring the project to completion* | **delay** | **be due for** *The bridge is due for completion in May.*
• COMPLETION + NOUN **date**
• PREP. **after/following ~** *Payment will be made following successful completion of the job.* **before/prior to ~** *The floorboards were replaced prior to completion of the sale.* **near ~** *The book is near completion.* **pending ~** *Development of the site has been delayed pending completion of the sewerage scheme.* **on/upon ~** *The committee will report back to us on completion of the study.*
• PHRASES **the date of completion**

complex noun

1 set of buildings
• ADJ. **huge, large, vast** | **conference, entertainment, factory, holiday, hospital, housing, industrial, leisure, museum, office, shopping, sports**
• VERB + COMPLEX **build**

2 mental/emotional problem
• ADJ. **real, terrible** | **inferiority, superiority** | **castration, guilt, Oedipus, persecution**
• VERB + COMPLEX **have, suffer from** | **develop, get** *Don't keep on at him about his handwriting or he'll get a complex.* | **give sb**
• PREP. **~ about** *She has a complex about her big ears.*

complex adj.

• VERBS **be, look, seem, sound** | **become**
• ADV. **enormously, especially, exceedingly, exceptionally, extraordinarily, extremely, highly, hugely, immensely, incredibly, infinitely, particularly, very** *This is a highly complex matter.* | **increasingly** | **fairly, quite, rather, relatively, somewhat** | **surprisingly** | **unnecessarily** | **technically** *technically complex surgery*

complexion noun

1 colour/quality of the skin/face
• ADJ. **clear, flawless, fresh, glowing, healthy, lovely, nice, perfect** | **bad, blotchy, dull, pallid, pasty, sallow** | **ageing** | **creamy, fair, milky, pale** | **dark, olive, swarthy, tanned** | **florid, pink, rosy, ruddy** *a young girl with a rosy complexion* | **yellow** | **pitted** | **smooth**
• VERB + COMPLEXION **have** | **give sb** *Years of heavy drinking had given Alison a florid complexion.*

2 general nature/character of sth
• ADJ. **serious** | **different, new** | **political, social** *a change in the political complexion of the council*
• VERB + COMPLEXION **put, take on** *What you have told us puts quite a different complexion on the situation.* ◇ *The joke took on a rather serious complexion when the police became involved.*

complexity noun

• ADJ. **considerable, enormous, extraordinary, extreme, great, immense** | **full, sheer** *Only now did he understand the full complexity of the problem.* | **growing, increasing** | **bewildering** | **unnecessary** | **added** | **economic, linguistic, structural, technical** *the linguistic complexity of Siberia*
• QUANT. **degree, level**
• VERB + COMPLEXITY **convey, highlight, illustrate, reveal** *It is difficult to convey the sheer complexity of the situation.* | **grasp, understand**
• COMPLEXITY + VERB **arise (from sth)**
• PREP. **of ... ~** *a pay system of unnecessary complexity*

complicate verb

• ADV. **enormously, greatly** *These events will greatly complicate the situation.* | **further**

• PHRASES **be complicated by the fact that** *The issue is complicated by the fact that a vital document is missing.*

complicated *adj.*

• VERBS **be, look, seem, sound** *It all sounds very complicated.* | **become, get** *This is where the story gets complicated.*
• ADV. **extraordinarily, extremely, fiendishly, highly, immensely, incredibly, particularly, terribly, very** | **increasingly** | **a bit, fairly, a little, quite, rather, somewhat** | **unnecessarily**

complication *noun*

1 problem
• ADJ. **major** | **added, additional, further** | **undue, unnecessary** | **political**
• VERB + COMPLICATION **add, cause** *The presence of an armed gang added a major complication.* | **avoid** *We always try to avoid any unnecessary complications.*
• COMPLICATION + VERB **arise, occur** *Further complications arose when the newspapers published an interview with the prisoner's family.*

2 medical
• ADJ. **acute, dangerous, serious, severe** | **chronic, long-term** | **minor** | **common** | **rare** | **local** | **potential** | **birth, diabetic, medical, post-operative**
• VERB + COMPLICATION **develop, have, suffer** *She developed complications two weeks after the treatment.* | **die from/of** | **avoid, prevent**
• COMPLICATION + VERB **develop, occur, arise** *Complications develop if the drug is not used properly.* | **result from sth**
• PHRASES **a risk of complications** *The treatment carries a high risk of complications.*
• PREP. **~with** *complications with her pregnancy.*

complicity *noun*

• ADJ. **alleged, apparent** *her alleged complicity in the bombing* | **active** | **government, police**
• PREP. **~between** *the complicity between the army and drug smugglers* **~in** *her complicity in a plot to kill the president* **~with** *She did not suspect him of complicity with the authorities.*
• PHRASES **an act of complicity**
⇨ Note at CRIME (for verbs)

compliment *noun*

1 expression of praise
• ADJ. **great, higher/highest, tremendous** *To listen to someone is the greatest compliment you can pay.* | **pretty** | **unexpected** | **backhanded, double-edged, dubious** *In a backhanded compliment she said he looked very good for his age.*
• VERB + COMPLIMENT **pay sb** | **mean sth as** *Please don't misunderstand me—I meant it as a compliment.* | **get, receive** | **accept, acknowledge** *She acknowledged their compliments with a big smile.* | **regard sth as, take sth as** *I'll take that as a compliment.* | **fish for** *She's always fishing for compliments about her looks.* | **repay, return** *He returned her compliment by saying how well she looked.*
• PREP. **~on** *She received several compliments on her speech.* **~to** *If Mark's wearing a suit, that'll be a compliment to you!*

2 your compliments good wishes
• VERB + COMPLIMENTS **give sb, present (sb with), send sb** *Please give my compliments to your wife.*
• COMPLIMENTS + NOUN **slip** *The only enclosure was a formal compliments slip from the accounts department.*
• PREP. **with sb's~** (= free) *All guests will receive a bottle of champagne with our compliments.* | **~to** *my compli-*

ments to the chef (= to show that you like a particular dish)

complimentary *adj.*

• VERBS **be**
• ADV. **extremely, highly, very** *She made some highly complimentary remarks about their school.* | **quite**
• PREP. **about**

comply *verb*

• ADV. **fully, strictly**
• VERB + COMPLY **fail to, refuse to** *When requested to leave, they refused to comply.*
• PREP. **with** *Candidates must comply strictly with these instructions.*

component *noun*

• ADJ. **basic, central, core, critical, crucial, essential, fundamental, important, integral, key, main, major, necessary, principal, significant, vital** | **minor** | **common** *The researchers discovered a common component in all types of the organism.* | **standard** *Our software is becoming a standard component of many computer systems.* | **individual, separate, simple** *Individual components for the car can be very expensive.* | **chemical, genetic** | **electrical, electronic** | **aircraft, engine, etc.** | **course**
• COMPONENT + NOUN **failure** *Component failure was the cause of the accident.* | **manufacturer, supplier**
• PREP. **~in** *a crucial component in our success.*

compose *verb*

• ADV. **specially** *music specially composed for the occasion*

composed *adj.*

1 composed of made up of sth
• VERBS **be**
• ADV. **entirely, exclusively, solely, wholly** *The committee was composed entirely of specialists.* | **chiefly, largely, mainly, mostly, overwhelmingly, predominantly, primarily** *Bones are largely composed of calcium.*

2 in control of your feelings
• VERBS **be, feel, look, seem**
• ADV. **extremely, remarkably, very** | **perfectly** *He was pale but perfectly composed.* | **fairly, quite** | **outwardly**

composer *noun*

• ADJ. **famous, great** | **minor** | **established, leading, successful** | **prolific** *Verdi was a prolific composer of operas.* | **classical** | **avant-garde, modern** | **contemporary, living** | **opera/operatic**
• COMPOSER + VERB **compose sth, write sth**
⇨ Note at JOB

composition *noun*

1 parts that form sth
• ADJ. **overall** *The overall composition of the Senate was Democrats 57 and Republicans 43.* | **internal** *the character of the state and its internal composition* | **exact, precise** | **changing** *the changing composition of the labour force* | **age, class, demographic, ethnic, family, gender, household, population, racial, social** *the ethnic composition of the region* | **species** | **chemical, mineralogical**
• VERB + COMPOSITION **determine** *elections to determine the composition of the assembly*
• COMPOSITION + VERB **change, differ** *Has household composition changed in the last decade?*
• PHRASES **a change in the composition of sth**

2 piece of music

● ADJ. **classical, instrumental, musical | original** *an original composition by a popular young composer*
● VERB + COMPOSITION **write | perform, play**
● PREP. **~by** *a composition by John Cage* **~for** *a composition for violin and piano*

3 art of writing music
● ADJ. **classical, free, instrumental, musical**
● PHRASES **a method of composition**
● VERB + COMPOSITION **study**

4 piece of writing
● ADJ. **literary, original, prose**
● VERB + COMPOSITION **do, write** *In the exam, you have to do a composition.*
● PREP. **~on** *a composition on the effects of crime*

5 art of writing
● ADJ. **literary, metrical, poetic, prose, written**
● PHRASES **a method of composition**

6 work of art
● ADJ. **abstract, figure, formal, pictorial | original | perfect**
● PREP. **~by** *a composition by the sculptor, Bernt Notke*

composure *noun*

● ADJ. **cool, perfect**
● VERB + COMPOSURE **keep, maintain | lose** *She totally lost her composure and began shouting.* **| recover, regain | ruffle** *Nothing could ruffle his composure.*
● PREP. **with~** *She answered with perfect composure.*

compound *noun*

1 chemical
● ADJ. **chemical** *Scientists have produced a new chemical compound.* **| inorganic, organic | synthetic | molecular, simple** *Dalton believed that the simplest compound of two elements must have one atom of each.* **| active, dangerous, potent, toxic, volatile | carbon, iron, etc.**
● VERB + COMPOUND **form, produce** *At the right temperature, the chemicals will form a compound.*
● COMPOUND + VERB **contain sth | be derived from sth, derive from sth, be found in sth, occur** *compounds derived from rainforest plants*
● PREP. **~of** *a compound of oxygen and hydrogen*

2 area of land and buildings
● ADJ. **palace, prison, military | walled, secure** *Police are investigating a raid on a secure compound.*
● PREP. **in/inside a/the~** *life inside the prison compound*

comprehend *verb*

● ADV. **fully**
● VERB + COMPREHEND **be able/unable to, cannot | fail to** *She failed to comprehend the seriousness of the situation.* **| be difficult to, be impossible to** *It is difficult to comprehend how far away the stars are.*

comprehensible *adj.*

● VERBS **be | become | make sth** *We changed the wording of the text to make it more comprehensible.*
● ADV. **easily, readily** *The instructions should be easily comprehensible to parents.* **| entirely, fully, perfectly | barely** *His French was barely comprehensible.*
● PREP. **to** *The system is perfectly comprehensible to most people.*

comprehension *noun*

1 understanding
● VERB + COMPREHENSION **have** *She has no comprehension of the seriousness of the situation.* **| check** *There are exercises for checking comprehension.*
● PREP. **beyond (your)~** *Why he can't do it himself is beyond my comprehension.* **without~**

● PHRASES **a lack of comprehension** *He showed a total lack of comprehension.*

2 language exercise
● ADJ. **listening, reading**
● VERB + COMPREHENSION **do** *We did a listening comprehension.*

comprehensive *adj.*

● VERBS **be**
● ADV. **extremely, very | fully, totally** *fully comprehensive insurance* **| increasingly | fairly, pretty, quite, reasonably** *The list is fairly comprehensive.* **| truly**

compromise *noun*

● ADJ. **acceptable, fair, good, happy, honourable, possible, pragmatic, reasonable, sensible, suitable | ideal | muddled, uneasy, unsatisfactory** *After months of negotiations, they have reached an uneasy compromise.* **| inevitable, necessary**
● VERB + COMPROMISE **agree on, arrive at, come to, find, make, reach, work out** *I'm not making any more compromises.* ◊ *They're still trying to work out an acceptable compromise.* **| look for, seek** *It is best to try to seek a compromise rather than a perfect solution.* **| offer, suggest** *After much discussion, she offered a compromise.* **| accept | reject**
● COMPROMISE + NOUN **agreement, deal, formula, proposal, resolution, solution | candidate** *He might be an attractive compromise candidate if both sides' first choices are rejected.*
● PREP. **~between** *It was a fair compromise between the two sides.* **~on/over** *They came to a compromise over the exact amount to be paid.* **~with** *There could be no compromise with the nationalists.*
⇨ Special page at MEETING

compromise *verb*

1 in order to reach agreement
● VERB + COMPROMISE **be prepared to, be ready to | refuse to** *He wanted his own way and refused to compromise.*
● PREP. **on** *Unions and management seem ready to compromise on the level of the pay increase.* **with** *They debated whether to compromise with the opposition parties.*

2 damage/put in danger
● ADV. **seriously** *The affair seriously compromised the party's prospects of electoral success.*
● VERB + COMPROMISE **be prepared to, be ready to | refuse to**
● PREP. **on** *We are not prepared to compromise on safety standards.*

compulsion *noun*

● ADJ. **strange | inner**
● QUANT. **element** *There is an element of compulsion in the new scheme for the unemployed.*
● VERB + COMPULSION **feel, have** *He felt an inner compulsion to write.*
● PREP. **under~** *You're under no compulsion to take part.*

computer *noun*

● ADJ. **powerful | desktop, home, laptop, mainframe, notebook, personal, portable** *the market for home computers* **| analogue, digital, parallel**
● VERB + COMPUTER **run, use | switch on | switch off | log onto | log off | boot up, start up | shut down | reboot, restart | program | link, network** *Computers can be networked using modems and telephone lines.* **| interface** *The software allows you to interface your computer and an OCR reader.* **| hold sth on, store sth on** *The data is all held on computer.*

COMPUTERS

installing software

- **boot up/start up** the **computer**
- **insert** the program **disk/CD-ROM**
- **follow** the set up **instructions**
- **reboot/restart** the **computer**

creating a document

- **select** the new document **option** from the **pull-down menus** or **click on** the new document **icon**
- **type**, **edit** and **format** the **document**
- **print out** the **document**
- **save** and **close** the **document**

resizing a window

cutting and pasting text

- **scroll down** the **text** to find the **block** of **text** you want to **move**
- **position** the **cursor** at the beginning of the block of text
- **hold down** the **left mouse button** and **drag** the **mouse** to **highlight** the block of **text**
- **release** the **left mouse button**
- **click on** the **right mouse button** and **select** the cut text **option from** the **pop-up menu**
- **move** the **cursor** to where you want the text to go
- **select** the paste text **option**

looking up something on the Internet

- **connect to** the **Internet**
- **type in** the **website address** or **click (on)/follow** a **link**
- **access** the **website**
- **browse/search** the **website** to find the information
- if necessary, **download** the **information**

running several applications at the same time

- **double click on** the different program **icons**
- **move** and **resize** the program **windows** as required
- **click on** a program's **window** to use that program
- when finished, **close** the **windows**

backing-up a file onto a floppy disk

- **insert** a **blank disk** and **format it** if necessary
- if using an old disk, **wipe** the **disk** or **delete/erase** some of the **files** to **create space**
- **compress/zip** the **file** if it is too large
- **copy/save** the **file** onto the disk
- if necessary, **rename** the backed-up **file**
- **eject/remove/take out** the **disk**

• COMPUTER + VERB **run** | **hold sth**, **store sth** *The computer stores data in a buffer until the printer can accept it.* | **crash** | **be down/up** *The computers are all down* (= not functioning) *at the moment.*
• COMPUTER + NOUN **network**, **program**, **system** | **equipment**, **hardware**, **software** | **language** | **science**, **technology** | **keyboard**, **screen**, **terminal**, **etc.** | **game**, **graphics**, **model** *A computer model is used to predict forces affecting the aircraft in flight.* | **expert**, **hacker**, **programmer**, **user** | **company**, **industry**, **manufacturer** | **time** *Such a large sorting operation can take up a lot of computer time.*
• PREP. **on (a/the)~** *It's all stored on the computer.*

computing *noun*

• COMPUTING + NOUN **skills**
• PREP. **in~** *He works in computing* ◇
⇨ Note at SUBJECT (for verbs and nouns)

con *noun*

1 (*also* **con trick**) trick
• ADJ. **big** *The scheme was all a big con.*
• CON + NOUN **artist**, **man**

2 (usually **the cons**) disadvantage
• VERB + CON **consider**, **discuss**, **weigh up** *Before making a decision, you need to weigh up the pros and cons of the situation.*
• PHRASES **the pros and cons**

conceal *verb*

• ADV. **completely** | **partially**, **partly** | **barely**, **scarcely** *He waited with barely concealed impatience.* | **carefully**, **cleverly**, **cunningly** | **dishonestly** | **effectively**, **successfully**
• VERB + CONCEAL **be able/unable to** *She was unable to conceal her surprise.* | **try to** | **manage to**
• PREP. **from** *He concealed the truth from her.*

concede *verb*

• ADV. **eventually**, **finally** | **readily** *She readily concedes that there is much work still to be done.* | **grudgingly**, **reluctantly** *He reluctantly conceded that he was not fit enough to play in the match.*
• VERB + CONCEDE **be forced to** | **be prepared to**, **be willing to** *He was not prepared to concede that he had acted illegally.* | **be reluctant to**, **be unwilling to** | **refuse to**
• PREP. **to** *The firm should concede a significant salary increase to its employees.*

conceivable *adj.*

• VERBS **be**, **seem** | **become**
• ADV. **entirely**, **perfectly**, **quite** *It's quite conceivable that she hasn't heard the news yet.* | **just** *I suppose it's just conceivable that we've made a mistake.* | **barely**, **scarcely**
• PHRASES **every conceivable sth** *We had to draw up plans for every conceivable emergency.*

conceive *verb*

1 think of/imagine
• ADV. **brilliantly**, **carefully** *The plan was brilliantly conceived.* | **poorly** | **broadly** *The course is very broadly conceived* (= it covers a wide range of topics). | **narrowly** | **originally** *The dam project was originally conceived in 1977.*
• VERB + CONCEIVE **can't/cannot** *I cannot conceive why you paid out so much money.* | **be difficult to**, **be impossible to** *It is difficult to conceive of a society without money.* | **be easy to**, **be possible to**
• PREP. **of** *We conceive of ourselves as individuals.*

2 become pregnant

• ADV. **naturally** *She was unable to conceive a child naturally and was offered fertility treatment.*
• VERB + CONCEIVE **be able/unable to**

concentrate *verb*

• ADV. **fiercely**, **hard**, **intently** *She was sitting at her desk concentrating hard.* | **fully**, **properly** | **mainly**, **predominantly**, **primarily** | **particularly** | **entirely**, **exclusively**, **purely**, **solely**
• VERB + CONCENTRATE **be unable to**, **can't**, **couldn't** *I tried to work but I found I couldn't concentrate.* | **be difficult to**, **be hard to**, **be impossible to** | **tend to** *UK banks tend to concentrate on short-term lending.* | **try to**
• PREP. **on/upon** *He concentrated mainly on the flying and spoke very little.*

concentrated *adj.*

1 of your attention
• VERBS **be**
• ADV. **totally** *Kate sat up fully, her attention now totally concentrated.*

2 of a substance
• VERBS **be**
• ADV. **highly**, **very** *The liquid is found in a highly concentrated form.*

3 found in one place
• VERBS **be**
• ADV. **heavily**, **highly**, **particularly**, **strongly**, **very** | **increasingly** | **largely**, **mainly**, **mostly**, **overwhelmingly**, **primarily** | **disproportionately** *These jobs are disproportionately concentrated in the service sector.* | **geographically** *The immigrant community is strongly concentrated geographically.*
• PREP. **at**, **in** *Most of the country's industry is concentrated in the north.* **within** *Childbearing is concentrated within the first decade of married life.*

concentration *noun*

1 giving all your attention/effort to sth
• ADJ. **deep**, **great**, **intense** | **total** *a look of total concentration on her face* | **poor** | **exclusive**
• VERB + CONCENTRATION **demand**, **require** *The game requires great concentration.* | **lose** | **break**, **disturb** *Don's voice from outside broke my concentration.*
• CONCENTRATION + NOUN **span**
• PREP. **~on** *his concentration on his writing*
• PHRASES **a lack of concentration**, **a lapse in/of concentration** *One momentary lapse in concentration could prove fatal.* **powers of concentration** *She has great powers of concentration for a child her age.*

2 large number/amount of sth in one place
• ADJ. **great**, **heavy**, **high**, **large** *The greatest concentration of traffic is in the city centre.* | **low** | **geographical**
• CONCENTRATION + VERB **increase**, **rise** *The concentration of nitrates in the drinking water has risen in recent years.* | **decrease**, **fall**

concept *noun*

• ADJ. **basic**, **simple** | **broad**, **general**, **overall**, **wider** *'Mental handicap' should be replaced with the broader concept of 'learning difficulties'.* | **entire**, **whole** *The whole concept of responsibility was alien to him.* | **central**, **core**, **essential**, **fundamental**, **important**, **key** | **clear**, **precise** | **ambiguous**, **elusive**, **nebulous**, **vague** *The concept of 'adequate medical care' is too vague.* | **complex**, **difficult**, **sophisticated** | **abstract**, **intellectual**, **theoretical** | **alien**, **bizarre** | **underlying** | **useful** | **modern**, **new**, **novel** | **old-fashioned**, **traditional** | **business**, **design**, **economic**, **historical**, **legal**, **mathematical**, **political**, **psychological**, **religious**, **scientific**
• VERB + CONCEPT **have** *Teachers should have a clear*

concept of what a multiracial society is. | **grasp, under-stand** *She finds it difficult to grasp abstract concepts.* | **define, formulate, frame** *the need to create new words to frame new concepts* | **introduce** | **develop**
● PREP. **~of** *He formulated the concept of imaginary time.*

conception *noun*

1 idea/understanding
● ADJ. **clear, distinct** *We now have a clearer conception of the problem.* | **broad, general** | **narrow** | **bold, grand** | **modern** | **traditional** | **popular** | **initial, original**
● VERB + CONCEPTION **have**
● PREP. **in~** *His work is strikingly fresh in conception.*
● PHRASES **have no conception of sth** *You have no conception of what her life is like.*

2 becoming/making sb pregnant
● VERB + CONCEPTION **prevent**
● PREP. **at~** *Sex identity is fixed at conception.*
● PHRASES **the moment of conception**

concern *noun*

1 feeling of worry
● ADJ. **considerable, deep, grave, great, major, serious** | **growing, mounting** | **common, widespread** | **national, public** *public concern about increased taxes*
● VERB + CONCERN **feel** *He felt some concern for her safety.* | **express, show, voice** | **cause** *The lack of firefighting equipment has caused concern.*
● PREP. **in sb's ~** *She forgot her own worries in her concern for him.* **out of ~** | **~ about/over** *She expressed her deep concern about conditions at the factory.* **~ for** *Out of concern for her health, we suggested she take a week off work.*
● PHRASES **be of (no) concern to sb** *Increased use of drugs is of great concern to parents.* **(a) cause for concern** *The president's health is giving serious cause for concern.* **a lack of concern** *I was surprised by her lack of concern.* **a matter of concern** *Stress at work is a matter of concern to staff and management.*

2 sth that worries/affects you
● ADJ. **chief, main, major, overriding, paramount, primary** *What are your main concerns as a writer?* | **common** *a common concern for new parents*
● PHRASES **be none of sb's concern** *How much we paid is none of your concern.*

concern *verb*

1 affect/involve
● ADV. **directly**
● PREP. **in** *Everyone who was directly concerned in (= had some responsibility for) the incident has now resigned.*

2 worry sb
● ADV. **a lot, really** *It really concerns me that he doesn't eat properly.* | **slightly**

concerned *adj.*

1 worried about sth
● VERBS **be, feel, look, seem, sound** | **become, get, grow** | **remain**
● ADV. **deeply, especially, extremely, genuinely, greatly, particularly, really, seriously, very** | **increasingly** | **a bit, a little, quite, rather, slightly, somewhat** | **(not) unduly** *She was not unduly concerned by the prospect of managing on her own.* | **naturally** | **rightly** | **simply**
● PREP. **about/at/by/over** *Doctors are concerned at the prospect of heart patients having to wait up to a year for surgery.* **for** *We are now deeply concerned for his safety.*

2 interested in sth
● VERBS **be**
● ADV. **especially, particularly, specifically** | **entirely, exclusively, solely** | **centrally, chiefly, essentially,**

largely, mainly, mostly, predominantly, primarily, principally *Mathematics is concerned essentially with understanding abstract concepts.* | **closely, directly, intimately**
● PREP. **with** *Social anthropology is centrally concerned with the diversity of culture.*

concert *noun*

● ADJ. **big** | **sell-out** | **evening, lunchtime** | **opening** | **closing, farewell, final** *He will be giving his farewell concert as Music Director of the Ulster Orchestra.* ◊ *The orchestra performs its final concert of the season tomorrow.* | **live, public** | **open-air, promenade** | **carol, classical, pop, rock** | **brass band, choral, orchestral, symphony** | **gala, subscription** *The Queen attended a gala concert at the Royal Festival Hall.* | **benefit, charity** | **tribute**
● QUANT. **series**
● VERB + CONCERT **attend, go to** | **give, perform (in), play (in)** | **have, hold, present, put on, stage** *The band is putting on its biggest concert of the year.* | **organize**
● CONCERT + NOUN **hall, platform, room, venue** | **performance, programme** | **artist, pianist** | **series, tour**
● PREP. **at a/the ~** | **~ of** *a concert of military music* **~for/in aid of** *organizing a concert for charity*

concerto *noun*

● ADJ. **piano, violin, etc.** | **D major, B minor, etc.**
● VERB + CONCERTO **compose, write** | **perform, play** | **conduct** | **record**
● PREP. **~for** *a concerto for clarinet and orchestra*
⇒ Special page at MUSIC

concession *noun*

1 sth you agree to in order to end an argument
● ADJ. **important, key, major, significant, substantial** | **limited, minor, small** | **special**
● VERB + CONCESSION **grant (sb/sth), make, offer (sb/sth)** | **get, obtain, win**
● PREP. **~ on** *The pressure group has won a number of concessions on environmental policy.* **~to** *The firm will be forced to make concessions to the union.*
● PHRASES **make no concessions to sb/sth** *They made no concessions to his disability.*

2 special right to do sth
● ADJ. **trade**
● VERB + CONCESSION **grant (sb/sth)** | **obtain, secure, win** *The company has just won a mining concession in the north of the country.*

3 lower charge for certain groups of people
● ADJ. **tax, travel**
● CONCESSION + VERB **be available to** *travel concessions available to older people*

conclusion *noun*

1 opinion reached after considering the facts
● ADJ. **correct** | **logical, reasonable, valid** | **inescapable, inevitable, obvious** | **erroneous, false, wrong** | **main** | **hasty**
● VERB + CONCLUSION **arrive at, come to, draw, reach** *I can't draw any conclusions from what she said.* | **jump to, leap to** *We don't want to jump to the wrong conclusion.* ◊ *Don't go jumping to conclusions before you know the facts.* | **lead to, point to** *It all points to the conclusion that nobody knew what was going on.*

2 ending of sth
● ADJ. **satisfactory, successful** | **foregone** *The result of the match was a foregone conclusion.* | **hasty**
● VERB + CONCLUSION **bring about, bring sth to** *The meeting was brought to a hasty conclusion.* | **come to**
● PREP. **in ~** *In conclusion, I would like to thank you all for your hard work.*
⇒ Special page at MEETING

conclusive *adj.*

- VERBS **appear, be, seem**
- ADV. **absolutely | fairly, pretty** *They produced some fairly conclusive evidence.* | **by no means, far from, hardly, not very** *The argument was far from conclusive.*

concrete *noun*

- ADJ. **solid | bare** *a floor made of bare concrete* | **wet | pre-cast, ready-mix/ready-mixed, reinforced**
- QUANT. **layer, slab**
- VERB + CONCRETE **mix | lay, pour | be made from/(out) of | set sth in** *The pathway is formed from large pebbles set in concrete.* ◇ *(figurative) I do not regard the constitution of the United Kingdom as set in concrete.*
- CONCRETE + VERB **set** *Before the concrete sets the surface can be given a final smoothing over.*

concur *verb*

- ADV. **strongly** *I strongly concur with that idea.* | **entirely, fully**
- PREP. **in, with** *Historians have concurred with each other in this view.*

concussion *noun*

- ADJ. **bad | mild, minor, slight**
- VERB + CONCUSSION **have, suffer**
- PREP. **with ~** *He was carried off the field with slight concussion.*

condemn *verb*

- ADV. **fiercely, roundly, strongly, vehemently, vigorously, vociferously | unequivocally, utterly | unanimously, universally | openly, publicly** *She publicly condemned the opposition leader.*
- PREP. **for** *He was roundly condemned for his mistake.*
- PHRASES **be widely condemned** *The action has been widely condemned by human rights groups.*

condemnation *noun*

- ADJ. **utter, wholesale | firm, severe, strong | universal, widespread | official, public** *There's been no official condemnation of the bombing.*
- VERB + CONDEMNATION **express, issue** *I can only express my strong condemnation of this dreadful behaviour.* ◇ *The United Nations issued a condemnation of the regime.* | **draw** *The violence has drawn firm condemnation from all the main political leaders.*
- CONDEMNATION + VERB **come from sb/sth** *Condemnation of this policy has come from all political parties.*

condition *noun*

1 state of sth
- ADJ. **excellent, good, immaculate, mint, peak, perfect, pristine | fair, reasonable | bad, poor | original** *The clock was restored to its original condition.* | **physical**
- PREP. **in ... ~** *The car is still in excellent condition.*

2 sb's state of health
- ADJ. **critical, serious | stable** *Doctors say his condition is now stable.* | **mental, physical** *There has been a serious deterioration in her mental condition.*
- CONDITION + VERB **get better, improve** *Without this treatment, her condition won't improve.* | **deteriorate, get worse**
- PREP. **in a ... ~** *He is still in a critical condition in the local hospital.* **out of ~** *I haven't been exercising much recently, so I'm a bit out of condition.*
- PHRASES **be in no condition to do sth** *You're in no condition to tackle the stairs.*

3 illness

- ADJ. **medical | serious | chronic | incurable | rare | heart, skin, etc. | mental** *She was unable to give informed consent because of a mental condition.*
- VERB + CONDITION **have, suffer from** *He has a rare skin condition.* | **be born with** *All three babies were born with an incurable heart condition.*

4 conditions situation/circumstances
- ADJ. **favourable, good, ideal, optimum** *Conditions are very favourable for starting a business.* | **adverse, appalling, awful, difficult, dreadful, freak** (only used about the weather), **harsh, poor, severe, terrible, treacherous** *adverse conditions for driving* ◇ *freak weather conditions* | **normal, prevailing | controlled** *The experiment is conducted under strictly controlled conditions.* | **experimental, laboratory | driving, housing, living, operating, working** *The working conditions in the factory are dreadful.* | **economic, market, political, social | climatic, environmental, physical, soil, weather**
- VERB + CONDITIONS **live in, work in/under** *An enormous number of people live in conditions of severe poverty.*
- CONDITIONS + VERB **exist, prevail** *As long as these weather conditions prevail, we are unable to rescue the climbers.* | **change | improve | deteriorate**
- PREP. **in ~** *in normal operating conditions* **under ~** *The samples are heated under experimental conditions.*

5 rule
- ADJ. **strict | special**
- VERB + CONDITION **attach, impose, lay down, set out** *the conditions attached to the grant of a residential licence* ◇ *The United Nations has imposed strict conditions on the ceasefire.* | **accept, agree to** *They would not agree to our conditions.* | **abide by, comply with, fulfil, meet, observe, satisfy** *To get a basic pension you must satisfy two conditions: ...* | **be subject to** *The bar was licensed subject to the condition that no children under 15 be admitted.* | **be in breach of** *He denied being in breach of bail conditions.*
- CONDITION + VERB **apply** *Special conditions apply to the use of the library's rare books.*
- PREP. **on ~ that** *They agreed to lend us the car on condition that* (= only if) *we returned it before the weekend.* **on ... ~** *I'll agree to the scheme on one condition: my name doesn't get mentioned to the press.* **under the ~s of** *Under the conditions of the agreement, all foreign troops will leave by May.*
- PHRASES **a breach of a condition, conditions of employment/sale, terms and conditions** *the terms and conditions of the contract*

6 necessary situation
- ADJ. **necessary, sufficient** *a necessary and sufficient condition for the eradication of unemployment*
- PREP. **~ for**

7 state of group
- ADJ. **human** *Work is basic to the human condition* (= the fact of being alive).
- VERB + CONDITION **improve** *aiming to improve the condition of the urban poor*

condolences *noun*

- ADJ. **heartfelt, sincere**
- VERB + CONDOLENCES **convey, express, extend, offer (sb), send (sb)** *We would like to take this opportunity to convey our heartfelt condolences to the families of the victims.* | **accept** *Please accept our sincere condolences.*

condom *noun*

- QUANT. **packet**
- VERB + CONDOM **unroll | put on, use, wear**

condone *verb*

- ADV. **tacitly**

● VERB + CONDONE **cannot/could not** *We cannot condone violence of any sort.*

conducive *adj.*

● VERBS **be**
● ADV. **highly, very** *Daylight is highly conducive to good plant growth.* | **hardly** *The noise was hardly conducive to a good night's sleep.*
● PREP. **to** *an environment conducive to learning*

conduct *noun*

1 behaviour
● ADJ. **good** *The prisoner was released early for good conduct.* | **discreditable, disgraceful, immoral, improper, ungentlemanly, unprofessional, unseemly | aggressive, violent | criminal, fraudulent, illegal, negligent, unlawful, wrongful | homosexual, sexual | personal | business, professional** *The business conduct of this bank will be subject to UK rules.* ◇ *Our organization sets high standards of professional conduct.* | **police | human** *It is tempting to think of morality as a guide to human conduct.*
● VERB + CONDUCT **engage in** *The committee concluded that the senators had engaged in improper conduct.* | **regulate** *Efforts were made to regulate the conduct of crowds at football games.* | **explain** *The minister was called to court to explain his conduct.*
● CONDUCT + VERB **constitute sth** *conduct constituting a crime*
● PREP. **~ by** *The violent conduct by the strikers was condemned.* **~ towards** *her conduct towards her husband*
● PHRASES **a code of conduct, rules of conduct, standards of conduct**

2 management of sth
● ADJ. **proper** *The elders were responsible for the proper conduct of community life.* | **day-to-day** *the day-to-day conduct of the business of the company*

conduct *verb*

1 organize sth/carry sth out
● ADV. **independently** *The enquiry must be independently conducted.* | **personally | properly | successfully**

2 lead/guide sb
● ADV. **personally** *How about a personally conducted tour of the house?*
● PREP. **along, around/round, down, through, to, etc.** *A guide conducted us around the museum.*

3 conduct yourself behave
● ADV. **honourably, well, with dignity** *She conducts herself with great dignity.*

4 heat/electricity
● ADV. **well** *a substance which conducts electricity well*

conductor *noun*

1 person who directs an orchestra
● ADJ. **great | famous | chief, principal | guest | opera/operatic, orchestra/orchestral**
● PREP. **~ of/with** *the principal conductor of the Berlin Symphony Orchestra*
● PHRASES **the conductor's baton**
⇨ Note at JOB

2 substance that allows heat/electricity to pass through
● ADJ. **good | bad, poor | electrical | lightning**

confederation *noun*

● ADJ. **loose** *The Franks were originally a loose confederation of Germanic tribes.*
● VERB + CONFEDERATION **establish, form, found | join**
● PREP. **~ between** *a confederation between two states* **~ of** *a confederation of employers*

conference *noun*

● ADJ. **national, international, regional, world | one-day, etc. | annual, quarterly, etc. | inaugural, preliminary, preparatory | consultative | joint | private | video | formal | full | successful | well-attended | high-level, summit | news, press | diplomatic, industry, inter-governmental, management, ministerial, multi-party, party, staff | constitutional, disarmament, education, environment, peace, trade, etc.**
● QUANT. **series**
● VERB + CONFERENCE **attend, go to | hold | organize | call, convene**
● CONFERENCE + VERB **meet, take place | begin, open | close, end | bring sb together** *The conference brought together historians working in a variety of fields.* | **be entitled sth** *a conference entitled 'Strategies for Epidemic Control'* | **be devoted to sth, examine sth, focus on sth, look at sth** *a conference devoted to the topic of peace* ◇ *an inter-governmental conference examining cross-border cooperation* | **hear sth** *The conference heard an appeal from a representative from one of the more deprived areas.* | **agree sth, decide sth, vote sth** *The conference agreed to adopt a set of compromise proposals.* | **adopt sth, approve sth, back sth, support sth** *The conference adopted a resolution on minority rights.* | **recommend sth | condemn sth, reject sth**
● CONFERENCE + NOUN **building, centre, complex, facilities, suite, venue | chamber, hall, room | table | platform** *The party leader made a morale-boosting speech from the conference platform.* | **chairman, speaker | guests, delegates, participants | organizer | agenda, programme | theme | debate, discussion, talks | speech | resolution | paper | report | session | season**
● PREP. **at a/the ~** *We met at an international conference.* **in ~ with** *He was in conference with (= in a meeting with) his lawyers all day.* | **~ about** *Few reporters turned up to his press conference about low pay.* **~ between** *a conference between the warring parties* **~ for** *a conference for catering managers* **~ on** *a conference on economic monetary union* **~ with** *Management had a joint conference with the union.*

confess *verb*

● ADV. **freely, openly | allegedly | ruefully, sheepishly**
● VERB + CONFESS **have to, must** *I must confess that I didn't have much faith in her ideas.*
● PREP. **to** *He was arrested and confessed to the murder.* ◇ *She confessed to me that she had known his true identity for some time.*

confession *noun*

1 admitting guilt
● ADJ. **detailed, full | honest, true** *It's difficult to believe it's an honest confession after all her lies.* | **false | alleged | uncorroborated | signed, taped/tape-recorded, written | deathbed**
● VERB + CONFESSION **make | sign | extract, get, obtain, secure** *He claims his confession was extracted under torture.* | **retract** *She made a false confession during the trial which she later retracted.* | **exclude** *The court excluded the confession wrongly obtained by the police.*
● PREP. **~ by** *an alleged confession by the defendant* **~ from** *a confession from the prisoner* **~ of** *a true confession of a terrible crime* **~ to** *a confession to murder*
● PHRASES **force/get a confession out of sb** *The police forced a confession out of him.*

2 embarrassing statement
● ADJ. **candid, open | shy**
● VERB + CONFESSION **made** *The government made open confession of its inability to cope with the crisis.*
● PREP. **~ of** *her shy confession of love*

● PHRASES **have a confession to make** *I have a confession to make. I read your private emails.*

3 to a priest

● VERB + CONFESSION **go to** *I used to go to confession every Saturday as a child.* | **hear** *The priest heard her confession and granted absolution.*

● CONFESSION + NOUN **box**

● PHRASES **an act of confession**

confetti *noun*

● QUANT. **shower**
● VERB + CONFETTI **shower (sb with), throw** *The winning team was showered with confetti.*
● CONFETTI + VERB **shower down** *Confetti showered down on the newly-weds.*

confidence *noun*

1 belief in others

● ADJ. **absolute, complete, full, total** *The company needs the full confidence of its investors.* | **great, high, real** *Confidence is high among the team's supporters.* | **reasonable** | **growing, increased, increasing** | **new, renewed** | **misplaced** *The general's confidence in his army proved misplaced.* | **international** | **popular, public** *public confidence in the government* | **business, consumer, customer, investor, market**
● VERB + CONFIDENCE **enjoy, feel, have** *This government no longer enjoys the confidence of the public.* ◇ *We all have complete confidence in this product.* | **express** *He expressed confidence in the new plans.* | **be lacking in, lack** | **share** *She wished that she shared his confidence.* | **maintain, preserve** *to maintain public confidence in the system of justice* | **bolster, boost, build (up), enhance, improve, increase, lift, raise** *Higher profits should raise business confidence.* | **gain** | **command, create, develop, encourage, engender, generate, give (sb), inspire, instil** *The training is designed to give staff confidence in managing problems.* ◇ *The company's record does not really inspire confidence.* | **rebuild, restore, revive** *Only if the chairperson resigns will we be able to restore the confidence of our members.* | **lose** *This government has lost the confidence of the public.* | **damage, dent, sap, shake, undermine, weaken** *Only one bank scandal is needed to shake the confidence in the financial markets.* | **destroy, shatter**
● CONFIDENCE + VERB **decrease** | **grow, increase, rise** | **return** *Confidence has returned to the market.*
● PREP. **~ about** *The captain was not lacking in confidence about his team's prospects.* **~ among** *a loss of confidence among investors* **~ between** *efforts to build confidence between employers and unions* **~ in** *They have no confidence in the legal system.*
● PHRASES **a crisis of confidence** *There is a crisis of confidence in the university about its future role.* **have every/little/no/some confidence** *The captain of the football team said he had every confidence in his men.* **a lack of confidence, a loss of confidence, a vote of (no) confidence** *This is a tremendous vote of confidence for the government.* **a (no) confidence motion/vote** *The government lost a parliamentary confidence vote.*

2 belief in yourself

● ADJ. **considerable, enormous, great** | **sublime, supreme, tremendous, utter** | **added, extra** | **fresh, newfound** | **increased, increasing, growing** | **calm, quiet** *giving an outward appearance of quiet confidence* | **easy** *She spoke in a tone of easy confidence.* | **false** *All his false confidence had drained away.* | **inner, personal** | **social**
● VERB + CONFIDENCE **have** *She has very little confidence in her own abilities.* | **show** | **feel** *'I can explain,' he said, with a confidence he did not feel.* | **brim with, exude, be full of, ooze, radiate** *Since she got the new job, she's been brimming with confidence.* ◇ *a man who exudes confidence* | **be lacking in, lack** *A lot of children are lacking in*

confidence. | **acquire, develop, gain, gather** *She's gained a lot of confidence over the last year.* | **grow in** *As the weeks went by he grew in confidence.* | **lose** *During his illness he really lost his confidence.* | **get back, rebuild, recover, regain, restore** *He's really striking the ball well and has got his confidence back.* | **bolster, boost, build (up), enhance** *Winning the competition really boosted her confidence.* | **give sb, instil** *to instil confidence in staff who feel nervous about taking on new roles* | **dent, sap, shake, undermine, weaken** *Failing his exams really dented his confidence.* | **destroy, shatter**
● CONFIDENCE + VERB **drain (away), evaporate, go** *My confidence went completely after my first major defeat.* | **grow, increase, rise** *Their confidence grew with each success.* | **return**
● CONFIDENCE + NOUN **boost, booster** *The home side badly need a confidence booster.* | **building** *Getting the certificate does a lot in terms of confidence building.*
● PREP. **with ~** *She answered the question with confidence.* | **~ about** *I lacked confidence about how I looked* **~ in** *his confidence in himself*
● PHRASES **a lack of confidence, a loss of confidence**

3 trust

● ADJ. **absolute, complete, full, total** | **mutual**
● VERB + CONFIDENCE **enjoy, have** *The Cabinet must enjoy the confidence of Parliament.* | **keep, retain** | **gain, get, win** | **build** *an environment which builds mutual confidence* | **betray, break** | **place, put** *Are we to place confidence in a minister who cannot remember a phone call he made last week?* | **withhold** | **take sb into** *She thought she might take Leo into her confidence.*
● CONFIDENCE + NOUN **trick, trickster**
● PREP. **in ~** *She told me in confidence—I couldn't break that confidence, could I?*
● PHRASES **a breach of confidence** *Telling other people what I'd said was a total breach of confidence.* **in strict confidence** *Enquiries will be dealt with in the strictest confidence.*

4 secret

● ADJ. **whispered**
● VERB + CONFIDENCE **exchange, share** *The girls exchanged whispered confidences.* | **keep** | **betray** *I could never forgive Mike for betraying a confidence.* | **encourage, invite** *She didn't encourage confidences.*
● PHRASES **an exchange of confidences**

confident *adj.*

● VERBS **appear, be, feel, look, seem, sound** | **become, get, grow** *He's got more confident as he's got older.* ◇ *She gradually grew more confident.* | **remain** | **make sb** *Going to university has made her more confident.*
● ADV. **extremely, really, remarkably, very** | **absolutely, completely, entirely, fully, perfectly, supremely, totally** | **increasingly** | **fairly, pretty, quite, reasonably** | **calmly, quietly, serenely** *He came out of the interview feeling quietly confident.* ◇ *She sauntered onto the set, looking serenely confident.* | **cautiously** | **socially** *You get young people who appear to be socially confident, but inside they are a bundle of neuroses.*
● PREP. **about** *We are confident about the future.* **of** *I'm fully confident of winning the title.*

confidential *adj.*

● VERBS **be** | **remain** | **keep sth, treat sth as** *The affair must be kept confidential.* ◇ *Information about prices is to be treated as confidential.*
● ADV. **extremely, highly** | **absolutely, completely, strictly, totally** *The findings are strictly confidential.* | **commercially** *commercially confidential data*

confidentiality noun

• ADJ. **absolute, complete, strict, total** *It is important to maintain strict confidentiality at all times.* | **commercial, professional**
• VERB + CONFIDENTIALITY **ensure, maintain, preserve, protect** *efforts to protect the confidentiality of the client* | **breach, break** *He breached confidentiality by releasing information on weapons tests.*
• CONFIDENTIALITY + NOUN **agreement**

confine verb

• ADV. **entirely, exclusively, solely, strictly, totally** | **increasingly** | **largely, mainly, principally** *The discussion will be confined largely to general principles.* | **generally, normally** | **effectively** | **by no means, not necessarily** *Poverty and deprivation are by no means confined to the north of the country.*
• PREP. **to** *Let's confine our attention to the problem of illegal drugs.*

confinement noun

• ADJ. **close** *The animals are kept in close confinement.* | **solitary**
• VERB + CONFINEMENT **be held in, be kept in** | **be placed in, be put in**
• PREP. **in ~** *He spent eleven years in solitary confinement.* | **~ to** *their confinement to army barracks*

confines noun

• ADJ. **close, cramped, limited, narrow, strict** *issues that go beyond the limited confines of the book* ◊ *within the strict confines of the law* | **immediate** | **comfortable, comfy, safe**
• VERB + CONFINES **leave** *It took him some effort to leave the comfy confines of his armchair.*
• PREP. **beyond/outside the ~ of** *She wanted to experience things outside the close confines of family life.* **in/within the ~ of** *He spent three years within the narrow confines of the prison.*

confirm verb

• ADV. **merely, only, simply** *This latest tragedy merely confirms my view that the law must be tightened.* | **officially** *The plans were officially confirmed yesterday.*
• VERB + CONFIRM **be able/unable to, can/could** | **appear to, seem to, tend to** *These new symptoms tend to confirm my original diagnosis.*

confirmation noun

• ADJ. **further** | **independent** | **direct** | **final** | **official, written**
• VERB + CONFIRMATION **ask for** | **need, require** | **seek** *The police are seeking independent confirmation of certain details of the story.* | **await, wait for** | **get, have, obtain, receive** | **give sb, provide (sb with)**
• CONFIRMATION + VERB **come** *Written confirmation came three days later.*
• PREP. **in ~** *She nodded in confirmation.*
• PHRASES **confirmation in writing** *We need confirmation in writing before we can send your order out.*

conflict noun

1 fight/argument
• ADJ. **big, great, major** | **bitter, serious, violent** | **growing, increasing** | **constant, continued, continuing, unresolved** *He is in constant conflict with the authorities.* | **open, overt** | **global, internal, regional** | **armed, military** | **civil, class, cultural, ethnic, family, industrial, political, social, religious**
• VERB + CONFLICT **bring sb/sth into, cause, come**

into, **create, lead to, provoke** *His work brought him into conflict with more conventional scientists.* ◊ *The decision led to a bitter conflict between the management and unions.* | **avert, avoid, prevent** *They hid their feelings to avoid conflict.* | **handle** | **end, resolve, settle, solve** *The United Nations are hoping to resolve the conflict quickly.*
• CONFLICT + VERB **arise (from sth), occur** *The conflict arose from different ambitions within the team.*
• PREP. **during/in a/the ~** *Thousands have been arrested in violent ethnic conflicts in the region.* **in ~** *They found themselves in conflict over the future of the firm.* **in ~ with** *in conflict with management* | **~ about/over** *a conflict over ownership of the land* **~ between** *conflicts between different ethnic groups* **~ with** *to end the conflict with France* **~ within** *serious conflicts within the ruling party*
• PHRASES **an area/a source of conflict, in direct conflict with sb**

2 difference between ideas/wishes, etc.
• ADJ. **fundamental, serious, sharp** | **direct** | **inherent** *the inherent conflict between the demands of farmers and wishes of environmentalists* | **inner** | **ideological**
• CONFLICT + NOUN **situation** | **management, resolution** *the key to successful conflict management*
• PREP. **in ~ with** *in direct conflict with his wishes* | **~ between** *the conflict between science and religion* **~ of** *a serious conflict of opinion*
• PHRASES **a conflict of interests/loyalties**

conflict verb

• ADV. **apparently** *how to reconcile apparently conflicting goals* | **potentially** *potentially conflicting values*
• PREP. **with** *His opinions conflicted with mine.*

conform verb

• ADV. **fully**
• VERB + CONFORM **be required to, must, should** | **fail to** *The toys fail to conform to current safety standards.*
• PREP. **to** *All companies are required to conform to these rules.* **with** *This equipment conforms fully with the latest safety regulations.*

conformity noun

• ADJ. **complete** | **strict** | **outward** *a society of outward religious conformity* | **political, religious, sexual, social**
• QUANT. **degree**
• VERB + CONFORMITY **achieve, bring sth into, ensure** *to bring national laws into conformity with European laws*
• PREP. **in ~ with** *The procedure is in strict conformity with standard international practices.* | **~ between** *to achieve conformity between all the schemes* **~ to** *conformity to the accepted standards* **~ with** *We work to ensure conformity with the customer's wishes.*

confront verb

• ADV. **directly** *He is willing to confront problems directly.* | **immediately, suddenly**
• PHRASES **be confronted with sth** *I was suddenly confronted by the task of rewriting the entire book.* **find yourself confronted by sth** *The demonstrators found themselves confronted by a line of police, blocking the road.*

confrontation noun

• ADJ. **full-scale, major, serious** *Their demands could lead to a serious confrontation with management.* | **direct, eyeball-to-eyeball, face-to-face, head-on, outright** | **open** | **bitter, bloody, heated, ugly, violent** | **armed, military** | **political**
• QUANT. **series**
• VERB + CONFRONTATION **have** | **cause, end in, lead**

to, provoke | bring sb into *His actions brought him into direct confrontation with the authorities.* | avoid
• CONFRONTATION + VERB arise, take place
• PREP. ~ between *a head-on confrontation between the two governments* ~ over *She had a series of heated confrontations with her parents over homework.* ~ with *a confrontation with the police*

confuse *verb*

1 make sb unable to think clearly; make sth unclear
• ADV. completely, totally *Seeing the two of them together totally confused me.* | slightly, somewhat | further *I will try to be brief and avoid further confusing the issue.*
2 mistake sb/sth for another person/thing
• ADV. easily *You can easily confuse the two paintings.*
• PREP. with *I sometimes confuse Jane with her sister.*

confused *adj.*

• VERBS appear, be, feel, look, seem, sound | become, get *He was beginning to get rather confused.* | remain | leave sb *He left his audience thoroughly confused.*
• ADV. extremely, highly, hopelessly, very *a highly confused picture of a complex situation* | completely, thoroughly, totally, utterly | increasingly | a bit, a little, rather, slightly, somewhat | momentarily *George paused, momentarily confused.*
• PREP. about *He was very confused about his feelings.* by *I'm confused by the whole thing.*

confusing *adj.*

• VERBS appear, be, look, seem, sound | become, get | make sth *Both teams were wearing the same colours, which made things confusing.* | find sth *I find the government policy extremely confusing.*
• ADV. extremely, highly, hopelessly, very | a bit, a little, pretty, rather, slightly, somewhat | potentially
• PREP. for *The new signs will be very confusing for tourists.* to *All this information can be confusing to the user.*

confusion *noun*

• ADJ. complete, total, utter | considerable, great | slight | general, widespread | administrative | mental
• VERB + CONFUSION cause, create, lead to, result in | add to *This latest decision has only added to the general confusion.* | clear up | plunge sb/sth into, throw sb/sth into *The local council has been thrown into total confusion by her resignation.*
• CONFUSION + VERB arise, reign *Confusion reigned when the two managers gave conflicting instructions.* | surround sth *The government needs to clear up the confusion surrounding its policy on water.*
• PREP. in (the)~ *She stared at them both in utter confusion.* ◊ *In the confusion that followed, she managed to slip away unnoticed.* | ~ about/over *There is widespread confusion about the government's transport policy.* ~ among *The announcement caused a lot of confusion among the students.* ~ as to *confusion as to the whereabouts of the man* ~ between *confusion between letters of the alphabet* ~with *the confusion of this book with her last one*
• PHRASES a scene/state of confusion, to avoid confusion *To avoid confusion, label each box clearly.*

congested *adj.*

• VERBS be | become, get
• ADV. heavily, highly, severely, very *The roads to Bordeaux were heavily congested.*
• PREP. with *The city streets were congested with vehicles.*

congestion *noun*

• ADJ. serious, severe | increased, increasing | road, traffic *Parking near the school causes severe traffic congestion.* | nasal
• VERB + CONGESTION cause, lead to | avoid, ease, reduce, relieve *measures to ease the increasing congestion in the centre of London* | increase

conglomerate *noun*

• ADJ. big, huge, large, vast | international, multinational | business, financial, industrial | food, media, mining, publishing, etc.

congratulate *verb*

• ADV. warmly
• VERB + CONGRATULATE must, wish to, would like to *I must congratulate you on your excellent exam results.*
• PREP. for *The employees should be congratulated for the part they have played in the success.* on *She congratulated me warmly on my performance.*
• PHRASES sb is to be congratulated *The company is to be congratulated on its success.*

congratulations *noun*

• ADJ. deepest | heartfelt, hearty, sincere, warm *May I offer my heartiest congratulations on your promotion?*
• VERB + CONGRATULATIONS express, extend, give (sb), offer (sb), send (sb) *Please give your parents my congratulations.* | accept
• PREP. ~ on/upon *Please accept my warmest congratulations on your engagement.* ~to *Congratulations to Tony on his new job!*

congregation *noun*

• ADJ. full | large | small
• VERB + CONGREGATION address *The vicar stood up to address the congregation.*
• PREP. in a/the~
• PHRASES a member of a congregation

congress *noun*

1 large formal meeting/series of meetings
• ADJ. international, national, world | annual | party | all-party | founding, inaugural | emergency | extraordinary | full
• VERB + CONGRESS attend, go to *Three hundred delegates attended the Liberal party congress.* | address | convene, hold | organize, schedule | open *The general secretary opened the congress on global warming.* | close
• CONGRESS + VERB take place | agree to sth, approve sth, adopt sth *The congress agreed to the tax-cutting package.* | call for sth | elect sb | vote
• CONGRESS + NOUN delegate, leader | debate
• PREP. at a/the ~ *We met again at the annual congress.* in ~ *It was a year before the association met again in congress.* | ~on *a congress on language in education*
2 Congress group of people elected to make laws
• CONGRESS + VERB approve sth *Congress approved most of the new powers.* | pass sth *Congress passed a series of important measures.* | vote *Congress voted to delay a decision.*
• PREP. in ~ *The Liberals in Congress felt the reforms did not go far enough.*
• PHRASES a member of Congress, a session of Congress *legislation for the next session of Congress*

conjecture *noun*

• ADJ. pure *Whether the business will survive another ten years is pure conjecture.*

● PREP. **~about/as to** *There was a lot of conjecture as to the extent of her wealth.*
● PHRASES **a matter for conjecture, open to conjecture** *Whether she will run for a second term in office is open to conjecture.*

conjunctivitis noun

⇨ Special page at ILLNESS

connect verb

1 join
● ADV. **directly** *Downstairs toilets were connected directly to the drains.* | **up** *We need to connect all the pipes up to the water tank.*
● PREP. **to** *Connect the machine to the power supply.* **with** *A corridor connects his office with the main building.*

2 link
● ADV. **closely, intimately** *Bad diet is closely connected with many common illnesses.* | **directly**
● PREP. **with** *The police were looking for evidence to connect him with the crime.*

connection noun

1 relationship between two things
● ADJ. **clear, close, direct, intimate, strong** *There is a close connection between family background and academic achievement.* | **tenuous** | **obvious** | **causal**
● VERB + CONNECTION **have** *His death had no connection with drugs.* | **discover, establish, find, make, see** *Researchers have now established a connection between air pollution and asthma.* ◇ *She did not make the connection between her diet and her poor health.* | **break, sever** *She wanted to sever all her connections with the firm.*
● PREP. **in ~ with** *I am writing in connection with your recent job application.* | **~ between** *the connection between crime and alcohol* **~ to/with** *What is your connection with the school?*
● PHRASES **in that/this connection** (= for reasons connected with sth recently mentioned)

2 place where wires/pipes join together
● ADJ. **loose** | **electrical, pipe**
● VERB + CONNECTION **break** *If you break the connection, the light won't come on.*
● CONNECTION + NOUN **charge**
● PREP. **~ to** *waiting for connection to the water mains*

3 bus/train/plane
● ADJ. **good** | **bus, rail/railway, train**
● VERB + CONNECTION **make** | **miss**
● PREP. **~ between** *There are good connections between the resort and major cities.* **~ to** *We'll be lucky if we make our connection to Paris.* **~ with** *good connections with New York*

4 person you know
● ADJ. **good** | **aristocratic** | **business, family, personal, political, professional, social**
● VERB + CONNECTION **have** *I have some good business connections in New York.* ◇ *He has connections* (= he knows important people who would be able to help him). | **use** *She used her connections to get the job.*

connoisseur noun

● ADJ. **great, real** *Only the real connoisseur could tell the difference between these two wines.* | **art, music, wine**
● PREP. **~ of** *a great connoisseur of Japanese art*

connotation noun

● ADJ. **strong** | **wider** *The notion of abuse has wider connotations than the physical.* | **negative, pejorative** | **positive** | **humorous** | **moral, racial, sexual**
● VERB + CONNOTATION **carry, have** *That word has* strong sexual connotations. | **attach, give sth** *the negative connotations attached to the word 'academic'*
● PREP. **~ of** *The word carries connotations of romance.*

conquest noun

● ADJ. **rapid** *the rapid conquest of Madrid* | **military** | **Norman, Roman, Spanish, etc.** *the Roman conquest of Britain* | **sexual**
● VERB + CONQUEST **make** *The army made many conquests in the east.* | **complete**
● PREP. **by/through ~** *He continued to expand his kingdom by conquest.*

conscience noun

● ADJ. **clear, easy, good** *I have a clear conscience.* | **bad, guilty, terrible, troubled, uneasy** | **civic, moral, political, social** *a government with no social conscience*
● VERB + CONSCIENCE **have** *He had no conscience about taking his brother's money.* | **appease, ease, salve, soothe** *After the feast she spent a week dieting to salve her conscience.* | **prick, trouble** | **appeal to, arouse, rouse, stir** | **wrestle with** *He wrestled with his conscience all night long.*
● CONSCIENCE + VERB **trouble sb** *Her conscience was troubling her a little.* | **dictate sth** *My conscience dictates that I resign.*
● PREP. **on your ~** *I'm sure she has something on her conscience.* ◇ *It was on his conscience that he hadn't called her.*
● PHRASES **a crisis of conscience, freedom of conscience, in (all/good) conscience** (= honestly) *We cannot in all conscience refuse to help.* **a matter of conscience** *This question is a matter of individual conscience.* **a pang/prick/twinge of conscience** *I had a sudden pang of conscience that I really ought to tell the truth.* **the voice of conscience** *She refused to listen to the voice of conscience.*

conscious adj.

1 aware of sth
● VERBS **be, seem** | **become** | **remain**
● ADV. **acutely, deeply** (*formal*), **extremely, highly, intensely, terribly, very** *She became acutely conscious that someone was watching her.* ◇ *We are now deeply conscious of these issues.* | **fully, perfectly** | **increasingly** | **hardly** *I was hardly conscious of my surroundings.* | **clearly** | **dimly, vaguely** *He fell, and was dimly conscious of Tara standing over him.* | **painfully** *All the time he was painfully conscious of how hard it was going to be to explain.* | **environmentally, politically, socially** *The company is extremely environmentally conscious* (= aware of environmental problems and how to deal with them).
● PREP. **of** *I am very conscious of the need for secrecy.*
● PHRASES **fashion/health/safety/security conscious** *fashion conscious teenagers*

2 able to see/hear/feel
● VERBS **be** | **become** | **remain** *She remained conscious throughout the operation.*
● ADV. **fully** *The patient is not yet fully conscious.* | **barely, hardly** *One man was so drunk as to be barely conscious.* | **half** *I was only half conscious.*

consciousness noun

1 being able to see/hear/feel things
● ADJ. **full** | **higher** *to aspire to a higher consciousness* | **individual** | **human**
● VERB + CONSCIOUSNESS **lose** *She hit her head on a rock and lost consciousness.* | **recover, regain** | **bring sb back to** *The cold water brought me back to full consciousness.* | **enter** *The words slowly entered her consciousness.*
● PHRASES **a level/state of consciousness** *an altered state of consciousness*

2 being aware of sth

• ADJ. **full** *I left the room with full consciousness of the impression I would make.* | **growing** | **altered** | **collective**, **public** | **national** | **modern** | **black** | **working-class** | **class**, **environmental**, **feminist**, **green**, **political**, **religious**, **social** *a new political consciousness among young people* | **false** *(technical) She sees racism as a form of false consciousness, where a society collectively believes untrue things about other races.*

• VERB + CONSCIOUSNESS **develop**, **raise** *They have succeeded in raising consciousness on many issues.* | **enter** *imagery that has entered the national consciousness through the media* | **be lodged in**, **lodge itself in** *The idea firmly lodged itself in the public consciousness.*

• PREP. **in (the)~** *a key position in feminist consciousness* | **~among**, **~of** *a growing consciousness of environmental issues among children*

conscription *noun*

• ADJ. **universal** | **military**
• VERB + CONSCRIPTION **introduce** | **abolish**, **end** | **avoid** *He injured himself to avoid conscription.*

consensus *noun*

• ADJ. **broad**, **clear**, **common**, **general**, **overwhelming**, **strong** | **emerging**, **growing** | **tacit**, **unspoken** | **international**, **national** | **political**, **social**
• QUANT. **degree**, **level**
• VERB + CONSENSUS **achieve**, **arrive at**, **reach** | **break** *He was the first to break the consensus and criticize the proposal.*
• CONSENSUS + VERB **exist** *No clear consensus exists over the next stage of the scheme.* | **emerge** *A general consensus on the problem is beginning to emerge.*
• CONSENSUS + NOUN **view**
• PREP. **by~** *They have always governed by consensus.* | **~about/on/over** *It is difficult to reach a consensus about electoral reform.* **~among/between** *no consensus among the members*
• PHRASES **a consensus of opinion** *The general consensus of opinion is that a high-fat diet is bad for you.* **a lack of consensus**

consent *noun*

• ADJ. **full** | **common**, **general**, **mutual** | **express** | **tacit** *Your silence implies tacit consent to these proposals.* | **informed** *Doctors must obtain the informed consent of all patients before giving any treatment.* | **prior** *No action can be taken without the prior consent of the owner.* | **formal**, **written** | **parental**
• VERB + CONSENT **give (sb)**, **grant (sb)** *You must give written consent before the documents can be released.* | **refuse (sb)**, **withhold** | **gain**, **get**, **have**, **obtain** *Do you have the consent of your employer?* | **require**, **seek**
• PREP. **by (common/general/mutual) ~** *The contract can only be broken by mutual consent.* **with/without sb's~** *Your property cannot be sold without your consent.* | **~for** *He gave his consent for treatment.* **~from** *consent from the parents* **~to** *He withheld his consent to the marriage.*
• PHRASES **the age of consent** (= the age at which sb is legally old enough to agree to have a sexual relationship)

consent *verb*

• ADV. **freely** | **kindly** *He has kindly consented to give us some of his valuable time.*
• PREP. **to** *Her father would not consent to the marriage.*

consequence *noun*

• ADJ. **full** | **far-reaching**, **important**, **profound** | **adverse**, **bad**, **catastrophic**, **damaging**, **dangerous**, **devastating**, **dire**, **disastrous**, **fatal**, **harmful**, **negative**, **serious**, **severe**, **terrible**, **tragic**, **unfortunate**, **unpleasant** |

beneficial, **good**, **positive** | **major**, **main** | **direct**, **immediate** | **indirect** | **inevitable**, **necessary** | **likely**, **possible**, **potential** | **logical**, **natural** | **long-term**, **short-term** | **unintended** | **ecological**, **economic**, **electoral**, **environmental**, **financial**, **legal**, **physical**, **political**, **social** *to face up to the physical consequences of ageing*

• VERB + CONSEQUENCE **have**, **lead to** *The practice had far-reaching environmental consequences.* | **accept**, **bear**, **face (up to)**, **suffer**, **take** *You must accept the full consequences of your behaviour.*
• CONSEQUENCE + VERB **arise**, **ensue**, **follow** *the important electoral consequences that will follow from this decision*
• PREP. **as a~** *Hundreds of people lost their jobs as a direct consequence of the merger.* **in ~ (of)** *(formal) The child was born deformed in consequence of an injury to its mother.* | **~ for** *This could have serious consequences for the economy.*

conservation *noun*

• ADJ. **energy**, **environmental**, **forest**, **nature**, **soil**, **water**, **wildlife** | **bird**, **elephant**, **etc.** | **architectural**, **building** | **art**, **painting/paintings**
• CONSERVATION + NOUN **body**, **group**, **organization** | **efforts**, **measure**, **policy**, **programme**, **project**, **scheme**, **work** | **area** *No new building is permitted in conservation areas.*

conservatism *noun*

• ADJ. **diehard**, **entrenched** | **moderate**, **relative** | **inherent**, **innate**, **natural** *the innate conservatism of British businessmen* | **economic**, **fiscal**, **ideological**, **political**, **religious**, **social**
• PREP. **~in** *people's conservatism in musical taste*

conservative *noun*

• ADJ. **diehard**, **dyed-in-the-wool**, **hardline**, **staunch** | **right-wing** | **back-bench** *disagreement among back-bench Conservatives* | **senior** *Senior Conservatives are opposed to the change.* | **political**

conservative *adj.*

• VERBS **be** | **become** | **remain**
• ADV. **deeply**, **extremely**, **highly**, **profoundly**, **very** | **increasingly** | **largely**, **predominantly** | **fairly**, **rather**, **relatively** | **basically**, **essentially** *She takes a basically conservative view of society.* | **generally** | **innately**, **instinctively**, **naturally** *the army's innately conservative values* | **notoriously** *Banks are notoriously conservative about their dealings with clients.* | **traditionally** *a traditionally conservative profession* | **culturally**, **morally**, **politically**, **socially** *the culturally conservative world of commerce and industry*

consider *verb*

• ADV. **carefully**, **seriously** *I'm seriously considering the possibility of emigrating.* | **briefly** *I did briefly consider going on my own.*
• PREP. **for** *We are considering her for the job of designer.*

consideration *noun*

1 careful thought about sth
• ADJ. **careful**, **detailed**, **full**, **serious** | **adequate**, **due**, **proper**, **sufficient** | **special**, **urgent** | **active**
• VERB + CONSIDERATION **give sth**, **take sth into** *We will give your proposals serious consideration.* ◇ *You must take the size of the room into consideration.* | **deserve**, **need**, **require** | **receive**
• PREP. **after~** *After due consideration, it was decided not to offer her the job.* **for sb's ~** *I enclose the report for your consideration.* **in ~ of** *(formal)* (= as payment for sth), **on ~**

On consideration, we have decided not to come. **under ~** *proposals under active consideration*

2 thinking about other people's wishes and feelings
● VERB + CONSIDERATION **have** *Have some consideration for those without a job.* | **show sb, treat sb with** *She showed little consideration for the beginners.*
● PREP. **out of ~** *He did it out of consideration for his daughter.* **~ for**

3 sth you think about when deciding sth
● ADJ. **main, major, important, prime | overriding, paramount | minor | aesthetic, commercial, economic, environmental, ethical, financial, health, legal, moral, personal, political, practical, safety, security**
● VERB + CONSIDERATION **take account of, take into account** *There are several important safety considerations that must be taken into account.*

consist *verb*

PHRASAL VERB
consist of sth
● ADV. **entirely, exclusively, merely, only, simply, solely** *Their conversation consisted almost entirely of gossip.* | **chiefly, essentially, largely, mainly, mostly, predominantly, primarily, principally**

consistency *noun*

1 always having the same standard/opinions, etc.
● ADJ. **absolute, complete, total | great, remarkable | internal**
● QUANT. **degree, level**
● VERB + CONSISTENCY **show** *He has shown remarkable consistency in his exam results.* | **achieve, ensure, maintain | lack**
● PREP. **~ in/of** *a consistency in/of approach* **~ with** *to maintain consistency with past practice*

2 thickness/firmness of a liquid substance
● ADJ. **thick, thin | soft, stiff | creamy, smooth | sticky | dropping** *Add milk to produce a soft dropping consistency.* | **correct, right** *Knead the dough to the right consistency.*
● VERB + CONSISTENCY **have** *The mixture should have the consistency of thick cream.* | **give, produce**

consistent *adj.*

1 always behaving in the same way
● VERBS **be | remain**
● ADV. **highly, remarkably, very | absolutely, completely, entirely, quite, wholly** *His attitude isn't absolutely consistent.* | **largely | fairly, reasonably**

2 in agreement with sth
● VERBS **be, seem | remain**
● ADV. **completely, entirely, fully, perfectly | broadly, largely | fairly, quite, reasonably | internally** *His argument is not even internally consistent* (= different parts of the argument contradict each other). | **mutually** *It is desirable that domestic and EU law should be mutually consistent.* | **logically**
● PREP. **across** *These findings are consistent across all the studies.* **with** *The figures are fully consistent with last year's results.*

consolation *noun*

● ADJ. **great | small**
● VERB + CONSOLATION **have** *She had the consolation of coming second in her last race of the day.* | **seek** *He went to seek consolation in the local pub.* | **draw, find, gain, take** *He drew little consolation from this fact.* ◇ *When her mother died, she found consolation in her religious beliefs.* ◇ *Although we lost the game, we took some consolation from the fact that we played well.* | **afford (sb), bring (sb),**

offer (sb), provide (sb with) *The next match will probably offer them the consolation of winning.*
● PREP. **~ for** *providing consolation for her loss* ◇ *There is some consolation for fans because the team still stands a chance of winning the local championship.* **~ to** *The children were a great consolation to me at that time.*
● PHRASES **be (of) little/small/some consolation to sb** *This news was of little consolation to us.* **if it is any consolation (to sb)** *If it's any consolation to you, the weather here is also awful.* **sb's one/only consolation** *When she lost her job, her only consolation was that she had some savings in the bank.*

conspicuous *adj.*

● VERBS **be, feel, seem | become | make sb** *Its colouring makes it highly conspicuous.*
● ADV. **highly, very | rather, somewhat** *The new building was rather conspicuous.* | **horribly, uncomfortably** *The stain on her dress was horribly conspicuous.*

conspiracy *noun*

● ADJ. **criminal, political** *charges of criminal conspiracy and corruption* | **alleged | international, worldwide**
● VERB + CONSPIRACY **be involved in, be part of** *I suspected that he was involved in the conspiracy.* ◇ *This action was part of a conspiracy to deceive the public.* | **organize** *Who organized the conspiracy against the president?* | **uncover** *Party officials have uncovered a conspiracy to discredit the prime minister.*
● PREP. **~ against** *a conspiracy against the king* **~ between** *a conspiracy between the police and the right-wing parties*
● PHRASES **a conspiracy of silence** *There is a conspiracy of silence about the killer* (= nobody will say what they know).
⇨ Note at CRIME (for more verbs)

constable *noun*

● ADJ. **police | Chief, Detective | beat, special, uniformed** *The force hopes to increase the number of its beat constables.* ◇ *Special constables provide part-time assistance for the regular police force.*
● PHRASES **the rank of constable**

constant *adj.*

● VERBS **be | remain, stay** *The level of unemployment remains fairly constant at around 10%.* | **hold sth** (technical), **keep sth** *All variables except one must be held constant.* ◇ *The temperature must be kept constant.*
● ADV. **remarkably | absolutely | almost, nearly, virtually | fairly, reasonably, relatively | more or less, roughly**
● PREP. **across** *These figures were virtually constant across the 1991 and 2001 censuses.*

consternation *noun*

● ADJ. **considerable, great | widespread**
● VERB + CONSTERNATION **cause, create, fill sb with** *The announcement created surprise and consternation.* ◇ *The thought of meeting him filled me with consternation.* | **express, feel, greet sth with** *Many greeted his resignation with consternation.*
● PREP. **in ~** *She stared at me in consternation.* | **~ among** *There is some consternation among business leaders.*

constipated *adj.*

● VERBS **be | become, get | make sb**
● ADV. **severely, very | a bit, slightly**

constipation noun

- ADJ. **severe | acute, chronic**
- QUANT. **bout**
- VERB + CONSTIPATION **have, suffer from | cause | prevent**
⇨ Special page at ILLNESS

constituency noun

1 district that elects an MP
- ADJ. **important, key | local | marginal** (= won or lost by only a small number of votes) *The Tories are concentrating their campaign in the key marginal constituencies.* | **target | electoral, parliamentary | inner-city, urban | suburban | county, rural | multi-member, single-member** *Japan's electoral system of multi-member constituencies*
- VERB + CONSTITUENCY **be elected for/to, represent** *She was elected to a rural constituency.* ◇ *He represents a constituency in the north of England.*
- CONSTITUENCY + NOUN **boundaries | MP**
- PREP. **in a/the ~** *the people in this constituency*

2 group in society likely to support a particular party
- ADJ. **broad, wider | natural, traditional** *These people are Labour's natural constituency.* | **political, social**
- VERB + CONSTITUENCY **appeal to** *The party needs to appeal to a broader constituency.*
- PREP. **in a/the ~**

constitution noun

1 laws/rules of a country
- ADJ. **federal, state | codified, written** *Britain does not have a written constitution.* | **unwritten | draft, proposed | interim**
- VERB + CONSTITUTION **draft, draw up, prepare** *plans to draft a new constitution* | **have | adopt, approve, enact, promulgate, ratify** *The new constitution will be adopted next year.* | **amend** *Parliament will vote to amend the constitution.* | **contravene, violate** *The president's actions violate the constitution.* | **suspend** *The constitution was suspended and the army was placed in full control.* | **be enshrined in** *These principles are enshrined in the country's constitution.*
- CONSTITUTION + VERB **forbid sth, guarantee sth, stipulate sth** *The constitution stipulated that a general election must be held within 120 days.*
- PREP. **according to/under a/the ~** *Under the constitution, an election must be called every five years.* **in a/the ~** *These rights are established in the federal constitution.*
- PHRASES **an amendment to a constitution, a clause in a constitution, the principles of a constitution, the provisions/terms of a constitution**

2 ability of the body to stay healthy
- ADJ. **good, strong | weak**
- VERB + CONSTITUTION **have** *The child had a weak constitution and was always ill.*

constrained adj.

- VERBS **be, feel**
- ADV. **severely, tightly** *She felt tightly constrained by her family commitments.*

constraint noun

- ADJ. **important, major | severe, tight** *The government has placed tight constraints on spending this year.* | **budget, financial**
- VERB + CONSTRAINT **impose, place, put | remove**
- PREP. **within a/the ~** *We have to work within severe constraints.* **without ~** *I felt free to speak to her without constraint.* | **~ on/upon** *There are major financial constraints on all schools.*

construction noun

1 roads/buildings
- ADJ. **gigantic, huge, large, massive** *massive constructions of bamboo and paper* | **basic, simple** *It has a basic construction of brick under a tiled roof.* | **complex | heavy** *the heavy construction industry* | **solid** *walls of solid construction* | **careful** *The drainage system needs careful construction.* | **brick, fibreglass, steel, timber, timber-frame, wooden** *a two-storey brick construction* ◇ *a schoolhouse of brick construction* | **bridge, building, canal, house/housing, railway, road** *Road and bridge construction is underway.*
- VERB + CONSTRUCTION **begin, start | complete** *Construction of the new road has now been completed.*
- CONSTRUCTION + VERB **be underway**
- CONSTRUCTION + NOUN **industry, sector | company, firm, group | project, programme | contract | job | work | worker | site, yard | costs | materials | method, process, technique**
- PREP. **during (the)~** *Major engineering challenges will be faced during construction.* **under ~** *A new factory is under construction.*

2 grammar
- ADJ. **grammatical, linguistic, sentence, syntactic | active, passive | adjectival, infinitive, predicative**

3 interpretation
- ADJ. **literal | logical, sensible | proper, true** *ruling on the proper construction to be given to section 78 of the Act* | **strict** *a strict construction of the clause* | **ideological, social, theoretical** *changes in the social construction of marriage* (= the meaning of marriage in society)
- VERB + CONSTRUCTION **give sth, put on sth** *What construction do you put on this letter* (= what do you think it means)?

consult verb

- ADV. **widely** *We consulted quite widely before deciding what to do.* | **closely | adequately, properly** *They felt they had not been properly consulted.*
- VERB + CONSULT **need to, should** *If the pain persists you should consult your doctor.*
- PREP. **about** *I need to consult my teacher about changing my course.* **with** *We are consulting closely with our partners and allies.*

consultant noun

1 sb who gives advice
- ADJ. **business, design, financial, management, public relations | independent, outside**
- VERB + CONSULTANT **act as** *He was happy to act as a consultant to the company.* | **bring in, employ (sb as), engage (sb as), hire (sb as), use** *We brought in a management consultant to sort out the mess.*
- PREP. **~in** *a consultant in design, printing and advertising* **~ on** *a consultant on business ethics* **~ to/with** *They work as consultants to a software company.*
⇨ Note at JOB

2 hospital doctor of high rank
- ADJ. **hospital, NHS** *She is now a hospital consultant.*
- CONSULTANT + NOUN **cardiologist, gynaecologist, obstetrician, paediatrician, pathologist, physician, psychiatrist, etc.**
- PREP. **~in** *a consultant in psychiatry*
⇨ Note at DOCTOR

consultation noun

- ADJ. **close | extensive, full, wide | proper | joint** *a joint consultation with doctors and patients* | **public** *There will be a period of public consultation before a decision is reached.*

● VERB + CONSULTATION **have, hold** *The prime minister will hold a consultation with all the relevant groups.*
● CONSULTATION + NOUN **document, paper | period**
● PREP. **in ~ with** *The scheme was developed in close consultation with the local community.* **without ~** *They have taken this decision without any consultation.* **~ about/on** *The company has promised wide consultation on its expansion plans.* **~ between** *a consultation between teachers and parents* **~ with** *We need more consultation with trade unions.*

consumer *noun*

● ADJ. **big, great, large** *The UK is the biggest consumer of tropical hardwoods after Japan.* **| average, ordinary | potential | passive** *Mass culture turns audiences into passive consumers, their participation limited to the choice between buying and not buying.* **| sophisticated | domestic, foreign | commercial, industrial | green** *Green consumers should be wary of manufacturers' claims that their products are environmentally friendly.* **| electricity, energy**
● VERB + CONSUMER **supply** *supplying domestic consumers* **| persuade | exploit** *to exploit consumers by charging a high price* **| protect** *What can be done to protect the ordinary consumer from unscrupulous service operators?* **| satisfy**
● CONSUMER + VERB **buy sth, spend sth**
● CONSUMER + NOUN **durables, electronics, goods, products, services** *the market for consumer durables* **| attitudes, awareness, behaviour, choice, confidence, demand, expenditure, needs, preferences, spending, tastes | protection, rights | group, organization, watchdog** *Consumer watchdogs have accused banks of 'appalling arrogance' in the way they treat customers.* **| society** *We are living in a consumer society.* **| market | prices | boom** *Government policy encouraged a consumer boom followed by a deep recession.* **| boycott** *The country could face a consumer boycott of its beef exports.*
● PREP. **among ~** *two years of research among consumers*

consumption *noun*

● ADJ. **heavy, high** *the country with the highest fuel consumption in the world* **| low | average | overall, total | excessive | conspicuous** (= buying expensive goods in order to impress people and show how rich you are) **| annual, daily** *Annual consumption of wine has risen from five to eleven litres per head.* **| per capita | domestic, local, home** *It is important that the recovery be export-led rather than led by domestic consumption.* ◇ *Half the small crop was kept for home consumption.* **| foreign, world | household | individual, personal | mass | public | private | future** *households that save for future consumption* **| alcohol, beer, cigarette, food, meat, tobacco, water | electricity, energy, fuel, gas, oil, petrol, power**
● QUANT. **level**
● VERB + CONSUMPTION **boost, encourage, increase, stimulate** *Doctors say that children need to increase their consumption of fruit and vegetables.* ◇ *The industry faced a serious challenge in trying to stimulate consumption.* **| cut down, reduce** *You need to reduce your alcohol consumption.*
● CONSUMPTION + VERB **go up, increase, rise | decline, decrease, fall, go down**
● CONSUMPTION + NOUN **expenditure, spending | figures, levels | habits, patterns**
● PREP. **for sb's ~** (= intended to be read or heard by sb) *The documents were for the committee rather than for public consumption.*
● PHRASES **fit/unfit for human consumption** (= safe/not safe to be eaten) *meat that is unfit for human consumption*

contact *noun*

1 meeting/talking/writing to sb
● ADJ. **close** *She is still in close contact with Sarah.* **| regular | direct** *Have you had any direct contact with the director of the company?* **| face-to-face**
● VERB + CONTACT **be in, have | come into, establish, get in, make** *In his job, he comes into contact with many different people.* ◇ *We first established contact with the organization in 1999.* ◇ *When I arrive in New York, I'll get in contact with him.* **| put sb in** *I put my cousin in contact with a friend who works at the company.* **| keep, maintain, stay in** *Maintaining contact after many years can be difficult.* **| break off | lose**
● PREP. **~ between** *There has been no contact between them for several years.* **~ with** *I have very little contact with Simon now.*

2 person you know who can help you
● ADJ. **good, useful, valuable | business, personal**
● VERB + CONTACT **have** *He has a lot of good contacts in the music industry.* **| build up, make** *It takes time to build up contacts.* ◇ *I made a lot of useful business contacts at the conference.*

3 when people/things touch each other
● ADJ. **physical, sexual** *The disease is transmitted through physical contact.*
● VERB + CONTACT **come into** *Do not let the glue come into contact with water.*
● PREP. **in ~** *For a brief moment their lips were in contact.* **on ~** *The light will go out on contact with water.* **| ~ between** *There should be no contact between the separate samples.* **~ with**

contact *verb*

● ADV. **immediately | directly | personally | by email, by phone/telephone** *He can be contacted by phone on the telephone number given below.*
● PHRASES **do not hesitate to contact sb** *Please do not hesitate to contact me if you have any questions.*

contact lens *noun*

● ADJ. **gas-permeable, hard, soft | daily-wear | tinted**
● VERB + CONTACT LENS **have in, wear | put in | remove, take out | clean, disinfect | rinse, soak**

contagious *adj.*

● VERBS **be, prove** *The new disease proved contagious.*
● ADV. **highly, very** *Enthusiasm is highly contagious.*

container *noun*

1 box/bottle/packet, etc.
● ADJ. **shallow | airtight, closed, sealed, watertight | insulated | empty | full | durable** *Store food in durable containers with lids.* **| recyclable, refillable | childproof, child resistant | ideal, suitable, useful** *Tubes are the ideal container for paint as air is excluded.* **| special | storage | aluminium, cardboard, glass, metal, plastic, steel, wooden | food, milk, water**
● VERB + CONTAINER **fill** *Fill the container with water.* **| store sth in**
● CONTAINER + VERB **contain sth, hold sth** *a container holding five litres*
● PREP. **in a/the ~** *Keep the seeds in an airtight container.* **| ~ for** *childproof containers for dangerous substances* **~ of** *a container of milk*

2 large metal box for transporting goods
● ADJ. **empty | full | bulk, cargo**
● CONTAINER + VERB **contain sth, hold sth** *containers holding shipments of bananas*
● CONTAINER + NOUN **lorry, ship, truck | port**

contaminated *adj.*

- VERBS **be | become | remain**
- ADV. **badly, heavily, highly** *A lot of our drinking water is now heavily contaminated.* | **potentially**
- PREP. **with** *The meat was believed to be contaminated with salmonella.*

contamination *noun*

- ADJ. **massive, serious, widespread | cross-** *Chopping boards can be a source of cross-contamination.* | **environmental, food | bacterial, radioactive**
- QUANT. **level** *There is already a high level of environmental contamination.*
- VERB + CONTAMINATION **avoid, prevent | reduce**
- PREP. **~by** *Always keep food covered to prevent contamination by flies.* **~ from** *There is a danger of serious contamination from radioactive waste.* **~ with** *Wash everything thoroughly to avoid contamination with bacteria.*
- PHRASES **a source of contamination**

contemplate *verb*

- ADV. **seriously** *She was seriously contemplating working abroad.*
- VERB + CONTEMPLATE **be prepared to, be willing to** *Are you prepared to contemplate retraining?* | **cannot, could not | refuse to**
- PHRASES **too awful/horrible/horrific to contemplate** *The thought of war was too awful to contemplate.*

contemplation *noun*

- ADJ. **quiet, silent | deep**
- VERB + CONTEMPLATION **be deep in, be lost in** *She was lost in contemplation of the scene in front of her.*
- PREP. **in ~ (of)** *He spent many hours in deep contemplation.* | **~ of** *the contemplation of beauty*

contemporary *adj.*

1 belonging to the same time as sb/sth else
- VERBS **be**
- ADV. **strictly** *She used only strictly contemporary documents to research the book.* | **almost, nearly | broadly, roughly** *a period broadly contemporary with the Shang dynasty*
- PREP. **with** *a composer contemporary with Beethoven*

2 modern
- VERBS **be**
- ADV. **very** *His work is very contemporary.*

contempt *noun*

1 lack of respect
- ADJ. **deep, utter, withering | cold, icy | healthy** *She'd developed what she considered a healthy contempt for authority.* | **barely/thinly disguised**
- VERB + CONTEMPT **feel, have, hold sb/sth in** *He felt nothing but contempt for them.* ◇ *Politicians seem to be generally held in contempt by the police.* | **betray, demonstrate, display, show** *His remarks betray an utter contempt for the truth* (= are completely false). | **develop | regard sb/sth with, treat sb/sth with | deserve** *I shall treat that suggestion with the contempt it deserves.*
- PREP. **~ for** *He has a deep contempt for racists.* | **beneath ~** *His treatment of his children is beneath contempt* (= so bad it is not even worth feeling contempt for). **with ~** *She looked at him with barely disguised contempt.*

2 (*also* **contempt of court**) refusal to obey a court
- ADJ. **civil, criminal**
- VERB + CONTEMPT **be held in** *She was held in contempt for refusing to testify.*
- PREP. **in~**

contemptuous *adj.*

- VERBS **be, feel, sound** *Her voice sounded almost contemptuous.*
- ADV. **savagely | utterly | almost | rather | openly**
- PREP. **of** *He was utterly contemptuous of her efforts.*

contender *noun*

- ADJ. **serious, strong | leading, main, major, number one, obvious, top | genuine, likely, possible**
- PREP. **~for** *a strong contender for the gold medal*

content *noun*

1 contents things inside sth
- VERB + CONTENTS **empty** *She emptied the contents of her bag on the floor*

2 amount of a substance that sth contains
- ADJ. **high** *foods with a high fibre content* | **low | alcohol, calorie, carbon, fat, fibre, moisture, protein, sugar, sulphur, vitamin, etc.**

content *adj.*

- VERBS **appear, be, feel, seem**
- ADV. **perfectly, quite, utterly** *I'm perfectly content just to lie in the sun.* | **fairly, reasonably, relatively | apparently | curiously, strangely** *She felt curiously content.*
- PREP. **with** *She seemed quite content with the idea.*

contented *adj.*

- VERBS **be, feel, look, seem**
- ADV. **deeply, extremely, very** *He gave a deeply contented sigh.* | **perfectly, quite**

contention *noun*

1 opinion that sb expresses
- ADJ. **main** *Her main contention is that staff should get better training.*
- VERB + CONTENTION **support** *There is no evidence to support her contention.* | **reject**

2 disagreement between people
- PREP. **~ between** *There is no contention between the two groups.*
- PHRASES **an area of contention, a bone/point/source of contention** *Where to go on holiday is always a bone of contention in our family.*

contentious *adj.*

- VERBS **be, prove | become | remain**
- ADV. **highly, very** *Abortion is a highly contentious issue.* | **rather, somewhat | politically**

contentment *noun*

- ADJ. **deep, quiet, real, true** *He gazed out to sea, with a feeling of deep contentment.*
- VERB + CONTENTMENT **find** *They finally found contentment in living a simple life.*
- PREP. **with~** *She sighed with contentment.*
- PHRASES **a feeling of contentment**

contest *noun*

- ADJ. **close, closely fought, equal, even | one-sided, unequal** *The contest was too one-sided to be exciting.* | **open** *This contest is wide open: any of half a dozen teams could win it.* | **fair** *The other bidders for the contract complained that it had not been a fair contest.* | **exciting, good, great, thrilling | bitter | head-to-head** *The contestants are eliminated one by one until the last two compete in a head-to-head contest.* | **global, international, local, national, regional | election/electoral, guberna-**

torial, leadership, political, presidential | beauty, song, sporting, talent
● VERB + CONTEST **have, hold, run** *We have three major beauty contests a year.* ◊ *Sporting contests are held in the arena.* | **compete in, enter, take part in** *A third candidate has entered the contest for the Republican nomination.* | **win, lose**
● CONTEST + VERB **take place**
● PREP. **during a/the ~** *During the election contest newspapers are not allowed to publish public opinion polls.* **in a/the ~** *Both sides are predicting victory in this close contest.* **out of a/the ~** *Jackson has injured his knee and is now out of the contest.* | **~against** *They won the doubles contest against the Williams sisters.* **~ between** *the contest between these two great boxers* **~for** *the contest for the leadership of the party* **~over** *In the animal kingdom intruders usually lose contests over territories.* **~ with** *The New Zealanders are looking forward to future contests with South Africa.*
● PHRASES **be no contest** (= used when one side in a contest is much stronger than the other and is sure to win), **the winner of a contest**

contest *verb*

1 in a competition
● ADV. **bitterly, fiercely, hotly, keenly** *The election was bitterly contested.* | **successfully, unsuccessfully**

2 oppose
● ADV. **fiercely, hotly, strongly, vigorously** *His views on evolution are strongly contested by other scientists.* | **successfully, unsuccessfully** *Defence lawyers successfully contested the case.*

context *noun*

● ADJ. **broad, general, larger, overall, wider** *You can't just look at it in terms of the immediate problem. You've got to see it in a wider context.* | **narrow** | **immediate** *A work which transcends its immediate historical context and speaks to later generations.* | **correct, proper, real, right** | **appropriate, realistic, relevant** *to present examples of language in use in an appropriate context* | **certain, given, particular, specific** *These actions only have meaning within certain specific contexts.* | **original** | **changed, changing, different, new, novel** | **meaningful** *Children need meaningful contexts for their work in science.* | **neutral** | **contemporary, modern | everyday, normal | global, international, local, national, regional | human** *It is natural to find conflict in the work environment, in the family, or any other human context.* | **communicative, conversational | experimental, practical, theoretical | classroom, school | business, commercial, cultural, economic, educational, fictional, geographical, historical, legal, literary, political, religious, social | Christian, Islamic, etc. | African, Asian, etc.**
● VERB + CONTEXT **offer (sb), provide (sb with)** *Institutions provide a context in which individuals can take on different roles.* | **place sth in, put sth into, set sth in** *This speech needs to be set in the context of Britain in the 1960s.* | **consider/examine/look at/see/understand/view sth in** *His decision can only be understood in context.* | **quote sth out of, take sth out of** *Her reply was quoted out of context and seemed to mean something quite different from what she had intended.*
● PREP. **in (a/the)~** *Similar problems have arisen in other contexts.* **within a/the~** *You've got to look at these remarks within the context of the recent scandals.* | **~for** *a neutral context for sharing and debating ideas*
● PHRASES **a range/variety of contexts**

continent *noun*

● ADJ. **Antarctic, Australian, African, etc.**

● VERB + CONTINENT **cross** *the first railway to cross the North American continent*
● CONTINENT + VERB **drift** *The evidence that the continents have drifted is overwhelming.*
● PREP. **across a/the ~** *He travelled across continents in his quest for adventure.* **on the ~** *Wolves are still found on the continent of Europe.*

contingent *noun*

● ADJ. **large, strong, substantial | military, naval, police | British, UN, etc.**
● PREP. **~from** *a strong contingent from Camberwell Art School* **~of** *a large contingent of American troops*

continuation *noun*

● ADJ. **direct | natural**
● VERB + CONTINUATION **see** *The years 2000–01 saw the continuation of the university's planned expansion.* | **ensure | be seen as** *His research could be seen as a natural continuation of the work done by Professor Lang.*

continuity *noun*

● ADJ. **greater | remarkable | unbroken** *After twelve or thirteen centuries of unbroken continuity the landscape was being changed out of all recognition.* | **underlying | historical, narrative**
● VERB + CONTINUITY **need | ensure, give sb/sth, maintain, provide (sb/sth with), secure** *More liaison between the old manager and the new one should ensure greater continuity.* | **break** *The author deliberately breaks the narrative continuity in order to confound the reader's expectations.*
● PREP. **~between** *There is often a lack of continuity between one government and the next.* **~in** *historical continuity in the feminist movement*
● PHRASES **a lack of continuity, a need for continuity** *the need for continuity of employment* **a sense of continuity** *giving children a sense of continuity*

contraception *noun*

● ADJ. **effective, safe | artificial | emergency | oral**
● VERB + CONTRACEPTION **practise, use** *A lot of couples now practise contraception.* ◊ *They never used any contraception.*
● PHRASES **the availability of contraception, a form/method of contraception** *a very reliable method of contraception*

contraceptive *noun*

● ADJ. **effective | oral**
● VERB + CONTRACEPTIVE **use**

contract *noun*

1 written agreement
● ADJ. **long-term, permanent | casual, fixed-term, short-term | three-year, two-year, etc. | formal, written | verbal | legal, valid | void** *The contract was declared void.* | **enforceable, unenforceable** (*law*) | **big, important, major | lucrative | business, commercial | employment, maintenance, research, service | catering, construction, haulage | marriage**
● VERB + CONTRACT **have** *Many workers do not have written contracts.* | **bid for, tender for** *Eighteen companies are bidding for the contract.* | **award (sb), give sb | get, win | lose** *The firm lost the contract to a large London company.* | **negotiate** *She managed to negotiate a permanent contract with the firm.* | **draw up, write | conclude, enter into, make, sign** *He entered into a contract with his former employer.* | **carry out, execute** *the firm carrying out the construction contract* | **cancel, end, repudiate** (*law*), **rescind** (*law*), **terminate** *Either party can*

terminate the contract at any time. | **be subject to** *The offer has been accepted, subject to contract* (= the agreement is not legally binding before contracts are signed). | **be in breach of, break, violate** *If you go on strike you will be in breach of contract.* | **enforce** *(law)* | **exchange** *(law) When a house is auctioned the successful bidder must exchange contracts immediately and pay a deposit.*
• CONTRACT + VERB **expire** *The contract expires at the end of next year.* | **be worth sth** *a series of major contracts worth millions of pounds*
• CONTRACT + NOUN **worker** (= one on a fixed-term contract) | **law**
• PREP. **in a/the ~** *They put a clause in the contract stipulating that the work should be finished by next month.* **on a ~** *He's on a three-year fixed-term contract.* **under ~ (to)** *At that stage of her career she was still under contract to one of the big Hollywood studios.* **under a/the ~** *Under her contract of employment, Mrs Lee could not be required to work at a different site.* | **~ between** *the contract between the employer and the employee* **~ for** *They won a contract for the delivery of five fighter planes.* **~ with** *Do you have a contract with your employer?*
• PHRASES **(a) breach of contract** *The company is being sued for breach of contract.* **a contract of employment/sale** *You should make sure that you have a formal contract of employment.* **the terms of a contract** *By using cheaper materials, the company has broken the terms of its contract.* **under the terms of a contract** *Under the terms of the contract the job should have been finished yesterday.*
2 agreement to kill sb
• VERB + CONTRACT **take out** | **have out** *He has a contract out on you.*
• CONTRACT + NOUN **killer, killing**
• PREP. **~ on** *She took out a contract on her ex-husband.*

contractor *noun*
• ADJ. **external, independent, outside, private** | **government** | **approved** *a list of approved contractors* | **building, defence, electrical, engineering, haulage**
• VERB + CONTRACTOR **employ, hire, use** *We'll need to employ a building contractor to do the work.*

contradict *verb*
• ADV. **clearly, completely, directly, flatly** *John's account of the event directly contradicts Stephen's.*
• VERB + CONTRADICT **appear to, seem to**

contradiction *noun*
• ADJ. **complete, direct, flat** | **flagrant, glaring, manifest, obvious** | **basic, fundamental** *There's a basic contradiction in the whole idea of paying for justice.* | **inherent** | **apparent** | **internal**
• PREP. **in ~ to/with** *That's in direct contradiction to what he said yesterday.* | **~ between** *There is an apparent contradiction between the needs of workers and those of employers.* **~ of** *That's a contradiction of what you just said.*
• PHRASES **a contradiction in terms** *The idea is almost a contradiction in terms.*

contradictory *adj.*
• VERBS **appear, be, seem, sound**
• ADV. **completely, directly, totally** *The evidence is completely contradictory.* | **quite, rather, somewhat** | **apparently, seemingly** *two apparently contradictory opinions* | **internally** *The argument is internally contradictory* (= contradicts itself). | **mutually** *The evidence demonstrates how easily people can hold mutually contradictory beliefs.*
• PREP. **to** *He did something contradictory to his orders.*

contrary *adj.*
• VERBS **be, run, seem** *These results run contrary to our expectations.* ◊ *It seems contrary to common sense.*
• ADV. **completely, directly, entirely, quite, totally** *My own experience is completely contrary.* ◊ *The new claim is directly contrary to what was originally stated.* | **clearly**
• PREP. **to** *Contrary to what the public was told, weapons were still being exported.*
• PHRASES **contrary to expectations** *Contrary to expectations, we didn't have any hold-ups on the journey.* **contrary to popular belief** *Contrary to popular belief, the economy is doing well.*

contrast *noun*
• ADJ. **clear, marked, sharp, stark, startling, striking, strong** *There is a stark contrast between the lives of the rich and those of the poor.* | **complete, direct**
• VERB + CONTRAST **make, offer, provide** *The fresh fruit provides a contrast to the rich chocolate pudding.*
• PREP. **by ~** *When you look at their new system, ours seems very old-fashioned by contrast.* **in ~ (to/with)** *The company lost $13 million this year, in contrast with a profit of $15 million last year.* | **~ between, ~ in** *The contrast in appearance between the sisters was striking.* **~ to** *This busy social life was a complete contrast to his old quiet life.*
• PHRASES **stand in ... contrast to sb/sth** *Their attitudes towards love and marriage stand in stark contrast to those of their parents.*

contrast *verb*
1 compare things in order to show differences
• ADV. **favourably, unfavourably** *He contrasted her brashness unfavourably with his mother's gentleness.*
• PREP. **with**
• PHRASES **compare and contrast** *Compare and contrast the two main characters in the play.*
2 be clearly different
• ADV. **markedly, sharply, starkly, strikingly, strongly, vividly** | **nicely** | **oddly** | **favourably, unfavourably** *The open approach contrasts favourably with the exclusivity of some universities.*
• PREP. **with** *This statement contrasts starkly with his previous statements.*

contravene *verb*
• ADV. **blatantly, clearly** *blatantly contravening the rules of civilized warfare*

contravention *noun*
• ADJ. **clear, direct**
• PREP. **in ~ of** *He was in direct contravention of the law.* | **~ of** *This was a clear contravention of the rules.*

contribute *verb*
1 give
• ADV. **enormously, generously, greatly, handsomely, heavily, substantially** *His research has contributed enormously to our understanding of this disease.* ◊ *Many people contributed generously to the appeal.* | **equally** *a situation where husband and wife contribute equally to the family budget* | **fully** | **financially**
• VERB + CONTRIBUTE **be asked to, be encouraged to**
• PREP. **to** *I would like to contribute to the church restoration fund.* **towards** *The company contributed £50 000 towards training costs.*
• PHRASES **have little/a lot/much to contribute (to sth)** *He had very little to contribute to the conversation.*
2 help cause sth
• ADV. **greatly, largely, significantly, substantially** *Parental involvement contributes significantly to children's*

learning. | **effectively** | **further** | **actively, directly** *Unemployment contributes directly to homelessness.* | **indirectly** | **undoubtedly** | **unwittingly**
• PREP. **to** *Several factors might contribute to the development of the disease.*

3 write for a newspaper, etc.
• ADV. **regularly** *a talented photographer who contributed regularly to 'The Face'*
• PREP. **to** *Students are encouraged to contribute articles to the university magazine.*

contribution *noun*

1 sth that helps cause/increase sth
• ADJ. **important, significant** | **big, enormous, great, huge, major, strong, substantial** | **minor, modest, small** | **invaluable, positive, useful, valuable** *We like to think that we are making a positive contribution to society.* | **notable, outstanding**
• VERB + CONTRIBUTION **make** *He made a major contribution to peace in the region.*
• PREP. **~to** *a valuable contribution to science*

2 money given to help pay for sth
• ADJ. **generous, large** | **small** | **voluntary** *We rely entirely on voluntary contributions.*
• VERB + CONTRIBUTION **make, offer, pay**
• PREP. **~to/towards** *I'd like to make a small contribution to the cost of the holiday.*

contributor *noun*

• ADJ. **important, significant** | **big, large** | **main, principal** | **net** *net contributors to the economy* | **regular** *The core of regular contributors is essential to the magazine.*
• PREP. **~to** *Carbon dioxide is the largest contributor to the greenhouse effect.*

contrived *adj.*

• VERBS **be, seem, sound**
• ADV. **highly, very** *highly contrived laboratory conditions* | **a little, rather, somewhat** | **carefully** *the carefully contrived image of party unity* | **cleverly, cunningly** | **artificially, deliberately**

control *noun*

1 power over sb/sth
• ADJ. **absolute, complete, full, total** | **effective, proper** | **close, strict** *Weeds should be kept under strict control.* | **direct** | **government, parental, political, state**
• VERB + CONTROL **have** | **assume, establish, gain, get, take, win** *A military junta took control of the country.* | **keep, maintain, retain** *She struggled to keep control of her voice.* | **lose, relinquish** *He lost control of the car when he swerved to avoid a cyclist.* | **wrest** *attempts to wrest control of the town from government forces* | **get out of, go out of** *The car went out of control on the icy road.* | **re-establish, regain** *Enemy forces have now regained control of the area.* | **give sb/sth** *The idea is to give councils full control of their own budgets.* | **exercise, exert** *Editors do not exercise control over large sections of their newspapers.* | **bring/get sth under** *They soon got the situation under control.*
• PREP. **beyond/outside your ~** *Parking is outside my control.* **in ~ (of)** *The elected government is back in control.* **out of ~** *I had this feeling that things were out of control.* **under (sb's) ~** *Everything is under control* ◇ *The department was under the control of Bryce Thompson.* | **~ over** *They have little control over that side of the business.*
• PHRASES **circumstances beyond sb's control** *The event has been cancelled due to circumstances beyond our control.*

2 limiting/managing sth
• ADJ. **air-traffic, arms, birth, budgetary, cost, crowd,** gun, pest, pollution, quality, rent, social, stock, traffic *The police are experts in crowd control.*

3 (usually **controls**) method of limiting/managing sth
• ADJ. **strict, stringent, tight, tough** | **lax** | **border, export, price** *calls for tougher export controls*
• VERB + CONTROL **impose, introduce** *The government has imposed strict controls on new building.* | **tighten** *The country has tightened its border controls.* | **ease, relax** *plans to relax price controls* | **lift, remove**
• PREP. **~ on** *They have introduced controls on public spending.*

4 for operating a machine
• ADJ. **remote** | **volume**
• VERB + CONTROL **take** *Once we were in the air, I was allowed to take the controls.*
• CONTROL + NOUN **panel**
• PREP. **at the ~s** *Chief Air Officer Sedley was at the controls of the Boeing 707.*

control *verb*

• ADV. **carefully, strictly, tightly** *Conditions in the greenhouse are carefully controlled.* ◇ *Expenditure within the company is tightly controlled.* | **effectively, properly** | **centrally, directly**

controller *noun*

• ADJ. **air traffic** | **programme** *He is the new programme controller for BBC2.* | **credit, financial, marketing, production** | **district, divisional, group, regional**
• PREP. **~ for** *the company's marketing controller for the north-west*
⇨ Note at JOB

controversial *adj.*

• VERBS **be, prove** | **become** | **remain**
• ADV. **extremely, highly, very** *a highly controversial subject* | **rather, somewhat** | **politically**

controversy *noun*

• ADJ. **considerable, great, major** | **bitter, fierce, raging, violent** | **lively** *His views have excited a lively controversy among fellow scientists.* | **fresh, further, new, renewed** | **continued, continuing, long-standing, prolonged** | **public** | **political** | **religious, theological** | **academic, critical, scholarly**
• VERB + CONTROVERSY **arouse, cause, create, excite, fuel, give rise to, provoke, spark (off), stir up** *What they are doing is bound to stir up controversy.* | **be dogged by, be marked by, be riven by, be surrounded by** *This year's championships have been dogged by controversy.* | **avoid** *The prime minister seemed anxious to avoid controversy about these appointments.* | **run into** *The network ran into controversy over claims of faked documentary footage.* | **be no stranger to** *The MP, who is no stranger to controversy herself, said the scandal could have serious repercussions.* | **court** *The singer deliberately courts controversy with his racist and sexist lyrics.*
• CONTROVERSY + VERB **arise, break out** *A fierce controversy has broken out over the issue.* | **rage** *Controversy is raging over the route of the new motorway.* | **exist** *Controversy exists as to how safe these drugs are.* | **centre on sth** *The controversy centred on the issue of compensation for the victims.* | **surround sth** *Much controversy surrounds the new exam.*
• PREP. **amid ~** *The minister has resigned amid continuing controversy over his education proposals.* | **~ about/concerning/over** *There has been a lot of controversy over the use of these drugs.* **~ among** *controversy among historians* **~ between** *controversy between the two leaders* **~ surrounding** *the bitter controversy surrounding*

the introduction of the new regulations ~ **with** her long-running controversy with fellow academics
- PHRASES **a matter/source/subject of controversy, a storm of controversy** The book raised a storm of controversy.

convenience noun

1 being useful/easy/suitable
- ADJ. **great** | **extra** All our holiday chalets include a microwave and food processor for extra convenience. | **administrative** The system is based on administrative convenience rather than public benefit.
- CONVENIENCE + NOUN **food** The children like convenience food such as sausages or fish fingers and chips. | **store**
- PREP. **at your ~** Can you telephone me at your convenience (= when it is convenient for you) to arrange a further meeting? **for (your) ~** I keep my cookery books in the kitchen for convenience. ◊ An order form is enclosed for your convenience.
- PHRASES **a marriage of convenience** (= a marriage for financial, political or practical reasons, not love), **at your earliest convenience** (business) (= as soon as possible), **comfort and convenience** In this resort you can enjoy all the comfort and convenience of modern tourism. **for the sake of convenience** We leave the keys near the front door for the sake of convenience.

2 sth useful
- ADJ. **great** It's a great convenience living next door to a post office. | **modern** They wouldn't like to live without modern conveniences such as microwaves.

convenient adj.

- VERBS **be, prove, seem, sound** | **make sth** | **find sth** I find the new system much more convenient.
- ADV. **extremely, highly, very** | **quite** | **mutually** We arranged a mutually convenient time to meet. | **politically**
- PREP. **for** Would this be convenient for you? ◊ The house is quite convenient for the shops.

convent noun

- ADJ. **Carmelite, Catholic, Franciscan, Ursuline, etc.**
- VERB + CONVENT **enter** She entered a convent (= became a nun) at the age of sixteen. | **leave** | **establish, found, set up** The nuns established a convent here in 1692.
- CONVENT + NOUN **building, wall** within the convent walls (= inside the convent) | **education, school**
- PREP. **in a/the ~** She spent her whole life in a convent. | **~ of** the Convent of St Saviour

convention noun

1 way sth is done
- ADJ. **accepted, established, long-standing, old, traditional, well-established** It's an established convention that the part of the prince is played by a woman. | **normal, standard, usual** | **polite** Her work refuses any concession to polite conventions of 'good taste'. | **arbitrary** | **rigid, strict** | **cultural, legal, social** the rigid social conventions of Victorian Britain | **dramatic, fictional, literary, narrative, operatic, poetic** The novel refuses to conform to the narrative conventions of 19th century realism. | **orthographic, punctuation, rhetorical**
- QUANT. **set**
- VERB + CONVENTION **adhere to, conform to, follow, keep to, observe** They followed the Greek convention of pinning gifts of money to the bride's dress. | **be bound by, be hidebound by** Life with the Leighs was not hidebound by rules or convention. | **break (with), cut through, defy, flout** She knew that she had broken an important social convention. ◊ He had the freedom of spirit to cut through

convention. ◊ No young politician can afford to flout convention in this way.
- CONVENTION + VERB **demand sth, dictate sth** Convention dictated that dangerous physical action is the part of heroes, not heroines.
- PREP. **according to/by ~** By convention, the Queen gives the Royal Assent to all measures passed by Parliament.
- PHRASES **a break with convention** In a surprising break with convention, she wore a red wedding dress. **a matter of convention**

2 conference
- ADJ. **annual** | **international, national** | **Democratic, Republican, etc.** | **careers, constitutional, party, political** A constitutional convention was elected to try to agree on a new form of government.
- VERB + CONVENTION **arrange, have, hold, organize** | **attend, go to** | **address** He addressed the annual Republican convention.
- CONVENTION + VERB **take place**
- CONVENTION + NOUN **centre** | **delegate**
- PREP. **at a/the ~** She was at the Democratic convention.
- PHRASES **delegates to a convention**

3 international agreement
- ADJ. **global, international** | **European, UN/United Nations, etc.** | **climate, human rights, etc.** | **draft**
- VERB + CONVENTION **adopt, ratify, sign** Over 60 countries have yet to ratify the climate convention. | **adhere to, comply with** Most countries have adhered to the convention. | **breach** This practice breaches the arms convention.
- CONVENTION + VERB **apply, govern sth** a convention governing the conditions under which mining is permitted | **establish sth** The convention established procedures for the transport of toxic waste. | **ban sth**
- PREP. **under a/the ~** This is forbidden under the European Convention on Human Rights. | **~ between** the 1869 convention between Turkey and Persia **~ for** the Berne Convention for the Conservation of European Wildlife **~ on** the 1951 United Nations Convention on refugees
- PHRASES **a breach of a convention**

conventional adj.

- VERBS **be, seem**
- ADV. **highly, very** | **entirely, quite, strictly** | **largely** | **fairly, pretty, rather, relatively, somewhat**

conversation noun

- ADJ. **brief, short** | **lengthy, long** We engaged in a long conversation. | **endless** listening to endless conversations about high prices and food shortages | **casual, everyday, general, informal, normal, ordinary** It's not a subject that often crops up in casual conversation. | **intimate, personal, private** | **face-to-face** | **overheard, recorded, taped** | **phone/telephone** | **civilized, polite** We sat making polite conversation and feeling rather uncomfortable. | **friendly, pleasant** | **animated** | **fascinating, good, intelligent, interesting, stimulating** He said that television had been the death of good conversation. | **proper, real, serious** There was no time for a proper conversation. | **simple** When you are struggling with an unfamiliar language, the simplest conversations can be misinterpreted. | **strange** | **chance** A chance conversation led to a brilliant new career for the young catering student. | **desultory, halting, stilted** We carried on a rather halting conversation. | **hushed, low-voiced, murmured, muted, muttered, quiet, whispered** | **shouted** | **one-sided, two-way** Think of prayer as a two-way conversation. | **imaginary** | **after-dinner** | **adult** Young children become quickly bored by adult conversation.
- QUANT. **snatch** I overheard snatches of a conversation between two doctors.
- VERB + CONVERSATION **carry on, have, hold, make**

You can't hold a private conversation there. ◇ *I tried to make conversation with the three silent people round the table.* | **begin, draw sb into, engage sb in, fall into, get into, open, start, strike up** *I got into conversation with one of the directors.* ◇ *He was waiting for her to open the conversation.* ◇ *I was keen to strike up a conversation with him.* | **be deep in, be engaged in** *They were deep in conversation and didn't notice the time.* | **continue, keep up** *Cara kept up a one-sided conversation.* | **control, dominate** | **bring around/round, steer, turn** *I managed to bring the conversation round to why they were leaving.* ◇ *He tried to steer the conversation away from the topic of money.* ◇ *She turned the conversation to her work.* | **enter, join (in)** | **break off** | **conclude, end, finish** | **avoid** *She avoided conversation with the other passengers.* | **encourage** *I was courteous but didn't encourage conversation.* | **hear, listen to, overhear** | **interrupt** | **resume** | **have no** *a plain girl who had no conversation* (= could not make conversation) *and no social graces*

• CONVERSATION + VERB **take place** *When did this conversation take place?* | **continue, proceed** *The conversation proceeded in French.* | **flow** *They all relaxed and conversation flowed freely.* | **come back/round to, drift, move on (to), switch, turn to, veer back/off** *The conversation drifted into family chat.* ◇ *The conversation moved on to other things.* ◇ *The conversation turned to holidays in France.* | **cease, end, stop** *All conversation ceased and everyone turned round.* ◇ *The conversation ended when the vacuum cleaner started up.* | **run out** *All too soon the stilted conversation ran out.*

• PREP. **during~** *In the Western world it is polite to maintain eye contact during conversation.* **in~ with** *In the programme tonight we hear Dr Chris Toole in conversation with the artist Mary Witherspoon.* | **~ about** *We had a long conversation about old cars.* **~ between** *a conversation between Jane and her parents* **~ on** *a conversation on the topic of activities for children* **~ with** *I had an interesting conversation with Dick Whortly.*

• PHRASES **an attempt at conversation** *She ignored all my attempts at conversation.* **be in close/deep/earnest conversation (with sb)** *Don was in close conversation with the girl on his right.* **a babble/buzz/hum of conversation** *She could hear him over the buzz of conversation and laughter.* **during the course of (the) conversation** *During the course of conversation, it emerged that Sheila had lived in Nigeria.* **keep the conversation going** *Our hostess did her best to keep the conversation going.* **a lull in the conversation, a topic of conversation** *The main topic of conversation was the big football match.*

conversion *noun*

1 change to a new form/system/use
• ADJ. **careful** *Today, after a careful conversion, it is a very comfortable and elegant country home.* | **barn, loft | office | currency** *There are no charges for currency conversion.* | **data, file | energy** *Cheap solar energy conversion has been the dream of some scientists since the 1970s.*
• VERB + CONVERSION **carry out, undertake**
• PREP. **~from, ~into** *A local building firm will carry out the conversion of the farm buildings into business units.* **~to** *conversion from analogue to digital data*

2 religious
• ADJ. **religious | deathbed | overnight, sudden** (*figurative*) *her overnight conversion to market economics*
• VERB + CONVERSION **experience, undergo** *In the late eighties he underwent a religious conversion.*
• CONVERSION + NOUN **experience**
• PREP. **~ from, ~ to** *her conversion from Buddhism to Christianity*

3 in rugby
• VERB + CONVERSION **kick | add** *The try came in the third minute and Jon Bland added the conversion.*

convert *noun*
• ADJ. **recent | enthusiastic | reluctant | Catholic, Jewish, etc.**
• VERB + CONVERT **become | gain, make, win** *an attempt to gain converts to Communism*
• PREP. **~from** *One of the early popes, Clement was a convert from paganism.* **~to** *a recent convert to Catholicism*

convey *verb*
• ADV. **clearly, vividly** *The novel vividly conveys the experience of growing up during the war.* | **accurately, adequately | effectively, successfully**
• VERB + CONVEY **can/could** *Gestures can convey meaning as well as words.* | **try to | manage to | fail to**
• PREP. **to** *He managed to convey his enthusiasm to her.*

convict *noun*
• ADJ. **escaped**

convict *verb*
• ADV. **rightly, wrongly**
• PREP. **for** *She was convicted for her part in the crime.* **of** *He was convicted of a serious driving offence.*

conviction *noun*

1 for a crime
• ADJ. **earlier, previous | spent** *You are not obliged to acknowledge spent convictions.* | **successful | unsafe, wrongful** *The men's convictions were declared unsafe.* | **criminal | manslaughter, murder, etc.**
• VERB + CONVICTION **have** *He has three previous criminal convictions.* | **lead to** *A reward is offered for information leading to the conviction of the attacker.* | **obtain, secure** *They need strong evidence to secure a conviction.* | **escape** *He believes that too many defendants are escaping conviction by claiming that they are insane.* | **appeal against** *He appealed against his conviction for murder.* | **overturn, quash | uphold**
• CONVICTION + NOUN **rate** *The conviction rate for rape is extremely low.*
• PREP. **on ~** *an offence which carries, on conviction, a sentence of not more than five years' imprisonment* | **~ against** *The appeal court overturned the conviction against her.* **~ for** *a conviction for murder*
• PHRASES **the rate of conviction**

2 belief/appearance of belief
• ADJ. **absolute, complete, total, unshakeable, utter | deep, deeply held, fervent, firm, fundamental, great, intense, passionate, real, strong** *It is the firm conviction of the governors that this child should not be admitted to the school.* ◇ *There was no great conviction in his voice.* | **growing | personal | inner | ideological, moral, political, religious | Catholic, Christian, etc.**
• VERB + CONVICTION **have** *She had this absolute conviction that what she liked others would like.* | **share** *The ex-leaders share a deep conviction that their views on world matters are still vitally important.* | **express | shake** *Nothing could shake her conviction that 'abroad' was a dangerous place.* | **strengthen | carry** *Her explanation failed to carry conviction in the face of the facts.* | **lack** *Her arguments lacked conviction.*
• CONVICTION + NOUN **politics** *The demise of consensus and the rise of conviction politics.*
• PREP. **with/without ~** *'Not true!' she said with conviction.* | **~ about** *He had a strong personal conviction about the power of the printed word.*
• PHRASES **have the courage of your convictions** (= to be brave enough to do what you feel to be right)

convinced *adj.*

- VERBS **appear, be, feel, seem, sound** | **become** *She became convinced that something was wrong.* | **remain**
- ADV. **deeply, firmly** | **absolutely, completely, fully, quite, totally, utterly** | **increasingly** | **almost** | **by no means, not altogether, not entirely, not fully, not wholly** | **fairly** | **half** *She was still only half convinced.* | **apparently** | **clearly**
- PREP. **of** *He was convinced of her innocence.*

convincing *adj.*

- VERBS **be, look, seem, sound** | **find sth** *I found his argument pretty convincing.*
- ADV. **extremely, very** | **completely, thoroughly, totally, utterly** | **hardly, not altogether, not entirely, not wholly** | **far from, not remotely** *He was far from convincing as a leader.* | **fairly, pretty, quite** | **enough, sufficiently** *She produced a convincing enough performance as the wronged wife.*

convoy *noun*

- ADJ. **armed, army, military, naval, troop** | **road, vehicle** | **aid, food, humanitarian, relief** *the proposal to send 500 armed soldiers to escort food convoys* | **UN/United Nations**
- VERB + CONVOY **lead** | **escort, protect** | **attack**
- CONVOY + VERB **carry sth** | **arrive**
- PREP. **in ~** *The ships travelled in convoy.* | **~ of** *a large convoy of lorries carrying medical supplies* **~ to** *the next aid convoy to the war-torn region*

convulsion *noun*

- ADJ. **violent** | **slight** | **sudden**
- VERB + CONVULSION **go into, have, suffer** *The patient lost consciousness and went into convulsions.* | **cause**
- CONVULSION + VERB **shake sb** *A sudden convulsion shook him, and he fell to the ground.*

cook *noun*

- ADJ. **excellent, good** *He's a very good cook* | **amateur, professional** *She wants to become a professional cook.*
- ⇨ Note at JOB

cook *verb*

- ADV. **thoroughly, well** *Make sure you cook the meat well.* | **evenly, gently, slowly** *Turn the fish over so that it cooks evenly.* | **quickly**
- PHRASES **be cooked through** *Ensure that the meat is cooked through.*

cooker *noun*

- ADJ. **electric, gas** | **pressure** | **free-standing**
- COOKER + NOUN **hood, point**

cookery *noun*

- ADJ. **basic** *Before he leaves home, he needs to learn some basic cookery.* | **step-by-step** *a step-by-step cookery series for beginners* | **vegetarian** | **cordon bleu** | **microwave** | **Chinese, Eastern, French, etc.**
- VERB + COOKERY **learn**
- COOKERY + NOUN **demonstration** | **class, course, lesson, school** | **book, column, magazine, programme** | **expert, writer**

cooking *noun*

- ADJ. **good, superb, wonderful** *Her cooking is wonderful.* | **home** *I miss my mother's good home cooking.* | **trad-**itional *traditional English cooking* | **regional** | **Chinese, Italian, etc.** *French regional cooking* | **vegetarian** | **slow**
- VERB + COOKING **do** *Who does most of the cooking in your house?*
- PREP. **during ~** *Stir the mixture to prevent the beans sticking to the bottom during cooking.* **in ~** *I use yogurt quite a lot in cooking.*

cool *verb*

1 become colder
- ADV. **completely, thoroughly** | **a little, slightly** | **down, off** *He went for a swim to cool off.*
- VERB + COOL **allow sth to, let sth** *Allow the cake to cool thoroughly before removing it from the tin.*

2 become calmer
- ADV. **considerably** | **slightly, somewhat**

cool *adj.*

1 fairly cold
- VERBS **be, feel, look** *The forest looked cool and shady.* | **become, get** *It will probably get cool later, so bring a coat.* | **keep sth** *Try to keep the drinks cool.*
- ADV. **very** | **fairly, quite, rather** | **beautifully, blissfully, deliciously, pleasantly, refreshingly, wonderfully** *The temple was light, spacious and blissfully cool.*

2 calm
- VERBS **appear, be, look** | **keep, remain, stay** *She managed to stay cool during the meeting.* | **act, play it** (*informal*) *He forced himself to count to ten and act cool.* ◊ *For once I felt uncertain about my real feelings. I decided to play it cool.*
- ADV. **very** | **completely** | **pretty** | **professionally** *Professionally cool, she went back to her patient.*
- PHRASES **cool, calm and collected** *He did his best to appear cool, calm and collected.*

3 not friendly/enthusiastic
- VERBS **appear, be, sound** | **remain**
- ADV. **distinctly, very** | **rather, somewhat**
- PREP. **about** *She was distinctly cool about their plans.* **towards** *He was cool towards me.*

cooperate *verb*

- ADV. **fully** *He has said he will cooperate fully with the police enquiries.* | **closely**
- VERB + COOPERATE **will/would** | **agree to, be prepared to, be willing to** | **refuse to**
- PREP. **in** *The two companies are cooperating in the development of a new engine.* **on** *cooperating on a research project* **with** *The firm has agreed to cooperate with the employment survey.*

cooperation *noun*

- ADJ. **close** | **full** | **greater, increased** | **active** | **effective** | **international, local** | **mutual** *a society founded on mutual cooperation and shared prosperity* | **cultural, economic, military, political, social, technical**
- VERB + COOPERATION **need, require** | **ask for, call for, seek** *She called for closer cooperation on drugs control.* ◊ *They are seeking the cooperation of senior medical staff.* | **enlist, get** *We are hoping to enlist the cooperation of women's groups.* | **give (sb), offer (sb)** | **encourage, promote** *promoting cooperation between universities and industry* | **ensure**
- PREP. **in ~ with** *The film was made in cooperation with the Sports Council.* **with/without sb's ~** *With the cooperation of the public, the police may be able to catch this man.* | **~ among** *increased technical cooperation among large companies* **~ between** *political cooperation between the two groups* **~ from** *You will need a bit of cooperation from your family.* **~ in** *We asked for their cooperation in the collection of data.* **~ on** *They offered*

their cooperation on the project. ~ **with** *We should like to thank you for your cooperation with us.*

• PHRASES **a lack of cooperation, a need for cooperation** *There is a need for greater economic cooperation.*

cooperative *noun*

• ADJ. **community, worker | agricultural, farmer/farming | production**

• VERB + COOPERATIVE **form | run sth as** *The family business is now run as a cooperative.*

coordinate *verb*

• ADV. **carefully** *a carefully coordinated policy*

• PREP. **with** *We try to coordinate our activities with those of other groups.*

• PHRASES **a coordinated approach/policy/programme**

coordination *noun*

1 working together

• ADJ. **better, greater | poor | international | economic, market, policy | colour** *advice on colour coordination* (= colours that look good together)

• VERB + COORDINATION **need, require | ensure, facilitate** *We must make a real effort to ensure greater coordination between the different groups.*

• PREP. **in ~ with** *a pamphlet produced by the government in coordination with the Sports Council* | **~ between** *to facilitate better coordination between departments* ~ **in** *a lack of coordination in government policy* ~ **with**

• PHRASES **a lack of coordination, a need for coordination** *a need for coordination with the training department*

2 ability to control your movements

• ADJ. **good | poor | physical | hand-eye** *You need good hand-eye coordination to play racket sports.*

• VERB + COORDINATION **have | lack**

• PHRASES **a lack of coordination**

cope *verb*

• ADV. **admirably, well** *She copes very well under pressure.* | **adequately** *Will the prison system cope adequately with the increasing numbers of prisoners?* | **easily**

• VERB + COPE **be able/unable to, can/can't** *She is unable to cope with her increasing workload.* ◇ *He felt that he couldn't cope any longer.* | **have to** *She had to cope without any help.* | **learn to | struggle to, try to** *struggling to cope with the demands of a new baby* | **be difficult to**

• PREP. **with** *Some people find unemployment very difficult to cope with.*

• PHRASES **sb's ability to cope, a way of coping** *a way of coping with bereavement*

copper *noun*

• ADJ. **molten | beaten | unalloyed | burnished** *Her hair shone like burnished copper.*

• VERB + COPPER **mine | produce | be alloyed with** *silver alloyed with copper*

• COPPER + VERB **be alloyed with sth** *copper alloyed with arsenic*

• COPPER + NOUN **mine | miner | mining, smelting | deposit, ore | alloy, sulphate | coin, ingot, pipe, plate, wire | engraving**

• PREP. **in ~** (= using copper) *She works mainly in copper.*

• PHRASES **an alloy of copper and/with sth** *Brass is an alloy of copper and zinc.*

copy *noun*

1 document/work of art

• ADJ. **accurate, faithful, good | cheap, crude, poor** *It was not the original painting, but a crude copy.* | **carbon, duplicate, exact, facsimile, identical, perfect, true** *The twins were carbon copies of each other.* ◇ *It must be certified as a true copy of the original document.* | **draft, working | clean, fair | master, original, top** *Take a photocopy of the master copy.* | **additional, extra, further, spare | multiple** *The photocopier had been set for multiple copies.* | **modern | certified | photographic, photostat | back-up** *Remember to make back-up copies of all your disks.* | **hard, paper, printed** (*computing*) *You will need to supply a hard copy version of all files.*

• VERB + COPY **make, print, run off, take** *I ran off a couple of copies of the letter.* | **attach, enclose, send** *I attach a copy of the report.* ◇ *Please find enclosed a copy of the draft document.* | **circulate, distribute, supply** *Copies of the article were circulated to members of the committee.* | **obtain, receive | keep** *Remember to keep copies of all your correspondence.*

2 book/newspaper/tape, etc.

• ADJ. **additional, extra, further, spare | back, old** *I have a few back copies of the newspaper.* | **advance** *Advance copies of the book were sent out to reviewers.* | **review | complimentary, free** *Free copies of the leaflet are available from the Department of the Environment.* | **illegal, illicit, pirate/pirated, unauthorized | manuscript, printed, proof | bound, hardback, leather-bound, paperback, presentation** *The candidate must submit two bound copies of his or her thesis.* | **battered, tattered, well-thumbed** *my battered copy of Shakespeare's plays* | **perfect, pristine | personal** *Charles I's personal copy of the psalter* | **signed**

• VERB + COPY **circulate, distribute | sign** *Author Bob Woodhouse will be signing copies of his new book.*

• COPY + VERB **circulate** *Even with the new legislation pirate copies will circulate.* | **be available**

3 written material

• ADJ. **good, great | advertising | editorial | knocking** (*informal*) *Knocking copy* (= writing that just says how bad sb/sth is) *is simply lazy journalism.*

• VERB + COPY **edit, prepare, produce, write** *The subeditors prepare the reporters' copy for the paper.* | **make** *This will make great copy for the advertisement.*

• COPY + NOUN **editor | date, deadline** *Copy date* (= the date for handing in copy) *for the next issue is 1 May.*

copy *verb*

1 make a copy

• ADV. **illegally** *illegally copied software*

• PREP. **from, onto** *Data can be copied from the computer onto floppy disks.*

2 write sth down exactly

• ADV. **carefully, laboriously, painstakingly | down, out** *I copied down several phone numbers from the list.* ◇ *laboriously copying out an old manuscript*

• PREP. **from, into** *She copied all the addresses into her address book.* **off** *copying a recipe off the packet* **onto** *He copied all the details from the brochure onto a piece of paper.*

3 do the same as sb else

• ADV. **slavishly** *She slavishly copies the older girl's style.*

• PREP. **from** *He's copied that mannerism from his brother.* **off** *She was caught copying off another student.*

copyright *noun*

• VERB + COPYRIGHT **have, hold, own** *The publisher has the copyright on all his books.* | **breach, infringe** *By publishing the book, they were guilty of infringing copy-*

right. | **be protected by** *Databases are generally protected by copyright.*
● COPYRIGHT + VERB **protect sth** *Copyright protects your work from being commercially exploited by someone else without your consent.*
● PREP. **in ~** *The songs remain in copyright.* **out of ~** *His work is now out of copyright.* | **~ in/on** *The family still holds the copyright on his works.*
● PHRASES **breach/infringement of copyright** *They sued her for breach of copyright.* **ownership of copyright** *Ownership of copyright can be transferred.*

cord noun

● ADJ. **thick, thin** | **strong** | **elastic, nylon, silk** | **gold** *a silk bag tied with a gold cord* | **dressing-gown, picture** | **nerve, spinal, vocal** (see also **umbilical cord**)
● QUANT. **length, piece** *You need a piece of thick cord about two metres long.*
● VERB + CORD **pull** | **knot, tie (sth with)** *He knotted the cord of his dressing-gown.* | **undo, untie**

cordial adj.

● VERBS **be** | **remain**
● ADV. **extremely, remarkably, very** | **not entirely** | **quite** *Relations between the two governments remained quite cordial.*

cordon noun

● ADJ. **tight** | **police, security**
● VERB + CORDON **form, throw** *Police officers threw a cordon around his car to protect him.* | **break through** *The crowd managed to break through the police cordon.*
● CORDON + VERB **prevent sth** *A police cordon prevented the marchers from entering the main square.*
● PREP. **~ around/round** *There is a tight security cordon around the area.*

core noun

● ADJ. **hollow** *Each fibre has a hollow core trapping still air and aiding warmth.* ◊ (figurative) *There was a hollow core of sadness inside me.* | **solid** | **copper, iron, etc.** | **reactor** *nuclear reactor cores* | **central, essential, inner, innermost, very** *This is seen as the central core of the government's policy.* ◊ *A new spirit welled up from the very core of the nation.* | **common** *a common core of shared understanding about law and government* | **hard** *A hard core of supporters, mostly teenage girls, gathered at the airport to see the star arrive.* | **emotional** *the emotional core of her music*
● VERB + CORE **form, make up** *These ideas formed the core of his philosophy.* | **get to** *We want to get to the core of the problem.*
● CORE + NOUN **activity, area, course, curriculum, discipline, module, programme, skill, subject** *the core area of management studies* ◊ *Students study five core subjects.* | **component, element, group** | **business, service** *We need to stop this expansion and concentrate on the core business.* | **belief, value** | **vocabulary**
● PREP. **at sth's ~** *At the core of our convictions is belief in individual liberty.* **to the ~** *She was shaken to the core by the news.* ◊ *He's a politician to the core* (= in all his attitudes, beliefs and actions).

corn noun

1 grain crops
● ADJ. **ripe** | **green** *The corn is still green.* | **young** | **standing** *a field of standing corn*
● QUANT. **ear, sheaf** | **bag, sack** | **field**
● VERB + CORN **grow** | **sow** | **cut, harvest, thresh** | **grind** | **eat**
● CORN + VERB **grow**

● CORN + NOUN **field** | **harvest** | **cob** | **mill**
● PHRASES **corn on the cob** (= maize cooked with all the grains still attached to the cob)
2 area of hard skin on the toe
● VERB + CORN **have, suffer from** | **treat**

corner noun

1 where two lines/edges meet
● ADJ. **bottom, top** | **left/left-hand, right/right-hand** | **back, front** | **lower, upper** | **southern, south-western, etc.** | **external, outer, outside** | **inner, inside, internal** | **opposite** | **overhanging, projecting** | **sharp** | **rounded** *Smooth rounded corners make cleaning easier.* | **awkward** *Make sure the staircase is well lit, with no awkward corners.* | **extreme, far, very** *He parked in the far corner of the car park.*
● CORNER + NOUN **cupboard, seat, table** *The waiter led us to a corner table.*
● PREP. **in a/the ~** *Put your address in the top right-hand corner of the page.*
2 of roads
● ADJ. **street** *There were a lot of young men hanging about on street corners.* | **sharp, tight** *It's a rather sharp corner and she took it a little too fast.* | **blind** *I hate coming out of that lane because it's a blind corner.*
● VERB + CORNER **round, take, turn** *As they turned the corner all the parcels slid to one side.*
● CORNER + NOUN **shop** *the local corner shop*
● PREP. **around/round a/the ~** *A white van came round the corner.* **at a/the ~** *at the corner of West Street and Park Street* ◊ *Turn right at the first corner.* **on a/the ~** *the shop on the corner of Mount Street*
3 place/region
● ADJ. **quiet** *He found a quiet corner and got on with his work.* | **little, small, tiny** *Welcome to our little corner of Surrey.* | **distant, far, far-flung, remote** *a remote corner of Afghanistan* | **picturesque** | **dark, gloomy, shadowed, shadowy** *She sat in a dark corner of the room.* | **shady, sheltered** *a cool shady corner of the garden* | **forgotten, hidden, obscure, odd, secret** *The box had been tucked away in an odd corner of the attic.*
● PREP. **in a/the ~** *She tucked herself away in a corner and read all day.*
● PHRASES **the corner of your mind** (figurative) *He pushed the thought back into the darkest corner of his mind.*
4 difficult situation
● ADJ. **tight** *He was used to having to talk his way out of tight corners.*
● VERB + CORNER **back/drive/force sb into** | **get sb/yourself into** *They had got her in a corner and there was nothing she could do about it.*
● PHRASES **be in a bit of a corner** *I'm in a bit of a corner over finding staff for Friday evening.*
5 in sport
● ADJ. **penalty** | **short**
● VERB + CORNER **award (sb)** *The referee awarded a corner.* | **take** *Beckham took the corner and Scholes headed it into the net.* | **force, win** *He put the goalkeeper under pressure and managed to force a corner.* | **concede** *James blocked the shot but conceded a corner.* | **miss** | **clear**
● CORNER + NOUN **kick**

coroner noun

● ADJ. **deputy**
● CORONER + VERB **issue sth** *The coroner issued a burial certificate.* | **order sth** *The coroner ordered an investigation into the man's death.* | **record a verdict of sth** *The coroner recorded a verdict of accidental death.*
● PHRASES **a coroner's court/inquest, a coroner's report/verdict**

corporal noun

⇨ Note at RANK

corporation noun

- ADJ. **big, giant, large, major | powerful | foreign | global, international, multinational, transnational | private, public | broadcasting, business, finance, industrial, oil**
- CORPORATION + NOUN **tax**
- ⇨ Note at ORGANIZATION (for verbs)

corps noun

- ADJ. **elite** *the elite corps of the Sultan's army* | **multinational** *a multinational corps under UK command* | **cadet, officer, volunteer | army, diplomatic, medical | media, press** *the UN press corps*
- CORPS + NOUN **commander**
- PREP. **in a/the~** *He's in the Royal Army Medical Corps.*

corpse noun

- ADJ. **human | naked | bloody, headless, mutilated | decaying, desiccated, rotting** *We passed the desiccated corpse of a brigand hanging on a gibbet.* | **shrouded | embalmed, mummified | living** *For over a year he lay in his hospital bed, a living corpse.*
- VERB + CORPSE **lay out** *The corpse had been laid out on a marble slab.* | **embalm | butcher, dismember, eviscerate, mutilate**
- CORPSE + VERB **be sprawled, lie, sprawl** *They saw the corpse sprawled on the steps.*
- PHRASES **be littered/strewn with corpses** *The ground was littered with the corpses of enemy soldiers.*

correct adj.

- VERBS **be, prove, seem** *His first idea proved correct.*
- ADV. **absolutely, completely, entirely, perfectly, quite** *What you say is perfectly correct, but it gives the wrong impression.* | **not entirely, not strictly** *He is not entirely correct in his assumptions.* | **basically, broadly, essentially, fundamentally, largely, more or less, substantially** *His estimate has turned out to be more or less correct.* | **clearly, undoubtedly | demonstrably** *None of the explanations offered is demonstrably correct—or demonstrably incorrect.* | **ideologically, politically** (*sometimes disapproving*) (= avoiding language or behaviour that may offend some groups of people) *He was an interesting speaker, if not always politically correct in his views.* | **legally, technically | morally | anatomically, botanically, factually, grammatically** *The flower drawings are all to scale and botanically correct.*
- PREP. **in** *The diagram is correct in every detail.* ◇ *I think I am correct in saying that this project is the first of its kind in this country.*

correction noun

- ADJ. **minor, small | necessary** *Make any necessary corrections before the text is printed.* | **error, spelling**
- VERB + CORRECTION **make | need, require** *There are some programming errors that need correction.*
- PREP. **~to** *I've got to make one or two small corrections to the text before it's finished.*

correctness noun

- ADJ. **grammatical, ideological, political** (*sometimes disapproving*) *Political correctness is the principle of avoiding language or behaviour that may offend certain groups of people.*
- VERB + CORRECTNESS **doubt, question** *She doubted the correctness of the information.* | **be convinced of** *She was convinced of the correctness of the decision.* | **confirm**

correlate verb

- ADV. **closely, highly, significantly, strongly, well | positively | inversely, negatively**
- VERB + CORRELATE **be found to, be shown to** *High morale among staff was found to correlate positively with productivity.*
- PREP. **to** *Property values are negatively correlated to the tax rate.* **with** *The average speed of the vehicles correlates closely with the severity of the accident caused.*

correlation noun

- ADJ. **close, good, high, remarkable, significant, strong | clear, obvious | direct, simple** *There is a direct correlation between exposure to sun and skin cancer.* | **broad, general, overall | low, poor, weak | positive | inverse, negative | statistical**
- VERB + CORRELATION **have** *The second group of measurements had a high correlation with the first.* | **discover, establish, find, observe, show** *The study showed a significant correlation between the baby's sleeping position and the risk of cot death.*
- CORRELATION + VERB **exist** *A strong correlation exists between the fatness of parents and their children.*
- PREP. **~between** *the correlation between speed and risk of accident* **~with** *the correlation of height with weight*
- PHRASES **lack of correlation**

correspond verb

1 be the same/match
- ADV. **closely | directly, exactly, precisely | approximately, broadly, roughly**
- PREP. **to** *Their nursery schools correspond roughly to our infant schools.* **with** *The movement of the dot on the screen corresponds exactly with the movement of the control lever.*

2 write letters
- ADV. **regularly**
- PREP. **with** *She corresponded regularly with her former music teacher.*

correspondence noun

1 letters exchanged
- ADJ. **confidential, personal, private | business, commercial, diplomatic, official | regular | voluminous | lively** *a lively correspondence in 'The Times' about ways of preparing tripe*
- QUANT. **item** *Numerous items of correspondence have been received on this subject.* | **pile** *He was leafing through piles of correspondence.*
- VERB + CORRESPONDENCE **enter into, have** *It would be foolish for a doctor to enter into correspondence with a patient.* ◇ *I have had correspondence with the company director on this matter.* | **carry on, keep up** *We kept up a correspondence for many months.* | **address, send** *Please send correspondence to 'Letters to the Editor, Model Railway Journal'.* | **receive | read | answer, deal with, handle** *The secretary deals with all the correspondence.* | **catch up on** *I would spend the time reading or catching up on my correspondence.* | **intercept** *The department intercepted the correspondence of foreign diplomats.*
- CORRESPONDENCE + NOUN **column** *the correspondence columns of the 'London Review of Books'* | **course** *I did a correspondence course in economics.*
- PREP. **by/through ~** *All our business is conducted by correspondence.* **in ~ with** *I have been in correspondence with the manager of the store.* | **~ about/on/concerning/regarding/relating to** *files full of confidential correspondence relating to the company's expansion plans* **~between** *I have seen the correspondence between the company and the local authority.* **~from** *The editor welcomes*

correspondence from readers on any subject. ~**with** *copies of his correspondence with the Queen*

2 connection
- ADJ. **direct, exact, one-to-one** *The child can see the one-to-one correspondence of the buttons and buttonholes.* | **close**
- PREP. ~**between** *a close correspondence between theory and practice*

correspondent *noun*

1 reporter
- ADJ. **newspaper, television** | **business, education, foreign, health, industrial, legal affairs, media, parliamentary, political, royal, science, sports, war** | **special** *A report from our special correspondent at the UN.* | **American, Moscow, New York Times, etc.**
- CORRESPONDENT + VERB **write (sth)**

corridor *noun*

- ADJ. **endless, long** | **short** | **broad, wide** | **narrow** | **labyrinthine** *the labyrinthine corridors of the ministry building* | **brightly-lit** | **badly-lit, dark, darkened, dim, gloomy, ill-lit** | **chilly, dank, draughty** | **bare, blank, featureless** | **deserted, empty** | **carpeted, lino-covered, marble-floored, stone, stone-flagged, tiled** | **picture-lined** | **white-walled, etc.** | **hospital, hotel, school** | **access** | **land, peace** *(both figurative) UN troops will secure the land corridor so that food supplies can reach the trapped civilians.*
- VERB + CORRIDOR **line** *Portraits line the corridors of the palace.*
- CORRIDOR + VERB **lead** *Narrow corridors lead off from the main hallway.* | **run along/down sth** *The corridor runs down the middle of the building.* | **link sth** *The corridor links the old part of the hospital with the new.*
- CORRIDOR + NOUN **wall**
- PREP. **along a/the ~, at/to the end of a/the ~, down a/the ~** *The office is just down the corridor on the left.* **in a/the ~** *I put my head down as I passed him in the corridor.*
- PHRASES **the corridors of power** *(figurative) She was a minister with considerable influence in the corridors of power.* **a labyrinth/maze of corridors** *She led us through a maze of hotel corridors to our room.*

corrode *verb*

- PHRASES **be badly corroded** *If the pipe is badly corroded, it should be replaced.*

corrosion *noun*

- VERB + CORROSION **cause** | **prevent** | **suffer from** *a building whose structure is suffering from corrosion*
- PHRASES **signs of corrosion**

corrosive *adj.*

- VERBS **be**
- ADV. **highly, strongly, very** *Many highly corrosive substances are used in the nuclear industry.*

corrupt *adj.*

- VERBS **be** | **become**
- ADV. **thoroughly, totally** *The whole regime is thoroughly corrupt.* | **notoriously** *one of the most notoriously corrupt city councils* | **morally, politically**

corruption *noun*

- ADJ. **gross, massive, serious** | **petty** | **endemic, rampant, rife, widespread** *Corruption was rife before the election.* | **high-level** | **alleged** | **financial, moral, political** | **official** | **government, police**
- QUANT. **case**

- VERB + CORRUPTION **attack, combat, curb, eliminate, fight, root out, stem, tackle** *He strongly attacked corruption and favouritism in the government.* ◊ *This police unit was established to fight corruption.* | **be involved in**
- CORRUPTION + NOUN **scandal** *She was brought down by a corruption scandal.* | **allegation** *The corruption allegations proved false.* | **investigation**
- PREP. ~**among** *corruption among high-ranking government officials*
- PHRASES **accusations/allegations of corruption, bribery and corruption**
⇨ Note at CRIME

cosmetic *noun* (usually **cosmetics**)

- ADJ. **expensive** | **cheap**
- VERB + COSMETIC **use, wear** | **apply, put on**
- COSMETIC + NOUN **business, company, industry**

cosmetic *adj.*

- VERBS **be**
- ADV. **merely, purely** *Opponents described the reforms as a purely cosmetic exercise.* | **largely**

cosmopolitan *adj.*

- VERBS **be**
- ADV. **distinctly, truly, very**

cost *noun*

1 money needed to buy sth
- ADJ. **considerable, enormous, great, high, huge, prohibitive** *The high cost of energy is a problem for consumers.* ◊ *The cost of repairs would be prohibitive.* | **low** | **escalating, rising** | **basic** | **full, overall, total** *You will have to bear the full cost of the building work.* | **additional, extra** *She was unwilling to pay the extra cost to get a room to herself.* | **average** *A total of 3.6 million tickets at an average cost of $58 are available for the Games.* | **gross, net** | **estimated** | **budgeted** | **likely, potential** | **real** | **annual, monthly, etc.** | **replacement** *What is the current replacement cost of these assets?* | **capital, start-up** *(business) The capital cost of these projects (= what it costs to set them up) is some $100 million—then there'll be the operating costs.* | **marginal** *(business) Competition will drive the price down near to the marginal cost (= the cost of the labour and materials to produce the product).* | **unit** *(business) (= the cost of producing one item)* | **fixed, variable** *(business) Fixed costs include rent.* | **direct, indirect**
- VERB + COST **bear, cover, meet, pay** *Allow £15 per day to cover the cost of meals.* ◊ *MPs receive allowances to meet the cost of travel.* | **increase, push up** *Inflation is pushing up the cost of living beyond our reach.* | **bring down, cut, lower, reduce** | **keep down** | **estimate, put** *I would put the cost of a new employee at £30 000 a year.* | **calculate, work out** | **reimburse**
- COST + VERB **escalate, go up, increase, rise** *The cost of dental treatment is increasing.* | **fall, go down**
- COST + NOUN **reduction, savings** *the pursuit of cost reduction* | **overrun** *There were cost overruns on each project.* | **base** *It is essential that we operate with the lowest possible cost base and most efficient facilities.*
- PREP. **at a ~ of** *A new computer system has been installed at a cost of £80 000.* | ~**to** *The cost to the government will be quite high.*
- PHRASES **an increase/a reduction in cost, at no extra cost** *The hotel offers tea and coffee at no extra cost.* **cost of living** *The cost of living has risen sharply in the last year.*

2 costs money needed to run a business/home, etc.
- ADJ. **considerable, enormous, great, high, huge** | **low** | **escalating, rising** *We have had to raise our prices because of rising costs.* | **administration/administrative,**

fuel, labour, operating, production, (research and) development, running, transport, travel
- VERB + COSTS **incur** *The corporation will pay all costs and expenses incurred with its written consent.* | **pay** | **increase** | **bring down, cut, lower, reduce** *The company has to find ways of cutting costs.* | **keep down** *The use of cheap labour helped to keep costs down.* | **cover** *We're hoping that we'll at least cover costs at the conference.*
- COSTS + VERB **be associated, be involved** *the costs associated with buying and selling property* | **escalate, rise**

3 effort/loss/damage to achieve sth
- ADJ. **considerable, enormous, great, heavy, huge** *They advanced a few hundred metres, but at a heavy cost in life.* | **dreadful, terrible** *the terrible cost of the war in death and suffering* | **real** | **environmental, financial, human, personal, political, social** *the environmental cost of nuclear power*
- VERB + COST **outweigh** *Do the benefits outweigh the costs?* | **count** *The town is now counting the cost of its failure to provide adequate flood protection.*
- PREP. **at (a)~(to)** *The raid was foiled, but at a cost: an injured officer who was lucky to escape with his life.* ◇ *He worked non-stop for three months, at considerable cost to his health.* **at the~of** *She saved him from the fire but at the cost of her own life.* | **~ in** *I felt a need to please people, whatever the cost in time and energy.*
- PHRASES **at all costs/at any cost** *You must stop the press finding out at all costs* (= whatever it takes to achieve this). **to your cost** *He's a ruthless businessman, as I know to my cost* (= I know from my own bad experience).

4 costs in a court case
- ADJ. **legal**
- VERB + COST **incur** *Both sides incurred costs of over £50 000.* | **pay** *He was fined £200 and ordered to pay costs.* | **be awarded** *If you win your case you will normally be awarded costs.*

cost *verb*

- ADV. **fully, properly** *The project has not been properly costed yet.*
- PREP. **at** *The programme was costed at £6 million.*

costly *adj.*

- VERBS **be, prove**
- ADV. **enormously, exceptionally, excessively, extremely, very** | **increasingly** | **fairly, pretty, quite, rather** | **potentially** | **relatively**
- PREP. **for** *The six-month delay will be costly for the company.* **in** *This process is costly in computer time.* **in terms of** *These teaching methods are too costly in terms of staff resources.* **to** *These measures could be costly to employers.*

costume *noun*

- ADJ. **full** *For the dress rehearsal, the cast will be in full costume.* | **colourful, elaborate, lavish** | **national, traditional** | **period** | **eighteenth-century, Victorian, etc.** | **clown, fairy, etc.**
- VERB + COSTUME **be dressed in, dress in, have on, wear** *He had a cowboy costume on.*
- COSTUME + NOUN **design** | **designer** | **drama** *The film is a costume drama based on a 19th-century novel.* | **change** *The main character had five costume changes.*
- PREP. **in~** *The battle was re-enacted by actors in period costume.*

cottage *noun*

- ADJ. **humble, little, small, tiny** | **charming, lovely, picturesque, pretty** | **country, rural** | **lonely** | **empty, unoccupied** | **derelict, run-down** | **half-timbered, thatched, thatch-roofed** | **detached, terraced, three-**

bed, three-bedroom, three-bedroomed, three-room, etc. | **rented** | **farm, estate, tied** (= owned by a farmer and rented to one of his/her workers) *They lived in a tied cottage on the estate.* | **holiday, summer, weekend** | **retirement** | **guest** *They put us up in a guest cottage next to their house.*
- VERB + COTTAGE **have, own** *It was her dream to have a little cottage in the country* | **live in, stay in** *We stayed in a cottage on a farm.* | **rent, take** *We rented a holiday cottage for a week.* | **let** | **buy** | **sell**
- COTTAGE + NOUN **home** | **garden**
- PREP. **in a/the~**

cotton *noun*

- ADJ. **pure** *a pure cotton T-shirt* | **light, thin** *shivering in her thin cotton nightdress* | **fine** | **rough** | **raw** | **printed** | **mercerized** | **sewing**
- QUANT. **reel** (= of cotton thread) | **bale, bolt** (= both of fabric)
- VERB + COTTON **grow** | **pick**
- COTTON + NOUN **thread** | **bud, wool** | **field, plantation** | **industry, manufacturing** | **mill** | **manufacturer** | **reel**

couch *noun*

- ADJ. **comfortable** | **wide** | **psychiatrist's** *She spends several hours a week on the psychiatrist's couch.*
- VERB + COUCH **lie (down) on, recline on, sink back on, sink into, sit (down) on, sprawl on, stretch (out) on** *They sat down on the wide couch.* | **get up from, rise from, slide off, swing your legs/yourself off**
- PREP. **on a/the~** *He slept on the couch.*
- COUCH + NOUN **potato** (*figurative*) (= sb who spends all their time sitting on a couch) *He's turned into a real couch potato since he subscribed to the sports channel.*

cough *noun*

- ADJ. **little, polite, slight** *The butler gave a little cough to announce his presence.* | **violent** | **bad, nasty** | **chesty, croupy** | **barking, dry, hacking, racking, rasping** | **persistent** | **smoker's** *He had a smoker's cough and nicotine-yellowed fingers.*
- VERB + COUGH **give** *He gave a slight, apologetic cough and said, 'Excuse me.'* | **have, suffer from** | **catch, develop, get**
- COUGH + NOUN **medicine, mixture, sweet**
- ⇨ Special page at ILLNESS

cough *verb*

- ADV. **a bit, a little, slightly** | **apologetically, discreetly, nervously, politely** | **loudly, violently** | **up** *He vomited and began coughing up blood.*
- PHRASES **cough and splutter** *The whisky made her cough and splutter.* **a coughing fit** *He had a coughing fit and couldn't speak for a few moments.* **cough into life** (*figurative*) *The old engine coughed into life.*

council *noun*

1 local government
- ADJ. **local** | **metropolitan, rural, urban** | **borough, city, community, county, district, municipal, parish, provincial, regional, town** | **elected**
- VERB + COUNCIL **elect** | **control** *Many county councils are now controlled by the Conservatives.* | **apply to** *Students should apply to their local council for a grant.*
- COUNCIL + NOUN **elections** | **member** | **meeting** | **chamber** | **tax**
- PREP. **on a/the~** *She's on the borough council.*
- PHRASES **a seat on a council** *Our party won the majority of seats on the city councils.*

2 group chosen to give advice, money, etc.

- ADJ. **advisory, funding, research | arts, sports**
- VERB + COUNCIL **create, establish, form, found, set up, start | apply to** *As a struggling young composer she applied to the Scottish Arts Council for a grant.*
- COUNCIL + VERB **award sb sth, give sb sth** *In Britain, the Arts Council gives grants to theatres.*
- COUNCIL + NOUN **member**
- PREP. **~ for** *setting up a new council for the arts*
⇨ Note at ORGANIZATION

councillor *noun*

- ADJ. **borough, city, county, district, local, parish, town | Conservative, Labour, Liberal Democrat, Tory,** etc. **| former | newly-elected**
- VERB + COUNCILLOR **elect sb (as)**
- PHRASES **the office of councillor**

counsel *noun*

1 advice
- ADJ. **good, wise**
- VERB + COUNSEL **give (sb), offer (sb) | accept, follow, get, listen to, take** *Listen to the counsel of your elders.*
- COUNSEL + VERB **prevail** *In the end, wiser counsels prevailed.*
- PREP. **~ on** *He is there to give you counsel on all matters.*
- PHRASES **a counsel of despair** (= advice not to try to do sth because it is too difficult), **a counsel of perfection** (= advice that is good but difficult or impossible to follow)

2 lawyer
- ADJ. **legal** *They were denied legal counsel or the right to call witnesses in their defence.* **| chief, senior | junior | leading** *The accused was represented by a leading counsel.* **| Crown, prosecuting/prosecution** *The witness was cross-examined by the prosecuting counsel.* **| defence/defending | King's/Queen's**
- VERB + COUNSEL **appoint | brief, instruct** *My solicitor will brief the senior counsel.*
- COUNSEL + VERB **represent sb | cross-examine sb, question sb | argue sth, claim sth, say sth, state sth, submit sth** *His counsel argued that he had not intended to harm the women.*
- PHRASES **counsel for the appellant/defendant/plaintiff/respondent, counsel for the defence/prosecution** *to be questioned by the counsel for the prosecution*

counselling *noun*

- ADJ. **group, individual | professional | proper | abortion, bereavement, business, career, debt, family, marriage guidance, retirement, stress**
- VERB + COUNSELLING **give sb, offer (sb), provide (sb with) | have, receive | be in need of, need** *Many of the victims of the tragedy still need counselling.* **| seek**
- COUNSELLING + NOUN **service** *the new student counselling and guidance service* **| session | skills**
- PREP. **~ for** *counselling for parents and children* ◇ *counselling for depression*

counsellor *noun*

- ADJ. **accredited, professional, trained | career, debt, marriage guidance, student**
- VERB + COUNSELLOR **see, talk to** *He talked to a counsellor about his marriage difficulties.*
⇨ Note at JOB

count *noun*

1 act of counting
- VERB + COUNT **do, have** *We did a quick count of the children and there were none missing.*
- PREP. **for a ~** *Raise your leg and hold it there for a count of ten.*

- PHRASES **at the last/latest count** *At the last count she had 43 cats!*

2 measurement/total
- ADJ. **high | low | blood, calorie, cell, pollen, sperm** *The pollen count is very high in the spring.* **| body, head** *The movie depends on good dialogue rather than violence and a high body count.* ◇ *The firm now has a head count of around 70 staff.*
- VERB + COUNT **keep** *Keep a count of your calorie intake for one week.* **| lose** *I've lost count of the times I've heard that joke.*
- COUNT + VERB **go up, increase, rise | drop, go down** *Her white cell count has gone down again.*

counter *noun*

1 long flat surface
- ADJ. **bar, delicatessen/deli, display, post office, reception, shop | kitchen | glass, mahogany, wooden, zinc**
- VERB + COUNTER **serve at/behind, work at/behind** *Mary served behind the counter at Bacon's for a few hours a week.* **| wipe (down)** *The barman wiped down the counter in silence.*
- COUNTER + NOUN **staff** *post office counter staff*
- PREP. **across a/the~** *He pushed the money across the counter to her.* **at/behind a/the ~** *The assistant behind the counter gave a curt nod.* **on a/the ~** *all the goods on the counter*

2 action used to prevent sth
- ADJ. **effective**
- PREP. **~ to** *The government's programme should be an effective counter to unemployment.*

counter-attack *noun*

- ADJ. **strong**
- VERB + COUNTER-ATTACK **launch, mount**
- PREP. **~ against** *The soldiers mounted a strong counterattack against the rebels.*

counterpart *noun*

- ADJ. **direct** *the difficulty of translating terms with no direct counterpart in the other language* **| modern** *the modern counterparts of those medieval writers* **| female, male** *Women soldiers will join their male counterparts at the army base.* **| older, younger | domestic, foreign | rural, urban | northern, southern,** etc. **| British, French,** etc.
- VERB + COUNTERPART **have** *British environmentalists have their counterparts in Europe.*

country *noun*

1 area of land with its own government
- ADJ. **beautiful, fascinating, great** *this great country of ours* **| hot, tropical | temperate | cold | foreign, overseas, strange** *It's difficult to live in a foreign country when you don't speak the language.* ◇ *students from overseas countries* ◇ *What must it be like, to grow old in a strange country?* **| home, native | adopted** *Many refugee servicemen gave their lives for their adopted country.* **| host** *The refugees do jobs that workers in the host country refuse to do.* **| neighbouring | distant, far, faraway | independent | occupied | free** *'It's a free country!' he shouted. 'I can do what I like.'* **| enemy, friendly | neutral, non-aligned | Arab, African,** etc. **| Eastern, Western,** etc. **| Anglophone, English-speaking,** etc. **| EU, NATO,** etc. **| member, non-member** *OECD member countries* **| developed, industrial/industrialized | developing, Third World, underdeveloped | advanced** *economically advanced countries* **| backward** *industrially backward countries* **| low-income, poor | affluent,**

rich | capitalist, communist, democratic, socialist | Catholic, Muslim, etc. | oil-exporting, oil-producing
- VERB + COUNTRY **govern, rule, run** *The country was ruled by a brutal dictatorship.* ◇ *the politicians who run the country* | **lead** *He accused the government of leading the country to disaster.* | **divide, split** *The issue of the single currency has divided the country.* | **flee, leave** *The former president has been forced to flee the country.* | **serve** | **love** *He loved his country deeply.* | **betray** | **play for, represent** *She represented her country at the Sydney Olympics.* | **tour, travel, visit** *He travelled the country on his motorbike.*
- COUNTRY + VERB **border sth** *countries bordering the Black Sea* | **export sth, import sth** *The country exports around 80% of its output.* | **agree sth, sign sth** *The two countries signed a basic treaty of cooperation.*
- PREP. **across a/the ~** *travelling across the country* **all over a/the ~** *They are holding special events all over the country.* **around/round a/the ~** *This is just one of 30 sites around the country.* **in a/the ~** *people who live in this country* **throughout a/the ~** *New schools are being built throughout the country.*
- PHRASES **country of origin** *All goods must be clearly labelled with their country of origin.* **a part of a country** *There will be rain in many parts of the country tomorrow.* **the country as a whole** *The rich benefited from the reforms, not the country as a whole.*

2 area of land with particular features
- ADJ. **desert, hill/hilly, mountain/mountainous, open, wooded** *The village is surrounded by miles and miles of open country.* | **rough, wild** | **farming** *This part of Africa is rich farming country.* | **hunting, walking** *superb walking country*
- QUANT. **stretch, tract** *a beautiful stretch of country* ◇ *Whole tracts of country, once fertile, have become arid.*

3 land away from towns/cities
- COUNTRY + NOUN **life | air | lane, road | area, district | town, village | cottage, estate, home, house, mansion, residence, retreat, seat | park | walk | boy, girl | gentleman, squire | dweller, folk, people**
- PREP. **across ~** *riding across country* **in the ~** *She lives in the country.*

countryside *noun*

- ADJ. **attractive, beautiful, delightful, glorious, lovely, lush, magnificent, picturesque, pleasant, spectacular, stunning, unspoilt, wonderful** *miles of unspoilt countryside* | **open** | **green, wooded** *a walk through the lush green countryside* | **flat | hilly, mountainous, rolling, rugged, undulating | wild | peaceful, quiet, tranquil | local, nearby, surrounding | native** *The feel for his native countryside comes through strongly in his photographs.* | **English, Kent, etc.**
- QUANT. **area, stretch, tract** *a delightful stretch of countryside* ◇ *vast tracts of countryside*
- VERB + COUNTRYSIDE **conserve, preserve, protect | destroy, ravage, ruin, spoil** *The countryside has been ravaged by pollution.* | **roam, wander (around/through)** *In the afternoons they roamed the countryside roundabout.*
- PREP. **in the ~** *living in the countryside* **surrounded by ~** *a small village surrounded by glorious countryside* **through (the) ~** *travelling through pleasant open countryside* | **~around** *the countryside around Oxford*

county *noun*

- ADJ. **border, coastal, rural** *the Welsh border counties* | **eastern, western, etc.** | **historic/historical** *the historic county of Westmorland* (= that no longer exists) | **home** *London and the home counties* (= the counties around London) | **native** *He was elected MP for his native county*

of Merioneth. | **neighbouring | dry** (= where it is illegal to sell alcohol)
- VERB + COUNTY **represent** *She represents the county in Parliament.*
- COUNTY + NOUN **boundary** *The river forms the county boundary.* | **town** *Trowbridge is the county town of Wiltshire* (= the town where the local government offices are). | **council, councillor | court | library | cricket | championship, match** (= in cricket)
- PREP. **in a/the ~** *people who live in this county*

coup *noun*

1 (*also* **coup d'état**) violent change of government
- ADJ. **abortive, attempted, failed, unsuccessful | successful | bloody | bloodless | army, military | palace, presidential** *He deposed his father in a palace coup in 1970.* | **communist | boardroom** *She lost her position in a boardroom coup* (= a sudden change of power among senior managers in a company).
- VERB + COUP **launch, mount, stage | foil, put down** *The coup was immediately put down and the plotters were shot.* | **plan, plot | lead | come to power in, seize power in** *He seized power in a military coup*
- COUP + NOUN **attempt, plot | leader, plotter**
- PREP. **~against** *an army coup against the president*

2 achievement
- ADJ. **big, brilliant, great, major, real, spectacular** *Winning that contract was her greatest coup.* | **diplomatic, financial, intelligence, propaganda, publicity**
- VERB + COUP **pull off** *He managed to pull off a major diplomatic coup.*

couple *noun*

- ADJ. **beautiful, handsome, lovely | elderly, middle-aged, retired, teenage, young | bridal, honeymoon, married, newly-married, newly-wed** *The bridal couple stood up for the first dance.* ◇ *The hotel was full of honeymoon couples.* | **cohabiting, unmarried | heterosexual | gay, homosexual, lesbian, same-sex | childless, infertile** *childless couples seeking to adopt*
- VERB + COUPLE **make** *They make a beautiful couple.*
- PHRASES **the happy couple** (= the bride and groom) *We stood and drank a toast to the happy couple.*

coupon *noun*

- ADJ. **valid** *This coupon is valid until 31 January.* | **money-off | entry** *To enter the competition, fill in the entry coupon on page 6.* | **clothing, petrol, etc.**
- VERB + COUPON **collect, save** *She had saved enough coupons to get a free flight.* | **complete, fill in | post, return, send (off)** *Cut out and return this coupon to claim your free holiday.*

courage *noun*

- ADJ. **considerable, great, outstanding, tremendous | moral, physical** *Caring for elderly relatives requires considerable moral courage.*
- VERB + COURAGE **require, take** *It takes courage to sing in public.* | **have** *I didn't have the courage to tell him.* | **show | find, pluck up** *I finally plucked up enough courage to speak to Rachel.*

courageous *adj.*

- VERBS **be, seem**
- ADV. **exceptionally, extraordinarily, extremely, highly, incredibly, tremendously, very | quite, rather**

courier *noun*

- ADJ. **diplomatic | drug | cycle, motorcycle**
- VERB + COURIER **act as** *He has admitted to acting as a*

drug courier. | **send sth by** *Urgent deliveries of medicine may be sent by motorcycle courier.*
⇨ Note at JOB

course noun

1 complete series of lessons/studies
- ADJ. **full-time, part-time** | **one-year, two-year, etc.** | **day, evening** | **crash, intensive** | **advanced, intermediate, etc.** | **foundation, introductory** | **refresher** | **academic** | **graduate, postgraduate, undergraduate** | **degree, diploma, honours** *a joint honours course in French and Russian* | **correspondence, external, sandwich** | **induction** | **training, vocational**
- VERB + COURSE **do, take** *He took a crash course in Italian.* | **enrol on, join, sign up for** | **withdraw from** *She withdrew from the course because of illness.* | **teach** | **offer, run** *The school runs courses all year round.* | **complete** *It took him five years to complete the course.* | **pass** | **fail**
- COURSE + VERB **run** *The course runs from 10–15 May.*
- PREP. **~ in** *a course in applied linguistics* **~ on** *a course on the development of capitalism*

2 route/direction
- VERB + COURSE **alter, change** *The boat altered course during the storm.* | **chart, plot, set** *We set course for Malta.* | **be blown off** | **follow** *The path follows the course of the river.*
- PREP. **off ~** *We're a long way off course* **on ~** *We're on course for our destination.*
- PHRASES **on a collision course** *The two planes were on a collision course.*

3 (*also* **course of action**)
- ADJ. **best, better**
- VERB + COURSE **adopt, follow, pursue, take** *It was the best course of action to take in the circumstances.*
- COURSE + VERB **be open to sb** *It was the only course open to him.*

4 development of sth over a period of time
- VERB + COURSE **change** *an event that changed the course of his life* | **follow, run, take** *Her career followed a similar course to her sister's.* ◇ *We could do nothing but let the disease run its course.*
- PREP. **during the ~ of** *during the course of the war* **in the ~ of** *In the course of time, I began to understand.*
- PHRASES **the course of history** *This was an event that changed the course of history.* **in due course** (= at the appropriate time; eventually), **in the normal/ordinary course of events** *In the normal course of events, you should get a reply by Monday.* **let nature take its course** *When the dog responded so badly to the treatment, we decided to let nature take its course* (= stop treating it and let it die naturally).

5 part of a meal
- ADJ. **main** | **first, second, etc.**
- PREP. **for a/the ~** *We had chicken for our main course.*
- PHRASES **a two-/three-course, etc. meal**

6 in sport/a race
- ADJ. **golf, obstacle, race**
- VERB + COURSE **complete** *Only ten yachts completed the course.*

7 series of medical treatments
- VERB + COURSE **give sb, put sb on** *She's been put on a course of injections.* | **prescribe (sb)** | **take**
- PREP. **~ of** *a course of antibiotics*

court noun

1 law
- ADJ. **high** *This is the highest court in the land.* | **appeal, civil, crown, high, juvenile, magistrates, military** *They took their case to the appeal court.* | **supreme** | **county, federal, etc.** | **European, French, etc.**
- VERB + COURT **go to, take sb/sth to** *We are prepared to go to court to get our compensation.* ◇ *Their neighbours took them to court.* | **come to, get to, go to** *The case should not be allowed to go to court.* | **bring sth to** *There wasn't enough evidence to bring the case to court.* | **settle sth out of** *The dispute was settled out of court.* | **appear before, appear in, attend** *She is too young to appear before the court.* ◇ *He will appear in court tomorrow charged with the murder.* | **preside over** *The court was presided over by Judge Owen.*
- COURT + VERB **hear sth** *The court heard how the mother had beaten the 11-year-old boy.* | **acquit sb, clear sb** *The court acquitted Reece of the murder of his wife.* | **dismiss sth, quash sth** *The court dismissed the appeal.* ◇ *The guilty verdict was quashed by the appeal court.* | **uphold sth** *The court upheld the plaintiff's claim of unfair dismissal.* | **hold sth, order sth, rule sth** *The court held that she was entitled to receive compensation.*
- COURT + NOUN **action, case, proceedings** | **hearing, trial** | **injunction, order, summons** *She tried to get a court order to prevent him from coming near her.* ◇ *He received a court summons for non-payment of tax.* | **decision, ruling** | **appearance** *Divorce no longer requires a court appearance.* | **battle** *They could now face a court battle for compensation.* | **bailiff, clerk, judge, official, registrar, staff, usher** *She was appointed a high court judge in 1998.* | **procedure, process** | **system** | **building**
- PREP. **at ~** *He was found guilty at Swindon Crown Court.* **before a/the ~** *The case is now before the court.* **in ~** *Relatives of the dead girl were in court.*
- PHRASES **contempt of court** *He was charged with contempt of court after shouting at a witness.* **a court of appeal** *The case will be heard by the court of appeal next month.* **a court of law** *I don't think that argument would stand up in a court of law.* **a ward of court** *The child was made a ward of court when her parents were jailed.*

2 for sport
- ADJ. **basketball, squash, tennis, etc.** | **clay, grass, hard** *Do you prefer playing tennis on grass courts or hard courts?*
- PREP. **off (the) ~** *Off court she is just as aggressive as she is on the court.* **on (the) ~** *The players have been on court for an hour.*

3 kings/queens
- ADJ. **royal**
- COURT + NOUN **circles** *Mozart quickly became a favourite in court circles.*
- PREP. **at (a/the) ~** *life at the court of Charles I* ◇ *life at court*

court verb

- ADV. **assiduously** *He spent three months assiduously courting a newspaper editor.*

courteous adj.

- VERBS **be, seem**
- ADV. **extremely, very** | **entirely, perfectly** | **always, invariably, unfailingly** *She was unfailingly courteous and helpful.* | **naturally**
- PREP. **to** *He was perfectly courteous to me.*

courtesy noun

- ADJ. **great, unfailing, utmost** | **common** *It's common courtesy to warn your neighbours if your children are going to have a party.* | **exaggerated** *He apologized with exaggerated courtesy.*
- VERB + COURTESY **do sb, have, show, treat sb with** *She might have done me the courtesy of replying to my letter.* ◇ *You could at least have had the courtesy to let me know.*
- PREP. **with ~** *He listened to all the complaints with great courtesy.* | **~ to** *her unfailing courtesy to everyone*

● PHRASES **a matter of courtesy** *It's a matter of courtesy to write and thank people after a party.*

court martial *noun*

● VERB + COURT MARTIAL **order** *The general ordered an immediate court martial.* | **hold** | **face**
● PREP. **at a/the ~** *The officer was convicted of desertion at a court martial.* **by ~** *He was tried by court martial.*

courtship *noun*

● ADJ. **long** | **brief, whirlwind** *After a whirlwind courtship, they married and went to live in Bath.*
● VERB + COURTSHIP **conduct** *Because of the war they were obliged to conduct their courtship by post.*
● COURTSHIP + NOUN **display, ritual** *the elaborate courtship display of the pigeon*
● PREP. **during a/the ~** *They went there together during their courtship.*

courtyard *noun*

● ADJ. **central, inner, interior, internal** | **outer** | **enclosed, walled** | **open** | **cobbled, paved**
● VERB + COURTYARD **surround** *The courtyard is surrounded on three sides by stables.*
● PREP. **around a/the ~** *The hotel is built around a paved central courtyard.* **in a/the ~** *sitting in the inner courtyard of the college*

cousin *noun*

● ADJ. **first** (= the child of the brother or sister of one of your parents), **second** (= the child of a cousin of one of your parents) | **distant, remote** | **close** *(figurative) These pigs are close cousins of the wild hog.* | **female, male** | **long-lost** *Completely out of the blue, she got a letter from her long-lost cousin in New York.*
● PHRASES **cousin once, twice, etc. removed** *She's my first cousin once removed* (= the daughter of my cousin).

cover *noun*

1 sth put on/over sth
● ADJ. **loose** *a sofa with a loose cover* | **protective** | **removable** | **dust** *We spread dust covers over the furniture while the builders were in.* | **cushion, duvet, mattress, seat** | **manhole**
● VERB + COVER **put on** | **take off**
● PREP. **~ for** *a cover for the swimming pool*

2 sth that is over sth
● ADJ. **thick** *a thick cover of snow* | **cloud, snow** *We descended into Heathrow through thick cloud cover.* | **forest, ground** *plants that provide good ground cover*

3 outside of a book/magazine
● ADJ. **back, front** | **hard, soft** | **book, magazine**
● COVER + NOUN **design** | **story** | **girl**
● PREP. **on a/the ~** *There's a picture of the author on the back cover.*

4 the covers blankets, sheets, etc.
● ADJ. **bed**
● VERB + COVERS **get under** | **pull up** | **pull back, throw back** *She threw back the covers and got out of bed.*
● PREP. **under the ~**

5 insurance against sth
● ADJ. **comprehensive, full** | **wide** *This company provides wider cover.* | **standard** | **additional** | **insurance** | **fire, health, indemnity, life, medical**
● VERB + COVER **have** | **give sb, provide (sb with)**
● PREP. **~ against** *cover against accidental damage* **~ for** *cover for contents*

6 shelter/protection from the weather/damage, etc.
● ADJ. **air** *The RAF provided air cover for the attack.*
● VERB + COVER **dive for, run for, take** *We ran for cover*

as it started to rain. | **seek** | **find** | **give sb, provide (sb with)** | **break** (= leave) *The deer broke cover as the hunters approached.*
● PREP. **under ~** *All the seats are under cover.* | **under ~ of** *We attacked at night, under cover of darkness.* | **~ from** *They sought cover from the wind.*

7 sth that hides the real nature of sth
● ADJ. **perfect** | **diplomatic** *spies operating under diplomatic cover*
● VERB + COVER **blow** (= reveal) *He realized his cover had been blown*
● PREP. **~ for** *The club is a cover for various criminal activities.*

cover *verb*

1 put sth over sth to hide/protect it
● ADV. **completely** | **loosely** | **up** *She used dried leaves and twigs to cover up the hole.*
● VERB + COVER **try to** *She tried to cover her face with her hands.* ◇ *(figurative) He tried to cover his embarrassment by starting to rub his hands together.* | **use sth to**
● PREP. **with** *He covered the body with a cloth.*

2 form a layer on sth
● ADV. **completely**
● PREP. **in** *The cars were all covered in snow.* **with** *The children were completely covered with mud.*

3 money/tax/insurance
● ADV. **barely, hardly** *The payments he gets barely cover his expenses.*
● VERB + COVER **help (to)** | **be intended to** | **be extended to** *VAT may be extended to cover books.*
● PREP. **against** *This policy should cover you against accidental injury.* **for** *a policy that covers you for fire and theft*

coverage *noun*

● ADJ. **considerable, extensive, massive** *There's been massive television coverage of the World Cup.* | **comprehensive, full** | **detailed, in-depth** | **wide, widespread** | **national, international, worldwide** | **limited** | **media, news, newspaper, press, radio, television/TV** *The television company was given a special award for its news coverage.* | **live** *There's live coverage of the match on BBC1.* | **exclusive**
● VERB + COVERAGE **give sth, provide (sth with)** *The minister's resignation was given widespread coverage.* | **attract, get, have, receive** *The wedding had wide press coverage.*
● COVERAGE + VERB **focus on sth** *Media coverage of the march focused on the few fights that broke out.*

covered *adj.*

● VERBS **be** | **become** | **remain** | **leave sb/sth** *The car sped past, leaving us covered in mud.*
● ADV. **well** *Make sure all cooked meat is well covered.* | **absolutely, completely, entirely, totally** | **closely, densely, thickly** *four sheets of paper closely covered in unfamiliar handwriting* | **evenly** | **sparsely, thinly** *the ground was sparsely covered with grass.* | **permanently, temporarily** *60% of the land is permanently covered in ice.* | **usually**
● PREP. **by** *Each body was covered by a blanket.* **in** *I was covered in blood.* **with** *The path was now completely covered with thick snow.*
● PHRASES **covered from head to foot/toe** *He crawled out, covered from head to foot in soot.*

cover-up *noun*

● ADJ. **big, major** | **government**
● VERB + COVER-UP **be engaged in, be implicated in,**

be involved in *Military leaders were involved in a major cover-up.* | **accuse sb of**
• PREP. **~ by** *cover-ups by the police* **~ over** *evidence of a cover-up over arms sales*
• PHRASES **allegations/claims of a cover-up**

cow *noun*

• ADJ. **beef** | **dairy, milch** (*often figurative*) | **sacred** (*often figurative*) *the sacred cow of free market economics*
• QUANT. **herd**
• VERB + COW **breed** | **milk**
• COW + VERB **low, moo** | **chew the cud, graze** | **calve** *The cow had difficulties calving.*
• COW + NOUN **byre, shed** (also **cowshed**) | **dung, manure, muck, pat** (also **cowpat**) | **bell**
• PHRASES **a breed of cow**

coward *noun*

• VERB + COWARD **brand sb, call sb, label sb** *He was branded a coward in some newspapers.*

cowardice *noun*

• ADJ. **moral** *It is an act of moral cowardice for a society to neglect its poor.*
• VERB + COWARDICE **display, show** | **accuse sb of**
• PHRASES **an act of cowardice, cowardice in the face of the enemy** *Any soldier displaying cowardice in the face of the enemy was shot.*

coy *adj.*

1 pretending to be shy
• VERBS **be** | **go**
• ADV. **all, extremely, very** *He went all coy when I mentioned her name.* | **a bit, a little, rather** *She gave him a rather coy look.*

2 unwilling to say sth directly
• VERBS **be** | **remain**
• ADV. **extremely, very** | **a little, rather** *Alicia was a little coy about how much the new dress had cost.* | **uncharacteristically**
• PREP. **about**

crack *noun*

1 line on the surface of sth where it has broken
• ADJ. **big, deep, huge, large, long, serious** | **short, small** | **fine, hairline, thin**
• CRACK + VERB **appear** | **develop, spread** | **run** *A fine crack ran up the wall.*

2 narrow opening
• ADJ. **narrow, small, tiny** | **wide**
• VERB + CRACK **fill** *We filled the cracks in the plaster before hanging the wallpaper.*
• CRACK + VERB **appear** *Wide cracks appeared in the ground during the drought.* | **open up, widen**
• PREP. **~ in** *There's a crack in the fence big enough to look through.*
• PHRASES **a crack of light** *a tiny crack of light under the door* **open a door/window a crack** *Could you open the window just a crack?*

3 sudden loud sound
• ADJ. **loud, sharp**
• VERB + CRACK **give, let out** *He gave a crack of laughter.* | **hear**
• PREP. **with a ~** *The chandelier hit the floor with a crack.* | **~ of**
• PHRASES **the crack of a whip, a crack of thunder**
⇨ Note at SOUND

crack *verb*

1 break
• ADV. **badly** *The dish had cracked quite badly.* | **slightly**

2 become mentally ill
• ADV. **completely** | **finally** *The stresses of her job became too great and she finally cracked.* | **up** *He thought he'd never get through the ordeal without cracking up.*
• PHRASES **crack under the pressure/strain, show signs of cracking** *He is under a lot of pressure but is showing no signs of cracking.*

PHRASAL VERB
crack down
• ADV. **hard**
• PREP. **on** *to crack down hard on crime*

crackdown *noun*

• ADJ. **bloody, violent** | **army, government, military, police**
• VERB + CRACKDOWN **promise, threaten** | **call for, demand, order** *The government has ordered a crackdown on truancy.* | **have, launch, mount**
• PREP. **~ on** *They're having a crackdown on private phone calls from the office.*

cradle *verb*

• ADV. **gently** *He picked the child up and gently cradled him in his arms.*
• PREP. **against** *She sat with the child cradled against her.*

craft *noun*

1 activity needing skill with your hands
• ADJ. **skilled** *Sheep shearing is a highly skilled craft.* | **ancient, traditional** | **country, local, rural**
• VERB + CRAFT **practise** *The men practised various traditional crafts, such as carving toys out of bone.*
• CRAFT + NOUN **activity, work** | **industry** | **worker** | **centre, exhibition, fair, shop, workshop** | **skill**
• PHRASES **art and craft** *Subjects taught include art and craft, drama, languages and maths.* **arts and crafts** *The gallery has major exhibitions of arts and crafts.*

2 all the skills needed for an activity
• VERB + CRAFT **learn, master, perfect** *It took her years to perfect her craft.*
• PHRASES **a master of your craft** *a carpenter who is a real master of his craft*

3 boat
• ADJ. **small** | **assault, fishing, landing, patrol, pleasure, river, sailing**

craftsman *noun*

• ADJ. **fine, good** | **master, skilled, trained** | **local** | **itinerant, travelling** | **independent**

craftsmanship *noun*

• ADJ. **exquisite, fine, skilled, superb** *We admired the superb craftsmanship of the furniture.*
• PREP. **with ~** *bowls made with exquisite craftsmanship*
• PHRASES **standard of craftsmanship** *a very high standard of craftsmanship*

cramp *noun*

• ADJ. **agonizing, painful** | **sudden** *She had a sudden painful cramp in her left leg.* | **abdominal, stomach**
• QUANT. **attack** *I was suddenly seized by an attack of cramp.*
• VERB + CRAMP **have**

crash noun

1 sudden loud noise
- ADJ. **almighty, deafening, great, loud, thunderous | distant | sickening, terrible** *There was a sickening crash as her head hit the ground.*
- VERB + CRASH **hear**
- PREP. **with a~** *The plates fell to the floor with an almighty crash.* | **~of** *a distant crash of thunder*
- PHRASES **a crash of thunder, the crash of the waves**

2 car/plane, etc. accident
- ADJ. **horrific, major, serious** *a major air crash* | **fatal | head-on | high-speed | car, coach, helicopter, plane, train | air, motorway, rail, road**
- VERB + CRASH **cause**
- CRASH + VERB **happen, occur | involve sth** *a crash involving two cars and a lorry* | **kill sb | claim sth** *The crash claimed three lives.*
- CRASH + NOUN **victim | site | landing | barrier**
- PREP. **in a/the~** *He was killed in a train crash.*

3 business failure
- ADJ. **financial | bank, property, stock market** *the stock market crash of 1987*
- PREP. **~in** *a crash in share prices*

crate noun

- ADJ. **sealed | upturned** *The cat was sitting on an upturned crate.* | **beer, milk, orange | shipping** *Their possessions had all been packed into shipping crates.*
- QUANT. **pile, stack**
- VERB + CRATE **pile, stack** *They stacked the crates in the corner of the yard.* | **pack (sth in/into), unpack** *They packed the crates with books.* | **load, unload | ship** *a company specializing in shipping crates*
- CRATE + VERB **contain sth**
- PREP. **~of** *a crate of oranges*

crater noun

- ADJ. **deep, gaping, huge, large** *The blast blew a gaping crater in the road.* | **shallow, small | bomb, shell | meteor | volcanic | lunar**
- VERB + CRATER **blow, form, leave, make**
- PREP. **in a/the~**
- PHRASES **the edge/lip/side of a crater** *We peered over the lip of the crater into the volcano.*

craving noun

- ADJ. **desperate**
- VERB + CRAVING **feel, have** *He had a craving to see the world.* | **satisfy** *She skipped normal meals to satisfy her craving for chocolate and crisps.* | **curb, reduce**
- PREP. **~for** *a desperate craving for affection*

crawl noun

1 very slow speed
- ADJ. **slow**
- PREP. **at a~** *The traffic was moving at a slow crawl.*
- VERB + CRAWL **be down to** *The traffic on the motorway was down to a crawl.* **slow (down) to**

2 swimming stroke
⇨ Note at STROKE

crawl verb

- ADV. **slowly | about, along, around/round, away, back, forwards, through** *We spent an hour crawling around on our hands and knees looking for the key.*
- VERB + CRAWL **manage to** *As night fell, we managed to crawl back to our lines.* | **start to** *Has the baby started to crawl yet?*

- PREP. **across, along, into, over, out of, under, up** *There's an insect crawling up your leg!*
- PHRASES **crawl on (your) hands and knees**

crayon noun

- ADJ. **coloured | wax**
- QUANT. **box**
- VERB + CRAYON **colour sth in with, draw (sth) with, use** *She coloured the picture in with crayons.*
- CRAYON + NOUN **drawing**
- PREP. **in~** *The notice was written in crayon.*

craze noun

- ADJ. **latest, new | passing** *Is this interest in health foods just a passing craze?* | **dance, fashion, fitness, etc.**
- VERB + CRAZE **start** *The princess started a craze for huge earrings.*
- CRAZE + VERB **sweep (across/through) sth** *Doctors warned of the latest drug craze to sweep America.* | **hit sth** *It's the latest craze to hit San Francisco.*
- PREP. **~among** *the latest craze among children* **~for** *the craze for fashionable sports clothing*

crazy adj.

1 mad/wild
- VERBS **be, seem, sound | go** *I'd go crazy if I lived here.* | **drive sb** *The group's performance always drives the audience crazy.*
- ADV. **really | absolutely, completely, totally | a bit, half, a little, pretty, quite, slightly**
- PREP. **with** *We were crazy with excitement.*

2 very angry
- VERBS **be | go | drive sb** *The kids would answer back, and that drove her crazy.*
- ADV. **absolutely, completely**
- PREP. **at** *He was crazy at me for letting the goal in.*

creak noun

- ADJ. **loud | little**
- VERB + CREAK **give, let out** *The gate gave a loud creak as he pushed it open.* | **hear**
- PREP. **with a~** *The gate swung open with a creak.* | **~of**
- PHRASES **the creak of a floorboard/door**
⇨ Note at SOUND

creak verb

- ADV. **slightly**
- PREP. **under** *The chair creaked under his weight.*
- PHRASES **creak and groan** *The ice creaked and groaned underfoot.* **creak open** *The door creaked open an inch.*

cream noun

1 fatty part of milk
- ADJ. **clotted, thick, whipped | double, single | fresh | sour/soured | pouring, whipping**
- QUANT. **dollop** *She piled great dollops of cream onto her apple pie.*
- VERB + CREAM **beat, whip, whisk** *Whisk the cream and icing sugar together.* | **fill sth with, serve sth with, top sth with** *Fill the meringues with whipped cream.*
- CREAM + VERB **go off** *This cream's gone off!*
- CREAM + NOUN **bun, cake, cheese, sauce | tea** (= a meal of tea with scones with jam and cream)
- PHRASES **and/with cream** *We had strawberries and cream for pudding.*
⇨ Special page at FOOD

2 substance that you rub into your skin
- ADJ. **face, hand | day, night** *She was massaging night*

cream into her face and neck. | **antiseptic, barrier, cleansing, shaving, sun**
● VERB + CREAM **apply, massage, put on** *Put a little antiseptic cream on the grazed skin.*

creamy adj.

● VERBS **be, look, seem, taste** *Stir the mixture until it looks creamy.* ◇ *It tastes deliciously creamy.*
● ADV. **deliciously, very, wonderfully**
● PHRASES **creamy white** *creamy white flowers*

crease noun

1 untidy line/fold
● ADJ. **deep**
● VERB + CREASE **have** *She had lots of deep creases at the corners of her eyes.* | **iron out, remove, smooth (out)** *She smoothed the creases from the tablecloth.*
● PREP. ~**in** *There were a lot of creases in her skirt.*

2 neat line that is put onto fabric/paper
● ADJ. **knife-edge, sharp**
● PREP. ~**in** *a sharp crease in his trousers*

crease verb

● ADV. **badly, easily** *This material creases very easily.* | **a bit, slightly** *His shirt had creased a bit in the suitcase.*
● PHRASES **be/get creased** *Her clothes were badly creased.*

creation noun

● ADJ. **employment, job** | **wealth**
● VERB + CREATION **advocate, call for, propose, recommend, urge** *They recommended the creation of a new government agency to be responsible for the environment.* | **encourage, foster, support** | **allow for** *The new Act allows for the creation of vocational schools.* | **allow, enable** | **avoid, prevent** | **lead to**

creative adj.

● VERBS **be, feel** *I don't always feel creative.* | **become**
● ADV. **highly, really, very** *a highly creative artist* | **genuinely, truly** *genuinely creative thinking*

creativity noun

● ADJ. **great** | **artistic, musical**
● VERB + CREATIVITY **develop, encourage, stimulate** *A good teacher can encourage artistic creativity.* | **inhibit, stifle** *This rigid approach stifles creativity.*
● PREP. ~**in** *This exercise encourages creativity in the use of language.*
● PHRASES **scope for creativity** *My job does not give me much scope for creativity.*

creature noun

● ADJ. **living** *All living creatures need food.* | **primitive, simple** | **complex** | **intelligent** | **cold-blooded, warm-blooded** | **wild** *the wild creatures of the forest* | **social** *Dogs are more social creatures than cats.* | **solitary** | **night, nocturnal** | **aquatic, marine, sea, underwater, water** | **land-based** | **woodland** *Woodland creatures such as foxes and owls are increasingly common in towns.* | **ape-like, bat-like, etc.** | **little, small, tiny** *These timid little creatures exude a pungent smell when threatened.* | **helpless** *The newborn young are helpless creatures and easy prey for birds.* | **dangerous** | **furry** | **magnificent** *It is awesome to see these magnificent creatures in flight.* | **exotic, strange** *a strange creature from another planet* | **mythical** | **evil** *I dreamt of evil creatures who were trying to catch me.*

crèche noun

● VERB + CRÈCHE **establish, set up** | **have, offer, provide, run**
● CRÈCHE + NOUN **facilities** | **worker**
● PREP. **in a/the** ~ *Younger children can be left in the crèche.*

credentials noun

1 qualities/training/experience
● ADJ. **excellent, impeccable, impressive, perfect** | **academic, educational** | **diplomatic, political, scientific, etc.** | **democratic, green, socialist, etc.**
● VERB + CREDENTIALS **have** *He has perfect credentials to make an officer.* | **establish, prove** *City established their championship credentials with a 6–0 win.* | **emphasize, strengthen, underline**
● PREP. ~**as** *First, he had to establish his credentials as a researcher.* ~**for** *She had excellent credentials for the job.*

2 documents
● VERB + CREDENTIALS **present** | **check, examine**

credibility noun

● VERB + CREDIBILITY **carry, have** *The certificate has great credibility in France and Germany.* | **be lacking in, lack** | **gain, regain** *The government is desperate to regain credibility with the public.* | **lose** | **establish, give, lend** *Recommendations from two previous clients helped to establish her credibility.* ◇ *Funding from the World Bank lends credibility to the project.* | **restore** | **add, enhance** *The use of computers adds credibility to the forecasts.* ◇ *BBC backing for the scheme will enhance its credibility.* | **damage, destroy, undermine**
● CREDIBILITY + VERB **suffer** *The prime minister's credibility suffered in his handling of the crisis.*
● CREDIBILITY + NOUN **gap** *Newspapers were talking of a credibility gap between her policies and her achievements.* | **problem** *Athletics' anti-dope campaigners are faced with a credibility problem.*
● PREP. ~**among**, ~**as** *her credibility as a witness* | ~**for** *There is little credibility among scientists for the book's claims.*

credible adj.

● VERBS **appear, be, seem** | **become** | **make sth** | **find sth** *I'm not sure that I find her story credible.*
● ADV. **highly, very** | **completely, fully, quite** *You need imagination to make what you write fully credible.* | **barely, hardly, scarcely** *It seems barely credible that anyone could have walked so far in a day.*

credit noun

1 buy now—pay later; money borrowed/lent
● ADJ. **long-term, short-term** | **interest-free** | **foreign** | **bank** | **consumer, export, trade**
● VERB + CREDIT **have, use** *When poorer people use credit, mail order is the key source.* | **get, obtain** *If you don't have a regular income you may be unable to get credit.* | **extend, give sb, grant (sb), offer (sb)** *Most shops selling furniture or electrical goods will offer credit.* | **deny sb, refuse sb** *The bank refused further credit to the company.* | **arrange** | **expand** *We propose to expand credit in order to create demand.*
● CREDIT + NOUN **account, agreement, arrangement, facilities, system, terms** | **limit** *Your credit limit is now £2 000.* | **period** | **sale, transaction, transfer** | **rating, scoring, standing** *He has a bad credit rating (= seems unlikely to pay the money back).* | **risk** *He's a bad credit risk.* | **control, crunch, squeeze** | **institution, market, union** | **note** *If damaged items have to be returned, the manufacturer may issue a credit note.*
● PREP. **on** ~ *I bought it on credit.*

- PHRASES **a letter of credit** (= a letter from one bank to another that enables you to obtain money) *I have arranged for my branch to send a letter of credit to the branch nearest the hotel.*

2 money in a bank account
- ADJ. **direct** *I'm paid by direct credit into my bank account.*
- VERB + CREDIT **have** *I have three credits on my bank statement.*
- CREDIT + NOUN **balance** *a credit balance of £265*
- PREP. **in~** *My account is in credit.* | **~of** *a credit of £35*

3 praise/approval
- ADJ. **great | full | eternal, everlasting | due** *We should give due credit to all who helped make the event a success.*
- VERB + CREDIT **give sb | claim, get, receive, take** *Why should she get all the credit?* | **do sb**, **reflect** *Your concern does you credit.* ◇ *The success of the venture reflects great credit on the organizers.* | **deserve**
- PREP. **to sb's ~** *To her eternal credit, she gave them a home.* | **~for** *At least give him credit for trying.*
- PHRASES **give credit where credit is due**

4 the credits list of people who worked on a film, etc.
- ADJ. **opening | final | film**
- CREDIT + VERB **roll** *We left the cinema before the final credits began to roll.*

5 sb/sth that brings honour to sb/sth else
- ADJ. **great**
- PREP. **~to** *He's a great credit to the school.*

credit *verb*

1 put money in the bank
- PREP. **with** *The bank credited the oil company with £500 000.*
- PHRASES **credit sth to sb's account**

2 with an achievement/quality
- PREP. **with** *I credited you with a little more sense.*
- PHRASES **be credited as/with sth** *She is generally credited as having written over 50 novels.* **be credited to sb** *The work has been credited to a sixteenth century bishop.* **be generally/widely credited with sth** *He is widely credited with having started the Middle East peace process.*

3 believe
- VERB + CREDIT **can/could hardly/scarcely** *I could hardly credit it when she told me she was leaving.* | **be hard to** *I find what he says rather hard to credit.*

creditable *adj.*

- VERBS **be, seem | make sth**
- ADV. **highly, very** *She gave a highly creditable performance as the wicked queen.*

credit card *noun*

- ADJ. **valid** *Your credit card is no longer valid.*
- VERB + CREDIT CARD **pay by, use** *We paid by credit card.* | **accept, take** *Do you accept credit cards?* | **issue | put sth on** *I put the bill on my credit card.*
- CREDIT CARD + VERB **expire** *My credit card expires at the end of June.*
- CREDIT CARD + NOUN **details, number** *Can you give me your credit card number?*
- PREP. **on your~** *He ran up a huge bill on his credit card.*

creditor *noun*

- VERB + CREDITOR **pay (off), repay** *They agreed to repay their creditors over a period of three years.*

credulity *noun*

- VERB + CREDULITY **strain, stretch** *The plot of the novel stretches credulity to the limit.*

creed *noun*

- ADJ. **political, religious**
- VERB + CREED **adopt, embrace** *Other countries have adopted this political creed enthusiastically.* | **reject**

creep *verb*

- ADV. **quietly | slowly | stealthily | about, around, back, in, out, up** *I could hear someone creeping around downstairs.* ◇ *He crept up behind me.*
- PREP. **along** *He crept stealthily along the corridor.* **down, into** (figurative) *Suspicion crept into her voice.* **over** (figurative) *A feeling of dread crept over him.* **out of, up on** *The cat quietly crept up on the pigeon.* ◇ (figurative) *Fatigue was creeping up on her.*

creepy *adj.*

- VERBS **be, feel, look, seem** *It feels a bit creepy in here.* | **get** *It can get pretty creepy in the cellar at night.*
- ADV. **a bit, pretty, slightly**

crescendo *noun*

- ADJ. **deafening**
- VERB + CRESCENDO **reach, rise to** *The music reached a deafening crescendo.*

crest *noun*

- VERB + CREST **gain, reach** *We finally reached the crest of the ridge.*
- PREP. **on a/the~** *We stood on the crest of the hill.*

crew *noun*

- ADJ. **experienced | inexperienced, novice | emergency, skeleton | aircraft, bomber, lifeboat, ship's, submarine, tank, train | cabin, flight, ground, maintenance, support | ambulance, camera, demolition, film, fire, gun, production, road, stage, television, TV** *Fire crews were called to the scene.*
- CREW + NOUN **member**
- PREP. **in a/the~** *all the men and women in the crew*
- PHRASES **a member of the crew**

cricket *noun*

1 sport
- ADJ. **county, international, school, village | club, first-class | professional | championship, league, test, World Cup | one-day, four-day, etc. | limited-over(s) | Sunday | attacking** *The crowd loves to watch attacking cricket.*
- QUANT. **game**
- VERB + CRICKET **play | watch | follow**
- CRICKET + NOUN **game, match | championship, competition | field, ground, pitch | ball, bat | pavilion | captain, manager, team | club | enthusiast, fan, lover | season | tour | scene** *This game marks his comeback to the international cricket scene.* | **commentator | memorabilia** *an auction of cricket memorabilia*
⇨ Special page at SPORT

2 insect
- CRICKET + VERB **chirp** *The only sound was a cricket chirping.*

crime *noun*

1 illegal act
- ADJ. **appalling, awful, barbaric, barbarous, bloody, brutal, despicable, dreadful, grave, great, heinous, hor-**

> **NOTE**
> ## Crimes
>
> **be guilty of, commit~**
> *Two key witnesses at her trial committed perjury.*
> **accuse sb of, charge sb with~**
> *He has been accused of her murder.*
> **convict sb of, find sb guilty of~**
> *She was found guilty of high treason.*
> **acquit sb of~**
> *The engineer responsible for the collapse of the bridge was acquitted of manslaughter.*
> **admit, confess to, deny~**
> *All three men have denied assault.*
> *She admitted 33 assault charges.*
> **plead guilty/not guilty to~**
> *He pleaded guilty to a charge of gross indecency.*
> **investigate (sb for)~**
> *She is being investigated for suspected bribery.*
> **be suspected for/of~**
> *He was the least likely to be suspected of her murder.*
> **be/come under investigation for~**
> *She was the second minister to come under investigation for corruption.*
> **be wanted for~, be wanted on charges of~**
> *He was wanted on charges of espionage.*
> **solve** a case, crime, murder, robbery, theft
> *The police and the public must work together to solve the murder.*
> **arrest sb for~**
> *Jean was arrested for arson.*
> **be tried for, stand trial for~**
> *to stand trial for extortion*
> **~case/trial**
> *The nurse's murder trial continues.*
> **~charge**
> *The police agreed to drop the conspiracy charges against him.*
> **a charge/count of~**
> *The jury convicted her on two counts of theft.*

rible, **horrific, serious, terrible, vicious** *one of the most horrific crimes of recent times* ◇ *(figurative) Not returning phone calls is a grave crime in today's culture.* | **big, major** *the biggest crime since the Great Train Robbery* | **lesser, minor, petty** *He was charged with the lesser crime of possessing a forged bond, rather than actually forging it.* | **real** *She claimed that the real crime is that burglars and muggers usually get a light sentence.* | **violent** | **non-violent** | **perfect** *He boasted of having carried out the perfect crime.* | **notorious** *one of the most notorious crimes in British history* | **capital** (= for which the penalty is death) *After the reforms the only capital crimes were treason and murder.* | **indictable** | **alleged** *She never faced trial for her many alleged crimes.* | **unsolved** | **copycat** *the danger of copycat crimes in the wake of the shootings* | **motiveless** *an apparently motiveless crime* | **victimless** *Insider dealing has been called a victimless crime.* | **white-collar** | **drug-related** | **sex/sexual** | **war** | **political** | **terrorist**
● VERB + CRIME **carry out, commit** | **report** *Many crimes are never reported to the police.*
● CRIME + VERB **involve sth** *crimes involving firearms* | **be punishable by sth** *crimes punishable by death*
● PREP. **~against** *crimes against humanity*
● PHRASES **a crime of passion/violence, the scene of the crime** *No weapon was found at the scene of the crime.*

2 illegal activity in general
● ADJ. **serious** | **petty** | **violent** | **non-violent** | **recorded** | **unrecorded** | **growing, mounting, rising** | **drug-related** | **middle-class, working-class, etc.** |

white-collar *Corporate crime—committed by businesses—should not be confused with white-collar crime, which refers to the occupation of the perpetrator and may be directed against a business.* | **business, corporate** | **organized** | **juvenile, youth** | **international, local, regional** | **rural, urban** | **car, computer, property, street** *attempts to prevent hacking and computer crime* | **sex/sexual**
● VERB + CRIME **carry out, commit** | **combat, fight, tackle** | **beat, crack** *(informal) Police forces will exchange ideas on cracking crime.* | **deter, prevent, stop** | **control, cut, reduce** | **detect, investigate** *The public have a crucial role to play in detecting crime.* | **solve** | **punish** | **cause** | **be driven to, turn to** *He says that bored youngsters turn to crime.*
● CRIME + VERB **double, increase, rise**
● CRIME + NOUN **figures, level, rate, statistics** | **control, prevention** | **problem, wave** *the country's crime problem* | **squad** *a senior detective with the serious crime squad* | **syndicate** *leading members of an organized crime syndicate* | **fiction, novel, series, story** *the latest TV crime series* | **reporter, writer** *the newspaper's crime reporter* ◇ *a new short story by the popular crime writer*
● PHRASES **a crackdown on crime** *a crackdown on drug-related crime* **crime and disorder, crime and punishment, fear of crime** *Fear of crime imprisons many elderly people in their homes.* **an increase in crime, a life of crime** *Unemployed young people were likely to be tempted into a life of crime.* **sb's partner in crime, a victim of crime** *Victims of crime may be able to obtain compensation.*

criminal *noun*

● ADJ. **dangerous, violent** | **serious** | **habitual, hardened** | **professional** | **master** | **petty** | **convicted** | **known** *He has been associating with known criminals.* | **notorious** | **common** *She was treated like a common criminal.* | **white-collar** | **war** *He was tried as a war criminal.*
● VERB + CRIMINAL **catch** *I told him to pass the information to the police so they could catch the criminals.*

crimson *adj.*

1 red
● ADJ. **dark, deep, rich** *a beautiful deep crimson colour*
⇨ Special page at COLOUR

2 red in the face
● VERBS **be** | **blush, flush, go, turn** *He flushed crimson and began to shout angrily at Frank.*
● ADJ. **bright, deep** *He turned bright crimson.*
● PREP. **with** *She was crimson with rage.*

cripple *verb*

1 injure
● ADV. **for life, permanently** *As a child she contracted polio and was crippled for life.*
● PHRASES **be crippled with** *He's eighty and crippled with arthritis.* **leave sb crippled** *The disease left him crippled.*

2 damage
● ADV. **financially** *The industry has been financially crippled by these policies.*

crisis *noun*

● ADJ. **acute, grave, major, serious, severe, terrible, worst** *the worst economic crisis for fifty years* | **growing, mounting** | **impending, looming** | **international, national** | **constitutional, economic, financial, fiscal, political** | **cash, debt, energy, hostage, housing, oil, refugee** *the Third World debt crisis* | **family, personal** | **identity** | **mid-life**
● VERB + CRISIS **be faced with, be hit by, face, go through, have** *(informal)*, **suffer** *With competition from*

cheap imports, the British coal industry is facing a serious crisis. ◇ *He's having a mid-life crisis.* | **cause, create, lead to, precipitate, provoke, spark off** | **deal with, defuse, ease, handle, overcome, resolve, respond to, solve, tackle** *Union leaders are taking immediate steps to defuse the crisis.* ◇ *attempts to ease the town's housing crisis* | **survive, weather** | **avert, prevent** | **aggravate**

● CRISIS + VERB **arise** *waiting for the next crisis to arise* | **deepen, worsen** | **be over** *As soon as the crisis was over, she relaxed.*

● PREP. **during a/the ~** *Three people died during the hostage crisis.* **in (a/the) ~** *The government is in crisis.* ◇ *She's no good in a crisis.* | **~ in** *the growing crisis in education* **~ over** *a crisis over pensions*

● CRISIS + NOUN **point** *The team's dismal season has reached crisis point.* | **management** *an expert in crisis management*

● PHRASES **a crisis of confidence** *The company is suffering a severe crisis of confidence.* **at/in moments/times of crisis** *In times of crisis it's good to have someone you can rely on for advice.*

crisp *noun* (usually **crisps**)

● ADJ. **potato** | **plain** | **cheese and onion, ready salted, salt and vinegar,** etc.

● QUANT. **bag, packet** *a packet of smoky bacon crisps*

● VERB + CRISP **eat**

● CRISP + NOUN **bag, packet**

⇨ Special page at FOOD

criterion *noun*

● ADJ. **sole** | **main** | **strict, stringent** | **objective** | **eligibility, selection**

● QUANT. **range, set**

● VERB + CRITERION **fulfil, meet, satisfy** *She failed to meet the stringent selection criteria.* | **establish, lay down** | **adopt, apply, use** *The other groups agreed to adopt our criteria.*

● PREP. **according to a/the ~** *Team members will be selected according to strict criteria.* **by a/the ~** *By this criterion, very few people are suitable.* | **~ for** *The report lays down criteria for disciplining staff.* **~ of** *What are the criteria of success for a training scheme?*

critic *noun*

1 says what is bad/wrong with sth
● ADJ. **bitter, fierce, harsh, hostile, severe, trenchant** *She is one of her husband's severest critics.* | **outspoken, vocal, vociferous** | **persistent** | **chief, great, leading, major** *He is now a major critic of the nuclear industry.*

● VERB + CRITIC **prove wrong** *She is looking for a chance to prove her critics wrong.*

● CRITIC + VERB **accuse sb** *Critics accused the government of giving in to pressure from the tobacco companies.* | **argue sth, believe sth, claim sth, charge sth, fear sth, point sth out, say sth, suggest sth** *Critics point out that poverty still exists.* | **be right/wrong**

● PREP. **~ of** *an outspoken critic of government policy*

2 gives opinions about plays/books/films, etc.
● ADJ. **good, great, incisive** | **distinguished, influential** | **art, drama, film, literary, music, restaurant, social, television, theatre**

● CRITIC + VERB **hail sth, praise sth** *The film was hailed by critics as a triumphant piece of realism.* | **attack sth, pan sth, slate sth** *The play was panned by critics.* | **describe sth** *Critics described the paintings as worthless rubbish.*

⇨ Note at JOB

critical *adj.*

1 disapproving
● VERBS **be** | **become** | **remain**
● ADV. **bitterly, deeply, extremely, fiercely, harshly, highly, severely, sharply, strongly, very** | **increasingly** | **a little, mildly, quite** | **openly** *She became openly critical of party policy.*

● PREP. **of** *The report was highly critical of the railway's poor safety record.*

2 important
● VERBS **be** | **become**
● ADV. **really** | **absolutely** | **increasingly**
● PREP. **for** *Maintaining control of the the budget is absolutely critical for success.* **to** *This reorganization is critical to the long-term future of the company.*

criticism *noun*

1 expressing disapproval of sb/sth
● ADJ. **bitter, fierce, harsh, heavy, serious, severe, sharp, strident, strong, trenchant** | **telling** *A more telling criticism is that he reduces ethics to interpersonal relationships.* | **adverse, damaging, damning, hostile, negative, scathing** | **constructive, fair, just, justifiable, legitimate, valid** *She made a number of valid criticisms.* | **considerable, extensive, widespread** | **constant** | **basic, fundamental** | **main, major, substantial** | **minor, moderate** | **general** | **direct, explicit, outspoken** | **implicit, implied, indirect** | **fresh** *Two successive defeats have brought fresh criticism.* | **growing, increasing, mounting** | **media, press** | **public**

● QUANT. **barrage** *The film star faced a barrage of criticism for his behaviour.*

● VERB + CRITICISM **direct, express, level, make, voice** *Criticism was levelled at senior managers.* | **attract, be open to, be singled out for, come in for, come under, draw, face, get, meet with, prompt, provoke, receive** *The government came under fierce criticism for its policies.* ◇ *The proposal is open to several important criticisms.* | **avoid, deflect, escape, forestall, ward off** *She sought to deflect criticism by blaming her family.* | **accept, meet, reply to, respond to, take** *He finds it hard to take criticism.* | **counter, dismiss, reject** *She countered my criticisms by saying we had no choice in the matter.* | **imply** *None of what has been said should be taken to imply criticism.* | **offer** *to offer criticism and receive it*

● CRITICISM + VERB **come from sb** *The harshest criticism came from right-wing ideologists.* | **centre on sth** *Criticism centred on the lack of information provided.*

● PREP. **~ about** *The main criticism about the information provided is that it arrives too late.* **~ against** *criticisms against the European single currency* **~ for** *They received criticism for continuing to supply the faulty goods.* **~ from** *We are bound to face criticism from both sides.* **~ of** *There has been serious criticism of the teaching methods used in the school.* **~ over** *We came in for some sharp criticism over this decision.*

2 of a play, book, film, etc.
● ADJ. **practical, textual** | **academic, art, biblical, cultural, film, historical, literary, music, scientific, social** | **feminist, Marxist, structuralist**

criticize *verb*

● ADV. **bitterly, fiercely, heavily, roundly, severely, sharply, strongly** | **openly, publicly** *She has openly criticized the government.* | **implicitly** | **justifiably, rightly** *Their record on human rights has been justifiably criticized.* | **constantly, frequently, repeatedly** | **reportedly**

● PREP. **for** *She criticized the system for being secretive.*

● PHRASES **be widely criticized (as sth)** *The law was widely criticized as racist.* **criticize sb/sth on the grounds that** *The film was criticized on the grounds that it glorifies violence.*

critique *noun*

- ADJ. **detailed, devastating, effective, far-reaching, penetrating, radical, searching, telling, thorough, trenchant, wide-ranging** | **feminist, social, structuralist**
- VERB + CRITIQUE **give, present, provide**
- PREP. **~of** *The book provides a thorough critique of current theories.*

crook *noun*

- ADJ. **small-time**
- VERB + CROOK **catch**

crop *noun*

1 plants grown for food
- ADJ. **agricultural** | **cash, commercial, export** | **fodder, food, forage** *Fodder crops are used to feed livestock.* | **subsistence** | **staple** | **traditional** *the replacement of traditional crops with cash crops for export* | **spring, winter** | **standing** *Rivers burst their banks and flooded standing crops.* | **arable, cereal, fruit, root, vegetable**
- VERB + CROP **grow, produce** *Most of the farmers grow arable crops.* | **plant, sow** | **bring in, gather, harvest, reap** | **damage, destroy** *Summer flash floods destroyed the crops.* | **rotate** | **spray** *Crops are sprayed with highly toxic chemicals to prevent insect damage.*
- CROP + VERB **fail** *Isolated communities were extremely vulnerable if crops failed.*
- CROP + NOUN **rotation** *Crop rotation helps prevent soil erosion.* | **damage, failure** | **production, yield** *to boost crop yields* | **spraying**
- PREP. **~of** *a crop of carrots*

2 total amount of grain, fruit, etc. grown
- ADJ. **abundant, bumper, excellent, good, heavy, record** | **poor** | **early** *Bring strawberry plants indoors for an early crop.* | **potato, rice, etc.**
- VERB + CROP **gather, get, harvest, have, reap** *a record crop was harvested ◊ We had a very good crop of apples last year.* | **bear, produce, yield** *It takes three to five years for a new plantation to bear a crop.*
- PREP. **~of**

crop *verb*

- ADV. **closely** *His hair was closely cropped.*
- PHRASES **crop sth short** *His hair had been cropped short and he looked different.*

cross *noun*

1 mark made by drawing one line across another
- VERB + CROSS **draw, put** *I've put a cross on the map to show where the hotel is.*

2 Christian symbol
- ADJ. **gold, silver, stone, wooden** *She wore a gold cross on a chain around her neck. ◊ The grave was marked with a stone cross.* | **market, village, wayside**
- PREP. **on the~** *a painting of Jesus Christ on the cross*
- PHRASES **(make) the sign of the cross** *The priest blessed her, and made the sign of the cross over her.*

3 in football or hockey
- ADJ. **deep, low, perfect**
- PREP. **~by/from** *a deep cross from Beckham*

cross *verb*

- ADV. **quickly, slowly** | **safely, successfully** *teaching children to cross the road safely* | **back, over** *Let's cross over now while the road is clear.*
- VERB + CROSS **try to** *They were arrested trying to cross the border.*
- PREP. **from, into** *They crossed from the States into Canada.* **over** *We crossed over the river into Sweden.* **to** *She crossed to the door.*

cross *adj.*

- VERBS **be, feel, look, seem, sound** | **become, get** *I'm going to get very cross before long.* | **make sb** *It really makes me cross to see people dropping litter in the street.*
- ADV. **extremely, really, very** | **a bit, quite, rather, slightly**
- PREP. **about** *Are you still cross about me forgetting the flowers?* **at** *She was very cross at the way she'd been treated.* **for, with** *She was quite cross with him for being late.*

cross-examination *noun*

- VERB + CROSS-EXAMINATION **be subject to, face** *Evidence is given on oath and witnesses are subject to cross-examination.* | **bear, stand up to, withstand** *His alibi would not have withstood cross-examination.*
- PREP. **during/in ~** *He was found to have lied twice in cross-examination.* **under ~** *The defendant broke down under cross-examination.*

cross-eyed *adj.*

- VERBS **be, look** | **go** *You'll go cross-eyed if you try to look at things so close to you.*
- ADV. **slightly**

crossing *noun*

1 journey across a stretch of water
- ADJ. **rough** | **smooth** | **ferry** *The price includes accommodation and ferry crossing.* | **river, sea** | **Atlantic, Channel, etc.**
- VERB + CROSSING **make** *You can only make the crossing in good weather.*
- PREP. **during a/the~** *We discussed our plans during the crossing.* | **~ from, ~ to** *a very rough crossing from England to Ireland*

2 place where you can cross sth
- ADJ. **border** | **level** (= over a railway) | **pedestrian, pelican, zebra** (These are all places where people walking can cross a road.)
- PREP. **at a/the~** *They were stopped and searched at the border crossing.* **on a/the~** *A passenger train smashed into a truck on a level crossing.*

crossroads *noun*

1 place where two roads cross
- VERB + CROSSROADS **come to**
- PREP. **at the~** *Turn right at the next crossroads.*

2 important point in your life/career, etc.
- ADJ. **important** | **historic**
- VERB + CROSSROADS **stand at** | **reach**
- PREP. **at a/the~** *We are standing at an important crossroads in the history of Europe.* | **~ in** *He had reached a crossroads in his career.*

cross section *noun*

- ADJ. **broad, fair, good, large, representative, wide**
- VERB + CROSS SECTION **be drawn from** *The contestants are drawn from a cross section of society.* | **represent**
- PREP. **~of** *We interviewed a wide cross section of people.*

crossword *noun*

- ADJ. **cryptic, quick**
- VERB + CROSSWORD **do, fill in, solve**
- CROSSWORD + NOUN **clue, puzzle**

crouch *verb*

- ADV. **low** *The hare crouches low on the ground.* | **down** *We crouched down to avoid being seen.*
- PREP. **behind** *crouching behind the sofa* **over** *They crouched over the dead animal.*

crow noun

- ADJ. **black | carrion**
- QUANT. **flock**
- CROW + VERB **fly | perch** *The black crow perched on the telephone pole.* | **caw, shriek**

crow verb

- ADV. **triumphantly, with delight** *She gave the purse to Ruby, who crowed with delight.*
- PREP. **about/over** *The company hasn't much to crow about, with sales down compared with last year.*

crowd noun

1 large number of people in one place

- ADJ. **big, bumper, capacity, good, great, huge, large, massive, record, sell-out, vast** *The show played to capacity crowds.* | **small | gathering, growing | assembled** *The president read a declaration to a vast assembled crowd.* | **jostling, madding, milling, surging** *We pushed our way through the milling crowds of guests.* | **admiring, appreciative, cheering, enthusiastic, excited, expectant | angry, hostile, partisan | rush-hour | motley** *the usual motley crowd of tourists, hawkers and pigeons* | **football, theatre | home** (at a football match)
- VERB + CROWD **attract, draw, pull (in)** *Boxing is a sport that always attracts large crowds.* | **break up, disperse** *Police were called to disperse the crowd.* | **control | address, play to | join, mingle with**
- CROWD + VERB **assemble, collect, gather** *An expectant crowd gathered outside his house.* | **grow, swell** *The crowd grew to over 15 000.* | **flock, mill, throng** *Crowds have been flocking to the beaches in this hot weather.* ◇ *A crowd thronged around the wounded man.* | **disperse, melt away, thin out** *After the ambulance drove off, the crowd dispersed.* | **cheer, roar | boo, hiss, jeer | line the street** *Crowds lined the streets of the city as the president's car approached.*
- PREP. **among a/the~** *A bewildered child was wandering among the crowd.* **in a/the~** *I saw some familiar faces in the crowd.* **through a/the~** *She fought her way through the crowd.* | **~of** *a big crowd of football supporters*
- CROWD + NOUN **control**
- PHRASES **the back/front/middle of a crowd**

2 the crowd ordinary people

- VERB + CROWD **be one of, follow** *She's happy to follow the crowd.* | **stand out from** *We all like to think we stand out from the crowd* (= are different from other people).

crowded adj.

- VERBS **be | become, get**
- ADV. **densely, extremely, very** *living in densely crowded conditions* ◇ *The shops were all very crowded.* | **increasingly | a bit, fairly, a little, pretty, quite, rather**
- PREP. **with** *The store was crowded with shoppers.*

crown noun

1 that a king/queen wears

- VERB + CROWN **wear | place, put on** *The crown was placed upon the new monarch's head.*

2 the crown position/power of a king/queen

- ADJ. **imperial, royal**
- VERB + CROWN **offer sb** *In 1688 the crown was offered to William and Mary.* | **refuse | succeed to** *He succeeded to the crown of Spain*
- CROWN + VERB **pass** *In 1553 the crown passed from Edward VI to Mary.*
- PHRASES **the heir to the crown**

3 the Crown the state as represented by a king/queen

- VERB + CROWN **serve**

- CROWN + NOUN **court | jewels | land** *a piece of Crown land*

4 honour of being the best in a sports competition

- ADJ. **Olympic, world, etc.**
- VERB + CROWN **take, win | lose** *He lost his Olympic crown to George Rice.* | **fight for | defend, retain**

5 top of the head

- ADJ. **bald**
- PREP. **at the ~** *She swept her hair into a bun at the crown of her head.* **on your~** *There were raindrops on his bald crown.*

crucial adj.

- VERBS **be, prove | become | remain | consider sth, deem sth, regard sth as, see sth as**
- ADV. **really | absolutely** *It's absolutely crucial that we get this right.* | **fairly, quite | hardly | clearly, obviously**
- PREP. **for** *The talks are crucial for the success of the plan.* **to** *Secrecy is crucial to this police operation.*

cruel adj.

- VERBS **be, seem, sound | become**
- ADV. **extremely, unspeakably, very** *an extremely cruel regime* | **a little, rather | deliberately | unnecessarily**
- PREP. **to** *I can't stand people who are cruel to animals.*

cruelty noun

- ADJ. **extreme, great** *an act of extreme cruelty* | **deliberate | mental | animal, child** *Cases of child cruelty occur more often than they are observed.*
- VERB + CRUELTY **inflict, show (sb)** *How can you inflict such cruelty on a child?* ◇ *Her stepmother showed her nothing but cruelty.* | **suffer** *The children suffered mental cruelty and neglect.*
- PREP. **~to/towards** *cruelty to animals*

cruise noun

- ADJ. **leisurely, luxury, pleasure** *a pleasure cruise around the bay* | **Caribbean, Mediterranean, world, etc.**
- VERB + CRUISE **go on, take** *She used all her savings to go on a world cruise.*
- CRUISE + NOUN **liner, operator, ship**
- PREP. **on a/the~** *They met on a cruise.* | **~along** *a cruise along the coast* **~around/round**

cruiser noun

- ADJ. **battle, heavy, light, merchant | cabin, motor, pleasure, sailing**
- PREP. **on a/the~** *He served on a merchant cruiser.*

crumb noun

- ADJ. **biscuit, bread** (also **breadcrumb**), **cake**
- VERB + CRUMB **brush (away), sweep (away)** *She brushed the cake crumbs off the table.* | **drop, scatter** *He bit into the roll, scattering crumbs.*
- PREP. **~of** *a few crumbs of bread*

crunch verb

- ADV. **loudly | underfoot** *Snow crunched underfoot.* | **up**
- PREP. **on** *He was crunching loudly on an apple*

crusade noun

- ADJ. **great | moral, personal**
- VERB + CRUSADE **embark on, launch, mount** *The charity tonight launched its great crusade against homelessness.* | **be engaged in, carry out, conduct, join** *She seems to be carrying out a personal crusade to stop this building work.* | **lead**

● PREP. **on a~** *He is on a crusade to take the church to the people.* | **~ against** *urging parents to join a crusade against crime* **~ for** *For 23 years he led a crusade for peace.*

crush noun

● ADJ. **huge** | **schoolgirl, teenage**
● VERB + CRUSH **have** | **develop, get**
● PREP. **~ on** *She had a huge crush on one of her teachers.*

crush verb

● ADV. **badly** *His hand was badly crushed in the accident.* | **slightly** | **finely** *Crush the biscuits finely before adding them to the mixture.* | **underfoot** *insects that had been crushed underfoot*
● PREP. **against** *She was crushed against the wall.* **beneath/under** *crushed beneath a bus* **between** *crushed between two cars*
● PHRASES **be/get crushed, crush sb to death**

crust noun

1 on a loaf of bread/pie
● ADJ. **thick, thin** | **pastry, pie**
● PHRASES **a crust of bread** *We saved a few crusts of bread for the birds.*
2 hard layer on the outside of sth
● ADJ. **thick, thin**
● VERB + CRUST **form** *The mud had formed a thick crust on the surface of the road.*
● CRUST + VERB **form** *Put the lid on properly, or a crust will form on the paints.*
● PREP. **~ of** *a thin crust of ice*
● PHRASES **the earth's crust**

crutch noun

● ADJ. **emotional, psychological** (*both figurative*) *He saw religion as a psychological crutch.*
● VERB + CRUTCH **need, use** *He needs crutches to walk.*
● PREP. **on/with~** *She can only walk with crutches.*

crux noun

● CRUX + VERB **lie** *The crux of the matter lies in our lack of expert knowledge.*
● PHRASES **the crux of the matter/problem**

cry noun

1 shout/loud noise
● ADJ. **great, loud** | **little, low, small** | **choked/choking, muffled, stifled, strangled** | **piercing, shrill** | **hoarse** *the hoarse cry of a crow* | **agonized, anguished, bitter, despairing, desperate, plaintive, terrible** | **startled** | **involuntary** | **battle, rallying, war, warning** | **animal, bird**
● VERB + CRY **give, let out, raise, utter** *She gave an agonized cry as they lifted the fallen branch from her leg.* ◊ *He was too weak to raise even the smallest of cries.* | **hear**
● CRY + VERB **go up** *A cry went up when it was discovered their man had escaped.* | **escape** *An involuntary cry escaped her as he entered the room.*
● PREP. **with a~** *He fell to the ground with a cry.* | **~ for** (*figurative*) *Her suicide attempt was really a desperate cry for help.* **~ of** *a cry of despair/delight*
⇨ Note at SOUND
2 act of crying
● ADJ. **good** | **little**
● VERB + CRY **have** *You'll feel better when you've had a good cry.*

cry verb

1 produce tears
● ADV. **a lot** | **a little** | **almost, nearly** | **never, rarely** | **bitterly** *He put his head on his arms and cried bitterly.* |

loudly | quietly, silently, softly | uncontrollably | alone
● VERB + CRY **begin to, start to** | **make sb** | **leave sb to** *children who are left to cry alone*
● PREP. **about** *What are you crying about?* **for** *a child crying for his mother* **over** *I wasn't going to waste time crying over him!* **with** *Anna was almost crying with frustration.*
● PHRASES **cry like a baby** *Finally he broke down and cried like a baby.* **cry your eyes out, cry yourself to sleep, feel like crying** *I felt like crying when I found out what had happened.* **a shoulder to cry on** (*figurative*) *He was a fatherly shoulder to cry on when things went wrong.*
2 shout
● ADV. **aloud, out** | **suddenly** | **angrily, indignantly** *'Never!' he cried angrily.* | **despairingly, desperately** | **excitedly** | **passionately, wildly**
● VERB + CRY **want to** *She wanted to cry out to him not to be so stupid.* | **hear sb** *I heard her cry out in her sleep.*
● PREP. **in** *'What do you mean?' she cried in agitation.* ◊ *'Who's there?' she cried in a shrill voice.*
● PHRASES **cry for help** *She cried for help as the fire spread.* **cry out in anguish/fear/pain**

crystal noun

● ADJ. **single** | **quartz, rock, etc.** | **ice, snow**
● CRYSTAL + VERB **form, grow** *Ice crystals had formed on the window.*

crystal ball noun

● VERB + CRYSTAL BALL **gaze into, look into** *I can't gaze into my crystal ball and tell you what will happen!*

cubicle noun

● ADJ. **small, tiny** | **screened-off, separate** | **changing, shower, toilet**
● CUBICLE + NOUN **curtain, door**
● PREP. **in a/the~**

cuddle noun

● ADJ. **big** *He gave her a big cuddle and told her not to worry.*
● VERB + CUDDLE **have** *They were having a cuddle on the sofa.* | **give** *Give Mummy a big cuddle.*
● PHRASES **a kiss and a cuddle** *He just wants a comforting kiss and a cuddle and he'll be all right.*

cue noun

● VERB + CUE **wait for** | **take** *Her husband took his cue, and said that it was time for them to leave.* | **miss** | **give sb** *She had not yet been given the cue to go on to the stage.*
● PREP. **on~** *I can't just cry on cue!* | **~ for** *This was the cue for him to come into the room.*
● PHRASES **right on cue** *Ella came in right on cue, just as they were being rude about her.* **take your cue from sb/sth** *They all took their cue from their leader.*

cuisine noun

● ADJ. **excellent, fine, superb** | **local, regional** *We sampled the local cuisine.* | **traditional** | **haute, nouvelle** | **French, Italian, etc.**
● VERB + CUISINE **offer, serve** *The hotel has a large dining room serving superb local cuisine.* | **sample, try**
● PHRASES **a standard of cuisine**

culmination noun

● ADJ. **logical** *This massive autobiographical work was the logical culmination of her long career.*
● VERB + CULMINATION **mark, represent** *The show marked the culmination of months of hard work.* | **reach**

The space race reached its culmination in the first moon walk. | see *2001 saw the culmination of the project.*
- PREP. **at the ~ of** *A decision will be taken at the culmination of the initial research.*

culpable *adj.*

- VERBS **be, seem** | **believe sb**
- ADV. **highly, very**
- PREP. **in** *The prime minister is highly culpable in this affair.* **of** *She believed him culpable of murder.*

culprit *noun*

- ADJ. **big, chief, main, major, prime, real, worst** *Keep the kitchen clear of all sources of bacteria, not forgetting the biggest culprit of all—the dishcloth.* | **likely, obvious**
- VERB + CULPRIT **hunt** *Police hunting the culprits have condemned the attack.* | **apprehend, catch, identify, find, track down**

cult *noun*

1 worship of a person/thing
- ADJ. **personality** *the personality cult of the president*
- CULT + NOUN **figure, hero** *He became a cult figure during the 1960s.* | **status** *The book achieved cult status as soon as it was published.* | **following** *The show has built up a cult following.* | **band, book, film**
- PREP. **~ of** *the cult of youth*

2 religious group
- ADJ. **religious** *the members of a religious cult*
- CULT + NOUN **leader, member** | **image, object, statue** | **practice**

cultivate *verb*

1 land
- ADV. **intensively** *The land here has been intensively cultivated for generations.*

2 crops
- ADV. **successfully** *Olives have been cultivated successfully in southern Australia.*

3 try to develop sth
- ADV. **actively, assiduously, carefully, deliberately** *This modern image is actively cultivated by the company.* | **successfully**

cultivated *adj.*

- VERBS **be**
- ADV. **highly** *a highly cultivated woman* | **carefully, deliberately** *a carefully cultivated image*

culture *noun*

1 customs/ideas/beliefs
- ADJ. **ancient** | **primitive** | **dominant** | **alien, foreign** | **indigenous, native** | **local, national** | **traditional** | **African, black, Greek, Western, world, etc.** *These ideas have always been central to Western culture.* | **rural, urban** | **mainstream** | **underground** | **wider** *Prisoners are isolated from the wider culture of society at large.* | **bourgeois, working-class, etc.** | **street, youth** *As young people started to have more money, a significant youth culture developed.* | **dance, drug, football, etc.** | **academic, business, company, corporate, intellectual, legal, political, professional, religious, scientific, etc.** *the political culture of the United States* | **capitalist, computer, consumer, enterprise, materialistic, etc.** *the development of the enterprise culture in Britain*
- VERB + CULTURE **assimilate (sb into)** *The Romans gradually assimilated the culture of the people they had conquered.* ◇ *Newcomers to the company are soon assimilated into the culture.* | **create, develop, foster, produce**

The new director is trying to foster a culture of open communication within the company.
- CULTURE + VERB **develop**
- CULTURE + NOUN **group** *a country containing many language and culture groups* | **shock** *She experienced great culture shock when she first came to Europe.*
- PREP. **in a/the ~** *In some cultures children have an important place.* | **~ of** *The social security system has been accused of producing a culture of dependency.*

2 art/literature/music, etc
- ADJ. **contemporary, modern** | **mass, pop, popular** | **folk** | **high** | **wide** | **literary, oral** *Jokes are an important part of our popular, oral culture.*
- PREP. **a man/woman of culture** *She is a woman of wide culture.*

cultured *adj.*

- VERBS **be, seem**
- ADV. **deeply, highly** *a highly cultured man*

cunning *noun*

- ADJ. **great** | **devious, low** | **animal** | **native** *She relied on her native cunning to survive.*
- VERB + CUNNING **have** *She had great cunning and ruthlessness.* | **show** | **use** *He had used cunning to get what he wanted.*
- PREP. **with~** *She managed him with great cunning.*

cup *noun*

1 container
- ADJ. **empty** | **full** | **half-empty, half-full** | **broken, chipped, cracked** | **china, paper, plastic** | **coffee, tea**
- QUANT. **set**
- VERB + CUP **fill, refill** | **drain, empty** *She was so thirsty that she drained her cup.* | **lift, pick up, raise** *She raised her cup to her lips.* | **place, put down, replace, set down** | **drink from/out of** *Customers didn't like drinking out of plastic cups.*
- CUP + VERB **contain sth**
- PHRASES **a cup and saucer**

2 drink
- ADJ. **strong** *I like a good strong cup of tea first thing in the morning.* | **fresh** *My coffee was cold, so I ordered a fresh cup.*
- VERB + CUP **offer sb** | **make (sb)** | **pour (sb)** *I'm making tea. Can I pour you a cup?* | **help yourself to** | **stir** *Enrique stirred his fourth cup of coffee of the day.* | **drink, sip** *I drink about ten cups of coffee a day.*
- PREP. **~ of**
- PHRASES **a nice cup of tea** *You sit down and I'll make you a nice cup of tea.*

3 in sport
- ADJ. **challenge, knockout** | **European, World, etc.**
- VERB + CUP **win** *Who won the cup?* | **lose** | **present (sb with)** *The cup will be presented to the winning team by the president himself.* | **lift** *He lifted the cup for the sixth time this year* (= it was the sixth time he had won).
- CUP + NOUN **competition** *They were the first Turkish team to win a major cup competition.* | **clash, match** *The team are ready for next week's World Cup clash with Italy.* | **final, quarter-final, semi-finals** | **win, winner**
- PHRASES **the first, etc. round of the cup**

cupboard *noun*

- ADJ. **big, deep, large** | **little, small, tiny** | **high, low** | **walk-in** | **built-in, fitted** | **private** | **bare, empty** | **wall** | **bathroom, bedside, kitchen, hall** | **airing, broom, coat, clothes, drinks, food, linen, medicine, stationery, storage, store** *There's a broom cupboard under the stairs.*
- VERB + CUPBOARD **open** | **close** | **look in** | **put sth in** *Put the clothes in the airing cupboard.* | **keep sth in**

● CUPBOARD + VERB **be full of sth** *The cupboard was full of old toys.*
● CUPBOARD + NOUN **door | unit** *We had some new cupboard units fitted in the kitchen.* | **space** *Do you have much cupboard space in your new house?*
● PREP. **in a/the ~** *Put the plates in the cupboard.*

curb noun

● VERB + CURB **impose, introduce, put | act as** *Counselling acted as a curb on his violent behaviour.*
● PREP. **~ on** *Many companies have imposed curbs on smoking in the workplace.*

curb verb

● ADV. **drastically, greatly** *This legislation will greatly curb the power of local authorities.*
● VERB + CURB **attempt to, try to | be designed to, be intended to** *a new law designed to curb harmful emissions from factories*
● PHRASES **aimed at curbing sth** *a range of policies aimed at curbing inflation* **an attempt/effort to curb sth, measures to curb sth**

cure noun

1 medicine/treatment that can cure an illness
● ADJ. **effective, instant, miracle, wonder** *There is no instant cure for this condition.* | **rest** *His new job was almost a rest cure after the stresses of the army.* | **cancer**
● VERB + CURE **look for, seek | develop, discover, find**
● CURE + VERB **work** *The cure works by boosting the body's immune system.*
● PREP. **~ for** *scientists seeking a cure for Aids* **~ from** *He was hoping for a cure from his debilitating illness.*
● PHRASES **no (known) cure** *There is no known cure for the disease.* **prevention is better than cure** *Prevention is better than cure, so start looking after your heart now.* **the search for a cure** *the search for a cure for the common cold*
2 return to good health
● ADJ. **miraculous | complete, permanent**
● VERB + CURE **bring about, effect, provide** *These drugs can sometimes effect miraculous cures.* ◇ *(figurative) Science cannot provide a cure for all the world's problems.*

cure verb

● ADV. **completely | miraculously** *She still believed that somehow she could be miraculously cured.*
● PREP. **of** *He was now completely cured of his illness.*

curfew noun

● ADJ. **strict | dusk-to-dawn, night, night-time, 24-hour, 7 p.m., etc.**
● VERB + CURFEW **declare, impose, order, place sth under** *A five-day curfew was declared by the government.* ◇ *The whole area has been placed under curfew.* | **lift** *The strict curfew has now been lifted.* | **break, defy** *Protesters defied the curfew and took to the streets.*
● CURFEW + VERB **be in force** *A dusk-to-dawn curfew was in force.*
● PREP. **under ~** *The city is still under curfew.* | **~ on** *Many people are in favour of a curfew on young people.*

curiosity noun

● ADJ. **great, intense | insatiable** *She has an insatiable curiosity about life.* | **mild | idle, mere, simple** *'Why do you ask?' 'Mere curiosity.'* | **natural** *School should awaken a child's natural curiosity.* | **open** *staring with open curiosity* | **morbid**
● VERB + CURIOSITY **have | arouse, awaken** *Their curiosity was aroused by his strange behaviour.* | **satisfy**

● CURIOSITY + VERB **get the better of sb, overcome sb** *Harry's curiosity got the better of him and he unlocked the cupboard*
● PREP. **out of ~** *We went to the show out of curiosity more than anything else.* **with ~** *The children watched us with mild curiosity.* | **~ about** *I needed to satisfy my curiosity about what it was like to make records.*
● PHRASES **a sense of curiosity**

curious adj.

1 eager to find out about sb/sth
● VERBS **be, feel, seem | became, get, grow | remain | make sb** *Her secretive manner had made me curious.*
● ADV. **deeply, extremely, intensely, very** *I was intensely curious to know more about him.* | **a little, mildly, rather, slightly | frankly** *She coped with the frankly curious looks of the men.* | **genuinely | idly** *He saw a book on the table and picked it up, idly curious.* | **naturally** *Puppies are naturally curious.*
● PREP. **about** *I was curious about how she would react.* **as to** *She was curious as to why he was there.*
● PHRASES **curious to find out/know/see sb/sth**
2 strange/unusual
● VERBS **be, feel, look, seem, smell, taste | find sb/sth**
● ADV. **extremely, very** *I find it very curious that you did not tell anyone.* | **a little, rather, slightly, somewhat** *The wine tasted rather curious.*

curl noun

1 piece of hair
● ADJ. **natural | soft | tight | corkscrew, spiral | auburn, blonde, dark, etc. | natural | stray** *She pushed a stray curl away from her eyes.* | **tangled, tumbling, unruly, untamed, wayward** *She smoothed down her tangled curls.* | **damp**
● VERB + CURL **press/push/stroke back, smooth back/down | ruffle, run your fingers through | tease** *He carefully teased his curls into place.* | **shake** *She shook her dark curls sadly.*
● CURL + VERB **fall, tumble** *Her auburn curls tumbled about her face.* | **bounce | frame sth** *Her face was framed by a mop of black curls.*
● PREP. **in ~s** *His hair spilled in curls over his forehead.* **through the/your ~s** *She raked a comb through her wayward curls.*
● PHRASES **a cascade/mass/mop of curls** *Her hair was styled into a cascade of spiral curls.* **lose its curl** *Her hair lost its curl as she got older.*
2 sth with a curved round shape
● ADJ. **faint, little, slight** *He acknowledged her remark with a faint curl of his lips.*
● PREP. **~ of** *a curl of smoke*

curl verb

● ADV. **tightly | slightly | up** *She curled her legs up under her.*
● PREP. **around/round** *His fingers curled tightly round the steering wheel.* **from** *Smoke was curling up from the chimney.* **into** *The cat curled into a ball and fell asleep.*
● PHRASES **be/lie/sit curled up** *She was lying curled up on her bed.* **curl (up) at the edges** *The photograph was brown and curling at the edges.*

curly adj.

● VERBS **be | go**
● ADV. **all** *(informal),* **very** *Your hair's gone all curly!* | **naturally** *She wished she had naturally curly hair.*

unit of money in a country

change/convert sth into/to~
I want to change 100 dollars into euros.
buy, sell~
The bank will sell you one Russian rouble for 4.14 Japanese yen.

Many of the collocates of MONEY (for example make, spend) can also be used with currencies:
The country spends millions of dollars on overseas aid every year.
50-, 100-, etc. ~coin/note
a pound coin
50-, 100-, etc. dollar bill
for a~
How many dinars will I get for a dollar?
in (the)~
The contract is denominated in euros.
a tax of 30p in the pound
~for~
The company promises to match any money the charity makes dollar for dollar.
~'s worth of sth
a million pound's worth of books

value of a currency compared with others

high, rising, strong~
Business should benefit from a stronger euro.
falling, low, weak~
The yen gained 10 points against a weak dollar.
over-valued~
Research suggests that the pound is over-valued.
float~
The UK floated sterling in June 1972.
devalue~
The Fiji dollar may have to be devalued.
defend, prop up, protect, shore up, support~
She dismissed suggestions that the central bank would intervene to prop up the euro.
~be worth sth
One Saudi Arabian riyal is worth approximately 0.27 US dollars.
~strengthen
The peso strengthened on the foreign exchanges.
~come under pressure
The pound came under pressure against the dollar.
~close, open
The pound closed yesterday at 1.4130 dollars.

~be fixed/pegged to
Many emerging countries have their currencies pegged to the dollar.
~value
The dollar value of the stock rose to $11.5 billion.
~terms
The rise in government spending was equivalent to only 9% in dollar terms.
~exchange rate
All prices are based on the South African rand exchange rate.
~traveller's cheques
sterling traveller's cheques
~equivalent
She was paid the dollar equivalent of £10 000.
against the~
The yen has strengthened against the pound.
to the~
How many dollars are there to the pound?
depreciation/devaluation/reflation of the~
the devaluation of the peso in 1994
a run on the~
The government increased interest rates to avoid a run on the rouble (= sudden large selling of the currency).
the value of the~
a rise in the value of the euro
⇨ See also the note at PER CENT

---

currency *noun*

1 money used in a particular country
- ADJ. **domestic | foreign** *They prefer to be paid in foreign currencies.* | **common, international** *US dollars are considered common currency in international transactions.* | **local** *You can convert sterling into the local currency.* | **national | European, Japanese, etc. | single** *the single European currency* | **major | stable, strong** *A stable currency means that your savings do not diminish in value* | **weak | hard | convertible**
- VERB + CURRENCY **change, convert sth into/to, exchange | buy, sell | devalue | support** *The fund supports weak currencies.* | **raise** *The country needs to raise enough hard currency to pay for its oil imports.*
- CURRENCY + VERB **rise | fall | float, fluctuate** *For four months all major currencies floated.* ◊ *The system allows currencies to fluctuate within certain limits.*
- CURRENCY + NOUN **conversion, exchange, translation** *The disappointing profits are due to unfavourable currency translations.* | **markets** *They make money by speculating on the currency markets.* | **deal, dealing, speculation, trade, trading | dealer, speculator, trader | crisis | fluctuation, movements | devaluation | system | reform | reserves**
- PREP. **in ... ~** *She had £50 in foreign currency.*

2 being believed/accepted/used by many people
- ADJ. **general, wide, widespread**
- VERB + CURRENCY **enjoy, have** *This belief has general currency.* | **gain** *How did the idea gain currency?*

current *noun*

1 continuous flowing movement of water
- ADJ. **fast, fast-flowing, powerful, strong | dangerous, treacherous | ocean | prevailing** *The prevailing current flows from east to west.* | **off-shore | tidal**
- CURRENT + VERB **flow | carry sb/sth, sweep sb/sth** *The strong current carried the boat downstream.* ◊ *She was swept away by the treacherous currents.*
- PREP. **against a/the ~** *He was swimming against the current.* **in a/the~** *The boat was carried along in the current.* **with a/the~** *It's easier to go with the current.*

2 flow of air
- ADJ. **warm | air** *Birds of prey use warm air currents to lift them high in the sky.*
- PHRASES **a current of air**

3 flow of electricity through a wire
- ADJ. **strong, weak | electric, electrical | alternating | direct | input, output**
- VERB + CURRENT **generate, produce | carry, pass, transmit | switch off/on** *Check all your wiring before switching on the current.*
- CURRENT + VERB **flow, pass through sth** *Measure the current flowing in the wire.*

curriculum *noun*

- ADJ. **broad, broadly-based, wide | narrow** *Teachers feel that the present curriculum is too narrow.* | **core** *Student choose from optional subjects in addition to the core curriculum.* | **national, official, statutory | mainstream** *His disability does not prevent him from following the mainstream curriculum.* | **academic, educational |**

higher education, primary, school, secondary, undergraduate | subject-based | English, geography, mathematics, etc. | hidden *Children learn many of their attitudes to life from the hidden curriculum at school.*
- VERB + CURRICULUM **design, develop, plan** | **broaden** | **introduce sth into** *Film Studies has been introduced into the curriculum as an option.* | **follow**
- CURRICULUM + NOUN **content, subjects** | **materials** | **design, development, planning** | **aims, objectives** | **change, reform, review**
- PREP. **across the~** *Pupils use computers across the curriculum* (= in all or most subjects). **on a/the~** *They all have to study French because it's on the curriculum.* **in a/the~** *More room should be given to foreign languages in the curriculum.* **within a/the~** *the balance of subjects within the curriculum*
- PHRASES **areas of the curriculum** *We cover all areas of the curriculum.*

curry *noun*

- ADJ. **hot** | **mild** | **beef, chicken, vegetable, etc.** | **Indian** | **madras, vindaloo, etc.**
- VERB + CURRY **eat, have** | **cook, make, prepare** | **go for** *Let's go for a curry after the film.*
- CURRY + NOUN **paste, powder** | **sauce** | **house** (= a restaurant that serves curry)
⇨ Special page at FOOD

curse *noun*

1 word used for expressing anger
- ADJ. **impatient**
- VERB + CURSE **mutter, utter**

2 wish that sth terrible will happen to sb
- VERB + CURSE **utter** | **put**
- PREP. **under a~** *She thought that she must be under a curse.* | **~ on/upon** *The witch is supposed to have put a curse on the house.*

curse *verb*

- ADV. **roundly** | **loudly** | **quietly, softly, under your breath** *He cursed under his breath as the spanner slipped.* | **inwardly, silently**
- PREP. **for** *I cursed her roundly for being late.*
- PHRASES **curse the day** *He was now cursing the day he had ever got involved in the project.* **curse your luck** *She cursed her luck that she had had to queue for so long.*

cursor *noun*

- VERB + CURSOR **insert, move, place, position, put**
⇨ Special page at COMPUTER

curtail *verb*

- ADV. **drastically, seriously, severely** *His power has been severely curtailed.* | **further** | **abruptly**

curtain *noun*

1 fabric that covers a window
- VERB + CURTAIN **close, draw, open, pull (across/aside/back/closed)** *They sat in the dark with the curtains drawn.* ◊ *She pulled back the curtains, and sunlight streamed in.*
- CURTAIN + VERB **hang** *Heavy red velvet curtains hung either side of the huge window.* | **billow** *The curtains billowed madly as the wind caught them.*
- PREP. **behind a/the~** *He took a bag from a shelf behind some curtains.*

2 in a theatre
- ADJ. **final**
- CURTAIN + VERB **go up, open, part, rise** | **close,**

come down, fall *At the end of the play the curtain came down to tremendous applause.*

curve *noun*

- ADJ. **gentle, graceful, slight, smooth** | **sharp, tight** *The road went round in a tight curve.* | **wide** | **sensual, voluptuous** *the voluptuous curve of her hips* | **downward, upward**
- VERB + CURVE **form, make** *The seats were arranged to form a curve.*
- PREP. **in a~** *The road follows the coast in a wide curve.*

curve *verb*

- ADV. **gently, slightly** *a gently curving stream* | **away, down, up** *The path curved down towards the village.*
- PREP. **around/round, towards, etc.** *The road curved away round the back of the hill.*

cushion *noun*

- ADJ. **plump, soft** *He sank back into the soft cushions of the sofa.* | **sofa**
- VERB + CUSHION **plump (up)** *She plumped up the sofa cushions before the guests arrived.*
- CUSHION + NOUN **cover**
- PREP. **on a/the~** *I rested my elbow on a cushion.*

custard *noun*

- ADJ. **creamy, thick** | **thin** | **smooth** | **lumpy** | **banana, egg, vanilla**
- VERB + CUSTARD **make** | **pour** | **strain** *Strain the custard to remove lumps.*
- CUSTARD + VERB **thicken** | **set**
- CUSTARD + NOUN **powder** | **pie**
- PHRASES **and/with custard** *some apple pie and custard*
⇨ Special page at FOOD

custody *noun*

1 legal right/duty to take care of sb/sth
- ADJ. **child** *a bitter child custody dispute* | **joint, sole** | **safe** *If valuables are placed in the safe, the hotel is responsible for their safe custody.*
- VERB + CUSTODY **ask for, claim, demand, fight for, seek** | **award sb, give sb, grant sb** *The parents were given joint custody of the two children.* | **gain, get** | **have**
- CUSTODY + NOUN **battle, dispute** | **hearing**
- PREP. **~of**

2 being guarded/kept in prison
- ADJ. **military, police** *The man died while in police custody.* | **protective** *The opposition leader has been taken into protective custody.*
- VERB + CUSTODY **be remanded in, be taken into** *A man has been remanded in custody charged with the murder of an eight-year-old girl.* | **be held in, be kept in, be/remain in** | **escape from** | **be released from**
- PREP. **in~** *She will remain in custody while reports are prepared about her mental condition.* **out of~** *trying to keep young people out of custody*

custom *noun*

- ADJ. **accepted, age-old, ancient, established, old, traditional** | **quaint** | **local** | **social**
- VERB + CUSTOM **follow, observe, respect** *They still follow the custom of pinning money to the bride's dress.* | **maintain, preserve, revive**
- CUSTOM + VERB **die out, disappear** *The custom died out in the nineteenth century.* | **prevail, survive** *These customs still prevail in remote areas.*
- PREP. **according to a/the ~, in accordance with (a/the ~)** *They poured wine round the trees in accordance*

with local custom. **through ~** *The rules have grown up through custom and are not laid down by law.* | **~of**
• PHRASES **as is/was the custom** *People threw coins onto the stage, as was the custom.*

customer *noun*

• ADJ. **big, favoured, good, important, key, large, major** *They are one of our biggest customers.* ◇ *They organized an evening's entertainment for favoured customers.* | **long-standing, long-time, loyal | regular | current, existing | potential, prospective, would-be** *There are a large number of potential customers for the new product.* | **dissatisfied, unhappy | satisfied** *We like to think that we have satisfied customers.* | **domestic | external, outside | international, overseas | personal, private | business, commercial, corporate, industrial**
• VERB + CUSTOMER **have | deal with, serve | attract, entice, get** *It's a special offer to attract new customers.* | **lose** *We can't afford to lose any more customers.*
• CUSTOMER + NOUN **care, relations, service, support** *If you have a complaint, contact the customer care unit.* ◇ *Part of good customer relations is knowing how to deal with complaints.* | **account, order | agreement** *The terms of the guarantee will be set out in the customer agreement.* | **demand/demands, needs, requirements, specifications** *This cheaper model was produced in response to customer demand.* | **reaction** *The questionnaire is to test customer reaction to the new store design.* | **dissatisfaction, satisfaction** *They carried out a customer satisfaction survey.* | **loyalty | complaints, enquiries | survey | profile, records | base** *They are hoping that TV advertising will increase their customer base.*

customs *noun*

• ADJ. **French, UK, etc.**
• VERB + CUSTOMS **clear, go through** *We cleared customs by five o'clock.* ◇ *You will have to declare these goods when you go through customs.* | **wave sb through** *We were waved through customs without a pause.*
• CUSTOMS + NOUN **control/controls, regulations** *the removal of European customs controls* | **duty/duties** *We had to pay customs duties on the beer.* | **building, hall, post** *the customs post on the border* | **agent, man, officer, official, staff | authorities | formalities, procedures | declaration, document, documentation, form** *We had to fill out customs forms on the plane.* | **clearance** *We were waiting for the goods to receive customs clearance.*
• PREP. **at ~** *We got stopped and searched at the Italian customs.* **through ~**

cut *noun*

1 hole/opening made by cutting
• ADJ. **clean, neat**
• VERB + CUT **make | give** *a high-quality blade that gives a clean cut*
• PREP. **~in** *Using sharp scissors, make a small cut in the material.*
2 wound
• ADJ. **bad, deep, nasty | minor, small, superficial** *He's got a small cut on his finger.* | **clean**
• VERB + CUT **have | get, suffer** *She got a bad cut over her right eye.* | **clean** *Clean the cut and cover it to prevent infection.* | **bandage, cover, dress**
• CUT + VERB **heal** *A clean cut heals quickly.*
• PREP. **~on** *a cut on her hand* **~to** *One man was attacked and suffered cuts to his face.*
• PHRASES **cuts and bruises**
3 act of cutting sth
• ADJ. **hair**
• VERB + CUT **have** *I've made an appointment to have a hair cut.*

4 reduction
• ADJ. **big, deep, drastic, large, major, massive, real, savage, severe, sharp, significant, substantial, swingeing | government | financial | budget, defence, education, expenditure, interest-rate, job, pay, price, service, spending, staff, tax, wage | power** *They get a lot of power cuts because they have overhead wires.*
• QUANT. **round** *The company has announced a new round of job cuts.*
• VERB + CUT **make** *They are planning to make substantial cuts in the service.* | **announce, propose** *proposed tax cuts* | **suffer, take** *The staff have all had to take a cut in salary.*
• CUT + VERB **come into effect** *The cuts will come into effect next May.*
• PREP. **~in** *cuts in public spending*
5 piece of meat
• ADJ. **choice, expensive, good, lean | cheap | cold ~s**
• PREP. **~of** *The recipe calls for a good lean cut of beef.*
6 share in the profits
• VERB + CUT **get, have, take** *By the time the organizers have had their cut, there won't be much left.*
• PREP. **~of** *He takes a cut of the profits.*

cut *verb*

1 with a knife/scissors, etc.
• ADV. **thick** *Make sure you cut the bread nice and thick.* | **thinly | cleanly** *Cut the stem cleanly, just beneath a leaf joint.* | **easily** *Sandstone cuts easily.* | **crossways, lengthways** *Cut the courgette in half lengthways.* | **away, down** *cutting down trees*
• PREP. **from** *They cut away all the dead branches from the tree.* **into** *She picked up the knife and cut into the meat.* ◇ *He cut the bread into thin slices.* **through** *I can't cut through this wood.*
• PHRASES **cut and paste** *(computing) You can cut and paste between different programs.* **cut sb/sth free** *Two survivors were cut free after being trapped for twenty minutes.* **cut sth into pieces** *Cut the cake into six pieces.* **cut sth in half/two** *She cut the loaf in two and gave me one of the halves.* **cut sth open** *She fell and cut her head open.*
2 reduce sth
• ADV. **considerably, drastically, significantly | short** *His career was cut short by injury.*
• VERB + CUT **try to | manage to** *We have managed to cut our costs quite drastically.* | **be forced to, have to**
• PREP. **by** *The department has to cut its spending by 30%.* **from, to** *The price has been cut from £250 to £175.*

PHRASAL VERBS
cut back
• ADV. **drastically, savagely, severely, significantly** *Social work services have been cut back drastically.*
• VERB + CUT BACK **be forced to, have to**
• PREP. **on** *Local authorities have been forced to cut back on expenditure.*
cut down
• ADV. **considerably, drastically | gradually**
• VERB + CUT DOWN **try to | manage to | advise sb to**
• PREP. **on** *I'm trying to cut down on fatty foods.*
cut sb/sth off
1 interrupt sb/sth
• ADV. **abruptly, suddenly** *His thoughts were abruptly cut off by a blinding flash of pain.*
2 prevent sb/sth leaving/reaching a place
• ADV. **completely, totally, utterly, wholly | effectively, largely, virtually**
• PREP. **from** *They were completely cut off from the outside world.*

cutback noun

- ADJ. **major, severe, sharp** | **budget, budgetary, economic, financial** | **government**
- VERB + CUTBACK **impose, make** *Many theatres are having to make major cutbacks.* | **announce**
- PREP. **~in** *a sharp cutback in military spending*

cutting noun

1 piece cut out from a newspaper
- ADJ. **newspaper, press** *She had kept all the press cuttings about the murder.*
- PREP. **~from** *a cutting from 'The Guardian'*

2 piece cut off from a plant
- ADJ. **leaf, root, stem**
- VERB + CUTTING **take**
- CUTTING + VERB **root, take** *After about four weeks you will be able to see whether the cuttings have taken.*
- PREP. **from a/the~** *These plants are easy to propagate from leaf cuttings.* | **~from** *Take cuttings from mature plants in the spring.*

cycle noun

1 series of events that happen repeatedly
- ADJ. **annual, daily, monthly, regular, seasonal, weekly** *the annual cycle of church festivals* | **complete, entire, whole** | **endless** *the endless cycle of birth, death and rebirth* | **natural** *Life is a natural cycle, just like the changing seasons.* | **vicious** *caught up in a vicious cycle of bingeing and dieting* | **lunar, solar** *the 76-year solar cycle* | **breeding, menstrual, reproductive** | **business, economic** | **water** *a diagram of the water cycle* | **life** *the life cycle of the butterfly*
- VERB + CYCLE **go through** *The European market is simply going through an economic cycle.* | **complete** *To complete the cycle, oxygen is necessary.* | **repeat**
- CYCLE + VERB **begin again** *Male and female adults mate, the female lays eggs, and the cycle begins all over again.* | **repeat (itself)** *This cycle of events continually repeats itself.*
- CYCLE + NOUN **length, time**
- PREP. **in a/the~** *at this point in the cycle* **per~** *The number of young produced per breeding cycle varies from species to species.*

- PHRASES **part of the cycle (of sth)** *part of the cycle of birth and death*

2 bicycle
- ADJ. **motor** (also **motorcycle**), **pedal**
- VERB + CYCLE **ride**
- CYCLE + NOUN **ride, tour** *We're going for a cycle ride this afternoon.* | **helmet** | **lane, path, route, track** *Cars are not allowed in the cycle lanes.* | **race**
- PREP. **by~** *They completed their journey by cycle.* **on a/the~** *lots of people in cars or on cycles*

cyclone noun

- ADJ. **violent** | **tropical**
- CYCLONE + VERB **hit sth, strike sth** *An exceptionally violent cyclone hit the town last night.* | **damage sth, destroy sth, devastate sth** *In 1974 Darwin was devastated by Cyclone Tracy.*
- PREP. **in a/the~** *trees damaged in the cyclone*
- PHRASES **the eye of the cyclone** (= the central point)

cymbal noun

- ADJ. **clashing, crashing**
- VERB + CYMBAL **clash, hit**
- CYMBAL + NOUN **crash** *The piece ends with a cymbal crash.*
- PHRASES **a clash/crash of cymbals**
⇨ Special page at MUSIC

cynical adj.

- VERBS **appear, be, feel, seem, sound** *I hope I don't sound unduly cynical.* | **become, get, grow** | **remain**
- ADV. **deeply, extremely, very** *his deeply cynical attitude* | **completely, totally, utterly** | **overly, unduly** | **a bit, fairly, a little, rather, slightly, somewhat**
- PREP. **about** *I'm a little cynical about her motives.*

cynicism noun

- ADJ. **bitter, weary** *He spoke in a tone of weary cynicism.* | **widespread**
- QUANT. **hint, note, touch, trace** *There was not a trace of cynicism in his voice.*
- PREP. **with~** *She viewed his new interest in her with cynicism.* | **~about** *There is now widespread cynicism about the political system.*

Dd

daft adj., adv.

- VERBS **be, feel, look, seem, sound** | **act, talk** (*both informal*) *Don't talk daft!*
- ADV. **bloody** (*taboo*), **really** | **completely, plain** *The decision is just plain daft.* | **a bit, pretty, rather**

dagger noun

- ADJ. **curved** | **ceremonial, jewelled, ornamental**
- VERB + DAGGER **draw** | **sheathe**

dam noun

- ADJ. **hydroelectric**
- VERB + DAM **build, construct** | **breach** *The dam has been breached and there is a danger of flooding.*
- DAM + VERB **burst** *The dam burst and the valley was flooded.* | **hold sth back** *The dam holds back the water.*
- PREP. **~ across/on** *a large hydroelectric dam on the River Danube*

damage noun

1 harm/injury

- ADJ. **considerable, enormous, great, serious, severe, substantial, untold** | **minor, slight** | **extensive, widespread** | **irreparable, irreversible, lasting, long-term, permanent** *The incident did permanent damage to relations between the two countries.* | **criminal, malicious, wilful** *He was prosecuted for criminal damage to a vehicle.* | **accidental** *The insurance policy covers the building for accidental damage.* | **emotional, environmental, mechanical, psychological, structural** | **brain** *She suffered serious brain damage at birth.*
- VERB + DAMAGE **cause, do, inflict** *The earthquake caused widespread damage to property.* ◊ *They inflicted severe psychological damage on their opponents.* | **suffer** | **repair** | **prevent**
- PREP. **~ by** *The palace suffered extensive damage by fire in 1825.* **~ from** *Crops are sprayed with chemicals to prevent damage from insects.* **~ to** *lasting damage to the environment*
- PHRASES **the cost/value of the damage** *The cost of the damage is estimated at around $2 billion.* **the extent of the damage** *At the moment it is difficult to assess the extent of the damage.*

2 damages money you can claim from sb

- ADJ. **heavy, substantial**
- VERB + DAMAGES **incur, suffer** *damages incurred by the unfairly sacked workers* | **claim, seek, sue (sb) for** *He decided to sue the company for damages.* | **assess** *The court will assess the damages.* | **apportion, award (sb)** | **pay (sb)** | **obtain, receive, recover, win** | **be liable for, be liable in** (*law*) *If goods are lost in transit, the carrier will be liable for damages.*
- DAMAGES + NOUN **action, claim** *A woman is to bring a civil damages action against the men she alleges murdered her son.* | **award**
- PREP. **in ~** *They are claiming £45 million in damages.* | **~ for** *He received damages for personal injury.* **~ of** *She was awarded damages of £90 000.*
- PHRASES **an action/a claim for damages** *The judge upheld her claim for damages against her former employer.*

damage verb

- ADV. **badly, seriously, severely** *The building was*

badly damaged by fire. | **slightly** | **irreparably, permanently** *She may have damaged her health irreparably.*

damaging adj.

- VERBS **be, prove** | **become**
- ADV. **deeply, extremely, gravely, highly, immensely, profoundly, seriously, severely, very** *This scandal could prove seriously damaging to the government.* | **quite, rather** | **possibly, potentially** | **positively** *These new measures will do nothing to raise school standards: they may be positively damaging.* | **economically, environmentally, politically, psychologically** *Building the proposed new road would be environmentally damaging.*
- PREP. **to** *Smoking is damaging to health.*

damp noun

- ADJ. **penetrating, rising**
- VERB + DAMP **have, suffer from** *The house had got woodworm and rising damp.* | **check for, look for** | **find** *The surveyor found damp in the kitchen.*

damp adj.

- VERBS **be, feel, look, smell** *The room smelled damp.* | **become, get** | **remain** | **make sth** *The rain had made the walls damp.*
- ADV. **very** | **a bit, a little, quite, rather, slightly** *Our clothes had got a bit damp.*

dance noun

1 series of steps/movements to music

- ADJ. **little** | **fast, lively** | **slow, stately** | **traditional** | **ritual** | **ballroom, folk, square** | **rain** | **mating** *pigeons performing their mating dance*
- VERB + DANCE **dance, do, perform** *In her delight she got up and did a little dance.* | **have** *May I have the next dance?* ◊ *I felt like having a dance.* | **like** *Would you like a dance?* | **sit out** *She had to sit out the last dance because of a twisted ankle.*
- DANCE + NOUN **music, rhythm** | **routine, sequence, step** | **class, teacher** | **floor, hall, studio**

2 social meeting with dancing

- ADJ. **barn** | **school** | **dinner, supper, tea**
- VERB + DANCE **go to** | **hold**
- DANCE + NOUN **band**
- PREP. **at a/the ~** *They met at a dance.*

3 dancing as a form of art/entertainment

- ADJ. **contemporary, modern** | **classical**
- DANCE + NOUN **company, troupe**
- PHRASES **a school of dance, a style of dance**

dance verb

- ADV. **almost** | **wildly** *They danced wildly down the street.* | **about, around, away** | **together**
- VERB + DANCE **ask sb to** | **want to**
- PREP. **for** *He was almost dancing for joy.* **to** *We danced to the music.* **with** *Will you dance with me?*

dancer noun

- ADJ. **brilliant, excellent, good, great, wonderful** *He's a brilliant dancer!* | **professional** | **trained** | **leading, principal** *a principal dancer with the Royal Ballet* | **male** | **ballet, ballroom, classical, clog, disco, flamenco, go-go, tap** *She's a very good flamenco dancer.*

• DANCER + VERB **perform (sth)** *dancers performing in the street* ◊ *classical dancers performing modern work*
⇨ Note at JOB

dancing *noun*

• ADJ. **wild | ballet, ballroom, belly, country, disco, flamenco, folk, line, maypole, morris, sequence, traditional** *She does line dancing and yoga in the evenings.*
• VERB + DANCING **do, go** *They liked to go dancing every Saturday night.*
• DANCING + NOUN **display | lesson** *She's taking dancing lessons.* | **school | career | partner**
• PHRASES **dancing in the streets** *There was dancing in the streets when we heard that the war was over.*

danger *noun*

• ADJ. **big, considerable, enormous, extreme, grave, great, mortal, obvious, real, serious, terrible** *They are in grave danger of losing everything.* ◊ *She knew that she was now in mortal danger.* ◊ *There is a real danger that the bridge will collapse from the weight of traffic.* | **acute, immediate, imminent, impending** *They are in imminent danger of attack.* | **constant, ever-present** *the ever-present danger of crime* | **long-term | inherent** *There are inherent dangers in the system.* | **slight | possible, potential | personal | physical | public** *The pollution from the factory is a public danger.*
• VERB + DANGER **be exposed to, face** *On their journey across the desert they faced danger of all sorts.* | **be fraught with, involve** *The task was fraught with danger.* | **cause** *He was convicted of causing danger to other road users.* | **pose** *the dangers posed by the possession of nuclear weapons* | **be aware of, foresee, identify, realize, recognize, see, sense, smell, spot** *No one foresaw the danger.* ◊ *The animal seemed to sense danger.* | **run** *A company must keep developing or it runs the danger of stagnating.* | **court** *Some people take crazy risks because they get a thrill from courting danger.* | **avert** *Vigorous action is needed to avert the danger of runaway inflation.* | **lessen, minimize, reduce | avoid, escape | ignore**
• DANGER + VERB **exist, face sb, lie (in sth), lurk, threaten sb** *One of the biggest dangers facing us may be climate change.* ◊ *The danger lies in becoming too complacent.* ◊ *Where would they hide if danger threatened?* | **arise, come (from sb/sth)** *The biggest danger to gorillas comes from humans.* | **pass** *We waited until all danger had passed.*
• DANGER + NOUN **area, spot, zone** *Despite the high levels of radiation, people are now moving back into the danger zone.* | **signals, signs** *He recognized the danger signs and gave up smoking.* | **money** *The divers were paid danger money for working in such hazardous conditions.* | **man** *The United manager believes Figo is the opposition's danger man.*
• PREP. **in ~** *We weren't in any danger.* **in ~ of** *The plant is now in danger of extinction.* **out of ~** *They ran until they were out of danger.* | **~ from, ~ of** *We're in serious danger of becoming a nation of worriers.* **~ to** *There is no danger to the public from these chemicals.*
• PHRASES **be off/on the danger list** *He was admitted to hospital in critical condition, but is now off the danger list.*

dangerous *adj.*

• VERBS **be, look, prove, seem, sound | become, get** *The situation could get quite dangerous.* | **remain | make sth** *The ice is making the roads very dangerous tonight.* | **consider sth, regard sth as**
• ADV. **bloody** (*taboo*)**, exceedingly, extremely, highly, incredibly, really, terribly, very** *a highly dangerous situation* | **increasingly | a bit, a little, quite, rather, slightly | possibly, potentially | downright, positively** *It's a risky idea, if not downright dangerous!* | **inherently |**

notoriously *This route through the mountains is notoriously dangerous.* | **politically** *Raising income tax is considered politically dangerous.*
• PREP. **for** *This treatment is extremely dangerous for the mother.* **to** *not dangerous to humans*

dare *verb*

• ADV. **hardly, scarcely** *I hardly dared breathe.*
• VERB + DARE **wouldn't** *I wouldn't dare go by myself.*

daring *adj.*

• VERBS **be, feel | become, get, grow** *He had grown more daring.* | **consider sth, think sth** *Her behaviour was considered very daring at the time.*
• ADV. **greatly, very** *Greatly daring, he covered her hand with his own.* | **a little, quite**

dark *noun*

• ADJ. **pitch** *I fumbled for the light switch in the pitch dark.* | **gathering** *We could just make out some figures in the gathering dark.*
• PREP. **after ~** *The girls weren't allowed out after dark.* **before ~** *We'd better try and finish this job before dark.* **in the ~** *I hate getting up in the dark.*
• PHRASES **afraid of the dark** *Many small children are afraid of the dark.*

dark *adj.*

• VERBS **be, look | get, go, grow** *It gets dark at about six o'clock.* ◊ *Suddenly the whole sky went dark.* ◊ *As it grew dark, they gathered round the fire.* | **remain, stay**
• ADV. **very | completely | almost, nearly** *It's only three o'clock and it's nearly dark already.* | **quite, rather**

darkness *noun*

• ADJ. **complete, pitch, total** *The building was in pitch darkness.* | **deep, inky** *the inky darkness of the tunnel* | **gathering** *It was becoming impossible to see the map in the gathering darkness.*
• VERB + DARKNESS **be plunged into** *The electricity failed and the house was plunged into darkness.* | **lie in, stand in** *The valley lay in darkness.*
• DARKNESS + VERB **come, close in, descend, fall, thicken** *We arrived at the village just as darkness fell.* | **lift** *waiting for the darkness to lift*
• PREP. **in (the) ~** *The building was in darkness.* ◊ *Her eyes seemed to glow in the darkness.* **into the ~** *The car disappeared into the darkness.* **out of the ~** *A figure appeared out of the darkness.*
• PHRASES **the hours of darkness** *The bombing took place during the hours of darkness.* **under cover of darkness** *They moved about under cover of darkness.*

dash *noun*

1 sudden quick movement
• ADJ. **quick, sudden | frantic, headlong, mad | final, last-minute**
• VERB + DASH **make**
• PREP. **~ across** *We had to make a frantic dash across town to get our plane* **~ for** *He made a sudden dash for the door.* **~ from, ~ through** *The book starts with a quick dash through the country's history.* **~ to** *He made a 200-mile dash to the hospital when a kidney donor became available.*

2 small amount of sth
• VERB + DASH **add** *Add a dash of lemon juice.*
• PREP. **~ of** *The food is European with a dash of Morocco.*

dash verb

1 go/run quickly
- ADV. **frantically | about, around, back, forward, off, out** *I've got to dash off now.*
- VERB + DASH **have to, must** *I must dash—I'm late.*
- PREP. **across, along, down, in, into, out of, through, to, up** *He dashed frantically across the road.*

2 destroy sth
- ADV. **quickly | cruelly** *Her hopes were cruelly dashed when her parents refused to let her go.*

data noun

- ADJ. **accurate, reliable | comprehensive, detailed, extensive | raw** *We have amassed the raw data and are about to begin analysing it.* | **factual, hard** *There is no hard data to support these theories.* | **empirical, experimental, numerical, observational, scientific, statistical | demographic, environmental, financial, geological, historical, technical**
- QUANT. **item, piece** *One vital item of data was missing from the table.* | **mass, set** *Special software is needed to manipulate the mass of data.* ◊ *Although we were using the same set of data, we obtained different results.*
- VERB + DATA **acquire, amass, capture, collect, gather, get, obtain** *We need to collect more data before we can do any more work.* | **enter, feed in | have, hold, record, store** *They are not allowed to hold data on people's private finances.* | **access, retrieve | analyse, examine, interpret, look at, study | handle, manage, manipulate, process** *The computer can manipulate massive amounts of data.* | **exchange, share, transfer | present (sb with) | provide (sb with)** *The government departments refused to provide the data that we required.*
- DATA + VERB **be derived from sth** *The data derived from this project has vastly increased our knowledge of how genes work.* | **indicate sth, reflect sth, show sth, suggest sth** *Data indicates that most crime is committed by young males.* ◊ *This data reflects the magnitude of the problem.* | **support sth**
- DATA + NOUN **acquisition, capture, collection | entry, input | storage | access, retrieval | analysis, handling, management, manipulation, processing | exchange, interchange, transfer, transmission | protection, security | source | archive, bank** (also **databank**), **base** (also **database**), **file | system**
- PREP. **in the ~** *We have found some very interesting things in the data.* | **~ about** *Data about patients is only released with their permission.* **~ for** *We have no data for southern Spain.* **~ from** *My aim is to synthesize data from all the surveys.* **~ on** *data on the effects of pollution*
- PHRASES **the acquisition/handling/storage, etc. of data, a source of data**

database noun

- ADJ. **large | comprehensive | national | computer, computerized, electronic | online**
- VERB + DATABASE **create, establish, set up** *We're trying to create our own computerized database.* | **add to, update** *The database is updated monthly.* | **access**
- DATABASE + VERB **contain sth** *The new database contains 200 000 images.*
- DATABASE + NOUN **application, engine, package, server, software, system | technology | creation, design, development | management | access | administrator, user**
- PREP. **on a/the ~** *The information is stored on a large database.* | **~ of** *a very large database of information*

date noun

1 particular day
- ADJ. **earlier, earliest** *She suggested an earlier date for*

the meeting. | **later, latest | exact, firm, specific** *I can't give you specific dates.* | **provisional, tentative | unspecified | significant** *7th May, 1999 was a very significant date in my life.* | **closing** *The closing date for applications is May 22.* | **expiry** *What's the expiry date on your credit card?* | **delivery | due** *The baby was born exactly on its due date.* | **birth | anniversary | sell-by** *This yogurt is past its sell-by date.* | **cut-off** *Historians disagree on the cut-off date for the medieval period.* | **commencement, completion** *The building was not finished by the completion date.*
- VERB + DATE **agree (on), arrange, decide (on), fix, set** *Can we fix dates for the holiday?* ◊ *Has a date been fixed for the meeting?*
- PREP. **after a/the ~** *We cannot accept applications received after this date.* **at a... ~** *The election is scheduled to take place at an unspecified date in the autumn.* **before a/the ~, by a/the ~** *The building must be finished by the date agreed.* **from a/the ~** *The agreement runs from that date.* **on a/the ~** *I've got two meetings on that date.* | **~ for** *We need to set a date for the wedding.* **~ of** *the date of the election*
- PHRASES **the/your big date** *Joe's getting ready for his big date on 3rd March, when he gets married.* **at a/some future date** *More money will be made available at some future date.* **at a later date** *We can do that at a later date.* **date of birth** *Please give your name, address and date of birth.* **of recent date** *The foundations are Roman, but the rest of the building is of more recent date.* **put a date on/to sth** *It's difficult to put a date on when this neighbourhood became fashionable.* **today's date** *What's today's date?*

2 appointment to meet sb socially
- ADJ. **dinner, lunch | blind** (= a date with sb you have not met before) *She met her husband on a blind date.* | **hot** (= exciting) *She had a hot date and wanted to look her best.*
- VERB + DATE **have** *I've got a date with Camilla on Friday night.* | **make** *We must make a date to have lunch.* | **keep** *She wanted to arrive in time to keep her date.* | **break, cancel** *He was late, and ended up breaking their dinner date.*
- PREP. **on a ~** *She's out on a date with her new boyfriend.* | **~ with**

date verb

- ADV. **accurately, precisely** *It has not yet been possible to date the paintings accurately.*

dated adj.

- VERBS **appear, be, look, seem, sound | become**
- ADV. **hopelessly, very | a bit, a little, rather, slightly, somewhat** *These ideas seem a bit dated now.* | **curiously** *This drama series is supposedly modern yet its characters live in a curiously dated world.*

daughter noun

- ADJ. **baby, newborn | little, small, young | teenage | grown-up | only | eldest, first-born, middle, oldest, youngest | elder, younger | illegitimate, legitimate | dutiful, good | long-lost | married, unmarried**
- VERB + DAUGHTER **have** *They've got three young daughters.* | **bear** (*formal*), **give birth to** *His wife recently gave birth to a daughter.* | **bring up** *Living alone and trying to bring up a small daughter is no easy task.*
- DAUGHTER + VERB **grow up**

dawn noun

1 early morning
- ADJ. **grey**
- VERB + DAWN **greet** (*literary*) *He always got up to greet the dawn.*

NOTE
Days of the week

last, next, that, this (coming)~
~last/next (week)
  The concert is this coming
  Wednesday.
  Are you free next Thursday?
  She's arriving on Friday next.
the~before, the previous~
  I'd been paid the previous Friday.
the following~
  She was due to start work the
  following Monday.
~of last/next/that/this week
  He arrived on Monday of last week.
the~before last
  We came here the Tuesday
  before last.
~week, a week on~
  I've bought tickets for Thursday
  week (= for the performance that is
  seven days after Thursday).
the first/second/third/last~in/of the
month
  The museum is free on the last
  Sunday of every month.
alternate~s, each, every~
  The competition is fixed for
  alternate Wednesdays.

all day~
  The restaurant is closed all day
  Saturday.
~afternoon, evening, morning,
night, etc.
  I'll see you on Friday evening.
  Saturday lunchtimes are very busy
  in the restaurant.
first thing (on)~
  I'll post it first thing on Monday
  morning.
late (on)~
  The crash occurred late on
  Tuesday night.
one~ (*written*)
  One Saturday morning, without
  telling anyone of my plan,
  I boarded a bus and headed out.
spend~
  She liked to spend Saturday
  afternoon shopping.
see sb~ (*informal*)
  So I'll see you Monday, then?
manage~ (*informal*)
  I could manage (= meet you on)
  Tuesday, say 11.30?

open/closed (on)~
  We're open every day except
  Sunday.
~arrive, come, dawn (*written*)
  Monday dawned still and
  misty, with a promise of
  autumn sunshine.
on (a)~
  A public meeting is to be held
  on Wednesday at the town hall.
  She was born on a Sunday.
  I like to just relax on Saturdays.
between~and~
(from)~to~
  The ticket office is open until 5 p.m.
  Monday to Friday.
by, no later than~
  Entries are to arrive no later than
  Monday, 1 October.
for~
  A special meeting is arranged for
  Friday 17 May.
~'s deadline, election, game,
meeting, performance, race, etc.
  He was not present at Tuesday's
  meeting.

- DAWN + VERB **break, come (up)** *Dawn was breaking over the valley.*
- DAWN + NOUN **light, sky | chorus** *The dawn chorus* (= birds singing) *woke Robyn at five.* | **patrol, raid** *Ammunition was seized during a dawn raid on the flat.*
- PREP. **at~** *That morning, she rose at dawn.* **before~, by~, till/until~, towards~**
- PHRASES **(at) the crack of dawn** (= as soon as it begins to be light), **from dawn to dusk** *He works from dawn to dusk, and often well into the night.*

2 beginning
- ADJ. **false** *This sudden success may prove to be a false dawn* (= not the beginning of continued success). | **new**
- PREP. **~of** *the dawn of civilization/history/a new era* ◇ *Let's think back to the dawn of time.*

dawn *verb*

1 begin
- PHRASES **dawn bright, sunny, clear, cold, etc.** *The day dawned bright and sunny.*

2 become clear
- ADV. **suddenly | gradually, slowly** *It slowly dawned on me that he might have been mistaken.* | **eventually, finally**
- VERB + DAWN **begin to** *It was beginning to dawn on her that she had been fooled.*
- PREP. **on** *The dreadful truth finally dawned on me.*

day *noun*

1 period of 24 hours
- ADJ. **the following, (the) next | the previous | the other** *I was in your area the other day* (= recently). | **one, some** *I hope we meet again some day.* | **the very** *It happened on the very day* (= the same day) *that Kemp was murdered.* ◇ *The parcel arrived the very next day.* | **auspicious, big, eventful, field, historic, memorable, red-letter, special** *The tabloid press had a field day with the latest government scandal.* | **fateful, sad** *those killed in the hail of bullets fired on that fateful day* | **Christmas,**

Mother's, etc. | feast, holy | election, opening, market, pay, polling, sports, visiting, wedding | rest, school, study, training *the pattern of the school day*
- DAY + VERB **pass** *He thought of her less as the days passed.*
- PREP. **by the~** *He's getting stronger by the day.* **for a/the~** *They stayed for ten days.* **in a/the~** *We hope to finish the job in a few days.* **on the~(of)** *On the day of his wedding he was very nervous.* | **~of** *It was the day of the big match.*

2 time between sunrise and sunset
- ADJ. **beautiful, bright, fine, glorious, hot, nice, sunny, warm | cold, grey, rainy, windy | autumn, spring, summer/summer's, winter/winter's** *a fine summer's day* | **fun, good, great, happy, lovely, wonderful** *Memories of happy days on the hills never fade.* | **bad** *On a bad day chaos reigns and nobody can predict when a plane will leave.* | **full** *I knew I had a full day's driving ahead of me.*
- VERB + DAY **spend** *We spent the day gardening.*
- DAY + VERB **break, dawn** *As day dawned I found her already hard at work.*
- PREP. **by~** *We travelled at night and rested by day.* **during the~, for a/the~** *We went to the seaside for the day.*
- PHRASES **all day (long), at the end of the day, day and night, one of those days** *It's been one of those days when everything's gone wrong.*

3 hours of the day when you work
- ADJ. **working | bad, busy, hard, long, tiring** *a hard day at the office* | **good, quiet | 7-hour, 8-hour, etc.** *a 9-hour working day*
- PHRASES **a good day's work**

4 (often **days**) particular period of time
- ADJ. **early, former, old, olden** *in the early days of the cinema* | **school, student, young** *in his younger days* | **golden, happy, heady** *the heady days of the 'swinging sixties'* | **dark** *the dark days of recession*
- PREP. **in sb's~** *Things were very different in my grandfather's day.* **of the~** *the government of the day* **since the~s of** *Much has changed since the days of my youth.*
- PHRASES **gone are the days when …** *Gone are the days when you could do a week's shopping and still have*

change from £20. **the bad/good old days** *That was in the bad old days of rampant inflation.* **in this day and age, in those days, the present day** (= the situation that exists in the world now) *a study of European drama, from Ibsen to the present day* **these days** *Kids grow up so quickly these days.* **those were the days** (= used to suggest that a time in the past was better than now)

daylight *noun*

• ADJ. **broad, full** *He was robbed in broad daylight.* | **natural** *I prefer to work in natural daylight.* | • VERB + DAYLIGHT **let in** *The thin curtains let in the daylight.* | **shut out** *The shutters were closed to keep out the daylight.* | **emerge into** *The prisoners emerged, blinking, into daylight.* | • DAYLIGHT + VERB **filter through sth, flood in, penetrate sth** *A little daylight was filtering through the curtains.* ◇ *He drew back the curtains and the daylight flooded in.* ◇ *The daylight penetrated to the far corners of the room.* | **break** *Towards 6 a.m. daylight broke.* | **fade** *The evening turned cool as daylight faded.* | • DAYLIGHT + NOUN **hours** *The public has access during daylight hours.* | • PREP. **before~** *She was up before daylight.* **by~** *By daylight the fire was almost under control.* **in~** *I can see better in daylight.* **into the~** *She went back out into the daylight.* | • PHRASES **the hours of daylight** *The machines roar incessantly during the hours of daylight.*

daytime *noun*

• DAYTIME + NOUN **phone number, telephone number** | **television** | **temperature** | **hours** | • PREP. **during the~, in the~** *Resist the temptation to nap in the daytime.*

dazed *adj.*

• VERBS **appear, be, feel, look, seem, sound** *She looked dazed and frightened.* | **leave sb** *The punch left him dazed and bleeding.* | • ADV. **almost** | **half** | **a bit, a little, slightly** *I still felt a little dazed.* | • PREP. **by** *half dazed by shock*

dead *adj.*

• VERBS **be, lie** *His wife lay dead beside him.* | **look** | **sham** *The animal will sometimes escape danger by shamming dead.* | **drop** *He just dropped dead one day in his garden.* | **shoot sb, strike sb** *Gunmen shot dead a policeman.* ◇ *She had been struck dead by lightning.* | **find sb** *The woman was found dead with a rope round her neck.* | **declare sb, pronounce sb** *She was declared dead on arrival at the hospital.* | • ADV. **quite** *I'm afraid he's quite dead.* | • PHRASES **dead and buried** *(figurative) In ten years he'll be dead and buried as a politician.* **dead and gone** *That won't happen until long after I'm dead and gone.* **dead or alive** *We didn't know whether the fish was dead or alive.* **more dead than alive** *Poor child, she looks more dead than alive.*

deadline *noun*

• ADJ. **strict, tight** | • VERB + DEADLINE **have, work to** *We're working to a very tight deadline.* | **impose, set** *The deadline set by the High Court is Monday 3rd March.* | **extend** *We're asking them to extend the deadline.* | **meet** *It will be a struggle to meet the deadline.* | **miss** | • DEADLINE + VERB **approach** *She began to panic as the deadline approached.* | **expire, pass** *The Wednesday deadline passed without any communication from the rebel leader.*

• PREP. **before a/the~, by a/the~** *I must get this report finished by tomorrow's deadline.* | **~for** *The deadline for entries is noon Thursday.*

deadlock *noun*

• ADJ. **complete** | **political** | • VERB + DEADLOCK **end in, reach** *The negotiations ended in deadlock.* ◇ *The strike appeared to have reached a deadlock.* | **break, resolve** | • PREP. **in~** *The negotiations were adjourned in deadlock last week.* | **~ between** *the deadlock between striking workers and their employer* **~in** *The summit called for an end to the deadlock in the peace talks.* **~over** *The government has called new talks in an attempt to break the deadlock over the issue of redundancy money.* | • PHRASES **a state of deadlock** *Talks between the two sides remain in a state of complete deadlock.*

deaf *adj.*

• VERBS **be** | **be born** *Their child was born deaf.* | **become, end up, go** *He eventually went deaf.* | **remain** *She remained deaf until she died.* | **leave sb, make sb** *Standing next to the machine all day left her deaf in one ear.* | • ADV. **very** | **profoundly** *(technical),* **stone, totally** *Many of these children are profoundly deaf.* ◇ *It's no good shouting—he's stone deaf.* | **a little, partially, rather, slightly** *She spoke loudly because her mother was a little deaf.* | **chronically** *helping chronically deaf patients* | • PREP. **~to** *(figurative) The committee remained deaf to our suggestions.* | • PHRASES **deaf in one ear**

deal *noun*

• ADJ. **fair, good** | **major** *They are hoping to clinch a major deal to supply computers to the army.* | **exclusive** *The TV station has signed an exclusive deal to show all United's home games.* | **lucrative** | **five-year, etc.** | **long-term** | **compromise** | **cut-price** *The company are offering cut-price deals on many flights.* | **shady** *He has been mixed up in several shady deals with arms dealers.* | **package** *The union accepted a package deal including higher pension and longer holiday allowance.* | **business, financial, political, trade** | **pay, sponsorship** | **arms, weapons** | **two-book, three-film, etc.** *The band signed a two-album deal with a record company.* | • VERB + DEAL **agree, arrange, close, complete, conclude, cut** *(informal),* **do, make, negotiate, reach, seal, sign, strike** *Management and unions have agreed a new deal on pay and productivity.* ◇ *I'll make a deal with you —I'll work evenings if you'll work weekends.* | **clinch, get, secure, win** *Nurses have taken to the streets to get a fair deal from the government.* | **have** *She has a lucrative deal with a cosmetics company.* | **pull out of** *Britain pulled out of the deal because of rising costs.* | **scupper** *Any sponsorship deal would be scuppered if Jones misses the Olympics.* | **offer (sb), propose** | **accept** *Staff have accepted a deal offering them a 2% share of profits.* | **reject** | • DEAL + VERB **go ahead** *The pay deal will not now go ahead.* | **fall apart, fall through** *The deal fell through when the author received a more attractive offer.* | • PREP. **in a/the ~** *They took over the company in a £750 000 deal.* **under a/the ~** *Under the deal, you save money if you repay the loan early.* | **~between** *a deal between France and Spain* **~from** *You may get a better deal from another bank.* **~on** *I got a very good deal on my new car.* **~ over** *The unions are ready to do a deal over pay.* **~with** *The company has done a deal with the catering staff.* | • PHRASES **get/have a bad/raw/rotten/rough deal** *Immigrants often get a bad deal when it comes to pay.* **get/have a fair/square deal** *The union tries to get a square deal for all its members.* **part of the deal** *Increased holiday allowance is part of the deal.* **the terms of the deal** *Under*

the terms of the deal, the band has to make two albums a year.
⇨ Special page at BUSINESS

deal *verb*

- ADV. **directly**
- PREP. **in** *The shop deals in second-hand books.* **with** *Our factory deals directly with its customers.*

PHRASAL VERB

deal with sth

- ADV. **quickly, speedily | at length, fully** *This topic is dealt with at greater length in the following chapter.* | **effectively | fairly, properly** *You have not dealt fairly with me.* | **easily** *Not all complaints are so easily dealt with.* | **separately** *The two issues should be dealt with separately.* | **together**
- PHRASES **a way of dealing with sth** *We discussed different ways of dealing with the problem.*

dealer *noun*

- ADJ. **licensed** *It is always a good idea to sell through a licensed dealer.* | **reputable** *Always buy from a reputable dealer.* | **shady, unscrupulous | antique/antiques, arms, art, car, drug**
- PREP. **through a/the ~** *She sold the painting through a London art dealer.* | **~ in** *a dealer in antiques*
⇨ Note at JOB

dealings *noun*

- ADJ. **extensive | personal | day-to-day** *The new arrangements will help the banks in their ordinary day-to-day dealings.* | **future | corrupt, fraudulent, illegal, underhand | business, commercial, financial**
- VERB + DEALINGS **have** *They had extensive dealings with officials in Rome.*
- PREP. **in your ~ with** *We need to be very careful in our dealings with these distressed young people.*

death *noun*

- ADJ. **early, premature, untimely** *The president's untimely death has thrown the country into chaos.* | **sudden, unexpected | immediate, instant | quick | slow | approaching, imminent, impending | certain** *He had been miraculously saved from almost certain death.* | **terrible | tragic** *the tragic death of their son* | **mysterious, suspicious** *Police are not treating the death as suspicious.* | **natural, unnatural | accidental** *a verdict of accidental death* | **violent** *Police report a decrease in violent deaths.* | **painful | cot, road | living** *(figurative) the living death of captivity*
- VERB + DEATH **bring, cause, lead to, mean, result in** *the drivers who bring death to our roads* ◇ *Poor living conditions can lead to early death.* ◇ *Touching the wires means instant death.* ◇ *The brutal attack resulted in the man's death.* | **die, face, meet** *She died a slow and painful death.* ◇ *He met his death two years later.* | **contemplate | risk | fear | approach, be near, near | cheat, escape** *He escaped death by inches when a tree fell on his tent.* | **save sb from | mourn** *mourning the death of their daughter* | **bleed to, burn to, choke to, freeze to, starve to | condemn sb to, sentence sb to | batter sb to, beat sb to, burn sb to, choke sb to, club sb to, crush sb to, flog sb to, hack sb to, kick sb to, put sb to, stab sb to, stone sb to, torture sb to, trample sb to | be punishable/punished by** *Incest was punishable by death.*
- DEATH + VERB **come, happen, occur** *Her death came at the age of 82.* ◇ *More deaths occur in winter.* | **result from** *deaths resulting from disease*
- DEATH + NOUN **rate** *The government's campaign aims to cut the death rate from heart attacks.* | **toll** *The death toll in the earthquake has been put at over one thou-*

sand. | **penalty, sentence** *If found guilty of drug trafficking, the pair could face the death penalty.* | **row** *There are currently over 3 000 prisoners on death row.* | **certificate | benefit** *Your next of kin will receive death benefit if you die in an accident.* | **duties** *After the death duties had been paid, there was little money left for the family.* | **threat** *The actor has received death threats since appearing in the controversial film.* | **wish** *He took drugs as if he had some kind of death wish.* | **agonies, throes** *The snake was writhing in its death agonies.* ◇ *(figurative) By 1740 European feudalism was in its death throes.* | **bed** (also **deathbed**) *On his deathbed, my father made me promise not to sell the house.* | **squad** *Paramilitary death squads are rumoured to be operating in the area.* | **warrant** *(often figurative) By publicly condemning the terrorists he was signing his own death warrant.* | **camp** *He died as a prisoner of war in an enemy death camp.*
- PREP. **after (sb's) ~** *Do you believe in life after death?* **at ~** *(formal) The average age at death of plague victims was 14.* **before (sb's) ~, in ~** *His face looked more peaceful in death than it had during his last days.* **near (to) ~** *It was clear that the dog was near death.* **on sb's ~** *On Samuel's death, the farm passed to his sons.* | **~ by** *death by starvation* **~ from** *Two deaths from cholera have been reported.*
- PHRASES **cause of death** *The coroner said the cause of death was a stroke.* **a matter of life and/or death** *Fulfilling orders on time is a matter of life and death for a small company.* **sentence of death** *Four prisoners were under sentence of death.*

debatable *adj.*

- VERBS **be | remain**
- ADV. **highly, very** *This is a highly debatable point.* | **somewhat**

debate *noun*

1 discussion

- ADJ. **considerable | fierce, heated, intense, lively, vigorous** *There has been heated debate about whether the film should be allowed.* | **wider** *You cannot separate unemployment from the wider debate about the economy.* | **public** *Television actually encourages public debate about such issues.* | **political**
- VERB + DEBATE **have | contribute to** *Many leading charities have contributed to the debate on world poverty.* | **encourage, promote** *A healthy society promotes vigorous debate.* | **provoke, spark off** *This accident has sparked off an intense debate on road safety.* | **stifle** *He accused the government of trying to stifle debate.* | **lose, win** *The environmentalists seem to have lost the debate over the building of this road.* | **be a matter for, be open to** *The benefits of the new law are open to debate.*
- DEBATE + VERB **rage, take place** *A debate about safety is taking place in schools everywhere.*
- PREP. **under ~** *The issue is still under debate.* | **~ about/on/over** *the debate on the environment* **~ among** *the debate among academics* **~ between, ~ surrounding** *the debate surrounding contemporary art* **~ with**
- PHRASES **the subject of debate** *The proposed changes to the law have been the subject of much debate.*

2 a formal discussion

- ADJ. **brief | lengthy, long | acrimonious, fierce, heated, lively, stormy** *a stormy debate in the House of Commons* | **congressional, parliamentary** *a parliamentary debate on the fishing industry*
- VERB + DEBATE **have, hold** *We had a brief debate about whether or not to accept the offer.* ◇ *The union holds debates for students.* | **participate in, speak in, take part in** *Do you ever speak in debates?* | **open** *The prime minister will open the debate.* | **close | lose, win** *The government lost the debate in the House of Commons.*

● PREP. **during/in a/the~ | ~ about/on** *Many of these points were raised during the debate on prison reform.*

debate *verb*

● ADV. **fully, properly, seriously, thoroughly | fiercely, hotly** *The issue is still being hotly debated.* **| openly, publicly** *The question of security needs to be debated publicly.* **| at length, endlessly, extensively**
● PREP. **with** *a presidential candidate debating with his opponent* ◇ *He sat there debating with himself what to do.*
● PHRASES **be widely debated** *The report has been widely debated in the industry.*

debit *verb*

● ADV. **automatically**
● PREP. **from** *The money will be debited from your account.* **with** *Your current account is automatically debited with the amount of your purchase.*

debris *noun*

● ADJ. **flying** *She was hit on the head by flying debris.* **| food, plant, rock** *These worms feed on plant debris.* **| garden, industrial, volcanic**
● QUANT. **piece | heap, pile**
● VERB + DEBRIS **scatter, shower** *The tank exploded, scattering debris all over the field.* **| clear (away/up), clear sth of, remove** *Teams of people are working to clear the debris.* ◇ *Remember to clear the drain of debris regularly.* **| search through, sift through** *Police have spent the day sifting through the debris for clues.*
● DEBRIS + VERB **accumulate** *Debris accumulates at the bottom of the bottle.*
● PREP. **among the~, in the~** *She found a pair of children's shoes among the debris.* **through the~**

debt *noun*

1 sum of money owed
● ADJ. **big, crippling, enormous, high, huge, large, massive, substantial** *He was burdened with crippling debts.* **| mounting** *a company faced with mounting debts* **| outstanding, unpaid** *She used her lottery winnings to pay off her outstanding debts.* **| overdue | bad** (= that cannot be repaid) *Bad debt has hit the bank's profits this year.* **| long-term, short-term | overall, total | gross, net | commercial, corporate | external, foreign, international | national, public** *The country has a national debt of 80% of GNP.* **| gambling**
● VERB + DEBT **be burdened with, have, owe (sb)** *the substantial debts that the company owed to the bank* **| incur, run up** *She ran up huge debts on her credit card.* **| clear, meet, pay (back/off), repay, settle** *Without a job, he'll never clear his debts.* ◇ *It'll take months to pay off all your debts.* **| reduce | tackle** *The new governments main aim is to tackle the country's massive debt.* **| default on** *The firm defaulted on its debt and its assets were seized.* **| cancel, wipe off/out, write off** *After a series of meetings, the banks were forced to write off the company's debts.* **| service** (= pay interest on) *The fall in exports has left the country unable to service its debts.* **| reschedule, restructure** *The company has reached a deal with its major creditors allowing it to restructure its debts.* **| secure** *a debt secured on property*
● DEBT + VERB **fall due | stand at sth, total sth** *The national debt stands at $7 000 million.* **| arise from sth** *debts arising from bad investments*
● DEBT + NOUN **collection, collector | burden**
● PREP. **of~** *$80 million of debt*
● PHRASES **a burden of debt** *Faced with a mounting burden of debt, he sold off the company.* **payment/repayment/settlement of a debt**

2 state of owing money

● ADJ. **serious**
● VERB + DEBT **go into, get into, slip into** *It is easy to get into serious debt with a credit card.* **| get out of** *You can get out of debt by strict economizing.*
● PREP. **in~** *He was heavily in debt by the time he sought advice.* **out of~** *struggling to stay out of debt*
● PHRASES **deeply/heavily in debt**

3 sth that you owe sb
● ADJ. **great**
● VERB + DEBT **owe | acknowledge, recognize**
● PREP. **in sb's~** *I am in Ruth's debt for the excellent advice she gave me.* **| ~ to** *In the introduction, the author acknowledges her debt to other writers on the subject.*
● PHRASES **owe a debt of gratitude to sb** *We owe a great debt of gratitude to our families for their support.*

decade *noun*

● ADJ. **present | coming, following, next | last, past, preceding, previous, recent**
● DECADE + VERB **elapse, go by, pass** *This decade has passed uneventfully.* **| begin, open, start** *This decade began badly for us.* **| close, end | see sth** *The past decade has seen a huge rise in the number of computer owners.*
● PREP. **during a/the ~, for a/the ~, in a/the ~, over a/the~, throughout a/the~, within a/the~**

decay *noun*

● VERB + DECAY **rapid | slow | dental, tooth | economic, industrial, urban | moral, physical, social**
● VERB + DECAY **cause** *Bacteria sticks to food debris in the teeth, causing decay.* **| stop** *Without a lot of money, the mayor won't be able to stop urban decay.* **| reverse** *This government promises to reverse industrial decay.* **| prevent** *The wood is treated with preservative to prevent decay.* **| fall into** *old buildings that had fallen into decay*
● PREP. **in~** *The derelict buildings are the signs of a town in decay.* **| ~ in** *Smoking accelerates age-related decay in the heart and arteries.* **~ of** *the slow decay of the castle and the surrounding buildings*
● PHRASES **the process of decay, signs of decay** *My dentist could not find any signs of decay.* **an odour/a smell/a stench of decay** *A smell of decay pervaded the air.* **a state of decay**

decayed *adj.*

● VERBS **be, look, smell | become**
● ADV. **badly** *Some of her teeth were very badly decayed.* **| completely** *The wood was completely decayed.* **| sadly** *New Shoreham, now sadly decayed, has barely 100 inhabitants.*

deceased *adj.*

● VERBS **be**
● ADV. **recently** *her recently deceased husband* **| sadly** *His mother is now sadly deceased.*

deceive *verb*

● ADV. **easily** *Human nature is such that we easily deceive ourselves.*
● VERB + DECEIVE **attempt to, try to**
● PREP. **into** *The public should not be deceived into buying inferior goods.*

December *noun*

⇨ Note at MONTH

decency *noun*

● ADJ. **common, human** *a lack of common decency* **| public** *Your behaviour is an affront to public decency.*

● VERB + DECENCY **have** *He might have had the decency to let us know.*
● PHRASES **a sense of decency, standards of decency**

decent *adj.*

1 good/acceptable
● VERBS **be, look** *The pub looked decent enough.*
● ADV. **really, very | perfectly | half/halfway, pretty, quite** *We had trouble finding a hotel that was halfway decent.* | **enough**
● PREP. **to** *My uncle has been pretty decent to me.*
2 honest/respectable
● VERBS **be**
● ADV. **very | perfectly, thoroughly**
● PHRASES **do the decent thing** *I think the minister should do the decent thing and resign.*

deception *noun*

● ADJ. **cruel | elaborate** *This elaborate deception fooled his family for ages.* | **deliberate**
● VERB + DECEPTION **practise, use** *He'll use deception to get what he wants.* | **see through** *She failed to see through his deception.* | **obtain sth by** *(especially law)* *She was charged with obtaining property by deception.*

deceptive *adj.*

● VERBS **be**
● ADV. **highly, very | dangerously**
● PHRASES **can be deceptive** *Appearances can be deceptive—dangerously deceptive.*

decide *verb*

● ADV. **finally** *We finally decided to stay where we were.* | **sensibly, wisely** *He decided very wisely to keep his money rather than spend it.*
● VERB + DECIDE **be able/unable to, can/can't could (not)** *I can't decide what to do.* | **have to, must** *You will have to decide soon.* | **try to | be difficult to**
● PREP. **against** *They decided against taking legal action* **between** *It was difficult to decide between the various options.* **in favour of** *They decided in favour of reducing the fees.* **on/upon** *We're still trying to decide on a venue.*
● PHRASES **decide for yourself** *She should be allowed to decide for herself.* **the task of deciding sth** *The committee will have the task of deciding whether more cash should be made available.* **to be decided** *The exact time of the meeting is still to be decided.*

decision *noun*

● ADJ. **big, crucial, fateful, important, key, landmark** *(law)*, **major, momentous** *It was a big decision to make.* ◊ *In a landmark decision, the court agreed to hear evidence from twenty years earlier.* | **difficult, hard, tough** *the difficult decision of whether to go to university or nurse her sick mother* | **firm** *We need a firm decision by Friday.* | **prompt, snap** *I had to make a snap decision about what to do with the money.* | **hasty, knee-jerk, rash | final, irreversible, irrevocable** *On Monday, the board of directors will meet to make their final decision.* ◊ *The decision is irreversible.* | **informed** *I need more facts before I can make an informed decision.* | **arbitrary | good, rational, right, sensible, wise | bad, poor, unwise, wrong | collective, joint, unanimous** *In the end, the decision to scrap the project was unanimous.* | **majority, split | court, government, etc. | investment, policy, etc.**
● VERB + DECISION **arrive at, come to, make, reach, take** *Key decisions are always taken by the editor.* | **announce, give (sb)** *The committee will give us their decision tomorrow.* | **abide by** *The decision has been made, and we must all abide by it.* | **affirm, uphold** *The management committee upheld her decision to fire two of her staff.*

| **reconsider | appeal against, challenge** *plans to challenge this decision in the High Court* | **overrule, overturn, quash, reverse** *Nobody has the authority to overrule his decision.* | **defer**
● DECISION + NOUN **maker**
● PREP. **~about/on** *a decision on her future*
⇨ Special page at MEETING

decisive *adj.*

● VERBS **be, prove**
● ADV. **absolutely | potentially** *He had one potentially decisive factor in his favour: the element of surprise.* | **ultimately** *It is the chief executive's opinion which is ultimately decisive.*

deck *noun*

1 top outside floor of a ship/boat
● ADJ. **open**
● VERB + DECK **go up on** *When we heard the alarm, we went up on deck.*
● PREP. **below~** *The passengers were trapped below deck.* **on~** *I joined the others on deck.*
2 one of the floors of a bus/ship
● ADJ. **lower, top, upper | aft/after, main, poop, promenade, saloon, sun** *(on a ship)*
● PREP. **on a/the~** *sitting on the top deck of the bus*

declaration *noun*

● ADJ. **formal, solemn | ringing** *The Russian leader received a ringing declaration of support yesterday.* | **joint | unilateral | public**
● VERB + DECLARATION **issue, make** *The government will issue a formal declaration tomorrow.* | **adopt, sign** *All four countries have adopted the declaration against hunting rare animals.*
● PREP. **~about/on** *the UN declaration on Human Rights* **~of** *a declaration of war*

declare *verb*

● ADV. **virtually** *He has virtually declared war on the right-wingers in his party.* | **immediately, promptly** *Martial law was immediately declared.* | **formally, officially | openly, publicly | grandly, proudly** *She proudly declared that she had once been introduced to the Queen.* | **loudly | boldly, confidently, firmly, roundly, stoutly | brightly** *'I'm as fresh as a daisy,' he declared brightly.* | **solemnly | unanimously | unilaterally** *The communists had unilaterally declared a ceasefire.* | **hereby** *(law or formal)* *We, the people of Indonesia, hereby declare Indonesia's independence.*
● PREP. **to** *He declared his true feelings to her.*

decline *noun*

● ADJ. **catastrophic, considerable, dramatic, drastic, massive, marked, precipitate, precipitous, rapid, serious, sharp, significant, steep, substantial | gentle, gradual, modest, slight, slow | continuing, progressive, steady** *a steady decline in manufacturing* | **general, long-term, overall | absolute, inevitable, inexorable, irreversible, terminal** *an industry in terminal decline* | **economic, industrial, moral, political, urban** *the moral decline of the nation* | **national**
● VERB + DECLINE **fall into, go into, suffer** *The cloth trade went into gradual decline.* | **cause, lead to** *The increased gold price lead to the decline of his jewellery business.* | **arrest, halt, stop** *We must halt this decline in health services.* | **prevent | reverse | accelerate | see** *We have seen a sharp decline in educational standards over recent years.*
● PREP. **in~** *The motor industry is still in decline.* **on the~**

This area has been on the decline for some years now. | *~in a steep decline in sales* **~of** *the decline of British farming*
• PHRASES **the decline and fall of sth** *the decline and fall of a great civilization*

decline *verb*

1 refuse
• ADV. **politely** | **absolutely** *I absolutely decline to discuss my dealings with him or anyone.*

2 become smaller/weaker
• ADV. **considerably, dramatically, drastically, markedly, sharply, significantly, steeply** *The economy has declined sharply in recent years.* | **a little, slightly** | **fast, rapidly** *The market for these products is declining fast.* | **steadily** | **gradually, slowly** | **further**
• PREP. **by** *Profits declined by 6% this year.* **from, to** *The number of full-time staff has declined from 300 to just 50.*
• PHRASES **decline in importance/numbers/size** *This section of the market has slowly declined in importance.*

decompose *verb*

• PHRASES **badly/partially/partly decomposed** *His badly decomposed body was found many weeks later.*

decorate *verb*

1 make sth attractive
• ADV. **beautifully, elaborately, elegantly, gaily, intricately, lavishly, ornately, richly** *The room was lavishly decorated with tinsel and holly.*
• PREP. **with** *Decorate the cake with raspberries and whipped cream.*

2 with paint/wallpaper
• ADV. **nicely, pleasantly, tastefully** *The bedrooms are tastefully decorated.*
• PREP. **in** *The room is decorated in pale blues and greens.*

3 give sb a medal
• PREP. **for** *He was decorated for bravery.*
• PHRASES **highly decorated** *the most highly decorated unit in the British Army*

decorative *adj.*

• VERBS **be, look**
• ADV. **extremely, highly, richly, very, wonderfully** *The style is ornate and highly decorative.* | **purely** *The items he makes are purely decorative.* | **quite**

decrease *noun*

• ADJ. **dramatic, large, sharp, significant** *There has been a sharp decrease in pollution since the law was introduced.* | **slight, small** | **gradual, progressive, steady** | **corresponding** *Fewer houses are available, but there is no corresponding decrease in demand.*
• VERB + DECREASE **show** *This year's figures show a decrease of 30% on last year.* | **report** *Half the companies in the survey reported a decrease in sales.* | **cause, lead to, result in**
• PREP. **on the ~** *Marriage is still on the decrease.* | **~from ... to ...** *a decrease from 62% to just under half* **~in** *The new treatment led to a huge decrease in the number of deaths.* **~of** *a decrease of 20%* | **~to**

decrease *verb*

• ADV. **considerably, dramatically, drastically, markedly, significantly** | **slightly** *Spending has decreased slightly this year.* | **rapidly** | **steadily** | **gradually**
• PREP. **by** *Crime has decreased by 20 per cent.* **from, to** *Average family size has decreased from five to three children.* **with** *The number of quarrels among children decreases with age.*

• PHRASES **decrease in number/size/value** *The heart gradually decreases in size.*

decree *noun*

• ADJ. **emergency** *The government had the power to legislate by emergency decree independently of Parliament.* | **papal, presidential, royal** | **court**
• VERB + DECREE **adopt, issue, pass, publish** *The president issued a decree prohibiting trade unions.* | **sign** | **enforce** *Local inspectors helped enforce presidential decrees.* | **revoke** | **defy** *10 000 demonstrators defied the decree and gathered in the square.* | **govern by, legislate by, rule by** *The general will rule by decree until a general election.*
• PREP. **in a/the~** *In an emergency decree, the government banned all rallies.* | **~on** *a decree on property rights*

dedicated *adj.*

• VERBS **appear, be, seem** | **become** | **remain**
• ADV. **highly, really, truly, very** *The workforce is small but highly dedicated.* | **absolutely, totally, utterly**
• PREP. **to** *She is totally dedicated to her job.*

dedication *noun*

• ADJ. **complete, total** | **great**
• VERB + DEDICATION **have** *Not everyone has the dedication and the talent to achieve this.* | **show** | **need, require** *You will need dedication and determination to complete the course.* ◇ *The job requires total dedication.*
• PREP. **~to** *I really admire Gina for her dedication to her family.*

deduce *verb*

• ADV. **easily** | **logically** *The total amount can be deduced logically from the figures available.*
• VERB + DEDUCE **be able to, can** | **be possible to** *Using the evidence available it is possible to deduce quite a lot about how these people lived.*
• PREP. **from** *We deduce from his behaviour that he is trying to gain attention.*

deduct *verb*

• ADV. **at source** *Tax is deducted at source.* | **automatically** *This amount will be deducted automatically from your salary.*
• PREP. **from**

deduction *noun*

1 working things out from the facts
• ADJ. **brilliant** | **logical** | **reasonable**
• VERB + DEDUCTION **make**
• PREP. **by~** *She arrived at this conclusion by logical deduction.* | **~about** *We can make some deductions about the history of the ruins.*
• PHRASES **powers of deduction** *a detective with excellent powers of deduction* **a process of deduction** *She arrived at the solution by a simple process of deduction.*

2 taking an amount from a total/the amount taken
• ADJ. **monthly, weekly** *monthly deductions for health insurance* | **tax**
• VERB + DEDUCTION **make** *The company automatically makes tax deductions from your salary.*
• PREP. **~for** *deductions for travel costs* **~from** *deductions from his wages*

deed *noun*

• ADJ. **brave, daring, glorious, good, great, heroic, mighty, noble** *She felt that she had done her good deed for the day.* | **dark, dastardly, dirty, evil, terrible** *The prince swore she would be punished for her dastardly deeds.*

● VERB + DEED **do, perform, perpetrate** *She would not be able to relax until the deed was done.* ◇ *warriors who performed glorious deeds* ◇ *evil deeds perpetrated by wicked people*
● PREP. **in ~(s)** *He frequently expressed his love for her in words if not in deeds.*

deep *adj.*

1 a long way from top to bottom/front to back
● VERBS **be, look** *The water looks quite deep there.*
● ADV. **really, very | fairly, pretty, quite**
● PHRASES **ankle/knee/waist deep** *She stood knee deep in the water.*

2 low in tone
● VERBS **be, sound** *Her voice sounded very deep on the telephone.* **| become**
● ADV. **very | fairly, quite**

3 strongly felt
● VERBS **be, go, run** *This suspicion runs very deep among some government members.* **| become**
● ADV. **very** *a very deep feeling of love* **| fairly, quite**

defeat *noun*

● ADJ. **bitter, catastrophic, complete, comprehensive, crushing, decisive, devastating, disastrous, heavy, humiliating, ignominious, overwhelming, resounding, serious, stunning** *Their party suffered a heavy defeat in the election.* ◇ *The battle ended in a humiliating defeat.* **| narrow** *They lost 4–3 in their second narrow defeat of the week.* **| consecutive, successive | election, electoral, political | military**
● VERB + DEFEAT **accept, admit, concede** *She is very determined, and will never admit defeat.* ◇ *The prime minister conceded defeat and resigned.* **| face | go down to, slump to, to suffer** *The team went down to their fifth consecutive defeat.* **| reverse** *A skilful politician can always reverse any defeats.* **| avoid** *We just need to avoid defeat in our last two matches.* **| inflict** *The army inflicted a heavy defeat on rebel forces.* **| end in | lead to**
● PREP. **~ against** *last week's crushing defeat against Manchester United* **~ by** *their defeat by the French*
● PHRASES **defeat at the hands of sb** *The team suffered defeat at the hands of their oldest rivals.*

defeat *verb*

● ADV. **comprehensively, convincingly, decisively, easily, heavily, soundly, totally** *The English were heavily defeated by the Scots in the battle that followed.* ◇ *The proposed bill was decisively defeated in Parliament.* **| narrowly** *Our team was narrowly defeated in the final.* **| eventually, finally, ultimately**
● PREP. **by** *The motion was defeated by 20 votes to 18.*

defect *noun*

● ADJ. **fundamental, important, major, serious** *a fundamental defect in the product* **| minor, slight, small** *Goods with slight defects are sold at half price.* **| building, mechanical, structural | birth, congenital, genetic** *All lambs are checked for birth defects when they are born.* **| eye, heart, physical, sight, speech, visual | character**
● VERB + DEFECT **contain, have, suffer from** *The book contains serious defects.* ◇ *He has a congenital heart defect.* **| find** *The inspector found defects in the aircraft's construction.* **| correct, cure, remedy, repair** *This is a physical defect that cannot be cured.* ◇ *The builders agreed to remedy the structural defects.*
● PREP. **~ in** *major defects in the education system* **~ of** *a defect of her character*

defective *adj.*

● VERBS **be, prove** *If the goods prove defective, the customer has the right to compensation.*
● ADV. **highly, seriously, severely** *Her vision is seriously defective.*

defence *noun*

1 action to protect sb/sth from attack
● ADJ. **adequate, effective | natural** *the body's natural defence against viruses* **| national | air | civil | nuclear**
● VERB + DEFENCE **organize, plan** *to plan the defence of harbour* **| come to, leap to, rush to, spring to** *He always sprang to Rose's defence when Ed tried to criticize her.*
● PREP. **in ~ of** *to fight in defence of your country* **| ~against** *defence against attacks from the north*
● PHRASES **weapons of defence**

2 sth that protects sb/sth from sth
● ADJ. **effective | coastal, sea**
● VERB + DEFENCE **put up** *They put up an effective defence against the guerrilla forces.* **| overcome, overwhelm** *With her tears and angry accusations she completely overwhelmed his defences.* **| build (up)** *They are building up defences along the river.* **| breach** *The sea breached the coastal defences in a number of spots.*
● DEFENCE + NOUN **mechanism**
● PREP. **~against**

3 forces, etc. for protecting a country
● DEFENCE + NOUN **force/forces, system | minister, ministry | policy, strategy | industry | budget, cuts, expenditure, spending**

4 legal argument
● ADJ. **good | robust, spirited, strong | adequate | legal**
● VERB + DEFENCE **conduct, make, mount, put up, raise | destroy**
● DEFENCE + NOUN **counsel, lawyer**
● PREP. **in sb's ~** *She spoke in his defence.* **| ~ of, ~ to** *a defence to murder*
● PHRASES **counsel for the defence**

5 in sport
● ADJ. **good, strong, stubborn**
● VERB + DEFENCE **put up | destroy | strengthen**
● PREP. **in ~** *to play in defence*

defenceless *adj.*

● VERBS **be, feel, lie** *The city lay defenceless before the most powerful fighting force on the continent.* **| leave sb** *They were left virtually defenceless against enemy attack.*
● ADV. **entirely, quite, totally, utterly** *She felt utterly defenceless.* **| almost, virtually**
● PREP. **against** *They were completely defenceless against enemy attack.*
● PHRASES **poor defenceless** *stealing money from a poor defenceless old lady*

defend *verb*

1 protect against attack
● PREP. **against**
● PHRASES **heavily defended** *The city was heavily defended against attack.*

2 support
● ADV. **fiercely, hotly, robustly, staunchly, stoutly, strenuously, strongly, vigorously** *The company has strenuously defended its decision to reduce the workforce.* **| publicly**
● PREP. **against** *She defended her department against accusations of incompetence.*

3 in sport/competitions
● ADV. **successfully**

● PREP. **against** *The champion successfully defended his title against the American challenger.*

defendant *noun*

● VERB + DEFENDANT **charge** *The defendant was charged with disturbing the peace.* | **sue** *a defendant being sued by an insurance company* | **convict, find guilty** *The defendant was convicted of murder.* ◇ *The jury found the defendant guilty on all counts.* | **sentence** *The defendant was sentenced to three years in prison.* | **acquit, find not guilty | release**
● DEFENDANT + VERB **plead guilty/not guilty**
● PREP. **against the~** *the plaintiff's claim against the defendant* **for the~** *Several witnesses gave evidence for the defendant.* | **~in** *a defendant in bankruptcy proceedings*

defensive *adj.*

1 protecting against attack
● VERBS **be**
● ADV. **purely** *These are purely defensive measures.* | **essentially, largely** *a largely defensive campaign*

2 showing you feel sb is criticizing you
● VERBS **be, feel, look, seem, sound | become, get** *Whenever anyone mentions women's rights, he gets rather defensive.*
● ADV. **extremely, fiercely, very** *He did not once glance at his listeners and seemed fiercely defensive.* | **a little, rather, slightly, somewhat | oddly** *Her manner was oddly defensive, as he hadn't intended any criticism at all.*
● PREP. **about** *He is extremely defensive about his work.*

defer *verb*

● ADV. **further | indefinitely** *The decision has been deferred indefinitely.*
● VERB + DEFER **agree to, decide to**
● PREP. **for** *Sentence was deferred for six months.* **pending** *Diagnosis was deferred pending further assessment.* **till/until** *We agreed to defer discussion of these issues until the next meeting.*

deference *noun*

● ADJ. **great**
● VERB + DEFERENCE **accord, show, treat sb with** *The actress was accorded all the deference of a visiting celebrity.* ◇ *Why do you treat your boss with such deference?*
● PREP. **in/out of~to** *The traditional menu was changed in deference to Western tastes.* | **with~** *She spoke with great deference.* | **~to, ~towards** *deference towards your elders*

defiance *noun*

● ADJ. **blatant, flagrant, open** *flagrant defiance of the rules* | **childish**
● PREP. **in~(of)** *She held up a clenched fist in defiance.* ◇ *They organized a street demonstration in defiance of the government ban.* **out of~** *I left the room untidy out of sheer defiance.*
● PHRASES **an act of defiance, a gesture of defiance**

defiant *adj.*

● VERBS **appear, be, feel, look, seem | become | remain** *Despite the criticisms, she remained defiant.*
● ADV. **very | slightly** *He had a slightly defiant air.* | **openly** *Sylvia tossed back her dark hair in a gesture that was openly defiant.* | **persistently**

deficiency *noun*

● ADJ. **major, serious, severe | slight, small | dietary, nutritional | enzyme, hormone, mineral, nutrient, vitamin | calcium, iron, etc.**

● VERB + DEFICIENCY **have, suffer from** *suffering from a severe vitamin deficiency* | **correct, make good, make up, overcome, remedy** *I've been prescribed iron tablets to make up the deficiency.* ◇ *An engineer could remedy the deficiencies in the design.*
● PREP. **~in** *serious deficiencies in the health service*

deficient *adj.*

● VERBS **be, prove | become**
● ADV. **sadly, seriously, severely, very, woefully** *An educational system which fails to teach basic arithmetic is seriously deficient.* | **totally | rather, slightly**
● PREP. **in** *Their food is deficient in iron.*

deficit *noun*

● ADJ. **huge, large, massive, serious, substantial | small | net, overall | balance-of-payments, budget, budgetary, financial, fiscal, trade**
● VERB + DEFICIT **face, have, run, show** *If the government didn't run such huge deficits, the country would not have financial problems.* ◇ *The trade balance shows a deficit of two million pounds.* | **go into, move into, run up, slip into** *to prevent the country moving into deficit* ◇ *The company has run up a deficit of £30 000.* | **cut, eliminate, make up, reduce, tackle, wipe out** *You cannot cut a budget deficit simply by raising taxes.* ◇ *We will find it hard to make up this deficit.* | **overcome, overturn** *United are hoping to overturn a two-goal deficit from the first leg.* | **finance, fund** *The government was forced to sell state-owned companies to fund the budget deficit.*
● DEFICIT + VERB **run at sth** *a budget deficit running at 7% of GDP* | **grow, increase, rise, widen | decrease, fall, narrow, shrink**
● PREP. **in~** *The UK remained in deficit with all countries outside the EU.* | **~with** *the US trade deficit with Japan*

define *verb*

● ADV. **accurately, carefully, correctly, exactly, explicitly, precisely, specifically** *It is important to define these terms accurately.* | **clearly, fully, strongly, well | adequately** *There may be problems if responsibilities are not adequately defined.* | **ill, poorly | broadly** *We have chosen to define the scope of our study quite broadly.* | **loosely, vaguely | closely, narrowly, rigidly, strictly, tightly | simply, solely | easily | formally, officially | traditionally | culturally, geographically, socially** *the culturally defined role of women* | **legally**
● VERB + DEFINE **be difficult to, be impossible to | be easy to** *Social values are not easy to define.*
● PREP. **in terms of** *The difficulty of a problem was defined in terms of how long it took to complete.*

definition *noun*

● ADJ. **careful, clear, concise, exact, precise, unambiguous** *The term 'partner' requires careful definition.* ◇ *The author provides a clear definition of cultural awareness.* | **comprehensive, exhaustive | adequate, satisfactory | broad, loose, wide | narrow, rigid, strict** *According to a strict definition, the expenses of a self-employed person can be deducted from tax.* | **official, statutory** *The firm falls within the statutory definition of a 'small company'.* | **conventional, standard | alternative | working** *We need a good working definition of 'pollution'.* | **dictionary**
● VERB + DEFINITION **give (sb), provide (sb with), offer (sb) | need, require | fit** *This unusual building barely fits the definition of a house.*
● DEFINITION + VERB **encompass sth, include sth**
● PREP. **according to a/the~** *According to a strict definition of 'assault', she was not assaulted.* **by~** *A clinic for women would, by definition, deal with pregnancy and*

childbirth. **under a/the ~** *Under the broader definition of 'poverty', thousands more people would be included.*

deformed *adj.*

- VERBS **be | be born | become**
- ADV. **badly, severely** *She had a badly deformed hand.* | **slightly | hideously, horribly**

deformity *noun*

- ADJ. **appalling, severe | slight | congenital, genetic | birth | physical | facial, hip, limb, etc.**
- VERB + DEFORMITY **have, suffer from**

defunct *adj.*

- VERBS **be | become | make sth** *The long-playing record was made defunct by the arrival of the CD.* | **consider sth** *These machines are now considered defunct.*
- ADV. **almost, virtually | largely | sadly** *He wrote many articles for the now sadly defunct newspaper, the Daily Correspondent.* | **long, now** *the ruined buildings of a long defunct mine*

defy *verb*

- ADV. **openly** *openly defying the authorities*
- VERB + DEFY **be prepared to, be ready to** *Campaigners have said that they are prepared to defy the law in order to achieve their aims.* | **continue to**

degenerate *verb*

- ADV. **rapidly | easily**
- PREP. **into** *The solemn event rapidly degenerated into farce.*

degrading *adj.*

- VERBS **be, seem | find sth** *He found the work extremely degrading.*
- ADV. **extremely, really, very | rather, slightly** *the rather degrading conditions in the prison* | **socially**
- PREP. **to** *pictures that are degrading to women*

degree *noun*

1 measurement of angles
- VERB + DEGREE **rotate (through), spin (through), turn (through)** *The car had spun through 180 degrees on impact.*
- DEGREE + NOUN **angle** *Place the shelf at a 90 degree angle to the wall.*
- DEGREE + NOUN **through ... ~s** *If you study the sky through 360 degrees you will see a whole range of colours.*

2 measurement of temperature
- VERB + DEGREE **reach** *Temperatures inside the burning building are estimated to have reached 600 degrees centigrade.*
- PREP. **at ... ~s** *Water boils at 100 degrees centigrade.*
- PHRASES **degrees above/below zero, degrees Celsius/centigrade/Fahrenheit, minus 10, 20, etc. degrees**

3 amount/level
- ADJ. **considerable, exceptional, extraordinary, great, high, large, remarkable, substantial, surprising, unusual, the utmost** *the utmost degree of freedom* | **fair, moderate, modest** *It was possible to date these remains with a fair degree of accuracy.* | **low, minimal, slight, small** *He would try anything to make her even the smallest degree happier.* | **lesser** *The tax changes will especially hit those on high incomes and, to a lesser degree, small businesses.* | **varying** *keen amateurs who work hard, with varying degrees of success* | **alarming, dangerous, extreme** *His arguments are simplistic to an extreme degree.* | **acceptable, adequate, meaningful, real, significant** *The book fails to answer the question with any acceptable de-*

gree of certainty. | **appropriate, necessary, proper, requisite, right | unacceptable**
- PREP. **in ... ~s** *The party leaders were all found to be corrupt in varying degrees.* **of ... ~** *employees of various degrees of ability* **to a ... ~** *The boss sometimes follows her instincts to a dangerous degree.* **with a ... ~ of** *We all tried to find out about the bus service, with varying degrees of success.* | **~ of** *There is a degree of risk in any sport.*
- PHRASES **by (slow) degrees** *By slow degrees, the company's turnover dwindled to nothing.* **in (an) equal degree** *I felt excitement and sadness in equal degree as I waved goodbye to my colleagues.* **a greater or lesser degree** *We were all disappointed to a greater or lesser degree.* **to the nth degree** (= to an extreme degree) *The children tested her patience to the nth degree.*

4 qualification
- ADJ. **college, university | first, ordinary, undergraduate | higher, master's, postgraduate, research | BA, BEd, BSc, MA, MSc, PhD, etc. | honours | pass | good, poor | first-class, (lower/upper) second-class, third-class** *Candidates must have at least an upper second class honours degree.* | **honorary | business, medical, history, law, philosophy, etc. | professional** *Candidates must hold a professional degree in architecture.* | **external | combined, joint, joint/combined subject, joint honours** *a joint honours degree in Business Studies and Modern Languages* | **modular | part-time**
- VERB + DEGREE **have, hold | do, take** *He took a degree in law then joined a law firm.* | **be awarded, gain, get, obtain, receive | award sb, confer on sb** *The university conferred on him the honorary degree of Doctor of Laws.*
- DEGREE + NOUN **course, level**
- PREP. **~ in** *a degree in economics*

dehydration *noun*

- ADJ. **severe** *He died from severe dehydration.*
- VERB + DEHYDRATION **suffer from | die from/of | cause | avoid**

deity *noun*

- ADJ. **major, supreme | lesser, minor** *one of the minor Greek deities* | **benevolent | patron** *a shrine to the patron deity of the city* | **female, male | heathen, local, pagan, Roman, etc.**
- VERB + DEITY **worship** *a tribe that worshipped two main deities*
- PHRASES **the incarnation/manifestation/representation of a deity** *Many animals were seen as the manifestation of a deity.*

dejected *adj.*

- VERBS **appear, be, feel, look** *She looked sorrowful and dejected.* | **become, grow**
- ADV. **completely, thoroughly, totally, utterly** *They were thoroughly dejected and miserable.* | **rather**
- PREP. **about** *feeling rather dejected about the future*

delay *noun*

- ADJ. **considerable, enormous, lengthy, long, major, serious, significant, substantial** *After a considerable delay, the government has agreed to accept the recommendations.* | **excessive, inordinate, undue, unnecessary** *Undue delays have been caused by people not doing their jobs properly.* | **inevitable, unavoidable | short, slight | unforeseen | frustrating | further | airport, flight, traffic, travel | time** *There is a five-minute time delay on the bank's safe.*
- QUANT. **series** *After a series of lengthy delays, the case finally came to court.*
- VERB + DELAY **be subject to** *Flights to New York may*

be subject to delay. | **be plagued by, experience, face, suffer** *Passengers have experienced long delays.* ◇ *The project has been plagued by delays.* | **cause, lead to** *The strike has led to some delays in train services.* | **avoid, prevent, reduce** *Please address your letters properly so as to reduce delays.* | **apologize for** *I apologize for the delay in replying to you.*
● DELAY + VERB **occur** *Travellers complained about lack of information when travel delays occurred.*
● PREP. **without ~** *Please send him the information without delay.* | **~ in** *delays in getting to the airport* **~ of** *a delay of several weeks* **~ to** *further delays to the scheme*

delay *verb*

● ADV. **seriously, significantly** *Mellanby's arrival was seriously delayed by a late train.* ◇ *These drugs can significantly delay the onset of the disease.* | **further** | **unduly** | **slightly, somewhat** | **inevitably, unavoidably** | **unaccountably** | **deliberately**

delegate *noun*

● ADJ. **conference, congress, convention** | **government, party, trade union**
● VERB + DELEGATE **elect** | **send** *They decided not to send a delegate to the conference.*
● DELEGATE + VERB **attend (sth)** *No fewer than 2 000 delegates attended the conference.*
● PREP. **~ from** *a delegate from the local Labour party* **~ to** *the British delegate to the United Nations*

delegation *noun*

1 people who represent a company, country, etc.
● ADJ. **large, small** | **high-level, high-powered, high-ranking, important** | **international** | **all-party, joint** *The prime minister met with an all-party delegation from the city council.* | **government, military, official, parliamentary, trade union** | **business, peace, trade**
● VERB + DELEGATION **send** | **head, lead** *A well-known academic will head the delegation.* | **form** | **invite** *The government invited an international delegation to inspect the plant.* | **meet**
● DELEGATION + VERB **represent sth** *a delegation representing the new regime* | **include sth** *The delegation included representatives from nine nations.* | **visit sb/sth** *The delegation will visit several Middle Eastern countries for talks* | **meet sb** | **walk out** *The British delegation walked out of the discussions in protest.*
● PREP. **in a/the ~** *all the ministers in the delegation* | **~ from** *an official delegation from Austria* **~ of** *a high-powered delegation of Asian businessmen*
● PHRASES **the chairman/head/leader of a delegation, a member of a delegation**

2 giving a job to sb with a lower rank
● ADJ. **effective, successful** *All managers should learn effective delegation.*
● PREP. **by ~** *Many of these tasks can be dealt with by delegation.* | **~ of** *delegation of responsibility*

delete *verb*

● ADV. **accidentally, by mistake, inadvertently** | **automatically**
● PREP. **from** *His name will be deleted from the list.*
● PHRASES **delete as appropriate** *Mr/Mrs/Ms (delete as appropriate)*

deliberation *noun*

1 careful consideration/discussion of sth
● ADJ. **careful** *After careful deliberation, it was agreed to abandon the project.* | **considerable** | **lengthy, long**
● PREP. **~ about/on** *your deliberations on his future*

2 speaking/moving slowly and carefully
● ADJ. **calm, cool, quiet, slow** | **great**
● PREP. **with ~** *With slow deliberation, he tore the letter into pieces.*

delicacy *noun*

1 rare and expensive type of food
● ADJ. **great** | **exotic, rare** | **local** *Have you tried any of the local delicacies?*
● VERB + DELICACY **be considered** *The eggs of this bird are considered a great delicacy.* | **sample, try**

2 care and sensitivity/requiring care and sensitivity
● ADJ. **extreme, great, utmost** *He handled the situation with extreme delicacy.*
● PREP. **with ~** *These objects are very old and should be treated with great delicacy.*
● PHRASES **a matter of (some) delicacy**

3 lightness and gentleness
● ADJ. **exquisite** *the exquisite delicacy of the embroidery*

delicate *adj.*

● VERBS **be, feel, look** *The glasses looked very delicate.* ◇ *Her bones felt as delicate as a bird's.* | **become**
● ADV. **extremely, very** | **quite, rather, somewhat** *a rather delicate child* ◇ *This is a somewhat delicate subject.* | **surprisingly** *He had a surprisingly delicate touch.* | **politically** *a politically delicate situation*

delicious *adj.*

● VERBS **be, look, smell, sound, taste** *The recipe sounds delicious.* ◇ *The beef tasted delicious.*
● ADV. **most, really, truly** *The meal was really delicious.* | **absolutely, quite** | **rather**

delight *noun*

1 feeling of great pleasure
● ADJ. **deep, great, intense** | **absolute, utter** | **pure, sheer** | **mischievous, perverse** | **childish/childlike** | **endless** | **evident, obvious** | **mutual** | **aesthetic, sensual, spiritual** *His mind was reeling with an almost aesthetic delight at the beauty of the thing.*
● VERB + DELIGHT **express** | **find, take** *She took evident delight in frightening the children with horror stories.* | **give sb** | **scream with, squeal with, whoop with** *Alice squealed with sheer delight when she saw the monkeys.* | **be greeted with** *The news was greeted with great delight.*
● PREP. **in/with ~** *We danced around with childish delight.* **of ~** *She gave a whoop of delight and dived into the water.* **to your ~** *To my great delight, they phoned and offered me the job.* | **~ at** *He expressed his delight at seeing us all again.* **~ in** *I find a perverse delight in listening to traffic.*
● PHRASES **a cry/gasp/squeal of delight, much to sb's delight** *Much to the delight of the crowd, the band came back and did three encores.*

2 sth that gives great pleasure
● ADJ. **real** | **constant, continual** *The baby was a constant delight and source of amazement.* | **unexpected** | **culinary, gastronomic**
● VERB + DELIGHT **explore, sample** | **enjoy, savour** *Savour the culinary delights of Morocco.*
● PREP. **to** *The old lady's reminiscences were a continual delight to Constance.*

delighted *adj.*

● VERBS **appear, be, feel, look, seem**
● ADV. **greatly, highly, only too, really** *Mrs Cartwright said she would be only too delighted to present the prizes.* | **absolutely, quite** | **clearly, obviously, plainly** | **secretly**

'Poor Gloria,' she said, although she was secretly delighted. | **genuinely**
● PREP. **at** *They were highly delighted at the court's decision.* **by** *I'm delighted by your news.* **with** *He's really delighted with his new CD player.*

delightful *adj.*

● VERBS **be, seem**
● ADV. **most, really** *It has been a most delightful evening.* | **absolutely, entirely, quite, truly**
● PHRASES **delightful little** *It was a delightful little fishing village.*

deliver *verb*

1 goods/letters
● ADV. **free of charge** *The company will deliver free of charge.* | **by hand** *The package had been delivered by hand.*
● PREP. **to** *The letter was delivered to his office.*
● PHRASES **have sth delivered** *You can either collect the goods or have them delivered.*

2 baby
● ADV. **safely** *The baby was delivered safely on Tuesday night.* | **by Caesarean (section)**

delivery *noun*

1 act of delivering sth
● ADJ. **express, fast, immediate, prompt, quick** | **late** | **morning, next-day** | **recorded, scheduled, special** *Ensure all photographic material is properly packed and sent by recorded delivery.* | **guaranteed** *guaranteed express delivery to over 170 countries* | **safe** | **mail, milk, newspaper** *All mail deliveries were suspended during the strike.* | **service** *The cuts will inevitably impact on service delivery.*
● VERB + DELIVERY **do, make** *We do all our deliveries in the mornings.* | **accept, take** *The government has now taken delivery of the new fighter planes.*
● DELIVERY + NOUN **van** | **date, schedule, time** | **boy, man** *He was employed at the local grocery store as a delivery boy.* | **charge** | **service**
● PREP. **for~** *completed orders for delivery* **on~** *Please pay the driver on delivery.* | **~to** *The company offers free delivery to your home.*

2 goods delivered
● ADJ. **large, small**
● VERB + DELIVERY **get, receive** *The shop receives only one delivery of books per week.*

3 giving birth to a baby
● ADJ. **difficult, easy** | **preterm** | **breech** | **vaginal** | **Caesarean** | **forceps, ventouse** | *The figures show an increase in forceps deliveries.*
● VERB + DELIVERY **have** *She had a very easy delivery with her second child.*
● DELIVERY + NOUN **room**

delusion *noun*

● ADJ. **dangerous** | **foolish** *I thought the whole idea was just a foolish and dangerous delusion.* | **paranoid**
● VERB + DELUSION **get, have, suffer (from)** *The psychiatrist said she was suffering from paranoid delusions.*
● PREP. **under a/the~** *He seemed to be under the delusion that he would make his fortune within a few years.* | **~about** *He had no delusions about his feelings for Kate.* **~of** *She had delusions of persecution.*
● PHRASES **delusions of grandeur** (= a belief that you are more important than you actually are) *Don't go getting delusions of grandeur.*

demand *noun*

1 firm request
● ADJ. **legitimate, realistic, reasonable** *I think your demand for higher wages is perfectly reasonable.* | **unrealistic, unreasonable** | **radical** | **urgent** | **central, main, major** | **fresh, new, renewed** *There have been renewed demands for the government to take action to reduce crime.* | **growing, increasing** | **final** *A final demand for payment had been issued.* | **written** | **financial, political** | **government, opposition, popular, public, royal, union** *The management had no intention of meeting union demands.* | **pay, ransom, tax, wage** *A ransom demand has been made for the kidnapped racehorse.*
● VERB + DEMAND **issue, make, present, press, put forward** *Demands have been made for the immediate distribution of food to the refugees.* | **renew, repeat, step up** *Campaigners have stepped up their demands for immediate government action.* | **face** | **respond to** | **agree to, give in to, meet, satisfy, yield to** *My government cannot give in to the demands of an illegal organization.* | **reject, resist**
● PREP. **on~** *Campaigners insist that abortion should be available on demand.* | **~for, ~from** *demands from the opposition for a recount of the votes*

2 need/desire for goods/services
● ADJ. **big, buoyant, considerable, enormous, great, heavy, high, huge, insatiable, peak, strong, unprecedented** *Demand for the product is buoyant.* ◇ *There's always a great demand for our soups in winter.* | **burgeoning, growing, increased/increasing, rising** | **excess, extra** | **constant, steady** *She is in constant demand to make public appearances and give interviews.* | **changing, fluctuating, seasonal** | **current, future** | **latent, likely, pent-up, potential, projected, prospective** | **overall, total** *We can estimate that total market demand for electrical goods will rise by 8%.* | **declining, falling, limited, low, reduced, sluggish** | **consumer, customer, market, popular, public** *By popular demand, the play will run for another week.* | **domestic, export, foreign, local, world, worldwide** *The slowdown in domestic demand was offset by an increase in exports.* | **electricity, energy, housing, labour, etc.**
● QUANT. **level** *a high level of demand*
● VERB + DEMAND **cope with, meet, satisfy** *The factories are staying open all weekend to try to meet the consumer demand for this product.* | **create, generate** *It is the job of the marketing manager to create demand for the new product.* | **boost, increase, stimulate** | **reduce** | **exceed, outstrip** *Supply normally exceeds demand for the bulk of consumer goods.* | **forecast** *It can be difficult to forecast demand in the construction industry.* | **manage** *policies aimed at managing demand*
● DEMAND + VERB **grow, increase, rise** *Demand for personal computers has risen sharply.* | **decline, fall, slow (down)** *As demand slows, the need to export will return.*
● PREP. **in~** *These old machines are still in demand.* | **~among** *the potential demand among children* **~for** *increased demand for health products* **~from** *the demand from consumers* **~on** *This section of the population makes a high demand on health care resources.*
● PHRASES **supply and demand** *the law of supply and demand*
⇨ Special page at BUSINESS

3 demands difficult/tiring things you have to do
● ADJ. **considerable, enormous, excessive, extra, great, heavy, high, impossible** *I think the demands of this job are excessive.* | **exacting, pressing** | **growing, increasing** | **competing, conflicting, contradictory** | **day-to-day, everyday** *the day-to-day demands of the job* | **immediate** *the need for scientific research freed from the immediate demands of industry* | **external** *The person who cannot say 'no' to others' requests is likely to be overwhelmed by external demands.* | **economic, emotional,**

financial, physical, practical, sexual, social, technical *Life is hard for nurses on children's wards, where the emotional demands can be overwhelming.*
• VERB + DEMANDS **impose, make, place** *My elderly parents make a lot of demands on me.* | **respond to** | **cope with** *coping with the conflicting demands of work and family life*
• PREP. **~ on/upon** *My work seems to make more and more demands on my time.*

demand *verb*

• ADV. **aggressively, angrily, coldly, fiercely, furiously, harshly, indignantly, irritably, roughly, sharply** *'Where are the keys?' she demanded angrily.*
• PREP. **from** *He had demanded money from her.* **of** *They failed to provide the information demanded of them.*

demanding *adj.*

• VERBS **be, seem** | **become, get**
• ADV. **extremely, highly, very** | **fairly, pretty, quite** | **physically, technically** *a technically demanding piece of music to play*

demise *noun*

• ADJ. **sad** | **rapid, sudden** *The war brought about the industry's sudden demise.* | **early, premature** *He praised the union's aims but predicted its early demise.* | **imminent** | **eventual, final, ultimate** | **apparent** | **virtual** | **political** *the events which contributed to his political demise*
• VERB + DEMISE **bring about, contribute to, lead to**

democracy *noun*

• ADJ. **genuine, true** | **political** | **constitutional, parliamentary** | **multi-party** | **Western**
• VERB + DEMOCRACY **believe in, support** *people who believe in true democracy* | **fight for** | **establish** | **restore** *The military regime has promised to restore democracy soon.*
• PREP. **in a/the ~** *We live in a multi-party democracy.*
• PHRASES **pro-democracy** *a pro-democracy demonstration in the capital* **the road to democracy** *the need to overcome political apathy and advance on the road to democracy* **the spread of democracy**

democratic *adj.*

1 favouring/practising democracy
• VERBS **be** | **become** | **remain** *There have been major changes in the constitution, but the system remains democratic.*
• ADV. **genuinely, truly** | **fully, thoroughly** *a fully democratic society* | **fairly, quite, reasonably** *They have a fairly democratic form of government.* | **dangerously** *In 1776 these were considered dangerously democratic principles.*
2 being fair to different sides
• VERBS **be, seem**
• ADV. **extremely, very** | **fairly, quite, reasonably** *I think it was a reasonably democratic decision.*

demolition *noun*

• VERB + DEMOLITION **be due for, be threatened with** *The church has been threatened with demolition for years.* | **prevent, save sth from** *They started a campaign to save the houses from demolition.*

demon *noun*

• ADJ. **evil** *tales of travellers attacked by evil demons*
• VERB + DEMON **be plagued by, be possessed by** *He is plagued by demons which go back to his traumatic childhood.* ◇ *The villagers believed the girl was possessed by*

demons. | **be pursued by** *He fled as if pursued by demons.* | **cast out, exorcise** *an ancient ritual to exorcise demons*

demonstrate *verb*

1 show
• ADV. **amply, beyond doubt, clearly, conclusively, convincingly, successfully, well** *Our study demonstrates beyond doubt that the play was written by Shakespeare.* | **adequately** | **further** | **easily** | **elegantly, neatly** | **empirically, experimentally** | **graphically, vividly** *This tragedy graphically demonstrates the dangers of walking on the fells after dark.*
• PREP. **to** *The prime minister must demonstrate to the country that he is really in control of his government.*
2 protest
• ADV. **peacefully**
• PREP. **against** *Campaigners were demonstrating against the slaughter of dolphins.* **for** *Their objective was to demonstrate peacefully for civil rights.*

demonstration *noun*

1 public protest/march
• ADJ. **big, huge, large, large-scale, major, massive** | **mass, popular, public** *mass demonstrations against cuts in the health service* ◇ *The president's decision provoked public demonstrations.* | **street** | **spontaneous** | **peaceful** *Thousands gathered for a peaceful demonstration.* | **violent** | **hostile** | **protest** *a protest demonstration against the war* | **student** | **opposition** | **anti-war, pro-democracy, etc.**
• VERB + DEMONSTRATION **hold, organize, stage** *Taxi drivers staged a demonstration against the new law.* | **go on, join, participate in, take part in** | **call off** *The demonstration was called off at the last minute.* | **break up, disperse** *Police in riot gear dispersed the demonstration.* | **ban, suppress** | **provoke, spark (off)** *The minister does not wish to provoke further demonstrations.*
• DEMONSTRATION + VERB **take place** | **call for sth** *demonstrations calling for an end to sanctions* | **greet** *The visiting president was greeted by hostile demonstrations.*
• PREP. **at a/the ~** *police intervention at demonstrations* **during a/the ~** *Hundreds were arrested during demonstrations in the capital.* | **~ against, ~ in protest at** *demonstrations in protest at the arrests* **~ in favour of, ~ in support of** *student demonstrations in favour of a multi-party system*
2 showing/explaining sth
• ADJ. **physical, practical** *physical demonstrations of affection* | **cookery, product, etc.**
• VERB + DEMONSTRATION **do, give sb** *I'll give a quick demonstration of some knitting techniques.* | **watch**
3 sth that shows clearly that sth is true
• ADJ. **clear, convincing, dramatic, impressive, perfect, vivid** *The strike was a dramatic demonstration of the power of the workforce.*

demonstrator *noun*

• ADJ. **angry** *Angry demonstrators threw stones.* | **peaceful** | **anti-government, pro-democracy, etc.**
• QUANT. **crowd, group** *Police opened fire on a crowd of peaceful demonstrators.*
• VERB + DEMONSTRATOR **disperse** *Troops were brought in to disperse the demonstrators.* | **clash with, fire on, open fire on, use sth against** *Water cannon and tear gas were used against the demonstrators.*
• DEMONSTRATOR + VERB **gather** *The demonstrators had gathered in the cathedral square.* | **march** *Demonstrators marched on the parliament building.* | **protest** *demonstrators protesting against the lack of housing* | **call for sth, demand sth** *demonstrators calling for the removal of the government* | **disperse** *The demonstrators dispersed when the soldiers arrived.* | **attack sb, clash**

with sb *Demonstrators clashed with government soldiers in the country's capital yesterday.* | **storm sth** *Demonstrators then tried to storm the police headquarters.*
• PHRASES **clashes between police and demonstrators**

denial noun

• ADJ. **firm, strong, vehement, vigorous** *When I asked if she had cheated in the exam, she answered with a vehement denial.* | **explicit** *The document contains an explicit denial that the company ever sold arms.* | **government, official** *Despite official denials, it appears the government did make a deal with the terrorists.*
• VERB + DENIAL **issue, make** *The chairman of the company issued a denial of the allegations.* ◇ *Jefferson made no denial of his actions on that night.*
• PREP. **~from** *a denial from senior officials*
• PHRASES **a chorus of denials** *His question was greeted with a chorus of denials.*

denounce verb

• ADV. **angrily, bitterly, fiercely, strongly** | **publicly** *He was publicly denounced as a traitor.* | **formally**
• PREP. **for** *The government was bitterly denounced for the emergency measures.* **to** *Someone in the village must have denounced them to the authorities.*
• PHRASES **be widely denounced** *These new regulations have been widely denounced.*

density noun

• ADJ. **high, low** | **average** *an average density of 2.4 people per hectare* | **population, traffic** *The population density in this city is very high.*
• VERB + DENSITY **calculate, measure**
• DENSITY + VERB **change, vary** | **increase, rise** | **decrease, fall**

dent noun

• ADJ. **big, great, large** | **considerable, serious, severe, significant** *(all figurative) The latest health scare has made a very considerable dent in the sales of beef.* | **little, slight, small**
• VERB + DENT **leave, make** *The impact of the stones made little dents in the metal.* | **have**
• PREP. **~in** *My side of the car had a large dent in it.*

dent verb

1 make a dent in sth
• ADV. **badly** *The car was quite badly dented on one side.* | **slightly**
2 damage sth
• ADV. **badly, seriously, severely** *Being turned down for the job dented his pride quite badly.* ◇ *The appearance of these cheap goods from abroad has severely dented the company's sales.* | **slightly**
• VERB + DENT **fail to** *The experience failed to dent her confidence.*

dentist noun

• ADJ. **good** | **qualified, registered** | **NHS, private**
• VERB + DENTIST **register with** *She couldn't get treatment because she wasn't registered with the dentist.* ◇ ⇨ Note at DOCTOR (for more verbs)

dentures noun

• ADJ. **ill-fitting**
• QUANT. **set** *a new set of dentures*
• VERB + DENTURES **have in, wear** *She doesn't wear her dentures at night.* | **put in** | **remove, take out** *Remember to clean your dentures after you take them out.*

denunciation noun

• ADJ. **angry, bitter, fierce, violent** | **public**
• VERB + DENUNCIATION **issue, make** *In his speech, he made a fierce denunciation of government policy.*
• PREP. **~of** *a public denunciation of the corrupt system*

deny verb

1 say sth is not true
• ADV. **emphatically, fiercely, firmly, hotly, strenuously, strongly, vehemently, vigorously** *Both women vehemently deny the charges against them.* | **angrily, indignantly** | **categorically, flatly** *He has categorically denied being involved in the fraud.* | **explicitly, expressly** | **implicitly** | **formally** | **publicly** | **immediately, promptly** | **simply** *If anyone accuses me I shall simply deny it.* | **consistently, repeatedly** *He has consistently denied murdering his estranged wife.*
• VERB + DENY **cannot** *You can't deny that it seems a very attractive idea.* | **try to** *I know it was you I saw, so there's no use trying to deny it.*
• PHRASES **no one could/would deny that** *No one would deny that there is a very great need for change.* **there is no denying sth** *There is no denying the fact that she is an excellent scholar.*
2 refuse sb sth
• ADV. **cruelly** *They were cruelly denied victory by an injury-time strike from Owen.* | **effectively** *Children could be compelled to work on the farm, effectively denying them schooling.*
• PREP. **to** *You cannot deny this opportunity to me.*

depart verb

• VERB + DEPART **be due to, be scheduled to** *The plane was scheduled to depart at 8.30.* | **be waiting to** | **prepare to** *They shook hands all round and prepared to depart.*
• PREP. **for** *He departs for New York tomorrow morning.* **from** *We depart from Heathrow at ten o'clock tonight.*

department noun

1 of a government
• ADJ. **government** | **education, health, social services, etc.** | **fire, police** *The Tokyo police department is clamping down on organized crime.*
• DEPARTMENT + NOUN **official, spokesman, spokesperson, spokeswoman, staff**
• PREP. **~of** *the Department of the Environment*
2 of an organization
• ADJ. **accident and emergency, casualty, outpatient, physiotherapy** | **design, finance, marketing, personnel, planning, publicity, sales, etc.** | **biology, English, maths, etc.**
• VERB + DEPARTMENT **manage, run** *Staff criticized the way the history department was run.*
• DEPARTMENT + NOUN **head, manager, staff**
• PREP. **in a/the~** *Complaints are dealt with in a different department.* **within a/the~** *to gain promotion within the department* | **~of** *the Department of Town Planning*
• PHRASES **the head of (a) department, a member of a department**

departure noun

1 leaving/going away from a place
• ADJ. **abrupt, sudden** *Everyone was a bit puzzled by her sudden departure.* | **hasty, speedy** | **early** | **imminent, impending** *The guard blew his whistle to warn of the train's imminent departure.* | **flight** *The last check-in time is 45 minutes before flight departure.*
• VERB + DEPARTURE **make** *He made a hasty departure.* | **hasten** *Her row with the MD probably hastened her departure.* | **delay**

● DEPARTURE + NOUN **point** *Atocha station was the departure point for our tour.* | **date** | **gate, lounge** *We sat in the departure lounge waiting for our flight to be called.*
● PREP. **before ~, prior to ~** *You should receive your flight tickets at least a week prior to departure.* **on ~** *All visitors must sign the book on arrival and again on departure.* | **~ for** *his departure for Naples* **~ from** *her departure from London*
● PHRASES **the day/time of departure, the point of departure** *(figurative) The author takes Freud's dream theories as the point of departure for his essay.*

2 sth different from what is usual/expected
● ADJ. **fresh, new** | **dramatic, fundamental, major, radical, revolutionary, significant**
● VERB + DEPARTURE **be, mark, represent**
● PREP. **~ from** *This document marks a radical departure from earlier recommendations.*

depend *verb*

PHRASAL VERB

depend on/upon sb/sth
1 be affected by sth
● ADV. **crucially, greatly, very much** *The future of the company will depend crucially on how consumers respond.* | **entirely, solely, largely, mainly** | **partly, rather, to some extent** | **ultimately** *Whether or not we can go ultimately depends on the weather.*
● VERB + DEPEND ON SB/STH **seem to** *The outcome seems to depend on the type of soil used.*

2 need
● ADV. **heavily** | **entirely, solely**
● PREP. **for** *She depends entirely on her parents for money.*

dependable *adj.*

● VERBS **be, seem** | **find sb** *I find him very dependable.*
● ADV. **extremely, very** | **absolutely, totally, utterly** *She is loyal and totally dependable.* | **not entirely**

dependence *noun*

1 needing sb's help/support
● ADJ. **great, heavy** *a heavy dependence on imported materials* | **absolute, complete, total** *his total dependence on his family* | **continuing, growing, increased, increasing** *The country has a growing dependence on foreign aid.* | **excessive** | **mutual** *Their relationship is based on a strong mutual dependence.* | **economic, financial** | **emotional, physical, psychological**
● VERB + DEPENDENCE **have** | **reduce** *The government wants to reduce industry's dependence on coal.*
● PREP. **~ on/upon** *her economic dependence on her husband*

2 being addicted to sth
● ADJ. **alcohol, drug, nicotine, etc.**
● PREP. **~ on** *dependence on alcohol*

dependent *adj.*

1 needing sb/sth
● VERBS **be, feel** | **become** | **remain**
● ADV. **closely, deeply, greatly, heavily, highly, very** *Many of the patients are closely dependent on staff for day-to-day emotional support.* ◇ *The country is heavily dependent on oil and gas imports.* | **critically, crucially** *Modern science is critically dependent on high-performance computing.* | **absolutely, completely, entirely, solely, totally, utterly, wholly** *Jane had never met anyone so utterly dependent.* ◇ *The land is dry and wholly dependent on irrigation.* | **increasingly** | **essentially, largely, mainly** | **partially, partly** *34% of people in the survey were at least partially dependent on public transport.* | **directly** | **mutually** *The various organs of the body do not function in isol-*

ation but are mutually dependent. | **economically, financially** | **emotionally**
● PREP. **on/upon** *Small firms are dependent upon the local economy.*

2 dependent on/upon influenced/decided by sth
● VERBS **be**
● ADV. **strongly** | **entirely, solely, totally** *The amount of benefit you receive is entirely dependent on the amount you have paid in.* | **essentially, largely, mainly** *Your access to a good education is largely dependent on where you live.* | **partially, partly**

depict *verb*

● ADV. **vividly** *The book vividly depicts French society of the 1930s.*

deplete *verb*

● ADV. **heavily, seriously, severely** *Both teams were severely depleted by injuries.*

depletion *noun*

● ADJ. **rapid** | **serious, severe, significant** | **resource** | **oxygen, ozone, etc.**
● VERB + DEPLETION **cause, lead to** *Increased consumption of water has led to rapid depletion of groundwater reserves.*

deploy *verb*

● ADV. **effectively** *Tanks were deployed effectively during the long campaign.*
● PREP. **against** *She rejected the arguments that had been deployed against her.*

deployment *noun*

● ADJ. **effective, efficient** | **rapid** | **full** *Without the full deployment of resources, we cannot achieve our aims.* | **staff** | **military, troop**
● VERB + DEPLOYMENT **be available for**

deport *verb*

● ADV. **forcibly**
● PREP. **(back) to** *Many refugees were forcibly deported back to the countries they had come from.* **from** *He was deported from Britain last week.*

deportation *noun*

● ADJ. **mass** *the mass deportation of refugees* | **forced**
● VERB + DEPORTATION **be threatened with, face** | **recommend sb for** *The Home Secretary has recommended the two drug dealers for deportation.*
● DEPORTATION + NOUN **order** *The government issued a deportation order against the four men.*
● PHRASES **the threat of deportation**

deposit *noun*

1 money paid into a bank account
● ADJ. **bank, building society** *Building society deposits have increased by 2.3%.* | **cash** | **dollar, sterling, etc.**
● VERB + DEPOSIT **make** *She made a deposit of £60 into her account.*
● DEPOSIT + NOUN **account**

2 money which is the first payment for sth
● VERB + DEPOSIT **pay, put down**
● PREP. **~ on** *We've put down the deposit on our new car.*

3 money paid when you rent sth
● ADJ. **refundable, returnable** *All deposits for holiday cottages are refundable.*
● VERB + DEPOSIT **give (sb), leave (sb), pay (sb)** *You have to pay a deposit of £100 as well as two months' rent.* |

get back *You'll get back your deposit once we've checked the bikes are all right.* | **forfeit, lose** *If furniture is damaged, you will forfeit your deposit.*
• PREP. **~on** *I had to leave a £50 deposit on the bike.*

4 layer of sth
• ADJ. **large | rich | thick, thin** *The floods left a thick deposit of mud over the fields.* | **gas, mineral, ore, etc.** *an area with large mineral deposits* | **geological, glacial, sedimentary**
• VERB + DEPOSIT **have** *The region has many deposits of valuable oil.* | **leave**

depot *noun*

• ADJ. **distribution, storage, supply | freight, goods | arms, fuel, gas, etc.** *an explosion at an arms depot* | **bus, tram** *on its way back to the bus depot*

depreciate *verb*

• ADV. **quickly, rapidly**
• VERB + DEPRECIATE **be expected to, be likely to**
• PREP. **against** *Sterling is expected to depreciate against the dollar.* **by** *The rupee depreciated by 9 per cent.*
• PHRASES **depreciate in value** *Cars depreciate in value fairly rapidly.*

depressed *adj.*

1 unhappy/mentally ill
• VERBS **be, feel, look, seem, sound | become, get** *You mustn't let yourself get depressed* | **remain, stay**
• ADV. **acutely, deeply, extremely, really, severely, terribly, very** *She became severely depressed after her mother's death.* | **thoroughly | increasingly | a bit, a little, mildly, quite, rather, slightly | clinically, suicidally** *There is medical evidence to show that he is suicidal and clinically depressed.*
• PREP. **about** *She's terribly depressed about losing her job.* **by** *I was depressed by our lack of progress.*

2 not economically successful
• VERBS **be | become | remain, stay**
• ADV. **badly, severely, very** *The shipping trade was badly depressed.* | **relatively | economically**

depressing *adj.*

• VERBS **be | become, get | find sth**
• ADV. **deeply, extremely, profoundly, really, very** *We found it a deeply depressing experience.* | **infinitely** *I find politics infinitely depressing: none of the parties appeal to me.* | **a bit, faintly, fairly, a little, pretty, quite, rather, slightly, somewhat**

depression *noun*

1 unhappiness/mental illness
• ADJ. **black, deep, serious, severe | acute, chronic | mild | clinical | manic | post-natal**
• QUANT. **bout, fit, period** *The actor says he suffers frequent bouts of depression.* ◇ *In a fit of depression, she threw away all her favourite books.* ◇ *A period of acute depression can sometimes follow childbirth.*
• VERB + DEPRESSION **develop, fall into, go into, succumb to** *She fell into a black depression and refused to leave her room.* | **experience, have, suffer (from)** *She was diagnosed as having clinical depression.* | **be treated for** *His wife had left him and he was being treated for depression.* | **come out of, get over** *She was gradually coming out of her depression.* | **cause, lead to** *Bereavement can often lead to depression.* | **relieve, treat** *a new drug used to treat depression*
• DEPRESSION + VERB **deepen | lift** *Her depression has lifted now.*
• PREP. **in ~** *He may have killed himself in depression.* **with ~** *He's been off work for months with depression.*

• PHRASES **(a) cause for depression** *These results should not be a cause for depression.* **the depths of depression** *I was in the depths of depression after receiving my exam results.* **feelings of depression, the onset of depression** *The onset of depression often follows a traumatic event.* **a state of depression** *He was in a state of acute depression.* **symptoms of depression, treatment for depression** *She had been receiving medical treatment for depression.*
⇨ Special page at ILLNESS

2 period of reduced economic activity
• ADJ. **great, major, serious, severe | economic** *The country is experiencing a severe economic depression.*
• VERB + DEPRESSION **be in the grip of, experience | go into** *The housing market has gone into depression.* | **face**
• DEPRESSION + VERB **deepen** *The depression seems to be deepening.* | **end**
• PREP. **during/in a/the ~** *Many people lost their jobs in the great depression of the 1930s.*
• PHRASES **the depths of a depression, a period of depression** *periods of severe economic depression*

3 hollow part in the surface of sth
• ADJ. **shallow, slight | deep**
• PREP. **~in, ~on** *From the air, the photos show a shallow depression on the planet's surface.*

deprivation *noun*

• ADJ. **acute, severe, terrible | sensory | emotional | economic, material, social** *an area of acute social and economic deprivation* | **inner-city, urban | rural | sleep** *a study of the effects of sleep deprivation*
• VERB + DEPRIVATION **experience, suffer** *Many of the people suffered terrible deprivation.*

deprived *adj.*

• VERBS **be, feel**
• ADV. **extremely, severely, terribly, very | totally | relatively | economically, emotionally, materially, socially** *emotionally deprived children*
• PREP. **of** *children who are deprived of love*

depth *noun*

• ADJ. **considerable, great** *going down to great depths below the surface* ◇ *Younger students cannot be expected to have great depth of understanding.* | **shallow** *Water normally moves more slowly at shallower depths.* | **abyssal** *the abyssal depths of the ocean* | **black, dark, murky | surprising, unexpected** *the unexpected depth of his feelings for her* | **emotional** *music of great emotional depth*
• PREP. **at~** *The camera must be strong enough to resist the immense water pressure at depth.* **at/from/to a ~ of** *These fish are found at a depth of over 100 metres.* **at/from/to a ... ~** *The clam burrows in the sand to a considerable depth.* | **in~** *I studied phonology in depth at university.* | **out of your~** *I don't like going out of my depth in the sea.* | **~s of** *The rejection plunged her into the dark depths of despair.*
• PHRASES **the depths (of the ocean/sea)** *sharks lurking in the murky grey depths of the sea* **depth of emotion/feeling** *The demonstration showed the depth of feeling against the war.* **the ocean depths**

deputation *noun*

• VERB + DEPUTATION **organize | send** *They sent a deputation to the ministry to complain.* | **meet, receive**
• PREP. **~from** *The managing director agreed to receive a deputation from the factory.* **~of** *A deputation of 40 strikers was organized.*

deputy noun

1 second most important person
- ADJ. **acting | former** *a former deputy chairman of the Democratic Party*
- VERB + DEPUTY **appoint (sb as)** *A new deputy has not yet been appointed.* | **act as**
- DEPUTY + NOUN **chair, chairman, director, governor, head, leader, manager, minister, president, etc.** *He was appointed deputy head of the school.*
- PREP. **~ to** *She is acting as deputy to the chairman of the board.*

2 member of a parliament
- ADJ. **congressional, parliamentary** *133 of the parliamentary deputies voted against the treaty.* | **opposition | right-wing, socialist, etc.**
- VERB + DEPUTY **elect** *Three women were among the 77 deputies elected.*

deranged adj.

- VERBS **be, seem | become**
- ADV. **a bit, slightly | mentally** *They took her into hospital because she was mentally deranged.*

derelict adj.

- VERBS **be, lie, look, seem, stand** *The land lay derelict for ten years.* | **become | make sth** *The houses were made derelict by the fire.*
- ADV. **totally | almost, virtually | partially, partly** *a partially derelict mill*

derive verb

- ADV. **clearly** *Females and cubs clearly derive some benefit from living in groups.* | **largely, mainly, primarily | partly | solely | directly** *This income was derived directly from his writing.* | **originally, ultimately**
- PREP. **from** *We can derive some comfort from this fact.*

descend verb

1 move downwards
- ADV. **quickly, rapidly | slowly**

2 lead downwards
- ADV. **sharply, steeply | gently, gradually**
- PREP. **into, to** *The path descends steeply to the village.*

3 be descended from sb/sth be related to sb/sth
- ADV. **directly** *The breed is almost directly descended from the Eurasian wild boar.*
- VERB + DESCEND **claim to** *He claims to be descended from a Spanish prince.*

descendant noun

- ADJ. **direct, lineal** *Quechua, the lineal descendant of the Inca language* | **collateral | immediate | distant, remote** *He was an O'Conor and a distant descendant of the last High King of Ireland.*

descent noun

1 movement down
- ADJ. **rapid, swift | slow | steep | gentle, gradual | difficult, easy** *They began the difficult descent of the mountain's south west face.* | **final** *The plane was making its final descent so we had to fasten our seat belts.*
- VERB + DESCENT **make**
- PREP. **on/during a/the ~** *The engines failed on the plane's descent to Orly.* | **~ down** *I made a slow and painful descent down the stairs.* | **~ from** *the descent from the top of the mountain* **~ into** *(figurative) his descent into alcoholism* **~ to** *The plane began its gentle descent to Heathrow.*
- PHRASES **a rate of descent** *We slowed the balloon's rate of descent.*

2 surface that goes downwards
- ADJ. **gentle | steep**

3 family origins
- ADJ. **direct, lineal** *She claims direct descent from Queen Victoria.* | **common** *Most European languages have a common descent.* | **mixed | Chinese, Irish, etc.**
- VERB + DESCENT **claim, have | trace | share** *groups sharing common descent*
- PREP. **by ~** *She is Hungarian by descent.* | **~ from** *He claims to have traced descent from Christopher Columbus.*
- PHRASES **a line of descent** *Humans and other apes followed separate lines of descent from a common ancestor.* **of Mexican, Scottish, etc. descent** *She is of mixed European and African descent.*

describe verb

- ADV. **accurately, exactly, in detail** *Their daily lives are described in detail.* | **fully** *This process is fully described in section three of the book.* | **adequately | briefly** *He described briefly what happened.* | **vividly**
- VERB + DESCRIBE **cannot** *Words cannot describe our feelings at that moment.* | **be difficult to, be hard to, be impossible to | go on to** *He goes on to describe very vividly how Caesar was stabbed to death.*

description noun

- ADJ. **complete, comprehensive, detailed, full** *The catalogue gives a full description of each product.* | **accurate, apt, exact, excellent, fair, fitting, good, perfect** *'Like a fish out of water' was an apt description of how I felt in my new job.* | **vivid** *a vivid description of life in Ancient Rome* | **graphic, lurid** *She gave us a lurid description of the birth.* | **lengthy, long | brief, short | basic, simple | vague | objective** *A report is generally an objective description rather than a statement of opinion.* | **physical | job** *There was no mention of any cleaning in my job description.*
- VERB + DESCRIPTION **give (sb), issue, provide (sb with)** *Police have issued a description of the gunman.* ◇ *She was able to provide a description of the intruder.* | **fit** *A man fitting your description was seen entering the building.* | **beggar, defy** *His face was so odd that it defies description.*
- DESCRIPTION + VERB **apply to sb, fit sb** *I realized to my horror that the description of the killer fitted me.*

descriptive adj.

- VERBS **be**
- ADV. **highly, very** *a highly descriptive account of her journey through Africa* | **entirely, purely** *The passage is purely descriptive.* | **merely, simply | essentially, largely, mainly**
- PREP. **of** *The terms are descriptive of strong emotion.*

desert noun

- ADJ. **arid, barren, dry** *green fields surrounded by arid desert* | **vast | inhospitable | Arctic, polar | cultural** *(figurative) The theatre and cinema closed and the town became a cultural desert.*
- VERB + DESERT **become, turn into/to** *The land loses its protective cover of vegetation and soon turns into desert.* | **cross** *He became the first person to cross the desert on foot.*
- DESERT + VERB **stretch** *The desert stretched for endless miles on all sides of us.*
- DESERT + NOUN **area, country, land, landscape, region** *vast tracts of desert land* | **conditions | heat | sand, soil | floor, surface | plain | animal, plant**
- PREP. **across/through the ~** *their journey across the desert* **in the ~** *cold nights in the desert* **into the ~** *He drove off into the desert.*

deserted adj.

- VERBS **appear, be, look, seem** | **become**
- ADV. **completely, quite, totally, utterly** *The streets were completely deserted.* | **almost, virtually** | **largely** | **apparently** | **temporarily**

deserve verb

- ADV. **certainly, really, surely** *You really deserve a medal!* | **justly, richly, rightly, truly** *He finally received the recognition that he so richly deserved.* | **fully, thoroughly** *This hotel fully deserves its four-star grading.* | **hardly, scarcely** *It's true she made a mistake but she hardly deserves to lose her job.*
- PREP. **for** *She deserves some reward for all her hard work.*
- PHRASES **deserve better** *His work received only a tiny mention in the journal; he deserves better.* **well deserved** *At last she managed to have a well-deserved rest.*

deserving adj.

- VERBS **be, seem**
- ADV. **eminently, very** | **fairly** | **equally** *All the causes seem equally deserving.*
- PREP. **of** *the areas most deserving of study*

design noun

1 making drawings of how sth should be made
- ADJ. **graphic** | **computer-aided** *a specialist in computer-aided design* | **architectural, industrial, interior**
- DESIGN + NOUN **business, company, consultancy, firm** | **consultant, engineer, staff, team** | **centre, department, studio** | **work** *She's done some design work for us in the past.* | **process** *The new CAD program really speeds up the design process.* | **program, software** | **project** | **ability, expertise, skills**
- PHRASES **art and design** *I'm doing a course in art and design.*

2 the way sth is made/a drawing of this
- ADJ. **basic, simple** | **complex, sophisticated** | **excellent, good** | **poor** | **adventurous, bold, innovative, original, revolutionary** | **attractive, beautiful, stylish** | **classical, conventional, traditional** | **ergonomic**
- VERB + DESIGN **come up with, create, produce** *He's come up with a really good design for a solar-powered car.* | **follow, use** *We followed the traditional design.*
- DESIGN + NOUN **feature** *The latest model incorporates some novel design features.* | **concept, idea, solution** *The architect put forward two alternative design concepts for the new library.* | **brief, requirements, specifications** *The chair she had sketched was far bigger than stipulated in the design brief.* | **fault** | **award** *The car wouldn't win any design awards, but it's very reliable.*
- PREP. **in~** *The machine is quite simple in design.* **of ... ~** *a vehicle of revolutionary design* **to a ... ~** *The other houses are built to a more conventional design.* | **~for** *the architect's designs for the cathedral*
- PHRASES **at the design stage** *Their new car is still at the design stage.*

3 pattern that decorates sth
- ADJ. **elaborate, intricate** | **simple** | **abstract, circular, floral, geometric, symmetrical**
- VERB + DESIGN **have** *The building has intricate geometric designs on several of the walls.*

4 intention
- ADJ. **evil, sinister** | **grand** *His grand design was to connect up every academic institution in the world.*
- VERB + DESIGN **harbour, have** *I suspected that he had some sinister designs.*
- PREP. **by~** *Had it happened by accident or by design?*

design verb

- ADV. **carefully, cleverly** *These shelves have been designed very cleverly to fit into corners.* | **specially, specifically** *They run specially designed courses for managers.*
- PREP. **for** *The instruments are designed for use in very cold conditions.*

designate verb

- ADV. **formally, officially** *The area has now been formally designated as a Site of Special Scientific Interest.* | **specially** | **clearly**
- PREP. **for** *These areas have been specially designated for children.*

designer noun

- ADJ. **good, talented** | **professional** | **chief, senior** *the company's chief fashion designer* | **dress, fashion, furniture, garden, graphic, industrial, interior, landscape, program, set, software, system/systems, textile, theatre** *They brought in an interior designer to suggest colour schemes for the house.* ◊ *She works as a set designer for the Royal Opera House.*
- VERB + DESIGNER **bring in**
- DESIGNER + NOUN **clothes, fashion** | **label, name**
  ⇨ Note at JOB

desirable adj.

1 to be wished for
- VERBS **be, seem** | **become** | **consider sth, deem sth, feel sth, regard/see/view sth as, think sth** *A new direction was felt desirable for both parties.* ◊ *This kind of work is seen as desirable.*
- ADV. **eminently, extremely, highly, very** *Experience of computers is highly desirable.* | **wholly** | **clearly, obviously** *It is clearly desirable that domestic and European law should be compatible.* | **inherently** | **theoretically** | **economically, morally, politically, socially**

2 causing sexual desire
- VERBS **be** | **become** | **find sb**
- ADV. **extremely, intensely, very** *He found her intensely desirable.* | **infinitely** | **sexually**

desire noun

- ADJ. **burning, deep, great, strong, urgent** | **insatiable, overwhelming** *Most children have an insatiable desire for knowledge.* | **genuine, real** | **natural** | **sexual**
- VERB + DESIRE **feel, have** *I suddenly felt an overwhelming desire to laugh* | **express** *The chairman expressed his desire to expand the company.* | **satisfy** | **be motivated by** *They were motivated by a deep desire for money and fame.*
- PREP. **~for** *Horses need to satisfy their desire for space and freedom.*
- PHRASES **an object of desire** *He felt he was nothing more to her than an object of desire.*

desire verb

- ADV. **greatly, really, sincerely, very much** *A home of her own was something she had always very much desired.*

desk noun

1 type of table
- ADJ. **big, enormous, high, huge, large, vast** | **leather-topped** | **antique** | **empty** *The empty desk suggested she had already gone home.* | **cluttered, untidy** | **writing** | **office, school**
- VERB + DESK **sit at** | **get up from** *He got up from his desk and went to the window.* | **clear** *My desk gets very cluttered if I don't clear it at the end of each day.* | **arrive**

on, land on *A very strange request landed on my desk this morning.*
● DESK + NOUN **drawer | diary, lamp | job**
● PREP. **at a/the ~** *He was sitting at his desk working when we got home.* **behind a/the~** *The manager sat frowning behind his desk throughout the whole interview.* **on a/the~** *I left the file on your desk.*

2 place in a building where a service is provided
● ADJ. **front, reception** *Leave your valuables at the reception desk.* **| cash, check-in, enquiry/enquiries, help, information, support** *She paid for the book at the cash desk.* ◇ *Staff experiencing problems with their computers should ring the help desk.*
● DESK + NOUN **clerk**
● PREP. **at the … ~** *There was a long queue at the check-in desk.* **on the … ~** *We asked the man on the information desk for a map of the city.*

desolate *adj.*

1 empty and depressing
● VERBS **be, seem, stand** *The house stands desolate and empty.* **| become | leave sth** *The land was left desolate.*
● ADV. **completely, quite** *The landscape was quite desolate.* **| rather** *a rather desolate place*
2 very unhappy
● VERBS **be, feel, look, sound** *He looked as desolate as Ruth felt.* **| become**
● ADV. **quite, utterly** *She was utterly desolate after losing her baby.* **| a little** *Her voice sounded a little desolate.*

despair *noun*

● ADJ. **black, bleak, deep | complete, total, utter**
● VERB + DESPAIR **feel | drive sb to** *The novel tells the story of a teenager driven to despair by the hypocrisy of the adult world.*
● PREP. **in~** *Robert shook his head in despair.* **of~** *She let out a cry of despair.* **with~** *He cried out with despair.* **| ~at** *I felt despair at being deceived.*
● PHRASES **the depths of despair** *When he became ill he sank to the depths of despair.* **in a moment of despair, a feeling/sense of despair** *I was overcome with a feeling of utter despair.*

desperate *adj.*

● VERBS **be, feel, look, seem, sound | become, get** *I was starting to get desperate.* **| make sb** *The sudden loss of his money had made him desperate.*
● ADV. **really | absolutely, utterly** *She felt utterly desperate.* **| increasingly | almost | a little, pretty, rather**
● PREP. **about** *I felt desperate about my future.*

desperation *noun*

● ADJ. **sheer | quiet | growing** *We realized with a sense of growing desperation that nobody knew we were in there.*
● QUANT. **hint, note** *There was a note of desperation in her voice.*
● VERB + DESPERATION **feel | drive sb to** *Driven to desperation by our noisy neighbours, we called the police.*
● PREP. **in (your) ~** *In desperation, I decided to try acupuncture.* ◇ *In his desperation to escape, Tom had slipped and broken a leg.* **out of~** *At the end of the film, the man becomes a thief out of sheer desperation.* **| ~ about/at** *Many of us feel a quiet desperation at the future.*
● PHRASES **an act of desperation** *The robbery was an act of desperation.* **courage, strength, etc. born of desperation** *With strength born of desperation, she managed to break down the door.*

despicable *adj.*

● VERBS **be, seem | condemn sth as, consider sth,**

find sth *Police have condemned the theft from an elderly widow as despicable.* ◇ *To fail was considered despicable.*
● ADV. **absolutely, quite** *It was an absolutely despicable thing to do.* **| pretty**

despise *verb*

● ADV. **thoroughly | clearly | secretly** *He secretly despised his father.* **| openly**
● PREP. **for** *She thoroughly despised him for his weakness.*

despondent *adj.*

● VERBS **be, feel** *Patients often feel despondent.* **| become, get, grow** *His work was rejected again and again, and he grew more and more despondent.*
● ADV. **very | utterly** *She was feeling utterly despondent.* **| a bit, pretty, rather, somewhat**
● PREP. **about** *He had become rather despondent about his lack of progress.*

dessert *noun*

● ADJ. **delicious | rich** *This chestnut pudding is a rich dessert with a festive flavour.*
● VERB + DESSERT **eat, have**
● DESSERT + NOUN **apple, wine | menu, trolley**
● PREP. **for~** *We had mousse for dessert.* **| ~of** *We finished off with a dessert of honey and nuts.*
⇨ Special page at FOOD

destination *noun*

● ADJ. **eventual, final, ultimate | favourite, popular** *The town is a popular destination for art lovers.* **| ideal, perfect | intended** *We got lost and ended up miles away from our intended destination.* **| exotic | holiday, tourist** *The island is an ideal holiday destination.* **| unknown**
● VERB + DESTINATION **arrive at, reach** *At around 1.00 p.m. we reached our final destination.*
● PREP. **to a/the~** *The deposed leader is reported to have fled the capital to an unknown destination.* **| ~for** *a popular holiday destination for golf enthusiasts*
● PHRASES **the country/port/state of destination** *The goods are examined by customs at the port of destination.*

destiny *noun*

● VERB + DESTINY **fulfil, meet** *She was convinced that sooner or later she would fulfil her destiny.* ◇ *The time was right for him to meet his destiny.* **| avoid, escape** *No man can escape his destiny.* **| shape** *Something was about to happen that would shape her destiny.*
● DESTINY + VERB **await sb, lie** *the destiny that awaited him* ◇ *Her destiny lay in that city.*
● PHRASES **be in control of your own destiny/be master of your own destiny** *She set up her own business because she wanted to be in control of her own destiny.* **a sense of destiny** *He was driven on by a strong sense of destiny.*

destroy *verb*

1 damage sth so badly that it no longer exists
● ADV. **completely, entirely, totally, utterly | all but, almost, effectively, practically, virtually** *Their lives have been virtually destroyed by this tragedy.* **| largely, partly | systematically** *The rainforest is being systematically destroyed.* **| by fire** *The building was destroyed by fire last year.*
● VERB + DESTROY **can/could** *Drugs can destroy the health and lives of young people.* **| threaten to** *This disease threatens to destroy many of our native trees.*
● PHRASES **an attempt to destroy sth** *a new attempt to destroy enemy positions* **be capable of destroying sth** *These weapons are capable of destroying the entire planet.*

be intent on destroying sth *She seemed intent on destroying everything they had built up together.*
2 kill an animal
• ADV. **humanely**
• PHRASES **have to be destroyed** *The horse broke a leg and had to be destroyed.*

destruction noun

• ADJ. **complete, total, wholesale | large-scale, mass, massive, widespread** *modern weapons of mass destruction* | **rapid | systematic | wanton** *the wanton destruction of public property* | **environmental, forest, habitat** *the environmental destruction caused by road building*
• VERB + DESTRUCTION **bring (about), cause, lead to, result in, wreak** *(formal) the destruction brought about by war.* ◊ *He gasped as he saw how much destruction she had wrought with the hammer.* | **prevent** *Some shopkeepers closed early to prevent the wholesale destruction of their property by the hooligans.*
• PHRASES **leave a trail of destruction** *The tornado left a trail of destruction behind it.* **the seeds of destruction** *By doubling its prices, the industry sowed the seeds of its own destruction.* **test sth to destruction** *Children will quickly test their toys to destruction.*

destructive adj.

• VERBS **be, seem | become**
• ADV. **extremely, highly, very | downright, wholly** *downright destructive behaviour* | **quite | potentially** *potentially destructive emotions* | **environmentally** *environmentally destructive policies*
• PREP. **of** *Clearing trees by burning is highly destructive of the forest environment.* **to** *These substances can be destructive to health.*

detachable adj.

• VERBS **be**
• ADV. **fully** *The lid is fully detachable.* | **easily, readily**
• PREP. **from** *The handle is detachable from the bag.*

detached adj.

• VERBS **be, feel, seem, sound | become | remain**
• ADV. **largely, very | completely, totally, wholly | rather, slightly | curiously, oddly, strangely** *He felt curiously detached from what was going on.* | **emotionally**
• PREP. **from** *She tries to remain emotionally detached from her patients.*

detachment noun

• ADJ. **complete | clinical, professional** *She gazed at the body with almost clinical detachment.* | **cool | critical | emotional**
• VERB + DETACHMENT **have, show** *He shows impartiality and detachment.*
• PREP. **with** ~ *She watched with complete detachment as the others made all the preparations.* | ~**from** *his increasing detachment from reality*
• PHRASES **an air of detachment, a feeling/sense of detachment**

detail noun

• ADJ. **little, minor, minute, small, tiny** *It is important to get even the small details right.* | **considerable, fine, great, meticulous** *Now let us examine this idea in greater detail.* ◊ *Every new animal or plant found was recorded in meticulous detail.* | **exact, precise** *I don't need to know the precise details of your quarrel.* | **colourful, vivid | graphic, sordid** *I can still remember the accident in graphic detail.* | **intimate** *The diary contains intimate details of their life together.* | **complete, full** *We'll give you full de-*

tails of how to enter our competition later.* | **bare, brief, sketchy** ~s *He only managed to give the police a few sketchy details of the robbery.* | **essential** *I only know the barest details of his plans.* | **practical** *I haven't sorted out the practical details of getting there yet.* | **complex, intricate | final** *Everyone must approve the basic plan before the final details are drawn up.* | **concrete** *Can you give me some concrete details of how you've been saving money?* | **factual, historical, technical**
• QUANT. **point** *I must correct some points of detail in your article on Barcelona.* | **wealth** *The book provides a wealth of detail on daily life in Ancient Rome.* | **level** *Ensure that your diagrams contain the appropriate level of detail.*
• VERB + DETAIL **give, go into, provide, send, supply** *Briefly describe the product, but do not give any technical details at this stage.* ◊ *I don't want to go into any more detail than absolutely necessary.* | **lay out, lay sth out in, set out, set sth out in, spell out, spell sth out in** *Details of the pension plan are set out below.* ◊ *The rules are set out in detail in chapter seven.* | **establish, finalize, work out, work sth out in** *We haven't yet worked out the travel details.* | **discuss, negotiate** *We still need to negotiate the details of the contract.* | **fill sb in on** *I'll give you a call later and fill you in on the details.* | **spare sb** *(informal)* '*We had a terrible time*—' '*Oh, spare me the details* (= don't tell me any more).' | **contain, have** *Tomorrow's papers will contain full details of the case.* | **show** *The receipt shows details of the item purchased.* | **disclose, pass on, release** ~s *The city council refused to disclose details of the proposed traffic ban.* | **find out** ~s *You can find out more details of the offer from your local travel agent.* | **enter** ~s *Enter your details in the form below then click on 'submit'.* | **take** ~s *The secretary took my details and said they would get back to me.* | **check** *Make sure you check the details of the policy before you sign it.* | **record** *The computer records the details of everyone entering the country.* | **be lacking in, lack** *The speech was well delivered but lacking in detail.*
• PREP. **for** ~s *For details contact Joanna Morland.* **in** ~ *I haven't looked at the proposal in detail yet.* **over a/the** ~ *They're still arguing over the details of the contract.* | ~**about** *I won't go into detail about the threats she made.* ~**on** *For more detail on how to obtain a visa, see page 8.*
• PHRASES **attention to detail** *The secret of their success lies in their attention to detail.* **down to the last detail** *an expedition planned down to the last detail* **every last detail** *She remembered every last detail of what I'd told her the month before.* **an eye for detail** *He has an excellent eye for detail.* **full of detail** *Her short stories are full of detail and humour.* **a lack of detail** *The report was criticized for its lack of detail.*

detailed adj.

• VERBS **be, seem**
• ADV. **extraordinarily, extremely, highly, immensely, very** *a very detailed account of the events* | **fully | increasingly | fairly, quite | meticulously, minutely | exquisitely, finely, richly** *the exquisitely detailed carvings on the cathedral door* | **unusually | unnecessarily**

detain verb

• ADV. **briefly** *He was kidnapped and briefly detained by a terrorist group.*
• VERB + DETAIN **need not** *This issue need not detain us long.*
• PREP. **for** *She was arrested and detained for distributing pro-democracy leaflets.* **in connection with** *Over 60 people have been detained in connection with the coup attempt.*
• PHRASES **be detained in custody/hospital** *Two people were detained in hospital following the crash.* **detain sb without charge/trial** *He has been detained without trial for nearly two years now.*

detect *verb*

• ADV. **early, late** *A lot of cancers can now be cured if they are detected early.* | **quickly** | **easily, readily** *Some substances can be detected fairly easily.* | **accurately**
• VERB + DETECT **be able to, be sensitive enough to, can** *a machine that is sensitive enough to detect tiny amounts of explosives* | **be unable to** | **be designed to** | **fail to** *The test failed to detect any illegal substances.* | **be difficult to, be hard to, be impossible to** | **be easy to, be possible to** | **be used to**
• PHRASES **be capable of detecting sth, a means/method/way of detecting sth**

detection *noun*

• ADJ. **early** *Our aim is the early detection and treatment of all cancers.*
• VERB + DETECTION **avoid, escape, evade** *Their prey can sometimes escape detection by remaining still.*
• DETECTION + NOUN **rate** *The latest figures show falling crime detection rates.*

detective *noun*

• ADJ. **private** *She hired a private detective to follow her husband.* | **undercover** | **store** *The store detective was keeping a close eye on a suspected shoplifter.*
• VERB + DETECTIVE **hire**
• DETECTIVE + VERB **investigate sth** *detectives investigating the case*
• DETECTIVE + NOUN **agency** | **work** *We are going to have to do some detective work on this.* | **fiction, novel, series, story**

detention *noun*

• ADJ. **arbitrary** *Opponents of the regime had been subject to arbitrary detention, torture and execution.* | **pre-trial** | **indefinite** *If found guilty of smuggling drugs, she could face indefinite detention.*
• VERB + DETENTION **be in, remain in** *147 of the illegal immigrants remain in detention.* | **hold sb in, place sb in, sentence sb to** *He was held in detention from 1991 to 2001.* ◊ *They were sentenced to 12 months' detention in a young offender institution.* | **be subject to, face** | **release sb from**
• DETENTION + NOUN **camp, centre**
• PREP. **in ~** *She spent 18 years in detention.* **under ~** *He made the confession while under detention.*
• PHRASES **a period/term of detention** *The judge will fix the period of detention.*

deter *verb*

• ADV. **hardly** *Her words of warning would hardly deter him.* | **effectively, sufficiently** *Will this harsher punishment effectively deter criminals?* | **easily**
• VERB + DETER **be likely/unlikely to** | **be enough to, be sufficient to** | **attempt to** | **be designed to** | **do little to, do nothing to** *The present system does little to deter corporate crime.*
• PREP. **from** *These new rules are likely to deter people from coming forward for help.*

deteriorate *verb*

• ADV. **badly, seriously** | **dramatically, sharply, quickly, rapidly** | **gradually** | **further**
• VERB + DETERIORATE **begin to** *His health began to deteriorate quite seriously.* | **continue to** | **be likely to**
• PREP. **into** *The unrest rapidly deteriorated into civil war.*

deterioration *noun*

• ADJ. **marked, serious, significant** *a serious deterior-* *ation in relations between the two governments* | **rapid, sharp** | **gradual, progressive** | **mental, physical** *Mental and physical deterioration both occur naturally with age.* | **environmental**
• VERB + DETERIORATION **cause, lead to, result in** *The stress led to a gradual deterioration in her health.* | **prevent** *Limits on the dumping of waste will at least prevent further environmental deterioration in the region.* | **arrest** *Steps need to be taken quickly to arrest the deterioration in the countries' relationship.*
• DETERIORATION + VERB **occur**
• PREP. **~ in** *a rapid deterioration in his condition*
• PHRASES **signs of deterioration** *The car's bodywork was already showing signs of deterioration.*

determination *noun*

• ADJ. **absolute, dogged, fierce, great, grim, gritty, ruthless, single-minded, steely, strong** | **clear** *The prime minister's speech revealed a clear determination to break the power of the unions.*
• VERB + DETERMINATION **be full of, have** *She was full of determination to achieve her goals.* ◊ *He has the determination to succeed.* | **reveal, show** *She has shown great determination and skill.* | **express, signal** *The government last night signalled its determination to resist tax cuts.* | **require** | **lack**
• PREP. **with ~** *He hung on with grim determination.*
• PHRASES **determination to succeed/win**

determine *verb*

• ADV. **exactly, precisely** *We need a detailed investigation to determine exactly why these cancers are occurring.*
• VERB + DETERMINE **try to** | **be used to, help to** *Computer models help to determine whether a particular area is likely to flood.* | **be easy to, be possible to** | **be difficult to, be impossible to** *It is difficult to determine the exact cause of the illness.* | **be necessary to** | **be able to**

determined *adj.*

• VERBS **appear, be, look, seem, sound** | **become** | **remain** | **make sb** *The opposition to her scheme made her more determined than ever.*
• ADV. **really, very** | **absolutely, quite, utterly** *They were quite determined that he wasn't going to do it.* | **fairly** | **clearly, obviously** | **fiercely, grimly** *His voice was grimly determined.* | **quietly** | **resolutely**

deterrent *noun*

• ADJ. **effective, good, great, powerful, real** | **the ultimate** *Defenders of the death penalty clearly regard it as the ultimate deterrent.* | **nuclear** *They stressed the need for an independent nuclear deterrent.*
• VERB + DETERRENT **act as, be** *a punishment that will act as a deterrent to other offenders*
• DETERRENT + NOUN **effect** *They were arguing about the deterrent effect of nuclear weapons.*
• PREP. **as a ~** *The bodies of executed criminals were hung on the city gates as a deterrent.* | **against** *a deterrent against cheating* **~ for** *There is no effective deterrent for these young criminals.* **~ to** *a deterrent to crime* ◊ *a deterrent to all but the most determined attacker*

detour *noun*

• ADJ. **lengthy, long** | **brief, short, small**
• VERB + DETOUR **make, take** *We had to make a lengthy detour through the backstreets.* | **be worth** *The monument is well worth a detour.*
• PREP. **~ around** *Trucks now face a five-mile detour around the bridge.* **~ through, ~ to** *The ship made a detour to the south.*

detrimental *adj.*

- VERBS be, prove, seem | become
- ADV. extremely, highly, seriously, very | positively *Sugar is positively detrimental to bodybuilding.* | rather
- PREP. to *This move could be seriously detrimental to the economy.*

devalue *verb*

- ADV. effectively
- PREP. against *The pound was devalued against the US dollar.* by *The Cambodian currency was effectively devalued by 25 per cent.*

devastation *noun*

- ADJ. complete, utter | widespread | ecological, environmental | economic
- VERB + DEVASTATION cause *The hurricane caused widespread devastation.*
- DEVASTATION + VERB be wrought *We surveyed the devastation wrought by the fire.*
- PHRASES a scene of devastation *He surveyed the scene of utter devastation beneath him.* a trail of devastation *The tornado left a trail of devastation in its wake.*

developed *adj.*

- VERBS be, seem
- ADV. highly, strongly, well *He's got a highly developed sense of humour.* | fully | partially | finely | poorly *She was born prematurely with poorly developed lungs.* | newly | economically *economically developed countries*

developer *noun*

- ADJ. big, major | local *A local developer is planning to build a supermarket on the site.* | private *The flats are being built by a private developer.* | speculative | housing, property *plans by a big property developer to build fifty new houses*
- DEVELOPER + VERB build sth, develop sth

development *noun*

1 developing sth
- ADJ. full *School should encourage the full development of a student's talents.* | gradual | rapid | sustainable | healthy | commercial, economic, industrial | evolutionary, historical | regional | rural, suburban, urban | human | educational, emotional, intellectual, linguistic, personal, physical, psychological, sexual, social, spiritual | software | child | property
- VERB + DEVELOPMENT aid, allow, assist, encourage, enhance, facilitate, favour, foster, permit, promote, stimulate, support *Education stimulates the development of rational thinking.* ◇ *A group of experts has been brought together to support the development of the project.* | accelerate, speed up *Environmental factors can accelerate the development of certain cancers.* | arrest, discourage, halt, hinder, inhibit, prevent, restrict, retard, slow *Too much emphasis on memorizing facts can inhibit the development of creative thinking.* | finance *The company went deep into debt to finance the development of the engine.* | monitor, oversee *A UN team is monitoring the development of the peace process.* | trace *In the opening chapter, the author traces the development of judo from its ancient roots.*
- DEVELOPMENT + VERB occur, take place
- DEVELOPMENT + NOUN initiative, plan, programme, project, scheme | aid, assistance | work *The invention requires more development work to make it viable.* | process *the lengthy development process of a new model of car* | budget, capital, fund, grant | costs, expenditure
- PREP. during~ *Cell divisions during development occur in a fixed sequence.* in ~ *A more powerful version of this*

electric bus in currently in development. under ~ *The new vaccine is still under development.*
- PHRASES research and development *I do quite a lot of research and development work in my job.* a stage in the development of sth *an important stage in the development of Anglo-Irish relations* a stage of development *This is a perfectly normal stage of development.*

2 new event/idea
- ADJ. exciting, important, major, radical, remarkable, significant, striking | the latest, new, recent | logical *The move from TV to film was a logical development in her career.* | unexpected | welcome | political, scientific, technical, technological
- DEVELOPMENT + VERB occur, take place *the significant developments taking place in the health service*
- PREP. ~in *new developments in film-making*

3 new buildings
- ADJ. housing, property | business, commercial | ribbon *Ribbon developments (= lines of buildings) extended along the main road.*

deviate *verb*

- ADV. considerably, significantly
- PREP. by *Output may deviate from the average by as much as 30%.* from *We had to deviate significantly from our usual route.*

device *noun*

- ADJ. clever, ingenious | labour-saving, useful | complex, sophisticated | simple | hi-tech | hand-held | automatic, electrical, electronic, mechanical | bugging, contraceptive, measuring, safety, timing, warning *Police found several bugging devices in the room.* | explosive, incendiary *An incendiary device exploded in the store, setting fire to furniture.*
- VERB + DEVICE be fitted with, have *All new cars are now fitted with these safety devices.* | design, develop, make | use *He measured the room using an ingenious new electronic device.*
- DEVICE + VERB consist of sth *The device consists of a large wheel mounted on a metal post.* | be designed to *a tiny device designed to trace telephone calls* | work *The device worked exactly as I'd hoped.*
- PREP. ~ for *a useful device for checking electrical circuits*

devil *noun*

- VERB + DEVIL believe in *Do you believe in the Devil?* | worship | be possessed by *He behaved like someone possessed by devils.* | exorcize
- DEVIL + NOUN worship | worshipper
- PHRASES the devil incarnate *(figurative) His strong left-wing views make him the devil incarnate to more extreme Conservatives.*

devoid *adj.* devoid of

- VERBS appear, be, seem | become | remain
- ADV. completely, entirely, quite, totally, utterly *Are you totally devoid of common sense?* | almost, largely, practically, virtually *The land is almost devoid of vegetation.*

devote *verb*

PHRASAL VERB

devote sth/yourself to sth
- ADV. entirely, exclusively, solely, specifically *She devoted herself entirely to writing.* | mainly

devoted adj.

- VERBS **be, seem | become | remain**
- ADV. **extremely, very | absolutely, completely, totally, utterly | passionately**
- PREP. **to** *They were totally devoted to each other.*

devotee noun

- ADJ. **ardent, committed, fervent, great, serious** *I'm a great devotee of jazz.*

devotion noun

- ADJ. **deep, enormous | great | fanatical, intense, passionate, single-minded** *Their single-minded devotion to the care of the dying was admirable.* | **total** *her total devotion to her husband* | **selfless | blind, dog-like** *He was mocked for his dog-like devotion to his boss.* | **lifelong, undying** *his lifelong devotion to his work* | **mutual** *a marriage rooted in mutual devotion and trust* | **religious** *a man of deep religious devotion*
- VERB + DEVOTION **show**
- PREP. **with ~** *He cared for his mother with great devotion.* | **~to** *They showed great devotion to each other.*
- PHRASES **devotion to duty** *The judge praised the firefighters for their bravery and devotion to duty.* **devotion to the cause** *She will be remembered for her selfless devotion to the cause of the poor.* **an object of devotion** *The statue of the emperor became an object of devotion.*

devour verb

- ADV. **eagerly, greedily, hungrily** *He devoured the food greedily.* | **quickly** *The animal quickly devoured its prey.*

dew noun

- ADJ. **heavy** *There was a heavy dew this morning.* | **morning** *The sun had dried the early morning dew.*
- QUANT. **drop** *Drops of dew shone on the grass.*
- DEW + VERB **fall, form**
- DEW + NOUN **drop** (also **dewdrop**)
- PHRASES **damp/heavy/wet with dew** *The grass was still wet with dew.*

dexterity noun

- ADJ. **great | manual**
- VERB + DEXTERITY **demand, require** *Video games demand great manual dexterity.* | **have** *I don't have the dexterity for juggling.*
- PREP. **with ~** *She handled the discussion with dexterity.*

diagnose verb

- ADV. **correctly | incorrectly, wrongly** *Her condition was wrongly diagnosed by the doctor.*
- PREP. **with** *He was diagnosed with leukaemia.*

diagnosis noun

- ADJ. **accurate, correct, right | incorrect, wrong | definite, definitive, firm, positive | provisional, tentative** *Without the results of the blood test, the doctor could only make a tentative diagnosis.* | **early** *Early diagnosis is critical for successful treatment.* | **initial | final | clinical, medical, psychiatric** *clinical diagnosis of schizophrenia* | **AIDS, cancer, etc. | fault**
- VERB + DIAGNOSIS **establish, give, make, reach** *The doctor cannot give a diagnosis without knowing the full medical history.* | **confirm** *Further tests have confirmed the diagnosis.*
- PREP. **after ~, before ~** *Patients may suffer from some of the symptoms years before diagnosis.* | **~ of** *the diagnosis of the disease* ◊ *a diagnosis of cancer*
- PHRASES **a method of diagnosis** *They are using new methods of diagnosis.*

diagram noun

- ADJ. **clear | detailed | rough | simple | flow, schematic | circuit, wiring**
- VERB + DIAGRAM **draw** *Draw a simple diagram of the leaf structure.*
- DIAGRAM + VERB **depict sth, illustrate sth, indicate sth, represent sth, show sth** *a flow diagram showing the stages in the printing process*
- PREP. **in a/the ~** *Compare this system to the one shown in diagram B.* **on a/the ~** *The trees will be planted at the points marked on the diagram.* | **~ of** *a diagram of the human nervous system*

dial noun

- VERB + DIAL **adjust, set, turn, twiddle, twist** *Set the dial for the number of copies required.*

dial verb

- ADV. **direct** *It is possible to dial direct to many countries.*

dialect noun

- ADJ. **local, native, regional | non-standard | northern, southern, etc. | Scottish, Ulster, etc.**
- VERB + DIALECT **speak (in)**
- DIALECT + NOUN **expression, form, word | speaker**

dialogue noun

- ADJ. **close** *There needs to be a closer dialogue between management and staff.* | **direct** *The government refused to engage in direct dialogue with the terrorists.* | **constructive, serious | political** *a serious political dialogue*
- VERB + DIALOGUE **engage in, have, hold** *Managers are willing to hold a dialogue with union leaders.* | **begin, enter into, open | resume**
- PREP. **~ about** *dialogue about concrete issues* **~ among** *The head encourages a climate of open dialogue among the teachers.* **~ between** *the need for dialogue between the two sides in the dispute* **~ on** *a constructive dialogue on pay and working conditions* **~ with** *They have agreed to resume their dialogue with the teachers.*

diameter noun

- ADJ. **inside, internal** *The tubes have an internal diameter of 2mm.* | **external, outside | large, small**
- VERB + DIAMETER **calculate, find, measure** *He used similar triangles to calculate the diameter of the earth.* | **have**
- PREP. **in ~** *The mirror is 25cm in diameter.*

diamond noun

1 precious stone
- ADJ. **flawless, perfect | real | paste | cut | uncut | industrial**
- VERB + DIAMOND **cut | polish | set | be encrusted with, be studded with** *a brooch encrusted with diamonds* | **drip with** *an old woman dripping with diamonds*
- DIAMOND + VERB **glitter, sparkle**
- DIAMOND + NOUN **mine | industry, trade | broker, dealer, merchant**

2 playing card
⇨ Note at CARD

diarrhoea noun

- ADJ. **severe | mild | acute, chronic | intermittent, persistent**
- VERB + DIARRHOEA **have, suffer from | develop, get**
⇨ Special page at ILLNESS

diary *noun*

1 for appointments
- ADJ. **appointments, bookings, engagement, social | desk, pocket | electronic**
- VERB + DIARY **have sth in** *I haven't got the meeting in my diary.* | **put sth in, write sth in** *Put it in your diary before you forget.*
- PREP. **in a/your~**

2 for writing down what happens each day
- ADJ. **detailed | daily | personal, private, secret | field, gardening, travel** *He jotted down observations on the animals' habits in his field diary.*
- VERB + DIARY **keep** *I starting keeping a diary when I was thirteen.* | **write sth in, note sth in, record sth in** *'It's all over,' he wrote in his diary for April 21.*
- DIARY + NOUN **entry**
- PREP. **in a/your~** *I've made a note in my diary.*
- PHRASES **an entry in a diary**

dice *noun*

- ADJ. **loaded**
- VERB + DICE **roll, throw** *You decide who's going to start by throwing the dice.*
- PREP. **on a/the ~** *You move forward according to the number on the dice.*
- PHRASES **a roll/throw of the dice** *The roll of the dice went against them.*

dictation *noun*

- VERB + DICTATION **do, have** *We did a French dictation in class.* | **give sb** *The teacher gave them a dictation.* | **take** *Her secretary is very good at taking dictation.*
- PREP. **at sb's ~** *I wrote some letters at his dictation.* **from ~** *I find it difficult to write letters from dictation.* **in a/the~** *We had some very difficult words in our dictation.*

dictatorship *noun*

- ADJ. **communist, fascist | left-wing, right-wing | military | totalitarian | benevolent**
- VERB + DICTATORSHIP **establish, set up** *The generals established a military dictatorship.* | **overthrow** *They succeeded in overthrowing the fascist dictatorship.*
- PREP. **during a/the~** *the atrocities that took place during his dictatorship* **under (a/the) ~** *These men had all lived under dictatorship.*

dictionary *noun*

- ADJ. **comprehensive, good | electronic, online | picture | pocket | English, French, etc. | English/French, French/English, etc. | bilingual, monolingual | learner's, native-speaker | standard | specialist, technical | collocation, etymological, historical, pronunciation | biographical, encyclopedic, medical** *I decided to consult a medical dictionary.*
- VERB + DICTIONARY **consult, look sth up in, use** *If you don't know the meaning of a word, look it up in the dictionary.* ◊ *teaching children how to use dictionaries* | **compile, write | edit | publish**
- DICTIONARY + NOUN **definition, entry**
- PREP. **in a/the ~** *I couldn't find the word in the dictionary.*

die *verb*

- ADV. **in childbirth | in infancy, prematurely, young** *One of their children died in infancy.* | **peacefully | suddenly | tragically** *Her father died tragically in a car crash.*
- VERB + DIE **be going to** *I thought I was going to die.* | **be allowed to** *She should be allowed to die peacefully.*

- PREP. **for** *to die for your country* **from** *The accident victim died from her injuries.* **of** *He died of a heart attack.*
- PHRASES **die a natural sudden, violent, etc. death**

diesel *noun*

- VERB + DIESEL **run on, use** *These buses run on diesel.*
- DIESEL + NOUN **power | fuel, fumes, oil | car, engine, locomotive, model, train** *The diesel model is noisier than the petrol model.*

diet *noun*

1 food sb/sth usually eats
- ADJ. **balanced, good, healthy, sensible | adequate** *People can fight infection more easily if they have an adequate diet.* | **bad, poor, unhealthy | staple** *a staple diet of cornmeal and vegetables* | **vegan, vegetarian**
- VERB + DIET **eat, have** *It is important to eat a balanced diet.* | **live on, survive on** *They had to survive on a diet of insects and berries.* | **feed sb on**
- DIET + VERB **consist of sth** *The animal's diet consists mainly of grasses.*
- PREP. **in a/the~** *the amount of fat in your diet* | **on a~** *These animals live on a mainly vegetarian diet.* | *~ of* *They were fed on a diet of rice and vegetables.*
- PHRASES **a diet high/rich in sth** *a diet rich in vitamins and minerals*

2 when you want to lose weight/are ill
- ADJ. **strict | slimming, weight-loss, weight-reducing | crash, starvation** *Crash diets are not the best way to lose weight.* | **calorie-controlled, low-calorie | restricted, special | fibre-rich, gluten-free, high/low-fibre, high/low-protein, low-fat, salt-free, etc.**
- VERB + DIET **follow, have** *If you follow this diet, you're bound to lose weight.* | **go on, start | stick to** *I have to stick to a low-fat diet.* | **be on** *I'd love some chips, but I'm on a diet.*
- DIET + NOUN **drink, food | plan** *Lose pounds with our new diet plan!*
- PREP. **on a~** *They're on a special high-protein diet.*

differ *verb*

1 be different
- ADV. **considerably, enormously, fundamentally, greatly, markedly, radically, sharply, significantly, substantially, widely** *The two approaches differ markedly* ◊ *Opinions differ widely on this issue.* | **little | slightly, somewhat | clearly**
- PREP. **according to** *Conditions of employment differ according to the type of company you are working for.* **between** *Social organization differs significantly between the different groups.* **from** *His ideas differ little from those of his father.* **in** *The models differ in size and shape.*

2 have a different opinion
- VERB + DIFFER **agree to** *In the end we agreed to differ.* | **beg to** *I beg to differ* (= I disagree with you).
- PREP. **about/over** *The two sides still differ over details of the plan.* **on** *The two parties differ on all the major issues.* **with** *It didn't seem right that I should differ with him.*

difference *noun*

1 way in which people/things are not the same
- ADJ. **big, broad, considerable, dramatic, enormous, great, huge, large, major, profound, radical, real, sharp, substantial, vast, wide** *A little extra care makes a big difference.* ◊ *I noticed a real difference in his attitude.* | **basic, essential, fundamental, crucial, important, key, significant | clear, distinct, marked, notable, noticeable, obvious, striking | minor, slight, subtle | national, regional | age, class, cultural, ethnic, gender, genetic, physical, psychological, racial, sex, social | historical,**

ideological, political | temperature, time *What's the time difference between London and Tokyo?*
- VERB + DIFFERENCE **make** *The new central heating has made an enormous difference to the house.* ◊ *What difference does it make if he doesn't have a car?* | **mean** *One tiny mistake when you're climbing could mean the difference between life and death.* | **exaggerate, emphasize, focus on, highlight, stress, underline** *We should be focusing on what we have in common rather than emphasizing our differences.* | **appreciate, be aware of, feel, know, notice, perceive, see, spot, tell** *Only an expert would know the difference between the male and the female.* ◊ *Can you spot the difference between these two photos?* ◊ *It's difficult to tell the difference between butterflies and moths.* | **explain, illustrate** | **examine, explore, look at** *The study explores the differences between the way girls and boys talk.* | **show** *The questionnaire showed vast differences in what kind of product people want.* | **reflect** *Our different attitudes to life reflect the differences in our backgrounds.*
- DIFFERENCE + VERB **be, lie** *The difference lies in the way the fruit is prepared.* | **arise (from sth), exist** *The differences in size arise from the amount of sunshine each plant gets.*
- PREP. **~between** *There's a big difference between reading about skiing and doing it yourself.* **~from** *He was very aware of his difference from the other children.* **~in** *The difference in price is not very significant.* **~of** *a crucial difference of emphasis* **~with** *There is one key difference with the earlier version of the software.* ◊ *The difference with this information service is that it's free.*
- PHRASES **a … with a difference** *If you want a holiday with a difference, come to Iceland.* **all the difference in the world** *There's all the difference in the world between choosing to do something and being forced to do it.* **a great deal of/a lot difference** *The extra money will make a lot of difference to us.* **make all the difference** *Just five minutes' exercise a day could make all the difference.* **no difference/not much difference** *There's not much difference between baseball and softball.*

2 sum of money in addition to the sum expected
- VERB + DIFFERENCE **pay** *If you decide you would prefer the more expensive model, you can bring this one back and pay the difference.* | **make up** *He hadn't got quite enough money, but his aunt agreed to make up the difference.* | **pocket** *He sold the car for more than he'd paid and pocketed the difference.* | **split** (figurative) *I wanted to leave early and Ian wanted to leave late, so we split the difference and left at noon.*

3 disagreement
- ADJ. **irreconcilable, major, serious, sharp** | **minor, slight** | **outstanding** *This round of talks aims to resolve the outstanding differences between the two sides.*
- VERB + DIFFERENCE **have** *They have had some minor differences, but in general they get on well together.* | **make up, patch up, put aside, reconcile, resolve, settle** *We're going to get the two sides together to see if they can't settle their differences.*
- DIFFERENCE + VERB **arise, emerge, occur** *Differences may arise when the young people do not have the same expectations as their parents.* | **remain** *Although the talks were generally successful, differences remain between the groups.*
- PREP. **~ as to/over** *There were some differences as to how to deal with the crisis.*
- PHRASES **a difference of opinion** *She and Luke had a difference of opinion over how much money they should spend.* **have your differences** *Like any married couple, we have our differences.*

different *adj.*
- VERBS **appear, be, feel, look, seem, sound, taste**
- ADV. **very** | **distinctly, markedly, radically, significantly, strikingly** *This school is radically different from*

most others. | **completely, entirely, quite, totally** | **rather, slightly** | **subtly** *The same colour can appear subtly different on different types of paper.* | **materially, qualitatively** | **refreshingly** *a refreshingly different approach to language learning*
- PREP. **from** *Human beings are different from other animals.* **to** *Their customs are very different to ours.*

differentiate *verb*
- ADV. **clearly**
- VERB + DIFFERENTIATE **be important to** | **be easy to, be possible to** | **be difficult to**
- PREP. **between** *It is not always possible to differentiate between the two diseases.* **from** *features which clearly differentiate this product from other similar ones*

difficult *adj.*
- VERBS **be, look, prove, seem, sound** | **become, get** *It is getting more and more difficult to find a job.* | **make sth** *The fog made driving very difficult.* | **find sth**
- ADV. **exceedingly, extraordinarily, extremely, incredibly, particularly, really, very** | **doubly** *Her disability made taking care of the home and raising a family doubly difficult.* | **increasingly** | **a bit, quite, rather** | **notoriously** *Birth rates are notoriously difficult to predict.*

difficulty *noun*
- ADJ. **considerable, enormous, grave, great, major, real, serious, severe** *We had enormous difficulty in getting hold of the right equipment.* | **insurmountable** | **increasing** *questions of increasing difficulty* | **inherent** *the difficulties inherent in treating overdose patients* | **particular, special** *English spelling presents special difficulties for foreign learners.* | **economic, financial** | **practical, technical** *I think we've managed to overcome most of the practical difficulties.* | **behavioural, emotional, learning** *children with learning difficulties*
- QUANT. **level** *The games have various different levels of difficulty.*
- VERB + DIFFICULTY **encounter, experience, face, get into, have, run into** *Among the difficulties encountered was a lack of cooperation on the part of the authorities.* ◊ *Anyone experiencing difficulty with radio reception should call us on the new helpline.* ◊ *Let me know if you have any difficulties.* ◊ *I had little difficulty in persuading the others to come.* ◊ *The scheme has run into serious difficulties.* | **cause, create, make, present** *Will it cause any difficulties if I go early?* ◊ *She is always making difficulties for herself.* | **cope with, deal with, overcome, resolve, solve, surmount** | **avoid** *how to avoid technical difficulties* | **be fraught with** *The situation was fraught with difficulty.*
- DIFFICULTY + VERB **arise, crop up** *Difficulties arise when people fail to consult their colleagues.* | **lie (in sth)** *The difficulty lies in identifying the precise nature of the problem.*
- PREP. **despite a/the~** *Despite all the difficulties, he still remains optimistic.* **in~** *We could see that the swimmer was in difficulties.* **with/without~** *We crossed the border without any difficulty.* ◊ *Life in the city was not without its difficulties.* | **~in** *She had difficulty in starting her car.* **~of** *the difficulty of finding affordable accommodation* **~with** *having difficulty with the engine*

dig *noun*

1 hard push
- ADJ. **sharp**
- VERB + DIG **give** *She gave him a sharp dig in the ribs.* | **feel, get**
- PHRASES **a dig in the ribs**

2 critical remark

● ADJ. **little** | **sly** *I resisted the temptation to get in a sly dig at Fred.*
● VERB + DIG **get in, have, make**
● PREP. **~ about, ~ at** *They were having a little dig at her about the way she tells everybody else what to do.*

3 in the ground
● ADJ. **archaeological**
● VERB + DIG **go on** *I went on an archaeological dig over the summer.*
● DIG + VERB **reveal sth** *The dig revealed the site of a Roman villa.*

dig *verb*

● ADV. **deep** *We'll have to dig quite deep to get at the roots.*
● PREP. **for** *digging for buried treasure* **through** *digging through solid clay*

digest *verb*

● ADV. **easily** *Some foods are digested more easily than others.* | **fully** | **partially** *The parent bird partially digests food in its crop.*
● VERB + DIGEST **can/can't** *He has to avoid fat because his body can't digest it.* | **be difficult to, be easy to** *Cheese is very difficult to digest.*

digestion *noun*

● ADJ. **good** | **poor**
● VERB + DIGESTION **have** *She's got very poor digestion.* | **aid, help** *Peppermint aids digestion.*

digit *noun*

● ADJ. **binary, decimal** *the decimal digits 0 to 9*
● QUANT. **sequence, series, set, string** *a sequence of binary digits*
● PHRASES **three, four, etc. digits long** *The number can be up to eight digits long.*

dignified *adj.*

● VERBS **be, look, seem** | **remain**
● ADV. **very** | **quite** | **quietly** *He remained quietly dignified in defeat.*

dignity *noun*

● ADJ. **enormous, great** | **calm, quiet** *She spoke to him with quiet dignity.* | **human, personal** *the importance of human dignity*
● VERB + DIGNITY **have, possess** *These people have enormous dignity.* | **keep, maintain, preserve, retain** *We all want to maintain our dignity in old age.* | **give sb** *Being treated in the privacy of your own room gives you more dignity.* | **lose** *The awful thing about old age is losing your dignity.* | **destroy, rob/strip sb of, threaten** *Slavery destroys human dignity.* ◇ *Keeping prisoners in such dreadful conditions strips them of all dignity.* | **muster** *With as much dignity as he could muster, he left the room.* | **stand on** (= insist on the respect you think you deserve) *She was never one to stand on her dignity.*
● PREP. **beneath your ~** *He clearly regarded manual work as beneath his dignity.* **with ~** *the right to die with dignity*
● PHRASES **an air of dignity** *His aristocratic voice gives him an air of dignity and power.* **lacking in dignity** *We felt that the way she was treated was lacking in dignity.* **a lack of dignity, a loss of dignity** *He hoped that he could change his mind without loss of dignity.* **a sense of dignity** *She had a strong sense of dignity.* **with your dignity intact** *He needed a way to retreat with his dignity intact.*

dilemma *noun*

● ADJ. **acute, appalling, big, difficult, genuine, great,**

impossible, real, serious, terrible, thorny | **central, essential, fundamental** *The fundamental dilemma remains: in a tolerant society, should we tolerate intolerance?* | **familiar, perennial** | **human** | **personal** | **ethical, moral** | **policy, political**
● VERB + DILEMMA **create, pose** *This poses a difficult dilemma for teachers.* | **be caught in, be faced with, confront, face, have** *They were caught in a real dilemma.* | **resolve, solve** *I could see no way of resolving this moral dilemma.*
● DILEMMA + VERB **arise, occur, present itself** *the dilemma that arises when a doctor has to decide whether or not to prescribe an expensive treatment* | **lie** *The dilemma over human cloning lies at the heart of the ethical choices facing society.* | **confront sb, face sb** *The dilemma facing the country's allies was even more serious.* | **remain**
● PREP. **in a/the~** *The minister is now in an impossible dilemma.* | **~ about/over** *She faced a dilemma about whether to accept the offer or not.* **~ between** *the perennial dilemma between getting on at work and fulfilling family commitments*
● PHRASES **a solution to a dilemma, a way out of a dilemma** *I couldn't see any way out of the dilemma.*

dilute *verb*

1 liquid
● ADV. **highly** *The fragrances are highly diluted.* | **slightly** *Dilute the juice slightly with water.*
● PREP. **in** *The perfumes are diluted in vegetable oils.* **with**
2 effect/quality
● ADV. **considerably, substantially** *The effect of this policy has now been considerably diluted.*

dimension *noun*

1 (often **dimensions**) measurements
● ADJ. **approximate** | **exact, precise** *It is important to measure the exact dimensions of the room.* | **overall** | **compact** *Despite the unit's compact dimensions, there's still plenty of room for expansion.* | **considerable** *a structure of considerable dimensions* | **fourth, second, third** *The fourth dimension, time, is also finite in extent.* | **physical, space/spatial, temporal/time** | **horizontal, vertical**
● VERB + DIMENSION **check, measure** *Can we just check the dimensions of the bedroom again?*
● PHRASES **in two/three dimensions** *a model in three dimensions*
2 aspect
● ADJ. **added, additional, different, extra, further, new** | **distinct** *In looking at population ageing we will consider two distinct dimensions.* | **wider** *There is a wider dimension to the question.* | **crucial, essential, important, main, major, significant** | **global, international, local, national, regional** *Communication via the Internet gives an important international dimension to the project.* | **aesthetic, class, cultural, economic, ethical, historical, human, ideological, moral, personal, political, religious, social, spiritual**
● VERB + DIMENSION **add, give (sth)** *Her illness adds an extra dimension to the problem.* | **have** *The affair had a different dimension now.* | **acquire, take on** *The crisis acquired a new dimension.*
● PREP. **~ to** *the spiritual dimension to our lives*

din *noun*

● ADJ. **awful, raucous, terrible** | **constant**
● VERB + DIN **make** *Who's making that awful din?* | **hear** | **hear sb above/over** *She could not be heard above the din of the crowd.*
● PREP. **above/over the~** *Charles shouted above the din.* | **~of**
● PHRASES **the din of battle**

dine verb

- ADV. **al fresco** *the joys of dining al fresco* | **in style** *We dined in style in the hotel restaurant.* | **out** *Dining out in attractive surroundings is one of life's great pleasures.*
- PREP. **on** *We dined on fresh local fish.*

dinghy noun

- ADJ. **inflatable, rubber** | **sailing**
- VERB + DINGHY **row, sail** *She sailed the dinghy across the bay.*
- DINGHY + NOUN **sailing, sailor**
- PREP. **in/into a/the~** *She rowed ashore in the dinghy.*

dining room noun

- ADJ. **large, spacious** | **cosy, small** | **elegant** | **formal** | **panelled** | **communal** | **guest, residents', staff**
- DINING ROOM + VERB **seat sb** *The dining room seats up to 60 guests.* | **serve sth** *a cosy dining room serving excellent home-prepared cooking*
- DINING ROOM + NOUN **chair, table**

dinner noun

1 main meal of the day
- ADJ. **delicious, excellent, good, slap-up, sumptuous** *We were treated to a slap-up meal with every kind of seafood imaginable.* | **four-course, three-course, etc.** | **leisurely** | **candlelit, romantic** | **intimate, quiet** | **Christmas, Sunday** | **school** | **convenience, TV** (= eaten while sitting watching the TV) | **chicken, seafood, turkey, etc.**
- DINNER + NOUN **table** *There was never much conversation at the dinner table in my family.* | **things** *We didn't wash up the dinner things until the morning after.* | **plates, service** *a bone-china dinner service* | **menu** *The school dinner menu always includes a balance of food types.* | **bell** | **money** *I always forgot to take my dinner money to school.* | **dance** *the society's annual dinner dance*
- ⇨ Note at MEAL (for verbs)

2 formal evening occasion, with dinner
- ADJ. **elegant, lavish** | **formal, official** | **informal** | **annual** *The rugby club's annual dinner is this week.* | **anniversary, celebratory** | **farewell** | **awards, prize-giving** | **charity, fund-raising** | **gala** *A gala dinner was held to celebrate the world premiere of the film.* | **literary** | **state** *A state dinner was held in honour of the visiting Japanese premier.*
- VERB + DINNER **give, hold, throw** *My old school is giving a fund-raising dinner* | **attend** *We're going to attend a formal dinner in aid of cancer research.* | **be invited to** | **change for, dress for** *Are we expected to dress for dinner?* | **speak at** *The former Olympic champion was invited to speak at a charity dinner.*
- DINNER + NOUN **party** *They invited three couples to a dinner party at their house.* | **engagement** | **dance** | **guests** | **jacket, suit**
- PHRASES **an after-dinner speaker/speech**

dip noun

- ADJ. **sharp** | **slight** | **sudden**
- VERB + DIP **suffer, take** *Share prices have taken a slight dip.*
- PREP. **~in** *a sharp dip in temperature*

dip verb

1 in liquid
- ADV. **lightly** *She dipped the brush lightly in the varnish.*
- PREP. **in, into** *He dipped his finger in the water*

2 go/move downwards
- ADV. **gently** *hills which dip gently to the east* | **steeply** | **down** *The road dipped steeply down into the town.*

- PREP. **below** *The sun dipped below the horizon.*

3 prices/support, etc.
- ADV. **slightly** | **sharply** *Support dipped sharply to 51%.*

diphtheria noun

- VERB + DIPHTHERIA **have, suffer from** | **catch, contract, get** | **immunize sb against** *Parents are advised to have their children immunized against diphtheria.*
- DIPHTHERIA + NOUN **epidemic** | **vaccine**
- ⇨ Special page at ILLNESS

diploma noun

- ADJ. **college, university** | **graduate, postgraduate, professional** | **higher** | **national** *The college offers the Higher National Diploma in computer studies.* | **full-time, part-time** | **one-year, two-year, etc.**
- VERB + DIPLOMA **study for, take** | **have, hold** | **be awarded, gain, get, obtain, receive** | **award (sb), confer (on sb)** *The university awards diplomas in higher education.* | **lead to** *The course leads to a diploma in psychiatric nursing.*
- DIPLOMA + NOUN **course, programme, studies** | **holder** *Diploma holders have a far better chance of employment than those with no qualification.*
- PREP. **~in** *a diploma in hotel management* **~of** *diploma of higher education*
- PHRASES **at diploma level** *Most students here are studying for a qualification at diploma level.*

diplomacy noun

1 managing international relations
- ADJ. **careful, shrewd** | **'gunboat ... '** *What they could not take by political intrigue they took by 'gunboat diplomacy'* (= threatening military action). | **international** | **secret** | **personal** *Churchill's highly personal diplomacy in seeking a meeting with the Russians* | **traditional** *a crisis lying outside the scope of traditional diplomacy* | **preventive** | **shuttle** *a round of shuttle diplomacy between Washington and Brussels* | **Anglo-French, European, Russian, etc.**
- VERB + DIPLOMACY **use** *preferring to use diplomacy rather than force*
- DIPLOMACY + VERB **go on** *Behind the scenes a lot of secret diplomacy was going on.*
- PREP. **by/through ~** *We must try and resolve this situation through diplomacy rather than conflict.*

2 skill in dealing with people
- ADJ. **great** | **quiet**
- VERB + DIPLOMACY **have** *We need someone who has tact and diplomacy.* | **exercise, show, use** *I thought you showed great diplomacy in dealing with him.* | **call for, need, require** *Trying to get the divorced couple to agree calls for a great deal of diplomacy.*
- PREP. **by/through ~** *The way forward in this situation is by diplomacy and negotiation.* **with ~** *She handled the awkward situation with her usual quiet diplomacy.*

diplomat noun

- ADJ. **senior** | **experienced, good, skilful, veteran** | **former, retired** | **foreign** | **career, professional** | **American, British, etc.**
- VERB + DIPLOMAT **be, serve as, work as** *He served as a diplomat in Russia before the war.*

direct verb

- ADV. **mainly, primarily, principally** *Tax cuts have been directed primarily at the better-off.* | **clearly** | **straight** *He directed the torch straight in her face.* | **specifically**
- PREP. **against** *anger directed specifically against ethnic minorities* **at** *criticism clearly directed at the Labour Party* **away from** *directing attention away from the real issues*

onto *The machine directs light onto a special film.* **to** *I directed my question to the chairman.* **towards** *We are directing our efforts towards helping young people.*

direct *adj.*

● VERBS **be**
● ADV. **extremely, very** *He asked me some very direct questions.* | **fairly, quite, rather** *Her manner can be rather direct.* | **disconcertingly** *his disconcertingly direct gaze*

direction *noun*

1 where to/from
● ADJ. **same** *They were both going in the same direction.* | **different, opposite** | **right, wrong** *Unfortunately, we were going in the wrong direction.* | **general** *I fired in the general direction of the officer's head and missed.* | **unexpected** *Support came from an unexpected direction.* | **anticlockwise, clockwise** *Turn the dial in a clockwise direction.* | **downward, upward** *These figures may have to be revised in an upward direction.* | **northerly, southerly, etc.** *The current flows in a south-easterly direction.* | **wind** *When sailing, keep a constant check on changes in wind direction.*
● VERB + DIRECTION **take** *Which direction do we have to take?* | **change, reverse** *The wind has changed direction.* ◇ *What happens if you reverse the direction of the current?* | **flow in, go (off) in | head in, move in, travel in** *The convoy is moving in the direction of the capital.* | **veer off in** *While he was studying in Paris, his thinking suddenly veered off in a new direction.* | **come from/in** *He was hit by a lorry coming in the opposite direction.* | **face (in)** *I didn't see the accident because I was facing in the opposite direction.* | **glance in, look in, nod in, point in** *She glanced in his direction.* ◇ *'Look!' she said, pointing in the direction of the coast.* | **nudge sb in, point sb in** *(figurative) We have to nudge politicians in the right direction.* ◇ *I can't come with you, but I can point you in the general direction.* | **pull (sb/sth) in** *(often figurative) There are different considerations, often pulling in different directions.*
● PREP. **from a/the ~** *There was shriek of laughter from the direction of Sarah's room.* ◇ *Let's approach the subject from a different direction.* **in a/the ~** *The aircraft was flying in a northerly direction.*
● PHRASES **the direction of flow/movement/travel** *I prefer to be facing the direction of travel.* **the direction of sb's gaze** *She followed the direction of his gaze.* **from/in all/both directions** *The blast sent debris flying in all directions.* ◇ *The road was blocked in both directions.* **a glance/nod in sb/sth's direction** *People passed by without a glance in her direction.* ◇ *(figurative) The report gives a brief nod in the direction of green issues before coming down firmly on the side of the market.* **a sense of direction** *I haven't got much sense of direction.*

2 development
● ADJ. **new** *The party must take a new direction if it is to survive.* | **right, wrong | clear** *No clear direction in policy can be identified.* | **future** *the debate about the future direction of socialism* | **policy**
● VERB + DIRECTION **take** *It is hard to know which direction the Church will take.* | **change** *It's time to change direction and find a new job.* | **go in, move in** *At least things are moving in the right direction now.*
● PHRASES **a change of direction** *This was a major change of direction for Britain's foreign policy.* **a step in the (right/wrong) direction** *The new law is undoubtedly a step in the right direction, but it doesn't go far enough.* ◇ *The first step in this direction will be by way of discussion with the unions.*

3 purpose
● ADJ. **clear** *Do not let the discussion fragment into a desultory conversation with no clear direction.*
● VERB + DIRECTION **be lacking in, lack** *Once again her life felt lacking in direction.*

● PHRASES **a sense of direction** *We are looking for somebody with a clear sense of direction.*

4 instructions
● ADJ. **clear, good, precise** *Isabel's directions are always very precise.* | **stage** *Shakespeare's famous stage direction, 'Exit, pursued by a bear.'*
● VERB + DIRECTION **ask for** *Let's stop and ask for directions.* | **give sb** *Can you give me directions for getting to John's?* | **get** *We got directions to the hall from a man in the village.* | **follow** *It's ever so easy to cook. You just follow the directions on the packet.*
● PREP. **~ for** *Are there any directions for putting up the tent?* **~ to** *Can you give me directions to the town centre?*

5 control/guidance
● ADJ. **clear** *In effective classrooms the teacher provided clear direction.* | **strategic** *the strategic direction of the company* | **spiritual** *The monarch looks to the archbishop for spiritual direction.* | **government** *All transport is under government direction.*
● VERB + DIRECTION **give sb, provide (sb with)**
● PREP. **under sb's ~** *working under the direction of a senior manager* | **~ from** *The new workers need direction from a supervisor.*

NOTE
Points of the compass

due ~ (of)
  The village is due north of Paris.
far ~
  a small village in the far north of Scotland.
  The reserve is a little further south on the coast.
down south, up north *(informal)*
  They have moved down south (= to the south of the country).
journey, way ~
  On our way south we travelled through several small villages.
road, track ~
  the road west out of the city
be/lie ~ of
  Brighton is south of London.
come, drive, fly, go, run, travel, walk ~
  From Fort William drive north for a couple of miles.
set off ~
  The troops set off north.
carry on, continue, proceed ~
  The road continues west for 10 miles.
bear, head ~
  Take the N1 motorway heading west from Bern.
turn ~
  When you reach the top of the hill turn north-east.
face, look ~
  The kitchen window faces south.
  The painting depicts the Grand Canal, Venice, looking north from the Rialto Bridge.
~ bank, coast, shore
  the south bank of the river
~ wind
  a bitter east wind
in the ~ (of)
  I live in the north.
  There are lakes in the north-east of Poland.
from the ~ (of)
  The wind is coming from the west.
to the ~ (of)
  Oxford is to the north-west of London.
towards the ~
  Towards the north the woods turn into pine forests.
Which way is ~?
  Which way is west?

directive *noun*

- ADJ. **clear** *Don't start anything without a clear directive from management.* | **general** | **important** | **draft, proposed** | **EU, European (Commission/Union), government, ministerial** | **policy, political** | **banking, environmental,** etc.
- VERB + DIRECTIVE **issue** *The EU issued a new drinking water directive.* | **adopt, agree (on/upon), approve, sign** | **comply with, implement** *All companies must comply with the new directive.* | **block, oppose**
- DIRECTIVE + VERB **come into force** *A new EU directive on maternity leave will come into force next month.* | **require sth** *The directive requires member states to designate sites of special scientific interest.*
- PREP. **in accordance with a/the ~** *They acted in accordance with the latest directive from Brussels.* **in a/the ~** *The proposals are contained in a European directive on wild birds.* **under a/the ~** *Private health services will be allowed under the directive.* | **~ from** *a directive from the European Commission* **~ on** *a directive on data protection*
- PHRASES **the provisions/terms of a directive**

director *noun*

1 controls a company/an organization
- ADJ. **company, managing** | **executive, non-executive** | **assistant, deputy** | **commercial, finance, marketing, production, sales**
- PHRASES **the board of directors, the post of director**
⇒ Note at JOB

2 of a film/play, etc.
- ADJ. **film, theatre** | **artistic, musical**
- PHRASES **the role of director** *He now felt ready to take on the role of director.*
⇒ Note at JOB

directory *noun*

- ADJ. **business, shopping, telephone, trade** *I found the company's name in a trade directory.*
- VERB + DIRECTORY **consult, look sb/sth up in** | **compile, create** | **edit** | **produce, publish**
- PREP. **in a/the ~** *Names are listed alphabetically in the directory.* **~ of** *a directory of names and numbers*

dirt *noun*

1 dust/soil/mud
- ADJ. **loose** *She brushed the loose dirt off her coat.* | **ingrained** | **dog**
- QUANT. **speck** | **streak** *He had streaks of dirt all over his face.* | **layer**
- VERB + DIRT **be covered in/with** *His shoes were covered in dirt.* | **brush off, clean off, remove, wash off** | **show** *The white rug really shows the dirt.*
- DIRT + VERB **accumulate** *Dirt had accumulated in the corners of the windows.*
- DIRT + NOUN **road, track** | **floor**
- PREP. **in the ~** *children playing in the dirt*

2 harmful/unpleasant information about sb
- VERB + DIRT **have**
- PREP. **~ on** *Do you have any dirt on the new guy?*
- PHRASES **dish the dirt** *She just loves to dish the dirt* (= tell people unkind/unpleasant things about sb).

dirty *adj.*

- VERBS **be, feel, look** | **get** *Go and play football if you like, but don't get dirty!* | **get sth, make sb/sth** *The soot had made everything dirty.* ◇ (*figurative*) *He's not frightened of getting his hands dirty* (= doing physical work).
- ADV. **extremely, filthy** (*informal*), **really, very** *Everything in the room was filthy dirty.* | **a bit, rather, slightly**

disability *noun*

- ADJ. **severe** | **permanent** | **learning, mental, physical** *children who have severe learning disabilities*
- VERB + DISABILITY **have** | **cope with, live with** *learning to live with disability*
- DISABILITY + NOUN **movement, organization** | **discrimination** | **allowance, pension**

disabled *adj.*

- VERBS **be** | **be born** | **become** | **leave sb** *The accident left him badly disabled.*
- ADV. **badly, profoundly, seriously, severely, very** *a new home for severely disabled people* | **partially, slightly** | **chronically, permanently** | **mentally, physically**

disadvantage *noun*

- ADJ. **big, considerable, distinct, grave, great, main, major, manifest, obvious, real, serious, severe** *Lack of qualifications is an obvious disadvantage.* | **minor, slight** | **added, additional, further** | **long-term** | **competitive** *These requirements will have to be standardized if some banks are not to suffer a competitive disadvantage.* | **economic, educational, financial, racial, social** *the problems of racism, racial disadvantage and poverty*
- VERB + DISADVANTAGE **experience, have, suffer (from)** *the disadvantage experienced by older people in the workplace* ◇ *The present system has the disadvantage that nobody really understands how it works.* ◇ *Competition has its disadvantages.* | **offset, outweigh** *The scheme's advantages outweigh the disadvantages.* | **overcome, remove** | **avoid** | **feel at a** *There was no reason for her to feel at a disadvantage.* | **place/put sb at a** *The fact that he didn't speak a foreign language put him at a disadvantage.*
- PREP. **at a ~** *We were at a distinct disadvantage compared with children from richer families.* **despite a/the ~** *Despite these disadvantages, many older people maintain an active social life.* **to sb's ~** *This change in the law will be to the disadvantage of small firms.* | **~ for** *another disadvantage for the night-worker* **~ in** *There are disadvantages in using this treatment.* **~ to** *There are disadvantages to all those schemes.*
- PHRASES **advantages and disadvantages** *Each plan has its own advantages and disadvantages.*

disadvantaged *adj.*

- VERBS **be** | **become** | **remain** *These social groups remain disadvantaged.*
- ADV. **badly, extremely, greatly, seriously, severely, very** | **doubly** *Part-time workers, the majority of whom are women, are doubly disadvantaged.* | **further** | **slightly** | **economically, educationally, financially, materially, socially**
- PREP. **by** *Many people will be greatly disadvantaged by the new tax system.*

disagree *verb*

- ADV. **profoundly, sharply, strongly, vehemently** *The only time we sharply disagreed was over the children's education.* | **completely, entirely, totally** *I disagree totally with this policy.* | **fundamentally**
- VERB + DISAGREE **be difficult to, be hard to, can/could hardly** *When I pointed out that it had been her idea in the first place, she could hardly disagree.*
- PREP. **about** *Jack and Robert disagree about everything.* **on** *We disagree on this matter.* **over** *Ministers disagree over the scale of the changes.* **with** *I disagree strongly with this idea.* ◇ *It is difficult to disagree with the chairman on this point.*

disagreement noun

- ADJ. **bitter, considerable, deep, major, serious, sharp, substantial, total, wide** *There is wide disagreement on this issue.* | **minor, slight** | **basic, fundamental** | **continuing** | **internal** *internal disagreements within the party* | **family** | **policy, political**
- VERB + DISAGREEMENT **be in, have** *They were in disagreement about the move to Cambridge.* ◇ *The things she said were always in disagreement, with the teacher or another member of the class.* ◇ *They had a disagreement about the best way to get to Manchester.* | **express** *She expressed disagreement with the government's policy.* | **resolve, settle, solve** *How is a basic disagreement of this nature to be resolved?* | **cause, lead to** | **be open to** *This view is subjective and therefore open to disagreement.*
- DISAGREEMENT + VERB **arise, occur** *A disagreement arose over who should pay for the trip.* | **exist** *Disagreement exists over the pattern of demand for coal.* | **remain** | **centre around/on sb/sth** *a disagreement centring on the link between crime and unemployment*
- PREP. **in ~** *He shook his head in disagreement.* | **~ about/over** *They had a major disagreement over who should clean the car.* **~ among/amongst, ~ as to** *There is considerable disagreement among archaeologists as to the age of the sculpture.* **~ between** *a serious disagreement between the two experts* **~ on** *There is fundamental disagreement on these matters.* **~ with** *He had a disagreement with his girlfriend.*
- PHRASES **an area of disagreement** *There are several areas of disagreement between the two governments.* **a source of disagreement** *Money was a constant source of disagreement.* **room/scope for disagreement** *There is plenty of room for disagreement in this controversial area.*

disappear verb

- ADV. **altogether, completely, entirely** | **all but, effectively, largely, practically, virtually** *The traditional way of life has all but disappeared.* | **gradually, slowly** | **overnight, quickly, soon** *He started the treatment and his symptoms disappeared overnight.* | **suddenly** | **eventually, finally** | **forever** *A number of species could soon disappear forever.* | **mysteriously, without trace** *Her father disappeared without trace when she was ten.* | **apparently** | **just, simply** *The plane suddenly just disappeared from the radar screen.*
- PREP. **behind** *The sun disappeared behind a cloud.* | **from** *Wildlife is fast disappearing from our countryside.* | **into, through, under,** etc.
- PHRASES **disappear from sight/view** *She watched until he had disappeared from view.* **fast/rapidly disappearing**

disappearance noun

- ADJ. **abrupt, sudden** *How could he explain his abrupt disappearance from the party?* | **rapid** *the rapid disappearance of our countryside* | **gradual** | **complete, total** | **virtual** | **apparent** | **mysterious**
- VERB + DISAPPEARANCE **lead to** *Modern farming practice has led to the virtual disappearance of this bird.* | **investigate** *Essex police are investigating the mysterious disappearance of two young men.* | **explain**
- PREP. **~ from** *the disappearance of money from my desk*

disappointed adj.

- VERBS **be, feel, look, seem, sound** | **leave sb** *The decision left them very disappointed.*
- ADV. **bitterly, deeply, desperately, extremely, greatly, hugely, really, sadly, sorely, terribly, very** *I was bitterly disappointed when I didn't get into university.* ◇ *If you think I'll agree to that, then you're going to be sadly disappointed.* | **almost** *He seemed almost disappointed when I agreed to go.* | **a bit, a little, mildly, pretty, quite, rather,**

slightly, somewhat | **clearly, obviously** | **naturally** | **oddly** *After convincing myself that the result didn't matter, I felt oddly disappointed when we lost.* | **visibly**
- PREP. **about** *I'm disappointed about John not coming.* **at** *They're disappointed at the result.* **by** *I was slightly disappointed by her attitude.* **in** *He's disappointed in his daughter.* **with** *We're disappointed with the new car.*

disappointing adj.

- VERBS **be, prove, seem** | **find sth**
- ADV. **bitterly, deeply, desperately, extremely, hugely, really, terribly, very** *The film was terribly disappointing.* | **a bit, a little, quite, rather, slightly, somewhat**

disappointment noun

1 sadness because sth has not happened, etc.
- ADJ. **bitter, considerable, deep, great, intense, sharp** | **slight** | **obvious**
- VERB + DISAPPOINTMENT **be aware of, feel** *He was aware of sharp disappointment and betrayal.* ◇ *She couldn't quite conceal the deep disappointment she felt.* | **express, voice** | **betray** *His voice betrayed his disappointment.* | **bite back, conceal, cover, hide, mask** *He bit back his disappointment.* ◇ *Her laugh covered her disappointment.* | **feign** *He feigned disappointment. Secretly, he was mightily relieved.* | **avoid** *To avoid disappointment, we recommend you book your holiday early.* | **be doomed to** *The scheme was doomed to disappointment.* | **share** *I know you will share our disappointment at the lack of progress on this issue.*
- DISAPPOINTMENT + VERB **show** *He let his disappointment show.* | **grip sb, surge through sb** *Disappointment gripped her.*
- PREP. **to your ~** *To her disappointment, they didn't go through Oxford but skirted round it.* | **~ at** *Paul couldn't hide his disappointment at not being asked to the party.* **~ over** *Campaigners have voiced disappointment over the government's decision.*
- PHRASES **a feeling/sense of disappointment, tears of disappointment**

2 sb/sth that is disappointing
- ADJ. **big, bitter, considerable, crushing, grave, great, huge, major, sad, serious, severe, terrible** *I'm afraid I was a sad disappointment to my mother.* | **slight** | **inevitable** | **personal**
- VERB + DISAPPOINTMENT **have** *She's had a lot of disappointments in the past.* | **come as** *This news has come as a disappointment to local business leaders.*
- DISAPPOINTMENT + VERB **come, follow sth** *His second disappointment came last year when he failed to get selected for the first team.* | **await sb** *A terrible disappointment awaited them.*
- PREP. **~ for** *The cancellation of the tour was a great disappointment for the many fans of the band.* **~ to** *It was a big disappointment to us when she left.*

disapproval noun

- ADJ. **strong** *Several countries have expressed their strong disapproval of the law.* | **faint, mild** | **widespread** | **official** | **public** *The decision met with widespread public disapproval.* | **moral, social**
- QUANT. **note** *There was more than a note of disapproval in her voice.*
- VERB + DISAPPROVAL **express, mark, register, show** *To mark his disapproval he refused to go to the wedding.* ◇ *Her face registered her disapproval.* ◇ *The students are showing their disapproval by refusing to attend lectures.* | **feel, sense** *Even at this distance she could sense his disapproval.*
- PREP. **in ~** *Her lip curled in disapproval.* **with ~** *Harold noted the boy's earring with disapproval.* | **~ at** *She was stiff with disapproval at the notion.* **~ of** *his disapproval of*

Wallace's conduct
● PHRASES **a chorus/roar of disapproval** *There was a chorus of disapproval from the crowd.* **an expression/a frown/a look of disapproval** *Seeing the look of disapproval on the doctor's face, I put out my cigarette.* **a murmur/sniff of disapproval** *Dr Ali gave a great sniff of disapproval.*

disapprove *verb*

● ADV. **strongly | thoroughly**
● PREP. **of** *He strongly disapproved of the way his daughter was behaving.*

disapproving *adj.*

● VERBS **be, look | become**
● ADV. **deeply, very | mildly, quite, rather, slightly | coldly** *her coldly disapproving smile*

disarmament *noun*

● ADJ. **nuclear** *They campaigned for nuclear disarmament.* **| international, multilateral** *The party supports multilateral disarmament.* **| unilateral**
● VERB + DISARMAMENT **campaign for | support**
● DISARMAMENT + NOUN **negotiations, talks, treaty**

disarray *noun*

● ADJ. **complete, total | some | financial**
● VERB + DISARRAY **fall into** *His personal life fell into disarray when his wife left him.* **| throw sth into** *Our plans were thrown into disarray by the rail strike.*
● PREP. **in ~** *The meeting broke up in disarray.* **| ~ within** *a period of disarray within the National Party*
● PHRASES **a state of disarray**

disaster *noun*

1 bad event/situation
● ADJ. **awful, big, dreadful, great, major, terrible, worst** *the biggest disaster in British mining history* **| near** *a near disaster in the city centre* **| imminent, impending** *It seemed that nothing could prevent the impending disaster.* ◇ *Everyone had the feeling that disaster was imminent.* **| potential | global, national | natural** *earthquakes, floods and other natural disasters* **| man-made | air, ecological, environmental, flood, military, mining, nuclear, rail** *fears of a nuclear disaster* **| business, economic, financial | personal**
● VERB + DISASTER **bring, cause, lead to, spell** *One person's mistakes can bring disaster to someone else.* ◇ *attempts to find out what caused the disaster* ◇ *The drought spelt economic disaster for the country.* **| avert, avoid, prevent, save sb/sth from, stave off, ward off** *A major disaster was averted only just in time.* ◇ *What can be done to ward off environmental disaster?* **| predict, prophesy** *Independent analysts in the market predicted disaster.* **| court, invite** *It's courting disaster to go into the mountains without proper weatherproof clothing.* **| be heading for** *his firm belief that the whole world was heading for disaster* **| face** *In the last match of the series England were facing disaster.* **| suffer** *There are many who have suffered personal disasters but managed to rebuild their lives.* **| survive** *It was a miracle any of the passengers or crew survived the worst air disaster in Portugal for 20 years.* **| end in** *The show ended in disaster when the tent collapsed.*
● DISASTER + VERB **happen, occur, strike** *finding out why the disaster occurred* ◇ *Everything was going fine. Then, without warning, disaster struck.* **| befall sb/sth, hit sb/sth, strike sb/sth** *the economic disaster that befell the country* **| loom, threaten** *We could all see that disaster loomed for the company.*
● DISASTER + NOUN **area, zone** *Only rescue workers are allowed into the disaster area.* **| relief | victim**

● PREP. **in a/the ~** *In a disaster everyone needs to keep calm.*
● PHRASES **a disaster waiting to happen** *Any one of these nuclear plants may be a disaster waiting to happen.* **in the aftermath of a disaster** *In the aftermath of the disaster people were too shocked to give a clear picture of what had happened.* **a recipe for disaster** *Letting her organize the party is a recipe for disaster* (= sth that is likely to go badly wrong). **a victim of a disaster** *providing help for the victims of the disaster*

2 a failure
● ADJ. **absolute, complete, real, total, unmitigated** *The play was a complete disaster from beginning to end.* **| economic, financial, social** *Buying that house turned out to be a financial disaster.*
● VERB + DISASTER **prove, turn out to be** *High-rise buildings proved a social disaster.*

disastrous *adj.*

● VERBS **be, prove | become**
● ADV. **absolutely, quite, utterly** *The policy was absolutely disastrous for the economy.* **| fairly, pretty | potentially | ecologically, electorally, financially**

disbelief *noun*

● ADJ. **complete, outright, total, utter | widespread | open | mock** *He raised his eyebrows in mock disbelief.* **| amused, astonished, furious, horrified, shocked, stunned**
● VERB + DISBELIEF **feel** *I felt disbelief first of all, then outrage.* **| express** *The president publicly expressed his disbelief at what had happened.* **| hide | greet sth with** *My stories were greeted with disbelief.* **| shake your head in, stare/watch in | suspend** *If you don't mind suspending your disbelief, you should enjoy this movie.*
● PREP. **in ~** *We could only watch in disbelief as the car rolled into the water.* **to your ~** *To my horrified disbelief, the animal was running towards me.* **| ~ at** *Hilary shook her head in disbelief at the news.*
● PHRASES **an expression/a look of disbelief** *with looks of utter disbelief on their faces* **suspension of disbelief** *The film version requires greater suspension of disbelief than the book.*

disc *noun*

1 computer disk
⇨ See DISK

2 CD/record
● ADJ. **vinyl** *I've got an old vinyl disc of her singing.*
● VERB + DISC **play | hear, listen to | produce, record**
● PREP. **on (a/the) ~** *He is one of the greatest opera singers on disc.* ◇ *The Prokofiev sonata comes first on the disc.* **| ~ of** *a disc of the two Mozart piano quartets*
⇨ See CD

3 part of the body
● ADJ. **prolapsed, slipped** *He's in bed with a slipped disc.*
● VERB + DISC **slip** *She's slipped a disc.*

discard *verb*

● ADV. **completely, entirely** *These ideas have now been completely discarded.*
● PREP. **in favour of** *Older managers have been discarded in favour of younger people.*

discern *verb*

● ADV. **clearly, easily** *She could clearly discern a figure walking up towards the house.* **| dimly, just**
● VERB + DISCERN **be able to, can/could | be difficult to, be hard to | be possible to**

discernible adj.

- VERBS **be** | **become**
- ADV. **clearly, easily, readily** *The difference between the two is readily discernible.* | **just** | **barely, scarcely** *Her face was barely discernible in the gloom.*

discharge noun

1 substance
- ADJ. **thick** | **nasal, vaginal, etc.** | **effluent, industrial, sewage, waste** | **electrical, radioactive** *thunder and lightning caused by an electrical discharge*
- PREP. **~from** *a thick discharge from the nose*

2 from court
- ADJ. **absolute** | **conditional**
- VERB + DISCHARGE **give** *He was given an absolute discharge but banned from driving for 12 months.*

discharge verb

1 from army/navy, etc.
- ADV. **dishonourably, honourably**
- PREP. **from** *He was found guilty and dishonourably discharged from the army.*

2 from prison/court
- ADV. **conditionally** *He was conditionally discharged after admitting the theft.*

3 gas/liquid
- ADV. **directly**
- PREP. **from, into** *Raw sewage was discharged from the treatment plant directly into the river.*

disciple noun

- ADJ. **ardent** *She was an ardent disciple of Freud.*
- VERB + DISCIPLE **become** | **make** *He commanded them to go out and make disciples of all nations.*

discipline noun

1 controlling behaviour
- ADJ. **effective, firm, good, strong** *We need better discipline in our schools.* | **harsh, iron, rigid, strict** *strict military discipline* | **lax, poor** *Discipline was too lax.* | **staff, team** | **military, naval, party, prison, school, work**
- VERB + DISCIPLINE **enforce, exercise, exert, impose** *the discipline that the party exercises over its members* | **keep, maintain** *The teacher was unable to maintain discipline.* | **accept, submit to** *They submitted to the discipline imposed by their leaders.* | **have** *The school was criticized for having very poor discipline.* | **lack** *Modern schools lack discipline.* | **tighten** *The new headmaster tightened discipline in the school.* | **relax** | **restore**
- PHRASES **a breach of discipline** *It's unfair to dismiss somebody for a single breach of discipline.* **a breakdown of discipline** *a breakdown of discipline in the classroom* **a lack of discipline**

2 controlling yourself
- ADJ. **good, great, useful, valuable** *It is good discipline to learn to delegate.* | **strict** | **personal** | **mental, spiritual** | **business, commercial, financial, fiscal, industrial, market, monetary** *The chancellor has stabilized the economy through strict fiscal discipline.*
- VERB + DISCIPLINE **have** *He'll never get anywhere working for himself—he's got no discipline.* | **show** | **lack** | **demand, require, take** *It takes great discipline to learn a musical instrument.*
- PHRASES **a lack of discipline**

3 subject of study
- ADJ. **core, main, major** *Students are to be tested on the three core disciplines: maths, English and science.* | **distinct, independent** *When did sociology emerge as a distinct discipline?* | **established, traditional** | **subject** | **academic, intellectual** *They established psychology as an*

academic discipline. | **professional** | **humanities, science/scientific**
- PREP. **across ~s** *There is a lack of communication across disciplines* (= between teachers and students of different subjects). **within a/the ~** *Within a discipline there may be more than one school of thought.*
- PHRASES **a range of disciplines** *The university offers a wide range of disciplines.*

disclose verb

- ADV. **fully** *He had not fully disclosed all his business dealings.* | **publicly**
- VERB + DISCLOSE **be obliged to, be required to, must** *Members of Parliament are required to disclose all their financial interests.* | **be reluctant to** | **fail to, refuse to** *He failed to disclose all the information.*
- PREP. **to** *She was accused of disclosing confidential material to a competitor.*

discomfort noun

1 slight pain
- ADJ. **acute, considerable, great, severe, growing** *He became conscious of a growing discomfort.* | **mild, minor, slight** *You may experience some slight discomfort after the operation.* | **bodily, physical**
- QUANT. **amount, degree**
- VERB + DISCOMFORT **complain of, experience, feel, get, have, suffer** *Some of the patients complained of discomfort.* ◇ *I didn't have much discomfort after the operation.* | **cause** | **ease, lessen, reduce, relieve** *Not eating late at night should help to relieve the discomfort.*
- PREP. **in ~** *He appeared to be in great discomfort.* **with/without~** *You should be able to drive without discomfort after about two weeks.*

2 embarrassment
- VERB + DISCOMFORT **cause** *The revelations caused some discomfort to the president.* | **enjoy** *Paula smiled, enjoying her sister's discomfort.*
- DISCOMFORT + VERB **grow, increase**

disconcerting adj.

- VERBS **be** | **become** | **find sth**
- ADV. **highly, very** | **a bit, a little, rather, slightly, somewhat** *I found all that noise rather disconcerting.*

discontent noun

- ADJ. **general, widespread** | **growing, increasing** | **popular, public** *Public discontent with the economy remained at a high level.* | **political, social**
- VERB + DISCONTENT **breed, cause, give rise to, lead to, provoke** *The higher tax provoked widespread discontent among the poor.* | **fuel** *Overcrowded conditions fuelled discontent and facilitated the spread of radical ideas.* | **feel** *the discontent that many people felt* | **seethe with** *The country was seething with discontent and the threat of revolution was real.* | **express, voice** *The peasants expressed their discontent.* | **stem** *The reforms failed to stem social discontent.*
- DISCONTENT + VERB **grow, spread** | **simmer** *Discontent simmered and then came to a head with the nationalist protests.* | **come to a head**
- PREP. **~among, ~about/at/over** *discontent among students about the lack of funding for education* **~with** *growing discontent with the government* **~within** *There were reports of growing discontent within the army.*
- PHRASES **a cause/source of discontent, murmurs/rumbles/rumblings of discontent**

discord noun

- ADJ. **internal** | **family, marital**

- QUANT. **hint, note** *A note of discord surfaced during the leaders' meeting.*
- VERB + DISCORD **avoid**
- PHRASES **a source of discord** *The contrasts between rich and poor nations are a source of discord.*

discount *noun*

- ADJ. **big, generous, good, high, huge, large, massive, substantial | low | special** *There is a special discount for staff.* | **staff, trade** *They offer a trade discount to builders.* | **cash, volume** *We offer a 5% cash discount for prompt payment.*
- VERB + DISCOUNT **allow sb, give (sb), offer (sb)** *They only give you a discount if you buy more than a certain amount.* | **get, obtain, receive | be entitled to, qualify for** *If you collect ten bonus points, you will be entitled to a discount.* | **negotiate** *It is important to negotiate a good discount and obtain books on approval.*
- DISCOUNT + NOUN **card, voucher** *Members are given a discount card which entitles them to 20% off.* | **scheme, system | price, rate | house, shop, store** (= that regularly sells good at a discount)
- PREP. **at a~** *Tickets are available to members at a discount.* | **~of** *a discount of 30%* **~on** *Customers are allowed a discount on orders over £500.*
- PHRASES **a rate of discount**

discourage *verb*

- ADV. **actively, firmly, positively, strongly** *Smoking is actively discouraged in the university.*
- VERB + DISCOURAGE **try to**
- PREP. **from** *We tried to discourage him from resigning.*
- PHRASES **be easily discouraged** *Children are easily discouraged from reading.*

discover *verb*

- ADV. **quickly, soon** *We soon discovered we'd been mistaken.* | **suddenly | subsequently | eventually**
- VERB + DISCOVER **be amazed to, be astonished to, be astounded to, be a surprise to, be surprised to** *She was surprised to discover he was perfectly capable around the house.* | **be alarmed to, be appalled to, be dismayed to, be horrified to, be a shock to, be shocked to** *It was a terrible shock to discover the full extent of the problem.* | **be delighted to, be fascinated to, be intrigued to | be fascinating to** *It would be fascinating to discover more about the town's history.* | **be difficult to | be possible to | aim to | attempt to, try to** *trying to discover the truth* | **be able/unable to**
- PHRASES **an attempt to discover sth, newly/recently discovered** *recently discovered evidence* **only to discover sth** *I arrived at the campsite, only to discover that it was closed for the winter.* **an opportunity to discover sth, waiting to be discovered** *There's great talent out there just waiting to be discovered.*

discovery *noun*

- ADJ. **amazing, big, exciting, great, important, major, remarkable, significant, startling, surprising, unexpected** *potentially the biggest archaeological discovery in Norway for fifty years* | **awful, chilling, grim, terrible** *the awful discovery that he had been deceiving her* | **latest, new, recent | accidental, chance** *All these were chance discoveries made by scientists engaged in other investigations.* | **archaeological, medical, scientific | personal** *The story tells of a man's journey of personal discovery up an African river.*
- VERB + DISCOVERY **make** *New scientific discoveries are being made all the time.* | **lead to** *Their work led to some important medical discoveries.* | **await** *There may be many unexpected treasures awaiting discovery.*

- PREP. **~by** *a discovery by a French scientist* **~of** *the discovery of oil in the North Sea*
- PHRASES **a process of discovery, a journey/voyage of discovery** *(figurative)* *To tour Sri Lanka is to take a voyage of discovery through a land of endless variety.*

discredit *noun*

- ADJ. **great**
- VERB + DISCREDIT **bring, reflect** *By telling lies he brought discredit upon Parliament.* ◇ *Your failure reflects no discredit upon you—you did your best.* | **bring sth into, do sb** *She brought the whole system into discredit.* ◇ *It does us great discredit to treat foreigners so badly.*
- PREP. **to sb's~** *His selfish decision is greatly to his discredit.* | **~to** *They were a discredit to their country.*

discrepancy *noun*

- ADJ. **glaring, great, huge, large, major, marked, material, serious, substantial, wide | minor, slight, small | apparent**
- VERB + DISCREPANCY **account for, explain** *How do you explain the apparent discrepancies between the money and the receipts?* | **find, note, notice, observe, perceive** *She failed to notice the discrepancy between the name on the cheque and the name on the driving licence.* | **ignore**
- DISCREPANCY + VERB **exist | arise, occur**
- PREP. **~between** *Discrepancies occurred between the written and electronic records.* **~in** *There were wide discrepancies in the evidence.*

discretion *noun*

1 freedom to make decisions
- ADJ. **considerable, full, greater, more, wide | absolute, complete, unfettered** *The school governors have absolute discretion over which pupils they admit.* | **executive, judicial, management/managerial, personal, professional** *The president used his executive discretion to pardon the two men.*
- VERB + DISCRETION **exercise, have, use** *The police exercise discretion in the area of minor traffic offences.* | **give sb** *They would like local authorities to be given greater discretion as to how the money is spent.* | **leave sth to** *'Do you want me to do the job myself or hire a photographer?' 'I leave it to your discretion.'*
- PREP. **at sb's~** *Bail is granted at the discretion of the court.* ◇ *There is no service charge and tipping is at your discretion.* | **~about** *We have discretion about how much to charge.* **~as to** *She has considerable discretion as to how the money is spent.* **~over** *giving judges more discretion over sentencing*
- PHRASES **the exercise/operation of discretion**

2 being discreet
- ADJ. **great, the utmost**
- VERB + DISCRETION **call for, need, require** *This case calls for the utmost discretion.* | **rely on** *This is confidential, but I know that I can rely on your discretion.*
- PREP. **with~** *to conduct enquiries with discretion.*
- PHRASES **a lack of discretion, a need for discretion**

discriminate *verb*

- ADV. **positively | unfairly**
- PREP. **against** *The present law discriminates unfairly against women.* **in favour of** *discriminating positively in favour of people from ethnic minorities* **on (the) grounds of** *Workers must avoid discriminating on the grounds of race or sex.*

discrimination *noun*

1 treating a person/group unfairly
- ADJ. **age, class, gender, race/racial, religious, sex/sexual | widespread** *There is widespread discrimin-*

ation against doctors of Asian origin. | **active, blatant, direct, explicit, overt** *evidence of active discrimination against black workers* | **covert, indirect** | **positive, reverse** *positive discrimination in favour of disadvantaged racial groups* | **illegal, unlawful** *Overt sex or race discrimination is illegal.* | **employment, job** | **government, institutional/institutionalized** *institutionalized discrimination against women within the police force*

● QUANT. **level** *Levels of discrimination against recent immigrants are high.*

● VERB + DISCRIMINATION **amount to, constitute** *Racist remarks by an employer to an employee can amount to unlawful discrimination.* | **experience, face, suffer (from)** *Many disabled people suffer discrimination at work.* | **practise** | **allege** *law suits alleging discrimination* | **be opposed to, combat, fight** | **ban, end, forbid, outlaw, prohibit, stop**

● DISCRIMINATION + VERB **occur** *The discrimination occurred at the shortlisting stage, not the interviews.*

● PREP. **~ against** *discrimination against women* **~ by** *Discrimination by age is as vicious as discrimination by race.* **~ in favour of** *Some firms practise discrimination in favour of older people.* **~ on the grounds of** *It's time we banned discrimination on the grounds of age.*

● PHRASES **a victim of discrimination**

2 judgement

● ADJ. **great** | **careful, fine**

● VERB + DISCRIMINATION **make** *Young children find it difficult to make fine discriminations.* | **show** *She showed great discrimination in rejecting the poor quality teas.*

● PREP. **~ between** *discrimination between right and wrong*

discuss *verb*

● ADV. **exhaustively, fully, in detail, thoroughly** *The plan was discussed in great detail.* | **at length, endlessly, extensively** *These ideas will be discussed at greater length in the next chapter.* | **briefly** | **further** | **openly** *This problem has never been discussed openly before.* | **informally** | **critically, intelligently** *Pupils should be encouraged to discuss critically the information they are given.*

● VERB + DISCUSS **convene (sth) to, meet to** *to convene a conference to discuss the country's political future* ◇ *The committee meets regularly to discuss these issues.* | **want to, wish to, would like to** | **refuse to** *He refused to discuss it with me.* | **be able to** | **be prepared to, be willing to** *I'm not prepared to discuss this on the phone.*

● PREP. **with** *I'd like to discuss this matter with you later.*

● PHRASES **an opportunity to discuss sth, widely discussed** *The proposals have been widely discussed in the media.*

discussion *noun*

● ADJ. **detailed, full, in-depth, lengthy, long** *They had a detailed discussion of the issues.* | **brief** | **considerable** *After considerable discussion, they decided to accept our offer.* | **initial, preliminary** | **further** *The plan was agreed without further discussion.* | **general, wide-ranging** *a wide-ranging discussion on women's rights* | **public** | **formal, informal** *After the lecture there will be an opportunity for informal discussion.* | **bilateral, group, one-to-one, round-table** *a series of bilateral discussions between Israel and neighbouring states* ◇ *Women were asked to take part in small group discussions.* | **candid, frank, open** | **animated, heated, intense, lively** *a heated discussion about politics* | **serious** | **reasoned** | **useful** | **inconclusive**

● VERB + DISCUSSION **have, hold** *We had a long discussion about the plans for next year.* ◇ *The two governments are to hold discussions on the border issue.* | **enter into** *We are hoping to enter into discussions with leaders of the*

prison service. | **be involved in, join in, participate in, take part in** *They refused to take part in the discussions.* | **generate, initiate, provoke, stimulate** *These latest findings have generated a lot of discussion of the moral issues involved.* | **set up** *ways of setting up discussions between children to explore each other's viewpoints* | **lead, open, start** *The discussion was led by the director of marketing.* ◇ *Who is going to start the discussion?* | **bring sth up for, come up for, open sth up for** *The issue should come up for discussion at the climate change conference.* ◇ *The topic must be opened up for general discussion.* | **open up** *We need to open up a discussion on the basic aspects of the theory.* | **confine** *I wish to confine the discussion to income taxation.* | **sum up** *Let us sum up the discussion so far.* | **break off, conclude, end** *The government has broken off discussions with the unions.* ◇ *We decided to end the discussion before it got out of hand.* | **defer, postpone** | **follow up** *Discussion should be followed up by a written report.*

● DISCUSSION + VERB **take place** *Discussions have taken place between the two leaders.* | **centre on** *Discussion centred on the contribution different groups would make to the project.* | **break out, ensue** *An intense discussion broke out about the importance of intuition.* ◇ *Adam raised the issue of multimedia applications and much useful discussion ensued.* | **continue**

● DISCUSSION + NOUN **group** | **document**

● PREP. **for ~** *the subject for discussion* **during/in a/the ~** *During our discussions we raised many issues that need deeper consideration.* **in ~ with** *The company had been in discussion with companies in Austria, Italy and Greece.* **under ~** *Plans for a new bypass are still under discussion.* | **~ about/on** *a discussion about reform of the health service* **~ as to** *Discussion continues as to the relative merits of the different schemes.* **~ between** *discussions between management and union officials* **~ of** *a discussion of the issues involved* **~ with** *discussions with the government*

● PHRASES **a basis for discussion** *We can use the draft document as a basis for discussion.* **a forum for discussion** *The group provides a forum for the discussion of ideas.* **the outcome of a discussion** *The outcome of the discussions is a decision to proceed with Phase 2 of the programme.* **a subject/topic for/of discussion**

⇨ Special page at MEETING

disdain *noun*

● ADJ. **great** | **utter** | **obvious** | **amused** | **cool, glacial** | **aristocratic, haughty**

● VERB + DISDAIN **feel, have** *She did not hesitate to express the disdain that she felt.* | **express, show** *Judges sometimes show great disdain for the law.* | **look on/upon sb/sth with, treat sb/sth with** *Traditionalists look upon the changes with disdain.*

● PREP. **in ~** *She turned her head away in disdain.* **with ~** *Why does he treat his father with such disdain?* | **~ for** *He has an aristocratic disdain for money.*

● PHRASES **an expression/a look of disdain**

disease *noun*

● ADJ. **common** | **obscure, rare** | **dangerous, serious** | **mild** | **chronic** | **acute** | **degenerative** | **deadly, fatal, incurable, killer, terminal** *fears of a new killer disease* | **curable** | **preventable** | **communicable, contagious, infectious** | **non-communicable** | **congenital, hereditary, inherited** | **childhood** *childhood diseases such as mumps and chicken pox* | **tropical** | **insect-borne, water-borne** | **occupational** | **bowel, (coronary) heart, liver, etc.** | **mental** | **sexually transmitted, social, venereal** *patients suffering from venereal disease* | **circulatory, respiratory** | **Alzheimer's, Crohn's, etc.**

● QUANT. **outbreak** *fears of an outbreak of Legionnaire's disease*

● VERB + DISEASE **have, suffer from** *He has a serious lung disease.* | **catch, contract, get** *You can't catch the disease just from physical contact.* ◇ *She got a rare liver disease when she was only twenty.* | **die from/of** *Children are still dying in their millions from preventable diseases.* | **cause** *a disease caused by a vitamin deficiency* | **carry, pass on, spread, transmit** *the ticks that carry the disease* ◇ *Such unhygienic practices spread disease.* ◇ *The disease is transmitted by mosquitoes.* | **diagnose** | **treat** | **combat, fight** *The government must take action to fight this deadly disease.* | **control, manage** *new drugs which help to control the disease* | **cure** | **prevent** *It's better to prevent disease by ensuring a clean water supply.* | **eradicate, stamp out, wipe out** *The disease has been eradicated from the world.*
● DISEASE + VERB **spread** *They want to stop the disease spreading.* | **afflict sb, strike sb** | **kill sb** *The disease has killed 500 people so far this year.*
● PREP. **with a/the ~** *the number of people with this disease* | **~ of** *a disease of the digestive system*
● PHRASES **a cure for a disease, the incidence of (a) disease** *the overall incidence of disease in the world* **a patient with/sufferer from a disease** *Sufferers from Alzheimer's disease can't cope at home.* **resistance to disease** *Tobacco lowers the body's resistance to disease.* **the risk of disease** *the risk of coronary heart disease* **the spread of (a) disease** *measures to prevent the spread of the disease* **the symptoms of a disease, the treatment for/of a disease**
⇨ Special page at ILLNESS

disfigure *verb* be disfigured

● ADV. **badly, grossly** *He was badly disfigured by the accident.* | **permanently**

disgrace *noun*

1 loss of respect
● VERB + DISGRACE **fall into** *Their father fell into disgrace and lost his business.* | **bring** *His crime had brought disgrace upon his whole family.* | **be sent away/home/off in** *She was sent home from the Olympics in disgrace.*
● PREP. **in ~** *He's in disgrace for having left his room in a mess.*
● PHRASES **there's no disgrace in sth** *There's no disgrace in being poor.*
2 disgraceful person/thing
● ADJ. **absolute, utter** *This room is an absolute disgrace (= because it is very dirty/untidy)!* | **national, public** *The state of our hospitals is a national disgrace.*
● PREP. **~ to** *The filthy streets are a disgrace to the town.*

disgraceful *adj.*

● VERBS **be**
● ADV. **absolutely, quite, utterly** *There's litter everywhere. It's absolutely disgraceful.*

disguise *noun*

● VERB + DISGUISE **adopt, put on, wear** *She adopted an elaborate disguise to help her pass through the town unrecognized.* | **see through** *We all saw through his disguise immediately.*
● PREP. **in ~** *The star travelled in disguise.*

disguise *verb*

● ADV. **cleverly, cunningly** *She was cleverly disguised as a policewoman.*
● VERB + DISGUISE **cannot/could not** | **try to**
● PREP. **from** *You cannot disguise what you are doing from your family.*
● PHRASES **an attempt to disguise sth** *He made no attempt to disguise his liking for her.* **heavily disguised**

speaking in a heavily disguised voice **barely/thinly disguised** *In her speech she made several thinly disguised attacks on the president.*

disgust *noun*

● ADJ. **great** | **utter** | **obvious** *Mr Haynes shook his head in obvious disgust and walked off.* | **public**
● VERB + DISGUST **feel** | **express, show** | **hide** *trying to hide the disgust that she felt* | **fill sb with** *Decent people were filled with disgust for whoever committed the crimes.* | **turn/walk away in** *He threw her one look, then turned away in disgust.* | **shake your head in, wrinkle (up) your nose in**
● PREP. **in ~** *Marion threw down the book in disgust.* **with ~** *They both looked with disgust at the men.* | **~ at** *I couldn't find the words to express my disgust at his actions.* **~ over** *expressions of public disgust over the affair* **~ with** *People are showing their disgust with the existing regime.*
● PHRASES **an exclamation/a snort of disgust** *He gave a snort of disgust.* **an expression/a gesture/a grimace/a look of disgust, a feeling/sense of disgust, much to your disgust** *Much to his disgust, he found himself sharing a carriage with a noisy young family.*

disgusted *adj.*

● VERBS **be, feel, look** | **become**
● ADV. **really** | **absolutely, quite, thoroughly, totally** | **rather, slightly** | **visibly** *She looked visibly disgusted.*
● PREP. **at** *I'm quite disgusted at the way he's treated you.* **by** *I was absolutely disgusted by the whole business.* **with** *I was thoroughly disgusted with her behaviour.*

disgusting *adj.*

● VERBS **be, look, smell, sound, taste** *That soup tastes disgusting!* | **find sth** *I find his behaviour disgusting.*
● ADV. **really** | **absolutely, quite** *I think the way she's treated him is absolutely disgusting.* | **pretty, rather** *He's got some rather disgusting habits.*

dish *noun*

1 container
● ADJ. **deep** | **flat, shallow** | **empty** | **baking, cooking, roasting, serving** | **fireproof, heatproof, ovenproof** | **china, glass, metal, silver** | **casserole, gratin, pie, soufflé, soup** | **butter, food, soap, vegetable** *your pet's food dish*
● PREP. **in a/the ~** *Arrange the chicken and salad in a serving dish.*
2 the dishes plates, bowls, etc.
● ADJ. **clean** | **dirty, unwashed** *The dirty breakfast dishes were still in the sink when we got home.* | **breakfast**
● VERB + DISHES **do, wash** *It's your turn to do the dishes.* | **dry** *He dried the dishes and put them away.* | **put away**
3 type of food
● ADJ. **main, side** *Serve one or two main dishes with a choice of salads and nibbles.* | **favourite** *Do you have a favourite dish?* | **delicious, tasty, wonderful** | **elaborate** | **simple** *a simple dish, beautifully prepared* | **classic, traditional** | **savoury, sweet** | **spiced/spicy** | **cold, hot** | **local, international, national, regional** *The national dish is 'bigos'—hunter's stew.* | **Chinese, French, etc.** | **vegetarian** | **cheese, egg, fish, meat, pasta, rice, seafood, vegetable** *Goulash is a meat dish.* | **breakfast, lunch, supper** *Kedgeree makes a wonderful supper dish.*
● VERB + DISH **cook, make, prepare** *She cooked us a delicious French dish with pork and tomatoes.* | **serve** *a restaurant that serves traditional Indian dishes* | **recommend** | **sample, try** *They sampled all the local dishes.*
● PHRASES **the dish of the day** *I can recommend the chef's dish of the day.*
⇨ Special page at FOOD

dishonest *adj.*

- VERBS **be, seem | become | consider** sth, **regard** sth **as** *What they are doing is not considered dishonest.*
- ADV. **very | downright** *I think he's downright dishonest!* | **rather, slightly | basically, fundamentally**

dishwasher *noun*

- VERB + DISHWASHER **load, stack | empty | run** *It wastes energy to run the dishwasher half empty.*
- DISHWASHER + NOUN **detergent, powder, salt**
- PHRASES **dishwasher proof/safe** *Are these glasses dishwasher safe?*

disillusioned *adj.*

- VERBS **be, feel | become, get, grow**
- ADV. **extremely, very | completely, thoroughly, totally, utterly | increasingly | rather | sadly** *If the king had hoped for peace, he was to be sadly disillusioned.*
- PREP. **by** *They felt bitter and disillusioned by the decision.* **with** *Later in life he grew rather disillusioned with communism.*

disillusionment *noun*

- ADJ. **general, public, widespread | growing**
- VERB + DISILLUSIONMENT **cause**
- PREP. **~ among** *causing widespread disillusionment among young people* **~ with** *There is growing public disillusionment with the present system of government.*

disintegrate *verb*

- ADV. **completely** *The plane completely disintegrated on impact.* | **slowly** *The social fabric of this country is slowly disintegrating.*
- VERB + DISINTEGRATE **begin to** *The bag had already begun to disintegrate.*
- PREP. **into** *The country has disintegrated into separate states.* **under** *He was a lawyer who had disintegrated under the strain.*

disintegration *noun*

- ADJ. **complete, total | gradual** *the gradual disintegration of traditional values* | **rapid | political, social** *indicators of social disintegration such as divorce, suicide and petty theft.*
- VERB + DISINTEGRATION **lead to, result in** *This defeat led to the disintegration of the empire.*

disk *noun*

- ADJ. **computer | hard | floppy | master** *The master disk can be duplicated as many times as required.* | **backup | program | server, system | blank | laser, magnetic, optical | high density**
- VERB + DISK **insert, put in** *Insert the disk into the drive slot.* | **remove, take out | format | read** *The computer reads the disk.* | **copy, duplicate** *I'll copy the disk into a file.* | **copy/save (sth) to, save sth on** *The program is set up so that you automatically save to disk every 15 minutes.* ◇ *Save the document to disk before closing it.* ◇ *The information can be saved on a disk.* | **wipe** *If you wipe that old disk, we can use it again.* | **hold sth on, store sth on** *The records will be stored on the computer's hard disk.*
- DISK + VERB **contain sth** *The disk contains the program you'll need.* | **hold sth** *Each disk holds 700 MB.*
- DISK + NOUN **capacity, space** *I'm running out of disk space on my computer.* | **drive | storage**
- PREP. **from ~** *The information required can then be retrieved from disk.* **on (a/the) ~** *Have you got the file on disk?* ◇ *the data on the disk* **onto ~** *It is safest to save your design onto disk.* **to ~** *You simply download the pages to disk.*
- ⇨ Special page at COMPUTER

dislike *noun*

1 feeling of not liking sb/sth
- ADJ. **acute, deep, great, hearty, intense, real, strong, violent** *Several committee members expressed their intense dislike of the chairman.* | **growing | particular | obvious, marked | instant | instinctive | open | active** *She threw him a look of active dislike.* | **cold** *He glanced at her with cold dislike.* | **pathological | personal | mutual** *In spite of their mutual dislike and hostility, they quite often worked together.*
- VERB + DISLIKE **feel, have** *She felt dislike rather than sympathy as he told his story.* ◇ *My grandfather has a great dislike of long hair on boys.* | **express, show | take** *I took an instant dislike to my new colleague.*
- PREP. **with ~** *Sonia stared at me with dislike and distrust.* | **~ for** *She had a deep dislike for Robert's wife.*
- PHRASES **a feeling/look of dislike**

2 sth you do not like
- PHRASES **your likes and dislikes** *I've told you all my likes and dislikes.*

dislike *verb*

- ADV. **cordially, greatly, heartily, intensely, positively, really, strongly** *She disliked her boss intensely.* | **particularly | simply** *He simply disliked working with committees and avoided it whenever possible.* | **instinctively | actively** *There are very few foods that I actively dislike.* | **clearly, obviously**
- PHRASES **be universally/widely disliked** *The new teacher was universally disliked.*

disloyalty *noun*

- VERB + DISLOYALTY **show | accuse sb of** *Her friends accused her of disloyalty.*
- PREP. **~ to** *He has shown disloyalty to the party and is not to be trusted.*

dismal *adj.*

- VERBS **be, look | become**
- ADV. **really** *It was a really dismal day.* | **a bit, fairly, pretty, rather** *Last year's results were fairly dismal.*

dismay *noun*

- ADJ. **deep, great** *The government has expressed 'deep dismay' at police violence against protesters.* | **growing, mounting | widespread**
- VERB + DISMAY **feel** *I felt a mounting dismay at the prospect.* | **express | hide** *It was impossible to hide my dismay at what I had seen.* | **cause** *The laws on hunting cause dismay to many animal lovers.* | **be regarded with, be greeted with, be viewed with** *The news was greeted with widespread dismay.*
- PREP. **in ~** *Louise stared at the torn letter in dismay.* **with ~** *I read of her resignation with some dismay.* | **~ at** *his dismay at her reaction* **~ over** *Brady made no secret of his dismay over his treatment.*
- PHRASES **(much) to your dismay** *Much to my dismay, she was out when I called.*

dismiss *verb*

1 decide sth is not important
- ADV. **quickly | out of hand, summarily** *He dismissed her suggestion out of hand.* | **easily, lightly, readily** *Children's fears should never be dismissed lightly.* | **contemptuously** *She contemptuously dismissed their complaints.*
- VERB + DISMISS **cannot/could not, unable to | be difficult to, be easy to, be possible to** *It was not easy to dismiss the matter from his thoughts.* | **try to**
- PREP. **as, from** *She dismissed their arguments as irrelevant.* ◇ *She tried to dismiss the idea from her mind.*

2 remove sb from a job
- ADV. **fairly** | **unfairly, wrongfully** *The court ruled that Ms Hill had been unfairly dismissed.* | **constructively** | **summarily**
- PREP. **from** *He was summarily dismissed from his job.*

dismissal *noun*

1 from a job
- ADJ. **automatic, immediate, instant, summary** *His attack on the manager led to his instant dismissal.* | **constructive, unfair, wrongful** *She won her claim for constructive dismissal because she had been pressured into resigning.*
- VERB + DISMISSAL **lead to** | **call for** *Crash victims are calling for the dismissal of the coach driver.* | **be faced with, be threatened with, face, risk** *They were warned that they risked dismissal if the strike continued.* | **appeal against, claim** *Cooke, who was with the firm 30 years, claims unfair dismissal.*
- PREP. **~for** *his dismissal for poor performance* **~ on the grounds of** *She is now faced with dismissal on the grounds of misconduct.*
- PHRASES **grounds/reason for dismissal**

2 refusing to consider sth
- ADJ. **arrogant, callous, casual, disdainful, easy**
- PREP. **~of** *his callous dismissal of her father's illness*

dismissive *adj.*

- VERBS **be, seem, sound**
- ADV. **very** | **completely, entirely** | **mildly, rather, slightly, somewhat** | **coldly** *Her manner was coldly dismissive.*
- PREP. **of** *She was very dismissive of his achievements.*

disobedience *noun*

- ADJ. **civil** *He called for a campaign of civil disobedience if the president did not honour the election results.*
- VERB + DISOBEDIENCE **punish (sb for)**
- PREP. **~to** *their disobedience to the king*
- PHRASES **an act of disobedience** *His behaviour was seen as another act of disobedience.*

disorder *noun*

1 untidy state
- ADJ. **complete**
- VERB + DISORDER **throw sth into** *The country was thrown into disorder by the strikes.*
- PREP. **in ~** *He died suddenly, leaving his financial affairs in complete disorder.*
- PHRASES **a state of disorder**

2 violent behaviour
- ADJ. **major, serious** | **widespread** | **violent** | **civil, crowd, public, social** | **political**
- QUANT. **outbreak** *There have been outbreaks of serious public disorder.*
- VERB + DISORDER **create, lead to** | **quell** *Troops were sent in to quell the disorder.* | **prevent** *new restrictions aimed at preventing social disorder*

3 illness
- ADJ. **serious, severe** | **chronic** | **common, rare** | **genetic, inherited** | **blood, brain, etc.** | **circulatory, eating, etc.** *Anorexia is a common eating disorder.* | **behavioural, emotional, mental, nervous, personality, physical, psychiatric, psychological**
- VERB + DISORDER **have, suffer from** *She suffers from a rare blood disorder.* | **treat**
- DISORDER + VERB **affect sth** *disorders affecting the very old, such as senile dementia*
- ⇨ Special page at ILLNESS

disorganized *adj.*

- VERBS **be, seem** | **become**
- ADV. **highly, hopelessly, very** *She never gets anywhere on time. She's hopelessly disorganized.* | **completely, totally** | **rather, somewhat**

disparity *noun*

- ADJ. **considerable, enormous, great, gross, wide** | **growing** | **clear, glaring, obvious**
- PREP. **~between** *The great disparity between the teams did not make for an entertaining game.* **~ in** *the disparity in their salaries* **~of** *a disparity of resources*

disperse *verb*

- ADV. **quickly, rapidly** | **quietly** | **widely** *The population in this area is quite widely dispersed.* | **geographically** *to decentralize and geographically disperse political and economic power*
- VERB + DISPERSE **begin to** *The crowd slowly began to disperse.*

display *noun*

1 arrangement of things
- ADJ. **attractive, beautiful, colourful, dazzling, excellent, eye-catching, fascinating, fine, good, interesting, stunning** | **special** | **public** | **permanent, temporary** | **static** *The locomotive is normally kept on static display in the National Railway Museum.* | **audio-visual, visual** *An audio-visual display gives visitors an idea of what life was like aboard a sailing ship.* | **floral, photographic** *a beautiful floral display outside the Town Hall* | **in-store, wall, window** | **museum, shop**
- VERB + DISPLAY **have** *The museum has a fine display of old medical instruments.* | **mount** *We plan to mount a display of the children's work in the lobby area.* | **go on** *Examples of her work will go on permanent display in the new museum.* | **put sth on** *The birds were put on display at the zoological society.*
- DISPLAY + VERB **illustrate sth, show sth** *The display illustrates the traditional industries of the town.*
- DISPLAY + NOUN **board, cabinet, case, stand** *a glass-fronted display cabinet*
- PREP. **on~** *Designs for the new sports hall are on public display in the library.* ◇ *On display are earrings, necklaces and bracelets made from jade, amber and amethyst.* | **~of** *a display of Roman coins*
- ⇨ Note at ART

2 performing a skill
- ADJ. **astonishing, awesome, breathtaking, brilliant, devastating, flamboyant, great, impressive, magnificent, outstanding, spectacular, spirited, superb, virtuoso** *a flamboyant display of footballing skills* | **disappointing, lacklustre, poor** | **firework** | **pyrotechnic** *The sun set in a pyrotechnic display that burnt up the whole western sky.* | **aerial, aerobatic, air, flying, parachute** | **courtship, mating, sexual**
- VERB + DISPLAY **give, perform, put on** *The male performs a magnificent courtship display.* ◇ *They put on a spectacular firework display.* | **treat sb to** *The crowd was treated to an impressive display of power tennis.* | **watch**
- DISPLAY + NOUN **team** *an aerobatic display team*
- PREP. **~ of** *They gave a virtuoso display of disco dancing.*

3 showing a particular feeling/quality
- ADJ. **brief** | **rare** | **impressive, incredible, striking** *Members of the community closed ranks in an impressive display of unity.* | **open, public** *an open display of affection for her husband* | **outward** *Despite his outward display of friendliness, I sensed he was concealing something.* | **ostentatious, overt** *an ostentatious display of wealth* |

aggressive *There may be specific events which trigger aggressive displays in your dog.*
- PREP. **~of** *She slammed the door behind her in a display of ill-temper.*

4 on a computer screen, etc.
- ADJ. **computer, screen | data, graphics, video, visual | colour, mono/monochrome | high resolution, low resolution** *a high resolution colour display* **| LCD/liquid crystal | analogue, digital | Windows**
- DISPLAY + NOUN **screen, terminal, unit** *display screen equipment* ◇ *a visual display unit*

display verb

- ADV. **clearly, prominently** *His football trophies were prominently displayed in the kitchen.* **| proudly**
- PREP. **to** *She proudly displayed her degree certificate to her parents.*

displeasure noun

- ADJ. **deep | divine, official, royal** *He saw the English victory as a sign of divine displeasure.*
- VERB + DISPLEASURE **cause, incur** *His tactless words had incurred his father's deep displeasure.* **| express, show, voice | conceal, hide** *He made no attempt to hide his displeasure.*
- PREP. **~ at** *his displeasure at being ignored* **~ with** *her displeasure with her colleagues*

disposal noun

- ADJ. **safe | routine | illegal | ultimate** *the problems of the ultimate disposal of nuclear waste* **| bomb, refuse, rubbish, sewage, waste | land, landfill, sea**
- DISPOSAL + NOUN **site | method | system, unit** *a kitchen waste disposal unit* **| company, expert, squad** *The device was defused by army bomb disposal experts.*
- PREP. **at your~** (= available for your use) *He will have a car at his disposal for the whole month.* ◇ *Well, I'm at your disposal* (= I am ready to help you in any way I can).

disposed adj.

- VERBS **be, feel, seem**
- ADV. **agreeably, favourably, kindly, well | naturally**
- PREP. **to** *She seems favourably disposed to the move.* **towards** *being naturally disposed towards speculation*

disposition noun

- ADJ. **cheerful, happy, pleasant, sunny | friendly, sociable | placid | nervous | jealous | aggressive, touchy | criminal**
- VERB + DISPOSITION **have, show** *These dogs show a very sociable disposition.*
- PREP. **of a ... ~** *This film is not recommended for those of a nervous disposition.*

disproportionate adj.

- VERBS **be, seem**
- ADV. **grossly, vastly | quite, totally, wholly**
- PREP. **to** *The punishment was grossly disproportionate to the crime.*

dispute noun

- ADJ. **considerable, major, serious** *There is considerable dispute over the precise definition of 'social class' as a term.* ◇ *The incident sparked off a major dispute between the two countries.* **| minor | acrimonious, bitter, fierce, heated | damaging | simmering** *The simmering dispute erupted in public when the two men came to blows at the party conference.* **| continuing, lengthy, long-running, long-standing, prolonged, protracted | outstanding** *He proposed a negotiated settlement of the outstanding dis-*

putes between the two countries. **| public | local, international | internal** *There were lengthy internal disputes between the two wings of the party.* **| domestic, family | labour, industrial, pay | border, boundary, land, territorial | legal | ideological, political | commercial, financial, trade | religious**
- VERB + DISPUTE **cause, lead to, provoke, spark (off)** *one of the many factors that led to the dispute* **| enter | be drawn into** *Governments are often drawn into disputes about matters of public taste and decency.* **| be embroiled in, be engaged in, be involved in** *They became embroiled in a dispute with their neighbours.* **| deal with, handle** *Police have difficulties in dealing with domestic disputes.* **| adjudicate, decide** *The purpose of industrial tribunals is to adjudicate disputes between employers and employees.* **| resolve, settle, solve | lose, win | avoid, prevent | be open to** *His theories are open to dispute* (= can be disagreed with).
- DISPUTE + VERB **arise, begin, erupt** *No one could remember exactly how the dispute had arisen.* **| escalate | concern sth** *disputes concerning environmental protection* **| involve sb/sth**
- PREP. **beyond ~** *The matter was settled beyond dispute by the court judgment* (= it could no longer be argued about). **in ~ (with)** *The actual sum of compensation due is still in dispute* (= being argued about). ◇ *The employees have been in dispute with management for three weeks.* **under ~** *the matters under dispute* **| ~ about/over, ~ among/amongst** *The exact relationship between the two languages is a matter of dispute amongst scholars.* **~ as to** *There is no dispute as to the facts.* **~ between** *a long-standing dispute between the families over ownership of the land.* **~ with**
- PHRASES **an area/a matter of dispute, potential/room/scope for dispute** *to minimize the scope for dispute over the meaning of the terms employed* **the resolution/settlement of a dispute**

dispute verb

- ADV. **fiercely, hotly** *The effectiveness of this treatment is still hotly disputed.*
- VERB + DISPUTE **can/cannot** *No one can dispute the fact that men still hold the majority of public offices.*

disregard noun

- ADJ. **complete, total, utter | blatant, flagrant | callous, cavalier, cynical | reckless, wanton** *their reckless disregard for human life* **| blithe, fine** (ironic) *With a fine disregard for geography, she decided to start her journey to Paris by sailing to the Hook of Holland.*
- VERB + DISREGARD **demonstrate, show**
- PREP. **~ for** *He showed complete disregard for the feelings of his family.* **~ of** *their flagrant disregard of the rules*

disrepair noun

- VERB + DISREPAIR **fall into** *The building had fallen into disrepair.*
- PREP. **in ~** *Much of the old building was still in disrepair.*
- PHRASES **a state of disrepair**

disreputable adj.

- VERBS **be, look, seem**
- ADV. **highly, very | rather, slightly, vaguely** *He had a vaguely disreputable appearance.*

disrepute noun

- VERB + DISREPUTE **fall into** *The old system had fallen into disrepute.* **| bring sth into** *The players' behaviour on the field is likely to bring the game into disrepute.*
- PREP. **in ~** *This theory is now in disrepute.*

disrespect noun

- ADJ. **total | healthy**
- VERB + DISRESPECT **have, show, treat sb/sth with** *She felt he had total disrespect for women.* | **mean no** *I mean no disrespect to the team, but their performance was poor.*
- PREP. **~for** *The new manager showed a healthy disrespect for formality.*
- PHRASES **no disrespect intended/to …** *No disrespect intended sir; it was just a joke.*

disrupt verb

- ADV. **badly, seriously, severely** *The bad weather has seriously disrupted supplies of food.* | **completely, totally**
- VERB + DISRUPT **threaten to | attempt to | be designed to** *The attacks are designed to disrupt plans for the elections.*
- PHRASES **an attempt to disrupt sth**

disruption noun

- ADJ. **considerable, enormous, great, major, massive, serious, severe | minimum** *how to organize the building work so as to cause minimum disruption* | **widespread | undue** *to allow the school to function without undue disruption* | **inevitable | economic, family, political, social** *the effects of family disruption during childhood* | **traffic**
- VERB + DISRUPTION **cause, create, lead to | suffer** *The city centre suffered some disruption due to a bomb scare.* | **avoid, prevent | minimize**
- DISRUPTION + VERB **occur**
- PREP. **~to** *The bombing campaign caused massive disruption to industry.*

disruptive adj.

- VERBS **be**
- ADV. **extremely, highly, very** *children with highly disruptive behaviour* | **slightly | potentially** *potentially disruptive elements in society* | **socially**
- PREP. **to** *Long working hours are very disruptive to home life.*

dissatisfaction noun

- ADJ. **considerable, deep | growing, increasing | general, widespread | popular, public | customer | political, sexual | job**
- VERB + DISSATISFACTION **cause, give rise to, lead to** *Pay cuts have led to widespread dissatisfaction.* | **express**
- PREP. **~about/over** *dissatisfaction over the slow progress of the peace process* **~among** *There was widespread dissatisfaction among the public.* **~at** *She expressed deep dissatisfaction at the way the interview had been conducted.* **~with** *There is growing dissatisfaction with the current style of management.*
- PHRASES **a feeling/sense of dissatisfaction, a cause/source of dissatisfaction**

dissatisfied adj.

- VERBS **be, feel | become | remain**
- ADV. **deeply, very** *The decision left us feeling deeply dissatisfied.* | **increasingly**
- PREP. **with** *She's very dissatisfied with her current job.*

dissent noun

- ADJ. **serious, strong** *He would brook no serious dissent.* | **growing | internal** *internal party dissent* | **political, religious** *Political dissent is not tolerated.*
- VERB + DISSENT **arouse, cause, provoke | express, show** *There are many ways of expressing dissent.* |

brook, tolerate | stifle, suppress *The regime ruthlessly suppresses all dissent.*
- PREP. **~against** *popular dissent against the Church* **~from** *His dissent from his family's religious beliefs caused a lot of ill-feeling.*
- PHRASES **a voice of dissent** *In the early 1960s, the voices of dissent began to rise.*

dissertation noun

- ADJ. **research | doctoral, Master's, undergraduate | MSc, PhD, etc. | 15 000-word, etc.**
- VERB + DISSERTATION **do, prepare, write** *Students can either do a dissertation or take part in a practical project.* | **complete, finish | hand in, present, submit** *Candidates are required to present a dissertation of between 8 000 and 12 000 words.*
- PREP. **~on** *He wrote his Master's dissertation on rats.*

disservice noun

- ADJ. **grave, great**
- VERB + DISSERVICE **do sb**
- PREP. **~to** *This violence will do a grave disservice to their cause.*

dissident noun

- ADJ. **leading, prominent | political, religious | exiled, imprisoned**

dissimilar adj.

- VERBS **appear, be, look**
- ADV. **very | quite, totally | not altogether, not entirely, not wholly**
- PREP. **from** *His views are not dissimilar from those of the Health Minister.* **to** *The way of life here is not altogether dissimilar to that in other parts of Europe.*

dissolve verb

1 become/make sth liquid
- ADV. **completely** *The tablet hasn't dissolved completely yet.* | **gradually, slowly | away** *The limestone has simply dissolved away.*
- PREP. **in** *Dissolve the sugar in water.*

2 end sth officially
- ADV. **formally, officially** *Their marriage was formally dissolved last year.*

distance noun

1 amount of space between two points
- ADJ. **appreciable, considerable, enormous, fair, good, great, huge, large, long, vast** *The town is a considerable distance from the coast.* ◊ *It's quite a good distance to the nearest village.* ◊ *The people travel vast distances to find food.* | **short, small | reasonable | certain, given | average, mean** *the average distance covered during pursuits by cheetahs* | **equal | maximum, minimum | optimum | correct, right | exact | full | extra | fixed | finite, infinite | careful, comfortable, convenient, discreet, respectful, safe** *The cat sat and watched us from a safe distance.* | **braking, stopping** *Allow for greater braking distances when pulling a loaded trailer.* | **geographical, physical** *These immigrants face problems of geographical distance and cultural isolation.*
- VERB + DISTANCE **cover, fly, go, travel, walk** *The young birds were soon flying distances of 200 feet or more.* ◊ *(figurative) Nobody thought he would last 15 rounds but he went the full distance.* | **keep** *I kept a comfortable distance behind the van.* | **determine, measure | gauge, judge** *It is very difficult to judge distances in the desert.*
- DISTANCE + NOUN **runner, running** *a long-distance runner*

● PREP. **at a~(from/of)** *When launching a kick it is essential to be at the correct distance from your opponent.* ◇ *The town is situated at a distance of twenty miles from Oxford.* ◇ *She followed them at a discreet distance.* **from a~(of)** *Visitors can only view the painting from a distance of three metres.* **over a~(of)** *The sound can be heard over a distance of more than five miles.* **within a~** *children living within a certain distance of the school* | **~away from** *The house is a short distance away from the bus station.* **~between** *What's the distance between London and Edinburgh?* **~from, ~to** *the distance from our house to the school*

● PHRASES **a ... distance ahead, away, apart, etc.** *A bomb exploded some distance away.* **within commuting/driving/strolling/travelling/walking distance** *The shops are within walking distance.* **within hailing/shouting/sniffing/spitting/striking/touching distance** *The cat was now within striking distance of the duck.* ◇ *(figurative) We came within spitting distance of winning the cup.*

2 point a long way away/being far away

● ADJ. **far, middle** *I could just see the hills in the far distance.* | **blue** *(literary) The moors stretched away into the blue distance* (= the sky).

● DISTANCE + NOUN **learning** *The Open University offers a wide range of distance learning programmes.* | **vision** *to have good distance vision*

● PREP. **at a~** *At a distance it is difficult to make out the detail on the building.* **from a~** *We admired the palace from a distance.* **in the~** *In the distance was a small village.*

3 not being too closely involved

● ADJ. **critical, professional** | **emotional, psychological, social**

● VERB + DISTANCE **keep, maintain** *She was warned to keep her distance from Charles if she didn't want to get hurt.* ◇ *Sociologists must maintain critical distance from the ideas of society at any particular time.*

● PREP. **~from** *He felt a sense of distance from the others.*

● PHRASES **a sense of distance**

distant *adj.*

1 far away in space

● VERBS **be, sound** | **become, grow** *The sound of the engine was growing more and more distant.*

● ADV. **far** *(literary),* **very** *in far distant lands* | **increasingly** | **unimaginably** *It was only a few miles away but it seemed unimaginably distant.* | **geographically** *geographically distant areas of the world*

● PREP. **from** *The stars are more distant from the earth than the sun.*

2 far away in time

● VERBS **be**

● ADV. **very** | **increasingly** | **fairly, not too** *in the not too distant future*

● PHRASES **the dim and distant past** *stories from the dim and distant past*

3 not friendly/not paying attention

● VERBS **be, seem** | **become** | **remain** | **find sb**

● ADV. **very** | **rather, slightly** | **strangely** *Even his children found him strangely distant and impersonal.*

distaste *noun*

● ADJ. **deep, extreme, great, intense, profound, strong** | **growing** | **evident, obvious** *She regarded the child with evident distaste.* | **irrational** | **mock**

● VERB + DISTASTE **feel, have** | **express, show** *trying not to show her distaste* | **conceal, hide** *He couldn't conceal the deep distaste that he felt for many of their customs.* | **look at sb/sth with, regard sb/sth with, view sb/sth with**

● PREP. **in ~** *She wrinkled her nose in mock distaste.* **with ~** *Jim looked with distaste at the cockroach in his*

soup. | **~at** *He couldn't hide his distaste at having to sleep in such a filthy room.* **~for** *Joe had a profound distaste for violence.*

● PHRASES **an expression/a look of distaste, a feeling of distaste**

distasteful *adj.*

● VERBS **be, seem** | **find sth**

● ADV. **extremely, highly** *I find his attitude highly distasteful.* | **thoroughly** | **fairly, rather**

● PREP. **to** *The work was thoroughly distasteful to her.*

distinct *adj.*

● VERBS **be** | **become** | **remain** | **keep sth** *It is necessary to keep these two issues distinct.* | **regard/see sth as**

● ADV. **very** | **completely, entirely, quite, totally, wholly** | **fairly** | **essentially, fundamentally** | **clearly** | **analytically, conceptually, formally** (= distinct in form), **qualitatively** *Political power should be regarded as analytically distinct from economic power.* | **anatomically, geographically, historically** *geographically distinct regions*

● PREP. **from** *The various dialects are quite distinct from one another.*

● PHRASES **as distinct from** *She was studying lung cancer, as distinct from other types of cancer.*

distinction *noun*

1 clear difference

● ADJ. **critical, crucial, important, key, main, major, vital** | **basic, essential, fundamental, underlying** | **clear, clear-cut, definite, marked, obvious, real, rigid, sharp, strong** | **fine, subtle** | **broad, general** | **crude, simple** | **logical, valid** | **useful** | **arbitrary, artificial** | **invidious** *making invidious distinctions between the 'deserving' and the 'undeserving' poor* | **absolute** *Is there always an absolute distinction between right and wrong?* | **conventional, old, traditional** *the conventional distinction between pure and applied science* | **formal** | **conceptual** | **theoretical** | **class, cultural, gender, moral**

● VERB + DISTINCTION **draw, make** *She draws an important distinction between the different kinds of illness.* | **recognize, see** *We can see a sharp distinction between ambition and greed.* | **blur** *blurring the distinction between amateur and professional players*

● DISTINCTION + VERB **lie** *Cultural distinctions lie at the heart of these issues.*

● PREP. **without ~** *All groups are entitled to this money without distinction* (= without a difference being made between them). | **~between**

2 excellence/fame

● ADJ. **considerable, great** | **modest** | **dubious** | **rare** | **unique** | **added** | **academic, intellectual, professional, social** *Wearing the county tie was a mark of modest social distinction.*

● VERB + DISTINCTION **have** *He has the dubious distinction of being the first railway baron to go bankrupt.* | **achieve** *She achieved distinction in several fields of scholarship.* | **add** *Fennel leaves add distinction to any dish.*

● PREP. **of~** *She is a historian of great distinction.* **with~** *He served with distinction in the First World War.*

distinctive *adj.*

● VERBS **be**

● ADV. **extremely, highly, very** *The shell has a highly distinctive pattern.* | **quite** | **fairly**

distinguish *verb*

● ADV. **clearly, sharply** | **carefully** | **easily, readily** *The adult can be readily distinguished by its orange bill.*

● VERB + DISTINGUISH **be able to, can/could** | **be unable to** | **be difficult to, be hard to, be impossible to, be**

possible to | be important to, be necessary to *It is important to distinguish between cause and effect.*
• PREP. between *It is often difficult to distinguish clearly between fact and fiction in this book.* from *She could not distinguish one child from another.*

distinguishable *adj.*

• VERBS be | become
• ADV. clearly, easily, readily | barely, hardly, scarcely
• PREP. by *The animal is easily distinguishable by the black stripes above its eye.* from *The male bird is barely distinguishable from the female.*

distort *verb*

• ADV. grossly, seriously, severely *He was accused of grossly distorting the facts.* | completely | slightly | deliberately

distortion *noun*

1 change in shape/sound
• ADJ. severe | slight | inevitable
• VERB + DISTORTION cause, create, lead to *The wrong chemical balance can cause severe distortion of the photographic image.* | avoid
2 changing sth so that it is shown falsely
• ADJ. gross, serious *His report was attacked as a gross distortion of the truth.* | deliberate

distract *verb*

• ADV. easily *He's easily distracted from his work* | momentarily *A noise outside momentarily distracted her.*
• PREP. (away) from *an attempt to distract attention away from the real problems in the country*

distracted *adj.*

• VERBS appear, be, look, seem | become, get *It's easy to get distracted when you're studying.*
• ADV. very | a little, slightly, somewhat *She seemed slightly distracted, as if something was worrying her.* | momentarily *Luke looked momentarily distracted.*

distraction *noun*

1 sth that takes your attention away
• ADJ. unwanted | welcome
• PREP. without~ *She worked hard all morning, without distraction.* | ~from *Work was a welcome distraction from her problems at home.*
2 being unable to think clearly
• VERB + DISTRACTION drive sb to *My kids drive me to distraction at times.* | be bored to | love sb to

distraught *adj.*

• VERBS appear, be, look, seem, sound *She sounded absolutely distraught.* | become | remain *Weeks after the accident she remained distraught.* | leave sb *His mother's death left him utterly distraught.*
• ADV. extremely, really, terribly, very | absolutely, completely, quite, utterly
• PREP. at *They were terribly distraught at the news of his accident.*

distress *noun*

• ADJ. acute, considerable, deep, extreme, great, immense, severe | genuine, real | obvious | unnecessary | emotional, mental, personal, physical, psychological *the physical distress of thirst and hunger* ◇ *the personal distress associated with unemployment* | economic, financial, social *The causes of social distress include inadequate housing.*

• VERB + DISTRESS cause (sb) | feel, suffer *the distress that she felt when her parents argued* ◇ *The animals suffer great pain and distress when hunted.* | show (signs of) *She seemed calm and showed no signs of distress.* | conceal *He tried to conceal his distress, but the tremor in his voice was unmistakable.* | avoid | alleviate, ease, relieve
• DISTRESS + NOUN call, signal *The sinking ship sent out a distress call.*
• PREP. in~ *The child was clearly in distress.* ◇ *a ship in distress* to sb's~ *He dropped out of college, to his family's distress.* | ~at *her obvious distress at hearing such bad news* ~over *The president issued a statement expressing her distress over the affair.*
• PHRASES a damsel in distress *medieval ballads about a knight saving a damsel in distress* a source of distress *Grief over ageing is a source of distress to men and women.*

distressing *adj.*

• VERBS be | become | find sth *I found the story deeply distressing.*
• ADV. deeply, extremely, highly, very | quite, rather | emotionally
• PREP. for *The divorce was extremely distressing for the children.*

distribute *verb*

1 give sth out
• ADV. equally, fairly | unequally | widely *The leaflets have been widely distributed.* | free *Copies of the book were distributed free to each school in the district.*
• PREP. among *We distributed the money equally among the team members.* between, to *distributing aid to people in need*
2 spread sth
• ADV. evenly, uniformly *Wealth is not evenly distributed between age groups.* | unevenly | randomly *Smokers were randomly distributed in the sample interviewed.* | patchily, sparsely
• PREP. among, between throughout *There are over 35 000 species of orchid distributed throughout the world.*

distribution *noun*

1 way sth is shared or exists over an area
• ADJ. egalitarian, equitable, fair *to ensure a fair distribution of wealth* | inequitable, unfair | equal *an equal distribution of wealth between people of different age groups* | unequal | even, uniform *After applying the cream, comb through to ensure even distribution.* | uneven *The country was noted for its uneven distribution of land resources.* | optimal, optimum | relative *the relative distribution of continents and oceans* | general, overall *the general distribution of earthquakes around the world* | broad, wide, widespread *the broad distribution of Bronze Age artefacts across Europe* ◇ *the wider distribution of wealth throughout society* | local, localized *Fish populations assume highly localized distributions within each river.* | global, regional, worldwide | spatial | income, wealth | weight | age, class, geographical, population, sex, social *the social class distribution of the male population* | normal, random, skewed, smooth *(all mathematics) a normal distribution with a bell-shaped frequency curve* | binomial, frequency, probability *(all mathematics)*
• VERB + DISTRIBUTION achieve, ensure *The engine is mounted in the middle to achieve a more even weight distribution.* | determine *Radiology was used to determine the distribution of the disease.* | have, show *(mathematics) These birds have a wide geographical distribution.* ◇ *IQs within the population show a normal distribution.*
• DISTRIBUTION + NOUN pattern *Animal herds may form in response to the distribution patterns of food.* |

map *an atlas containing distribution maps of the most important tropical diseases*
• PREP. **~across** *the distribution of resources across society* | **~ among** *data on wealth distribution among age groups* **~between** *a disparity in age distribution between groups* **~ over** *the distribution of trees over the estate* **~ throughout** *uniform distribution of the chemical throughout the timber*
• PHRASES **a change in distribution** *changes in the distribution of wealth and income*

2 giving/delivering sth to people
• ADJ. **free** *The document contains sensitive information and is not suitable for free* (= unrestricted) *distribution.* ◇ *The previously free* (= not paid for) *distribution of textbooks will now be confined to students who are needy.* | **general** *Our catalogue lists all our books that are available for general distribution.* | **selective** | **exclusive** *The publisher has signed an agreement for the exclusive distribution of the books in the US.* | **proper** | **electronic** *the electronic distribution of software to customers* | **global**, **international**, **local**, **national**, **worldwide** *Roads are used for local distribution of goods.* | **electricity**, **food**, **fuel**, **gas**, **land**, **milk**, **water** *the creation of 1 500 smallholdings as part of a land distribution programme* | **retail**, **wholesale** *the wholesale and retail distribution of a huge variety of goods*
• VERB + DISTRIBUTION **control**, **handle**, **organize** *The company is to handle the distribution of the product in Europe.* | **available for** *2 000 copies of the booklet have been printed and are available for distribution.* | **ensure** *to ensure the proper distribution of medical aid* | **allow** (**for**) *to allow for the distribution of aid*
• DISTRIBUTION + NOUN **agreement**, **arrangement**, **deal** *Her company has signed a non-exclusive distribution agreement.* | **list** *I attach a copy of the distribution list so you can see who got the last edition.* | **rights** | **costs** | **channel** *We have many distribution channels for our software, including electronic distribution.* | **network** | **method** | **system** | **facilities** *The company wants to invest in new distribution facilities.* | **base**, **centre**, **depot**, **outlet**, **point** *The company has decided to use Belfast as its distribution base.* | **operation** *The company has manufacturing or distribution operations in 33 countries worldwide.* | **business**, **company** | **industry**
• PREP. **for~** *free colour leaflets for distribution overseas* | **~among** *food for distribution among the villagers* **~between** *the distribution of the health budget between various hospitals* **~by** *the distribution by the government of a leaflet explaining the new tax* **~ through** *distribution through department stores* **~to** *The food was parcelled up for distribution to outlying communities.*
• PHRASES **a/the chain of distribution** *There are savings to be made where retailers are bypassed in the chain of distribution.* **a channel of distribution**

3 payment
• ADJ. **capital**, **dividend**, **share** | **cash**
• VERB + DISTRIBUTION **make** *When are distributions likely to be made to creditors?* | **be available for** *These are company reserves available for distribution as the directors may determine.*
• PREP. **~to** *The promissory notes were purchased for distribution to investors.*

distributor *noun*

• ADJ. **global**, **international**, **overseas**, **worldwide** | **local**, **national** | **exclusive**, **sole** | **authorized**, **licensed** | **independent**, **third party** *Third party distributors are used to distribute the product in areas where the group does not have offices.* | **large**, **leading**, **main**, **major**, **primary** *We are the primary distributor of the system in France.* | **car**, **computer**, **film**, **food**, **software** | **electricity** *the national electricity distributor*

• VERB + DISTRIBUTOR **appoint** (**sb**) **as** *We have been appointed sole UK distributor of a number of Hungarian wines.* | **act as** *We will act as the exclusive distributor for these Russian goods to the world market.*
• PREP. **through a/the ~** *You can get the book through your local distributor.* | **~for** *the exclusive distributor for these goods* ◇ *a distributor for the German market* ◇ *a distributor for Hewlett-Packard Co*

district *noun*

• ADJ. **neighbouring**, **surrounding** *Fire crews from all the surrounding districts helped to fight the fires in the city.* | **central** *Every city has its central business district.* | **outlying**, **remote** *a new railway station to help people commuting from outlying districts* | **northern**, **southern**, **etc.** | **affluent**, **exclusive**, **rich**, **wealthy** | **poor**, **working-class** *the shacks in the poorest districts of the city* | **slum** | **coastal**, **country**, **local**, **metropolitan**, **rural**, **suburban**, **urban** | **agricultural**, **business**, **commercial**, **financial**, **industrial**, **mining**, **residential**, **shopping** | **administrative**, **electoral**, **federal**, **health**, **military**, **polling**, **postal** *a federal district court in New York* ◇ *He has been transferred to a hospital in a different health district.*
• DISTRICT + VERB **stretch** *Their district stretches nearly 150 miles, from the mountains to the sea.*
• DISTRICT + NOUN **authority**, **council** *the district health authority* | **councillor**, **judge**, **nurse**, **etc.** | **court**, **hospital**, **etc.** | **boundary** *Redrawing district boundaries would change the election results.*
• PREP. **in/within a/the~** *The hospital is only responsible for patients within its own district.*

distrust *noun*

• ADJ. **deep**, **deep-seated**, **profound** | **growing** | **widespread** | **popular**, **public** *the popular distrust of foreigners after the war* | **mutual** | **healthy** *She has a healthy distrust of door-to-door salesmen.*
• VERB + DISTRUST **feel**, **have** | **express**, **show** | **create** *The many policy changes have created growing distrust among employees.* | **overcome** *Great efforts were made to overcome public distrust.* | **retain** *Nonconformists retained a deep distrust of their Anglican neighbours.*
• PREP. **~between** *distrust between the two police forces* **~in** *his distrust in politics* **~of** *a distrust of the media*
• PHRASES **a climate of distrust**

disturbance *noun*

1 actions that upset the normal state of sb/sth
• ADJ. **considerable**, **major**, **serious** | **minimal**, **minimum**, **minor**, **slight**
• QUANT. **level** *an unacceptable level of disturbance to occupiers of adjacent properties*
• VERB + DISTURBANCE **cause**, **create**, **make** *The traffic causes serious disturbance to residents.* | **suffer** | **prevent** *She moved the nest very carefully to prevent disturbance to the birds.*
• PREP. **without~** *a place where you can work without disturbance* | **~from** *disturbance from noisy lorries* **~of** *the major disturbance of marine life caused by oil spillages* **~to** *Buildings should create minimum disturbance to the environment.*

2 violent public event
• ADJ. **serious** *The decision led to serious disturbances in all the country's main cities.* | **violent** | **public** | **crowd**, **mass** | **serious** | **civil**, **ethnic**, **political**, **racial**, **social** | **inner city**, **rural**, **urban**
• VERB + DISTURBANCE **cause**, **give rise to**, **lead to**, **provoke**, **trigger** (**off**) *He was arrested and charged with causing a disturbance in a public place.* ◇ *An influx of refugees has triggered off disturbances.* | **be involved in** *Large numbers of workers involved in the disturbances*

have been arrested. | **deal with, put down, quell** *Troops were brought in to put down the disturbance.*
● DISTURBANCE + VERB **occur** | **involve sb** *disturbances involving members of a crowd of 550 demonstrators*
● PREP. **during/in a/the ~** *Several people were injured during a disturbance in the capital city.* | **~among** *There had been violent disturbances among the prisoners.* **~between** *disturbances between members of two rival factions*
● PHRASES **a disturbance of the peace** *The government advocated strong action against Mussolini's disturbance of the peace.*

3 emotional/physical upset
● ADJ. **serious, severe** | **behavioural, emotional, mental, psychiatric, psychological** *teenagers suffering from a kind of psychological disturbance* | **bowel, menstrual** | **sleep**
● VERB + DISTURBANCE **suffer from**
● PREP. **~in** *a disturbance in liver function* ◇ *behavioural disturbances in children*

disturbed *adj.*

1 mentally ill
● VERBS **be, seem** | **become**
● ADV. **acutely, deeply, highly, seriously, severely, very** *Many of our patients are severely disturbed.* | **behaviourally, emotionally, mentally, psychiatrically, psychologically** *emotionally disturbed children*

2 very anxious
● VERBS **be, feel** | **become**
● ADV. **deeply, greatly, profoundly, very** | **a little, slightly, vaguely** | **oddly**
● PREP. **by** *I felt oddly disturbed by the incident.*

disturbing *adj.*

● VERBS **be** | **become** | **remain** | **find sth**
● ADV. **deeply, extremely, highly, profoundly, very** *a profoundly disturbing experience* | **rather, slightly, somewhat, vaguely** | **oddly, strangely** | **unexpectedly**

disuse *noun*

● VERB + DISUSE **be in** *The workforce has shrunk to less than a thousand and much of the plant is in disuse.* | **fall into** *A new bridge was built ten years ago and the old one has fallen into disuse.*
● PREP. **from/through/with ~** *Her muscles had become weak through disuse.*
● PHRASES **a period of disuse**

ditch *noun*

● ADJ. **deep, wide** | **shallow, small** | **open** *The drainage system consisted of a few open ditches to facilitate run-off.* | **muddy** | **drainage, irrigation** | **roadside**
● VERB + DITCH **dig**
● DITCH + VERB **run** *The ditch ran parallel to the road.* | **surround sth** *His lettuce garden was surrounded by a deep ditch.*
● PREP. **in/into a~** *I tripped and fell into a muddy ditch.*

dive *noun*

1 of an aircraft
● ADJ. **steep, vertical** | **gentle, shallow** | **spiral**
● VERB + DIVE **go into** *The plane went into a steep dive.* | **pull out of** *The pilot seemed to be having difficulty in pulling out of the dive.*

2 move/jump/fall
● ADJ. **headlong, nose** (also **nosedive**) (*both often figurative*) *The economy is on a headlong dive to disaster.* ◇ *His acting career took a nosedive and he turned to drink for solace.* | **sudden** | **running** *She made a running dive to get across the crevasse.*

● VERB + DIVE **make, take** *She made a dive for the door.* ◇ *He took a dive in the penalty area and won his team a controversial penalty.* ◇ (*figurative*) *The market is volatile and profits could take a dive.*
● PREP. **~for** *There would be a dive for the bar as soon as the show finished.*

dive *verb*

1 jump into water
● ADV. **deep, head first** | **down**
● PREP. **for** *diving for pearls* **from** *She dived from the top diving board.* **into** *He dived head first into the water.* **off**
● PHRASES **go diving** *The main purpose of his holiday to Greece was to go diving.*

2 of birds/aircraft
● ADV. **suddenly** | **vertically** *Unlike some birds, it does not dive vertically.*
● PREP. **from, to** *The plane suddenly dived from 10 000 feet to 5 000.*

3 move/jump/fall
● ADV. **head first, headlong**
● PREP. **beneath, into** *He dived headlong into the ditch.* **through, under**
● PHRASES **dive for cover** *We heard an explosion and dived for cover.*

diverge *verb*

● ADV. **considerably, markedly, widely**
● PREP. **from** *This country's interests diverge considerably from those of other European countries.*

diverse *adj.*

● VERBS **be, seem** | **become**
● ADV. **enormously, exceptionally, extremely, highly, remarkably, very, widely** | **increasingly** | **quite, relatively** | **apparently** | **culturally, ethnically, socially** *an ethnically diverse population*

diversion *noun*

1 change of direction
● ADJ. **brief, short** | **major**
● VERB + DIVERSION **make, take** *From Poiso we make a short diversion to drive to the top of the mountain.*
● PREP. **~from** *the diversion of water from the river into the reservoir* **~to** *The pilot set the aircraft up for a diversion to the nearest suitable airfield.*

2 temporary route
● ADJ. **temporary** *A temporary diversion has been set up to take traffic away from the accident site.* | **traffic**
● VERB + DIVERSION **set up** | **signpost** *The road will be closed for two days; diversions have been signposted.*
● DIVERSION + VERB **be in operation** *The main road is now closed and diversions are in operation.*

3 distraction
● ADJ. **welcome**
● VERB + DIVERSION **create, provide** *The fire was started to create a diversion, allowing some prisoners to escape.*
● PREP. **~from** *The cinema provided a welcome diversion from camp routine.*

4 pleasant activity
● ADJ. **pleasant, pleasurable** | **minor**
● VERB + DIVERSION **make, provide** *The party would make a pleasant diversion in his rather dull social life.*

diversity *noun*

● ADJ. **considerable, enormous, extraordinary, great, immense, rich, wide** *There is need for greater diversity and choice in education.* ◇ *the rich diversity of the city's cultural life* | **growing, increased, increasing** | **bio-**

logical, genetic *the need to preserve biological diversity* |
cultural, ethnic, linguistic, political, regional
• VERB + DIVERSITY **create | encourage | promote**
*Our party believes in encouraging cultural diversity, not
division.* | **maintain, preserve, protect** *The producer was
under pressure to maintain a diversity in his output.* | **de-
crease, increase | allow (for)** *Tyrannies do not allow di-
versity and disagreement.*
• PREP. **~ in** *diversity in the style of the reports* **~ of** *There
is a wide diversity of views on this subject.*

divide *noun*

• ADJ. **great,   sharp | growing | north-south,   etc. |
class, cultural, ideological, religious, sectarian | party**
• VERB + DIVIDE **close**
• DIVIDE + VERB **widen | narrow | open (up)**
• PREP. **~ between** *the sharp divide between rich and
poor regions* **~ in** *The leader's speech aimed to close the embarrassing divide in party ranks.*

divide *verb*

1 separate into parts
• ADV. **broadly, roughly** *This report is divided broadly
into two parts.* | **exactly | clearly | conveniently, neatly**
Railway enthusiasts divide neatly into two groups. |
evenly | up *The country is divided up into nine regions.*
• PREP. **into** *The children divided into three teams.*
• PHRASES **divide in two** *the point where the river div-
ides in two*

2 share
• ADV. **equally | up**
• PREP. **among/amongst** *The money was divided equally
among his sons.* | **between** *They divided their time between
London and their country cottage.*

3 cause disagreement
• ADV. **bitterly, deeply, hopelessly, seriously, sharply**
This issue has bitterly divided the community. | **evenly**
• PHRASES **be divided about/on/over sth** *Cabinet min-
isters were deeply divided on the issue.*

dividend *noun*

1 payment on a company share
• ADJ. **high | 10%,   etc. | fixed | increased | gross,
total | net | expected** *a method of valuing shares based
on expected dividends* | **annual, quarterly | interim |
final | company | share** *Investors will still pay tax on
their foreign share dividends.* | **cash**
• VERB + DIVIDEND **pay | receive | announce,   de-
clare** *The company has not yet declared its dividends for
this year.* | **recommend** *The board has recommended a
final dividend of 6 pence per share.* | **boost, increase, lift,
raise | hold, maintain** *The interim dividend is main-
tained at 2.5 cents per share.* | **cut, reduce, slash | pass**
*During that time, dividends were cut or passed (= not paid)
and there were plenty of closures.*
• DIVIDEND + VERB **be up** *The dividend is up 10.6% to
11.3p.* | **go up, grow, jump, rise** *The dividend should
jump to 5p.* | **stay** *The dividend stays at 0.5p.* | **be payable**
The final dividend, payable on July 1, is reduced to 1p.
• DIVIDEND + NOUN **payment,   payout | growth,   in-
crease | cut | income, total, yield | policy**
• PREP. **~ on** *They have announced the quarterly divi-
dend on the shares.*
• PHRASES **an increase in a dividend**

2 benefit/reward
• ADJ. **considerable, enormous, great, handsome, rich
| economic**
• VERB + DIVIDEND **bring, pay, produce, reap, yield**
*Her hard work paid dividends when she won the school
dancing competition.* ◇ *The company reaped rich divi-
dends with its new strategy for packaging holidays.*

• PREP. **~ in** *The chain's investment in new stores is bringing dividends in new customers.*

diving *noun*

• ADJ. **deep-sea, scuba, sub-aqua | commercial**
• VERB + DIVING **go**
• DIVING + NOUN **board | display** *The crowd enjoyed a
diving display before the swimming races.* | **equipment,
gear, suit | bell** *A diving bell is usually used for oper-
ations below 50 metres.*

divisible *adj.*

• VERBS **be**
• ADV. **infinitely** *He argued that all matter was infinitely
divisible.*
• PREP. **by** *Twelve is divisible by four.* **into** *Plants are divisible into three main groups.*

division *noun*

1 dividing sth into separate parts
• ADJ. **clear, distinct, simple** *Sometimes there is no sim-
ple division between good and evil.* | **complex, elaborate
| rigid | broad, rough | equal, fair | unequal, unfair** *an
unequal division of the cake* ◇ *an unfair division of labour*
| **conventional, time-honoured** *the conventional division
of language into grammar and vocabulary* | **theoretical
| hierarchical** *hierarchical division between 'workers'
and 'management'* | **threefold,   three-way,   tripartite |
cell**
• VERB + DIVISION **make** *You can make a rough division
of his music into 'light' and 'serious'.*
• PREP. **~ among** *His will detailed his assets and gave instructions for their division among his children.* **~ between** *the division of the money between the members*
~ into *In selling there is a broad division into direct and indirect methods.*
• PHRASES **the division of labour, the division of
wealth**

2 differences between two groups/things, etc.
• ADJ. **bitter, deep, great, sharp** *There are sharp divisions within the party over the privatization of the rail-
ways.* | **fundamental | factional, internal** *factional div-
isions   within   the   party* | **traditional | north-south |
class, cultural, ethnic, gender, ideological, linguistic,
political, sexual, social, societal**
• VERB + DIVISION **create,   provoke | exploit | heal**
*The prime minister's speech will attempt to heal divisions
within his party.*
• PREP. **~ among** *There are reports of serious divisions
among senior party members.* **~ between, ~ within** *division within the government*

3 section of an organization
• ADJ. **regional | industrial, manufacturing, market-
ing, retail, sales, training, wholesale | administrative**
the administrative divisions of the Roman Empire | **air-
borne, armoured, infantry, etc. | first, high, low, prem-
ier, second, senior, top, etc.** *(sport) He's now playing foot-
ball in the higher divisions.* | **heavyweight, lightweight,
middleweight, etc.** (= in boxing, etc.)
• PREP. **in the ... ~** *They compete in the senior division of
the chess league.*

4 dividing one number by another
• ADJ. **long**
• VERB + DIVISION **do** *Can you do long division?*
• PREP. **~ by** *division by three*

divisive *adj.*

• VERBS **be | become | remain**
• ADV. **deeply | potentially | economically, politically,
socially** *He believes that unemployment is socially div-
isive and is leading to the creation of an underclass.*

divorce noun

- ADJ. **amicable, uncontested | acrimonious, bitter | messy, painful | quick**
- VERB + DIVORCE **want | apply for, ask for, file for, petition for, seek, sue for** *She filed for divorce in 1996.* | **get, obtain** *He told her that he was married but getting a divorce.* | **experience, go through** *She watched her parents go through an acrimonious divorce.* | **agree to, consent to | contest** *These days divorce is rarely contested.* | **grant (sb)** *Over 50 000 divorces were granted last year.* | **end in** *An increasing number of marriages end in divorce.*
- DIVORCE + VERB **come through** *He is waiting for the divorce to come through before he remarries.*
- DIVORCE + NOUN **court | case, proceedings | decree, settlement | figures, rate, statistics** *The divorce rate has been growing steadily since 1971.* | **law**
- PREP. **~ from** *her divorce from the pop star* **~ on the grounds of** *seeking a divorce on the grounds of cruelty*
- PHRASES **grounds for divorce** *He cited adultery as grounds for divorce.*

dock noun

1 place for loading/unloading ships
- ADJ. **commercial | coal, fish, etc.**
- VERB + DOCK **build, construct | arrive at/in | enter**
- DOCK + NOUN **company | strike | worker**
- PREP. **at a/the ~** *A car pulled up at the dock.* **in ~** *The ship is in dock for repairs.* **on a/the ~** *the cargo stacked on the dock*

2 the dock in a court of law
- VERB + DOCK **enter, go into, step into | appear in, be in** *She was in the dock on charges of attempted fraud.* | **be put in, end up in, land in** *After a night of drunken revelry they ended up in the dock.*
- PREP. **from the ~** *an outburst from the dock* **in the ~** *The defendant stood in the dock.*

doctor noun

- ADJ. **excellent, good | qualified | experienced | family, local** *Who is your family doctor?* | **hospital, school | NHS | private**
- VERB + DOCTOR **register with** *You should register with a doctor as soon as possible.* | **call, fetch, get, send for** *We called the doctor immediately.* (For more verbs see note.)

doctorate noun

- ADJ. **honorary | engineering, music, etc.**
- VERB + DOCTORATE **do, study for, take, write** *She's doing a doctorate in ancient history.* | **complete** *He's completed his doctorate on Victorian sexuality.* | **have** *The applicants all have doctorates from good universities.* | **be awarded, be granted, gain, get, obtain, receive**
- DOCTORATE + NOUN **degree | thesis, work**
- PREP. **~ from** *a doctorate from Edinburgh University* **~ in** *a doctorate in Business Administration* **~ of** *a doctorate of divinity* **~ on** *a doctorate on post-colonial development*

doctrine noun

- ADJ. **Catholic, Islamic, etc. | economic, legal, political, religious | revolutionary | classical, conventional, established, orthodox, traditional | high** *He expounded traditional Calvinism with its high doctrine of church order* (= its doctrine that church order is very important). | **old | prevailing | central, essential | general | false, untenable | influential**
- QUANT. **point** *communities divided on points of doctrine* | **body** *an influential body of doctrine*
- VERB + DOCTRINE **advocate, expound, preach, pro-**

---

be, practise as~
  He practises as a clinical psychologist.
have a dentist, doctor, psychiatrist, psychologist, therapist
  Do you have a family doctor?
need~
  She took good care of her teeth and never needed a dentist.
find~
  What's the best way to find a therapist?
consult, go to, see, visit~
  I think you ought to see a psychologist.
refer sb to~
  referring patients to a specialist
~practise
  doctors who practise from home
~examine sb/sth, see sb
  I had an ear, nose and throat specialist examine my sinuses.
  The doctor will see you now.
~treat sb/sth
  He is being treated by the physiotherapist.
~advise sb/sth
  The optician has advised that I wear contact lenses.
a dentist, doctor, psychiatrist, specialist **prescribes (sb) sth**
  The psychiatrist prescribed anti-depressants.
⇒ See also the note at JOB

---

claim, teach | defend | develop, establish, formulate, produce | accept, adhere to, adopt, be committed to, believe (in), embrace, subscribe to, support, uphold *They were all committed to the doctrine of social equality.* | **abandon, condemn, oppose, reject, undermine** *She rejected the traditional Christian doctrines.* | **apply, invoke | reconcile** *Thompson reconciled the doctrine of heat with that of mechanics in 1851.*
- DOCTRINE + VERB **advocate sth | allow sth** *Their doctrine allows the use of violence.*
- PREP. **in ~** *The Church welcomed all who were considered sound in doctrine.*

document noun

1 official paper/book
- ADJ. **important, key, seminal** *one of the key documents in this case* | **relevant | large, lengthy, long, weighty | brief, short | 10-page, etc. | complete, entire, whole** *This statement must be understood in the context of the entire document.* | **summary | detailed | draft | revised | final | original** *The original document has been lost or destroyed.* | **electronic, paper, printed, written | published, unpublished | enclosed** *Please sign the enclosed document and return it to me.* | **single** *A constitution need not be a single document.* | **classified, confidential, privileged** *(law),* **(top) secret | private | public | available** *Documents will be available at the news conference.* | **internal** *details of internal UN documents* | **approved, signed | unsigned | authentic, genuine | forged | disclosed, leaked | government, legal, official | policy, strategy | travel** *Keep your travel documents in a secure place.* | **registration** *a car's registration document* | **contract, offer, tender** *(all business) He has promised to post a formal offer document to shareholders by Monday.* | **briefing | consultation, consultative, discussion, proposal, working** *a working document in the discussions for a final treaty* | **basic, framework | guidance | supporting | (legally) binding** *A document signed abroad is as legally*

binding as one signed at home. | **constitutional, contractual | historical**
- QUANT. **copy**
- VERB + DOCUMENT **draft, draw up, prepare, produce, publish, type, write** *The government has produced an important new policy document.* | **revise | disclose** *(law)*, **issue** *a consultative document issued by the Department of Trade and Industry* | **receive | obtain | file** *Copies of the relevant documents must be filed at court.* | **hand over/sb, present, submit** *Supporting documents must be submitted to the supervisory authority.* | **produce** *He was unable to produce the document that he claimed would prove his case.* | **keep | circulate, send (out) | leak** *documents leaked from the government to the press* | **read | go through, read through** *Go through the document checking for errors.* | **search through, sort through** *I had to search through 4 000 documents to find the information I needed.* | **consider, examine, study | accept, adopt, approve, endorse, execute** *(law)*, **sign** *The conference adopted a document on minority rights.* | **authenticate | forge | refer to | address | attach, enclose** *The relevant documents are enclosed for your information.* | **scan** *Existing paper documents could be scanned into a computer.*
- DOCUMENT + VERB **be concerned with sth, concern sth, deal with sth, focus on sth, relate to sth | contain sth, cover sth, include sth** *documents covering various points of concern* | **refer to sth | acknowledge sth, describe sth, detail sth, explain sth, indicate sth, list sth, note sth, outline sth, record sth, say sth, set out sth, state sth, tell sb sth** *The document says they are against tax rebates.* | **call for sth, propose sth, suggest sth** *a document calling for a ceasefire* | **aim at sth, envisage sth, seek sth** *documents aimed at stimulating discussion* | **reveal sth, show sth | purport sth** *Documents leaked to this newspaper purport to reveal that radioactive waste is being illegally dumped on the site.* | **summarize sth | confirm sth | be agreed (on/upon)** *a document agreed with the District Council* | **be called sth, be entitled sth, be headed sth, be known as sth** *a document entitled 'Guidelines for Good Practice'* | **be written** *The document is written in Chinese.* | **exist** *No other genuine document exists.* | **date back from/to … , be dated …** *documents dating back to the 1920s* ◇ *The document is dated 775.*
- PREP. **according to a/the~** *According to leaked cabinet documents, no compensation would be paid.* **in a/the~** *He particularly criticized the terminology in the document.* **throughout a/the~** *There is a disclaimer throughout the official documents.* | **~ about/concerning** *a document concerning arbitration procedures in Cairo* **~ of** *a document of 2 000 words* ◇ *a document of 1999* ◇ *Her journal is an important document of Victorian rural life* **~ on** *a government document on transport policy*
- PHRASES **a draft/version of a document**

2 computer file
- ADJ. **active, current** *Highlight a passage in the active document and click on the print icon.* | **printed**
- VERB + DOCUMENT **open | close | display** *to display documents on screen* | **retrieve | scroll through** *Scroll through the document using the slider bar on the right of the window.* | **search** *a software tool for searching documents and retrieving information* | **create** *To create a new document, select New from the File menu.* | **edit | save** *Save the document before closing.* | **format | spell check | send** *Send and receive documents at the click of a button.* | **receive | print (out)**
- PREP. **in a/the~** *Cut and paste is used to move text to a new place in the document.*
⇨ Special page at COMPUTER

documentary *noun*

- ADJ. **dramatized | fly-on-the-wall | film, radio, television/TV | controversial | science, wildlife, etc. | half-hour, hour-long, forty-minute, etc.**
- VERB + DOCUMENTARY **make** *She has made a television documentary on poverty in our cities.* | **film | show | see, watch**
- DOCUMENTARY + NOUN **feature, film, programme, series**
- PREP. **in a/the~** *There were some interesting interviews in the documentary.* | **~ about/on** *a documentary about identical twins*

dog *noun*

- ADJ. **domestic, family, household, pet | feral, wild | stray | mongrel | pedigree | lap, toy** *The lady was kissing a little lap dog.* | **faithful, friendly | good, well-behaved, well-trained | bad** *Bad dog! What are you doing there?* | **dangerous, fierce, killer, savage | mad, rabid | mangy | show | fighting, hunting, working | farm, guard, guide, gun, police, sheep, sledge, sniffer, tracker** *Sniffer dogs were used to find the drugs.* | **top** *(often figurative) The team wanted to prove that they were top dogs in the region.*
- QUANT. **pack**
- VERB + DOG **have, keep, own** *The dog's owner was fined £500 and banned from keeping dogs for five years.* | **breed** *These dogs have been bred to work as guide dogs for the blind.* | **train** *He's trained his dog to sit on the back of his bike.* | **feed | take for a walk, walk** *I'm just going to walk the dog.* | **neuter** *We didn't want puppies so we had the dog neutered.* | **worm** *The stray dogs are wormed and treated with flea powder.* | **muzzle | destroy, put down** *A dog that savaged a five-year-old child was later destroyed, police have confirmed.*
- DOG + VERB **bark, bay, growl, howl, pant, snarl, whine, yap, yelp** *The dog barked loudly at the stranger.* ◇ *The little dogs were yapping at my ankles.* | **bound, roam (sth), run, scamper, trot, walk, wander** *The dog bounded up to me and started licking my hand.* ◇ *Stray dogs roamed the streets at night.* | **come/walk to heel | attack sb/sth, bite sb/sth, go for sb/sth, maul sb/sth, savage sb/sth, set upon sb/sth, snap | lie, stretch (out) | lick | chew sth (up), gnaw (at) sth** *The dog chewed up one of my shoes.* ◇ *A dog was gnawing at an old bone.* | **sniff, snuffle** *A dog was sniffing round my heels.* | **prick up its ears, wag its tail | scratch** *The dog was scratching at the door to be let in.* | **foul sth** *Owners who allow their dogs to foul the footpath will be fined.*
- DOG + NOUN **basket | biscuit, food | collar | dirt, excrement, faeces, mess, poo, shit, turd | breeder, handler, lover, owner, trainer, warden** *The dog warden rounds up stray dogs and takes them to the dog pound until claimed.* | **fight | pound | show | racing | track** *Races have been held at this dog track for seventy years.*

dogma *noun*

- ADJ. **old | rigid | party, political, religious** *The newspaper seeks to be independent of political dogma.*
- VERB + DOGMA **accept | question, reject** *People are beginning to question the old dogmas.*

dole *noun*

- VERB + DOLE **claim, go on, sign on** *She lost her job and had to claim dole.* ◇ *As soon as he was made redundant, he signed on the dole.* | **draw, get** *The factory closure will mean another few hundred people drawing the dole.*
- DOLE + NOUN **money | queue** *School leavers were joining the dole queue every day.* | **office**
- PREP. **off the~** *Many had come off the dole and set up their own small businesses.* **on the~** *She was on the dole for three years before she got a job.*

doll *noun*

- ADJ. **little, tiny | china, paper, plastic, porcelain, rag,**

rubber, wooden *a child playing with a rag doll* | baby | Barbie | mechanical | Russian
- VERB + DOLL   play with
- PHRASES   a dolls' house, dolls' clothes

dollar *noun*

⇨ Note at CURRENCY

domain *noun*

- ADJ.   private, public | Internet
- DOMAIN + NOUN   name *Register a domain name if you want people to find your website.* | registration
- PREP.   in a/the ~, within a/the ~ *This information is all in the public domain.* outside a/the ~ *things that happen outside the domain of the home*

domesticated *adj.*

1 used to living with people
- VERBS   be *These animals are only partly domesticated.*
- ADV.   fully | partly

2 able to cook/clean, etc.
- VERBS   be, seem | become
- ADV.   very | thoroughly *He is thoroughly domesticated and cooks a delicious chicken casserole.* | quite

dominance *noun*

- ADJ.   clear, complete, overwhelming, total | growing, increasing | cultural, economic, military, political, territorial | market | male
- VERB + DOMINANCE   achieve, assert, assume, establish, exert, gain *The firm soon achieved complete dominance in the marketplace.* | have, maintain, retain *The firm is determined to maintain dominance in the market.* | challenge, undermine *Ex-colonial countries began to challenge the cultural dominance of Europe.*
- PREP.   ~ in *black American dominance in heavyweight boxing* ~ over *He asserted his dominance over the other party members.*

dominant *adj.*

- VERBS   be, seem | become | remain
- ADV.   extremely, very | completely, overwhelmingly, totally | increasingly | fairly, relatively | economically, politically, socially *the economically dominant class*

dominate *verb*

- ADV.   completely, entirely, totally *She completely dominated the conversation.* | increasingly *His work increasingly dominates his life.* | largely | overwhelmingly

domination *noun*

- ADJ.   complete, total | cultural, economic, ideological, political | class, male | colonial, foreign, imperial | world | market
- VERB + DOMINATION   seek *countries that seek world domination* | achieve, establish *They achieved political domination of the area.* | maintain, retain *The company has struggled to maintain its domination in the marketplace.* | come under, fall under *The country came under foreign domination.* | be free from/of *The country longs to be free of colonial domination.*
- PREP.   under sb's ~ *The country is still under foreign domination.* | ~ over *their economic domination over the Far East*

donation *noun*

- ADJ.   generous, handsome, large, substantial | small | company, corporate | personal, private | public *The project is funded by public donation.* | voluntary | charit-

able, political | cash, financial | blood, organ
- VERB + DONATION   give, make, send *He made a generous donation to the charity.* | get, receive | appeal for, ask for | depend on, need, rely on
- PREP.   in ~s *The charity has received over $10 million in donations.* | ~ to *a donation to a charity* ~ towards *a donation towards the building of a new hospital*

donkey *noun*

- VERB + DONKEY   ride
- DONKEY + VERB   bray | graze
- DONKEY + NOUN   cart | ride

donor *noun*

1 gives a part of their body
- ADJ.   blood (transfusion), bone marrow, kidney, organ, etc. | potential | suitable *The operation will go ahead as soon as a suitable donor can be found.*
- DONOR + VERB   donate sth, give sth *Donors give blood twice a year.*
- DONOR + NOUN   blood, organ *Donor organs are constantly required for transplant operations.* | card

2 gives money/goods
- ADJ.   anonymous *The charity received £50 000 from an anonymous donor.* | aid *Japan has been one of the country's biggest aid donors.*
- DONOR + VERB   give sth, make a donation, pledge sth *Donors pledged a total of $1 000 million in relief aid.*
- DONOR + NOUN   country, government *loans from rich donor countries to developing nations*

doom *noun*

- ADJ.   approaching, impending
- VERB + DOOM   spell *Fuel shortages spelt the doom of such huge gas-guzzling cars.*
- PHRASES   a feeling/sense of doom *As I approached the exam room, I had a feeling of impending doom.*

doomed *adj.*

- VERBS   be, seem
- ADV.   inevitably | ultimately
- PREP.   to *The species was doomed to extinction.*
- PHRASES   doomed to disappointment/extinction/failure *The project was doomed to failure from the start.*

door *noun*

- ADJ.   open | closed, shut | locked, unlocked | ajar, half-open *He had left the door ajar.* ◇ *The door was half-open when we got there.* | back, front, rear, side *the back door of a house* ◇ *the rear door of a car* | inner, internal *The inner door leads to the safe and is always locked after 5 p.m.* | external, outer *All external doors should be bolted top and bottom.* | big, great, heavy, huge, massive, solid, stout, thick *She had trouble pushing the heavy door open.* | narrow, wide | glass-panelled, glazed | double *Go along the corridor and through the double doors.* | unmarked | automatic, folding, revolving, sliding, swing *He got stuck in a revolving door.* ◇ *She pushed her way through the swing doors.* | bathroom, flat, kitchen, etc. | car, fridge, garage, lift, stage | trap (also trapdoor) | magic, mysterious, secret
- VERB + DOOR   fling/throw open, open, pull/push open *He flung the door open and caught them stuffing a document back into a briefcase.* | bang, close, pull closed/shut, pull/push to, push closed/shut, shut, slam (shut) *He pulled the door to.* | bar, bolt, lock *He arrived home to find the door barred.* ◇ *Remember to bolt the door before you go to bed.* | unbar, unbolt, unlock | keep/leave closed/open/shut, keep/leave on the latch (= closed but not locked), prop ajar/open *I left the door on the latch so that I could sneak back in later.* ◇ *Someone had*

propped the fire door open with a pile of books. | **come/go in (through), come/go out (of/through), come/go through, slip out of/through** He came in the side door. | **bang on, knock at/on** I banged on the door for ages but still couldn't wake them. | **answer** Go and answer the door (= open the door to sb who has knocked on it). | **see sb to** (= accompany sb who is leaving to the door) | **break down/in** They had to break the door down to get into the flat.

• DOOR + VERB **creak** | **burst open, clatter open, creak (open), fly open, open, slide open, swing open/shut/to** The door burst open and a little boy ran in. | **flap open, hang open** The car drove off with its rear door flapping open. | **be/stand ajar, be/stand open** The door stood ajar so I could see a narrow section of the room. | **be closed/shut, be jammed (open/shut), be stuck** | **bang (open/shut), clang open/shut, crash open/shut, rattle, shake** I was woken by a door banging in the wind. | **click (shut/to), close, shut, slam (shut)** | **connect sth, face sth, lead to sth, open onto sth** The door connecting the two offices is kept locked. ◇ This door leads to my bedroom. ◇ The door opens onto a sunny terrace. | **be set in/into the wall** I stopped at a low oak door set into the stone wall. | **bear a notice/plate/sign, be marked sth** I went through the door marked 'Enquiries'.

• DOOR + NOUN **handle, knob** | **frame, jamb** | **knocker** | **bolt, catch, chain, latch, lock** | **key** | **mat** (also **doormat**) | **stop** (also **doorstop**) This big fat dictionary would make a good doorstop. | **mirror, panel, pillar** (on a car)

• PREP. **at the ~** There's someone at the door. **in the ~** He stood in the door for several minutes before deciding whether he'd stay. **through the ~** He looked through the door to make sure the children were all right. | **~ into/to** the door into the back garden

• PHRASES **close/shut, etc. the door behind you** He banged the front door behind him as he left. **hold/open the door for sb, pop/stick you head round/through the door** She popped her head through the door to say goodbye. **shut/slam the door in sb's face**

doorbell noun

• VERB + DOORBELL **press, ring (on)** | **answer** He refused to answer the doorbell.
• DOORBELL + VERB **ring, sound** I heard the doorbell ring, and went to see who was there.
• PHRASES **a ring at/on the doorbell**

doorway noun

• ADJ. **open** | **shop** We sheltered in a shop doorway.
• PREP. **in a/the ~** A tall figure was standing in the doorway. **through a/the ~** We passed through the doorway and found ourselves in a walled garden.

dope noun

• VERB + DOPE **smoke** | **peddle**
• DOPE + NOUN **fiend** | **scandal** | **peddler** | **test** She was disqualified from competing for a year after failing a dope test.
⇨ Note at DRUG

dosage noun

• ADJ. **high, low** | **correct, recommended**
• VERB + DOSAGE **give (sb), take** Always take the correct dosage. | **increase** | **reduce**

dose noun

• ADJ. **hefty, high, large, massive, strong** a strong dose of painkillers ◇ (figurative) The film also contains a hefty dose of comedy. | **low, small** | **correct** | **double, full, sin-**

gle, standard | **daily, frequent** | **fatal, lethal** a lethal dose of radiation
• VERB + DOSE **receive, take** patients who receive high doses of this drug ◇ I had forgotten to take my dose of antibiotic. | **administer, give sb** The nurse will administer the correct dose. ◇ She needs to be given a daily dose of the medicine. | **increase** | **reduce**

double verb

• ADV. **more than** Our profits have more than doubled this year. | **almost, nearly, practically, virtually** The price of houses has nearly doubled in the last ten years. | **effectively** | **approximately, roughly**
• PREP. **in** The village has approximately doubled in size since 1960. **to** The party almost doubled its share of the vote to 21.5%.

double bass noun

⇨ Special page at MUSIC

doubt noun

• ADJ. **considerable, grave, real, serious, severe** | **slight** Without the slightest doubt this is a remarkable exhibition. | **gnawing, lingering, nagging, niggling** | **growing, increasing** | **personal, private** He made clear his own private doubts about it. | **reasonable** We have established beyond all reasonable doubt that the painting was indeed by Rembrandt. | **religious**
• VERB + DOUBT **arouse, raise** His failure to appear raises serious doubts as to his reliability. | **entertain, feel, harbour, have** She still felt the same niggling doubt: was he really telling the truth? | **express, voice** | **clear up, dispel, remove, resolve** The announcement dispelled any doubts as to the prince's intentions. | **cast, throw** Her record of dismissals casts doubt on her ability to hold down a job. | **call sth into, throw sth into** The proposed development has been thrown into doubt by the decision. | **be open to** Their honesty is open to doubt.
• DOUBT + VERB **appear, arise** Doubts have arisen over the viability of the schedule. | **exist** Considerable doubt exists as to the precise origin of this custom. | **persist, remain** | **surround sth** From the start, doubts surrounded her claim to be the missing heiress.
• PREP. **beyond (a/all/any) ~** The evidence proves beyond doubt that he is innocent. **in ~** The arrangements for the event still seemed to be in doubt. ◇ If in doubt, consult your doctor. **without (a) ~** She is without a doubt the best tennis player I know. | **~ about/over** Some committee members still harboured doubts about the plans.
• PHRASES **beyond/without a shadow of (a) doubt** This proves without a shadow of doubt that we were right. **have your doubts about sth** They say they'll be here on time, but I have my doubts about that.

doubt verb

• ADV. **seriously, very much** I never seriously doubted his story. | **privately** Lee privately doubted the truth of this statement.

doubtful adj.

1 feeling doubt
• VERBS **be, feel, look, seem, sound** Eric was far from sure and Marion looked doubtful. | **become** | **remain**
• ADV. **extremely, very** | **a bit, a little, rather**
• PREP. **about** She was rather doubtful about the wisdom of eating the two-day-old food.

2 unlikely
• VERBS **be, look, seem** | **remain**
• ADV. **extremely, highly, very** Even if we could go, which is highly doubtful, John wouldn't be able to come with us. | **increasingly** | **a bit, a little, rather, somewhat**

dough noun

- ADJ. **firm | soft | smooth | sticky | bread, pizza**
- QUANT. **ball, lump, piece**
- VERB + DOUGH **make | knead, shape** *Knead the dough lightly, then shape it into a round loaf.* | **roll out, turn out** *Turn the dough out onto a lightly floured surface.*
- DOUGH + VERB **rise** *Leave the dough to rise.*

downfall noun

- ADJ. **eventual, ultimate**
- VERB + DOWNFALL **bring about, cause, lead to** *a scandal that brought about his downfall* | **contribute to, hasten** *The failure of this scheme contributed to her eventual downfall.* | **plot** *They were found guilty of plotting the downfall of the government.*
- DOWNFALL + VERB **come** *The movement's downfall came with the failed coup d'état.*
- PHRASES **be sb's downfall** *His greed was eventually his downfall.*

downpour noun

- ADJ. **heavy, torrential | continuous, incessant, relentless, steady | sudden**
- PREP. **in~** *We got caught in a torrential downpour.*

downturn noun

- ADJ. **serious, severe, sharp, significant | mild, slight | economic**
- VERB + DOWNTURN **experience, suffer** *The building industry is experiencing a severe downturn in its workload.* | **see, witness**
- PREP. **~in** *The 1990s witnessed a sharp downturn in the party's fortunes.*

dowry noun

- ADJ. **large, substantial | small**
- VERB + DOWRY **give sb, pay (sb)** | **bring** *His family hoped that his bride would bring a large dowry.*
- DOWRY + NOUN **system**

doze noun

- VERB + DOZE **have** *She had a little doze after lunch.* | **drift into, fall into** *Sitting in an armchair in front of the fire, I soon fell into a doze.*

doze verb

- ADV. **fitfully** *I dozed fitfully for a few hours.*

draft noun

- ADJ. **early, first, initial, original, preliminary | rough | final**
- VERB + DRAFT **draw up, prepare, produce, write** *She produced an initial draft of her plans.* | **approve** *The preliminary draft of the agreement has been approved.*
- DRAFT + NOUN **agreement, bill, budget, constitution, contract, document, law, legislation, letter, plan, proposal, report, treaty**
- PREP. **in a/the ~** *These details were not included in the preliminary draft.*
- PHRASES **in draft form** *The document is still in draft form.*

draft verb

- ADV. **carefully, properly | badly, poorly** *Some of the clauses in the contract had been very poorly drafted.*

drain noun

1 pipe/hole that dirty water goes down
- ADJ. **blocked**
- VERB + DRAIN **block | clear, unblock | lay** *They were busy laying the drains for the new houses.*

2 sth that uses up time/money/resources
- ADJ. **heavy, major, serious | brain** *scientists joining the brain drain* (= moving to a country where they can work in better conditions and earn more)
- PREP. **~on** *These losses have been a major drain on the company's resources.*

drain verb

1 make sth empty/dry
- ADV. **thoroughly, well** *Remove the artichokes, drain thoroughly and allow to cool.* ◇ *well-drained soil*

2 make sb/sth weaker/poorer, etc.
- ADV. **totally, utterly | emotionally, physically | away** *draining away the country's coal reserves*
- PREP. **of** *His voice was utterly drained of emotion.*
- PHRASES **be/feel drained** *Sue felt exhausted and emotionally drained.*

drama noun

1 play/theatre
- ADJ. **powerful | classical, contemporary, modern | musical | radio, television/TV | costume, historical | courtroom, hospital, police** *Millions follow this hospital drama twice a week.*
- VERB + DRAMA **write** *It is very difficult to write good drama.* | **produce** *the first episode of a new police drama produced for television*
- DRAMA + NOUN **production | serial, series | festival | critic** *the drama critic for the 'Sunday Times'* | **school, training**
- PREP. **in a/the ~** *the actors in a drama* | **~ about** *a powerful television drama about inner-city life*
- ⇨ Note at SUBJECT

2 exciting event
- ADJ. **human | real-life** *The actor was involved in a real-life drama when he was held up at gunpoint last night.*
- DRAMA + VERB **unfold** *a collection of people watching the drama unfold outside the nightclub*

3 excitement
- ADJ. **high**
- QUANT. **touch** *The argument added a touch of drama to an otherwise dull day.*
- VERB + DRAMA **be full of** *The afternoon was full of drama and excitement.* | **heighten** *The arrival of the police heightened the drama further.*
- PHRASES **a moment of drama**

dramatic adj.

- VERBS **be, sound**
- ADV. **extremely, highly, intensely, very | fairly, quite, rather | suitably** *Her entrance was accompanied by suitably dramatic music.*

drape verb

- ADV. **casually, loosely | elegantly | beautifully** *Some silk fabrics will drape beautifully.*
- PREP. **across, around/round, over** *He sat with his arm draped casually around her shoulders.*
- PHRASES **be draped in/with sth** *The body was draped in a blanket.*

draught noun

- ADJ. **cold, icy** *A cold draught of air blew in from the open window.*

- VERB + DRAUGHT **create | prevent**
- DRAUGHT + VERB **blow, come, whistle** *a draught coming under the door*
- DRAUGHT + NOUN **excluder, proofing** *Fit draught excluders to the bottoms of doors.*
- PREP. **~from** *the draught from the window*
- PHRASES **a draught of air**

draw *noun*

- ADJ. **goalless, one-all, three-three, etc.**
- VERB + DRAW **end in** *The game ended in a two-all draw.* | **earn, get, hold sb to** *San Marino held them to a goalless draw.*
- PREP. **~against, ~with** *their 1–1 draw with United*

draw *verb*

1 make pictures
- ADV. **accurately, beautifully, carefully, clearly, well** *a beautifully drawn picture* ◊ *He draws very well.* | **badly, crudely, roughly** *a crudely drawn child's face*

2 pull
- ADV. **half, partly** *The blinds were partly drawn.* | **back** *She drew back the curtains and let the sunlight in.* | **up | aside, to one side** *I tried to draw him aside so I could talk to him in private.* | **together** (*figurative*) *The project enables students to draw together their knowledge, skills and experience.*
- PREP. **onto** *She drew me onto the balcony* **out of** *He drew the cork out of the bottle.* **to** *I drew my chair up to the fire.* **towards**

3 attract
- ADV. **immediately | inevitably, inexorably, irresistibly** *Her gaze was drawn irresistibly to the scene outside.*
- PREP. **from** *The scheme has drawn interest from local businessmen.* **to** *We asked the surfing champion what first drew him to the sport.*

PHRASAL VERBS

draw on/upon sth
- ADV. **heavily** *The novelist draws heavily on her personal experiences.*

draw sth up
- ADV. **professionally, properly** *Make sure the contract is properly drawn up.*

drawback *noun*

- ADJ. **big, main, major, real, serious | minor, slight | obvious | possible, potential**
- VERB + DRAWBACK **have (its/their), suffer from** *This strategy has its drawbacks.* ◊ *The system suffers from two major drawbacks.* | **overcome** *We have to find ways of overcoming these drawbacks.*
- PREP. **~ to** *Bad weather was the main drawback to camping in the far north.* **~ with** *The one big drawback with the planned scheme was its high cost.*

drawer *noun*

- ADJ. **deep, shallow** *a desk with two deep drawers either side* | **open | locked | bottom, middle, top | kitchen | desk, dresser, dressing table | cash, cutlery, filing | secret**
- VERB + DRAWER **open, pull open/out, slide open** *She pulled open the second drawer down to find the money had gone.* | **close, push in/shut, shut** *He pushed the drawer shut with a bang.* | **reach into** *She reached into the drawer and found the key to the safe.* | **go through, look through, ransack, rummage in/through** *What do you think you are doing, rummaging through my drawers?*
- PREP. **from/out of a/the ~** *She took the gun from the drawer.* **in a/the~** *He put the letters in the drawer.*

drawing *noun*

- ADJ. **charcoal, ink, line, pencil** *a set of charcoal drawings by a local artist* | **scale** *a scale drawing of a jumbo jet* | **engineering, technical, working** *a working drawing of the proposed power station* | **life** *He earned money modelling for life drawing classes.*
- VERB + DRAWING **do, make** *He made a drawing of how the Roman villa must have looked.*
- DRAWING + VERB **show sth** *The drawing shows the Market Square.*
- DRAWING + NOUN **board** *These days, designers spend more time at the computer than at the drawing board.*
- PREP. **in a/the ~** *The door opened onto a courtyard, as shown in the drawing.* | **~by** *a pencil drawing by Picasso* ⇨ Note at ART

drawl *noun*

- ADJ. **flat, nasal, slow, soft | Brooklyn, Southern, etc.**
- PHRASES **in a~** *'Howdy, pardner,' he said in his slow Texan drawl.* **with a~** *She spoke with soft Southern drawl.*

drawl *verb*

- ADV. **lazily, sardonically, slowly, softly** *'Come in,' he drawled softly.*

dread *noun*

- ADJ. **great, mortal** *Her greatest dread was that she would lose her job.* | **constant**
- VERB + DREAD **feel, have** *He had a dread of hospitals.* ◊ *the dread she felt at the thought of meeting him again* | **live in** *He lived in constant dread that one day he might be found out.* | **fill sb with** *Does the thought of flying fill you with dread?*
- PREP. **in~of** *After her shoplifting spree she lived in mortal dread of being found out.* | **~of** *her dread of discovery*
- PHRASES **a feeling/sense of dread**

dread *verb*

- ADV. **absolutely** *I've got to go and tell the headmaster tomorrow and I'm absolutely dreading it!* | **rather | always** *He had always dreaded being singled out.*

dreadful *adj.*

- VERBS **be, feel, look, smell, sound, taste** *Poor thing! You look absolutely dreadful!* (= very ill)
- ADV. **really** *I feel really dreadful about letting you down.* | **absolutely, quite, truly** *To be honest, her singing was quite dreadful.* ◊ *a truly dreadful hat* | **pretty, rather**
- PREP. **for** *It must have been dreadful for you!*

dream *noun*

1 while you are asleep
- ADJ. **awful, bad, disturbing, strange** *a child frightened by a bad dream* | **pleasant | vivid | recurrent | erotic, wet | prophetic** *He had a prophetic dream about a train crash the night before the rail disaster.*
- VERB + DREAM **dream, have** *She fell asleep and dreamed strange dreams.* ◊ *I had a very disturbing dream last night.* | **awake/wake from, be awoken/woken from** *I was awoken from my dream by a knock at the door.* | **interpret | haunt** *Images of the crash still haunted his dreams years later.*
- DREAM + VERB **come true** *I hope my dream about prison won't come true!* | **haunt sb** *vivid dreams that regularly haunted him*
- DREAM + NOUN **interpretation**
- PREP. **in a/the ~** *In her dream, she was on board a ship heading for America.* | **~ about** *a recurrent dream about being late for an exam*
- PHRASES **as (if) in a dream** *She found herself standing*

in front of the crowded hall and making her speech, as if in a dream. **sweet dreams** *'Sweet dreams,' she said, turning off the light.*

2 sth that you want very much to happen

- ADJ. **big, great** *Her biggest dream was to become a singer.* | **lifelong** | **distant** *His plans to travel the world now seemed like a distant dream.* | **impossible** *Peace no longer seemed an impossible dream.* | **utopian** | **romantic** *She had this romantic dream of living in a windmill.*
- VERB + DREAM **cherish, have** *the great utopian dream that they have cherished for so long* | **achieve, fulfil, realize** *At last his dreams were fulfilled.* | **shatter** *The injury shattered her dream of running in the Olympics.* | **keep alive** *The victory keeps San Marino's dream of a World Cup place alive.*
- DREAM + VERB **come true** *He put all his efforts into making his dream of a united country come true.* | **turn into a nightmare, turn sour** *Their dream turned into a nightmare as the cruise ship began to sink.*
- DREAM + NOUN **holiday, home, house** *After Betty retired, she and her husband designed and built their dream house.* | **world** *The government is living in a dream world if they think voters will agree to higher taxes.*
- PREP. **~ of** *their dream of a fairer world*
- PHRASES **the ... of sb's dreams** *the house of her dreams* **beyond sb's wildest dreams** *They achieved a success beyond their wildest dreams.* **a dream come true** *Their holiday in the Bahamas was a dream come true.*

dream *verb*

- ADV. **always** *As a child she always dreamt of working with animals.* | **never** *I never dreamt I'd actually get the job.* | **still** | **long** *People have long dreamt of an egalitarian society.* | **just, only** *It was the kind of trip most of us can only dream about.*
- VERB + DREAM **wouldn't** *I wouldn't dream of going without you* (= I would never go without you).
- PREP. **about, of**

dress *noun*

1 piece of clothing

- ADJ. **ankle-length, full-length, long** | **short** | **skimpy** | **clinging, figure-hugging, tight, tight-fitting** | **loose-fitting, shapeless** | **full-skirted** | **backless, high-necked, low-cut, off-the-shoulder, revealing, sleeveless, strapless** | **slinky** | **cotton, silk,** etc. | **day, evening, Sunday** | **ball, cocktail, dinner, maternity, party, wedding**
- VERB + DRESS **zip (up)** | **unzip** | **hitch up, lift, pull up** *She hitched up her long dress so it wouldn't drag in the mud.* | **pull down** | **smooth** *She sat down and smoothed her dress over her legs.*
- DRESS + NOUN **material** | **shop** | **designer** | **size**
- PREP. **in a/the ~** *She appeared in a slinky satin dress.*
- ⇨ Special page at CLOTHES

2 clothes for either men or women

- ADJ. **ceremonial, formal** | **casual, informal** | **correct** | **evening** | **modern** | **period** | **national, traditional** *He was wearing traditional Scottish dress.* | **fancy** | **battle, military** | **civilian**
- DRESS + NOUN **code** *The club has a strict dress code.* | **sense** *He's got poor dress sense.* | **shirt** | **uniform** *in full dress uniform*
- PREP. **in ... ~** *a performance of 'Hamlet' in modern dress*

dress *verb*

1 put on clothes

- ADV. **hurriedly, quickly** | **slowly** | **carefully**
- PREP. **in** *He dressed carefully in the brown suit he had been married in.*

- PHRASES **be fully dressed** *She lay down on her bed, fully dressed.* **get dressed** *She got dressed quickly.*

2 wear clothes

- ADV. **beautifully, elegantly, fashionably, immaculately, impeccably, neatly, nicely, smartly, well** *Susan always dresses very elegantly.* ◇ *She was determined to be the best dressed woman at the wedding.* | **badly, poorly, shabbily** | **appropriately, suitably** | **unsuitably** | **decently, properly, respectably** | **improperly** | **plainly, simply, soberly** | **ostentatiously, nattily, richly** | **casually** | **formally** | **expensively** | **warmly** | **scantily** | **identically** *The twins were dressed identically.*
- PREP. **for** *I have to dress smartly for work.* **in** *The women were all dressed in blue skirts and white blouses.*

dressing *noun*

1 covering put on a wound

- ADJ. **clean, fresh, sterile** | **surgical, wound**
- VERB + DRESSING **apply, put on** *Clean the wound and put on a fresh dressing.* | **change** | **remove**

2 sauce for food, especially salads

- ADJ. **salad** | **French** | **herb** | **vinaigrette**
- PREP. **in a~, with a~** *salad with a vinaigrette dressing* | **~for** *a herb dressing for fish*

drift *noun*

1 slow movement towards sth

- ADJ. **gradual, slow**
- PREP. **~ (away) from** *the drift of people away from rural areas into urban slums* **~ (back) to** *As the strike went on, there was a gradual drift back to work.* **~ into** *his drift into crime* **~ towards**

2 general meaning of sth

- ADJ. **general, main**
- VERB + DRIFT **catch, follow, get** *I didn't follow the speech exactly, but I caught the main drift of what was being said.* | **lose** *I lost the drift of what she was saying.*

3 pile of snow/sand made by the wind

- ADJ. **deep, great** | **sand, snow** (also **snowdrift**)

drift *verb*

1 be carried along by the wind/water

- ADV. **slowly** | **helplessly** *Cold and hungry, they drifted helplessly towards the Arctic.* | **downriver, downstream, downwind** *The boat drifted slowly downstream.* | **along, back, down, out**
- PREP. **from, to, towards,** etc. *drifting out to sea*

2 move slowly/without purpose

- ADV. **aimlessly** | **slowly** | **quietly, silently** | **about, around/round, apart, away, back, down, off, up** *Voices drifted up through the floorboards.*
- VERB + DRIFT **begin to** | **seem to** | **allow sth to** *He allowed his thoughts to drift back to his conversation with Carrie.*
- PREP. **about/around/round** *He spent the day drifting aimlessly about the house.* **across** *She drifted across the room to where we were standing.* **between** *She began to drift between sleep and wakefulness.* **from** *We seem to be drifting away from the point.* **in, into** *He drifted into teaching, but never really enjoyed it.* **out of** *He drifted in and out of consciousness.*

drink *noun*

- ADJ. **cold, cool, iced, refreshing** *I could do with a nice cool drink.* | **hot, warm** | **milky** | **fizzy** | **low-alcohol, non-alcoholic, reduced-alcohol, soft** | **alcoholic, stiff, strong** | **diet, low-calorie** | **long** *She took a long drink of cold water.* | **celebratory** | **welcome** *You will be offered a welcome drink on arrival at the hotel.* | **farewell** | **early-**

evening, lunchtime | leisurely *We were enjoying a leisurely drink before dinner.* | quick | quiet
● QUANT. **round** *We ordered a round of drinks while waiting for a table.*
● VERB + DRINK **drink, have** *I'll just drink my drink then we can go.* ◇ *She had a hot drink and went to bed.* | **sip** | **down, finish, knock back** *He knocked back his drink in one go and ordered another one.* | **take** *He took a drink of his beer and sat down.* | **go for** *Would you like to go for a drink after work?* | **buy (sb), get (sb), offer (sb), order (sb)** *Can I buy you a drink?* | **pour (sb), serve (sb)** *He poured himself a stiff drink to calm his nerves.* | **spike** *The robbers spiked his drink before taking his wallet and passport.* | **drive sb to** *Her money problems drove her to drink* (= made her start drinking a lot of alcohol). | **turn to** *After his wife died, he turned to drink.*
● DRINK + NOUN **drinks party** *We've been invited to a drinks party.* | **drinks cabinet/cupboard** *She took a bottle from the drinks cabinet.* | **problem** *She suspected her boss had a drink problem.*
● PREP. **in a/the ~** *Do you want ice in your drink?* | **~ of** *I'll have a drink of milk, please.*

drink *verb*

1 take liquid into the body
● ADV. **greedily** *I pulled the ring-top from the can and drank greedily.* | **down, up** *He filled a cup with water and drank it down in one gulp.* ◇ *Drink up, and let's go home.*
● VERB + DRINK **get yourself sth to, find sth to, have sth to** *Go and get yourself something to eat and drink.*
● PREP. **from** *He drank from a tumbler.* | **through** *drinking lemonade through a straw*
● PHRASES **eat and drink**

2 drink alcohol
● ADV. **excessively, heavily, to excess, too much** *He's been drinking heavily since he lost his job.* | **in moderation, moderately, sensibly** *One way of persuading people to drink sensibly is to provide good-tasting alternatives with less alcohol.* | **steadily** *She had been drinking steadily since the early morning.*
● PHRASES **drink and drive** *The campaign aims to persuade people not to drink and drive.* **drink like a fish** (= drink a lot) *Simon was drinking like a fish that evening.* **drink yourself to death** *He knew that he was probably drinking himself to death.*

drinker *noun*

● ADJ. **habitual, hard, heavy** *This liver condition is common in heavy drinkers.* | **moderate** | **problem** *help for the families and friends of problem drinkers* | **social** *She is a social drinker only—she never drinks at home.* | **beer, coffee, tea, etc.** *I'm not a big tea drinker.*

drinking *noun*

● ADJ. **excessive, heavy** *the health problems associated with heavy drinking* | **moderate** | **underage** *new measures aimed at preventing underage drinking*
● VERB + DRINKING **cut down on, limit** *His doctor had advised him to limit his drinking.*
● DRINKING + NOUN **session** | **companion**
● PHRASES **a bout of drinking**

drip *noun*

1 water dripping
● ADJ. **slow, steady**
● PREP. **~ of** *the steady drip of water from the tap*

2 drop of water that falls down from sb/sth
● VERB + DRIP **catch** *There were buckets to catch the drips from the ceiling.*
● DRIP + VERB **fall** *Drips fell from the roof of the cave.*
● PREP. **~ from** *drips from the tap*

3 medical equipment
● ADJ. **intravenous** | **saline**
● VERB + DRIP **fix up, set up** | **be attached to, be on** *He is on a saline drip.* | **attach sb to, put sb on** | **take sb off** *He was taken off his drip last night.*

drive *noun*

1 car journey
● ADJ. **long, easy, short** | **eight-hour, sixty-mile, etc.** | **leisurely** | **pleasant, scenic** *It's a pleasant drive to the coast.* | **test**
● VERB + DRIVE **go for, take** *Let's go for a drive.*
● PREP. **within a ~** *All my family live within an hour's drive.*
● PHRASES **a ... drive away** *The lakes are only a short drive away.*

2 way a vehicle is moved
● ADJ. **all-wheel, four-wheel, front-wheel, rear-wheel** | **left-hand, right-hand** *Left-hand drive cars make driving in Britain difficult.*

3 path/road outside a house
● ADJ. **sweeping, winding** | **gravel/gravelled** | **tree-lined** | **private** | **front**
● DRIVE + VERB **sweep, swing** *A gravel drive swept between manicured lawns.*
● PREP. **down the ~, in the ~, on the ~** *There was a car parked on the drive.* **up the ~** *He walked up the front drive of the vicarage.*

4 energy/determination
● ADJ. **competitive** | **personal** | **narrative** *A lack of narrative drive leaves the reader with piecemeal vignettes.*
● VERB + DRIVE **have** | **lack** *He lacks the competitive drive needed to succeed.*

5 desire/need
● ADJ. **innate, inner, instinctive/instinctual** | **creative** | **emotional, sex/sexual**

6 effort
● ADJ. **big** | **relentless** | **national, nationwide** | **cost-cutting, efficiency, export, fundraising, marketing, membership, modernization, recruitment, sales** | **anti-corruption, anti-drug, etc.**
● VERB + DRIVE **launch** *We're going to launch a big recruitment drive in the autumn.*
● PREP. **~ against** *a drive against corruption* **~ by** *the recent recruitment drive by the police* **~ for** *the country's drive for modernization* **~ towards** *a drive towards higher safety standards*

7 computing
● ADJ. **CD-ROM, disk, DVD, floppy, hard, zip**

8 in sport
● ADJ. **powerful, strong, thunderous** | **angled, crisp** | **left-foot, right-foot** (in football) *Cole scored with a thunderous left-foot drive.* | **backhand, forehand** (in tennis) *a forehand drive down the line*
● VERB + DRIVE **hit** | **hook, slice** (in golf)
⇨ Special page at SPORT

drive *verb*

● ADV. **fast, quickly** *You shouldn't drive so fast!* ◇ *She drove quickly back to the office.* | **slowly** | **carefully** | **recklessly** *He was arrested for driving recklessly.* | **around, away, back, off, on** *She got into the car and drove away.*
● PREP. **from, to** *driving from London to Manchester*
● PHRASES **drink and drive**

driver *noun*

● ADJ. **careful, good, safe** | **bad, dangerous, reckless** | **drunk/drunken, hit-and-run** *He was killed by a drunken driver.* | **experienced, inexperienced** | **learner** *Learner*

drivers are not allowed on the motorways. | **racing, rally** | **ambulance, bus, cab, car, coach, engine, lorry, tanker, taxi, train, truck, van**
⇨ Note at JOB

driving noun

● ADJ. **good, safe** *a new campaign to promote safe driving* | **aggressive, bad, careless, dangerous, reckless** *She was charged with reckless driving.* | **drink, drunk, drunken** *Police stopped 30 motorists for drink driving on New Year's Eve.*
● VERB + DRIVING **be banned from, be disqualified from** *He was banned from driving for six months after failing a breath test.*
● DRIVING + NOUN **seat** | **instructor, lesson** | **test** | **offence** | **charge** *There wasn't enough evidence for a dangerous driving charge.* | **ban** *She was given a large fine and a two-year driving ban.*

driving licence noun

● ADJ. **current** | **clean** | **full** | **provisional**
● VERB + DRIVING LICENCE **have, hold** | **lose**

drizzle noun

● ADJ. **fine, light, thin** | **steady** | **patchy**
● DRIZZLE + VERB **fall** *Light drizzle fell all afternoon.*
● PREP. **in/through a/the ~** *We walked home through the drizzle.*

drone noun

● ADJ. **faint** | **low** | **distant** | **constant, continuous, steady**
● VERB + DRONE **hear**
● PREP. **with a ~** *The planes flew overhead with a low drone.* | **~ of** *the continuous drone of the engine*

drop noun

1 reduction
● ADJ. **big, considerable, dramatic, huge, large, massive, significant, substantial** | **slight, small** | **rapid, sharp, sudden** | **steady** | **catastrophic**
● VERB + DROP **suffer** *The restaurant has suffered a big drop in trade.* | **cause, lead to**
● PREP. **~ in** *The glut of coffee led to a sharp drop in prices.*

2 vertical distance down from a place
● ADJ. **sheer, steep, vertical** *The cliff plunged in a sheer drop down to the beach.* | **long**

3 small round mass of liquid
● DROP + VERB **fall** *Great drops of rain started to fall.* | **roll down sth**
● PREP. **~ of** *Large drops of sweat rolled down her face.*

drop verb

1 allow sth to fall
● ADV. **accidentally, carelessly** | **almost, nearly** | **promptly** *He saw Emma and promptly dropped his tray of drinks.*
● PREP. **in/into, on/onto** *I accidentally dropped my glasses into the water.*

2 jump/move downwards
● ADV. **heavily** | **gently, lightly** | **quickly** | **limply, uselessly** *His arms dropped uselessly to his sides.* | **down, open** *Her mouth dropped open in disbelief.*
● VERB + DROP **let sth** *She smiled and let her eyes drop again.* | **be/feel ready to** *I feel ready to drop* (= because I am so tired).
● PREP. **into, onto, to** *He dropped lightly down onto the lawn beneath.*
● PHRASES **drop like a stone** (*figurative*) *Her heart dropped like a stone at this news.*

3 become lower
● ADV. **considerably, dramatically, drastically, sharply, significantly** *The price of oil has dropped significantly.* | **slightly** | **fast, rapidly** | **steadily** | **further**
● VERB + DROP **be likely/unlikely to** *Sales are likely to drop further.*
● PREP. **below** *The temperature rarely drops below 30°C.* **by** *The price has dropped by 15 per cent.* **from, to** *The number of children in the class has dropped from 25 to 18.*

4 slope downwards
● ADV. **sharply, steeply** | **away**
● PREP. **into/to/towards** *The land dropped steeply away into a small valley.*

5 no longer include sb in sth
● ADV. **quietly**
● PREP. **from** *He has been quietly dropped from the England team.* **in favour of**

6 stop doing sth/be stopped
● ADV. **quietly** *The subject was quietly dropped.* | **suddenly** *He suddenly dropped his habitual banter.* | **eventually, finally** | **altogether** *When nobody volunteered, the idea was finally dropped altogether.*
● VERB + DROP **let sth** *Can't we just let the matter drop?* | **agree to, decide to** *Both countries have agreed to drop border controls.*
● PREP. **in favour of** *The formal grade of Geologist was dropped in favour of Scientific Officer.*

drought noun

● ADJ. **severe, terrible, worst** *It has been the worst drought in the country's history.* | **long, prolonged** | **summer**
● VERB + DROUGHT **have** *England has had several summer droughts in recent years.* | **cause** | **break** *A week of good rains has broken the drought.*
● DROUGHT + VERB **affect sth** *Large areas of Africa are affected by severe drought.*
● DROUGHT + NOUN **conditions**
● PREP. **during/in ~** *Some of the newer plants in the garden died during the drought.*
● PHRASES **in times of drought, months/years of drought**

drug noun

1 substance used as a medicine
● ADJ. **powerful, strong** | **modern, new** | **wonder** *They're hailing it as the new wonder drug.* | **sedative** | **anti-cancer, anti-inflammatory, anti-malarial, etc.** | **prescription** *You used to be able to buy this medicine over the counter, but it is now a prescription drug.*
● QUANT. **course, dose**
● VERB + DRUG **be on, take** *Are you taking any other drugs at present?* | **prescribe (sb), put sb on** *The doctor put me on anti-inflammatory drugs.* | **give sb, treat sb with** | **administer, give sb** *The nurses came round to give the patients their drugs.* | **develop** *new drugs that have been developed recently* | **be resistant to, not respond to** *Some infections are now resistant to drugs.*
● DRUG + VERB **cure sth, help sth, treat sth** *drugs that help the growth of skin tissue*
● DRUG + NOUN **company**
● PREP. **~ against** *a powerful drug against tuberculosis* **~ for** *He's taking drugs for depression.*

2 illegal substance
● ADJ. **illegal** | **addictive, hallucinogenic** | **dangerous, hard** *heroin and other hard drugs* | **soft** (= not considered very dangerous) *Many addicts start on soft drugs, such as cannabis.* | **designer** (= artificially produced) *She took a tablet of the designer drug Ecstasy.*
● VERB + DRUG **inject** (See note for more verbs.)
● DRUG + NOUN **baron, pusher** | **cartel** | **misuse** |

drug/drugs charges, offence | squad | war *the latest moves in the drug war* (See note for more nouns.)
• PHRASES drink and drugs *the dangers of drink and drugs*

> **NOTE**
> **Illegal Drugs**
>
> do (*informal*), experiment with, take, try, use ~
> *The minister confessed to having experimented with cannabis in her youth.*
> be/get high on ~
> *They committed the crime while high on drugs.*
> be addicted to, be dependent on, be/get hooked on, be on (*informal*)
> *He seemed to be on acid most of the time.*
> be/come off ~
> *He's tried several times to come off cocaine.*
> possess ~
> *arrested on charges of possessing narcotics*
> deal (in), sell, smuggle, supply, traffic (in) ~
> *The country imposes the death penalty for trafficking in marijuana.*
> seize ~
> *The heroin seized has an estimated street value of £600 000.*
> ~ abuse, addiction, consumption, use
> *Cannabis consumption has increased sharply.*
> ~ habit, problem
> *She allegedly has a $500-a-day coke habit.*
> ~ overdose
> *Heroin overdose is a major cause of death among heroin users.*
> ~ addict, user
> ~ dealer, trafficker, smuggler
> ~ production, smuggling, trade, trafficking
> *The authorities have been accused of active involvement in the narcotics trade.*
> addiction to, dependence on, use of ~
> *the use of cocaine*
> trade in ~
> *measures to combat the trade in narcotics*

---

drum noun

• ADJ. bass, kettle, side, snare
• VERB + DRUM bang, beat, hit
• DRUM + NOUN kit, machine | beat, pattern, rhythm, roll | major, majorette
• PHRASES a roll of drums
⇨ Special page at MUSIC

drunk adj.

• VERBS be, feel, look, sound *I was beginning to feel very drunk.* | get *Harry went out and got drunk last night.* | get sb, make sb *Andrew decided to try and get Sharon drunk.* ◇ *The wine had made him drunk.*
• ADV. blind, completely, extremely, hideously, hopelessly, horribly, really, roaring, very *He came home blind drunk, as usual.* | almost (*often figurative*) *She was almost drunk with all these new impressions.* | fairly, half, a little, pretty, quite, rather, slightly *He was still half drunk.*
• PREP. with (*figurative*) *drunk with fatigue*

dry verb

• ADV. carefully, completely, thoroughly *Wait until the paint has completely dried.* ◇ *Always dry clothes thoroughly before you wear them again.* | quickly | slowly | naturally | off, out *We left the wood in the shed to dry out.*
• VERB + DRY allow sth to, leave sth to, let sth *It's best to let your hair dry naturally.*

PHRASAL VERB
dry up
1 become empty of water
• ADV. completely *It's been so hot this year that the pond has dried up completely.*
2 be no longer available
• ADV. completely *Funds have completely dried up.* | virtually

dry adj.

• VERBS be, feel, look, seem | become, get, go, run *Come into the warm and get dry, both of you.* ◇ *Ruth felt her mouth go dry.* ◇ *The wells in most villages in the region have run dry.* ◇ (*figurative*) *Vaccine supplies started to run dry as the flu outbreak reached epidemic proportions.* | keep, remain, stay *We managed to keep dry by huddling in a doorway.* ◇ *There is every prospect of the weather remaining dry this week.* | pat sb/sth, rub sb/sth, towel sb *Rinse the mushrooms and pat dry.* ◇ *He towelled himself dry.* | bleed sb, milk sb, squeeze sb, suck sb (*all figurative*) *The big corporations are bleeding some of these small countries dry* (= taking all their money). | keep sth *This type of wound is best kept dry without a dressing.*
• ADV. excessively, extremely, very | bone, completely, perfectly, quite, thoroughly, totally *The river was bone dry.* ◇ *Make sure the paint is thoroughly dry.* | almost, nearly | barely, hardly, scarcely (*often figurative*) *The ink was scarcely dry on the ceasefire agreement before fighting broke out again.* | mainly, mostly *The day will start bright and mainly dry.* | a bit, a little, rather, reasonably, relatively

dubious adj.

• VERBS be, seem, sound | become
• ADV. distinctly, extremely, highly, very *some highly dubious information* | rather, somewhat | morally *It sounds a morally dubious proposition.*

duck noun

• ADJ. wild | plastic, rubber *A rubber duck floated in the bath.* | roast
• QUANT. flock, flotilla (only used for ducks that are swimming) *A flotilla of ducks bobbed near the shore.*
• VERB + DUCK feed *Every afternoon they went to the park to feed the ducks.*
• DUCK + VERB quack | paddle, swim *The ducks paddled furiously towards the bread.* | bob | dive | dabble *Some species of duck dive for food, while others dabble in plants and insects near the surface.* | waddle *A family of ducks waddled along the river bank.* | nest | migrate
• DUCK + NOUN breast *Slice the duck breast and serve.* | egg | pond

duke noun

⇨ Note at PEER

dull adj.

• VERBS appear, be, look, seem, sound | become, get *The work gets a bit dull at times.* | make sth *The long lectures made the afternoon dull.* | find sth
• ADV. deadly, extremely, stupefyingly, very *The film was long and deadly dull.* | a bit, a little, fairly, pretty, rather, somewhat | disappointingly

dumb adj.

1 unable to speak
• VERBS be | become, be struck *They were struck dumb by some sort of shock.*
• PREP. with *She sat there, dumb with rage.*
• PHRASES deaf and dumb

2 stupid

- VERBS **be, feel, look, seem, sound** *I'm sure my question sounded really dumb.* | **act, play** *I decided to act dumb.*
- ADV. **really, very** | **pretty, rather**

dump *noun*

- ADJ. **garbage, refuse, rubbish, waste** *cleaning up a toxic waste dump* | **nuclear**
- DUMP + NOUN **site** *Local residents have organized a protest against the planned dump site.*
- PREP. **at a/the ~** *Radioactive waste has been found at the dump.* **to a/the ~** *taking rubbish to the dump* | **~ for** *a new dump for nuclear waste*

dump *verb*

- ADV. **illegally** *The firm had illegally dumped toxic waste.* | **legally** | **unceremoniously** *They carried him down to the beach and dumped him unceremoniously in the freezing water.* | **at sea** *dumping sewage at sea* | **down** *He dumped the boxes down in the kitchen.*

duplicate *noun*

- VERB + DUPLICATE **make** *We made a duplicate of the key.*
- PREP. **in ~** *The contract is prepared in duplicate, so that both parties can sign it.*

duplicate *verb*

- ADV. **exactly** *The original experiment cannot be exactly duplicated.* | **simply** *I wanted to avoid simply duplicating work that had already been done.*

duplication *noun*

- ADJ. **unnecessary, wasteful** *Duties have been reassigned to avoid wasteful duplication of work.*
- VERB + DUPLICATION **avoid, eliminate, prevent, reduce** *The new procedures should reduce duplication of medical care and treatment.*

duration *noun*

- ADJ. **brief, short | long | indefinite | maximum | overall, total** *We took four trains, and the overall duration of the journey was 72 hours.* | **average, expected, likely** *the expected duration of the disease*
- PREP. **for the ~ (of)** *She stayed there for the duration of the journey.* **of … ~** *The next contract will be of shorter duration.* **throughout the ~ of** *This continued throughout the duration of their marriage.*

dusk *noun*

- ADJ. **approaching, gathering**
- DUSK + VERB **approach, fall, gather** *Dusk was falling as we drove home.*
- PREP. **after ~, at ~, before ~, in the ~** *The lamps twinkled in the gathering dusk.*
- PHRASES **from dawn to dusk**

dust *noun*

- ADJ. **fine | brick, coal, radioactive**
- QUANT. **cloud, layer** *The tractor came up the track in a cloud of dust.* ◇ *There was a layer of fine dust on the table.* | **particle, speck** *Remove any particles of dust on the surface of the paint.* ◇ *microscopic specks of dust*
- VERB + DUST **gather** *Her chess set lay on a shelf gathering dust.* | **be covered in/with**
- DUST + VERB **lie** *The dust now lay in a thick layer on her piano.*
- DUST + NOUN **cloud | particle | storm**

dustbin *noun*

- VERB + DUSTBIN **chuck sth in, dump sth in, throw sth in** *She chucked the mouldy potatoes in the dustbin.* | **go in** *These old shoes can go in the dustbin now.* | **be consigned to, be destined for** *(figurative)* *The politicians who lost the elections will be consigned to the dustbin of history.* | **empty** *How regularly are the dustbins emptied?* | **put out** *We put out the dustbins on a Wednesday morning before the van comes.*
- DUSTBIN + NOUN **bag, liner | lid | man** *The dustbin men forgot to empty our bin this morning.*
- PREP. **~ of** *(figurative)* *The pollution in this country makes it the dustbin of Europe.*

duty *noun*

1 sth that you have to do because it is right or expected

- ADJ. **contractual, legal, mandatory, statutory** *Retailers have a statutory duty to provide goods suitable for their purpose.* | **general, primary** *the general duty of the police to preserve the peace* | **professional | civic, public** *I feel it is my civic duty to vote.* | **patriotic | family, filial, parental | ethical, moral** *He felt it was his moral duty to help his neighbour.* | **absolute, bounden, fundamental, sacred, solemn** *I feel it's my bounden duty to try and help her.*
- VERB + DUTY **have, owe** *(law)* *You have a legal duty to take reasonable care.* ◇ *The railway company owes a duty of care to all its customers.* | **carry out, do, fulfil, meet, perform** *She put down the phone and went out, her duty done.* ◇ *She felt she had fulfilled her duty by providing him with a son.* | **fail in** *He had failed in his duty towards his daughter.* | **neglect, shirk** *I'd be shirking my duty if I didn't warn him.* | **assign, charge sb with, impose** *It was a duty imposed by her father.* | **assume, take on** *He took on the duty of maintaining the family home.*
- DUTY + VERB **call** *I wanted to stop and chat, but duty called and I went back to the office.*
- PREP. **under a/the ~** *You are under a statutory duty to keep accurate records.* | **~ of** *It's the duty of each and every one of us to do their best for the team.* ◇ *They have a duty of confidentiality.* **~ to, ~ towards** *They have a duty to their parents to work hard.*
- PHRASES **a breach of duty** *It was a clear breach of professional duty.* **do your duty** *I suppose we'd better do our duty and report the accident.* **do your duty by sb** *You feel that you have to do your duty by your children.* **be duty bound to do sth** *An employer is not duty bound to provide a reference when an employee leaves.* **(above and) beyond the call of duty** *The time he put in helping new recruits went beyond the call of duty.* **feel it your duty to do sth** *I felt it my duty to go to the police.* **in breach of a duty** *(formal)* *It was ruled that the injured man was in breach of his duty by not wearing the safety equipment provided.* **a sense of duty** *I did it out of a sense of duty.*

2 tasks that you do when you are at work

- ADJ. **light** *When I returned to work after my illness I was put on light duties.* | **onerous | day, night** *At 10.45 p.m. she reported for night duty.* | **beat, escort, guard, point, sentry** *Police usually do beat duty in pairs.* ◇ *The traffic lights were not working so there was a policeman on point duty.* | **daily, routine | official | administrative, professional, secretarial | domestic, household** *My household duties were not particularly onerous.* | **military**
- VERB + DUTY **have** *The members of staff each have their own duties.* | **carry out, discharge, do, perform** *She was unable to carry out her duties because she was too ill.* | **come on, go on, report for** *Colleagues became suspicious when he failed to report for duty.* | **come off, go off** *What time do you go off duty?* | **neglect, shirk** *He was accused of neglecting his professional duties.* | **resume, return to** *He leaves hospital tomorrow and is expected to resume his duties at the beginning of next month.* | **be released from** *Her son was released from duty in the army to visit her in*

hospital. | **be relieved of, be suspended from** *When he failed to turn up for training, he was relieved of his duties as captain.*
- DUTY + NOUN **doctor, nurse, officer, pharmacist** *He went to the police station and spoke to the duty officer.*
- PREP. **off~** *I'm off duty tomorrow night.* **on~** *You're not allowed to drink alcohol on duty.*
- PHRASES **the execution/performance of your duties** *The company is liable if you are injured during the execution of your duty.*

3 tax
- ADJ. **heavy, high** *the heavy duty on cigarettes* | **low** | **customs, excise, export, import** *excise duty on spirits* | **alcohol, fuel, tobacco, etc.** *Tobacco duty is a major source of revenue for the government.* | **death**
- QUANT. **amount** *We tried to estimate the amount of duty we would have to pay.*
- VERB + DUTY **put on, slap on** *They are going to put duty on foreign cars.* | **take off** | **increase, put up, raise** *They're going to put up the duty on tobacco.* | **cut, lower, reduce** | **pay** | **avoid, evade** *They claim that the wine is for personal use and so evade the duty.* | **be liable to** *Perfume is liable to import duty.* **carry** *Cider carries duty at the lower rate.* | **be exempt from** *Beer for personal use is exempt from duty.*
- PREP. **in~** *By changing its supplier, the company saved thousands of pounds in import duty.* | **~on** *You have to pay duty on all electrical goods.*

duvet *noun*
- ADJ. **double, king-size, single** | **light, lightweight, thick, thin** | **warm**
- VERB + DUVET **pull** *She climbed into bed and pulled the duvet over her.* | **fling back, kick off, throw back** *He flung back the duvet and got out of bed.*
- DUVET + NOUN **cover**
- PREP. **beneath/under a/the ~** *He snuggled down under the warm duvet.*

dweller *noun*
- ADJ. **city, town, urban** | **country, rural** | **slum** *the poor slum dwellers of the capital city* | **cave, forest, hill**

dwelling *noun*
- ADJ. **permanent** | **private** | **family** | **human** *The building looked more like a doll's house than a human dwelling.* | **characterful, elegant**
- VERB + DWELLING **convert sth into** *an application to convert the old barn into a dwelling* | **occupy**
- DWELLING + NOUN **house, place**

dwindle *verb*
- ADV. **fast, quickly, rapidly** *Supplies of coal are dwindling fast.* | **gradually, slowly** | **steadily** | **away** *Membership of the club had dwindled away to nothing.*
- PREP. **to** *Profits slowly dwindled to nothing.*

dye *noun*
- ADJ. **fabric, food, hair, wood, etc.** | **chemical, synthetic** | **natural, plant, vegetable**
- PREP. **in (a/the)~** *The cloth is then soaked in blue dye.*

dynamic *adj.*
- VERBS **be, seem** | **become** | **remain** *The business has managed to change and remain dynamic.*
- ADV. **highly, truly** *These countries are characterized by highly dynamic economies.* | **fully** | **increasingly** | **essentially, fundamentally** *The process is essentially dynamic with ideas and feedback flowing both ways.*

dynamite *noun*

1 explosive
- QUANT. **stick**
- VERB + DYNAMITE **blow sth up with, use** *They used five tons of dynamite to blow up the rock.* | **detonate**
- DYNAMITE + VERB **explode**

2 sb/sth that causes great excitement/shock, etc.
- ADJ. **absolute, pure** | **political** *Don't mention the single currency—it's political dynamite.*

dynasty *noun*
- ADJ. **ancient** *Scotland's ancient dynasty* | **great** | **royal** | **ruling** *the ruling dynasties of the Visigoths*
- VERB + DYNASTY **establish, found** | **bring to an end, overthrow**
- DYNASTY + VERB **begin** | **come to an end, end** | **last, reign**
- PREP. **during a/the~** *a porcelain figure made during the Tang dynasty* **from a/the~** *bowls and pots from the twelfth dynasty* **under a/the ~** *The civil service was established under the previous dynasty.*
- PHRASES **the end/fall of a dynasty, the founder of a dynasty, a member of a dynasty, the rise of a dynasty** *the rise and fall of the Habsburg dynasty*

dysentery *noun*
- ADJ. **amoebic**
- QUANT. **attack** | **outbreak**
- ⇨ Special page at ILLNESS

Ee

eager *adj.*

- VERBS **appear, be, look, seem, sound | become**
- ADV. **only too, really, very** *They were only too eager to help us.* | **increasingly | quite**
- PREP. **for** *We were eager for news.*

eagle *noun*

- EAGLE + VERB **circle, fly, soar | swoop | catch sth, prey on sth | nest | breed**
- EAGLE + NOUN **eye** (*figurative*) *The tiny error didn't escape the eagle eye of her boss.*

ear *noun*

1 part of the body

- ADJ. **left, right | inner, middle, outer | big, large | long** *a rabbit with long floppy ears* | **pointed/pointy | floppy | torn** *Blood from his torn ear was soaking his collar.* | **sharp** *His sharp ears had picked up the uncertainty in her voice.* | **trained** *To the trained ear the calls of these birds sound quite different.* | **listening** *In the silence everyone seemed to be aware of listening ears.* | **receptive, sympathetic** *She did not like the scheme, as she made clear every time she found a receptive ear* (= sb willing to listen). ◇ *The counsellor provided a sympathetic ear for students with problems.*
- VERB + EAR **plug** *He plugged his ears with tissue paper to drown out the music.* | **close, shut, stop** *At first I stopped my ears to what I did not want to hear.* | **strain** *I strained my ears to catch the conversation in the other room.* | **prick up** *The dog pricked up its ears.* | **flatten, lay back, put back** *A horse may show annoyance by putting its ears back.* | **pierce** *I've just had my ears pierced so I'm going to buy some earrings.* | **syringe** *He could hear much better after having his ears syringed.* | **echo in, ring in** *The voices buzzing all around echoed in her ears.* ◇ *He went home with the teacher's warning ringing in his ears.* | **hiss in, whisper (sth) in | reach** *If news of the break-in reaches the boss's ears, we're in trouble.*
- EAR + VERB **hear sth, pick sth up** *When the notes are played so close together the ear hears no space between them.* | **prick (up), twitch** *His ears pricked up when he heard his name mentioned.* | **be alert** *He waited in the darkness, his ears alert for the slightest sound.* | **strain** *She stood outside the room, her ears straining to hear what they were saying.* | **pop** *If you suck a sweet as the plane takes off it stops your ears popping.* | **ring** *The explosion set my ears ringing and even made me jump a bit.*
- EAR + NOUN **canal, drum, lobe | infection | plug, protector | flap, muffs** *She put on her ear muffs and went out into the snow.* | **wax**
- PREP. **in your~** *'Taxi?' said a voice in my ear.*
- PHRASES **beam/grin/smile from ear to ear, can't believe your ears** *She actually apologized. I couldn't believe my ears!* **(drop/have) a word in sb's ear** *Drop a quiet word in her ear about it before it's too late.* **fall on deaf ears** *Their complaints about the poor service fell on deaf ears* (= were ignored). **for sb's ears alone** *I have a few words for your ears alone.* **keep your ears open** *I'll keep my ears open for a second-hand bike for you.* **music to sb's ears** *He arrived home hungry, and the noise of saucepans from the kitchen was music to his ears.* **turn a deaf ear to sth** *The teacher turned a deaf ear to the boy's swearing* (= ignored it). **with half an ear** *He listened to her with only half an ear as he watched TV.*

2 ability to recognize sounds

- ADJ. **fine, good**
- VERB + EAR **have**
- PREP. **by ~** *She usually plays the guitar by ear, rather than reading the music.* | **~ for** *He has a good ear for accents and can usually tell where a speaker comes from.*

earl *noun*

⇨ Note at PEER

early *adj.*

- VERBS **be, feel, seem**
- ADV. **extremely, really, very | a bit, fairly, a little, quite, rather, relatively** *I'm sorry I'm a bit early.* | **surprisingly** *These discoveries were made at a surprisingly early date.*
- PREP. **for** *It's a little early for lunch.* **in** *He discovered these pleasures early in life.*

earn *verb*

- ADV. **really** *'I feel I've really earned this,' she said, taking up her mug of tea.* | **deservedly, richly, rightly** *He deservedly earned the admiration of his colleagues.*
- VERB + EARN **have to, need to** *First you have to earn their respect.* | **seek to, try to**

earnings *noun*

- ADJ. **high | low, meagre | average | annual, hourly, weekly | gross, pre-tax, taxable | pensionable | after-tax, net** *Her net earnings last year were £15 000.*
- QUANT. **level** *Levels of earnings are still rising.*
- VERB + EARNINGS **have** *People with a university education tend to have higher earnings than those with a basic education.* | **calculate | declare** *You must declare all earnings to the tax office.* | **tax**
- PREP. **~ from** *Germany's earnings from exports rose by 2%.* **~ of** *annual earnings of £20 000*
- PHRASES **earnings-related** *an earnings-related pension scheme* **growth in earnings** *the growth in average earnings over the last ten years* **loss of earnings** *She is also claiming compensation for loss of earnings.*
⇨ Note at PER CENT (for more verbs)
⇨ Special page at BUSINESS

earphones *noun*

- ADJ. **radio**
- QUANT. **pair, set**
- VERB + EARPHONES **have on, wear | put on | remove, take off**
- PREP. **through ~** *She was listening to a personal stereo through earphones.*

earring *noun*

- ADJ. **dangling, dangly | drop, hoop/hooped, stud**
- QUANT. **pair** *She wore a pair of dangly earrings.*
- VERB + EARRING **have on, wear | clip on, put in/on | take off**

earth *noun*

1 the world

- VERB + EARTH **orbit** *satellites orbiting the earth*
- EARTH + VERB **orbit sth, revolve, rotate** *The earth orbits the sun.* ◇ *The earth revolves on its axis.*

• EARTH + NOUN **tremor** *Furniture fell over as the room was shaken by an earth tremor.* | **sciences**
• PREP. **above the ~** *We are flying at 30 000 feet above the earth.* **around/round the ~** *the moon's orbit around the earth* **on (the) ~** *The island was there before there was life on earth.* **to ~** *The astronauts were able to send the information back to earth.*
• PHRASES **the centre/surface of the earth, the earth's core/crust/mantle/surface, (the) planet earth**

2 soil

• ADJ. **bare** *The fields had been ploughed, and there was nothing but bare earth to be seen.* | **fertile** | **barren, infertile** | **soft** | **solid** | **damp, moist, wet** | **fresh, freshly-dug** | **loose** *I filled the pot with a handful of loose earth.* | **baked** *The sun beat down on the baked earth.* | **scorched** *The wreckage of the plane was scattered across the scorched earth.* | **chalky, sandy**
• QUANT. **clod, clump, lump** *My boots were caked in big clods of wet earth.*
• EARTH + NOUN **bank, mound** *I scrambled to the top of the steep earth bank.*
• PREP. **in the ~** *The plants must have their roots in the earth.* **under the ~** *in mines deep under the earth*

earthquake *noun*

• ADJ. **big, great, huge, major, massive, severe** | **minor, small**
• EARTHQUAKE + VERB **happen, hit sth, occur, strike (sth)** *The earthquake hit the city at two in the morning.* | **shake sth** *The earthquake shook buildings throughout the business district.* | **destroy sth, devastate sth, kill sb, leave sb homeless** | **measure sth** *an earthquake measuring 5.8 on the Richter scale*
• EARTHQUAKE + NOUN **zone**
• PREP. **in a/the ~** *The block of flats was destroyed in an earthquake.*
• PHRASES **the epicentre of an earthquake, the magnitude of an earthquake**

ease *noun*

• ADJ. **alarming, astonishing, consummate, great, remarkable** *I obtained the drugs with alarming ease.* | **comparative, relative** | **apparent** *I was surprised at the apparent ease with which he had got into the building.* | **contemptuous** *She returned her opponent's serve with contemptuous ease.* | **practised**
• PREP. **for ~ in** *The back of the garment is split for ease in walking.* **for ~ of** *The whole machine is designed for ease of use.* **with ~** *They passed the exam with ease.* | **~ of** *The car brings ease of access to the countryside.*

ease *verb*

1 make sth less painful/serious/difficult

• ADV. **considerably, greatly** *The situation would be considerably eased if more money were made available.* | **slightly, somewhat** | **gradually, slowly** | **away** *The pain in my leg gradually eased away.*
• VERB + EASE **help (to)** *The new road should help ease traffic problems.* | **begin to** *Tensions between the two countries are beginning to ease.* | **try to**

2 move carefully

• ADV. **carefully, gently** | **away, back, down, forward, etc.** *Jean eased back on the pillows and relaxed.*
• PREP. **away from, into** *He eased himself into the driving seat.* **out of** *She carefully eased the car out of the garage*

east *noun, adj.*

⇨ Note at DIRECTION

Easter *noun*

• ADJ. **early, late** *Easter is early this year.*

• VERB + EASTER **have, spend** *Have a good Easter.* ◇ *I prefer to spend Easter at home.* | **celebrate**
• EASTER + NOUN **egg** | **break, holiday/holidays, vacation** | **Day, weekend, Monday, Saturday, Sunday, week** | **festival** | **celebrations**
• PREP. **at ~** *Our next holiday is at Easter.* **for ~** *We usually go away for Easter.* **over ~** *The library is closed over Easter.*
• PHRASES **Happy Easter!, wish sb a happy Easter**

easy *adj.*

• VERBS **be, look, seem, sound** | **become, get** *Life is getting easier for us.* | **remain** | **make sth** *These changes should make your job easier.* | **find sth** *I found the exam quite easy.*
• ADV. **extremely, really, very** | **enough, fairly, quite, rather, relatively** *It is easy enough to see how it happened.* | **incredibly, ridiculously, surprisingly** *The written test was ridiculously easy.*
• PREP. **for** *Writing is not easy for her.*
• PHRASES **all too easy** *It was all too easy to forget why we had been sent there.* **the easiest thing in the world** *It is the easiest thing in the world to blame your parents.* **be no easy task** *Contacting everyone was no easy task.* **quick and easy** *a book designed for quick and easy reference*

eat *verb*

• ADV. **well** *We ate very well most of the time (= had lots of nice food).* | **healthily, properly, sensibly** *trying to eat more healthily* ◇ *He had not eaten properly for days.* ◇ *She doesn't eat sensibly (= doesn't eat food that is good for her).* | **hungrily** | **sparingly** *Barton did not feel very hungry and ate sparingly.* | **up** *Come on, eat up your lunch.*
• VERB + EAT **get yourself sth to, find sth to, have sth to** *Have you got anything to eat?* | **have enough to** | **try and/to** *Try and eat something. It will do you good.*
• PHRASES **eat and drink** *Go and get yourself something to eat and drink.* **eat like a horse** (= eat a lot) *She's very thin but she eats like a horse!*

eater *noun*

• ADJ. **meat** | **big, good, great, hearty** *All my children are big eaters.* | **fussy, picky** *He eats anything—he's not a fussy eater.* | **healthy** | **compulsive** | **messy**

ebb *noun*

• ADJ. **strong**
• EBB + NOUN **tide** *They left the harbour on the ebb tide.*
• PREP. **against an/the ~** *It was difficult sailing upstream against a strong ebb.* **on an/the ~** *By this time, the tide was on the ebb.* ◇ *We floated away from the beach on the ebb.* **with an/the ~** *They went out to sea with the ebb.*
• PHRASES **the ebb and flow of the tide**

ebb *verb*

• ADV. **away** *He knew that his life was ebbing away.*
• VERB + EBB **begin to** *Her strength began to ebb.* | **seem to**

eccentric *adj.*

• VERBS **be, look, seem** | **become, get** *The old lady was getting very eccentric.* | **consider sb, find sb, regard sb as** *We were definitely regarded as eccentric.*
• ADV. **extremely, highly, very, wildly** | **a bit, faintly, fairly, a little, rather, slightly, somewhat** | **endearingly, engagingly** *his engagingly eccentric brother*

echo *noun*

• ADJ. **distant, faint** | **clear, distinct, strong** *(often figurative)* *There are distinct echoes of Elvis Presley in his*

vocal style. | **hollow** | **returning** *The bat compares the sound of its cry with the sound of the returning echo.*
● VERB + ECHO **hear, listen for/to** *We could just hear a faint echo.* | **produce, send back, send out** *Their footsteps on the bare boards sent out hollow echoes.* | **find** *(figurative) The political upheavals find an echo in the art of the time.*
● ECHO + VERB **sound** *A faint echo sounded in the cave.* | **die (away)** *The echo slowly died away.* | **come back, return** *An echo came back from the walls of the building.*
● PREP. **~from** *the echo from a brick wall*

echo *verb*

1 come back as an echo
● ADV. **faintly | loudly | eerily, strangely, weirdly | flatly, hollowly** *The sound echoed hollowly through the tall empty house.* | **still | back** *Their voices echoed back across the water.*
● VERB + ECHO **seem to**
● PREP. **across** *The protest seemed to echo across the room.* **around/round** *His voice echoed around the room.* **down** *Her footsteps echoed down the corridor.* **in** *Her screams still echoed in his ears.* **off** *The call echoed off the walls of the cave.* **through** *Laughter echoed through the house.* **with** *The great hall echoed with laughter.*

2 repeat/agree with sb/sth
● ADV. **exactly | faithfully, wholeheartedly | widely** *an opinion that is widely echoed in the tabloid press* | **clearly | merely, only, simply** *In his statement, the minister merely echoed the views of the chief police officer.* | **disbelievingly, incredulously** *'He's gone!' Viv echoed incredulously.*
● VERB + ECHO **seem to** *They had ideas which seem to echo our own.*

eclipse *noun*

● ADJ. **lunar, solar | partial, total** *a total lunar eclipse*
● PHRASES **an eclipse of the moon/sun**

ecology *noun*

● ADJ. **fragile | animal, human, marine, plant**
● VERB + ECOLOGY **damage, disrupt**
● ECOLOGY + NOUN **movement**

economical *adj.*

● VERBS **be, seem** *Solid fuel would be more economical.*
● ADV. **extremely, highly, remarkably, very** *This new oven is highly economical.* | **fairly, quite**
● PREP. **in** *This arrangement is more economical in its use of staff.* **of** *more economical of time and resources* **with** *This arrangement is more economical with space.*

economics *noun*

● ADJ. **applied, theoretical | classical, free-market, Keynesian, liberal, market, neo-classical, supply-side | business, development, environmental, health, industrial, welfare**
● PHRASES **a school of economics**
⇨ Note at SUBJECT (for verbs and nouns)

economist *noun*

● ADJ. **chief, leading, senior | distinguished, respected | academic, government, professional | classical, free-market, Keynesian, liberal, neo-classical | agricultural, business, development, environmental, health, political**
⇨ Note at JOB

economy *noun*

1 operation of a country's money supply
● ADJ. **booming, buoyant, dynamic, healthy, sound, stable, strong | ailing, depressed, flagging, fragile, stagnant, weak** *The government devalued the currency to try to revive the flagging economy.* | **advanced, developed, modern | agrarian, agricultural, capitalist, industrial, liberal, market, mixed, monetary, planned, rural, service-based, socialist** *a modern industrial economy* | **domestic, global, internal, international, local, national, world** *the increasingly competitive global economy* | **black, informal, underground** *The black economy booms when there is high unemployment.*
● VERB + ECONOMY **build, rebuild** *Each party has its own strategy for building a strong economy.* | **control, handle, manage, manipulate, operate, regulate, run** *The government was accused of failing to run the economy competently.* | **boost, develop, expand, help, improve, kick-start, reinvigorate, rescue, revive, stabilize, stimulate, strengthen | liberalize | damage, harm, weaken, wreck**
● ECONOMY + VERB **develop, expand, flourish, grow | be in/go into recession, collapse, contract, fail, slow, stagnate | pick up, recover, stabilize**
● PHRASES **an area/a sector of the economy** *Transport workers are employed in all sectors of the economy.* **the backbone/mainstay of the economy** *Agriculture was the backbone of the economy.* **growth in/of the economy** *A small manufacturing sector inhibits growth in the economy.* **control/handling/management of the economy** *37% approved the president's handling of the economy.* **the size of the economy, the state of the economy** *The government has been criticized over the state of the economy.*
⇨ Special page at BUSINESS

2 careful use of money/time/resources
● ADJ. **important, major, significant | false** *Buying cheap shoes is a false economy.*
● VERB + ECONOMY **achieve, make** *We could achieve major economies in time with this new machinery.*
● ECONOMY + NOUN **drive** *Savings are being planned as part of a huge economy drive.*
● PREP. **~in** *possible economies in telephone costs*
● PHRASES **economy of effort/movement** *It was impressive to see her economy of movement as she worked the machine.* **economy of scale** *Large firms can benefit from economies of scale.*

ecstasy *noun*

1 feeling
● ADJ. **pure, sheer | religious, sexual**
● PREP. **in ~** | **~ at** *Kate closed her eyes in ecstasy at the thought of a cold drink.* **~ over** *I was in sheer ecstasy over the prospect of meeting my idol.*

2 Ecstasy drug
● ECSTASY + NOUN **tablet**
⇨ Note at DRUG (for more verbs and nouns)

ecstatic *adj.*

● VERBS **appear, be, feel, look | become**
● ADV. **absolutely | not exactly**
● PREP. **about** *Annie was ecstatic about the idea.* **at** *Martin was not exactly ecstatic at the news.*

edge *noun*

1 place where sth ends
● ADJ. **top** *the top edge of the picture frame* | **bottom, lower | inner, inside | outer, outside | front | northern, southern, etc.** | **very** *Erosion has left the house perched on the very edge of the cliff.* | **cliff, water's** *A row of boats was beached at the water's edge.*
● VERB + EDGE **reach** *We had reached the edge of the*

map and didn't know which way to go. | **skirt** *The road skirts the western edge of the forest.*
• PREP. **along the ~, around/round the ~** *Smoke was making its way around the edges of the door.* **at the ~** *Soon we were at the edge of the woods.* **on the ~** *She sat on the edge of her bed.* **over the ~** *The car rolled over the edge of the cliff.*
• PHRASES **right on the edge** *They live right on the edge of town.*
2 sharp side of sth
• ADJ. **sharp | cutting | serrated** *a knife with a serrated edge* | **jagged, ragged, rough | smooth | blunt**
• VERB + EDGE **sharpen**
3 advantage
• ADJ. **competitive | slight | decided**
• VERB + EDGE **give sb/sth | gain, have** *to gain a competitive edge over rival suppliers*
• PREP. **~ over** *The intensive training she had done gave her the edge over the other runners.*

edge *verb*

• ADV. **carefully, cautiously, nervously | quietly | slowly**
• PREP. **along** *He edged carefully along the narrow ledge.* **towards** *We slowly edged our way towards the exit.*
• PHRASES **edge your way**

edgy *adj.*

• VERBS **appear, be, feel, seem, sound | become, get** *He began to get very edgy.* | **make sb** *She made Jeff edgy with her constant demands.*
• ADV. **all, very** *She was all edgy that evening.* | **a bit, rather** *She had been a bit edgy all day.*
• PREP. **about** *Hester seemed edgy about something.* **with** *He was rather edgy with her.*

edition *noun*

• ADJ. **first** *a bookshop that specializes in rare first editions* | **limited, special** *The book appeared in a limited edition of 3 000.* | **cheap | hardback, leather-bound, paperback | pocket | abridged** *They have brought out an abridged edition of the encyclopedia.* | **illustrated | revised | critical** *a critical edition of Shakespeare's plays* | **facsimile** *a facsimile edition of Dr Johnson's Dictionary of 1755* | **electronic | morning, evening** *The story made it into the evening edition of the newspaper.*
• VERB + EDITION **bring out, issue, produce, publish**
• EDITION + VERB **appear, be out, come out** *The first edition of the newspaper appeared in 1859.*
• PREP. **in a … ~** *The encyclopedia will shortly be out in a revised edition.* | **~ of** *the November edition of 'Vogue'*

editor *noun*

1 prepares a book, television or radio programme
• ADJ. **commissioning | assistant, senior | copy | freelance | film, programme | art, cookery, fiction, music, picture**
2 in charge of a newspaper/part of a newspaper
• ADJ. **chief, executive, managing | deputy | assistant, associate | contributing | joint | magazine, newspaper, tabloid | features, news, picture | specialist | City, economics, fashion, financial, foreign, industrial, literary, political, sports, travel** *On page 12, our City editor comments on the takeover bid.*
• PHRASES **a letter to the editor**
⇨ Note at JOB

editorial *noun*

• ADJ. **newspaper | lengthy | hard-hitting**
• VERB + EDITORIAL **write | carry, publish, run** *The*

paper only occasionally carries editorials.* ◇ *The newspaper ran a hard-hitting editorial criticizing the government's economic policies.*
• PREP. **in an/the ~** *He declared his support for the minister in an editorial.* | **~ on** *an editorial on the problem of crime*

educated *adj.*

• VERBS **be, seem, sound**
• ADV. **highly, impeccably, well** *She seemed intelligent and well educated.* | **badly, ill, poorly | reasonably, sufficiently | properly, suitably | fully | broadly** *the need for a broadly educated workforce* | **formally, traditionally** *Less formally educated people can acquire professional competence.* | **privately | expensively**

education *noun*

• ADJ. **decent, excellent, first-class, good | poor | compulsory | formal** *Although he had had little formal education, he could read and write well.* | **adult, further, higher, pre-school, primary, secondary** *a college of further education* | **university | professional, vocational | all-round | health, religious, sex | full-time, part-time | public, state | private** *parents who choose private education for their children*
• VERB + EDUCATION **have, receive** *He was at a disadvantage because of the poor education he had received.* | **give sb, provide (sb with)** *The school provides an excellent all-round education.* | **enter** *students entering higher education* | **continue, extend** *She went to college to continue her education.* | **leave** *young people who are just leaving full-time education* | **complete, finish** *He went to America to complete his education.*
• EDUCATION + NOUN **authority, committee, department, ministry, sector, service, system** *funds provided by the local education authority* | **minister, officer, official | policy | reform | campaign, initiative, programme, project, scheme** *The council has launched a new health education campaign.* | **facilities, materials, resources | class, course** *adult education courses* | **centre, college, establishment, institution**
• PREP. **in ~** *students in full-time education* **through ~** *We acquire much of our world knowledge through education.* | **~ about** *education about danger on the roads*

eerie *adj.*

• VERBS **be, feel, look, sound**
• ADV. **distinctly, downright** *This place has a distinctly eerie atmosphere.* | **almost** *a silence so long that it was almost eerie* | **rather, slightly**

effect *noun*

1 change that is caused by sth
• ADJ. **decisive, dramatic, far-reaching, important, marked, powerful, profound, significant, strong | marginal, minimal, modest, negligible | chief, main, major, principal | full** *The full effects of the new tax have not yet been felt.* | **apparent, appreciable, detectable, discernible, measurable, noticeable, visible | likely, possible, potential, predictable, probable | subtle | disproportionate | residual | adverse, catastrophic, crippling, damaging, debilitating, deleterious, destructive, detrimental, devastating, disastrous, harmful, ill, negative, serious, traumatic, undesirable, unfortunate** *the crippling effect of sanctions on the economy* ◇ *He didn't seem to have suffered any ill effects from his fall.* | **beneficial, positive, salutary | the desired** *We had problems with mosquitoes, but this spray had the desired effect.* | **magical, remarkable** *Giving up smoking had a magical effect on his stamina.* | **immediate | direct, indirect | short-term | lasting, long-term, permanent | domino, knock-on, ripple, spin-off** *Any delay in delivery of materials will*

have a knock-on effect throughout the production process. (see also **side effect**) | **practical** | **aggregate**, **combined**, **cumulative**, **net**, **overall** | **qualitative**, **quantitative** | **cohesive** | **divisive** | **deterrent**, **disincentive** *The deterrent effect of the death penalty has long been questioned.* ◇ *Heavy taxation has a disincentive effect.* | **calming**, **hypnotic**, **soothing**, **soporific** | **curative**, **restorative**, **therapeutic** | **placebo** | **inflationary** | **corrosive** | **greenhouse** *policies to reduce emissions of gases which cause the greenhouse effect*

• VERB + EFFECT **bring about**, **exert**, **have**, **produce** *The drug exerts a powerful effect on the brain.* | **take** *The medicine started to take effect after a few minutes.* | **feel**, **experience**, **suffer** (**from**) *Women feel the effects of alcohol more quickly than men.* | **recover** **from** | **observe** | **show** | **assess**, **determine**, **estimate**, **examine**, **measure**, **study** | **ameliorate**, **cushion**, **lessen**, **minimize**, **mitigate**, **reduce**, **soften** *to minimize the effects of economic change* | **cancel out** | **counter**, **counteract**, **offset** | **compound**, **magnify**, **maximize** | **avoid** | **aim at** *That is precisely the effect I was aiming at.* | **be worried about**, **fear** | **underestimate** | **ignore**

• EFFECT + VERB **spread** | **last** | **wear off** *How soon will the effects of the drug wear off?*

• PREP. **in ~** *The border closure meant, in effect, that no trade took place between the countries.* **to this/that~** *They told us to go away, or words to that effect.* **with ... ~** *The plague struck London again with devastating effect.* | **~on/upon** *The dry weather had an adverse effect on the potato crops.*

• PHRASES **cause and effect** *key historical concepts such as cause and effect* **to little/no effect** *The air-conditioning came on, to little effect.*

2 use of an official rule/plan, etc.
• ADJ. **immediate**
• VERB + EFFECT **come into** *The new regulations come into effect next month.* | **bring sth into**, **put sth into** *The recommendations will soon be put into effect.*
• PREP. **in ~** *Some laws from the eighteenth century are still in effect.* **with ~** *The bank has cut interest rates with immediate effect.*

3 impression that a speaker/book/film, etc. gives
• ADJ. **dramatic**, **startling**, **striking**, **stunning** | **maximum**, **optimum** | **the desired** *I found that by adding white I could achieve the desired effect.* | **overall** *The overall effect of the painting is overwhelming.*
• VERB + EFFECT **give** (**sth**), **have** *The stage lighting gives the effect of a moonlit scene.* | **achieve**, **create** | **enhance**, **heighten** *The dramatic effect was heightened by her black dress and dead white face.* | **mar**, **spoil**
• PREP. **for ... ~** *'You know why I'm here?' Doug paused for maximum effect.* **to ... ~** *She uses animal sounds to startling effect in her music.*

4 techniques used when making sth
• ADJ. **special** | **cinematic** | **audio**, **sound** | **optical**, **visual** | **lighting** | **elaborate** | **digital**

effective *adj.*

1 producing the result you want
• VERBS **be**, **look**, **prove**, **seem** | **make sth** | **find sth** *We find advertising on the radio very effective.*
• ADV. **brilliantly**, **especially**, **extremely**, **highly**, **particularly**, **really**, **remarkably**, **very** *a highly effective technique* | **completely**, **fully**, **perfectly** | **increasingly** | **fairly**, **moderately**, **partially**, **pretty**, **quite**, **rather**, **reasonably** | **enough** *This method is effective enough with greenfly.* | **not sufficiently** | **immediately** | **potentially** | **devastatingly**, **powerfully**, **surprisingly** *Sneezes are devastatingly effective at spreading infection.* | **politically** *What makes a TV programme politically effective?*
• PREP. **at** *effective at keeping out the wind* **in** *effective in helping people to stop smoking*

2 of laws/rules
• VERBS **be** | **become** | **remain**
• ADV. **fully** | **partially** | **directly**, **immediately** *directly effective treaty provisions* | **legally**

effectiveness *noun*

• ADJ. **overall** | **limited** | **operational**, **organizational**, **practical** | **educational**, **military**, **political** | **cost** *This hard-wearing material combines cost effectiveness with quality.*
• VERB + EFFECTIVENESS **assess**, **check**, **determine**, **evaluate**, **judge**, **measure**, **monitor**, **test** | **demonstrate** *The exam results demonstrated the effectiveness of personal tuition.* | **enhance**, **improve**, **increase**, **maximize** | **destroy**, **impair**, **limit**, **reduce** | **lose** *The drugs work well at first but gradually lose their effectiveness.*
• PREP. **~ as** *They're doing tests to evaluate the effectiveness of this herb as an antiseptic.* **~ in** *the effectiveness of penicillin in controlling bacterial infection*

efficiency *noun*

• ADJ. **ruthless** | **great**, **high** *attempts to achieve greater efficiency in the production process* | **maximum**, **optimum** | **low** | **cost** | **energy**, **fuel** | **mental**, **physical** | **administrative**, **business**, **economic**, **industrial** | **management**, **operational**, **organizational**, **production**, **productive**, **technical**
• VERB + EFFICIENCY **achieve** | **boost**, **enhance**, **improve**, **increase**, **maximize**, **promote** | **decrease**, **impair**, **reduce**
• EFFICIENCY + NOUN **drive**, **measures** *New timekeeping procedures had been introduced as part of an efficiency drive.* | **gains**, **improvements**, **savings** *the efficiency gains resulting from improved technology*
• PREP. **with ~** *The uprising was put down with ruthless efficiency.* | **~ in** *greater efficiency in energy use*

efficient *adj.*

• VERBS **appear**, **be**, **look**, **seem**, **sound** | **become** | **make sth**
• ADV. **extremely**, **highly**, **really**, **remarkably**, **very** | **fully**, **perfectly** *The procedure is not fully efficient: improvements could be made.* ◇ *We already have a perfectly efficient system—why change it?* | **increasingly** | **fairly**, **pretty**, **quite**, **reasonably**, **relatively** | **briskly**, **quietly** *The receptionist was briskly efficient.* ◇ *A quietly efficient manservant brought them coffee and brandy.* | **formidably**, **incredibly**, **superbly**, **supremely** *His secretary was formidably efficient: her minutes were works of art.* | **economically**, **mechanically**, **technically**
• PREP. **at** *Their equipment was not as efficient at finding gold as today's machinery.* **in** *The heating system is very efficient in its use of of fuel.*

effort *noun*

1 physical/mental energy needed to do sth
• ADJ. **considerable** | **hard** *It took a whole day of hard effort to knock down the wall.* | **constant**, **sustained** | **extra** | **physical** | **intellectual**, **mental**
• QUANT. **amount** *the amount of effort required*
• VERB + EFFORT **demand**, **need**, **require**, **take** *It takes constant effort to become fluent in a language.* | **devote**, **expend**, **put in** *All the team members have put in a great deal of effort.* | **spare no** *No effort has been spared to make this hotel a welcoming, comfortable place.* | **be** (**well**) **worth** *The walk is difficult but well worth the effort.*
• EFFORT + VERB **go into** *A lot of effort went into making the costumes.*
• PREP. **with/without~** *This can be done quickly and with very little effort.*
• PHRASES **a great deal of effort**

2 attempt to do sth
- ADJ. **all-out, big, brave, determined, enormous, great, herculean, heroic, huge, major, remarkable, special, strenuous, superhuman, tremendous, valiant** *I can see you have made a big effort to clean up.* | **desperate, frantic** *their frantic efforts to put out the fire* | **final, last, last-ditch** *The UN General Secretary flew in in a last-ditch effort to save the talks.* | **genuine, positive, real, serious** | **feeble** *She made a feeble effort to smile, then started crying again.* | **sporadic** *I make sporadic efforts to sort out my files.* | **successful** | **fruitless, futile, unsuccessful** | **collaborative, collective, concerted, cooperative, joint, team** *Students, teachers and families got together in a team effort to decorate the school.* | **conscious, deliberate** *I have to make a conscious effort to be polite so early in the morning.* | **voluntary** *The museum relies on the voluntary efforts of enthusiasts.* | **fund-raising**
- VERB + EFFORT **make** | **increase, intensify, redouble, renew, step up** *The police have renewed their efforts to find the murderer.* | **channel, concentrate, focus** *The police channelled their efforts into searching around the river.* | **fail in** *He failed in his efforts to give up smoking.* | **resist** *The wound resisted all my efforts to stop it bleeding.* | **abandon** | **be rewarded for, reward** *Her efforts were rewarded when she won an Oscar.* | **applaud** *The gallery owner applauded the efforts of firefighters to save the exhibits.*
- EFFORT + VERB **come to nothing, fail**
- PREP. **in an/your~** *The club has changed the rules in an effort to make them fairer.* **through sb's~** *Through their efforts, enough money was raised to buy the equipment.*
- PHRASES **your best efforts** *Despite our best efforts, we didn't manage to win the match.* **a reward for your efforts** *Second prize was a fair reward for his efforts.* **make every effort** *We are making every effort to obtain the release of the hostages.*

effortless *adj.*

- VERBS **appear, be, look, seem** *Burton made the jump look effortless.*
- ADV. **apparently, seemingly** *her apparently effortless performance*

egg *noun*

1 of birds/as food
- ADJ. **fresh** | **addled, bad, rotten** | **free-range, organic** | **chicken, duck, hen's, quail's, etc.** | **chocolate, Easter** | **boiled, fried, hard-boiled, poached, scrambled, soft-boiled** | **Scotch**
- QUANT. **clutch** *She lays a clutch of four eggs on average.* | **box**
- VERB + EGG **lay,** **produce** | **hatch** | **incubate** | **emerge from, hatch from** | **boil, cook, fry, poach, scramble** | **break, crack** *Crack two eggs into the mixture.* | **separate** *Separate the eggs, putting the whites to one side.* | **beat, whisk** | **brush sth with, glaze sth with** *Brush the pastry with a little beaten egg.*
- EGG + VERB **hatch** | **break, crack**
- EGG + NOUN **shell** (also **eggshell**) | **white, yolk** | **box** | **mayonnaise, noodles, pasta, sandwich**
- PHRASES **the white/yolk of an egg**
⇨ Special page at FOOD

2 cell from which a new young creature is formed
- ADJ. **fertilized** | **unfertilized**
- VERB + EGG **fertilize** *Only one sperm fertilizes an egg.*
- EGG + NOUN **donor**
- PHRASES **the nucleus of an egg**

ego *noun*

- ADJ. **big, enormous, huge, inflated, massive, strong** *a conceited man with a very big ego* | **fragile, weak**
- VERB + EGO **bolster, boost, feed, flatter, massage** *She likes to mix with people who flatter her ego.* | **bruise, damage, deflate, dent, wound** *He was lucky to escape with just a bruised ego when he fell off his bike.*
- PHRASES **a blow to your ego** *It was a huge blow to his ego to find out he was so unpopular.* **a boost to your ego**

eject *verb*

1 push/send sth out
- ADV. **forcibly** | **summarily** *They were summarily ejected by the security guard.*
- PREP. **from** *He was forcibly ejected from the restaurant.*

2 make an emergency exit
- ADV. **safely**
- PREP. **from** *All the crew members ejected safely from the plane.*

elaborate *verb*

- ADV. **further** *This point will be elaborated further in the next chapter.* | **at length**
- VERB + ELABORATE **attempt to, try to** | **refuse to**
- PREP. **on/upon** *They refused to elaborate on the reasons for their decision.*

elaborate *adj.*

- VERBS **be, look, seem, sound** *The plans looked very elaborate.* | **become**
- ADV. **exceptionally, extremely, highly, very** *highly elaborate carvings* | **increasingly** | **fairly, quite, rather**

elastic *noun*

- ADJ. **loose, tight** *an old skirt with loose elastic*
- QUANT. **length, piece** *The trousers are held up by a length of elastic around the waist.*
- ELASTIC + VERB **break, go, snap** *The elastic in these socks has gone.*

elated *adj.*

- VERBS **be, feel, look, seem, sound**
- ADV. **very** | **strangely**
- PREP. **at** *I felt strangely elated at the news.* **by** *elated by our victory* **with** *elated with his success*

elation *noun*

- ADJ. **great, sheer** | **unbelievable** | **mild** | **curious**
- VERB + ELATION **experience, feel** | **show**
- PREP. **~ at** *She showed her elation at having finally achieved her ambition.*
- PHRASES **a feeling/mood/sense/surge of elation** *I felt a strange sense of elation.* **tears of elation**

elbow *noun*

- ADJ. **dislocated, fractured**
- VERB + ELBOW **lean, place, rest** *He rested one elbow on the wall as he spoke.* | **lean on, prop/raise yourself up on** *She opened her eyes and propped herself up on one elbow to look at him.* | **catch, grasp, take** *He caught her elbow to steady her.* | **thrust** *She thrust her elbow into her attacker's face.* | **bang** *I banged my elbow on the table as I got up.* | **dislocate, fracture, injure**
- ELBOW + NOUN **joint** | **injury** | **room** *The tiny toilet compartment gives you hardly any elbow room.*
- PREP. **above the~, at your~** *A voice at my elbow said, 'Would Sir care to be seated?'* **below the~** *The whole of his arm below the elbow was badly burnt.* **beneath/under your~** *She slid a hand under his elbow to guide him into the shop.* **by the~** *He took his guest by the elbow and steered him in the direction of the bar.* **on one~** *He raised himself on one elbow and looked at the bedside clock.*
- PHRASES **be up to your elbows in sth** *He was up to his elbows in hot water, doing the washing-up.* **the crook of**

your elbow *She was cradling a small parcel in the crook of her elbow.* **dig your elbow into sb's ribs** *She dug her elbow into Jim's ribs to remind him not to give the secret away.*

elect *verb*

- ADV. **annually** *Members of the council are elected annually.* | **locally, nationally** | **democratically, freely, popularly** | **unanimously** | **directly, indirectly** *It was decided that the president should be elected directly in free elections.* | **duly, formally** | **lawfully, legally, legitimately**
- PREP. **to** *She has been elected to Parliament.*
- PHRASES **be/get elected** *What changes will he make if he gets elected?* **be declared elected** *Any candidate with more than half the votes shall be declared elected.* **be elected unopposed** *Five were successful, three being elected unopposed.* **newly elected** *the newly elected chairman*

election *noun*

- ADJ. **fair, free** | **democratic, multi-party** | **rigged** | **direct, indirect** | **fresh, new** | **early** *The prime minister may decide to call an early election.* | **primary, run-off** | **federal, local, municipal, national, regional, state** | **congressional, council, general, gubernatorial, leadership, legislative, local government, mayoral, parliamentary, party, presidential, Senate**
- VERB + ELECTION **have, hold** | **call** | **contest, fight** | **stand for** | **lose, win** | **rig**
- ELECTION + VERB **take place** | **be due, be scheduled for** *Elections are scheduled for November.*
- ELECTION + NOUN **campaign** | **manifesto, pledge, promise** | **broadcast** | **candidate** | **defeat, victory, result** | **day, night, year** | **fraud**
- PREP. **at/in a/the~** *in the 2001 general election* **by~** *Membership of the committee is by election.* | **~to** *her election to the Senate*
- PHRASES **the outcome of an election, the run-up to an election** *opinion poll results in the run-up to elections*

elector *noun*

- ADJ. **eligible** | **registered**
- ELECTOR + VERB **choose sb, vote (for sb)** *Not all the registered electors actually voted.*
- PHRASES **the register of electors** *If your name is not on the register of electors, you will not be able to vote.*

electorate *noun*

- ADJ. **registered** | **total** | **local, national** | **mass** *The rise of a mass electorate forced politicians to try and broaden their appeal.* | **middle-class, working-class, etc.** | **American, British, etc.**
- ELECTORATE + VERB **choose sb, elect sb, go to the polls, vote** *the representative chosen by the electorate*
- PHRASES **the electorate as a whole/the electorate at large** *the need to appeal to the electorate at large*

electrician *noun*

- ADJ. **apprentice, qualified**
- VERB + ELECTRICIAN **call in** *We need to call in an electrician to sort out the wiring.*
- ELECTRICIAN + VERB **rewire sth, wire sth** *You'll need a qualified electrician to rewire your house.*
- ⇨ Note at JOB

electricity *noun*

- ADJ. **high-voltage, low-voltage** | **mains** | **static** | **off-peak** *We run the washing machine at night because off-peak electricity is much cheaper.*
- VERB + ELECTRICITY **generate, produce** | **provide, supply** *The hydroelectric plant provides electricity for half the island's population.* | **conduct** *Metals conduct electri-*

city well. | **be powered by, use** | **cut off, disconnect** *Her electricity was cut off when she didn't pay her bill.* | **save** *I switched the light off to save electricity.*
- ELECTRICITY + VERB **flow** *Electricity flows through the wires in the circuit.*
- ELECTRICITY + NOUN **bill** *Insulating your house could cut your electricity bill by half.* | **charges, costs, prices** *a 10% drop in electricity prices* | **meter** | **board, company, industry** | **supply** | **grid** *The village will soon be connected to the national electricity grid.* | **consumption, demand** | **generator** | **pylon** | **cable, line, wire**

electric shock *noun*

- ADJ. **massive, severe, strong** | **mild**
- VERB + ELECTRIC SHOCK **get, receive** | **give sb**
- ELECTRIC SHOCK + NOUN **therapy, treatment**

electronics *noun*

- ADJ. **high-tech, state-of-the-art** | **consumer, defence, medical**
- VERB + ELECTRONICS **work in** *About 45 000 people worked in electronics in Scotland.*
- ELECTRONICS + NOUN **company, firm, giant, group** *Their firm merged with a Japanese electronics giant.* | **industry, manufacturer** | **market, sector** | **product** | **engineer, specialist**
- ⇨ Note at SUBJECT (for more verbs and nouns)

elegance *noun*

- ADJ. **great** | **classical** | **sartorial** *John has never been known for his sartorial elegance.*
- QUANT. **touch** *The ornamental ironwork lends a touch of elegance to the house.*
- VERB + ELEGANCE **display, have** *The building has great elegance and charm.* | **lack** | **add, give sth, lend sth** *The pillars give a classical elegance to the room.*

elegant *adj.*

- VERBS **be, feel, look**
- ADV. **extremely, very** | **quite, rather** | **beautifully** *the beautifully elegant spire of the church* | **casually, quietly** *the quietly elegant wives of the directors* | **impossibly, supremely** *the foyer of an impossibly elegant Paris hotel*

element *noun*

1 one part of sth
- ADJ. **basic, critical, crucial, decisive, essential, fundamental, important, key, main, major, necessary, principal, significant, vital** | **dominant** *The promise of tax cuts became the dominant element in the campaign.* | **considerable, large** *There is a considerable element of danger in her job.* | **competitive** *There is too much of a competitive element in the sales department.* | **racial, sexual** *Police say there may have been a racial element to the attacks.*
- VERB + ELEMENT **be, constitute, form** | **contain, have, include, involve** *These rumours do contain an element of truth.* | **introduce**
- PREP. **~in** *This constitutes one of the key elements in this reform programme.* **~of** *Practical work will form a major element of the syllabus.* ◇ *There may have been an element of jealousy in her response.*

2 the elements bad weather
- VERB + ELEMENTS **brave** *I put on my thick coat ready to brave the elements.* | **battle (against)** *He told us stories of how he had battled the elements on his mountaineering trips.* | **be exposed to, be open to** *The place was completely exposed to the elements.* | **be protected from, be sheltered from**
- PHRASES **protection/shelter from the elements**

elephant *noun*

- ADJ. **African | Asian, Indian | bull, cow | baby | trained | wild | rogue**
- QUANT. **herd**
- VERB + ELEPHANT **hunt, poach | cull | drive, herd, round up**
- ELEPHANT + VERB **trumpet | charge, stampede | trample sb**
- ELEPHANT + NOUN **herd | tusk | conservation**

eliminate *verb*

- ADV. **altogether, completely, entirely, totally** *The risk cannot be eliminated altogether.* ◊ *This procedure does not completely eliminate the possibility of an accident.* | **virtually | largely | effectively** *Getting this job has effectively eliminated his financial worries.*
- VERB + ELIMINATE **seek to, take steps to, try to | help (to) | be designed to** *The single market is designed to eliminate barriers to the free movement of goods, services and people.* | **be impossible to**
- PREP. **from** *Try to eliminate fatty foods from your diet.*

elite *noun*

- ADJ. **governing, ruling | business, political, social**
- VERB + ELITE **create, form** *These people form an elite who have the power to make decisions.* | **join**
- PHRASES **a member of an elite** *a club for members of the business elite*

eloquent *adj.*

- VERBS **be | become, grow, wax** *He waxed eloquent about her talents as an actress.*
- ADV. **extremely, very** *a very eloquent speaker* | **quite**
- PREP. **about, on** *He grew quite eloquent on the subject.*

elusive *adj.*

- VERBS **be, prove** *Further movie roles have proved somewhat elusive for the young actor.* | **become | remain**
- ADV. **extremely, very | rather, somewhat | strangely** *Sleep was strangely elusive.* | **notoriously** *Truth is a notoriously elusive quality.*

emaciated *adj.*

- VERBS **be, look | become, grow**
- ADV. **painfully, severely** *his severely emaciated body*

email *noun*

- VERB + EMAIL **write | send, fire off** *When I saw what he'd written I fired off an angry email.* | **get, receive | read | reply to | delete | archive**
- EMAIL + NOUN **address | message**
⇒ Special page at COMPUTER

embargo *noun*

- ADJ. **complete, strict, total | selective | international | economic | arms, oil, trade**
- VERB + EMBARGO **impose, place, put | enforce, tighten | lift** *The government has agreed to lift the embargo imposed ten years ago.* | **break, violate** *We knew the arms embargo was being broken.*
- PREP. **~ against** *the international embargo against the country* **~ on** *a strict embargo on oil imports*

embark *verb*

PHRASAL VERB

embark on/upon sth
- ADV. **immediately | seriously** *some advice for anyone seriously embarking on a career in the music business*

- VERB + EMBARK ON/UPON STH **be about to, be ready to** *She was now ready to embark on her journey of adventure.*

embarrassed *adj.*

1 shy/awkward/ashamed
- VERBS **be, feel, look, seem, sound | become**
- ADV. **acutely, deeply, excruciatingly, extremely, highly, particularly, really, terribly, very | almost | a bit, faintly, a little, quite, rather, slightly, somewhat** *He looked a bit embarrassed.* | **clearly, obviously, visibly**
- PREP. **about** *She's embarrassed about her height.* **at** *He felt acutely embarrassed at being the centre of attention.* **by** *She seemed almost embarrassed by her own outburst.* **for** *His colour had risen and Isobel felt embarrassed for him.*

2 not having any money
- VERBS **be**
- ADV. **financially**

embarrassing *adj.*

- VERBS **be, prove, sound | become, get | make sth** *My mother's presence made the situation even more embarrassing.* | **find sb/sth** *I found the whole evening intensely embarrassing.*
- ADV. **acutely, bloody** (*taboo*), **deeply, excruciatingly, extremely, highly, intensely, really, seriously, terribly, very** *a deeply embarrassing moment* | **increasingly | almost | a bit, a little, pretty, quite, rather, slightly, somewhat | potentially | politically, socially**
- PREP. **for** *It was acutely embarrassing for us all.* **to** *This latest incident could be embarrassing to the government.*

embarrassment *noun*

1 feeling of being embarrassed
- ADJ. **acute, considerable, great, intense, severe | total | slight** *She smiled to hide her slight embarrassment.* | **further | obvious | silent**
- VERB + EMBARRASSMENT **feel** *I felt some embarrassment as we shook hands.* | **cover, hide | cause | avoid** *The government wishes to avoid further embarrassment over the affair.* | **blush/flush with, giggle with, squirm with** *I still squirm with embarrassment at the thought of it.* | **die from/of** (*figurative*) *I could have died of embarrassment when I saw her standing behind me.* | **ease, relieve | save sb, spare sb** *Helen changed the subject to save me the embarrassment of replying.*
- PREP. **in ~** *We all watched in silent embarrassment as Mr Rogers started to cry.* **with/without ~** *I could finally talk about my problem without embarrassment.* | **~ at** *her embarrassment at being found out* **~ over** *the government's embarrassment over the affair*
- PHRASES **(much) to sb's embarrassment** *Much to his embarrassment, Mike realized that a small crowd was watching him.* **feelings of embarrassment, a flush of embarrassment** *A flush of embarrassment came to her cheeks.* **a source of embarrassment**

2 sb/sth that makes you embarrassed
- ADJ. **considerable, great, huge, major, serious, severe | potential | financial, political, social**
- VERB + EMBARRASSMENT **be, become, prove** *The protests were becoming something of an embarrassment to the government.* | **consider sb/sth**
- PREP. **~ for** *The episode was a huge embarrassment for all concerned.* **~ to** *The poor child was considered an embarrassment to his family.*

embassy *noun*

- ADJ. **foreign | British, Chinese, etc.**
- VERB + EMBASSY **open, set up | close** *They broke off diplomatic relations and closed the embassies in each other's country.*

● EMBASSY + NOUN **building,   grounds | official, spokesman/spokeswoman, staff**
● PREP. **at a/the~** *She works at the Malaysian embassy in London.* **in a/the~** *a fire in the Spanish embassy* **outside a/the~** *a protest outside the American embassy*

embedded *adj.*

● VERBS **be | become**
● ADV. **deeply, firmly**
● PREP. **in/within** *These ideas are deeply embedded in our culture.*

embrace *noun*

● ADJ. **close, passionate, tight, warm** *the comfort of her warm embrace*
● VERB + EMBRACE **be locked in, hold sb in** *They were locked in a passionate embrace on the station platform.* | **escape (from), extract yourself from, free yourself from** *He managed to free himself from her embrace.* | **release sb from** *He released her from his embrace.*
● PREP. **in an~** *two lovers in a tight embrace* **into an~** *He drew her into his embrace.*

embrace *verb*

1 put your arms round sb
● ADV. **tightly, warmly** *He rose from his chair and embraced her warmly.*

2 accept sth
● ADV. **fully, genuinely** *the only party which fully embraces the concept of a united Europe* | **enthusiastically, wholeheartedly, with enthusiasm** *She embraced the feminist cause with enthusiasm.*

embroider *verb*

● ADV. **beautifully, delicately, exquisitely | heavily, richly** *a robe of richly embroidered silk*
● PREP. **on** *She embroidered flowers on the front of the dress.* **with** *She embroidered the dress with flowers.*

embryo *noun*

● ADJ. **developing | early** *the cells of an early embryo* | **human, frog, etc.**
● VERB + EMBRYO **implant** *Two or three embryos are implanted into the woman's body.*
● EMBRYO + VERB **develop**

emerge *verb*

1 come out
● ADV. **slowly | suddenly | finally, eventually**
● PREP. **from** *The world is only slowly emerging from recession.* **into** *They suddenly emerged into brilliant sunshine.* **out of** *the musical forms that emerged out of the American black experience*

2 become known
● ADV. **clearly, strongly** *One thing emerges very clearly from this study.* | **gradually | quickly** *The answer to the problem quickly emerged.* | **recently | later, subsequently** *It subsequently emerged that he had known about the deal all along.* | **eventually, ultimately** *What eventually emerged from the election disaster was a realization that it was time for change.*
● VERB + EMERGE **begin to, start to** *Problems with this drug are now beginning to emerge.*
● PREP. **from** *Several facts started to emerge from my investigation.*

3 start to exist
● ADV. **rapidly** *The Pacific region has rapidly emerged as a leading force on the world stage.* | **gradually, slowly**
● PHRASES **newly emerged/emerging** *newly emerging areas of science*

emergence *noun*

● ADJ. **gradual | rapid, sudden**
● VERB + EMERGENCE **lead to** *Conditions after the war led to the emergence of a new type of political party.* | **herald, mark, signal | see, witness** *The last decade saw the emergence of a dynamic economy.* | **encourage** *The annual competition has encouraged the emergence of several talented young musicians.* | **prevent**
● PREP. **~as** *his emergence as the party's leader* **~from** *the island's emergence from the sea*

emergency *noun*

● ADJ. **extreme** *(formal)*, **major, real, serious** *Don't call me unless its a real emergency.* | **sudden, unexpected, unforeseen | international, national** *in times of national emergency* | **medical | military**
● VERB + EMERGENCY **cope with, deal with, handle, respond to** *firefighters on call to respond to emergencies*
● EMERGENCY + VERB **arise** *Call this number if any unforeseen emergency should arise.*
● EMERGENCY + NOUN **action, measures, procedures | laws, legislation, regulations | powers** *The police have been given emergency powers to deal with the crisis.* | **rule | meeting, session, talks | cover** *The army provided emergency cover when the ambulance service went on strike.* | **services** *The emergency services are struggling to cope with the number of call-outs.* | **aid, assistance, funds, relief, supply** *Emergency supplies of food have been flown to the area.* | **fund | call** *The ambulance crashed while answering an emergency call.* | **admission, case** *Emergency admissions to hospital are given top priority.* | **surgery, treatment | repairs | exit | landing**
● PREP. **for~** *She told me to keep the money for emergencies.* **in an~** *I need to know what to do in an emergency.*
● PHRASES **the accident and emergency department** *the closure of the hospital's accident and emergency department* **in case of emergency/emergencies** *There's a fire blanket on the kitchen wall in case of emergencies.* **a state of emergency** *The president immediately declared a state of emergency.*

emigration *noun*

● ADJ. **mass, massive**
● QUANT. **wave** *He called for a halt to the recent wave of emigration.*
● PREP. **~from** *emigration from Europe to America* **~to**

emission *noun*

● ADJ. **harmful, noxious, toxic | gaseous | exhaust, vehicle | industrial | atmospheric | acid, carbon, carbon dioxide, lead, sulphur, sulphur dioxide, etc.**
● VERB + EMISSION **cut, reduce** *We must take action to cut vehicle emissions.* | **control, limit, stabilize**
● EMISSION + VERB **increase | decrease, fall**
● EMISSION + NOUN **levels**
● PREP. **~s from** *measures to reduce harmful emissions from traffic*

emotion *noun*

● ADJ. **deep, extreme, intense, overwhelming, powerful, profound, strong, violent | complex | conflicting, contradictory, mixed, tangled** *She felt torn by conflicting emotions.* | **destructive, negative** *Counselling can teach people to handle negative emotions such as fear and anger.* | **positive | inner, innermost | painful | fragile** *The nurse was handling his fragile emotions very carefully.* | **raw** *a moving performance full of raw emotion* | **pent-up, suppressed** *Years of pent-up emotion came out as he sobbed.* | **human** *Fear is a normal human emotion.*
● QUANT. **flicker, hint, trace** *There wasn't a hint of emotion in his eyes.* | **flood, rush, surge, wave** *She felt a sud-*

den rush of emotion at the thought of seeing him again. |
display *She could not cope with such public displays of
emotion.*
● VERB + EMOTION **experience, feel** *the emotions that
we experience as children* ◇ *He felt no emotion as she left.* |
be choked with, be filled with, be overcome with *Her
voice was choked with emotion.* | **be devoid of, be
drained of** | **display, express, show** *Drama can help
children to express their emotions.* ◇ *The woman's face
showed no emotion.* | **release** *Releasing these emotions is
part of the healing process.* | **betray** | **shake with, trem-
ble with** *She realized she was shaking all over with emo-
tion.* | **bottle up, control, hide, stifle, suppress** | **cope
with, deal with, handle** | **confront** *Counsellors encourage
victims of crime to confront their emotions.* | **arouse, pro-
voke, stir (up)** *an incident that has aroused strong emo-
tions locally* | **be charged with, be full of** *a speech that
was charged with emotion*
● PREP. **with/without~** *She spoke with deep emotion.*
● PHRASES **depth/intensity of emotion** *The film has a
surprising depth of emotion for a comedy.* **a gamut/range
of emotions** *Her performance in the play covered the
whole gamut of emotions.*

emotional *adj.*

● VERBS **be, feel, look, sound** | **become, get, grow** *He
got quite emotional during the speech.* | **make sb** *Having
all her friends around her made her very emotional.*
● ADV. **deeply, extremely, highly, very** | **quite, rather**
● PREP. **about** *Don't be so emotional about everything!*
● PHRASES **in an emotional state** *He was in a very emotional state.*

emotive *adj.*

● VERBS **be, seem** | **become**
● ADV. **highly, powerfully, very** *He raised the highly emo-
tive issue of bullfighting.* | **rather**

empathy *noun*

● ADJ. **deep, great, real** | **total**
● VERB + EMPATHY **feel, have** | **demonstrate, show** |
develop, establish
● PREP. **~between** *The nurse should try to develop empathy between herself and the patient.* **~for** *I felt real empathy for my mother and what she had been through.*
~with *She had a deep empathy with animals.*
● PHRASES **a feeling of empathy, a lack of empathy**

emperor *noun*

● ADJ. **reigning**
● VERB + EMPEROR **crown** sb *Charlemagne was
crowned Emperor on Christmas Day 800 AD.*
● PREP. **under an/the ~** *It was under the emperor
Justinian that these advances were made.* | **~ of** *the em-
peror of Japan*
● PHRASES **the reign of an emperor** *during the reign of
the last emperor*

emphasis *noun*

1 special importance/attention
● ADJ. **considerable, great, heavy, increased** *schools
that put a heavy emphasis on sporting achievement* |
strong | **main** *discussing where the main emphasis
should be placed* | **particular, special** *Examine the events
leading to the war, with particular emphasis on France's
role in them.*
● VERB + EMPHASIS **give, lay, place, put** *The company
lays great emphasis on customer care.* | **shift** *The Demo-
crats shifted the emphasis away from direct taxation.*
● EMPHASIS + VERB **move, shift** *In recent years, the em-*

phasis has moved away from punishing drug addicts towards helping them.*
● PREP. **~on/upon** *The emphasis is on keeping fit rather
than developing lots of muscles.*
● PHRASES **a change/shift of emphasis**
2 stress on a word/phrase
● ADJ. **great** *'I', he said with great emphasis, 'was the
one.'* | **slight** *His slight emphasis on the word 'Lady' was
definitely mocking.*
● VERB + EMPHASIS **put**
● PREP. **with~** *She repeated the question with emphasis.* |
~on *Put the emphasis on the second syllable.*

emphasize *verb*

● ADV. **strongly** | **rightly** *The new law rightly empha-
sizes parental responsibility.*
● VERB + EMPHASIZE **must, should** *I must emphasize
that this is only a summary, and the full report will not be
available until next week.* | **be important to** *It is
important to emphasize this point.* | **seem to, serve to,
tend to** *All the arguments and counter-arguments serve to
emphasize the controversy surrounding this disease.* | **fail
to** | **be at pains to, be keen to** *I have been at pains to em-
phasize the positive aspects of discipline.*

emphatic *adj.*

● VERBS **be** | **remain**
● ADV. **most, quite, very**
● PREP. **about** *He was most emphatic about me leaving.*

empire *noun*

1 group of countries
● ADJ. **big, great, large, mighty, vast** | **colonial, over-
seas** *the decline of the old colonial empires*
● VERB + EMPIRE **establish, found** | **dismantle** *The
Japanese empire was quickly dismantled.* | **expand** |
lose *By now Britain had lost its empire.*
● EMPIRE + VERB **grow** | **collapse, crumble, disinte-
grate** *The mighty empire finally crumbled.*
● PHRASES **the break-up/decline/fall of an empire, part
of an empire** *a country that is still part of the empire*
2 group of companies/organizations
● ADJ. **big, huge, large** | **little** (= used to criticize sb's at-
titude to the things they control) *All the bureaucrats jeal-
ously guarded their own little empires.* | **business, com-
mercial, financial, industrial, media**
● VERB + EMPIRE **build (up), create** *He has built a huge
business empire from humble beginnings.*
● EMPIRE + VERB **collapse, crumble**
● PHRASES **the collapse of an empire**

employ *verb*

1 pay sb to work
● ADV. **directly, indirectly** *By 1960 the arms industry in
America directly employed 3.5 million people.*
● PREP. **in** *A large part of the workforce is employed in
agriculture.*
● PHRASES **be fully employed** *10% of 10–15-year-old
girls were fully employed as late as 1911.* **be gainfully employed** *Those not gainfully employed are dependent on
their savings.* **be permanently/temporarily employed, be
regularly/irregularly employed**
2 use
● ADV. **commonly, extensively, frequently, often, widely** *The safety net is an image commonly employed in
everyday life.* | **generally, usually** | **actively, deliberate-
ly** *teaching that actively employs computers in innovative
and fruitful ways* | **successfully, usefully**
● VERB + EMPLOY **can/could** *The army has far more
junior officers than it can usefully employ.*

3 be employed be busy doing sth
- ADV. **better** *You'd be far better employed taking care of your own affairs.* | **busily, usefully**
- PREP. **in** *Will and Joe were busily employed in clearing out all the furniture.*

employee *noun*

- ADJ. **salaried | full-time, part-time | permanent, temporary | retired | junior, senior | key | long-serving, loyal | potential, prospective | manual | skilled, unskilled | blue-collar, white-collar**
- VERB + EMPLOYEE **have** *The company has only 60 employees.* | **recruit | dismiss, lay off, make redundant, sack** *a fair reason for dismissing an employee* ◊ *The company made hundreds of employees redundant.*
- EMPLOYEE + VERB **join sth | work** *employees who work more than 20 hours per week* | **leave | earn sth**
- EMPLOYEE + NOUN **benefits** *In addition to a competitive salary, the company offers attractive employee benefits.* | **status** *Freelance workers do not enjoy the benefits of employee status.* | **relations**

employer *noun*

- ADJ. **big, large, large-scale, major** *one of the region's major employers* | **good** *The hotel prides itself on being a good employer that treats its staff well.* | **unscrupulous** *the use of illegal workers by unscrupulous employers* | **potential, prospective, would-be**
- VERB + EMPLOYER **have, work for**

employment *noun*

- ADJ. **paid, salaried | full-time, part-time | lifelong, lifetime, long-term, permanent, stable | short-term, temporary | regular | casual | seasonal | gainful, meaningful** *The company was one of the first to offer meaningful employment to the blind.* | **full, total** *The government aims to achieve full employment within three years.* | **high, low** *an area of very low employment* | **large-scale** *Steel making is the only local industry offering large-scale employment.* | **manual | skilled, unskilled | blue-collar, white-collar | factory, office**
- QUANT. **level** *policies aimed at maintaining a high level of employment*
- VERB + EMPLOYMENT **look for, seek** *recent graduates seeking employment* | **find, gain, get, obtain, secure** *He finally secured employment in a local factory.* | **take up** *(formal) He took up employment with the company in May 2002.* | **give up, lose** *She lost her employment when the firm closed.* | **give sb, offer sb | create, generate, provide** *This investment will certainly create employment in the area.* ◊ *The steelworks provided employment for thousands of people.* | **boost, increase, raise, stimulate** *policies designed to stimulate employment*
- EMPLOYMENT + VERB **increase, rise | fall**
- EMPLOYMENT + NOUN **opportunities, possibilities, prospects** *There are few employment prospects in the town for unqualified young people.* | **rights | training | status** *The survey studied the employment status and lifestyle of people within the community.* | **agency | contract | conditions, terms | figures, records, statistics | levels | patterns, trends | market** *school-leavers entering the employment market* | **policy** *the government's full-employment policy* | **practices** *The firm's employment practices have been widely criticized.*
- PREP. **in~** *Most of last year's graduates are now in employment.* **out of~** *She had been out of employment for three years.*
- PHRASES **conditions of employment** *trade union concerns such as conditions of employment and health and safety* a **contract of employment, patterns/trends of employment** *significant changes in patterns of employment*
⇨ Special page at BUSINESS

empty *verb*

1 make sth empty
- ADV. **completely** *The cupboards had all been completely emptied.* | **half | out** *We emptied out the tank.*
- PREP. **of** *He emptied the bottle of its contents.*

2 become empty
- ADV. **completely | half** *The hall half emptied as bored businessmen raced for the buffet tables.* | **out** *The room gradually emptied out.*
- PREP. **into** *The castle had a deep moat which emptied into the lake.* **of** *The streets soon emptied of shoppers.*

empty *adj.*

- VERBS **appear, be, feel, lie, look, seem** *The box lay empty on the bed.* | **become, end up** *The reservoirs could end up empty if this dry weather continues.* | **remain, stand, stay** *The council is letting useful housing stand empty.* | **leave sth** *The house had been left empty for several weeks.*
- ADV. **completely, quite, totally, utterly** *There was a vast expanse of utterly empty sky to look at.* | **almost, nearly, practically, virtually | largely, mostly | half** *a half-empty box of chocolates* | **fairly, relatively** *Some parts of the city are desperately overcrowded while others are relatively empty.* | **apparently | curiously, horribly** *The house felt curiously empty without the children.*
- PREP. **of** *The streets were empty of people.*

enclose *verb*

- ADV. **completely, fully, totally** *The garden is fully enclosed.* | **partially**
- PREP. **in/within** *The ring is enclosed in a plastic case.*

encore *noun*

- VERB + ENCORE **give, play, take** *The singer gave four encores.* ◊ *He took several encores before the crowd finally began to leave.* | **get** *You'll never get an encore if you perform like that!* | **call for** *The audience called for an encore.*
- PHRASES **as/for an ~** *For an encore, he sang an unaccompanied folk song.*

encounter *noun*

- ADJ. **brief** *I did not see him again except for a brief encounter on a train.* | **casual, chance, unexpected** *It was a chance encounter that led to the setting up of the new political party.* | **close** *I decided not to risk a second close encounter with the snakes.* | **face-to-face | direct** *The press conference was her first direct encounter with the media.* | **unpleasant, violent | social** *the language we use in everyday social encounters* | **sexual**
- VERB + ENCOUNTER **have** *I had my first encounter with the president two years ago.*
- ENCOUNTER + VERB **take place**
- PREP. **~between** *violent encounters between police and protesters* **~with** *my first encounter with my new boss*

encounter *verb*

- ADV. **commonly, frequently, often, regularly** *Walruses were commonly encountered in the Shetland Islands until quite recently.* | **rarely | inevitably**
- VERB + ENCOUNTER **be likely to** *What are the difficulties you are most likely to encounter?*

encourage *verb*

- ADV. **greatly, strongly** *We were greatly encouraged by the support we received.* | **actively, positively** *The government must actively encourage investment in these areas.*
- VERB + ENCOURAGE **aim to | try to | be designed to** *These questions are designed to encourage debate.* | **be likely to** *Newspapers should not publish material that is*

likely to encourage discrimination on the grounds of race or colour.
- PREP. **in** *Her head of department encouraged her in her research work.*

encouragement *noun*

- ADJ. **considerable, great | active, positive | the slightest** *Given the slightest encouragement, he'd be on his knees swearing eternal devotion.*
- VERB + ENCOURAGEMENT **give sb, offer (sb), provide (sb with)** *Mick was always ready to offer advice and encouragement.* | **need | draw, get, have, receive, take** *I draw great encouragement from the fact that the classroom is always full.*
- PREP. **with ~** *With a bit of encouragement, she could do really well.* | **~ by/from** *You need encouragement from people who understand what you are trying to do.* **~ to** *Getting the support of the Queen was a great encouragement to those involved in the project.*
- PHRASES **words of encouragement** *Perhaps I can offer a few words of encouragement to those who did not win any prizes this time.*

encouraging *adj.*

- VERBS **be, look, seem, sound | remain**
- ADV. **extremely, highly, immensely, most, really, tremendously, very** *This news is most encouraging.* | **mildly, quite, reasonably | positively | hardly**

encyclopedia *noun*

- VERB + ENCYCLOPEDIA **consult, look sth up in, use | compile, write | edit | publish**
- PREP. **in an/the ~** *I looked the Civil War up in my encyclopedia.*
- PHRASES **an entry in an encyclopedia** *There are over 20 000 entries in the encyclopedia.*

end *noun*

1 furthest part of sth
- ADJ. **bottom, lower | top, upper | back, rear, tail** *(figurative) I just caught the tail end of the movie.* | **front | extreme, very | far, opposite, other** *That's his wife sitting at the far end of the table.* | **round, square, etc. | pointed, sharp | cheap** *housebuyers at the cheap end of the market* | **dear, expensive | dead** *We tried cutting through a back road but it was a dead end.* ◇ *(figurative) a dead-end job* | **deep, shallow** *(of a swimming pool) (figurative) The company believes in throwing new employees in at the deep end with no training.* | **free, knotted, loose** *Take the free end of the rope and pass it through the hole.* ◇ *(figurative) The author tied up all the loose ends of the story in the final chapter.* | **west, western, etc.** *the southern end of the lake*
- VERB + END **come to, get to, reach** *Continue until you reach the end of the road.* | **change** *The teams changed ends at half time.*
- PREP. **at the ~** *Turn into Hope Street and our house is right at the end.* **on ~** *Stand it on end (= upright).*
- PHRASES **end of the spectrum** *The two parties represent opposite ends of the political spectrum.* **(from) end to end** *We walked along the whole promenade, from end to end.* ◇ *They arranged the tables end to end.*

2 last part of sth
- ADJ. **abrupt, sudden | dramatic | early** *The injury brought her career to an early end.* | **fitting** *The award was a fitting end to a distinguished career.*
- VERB + END **come to, get to, reach** *The meeting finally came to an end at six.* ◇ *I'll never get to the end of this book!* | **approach, draw to, near** *As the evening was drawing to an end, the firework display took place.* | **bring**

(sth to), put *Talks were in progress to bring an end to the fighting.* | **call for** *call for an end to the violence*
- END + VERB **be in sight** *There's no end in sight to the present crisis.*
- END + NOUN **product, result** *The film's backers were delighted with the end product.*
- PREP. **at an ~** *The proceedings are expected to be at an end by 6 p.m.* **at the ~** *They get married at the end of the movie.* **by the ~** *He wants the reports by the end of the month.* **in the ~** *In the end, they decided to spend the holiday at home.* **to the ~** *He won't win, but he'll keep fighting to the end.* **towards the ~** *I was getting bored towards the end of the talk.* **till/until the ~** *I'm staying until the end of this week.* **up to the ~** *It stayed hot right up to the end of September.* **~ to** *What the business community wants is an end to the recession.*
- PHRASES **the end of an era** *Her death marks the end of an era.* **the end of the line/road** *(figurative) The loss of this contract could signal the end of the line for the shipyard.* **from beginning to end** *His story was one big lie from beginning to end.* **to/until the bitter end** *We will fight this court case to the bitter end.*

3 aim/purpose
- ADJ. **beneficial, desirable, worthwhile, worthy | destructive | practical, pragmatic | common** *Despite our differences, we were working to a common end.* | **selfish | commercial, economic, educational, ideological, political, social, utilitarian**
- VERB + END **achieve, further, pursue** *She was prepared to lie in order to achieve her ends.* | **work to**
- PREP. **to ... ends** *The money might have been used to more beneficial ends.* **to this ~** *She wished to have a house built, and to this end she engaged a local architect.*
- PHRASES **an end in itself** *For her, travelling had become an end in itself rather than a means of seeing new places.* **a means to an end** *I don't enjoy studying computing—it's just a means to an end.* **the end justifies the means** *He defended a morality in which the end justifies the means.* **to/for your own ends** *She is exploiting the current situation for her own ends.* **with this end in view** *(= in order to achieve this)*

4 death
- ADJ. **sad, tragic | bad, sticky** *to come to a sticky (= unpleasant, but deserved) end* | **untimely**
- VERB + END **come to, meet** *(literary) He met his end at the Battle of Waterloo.*
- END + VERB **come** *The end came when he collapsed after playing golf.*

end *verb*

- ADV. **abruptly, suddenly** *The meeting ended abruptly when the chairman was called away.* | **prematurely | at last, eventually, finally** *At last the war ended.* | **all but, effectively, virtually** *A back injury effectively ended her career.* | **inconclusively** *The peace talks have ended inconclusively, with neither side prepared to give way on key points.* | **peacefully | disastrously, tragically | disappointingly, unhappily**
- PREP. **in** *The attempt finally ended in failure.* **with** *The show ended with a song.*
- PHRASES **end in disaster** *The military action could end in disaster.* **end in tears** *(figurative) After all that excitement the day was bound to end in tears (= unhappily).*

endanger *verb*

- ADV. **greatly, seriously** *Taking these drugs could seriously endanger your health.*
- VERB + ENDANGER **be likely to** *They are accused of causing an explosion likely to endanger life.*
- PHRASES **highly endangered** *14 per cent of primate species are highly endangered.*

endear verb

● ADV. **hardly, not exactly**
● VERB + ENDEAR **(not) be calculated to** '*All better now, are we?' he enquired in a patronizing manner hardly calculated to endear.*
● PREP. **to** *She had an unfriendly manner which did not exactly endear her to her colleagues.*

endeavour noun

● ADJ. **cooperative, joint | brave, gallant, heroic | earnest, honest** *the government's honest endeavours to improve the lives of the poor* | **lifelong** *Learning a foreign language well can be a lifelong endeavour.* | **fruitless, futile, unsuccessful | successful | human** *Enthusiasm is a vital ingredient in all human endeavour.* | **artistic, creative, educational, intellectual, political, scientific** *She always encourages her children in their artistic endeavours.*
● VERB + ENDEAVOUR **make** *You must make an endeavour to work harder.*
● PREP. **in an ~** *We wish her every success in this endeavour.* ◇ *In an endeavour to improve the service, they introduced free parking.*
● PHRASES **your best endeavours** *Despite her best endeavours, she couldn't persuade anyone to volunteer.* **a field of endeavour** *He has the ability to achieve success in whatever field of endeavour he should choose.* **make every endeavour** *We will make every endeavour to obtain sufficient supplies.*

ending noun

● ADJ. **happy | sad, tragic, unhappy | dramatic | fairy-tale** *The crowd cheered on the unknown Tunisian, hoping for a fairy-tale ending to the race.* | **perfect** *The meal was the perfect ending to a great weekend.* | **abrupt** *I was surprised by the abrupt ending to the conversation.*
● VERB + ENDING **have** *The book has a sad ending.*
● PREP. **~to** *This is a happy ending to a rather sad story.*

endless adj.

● VERBS **be, seem** *The long walk back seemed endless.*
● ADV. **almost, virtually | apparently, seemingly** *a seemingly endless list of repairs to be carried out*

endorse verb

● ADV. **enthusiastically, firmly, heartily, strongly, warmly, wholeheartedly | entirely, fully | overwhelmingly, unanimously | broadly** *The government has broadly endorsed a research paper proposing new educational targets for 14-year-olds.* | **explicitly, implicitly** *The plan does not explicitly endorse the private ownership of land.* | **formally, officially | publicly | effectively**
● VERB + ENDORSE **fail to, refuse to**

endorsement noun

● ADJ. **enthusiastic, full, overwhelming, ringing, strong, unanimous | lukewarm** *The new design only received a lukewarm endorsement from head office.* | **official**
● VERB + ENDORSEMENT **give sth** *We are happy to give the product our full endorsement.* | **withdraw, withhold | require | seek** *They are now seeking endorsement for their ideas.* | **get, receive, win | have** *These measures have the strong endorsement of the Labour party.*
● PREP. **~as** *her endorsement as leader of the delegation* **~by** *endorsement of the product by the Consumer Council* **~for** *endorsement for the plan* **~from** *His presidential campaign won endorsement from several celebrities.*

endurance noun

● ADJ. **great, remarkable | sheer | mental, physical**
● VERB + ENDURANCE **have, show** *She showed great endurance in the face of pain.* | **test** *The astronauts will undergo a series of trials to test their physical and mental endurance in space.* | **build (up)** *Swimming a little further each session will build endurance.*
● ENDURANCE + NOUN **test**
● PREP. **beyond~** *This behaviour is beyond endurance.*
● PHRASES **a feat of endurance** *They are capable of amazing feats of endurance.* **the limit/limits of your endurance** *She was almost at the limits of her endurance.* **powers of endurance** *The task was a test of their powers of endurance.* **a test of endurance** *Running a marathon is seen by many as the ultimate test of endurance.*

enemy noun

● ADJ. **arch, bitter, deadly, great, implacable, mortal, sworn | dangerous, formidable, powerful | ancient, old, traditional** *In today's match England play their old enemy, Scotland.* | **chief, main, principal** *The lion is the zebra's chief enemy.* | **natural** *The Church and the Communist Party were natural enemies.* | **common** *They united in the face of a common enemy.* | **political**
● VERB + ENEMY **have** *She didn't have an enemy in the world.* | **make** *He made many enemies during his brief reign.* ◇ *I didn't want to make an enemy of Mr Evans.* | **attack, fight (against)** *He was prepared to use any weapon to fight against his enemies.* | **defeat, destroy | confront, face** *He turned to face his enemy.* | **defend sth against, protect sb/sth against/from** *The cat uses its claws to protect itself against enemies.* | **deter** *The skunk releases a pungent smell to deter the enemy.*
● ENEMY + VERB **attack sb/sth**
● ENEMY + NOUN **army, forces, soldiers, troops, unit | defences, lines | lines, positions, ranks** *The spies managed to penetrate behind enemy lines.* | **camp | action, bombing, fire** *The men came under enemy fire.* ◇ *the first casualty from enemy action* | **activity** *Intelligence reported enemy activity just off the coast.* | **country | territory | aircraft, fighter, plane, ship | propaganda**
● PREP. **against an/the~** *They decided to use the weapon against the enemy.*
● PHRASES **fall into enemy hands** *The document must not at any price fall into enemy hands.* **in the face of the enemy** *He was shot for desertion in the face of the enemy.* **public enemy (number one)** *Since the scandal, the former minister has become public enemy number one.*

energetic adj.

● VERBS **be, feel, seem**
● ADV. **extremely, highly, really, remarkably, very** *Quasars are the highly energetic cores of distant galaxies.* ◇ *She seems remarkably energetic for a woman her age.* | **quite** *I'm feeling quite energetic today.*

energy noun

1 ability to be active/work hard

● ADJ. **boundless, indefatigable, inexhaustible, unflagging** *I admire her boundless energy.* | **surplus | nervous, restless | youthful | creative** *There was a lack of creative energy in the British film industry.*
● QUANT. **amount, level** *You can judge how healthy you are by the amount of energy you have.* | **great deal** *Bringing up twins requires a great deal of energy.* | **burst** *With a sudden burst of energy, he ran to the top of the hill.*
● VERB + ENERGY **be bursting with, be full of, have** *The children are always full of energy.* ◇ *I don't seem to have any energy these days.* | **lack** *He never seems to lack energy.* | **expend, put** *She put all her energies into her work.* | **channel, devote, direct, turn** *We're trying to deal with young offenders by channelling their energy into*

sport rather than crime. | **conserve, save** | **work off** *The kids were running around crazily, working off their surplus energy.* | **waste** *We don't want to waste our energy trying to persuade people who are just not interested.* | **sap** *The hills sapped his energy and he got off his bike for frequent rests.* | **dissipate** *The volunteers' energy was dissipated by the enormous amounts of paperwork involved in the project.*

• ENERGY + VERB **flag** *It was late and my energy was beginning to flag.*

• PHRASES **an outlet for your energy** *Football gives them an outlet for their energy.* **a waste of energy** *It's a waste of energy cutting this grass—nobody's going to see it.*

2 source of power

• ADJ. **renewable** *the change from fossil fuels to renewable energy* | **atomic, nuclear, solar, wave, wind**

• QUANT. **amount** *The new power station produces vast amounts of energy.*

• VERB + ENERGY **generate, produce** | **harness** *attempts to harness solar energy* | **provide, supply** | **consume, use** | **store** *No battery could store enough energy to turn over a car's engine.* | **conserve, save** | **waste** | **need, require**

• ENERGY + NOUN **production** | **consumption, use** | **demand, needs, requirements** *total energy requirements for the coming year* | **supply** *The nuclear plant provides a fifth of the nation's energy supplies.* | **resources, sources** | **conservation, savings** *equipment that offers long-term energy savings* | **efficiency** | **bill, costs, prices** | **crisis, problem, shortage** *The country could face an energy crisis if demand continues to rise.* | **company, industry, sector** *state control of the energy industries* | **market** *The cost of solar power needs to fall before it makes an impact on the energy market.* | **management, plan, policy, programme, project, strategy** *a government-sponsored renewable energy project*

• PHRASES **a demand for energy** *The demand for energy and fuel is expected to increase dramatically.* **energy-saving** *energy-saving features that can reduce energy bills by 50%* **a form of energy, a source of energy**

enforce *verb*

• ADV. **fully, properly, rigidly, rigorously, strictly, vigorously** *The rules were strictly enforced.* | **legally**

• VERB + ENFORCE **can/cannot, could/could not** *The ban cannot be legally enforced.* | **be difficult to, be hard to, be impossible to** | **help (to)** *a system of local inspectors to help enforce presidential decrees* | **seek to, take steps to** *The government may take steps to enforce compliance with the new measures.* | **decline to, refuse to**

enforcement *noun*

• ADJ. **effective, proper** | **rigorous, strict, stringent, tighter, tougher, vigorous** *MPs called for tougher enforcement of the existing laws on drugs.* | **law** | **legal, police**

• ENFORCEMENT + NOUN **agent, officer** | **authority, body** *law enforcement bodies* | **machinery, mechanism, powers, system** *The court is ineffective because it lacks the necessary enforcement machinery.* | **measures, methods, practices, procedures, proceedings**

engage *verb*

• ADV. **directly, fully**

• VERB + ENGAGE **fail to, refuse to**

• PREP. **with** *acknowledging the need to engage directly with these problems*

PHRASAL VERB

engage (sb) in sth

• ADV. **actively** *people who actively engage in shaping the world they live in*

• VERB + ENGAGE (SB) IN STH **attempt to, seek to, try to** *He tried to engage me in conversation.* | **be eager to, be willing to** | **be reluctant to, be unwilling to**

engaged *adj.*

1 doing sth

• VERBS **be**

• ADV. **deeply, heavily** *those who are deeply engaged in party politics* | **fully, totally** | **largely, mainly, primarily** | **directly** | **constantly** | **currently** | **actively, busily** | **otherwise** *I'm afraid Mr Wilson cannot see you now as he is otherwise engaged.*

• PREP. **in** *She was engaged in conversation with a client.* **on** *He is actively engaged on several projects.* **with** *Mrs Scott is engaged with a customer at the moment.*

2 having promised to marry sb

• VERBS **be** | **become, get** *The couple got engaged last month.*

• PREP. **to** *She's engaged to an actor.*

engagement *noun*

1 appointment

• ADJ. **previous, prior** *Mrs Spratt regrets that she is unable to attend owing to a previous engagement.* | **important** | **business, official, public, social** | **dinner, lunch**

• VERB + ENGAGEMENT **have** | **keep** *It is important that I keep this engagement.* | **carry out** *(formal) The prime minister will carry out no official public engagements during the month of August.* | **cancel, fail to keep** *The president fell ill and was forced to cancel all public engagements.*

• ENGAGEMENT + NOUN **diary**

• PREP. **~with** *He had an important engagement with his financial adviser.*

2 agreement to get married

• ADJ. **long** | **broken**

• VERB + ENGAGEMENT **announce** | **break (off)**

• ENGAGEMENT + NOUN **ring**

• PREP. **~ to** *He announced his engagement to his long-time girlfriend.*

engine *noun*

1 part of a vehicle that produces power

• ADJ. **big, powerful** | **small** | **twin~s** *a large plane with twin engines* | **1.4-litre, 1200cc, 20-valve, four-cylinder, two-stroke, etc.** | **diesel, internal-combustion, jet, outboard, petrol, piston, turbine, turbo/turbocharged** | **aircraft, car, rocket**

• VERB + ENGINE **crank (up), start, switch on** | **cut** *(informal),* **kill** *(informal),* **switch off** *He pulled up under some trees and cut the engine.* | **rev (up), run** *She sat at the traffic lights revving the engine.* | **repair, service, tune** | **lubricate** | **fit (sth with)** *The new model is fitted with a more powerful engine.*

• ENGINE + VERB **run** *She waited with the engine running while he bought a paper.* ◇ *The engine runs on unleaded petrol.* | **idle, tick over, turn over** *The engine was just ticking over.* | **catch, start** *I pressed the starter and the engine caught first time.* | **stop** | **fire** *The engine's firing on all four cylinders now.* | **break down, die, fail, misfire, overheat, seize up, stall** | **cough, splutter** *The engine coughed and died.* | **roar, scream** *The plane's engine roared as it prepared for take-off.* | **race, rev (up)** *He heard a car engine racing behind him.* | **power sth** *This model is powered by a 1.8-litre petrol engine.*

• ENGINE + NOUN **capacity, power, speed** | **compartment, room** *the ship's engine room* | **component** | **failure, problems, trouble** *It looks as if we've got a spot of engine trouble.* | **noise**

• PREP. **in an/the~** *You need more oil in the engine.*

• PHRASES **the noise/roar/sound of the engine**

2 vehicle that pulls a train
- ADJ. **large, powerful | diesel, electric, steam | railway, tank**
- VERB + ENGINE **build**
- ENGINE + VERB **break down, fail** *The engine broke down just outside the station.*
- ENGINE + NOUN **driver | failure | speed | shed**

engineer *noun*

1 designs/builds engines/roads, etc.
- ADJ. **chief | chartered, qualified, skilled, trained** *You need the advice of a qualified engineer.* **| consultant/consulting, production | aeronautical, agricultural, aircraft, chemical, civil, design, electrical, electronics, flight, marine, mechanical, mining, railway, recording, software, sound, structural**
- VERB + ENGINEER **produce, train** *Britain isn't producing enough engineers.*
- ⇨ Note at PROFESSIONAL (for more verbs)

2 repairs machines/equipment
- ADJ. **qualified, registered, skilled, trained | maintenance, service | heating, lighting, telephone**
- VERB + ENGINEER **call in/out**
- ⇨ Note at JOB (for more verbs)

engineer *verb*

1 manage to arrange sth
- ADV. **brilliantly, carefully** *She carefully engineered a meeting with the chairman.*
- VERB + ENGINEER **seek to, try to**

2 design and build sth
- ADV. **carefully, finely, precisely, superbly** *the car is superbly engineered and a pleasure to drive.*

engineering *noun*

- ADJ. **heavy, light | conventional | precision | advanced | aeronautical, agricultural, chemical, civil, design, ecological, electrical, electronic, genetic, mechanical, process, software, systems, etc.**
- QUANT. **piece** *The bridge is a fine piece of engineering.*
- ENGINEERING + NOUN **company, firm, group | industry | services | work/works** *Train services on Sunday will be restricted, because of engineering works.*
- PHRASES **a feat of engineering** *The new building is a remarkable feat of engineering.* ◊
- ⇨ Note at SUBJECT (for more verbs and nouns)

English *noun*

- ADJ. **plain** *You'd have no trouble understanding his point if he'd written the article in plain English!* **| spoken, written | American, British, Indian, etc. | BBC, the Queen's | Early, Middle, Modern, Old**
- ⇨ Note at LANGUAGE (for more collocates)

engrossed *adj.*

- VERBS **appear, be, look, seem | become, get**
- ADV. **deeply, very | completely, entirely, thoroughly, totally | apparently | happily**
- PREP. **in** *He seemed completely engrossed in his book.*

enhance *verb*

- ADV. **considerably, dramatically, enormously, greatly, much, significantly, substantially** *The attractiveness of the book is much enhanced by Mark Stevens's drawings.* **| directly | further | undoubtedly**
- VERB + ENHANCE **can/could, may/might** *things that can significantly enhance the quality of your life* **| help (to), serve to | be designed to, seek to** *reforms designed to enhance market efficiency*

enigmatic *adj.*

- VERBS **be | remain**
- ADV. **highly, very** *His reply was highly enigmatic.* **| slightly, somewhat | curiously, strangely**

enjoy *verb*

- ADV. **enormously, greatly, hugely, immensely, really, thoroughly, tremendously** *She greatly enjoys her work.* ◊ *We enjoyed the game immensely.*
- VERB + ENJOY **be able to | seem to** *The kids all seemed to enjoy themselves.* **| begin to** *I was just beginning to enjoy it when the rain came down.*

enjoyable *adj.*

- VERBS **be, look, sound | become | make sth** *I always try to make my lessons enjoyable.* **| find sth**
- ADV. **enormously, extremely, highly, hugely, immensely, most, really, very** *We had a most enjoyable evening.* **| thoroughly | quite**

enjoyment *noun*

- ADJ. **full, great, huge, maximum, real** *A large income is not necessary for the full enjoyment of life.* **| pure, sheer** *For sheer enjoyment, you can't beat this game.* **| evident, obvious | quiet, simple**
- VERB + ENJOYMENT **derive, find, get, have** *They found real enjoyment just in being together.* **| bring (sb), give sb, provide (sb with)** *The show brought enjoyment to millions of viewers.* **| add to, enhance, increase** *Food is there to keep you healthy and enhance your enjoyment of life.* **| spoil**
- PREP. **for (sb's)** ~ *I play rugby purely for enjoyment.* **with** ~ *Mackie was smiling with enjoyment.* **| ~ in** *The noise really spoilt her enjoyment in living there.*
- PHRASES **a source of enjoyment** *Her little grandson has been a source of great enjoyment to her.*

enlarge *verb*

- ADV. **considerably, greatly** *The castle was enlarged considerably in the fifteenth century.* **| slightly**
- VERB + ENLARGE **seek to** *The gallery is seeking to enlarge its holdings of Danish art.*

enmity *noun*

- ADJ. **bitter, fierce | lasting, long-standing, old, traditional** *He had earned their lasting enmity.*
- VERB + ENMITY **earn (sb), incur**
- PREP. ~ **between** *the fierce enmity between the two groups* ~ **towards** *his enmity towards the Church*

enormity *noun*

- ADJ. **full, sheer**
- VERB + ENORMITY **appreciate, grasp, realize** *It's difficult to grasp the sheer enormity of the tragedy.* **| bring home** *Her words brought home the enormity of what was happening.*

enquire *(also* inquire*) verb*

- ADV. **further | pleasantly, politely** *Adam enquired politely whether they had enjoyed the show.* **| anxiously, solicitously | eagerly, hopefully | casually, evenly, mildly | coldly, coolly** *'You wish to speak with me?' he enquired coldly.* **| drily, sarcastically, sweetly** *(ironic)* **tartly** *'Do you mean blackmail?' she enquired sweetly.*
- PREP. **about** *To enquire about tickets, phone the number below.* **after** *Rose was enquiring after you* (= asking how you were). ◊ *She enquired after my mother's health.* **as to** *He didn't enquire as to my identity.* **into** *A commission has been set up to enquire into alleged malpractice.*

enquiry (*also* inquiry) *noun*

1 official investigation

- ADJ. **full/full-scale**, **major** | **detailed** | **preliminary** | **immediate** | **open**, **public** | **confidential** | **internal** | **joint** *a joint enquiry undertaken by the Department of Health and the Dental Association* | **impartial**, **independent** | **informal** | **formal**, **official** | **congressional**, **government**, **judicial**, **parliamentary**, **police** | **disciplinary** | **fatal accident**, **murder**, etc.
- VERB + ENQUIRY **carry out**, **conduct**, **have**, **hold**, **undertake** | **announce** *The governor announced an enquiry into the events.* | **initiate**, **launch**, **open (up)**, **set up**, **start** *Police have launched a murder enquiry.* | **adjourn** | **reopen** | **call for** *Local MPs are calling for a full independent enquiry into the way the police handled the affair.* | **demand**, **order** *The government has ordered a public enquiry into the affair.* | **be subjected to**, **face** *You may be subjected to a disciplinary enquiry.* | **attend** | **be involved in** | **chair**, **head**, **lead** *The enquiry will be chaired by a judge.*
- ENQUIRY + VERB **be underway**, **take place** *A major enquiry is underway after the death of a union official.* ◇ *The enquiry will take place behind closed doors.* | **begin**, **commence**, **start** | **hear sth** *The enquiry heard this week that the crash was unavoidable.* | **consider sth**, **examine sth**, **investigate sth** | **reveal sth** | **conclude sth**, **establish sth**, **find sth** *An enquiry found that the vintage plane was in good working order.* | **rule sth** *The enquiry ruled that the cars should be fitted with bigger bumpers.* | **blame sb/sth**
- ENQUIRY + NOUN **report** | **team**
- PREP. **at an/the ~** *At the enquiry the minister maintained that nothing illegal had been done.* **during/in an/the~** *arguments during the enquiry* **pending an~** *The director has been suspended on full pay, pending an internal enquiry.* | **~ by** *an enquiry by the Charity Commission* **~ into** *a public enquiry into the environmental effects of the proposed new road*
- PHRASES **the outcome/result of an enquiry**, **the subject of an enquiry** *He now finds himself the subject of an enquiry after reports of financial irregularities.*

2 request for information

- ADJ. **exhaustive**, **extensive**, **thorough** *I've made exhaustive enquiries, but haven't been able to find what I want.* | **detailed** | **specific** | **general** *Our national enquiry centre is open every day and can help you with all your general enquiries.* | **discreet** | **informal** | **routine** | **preliminary** | **customer** | **house-to-house**, **phone/telephone**, **written**
- QUANT. **flood**, **stream** *After the disaster, the police had a flood of enquiries about missing relatives.*
- VERB + ENQUIRY **make**, **pursue**, **direct**, **undertake** *The police are still pursuing their enquiries.* ◇ *The committee directed its enquiries to Mrs Taylor.* | **complete** | **welcome** *The faculty welcomes enquiries from prospective entrants.* | **get**, **have**, **receive** | **be inundated with** | **answer**, **respond to**, **deal with**, **handle** | **assist (sb) in/with**, **help (sb) in/with** *Police believe he can help them with their enquiries into a robbery.*
- ENQUIRY + NOUN **desk**, **office** | **service** | **form** *You are requested to complete an enquiry form.*
- PREP. **pending an/the ~** *She has been released on bail pending further enquiries.* | **~ about/as to/concerning/regarding/relating to/with regard to** *enquiries as to the whereabouts of Erin Smith* **~ by** *enquiries by police* **~ from** *enquiries from the public* **~ into** *I'm making enquiries into the possibility of going by train.*

3 asking questions/collecting information

- ADJ. **careful** | **further** | **critical** | **intellectual** | **empirical** | **historical**, **philosophical**, **scientific**, **sociological** *The purpose is one of scientific enquiry.*
- VERB + ENQUIRY **encourage** *The subjects on the curriculum encourage intellectual enquiry.*

- PREP. **~ concerning/into** *enquiry into the origins of the universe*
- PHRASES **an area of enquiry** *The purpose of the research is to put this area of enquiry on a sound experimental footing.* **a board/commission/committee of enquiry**, **a line of enquiry** *No one has yet been arrested but the police have assured us that all possible lines of enquiry are being pursued.* **a method of enquiry** *Methods of enquiry vary from subject to subject.* **a spirit of enquiry** *Children are born with a spirit of enquiry.*

enrolment *noun*

- ADJ. **high**, **low** | **total** *Total enrolment fell between 1991 and 1997.* | **open** (= not restricted) | **school** | **candidate**, **student**
- ENROLMENT + VERB **take place** *Enrolment will take place in the main hall.* | **be/go up**, **rise** | **be/go down**, **fall**
- PREP. **at ~** *You will be given a reading list at enrolment.* **on ~** *The full fee is payable on enrolment.* | **~ for** *Enrolment for engineering courses is low this year.* **~ in** *enrolments in evening classes* **~ on** *enrolment on a computer course*

ensure *verb*

- VERB + ENSURE **must** | **aim to**, **try to** | **take action/care/steps to** *We must take steps now to ensure the survival of these animals.* | **be designed to** *provisions designed to ensure safe conditions of work* | **help (to)** | **be important to**, **be necessary to**, **be sufficient to** *It is important to ensure that delegates have been properly briefed.*
- PHRASES **an attempt to ensure sth**, **efforts/measures to ensure sth**

entail *verb*

- ADV. **actually** *What does the job actually entail?* | **inevitably**, **necessarily** *Restructuring will inevitably entail compromises.*

entangled *adj.*

- VERBS **be** | **become**, **get** *The fishing lines had become hopelessly entangled.*
- ADV. **hopelessly**
- PREP. **in** *He became entangled in legal disputes.* **with** *Sara had got entangled with some political group.*

enter *verb*

1 come/go into a place

- ADV. **illegally** *people who enter the country illegally*
- VERB + ENTER **allow sb/sth to**, **permit sb/sth to** *He stood back to allow us to enter.* | **forbid sb to**
- PREP. **by/through** *We entered through a large iron gate.*

2 add information to sth

- ADV. **manually** *You may need to enter this information manually.*
- PREP. **in** *Your details have been entered in our database.* **into**, **on** *Please enter all your personal details on the form provided.* **onto** *Enter the data onto the computer.*

enterprise *noun*

1 plan/project

- ADJ. **great** | **exciting** | **ambitious**, **difficult**, **hazardous** | **common**, **cooperative**, **joint** *The programme is a joint enterprise with the National Business School.*
- VERB + ENTERPRISE **embark on/upon**, **start**, **undertake** *They are willing to undertake a new enterprise.* | **abandon**
- ENTERPRISE + VERB **fail**, **succeed**
- PREP. **in an/the ~** *The team leader will be the most important factor in this difficult enterprise.*

2 a business

- ADJ. **large, large-scale, medium-sized, small, small-scale | profitable, successful | family, private | public, state, state-owned | multinational | agricultural, business, commercial, economic, farming, industrial, manufacturing** *the complex organization of a business enterprise*
- VERB + ENTERPRISE **control, manage, run** *He runs a successful small enterprise.* | **invest in**
- ENTERPRISE + VERB **expand, grow, succeed | fail**
- PREP. **in/within an ~** *something that affects all the workers in the enterprise*

3 development of businesses

- ADJ. **free, private** *The Act will encourage private enterprise.* | **local | corporate, individual, municipal**
- VERB + ENTERPRISE **encourage, promote**
- ENTERPRISE + NOUN **culture** *The government has promoted the small firm and the enterprise culture.*

4 abilities/imagination

- ADJ. **great** *I thought she showed great enterprise.*
- VERB + ENTERPRISE **show**
- PHRASES **a spirit of enterprise**

entertain verb

1 invite sb to eat/drink with you

- ADV. **lavishly** *The Bradfords always entertained lavishly at Christmas.*
- PREP. **to** *They entertained us to lunch in their new house.*

2 interest/amuse sb

- ADV. **thoroughly** *Everyone was thoroughly entertained.*
- PREP. **with** *She entertained us with stories of her travels.*
- PHRASES **keep sb entertained** *We hired a magician to keep the children entertained.*

3 think about an idea/hope/feeling

- ADV. **seriously** *I am amazed that such a crackpot scheme could be seriously entertained.* | **briefly** *briefly entertaining hopes that he might keep the affair a secret*
- VERB + ENTERTAIN **be prepared to, be willing to** *She would make no promises, but was prepared to entertain the idea.* | **refuse to**

entertaining adj.

- VERBS **be, sound | become | make sth** *He tried to make his speech more entertaining.* | **find sth** *The others seemed to find my discomfort hugely entertaining.*
- ADV. **extremely, highly, hugely, marvellously, vastly, very, wonderfully** *It was highly entertaining for the people around them.* | **thoroughly | fairly, quite**

entertainment noun

- ADJ. **lavish | pure** *Soaps like 'Neighbours' are pure entertainment and there is nothing wrong with that.* | **free | live | evening, nightly** *The hotel has a varied programme of nightly entertainment.* | **mass, popular** *Cinema is a medium of mass entertainment.* | **family, light, musical** *Vote for your top light entertainment show.* | **home, public, street**
- VERB + ENTERTAINMENT **lay on, offer, provide, put on** *They laid on lavish entertainment for their guests.*
- ENTERTAINMENT + NOUN **business, industry, world | centre, venue | programme | value** *The films were bought chiefly for their entertainment value.*
- PREP. **for sb's ~** *Ladies and gentlemen, for your entertainment, we present Magic Man.*
- PHRASES **a form of entertainment, a place of entertainment** *places of entertainment such as cinemas*

enthral verb

- PHRASES **be enthralled by/with sth** *They were enthralled with the play.* **hold/keep sb enthralled** *She kept her audience enthralled throughout her twenty-minute performance.* **listen/watch enthralled** *The children listened enthralled as the storyteller unfolded her tale.*

enthusiasm noun

- ADJ. **burning, considerable, enormous, extraordinary, great, immense, passionate, tremendous | genuine, real | growing | boundless, unbounded, unbridled | undiminished | excessive | spontaneous, sudden | new, new-found, renewed** *We went about our task with renewed enthusiasm.* | **early, initial | general, widespread | popular, public | personal | infectious | boyish, youthful | innocent | natural | religious**
- QUANT. **burst, surge** *After an initial burst of enthusiasm for jogging, I gradually lost interest.*
- VERB + ENTHUSIASM **be full of, feel, have** *Her voice was full of enthusiasm.* | **convey, express, show** *She managed to convey an enthusiasm she did not feel.* ◇ *The team have shown enthusiasm and commitment.* | **summon up | feign** *He accepted the invitation with feigned enthusiasm.* | **conceal, hide | share | maintain | lose | arouse, engender, fire (sb with), generate** *The trip has fired his enthusiasm for all things French.* | **dampen, dent** *This weather would dampen anyone's enthusiasm for swimming.*
- ENTHUSIASM + VERB **bubble over/up** *trying to hide the boyish enthusiasm bubbling up inside him* | **grow | fade, wane, wear off**
- PREP. **with/without ~** *I look forward to the challenge ahead with great enthusiasm.* | **~ about** *Few people expressed enthusiasm about the current leaders.* **~ among** *The idea aroused immense enthusiasm among party workers.* **~ for** *The initial enthusiasm for the project was wearing off.*
- PHRASES **a lack of enthusiasm** *Both sides have shown a distinct lack of enthusiasm for discussion.*

enthusiastic adj.

- VERBS **be, feel, look, seem, sound | become, get**
- ADV. **all, extremely, highly, immensely, incredibly, really, very, wildly** *She's all enthusiastic about China now that she's been there.* ◇ *The audience was wildly enthusiastic.* | **less than, not overly, not particularly** *Mrs Neil did not seem particularly enthusiastic about her job.* | **largely** *Film critics are largely enthusiastic about the thriller.* | **fairly, quite | genuinely**
- PREP. **about** *He was quite enthusiastic about the idea.* **in** *enthusiastic in their support of him*

entity noun

- ADJ. **discrete, distinct, independent, separate, single** *Church and empire were fused in a single entity.* | **basic | abstract | artificial | physical | living | business, corporate, economic, legal, national, political, social** *A company is a separate legal entity.*
- VERB + ENTITY **form** *The two companies will combine to form a new entity.*

entrance noun

1 door/place through which you enter sth

- ADJ. **narrow, wide | main | back, front, rear, side | cave, church, harbour, school, tunnel, etc.**
- VERB + ENTRANCE **use** *While the front door is being repaired, please use the side entrance.* | **mark** *The little porch marked the entrance to a churchyard.* | **have** *The building has only one entrance.* | **block** *She stood firm, blocking the entrance.*

● ENTRANCE + NOUN **area, foyer, hall, lobby | door, doorway, gate, porch | passage**
● PREP. **at the~, by a/the~** *The band left by the rear entrance to escape photographers.* **in the~** *She stood in the entrance to the ward.* **through the~** *Go through the main entrance into the yard.* **| ~ from** *There is a back entrance from West Street.* **~ into** *the entrance into the car park* **~ to** *He was waiting at the entrance to the cave.*

2 act of coming in
● ADJ. **dramatic, grand**
● VERB + ENTRANCE **make** *She made a grand entrance once all the guests were assembled.* **| gain** *Some of the protesters tried to gain entrance to the meeting.*
● PREP. **~ into** *her entrance into politics*

3 right to enter a place
● VERB + ENTRANCE **gain** *students hoping to gain entrance to university*
● ENTRANCE + NOUN **charge, fee | ticket** *an entrance ticket to the zoo* **| requirements | exam/examination**

entrant *noun*

● ADJ. **school, university | competition | winning** *The winning entrant received tickets to the theatre.*
● VERB + ENTRANT **attract** *The essay competition attracted 46 entrants.*
● PREP. **~ for** *the entrants for the award* **~ in** *You will automatically be registered as an entrant in the Prize Draw.* **~ into** *another new entrant into the multimedia market* **~ to** *the number of entrants to higher education*

entrepreneur *noun*

● ADJ. **good, great, successful | creative, innovative | ambitious, dynamic | large-scale, small/small-scale | individual, private | budding, potential, would-be | business, music, property, etc.**

entry *noun*

1 right to enter sth
● ADJ. **free** *The club offers free entry to women on Thursdays.* **| school, university**
● VERB + ENTRY **apply for | gain | allow sb, grant sb** *They were later allowed entry into the country.* **| refuse sb, restrict** *It has been necessary to restrict entry into the club.* **| guarantee sb**
● ENTRY + NOUN **criteria, qualifications, requirements, standard | visa | ticket** *Entry tickets to most attractions are included in the price of the holiday.*
● PREP. **~ into** *These qualifications will not guarantee you entry into the police force.* **~ to** *She applied for entry to Nottingham University.*
● PHRASES **right of entry** *The landlord had the right of entry to the flat with due warning.*

2 act of coming in
● ADJ. **forced, forcible** *The house was quiet, and there were no signs of a forced entry.* **| unauthorized** *The sign on the gates read 'No Unauthorized Entry'.* **| illegal | dramatic | triumphal** *Caesar's triumphal entry into Rome*
● VERB + ENTRY **force, gain** *He found the door locked, but he forced an entry.* **| make** *The champion made his usual dramatic entry into the arena.*
● ENTRY + NOUN **point** *Drugs are believed to come into the country through five main entry points.*
● PREP. **~ into** *Hungary's entry into the EU* **~ to** *She wondered how she could gain entry to the building.*

3 sb/sth that enters a competition
● ADJ. **winning** *The winning entry will be published in next month's issue.*
● VERB + ENTRY **post, send (in)** *Send in your entry as soon as possible!* **| attract, get, have, receive** *The show attracted entries from all over the country.* ◇ *We have had a lot of entries this year.* **| judge**

● ENTRY + NOUN **coupon, form | fee**
● PREP. **~ for** *We had too many entries for this event.* **~ in** *There were a record 2 000 entries in the under-17 section.* **~ to** *one of the best entries to our competition*

4 one item in a list/book
● ADJ. **diary | dictionary**
● VERB + ENTRY **make, write**
● PREP. **in an/the~** *Very little information is given in the diary entries.* **| ~ for** *Look at the dictionary entry for 'welcome'.* **~ in** *the last entry she made in her diary* **~ on** *First examine the entries on the marriage register.*

envelope *noun*

● ADJ. **bulky, fat, thick | self-addressed, stamped addressed** *Please enclose a stamped addressed envelope if you would like a reply.* **| post-paid, pre-paid, reply-paid** *To apply, use the enclosed reply-paid envelope (no stamp needed).* **| padded | airmail | brown, buff, manila, plain, white** *an official-looking manila envelope*
● VERB + ENVELOPE **open, rip open, slit open, steam open, tear open** *The letter was suspicious, and I considered steaming open the envelope.* **| address, mark** *an envelope addressed in my mother's round handwriting* ◇ *The envelope was marked 'Personal'.* **| seal**
● ENVELOPE + VERB **contain sth**
● PREP. **in an/the~** *I had put the letter in the wrong envelope.* **into an/the~** *He quickly stuffed the money back into the envelope.* **on an/the~** *I couldn't read the address on the envelope.* **| ~ of** *He gave her the envelope of certificates.*
● PHRASES **the back of an envelope** *I scribbled his phone number on the back of an envelope.*

envious *adj.*

● VERBS **appear, be, feel, look, seem, sound** *She tried not to appear envious.* **| become | make sb** *Don't tell me any more—you're making me envious!*
● ADV. **extremely, very | almost | a little, quite, rather, slightly, somewhat**
● PREP. **of** *He had always felt envious of his brother.*

environment *noun*

1 conditions of the place where you are
● ADJ. **immediate** *Cold-blooded animals depend on the temperature of their immediate environment.* **| alien, new, unfamiliar | changing | protected, safe, secure, stable | friendly | pleasant | clean, healthy | stimulating | favourable** *This period provided a favourable environment for the spread of communism.* **| uncertain, unstable | dangerous | noisy | competitive | hostile | extreme, harsh | fragile** *Walkers can unwittingly damage the fragile environment in which the birds live.* **| rural, urban | arid, cold, warm | aquatic, coastal, forest, mountain | domestic, family, home** *Children learn best in their home environment.* **| physical | cultural, emotional, social | office, work, working, workplace** *A comfortable working environment will increase productivity.* **| classroom, educational, learning, school, teaching, training | economic, financial** *Investors are showing more caution in the current economic environment.* **| political | business, commercial, corporate** *She now had to transfer her design skills to a commercial environment.* **| professional**
● VERB + ENVIRONMENT **create, provide** *parents who strive to provide a stimulating environment for their children to grow up in* **| adapt to** *creatures that have adapted to hostile desert environments* **| improve | explore** *The cat walked round, exploring its new environment.*
● PREP. **in an/the ~** *people working in increasingly competitive environments*

2 the environment the natural world
● ADJ. **natural | global, world | local**

● VERB + ENVIRONMENT **preserve, protect, safeguard** *The government should do more to protect the environment.* | **clean up, improve** | **have an impact on** *factors that have a huge impact on the environment* | **damage, harm, pollute** *industries which damage the environment*
● ENVIRONMENT + NOUN **agency, committee, department, group, ministry** | **minister, official, spokesman, spokeswoman** | **policy** | **conference** | **protection** | **issues**
● PREP. **in the ~** *the amount of carbon in the environment*
● PHRASES **conservation/protection of the environment, damage to the environment** *farming methods that minimize damage to the environment* **harmful to the environment** *The label identifies the products that are least harmful to the environment.* **pollution of the environment**

envisage *verb*

● ADV. **originally** *It was originally envisaged that the talks would take place in the spring.* | **always, never**
● VERB + ENVISAGE **can/could** *I can envisage difficulties if we continue with this policy.* | **be difficult to, be hard to, be impossible to** | **be easy to, be possible to**

envoy *noun*

● ADJ. **papal, personal, royal, special** | **diplomatic, peace** | **UN/United Nations** | **American, British, etc.**
● VERB + ENVOY **be, serve as** | **appoint (sb as)** *The government has not yet appointed an envoy to the area.* | **dispatch, send** *A special peace envoy was sent to the area.*
● PREP. **~ from** *a special envoy from the American president* **~ to** *He served as envoy to the French government.*

envy *noun*

● ADJ. **extreme** | **unconscious** | **class, social**
● QUANT. **tinge, touch** *I detected a tinge of envy in her tone.* | **pang, stab, twinge** *I felt a twinge of envy for the people who lived there.*
● VERB + ENVY **be consumed with, be green with, feel, have** *I had no envy of his success.* | **express, show** | **arouse, excite, fill sb with, inspire** *Her youth and looks aroused extreme envy in her rivals.*
● PREP. **with ~** *I look with envy on those lucky people with big families.* | **~ at** *I was filled with envy at their adventurous lifestyle.* **~ for** *the envy she felt for her sister*
● PHRASES **be the envy of sb/sth** *British television is the envy of the world* (= is admired by everyone). **an object of envy** *Her car was an object of envy in the neighbourhood.*

envy *verb*

● ADV. **greatly, really** | **secretly**
● PREP. **for** *I secretly envied her for her good looks.*

epidemic *noun*

● ADJ. **major** | **widespread, worldwide** | **cholera, flu, typhoid, etc.**
● EPIDEMIC + VERB **break out, strike (sth)** *A typhus epidemic struck in the winter of 1919–20.* | **spread, sweep (sth)** *the flu epidemic sweeping the country*
● PREP. **during/in an/the ~** *Over fifty people died during the flu epidemic last winter.* **~ of** *an epidemic of cholera*
● PHRASES **reach epidemic proportions** *Marriage breakdown in the West has reached epidemic proportions.*

episode *noun*

1 one separate event in sb's life/a story
● ADJ. **dramatic, exciting** | **bizarre, extraordinary** | **sad, tragic, unfortunate, unpleasant** | **major** | **brief** | **acute, severe** (*medical*) *an acute episode of pneumonia* | **latest** *She has only told you about the latest episode in a long history of mental illness.*

● VERB + EPISODE **remember** | **forget**
● PREP. **during an ~** *during a brief episode of socialist rule* | **~ from** *remembering episodes from our childhood* **~ in** *an extraordinary episode in American history*
● PHRASES **the entire/whole episode** *He says he just wants to forget the whole unfortunate episode.*

2 one part of a TV/radio drama
● ADJ. **exciting, thrilling** *Don't miss next week's exciting episode!* | **next** | **final, last**
● VERB + EPISODE **see, watch** | **miss** | **film, make** *The next episode has not yet been filmed.*
● PREP. **during/in an/the ~** *It happened in the final episode of 'Star Trek'.*

epitaph *noun*

● ADJ. **fitting, perfect**
● VERB + EPITAPH **write** | **make, stand as** *These films stand as an epitaph to the great director.*
● PREP. **as an ~** *He wanted these lines as his epitaph.* | **~ for** *She wrote the perfect epitaph for the poet.* **~ on** *Joyce's epitaph on King Edward VIII* **~ to** *It makes a fitting epitaph to a great career.*

epoch *noun*

● ADJ. **new** | **present** | **past** | **historical**
● VERB + EPOCH **mark** *The dropping of the first atom bomb marked a new epoch in warfare.*
● PREP. **during/in an/the ~** *the importance of the computer in the present epoch* **~ of** *an epoch of great social change*
● PHRASES **the beginning/end of an epoch**

equal *noun*

● ADJ. **intellectual, social**
● VERB + EQUAL **regard sb as, treat sb as** *He did not regard himself as her intellectual equal.*
● PREP. **as an ~** *He talks even to small children as equals.* **between ~s** *An interview should be a conversation between equals.* **without ~** *His guitar playing is without equal.*
● PHRASES **be sb's equal** *I shall never be his equal at chess.* **first among equals** *He was regarded as the 'first among equals' by the other office clerks.* **have few equals** *When it comes to plain speaking, she has few equals.* **have no equal** *In fighting, they had no equals.*

equal *adj.*

1 same in size/quantity/value, etc.
● VERBS **be** | **become** | **make sth** *We moved some of the better players to make the two sides equal.*
● ADV. **absolutely, exactly, in every way, precisely** *Their test results were equal in every way.* | **almost, nearly, virtually** | **about, approximately, more or less, roughly** *The EU nations together have an economy about equal in size to that of the US.* | **just** | **at least** *Fitness is important in sport, but of at least equal importance are skills.*
● PREP. **in** *The two books are more or less equal in length.* **to** *Three feet is roughly equal to one metre.*

2 having the same rights
● VERBS **be** | **be born** *I believe everyone is born equal.*
● ADV. **genuinely, truly**

3 equal to sth able to do sth
● VERBS **be, feel, prove, seem** *I hope that he proves equal to the challenge.* | **become** | **make sb** *I felt that nothing could make me equal to the demands being made of me.*
● ADV. **more than** *I felt more than equal to the task.*

equality noun

- ADJ. **complete, full, genuine, true | greater | economic, legal, political, racial, sexual, social**
- VERB + EQUALITY **have** *Women do not yet have true equality in the company.* | **achieve | demand, fight for, strive for | promote | establish | ensure, guarantee**
- PHRASES **equality of opportunity** *People from these minority groups must have equality of opportunity.*
- PREP. **~ between** *fighting for greater equality between the sexes* **~ for** *the task of achieving equality for gay men* **~ in** *These women are demanding fairness and equality in their pay.* **~ with** *The women are demanding full equality with the men of their tribe.*

equate verb

- ADV. **directly** *The constellations in the night sky cannot be directly equated with the heroes of Greek mythology.* | **roughly | simply | crudely** *crudely equating happiness with a high income*
- VERB + EQUATE **can/cannot, could/could not | be difficult to, be hard to** *It's hard to equate this gentle woman with the monster portrayed in the newspapers.*
- PREP. **with** *We are taught to equate beauty with success.*

equation noun

1 mathematical statement
- ADJ. **complicated, simple** *This can be shown by a simple equation.* | **algebraic, mathematical**
- VERB + EQUATION **solve, work out** *I could not find a way of solving the equation.* | **satisfy** *the range of values of χ which would satisfy this equation*
- PREP. **~ for** *the equation for a straight line*
- PHRASES **a side of the equation** *the numbers on the right-hand side of the equation*

2 situation
- VERB + EQUATION **be a part of, come into, enter (into)** *The availability of public transport is also part of the equation.* ◇ *Money also comes into the equation.*

equator noun

- VERB + EQUATOR **cross**
- PREP. **around the ~** *Rainforests occur around the equator.* **at the ~** *The sun heats the sea more at the equator than at the poles.* **close to/near the ~** *in an area near the equator* **on the ~** *The lake lies exactly on the equator.*
- PHRASES **north/south of the equator** *The island is just 80 miles north of the equator.*

equip verb

- ADV. **lavishly, splendidly, superbly, well** *The centre is well equipped for sailing.* | **badly, poorly | comprehensively, fully, properly | adequately, suitably | specially**
- VERB + EQUIP **seek to, try to**
- PREP. **for** *The hostel is specially equipped for wheelchair access.* **with** *The flat is fully equipped with a cooker and fridge.*
- PHRASES **come equipped with** *Rooms vary in size and come equipped with hairdryers, television and telephone.*

equipment noun

- ADJ. **the latest, modern, state-of-the-art, up-to-date | sophisticated | sensitive | heavy | portable | basic, standard | essential, necessary, vital** *Hospitals are increasingly depending on charity for vital equipment.* | **specialist | defective, faulty | outdated | labour-saving | domestic, household, kitchen | school | sports | play** *The local council is supplying new play equipment for the playground.* | **business, office | laboratory, scientific | computer, electrical, electronic, high-tech, technical | medical | military | communi-** cation, navigation, radar, radio, telecommunications | camera, photographic, video | life-saving, protective, safety, security | rescue | garden, gardening | **intellectual, mental, physical, sensory** *He lacks the intellectual equipment to succeed in politics.*
- QUANT. **item, piece**
- VERB + EQUIPMENT **provide, supply | use** *The plane uses state-of-the-art navigation equipment.* | **install | need, require** *No specialist equipment is needed.*
- EQUIPMENT + VERB **consist of sth** *The basic equipment consists of a plastic mask and a length of rope.*
- PREP. **~ for** *high-tech equipment for keeping the temperature steady*

equivalent noun

- ADJ. **direct, exact, nearest** *the nearest equivalent we have to a carnival* | **approximate | modern** *the modern equivalent of the village inn* | **American, British, etc.**
- VERB + EQUIVALENT **have** *a word which has no direct equivalent in English*
- PREP. **~ for** *There is no exact male equivalent for witches.* **~ in** *It is the approximate equivalent in height to the Matterhorn.* **~ of** *This qualification is the equivalent of a degree.* **~ to** *This concert hall has been described as the American equivalent to London's Albert Hall.*

equivalent adj.

- VERBS **be, seem | become**
- ADV. **exactly, precisely | almost, closely, essentially, practically | approximately, broadly, more or less, roughly** *the price we would pay elsewhere for a broadly equivalent house*
- PREP. **in, to** *These first computers were equivalent in power to a modern calculator.*

era noun

- ADJ. **golden, great** *the golden era of radio* | **new | present | modern | bygone, past, previous** *The room had the elegance of a bygone era.* | **post-imperial, post-war | Edwardian, Victorian, etc. | Clinton, Thatcher, etc. | Christian, Common** *the early centuries of the Christian/Common Era*
- VERB + ERA **usher in** *The fall of the Berlin Wall ushered in a whole new era.* | **enter, move into** *The country has entered an era of high unemployment.*
- ERA + VERB **begin | end**
- PREP. **during/in an/the ~** *We live in an era of religious uncertainty.* **into ~** *a practice that has survived into the present era* | **~ in** *a new era in the history of art*
- PHRASES **the beginning/dawn/dawning of a (new) era, be on the threshold of a new era, the end of an era**

eradicate verb

- ADV. **completely, entirely, totally | successfully**
- VERB + ERADICATE **try to | help (to) | be difficult to, be impossible to** *These insects are very difficult to eradicate.*
- PREP. **from** *The disease has now been successfully eradicated from the world.*
- PHRASES **an attempt/effort to eradicate sth**

erase verb

- ADV. **completely | virtually | partially**
- VERB + ERASE **try to | be determined to** *They are determined to erase the bad memories of last year's defeats.*
- PREP. **from** *These people have been virtually erased from the history book.*

erect verb

- ADV. **hastily, quickly | specially** *The event will take place in a specially erected marquee.*

● PHRASES **newly/recently erected** *the newly erected station buildings*

erect *adj.*

1 standing/sitting straight up
● VERBS **be, sit, stand** *He sat very erect, listening intently.* | **hold sth** *She held her head erect as she walked proudly up to the platform.*
● ADV. **very**

2 stiff
● VERBS **be** | **become**
● ADV. **completely, fully** | **stiffly**

erection *noun*

● VERB + ERECTION **get, have** | **lose** | **give sb**

erode *verb*

● ADV. **badly, deeply, seriously, severely** *Walkers should stick to obvious paths, even if they are badly eroded.* ◇ *The experience had seriously eroded his confidence in himself.* | **completely** | **further** | **gradually, slowly** *The distinction between social classes is slowly being eroded.* | **steadily** *The river bank had been steadily eroded over the years.* | **rapidly** | **easily** | **away** *The rocks have eroded away over time.*
● VERB + ERODE **threaten to** *The pressure towards uniformity that constantly threatens to erode local traditions.* | **tend to**

erosion *noun*

● ADJ. **serious, severe** *Acid rain has caused severe erosion on the hillside.* | **rapid** | **gradual, steady** *the steady erosion of their civil liberties* | **coastal, soil** | **glacial, water, wind**
● VERB + EROSION **cause, contribute to, lead to, result in** | **protect sth from, reduce** | **suffer (from)** *The area suffers badly from coastal erosion.*
● EROSION + VERB **affect sth** *the areas worst affected by soil erosion*
● PHRASES **the rate of erosion**

erotic *adj.*

● VERBS **be, feel** | **become** | **find sth**
● ADV. **highly, powerfully** | **mildly** | **blatantly, overtly** *There were some overtly erotic scenes in the film.*

errand *noun*

● ADJ. **little, simple**
● VERB + ERRAND **do, go on, run** *She made her brother run some little errands for her.* | **send sb on** *My boss kept sending me out on errands.*
● PREP. **on an ~** *She's gone on an errand for her mother.*

erratic *adj.*

● VERBS **be, seem** | **become** | **remain**
● ADV. **extremely, very, wildly** | **completely** | **increasingly** *her increasingly erratic behaviour* | **fairly, a little, rather, slightly, somewhat**

error *noun*

● ADJ. **fundamental, glaring, grave, great, major, monumental, serious** *The report contained some glaring errors.* | **fatal** *He made the fatal error of borrowing more than he could pay back.* | **minor, small** | **embarrassing, unfortunate** | **past** *The ability to learn from past errors is vital in business.* | **common** | **grammatical, spelling, typing** | **factual** | **tactical** *The Kenyan athlete made a tactical error in starting too fast.* | **administrative, clerical** |

human, pilot *The plane crash was caused by human error, not mechanical failure.*
● VERB + ERROR **commit, make** *He had committed a grave error in letting them see the document.* ◇ *She made several serious errors during the race.* | **contain** *The document contained a lot of typing errors.* | **detect, discover, find, spot** *I found several factual errors in the report.* | **point out** *The error was pointed out to her by one of her colleagues.* | **realize** *I only realized my error when it was too late.* | **avoid** *She has avoided the common error of writing too much.* | **correct, rectify** *Glasses can correct most errors in your vision.* | **compound** *The paper accidentally printed the victim's address, then compounded their error by printing her name the next day.*
● ERROR + VERB **arise (from sth), occur** *errors arising from inadequate information*
● ERROR + NOUN **detection** | **correction** | **message** *An error message comes up when I try to open the program.*
● PREP. **in ~** *The machine had been switched off in error* (= by mistake). | **~ in** *He checked his letter for errors in spelling.* ◇ *He realized his error in not attending the funeral.* **~ of** *The speech contained many errors of fact.*
● PHRASES **a comedy of errors** *His attempts to arrange a party ended up as a comedy of errors.* **an error of judgement** *The minister had made an amazing error of judgement.* **a margin of error** *The margin of error for a racing driver is tiny.*

erupt *verb*

● ADV. **violently** *the volcano which erupted violently last month* | **suddenly** *His anger suddenly erupted into furious shouting.*
● VERB + ERUPT **threaten to**
● PREP. **into** *violence that threatened to erupt into a full-scale war*

eruption *noun*

1 explosion of a volcano
● ADJ. **big, great, major, violent** *It was the biggest eruption of Vesuvius for some years.* | **minor** | **volcanic**
● VERB + ERUPTION **predict**
● ERUPTION + VERB **happen, occur, take place**
● PREP. **in an/the ~** *The temple was destroyed in the violent eruption of 1470 BC.*

2 sudden start of sth loud/violent
● ADJ. **sudden** *a sudden eruption of fighting*
● PREP. **~ of**

escalate *verb*

1 become/make sth worse
● ADV. **rapidly** | **steadily** *Violence between the two sides has been steadily escalating.* | **suddenly**
● PREP. **into** *The conflict could escalate rapidly into a full-scale war.*

2 increase
● ADV. **sharply** *The cost of raw materials has escalated sharply.*

escalation *noun*

● ADJ. **dramatic, major, serious** | **further** | **rapid**
● VERB + ESCALATION **lead to** *The reorganization has led to a dramatic escalation in costs.* | **prevent**
● PREP. **~ in** *a serious escalation in the fighting* **~ into** *the escalation of the conflict into an all-out war*

escalator *noun*

● ADJ. **down, up** *kids running up a down escalator*
● VERB + ESCALATOR **take** *Take the escalator down to the lower level.* | **go up** | **descend, go down**
● ESCALATOR + VERB **carry sb** *Passengers are carried by escalator to the first floor.*

escape *noun*

1 getting away from a place

- ADJ. **attempted | successful | great** *one of the greatest escapes of all time*
- VERB + ESCAPE **effect, make, make good** *He made his escape through the window.* ◇ *I found an open door and made good my escape.* | **plan | foil, prevent**
- ESCAPE + NOUN **attempt, bid | route**
- PREP. **~from** *his escape from the prison camp*
- PHRASES **a means/way of escape** *She looked round for a means of escape.* **a possibility of escape** *There was clearly no possibility of escape.*

2 avoiding sth unpleasant or boring

- ADJ. **close, narrow, near | lucky, miraculous, remarkable** *A driver had a lucky escape after a brick was dropped on his car from an overhead bridge.*
- VERB + ESCAPE **have**
- PREP. **~from** *He had a narrow escape from gunfire.*

escape *verb*

- ADV. **narrowly** *They narrowly escaped being killed in the fire.* | **not entirely** *The head of department cannot entirely escape responsibility for this situation.*
- VERB + ESCAPE **cannot/could not | attempt to, try to | manage to | let sb** *It was stupid of Lee to let them escape.* | **help sb (to)**
- PREP. **from** *to escape from prison* **into** *They escaped into the forest.* **to** *The family escaped to England.* **with** *Thieves escaped with property worth over £5 000.*
- PHRASES **escape alive** *Only two of the men escaped alive.* **escape sb's clutches** *He had managed to escape the clutches of the police yet again.* **escape unharmed/unhurt/uninjured/unscathed, escape with your life** *She was very lucky to escape with her life.*

escort *noun*

- ADJ. **armed, military, motorcycle, police**
- VERB + ESCORT **be accompanied by, have** *She had a police escort to the hospital.* | **give sb, provide (sb with), send** *Can you give us an escort?* ◇ *The army provided a small armed escort for the delegation.* | **need** *The referee needed a police escort as he left the stadium.*
- ESCORT + NOUN **vehicle**
- PREP. **under~** *The opposition leader was arrested and taken to the capital under escort.* **with/without an~** *They left with a small escort.* | **~for** *an escort for the Queen's car* **~of** *an escort of ten soldiers*

espionage *noun*

- ADJ. **industrial** *The big computer companies are very worried about industrial espionage.* | **international | American, British, etc.**
- VERB + ESPIONAGE **be engaged in, be involved in, engage in | be executed for, be expelled for, be imprisoned for** *Two members of the embassy staff had been expelled for espionage.*
- ESPIONAGE + NOUN **activities**
- PREP. **~against** *She was found guilty of espionage against the United States.* **~on behalf of** *espionage on behalf of foreign states*
- PHRASES **the world of espionage** *the shadowy world of espionage*
- ⇨ Note at CRIME (for more verbs)

essay *noun*

- QUANT. **collection** *In 2001 she published a collection of essays.*
- VERB + ESSAY **do, write** *Have you done your essay yet?* | **give in, hand in** *Essays handed in late will not be accepted.*
- ESSAY + NOUN **question, title, topic** *You have to answer 3 out of 8 essay questions in the exam.*
- PREP. **in an/the~** *He made some very good points in his essay.* | **~about/on** *We've got to write an essay on the environment.* **~by** *an essay by Montaigne*

essence *noun*

1 basic/most important quality of sth

- ADJ. **real, true, very**
- VERB + ESSENCE **capture, convey, embody, encapsulate, represent** *His paintings embody the very essence of the immediate post-war years.*
- PREP. **in~** *His theory was not new in essence.*

2 concentrated substance

- ADJ. **almond, vanilla, etc.**
- QUANT. **dash, drop** *Add a few drops of vanilla essence.*
- VERB + ESSENCE **add, use**

essential *adj.*

- VERBS **appear, be, seem | become** *It is becoming almost essential for students to have a second language.* | **remain | make sth** *Increased competition makes it essential for the business to innovate.* | **consider sth, deem sth, regard sth as, see sth as, think sth** *Do you consider these textbooks essential for the course?*
- ADV. **really | absolutely | almost, virtually | fairly | by no means** *Although useful, the accessories are by no means essential.*
- PREP. **for** *the skills essential for success* **to** *He believed that some form of religion was essential to human life.*

essentials *noun*

- ADJ. **bare, basic** *the bare essentials for existence*
- VERB + ESSENTIALS **grasp** *Just try and grasp the essentials of the argument.* | **provide** *The relief agencies are trying to provide food and other basic essentials.* | **concentrate on** *Don't let's worry about the details at this stage. Let's concentrate on the essentials.*

establish *verb*

1 start/create sth

- VERB + ESTABLISH **attempt to, seek to, try to** *trying to establish links with local schools* | **help (to), help sb (to)** | **agree to** *The two countries agreed to establish full diplomatic relations.* | **be able to** | **be important to**
- PHRASES **an attempt/effort to establish sth, newly/recently established** *He was appointed to the newly established Department of the Environment.*

2 make sth known and accepted

- ADV. **firmly, securely** *His position in the organization is now firmly established.*
- VERB + ESTABLISH **attempt to, seek to, try to | help (to), help sb (to)** *The exhibition helped her establish herself as an artist.*
- PREP. **as** *He has now established his reputation as a popular musician.*
- PHRASES **become/get established** *The festival has become established as one of the town's annual events.*

3 make certain of sth

- ADV. **conclusively, definitely | empirically**
- VERB + ESTABLISH **attempt to, seek to, try to** *Police are still trying to establish the identity of the dead man.* | **help (to) | be able to | be possible to | be difficult to | be important to**
- PHRASES **an attempt/effort to establish sth**

establishment *noun*

1 act of starting sth

- ADJ. **formal** *the formal establishment of the republic in 1948* | **gradual, rapid**

• VERB + ESTABLISHMENT **call for, support** *Opposition MPs are calling for the establishment of an independent food and drugs agency.* | **agree to, consent to** | **lead to** *This report led to the establishment of a special committee to investigate the matter.* | **allow (for), enable, provide for** *a law allowing the establishment of private television stations* | **announce** | **see** *The months that followed saw the establishment of a strong military presence in the region.*

• PREP. **with the~of** *With the establishment of major new markets, the economy is thriving.*

2 shop/business/organization
• ADJ. **catering, educational, military, research, training** *She's now running a small government research establishment.*
⇨ Note at ORGANIZATION (for verbs)

3 the establishment people in positions of power
• ADJ. **academic, art, literary, medical, musical, political, religious, scientific** | **British, French,** etc. *The British Establishment is very slow to accept change.*
• VERB + ESTABLISHMENT **offend** *His abstract paintings offended the art establishment.*

estate noun

1 land owned by a person/family/organization
• ADJ. **big, great, large, substantial, vast** | **small**
• VERB + ESTATE **have, own** *The family owns a large estate in the north of the country.* | **buy** *Queen Victoria bought the estate in 1848.* | **manage, run**
• ESTATE + NOUN **employee, manager, owner, worker** | **management**
• PREP. **on an/the~** *the number of people living on the estate* | **~of** *an estate of 20 000 acres*
• PHRASES **an heir to an estate** *The young prince is the heir to a vast estate in the west of the country.*

2 land with a lot of buildings of the same type
• ADJ. **large, massive** | **small** | **council, housing** | **private** | **industrial, trading** *The factory is on a large industrial estate on the outskirts of town.*
• VERB + ESTATE **build**
• PREP. **on an/the~** *She lives on a council estate in Leeds.*

3 property that sb leaves when they die
• ADJ. **personal**
• VERB + ESTATE **leave** *She left her whole estate to her niece.* | **inherit** *She inherited her father's estate.* | **own** *He owns personal estate worth $30 million.*
• ESTATE + VERB **be valued at sth, be worth sth**

esteem noun

• ADJ. **great, high** | **low** | **personal, self-** *I needed to do it for my own personal esteem.* | **popular, public, social**
• VERB + ESTEEM **earn** *She had earned the esteem of everyone in the town.* | **lose** *It is easy for children to lose their self-esteem.* | **accord sb** *the level of social esteem accorded to doctors* | **fall in, rise in** *He fell in public esteem following the scandal.*
• PREP. **in … ~** *the status of teachers in the public esteem* | **~ for** *the public's esteem for the prime minister* **~ of** *The school's aim is to build the self-esteem of the children.*
• PHRASES **hold sb/sth in great/high/low esteem** *He is held in the highest esteem by all who know him.* **a mark/token of esteem** *We would like to offer you this gift as a mark of our esteem.*

estimate noun

• ADJ. **official, unofficial** | **current, recent** *Current estimates suggest that supplies will run out within six months.* | **early, initial, preliminary** | **accurate, fair, good, realistic, reasonable, reliable** | **best** *Flight times in the brochure are based on our best estimate, and will be confirmed as soon as possible.* | **approximate, rough** |

conservative, low *I think 15 000 will turn out to be a very low estimate.* | **high** *According to the highest estimate, over 100 000 men died in the battle.* | **optimistic, pessimistic** | **cost**
• VERB + ESTIMATE **make** *Can you make an estimate of the numbers involved?* | **give (sb), provide (sb with), submit** *Three firms submitted estimates for the work.* | **revise**
• ESTIMATE + VERB **be based on sth** | **indicate sth, predict sth, show sth, suggest sth** *One estimate suggests that 30 000 jobs may be lost.* | **put sth at** *Some estimates put the figure as high as 50%.* | **range, vary** *Cost estimates vary from $50 000 to $200 000.*
• PREP. **according to an/the~** *According to the revised estimate, four million people will be without homes.* **at an~** *Even at a conservative estimate, there is a lot of work to be done.* **in an/the~** *In his first estimate, he suggested a figure of £5 000.* | **~by, ~from** *According to an estimate by a leading newspaper, she earns £40 million a year.* **~ for** *We will send you an estimate for the repairs.* **~ of** *an estimate of profits* ◇ *an estimate of £300*

estimate verb

• ADV. **currently** | **accurately, reliably** | **provisionally** | **conservatively** *It is conservatively estimated that not less than half a million people died in the famine.* | **officially, unofficially** *The strike was officially estimated to have cost $80 million.*
• VERB + ESTIMATE **be difficult to, be hard to, be impossible to** | **be used to** *The results of the survey were used to estimate the preferences of the population at large.*
• PREP. **at** *We estimated the cost at £50 000.*

estimation noun

• VERB + ESTIMATION **go up in, rise in** *He went up in my estimation when I heard about his charity work.* | **go down in**
• PREP. **in sb's ~** *In my estimation, you've done a good job.*

estranged adj.

• VERBS **be, feel** | **become**
• ADV. **deeply** | **completely** | **increasingly**
• PREP. **from** *He felt deeply estranged from the society he lived in.*

ethics noun

• ADJ. **personal** *She resigned over an issue of personal ethics.* | **Christian** | **business, medical, professional** *The study was approved by the medical ethics committee.*
• PHRASES **a code of ethics** *There should be a code of business ethics which indicates how clients are to be served.* **a matter/question of ethics.** *It's the committee's job to decide on matters of ethics.*

etiquette noun

• ADJ. **professional, social** *He showed his contempt for social etiquette by not wearing a tie.* | **correct** *What's the correct etiquette when addressing a judge?* | **strict** *the strict etiquette of palace life*
• VERB + ETIQUETTE **breach** *He had breached etiquette by not informing his superiors of his decision.*
• ETIQUETTE + VERB **require sth** *Etiquette requires that the bride's father makes a speech.*
• PHRASES **a breach of etiquette** *The solicitor was accused of a breach of professional etiquette.* **matters of etiquette** *He is an expert on matters of etiquette.* **the rules of etiquette** *She knew how to address bishops according to the rules of etiquette.* **a stickler for etiquette** *She's a real stickler for etiquette, so you'd better ask her advice.*

euphoria *noun*

- ADJ. **early, initial** *after the initial euphoria* | **general**
- QUANT. **wave** *The news sparked a wave of euphoria across the country.*
- VERB + EUPHORIA **feel** *the euphoria we all felt when they were finally defeated*
- EUPHORIA + VERB **evaporate, fade**
- PREP. **~ about** *All the euphoria about the 'new methods' soon faded.* **~ over** *By then, the euphoria over the fall of the Berlin Wall had evaporated.*
- PHRASES **a feeling of euphoria, a state of euphoria**

euro *noun*

⇨ Note at CURRENCY

euthanasia *noun*

- ADJ. **voluntary** | **involuntary**
- VERB + EUTHANASIA **perform, practise** | **legalize**

evacuate *verb*

- ADV. **safely**
- VERB + EVACUATE **help (to)** *to provide aircraft to help evacuate refugees*
- PREP. **from** *Helicopters were used to evacuate people from their homes.* **to** *The man has now been safely evacuated to the mainland.*

evacuation *noun*

- ADJ. **large-scale, mass** | **emergency, immediate** | **casualty** | **wartime**
- EVACUATION + NOUN **area, zone** | **order** | **plan, programme, scheme** | **procedures**
- PREP. **~ from** *the evacuation of civilians from the area*

evade *verb*

1 escape
- ADV. **narrowly** *They narrowly evaded a police car which was approaching.* | **successfully**
- VERB + EVADE **attempt to, try to** | **manage to** *He managed to evade capture and escaped over the border.*

2 avoid dealing with sth
- ADV. **simply** *Her response was simply to evade the problem altogether.* | **carefully, skilfully** | **easily** *Responsibility could not be so easily evaded.* | **altogether**
- VERB + EVADE **attempt to, try to**

evaluate *verb*

- ADV. **fully, properly, thoroughly** | **carefully, systematically** *The evidence should be carefully evaluated.* | **critically** | **positively** *The role of stay-at-home mother is more positively evaluated in working-class communities.*
- VERB + EVALUATE **aim to, attempt to, be designed to** | **help (to)** *to help evaluate the success of the campaign* | **be used to** *criteria used to evaluate employees' performance* | **be difficult to, be hard to**

evaluation *noun*

- ADJ. **comprehensive, thorough** | **objective** | **critical** *a critical evaluation of the film* | **job** *a new pay structure based on job evaluations*
- VERB + EVALUATION **carry out, make** *We've still got to carry out an evaluation of the results.*
- EVALUATION + NOUN **procedure, process** | **study**
- PREP. **in an/the ~** *In their evaluation of the project, they considered only certain aspects of it.* **under ~** *The new scheme is still under evaluation.*

eve *noun*

- ADJ. **Christmas, Midsummer's, New Year's**

- PREP. **on the ~ of** *opinion polls published on the eve of the election*

even *adj.*

1 level/smooth
- VERBS **be, look** *The floor isn't completely even.*
- ADV. **very** | **absolutely, completely**

2 same size/level
- VERBS **be** | **become** | **keep sth** *Try to keep your stitches absolutely even.*
- ADV. **very** | **absolutely, completely** | **fairly** *Try to keep the room at a fairly even temperature.*

3 equal
- VERBS **be, seem** | **remain**
- ADV. **very** | **fairly, more or less** *The scores remained more or less even throughout the competition.*

evening *noun*

1 part of the day
- ADJ. **this, tomorrow, yesterday** | **Friday, Saturday, etc.** | **April, May, etc.** | **spring, summer, etc.** | **long** *the long winter evenings* | **dark** | **quiet** | **balmy, beautiful, fine, golden, warm** | **cold, cool, dry** | **early, late** *It was early evening and very still.*
- VERB + EVENING **spend** *We spent the evening walking round the town.*
- EVENING + VERB **progress, wear on** *As the evening wore on, Phil became very drunk.*
- EVENING + NOUN **light, star** | **meal** | **shift, work** | **class, course** | **entertainment, performance** | **prayer, service** | **rush hour** | **news, newspaper, paper**
- PREP. **during the ~, for an/the ~** *Her parents were out for the evening.* **in the ~, on Friday, etc. ~**
- PHRASES **an/the evening off/out** *You deserve an occasional evening out.* **good evening**

2 event happening in the evening
- ADJ. **gala, musical, social** | **open, parents'** *Prospective students were invited to the school's open evening.* | **convivial, enjoyable, lovely, memorable, pleasant, successful, wonderful**
- VERB + EVENING **hold** *The club will hold a social evening to welcome new members.*
- EVENING + NOUN **clothes, dress, gown, wear**
- PREP. **during the ~, for the ~**

event *noun*

1 sth that happens
- ADJ. **big, great, historic, important, key, main, major, momentous, significant** *Tonight's programme looks back at the main events of the year.* | **dramatic, remarkable** | **happy** | **sad, tragic, traumatic** | **rare** *Outside big cities, murder is a rare event.* | **subsequent** *Subsequent events proved him wrong.* | **historical, political**
- VERB + EVENT **witness** *When the ship finally reached land, only a few of the crew were left to witness the event.* | **record** *We had a huge party, and hired a photographer to record the event.* | **celebrate, commemorate, mark** *Today is the hospital's fiftieth anniversary, and there will be a party to mark the event.*
- EVENT + VERB **happen, occur, take place, unfold** *TV viewers watched in horror as events unfolded.* | **lead to sth** *These events quickly led to confusion.* | **lead up to sth** *The police are trying to establish a picture of events leading up to the killing.*
- PHRASES **a chain/sequence/series of events, the course of events** *Would it have been possible to change the course of events?*

2 planned social occasion
- ADJ. **big, important, main, major, special** | **popular** | **prestigious** *The Birmingham meeting is one of the most prestigious events in the racing calendar.* | **inaugural** |

annual, regular | forthcoming *Forthcoming events are listed on the back page of the local newspaper.* | fundraising, musical, social, sporting
• VERB + EVENT **hold, organize, stage** *The event will be held in the grounds of the manor house.* | **publicize** | **attend, support** *I would like to thank everyone who attended our charity evening for supporting the event.* | **boycott** *Several leading players boycotted the event in protest at the reduced prize money.*
• EVENT + VERB **take place**

3 race/competition
• ADJ. **big, main** *This race will be the main event of the afternoon.* | **individual, team** | **men's, women's** | **field, track** | **jumping, running, throwing** | **distance, long-distance, middle-distance, sprint**
• VERB + EVENT **enter (for), take part in** *A record number of teams have entered the event.* | **win**
• EVENT + VERB **take place** *The team events will take place later this week.*
• PREP. **in an/the ~** *African runners swept the medals in the distance events.*

evict *verb*

• ADV. **forcibly** | **unlawfully**
• VERB + EVICT **seek to, try to**
• PREP. **from** *They were forcibly evicted from their home.*

eviction *noun*

• ADJ. **illegal, unlawful** *He claimed damages for unlawful eviction.* | **forcible**
• VERB + EVICTION **be threatened with, face** | **resist**
• EVICTION + NOUN **notice, order, warrant**
• PREP. **~from** *They are facing eviction from their home.*

evidence *noun*

• ADJ. **abundant, ample, considerable, extensive, plentiful, substantial, widespread** | **growing** | **clear, compelling, conclusive, convincing, decisive, good, hard, incontrovertible, irrefutable, overwhelming, persuasive, positive, powerful, solid, striking, strong, unambiguous, unequivocal** | **adequate** | **flimsy, inadequate, insufficient, scant** | **concrete, direct, firm, first-hand, objective, tangible** *The figures provide concrete evidence of the bank's claim to provide the best service.* | **indirect** | **available, current, present** *Available evidence points to pilot error as the cause of the crash.* | **fresh, further, more, new** | **crucial, important, valuable, vital** *The defence accused the prosecution of withholding crucial evidence.* | **corroborative** *They convicted the wrong man on the basis of a signed confession with no corroborative evidence.* | **conflicting** *Another team of scientists has come up with conflicting evidence.* | **damning** *The scandal is damning evidence of the government's contempt for democracy.* | **anecdotal, archaeological, circumstantial, documentary, empirical, experimental, factual, forensic, formal, historical, material, medical, photographic, scientific, statistical, video, visible, visual** *There was a mass of circumstantial evidence linking Watson to the murder.* | **false** *She admitted giving false evidence to the court.*
• QUANT. **piece** | **body, mass** *A body of evidence emerged suggesting that smoking tobacco caused serious diseases.*
• VERB + EVIDENCE **have** *We do not have the evidence to prove these claims.* | **look for, search for** | **accumulate, collect, come up with, find, gather, obtain, produce** *Scientists have found fresh evidence to suggest that a huge explosion led to the death of the dinosaurs.* | **offer (sb), provide (sb with), show (sb)** *The tapes provided evidence of her intentions.* | **give, present (sb with)** *She was hoping she would not have to give evidence in court.* | **see** *He says he's been working hard, but I haven't seen any evidence of*

it. | **consider, examine, study** | **review** | **cite (sth as)** *The team cited evidence from a recent earthquake to back up their idea.* ◊ *The rise in crime is often cited as evidence of a general breakdown of authority.* | **use sth in** *The police officer took a statement which was later used in evidence.* | **hear** *We must wait to hear his evidence before we make any judgement.* | **admit, allow** *The judge can decide whether to admit or exclude evidence.* | **exclude**
• EVIDENCE + VERB **exist** | **come to light, emerge** | **accumulate, grow** *Evidence is accumulating that a defective gene may be responsible for this disease.* | **confirm sth, demonstrate sth, establish sth, point to sth, show sth, suggest sth, support sth** *The evidence pointed to the existence of an international smuggling network.* | **be based on sth, be derived from sth, come from sth** *evidence of growing poverty based on extensive surveys* | **implicate sb/sth, link sb/sth** *evidence linking her to the crime*
• PREP. **as ~** *He cited Australia's sporting success as evidence for his theory.* **in ~** *A photo of the victim's injuries was produced in evidence.* **on ... ~** *On present evidence the team will be lucky to make the final.* **on the ~ of** *On the evidence of his latest exhibition, Miller is an artist who is past his best.* | **~ about, ~ concerning, ~ regarding, ~ relating to** *The team have been collecting evidence about war crimes.* **~ against** *The woman went to court to give evidence against her attacker.* **~ for** *What evidence do you have for that claim?* **~ of** *Archaeologists found evidence of a rich and varied culture at the settlement.* **~ on** *The first chapter reviews the evidence on how children learn language.*
• PHRASES **in the face/teeth of evidence** *The company denies, in the face of overwhelming evidence, that smoking causes cancer.* **in the light of evidence** *In the light of new evidence, a new enquiry into the crash is likely to take place.* **lack of evidence** *The kidnapping charge was dropped because of lack of evidence.* **not a scrap/shred of evidence** *He made the accusations without a shred of evidence to back them up.*

evident *adj.*

• VERBS **be, seem** | **become** | **remain** | **make sth** *The silence of the forest was made evident by the occasional snap of a twig.*
• ADV. **clearly, plainly, strongly, very** | **perfectly, quite** | **increasingly** | **especially, particularly** | **fairly** | **sufficiently** | **immediately** | **already** *It is already evident that new roads only generate new traffic.* | **painfully** *The strain of her work schedule became painfully evident as she jetted from New York to London and on to Milan.*
• PREP. **from** *It was fairly evident from her tone of voice that she disapproved.* **in** *His anger was evident in his attitude to the others.* **to** *It was evident to me that the mission would fail.*

evil *noun*

• ADJ. **great** | **lesser** *This sort of job is a lesser evil than unemployment.* | **moral, social** *combating the social evils of poverty, disease and ignorance*
• VERB + EVIL **do** *His simple message was that God will punish those that do evil.* | **combat, fight, resist, turn (away) from** *You can always choose to resist evil.*
• PHRASES **the forces of evil** *a perpetual struggle between the forces of good and the forces of evil* **good and evil** *not a simple choice between good and evil* **the root of all evil** *He sees money as the root of all evil.*

evil *adj.*

• VERBS **be, look, seem** | **become**
• ADV. **really, truly, very** | **wholly** | **basically, inherently, intrinsically** *He believes that all people are basically evil.*

evoke verb

● ADV. **clearly, vividly | still** *Her face, though sad, still evoked a feeling of serenity.*
● VERB + EVOKE **try to | be designed to, be intended to** *narrative techniques that are intended to evoke sympathy from the reader*

evolution noun

● ADJ. **gradual | rapid | continuous | natural | peaceful** *the peaceful evolution to democracy* | **biological, cultural, historical, political, social, technological | animal, human | Darwinian**
● VERB + EVOLUTION **trace** *a book tracing the evolution of the English language*
● EVOLUTION + VERB **occur, proceed, take place** *Evolution proceeds by a series of small changes.*
● PREP. **~ from … to …** *his evolution from comedian to serious actor* **~ towards** *the country's gradual evolution towards democracy*
● PHRASES **the theory of evolution** *people who reject the theory of evolution*

evolve verb

● ADV. **gradually, slowly | rapidly | eventually** *the theory which eventually evolved from this study* | **constantly, continually | naturally | independently, separately** *Monkeys in the New World evolved quite separately from those in the Old World.*
● VERB + EVOLVE **continue to**
● PREP. **from** *More complex animals gradually evolved from these very simple creatures.* **into** *The protest movement has evolved into a well organized political party.*
● PHRASES **fully/highly evolved** *These are very highly evolved animals.*

exaggerate verb

● ADV. **greatly, grossly, vastly, wildly** *These figures have been greatly exaggerated.* | **a little, rather, slightly, somewhat | further | easily** *The historical significance of these events can be easily exaggerated* (= it is easy to think they are more significant than they are). | **artificially, deliberately**
● VERB + EXAGGERATE **tend to** *John does tend to exaggerate slightly.* | **be easy to | be difficult to, be hard to, be impossible to** *It is difficult to exaggerate the importance of developing good study habits.*

exaggeration noun

● ADJ. **great, gross, wild | mild, slight**
● QUANT. **degree** *There was a degree of exaggeration in his description of events.*
● VERB + EXAGGERATION **be given to, be prone to** *John is rather given to exaggeration.* | **allow for** *Their results, even allowing for exaggeration, are impressive.*
● PREP. **without ~** *There were, without exaggeration, hundreds of applications for the job.*
● PHRASES **a bit of an exaggeration** *It would be a bit of an exaggeration to say that I'm desperate to leave.* **it is no exaggeration to say sth** *It is no exaggeration to say that having a baby changes your life.*

exam noun

● ADJ. **difficult, stiff | easy | entrance, matriculation, placement | end of term/year, final | professional, school | chemistry, French, geography, etc. | external | mock** *I did badly in the mock exam but passed the real thing.* | **multiple choice, oral, practical, written**
● VERB + EXAM **prepare for, revise for, study for** *I can't go out because I'm revising for end of year exams.* | **do, sit, take** *When do you sit your final exams?* | **resit, retake | do well in, pass, scrape through** *In spite of her*

worries, she passed the exam with flying colours. ◇ *I wrote two awful essays and was lucky to scrape through the exam.* | **do badly in, fail, flunk | cheat in** *Candidates found cheating in any exam will be disqualified from all their exams.* | **set** *The final exam is set by a board of professors.* | **administer, invigilate | mark**
● EXAM + VERB **begin, start | be over, finish** *As soon as the exams are over I'm going on holiday.*
● EXAM + NOUN **practice, preparation, revision | paper, question | marks, results | failure, pass | technique | nerves** *Most students suffer from exam nerves to some extent.* | **fee | time** *There is a subdued atmosphere in the school at exam time.* | **format** *The exam format has been changed to include multiple choice questions.* | **board** *The regional exam boards all get together regularly to ensure equal standards.*
● PREP. **in an/the ~** *He did badly in his maths exam.* | **~ for** *an exam for school leavers* **~ in** *an exam in chemistry*

examination noun

1 exam
● ADJ. **difficult, stiff** *The stiff entrance examination removes 60 per cent of prospective students.* | **easy | important | entrance, matriculation, selection | end of term/year, final** *He has just completed his final examinations at London University.* | **professional, school | formal | competitive | external, public** *One of the teacher's principal duties is to prepare students for external examinations.* | **A level, GCSE, etc. | mock | multiple choice, oral, practical, written, viva voce**
● VERB + EXAMINATION **prepare for, revise for, study for | enter for** *Students may enter for both examinations.* | **do, sit, take** *She will take her professional examinations later this year.* | **resit, retake | do well in, pass | do badly in, fail | set** *The examinations are set by individual teachers.* | **administer, invigilate | mark**
● EXAMINATION + NOUN **paper, question | syllabus | candidate | grades, marks, results | certificate | hall, room | fee | technique | success**
● PREP. **~ in** *He failed his examination in history.* **~ on** *an examination on human anatomy*

2 looking at sth carefully
● ADJ. **careful, close, detailed, full, lengthy, rigorous, thorough** *Each of the proposals deserves careful examination.* | **brief, cursory, superficial | initial, preliminary | critical** *The school curriculum has undergone critical examination in recent years.* | **clinical, forensic, medical, physical, post-mortem, psychiatric, scientific**
● VERB + EXAMINATION **carry out, conduct, do, make, perform** *He carried out a post-mortem examination.* ◇ *We will make a more thorough examination of the area later.* | **come under, have, be subject/subjected to, undergo** *I was advised to have a full eyesight examination.* | **stand up to** *His ideas about social change do not stand up to close examination.*
● EXAMINATION + VERB **reveal sth, show sth** *A medical examination showed no signs of hypertension.*
● EXAMINATION + NOUN **couch** *She lay on the examination couch and waited for the doctor to return.*
● PREP. **on ~** *On closer examination the wood was found to be rotten.* **under ~** *Several items of clothing are still under examination.* | **~ by** *The school's controversial methods have come under examination by the local authority.*
⇨ See CROSS-EXAMINATION

examine verb

1 consider/look at sb/sth carefully
● ADV. **carefully, closely, in detail, minutely** *Each case must be carefully examined.* ◇ *We shall now proceed to examine these two aspects of the problem in detail.* | **ex-**

haustively, fully, properly, thoroughly | briefly | further | critically *Critically examine your work as if you were looking at someone else's efforts.* | medically
● VERB + EXAMINE **aim to, be designed to, seek to, set out to** *This study sets out to examine the possible effects of climate change.* | **proceed to** | **stop to** *Anna stopped to examine a plant growing by the stream.* | **be necessary to, need to** | **want to, wish to**
● PREP. **for** *The room was examined minutely for clues.*
● PHRASES **let us examine ...** *Let us examine the implications of this theory.*

2 test what sb knows/can do
● ADV. **externally, internally** *The course is externally examined* (= by people from outside the college, university, etc.).
● PREP. **in** *The students will be examined in all subjects at the end of term.* **on** *You are only being examined on this semester's work.*

example *noun*

1 sth that is typical/demonstrates a point
● ADJ. **characteristic, classic, prime, representative, typical** *This is a classic example of a badly designed building.* | **excellent, fine, good, impressive, magnificent, outstanding, perfect, superb, wonderful** *a magnificent example of sixteenth-century architecture* | **fascinating, interesting, intriguing** | **notable, remarkable, striking** | **graphic, vivid** | **dramatic, extreme, spectacular** | **clear, obvious, simple, straightforward** | **blatant, flagrant, glaring** *His treatment of his secretary was a blatant example of managerial arrogance.* | **familiar, famous, well-known** | **notorious** | **common** | **rare** | **much-quoted, oft-quoted, often-quoted** *The oft-quoted example of Nero playing the violin as Rome burned shows the Emperor's detachment from reality.* | **illustrative** | **helpful, illuminating, instructive, useful** | **practical** *The book is full of practical examples of classroom activities.* | **concrete** *Let me give a concrete example of what I mean.* | **hypothetical**
● VERB + EXAMPLE **give sb, provide (sb with)** *Let me give you a few examples of what I mean.* | **contain, include** *The leaflet includes several examples of bad grammar.* | **cite, draw, take (sth as)** *She illustrates her point with examples drawn from contemporary newspaper accounts.* ◇ *To take an obvious example, if there is a good harvest the price of grain will fall.* | **find**
● EXAMPLE + VERB **illustrate sth, show sth**
● PREP. **for ~** *A touring cyclist, for example, might turn the pedals 80 times a minute.* **in an/the ~** *The teacher in our example is clearly wrong.* | **~ of** *We can still find examples of discrimination today.*

2 sb whose behaviour is good and should be copied
● ADJ. **good, great, inspiring, shining** *She is a shining example of how to organize your time.* | **bad, poor**
● VERB + EXAMPLE **set, show** *You must set a good example to the children.* | **follow** *I think all schools should follow the example of this one.* | **hold sb/sth up as** *The film was held up as an example of good cinema.*
● PREP. **by ~** *Children learn by example.* | **~ to** *His generosity is an example to us all.*
● PHRASES **make an example of sb** *The headmaster had made an example of him by scolding him in front of the whole school.*

exasperation *noun*

● ADJ. **sheer** | **mild**
● QUANT. **hint**
● VERB + EXASPERATION **feel** | **express, give vent to** *The organization has expressed its exasperation with the government.* | **control, hide, suppress**
● PREP. **in ~** *She rolled her eyes in sheer exasperation.* **with ~** *He snorted with exasperation.* | **~ at** *the exasper-*

ation he felt at his failure* ~ **with** *their exasperation with the government rules*
● PHRASES **a groan/grunt/sigh of exasperation** *With a groan of exasperation, he picked up the luggage himself.*

excavate *verb*

● ADV. **completely, fully** *The area has not yet been fully excavated.* | **extensively** | **partially, partly** | **carefully**
● PREP. **from** *Pottery has been excavated from the site.*

excavation *noun*

● ADJ. **archaeological**
● VERB + EXCAVATION **carry out, conduct** *Further archaeological excavations are now being carried out.*
● EXCAVATION + VERB **reveal sth, uncover sth, unearth sth** *Excavations of the site have revealed an Iron Age settlement.* | **proceed, take place** *More discoveries were made as the excavation proceeded.*

exceed *verb*

● ADV. **considerably, far, greatly, significantly, substantially** | **comfortably, easily** *The House voted by 327 votes to 93, comfortably exceeding the required two-thirds majority.* | **slightly** | **clearly** | **regularly** | **rarely** *Summer temperatures rarely exceed 27°C.* | **generally, normally, usually**
● VERB + EXCEED **be expected to, be likely to** *Income is expected to exceed expenditure.* | **be unlikely to**

excellence *noun*

● ADJ. **all-round** | **academic, artistic, culinary, educational, manufacturing, scientific, sporting, technical**
● VERB + EXCELLENCE **pursue, strive for** *The school strives for academic excellence.* | **achieve**
● PREP. **~ in** *The Business School has a reputation for excellence in research.*
● PHRASES **a centre of excellence** *The college aims to be a world centre of excellence in the field of marine biology.* **levels/standards of excellence** *The restaurant's standards of excellence have won it several awards.* **the pursuit of excellence** *her relentless pursuit of sporting excellence*

excellent *adj.*

● VERBS **appear, be, look, prove, seem, sound** | **become** | **consider sth** *The school is considered excellent.*
● ADV. **most, really, truly** | **absolutely, quite** | **rather** | **generally** *The meals are generally excellent.* | **uniformly** *The performances and recordings are uniformly excellent.* | **apparently** | **potentially** | **otherwise** *In an otherwise excellent issue about global warming, I found Jeremy Creed's article very unconvincing.*
● PREP. **at** *Clancey was excellent at keeping the kids under control.* **for** *These potatoes are excellent for baking.*

exception *noun*

● ADJ. **conspicuous, important, major, notable, obvious, significant, striking** *Most industries have suffered badly in the recession, but there have been a few notable exceptions.* | **minor, rare** | **honourable** *With a few honourable exceptions, MPs kept quiet about the corruption.*
● VERB + EXCEPTION **make** *No parking is allowed, but an exception is made for disabled drivers.*
● PREP. **with the ~ of** *The whole of the island was flooded with the exception of a small area in the north.* **without ~** *Without exception, all employees must carry their identity card with them at all times.* | **~ to** *Guide dogs are the one exception to the store's ban on dogs.*
● PHRASES **be no exception** *The weather had been rainy for days, and the day of the race was no exception.* **be the exception rather than the rule** *Nowadays a job for life is very much the exception rather than the rule.* **be the**

exception to the rule *Most of his family are sports enthusiasts, but he's the exception to the rule.*

exceptional *adj.*

- VERBS **be** | **remain** | **consider sb/sth** *The head teacher considers Jamie's performance altogether exceptional.*
- ADV. **highly, really, very** | **altogether, quite, wholly**

excerpt *noun*

- ADJ. **short**
- VERB + EXCERPT **feature, give, include, play, publish, quote, show** *The programme included excerpts from Verdi's operas.*
- PREP. **~from** *The paper published some short excerpts from Mandela's memoirs.*

excess *noun*

1 large amount of sth
- ADJ. **large**
- PREP. **in ~** *The drug can be harmful if taken in excess.* **in~of** *The vehicle had been travelling at speeds in excess of 90 miles per hour.* **to ~** *They never smoked or drank to excess.* | **~of** *a large excess of gas*

2 excesses harmful actions
- ADJ. **worst**
- VERB + EXCESSES **avoid, curb** | **commit, perpetrate** *the worst excesses committed by the occupying army*

excessive *adj.*

- VERBS **appear, be, seem** | **become** | **consider sth, regard sth as, see sth as** *He considered the level of tax excessive.*
- ADV. **grossly** | **a bit, a little, rather, somewhat**

exchange *noun*

1 giving/receiving sth in return for sth else
- ADJ. **fair** | **mutual, two-way** *We get together once a month for a mutual exchange of ideas.*
- PREP. **in ~ (for)** *Woollen cloth and timber were sent to Egypt in exchange for linen or papyrus.* | **~ between** *There were exchanges of goods between the two regions.* **~ for** *She considered free language lessons a fair exchange for free accommodation.*

2 angry conversation/argument
- ADJ. **brief** | **acrimonious, angry, bitter, heated, sharp** | **verbal** *a bitter verbal exchange*
- PREP. **~ about** *angry exchanges about the problem of unemployment* **~between** *There were many acrimonious exchanges between the two men.* **~ with** *Opposition MPs were involved in heated exchanges with the prime minister.*
- PHRASES **an exchange of views** *She had a full and frank exchange of views with her boss before resigning.*

3 of foreign currencies
- EXCHANGE + NOUN **rate**

4 visit
- ADJ. **academic, cultural** | **student, youth** | **official**
- VERB + EXCHANGE **go on**
- PREP. **on an/the ~** *She is in France on a student exchange.* | **~to** *He's gone on an exchange to Rome.* **~with** *an exchange with a German student*

excise *noun*

- VERB + EXCISE **impose, levy** *the excise levied on beer and tobacco* | **pay** | **increase, raise** | **cut, reduce**
- EXCISE + NOUN **duty, revenue, tax** | **licence** *applications for vehicle excise licences* | **officer**
- PREP. **~on** *to increase the excise on whisky*

excitable *adj.*

- VERBS **be, seem** | **become**
- ADV. **highly, very** | **quite, rather, somewhat** | **easily** *The horses have easily excitable nervous systems.*

excited *adj.*

- VERBS **be, feel, look, seem, sound** | **become, get, grow** | **get sb** *Don't get the children too excited.*
- ADV. **all, extraordinarily, extremely, highly, really, terribly, tremendously, very, wildly** *He was all excited about his new car.* ◊ *By now the crowd was wildly excited.* | **increasingly** | **a bit, a little, pretty, quite, rather** | **strangely** | **sexually**
- PREP. **about** *The kids seem pretty excited about the holiday.* **at** *excited at the news* **by** *He was puzzled but strangely excited by the commotion.*

excitement *noun*

- ADJ. **considerable, fierce, great, high, intense, tremendous** | **breathless, febrile, feverish, heady, wild** | **genuine, real, sheer** | **initial** | **sudden** | **growing, heightened, mounting** | **added, further** | **suppressed** | **nervous, restless** | **guilty** | **pleasurable** | **strange** | **vicarious** *The reader of adventure stories wants romance and vicarious excitement.* | **youthful** | **intellectual, physical, political, sexual**
- QUANT. **flicker, flurry, flush, frisson, ripple, surge** *She felt a surge of excitement when she heard the song.*
- VERB + EXCITEMENT **be bubbling with, be filled with, be flushed with, be sick with, be trembling/tingling with, feel** *Her face was flushed with excitement.* ◊ *She was almost sick with excitement and apprehension.* | **cause, generate** *The news caused tremendous excitement among scientists.* | **conceal, control, hide, suppress** *He couldn't suppress the excitement in his voice.* | **add** *The element of risk just adds excitement.*
- EXCITEMENT + VERB **build up, grow, mount, rise** *The tension and excitement built up gradually all day.* | **die down, evaporate, wear off**
- PREP. **in ~** *clapping her hands in excitement* | **~among** *The news has caused great excitement among scientists.* **~at** *her excitement at the prospect of a new job* **~of** *the excitement of meeting new people*
- PHRASES **an air of excitement** *There was an air of excitement about the place.* **a feeling/sense of excitement, a fever/state of excitement**

exciting *adj.*

- VERBS **be, look, seem, sound** | **become, get** *The film was just getting exciting when we had to leave.* | **find sth** *She found the idea terrifically exciting.*
- ADV. **enormously, extraordinarily, extremely, immensely, incredibly, really, terribly, terrifically, tremendously, unbelievably, very, wildly, wonderfully** | **pretty, quite, rather** | **potentially** *the germ of a potentially exciting innovation* | **undeniably** | **visually** *a book that is attractive and visually exciting* | **sexually**
- PHRASES **exciting new** *an exciting new magazine*

exclaim *verb*

- ADV. **loudly, softly** | **angrily, indignantly** | **helplessly, weakly** | **triumphantly** | **suddenly**
- PREP. **at, in** *They exclaimed in horror at the price.* **over** *standing in front of shop windows exclaiming over the beautiful clothes* **with** *She exclaimed with delight at the sight of the presents.*

exclamation *noun*

- ADJ. **sharp, sudden** | **loud** | **muffled, small**
- VERB + EXCLAMATION **give, let out, utter** *She gave a loud exclamation of delight.* | **stifle, suppress**

exclude *verb*

- ADV. **rigorously | altogether, completely, entirely, totally | not absolutely, not wholly** *The possibility of error cannot be absolutely excluded.* | **virtually | largely | permanently | apparently | clearly | automatically** *Unlawfully obtained evidence is not automatically excluded from a criminal trial.* | **necessarily | deliberately | explicitly, expressly, specifically | effectively** *By excluding children from pubs we are effectively excluding many parents.* | **systematically | unfairly**
- VERB + EXCLUDE **attempt to, be designed to, purport to, seek to** *a clause that seeks to exclude liability for death or serious injury* | **tend to** *tending to exclude certain groups from full participation in society*
- PREP. **from** *Women were excluded from the council.*
- PHRASES **feel excluded** *Many local people felt excluded from decisions that affected their own community.*

exclusion *noun*

- ADJ. **complete, total | virtual | continued** *women's continued exclusion from political life* | **social** *the problem of social exclusion*
- EXCLUSION + NOUN **zone** *A 20-mile exclusion zone was set up around the power station to guard against further explosions.*
- PREP. **to the ~ of** *Don't revise a few topics to the exclusion of all others.* | **~ from** *disciplinary measures including exclusion from school*

exclusive *adj.*

1 belonging to/used by only one person/group
- VERBS **be**
- ADV. **almost** *the course's almost exclusive concentration on grammar* | **not necessarily** *The recording deal is not necessarily exclusive. The band can record material for other companies as well.*
- PREP. **to** *These products are exclusive to our shops.*

2 not welcoming to everyone
- VERBS **be | become | remain | keep sth** *The owners of the golf club are determined to keep it exclusive.*
- ADV. **very | quite, rather, somewhat** *a somewhat exclusive venue* | **necessarily** *The school is expensive and necessarily exclusive.* | **racially, socially**

3 not able to exist/be true at the same time
- VERBS **be**
- ADV. **mutually** *The two options are not mutually exclusive* (= you can have them both).

excursion *noun*

- ADJ. **brief, short | day, evening, full-day, half-day, weekend | annual | organized | boat, coach, train | holiday, shopping, sightseeing**
- VERB + EXCURSION **go on, make** *We decided to make an all-day excursion to the island.* | **arrange, organize | take sb on**
- PREP. **~ to** *He took us on an excursion to the ruined city.*

excuse *noun*

1 reason given
- ADJ. **perfect, wonderful | good, legitimate, valid | convincing, plausible, reasonable | feeble, flimsy, lame, pathetic, poor | convenient, easy** *The children provided a convenient excuse for missing the party.* | **standard, usual | every** *She seized on every excuse to avoid doing the work.* | **the slightest** *He became moody and unreasonable, flailing out at Katherine at the slightest excuse.*
- VERB + EXCUSE **have** *He had no excuse for being so late.* | **give, make, offer** *She made some feeble excuse about the car having broken down.* ◇ *You don't have to make excuses for her* (= try to think of reasons for her be-

haviour). ◇ *It's late. I'm afraid I'll have to make my excuses* (= say I'm sorry, give my reasons and leave). | **give sb, offer sb, provide (sb with)** *Delivering the stuff for Rodney gave me an excuse to take the car.* ◇ *Her mother's illness provided her with an excuse to stay at home.* | **need | look for | find, invent, make up, seize on, think up** *She had to find a valid excuse for leaving the room.* ◇ *He made up a rather lame excuse for the work being late.* | **use sth as** *The political crisis is being used as an excuse to dock people's pay.* | **run out of** *He's run out of excuses for not tidying his room.* | **accept, believe | reject**
- PREP. **~ about** *He invented a pathetic excuse about losing his watch.* **~ for** *It's just an excuse for a party.*
- PHRASES **there is no excuse for …** *There's no excuse for such behaviour.*

2 bad example of sth
- ADJ. **pathetic, poor**
- PREP. **~ for** *Why get involved with that pathetic excuse for a human being?*

execute *verb*

1 kill sb as an official punishment
- ADV. **summarily | extrajudicially, illegally | publicly | wrongly** *innocent people who are wrongly executed*
- PREP. **for** *He was executed for treason.*

2 perform/carry out sth
- ADV. **beautifully, boldly, brilliantly, cleanly, meticulously, neatly, skilfully, successfully, well** *The movement was beautifully executed.* | **poorly**

execution *noun*

1 killing sb as an official punishment
- ADJ. **public | mass | judicial | extrajudicial | summary | political | mock**
- VERB + EXECUTION **order** *The tribunal ordered the execution of 42 coup plotters.* | **carry out** *Executions were carried out in the prison yard.* | **face** *If caught, the men could face execution.* | **await** *prisoners who are on death row awaiting execution* | **suffer** *(formal)* *She was taken prisoner and suffered eventual execution.* | **attend, watch, witness**
- EXECUTION + VERB **take place** *A bell was tolled when executions took place.*
- PREP. **~ by** *execution by hanging*
- PHRASES **a stay of execution** (= a delay in an execution being carried out) *The judge had granted a stay of execution.*

2 carrying out a plan/order
- ADJ. **successful** *the successful execution of the contract*
- VERB + EXECUTION **stay, suspend** *The court has discretion to stay or suspend execution of the order.*
- PHRASES **the execution of your duty** *She was charged with obstruction of a police officer in the execution of his duty.* **a stay of execution** (= a delay in an order being carried out)

executive *noun*

1 person with an important job in business
- ADJ. **chief, senior, top** *a top executive in a large corporation* | **junior | key** *contracts to prevent the loss of key executives* | **busy | high-flying, high-powered | female, woman** *The contract gives a female executive maternity leave rights.* | **business, company, corporate, industry | advertising, legal, marketing, media, public relations, sales, television**

2 group of people who run a company/organization
- ADJ. **central, national | political | government, party, union** *She is a member of the party's national executive.* | **strong** *Conservatives are by tradition believers in a strong executive.* | **elected**

- VERB + EXECUTIVE **control** *Parliament's ability to control the executive*
- EXECUTIVE + VERB **decide sth**
- EXECUTIVE + NOUN **member | meeting**
- PHRASES **a member of an executive**

exemplify *verb*

- ADV. **clearly, well**

exempt *verb*

- ADV. **expressly, specifically**
- PREP. **from** *Small businesses are expressly exempted from the requirements of this legislation.*

exempt *adj.*

- VERBS **be | become | remain**
- ADV. **completely, entirely, totally, wholly | partially | automatically** *Pensioners are automatically exempt from prescription charges.*
- PREP. **from** *This income is totally exempt from taxation.*

exemption *noun*

- ADJ. **complete, full, total | blanket** *The bill gives sensitive police files a blanket exemption.* **| partial | temporary | special | tax**
- VERB + EXEMPTION **be entitled to, be subject to, enjoy, qualify for** *These goods are subject to exemption from tax.* ◇ *They enjoyed exemption from customs duties on goods to be used by themselves.* **| apply for, claim, seek | gain, get, obtain | give (sb), grant (sb) | refuse | waive** (*law*)
- EXEMPTION + VERB **apply (to sb/sth), cover sb/sth, relate to sb/sth** *The exemption which applies to home-buyers.*
- EXEMPTION + NOUN **clause**
- PREP. **~ for** *There are parking restrictions in the city centre with exemptions for disabled drivers.* **~ from** *You may be able to apply for exemption from local taxes.* **~ on** *tax exemptions on gifts to spouses*

exercise *noun*

1 use of the body to keep healthy
- ADJ. **good, healthy | hard, strenuous, vigorous | gentle, light, moderate** *Try to do fifteen minutes of gentle exercise every day.* **| regular | daily, morning | adequate | aerobic | mental, physical**
- VERB + EXERCISE **do, get, take** *John never does any exercise.* ◇ *Do you take enough exercise?* **| need**
- EXERCISE + NOUN **programme, regime, routine | class | bike | video**
- PREP. **during ~** *Stop frequently to rest during exercise until you are fitter.*
- PHRASES **a form/kind/type of exercise, lack of exercise** *Lack of exercise is a risk factor in heart disease.*

2 set of movements/activities
- ADJ. **basic, simple | keep-fit | warm-up | breathing, relaxation, strengthening, stretching | chest, leg, etc.**
- QUANT. **set**
- VERB + EXERCISE **do, perform** *Remember to do your breathing exercises every day.* ◇ *You may find it helpful to perform this exercise in front of the mirror.* **| devise** *You can devise your own exercises to music.* **| repeat**

3 set of questions
- ADJ. **easy, simple | difficult, hard | oral, practical, written | practice | comprehension, grammar, listening, translation, writing**
- QUANT. **set**
- VERB + EXERCISE **do | give sb, set (sb) | create**
- PREP. **~ in** *an exercise in translation*

4 use of a power/a right/a quality
- ADJ. **effective** *the effective exercise of power by the government* **| free** *the free exercise of informed choice* **| peaceful | legitimate, proper | improper**
- VERB + EXERCISE **limit, regulate | justify**
- PHRASES **the exercise of authority/power** *to limit the exercise of political power* **the exercise of discretion**

5 for a particular result
- ADJ. **simple, straightforward | major, massive | successful | interesting, useful, valuable, worthwhile | arbitrary, cosmetic, cynical, fruitless, futile, pointless** *In the end it proved a pointless exercise.* **| academic, intellectual, mental, (pen and) paper, technical, theoretical** *This is not a purely academic exercise: it should have a real impact on the way we work as a department.* ◇ *Role-playing situations allows a finer assessment to be made than in pen and paper exercises.* **| costly, expensive | political** *The whole consultation process was just a cynical political exercise.* **| joint | pilot** *After a successful pilot exercise last year, the new system is being introduced throughout the company.* **| consultation, cost-cutting, costing, damage limitation, evaluation, marketing, propaganda, publicity, public relations, research**
- VERB + EXERCISE **carry out, conduct, perform** *The company has just carried out a major cost-cutting exercise.* **| embark on, mount** *Before embarking on any exercise, you should conduct a cost-benefit analysis.* **| devise**
- PREP. **~ in** *The seminar was a valuable exercise in information exchange.*
- PHRASES **the aim/object of the exercise** *The object of the exercise is to increase public awareness of environmental issues.*

6 for soldiers/police
- ADJ. **training | flying, military, naval | joint** *US forces took part in joint exercises with the British Navy.*
- VERB + EXERCISE **do, go on, take part in** *The troops go on exercises twice a year.* **| mount**
- PREP. **on ~** *Half the regiment was away on exercise.*

exercise *verb*

- ADV. **effectively | properly | lawfully, rightfully** *the purposes for which power can be rightfully exercised*
- VERB + EXERCISE **be able to | be free to** *Managers are free to exercise their discretion in these cases.* **| be necessary to, need to** *It is necessary to exercise caution when making recommendations.* **| continue to** *The all-powerful steering committee continued to exercise control.* **| fail to** *You need to prove that the company's representative failed to exercise due care.*

exertion *noun*

- ADJ. **considerable, great | mental, physical** *Try to avoid physical exertion.*
- PREP. **from the ~** *She was hot and breathless from the exertion of cycling uphill.* **with ~** *flushed and sweating with exertion after digging the garden*

exhaust *noun*

- ADJ. **car, vehicle | diesel, petrol** *Diesel exhaust contains a lot of soot.*
- EXHAUST + NOUN **emission, fumes, gas, pollution, smoke | pipe, system**
- PREP. **from an/the ~** *pollution from car exhausts*

exhaust *verb*

1 make sb very tired
- ADV. **absolutely, completely, totally, utterly** *The swimming had completely exhausted him.* **| emotionally, mentally, physically** *The experience had exhausted her physically and emotionally.*

2 use sth up completely

exhausted

- ADV. **completely, totally | almost, nearly** *The funds are nearly exhausted.* | **quickly, rapidly** *Their limited resources were quickly exhausted.*

exhausted *adj.*

- VERBS **be, feel, look, seem, sound | become, get | leave sb** *The row had left him physically exhausted.*
- ADV. **really | absolutely, completely, quite, thoroughly, totally, utterly** *He fell into bed utterly exhausted.* | **pretty, rather | emotionally, financially, mentally, physically** *financially exhausted countries*
- PREP. **from** *I was exhausted from the day's work.*

exhausting *adj.*

- VERBS **be, prove | become | find sth**
- ADV. **really, very** *a really exhausting day* | **quite | a bit, fairly, pretty | emotionally, mentally, physically**

exhaustion *noun*

- ADJ. **complete, sheer, total, utter | emotional, mental, nervous, physical | heat**
- VERB + EXHAUSTION **suffer from** *She was taken to hospital suffering from exhaustion.* | **be close to** *He was hollow-eyed and seemed very close to exhaustion.* | **be overcome by, collapse from/with** *Two of the horses collapsed with exhaustion.* | **drive sb to, lead to** *Don't work too hard and drive yourself to exhaustion.* | **die from/of**
- PREP. **in ~** *He fell silent, with his head bowed in exhaustion.* **with ~** *She was faint with exhaustion.*
- PHRASES **at/to the point of exhaustion** *driven to the point of complete exhaustion* **a state of exhaustion**

exhaustive *adj.*

- VERBS **be**
- ADV. **by no means, not necessarily** *This list is by no means exhaustive.* | **fairly** *After a fairly exhaustive investigation, they were able to put things right.*

exhibition *noun*

- ADJ. **big, large | small | important, major** *a major exhibition of the painter's work* | **annual, summer | international, local | private, public | permanent | changing, special, temporary** *The library has a policy of mounting changing exhibitions.* ◇ *There is a series of special exhibitions throughout the year.* | **touring, travelling** *a touring exhibition of Impressionist drawings* | **collaborative, joint | one-man, one-person, one-woman, solo** *By 1914 Picasso had held one-man exhibitions in England, Germany and Spain.* | **retrospective | art, craft, photographic, etc. | trade** *the international food trade exhibition in Cologne*
- VERB + EXHIBITION **have, hold, host** *The museum hosted a big exhibition of her work last year.* | **house** *The old factory has been converted to house an exhibition.* | **attend, go to, see, visit | arrange, organize, plan | display, mount, present, put on, show, stage** *They plan to stage an art exhibition in a nearby town.* | **launch, open** *The mayor will open the exhibition next week.* | **sponsor | go on** *The Mappa Mundi will go on permanent exhibition at Hereford Cathedral.*
- EXHIBITION + VERB **open** *The exhibition opens at the Tate Gallery in July.* | **close, end | be on, be on view, run, take place** *The exhibition runs from 11 April to 5 July.* | **continue | move (on) to** *The exhibition moves on to the National Gallery, Washington, next month.* | **be called sth, be entitled sth | comprise sth, cover sth, feature sth, include sth, show sth** *The exhibition includes drawings by Rembrandt.* | **illustrate sth, trace sth** *an exhibition illustrating the history and development of the university* | **be dedicated to sb/sth, be devoted to sb/sth** *an exhibition devoted to female painters*
- EXHIBITION + NOUN **centre, gallery, hall, venue | space** *The new wing will provide 20 000 more square feet of exhibition space.* | **stand** *Hundreds of firms had exhibition stands.* | **catalogue | programme** *the gallery's exhibition programme for next year*
- PREP. **on ~** *A selection of her paintings is on exhibition at the Whitechapel Art Gallery.* | **~ of** *an exhibition of contemporary art* **~ on** *an exhibition on local history*
⇒ Note at ART

exile *noun*

1 being sent to live in another country
- ADJ. **long | permanent | enforced | self-imposed, voluntary | internal** *Many spent decades in labour camps or in internal exile.*
- VERB + EXILE **be driven/forced/sent into | flee into, go into** *The king went into exile after the overthrow of his government.* | **live in** *They joined the many other Armenians living in exile.* | **die in | return from** *He still hopes to return from exile one day.*
- PREP. **in ~** *She had spent 40 years in exile.* | **~ from** *Dante died in exile from Florence.*
- PHRASES **a place of exile**

2 person forced to live in another country
- ADJ. **political | tax** (= a rich person who moves to another country where taxes are lower)
- EXILE + VERB **return** *A general amnesty was granted, allowing political exiles to return freely.*
- PHRASES **the recall of exiles, the return of exiles**

exile *verb*

- ADV. **permanently, temporarily | effectively** *He was effectively exiled after a failed bid for power.*
- PREP. **from** *The family was exiled from France.* **to** *He was exiled to Siberia.*

exist *verb*

- ADV. **actually, really** *Do these creatures really exist?* | **already, still** *Few of these monkeys still exist in the wild.* | **currently | independently** *He argued that ideas do not exist independently of the language that expresses them.*
- VERB + EXIST **be known to** *the enormous volcanoes now known to exist on Mars* | **continue to | cease to**

existence *noun*

1 state of existing
- ADJ. **actual, real** *El Cid's actual existence is not in doubt.* ◇ *Since her illness, other people had become shadowy and had no real existence for her.* | **brief | continued, future | very** *The peasants depend on a good harvest for their very existence* (= in order to continue to live). | **mere** *The mere existence of these strange creatures fascinated him.* | **autonomous, independent, separate** *any organism capable of independent existence* | **human** *the mystery of human existence* | **material, physical | social**
- VERB + EXISTENCE **be in** *The idea of God in nature has been in existence for as long as human beings have worshipped.* | **come into, spring into** *The organization came into existence ten years ago.* ◇ *What are the chances of these molecules springing spontaneously into existence?* **be crushed out of, go out of** *If you jump into a black hole you will get torn apart and crushed out of existence.* ◇ *There was a fear that the club might go out of existence for lack of support.* | **bring sth into, call sth into** *striving to bring into existence a new kind of society* | **be aware of, know of | be unaware of | assert | assume, postulate, presuppose** *The theory assumes the existence of a 'meritocracy'—that there is equal opportunity for all.* | **accept, acknowledge, believe in, recognize** *He didn't believe in the existence of God.* | **deny | doubt | imply, indicate, suggest | discover, reveal | confirm, demon-**

strate, establish, prove | disprove | explain *How do you explain the existence of closely related species in widely separated locations?* | justify | forget, ignore *The girl's parents continued to ignore her very existence.* | resent *Deep down I resented his existence.* | jeopardize, threaten *Climate changes threaten the continued existence of the species.* | owe *The school owed its existence to the generosity of one man.* | be vital to *A super-efficient sense of smell is no longer vital to our existence.*

• EXISTENCE + VERB **depend on/upon sth** *The company's existence depends on continued growth.*
• PREP. **in~** *the only instrument of its kind in existence*
• PHRASES **a mode of existence** *the nature and significance of the temporal mode of existence* **the struggle for existence** *Darwin viewed the struggle for existence as being the major promoter of evolution.*

2 way of living

• ADJ. **bare, frugal, hand-to-mouth, miserable, precarious** *He lived a hand-to-mouth existence in the less attractive areas of London.* | **comfortable, ordered, peaceful, quiet** | **dull, humdrum, routine** | **isolated, lonely, solitary** | **nomadic** | **rural, suburban, urban** | **daily, day-to-day, everyday, previous, prior** *He claimed to be able to remember a previous existence.*
• VERB + EXISTENCE **enjoy, have, lead, live** | **eke out, endure** *They eke out a precarious existence foraging in rubbish dumps.*

exit *noun*

1 way out

• ADJ. **front, rear, side** | **emergency, fire** | **the nearest** *She headed for the nearest exit.*
• VERB + EXIT **head for, make for** | **bar, block** *Do not leave bags lying around which could block the emergency exits.*
• EXIT + NOUN **door, gate, route**
• PREP. **to/towards the~** *They moved to the exits.*

2 act of leaving

• ADJ. **fast, hurried, quick, swift** | **dignified** | **early** *her early exit from the tournament, in only the second round* | **mass**
• VERB + EXIT **make** *She turned on her heel and made what she hoped was a dignified exit.*
• EXIT + NOUN **visa**
• PREP. **~from** *a mass exit of members from the party*

3 for traffic

• ADJ. **motorway** | **northbound, southbound, etc.**
• VERB + EXIT **take**
• PREP. **~for** *At the roundabout, take the exit for Swindon and Bristol.* **~from** *Traffic lights control the exit from the M8 at Newbridge.*

exorbitant *adj.*

• VERBS **be, seem**
• ADV. **grossly** | **quite** *The hotel charges quite exorbitant prices.* | **pretty**

expand *verb*

• ADV. **considerably, dramatically, enormously, greatly, hugely, massively, significantly, vastly** *The business has expanded greatly over the last year.* | **further** | **fast, quickly, rapidly** | **gradually, slowly** | **suddenly** | **steadily**
• VERB + EXPAND **aim to, be eager to, be keen to, hope to, look to, plan to, seek to, want to** *The firm is looking to expand its operations overseas.* | **help (to)** *The store has helped expand the British cheese market by encouraging small dairy farmers.* | **begin to** | **continue to** | **seem to**
• PREP. **from** *The number of managers has expanded*

from 700 to 1 300. **into** *The village has expanded into a town.* **to**

expanse *noun*

• ADJ. **broad, endless, great, huge, large, vast, wide** *a vast expanse of sand* | **barren, bleak, empty** *a bleak expanse of concrete* | **flat** *looking out over the flat expanse of blackened fields* | **open** | **cold** | **grey, white** *the white expanses of the frozen north* | **shining** *the desk's shining expanse of polished wood*
• PREP. **~of**

expansion *noun*

• ADJ. **big, considerable, enormous, great, huge, major, massive, significant, substantial, vast** *The company was now set for major expansion.* | **maximum** | **dramatic, marked, remarkable, unprecedented** *an unprecedented expansion in linguistic studies at British universities* | **rapid** | **gradual** | **steady** | **continued, further, sustained** | **eastward, westward, etc.** | **global, international, overseas, worldwide** | **successful** | **aggressive** *The board decided to embark on aggressive overseas expansion.* | **healthy** | **planned, proposed** | **uncontrolled** | **business, commercial, company** | **economic, industrial** | **colonial, imperial, territorial** | **population** | **urban**
• VERB + EXPANSION **show** *The economy is still showing healthy expansion.* | **allow (for), provide for** *The design of the front pockets allows for expansion.* | **be ripe for** *a ready-made hotel chain ripe for further expansion* | **be set for** *The company is set for further expansion into niche areas.* | **call for** | **go for, look for** *We are going for maximum expansion.* | **encourage, facilitate, promote** | **impede, limit, restrict** | **halt, stop** | **prevent** | **embark on** | **finance, fund** *In order to finance expansion on this scale, the government has relied heavily on borrowing.*
• EXPANSION + VERB **occur, take place**
• EXPANSION + NOUN **plan, programme**
• PREP. **~into** *expansion into the luxury car market* **~in** *a great age of expansion in trade and science*
• PHRASES **a period of expansion** *a period of rapid economic expansion* **the rate of expansion** *The rate of expansion of our overseas trade has been spectacular.* **potential/room/scope/space for expansion** *The company believes there is scope for expansion in this sector.*

expect *verb*

• ADV. **confidently** *She confidently expects to win.* | **fully** *My parents fully expect us to get married.* | **not really** *I didn't really expect them to come.* | **half** *I was half expecting to see Jim at the concert.* | **honestly** *Did you honestly expect me to believe that?*
• VERB + EXPECT **be reasonable to, can, can realistically, can reasonably** *We can expect to see an improvement in the weather over the next few days.* | **be unrealistic to, be unreasonable to, can hardly** *It would be unreasonable to expect them to do all that work for free.* ◇ *You can hardly expect to learn a foreign language in a few months.* | **would, would normally** *I would expect the factory to be working again as normal by next week.* | **be entitled to** *You are entitled to expect certain minimum standards of accommodation.*
• PREP. **from** *We expect good results from our employees.*
• PHRASES **(only) to be expected** *This kind of behaviour is to be expected from a two-year-old.* **expect a lot/too much of sb** *I think my parents always expected too much of me.* **when you least expect sth** *An accident can happen anywhere, at any time, just when you least expect it.*

expectation *noun*

• ADJ. **great, high** | **low** *Many children start with low expectations.* | **growing, rising, heightened, increased**

Heightened expectations for educational progress had not been realized. | **lowered** | **optimistic**, **positive** | **negative**, **pessimistic** | **normal** *The plaintiff is aged 30 and has a normal expectation of life.* | **clear**, **confident** | **legitimate** (*law*), **reasonable** | **false**, **naive**, **over-high**, **over-optimistic**, **unrealistic**, **unreasonable** | **disappointed** *There were disappointed expectations all round when the contents of his will became known.* | **wild** *This realization of our dreams surpassed even our wildest expectations.* | **future** | **general**, **widespread** *There is still a general expectation that married couples will have children.* | **popular**, **public** | **traditional** | **family**, **parental**, **social**, **teacher** | **market** | **economic** | **career**, **life**

● VERB + EXPECTATION **have**, **hold** *You have unrealistic expectations.* ◊ *differences in the expectations held by different social groups* | **form** *the way in which expectations are formed* | **arouse**, **build up**, **create**, **raise**, **set up** *the high expectations aroused by civil rights legislation* | **heighten** | **lower**, **reduce** *Her approach to welfare sought to lower people's expectations and impose work discipline.* | **influence**, **shape** *trying to influence public expectations of the police* | **come/live up to**, **fulfil**, **match**, **meet**, **realize**, **satisfy** *Her new car has not lived up to her expectations.* | **exceed**, **go beyond**, **surpass** | **fall short of** *The reality of the holiday fell short of our expectations.* | **confound** *The rise in share price confounded expectations.*

● EXPECTATION + VERB **rise**, **soar** *Once the government's promise was made, popular expectations soared.*

● PREP. **against~** *Against all expectations, she was enjoying herself.* **contrary to ~** *The building work was completed on time, contrary to expectation.* **below ~** *What should you do when an employee's performance is disappointing and below expectation?* **beyond~** *The scheme has produced results way beyond expectation.* ◊ *He had been successful beyond his expectations.* **in the ~ of/that** *The article was written before the election result in the clear expectation of a Labour victory.* | **~ about** *the government's expectations about the economy* **~ for** *We have high expectations for her future.* **~ of** *We certainly had a reasonable expectation of success.*

● PHRASES **have every expectation** *I have every expectation of cheering the team on to victory in the final.* **in line with expectations** *The various categories of operating expenditure are broadly in line with expectations.*

expedient *adj.*

● VERBS **be**, **prove** | **become** | **consider sth**, **deem sth**, **think sth** | **find sth** *The government found it expedient to relax censorship a little.*

● ADV. **politically**

expedition *noun*

● ADJ. **great**, **major** *Finally, the great expedition set off for the long journey to the Holy Land.* | **small** | **joint**, **international** *The British agreed to a joint expedition with the French.* | **foreign** | **successful** | **collecting**, **fishing**, **foraging**, **hunting**, **shopping** | **archaeological**, **scientific** | **military**, **naval** | **punitive** *In response, Charles VI sent a punitive expedition to Brittany, raping and killing the populace.* | **Antarctic**, **Everest**, etc.

● VERB + EXPEDITION **go on**, **make** *He had made two expeditions to Spain to study wild plants.* | **embark on**, **set off/out on**, **undertake** *She was about to embark on a major expedition.* | **head**, **lead** | **join** | **organize**, **plan** | **launch**, **mount** *They plan to launch an expedition into the mountains.* | **send**

● EXPEDITION + VERB **leave**, **set off/out**, **start** | **return** *The expedition returned only two weeks after it had left.* | **reach sth** *On 21 January the expedition reached the South Pole.*

● EXPEDITION + NOUN **leader**, **member**

● PREP. **on an/the ~** *She was out on a shopping expedition.* | **~ against** *He led a military expedition against the*

rebels. **~ into** *an expedition into the interior of Australia* **~to** *a naval expedition to West Africa*

● PHRASES **a leader/member of an expedition**

expel *verb*

● ADV. **forcibly** *They were forcibly expelled from their farm by the occupying authorities.*

● PREP. **for**, **from** *He was expelled from school for disruptive behaviour.*

expenditure *noun*

● ADJ. **considerable**, **heavy**, **high**, **huge**, **major**, **massive** *The group is calling for higher expenditure on education.* | **low**, **modest** | **average** *the family's average expenditure on food* | **aggregate**, **overall**, **total** | **gross**, **net** | **additional**, **extra**, **further** | **increased** | **excessive** | **necessary**, **unnecessary** | **budget**, **budgeted**, **estimated**, **planned**, **projected**, **proposed** | **actual** *The next two items refer to actual expenditures incurred, rather than estimated needs.* | **current**, **future** *Pay constitutes two-thirds of all current expenditure.* | **annual** | **per capita** *the country with the highest per capita expenditure on health care in the EU* | **direct** *the total direct expenditure on training* | **operating** | **capital** *Capital expenditure can be financed by borrowing; operating expenditure should not.* | **local**, **national** | **federal**, **government**, **public**, **state** *Public expenditure was running at 44.6% of GNP.* | **departmental**, **household**, **personal** | **consumer** | **advertising**, **research and development** | **defence**, **health**, **military**, **social**, **welfare**

● QUANT. **item** *You may wish to take out a loan for a major item of expenditure.* | **level**

● VERB + EXPENDITURE **increase** | **control**, **curb**, **cut**, **limit**, **reduce** *plans to cut health expenditure* | **allow for**, **budget**, **provide for**, **plan**, **set** *The budget provided for expenditure of $2 billion.* ◊ *Expenditure was set at £16 million.* | **estimate**, **project**, **put** *Expenditure was put at 100 million euros.* | **incur** | **finance**, **meet** *Make sure you have enough in the current account to meet expenditure.* | **have** *Both brands had heavy advertising expenditure.* | **monitor**

● EXPENDITURE + VERB **go up**, **grow**, **increase**, **rise** | **fall**, **go down** | **amount to sth** *Total expenditure amounted to approximately £1 million.* | **run at sth** | **exceed sth** *people whose annual expenditure exceeds their income* | **arise from sth** *extra expenditure arising from the commission's report into health and safety*

● EXPENDITURE + NOUN **cut** *public expenditure cuts* | **level** | **pattern**

● PREP. **~ of** *government expenditure of more than £500 million* **~ on** *increased expenditure on the railway network*

● PHRASES **a cut/reduction in expenditure**, **an increase/a rise in expenditure**

expense *noun*

1 cost/money spent on sth

● ADJ. **considerable**, **enormous**, **great**, **vast** | **additional**, **extra** | **unexpected** | **unnecessary** | **public** *The bridge was built at public expense.* | **personal**

● VERB + EXPENSE **go to**, **incur** *They went to all the expense of redecorating the house and then they moved.* | **put sb to** *Their visit put us to a lot of expense.* | **bear**, **cover**, **meet** *She had to meet the expense herself.* | **spare no** *No expense was spared* (= they spent as much money as was needed) *to make the party a success.* | **avoid** | **be worth** *The results are well worth the expense.*

● EXPENSE + VERB **arise**

● PREP. **at sb/sth's ~** *They had to repair the damage at their own expense.* ◊ *He built up the business at the expense of his health.* **at ... ~** *The garden was transformed at great expense.* ◊ *The accommodation package includes admission to the golf course at no extra expense.*

2 sth that makes you spend money
- ADJ. **big, considerable** | **incidental** *Relocated employees received grants towards incidental expenses like buying carpets.* | **business, management** *Meetings, and the time for them, are a considerable management expense.*

3 expenses money spent for a particular purpose
- ADJ. **high** *Medical expenses can be quite high if you are not insured.* | **allowable, legitimate, reasonable** *You can claim back the tax on legitimate business expenses.* | **basic** *The guides are unpaid except for basic expenses.* | **out-of-pocket** (= paid for by an employee, to be claimed back later from the employer) *Any out-of-pocket expenses incurred on the firm's business will be reimbursed.* | **personal** | **living** | **household** | **operating, overhead, running** | **business, work-related** | **travel/travelling** | **relocation, removal** | **legal, medical** | **funeral**
- VERB + EXPENSE **incur** | **cover, defray, meet, pay, refund, reimburse** *He was given a sum of money to cover his travel expenses.* | **claim (back)** *They are claiming expenses for travel and overnight accommodation.* | **deduct** *You will have to pay income tax on the rent you receive, although you can deduct expenses such as insurance.*
- EXPENSES + VERB **arise** *You can expect to receive compensation for all expenses arising out of the accident.*
- EXPENSES + NOUN **expense account** *Put the cost of the meal on your expense account.* | **expense/expenses claim**
- PREP. **on ~** *a commercial traveller staying at the hotel on expenses*
- PHRASES **all expenses paid** *a two-day, all expenses paid trip to London*

expensive *adj.*

- VERBS **be, look, prove, seem, sound** *Her suit looked extremely expensive.* | **become, get** *Holidays in this country are getting very expensive.* | **make sth** *Adding these safety features would make the cars too expensive.* | **find sth** *I found the food very expensive.*
- ADV. **amazingly, astronomically, enormously, exceedingly, extortionately, extremely, frighteningly, hideously, highly, horrendously, horribly, hugely, immensely, incredibly, inordinately, ludicrously, massively, outrageously, ridiculously, ruinously, terribly, vastly, very** *Some of these legal cases are enormously expensive.* | **impossibly, prohibitively** *Giving every patient an annual anti-flu injection would be prohibitively expensive.* | **increasingly** | **a bit, comparatively, fairly, moderately, pretty, quite, rather, relatively, correspondingly** *Walls are generally the greatest source of heat loss and correspondingly expensive to tackle.* | **needlessly, unduly, unnecessarily** | **notoriously** | **obviously** | **discreetly** *discreetly expensive perfume*

experience *noun*

1 knowledge/skill got from seeing/doing sth
- ADJ. **considerable, extensive, long, wide** | **good, invaluable, relevant, unrivalled, valuable** *She didn't get paid much but it was all good experience.* ◇ *Both candidates for the presidency were short of relevant experience.* ◇ *Rolls Royce's unrivalled experience in high technology manufacturing* | **previous** *Do you have any previous experience of this type of work?* | **direct, first-hand, hands-on, practical** *the importance of hands-on experience as well as academic training* | **professional, work**
- VERB + EXPERIENCE **have** | **lack** | **gain,   get** | **broaden** *She wanted to broaden her experience in international affairs.*
- PREP. **~of** *She has considerable professional experience of translation.*
- PHRASES **a lack of experience, a wealth of experience** *The veteran goalkeeper will bring a wealth of experience to the team.*

2 the things that have happened to you
- ADJ. **past** *We're in for a difficult couple of weeks, if past experience is anything to go by.* | **direct, first-hand, hands-on, personal** | **subjective** *Experience is subjective and very hard to measure.* | **vicarious** *I love reading: I have an insatiable appetite for vicarious experience.* | **common, shared** *his peers, with whom he shares the common experience of being black in a white society* | **common** *It is a matter of common experience that disorder will increase if things are left to themselves.* | **everyday** *Choose illustrative examples from the children's everyday experience.* | **human** *There are few areas of human experience that have not been written about.* | **sensory**
- VERB + EXPERIENCE **have** | **share** | **draw on, learn by/from/through** *In her book, she draws on her first-hand experience of mental illness.* ◇ *We all learn by experience.* | **be based on** *The book is based on personal experience.*
- EXPERIENCE + VERB **suggest sth, teach (sb) sth** *Experience has taught me that life can be very unfair.*
- PREP. **by/from ~** *We know from experience that hot objects are painful to touch.* **in sb's ~** *In my experience, very few people really understand the problem.* **~ of** *He has direct experience of poverty.*

3 event/activity that affects you
- ADJ. **enjoyable, exhilarating, good, interesting, memorable, pleasant, rewarding, unforgettable, valuable** | **bad, harrowing, painful, traumatic, unnerving, unsettling** *I had a bad experience with fireworks once.* | **hair-raising, nerve-racking** *a hair-raising experience of white-water rafting* | **humbling, salutary, sobering** | **personal, subjective** | **common, shared** *The use of drama can motivate students by allowing them to share a common experience.* | **common** *It is a common experience to feel that an author writes well, without being able to say why.* | **real-life** | **past** | **childhood, early, formative** *Early experiences shape the way we face up to and deal with crises in later life.* | **educational, learning** | **mystical, religious, visionary** | **psychic** | **sexual** | **near-death**
- VERB + EXPERIENCE **enjoy, go through, have, undergo** *She has been through a very traumatic experience.* ◇ *I think you will enjoy the experience of taking part in the show.* | **come through, get over** *It could take him years to get over this experience.* | **describe, recount, talk about** | **share, swap** *Does anyone have any experiences—good or bad—that they would like to share with the group?* | **relive** *Reliving past experiences can release powerful feelings that have been pent up too long.* | **be based on** *The novel is based on his experiences in the war.*
- PHRASES **quite an experience** *It was quite an experience being involved in making a television programme.*

experience *verb*

- ADV. **actually** | **directly, first-hand** *He hadn't directly experienced the fighting in the city.* ◇ *people who have actually experienced these problems first-hand* | **subjectively**

experienced *adj.*

- VERBS **be, seem, sound** | **become**
- ADV. **extremely, highly, immensely, really, vastly, very** *The staff are all highly experienced.* | **fully** | **quite** | **sufficiently, suitably** *The task needs the skills of a suitably experienced engineer.* | **widely** *a widely experienced and articulate politician* | **sexually**
- PREP. **in** *She's very experienced in looking after children.*

experiment *noun*

- ADJ. **animal** *protesting against animal experiments* | **field, laboratory** | **educational, medical, psychological, scientific** | **practical** | **thought** *His efforts involved thought experiments and analogies, rather than detailed experimentation.* | **simple** | **brief** | **careful, control** (*sci-*

ence), controlled | interesting | ingenious | pioneering | bold *the country's bold experiment with economic reform* | successful, unsuccessful | pilot, preliminary | further *Further experiments will be carried out to verify this result.* | celebrated, classic/classical, famous, well-known *Pavlov's famous experiment with the dog and the dinner bell* | unique *Brazil's unique experiment with alcohol-fuelled cars*

● VERB + EXPERIMENT **carry out, conduct, do, perform** | **try** *The school decided to try an experiment in single-sex teaching.* | **design** | **set up** | **describe, report** *a classic experiment reported in 1964*

● EXPERIMENT + VERB **confirm sth, demonstrate sth, find sth, illustrate sth, prove sth, show sth** | **indicate sth, suggest sth** | **be aimed at sth, be designed to do sth** *an experiment aimed at cutting road deaths resulting from excessive speeding* | **involve sth, use sth** | **be successful, work** *If the conditions are not right, the experiment will not work.* | **fail**

● PREP. **by~** *The appropriate concentration of the drug is best determined by experiment.* **during an/the ~** *The animals seemed healthy during the experiment.* **in an/the ~** *In these experiments, chilling is necessary.* | **~ in** *the country's brief experiment in multi-party democracy* **~ on** *The team carried out experiments on cancer tissue.* **~ with** *conducting an experiment with zinc chips and hydrochloric acid*

experiment *verb*

● ADV. **successfully**
● VERB + EXPERIMENT **begin to** | **continue to**
● PREP. **on** *They experimented successfully on the plants to discover disease-resistant varieties.* **with** *We have experimented with various different designs of kite.*

expert *noun*

● ADJ. **real** | **leading** | **acknowledged, recognized** | **professional, qualified** | **self-proclaimed, self-styled** | **so-called** | **international, world** *She is a world expert on butterflies.* | **local** | **independent, outside** | **computer, financial, gardening, health, legal, marketing, medical, military, scientific, technical, etc.**

● QUANT. **committee, panel, team** *A panel of experts will answer questions from the television audience.*

● VERB + EXPERT **consult, take advice from, talk to**
● EXPERT + VERB **advise sb/sth, agree sth, argue sth, believe sth, claim sth, fear sth, predict sth, reckon sth, recommend sth, say sth** *Experts agree that a balanced diet is the key to great health.*

● PREP. **~ at** *He's an expert at getting his own way.* **~ in** *an expert in skin care* **~ on** *an expert on European art*

expertise *noun*

● ADJ. **considerable, extensive, great** | **limited** | **appropriate, relevant** *Each area of the curriculum should be led by a staff member with appropriate expertise.* | **necessary** *MPs may lack the necessary expertise to scrutinize legislation effectively.* | **established, existing** | **particular, special/specialist, specific** *areas of special expertise* | **collective, combined, shared** *They met regularly to share experiences and develop their collective expertise.* | **in-house, local, outside** *We sometimes have to call on outside expertise.* | **staff** | **subject** | **academic, business, clinical, engineering, financial, legal, management/managerial, marketing, medical, professional, scientific, technical, technological**

● QUANT. **degree, level** *A high degree of expertise is required for this stage of the manufacturing process.*

● VERB + EXPERTISE **have** *She has great expertise in these matters.* | **lack** | **need, require** | **acquire, develop, gain** | **build on** *This project builds on the existing expertise of staff at the centre.* | **provide** *Professor Simpson pro-*

vided expertise in engineering. | **apply, bring, bring to bear, use** *How could he apply his academic expertise to practical matters?* ◊ *He will bring a great deal of expertise to bear on this issue.* | **bring together, call on, draw on** *The project brings together expertise in teaching and library provision.* ◊ *We need to draw on the professional expertise of a large number of teachers.* | **rely on** | **pass on, share** *The teachers would be available to share expertise and offer advice.*

● EXPERTISE + VERB **be available** *We need to discover what relevant expertise is available to us.*

● PREP. **~ in** *gaining expertise in specialist financial areas* **~ on** *She brings expertise on general financial and technical matters.*

● PHRASES **an area/a field of expertise, a range of expertise** *The variety of technology requires a wide range of expertise.*

expire *verb*

● VERB + EXPIRE **be due to** *His contract is due to expire at the end of this year.*

explain *verb*

● ADV. **in detail** *I wrote explaining the issues in great detail.* | **fully** *The reasons for the accident have not been fully explained.* | **adequately, properly, satisfactorily** | **partly** *This partly explains why he was so late.* | **briefly** | **easily, readily** *This phenomenon can be easily explained.* | **clearly** | **carefully** | **patiently** *The doctor explained patiently what the treatment would be.* | **earnestly** | **concisely, succinctly, tersely** *The general principles behind the method used are explained clearly and concisely.* ◊ *'We've already paid,' I explained tersely.* | **awkwardly, lamely** | **breathlessly, excitedly**

● VERB + EXPLAIN **be able/unable to, can/could** *I know I'm late, but I can explain why.* | **attempt to, seek to, try to** | **help (to)** | **purport to** *Many theories purport to explain growth in terms of a single cause.* | **be difficult to, be hard to** *It's difficult to explain exactly how the system works.* | **hasten to** *She saw his quick frown and hastened to explain.* | **let sb** *Let me explain what I mean.*

● PREP. **about** *She tried to explain about her fears and anxieties.* **to** *She explained the plan to me very carefully.*

● PHRASES **explain everything** *I've got a letter here which explains everything.* **go a long way/some way towards explaining sth** *This goes some way towards explaining the hostility between the two groups.*

explanation *noun*

● ADJ. **convincing, credible, good, likely, logical, natural, obvious, plausible, probable, rational** *The most likely explanation is that his plane was delayed.* | **implausible, inadequate, unlikely** | **acceptable, adequate, reasonable, satisfactory, sufficient** | **no apparent** *There was no apparent explanation for the attack.* | **clear, coherent** | **complete, comprehensive, detailed, full** | **partial** | **complex, complicated** | **easy, simple** | **innocent, prosaic** *There's sure to be a perfectly innocent explanation for all this—though I admit it looks bizarre.* | **convenient** | **accepted, traditional** *There is no generally accepted explanation of this practice.* | **official** | **possible** | **correct, real, true** | **brief** | **lengthy, long** | **verbal** | **general** | **common** *the common explanations for hooliganism* | **only, sole** *It's the only explanation that makes any kind of sense.* | **causal** *The causal explanation must be that old age causes poverty, not that poverty causes people to be old.* | **ad hoc, post hoc** *post hoc (= after the event) explanations of historical changes that would have made no sense to anyone living at the time* | **cultural, historical, political, psychological, scientific, sociological, technical, theoretical**

● VERB + EXPLANATION **have** *I had no explanation for*

her strange behaviour. | **give (sb), offer (sb), provide (sb with)** *He only offered a partial explanation for his lateness.* | **enter into, go into, launch into** *She launched into a detailed explanation of every aspect of her work.* | **advance, propose, put forward** *one explanation advanced by Marxist historians* | **call for, need, require** *An explanation is clearly called for.* | **look for, seek | find, think of** *I can think of one possible explanation for her behaviour.* | **ask for, demand** *She wrote to the company demanding an explanation.* | **wait for | deserve, merit** *I suppose you deserve an explanation.* | **owe sb** *I think you owe me an explanation.* | **accept | defy** *Her success has been so remarkable as to defy explanation.*

• EXPLANATION + VERB **lie** *The simplest explanation for his achievements lies in his greater ability and superiority over his contemporaries at university.* | **emerge, occur to sb, present itself, suggest itself** *No single clear explanation emerged from the experiments.* ◇ *A more credible explanation now occurred to her.* ◇ *Another quite plausible explanation presented itself.*

• PREP. **in ~** *'I've worked with them before, you see,' he added, in explanation.* **without ~** *She left suddenly and without explanation.* | **~ about** *He entered into a technical explanation about software and programming.* **~ as to** *He provided no explanation as to why he was late.* **~ for** *There is probably some perfectly logical explanation for their behaviour.* **~ from** *We are still waiting for a full explanation from the teacher concerned.*

• PHRASES **an attempt at explanation** *The men left quickly with no attempt at explanation.* **by way of explanation** *'I had to see you,' he said, by way of explanation.*

explicable *adj.*

• VERBS **be, seem | become**
• ADV. **easily, readily** *The sudden increase in sales is easily explicable.* | **entirely, perfectly, wholly** *His behaviour is entirely explicable.* | **largely | partly**
• PREP. **by** *The delay is partly explicable by the roadworks.* **in terms of** *The differences in the children's achievements were not wholly explicable in terms of their social backgrounds.*

explicit *adj.*

• VERBS **be | become | make sth, render sth** *We think such information should be made explicit and not left vague.*
• ADV. **highly** *a highly explicit description of torture* | **absolutely, fully, quite** *Our orders were quite explicit.* | **increasingly | fairly, relatively | sufficiently | sexually**
• PREP. **about** *The government has been quite explicit about its intentions.* **as to** *She told him he needed to be more creative, without being explicit as to what this meant in practice.*

explode *verb*

1 blow up
• VERB + EXPLODE **be liable to** *The chemical is liable to explode on contact with water.* | **fail to** *A blast bomb was thrown but the device failed to explode.*

2 get angry/dangerous/moving
• ADV. **literally | suddenly**
• VERB + EXPLODE **be about to, be ready to, be set to** *A row over public spending is set to explode.* | **be liable to, be likely to | seem to**
• PREP. **into** *He suddenly exploded into action.* **with** *She literally exploded with anger.*

exploit *noun*

• ADJ. **dare-devil, daring | legendary** *His courage and exploits were legendary.* | **military, sexual, sporting** *bragging about his sexual exploits*

exploit *verb*

1 treat sb unfairly for your own advantage
• ADV. **mercilessly, ruthlessly** *The workers are ruthlessly exploited by their employers.* | **cynically** *He pursued his own interests, cynically exploiting his privileged position as trustee.* | **deliberately | sexually**

2 make the best use of sth
• ADV. **extensively, heavily | fully, to the full** *The firm has been successful in exploiting new technology to the full.* | **further | widely | effectively, profitably, successfully | properly | quickly | easily | cleverly, skilfully** *The architect has cleverly exploited new materials and building techniques.* | **commercially** *She was keen to exploit her discovery commercially.*
• VERB + EXPLOIT **be determined to, be keen to, hope to, seek to | be quick to** *The team were quick to exploit their competitive advantage.* | **attempt to | fail to**

exploitation *noun*

1 unfair use of sb
• ADJ. **brutal, ruthless** *her ruthless exploitation of popular fear* | **capitalist, class, economic, industrial, sexual**
• VERB + EXPLOITATION **prevent | struggle against** *The party's avowed aim was to struggle against capitalist exploitation.* | **be open to, be vulnerable to** *Migrant workers are vulnerable to exploitation.* | **be based on** *societies based on the exploitation of slaves*

2 use of sth
• ADJ. **effective, efficient, full, successful | direct** *the direct exploitation of natural forests* | **large-scale | sustainable | commercial | mineral**
• VERB + EXPLOITATION **be open for, be ripe for** *Emergent democracies created markets that were ripe for exploitation.*

exploration *noun*

1 of a place
• ADJ. **gas, mineral, oil, petroleum | polar, space | offshore** *the heavy cost of offshore oil exploration* | **archaeological, scientific | speculative | extensive | detailed**
• VERB + EXPLORATION **carry out** *Extensive exploration was carried out using the latest drilling technology.* | **continue**
• EXPLORATION + VERB **take place** *areas where mineral exploration is taking place*
• EXPLORATION + NOUN **activity, drilling** *Exploration activity slowed during the 1970s.* | **programme | company** *an oil exploration company*
• PREP. **~ for** *speculative exploration for oil*

2 of an idea/subject
• ADJ. **brief | extensive | deep, full | careful, detailed** *My ideas on semantics needed more careful exploration.* | **creative, critical** *creative exploration of music as a medium in education* | **intellectual | personal** *her personal exploration of spirituality*
• VERB + EXPLORATION **need | continue**

explore *verb*

1 travel around an area
• VERB + EXPLORE **be keen to, want to, wish to | be free to** *In the afternoon you'll be free to explore a little on your own.*
• PREP. **for** *exploring for oil*

2 think about sth in detail
• ADV. **extensively | briefly | fully, thoroughly** *These questions have not been fully explored yet.* | **properly, systematically | carefully, in detail** *This idea is worth exploring in some detail.* | **further | usefully** *The film usefully explores some of the issues surrounding adoption.*
• VERB + EXPLORE **need to | be keen to, want to, wish to | aim to, seek to | begin to, continue to**

explorer *noun*

● ADJ. **great** *the great British explorers of the sixteenth century* | **intrepid** | **Antarctic, Arctic, polar**

explosion *noun*

1 sudden loud bursting/exploding

● ADJ. **almighty, big, deafening, enormous, huge, loud, major, massive, powerful, serious, tremendous, violent** | **minor, small** | **muffled** *There was a muffled explosion somewhere on their right.* | **distant** *The floor shook with a distant explosion.* | **controlled** | **test** *a nuclear test explosion* | **accidental** | **bomb, chemical, gas, mine, volcanic** | **atomic, nuclear** | **terrorist** | **political, social** *(figurative) The shock waves of this political explosion engulfed the whole of Europe.*

● VERB + EXPLOSION **cause, set off, trigger** *The build-up of gas caused a small explosion.* | **carry out** *Bomb disposal experts carried out a controlled explosion on the suspect package.* | **hear** | **prevent**

● EXPLOSION + VERB **come, happen, occur, take place** *The explosion came 20 minutes after a coded warning to the police.* ◇ *The explosion occurred just after midday.* | **shake sth** *The explosion shook nearby homes.* | **destroy sth, rip through sth, wreck sth** *A massive explosion ripped through the chemical works.* | **injure sb, kill sb** | **echo** *A loud explosion echoed round the valley.*

● PREP. **in an/the~** *3 people were injured in the explosion.*

2 sudden large increase

● ADJ. **sudden** | **veritable** *In the 1860s a veritable explosion of major scientific publications took place.* | **population** | **information** *trying to keep up with the information explosion* | **price, wage**

● EXPLOSION + VERB **occur, take place**

● PREP. **~in** *a sudden explosion in the number of students* **~of** *an explosion of interest in learning Japanese*

explosive *noun*

● ADJ. **high** *a bomb containing 200 lb of high explosive* | **commercial, home-made** | **chemical, conventional, plastic, semtex**

● VERB + EXPLOSIVE **make, manufacture** | **plant** *They planted explosives in the tunnel.* | **detonate, set off**

● EXPLOSIVE + NOUN **explosives expert**

explosive *adj.*

1 capable of exploding

● VERBS **be**

● ADV. **highly** *a highly explosive mixture of gases*

2 causing strong feelings

● VERBS **be** | **become**

● ADV. **highly** *Race is a highly explosive issue.* | **potentially** *The political situation is potentially explosive.*

exponent *noun*

● ADJ. **chief, foremost, leading, main, principal** | **great, outstanding** | **famous, well-known** | **early** *He was an early exponent of multimedia in the classroom.*

● PREP. **~of** *a leading exponent of the Japanese flute*

export *noun*

● ADJ. **important, main, major, principal, staple** *Coconut is one of the staple exports of the islands.* | **record** *The industry has achieved record exports in the past year.* | **total** *In 2001 total exports were valued at $2 billion.* | **British, US, etc.** | **world** *The US share of world exports has declined.* | **illegal, illicit** *stopping the illegal export of live animals* | **live** *lambs for live export* | **invisible** *Earnings from the sale of banking, insurance and other services to foreigners are described as 'invisible exports'.* | **capital, commodity** | **agricultural, industrial, manufactured,**

manufacturing | **arms, art, banana, beef, coal, coffee, food, grain, oil, timber, etc.**

● QUANT. **level, value, volume**

● VERB + EXPORT **boost, encourage, expand, increase, promote** | **reduce, restrict** *plans to restrict the export of arms to certain countries* | **allow** | **ban, prohibit** | **achieve** | **prevent, stop** | **await** *yards where thousands of cars await export*

● EXPORT + VERB **grow, increase, rise** *Oil exports have risen steadily.* | **drop, fall** | **be valued at sth, total sth** *Exports totalled $10 billion in 2002.* | **account for sth** *Oil exports account for nearly 80% of the country's foreign earnings.* | **be destined for sth** *Scottish exports destined for Western Europe*

● EXPORT + NOUN **crop, goods** | **business, industry, trade** | **market, sector** | **earnings, revenue, sales** | **figures, performance** *a strong export performance* | **growth** | **controls, licence, quota, restrictions** *a call for tougher art export controls* | **ban** *an export ban on live cattle* | **drive** *the export drive by Japanese industry* | **order** *how to win more export orders*

● PREP. **for~** *This is where the fruit is packaged for export.* | **~from** *exports from the EU to Canada* **~to**

● PHRASES **a ban on exports** *to place a ban on exports of toxic waste* **a decline/fall in exports, an increase/a rise in exports**

⇨ Note at PER CENT (for more verbs)

export *verb*

● ADV. **widely** *a French breed of cattle that has been exported widely* | **illegally** *illegally exported works of art*

● PREP. **from** *Last year 2 000 birds were exported from the island.* **to** *The country exports sugar to Europe.*

exporter *noun*

● ADJ. **big, large** | **leading, major** | **food, oil** *the biggest oil exporter in the world* | **net** *The country is a net exporter of food.*

expose *verb*

1 uncover sth

● ADV. **completely, fully** | **briefly** | **suddenly** | **deliberately** *She lifted her chin in a gesture that deliberately exposed the line of her throat.*

● PREP. **to** *These drawings must not be exposed to the air.*

2 show the truth

● ADV. **fully** | **clearly** *a report which clearly exposes the weakness of the government's economic policy* | **publicly** *He was publicly exposed as a liar and a cheat.* | **cruelly** *He was outclassed by an Aston Villa side that cruelly exposed his lack of pace.*

● VERB + EXPOSE **threaten to** | **seek to, try to**

3 to sth harmful

● ADV. **directly** | **constantly** *The general public is constantly exposed to radiation.* | **regularly**

● PREP. **to**

exposed *adj.*

● VERBS **be, feel** | **become** | **leave sb/sth** *Depletion of the ozone layer leaves the earth's surface increasingly exposed to harmful radiation from the sun.*

● ADV. **extremely, heavily** *(business)*, **highly, very** *The country became highly exposed to the vagaries of international markets.* | **completely, fully, totally** | **increasingly** | **fairly, rather, relatively** | **dangerously, painfully** *The postponement of difficult decisions left the government dangerously exposed to American influence.*

● PREP. **to** *The garden was very exposed to westerly winds.*

exposure noun

1 to sth harmful
- ADJ. **high, massive | maximum | excessive | low-level | long, long-term, prolonged | brief | constant, continued, continuous, repeated | chemical, radiation, sun | human** *human exposure to asbestos*
- VERB + EXPOSURE **receive, suffer** *She suffered a massive exposure to toxic chemicals.* | **increase | limit, minimize, reduce** *Banks will seek to minimize their exposure to risk.* | **avoid**
- PREP. **~ to** *The report recommends people to avoid prolonged exposure to sunlight.*

2 to experience
- ADJ. **brief | greater | limited**
- VERB + EXPOSURE **give sb | get, have | increase**
- PREP. **~ to** *giving children greater exposure to other cultures*

3 showing the truth
- ADJ. **full** *full exposure of the links between government officials and the arms trade* | **public**

4 on TV/in newspapers, etc.
- ADJ. **regular | media, press, television**
- VERB + EXPOSURE **give sb/sth** *The magazine aims to give exposure to the work of women artists.* | **gain, get, have, receive** *a would-be television personality who is constantly trying to get media exposure*

express verb

- ADV. **well** *Perhaps I have not expressed myself very well.* | **fully** *She expresses herself most fully in her paintings.* | **openly** *He expressed his anger openly.* | **clearly | cogently** *Students must learn to express a point of view cogently and with clarity.* | **exactly, precisely | concisely, succinctly | eloquently** *The poet eloquently expresses the sense of lost innocence.*
- VERB + EXPRESS **be/feel able/unable to** *Many patients feel unable to express their fears.* | **find it difficult to**
- PHRASES **a chance/an opportunity to express sth**

expression noun

1 showing feelings/ideas
- ADJ. **clear, coherent** *Her statement was a clear expression of her views on this subject.* | **concrete, material, practical, tangible** *The report gave concrete expression to the fears of many immigrants.* | **direct** *Just because there is no direct expression of prejudice, that does not mean the prejudice does not exist.* | **full** *The new concept of form reached its fullest expression in the work of Picasso.* | **highest, perfect, ultimate** *His highest expression of praise was 'Not bad!'* ◇ *the highest expression of human creativity* | **effective, powerful | simple | natural** *He wanted to write a verse drama in which the verse would seem a natural expression of modern life.* | **spontaneous | free** *the right of free expression* | **open, overt, public** *the open expression of emotion* | **outward** *the outward expression of inner emotional feelings* | **formal | characteristic, classic** *Modernism was the characteristic expression of the experience of modernity.* | **unique | collective** *Harvest festival was the occasion for the collective expression of a community's religious values.* | **individual, personal** *to allow scope for individual expression* | **visible, visual | emotional, physical, sexual, verbal | artistic, creative, cultural, linguistic, literary, musical, poetic, political, religious | human**
- VERB + EXPRESSION **achieve, find, reach, receive** *an anger and frustration that finds expression in (= is shown in) violence* | **allow sth, give sth** *The method is to listen to the music and allow expression to whatever comes to you.* ◇ *Only in his dreams does he give expression to his fears.* | **demand, need, require** *Suddenly her deeper feelings demanded expression.*
- PREP. **beyond ~** *She suddenly felt happy beyond expression* (= so happy that she could not express it).
- PHRASES **freedom of expression** *Freedom of expression* (= freedom to say what you think) *is a basic human right.* **a means of expression** *Words, as a means of expression, can be limiting.*

2 on sb's face
- ADJ. **bland, blank, frozen, set, vacant | dazed, glazed | deadpan** *cracking jokes with a deadpan expression on his face* | **curious, enigmatic, inscrutable, odd, strange, unreadable | guarded | searching | faraway | thoughtful, wistful | doubtful, wary | anxious, troubled, worried | bleak, grim, serious | angry, fierce, furious, stern | hangdog, hunted, lugubrious, melancholy, mournful, pained, sad | brooding, intense, rapt | surprised, shocked | baffled, bemused, bewildered, puzzled, quizzical | alert | amused, wry | benign, sympathetic | satisfied, smug | innocent | fleeting | facial**
- VERB + EXPRESSION **have, wear** *She had a very bewildered expression on her face.* ◇ *The children's faces all wore the same rapt expression.* | **assume, put on** *She carefully put on her most innocent expression.* | **take on** *Rose's face took on the fierce expression of a schoolgirl talking about her most hated teacher.* | **catch, see** *Catching a fleeting expression on Lucy's face, she persisted with her question.* | **watch | gauge, read** *I looked at her, trying to read the expression on her face.* | **change** *His face never changed expression.*
- EXPRESSION + VERB **alter, change** *His expression changed to embarrassment.* | **relax, soften** *His expression softened when he saw her.* | **darken, harden** *Her expression hardened into one of strong dislike.* | **freeze | betray sth, reveal sth, show sth, suggest sth, tell sb sth** *Her expression betrayed nothing of her thoughts.* ◇ *His grim expression told her it would be useless.* | **give nothing away | cross sth, flit across sth** *She had been watching the expression that crossed his face.*
- PREP. **without ~** *'Go on,' she said, without expression.* | **~ of** *He wore an expression of anxiety on his face.*
- PHRASES **the expression in sb's eyes/on sb's face** *He looked at her with a very strange expression in his eyes.*

3 words
- ADJ. **common | outdated | colloquial, slang | favourite | memorable | strange, unusual | figurative, idiomatic | coarse, vulgar | American, English, etc. | geographical** *Until the mid-nineteenth century, 'Italy' was just a geographical expression.*
- VERB + EXPRESSION **use** *He tends to use strange expressions like 'It's enough to make a cat laugh'.*
- EXPRESSION + VERB **mean sth**

expressive adj.

- VERBS **be | become**
- ADV. **deeply, highly, very, wonderfully** *She has a wonderfully expressive voice.* | **emotionally**
- PREP. **of** *His art is deeply expressive of emotions.*

expulsion noun

- ADJ. **automatic | immediate | mass | forced**
- VERB + EXPULSION **lead to, result in** *Copying from another candidate results in automatic expulsion.* | **call for, demand | order** *The government ordered the immediate expulsion of the two men.* | **be threatened with, face** *Several pupils now face expulsion.* | **appeal against** *an ex-party member who intends to appeal against his expulsion*
- PREP. **~ from** *her expulsion from the society*
- PHRASES **ground(s) for expulsion** *His disruptive behaviour was felt to be sufficient grounds for his expulsion.*

extend *verb*

- ADV. **greatly, significantly** *Next year we will greatly extend the range of goods that we sell.*
- PREP. **from, to** *The repayment period will be extended from 20 years to 25 years.*

extension *noun*

1 part added to a building
- ADJ. **planned, proposed | home, kitchen | one-storey, two-storey, etc.**
- VERB + EXTENSION **add, build**
- PREP. **~to** *They're building an extension to their house.*

2 extra time
- ADJ. **one-week, two-year, etc.**
- VERB + EXTENSION **apply for, ask for, request** *He's applied for an extension of his visa.* | **get, receive** *She got an extension for writing her essay.* | **give sb, grant sb**

3 making sth larger/taking sth further
- ADJ. **considerable, great, major, massive, significant | modest | further** *This new job is a further extension of his role as a manager.* | **general | gradual** *a gradual extension of the powers of central government* | **hair** *Hair extensions are pieces of artificial hair that are added to your hair to make it longer.*

4 taking an argument/a situation further
- ADJ. **logical, natural, obvious** *The team appraisal is a logical extension of the individual appraisal interview.*
- PREP. **by ~** *The blame lies with the teachers and, by extension, with the Education Service.*

extent *noun*

- ADJ. **full, greatest, maximum, overall** *The overall extent of civilian casualties remained unclear.* | **actual, exact, precise, true | geographical, territorial**
- VERB + EXTENT **reach** *The railway network had reached its greatest extent in route mileage.* | **see | consider, examine, explore, investigate | assess, calculate, estimate, evaluate, gauge, judge, measure | define, determine, establish, identify** *a statement defining the extent of Latvia's territory* | **discover | acknowledge, appreciate, realize, recognize | know, understand** *We do not yet know the extent of her injuries.* | **demonstrate, illustrate, indicate, make clear, reflect, reveal, show** *The operation revealed the extent of the cancer.* | **outline** *a lengthy agenda outlining the extent of global environmental problems* | **discuss | clarify, explain | emphasize, highlight, underline** *The victory underlined the extent to which Prussia had become a major power.* | **exaggerate, overstate** *She was exaggerating the true extent of the problem.* | **overestimate | underestimate | play down, underplay, understate** *The government sought to play down the extent of the problem.* | **ignore | conceal, obscure | limit, reduce, restrict** *to reduce the extent of deforestation*
- PREP. **in ~** *The park is about 20 acres in extent.* **to an ~** *To an extent* (= to some degree) *East-West distrust continued throughout the war.* **to a … ~** *He had withdrawn from the company of his friends to an alarming extent.*
- PHRASES **at sth's fullest/greatest extent** *At its fullest extent the Angevin Empire comprised most of western France.* **to a considerable/great/large/significant extent, to a certain/to some extent** *To some extent, we are all responsible for this tragic situation.* **to a lesser/limited/small extent** *The pollution of the forest has seriously affected plant life and, to a lesser extent, wildlife.* **to the same extent** *People no longer live in small communities to the same extent as they used to.*

exterior *noun*

1 outside of a building
- ADJ. **elegant | plain**

- PREP. **behind an/the ~** *Hidden behind a plain exterior is a wonderful hotel.* **on the ~** *There is an abundance of fine sculpture, both on the exterior and inside.*

2 sb's outward behaviour
- ADJ. **bland, bluff, calm, charming, confident, cool, glacial** *Her calm exterior hides very passionate feelings.*
- EXTERIOR + VERB **belie, conceal, hide** *His bluff exterior belied a connoisseur of antiques.*
- PREP. **behind sb's ~** *Behind his cool exterior lurks a reckless and frustrated person.* **beneath/underneath sb's ~** *Beneath her charming exterior lies a very determined woman.*

extinct *adj.*

- VERBS **be | become, go | presume sth, think sth** *The species was presumed extinct.*
- ADV. **completely, totally | all but, almost, nearly, practically, virtually** *The numbers of these animals have been falling steadily and they are now almost extinct.*

extinction *noun*

- ADJ. **mass, total, widespread** *the mass extinction of the dinosaurs* | **near, virtual | imminent, impending**
- VERB + EXTINCTION **cause, lead to** *Modern farming methods have led to the total extinction of many species of wild flowers.* | **be doomed to, be in danger of, be on the brink/edge/verge of, be threatened with, face** *The island's way of life is doomed to extinction.* ◊ *These animals are now on the verge of extinction.* | **be saved from**

extortion *noun*

- ADJ. **attempted | alleged**
- EXTORTION + NOUN **racket** *He was known for running a brutal extortion racket.*
- ⇨ Note at CRIME (for verbs)

extra *noun*

- ADJ. **little** *There was no money left over for luxuries or little extras.* | **optional | hidden** *£400 is a lot to pay for a weekend break, but there are no hidden extras.* | **added** *Regular guests also get added extras like free room service.*
- EXTRA + VERB **include sth** *Optional extras include anti-lock brakes and an electric sunroof.*

extract *noun*

1 passage from a book/piece of music
- ADJ. **brief, short | long | literary**
- VERB + EXTRACT **read | publish**
- EXTRACT + VERB **be from, be taken from** *The extract is taken from a long essay.*
- PREP. **~ from** *He read out a brief extract from his book.*

2 substance taken from another substance
- ADJ. **natural** *conditioners made from natural plant extracts* | **herbal, malt, meat, plant, vanilla, yeast** *Add a few drops of vanilla extract.*
- PREP. **~ of** *extract of apricot*

extradition *noun*

- VERB + EXTRADITION **avoid, escape** *It won't be easy for them to escape extradition.* | **ask for, call for, demand, request, seek** *The new government will seek the extradition of the suspected terrorists.* | **allow, order** *A judge ordered her extradition to Britain.* | **await, face** *The smuggler is in prison tonight, awaiting extradition to Britain.* | **fight, resist** *His lawyer announced that he will fight extradition.*
- EXTRADITION + NOUN **hearing, proceedings | agreement, treaty** *There is no extradition agreement between the two countries.* | **request**
- PREP. **~ from, ~ to**

extraordinary adj.

• VERBS **appear, be, feel, look, seem, sound | make sth** *What makes it so extraordinary is that the experts had all dismissed her theories as rubbish.* | **find sth** *I find her attitude quite extraordinary.* | **regard sth as, see sth as**
• ADV. **most, really, truly | absolutely, altogether, quite** *It seems altogether extraordinary.* | **rather**

extravagant adj.

• VERBS **be, feel, seem** *I go to that restaurant for lunch if I'm feeling extravagant.* | **become**
• ADV. **terribly, very, wildly** *He had a wildly extravagant lifestyle.* | **a bit, a little, rather, somewhat**
• PREP. **with** *You mustn't be so extravagant with other people's money.*

extreme noun

• ADJ. **opposite, polar** *Their views are at opposite extremes from each other.* | **climatic, political, temperature** *It's a difficult place to live because of its climatic extremes.*
• VERB + EXTREME **avoid** *Avoid any extremes of emotional behaviour.* | **go to** *He went to the extreme of adulation, describing Churchill as the greatest man who ever lived.* | **carry sth to, take sth to** *It's foolish to take any dieting to extremes.*
• PREP. **at an/the** *At the extreme, some nuclear waste is so radioactive it has to be kept isolated for thousands of years.* **between~s** *There has to be a solution between these extremes.* **in the~** *His voice was scornful in the extreme.* **to the~** *She was always kindly and generous to the extreme.* | **~s of** *These photographs show extremes of obesity and emaciation.*
• PHRASES **at one extreme, at the other extreme** *At the other extreme, women still childless at 32 were more likely to be from a professional background.* **go from one extreme to the other** *She goes from one extreme to the other, and either works very hard or does absolutely nothing.*

extreme adj.

• VERBS **be, seem, sound | become**
• ADV. **very | a bit, fairly, a little, quite, rather, somewhat** *Some of his views seem rather extreme.* | **dangerously | politically**
• PHRASES **at its most extreme** *This is hero-worship at its most extreme.*

extremist noun

• ADJ. **left-wing, right-wing** *an attack by right-wing extremists* | **political, religious | Muslim, Republican, etc.**
• EXTREMIST + NOUN **group, party**

exuberance noun

• ADJ. **sheer** *She was laughing from the sheer exuberance of the performance.* | **natural, youthful**
• VERB + EXUBERANCE **curb** *He has to learn to curb his natural exuberance.*

eye noun

1 part of the body
• ADJ. **left, right | amber, blue, brown, dark, golden, green, grey, hazel | big, huge, large, enormous, wide** *She just looked at me with those big blue eyes of hers.* ◇ *His eyes were wide with horror.* | **narrow | close-set | wide-apart, wide-set | deep/deep-set, heavy-lidded, hollow, hooded, sunken | protuberant | beady, piggy | baggy, puffy, swollen | bleary, bloodshot, dark-ringed, exhausted, red, red-rimmed, sleepy, tired, weary** *Her dark-ringed eyes showed that she hadn't slept.* | **bright, brilliant, luminous, lustrous, sparkling, starry | clear, limpid, liquid | soft, velvety, warm | cloudy, misty, moist,** rheumy, tear-filled, tearful, watery | dry | sightless, unseeing | short-sighted | half-closed, narrowed | unblinking | dazed, unfocused | mad, staring, wild | angry, cruel, fierce | anxious | greedy, hungry *The dog's hungry eyes were on my sandwich.* | **curious, prying** *He drew the curtains to make sure no prying eyes saw what he was doing.* | **intelligent, keen, sharp, shrewd | penetrating, piercing | cold, expressionless, glassy, glazed, lifeless, steely, vacant | downcast, sad, solemn, soulful**
• VERB + EYE **open· | close, shut | lift, raise | cast, turn** *I cast my eyes around the room but couldn't see any familiar faces.* ◇ *He turned his eyes to the door when he heard the handle turning.* | **avert** *She averted her eyes from his face.* | **screw up** *He screwed up his eyes against the glare of the sun.* | **strain** *I didn't want to strain my eyes to read, so I put the light on.* | **protect** *Skiers wear goggles to protect their eyes from the sun.* | **shade, shield** *He held up the newspaper to shield his eyes from the sun.* | **test | gouge** *She reached up and tried to gouge her attacker's eyes.* | **catch** *A movement in the reeds caught my eye* (= attracted my attention). | **look sb (straight) in, meet** *She looked her father straight in the eye and answered his question truthfully.* ◇ *He seemed unwilling to meet my eye.*
• EYE + VERB **dilate, fly open, grow wide, open, round, widen** *Her eyes dilated with horror at what she had done.* ◇ *Her eyes flew open in surprise.* ◇ *His eyes rounded in mock amazement.* | **close, shut | stream, water** *My eyes stream when I chop onions.* | **hold sth** *His eyes held a sceptical gleam.* | **be alight with sth, blaze, flare, flash, gleam, glint, glisten, glitter, glow, light up, shine, smoulder, spark, sparkle, twinkle** *She laughed, her eyes alight with excitement.* ◇ *His eyes blazed with menace.* | **mirror sth, reflect sth** *His eyes reflected his anguish.* | **blur, cloud, brim/fill with tears, mist | darken, dim, dull, glaze (over)** *Her eyes glazed over when I said I worked in dictionaries.* | **harden** *His eyes hardened as he remembered how they had laughed at him.* | **narrow, sharpen | burn, hurt, prick, prickle, smart, sting** *Her eyes prickled with unshed tears.* | **be drawn to sb/sth, follow sb/sth, turn to sb/sth** *His eyes were drawn to a bundle of papers in the corner.* ◇ *My eyes followed his every move.* | **fall on sb/sth, settle on sb/sth | dwell on sb/sth, fix on sb/sth, be fixed on sb/sth, be intent on sb/sth, focus on sb/sth, gaze (up) at sb/sth, be glued to sb/sth, linger on sb/sth, lock on sb/sth, rest on sb/sth, be riveted on/to sb/sth, stare (at) sb/sth, be trained on sb/sth, watch sb/sth** *She tried to sit up, her eyes fixed on Jean's face.* | **look at sb/sth, peer at sb/sth, regard sb/sth | glare at sb/sth | lock (together), meet** *Their eyes locked together in a battle of wills.* | **dart, flick, flicker, flit, glance, go, leap, move, run, shift** *His eyes darted from face to face.* | **roll, swivel** *She tried the door, her eyes rolling in panic.* | **dance** *Her eyes danced with amusement.* | **roam, rove** *He let his eyes roam round the scene.* | **drift, slide, slip, stray, wander** *His eyes drifted over to Helen's chair.* | **probe sth, rake sth, scan sth, scour sth, search sth, sweep sth** *His eyes scanned the room as he entered.* | **drop, fall, lower** *Her eyes dropped to her lap as she answered.* | **lift | bore into sb, lance (through) sb, pierce sb** *She could feel the old lady's eyes bore into her.* | **accustom to sth, adjust to sth, become/grow accustomed to sth** *As my eyes accustomed to the darkness, I could make out a shape by the window.* | **blink | crinkle (up), squint, wrinkle** *His eyes crinkled up at the corners as he smiled.* ◇ *Her eyes squinted against the brightness.* | **strain** *My eyes strained to make anything out in the darkness.* | **slant | bulge, pop** *His eyes bulged in fury.* | **betray sb/sth, give away sb/sth** *His narrow eyes betrayed his impatience.* | **question sb, quiz sb | smile | mock sb | appraise sb/sth, examine sb/sth, scrutinize sb/sth, study sb/sth, survey sb/sth | take sth in** *My eyes took in every detail as I entered the house for the first time in twenty years.*

- EYE + NOUN **muscles, socket | contact** *I knew he was lying because he wouldn't make eye contact with me.* | **movement** *Rapid eye movements frequently accompany dreaming.* | **doctor, specialist, surgeon | hospital | operation, surgery, treatment | examination, test | complaint, damage, defect, disease, disorder, infection, injury, strain, trouble | drops** *The doctor gave me eye drops to put in three times a day.* | **protection** *It is essential to wear some form of eye protection.* | **make-up | level** *Your computer screen should be at eye level so that you can work with your neck straight.*
- PREP. **in your~s** *There were tears in his eyes as he spoke.* ◇ *The sun was in my eyes and I couldn't see the road.* **under sb's~** *I want you under my eye* (= where I can see you).
- PHRASES **as far as the eye can see** *The tide was out, leaving nothing but mud as far as the eye could see.* **before your very eyes** *Before our very eyes, the bird snatched the fish from the plate and flew off.* **can't keep/take your eyes off sb/sth** *He couldn't keep his eyes off the girl sitting opposite him.* **cast/raise/roll your eyes heavenwards** (= to show that you are annoyed or impatient) *She rolled her eyes heavenwards when she saw what her husband was wearing.* **a gleam/glint/twinkle in sb's eye** *He looked at me with a twinkle in his eye.* **have an eye on sb/sth** (= be watching) *The store detective had his eye on a group of boys who were acting suspiciously.* **keep an eye on sb/sth** (= watch) *Could you keep an eye on my bag while I go to the toilet?* **keep an eye open/out for sb/sth** (= watch out for) *I walked round the shops, keeping an eye out for bargains.* **out of the corner of your eye** *Out of the corner of her eye, she saw Harry start forward.* **set eyes on sb/sth** *From the moment he set eyes on her he knew that he wanted to marry her.* **to/with the naked/unaided eye** *The planet should be visible to the naked eye* (= without a telescope). **under sb's critical, watchful, etc. eye** *The team went through their paces under their trainer's critical eye.* **with your own eyes** *If I hadn't seen his jump with my own eyes, I would never have believed it possible.*

2 ability to see
- ADJ. **eagle, good, keen, quick, sharp** *The children's eagle eyes spotted an ice-cream shop half a mile away.* ◇ *A surgeon needs a good eye and a steady hand.*
- PREP. **~for** *Her skill at working with wood is coupled to a keen eye for design.*

3 way of seeing
- ADJ. **careful, cautious, close, suspicious, wary, watchful | critical, stern | jaundiced | fresh, new** *He saw his students with new eyes now that he had a child of his own.* | **kindly, sympathetic | fatherly | discerning | experienced, expert, practised** *To an expert eye, the painting is an obvious fake.* | **inexperienced, untrained | artistic**

- PREP. **in sb/sth's ~** *She can do no wrong in his eyes.* ◇ *In the eyes of the law his knife was an offensive weapon.* **through sb's~s** *You need to look at your website through the user's eyes.* **to sb's~** *To my eye, the windows seem out of proportion.* **with a ... ~** *She viewed the findings with a critical eye.* **with the~of** *He looked at the design with the eye of an engineer.*
- PHRASES **in your mind's eye** (= your imagination) *He pictured the scene in his mind's eye.*

eye *verb*

- ADV. **keenly, narrowly, sharply, shrewdly | curiously, speculatively, thoughtfully | carefully, cautiously, suspiciously, warily | doubtfully, uncertainly | coldly, contemptuously, coolly | greedily, hungrily** *The children eyed the cakes greedily.*

eyebrow *noun*

- ADJ. **heavy, thick | thin | bushy, shaggy, unkempt | plucked, shaped | winged | dark, jet-black | lifted, raised | surprised | amused | derisive, mocking | cynical, sardonic, sceptical | enquiring, querying, questioning, quizzical**
- VERB + EYEBROW **arch, cock, lift, quirk, raise** *'Really?' she said, raising a sardonic eyebrow.* | **pluck** *She spent hours in front of the mirror, plucking her eyebrows.*
- EYEBROW + VERB **lift, rise** *His dark eyebrows lifted in surprise.*
- EYEBROW + NOUN **pencil**

eyelash *noun*

- ADJ. **thick | long | curling | artificial, false**
- VERB + EYELASH **bat, flutter** *She smiled and fluttered her eyelashes at the ticket inspector.*
- EYELASH + VERB **flicker, flutter**

eyelid *noun*

- ADJ. **lower, upper | closed, half-closed, lowered | drooping, heavy, hooded**
- VERB + EYELID **lift** *She lifted one eyelid to see what he was doing.*
- PREP. **behind (your)~** *She watched him from behind half-closed eyelids.*

eyesight *noun*

- ADJ. **good, keen | bad, deteriorating, failing, poor** *Failing eyesight finally forced her into an old people's home.*
- VERB + EYESIGHT **have** *Owls have good eyesight.*
- EYESIGHT + VERB **deteriorate, fail**

Ff

fabric noun

1 cloth
- ADJ. **beautiful, rich** *rich fabric wall coverings* | **delicate, fine, lightweight, sheer, soft, thin** | **coarse, firm, hard-wearing, thick** | **stretch** | **floral, patterned, plain, printed, striped** | **knitted, woven** | **cotton, nylon, woollen, etc.** | **synthetic** | **curtain, dress, furnishing**
- QUANT. **length, piece, strip**
- VERB + FABRIC **produce, weave** *The fabric is woven on these machines.*

2 basic structure of a society/way of life
- ADJ. **basic** *the basic fabric of family life* | **economic, political, social**
- VERB + FABRIC **destroy** *The government's policies have destroyed the social fabric.*
- PHRASES **the very/whole fabric of sth** *a threat to the very fabric of society*

face noun

1 front part of the head
- ADJ. **angelic, beautiful, handsome, lovely, pleasant, pretty, sweet** | **plain, ugly, terrible** | **colourless, grey, pale, pallid, white** | **flushed, pink, red, ruddy** *Her face was flushed after her run.* | **tanned** | **dark** | **sallow** | **heart-shaped, oval, round, square** | **bearded, freckled, unshaven** | **lined, wrinkled** | **pock-marked, raddled** | **fat, plump** *She had a plump, pretty face.* | **gaunt, haggard, lean, pinched, thin, wizened** | **craggy, rugged** *a craggy face with deep-set eyes and bushy brows* | **elfin** *Her short hair suited her elfin face.* | **painted** | **happy, smiling** | **tear-stained, tear-streaked** | **human**
- VERB + FACE **tilt, turn** *She turned her face away.* ◊ *He tilted her face up to his.*
- FACE + VERB **look, peer, stare** *A face peered round the door at him.*
- PREP. **in the/sb's ~** *The ball hit him in the face.* ◊ *His eyes were sunken in his gaunt face.* **on the/sb's ~** *She put some powder on her face.*
- PHRASES **a sea of faces** (= a large crowd of faces) *From the stage, he looked down at a sea of faces.*

2 expression on sb's face
- ADJ. **animated, cheerful, friendly, grinning, happy, radiant, smiling** | **anxious, frightened, troubled** | **angry, furious** | **hard, set, stern** *His face was set and hard.* | **grave, serious** | **long, sad** *The news for the company isn't good, judging from the long faces in the boardroom.* | **funny** *She made a funny face and gave a snorting sort of laugh.* | **honest, kind** | **expectant** | **rapt** | **expressive, open** *She looked at the honest, open face of her husband.* | **blank, expressionless, impassive** *His face remained impassive, so strong was his self-control.*
- VERB + FACE **make, pull** *What are you pulling a face at now?* | **search** *He searched her face for some clue as to what she meant.*
- FACE + VERB **brighten, glow, light up** *Her little face lit up when I gave her the present.* | **beam, smile** *The face smiled benignly at him.* | **cloud, crumple, drop, fall** *Her face crumpled and she started crying.* ◊ *'I can't come,' she said. His face fell.* | **clear** *His face cleared and she smiled back.* | **darken, harden, set** *Her face darkened with anger.* ◊ *His face set in grim lines.* | **soften** *The father's face softened as he hugged his little boy.* | **flame, flush, go red, redden** *Jack's face flushed with embarrassment.* | **pale** *Her face paled with fright.* | **contort, crease, pucker,**

tighten, twist *Her face contorted in pain.* | **betray sth, reveal sth** *Her face betrayed no emotion at all.*
- PREP. **on sb's ~** *She had a big smile on her face.*
- PHRASES **a face like thunder** (= a very angry face) *Mr Hibbs came in with a face like thunder.*

3 front part/side of sth
- ADJ. **front, rear** | **North, South, etc.** | **steep** *We slowly climbed the steep face of the crag.* | **cliff, rock** | **clock**
- PHRASES **face down/downwards, face up/upwards** *She placed the cards face downwards on the table.*

4 person
- ADJ. **familiar, (same) old** *I looked around for a familiar face.* ◊ *I'm so bored with seeing the same old faces!* | **different, fresh, new, strange, unfamiliar** | **famous, well-known** *a restaurant where you often see famous faces*
- VERB + FACE **see**

5 particular character/aspect of sth
- ADJ. **human** *bureaucracy with a human face* | **acceptable** | **unacceptable** *Social deprivation is the unacceptable face of capitalism.* | **true** | **changing** *the changing face of Britain*

facet noun
- ADJ. **essential, important** | **common** | **tiny** | **interesting** | **hidden**
- VERB + FACET **have** *She has another important facet to her personality.*

facilitate verb
- ADV. **greatly** *The use of computers has greatly facilitated the firm's ability to keep accurate records.* | **further**
- VERB + FACILITATE **be designed to, help (to)**

facility noun

1 facilities buildings/services/equipment
- ADJ. **excellent, first-class, good** | **adequate, appropriate, proper, suitable** | **inadequate, poor** | **basic, limited** *a hotel with only basic facilities* | **modern, up-to-date** | **extensive** | **extra, available, existing** *We are looking to upgrade the existing facilities.* | **essential, necessary** *to improve access to essential facilities* | **local, community** *hospitals, schools and other major community facilities* | **communal, shared** *The toilets and other communal facilities were in a shocking state.* | **public** | **disabled** *The railway station was criticized for its lack of disabled facilities.* | **conference, airport, hotel** | **bar, holiday, leisure, play, recreational, social, sporting/sports** | **transport, travel** | **parking, shopping** | **storage** | **canteen, dining, restaurant** | **catering, cooking, kitchen** | **baby changing, bathroom, laundry, sanitary, shower, toilet, washing** | **en suite, private** *All bedrooms offer private facilities* (= a private bathroom). | **health, health care, hospital, medical** | **childcare, crèche, day care, nursery** | **educational, training** | **library, research** | **laboratory** | **computing**
- VERB + FACILITIES **have, offer, provide** | **improve, upgrade** | **make use of, use** *I made full use of the computing facilities.*
- FACILITIES + VERB **be available, exist** | **include sth** *Facilities include a large indoor pool, jacuzzi and sauna.*
- PREP. **~ for** *The school has no facilities for the teaching of music.* ◊ *The hotel provides excellent facilities for children.*
- PHRASES **a range of facilities**

2 special feature of a machine/service

- ADJ. **central** *The archive offers a central facility for cataloguing and indexing data.* | **back-up** *The report warns that there are no back-up facilities if the reprocessing plant breaks down.* | **support** *training and other support facilities* | **special** | **useful** | **flexible** *A First National Bank loan is an extremely flexible facility.* | **technical** | **cheque book, credit, loan, overdraft** *a bank account with an overdraft facility* | **editing, graphics, help, mail, search, word processing** *(all computing)*
- VERB + FACILITY **have, offer, provide** | **use**
- FACILITY + VERB **allow (for) sth** *The cheque book facility allows for a minimum withdrawal of £200.*
- PREP. **~ for** *The device has a facility for storing any sound you like.*

3 natural ability

- ADJ. **amazing, great**
- VERB + FACILITY **have** | **show**
- PREP. **with ~** *He played with great facility.* | **~ for** *She showed an amazing facility for mind-reading.*

fact *noun*

- ADJ. **important, interesting, relevant, salient** *looking at all the relevant facts* | **basic** | **concrete, hard, incontrovertible, inescapable, observable, obvious, plain, straightforward, true, undeniable** *The police have to support their case with hard facts.* ◇ *These are all incontrovertible facts.* | **bare, brute, disturbing, harsh, sad, stark, unpalatable, unpleasant** *the bare facts of war* ◇ *a rather harsh fact of life* | **little-known, well-known** *It is a well-known fact that girls do better than boys at school.* | **mere** *The mere fact of your being there will arouse their suspicions.* | **historical**
- VERB + FACT **be aware of, have, know** *We haven't got all the facts yet.* ◇ *She already knew the facts she needed.* | **ascertain, establish, find out** *the best way of establishing the facts* | **check, examine, look at** *I think you need to check your facts.* ◇ *For God's sake, look at the facts!* | **prove** *These facts have not yet been proved.* | **collect, gather** | **select** *Historians must select the facts that they present.* | **give, impart, present, state** *The job of the teacher is not simply to impart facts.* ◇ *I'm not making excuses—I'm just stating a fact.* | **interpret** *different ways of interpreting the facts* | **account for, explain** *How do you account for the fact that unemployment is still rising?* | **accept, acknowledge, face, recognize** *She wouldn't accept the fact that she had lost.* ◇ *I'm afraid you'll have to face facts. She'll never marry you.* | **grasp** *He doesn't seem able to grasp this basic fact.* | **learn** | **assimilate** *Students need time to assimilate the facts.* | **deny, dispute** *No one can deny this fact.* | **ignore, overlook** *This approach ignores the fact that people, not computers, commit crimes.* | **be oblivious to** | **conceal, disguise, hide** *If he was bored, he managed to hide the fact very well.* | **obscure** *The recent improvements should not obscure the fact that general standards are still far too low.* | **draw attention to** *The report draws attention to the fact that the country is now a net exporter of the product.* | **emphasize, underline** | **confine yourself to, keep to, stick to** *Just stick to the facts.* | **be based on** *a novel based on historical fact* | **reflect** *Prices reflect the fact that the company is aiming at the luxury market.* | **stem from** *He knew their bitterness stemmed from the fact that he was in charge.* | **be explained by** | **be complicated by, be compounded by, be exacerbated by** *The problem was compounded by the fact that I had no idea what I was looking for—only 'some sort of clue'.* | **lament, regret, resent** *We sat miserably in the pub, lamenting the fact that our dry clothes were a 60-mile bus journey away.* ◇ *She resented the fact that I was older and had more freedom than her.*
- FACT + VERB **remain** *The fact remains that we are still two teachers short.*
- PREP. **after the ~** *On some vital decisions employees were only informed after the fact* (= when it was too late to change them). **apart from the ~** *She was happy, apart from the fact that she could not return home.* **despite/in spite of/notwithstanding the ~** *She's taking her children on holiday, despite the fact that school starts tomorrow.* **due to the ~** *Due to the fact that they did not read English, the prisoners were unaware of what they were signing.* **given the ~** *The findings are not surprising, given the facts:* ... **in ~** *I used to live in France; in fact, not far from where you're going.* | **~ about** *We learned several interesting facts about elephants.*
- PHRASES **(as) a matter of fact** *It's not wild speculation! It's plain matter of fact.* ◇ *'I suppose you'll be leaving soon, then?' 'No, as a matter of fact I'll be staying for another two years.'* **facts and figures** *presenting all the facts and figures to the meeting* **the fact of the matter** *A new car would be wonderful but the fact of the matter is that we can't afford one.* **the facts of the case** *The facts of the case are quite straightforward.* **a fact of life** (= a situation that cannot be changed) *It is an unpalatable fact of life that the most deserving people do not often achieve the most success.* **the facts of life** (= the details about sex and how babies are born, especially as told to children), **fact or fiction?** *The Loch Ness Monster: fact or fiction?* **the facts speak for themselves** (= further explanation about sth is unnecessary because the facts prove it is true), **get your facts right/wrong** *If you're going to make accusations, you'd better get your facts right.* **have the facts at your fingertips** *When making your presentation, it is important to have all the facts at your fingertips* (= to have the information you need and be able to find it and use it quickly). **in actual fact/in point of fact** *I thought the work would be difficult. In actual fact, it's very easy.* **in view of the fact that** ... *Voluntary work was particularly important in view of the fact that women were often forced to give up paid work on marriage.* **know for a fact** *Do you know for a fact that he is in London?* **a question/statement of fact** *It's a simple statement of fact.* **a recognition of the fact that** ... *a growing recognition of the fact that learning may take different forms*

faction *noun*

- ADJ. **dominant, leading, main, major** | **internal** | **competing, opposing, rival, warring** | **breakaway** | **dissident, rebel** | **disaffected** | **military, parliamentary, political** | **conservative, hard-line, left-wing, liberal, moderate, radical, right-wing** | **anti-reform, anti-talks, etc.**
- VERB + FACTION **lead**
- PREP. **~ in** *the largest faction in the civil war* **~ within** *the dominant faction within the government*

factor *noun*

- ADJ. **important, main, major, relevant, significant** *one of the most significant factors* | **critical, crucial, deciding, decisive, determining, key, vital** *This is regarded as the crucial factor in deciding who should get priority.* ◇ *Money proved to be the deciding factor.* | **contributing, contributory** *Poor organization was certainly a contributory factor to the crisis.* | **complicating, distorting** *A complicating factor is her parents' refusal to cooperate with the police.* | **limiting** | **mitigating** *The appeal judges spoke of strong mitigating factors in the case.* | **aggravating** | **additional** | **single** *The closure of the mine was the single most important factor in the town's decline.* | **common** *Look for the common factor in all these cases.* | **external, extraneous, extrinsic** *External factors in the production of disease include pollution of the environment.* | **internal, intrinsic** | **causal, causative** | **risk** *Studies have established that smoking is a risk factor for cancer.* | **contextual, demographic, economic, environmental, genetic, political, psychological, situational, social**

● VERB + FACTOR **consider, take into account** *A variety of other factors will be taken into account.* | **depend on**
● FACTOR + VERB **be involved, operate** *the contextual factors which operate to hinder understanding* | **affect sth, be responsible for sth, contribute to sth, determine sth, influence sth, precipitate sth, predispose sb/sth to sth** *environmental factors which predispose children to middle-ear infections* | **constrain sth, inhibit sth, militate against sth** *one of the factors that influenced his decision* | **interact** *looking at how economic and social factors interact* | **include sth**
● PREP. **~ behind** *the main factors behind the dollar's weakness* **~ in** *a key factor in the decision*
● PHRASES **a combination/number/range/variety of factors** *The outcome will depend on a number of factors.*

factory *noun*

● ADJ. **large** | **small** | **modern** | **disused** | **aircraft, car, chemical, clothing, munitions, etc.**
● VERB + FACTORY **open, set up** *capital to set up a ceramics factory* | **close (down), shut (down)** *They had to close the factory down in the recession.* | **manage, run**
● FACTORY + VERB **make sth, produce sth** | **open** | **close (down), shut (down)** *The factory closed down ten years ago.*
● FACTORY + NOUN **manager, owner, worker** | **job, production, work** | **buildings** | **closure**
● PREP. **at/in~** *He works in a shoe factory.*

factual *adj.*

● VERBS **be** | **keep sth** *Try to keep your account as factual as possible.*
● ADV. **entirely, purely, strictly** | **basically, largely** | **supposedly** *the speculative nature of the supposedly factual information conveyed through the media*

faculty *noun*

1 natural ability of the body/mind
● ADJ. **higher** *the evolution of man's higher faculties* | **cognitive, intellectual, mental, rational** *He is not in full possession of all his mental faculties.* | **creative, critical, imaginative, moral** | **human**
● VERB + FACULTY **be in possession of, have** *She is over eighty but still has all her faculties.* | **lose** | **develop** *trying to develop the student's critical faculties*
● PREP. **~ for** *our faculty for picking up speech even in noisy environments*

2 university department
● ADJ. **Arts, English, law, medical, etc.**
● FACULTY + NOUN **board, head, member**
● PREP. **across~** *collaboration across faculties* **in a/the~** *students who are doing degrees in the Arts Faculty* | **~ of** *the Faculty of Arts*

fad *noun*

● ADJ. **current, latest, new** | **passing** | **management** | **food** *Most children have food fads at some time.*
● PREP. **~for** *the fad for cookery programmes*

fade *verb*

● ADV. **fast, quickly, rapidly** *Hopes of a peace settlement were fading fast.* | **gradually, slowly** | **quietly** *It was impossible for her to fade quietly into the background.* | **away**
● VERB + FADE **begin to** | **seem to** *All else seemed to fade into insignificance.*
● PREP. **from** *The smile faded from his face.* **into** *Their voices faded into the distance.*

faeces *noun*

● ADJ. **fresh** | **dog, human, etc.**
● QUANT. **mass, piece**
● VERB + FAECES **be excreted in, be expelled in, be passed in** *The larvae may be excreted in the faeces.* | **collect** *A sample of fresh faeces should be collected each day.*
● FAECES + NOUN **sample**
● PREP. **in the ~** *The amount of blood in the faeces was measured.*

fail *verb*

1 not succeed
● ADV. **dismally, miserably** *I tried to cheer her up, but failed miserably.* | **spectacularly** *The show didn't just fail, it failed spectacularly.*
● VERB + FAIL **cannot/could not, can/could hardly** *The song can't fail to be a hit* (= will definitely be a hit). | **be bound to, be destined to, be doomed to** *an enterprise that was doomed to fail from the start*
● PREP. **in** *Doctors are failing in their duty if they do not warn their patients of the dangers.*

2 fail to do sth not do sth
● ADV. **totally** *The authorities have totally failed to address this problem.*

failing *noun*

● ADJ. **major, worst** *Vanity is her worst failing.* | **common, human** *the very human failing of wanting to tell other people what to do* | **moral** | **personal**
● VERB + FAILING **have** *We all have our failings.*

failure *noun*

1 lack of success
● ADJ. **complete, total** | **abject, humiliating, ignominious** *The attempt ended in abject failure.* | **inevitable** | **costly** | **alleged, apparent, perceived** | **evident** | **comparative, relative** | **initial** *Initial failure was followed by unexpected, if modest, success.* | **ultimate** *War is the ultimate failure of public communication.* | **personal** | **moral** | **academic** | **economic, financial** | **military**
● VERB + FAILURE **be doomed to, end in, result in** *All her efforts were doomed to failure.* | **admit, confess** *He was too proud to admit failure.* | **expect** *Children who are doing badly tend to expect failure and criticism.* | **fear** | **avoid**
● FAILURE + NOUN **rate** *There is a high failure rate with this treatment.*
● PHRASES **fear of failure** *Fear of failure should not deter you from trying.* **a history of failure** *John had a long history of academic failure.* **a possibility/risk of failure, a sense of failure**

2 unsuccessful person/thing
● ADJ. **great, serious** | **complete, total, utter** | **catastrophic, disastrous** | **abject, conspicuous, dismal, humiliating, ignominious, lamentable, miserable** | **costly** | **heroic** *Her ideas were large: if she could not succeed, she would at least be a heroic failure.* | **alleged, apparent, perceived** | **evident** | **comparative, relative** | **past** *to learn from past failures* | **rare** *The film was one of the rare failures in his career.* | **unexpected** | **personal** | **collective** | **moral** | **academic** | **economic, financial** *economic failure and increasing unemployment* | **military**
● VERB + FAILURE **be, represent** | **prove** *The venture proved a costly failure.* | **feel** *I felt a complete failure.* | **consider sb/sth, regard sb/sth as** | **brand sb/sth, pronounce sb/sth** *Her parents had long since branded her a failure.*
● FAILURE + VERB **arise from sth** *failures arising from circumstances beyond your control*
● PREP. **~ of** *The decision to withdraw funding represents a failure of imagination.*

3 not doing sth

• ADJ. **fundamental | general | manifest | consistent, constant, continued/continuing, persistent, repeated | government, management** *government failure to listen to the voice of the electorate*

• VERB + FAILURE **excuse, justify** *seeking to excuse his failure to ask her permission*

4 of a machine/system/part of the body, etc.

• ADJ. **battery, brake, component, computer, engine, equipment, mechanical, power, system, technical | bank, business, commercial, company, corporate, market** *Business failures rose by 30% in 2001.* | **brain, heart, kidney, liver | crop, harvest | communication**

• VERB + FAILURE **cause, lead to, result in** *a rare viral infection that can lead to heart failure*

• FAILURE + VERB **occur** *A power failure occurred between 4 and 5 p.m.*

• PREP. **~ in** *a failure in the computer system*

faint *verb*

• ADV. **almost, nearly**

• VERB + FAINT **be about to, be going to** *He was so pale she thought he was going to faint.*

• PREP. **at** *He would faint at the sight of blood.* **from** *She fainted from lack of air.* **with** *She almost fainted with shock.*

faint *adj.*

1 not strong or clear

• VERBS **be, look, sound** *His voice sounded faint and far away.* | **become, grow** *The whispers grew fainter and fainter, then stopped altogether.*

• ADV. **extremely, very** *I can't make out the number—it's very faint.* | **rather**

2 near to losing consciousness

• VERBS **be, feel, look**

• ADV. **extremely, very | almost | a bit, a little, quite** *I was beginning to feel a little faint.*

• PREP. **with** *I was faint with hunger.*

fair *noun*

• ADJ. **major | annual | trade | antiques, book, craft, horse**

• VERB + FAIR **attend, go to, visit | have, hold, host** *The city is holding its annual trade fair in May this year.* | **organize** *She is organizing next year's book fair.*

• FAIR + VERB **take place**

• PREP. **at a/the ~** *I bought it at a local craft fair.*

fair *adj.*

• VERBS **be, seem | make sth** *I'll give you ten pounds each to make it fair.* | **consider sth, think sth** *I didn't think it fair that the others should be allowed to go but not me.*

• ADV. **scrupulously, very** *It's important to be scrupulously fair when marking the final exam paper.* | **absolutely, completely, entirely, perfectly, quite, totally** *I don't care what he thinks. It seems perfectly fair to me.* ◇ *That doesn't seem quite fair.* | **hardly** *It's hardly fair that I should be working while everyone else is enjoying themselves!* | **pretty, reasonably**

• PHRASES **to be fair** *To be fair, we hadn't really spent enough time on the job.*

• PREP. **to** *That seems fair to all sides.*

fairness *noun*

• ADJ. **strict**

• VERB + FAIRNESS **achieve, ensure, guarantee** *a way of achieving fairness to the accused*

• FAIRNESS + VERB **call for sth, demand sth, require sth** *Fairness demanded an equal division of the winnings.*

• PREP. **in (all) ~** *In all fairness to him, I should say that most of his story is true.* **with ~** *They were all treated with strict fairness.* | **~ in** *the need for fairness in applying these rules* **~ to** *The new system of waiting lists should guarantee fairness to all patients.*

• PHRASES **a sense of fairness** *Children have a very strong sense of fairness.*

fairy *noun*

• ADJ. **good | bad, wicked**

• VERB + FAIRY **believe in**

faith *noun*

1 trust in sb/sth

• ADJ. **enormous, great, tremendous | absolute, complete, implicit, total, unshakeable | blind** *He seems to have a blind faith in his boss.* | **abiding** *an artist whose work reflects his abiding faith in humanity* | **touching** *She showed a touching faith in my ability to resolve any and every difficulty.* | **public** *Business crime undermines public faith in the business system.*

• VERB + FAITH **have | place, pin, put** *He distrusted political systems and placed his faith in the genius of individuals.* ◇ *She did not pin much faith on their chances of success.* | **show | lose** *people who lose faith in themselves* | **shake, undermine | destroy | restore** *trying to restore faith in the political system* | **regain | retain** *If the company can retain its customers' faith it could become the market leader.* | **affirm, express, proclaim**

• PREP. **~ in** *Her faith in human nature had been badly shaken.*

• PHRASES **an act of faith, a leap of faith** *These reforms are totally untested and will require a leap of faith on the part of teachers.* **have every faith in sb**

2 strong religious belief

• ADJ. **religious | genuine, strong, true | simple | unquestioning | active** *a large decline in the number of people who have an active faith of any sort* | **personal**

• VERB + FAITH **have | come to, find** *He found faith gradually, rather than in a sudden conversion.* | **lose | shake, undermine | regain | proclaim**

• FAITH + NOUN **healer, healing**

• PREP. **through ~** *They believe that people can come to salvation through faith.* | **~ in** *After her son's death she lost her faith in God.*

• PHRASES **an article of faith** *(often figurative) Manchester United's greatness was an article of faith for him (= a belief that could not be questioned).*

3 religion

• ADJ. **living** *Christianity is a living faith which has shaped the history of Britain.* | **world** *The study of other world faiths is an important part of religious education.* | **Catholic, Jewish, Muslim, etc.**

• VERB + FAITH **profess | practise** *Christians were allowed to practise their faith unmolested by the authorities.* | **keep alive, uphold** *Their aim was to keep alive the traditional Jewish faith.* | **hand on, pass on, preach, spread, teach** *the role of parents in passing on the faith to their children* ◇ *feeling the call to preach the faith to others*

• PHRASES **people of different faiths**

4 intention to do right

• ADJ. **bad, good** *The judge did not find any bad faith (= intention to do wrong) on the part of the defendants.*

• VERB + FAITH **keep** *As club manager he was not prepared to keep faith with (= keep a promise to) the players who had failed him.* | **break** (= break a promise to sb)

• PREP. **in ... ~** *We printed the report in good faith, but have now learnt that it was incorrect.*

faithful *adj.*

1 loyal
- VERBS **be | remain, stay** *soldiers who stayed faithful to the king*
- ADV. **extremely, very** *He has been a very faithful friend to me.* | **absolutely, entirely, utterly**
- PREP. **to** *He had remained entirely faithful to his wife.*

2 accurate
- VERBS **be**
- ADV. **remarkably, very | fairly, quite**
- PREP. **to** *The film is quite faithful to the original novel.*

fall *noun*

1 accident
- ADJ. **bad, nasty, terrible** *She took a bad fall while out riding.* | **accidental**
- VERB + FALL **have, suffer, take** *The doctor says she's had a very nasty fall.* | **break, cushion** *Luckily a bush broke his fall.* | **survive** *The chances of surviving a fall under a train are almost nil.*
- PREP. **in a/the** *He was hurt in a fall at his home yesterday.* | **~from** *She broke her neck in a fall from a horse.*

2 of snow/rocks
- ADJ. **heavy | light | fresh** *a fresh fall of snow* | **rock, snow** (also **snowfall**)
- PREP. **~of** *covered by a light fall of volcanic ash*

3 decrease
- ADJ. **big, dramatic, great, large, marked, massive, significant, substantial** *a big fall in house prices* ◇ *This triggered the recent dramatic falls on the Tokyo stock exchange.* | **modest, slight, small | steady | rapid, sharp, steep, sudden, swift | expected, projected** *a projected fall of 2%* | **unexpected | continuing, further | overall | catastrophic**
- VERB + FALL **bring, cause, contribute to, lead to, trigger | see, suffer** *Share prices suffered a slight fall yesterday.* | **record, reveal, show** *The opinion polls show a significant fall in her popularity.* | **report** *Both companies reported a fall in profits in the first quarter of this year.* | **represent** *This figure represents a fall of 21% on the same period last year.*
- FALL + VERB **occur** *The fall in age at first marriage occurred during the second half of the 18th century.*
- PREP. **~in** *a large fall in share prices*

4 defeat
- VERB + FALL **bring about, cause, contribute to, lead to** *the actions that led to his eventual fall from power*
- PREP. **~from**
- PHRASES **the rise and fall of sth** *a book charting the rise and fall of the Habsburg Empire*

fall *verb*

1 drop down towards the ground
- ADV. **heavily** *She fell heavily to the ground.* | **steadily** *The rain was falling steadily.* | **down, off, overboard** *A tile fell off the roof.* ◇ *He fell overboard in heavy seas.*
- VERB + FALL **be about to | let sb/sth** *She lifted her arm, but then let it fall.*
- PREP. **from, into** *One of the kids fell into the river.* **on** *the snow falling on the fields* **onto** *Loose bricks were falling down onto the ground.* **to** *The plate fell to the floor.*

2 suddenly stop standing
- ADV. **almost, nearly** *He stumbled and almost fell.* | **headlong** *She fell headlong, with a cry of alarm.* | **down, over** *One of the children fell over.*
- VERB + FALL **be about to** *The house looked as if it was about to fall down.*
- PHRASES **stumble/trip and fall**

3 decrease
- ADV. **dramatically, sharply, significantly, steeply** *The price of coal fell sharply.* | **slightly | steadily**

- VERB + FALL **be expected to, be likely to** *Demand is likely to fall by some 15%.* | **continue to**
- PREP. **below** *Winter temperatures never fall below 10°C.* **by** *Expenditure on education fell by 10% last year.* **from** *The number of people unemployed has fallen from two million to just over one and a half million.* **to** *Her voice fell to a whisper.*

4 belong to a group
- ADV. **squarely**
- PREP. **into** *Out of over 400 staff there are just 14 that fall into this category.* **outside** *That topic falls outside the scope of this thesis.* **under** *This falls under the heading of scientific research.* **within** *This case falls squarely within the committee's jurisdiction.*

false *adj.*

1 not true, genuine or real
- VERBS **be, look, prove, sound**
- ADV. **absolutely, completely, entirely, quite, totally, utterly** *The gossip about her later proved to be entirely false.* | **partly | certainly, definitely | blatantly, clearly, obviously, patently, undoubtedly** *Their claim was patently false.*
- PHRASES **true or false** *Lagos is the capital of Nigeria. True or false?*

2 not showing your true feelings
- VERBS **be, ring, sound** *Ella's enthusiasm rang false.*
- ADV. **horribly, very** *She managed a horribly false smile.* | **slightly** *Helen's voice sounded slightly false.*

falter *verb*

- ADV. **slightly | never** *His courage never faltered.*
- VERB + FALTER **begin to** *The economy is beginning to falter.*

fame *noun*

- ADJ. **considerable, great** *the years of his greatest fame* | **widespread | local | national | international, world/worldwide** *She gained international fame as a dancer.* | **lasting, undying | brief | instant, sudden | newfound | posthumous** *Largely unknown in his lifetime, Mendel's discoveries earned him posthumous fame.*
- VERB + FAME **enjoy** *He was enjoying his new-found fame.* | **achieve, come to, find, gain, rise to, shoot to, win** *She found fame on the stage.* ◇ *He shot to fame in 1997 when he won the US Open.* | **bring sb, earn sb** *His adventure brought him both fame and notoriety.* | **seek**
- FAME + VERB **rest on sth** *Her fame rests on a single book.* | **come to sb** *a man to whom fame came very late* | **grow, spread** *The restaurant's fame spread quickly.*
- PHRASES **at the height of sb/sth's fame** *In 1934, when at the height of his fame, he disappeared.* **sb/sth's (chief/main/only) claim to fame** *The town's main claim to fame is being the home of one of the strangest buildings in the world.* **fame and fortune** *After this concert she was firmly on the road to fame and fortune.* **a/sb's rise to fame**

familiar *adj.*

1 well-known
- VERBS **be, feel, look, seem, smell, sound** *The place felt faintly familiar to me.* | **become | make sth**
- ADV. **distinctly, very** *The room looked distinctly familiar.* | **entirely | increasingly | faintly, fairly, quite, rather, reasonably, slightly, vaguely | enough** *The report's conclusions were already familiar enough to the government.* | **already | immediately, instantly** *His face was instantly familiar, even after all those years.* | **somehow** *a name that was somehow familiar* | **curiously, disconcertingly, oddly, strangely** *Her face looked strangely familiar.* | **blessedly, comfortingly** *The kitchen smelled warm and inviting and blessedly familiar.* | **all too, de-**

pressingly, horribly, painfully, sickeningly *a situation which has become all too familiar to most teachers*
- PREP. **to** *The name sounded vaguely familiar to her.*

2 familiar with sth having a good knowledge of sth
- VERBS **be, seem | become, get, grow** *I was now getting much more familiar with the local area.*
- ADV. **extremely, intimately, very | completely, fully, perfectly, thoroughly** *You will need to be thoroughly familiar with our procedures.* | **increasingly | fairly, pretty, quite, reasonably | already**

familiarity *noun*

1 knowing sb/sth well
- ADJ. **detailed, greater, intimate | basic**
- VERB + FAMILIARITY **have** *I had only a basic familiarity with computers.* | **acquire, gain** *Over the years, he gained greater familiarity with the culture and way of life in the country.*
- PREP. **~with** *her detailed familiarity with her subject*
- PHRASES **a lack of familiarity**

2 friendly informal manner
- ADJ. **easy** *He treated her with the easy familiarity of an equal.*

family *noun*

1 group of people related to each other
- ADJ. **large | old, old-established | land-owning, wealthy, well-to-do | hard-up, low-income, poor** *tax incentives for low-income families* | **homeless | close, close-knit** *We are a very close-knit family and support each other through any crises.* | **immediate** *We've only told the immediate family* (= the closest relations). | **conjugal, nuclear** *the nuclear family of parents and children* | **extended** *maintaining contact with members of his extended family* | **lone-parent, one-parent, single-parent** *the difficulties faced by one-parent families* | **two-parent | adoptive** *helping emotionally damaged children to find placements with adoptive families* | **patriarchal | middle-class, working-class, etc. | royal | bereaved** *a counselling agency to help bereaved families*
- VERB + FAMILY **belong to, be one/part of, come from** *He belonged to an old-established family.* ◇ *We all knew her so well that we felt she was almost part of the family.* ◇ *Many of our students come from poor families.* | **marry into** *She married into a wealthy family.* | **run in** *a medical condition which runs in the family* | **be in** *This painting has been in our family for generations.*
- FAMILY + NOUN **background, history** *Do you know anything about her family background?* ◇ *a family history of heart disease* | **connections, relationships, ties** *They prefer to stay in their home country because of family ties.* | **member | life | business | home | commitments** *The job wouldn't really fit in with my family commitments.* | **income | doctor | holiday | feud | heirloom | motto | name** (= surname) | **planning** (= controlling the number of children you have by using contraception)
- PREP. **in a/the~** *These problems occur in all families.* | **within a/the~** *creating conflict within the family*
- PHRASES **family and friends** *The support of family and friends is vital.* **a member of a family**

2 children
- ADJ. **large, small | young** *parents with young families*
- VERB + FAMILY **have** *I always wanted to have a large family.* | **start** *They got married last year and plan to start a family* (= have children) *soon.* | **bring up, raise** *struggling to bring up a family on a low income* | **feed, support** *It is difficult for them to earn enough to feed their families.*
- FAMILY + NOUN **size** *Average family size has decreased since the Victorian era.* | **man** *a good family man, completely devoted to his wife and kids*

famine *noun*

- ADJ. **great, severe, terrible | widespread | imminent, impending** *Against a background of impending famine, heavy fighting took place.*
- VERB + FAMINE **face, suffer** *Four million people are now facing famine.* ◇ *countries that regularly suffer famines* | **cause, produce | relieve**
- FAMINE + VERB **strike** *When famine strikes, it is often women and children who suffer the most.*
- FAMINE + NOUN **relief | victim**
- PREP. **during a/the~** *Thousands of people died during the terrible famine of that year.*
- PHRASES **a threat of famine**

famous *adj.*

- VERBS **be | become | make sb/sth** *The school was made famous by its association with Charles Dickens.*
- ADV. **really, very | quite | internationally, locally** *internationally famous rock stars* | **justly, rightly** *The city is justly famous for its nightclubs.*
- PREP. **as** *He was famous as both a teacher and a scientist.* **for** *The town became famous for its lace.*
- PHRASES **rich and famous** *One day I'll be rich and famous, you'll see!* **world famous** *He became a world famous conductor.*

fan *noun*

1 enjoys watching/listening to sb/sth very much
- ADJ. **adoring, ardent, avid, big, dedicated, devoted, great, keen, loyal, number one, real** *I'm a big fan of Italian food.* ◇ *one of the team's biggest fans* ◇ *The singer says her dad is her number one fan.* | **lifelong | armchair** *For armchair fans back home, it was one of the highlights of the Sydney Olympics.* | **obsessive** *The actress is asking the court to protect her from an obsessive fan who is making her life a misery.* | **cricket, football, rugby, soccer, sports, etc. | jazz, music, pop, etc. | film, movie | home** *The goal was greeted by jubilation from the home fans.* | **away, travelling, visiting | opposing/opposition, rival** *There were clashes between rival fans after the match.*
- VERB + FAN **delight** *The big band sound of Syd Lawrence and his Orchestra will delight fans.* | **disappoint, let down** *Fans will not be disappointed.*
- FAN + VERB **converge on sth, gather, turn out/up** *Soccer fans converged on the capital for the cup final.* ◇ *More than 40 000 fans turned up for the 12-hour event.* | **watch sth | applaud (sb/sth), boo (sb/sth), chant sth** *Over 25 000 fans applauded both teams off the field.* | **besiege sth** *Hundreds of fans besieged the star's hotel.*
- FAN + NOUN **club, letter, mail**

2 machine that creates a current of air
- ADJ. **electric | cooling | extractor | ceiling, overhead**
- FAN + NOUN **belt, heater**

fanatic *noun*

- ADJ. **real | cricket, fitness, football, keep-fit, health, sports** *He's a real football fanatic.* | **religious**

fancy dress *noun*

- VERB + FANCY DRESS **don, wear** *Several of the managers donned fancy dress for the office party.*
- FANCY DRESS + NOUN **ball, party**
- PREP. **in~** *Many of the marathon runners compete in fancy dress.*

fanfare *noun*

- ADJ. **great** (*often figurative*) *The new building was opened with great fanfare in January 1895.* | **trumpet**

- VERB + FANFARE **give, play**
- FANFARE + VERB **sound** *A trumpet fanfare sounded and the procession began.*
- PHRASES **a fanfare of trumpets**

fang *noun*

- ADJ. **long** | **sharp**
- VERB + FANG **bare, show** *The wolf growled and bared its sharp fangs.* | **sink** *The snake sank its fangs into its victim.*

fantastic *adj.*

1 very good

- VERBS **be, feel, look, smell, sound, taste** *I felt fantastic after my swim.* ◇ *This cake tastes fantastic.*
- ADV. **really, truly** *We had a really fantastic holiday.* | **absolutely, just, quite** *The sense of freedom was absolutely fantastic.*

2 strange

- VERBS **be, look, sound**
- ADV. **rather** *It may sound rather fantastic, but it's the truth.* | **increasingly** *The plot gets increasingly fantastic as the film goes on.*

fantasy *noun*

- ADJ. **pure, sheer** *Most of what they told us was pure fantasy.* | **wild** *She dismissed the idea as a wild fantasy.* | **personal, private** | **childhood, childish** | **erotic, romantic, sexual** | **male**
- VERB + FANTASY **enjoy, have, indulge in** | **build, weave** *She had woven a whole fantasy about living in a cottage by the sea.* | **cherish, nourish** *I cherished the fantasy that I might one day have a son who would fulfil the dream.* | **act out** *Children can act out their fantasies in a secure environment.* | **fulfil, live (out), play out, satisfy** *My childhood fantasies were finally fulfilled.* ◇ *He was able to play out his fantasy of pop stardom.*
- FANTASY + NOUN **life, world** *living in a fantasy world*
- PREP. **~about** *She had a fantasy about going to live on a South Pacific island.*
- PHRASES **the realms of fantasy** *The idea belonged in the realms of fantasy.* **a world of fantasy** *She felt she had entered a world of fantasy.*

farce *noun*

- ADJ. **complete, total** *The whole procedure has become a complete farce.* | **French, Whitehall** (*both figurative*) *It was like a Whitehall farce the way I was sent from department to department and everyone said it was someone else's job to help me.*
- VERB + FARCE **become, degenerate into, end in, turn into** *The debate degenerated into farce when opposing speakers started shouting at each other.*

fare *noun*

1 money paid to travel by bus, taxi, etc.

- ADJ. **expensive, high** | **cheap, low** | **adult, full, normal, standard** | **children's, concessionary, discounted, half, reduced** | **return, single** | **first-class, second-class** | **air, bus, cab, coach, ferry, rail, taxi, train**
- VERB + FARE **pay** *I'm afraid you will have to pay the full fare.* | **charge** *Buses charged a standard fare of about 20 pence per mile.* | **increase, put up** | **bring down, cut, reduce, slash** *air fares slashed by a massive 30%* | **introduce, offer** *The airline has introduced a cheap return fare to New York.* | **dodge** *He faces charges of dodging taxi fares.*
- FARE + VERB **cost (sb) sth** *The return fare will cost you less than two single tickets.* | **go up, increase, rise** | **come down**

- FARE + NOUN **increase, rise** | **reduction** | **deal** *a special fare deal for air travellers*
- PREP. **at...~** *Children travel at half fare.*
- PHRASES **an increase/a rise in fares, a reduction in fares** *The company is promising reductions in fares.*

2 passenger in a taxi

- VERB + FARE **pick up** *The taxi driver picked up a fare outside the opera house.*

3 food; material for listening to, reading, etc.

- ADJ. **delicious, rich, wholesome** | **plain, rough, simple** | **daily, standard, staple, traditional, typical** *Court trials involving famous people are the daily fare of newspapers.* ◇ *The band's music was standard rock fare.* | **local** | **vegetarian** | **Chinese, English, French, etc.** | **Christmas, farmhouse**
- VERB + FARE **offer, serve** *a restaurant serving traditional Scottish fare* | **sample** *tourists seeing the sights and sampling the local Spanish fare*

fare *verb*

- ADV. **badly, well** *She should fare better in this competition.* ◇ *He fared well against his main rival.*

farewell *noun*

- ADJ. **fond** | **emotional, tearful** | **sad** | **silent** *I said a silent farewell to my village as I left for the city.* | **final**
- VERB + FAREWELL **bid sb/sth, say, wish sb** *We bade them a final farewell.* | **wave** *I waved farewell to my friends from the deck of the ship.* | **make** *The court dignitaries made their farewells to the emperor.* | **exchange** *They exchanged fond farewells at the railway station.* | **be** *Is this farewell or will we see each other again?*
- FAREWELL + NOUN **appearance** *This famous warplane is about to make its farewell appearance.* | **address, speech** | **performance, tour** *the band's farewell tour* | **dinner, party** | **card, gift, present**
- PREP. **in~** *He raised his hand in farewell.* | **~to** *She was sorry to bid farewell to Portugal.*

far-fetched *adj.*

- VERBS **be, seem, sound**
- ADV. **extremely, impossibly, very** *The whole story was impossibly far-fetched.* | **a bit, a little, pretty, rather**

farm *noun*

- ADJ. **large** | **little, small** | **100-acre, 200-hectare, etc.** | **neighbouring, next** *She lives on the next farm.* | **local, nearby, surrounding** | **isolated, outlying, remote** | **border** | **hill** | **organic** | **intensive** | **commercial** | **factory** | **model** *Ten model farms have been set up to showcase modern production methods.* | **working** *The area combines a working farm and a farming museum.* | **family, home** | **traditional** | **private** | **state** | **cooperative, collective** | **arable, livestock, mixed** | **dairy, fur, stud** | **fish, fruit, pig, poultry, sheep, trout, turkey, etc.**
- VERB + FARM **have, own** | **manage, run** | **work (at/on)** *During the war, few men were left to work the farm.* ◇ *The children had to work on the family farm.* | **set up** | **live at/on** | **be brought up on** | **visit**
- FARM + VERB **lie** *The farm lies on the hills above the lake.* | **produce sth** *a dairy farm producing speciality cheeses*
- FARM + NOUN **produce, product** *Farm produce, including fruits and grains, was their principal export.* ◇ *farm products such as eggs and vegetables* | **animal** | **labourer, worker** | **labour, work** | **manager, owner** | **management** | **land** (also **farmland**) | **building** | **equipment, implements, machinery** | **policy** *the EU farm policy* | **subsidies, support** *The EU has decided to cut farm subsidies.* | **life** *village and farm life* | **cottage, house** (also **farmhouse**) | **shop** | **road, track**

● PREP. **at a/the~** *The police are investigating a fire at a farm near Whitby.* **down on the~** *The myth of happy and contented animals down on the farm is now far from the truth.* **on a/the~** *He had lived on that farm all his life.*

farm *verb*

● ADV. **heavily, intensively** *The land has been intensively farmed.* | **organically** *They farm organically now.*

farmer *noun*

● ADJ. **big, large** | **small** *a new scheme to help the small farmer* | **peasant, tenant** | **gentleman** | **commercial** | **hill** | **organic** | **arable, livestock** | **dairy** | **cattle, chicken, pig, sheep, etc.**

farming *noun*

● ADJ. **commercial** | **intensive** | **battery, factory** | **subsistence** | **hill** | **organic** | **arable, livestock, mixed** | **dairy** | **fish, fruit, poultry, sheep, etc.**
● VERB + FARMING **be engaged in, work in**
● FARMING + NOUN **community** | **industry** | **land** | **method, practice**

fascinating *adj.*

● VERBS **be, look, sound** | **become** | **make sth** | **find sth**
● ADV. **deeply, most, really, terribly, truly, very** *a most fascinating book* ◇ *'This is all very fascinating,' said Wilcox, 'but I've got a meeting in five minutes.'* | **absolutely, quite** | **endlessly** *I find the natural world endlessly fascinating.*
● PREP. **to** *What was fascinating to me was the way the creatures moved.*

fascination *noun*

● ADJ. **deep, great** | **growing** | **particular, peculiar, special** | **endless, enduring, lifelong, perennial** | **awful, horrible, horrified, morbid, unhealthy** | **strange** *a morbid fascination with death*
● VERB + FASCINATION **have, hold** *The sea holds a fascination for all children.* | **develop, feel, find, have** *He had a deep fascination with all forms of transport.* | **exercise, exert** *These exotic plants exert a fascination all of their own.* | **share** *She shared his fascination for motorbikes.* | **gaze in/with, look (on) in/with, stare in/with, watch in/with** | **listen in/with** *He looked on in horrified fascination as the ship drew nearer to the rocks.*
● PREP. **in/with ~** *She watched in fascination as the cat pounced on the mouse.* | **~for** *She developed a fascination for these creatures.* **~ in** *He found great fascination in her quiet, frank manner.* **~ with** *a lifelong fascination with Baroque music*
● PHRASES **part of the fascination** *Seeing over a thousand species of fish is part of the fascination of the reef.* **a source of fascination to sb** *His letters have been a source of fascination to a wide audience.*

fashion *noun*

1 style of dressing, etc. popular at a particular time
● ADJ. **current, latest, modern, new** | **growing** | **changing, passing** *changing fashions in education* ◇ *This theory, though recent, is more than a passing fashion.* | **high** *The store sells everything from sports clothes to high fashion.* | **designer** *the influence of Italian designer fashion on the clothes industry* | **female, street, youth** | **architectural, cultural, intellectual**
● VERB + FASHION **be, be in** *She wore a powdered wig, as was the fashion of the day.* ◇ *Black is always in fashion.* | **become, come into** *Pessimism has become the fashion.* ◇ *When did flares first come into fashion?* | **fall out of, go out of** *Careful spending has gone out of fashion in our con-*

sumer society. | **be out of** | **come back into** | **be back in** | **introduce, set, start** *He set a fashion for large hats.* | **follow, keep (up) with, keep pace with** *I've given up trying to keep up with the latest fashions.*
● FASHION + VERB **change** *watching how fashions change over the years*
● FASHION + NOUN **statement** *Flared trousers were a fashion statement of the seventies.* | **model** *She started her career as a fashion model.* | **show** | **shoot** *photographers at fashion shoots* | **magazine** | **scene** *fresh interest in the New York fashion scene* | **capital** *Paris, the world's fashion capital* | **business, industry, market, trade, world** *Her summer collection took the fashion world by storm.* | **company, house, label** *one of the most successful fashion houses in Milan* | **retailer, shop** | **design, photography** | **designer, editor, photographer** | **accessory, clothes, garment** | **victim** *this season's must-have accessories that no fashion victim will be seen without*
● PREP. **after the ~ of** *She spoke in French after (= copying) the fashion of the court.* | **~ for** *the fashion for long dresses* **~ in** *Fashions in art come and go.*
● PHRASES **changes in fashion, the fashion of the day, the height of fashion** *The palazzo represents the height of architectural fashion for the mid-17th century.* **the world of fashion** *household names in the world of fashion and design*

2 way you do sth
● ADJ. **true** ... *The inspector insisted the meeting be held, in true spy novel fashion, in the open air.* | **normal, orthodox, usual** *Application for the course can be made in the normal fashion.* | **conventional, time-honoured, traditional** *They celebrated their win, in time-honoured fashion, by spraying champagne everywhere.* | **typical** *We had just gone out when, in typical fashion, the rain came down.* | **limited** *He has a small vocabulary and is only able to express himself in a limited fashion.* | **positive** | **no uncertain** *Karpov struck back in no uncertain fashion to win the seventh game.* | **meaningful** | **parrot** *Students become frustrated with learning verbs parrot fashion.* | **best** *(often ironic),* **exemplary** *batons ready in best police fashion* | **civilized** | **appropriate** | **cavalier** | **controlled, orderly, organized, regular, systematic** | **ad hoc, desultory, haphazard, piecemeal, random, roundabout** | **arbitrary** | **straightforward** | **logical, predictable** | **linear** *Costs and revenues are assumed to behave in a linear fashion.* | **easy, leisurely, relaxed** *The descent of the footpath starts in easy fashion.* | **dramatic, spectacular** | **bizarre, peculiar** | **mysterious** | **friendly** | **jocular** | **businesslike** | **democratic**
● VERB + FASHION **behave in**
● PREP. **after a~** *So they became friends, after a fashion (= to some extent).* **in a~** *Why are they behaving in such a ridiculous fashion?* **in ... ~** *The troops embarked in orderly fashion.*

fashionable *adj.*

● VERBS **be, look** | **become** | **remain** | **make sth** | **consider sth**
● ADV. **extremely, highly, very** *Furnishings of this sort are now highly fashionable.* | **increasingly** | **quite, rather** | **currently** | **newly** | **suddenly** *a young and suddenly fashionable actor* | **no longer**
● PREP. **among** *These cars are no longer fashionable among the young.*

fast *noun*

● ADJ. **long** | **brief**
● VERB + FAST **go on, keep, observe** *All members of the religious community keep these fasts.* | **break** *In the evening the people break their fast.*

fast *adj., adv.*

- VERBS **be, seem** *Her pulse seemed very fast.*
- ADV. **exceptionally, extremely, really, remarkably, surprisingly, very** *I should make a very fast profit on these.* | **a bit, fairly, a little, pretty, quite, reasonably, relatively** *I suppose delivery in two days is quite fast really.* | **amazingly, blindingly, incredibly, unbelievably** *He came round the corner blindingly fast.* | **dangerously**

fasten *verb*

- ADV. **firmly, properly, securely, tightly** *We fastened all the windows securely.* | **up** | **together** *She fastened the papers together with a paper clip.*
- PREP. **to** *She fastened the rope to a tree.*

fat *noun*

1 substance directly under your skin
- ADJ. **excess, surplus** | **body** | **puppy** *It wasn't easy to lose puppy fat when Mum fed her on stodgy home cooking.*
- VERB + FAT **go to, put on, run to** *If you eat too much you will put on fat.* ◊ *She was middle-aged and running to fat.* | **burn (off), lose, shed** *Exercise helps you burn off excess fat.* | **break down** *Claims that anti-cellulite creams can break down fat are controversial.*
- FAT + VERB **accumulate** *The waistline is usually the first area where fat accumulates.*
- PHRASES **not an ounce of fat** *His body was all muscle, with not an ounce of fat.* **a roll of fat** *He had great rolls of fat round his middle.*

2 in your diet/used in cooking
- ADJ. **dietary** | **added, excess, extra, surplus** | **visible** | **animal, vegetable** | **mono-unsaturated, polyunsaturated, saturated, unsaturated** *margarines that contain polyunsaturated fats* | **cooking** | **bacon, beef, etc.** | **hot** *Put the chicken in hot fat and braise thoroughly.*
- VERB + FAT **contain, have** *This cheese has a lot of fat in it.* | **be high/low in fat** *Ice cream is high in fat and sugar.* | **eat** *The amount of fat you eat can affect the health of your heart.* | **cut down on** *It's easy to cut down on fat without changing your diet too much.* | **cut out** *She has cut out fat altogether in an effort to lose weight.* | **cut, trim** *Trim any visible fat off the meat before cooking.* | **drain (off), pour off, skim off** *Remove the turkey from the pan and drain off the excess fat.*
- FAT + VERB **contain sth** *Fats contain more calories than carbohydrates for the same weight.* | **spit** *The only sound from the kitchen was the lamb fat spitting.*
- FAT + NOUN **intake** *the relationship between fat intake and cholesterol levels* | **content** *Despite its very low fat content, it is deliciously creamy.*

fat *adj.*

- VERBS **be, feel, look** | **become, get, grow** | **make sb** *Try to cut out the foods that are making you fat.*
- ADV. **enormously, hugely, immensely, really, very** | **quite, rather** | **grossly, monstrously**
- PHRASES **big/great fat** *sitting next to a big fat woman* ◊ *a big fat envelope stuffed with banknotes*

fatal *adj.*

1 causing death
- VERBS **be, prove**
- ADV. **near** *He has not driven since his near fatal crash earlier this year.* | **always, invariably, universally** | **often, sometimes, usually** | **rarely** | **potentially** *The disease is potentially fatal.*
- PREP. **for** *This kind of accident is almost always fatal for the pilot.* **to** *a chemical which is invariably fatal to small mammals*

2 causing serious trouble

- VERBS **be, prove**
- ADV. **absolutely** | **ultimately** *Her disregard of this advice was ultimately fatal.*
- PREP. **to** *Tax increases have proved fatal to the nation's business community.*

fate *noun*

1 sb/sth's future
- ADJ. **awful, dreadful, grim, terrible** | **cruel, unhappy** | **tragic** | **worse** *They decided to kill themselves rather than suffer a worse fate at the hands of their enemy.* | **common, normal, usual** | **likely** *Under-representation is the likely fate of small parties.* | **ultimate** | **unknown** *The ultimate fate of the captured troops is unknown.* | **the same, similar** *She broke her ankle before the big match, then suffered the same fate a month later.*
- VERB + FATE **face** *He faces a grim fate if he is sent back to his own country.* | **meet, suffer, undergo** | **share** *He had no desire to share the fate of his executed comrades.* | **avoid, escape** *She managed to escape the fate of the other rebels.* | **deserve** *What had he done to deserve such a terrible fate?* | **accept, be resigned to** *The condemned men were resigned to their fate.* | **bemoan, bewail** *Instead of just bemoaning your fate, why not do something to change it?* | **ponder** | **seal** *He had signed his confession and sealed his own fate.* | **decide** *An extraordinary general meeting to decide the company's fate will be held on Thursday.* | **abandon sb/sth to, leave sb/sth to** *The generals abandoned the men to their fate.* | **rescue/save sb/sth from** | **discover, hear (of), know (of), learn (of)** *He will learn of his fate in court tomorrow.* | **await** *The convicts awaited their fate in prison.*
- FATE + VERB **await sb/sth, be/lie in store for sb/sth** *They were warned of the dreadful fate that awaited them if ever they returned to their homes.* | **befall sb/sth** *Worst of all was the fate that befell the captured rebel general.* | **be/hang in the balance** *The fate of the African wild dog hangs in the balance* (= is uncertain).
- PHRASES **hold/have sb/sth's fate in your hands** *The jury held the fate of the accused in their hands.* **leave/place/put your fate in sb's hands, a fate worse than death** (*often humorous*) *Obeying her parents' wishes for her life seemed a fate worse than death.*

2 power controlling everything
- ADJ. **cruel** *He believed that the universe was controlled by the whims of a cruel fate.* | **kind** *Fate was kind to me.*
- VERB + FATE **believe in** *Such coincidences are almost enough to make one believe in fate.* | **tempt** *It would be tempting fate to say that we will definitely win the game.* | **leave sth to** *I have a great deal of trust and I leave everything to fate.*
- FATE + VERB **decide sth, decree sth** *Fate decreed that she would never reach America.* | **intervene** *He secretly hoped that fate would intervene and save him having to meet her.* | **strike** *Only weeks after her previous injury, fate struck again, leaving her unable to compete.* | **deal a/its hand, deal sb a hand** *Anne accepted the cruel hand that fate had dealt her.* | **take a hand** *Fate took a hand in* (= influenced) *the outcome of the championship.*
- PHRASES **an accident/quirk/turn/twist of fate** *It seemed a cruel twist of fate that the composer should have died so young.* **the hand of fate** *The new job had come at just the right time for him. Was it the hand of fate?*

father *noun*

- ADJ. **lone, single** *As a single father, he found it a struggle bringing up three children.* | **widowed** | **absent** | **biological, natural, real** | **adoptive, foster, step-** | **surrogate** *Elena's brother was a surrogate father to her kids after her husband died.* | **elderly, old** | **dead, deceased, late** | **caring, devoted, good, loving, marvellous** *He is very good with children and would make a marvellous* *father.* | **adoring, doting, indulgent** | **beloved** *She kept the books that had belonged to her beloved father.* | **proud** *He has just become the proud father of a baby girl.* | **domineering, overbearing, possessive** | **drunken, violent** | **doctor, engineer, immigrant,** etc. *Their musician father encouraged their love of music.*

● VERB + FATHER **resemble, take after** *The two boys were like their mother in character, but Louise took after her father.* | **follow, succeed** *She followed her father into the legal profession.* ◇ *He succeeded his father as Professor of Botany.* | **inherit sth from** *She inherited the urge to travel from her father.*

● FATHER + NOUN **figure** *Some of his students regard him as a father figure.*

● PHRASES **a father of two,** etc. *Boland, a father of two, was arrested on charges of theft.* **follow in your father's footsteps** *He followed in his father's footsteps and became a motor mechanic.* **the death/loss of your father**

fatigue *noun*

1 great tiredness
● ADJ. **extreme, severe** | **growing** | **general** | **mental, physical** | **battle, compassion** *soldiers suffering from battle fatigue* ◇ *Compassion fatigue among donor countries means there is less money for worthy causes.* | **driver** *car accidents caused by driver fatigue*

● VERB + FATIGUE **suffer from, drop (down) with** | **combat, fight (off), reduce** *The right vitamins help you combat fatigue.*

● FATIGUE + VERB **set in** *She had to stop work when fatigue set in.* | **overcome sb**

● PREP. **from** *~ crying from cold and fatigue* **with** *~ The man was shivering with fatigue.*

● PHRASES **a feeling of fatigue, signs of fatigue**

2 fatigues clothes worn by soldiers
● ADJ. **army, battle, combat** | **camouflage**
● PHRASES **in** *~ soldiers in combat fatigues*
⇨ Special page at CLOTHES

fault *noun*

1 responsibility for sth wrong
● ADJ. **stupid** *It's his own stupid fault his car was stolen—he should have kept it locked.*

● FAULT + VERB **lie with sb** *The fault lay not with her but with her manager.*

● PREP. **at** *~ The party at fault in a court case usually pays the other party's legal costs.* **through sb's** *~ Many of the soldiers died through his fault.* **without** *~ Having made an error of judgement she was not without fault in the matter.*

● PHRASES **all/entirely your (own) fault** *It's all your own fault, you know.* **be largely/partly your (own) fault, be hardly your (own) fault, fault on sb's part** *(law) the absence of fault on the part of the prosecution* **through no fault of your own** *helping people who, through no fault of their own, have lost their homes*

2 weakness in sb's character
● ADJ. **great** *Her great fault was that she thought too well of herself.* | **moral**

● VERB + FAULT **have** *We all have our faults.* | **be blind to, overlook** *He is blind to his son's faults.* ◇ *She was prepared to overlook his faults.*

● PREP. *~* **in** *Incorrectness in speech was considered a great fault in a gentleman.*

● PHRASES **for all sb's faults** *For all her faults (= in spite of her faults) she was a great woman.* **to a fault** *He is generous to a fault (= very generous and perhaps too generous).*

3 sth wrong or not perfect with sth
● ADJ. **bad, major, serious** | **basic** *There is a basic fault in the design of the engine. It cannot be fixed.* | **dangerous** | **minor** | **common** *a common fault with this type of machine* | **real** *The only real fault of the book is its looseness of structure.* | **obvious** | **possible** | **design** | **technical**

| **electrical, engine, mechanical, structural** *Of course, minor mechanical faults sometimes occur.*

● VERB + FAULT **have** *The engine has a serious fault.* | **develop** *The car soon developed another fault.* | **look for** | **diagnose, discover, find, identify, locate** *They've found a major fault with the electrical system.* ◇ *When she tested the recorder she could find no fault with it.* | **find, pick** *My mother did nothing but find fault with my schoolboy manners.* ◇ *He's deliberately picking fault with the meal to get a reduction on the bill.* | **correct, fix, rectify, repair** *trying to correct the faults in the program* | **report** *You should report any fault directly to the phone company.*

● FAULT + VERB **occur** | **lie in sth** *The fault lay in the structure of the economy.*

● FAULT + NOUN **detection, diagnosis, finding**

● PREP. *~* **in** *Diabetes is caused by a fault in the insulin production of the body.* *~* **with** *She was always finding fault with his manners.*

● PHRASES **for all its faults** *For all its faults (= in spite of the faults), we love this city.*

4 in tennis
● ADJ. **double** | **foot**
● VERB + FAULT **serve** *Even tennis champions sometimes serve double faults.*

5 geology
● ADJ. **geological**
● FAULT + NOUN **line** | **scarp** | **system, zone**

favour *noun*

1 sth that helps sb
● ADJ. **big, great** | **little, small** | **special** | **personal** *As a personal favour to me, please don't release my story to the press.* | **political, sexual**

● VERB + FAVOUR **ask** *I came here to ask you a favour, a big favour.* | **expect** *Although I am friends with the tennis ace, I don't expect any favours from him on court.* | **bestow, do, grant sb** *Rodrigo accepted the favours bestowed on him by the new king.* ◇ *Do yourself a favour and cut your credit cards in half.* | **owe sb** *I'll ask Jane. She owes me a favour.* | **return** *Thanks very much. I'll return the favour one day.* | **seek** | **obtain** | **accept, receive**

2 approval or support for sb/sth
● ADJ. **great, high, particular** *Traditionally, vigilante groups have found greater favour on the political right.* ◇ *He stood in high favour at the court of Lewis the Pious.* | **divine, government, political, royal** *In the Christian tradition, the world exists only as an act of divine favour.*

● VERB + FAVOUR **be in, enjoy, have, stand in** *The bishop was said to have enjoyed the king's favour.* | **find, gain, win** *Her political views have not found favour in recent years.* | **curry** *trying to curry favour with the teachers* | **show** *As an examiner, she showed no favour to any candidate.* | **be out of** | **fall from, fall out of, lose** *The senior officials were punished and rapidly fell from favour.* ◇ *This idea has long since fallen out of favour.* | **be back in, bring sth back into, come back into** *A style of art can go out of fashion and then come back into favour fifty years later.* | **argue in, speak (out) in** *to argue in favour of this policy* | **come down/out in, decide in, find in, resolve in, rule in, vote in** *The committee came down in favour of setting up a national body.* ◇ *The High Court found in favour of the plaintiffs.* | **work in** *Environmental conservation generally works in favour of maintaining the status quo.* | **go in** *The golf tournament went in the Americans' favour (= they won).*

● PREP. **in** *~* **of** *He is strongly in favour of capital punishment.* ◇ *Early in his musical career he abandoned blues in favour of jazz.* **in sth's** *~ This piece of software has two points in its favour: it's fast and inexpensive.* | *~* **with** *She is too popular with the public to find much favour with the critics.*

● PHRASES **an argument in sb/sth's favour** *an argu-*

ment in favour of censorship **a bias in sb/sth's favour,
look with favour on/upon sb/sth** *Depth of training is
looked upon with favour by many employers.* **without fear
or favour** (= in a fair way)

favour *verb*

• ADV. **strongly** *We strongly favour reform of the system.*
• VERB + FAVOUR **appear to, be known to, be likely to,
be thought to, seem to, tend to** *The prime minister is
thought to favour an early referendum on the issue.*
• PREP. **at the expense of** *He favoured some individuals
at the expense of others.* **over** *News coverage should not favour one party over another.*

favourable *adj.*

• VERBS **be, look, seem | become | remain**
• ADV. **exceptionally, extremely, highly, very** *She
gained a highly favourable impression of the company.* |
**extraordinarily, overwhelmingly | fairly, moderately,
quite | broadly, generally** *His proposals met with a
broadly favourable response.* | **uniquely**
• PREP. **for** *Conditions are now favourable for skiing.* **to**
The court's judgement was favourable to their client.

favourite *noun*

1 sb/sth that you like more than others
• ADJ. **firm, great, huge, particular, special, very** *This
painting is a particular favourite of mine.* ◇ *My very fa-
vourite film is 'The Wizard of Oz'.* | **all-time, established,
old, perennial, traditional** *This movie is my all-time favourite.* ◇ *You will find all your old favourites in this book
of poems.* | **family, personal, popular**
• VERB + FAVOURITE **choose** *If I had to choose a favourite, it would be Monet's 'Water Lilies'.*
• PREP. **~for** *The woods surrounding the estate were a favourite for family walks.* **~among** *He is a favourite among
his teammates.* **~with** *The song is a firm favourite with
their fans.*

2 competitor expected to win
• ADJ. **clear, firm, hot, odds-on, overwhelming, red-hot**
She is odds-on favourite to win a coveted Academy Award.
| **second | joint | even money** *The horse is an even
money favourite.* | **2–1, etc.** *Tiger Woods is 3–2 favourite
to win the Million Dollar Challenge.* | **home, local | cup,
race, title**
• VERB + FAVOURITE **look, start (as)** *The Brazilians
still look firm favourites to take the title.* | **emerge as**
• PREP. **~for** *Jopanini is second favourite for Saturday's
race, behind Bright Spark.*
• PHRASES **favourite to win** *The Spanish are the favourites to win.*

favouritism *noun*

• VERB + FAVOURITISM **show | accuse sb of**
• PREP. **~ to/towards** *She denied showing favouritism to
any of her students.*
• PHRASES **accusations of favouritism** *He resigned over
accusations of favouritism.*

fax *noun*

• ADJ. **incoming**
• VERB + FAX **send (sb) | get, receive**
• FAX + NOUN **machine | number | line | signal** *Our
fax machine differentiates between an incoming fax signal
and a voice call.* | **message | modem, software**
• PREP. **by~** *There was still time to receive copies by fax.* |
~from, ~to

fear *noun*

• ADJ. **deep, great, real, terrible** *It was the first time she*

had experienced real fear. | **growing | irrational | un-
founded, well-founded** *Our fears proved unfounded.*
• VERB + FEAR **experience, feel, have** *She did not know
why she should feel such fear.* | **be filled with, be gripped
by, be paralysed by/with, be trembling with | express,
show, voice** *The boy showed no fear.* ◇ *Doctors have voiced
fears that we may be facing an epidemic.* | **cause, fuel, in-
stil** *This incident has fuelled fears of a full-scale war.* ◇ *the
fear that her mother had instilled in her* | **allay, dispel,
overcome** *The government is keen to allay the public's
fears.* ◇ *She managed to overcome her fear.* | **live in** *The
people live in fear of attack by the bandits.*
• FEAR + VERB **abate, subside** *When she heard the
news, some of her fear subsided.* | **grip sb, haunt sb** *A sud-
den fear gripped him.*
• PREP. **for~** *Nobody refused for fear of losing their job.*
in ~ *He ran away in fear.* **out of ~** *He lied out of fear.*
through ~ *The pupils obeyed through fear of punishment.*
without ~ *She stared at him without fear.* **with ~** *His face
was white with fear.* | **~about** *his fear about what might
happen* **~for** *my fear for her safety* **~of** *They have a terrible
fear of failure.*
• PHRASES **fear and trepidation** *The men set off in fear
and trepidation.* **strike fear into (the heart of) sb** *The
sound of gunfire struck fear into the hearts of the villagers.*

fear *verb*

• ADV. **genuinely, greatly, really, seriously** *This disease
is greatly feared.* ◇ *I really feared that this might be the
end.* | **rightly** *Everyone rightly feared the coming war.*
• VERB + FEAR **seem to | begin to | have little/noth-
ing to** *You have nothing to fear from him.* | **have reason
to** *I have reason to fear that you might abuse your power.*
• PREP. **for** *We feared for their safety.*

fearful *adj.*

• VERBS **appear, be, feel, look, seem | become, grow |
remain | leave sb, make sb** *The experience had left her
fearful and uncertain.*
• ADV. **extremely, very | almost | a bit, a little, rather,
slightly | understandably**
• PREP. **about** *understandably fearful about the future*
for *I felt fearful for my life.* **of** *He was fearful of every
shadow.*

fearless *adj.*

• VERBS **be, seem | make sb**
• ADV. **absolutely, completely, quite, totally, utterly**
• PREP. **in** *She was fearless in her attacks on public
figures.*

feasibility *noun*

• ADJ. **economic, technical**
• VERB + FEASIBILITY **consider, discuss, examine,
explore, investigate, look at, study | assess, deter-
mine, evaluate, test** *a drilling project to assess the feasibil-
ity of bringing the water four miles into the village* | **dem-
onstrate | prove | doubt, express doubts about, ques-
tion** *Some of them doubted the feasibility of the proposal.*
• FEASIBILITY + NOUN **study** *The local council called
for a feasibility study into the new road scheme.*

feasible *adj.*

• VERBS **be, look, seem | become | consider sth** *A
tunnel was not considered economically feasible.*
• ADV. **entirely, perfectly, quite** *It's perfectly feasible to
produce electricity without creating pollution.* | **barely,
hardly, not really, scarcely | administratively, econom-
ically, financially, politically, technically**

feast *noun*

1 special meal
- ADJ. **delicious** | **great, sumptuous** *Villagers used to hold a great feast at harvest time.* | **village, wedding**
- VERB + FEAST **give, have, hold** | **make, prepare** *The women were busy preparing the wedding feast.* | **provide (sb with)** *The migrating salmon provide a delicious feast for the brown bear.* | **attend**
- PREP. **at a/the~** | **~of** *a feast of Spanish food and wine*

2 religious festival
- ADJ. **moveable** (the date of which varies from year to year)
- VERB + FEAST **celebrate**
- FEAST + NOUN **day**
- PREP. **on the~ of** *on the feast of St John* | **~of** *the feast of the Passover*

feat *noun*

- ADJ. **amazing, astonishing, brilliant, extraordinary, incredible, remarkable** | **considerable, great** | **major** | **difficult, no mean** *Dragging the fully laden boat across the sand dunes was no mean feat.* | **easy** | **impossible** | **acrobatic, intellectual** | **engineering** *The tunnel was one of the greatest engineering feats of the 19th century.*
- VERB + FEAT **accomplish, achieve, bring off, perform, pull off** *He has pulled off an extraordinary feat in completing the voyage single-handedly.* | **be capable of** *She was capable of remarkable feats of endurance.* | **repeat** | **emulate** *He emulated the feat of the legendary athlete Jesse Owens.*
- PREP. **~of** *a remarkable feat of strength*

feather *noun*

- ADJ. **breast, neck, tail** | **ostrich, peacock, etc.** | **downy** *the downy feathers on the duck's breast*
- VERB + FEATHER **preen** *a swan preening its feathers* | **fluff (out/up)** *The owl fluffed out its feathers.* | **ruffle** *Its feathers were ruffled by the chill breeze.* | **pluck** *plucking the dead hen's feathers*
- FEATHER + NOUN **duster, pillow**
- PHRASES **as light as a feather**

feature *noun*

1 important part of sth
- ADJ. **basic, central, essential, important, key, main, major, significant** | **conspicuous, distinctive, distinguishing, dominant, notable, noteworthy, noticeable, predominant, prominent** *a distinctive feature of his poems* | **outstanding, remarkable, striking** | **attractive, endearing, eye-catching** | **interesting, special, unusual** | **salient** *He took me around our new offices, pointing out all the salient features.* | **useful** | **characteristic, typical** | **unique** | **common** *the common feature in all these cases* | **permanent, regular** *These walks became a regular feature of his day.* | **recurring** *Self-deprecation is a recurring feature as Stevenson talks.* | **redeeming** *The one redeeming feature of the scheme was its low cost to the council.* | **original** *The house retains most of its original features.* | **built-in** | **additional** | **constructional, design, physical, structural** | **energy-saving, safety** *a car with new built-in safety features*
- VERB + FEATURE **have** *The site had a number of interesting features.* | **retain** | **point out**
- FEATURE + VERB **distinguish sth** *the essential feature that distinguishes anorexia nervosa from other eating disorders* | **characterize sth** *A feature that characterizes all anteaters is an extremely slow metabolic rate.* | **include sth** *Special features include passenger airbags and an electric sunroof.*

2 features sb's face
- ADJ. **handsome** | **delicate, fine** | **rugged** *admiring his rugged features* | **chiselled** *a slim figure with strongly chiselled features* | **aquiline, hawk-like** | **facial**
- VERB + FEATURES **have** *She's got very delicate features.*
- PREP. **with~** *a young woman with fine features*

3 newspaper article/television item
- ADJ. **big, major, special** | **regular** *The magazine runs a regular feature on ethnic cooking.* | **in-depth**
- VERB + FEATURE **do, have, publish, run** *Next month they will publish a special feature on computer books.*
- FEATURE + NOUN **writer**
- PREP. **~on** *an in-depth feature on the Italian fashion scene*

feature *verb*

1 include sth as an important part
- ADV. **regularly** *Women's magazines regularly feature diets and exercise regimes.* | **rarely**
- PHRASES **be featured in/on sth** *His work is featured in a special documentary tonight.* ◇ *The school has been featured on television.*

2 have a part in sth
- ADV. **heavily, highly, largely, prominently, significantly, strongly** *Reading over his past speeches, you'll see that housing, public health and education feature strongly.*
- PREP. **in** *Garlic features prominently in her recipes.*

February *noun*

⇨ Note at MONTH

federation *noun*

- ADJ. **loose** *He proposed a loose federation of small, local groups.* | **national** | **international, world** *the International Federation of Football Clubs* | **athletics, soccer, etc.** *the British Athletics Federation* | **employers', industry, labour, police, trade union**
- VERB + FEDERATION **create, form, set up** *They were now ready to create a national labour federation.*
- FEDERATION + VERB **break up** *The federation broke up in 1989.*
- PREP. **in a/the~** *the six republics in the federation* | **within a/the~** *He urged them to remain within the federation.* | **~of** *a federation of over 3 000 organizations*
- PHRASES **a member of a federation**

fed up *adj.*

- VERBS **be, feel, look, seem, sound** | **become, get** *The children were starting to get a bit fed up.*
- ADV. **really, very** *You look really fed up!* | **absolutely, thoroughly, totally** | **a bit, a little, pretty, rather**
- PREP. **about** *He still sounds pretty fed up about everything.* **with** *I'm absolutely fed up with the whole thing.*

fee *noun*

- ADJ. **exorbitant, fat** (*informal*)**, hefty, high, huge, large, substantial** *I expect you had to pay a fat fee to your divorce lawyers.* | **low, modest, nominal, reasonable, small** *We had to pay a nominal fee to join the club.* ◇ *Their fees are quite reasonable.* | **fixed, flat, set** *Many tax advisers now offer fixed fee interviews.* | **full** | **concessionary, reduced** | **normal, standard, usual** | **appropriate** *Send the form, together with the appropriate fee, to the Land Registry.* | **additional, extra, top-up** *There is no additional fee or paperwork for this insurance cover.* | **outstanding, unpaid** *We will be taking active steps to collect the outstanding fees.* | **annual, hourly, monthly** | **court, legal** | **consultancy, professional** *the professional fees of the solicitors and accountants involved* | **admission, entrance, entry, joining, membership, subscription** *a £30 membership fee* | **administration, arrangement, booking, cancellation, handling, licence, regis-**

tration | college, course, school, student, tuition | transfer (= charges paid by a football club 'buying' a player from another team) | green (= a charge to use a golf course)

• VERB + FEE charge, impose *They charge higher fees to overseas students.* | incur *Employees are reimbursed for any legal fees incurred when they relocate.* | pay | collect | waive *He agreed to waive his usual fee.* | refund, reimburse | increase, reduce | agree, negotiate *She negotiated a fee of $1 800 a week.* | cover *You'll need money to cover fees and expenses.* | afford

• FEE + VERB be due, be payable *All fees are payable when the invoice is issued.* | cover sth, include sth *The fee includes the cost of testing the electric wiring.* | go up *The admission fee has gone up.*

• FEE + NOUN income *The firm's consultancy fee income rose by 3% last year.* | structure

• PREP. for a ~ *For a small fee, anyone can use these facilities.* | ~ for *We now charge a fee for museum entrance.*

feed verb

1 give food to a person/animal/plant
• ADV. properly, well *Have they been feeding you well?* | regularly
• VERB + FEED help (to) *Let us discipline ourselves so as to help feed a hungry world.*
• PREP. on *She fed the children on baked beans and fish fingers.* to *Most of the crop is fed to the cattle.* with *The animals are fed with hay and grass.*
• PHRASES a mouth to feed *He saw the new baby as just another mouth to feed.*

2 eat
• ADV. voraciously *The bears feed voraciously in summer and store energy as fat.* | busily *Egrets and a solitary grey heron were busily feeding.* | mainly, predominantly | exclusively
• PREP. on *The seals feed mainly on fish and squid.*

3 supply sth
• ADV. directly
• PREP. into *The data is fed directly into a computer.* through *This feeds the paper through to the printer.* to, with *feeding the media with rumours and accusations*

feedback noun

• ADJ. constructive, favourable, good, positive, useful, valuable | negative | appropriate, relevant | direct | immediate, instant *The writer gets no immediate feedback and simply has to imagine the reader's reaction.*
• VERB + FEEDBACK give sb, provide (sb with) | get, have, obtain, receive | collect
• PREP. ~ about/on *They will be given feedback on their performance.* ~ from *I've had a lot of very constructive feedback from the students about this.*

feel verb

• ADV. deeply, strongly *She felt her mother's death very deeply.*
• PREP. about *He feels very strongly about a lot of issues.*

feeling noun

1 sth that you feel/sense/believe
• ADJ. strong | definite, distinct | nagging, sneaking/sneaky, vague *I had a nagging feeling that I had forgotten something.* | glorious, good, great, marvellous, warm, wonderful *It was a good feeling to be arriving home again.* | horrible, nasty, queasy, sick, sinking, terrible, tight, uncomfortable, uneasy *He suddenly had a terrible sinking feeling in the pit of his stomach.* ◇ *I've got a tight feeling in my stomach.* | guilty | curious, eerie, odd, peculiar, strange | gut, instinctive *My gut feeling was that*

we couldn't trust her. | general, popular, public *The general feeling of the meeting was against the decision.*
• VERB + FEELING feel, get, have *He felt a wonderful warm feeling come over him.* ◇ *Do you get the feeling that we're not welcome here?* | give sb, leave sb with *She was left with the feeling that he did not care.* | know (*informal*) *'I really resent the way he treated me.' 'I know the feeling* (= I know how you feel).' | arouse, evoke, inspire *a case that has aroused strong public feeling*
• FEELING + VERB come over sb | be mutual *'I'm going to miss you.' 'The feeling's mutual* (= I feel exactly the same).'
• PREP. ~ about *I don't have any strong feelings about it one way or the other.* ~ of *a feeling of excitement* ~ on *What are your feelings on this issue?*

2 feelings emotions
• ADJ. deep, intense, strong | ambivalent, mixed *I had mixed feelings about meeting them again.* | positive, warm | hostile, negative | hurt, injured | inner, innermost, real, true | pent-up *releasing her pent-up feelings* | personal | religious | sexual
• VERB + FEELINGS experience, harbour, have, suffer *She experienced a whole range of feelings.* ◇ *He still harboured feelings of resentment.* ◇ *She was lucky that she had suffered no more than hurt feelings.* | express, give vent to, release, show, vent *He finds it difficult to express his feelings.* ◇ *I finally gave vent to my feelings and started yelling at him.* | articulate, describe, discuss, talk about *discussing his innermost feelings with me* | bottle up, hide, mask, repress, suppress *trying to hide her true feelings* | banish *He was determined to banish all feelings of guilt.* | hurt *I'm sorry if I've hurt your feelings.* | spare *We didn't tell Jane because we wanted to spare her feelings.* | arouse, engender, evoke, inspire *The debate aroused strong feelings on both sides.* | heighten *It was the practical aspect of life that heightened her feelings of loneliness and loss.* | understand | reciprocate, return *Although she did not reciprocate his feelings, she did not discourage him.*
• FEELINGS + VERB come into sth *Personal feelings don't come into it—we have to do what's right.* | run high *Feelings were running high* (= people became very angry or excited) *as the meeting continued.*
• PREP. ~ about, ~ for *It makes no difference to my feelings for you.* ~ of *his feelings of grief* ~ towards *her feelings of anger towards him*
• PHRASES no hard feelings (*informal*) *Someone's got to lose. No hard feelings, Dave, eh?*

3 understanding/sensitivity
• ADJ. great, wonderful
• VERB + FEELING have | develop *He had developed a feeling for when not to disturb her.*
• PREP. with ~ *She spoke with feeling about the plight of the homeless.* | ~ for *She has a wonderful feeling for colour.*

4 sympathy/love
• VERB + FEELING have *You have no feeling for the sufferings of others.*
• PREP. ~ for *She still had a lot of feeling for David.*

5 anger
• ADJ. bad, ill
• VERB + FEELING cause, create, lead to | stir up
• PREP. ~ against *Their aim was to stir up feeling against the war.* ~ between *There was a lot of bad feeling between the two groups of students.*

6 ability to feel physically
• VERB + FEELING lose | regain
• PREP. ~ in *After the accident he lost all feeling in his legs.*

7 atmosphere
• VERB + FEELING create, recreate *They have managed to recreate the feeling of the original theatre.*
• PREP. ~ of *Light colours create a feeling of spaciousness.*

fellow *noun*

1 man
- ADJ. **old, young | big, little | handsome | charming, fine, good, nice, splendid | lucky, poor** (= unlucky)

2 member of an academic society/college
- ADJ. **junior, senior | honorary, research, teaching**
- VERB + FELLOW **elect sb**
- PREP. **~ of** *He was elected a fellow of the Royal Society.*

feminine *adj.*

- VERBS **be, feel**
- ADV. **really, very | almost | traditionally** *Girls may be given fancier names because this fits in with a traditionally feminine image.*

feminism *noun*

- ADJ. **contemporary, modern | egalitarian, liberal, socialist | militant, radical, revolutionary | Western**

feminist *noun*

- ADJ. **active, committed | egalitarian | militant, radical | Western**

fence *noun*

- ADJ. **high | low | barbed-wire, chain-link, iron, mesh, metal, picket, wire, wooden** *There was a cottage garden at the front and a white picket fence.* | **electric | boundary, garden, perimeter, security** *the airport perimeter fence* | **political** (*figurative*) *a proposal favoured by people on both sides of the political fence*
- VERB + FENCE **build, erect, put up | climb** (**over**), **jump** (**over**)
- FENCE + NOUN **post**
- PREP. **over a/the ~** *She leaned over the fence.* | **~ around/round** *a fence around the site*

fend *verb*

PHRASAL VERB
fend for yourself
- VERB + FEND FOR YOURSELF **be able to | be left to, have to** *The children were left to fend for themselves.*

ferment *noun*

- ADJ. **heady, intense | artistic, creative, cultural, intellectual | political, revolutionary** *a period of intense political ferment*
- PREP. **in (a) ~** *The country was in ferment.*

ferocity *noun*

- ADJ. **great, sheer | unexpected**
- PREP. **with ~** *It attacks its prey with great ferocity.*

ferry *noun*

- ADJ. **cross-channel | night | car, passenger**
- VERB + FERRY **get, go on, take, travel on, use | wait for | catch | board, drive onto | drive off, get off**
- FERRY + VERB **carry sb, take sb** *a ferry carrying more than a thousand people* | **arrive, come in, dock** *We watched the ferry dock.* | **depart, go, leave, sail** *The last ferry sails at 4 p.m.* | **cross sth** *the ferries that cross the River Mersey* | **run** *Ferries run every hour or so.*
- FERRY + NOUN **crossing, journey | route | boat | passenger | port, terminal | line, operator, service**
- PREP. **aboard/on/on board a/the ~** *the people on the ferry* **by ~** *We went by night ferry.* | **~ across/over** *We caught the ferry across the river.* **~ between** *the ferry between Dundee and Tayport* **~ for/to** *the ferry for Italy* **~ from** *the ferry from Ramsgate to Dunkirk*

fertile *adj.*

- VERBS **be, look | become | remain, stay**
- ADV. **extremely, highly, very** *a highly fertile soil*

fertilizer *noun*

- ADJ. **natural | artificial, chemical | liquid**
- VERB + FERTILIZER **spray, spread, use** *He spread fertilizer on the field with a rake.*

fervour *noun*

- ADJ. **great | evangelical, moral, religious | nationalist, patriotic, revolutionary**
- VERB + FERVOUR **arouse** *The speech aroused nationalist fervour.*
- PREP. **with ~** *He took up the cause with evangelical fervour.* | **~ for** *their fervour for the cause*

festival *noun*

1 series of performances/events
- ADJ. **big, major | annual | autumn, spring, etc. | international, local | arts, beer, cultural, dance, drama, film, flower, folk, jazz, literary, music, rock, theatre**
- VERB + FESTIVAL **have, hold | attend, go to, visit | organize | appear at, take part in** *The school has taken part in the festival since 1997.*
- FESTIVAL + VERB **take place | begin, open, start | attract sb** *The festival attracts thousands of visitors every year.*
- FESTIVAL + NOUN **organizer | events, programme**
- PREP. **at a/the ~** *He's appearing at a local folk festival tonight.* **during a/the ~** *the movies shown during the eight-day festival* **in a/the ~** *the events in this year's festival*

2 religious celebration
- ADJ. **great, important, major | annual | pagan, religious | Christian, Muslim, etc. | harvest**
- VERB + FESTIVAL **celebrate, observe** *The family always observes the Jewish festivals.*
- PREP. **at/on a/the ~** *the pilgrims who arrived on major festivals*

festivities *noun*

- ADJ. **Christmas, seasonal**
- VERB + FESTIVITIES **join in, take part in | enjoy**
- PREP. **during the ~** *She managed to disappear during the festivities.*

feud *noun*

- ADJ. **long, long-running, long-standing, old | bitter | petty | blood** *Blood feuds and general gangsterism added to the local crime rate.* | **family, internecine, personal, private** *a long-standing family feud*
- VERB + FEUD **have | start** *The incident started a family feud.* | **settle** *a time to settle old feuds*
- PREP. **~ between** *the feuds between rival companies* **~ over** *They had a long-running feud over money.* **~ with** *his personal feud with the city authorities*

fever *noun*

1 high temperature
- ADJ. **high, raging** *She had a very high fever.* | **slight | glandular, rheumatic, scarlet, etc.**
- QUANT. **bout** *He suffered from recurrent bouts of fever.*
- VERB + FEVER **have, run, suffer from** *He put his hand to my forehead as if I was running a fever.* | **catch, come/go down with, develop** *James has gone down with a fever.* | **die of | bring down, reduce** *drugs which can help to bring down the fever* | **be accompanied by** *Inflammation is frequently accompanied by fever.*
- PREP. **with a ~** *He was in bed with a fever.*
- ⇒ Special page at ILLNESS

2 nervous excitement
- ADJ. **election, World Cup**
- FEVER + VERB **grip sb** *Election fever suddenly gripped the nation.*
- PREP. **in a ~ of** *She was in a fever of anxiety about him.*

fib noun

- VERB + FIB **tell** *Don't tell fibs!*

fibre noun

1 in food
- ADJ. **dietary** *your total daily intake of dietary fibre* | **vegetable**
- VERB + FIBRE **be high/rich in** *foods that are rich in fibre*
- FIBRE + NOUN **content** *foods that have a high fibre content* | **intake**
- PHRASES **a high/low fibre diet** *the problems associated with a low fibre diet* **an intake of fibre, a source of fibre** *Peaches are a good source of fibre.*

2 material/body tissue
- ADJ. **coarse** *Mechanical filters draw air through flat, coarse fibres.* | **hollow** | **strong** | **natural** | **artificial, man-made, synthetic** | **carbon, coconut, cotton, nylon, paper, polyester, textile, wood** | **glass, optical** | **muscle, nerve** | **moral** *(figurative) It isn't just a lack of moral fibre that leads to a rising divorce rate.*
- VERB + FIBRE **be made from/of** *Wear underwear that is made from natural fibres.*
- FIBRE + NOUN **optics**

fickle adj.

- VERBS **be**
- ADV. **very** | **a bit, rather** | **notoriously** *The television world was a notoriously fickle one.*

fiction noun

1 stories that are not true
- ADJ. **contemporary, modern** | **classic** | **light, popular, pulp** | **literary, serious** | **crime, detective, historical, romantic, science**
- VERB + FICTION **publish, write** | **read**
- PHRASES **a work of fiction** *He has written over 20 works of fiction.* **a writer of fiction** *a well-known writer of crime fiction*

2 sth that is not true
- ADJ. **pure** *Don't believe what she says—it's pure fiction!*
- VERB + FICTION **keep up, maintain** *She still tries to maintain the fiction that she is happily married.*
- PHRASES **fact and fiction** *Fact and fiction became all jumbled up in his report of the robbery.*

fictional adj.

- VERBS **be** *The names of the shops are entirely fictional.*
- ADV. **entirely, purely, wholly**

fictitious adj.

- VERBS **be** *His story is wholly fictitious.*
- ADV. **entirely, purely, totally, wholly** | **largely**

fidelity noun

- ADJ. **great** | **absolute** | **marital**
- PREP. **with ~** *telling the story with great fidelity to the original* | **~ to** *They swore an oath of fidelity to their king.*

fidget verb

- ADV. **nervously**
- PREP. **with** *She was fidgeting nervously with her pen.*

field noun

1 on a farm
- ADJ. **cultivated, green, ploughed** *looking out on the green fields of Shropshire* ◊ *We had to walk across a ploughed field.* | **enclosed** | **open** | **surrounding** | **fertile** | **arable** | **paddy, rice** | **corn, wheat, etc.**
- VERB + FIELD **work in** *People were working in the fields.* | **cultivate, work** *Despite the war, they continued to work the fields.* | **plough** | **plant** *He planted fields full of sunflowers.* | **graze in**
- PREP. **across/through a/the ~** *walking across the field* **(out) in a/the ~** *tractors working out in the field* | **~ of** *a field of wheat*

2 subject/activity
- ADJ. **chosen, specialist** *All of them are experts in their chosen field.* | **research**
- VERB + FIELD **work in** *people who work in this field* | **open up** *This discovery has opened up a whole new field of research.*
- PREP. **in a/the ~** *There has been no solid research in this field.* **outside a/sb's ~** *I can't answer that—I'm afraid it's outside my field* (= outside the subject I am studying/know sth about). | **~ of** *now working in the field of computer science*
- PHRASES **an expert/a leader in the field, a field of research/study**

3 practical work
- VERB + FIELD **work in**
- FIELD + NOUN **investigation, research, study, trial** | **methods** | **trip** *We went on a geology field trip.*
- PREP. **in the ~** *essential reading for those working in the field*

4 for playing a sport
- ADJ. **playing, sports** | **football, rugby, etc.**
- VERB + FIELD **take** *Today they take the field* (= go on to the field to play a match) *against county champions Essex.*
- PREP. **on a/the ~** *people walking their dogs on the school's playing field* **off the ~** *Players need discipline both on and off the field* (= when playing and in other areas of their lives).

5 the field competitors in a sport/business
- ADJ. **strong**
- VERB + FIELD **head, lead** *She managed to head the field across the finishing line of the London Marathon.* ◊ *They lead the field in home entertainment systems.*
- FIELD + VERB **include sb** *The strong field includes three world record holders.*
- PREP. **ahead of the ~** *His superb technique puts him head and shoulders ahead of the field.*

6 in science
- ADJ. **electric, electromagnetic, energy, force, gravitational, magnetic** *the earth's magnetic field*
- FIELD + NOUN **strength**

7 computing
- ADJ. **display, input**
- VERB + FIELD **create** *You will need to create separate fields for first name, surname and address.* | **move between** *the use of keys to move between fields*
- ⇨ Special page at COMPUTER

fieldwork noun

- ADJ. **extensive, intensive** | **detailed**
- VERB + FIELDWORK **be engaged in, carry out, conduct, do, participate in, undertake**
- FIELDWORK + NOUN **student**
- PREP. **during/in the course of ~** *evidence obtained during fieldwork* | **~ on** *extensive fieldwork on chimpanzees*

fifty-fifty adj., adv.

- VERBS **be | divide sth, go, split sth** *We'll divide the profit fifty-fifty.* ◇ *We went fifty-fifty on the meal.*
- ADV. **about, roughly** *The chances of reaching the survivors in time are about fifty-fifty.*

fight noun

1 struggle using physical force

- ADJ. **big | fierce, furious | real** *Suddenly the argument developed into a real fight.* | **good** *There's nothing he likes so much as a good fight.* | **fair** *It was a fair fight and Stephen won.* | **free** *They inadvertently got mixed up in a free fight involving some 20 people.* | **running** *He was killed during a series of running fights outside a disco.* | **stand-up, straight** *In a straight fight the crusaders usually won; in skirmishes, the Saracens often overcame their more numerous opponents.* | **pub, street | gang | fist | food, pillow, water | championship, title** *watching the world title fight between Tyson and Lewis* | **professional | heavyweight, etc.** | **bull** (also **bullfight**), **cock, dog**
- VERB + FIGHT **pick, start** *He tried to pick a fight with me.* ◇ *I don't know who started the fight.* | **be looking for, be spoiling for, want** *Andy was drunk and spoiling for a fight.* | **be in, get into, get involved in, get mixed up in, have** *Don't get into any more fights!* | **break up, stop** *The fight was broken up by a teacher.* | **win | lose | watch**
- FIGHT + VERB **take place** *The dog fights took place every Sunday morning.* | **break out, erupt, start | ensue** *A fight ensued which left one man dead.*
- PREP. **in a/the ~** *He killed a man in a fight.* | **~ about/over** *They nearly had a fight over who should move first.* | **~ between** *fights between police and football fans* | **~ with** *They got involved in a fight with some older boys.*

2 trying to get/do sth

- ADJ. **brave, good, strong** *She died at the age of 43 after a brave fight against cancer.* | **hard, long, real, tough** *a long fight to beat inflation* | **bitter, desperate | legal**
- VERB + FIGHT **put up** *Coal workers are determined to put up a fight to save their jobs.* | **lead, spearhead** *leading the fight for compensation for the sacked workers* | **join (in)** *Doctors have now joined in the fight to make this treatment available to all.* | **face** *Now he is facing his toughest fight yet—back to fitness after a series of injuries.* | **be engaged in** *He is still engaged in a bitter fight with his old firm.* | **carry on, continue, keep up** *She said they would continue their fight to find a cure for Aids.* | **step up** *The government has vowed to step up the fight against crime.* | **take** *She vowed to take her fight to the High Court.* | **win | lose** *Are we losing the fight against illegal drugs?* | **give up** *She just gave up her fight for life.*
- FIGHT + VERB **be on** *The fight is on to have this brutal practice stamped out.* | **continue, go on** *The fight for justice goes on.*
- PREP. **without a ~** *I'm not giving up without a fight!* | **~ against** *a new weapon in the fight against car crime* | **~ for** *their fight for a fair deal*
- PHRASES **a fight for life/survival** *the firm's desperate fight for survival in a cut-throat market* | **have a fight on your hands** *Union leaders know that they have got a real fight on their hands.*

3 competition

- ADJ. **brave, good, great, strong, tremendous | straight**
- VERB + FIGHT **put up** *The team put up a good fight (= they played well) but were finally beaten.*
- FIGHT + VERB **be on**
- PREP. **~ between** *This will be a straight fight between Labour and the Conservatives: the other parties are nowhere.* | **~ for** *The fight for supremacy in the sport is on.*
- PHRASES **a fight to the death** (figurative) *By 1807 politics had become a fight to the death between the two fac-*

tions. **a fight to the finish** *If the polls are wrong and it's a fight to the finish, the result may not be known until all the votes have been counted.* **have a fight on your hands** *She now has a fight on her hands (= will have to play very well) to make it through to the next round.* **make a fight of it** *No doubt Ferguson wants his team to make a fight of it.*

fight verb

1 in a war/battle

- ADV. **bravely, gallantly, valiantly | bitterly, hard | back, off**
- VERB + FIGHT **be prepared to, be ready to** *He did not believe that the enemy was ready to fight.* | **continue to**
- PREP. **against** *They fought bravely against the enemy.* **alongside** *fighting alongside his comrades* **for** *They fought for control of the island.* **over** *fighting over disputed land*

2 struggle against/hit sb

- ADV. **bitterly, hard | back, off** *The jeweller was stabbed as he tried to fight the robbers off.*
- VERB + FIGHT **be prepared to**
- PREP. **against** *She fought hard against his strong grip.* **with** *Riot police fought with militants demonstrating in support of the uprising.*

3 in a contest

- ADV. **bitterly, hard | successfully**
- VERB + FIGHT **be determined to, be prepared to, be ready to** *We need a good manager who is prepared to fight for a fair share of the funds.* | **continue to**
- PREP. **for** *Regional monopolies were bitterly fought for.*
- PHRASES **fiercely/keenly fought** *The second half was keenly fought, but neither side managed to score.*

4 try to stop/achieve sth

- ADV. **hard, like a tiger, tooth and nail** (= in a very determined way) *He fought hard to overcome his disability.* ◇ *She'll fight like a tiger to protect her children.* ◇ *The residents are fighting tooth and nail to stop the new development.* | **doggedly, stubbornly, tenaciously | desperately | successfully | back, off** *It is time to fight back against street crime.*
- VERB + FIGHT **be determined to, be prepared to, be ready to, vow to | continue to | help (to)**
- PREP. **against** *They are committed to fighting against racism.* **for** *fighting for equal rights*

5 argue

- ADV. **bitterly**
- PREP. **about** *It's a trivial matter and not worth fighting about.* **over** *The children will fight over quite small things.* **with** *He's always fighting with his brother.*

fighting noun

- ADJ. **bitter, fierce, hard, heavy, intense, serious | continued/continuing | fresh, renewed | spasmodic, sporadic | hand-to-hand** *The sword and mace were favourite weapons for hand-to-hand fighting.* | **street**
- VERB + FIGHTING **end, halt, stop** *holding talks designed to end the fighting* | **take part in** *The conspirators took no part in the fighting which ensued.* | **be killed in, die in | escape, flee** *refugees fleeing the fighting*
- FIGHTING + VERB **take place | begin, break out, erupt, flare, start** *Fierce fighting broke out among the refugees.* | **ensue, follow | continue | rage** *For nearly two months the fighting raged.* | **intensify | die away/down, diminish** *Even if the fighting dies down, no answer is in sight to the political crisis.* | **stop | resume**
- PREP. **during/in the ~** *He was badly wounded during the fighting.* | **~ between** *There has been renewed fighting between the government forces and the rebels.*
- PHRASES **a lull in the fighting**

figure noun

1 amount/price
- ADJ. **high | low | double, single | accurate, exact | approximate, ballpark, rough, round | real, reliable, true | official | latest | inflated | target | sales, trade, unemployment, viewing,** etc.
- VERB + FIGURE **reach** *The rate of inflation has now reached double figures.* | **add (together/up) | release** *The government has just released new unemployment figures.*
- FIGURE + VERB **add up** *These figures don't add up.* | **be bandied about** *Lots of different figures were being bandied about.*
- PHRASES **according to (the) figures** *The industry remains in the doldrums, according to official figures out today.* **in round figures**

2 figures arithmetic
- PHRASES **good/bad at figures** *I was never very good at figures.* **have a head for figures**

3 person
- ADJ. **great | central, important, influential, key, leading, prominent, respected, well-known** *a key figure on the committee* | **public | national | senior | familiar** *He was a familiar figure in the local pub.* | **unlikely** *They were visited by the unlikely figure of Bill Clinton.* | **authority, dominant | father, mother, parental | tragic | comic, ridiculous | cult, legendary | historical | political, religious | government, opposition**
- PREP. **~of** *a figure of authority/fun*

4 shape of a person
- ADJ. **life-size | dark, shadowy | seated, standing,** etc. *The seated figure in the corner beckoned me over.* | **central** *the central figure in the photo* | **solitary | human**
- FIGURE + NOUN **painter, painting**

5 shape of sb's body
- ADJ. **beautiful, fine, good, handsome, hour-glass, lovely** *She's still got a lovely figure.* | **slender, slim | ample, bulky, full, large, stocky | tall | dashing, imposing, striking | neat, slight, small, tiny, trim | lithe**
- VERB + FIGURE **cut, have** *He cut a dashing figure in his uniform.* | **keep** *She's kept her figure after all these years.* | **watch** *You need to watch your figure.* | **lose**
- PHRASES **a fine figure of a man/woman**

6 picture/diagram
- VERB + FIGURE **see** *See Figure 8.*
- FIGURE + VERB **show sth**

figure verb

- ADV. **largely, prominently, significantly, strongly | hardly, scarcely** *Vegetables hardly figure at all in their diet.*
- PREP. **among** *This man did not figure among the suspects.* **in** *The issue figured prominently in our discussion.*

file noun

1 collection of papers
- ADJ. **bulging, bulky, fat, thick | card, box, lever-arch, Manila, paper** *six box files bulging with notes* | **official | confidential, personal, secret | detailed | case** *The work involves preparing case files and attending court.* | **information | client, customer, personnel | court, newspaper, office, police, security**
- QUANT. **stack** *A stack of files awaited me on my desk.*
- VERB + FILE **have, keep** *The company keeps secret files on all its employees.* ◇ *Personnel files are kept in secure storage.* | **keep sth on** *Your application will be kept on file* (= in a file). | **collate, compile, prepare** *He had compiled a file of largely circumstantial evidence.* | **enter sth into** *The details of the incident will be entered into the file.* | **open** *The police have opened a file on the case.* | **close** *The file on the murder was closed five years ago.* ◇ *She closed*

the file and put it aside. | **reopen** *Police have reopened the file on the missing girl.* | **update** *It is important to update customer files.* | **pull out, take out** *She went to the filing cabinet and took out a file.* | **check, go through, look at, read** *I'll check the files for any information on the case.*
- FILE + VERB **contain sth**
- PREP. **in a/the~** *the information contained in the police files* **on~** *All the details of the transaction are on file.* | **~on** *The police already have a thick file on that family.*

2 on a computer/disk
- ADJ. **large | computer | data, database, document, graphics, program, spreadsheet, system, text | master | back-up** *to make/take a back-up file* (When talking about a new file, not a back-up file or a copy, the correct verb is **create**.) | **Unix, ZIP,** etc.
- VERB + FILE **create | hold sth in, store sth in** *the information held in this file* | **enter sth into** *entering data into a file* | **open | close | save | load | access, read, view** *You need a special password to access this file.* | **back up, copy | edit | delete, erase | delete sth from** *deleting data from a file* | **name, rename | recover, retrieve** *how to recover deleted files* | **hold, store** *The files are stored in Mac format.* | **compress, stuff | transfer** *transferring files between workstations*
- FILE + VERB **contain sth**
- FILE + NOUN **name | format | server**
- PREP. **in a/the~** *The names and addresses are all kept in computer files.*
⇨ Special page at COMPUTER

file verb

1 put sth in a file
- ADV. **carefully | alphabetically | away** *These notes should be carefully filed away for future reference.*
- PREP. **under** *The card is filed alphabetically under the name of the editor.*

2 record sth officially
- ADV. **formally** *He has now formally filed a complaint against the police.*
- PREP. **for** *to file for bankruptcy/divorce* **with** *A copy of the notice must be filed with the court.*

3 walk in line
- ADV. **silently | out, past** *The long line of mourners filed silently past.*
- PREP. **in, into, out of, past, through**

fill verb

- ADV. **fast, quickly, rapidly** *At the moment, most reservoirs are filling fast.* | **gradually, slowly | up**
- VERB + FILL **begin to** *The sails began to fill.* | **seem to** *He seemed to fill the room with his presence.*
- PREP. **with** *Fill the bucket with water.*
- PHRASES **be filled to capacity** *The school is filled to capacity—we simply can't take any more students.* **be filled to the brim (with sth)** *The drawers were all filled to the brim.*

fillet noun

- ADJ. **anchovy, cod, haddock, salmon,** etc. | **beef, pork**
- FILLET + NOUN **steak**
- PREP. **~of** *fillet of beef with a red wine sauce*
⇨ Special page at FOOD

filling noun

- ADJ. **dental | amalgam, gold**
- VERB + FILLING **have** *She's only eight years old and she's already got five fillings.* ◇ *I went to the dentist yesterday and had two fillings.* | **do, give sb** *The dentist said she would do the filling straightaway.* | **replace**
- FILLING + VERB **come out, fall out**

film noun

1 movie
- ADJ. **long | short | exciting, good, interesting | successful | awful, bad, boring | epic | violent** *She thought the film far too violent to show to children.* | **X-rated | silent | black-and-white | low-budget | Hollywood, independent | television, video | adventure, children's, comedy, documentary, feature, gangster, horror, pornographic**
- VERB + FILM **see, watch | go to (see), take sb to (see)** *We went to an awful film last night.* | **direct, make, produce, shoot** *She makes children's films.* ◇ *The film was shot on location in Kenya.* | **take** *film taken by security cameras* | **cut, edit** *The film was heavily edited for screening on television.* | **distribute, release, screen, show** *The film was finally released after weeks of protest by religious groups.* | **ban, censor**
- FILM + VERB **be on, show** *There's an interesting film on at the local cinema.* | **come out, open, premiere** *The film came out last week.* | **be based on sth** *a film based on the novel by Charles Potter* | **be called sth, be entitled sth** *a film entitled 'Bitter Moon'* | **capture sth** *The film manages to capture the mood of the times.* | **contain sth, include sth** *The film contains explicit scenes of violence.* | **depict sth, present sth, represent sth, show sth** *The film depicts immense courage amid the horrors of war.* | **tell sth** *This film tells the remarkable story of a disabled actor.* | **feature sb, star sb** *The film stars Nicole Kidman as a nightclub singer.* | **record sth** *a film recording the first powered flight* | **deal with sth** *a film dealing with old age* | **open** *The film opens with a bird's-eye shot of London.* | **end**
- FILM + NOUN **crew, director, editor, maker, people, producer, team, unit, writer** *The film has plenty of what film people call 'bankability'.* | **world | actor, actress, legend, star | part, role | career, debut, work | credits** *His film credits* (= the films he has made) *as director include 'Mood Music' and 'Lies'.* ◇ *We stayed for the film credits* (= the names of people involved in the making of a film) *to see who the music was by.* | **critic | buff, fan | premiere | censor, censorship | screenplay, script | music, score, soundtrack | narrative | scene | stunt** *He was killed when a film stunt went wrong.* | **poster | studio | set** *They built a massive film set of an airport.* | **props | adaptation, version** *the film version of the bestselling novel* | **classic** *the film classic 'Fantasia'* | **documentary, drama | genre | clip, footage, sequence | report** *The news always contains several film reports.* | **series** *the 'Star Wars' film series* | **archives, library | business, company, industry | mogul** *Tyrannical Hollywood film moguls ruled their stars' lives.* | **distributor | making, production | festival | show | awards | camera, equipment, projector, recorder | rights** *The scramble for the film rights to her next novel has already begun.* | **school, student**
- PREP. **in a/the ~** *There is a great car chase in the film.* **on ~** *They captured the incident on film.* | **~ about** *a film about Queen Victoria* **~ of** *They've just started shooting a film of the novel.*
- PHRASES **the beginning/end of the film, be in films** (= work in the film industry), **a film with subtitles, the screening/showing of a film**

2 used for taking photographs
- ADJ. **black-and-white, colour | fast** *Fast film would be best for such action shots.* | **35 millimetre, etc.**
- QUANT. **length, reel, roll** *a roll of 35 millimetre film*
- VERB + FILM **load, put in | remove, take out | rewind | develop, process** *I get my films developed at a local shop.* | **expose** *In the darkroom they found that only half the film had been exposed.* | **splice** *He spliced the two lengths of film together.*

3 thin layer of a substance/material
- ADJ. **fine, thin**
- VERB + FILM **be covered in/with** *The books were covered in a thin film of dust.*
- PREP. **~ of** *There was a fine film of sweat on her forehead.*

film verb

- ADV. **secretly** *The controversial experiment involved secretly filming a group of children.* | **on location** *The serial was filmed on location in Italy.*
- PHRASES **beautifully filmed** *fast-paced, well acted and beautifully filmed in the Blue Ridge Mountains*

filthy adj.

- VERBS **be, feel, look, smell | get | leave sth, make sth** *He always leaves the bath absolutely filthy!*
- ADV. **really | absolutely, completely | pretty**

final noun

1 last game/match in a competition
- ADJ. **grand** *He got through to the grand final of the competition.* | **area, national, regional, world | men's, women's | championship, cup**
- VERB + FINAL **hold, stage | be/get through to, go through to, make it to, qualify for, reach** *If we play well, we hope to make it to the final.* | **compete in, meet sb in, play in** *Scotland met Wales in the final at Twickenham.*
- FINAL + VERB **be played, take place**
- PREP. **in the ~** *Who is in the men's final?*

2 finals final exams at university
- VERB + FINALS **do, sit, take | fail, pass**

finale noun

- ADJ. **dramatic, exciting, grand, rousing, thrilling** *The evening ended with a grand finale of fireworks and music.* | **fitting**
- VERB + FINALE **end in/with, have, reach** *The match had a thrilling finale, with three goals scored in the last five minutes.* | **provide** *This victory provided a fitting finale to a brilliant season for the club.*
- PREP. **~ to** *a rousing finale to an evening of enthralling music*

finance noun

1 money needed to fund sth
- ADJ. **cheap** (= borrowed at low interest) | **necessary | additional, extra, further** *the need to obtain additional finance* | **long-term, medium-term, short-term | independent | joint | external, outside | international | private (sector), public (sector) | bridging** *You may require bridging finance until the sale of your own property is completed.* | **capital** (= money that is paid) | **credit, debt, loan** (= money that is borrowed) | **equity** (= money from issuing shares) | **bank** *the availability of bank finance* (= bank loans) *for small businesses* | **housing, mortgage**
- VERB + FINANCE **get, obtain, raise** *She struggled to get the necessary finance for her training.* | **allocate, arrange, provide | need, require**
- FINANCE + VERB **be available** *the finance available to local government*
- FINANCE + NOUN **company, house | sector** *The banking and finance sector was booming.*
- PREP. **~ for** *Several banks are providing finance for the housing programme.*
- PHRASES **a source of finance**

2 managing money
- ADJ. **high** *the world of high finance* (= finance involving large companies or countries) | **company, corporate | (local) government, public, state | consumer, personal** *that most emotive of personal finance issues—*

taxation | **international** | **capital** (= paying money for sth) | **credit, debt, loan** (= borrowing money for sth) | **equity** (= issuing shares to get money)
• FINANCE + NOUN **director, minister, officer** *Local government finance officers found the tax very difficult to administer.* | **committee, department**

3 finances money available
• ADJ. **healthy, sound** *Our family finances are not very healthy at the moment.* | **shaky** *The company's finances are looking a bit shaky.* | **company** | **government, public, state** | **family, household, personal, private**
• VERB + FINANCES **have** *We don't have the finances to go on holiday this year.* | **lack** | **raise** *They are not sure how they will raise the finances to go on the trip.* | **deal with, handle, manage, plan, run** *how to plan your finances for a comfortable retirement* | **get/keep in order, sort out** *The company was under pressure to get its finances in order.* | **boost, improve** | **be a drain on, put a strain on, strain, stretch** *Buying a new car need not put a strain on your finances.*
• FINANCES + VERB **be in a mess** *Their finances are in a mess: they plan to call in an accountant.*
• PHRASES **the state of sb's finances**
⇨ Special page at BUSINESS

finance *verb*
• ADV. **entirely, wholly** | **largely, mainly** | **partially, partly** | **privately, publicly** *The new roads will be financed privately.* | **jointly** *financed jointly by the British and French governments* | **directly** | **properly** *the introduction of a properly financed dog warden scheme*
• VERB + FINANCE **help (to)** | **be needed to, be required to** *the £37 million needed to finance the redevelopment* | **be used to**

find *noun*
• ADJ. **exciting, good, great, important, interesting, real, remarkable, significant, spectacular, startling** *The letters were a real find and James went on to publish two volumes of them.* | **small** | **lucky** *A lucky find in the Cotswolds is helping archaeologists discover what life was like in Roman Britain.* | **unexpected** | **stray** *Stray finds are more commonly discovered than whole new sites.* | **archaeological** | **medieval, prehistoric**
• VERB + FIND **discover, make, unearth** *prehistoric finds made in an unexplored cave* | **yield** *To date the site has yielded many interesting finds.* | **report** *I reported my find to the landowner.*

finding *noun*
1 result of research into sth
• ADJ. **important, key, significant** | **main** | **general** | **interesting** | **striking, surprising, unexpected, novel** | **positive** | **conflicting** | **early, initial, original** *The original findings conflict with more recent findings.* | **interim, preliminary** | **new, recent** | **scientific** | **empirical, experimental, research** | **survey**
• VERB + FINDING **record, write up** *Students were asked to conduct a survey and write up their findings in the form of a report.* | **summarize** | **announce, make public, present, publish, report** *The findings of the commission have not yet been made public.* ◊ *They will present their findings to senior police officers.* | **explain, interpret** | **examine** | **comment on, discuss** | **confirm, support** *UN official reports supported the preliminary findings that the plane was brought down by a missile.* | **challenge** *Sociologists have challenged the findings of criminologists on the behaviour of prisoners.*
• FINDING + VERB **be based on sth** *The findings are based on interviews with more than 2 000 people.* | **relate to sth** *Our findings relate to physically rather than the visually handicapped pupils.* | **apply to sth** *The findings*

from the case study school may apply to schools elsewhere. | **indicate sth, point to/towards sth, reveal sth, show sth, suggest sth** *Our findings point to a lack of training among social services staff.* | **agree with sth, be consistent with sth, be in agreement with sth, be in line with sth, confirm sth, support sth** *Our recent findings are in line with those of an earlier study.* | **conflict (with sth)** | **lead to sth** *The findings led to the conclusion that ...* | **provide sth** *The research findings will provide practical assistance for teachers.* | **be made** *Similar findings were made in Spain.* | **emerge** *A similar finding emerged from a later experiment.*
• PREP. **~about** *recent scientific findings about sleep patterns* **~for** *The findings for one group can be applied to the others.* **~from** *findings from a recent research project* **~on** *findings on the depopulation of the countryside*

2 decision by a court
• VERB + FINDING **make** | **justify** *The facts of this case do not justify a finding of negligence.* | **uphold** *The appeal court upheld a finding that the agreement was unlawful.*
• PREP. **~against** *a finding against him by the Independent Commission Against Corruption* **~in favour of** *The court made a finding in favour of the defendant.*

fine *noun*
• ADJ. **big, heavy, hefty, large, massive, stiff, substantial** | **maximum** | **parking**
• VERB + FINE **get** *I got a parking fine for parking on double yellow lines.* | **pay** | **give (sb), impose, levy** *Heavy fines were levied on motoring offenders.* | **be liable for/to, face, risk** *Drivers risk heavy fines for driving without a licence.* | **be punishable by, carry, lead to** *The offence carries a maximum fine of £500.* | **increase**
• PREP. **in~** *The club is struggling to pay £75 000 in fines to the football league.* | **~for** *a fine for water pollution*

fine *verb*
• ADV. **heavily** *Any company found to be breaking these rules will be heavily fined.*
• PREP. **for** *He got fined £200 for parking illegally.*
• PHRASES **get fined**

fine *adj.*
1 good enough/suitable
• VERBS **be, look, seem, smell, sound, taste** | **turn out** *I knew that everything would turn out fine in the end.*
• ADV. **absolutely, just** *Don't worry. Your voice sounds absolutely fine.*
• PREP. **for** *This paper's not very good quality, but it's fine for rough work.*
2 in good health/happy and comfortable
• VERBS **be, feel, look, seem** *George looks fine now.*
• ADV. **absolutely** *I feel absolutely fine.*
3 bright and sunny/not raining
• VERBS **be** | **turn out** *It's turned out fine again today.* | **keep, remain, stay** *Let's hope it stays fine for the wedding this afternoon.*
4 thin/small
• VERBS **be**
• ADV. **extremely, very** *Her hair is very fine.* ◊ *a very fine distinction* | **quite**

finger *noun*
• ADJ. **first, index** | **middle** | **ring, third, wedding** *I noticed the ring on the third finger of her left hand.* | **little** | **ringed** | **broken, dislocated, injured** | **pointing** | **accusatory, accusing, admonitory, warning** *The teacher raised a warning finger and we stopped talking.* | **prying** *The ornaments had been put out of reach of the children's prying fingers.* | **delicate, elegant, slender, slim** | **bony, lean, skeletal, skinny** | **chubby, fat, plump, podgy** |

blunt, spatulate, square-tipped | gnarled | arthritic | gentle *She took off his bandages with gentle fingers.* | capable, deft, nimble, skilful, skilled *Her nimble fingers undid the knot in seconds.* | nerveless | nervous | clumsy *His clumsy fingers struggled with the buttons.* | dirty, filthy, grubby, sticky

● VERB + FINGER **point** *'It was them!', she cried, pointing an accusing finger at the boys.* ◇ *(figurative) The enquiry pointed the finger of blame at the driver of the crashed coach.* | **draw** *The man drew a finger across his throat in a threatening gesture.* | **jam, poke, put, stick** *Everyone put their fingers in their ears when the shooting started.* | **jab, stab** *The protester was jabbing a finger aggressively at a policeman.* | **hold up, raise** *She raised a finger to her lips to ask for silence.* | **wag, waggle** *'None of that!' cried the teacher, wagging her finger.* | **dip** *I dipped my finger in the sauce and licked it.* | **run** *She ran her finger along the dusty shelf.* | **drum, tap** *He was drumming his fingers nervously on the arm of the chair.* | **click, snap** *We were swaying and clicking our fingers in time to the music.* ◇ *He snapped his fingers and the waiter came running.* | **stub** *I stubbed my finger painfully while reaching for a book.* | **shut, trap** *The child needed treatment after trapping her finger in the car door.* | **crook** *He crooked a finger to tell us to go over to him.* | **extend** *He held up his hand with the fingers extended.* | **prick** *The nurse pricked my finger to get some blood.* | **count (sth) on** *Although she knew lots of people, she could count her friends on the fingers of one hand.*

● FINGER + NOUN **bones, joints | movement | injury**

● PREP. **with your ~s** *It's easiest to eat chicken legs with your fingers.*

● PHRASES **the finger of fate/suspicion** *(figurative) The finger of suspicion was pointed at the chicken served for lunch.* **the tips of the fingers**

fingernail *noun*

● ADJ. **long | black, dirty | broken, torn | manicured, well-manicured | painted, red, scarlet**

● VERB + FINGERNAIL **cut, manicure, polish | bite, chew | break, tear | dig in** *She dug her fingernails into my neck.* | **drag, draw, rake, scrape** *the sound of fingernails being dragged down a blackboard* | **examine** *'Actually, I'm leaving you', she said, continuing to examine her fingernails.*

● FINGERNAIL + VERB **dig in**

● PREP. **under the/your ~s** *I noticed I had dirt under my fingernails.*

fingerprint *noun*

● QUANT. **set** *The police were able to obtain a set of fingerprints from the suspect.*

● VERB + FINGERPRINT **leave** *She was careful not to leave any fingerprints.* | **check (sth) for, dust sth for, examine sth for, look for** *The car is being examined for fingerprints.* | **find | obtain, take** *The investigator questioned him and took his fingerprints.* | **match** *The suspect's fingerprints have been matched with those found at the scene of the crime.*

finish *noun*

1 last part/end of sth

● ADJ. **exciting, good, great, thrilling, tremendous** *His best finish was 11th in the Hungarian Grand Prix.* | **perfect** *It was the perfect finish to a wonderful day.* | **sprint, storming, strong** *The runners came round the bend for a sprint finish in the home straight.* | **close, dramatic, nailbiting, photo, tight** *It was a photo finish, with three horses neck and neck at the finishing line.*

● VERB + FINISH **provide** *The rules of the game were changed to provide a more exciting finish for the television*

audience. | **be in at** *Her car suffered from gearbox trouble, but she was still in at the finish.*

● FINISH + NOUN **line**

● PREP. **at the~** *Several runners needed medical attention at the finish.* **to a/the~** *They fought bravely right to the finish.* | **~ to** *a dramatic finish to the match*

● PHRASES **from start to finish** *He was in the lead from start to finish.*

2 look/feel of sth

● ADJ. **good, neat, professional | perfect | attractive | decorative | fine, smooth | textured | natural | paint/painted | eggshell, gloss/glossy, matt, satin, shiny | brass, metallic, wood** *a guitar with a natural wood finish* | **surface | floor, wall, etc.** *The wall and floor finishes are all of the the highest standard.*

● VERB + FINISH **have** *This paint has a gloss finish.* | **achieve, get, obtain** *With our new tool for putting up wallpaper you can get a perfect finish every time.* | **create, give (sth), produce, provide** *This trim really does give the garment a professional finish.* | **match** *The steel roof has been coloured to match the finish of the original wrought iron.* | **apply** *Make sure the surface is clean and smooth before the finish is applied.*

● PREP. **to a ~** *Sand the wood to a fine finish using steel wool.* **with a ~** *a door handle with a brass finish* | **~ on** *How did you achieve that finish on the wood?*

finish *verb*

● ADV. **almost, nearly | just** *She had just finished dressing when the telephone rang.* | **soon | eventually, finally | off** *He finished off by welcoming new arrivals to the school.*

● VERB + FINISH **let sb** *Let me just finish what I'm doing.*

● PREP. **by** *He finished by telling us about his trip to Spain.* **with** *The evening finished with a few songs.* ◇ *Have you finished with the vacuum cleaner yet? I need it.*

fire *noun*

1 destructive flames

● ADJ. **big, huge | fierce | serious | disastrous | bush, forest, house**

● VERB + FIRE **be on** *The house is on fire!* | **catch** *A lantern was knocked over and the barn caught fire.* | **cause, set sth on, start** *Groups of rioters attacked and set the police headquarters on fire.* | **fan** *Strong winds fanned the fire.* | **add fuel to, fuel** *(both figurative) Frustrated ambitions can fuel the fire of anger and resentment.* | **extinguish, put out | fight** *He joined the crowds of men and women fighting the fire.* | **contain, control** *Firefighters struggled to control the fire.* | **be damaged by/in, be destroyed by/in** *The factory was destroyed in a fire started by arsonists.* | **be killed by/in, die in**

● FIRE + VERB **break out, start** *A fire broke out in the mail room.* | **go out | blaze, burn, rage** *The fire burnt for three days before it was finally contained.* | **spread, sweep through sth** *In 1925 a disastrous fire swept through the museum.* | **damage sth | destroy sth, gut sth** *The fire gutted the building, leaving just a charred shell.*

● FIRE + NOUN **safety** *legislation related to fire safety* | **hazard, risk** *Foam-filled couches are a serious fire hazard.* | **drill** *We have regular fire drills to ensure that the staff know how to evacuate the building.* | **alarm | brigade, department, service | station | engine | hydrant | hose | extinguisher | escape** *The thief got away down the fire escape.* | **door**

● PHRASES **bring a fire under control** *Firefighters have now managed to bring the fire under control.* **set fire to sth** *Someone had set fire to her car.*

2 burning fuel for cooking/heating

● ADJ. **blazing, crackling, hot, roaring, warm | dying,**

smouldering | little | open | charcoal, coal, log, oil, peat, wood
• VERB + FIRE **build, make** | **kindle, light** *Kim had managed to kindle a little fire of dry grass.* | **poke, stir, stoke (up)** *On cold nights we stoked up the fire to a blaze.* | **put sth on** *Put some more wood on the fire.* | **cook on/over** *When we go on safari we like to cook on an open fire.*
• FIRE + VERB **burn** *Although it was summer a fire burned in the great stone hearth.* | **kindle, light** *We had plenty of dry wood, so the fire lit easily.* | **die (down)** *The fire was beginning to die down.* | **burn (itself) out, go out** | **crackle** | **glow** | **smoke** *The fire smoked instead of burning properly.*
• PHRASES **the glow from/of a fire** *The interior was only lit by the golden glow of the fire.*

3 apparatus for heating rooms
• ADJ. **electric, gas**
• VERB + FIRE **light, switch on, turn on** *Use a match to light the gas fire.* | **switch off, turn off**
• FIRE + VERB **be off/on** *Is the fire still on?*

4 shots from guns
• ADJ. **heavy** | **anti-aircraft, covering, friendly** *The commandos pushed forward under the covering fire of their artillery.* ◇ *Several soldiers were killed in friendly fire due a mistake by allied forces.* | **artillery, sniper** | **cannon, machine-gun, mortar, rifle**
• QUANT. **burst** *a burst of machine-gun fire*
• VERB + FIRE **open** *The troops opened fire on the crowd.* | **return** *She returned fire from behind the low wall.* | **cease, hold** *They were told to hold their fire until the enemy came closer.* | **be/come under** *We were under constant fire from enemy snipers.* ◇ *(figurative) The minister of transport came under fire* (= was heavily criticized) *for forcing increases in rail fares.* | **draw** *A few soldiers were sent out to draw* (= attract) *the enemy's fire.*
• PHRASES **be in the line of fire** *Unfortunately he was in the line of fire* (= between the people shooting and what they were shooting at) *and got shot.*

fire *verb*
• ADV. **blindly, wildly** *She fired blindly into the mass of shadows.* | **wide** *Whitlock purposely fired wide.* | **back** | **off** *They fired off a volley of shots.*
• VERB + FIRE **be ready to** *He grabbed the shotgun and levelled it, ready to fire if anyone entered.* | **order sb to** *He ordered the troops to fire over the heads of the crowd.*
• PREP. **at** *She fired a revolver at her attacker.* **into** *He fired the gun into the air.* **on/upon** *The police fired on protesters in the city centre.*

fire alarm *noun*
• VERB + FIRE ALARM **set off** *It was thought that the fire alarm had been set off as a prank.* | **install** *Fire alarms have been installed in the building.*
• FIRE ALARM + VERB **go (off), sound**

firearm *noun*
• ADJ. **imitation, replica** | **unlicensed**
• VERB + FIREARM **be in possession of, possess** *The police charged her with possessing a firearm with intent to endanger life.* | **carry**
• FIREARMS + NOUN **training** | **expert** | **certificate, licence** | **offence** *He is wanted for robbery and firearms offences.*

fire brigade *noun*
• ADJ. **local**
• VERB + FIRE BRIGADE **call (out), phone** *Dial 999 to call the fire brigade.* | **join**
• FIRE BRIGADE + VERB **put sth out** *The fire brigade have put out a blaze in a local post office.*

firefighter, fireman *noun*
• ADJ. **full-time, part-time**
• VERB + FIREFIGHTER, FIREMAN **call (out)** *Firefighters were called to a house in Chaucer Avenue.*
• FIREFIGHTER, FIREMAN + VERB **fight sth, tackle sth** *Firefighters from three counties tackled a warehouse blaze.* | **put sth out** | **rescue sb** *Firemen rescued a driver trapped in the wreckage of his car.*
⇨ Note at JOB

fireplace *noun*
• ADJ. **big, enormous, great, huge** | **empty** | **open** | **brick, cast-iron, marble, stone, etc.**
• VERB + FIREPLACE **have** *Every room in the house has a fireplace.* | **build, install**
• PREP. **in a/the~** *A log fire crackled in the fireplace.*

firework *noun*
• VERB + FIREWORK **light** *Be very careful when lighting fireworks.* | **let off, set off** *They set off fireworks in their back garden.*
• FIREWORK + VERB **explode, go off**
• FIREWORK + NOUN **display, show**

firing squad *noun*
• VERB + FIRING SQUAD **face** *He could face a firing squad if found guilty of the charges.* | **be executed by, be shot by** *She was executed by firing squad.*
• PREP. **before/in front of a/the ~** *Many died in front of the firing squad.*

firm *noun*
• ADJ. **big, large, major** | **medium-sized** | **small** | **well-known** | **successful** | **established** | **start-up** *start-up firms in the booming computer market* | **private** | **family** | **international, multinational** | **foreign** | **local** | **accountancy, audit/auditing, broking, consulting, engineering, law, manufacturing, software, stockbroking, telecommunications** | **mail order**
• VERB + FIRM **establish, found, set up, start (up)** *She set up her own software firm.* | **manage, run** | **merge with** *They are likely to merge with a bigger firm.* | **acquire, buy (out), take over** *The firm was taken over by a multinational consulting firm.* | **close (down), dissolve** *the decision to close down the firm* | **own** | **work for** | **join, leave** | **employ, hire** *She hired a firm of private detectives to follow him.*
• FIRM + VERB **be based in sth** *a firm called Data Incorporated, based in Chicago* | **expand, grow** | **merge** | **compete** *Local firms are finding it difficult to compete in the international market.* | **close (down), collapse, fail, go bust, go into liquidation** *The well-established firm closed down with the loss of 600 jobs.* | **develop sth, make sth, manufacture, produce sth** | **specialize in sth** *a firm specializing in high-technology products*
• PREP. **in/within a/the~** *the different departments within the firm*
• PHRASES **a client of a firm, a firm of accountants/consultants/solicitors, a partner in a firm**
⇨ Note at ORGANIZATION
⇨ Special page at BUSINESS

firm *adj.*
1 solid/strong
• VERBS **be, feel, look, seem** | **remain, stay** *Exercise is important if you want your muscles to stay firm.* | **make sth** *Use extra stuffing to make the cushions firmer.* | **keep sth** *exercises to keep your muscles firm*
• ADV. **very** | **fairly, quite, reasonably**
2 not likely to change

• VERBS **be, sound | hold, remain, stand** *Jo held firm: nothing else would do.* ◇ *We stand firm on these principles.*
• ADV. **very | fairly, quite**
• PREP. **with** *I have always been quite firm with my children.*

first *noun*

1 (*also* **first gear**) lowest gear on a bicycle/vehicle
• VERB + FIRST **engage** *She engaged first gear and pulled off.* | **get into, move into, slam into** *As he moved into first the gear-lever knob came off in his hand.* | **put sth into** *Put the car into first and pull off slowly.* | **find** *It's very difficult to find first on this car.*
• PREP. **in** ~ *There was something wrong with the gearbox and I had to drive all the way home in first.*

2 highest level of university degree
• ADJ. **double** *She did Philosophy and English Literature and got a double first.*
• VERB + FIRST **be awarded, gain, get, obtain**
• PREP. ~ **in** *He got a first in modern history.*

first aid *noun*

• ADJ. **emergency**
• VERB + FIRST AID **administer, give** *While one of you gives first aid, the other should call an ambulance.* | **receive** | **be trained in** *At least one member of staff should be trained in first aid.*
• FIRST AID + NOUN **box, kit, manual | course | post** *Medics were bringing casualties to the first-aid post.*

fish *noun*

1 animal that lives and breathes in water
• ADJ. **freshwater, marine, salt-water, sea | tropical | predatory**
• QUANT. **school, shoal**
• VERB + FISH **catch, land** *He landed one very big fish.* | **breed, farm, have, keep** *fish farmed in Scotland* ◇ *He keeps tropical fish.*
• FISH + VERB **swim | hatch | bite** *The fish aren't biting* (= biting at the bait) *today.*
• FISH + NOUN **species | bowl, pond, tank | food | stocks** *the depletion of fish stocks*

2 fish as food
• ADJ. **fresh | dried, frozen, salted, smoked | oily | red, white**
• QUANT. **bit, piece | fillet**
• VERB + FISH **eat, have | clean, fillet, gut, prepare, skin** *I cleaned and filleted the fish.* | **marinade | bake, cook, fry, grill, poach, steam | flake** *Remove the skin and flake the cooked fish.*
• FISH + VERB **taste** *This fish tastes funny.*
• FISH + NOUN **bone | cake, dish, finger, oil, paste, pie, sauce, soup, stock | market, shop | knife, slice**
• PHRASES **fish and chips, fish in batter**
⇨ Special page at FOOD

fisherman *noun*

• ADJ. **keen | expert, skilled | local** *Local fishermen are protesting about the latest government regulations.* | **commercial | deep-sea | fly-** *A keen fly-fisherman caught a record-sized salmon.*
• FISHERMAN + VERB **catch sth**
⇨ Note at JOB

fishing *noun*

• ADJ. **good, great** *This stretch of the river is renowned for its good fishing.* | **coarse, deep-sea, drift-net, fly-, sea** *One of his hobbies was fly-fishing.* | **game, salmon, shark, trout, etc.** *She has been big game fishing off the coast of Kenya.* | **commercial, industrial**
• VERB + FISHING **go** *He goes fishing every weekend.*
• FISHING + NOUN **basket, equipment, gear, line, rod, stool, tackle | boat, craft, fleet, smack, trawler, vessel | hamlet, harbour, port, station, town, village | area, grounds, spot, zone** *the rich fishing grounds off the coast of Namibia* ◇ *Just below that bridge is a good fishing spot.* | **activity** *controls on fishing activity* | **quotas | agreement** *The two countries have signed a new fishing agreement.* | **ban | rights** *Fishing rights are held by the local angling club.* | **licence** *You need a fishing licence to fish in the lake.* | **expedition, holiday, trip | club | lodge | business, industry, trade | methods, techniques**
• PREP. ~ **for** *Ecuador announced a ban on fishing for shrimps.*

fishy *adj.*

• VERBS **be, look, seem, smell, sound** *It all sounds very fishy to me.*
• ADV. **very | definitely, distinctly | a bit**
• PHRASES **something fishy** *There was definitely something fishy going on.*

fist *noun*

• ADJ. **clenched, tight | gloved**
• VERB + FIST **clench | bang, pound, slam, smack, smash, strike, thump** *He banged his fist loudly on the table.* | **shake, wave** *The man was shaking his fist at us through the window.* | **swing** *He swung his fists wildly at his attacker's head.* | **draw back** *She drew back her fist and threw a punch at his nose.*
• FIST + NOUN **fight**
• PREP. **in your** ~ *She was holding a hammer in her fist.*
• PHRASES **clench/make your hand into a fist**

fit *noun*

1 sudden attack of illness
• ADJ. **bad, major | convulsive, epileptic, fainting**
• VERB + FIT **be seized by/with** (*literary*)**, have, suffer** *She suffered a major fit last year.* | **suffer from** *He suffers from fits of depression.* | **die of | bring on, cause, trigger** (**off**) *He suffers from a brain disorder that can trigger off convulsive fits.* | **control** *new drugs that can control fits* | **prevent**
• FIT + VERB **happen, occur** *The fits usually occur at night.*
• PREP. **during/in a** ~ *She hurt her arm during one of her fits.*

2 short period of coughing/laughter/strong feeling
• ADJ. **coughing, screaming, sneezing**
• VERB + FIT **have, throw** *My dad will throw a fit if he finds out!* | **burst into, collapse in/into, erupt in/into, fall into** *She collapsed in a fit of laughter.* | **bring on** *The cold air brought on one of his coughing fits.*
• FIT + VERB **be over, pass** *When her coughing fit was over she continued to speak.*
• PREP. **in a** ~ *He pushed the referee in a fit of temper* | ~ **of** *a fit of anger/giggles*
• PHRASES **have sb in fits** (**of laughter**) *The comedian had them all in fits of laughter.*

3 way sth fits/way two things match
• ADJ. **good** *We need to achieve the best fit between the staff required and the staff available.* | **correct, exact, perfect | poor** *The door was a poor fit and didn't open properly.* | **close, snug, tight | loose | comfortable** *The jersey is a comfortable fit—not too tight and not too loose.* | **statistical**
• VERB + FIT **achieve, get, produce** *File away any excess metal until a snug fit is achieved.* | **ensure** *The shoe has a special strap to ensure correct fit.* | **give** (**sth**) *The formula gives a much better fit to the experimental data.*
• PREP. ~ **between** *the statistical fit between the interest rate and investment*

● PHRASES **a lack of fit** *He argues that there is a lack of fit between our system of values and capitalism.*

fit *verb*

1 right size/type
● ADV. **neatly, nicely, securely, snugly, tightly, well** *The pencils fit neatly into this box.* | **exactly, perfectly** *The screws fitted the holes exactly.* | **badly** *The top of the box fitted badly and some of the contents had spilled out.* | **easily** *That chair should fit into the room easily.* | **together** *These two pieces of wood fit together to make the base.*
● VERB + FIT **be designed to** *The waste unit is designed to fit under the sink.*
● PREP. **in, into, onto, over, under, etc.** *Will this box fit into the cupboard?*

2 agree/match
● ADV. **perfectly**
● PREP. **for** *Your experience fits you perfectly for the job.*

fit *adj.*

1 healthy
● VERBS **be, feel, look, seem** | **become, get** *the struggle to get fit and stay fit* | **keep, stay** *Go for a little jog to keep fit.* | **make sb** *Exercising once a week is not enough to make you fit.* | **keep sb** *gentle exercises designed to keep you fit*
● ADV. **extremely, fighting, really, very** *He seemed fighting fit and ready for action.* | **fully** *John isn't fully fit yet after his operation.* | **fairly, pretty, quite, reasonably | physically** *She felt physically fitter and more alive than she could ever remember.*
● PREP. **for** *The doctor said she was now fit for work.*
● PHRASES **as fit as a fiddle** (= very healthy), **fit and healthy/well** *She looks really fit and well.* **fit and ready**

2 suitable
● VERBS **consider sth, see, think** *The newspaper did not see fit to publish my letter* (= and I criticize it for that). ◇ *You must do as you think fit* (= but I don't agree with your decision).
● PREP. **for** *The food was not fit for human consumption.*
● PHRASES **fit and proper** (*law*) *circumstances in which someone is not considered a fit and proper person to run a bank* **fit for a king** *It was a meal fit for a king* (= of very good quality). **in no fit state** *He's so angry he's in no fit state to see anyone.*

fitness *noun*

● ADJ. **full, peak | low | all-round, general, overall | individual, personal | aerobic, physical | match** *Hendry is back to match fitness and is expected to play.*
● QUANT. **degree, level** *You need a good level of physical fitness for this sport.*
● VERB + FITNESS **attain** *He has attained peak fitness this season.* | **maintain** *Regular exercise helps to maintain physical fitness.* | **be back to, get (sb) back to, regain, return to | build (up), enhance, improve, increase, work on** *A special trainer has been brought in to work on the tennis player's fitness.* | **prove** *The coach has given him until next week to prove his fitness.*
● FITNESS + NOUN **level** *First, determine your present fitness level.* | **training | programme, regime | check, test | fanatic, freak** *She's a bit of a fitness freak. She goes running every night.* | **centre** *a fitness centre with gymnasium and squash courts*
● PHRASES **health and fitness** *Walking is good for health and fitness.*

fitting *noun*

● ADJ. **original | standard | special | interior, internal | electrical, plumbing | bathroom, kitchen | lamp, light | metal, plastic, etc. | brass, copper, etc.**
● VERB + FITTING **install** *Our bathroom fittings are easy to install.* | **remove | make | use** *a fitting used to join copper pipe*
● PHRASES **fixtures and fittings** *The room still has the original fixtures and fittings.*

fitting *adj.*

● VERBS **be, seem** *It seemed entirely fitting that she should be wearing black.* | **consider sth, regard sth as, think sth** *I did not think it fitting to ask James about his daughter's death.*
● ADV. **very | entirely, perfectly**

fix *noun*

1 solution to a problem
● ADJ. **quick** *There is no quick fix to the breakdown in negotiations between the two companies.* | **technical, technological | bug** *The new software incorporates many bug fixes and product improvements.*

2 amount of sth, especially a drug
● ADJ. **regular**
● VERB + FIX **have** *He gets withdrawal symptoms if he hasn't had his regular fix.* | **need | get**

3 difficult situation
● VERB + FIX **be in** *I was in a fix.* | **get in/into** *How did you get into such a fix?* | **put sb in** *The power cut put us in a fix because we had invited people to dinner.* | **get (sb) out of** *I lent her the money to get her out of a fix.*

fix *verb*

● ADV. **firmly, securely | directly**
● PREP. **onto, to** *The handrail can be fixed directly to the wall.*
● PHRASES **fix sth in place/position** *Fix the bars in position with the screws provided.*

fixed *adj.*

● VERBS **be, seem | become | remain, stay**
● ADV. **very | firmly, securely** *Check that the boards are all securely fixed.* | **rigidly** *His gaze was rigidly fixed ahead.* | **relatively | irrevocably, permanently**

fixture *noun*

1 sporting event
● ADJ. **important, major | difficult | away, home | annual, regular | opening | final | international | friendly | league | sporting**
● VERB + FIXTURE **play** *playing an important fixture this evening* | **fulfil** *The club was fined for not fulfilling its fixtures at the weekend.* | **make sth** *There are plans to make the race an annual fixture.* | **arrange, schedule | stage** *The golf club has staged many international fixtures.* | **postpone**
● FIXTURE + NOUN **list** *a full fixture list of friendly matches*
● PREP. **~against** *a home fixture against Leeds*

2 sth fixed in a house
● ADJ. **original** *an exceptional example of Victorian architecture with the original fixtures and fittings intact* | **permanent** (*often figurative*) *The new conductor is now a permanent fixture in the orchestra.*
● PHRASES **fixtures and fittings**

flag *noun*

● ADJ. **national | chequered** *Schumacher took the chequered flag to win his fourth Grand Prix of the season.* | **tattered** *A tattered flag hung from the roof of the burnt-out building.*

• VERB + FLAG **fly, hang (out), hoist, raise, run up** *a ship flying a Russian flag* | **lower** | **wave** *The crowd all waved flags as the president came past.* | **unfurl** | **carry**
• FLAG + VERB **hang** | **flap, flutter, fly, wave** *a flag fluttering in the breeze* | **be/fly at half mast**
• FLAG + NOUN **pole** (also **flagpole**)
• PREP. **under a/the~** *a ship sailing under a British flag* | **~of** *a flag of truce*

flail *verb*

• ADV. **desperately, helplessly, wildly** *She ran along, her arms flailing wildly.* | **about, around** *He flailed about in the water, shouting 'I can't swim!'*

flair *noun*

• ADJ. **considerable, great** | **real** | **natural** | **artistic, creative, design, entrepreneurial, imaginative**
• VERB + FLAIR **have** *She has a natural flair for languages.* | **show** | **lack** *His designs are all right, but he lacks artistic flair.* | **develop**
• PREP. **with~** *jazz guitarists who improvise with flair* | **~for** *an activist with a flair for publicity*

flame *noun*

1 hot bright stream of fire
• ADJ. **hot** | **small** | **bright** | **pale** | **dancing, flickering, leaping** | **steady** | **naked** *Never smoke or use spray paint near a naked flame.* | **candle, gas** | **Olympic**
• QUANT. **ball, sheet, tongue** *The plane crashed in a ball of flames.* ◊ *Sheets of flame shot into the air.*
• VERB + FLAME **ignite, spark** *(often figurative)* *His childhood interest in the game had ignited a flame of passion for football.* | **rekindle** *(often figurative)* *They tried to rekindle the flames of romance.* | **douse, extinguish, quench, snuff (out)** | **feel** *(often figurative)* *She felt a flame of anger flicker and grow.*
• FLAME + VERB **burn** *The flame burnt brightly.* | **grow** | **die, go out** *The candle flame flickered and went out.* | **leap, rise, shoot** *Flames leapt from the burning house.* ◊ *Flames shot high into the air.* | **lick (sth)** *Orange flames were already licking round the foot of the stairs.* | **dance, flicker** *Flames danced in the gas lantern.*
• FLAME + NOUN **thrower** *The infantry were equipped with flame throwers.*
• PHRASES **the crackle of flames**

2 flames fire
• ADJ. **roaring**
• VERB + FLAMES **be engulfed in, be in** *A large part of the building was in flames.* | **go up in** *All the historical records have gone up in flames* (= have been destroyed by fire). | **burst into, erupt in, explode in/into** *The helicopter burst into flames.* | **fuel** *Oxygen tanks fuelled the flames.* | **fan** *Winds fanned the flames.* | **shoot sb/sth down in** *The aircraft was shot down in flames.* | **fight** *He fought the flames for two hours.* | **control** *Firefighters have been trying to control the flames.* | **douse, extinguish, put out, quench, smother** *Men came with buckets of water and began to douse the flames.* | **be beaten back by** *They tried to get into to the house but were beaten back by the flames.*
• FLAMES + VERB **die down** | **spread, sweep through sth** *They watched the flames sweep through the old wooden barn.* | **engulf sth** *The flames quickly spread and engulfed their home.* | **light sth (up)** *The flames lit up the skyline.*

flammable *adj.*

• VERBS **be**
• ADV. **highly** *These materials are highly flammable.*

flank *noun*

• ADJ. **left, right** | **north, northern, etc.** | **lower** *the lower flanks of Vesuvius* | **mountain**
• VERB + FLANK **attack** *They decided to attack their enemy's southern flank.* | **defend, protect** | **expose** *West Ham exposed the right flank of Norwich's defence* (= showed that it could be attacked easily).
• FLANK + NOUN **attack**
• PREP. **along a/the~** *along the eastern flank of Greenland* **down the~** *a beautiful pass down the right flank* **on a/the~** *The army was attacked on the left flank.*

flannel *noun*

• ADJ. **damp, wet** | **cold** | **face**
• VERB + FLANNEL **use** *Use a damp flannel to clean the skin.*
• PREP. **with a~** *She wiped his eyes and nose with a wet face flannel.*

flap *noun*

1 flat piece of paper, metal, etc.
• ADJ. **small** | **hinged** | **loose** *a loose flap of skin* | **tent** | **pocket** *a stylish jacket with leather cuffs and pocket flaps*
• VERB + FLAP **undo** *The officer undid the flap of his holster and drew his gun.* | **draw back, lift back/up, open, pull back** *He drew back the tent flap.* | **close** | **lower** *The pilot lowered the flaps as the aircraft came into land.*

2 state of worry/excitement
• ADJ. **real**
• VERB + FLAP **get in/into** *Far from getting into a flap over the controversy, the government has used the media attention to its advantage.* | **put sb in/into** *Having to cook for everyone at Christmas put his mother in a real flap.*
• PREP. **in a~** *I've never seen her in a flap; she's always so calm.* | **~over** *a flap over nuclear issues*

flap *verb*

• ADV. **gently** | **wildly** *The sails flapped wildly in the stiff breeze.* | **about, around**

flare *noun*

1 bright unsteady light/flame; sudden feeling
• ADJ. **brief, sudden** *There was a sudden flare as a fuel tank exploded.* | **bright** | **solar** *Radiation comes from the sun during solar flares.*
• VERB + FLARE **see** | **feel** *She felt a sudden flare of anger.*

2 device producing a bright flame
• ADJ. **distress**
• VERB + FLARE **see** *If they did not see a green flare in ten minutes, they were to launch the attack.* | **fire, send up, set off** *The ship's crew sent up a distress flare.* | **drop** *The bomber dropped a flare to illuminate the target.*
• FLARE + VERB **go up** *The flare to mark the start of the attack went up at 0440.* | **burn** *They could see orange flares burning in the distance.* | **explode** | **hit sb/sth** *A flare fired by a supporter hit the referee in the face.* | **illuminate sth, light sth (up)** *Flares lit up the night sky.*
• FLARE + NOUN **gun**

flare *verb*

• ADV. **suddenly** *Anger suddenly flared in his eyes.* | **briefly** *A light flared briefly, then went out.* | **up** *Violence flared up in the capital last night.*
• PHRASES **flare into life** *The fire flared into life again.*

flash *noun*

1 sudden bright light; sudden idea/emotion/action
• ADJ. **great** | **blinding, bright, brilliant** | **sudden** |

brief, momentary, quick | occasional | rare *a rare flash of humour* | light, lightning | news (also newsflash)
- VERB + FLASH feel, have *He felt a brief flash of jealousy.* ◊ *She had a sudden flash of inspiration.* | catch, detect, notice, see *We caught a flash of white in the bushes.*
- FLASH + VERB illuminate sth, light sth (up) *A bright flash of lightning lit up the sky.*
- PREP. ~from *The flashes from the guns illuminated the sky.* ~of *a sudden flash of light*

2 bright light for a camera
- ADJ. built-in | camera
- VERB + FLASH use *I don't think the picture will come out in this light. Try using the flash.*
- FLASH + VERB go off, work *The flash didn't go off.*
- FLASH + NOUN photography | bulb | unit *a camera with a built-in flash unit*
- PREP. with (a)~ *I took it with flash.*

flash *verb*

1 shine
- ADV. briefly *It was only the sun, flashing briefly on her bleached hair.*
- PREP. at *A car flashed its headlights at me.*

2 show emotion
- ADV. suddenly | angrily *Her eyes flashed angrily.*
- PREP. with *Her eyes suddenly flashed with anger.*

flashback *noun*

- ADJ. sudden
- VERB + FLASHBACK get, have
- PREP. in (a)~ *The story is told in flashback.* | ~to *I had a sudden flashback to the time immediately after the war.*

flask *noun*

- ADJ. Thermos™, vacuum | hip | metal, silver | conical, culture, round bottom (*all science*)
- VERB + FLASK fill | carry *When he climbed in the snow he always carried a silver flask of brandy for emergencies.* | pull out *She pulled out her flask and drank from it.* | uncork, unscrew | drink (sth) from, take a swallow from, take a swig from
- FLASK + VERB contain sth *a culture flask containing 4ml of the medium*
- PREP. ~of *We took a flask of tea with us.*

flat *noun*

1 set of rooms
- ADJ. big, spacious | modest | cramped, little, poky, small, tiny | comfortable, cosy | beautiful, nice | luxury, posh | shabby | modern | self-contained | purpose-built | furnished, unfurnished | one-room, studio | one-bedroomed, two-room, etc. | bachelor, granny *Even the prices of small bachelor flats are unbelievable.* ◊ *They converted two rooms of their house into a granny flat for Tony's elderly mother.* | attic, basement, bottom, downstairs, first-floor, ground-floor, penthouse, top, top-floor, upstairs *the people who lived in the downstairs flat* | high-rise *a block of high-rise flats* | empty, unoccupied, vacant | privately-owned | rented | council | holiday | next *They live in the next flat.*
- QUANT block *The tall blocks of flats dominated the skyline.*
- VERB + FLAT have, own *They have a flat in Paris and a house in Normandy.* | rent, take *The musician took a flat in a fashionable area of London.* | let, sublet *The landlady found they had been illegally subletting the flat.* | buy | sell | find (sb) | look for *Do you think that the council could find me another flat?* | get (sb) *We got her a flat in the same block as ours.* | live in, occupy, stay in *Our flat is one of the two occupied in the block.* | share | move into, move (out) from, move out of (of) | build | dec-

orate, refurbish *a contract to refurbish 18 council flats* | lock (up) | let sb/yourself into *She let herself into the flat with the spare key.* | leave, let sb/yourself out (of) | break (into) | evict sb from
- FLAT + VERB be located *The flat is located in a modern development.* | face sth, overlook sth *a luxury block of flats overlooking the marina*
- PREP. at a/the~ *I'll meet you back at your flat.* in a/the~ *She lives in the top flat.*
- PHRASES convert/divide/make/turn sth into flats *The house has now been converted into flats.*

2 land
- ADJ. coastal | tidal | mud (also mudflat), sand, salt *mud and sand flats rich in animal life*
- PREP. on the~ *These birds live on the coastal flats.*

3 musical note
- ADJ. A, B, etc.
- VERB + FLAT have *The key of E flat major has three flats.* | play
- PREP. in ... ~ *Mendelssohn's Quintet in B flat*

flat *adj.*

- VERBS be, look | become | lie, stay *I can't get this material to lie flat.* ◊ *She lay flat on the ground.* | fold sth, get sth, make sth, press sth *Shall I fold the paper flat or roll it up?*
- ADV. very | absolutely, completely, quite *The sea was almost completely flat.* | almost | fairly, quite, rather

flattered *adj.*

- VERBS be, feel
- ADV. immensely, very | rather | a little, vaguely
- PREP. at *She felt vaguely flattered at the suggestion.*

flattering *adj.*

- VERBS be | find sth
- ADV. enormously, extremely, tremendously, very | far from, hardly, less than, not entirely *The descriptions of her were less than flattering.* | quite, rather
- PREP. to *This style of dress is flattering to most women.*

flattery *noun*

- ADJ. artificial
- VERB + FLATTERY use *Salespeople are often accused of using artificial flattery.* | fall for *She falls for his flattery every time.*
- PREP. through~ *He thinks he can get his way through flattery.* with~ *She persuaded him with flattery.*

flaunt *verb*

- ADV. deliberately, openly *openly flaunting their wealth*
- PREP. in front of *She flaunted her success in front of the others.*

flavour *noun*

1 taste of food
- ADJ. delicious, exquisite, fine, good, lovely, pleasant, wonderful | characteristic, distinctive, particular, unique, unmistakable | true | full, pronounced, rich, strong | mellow, rounded | delicate, mild, subtle | bland | extra | fresh | sweet | bitter, sharp, sour, tangy, tart | salty | hot, spicy | smoky | exotic | cheese/cheesy, chocolate, fruit, lemon/lemony, minty, nutty, etc.
- VERB + FLAVOUR have *It's got a very mild flavour.* | take on *Coffee takes on a flavour all of its own when enjoyed with freshly cooked pastry.* | keep *Delicate herbs keep their flavour better when frozen.* | lose | add, give sth, impart, lend (sth), provide *a herb that adds a charac-*

teristic flavour to a range of dishes | **bring out, release** *The lemon juice brings out the natural fruit flavours.* ◊ *Bay leaves should be broken to release their flavour.* | **enhance, improve** | **spoil** | **destroy** *Cooking the vegetable destroys its wonderful delicate flavour.* | **appreciate, enjoy, savour** *Enjoy the flavour of fresh fish.*

• FLAVOUR + NOUN **enhancer** *Salt is a common flavour enhancer.*

• PREP. **for ~** *Cream may be added to the sauce for extra flavour.* **with a ~** *a dish with a strong spicy flavour*

• PHRASES **full of flavour** *vegetables that are fresh and full of flavour*

2 particular quality/atmosphere

• ADJ. **distinctive, particular, true, unique** | **pronounced, strong** | **international, local, oriental, regional** | **American, Scandinavian, etc.** | **political**

• VERB + FLAVOUR **have** *The college has a truly international flavour.* | **acquire, take on** *The music festival has taken on a distinctly German flavour.* | **lose** | **add, give sth, impart, provide** *The intervention of the authorities gave union struggles a decidedly political flavour.* | **experience, get** *The children experienced the flavour of medieval life.* ◊ *She rotated around the departments to get a flavour of all aspects of the business.* | **appreciate, enjoy** | **capture** *The film captures the flavour of rural life in this area.* | **convey**

• PREP. **with a ... ~** *a TV show with an American flavour*

flavoured *adj.*

• VERBS **be** *The food they eat is very highly flavoured.*

• ADV. **full, highly, richly, strongly, well** | **delicately** *a delicately flavoured clear soup*

• PREP. **with** *This dish is flavoured with lemon grass and garlic.*

flavouring *noun*

• ADJ. **artificial, natural** *This product contains only natural flavourings.* | **food** | **peppermint, vanilla, etc.**

• QUANT. **drop** *Add a few drops of peppermint flavouring.*

• VERB + FLAVOURING **contain** | **use** *We don't use any artificial flavourings in our products.* | **add**

flaw *noun*

• ADJ. **main, major, serious** | **basic, fatal, fundamental** | **minor, slight, small** | **obvious** | **design**

• VERB + FLAW **have** *Unfortunately, this plate has a slight flaw in it.* | **look for** | **discover, find, identify, see** *It took me a long time to find the flaw in her logic.* ◊ *Engineers have identified serious design flaws in the proposed nuclear waste dump.* | **expose, highlight, point out/to, reveal** *The markets have exposed the fatal flaw in the government's economic policy.*

• FLAW + VERB **appear** *Flaws have appeared in the new version of the software.*

• PREP. **~ in** *one of the major flaws in his character*

flawed *adj.*

• VERBS **be, seem** | **remain**

• ADV. **badly, deeply, hopelessly, seriously** | **fatally** *a series of fatally flawed judgements* | **crucially, fundamentally** | **slightly, somewhat** | **conceptually, methodologically** *The study was methodologically flawed.*

flea *noun*

• ADJ. **cat, dog, etc.**

• VERB + FLEA **get, have** | **be riddled with** | **control** *This drug is given to dogs to control fleas.*

• FLEA + VERB **jump** | **bite** | **carry/spread disease**

• FLEA + NOUN **bite** | **collar, powder**

flee *verb*

• ADV. **abroad, across the border, into exile** *Hundreds of refugees fled across the border to escape the fighting.* | **north, south, etc.** | **in panic**

• VERB + FLEE **be forced to, have to** *They were forced to flee the country.* | **try to** | **manage to** | **turn** *They turned and fled when they saw the gang of youths approaching them.*

• PREP. **from** *She dropped the phone and fled from the office.* **into/to** *They fled to Britain when the war started.*

• PHRASES **flee empty-handed** *When the police arrived the burglars fled empty-handed.* **flee for your life** *She had to flee for her life when soldiers attacked her village.* **flee in panic/terror** *The children fled in terror as the hay caught fire.* **flee like the wind** *When danger threatens, collect your possessions and flee like the wind.* **flee to safety** *The family managed to flee to safety.*

fleet *noun*

• ADJ. **great, huge, large** *a large fleet of gunboats* | **small** | **fishing, whaling** | **merchant, shipping** | **battle, invasion** | **enemy, foreign** | **submarine, tanker, car, vehicle** *the company car fleet*

• VERB + FLEET **operate, own** *He operated a small fishing fleet.* | **command** | **mobilize, send (in)** *The fleet was mobilized and the country prepared for war.* | **disband, ground** | **defeat, destroy** | **join** *The ship sailed to join the fleet at Barbados.* | **maintain** *The fleet was is very expensive to maintain.*

• PREP. **in a/the ~** *There were over 500 ships in the enemy fleet.* | **~ of** *a fleet of taxis*

flesh *noun*

1 soft part of sb's body

• ADJ. **firm, smooth, soft, tender** | **pale, pink, white** | **bare, exposed** | **raw** | **torn** | **burning, burnt** | **rotting** | **living** | **dead** | **female, male** | **animal, human**

• VERB + FLESH **touch** | **cut (into)** *His shirt was too small for him and cut into the tender flesh at his armpit.* | **strip, tear at/off** *Peregrine falcons usually pluck the feathers and strip the flesh off their bird prey.* ◊ *African hunting dogs will tear at the flesh of their victim until it is weak.* | **dig into, pierce (into), tear (into)** *Cook the duck until the juices run pale yellow when the flesh is pierced.* ◊ *The weapon tore into his flesh.* | **eat** *According to Greek mythology, the minotaur would only eat human flesh.* | **become, make sth** *(literary) In the Christian tradition, God is made flesh* (= becomes human).

• FLESH + VERB **tingle** *My flesh tingled as I got out of the ice cold pool.* | **crawl, creep** *(both figurative) The scary story made his flesh creep* (= made him feel afraid).

• FLESH + NOUN **wound** *The injury was only a flesh wound and would heal in ten days or so.* | **tone** *In the centre of the painting there is a woman painted in blues, reds and flesh tones* (= colours used to paint human skin).

• PREP. **in the ~** *Thousands of fans gathered to see the band in the flesh* (= see the band in reality and not just in a picture).

• PHRASES **flesh and blood** *She wasn't a ghost. She was flesh and blood* (= alive/real). **flesh and bone** *Babies are born not just as bundles of flesh and bone* (= not simply living bodies without thoughts or feelings) *but with already distinctive personalities.* **the lusts/pleasures/sins/temptations of the flesh** *His moral sermons always denounced the lusts of the flesh* (= the fulfilment of purely physical or sexual desires). **the smell of flesh** *the smell of rotting flesh*

2 soft part of fruit/vegetables

• ADJ. **soft** | **sweet** | **juicy**

• VERB + FLESH **chop, cut** *Pare the mangoes and cut the flesh away from the stone.* | **scoop (out)** *Cut the melon in half, remove the seeds and scoop out the flesh.*

flex *noun*

- ADJ. **long | trailing** *Long trailing flexes are a serious trip hazard.* | **electric/electrical | kettle, telephone, etc.**
- QUANT. **length**
- VERB + FLEX **cut** *Side cutters are useful for cutting electrical flex to length.*

flexibility *noun*

- ADJ. **considerable, enormous, great | added, additional, extra, increased, more | maximum, total | enough, sufficient | financial**
- QUANT. **degree** *Police work involves a considerable degree of flexibility and discretion.*
- VERB + FLEXIBILITY **have** *You have considerable flexibility in this job and can choose how to do things.* | **show | obtain** *Flexibility of labour was obtained through the break up of old trade union structures.* | **maintain, retain | restore** *She had physiotherapy to restore the flexibility of her muscles.* | **bring (sb/sth), give (sb/sth), introduce, provide (sb/sth with)** *The new range of machines will bring flexibility to your business computing.* | **allow (sb/sth), allow for, offer (sb/sth), permit (sb/sth)** *The courses are designed to allow maximum flexibility.* | **build, create** *reforms to build flexibility into the system* | **enhance, improve, increase | encourage** *an initiative to encourage greater flexibility in teaching and learning* | **reduce | need, require**
- PREP. **~ in** *This will give schools greater flexibility in their use of resources.* **~ over** *flexibility over the deadline*
- PHRASES **a need for flexibility** *There is a need for greater flexibility in the way the network is managed.*

flexible *adj.*

- VERBS **be, seem | become | remain | make sth** *We need to make the working day more flexible.* | **keep sth**
- ADV. **extremely, highly, very | completely, fully, perfectly, totally | infinitely** *Human beings are infinitely flexible and able to adjust when survival depends on it.* | **fairly, pretty, quite, reasonably, relatively | enough, sufficiently | insufficiently**
- PHRASES **about** *My mother is fairly flexible about what time I need to be home.*

flick *noun*

- ADJ. **quick**
- VERB + FLICK **give (sth)** *The fish gave a quick flick of its tail.*
- PREP. **with a ~** *With a flick of his wrist he removed the ash from the end of his cigarette.* | **~ of**
- PHRASES **at the flick of a switch** *Heat is available at the flick of a switch* (= instantly, by simply switching on the electricity).

flick *verb*

- ADV. **casually | nervously | quickly | away, back**
- PREP. **across** *His tongue flicked nervously across dry lips.* **from** *He casually flicked away some dust from his jacket.* **off** *She flicked the ash off her cigarette.* **over** *His eyes flicked quickly over the screen.*
- PHRASES **flick sth open** *She snatched up her briefcase and flicked it open.*

PHRASAL VERB

flick through sth

- ADV. **absent-mindedly, casually, idly** *She flicked idly through a magazine.* | **quickly**

flicker *noun*

- ADJ. **faint, slight, small, tiny** *She caught the faintest flicker of amusement on his face.* | **brief, momentary |**

last (*often figurative*) *The secret police were determined to stamp out the last flickers of academic freedom.*
- VERB + FLICKER **give** *The candle gave one last flicker and went out.* | **show | catch, notice, see | detect, feel** *She felt a brief flicker of jealousy.*
- FLICKER + VERB **cross sth** *A flicker of guilt crossed his face.* | **catch your eye** *A flicker of movement caught her eye and she turned her head.*
- PREP. **with a ~ of** *'He'll soon be here,' she thought, with a flicker of excitement.* **without a ~ of** *She spoke without any flicker of fear.* | **~ of**
- PHRASES **the flicker of a candle/flame** *The brief flicker of a candle flame caught our eyes.* **the flicker of an eyelid, a flicker of sb's/the eyes** *Her only reaction was a slight flicker of her eyes.* **a flicker of hope/interest** *European stock markets showed barely a flicker of interest in the election result.* **a flicker of light/movement** *He saw a flicker of light in the darkness.* **a flicker of recognition** *The witness stared at the accused but she showed not a flicker of recognition.* **a flicker of a smile** *I noticed a flicker of a smile on her face.*

flicker *verb*

- ADV. **briefly, for a moment, momentarily | nervously** *Her eyes flickered nervously in anticipation.* | **(on and) off, out** *The lights flickered on and off.*
- PREP. **across/over** *His gaze flickered over her.*
- PHRASES **flicker into life** *The television screen flickered into life.* **flicker open** *Katherine's eyes flickered open.*

flight *noun*

1 journey by air; plane making journey

- ADJ. **return** *The first prize is a return flight to Delhi.* ◇ *The outbound flight was smooth but the return flight was held up by six hours.* | **outbound | connecting | shuttle | regular, scheduled | charter | commercial | direct, non-stop | special | delayed | domestic, internal, local | long, long-distance, long-haul | intercontinental, international, transatlantic | first** *I got to the airport early to be ready for the first flight out.* | **last** *She flew into London on the last flight from Frankfurt.* | **first, maiden** *The Wright Brothers made their first flight in the Kitty Hawk in 1903.* | **final, last** *This will be the last flight of the vintage aircraft before it is installed in the museum.* | **early | evening, morning, night | bumpy** *The bumpy flight brought on a bout of airsickness.* | **smooth | pleasure | mercy, relief | military | reconnaissance, surveillance | routine | training** *a routine air-force training flight* | **solo | air, space | airline, (hot-air) balloon, helicopter | cargo, passenger | cheap**
- VERB + FLIGHT **catch, take, travel on** *They caught an early flight back to London.* | **miss | have** *Did you have a good flight?* | **make** *The aeroplane made its maiden flight in 1976.* | **be booked on/onto, be on** *I'm on the first flight to Milan in the morning.* | **book (sb), book sb/yourself on/onto, get** *He asked her to book him on the next available flight to Geneva.* ◇ *We managed to get a non-stop flight to New York.* | **charter** *The club has chartered a special flight from Manchester to Bologna for their fans.* | **confirm | cancel, suspend** *The UN has suspended relief flights because of shelling around the airport.* | **change | board | operate** *The airline operates regular flights to Greece.* | **delay, hold up | divert** *The flight was diverted to Gatwick because of a bomb scare.* | **blow up** *She was accused of planting the bomb that blew up flight 217.*
- FLIGHT + VERB **be bound for sth** *a flight bound for Antigua* | **leave, take off | arrive | land | be full** *I'm afraid I can't book you onto that flight—it's full.*
- FLIGHT + NOUN **number** *We need your time of arrival and flight number.* | **time** *The flight time from Heathrow to Marseilles is less than two hours.* | **delay** *Your travel insurance compensates you for flight delays.* | **attendant, crew | commander, engineer** (*both military*) | **instru-**

ments | **recorder** *The flight recorder should help to establish why the plane suddenly crashed.* | **simulator** | **path** *They have persuaded the authorities to divert the flight path of the military jets away from their village.*
● PREP. **aboard/on/on board a/sth ~** *passengers aboard a flight bound for Johannesburg* **during a/the ~** *Please refrain from smoking during the flight.* | **~ for** *She took a flight for Los Angeles.* **~ from,** *~* **out of** *They waited for the first flight out of Lisbon.* **~ to** *a flight from Sidney to Tokyo*

2 action of flying
● ADJ. **sustained | steady | normal | forward | soaring | low-level | horizontal, level | vertical | circular, curving | high-speed, supersonic**
● VERB + FLIGHT **be capable of** *Barn owls are capable of flight at 56 days.* | **achieve** *Bats are the only mammals to have wings and to achieve sustained flight.* | **take** *They watched the young eagles take flight.*
● PREP. **during ~** *The wings vibrate during flight.* **in ~** *a flock of geese in flight*
● PHRASES **the line of flight** *Don't get into the line of flight of the bees—you'd be sure to get stung.*

3 number of stairs/steps
● ADJ. **long | short | steep | shallow | broad | narrow | double** *The villa is fronted by a double flight of stairs.*
● VERB + FLIGHT **climb (up), go/run/walk up | descend, go/run/walk down | fall down**
● FLIGHT + VERB **lead ...** *a flight of steps leading to the foyer* | **go down/up sth** *A flight of steps goes up the left-hand side of the room.*
● PREP. **down/up a/the ~** *The office is just round that corner and up a short flight of stairs.*
● PHRASES **(at the bottom/top of) a flight of stairs/steps**

4 running away
● ADJ. **headlong, panicked**
● VERB + FLIGHT **put (sb/sth) to** *(literary) The army was defeated and the king put to flight.* | **take** *As soon as they detected the cheetah the antelope took flight.*
● PREP. **in ~** *Left-wing opposition leaders, in flight from persecution, went across the border.* | **~ from** *a headlong flight from danger* **~ into** *a flight into the unknown* **~ to** *The story tells of his flight from East to West Berlin.*

flinch *verb*

● ADV. **violently | almost | hardly** *He hardly flinched when he was hit.* | **slightly | visibly | inwardly** *She flinched inwardly as he took her hand.* | **away**
● VERB + FLINCH **make sb** *Her finger touched the scar on his forehead, making him flinch.*
● PREP. **at** *She flinched visibly at the sight of the body.* **from** *She flinched away from him.* ◇ *(figurative) She won't flinch from speaking her mind.* **with** *He flinched with the force of the blow.*

fling *noun*

● ADJ. **brief | (one) final, (one) last** *The athlete will have one final fling (= participate in one final competition) before retirement.*
● VERB + FLING **have** *She's had her fling and now she's got to settle down.*
● PREP. **~ with** *He had a fling with his neighbour's wife.*

float *verb*

1 on water/in air
● ADV. **gently | downstream, downwards | upwards** *In the dream my feet leave the ground and I start to float upwards.* | **about, around, away, off**
● VERB + FLOAT **seem to** *Her voice seemed to float on the water as gently as a slight mist.*
● PREP. **across** *A few small clouds floated across the sky.* **down** *chunks of ice floating down the river* **in** *pieces of*

wood floating in the water **on** *A few leaves floated on the surface of the water.*

2 currency
● ADV. **freely** *The government decided to allow the peso to float freely.*
● VERB + FLOAT **allow sth to**

flog *verb*

● ADV. **publicly** *Offenders were publicly flogged.*
● PHRASES **flog sb to death**

flood *noun*

1 large amount of water
● ADJ. **devastating, great, heavy, severe | summer, winter**
● VERB + FLOOD **cause** *Heavy rainfall in the mountains caused the floods.*
● FLOOD + VERB **hit sth, strike sth** *This summer the region was struck by devastating floods.* | **inundate sth** *The meadowland was inundated by heavy floods.* | **cause sth** *The flood caused widespread destruction.* | **subside** *The floods are slowly subsiding.*
● FLOOD + NOUN **water/waters | alert, damage, victim | control, defence, prevention, protection, relief**
● PHRASES **be in (full) flood** *The river was in full flood (= had flooded its banks).*

2 large number/amount
● ADJ. **great | constant | sudden**
● FLOOD + VERB **inundate sb/sth** *She was inundated by floods of fan mail.*
● PREP. **~ of** *a great flood of refugees*
● PHRASES **in floods of tears** (= crying a lot) *The little girl was in floods of tears.*

flood *verb*

● VERB + FLOOD **be liable to** *The area near the river is liable to flood.*
● PHRASES **be badly flooded** *The village had been badly flooded.*

floor *noun*

1 lower surface of a room
● ADJ. **bare** *I can't sleep on the bare floor!* | **carpeted, parquet, tiled, wood, wooden | polished | bathroom, kitchen, etc.**
● VERB + FLOOR **clean, mop, polish, scrub, sweep, wash, wax, wipe | drop to, fall to** *His glass fell to the floor and broke.*
● FLOOR + NOUN **covering, tile | space**
● PREP. **on the ~** *Do you mind sitting on the floor?*
● PHRASES **from floor to ceiling** *Bookcases lined the walls from floor to ceiling.*

2 bottom of the sea, a forest, etc.
● ADJ. **cave, forest, ocean, sea, valley**

3 level in a building
● ADJ. **bottom, ground | top | first, second, etc. | mezzanine | lower, upper**
● VERB + FLOOR **occupy** *The offices occupy the two top floors of the building.*
● PREP. **on the ~** *a cafe on the mezzanine floor*

floorboard *noun*

● ADJ. **wooden | bare | polished | loose | creaking, squeaky**
● VERB + FLOORBOARD **lay** *The builders are still laying the floorboards.* | **lift (up)** *Lift some loose floorboards to get at the pipes.*
● FLOORBOARD + VERB **creak** *The wooden floorboards creaked as he walked down the corridor.*

● PREP. **beneath/under/underneath the~** *They said that he kept his money under the floorboards.*
● PHRASES **a gap between/in the floorboards** *She could hear voices through the gaps in the floorboards.*

flop *noun*

● ADJ. **almighty, big, resounding, spectacular** *The show was the biggest flop in TV history.* | **complete** | **expensive** *The concert may prove an expensive flop unless more people decide to go.*

flour *noun*

● ADJ. **strong** | **plain, self-raising** | **white, wholemeal** | **stoneground** | **unbleached** | **rice, rye, wheat, etc.**
● QUANT. **bag, packet, sack**
● VERB + FLOUR **use** | **add, blend, fold in, mix (in), rub sth in/into, stir (in)** *Blend the flour with a little milk to make a smooth paste.* ◇ *Rub the butter into the flour.* | **sieve, sift** *Sift the flour and salt into a bowl.*
● FLOUR + NOUN **mill**
⇨ Special page at FOOD

flourish *noun*

● ADJ. **final** | **dramatic, rhetorical, theatrical** *a speech full of rhetorical flourishes*
● VERB + FLOURISH **end in/with, finish with** | **start (off) with** | **sign with** *Bill signed on the bottom line with a flourish.*
● PREP. **with a~** *With a final flourish she laid down her pen.*
● PHRASES **a flourish of trumpets**

flout *verb*

● ADV. **deliberately, openly** *The protesters have openly flouted the law.*

flow *noun*

● ADJ. **heavy, large, massive** | **good** | **adequate** | **poor** *Our shower doesn't work very well because of the poor water flow.* | **main** | **increased, increasing** | **ceaseless, constant, continuous, endless** | **free, uninterrupted** *the uninterrupted flow of traffic* | **even, smooth, steady** *to maintain an even flow of work through the department* | **easy, natural** *I liked the concerto for its natural flow.* | **outward** *the outward flow of investment from the country* | **annual, daily, seasonal** | **data, information** | **air, blood, gas, lava, menstrual, river, water** | **capital, cash, financial, investment, production, trade**
● VERB + FLOW **have** *Big pension funds have a constant flow of cash.* | **get, obtain** *Squeeze the tube of sealant slowly to obtain an even flow.* | **allow** *We like to allow a free flow of ideas in our company.* | **produce, provide** *The system provides a continuous flow of information to the market.* | **keep, maintain** *He kept up a flow of chatter.* | **ensure** *You must use a wide pipe to ensure an adequate flow of water.* | **control, regulate** | **assist, encourage, facilitate, stimulate** *to encourage the flow of revenue into the country* | **enhance, improve, increase** *The company is trying to enhance its cash flow.* | **disrupt, impede, reduce, restrict, slow (down)** *The continual bombing disrupted the flow of supplies to the ground troops.* | **block, break (up), cut (off), halt, interrupt, staunch, stem, stop** *They tried to staunch the flow of blood.* | **divert** *The main flow of water has been diverted to a new course.* | **join** | **measure**
● FLOW + NOUN **rate** *The flow rate was measured at 9.5 litres per second.* | **chart, diagram**
● PREP. **against the~** *They have to swim against the flow of the river.* | **~around/round** *air flows around the wings of an aircraft* **~from** *First cut off the water flow from the*

boiler. **~into** *She joined the flow of immigrants to the country.* **~through** *the flow of data through the system*
● PHRASES **changes in the flow** *Changes in the flow of patients have reduced the number of beds available.* **the ebb and flow** *the ebb and flow of the tide* ◇ *(figurative) He was at the mercy of the ebb and flow of public opinion.* **in full flow** *She tried to interrupt his speech, but he was already in full flow* (= talking continuously and not thinking of stopping). **the rate of flow** *the rate of flow of water*

flow *verb*

● ADV. **easily, freely, smoothly** *We talked, and the conversation flowed freely.* ◇ *Wine and beer flowed freely.* | **fast, swiftly** *The river flows quite fast here.* | **slowly** | **naturally** *In a good production of the play, the action and the words flow naturally.* | **directly** *Some of these changes will flow directly from the legislation.* | **constantly, continuously** | **away, back, in, out, past**
● VERB + FLOW **seem to** | **begin to, start to** | **continue to** *Imported food aid continued to flow in.*
● PREP. **across, along, between, down** *a small stream that flowed down the hillside* **from** *Blood was still flowing from the wound.* **into** *One day seemed to flow into the next.* **out of, over, through** *Information flows continuously through the network.* **to** *to get blood flowing to the brain*

flower *noun*

● ADJ. **bright, brilliantly-coloured, colourful** | **fragrant, scented, sweet-scented, sweet-smelling** | **delicate, tiny** | **huge** | **lily-like, star-shaped, etc.** | **exotic, rare** | **alpine, garden, wild, woodland** | **autumn, spring, etc.** | **seasonal** | **out-of-season** | **beautiful, lovely, pretty** *What lovely flowers!* | **fresh** | **cut** *They sell a few pot plants, but they mainly sell cut flowers.* | **dried, pressed** | **dead** | **artificial, fake** | **closed, open** *The flowers were still tightly closed.* | **daffodil, tulip, etc.**
● QUANT. **bouquet, bunch**
● VERB + FLOWER **have, produce** *It has deep pink scented flowers.* ◇ *It was the first year that the cactus had produced flowers.* | **come into** *If the winter weather is mild, plants may come into flower too early.* | **pollinate** *The flowers are pollinated by insects.* | **press**
● FLOWER + VERB **go to seed, seed**
● FLOWER + NOUN **bud, head, petal, seed, stalk, stem** | **bed, border** | **arrangement, arranger, arranging** *I'm learning flower arranging.* | **display** | **pot** (also **flowerpot**) | **basket, container, vase** | **garden** | **festival, show** | **market, seller, shop, stall** | **garland, wreath**
● PREP. **in~** *It was June and the roses were in flower.*
● PHRASES **a bank/carpet/mass of flowers** *The alleys were adorned with banks of flowers.* ◇ *The forest floor was a carpet of wild flowers.* **covered in flowers** *The bush was absolutely covered in flowers.*
⇨ Note on page 316.

flu *noun*

● ADJ. **mild** | **gastric** | **summer**
● QUANT. **bout, dose** *She's had a nasty dose of flu.*
● VERB + FLU **be in bed with, be laid up with, have, suffer from** | **catch, contract, get, go down with**
● FLU + NOUN **bug, virus** | **epidemic** | **victim** | **vaccine** | **jab**
⇨ Special page at ILLNESS

fluctuate *verb*

● ADV. **considerably** | **sharply, widely, wildly** *Prices have fluctuated wildly in recent years.* | **constantly, continually** *constantly fluctuating patterns*
● PREP. **according to** *Traffic congestion fluctuates according to the time of day.* **around** *The number of boys at the school fluctuates around 100.* **between** *The number of unemployed fluctuates between two and three million.*

> **NOTE**
> **Flowers**
>
> **grow~**
> *Tulips are grown everywhere.*
> **breed~**
> *She breeds orchids in her greenhouse.*
> **plant, put in~**
> *Autumn is the best time to plant peonies.*
> **dig out/up, take out~**
> *Dig up your geraniums before the first frosts.*
> **spray, water~**
> *It's a good idea to spray your roses against greenfly.*
> **prune** roses
> **deadhead~**
> *Don't forget to deadhead the pansies.*
> **pick (sb)~**
> *I picked some daffodils for you.*
> **smell~**
> *He stopped to smell the flowers.*
> **arrange~**
> *She arranged the tulips in a vase.*
> **bring/give/send/take (sb)~**
> *He took her flowers and chocolates.*
> **~grow**
> *Daffodils grow wild in the mountains.*
> **~be in flower, be/come out, (be in) bloom, come into**
> **flower, come out, flower**
> *The spring flowers were just coming out.*
> *What time of year do daffodils flower?*
> **~smell**
> *Some of these roses smell absolutely wonderful.*
> **~close/open (up)**
> *You know it's summer when the first daisies open.*
> **~droop, wilt, wither**
> *The petunias were already wilting in the hot sun.*
> **~be over**
> *It was April and the snowdrops were long over.*
> **a bouquet/bunch/garland/posy/spray/vase of~**
> *a spray of mixed violets and primroses*

fluctuation *noun*

• ADJ. **considerable, large, marked, sharp, violent, wide, wild | local, minor | rapid | short-term | cyclical, periodic, regular, seasonal** *seasonal fluctuations in the demand for labour* **| random | climatic, currency, economic, exchange rate, market, price, temperature**
• VERB + FLUCTUATION **cause, produce** *factors which cause these exchange rate fluctuations* **| be subject to** *The number of students at a college can be subject to considerable fluctuation.*
• FLUCTUATION + VERB **occur** *the climatic fluctuations that have occurred over the last ten years*
• PREP. **~in** *There have been quite wide fluctuations in oil prices in recent years.*

fluency *noun*

• VERB + FLUENCY **achieve, acquire** *Some young children achieve great fluency in their reading.*
• PREP. **~in** *Fluency in spoken English is essential.*

fluid *noun*

• ADJ. **excess | amniotic, bodily/body, intravenous | brake, cleaning**
• VERB + FLUID **drink** *Change your diet and drink plenty of fluids.* **| lose | replace** *replacing vital body fluids and salts that are lost when you sweat* **| retain** *Retaining excess fluid could be a problem.*

fluid *adj.*

• VERBS **be | become | remain | keep sth** *I think we should try and keep our arrangements fluid at this stage.*
• ADV. **extremely, highly, very** *It's a highly fluid situation.* **| fairly, quite, rather, relatively**

flurry *noun*

1 small amount of rain/snow
• ADJ. **snow**
• PHRASES **a flurry of rain/snow**

2 short sudden burst of sth
• ADJ. **brief, sudden** *There was a sudden flurry of interest in the book.*
• PREP. **~of**
• PHRASES **a flurry of activity/excitement**

flush *noun*

• ADJ. **faint, slight | deep, dull, pink, red, scarlet, warm | hectic, sudden** *a hectic flush of rising excitement* **| hot** *Hot drinks can cause sweating and hot flushes in the face and head.*
• VERB + FLUSH **feel** *She felt a dull flush of anger creeping into her face.* **| bring** *The promise in his voice brought a warm flush to her cheeks.*
• FLUSH + VERB **creep, rise, spread, suffuse sth** *A flush of embarrassment rose to her cheeks.*
• PREP. **~of** *There was a faint flush of colour on those pale cheeks.*
• PHRASES **(in) the first flush of enthusiasm, passion, youth, etc.** (= a time when enthusiasm, etc. is new, exciting and strong)

flush *verb*

• ADV. **deeply | a little, slightly | angrily, guiltily, painfully** *He made his excuses, flushing guiltily.*
• PREP. **with** *He flushed scarlet with embarrassment.*

flushed *adj.*

• VERBS **appear, be, feel, look | become**
• ADV. **deeply, extremely, very | a bit, faintly, a little, quite, slightly | unnaturally**
• PREP. **with** *Her face was flushed with embarrassment.*

flute *noun*

⇒ Special page at MUSIC

flutter *noun*

1 quick, light movement
• ADJ. **little**
• VERB + FLUTTER **give** *His heart gave a little flutter as the ladder slipped a couple of inches.*

2 state of nervous excitement
• VERB + FLUTTER **be in, feel** *She felt a flutter of excitement.* **| get in | cause**
• PREP. **in a~** *They arrived in a flutter.* **| ~of**

fly *noun*

1 insect
• VERB + FLY **swat** *I swatted the fly with a newspaper.*
• FLY + VERB **buzz** *A fly was buzzing against the window.* **| crawl | land (on sth), settle (on sth)** *A fly settled on the butter.*
• FLY + NOUN **larva | repellent, spray**

2 (also **flies**) on trousers
• ADJ. **button/button-up, zip/zipped**
• VERB + FLY **button (up), do up, zip up | undo, unzip** *Do you know your flies are undone?*
• FLY + NOUN **button**
⇒ Special page at CLOTHES

fly *verb*

- ADV. **high, low | fast, slowly | about, around, past**
- PREP. **above** *We watched the birds flying high above us.* **over** *an aeroplane flying low over the sea*

focal point *noun*

- VERB + FOCAL POINT **act as, become, form, make, provide (sth with), serve as**
- PREP. **~for** *The school provides a focal point for the local community.* **~in** *In what sense was the discovery of America a focal point in history?*

focus *noun*

1 centre of interest/attention
- ADJ. **central, main, major, primary, prime, principal | important, special | greater, increased | clear, sharp, strong** *The company's restructuring is designed to give a sharper focus on key growth markets.* **| narrow** *I found the focus of the debate too narrow.*
- VERB + FOCUS **act as, give sb/sth, provide (sb/sth with), serve as** *Cities have always acted as the principal focus of political life.* **| change, shift** *At this stage of the trial the defence lawyer often shifts the focus onto the victim.* **| bring sth into** *This case has brought the problem of drug abuse in schools into sharp focus.* **| come into** *The question of compensation comes into focus.*
- FOCUS + VERB **be on sb/sth** *Our primary focus this term will be on group work.* **| shift** *The focus has now shifted towards the problem of long-term unemployment.*
- PREP. **~for** *She became a focus for all his anger.* **~on** *an increased focus on younger people*
- PHRASES **a change/shift of focus, the focus of attention** *He found he was now their main focus of attention.*

2 point/distance at which sth is clearly seen
- ADJ. **sharp | soft** *soft focus shots of cuddly animals*
- VERB + FOCUS **come into** *When I got glasses suddenly the whole world came into focus* (= became clear to see).
- PREP. **in~** *The binoculars were not in focus* (= were not showing things clearly). **out of~** *The children's faces are badly out of focus* (= not clearly shown) *in the photograph.*

focus *verb*

1 give attention to sth
- ADV. **heavily, largely, mainly, particularly, primarily, principally | entirely, exclusively, solely** *The study focuses exclusively on secondary schools.* **| increasingly | fully | firmly** *The attention of the news media was firmly focused on the elections.* **| specifically | clearly | directly | closely, sharply | narrowly | initially | inevitably** *He inevitably focused on his own concerns, with only a passing query about Jeff.* **| traditionally** *Degree courses have traditionally focused on the established great writers of the past.*
- VERB + FOCUS **need to | try to | decide to | tend to | help (to)** *Think of some questions that will help focus the discussion.*
- PREP. **on/upon** *We need to focus upon the main issues.*
- PHRASES **highly/tightly focused** *The department undertakes highly focused research.* **narrowly focused** *The study was criticized for being too narrowly focused.*

2 direct your eyes towards sth
- ADV. **automatically**
- VERB + FOCUS **try to** *She blinked and tried to focus.*
- PREP. **on/upon** *The eye will automatically focus on the small group in the foreground.*

foe *noun*

- ADJ. **bitter, dangerous, deadly, formidable, implacable, terrible** *He knew that Carlton could be an implacable foe.* **| common | old** *playing in the final against their old foes Italy*
- VERB + FOE **vanquish** (*figurative*) *She had fought many battles, vanquished many foes.*
- PREP. **against a~** *to join forces against a common foe*
- PHRASES **friend and foe** *His newspaper articles criticized friend and foe alike.* **friend or foe** *She was unsure as yet whether he was friend or foe.*

fog *noun*

- ADJ. **dense, heavy, thick | freezing | patchy** *Drizzle and patchy fog are forecast.* **| swirling**
- QUANT. **bank, blanket, patch** *The town was shrouded in a thick blanket of fog.*
- VERB + FOG **be shrouded in**
- FOG + VERB **cover sth, lie, shroud sth** *A freezing fog lay over the valley.* **| close in, come down, descend, roll in** *A dense fog came down in the afternoon.* ◊ *A heavy fog rolled in from the sea.* **| thicken | clear, disperse, lift** *The fog had lifted by late morning.* **| drift, swirl** *fog drifting over the water* **| obscure sth** *A bank of fog obscured the farmhouse.*
- FOG + NOUN **patches**
- PREP. **in/into (a/the)~** *We got lost in the fog.* **through (a/the)~** *We drove slowly through the fog.*

foil *noun*

1 metal in a thin sheet
- ADJ. **aluminium, gold, silver, tin | kitchen**
- QUANT. **piece, sheet | roll**
- VERB + FOIL **cover sth with, wrap sth in** *I wrapped the sandwiches in kitchen foil.*

2 sth that shows off the qualities of sth else
- ADJ. **good, ideal, perfect**
- VERB + FOIL **be, provide**
- PREP. **as a~** *She has used mosses as a foil for the brightly coloured flowers in the bed.* **| ~for/to** *The couple provided the perfect foil for one another.*

fold *noun*

1 part of sth folded
- ADJ. **billowing, loose, soft** *billowing folds of clouds* **| deep, heavy | neat | vertical**
- VERB + FOLD **be hidden behind/by/in** *The troops were hidden by the deep folds of the ground.* **| fall in, hang in ~s** *The fabric fell in soft folds.* ◊ *His face hung in heavy folds.*
- PREP. **in a/the~** *It was a solitary spot in a fold between two hills.* **| ~in** *a fold in the land*
- PHRASES **folds of flesh/skin** *the loose folds of flesh under her chin*

2 the fold group of people who feel they belong
- ADJ. **international | family | Anglican, Catholic, etc.**
- VERB + FOLD **join | leave | come back into/to, return to | be back in** *The country is now firmly back in the international fold.* **| bring sb (back) into/to** *The indigenous people were brought into the Catholic fold.* **| accept sb back into, welcome sb (back) into/to** *His father finally accepted him back into the family fold.*
- PREP. **within a/the ~** *opposing viewpoints within the Anglican fold*

fold *verb*

- ADV. **carefully, neatly | deftly** *He deftly folded the typed sheets and replaced them in the envelope.* **| gently** *Her hands lay gently folded in her lap.* **| in half, in two** *She folded the piece of paper in half.* **| back, down, over | up** *I folded up the clothes and put them away.*
- PREP. **into** *She folded the clothes into a neat bundle.*

foliage *noun*

- ADJ. **bright | dense, heavy, luxuriant | dead | ever-**

green, year-round | grassy | spring, summer, etc. |
tropical

folk (also folks) noun

● ADJ. **decent, good, honest, law-abiding** | **common,
everyday, ordinary** *It's the ordinary everyday folk who
come to shop at this market.* | **humble, simple** | **friendly**
| **rich** | **poor** | **working, working-class** | **elderly, old** |
young | **black, white** | **men** (also **menfolk**) *He described
the customs of the menfolk of his family.* | **city, country**
places that appeal to city folk | **local**
● VERB + FOLKS **visit** *I am going to visit my folks* (= parents) *at the weekend.*
● FOLK + VERB **live** *ordinary working-class folk who
live near the factory* | **say sth, talk (of sth), tell (sb) sth**
Folks say that he is a hard man. ◇ *If only I'd listened to the
old folk telling their stories.*
● FOLK + NOUN **culture, customs, memory, myth,
tradition, wisdom** *She had an interest in the folk customs
of ancient societies.* | **story, tale** | **hero** *He is something of
a folk hero in these parts.* | **art, dancing, music, singing** |
dance, song | **musician, singer** | **festival** | **medicine,
remedy**
● PHRASES **the folks back home** *The visiting team lost
3–0, dismaying the folks back home* (= the people from the
place the team had come from).

folklore noun

● ADJ. **popular** | **local** | **cricket, sporting, etc.**
● VERB + FOLKLORE **be part of** | **become part of,
enter (into), pass into** *The victory became part of sporting
folklore.*
● FOLKLORE + VERB **have it that …** *Local folklore has
it that prehistoric men drove cattle over these cliffs.*
● PREP. **according to** ~ *According to popular folklore,
anyone who owns such a picture will have bad luck.* **in … ~**
a character in American folklore

follow verb

1 go after sb/sth
● ADV. **closely** *Johnson finished first, closely followed by
Stevens and Higgins.* | **dutifully, obediently** *The dog fol-
lowed obediently at her heels.* | **blindly** *She followed blind-
ly, stumbling over stones in her path.* | **on** *You go ahead
and we'll follow on later.*
● VERB + FOLLOW **beckon (to) sb to** *She beckoned him
to follow her.*
2 happen after sth
● ADV. **closely, quickly, shortly, swiftly** *The next pro-
gramme will follow shortly.* | **immediately** *in the period
immediately following the election*
3 happen/be true as a result of sth
● ADV. **not necessarily** *It does not necessarily follow that
sleep loss would cause these symptoms.*
● PREP. **(on) from** *Several conclusions follow on from his
statement.*
4 accept advice/instructions
● ADV. **carefully** *Follow my instructions very carefully.* |
dutifully, obediently
5 copy
● ADV. **faithfully** *The film follows the book faithfully.* |
blindly, slavishly *It wasn't in his nature to follow blindly.*
◇ *slavishly following the views of his teachers*
● VERB + FOLLOW **be expected to, be likely to** *Banks
are expected to follow the building societies in raising
mortgage rates.*
● PHRASES **follow suit** (*figurative*) (= act or behave in
the way that sb else has just done)
6 understand sth
● ADV. **not quite** *I'm sorry but I don't quite follow you*
(=understand what you are saying).

● VERB + FOLLOW **be easy to** | **be difficult to, be hard
to, be impossible to** *His argument was difficult to follow.*

follower noun

● ADJ. **ardent, close, enthusiastic, keen** *a keen follower
of football* | **dedicated, devoted, devout, faithful, loyal,
true** *a true follower of Islam* | **local** | **sports** | **cricket,
football, rugby, etc.**
● QUANT. **band**
● VERB + FOLLOWER **have** *She still has many loyal fol-
lowers.* | **attract** | **lead** *The myth says that he led a small
band of followers to seek their fortune in distant lands.*
● PREP. **among sb's** ~ *The king was not powerful enough
to command respect among his followers.*

following noun

● ADJ. **big, considerable, great, large, mass, strong** |
limited, small | **local** | **dedicated, devoted, faithful, fan-
atical, loyal** | **enthusiastic** | **personal** | **cult** *They enjoy
a cult following in the UK.*
● VERB + FOLLOWING **command, enjoy, have** | **ac-
quire, attract, build up, create, gain, gather**
● PREP. ~**among** *Top of the range Scotches attract a fan-
atical following among whisky buffs.*

follow-up noun

● ADJ. **long-term** | **immediate** | **six-month, two-year,
etc.** | **regular**
● VERB + FOLLOW-UP **plan** | **write** *She is writing a
follow-up to her best-selling novel.*
● FOLLOW-UP + NOUN **period** | **action, work** *After the
report, advisers are expected to carry out follow-up work.* |
discussion, interview, meeting, session | **visit** *You will
receive a follow-up visit from the person conducting the as-
sessment.* | **operation** *a follow-up operation to consolidate
military successes* | **treatment** *They were attending hos-
pital for follow-up treatment.* | **report, study, survey** *a
long-term follow-up study of all children born in Great
Britain in one week*
● PREP. ~**to** *We are planning a follow-up to today's event.*

folly noun

1 lack of good judgement
● ADJ. **absolute, sheer** | **ultimate** | **youthful** | **human**
| **economic, political**
● VERB + FOLLY **realize, recognize, see** *Suddenly she
saw the folly of it all.* | **demonstrate, show** *These facts
demonstrate the folly of the policy.* | **underline**
● PHRASES **an act of folly** *That would be an act of sheer
folly!* **the folly of your ways** *They have finally seen the
folly of their ways.* **the height of folly** *To sign away his
rights to the book would have been the height of folly.*
2 building
● ADJ. **Gothic, Victorian** | **monumental** | **architectural**
● VERB + FOLLY **build**

fond adj. fond of sb/sth

● VERBS **be, feel, seem** | **become, grow** | **remain**
● ADV. **especially, extremely, genuinely, immensely,
particularly, really, very** *She seems genuinely fond of the
children.* | **quite, rather**

fondness noun

● ADJ. **great** | **certain, special**
● VERB + FONDNESS **feel, have**
● PREP. ~**for** *I've always had a certain fondness for her.*

food noun

● ADJ. **delicious, excellent, good, superb, tasty, won-
derful** | **favourite** | **decent** | **adequate, enough, suffi-**

FOOD AND COOKING

describing food

- moist, rich, sticky **cake**
- a delicious, rich **dessert**
- a classic, delicious, savoury, tasty **dish**
- a/an appetizing, delicious, excellent, healthy, nourishing, substantial, tasty, wholesome **meal**
- crisp, crunchy, fresh, green **salad**
- creamy, piquant, rich, spicy, sweet and sour, tangy, thick **sauce**
- a healthy, light, quick, savoury, tasty **snack**
- chunky, clear, creamy, hearty, thick, thin **soup**

a substantial meal

quantifiers

- a **clove** of garlic
- a **fillet** of fish
- a **knob** of butter
- a **pinch** of salt
- a **rasher** of bacon
- a **sprig** of parsley
- a **stick** of celery
- a **wedge** of lemon

cooking

- melt, soften **butter**
- (hard/soft-)boil, fry, poach, scramble **eggs**
- bake, fry, grill, poach, steam **fish**
- brown, soften **onions**
- heat up, simmer **soup**; bring **soup** to the boil
- boil, parboil, steam **vegetables**
- preheat **the oven** to 450°
- lower, remove the pan from, take the pan off, turn down/up **the heat**

preparation

- sprinkle, top with grated **cheese**
- beat, whisk **eggs**
- clean, fillet, gut, skin **fish**
- chop, cube, dice, marinate, mince, tenderize **meat**
- add, blend, combine, mix, pour in, stir in **ingredients**
- chop, peel **vegetables**

serving

- garnish with **herbs**
- sprinkle with **lemon juice**
- drizzle, pour **oil**
- drain **pasta**
- dress, toss a **salad**
- season (with **salt** and **pepper**) to taste

---

cient *Everyone has the right to adequate food and clean water.* | ample | basic, everyday, staple *lower fat alternatives to everyday foods ◊ Retail prices of staple foods remain unchanged.* | plain, simple | exotic, speciality | fine, gourmet, quality *Our restaurant serves the finest food.* | cheap | bad, poor, unhealthy | healthy, nourishing, nutritious, proper, the right, wholesome *Healthy food can and should be delicious ◊ Lack of proper food led to much illness among seamen. ◊ It's is important to get plenty of exercise and to eat the right foods.* | diet, health *Essential oils can be bought from most good health food shops* | rabbit (*informal, disapproving*) *My father preferred to eat meat and hated rabbit food* (= lettuce and other raw vegetables normally found in salads). | fast, junk, snack, takeaway | hot | cold | raw, uncooked | leftover | rotten | fresh | natural | organic | frozen | canned, tinned | processed | convenience, ready-made, ready-prepared | fatty, fried, starchy, stodgy *She is trying to cut down on fatty foods.* | high-calorie, rich *Avoid rich foods like pastries.* | sugary, sweet | savoury, spicy | Greek, Indian, etc. | vegetarian | genetically-modified *Campaigners are challenging the safety of genetically-modified food.* | animal, vegetable *Omnivores are able to eat animal or vege-table food.* | **solid** *The baby refuses to swallow any solid food.* | **baby** | **cat**, **dog**, **fish**, **pet** | **hospital**, **party**, **prison**, **pub**, **restaurant** | **imported**

● QUANT. **portion**, **plate** | **morsel**, **scrap** *They moved from village to village begging scraps of food.*

● VERB + FOOD **consume**, **eat**, **have** *the amount of food that an average family consumes in a week* ◇ *You should eat more fresh foods.* ◇ *She had had no food for two days.* | **enjoy**, **like** *He obviously enjoys good food.* | **live on** *people who live on junk food.* | **be off**, **go off** *The dog has gone off its food.* | **avoid**, **cut down on**, **cut out** | **be/go short of**, **run short of** *The city was under siege and began to run short of food.* | **be without**, **go without**, **live without** *We had been days without food.* | **offer (sb)** *The centre offers food and accommodation for students.* | **give sb**, **provide (sb with)**, **serve (sb)**, **supply (sb with)** *a restaurant that serves good healthy food* ◇ *Thanks to international aid, the town had been supplied with food for nine months.* | **feed sb/sth (on)** *He always fed Whiskers the best cat food.* ◇ *She fed her baby on wholesome food.* | **handle** *Always take great care when handling food.* | **cook**, **do**, **make**, **prepare** *A lot of people can't be bothered to cook good food.* ◇ *Who's doing the food for the party?* | **smell**, **taste** *Taste the food and tell me what you think.* | **cut (up)** *Please cut up the food for your baby sister.* | **pick at** *He had lost his appetite and picked at his food.* | **play with** *Stop playing with your food like a baby!* | **chew** | **swallow** | **bolt**, **gulp (down)** *She told the kids not to gulp down their food.* | **digest** | **order** *They sat down at the restaurant table and immediately ordered their food.* | **grow** | **import** | **beg (for)**, **hunt for**, **look for**, **search for**, **scavenge for** *The female eagle broods and the male hunts for food.* | **find** *Most mammals use their sense of smell to find food.* | **keep**, **store** *Keep food fresher for longer with our new sealable containers.* ◇ *Bears store food for the winter.* | **put out** *He put out food for the birds.* | **share**

● FOOD + VERB **smell**, **taste** *Does the food taste good?* | **be in short supply**, **be short** *We have strikes, food is short and the queues grow longer.* | **run out**

● FOOD + NOUN **resource**, **source**, **supply** *Fruits are an important food source for bats.* ◇ *The seaside fish market is a ready food supply for scavenging seabirds.* | **supplies** *The UN has been issuing emergency food supplies to the refugees.* | **stuff** (also **foodstuff**) *Many basic food-stuffs, such as bread and milk, are tax-free.* | **crop**, **plant** *Peasants were encouraged to grow basic food crops such as beans and corn.* | **product** *The labels on food products give a lot of information about their nutritional content.* | **consumption** | **intake** *His doctor warned him to reduce his daily food intake.* | **preparation** | **hygiene**, **safety** | **scare** *There has been a food scare over salmonella in eggs.* | **distribution** | **crisis**, **shortage** | **rationing**, **rations** | **industry**, **market** *The country intends to increase its share of the European food market.* | **manufacturing**, **production** | **company**, **manufacturer**, **producer** | **market**, **outlet**, **retailer**, **shop**, **store**, **supplier** *Britain's first organic food market* ◇ *a fast food outlet* | **prices** | **bill** *I am trying to cut my weekly food bill by one third.* | **policy** *EU food policy* | **poisoning** | **additives** | **colouring** | **processor** *Blend the egg yolks, lemon juice and herbs in a food processor.* | **chain** *Plankton is at the bottom of the marine food chain.*

● PREP. **for ~** *killing animals for food* **without ~** *After three days without food, the men were close to starvation.*

● PHRASES **food and drink** *Gina had prepared food and drink for the work party.* **food and water** *Food and water were running out.* **food and wine** *The Dordogne region is famous for its food and wine.* **a smell of food** *There was a smell of food from the kitchen* **a supply of food** *The ocean provided the villagers with an endless supply of food.* **the taste of food** *the characteristic taste of our food*

fool noun

● ADJ. **awful**, **big**, **bloody** (*taboo*), **damned**, **great**, **silly**, **stupid** *You're an even bigger fool than I thought.* | **absolute**, **complete**, **utter** | **poor** (= unfortunate) | **old** (= used to show sympathy, affection or a lack of respect) *The poor old fool was imprisoned on my account.* | **young** | **little** *You silly little fool!* | **court** *court fools who used to provide entertainment in the royal court*

● VERB + FOOL **feel (like)** *I felt such a fool when I realized what I'd done.* | **look (like)** *They had left me looking like a fool.* | **act (like)**, **behave like**, **play** *Stop behaving like a fool!* ◇ *He thought that being an actor only involved tap dancing and playing the fool* (= acting in a childish/funny way). | **suffer**, **tolerate** *She doesn't suffer fools gladly.* | **call sb** | **take sb for** *He had taken me for a complete fool.* | **be no/nobody's** (= be too clever to be deceived by sb/sth) *She's nobody's fool. She had the car checked by a mechanic before buying it.*

● PREP. **like a ~** *Like a fool, I told her everything.* | **~ of a sth** *That fool of a doctor has prescribed me the wrong medicine!*

● PHRASES **make a fool (out) of sb/yourself** *She was angry at having been made a fool of.* **more fool (sb)** *I thought it was safe to leave my suitcase there. More fool me* (= I was stupid to think so).

fool verb

● ADV. **completely** | **easily** *I'm not easily fooled by anyone, least of all you.*

● VERB + FOOL **can't/couldn't** | **try to**

● PREP. **into** *He fooled them into thinking he was a detective.* **with** *You can't fool me with all that nonsense!*

● PHRASES **have sb fooled** *She had me completely fooled for a moment.*

foolish adj.

● VERBS **appear**, **be**, **feel**, **look**, **seem**, **sound**

● ADV. **exceedingly**, **extremely**, **incredibly**, **really**, **singularly**, **very** | **utterly** | **a bit**, **a little**, **quite**, **rather**, **slightly**, **vaguely**

foolproof adj.

● VERBS **be**, **look**, **seem** | **make sth** *We're trying to work out a way to make the system foolproof.*

● ADV. **absolutely**, **quite** | **nearly**, **pretty well**, **virtually** *The system is pretty well foolproof.*

foot noun

1 part of the body

● ADJ. **left**, **right** | **back**, **front** *He shifted his weight onto his back foot.* | **dainty (little)**, **small** | **big**, **enormous** | **narrow**, **wide** | **flat** *He was excused military service because of his flat feet.* | **bare** *It's dangerous to walk on the beach in/with bare feet.* | **blistered**, **swollen** | **dirty**, **smelly**, **unwashed** | **booted**, **stockinged** *the rumble of many booted feet on the bridge* ◇ *He padded across the room in his stockinged feet* (= wearing socks but no shoes). | **webbed** *Ducks' webbed feet help them to swim.* | **silent** *He slipped across the corridor on silent feet.* | **leaden** (*figurative*) *He walked towards the examination room with leaden feet* (= slowly). | **winged** (*figurative*) *She flew on winged feet* (= fast) *up the narrow stair.*

● VERB + FOOT **get to**, **jump to**, **leap to**, **rise to**, **scramble to** *He got shakily to his feet.* | **be on** *I've been on my feet all day and I need to sit down for a rest.* | **plant**, **put** *I planted my feet firmly on the chair and reached up to the top window.* ◇ *She put her foot down on the accelerator and the car lurched forward.* | **raise** *He raised his foot off the accelerator pedal.* | **stamp** | **swing** *He swung a foot at the ball but missed completely.* | **shuffle** | **drag** *She dragged her* feet as she reluctantly followed her parents. | **wipe** Wipe your feet when you come in from the street. | **tread on** That man trod on my foot and he didn't even apologize.

● FOOT + VERB **catch** His foot caught in the cable and he fell under the train. | **slip** My foot slipped as I was about to shoot and I missed the ball. | **crunch, patter, pound, shuffle** I heard feet crunching over the gravel outside the house. | **dangle** I sat by the river with my feet dangling in the water. | **kick** They carried him out of the room with his feet kicking. | **sink** My feet sank deep into the mud.

● FOOT + NOUN **massage** | **injury** | **passenger, soldier** Foot passengers were allowed to leave the ferry before the vehicles. | **patrol** soldiers on foot patrol

● PREP. **beneath/under your ~** The snow crunched beneath her feet. **from ~ to ~** They looked unsure and shifted uneasily from foot to foot. **on ~** The city is best explored on foot. **in the/your~** He's broken several bones in his left foot. **with the/your~** She kicked the ball with her right foot.

● PHRASES **the ball of the/your foot** I squatted down to speak to the boy, balancing on the balls of my feet. **from head to foot** She was dressed from head to foot in green velvet. **put your feet up** He likes to put his feet up and watch TV when he gets home. **set foot in/on sth** Cook claimed to be the first European to set foot in Australia. **the sole of the/your foot** The soles of my feet were covered in blisters.

2 measurement
⇨ Note at MEASURE

football noun

● ADJ. **adventurous, attractive, classy, creative, entertaining, exciting, fine, fluent, good, great, neat** | **one-touch** The Dutch team impressed the fans with their classy one-touch football. | **amateur, professional** | **junior** | **first-team** | **club, league** | **international, world** | **domestic** | **five-a-side** | **indoor** | **live** | **American, Aussie rules/Australian rules, Gaelic**

● QUANT. **game**

● VERB + FOOTBALL **play** | **watch** | **follow** Young Italians follow football like we follow the royal family.

● FOOTBALL + NOUN **club, league, squad, team** | **hero, player, star** | **field, ground, pitch, stadium** | **terraces** The government is trying to tackle violence on the football terraces. | **boots, kit, shirt, shorts, strip** | **agent, management, manager** | **authorities** The police say the players' behaviour is a matter for the football authorities. | **enthusiast, fan, follower, supporter** | **crowd** | **programme** | **championship, game, match, tournament** | **training** | **career** | **hooliganism, riot, violence** | **hooligan** | **chant** Obscene football chants stop people taking their children to matches. | **commentator, writer** | **action, coverage** Join Radio 5 for all the top football action. | **world** The football world was rocked by the scandal. | **culture** The World Cup is fascinating for its clash of football cultures.

⇨ Special page at SPORT

footballer noun

● ADJ. **brilliant, good, skilful, talented** | **famous** | **keen** | **amateur, professional** | **international**

● FOOTBALLER + VERB **play**

foothold noun

1 place to put your foot when climbing
● ADJ. **firm, secure**
● VERB + FOOTHOLD **have** | **find, get, scrabble for** He found a secure foothold and pulled himself up. ◇ scrabbling for a foothold on the steep grassy bank | **give sb** The bench gave me the foothold I needed to climb into the tree.

2 strong position for making further progress
● ADJ. **firm, secure** | **permanent** | **big** | **small**
● VERB + FOOTHOLD **have** | **establish, gain, get, obtain, secure** The company is trying to gain a foothold in

the European market. | **maintain** | **lose** | **regain** | **give (sb/sth), provide (sb with)** I hope the textbook will provide a foothold for students of the subject.

● PREP. **~ in** The firm has a firm foothold in this market.

footing noun

1 secure grip with your feet
● ADJ. **firm, sure**
● VERB + FOOTING **keep** He struggled to keep his footing on the slippery floor. | **be sure of** She looked over her shoulder to be sure of her footing. | **struggle for** | **lose, miss** | **give (sb), provide (sb with)** The sole of this shoe will give a firm footing even on slippery surfaces.

2 basis on which sth exists/operates
● ADJ. **firm, proper, right, secure, solid, sound** | **wrong** | **equal, the same** All claimants stand on an equal legal footing. | **different, unequal** | **normal** | **permanent** The arrangement was put on a permanent footing earlier this year. | **commercial, competitive, financial, legal** | **war** The army was placed on a war footing (= prepared for war).

● VERB + FOOTING **be on, stand on** The two teams stand on an equal footing. | **be back on** | **gain** Town planning procedures gained a footing in local government. | **get (sb/sth) off** on Being inconsiderate to the doctor will get you off on the wrong footing. | **get (sth) on, place sth on, set sth on** We need to get the business on a sound footing. | **get (sth) back on, put sth back on**

● PREP. **on a … ~** an attempt to put the economy on a more secure footing

footpath noun

● ADJ. **public** | **long-distance**
● VERB + FOOTPATH **follow, take, use** | **keep to**
● FOOTPATH + VERB **follow sth, lead, run** The footpath runs along the canal. | **cross sth** a footpath crossing farmland | **link sth** the footpath linking Sprotton and Lumm
● FOOTPATH + NOUN **network, system**
● PREP. **along a/the ~** We walked along the footpath. **by (a/the) ~** The monastery is an hour away by footpath. **down a/the~, on the~** We stood on the footpath and waited for a gap in the traffic. **up a/the ~** | **~ across, ~ along, ~ alongside, ~ from, ~ over, ~ through, ~ to** the footpath through the wood

footprint noun

● ADJ. **clear** | **fresh** | **muddy, wet**
● VERB + FOOTPRINT **leave, make** The intruder had left some clear footprints in the flower beds. ◇ Her wet boots made footprints on the dusty floor. | **find** The detective found fresh footprints in the mud next to the victim. | **follow** They had fled through the snow, and police had followed their footprints.

footstep noun (usually footsteps)

● ADJ. **heavy** | **light** | **dragging** He heard the sound of heavy, dragging footsteps in the corridor. | **measured, slow** | **brisk, hurried, hurrying, quick, rapid, running** | **loud** | **soft** | **uncertain** | **approaching** | **receding**

● VERB + FOOTSTEPS **hear, listen to** | **listen for** listening for her mother's footsteps | **retrace** I am retracing the footsteps of the lost expedition.

● FOOTSTEPS + VERB **run, walk** | **halt, stop** The footsteps halted in the doorway. | **approach, come** The footsteps came closer as she listened. | **recede** | **pass (on)** The footsteps passed on, receding down the corridor. | **descend the stairs** | **falter** | **die away, fade (away)** Her footsteps died away as she walked down the path. |

crunch, echo, pound, sound *Hurried footsteps sounded on the stairs.*
• PHRASES **the sound of (sb's) footsteps**

footwork *noun*

• ADJ. **deft, fancy, fine, good, neat, nimble**
• VERB + FOOTWORK **show** *She showed some nimble footwork and looked a promising player.*

forbid *verb*

• ADV. **strictly** *Smoking is strictly forbidden.* | **absolutely, totally, utterly** *You cannot do that. I absolutely forbid it.* | **expressly, specifically**
• PREP. **from** *He was forbidden from leaving the country.*

force *noun*

1 physical strength, power or violence
• ADJ. **considerable, great, terrible, tremendous | full, maximum | brute, sheer | reasonable | sufficient | excessive | unlawful | deadly, lethal | explosive | physical | gale** *The wind was increasing to gale force.*
• VERB + FORCE **resort to, use** *In the end, we had to resort to brute force to get the door open.* | **take sth by** *The troops marched in and took the city by force.* | **feel** *Even the opposition MPs felt the force of the prime minister's argument.*
• PREP. **by ~** *The king made laws and imposed them by force.*
• PHRASES **catch/experience/feel/meet/take the full force of sth** *Our shop took the full force of the bomb blast.* ◊ *I felt the full force of her criticism.* **meet force with force** *The country's attempts to meet force with force (= resist an attack using force) led to the outbreak of war.* **the use of force** *The regulations allow the use of force if necessary.*

2 effect that causes sth to move
• ADJ. **powerful, strong | weak | attractive | repulsive | balanced | external, internal** *Deep internal forces cause movements of the earth's crust.* | **lateral | centrifugal, centripetal, electromagnetic, electromotive, gravitational, mechanical, nuclear, tidal**
• VERB + FORCE **exert** *The sun exerts a force on the earth.* | **increase | decrease | balance** *The forces of expansion are balanced by forces of contraction.*
• FORCE + VERB **balance sth**
• FORCE + NOUN **field** *the force field of a magnet* ◊ *(figurative) It was as if an invisible force field kept us apart.*
• PREP. **~ between** *the attractive and repulsive forces between individual particles*
• PHRASES **a balance of forces** *the balance of nuclear forces in atoms* **the force of gravity**

3 authority of sth
• ADJ. **binding, legal, statutory** *The contract was not signed and has no binding force.*
• VERB + FORCE **come into** *The new law comes into force as from midnight tomorrow.* | **bring sth into**
• PREP. **in ~** *Some laws relating to obsolete customs are still in force.*
• PHRASES **the force of law** *Professional standards often do not have the force of law (= cannot be enforced).*

4 sb/sth with power/influence
• ADJ. **considerable, formidable, great, irresistible, major, overwhelming, potent, powerful, significant, strong | active, controlling, dominant, driving, moving | motivating | persuasive | constructive, creative, dynamic, positive, progressive | destructive, disruptive, negative, subversive** *She was seen as a potentially subversive force within the party.* | **cohesive, unifying | competitive, conflicting, countervailing, reactionary | internal | external, international, outside** *The play portrays a marriage torn apart by external forces.* | **natural** *powerful natural forces such as earthquakes and drought*

| **spiritual, supernatural | dark, demonic, evil, malevolent** *'There are dark forces in the universe,' he raved, 'and we are powerless against them!'* | **cultural, economic, intellectual, market, moral, political, productive, revolutionary, social** *powerful social and economic forces*
• VERB + FORCE **remain** *Though officially retired, she remains the creative force behind the design business.* | **balance** *This is a politician who does not like to balance market forces.*
• PREP. **~ behind** *Local parents were the driving force behind the project.* **~ for** *Competition is a force for change in industry.*
• PHRASES **a balance of forces** *shifts in the balance of political forces in Europe* **a force to be reckoned with** *With its new players, the team is now very much a force to be reckoned with.*

5 group of people trained for a particular purpose
• ADJ. **large | small, token** *a token force of only 300 men* | **100-strong, etc. | crack, elite, special** *These elite forces are the best equipped and trained in the world.* | **combined, joint** *the combined forces of MI5 and Scotland Yard* ◊ *a joint task force* | **allied, coalition, multinational | strategic | labour, sales** *a company's labour force* ◊ *the country's labour force* | **armed, military, paramilitary | government, loyal | enemy, guerrilla, hostile, occupying, opposition, rebel | regular | reserve | volunteer | conventional | nuclear | assault, defence, expeditionary, fighting, invasion, peace, peacekeeping, police, security, strike** (See also **task force**.) | **air, airborne, amphibious, ground, land, naval**
• VERB + FORCE **assemble, create, form, mobilize, set up** *A large expeditionary force is now being assembled.* | **send** *the decision to send armed forces over the border* | **deploy, use** *A small peacekeeping force will be deployed in the area.* | **withdraw | demobilize | command, head (up), lead | join** *She decided to join the armed forces.* | **combine, join** *The two companies have joined forces to form a new consortium.*
• FORCE + VERB **control sth** *Rebel forces now control most of the capital.*
• PREP. **in a/the ~** *people in the security forces*
• PHRASES **a member of a force, the withdrawal of a force** *a UN deadline for the withdrawal of forces*

foreboding *noun*

• ADJ. **deep, gloomy**
• VERB + FOREBODING **feel, have** *I felt a gloomy foreboding that something was going to go wrong.* | **be full of** *He returned, full of foreboding, to the scene of the accident.* | **fill sb with**
• PREP. **with (a) ~** *The sky was dull, with a foreboding of rain.* | **~ of** *She had a foreboding of danger.*
• PHRASES **a feeling/sense of foreboding**

forecast *noun*

• ADJ. **good, optimistic, promising | gloomy, pessimistic | conservative | accurate, correct | detailed | revised | annual | early | long-range, long-term** *a long-range weather forecast* | **short-term** *a short-term forecast of the UK economy* | **official | economic, financial, market, traffic, weather | cash-flow, cost, earnings, growth, profit, revenue, sales**
• VERB + FORECAST **prepare, produce | give, issue, make, provide** *The government has issued a pessimistic economic forecast.* | **revise, update | rely on | be in line with** *The interest rate is in line with the forecast.*
• FORECAST + VERB **predict sth, say sth, suggest sth** *Some forecasts suggest that the increase in heart disease will continue for some time.* | **assume sth | be based on sth** *forecasts based on a complicated procedure*
• PREP. **~ about** *Forecasts about the economy are often*

misleading. ~ **for** *forecasts for earnings* ◊ *forecasts for different sectors of the industry* ◊ *forecasts for the year*

forecast *verb*

- ADV. **accurately, correctly | originally** *higher costs than those originally forecast*
- VERB + FORECAST **be difficult to, be hard to**
- PHRASES **be widely forecast** *a result that was widely forecast*

forefront *noun* the forefront

- VERB + FOREFRONT **remain at/in** *Education remains at the forefront of the state's planning.* | **keep sb/sth at/in/to** | **come into/to** *She came to the forefront as governor after the political change.* | **bring sb/sth to, place sb/sth at/in/to, push sb/sth into/to, put sb/sth (back) at/in, take sb/sth into/to, thrust sb/sth into/to** *The new factory could put the town back at the forefront of steelmaking.*
- PREP. **at/in the ~ (of)** *issues at the forefront of government policy*
- PHRASES **at/in/to the forefront of sb's mind** *This question remained at the forefront of her mind.*

foreground *noun*

- VERB + FOREGROUND **occupy** *A happy family occupies the foreground of the painting.*
- PREP. **in the ~** *This issue is very much in the foreground.*

forehead *noun*

- ADJ. **broad, high, wide | domed | sloping | bald | furrowed, wrinkled | smooth**
- VERB + FOREHEAD **wrinkle | mop, wipe | hit, rub, slap, smack, tap** *He groaned and slapped his forehead, as if suddenly remembering something obvious.*
- PREP. **across your ~** *He rubbed a hand across his forehead as though he were tired.* **from your ~** *He wiped the sweat from his forehead.* **in the ~** *He went to bed complaining of a pain in the forehead.* **off your ~** *She pushed her wet hair off her forehead.* **over your ~** *His hair fell over his forehead.*

foreign *adj.*

1 not coming from your own country
- VERBS **be, look, sound** *The name sounded foreign.*
- ADV. **slightly** *a slightly foreign accent* | **distinctly** *He was a small man, distinctly foreign in appearance.*

2 foreign to sb not typical of sb/not known to sb
- VERBS **be, feel, seem**
- ADV. **very | completely, entirely, quite, totally, utterly** *This kind of behaviour is completely foreign to her.*

forerunner *noun*

- ADJ. **early, immediate** *an early forerunner of the modern jet engine* | **direct**

foresee *verb*

- ADV. **clearly | reasonably** *He could not reasonably have foreseen the consequences.*
- VERB + FORESEE **can/could** *We could foresee no difficulties with these proposals.* | **be difficult to, be impossible to** *It is impossible to foresee the future.*

foresight *noun*

- ADJ. **considerable, great**
- VERB + FORESIGHT **have** *He had had the foresight to bring in the washing before the rain started.* | **show** *The plans showed great foresight.* | **lack**
- PHRASES **a lack of foresight**

forest *noun*

- ADJ. **dense, thick | impenetrable | dark | native, natural | ancient, primeval, virgin | rain** (also **rainforest**), **tropical | coniferous, deciduous | beech, birch, pine,** etc.
- QUANT. **stretch, tract** *a large stretch of virgin forest*
- VERB + FOREST **plant | chop down, clear, cut down, destroy** *Forest is being cleared to make way for new farming land.* | **be covered by/in/with** *Much of Europe was once covered in forest.*
- FOREST + VERB **stretch** *Thick forest stretched as far as the eye could see.*
- FOREST + NOUN **tree | floor | land | fire**
- PREP. **in a/the ~** *They got lost in the forest.* **through a/the ~** *We slashed our way through the dense forest.*
- PHRASES **the edge/heart/middle of the forest**

forestry *noun*

- ADJ. **commercial, plantation | sustainable | tropical**
- FORESTRY + NOUN **plantation | practice | track | worker | industry, management | policy, programme, project, strategy | department**

forethought *noun*

- VERB + FORETHOUGHT **have** *We had had the forethought to book places in advance.*
- PREP. **with/without ~** *He had made the remark completely without forethought.*
- PHRASES **a lack of forethought**

forgery *noun*

⇨ Note at CRIME

forget *verb*

- ADV. **clean, completely, entirely, quite, totally** *I'm terribly sorry—I clean forgot to give your brother the message.* | **almost, nearly | never** *I'll never forget the expression on his face.* | **quickly, soon | instantly, promptly** *'I will,' she promised, and promptly forgot about it.* | **momentarily, temporarily** *Her joy was so infectious that he momentarily forgot his own fears for the future.* | **easily** *The experience of nearly getting killed is not easily forgotten.* | **conveniently** *(ironic)* *He conveniently forgot to tell me he was married.*
- VERB + FORGET **seem to** *You seem to forget that it was your idea in the first place.* | **tend to | want to | try to | be easy to** *It is easy to forget that not all countries have these advantages.* | **let sb** *Let's forget last night, shall we?* | **make sb**
- PREP. **about** *Oh yes! I almost forgot about the party.*
- PHRASES **forget all about sth** *In the excitement I forgot all about my little brother.* **forgive and forget** *It was all a long time ago and now Ellen found she could forgive and forget.* **keep forgetting** *She keeps forgetting where she's put her glasses.* **largely forgotten** *His pioneering work in the field was largely forgotten until the late 1940s.*

forgive *verb*

- ADV. **quite** *I suspect that Rodney has never quite forgiven either of them.* | **never | easily** *Donna would not easily forgive Beth's silly attempt to trick her.*
- VERB + FORGIVE **be able/unable to, can/could** *I couldn't forgive him.* | **be easy to** *An insult like that isn't easy to forgive.* | **ask sb, beg sb to** *He fell to his knees and begged God to forgive him.* | **try to**
- PREP. **for** *She never forgave him for losing her ring.*
- PHRASES **forgive and forget** *He was not the sort of man to forgive and forget.*

forgiveness *noun*

- ADJ. **complete**
- VERB + FORGIVENESS **find, have, receive** *Do I have your forgiveness?* | **ask (for), beg (for), pray for, seek** | **find** *victims of violence who can nevertheless find forgiveness in their hearts* | **offer (sb), show (sb)**
- PREP. **~for** *He begged her forgiveness for his mistake.*

forgo *verb*

- ADV. **willingly** *She would willingly forgo a birthday treat if only her warring parents would declare a truce.*
- VERB + FORGO **have to** *Time to prepare was a luxury he would have to forgo.* | **decide to** | **be prepared to, be willing to**

fork *noun*

1 tool for eating
- ADJ. **toasting**
- VERB + FORK **pick up** | **put down** | **use**
- PREP. **on a/the~** *She impaled a piece of meat on her fork.* **with a~** *Mash the mixture with a fork.*
- PHRASES **a knife and fork** *He put the knives and forks on the table.*

2 place where sth divides into two parts
- ADJ. **left/left-hand, right/right-hand**
- VERB + FORK **take** *As you pass the farm, take the right fork of the track up the hill.*
- PREP. **at a/the~** *Bear left at the fork in the road.* | **~in** *sitting in the fork of the tree*

forlorn *adj.*

- VERBS **be, feel, look, seem, sound, stand** *The house stood forlorn and empty.* | **become**
- ADV. **very** | **quite, utterly** *She didn't belong, and felt utterly forlorn.* | **almost** | **rather, somewhat**

form *noun*

1 type of sth/way of doing sth
- ADJ. **common** *Strikes are the most common form of industrial protest.* | **extreme** *an extreme form of socialism* | **pure** *In its purest form, the substance is highly explosive.* | **complex, simple** | **mild** | **virulent** *a virulent form of flu* | **early, final** *an early form of bicycle* ◇ *The document was edited before being circulated in its final form.* | **art, literary, musical** *Story-telling has acquired the status of an art form.* | **life** *primitive life forms at the bottom of the sea* | **digital, electronic** *The data is stored in digital form.* | **graphic, tabular** *The results of the survey are shown below in tabular form.* | **liquid**
- VERB + FORM **take** *Bullying can take many forms.*
- PREP. **in ... ~** *The gas is stored in liquid form.* **in the~of** *These costs were passed on to the tenants in the form of higher rents.* | **~of** *Swimming is one of the best forms of exercise.*
- PHRASES **in any shape or form** *The company will not tolerate discrimination in any shape or form.* **in some form or other** *We spend most of our time communicating in some form or other.*

2 shape
- ADJ. **human** *paintings of the human form* | **adult**
- VERB + FORM **alter, change** *a mythical creature that could change its form* | **assume, take on** *a god who could take on human form*
- PREP. **in a/the~** *Two weeks later the moth will emerge in its adult form.*

3 piece of paper with questions on it
- ADJ. **application, booking, entry, order**
- VERB + FORM **complete, fill in/out** *Please complete the application form and return it to us.* | **sign** | **return**

4 strength/fitness

- ADJ. **fine, good** | **poor** | **current, present**
- VERB + FORM **maintain** *The team is hoping that it can maintain its current form.*
- PREP. **in ~** *She was in fine form for the tournament.* ◇ *Barcelona are the team in form.* **off~** *Her recent illness possibly explains why she was off form in this race.* **on (sb's)~** *He'll be a difficult opponent to beat; he's really on form today.* ◇ *On his present form it seems likely that he will win the match.* **out of ~** *The team was out of form and did not play as well as expected.*

form *verb*

1 make/organize sth
- VERB + FORM **attempt to, try to** | **agree to, decide to** | **ask sb to, invite sb to** *The leader of the party with the most seats is invited to form a government.* | **help (to)**
- PHRASES **newly/recently formed** *a newly formed political party*

2 make sth into a shape
- PREP. **into** *She formed the clay into a ball.*
- PHRASES **fully formed** *The plan came in a flash of inspiration, fully formed.* **perfectly formed** *a perfectly formed body*

formal *adj.*

1 very correct/official
- VERBS **be, seem, sound** | **become**
- ADV. **extremely, very** | **strictly** *Learning was by rote and strictly formal.* | **almost** *The greeting was polite, almost formal.* | **fairly, quite, rather, relatively** | **oddly** *Her words sounded oddly formal.* | **stiffly** *His manner was stiffly formal.*

2 concerned with the way sth is done
- VERBS **be**
- ADV. **merely, purely** *Getting approval for the plan is a purely formal matter: nobody will seriously oppose it.* | **largely** *The monarch retains largely formal duties.*

formality *noun*

1 action that is necessary according to custom/law
- ADJ. **mere, simple** *Your acceptance into the club will be a mere formality.* | **customs, immigration, legal**
- VERB + FORMALITY **complete, deal with, go through** *It only took a few minutes to complete the legal formalities.* | **dispense with** *Let's dispense with the formalities and get down to work.*
- PHRASES **just/merely/only a formality** *She was clearly the best candidate for the job, so her interview was just a formality.*

2 polite formal behaviour
- ADJ. **cold, cool, icy, stiff**
- QUANT. **degree, level** *It is important to be aware of the level of formality required at any social function.*
- VERB + FORMALITY **maintain** *She preferred to maintain a cool formality in her dealings with her manager.*

format *noun*

- ADJ. **large, small** | **standard**
- VERB + FORMAT **change** *For this year, we have decided to change the format of the conference slightly.*
- PREP. **in a/the~** *The book is now available in a slightly smaller format.*

formation *noun*

1 making/developing sth
- ADJ. **policy** *the top civil servants who are responsible for policy formation*
- VERB + FORMATION **lead to, result in** *This dispute led to the formation of a new breakaway group.*

2 arrangement/group/pattern

● ADJ. **close, tight** | **battle** *The troops advanced in battle formation.* | **family, household, social** *changing patterns of marriage and family formation*
● FORMATION + NOUN **dancing, flying**
● PREP. **in a … ~** *The men were grouped in a close formation.* **in ~** *a squadron of planes flying in formation*

3 sth that has been formed
● ADJ. **cloud, geological, rock** | **military, political**

formidable *adj.*

● VERBS **be, look, seem, sound** *The task looks formidable.* | **remain** | **find sth** *Men found her formidable.*
● ADV. **really, truly, very** *a very formidable opponent* | **a bit, pretty, quite, rather, somewhat**

formula *noun*

1 group of signs/letters/numbers
● ADJ. **complex, complicated** | **simple** | **algebraic, chemical, mathematical, scientific**
● VERB + FORMULA **devise, work out** *A simple mathematical formula has been devised to allow you to calculate the interest due.* | **apply, use**
● PREP. **~ for** *Do you know the formula for finding the area of a circle?*

2 method of solving a problem
● ADJ. **good, magic, successful, winning** | **time-honoured, traditional** | **face-saving** *The government was forced to find a face-saving formula to cover its misjudgement.* | **peace** *No one has yet come up with a successful peace formula.* | **political**
● VERB + FORMULA **have** *No one has a magic formula for keeping youngsters away from crime.* | **come up with, devise, find, hit on, provide, work out** *We think we might have hit on a winning formula.*
● PREP. **~ for** *What is their formula for success?*

formulate *verb*

● ADV. **fully** | **carefully, properly** *His ideas are always very carefully formulated.* | **clearly, explicitly** | **consciously** *He claims that Marx never consciously formulated his own theoretical position.*
● VERB + FORMULATE **try to** | **help (to)**

fort *noun*

● ADJ. **hill** | **Iron Age, Roman, Saxon, etc.** *an Iron Age hill fort*
● VERB + FORT **attack, besiege** | **hold** *Government forces managed to hold the fort.*
● FORT + VERB **be/come under attack, be/come under siege** *The fort was under attack for three days.* | **fall** *The fort finally fell after a week of intense fighting.*
● PREP. **at/in a/the ~** *All was calm at the fort that night.*

forthcoming *adj.*

1 available
● VERBS **be** *Help was duly forthcoming.*
● ADV. **duly** | **readily** | **immediately**
2 willing to give information
● VERBS **be**
● ADV. **unusually** | **not very**
● PREP. **about** *She wasn't very forthcoming about where she'd been.*

forthright *adj.*

● VERBS **be, seem**
● ADV. **very** | **pretty** | **characteristically** *MacTavish was characteristically forthright in his reply.*
● PREP. **about** *She's always been very forthright about her preferences.*

fortified *adj.*

● VERBS **be**
● ADV. **heavily, strongly**
● PREP. **against** *The town was heavily fortified against attack.*

fortnight *noun*

● ADJ. **next** | **last, past, previous** | **whole**
● VERB + FORTNIGHT **spend** *We've spent the last fortnight in Spain.*
● FORTNIGHT + VERB **elapse, go by, pass** *A fortnight passed and we still hadn't heard from them.*
● PREP. **after a/the ~, during a/the ~, for a/the ~, in a/the ~** *We hope to leave in the next fortnight.* **over a/the ~, within a/the ~**

fortress *noun*

● ADJ. **great** | **formidable, impregnable, strong** | **grim**
● VERB + FORTRESS **attack, besiege, lay siege to** | **take** *Greek warriors took the fortress with little effort.* | **hold, occupy**
● FORTRESS + VERB **be/come under attack, be/come under siege** | **fall** *The fortress fell after a nine-day siege.*
● FORTRESS + NOUN **town**
● PREP. **in a/the ~** *They took refuge in the fortress.*

fortunate *adj.*

● VERBS **be, feel, seem** | **consider sb, count yourself, think sb** *We consider ourselves extremely fortunate.*
● ADV. **extremely, particularly, really, very** | **comparatively, quite, rather** | **indeed** *He was indeed fortunate in his friends.*
● PREP. **for** *It was fortunate for us that the rain stopped.* **in** *We are fortunate in having quite a lot of land.*

fortune *noun*

1 luck
● ADJ. **good** | **ill**
● QUANT. **piece, stroke** *By a stroke of good fortune, Steven was still in his office.*
● VERB + FORTUNE **have** | **bring (sb)** *A horseshoe nailed to your door is supposed to bring good fortune.*
● FORTUNE + VERB **be on sb's side, favour sb** *For once, fortune was on our side: the weather improved in time for the match.* **smile on sb** *Fortune smiled on me that day* (= I had good fortune).
● PHRASES **as good/ill fortune would have it** *As good fortune would have it, a bus came along just when I needed it.* **a change in/of fortune** *All we can do is hope for a change in fortune.* **have the good fortune to do sth** *I had the good fortune to work with people I liked.*

2 fortunes what happens to sb/sth
● ADJ. **declining, flagging** | **changing, fluctuating, mixed** *a year of mixed fortunes for the company* | **economic, electoral**
● VERB + FORTUNES **revive** *The party still hopes to revive its flagging electoral fortunes.* | **follow** *fans who follow the fortunes of their chosen team*
● FORTUNES + VERB **change, fluctuate** *A company's fortunes can change overnight.* | **improve, rise** | **decline, fall** *as the country's fortunes rose and fell*
● PHRASES **a reversal of fortunes** *The company suffered a great reversal of fortunes when public taste changed.*

3 what is going to happen to sb in the future
● VERB + FORTUNE **read, tell** *They went to have their fortunes read.*
● FORTUNE + NOUN **teller, telling**

4 very large amount of money
● ADJ. **considerable, enormous, great, immense, large, substantial, vast** | **small** (= quite large) *Rebuild-*

ing the house must have cost a small fortune. | **family, personal**

• VERB + FORTUNE **accumulate, acquire, amass, build (up), make, win | inherit | leave (sb)** *Her aunt died and left her a fortune.* | **lose, squander** *He lost his fortune in the stock market crash of 1929.* ◇ *squandering the family fortune* | **seek** *They went to seek their fortune abroad.* | **be worth** (*informal*) *Some of those old toys are worth a fortune now.* | **cost** (*informal*) | **pay, spend** (*both informal*) *She spends a fortune on clothes!*

• PREP. **~from** *He built his fortune from breeding horses.* **~in** *She made a fortune in the property boom.* **~on** *They sold their house at the right time and made a fortune on it.* **~out** *He has amassed a considerable fortune out of trading shares.*

• PHRASES **fame and fortune** *They went to America in search of fame and fortune.* **heir/heiress to a fortune** *He was sole heir to the family fortune.*

forum *noun*

1 way people can exchange ideas
• ADJ. **important, useful, valuable | public**
• VERB + FORUM **create, provide (sb with) | act as, be used as, serve as**
• PREP. **~for** *The conference provides a useful forum for the exchange of views and ideas.*

2 meeting at which people can exchange ideas
• ADJ. **open** *The film show was followed by an open forum on editing techniques.* | **international, national**
• VERB + FORUM **hold | attend, go to**
• FORUM + VERB **take place**
• PREP. **~on** *An international forum on economic development took place in Brussels.*

foster *verb*

• ADV. **carefully, deliberately** *The school has carefully fostered its progressive image.* | **energetically**
• VERB + FOSTER **help (to) | be designed to**

foul *noun*

• ADJ. **blatant, clear, deliberate, nasty**
• VERB + FOUL **commit** *He committed a second clear foul and was sent off.*
• PREP. **~on** *He was sent off for a blatant foul on Giggs.*

foul play *noun*

1 criminal activity
• VERB + FOUL PLAY **suspect | rule out** *The police have ruled out foul play in the case of his death.*

2 play that is against the rules
• ADJ. **deliberate, serious**
• VERB + FOUL PLAY **be guilty of** *He was clearly guilty of foul play and deserved to be sent off.*

foundation *noun*

1 organization that provides money for sth
• ADJ. **charitable, private**
• VERB + FOUNDATION **establish, set up** *a charitable foundation established in 1983*
• PREP. **~for** *a private foundation for sport and the arts*

2 foundations parts of a building below the ground
• ADJ. **deep | concrete**
• VERB + FOUNDATIONS **dig, lay** *digging trenches and laying concrete foundations* | **shake, undermine** *The thunder seemed to shake the very foundations of the building.* ◇ *They had dug too deep and undermined the foundations of the house.*
• FOUNDATION + NOUN **stone** *In 1853 Queen Victoria laid the foundation stone of the new palace.*

3 basis for sth

• ADJ. **excellent, firm, good, secure, solid, sound, strong | insecure, shaky, weak | ideological, intellectual, philosophical, political, theoretical | economic**
• VERB + FOUNDATION **build, lay, provide (sth with)** *This agreement laid a sound foundation for future cooperation between the two countries.* | **build on** *We now have a firm foundation to build on.* | **rest on** *The peace treaty rests on shaky foundations.* | **rock, shake, strike at, threaten, undermine** *an event which rocked the foundations of British politics*
• FOUNDATION + NOUN **course, year** *The Fine Arts degree starts with a foundation year.* | **subjects** *All students have to do the foundation subjects of maths and English.*
• PREP. **~for** *providing a solid foundation for this new democracy*
• PHRASES **rock/shake sth to its foundations** *The scandal rocked the legal establishment to its foundations.*

4 facts that show that sth is true
• VERB + FOUNDATION **have no** *malicious rumours which have no foundation*
• PREP. **without~** *Rumours of his resignation are entirely without foundation.*

founder *noun*

• ADJ. **original | joint** *a wife and husband who are joint founders of the company* | **company**
• FOUNDER + NOUN **member** *a founder member of the band*

fountain *noun*

• ADJ. **ornamental | drinking** *Children were queuing at the drinking fountain.*
• FOUNTAIN + VERB **play, splash** *A white marble fountain played in the middle of the square.*

fox *noun*

• ADJ. **urban | rural**
• VERB + FOX **hunt**
• FOX + VERB **bark** *I heard a fox bark in the dark.*
• FOX + NOUN **cub | hunt, hunting**

foyer *noun*

• ADJ. **entrance, reception | cinema, hospital, hotel, school, station, theatre | crowded, deserted**
• PREP. **across the~, in the~** *We arranged to meet up in the foyer of the Hyatt hotel.*

fraction *noun*

1 part/amount
• ADJ. **large, significant, sizeable, substantial | mere, small, tiny** *A mere fraction of available wind energy is currently utilized.*
• PREP. **~of** *Why not grow your own fruit at a fraction of the price?*
• PHRASES **just/only a fraction** *The average income is high, though many people earn just a fraction of that average.*

2 exact part of a number
• ADJ. **vulgar | decimal | improper** *11/8 is an improper fraction, equivalent to one and three-eighths.*
• VERB + FRACTION **express sth as** *Express 25% as a fraction.*

fracture *noun*

• ADJ. **fatigue, stress** *He suffered a stress fracture of the right foot.* | **hairline | compound, depressed, double, multiple, simple, spiral | hip, leg, skull, spinal, etc.**
• VERB + FRACTURE **suffer, sustain**

fragile *adj.*

- VERBS **be, feel, look, seem** | **remain**
- ADV. **exceedingly, extremely, very** | **a little, rather** | **ecologically** *the ecologically fragile mountain forests*

fragrance *noun*

- ADJ. **exquisite, fresh, pleasant, sweet** | **delicate, faint, gentle, light, soft, subtle** | **floral**
- VERB + FRAGRANCE **have** *This perfume has a light, fresh fragrance.* | **smell**
- FRAGRANCE + VERB **fill sth** *The fragrance of lavender filled the room.* | **be reminiscent of sth** *Geranium oil has a sweet fragrance reminiscent of roses.*
- PHRASES **full of fragrance** *fruits full of exquisite fragrance and flavour*

fragrant *adj.*

- VERBS **be, smell** | **become**
- ADV. **extremely, very, wonderfully** *a garden full of wonderfully fragrant flowers* | **mildly, slightly, subtly**
- PREP. **with** *The air was fragrant with lavender.*

frail *adj.*

- VERBS **be, look, seem** | **become, get, grow**
- ADV. **extremely, very** | **increasingly** | **rather** | **mentally, physically** *Many old people become mentally frail.*
- PHRASES **old and frail** *She looked old and frail.*

frailty *noun*

- ADJ. **increasing** *Despite increasing physical frailty, he continued to write stories.* | **human** *a figure of authority, but one all too prone to human frailties* | **mental, physical**

frame *noun*

1 of a door/picture/window
- ADJ. **door, window** | **photo, photograph, picture**
- PREP. **in a/the~** *pictures in gold frames*

2 shape of sb's body
- ADJ. **athletic, big, bony, large, lean, muscular, powerful, skinny, slender, slight, small, tall, wiry**
- VERB + FRAME **have** *She has quite a small frame.*
- PREP. **with a ... ~** *a man with a lean, athletic frame*

framework *noun*

- ADJ. **basic, broad, general** | **wider** *The needs of individual schools need to be considered in a wider framework.* | **existing** | **flexible** | **comprehensive** | **coherent** | **analytical, conceptual, theoretical** | **legal, political** | **administrative, management, policy** | **economic, financial** | **chronological, historical** *Carbon dating provides the archaeologist with a basic chronological framework.*
- VERB + FRAMEWORK **establish, have, set** *They established a basic framework of ground rules for discussions.* | **offer (sb), provide (sb with)**
- PREP. **outside a/the~** *Negotiations were also conducted outside the framework of the treaty talks proper.* **within a/the ~** *The committee will work within the framework of certain broad objectives.* | **~for** *a legal framework for the regulation of public access to databases*

franchise *noun*

1 right to vote in elections
- ADJ. **democratic** | **universal** *the fight for a universal franchise* | **limited, restricted** | **parliamentary**
- VERB + FRANCHISE **qualify for** *It was decided that all men in the armed forces should qualify for the franchise.* | **exercise** *He had to exercise the franchise on behalf of other council members.* | **enlarge, extend, widen** *After the Second World War the franchise was extended to all adults over eighteen.* | **restrict**

2 permission to sell a company's goods/services
- ADJ. **catering, fast food, rail, television, etc.**
- VERB + FRANCHISE **have, hold** *the company that holds the rail franchise for the south-east of the country* | **acquire, buy, win** *The company has just won a television franchise.* | **award (sb), give sb, grant sb** *The franchise was awarded to a French company.* | **auction, sell** *TV franchises will be auctioned to the highest bidder.* | **retain** | **lose** *The ITV licensee lost its franchise to Carlton TV.*
- FRANCHISE + NOUN **system** | **business, company, operation** | **holder** | **agreement** | **auction, bid** | **fee**
- PREP. **~for** *The diving school has acquired a franchise for scuba equipment.*
- PHRASES **on a franchise basis** *Catering in the schools is run on a franchise basis.*

frank *adj.*

- VERBS **be**
- ADV. **extremely, remarkably, very** | **absolutely, perfectly, quite** *Let me be perfectly frank with you.* | **fairly** | **delightfully, disarmingly, refreshingly** *She surveyed Sophie from top to toe in a disarmingly frank way.* | **brutally** *She was brutally frank in her assessment of our chances.* | **surprisingly**
- PREP. **about** *Macmillan was quite frank about his concerns.* **with** *To be frank with you, I don't really think you've got a chance.*
- PHRASES **full and frank** *a full and frank exchange of views*

frantic *adj.*

- VERBS **be, seem** | **become, get, go** | **drive sb** *The children have been driving me frantic all day!*
- ADV. **really** | **absolutely, quite** *He was quite frantic by the time we got home.* | **increasingly** | **almost**
- PREP. **with** *We were starting to get frantic with worry.*

fraud *noun*

- ADJ. **serious** | **massive** | **complex, sophisticated** | **attempted** | **alleged** | **computer** *A bank lost several million pounds through a sophisticated computer fraud.* | **electoral, financial, insurance, tax, etc.**
- FRAUD + NOUN **squad** *detectives from the fraud squad*
⇨ Note at CRIME (for verbs)

freak *noun*

1 strange/unusual event
- FREAK + NOUN **accident, result, storm, wave** *A driver was killed in a freak accident when a cow fell from a bridge.* ◇ *The manager described the 8–0 defeat as a freak result.*
- PREP. **~of** *This was no more than a freak of history.*
- PHRASES **by some freak of sth** *By some freak of fate, she won an enormous sum of money.*

2 person with a very strong interest in sth
- ADJ. **computer, fitness, health, speed** *For the real speed freak, there is a 2-litre, fuel-injection version of the car.* | **control** *Her dad seems to be a bit of a control freak, always keeping a close watch on what anybody's doing.*
- PHRASES **a bit of a freak**

3 sb who is considered to be strange
- VERB + FREAK **feel** | **regard sb as** *Other students regarded him as a freak.*
- PHRASES **a bit of a freak** *I felt a bit of a freak in my strange clothes.*

freckle *noun*

- ADJ. **brown, dark, golden, light, pale**

- VERB + FRECKLE **be covered with, have**
- PHRASES **a crop/sprinkling of freckles** *She had wonderful clear skin with an attractive sprinkling of freckles.*

free *verb*

- VERB + FREE **struggle to, try to** *She struggled to free herself from his grip.* | **manage to**
- PREP. **from** *They succeeded in freeing their friends from prison.* **of** *He had finally been freed of his responsibilities.*
- PHRASES **be freed on bail** *The court ruled that he should be freed on bail of $50 000.*

free *adj., adv.*

1 not controlled by rules
- VERBS **be, feel, seem | become | remain | leave sb** *The government wants to leave companies free to make their own decisions.*
- ADV. **completely, entirely, quite, totally** *The students are entirely free to choose their own courses.* | **fairly, reasonably, relatively**
- PREP. **from** *The organization wants to remain free from government control.*

2 not in prison; not restricted/trapped
- VERBS **be, roam** *animals roaming free across the plains* | **break, get, pull, walk** *The ship broke free from its moorings.* ◇ *They tied him up but he managed to get free.* ◇ *She managed to pull free of her attacker.* ◇ *She walked free from jail.* | **remain | cut sb/sth, let sb/sth, pull sb/sth, set sb/sth** *He was trapped by his leg, but his rescuers cut him free.* ◇ *They let their prisoner free.* ◇ *The birds were set free.*
- ADV. **completely, entirely, totally**

3 costing nothing
- VERBS **be, come** *This full-colour poster comes free with the magazine.*
- ADV. **absolutely, completely, entirely, totally**
- PHRASES **for free** *We might be able to get some plants for free.* **free of charge** *We will send you our booklet free of charge.*

4 free from/of sth without sth
- VERBS **be | become | remain, stay | keep sth** *We've managed to keep the garden free of weeds this year.*
- ADV. **completely, entirely, totally** *At last he's totally free from pain.* | **relatively**

5 not being used
- VERBS **be, look, seem | become | keep sth** *The hospital needs to keep some beds free for emergencies.*
- ADV. **completely**

6 not busy
- VERBS **be** *Are you free this afternoon?* | **keep sth** *We try and keep Sundays free.*
- ADV. **completely, entirely, totally | fairly, pretty, reasonably**

freedom *noun*

- ADJ. **complete, full, maximum, perfect, total | considerable, great** *The new syllabus allows students greater freedom of choice.* | **comparative, relative | basic, fundamental** *Living without war is a fundamental freedom.* | **individual, personal** *Individual freedom should be balanced against the rights of the community.* | **new-found** *When she lost her job, she at first relished her new-found freedom.* | **academic, artistic, creative, economic, intellectual, political, press, religious, sexual** *Without academic freedom, we cannot do any research.*
- QUANT. **measure** *Teachers can exercise a measure of freedom in their choice of materials.*
- VERB + FREEDOM **enjoy, have** *Publishers here enjoy comparative freedom to publish what they want.* | **enjoy, relish** *I was enjoying the freedom of not having to go to work.* | **exercise | achieve, gain, obtain, secure, win**

The women have won many new freedoms for themselves. | **maintain, retain | give up, lose, surrender** *As Mike saw it, marriage would mean giving up his freedom.* | **cost sb** *His inability to resist temptation would eventually cost him his freedom.* | **allow sb, give sb, permit sb | curtail, inhibit, reduce, restrict, threaten** *I don't want to curtail my daughter's freedom.* ◇ *Our freedom was threatened by press censorship.*
- PREP. **~ from** *freedom from fear and pain* **~ in** *Branch managers have considerable freedom in running their offices.* **~ of** *The Official Secrets Act was amended to allow greater freedom of information.*
- PHRASES **freedom of choice, freedom of expression/speech, freedom of movement, freedom of the press**

freelance *adj., adv.*

- VERBS **be, work** *He's been freelance for several years.* ◇ *She works freelance from home.* | **go, turn** *She decided to give in her notice and go freelance.* | **remain, stay**
- PHRASES **on a freelance basis** *She continued to work for the company on a freelance basis.*

freeze *noun*

1 period of weather with a temperature below 0°
- ADJ. **big** *The weather report advised us to prepare for a big freeze.*

2 putting a particular level on sth
- ADJ. **immediate | complete, total** *a total freeze on gas emissions* | **virtual | pay, price, wage**
- VERB + FREEZE **bring in, impose** *The government has imposed a price freeze on petrol.* | **announce, declare | lift** *It's too expensive to lift the freeze on pay.*
- PREP. **~ on** *a freeze on bus fares*

freeze *verb*

1 become ice/extremely cold
- ADV. **solid** *The pond had frozen solid.* | **over, up** *The lake has frozen over.* ◇ *The pipes have frozen up.*
- PHRASES **freeze to death** *Hundreds of homeless people could freeze to death this winter.*

2 preserve food
- ADV. **well** *Many vegetables freeze very well.*

3 stop moving
- ADV. **suddenly | for a moment/second, momentarily** *His smile froze for a moment.*
- VERB + FREEZE **seem to** *Suddenly, Ronny seemed to freeze.*
- PREP. **in/with** *She froze with horror when she saw the body.* **into** *Maggie's face had frozen into a cold mask.*
- PHRASES **freeze to the spot** *He was so surprised he froze to the spot.*

4 wages/prices
- ADV. **effectively** *Wages were effectively frozen for six months.*
- PREP. **at** *Prices have been frozen at this level for over a year now.*

freezer *noun*

- ADJ. **domestic | fridge | chest | deep**
- VERB + FREEZER **fill, stock | defrost**
- FREEZER + NOUN **cabinet, compartment | bag, container | centre** *They bought all their frozen food from the same freezer centre.* | **contents** *Your freezer contents can be insured against loss.*

freezing *adj.*

- VERBS **be, feel, look** *That water looks freezing.*

• ADV. **bloody** (*taboo*) | **absolutely** *It's absolutely freezing out there!*
• PHRASES **freezing cold** *It was a freezing cold day.*

freezing point *noun*

• VERB + FREEZING POINT **get to, reach**
• PREP. **above ~** *In the Antarctic, the temperature rarely rises above freezing point.* **at~** *the changes that take place at freezing point* **below ~** *The temperature dropped below freezing point this afternoon.*

freight *noun*

• ADJ. **heavy** | **air, rail, road**
• VERB + FREIGHT **carry, handle, haul, move, transfer, transport** *All vehicles carrying freight need a special licence.* ◇ *an agent handling freight and passengers* ◇ *The freight was transferred to a train at Rotterdam.*
• FREIGHT + NOUN **car, locomotive, train, transport, wagon** *The train's freight wagons can carry a fully-laden lorry.* | **traffic** | **depot, terminal, yard** | **carrier, company** | **business, industry** | **service** | **charges, costs**

French *noun*

⇨ Note at LANGUAGE

frenzy *noun*

• ADJ. **erotic** | **feeding** *The smell of blood sent the sharks into a feeding frenzy.*
• VERB + FRENZY **drive sb/sth into, send sb/sth into, throw sb/sth into, whip sb/sth (up) into, work sb/sth into** *He was so angry that he worked himself into a frenzy.*
• PREP. **in a/your~** *She tore the letter open in a frenzy.*
• PHRASES **a frenzy of activity, in a frenzy of excitement/rage/violence**

frequency *noun*

1 rate at which sth happens
• ADJ. **great** | **increased, increasing** | **relative** *The relative frequency of this illness in the area is of concern to all doctors.* | **alarming** *Bullets bounced off the rock with alarming frequency.*
• VERB + FREQUENCY **decrease in, increase in** *Crime increases in frequency in less settled neighbourhoods.* | **decrease, increase, reduce** *The drug can reduce the frequency and severity of attacks.*
• PREP. **with ~** *Accidents of this sort are happening with increasing frequency.*
2 of a wave
• ADJ. **high, low** | **ultrasonic** | **microwave, radio, television, vibration, wave** | **signal**
• FREQUENCY + NOUN **range** | **band**

frequent *adj.*

• VERBS **be, seem** | **become** *The attacks have become increasingly frequent.*
• ADV. **extremely, very** | **increasingly** | **fairly, quite, relatively** *She was a fairly frequent visitor to the house.*
• PREP. **among** *Coughs and colds are frequent among young children.*
• PHRASES **at frequent intervals** *She phoned home at frequent intervals.*

fresh *adj.*

• VERBS **be, look, smell, taste** | **stay** *Mushrooms don't stay fresh for long.* | **eat sth, have sth** *It's best to eat them fresh.* | **keep sth** *Put it in the fridge to keep it fresh.*
• ADV. **really, very** | **quite**
• PHRASES **lovely/nice (and) fresh** *There's some cold beef and a nice fresh loaf.*

friction *noun*

1 disagreement between people/groups
• ADJ. **considerable, serious** | **increasing** | **constant** *I'm exhausted from the constant friction between my boss and my colleagues.*
• VERB + FRICTION **cause, create, generate, lead to, produce** *His decision led to considerable friction in his family.* | **prevent**
• PREP. **~ between** *friction between neighbours* **~ with** *Her requests for time off created friction with her boss.*
• PHRASES **a cause/source of friction**
2 rubbing of one thing against another
• VERB + FRICTION **cause, generate, produce** *Rubbing the stones together produces friction.* | **reduce**

Friday *noun*

⇨ Note at DAY

fridge *noun*

• ADJ. **domestic**
• VERB + FRIDGE **raid** *The kids tend to raid the fridge when they get home from school.* | **fill, stock** *The fridge was stocked with food and drink.* | **defrost**
• FRIDGE + NOUN **freezer** | **door**

friend *noun*

• ADJ. **best, bosom, close, dear, good, great, intimate, real, special** *Her best friend at school was called Anna.* ◇ *I'm inviting only my closest friends to the party.* | **faithful, loyal, true** | **lifelong, long-standing, old** *It was so relaxing to be among old friends.* | **female, male, woman** *He was last seen leaving a restaurant with a female friend.* | **fair-weather** *People he had trusted turned out to be only fair-weather friends* (= stopped being his friends when he was in trouble). | **mutual** *We met each other through a mutual friend.* | **family, personal** | **childhood, school** *Do you keep in touch with any school friends?*
• VERB + FRIEND **become** *They became friends after meeting on holiday.* | **remain, stay** *We stayed friends even after we grew up and left home.* | **find, make** *He finds it difficult to make friends.* ◇ *She's made friends with the little girl who lives next door.* | **win** *He won't win any friends if he carries on talking like that.* | **have** *She doesn't have many good friends.*
• PHRASES **a circle of friends** *He introduced me to his circle of friends.* **a friend of mine, yours, etc.** *I was given this necklace by a good friend of mine.*

friendless *adj.*

• VERBS **be, feel** | **leave sb** *With the departure of his remaining colleague he was left friendless.*
• ADV. **totally, utterly** | **virtually**

friendly *adj.*

1 behaving in a kind/pleasant way
• VERBS **appear, be, look, seem** | **become**
• ADV. **exceptionally, extremely, genuinely, really, very** *Frank was a genuinely friendly sort.* | **perfectly** *He seemed detached, almost bored, but perfectly friendly.* | **almost** *For once he seemed almost friendly.* | **quite, reasonably** | **not exactly, not particularly** *Her manner was not exactly friendly* | **naturally**
• PREP. **to, towards** *He was always friendly towards me.*
2 being friends
• VERBS **be, seem** | **become, get** | **remain**
• ADV. **very** | **pretty, quite** *They were quite friendly when they worked together.*
• PREP. **with** *She's very friendly with Maureen.*
• PHRASES **be on friendly terms (with sb)** *We have managed to remain on friendly terms.*

3 easy to use/helpful/not harmful
- VERBS **be**
- ADV. **environmentally** *environmentally friendly cleaning products*
- PHRASES **child-/family-friendly** *Employers are being encouraged to adopt family-friendly measures like flexible hours.* **ozone-friendly, user-friendly**

friendship *noun*

- ADJ. **beautiful, close, intimate, deep, firm, great, warm** *Their quarrel meant the end of a beautiful friendship.* ◇ *They formed a close friendship at university.* | **innocent** *Their affair had started out as an innocent friendship.* | **eternal, lasting, lifelong, long, long-standing** *They made vows of eternal friendship to each other.* ◇ *It was a period of her life when she made some lifelong friendships.*
- VERB + FRIENDSHIP **develop, establish, form, make, start up, strike up** *He finds it difficult to make lasting friendships.* ◇ *Jo struck up a friendship with a girl on her course.* | **cement** *We cemented our friendship with a meal and a few drinks.* | **cultivate** *He's keen on cultivating his friendship with the Edwards family.* | **promote** *The aim of the culture festival is to promote friendship between the two countries.* | **renew** *It will be a pleasure to renew our friendship.* | **destroy, spoil, wreck** *How can you let such a silly incident wreck your friendship?* | **betray** *He betrayed our friendship by revealing my secret to his cousin.*
- FRIENDSHIP + VERB **develop** *Friendships need time to develop.*
- PREP. **~ between** *He was jealous of the friendship between his wife and daughters.* **~ with** *Her mother did not approve of her friendship with Ahmed.*
- PHRASES **bonds/ties of friendship** *The ties of friendship between us will never be broken.* **the hand of friendship** *The president extended the hand of friendship towards the country's former enemy.* **a gesture of friendship** *In a gesture of friendship, the president invited his former enemies to a reception.* **an offer of friendship** *She offended them by turning down their offer of friendship.* **a spirit of friendship** *We hope the spirit of friendship and cooperation between our countries will remain strong.* **a token of your friendship** *Please accept this gift as a token of our friendship.*

fright *noun*

1 fear
- VERB + FRIGHT **take** | **be shaking/trembling with** | **die of** (*informal*) *He almost died of fright when the fish jumped out of the water.*
- PREP. **in ~** *She cried out in fright.* **with ~** *They were paralysed with fright.* | **~ at** *The birds took fright at the sight of the cat and flew off.*

2 sudden feeling of fear
- ADJ. **awful, bad, dreadful, nasty, terrible**
- VERB + FRIGHT **get, have** *Emma got such a fright that she dropped the tray.* ◇ *I had a terrible fright this morning when I saw you there.* | **give sb**
- PHRASES **a bit of a fright, the fright of your life** *You gave me the fright of my life, jumping out like that!* **quite a fright**

frighten *verb*

- ADV. **really** *The prospect of war really frightens me.* | **quite** | **almost** | **easily** *a man who doesn't frighten easily* (= become frightened easily)
- VERB + FRIGHTEN **want to** | **not mean to** *I didn't mean to frighten you.* | **try to**
- PHRASES **frighten sb out of their wits, frighten sb to death, frighten the life out of sb** (*all informal*) *Don't creep around like that! You frightened the life out of me!*

frightened *adj.*

- VERBS **be, feel, look, seem, sound** | **become, get** *I got quite frightened when he lost his temper.* | **remain**
- ADV. **badly, desperately, extremely, genuinely, really, terribly, very** | **thoroughly** | **almost** | **a bit, a little, pretty, quite, rather** | **suddenly** | **physically** *I felt frightened, physically frightened.*
- PREP. **about** *I was nervous and frightened about the future.* **at** *Simon was badly frightened at the result of his action.* **by** *Most of us are frightened by our emotions.* **of** *I'm rather frightened of dogs.*
- PHRASES **frightened out of your wits, frightened to death** (*both informal*) *She was frightened to death when she saw her small daughter on the edge of the cliff.*

frightening *adj.*

- VERBS **be, feel, look, seem, sound** | **become, get** *The situation was getting quite frightening.* | **make sth** *What can we do to make the experience less frightening?* | **find sth** *He found the responsibility rather frightening.*
- ADV. **extremely, genuinely, positively, really, truly, very** | **almost** | **a bit, fairly, a little, pretty, quite, rather**
- PREP. **for** *This is extremely frightening for elderly people.* **to** *It was all very frightening to a small boy.*

fringe *noun*

1 hair
- ADJ. **heavy, thick** | **light, wispy**
- VERB + FRINGE **grow** | **cut, trim** *My fringe needs trimming.* | **brush, push** *She kept brushing her fringe off her forehead.*
- PREP. **from beneath/under your ~** *She stared at us from beneath her fringe.* **in a ~** *She has her hair pulled forward in a fringe.*

2 outer edge of a place/group/society, etc.
- ADJ. **outer** | **marginal** | **eastern, western, etc.** | **coastal, urban** | **delinquent, lunatic** *the delinquent fringe of the Nationalist Party*
- VERB + FRINGE **keep to, remain on, stand on** *He has always remained on the fringes of mainstream politics.*
- FRINGE + NOUN **area** | **group** | **meeting** | **theatre, venue** *He moved from fringe theatre to mainstream when he was chosen to play a leading role on Broadway.*
- PREP. **along the ~** *the forests along the eastern fringe of the Andes* **around the ~** *new housing around the urban fringe* **at the ~** *They pitched their tents at the fringe of the open fields.* **beyond the ~** *Beyond this marginal fringe no agriculture is possible.* **on the ~(s)** *These people live on the fringes of society.*

frog *noun*

- FROG + VERB **hop, jump, leap, plop into sth** *The frog plopped into the pond.* | **croak**
- FROG + NOUN **spawn** (also **frogspawn**)

front *noun*

1 line/area where fighting takes place in a war
- ADJ. **eastern, western, etc.** *Thousands were killed on the eastern front.*
- VERB + FRONT **send sb to** *Even young teenagers were sent to the front.*
- PREP. **at the ~** *A new battalion arrived at the front.* **on the ~** *They had to fight on two fronts.*

2 way of behaving that hides your true feelings
- ADJ. **bold, brave**
- VERB + FRONT **put on** *She put on a brave front, but I knew how miserable she was.*
- PREP. **~ for** *Her aggressive behaviour is just a front for her shyness.*
- PHRASES **present a united front** *However much the*

directors disagree with each other, they always present a united front to the world.

frontier *noun*

1 border between countries
- ADJ. **common** *Neither country would guarantee the integrity of their common frontier.* | **eastern**, **northern**, etc. *There were very few border controls on the south-western frontier.* | **Franco-Spanish**, **Hispano-French**, **Spanish-French**, **French**, etc.
- VERB + FRONTIER **cross** *The army crossed the frontier in the middle of the night.* | **control**, **defend**, **guard** *The rebels control the frontier and the surrounding area.*
- FRONTIER + NOUN **controls**, **post** | **guard** | **area**, **province**, **region**, **town**, **zone** | **line**
- PREP. **across the** ~ *Many people travelling across the frontier were illegal immigrants.* **along the** ~ *an army grouping along the frontier* **at the** ~ *There was an army checkpoint at the frontier.* **on the** ~ *people living on the German frontier* **over the** ~ *They were forced to retreat back over the frontier.* | ~ **between** *the frontier between India and Pakistan* ~ **with** *France's frontier with Germany*

2 border between what we know and do not know
- ADJ. **final**, **new**
- VERB + FRONTIER **explore** *Space is the final frontier for us to explore.* | **advance**, **push back** *The scientists' work will push back the frontiers of physics.*

frost *noun*

1 weather condition
- ADJ. **bitter**, **great**, **hard**, **heavy**, **severe**, **sharp** | **light** | **early**, **first**, **late** *The young plants all died in the late frost.* | **autumn**, **spring**, **winter** | **ground** *a heavy ground frost* | **night**
- QUANT. **touch** *There was just a touch of frost in the air.* | **degree** *There were ten degrees of frost last night.*
- FROST + VERB **set in** *The winter frosts have set in up north.* | **nip at sth** *The sharp frost nipped at our noses.*

2 very thin layer of little pieces of ice
- ADJ. **bitter**
- VERB + FROST **be covered in/with** *The windows were covered in frost.*
- VERB + FROST **melt** *The car was wet with melting frost.*

frosty *adj.*

1 cold enough for frost
- VERBS **be**, **look** | **become**, **get**, **turn** *when the weather turns frosty* | **remain**, **stay**
- ADV. **very**
- PHRASES **cold and frosty** *The day dawned cold and frosty.*

2 unfriendly
- VERBS **be**, **look**, **seem** | **become**, **turn** *He cool green eyes became positively frosty.* | **remain**
- ADV. **decidedly**, **distinctly**, **positively**, **very** *The atmosphere in the room was decidedly frosty.* | **pretty**

frown *noun*

- ADJ. **deep**, **heavy** | **faint**, **quick**, **slight**, **small**, **tiny** | **puzzled**, **thoughtful**, **worried** | **angry**, **black**, **fierce**, **grim**, **warning** | **deepening**
- VERB + FROWN **give** *The boy gave a small frown.* | **wear** *She wore a worried frown.* | **crease into**, **pucker into**, **wrinkle in** *Her face creased into a frown.* | **be drawn/draw together in** *His brows drew together in a frown.*
- FROWN + VERB **deepen**, **grow darker/deeper** *Her frown grew deeper at the memory.* | **crease sth** *Her frown creased her forehead.* | **mar sth** *A frown marred his hand-*

some features. | **cross sth**, **touch sth** *A frown crossed her brow.*
- FROWN + NOUN **line**
- PREP. **with a** ~ | ~ **of** *a frown of concentration/disapproval/puzzlement*
- PHRASES **a frown in your eyes** *He looked at her with a puzzled frown in his eyes.* **a frown on your face**

frown *verb*

- ADV. **darkly**, **deeply**, **heavily**, **sharply** | **slightly** | **impatiently** | **thoughtfully** *She studied the letter, frowning thoughtfully.*
- PREP. **at** *She turned and frowned at him.* **in** *He looked at the coded message, frowning in concentration.* **with** *He frowned with annoyance.*

fruit *noun*

1 part of a plant
- ADJ. **fresh** | **ripe**, **unripe** | **rotten** | **candied**, **crystallized**, **dried** | **canned**, **tinned** | **exotic**, **tropical** | **citrus** *citrus fruits such as limes and lemons*
- QUANT. **piece** *Finish the meal with a piece of fresh fruit.*
- VERB + FRUIT **eat**, **have** | **bear** *The crab apple bears a small, bitter fruit.* | **pick** | **core**, **peel**, **prepare**
- FRUIT + NOUN **tree** | **juice**, **salad**

2 the fruits good result/reward
- VERB + FRUITS **enjoy** *Their work left them enough time to enjoy the fruits of their success.* | **reap** *He was now reaping the fruits of all his hard work.*
- PHRASES **the first fruits of sth** *the first fruits of the government's health campaign*
- ⇨ Special page on page 332.

fruitful *adj.*

- VERBS **be**, **prove**
- ADV. **enormously**, **extremely**, **remarkably**, **very** | **quite**, **reasonably** | **potentially**
- PREP. **in** *This research has been enormously fruitful in helping our understanding of the disease.*

fruition *noun*

- ADJ. **full**
- VERB + FRUITION **come to**, **reach** *Their efforts came to fruition many years later.* | **bring sth to** *It was left to her successor to bring the plan to its full fruition.*

fruitless *adj.*

- VERBS **be**, **prove**, **seem** | **render sth** *Dunbar's departure rendered the whole operation quite fruitless.*
- ADV. **quite**, **utterly** | **largely** | **apparently**

frustrated *adj.*

- VERBS **appear**, **be**, **feel**, **look**, **seem**, **sound** | **become**, **get** *starting to get frustrated* | **leave sb**, **make sb** *This failure leaves the child depressed and frustrated.*
- ADV. **deeply**, **extremely**, **really**, **very** | **completely**, **totally** | **increasingly** | **a bit**, **a little**, **quite**, **rather**, **slightly** *She sounded rather frustrated to me.* | **sexually**
- PREP. **at** *Both sides in the dispute appeared very frustrated at the lack of progress.* **by** *We were frustrated by the long delays.* **with** *Sometimes he gets really frustrated with his violin playing.*

frustrating *adj.*

- VERBS **be**, **prove** | **become**, **get** | **make sth** | **find sth** *I found the delays intensely frustrating.*
- ADV. **deeply**, **extremely**, **incredibly**, **intensely**, **particularly**, **really**, **terribly**, **very** | **increasingly** | **a bit**,

FRUIT

growing

Pineapples **grow** in tropical climates.

We have been **growing** redcurrants for many years.

Blackberries **ripen** in the autumn.

We haven't **had** any pears yet this year.

This tree **produces** very sweet plums.

She **picked** a ripe apricot and started to eat it.

Growers are expecting a bumper apple **harvest** this year.

a bumper apple **crop/crop of** apples

He's a peach **grower**.

a bumper crop of apples

plants

- apple, cherry, lemon, lime, mango, mulberry, olive, orange, peach, pear, plum **trees**
- blackcurrant, bramble, gooseberry **bushes**
- banana, strawberry **plants**
- grape **vines**
- raspberry **canes**

seeds

- apple, orange **pips**
- cherry, peach, plum **stones**
- melon **seeds**
- apple **cores**

flowers

- apple, cherry, lemon, orange **blossom**
- banana, lemon, melon **flowers**

plantations

- apple, cherry **orchards**
- citrus, lemon, olive, orange **groves**
- banana **plantations**

skin

- citrus, grapefruit, lemon, orange **peel**
- banana **skin**

---

quite, rather, slightly | ultimately *It was a demeaning and ultimately frustrating experience.*
- PREP. **for** *It was rather frustrating for all of us.*

frustration noun

- ADJ. **considerable, great** | **sheer** *I shouted at him in sheer frustration.* | **angry, bitter** | **pent-up** | **sexual**
- VERB + FRUSTRATION **experience, feel, seethe with** *He was still seething with angry frustration.* | **express,**

show, take out, vent *He took his pent-up frustration out on his family.* | **hide** | **cause, lead to** *These petty rules can lead to frustration and anger.*
- PREP. **in ~** *He clenched his fists in frustration.* **out of ~** *crying out of bitter frustration* **through ~** *Several people resigned through frustration.* **with ~** *weeping with frustration* | **~ at** *Many have expressed frustration at the delays.* **~ over** *showing frustration over the lack of progress* **~ with** *their frustration with bureaucracy*

● PHRASES **a feeling/sense of frustration, tears of frustration** *There were tears of frustration in her eyes.*

fry *verb*

● ADV. **gently, lightly**
● PREP. **in** *Fry the vegetables gently in oil.*

fuel *noun*

● ADJ. **clean, smokeless, unleaded | fossil, nuclear, solid | domestic, household | aviation | spent** *The plant reprocesses spent fuel from nuclear power stations.*
● VERB + FUEL **burn, run on, use** *power stations which burn fossil fuels ◇ What sort of fuel does the car run on? |* **burn sth as, use sth as** *The power plant burns used vehicle tyres as fuel. |* **save, waste | process, reprocess**
● FUEL + NOUN **bill, costs, prices | consumption** *a car with high fuel consumption |* **economy, efficiency** *The engine gives good fuel economy. |* **pump, tank**

fugitive *noun*

● ADJ. **hunted, wanted** *one of the most wanted fugitives sought by the Italian police*
● PREP. **~ from** *a sanctuary where fugitives from justice could shelter*

fulfil *verb*

● ADV. **amply, really** *He amply fulfilled the weight of expectation that they had placed on him. |* **completely | not quite** *Turkey is a market that has never quite fulfilled its potential. |* **adequately | properly | effectively | successfully | admirably** *The building is still fulfilling its original purpose admirably. |* **finally, ultimately**
● VERB + FULFIL **be able/unable to, can/could** *Alan was finally able to fulfil his promise to Sarah. |* **must** *Students must fulfil the following entry criteria. |* **seek to, try to | fail to**

fulfilment *noun*

1 doing sth to the required standard
● ADJ. **proper** *the proper fulfilment of their duties*
2 feeling of satisfaction
● ADJ. **great** *She needed greater fulfilment in her job. |* **complete, perfect | partial | personal** *her search for personal fulfilment |* **intellectual, physical, sexual | wish** *Most computer games provide some kind of wish fulfilment.*
● VERB + FULFILMENT **derive, find, gain, obtain | provide (sb with)**
● PREP. **~ from** *He derives a lot of fulfilment from his charity work. ~* **in** *I can't find fulfilment in doing housework.*
● PHRASES **a desire/need for fulfilment, a sense of fulfilment** *They gain a sense of fulfilment from their work.*

full *adj.*

1 holding/containing as much as it will hold
● VERBS **be, look, seem | become, get** *The garage has got full of junk again. |* **leave sth** *He left the bath full of water.*
● ADV. **absolutely, completely** *The kitchen was absolutely full of flies! |* **almost, nearly, virtually** *The reservoirs are all virtually full. |* **half**
● PREP. **of** *The bottle was half full of mineral water.*
2 containing a lot of sth
● VERBS **be, look, seem**
● ADV. **extremely, very | fairly, pretty, quite** *Her wine glass was still quite full.*
3 having had enough to eat or drink
● VERBS **be, feel**
● ADV. **absolutely | rather**
● PHRASES **full up** *I'm full up. I can't eat another thing.*

fume *verb*

● ADV. **inwardly, quietly**
● PREP. **about/over** *She was still quietly fuming about Peter's remarks.* **at** *We were all fuming at the delay.*
● PHRASES **be left fuming** *Motorists were left fuming as police closed the motorway for six hours.* **sit/stand (there) fuming** *He sat fuming over what he had just learnt.*

fumes *noun*

● ADJ. **acrid, choking, dangerous, noxious, poisonous, toxic | diesel, exhaust, petrol, traffic | cooking | petrol, solvent | carbon monoxide, sulphurous, etc.**
● QUANT. **cloud** *Clouds of toxic fumes escaped from the chemical plant.*
● VERB + FUMES **give off, produce** *The fire gave off choking fumes. ◇ an industrial process which produces toxic fumes |* **breathe (in), inhale**
● FUMES + VERB **kill sb, overcome sb** *A firefighter was overcome by fumes at a blaze in a plastics factory. |* **escape** *Sometimes exhaust fumes escape into the vehicle.*

fun *noun*

● ADJ. **enormous, excellent, good, great, terrific, tremendous, wonderful | harmless, innocent** *The boys' game started as harmless fun but ended in tragedy.*
● VERB + FUN **have** *We had a lot of fun at Mick's party. |* **spoil** *We won't let a bit of rain spoil our fun.*
● FUN + NOUN **day** *She organized an annual fun day for local children.*
● PREP. **for ~** *I write for fun, not because I expect to make money.* **in ~** *She only said that in fun—please don't take it seriously!*
● PHRASES **be no fun** *It's no fun getting up at 4 a.m. on a cold, rainy morning.* **a bit of fun** *I was only having a bit of fun.* **just for fun, just for the fun of it** *They took up motor racing just for the fun of it, rather than to win anything.* **a sense of fun** *You have to have a sense of fun to be a good teacher.*

function *noun*

1 purpose/special duty of sb/sth
● ADJ. **crucial, essential, important, useful, valuable, vital | chief, main, major, primary, prime | dual** *The committee has a dual function, both advisory and regulatory. |* **bodily, brain, liver, mental, etc.** *Fortunately, his head injuries left his bodily functions unimpaired.*
● VERB + FUNCTION **have | carry out, fulfil, perform, serve** *All members carry out their own particular functions. ◇ The club serves a useful function as a meeting place.*
2 important social event
● ADJ. **charity, official, social** *The princess attended a charity function in aid of cancer research.*
● VERB + FUNCTION **hold | attend, go to**
● FUNCTION + NOUN **room** *The wedding reception will be held in the Swan Hotel's function room.*

function *verb*

● ADV. **effectively, efficiently, smoothly, successfully, well | perfectly | correctly, normally, properly** *All the instruments were functioning normally. |* **adequately, satisfactorily** *Problems arise when the body's immune system is not functioning adequately. |* **independently** *Can we devise a system in which judges function independently of party politics? |* **actually** *This model does not describe accurately the way a market economy actually functions. |* **still** *The bombs continued to fall, but somehow the city still functioned.*
● VERB + FUNCTION **be able/unable to, can/could** *When nutrients are in short supply the body cannot function properly. |* **begin to | continue to | cease to**

● PHRASES **fully functioning** *The group has now become a fully functioning political organization.*

fund *noun*

1 sum of money collected for a particular purpose

● ADJ. **large | appeal, charitable, charity** *The newspaper launched an appeal fund for victims of the disaster.* | **benevolent, campaign, investment, memorial, pension, prize, social, trust** *a benevolent fund for retired actors*

● VERB + FUND **create, establish, launch, set up, start** *They set up an investment fund to provide money for their retirement.* | **administer, manage | draw on** *They don't want to draw on the fund unless they have to.*

● PREP. **in a/the ~** *There is currently over £200 000 in the fund.* | **into a/the ~** *The money received is paid directly into a pension fund.*

● FUND + NOUN **holder, manager**

2 funds money that is available and can be spent

● ADJ. **sufficient | insufficient | limited** *There are only limited funds available.* | **unlimited | surplus | available | government, private, public**

● VERB + FUNDS **have** *We have insufficient funds to pay for the building work.* | **be out of, be short of** *We are short of funds at the moment, so we are not going on holiday.* | **appeal for** *The school is appealing for funds to invest in new equipment.* | **borrow, boost, build up, collect, generate, get, obtain, raise, receive, secure | allocate, lend, make available, provide, release** *Funds will be made available to ensure the provision of hospital services.* | **channel, direct, use** *The government is to channel more funds into local development schemes.*

● FUND + NOUN **raiser** (also **fund-raiser**), **raising** (also **fund-raising**)

● PREP. **~ for** *a charity event to raise funds for local schools* **~ from** *Funds from the event will support the work of the hospice.*

● PHRASES **access to funds** *The current account offers savers instant access to funds.* **a flow of funds** *the flow of funds between various economic sectors* **a lack/shortage of funds** *The project was hampered by lack of funds.*
⇨ Special page at BUSINESS

fund *verb*

● ADV. **largely, mainly | entirely** *The venture is funded entirely by its board of directors.* | **partially, partly | generously, properly, well | fully** *a new, fully funded training scheme* | **adequately | inadequately, poorly | centrally, directly** *The school opted out of local authority control and is funded directly by the government.* | **publicly | externally, independently, privately | jointly** *a scheme jointly funded by central and local government*

● VERB + FUND **be used to, help (to)** *This money will help to fund administration costs.* | **agree to | refuse to**

fundamental *adj.*

● VERBS **be, seem | remain | consider sth, regard sth as** *We consider these freedoms fundamental to democracy.*
● ADV. **truly, very | absolutely, quite** *This principle is clear and absolutely fundamental.* | **fairly, rather**
● PREP. **to** *Improved funding is fundamental to the success of the project.*

fundamentals *noun*

● ADJ. **basic | very** *The new law strikes at the very fundamentals of a free press.*
● VERB + FUNDAMENTALS **teach | grasp, learn, master** *We quickly mastered the basic fundamentals of navigation.* | **go back to, return to** *The government went back to fundamentals, concentrating on avoiding food shortages.*

funding *noun*

● ADJ. **adequate, proper | generous, substantial | inadequate | additional, extra, further | direct | long-term | annual, three-year, etc.** *the airline industry's annual funding requirement* | **emergency, short-term, stop-gap | official | clandestine, illegal, secret** *the clandestine funding of an illegal group* | **core | central | internal | external, outside** *Half the university research posts depend on outside funding.* | **international, local, national | foreign | government, public/public-sector, state | private/private-sector | corporate | development, education, research, science, venture, etc. | hospital, library, university, etc.**

● VERB + FUNDING **give sb/sth, grant sb/sth, provide (sb/sth with)** *The refusal to grant extra funding to schools in the poorest areas caused a political storm.* | **attract, secure, seek, win | get, obtain, receive | increase | cut, reduce | withdraw, withhold**

● PREP. **... in/of ~** *£25 million in funding* | **~ for** *The president called for greater funding for housing for the poor.* **~ from** *The school has attracted funding from a number of sources.* **~ to** *an increase in funding to drug rehabilitation clinics*

● PHRASES **a cut/an increase in funding, a lack of funding, a level of funding** *Present levels of funding have forced the school to cut its teaching staff.* **a means/source of funding**

funeral *noun*

● ADJ. **church | family | simple | state | respectable** *His savings were just enough to pay for a respectable funeral.* | **mass** *a mass funeral of the victims of the fire*

● VERB + FUNERAL **attend, come to, go to | arrange** *The dead man's son arranged the funeral.* | **conduct** *A clergyman friend of the family conducted the funeral.* | **have** *She had a simple funeral, as she had requested.*

● FUNERAL + VERB **take place**

● FUNERAL + NOUN **ceremony, mass, rites, service | oration, sermon | cortège, procession | gathering** *Everyone went back to the house after the service for the funeral gathering.* | **car | director | home, parlour | costs, expenses | arrangements | business, industry | pyre** *the flames of the funeral pyre*

● PREP. **at a/the ~** *He gave the address at her funeral.*

funny *adj.*

1 making you laugh

● VERBS **be, look, seem | become, get** *The movie gets funnier towards the end.* | **find sth**

● ADV. **achingly, bloody** (*taboo*), **brilliantly, dead, extraordinarily, extremely, genuinely, hilariously, hysterically, really, riotously, terribly, uproariously, very, wickedly, wildly, wonderfully** *At last, a genuinely funny comedy show!* ◇ *His performance was hilariously funny.* ◇ *You should have seen it—it was terribly funny!* | **almost | pretty, quite | unintentionally**

2 strange

● VERBS **be, feel, look, seem, smell, sound, strike sb as, taste** *Didn't it strike you as funny that Adam wasn't there?* ◇ *This wine tastes funny.* | **find sth** *Don't you find it a bit funny that she never mentions her husband?*

● ADV. **extremely, really, very | a bit, a little, pretty, rather** *Helen gave me a rather funny look.*

● PHRASES **funny little** *He's a funny little man.* **funny old** *It's a funny old world, isn't it?*

fur *noun*

● ADJ. **thick | soft | real | artificial, fake, imitation, synthetic | matted** *The cat's fur was matted with blood.* | **fox, rabbit, etc.**

● VERB + FUR **be wrapped in, wear** *She was wearing*

her fur (= for example, a fur coat). | **be lined with, be trimmed with** *a cloak lined with fur*
• FUR + NOUN **trade | farm**
• PREP. **in a/sb's ~** (= wearing a fur coat, etc.) *elegant women in furs* **of ~** *a collar of fur*

furious *adj.*

• VERBS **be, feel, look, seem, sound | become, get | make sb** *Their incompetence made me furious.*
• ADV. **absolutely | simply | coldly | suddenly**
• PREP. **about** *He was simply furious about what had happened to his mother.* **at** *The prime minister is said to be furious at the newspaper report.* **over** *She was still furious over suggestions that she had lied to the public.* **with** *I got absolutely furious with him.*

furnace *noun*

• ADJ. **blazing, fiery, hot, red-hot | electric, gas | glass, steel | blast**
• VERB + FURNACE **fire** *enough coal to fire the furnaces*
• FURNACE + VERB **burn, glow** *The furnaces glowed fiercely.* | **roar** *A dark shed, lit only by the glow of roaring furnaces.*

furnished *adj.*

• VERBS **be**
• ADV. **fully** *The flat is fully furnished.* | **partially, partly | attractively, beautifully, charmingly, comfortably, elegantly, expensively, luxuriously, nicely, ornately, pleasantly, prettily, richly, sumptuously, tastefully, well** *His rooms were comfortably furnished.* ◇ *The villa was expensively furnished throughout.* | **basically, modestly, plainly, simply** *a simply furnished room* | **adequately | barely, sparsely | individually** *Each of the ten bedrooms is individually furnished.*

furniture *noun*

• ADJ. **antique, period** *an eighteenth-century town house, complete with period furniture* | **modern | fine** *The wood is used for making fine furniture.* | **cheap, second-hand | foam-filled, upholstered | bedroom, garden, office, outdoor | cane, pine, rattan, wooden, etc.**
• QUANT. **piece**
• VERB + FURNITURE **arrange, move around, rearrange** *The room would look bigger if we rearranged the furniture.*

furore *noun*

• ADJ. **considerable | public | political**
• VERB + FURORE **cause, create, provoke** *His choice of words created quite a furore.*
• FURORE + VERB **surround sth** *the furore which surrounded her appointment as chairman* | **follow, result from sth | die down**
• PREP. **amid a/the ~ (of)** *His resignation passed almost unnoticed amid the furore of the elections.* | **~ about/over/surrounding** *the furore over the proposed introduction of tax on fuel* **~ among** *The sale of the two best players caused a furore among the fans.*

furtive *adj.*

• VERBS **be, feel, look, seem, sound | become** *The look in his eyes became furtive.*
• ADV. **very | almost** *The secretary looked almost furtive when I walked in.* | **slightly | oddly** *He cast an oddly furtive glance at her.*

fury *noun*

• ADJ. **cold | controlled, inner, pent-up** *He growled with barely controlled fury.*
• VERB + FURY **be beside yourself with, be shaking with, feel** *He was beside himself with fury.* ◇ *I had never felt such fury before.* | **vent** *He vented his fury on a telephone box.* | **arouse, drive sb to, provoke** *That kind of treatment would drive anyone to fury.* ◇ *The decision to close the factory has provoked fury.*
• FURY + VERB **mount, rise | drain, fade** *His face and body sagged as the fury drained from him.*
• PREP. **in (a) ~** *She turned on him in a fury.* **with ~** *He reacted with cold fury.* | **~ against** *Her fury against him rose.* **~ at** *He kicked the tree in fury at his own stupidity.*
• PHRASES **turn your fury on sb** *I hoped she wouldn't turn her fury on me.*

fuse *noun*

1 device that makes a bomb explode
• ADJ. **short | long, slow | safety**
• VERB + FUSE **set** *He set the fuse to thirty minutes.* | **light**

2 in an electric circuit
• ADJ. **5-amp, 10-amp, 13-amp, etc.**
• VERB + FUSE **fit** *Make sure that the correct fuse is fitted.* | **change, replace | blow** *When the machine was switched on it blew a fuse.*
• FUSE + VERB **blow** *Fuses blow if they are overloaded.*
• FUSE + NOUN **wire | box** *The fire started in the fuse box downstairs.*

fuss *noun*

• ADJ. **awful, big, great, terrible**
• VERB + FUSS **cause, kick up, make** *She kicked up an awful fuss when she heard about it.*
• FUSS + VERB **blow over, die down** *Once the fuss has blown over, we'll be able to get on with work as usual.*
• PREP. **without ~** *They left quietly, without fuss.* | **~ about** *She made a big fuss about not having a window seat on the plane.* **~ over** *I think it's all a lot of fuss over nothing.*
• PHRASES **make a fuss of sb** *The children were all making a great fuss of the new baby.* **with the minimum of fuss** *The job was done with the minimum of fuss.*

futile *adj.*

• VERBS **be, prove, seem | consider sth, describe sth as** *The president described these activities as futile.*
• ADV. **absolutely, completely, quite, totally, utterly** *an utterly futile struggle for justice* | **largely, rather | apparently, seemingly | ultimately** *Their attempts were impressive but ultimately futile.*

futility *noun*

• ADJ. **complete, utter**
• VERB + FUTILITY **know, realize, see, sense** *She could see the utter futility of trying to protest.*
• PHRASES **a feeling/sense of futility**

future *noun*

1 time that will come after the present
• ADJ. **foreseeable, immediate, near, not-too-distant** *Things will continue as they are for the foreseeable future.* ◇ *A new branch of the shop will be opening in the near future.* | **distant, remote**
• VERB + FUTURE **look to, plan for** *Don't think too much about past troubles—look to the future.* | **foretell, look into, predict**
• FUTURE + VERB **bring (sb), hold** *whatever the future may bring you* ◇ *Who can tell what the future holds?*

● PREP. **for the** ~ *What are your plans for the future?* **in (the)** ~ *In future, employees will park their vehicles away from the works entrance.* ◇ *The possibility of travel to other solar systems still lies in the distant future.* **of the** ~ *The stars of the future are competing in the world junior athletics championships this month.*

● PHRASES **a vision for/of the future** *In her speech, the director outlined her vision for the future.*

2 what will happen to sb/sth

● ADJ. **bright, great, promising, rosy, secure** *He has a great future as a designer.* | **bleak, dire, gloomy, grim, uncertain** *He forecasts a dire future for the industry.* | **long-term** | **economic, financial, political**

● VERB + FUTURE **face, have** *The firm faces a very uncertain future.* | **determine, shape** *the right to determine their own future in a democratic fashion* | **forecast, predict, see** | **consider, ponder (on)** *After being dropped from the team the young defender is considering his future.*

| **invest in** *She decided to invest in her future by taking a management course.*

● PREP. **~ as** *She has a very promising future as a musician.* **~ in** *He could see no future in his job.*

● PHRASES **a question mark over the future of sb/sth** *A question mark hangs over the future of the company after shares plunged to a record low.*

fuzzy *adj.*

1 unclear

● VERBS **be, feel, look, seem, sound** | **become, go** *The screen suddenly went fuzzy.*

● ADV. **all, extremely, very** *The truck's headlights were all fuzzy and ghostlike.* | **a bit, rather, slightly**

2 sticking up

● VERBS **be** | **go**

● ADV. **all** *My hair's gone all fuzzy!* | **a bit, rather**

Gg

gadget *noun*

- ADJ. **little** | **clever**, **neat**, **nifty** | **useless** | **latest**, **modern**, **new** | **electrical**, **electronic** | **kitchen**
- VERB + GADGET **invent**
- PREP. **~for** *She has invented a nifty little gadget for undoing stubborn nuts and bolts.*

gag *noun*

1 piece of cloth
- VERB + GAG **put on** *They tied him up and put a gag on him.* | **take off**

2 joke
- ADJ. **good**, **great** | **sight**, **visual** *a mixture of wit and instant visual gags* | **running** *There was this running gag about a penguin* (= they kept telling penguin jokes).
- VERB + GAG **crack** *a non-stop comedian, cracking gags by the dozen*
- PREP. **~about**

gag *verb*

- PHRASES **bind and gag sb** *The men left the security guards bound and gagged.*

gain *noun*

- ADJ. **big**, **considerable**, **huge**, **major**, **real**, **significant**, **substantial** *This change in the tax system will mean big gains for some companies.* | **modest**, **small** | **long-term**, **short-term** | **potential** | **pre-tax** | **net**, **overall** *Labour made an overall gain of 39 seats.* | **ill-gotten** *She tucked her ill-gotten gains into her purse and left.* | **personal**, **private** *using the investments for their private gain* | **commercial**, **economic**, **financial**, **material** *There will be no financial gain for mothers from this new scheme.* | **electoral**, **political** *the far right made huge electoral gains* | **military**, **territorial** | **weight** *She was most upset by her recent weight gain.* | **efficiency**, **productivity** *There is still scope for efficiency gains* (= gains to be made by being more efficient).
- VERB + GAIN **make** | **bring (sb)** *Better workplace design can bring real gains in productivity.*
- PREP. **for ~** *It's amazing what some people will do for gain.* | **~from** *£3.9 million gains from the sale of stock* **~in** *Last year there was only a modest gain in earnings.*

gain *verb*

- ADV. **certainly**, **undoubtedly** *Consumers have certainly gained from the increased competition in the telecommunications industry.* | **clearly** | **quickly**, **rapidly** | **gradually**, **slowly** *His ideas gradually gained acceptance.* | **steadily** | **eventually**, **finally**, **ultimately** | **successfully** | **automatically** *Husbands and wives of British nationals do not automatically gain citizenship.* | **easily**
- VERB + GAIN **stand to** *The company stands to gain* (= is likely to gain) *quite a lot from this government scheme.* | **expect to**, **hope to** *What do you hope to gain by this action?* | **attempt to**, **seek to**, **strive to**, **try to** *Protesters tried to gain access to the presidential palace.* | **fail to**
- PREP. **by** *There is nothing to be gained by forcing people to comply.* **from** *We all gained a lot from the experience.*
- PHRASES **have everything/much/little/a lot/nothing to gain/be gained** *Why not give it a go? You've nothing to lose and everything to gain.* ◇ *I don't think there's anything to be gained from this course of action.*

gait *noun*

- ADJ. **rolling**, **strolling**, **stumbling**, **waddling**
- PREP. **with a ~** *He walked with a rolling gait.*

gala *noun*

- ADJ. **charity**, **Royal** | **swimming**
- VERB + GALA **have**, **hold** | **attend**, **go to**
- GALA + NOUN **concert**, **day**, **dinner**, **evening**, **event**, **night**, **occasion**, **performance**, **weekend**

galaxy *noun*

- ADJ. **distant** | **nearby**, **nearest**, **neighbouring**
- PREP. **in a/the ~** *scientists observing phenomena in nearby galaxies*

gale *noun*

- ADJ. **fierce**, **full**, **great**, **heavy**, **howling**, **severe**, **strong** | **Force 9**, **Force 10**, **etc.** | **northerly**, **westerly**, **etc.** | **autumn**, **winter**, **etc.** | **equinoctial** | **Atlantic**, **North Sea**, **etc.**
- VERB + GALE **blow** *It was blowing a gale outside.* | **get caught in** *We got caught in a howling gale.*
- GALE + VERB **blow** *A severe gale was blowing along the coast.*
- GALE + NOUN **force** *gale force winds* | **warning**
- PREP. **in ~** *The tree had come down in a fierce gale the night before.*

gallantry *noun*

- ADJ. **great**, **outstanding**
- VERB + GALLANTRY **demonstrate**, **show** *a soldier who had demonstrated outstanding gallantry*
- GALLANTRY + NOUN **award**, **medal**

gallery *noun*

1 for art
- ADJ. **art**, **exhibition**, **picture**, **portrait** | **commercial**, **private**, **public** | **national** *He offered ten major paintings to start a national gallery of modern British art.*
- VERB + GALLERY **go to**, **visit**
- GALLERY + VERB **exhibit sth**, **show sth** *Some of his work has been exhibited by local art galleries.* | **specialize in sth** *a gallery specializing in ceramics* | **close**, **open**
- GALLERY + NOUN **space** *The extension will provide 600 square metres of new gallery space.*
- PREP. **at a/the ~** *The painting is now on display at the National Gallery in London.* **in a/the ~** *There were very few people in the gallery.*

2 in a hall
- ADJ. **long**, **wide** | **first-floor**, **upper** | **public** *The packed public gallery at Teesside Crown Court erupted in a roar of approval.*
- PREP. **in a/the ~** *I found myself in a wide gallery looking down on the floor below.*

gallon *noun*

⇨ Note at MEASURE

gallop *noun*

- ADJ. **fast**, **good**, **head-down**, **mad** | **steady**

● VERB + GALLOP **break into** *The horses broke into a mad gallop when they heard the gunshot.*
● PREP. **at a~** *They reached the farm at a gallop.* **into a~** *The noise startled the horse into a gallop.* | **~through** *(figurative) The programme starts with a gallop through the history of the railway.*
● PHRASES **at full gallop** *riders coming at full gallop*

gamble *noun*

● ADJ. **big, huge, major** | **calculated** | **desperate** *It was time for a last desperate gamble.* | **political**
● VERB + GAMBLE **take**
● GAMBLE + VERB **pay off, work** *I took a calculated gamble and it paid off.*
● PREP. **~on** *Backpackers with a heavy load should resist taking a gamble on the weather.*
● PHRASES **a bit/something of a gamble** *Trying to find the right pension can be a bit of a gamble.*

gambler *noun*

● ADJ. **compulsive, heavy, inveterate** *Most compulsive gamblers are not successful.* | **notorious** | **professional**

gambling *noun*

● ADJ. **compulsive** *He went to a psychiatrist about his compulsive gambling.* | **illegal** *The police are trying to stop all illegal gambling.* | **legalized, legitimate**
● GAMBLING + NOUN **casino, club, den** | **table** | **debt** *She ran up gambling debts worth a million pounds.* | **man** *If I were a gambling man, I'd put my money on him resigning soon.*

game *noun*

1 activity/sport
● ADJ. **ball, board, card, computer, video** | **good** *This is a good game for getting people to mix.* | **competitive** *competitive games in which there is always a winner and a loser* | **team** *How I hated team games at school!* | **party** | **children's** *children's party games like Musical Chairs* | **indoor, outdoor** *finding good indoor games for children*
● VERB + GAME **have, play** *Shall we have a game of chess?* | **draw, lose, win**
● PREP. **~against/with, ~of** *To pass the time, we played a game of cards.*
2 sports match
● ADJ. **big** (= important) *The team are in training for their big game.* | **first, opening** | **final, last** | **away, home** | **Cup, League** *their first League game of the season*
● VERB + GAME **have, play** *United are playing a home game this week.* | **draw, lose, win** *We won the first game and drew the second.*
● PREP. **~against/with** *He's hoping to be fit before next week's game with Liverpool.* **~of** *a game of tennis*
3 how sb plays
● ADJ. **good, great** *That girl plays a great game of bridge.*
● VERB + GAME **have, play** *Trescothick had a good game and was man of the match.* | **improve, raise** *Hendry raised his game to collect the £40 000 first prize.*
4 games sports competition
● ADJ. **Commonwealth, Olympic**
● VERB + GAMES **compete in, participate in, take part in** *She's hoping to participate in the next Olympic Games.* | **host** *Beijing's bid to host the Olympic Games*
5 business/activity
● VERB + GAME **be in** *How long have you been in this game?*
● PREP. **~of** *the game of life/politics*
● PHRASES **all part of the game** *Getting dirty was all part of the game to the kids.* **new to this game** *I'm new to this game myself.*

6 secret plan
● ADJ. **little, silly, stupid**
● VERB + GAME **play** *I realized that he had been playing a stupid game with me.* | **put an end to, put a stop to** *I'll soon put an end to her silly little games.* | **give away** *Don't let him talk to anybody or he'll give the game away.*

gamut *noun*

● ADJ. **complete, entire, full, whole**
● VERB + GAMUT **cover, run** (through)
● PREP. **~of** *The exhibition runs the whole gamut of artistic styles.*

gang *noun*

1 group of criminals
● ADJ. **street** *a street gang known as the Hooligans* | **armed, criminal, organized, terror/terrorist** *The robbery was carried out by an armed gang.* | **teenage** | **rival** *Fights had ensued between rival gangs of football fans.*
● VERB + GANG **belong to, join** *A lot of the lads belong to gangs.* ◇ *He pressed me to join his gang.*
● GANG + NOUN **attack, fight, violence, warfare** *a gang fight between two rival teenage gangs* | **leader, member** | **life** *a tale of LA gang life* | **rape**
● PREP. **in a/the~** *We were in the same gang.* | **~of** *a gang of skinheads*
● PHRASES **a member of a gang**
2 group of friends
● PREP. **~of** *You probably go with a gang of friends to the same pub most Saturdays.*
● PHRASES **one of the gang** *Her friends made me feel welcome and treated me as one of the gang.*

gangrene *noun*

● VERB + GANGRENE **have, suffer from** | **develop**
● GANGRENE + VERB **set in** *The wound was not properly disinfected and gangrene set in.*
⇨ Special page at ILLNESS

gaol *noun*

⇨ See JAIL

gap *noun*

1 space between things
● ADJ. **big, huge, large, wide** | **narrow, small** | **awkward** *an awkward gap between the bed and the door*
● VERB + GAP **leave** | **fill, seal** *Seal the gaps around the windows with an exterior-quality sealant.*
● GAP + VERB **appear, open up** *He flashed his headlights and jumped lanes whenever a gap opened up.*
● PREP. **through a/the~** *A rabbit ran along the fence and darted through a gap.* | **~between** *Position the tiles, leaving a narrow gap between the edges.* **~in** *A huge gap had appeared in the hedge.*
2 period of time
● ADJ. **awkward** | **long, short** | **time**
● VERB + GAP **fill** *wondering how to fill an awkward gap in the conversation*
● GAP + NOUN **year** *I'm planning to travel in my gap year* (= the year between school and university).
● PREP. **after a/the ~** *She returned to teaching after a twelve-year gap.* | **~between** *a job to fill the gap between school and university* **~in** *a gap in his career*
3 difference
● ADJ. **big, huge, large, significant, substantial, wide, yawning** | **unbridgeable** *the unbridgeable gap between the two cultures* | **growing, widening** | **narrow** | **age, generation** *Despite the age gap, romance blossomed.* | **cultural/culture** | **gender** *the gender gap in earnings* |

credibility *Newspapers were talking of a credibility gap between what he said and what he did.* | **information, knowledge, skills** *the knowledge gap between doctor and patient* | **trade** (= the gap between export and imports; used in journalism)

• VERB + GAP **bridge** *an attempt to bridge the gap between the academic world and industry*

• GAP + VERB **widen** | **narrow** | **separate sb/sth** *He realized how narrow was the gap separating him from his pagan ancestors.*

• PREP. **~ between** *The gap between rich and poor widened.*

4 where sth is missing

• ADJ. **big, enormous, great, huge, important, large, serious, significant, terrible, yawning** *serious gaps in their knowledge*

• VERB + GAP **create, leave** *His death left a huge gap in my life.* | **identify** | **close, fill (in), plug** *Her appointment will fill the gap created when the marketing manager left.*

• PREP. **~in** *legislation to close a gap in the law*

• PHRASES **a gap in the market** *We think we've identified a gap in the market* (= a business opportunity to make or sell sth that is not yet available).

gape *verb*

• PREP. **at** *What are you gaping at?*

• PHRASES **gape open** *She watched him, her mouth gaping open.* ◇ *(figurative) The empty cash box lay gaping open in one corner.*

garage *noun*

1 for keeping cars in

• ADJ. **double, single** | **detached, integral, lean-to, lock-up** | **underground** | **bus**

• GARAGE + NOUN **door**

• PREP. **in a/the~** *Don't forget to put the car in the garage.*

2 for repairing cars/buying petrol

• ADJ. **local**

• VERB + GARAGE **own, run** | **take sth to** *I took the car to the local garage to get it fixed.*

• GARAGE + NOUN **mechanic, owner**

• PREP. **at a/the~** *The car's still at the garage.*

garden *noun*

• ADJ. **beautiful, lovely, pretty** | **big, large** | **small, tiny** | **back, front** *people hanging out washing in their back gardens* | **flower, herb, kitchen, rose, vegetable** *Most of the hotel's salads are grown in its own kitchen garden.* | **rock, water** *a rock garden with an astonishing variety of alpine plants* | **botanical, cottage, formal, landscaped, public, town, walled** *a large country house with beautiful landscaped gardens* ◇ *plants suitable for a small town garden* ◇ *a lovely Victorian walled garden*

• VERB + GARDEN **create, design, lay out, plan, plant** *creating a garden out of a wilderness* ◇ *We got someone to design the garden for us.* ◇ *The garden is laid out in eighteenth century style.* | **plant** *We planted the garden with herbs and wild flowers.* | **dig, do, tend, tidy (up), weed** *Weekends were spent doing the garden.*

• GARDEN + NOUN **flower, plant** | **pest** *aphids, one of the commonest garden pests* | **tools** | **gate, path, shed, wall** | **furniture, seat** | **centre** *We got the gravel at our local garden centre.*

• PREP. **in/into a/the~** *Mary's out in the garden.*

• PHRASES **the bottom/end of a garden**

gardener *noun*

• ADJ. **enthusiastic, keen** | **experienced, expert, good** | **amateur** | **jobbing** *She employs a jobbing gardener to keep the garden tidy.* | **assistant, head** *head gardener to*

the Duke of Devonshire | **organic** *The organic gardener avoids the use of pesticides.* | **landscape, market**
⇨ Note at JOB

gardening *noun*

• ADJ. **organic** | **landscape, market**

• VERB + GARDENING **do** *It's my husband who does the gardening.*

• GARDENING + NOUN **business** *She started up her own market gardening business two years ago.* | **book, magazine** | **programme, show** *a TV gardening show* | **equipment, gloves, tools** | **expert**

garlic *noun*

• ADJ. **wild**

• QUANT. **clove**

• VERB + GARLIC **peel** | **chop, crush**

• GARLIC + NOUN **clove** | **bread** | **sausage**
⇨ Special page at FOOD

garment *noun*

• ADJ. **heavy** | **shapeless** | **knitted, woollen**

• VERB + GARMENT **have on, wear** *She wore a shapeless knitted garment.*

gas *noun*

1 substance like air

• ADJ. **noxious, poisonous, toxic** | **explosive, inflammable, radioactive** | **inert** | **exhaust, greenhouse** *pollution from greenhouse gases* | **nerve, tear** *Police used water cannon and tear gas against demonstrators.*

• VERB + GAS **give off, produce** *It gives off a poisonous gas as it rots down.*

• GAS + VERB **build up** *Noxious gases had built up in the sewer.* | **escape, leak** *Toxic gases can escape through one of the pipes.*

2 for heating/cooking

• ADJ. **butane, coal, natural, propane** | **bottled, Calor**

• VERB + GAS **cook with** *I prefer to cook with gas.* | **light, turn on** *I lit the gas and put the soup on to warm.*

• GAS + NOUN **appliance, boiler, central heating, cooker, fire, lamp, oven** | **bottle, cylinder, pipeline** | **board** | **industry** | **field** *tapping the North Sea gas fields* | **supply** | **works** *Local gas works were closed as natural gas became available.* | **leak** *All gas leaks should be reported as soon as possible.*

• PHRASES **gas mark 2, 3, etc.** *Set the oven at gas mark 4.*

gash *noun*

1 deep wound

• ADJ. **deep, great, long** | **nasty, terrible**

• VERB + GASH **get, have**

• PREP. **on the~** *She got a nasty gash on the head.*

2 large hole

• ADJ. **deep, great, long**

• VERB + GASH **carve, cut, tear** *The bulldozers carved a great gash through the forest.* ◇ *The rocks tore a long gash in the ship's hull.*

gasp *noun*

• ADJ. **big, great** | **little, short, small** | **quick, sharp, sudden** | **loud** | **low** | **audible** | **shocked** | **strangled** | **involuntary**

• VERB + GASP **give, let out** | **stifle** | **bring** *The stunt brought shocked gasps from the audience.* | **hear** | **take (in)** *taking in great gasps of air*

• GASP + VERB **escape sb**

• PREP. **between ~s** *'Listen carefully,' he said, between gasps of breath.* **in ~s** *He leant against the railing, his*

breath coming in short gasps. **with a ~** *She spun round with a little gasp of delight.* | **~of**
⇨ Note at SOUND

gasp *verb*

• ADV. **almost | aloud | breathlessly**
• VERB + GASP **make sb** *The cold made her gasp.* | **manage to** *'No!' she managed to gasp.*
• PREP. **at** *She gasped at his boldness.* **in** *Denis almost gasped aloud in astonishment.* **with** *gasping with pain*
• PHRASES **gasp for air/breath, leave sb gasping** *Her breath went and left her gasping for air.*

gate *noun*

• ADJ. **entrance, front, main | back, postern** (in a castle), **side | inner, outer | double, five-bar/five-barred, portcullis** *a wide driveway with double gates* | **great** *The great gates of the abbey were shut fast.* | **heavy | high | narrow | ornamental | open | iron, metal, steel, wooden, wrought-iron | city, factory, farm, garden, park, prison, school, etc. | security | sluice**
• QUANT. **set** *a set of ornamental gates*
• VERB + GATE **open | bar, close, fasten, lock, shut** *Don't forget to shut the gate when you leave.* ◇ *The defenders had closed and barred all the city gates.* | **go through** *Go through the gate and continue down the track.*
• GATE + VERB **open, swing open** *The heavy gate swung open.* | **close, shut** *The gate shut behind him.*
• PREP. **through a/the ~** *He led us through a gate into a little garden.*

gather *verb*

1 come together in a group
• ADV. **quickly | around/round, together**
• PREP. **about/around/round** *The boys gathered around the car.* **for** *They are all gathering for a major conference.*
2 bring people/things together
• ADV. **hastily, quickly** *She hastily gathered all her belongings together.* | **carefully | together, up**
3 increase
• ADV. **quickly, rapidly** *The movement for reform rapidly gathered momentum.* | **slowly | steadily**
• VERB + GATHER **begin to, start to** *As the weeks passed, Charlotte began to gather strength.*

gathering *noun*

1 meeting
• ADJ. **big, large | small | informal, private, public | illegal | family, political, religious, social**
• VERB + GATHERING **attend, go to** *Women are not allowed to attend public gatherings.* | **have, hold, organize** *We're having a small family gathering to mark our wedding anniversary.* | **address**
• GATHERING + VERB **take place**
• PREP. **~of** *The prime minister addressed a gathering of local government officials.*
• PHRASES **a gathering of the clan/clans** (*humorous*) *All the children and grandchildren are going to my parents' at Christmas for the annual gathering of the clan.*
2 collecting
• ADJ. **information, intelligence**

gauge *noun*

1 measuring instrument
• ADJ. **accurate | fuel, oil, petrol | depth, pressure, temperature**
• VERB + GAUGE **check, glance at, look at, read** *The pilot checked the fuel gauge frequently.*
• GAUGE + VERB **read sth, show sth, tell sb sth** *The*

petrol gauge was reading 'full'. ◇ *The depth gauge tells you how deep you have dived.*
2 distance between rails
• ADJ. **broad, narrow, standard**
• VERB + GAUGE **adopt** *Eventually all the British railway companies adopted the standard gauge of 4 feet 8½ inches.*
3 fact for judging sth
• ADJ. **reliable, useful**
• VERB + GAUGE **be seen as, serve as** *This company is seen as a gauge of Britain's industrial well-being.*
• PREP. **~of**

gauge *verb*

• ADV. **accurately, correctly | carefully**
• VERB + GAUGE **be able to, can/could | try to | be difficult to, be hard to, be impossible to** *It is difficult to gauge accurately how much fuel is needed*

gay *adj.*

• VERBS **be, look, sound**
• ADV. **openly** *He is now openly gay.*

gaze *noun*

• ADJ. **direct, fixed, level, steady, unblinking, watchful** *She felt embarrassed under his steady gaze.* | **intense, intent, penetrating, piercing, searching | clear | cold, cool, hard, steely, stony | admiring, angry, critical, etc. | blue, brown, dark, grey** *His deep blue gaze held hers.* | **public** (*figurative*) *Pop stars are constantly exposed to the public gaze.*
• VERB + GAZE **direct, fix (sb with), focus, turn** *They fixed their gaze on the dark line of the coast ahead.* ◇ *She fixed him with a level gaze.* ◇ *He turned his gaze on me.* | **meet** *She refused to meet my gaze.* | **hold | follow** *I followed her gaze and spotted a new arrival at the far side of the room.* | **avert, drop, lower** *She deliberately averted her gaze when he came in.* | **avoid** *She avoided his gaze.*
• GAZE + VERB **drift, flick, flicker, fly, move, rake (sth), roam (sth), run, shift, slide, sweep (sth), travel, wander** *His gaze flickered an instant.* ◇ *His gaze flickered over the room.* | **follow sth** *Her gaze followed Simon's through the archway.* | **fix on sth, lock (with sth), meet sth** *Her gaze fixed on his and held it unblinkingly.* ◇ *His gaze locked with hers.* | **hold sth | linger, rest** *Rebecca's gaze rested on the child thoughtfully.* | **fall** *Her gaze fell on Kate's tousled hair.* | **narrow** *The dark gaze narrowed.*
• PREP. **under sb's~** *He blushed under her angry gaze.*

gaze *verb*

• ADV. **calmly, steadily | intently, unblinkingly** *He gazed unblinkingly into the distance.* | **absently, blankly, unseeingly** *He gazed absently at the passing crowd.* | **thoughtfully | admiringly, adoringly, fondly, longingly, lovingly** *She gazed admiringly up at him.* | **down, out, up** *gazing out over the lake*
• PREP. **at** *gazing at her beautiful jewellery* **in** *They gazed in wonder at the mighty peaks.* **into** *She gazed steadily into his face.*

gear *noun*

1 in a vehicle
• ADJ. **bottom, top** *driving along in top gear* | **high, low | first, second, etc. | reverse**
• VERB + GEAR **engage, select** *Engage first gear and move off.* | **change, change into, move into, put/slam/slip sth into, shift (into), switch** *It's difficult to steer and change gear at the same time.* ◇ *She put the car into first gear and drove off.* ◇ (*figurative*) *The party organization is moving into top gear as the election approaches.* | **move up, step up** (*often figurative*) *Coming out of the*

final bend, the runner stepped up a gear to overtake the rest of the pack. | **crash, grind** *He was crashing the gears because he was so nervous.*
• GEAR + NOUN **change** *She made a smooth gear change.* | **lever, stick** (also **gearstick**)
• PREP. **in (a/the)** ~ *driving along in third gear* ◇ *Some drivers leave the car in gear when parking on hills.* **out of** ~ *Leave the car out of gear.*

2 equipment/clothes
• ADJ. **camping, climbing, fishing, running, sports, swimming, walking** | **breathing** *firemen in breathing gear* | **landing, winding** *the plane's landing gear* | **combat, riot** | **outdoor** | **designer** *wearing expensive designer gear*
• VERB + GEAR **be dressed in, have on, wear** *She had her running gear on.* | **put on, take off**
• PREP. **in ...** ~ *a group of young men in combat gear*

gear *verb* **be geared to/towards sth**
• ADV. **completely, entirely, exclusively, totally** *an economy exclusively geared towards tourism* | **primarily** | **specifically** *Our training programmes are geared specifically to the needs of older workers.* | **clearly**

gem *noun*
1 jewel
• ADJ. **precious, priceless**
• PHRASES **dripping with gems** *a millionairess dripping with gems and pearls* **encrusted/studded with gems** *a belt studded with priceless gems*
2 person/thing
• ADJ. **little** | **absolute, real** *The second side of their new album contains some real gems.* | **hidden** *She worked in the antiques trade, searching out hidden gems in the most unlikely places.* | **architectural** *architectural gems like York Minster*
• PHRASES **a gem of a sth** *This is a little gem of a flower.*

gender *noun*
• GENDER + NOUN **relations** | **differences, divisions** *She examines the interplay between changing gender divisions and urban change.* | **bias, imbalance, inequality** *The government is working on tackling gender inequalities in employment.* | **identity, role, stereotype** *Managers may value different qualities in men than in women, reinforcing gender stereotypes.* | **issues, politics**

gene *noun*
• ADJ. **dominant, recessive** | **abnormal, defective, mutant** | **human**
• VERB + GENE **carry, have** *people who carry the gene that causes this disease* | **pass on** *The gene is passed on to their children.*
• GENE + VERB **be responsible for sth, cause sth, control sth, influence sth** *Genes control the development of an embryo.* | **mutate**
• GENE + NOUN **pool** *Scientists have estimated that a gene pool of at least 300 animals is necessary to maintain a healthy tiger population.* | **defect, mutation** *Gene mutations are alterations in the DNA code.* | **sequence** | **therapy**
• PREP. ~ **for** *An individual may pass on to future generations its genes for tallness.*

general *noun*
• GENERAL + VERB **command sth, lead sth** *Both generals had commanded units in that area.*
⇨ Note at RANK

generalization *noun*
• ADJ. **broad, sweeping** | **abstract** | **useful, valid**
• VERB + GENERALIZATION **make**
• PREP. ~ **about** *The author makes several sweeping generalizations about the causes of the crisis.*

generalize *verb*
• VERB + GENERALIZE **can/could** | **be easy to, be possible to** | **be difficult to, be hard to, be impossible to** | **be dangerous to, be unsafe to, be unwise to**
• PREP. **about** *It is impossible to generalize about such a complicated subject.* **from** *We cannot generalize from these few examples.*

generate *verb*
• ADV. **quickly** | **automatically, spontaneously** *People used to believe that dirt spontaneously generated disease.* | **randomly** *a sequence of randomly generated fractions* | **externally, internally** *internally generated revenue* | **locally**
• VERB + GENERATE **help (to)** *the opportunity to help generate ideas* | **be used to** *The wind turbines are used to generate electricity.* | **be expected to, be likely to** *The lottery is expected to generate substantial funds for charities.*
• PREP. **from** *Living cells generate energy from food.* ◇ *profits generated from the company's activities*

generation *noun*
1 people/period of time
• ADJ. **current, present** | **new, younger** | **older** *The older generation prefer a darker and more traditional kind of clothing.* | **coming, future, later, next, rising** *The forest will be preserved for future generations.* | **earlier, former, last, past, preceding, previous** *These children seem to have a stronger sense of purpose than the previous generation.* ◇ *the wisdom of past generations* | **first, second, etc.** *The second generation of immigrants often adopted British forenames.* | **subsequent, succeeding, successive** *Succeeding generations have added to the stock of stories and legends.* | **whole** *The First World War slaughtered a whole generation.*
• VERB + GENERATION **belong to** *people who belong to a younger generation*
• GENERATION + NOUN **gap** *I was aware of a real generation gap between us.*
• PREP. **for a** ~ *The consequences of the radioactive leakage may not become apparent for a generation or more.* **for** ~**s** *This kind of apple has been grown for generations.*
• PHRASES **from generation to generation** *The recipe for making the liqueur has been handed down from generation to generation.* **from one generation to the next**
2 production of sth
• ADJ. **electricity, gas, income, power** *different methods of power generation*

generator *noun*
• ADJ. **diesel, gas, petrol, steam, wind** | **electrical, electricity, power**
• VERB + GENERATOR **drive, power** *A water turbine drives the generator.*
• GENERATOR + VERB **deliver sth** *The wind generator delivers 120 watts in a strong breeze.*

generosity *noun*
• ADJ. **extraordinary, great, unusual**
• VERB + GENEROSITY **show (sb)** *He thanked them for the extraordinary generosity they had shown.* | **take advantage of** *Their guests took advantage of their generosity, overstaying their welcome by several days.*
• PREP. ~ **to/towards** *their great generosity to the school*

• PHRASES **an act of generosity, generosity of spirit** *She showed an unusual generosity of spirit to those who had opposed her.* **thanks to the generosity of sb** *The hospital has now bought a new body scanner, thanks to the generosity of local fund-raisers.*

generous *adj.*

• VERBS **appear, be, feel, seem, sound | become, get** *John's getting very generous with the wine!*
• ADV. **amazingly, exceedingly, exceptionally, extraordinarily, extremely, incredibly, most, very, wonderfully** *You have been most generous.* | **excessively, overly** *The review panel criticized the payments as overly generous.* | **fairly, pretty, quite, rather, reasonably, relatively**
• PREP. **of** *Thank you for your donation. It was very generous of you.* **to** *They have been extremely generous to the mosque.* **with** *She's quite generous with her praise.*

genetics *noun*

• ADJ. **evolutionary | molecular | medical | human, plant | population | Mendelian**
• PHRASES **the science of genetics**
⇨ Note at SUBJECT (for verbs and nouns)

genitals *noun*

• ADJ. **female, male**
• VERB + GENITALS **cover | display, exhibit, expose**

genius *noun*

1 very great and unusual ability
• ADJ. **great, pure, real | natural**
• QUANT. **flash, stroke, touch** *In a flash of pure genius, she realized the answer to the problem.* ◊ *It was a stroke of genius on my part to avoid such awkward questions.*
• VERB + GENIUS **have** *She has a genius for sorting things out.* **show** *a work which shows real genius*
• GENIUS + VERB **lie in sth** *His genius lies in his ability to convey pure terror in his work.*
• PREP. **of~** *a writer of genius* | **~for** *his genius for pinpointing the absurd*
2 person with great and unusual ability
• ADJ. **great | natural | eccentric, wayward | artistic, comic, creative, literary, mathematical, military, musical, etc.**

genocide *noun*

• ADJ. **mass** *Refugees gave accounts of the mass genocide.* | **cultural**
• PREP. **~against** *genocide against ethnic minorities*
⇨ Note at CRIME (for verbs)

gentle *adj.*

• VERBS **appear, be, look, seem, sound | become**
• ADV. **extremely, very | almost | fairly, quite | surprisingly, unusually | deceptively** *His mouth looked deceptively gentle.*
• PREP. **on** *The new treatments are gentle on your hair.* **with** *She was very gentle with the children.*

gentleman *noun*

1 man who is polite/behaves well towards others
• ADJ. **perfect, real, true** *He's a real gentleman, always kind and considerate.*
• PHRASES **be no gentleman** *He may be a lord, but he's no gentleman.* **too much of a gentleman** *He was too much of a gentleman to ask them for any money.*
2 rich man with a high social position
• ADJ. **country, landed** *He retired to his estate in Norfolk, and lived the life of a country gentleman.*
• GENTLEMAN + NOUN **farmer**

genuine *adj.*

1 real
• VERBS **be, look, prove | consider sth** *The document is not considered genuine.*
• ADV. **absolutely, completely, perfectly, quite** *Her happiness was perfectly genuine.* | **apparently | obviously | undoubtedly**
2 sincere
• VERBS **appear, be, look, seem, sound**
• ADV. **really, very | absolutely, completely, perfectly, quite** *I'm convinced she is absolutely genuine.* | **enough** *His offer sounded genuine enough.* | **apparently | obviously | undoubtedly**

geography *noun*

• ADJ. **economic, historical, human, physical, political, social**
⇨ Note at SUBJECT (for verbs and nouns)

geology *noun*

• ADJ. **applied, engineering | physical, structural | environmental, marine | petroleum | Pleistocene, Quaternary, etc.**
• PHRASES **the science of geology**
⇨ Note at SUBJECT (for verbs and nouns)

geometry *noun*

• ADJ. **algebraic, co-ordinate, differential, fractal, solid, three-dimensional | Euclidean | basic | internal, local | sacred** *Pre-Christian sacred geometry was incorporated into church architecture.*
⇨ Note at SUBJECT (for verbs and nouns)

germ *noun*

• ADJ. **virulent** *The epidemic was caused by a particularly virulent flu germ.* | **flu, typhoid, etc.**
• VERB + GERM **carry** *Children carry all kinds of germs home from school.* | **harbour** *Cracks and scratches in work surfaces can harbour germs.* | **destroy, kill** *They used bleach to kill any germs in the sink and drain.*
• GERM + NOUN **warfare**

German *noun*

⇨ Note at LANGUAGE

German measles *noun*

⇨ Special page at ILLNESS

gesticulate *verb*

• ADV. **wildly** *He gesticulated wildly as he tried to make her understand.*
• PREP. **at** *The other woman was gesticulating at the ambulance.* **to** *gesticulating to me with her hands* **towards** *The officer gesticulated towards the refugees.* **with**

gesture *noun*

1 movement that expresses sth
• ADJ. **dramatic, expansive, expressive, extravagant, flamboyant, melodramatic, sweeping, theatrical** *She made an expansive gesture with her arms.* | **abrupt | careless, vague** *He responded with a vague gesture in the direction of the pub.* | **obscene, rude | angry, defiant, threatening | dismissive, impatient, irritable | helpless | imperious | placatory**
• VERB + GESTURE **make** *The children made rude gestures at them.*
• PREP. **by~** *They communicate entirely by gesture.* **in a~** *He waved his arms in a melodramatic gesture.* **with a~** *She*

waved us away with an impatient gesture. | ~ of a gesture of despair

2 sth that shows other people what you think/feel
- ADJ. **nice** I thought it was a nice gesture to send everyone a card. | **bold** a bold gesture of reconciliation | **dramatic, extravagant, grand** He had the respect of his people without the need for grand gestures. | **conciliatory, friendly, goodwill** | **charitable, philanthropic** | **empty, small, symbolic, token** Words and empty gestures are not enough—we demand action! ◇ a token gesture of their good intentions | **futile** | **political**
- PREP. **as a~** Several hostages were released as a goodwill gesture. **in a~** In a dramatic gesture, the prime minister refused to attend the meeting. | **~against** The invasion attempt was intended as a political gesture against his opponents. **~ of** His gift was a gesture of friendship. **~ towards** The president's speech was seen as a conciliatory gesture towards former enemies.

gesture verb
- ADV. **vaguely** | **wildly** | **expansively** | **abruptly, impatiently** | **helplessly**
- PREP. **at** She gestured at him to step back. **about/around** He gestured around the room, lost for words. **for** He gestured abruptly for Virginia to get in the car. **to** Mrs Davis gestured to the waiter. **towards** He gestured vaguely towards the house. **with** gesturing wildly with her hands

ghost noun
- VERB + GHOST **see** You look as if you've seen a ghost! | **believe in** I don't believe in ghosts. | **exorcise, lay to rest** A priest was called in to exorcise the ghost.
- GHOST + VERB **appear, haunt sth, walk** dark, cold nights when ghosts walk
- GHOST + NOUN **story**
- PREP. **~ of** The ghost of a hanged poacher is said to haunt the manor house.
- PHRASES **as pale/white as a ghost** He looked as pale as a ghost as he climbed out of the wrecked car.

giant noun
1 very large man
- PHRASES **a gentle giant** Some people are intimidated by his size, but in fact he's a gentle giant. **a giant of a man** He was a giant of a man, standing nearly seven feet tall.

2 sth that is very large/important
- ADJ. **corporate, multinational** | **car, chemicals, financial, food, industrial, oil, retail, etc.** The oil giant Esso is planning to set up a new refinery in the port. | **literary** Camus is considered to be one of the twentieth century's literary giants.
- PREP. **~ among/amongst** The Amazon is a giant amongst rivers. **~ of** The company is now one of the giants of the computer industry.

giddy adj.
- VERBS **be, feel** | **become, come over all** (informal), **get** My mum came over all giddy and had to sit down. | **leave sb, make sb** Steep stairs may leave you giddy and faint.
- ADV. **quite** | **a bit, rather, slightly**
- PREP. **from** He felt tired and giddy from the sleeping pill. **with** I was giddy with the heat.

gift noun
1 sth that you give to sb
- ADJ. **expensive, generous, kind, lavish, valuable** Thank you all for your kind gifts. ◇ She received lavish gifts of jewellery and clothes. | **perfect** | **small** | **free** When you place your first order with us, we will send you

the free gift of your choice. | **birthday, Christmas, parting, retirement, wedding** | **unwanted** the problem of what to do with unwanted gifts
- VERB + GIFT **bear, bring (sb), exchange, give sb, make sb, offer sb** He arrived home bearing gifts for everyone. ◇ They gave each other gifts at Christmas. ◇ She wanted to make a gift to her grandchildren. | **accept, get, receive** Please accept this small gift. ◇ The children all received gifts.
- GIFT + NOUN **shop** | **box, pack, set, token, voucher** New customers will receive a free gift pack containing a selection of our products. ◇ a gift set of shampoo, soap and hand cream | **token, voucher**
- PREP. **as a~** The messengers brought the king a fine suit of armour as a gift. | **~for** There were gifts for all the children. **~from** This vase was a gift from my mother. **~to** The golf clubs were her gift to her husband.
- PHRASES **shower gifts on sb, shower sb with gifts**

2 natural ability
- ADJ. **great, outstanding, remarkable, special, wonderful** his great gifts as a teacher | **rare** | **God-given, innate, natural, special** | **artistic, musical**
- VERB + GIFT **have, possess**
- PREP. **~for** She has a natural gift for music.

gifted adj.
- VERBS **be**
- ADV. **exceptionally, extremely, highly, immensely, prodigiously, supremely, very** | **undeniably** | **naturally** a naturally gifted sportswoman | **uniquely** | **precociously** | **academically, athletically, intellectually, musically** academically gifted children
- PREP. **at** He's very gifted at maths. **in** gifted in the art of healing **with** Their helpers are gifted with amazing powers of patience.

gig noun
- ADJ. **benefit, charity** | **free** | **live** | **pub**
- VERB + GIG **do, play (in)** They're doing a gig in Leeds tonight. | **go to**
- PREP. **at a/the~** They're performing at a local pub gig.

giggle noun
- ADJ. **little** | **high-pitched** | **nervous** | **girlish**
- VERB + GIGGLE **give, have, let out** | **collapse into, dissolve into, get ~s** We all collapsed into giggles. ◇ Susan tends to get the giggles at the most inappropriate moments. | **stifle, suppress** I just managed to stifle a giggle at the absurd idea. | **hear**
- PREP. **with a~** 'Age before beauty!' she said with a giggle. | **~about/at** We had quite a giggle about the new office romance.
- PHRASES **a fit of (the) giggles**

giggle verb
- ADV. **helplessly, hysterically, nervously** The children giggled hysterically.
- PREP. **about** They giggled about their teacher's accident. **at** We giggled at the picture. **over** giggling over old photographs **with** The children giggled with delight.
- PHRASES **a fit of giggling**

gimmick noun
- ADJ. **latest, new** a new gimmick to encourage people to go to the cinema | **election, marketing, publicity, sales** The promise of lower taxation may have been just an election gimmick to gain votes.
- PHRASES **just/nothing more than/only a gimmick** He dismissed the event as just a publicity gimmick.

gin noun

- ADJ. **stiff** | **double, large** | **small** | **pink, sloe**
- VERB + GIN **drink, have** *'What are you drinking?' 'I'll have a gin and tonic, please.'* | **sip** | **pour** (sb) *She poured herself a large gin.*
- PHRASES **a gin and tonic**

girl noun

- ADJ. **baby** *They've had a baby girl.* | **little, small, young** *When she was a little girl, she dreamed of becoming a ballerina.* | **adolescent, teenage** | **bubbly, happy, lively** | **lovely, nice** | **attractive, beautiful, good-looking, gorgeous, handsome, pretty, stunning** | **single, unmarried**

girlfriend noun

- ADJ. **current, latest, new** | **ex-, former, old** | **long-standing, long-term, serious, steady** | **live-in** | **pregnant** | **jealous** | **jilted**
- QUANT. **string, succession**
- VERB + GIRLFRIEND **have** | **meet** | **live with** | **sleep with** | **propose to** | **marry**

gist noun the gist

- ADJ. **general**
- VERB + GIST **convey, give** (sb) *It is difficult to convey the gist of Reich's ideas simply.* | **follow, get, understand**
- PREP. **~ of** *I could follow the general gist of their conversation.*

glad adj.

- VERBS **be, feel, look, seem, sound** | **make sb** *The smell of the sea air makes you glad to be alive!*
- ADV. **awfully, extremely, heartily, only too, really, terribly, very** *She was only too glad to escape them all.* | **just** *I'm just glad it's all over.* | **almost** *Danny looked almost glad to be going.* | **quite, rather** | **secretly** *She was secretly glad of his company.*
- PREP. **about** *What have I got to be glad about?* **for** *We're glad for you both.* **of** *I was quite glad of his help.*

glamorous adj.

- VERBS **be, feel, look, seem, sound** | **become** | **consider sth, regard sth as, see sth as** *Canoeing is not seen as glamorous in the way that skiing is.*
- ADV. **really, very** | **less than, not exactly, not in the least** *Working in publishing turned out to be less than glamorous.* | **quite, rather**

glamour noun

- QUANT. **touch** *Several film stars were invited to add a touch of glamour to the occasion.*
- VERB + GLAMOUR **have** *He had a glamour about him that she found very attractive.* | **lack** *Jumbo jets somehow lack the glamour of the transatlantic liner.* | **add, give sb/sth, lend sb/sth** *Her long dark hair lent her a certain glamour.*
- PHRASES **a certain glamour**

glance noun

- ADJ. **backward, sidelong, sideways** *She cast a sidelong glance at Fern.* | **brief, cursory, fleeting, quick, swift** *After a cursory glance at the report he frowned.* | **casual** | **covert, furtive, surreptitious** *The man walked slowly along, casting furtive glances behind him.* | **accusing, angry, baleful, disapproving, mocking, reproachful, scornful, sharp, suspicious, withering** *Meena threw him an angry glance.* | **curious, puzzled, questioning, quizzical** | **admiring, approving** | **knowing** | **meaningful** *The couple exchanged meaningful glances but said nothing.* | **amused, wry** | **anxious, nervous, worried** | **plaintive**
- VERB + GLANCE **cast (sb), dart, give (sb/sth), have, shoot (sb), steal, take, throw (sb)** *He gave her a mocking glance.* ◇ *I had a quick glance at the article, but I haven't read it yet.* ◇ *He stole a sidelong glance at the young woman sitting next to him on the train.* ◇ *She took one last glance in the mirror and then left.* | **exchange** *They exchanged knowing glances.* | **catch** *I caught the teacher's glance and nearly burst into nervous laughter.* | **attract, draw** *Their vintage car attracted admiring glances wherever they went.*
- GLANCE + VERB **flick, flicker, move** *Her glance flickered briefly across to the group standing at the other side of the street.* | **meet** *Their glances met, then they both looked away.* | **fall on sb/sth, rest on sb/sth** *His glance fell on a pile of papers at one side of the desk.*
- PREP. **at a ~** *The software allows you to see at a glance what fonts you have on the computer.* **with a ~** *With a quick glance at the time, she stood up and prepared to leave.* **without a ~** *He left without a backward glance.* | **~ at** *A glance at my watch told me it was already past six o'clock.* **~ of** *He ignored my glance of disapproval.* **~ over** *He kept throwing nervous glances over his shoulder.*

glance verb

- ADV. **briefly, quickly, sharply** *Norton glanced sharply at him.* | **anxiously, fearfully, nervously** *She glanced nervously over her shoulder.* | **curiously** *glancing curiously about him* | **covertly** *He glanced covertly at his watch.* | **barely, hardly** *She barely glanced at him.* | **down, up** *She glanced up at him.*
- VERB + GLANCE **pause to, turn to** *He turned to glance in our direction.* | **happen to** *At that moment she happened to glance up.*
- PREP. **about/around/round** *She glanced around the room.* **across/over** *She glanced across to where the others were standing chatting.* **at** *She glanced briefly at his lapel badge.* **towards** *He glanced towards the kitchen.*

gland noun

- ADJ. **enlarged, swollen** *She's gone to bed with swollen glands and a temperature.* | **adrenal, endocrine, exocrine, pineal, pituitary, prostate, sebaceous, thyroid** | **poison, salivary, scent, sweat, venom** *Female ants release pheromones from their scent glands.*
- GLAND + VERB **release sth, secrete sth**

glandular fever noun

⇨ Special page at ILLNESS

glare noun

1 strong light

- ADJ. **blinding, full, harsh, hot** | **sudden** *A sudden glare of headlights lit the driveway.*
- VERB + GLARE **reflect** *The walls were whitewashed to reflect the glare of the sun.* | **reduce** *We wore sunglasses to reduce the glare from the road.* | **be blinded by, be dazzled by** *For a moment she was blinded by the harsh glare of the sun.* | **be caught in** *The rabbit was caught in the glare of the car's headlights.*
- PREP. **against the ~** *We screwed up our eyes against the blinding glare from the searchlights.* **in/under the ~ of** *Under the glare of the street lamps, visibility was good.* | **~ from**
- PHRASES **the glare of publicity** *(figurative) The divorce was conducted in the full glare of media publicity.*

2 angry look

- ADJ. **angry, baleful, defiant, furious, hostile, malevolent, menacing, withering** | **icy, steely, stony** | **warning**
- VERB + GLARE **fix sb with, give sb, send sb, shoot**

(sb), **turn on sb** *She fixed her questioner with an icy glare.* ◇ *He sent her a glare that was full of suspicion.* ◇ *She shot a warning glare at her companion.* ◇ *He turned his baleful glare on the cowering suspect.*

glare *verb*

- ADV. **angrily, balefully, fiercely, furiously** | **back** *I looked at her and she glared angrily back.*
- PREP. **(down/up) at** *He stood at the bottom of the stairs, glaring up at us.*

glass *noun*

1 transparent substance
- ADJ. **clear, coloured, opaque, plain, smoked, tinted** | **broken** | **flying** *A bomb went off, and many people were injured by flying glass.* | **bulletproof, cut, frosted, plate, safety, stained, toughened**
- QUANT. **piece** | **pane, sheet** | **fragment, sliver, splinter** *The floor was littered with fragments of broken glass.*
- VERB + GLASS **blow, make** *watching the Venetian craftsmen blowing glass* ◇ *The factory makes safety glass.* | **break, crack, shatter, smash**
- GLASS + VERB **break, crack, shatter, smash, splinter** *the sound of breaking glass*
- GLASS + NOUN **beads, bottle, bowl, eye, jar, vase** | **cabinet, case** | **door, panel, partition, roof, wall** | **fibre** *a boat made of glass fibre*
- PREP. **behind ~** *The books were all behind glass* (= in glass cases). **on ~** *She cut her foot on some glass.* **under ~** *growing fruit under glass* (= in a glasshouse) **through ~** *He could see the light through the frosted glass.*

2 for drinking
- ADJ. **brimming, full** | **half-empty, half-full** | **empty** | **beer, brandy, champagne, sherry, whisky, wine** | **crystal** *a set of crystal glasses* | **tall** *a tall glass of milk* | **fresh** *He poured her a fresh glass of sherry.* | **pint** *beer in a pint glass*
- VERB + GLASS **have** *He had a small glass of lager with his meal.* | **drink, sip** *She sat sipping a glass of champagne.* | **drain, empty** | **fill, pour, refill, top up** *The waiter filled their glasses.* | **clean, polish, wash** *The butler was polishing the brandy glasses.* | **raise** *She raised the glass to her lips.* | **hand sb** *I handed her a glass of wine.* | **put down, set down** *I put my glass down on the table.* | **clink** *They clinked glasses, still laughing.*
- GLASS + VERB **clink** *He heard glasses clinking in the other room.*
- PREP. **in a/the/sb's ~** *the red liquid in his glass* | **~ of** *She had had three glasses of whisky already.*
- PHRASES **(a) glass in (your) hand** *He sat back, glass in hand.*

glasses *noun*

- ADJ. **dark, sun** (also **sunglasses**), **tinted** *I wear blue-tinted glasses on sunny days.* | **reading** | **half-moon, (little) round** | **pebble, thick, thick-lensed** *a short, fat man with greasy black hair and thick pebble glasses* | **granny** | **owlish** | **heavy** | **gold-rimmed, horn-rimmed, steel-rimmed, wire-framed/wire-rimmed** | **rimless** | **field, opera**
- QUANT. **pair**
- VERB + GLASSES **have on, wear** | **put on** | **remove, take off** | **look over, peer over** *Her father lowered his paper and peered over his glasses at her.* | **adjust, push up** *She pushed her glasses up and rubbed the bridge of her nose.* | **clean, polish, wipe**
- GLASSES + VERB **steam up** *His glasses steamed up as soon as he came indoors.* | **be perched on sth, perch on sth** *Horn-rimmed glasses perched on the bridge of her nose.*
- PREP. **behind (your) ~** *She blinked behind her glasses.* ◇ *Their anxious faces were hidden behind dark glasses.*

gleam *noun*

1 soft light
- ADJ. **dull, faint** | **distant**
- PREP. **~ of** *the distant gleam of the sea*
- PHRASES **a gleam of light** *a faint gleam of light from the doorway*

2 in sb's eyes
- ADJ. **cold, dark, strange** | **predatory, speculative** | **mischievous, sardonic, wicked** | **sudden**
- VERB + GLEAM **have** *He had a speculative gleam in his eyes.*
- GLEAM + VERB **come into/enter/light sb's eye/eyes** *A sudden gleam came into her eye as she remembered that tomorrow was her day off.*
- PREP. **~ of** *A gleam of laughter lit his eyes.*
- PHRASES **a gleam in sb's eye/eyes**

gleam *verb*

- ADV. **dully, faintly, softly** *The knife's blade gleamed dully in the dark.*
- PREP. **with** *The long oak table gleamed with polish.*
- PHRASES **gleam golden, white, etc.** *The pebble beach gleamed white in the moonlight.*

glimmer *noun*

- ADJ. **faint, tiny** *In the east we could see the first faint glimmer of dawn.* ◇ *(figurative) The faint glimmer of an idea had crept into his mind.*
- PREP. **~ of**

glimpse *noun*

1 brief sight of sb/sth
- ADJ. **brief, fleeting, the merest, momentary, quick** | **occasional** *They caught occasional glimpses of great birds circling.* | **tantalizing** *This was my first tantalizing glimpse of the islands.*
- VERB + GLIMPSE **catch, get, have, take** *Thousands of people had gathered, hoping to catch a glimpse of the Queen.* ◇ *We only had a fleeting glimpse of the sun all day.* | **afford sb**
- PREP. **~ at** *He took a quick glimpse at the map.* **~ of** *We got just a brief glimpse of the car as it rushed by.*

2 brief experience of sth
- ADJ. **brief** | **fascinating, intriguing** | **rare** *This scene may give a rare glimpse of Charles's personal style as king.*
- VERB + GLIMPSE **get, have, take** | **afford sb, allow sb, give sb, offer (sb), provide** *That smile afforded her a brief glimpse of the other side of Adam Burns.*
- PREP. **~ at** *The exhibition offers a fascinating glimpse at life beneath the waves.* **~ into** *Take a glimpse into the future of rail travel.* **~ of** *She got a glimpse of a very different way of life.*

glint *noun*

1 flash of light
- ADJ. **golden, metallic**
- VERB + GLINT **catch, see** *Among the trees I caught a glint of blue.*
- PREP. **~ of**

2 in sb's eye
- ADJ. **dangerous, determined** | **mischievous, playful, teasing**
- VERB + GLINT **have** *He had a dangerous glint in his eyes.*
- GLINT + VERB **appear in sb's eye/eyes, come into/to sb's eye/eyes** *A determined glint appeared in her eye.*
- PREP. **~ in, ~ of** *There was a glint of amusement in her eyes.*

glint verb

- ADV. **angrily** *His eyes glinted angrily.*
- PREP. **with** *Her eyes glinted with amusement.*

glitter verb

1 shine brightly
- ADV. **brightly** *Crystal chandeliers glittered brightly above them.*
- PREP. **in** *His metal buttons glittered in the sunlight.* **with** *Trees and grass glittered with dew.*

2 show emotion
- ADV. **coldly, dangerously, darkly, fiercely, strangely** *His deep-set eyes glittered coldly.*
- PREP. **with** *Her eyes glittered with delight.*

globe noun the globe

- VERB + GLOBE **span** *a commercial service that will soon span the globe* | **circumnavigate, travel** *one of the first boats to circumnavigate the globe* ◇ *She travelled the globe in search of good writers of children's stories.*
- PREP. **across the ~** *The railway network soon spread across the globe.* **all over the ~** *Motor vehicles are found all over the globe.* **around/round the ~** *Chess fans around the globe watched the match with breathless interest.*
- PHRASES **all parts of the globe, every corner of the globe** *Athletes from every corner of the globe competed in the Games.*

gloom noun

1 sadness
- ADJ. **black, deep** *She was in deep gloom because not even a postcard had arrived from Ricky.* | **general** | **economic** *the general economic gloom*
- VERB + GLOOM **be filled with, be sunk in, sink into** *He was sunk in deep gloom at the prospect of being alone.* ◇ *I sank into gloom and depression.* | **fill sb with** *The news filled me with gloom.* | **cast** *Rumours of his ill health cast gloom over the celebrations.* | **combat, dispel, lift** *efforts to dispel their gloom*
- GLOOM + VERB **deepen, descend** *Their gloom deepened as the election results came in.* ◇ *She felt gloom descend on her shoulders.* | **lift** *When the gloom finally lifts, the pessimists will be surprised at how much has been going right.*
- PREP. **in ~** *The nation was deep in gloom.* | **~ about** *There is a general gloom about the farming industry.*
- PHRASES **doom and gloom** *Despite falling demand, the year has not been all doom and gloom.* **gloom and despondency** *the darkest feelings of gloom and despondency*

2 darkness
- ADJ. **deep | deepening, descending, gathering** *He peered into the gathering gloom.* | **cold, damp, dingy | evening** *The fog looked ominous in the evening gloom.*
- VERB + GLOOM **penetrate, pierce** *The sound of distant police whistles pierced the gloom.* | **adjust to, become/get accustomed to** *Slowly, my eyes became accustomed to the gloom.* | **peer into/through | be shrouded in** *The sun went in and the house was again shrouded in gloom.*
- GLOOM + VERB **deepen, descend** *We sat and watched as the gloom descended.*
- PREP. **in the ~** *We lost sight of them in the gloom.* **into the ~** *The tram rattled off into the gloom.* **out of the ~** *Two figures materialized out of the gloom.* **through the ~** *She could see the house faintly through the gloom.*

gloomy adj.

- VERBS **be, feel, look, seem, sound | become, get** *Now, don't start to get gloomy.* | **remain**
- ADV. **decidedly, very** *The future looked decidedly*

gloomy. | **far from** *The committee's view was in fact far from gloomy.* | **pretty, rather**
- PREP. **about** *Her trainer was even more gloomy about the prospects for British tennis.*

glory noun

1 fame/honour
- ADJ. **personal** *They are driven by a craving for personal glory.* | **reflected** *She basked in the reflected glory of her daughter's success.* | **greater** *The force behind all Peter's reforms was the greater glory of the Russian state.* | **military** *young soldiers keen to win military glory*
- VERB + GLORY **cover yourself in/with, get, win** *He covered himself in glory and came home a rich man.* ◇ (*informal*) *Typical! I do all the work and she gets all the glory.* | **bring (sb)** *Victory brought them glory, fame and riches.* | **bask in | steal, take** *It was 19-year-old David Hagan who stole the points and the glory with a brilliant goal in the closing minutes of the game.*
- GLORY + NOUN **days** *We remember the team's glory days in the 1960s, when they won the World Cup.*
- PREP. **for/to the ~ of** *They built many churches, great and small, to the glory of God.*
- PHRASES **a blaze of glory** *It's my last ever tournament and I hope to go out in a blaze of glory!* **sb's moment of glory** *His moment of glory came when he won the Olympic downhill skiing event.*

2 beauty/beautiful feature
- ADJ. **full** *You cannot appreciate the bridge's full glory by going over it; it is best viewed from below.* | **crowning** *The city's crowning glory is its Gothic cathedral.*
- PHRASES **in all her/his/its/their glory** *Autumn is the time to see the beech woods in all their glory.* **restore sth to its former glory** *The eighteenth-century building has been restored to its former glory.*

gloss noun

- ADJ. **clear, high** *Use a high gloss paint.* | **healthy, natural** *Your hair has lost its natural gloss.*
- VERB + GLOSS **add** *We used a gel to add gloss to her hair.* | **lose**
- GLOSS + NOUN **finish, paint, varnish** *furniture with a dark gloss finish*

glove noun

- ADJ. **long | fingerless | protective | cotton, kid** (*often figurative*), **latex, leather, rubber, woollen** *Treat her with kid gloves—she's very sensitive.* | **boxing, driving, evening, gardening, oven, surgical**
- QUANT. **pair**
- VERB + GLOVE **pull on | peel off, pull off** *She peeled off her glove to reveal a wedding ring.*
- GLOVE + NOUN **compartment** *Don't keep important documents in the glove compartment of your car.*
⇨ Special page at CLOTHES

glow noun

1 steady light
- ADJ. **cosy, rich, soft, warm | dim, dull, faint, pale | fierce | steady | eerie, ghostly**
- VERB + GLOW **cast, give sth, throw** *The lamplight gave a cosy glow to the room.* ◇ *The sunset threw an orange glow on the cliffs.* | **be bathed in** *The whole village was bathed in the glow of the setting sun.*
- GLOW + VERB **light sth** *Our faces were lit by the faint green glow of the dashboard lights.*
- PREP. **~ from** *the soft glow from the lamp* **~ of**

2 in sb's face
- ADJ. **healthy, pink, rosy, warm**
- VERB + GLOW **have** *Her cheeks had a healthy glow.*

- PHRASES **bring a glow to sb's cheeks/face** *The wine had brought a warm glow to her cheeks.*

3 feeling
- ADJ. **rosy, warm**
- VERB + GLOW **bask in, bathe in, feel** *She bathed in the warm glow of first love.*
- PREP. **~of** *He felt a glow of pride as he watched them.*

glow *verb*

1 give out light/heat
- ADV. **dully, faintly, softly** *Two lamps glowed softly in the lounge.*
- PHRASES **glow orange, red, etc.** *The stones around the bonfire glowed red with the heat.*

2 look healthy, happy, angry, etc.
- ADV. **positively**
- PREP. **with** *She was positively glowing with happiness.*

glue *noun*

- QUANT. **pot, tube** *All you will need is a sharp knife and a pot of glue.*
- VERB + GLUE **apply, put on** *Put glue on both the surfaces.* | **sniff** *He took to drinking and sniffing glue.*
- GLUE + VERB **dry, set** *It takes about half an hour for the glue to set.*

glue *verb*

- ADV. **firmly | down, in/into place, together** *Glue the pieces firmly together.*
- PREP. **onto/to** *Someone's glued this coin to the table!*

go *verb*

1 happen
- ADV. **smoothly, well** *Everything went very smoothly.* | **badly**

2 pass
- ADV. **quickly, slowly** *The holiday went very quickly.* | **by** *The days seemed to go by very slowly.*

3 look/taste good with sth
- ADV. **well | together** *Leeks and potatoes go well together in a soup.*
- PREP. **with** *That tie goes well with that shirt.*

PHRASAL VERBS

go down
- ADV. **badly, well**
- PREP. **with** *The novel went down well with the public.*

go on
- ADV. **endlessly**
- PREP. **about** *He goes on endlessly about his health problems.* **at** *Stop going on at me about that money.* **with** *We'll go on with the presentations after lunch.*
- PHRASES **go on and on** *The journey just seemed to go on and on.*

goal *noun*

1 wooden frame into which a ball is kicked/hit
- ADJ. **open** *He kicked the ball into an open goal.*
- VERB + GOAL **go in, play in** *The goalkeeper was injured so a defender had to go in goal.*
- PREP. **in~** *Who's in goal for Arsenal?*

2 point scored in a game
- ADJ. **brilliant, excellent, good, great, spectacular, stunning, superb, well-taken | scrappy, soft** *The fans were annoyed that the team gave away such a soft goal.* | **decisive, winning | equalizing | important, useful, vital | own** *Vega scored an unfortunate own goal when he slipped as he tried to clear the ball.*
- VERB + GOAL **get, score | kick** (in rugby) | **head** (in) | **make** *Visconti scored one goal himself and made two for*

Lupo. | **concede, give away, let in | allow, disallow** *The referee disallowed the goal.*
- GOAL + VERB **come from sb/sth** *The equalizing goal came from Cole.* ◇ *The second goal came from a penalty.*
- PREP. **~against** *They scored three goals against the home team.* **~for** *his first goal for Spain* **~from** *A late goal from Owen won the game for Liverpool.*
  ⇨ Special page at SPORT

3 aim
- ADJ. **immediate, short-term** *Our immediate goal is to earn enough money to keep the business going.* | **long-term, ultimate | main, major, primary, prime | clear, explicit, specific | ambitious** *They have set themselves some ambitious goals.* | **modest | desirable | achievable, attainable, realistic | unattainable, unrealistic | elusive | personal | common** *We are all working towards a common goal.* | **twin** *The prison service pursues the twin goals of the punishment and rehabilitation of offenders.* | **strategic | political**
- VERB + GOAL **have** *It is important to have explicit goals.* | **establish, set (sb) | pursue, strive for, work towards | achieve, attain, reach**
- PREP. **~of** *their goal of providing free university education for everyone*

goalkeeper *noun*

- ADJ. **brilliant, excellent, good | England, Liverpool, etc.** *The England goalkeeper played brilliantly.* | **international | reserve, substitute | veteran, young**
- PREP. **~for** *He now plays as goalkeeper for Liverpool.*

goat *noun*

- ADJ. **billy, male | female, nanny | wild | mountain**
- QUANT. **flock, herd**
- VERB + GOAT **keep | milk | tether** *Tethered goats grazed among the apple trees.*
- GOAT + VERB **bleat | graze | wander**
- PHRASES **goat's cheese/milk**

god *noun*

- ADJ. **pagan | Christian, Greek, Roman, etc. | heathen, false** *those who follow false gods* | **fertility | sun**
- VERB + GOD **believe in, follow, have** *Do you believe in God?* ◇ *Muslims have only one God.* | **praise, pray to, thank, worship** *The people worshipped pagan gods.*
- GOD + VERB **exist** *Can we prove that God exists?*
- PREP. **~of** *the Roman god of war*
- PHRASES **faith in God** *Nothing ever shook her faith in God.* **the will of God** *He saw the accident as the will of God.*

goddess *noun*

- ADJ. **pagan | Egyptian, Roman, etc. | fertility, mother | moon, sun | screen** (*figurative*) *She dreamed of becoming a Hollywood screen goddess.*
- VERB + GODDESS **pray to, worship**
- PREP. **~of** *Aphrodite, the goddess of love*

goggles *noun*

- ADJ. **protective, safety | driving, flying, motorcycle, ski, snow, swimming**
- QUANT. **pair**
- VERB + GOGGLES **have on, wear | put on, take off**
- GOGGLES + VERB **steam up** *My swimming goggles keep steaming up so I can't see.*

gold *noun*

1 yellow metal
- ADJ. **pure | real | solid | fool's | 9-carat, 18-carat, etc. | molten | beaten, rolled | burnished | tarnished**
- VERB + GOLD **extract, mine, produce | look for, pan**

for, prospect for *He spent weeks panning for gold in the river.* | **discover, find, strike** | **be set in** *The rubies were set in 18-carat gold.*

● GOLD + NOUN **mine, miner, mining, prospecting, prospector** | **rush** *a gold rush town* | **deposit, dust, nugget** | **bar, bullion, ingot** | **leaf, plate** | **market, reserves, stocks** *falling government gold stocks* | **standard** *The currency was tied to the gold standard.*

● PHRASES **a vein of gold** *In the afternoon he struck a rich vein of gold.*

2 (*also* **gold medal**) in sports

● ADJ. **Olympic**

● VERB + GOLD **get, take, win** *She got a gold in the long jump.* | **go for** *She's going for gold this time.*

golden *adj.*

● VERBS **be, gleam, look** *The abbey walls gleamed golden in the light of the setting sun.* | **turn** *The whole sky turned golden and red.*

● ADV. **faintly, softly** *the faintly golden afternoon light*

golf *noun*

● ADJ. **amateur, pro, pro-am, professional** *Amateur golf is very competitive.* | **mini/miniature** *The hotel offers miniature golf and other activities for children.*

● QUANT. **game, round**

● VERB + GOLF **play** | **take up** | **watch**

● GOLF + NOUN **course, links** | **hole** *The eighth at Banff is one of the world's great golf holes.* | **club** *She decided to join a golf club.* | **ball, bag, buggy, cart, club, equipment, glove, shoes, tee, umbrella** *You can borrow golf clubs if you want a game.* | **swing** *His coach says his golf swing needs improving.* | **game, match, tournament** | **title** | **handicap** *She has a golf handicap of 18.* | **professional, star** | **fan/fanatic** | **season** | **circuit, scene, tour** | **clinic, lesson** *The club is holding a golf clinic next week, where golfers can get advice from the pros.* | **correspondent, journalist, reporter, writer** | **magazine** | **holiday, package** *Choose from over 100 golf packages in our brochure.* | **widow** *She's been a golf widow since she gave her husband his first set of clubs.*

⇨ Special page at SPORT

golfer *noun*

● ADJ. **brilliant, good** | **experienced** | **handicap** *a low handicap golfer* | **champion, top** | **keen** | **amateur, professional** | **club**

● GOLFER + VERB **play**

good *noun*

● ADJ. **common** *The results of the research should be used for the common good rather than for individual profit.*

● VERB + GOOD **do (sb)** *You can try talking to her, but I don't think it will do much good.* ◇ *It will do you good to get out of the house more often.*

● PREP. **for sb/sth's ~** *When the prime minister's health problems continued, he resigned for the good of the party.*

● PHRASES **a force for good** *In disadvantaged areas, schools can be a force for good.* **for sb's (own) good** *I know you don't want to go into hospital, but it's for your own good.* **for the good of sth, good and evil** *the struggle between good and evil* **a power of good** *That holiday has done me a power of good.*

good *adj.*

● VERBS **be, feel, look, seem, smell, sound, taste** | **become, get** *She's getting quite good at reading now.*

● ADV. **dead, extremely, really, very** *a really good film* | **fairly, pretty, quite** *You've done a pretty good job.*

● PREP. **at** *He's very good at music.* **for** *Vegetables are*

good for you. **to** *She was very good to me when my husband died.* **with** *She's good with figures.*

good-looking *adj.*

● VERBS **be**

● ADV. **extraordinarily, extremely, really, strikingly, terribly, very** | **not exactly, not particularly** *She was not exactly good-looking, but definitely attractive.* | **quite, rather, reasonably** *He was tall and quite good-looking.*

goods *noun*

● ADJ. **consumer, electrical, electronic, household, luxury** *a shop selling electrical goods* | **durable, perishable** *A 'use by' date must be stamped on all perishable goods.* | **mass-produced** | **cheap, low-priced** | **branded, own-label** *The supermarket's own-label goods are cheaper than branded goods.* | **duty-free** | **second-hand** | **defective, faulty, shoddy** | **stolen** *He was accused of handling stolen goods.* | **counterfeit, fake**

● VERB + GOODS **make, manufacture, produce** *factories which produce luxury goods for the export market* | **buy, purchase** | **export, import** | **sell, supply** | **deliver** *The goods will be delivered within ten days.* | **transport**

● GOODS + NOUN **train, vehicle, wagon** | **depot, yard**

goodwill *noun*

● VERB + GOODWILL **enjoy, have** | **create** *Addressing customers in their own language helps create goodwill.* | **win** | **lose** *They are in danger of losing the government's goodwill.* | **depend on, rely on** | **express, show**

● PREP. **~ to, ~ towards** *He expressed goodwill towards his former colleagues.*

● PHRASES **a gesture of goodwill** *The government released him as a gesture of goodwill.* **in a spirit of goodwill** *They made the offer in a spirit of goodwill.*

goose *noun*

● ADJ. **wild** | **roast**

● QUANT. **flock, gaggle** (only used for geese on the ground), **skein** (only used for geese that are flying)

● GOOSE + VERB **waddle** | **hiss, honk** | **feed, graze** | **migrate**

gorgeous *adj.*

● VERBS **be, look, sound** *Doesn't Kate look gorgeous?*

● ADV. **really** | **absolutely, drop-dead, simply** *a drop-dead gorgeous Hollywood icon* | **rather**

gospel *noun* the gospel

● ADJ. **Christian**

● VERB + GOSPEL **bring, preach, proclaim, spread, take** *She preached the Christian gospel to the poor and destitute.* | **hear** *Thousands came to hear the gospel.*

● GOSPEL + NOUN **message, story**

gossip *noun*

1 rumours about other people

● ADJ. **latest** | **common** *It's common gossip in the office that she's about to leave her husband.* | **idle, malicious, salacious, silly**

● QUANT. **bit, piece, titbit** *I heard an interesting bit of gossip yesterday.*

● VERB + GOSSIP **spread** *Someone has been spreading malicious gossip about me.* | **exchange, swap** | **hear, listen to, pay attention to** *You shouldn't listen to idle gossip.*

● GOSSIP + VERB **circulate, go around/round** *A piece of silly gossip was going round the school.*

● GOSSIP + NOUN **column, columnist** *I saw it in the gossip column of the local newspaper.*

● PREP. ~ **about** *a magazine full of gossip about famous people*

2 conversation about other people
● ADJ. **good**
● VERB + GOSSIP **have**
● PREP. ~ **about** *We had a good gossip about the boss.* ~**with** *She's having a gossip with Maria.*

govern *verb*

● ADV. **well** | **directly** *The colony was governed directly from Paris.*
● VERB + GOVERN **be fit/unfit to** *He accused the opposition party of being unfit to govern.*

government *noun*

1 people in control of a country
● ADJ. **central, federal, local, national, provincial, regional** | **Communist, Conservative, Labour, etc.** *the country's new Communist government* | **left-wing, right-wing** | **coalition** | **minority** *The socialists won 42% of the seats and formed a minority government.* | **caretaker, interim, transitional** *The president dissolved the assembly and swore in an interim government.* | **military** | **puppet** | **French, Western, etc.** *The report on world poverty calls for urgent action from Western governments.*
● VERB + GOVERNMENT **elect** *The present government was elected last year.* | **form** *A new government was formed in September of that year.* | **install** *A puppet government was installed as the occupying forces withdrew.* | **swear in** | **head, run** *a new government headed by a former military leader* | **bring down, destabilize, oust, overthrow, topple** *This crisis could bring down the British government.* ◇ *The group aims to overthrow the military government.*
● GOVERNMENT + VERB **come to power** | **take office** *On May 23 a coalition government took office.* | **fall, resign** *a national emergency that could cause the government to fall* | **announce sth** *The government announced the cancellation of the dam project.* | **introduce sth, launch sth**
● GOVERNMENT + NOUN **agency, body, department** | **funds, money** | **aid, assistance, backing, funding, grant, subsidy, support** | **expenditure, spending** | **cuts** *The hospital has been hit by government cuts.* | **control** | **intervention, involvement** *calls for government intervention in the dispute* | **minister, official, representative, spokesman** | **sources** *According to government sources, two people died in the incident.* | **figures, statistics** | **post** | **reshuffle** *The former minister was relieved of his post in last month's extensive government reshuffle.* | **decisions, legislation, measures, plans, policy, proposals** | **report** | **propaganda**
● PREP. **in** ~ *a problem facing whichever party is in government* **under a/the** ~ *measures that were introduced under the last government*
● PHRASES **a change of government** *It is time we had a change of government.* **the government of the day** *This was a decision taken by the government of the day.* **a member of a government** *The prime minister has been meeting members of the French government.*

2 act of governing
● ADJ. **democratic, representative** | **firm, good, strong** *We need strong government to take the country through this crisis.* | **weak**

governor *noun*

● ADJ. **deputy** | **acting, interim** *She was appointed as acting governor until an election could be held.* | **colonial, district, provincial, regional, state** | **imperial** | **military** | **prison, school** | **parent** *She served as a parent governor at her children's school.*
● VERB + GOVERNOR **appoint, appoint sb (as), co-opt,**

co-opt sb (as), elect, elect sb (as) | **serve as**
● PHRASES **a board of governors**

gown *noun*

1 woman's long dress
● ADJ. **long** | **flowing** *She was dressed in a long flowing gown.* | **ball, bridal, evening, wedding**
● GOWN + VERB **be trimmed with sth** *She wore a white satin gown trimmed with lace.*
● PREP. **in a/the~**

2 worn by judges, surgeons, etc.
● ADJ. **academic** | **hospital, surgical**
● PREP. **in a/the~**
● PHRASES **town and gown** (= the permanent members of a university town and the members of its university)
⇨ Special page at CLOTHES

GP *noun*

● ADJ. **excellent, good** | **qualified** | **experienced** | **family, local** *Who is your local GP?*
● VERB + GP **register with** *You should register with a GP as soon as possible.*
● GP + VERB **refer sb** *The GP referred her to a specialist.*
⇨ Note at DOCTOR (for more verbs)

grab *verb*

● ADV. **suddenly**
● VERB + GRAB **try to** | **manage to** *He managed to grab a couple of hours' sleep.*
● PREP. **at** *I grabbed at his arm as he ran past.* **by** *As he walked past the boys, one of them grabbed him by the arm.* **from** *Somebody tried to grab her handbag from her.*
● PHRASES **grab hold of sth** *He grabbed hold of a handrail to save himself from falling.*

grace *noun*

● ADJ. **easy, lithe, supple** | **natural** | **feline**
● VERB + GRACE **have, move with**
● PREP. **with**~ *Ann moved with easy grace.*

grade *noun*

1 level/quality
● ADJ. **high, top** *a piece of high grade building land* ◇ *He still wants to play top grade football.* | **low, poor** *low grade steel*

2 mark given for a piece of work/an exam
● ADJ. **final** *The oral exam constitutes 10% of the final grade.* | **excellent, good, high** | **low, poor**
● VERB + GRADE **achieve, attain, get, receive** *She got very good grades in her exams.* | **award (sb)**

3 level of importance/level of pay at work
● ADJ. **high, senior** *He has asked to be put onto a higher grade.* ◇ *large pay rises for senior grades* | **junior, low** | **management** | **manual**
● PREP. **at a/the ...** ~ *She was offered a job at a lower grade.* **on a/the ...** ~ *the people on management grades*

grade *verb*

● ADV. **carefully** *a series of modern stories carefully graded for beginner to intermediate students*
● PREP. **according to** *The timber is graded according to its thickness.* **by** *The containers are graded by size.* **from ... to ...** *Eggs are graded from small to extra large.*

gradient *noun*

● ADJ. **steep** | **gentle, slight** | **downhill, uphill**
● VERB + GRADIENT **have** *The road has a fairly steep gradient.*
● PREP. **on a**~ *The football pitch was on a slight gradient.*

graduate *noun*

- ADJ. **college, university** *job opportunities for university graduates* | **arts, engineering, history, law, medical, science, etc.** | **new, recent**
- GRADUATE + NOUN **course, degree, diploma** | **school** | **student** | **recruit, trainee** *He joined the company as a graduate trainee.* | **employment, recruitment** *The company places great importance on graduate recruitment and training.* | **unemployment**
- PREP. **~in** *a graduate in sociology*

graduation *noun*

- ADJ. **college, university**
- GRADUATION + NOUN **ceremony, day** *Mark's whole family attended his graduation ceremony.*
- PREP. **after ~** *She managed to find a job immediately after graduation.* **on/upon ~** *On graduation, he plans to travel around Asia.*

graffiti *noun*

- ADJ. **political, racist**
- QUANT. **piece**
- VERB + GRAFFITI **daub, draw, scrawl, scribble, spray, write** *Graffiti was scribbled all over the walls.* | **be covered with, be daubed with, be sprayed with** *The buildings were covered with racist graffiti.*
- GRAFFITI + NOUN **artist** *a fashionable graffiti artist*

graft *noun*

1 on part of the body
- ADJ. **bone, skin**
- VERB + GRAFT **do** *Doctors are hoping to do a bone graft to repair the damaged bone.*
- GRAFT + VERB **take** *If the skin graft takes, then surgeons will do another operation a few weeks later.*

2 hard work
- ADJ. **hard** *Starting a new business involves a lot of hard graft.*
- VERB + GRAFT **do** *Most of the graft was done for them by their assistants.*

grain *noun*

1 seeds of wheat, etc.
- VERB + GRAIN **grow, produce** | **sow** | **store**
- GRAIN + NOUN **harvest, production, yield** | **exports, imports**

2 natural pattern of lines in wood
- ADJ. **fine, smooth** | **coarse, rough** | **natural** *This wood has a beautiful natural grain.*
- PREP. **across/against the ~, along/with the ~** *Cut the wood along the grain.*

gram *noun*

⇨ Note at MEASURE

grammar *noun*

- ADJ. **correct, good** *Spelling and good grammar are both very important.* | **bad, incorrect** | **Arabic, French, Latin, etc.** *the complexities of English grammar*
- VERB + GRAMMAR **correct, teach** *People were too polite to correct my grammar when spoke I German.* | **learn**
- GRAMMAR + NOUN **rules**
- PHRASES **the rules of grammar**

grammatical *adj.*

- VERBS **be, sound**
- ADV. **perfectly** *This sentence is perfectly grammatical.*

grandeur *noun*

- ADJ. **rugged** *the rugged grandeur of the mountains* | **breathtaking, dramatic, majestic, sheer** *the breathtaking grandeur of the cathedral* | **faded, former**

grandfather, grandmother *noun*

- ADJ. **maternal, paternal** | **doting**

grandparent *noun*

- ADJ. **maternal, paternal** | **doting** *a present from his doting grandparents*
- QUANT. **set** *I've sent photos of the children to both sets of grandparents.*

grant *noun*

- ADJ. **large, substantial** | **small** | **full** *The full student maintenance grant was rather less than £2 000.* | **annual** | **capital, lump-sum, purchase** *The school has received a large capital grant to improve its buildings.* | **maintenance** | **emergency** *emergency grants for special needs for items such as cookers and clothing* | **discretionary** | **mandatory** | **student** | **project, research** *There is a lot of competition for research grants.* | **clothing, conservation, (home) improvement, land, maternity, renovation, training, etc.** | **Arts Council, EU, government, local authority, etc.**
- VERB + GRANT **apply for** | **be eligible for, qualify for** *You may be eligible for a clothing grant.* | **get, obtain, receive** *You can get a grant if you've lived in the area for three years.* | **award (sb), give sb, make (sb), offer (sb), provide (sb with)** *The government has awarded a 3.5 million pound grant for the restoration of the opera house.* | **refuse sb** | **cut** *The theatre's annual grant from the Arts Council has been cut.*
- PREP. **~ for** *a grant for a youth project* **~ from** *a grant from the local authority*

grant *verb*

- ADV. **expressly, specifically** *the rights expressly granted by the terms of the lease* | **effectively** *The law effectively grants the company immunity from prosecution.*
- VERB + GRANT **agree to, decide to** | **refuse to** *The judge refused to grant him bail.* | **be willing to**

grape *noun*

- ADJ. **juicy, sweet** *lovely sweet grapes* | **black, green, purple, white** | **seedless**
- QUANT. **bunch**
- VERB + GRAPE **eat, have** | **harvest, pick** *The first grapes are harvested in mid-August.* | **crush, tread** *The peasants were treading the grapes in huge vats.*
- GRAPE + NOUN **harvest**
⇨ Special page at FRUIT

graph *noun*

- ADJ. **bar, line**
- VERB + GRAPH **draw, produce** | **depict sth as/on, show sth as/in/on** *The statistics can be depicted as a graph.* | **plot sth on** *The figures are all plotted on a graph.*
- GRAPH + VERB **show sth** *She drew a graph showing the relationship between costs and sales.*
- GRAPH + NOUN **paper**
- PREP. **in a/the ~** *I decided to show the results in a bar graph.* **on a/the ~** *We can see on this graph how the company has grown over the last year.*
- PHRASES **in graph form** *Results can be shown in numeric or graph form.*

graphics *noun*

- ADJ. **computer** | **basic, simple** *The screen can display simple graphics as well as text.* | **colour** | **high-resolution** | **three-dimensional, two-dimensional**
- VERB + GRAPHICS **produce** | **display** | **manipulate** *The program can produce and manipulate text and graphics.* | **support** *The editor's PC should support desktop publishing and graphics.*
- GRAPHICS + NOUN **application, package, program, software, system** | **capability, performance** | **card, file, tablet, workstation** | **design, designer**
⇨ Special page at COMPUTER

grasp *noun*

1 holding sth
- ADJ. **firm, strong** *She felt a firm grasp on her hand.*
- VERB + GRASP **slip from** *As she jumped forward, the ball slipped from her grasp.* | **prise sth from, rip sth from, snatch sth from, wrench sth from, wrest sth from** *She wrenched the bottle from his grasp.*
- PREP. **beyond your ~** *The key was on a high shelf, just beyond her grasp.* **in your ~** *He kept the letter firmly in his grasp.* **from sb's ~** *The robber tried to free the case from her grasp.* **out of sb's ~** *She kicked the gun out of his grasp.* **within (your) ~** *(often figurative) Just when victory seemed within grasp, the referee blew his whistle.*

2 understanding
- ADJ. **fine, firm, good, impressive, proper, sound** | **limited, poor** | **intellectual** *The task was beyond the intellectual grasp of some of the students.* | **intuitive** *We have no intuitive grasp of the immensity of time.*
- VERB + GRASP **have** | **get** *Working with native speakers helped me get a good grasp of the language.*
- PREP. **beyond your ~** *These ideas are all beyond his grasp.* **within your ~** | **~ of** *a poor grasp of mathematics*

grasp *verb*

1 take hold of sb/sth suddenly and firmly
- ADV. **firmly, tightly**
- PREP. **at** *Her hands were grasping at his coat.* **by** *She grasped him tightly by the wrist.*
- PHRASES **grasp hold of sb/sth** *She grasped hold of the banister to support herself.*

2 understand sth
- ADV. **fully** *He had not fully grasped the fact that he was the one who would pay for all this.* | **not really** *I hadn't really grasped what they were talking about.* | **quickly** | **easily, readily** *a means by which students can more easily grasp the basics of science*
- VERB + GRASP **try to** | **be unable to, fail to** *She failed to grasp the significance of these facts.* | **quick to** *He was quick to grasp the basic principles.* | **be difficult to, be hard to** *Some of these concepts are very difficult to grasp.*

grass *noun*

- ADJ. **green** | **coarse, rough, thick** | **lush** | **long, tall** | **short** | **fresh-cut, freshly-cut, freshly-mown** | **damp, wet** | **dry** | **wild**
- QUANT. **blade** *I've walked along that path for so many years I know every blade of grass.* | **clump, tuft** *There were only a few clumps of coarse grass for the animals to eat.*
- VERB + GRASS **eat** | **cut, mow** | **sow**
- GRASS + VERB **grow**
- GRASS + NOUN **clippings, cuttings** | **seed** | **verge** *We parked on the grass verge by the side of the road.*
- PREP. **across the ~** *They all set off across the grass.* **in the ~** *I found the wallet lying in the grass.* **on the ~** *You're not allowed to walk on the grass.* **through the ~** *The dog came running through the long grass.*

grate *verb*

1 rub sth into small pieces
- ADV. **coarsely** | **finely** *Sprinkle the top of the dish with some finely grated cheese.*
- PHRASES **freshly grated** *a teaspoon of freshly grated nutmeg*

2 make a sharp unpleasant sound
- ADV. **harshly**
- PREP. **against** *The steel of the helmet grated against the door.* **on** *The grit beneath her soles grated harshly on the wooden deck.*

grateful *adj.*

- VERBS **be, feel, look, seem, sound** | **remain**
- ADV. **deeply, enormously, especially, extremely, genuinely, immensely, more than, most, particularly, profoundly, really, terribly, truly, very** *We are deeply grateful to you and your family.* ◇ *I am more than grateful for their generous response.* ◇ *Thank you for your help. I really am most grateful.* | **almost** *His father looked almost grateful for once.* | **quite, rather** | **just, simply** *I'm just grateful the injury is not as bad as we'd feared.* | **always** | **eternally** *I'm eternally grateful that we managed to go there before the war.*
- PREP. **for** *I'm really grateful for your help.* **to** *I'm immensely grateful to you for your support.*

gratifying *adj.*

- VERBS **be** | **find sth**
- ADV. **extremely, most, particularly, very**
- PREP. **for** *It is most gratifying for me to know that my work has been useful.*

gratitude *noun*

- ADJ. **deep, profound** | **heartfelt, real, sincere** | **eternal, undying**
- VERB + GRATITUDE **feel** *the very deep gratitude I felt towards her* | **express, show** | **earn (sb)** *His kindness and support earned him her eternal gratitude.*
- PREP. **in ~** *He almost wept in gratitude when he saw the money.* **with ~** *I remember them with gratitude.* | **~ at** *my gratitude at her thoughtfulness* **~ for, ~ to/towards** *I would like to express my deep sense of gratitude to the staff for their patience.*
- PHRASES **as a token of your gratitude** *I sent him some money as a token of my gratitude.* **owe a debt of gratitude to sb** *We owe her a deep debt of gratitude for her services.* **a feeling/sense of gratitude**

grave *noun*

- ADJ. **deep, shallow** *The body was found in a shallow grave in a nearby wood.* | **open** *The mourners threw flowers into the open grave.* | **freshly-dug** | **unmarked** *His body is buried in an unmarked grave.* | **mass** *A mass grave has been discovered in a wood outside the village.* | **watery** *He rescued her from a watery grave (= saved her from drowning).*
- VERB + GRAVE **dig** | **mark** *The grave was marked by a simple headstone.* | **desecrate** *Some of the graves have been desecrated by vandals.*
- PREP. **beyond the ~** *The old lady still influences the family from beyond the grave.* **in a/the ~** *I'll be in my grave by the time that happens!* **on a/the ~** *She puts fresh flowers on her husband's grave every Sunday.*

gravity *noun*

1 natural force
- ADJ. **weak, zero** *the weak gravity on the moon* | **strong**
- VERB + GRAVITY **be subject to** *All objects are subject*

to gravity. | **defy** *The building leans so much that it seems to defy gravity.*
● PREP. **by ~** *The water flows from the tank by gravity to the houses below.*
● PHRASES **centre of gravity** (*often figurative*) *Europe's economic centre of gravity shifted northwards.* **the force of gravity, the law/laws of gravity**

2 seriousness
● ADJ. **extreme** *I don't think you realize the extreme gravity of this offence.*
● VERB + GRAVITY **appreciate, realize, understand**
● PREP. **with ~** *Criminal law does not treat traffic offences with the gravity they deserve.*

graze *noun*
● ADJ. **minor, slight, small**
● VERB + GRAZE **get, have, suffer** *She suffered only minor grazes in the crash.*
● PREP. **~ on** *I've got a graze on my leg.*

graze *verb*
1 of animals
● ADV. **peacefully, quietly** *Sheep were grazing peacefully in the fields.*
● VERB + GRAZE **allow sth to, turn sth out to** *The cattle were turned out to graze.*
● PREP. **on/upon** *lambs grazing on the rough moorland pasture*

2 break the surface of your skin
● ADV. **badly** *She had grazed her elbow quite badly.*
● PREP. **on** *He fell and grazed his knees on a rock*

grease *noun*
● VERB + GREASE **be covered in/with, be smeared in/with** *The kitchen surfaces were all smeared with grease.* | **dissolve, remove**
● GREASE + NOUN **mark, spot, stain**
● PHRASES **a blob/smear of grease**

grease *verb*
● ADV. **well** | **lightly** *Place the cakes on a lightly greased baking tray.*

great *adj.*
1 large in amount/degree/size, etc.
● VERBS **be** | **become**
● ADV. **very** *The play was a very great success.*
● PHRASES **great big** *There's a great big hole in this sleeve.* **no great** *Don't worry. It's no great problem.*

2 admired
● VERBS **be**
● ADV. **really, truly, very** *He was a truly great man.*

3 very good/pleasant
● VERBS **be, feel, look, seem, smell, sound, taste** *You're looking great. Marriage must suit you!*
● ADV. **really** *That's really great news!* | **absolutely** *The food smells absolutely great.*

greatness *noun*
● ADJ. **true** *This book tells you nothing about the true greatness of his paintings.*
● VERB + GREATNESS **achieve** *those people who have achieved greatness* | **be destined for** *a woman who was destined for greatness*
● GREATNESS + VERB **lie** *Her greatness lies in her deep understanding of human nature.*

greed *noun*
● ADJ. **pure, sheer, simple** | **human, personal**

● VERB + GREED **satisfy** *She killed him to satisfy her greed.* | **be consumed by, be driven by**
● PREP. **~ for** *He was driven by greed for money and power.*

Greek *noun*
● ADJ. **ancient, classical** | **New Testament** | **modern**
● GREEK + NOUN **alphabet**
⇨ Note at LANGUAGE

green *adj.*
● ADV. **very** | **quite, slightly** *The cloth looked slightly green in that light.*
● ADJ. **bottle, dark** | **light, pale** | **bright, brilliant, emerald, lime, lush, rich, vivid** *wearing an emerald green dress* ◇ *the lush green grass* | **dull** | **olive** *an olive green carpet*
⇨ Special page at COLOUR

greet *verb*
1 say hello to sb
● ADV. **cheerfully, enthusiastically, pleasantly, warmly** *The two men greeted one another warmly.* | **courteously, politely** | **coolly** *Stella greeted her mother coolly.*
● VERB + GREET **be there to, be waiting to** *You must be there to greet your guests.* ◇ *My parents were waiting to greet us at the door.* | **come to, rise to, turn to** *The president rose to greet his guests.*
● PREP. **with** *She greeted him with a quick kiss.*
● PHRASES **greet sb by name** *The head teacher greeted all the pupils by name.*

2 react to sth in particular way
● ADV. **enthusiastically** | **coolly** | **angrily** *The announcement was greeted angrily by the workers.*
● PREP. **with** *The news was greeted with astonishment.*

greeting *noun*
1 first words you say when you meet sb
● ADJ. **formal, friendly, polite**
● VERB + GREETING **call (out), nod, shout, smile, wave** *He jumped to his feet and called out a greeting.* ◇ *They said nothing, but nodded a polite greeting.* | **exchange** *The delegates shook hands and exchanged greetings.* | **acknowledge, respond to, return** *I said 'Good morning!', but she didn't return the greeting.* | **ignore**
● PREP. **in ~** *He held out his hand in greeting.*

2 greetings good wishes
● ADJ. **affectionate, personal, warm** | **birthday, Christmas, New Year, seasonal**
● VERB + GREETINGS **bring, extend, send (sb)** *He brought Christmas greetings from the whole family.* ◇ *We extend our greetings to you and thank you for listening to us.*
● GREETINGS + NOUN **card**

gregarious *adj.*
● VERBS **be, seem** | **become**
● ADV. **highly, very** *These animals are highly gregarious.*

grenade *noun*
● ADJ. **hand, smoke, stun** | **rocket-propelled** | **live**
● VERB + GRENADE **be armed with, carry, have** *The hijackers were armed with hand grenades.* | **hold** *She was holding the grenade above her head, ready to throw.* | **hurl, lob, throw, toss** *I tossed the grenade through the open door.* | **pull the pin out of**
● GRENADE + VERB **fall, land** | **explode, go off**
● GRENADE + NOUN **attack** | **launcher**

grey adj.

1 of the colour between black and white
- ADV. **very** *The sky looks very grey. I think it's going to rain.* | **quite, rather, slightly**
- ADJ. **dark** | **light, pale** *a light grey suit* | **silvery, slate**
⇨ Special page at COLOUR

2 with grey hair
- VERBS **be** | **go, turn** *He went grey before he was forty.*
- ADV. **very** | **completely** *She was completely grey by the age of thirty.*

grid noun

1 pattern of lines that cross each other
- ADJ. **rectangular, square** | **regular**
- GRID + NOUN **line, pattern, square, system** *The artist drew a set of grid lines over the area to be painted.*

2 system of squares drawn on a map
- GRID + NOUN **line, reference, square** *The grid lines on the map run north-south.* ◇ *An Ordnance Survey grid reference gives the position of a place to within 100 metres.*

3 system of electric cables
- ADJ. **national** | **electricity**
- GRID + NOUN **system** *Power can be fed from wind generators into the electricity grid system.*

grief noun

- ADJ. **considerable, deep, great, inconsolable, real** | **private** *I felt awkward at intruding on their private grief.*
- VERB + GRIEF **be overcome with, be stricken with, experience, feel** *Her parents were stricken with grief.* | **express, show** | **die from/of** | **come to terms with, cope with, deal with** *struggling to come to terms with their grief* | **cause (sb)** *Such behaviour can cause considerable grief.*
- PREP. **~at** *Children can feel real grief at the loss of a pet.* **~for** *her grief for her dead husband*
- PHRASES **a feeling/sense of grief**

grievance noun

- ADJ. **genuine, legitimate, real** *Some people will complain even if they have no genuine grievance.* | **imaginary, imagined** | **long-standing, old** | **individual, personal** | **economic, social** *By the 1530s social grievances were again being voiced.*
- VERB + GRIEVANCE **harbour, have, nurse** *She still nursed her old grievance.* | **air, express, vent, voice** | **hear** *(formal),* **listen to** *MPs spend many hours listening to the real or imagined grievances of their constituents.* | **redress, remedy, settle** *Managers would make every effort to remedy individual grievances as they arose.*
- PREP. **~about/over** *The meeting will be a chance to air your grievances about the organization.* **~against** *He had a personal grievance against the professor.*
- PHRASES **a sense of grievance**

grieve verb

- ADV. **deeply** *She had grieved deeply for her father.* | **still**
- PREP. **for** *They are still grieving for their child.* **over** *grieving over the loss of his daughter*

grill noun

1 part of a cooker
- ADJ. **hot** *Cook under a hot grill for 7 minutes.* | **eye-level** | **electric, gas**
- VERB + GRILL **preheat** *Preheat the grill to medium.*
- GRILL + NOUN **pan**
- PREP. **under a/the~** *Place the chops in the grill pan, and put it under the grill.*

2 framework of metal bars that you cook food on

- ADJ. **charcoal**
- PREP. **on a/the~** *Once the charcoal is glowing, place the food on the grill, turning it regularly.*

grimace noun

- ADJ. **little, slight, small** | **ugly** | **rueful, wry** | **facial**
- VERB + GRIMACE **give, make** *She made a wry grimace.* | **twist into** *His face twisted into a grimace.*
- GRIMACE + VERB **twist sth** *An ugly grimace twisted her face.*
- PREP. **with a~** *He acknowledged his mistake with a wry grimace.* | **~of** *a grimace of disgust/pain*

grimace verb

- ADV. **slightly** | **ruefully, wryly**
- PREP. **at** *He grimaced slightly at the pain.* ◇ *She grimaced at him.* **in** *She grimaced in disgust.*

grime noun

- VERB + GRIME **be covered in/with**
- PHRASES **a layer of grime** *Over the years, the painting has become covered in a thick layer of grime*

grin noun

- ADJ. **big, broad, huge, large, wide** | **faint, feeble** | **friendly, sympathetic** | **infectious** | **lazy** | **fatuous, foolish, goofy, silly** | **boyish, cheeky, impish, mischievous, sly** *Edmund looked up with an impish grin.* | **bashful, sheepish** | **sickly** | **rueful, sardonic, wry** | **self-deprecatory, self-mocking** | **knowing** | **insane, manic** | **grim, humourless, mirthless** | **evil, ferocious, hideous, wicked, wolfish** | **crooked, lopsided** | **gap-toothed, toothless, toothy**
- VERB + GRIN **crack, force, give (sb)** *He gave the photographer a big grin.* | **break into, split into** *The old man's face broke into a grin.* | **hide, restrain, stifle** *She tried to stifle a grin.*
- GRIN + VERB **broaden, grow broader/wider, widen** | **appear, spread across/over sth** *A mischievous grin spread across the little girl's face.* | **disappear, fade** *His wry grin faded.*
- PREP. **with a~** *'Fooled you!' he said, with a cheeky grin.* | **~at** *a grin at his wife* **~of** *a grin of triumph*
- PHRASES **take/wipe the grin off your face** *Take that grin off your face!* **wipe the grin off sb's face** *I'll soon wipe that silly grin off her face.*

grin verb

- ADV. **broadly, widely** *He appeared in the doorway grinning broadly.* | **weakly** | **crookedly** | **cheerfully, happily** | **amiably** | **cheekily, impishly, mischievously** | **triumphantly** | **inanely** | **sheepishly** *He just stood there, tongue-tied and grinning sheepishly.* | **apologetically, ruefully, wryly** *She grinned apologetically when she saw him.* | **unrepentantly** | **conspiratorially** | **wickedly** | **maliciously, wolfishly** | **sourly** | **back, down, up** *She relaxed and grinned wickedly back at him.* ◇ *He lay grinning impishly up at me.*
- PREP. **at** *He stopped eating to grin at me.* **to** *She grinned to herself at the thought.* **with** *They grinned with pleasure.*
- PHRASES **grin from ear to ear** *She looked at us, grinning from ear to ear.*

grind verb

- ADV. **coarsely** | **finely** *The cement need not be finely ground.* | **down, up** *Grind the seeds down to a powder.*
- PREP. **into** *machinery for grinding wheat into flour* **to** *The coffee is ground to a fine powder.*
- PHRASES **freshly ground** *freshly ground black pepper*

grip noun

1 hold on sth
- ADJ. **firm, good, secure, strong, tight | cruel, crushing, fierce, iron, painful, punishing, vice-like** *Her upper arms were seized in an iron grip.* | **restraining**
- VERB + GRIP **have** *He still had a firm grip on my arm.* | **get, take** *Taking a tight grip on the hook, he began to pull it towards himself.* | **keep** *Keep a secure grip on the rope at all times.* | **lose** *She slipped and lost her grip of the rope.* | **tighten** *Robert tightened his grip on her shoulder.* | **loosen, relax, release, slacken**
- GRIP + VERB **tighten | loosen, relax, slacken** *His grip slackened and she tore herself away.*
- PREP. **in a/sb's ~** *Hold the microphone in a firm grip.* ◇ *She was powerless in his vice-like grip.* | **~ on** *She relaxed her grip on the door frame.*

2 power/control
- ADJ. **firm, iron, powerful, strong, tight, vice-like**
- VERB + GRIP **have** *The Church does not have a strong grip on the population.* | **get, take** *The government needs to get a grip on this problem.* ◇ *(informal) Get a grip!* (= take control of yourself, your life, etc.) | **keep** *We need to keep a tight grip on costs.* | **strengthen, tighten** *They managed to strengthen their grip on the southern part of the country.* | **lose** *(informal) Sometimes I feel I'm losing my grip* (= losing control of my life, etc.)
- PREP. **in sth's ~** *Winter still held them in its iron grip.* ◇ *a country in the grip of recession* | **~ on** *The government does not seem to have a very firm grip on the economy.*
- PHRASES **come/get to grips with sth** (= to begin to take control of sth or understand sth difficult) *I'm slowly getting to grips with the language.*

grip verb

- ADV. **firmly, hard, tightly | gently, lightly**
- PREP. **at** *She gripped hard at the arms of her chair.* **by** *He gripped her gently by the shoulders.*

grit noun

1 small pieces of stone
- QUANT. **bit, piece** *A bit of grit had got into my eye.*

2 courage/determination
- ADJ. **sheer, true**
- VERB + GRIT **have** *Don't give in yet. You have more grit than that.* | **display, show** *The team showed their true grit and played a magnificent game.* | **take** *It takes sheer grit to stand up to a bully like that.*

groan noun

- ADJ. **loud** *He let out a loud groan of frustration.* | **little, small | deep, low | harsh, hoarse | muffled**
- VERB + GROAN **give, let out, utter | stifle, suppress | hear**
- PREP. **with a ~** *He stood up slowly with a groan of pain.* | **~ of**
- ⇨ Note at SOUND

groan verb

- ADV. **loudly | quietly, softly | aloud, out loud | inwardly** *He groaned inwardly at the thought of spending another day in that place.*
- PREP. **at, in** *She groaned out loud in protest.* **with** *Some of the patients were groaning with pain.*
- PHRASES **moan and groan** *There's no point in moaning and groaning about not having any money.*

groomed adj.

- VERBS **be, look** *She is always perfectly groomed.*
- ADV. **well | immaculately, impeccably, meticulously, perfectly | beautifully, sleekly, smoothly**

groove noun

- ADJ. **deep, shallow | narrow, wide**
- VERB + GROOVE **carve, cut, make** *Running water had carved a groove down the face of the wall.*
- PREP. **~ in** *a deep groove in the surface of the rock*

grope verb

- ADV. **blindly | vaguely | about/around/round**
- PREP. **for** *She groped blindly for the door handle.*
- PHRASES **grope your way** *I groped my way across the pitch-black stage.*

ground noun

1 solid surface of the earth
- ADJ. **firm, hard | muddy, soft, wet | dry, dusty | fertile** *(often figurative) The fall of the old regime provided fertile ground for opportunism.*
- VERB + GROUND **fall to, hit** *The helicopter burst into flames when it hit the ground.* | **reach** *She's so short, her feet don't reach the ground when she sits down.* | **get off, leave** *The plane was so overloaded it couldn't leave the ground.* ◇ *(figurative) His plan is too costly to ever get off the ground.*
- GROUND + NOUN **level** *A waterproof membrane is built into the wall just above ground level.*
- PREP. **above/below ~** *The roots may spread as far below ground as does the foliage above ground.* **in the ~** *a hole in the ground* **on the ~** *He sat down on the ground.* **under the ~** *The tunnel goes deep under the ground.*

2 area of land
- ADJ. **high, low** *The village stands on high ground and is not prone to flooding.* | **open | difficult, rocky, rough, stony, uneven | marshy**
- QUANT. **patch, piece** *We found a patch of open ground in the middle of the woods.*

3 piece of land used for a particular purpose
- ADJ. **burial | dumping | cricket, football, practice, rugby, sports, training | parade | breeding, feeding, hunting**
- PREP. **at a/the ~** *I'll meet you at the football ground.* **in a/the ~** *all the graves in the burial ground*

4 grounds land surrounding a large building
- ADJ. **extensive | castle, hospital, palace, school, etc.**
- VERB + GROUNDS **be set in, have** *The palace is set in extensive grounds.*
- PREP. **in the ~ (of)** *Many estate workers lived in cottages in the grounds of the castle.*

5 area of interest/study/discussion
- ADJ. **familiar, firm, home** *I was on more familiar ground now that we were talking about our own system.* | **dangerous, shaky** *Legally, we're on very shaky ground* (= our actions may not be legal). | **safe | common** *Both parties in the debate shared some common ground.*
- VERB + GROUND **cover, go over** *Several researchers have published articles covering this ground.* ◇ *We just seem to be going over the same ground that we covered last year.*
- PREP. **on ... ~** *He knew he was on dangerous ground talking about money.*
- PHRASES **break new ground** *Her architectural designs have broken new ground.*

6 grounds reason for sth
- ADJ. **good, reasonable, sufficient, valid**
- VERB + GROUNDS **have** *The constable had reasonable grounds for arresting her.* | **give (sb)** *His evasiveness gave grounds for the suspicion that he knew more than he was saying.*
- PREP. **on ... ~s** *Permission to open a mine was denied on environmental grounds.* **on the ~s of** *He resigned from his post on the grounds of ill health.* | **~ for** *Drunkenness at work was sufficient grounds for instant dismissal.*

ground *verb* be grounded in/on sth

- ADV. **firmly** *His book is firmly grounded in memories of his own childhood.*

grounding *noun*

- ADJ. **good, solid, thorough | basic**
- VERB + GROUNDING **have** *All applicants for the job should have a basic grounding in computer skills.* **| get | give (sb), provide (sb with)** *The course should give you a thorough grounding in financial matters.*
- PREP. **~in** *to get a good grounding in science*

groundless *adj.*

- VERBS **be, prove, seem**
- ADV. **completely, entirely, quite, totally, utterly** *Our fears proved totally groundless.* **| largely**

groundwork *noun*

- ADJ. **basic**
- VERB + GROUNDWORK **do, lay, prepare, provide (sb with)** *The first meeting laid the groundwork for the final agreement.* ◇ *The first year provides the basic groundwork for the pupils' study of maths.*
- PREP. **~for** *We are already doing the groundwork for the introduction of the scheme next year.*

group *noun*

- ADJ. **big, large, wide** *She has a very wide group of friends.* **| select, small** *The president met with a select group of senior ministers.* **| coherent, cohesive, tight, tightly-knit** *The strangers who came together for the course soon became a cohesive group.* **| minority** *Disabled drivers are an ever-growing minority group.* **| cultural, ethnic, racial | family** *The animals live in family groups of 10–20 individuals.* **| age, peer** *young people in this age group* ◇ *He started smoking because of peer-group pressure.* **| discussion** *a discussion group that meets once a month* **| self-help | action, pressure** *Local parents have formed an action group to campaign for better road safety.* **| splinter** *A few members of the party broke away to form a splinter group.* **| theatre | pop, rock | blood** *What blood group are you?*
- VERB + GROUP **form, found, set up, start | divide sb/sth into** *We divided the class into small groups.* **| manage, run | become a member of, join | leave** *He left the group last year to pursue a solo career.*
- GROUP + VERB **form** *The group formed back in 1992.* **| split up** *The group has split up and re-formed several times with different musicians.*
- GROUP + NOUN **member**
- PREP. **as a~** *The gorillas go foraging for food as a group.* **in a/the~** *There are fifteen of us in the group.* **within a/the~** *Within a group, each individual had a definite status.* **| ~of** *a group of young mothers*
- ⇨ Note at ORGANIZATION

group *verb*

- ADV. **closely | loosely | thematically** *Works in the exhibition are grouped thematically.* **| together**
- PREP. **according to** *Eggs were grouped according to colour and size.* **around/round** *They sat grouped around the fire.* **by** *The children were grouped by age.* **in/into** *These stories can be loosely grouped into three types.* **with** *The England team was grouped with Uruguay and Holland.*
- PHRASES **group sth under a heading** *The names were grouped under four different headings.*

grow *verb*

1 increase

- ADV. **fast, quickly, rapidly | slowly | steadily | expo-** nentially *Well before a billionth of a second had elapsed the universe started to grow exponentially.*
- VERB + GROW **seem to | begin to, start to | continue to | be expected to**
- PREP. **by** *Profits are expected to grow by 10% next year.* **from** *Her media empire grew from quite small beginnings.* **in** *She continued to grow in confidence* **into** *The village grew into a town.*

2 of a person/animal

- ADV. **fast, quickly, rapidly | slowly**
- PREP. **into** *The small puppy quickly grew into a very large dog.*

3 of plants/hair

- ADV. **well** *Tomatoes grow best in direct sunlight.* **| fast, quickly, rapidly | slowly | steadily | thickly** *the nettles that grew thickly round the boathouse* **| outwards, upwards** *As the island subsided the reef grew upwards and outwards.*
- VERB + GROW **allow sth to, let sth** *She decided to let her hair grow.*
- PREP. **from** *The tree grew from a small acorn.* **into** *Small acorns grow into great oak trees.*
- PHRASES **grow unchecked** *A rose in full bloom had been allowed to grow unchecked up one of the walls.*

4 make plants grow

- ADV. **organically** *organically grown produce*
- VERB + GROW **be easy to** *an attractive plant which is very hardy and easy to grow*

growl *noun*

- ADJ. **low | husky, soft, throaty | aggressive, threatening** *The dog gave a threatening growl.*
- VERB + GROWL **give, let out | hear**
- PREP. **with a~** *He spoke with a deep soft growl in his throat.* **| ~of** *The growl of the engine.*
- ⇨ Note at SOUND

growl *verb*

- ADV. **angrily, savagely** *'I'm a desperate man,' he growled savagely.* **| softly, throatily**
- PREP. **at** *The dog growled softly at me.* **with** *Her stomach was growling with hunger.*

growth *noun*

1 increase in sth

- ADJ. **considerable, dramatic, enormous, exponential, impressive, phenomenal, significant, spectacular, strong, tremendous** *the exponential growth in world population* **| explosive, fast, rapid** *the explosive growth of personal computers in the 1990s* **| modest, slow, steady** *The factory has achieved a steady growth in output.* **| low** *a vicious circle of low growth and low productivity* **| long-term | economic, industrial | population**
- VERB + GROWTH **achieve | maintain, sustain | encourage, promote, stimulate | control** *new measures to control the growth of traffic on the roads*
- GROWTH + NOUN **rate** *The economy enjoyed the highest growth rate in Asia.* **| area, industry** *Communications technology has proved to be a growth area.*
- PREP. **~in** *There was a rapid growth in the numbers of private cars.*
- PHRASES **a rate of growth**
- ⇨ Special page at BUSINESS

2 growing

- ADJ. **healthy, normal** *A good diet is vital for healthy growth.* **| excessive** *the excessive growth of algae in rivers* **| intellectual, personal, spiritual**
- VERB + GROWTH **encourage** *Give the plants a good pruning to encourage growth.* **| stunt** *Lack of food had stunted his growth.*
- GROWTH + NOUN **hormone**

3 abnormal lump in the body
- ADJ. **cancerous, malignant | benign**
- VERB + GROWTH **have**
- PREP. **~on** *He had a cancerous growth on his lung.*

grudge *noun*

- ADJ. **long-standing, old** *It's time to forget old grudges.* **| personal**
- VERB + GRUDGE **bear, harbour, have, hold, nurse** *I don't hold grudges for very long.*
- PREP. **~ against** *Do you know anyone who might harbour a grudge against you?*

gruesome *adj.*

- VERBS **be**
- ADV. **horribly, particularly, truly | pretty, rather** *a rather gruesome sight*

grunt *noun*

- ADJ. **little | low | non-committal** *He gave a non-committal grunt in reply.*
- VERB + GRUNT **give, let out | hear**
- PREP. **with a ~** *He lifted the heavy box with a grunt.* **| ~of** *a grunt of pain*
- ⇨ Note at SOUND

grunt *verb*

- ADV. **loudly | merely, only** *He merely grunted at her and nodded his head.*
- PREP. **at** *His father grunted at him as he left the room.* **in** *She asked him a question and he grunted in reply.* ◇ *He grunted in pain.* **with** *She stirred the soup, grunting with satisfaction.*
- PHRASES **grunt and groan** *Grunting and groaning, they heaved the wardrobe up the stairs.*

guarantee *noun*

1 written promise by a company
- ADJ. **full | lifetime, three-year, two-year, etc. | money-back**
- VERB + GUARANTEE **carry, come with, have** *All our products come with a two-year guarantee.* **| give (sb), issue, offer (sb)**
- PREP. **under~** *The car is still under guarantee, so you should be able to get it repaired free of charge.* **| ~against** *The window frames carry a 20-year guarantee against rot or decay.* **~for** *The garage gives a year's guarantee for all repair work.* **~on** *The contractors offer a full money-back guarantee on all their work.*

2 promise that sth will be done/will happen
- ADJ. **absolute, cast-iron, firm, reliable | long-term | constitutional, personal** *The country gives a constitutional guarantee of the rights of minorities.*
- VERB + GUARANTEE **give (sb), offer (sb), provide (sb with) | demand, want | get** *We didn't get any firm guarantee of a loan.*
- PREP. **~against** *There was no guarantee against misuse of the king's power.* **~for** *The demonstrators were demanding guarantees for fair elections.* **~of** *Driving into town early is no longer a guarantee of getting a parking space.*

guarantee *verb*

1 promise to do sth/promise sth will happen
- ADV. **absolutely** *I can absolutely guarantee that you will enjoy the show.* **| personally** *I personally guarantee total and immediate support in all measures undertaken.*
- VERB + GUARANTEE **be able to, can**

2 give a written promise about the quality of sth

- PHRASES **be fully guaranteed** *All our electrical goods are fully guaranteed.*

3 make sth certain to happen
- ADV. **absolutely | almost, practically, virtually | effectively** *The complicated electoral system effectively guarantees the president's re-election.* **| automatically** *The process of training and qualification does not automatically guarantee you a job.* **| by no means, not necessarily** *The outcome is by no means guaranteed.*

guard *noun*

1 person who guards sb/sth
- ADJ. **armed, uniformed** *The building is protected by armed guards.* **| border, prison, security**
- VERB + GUARD **post** *Guards had been posted all around the radio station.*
- GUARD + VERB **patrol sth** *Guards patrolled the perimeter fence.* **| protect sth**
- GUARD + NOUN **duty | dog**

2 being ready to prevent attack or danger
- ADJ. **close | constant | armed** *The accused was taken to court under armed guard.* **| police**
- VERB + GUARD **keep, mount, stand** *Soldiers stood guard on the city gates.*
- PREP. **off your~** *The question seemed to catch him off his guard.* **on (your)~** *Several police officers were on guard outside the factory.* ◇ *He was always on his guard against moneymaking schemes.* **under~** *The prisoners were under close guard.* **| ~ against, ~ over** *Two police officers kept guard over the burnt-out building.*

3 group of soldiers/policemen who guard sb/sth
- ADJ. **civil, national, palace, presidential | advance**
- VERB + GUARD **change** *The guard was changed every two hours.* **| call out** *It would only be a matter of minutes before the alarm was raised and the guard called out.*
- PHRASES **guard of honour** *Fellow soldiers from Corporal Smith's regiment formed a guard of honour at his wedding.*

guard *verb*

- ADV. **well** *The mountain pass is well guarded.* **| carefully** *a bird carefully guarding its eggs* **| fiercely, jealously** *She jealously guarded her position of power.*
- PREP. **against** *guarding the city against attack* **from** *pop stars who need to be guarded from their fans*
- PHRASES **closely/heavily/securely guarded** *The military base is closely guarded.* **guard sb/sth with your life** *He was under instructions to guard the key with his life.* **strictly/tightly guarded** *strictly guarded privacy*

guardian *noun*

1 person/institution that guards/protects sth
- ADJ. **self-appointed** *She has become the self-appointed guardian of the nation's conscience.* **| moral**
- VERB + GUARDIAN **act as** *The village people act as guardians of the land.*

2 person who is responsible for a child
- ADJ. **legal**
- VERB + GUARDIAN **appoint, appoint sb (as)** *The court appoints a legal guardian for the child.* **| act as**

guerrilla *noun*

- ADJ. **armed | urban** *Urban guerrillas detonated a car bomb in front of the company's headquarters.* **| communist, opposition, right-wing, separatist, etc.**
- GUERRILLA + NOUN **army, band, force, group, movement, organization, unit | commander, fighter, leader | activity, attack, campaign, offensive, raid, resistance, struggle, war, warfare** *Ten years of guerrilla resistance followed the occupation.* **| tactics**

guess noun

- ADJ. **fair, good, reasonable, safe** *April is the best guess for first deliveries.* | **calculated, educated, informed, inspired, intelligent** *As a vet, he could make an educated guess as to what was wrong with his stomach.* | **rough, wild** *At a rough guess, I'd say we're about twenty miles from home.* | **lucky** *'How did you know?' 'It was just a lucky guess.'*
- VERB + GUESS **have, hazard, make, take** *If you don't know the answer, have a guess.* ◇ *If I might hazard a guess …* | **give sb** *'Where's Tom?' 'I'll give you three guesses!'* (= the answer is fairly obvious and you should guess it easily)
- PREP. **at a~** *At a guess, I'd say there's a problem with the fuel pump.* | **~ about/as to/at** *He made a wild guess as to how much the piano might cost.*

guess verb

- ADV. **correctly, right** | **incorrectly, wrong** *Jane had guessed wrong about who was responsible for the fire.* | **never** *You'll never guess what she told me.*
- VERB + GUESS **can/could** *Can you guess his age?* | **can only** *We can only guess how fast a dinosaur might have run.* | **try to** | **be easy to, not be difficult to, not be hard to** *It's not hard to guess where they went.*
- PREP. **at** *I was only guessing at her age.* **from** *She guessed from his expression that he had not won.*
- PHRASES **could/might/should have guessed** *So it was Rob who broke the window? I might have guessed!* **let me guess** *What star sign are you? No, let me guess.*

guesswork noun

- ADJ. **pure** | **informed, inspired** *Their results owe more to informed guesswork than to actual knowledge.*
- VERB + GUESSWORK **be based on** *Their price estimates are based on pure guesswork.*
- PHRASES **a matter of guesswork** *Long-term forecasts were largely a matter of guesswork.*

guest noun

1 person that you invite to your home
- ADJ. **house** | **honoured, welcome** *She was treated as an honoured guest.* ◇ *You are always a welcome guest in our house.* | **unexpected, uninvited** *She tactfully discouraged their uninvited guests from staying longer.* | **unwanted, unwelcome** *The refugees were made to feel like unwanted guests in the country.*
- VERB + GUEST **invite** *She had invited six guests.* | **entertain** *She felt that she had to entertain her guests.*
- GUEST + NOUN **room**

2 person invited to an event
- ADJ. **chief, principal** *The athlete was chief guest at the schools sports day.* | **dinner, party, reception, restaurant, wedding** *The best man and his assistants welcomed the reception guests as they arrived.*
- VERB + GUEST **greet, welcome**
- GUEST + VERB **attend sth** *The banquet was attended by 200 guests.*
- GUEST + NOUN **list**
- PHRASES **a guest of honour**

3 person who is staying at a hotel
- ADJ. **hotel** | **frequent, regular**

4 at a public event/on a radio or television show
- ADJ. **special** *Film star Matt Damon is one of the special guests on tonight's programme.*
- GUEST + NOUN **artist, celebrity, star** *Guest artists from all over Europe will take part in the concert.* | **speaker** | **appearance** *She made a rare guest appearance on the programme.*

guidance noun

- ADJ. **careful, clear, detailed, precise** | **firm** *Parents need to provide their children with firm guidance.* | **gentle** | **helpful** *The handbook gives helpful guidance on writing articles.* | **practical, general** *These notes are for general guidance only.* | **divine, expert, parental** *She prayed for divine guidance.* | **technical** | **marriage** | **career, vocational** | **ethical, moral**
- VERB + GUIDANCE **give (sb), offer (sb), provide (sb with)** *We can give guidance to students on which courses to choose.* | **need** | **ask for, look to sb for, seek** *Children look to their parents for guidance.* ◇ *I think you should seek guidance from your solicitor on this matter.*
- PREP. **under … ~, under the ~ of** *Volunteers are restoring the building under expert guidance.* | **~ about** *The Careers Officer also offers guidance about university courses.* **~ as to** *Guidance must be given as to what tasks the learner should attempt.* **~ on** *The Safety Officer provides guidance on firefighting and office safety.*

guide noun

1 sth that helps you plan what you are going to do
- ADJ. **approximate, rough** | **accurate**
- VERB + GUIDE **give (sb), provide (sb with)** | **use sth as** *Use the table below as a guide to how much washing powder to use.*
- PREP. **~ as to** *These figures give a rough guide as to the sales we can expect.* **~ to**

2 book that gives information about a subject
- ADJ. **essential, good, helpful, informative, invaluable, practical, reliable, useful, valuable** | **brief, quick, short, simple** | **complete, comprehensive, definitive, in-depth** *This book is the definitive guide to world cuisine.* | **step-by-step** *a step-by-step guide to creating your own website* | **reference** *The book contains a quick reference guide to essential grammar at the back.*
- PREP. **~ to** *a guide to British birds*

3 person
- ADJ. **tour, tourist** *Our tour guide showed us around the old town.*
- VERB + GUIDE **act as, be** *He agreed to go with them and act as their guide.*

4 book for tourists
- ADJ. **holiday, travel** | **hotel** | **street**
- VERB + GUIDE **consult** *We consulted our guides as we walked around the cathedral.* | **write** | **publish**

guide verb

1 influence sb's behaviour
- ADV. **firmly**
- VERB + GUIDE **help (to)** *the information and data which help guide the affairs of the business* | **try to**
- PREP. **into** *the ways in which young people are guided into employment* **on** *Schools were firmly guided on the details of the curriculum*

2 explain sth/help sb
- ADV. **carefully** *Their teacher Phil Bailey carefully guides them through rehearsals.*
- VERB + GUIDE **help (to)**
- PREP. **in** *He guided me in my research.* **on** *guiding teachers on how to maintain discipline* **through** *He guided us through the intricacies of the divorce law.*

3 help sb move
- ADV. **gently** *He took her arm, gently guiding her.*
- PREP. **across, along, etc.** *She guided him across the busy road.* **to/towards** *He guided her hand to his face.*

guideline noun

- ADJ. **clear, good, helpful, practical, reliable, useful** | **broad, general, simple** | **detailed, explicit** | **strict, tight**

| EU, government | planning, safety | ethical, financial, legal

• QUANT. **set** *The organization has issued a set of guidelines for builders to follow.*

• VERB + GUIDELINE **develop, draw up, lay down, set out | give (sb), issue, offer (sb), provide (sb with), suggest** *The document gives clear guidelines on the use of pesticides.* | **adhere to, apply, follow, stick to** *We have to follow the safety guidelines laid down by the government.* | **breach, ignore** *The minister is accused of allowing the company to breach guidelines on arms sales.*

• GUIDELINE + VERB **apply** *The same general guidelines on when to dress formally apply to both men and women.*

• PREP. **within ~** *Within clear guidelines, managers can use their budget to entertain clients.* | **~ about** *detailed guidelines for doctors about how to deal with difficult patients* **~ for** *The article suggests some guidelines for healthy eating.* **~ from** *guidelines from the Department of Health* **~ on** *new EU guidelines on food hygiene*

guilt *noun*

1 feeling
• ADJ. **dreadful, terrible**
• QUANT. **pang, twinge**
• VERB + GUILT **be consumed with, be haunted by, be overwhelmed with, be racked with, feel, suffer** *I knew that the next day I would be consumed with guilt.* ◇ *You needn't feel any guilt about me.* | **assuage** *Talking to her helped to assuage my guilt.*
• GUILT + VERB **sear sb, sweep over sb, wash over sb** *Guilt swept over her.*
• GUILT + NOUN **complex | feelings**
• PREP. **~ about/at/over** *He had no feelings of guilt over what he had done.*
• PHRASES **a burden of guilt** *the burden of guilt that she carried with her* **a feeling/sense of guilt**

2 fact of having broken a law/done sth wrong
• VERB + GUILT **admit | establish, prove** *It might be difficult to prove his guilt.*
• GUILT + VERB **lie** *There is no doubt as to where the guilt lies.*
• PHRASES **an admission of guilt** *I took his silence as an admission of guilt.* **proof of guilt**

guilty *adj.*

1 feeling/showing guilt
• VERBS **feel, look**
• ADV. **extremely, incredibly, really, terribly, very** *She's got a terribly guilty conscience about it.* | **almost** *I feel almost guilty that so many good things are happening to us.* | **a bit, faintly, a little, rather, slightly, somewhat, vaguely** *She was looking rather guilty when I came into the room.* | **oddly, ridiculously**
• PREP. **about** *I feel very guilty about leaving her.*

2 having broken the law/done sth wrong
• VERBS **be, plead** *He pleaded guilty to starting the fire.* | **believe sb, presume sb** *No one believed him guilty of this terrible crime.* ◇ *A person should never be presumed guilty.* | **deem sb, find sb, hold sb, prove sb** *Company directors may be deemed guilty of an offence if their company causes pollution.* ◇ *He was found guilty of murder.*
• ADV. **certainly, clearly** *She was certainly guilty, but the police couldn't prove it.*
• PREP. **of** *She was guilty of fraud.*

guinea pig *noun*

• VERB + GUINEA PIG **act as** *Twenty students volunteered to act as guinea pigs.* | **use sb as**
• PREP. **~ for** *Dealers used their clients as guinea pigs for their untried techniques.*

guitar *noun*

• ADJ. **acoustic, electric | bass, lead, rhythm | classical, jazz, rock | 6/12-string**
• VERB + GUITAR **strum (on)** *As she sang, she strummed her guitar.* | **tune (up) | build, make**
• GUITAR + NOUN **string | lick, riff**
⇨ Special page at MUSIC

Gujarati *noun*

⇨ Note at LANGUAGE

gulf *noun*

• ADJ. **deep, great, huge, unbridgeable, wide, yawning | growing, widening** *There appeared to be a growing gulf between the prosperous south and the declining towns of the north.*
• VERB + GULF **cause, create** *This atrocity has created a huge gulf between the two groups.* | **widen** *Other factors widened the gulf that separated rich from poor.* | **emphasize, illustrate** *The documentary illustrated the gulf between industrialized and developing countries.* | **bridge, span** *The new degree course aims to bridge the gulf between education and industry.*
• GULF + VERB **exist | separate sb/sth** *the yawning gulf that separates the two cultures* | **open up** *A gulf had opened up between the former friends.*
• PREP. **~ between** *For many teachers, there existed an unbridgeable gulf between home and school life.* **~ in** *the huge gulf in level between professional and amateur teams*

gull *noun*

⇨ See SEAGULL

gulp *noun*

1 amount you swallow when you gulp
• ADJ. **deep, great, huge, large, long**
• VERB + GULP **take** *She took a large gulp of wine from the bottle.*
• PREP. **in ~s** *She drank the tea in great gulps.* | **~ of**

2 act of gulping
• ADJ. **loud, noisy**
• VERB + GULP **give** *He gave a loud gulp and stopped mid-sentence.*
• PREP. **with a ~** *'I'm afraid I've broken it,' she said with a gulp.*
• PHRASES **at a/one gulp, in one/a single gulp** *He downed half the contents of the glass in one loud gulp.*

gulp *verb*

1 eat/drink sth quickly
• ADV. **greedily | noisily | down** *She gulped down her coffee and left.*

2 make a swallowing movement
• ADV. **nervously** *'Do you know where she is?' asked Chris. The man gulped nervously and nodded.*
• PHRASES **gulp for air/breath** *Keith swam to the surface and gulped for air.*

gum *noun*

• ADJ. **lower, upper | toothless** *The old man smiled to reveal toothless gums.* | **bleeding, swollen**
• GUM + NOUN **disease**

gun *noun*

• ADJ. **big, heavy | enemy** *They succeeded in silencing the enemy guns.* | **replica, toy | anti-aircraft, anti-tank, Bren, field, hand, harpoon, laser, machine, spear, Sten, stun, sub-machine | grease, spray, staple**
• VERB + GUN **be armed with, carry, have** *Look out!*

He's got a gun! | **load** *I loaded the gun with my last two bullets.* | **draw, produce, pull (out)** | **aim, hold, point, raise** *He raised his gun, aimed and fired.* | **man** *Enemy ship approaching! Man the guns!* | **handle, use** | **fire, shoot sb/sth with** | **lay down, put down** | **silence**
- GUN + VERB **blaze, fire, go off** *Guns were firing and grenades going off all around.* | **shoot sth** *This new gun shoots a laser beam at the target.* | **jam** | **be mounted** *There were several guns mounted in the back of the vehicle.*
- GUN + NOUN **club** | **control, law** *a state that has strict gun controls* | **lobby** *the powerful gun lobby in the US* | **emplacement, position** | **attack, battle** | **crew** | **barrel** | **rack**
- PHRASES **the barrel of a gun** *I found myself looking down the barrel of a gun.* **guns and ammunition** *We're very short of guns and ammunition.* **hold a gun on sb, hold a gun to sb's head** *Two armed men held a gun to his head and made him empty the safe.* **turn a gun on yourself** *The gunman then turned the gun on himself and blew his brains out.*

gunfire *noun*

- ADJ. **heavy, intense** | **scattered, sporadic** | **indiscriminate** *Seventy protesters were killed by indiscriminate gunfire.* | **distant** | **automatic** *We heard the rapid crackle of automatic gunfire.*
- QUANT. **burst** *A burst of gunfire echoed across the square.*
- VERB + GUNFIRE **hear** | **spray sb/sth with** *The terrorists boarded the bus and sprayed the passengers with gunfire.* | **be hit/wounded by** *A convoy was hit by gunfire.*
- GUNFIRE + VERB **break out** *Heavy gunfire broke out in the capital last night.* | **echo**
- PHRASES **the crack/crackle/rattle/sound of gunfire, an exchange of gunfire** *They were killed in an exchange of gunfire between riot police and demonstrators.*

gunshot *noun*

- VERB + GUNSHOT **hear** *We heard gunshots round about midnight.*
- GUNSHOT + NOUN **wound** *He died of gunshot wounds to the chest.*
- PHRASES **the noise/sound of a gunshot**

gurgle *noun*

- ADJ. **little** | **low**
- VERB + GURGLE **give, let out** | **hear**
- PREP. **with a~** *The water emptied with a gurgle.* | **~ of** *He gave a low gurgle of laughter.*
- ⇨ Note at SOUND

gust *noun*

- ADJ. **great** | **little** | **strong** | **sudden** | **occasional**
- PREP. **~of** *a sudden gust of wind*
- PHRASES **blow/come in gusts** *The wind came in great gusts off the Pacific.*

gut *noun*

1 tube in the lower part of the body
- ADJ. **healthy**
- VERB + GUT **pass through**
- GUT + NOUN **flora, wall**
- PREP. **in the/your~**

2 guts organs inside the body
- PHRASES **blood and guts** *(figurative) I don't like films that are full of blood and guts.* **a pain in your guts** *I had a terrible pain in my guts after eating too many plums.*

3 guts courage/determination
- VERB + GUTS **have** *She had the guts to stand up to the school bully.* | **take** *It takes guts to keep on running even though you have blistered feet.*

gut *verb*

- ADV. **completely** *The hotel was completely gutted by fire last year.*

guy *noun*

- ADJ. **decent, friendly, funny, good, great, nice, sweet, wonderful** | **bad** | **ordinary, regular** *Neighbours described the killer as 'just a regular guy'.* | **big, little** | **middle-aged, old, young** | **black, white** | **gay** | **tough** | **crazy**

gym *noun*

- ADJ. **fully-equipped** | **school**
- GYM + NOUN **session, workout** | **equipment**

gymnast *noun*

- ADJ. **brilliant, expert, good** | **Olympic**
- GYMNAST + VERB **train** *young gymnasts who have to train for up to five hours a day* | **compete, perform**

gymnastics *noun*

- ADJ. **rhythmic**
- VERB + GYMNASTICS **do** *She does gymnastics at school.*
- GYMNASTICS + NOUN **display, exhibition** | **championships** | **coach**
- PREP. **in (the)~**
- ⇨ Special page at SPORT

Hh

habit noun

● ADJ. **annoying, anti-social, bad, dirty, disconcerting, horrible, irritating, nasty, unfortunate** *Life has a nasty habit of repeating itself.* | **charming** (*often ironic*), **endearing, good** *one of his more endearing habits* ◇ *her charming habit of setting fire to cats* | **eccentric, odd** | **old** | **daily, regular** | **personal, sexual, social** *I found some of his personal habits rather disconcerting.* | **buying, shopping, spending** *an effort to change the buying habits of the British public* | **dietary, drinking, eating, feeding, reading, viewing** *women's television viewing habits* | **drug, smoking** *trying to kick the smoking habit*
● VERB + HABIT **be in, have** *She had been in the habit of drinking five or six cups of coffee a day.* ◇ *She's got some very annoying habits.* ◇ *He had an irritating habit of singing tunelessly about the house.* | **acquire, develop, fall into, form, get into, make** *I had fallen into my old bad habit of leaving everything until the last minute.* ◇ *Try to get into good habits and eat regular healthy meals.* ◇ *Make a habit of noting down any telephone messages.* | **become** *Don't let eating between meals become a habit.* | **break (yourself of), get out of, give up, kick** *a difficult habit to break* ◇ *You must break yourself of the habit.* ◇ *I had got out of the habit of going to the pub.* | **change**
● HABIT + VERB **change** *Even last year the nation's eating habits changed significantly.*
● PREP. **by ~** *Much of what we do in daily life is done by habit.* **out of ~** *I sat in my old seat purely out of habit.*
● PHRASES **a creature of habit** *Horses are creatures of habit and like to have a daily routine.* **force of habit** *Mr Norris bellowed from force of habit.* **the habit of a lifetime** *It's hard to change the habits of a lifetime.*

habitable adj.

● VERBS **be** | **remain** | **make sth, render sth** *They've done their best to make the house habitable.* | **consider sth** *The houses were not considered habitable.*
● ADV. **barely** *The room was barely habitable.*

habitat noun

● ADJ. **native, natural** *her observations of wild chimps in their natural habitat* | **important** | **endangered, fragile, threatened** *Peat bogs are one of Europe's most threatened habitats.* | **coastal, forest, wetland, wildlife, woodland**
● VERB + HABITAT **provide** *The forest provides a habitat for hundreds of species of plants and animals.* | **conserve, protect** *new measures to protect wildlife habitats* | **damage, destroy, disrupt** *Development is destroying the animal's native habitat.*
● HABITAT + VERB **support sth** *The many different habitats support a wide variety of birds.*
● HABITAT + NOUN **destruction, loss** *Many species are threatened in the wild due to habitat destruction by man.*
● PREP. **in a/the ~** *the animals and plants in this woodland habitat* | **~ for** *The moorland is an important habitat for many rare bird species.*
● PHRASES **loss of habitat** *The greatest danger to tigers now is through loss of habitat.*

hack verb

● ADV. **away, off** *They hacked away at the dense vegetation.* ◇ *hacking off the dead branches*
● PREP. **at** *She hacked at the hedge with the shears.*
● PHRASES **hack sth to bits/pieces** *The body had been hacked to pieces.* **hack sb to death** *He was hacked to death*

by the mob. **hack your way** *The explorers had to hack their way through dense jungle.*

haemorrhage noun

● ADJ. **massive, severe** | **recurrent** | **acute** *The patient died from acute cerebral haemorrhage.* | **brain, cerebral**
● VERB + HAEMORRHAGE **have, suffer** *Twelve hours later she suffered a massive brain haemorrhage.* | **die from/of** | **halt, stop** (*both usually figurative*) *The company is desperate to halt the haemorrhage of skilled staff.*

hail noun

● HAIL + VERB **fall** *Hail fell shortly after lunch.* | **melt** *The hail melted once the sun came out.*
● PREP. **in (the) ~** *We got caught in the hail.* **through (the) ~** *driving through the hail*

hair noun

● ADJ. **auburn, black, blond, brown, chestnut, dark, fair, ginger, golden, grey, grizzled, jet-black, red, sandy, white, yellow** | **bushy, coarse, crinkly, curly, fine, frizzy, smooth, straight, thick, wavy, wiry** | **beautiful, glossy, shiny, sleek** | **dishevelled, dry, dull, fuzzy, greasy, scruffy, tousled, unruly, untidy, windswept** *a new shampoo for dull or dry hair* ◇ *His hair was tousled and he looked as if he'd just woken up.* | **cropped, long, short, shoulder-length** *She had shoulder-length black hair.* | **body, facial, pubic** | **cat, dog, etc.** *The rug was covered with cat hairs.*
● QUANT. **lock, wisp**
● VERB + HAIR **have** *She had beautiful auburn hair.* | **lose** *He had turned forty and was beginning to lose his hair.* | **wear** *She wore her long hair loose on her shoulders.* | **arrange, do, tidy** *I don't like the way she's arranged her hair, do you?* ◇ *I'll be down in a minute, I'm just doing my hair.* | **plait, put up, tie back** *Why don't you put your hair up for this evening?* | **brush, comb** | **shampoo, wash** | **cut, trim** *He went to the barber's to have his hair cut.* | **curl, perm** *I've decided to have my hair permed.* | **grow** *I'm trying to grow my hair.*
● HAIR + VERB **grow** *Why don't you let your hair grow?* | **curl** *His hair curls naturally.* | **fall, hang, lie** *Her blond hair fell over her eyes.* | **gleam, glint, glisten**
● HAIR + NOUN **loss** *how to cope with hair loss*

haircut noun

● ADJ. **decent, good** | **new** | **short, skinhead**
● VERB + HAIRCUT **get, have** *You ought to smarten up and have a haircut before the interview.* | **need** *He was unshaven, and badly needed a haircut.*

half noun

● ADJ. **first, second** | **last, latter** *in the latter half of the nineteenth century* | **top, upper** | **bottom, lower** *the lower half of the window* | **front** | **back, rear** *the rear half of the car* | **left, right** *the left half of the brain* | **northern, western, etc.** *the northern half of the country*
● PREP. **by a ~** *Costs rose by a half.* **in ~** *We divided the money in half.* **in the … ~** *He played well in the second half of the match.* | **~ of** *the first half of the concert* ◇ *Over a half of all accidents happen in the home.*
● PHRASES **about/almost/at least/over a half** *Over a half of all the people interviewed said they were disappointed in the government.* **half and half** *We split the work*

half and half. **one/two/three, etc. and a half** *She's four and a half years old now.*

hall *noun*

1 inside the front entrance of a house/building
- ADJ. **entrance | reception | narrow | dark, darkened, unlit** *He hurried them along the narrow, dark hall.*
- VERB + HALL **lead to** *The hall led to a locked door.*
- PREP. **across the~** *the room across the hall* **along the~, at/to the end of the ~, down the ~** *There were strange noises coming from the room down the hall.* **in the~**

2 building/large room
- ADJ. **cavernous, huge, spacious, vast | magnificent | bare** *Our voices echoed round the huge bare hall.* | **gloomy | cold, draughty | crowded, packed | main** *More than 200 members of the public packed the main hall at the community centre.* | **baronial, great | assembly, conference, congress, meeting | booking, ticket | banquet, banqueting, dining | concert, dance, examination, exhibition, lecture, market, sports | church, city, communal, community, council, county, parish, public, school, village | bingo, pool, snooker**
- VERB + HALL **crowd into, fill, pack** *The strains of the national anthem filled the hall.*
- PREP. **in the~, into the~, through the~** *His voice echoed through the hall.*
- PHRASES **hall of residence** *Most first-year students live in the halls of residence.*

hallucination *noun*

- ADJ. **mild | weird | auditory, visual | drug-induced**
- VERB + HALLUCINATION **have** *For a moment I thought I was having hallucinations.* | **cause, induce**

halt *noun*

- ADJ. **abrupt, sudden** *The bus came to an abrupt halt outside the school.* | **grinding, shuddering** *The strike brought the capital city to a grinding halt.* | **temporary | immediate**
- VERB + HALT **come to, draw to, grind to, jolt to, lurch to, scream to, screech to, shudder to, skid to, slide to, slither to** *The economy seems to be grinding to a halt.* ◇ *The car skidded to a halt just inches from the river.* | **bring sth to** *Production was brought to a temporary halt when power supplies failed.* | **call** *Scientists have decided to call a halt to the tests.* | **call for, demand**
- PREP. **~ in** *a halt in nuclear testing* **~ to** *The protesters are calling for a halt to the export of live animals.*

halt *verb*

- ADV. **virtually | effectively** *The strike effectively halted production at the factory.* | **abruptly** *All these ideas for expansion were abruptly halted by the outbreak of war.* | **briefly, temporarily | finally**
- VERB + HALT **try to | threaten to | fail to** *failing to halt the destruction of the rainforest*
- PHRASES **halt in your tracks** *A sudden shout made them halt in their tracks and look round.* **halt sth in its tracks** *The development programme has been halted in its tracks by this intervention.*

halve *verb*

- ADV. **more than | almost, nearly, virtually | approximately, roughly | effectively**
- PREP. **in** *The shares have more than halved in value since the summer high of 572p.* **to** *Overall operating profits halved to $24 million.*

ham *noun*

- ADJ. **lean | baked, boiled, cooked, cured, honey-roast, Parma, smoked | cold** *cold ham and salad* | **sliced**
- QUANT. **bit, piece, slice | joint, leg**
- VERB + HAM **eat, have | boil, cook, roast | carve, slice**
- HAM + NOUN **roll, salad, sandwich**
- PHRASES **ham on the bone** *We had boiled ham on the bone for dinner.*
- ⇨ Special page at FOOD

hammer *noun*

- VERB + HAMMER **hit sth with, tap sth with, use, wield | swing** *He swung the hammer with all his strength.*
- HAMMER + NOUN **blow** (*often figurative*) *The decision is a hammer blow for the coal industry.*
- PHRASES **a hammer and chisel, a hammer and nails, hammer and sickle** *the hammer and sickle of the Soviet flag*

hammering *noun*

1 noise
- ADJ. **loud**
- VERB + HAMMERING **hear**
- PREP. **~ at/on** *a loud hammering on the door*

2 very bad defeat
- ADJ. **real**
- VERB + HAMMERING **give sb | take** *They took a real hammering at the hands of their opponents.*

hamper *verb*

- ADV. **badly, greatly, seriously, severely** *Rescue efforts were severely hampered by the bad weather.* | **further**

hand *noun*

1 part of the body
- ADJ. **left, right | beautiful, delicate, long-fingered, pretty | well-manicured | coarse, rough, work-reddened, work-roughened, work-worn | soft | firm, strong | limp** *He offered a limp hand to shake.* | **frail | arthritic | gnarled, knotted | claw-like | hairy | clammy** *He clutched the cane in his clammy hand.* | **cool** *His hand, when she shook it, was cool and firm.* | **dirty, filthy, greasy, grubby, sticky, sweaty, unwashed** *He wiped his greasy hands on the front of his overalls.* | **clean | gloved | ringed | ringless | open, outspread** *She gestured towards the window with an open hand.* | **outstretched** *She walked towards him with her hand outstretched to take his.* | **free** *With his free hand he took hold of the knife.* | **cupped** *She rested her chin in her cupped hand.* | **busy, deft** *Her busy hands had transformed the tiny room into a work of art.* | **willing** *There's plenty of work for willing hands* | **eager** *Eager hands reached out to help him.* | **nervous, shaking, trembling, unsteady | steady** *A surgeon needs a good eye and a steady hand.* | **friendly, sympathetic** *He put a friendly hand on his friend's knee.* | **generous, liberal** (*both figurative*) *She filled our glasses with a generous hand.* | **capable, expert, practised, skilful, skilled** *With a practised hand he motioned a waiter to bring a fresh pot of coffee.* | **careless, clumsy**
- VERB + HAND **take** *She took the child's hand and helped him climb the steps.* | **hold, hold on to** *They walked along, holding hands.* ◇ *She held on to my hand as I tried to leave.* | **reach for** *He reached for her hand and held it tightly.* | **press, squeeze, touch** *She pressed his hand. 'I know,' she said softly.* | **shake** *He shook Blake's hand as if they were long lost friends.* ◇ *He shook hands with all of us before leaving.* | **feel** *I felt a hand on my shoulder.* | **extend, hold out, put out, reach out** *She smiled and extended a hand in welcome.* ◇ *He put out a hand as if to touch her.* | **lay, place, press, put** *He laid a*

hand on her arm. ◇ *She put her hands to her cheeks in embarrassment.* | **slide** *He slid his hands into his pockets.* | **withdraw** *Slowly Ruth withdrew her hand from his.* | **hold up, lift, put up, raise, throw up** *He lifted his hand to her face.* ◇ *Several students put up their hands to answer the question.* ◇ *She raised her hand in farewell.* ◇ *He threw up his hands in despair when he saw the damage.* | **spread** *She shrugged and spread her hands. 'That's all I can tell you.'* | **wave** | **clap** *We were all clapping our hands in time to the music.* | **clasp, clench, rub, wring** *He had his hands clasped behind his head.* ◇ *She clenched her hands in her lap to hide their trembling.* ◇ *He rubbed his hands together in satisfaction.* ◇ *He was sobbing and wringing his hands by the grave.* | **beat** *He beat his hands on the steering wheel in frustration.* | **cup** *I cupped my hand over the mouthpiece of the phone so they couldn't hear me.* | **wash** | **wipe**

● HAND + VERB **shake, tremble** *Her hand shook as she lifted the glass to her lips.* | **reach out, shoot out** *A strong hand reached out and caught hold of her arm.* | **grope for sth, reach for sth, seek sth** *My hand groped for the door handle.* ◇ *His hand sought hers.* | **find sth** *His hand eventually found the light switch.* | **catch sth, clamp, clasp sth, close around/on/round sth, fasten around/on/round sth, grab sth, grasp sth, seize sth** *The policeman kept a firm hand clamped on his shoulder.* | **clutch sth, grip sth, hold sth** | **claw (at) sth, pull sth, tug sth** *His hands clawed at the muddy earth.* | **push sth** | **squeeze sth, tighten sth** | **brush (across/against) sth, caress sth, stroke sth, touch sth** *His hand brushed against hers.* | **creep, go, move, slide, slip, steal, stray** *Muriel's hand crept to her neck to hold her pearls.* | **fly** *Her hand flew to her mouth. 'Oh no!'* | **jerk, twitch** | **run over/through sth, trail** *Her hand ran over the surface, feeling the different textures.* | **freeze, still** *His hand froze in mid-gesture.* | **hover, waver** *My hand hovered over the switch for a moment.* | **lie, rest** *His hand rested on her shoulder.* | **go up, shoot up** | **come down, descend, drop** *A large hand descended on his shoulder.* ◇ *His hands dropped to his sides and he fell to the floor.* | **withdraw** | **lift, rise** *Her hand lifted to place a cigarette in her mouth.* | **cover sth** *Her hand moved to cover his.*

● HAND + NOUN **gesture, movement, position, signal** | **dryer, towel** | **drill, saw** (also **handsaw**), **tools** | **pump** | **mirror** | **baggage, luggage** *You can take your laptop on the plane as hand luggage.* | **cream** | **delivery** *Mail for hand delivery is put in a separate tray.* | **grenade, gun** (also **handgun**) | **injury**

● PREP. **by** ~ *Delicate clothes should be washed by hand.* **by ... ~s** *The rocks looked like they had been shaped by human hands.* **in your** ~ *She had a piece of paper in her hand.* ◇ *(figurative) Can I leave these queries in your capable hands?* **on your** ~ *She had large rings on both hands.* **with your** ~ *Operate the gears with your left hand.*

● PHRASES **fall into the wrong hands** *(figurative) Guards made sure that the food supplies didn't fall into the wrong hands.* **get/keep/take your hands off sb/sth** *She warned her brother to keep his hands off her bag.* **get/lay your hands on sth** *I desperately need to lay my hands on some money by Monday.* **hand in hand** *They walked hand in hand along the path.* **hands on hips** *She stood in the doorway, hands on hips.* **in safe hands** *(figurative) He retired feeling confident that his company was in safe hands.* **on (your) hands and knees** *He was on his hands and knees, looking for a contact lens.* **out of sb's hands** *(figurative) I don't work in that department any more, so the problem is out of my hands.* **the palm of your hand** *She studied the object in the palm of her hand.* **run a hand/your hands over/through, etc. sth** *Clive ran a hand through his hair.* **with your bare hands** *He killed the lion with his bare hands.*

2 a hand help

● VERB + HAND **give sb, lend (sb)** *Can you give me a hand with loading the van?* ◇ *At harvest time all the villa-*

gers lend a hand. | **need** *Do you need a hand with those invoices?*

3 role in a situation

● VERB + HAND **have** | **strengthen** *The strategic alliance served to strengthen the country's hand in the region.*

● PREP. ~ **in** *Several of his colleagues had a hand in his downfall.*

4 in card games

● ADJ. **bad, good**

● VERB + HAND **deal (sb)** *Who dealt the last hand?* ◇ *(figurative) She felt that life had dealt her a bad hand.* | **get, have** | **play**

hand *verb*

● ADV. **effectively** | **formally, officially** *formally handing over power to the new government* | **personally** *She wanted to hand the petition to the prime minister personally.* | **just, merely, simply** *They would simply hand her over to the magistrate as a thief.* | **quickly** | **immediately, promptly** | **grudgingly, reluctantly** *He grudgingly handed me the money.* | **silently** | **back, in, out, over** *She handed out the exam papers.*

● VERB + HAND **be prepared to, be ready to, be willing to** | **refuse to** | **force sb to**

● PREP. **to** *He handed the book to Sally.*

handbag *noun*

● ADJ. **big, capacious, large**

● VERB + HANDBAG **clutch, hold** | **carry** | **swing** | **delve into, fish about/around in, fumble in, reach into, rummage (around) in, search (in/through)** *She was rummaging in her handbag for her keys.* | **snatch** *She had her handbag snatched as she sat having a coffee.*

● PREP. **from a/the** ~, **out of a/the** ~ *She took a pen out of her large leather handbag.* **in a/the** ~, **into a/the** ~ *She put her purse into her handbag.*

● PHRASES **the contents of a handbag**

handcuffs *noun*

● QUANT. **pair, set** *The policeman slipped a pair of handcuffs on his wrists.*

● VERB + HANDCUFFS **have on, wear** | **put on, slip on** *The other policeman put the handcuffs on him.* | **remove, take off, undo, unfasten, unlock**

● PREP. **in** ~ *He was taken away in handcuffs.*

handful *noun*

1 amount that can be held in one hand

● ADJ. **good** | **double** *She bent and pulled up a double handful of weeds.*

● PREP. ~ **of** *She grabbed handfuls of the dirty snow.*

2 small number of people/things

● ADJ. **small, tiny** | **mere** *having to cope with a mere handful of staff* | **good** *He has a good handful of letters after his name.*

● PREP. ~ **of** *a handful of people*

● PHRASES **just/only a handful of sth** *We have received only a small handful of letters on this subject.*

handicap *noun*

1 physical/mental disability

● ADJ. **serious, severe** | **mild** | **mental, physical, visual** *She can't drive because of her visual handicap.*

● VERB + HANDICAP **be born with, have, suffer (from)** *Over a million people in Great Britain suffer from mental handicap.* | **cause** | **cope with, overcome** *She has managed to overcome her physical handicaps.*

● PREP. **despite a/the** ~ *Despite her handicap, Jane is able to hold down a full-time job.*

2 disadvantage
- ADJ. **big, considerable, great, major, real, serious, severe, terrible** *Lack of transport was a major handicap.*
- VERB + HANDICAP **have, suffer** *If you don't speak the language, you've got a real handicap.* | **prove** *His lack of height can prove a handicap against tall players.*
- PREP. **despite a/the ~ | ~ to** *This could be a serious handicap to her education.*

handicapped adj.
- VERBS **be, be born** *Steven was born severely handicapped.* | **leave sb** *An accident at birth left him badly handicapped.*
- ADV. **badly, profoundly, seriously, severely | mildly, slightly | permanently | mentally, physically, visually** *special equipment for visually handicapped children*

handkerchief noun
- ADJ. **clean | crumpled, dirty, grubby, used | pocket | lace, linen, paper, silk | embroidered**
- VERB + HANDKERCHIEF **blow your nose on, use** *He blew his nose on a grubby handkerchief.* | **wave**

handle noun
- ADJ. **long, short | carrying** *The table folds up and comes complete with a carrying handle.* | **door | knife, fork, pickaxe, etc.**
- VERB + HANDLE **have | pull, push, try, turn** *You have to turn the handle and then pull it towards you.* ◇ *He tried the handle but the door was locked.*
- PREP. **on a/the ~** *His initials were on the knife handle.*

handle verb
1 touch sth with your hands
- ADV. **carefully, with care** *A label on the crate read: 'Handle with care'.* | **carelessly** *Garden tools can be hazardous if carelessly handled.* | **roughly** *Many of the prisoners were roughly handled; some were killed.*

2 deal with sb/sth
- ADV. **competently, efficiently, properly, skilfully, successfully, well** *I think you handled that situation very well.* | **badly | carefully, delicately** *This issue may need to be handled carefully.* | **easily** *Her next question was not so easily handled.* | **routinely** *The library routinely handles a wide variety of enquiries.*
- VERB + HANDLE **be able/unable to, can/could, know how to** *This was a problem that I just couldn't handle.* ◇ *She knew how to handle publicity.* | **be designed to, be equipped to** *He wasn't mentally equipped to handle this situation.* | **learn how to | be easy to | be difficult to, be hard to** *Large meetings are notoriously less productive and more difficult to handle.*
- PREP. **with** *She handled the crisis with total assurance.*

handling noun
- ADJ. **careful, delicate, gentle** *Timid children need gentle handling to build up their confidence.* | **careless, clumsy | sensitive, sympathetic** *Issues such as drug addiction require sensitive handling when featured in TV dramas.* | **insensitive | competent** *She was praised for her competent handling of the crisis.* | **baggage, cargo, freight, stock | customer, passenger** *a small airport with limited passenger handling facilities* | **food** *hygienic food handling practice* | **data, information**
- VERB + HANDLING **need, require**

handout noun
1 food/money given to people who need it badly
- ADJ. **free | government, state | cash**
- VERB + HANDOUT **give (sb) | get, receive** *All those eligible will receive a cash handout.*
- PREP. **~ from** *a handout from the government* **~ to** *state handouts to the poor*

2 sheet/leaflet
- VERB + HANDOUT **distribute, give sb, give out**
- PREP. **in a/the ~** *More information can be found in the handout.* | **~ on** *We were given a handout on job hunting.*

handshake noun
- ADJ. **firm, hearty | limp** *She wasn't impressed by his limp handshake.*
- VERB + HANDSHAKE **have** *He had a firm handshake.* | **give sb** *Fawcett gave me a hearty handshake.*
- PREP. **with a ~** *They sealed the agreement with a handshake.* | **~ from** *a handshake from the chairman*

handsome adj.
- VERBS **be, look | become, grow**
- ADV. **devastatingly, exceedingly, extraordinarily, extremely, incredibly, strikingly, very, wonderfully** *He was young and devastatingly handsome.* | **almost | quite, rather | classically, darkly, elegantly, ruggedly, youthfully** *his ruggedly handsome features*
- PHRASES **tall, dark (and) handsome** *a tall, dark, handsome stranger*

handwriting noun
- ADJ. **clear, good, legible, neat** *Her handwriting was neat and legible.* | **awful, bad, illegible, poor, terrible** *Why do doctors have such terrible handwriting?*
- VERB + HANDWRITING **have | read** *Her handwriting is very difficult to read.* | **recognize** *I didn't recognize the handwriting on the envelope.*
- PREP. **in your ~** *She copied out the lines in her best handwriting.*

handy adj.
1 useful
- VERBS **be | come in** *I advise you to buy one—it may come in handy one day.*
- ADV. **very | quite**
- PREP. **for** *The arrangement was handy for both of us.*

2 nearby
- VERBS **be | keep sth** *Always keep a cloth handy to wipe up any mess.*
- ADV. **very | quite**
- PREP. **for** *The house was near Drury Lane, very handy for the theatre.*

3 good at using sth
- VERBS **be**
- ADV. **very | fairly, pretty, quite**
- PREP. **at** *'I'm pretty handy at giving out advice,' claimed Mark.* **with** *Lucy is quite handy with a drill!*

hang verb
- ADV. **limply, loosely** *He had lost weight and the suit hung loosely on him.* | **uselessly** *Her injured arm hung uselessly at her side.* | **upside down** *The sloth spends most of its time hanging upside down from the branches.* | **down** *Large leaves hung down from the branches of the trees.*
- PREP. **by** *The monkey was hanging by its tail from the beams overhead.* **from** *Banners hung from every window.*

PHRASAL VERB

hang on
1 keep hold of sth
- ADV. **tight** *Hang on tight—we're off.*
- VERB + HANG ON **try to**

- PREP. **for** *She hung on for dear life.* **to** *Hang on to* (= keep) *those old photographs—they may be valuable.* **with** *Martin tried to hold on with his toes as well as his feet.*

2 wait
- ADV. **a minute** *Hang on a minute—I'll just see if he's here.*

hanker *verb*

- ADV. **secretly | always | still**
- PREP. **after** *She's always hankering after excitement.* **for** *I still hankered for the farm life.*

haphazard *adj.*

- VERBS **be, seem | become**
- ADV. **very | entirely, totally** *The local authority's approach to health care seems totally haphazard.* | **fairly, rather, somewhat | apparently, seemingly**
- PHRASES **in a haphazard fashion/manner/way** *The town had grown in a somewhat haphazard way.*

happen *verb*

- ADV. **actually, really** *She couldn't quite believe that all this was actually happening to her.* | **just** *I don't remember learning to swim, it just happened.* | **spontaneously** *Sometimes fun activities just happen spontaneously; at other times they take careful planning.* | **overnight** *Change doesn't happen overnight.*
- VERB + HAPPEN **be going to** *They could only wait and see what was going to happen.* | **be likely to | be bound to** *Mistakes are bound to happen sometimes.* | **tend to** *What tends to happen is that students spend the first week of the course in a blind panic, but settle down by the second or third week.* | **want sth to | make sth** *You have to make things happen if you want them to happen.* | **let sth** *Don't just sit back and let it happen.*
- PREP. **to** *She didn't know what was happening to her.*

happiness *noun*

- ADJ. **deep, great | perfect, pure, sheer, true | eternal, lasting | future** *Living together before you marry is no guarantee of future happiness.* | **earthly | human | personal | domestic, family, marital**
- VERB + HAPPINESS **be filled with, feel | glow with** *Her face was glowing with happiness.* | **cry with, sigh with, weep with | achieve, find** *She seems to have found happiness with her new husband.* | **bring (sb)** *It is easy to believe that money brings happiness.* | **buy (sb)** *You cannot buy happiness.* | **wish sb**
- PREP. **with ~ | ~ at** *He was weeping with happiness at being free.*
- PHRASES **a feeling of happiness, wish sb every happiness** *We wish them every happiness in their new life.*

happy *adj.*

1 feeling pleasure
- VERBS **appear, be, feel, look, seem, sound** *Outwardly the couple appeared happy.* ◇ *Andrew felt happier than he had been for a long time.* | **become | make sb** *Money won't make you happy.* | **keep sb** *He went home from time to time, to keep his mother happy.*
- ADV. **extremely, only too, particularly, really, very** *We'd be only too happy to accept your invitation.* | **completely, perfectly, quite** *Mum seemed perfectly happy with my explanation.* | **genuinely, truly** *For the first time in her life, she felt truly happy.* | **far from, not altogether, not at all, not entirely, not exactly, not particularly, not too, not totally** *Her boss was not entirely happy about the situation.* | **fairly, pretty, reasonably, relatively | just** *I'm just happy to be back home.* | **absurdly, amazingly, blissfully, deliriously, ecstatically, radiantly, ridiculously, strangely, surprisingly | clearly, obviously**

- PREP. **about** *I'm not too happy about her attitude.* **for** *So you're getting married, I hear. I'm really happy for you!* **with** *I was quite happy with the way things went.*

2 giving pleasure
- VERBS **be, seem**
- ADV. **extremely, gloriously, particularly, very, wonderfully** *It had been a gloriously happy time.* | **quite**

harass *verb*

- ADV. **racially, sexually** *She had been sexually harassed at work.*

harassment *noun*

- ADJ. **racial, sexual | police | constant, continual**
- VERB + HARASSMENT **be subject to, be subjected to, suffer** *She had been subjected to continual sexual harassment.*
- PREP. **~ by** *They are complaining about harassment by the police*
- PHRASES **a victim of harassment**
- ⇒ Note at CRIME (for more verbs)

harbour *noun*

- ADJ. **deep, deep-water | good, safe, sheltered | natural | busy | picturesque, pretty | fishing**
- VERB + HARBOUR **have** *The town has a small natural harbour.* | **come into, go into, enter** *They entered the harbour with flags flying.* | **go out of, leave**
- HARBOUR + NOUN **wall**
- PREP. **in (a/the)~** *The fishing fleet is in harbour.* ◇ *the activity in the harbour* **into (a/the) ~** *The damaged vessel was towed into harbour.* **out of a/the~** *We sailed out of the harbour at daybreak.*
- PHRASES **the entrance to/the mouth of a harbour**

hard *adj.*

1 solid/stiff
- VERBS **be, feel, look, seem** *The chairs felt hard and uncomfortable.* | **become, go** *Don't leave the cake uncovered or the icing will go hard.* | **stay**
- ADV. **extremely, very | a bit, fairly, quite, rather**
- PHRASES **rock hard** *The toffee was rock hard.*

2 difficult
- VERBS **be, look, seem | become, get** *Life got very hard.* | **make sth** *If you tell the children the answers, it only makes it harder for them to do the work on their own.* | **find sth** *I found the exam quite hard.*
- ADV. **extremely, really, very | a bit, fairly, pretty, quite, rather**

hardback *noun*

- VERB + HARDBACK **publish | come out in** *His second book came out in hardback last month.*
- HARDBACK + NOUN **book, edition**
- PREP. **in ~** *It's only available in hardback.*

hardship *noun*

- ADJ. **appalling, considerable, dreadful, extreme, genuine, great, immense, real, severe | widespread | undue, unnecessary | economic, financial, material, personal, physical**
- VERB + HARDSHIP **cause | bear, endure, experience, face, suffer, survive** *a close community which makes these hardships easier to bear* ◇ *Students may suffer severe financial hardship as a result of the government's decision.* ◇ *They have already survived considerable hardship.*
- HARDSHIP + NOUN **payment** *The union made hardship payments to some of the sacked workers.*
- PREP. **in ~** *They are living in genuine hardship.* **with-**

out~ *Rail services to rural areas could be withdrawn without undue hardship.* | ~ among *widespread hardship among students* ~to *The cold was no real hardship to me.*
● PHRASES **times of hardship** *In times of economic hardship, firms cut back on training.*

hardware *noun*

1 of a computer
● ADJ. **computer**
● QUANT. **piece** *The laptop drawing tablet is a very useful piece of hardware.*
● VERB + HARDWARE **design, develop | provide, supply** *supplying computer hardware to business*
● HARDWARE + NOUN **component, device, product | environment, platform, system** *This application runs on a wide variety of hardware platforms.* | **configuration | design, development | company, manufacturer, supplier, vendor**
⇨ Special page at COMPUTER
2 heavy machinery/weapons
● ADJ. **military** *firms selling military hardware*

harm *noun*

● ADJ. **considerable, great, serious, untold** *He was clearly intent on inflicting serious harm on someone.* | **irreparable, lasting, permanent | emotional, mental, physical, psychological** *elderly people in danger of physical or emotional harm* | **economic, environmental**
● VERB + HARM **cause, do, inflict** *The huge fall in exports has done a great deal of harm to the economy.* | **mean (sb), wish sb** *I'm sorry if I upset you—I didn't mean any harm.* ◇ *No one wishes you harm.* | **come to, suffer** *I don't think he'll come to any harm if his mother is with him.* | **keep sb from, prevent, protect sb from, shield sb from** *The children were removed from their parents to prevent harm to them.* ◇ *She tried to shield her child from harm.*
● HARM + VERB **come to sb/sth** *I don't want any harm to come to these pictures.*
● PREP. ~from *babies at risk of serious harm from their parents* ~to *the harm done to the environment*
● PHRASES **more harm than good** *The drugs he was prescribed did him more harm than good.* **out of harm's way** *The younger children were kept out of harm's way.*

harm *verb*

● ADV. **seriously** *Misusing drugs in pregnancy can seriously harm your baby.* | **deliberately | physically**
● VERB + HARM **intend to, want to** *He claimed that he had not intended to harm the girl.* | **try to**

harmful *adj.*

● VERBS **be | become | consider sth** *She actually considered fresh air harmful.*
● ADV. **extremely, particularly, positively, very** *These products are often positively harmful.* | **quite | possibly, potentially** *A lot of these chemicals are potentially very harmful.* | **allegedly | (not) necessarily** *Not all virus infections are necessarily harmful to vines.* | **intrinsically | environmentally, socially** *These pesticides are environmentally harmful.*
● PREP. **to** *pesticides that are harmful to the environment*

harmless *adj.*

● VERBS **appear, be, look, seem, sound | make sth, render sth** *chemical wastes which have to be rendered harmless* | **consider sth**
● ADV. **absolutely, completely, perfectly, quite, totally | almost, virtually | enough** *He looks harmless enough.* | **comparatively, fairly, pretty, reasonably, relatively |**

apparently, seemingly *a small and seemingly harmless creature* | **environmentally**
● PREP. **to** *The substance is harmless to people.*

harmony *noun*

1 state of agreement
● ADJ. **absolute, complete, perfect | reasonable, relative** *They've lived together in reasonable harmony for many years.* | **domestic, political, racial, social** *On the surface, their life seemed a model of domestic harmony.*
● VERB + HARMONY **achieve | maintain, preserve** *They try to maintain harmony between the two communities.* | **foster, promote** *The Church tries to promote racial harmony.* | **live in**
● PREP. **in~** *They work together in harmony.* | ~between *They try to foster harmony between different groups of people.* ~with *living in perfect harmony with nature*
● PHRASES **a sense of harmony** *A new sense of harmony developed in the community.*
2 pleasant combination of different musical notes
● ADJ. **musical | five-part, four-part, etc.** *an arrangement with four-part harmony*
● PREP. **in~** *to sing in harmony*

harness *noun*

1 for a horse
● ADJ. **leather**
● VERB + HARNESS **put on | remove, take off**
● PREP. **in (a)~** *a horse in harness*
2 for a person
● ADJ. **child | safety | climbing, parachute**
● VERB + HARNESS **have on, wear | do up, fasten** *She fastened the safety harness tightly round her waist before starting the descent.* | **undo, unfasten**
● PREP. **in a/the~** *Another man in a harness was being lowered from the helicopter.*

harness *verb*

● ADV. **effectively, successfully | fully**
● VERB + HARNESS **attempt to, seek to, try to** *attempting to harness the power of the sun* | **manage to**
● PREP. **for** *How can this energy be harnessed effectively for the good of humankind?*

harp *noun*

● VERB + HARP **set, tune** *By means of pedals, a harp can be set in any desired key.*
⇨ Special page at MUSIC

harp *verb*

PHRASAL VERB
harp on
● ADV. **always, constantly** *He is always harping on about the war.* | **still**
● PREP. **about**
● PHRASES **keep harping on** *Don't keep harping on about my age!*

harsh *adj.*

● VERBS **appear, be, prove, seem, sound** *It may seem harsh to criticize him after his death.* | **become**
● ADV. **exceptionally, extremely, particularly, very | increasingly | a bit, a little, rather, somewhat | unduly, unnecessarily** *He accused her of being unduly harsh.* | **surprisingly**

harvest *noun*

● ADJ. **abundant, bumper, good, large, rich** *We've had a bumper harvest of apples this year.* ◇ *(figurative) She re-*

turned from the conference with a rich harvest of knowledge. | **bad, disastrous, poor** *a series of poor harvests in the 1830s* | **cereal, corn, grain, potato, wheat, etc.**
• VERB + HARVEST **bring in, gather (in), get in, reap** *They were busy getting the harvest in.* ◊ *(figurative) We are now reaping the harvest of our hard work last year.*
• HARVEST + VERB **fail** *The strawberry harvest failed because of the drought.*
• HARVEST + NOUN **time** | **feast, festival**
• PREP. **after (the)** ~ *Potatoes are normally sprayed after harvest.* **during (the)** ~ *During harvest they work from dawn to dusk.* | ~**of** *a good harvest of potatoes*

hassle noun

• ADJ. **legal** *They faced interminable legal hassles if they wanted to claim compensation.*
• VERB + HASSLE **get, have** *I started to get all this hassle from my boss about increasing productivity.* | **give sb** *He gave me so much hassle I decided it wasn't worth it.* | **save** *It saves a lot of hassle if you buy them by post.* | **be worth** *Camping holidays aren't really worth all the hassle.*
• PREP. **with no/without** ~ *She got the computer set up with no hassle at all.* | ~**about/over** *I've had so much hassle over this business.*
• PHRASES **take the hassle out of sth** *Package holidays take all the hassle out of travel arrangements.*

haste noun

• ADJ. **blind, breathless, frantic, great** *She worked with frantic haste.* | **indecent, reckless, undue** *He accused the government of undue haste in bringing in the new law.*
• VERB + HASTE **make** *I had to make haste if I wasn't to be late.*
• PREP. **in (your)** ~ *They obviously left in great haste.* ◊ *In his haste to get home, he forgot to go to the library.* **with** ~ *He married again with almost indecent haste.* **without** ~ *They approached without haste.*
• PHRASES **with all haste** *The ships were ordered to sea with all haste.*

hat noun

• ADJ. **broad-brimmed, wide-brimmed** | **floppy** | **battered** | **pointed** | **fur, straw, woollen, woolly** | **bobble, bowler, hard, panama, party, peaked, picture, riding, sun** (also **sunhat**), **ten-gallon, three-cornered, top**
• VERB + HAT **don, place** *He placed a battered felt hat on his head.* | **doff, remove** | **raise, tip, touch** *The doorman tipped his hat as we entered.*
• HAT + VERB **be trimmed with sth** *The governor wore a cocked hat trimmed with white feathers.*
• HAT + NOUN **box** | **shop** | **stand**
• PHRASES **pull a hat (down) over your ears/eyes/face**
⇨ Special page at CLOTHES

hatch noun

• ADJ. **closed, open** *Leave the hatch open.* | **escape** | **inspection, service** *The engineer was peering into the service hatch.* | **serving** *She opened the serving hatch and put the soup on the counter.* | **kitchen, loft**
• VERB + HATCH **lift, open, raise** *She lifted the hatch and slid it away from the opening.* | **batten down, close, shut** *They battened down the hatches and prepared for the storm.* ◊ *He ordered the hatches to be closed.*
• PREP. **through a/the** ~ *They got out through the escape hatch.* | ~**between** *a hatch between the kitchen and the dining room* ~**to** *a hatch to the dining room*

hate noun

1 strong feeling of dislike
• ADJ. **absolute, naked, pure** *In her eyes he could see naked hate.*

• VERB + HATE **be filled with, be full of, burn with** *He burned with hate for everyone and everything.*
• HATE + NOUN **campaign, figure, mail** *victim of a vicious hate campaign* ◊ *She became a hate figure for politicians on the left.*
• PREP. ~**for** *full of hate for the people who had betrayed her*

2 sb/sth you hate
• ADJ. **pet** *Jazz has always been a pet hate of mine.*

hate verb

• ADV. **particularly, really** | **absolutely** *I absolutely hate cooking.* | **almost** *For a moment she almost hated him.* | **just** *Don't you just hate people who are always right?* | **always** *I always hated school.* | **still**
• VERB + HATE **begin to, come to, grow to** *He came to hate the town, with its narrow prejudices.* | **love to** *the media baron all the socialists love to hate*
• PREP. **for** *He hated me for standing up to him.*
• PHRASES **hate it when** *I hate it when you lose your temper like that.*

hatred noun

• ADJ. **bitter, deep, intense, passionate, pure, violent** *She shot him a look of pure hatred.* | **absolute, implacable** | **blind, irrational** | **class, ethnic, racial, religious**
• VERB + HATRED **be filled with, be full of, feel, have** *She was full of hatred and bitterness.* ◊ *He has a deep hatred of the police.* | **incite, stir up** *He is accused of stirring up racial hatred.*
• HATRED + VERB **flare (up)** *Hatred flared up inside her.*
• PREP. **in/with** ~ *She stared at it in hatred.* | ~**against** *inciting religious hatred against the Catholic minority* ~**between** *the intense hatred between the two communities* ~**for** *I felt no hatred for him.* ~**of** *his hatred of women* ~**towards** *their hatred towards the oppressors*
• PHRASES **a feeling of hatred**

haul noun

1 act of hauling
• VERB + HAUL **give sth**
• PREP. ~**on** *When I shout, give a haul on the rope.*

2 distance to be travelled
• ADJ. **long, short** *the long haul back to Cape Town* ◊ *a short-haul passenger plane* | **final, last** *the final haul up the hill to the finishing line*
• PREP. ~**from, ~to**

3 of fish/stolen goods, etc.
• ADJ. **big, large, record** *The thieves got away with a record haul of £25 million.* | **arms, drugs**
• VERB + HAUL **get, get away with** *The gang did not expect to get such a large haul.*
• HAUL + VERB **be worth sth** *a haul worth £30 000*
• PREP. ~**of** *the biggest ever haul of illegal drugs*

haunt noun

• ADJ. **favourite, old, popular, regular, usual** | **tourist** *The area was a popular tourist haunt.*
• VERB + HAUNT **go back to, return to, revisit** *We've been back to some of our old haunts.*

haunt verb

1 appear as a ghost in a place
• ADV. **reputedly, supposedly** *a Norman castle which is reputedly haunted*
• VERB + HAUNT **come back to, return to** *He said he would come back to haunt her.* ◊ *(figurative) That decision came back to haunt him in later life.*

2 be always in your mind
• ADV. **still** *the great fear that still haunts her*

● VERB + HAUNT **continue to** *These visions continued to haunt her for many years.*

haven *noun*

● ADJ. **safe** *The aim is to create a safe haven for the thousands of refugees.*
● VERB + HAVEN **create, offer (sb), provide (sb with)**
● PREP. **in a/the ~** *They were living in a safe haven away from the fighting.* | **~ for** *The wood is a haven for wildlife.* **~ of** *This house is a haven of peace compared with ours.*

havoc *noun*

● VERB + HAVOC **cause, create, play, wreak**
● PREP. **~ among** *The new tax could wreak havoc among smaller companies.* **~ for** *High winds have been creating havoc for farmers.* **~ in** *The disease can cause havoc in commercial orchards.* **~ on** *The flood wrought havoc on the countryside.* **~ to** *The storm caused havoc to wildlife.* **~ with** *The fog played havoc with flight schedules.*

hawk *noun*

● HAWK + VERB **hover** | **swoop (down)** *The hawk swooped low over the field.*
● PHRASES **watch (sb) like a hawk** *He waited, watching her like a hawk.*

hay *noun*

● QUANT. **bale**
● VERB + HAY **cut, harvest, make** *The freshly harvested hay was taken into the big hay barn.* ◇ *They make hay to feed the cattle in winter.*
● HAY + NOUN **meadow** | **bale** | **barn, loft**
● PREP. **in the ~** *The children were playing in the hay.*

hazard *noun*

● ADJ. **big, great, major, real, serious** | **constant** | **possible, potential** | **hidden, unexpected, unseen** | **environmental, industrial, natural, occupational** *industrial hazards such as excessive noise and pollution* ◇ *Loneliness is one of the occupational hazards of being a writer.* | **health** *Other people's smoke is now seen as a health hazard.* | **fire** *The rubbish under the flooring is a serious fire hazard.*
● VERB + HAZARD **cause, create, pose** *Production of these chemicals poses serious environmental hazards.* | **be exposed to, encounter, face, meet** *The worst hazard we faced was having our money stolen.* | **avoid** *Go in September if you want to avoid the hazard of extreme heat.* | **eliminate, minimize** | **cope with, deal with, negotiate** *Companies should have systems for dealing with work hazards.*
● PREP. **~ for** *Holes in the pavement are a hazard for blind people.* **~ to** *The burning of industrial waste is a major hazard to human health.*
● PHRASES **exposure to a hazard** *Try and reduce your exposure to hazards such as poor quality air.*

hazardous *adj.*

● VERBS **be, prove** | **become** | **consider sth**
● ADV. **extremely, highly, particularly, very** | **rather, somewhat** | **potentially** *burning potentially hazardous medical waste* | **environmentally** *environmentally hazardous substances*
● PREP. **for** *These conditions are very hazardous for shipping.* **to** *chemicals that are hazardous to human beings*

haze *noun*

● ADJ. **thick** *a thick haze of smoke* | **faint, thin** *The sun now had a faint golden haze around it.* | **shimmering** | **heat** *A heat haze shimmered above the fields.*

● HAZE + VERB **hang, shimmer** *In the evenings a blue haze hung in the valleys.*
● PREP. **in a/the ~** *Meetings are always conducted in a haze of cigarette smoke.* **through a/the ~** *He watched the world through a haze of tobacco smoke.*

hazy *adj.*

1 not clear because the air is difficult to see through
● VERBS **be, look** *The distant mountains looked hazy and mysterious.* | **become** | **remain**
● ADV. **very** | **a little, quite, rather, slightly** *Generally, it will be rather hazy today, with some hill fog.*
● PREP. **with** *The summers were hazy with pollution.*

2 confused
● VERBS **be** | **become** | **remain**
● ADV. **extremely, very** *I have only a very hazy idea about how the economy works.* | **a bit, fairly, a little, rather, somewhat** *My memory of that day is somewhat hazy now.*
● PREP. **about** *I'm a bit hazy about my family history.*

head *noun*

1 part of the body
● ADJ. **bare** | **bald** | **shaved** | **blonde, dark, fair, grey, greying** | **bent, bowed** *She sat with bowed head.* | **severed** *The city gates were adorned with severed heads.*
● VERB + HEAD **poke, pop, put, stick** *He put his head round the door.* | **bob, cock, crane, incline, jerk, tilt, turn** *She jerked her head in the direction of the door.* | **lift, raise** | **bend, bow, drop, duck, hang, lower** *He hung his head in shame.* | **swing, throw back, toss** *He threw his head back and laughed out loud.* | **nod, shake** *They nodded their heads in agreement.* ◇ *She shook her head in disbelief.* | **scratch** *He scratched his head. 'I don't understand,' he said.* ◇ *(figurative) Detectives have been left scratching their heads over the stolen painting's sudden reappearance.* | **clutch, hold** *He lay writhing on the ground, clutching his head in pain.* | **bury** *She buried her head in the pillow.* | **shave**
● HEAD + VERB **ache, throb** | **bob, jerk, nod, tilt, turn** *Her head tilted to one side as she considered the question.* | **droop, drop, hang down, hang low** *His head drooped and tears fell into his lap.*
● HEAD + NOUN **injury** | **cold**
● PREP. **above your ~** *The thunder burst with a grand crash above our heads.* **over your ~** *The soldiers were ordered to fire over the heads of the crowd.*
● PHRASES **from head to foot/toe** *We were covered from head to foot in mud.* **a fine/good, etc. head of hair** (= a lot of hair) *a woman with a lovely head of chestnut hair* **have/hold/put, etc. your head in your hands** *He put his head in his hands, exasperated.* **head first** *He dived head first into the water.* ◇ *(figurative) She got divorced and rushed head first into another marriage.* **a nod of the head** *The ambassador dismissed him with a curt nod of the head.* **a shake of the head** *She declined with a brief shake of the head.*

2 mind
● ADJ. **clear, cool, level** *She needed to keep a clear head if she was to remain in control.* | **good** *I have a good head for figures.*
● VERB + HEAD **use** *I wish you'd use your head* (= think carefully before doing or saying something). | **enter** *It never entered my head that he might be lying.* | **get it into** *When will you get it into your head* (= understand) *that I don't want to discuss this any more!* ◇ *For some reason she's got it into her head* (= believes) *that the others don't like her.* | **put sth into** *Who's been putting such weird ideas into your head?* | **get sth out of, put sth out of** *I can't get that tune out of my head.* ◇ *Try to put the exams out of your head for tonight.* | **bother** *Don't bother your pretty little head with things like that!*

● HEAD + VERB **spin** *He could feel his head spinning after only one drink.*
● PREP. **in your~** *I can't work it out in my head—I need a calculator.* **inside your~** *It was an accident, said a voice inside his head.*
● PHRASES **can't get your head round sth** (= can't understand sth) *She's dead. I can't get my head round it yet.* **need your head examined** *He looked at me as if I needed my head examined* (= as if I were crazy).

3 heads side of a coin
● VERB + HEADS **call** *I called heads and it came down tails.* | **come down/up**
● PHRASES **heads or tails?**

4 of a group/organization/school, etc.
● ADJ. **deputy | departmental | nominal, titular** *The Queen is titular head of the Church of England.* | **crowned** *The message was sent to all the crowned heads* (= kings and queens) *of Europe.*
● HEAD + NOUN **gardener, teacher, waiter | boy, girl** (= in a school)
● PHRASES **a head of department, the head of the family, a head of government/state** *a summit meeting of heads of state* **a head of (the) household**
⇨ Note at JOB

head *verb*

1 go
● ADV. **north, northwards, etc.** *We headed west for two days.* | **back** *Let's head back home.*
● PREP. **back to** *We headed straight back to school.* **for** *He turned and headed for the door.* **towards** *heading towards London*

2 be in charge of sth
● ADV. **jointly** *The committee will be headed jointly by two men.* | **up**
● VERB + HEAD **appoint sb to** *She has been appointed to head up the research team.*

headache *noun*

1 pain in the head
● ADJ. **bad, severe, terrible, violent | mild, slight | dull | pounding, splitting, throbbing | migraine, tension** *He developed a severe migraine headache.*
● VERB + HEADACHE **have, suffer from** *I've got a splitting headache.* | **get, develop** *We all get headaches from time to time.* | **complain of** *The workers had complained of headaches and nausea.* | **bring on, cause, give sb** *Exhaust fumes made him drowsy and brought on a headache.* ◇ *Red wine gives me a headache.* | **plead** *She had left the party early, pleading a headache.*
● HEADACHE + NOUN **pill, tablet**
⇨ Special page at ILLNESS

2 sb/sth that causes worry/difficulty
● ADJ. **big, major, real | constant**
● PREP. **~for** *Uneven cash flow proved to be a major headache for the company.*

heading *noun*

● ADJ. **broad, general** *Books on bridges should be listed under 'bridges' and not under a broader heading such as 'engineering'.* | **main, major | chapter, page, section | subject, topic | letter** *With the computer, we can print our own letter headings.*
● VERB + HEADING **come under, fall under** *These drugs come under the heading of non-medical substances.*
● PREP. **under a/the~** *I've organized what I have to say about unemployment under three main headings.*

headlights *noun*

● ADJ. **dimmed, undimmed** *I kept my headlights undimmed along the country lanes.*

● VERB + HEADLIGHTS **put on, switch on, turn on | dip | flash** *He flashed his headlights at the oncoming car.*
● HEADLIGHTS + VERB **be (full) on | blaze, flash, shine** *The headlights shone on empty streets as we drove through the town.* | **pick sth out** *My headlights finally picked out a road sign.* | **sweep** *The car's headlights swept across the front of the house.*
● PHRASES **the glare of headlights**

headline *noun*

1 title of an article in a newspaper
● ADJ. **newspaper, tabloid** *'Carnage at Airport', screamed the tabloid headline.* | **banner, front-page | screaming | lurid** *lurid headlines about the sex lives of the stars* | **sporting, sports**
● VERB + HEADLINE **carry, have, run** *The Guardian carried the front-page headline 'Drugs Firms Shamed'.* | **read, scan, see** *I just had time to scan the headlines before leaving for work.* | **be in, capture, dominate, grab, hit, hog, make ~s** *She's always in the headlines.* ◇ *He always manages to grab the headlines.* ◇ *The hospital hit the headlines when a number of suspicious deaths occurred.* ◇ *The story has been hogging the headlines for weeks.* ◇ *The story was important enough to make the headlines.*
● HEADLINE + VERB **proclaim sth, read sth, say sth, scream sth** *The Sunday Observer had a headline saying, 'Pop Star Arrested on Drugs Charges'.*
● HEADLINE + NOUN **news** *'Queen Mother goes on Holiday' is hardly headline news!*
● PREP. **in a/the~** *The most unusual fact in the story is often used in the headline.* **under a/the~** *The Daily Gazette ran a story under the headline 'Pope's Last Words'.* **with a/the~** *a story in the newspaper with the headline 'Woman Gives Birth on Train'* | **~about** *There was a banner headline about drugs in schools.*
● PHRASES **make headline news** *The engagement of the two tennis stars made headline news.*

2 the headlines main news stories on TV/radio
● ADJ. **news**
● VERB + HEADLINES **hear, listen to** *Let's just hear the news headlines.* | **look at, see, watch**

headquarters *noun*

● ADJ. **international, local, national, regional | permanent | temporary | field | enemy | rebel | administrative, campaign, operational | army, military | police | business, company, corporate, group | party**
● VERB + HEADQUARTERS **have** *The organization has its headquarters in Brussels.* | **establish, set up** *The company has set up its European headquarters in the UK.* | **open | close** *They're planning to close their headquarters in Washington.*
● PREP. **at (the)~** *They're very worried about this at headquarters.* ◇ *She works at the company's headquarters.*

heal *verb*

● ADV. **completely, properly** *The wound hasn't healed properly yet.* | **partially | beautifully, nicely, well | gradually, slowly | quickly | eventually, finally | up** *The wound healed up very nicely.*

health *noun*

● ADJ. **excellent, full, good, perfect | bad, declining, delicate, failing, fragile, frail, ill, poor** *He had to retire due to ill health.* | **general, mental, physical, sexual | environmental, occupational** *environmental health officers* | **public** *The poisoned food has been removed from the shops and there is no threat to public health.* | **human**
● VERB + HEALTH **enjoy, have** *She's never really enjoyed good health.* | **look after, maintain** *You need to maintain your physical and mental health.* | **improve**

ways to improve the nation's general health | **promote** *a programme to promote better health in the workplace* | **recover, regain** | **nurse sb back to** *She was nursed back to full health.* | **damage, harm, ruin, undermine** | **risk**

● HEALTH + VERB **improve** *Her health gradually improved.* | **deteriorate, fail, worsen** *His health began to fail under the heavy pressures of the job.*

● HEALTH + NOUN **care** *How is primary health care best delivered?* | **authority, board** *the district/local/regional health authority* | **issue, needs, problem** | **hazard, risk** | **education** | **centre** *a community health centre* | **insurance** *private health insurance* | **food** *health food stores* | **professional, visitor, worker** *Your doctor, midwife or health visitor will advise.* | **warning** *The air quality was so bad that the government issued a health warning.* | **minister**

● PHRASES **bad/good for your health** *Smoking is bad for your health.* **health and safety** *health and safety at work* **(not) in the best of health, in good/poor health** *He felt in much better health.* **sb's state of health** *He is unable to travel far because of his state of health.*

health service *noun*

● ADJ. **comprehensive, good** | **free** | **community, family, national, public**

● VERB + HEALTH SERVICE **manage, run** *the problems of managing the health service* | **establish, introduce, set up** *plans to set up a national health service* | **improve, reform** | **finance, pay for** | **nationalize, privatize**

● HEALTH SERVICE + VERB **provide sth** *The health service can't provide cosmetic surgery.*

● HEALTH SERVICE + NOUN **employee, manager, official, staff, worker**

● PREP. **in the ~** *a shortage of labour in the health service* **on the ~** *Are you going to have your operation done on the national health service?* **under the ~** *This treatment is difficult to obtain under the national health service.* **within the ~** *decision-making within the health service*

healthy *adj.*

1 not ill

● VERBS **appear, be, be born, feel, look, seem** | **become** | **keep, remain, stay** | **make sb** *Working in the open air has made him very healthy.* | **keep sb** *Her good diet had kept her healthy.*

● ADV. **extremely, fantastically, really, very** | **perfectly** *He's a perfectly healthy child.* | **fairly, quite, reasonably** | **apparently** *The rare disorder strikes apparently healthy boys between the ages of five and twelve.* | **disgustingly** *(informal, ironic) You look disgustingly healthy! How do you manage it?* | **otherwise** *She looked pale, but otherwise healthy.* | **mentally, physically**

● PHRASES **fit and healthy**

2 producing good health

● VERBS **be** | **consider sth** *a new diet which is considered much healthier than previous ones*

● ADV. **extremely, very** *We have a very healthy diet.* | **quite** *Their lifestyle is quite healthy.* | **generally**

3 working well

● VERBS **be** | **remain**

● ADV. **extremely, very** *The economy is extremely healthy at the moment.* | **fairly, quite, reasonably, relatively** | **basically, fundamentally, generally** | **financially**

heap *noun*

● ADJ. **big, great, large** | **little, small** | **crumpled, untidy** | **compost, manure, muck, rubbish, scrap, slag, spoil** *colliery spoil heaps*

● VERB + HEAP **be piled in** *Papers were piled in great heaps on the desk.* | **collapse in, fall (down) in** *(both figurative) He collapsed in an exhausted heap on the floor.*

● PREP. **in a/the ~** *His clothes lay in a crumpled heap on the floor.* **on/onto a/the ~** *Throw the potato peelings on the compost heap.* | **~ of** *a great heap of stones*

● PHRASES **the bottom/top of the heap** *(figurative) These workers are at the bottom of the economic heap.*

hear *verb*

1 be aware of sounds

● ADV. **clearly, well** *He's getting old and he can't hear very well.* | **just** *I could just hear the music in the distance.* | **distantly** *Distantly he heard the report of another gun.* | **aright, correctly** *'Sheep?' It sounded so unlikely that Julia did not think she could have heard aright.*

● VERB + HEAR **can/could** *Can you hear me clearly at the back?* | **pretend not to** | **strain to**

2 be told about sth

● VERB + HEAR **be delighted to, be glad to, be gratified to, be pleased to** *I was delighted to hear about your promotion.* | **be sorry to** *I was sorry to hear of your father's death.* | **be interested to, be surprised to** *I was surprised to hear that she was married.* | **want to** *I told Michael what he wanted to hear.* | **let sb** *Let's hear you sing, then.* ◇ *You'd better not let Dad hear you say that.*

● PREP. **about** *I've heard about this sort of thing before.* **of** *On hearing of his plight, the council offered him a home.*

● PHRASES **hear little, a lot, nothing, etc. about sth** *We hear very little about these issues nowadays.*

hearing *noun*

1 ability to hear

● ADJ. **acute, excellent, good, normal, sharp** | **bad, impaired, poor**

● VERB + HEARING **have, possess** *Whales have acute hearing.* | **lose** *She lost her hearing when she was a child.* | **get back, regain** *Is there any chance that he'll get his hearing back?* | **affect, impair, make worse**

● HEARING + VERB **deteriorate, get worse, go** *His hearing began to deteriorate.* ◇ *Her hearing was already going.* | **come back, get better, improve** *Two months after the accident her hearing came back.*

● HEARING + NOUN **impairment, loss, problems** | **aid** *to have/wear a hearing aid* | **person** *a course in sign language for both deaf and hearing people*

● PHRASES **hard of hearing** *You'll have to speak more loudly. I'm afraid she's rather hard of hearing.*

2 trial in a court of law/similar investigation

● ADJ. **final, preliminary** | **fair** | **formal, full** | **open, public** | **private, secret** | **oral** | **appeal, custody, disciplinary, petition, pre-trial** | **committee, congressional, court, tribunal**

● VERB + HEARING **conduct, hold** *Most councils hold hearings in public.* | **ask for, call for, demand** *Protesters are calling for a public hearing.* | **get, have** *She said that she had had a very fair hearing from the disciplinary tribunal.* | **attend** | **adjourn** | **tell** *The hearing was told that the child had been left with a 14-year-old babysitter.*

● HEARING + VERB **take place** | **begin, open**

● PREP. **at a/the ~** *At a preliminary hearing the judge announced that the trial would begin on March 21.* **in a/the ~** *She was granted a divorce in a five-minute hearing.* **pending a/the ~** *Pending the hearing of the case by the court, the business will be allowed to continue trading.* **without a ~** *A High Court judge dismissed the case without a hearing.*

3 chance for an opinion to be considered

● ADJ. **fair, sympathetic**

● VERB + HEARING **give sb/sth** *At least give our ideas a fair hearing before you reject them.* | **get** *You haven't got much chance of your plan getting a sympathetic hearing.* | **deserve** *Their views deserve a hearing.*

● PREP. **~ for** *All I'm asking is a fair hearing for my ideas.*

hearsay *noun*

- VERB + HEARSAY **be based on, rely on** *Her judgements are based on hearsay rather than evidence.*
- HEARSAY + NOUN **evidence**
- PREP. **by** ~ *She discovered a world of parties and pleasure she had hitherto only known by hearsay.* **from** ~ *They started to piece the story together from hearsay.*

heart *noun*

1 part of the body
- ADJ. **healthy, strong | bad, weak | artificial | human**
- HEART + VERB **beat | pump sth** *The heart pumps blood through the body.* **| fail, stop | hammer, palpitate, pound, race, throb, thud, thump**
- HEART + NOUN **rate | complaint, condition, defect, disease, failure, murmur, problem, trouble | bypass, operation, surgery, transplant** *a triple heart bypass operation* ◇ *open-heart surgery*

2 feelings/emotions
- ADJ. **big, good, kind, soft, tender, warm | cold, hard | broken | heavy, sinking** *With a heavy heart, she watched him go.* **| light** *He set off with a light heart.*
- VERB + HEART **have** *She has a kind heart.* ◇ *Have you no heart?* **| break** *He broke her heart.* **| gladden | steal, win | harden | open, pour out** *Finally, he broke down tears and poured out his heart to her.*
- HEART + VERB **jump, leap, lurch, miss/skip a beat** *Her heart leapt with joy.* **| ache** *My heart aches when I think of their sorrow.* **| desire sth** *everything your heart could desire* **| sink | go out** *Our hearts go out to* (= we sympathize deeply with) *the families of the victims.*
- PREP. **at** ~ *At heart he is a republican.* **from the** ~ *I could tell he spoke from the heart.* **in your** ~ *In my heart, I knew it wasn't true.*
- PHRASES **an affair of the heart** (= a romance) *Her novels tend to deal with affairs of the heart* **a change of heart** (= a change of attitude) *He could have a change of heart and settle down to family life.* **from the bottom of your heart** *I beg you, from the bottom of my heart, to spare his life.* **heart and soul** *He committed himself heart and soul to the cause.* **have a heart of gold/stone** (= to be a kind/cruel person) (= no sympathetic feelings), **the hearts and minds of sb** *to win the hearts and minds of the nation's youth* **in good heart** (= cheerful and well), **put some/more heart into sth** *Let's sing it one more time from the beginning—and put some heart into it!* **sick at heart** (= very unhappy), **with all your heart** *I wish you well with all my heart.*

3 important/central part
- ADJ. **very**
- VERB + HEART **lie at** *The distinction between right and wrong lies at the heart of all questions of morality.* **| go to** *The committee's report went to the heart of the government's dilemma.*
- PREP. **at the** ~ *the issue at the heart of modern government* **| ~ of** *We live in the very heart of the city.*
- PHRASES **the heart of the matter/problem**

4 playing card
⇨ Note at CARD

heart attack *noun*

- ADJ. **fatal | massive, serious** *She died of a massive heart attack.* **| mild, minor | suspected**
- VERB + HEART ATTACK **have, suffer** *He suffered a fatal heart attack while cycling.* **| die from/of**
⇨ Special page at ILLNESS

heartbeat *noun*

- ADJ. **irregular, regular | racing** *She was suddenly aware of her racing heartbeat.*
- VERB + HEARTBEAT **monitor | feel**

- PHRASES **the sound/thud of a heartbeat** *I could feel the thud of my heartbeat.*

heartland *noun*

- ADJ. **agricultural, industrial** *the industrial heartland of Germany* **| Conservative, Labour, etc. | traditional**
- PREP. **in a/the** ~ *The party has lost seats in its traditional heartland of southern Thailand.*

heat *noun*

1 being hot/level of temperature
- ADJ. **burning, fierce, great, intense, searing, terrible, tremendous** *The soil is baked dry by the fierce heat of the sun.* **| gentle | excess, excessive** *If circulation is impaired, the body cannot lose excess heat.* **| red, white** (often figurative) *Everything he did was at white heat and lightning speed.* **| blood, body**
- VERB + HEAT **feel** *We could feel the tremendous heat coming from the fire.* **| disperse, dissipate, give out, lose** *Even after the sun had set, the stones continued to give out heat.* **| conserve, retain** *The thick walls retain the heat.* **| absorb** *Darker surfaces absorb heat.* **| conduct** *Being a metal, aluminium readily conducts heat.* **| generate, produce, provide, radiate** *Computers, faxes and photocopiers all generate heat of their own.* **| withstand** *a material which can withstand heats of up to 2 000°C*
- HEAT + VERB **build up, increase** *He tried to ignore the heat building up in the confined space.*
- HEAT + NOUN **loss | exhaustion, stress, stroke** (also **heatstroke**) *She slumped to the ground, near to heat exhaustion.*
- PREP. **~ from** *the heat from the fire*

2 hot weather/conditions
- ADJ. **baking, blazing, blinding, blistering, boiling, extreme, great, intense, oppressive, scorching, searing, shimmering, stifling, suffocating, sweltering** *We walked more than ten miles in the blistering heat.* **| dry | humid, steamy, sultry** *the steamy heat of New York in summer* **| 80-degree, 90-degree, etc. | afternoon, midday, morning | summer | desert, tropical**
- HEAT + VERB **grow** *Daily the heat grew.*
- HEAT + NOUN **haze** *A heat haze shimmered above the fields.*
- PREP. **in the** ~ *I can't work in this heat.*
- PHRASES **the heat of the day** *To avoid the heat of the day we went out in the mornings.*

3 source of heat
- ADJ. **high | gentle, low | medium, moderate | direct** *Chocolate should never be melted over direct heat.* **| dry**
- VERB + HEAT **turn up** *Towards the end of the cooking, turn up the heat to brown the outside.* **| lower, reduce, turn down | remove sth from, take sth off** *Bring to the boil slowly, then remove from the heat.* **| return sth to** *Return the pan to the heat and stir.*
- PREP. **off the** ~ *Make sure the pan is off the heat.* **on a** ~ *Cook on a low heat for five minutes.* **over a** ~ *Simmer the sauce over a gentle heat.*

4 strong feelings
- ADJ. **sudden** *He stared at her, sudden heat in his eyes.*
- HEAT + VERB **flare, flood sth, rise** *Heat flooded her cheeks.*
- PREP. **in the ~ of** *in the heat of battle/passion* **with** ~ *'It was your hare-brained idea,' Henry said with heat.* **without** ~ *She spoke without heat.*
- PHRASES **in the heat of the moment** *Michael bitterly regretted those angry words, spoken in the heat of the moment.*

5 race/competition
- ADJ. **qualifying, regional | dead** *Competition was fierce, with a dead heat in one of the races* (= with two competitors finishing in exactly the same time).

● VERB + HEAT **win** *She won her heat.*
● PREP. **in a/the~** *He fell in the first heat.*

heat *verb*

● ADV. **gently** *Heat the sauce gently for a few minutes.* |
through, up *Allow the food enough time to heat through.* ◇
They heat up the food in a microwave oven.

heated *adj.*

● VERBS **be**
● ADV. **adequately, properly, well** | **badly, inadequately** | **slightly** *a slightly heated aquarium* | **centrally** *modern, centrally heated homes* | **electrically**

heater *noun*

● ADJ. **convector, fan, immersion, instantaneous, multi-point, storage** | **electric, gas, oil, paraffin** | **aquarium, car, greenhouse, pool, room, water**
● VERB + HEATER **have** | **off/on** | **turn off/on** | **turn down/up**
● HEATER + VERB **be off/on** *Even with the heater full on, the room felt cold.*

heating *noun*

● ADJ. **electric, gas-fired, solar** | **central, domestic, home, underfloor** | **water**
● VERB + HEATING **have** *The flat has gas-fired central heating.* | **have on, keep on, leave on, run, use** *We haven't had the heating on this evening.* | **put on, switch on, turn on** *They are afraid to put the heating on because it's so expensive.* | **switch off, turn off** *They have their heating turned off during the morning.* | **turn down/up** | **fit, install, put in** *We're having central heating installed.*
● HEATING + VERB **be (full) on, be on high/low** *The heating was on but the window was open.* ◇ *The heating's on low.* | **be off** | **come on** | **go off** *Our heating goes off at eleven o'clock and comes on again at seven.* | **work** *The heating doesn't work.* | **break down** *The house was very cold because the heating had broken down.*
● HEATING + NOUN **bill** | **system** *What sort of heating system has your new flat got?*

heave *noun*

● ADJ. **great, mighty**
● VERB + HEAVE **give (sth)** *She gave a great heave and the box inched forward.*

heaven *noun*

1 believed to be the home of God
● VERB + HEAVEN **ascend to, go to** *I feel like I've died and gone to heaven.*
● PREP. **from~** *Our child seemed a gift from heaven.* **in~** *(figurative) It was a marriage made in heaven.*
● PHRASES **the kingdom of heaven**

2 place/situation in which you are very happy
● ADJ. **absolute, sheer** *It was sheer heaven being alone at last.*
● PREP. **in~** *The kids were in absolute heaven at the fair.*
● PHRASES **a heaven on earth** *The island is truly a heaven on earth.* **sb's idea of heaven** *Building up a tan by the pool with a good book is my idea of heaven.*

heavy *adj.*

1 weighing a lot
● VERBS **be, feel, look, seem** *My suitcase was beginning to feel very heavy.* | **become, get** *You're getting too heavy to carry!* | **make sth** *The bottles of wine made the bag even heavier.* | **find sth** *I didn't find it too heavy to carry.*
● ADV. **extremely, really, very** | **fairly, pretty, quite, rather** *Be careful. That box is rather heavy.*

2 worse than usual
● VERBS **be** | **become, get** *The rain was getting quite heavy.*
● ADV. **extremely, really, very** *The traffic's really heavy on the bypass.* | **fairly, pretty, quite**

Hebrew *noun*

● ADJ. **ancient, biblical** | **medieval** | **modern**
● HEBREW + NOUN **alphabet, script** | **scripture**
⇨ Note at LANGUAGE

hedge *noun*

● ADJ. **high, low, tall, thick** | **boundary, garden, roadside** *Establish which boundary hedges are yours, and which belong to a neighbour.* | **beech, box, hawthorn, privet, yew, etc.** *a thick hawthorn hedge*
● VERB + HEDGE **plant** | **clip, trim** *Trim the hedge and collect the trimmings.*
● HEDGE + NOUN **clippings, trimmings** | **trimmer**

heel *noun*

1 back part of the foot
● VERB + HEEL **lean back on, sit back on, squat on** *She took a potato from the fire and sat back on her heels.* | **rock (back) on** *The punch rocked him back on his heels.* ◇ *He rocked back and forth on his heels as he laughed.* | **pivot on, spin on, turn on** *He turned on his heel and marched away angrily.* | **click (together)** *The officer clicked his heels together and saluted.* | **catch** *She caught her heel and tripped.* | **injure**
● HEEL + VERB **click**
● HEEL + NOUN **injury**
● PREP. **at your~s** *She came up the path with two little dogs at her heels.* **under the~** *(figurative) For years the nation had been under the heel of a dictatorial regime.*
● PHRASES **(close/hard/hot) on your heels** *(figurative) They reached the border with the police hot on their heels.*

2 part of a shoe/sock
● ADJ. **flat, low** | **high, spike, stiletto** | **three-inch, etc.**
● HEEL + NOUN **bar** *I took my shoes to a heel bar to have them repaired.*

height *noun*

1 how tall sb/sth is
● ADJ. **full, maximum** *He drew himself up to his full height and glared at us.* | **considerable, great, towering** *Her great height was rather a handicap.* | **average, medium, middle** *a man of middle height*
● VERB + HEIGHT **measure** | **grow to, reach** *The plants grow to a maximum height of 24 inches.*
● PREP. **in~** *The wall is 2.5 metres in height.*

2 distance above the ground/sea level
● ADJ. **considerable, great** *The object had clearly fallen from a considerable height.* | **ceiling, chest, head, shoulder, waist, etc.** *Bring your hands to shoulder height.*
● VERB + HEIGHT **gain** | **lose** *The plane was beginning to lose height.* | **maintain** *The pilot was unable to maintain height.* | **attain, climb to, reach, rise to** *The balloon reached a height of 20 000 feet.*
● PREP. **at a~ of** *The animal lives in lakes near Mexico City, at a height of 6 000 to 7 000 feet above sea level.*

3 (usually **heights**) high place
● ADJ. **mountain, rocky** *The condor soars above the mountain heights.*
● VERB + HEIGHT **scale** *They were the first expedition to scale the heights of Everest.* | **have no head for** | **have a head for** *A steeplejack has to have a good head for heights.* | **be afraid of, have no head for**
● PREP. **from a~** *The pattern of the ancient fields is clearly visible from a height.*
● PHRASES **a fear of heights**

4 heights high level of achievement
- ADJ. **commanding, dizzy, giddy, lofty** *They have risen to the dizzy heights of the semi-finals.* | **new** *The group's popularity reached new heights when they got a top ten hit.*
- VERB + HEIGHTS **reach, rise to, scale** *She rose to undreamed-of heights of power and fame.*

heighten *verb*
- ADV. **greatly** *This latest attack has greatly heightened fears of an all-out war.* | **further**
- VERB + HEIGHTEN **serve to** *Seeing others enjoying themselves only served to heighten his sense of loneliness.* | **seek to** *an exercise which seeks to heighten people's awareness of the problems*

heir *noun*
- ADJ. **lawful, legal, legitimate, rightful** *the rightful heir to the throne* | **natural, real, true** *The socialists saw themselves as true heirs of the Enlightenment.* | **direct** *When the Earl of Surrey died in 1347 he left no direct heir.* | **immediate** | **designated** | **apparent, presumptive** (both only after **heir**) *On his brother's death he became heir apparent to the title.* | **sole** | **female, male** | **political, spiritual** *The house was her spiritual home for which she sought a spiritual heir.*
- VERB + HEIR **have** *He has no heir to leave his fortune to.* | **beget, get, produce** *He planned to marry and produce an heir for his estate.* | **became, fall** *At the age of twenty he fell heir to a large estate.*
- PREP. **~ to** *He is the sole heir to a large mining fortune.*
- PHRASES **the heir to the throne, sb's son and heir** *He left most of his property to his eldest son and heir.*

heirloom *noun*
- ADJ. **family** | **ancient**
- HEIRLOOM + VERB **be passed down, come down** *The brooch is a family heirloom which came down to her from her great-grandmother.*

helicopter *noun*
- ADJ. **air force, military, police** | **civilian, private** | **rescue** | **model**
- VERB + HELICOPTER **fly** *He flew helicopters during the Gulf War.*
- HELICOPTER + VERB **fly** | **hover** *The helicopter hovered above the air strip.* | **take off** | **land** | **crash** | **carry sb** *a helicopter carrying troops*
- HELICOPTER + NOUN **flight** | **pad** | **pilot** | **gunship**
- PREP. **by ~** *The victims were flown to hospital by helicopter.* **in a/the ~** *There were three people in the helicopter when it crashed.*

hell *noun*
1 place bad people are said to go to when they die
- VERB + HELL **go to** *He was terrified of going to hell when he died.*
- HELL + NOUN **fire**
- PREP. **in~** *tormented souls in hell*
- PHRASES **the fires/flames of hell** *Lava poured out of the volcano, glowing like the fires of hell.*

2 very unpleasant place/situation
- ADJ. **absolute, pure, sheer** *It was sheer hell having to sit through hours of boring lectures!* | **living** *The last few weeks have been a living hell for the refugees.*
- VERB + HELL **go through** *She's been going through hell with that bad tooth.* | **give sb, make sb's life** *Her boss is making her life hell.*
- PREP. **in~** *'We're living in hell,' said one of the refugees.*
- PHRASES **the ... from hell** *It really was the holiday from hell—it rained all the time, we all got colds, and we*

missed the plane home. **hell on earth** *For someone who doesn't like heat, Florida would be hell on earth.*

helmet *noun*
- ADJ. **visored** | **crash, cycle, flying, motorcycle, safety** | **fireman's, policeman's,** etc.
- VERB + HELMET **have on, wear** | **put on** | **remove, take off**

help *noun*
- ADJ. **big, enormous, great, invaluable, real, substantial, tremendous, valuable** *You've been a big help—thanks.* ◇ *It's a great help having you around.* ◇ *This is the first scheme to offer real help to working mothers.* | **generous** | **direct** *The careers officer gives direct help as well as advice.* | **mutual, self-** *The system is based on mutual help rather than on payment for services.* ◇ *a best-selling author of self-help books* | **voluntary** *The homeless centre relies entirely on voluntary help.* | **immediate** | **individual** *Teachers have little time to give individual help to students.* | **expert, skilled, technical** | **outside** *They can usually manage by themselves, but occasionally need outside help.* | **financial, legal, medical, practical, professional** *When the symptoms persisted, I decided to seek medical help.*
- VERB + HELP **appeal for, ask for, beg for, call for, scream for, seek, send for, shout for, summon** *Police are appealing for help in catching the killers.* ◇ *I opened the window and called for help.* | **bring, enlist, fetch, find, get** *He enlisted the help of a private detective in his search for the truth.* ◇ *He ran to get help.* | **need, want** *Do you need any help unloading the car?* | **get, receive** | **accept** *He's too proud to accept help.* | **come to, give sb, offer (sb), provide (sb with)** *Passers-by came to the woman's help when she was mugged.*
- HELP + VERB **arrive, come** *He lay injured for four hours before help arrived.* | **be at hand** (*informal*) *Don't panic—help is at hand.*
- HELP + NOUN **desk, line** (also **helpline**) *For further information, phone our helpline.*
- PREP. **beyond ~** *Some of the injured animals were beyond help and had to be destroyed.* **of ~** *The manual is too technical to be of help to the inexperienced user.* **with ~** *With a little help, I think I could fix the computer myself.* ◇ *We broke open the lock with the help of a spanner.* | **~ for** *The training centre provides special help for the long-term unemployed.* **~ from** *With help from a parent, a child can do simple cooking.* **~ in** *Local teachers provided invaluable help in developing the material.* **~ to** *She's been a big help to her father.* **~ with** *He'll need help with this homework.*
- PHRASES **an appeal/a plea/a request for help** *The family's request for help went unanswered.* **a cry for help** *I heard a cry for help from inside the building.* **in need of help** *The man was clearly in need of urgent medical help.* **an offer of help** *He rudely rejected her kind offer of help.*

help *verb*
1 do sth for sb
- ADV. **a lot** *My mother helps me a lot.* | **a bit** | **solicitously** *He solicitously helped her back into the chair.* | **out**
- VERB + HELP **be able/unable to, can/could** *Can you help me with my homework?* | **try to** *I was only trying to help out.*
- PREP. **across** *I helped her across the road.* **into, out of** *She helped the old man out of the car.* **with** *We all help with the housework.*
- PHRASES **help sb to their feet** *Mike helped the old lady to her feet.* **a way of helping** *the best way of helping your child*

2 make sth easier/better
- ADV. **enormously, greatly, immeasurably, a lot, really, tremendously** *Talking to a counsellor helped her enor-*

mously. ◇ *The whole process was greatly helped by the widespread availability of computers.* | **a bit, a little** | **certainly** *It certainly helped that her father is a duke!*
• VERB + HELP **be designed to** *The minimum wage is designed to help people in low-pay service industries.*
• PREP. **in** *Iron helps in the formation of red blood cells.*

helper *noun*

• ADJ. **voluntary, volunteer** | **willing**
• QUANT. **band** *He recruited a band of willing helpers.*

helpful *adj.*

• VERBS **be, prove** | **consider sth, find sb/sth**
• ADV. **enormously, especially, extremely, immensely, most, particularly, really, unusually, very** *Thank you, you have been most helpful.* | **not at all, not particularly** *Demanding peace short of victory would not be at all helpful.* | **fairly, quite** | **immediately** *indulging in ambitious, but not immediately helpful plans* | **generally, usually** | **always, invariably**
• PREP. **for** *This information would be extremely helpful for teenagers.* **in** *Graphs are helpful in presenting the information.* **on** *He was quite helpful on how to do the accounts.* **to** *The lifts will be helpful to the older patients.*
• PHRASES **friendly and helpful** *I found all the staff friendly and helpful.*

helping *noun*

• ADJ. **big, generous, huge, large** *a generous helping of potatoes* | **small** | **extra, second**
• VERB + HELPING **eat, have**
• PREP. **~of** *I had an extra helping of meat.*

helpless *adj.*

• VERBS **be, feel, lie, look, seem, stand, watch** *John felt completely helpless.* ◇ *He lay helpless in the hospital ward.* | **become** | **leave sb, render sb** *He was left helpless and alone.* ◇ *She was rendered helpless by panic.*
• ADV. **absolutely, completely, quite, totally, utterly** | **apparently, seemingly** | **physically**
• PREP. **against** *She was helpless against his strength.* **before** *Kirk stood helpless before this giant of a man.* **in the face of** *feeling helpless in the face of all these rules and regulations* **with** *She was helpless with anger.*

helplessness *noun*

• ADJ. **utter**
• PHRASES **a feeling/sense of helplessness** *A feeling of utter helplessness washed over him.*

hen *noun*

• ADJ. **speckled** | **battery, free-range** | **mother** *She fussed around like mother hen.* | **broody**
• VERB + HEN **keep**
• HEN + VERB **lay (eggs)** *The hen layed three beautiful speckled eggs.* | **cackle, cluck, squawk** *I could hear the hens clucking in the farmyard.* | **roost** | **peck, scratch** *The hens pecked hopefully at the dusty floor.*
• HEN + NOUN **coop, house, roost**

hepatitis *noun*

• ADJ. **severe** | **acute, chronic** | **active** | **viral**
• VERB + HEPATITIS **have, suffer from** | **be infected with, contract, get**
• HEPATITIS + NOUN **virus** | **patient**
• PHRASES **hepatitis A/B/C**
⇨ Special page at ILLNESS

herb *noun*

• ADJ. **dried, fresh** | **mixed** *Add a teaspoonful of mixed herbs.* | **aromatic, fragrant** | **culinary, medicinal**
• QUANT. **bunch**
• VERB + HERB **garnish sth with** *Serve cold, garnished with fresh herbs.*
• HERB + NOUN **bed, border, garden**
⇨ Special page at FOOD

herd *noun*

1 group of animals
• ADJ. **great, large** | **small** | **beef, breeding, dairy** *The farm has only a small dairy herd.* | **cattle, elephant, etc.**
• HERD + NOUN **instinct**
• PREP. **in a/the~** *The animals tend to graze in a herd.* | **~of** *a large herd of cows*
• PHRASES **a member of a herd**

2 group of people
• ADJ. **common**
• VERB + HERD **follow** *If you feel so strongly, why follow the herd* (= do the same as everybody else)? | **stand out from** *She prided herself on standing out from the common herd* (= being different from ordinary people).
• HERD + NOUN **instinct**

heritage *noun*

• ADJ. **rich** | **natural** | **common, national** *Folk songs are part of our common heritage.* | **architectural, artistic, cultural, historical, literary**
• VERB + HERITAGE **have** *The city has an exceptionally rich heritage of historic buildings.* | **preserve, protect** *protecting our heritage of wild plants*
• HERITAGE + NOUN **centre, museum, site**

hernia *noun*

• VERB + HERNIA **have, suffer from** | **remove, repair**
• HERNIA + NOUN **operation, repair**
⇨ Special page at ILLNESS

hero *noun*

• ADJ. **big, great** *He was one of the great football heroes of his day.* | **real** | **all-time** *Einstein is the all-time hero of many scientists.* | **unsung** *She was an unsung hero of the British film industry.* | **reluctant, unlikely** | **brave, gallant** *The song remembers the brave heroes who died for their country.* | **romantic, tragic** *Being short and overweight, he was an unlikely romantic hero.* | **square-jawed, swashbuckling** *Tired of playing the square-jawed hero, he sought out more challenging roles.* | **all-conquering, conquering** *In his war stories he portrayed himself as the all-conquering hero.* ◇ *He returned home from the tournament a conquering hero.* | **fallen** *a fallen hero trying to regain his position* | **cult** *James Dean was a cult hero of the fifties.* | **folk, local, national, popular** | **fictional, legendary, mythical** | **eponymous** *Don Quixote, the eponymous hero of the novel by Cervantes* | **boyhood, childhood** *Bugs Bunny was one of my childhood heroes.* | **proletarian, working-class** | **military** | **celluloid** | **musical** *In this album she pays tribute to her musical heroes.* | **film, football, guitar, sporting, war** *Jimi Hendrix was her guitar hero.*
• VERB + HERO **be hailed (as)** *He was hailed as a hero after the rescue.* | **become, make sb into, turn sb into** *The fight to save the forest turned him into a local hero.* | **die** *He died a national hero.*
• PREP. **~to** *He was a hero to all his schoolmates.*
• PHRASES **be no hero** *John was no hero—he stood back as his friends approached the two armed border guards.* **give sb/receive a hero's welcome, hero of the hour** *Everyone played brilliantly, but Jones was the hero of the hour.* **(die) a hero's death**

heroic *adj.*

- VERBS **be**
- ADV. **truly** *a truly heroic battle* | **suitably** *He struck a suitably heroic pose.*

heroin *noun*

- ADJ. **pure** | **street**
- QUANT. **dose, gram, ounce, shot, wrap**
- VERB + HEROIN **fix, inject, smoke**
- HEROIN + NOUN **injector** | **possession** | **injection** | **overdose** *a fatal heroin overdose* | **dealing**
⇒ Note at DRUG (for more verbs and nouns)

heroine *noun*

- ADJ. **great** *Violetta is one of the great tragic heroines of Verdi's operas.* | **national** | **romantic, tragic** | **unsung** *She remains one of the unsung heroines of the Second World War.* | **childhood** *She was thrilled to be interviewing her childhood heroine.* | **eponymous** *Jane Eyre, the eponymous heroine of the novel by Charlotte Brontë* | **sporting**

heroism *noun*

- ADJ. **great, real, true**
- PHRASES **an act of heroism**

herring *noun*

- ADJ. **fresh** | **pickled, salted, smoked, soused**
- VERB + HERRING **catch** | **eat, have**
- HERRING + NOUN **fillet**
⇒ Special page at FOOD

hesitate *verb*

- ADV. **briefly, a little, (for) a minute/moment/second, momentarily** *Alison hesitated a moment, as if she were waiting for him.*
- VERB + HESITATE **appear to, seem to** | **make sb** *Something about his smile made her hesitate.*
- PREP. **about** *I didn't hesitate about working with Craig.* **between** *He was hesitating between a glass of wine and an orange juice.* **over** *He stood hesitating over whether to join the fight.*

hesitation *noun*

- ADJ. **brief, fractional, momentary, slight** *There was a momentary hesitation before he replied.* | **initial** *After some initial hesitation, teachers seem to have accepted the new system.*
- PREP. **after ... ~** *After much hesitation, they decided to leave.* **without ~** *She answered immediately, without any hesitation.*
- PHRASES **have no hesitation in doing sth** *I have no hesitation in recommending him for the job.* **a moment's hesitation, a moment of hesitation** *After a moment's hesitation, he nodded.*

hibernation *noun*

- ADJ. **long** | **winter**
- VERB + HIBERNATION **go into** *At the first cold of autumn, many insects go into hibernation.* | **emerge from**
- PREP. **in ~** *The tortoise spends the winter months in hibernation.*

hiccup *noun*

1 sound made in the throat
- ADJ. **small** | **loud**
- VERB + HICCUP **give, let out** *She gave a loud hiccup.*

2 (the) hiccups series of hiccups

- QUANT. **attack** *He suddenly had an attack of the hiccups.*
- VERB + HICCUPS **get, suffer from** *I ate too quickly and got hiccups.*

3 small problem
- ADJ. **little, slight** | **occasional** | **temporary**
- PREP. **~ in** *This one defeat was the only hiccup in the team's steady progress up the League.*

hide *noun*

- ADJ. **thick, tough** *Elephants have a very tough hide.* | **buffalo, elephant, elk, ox, rhino**
- VERB + HIDE **tan** *The hide is tanned for leather.*

hide *verb*

1 go/put sth where you/it cannot be seen
- ADV. **away** *She hid the documents away in a drawer.*
- VERB + HIDE **prefer to, want to** *She wanted to run away and hide.* ◇ (figurative) *He accused the prime minister of preferring to hide from the truth.*
- PREP. **among** *hiding among the bushes* **behind** (figurative) *He hid behind a false identity.* **beneath** *He had a weak mouth which he hid beneath a moustache and beard.* **from** *hiding from their enemies* **in** *hiding in the shadows* **under** *He hid the book under his bed.*
- PHRASES **carefully/completely/well hidden** *The letters were well hidden in the back of the cupboard.* **half hidden** *The buildings were half hidden by the trees.* **hidden deep beneath/in sth** *tiny villages hidden deep in the softly rolling hills* **hidden from sight/view** *The house was hidden from view by a large hedge.* **lie/remain hidden** *treasures which have lain hidden in bank vaults since the war* **partially/partly hidden** *The house was partially hidden behind some trees.* **a place to hide (sth)** *I'll find a better place to hide it.*

2 keep sth secret
- ADV. **well** | **completely**
- VERB + HIDE **be able/unable to** *She was unable to hide her delight at his failure.* | **try to** | **make no attempt to** *He made no attempt to hide his anger* | **manage to**
- PREP. **from** *The government tried to hide the evidence from the public.*
- PHRASES **keep sth hidden** *feelings that she had kept completely hidden all these years* **remain/stay hidden** *The truth may well remain hidden for ever.*

hiding *noun*

- VERB + HIDING **go into** *He had gone into hiding just after war broke out.* | **come out of** *After the car had passed by they came out of hiding.*
- PREP. **in ~** *The fugitive had spent five weeks in hiding.*

hierarchical *adj.*

- VERBS **be** *The company's structure is rigidly hierarchical.* | **become**
- ADV. **extremely, rigidly, strictly, strongly, very** | **fairly** | **essentially**

hierarchy *noun*

- ADJ. **complex** | **rigid, strict** *the rigid class hierarchy of rural society* | **administrative, bureaucratic, corporate, management, managerial, organizational** | **class, social** | **church, ecclesiastical** | **party, political** *high up in the party hierarchy* | **military**
- VERB + HIERARCHY **create, establish** *A new management hierarchy was created within the company.* | **move up, rise in/through** *He joined the party in 1966 and quickly moved up the hierarchy.*
- PREP. **in a/the ~** *She is above me in the hierarchy.* **within a/the ~** *There was a range of opinion within the ecclesias-*

tical hierarchy on the issue. | ~ **of** There was a clear hierarchy of power in the company.
- PHRASES **sb's level/position/status in a hierarchy**

high noun

1 high level or point
- ADJ. **all-time, new, record**
- VERB + HIGH **hit, reach** Share prices reached an all-time high yesterday.

2 feeling of great pleasure or happiness
- ADJ. **real, tremendous | emotional**
- VERB + HIGH **experience, get** the high she got from cocaine | **give sb** The drug gives you a tremendous high.
- PREP. **on a ~** She's been on a real high since she got her exam results. ◇ This show is our swansong—we want to finish on a high.
- PHRASES **the highs and lows** the emotional highs and lows of an actor's life

highlight noun

- ADJ. **real, undoubted** The real highlight of the trip for me was the visit to the Tower of London. | **personal | edited, recorded ~s** (used to talk about sports broadcasts) Recorded highlights of the match will be shown later tonight.
- PHRASES **the highlight of the day, week, year, etc.** The highlight of the week was Saturday's firework display.

highlight verb

- ADV. **clearly** These figures clearly highlight the difference in world living standards. | **dramatically, graphically** The needs of these children were dramatically highlighted by the Child Poverty Action Group. | **merely, only, simply** The peace talks merely highlighted the great gulf in understanding between the two sides.
- VERB + HIGHLIGHT **serve to** The incident has sadly only served to highlight the differences within the party.

highway noun

- ADJ. **broad | three-lane, two-lane, etc.** a four-lane highway | **public** (formal) He was fined for obstructing the public highway. | **main, major, national | trans-Amazon, trans-European, etc. | coastal, desert | east-west, north-south**
- VERB + HIGHWAY **pull off** We pulled off the highway and stopped for a break. | **obstruct**
- PREP. **along the ~** They tore along the highway. **down the ~, off the ~, on the ~, onto the ~, up the ~ | ~ to** the highway to Sydney

hike noun

- ADJ. **long | strenuous | ten-mile, two-day, etc.**
- VERB + HIKE **go on** The boys have gone on a long hike with the Boy Scouts.
- PREP. **on a ~** They met on a hike. | **~ from, ~ to** It's a hell of a hike from Sydney to Perth.

hill noun

- ADJ. **big, high, long** The bus sped down the long hill. | **little, low, small** The village is set on a small hill. | **steep | gentle | rolling, undulating ~s** The landscape is made up of low, rolling hills. | **conical, rounded | blue, dark, green, purple | bare, forested, grassy, open, rocky, rugged, wooded | distant, far** the distant blue hills | **isolated, lonely | encircling, surrounding ~s** Troops forced villagers to flee to the surrounding hills. | **prominent | coastal | chalk** the chalk hills of southern England
- VERB + HILL **climb (up), go up** They climbed a steep hill and came to the village. | **come down | take to ~s**

(literary) We took to the hills in a variety of four-wheel-drive vehicles.
- HILL + VERB **overlook sth, rise** a hill overlooking the wide valley below ◇ Wooded hills rise behind the town.
- HILL + NOUN **climbing, walking | walker | farming | farmer | farm, fort, station** (= a small town in the hills, especially in India), **town, village** In the heat of summer the rich fled to the hill stations. | **country | top** (= also **hilltop**) | **start** (= starting a vehicle on a slope)
- PREP. **down a/the ~** A grassy path led down the hill. **in the ~s** There are several lead mines in the hills above Grassington. **on a/the ~** The church is perched on a hill. **over a/the ~** Over the hill lies another village. **up a/the ~** A few yards up the hill, on the left, was a turning. | **~ above** the hills above the town
- PHRASES **the bottom/foot of a/the hill** A spring emerges at the bottom of the hill. **the top of a/the hill**

hillside noun

- ADJ. **steep | bare, exposed, open, rocky | grassy, green, wooded** On our left was a wooded hillside. | **terraced** I was back in wine country, with terraced hillsides on both sides of the road. | **distant**
- VERB + HILLSIDE **be set on** Many of the chalets are set on a hillside reached by steps.
- PREP. **down a/the ~** A stream tumbles down the steep hillside. **on a/the ~** The house was on a hillside outside the town. **up a/the ~** We clambered up the hillside to the ridge above. | **~ above** the hillside above the village

hinder verb

- ADV. **greatly, seriously** These killings have seriously hindered progress towards peace.
- VERB + HINDER **be likely to, tend to** Bulky clothes tend to hinder movement.
- PHRASES **help or hinder sth** factors which might help or hinder a child's progress at school

hindrance noun

- ADJ. **great**
- VERB + HINDRANCE **be, prove** Having a car in the city might prove a hindrance.
- PREP. **without ~** (formal) The cook needs room to get at the cooker, sink and cupboards without hindrance. | **~ to** The new regulations are actually a great hindrance to teachers.
- PHRASES **without let or hindrance** (law)

hindsight noun

- PREP. **in ~** Their first scheme was deemed, in hindsight, a mistake. **with ~** This all seems obvious with hindsight.
- PHRASES **(with) the advantage/benefit/wisdom of hindsight** It is easy to criticize others when you have the benefit of hindsight.

Hinduism noun

⇨ Note at RELIGION

hint noun

1 suggestion
- ADJ. **broad, clear, heavy, strong** He gave a broad hint that he was on the verge of leaving. | **gentle, subtle, veiled | tantalizing**
- VERB + HINT **drop, give (sb)** I dropped a few subtle hints about the payment being due. | **get, take** OK, I get the hint! ◇ Can't you take a hint and leave me alone?
- PREP. **~ about, ~ from** a hint from my boss about my absences from the office **~ to** Is that a hint to me to leave?

2 small amount of sth

● ADJ. **strong** *a dish with a strong hint of garlic* | **faint, merest, slightest** *The slightest hint of gossip upset her.*
● PREP. **~of** *There was a hint of amusement in his voice.*
● PHRASES **at the first hint of sth** *At the first hint of trouble, I will call the police.*

3 piece of advice
● ADJ. **handy, helpful, practical, useful**
● VERB + HINT **give (sb)**
● PREP. **~about** *The book gives some useful hints about how to plan your garden.* **~on** *a book full of handy hints on painting and decorating*

hint *verb*

● ADV. **strongly** *He hinted strongly that he would be resigning soon.* | **discreetly** | **darkly** *She hinted darkly that all was not well.* | **only**
● PREP. **at** *The problems are only hinted at in the report.*

hip *noun*

● ADJ. **lean, narrow** *Her hips were still narrow like a girl's.* | **sturdy, wide** | **broken, dislocated, fractured** | **arthritic** | **artificial**
● VERB + HIP **have/put your hands on** *He put his hands on his hips and sighed.* | **roll, sway, swing, wiggle** *She wiggled her hips seductively as she walked.* | **rotate, turn, twist** *Twist your hips towards your opponent as you punch.* | **thrust** | **break, dislocate, fracture**
● HIP + VERB **spread** *Her hips had spread since having a baby.*
● HIP + NOUN **fracture, injury** | **deformity** | **operation, replacement** *My grandmother's having a hip replacement.* | **bone, joint, socket** | **flask** *He took a swig of whisky from his hip flask.* | **pocket** *Don't carry money or documents in your hip pocket.*
● PREP. **across the ~s** *She was wearing a short blue dress, belted across the hips.* **at the ~** *He had his leg amputated at the hip.* **from the ~** *The gun could be fired from the shoulder or from the hip.* **on the ~** *She was carrying a baby on her hip.* **to the ~** *The skirt is slit to the hip on one side.*
● PHRASES **hands on hips** *He leaned casually against the door frame, hands on hips.*

hire *noun*

● ADJ. **bicycle, car, equipment, etc.**
● HIRE + NOUN **car** *Our hire car broke down after only an hour.* | **charge, cost** | **company, firm, shop**
● PREP. **for ~** *There are boats for hire on the lake.* **on ~ (from/to)** *The equipment is on hire from a local company.* | **~of** *The main expense was the hire of a car.*

hire *verb*

● ADV. **promptly** *The entire workforce was laid off and a fresh one promptly hired.* | **by the day, week, etc.** *What's the cost of hiring by the day?* | **locally** *Ski equipment can be hired locally.*
● PREP. **from** *Bicycles can be hired from several local shops.*

hiss *noun*

● ADJ. **sharp** | **faint, soft, low** *There was a low hiss on the tape.* | **audible**
● VERB + HISS **give, let out** *The snake gave a hiss.* | **hear**
● PREP. **with a~** *She drew in her breath with a hiss.* | **~of** *We could hear the faint hiss of escaping gas.*
● PHRASES **boos and hisses, a hiss of air, the hiss of a snake**
⇨ Note at SOUND

hiss *verb*

1 make a sound like a long 's'
● ADV. **gently** *The gas lamp hissed gently.*
2 say sth in an angry, hissing voice
● ADV. **angrily, furiously** *'Don't be stupid!' she hissed furiously.* | **quietly**
● PREP. **at** *She hissed at me to be quiet.*
● PHRASES **hiss (sth) through your teeth** *'Go away!' he hissed through clenched teeth.*

historian *noun*

● ADJ. **distinguished, eminent, great, leading, respected** *a talk given by an eminent social historian* | **serious** *No serious historian today accepts this theory.* | **academic, professional** | **amateur** | **official** *the official historian of the Labour Party* | **contemporary, early, future** *The oldest tradition goes back to the contemporary historian John Foxe.* ◊ *What will future historians make of the late twentieth century?* | **ancient, medieval, modern** *She is a writer as well as a distinguished modern historian.* | **local** | **family** | **art, church, cultural, economic, human, literary, military, political, social, etc.** | **revisionist** *Revisionist historians have questioned the accepted version of events.*

history *noun*

1 the past, especially as a subject of study
● ADJ. **contemporary, early, recent** *the early history of the trade union movement* ◊ *things that happened in recent history* | **ancient, medieval, modern** | **local** | **family** | **British, world, etc.** | **official** *the official history of the Labour Party* | **recorded** *The debate about the origins of the universe has been going on throughout recorded history.* | **oral** *Oral history enables us to take account of those many aspects of history that are not recorded in documents.* | **art, church, cultural, economic, human, literary, military, political, social, etc.**
● QUANT. **piece** *She created a piece of history by winning her fourth title.*
● VERB + HISTORY **be steeped in** *a building that is steeped in history* | **go down in, make, pass into** *He will go down in history as a wise adviser and a kind man.* ◊ *He made history by being the first man to walk on the moon.* | **trace** *The regiment traces its history back to 1803.* | **distort, rewrite** *her attempt to rewrite history with herself in the role of heroine*
● HISTORY + VERB **go back (to)** … *The town's history goes back to Roman times.* | **reveal sth, show sth** *History shows that New Zealand are almost unbeatable by British teams on their own turf.* | **repeat itself** *Years later, family history repeated itself with Eve's daughters.*
● HISTORY + NOUN **book** *(figurative) She has earned her place in the history books.*
● PREP. **during sth's ~** *The country has suffered several invasions during its history.* **in (sth's) ~** *the most extraordinary royal meeting in history* ◊ *the best player in the sport's history* **throughout ~** *There have been conflicts such as this throughout history.*
● PHRASES **change the course of history** *events that could change the course of history* **a period of history** *This is a fascinating period of history.* **the rest is history** (= the rest of the story does not need to be told because it is well-known) **a sense of history** *a people with no sense of history* **a slice of history** *The team grabbed a slice of history here today* (= achieved sth that will be remembered).
⇨ Note at SUBJECT (for more verbs and nouns)

2 facts about sb/sth's life/existence in the past
● ADJ. **chequered, colourful, fascinating, interesting, rich** *The city has a rich and colourful history.* | **long** *She has a long history of mental illness.* | **previous, subsequent** | **case** *She familiarized herself with the case history of her new patient.* | **employment, family, life, med-**

ical, personal, sexual *The doctor will need some details of your medical history.* ◊ *I know nothing about his personal history.*
- VERB + HISTORY **have**
- PREP. **~of** *a history of heart disease in the family*

3 sth in the past that is no longer important
- ADJ. **past** *They had an affair once, but that's past history now.*

hit *noun*

1 act of hitting sth/sb
- ADJ. **direct**
- VERB + HIT **give sth, make, score** *Give it a good hit* ◊ *At last he managed to score a hit.* | **receive, suffer, take** *One of the tanks took a direct hit.*
- HIT + NOUN **list** *She was at the top of the terrorists' hit list* (= the list of people they intended to kill) *for over two years.* ◊ *Which services are on the government's hit list?* | **man, squad** *He claimed that a hit man had been paid £20 000 to kill him.*

2 sb/sth that is very popular
- ADJ. **big, greatest, huge, massive, real, smash** *The show has been a smash hit.* | **immediate, instant** | **box-office, chart** *The band are here to promote their latest chart hit.*
- HIT + NOUN **album, film, movie, record, show, single, song** | **parade** (*old-fashioned*) *The single was number one in the British hit parade*
- PREP. **~with** *The series has been a big hit with children.*

hit *verb*

1 touch sb/sth with a lot of force
- ADV. **hard** *She didn't hit me very hard.* | **almost, nearly** *A taxi almost hit him as he was crossing the street.* | **accidentally** *I accidentally hit my knee on the desk.*
- VERB + HIT **want to** *I was so angry, I wanted to hit him.* | **be going to** *I was afraid he was going to hit me.*
- PREP. **in** *She hit him in the face.* **on** *I hit my head on the low doorway.* **with** *He hit her with a stick.*
- PHRASES **hit sb over the head** *He was hit over the head with a broken bottle.*

2 have a bad effect on sb/sth
- ADV. **badly, hard, heavily, severely** *Our department has been badly hit by the cutbacks.* ◊ *Some businesses have been hit very hard by the rise in interest rates.*

PHRASAL VERB
hit out
- ADV. **hard** | **wildly** *I just hit out wildly in all directions.*
- PREP. **at** *In a rousing speech the minister hit out at racism in the armed forces.*

hitch *noun*

- ADJ. **slight** | **last-minute** *There are always a few last-minute hitches at the dress rehearsal.* | **legal, technical** *There was a slight technical hitch which delayed the plane's take-off.*
- PREP. **without a~** *Everything went without a hitch.* | **~in** *There's been a hitch in the plans.*

HIV *noun*

- VERB + HIV **be at risk from** | **contract, get** | **have, suffer from** *people suffering from HIV and Aids* | **be affected by, be infected by** | **spread, transmit** | **be/test negative for, be/test positive for** | **test sb/sth for, screen sth for** *screening blood for HIV* | **treat**
- HIV + NOUN **infection** | **antibody,   virus** | **carrier, sufferer** | **status** *If you are unsure of your HIV status, consider having a test.* | **test**
- PHRASES **HIV negative/positive**
⇨ Special page at ILLNESS

hoard *noun*

- ADJ. **big, large, major, vast** *one of the biggest hoards of Roman coins ever found* | **small** | **secret** *her secret hoard of food*
- PREP. **in ~s** *Gold coins have been found in hoards in many parts of the country.* | **~of** *a vast hoard of treasure*

hoarse *adj.*

- VERBS **be, sound** | **become, get, go** | **leave sb, make sb/sth, scream yourself, shout yourself** *All the shouting had left her rather hoarse.* ◊ *Excitement made her voice hoarse.* ◊ *He shouted himself hoarse, but still no one came.*
- ADV. **extremely, very** | **rather, slightly**
- PREP. **from** *Her voice was hoarse from shouting.* **with** *His voice was hoarse with anxiety.*

hoax *noun*

- ADJ. **elaborate** *It turned out to be an elaborate hoax.* | **cruel** *He described the deception as a cruel hoax.* | **bomb**
- VERB + HOAX **perpetrate, play, stage** *a hoax perpetrated by the British government*
- HOAX + NOUN **call, caller**
- PREP. **~on** *The organizers staged a hoax on some of the competitors.*

hobby *noun*

- ADJ. **absorbing, enjoyable, relaxing, satisfying** | **favourite, pet** *Cooking is her pet hobby.*
- VERB + HOBBY **have** *Have you got any hobbies?* | **enjoy, follow, indulge (in), pursue** *She never had any time to pursue her hobbies.* | **start, take up** *Why don't you take up a new hobby?*
- PREP. **among your ~s** *Cycling and karate are among her hobbies.* **as a~** *He takes photographs as a hobby.*

hockey *noun*

- ADJ. **field, ice, indoor, roller** | **ladies', mens', mixed** | **senior, under-18, etc.**
- VERB + HOCKEY **play** *She plays hockey in the winter.*
- HOCKEY + NOUN **stick** | **pitch** | **match, tournament** | **coach, player** | **star** | **club, squad, team** *the Olympic hockey squad* | **league, tournament**
⇨ Special page at SPORT

hold *noun*

1 act/way of holding sth
- ADJ. **firm, tight** *He still had me in a tight hold.*
- VERB + HOLD **catch, get, grab, grasp, seize, take** *Take hold of the handle and give it a hard pull.* | **have, keep** *He kept a firm hold on my hand.* | **lose** *He lost his hold on the rock and was swept away by the tide.* | **tighten** | **relax, release** *She finally released her hold on me.*
- PREP. **~on** *He tightened his hold on her.*

2 influence/control over sb
- ADJ. **firm, powerful, strong, tight** *He still has a firm hold on the party.* | **increasing** | **fragile, tenuous, weak** *Her hold on power was now quite tenuous.*
- VERB + HOLD **have** | **lose** *The allies lost their hold on northern France.* | **consolidate, strengthen, tighten** *Enemy forces have consolidated their hold on the northern province.* | **break, weaken** *an attempt to break the hold of the Church*
- PREP. **~on** *This had weakened his hold on power.* **~over** *He no longer had any hold over her.*

holder *noun*

- ADJ. **licence, passport, ticket** *Only ticket holders will be allowed into the ground.* | **account, credit card, policy** *Account holders with the bank qualify for a discount on loans.* | **championship, cup, record, title** *the current 800* *metres record holder* | **job, office, post** *She wondered why the previous job holder had left.*

hold-up *noun*

1 robbery
- ADJ. **armed** | **bank**
- VERB + HOLD-UP **carry out**

2 delay
- ADJ. **lengthy** | **traffic**

hole *noun*

- ADJ. **big, deep, gaping, great, huge, large, massive, yawning** | **small, tiny** | **circular, round** | **jagged, ragged** *The missile had torn a jagged hole in the side of the ship.* | **neat** | **bullet** *The wall was full of bullet holes.* | **mouse, rabbit,** etc.
- VERB + HOLE **bore, break, cut, dig, drill, make, punch, tear, wear** *We dug a deep hole to bury the animals in.* ◇ *She punched two holes in each sheet of paper.* ◇ *He had worn a hole in the knees of his trousers.* | **fill (in), plug** *I uprooted the tree and filled the hole with earth.* ◇ *We used cement to plug the holes.*
- PREP. **down a/the ~** *The snake disappeared down a hole.* **in a/the ~** *There was water in the hole.* **through a/the ~** *We climbed through the hole.* | **~ in** *I used a skewer to make an extra hole in my belt.*
- PHRASES **full of holes** *The old blankets were now full of holes.* **riddled with holes** *The car was riddled with bullet holes.*

holiday *noun*

1 period of time away from home for pleasure
- ADJ. **enjoyable, exciting, fun-filled, good, lovely, wonderful** | **disastrous** *We had a disastrous camping holiday.* | **dream** *What would be your dream holiday?* | **foreign, overseas** | **summer, winter** | **7-night, two-week,** etc. | **package** | **family** | **activity, adventure, camping, skiing** *I learned to windsurf on an activity holiday.*
- VERB + HOLIDAY **go on, have, take** *We're going on holiday to France this summer.* ◇ *Are you having a holiday this year?* | **book** *Have you booked your summer holiday yet?* | **cancel** *I got ill and had to cancel my holiday.*
- HOLIDAY + NOUN **destination, resort, venue** *a popular seaside holiday resort* | **accommodation, cottage, home** *They also have a holiday home at the seaside.* | **camp, complex, village** | **period, season** *The pool is open throughout the holiday season.* | **brochure** | **business, company, firm** *The recession hit the package holiday business hard.* | **insurance** *You should take out holiday insurance before you leave.* | **arrangements, plans** | **romance** *Their holiday romance turned into a lasting relationship.* | **photos, snaps**
- PREP. **on (a) ~** *They met while on holiday in Spain.*
- PHRASES **a holiday of a lifetime** *This is your chance to win the holiday of a lifetime.*

2 period of rest from work/school
- ADJ. **annual, Christmas, Easter, summer** *The centre is now closed for the Christmas holidays.* | **school** | **paid**
- VERB + HOLIDAY **be entitled to, get, have** *You are entitled to 24 days' paid holiday per year.* ◇ *I have three weeks' holiday a year.* | **take** *I'm taking the rest of my holiday in October.* | **spend** *She spent her holiday decorating the flat.* | **need** *I really need a holiday!*
- HOLIDAY + NOUN **time** | **entitlement** | **pay** | **job** *She had a holiday job as a gardener when she was a student.*
- PREP. **during the ~s** *It can be difficult to keep children occupied during the long summer holidays.* **in the ~s** *My aunt's coming to stay in the holidays.* **on ~** *I'm afraid Mr Adamek is on holiday this week.*

3 day when people do not go to work/school

- ADJ. **bank, national, public, religious**
- HOLIDAY + NOUN **weekend** *The roads will be busy on Monday as it's a holiday weekend.*

hollow *noun*

- ADJ. **deep** | **little, shallow, slight** | **damp, dark, grassy** | **sheltered** | **natural**
- PREP. **in a/the ~** *Snow lay in dark hollows.* | **~ in** *a hollow in the ground* **~ of** *the hollow of her throat*

home *noun*

1 place where sb/sth lives
- ADJ. **boyhood, childhood, family, marital, matrimonial, natural, parental** *Placing a child in public care is sometimes the only solution to ill-treatment in the natural home.* ◇ *It's unusual for young people over 25 to still live in the parental home.* | **native** *She left her native home in Ireland and went to America.* | **permanent, temporary** *a shelter for people with no permanent home* | **comfortable, luxurious, luxury, magnificent, nice, pleasant** | **humble** | **happy, secure, stable, supportive** *These children badly need a stable and secure home life.* ◇ *The lock-up garage provides a secure home for your car.* | **broken** *children from a broken home* (= whose parents are no longer together) | **single-parent** *More and more children in the school are from single-parent homes.* | **middle-class, working-class,** etc. | **dream** *They found their dream home on the shore of a lake.* | **detached, semi-detached, terrace/terraced** | **rented** | **council** | **country, island, mountain, riverside, seaside, suburban, valley, village** *He used to spend the summer painting at his country home.* | **holiday, weekend** *They also have a holiday home in Spain.* | **caravan, mobile, motor** *The storm wrecked the family's caravan home.* | **ancestral** | **stately** *Priceless antique furniture was destroyed in the fire at the stately home.* | **forest** *These birds are in danger of becoming extinct as their forest home disappears.* | **winter** *The mudflats offer a winter home to thousands of migrating swans.* | **legendary** *The hill is the legendary home of King Arthur.* | **spiritual** *The first time he visited New Orleans he knew he had found his spiritual home.*
- VERB + HOME **arrive, come, get, go, make your way** *Let's go home—I'm tired.* | **bring sb/sth, take sb/sth** | **be away from, get away from, leave** *He didn't leave home until he was 24.* | **abandon** *The people abandoned their homes and headed for the hills.* | **find (sb/sth), give sb/sth** *Perhaps we could find a home for the kitten.*
- HOME + NOUN **address, number** *Try phoning me on my home number after six o'clock.* | **buyer, owner** | **ownership** | **purchase** | **sales** | **background, conditions, environment, life, situation** *He came from an appalling home background.* ◇ *She had never had a stable home life.* | **area, base, country, district, state, town** | **territory, turf** *I arranged to meet her in her office, as she seemed more relaxed on her home territory.* | **improvement, maintenance, repairs** | **extension** | **loan** | **help** *My grandmother has a home help who comes and cleans twice a week.* | **appliance** | **computer** | **furnishings** | **contents** *Make sure you insure your home contents for an adequate amount.* | **comforts** *She desperately missed her home comforts while camping.* | **insurance** | **security** *Fitting a burglar alarm is the most effective way to increase home security.* | **entertainment** *the market for home entertainment systems* | **use** *This video is for home use only.* | **user** *a laser printer aimed at the home user* | **trial** *We are offering a free 15-day home trial on our software.* | **student, study** *The course is suitable for classroom or home study.* | **tutor** | **work, worker** *He supplements his income with part-time or home work.* | **baking, cooking** *She missed her mother's home cooking.* | **nursing** | **visit** *The doctor was assaulted on a home visit.* | **remedy, treatment** *I've tried all the home remedies for headaches without success.* | **leave** *He went missing while on home leave from prison.*

| **movie**, **video** *We have a home movie of my dad teaching me to swim.* | **consumption** *He claimed he had bought the cigarettes for home consumption, not to sell them.* | **market** *They hope to sell as many computers on the home market as they export.* | **affairs**, **news** *the party's spokesman for home affairs* ◊ *The newspaper gives priority to home news over international news.* | **port**, **waters** *seamen serving in home waters*

• PREP. **at~**, **away from~** *Her job means she's away from home for weeks at a time.* **back ~**, **in your own ~** | **~ of** *Andalusia, the home of flamenco*

• PHRASES **a home from home** *The hotel's friendly atmosphere makes it a real home from home.* **home-grown** *home-grown vegetables* ◊ *(figurative) The show gives home-grown musical talent the chance to show what they can do.* **home-made** *home-made bread* **on the home front** (= used to introduce domestic news) *On the home front, the fuel crisis continues to worsen.* **welcome home** *The banner said 'Welcome home dad!'*

2 place that provides care for sb/sth

• ADJ. **care**, **charity**, **children's**, **convalescent**, **foster**, **nursing**, **old people's**, **remand**, **residential**, **rest**, **retirement** | **purpose-built** *Work begins this week on a purpose-built home for the city's homeless.*

• VERB + HOME **provide (sb with)** *We have to provide a good home for the children.* | **run** *They run a retirement home for the elderly.*

homeland noun

• ADJ. **beloved** *They were devastated that they had to leave their beloved homeland.* | **ancient**, **traditional** *the struggle to defend their ancient homeland* | **former** | **tribal** | **adopted** *He wants his children to grow up in his adopted homeland.* | **Jewish**, **Palestinian**

• VERB + HOMELAND **flee**, **leave** *During the war, they were forced to flee their homeland.* | **go back to**, **return to**, **visit** *He longs to return to his homeland.*

• PREP. **in a/sb's ~** *They hope to remain in their homeland.*

homeless adj.

• VERBS **be** | **become**, **end up**, **find yourself** *He found himself homeless after his marriage broke up.* | **leave sb**, **make sb**, **render sb** *Three hundred people were made homeless by the earthquake.*

• ADV. **officially** | **intentionally**, **voluntarily** *The local authority ruled that he had made himself intentionally homeless and was therefore not entitled to be rehoused.*

homesick adj.

• VERBS **be**, **feel** | **become**, **get** | **make sb** *Seeing other families together made him terribly homesick.*

• ADV. **desperately**, **terribly**, **very** | **a bit**, **a little**

homework noun

• ADJ. **English**, **science**, **etc.**

• QUANT. **piece**

• VERB + HOMEWORK **do** *Have you done your maths homework yet?* | **finish** | **hand in** *I want you to hand in this homework on Friday.* | **get**, **have** *They get masses of homework at secondary school.* | **give (sb)**, **set (sb)** *The science teacher always sets a lot of homework.* | **correct**, **mark**

• PREP. **for~** *We had to write out one of the exercises for homework.* | **~ on** *I've got some homework to do on the Industrial Revolution.*

homicide noun

• ADJ. **criminal**, **culpable**, **unlawful** | **justifiable** *The jury returned a verdict of justifiable homicide.*

⇨ Note at CRIME (for verbs)

homogeneous adj.

• VERBS **be** | **become**

• ADV. **remarkably**, **very** | **totally** | **largely** | **fairly**, **relatively** | **increasingly** | **apparently** | **supposedly** | **internally** | **culturally**, **ethnically**, **linguistically**, **racially**, **socially** *a culturally homogeneous society*

homosexual noun

• ADJ. **practising** | **closet**, **repressed** | **female**, **male**

• VERB + HOMOSEXUAL **come out as** *He came out as a homosexual after his mother died.*

• HOMOSEXUAL + VERB **come out of the closet**

• PHRASES **discrimination against homosexuals**

honest adj.

• VERBS **be**, **seem**

• ADV. **extremely**, **really**, **scrupulously**, **truly**, **very** | **absolutely**, **completely**, **perfectly**, **quite**, **totally** | **less than**, **not altogether**, **not entirely** *I don't think you've been altogether honest with me.* | **basically**, **enough**, **reasonably** *She seems honest enough.* | **refreshingly** | **brutally**, **painfully**, **ruthlessly** *Let's be brutally honest about this: you haven't a hope of succeeding.*

• PREP. **about** *Try to be honest about how you feel.* **in** *He is always scrupulously honest in his business activities.* **with** *My parents were always completely honest with me.*

• PHRASES **to be honest (with you)** *To be quite honest with you, I don't think he's the right person for the job.* **open and honest** *She was totally open and honest about her feelings.*

honesty noun

• ADJ. **absolute**, **complete**, **scrupulous**, **total** *I always expect total honesty from my employees.* | **transparent** | **brutal**, **painful**, **ruthless** *'Don't you believe me?' 'I don't know,' she said with painful honesty.* | **disarming** | **intellectual** *You need ruthless intellectual honesty about your own skills, weaknesses and motives.*

• VERB + HONESTY **have** *She had the honesty to admit her mother was right.* | **lack** | **expect**

• PREP. **in ~** (= honestly) *Who in honesty can blame her?* **with~** *She answered the questions with complete honesty.* | **~ about** *I appreciate your honesty about this.*

• PHRASES **honesty and integrity** *He has the honesty and integrity to be chairman.* **in all honesty** (= used to say sth which, though true, may seem disappointing) *In all honesty, the book was not as good as I expected.*

honey noun

• ADJ. **clear** | **runny** | **wild**

• QUANT. **dollop** | **jar**, **pot**

• VERB + HONEY **make**, **produce** *learning how bees make honey* ◊ *a jar of locally-produced honey* | **gather** *to gather honey from the hive* | **spread (sth with)** *He spread some honey on his bread.*

• HONEY + NOUN **bee**

• PHRASES **as sweet as honey**

⇨ Special page at FOOD

honeymoon noun

• ADJ. **brief**, **short** *We had a brief honeymoon in Paris.* | **long** | **second** *After so many years of marriage, we're planning a second honeymoon.*

• VERB + HONEYMOON **go on**, **have**, **leave for**, **spend** *They go on honeymoon the day after the wedding.*

• HONEYMOON + VERB **be over** (*usually figurative*) *The honeymoon was over and the reality of what she had taken on began to dawn.*

• HONEYMOON + NOUN **couple** | **suite** | **period** (*figurative*) *There was always a honeymoon period when Mum started a new job.*

• PREP. **for a~** *They can't decide where to go for their honeymoon.* **on~** *While on honeymoon in Bali, she learned to scuba dive.*

honour *noun*

1 sth that makes you feel proud
• ADJ. **great, rare, signal, special, tremendous | doubtful, dubious** *Max was given the dubious honour of organizing the children's party.*
• VERB + HONOUR **have** *I had the rare honour of being allowed into the artist's studio.* **| do sb** (*formal*)**, give sb** *Will you do me the honour of dining with me?* **| share** *He shared the honour of being the season's top scorer with Andy Cole.*

2 great respect
• PREP. **in sb's~** *They organized a party in his honour.*
• PHRASES **a guard of honour** *The princess's coffin was accompanied by a guard of honour.* **(the) guest of honour** *The president was guest of honour at the society's banquet.* **a lap of honour** *The crowd cheered while the athletes ran their lap of honour.* **a mark of honour** *They stood in silence as a mark of honour to the drowned sailors.* **the place/seat of honour, a roll of honour** *The school's roll of honour lists everyone killed in the war.*

3 good reputation
• ADJ. **family, national, personal, professional** *He was now satisfied that the family honour had been restored.*
• VERB + HONOUR **defend, fight for, save, uphold** *She felt she had to defend the honour of her profession.* **| restore | do, bring** *This biography does great honour to the poet's achievements.* ◊ *She brought honour to her country as an Olympic medal-winner.*
• HONOUR + VERB **be satisfied** *In the return match the home team won 3–0 and honour was satisfied.* **| be at stake** *National honour is at stake in this match between France and England.*
• PREP. **on your ~** (*old-fashioned*) *I swear on my honour* (= very seriously) *that I knew nothing about this.* **with ~** *The prime minister sought an agreement that would bring peace with honour.* **without ~** *a man without honour*
• PHRASES **be/feel (in) honour bound (to ...)** *He felt honour bound to help her.* **a code of honour** *Knights in the Middle Ages had a strong code of honour.* **a man of honour, a matter/point of honour** *It is a matter of professional honour to keep our standards as high as possible.* **a sense of honour, sb's word of honour** *I give you my word of honour I will not forget what I owe you.*

4 award/official title, etc.
• ADJ. **full ~s, highest, major, top** *the stars who took top honours at the MTV Awards* **| academic, battle, civilian, military, political, royal**
• VERB + HONOUR **award (sb), bestow, confer, give sb** *The Order of Merit is the highest civilian honour that can be conferred on someone.* **| accept, pick up, receive, scoop, take, win** *She has confirmed that she will accept the honour of a peerage.* ◊ *It was the British who scooped the honours at last night's Oscars.*
• HONOUR + NOUN **list, system** *He was made a life peer in the New Year's honours list.*
• PHRASES **with full military honours** *He was buried with full military honours.*

5 honours type of degree course
• ADJ. **combined, joint**
• VERB + HONOURS **do, take** (*formal*) *All students taking honours in Greek may also study Modern Greek.*
• HONOURS + NOUN **course, degree** *He's in the third year of his honours course.* **| graduate, student**
• PREP. **~ in** *joint honours in mathematics and statistics*

6 honours high mark in a degree course
• ADJ. **first-class, second-class, third-class**
• HONOURS + NOUN **degree | graduate**
• PREP. **with ~** *She passed with second class honours.*

honourable *adj.*

• VERBS **be**
• ADV. **very** *a very honourable man* **| completely, entirely, perfectly** *My intentions were perfectly honourable.*

honoured *adj.*

• VERBS **be, feel**
• ADV. **deeply, greatly, highly, truly** *I am deeply honoured to be invited to this momentous occasion.*

hood *noun*

• VERB + HOOD **pull back, pull off, pull up, put up** *He walked into the room and pulled off his hood.* ◊ *She put up her hood when it started to rain.*
• PHRASES **with the hood down/up** *He was wearing a blue anorak with the hood up.*
⇨ Special page at CLOTHES

hooked *adj.*

• VERBS **be | become, get** *I first got hooked on scuba diving when I was twelve.* **| get sb | keep sb** *a master storyteller who knows how to keep his readers hooked*
• ADV. **truly** *People who are truly hooked will go to any lengths to satisfy their craving for the drug.* **| completely, totally**
• PREP. **on** *She's completely hooked on soap operas.*

hope *noun*

1 belief that sth you want will happen
• ADJ. **considerable, fervent, great** *a feeling of considerable hope* ◊ *It is my fervent hope that you will be able to take this project forward.* **| high** (only used with **hopes**) *Hopes are high that a resolution to the conflict can be found.* **| best, main** *Privatization seems to offer the best hope for the industry.* **| faint, frail, slight, vague** *There was still a faint hope that they would accept the offer.* **| real, sincere** *without any real hope of success* ◊ *It is my sincere hope that she will find happiness at last.* **| realistic, reasonable | desperate, wild | false, forlorn, vain** *He wasn't trying to give her false hope.* ◊ *It seemed a forlorn hope that we would find a taxi.* **| early** *His early hopes of freedom were now gone.* **| last, only** *He had one last hope to cling to.* **| fresh, renewed** *the treatment gave him renewed hope* **| sudden** *Her dark eyes lit with sudden hope.* **| lingering, remaining** *These figures kill off any lingering hopes of an early economic recovery.* **| personal**
• QUANT. **flicker, glimmer, ray, spark** *I looked at her and felt a glimmer of hope.*
• VERB + HOPE **be full of, cherish, entertain, have, see** *Lord Mountbatten secretly cherished hopes that Charles would marry his granddaughter.* ◊ *Political leaders do now entertain the hope that a settlement can be found.* ◊ *She saw little hope of meeting the targets.* **| express, voice** *The Mexican president expressed hope for cooperation on trade.* **| share | pin** *He pinned all his hopes on getting that job.* **| cling to, keep alive, live in** *keeping alive the hope that a peace settlement might be found* ◊ *I haven't yet found a flat, but I live in hope.* **| not hold out** *I don't hold out much hope of finding a buyer.* **| abandon, give up, lose** *I didn't give up hope of being released.* **| arouse, bring sb, give sb, offer (sb), raise** *The use of fish oil to treat cancer has brought fresh hope to millions of sufferers.* ◊ *This announcement has raised hopes that the crisis may be coming to an end.* **| boost** *The latest jobs figures have boosted hopes for the economy.* **| jeopardize | dash, destroy, kill (off), shatter, wreck** *Her hopes of going to university have now been dashed.*
• HOPE + VERB **lie, rest** *Her only hope lay in escape.* ◊ *Their main hopes rest on their new striker.* **| grow, rise** *Hopes of a peaceful end to the strike are now growing.* **|**

flare (up), spring (up), surge *Hope flared up inside her.* | disappear, fade *Hope faded after wrecked remains of the ship were washed onto the shore.*
• PREP. **beyond~** *damaged beyond hope of repair* **in ~ of, in the ~ that** *I am writing to you in the hope that you can help me obtain some information.* **without~** *She felt weak and without hope.* | **~ for** *young people who are full of hope for the future* **~ of** *I have no hope of winning.*
• PHRASES **every/little/no/some hope of sth** *We have every hope of completing the project this year.* ◇ *There is little hope that they will be found alive.* **grounds/reason for hope** *We now have good grounds for hope.* **(not) a hope in hell** *You haven't got a hope in hell of finding a job.* **a sign/symbol of hope**

2 sth you wish for
• ADJ. **high ~s** *They have high hopes for their children.* | **future** | **distant** *Peace is a distant hope in this war-torn region.* | **personal** | **disappointed, unfulfilled** *a bitter tale of disappointed hopes* | **championship, medal, Olympic,** etc. *the team's championship hopes*
• PREP. **~ for, ~ of**
• PHRASES **your hopes and dreams/expectations/fears** *She told me all her hopes and dreams.*

3 sb/sth that will help you get what you want
• ADJ. **bright** | **last, only** *He turned to her in despair and said, 'You're my last hope.'* | **medal**
• PREP. **~ for** *She is Britain's brightest hope for a medal.* **~ of** *The operation was Kelly's only hope of survival.*

hope *verb*

• ADV. **desperately, fervently, really, sincerely, very much** *hoping desperately that their missing son would come home* ◇ *I sincerely hope that you will be successful.*
• VERB + HOPE **(not) dare (to)** *I scarcely dared hope the plan would succeed.* | **begin to** | **continue to**
• PREP. **for** *We are hoping for good weather.*
• PHRASES **hope against hope** (= to continue to hope for sth even though it is very unlikely), **hope for the best** (= to hope that sth will happen successfully, especially where it seems likely that it will not)

hopeful *adj.*

1 thinking that sth good will happen
• VERBS **be, feel, seem, sound** *I feel quite hopeful that a peaceful solution will be found.* | **become, get** *Don't get too hopeful. We may not be able to go.* | **remain** *The police remained hopeful that she would be found alive.*
• ADV. **extremely, very** | **almost** | **fairly, pretty, quite** | **eternally** *Only Janet, eternally hopeful, thought it was worth trying again.*
• PREP. **about** *She was not very hopeful about her situation.* **of** *The police are quite hopeful of catching the thieves.*

2 making you think that sth good will happen
• VERBS **be, look, seem** *Things aren't looking very hopeful at the moment.*
• ADV. **extremely, very** | **fairly, quite** *There are some fairly hopeful signs of recovery in the US market.*

hopeless *adj.*

1 giving no hope
• VERBS **be, look, seem**
• ADV. **completely, quite, utterly** *The situation seemed completely hopeless.* | **apparently, seemingly**

2 feeling no hope
• VERBS **feel** *She felt lonely and completely hopeless.*
• ADV. **completely** | **rather**

3 very bad
• VERBS **be**

• ADV. **absolutely** | **pretty** *He's a pretty hopeless dancer.*
• PREP. **at** *I'm absolutely hopeless at languages.* **with** *I've always been hopeless with machinery.*

horizon *noun*

1 line where earth and sky meet
• ADJ. **northern, southern, etc.** | **distant, far** *The sea stretched away to the distant horizon.*
• VERB + HORIZON **scan** *The captain scanned the horizon for any sign of other vessels.*
• PREP. **above the ~** *I watched the pale sun climb over the horizon.* **below the ~** *The sun was sinking rapidly below the western horizon.* **beyond the ~** *Land was still out of sight beyond the horizon.* **on the ~** *A cloud of dust on the horizon announced the arrival of the cavalry.* **over the ~** *The moon was rising over the horizon.*

2 horizons limits to knowledge/experience
• ADJ. **limited, narrow** | **new** | **cultural, intellectual, musical** *My first trip to the theatre broadened my cultural horizons.*
• VERB + HORIZONS **broaden, expand, open up, widen** *It is hoped that the course will open up new horizons for students.* | **limit, narrow, restrict** *Their horizons were limited to events within the village community.*
• HORIZONS + VERB **stretch** *His horizons didn't stretch beyond his next night out.*
• PREP. **beyond your~** *They had become aware of possibilities beyond their own limited horizons.*

hormone *noun*

• ADJ. **female, male** | **growth, sex** *children who do not produce enough growth hormone*
• VERB + HORMONE **produce, release, secrete** *Hormones are secreted into the bloodstream.*
• HORMONE + NOUN **production** | **replacement therapy, treatment** | **deficiency, imbalance** | **balance, level**

horn *noun*

1 part of an animal
• ADJ. **buffalo, bull's, cow's, rhino, etc.** *ornaments made of rhino horn* | **curled, curved** *a large bull with curved horns* | **sharp**

2 warning device on a vehicle
• ADJ. **car**
• VERB + HORN **blow, honk, sound, toot** *Passing motorists honked their horns.*
• HORN + VERB **beep, blare, hoot, sound** *Another horn blared behind me.*
• HORN + NOUN **blast** *Impatient horn blasts began to sound behind him.*
• PREP. **on a/the~** *He gave a furious blast on his horn.*

3 musical instrument
• VERB + HORN **blow**
• HORN + NOUN **section**
⇨ Special page at MUSIC

horoscope *noun*

• VERB + HOROSCOPE **cast, draw up** *To draw up someone's horoscope, you need to know their date and exact time of birth.* | **consult, read** | **believe in** *Do you believe in horoscopes?*
• HOROSCOPE + VERB **say sth** *What does your horoscope say?*

horrible *adj.*

• VERBS **be, feel, look, seem, smell, sound, taste**
• ADV. **bloody** (*taboo*), **really** *That was a really horrible thing to say!* | **absolutely, perfectly, quite, truly** *a truly horrible sight* | **pretty, rather** *a pretty horrible experience*
• PREP. **to** *My sister has always been horrible to me.*

horrific adj.

- VERBS **be, look** | **describe sth as** *Police described the attack as horrific.*
- ADV. **really** | **absolutely, quite, truly** *Some of the scenes we witnessed were quite horrific.* | **fairly, pretty**

horror noun

1 feeling of fear/shock

- ADJ. **abject, absolute, utter** *The thought of working nights fills me with abject horror.* | **mock** *She raised her hands in mock horror when she saw my new haircut.*
- VERB + HORROR **feel, have** *She felt horror and pity at seeing Marcus so ill.* ◊ *She had a horror of pubs.* | **fill sb with** *The possibility of meeting him again filled me with horror.* | **overcome** | **recoil in** *Anna recoiled in horror as the snake approached.*
- HORROR + NOUN **film, story** *They were trying to scare each other with horror stories about going to the dentist.*
- PREP. **in ~** *They watched in horror as the aircraft crashed to the ground.* **to your ~** *To his horror, he saw a dead body lying beside the road.* **with ~** *He realized with absolute horror that he no longer had the money.* | **~ of** *I'm trying to overcome my horror of insects.*
- PHRASES **a look of horror, shock horror** *newspapers full of shock horror headlines*

2 sth frightening/shocking

- ADJ. **full** *He never experienced the full horrors of trench warfare.* | **ultimate** *I used to regard public speaking as the ultimate horror.*
- VERB + HORROR **commit, inflict, perpetrate** *He had witnessed horrors committed by the enemy.* | **experience, suffer** | **witness**

horse noun

- ADJ. **beautiful, fine, good, lovely, magnificent** *He was mounted on the finest horse you could ever see.* | **bay, black, chestnut, grey, piebald, roan, skewbald** | **thoroughbred** | **feral, wild** | **unbroken** | **highly-strung, nervous, restless, skittish** | **frightened, startled, terrified** | **placid** | **fancied** *The race organizers became suspicious when the two most fancied horses finished last.* | **loose, riderless, runaway** *Three horses fell when a loose horse ran across the track.* | **fresh** *They would need fresh horses if they were to reach the border the next day.* | **lame** | **heavy, shire** *The brewery had 25 heavy horses delivering beer in London.* | **riding, saddle** | **carriage, cart** (also **carthorse**), **draught, dray** | **pack** | **cavalry, police** | **race** (also **racehorse**) | **pantomime** *He got a part as the rear end of a pantomime horse.* | **rocking**
- VERB + HORSE **breed** | **get ready** *Get my horse ready and wait for me.* | **saddle** | **be mounted on, mount** | **ride** | **lead** | **brush down, groom** | **shoe** | **stable** | **handle** *She has a knack for handling horses.* | **ill-treat** | **frighten** | **hobble, tether** | **nobble** *He was jailed for 15 years for nobbling a horse that had been going to run in the Derby.*
- HORSE + VERB **canter, gallop, trot, walk** *Several horses trotted past us.* | **prance** | **run** *There are ten horses running in the next race.* | **plod** *The weary horse plodded up the hill.* | **neigh, snort, whinny** | **bolt** | **rear (up), shy** | **plunge** *The cart overturned, the horse plunging and rearing in its traces.* | **fall, slip, stumble** *The horse stumbled and threw its rider.* | **throw sb** | **jump** | **pull sth** *They passed an old horse pulling a cart full of apples.* | **prick up its ears** | **graze**
- HORSE + NOUN **box** *The car in front was pulling a horse box.* | **breeder, dealer, owner, rider, trainer** | **droppings, dung, manure, shit** (*taboo*) | **fair** *Hundreds of horses are bought and sold at the annual horse fair.* | **race** | **racing, riding, show, trials** *He won second prize in a horse show.* | **trough** *The horse trough was full of stag-*

nant water. | **whip** | **trading** (also **horse-trading**) (*figurative*) *political horse-trading*

- PREP. **on a/the ~**
- PHRASES **a horse and carriage/cart, horse-drawn** *horse-drawn vehicles*

hospital noun

- ADJ. **community, district, local** | **NHS, private** | **day, long-stay** | **general** | **children's, maternity, mental, psychiatric, etc.** | **teaching**
- VERB + HOSPITAL **go into/to** *He's had to go into hospital rather suddenly.* | **rush sb to, take sb to** | **admit sb to, readmit sb to** | **stay in** | **come out of, leave** *She came out of hospital this morning.* | **discharge sb from**
- HOSPITAL + NOUN **doctor, staff** | **inpatient, outpatient, patient** | **care, services, treatment** | **clinic, unit, ward** | **bed** | **admission, stay**
- PREP. **at a/the ~** *She works at the John Radcliffe Hospital.* **in (a/the) ~** *He is in hospital recovering from a heart operation.* ◊ *I used to work as a cleaner in a hospital.* **to (a/the) ~** *He's been taken to hospital for tests.* ◊ *We went to the hospital to visit my gran.*
- PHRASES **admission to hospital, a stay in hospital**

hospitality noun

- ADJ. **generous, lavish, warm** | **corporate** *the company's corporate hospitality budget*
- VERB + HOSPITALITY **extend, offer (sb), provide (sb with), show sb** *We wish to thank the people of Norway for the warm hospitality extended to us during our recent visit.* | **accept** *We were glad to accept their generous hospitality.* | **repay, return** *You must allow me to repay your hospitality.* | **abuse**

host noun

1 person who receives and entertains visitors

- ADJ. **charming, generous, genial, good, perfect, welcoming** *George was a perfect host.*
- VERB + HOST **act as, play** *The village is playing host to a film crew.*
- HOST + NOUN **club, community, country, family, government, nation, society, state** *The host club is to be congratulated on its organization of the tournament.*
- PREP. **~ to** *The acre of garden is host to a splendid bank of rhododendrons.*

2 person who introduces a television or radio show

- ADJ. **chat-show, game-show, talk-show, television, TV** *The event will be opened by television host Bill Punter.*

host verb

- ADV. **jointly** *The tournament is to be jointly hosted by India, Pakistan and Sri Lanka.*
- VERB + HOST **agree to, offer to** | **be keen to** *The country is very keen to host the Winter Olympics in six years' time.*
- PHRASES **a bid to host sth** *the city's bid to host the Olympic Games in the year 2008*

hostage noun

- VERB + HOSTAGE **hold (sb)** *Eight people were held hostage for four months.* | **seize, take (sb)** *The gunmen took 24 hostages.* | **free, release, set free** *diplomatic efforts to get the hostages released*

hostel noun

- ADJ. **refugee, student, youth** | **bed and breakfast** | **bail, probation** *a probation hostel for young offenders*
- VERB + HOSTEL **stay at/in** *homeless families staying in bed and breakfast hostels*
- HOSTEL + NOUN **accommodation**

● PREP. **at a/the~** *We stayed at a student hostel during the conference.* **in a/the~** *He lives in a hostel for the homeless.*

hostile *adj.*

● VERBS **appear, be, feel | become | remain | make sb** *The experience has made him generally hostile towards women.* **| consider sth, construe sth as, deem sth, perceive sth as, regard sth as, see sth as** *They were reluctant to take any step that might be regarded as hostile.*
● ADV. **bitterly, decidedly, deeply, downright, distinctly, extremely, fiercely, markedly, positively, uncompromisingly, unremittingly, very** *He was deeply hostile to the idea of psychotherapy.* ◇ *The audience gave him a downright hostile reception.* **| entirely, totally | increasingly | almost | apparently | potentially | basically, generally | actively, openly | mutually | uniformly** *The press became uniformly hostile to the new administration.* **| politically** *politically hostile newspapers*
● PREP. **to** *Many people were openly hostile to the idea.* **towards** *He was extremely hostile towards her.*

hostility *noun*

1 opposition/aggressive feelings or behaviour
● ADJ. **bitter, considerable, deep, extreme, great, implacable | downright, open, outright** *Mixed-race couples faced open hostility.* **| veiled** *There was a barely veiled hostility in her tone.* **| general, widespread | popular, public** *the widespread popular hostility towards the war* **| personal | mutual**
● VERB + HOSTILITY **feel** *the deep hostility felt by many teenagers against the police* **| express, show | arouse, attract, provoke** *The prime minister was concerned that such a move would arouse public hostility.* **| be greeted with, be met with, encounter, face, meet with** *The proposal was met with outright hostility.*
● PREP. **~between** *You could almost feel the hostility between her and her mother.* **~against/to/towards** *the bitter hostility towards the occupying forces*

2 hostilities fighting in a war
● VERB + HOSTILITIES **cease, end, suspend** *Both sides finally agreed to suspend hostilities.* **| resume** *Hostilities were resumed later that year.*
● HOSTILITIES + VERB **begin, break out | cease, end** *On the 11th of November 1918 hostilities ceased.* **| resume**
● PREP. **~against** *the beginning of hostilities against Germany in 1914* **~between** *Hostilities broke out between the two provinces later that year.*
● PHRASES **the cessation of hostilities, an outbreak of hostilities**

hot *adj.*

1 of the weather
● VERBS **be | become, get, grow** *The sun shone fiercely down and it grew hotter and hotter.*
● ADV. **baking, blazing, bloody** (*taboo*), **boiling, exceedingly, exceptionally, extremely, incredibly, insufferably, intensely, oppressively, really, scorching, stiflingly, swelteringly, unbearably, uncomfortably, unusually, very** *a boiling hot summer's day* ◇ *It was unbearably hot in the car.* **| a bit, fairly, pretty, quite, rather** *This weather's a bit hot for me.*

2 of a person
● VERBS **be, feel, look** *Don't you feel hot so close to the fire?* **| get, grew** *They had been going steadily up for half an hour and she was beginning to get uncomfortably hot.* ◇ *His face grew hot at the memory of his embarrassment.*
● ADV. **boiling, burning, extremely, really, uncomfortably, very** *I was boiling hot and sweaty.* ◇ *His forehead was burning hot.* **| a bit, quite, rather**

3 of a thing
● VERBS **be, feel, look, seem | get**

● ADV. **extremely, really, red-, scalding, very, white-** *white-hot metal* **| a bit, fairly, moderately, quite, rather, slightly** *Wash the tablecloth in fairly hot soapy water.* ◇ *Bake in a moderately hot oven.* **| enough, sufficiently** *The ground was hot enough to fry an egg on.*

4 of food: not cold
● VERBS **be | keep, stay** *The food should stay hot until we're ready to eat.* **| keep sth** *The containers keep the food hot for five hours.* **| eat sth, serve sth** *Serve hot or cold accompanied by bread and a salad.*
● ADV. **piping, really, scalding, sizzling, steaming, very** *a bowl of piping hot soup* ◇ *Make sure the fat is sizzling hot.* **| a bit, fairly, quite, rather**

5 of food: spicy
● VERBS **be, taste**
● ADV. **extremely, really, very** *I love really hot food.* **| a bit, pretty, quite, slightly** *That was a pretty hot curry!*

hotel *noun*

● ADJ. **big, large | little, small | cheap, expensive | five-star, four-star, etc. | attractive, beautiful, comfortable, delightful, deluxe, good, grand, elegant, excellent, fine, first-class, luxurious, luxury, pleasant, posh, quality, smart, top** *all the style and comfort that only the best hotels can provide* ◇ *It was a luxury hotel with its own swimming pool and restaurant.* **| seedy | modern | air-conditioned** *The hotel is fully air-conditioned.* **| traditional | friendly | family, family-run** *a family hotel with a playground for small children* ◇ *a friendly family-run hotel* **| independent, private | international | country, country-house** *a small country hotel* **| holiday, resort, tourist | seafront, seaside | local, nearby | bed and breakfast** *homeless families living in bed and breakfast hotels*
● VERB + HOTEL **stay at/in** *We're staying at a cheap hotel near the station.* **| book in at/into, check in at/into, check out of** *We checked into the hotel, then went for a walk along the beachfront.* **| own | manage, run**
● HOTEL + VERB **be located, be situated** *The hotel is situated in the historic heart of the city.* **| feature sth, have sth, offer sth, provide sth** *The hotel features a lovely dining room overlooking the lake.* ◇ *The hotel offers excellent facilities.*
● HOTEL + NOUN **accommodation, bedroom, room, suite | restaurant | foyer, lobby | guest, manager | industry | chain, group**
● PREP. **at a/the~** *We met at the hotel.* **in a/the~** *We're staying in a two-star hotel in the centre of the city.*

hotline *noun*

● ADJ. **24-hour | information, technical support, ticket | credit card | telephone**
● VERB + HOTLINE **call, dial, phone, ring** *Dial our 24-hour hotline to find out if you have won a prize.* **| establish, set up** *A telephone hotline has been set up to give information about the changed train services.* **| operate, run** *The company will be operating an information hotline that customers can call if they are worried about products.*

hound *noun*

● ADJ. **hunting**
● QUANT. **pack**
● HOUND + VERB **bark, bay** *We could hear the hounds barking at the fox.* **| pick up the scent** *The hounds picked up the scent of the fox.* **| chase sth, follow sth, pursue sth** *In drag hunting, hounds chase an artificial scent.* **| run**
● PHRASES **ride to hounds** *Days off were spent riding to hounds* (= hunting).

hour noun

1 period of sixty minutes
- ADJ. **solid** *I slept for eight solid hours.*
- VERB + HOUR **take** *It takes two hours to get to London.* | **spend** | **last** *The performance lasted three hours.* | **gain, lose** *You gain five hours when you fly from New York to London.*
- HOUR + VERB **go by, pass** *An hour passed and she still hadn't arrived.*
- PREP. **by the ~** *They're paid by the hour.* **for an ~** *She worked for three hours.* **in/within an ~** *I should be back within a couple of hours.* **over/under an ~** *He's been gone for over an hour.* **per~** *Top speed is 120 miles per hour.* **within the ~** *We hope to be there within the hour* (= in less than an hour). | **~ of** *There are still two hours of daylight left.*
- PHRASES **half an hour, hour after hour, an hour's time, with every passing hour** *She grew more worried with every passing hour.*
⇨ Note at MEASURE

2 the hour time when a new hour starts
- VERB + HOURS **chime, strike** *The clock struck the hour.*
- PREP. **on the ~** *Buses leave every hour on the hour.* **past the ~** *ten minutes past the hour* **to the ~** *ten minutes to the hour*

3 time when you do a particular activity
- ADJ. **lunch** | **peak, rush** *rush-hour traffic*
- VERB + HOUR **spend** *I spent my lunch hour shopping.*
- PREP. **~ of** *an hour of rest*

4 hours time when sb is working/a shop is open
- ADJ. **office, opening, working** | **licensing, visiting** *Britain's licensing hours* (= when pubs are allowed to open) ◊ *the hospital's visiting hours* | **flexible** | **long** | **regular**
- VERB + HOURS **work** *She works very long hours.* | **keep** *He keeps regular hours.*
- PREP. **after ~** *He spends a lot of time in his office after hours.* **out of ~** *Doctors often have to work out of hours.*

5 time when sth happens
- ADJ. **darkest, finest** *This was often thought of as the country's finest hour.* | **antisocial, unearthly, ungodly, unsocial** *I apologize for phoning you at this ungodly hour.*
- HOUR + VERB **come** *The hour had come for us to leave.*
- PREP. **between the ~s of** *The office is closed between the hours of twelve and two.* | **~ of** *the hours of darkness*
- PHRASES **your hour of need** *She helped me in my hour of need.*

house noun

1 building that is made for one family to live in
- ADJ. **beautiful, comfortable, delightful, elegant, fine, grand, handsome, lovely, luxurious, magnificent, posh, pretty, splendid** | **dream** *They built their own dream house overlooking the river.* | **depressing, dingy, gloomy, ugly** | **derelict, dilapidated, ramshackle, shabby, untidy** | **detached, semi-detached, terrace/terraced** | **big, enormous, gigantic, huge, large, palatial, spacious** | **rambling** *It was easy to get lost in the rambling house.* | **little, modest, small, tiny** *They lived in a modest semi-detached house in the suburbs.* | **single-storey, single-storeyed, two-storey, etc.** | **four-bedroom, four-bedroomed, eight-room, eight-roomed, etc.** | **gabled, half-timbered, red-brick, thatched** | **exclusive, expensive** | **private** | **council** (= rented from the local council) | **rented** | **empty, unoccupied, vacant** | **country, suburban, town** | **great, manor, mansion** *The great house stood on the edge of the village.* | **farm** (also **farmhouse**), **ranch** | **ancestral** | **communal** | **summer** | **tree** | **halfway, safe** *a halfway house for prisoners returning to society* ◊ *The police provided a safe house for the informer.*

- VERB + HOUSE **live in, occupy** *a house occupied by students* | **share** *She shares a house with three other nurses.* | **buy, rent, sell** | **let (out)** *We let out our house when we moved to America.* | **repossess** *Their house was repossessed when they couldn't keep up their mortgage payments.* | **move, move into, move out of** *It's stressful moving house.* | **set up** *They want to set up house together* | **keep** *She kept house* (= cooked, cleaned, etc.) *for her elderly parents.* | **play (at)** *The children were playing house, giving dinner to their teddies.* | **build** | **demolish, knock down, tear down** | **maintain** | **decorate, do up, redecorate, refurbish, renovate** *They bought a dilapidated house when they got married, and are gradually doing it up.* | **furnish** | **insulate, rewire** | **extend** *We're hoping to extend the house.*
- HOUSE + VERB **be situated, lie, stand** *The house stood a short distance from the wood.* | **face sth, overlook sth** *The house faces south, making the most of the sun.* ◊ *houses overlooking the park* | **loom** *The house loomed over him as he waited at the front door.* | **be worth sth** | **collapse, fall down** | **burn down, catch fire** | **come into view**
- HOUSE + NOUN **agent** | **buyer, owner** *The bank offers attractive rates to first-time house buyers.* | **tenant** | **building, construction** | **decoration, improvement, renovation, repairs** | **builder, decorator, painter** | **contents** | **design, plan, planning** | **hunting** | **move** *They helped us with our house move.* | **prices, rents, values** | **purchase** | **sales** | **mortgage** | **insurance** | **repossession** | **front, interior** | **number** | **keys** | **guest** | **call** *In the morning, the doctor makes house calls.* | **arrest** *The former dictator is under house arrest in his country mansion.* | **dust** | **blaze, fire** | **party, -warming** *They've moved house and have invited us to their house-warming on Saturday.* | **husband** *He's happy being a house husband while his wife goes out to work.* | **plant** | **fly, mouse, sparrow, etc.**
- PREP. **at sb's/the ~** *I finally tracked him down at his house in London.* **from ~ to ~** *She went from house to house collecting signatures for her campaign.* **in a/the ~** *It was so hot outside we stayed in the house.*
- PHRASES **house-to-house** *Police are making house-to-house enquiries following the discovery of the body.*

2 all the people who live in one house
- ADJ. **friendly, happy**
- VERB + HOUSE **wake (up)** *You'll wake up the whole house with that noise.*

3 in a theatre/cinema
- ADJ. **empty** | **full, packed**
- VERB + HOUSE **play to** *They played to a packed house.*
- HOUSE + NOUN **lights** | **manager**
- PHRASES **bring the house down** (= please the audience very much) **front-of-house** (= the parts of a theatre used by the audience) *the front-of-house staff*

house verb

- ADV. **adequately** *At no time in the 19th century were the working classes adequately housed.* | **badly, inadequately** *The losers in this society are the old, the sick, the jobless, the homeless and badly housed.* | **temporarily** *The fish can be temporarily housed in a smaller aquarium.*

household noun

- ADJ. **average** *The average household pays 27p a day in water rates.* | **domestic, private, etc.** | **rural, urban** | **middle-class, working-class, high-income, low-income, poor, etc.** | **family, married-couple, single-person, etc.**
- VERB + HOUSEHOLD **manage, run** | **set up** *Becoming an adult and setting up a household no longer mean the same thing.*
- HOUSEHOLD + NOUN **appliance, contents, furniture,**

goods, **item, product** *The household contents are covered by a separate insurance policy.* | **bills, budget, expenditure, expenses, income** | **chore, duties, task** | **rubbish, waste**
• PHRASES **the head of the household** *The head of the household is responsible for completing the Council Tax form.*

housekeeping noun

• ADJ. **careful, good, prudent** *The company has made considerable savings through good housekeeping, such as avoiding wastage.* | **bad, poor** *My financial problems were made worse by my bad housekeeping.*
• HOUSEKEEPING + NOUN **allowance, money** *Her husband spent the housekeeping money on gambling.*

housework noun

• VERB + HOUSEWORK **do** *I spent all morning doing housework.* | **share** *The cook their own meals but they share the housework.* | **help with** *Her husband never helps with the housework.*

housing noun

• ADJ. **affordable, cheap, good, low-cost** *The aim of the scheme was to provide good low-cost housing for workers.* | **decent, good** | **adequate** | **bad, inadequate, poor, substandard** *Many health problems are made worse by poor housing.* | **permanent, temporary** | **council, local authority, public, social** *Public expenditure on social housing provision has doubled in the last five years.* | **rented** | **private** | **sheltered** *sheltered housing for old people* | **high-rise** | **rural, urban**
• VERB + HOUSING **provide**
• HOUSING + NOUN **association, authority, committee, department, office** | **conditions** | **development, estate, scheme** *Many new housing developments had sprung up around the city.* | **construction** | **provision** | **market** | **crisis, shortage** | **allowance, benefit** *She receives a substantial housing allowance on top of her salary.* ◊ *I received housing benefit when I was unemployed.*
• PREP. **in ... ~** *Too many families are still living in substandard housing.*

hover verb

• ADV. **nearby** | **anxiously, uneasily** *He was hovering anxiously outside.* | **indecisively, uncertainly** *She hovered uncertainly near the front door.* | **impatiently**
• PREP. **about/around, behind, by, near** *She couldn't bear him hovering around her.*
• PHRASES **hover in the background** *Phoebe was hovering in the background, uncertain what to do.* **hover in the doorway**

howl noun

• ADJ. **deep** | **mournful** *The dog gave a mournful howl.*
• VERB + HOWL **give, let out** | **hear**
• PREP. **with a ~** *With a howl he leapt at his foe.* | **~ of** *howl of laughter/protest*
• PHRASES **be greeted/met with howls of sth** *His comments were met with howls of outrage.* **the howl of the wind/a wolf, howls of laughter, howls of outrage/protest/rage**
⇨ Note at SOUND

huddle noun

• ADJ. **little, small, tight**
• VERB + HUDDLE **get into, go into** *The team went into a huddle at half-time to discuss their tactics.*
• PREP. **in a ~** *They stood in a tight huddle, whispering.* | **~ of** *A little huddle of men stood in one corner.*

huddled adj.

• VERBS **be, lie, sit, stand** *Phil sat huddled miserably in his chair.* | **find sb** *She found him huddled in a corner, shaking violently.*
• ADV. **miserably**
• PREP. **against** *Karen was huddled against the wall.* **beneath/under** *She lay huddled under the blankets.* **in** *He slept, huddled in an armchair.*

huff noun

• VERB + HUFF **get in, go into** | **go off in, march off in, storm off in, walk off in** *She went off in a huff after losing the game.*
• PREP. **in a ~** *He's in a huff because he wasn't invited.* | **~ at** *She got in a huff at being doubted.* **~ over** *Alison's in a huff over the joke they played on her.*

hug noun

• ADJ. **big** | **affectionate, comforting, friendly, loving, reassuring, warm** | **quick**
• VERB + HUG **give sb** *He gave the children a quick hug, then got into the car.*

hug verb

• ADV. **close, tight/tightly** *James went to his daughter and hugged her tightly.* | **gently** | **fiercely**
• PREP. **to** *He reached out and hugged her to him.*
• PHRASES **hug and kiss sb**

huge adj.

• VERBS **be, look** | **become, grow** *Her eyes grew huge.*
• ADV. **really** *This is a really huge amount of money.* | **absolutely, simply** *Their house is absolutely huge!* | **potentially** *There's a potentially huge demand for this product.*

hum noun

• ADJ. **faint, soft** | **low** | **high-pitched** | **constant, continuous, steady** *I could hear the constant hum of distant traffic.* | **background**
• VERB + HUM **hear**
• PREP. **~ of** *the background hum of the air-conditioning*

hum verb

• ADV. **quietly, softly** | **happily** | **tunelessly** | **along** *humming along with the music*
• VERB + HUM **begin to** *He began to hum, somewhat tunelessly.*
• PHRASES **hum to yourself** *She was humming softly to herself.*

humanitarian adj.

• VERBS **be**
• ADV. **purely** *Both countries say their intervention is purely humanitarian.* | **essentially**

humanity noun

• ADJ. **great, true** | **common** *Guilt and a sense of common humanity make people less harsh.*

humidity noun

• ADJ. **high, low** | **ambient, relative** *in dry weather, when the ambient humidity is low*
• QUANT. **level**
• HUMIDITY + VERB **increase, rise** | **decrease, fall**
• HUMIDITY + NOUN **level** | **control** *The museum is equipped with sophisticated humidity controls.*

humiliate *verb*

- ADV. **deeply | totally, utterly | publicly** *Lowe was publicly humiliated by his colleagues.*
- PREP. **in front of** *I had been assaulted and deeply humiliated in front of all my friends.*
- PHRASES **feel humiliated** *I have never felt so humiliated in all my life.*

humiliating *adj.*

- VERBS **be | find sth**
- ADV. **deeply, profoundly, very | utterly** *He found the experience utterly humiliating.* | **somewhat**
- PREP. **for** *The whole experience was somewhat humiliating for us.* **to** *a settlement that was deeply humiliating to their country*

humiliation *noun*

- ADJ. **great, intense, painful | total | further | public | national | final, ultimate** *He was forced to face the ultimate humiliation the next morning.* | **military**
- VERB + HUMILIATION **be subjected to, endure, face, suffer** *She suffered the humiliation of having her house searched.* | **feel** *feeling the intense humiliation of having failed*
- PHRASES **a feeling/sense of humiliation**

humorous *adj.*

- VERBS **be, look, sound | become | find sth**
- ADV. **extremely, very | mildly, quite, slightly** *She has written her description of him in a mildly humorous vein.* | **delightfully** *The film is delightfully humorous in the best traditions of romantic comedy.* | **darkly**

humour *noun*

1 amusing quality/ability to find things funny

- ADJ. **wry** *With wry humour, they laugh at their misfortunes.* | **irreverent | caustic, sardonic | black, dark, gallows, grim | self-deprecating | gentle | tongue-in-cheek | slapstick, visual | unconscious, unintentional | deadpan, dry | schoolboy** *His colleagues soon got fed up with his schoolboy humour.* | **lavatorial**
- QUANT. **touch** *Her speech was serious, but not without the occasional touch of humour.*
- VERB + HUMOUR **be full of, contain** *The stories are full of humour.* | **appreciate, see** *The man who lost his shoes failed to see the humour of the situation.*
- PHRASES **a brand of humour** *a television sitcom with its own peculiar brand of humour* **sense of humour** *to have a dry/good/great/warped/weird/wicked sense of humour*

2 mood

- ADJ. **good** *Her good humour was restored by the excellent meal.*
- PHRASES **in (a) good humour** *The remarks were made in good humour.* ◇ *He was obviously in a good humour this evening.*

hunch *noun*

- VERB + HUNCH **have** *I had a hunch that she was not telling the truth.* | **act on, follow, play** *Acting on a hunch, I waited outside her house to see if she went out.* ◇ *I decided to follow my hunch and come and see you.* | **back, confirm** *They now have a database of information to back their hunches about customers' preferences.*
- PREP. **on a~** *I phoned on a hunch to ask if they had any work for me.*

hunger *noun*

1 feeling of wanting to eat

- ADJ. **extreme** *Any good weight loss regime should not lead to extreme hunger.* | **world**
- VERB + HUNGER **feel** *It is usual to feel hunger during exercise.* | **be weak with | die from/of** *Thousands of people have died of hunger.* | **alleviate, relieve, satisfy** *looking for ways to alleviate world hunger* ◇ *Perhaps the cat was killing to satisfy hunger.*
- HUNGER + NOUN **pangs** *The new snack bar will keep those hunger pangs at bay.* | **strike** *About 60 prisoners have gone on hunger strike.*
- PHRASES **pangs of hunger**

2 strong desire for sth

- ADJ. **great, insatiable | land** *Peasant land hunger grew ever more acute as the population swelled.*
- VERB + HUNGER **feel, have | satisfy**
- HUNGER + VERB **grow**
- PREP. **~for** *She has an insatiable hunger for knowledge.*

hungry *adj.*

- VERBS **be, feel, go, look** *the number of children who have to go hungry* | **become, get | make sb** *Seeing everyone eating had made him extremely hungry.*
- ADV. **desperately, dreadfully, extremely, ravenously, really, starving** (*informal*), **terribly, very** *We were all ravenously hungry after the walk.* | **a bit, quite, rather | always, permanently**

hunt *noun*

1 hunting wild animals

- ADJ. **fox, seal, tiger,** etc.
- VERB + HUNT **take part in** *She had never taken part in a fox hunt before.*
- HUNT + NOUN **follower, supporter** *Hunt followers deny the sport is cruel.* | **saboteur** *clashes between hunt supporters and hunt saboteurs* | **meeting**

2 searching for sb/sth

- ADJ. **massive, nationwide** *Police launched a nationwide hunt for the woman, amid fears for her safety.* | **police | murder** *Police forces in five counties are now involved in the murder hunt.* | **treasure | witch** (*often figurative*) *The investigation turned into a full-scale Communist witch hunt.*
- HUNT + VERB **begin, launch** *A massive police hunt was launched for the missing child.* | **lead** *Detectives leading the hunt for the killer believe he may be in hiding.* | **step up** *The mountain rescue team is stepping up its hunt for the missing climbers.* | **call off** *The hunt for survivors has now been called off.*
- HUNT + VERB **begin, be on** *The hunt is on for potential employees with experience of electronic publishing.*
- PREP. **~for**

hunting *noun*

1 chasing wild animals

- ADJ. **big-game, deer, fox** (also **fox-hunting**), etc. *He was killed by a lion while big-game hunting in Africa.* | **commercial** *commercial hunting of minke whales*
- VERB + HUNTING **go** *Local people go hunting in the woods.* | **ban** *Should fox-hunting be banned?*
- HUNTING + NOUN **knife, rifle | ground** *These waters are a hunting ground for sharks.* | **lodge** *The king built a large hunting lodge in the mountains.* | **trip | season**

2 trying to find sth

- ADJ. **bargain, house, job, treasure** *Archaeologists have called for a ban on treasure hunting in the region.*
- VERB + HUNTING **go** *We went bargain hunting at the antique market.*
- HUNTING + NOUN **ground** (*figurative*) *Crowded markets are a happy hunting ground for pickpockets.*

hurdle *noun*

1 in a race

- VERB + HURDLE **clear, jump (over)** *She cleared the first few hurdles easily.* | **fall at, hit** *His horse fell at the final hurdle.*

2 problem/difficulty

- ADJ. **big, difficult | main, major | final, first, last, next** *The first big hurdle in putting your car on the road is getting insurance.*
- VERB + HURDLE **face** *This is perhaps the most difficult hurdle that we face.* | **clear, jump, overcome, pass** *We'll jump each hurdle as we come to it.* ◊ *You have already overcome the first major hurdle by passing the entrance exam.* | **fall at** *The plan fell at the first hurdle.*

hurricane *noun*

- HURRICANE + VERB **hit sth, strike (sth)** *A hurricane hit the city yesterday at 5 p.m.* | **damage sth, destroy sth, devastate sth** *The fields were devastated by the hurricane.* | **blow, blow itself out** *The hurricane took several days to blow itself out.*
- HURRICANE + NOUN **force** *hurricane-force winds*
- PREP. **in a/the ~** *The roof blew off in a hurricane.*
- PHRASES **the eye of the hurricane** (= the central point)

hurry *noun*

- ADJ. **big, desperate, great, tearing, terrible** *I was late for the match and in a tearing hurry.*
- PREP. **in a ~** *They were in a hurry to set off.* **in no ~** *She's in no hurry to find out how much her phone bill comes to.* **in your ~** *In his hurry to leave, he forgot his briefcase.*

hurt *noun*

- ADJ. **bitter, deep, great**
- VERB + HURT **feel** *the deep hurt that he felt when Jane left him* | **cause** *She knew that she had caused her husband a lot of hurt.*

hurt *verb*

1 cause pain/injury

- ADV. **badly, seriously** *She fell and hurt her leg quite badly.* ◊ *No one was seriously hurt in the accident.* | **slightly**

2 be/feel painful

- ADV. **badly, a lot, really** *My ankle still hurts quite badly.* ◊ *Does it hurt a lot?* ◊ *Ouch! It really hurts.* | **slightly**
- VERB + HURT **be going to** *I knew it was going to hurt—but not that much!* | **begin to**

3 upset sb

- ADV. **badly, deeply, really, terribly** *Her remarks hurt him deeply.* ◊ *They never told me why and that really hurt.*
- VERB + HURT **attempt to, try to** *Are you deliberately trying to hurt me?* | **want to** *Why would I want to hurt her?* | **not mean to** *I never meant to hurt anyone.*

hurt *adj.*

1 injured

- VERBS **be, look | get** *Stop that or you'll get hurt!*
- ADV. **badly, seriously** *Steve didn't look seriously hurt.* | **slightly**

2 upset

- VERBS **be, feel, look, seem, sound | get**
- ADV. **bitterly, deeply, extremely, really, terribly, very | a bit, quite, rather, slightly**
- PREP. **by** *Roy seemed deeply hurt by this remark.*

hurtful *adj.*

- VERBS **be | find sth** *I found some of his comments rather hurtful.*
- ADV. **deeply, very** *She made some very hurtful remarks.* | **a bit, rather**
- PREP. **to** *What he said was deeply hurtful to me.*

husband *noun*

- ADJ. **future, prospective | suitable | ex-, former | dead, deceased, late | good, loving, wonderful | faithful | errant, unfaithful | estranged | absent | jealous | dominant, domineering | brutal, violent | house** (= a man who stays at home to look after children, cook, clean, etc. while his wife works)
- VERB + HUSBAND **meet** *That was the day she met her future husband.* | **marry | be divorced from, be separated from, divorce, leave, walk out on** *She suddenly walked out on her husband, leaving him to bring up the children.*
- PHRASES **husband and wife** *They lived together as husband and wife for over thirty years.* **husband-to-be**

hush *noun*

- ADJ. **sudden | breathless, deathly | expectant**
- HUSH + VERB **descend, fall** *A sudden hush fell over the room as the head teacher entered.* | **follow sth** *A deathly hush followed the explosion.*

hut *noun*

- ADJ. **makeshift | prefabricated | bamboo, metal, mud, stone, straw, wooden | thatched | circular, round | single-storey/single-storeyed | ramshackle, rickety | derelict | beach, garden, mountain | fisherman's, fishing, shepherd's, etc. | army, barrack | site** *The builders were collecting their wages from the site hut.* | **refreshment | changing**
- VERB + HUT **build** *huts built with mud bricks*
- HUT + VERB **stand** *The wooden hut stood on a lonely stretch of beach.*
- PREP. **in a/the ~** *The scheme housed children in large numbers in prefabricated huts.*

hygiene *noun*

- ADJ. **good, scrupulous | poor** *infections that are the result of poor food hygiene* | **dental, food, oral, personal, public** *Many skin diseases can be prevented by good personal hygiene.*
- HYGIENE + NOUN **practices, regulations, standards**
- PHRASES **standards of hygiene**

hymn *noun*

- ADJ. **rousing** *The service began with a rousing hymn.* | **traditional | modern**
- VERB + HYMN **play, sing**
- HYMN + NOUN **book | tune**

hype *noun*

- ADJ. **media | marketing | pre-match, pre-race, pre-season, etc.**
- VERB + HYPE **live up to** *The movie failed to live up to all the hype.* | **believe**
- HYPE + VERB **surround sth** *the hype surrounding her latest book*
- PREP. **~ about** *I don't believe all the hype about how good the French team will be this season.*

hypnosis *noun*

- VERB + HYPNOSIS **be given, have, undergo | practise, put sb under** *I decided to put him under hypnosis and ask him again.* | **induce | be susceptible to**

● HYPNOSIS + NOUN **session**
● PREP. **during** ~ *changes in breathing observed during hypnosis* **under** ~ *the things that people remember under hypnosis*

hypothesis *noun*

● ADJ. **acceptable, plausible** | **bold** *Scientists have proposed a bold hypothesis.* | **unlikely** | **speculative** | **testable** | **working** *These observations appear to support our working hypothesis.* | **scientific**
● VERB + HYPOTHESIS **construct, form, formulate, have, make, propose, put forward, suggest** *It is possible to make a hypothesis on the basis of this graph.* ◇ *A number of hypotheses have been put forward.* | **consider, discuss, examine, test (out)** *using this data to test her hypothesis* | **confirm, prove, support** | **accept** | **reject** *None of the hypotheses can be rejected at this stage.*
● VERB + HYPOTHESIS **concern sth** *Her hypothesis concerns the role of electromagnetic radiation.* | **predict sth** *The hypothesis predicts that children will perform better on task A than on task B.*
● PREP. **on a/the** ~ *Her study is based on the hypothesis that language simplification is possible.* | ~ **about** *an interesting hypothesis about the development of language* ~ **on** *The results confirmed his hypothesis on the use of modal verbs.*

hypothetical *adj.*

● VERBS **be** *This is a purely hypothetical situation.*
● ADV. **entirely, purely, totally**

hysteria *noun*

● ADJ. **mass, public** | **mild, near** | **rising** | **media, tabloid** *Unnecessary anxiety has been caused by media hysteria and misinformation.* | **religious**
● QUANT. **fit** *She smashed the place up in a fit of hysteria.* | **note, touch** *the touch of hysteria in her voice*
● VERB + HYSTERIA **border on** *Sam arrived in a state of excitement bordering on hysteria.* | **bring on, engender, generate** *That thought was enough to bring on near hysteria.*
● HYSTERIA + VERB **mount, rise** *She felt hysteria rising.* | **die down, diminish** *Eventually the hysteria died down.* | **sweep (across/through)** sth *the hysteria that swept through the country*
● PREP. ~ **about** *public hysteria about the bombings* ~ **over** *hysteria over Aids*
● PHRASES **on the brink/point/verge of hysteria** *She was babbling, on the verge of hysteria.*

hysterical *adj.*

1 suffering from/caused by hysteria
● VERBS **be, feel, sound** *Emily realized that she sounded hysterical.* | **become, get** *Calm down, you're getting hysterical.*
● ADV. **completely** | **almost, nearly** *By this time Mary was almost hysterical.* | **faintly, mildly, rather, slightly**

2 very funny
● VERBS **be**
● ADV. **absolutely, totally** *The whole episode was absolutely hysterical!*

Ii

ice noun

- ● ADJ. **thick** *Is the ice thick enough to walk on?* | **thin** | **black** *Motorists have been warned about black ice on the roads.*
- ● QUANT. **block, slab** *The spray froze and formed great blocks of ice on the front of the ship.*
- ● VERB + ICE **form**
- ● ICE + VERB **form** *Ice had formed on the pond.* | **crack, melt** *The ice was beginning to melt.*
- ● PREP. **on the~** *skating on the ice*

ice cream noun

- ● ADJ. **chocolate, strawberry, vanilla, etc.**
- ● QUANT. **scoop** | **carton, tub**
- ● VERB + ICE CREAM **eat, have**
- ● ICE CREAM + VERB **melt**
- ● ICE CREAM + NOUN **carton, cone** | **parlour, van**
- ● PHRASES **and/with ice-cream** *apple pie with ice cream*
⇨ Special page at FOOD

icing noun

- ● ADJ. **fondant, gelatine, royal, sugar paste** | **chocolate, lemon, etc.**
- ● VERB + ICING **roll out** *Roll out the icing into a large square.* | **cover sth with, pipe, smooth, spread, squeeze** *Pipe a little green icing around the strawberries.* | **trim off** *Trim off excess icing around the base.* | **colour** *Colour the remaining icing red.*
- ● ICING + VERB **dry**
- ● ICING + NOUN **sugar** | **bag**

icon noun

1 small symbol on a computer screen
- ● ADJ. **folder, network, printer, program, window, etc.**
- ● VERB + ICON **click (on), double-click (on), right-click (on)** *Click the 'modems' icon.* | **drag**
⇨ Special page at COMPUTER

2 person considered to be a symbol
- ● ADJ. **national** | **cultural** | **gay, lesbian** | **fashion, pop, sporting, style**

idea noun

1 plan/suggestion
- ● ADJ. **bright, brilliant, clever, excellent, good, great, marvellous** | **valuable, worthwhile** | **exciting, inspirational, interesting, stimulating** | **constructive, positive** | **creative, imaginative, innovative, original** | **wacky** | **big** *The latest big idea is to make women more interested in sport.* | **alternative** *Group counselling is used as an alternative idea to punishment.* | **fresh, new** | **absurd, bad, mistaken, ridiculous** | **crackpot, crazy, mad, outlandish, wild** | **half-baked** | **ambitious, big, grand** *He joined the company as an office assistant with big ideas.* | **grandiose** | **basic** *The basic idea is that we all meet up in London.*
- ● VERB + IDEA **have** *Do you have any ideas for a present for Lara?* | **come up with, dream up, hit on/upon, produce, think up** | **draw, get** *Her ideas are drawn mainly from Chinese art.* | **contribute, input** | **moot, put forward** | **promote, push (forward), sell** *They managed to push the idea of moving office through the committee.* | **welcome** *Most employees welcome the idea of a ban on smoking.* | **consider, entertain, flirt with, toy with** *I'm toying with the idea of packing in my job.* | **mull over, turn**

over *He kept turning the idea of resigning over in his mind.* | **encourage, generate** *Brainstorming is a good way of generating ideas.* | **stifle** *a system of decision-making that stifles original ideas* | **reject, scoff at, veto** | **test, try out** | **bounce around, bounce off sb, brainstorm, discuss, explore, talk about** *I met up with a designer to bounce a few ideas around.* ◇ *It's useful to have someone to bounce ideas off.* | **exchange, pool, share** | **give sb** *What gave you the idea to go freelance?* | **apply, implement, put into action/effect/practice** *The idea had long been mooted but nothing had been done to put it into practice.* | **transform, translate** *How could we translate the idea into business reality?* | **steal** *She accused the company of stealing her idea.* | **impose** *She always tries to impose her own ideas on the rest of the team.*
- ● IDEA + VERB **come into sb's head/mind, come to sb, flash across/into sb's mind/brain, hit sb, occur to sb, pop into sb's head, strike sb** *The idea for the invention came to him in the bath.* | **emerge, evolve, form, grow** *An idea began to form in his mind.* | **flow** *His ideas flowed faster than he could express them.* | **come from sb/sth, date back from/to sth, originate, start, stem from sth** *The idea for the Olympics originated with Pierre de Coubertin.* | **blossom, work (out)** *The idea has now blossomed into a successful mail-order business.* | **lead** *The idea eventually led to the invention of the telephone.* | **come to nothing**
- ● PREP. **~ about** *I have an idea about how to tackle the problem.* **~ for** *We were asked to suggest ideas for improving efficiency.* **~ of** *She had the idea of advertising on the Internet.*
- ● PHRASES **be open to ideas** *I don't know what to do, but I'm open to ideas.* **the germ/glimmering of an idea** *The germ of his idea came from watching a bird make a nest.* **have other ideas** *I wanted to take the week off, but my boss had other ideas.* **it might be an idea** *It might be an idea to leave a note on the door for Mark.*

2 thought/impression
- ● ADJ. **clear, concrete, precise** | **abstract** | **theoretical** | **basic, rough, vague** *He gave me a rough idea of what was wanted.* | **key, main** *The book introduces the key ideas of sociology.* | **dominant** | **fixed, inflexible, preconceived** | **definite, firm, strong** *She has very definite ideas about what kind of a job she wants.* | **complex, difficult** | **simplistic** | **conventional, traditional** | **radical, revolutionary** | **contradictory** | **erroneous, false, wrong** *I don't want anyone getting the wrong idea about me.* | **funny, strange** | **utopian** | **romantic** *People have a romantic idea of the police force.* | **new-fangled** | **outdated** | **not the faintest/foggiest/remotest/slightest** (*informal*) *I haven't got the faintest idea what she meant.* | **artistic, economic, intellectual, moral, musical, philosophical, political, scientific** | **fascist, feminist, nationalist, socialist**
- ● VERB + IDEA **get** *They seem to have got the idea that we will be giving them a lift.* ◇ *You'll soon get the idea (= understand).* | **espouse, have, hold** *He holds very different ideas to mine about discipline.* | **develop, form, shape** *the experiences that shaped her ideas* | **express** | **communicate, convey, get across, get over, present, put across** *The book puts across complex ideas in a way anyone can understand.* | **demonstrate, explain, expound, illustrate** | **clarify, formalize, formulate, organize, structure** *Give careful thought to how to structure your ideas in the essay.* | **change, reconsider, reshape, revise** *They had to reconsider their ideas in the light of new evi-*

dence. | **accept** | **dismiss, reject** | **harbour** *I hope he's not still harbouring ideas about asking me out.* | **be obsessed with** *He's obsessed with the idea of getting a motorbike.* | **relish** *I don't relish the idea of sharing an office with Tony.*

● IDEA + VERB **amuse sb, appeal to sb, please sb** *The idea of going to his rescue amused her.* | **catch on, take hold** *Some students started wearing denim, and the idea caught on.*

● PREP. **~about** *She's got some funny ideas about how to motivate staff.* **~behind** *The idea behind the ceremony is to keep the gods happy to ensure a good crop.* **~of** *Swimming in an icy river is not my idea of fun.*

ideal noun

● ADJ. **high, lofty, noble** *Sam was a real leader who had high moral ideals.* | **unattainable** *This is not an unattainable ideal.* | **aesthetic, artistic, ethical, moral, political** | **democratic, liberal, revolutionary, socialist**

● VERB + IDEAL **be committed to, be devoted to, believe in, cling to, espouse, have, support** *They still clung to the old ideals.* | **pursue, strive for** | **achieve, attain, be true to, conform to, live up to** *A journalist should always live up to the ideals of truth, decency, and justice.* | **fall short of** *This agreement falls far short of the ideal.* | **abandon, betray** *She was accused of betraying her political ideals.* | **embody, reflect** *the democratic ideals embodied in the charter*

ideal adj.

● VERBS **be, look, seem, sound** | **make sth** *The hotel's size makes it ideal for large conferences.* | **consider sth**

● ADV. **absolutely, almost** | **less than** *Language learning often takes place in a less than ideal environment.*

● PREP. **for** *The houses are absolutely ideal for families with young children.*

identical adj.

● VERBS **appear, be, look, seem** | **remain**

● ADV. **absolutely, completely, exactly** | **not necessarily** *Different spreadsheet packages tend to be similar, though not necessarily identical.* | **almost, more or less, nearly, practically, virtually** *The two houses were more or less identical.* | **effectively** | **apparently** | **basically, essentially** | **chemically, formally, genetically**

● PREP. **to** *This knife is identical to the one used in the attack.* **with** *offspring that are genetically identical with the parents*

identification noun

1 act of identifying sb/sth

● ADJ. **accurate, correct** | **positive**

● VERB + IDENTIFICATION **make** *She was unable to make a positive identification of the suspect.*

● IDENTIFICATION + NOUN **parade** *A witness picked him out of an identity parade as the robber.*

2 proof of identity

● VERB + IDENTIFICATION **carry, have** *Always carry some identification.* ◊ *Do you have any identification?* | **ask for, check** *The police checked their identification.*

● IDENTIFICATION + NOUN **card, papers** | **code, number** *The vehicle's identification number is stamped on the engine.*

● PHRASES **a means of identification** *My only means of identification was my cheque book.*

identify verb

● ADV. **accurately, correctly** *The new test will enable us to identify more accurately patients who are most at risk.* ◊ *Did you identify all the pictures correctly?* | **falsely, incorrectly, wrongly** | **positively** | **clearly, unambiguously,**

unequivocally *We have not yet clearly identified the source of the pollution.* | **formally** *Someone has to formally identify the body.* | **easily, readily** *I could identify him easily if I saw him again.* | **tentatively** *All three structures dated to the third century and were tentatively identified as shrines.*

● VERB + IDENTIFY **be able/unable to, can** *tests that can identify people at risk of cancer* | **be easy to, be possible to** | **be difficult to** | **be necessary to** | **attempt to, seek to, try to** | **be used to, enable sb to, help to** | **decline to** *The newspaper declined to identify the source of the allegations.*

● PHRASES **a means/way of identifying sb/sth** *one means of identifying the disease in its early stages*

PHRASAL VERBS

identify with sb

● ADV. **closely, strongly** *She identified strongly with the main character in the play.*

● VERB + IDENTIFY WITH SB **can/could** *I can't identify with men like him.*

identify sb with sth

● ADV. **closely** *The policy is closely identified with the prime minister himself.* | **clearly**

identity noun

● ADJ. **true** | **assumed, false** *He was discovered living under an assumed identity in South America.* | **mistaken** *This is obviously a case of mistaken identity.* | **new** | **common, corporate, cultural, national, personal, political, racial, sexual**

● VERB + IDENTITY **create, develop, establish, forge** *They are still struggling to establish their identity as a political party.* ◊ *The company forged its own identity by producing specialist vehicles.* | **give sb/sth** *He felt that having a job gave him an identity.* | **maintain, preserve** *Many minority groups are struggling to maintain their cultural identity.* | **lose** | **change** *He changed his identity and moved abroad on his release from prison.* | **assume** *She was given a false passport and assumed a new identity.* | **disclose, reveal** *He refused to reveal the identity of his client.* | **discover, find out** | **guess** *It was easy to guess the identity of the thief.* | **conceal, hide, keep secret, protect** *Her voice was disguised to conceal her identity.*

● IDENTITY + NOUN **bracelet, tag** | **card, documents, papers** | **code** | **parade** *The victim picked out her attacker in an identity parade.* | **crisis** *The country suffered from an identity crisis for years after the civil war.*

● PREP. **~as** *Scotland has never lost its identity as a separate nation.*

● PHRASES **proof of identity** *The police officer asked him for proof of identity.* **a search for identity** *His search for his cultural identity took him to where his parents were born.* **a sense of identity**

ideology noun

● ADJ. **dominant** | **official** | **coherent** *The party's policies were based on prejudice rather than on any coherent ideology.* | **strong** | **cultural, economic, educational, political, religious** | **bourgeois, capitalist, communist, Marxist, revolutionary, socialist, etc.**

● VERB + IDEOLOGY **have** *The party had a Marxist ideology.* | **adopt** *They distanced themselves from the upper class and adopted a communist ideology.* | **reject**

idiot noun

● ADJ. **blithering, complete, gibbering, prize, right, silly, stupid** *What stupid idiot left their shoes on the stairs?*

● VERB + IDIOT **be, feel (like), look like** *I felt a right idiot, standing there in front of all those people!*

● PHRASES **make an idiot of yourself** *He's made a complete idiot of himself over this woman!*

idle *adj.*

1 lazy
- VERBS **be** | **become**
- ADV. **very** | **bone** (*informal*), **totally** *She never lifts a finger to help. She's bone idle.* | **rather**

2 not in use
- VERBS **be, lie, sit, stand** *Half their machines are lying idle.* ◇ *The pumps are standing idle.* | **remain** | **leave sth, make sth** *The land was left idle for years.*

idol *noun*

- ADJ. **film, football, pop, rock, sports, etc.** | **teen, teenage** *By this time Pitt had become a teenage idol.*
- VERB + IDOL **make (sb)** *Teenagers made Dean their idol.* ◇ *The film made an idol of her.*

ignite *verb*

- ADV. **spontaneously** *The burning foam generates such heat that other items in the room can ignite spontaneously.*
- VERB + IGNITE **fail to** *The gunpowder sometimes fails to ignite.*

ignition *noun*

- VERB + IGNITION **switch on, turn on** *She got into the car and switched on the ignition.* | **switch off, turn off**
- IGNITION + NOUN **key** *He turned the ignition key.*
- PREP. **in the~** *I must have left my key in the ignition.*

ignorance *noun*

- ADJ. **complete, total** | **remarkable** | **widespread** | **blissful**
- VERB + IGNORANCE **betray, show** *I tried not to betray my ignorance.* ◇ *He showed a remarkable ignorance of the facts.* | **admit, confess, plead** *I had to confess my ignorance.* ◇ *He pleaded ignorance of any wrongdoing.* | **live in, remain in** *The sisters lived in total ignorance of each other.* | **keep sb in** *He was kept in ignorance of his true identity.* | **be based on** *These attitudes are based on ignorance and fear.*
- PREP. **due to~** *mistakes due to ignorance* **in~(of)** *She remained in blissful ignorance of these events.* **through~** *Many lives are lost through ignorance.* | **~about** *There is still widespread ignorance about this disease.*

ignorant *adj.*

- VERBS **appear, be, feel, seem** | **remain** *The general public remained totally ignorant of the danger.* | **keep sb** *We were kept ignorant of the facts.*
- ADV. **completely, entirely, pig** (*informal*), **quite, totally, utterly, very, wholly** *Don't ask Paul. He's pig ignorant.* | **largely** | **rather** | **blissfully** *We went to bed that night blissfully ignorant of the storm to come.* | **grossly, lamentably, woefully**
- PREP. **about** *He was completely ignorant about the country's political system.* **of** *We are still woefully ignorant of the causes of this disease.*

ignore *verb*

- ADV. **altogether, completely, entirely, quite, totally** | **almost, practically, virtually** | **largely** | **generally** | **just, simply** *The government has simply ignored the problem altogether.* | **consistently** | **apparently** | **duly** *Her mother's opinions on how babies should be cared for were freely given and duly ignored.* | **easily** *The diesel fumes from Oxford's buses are not easily ignored.* | **conveniently** (*ironic*) *The managers have conveniently ignored these statistics.* | **blatantly** *Safety guidelines had been blatantly ignored.* | **assiduously, carefully, deliberately, determinedly, pointedly, resolutely, steadfastly, studiously** *She sat at her desk and studiously ignored me.* | **blithely,**

cheerfully *He blithely ignored her protests and went on talking as if all were agreed between them.* | **coldly**
- VERB + IGNORE **cannot (afford to)** *a warning the prime minister cannot afford to ignore* | **be difficult to, be hard to, be impossible to** | **tend to** *Scientists have tended to ignore these creatures.* | **try to** | **choose to** *The judge chose to ignore the views of the doctors.*
- PHRASES **be widely ignored** *Safety standards are widely ignored in the industry.* **ignore sth at your peril** *The pernicious effect of this advertising on children is a problem that we ignore at our peril.* **ignore the fact that** ... *Did you think I'd ignore the fact that you were suffering from shock?* **sth can be safely ignored** (*ironic*) *These people occupy such a marginal position in society that the authorities think they can be safely ignored.*

ill *adj.*

- VERBS **be, feel, look** | **become, be taken, fall, get** | **make sb** *I can't eat bananas. They make me ill.*
- ADV. **critically, dangerously, desperately, extremely, gravely, really, seriously, severely, terribly, very** *His mother is seriously ill in hospital.* | **almost** *Robyn was almost ill with excitement and outrage.* | **pretty, quite, rather, slightly** | **genuinely** | **violently** *She was taken violently ill and had to be put to bed.* | **acutely** | **chronically** *chronically ill patients* | **fatally, incurably, mortally, terminally** *a hospice for the terminally ill* | **mentally, physically** *the problems faced by mentally ill people*

illegal *adj.*

- VERBS **be** | **become** | **remain** | **declare sth, deem sth, judge, make sth, pronounce sth, rule sth** *Their action was judged illegal by the International Court.* ◇ *The sale of these knives should be made illegal.*
- ADV. **highly** | **absolutely, quite, strictly, totally** | **allegedly** | **technically** *Prize-fighting remained popular, though technically illegal, until the 1880s.*

illegitimate *adj.*

- VERBS **be** | **consider sth, regard sth as**
- ADV. **absolutely, completely, entirely, quite, wholly** *It is quite illegitimate to argue that the government had no choice.*

illiteracy *noun*

- ADJ. **widespread** *Illiteracy was widespread at that time.*
- QUANT. **level, rate**
- ILLITERACY + NOUN **rate** *Illiteracy rates have fallen in recent years.*

illiterate *adj.*

- VERBS **be**
- ADV. **completely, totally** | **almost, largely, virtually** | **functionally** *People judged to be functionally illiterate lack the basic reading and writing skills required in everyday life.* | **economically, politically** *Is it surprising that young people who are politically illiterate do not bother to vote?*

illness *noun*

- ADJ. **fatal, incurable, terminal** | **debilitating, life-threatening, major, serious, severe** | **minor** | **lingering, long, long-standing, long-term, prolonged** | **brief, short** | **final, last** | **acute, chronic** | **infectious** | **painful** | **depressive, mental, psychiatric, psychotic** | **psychosomatic** | **physical** | **respiratory** | **childhood**
- QUANT. **bout, episode** *an acute episode of mental illness*
- VERB + ILLNESS **have, suffer (from)** *Badly fed children suffer a lot of minor illnesses.* ◇ *people who suffer*

ILLNESSES

You can **have** any illness or disease:
I'm warning you—I've got a bad cold.
Have the kids had chickenpox yet?

Get can be used with diseases or illnesses that you often have:
He gets really bad hay fever every summer.

Suffer from is used in more formal contexts and with more serious diseases:
This medicine is often recommended for patients who suffer from arthritis.

You can also:

a heavy cold

catch	develop	come/go down with	contract	suffer
chickenpox	Aids	appendicitis	Aids	a breakdown
a cold	an allergy (to sth)	bronchitis	cancer	a heart attack
a cough	arthritis	chickenpox	conjunctivitis	a stroke
flu	cancer	diarrhoea	hepatitis	
German measles	cataracts	flu	HIV	
glandular fever	epilepsy	food poisoning	meningitis	
measles	heart/liver trouble	measles	pneumonia	
mumps	high blood pressure	mumps		
a stomach bug	an infection			
whooping cough	pneumonia			
	rheumatism			

an **attack of** flu, nerves, shingles; an asthma **attack**
a **bout of** bronchitis, coughing, flu, pneumonia, sickness
a coughing, an epileptic **fit**

Is it serious?

no	yes
a bit of a cold, a cough, an infection	a **bad/heavy/nasty** cold
mild depression	a **bad/nasty/severe** attack of sth, bout of sth
a **mild** attack of sth, bout of sth	a **bad/hacking/racking** cough
a **mild** heart attack, infection	a **bad/splitting** headache
a **slight** cold, headache	a **massive/serious** heart attack, stroke

What's the treatment?

take	be given/ be on/take	have/undergo	have/be given	have/be given/ undergo
medicine	antibiotics	an operation	acupuncture	hypnosis
pills	drugs	surgery	an anaesthetic	therapy
tablets	medication	a transplant	a blood transfusion	treatment
	painkillers		an injection	
			a scan	
			an X-ray	

from mental illness | **contract, develop, get** *He contracted a serious illness and died a month later.* | **diagnose** | **treat** *The drug is used to treat a wide range of illnesses.* | **cause** *illnesses caused by poverty* | **prevent** *a drug that may be helpful in preventing illnesses such as cancer* | **recover from** | **fight (off)** *The immune system enables the body to fight off illness.* | **feign** *She feigned illness so that she wouldn't have to go to school.* | **nurse sb through** *She nursed her father through his final illness.*

• ILLNESS + VERB **affect sb** *The mystery illness affected hundreds of people in the city.*

• PREP. **after~** *He's just returned to work after illness.* **because of/due to/through ~** *earnings lost due to illness* **with ~** *people with serious psychological illnesses* | **~among** *a high rate of illness among the workers* **~associated with** *the illnesses associated with HIV infection* **~in** *episodes of illness in children*

• PHRASES **the onset of illness** *the sudden onset of illness in a parent* **a smoking-/Aids-, etc. related illness** *the most common stress-related illnesses*

illogical *adj.*

• VERBS **be, seem, sound**
• ADV. **completely, entirely, quite, totally** | **rather, slightly** | **apparently** | **strictly** *Although strictly illogical, Martin's interpretation of this paradox seems the best.*

ill-treatment *noun*

• VERB + ILL-TREATMENT **suffer**
• PHRASES **ill-treatment at sb's hands** *They suffered ill-treatment at the hands of the guards.*

illuminate *verb*

1 give light to sth
• ADV. **brightly, clearly** | **dimly, faintly, softly** *The room was dimly illuminated by the soft glow of his bedside lamp.* | **briefly** | **suddenly**

2 make sth clear
• ADV. **greatly, vividly** *an incident which vividly illuminated the problems we faced*
• VERB + ILLUMINATE **help (to)** *The study of the present also helps to illuminate the past.*

illuminating *adj.*

• VERBS **be, prove** | **find sth**
• ADV. **extremely, highly, most, very** *I found his talk most illuminating.* | **not particularly** | **quite**

illumination *noun*

• ADJ. **bright, good, strong**
• QUANT. **level** *providing an excellent level of illumination*
• VERB + ILLUMINATION **provide** *The skylight will provide good illumination from above.*
• ILLUMINATION + VERB **come from sth** *Most of the illumination came from candles.*
• PHRASES **a source of illumination** *The only source of illumination was a single small window.*

illusion *noun*

• ADJ. **dangerous** *To believe you have nothing more to learn is a dangerous illusion.* | **optical, visual** *The road ahead looks wet, but in fact this is an optical illusion.*
• VERB + ILLUSION **be under, entertain, have** *They are under no illusions about the difficulties ahead of them.* | **create, give (sb)** *The huge size of the vehicle gives the illusion of safety.* | **foster, maintain, preserve, sustain** *They are trying to maintain the illusion that the company is in good shape.* | **break, destroy, dispel, shatter** *Within the*

first week at university all my illusions were shattered. | **shed** *Now is the time to shed our illusions.*

• PREP. **~about/as to** *She had no illusions about her attractiveness to men.*

• PHRASES **be all an illusion** *It turned out that their happy marriage was all an illusion.*

illustrate *verb*

1 put pictures in sth
• ADV. **heavily, lavishly, richly** | **fully** | **attractively, beautifully, delightfully, handsomely, superbly**
• PREP. **with** *The new edition is heavily illustrated with photographs of aircraft.*

2 make sth clear using examples/pictures
• ADV. **amply** | **admirably, aptly, neatly, nicely, well** *The dire consequences of chronic underfunding are nowhere better illustrated than in the nation's schools.* | **perfectly** | **merely, simply** *His question merely illustrates his ignorance of the subject.* | **clearly, dramatically, graphically, strikingly, vividly** | **brutally, starkly, tragically** *The case tragically illustrates the dangers of fireworks.*
• VERB + ILLUSTRATE **serve to** *Two examples serve to illustrate this point.* | **be chosen to, be designed to, be intended to**
• PREP. **to** *a way of illustrating to the chairman the folly of his decision*

illustration *noun*

1 picture in a book etc.
• ADJ. **black and white, colour/coloured, full-colour** | **beautiful, lively** *The clear, lively illustrations are in full colour.* | **clear** | **book, cover**
• ILLUSTRATION + VERB **show sth** | **accompany sth** *the illustrations accompanying the text*
• PREP. **in an/the ~** *The kite is assembled as shown in the illustration.* **with an/the ~** | **~ by** *'The Black Cat' by Alan Ahlberg, with illustrations by Arthur Robins*

2 example
• ADJ. **good, excellent, perfect** | **clear, dramatic, graphic, striking, vivid** *These events are a graphic illustration of the fact that their promises cannot be trusted.* | **simple** *Let us take a very simple illustration.* | **classic**
• VERB + ILLUSTRATION **serve as** *Chicago serves as an illustration of the problems faced by such cities.* | **give (sb), provide** *Explain the policy of détente and provide some illustrations of how it worked in practice.* | **take, use sth as/for** *I will use one recent example as an illustration.*
• PREP. **as an~** *As an illustration of this point, I'm going to tell you a true story.* **by way of~** *He quoted several famous writers by way of illustration.*

image *noun*

1 impression of sb/sth given to the public
• ADJ. **positive** | **negative** | **upmarket** | **downmarket** | **tarnished** *The party needs to clean up its somewhat tarnished image.* | **clean-cut, girl-next-door, wholesome** *She was aiming for a wholesome, girl-next-door image.* | **macho** | **hackneyed** *the hackneyed image of the poor student* | **media, public, screen** *In real life she looks nothing like her screen image.* | **brand, corporate** *Champagne houses owe their success to brand image.*
• VERB + IMAGE **create** *The company needs to create a new image for itself.* | **present, project, promote** *a book which presents positive images of older people* | **aim for, go for** | **change** | **clean up, enhance, improve, polish, revive** *an effort to improve the organization's public image* | **keep up, live up to** *The group has failed to live up to its macho image.* | **discard, shed** *The industry is trying to shed its negative image.* | **tarnish**

2 mental picture of sb/sth
• ADJ. **powerful, vivid** | **sudden** *She had a sudden*

mental image of herself in a wedding dress. | **positive** | **negative** | **distorted** the distorted images in his dreams | **popular** | **stereotyped/stereotypical** | **mental** | **literary, poetic** | **dream**
- VERB + IMAGE **have** | **conjure up, summon up** Dieting always seems to conjure up images of endless cottage cheese salads. ◇ the ability to summon up images in the mind | **build up** I like to build up images of the characters and setting before I start to write. | **use** | **reinforce** Treating disabled people like children only reinforces negative images of disability.
- PREP. **~ from** images from his past

3 copy
- ADJ. **living, spitting** He's the spitting image of his father! | **mirror** Charity was a mirror image of her twin. ◇ (figurative) The return journey was almost a mirror image of the outward one (= the same things happened in the reverse order).

4 picture
- ADJ. **disturbing, poignant, powerful, striking** powerful and disturbing images of the war | **visual** The visual image is steadily replacing the written word. | **flickering, moving** flickering images on a screen | **still** the use of still and moving video images | **colour** | **black-and-white, monochrome** | **photographic, video** | **screen** Each illustration is displayed as a complete screen image. | **digital** | **graven** (literary) It was forbidden to worship graven (= carved) images. | **religious** | **pornographic**
- VERB + IMAGE **produce** the images produced on laser printers | **capture, scan** She longed to capture the image on film. | **edit** | **display, show** the pixel information used to display a digital image | **store** You can store these images in a separate computer file. | **juxtapose** The display juxtaposed images from serious and popular art.
- IMAGE + VERB **show sth** heat images that show where most of the activity in the brain is
- IMAGE + NOUN **capture, processing** | **database**
- ⇨ Special page at COMPUTER

imagery noun
- ADJ. **powerful, resonant, telling, vivid** the vivid visual imagery of dreams | **slick** the slick imagery of rock stardom | **popular** drawing on popular imagery from newspapers and magazines | **visual** | **mental** Illustration may come between the text and the reader's own mental imagery. | **religious, sexual**
- VERB + IMAGERY **draw on, use**

imaginable adj.
- VERBS **be**
- ADV. **barely, hardly, scarcely** To such poor people, the idea of having a choice of food is barely imaginable.
- PHRASES **the best/worst … imaginable** They live in the worst conditions imaginable. **every imaginable** They had every imaginable colour. ◇ They had every colour imaginable. **the most … imaginable** It was the most boring film imaginable!

imaginary adj.
- VERBS **be**
- ADV. **completely, purely, wholly** The characters in this book are purely imaginary.

imagination noun
- ADJ. **great** | **active, creative, fertile, vivid** | **fevered, overactive, overheated** It's just a product of your fevered imagination! | **collective, popular, public** a popular hero who inspired the collective imagination | **visual** I was no good at art—I have a very poor visual imagination. | **historical, literary** It requires a strong effort of historical

imagination to understand the Roman attitude to death. | **human** the powers of the human imagination
- VERB + IMAGINATION **have** | **show** | **lack** Today's pop music lacks imagination. | **require, take** It does not take great imagination to guess what happened next. | **use** I haven't got a picture of this so you'll just have to use your imagination. | **capture, captivate, catch, excite, fire, inspire, seize, stimulate, stir** Victorian writers fired the popular imagination with their tales of adventure. | **grip, hold** Dinosaurs caught and have held the imagination of us all because they seem like dragons. | **stretch, tax** | **defy** The scale of the disaster defied imagination (= was greater than you could imagine). | **leave sth to** As for their reaction, I'll leave that to your imagination!
- IMAGINATION + VERB **conjure sth up** His imagination conjured up a vision of the normal family life he had never had. | **run away with you, run riot/wild**
- PREP. **beyond (your) ~** misery that is beyond most people's imagination **in the/your ~** Nobody hates you—it's all in your imagination! **with/without ~** He was totally without imagination.
- PHRASES **a lack of imagination, a figment/product of sb's imagination** The figure vanished as silently as if it had simply been a figment of her imagination. **not by any/by no stretch of the imagination** Not by any stretch of the imagination could she be called beautiful (= she was definitely not beautiful in any way). **only your imagination** Is it only my imagination or have you lost weight? **with a little imagination** With a little imagination you can create a delicious meal from yesterday's leftovers.

imaginative adj.
- VERBS **be, seem**
- ADV. **brilliantly, extremely, highly, most, very, wonderfully** a wonderfully imaginative story | **quite**

imagine verb
1 form a picture of sth in your mind
- ADV. **clearly, easily, readily** I could clearly imagine the scene in the office. | **hardly, scarcely** I could hardly imagine living in such a remote and desolate spot. | **just** She could just imagine her mother's look of horror. | **actually** I can't actually imagine her falling for that trick. | **always** I always imagined him following in his father's footsteps. | **fondly, naively** I had fondly imagined that riding a mule would be easy.
- VERB + IMAGINE **can/could (well)** I can well imagine the atmosphere at home at this moment. | **can/could not (possibly)** There's more at stake here than you can possibly imagine. | **try to** | **be difficult to, be hard to, be impossible to** It is difficult to imagine Blackpool without its famous Tower. | **be easy to**
- PHRASES **let us imagine** Let us imagine what really might have happened.

2 see/hear/think sth that is not true/does not exist
- ADV. **really, seriously** You don't seriously imagine I'll agree to that? | **almost** I could almost imagine you were jealous. | **actually** | **fondly, naively**
- VERB + IMAGINE **be easy to**
- PHRASES **be imagining things** Had I really heard a noise, or was I just imagining things? **real or imagined** He was always keen to avenge insults, real or imagined.

imbalance noun
- ADJ. **growing** | **regional** | **gender, power, trade** | **chemical, hormonal**
- VERB + IMBALANCE **cause, create** | **correct, redress** Increased recruitment of women engineers will help correct the gender imbalance in the profession.
- IMBALANCE + VERB **arise, occur**
- PREP. **~ between** an imbalance between imports and

exports ~ in *An imbalance in certain chemicals leads to disturbances in the brain's function.*

imitation *noun*

1 copy of a thing
- ADJ. **accurate, good, passable | cheap, crude, pale, poor** *Accept no cheap imitations of our product!* ◊ *Their version of jazz funk is a pale imitation of the real thing.*

2 act of copying sth
- ADJ. **faithful, slavish | direct** *Children are seen as learning to write by direct imitation of adult models.*
- PREP. **in ~ of** *The poems, some in imitation of Ossian, are graceful if unremarkable.*

3 copy of sb's speech/behaviour
- ADJ. **fair, good, passable | poor**
- VERB + IMITATION **do, give, perform** *He does a very good imitation of George W. Bush.*

immaculate *adj.*
- VERBS **be, look | keep sth**
- ADV. **absolutely, totally**

immaterial *adj.*
- VERBS **be, prove, seem | become**
- ADV. **completely, entirely, quite, wholly** *The condition of the car is quite immaterial as long as it works.* | **almost, virtually | relatively**
- PREP. **to** *These facts are immaterial to the problem.*

immature *adj.*
- VERBS **be, seem**
- ADV. **very | rather, relatively | emotionally, physically, politically, sexually**

immediacy *noun*
- VERB + IMMEDIACY **lack**
- PHRASES **a lack of immediacy, a loss of immediacy** *Television allows viewers to experience an event without any loss of immediacy.*

immediate *adj.*
- VERBS **be, seem** *The effect seems immediate.*
- ADV. **almost** *The painkillers brought almost immediate relief.*

immerse *verb*

1 put sth in liquid
- ADV. **completely, fully, totally | partially**
- PREP. **in** *The seeds need to be completely immersed in water.*

2 concentrate completely on sth
- ADV. **deeply** *Clare and Phil were deeply immersed in conversation.* | **completely, totally | in** *For six months I totally immersed myself in my work.*

immigrant *noun*
- ADJ. **illegal | foreign | Irish, Italian, Jewish, etc. | recent | would-be | first-generation, second-generation** *First-generation immigrants may dream of returning 'home'; their children say Britain is their home.*
- QUANT. **flood, influx, wave**
- VERB + IMMIGRANT **accept, welcome | deport, return** *ships laden with would-be immigrants who were forcibly returned*
- IMMIGRANT + VERB **arrive, enter sth** *immigrants seeking to enter the country* | **come from sth | settle (sth)** *European immigrants settled much of Australia.*
- IMMIGRANT + NOUN **community, family, group, population | worker | labour**

- PREP. **~ from, ~ to** *She was the daughter of Chinese immigrants to America.*

immigration *noun*

1 coming to live in a country
- ADJ. **illegal | large-scale, mass**
- VERB + IMMIGRATION **control, restrict** *laws restricting immigration into the US*
- IMMIGRATION + NOUN **control, law, policy, rules | authority, officer, official, service**
- PREP. **~ from** *There was a sudden increase in immigration from Eastern Europe.*

2 (*also* **immigration control**) at a port/airport
- VERB + IMMIGRATION **go/pass through** *We landed at Heathrow and went through customs and immigration.*
- IMMIGRATION + NOUN **checks, formalities, procedures** *calls for tighter immigration procedures*

immobile *adj.*
- VERBS **lie, remain, sit, stand** *She seemed scarcely to breathe as she lay immobile.* | **become | hold sb, leave sb** *For a moment shock held her immobile.* ◊ *The accident left him totally immobile.*
- ADV. **completely, perfectly, totally, utterly | almost, virtually | relatively**

immoral *adj.*
- VERBS **be, seem, sound | condemn sth as, consider sth, regard sth as, think sth** *He condemned the government's action as immoral.*
- ADV. **downright, quite, totally, utterly | rather, slightly, vaguely** *That sounds vaguely immoral.*

immortal *adj.*
- VERBS **be, seem | become**
- ADV. **almost, virtually | effectively** *The wild cocoa tree is effectively immortal.* | **potentially**

immortality *noun*
- ADJ. **personal** *Some religions include a doctrine of personal immortality.*
- VERB + IMMORTALITY **achieve | confer, give sb** *It was in the power of the gods to confer immortality upon mortals.*
- PHRASES **the immortality of the soul** *They believe in the immortality of the soul.*

immune *adj.*

1 protected against a disease
- VERBS **be, seem | become | remain, stay | make sb** *The vaccination doesn't necessarily make you completely immune.*
- ADV. **completely, totally**
- PREP. **to** *Many people are immune to this disease.*

2 not affected by sth
- VERBS **appear, be, prove, seem | become | remain**
- ADV. **completely, entirely, quite, totally, wholly | by no means, far from** *Children are far from immune to the virus of cruelty that is latent in all human beings.* | **almost, largely, virtually | relatively**
- PREP. **to** *She's quite immune to criticism.*

immunity *noun*

1 protection against disease
- ADJ. **strong | acquired, natural**
- VERB + IMMUNITY **have** *The island's inhabitants had no immunity to the diseases carried by the explorers and quickly succumbed.* | **lack | acquire, build up, develop** *Once you have had a cold you build up immunity to that particular virus.* | **stimulate** *the use of vaccines to stimu-*

late immunity | **boost** | **lower** *High levels of stress may lower your immunity to common illnesses.*
• IMMUNITY + VERB **develop** *A strong immunity to reinfection develops after one year.*
• PREP. **~ against/to** *The newcomers lacked immunity against local strains of the disease.*

2 protection from danger/punishment
• ADJ. **complete**, **total** | **effective** | **diplomatic**, **legal**, **parliamentary** *Several ministers were stripped of parliamentary immunity as a prelude to facing corruption charges.* | **public interest** *The newspaper claimed public interest immunity when threatened with prosecution for publishing the story* (= claimed that the public had a right to know about the story).
• VERB + IMMUNITY **enjoy** | **claim**, **seek** | **confer**, **give sb**, **grant** (**sb**), **guarantee** (**sb**), **provide** | **abolish**, **lift**, **strip sb of** *The Supreme Court lifted the company's immunity from criminal prosecution.* | **lose**
• PREP. **~ from** *Unions were granted immunity from prosecution for non-violent acts.*

immunize *verb*

• ADV. **routinely**
• PREP. **against** *Children have been routinely immunized against polio since 1958.* **with** *They immunized some mice with a dose of the live vaccine.*

impact *noun*

1 effect/impression
• ADJ. **big**, **considerable**, **dramatic**, **enormous**, **great**, **high**, **huge**, **important**, **main**, **major**, **massive**, **powerful**, **profound**, **real**, **significant**, **strong**, **substantial**, **tremendous** *a high-impact message aimed at changing high risk behaviour among drug-users* | **limited**, **marginal**, **minimal/minimum**, **negligible** | **full** *The industrial north of the country felt the full impact of the recession.* | **maximum** *We'll show you how to dress for maximum impact at the all-important audition.* | **overall**, **total** | **growing**, **increasing** | **added** | **disproportionate** | **uneven** *the uneven impact of the debt crisis on developing countries* | **aggregate**, **combined**, **cumulative** *considering the cumulative impact of a series of damaging events* | **decisive** | **direct** *The railways made a direct physical impact on the landscape.* | **immediate**, **instant** | **initial**, **short-term** | **lasting**, **long-term** | **far-reaching**, **wider** *It is important to appreciate the wider impact and implications of this proposal.* | **future**, **likely**, **possible**, **potential** | **beneficial**, **favourable**, **positive** | **adverse**, **catastrophic**, **damaging**, **devastating**, **disastrous**, **heavy**, **negative**, **serious**, **severe** | **human** *The severest human impact on the dolphins has been the loss of habitat.* | **personal** *The personal impact of party leaders has been very important.* | **physical**, **visual** *seeking to reduce the visual impact of wind farms on the landscape* | **cultural**, **ecological**, **economic**, **emotional**, **environmental**, **financial**, **health**, **political**, **psychological**, **social** *The environmental impact of power generation is being assessed.*
• VERB + IMPACT **achieve**, **create**, **exert**, **have**, **make** *Variations in the interest rate will have an impact on the whole housing market.* ◊ *You certainly made a big impact on Carter.* | **feel** *The initial impact of the reforms will be felt most keenly in primary schools.* | **analyse**, **assess**, **consider**, **evaluate**, **examine**, **explore**, **judge**, **measure**, **monitor**, **study** *It is difficult to judge the likely impact of the changes on employment patterns.* | **enhance**, **increase**, **maximize** | **alleviate**, **cushion**, **lessen**, **minimize**, **reduce**, **soften** *We are trying to minimize the impact of price rises on our customers.* | **diminish**, **lessen**, **reduce**, **weaken** *Listening to the speech through an interpreter lessened its impact somewhat.* | **lose** *When peace returned, the hardline message lost much of its impact.* | **resist**, **withstand** *This section explores how mothers resist*

the impact of poverty on the health of their children. | **be concerned about** | **appreciate** | **highlight** | **address** | **predict** | **reflect** *Architecturally, these churches reflected the impact of the Renaissance.*
• PREP. **under the ~ of** *Manufacturing fell sharply under the impact of the recession.* | **~ on/upon** *to highlight the impact of technology on working practices*

2 act/force of one object hitting another
• ADJ. **full** | **initial**
• VERB + IMPACT **take** *The front coach of the train took the full impact of the crash.* | **feel** | **absorb** *A well-designed sports shoe should absorb the impact on the 28 bones in each foot.* | **lessen**, **soften** *Air bags are designed to soften the impact for crash victims.* | **survive**, **withstand** *The crew of six may have survived the initial impact, but the whole plane went up in flames seconds later.*
• IMPACT + VERB **occur** *Impact occurred seconds after the pilot signalled for help.* | **knock sb/sth ...** *The impact knocked him off balance.*
• IMPACT + NOUN **speed** | **crater** *Small meteorites have left impact craters all over the planet's surface.*
• PREP. **on ~** *The front of the car had crumpled on impact.*
• PHRASES **the moment/point/time of impact**

impair *verb*

• ADV. **dramatically**, **gravely**, **greatly**, **seriously**, **severely**, **significantly**, **substantially** | **directly** *factors which directly impair memory*
• PHRASES **badly impaired** *Her sight is badly impaired.* **hearing/mentally/visually impaired** *the problems faced by people who are hearing impaired*

impartial *adj.*

• VERBS **be** | **remain** *The judge must remain impartial.*
• ADV. **completely**, **quite**, **strictly**, **totally** | **fairly**, **reasonably**, **relatively**

impartiality *noun*

• ADJ. **complete** | **due** *The BBC must ensure that due impartiality is preserved in its news programmes.*
• VERB + IMPARTIALITY **guarantee**, **maintain**, **preserve** | **compromise**, **prejudice** *The newspaper sought to present a range of opinions without compromising its impartiality.*

impassable *adj.*

• VERBS **be** | **become** | **remain** | **make sth** | **think sth** *The river's broad mudflats were thought completely impassable.*
• ADV. **completely**, **totally** *The mud made the roads impassable.* | **almost**, **virtually**

impasse *noun*

• ADJ. **diplomatic**, **legal**, **political**
• VERB + IMPASSE **reach** *Negotiations seemed to have reached an impasse.* | **break**, **end**, **overcome**, **resolve**
• PHRASES **a way out of an impasse** *The proposal offered both sides a way out of the diplomatic impasse.*

impassive *adj.*

• VERBS **be**, **sit**, **stand** | **become** | **remain**
• ADV. **completely**, **quite**, **totally** | **almost** *Her expression was cool, almost impassive.* | **rather** | **usually** *A smile transformed her usually impassive face.*

impatience *noun*

• ADJ. **growing**, **mounting** | **slight** | **barely concealed/controlled**
• QUANT. **hint**, **note**, **touch**
• VERB + IMPATIENCE **feel** *She felt a growing impa-*

tience. | **express**, **show** *He was trying hard not to show his impatience.* | **contain**, **control**, **curb**, **restrain** *unable to contain her impatience* | **conceal**, **hide**
- IMPATIENCE + VERB **grow**
- PREP. **with** ~ *He stamped his feet as he waited with barely concealed impatience for the telephone.* | ~ **at** *He expressed impatience at the slow rate of progress.* ~ **for** *his impatience for her to return* ~ **with** *impatience with the slowness of change*
- PHRASES **a gesture of impatience** *He shook his head in a gesture of impatience.* **a sigh of impatience** *He bit back a sigh of impatience.* **signs of impatience** *The children were beginning to show signs of impatience.*

impatient *adj.*

- VERBS **appear**, **be**, **feel**, **seem**, **sound** | **become**, **get**, **grow** *The children were growing impatient.*
- ADV. **extremely**, **really**, **very** | **increasingly** | **almost** | **a bit**, **a little**, **rather**, **slightly**, **somewhat**, **a touch** *He spoke in a somewhat impatient tone.* | **suddenly**
- PREP. **about** *She's getting impatient about the delays.* **at** *Sean was a touch impatient at the time Valerie devoted to her mother.* **for** *impatient for change* **with** *Sometimes he is very impatient with his wife.*

impede *verb*

- ADV. **greatly**, **seriously**, **significantly** *The bad weather seriously impeded our progress.*

impediment *noun*

- ADJ. **great**, **major**, **serious** | **absolute** | **chief**, **main** | **lawful**, **legal** *There are no legal impediments to their appealing against the decision.*
- VERB + IMPEDIMENT **be**, **constitute**, **provide** | **remove** *The agreement is designed to remove impediments to trade between the two countries.*
- PREP. ~**to** *Their boycott of the talks constitutes a serious impediment to peace negotiations.*

impenetrable *adj.*

1 impossible to enter/get through
- VERBS **appear**, **be**, **look**, **seem** | **become** | **find sth** *They found the jungle virtually impenetrable.*
- ADV. **almost**, **nearly**, **virtually**

2 impossible to understand
- VERBS **be**, **seem** | **become** | **remain** | **find sth**
- ADV. **almost**, **virtually** | **somewhat** *I find his style somewhat impenetrable.* | **seemingly**
- PREP. **to** *The language of this document would be impenetrable to anyone except a specialist.*

imperative *adj.*

- VERBS **be**, **seem** | **become** | **remain** *It remains imperative that all sides should be involved in the talks.* | **make sth** *The collapse of the wall made it imperative to keep the water out by some other means.* | **consider sth** *We consider it absolutely imperative to start work immediately.*
- ADV. **absolutely**

imperceptible *adj.*

- VERBS **be**
- ADV. **almost**, **virtually** *His head moved in an almost imperceptible nod.*
- PREP. **to** *The slight change in the taste was imperceptible to most people.*

imperfect *adj.*

- VERBS **be** | **remain** *Our understanding of cancer remains imperfect.*

- ADV. **highly**, **very** *The system is highly imperfect.* | **rather**, **slightly** *These goods are slightly imperfect.*

imperfection *noun*

- ADJ. **moral**, **physical**
- VERB + IMPERFECTION **cover up** | **reveal**, **show up**
- PREP. ~ **in** *Careful inspection in daylight revealed imperfections in the paintwork.*

imperialism *noun*

- ADJ. **American**, **British**, **Roman**, **Western**, etc. | **capitalist**, **cultural**, **economic**

impersonal *adj.*

1 not showing friendly human feelings
- VERBS **be**, **seem** | **become** | **find sth** *I find the atmosphere there rather impersonal.*
- ADV. **very** | **totally** | **a bit**, **rather** | **coldly**, **coolly** *His voice was coolly impersonal.* | **oddly**

2 not referring to any particular person
- VERBS **be** | **keep sth** *I think we should keep things entirely impersonal.*
- ADV. **absolutely**, **completely**, **entirely**, **totally**

impertinence *noun*

- ADJ. **gross** *I consider his remark a gross impertinence.*
- VERB + IMPERTINENCE **have** *She had the impertinence to suggest I needed a holiday.*
- PHRASES **the height of impertinence**

impertinent *adj.*

- VERBS **be**, **seem** | **get** *Don't you get impertinent with me!* | **find sth** *She found the question highly impertinent.*
- ADV. **highly**, **very** | **slightly**, **somewhat**

impervious *adj.*

- VERBS **appear**, **be**, **seem** | **become** | **remain**
- ADV. **completely**, **quite**, **totally**, **wholly** *He was completely impervious to criticism.* | **almost**, **largely**, **virtually** | **apparently**
- PREP. **to** *She was impervious to his charms.*

impetus *noun*

- ADJ. **considerable**, **great**, **powerful**, **strong** | **main**, **major** | **immediate**, **initial**, **original** | **fresh**, **new**, **renewed** *Each new rumour added fresh impetus to the smear campaign.* | **added**, **extra**, **further** | **necessary** *His disappointment in the World Championships provided the necessary impetus to give everything for this final race.*
- VERB + IMPETUS **add**, **give sb/sth**, **provide** (**sb/sth with**) *The slope added impetus to his speed.* | **gain**, **gather**, **receive** *The movement is steadily gaining impetus.* | **lose** *With the death of its founder, the campaign lost much of its impetus.*
- IMPETUS + VERB **come from sth** *Much of the impetus for change came from customers' opinions.*
- PREP. ~ **behind sb/sth** *The main impetus behind the move west was to find gold and other minerals.* ~ **for** *the impetus for arms control agreements* ~ **towards** *the impetus towards urban development*

impinge *verb*

- ADV. **seriously** *actions which seriously impinge on other people's personal freedoms* | **hardly** | **directly**, **indirectly**
- PREP. **on/upon** *measures which directly or indirectly impinge upon women's lives*

implausible adj.

● VERBS **be, seem, sound | consider** sth, **deem** sth *These results might be considered implausible.*
● ADV. **highly | quite, totally, wholly** *This idea is totally implausible.* | **increasingly** *He gave a series of increasingly implausible excuses.* | **not altogether, not entirely | pretty, rather, somewhat | inherently**

implement noun

● ADJ. **agricultural, farm, garden, kitchen, surgical | sharp** *Make sure that all sharp implements, such as scythes, have covers.* | **flint, metal, stone, wooden**

implement verb

● ADV. **fully, properly** *These policies have never been fully implemented.* | **partially | adequately | actually** *The proposed changes were never actually implemented.* | **widely** *These reforms have now been widely implemented in schools.* | **effectively, successfully | quickly**
● VERB + IMPLEMENT **agree to, decide to, intend to, promise to | attempt to, seek to, try to | fail to** *The government failed to implement the plan.* | **refuse to | be forced to, be obliged to | be difficult to, be hard to** *The decision will be difficult to implement.*

implementation noun

● ADJ. **effective, successful | complete, full | detailed** *Detailed implementation of the plans was left to the regional offices.* | **strict | smooth** *We will consult widely to ensure smooth implementation.* | **practical** *The practical implementation of the regulations proved difficult.* | **early, immediate | gradual | policy**
● VERB + IMPLEMENTATION **achieve, ensure, secure** *To achieve implementation of the programme is a long, slow task.* | **monitor, oversee, supervise** *The UN is to supervise the implementation of the peace treaty.* | **consider, discuss**
● IMPLEMENTATION + NOUN **plan | process** *The restructuring will take place in phases, to simplify the implementation process.* | **problem**

implicate verb be implicated in sth

● ADV. **deeply, heavily, strongly** *These groups are very strongly implicated in the violence.* | **directly**

implication noun

1 possible effect/result
● ADJ. **considerable, crucial, enormous, important, major, massive, strong | main | deeper, fundamental, profound | broad, far-reaching, wider** *discussing the broader implications of the medical plan* | **full** *Now they realized the full implications of the new system.* | **direct | clear, obvious | underlying | general | further | possible, potential | future, long-term | grave, serious | disturbing, frightening, ominous, sinister | adverse, damaging, negative | interesting | radical, revolutionary | practical** *These results have important practical implications.* | **commercial, constitutional, economic, educational, environmental, ethical, financial, ideological, legal, moral, philosophical, political, psychological, social** *the constitutional implications of a royal divorce* | **cost, health, policy, resource, safety, security, tax**
● VERB + IMPLICATION **carry, have** *The emphasis on testing leads to greater stress among students and carries implications of failure.* | **grasp, realize, understand | assess, consider, examine, explore, ponder, study** *You need to consider the legal implications before you publish anything.* | **digest | discuss | explain | accept** *a society that fully accepts the implications of disability* | **reject | ignore**

● IMPLICATION + VERB **arise** *Several interesting implications arise from these developments.* | **be involved** *Given the resource implications involved, the plan will have to be scaled down.*
● PREP. **~ about** *disturbing implications about the company's future* **~ for** *The research has far-reaching implications for medicine as a whole.*

2 sth suggested but not said openly
● ADJ. **clear, obvious** *The implication is clear: young females do better if they mate with a new male.* | **possible** *His remark seemed to have various possible implications.* | **unspoken**
● VERB + IMPLICATION **carry, have | understand | digest** *Brian paused for a moment while he digested the implications of this statement.* | **resent** *I resent the implication that I don't care about my father.*
● PREP. **by ~** *In refusing to believe our story, he is saying by implication that we are lying.*

imply verb

● ADV. **clearly, heavily, strongly | simply | generally, normally, usually | automatically | not necessarily** *This does not necessarily imply that children achieve better results in private schools.* | **in no way** *They believe that submission in no way implies inferiority.*
● VERB + IMPLY **seem to** *The letter seems to imply that the minister knew about the business deals.* | **intend to, mean to** *I never meant to imply any criticism.* | **take sth to** *This statement should not be taken to imply that the government is exonerated of all blame.*
● PHRASES **express or implied** *the express or implied terms of the contract*

import noun

● ADJ. **main, major | foreign, overseas | cheap | annual** *The value of annual imports rose rapidly.* | **net** *the UK's net imports of food* | **total | essential | luxury | illegal | agricultural, car, coal, energy, food, grain, oil, steel, etc.**
● VERB + IMPORT **boost, increase** *pressure on the government to stimulate the faltering economy and boost imports* | **curb, cut, reduce, restrict | discourage | control | block, prevent, stop | ban, prohibit** *The government decided to prohibit the import of toxic waste.* | **finance** *Most of their oil revenues are used to finance imports of consumer and capital goods.* | **replace** *The industry aims both to increase exports and replace imports.*
● IMPORT + VERB **grow, increase, rise | drop, fall | be valued at sth, total sth** *Imports were valued at £516 million last month.* | **account for sth** *Imports of foodstuffs accounted for a small proportion of total imports.*
● IMPORT + NOUN **ban, control, restrictions | duty, tariff | price** *rising import prices* | **licence | quota** *A restricted import quota was set for meat products.* | **penetration** *greater import penetration of the domestic market*
● PREP. **~ from** *America has cut its oil imports from the Middle East by 73%.* **~ into** *Special duties were imposed on imports into the republic.*
● PHRASES **a ban/restriction on imports, the demand for imports, a fall/rise in imports**
⇒ Note at PER CENT (for more verbs)

import verb

● ADV. **directly | illegally, legally | specially**
● PREP. **from** *The store's croissants are imported directly from France.* **into** *These dogs are illegally imported into the country.* **to** *goods that are imported to Britain*

importance noun

● ADJ. **cardinal, central, considerable, critical, crucial, enormous, especial, extreme, fundamental, great, high,** immense, key, major, outstanding, overriding, overwhelming, paramount, particular, primary, prime, profound, real, special, supreme, tremendous, vital | first, greatest, highest, utmost *This information is of the first importance.* ◇ *It is of the utmost importance that you arrive on time.* | growing, increasing | declining *the declining importance of manufacturing industry* | lesser, limited, marginal, minor, secondary | direct | general | added | immediate | continued/continuing, lasting | equal | relative | intrinsic | obvious | perceived *differences in the perceived importance of the different subjects in the curriculum* | potential | public | international, national | practical | theoretical | symbolic *the symbolic importance of iron in German culture* | archaeological, commercial, constitutional, cultural, ecological, economic, environmental, historical, legal, military, political, social, strategic

• VERB + IMPORTANCE **have** *These finds have considerable archaeological importance.* | **assume, take on** *Childcare schemes take on an added importance at a time of national recession.* | **grow in, increase in, rise in** | **decline in, diminish in, fall in** *The overseas markets have now declined in importance.* | **attach, give sth, place** *To what objectives do you attach most importance?* ◇ *the importance placed on cleanliness* | **accept, acknowledge, appreciate, be aware of, grasp, realize, recognize, see, understand** *People were aware of the importance of working with nature.* | **demonstrate, illustrate, indicate, point to, reflect, show, suggest** *Figure 2.2 shows the relative importance of the different service industries.* | **assert** | **deny** | **confirm** | **draw attention to, emphasize, highlight, point up, promote, stress, underline** *The manual stresses the importance of regular maintenance.* | **diminish, downplay, minimize, play down, underplay** *She was inclined to play down the importance of her own role in the affair.* | **exaggerate, overestimate** | **underestimate, undervalue** *Don't underestimate the importance of neat presentation.* | **increase** | **reduce** | **consider, discuss** | **explain** | **cast/throw doubt on, doubt, question** *No one can seriously question the political importance of the environment.* | **forget, ignore, overlook**

• IMPORTANCE + VERB **arise from sth, lie in sth** *The town's importance lies in the richness and quality of its architecture.* | **depend on sth**

• PREP. **of … ~** *The railways were of crucial importance in opening up the American West.* | **~ for** *an area of enormous importance for wildlife* **~ to** *the importance to the country of a healthy economy*

• PHRASES **in order of importance** *Deal with the issues in order of importance.* **a matter of importance**

important *adj.*

• VERBS **be, seem** | **become** | **remain** | **make sth** *This is what makes our work so important.* | **believe sth, consider sth, deem sth, regard sth as, see sth as, think sth** *These ideas are considered enormously important.*

• ADV. **critically, crucially, enormously, especially, extremely, hugely, most, particularly, really, terribly, very, vitally** *This is most important: you must deliver the letter to Johnson himself.* | **increasingly** | **doubly** | **fairly, quite** | **equally** *These two factors are equally important.* | **internationally, regionally** *an internationally important site for these rare birds* | **economically, functionally, historically, politically, strategically** *historically important buildings*

• PREP. **for** *It's important for you to understand this.* **to** *Spending time with my children is important to me.* ◇ *The work of the intelligence services was crucially important to victory in the war.*

impose *verb*

• ADV. **effectively** *The terms of the contract were effectively imposed rather than agreed.* | **simply** *New technology* cannot be used successfully if it is simply imposed on an unwilling workforce. | **centrally** *a centrally imposed school curriculum* | **externally** *the pressure of having to meet externally imposed targets* | **artificially** *Motivation to learn must come from the child; it cannot be artificially imposed.*

• VERB + IMPOSE **seek to, strive to, try to**

• PREP. **on/upon** *The government has imposed a ban on the sale of handguns.*

imposition *noun*

1 act of imposing sth

• VERB + IMPOSITION **justify** *Several reasons were put forward to justify the imposition of censorship.* | **oppose, resist** | **resent**

• PREP. **~ on** *resisting the imposition of VAT on fuel*

2 unreasonable thing sb expects you to do

• ADJ. **unacceptable, unwelcome**

• PREP. **~ on** *She felt the journey to be an unwelcome imposition on her time.*

impossible *adj.*

1 not possible

• VERBS **appear, be, look, prove, seem, sound** | **become** | **remain** | **make sth, render sth** *Darkness made it impossible to continue.* | **believe sth, consider sth, deem sth, find sth, regard sth as, see sth as, think sth** *I found his offer impossible to resist.*

• ADV. **absolutely, completely, quite, totally, utterly** | **frankly** *Cooking for forty would be frankly impossible without my new assistant.* | **just, simply** *I'm really sorry. It's just impossible.* | **by no means, far from, not altogether** *a desirable and far from impossible objective to achieve* | **almost, more or less, near, nearly, next to, nigh on, practically, virtually, well-nigh** *It was well-nigh impossible for him to convince her that he was right.* | **pretty** | **effectively** | **literally** | **apparently, seemingly** | **theoretically** | **clearly, obviously** | **equally** *Both options are equally impossible.* | **generally** | **hitherto, previously** *With the new equipment we will be able to accomplish hitherto impossible tasks.* | **ultimately** | **economically, financially, logically, logistically, mathematically, politically, physically, scientifically, socially, technically** *The high cost of childcare made returning to work economically impossible.*

• PREP. **for** *The situation is quite impossible for us.* ◇ *It's impossible for me to say.*

2 bad-tempered; difficult to talk to/deal with

• VERBS **be** | **become** | **find sb** *I find her impossible.*

• ADV. **bloody** (*taboo*), **really** | **absolutely, completely, quite, totally** *You can be absolutely impossible at times!* | **just**

impotence *noun*

• ADJ. **total** | **relative** | **male** | **political, sexual**

• PHRASES **a feeling/sense of impotence** *Violence may result from a sense of impotence.*

impotent *adj.*

1 without enough power/influence

• VERBS **be, feel, prove** | **remain** | **leave sb, make sb, render sb** *Companies are rendered impotent by all the rules and regulations.*

• ADV. **completely, quite, totally** | **virtually** | **politically**

• PREP. **against** *They were virtually impotent against the power of the large companies.*

2 not capable of having sex

• VERBS **be** | **become** | **leave sb, make sb** *The operation left him impotent.*

• ADV. **sexually**

impracticable adj.

- VERBS **be, prove, seem | become | make sth, render sth** *The damage it would cause makes the idea utterly impracticable.* | **consider sth, find sth** *This idea was considered completely impracticable.*
- ADV. **highly | completely, quite, totally, utterly**

impractical adj.

1 not sensible or reasonable
- VERBS **be, prove** *Such a solution proved impractical.* | **become | make sth** *The weight of the machine makes lifting it impractical.* | **consider sth, deem sth, find sth, regard sth as** *They found his ideas impractical.*
- ADV. **highly, hopelessly** *The long flowing dress was highly impractical.* | **completely, downright, entirely, quite, totally, wholly | rather, somewhat | fundamentally** *a fundamentally impractical design* | **obviously**

2 not good at everyday jobs
- VERBS **be, seem**
- ADV. **hopelessly** *He was hopelessly impractical when it came to planning new projects.*

imprecise adj.

- VERBS **be, seem | become**
- ADV. **extremely, very | fairly, rather, somewhat | notoriously** *'Breach of the peace' is a notoriously imprecise notion.*
- PREP. **about** *She was rather imprecise about the cost of the trip.*

impress verb

- ADV. **really** *His work really impressed me.*
- VERB + IMPRESS **be determined to, be keen to, hope to, want to | attempt to, seek to, try to | be designed to | fail to** *The results failed to impress us.*
- PREP. **with** *She impressed us with both the depth and range of her knowledge.*
- PHRASES **an attempt/effort to impress sb, be easily impressed** *I was young and easily impressed.*

impressed adj.

- VERBS **be, look, seem, sound**
- ADV. **deeply, enormously, especially, extremely, greatly, immensely, mightily, much, overwhelmingly, particularly, profoundly, really, terribly, tremendously, very (much)** *I was not overly impressed by the proposals.* | **fairly, mildly, quite | enough, sufficiently** *The prince was impressed enough to commission a portrait from the artist.* | **genuinely | immediately, instantly | favourably | duly, suitably** *He mentioned a few famous acquaintances, and we were suitably impressed.* | **clearly, obviously**
- PREP. **by** *The manager was favourably impressed by Jo's work.* **with** *He was very impressed with her house.*

impression noun

1 idea/feeling/opinion about sth
- ADJ. **distinct, firm, strong | main, overriding, overwhelming | convincing | clear, vivid | fleeting, vague | accurate | distorted, erroneous, false, mistaken, misleading, spurious, wrong | good** *The village gives a good impression of what a medieval city would have looked like.* | **favourable | negative | opposite | early, first, immediate, initial** *First impressions can be misleading.* | **final | general, overall | general, widespread** *There is a widespread impression that schooling needs to be improved.* | **public | personal, subjective**
- VERB + IMPRESSION **form, gain, get, have, obtain, receive** *I got the distinct impression that you disliked her.* | **convey, create, give (sb), leave sb with, provide (sb**

with) *The book leaves you with a distorted impression of politics.* | **maintain** *She was trying to maintain the impression that she was in control.* | **confirm | heighten, reinforce, strengthen | avoid** *It was difficult to avoid the impression that he was assisting them for selfish reasons.* | **correct** *I must correct a false impression that I gave you just now.* | **record** *She recorded her impressions of the city in her diary.*
- IMPRESSION + VERB **count** *When it comes to finding a partner, first impressions do count.*
- PREP. **under a/the** *~ I was under the impression that you weren't coming until tomorrow.* | *~ about I had the wrong impression about him.* *~ as to mistaken impressions as to the strength of the market*

2 effect that an experience/person has on sb/sth
- ADJ. **considerable, deep, powerful, profound, strong, tremendous | superficial | abiding, indelible, lasting | excellent, favourable, good, great | bad, poor, unfavourable | false, misleading, wrong | right** *If you want to create the right impression, I suggest you wear a suit.* | **first, immediate** *The new striker failed to make an immediate impression on the team.*
- VERB + IMPRESSION **create, leave, make**
- PREP. **~on/upon** *The day's events left a lasting impression on them.*

3 drawing
- ADJ. **artist's**
- VERB + IMPRESSION **issue** *The police have issued an artist's impression of the attacker.*

4 amusing copy of sb
- ADJ. **good, reasonable**
- VERB + IMPRESSION **do** *He does some very good impressions of pop stars.*

5 mark left on an object
- VERB + IMPRESSION **bear** *The sealing wax bore the impression of a sailing ship.*

impressionable adj.

- VERBS **be, seem**
- ADV. **highly, very** *He is in a highly impressionable state.*

impressive adj.

- VERBS **be, look, seem | become | remain | make sth** *The fact that he is so young makes his achievements even more impressive.* | **find sth**
- ADV. **decidedly, enormously, extremely, highly, hugely, immensely, mightily, most, particularly, really, tremendously, truly, very** *The new building looks most impressive.* | **far from, hardly, not unduly** *He was far from impressive in his semi-final against Federer.* | **fairly, pretty, quite, rather | undeniably, undoubtedly | suitably** *A large portico provides a suitably impressive entrance to the chapel.* | **equally, similarly** *The scenery to the north of the lake is equally impressive.* | **consistently | technically, visually** *The film is technically impressive, but lacks real excitement.*

imprint noun

- ADJ. **indelible, permanent | unmistakable**
- VERB + IMPRINT **bear** *The ceramics bore the imprint of Luca della Robbia.* | **leave, make** *Glaciation has left a permanent imprint on the landscape.* ◇ *(figurative) The sinister atmosphere of the place left an indelible imprint on my memory.*
- PREP. **~on/upon**

imprison verb

- ADV. **virtually** *Her fear virtually imprisoned her in her home.* | **falsely, unlawfully, wrongfully, wrongly** *working on behalf of people who have been wrongly imprisoned* | **briefly, temporarily**

- PREP. **for** *He was imprisoned for debt.* **in** *He was imprisoned in a local castle.*

imprisonment noun

- ADJ. **six months', ten years', etc.** | **life** | **indefinite** | **immediate** | **false, unlawful, wrongful**
- VERB + IMPRISONMENT **be liable to, face** *The Act states that anyone committing the offence is liable to imprisonment.* ◇ *The coup leaders could face life imprisonment.* | **receive, suffer** *Those who were captured suffered imprisonment.* | **be released from** | **sentence sb to**
- IMPRISONMENT + VERB **be suspended for sth** *The judge sentenced her to 6 months imprisonment suspended for 15 months.*
- PREP. **~ for** *imprisonment for illegal possession of weapons*
- PHRASES **(carry) a penalty of ... imprisonment** *The offence carries a penalty of 2 years' imprisonment.* **imprisonment without trial, a period/sentence/term of imprisonment, punishable by imprisonment** *a felony punishable by imprisonment*

improbable adj.

- VERBS **appear, be, look, seem, sound** | **become** | **make sth** *These new facts make the theory improbable.*
- ADV. **extremely, highly, very, wildly** *a wildly improbable idea* | **completely, quite** | **not altogether** | **fairly, rather, slightly** | **inherently, intrinsically** *There is nothing inherently improbable in the idea.*

improper adj.

- VERBS **be, seem** | **consider sth, regard sth as, think sth** *She thought it quite improper for a woman to ride a motorbike.*
- ADV. **highly, most** | **entirely, quite**

impropriety noun

- ADJ. **gross** | **constitutional, financial, procedural** *(law),* **sexual**
- VERB + IMPROPRIETY **commit** *Several employees were suspended amid allegations that financial improprieties had been committed.* | **accuse sb of** *Parliament was accused of constitutional impropriety.*
- PHRASES **a suggestion of impropriety** *There is no suggestion of impropriety by the minister.*

improve verb

- ADV. **considerably, dramatically, greatly, immeasurably, materially, radically, significantly, substantially, vastly** | **markedly, noticeably** | **marginally, slightly** | **rapidly** | **steadily**
- VERB + IMPROVE **continue to** *The weather should continue to improve over the weekend.* | **strive to, try to** *trying to improve their working conditions* | **help to** | **be designed to**
- PHRASES **aimed at improving sth** *measures aimed at improving government efficiency* **an attempt/effort to improve sth, an incentive to improve sth** *Workers need to be given an incentive to improve their performance.* **much improved** *We now offer a much improved service to our customers.*

improvement noun

- ADJ. **big, considerable, enormous, great, huge, marked, massive, material, radical, remarkable, significant, substantial, vast** | **marginal, minor, modest, slight, small** | **noticeable, obvious, visible** | **actual, definite, distinct, genuine, real, tangible** | **measurable** | **dramatic, rapid, sharp** | **gradual, incremental, steady** | **constant, continued, continuing, continuous, progressive, sustained** | **long-term** | **short-term** | **temporary** |

further | **all-round, general, overall** | **important, notable** | **much-needed, necessary** | **welcome, useful** | **positive, recent** | **immediate** | **desired, expected** | **suggested** *If suggested improvements are not carried out, we have the right to suspend the insurance cover.* | **intended** | **possible, potential** | **underlying** *Their policies have resulted in a definite underlying improvement in the economy.* | **moral** | **economic, educational, environmental, health, safety, social** | **organizational, productivity, quality, service, technical, technological** | **agricultural, land** | **ground, home, housing, rail, road, school** *The club will spend £300 000 on ground improvements.*
- VERB + IMPROVEMENT **be, constitute, reflect, represent** *The country's economic record since 1945 represents an improvement on the period between the world wars.* | **show** *Exports have showed some improvement.* | **need, require** | **carry out, effect, make** *He made a steady improvement and was released within 10 days of admission.* | **lead to, produce, provide, result in, yield** *The drug produced an improvement in all but one case.* | **achieve, bring (about), secure** *steps taken to secure improvement in pupils' attendance* | **seek** | **call for, demand** | **recommend, suggest** | **encourage, promote** | **announce, report** *Wholesalers reported an improvement in sales for the third quarter.* | **notice, see, witness** *With this exercise plan you will notice an enormous improvement in your stamina.* | **find** *No improvement was found after the tenth day of treatment.*
- IMPROVEMENT + VERB **take place** | **result from sth**
- IMPROVEMENT + NOUN **programme, scheme** *The proposed road improvement scheme involves bypassing several villages.* | **work** *The improvement work to houses will create jobs.*
- PREP. **~ in** *The new factory brought a huge improvement in working conditions.* **~ on/over/upon** *These results are a distinct improvement on last year's.* **~ to** *Several improvements were made to the design during its production run.*
- PHRASES **an area for/of improvement** *The new assessment system could pinpoint areas for improvement within the company.* **room/scope for improvement** *Their average marks have risen, but there is still room for improvement.* **signs of improvement** *The economy is showing signs of improvement.*

improvisation noun

- ADJ. **spontaneous** *Most of their music was spontaneous improvisation.* | **dramatic, musical** | **jazz** | **piano**

improvise verb

- ADV. **hastily** *We hastily improvised a screen out of an old blanket.*
- VERB + IMPROVISE **have to** *There isn't much equipment. We're going to have to improvise.*

impulse noun

1 sudden strong wish

- ADJ. **strong** | **irresistible** | **first, original** *My first impulse was to run away.* | **sudden** | **basic** | **instinctual, natural** | **repressed** | **conflicting, contradictory, contrary** | **aggressive, violent** | **creative** | **sexual**
- VERB + IMPULSE **feel, have** *She felt a sudden impulse to look to her left.* | **be subject to** *We are all subject to aggressive impulses.* | **be driven by** | **check, control, deny, fight (back/down), resist, restrain, stifle, suppress** *He fought down an impulse to scream.* | **give in to, obey, yield to** *She gave in to an impulse and took the money.* | **act on** *Acting on impulse, he picked up the keys and slipped them into his pocket.* | **buy sth on** *Some people will buy a puppy on impulse without any idea of what is involved.*

• IMPULSE + VERB **arise** *Impulses that are repeatedly denied can arise in other forms.*
• IMPULSE + NOUN **buy, purchase** *The little black designer dress had been an impulse buy.* | **buying** | **buyer**
• PREP. **on (an)~** *On an impulse, I went into the shop and bought a box of chocolates.* | **~towards** *basic impulses towards things such as food and drink*

2 movement of energy
• ADJ. **electrical, nerve/nervous**
• VERB + IMPULSE **transmit** *Nerve impulses are transmitted to the brain.* | **convert sth into, transform sth into** *Radio waves are converted into electrical impulses.*

3 sth that causes sb/sth to do sth
• ADJ. **positive** | **political, social**
• IMPULSE + VERB **lead (sb/sth) to sth, prompt (sb/sth to sth)** *the impulse that prompted economic change*
• PREP. **~ behind** *the impulse behind a concept* **~ for** *the impulse for social reform* **~ toward** *the political impulses towards joining a trade union*

inability noun

• ADJ. **apparent** | **complete, total** | **chronic** *the government's chronic inability to face facts* | **physical**
• VERB + INABILITY **be/feel frustrated by** *She felt increasingly frustrated by her inability to demonstrate her ideas.* | **overcome** *He has to overcome his inability to assert himself.*

inaccessible adj.

• VERBS **be, prove, seem** *The mouth of the river proved inaccessible.* | **become** | **remain** | **make sth, render sth** *A high wall made the building inaccessible.*
• ADV. **very** | **completely, entirely, quite, totally, utterly** | **almost, practically, virtually, largely** | **rather** | **effectively** | **otherwise**
• PREP. **by** *areas inaccessible by road* **to** *The hall is inaccessible to wheelchair users.*

inaccuracy noun

• ADJ. **major, material, significant** | **factual, historical**
• VERB + INACCURACY **contain** | **be fraught with, be full of** *Reference works on that country, when available, are full of inaccuracies.* | **correct** *I am writing to correct factual inaccuracies contained in your article of June 3rd.*
• PREP. **~in** *inaccuracies in reporting*

inaccurate adj.

• VERBS **be, prove** | **become**
• ADV. **extremely, grossly, hopelessly, seriously, terribly, very, wildly** *a wildly inaccurate account of events* | **quite, totally, wholly** | **a bit, rather, slightly, somewhat** *These figures are somewhat inaccurate.* | **notoriously** *Maps of the region are notoriously inaccurate.* | **historically** *It was good drama, but historically inaccurate.*

inactive adj.

• VERBS **be** | **become** | **remain**
• ADV. **totally** *He had been totally inactive for two weeks.* | **fairly, relatively** | **physically, sexually** | **economically, politically**

inactivity noun

• ADJ. **relative** *Her most brilliant work was done during several months of relative inactivity.* | **economic, political** | **enforced** *It was good to be home again after the enforced inactivity of the hospital bed.*
• PHRASES **a period of inactivity** *The job entailed long periods of inactivity.*

inadequacy noun

• ADJ. **total** | **fundamental** | **glaring, obvious** | **personal** | **sexual, social** | **theoretical**
• VERB + INADEQUACY **demonstrate, expose, highlight, point out/to, reveal, show (up)** *She rightly points to the inadequacy of the argument.* ◇ *The test soon revealed several inadequacies in the equipment.* | **realize, recognize, see** *I now see the inadequacy of the explanation.* | **admit to** *His advice was to be defensive and never admit to any inadequacy.* | **cover up, disguise, hide** *They possibly falsified the results to cover up the inadequacies of their theory.* | **overcome** *Clear legislative reform is needed to overcome the inadequacies of the current situation.*
• INADEQUACY + VERB **arise from sth, stem from sth**
• PREP. **~in** *inadequacies in educational facilities*
• PHRASES **a feeling/sense of inadequacy**

inadequate adj.

1 not good enough
• VERBS **appear, be, look, prove, seem** | **become** | **consider sth, find sth, judge sth, regard sth as, think sth** *These precautions have been judged inadequate.*
• ADV. **deeply, grossly, hopelessly, ludicrously, pitifully, ridiculously, seriously, very, woefully** *His wages were pitifully inadequate for the needs of his growing family.* | **completely, entirely, quite, totally, utterly, wholly** | **increasingly** | **somewhat** | **clearly, manifestly, obviously, patently, plainly** | **curiously** | **notoriously**
• PREP. **at** *People, despite their intelligence, are curiously inadequate at communicating with horses.* **for** *This computer is clearly inadequate for my needs.*

2 not able to deal with a situation
• VERBS **be, feel, seem** *I felt dreadfully inadequate.*
• ADV. **deeply, dreadfully, hopelessly, very** | **quite, totally, wholly** | **rather** | **generally** | **personally, professionally, sexually** *The staff at the consulate seemed not only insensitive, but professionally inadequate.*
• PREP. **to** *She was inadequate to the demands that were made on her.*

inadvisable adj.

• VERBS **be, seem** | **become** | **make sth** *Her condition made surgery inadvisable.* | **feel sth, think sth**
• ADV. **highly** *It was thought highly inadvisable for young women to go there alone.*

inappropriate adj.

• VERBS **be, seem** | **become** | **make sth** *The size of the machines makes them inappropriate for domestic use.* | **consider sth, feel sth, judge sth, regard sth as, see sth as, think sth** *It was felt inappropriate by some that such a serious occasion should include dancing.*
• ADV. **highly, particularly, singularly, very** *This treatment was singularly inappropriate in her case.* | **completely, entirely, quite, totally, utterly, wholly** | **increasingly** | **somewhat** | **clearly** | **embarrassingly, grotesquely** | **culturally**
• PREP. **for** *Your bright red coat would be quite inappropriate for a funeral.* **to** *The existing library is totally inappropriate to our needs.*

inattention noun

• ADJ. **momentary**
• PREP. **~to** *He was dismissed for inattention to his duty.*
• PHRASES **a moment of inattention** *One moment of inattention when driving could be fatal.*

inaudible adj.

• VERBS **be** | **become**

- ADV. **quite, totally** | **almost, practically, virtually** *His voice was almost inaudible.* | **largely**
- PREP. **to** *The sound is inaudible to the human ear.*

inaugurate *verb*

- ADV. **formally, officially** *The assembly was formally inaugurated on December 13.*

inauguration *noun*

- ADJ. **formal** | **presidential**
- VERB + INAUGURATION **attend** | **mark** *a ceremony to mark the inauguration of the president's third term in office*
- INAUGURATION + VERB **be held, take place**
- INAUGURATION + NOUN **ceremony** | **speech**

incapable *adj.*

- VERBS **appear, be, feel, prove, seem** | **become** | **make sb, render sb** *The wine had made him incapable of thinking clearly.* | **adjudge sb, deem sb**
- ADV. **absolutely, completely, quite, totally, utterly, wholly** | **almost** | **largely** | **clearly** | **inherently** | **constitutionally, temperamentally** *She was constitutionally incapable of bad temper.* | **physically** *He was apparently physically incapable of lowering his voice.* | **mentally** *This type of arrangement remains valid even if you become mentally incapable.*
- PREP. **of** *Computers are incapable of creative thought.*

incapacitate *verb* **be incapacitated**

- ADV. **severely** | **totally** *By this time my father was totally incapacitated by his illness.* | **temporarily** | **mentally, physically**

incarnation *noun*

- ADJ. **current, latest, modern, new, present** *(figurative) In its new incarnation, the car has a more rounded body shape.* | **last** | **earlier, previous** | **future**
- PREP. **~as** *her previous incarnation as a Norse explorer*

incense *noun*

- ADJ. **fragrant**
- VERB + INCENSE **burn**
- INCENSE + NOUN **stick** | **burner**
- PHRASES **a scent/smell of incense**

incentive *noun*

- ADJ. **big, considerable, great, massive** | **powerful, strong** | **adequate, sufficient** | **main, major** | **added, additional, extra, more** | **less** | **real** | **direct** *The most direct financial incentive to prevent rubbish is to charge people by the amount of rubbish they put out.* | **important** | **positive** | **special** | **commercial, economic, financial, fiscal, monetary** | **cash** | **price, tax** | **sales** | **work** | **government**
- VERB + INCENTIVE **act as, be** *He argues that the free supply of skilled labour will act as an incentive for employees to be more diligent.* | **have** *She had the added incentive of being within reach of the world record.* | **need** | **give (sb/sth), offer (sb/sth), provide (sb/sth with)** | **create** *The government has created tax incentives to encourage investment.* | **increase** | **reduce** | **undermine** *High taxation rates have undermined work incentives.* | **remove**
- INCENTIVE + NOUN **programme, scheme, system** *The company operates a share incentive scheme for its workers.* | **payment**
- PREP. **~to** *an incentive to investment*
- PHRASES **have every incentive** *The absence of penalties for anti-competitive behaviour means that firms have every incentive to engage in price-fixing.* **a lack of in-**

centive *Low levels of profitability mean there is a lack of incentive to undertake new investment.*

incest *noun*

- ADJ. **brother-sister, father-daughter, etc.**
- VERB + INCEST **criminalize, forbid, prohibit** *taboos forbidding incest*
- INCEST + NOUN **survivor, victim** | **taboo**
- PREP. **~between** *incest between brother and sister*
- ⇒ Note at CRIME (for more verbs)

inch *noun*

⇒ Note at MEASURE

incidence *noun*

- ADJ. **great, high** *There is a greater incidence of cancer in the families of radiation workers.* | **low** | **increased/increasing, rising** | **actual** | **overall** | **annual** | **recorded** *the highest recorded incidence of air pollution*
- VERB + INCIDENCE **have, show** *The country had the lowest incidence of Aids cases proportional to its population.* ◊ *The medical histories of our patients show a high incidence of past diseases.* | **increase, raise** | **reduce** | **find** *They found an increased incidence of childhood leukaemia in some areas.* | **measure** | **compare** *We compared the incidence of coronary heart disease and total mortality.* | **analyse, consider, investigate** | **explain** *The lack of vitamins may explain the higher incidence of heart disease.*
- INCIDENCE + VERB **increase** | **decrease, fall**
- INCIDENCE + NOUN **rate** *an incidence rate of 4 or 5 per 10 000 of the population*
- PREP. **~among** *The report analyses the incidence of cancer among people aged 0–24.* **~in** *The study noted an increased incidence of heart disease in women.*
- PHRASES **a decrease/an increase/a variation in the incidence of sth**

incident *noun*

- ADJ. **major, serious** | **little, minor, small, trivial** | **further** *After nearly falling twice, she managed to make it to the top of the cliff without further incident.* | **whole** *He came to regret the whole incident.* | **actual, real/real-life** *The story is based on an actual incident.* | **alleged** | **reported** | **recorded** | **latest, recent** | **past** | **bad, horrific, horrifying, nasty, terrible, ugly, unpleasant, unsavoury** *some of the worst incidents of urban violence* | **violent** | **fatal, tragic** | **dramatic** | **controversial** | **famous** | **regrettable, unfortunate** | **embarrassing** | **bizarre, curious, mysterious, strange, unusual** | **amusing** | **unrelated, separate** *The police said that two men had been arrested after the match in unrelated incidents.* | **isolated** *It is feared that the attack may not have been an isolated incident.* | **scattered** *scattered incidents of violence across the country* | **domestic** | **international** | **border** *Talks between the neighbouring countries were called off following a border incident.* | **racial** | **diplomatic** *An error in the translation nearly caused a diplomatic incident.* | **terrorist** | **nuclear** | **bomb/bombing, shooting, stabbing** | **pollution** | **off-the-ball** *(sport) She received a serious jaw injury in an off-the-ball incident.*
- VERB + INCIDENT **cause, provoke** | **be responsible for** *The group is believed to have been responsible for several terrorist incidents.* | **be involved in** *The hot-headed tennis star became involved in an incident with the umpire.* | **deal with, handle** *The incident was extremely well handled.* | **avoid, prevent** | **regret** | **see, witness** | **recall, remember** *He recalled a similar incident 14 months earlier.* | **forget** | **describe, recount** *She described the incident as outrageous.* ◊ *They all laughed as he recounted the amusing incident.* | **discuss, talk about** | **play down** *the government's desire to play down the incident* | **report**

The pedestrian who had nearly been run over reported the incident to the police. | **investigate** | **be hurt in, be injured in, be killed in** | **pass (off) without, proceed without, take place without** *The demonstration passed without incident.*

● INCIDENT + VERB **happen, occur, take place** | **arise (from/out of sth)** *incidents arising out of an industrial dispute* | **involve sb/sth** *a minor incident involving a petrol tanker* | **cause sth, lead to sth, spark sth (off)** *The incident sparked off a riot which lasted three days.*

● INCIDENT + NOUN **room** *An incident room was set up at a police station near the site of the crash.*

● PREP. **following an/the ~** *He was asked to leave the club following an incident at a training camp.* **in an/the ~** *Three soldiers were wounded in the incident.* **over an/the ~** *She was never disciplined over the incident.* **without ~** *The patrol had covered 200 miles without incident.*

incidental *adj.*

● VERBS **be** | **become** | **consider sth, declare sth, deem sth** *The fact that the concert made a profit was considered incidental.*

● ADV. **completely, entirely, purely** *Any resemblance of a character in this book to a living person is purely incidental.* | **merely** *Information skills are not merely incidental to the curriculum but central to it.* | **almost** | **seemingly**

● PREP. **to** *It's just a risk incidental to the job.*

incision *noun*

● ADJ. **deep** | **small, tiny** | **abdominal, etc.** | **surgical**

● VERB + INCISION **make** *The surgeon made a small incision in the patient's cornea.*

incite *verb*

● ADV. **deliberately**

● PREP. **to** *deliberately inciting the crowd to violence*

inclination *noun*

● ADJ. **strong** | **slight** *I did not feel the slightest inclination to hurry.* | **true** | **natural, own, personal** *The king's own inclination was always towards a pro-French policy.* | **homosexual, sexual** | **artistic, political**

● VERB + INCLINATION **feel, have** | **show** | **lack** | **curb** *Hopes of advancement in the company may curb any inclination to deviate from the requirements of superiors.* | **follow** *In matters of dress she followed her personal inclinations rather than fashion.*

● PREP. **by ~** *He is a teacher by occupation but a philosopher by inclination.* | **~ for** *an inclination for war* **~ towards** *She has no inclination towards mysticism.*

● PHRASES **the time nor/or the inclination** *I have neither the time nor the inclination to play stupid games!*

incline *verb*

1 bend forward

● ADV. **slightly** *Luke inclined his head slightly in acknowledgement.* | **graciously, politely**

2 lean/slope

● ADV. **gently, steeply**

● PREP. **towards** *The land inclined gently towards the shore.*

inclined *adj.*

1 wanting to do sth

● VERBS **be, feel, seem** *I only write when I feel inclined to.* ◊ *There's time for a swim if you feel so inclined.*

● ADV. **strongly, very** | **rather** *I'm rather inclined to wait a few days before deciding.* | **favourably**

● PREP. **towards** *Advertising aims to make people aware of a product and favourably inclined towards it.*

2 tending/likely to do sth

● VERBS **appear, be, seem** | **become, grow**

● ADV. **strongly, very** | **increasingly** | **a bit, half, a little, rather, slightly** *I'm half inclined to believe you.* ◊ *She's rather inclined to become impatient.* | **naturally** | **criminally, liberally, mystically, romantically, suicidally** *The club was a notorious hang-out for the criminally inclined.*

● PREP. **to** *(formal) people who are naturally inclined to melancholy*

● PHRASES **that way inclined** *(informal) What's that? The 'Model Railway Journal'? I didn't know you were that way inclined* (= interested in model railways).

3 having a natural ability for sth

● VERBS **appear, be, seem**

● ADV. **academically, artistically, musically** *children who are academically inclined*

inclusion *noun*

● ADJ. **possible** *We welcome readers' letters for possible inclusion on this page.*

● VERB + INCLUSION **be worthy of, justify, merit, warrant** *Some words are too infrequent to be worthy of inclusion in the dictionary.* | **be eligible for, be suitable for, qualify for** *All work by current students is eligible for inclusion in the journal.* | **be unsuitable for** | **be available for** | **consider sth for, welcome sth for** | **welcome, accept** *The rebels refused to accept the inclusion of representatives of the existing regime in the negotiations.* | **prevent** *They tried to prevent the inclusion of any wording in the statement that would cause offence.*

● PREP. **for ~** *an article for inclusion in the newsletter*

● PHRASES **criteria for inclusion** *There are strict criteria for inclusion in the competition.*

inclusive *adj.*

● VERBS **be**

● ADV. **fully** *a fully inclusive price*

● PREP. **of** *The charge is inclusive of food.*

● PHRASES **all inclusive** *The price is all inclusive.*

income *noun*

● ADJ. **above-average, high, large** | **sufficient** | **average** *Average incomes are rising more slowly.* | **below-average, low, meagre, small** | **rising** | **additional** *They hope that the lottery will provide additional income for charities.* | **total** | **future** | **permanent, secure** | **regular, steady** | **annual, monthly, weekly** | **national** | **per capita** *the average per capita income* | **personal, private** *He has a large private income on top of what he earns as a teacher.* | **family, household** | **gross, pre-tax** | **taxable** | **after-tax, net, post-tax** | **disposable** | **real** | **earned** | **unearned** | **money** *the money incomes of individuals* | **retirement** | **capital, fee, foreign, investment**

● VERB + INCOME **have** | **receive** *She received an income for life as a result of her father's will.* | **earn, generate, provide (sb with)** *Financial assets have the advantage of earning income.* ◊ *The return on your investment can provide you with regular income.* | **boost, increase, supplement** *ways of boosting your retirement income* ◊ *She supplements her income by doing an evening job.* | **reduce** | **exceed** *For 2001, expenditure exceeded income by £10 000.* | **depend on** | **live on** *A large number of families in the area are living on below-average incomes.* | **redistribute** *They aim to redistribute income from the rich to the poor.* | **treat sth as** *Interest is treated as income for tax purposes.*

● INCOME + VERB **arise (from sth), come from sth, derive from sth** *If a person's income arises in the UK it is subject to UK income tax.* ◊ *A lot of our income comes from bank interest.* | **grow, increase, rise** | **drop, fall** | **exceed sth**

● INCOME + NOUN **bracket, group, level** *Elderly people*

often belong to a low income group. | **distribution, redistribution** | **incomes policy** *There are internal disputes over the party's incomes policy.* | **support** *A single mother of three, she relies on income support.* | **statement** *a company's income statement* | **tax**
● PREP. **on an ~** *Many families on a low income are dependent on state support.* | **~from** *income from tourism*
● PHRASES **the distribution/redistribution of income, a drop in income, income and expenditure** *Every company must keep control of its income and expenditure.* **income per capita/head** *Real income per head of population was at a low point five years ago.* **a source of income**
⇨ Note at PER CENT (for more verbs)
⇨ Special page at BUSINESS

incompatibility *noun*

● ADJ. **basic** | **inherent** | **mutual** *the mutual incompatibility of socialist and capitalist economic systems*
● VERB + INCOMPATIBILITY **demonstrate** *The disastrous merger demonstrated the incompatibility of the two companies.*
● PREP. **~between** *Incompatibility between systems has been a major problem for video users.* **~with** *Critics of the new machine point to its incompatibility with other products on the market.*
● PHRASES **grounds of incompatibility** *A divorce was sought and granted on grounds of incompatibility.*

incompatible *adj.*

● VERBS **appear, be, prove, seem** | **become** | **consider sth, see sth as**
● ADV. **completely, entirely, quite, totally, wholly** | **increasingly** | **by no means, not entirely, not necessarily** *Scepticism and trust are not necessarily incompatible.* | **largely** | **somewhat** | **apparently, seemingly** | **potentially** | **simply** | **basically, fundamentally** | **clearly** | **mutually** *The two systems are mutually incompatible.*
● PREP. **with** *This behaviour is completely incompatible with his role as a teacher.*

incompetence *noun*

● ADJ. **gross, monumental** | **sheer** | **alleged** | **economic, professional, technical** | **government, managerial, police**
● VERB + INCOMPETENCE **display** *He displayed his incompetence by turning in a report that was full of errors.* | **tolerate** *I will not tolerate your incompetence any longer!* | **accuse sb/sth of, allege** | **be dismissed for**
● PREP. **~at/in** *incompetence in writing* **~on the part of** *Several officers had alleged incompetence on the part of the general.*

incompetent *adj.*

● VERBS **appear, be** | **adjudge sb/sth, consider sb/sth** *I know my boss considers me incompetent.*
● ADV. **grossly, hopelessly, singularly** *a grossly incompetent piece of reporting* | **completely, totally, utterly** | **managerially, socially, technically** | **mentally**
● PREP. **at** *He is utterly incompetent at his job.*

incomplete *adj.*

● VERBS **be** | **remain** *Her collection remained incomplete.* | **leave sth** *The building was left incomplete.*
● ADV. **seriously, very, woefully** *Any view of Shostakovich is seriously incomplete without knowledge of these recordings.* | **somewhat** | **inevitably, necessarily** *We begin with a brief and necessarily incomplete review of UK statistics.* | **unfortunately**

incomprehensible *adj.*

● VERBS **be, seem** | **remain** | **find sth** *She found his accent virtually incomprehensible.*
● ADV. **completely, quite, totally, utterly** | **almost, nearly, virtually** | **largely** | **pretty**
● PREP. **to** *Latin verse remained completely incomprehensible to me.*

inconceivable *adj.*

● VERBS **appear, be, seem** | **become** | **find sth** *She found the idea quite inconceivable.*
● ADV. **quite, totally, utterly, wholly** | **almost, practically, virtually**
● PREP. **to** *The thought of leaving her family was inconceivable to her.*

inconclusive *adj.*

● VERBS **be, prove** | **remain**
● ADV. **largely** | **fairly, rather, somewhat** | **apparently** | **ultimately** | **curiously** *the curiously inconclusive finish to the symphony*

incongruous *adj.*

● VERBS **be, look, seem** | **find sth**
● ADV. **entirely, utterly** | **doubly** | **a little, rather, somewhat** *I found the scene somewhat incongruous.*

inconsistency *noun*

● ADJ. **serious** | **glaring** | **apparent** | **internal** *Researchers have found that internal inconsistencies in hospital case notes are common.* | **logical**
● VERB + INCONSISTENCY **contain** | **be filled with** *The script is filled with logical inconsistencies.* | **lead to, result in** *The lack of a clear set of competition rules resulted in inconsistency in the awarding of prizes.* | **find, see, spot** *The program has found an inconsistency in the database files.* ◇ *She was quick to spot the inconsistencies between his two reports.* | **point out, reveal** *Commentators have pointed out the inconsistencies in the government's financial policy.* | **remove, resolve** *The amendment will remove the inconsistency between the two laws.*
● INCONSISTENCY + VERB **emerge** | **creep in, creep into sth** *Inconsistencies began to creep into his testimony.*
● PREP. **~in** *inconsistencies in the evidence*

inconsistent *adj.*

● VERBS **appear, be, seem**
● ADV. **highly, very** | **quite, totally, wholly** | **not necessarily** | **rather, somewhat** | **apparently** | **clearly, plainly** | **internally, logically** *Her argument is internally inconsistent.* | **mutually** *The two accounts are mutually inconsistent.*
● PREP. **in** *The company is inconsistent in the way it disciplines staff.* **with** *His statement was inconsistent with other accounts of the events.*

incontinence *noun*

● ADJ. **faecal, urinary** | **stress**
● VERB + INCONTINENCE **suffer from**
● INCONTINENCE + NOUN **pad**

inconvenience *noun*

● ADJ. **considerable, great, serious** | **minor** | **public** *The rail strike is likely to cause considerable public inconvenience.* | **administrative**
● VERB + INCONVENIENCE **have, suffer** | **avoid** *I chose a different route to avoid the inconvenience of going through the town centre.* | **cause (sb), put sb to** *I don't want to put you to any inconvenience.* | **minimize, save (sb)** *You could have fetched me from the airport and saved*

me the inconvenience of having to take the bus! | apologize for, **regret** *This shop is closed today for staff training. We regret any inconvenience caused.*
- INCONVENIENCE + VERB **arise from sth** *inconvenience arising from errors in the timetable*
- PREP. **~ to** *Every effort will be made to minimize inconvenience to customers while work is in progress.*
- PHRASES **with a minimum of inconvenience** *The club management will try to ensure that the building work is carried out with the minimum of inconvenience to guests.*

inconvenience *verb*

- ADV. **greatly** *The general public has been greatly inconvenienced by this strike.*

inconvenient *adj.*

- VERBS **be, prove** | **become** | **find sth**
- ADV. **extremely, highly, most, terribly, very** *She called at a most inconvenient time.* | **a bit, rather, somewhat** | **politically** *Further environmental legislation could be politically inconvenient for the government.*
- PREP. **for** *Would this afternoon be inconvenient for you?* **to** *This is a time of the evening that is inconvenient to many viewers.*

incorporate *verb*

- ADV. **fully** | **largely** | **clearly** | **expressly** *These conditions must be expressly incorporated into the contract of employment.* | **properly** | **gradually** | **quickly** | **eventually, finally** | **easily, readily** *These new features can easily be incorporated.* | **neatly** | **effectively** | **satisfactorily, successfully** | **necessarily** | **forcibly** *the countries which Stalin forcibly incorporated into the Soviet empire*
- PREP. **as** *In 1940 the area was incorporated as part of the city of London.* **in** *The data is now incorporated in the total figures.* **into** *We can incorporate this information into our report.* **within** *Results are incorporated within personalized medical records.*

incorrect *adj.*

- VERBS **be, prove** | **consider sth**
- ADV. **quite, totally** | **clearly, obviously** | **simply** *That statement is simply incorrect.* | **factually, grammatically, politically, technically** *a factually incorrect statement*

increase *noun*

- ADJ. **big, considerable, dramatic, enormous, exponential, huge, large, major, marked, massive, significant, substantial, vast** | **moderate, modest, small** | **apparent** | **rapid, sharp** | **gradual, steady** | **fivefold, tenfold, etc.** | **10%, etc.** | **net, overall** | **across-the-board** *The pay rise represented an across-the-board increase of between 9% for the highest paid and 32% for the lowest paid worker.* | **annual, monthly, etc.** | **dividend, fare, pay, price, rent, salary, tax, temperature, wage**
- VERB + INCREASE **experience, see, show** *Many parts of the country have experienced an increase in unemployment.* ◇ *This year saw an increase in the number of job applicants.* ◇ *Profits show a steady increase.* | **enjoy** *The country is enjoying the biggest increase in business confidence for years.* | **achieve** *We achieved a small increase in profits of £3 257.* | **bring (about), cause, lead to, result in** *Intensive farming has brought about an increase in outbreaks of food poisoning.* ◇ *The war resulted in a massive increase in government spending.* | **reflect, represent** | **entail, involve, mean** *The measures to improve the health service will involve an increase in government spending.* | **announce, report** *The company reported a 9.5% increase in third quarter losses.*
- INCREASE + VERB **occur**
- PREP. **on the ~** *Burglaries in the area are on the in-*

crease. | **~ in** *There has been an increase in demand for two-bedroom flats.* **~ on/over** *The figures show a sharp increase on last year's turnover.* **~ to** *a dividend increase to 11.4 pence*
- PHRASES **a rate of increase**

increase *verb*

- ADV. **considerably, dramatically, enormously, greatly, significantly, substantially** | **slightly** | **gradually** | **rapidly, sharply, steeply** | **steadily** | **twofold, threefold, etc.** *Sales increased almost fourfold in this period.*
- VERB + INCREASE **be expected to, be likely to** *Demand is expected to increase over the next decade.*
- PREP. **by** *The budget has increased by more than a third in the last year.* **from, in** *to increase in amount/number/price/size* **to** *Last month the reward was increased from £20 000 to £40 000.* **with** *Disability increases with age.*

incredible *adj.*

1 impossible to believe
- VERBS **be, seem, sound** | **find sth** *I find this quite incredible!*
- ADV. **really, truly** | **absolutely, quite** | **just, simply** | **almost**
- PREP. **to** *It seems incredible to me that we didn't think of this before.*

2 extremely good/extremely large
- VERBS **be, look, smell, taste** | **find sth**
- ADV. **really, truly** | **absolutely, quite** | **just, simply** | **pretty** *You're pretty incredible, Belinda.*

indebted *adj.*

1 feeling grateful to sb
- VERBS **be, feel** | **remain**
- ADV. **deeply, greatly, much, profoundly**
- PREP. **to** *I am deeply indebted to all the doctors and nurses who treated me.*

2 owing money to sb
- VERBS **be** | **remain**
- ADV. **heavily, highly, severely** *The company is heavily indebted.* ◇ *highly indebted countries*
- PREP. **to** *indebted to the bank*

indecency *noun*

- ADJ. **gross** | **public**
- PHRASES **an act of indecency**
⇨ Note at CRIME (for verbs)

indecent *adj.*

1 involving naked people, sex, etc.
- VERBS **be** | **class sth as, consider sth, regard sth as, think sth** *photographs that are classed as indecent*
- ADV. **grossly, positively** *That skirt of hers is positively indecent.*

2 not morally right
- VERBS **be, seem**
- ADV. **positively** *The rush to get hold of their father's money seemed positively indecent.* | **almost** *She started a new relationship with almost indecent haste.*

indefensible *adj.*

- VERBS **be** | **find sth** *I find such behaviour indefensible.*
- ADV. **totally** | **morally, politically** *It would be morally indefensible for her to desert her father now.*

independence *noun*

- ADJ. **considerable, great** | **complete, full, total** | **relative** *The council's relative independence of the government means it can negotiate its own agreements.* | **nomin-**

al | **genuine, real, true** | **de facto** *Aquitaine's de facto independence from the king of France* | **continued/continuing, growing** | **hard-won** | **local, national** | **academic, economic, editorial, financial, judicial, personal, political, professional**
- QUANT. **degree, measure**
- VERB + INDEPENDENCE **have** *Young people have more independence these days.* | **lack** | **enjoy, value** *I value my independence too much to get married.* | **display, show** *She displayed independence of judgement in choosing a career quite different from that of her parents.* | **assert** *Edward III tried to assert his independence of the regime at court.* | **achieve, gain, win** *Mexico achieved independence from Spain in 1821.* | **bring (about)** *the need to bring independence to the country* ◇ *a colonial crisis which brought about independence* | **declare, proclaim** | **ensure, maintain, preserve, retain, sustain** *The army is committed to ensuring the independence of the country.* | **give up, lose** *She doesn't want to lose her hard-won independence.* | **regain, restore** | **encourage, promote** *Parents should encourage independence in their children.* | **undermine** *Economic aid tends to undermine the national independence of third world countries.* | **seek** | **call for, demand** | **vote for** | **give sb/sth, grant sb/sth** | **recognize** *They have agreed to recognize the breakaway republic's independence.*
- INDEPENDENCE + VERB **come** *Independence came to the British colonial territories in Africa in the late fifties and early sixties.*
- INDEPENDENCE + NOUN **day** | **celebrations** | **movement** | **struggle**
- PREP. **at ~** *Namibia became a full member of the UN at independence.* | **~ from** *independence from Spain* **~ of** *the church's independence of the state* ◇ *independence of mind*
- PHRASES **a declaration of independence, a lack of independence, the loss of independence, a sign/symbol of independence** *The car became a symbol of independence.* **the struggle for independence, a war of independence** *the American War of Independence*

independent *adj.*

1 not needing other people
- VERBS **be, feel, seem** | **become** | **remain** | **make sb** *Travelling in Asia has made her a lot more independent.*
- ADV. **fiercely, sturdily, very** *Many disabled people are fiercely independent.* | **completely** | **fairly, pretty, quite** | **economically, financially**
- PREP. **of** *By the age of eighteen he was completely independent of his parents.*

2 not influenced or controlled by anyone else
- VERBS **be** | **become** | **remain** | **make sth** | **declare sth** *In 1961 the country was declared independent.*
- ADV. **completely, entirely, fully, genuinely, quite, totally, truly, wholly** | **almost, fairly, largely, virtually** | **increasingly** | **effectively, essentially** *The country has pursued an effectively independent line on military issues.* | **nominally, supposedly** | **newly** *newly independent countries* | **politically**
- PREP. **from** *The country became fully independent from France in 1960.* **of** *an organization that is independent of the government*

indestructible *adj.*

- VERBS **be, prove, seem**
- ADV. **completely** | **almost, virtually** *Their shells are so hard they are virtually indestructible.* | **seemingly**

index *noun*

1 list of names/topics in a book
- ADJ. **comprehensive, complete** | **detailed** | **general** | **alphabetical**
- VERB + INDEX **appear in, be in** *Although the book*

was devoted to cancer, the word 'cancer' did not even appear in the index.* | **consult, look (sth up) in** *Why don't you look up her name in the index?* | **compile**
- INDEX + VERB **give sth, list sth** *The index only gives the main towns.*
- PREP. **in a/the ~** *Is there any reference to it in the index?* | **~ to** *It's a general index to the whole work.*

2 ordered record of books/files
- ADJ. **subject, title** | **card** | **computer, computerized**
- VERB + INDEX **have, keep** *We keep a card index of all the titles on the shelves.* | **compile, create** | **consult, look (sth up) in, search** *Look up 'The Waste Land' in the index.* ◇ *Search the index to find the address of the data file.*
- INDEX + NOUN **card**
- PREP. **in a/the ~** *cards in a card index*

3 system showing the level of sth; measure of sth
- ADJ. **good, reliable, sensitive** | **high** | **low** | **weighted** | **official** | **general** *a general index calculated from death and population information* | **world** *The world index fell 3.1%.* | **cost-of-living, market, retail price** | **futures, share, stock** | **Dow Jones, FT-SE 100, etc.**
- VERB + INDEX **have** *Those who lived in the inner cities had a high index of deprivation.* | **use (sth as)** *The test results were used as an index of language proficiency.* | **compile, construct, create** | **calculate, compute** *The index was calculated with a computer.* | **publish** *The retail price index is published monthly.* | **drag, drive, push, take** *A wave of frenzied buying pushed the index up 136.2 points.*
- INDEX + VERB **measure sth** *an index designed to measure monthly changes in the volume of industrial production* | **be based on sth** *an index based on incidents causing a loss of production* | **be linked to sth** *The increase in our standard rates will be linked to the retail price index.* | **cover sth** *an index covering some 1 700 companies* | **open** | **close, end** *The hundred shares index closed down 15 points.*
- PREP. **in an/the ~** *dividends on shares in the index* **on an/the ~** *people dealing in options on the FT-SE 100 index*
- PHRASES **a drop/fall in an index** *a 28.2 point drop in the FT-SE 100 index* **changes in an index, an increase in an index, as measured by an index** *Inflation, as measured by the retail price index, is expected to drop.*
- ⇨ Note at PER CENT (for more verbs)

indicate *verb*

- ADV. **clearly** | **not necessarily** *Expense does not necessarily indicate worth.*
- VERB + INDICATE **appear to, seem to** *These facts would seem to indicate that the family was wealthy.* | **be used to** *Symbols are used to indicate the facilities available at each hotel.*
- PREP. **to** *These figures indicate to me that the company is in serious trouble.*

indication *noun*

- ADJ. **firm, good, great, strong** | **accurate, reliable, true** | **clear, definite, sure** | **important** | **useful, valuable** | **sufficient** | **approximate, broad, fair, general, reasonable, rough** | **simple** | **positive** | **initial, preliminary** | **outward, visual, visible** *Rising interest rates were an outward indication of the change in government attitude to economic controls.* ◇ *Some car alarms have no visual indication that they are in operation.*
- VERB + INDICATION **be, constitute, serve as** *The popularity of the government building project served as an indication of public support.* | **have** *A government spokesperson said they had no indication who was responsible for the attack.* | **give (sb), provide (sb with)** *His early successes gave some indication of his ability.* | **get, receive** | **find, see** *The researchers say they can find no indication that television has harmful physical effects on children.* |

dren. | **regard sth as, see sth as, take sth as** *The comments made by management may be taken as an indication of how they felt about their workers.*

● INDICATION + VERB **show sth, suggest sth** *Indications show that at least 2 000 more businesses will go bankrupt before the end of the year.*

● PREP. **amid ~s of** *Amid indications of growing disorder in the capital, the president is to make a speech on television tonight.* | **~ as to** *He gave us no indication as to what was the matter.* **~ to** *This is an indication to drivers who break the law that they will be punished*

● PHRASES **(all) the indications are that …** *All the indications are that she will make a full recovery.* **there is every indication that …** *There's every indication that the operation has been a success.*

indicative *adj.*

● VERBS **be** | **consider sth, interpret sth as, regard sth as, see sth as, take sth as** *The rise in unemployment is seen as indicative of a new economic recession.*

● ADV. **clearly** | **(not) necessarily** *Recurrent dreams are not necessarily indicative of psychological problems.*

● PREP. **of**

indicator *noun*

1 sign showing what sth is like

● ADJ. **good, reliable, sure** | **poor, unreliable** *Level of education is actually quite a poor indicator of ability to run a business well.* | **sensitive** | **crude, partial, rough** | **simple** | **key, leading, main, major** | **important, significant** | **useful, valuable** | **economic, financial, performance, social, socio-economic** *performance indicators such as language and numeracy skills*

● VERB + INDICATOR **be, serve as** *These warts can serve as an indicator of other infections.* | **provide (sb with)** | **regard sth as, see sth as, take sth as** *Gold prices are often seen as an indicator of inflation.* | **use (sth as)** | **develop** *It is still difficult to develop indicators for many concepts used in social science.*

● INDICATOR + VERB **show sth, suggest sth** *Economic indicators suggest that a recovery is on the way.*

● PREP. **~ for** *an indicator for the presence of minerals*

indictment *noun*

1 sign that sth is bad/wrong

● ADJ. **powerful** | **damning, scathing, terrible** *Her speech was a scathing indictment of the government's record on crime.* | **sad**

2 accusing sb of a crime

● ADJ. **criminal** | **fresh**

● VERB + INDICTMENT **issue, bring** *A New York jury brought criminal indictments against the founder of the organization.* | **be charged on, be convicted on, be tried on** | **plead (not) guilty to**

● INDICTMENT + VERB **charge (sb/sth with sth)** *an indictment charging theft*

● PREP. **in a/the ~** *Two men were named in the indictment.* **on ~** *a trial on indictment* | **~ against** *They issued an indictment against them.* **~ for** *She was convicted on an indictment for conspiracy.*

indifference *noun*

● ADJ. **complete, supreme, total** | **a certain** | **growing** | **studied** | **apparent, feigned, pretended, seeming** | **bland, casual** | **callous, cold, cool, cruel** | **public**

● VERB + INDIFFERENCE **feel** | **express, show** *She showed total indifference to his fate.* | **affect, assume, feign, pretend** *He feigned indifference to criticism of his work.* | **regard sb/sth with** *The more recent members of staff regard the change in corporate culture with a certain indifference.* | **treat sb/sth with** | **be met with** *Con-*

stable's landscapes met with indifference when they were first exhibited. | **be resigned to** *The president is resigned to public indifference to his latest initiative.*

● PREP. **with an ~** *Ellis spoke with a casual indifference that he did not feel.* | **~ to/towards** *his indifference towards art*

● PHRASES **an attitude of indifference** *She adopted an attitude of supreme indifference.* **a matter of indifference** *It's a matter of indifference to me whether he goes or not.*

indifferent *adj.*

1 not interested

● VERBS **appear, be, feel, seem, sound** *He appeared indifferent to her suffering.* | **become** | **remain**

● ADV. **completely, quite, totally** | **almost** *Pat sounded almost indifferent.* | **largely** | **apparently** | **coldly**

● PREP. **about** *Most staff were indifferent about the plans.* **to** *He was coldly indifferent to other people.*

2 of low quality

● VERBS **be**

● ADV. **very** *We enjoyed the day, in spite of very indifferent weather.* | **rather** *a rather indifferent performance*

● PHRASES **good, bad and indifferent** *The festival has the usual mix of films—good, bad and indifferent.*

indigenous *adj.*

● VERBS **be**

● ADV. **truly** *examples of truly indigenous music*

● PREP. **to** *The tree is indigenous to China.*

indigestion *noun*

● ADJ. **serious, severe** | **acute, chronic** | **slight**

● VERB + INDIGESTION **get, have, suffer from** | **give sb** *Rich food always gives me indigestion.*

● INDIGESTION + NOUN **tablet**

⇒ Special page at ILLNESS

indignant *adj.*

● VERBS **be, feel, look, seem, sound** | **become, grow, wax** *She waxes righteously indignant if anyone tries to contradict her.* | **make sb**

● ADV. **extremely, fiercely, highly, very** *'He deserves to be thrashed,' she protested, fiercely indignant.* | **almost, mildly, quite, rather** | **justly, righteously**

● PREP. **about/over** *She became rather indignant over suggestions that she had lied.* **at** *They were quite indignant at his remarks.*

indignation *noun*

● ADJ. **considerable, great, high** *His response was one of high indignation.* | **widespread** | **public** | **moral, righteous** | **mock**

● VERB + INDIGNATION **be filled with, be full of, feel** *They were full of righteous indignation at the thought of being cheated.* | **express, show** | **blush/burn/flush with, quiver/shudder/tremble with** *His plump face flushed with indignation.* ◇ *Bertha's voice quivered with indignation.* | **arouse, cause, provoke**

● INDIGNATION + VERB **grow, rise** *Indignation grew as more nightclubs opened.* ◇ *She could feel her indignation rising.*

● PREP. **in ~** *She turned to him in indignation.* **with ~** *He refused it with some indignation.* | **~ about/at/over** *The government expressed its indignation over the way the incident had been handled.* **~ against** *public indignation against the government*

indiscretion *noun*

● ADJ. **serious** | **minor, slight, small** | **personal** | **political** | **youthful** | **dietary, sexual**

• VERB + INDISCRETION **commit** *He had committed a minor sexual indiscretion.* | **regret** *I instantly regretted my indiscretion and asked her to keep the news to herself.* | **report** *He had never forgiven her for reporting his indiscretion in front of his friends.*

indispensable *adj.*

• VERBS **be, prove** | **become** | **make sb/sth** *He had soon made himself indispensable.* | **consider sb/sth**
• ADV. **absolutely** | **almost, virtually**
• PREP. **for** *Written sources are considered virtually indispensable for today's history teaching.* **in** *These drugs are almost indispensable in the fight against the disease.* **to** *skills which turned out to be indispensable to her career*

individual *noun*

• ADJ. **outstanding, talented** | **key** | **powerful** | **creative** | **average, ordinary** *Their research shows that the average individual watches around three and a half hours of television per day.* | **private** *He was carrying out his functions as a trustee in the course of his business, rather than as a private individual.* | **single** | **particular, certain** *The motives influencing a particular individual may change from time to time.* | **autonomous, independent** *His philosophy is about becoming aware of oneself as an autonomous individual.* | **isolated** *Society does not consist of isolated individuals, but people in a network of relationships.* | **unique** *She saw the artist as a unique individual, possessing a heightened awareness of reality.* | **like-minded** *a group of like-minded individuals* | **named** *The book recommends that you sign 'Yours sincerely' if you are sending the letter to a named individual.* | **qualified** *We welcome applications from suitably qualified individuals.* | **human** *We know that all human individuals are unique.*
• VERB + INDIVIDUAL **treat sb as** *The teacher should treat each pupil as an individual.*
• INDIVIDUAL + VERB **vary** *Although individuals vary widely, the bones of the average female skeleton are smaller and lighter than the male.*
• INDIVIDUAL + NOUN **level** *His writings are concerned with religious phenomena at the individual level.*
• PHRASES **any/no/one individual** *No single individual had done so much for the development of the motor vehicle.* **concern for the individual, the freedom of the individual** *the issue of the freedom of the individual versus the intervention of the state* **a group of individuals** *She had taken a group of individuals and made them into a superb team.* **the individual concerned** *It's up to the individual concerned to contact the police.* **the needs of the individual** *Each course has to be tailored to the needs of the individual.* **respect for the individual, vary from individual to individual** *Eating habits are bound to vary from individual to individual.*

individuality *noun*

• ADJ. **human**
• VERB + INDIVIDUALITY **have** *Each song has its own individuality.* | **express, reflect, show** *clothes that reflect your individuality* | **give sth** *The small items of handcrafted furniture give individuality to the room.* | **recognize** *This book will help you recognize your individuality.* | **retain** | **lose**
• PHRASES **a feeling/sense of individuality, the suppression of individuality** *Becoming part of a team should not mean the suppression of individuality.*

inducement *noun*

• ADJ. **big, massive, powerful, strong** | **sufficient** | **extra, further** | **positive** | **cash, financial**
• VERB + INDUCEMENT **offer (sb/sth as), provide (sb/sth as)** *The higher payments were offered as an inducement.* | **receive**

• PREP. **~for** *The reduced tax is a major inducement for first-time buyers.* **~to** *an inducement to crime and violence* ◇ *inducements to employees*

indulge *verb*

• VERB + INDULGE **be able to, be free to, can**
• PREP. **in** *She was free to indulge in a little romantic daydreaming.* **with** *For a special treat indulge yourself with one of these luxury flavours of ice cream.*

indulgence *noun*

1 having whatever you want
• ADJ. **excessive** | **personal, self-** *guilty of self-indulgence* | **sexual**
• PREP. **~in** *She allowed herself only a few moments' indulgence in self-pity.*
• PHRASES **a life of indulgence**

2 sth you allow yourself
• ADJ. **expensive, private, small**
• VERB + INDULGENCE **allow yourself** *As a relief from work she allowed herself a few small indulgences.*

3 acceptance of change to the normal way of doing sth
• VERB + INDULGENCE **ask, beg, request** *He begged the audience's indulgence to read some passages from his latest book.* | **grant** *(law),* **show (sb)** *He attacked the indulgence shown to religious dissenters.*

industrial action *noun*

• ADJ. **continuing** | **unlawful**
• VERB + INDUSTRIAL ACTION **take** | **threaten** | **call for** | **vote for** | **start** | **step up** *The union is considering stepping up its industrial action.* | **suspend** | **stop** | **take part in, be/become involved in** *His research indicates an increase in the number of women involved in industrial action.* | **support**
• PREP. **~against** *The union is threatening industrial action against the company.* **~by** *industrial action by railway workers* **~in support of** *industrial action in support of demands for a ten per cent salary adjustment* **~over** *to take industrial action over pay*

industrialist *noun*

• ADJ. **leading, prominent, top** | **local** | **wealthy**

industry *noun*

• ADJ. **thriving** | **important, key, major** | **(fastest) growing** | **declining** | **modern** | **traditional** | **cottage** *Weaving and knitting are traditional cottage industries.* | **domestic, international, local, national** | **private, privatized** | **government-owned, nationalized, state-run** | **heavy** | **light** | **strategic** *strategic industries such as the extraction of oil and natural gas* | **manufacturing, service** *the shift away from manufacturing to service industry* | **labour-intensive** | **high-tech/high-technology** | **building, construction** | **engineering** | **shipbuilding** | **chemical, coal, electricity, energy, gas, mining, nuclear, oil, petrochemical** | **agricultural, fishing, food, timber** | **pharmaceutical** | **automobile, automotive, car, motor** | **computer, electronics** | **textiles** | **advertising** | **insurance** | **entertainment, film, music/record** | **catering, hospitality, hotel, leisure, tourist**
• VERB + INDUSTRY **assist, develop, encourage, help, stimulate** *The government decided to encourage industries based on biotechnology.* ◇ *government measures to stimulate new industry* | **run down** *Running down the nuclear industry will result in heavy job losses.* | **damage** *They claim that a commercial port would damage the local tourist industry.* | **cripple, destroy, ruin** | **nationalize** | **privatize** | **regulate** | **protect** *trade barriers erected to protect domestic industry* | **subsidize** *The state's timber industry is heavily subsidized.* | **interfere in/with** *The*

government has interfered in industry, with disastrous results, by attempting to alter economic trends. | **be involved in/with** More than 140 000 people are directly involved in the industry. | **enter, go into** students training to enter the catering industry ◊ She decided to leave teaching and go into industry.
● INDUSTRY + VERB **develop, grow up, spring up** In the favourable economic environment, new light industries are constantly springing up. | **boom, expand, grow** The tourist industry is still expanding rapidly. | **decline, shrink** | **close down, disappear** When the railway disappeared, other industries associated with it closed down. | **compete** | **produce sth**
● INDUSTRY + NOUN **leader** | **standard** They hope that the disk drive will become an industry standard.
● PREP. **in/within ~** In the computer industry, change comes about very rapidly.
● PHRASES **a captain of industry, commerce and industry** The banks lend money to commerce and industry. **regulation of (an) industry** proposals for regulation of the water industry **the revival of (an) industry** the revival of the British film industry **a sector of industry, trade and industry** the Department of Trade and Industry

inedible adj.

● VERBS **be, look** | **become** | **make sth** These chemicals make the fruit inedible.
● ADV. **totally** The food was totally inedible. | **almost**

ineffective adj.

● VERBS **be, prove, seem** These policies have proved ineffective. | **become** | **make sth, render sth** The contract was rendered ineffective by this careless wording.
● ADV. **highly, singularly, very** | **completely, entirely, totally, wholly** | **largely** | **pretty, rather, relatively, somewhat** | **apparently** | **politically**
● PREP. **against** These weapons are totally ineffective against tanks. **in** chemicals that are very ineffective in killing weeds

inefficiency noun

● ADJ. **gross** | **inherent** | **bureaucratic, economic, managerial**
● VERB + INEFFICIENCY **cause, create, lead to, make for** Conflict between management and workers makes for inefficiency in the workplace. | **minimize, reduce** | **overcome, root out** We need to root out inefficiencies in the production process.
● INEFFICIENCY + VERB **arise** This type of inefficiency arises because workers and management are ill-equipped.

inefficient adj.

● VERBS **be, seem** | **become**
● ADV. **extremely, grossly, highly, hopelessly, terribly, very** | **quite, rather, relatively, somewhat** | **generally** | **potentially** | **inherently** | **notoriously** | **economically** an economically inefficient system

ineligible adj.

● VERBS **be** | **become** | **make sb/sth** | **consider sb/sth, declare sb/sth, deem sb/sth** The country had been declared ineligible for World Bank lending.
● PREP. **for** The new rules have made thousands more people ineligible for legal aid.

inept adj.

● VERBS **be, prove** | **become**
● ADV. **very** | **quite** | **rather** | **politically, socially** It would be politically inept to cut these training programmes now.
● PREP. **at** He was rather inept at word games.

inequality noun

● ADJ. **considerable, great, marked, substantial** Inequalities of income would lead to even greater inequalities in access to health care. | **real** | **growing, increased/increasing** | **global, regional** | **class, economic, educational, gender, income, pay, racial, sex/sexual, social, socio-economic, structural**
● VERB + INEQUALITY **cause, create, lead to** The introduction of school fees would create inequality between schools. | **maintain, perpetuate** Many sociologists have regarded education as central in perpetuating inequality. | **reinforce** Sex inequality in pay reinforces class inequality. | **increase** | **reduce** | **remove** They can build a more harmonious society once inequality and exploitation are removed. | **rectify, redress** The country has had some success in redressing racial inequalities.
● INEQUALITY + VERB **exist** inequalities that exist in wealth and income | **arise from sth, be based on sth** inequalities based on racism and social class | **persist, remain** Even in the age of compulsory school, inequalities have remained. | **increase** | **decline**
● PREP. **~ between** economic inequality between men and women **~ in** gender inequality in education
● PHRASES **inequalities of opportunity/power/wealth, a pattern of inequality**

inert adj.

● VERBS **be, lie, remain** | **become**
● ADV. **completely** She lay completely inert on her bed. | **relatively** | **chemically** chemically inert radioactive waste

inertia noun

● ADJ. **sheer** | **bureaucratic, institutional, organizational, political**
● VERB + INERTIA **lapse into** She lapsed into inertia and lay there as if asleep. | **overcome** The forces for change in the government are not sufficient to overcome bureaucratic inertia.
● PREP. **out of ~** He stayed where he was, not because he really wanted to, but out of inertia. **through ~** Projects were frequently abandoned through sheer inertia.
● PHRASES **a state of inertia**

inevitability noun

● ADJ. **terrible, tragic** | **a certain** | **historical**
● VERB + INEVITABILITY **have** | **accept** She was learning to accept the inevitability of death.
● PREP. **~ about** The tragedy had a certain inevitability about it.
● PHRASES **a feeling/sense of inevitability**

inevitable adj.

● VERBS **appear, be, look, seem** | **become** | **make sth** The scandal made her resignation inevitable. | **regard sth as, see sth as** They came to see defeat as inevitable.
● ADV. **absolutely, quite** | **almost, virtually** | **apparently, seemingly** | **probably** | **historically, politically**
● PHRASES **bow to the inevitable** She bowed to the inevitable (= accepted a situation in which she had no choice) and resigned.

inexhaustible adj.

● VERBS **be, seem** Her energy seemed inexhaustible.
● ADV. **virtually** | **apparently, seemingly**

inexpensive adj.

● VERBS **be**
● ADV. **very** | **comparatively, fairly, quite, reasonably, relatively** Paper is relatively inexpensive here.

inexperience noun

- ADJ. **relative** | **youthful** | **political**
- VERB + INEXPERIENCE **reveal, show** *She showed her inexperience by asking lots of trivial questions.* | **be down to** *The team's defensive errors were down to* (= a result of their) *inexperience.* | **put sth down to** *He put his mistakes down to* (= believed they were caused by his) *inexperience.*
- INEXPERIENCE + VERB **show** *Her inexperience in politics did not show as she debated with the other candidates.*
- PREP. **because of/from/through~** *They made mistakes through inexperience.* | **~in** *inexperience in teaching*

inexperienced adj.

- VERBS **be, feel, seem**
- ADV. **hopelessly, very** | **totally** *He was unqualified and totally inexperienced.* | **relatively** *She was still a relatively inexperienced pilot.* | **politically, sexually**
- PREP. **in** *She was inexperienced in teaching art.* **with** *men who are inexperienced with children*
- PHRASES **young and inexperienced**

inexplicable adj.

- VERBS **be, seem** | **remain** | **find sth**
- ADV. **completely, quite, totally** *Their actions are completely inexplicable.* | **apparently** | **otherwise** *This theory makes sense of an otherwise inexplicable phenomenon.*

infancy noun

- ADJ. **early** *The vaccination is given in early infancy.*
- VERB + INFANCY **survive (beyond)** *Their first child did not survive infancy.* | **die in** *She died in infancy.*
- PREP. **during/in ~** *Deaths during infancy have fallen dramatically in the last hundred years.* ◇ (figurative) *The new company is still in its infancy.* **from~** *from infancy to late childhood* **since (sb's)~** *Since her infancy she has been a healthy baby.* **throughout (sb's)~** *He was ill many times throughout his infancy.*

infant noun

- ADJ. **young** *He is studying hearing in very young infants.* | **newborn** | **unborn** | **stillborn** | **pre-term, premature** *jaundice in premature infants* | **full-term** | **healthy, normal** | **low birthweight** | **human** *a book on intellectual development in the human infant* | **female, male** | **screaming, sleeping** *Marjorie looked down at the sleeping infant in her arms.*
- INFANT + NOUN **death, mortality** *countries with high infant mortality* | **child, daughter, son**
- PHRASES **sudden infant death syndrome**

infected adj.

- VERBS **be** | **become, get**
- ADV. **badly, heavily** | **chronically**
- PREP. **with** *patients who are infected with this virus*

infection noun

- ADJ. **heavy, nasty, serious, severe** | **mild, minor, moderate** | **acute** | **chronic** | **recurrent** | **further** | **primary, secondary** *If the primary infection is not treated further outbreaks may occur.* | **new** *Over 90% of all new infections occur in the developing world.* | **rare** | **bacterial, fungal, viral** | **chest, ear, etc.** | **respiratory, urinary, etc.** | **herpes, HIV, etc.**
- VERB + INFECTION **have, suffer (from)** *He's suffering from an acute infection of the lower respiratory tract.* | **be at risk from/of, be prone/susceptible/vulnerable to** *Goats appear to be more susceptible to the infection than sheep.* | **be exposed to** *Vaccination is essential to protect people exposed to hepatitis B infection.* | **acquire, catch,** contract, develop, get *She's always getting chest infections.* | **pass (on), spread, transmit** *The infection is passed on through the horse feed.* | **carry** *Almost all the sheep on the farm carried the infection.* | **guard against, protect sb/sth from** *to protect the body from infection* | **avoid, prevent** | **combat, fight** *The virus affects the body's immune system so that it cannot fight infection.* | **fight off, kill** *Normally, white blood cells fight off and kill infections.* | **recover from** | **leave/make sb susceptible to, leave/make sb vulnerable to** | **die from/of** | **diagnose (sb with)** | **treat (sb for)**
- INFECTION + VERB **develop, occur** *an infection that occurs in swans* | **spread** *They want to prevent the infection spreading to other parts of the body.* | **cause sth, result in sth** *Heavy lung infections may result in pneumonia.*
- PREP. **in~** *In acute infections of the urinary tract the patient may suffer severe pain.* | **~by** *infection of people by the virus* **~from** *infection from sewage water* **~through** *infection through unsafe sex* **~with** *infection with bacteria*
- PHRASES **a cause of infection, the onset of infection** *The drug must be taken from the onset of the infection.* **resistance to infection** *Taking vitamin C builds up your resistance to infection.* **a risk of infection, a site of infection** (medical) *The urethra was the primary site of infection* **a source of infection** *We are trying to trace the source of infection.* **the spread of infection**
- ⇨ Special page at ILLNESS

infectious adj.

- VERBS **be, remain**
- ADV. **highly, very** | **potentially**

infer verb

- ADV. **reasonably**
- VERB + INFER **can/could** | **be possible to** | **be difficult to, be hard to** *It is difficult to infer anything from such scanty evidence.* | **be reasonable to** | **be wrong to**
- PREP. **from** *From this study we can reasonably infer that this behaviour is inherited.*

inference noun

- ADJ. **fair, logical, reasonable** | **obvious**
- VERB + INFERENCE **draw, make**
- INFERENCE + VERB **be based on sth** *inferences based on their answers to a number of set questions*
- PREP. **~about** *In the absence of detailed documentary evidence, we can only make inferences about Minoan religion.* **~from** *The value of data depends on our skill in drawing inferences from it.*

inferior noun

- ADJ. **intellectual, social**
- VERB + INFERIOR **consider sb** *She considered everyone her intellectual inferior.*

inferior adj.

- VERBS **be, feel, seem** *Her obvious popularity made me feel inferior.* | **consider sb/sth, regard sb/sth as, see sb/sth as** *Women are often regarded as inferior.*
- ADV. **decidedly, distinctly, greatly, markedly, significantly, vastly, very** | **slightly, somewhat** | **demonstrably** | **intrinsically** | **intellectually, morally, socially, technically**
- PREP. **in** *These later paintings are slightly inferior in value.* **to** *His later work was vastly inferior to his early work.*

inferiority noun

- ADJ. **moral, racial, social** *the myth of racial inferiority* | **numerical** *The invading force, conscious of their numerical inferiority at sea, decided on an airborne attack.*

- VERB + INFERIORITY **accept**
- INFERIORITY + NOUN **complex** *He had an inferiority complex about his looks.*
- PREP. **~ to** *She accepted her inferiority to her rivals.*
- PHRASES **a feeling/sense of inferiority, a position of inferiority, a sign of inferiority** *Using a false accent over the phone is a sign of inferiority.*

infertility *noun*

- ADJ. **female, male**
- VERB + INFERTILITY **cause, lead to** | **treat**
- INFERTILITY + NOUN **clinic, treatment**

infested *adj.*

- VERBS **be** | **become**
- ADV. **badly, heavily** *The building was heavily infested with cockroaches.*
- PREP. **with**

infiltration *noun*

- ADJ. **large-scale** | **communist, right-wing, etc.**
- VERB + INFILTRATION **reduce** | **prevent**
- PREP. **~ by** *The police tried to prevent infiltration by drug traffickers.* **~ into** *the infiltration of rain into the soil*

infinite *adj.*

- VERBS **be** | **become**
- ADV. **almost, practically, virtually** *an almost infinite variety of colours* | **apparently** | **potentially**

infinitive *noun*

- ADJ. **bare** *Modal verbs generally take the bare infinitive.* | **perfect** *You use 'have' to form the perfect infinitive of a verb.* | **passive** | **split** *The use of the split infinitive is now generally acceptable.*
- VERB + INFINITIVE **form** | **take** | **split**

infinity *noun*

1 endless space/time
- VERB + INFINITY **extend into/to, stretch into/to** *Theoretically, a line can extend into infinity.*
- PREP. **at ~** *Parallel lines meet at infinity.* **into ~** *In this weather the cliff face was a foggy drop into infinity.*

2 number larger than any other
- VERB + INFINITY **approach, tend to/towards** *As x approaches infinity y approaches zero.*
- PREP. **at ~** *The usual convention is to choose the reference point at infinity.*

infirm *adj.*

- VERBS **be** | **become**
- ADV. **mentally, physically**

infirmity *noun*

- ADJ. **mental, physical** | **increasing**
- PHRASES **age and infirmity** (*literary*) *those incapable of supporting themselves by reason of age and infirmity*

inflamed *adj.*

- VERBS **be** | **become, get**
- ADV. **highly, severely, very** *Her joints are severely inflamed.* | **further** | **acutely** | **chronically**

inflammable *adj.*

- VERBS **be**
- ADV. **highly, very** *These gases are highly inflammable.*

inflammation *noun*

- ADJ. **painful, severe** | **mild** | **acute, chronic** | **colonic, intestinal, etc.**
- VERB + INFLAMMATION **reduce** *Steroids often help reduce the inflammation and itching in the skin.*
- PREP. **~ of** *inflammation of the stomach*
- PHRASES **signs of inflammation**

inflate *verb*

- ADV. **fully** | **partially**
- PREP. **with** *The balloon was kept fully inflated with hydrogen.*

inflated *adj.*

- VERBS **be**
- ADV. **greatly, grossly, hugely, vastly** | **artificially, falsely** *The prices of meals are often artificially inflated.*

inflation *noun*

- ADJ. **high** | **low, moderate** | **zero** | **galloping, raging, rampant, rising, runaway, soaring, spiralling, uncontrollable** | **double-digit** (= 10 per cent or more) | **consumer-price, price, wage** | **domestic**
- VERB + INFLATION **cause** | **fuel, push up, raise** | **beat, bring down/under control, check, combat, control, curb, cut, fight, get down/under control, keep down, keep in check, keep under control, reduce** *policies to beat inflation* ◇ *It is vital that inflation is kept in check.* | **keep pace with** *Wages are not keeping pace with inflation.*
- INFLATION + VERB **be up** | **be down** *Inflation is down to its lowest level in three years.* | **exceed sth, reach sth** *Inflation reached a monthly rate of 5%.* | **average sth, be at sth, run at sth, stand at sth** *Inflation is running at 4%.* | **edge up, go up, increase, rise** | **fall, go down, slow** *Inflation has slowed to 7%.* | **erode sth** *savings eroded by inflation*
- INFLATION + NOUN **figures, rate** *an inflation rate of 2%* | **forecast, target**
- PHRASES **the battle/fight against inflation, a drop/fall in inflation, an increase/a rise in inflation** *an increase in inflation to 3.5%* **a rate of inflation**

inflexible *adj.*

- VERBS **be, prove, seem** *The rules seemed arbitrary and inflexible.* | **become** | **remain**
- ADV. **highly, very** | **completely, totally** *The seven-year period is not totally inflexible.* | **rather, relatively, somewhat** *She's a good teacher, but she can be rather inflexible.*

inflict *verb*

- ADV. **deliberately** *When someone deliberately inflicts damage, it is a matter for the police.* | **maliciously, negligently** (*both law*) *He was charged with maliciously inflicting grievous bodily harm.*
- PREP. **on/upon** *They inflicted a humiliating defeat on their rivals.*

influence *noun*

1 effect sb/sth has; power to control sb/sth
- ADJ. **big, considerable, enormous, great, significant** | **growing** | **chief, dominant, major, overwhelming, powerful, profound, strong** *He had a profound influence on modern poets.* | **important** | **crucial, decisive** | **undue** (*law*) *The court found that the bank exerted undue influence over Mrs Black in getting her to sign the contract.* | **beneficial, positive** | **adverse, corrupting, destructive, disruptive, evil, negative** | **stabilizing, steadying** | **calming, restraining** | **civilizing** | **direct** | **pervasive, wide** | **external, outside** *The religious community wished*

to be independent of outside influence. | **foreign** | **cultural, economic, genetic, political**
- VERB + INFLUENCE **have** | **give sb** *Her wealth gave her influence over affairs of state.* | **exercise, exert, use, wield** *Can you use your influence with the director to get me a part in the film?* ◊ *Drug cartels wielded enormous influence in the city.* | **extend** *The unions have been able to extend their influence over all industries.* | **be under** *The court was told that he was under the influence of alcohol when he committed the offence.* | **come/fall under** *She came under the influence of Sartre at this period.* | **be independent of** | **show** *Spanish architecture shows Moorish influence.* | **attribute sth to** *Much of his writing can be attributed to the influence of Freud.*
- INFLUENCE + VERB **extend** *Their influence extended as far as China.*
- PREP. **under the~** *The town grew under the influence of colonialism.* | **~from** *There was no influence from outside.* **~ in** *She has a certain amount of influence in the way things are organized.* **~on/upon** *They were a major influence upon the development of the sport.* **~over** *I have absolutely no influence over him.* **~with** *Queen Isabella was urged to use her influence with the French monarch.*
- PHRASES **a sphere of influence** *Rome's sphere of influence extended across Europe, North Africa and the Middle East.* **bring your influence to bear on sb/sth** *The king tried to bring his influence to bear on* (= tried to influence) *the parliament.* **under the influence (of alcohol/drink)** *He was arrested for driving under the influence.*

2 sb/sth that affects the way sb behaves/thinks
- ADJ. **big, considerable, great, significant** | **dominant, major, overwhelming** | **powerful, profound, strong** | **important** | **early** *Who were your early influences* (= influences at the start of your career)*?* | **formative** *The massive intellect of his mother had been a formative influence from his earliest years.* | **diverse** *He is a writer of Indian descent and draws upon diverse cultural influences.* | **outside** *Parents often seek to shelter their children from outside influences* | **good** | **adverse, bad, corrupting, destructive, disruptive, harmful, negative** | **stabilizing, steadying** | **calming, restraining** | **civilizing** | **environmental, genetic** | **artistic, cultural, musical**
- VERB + INFLUENCE **be, represent** *The legacy of Ancient Rome represented the overwhelming influence on Romanesque architecture.* | **have** *The band had many influences.* | **be exposed to** *a study of children exposed to different cultural influences* | **draw from/on/upon**
- INFLUENCE + VERB **be at work** *There were a number of influences at work in Gaudí's architecture.*
- PREP. **~ on** *She's by far the biggest influence on my writing.*

influence *verb*

- ADV. **considerably, deeply, enormously, greatly, heavily, powerfully, profoundly, strongly** *This book influenced her profoundly.* | **increasingly** | **largely, mainly, primarily** | **partly, slightly** | **directly, indirectly** *Pressure from industry bosses has directly influenced government policy.* | **clearly, obviously, undoubtedly** | **actively** | **critically, crucially, decisively, significantly** | **inevitably** | **positively** *actions that positively influence health* | **adversely** | **unduly** *Try to be aware of external factors which may unduly influence your judgement.*
- VERB + INFLUENCE **seem to** | **attempt to, seek to, try to** *seeking to influence university appointments*
- PREP. **in** *Her parents tried to influence her in her choice of university.*
- PHRASES **be easily/readily influenced** *He was naïve and easily influenced by his friends.*

influential *adj.*

- VERBS **be, prove** | **become**
- ADV. **deeply, enormously, especially, extraordinarily, extremely, highly, hugely, immensely, particularly, really, very** *This was a highly influential work.* ◊ *As a writer she was hugely influential.* | **increasingly** | **fairly, quite** | **widely** | **politically**
- PREP. **in** *The group was influential in setting up the new schools.*

influenza *noun*

- QUANT. **attack, bout**
- VERB + INFLUENZA **have, suffer from** | **catch, contract**
- INFLUENZA + NOUN **epidemic** | **virus**
- ⇒ Special page at ILLNESS

influx *noun*

- ADJ. **great, huge, large, massive, vast** | **small** | **new** | **sudden** | **continuing** | **steady** | **daily** *the daily influx of sightseers to the city*
- VERB + INFLUX **have, receive** *The hotel has received a large influx of guests.* | **prevent** *The country sealed its borders to prevent the influx of illegal immigrants.* | **cope with** *They didn't know how they were going to cope with the sudden influx of refugees.*
- PREP. **~ into/to** *a massive influx of foreign tourists into London*

inform *verb*

- ADV. **merely, simply** *I am not advising you. I am merely informing you of the situation.* | **regularly** | **immediately** | **officially** | **personally** | **kindly, politely** *Next time you decide to take some action, kindly inform me.* | **bluntly** *'I won't do it!' she informed him bluntly.* | **coldly, coolly**
- VERB + INFORM **be pleased to** | **regret to** *I regret to inform you that you have been unsuccessful in your application.* | **be required to** *The clinic is required to inform the patient about possible alternative treatments.*
- PREP. **about** *efforts to inform young people about the dangers of drugs* **of** *We will immediately inform you of any changes to the programme.*

informal *adj.*

- VERBS **be** | **become** | **remain**
- ADV. **extremely, highly, very** | **fairly, quite, rather, relatively** *Our meetings are relatively informal.* | **purely** *These meetings should remain purely informal, with no obligation on either side.* | **cheerfully, delightfully**

information *noun*

- ADJ. **accurate, correct, precise** | **false** *It is alleged that he gave false information to the tax authorities.* | **relevant, useful, valuable** | **useless** | **available** *Further information is available on request.* | **missing** | **fresh, new** | **latest, up-to-date** *the latest information on lung conditions* | **additional, extra, further** | **general** *general information about the company as a whole* | **basic** *basic information like date of birth, doctor's name and phone number* | **background** | **detailed** | **factual** | **classified, confidential, secret** | **price-sensitive** *There are legal constraints on the use of price-sensitive information.* | **bibliographic, economic, educational, financial, social, technological, etc.**
- QUANT. **item, piece** *an interesting piece of information* | **bit, fragment, nugget, scrap, snippet** *She let slip a few nuggets of information about herself.* | **mine, wealth** *This book is a mine of information on the Romans.*
- VERB + INFORMATION **contain** | **have** *Do you have the information I need?* | **retain, store** *James is able to retain an enormous amount of factual information in his head.* ◊ *database systems that process and store information* | **need, require** | **ask for, request** | **look for, seek** |

find, gain, get, obtain *information gained from research* | collect, gather *The police are still questioning witnesses and gathering information.* | receive | dig up *Have you dug up any further information on the suspect?* | extract, retrieve *the difficulties of extracting information from government officials* ◊ *software that retrieves information from a variety of different sources* | access *Portable computers are good for accessing information while travelling.* | download | disclose, give, impart, make available, provide (sb with), supply (sb with) *a court order preventing an ex-employee from disclosing confidential information* | leak *Someone leaked information to the press.* | pass on *They passed on the information about the crime to the police.* | circulate, disseminate *an organization that collects and disseminates information about women in science* | exchange *The French and British police will exchange information on wanted criminals.* | withhold *It was improper of the broker to withhold the information from the stock exchange.* | cover up, suppress | collate, organize | check | analyse | present *The way you present the information is important.* | publish | act on, go on *At the moment we've very little information to go on.*
• INFORMATION + VERB relate to sth *information relating to the social background of the child* | lead to sth *a reward for information leading to an arrest*
• INFORMATION + NOUN service | bureau, desk, office, centre | source | system | processing
• PREP. according to ~ *According to information received by the police, the terrorists have left the country.* for sb's ~ *This leaflet is produced for the information of our customers.* | ~ about/concerning/on/regarding *financial information concerning a company*
• PHRASES access to information, the exchange of information, the flow of information *to improve the flow of information within the company* a lack of information, a request for information, a source of information

informative *adj.*

• VERBS be, prove | find sth
• ADV. extremely, highly, most, particularly, very, wonderfully *The survey proved most informative.* | quite
• PREP. about *The book is extremely informative about life in Roman times.*

informed *adj.*

• VERBS be | keep | keep sb
• ADV. closely, well *The kids are much better informed than I was at their age.* | fully, properly *Consumers must be fully informed of the services available.* | adequately, reasonably *I offer my observations as those of an interested and reasonably informed member of the general public.* | badly, ill, poorly | reliably *I am reliably informed that there are plans to close this school.* | politically *a politically informed public* | theoretically *theoretically informed research*
• PREP. about *They were poorly informed about their rights.* of *We will keep you informed of any developments.* on *Keep me informed on progress.*

informer *noun*

• ADJ. police *He later became a police informer.*
• VERB + INFORMER become, turn *One of the gang members had turned informer.*
• PHRASES a network of informers

infrequent *adj.*

• VERBS be | become
• ADV. very | comparatively, fairly, rather, relatively *Disturbances are relatively infrequent in British prisons.*

infringement *noun*

• ADJ. serious | minor | clear | alleged | possible | copyright, patent, trademark
• VERB + INFRINGEMENT be, constitute *The committee ruled that the US ban constituted an infringement of free trade.* | commit *sympathy for people who commit minor infringements under difficult circumstances*
• PHRASES an infringement of copyright/the law

ingenious *adj.*

• VERBS be, sound *The idea sounds quite ingenious*
• ADV. extremely, highly, most, quite, very *a most ingenious device*

ingenuity *noun*

• ADJ. considerable, great | intellectual, technical | human
• QUANT. amount, degree *Getting out of this mess was going to require a fair degree of ingenuity.*
• VERB + INGENUITY have *someone who has the ingenuity to solve problems* | apply, use *There is always a solution, so long as you are prepared to use your ingenuity.* | display, show *The children showed a lot of ingenuity.* | admire | call for, need, require, take *Considerable ingenuity is needed to minimize costs.* ◊ *It didn't take much ingenuity to transform the door into a table.*
• PREP. with~ *They adapted the available materials with great ingenuity.* | ~ in *We have to admire his ingenuity in redesigning the machinery.*

ingrained *adj.*

• VERBS be | become | remain
• ADV. deeply *Prejudice remains deeply ingrained in many organizations.*
• PREP. in

ingredient *noun*

1 thing from which sth is made
• ADJ. excellent, good *It always pays to use the best ingredients when cooking.* | main, major, principal *the principal ingredient of smog* | important, vital | secret, special | basic | common | active *salicylic acid, the active ingredient in aspirin* | remaining *Add all the remaining ingredients and bring to the boil.* | fresh | natural | artificial | exotic | dry *Use a spoon to mix the dry ingredients.* | raw | food
• VERB + INGREDIENT use *I only use natural ingredients.* | add, pour in/on/over *Mix the marinade ingredients and pour over the goose.* | blend, combine, mix, stir (in) *Blend all the ingredients together in a bowl.*
• PHRASES a list of ingredients *All food products should carry a list of ingredients on the packet.*
⇨ Special page at FOOD

2 thing/quality necessary to make sth successful
• ADJ. crucial, essential, fundamental, important, key, vital *Hard work is a vital ingredient for success.* | main, major, principal | basic, necessary *Forecasting is a basic ingredient of business planning.* | right *The little town has all the right ingredients for a murder mystery.* | magic, secret, special | added/additional, extra | missing
• VERB + INGREDIENT have *The Australian team had the added ingredient of perseverance.* | provide, supply *She hopes the change of career will supply the missing ingredient in her life—excitement.*
• PREP. ~ for *Tolerance is an essential ingredient for a happy marriage.* ~ in *Individualism has been the secret ingredient in developing his chain of fashion stores.*
• PHRASES an ingredient for success

inhabitant noun

● ADJ. **local** | **old** *He is Brixham's oldest inhabitant.* | **younger** | **present** | **permanent** | **early** *The island's earliest inhabitants came from India.* | **original** | **indigenous, native** | **rural, village** | **human**
● VERB + INHABITANT **have** *London has over seven million inhabitants.*
● INHABITANT + VERB **live** *77% of the inhabitants lived in the countryside.*
● PREP. **of/with ... ~** *towns of about 10 000 inhabitants*

inhale verb

● ADV. **deeply** | **sharply** *Janet inhaled sharply when she saw him.* | **slowly**

inherit verb

● VERB + INHERIT **stand to** *He stood to inherit (= was likely to inherit) property worth £5 million.*
● PREP. **from** *She inherited some money from her mother.*
● PHRASES **be genetically inherited** *How many of these traits are genetically inherited?*

inheritance noun

1 money/property
● ADJ. **large** | **small** | **rightful** *(literary) He accused his younger brother of trying to steal his rightful inheritance.* | **shared**
● VERB + INHERITANCE **leave sb** *She left him an inheritance of £100 000.* | **come into, enter (into/on/upon)** *(literary), receive When he was 21 he came into a large inheritance.* | **claim** *When his father died, he returned to England to claim his inheritance.* | **renounce** | **challenge** *Jealous relatives tried to challenge her inheritance.* | **steal** | **restore (sb to)** *The Earl of Arundel's heir was restored to his inheritance and granted the lordship of Chirk.* | **divide** *The inheritance was divided equally among all the sons.* | **share (in)** *Under their law, all children shared in the inheritance.*
● INHERITANCE + NOUN **tax** | **law**
● PREP. **~by** *The system involved inheritance by the eldest son.* **~through** *inheritance through marriage*
2 sth from the past/your family
● PREP. **common** *a common inheritance of language and culture* | **cultural** | **genetic, physical** | **classical** *the influence of the classical inheritance (= the culture of ancient Greece and Rome) on Renaissance thought*

inhibit verb

● ADV. **seriously, severely, significantly** *Alcohol significantly inhibits the action of the drug.* | **completely** | **slightly**
● VERB + INHIBIT **tend to** *A large service sector and a small manufacturing sector would tend to inhibit growth in the economy.*
● PREP. **from** *The fear of dismissal inhibited employees from raising problems.*

inhibited adj.

● VERBS **be, feel** | **become**
● ADV. **very** | **rather, slightly** | **emotionally**
● PREP. **about** *He was rather inhibited about discussing politics.* **by** *She felt very inhibited by her own lack of experience.* **from** *No one should feel inhibited from taking part in the show.*

inhibition noun

● VERB + INHIBITION **have (no)** | **show (no)** | **get rid of, lose, overcome** *The children, at first shy, soon lost their inhibitions.*
● PREP. **without ~** *Young children will participate in a drama class without inhibition.* | **~about** *They had no inhibitions about voicing their feelings.* **~against** *an inhibition against certain behaviour*

inhuman adj.

● VERBS **be** | **consider sth, regard sth as** *We regard their treatment of the prisoners as inhuman.*
● ADV. **positively** *What she proposes is positively inhuman!* | **totally, utterly** | **almost**

initial noun

● VERB + INITIAL **have** *The two authors have the same initials.* | **be/become known by** *She's always been known by her initials.* | **use** | **bear, carry** *A stone over the door bears the initials 'R.P.', which stand for 'Ralph Piggot'.* | **carve, embroider, engrave (sth with), mark sth with, monogram sth with, put, sign, stamp (sth with), write** *He carved his girlfriend's initials in the rock.* ◇ *Now that she was managing director she could put the initials MD after her name.*
● INITIAL + VERB **stand for sth**
● PREP. **~for** *When writing, if you use initials for a long name, make sure you spell out the name at least once.*

initiate verb

● ADV. **formally** *The enquiry was formally initiated last month.*

initiation noun

● INITIATION + NOUN **ceremony, rite, ritual** *an initiation ceremony for new members of the organization*
● PREP. **~into** *It was my initiation into the world of high fashion.*
● PHRASES **a ceremony/rite of initiation**

initiative noun

1 new plan
● ADJ. **fresh, new** *fresh initiatives to find a peaceful end to the conflict* | **pioneering** *pioneering initiatives in bioengineering* | **current, latest, recent** | **important, major** | **welcome** | **successful** | **practical** | **exciting** | **private** | **co-operative, joint** | **international, local, national, regional** | **government** | **business, diplomatic, economic, education/educational, environmental, marketing, peace, policy, political, research, training**
● QUANT. **range, series**
● VERB + INITIATIVE **undertake** *The research initiative is being undertaken by a group of environmentalists.* | **plan** | **develop** | **announce** | **introduce, launch, set up, start** *The government has launched a new policy initiative.* | **be/become involved in** *Ten schools have been involved in the initiative.* | **lead** | **approve** | **reject** *The peace initiative was rejected out of hand.* | **sponsor** *a peace initiative sponsored by the Organization of African Unity* | **endorse, support** *The committee endorsed an initiative by the chairman to enter discussion about a possible merger.* | **welcome** *We welcome the government's initiative to help the homeless.* | **praise** | **encourage**
● INITIATIVE + VERB **be aimed at sth, be designed to** *a local initiative aimed at economic regeneration* ◇ *an initiative designed to promote collaborative research* | **involve sth, relate to sth** | **founder** *The initiative foundered because there was no market interest in redevelopment.*
● PREP. **~against** *a new initiative against car theft* **~by** *the latest initiative by the UN Secretary General* **~for** *an initiative for peace and human rights* **~on** *the government's major new initiative on crime*
⇨ Special page at BUSINESS
2 ability to decide/act independently
● ADJ. **considerable, great, real** | **individual, personal,**

private *It is a very hierarchical company and there's little place for individual initiative.* | **entrepreneurial**
● VERB + INITIATIVE **have** *He had the initiative to ask what time the last train left.* | **display, show | act/work on your own, use** *He acted on his own initiative and wasn't following orders.* ◇ *Don't ask me what you should do all the time. Use your initiative!* | **lack | encourage, promote | stifle** *Raising taxes on small businesses will stifle initiative.*
● PREP. **on sb's~** *The project was set up on the initiative of a local landowner.* | **~in** *Some scientists show little initiative in applying their knowledge.*
● PHRASES **a lack of initiative, on your own initiative** *In an unprecedented action, the army, on its own initiative, arrested seven civilians.*

3 the initiative opportunity to gain an advantage
● VERB + INITIATIVE **have, hold** *After their latest setback, the rebel forces no longer hold the initiative.* | **gain, seize, take | regain** *In the second half, Manchester United regained the initiative.* | **lose**
● INITIATIVE + VERB **comes from sb/sth, lie with sb** *The initiative to re-open negotiations came from Moscow.*
● PREP. **~in** *She took the initiative in asking the board to conduct an enquiry.*

injection noun

1 act of injecting sb
● ADJ. **intramuscular, intravenous | anti-tetanus/tetanus, flu, pain-killing | insulin, penicillin, etc. | booster** *Can I bring my dog in for his booster injection?* | **lethal** *In some US states execution is by lethal injection.* | **regular | daily**
● VERB + INJECTION **have** *He had to have a tetanus injection after injuring himself with a shovel.* | **administer, give sb, perform** *They gave her an injection to stop the pain.* | **receive** *The rats received a daily injection of the drug.*
● PREP. **by~** *The best treatment is antibiotics, preferably by injection.* | **~against** *an injection against whooping cough* | **~for** *injections for diabetes* | **in/into** *an injection into the vein* | **~with** *Both groups received a second injection with the same solution.*

2 money
● ADJ. **massive, substantial | much-needed | capital, cash** *An undisclosed buyer will provide a much-needed cash injection for the fragile balance sheet.*
● VERB + INJECTION **need, require | give sth, provide (sth with) | receive**
● PREP. **~from** *a cash injection from the Belgian state* | **~into** *an injection of cash into the economy*
● PHRASES **an injection of capital/cash/money/resources** *The company had reached the size where it needed an injection of capital.*

injunction noun

1 court order
● ADJ. **interim, preliminary | temporary | permanent | court**
● VERB + INJUNCTION **apply for, seek | get, obtain, take out, win** *She took out an injunction to prevent the press publishing the information.* | **grant (sb), issue | refuse (sb/sth) | vary** *an application to court to vary an injunction* | **lift** *It was agreed that the temporary injunction should be lifted.* | **uphold | overturn | ignore**
● INJUNCTION + VERB **order sth, require sth | ban sth, bar sth, forbid sth, prohibit sth, restrain sb/sth** *The court upheld an injunction barring protesters from blocking access to the company.* ◇ *an injunction restraining the disclosure of company secrets* | **prevent sth**
● PREP. **~against/on** *They got an interim injunction against the union.*
● PHRASES **a breach of an injunction**

2 warning/order from sb in authority
● ADJ. **stern**
● VERB + INJUNCTION **follow, obey** *The rank and file members will follow the injunction of the party leadership.* | **ignore**

injure verb

1 harm yourself/sb physically
● ADV. **badly, seriously, severely | slightly | accidentally** *insurance to cover you in case one of your employees accidentally injures someone* | **deliberately**

2 damage sb's reputation, pride, etc.
● ADV. **seriously, severely** *This incident could seriously injure the company's reputation.*
● VERB + INJURE **be calculated to** (*law*), **be likely to** *espionage activity which was likely to injure the national interest*

injured adj.

● VERBS **be, lie** *He could have been lying injured on the moors after a fall from his horse.* | **get**
● ADV. **badly, critically, gravely, seriously, severely** *her badly injured ankle* ◇ *Several people were seriously injured.* | **slightly** *a slightly injured arm* | **fatally**

injury noun

● ADJ. **appalling, bad, horrendous, major, nasty, serious, severe, terrible | crippling | fatal | multiple | extensive | minor, slight, superficial | old | nagging, niggling, recurring | long-term | permanent** *Researchers have determined that heading a football can cause permanent injury.* | **accidental | internal | visible | facial, head, knee, leg, spinal, etc. | sports | industrial | bodily, emotional, personal** (*all law*)
● QUANT. **run, series, spate** *He missed most of the season with a spate of injuries.*
● VERB + INJURY **do yourself, incur, pick up, receive, suffer** *You'll do yourself an injury riding that old bike.* ◇ *She picked up an injury during the quarter-final.* | **risk** *The doctor said he would risk serious injury if he were to fall again.* | **cause (sb/sth), inflict** *The car turned right over, causing severe injury to the driver.* ◇ *Please help me before our dogs inflict serious injury on each other!* | **carry, have, nurse, suffer from** *She has replaced him in the team while he nurses a shoulder injury.* | **be prone to | feign** *He was accused of feigning injury.* | **aggravate** *He aggravated a neck injury while playing for Derby County.* | **die from/of** *The inquest heard that he died from multiple injuries.* | **avoid, escape** *Stretching exercises can help avoid injury.* ◇ *Fortunately, the passengers escaped serious injury.* | **overcome, shake off** *She has failed to shake off her stomach injury.* | **recover from | deal with, treat, be treated for** *Finger injuries should be dealt with immediately.* ◇ *He is still being treated for injuries to his legs.* | **go off with** *He went off* (= off the playing field) *with an injury in the second half.* | **be out with** *She is out* (= out of the competition/team) *for six weeks with a hamstring injury.* | **pull out because of/due to/with** *He pulled out with* (= decided not to compete because of) *an injury at the last moment.* | **be back after/from, come back from, return after/from** *She should be back from injury.* | **have sb back after** *India had wicketkeeper More back after injury.*
● INJURY + VERB **happen (to sb), occur** *This type of injury could happen to any player at any time.* | **result from sth** *injuries resulting from exposure to harmful substances* | **heal | dog sb/sth, hamper sb/sth, trouble sb** *Her athletics career has been dogged by injury.* | **sideline sb** *Both defenders have been sidelined by injury.* | **force sb to** *The knee injury forced him to give up playing at the age of 23.* | **arise from/out of** (*law*) *personal injuries arising from negligence*

• INJURY + NOUN **problems** *The team has a lot of injury problems.* | **time** *They scored two goals in injury time* (= time added at the end of a game because the game has been interrupted by injured players needing treatment).
• PREP. **because of** ~ *She's unable to play because of injury.* **through** ~ *He has pulled out of the match through injury.* **with** ~ *She slumped to the floor with injuries to her back and neck.* **without** ~ *a step-by-step guide to lifting without injury* | **~from** *injuries from the fire* **~to**
• PHRASES **add insult to injury** *It adds insult to injury* (= it make things worse) *that banks are allowed to increase their charges without our knowledge or consent.* **a claim for injury** (*law*) *a claim for personal injury* **a risk of injury** *There is a real risk of injury in sports such as climbing.*

injustice *noun*

• ADJ. **cruel, grave, great, gross, terrible** | **perceived** | **racial, social**
• VERB + INJUSTICE **experience, suffer** *He suffered the injustice of being punished for a crime which he did not commit.* | **regard sth as** *The trial was regarded as the greatest injustice of the post-war criminal justice system.* | **cause** (*law*), **commit, do** (**sb/yourself**) *She remains adamant that an injustice was done.* ◇ *We may have been doing him an injustice* (= criticizing him unfairly). *This work is good.* | **expose** *a novel that sets out to expose social injustice* | **fight against, protest against, speak out against, struggle against, work against** *She was acclaimed for speaking out against injustice.* | **correct, remedy** *people who work hard to correct society's injustices* | **stop**
• PREP. **~by** *a terrible injustice by the police* **~to** *It would be an injustice to the man to imprison him for life.*
• PHRASES **the injustice of it all** *She was overwhelmed by the injustice of it all* (= of the situation). **a sense of injustice, a victim of injustice**

ink *noun*

• ADJ. **wet** *Be careful. The ink is still wet.* | **coloured** | **India/Indian** | **indelible, permanent, waterproof** | **washable** | **invisible** | **printing**
• VERB + INK **use** *Most people now use ballpoints rather than ink.* | **write in** *He wrote very neatly in blue ink.* | **spill**
• INK + VERB **dry** *Allow the ink to dry.* | **smudge** *The drawback of this printer is that the ink tends to smudge.*
• INK + NOUN **blot, spot** | **pen** | **cartridge** *We need to replace the ink cartridge in the printer.* | **drawing**
• PREP. **in~** *There were several alterations in ink.*
• PHRASES **pen and ink** *a pen and ink drawing*

inkling *noun*

• ADJ. **first** *The first inkling we had of Cliff's problem was when he didn't come to work.* | **faintest, slightest** *We didn't have the slightest inkling of the dramatic news we were about to hear.*
• VERB + INKLING **have** (**no**) | **get** | **give** (**sb**) *She never gave us any inkling of what she was planning.*
• PREP. **~of**

inmate *noun*

• ADJ. **fellow** | **former** *a former inmate of Gloucester jail* | **young** | **male, female** | **camp, prison**
• VERB + INMATE **move, transfer** *The inmates were moved to an undisclosed location.*
• INMATE + VERB **escape**
• INMATE + NOUN **population**
• PREP. **among** ~ *drug and alcohol misuse among inmates*

innocence *noun*

1 being not guilty of a crime, etc.
• ADJ. **total**
• VERB + INNOCENCE **declare, proclaim** *The prisoners passionately proclaimed their innocence in front of the jury.* | **claim** *She claimed total innocence of all charges.* | **protest** *Hayes has protested his innocence throughout the case.* | **demonstrate, establish, prove** | **be convinced of** *The solicitors were convinced of his innocence and urged him to appeal the conviction.*
• PHRASES **in all innocence** *I asked her the question in all innocence. I didn't know it was going to upset her.* **the presumption of innocence** (*law*)

2 lack of knowledge/experience
• ADJ. **childlike, wide-eyed** | **lost** | **injured** *She replied to her father's accusations in tones of injured innocence.* | **apparent** | **mock**
• VERB + INNOCENCE **lose** *He had lost the innocence of childhood.* | **retain** | **take advantage of** *She had taken advantage of his innocence.*
• PREP. **in your** ~ *In his innocence he had allowed the salesman in to discuss vacuum cleaners.* **with … ~** *He grinned with apparent innocence.* | **~about** *There is an innocence about the story.*
• PHRASES **an air of innocence** *There was a touching air of innocence about the boy.* **a look of innocence, the picture of innocence** *'You cheated!' 'I what?' asked David, the picture of innocence* (= pretending to look innocent). **a state of innocence**

innocent *adj.*

1 not guilty
• VERBS **be, plead** *He pleaded innocent to the charges.* | **believe sb, presume sb** *I had always believed her innocent.* ◇ *The accused person should always be presumed innocent until proved guilty.* | **declare sb, find sb, prove sb** *The court found her innocent of the crime.*
• ADV. **completely, entirely, totally, wholly**
• PREP. **of** *I am totally innocent of this crime.*

2 not intended/intending to cause harm
• VERBS **be, look, play, seem, sound** *Stop playing innocent and answer my questions, please.*
• ADV. **very** | **all, altogether, perfectly** *She tried to sound all innocent as she asked the question.* ◇ *The circumstance could be altogether innocent, but suspicions have been raised.* | **relatively** | **apparently, seemingly**

3 with no experience of the world
• VERBS **be, seem** *She was sixteen and sweetly innocent.*
• ADV. **remarkably, very** | **sweetly** | **strangely** *the strangely innocent world of her childhood* | **sexually**

innocuous *adj.*

• VERBS **appear, be, look, seem**
• ADV. **perfectly, totally, wholly** *His comment seemed perfectly innocuous.* | **fairly, pretty, quite, relatively** *The liquid looked fairly innocuous.* | **enough** *The question appeared innocuous enough, but I still did not trust her.* | **apparently, seemingly**

innovation *noun*

1 introduction of new ideas
• ADJ. **constant, continuous** | **successful** | **cultural, educational, industrial, scientific, technical, technological** | **design, policy, product** *industries where constant product innovation is a criterion for survival*
• VERB + INNOVATION **encourage, facilitate, foster, stimulate** | **stifle** *Too strict a regulatory system will stifle innovation.*
• INNOVATION + VERB **occur** *Technical innovation may occur directly in the factory.*
• INNOVATION + NOUN **process**

- PREP. **~in** *innovation in engineering*
- PHRASES **scope for innovation**

2 new idea

- ADJ. **great, major, important, significant | successful | welcome | interesting | latest, new | recent | scientific, technical, technological**
- VERB + INNOVATION **come up with** *She believed she had come up with one of the greatest innovations of modern times.* | **introduce** *Many innovations were introduced by the 1919 Act.* | **design, develop** *technological innovations designed to save energy*
- INNOVATION + VERB **occur**
- PREP. **~ by** *Mathematical astronomy was the great innovation by the Greeks of the 5th century BC.* **~ in** *innovations in machinery and instruments*

input *noun*

1 of time/knowledge/ideas

- ADJ. **considerable, great, important, major, significant, substantial | additional | direct | regular | local | specialist, technical**
- VERB + INPUT **have | need | get, receive | provide** *constructive criticism which provided an input into the school's decision-making process*
- PREP. **~ by** *The report contains a substantial input by the police.* **~ from** *input from various interested parties* **~ in** *They all had some input in the discussion.* **~ into** *her input into the survey* **~ on** *The union would like more input on redundancies.* **~ to** *an additional input to market analysis*

2 for a computer

- ADJ. **data | user | keyboard | computer**
- VERB + INPUT **require** *Early computers required input in the form of punched cards.* | **accept** *The software will accept input from a variety of other programs.* | **process** *It may be beyond the capability of the hardware to process the input.* | **be used as/for** *Decision tables can be used as computer input.* | **check** *Check your input and make sure you have selected only one item.*
- INPUT + NOUN **data | file | field, form, screen** *The cursor is positioned on the first input field of the page.* | **device** *an input device such as a keyboard*
- PREP. **~ for** *inputs for the printers* **~ from** *input from a mouse* **~ to** *input to a computer database*
- PHRASES **input and output**

inquest *noun*

- ADJ. **full | fresh | coroner's**
- VERB + INQUEST **conduct, hold | order** *The court ordered a fresh inquest into the tragedy.* | **open | adjourn | attend**
- INQUEST + VERB **open | hear sth** *An elderly woman froze to death, an inquest heard yesterday.* | **decide sth, find sth** *An inquest found that the deceased had died of a drugs overdose.* | **return a verdict** *The inquest returned a verdict of accidental death.*
- INQUEST + NOUN **jury | verdict**
- PREP. **at a/the** *A verdict of suicide was recorded at the inquest.* | **~ into** *an inquest into the team's poor performance* **~ on** *an inquest on three fishermen*

inquire, inquiry

⇨ See ENQUIRE, ENQUIRY

inquisitive *adj.*

- VERBS **appear, be, seem | become**
- ADV. **highly, very** *a highly inquisitive mind* | **naturally** *Children are naturally inquisitive.* | **incurably**
- PREP. **about** *We try not to be too inquisitive about what he's doing.*

insane *adj.*

1 mentally ill/crazy

- VERBS **be, look | become, go** *He later became insane and was confined to an asylum.* ◊ *He went almost insane when he heard that his daughter had died.* | **drive sb** *You're driving me nearly insane with that noise.* | **certify sb, declare sb** *In 1975 she was certified clinically insane and sent to a mental hospital.*
- ADV. **completely, totally | almost, nearly | a little | dangerously | clinically | criminally** *He is criminally insane, unable to stop himself attacking women.*

2 very stupid/dangerous

- VERBS **be, seem** *It seems insane to cut the budget now.*
- ADV. **quite, totally** *The whole idea is quite insane.*

insanity *noun*

- ADJ. **total**
- VERB + INSANITY **plead** *At the murder trial, he pleaded insanity.*

inscribe *verb*

- ADV. **personally** *The volume had been personally inscribed by the author.* | **suitably** *He sent me a number of his books, all suitably inscribed.*
- PREP. **on** *Her name was inscribed on the watch.* **with** *The watch was inscribed with her name.*

inscription *noun*

- ADJ. **faded | famous | dedicatory, funerary, memorial, monumental | Greek, Latin, etc.**
- VERB + INSCRIPTION **bear, carry, have** *The monument carries the inscription: 'To the fallen in two world wars'.* | **carve, engrave** *an inscription carved in the stone*
- INSCRIPTION + VERB **bear sth, read sth, record sth, say sth, show sth, tell sb sth** *The inscription bears the date 1655.* ◊ *The simple inscription on her grave reads: 'She sleeps in peace.'*

insect *noun*

- ADJ. **flying, winged | aquatic | beneficial** *Unfortunately, pesticides kill off beneficial insects as well as harmful ones.* | **harmful, poisonous | social** *Social insects, such as ants, live in large colonies.*
- QUANT. **swarm**
- INSECT + VERB **buzz** *An insect was buzzing around the room.* | **fly | crawl | swarm | bore** *Insects had bored deep into the wood.* | **bite, sting**
- INSECT + NOUN **attack** *The wood should be treated against insect attack.* | **bite | eggs, larva | pests** *Gardeners welcome birds as they control insect pests.* | **repellent, spray | species | world** *Wasps are the master builders of the insect world.*

insecure *adj.*

1 not safe

- VERBS **appear, be, look, seem | become | remain**
- ADV. **extremely, very | increasingly | a little, rather, somewhat | financially** *men who are worried about losing their jobs and becoming financially insecure*

2 anxious

- VERBS **be, feel | become, grow**
- ADV. **deeply, extremely, profoundly, really, very | increasingly | a bit, a little, quite, rather | basically | notoriously** *a star who is notoriously insecure about her looks*
- PREP. **about** *He felt a bit insecure about being left alone.*

insecurity *noun*

- ADJ. **deep, great | growing, increased | general** *The*

prime minister spoke of the general insecurity in the country. | **economic, emotional, financial** | **job**
- PREP. **~about** *her insecurities about her abilities*
- PHRASES **a feeling/sense of insecurity**

insensitive adj.

1 not knowing or caring how sb else feels
- VERBS **appear, be, seem** | **become, grow** | **make sb** | **think sb** *I don't want to be thought insensitive, but I do think we should go ahead despite the accident.*
- ADV. **extremely, highly, incredibly, remarkably, very** | **totally** | **a bit, rather, somewhat**
- PREP. **to** *Years of abuse at boarding school had made him insensitive to others' suffering.*

2 not able to feel/be influenced by sth
- VERBS **be** | **remain**
- ADV. **completely, totally** | **almost** | **largely** | **fairly, relatively**
- PREP. **to** *The machine is relatively insensitive to changes in the atmosphere.*

insensitivity noun

- ADJ. **complete** | **crass**
- VERB + INSENSITIVITY **display, show**
- PREP. **~ to/towards** *The government has shown complete insensitivity to the refugees.*

inseparable adj.

- VERBS **be, seem**
- ADV. **absolutely, quite** | **almost, practically, virtually** *The two brothers are almost inseparable.* | **effectively**
- PREP. **from** *Religion is inseparable from politics.*

insert verb

- ADV. **carefully, gently**
- PREP. **between** *The English translation is inserted between the lines of text.* **in/into** *Fine needles are gently inserted into the patient's skin.* **through** *A probe was inserted through his mouth.*

insight noun

- ADJ. **considerable, great, real, significant** | **deep** | **detailed** | **brief** | **good, remarkable** *The objective of the research is to gain a better insight into labour market processes.* | **penetrating, profound, revealing, illuminating** | **crucial, important, invaluable, valuable** | **useful** | **fascinating, interesting** | **startling** | **fresh, new** | **original, unique** *Freud's original insights into the working of the mind* | **rare** | **clear** | **basic** | **direct** *The research will provide direct insight into molecular mechanisms.* | **further** | **sufficient** | **individual, personal** | **critical, historical, theoretical**
- QUANT. **flash** *With a flash of insight, she found the solution to the problem.* | **degree**
- VERB + INSIGHT **have** *The experienced specialist has professional skills and insight.* | **be lacking in, lack** | **show** | **allow (sb), afford (sb), give (sb), offer (sb), provide (sb with), produce, yield** | **gain, get, obtain** | **apply** *Teachers have to apply in the classroom the insights that they gain in educational courses.*
- PREP. **~ about** *Schopenhauer's insight about music* **~ into** *a fresh insight into Picasso's mind* **~ (as) to** *an insight as to how the gene works*
- PHRASES **a lack of insight**

insignificance noun

- ADJ. **comparative, relative**
- VERB + INSIGNIFICANCE **pale into, fade into** *Her achievements fade into insignificance beside those of her sisters.*

insignificant adj.

- VERBS **appear, be, feel, look, seem** *He made her feel insignificant.* | **become** | **remain** | **consider sth** *an event that was considered insignificant*
- ADV. **very** | **completely, quite** | **almost** | **comparatively, fairly, rather, relatively** | **apparently, seemingly** | **statistically** *These results are statistically insignificant.* | **socially**

insinuation noun

- ADJ. **veiled**
- VERB + INSINUATION **make** | **resent** *I deeply resent the insinuation that I'm only interested in the money.*
- PREP. **~ about** *Why did you make those veiled insinuations about me?* **~ against** *insinuations against the unsuccessful candidate*

insist verb

- ADV. **firmly, strongly** | **stubbornly** *He stubbornly insisted on doing it all himself.* | **absolutely** *I'm paying for this—no, I absolutely insist.* | **gently, quietly** *He quietly but firmly insisted.* | **always** | **repeatedly** | **still** *She still insists her critics are wrong.* | **rightly** *People rightly insist on being treated as individuals.*
- VERB + INSIST **continue to** | **try to** | **be entitled to** *Employers are entitled to insist that employees honour the terms of their agreement.*
- PREP. **on/upon** *He insists on speaking to you personally*

insistence noun

- ADJ. **strict** | **gentle** | **earlier, previous**
- VERB + INSISTENCE **abandon, drop** *The union has dropped its earlier insistence that workers should receive bonus payments.*
- PREP. **at/on sb's ~** *At the insistence of his father, he bought himself a new suit.* | **~ by** *insistence by the government that 25% of all household waste be recycled* **~ on/upon** *an insistence upon the highest standards of grammatical correctness*

insistent adj.

- VERBS **be** | **become, grow** | **remain**
- ADV. **extremely, most, very** *She was most insistent that we shouldn't leave the door unlocked.* | **fairly, quite**
- PREP. **about** *She was insistent about inviting him.* **on/upon** *He was insistent on a formal written agreement.*

insoluble adj.

1 that cannot be solved/explained
- VERBS **be, seem** | **remain**
- ADV. **absolutely** | **almost** | **apparently, seemingly**

2 impossible to dissolve in a liquid
- VERBS **be**
- ADV. **highly** | **practically, virtually**
- PREP. **~ in** *These chemicals are practically insoluble in water.*

inspect verb

- ADV. **carefully, closely, thoroughly** | **regularly**
- VERB + INSPECT **allow sb to, be entitled to** *Each party in the case is entitled to inspect the documents held by the other.*
- PREP. **for** *He inspected the water tank carefully for cracks.*

inspection noun

- ADJ. **careful, close, detailed, thorough** | **full** | **brief, cursory** | **routine** | **frequent, regular** | **annual, daily, etc.** | **surprise** *a surprise inspection of the premises by the*

health inspector | **preliminary** | **public** *The records are open to public inspection.* | **independent** | **international** *They have refused to allow international inspection of their nuclear facilities.* | **physical, visual** | **safety** | **medical** | **on-site, site** *Following an on-site inspection, the surveyor prepared a written report on the property.*
• VERB + INSPECTION **be available for, be open for/to, be subject to** *A company's accounting records must be open for inspection at all times.* ◇ *Nursing agencies are subject to inspection by the health authority.* | **bear** (*literary*) *He knew that his motives would not bear too close an inspection* (= that his motives were not good). | **carry out, conduct, make** *The architect is carrying out a thorough inspection of the building.* | **allow** | **pass** *The hotel passed its annual inspection.* | **fail**
• INSPECTION + VERB **reveal sth, show sth, suggest sth** *Closer inspection of the vase revealed it to be a fake.* | **take place**
• INSPECTION + NOUN **visit** | **report** | **team** | **hatch, panel**
• PREP. **for** ~ *He held out the saucepan for inspection.* **on/upon** ~ *The report seemed impressive at first, but on closer inspection there were several inaccuracies.* | **~by** *an inspection of the troops by the commander-in-chief*
• PHRASES **a tour of inspection** *The head went on a tour of inspection of all the classrooms.*

inspector *noun*

1 official who inspects sth
• ADJ. **chief, principal** | **deputy** | **local** | **independent** | **official** | **government, ministry, RSPCA, UN/United Nations, etc.** | **building, factory, (health and) safety, planning, (public) health, school, tax, ticket, weapons** *UN weapons inspectors*
• VERB + INSPECTOR **call in** *The school inspectors were called in.*
• INSPECTOR + VERB **be in charge of sth** *the inspector in charge of producing the report* | **look at sth** | **report (on) sth**
• PREP. **~of** *an inspector of prisons*
⇨ Note at JOB
2 police officer
• ADJ. **police** | **Chief, detective**
• PHRASES **the rank of inspector**

inspiration *noun*

• ADJ. **great, sheer** | **direct** *His wife was the direct inspiration for the main character in the book.* | **sudden** | **fresh** | **artistic, creative, poetic** | **divine**
• QUANT. **flash, moment** *In a flash of sheer inspiration, I decided to paint the whole house white.*
• VERB + INSPIRATION **derive, draw, find, gain, get, owe, take** *The movement draws much of its inspiration from the Greek philosophers.* ◇ *Many of us found inspiration in her teaching.* ◇ *Where did you get the inspiration for the book?* ◇ *Her latest book owes its inspiration to childhood memories.* | **give sb, provide (sb with)** | **look for, seek** *He peered into his glass, as if seeking inspiration there.* | **be lacking (in), lack**
• INSPIRATION + VERB **come (from sth)** *One day the inspiration just came.* ◇ *Her inspiration comes from Asia.*
• PREP. **~ behind** *He was the inspiration behind last week's victory.* **~for** *The sea has provided an inspiration for many of his paintings.* **to** *She's been a great inspiration to me.*
• PHRASES **a source of inspiration**

inspired *adj.*

• VERBS **be, feel, seem** | **become**
• ADV. **divinely** *divinely inspired wisdom* | **ideologically, politically** *politically inspired violence*

inspiring *adj.*

• VERBS **be, seem** *None of the leaders seems very inspiring.* | **find sth/sb** *People find her inspiring.*
• ADV. **deeply, really, very** *a very inspiring sight* | **far from, hardly, less than, not particularly** *A pile of ironing is hardly inspiring.*

instability *noun*

• ADJ. **increased** | **growing, increasing** | **continuing** | **inherent, internal** | **economic, financial, political, social** | **emotional, mental**
• QUANT. **degree** *The increased inflation will inject a degree of instability into the economy.*
• VERB + INSTABILITY **cause, create** *Racism causes political instability and violence.* | **avoid** *The law was introduced to avoid instability during the transition.*
• INSTABILITY + VERB **arise, occur** *Instability may arise at times of change.*
• PHRASES **a period of instability** *a long period of economic instability* **a source of instability**

install *verb*

• ADV. **properly, safely** *Make sure the equipment is properly installed.* ◇ (*figurative*) *She saw her guests safely installed in their rooms and then went downstairs.* | **easily** *The loft ladder is easily installed.* | **successfully** | **professionally** *A professionally installed alarm will cost from about £500.*
• VERB + INSTALL **be easy to, be simple to** *The switches are cheap to buy and easy to install.*
• PHRASES **newly/recently installed** *a recently installed swimming pool*

instalment *noun*

1 regular payment
• ADJ. **fixed** | **equal** *a loan repaid in equal annual instalments* | **first, initial** | **second, third, etc.** | **final, last** | **next** | **annual, monthly, weekly, quarterly**
• VERB + INSTALMENT **pay (off), pay (sth) by/in, pay sth off in** *She sold the car before she had paid the instalments.* ◇ *The tenants agreed to pay off the arrears in instalments.* | **repay (sth) by/in**
• INSTALMENT + VERB **be/become due, be payable by/in** *The next instalment is not due until July.*
• INSTALMENT + NOUN **payment** | **plan, terms** *We offer an instalment plan.*
• PREP. **by** ~ *The amounts are repayable by instalment.* **in** ~ *Repayment is in ten instalments.*
2 part of a story
• ADJ. **first, second, etc.** | **final, last** | **daily, weekly** | **next**
• VERB + INSTALMENT **publish (sth in)** *The 'Screwtape Letters' were published in instalments from May to November 1941.*
• PREP. **~in** *the final instalment in the trilogy*

instance *noun*

• ADJ. **countless, innumerable, numerous** | **occasional, rare** | **isolated** | **(any) given, particular, specific** *Further information is required to determine the correct answer in any given instance.* | **extreme** | **striking** | **classic** *This is a classic instance of Dostoevsky's writing operating on two levels.*
• VERB + INSTANCE **give, provide** *North America provides the most striking instance of European settlement on a grand scale.* | **cite (sth as), take** *Experts cite the country as an instance where human rights violations could lead to international intervention.* ◇ *To take a particular instance of this problem: …* | **recall** *I cannot recall any other instance in modern times in which a huge and mighty state crumbled to dust.*

• INSTANCE + VERB **occur** *An instance of this controversy occurred last year.* | **show sth** *This instance shows how important it is to check that the machine is working properly before you use it.*
• PREP. **for ~** (= for example) *Murder, petty theft and tax evasion, for instance, all have different motives and consequences.* **in … ~** *In one instance, several people had their mobile phones stolen.* ◇ *It is not always helpful to draw analogies between sexism and racism, but in this instance it is useful.* **~ of** *This is an instance of his general attitude to his employees.*
• PHRASES **in the first instance** (*formal*) *In the first instance, a letter from your employer may be all you need.*

instant noun

1 short period of time
• ADJ. **brief, fleeting** *For a brief instant, I thought she was going to fall.* | **one, single** *His news was too important to be contained for a single instant longer.*
• VERB + INSTANT **pause for** *He paused for an instant before continuing.*
• PREP. **for an ~** *Just for an instant I thought he was going to refuse.* **in an ~** *It was all over in an instant.* | **~ after/before** *She woke up in the instant before the phone rang.*

2 single point in time
• ADJ. **(any) given, (any) one** *At any given instant the distribution of molecular speeds is always constant under the same conditions.* | **very** *He took out his keys to lock the door. At that very instant the door flew open and a man ran into the room.*
• PREP. **at … ~** *The bomb could go off at any instant.*

instant adj.

• VERBS **be**
• ADV. **almost** *His response was almost instant.*

instantaneous adj.

• VERBS **be** *Her death was almost instantaneous.*
• ADV. **almost, virtually**

instinct noun

• ADJ. **deep, powerful, strong** | **gut** | **first, initial** *His first instinct was to run away from danger.* | **good, unerring** *Against her better instincts, she ran back into the burning house to save some of her jewellery.* ◇ *He had an unerring instinct for when people were lying to him.* | **base** | **basic** | **natural** | **primitive** | **creative** | **aggressive, competitive** | **maternal, mothering, protective** | **fighting, hunting, killer, predatory** (*often figurative*) *He plays well but lacks that killer instinct that wins matches.* | **survival** | **herd** *What makes all these people come to the club? In my view it's the herd instinct.* | **sexual** | **business, commercial, political** | **animal, human**
• VERB + INSTINCT **have** | **lack** | **develop** *In negotiating you have to develop an instinct for when to be tough and when to make a deal.* | **follow, go on, obey, rely on, trust** *Why don't you just follow your natural instincts?* | **ignore, suppress** | **satisfy** | **appeal to** *They accused the campaign of appealing to the electorate's baser instincts.* | **share** *Both superpowers shared the same instinct for self-preservation.*
• INSTINCT + VERB **tell sb sth** *Her instinct told her that she was being followed.* | **guide sb** *Artists have to learn to be guided by their instincts.* | **take over** *Her instincts took over and she dived on the escaping thief.* | **be right/wrong** *I've trusted my instincts in the past and they've usually been right.*
• PREP. **by ~** *Babies know by instinct who their mother is.* **on ~** *I acted purely on instinct.* | **~ for** *He's got an instinct for survival in a tough job.*

instinctive adj.

• VERBS **be, seem** | **become**
• ADV. **totally** | **purely** *My reaction was purely instinctive.* | **almost**

institute noun

• ADJ. **professional** | **independent** | **government** | **international, national** | **economic, education, educational, research, scientific, technical**
• VERB + INSTITUTE **establish, found, set up** | **open** | **belong to** *She belongs to the Chartered Institute of Management.* | **join**
• INSTITUTE + VERB **find sth** *The environmental research institute found that the global average temperature had risen by 1.2°C.* | **claim sth, say sth** *The Institute says that an unidentified virus is to blame for the syndrome.* | **publish sth** | **provide sth** *an institute providing opportunities to veterinary graduates*
• PREP. **at an/the ~** *She used to give lectures at the Mechanics' Institute.* **in/within an/the ~** *He is a key figure in the Institute of Mathematics.* | **~ for** *the International Institute for Economic Development* **~ of**
• PHRASES **a founder of an institute, a member of an institute**
⇨ Note at ORGANIZATION

institution noun

1 large organization
• ADJ. **central, major** *Parliament remains the central institution of the constitution of the United Kingdom.* | **established** | **existing** *They argue for the reform of existing political institutions.* | **traditional** | **public** | **private** | **government, governmental, state** | **international, national** | **local** | **democratic** | **academic, administrative, charitable, cultural, economic, educational, financial, legal, lending, political, religious, research** *cultural institutions such as the Danish Institute*
• PREP. **at a/the ~** *a course at an institution of higher education* **in/within ~** *examination procedures within educational institutions*
⇨ Note at ORGANIZATION (for verbs)

2 building for people with special needs
• ADJ. **mental, penal**
• VERB + INSTITUTION **be admitted to, be placed in** *Many people with dementia would rather remain at home than be placed in an institution.* | **be kept in**
• PREP. **at/in ~** *patients in mental institutions* | **~ for** *an institution for mentally ill offenders*

3 custom
• ADJ. **national** *Fish and chips became a national institution in Britain.* | **cultural, economic, legal, political, religious, social** *cultural institutions such as religious and legal codes*

instruct verb

• ADV. **carefully** | **explicitly, specifically** *You were explicitly instructed to wait here.*
• PHRASES **as instructed** *I took the pills as instructed.*

instruction noun

1 instructions information on how to do sth
• ADJ. **comprehensive, full** | **adequate** | **clear, explicit** | **detailed, precise, specific, step-by-step** | **complex** | **simple** | **general** | **special** | **careful** | **printed, verbal, written** | **pack, packet** | **technical** | **safety** | **operating, cooking, washing** | **manufacturer's**
• QUANT. **list, series, set**
• VERB + INSTRUCTIONS **read** *You should always read the instructions on medicines thoroughly.* | **understand** | **follow** *These fondant decorations are easy to master if you follow our simple step-by-step instructions.* | **give (sb),**

leave (sb), supply *He gave her detailed instructions on the procedure to be followed.* ◇ *instructions supplied with a product* | repeat | come with *Did it come with any instructions about assembling it?*
• INSTRUCTIONS + VERB tell sb sth *instructions that tell you where everything goes*
• INSTRUCTION + NOUN book/booklet, leaflet, manual *I had to refer to the instruction booklet.*
• PREP. according to the ~ *Microwave ovens should be serviced according to the manufacturer's instructions.* in accordance with the ~, in the ~ *It tells you in the instructions not to let the machine get too hot.* | ~ about, ~ as to *The organizer will give instructions as to what to do.* | ~ on *instructions on how to use the photocopier*
• PHRASES follow (sb's) instructions to the letter *The jockey followed his trainer's instructions to the letter* (= followed them in every detail).

2 instructions sth that sb tells/permits you to do
• ADJ. clear, explicit, express, specific | firm, strict *I have strict instructions not to let anyone else in.* | direct | special | fresh, new | further | final | written
• VERB + INSTRUCTIONS be under, have | act on/under *She is acting under direct instructions from the president.* | carry out, comply with, follow, obey *Failure to obey a policeman's instructions may amount to an offence.* | disobey | ignore | await, wait (for) *He remained under cover and waited further instructions from headquarters.* | accept *Solicitors may not accept instructions in cases where they would have a conflict of interests.* | receive | give (sb), issue, leave (sb), send (sb) *The government has issued specific instructions on reducing waste disposal.* | bark (out), shout, yell *The director sat in his chair barking instructions at the cast.* | repeat
• PREP. according to the ~ *We acted according to the instructions we received.* in accordance with the ~, on (sb's) ~ *She was released on instruction from the Foreign Ministry.* under (sb/sth's) ~ *Under Charlemagne's instructions, many classical texts were recopied.* with/without ~ *They were not empowered to negotiate without instructions.* | ~ from, ~ to *an instruction to Lieutenant-General Gough from General Clark*
• PHRASES carry out/follow/obey (sb's) instructions to the letter (= follow them in every detail)

3 in a computer
• QUANT. series, set
• VERB + INSTRUCTION carry out, execute *The chip runs at speeds of up to 100MHz and executes two instructions per clock cycle.*

4 teaching
• ADJ. proper | formal, informal | advanced, basic | further | individual, individualized | practical, professional, technical | moral, religious | flying
• QUANT. course
• VERB + INSTRUCTION get, have, receive *She had no formal instruction in music.* | need | offer (sb) *The Cleveland Clog Dancers were on hand to offer instruction on the important steps.* | give (sb), provide (sb with)
• PREP. for the ~ of *The information is for the instruction of passengers.* under ~ *drivers under instruction* | ~ by *The two-day course features instruction by leading professionals and academics.* ~ in *He claimed that he was not capable of giving instruction in poetry.* ~ on *basic instruction on using the Internet*
• PHRASES a medium of instruction *The medium of instruction throughout the course is English.*

instructive adj.

• VERBS be
• ADV. extremely, highly, most, particularly, very *It was a most instructive day.* | quite

instructor noun

• ADJ. qualified, trained | experienced | chief, senior | driving, flying, parachute, riding, ski, swimming, etc.
• INSTRUCTOR + VERB teach sb/sth
⇨ Note at JOB

instrument noun

1 tool for a particular task
• ADJ. precision | sophisticated | reliable | crude | blunt *The autopsy revealed that the deceased had been hit with a blunt instrument.* ◇ *(figurative) Even though it was a somewhat blunt instrument* (= not very precise), *our questionnaire provided us with some interesting ideas.* | sharp | small | delicate | appropriate | research | drawing, measuring, writing | astronomical, flight, flying, mathematical, medical, navigation, navigational, optical, scientific, surgical | cockpit
• QUANT. set *a set of mathematical instruments*
• VERB + INSTRUMENT use *All pupils should learn to use drawing instruments.* | check, read *to read the instruments and make a note of the wind speed and direction* | design, develop, devise, invent | build, make *All the instruments are made from glass capillary tubing.*
• INSTRUMENT + VERB measure sth *an instrument that measures light intensity*
• INSTRUMENT + NOUN check *The pilot did his instrument checks and taxied towards the runway.* | maker | panel *There was a warning light flashing on the instrument panel.*
• PHRASES an instrument of torture *medieval instruments of torture such as the rack and the wheel*

2 for playing music
• ADJ. musical | beautiful, fine | classical | modern | period *baroque music played on period instruments* | solo | orchestral | brass, keyboard, percussion, string/stringed, wind, woodwind | acoustic, electric, electronic
• VERB + INSTRUMENT play (on) *She plays three musical instruments.* ◇ *The score was written to be played on a keyboard instrument.* | learn, learn (how) to play | tune *Ensure the instrument is tuned to concert pitch.* | make *an instrument made by a woman guitar maker in Canada*
• INSTRUMENT + VERB sound *The instrument sounds like a cello.*
• INSTRUMENT + NOUN maker
⇨ Special page at MUSIC

3 sb/sth used to make sth happen
• ADJ. chief, key, main, major, prime, principal | good, great *They agreed that the UN was the best instrument for reaching agreement.* | ideal | important, valuable | powerful | useful | effective | flexible | mere *Some cynics say that sport is a mere instrument of capitalist domination.* | chosen *The despot claimed to be the chosen instrument of divine providence.* | divine | political
• VERB + INSTRUMENT perceive sb/sth as, regard sb/sth as, see sb/sth as, view sb/sth as *They saw criminal law as an instrument for improving public morals.* | use sb/sth as | make sb/sth
• PREP. ~ for *Criminal law is not the best instrument for dealing with family matters.* ~ of *She was accused of making a public service an instrument of private advantage.*

instrumental adj.

1 important in making sth happen
• VERBS be | become
• ADV. highly | largely | partly
• PREP. in *They were highly instrumental in bringing the business to Newtown.*

2 being only a means to an end
• VERBS be
• ADV. very | purely | merely | essentially

insufficient adj.

- VERBS **be, prove**
- ADV. **quite, wholly | simply | clearly**
- PREP. **for** *The resources available are quite insufficient for the task.*

insulated adj.

1 protected against the cold, sound, etc.
- VERBS **be**
- ADV. **well | badly, poorly | heavily | properly**
- PREP. **against** *The laboratory was well insulated against all outside noise.* **with** *The hot water tank should be insulated with proper insulating materials.*

2 protected from unpleasant experiences
- ADV. **completely, totally | largely**
- PREP. **from** *The community was totally insulated from the outside world.*

insult noun

- ADJ. **bad, terrible** *one of the worst insults you can throw at somebody* | **ultimate** *Whatever you do, don't call a 'railway enthusiast' a trainspotter—it's the ultimate insult.* | **calculated, deliberate** | **personal**
- VERB + INSULT **hurl, offer** (*literary*), **shout, throw** *They were hurling insults at the police.* ◇ *The king is unlikely to forgive the insult offered to his ambassador.* | **mean sth as** *I don't mean this as an insult, but I think the team would play better without you.* | **take sth as** *I meant it as a bit of constructive advice, but he took it as a personal insult* | **endure, suffer** *Foreigners have to suffer constant insults from the local population.* | **exchange, trade** *The two groups of fans exchanged insults.*
- INSULT + VERB **fly** *Insults were flying back and forth.*
- PREP. **~to** *It was an insult to his wife.*
- PHRASES **add insult to injury** *Only 300 people came to the match and to add insult to injury (= to make things worse), the floodlights went out during the second half.* **an insult to your intelligence** *The questions were a real insult to our intelligence* (= because they were too easy).

insult verb

- ADV. **publicly** *He was dismissed for publicly insulting prominent politicians.*
- PHRASES **be/feel (deeply) insulted** *I felt deeply insulted that she hadn't asked me to the meeting.*

insulting adj.

- VERBS **be, seem, sound | become | find sth, regard sth as** *I find it insulting to be spoken to in that way.*
- ADV. **highly, very | quite | almost** *He made the question sound almost insulting.* | **a little, rather, vaguely | deliberately** *Her tone was deliberately insulting.*
- PREP. **to** *His opinions are highly insulting to women.*

insurance noun

- ADJ. **(fully) comprehensive | adequate | additional | long-term, short-term | national, social, state | personal, private | commercial | compulsory | voluntary | life | health, medical | animal, car, home, house, household, marine, motor | travel | accident, fire, legal expenses, unemployment | civil liability, liability, professional indemnity, public liability, third party | general | special**
- VERB + INSURANCE **have, maintain** *Have you got fully comprehensive insurance?* ◇ (*formal*) *The company maintains liability insurance for its directors and officers.* | **apply for | arrange, buy, get, obtain, purchase, take out** *The contract requires me to arrange my own insurance.* ◇ *The travel agent recommended that I take out travel insurance.* | **sell | pay** *I haven't paid the insurance*

yet this month. | **claim (on)** *She set fire to her house and then claimed insurance.* ◇ *We claimed for the car repairs on the insurance.* | **offer (sb) | provide (sb with)**
- INSURANCE + VERB **cover sb/sth, pay for sth** *Does your personal accident insurance cover mountain rescue?* ◇ *Millions of people in the US are not covered by health insurance.* ◇ *The insurance will pay for the damage.*
- INSURANCE + NOUN **cover** *insurance cover for bodily injury to third parties* | **policy** *a personal insurance policy* | **scheme** *a national insurance scheme* | **contribution, payment, premium** *a monthly insurance premium* | **costs** *rising insurance costs* | **claim | money, payout** *He bought a new suit out of the insurance money.* | **broking, services | business, industry, market, sector | company, firm, fund, group | agent, broker, salesman, underwriter | certificate**
- PREP. **~ against** *More people are taking out insurance against the high cost of dental care.* **~ for** *compulsory insurance for personal injury to employees* **~ on** *The court heard that he stood to gain millions in insurance on his wife.* **~ with** *Her insurance is with General Accident.*
- PHRASES **a certificate of insurance, a contract of insurance, a period of insurance** *If you make more than two claims in any period of insurance you may lose your no claim bonus.*

insured adj.

- VERBS **be**
- ADV. **fully | adequately | inadequately | privately** *There is evidence that privately insured patients are offered a higher level of care.*
- PREP. **against** *Your video is not insured against accidental damage.* **for** *I was not adequately insured for the damage my tenants caused.*

insurmountable adj.

- VERBS **appear, be, prove, seem** *The age barrier appeared insurmountable.* | **become | remain**
- ADV. **nearly, virtually | apparently, seemingly** *They were now faced with seemingly insurmountable technical problems.*

insurrection noun

- ADJ. **armed** *Years of discontent turned into armed insurrection.* | **popular** *There was a popular insurrection against the police.*
- VERB + INSURRECTION **plan, plot** *They were accused of plotting insurrection against the government.* | **lead | launch | crush, put down**
- PREP. **~ against** *insurrection against the monarchy*

intact adj.

- VERBS **appear, be | remain, stay, survive** *The building survived almost intact.* | **emerge** *a hero who always escaped by the skin of his teeth, emerging miraculously intact after each cliff-hanging episode* | **find sth** *We found the tomb perfectly intact.* | **keep sth, maintain sth, preserve sth** *The collection should be kept completely intact.* | **leave sth** *a group of old army buildings that had been left largely intact*
- ADV. **remarkably, substantially, very much** *The character of the original house is very much intact.* | **completely, entirely, perfectly, wholly | almost, nearly, virtually | basically, essentially, largely, more or less | fairly, reasonably, relatively | apparently | still** *The mill machinery is still intact.* | **miraculously**

intake noun

1 amount of food/drink taken into the body
- ADJ. **high | moderate | low | increased | total | good | excessive | adequate | balanced | normal |**

average | (recommended) daily | regular | dietary, nutritional | calorie | alcohol, calcium, energy, fat, fibre, fluid, food, oxygen, protein, salt, sugar, water
• VERB + INTAKE **have** *Make sure you have a balanced intake of vitamins A, B, C and D.* | **maintain** *You should maintain a low intake of fat.* | **increase, raise** | **control, watch** *You need to watch your alcohol intake.* | **cut, cut down (on), limit, lower, reduce, restrict** *One of the best ways to get to your ideal size is to cut fat intake right down.*

2 number of students in a year
• ADJ. **high | low | new | annual | graduate, student**
• VERB + INTAKE **have** *The school has an annual intake of 20 to 30.* | **cut, reduce | increase**

3 where liquid/air enters a machine
• ADJ. **air, water | pump**
• VERB + INTAKE **clog (up)** *Algae has clogged the intake to the water turbine.*

4 of breath
• ADJ. **harsh, sharp** *She gave a sharp intake of breath.*
• VERB + INTAKE **give**
• PHRASES **an intake of breath**

integrate *verb*

1 combine two things
• ADV. **closely, tightly, well** *They called for the defence system to be more closely integrated.* | **completely, fully, seamlessly, thoroughly | properly | successfully** *The department has successfully integrated new ideas into the traditional course structure.*
• PREP. **into** *The results should be integrated into the final report.* **with** *This computer program can be integrated with existing programs.*
• PHRASES **highly integrated** (= with many different parts working successfully together) *a highly integrated approach to planning* **poorly integrated**

2 mix with other people
• ADV. **well** *The lower primary pupils are well integrated into the life of the school.* | **completely, fully | quickly**
• PREP. **into** *They soon became fully integrated into the local community.* **with** *They didn't integrate with the other children.*

integration *noun*

• ADJ. **true | complete, full | close, seamless | further, greater, improved, increased | rapid | economic, monetary, political, racial, social** *We are working to bring about closer political integration in the EU.* | **internal | systems** (*computing*)
• QUANT. **degree, level**
• VERB + INTEGRATION **achieve, bring about | accelerate, encourage, facilitate, promote, speed up, stimulate** *measures to promote the social integration of mentally handicapped people* | **require | lead to**
• PREP. **~ between** *integration between research and higher education* **~ into** *the integration of disabled pupils into the general education system* **~ with** *He called for greater integration with Europe.* **~ within** *economic integration within the three communities*
• PHRASES **a move towards integration** *a move towards greater internal integration in Europe* **a need for integration, a process of integration**

integrity *noun*

• ADJ. **great, high | absolute, complete | personal | artistic, financial, moral, political, professional | physical, structural, territorial** *The country is fighting to preserve its territorial integrity.* | **data** (*computing*)
• VERB + INTEGRITY **have** *Her photography had great artistic integrity.* | **lack | lose | restore** *The minister promised to restore the honesty and integrity of the government.* | **ensure** *It's up to the user to ensure the integrity of*

the data they enter. | **maintain, retain** *We all have an interest in maintaining the integrity of the ecosystem.* | **defend, preserve, safeguard | threaten** *The project threatens the integrity of one of the world's most important wetlands.* | **compromise, impair, undermine** *I would never do anything to compromise the integrity of the company.* | **destroy** *Nuclear weapons have the capability to destroy the physical integrity of the planet.* | **question** *She questioned his integrity as a councillor.*
• PREP. **with ~** *The code calls on members to behave with integrity at all times.*
• PHRASES **an attack on sb/sth's integrity, a challenge/threat to sb/sth's integrity**

intellect *noun*

• ADJ. **brilliant, considerable, formidable, keen, powerful, superior, sharp | limited, low, weak | creative, rational, scientific | human**
• VERB + INTELLECT **have** *She has a formidable intellect.* | **exercise** *He enjoyed exercising his intellect in analysing the controversies of his day.*

intelligence *noun*

1 ability to understand
• ADJ. **acute, considerable, great, high** *a writer with an acute intelligence* ◊ *This essay shows considerable intelligence.* | **quick | average, normal | limited, low | innate, native | human | artificial** *Computer scientists study artificial intelligence.*
• VERB + INTELLIGENCE **have** *At least he had the intelligence to turn off the gas.* | **demonstrate, show | use**
• INTELLIGENCE + NOUN **test**

2 information
• ADJ. **secret** *We've obtained secret intelligence about enemy plans.* | **reliable | military** *Military intelligence is gathered using sophisticated technology.* | **criminal**
• VERB + INTELLIGENCE **collect, gather**
• INTELLIGENCE + NOUN **agency, service** *He works for the French intelligence service.* | **officer | gathering** *His unit was responsible for intelligence gathering in North Africa.* | **report | operation**

intelligent *adj.*

• VERBS **be, look, seem**
• ADV. **extremely, highly, incredibly, most, remarkably, very** *a highly intelligent woman* | **fairly, quite, reasonably** *He should be able to solve the problem. He's reasonably intelligent.* | **obviously | seemingly**

intelligible *adj.*

• VERBS **be | become | make sth** *They do their best to make science intelligible to young children.* | **find sth** *She found his motives perfectly intelligible.*
• ADV. **perfectly | easily, immediately, readily | barely, scarcely** *His reply was barely intelligible.* | **mutually** *Czech and Slovak are separate languages but they are mutually intelligible.*
• PREP. **to** *We need an explanation that is readily intelligible to ordinary people.*

intend *verb*

• ADV. **fully** *She fully intends to continue her sporting career once she has recovered from her injuries.* | **clearly | originally** *He had originally intended to stay in the country for only a year or two.*
• PREP. **for** *It was thought that the bomb might have been intended for a visiting MP.*

intense *adj.*

• VERBS **be | become | remain**

● ADV. **extremely, incredibly, particularly, really, very** | **fairly, pretty, quite**

intensify verb

● ADV. **greatly** | **sharply** *The fighting in the area has intensified sharply.* | **further**
● VERB + INTENSIFY **appear to, seem to** *The extreme cold seemed, if anything, to intensify.* | **tend to** | **be likely to** | **serve to** *The reforms served only to intensify the misery of the poorer peasants.*

intensity noun

● ADJ. **high, low** *a band of light with high intensity* | **fierce, great** *The sun beat down with fierce intensity.* ◇ *He studied the report with great intensity.* | **emotional** | **passionate**
● VERB + INTENSITY **decrease (in), reduce (in)** | **grow in, increase (in)** *Her headaches started to increase in intensity.* | **vary in**
● PREP. **in~** *The pain was growing in intensity.*

intensive adj.

● VERBS **be**
● ADV. **highly, very** *highly intensive courses for business and professional people* | **increasingly**
● PHRASES **labour intensive** *Rice production is very labour intensive* (= requires a lot of labour).

intent adj.

1 determined to do sth
● VERBS **appear, be, seem**
● ADV. **apparently, seemingly** | **clearly, evidently, obviously** *They are clearly intent on maintaining standards.*
● PREP. **on/upon** *He was intent on murder.*

2 concentrating on sth
● VERBS **be** | **become**
● ADV. **very** | **suddenly** *Her gaze was suddenly intent.*
● PREP. **on** *She was very intent on her work.*

intention noun

● ADJ. **original** *My original intention was to study all morning, but this turned out to be impractical.* | **declared, stated** | **firm** | **general** | **deliberate**
● VERB + INTENTION **have** *I have no intention of changing jobs.* | **announce, declare, state** *The council has announced its intention to crack down on parking offences.*
● PREP. **with a/the~ of** *I went to the bank with the intention of getting some traveller's cheques.* | **~ behind** *The general intention behind the project is a good one.* **~ by** *The intention by the local authority to build 2 000 new houses is unrealistic.* **~ in** *His intention in inviting us to dinner was to persuade us to back his project.*
● PHRASES **good/the best intentions** *It was done with the best intentions, I assure you* **have every/no intention of doing sth** *We have every intention of winning the next election.* **make your intention clear** *He didn't make his intentions clear in his letter.*

interact verb

1 have an effect on each other
● ADV. **closely** | **directly**
● PREP. **with** *This hormone interacts closely with other hormones in the body.*

2 mix with other people
● ADV. **well** | **socially**
● PREP. **with** *He interacts very well with other children.*

interaction noun

● ADJ. **complex** | **informal** | **social** | **human** | **face-to-face, group** | **classroom**

● INTERACTION + NOUN **processes** *the interaction processes of chimpanzees*
● PREP. **~ among** *Informal interaction among employees is seen as part of the ongoing training process.* **~ between** *the complex interaction between animals and their environment* **~ with** *What is her interaction with her boss like?* **~ within** *interaction within the group*
● PHRASES **patterns of interaction** *Specific patterns of interaction in the family have been observed.*

interactive adj.

● VERBS **be** | **become**
● ADV. **highly** | **fully** *The program is fully interactive.*

interchangeable adj.

● VERBS **be, seem** | **become**
● ADV. **fully, totally** | **almost, virtually**
● PREP. **with** *These parts are fully interchangeable with those in other machines.*

intercom noun

● INTERCOM + VERB **buzz, sound**
● INTERCOM + NOUN **system**
● PREP. **on the~** *I spoke to her on the intercom and said I'd call round later.* **over the~** *Mr Jack's arrival was announced over the intercom.*

intercourse noun

1 sex
● ADJ. **sexual** | **heterosexual, homosexual** | **anal, vaginal** | **non-consensual** | **unlawful**
● VERB + INTERCOURSE **engage in, have, indulge in** *She never had sexual intercourse before she was married.* | **consent to** *The judge asked if she had consented to intercourse.*
● INTERCOURSE + VERB **occur, take place** *He admitted that intercourse had taken place.*
● PREP. **~ between** *intercourse between consenting adults* **~ with** *He accused her of intercourse with another man.*

2 exchange of ideas, feelings, etc.
● ADJ. **social** *Life is a pleasant blend of work and social intercourse.*

interest noun

1 desire to learn/hear more about sb/sth
● ADJ. **avid, burning, close, considerable, consuming, deep, great, intense, keen, lively, passionate, strong** *The police were starting to take a close interest in the company's activities.* ◇ *She always had a great interest in the supernatural.* | **particular** | **growing, increasing** | **slightest** *He's never shown the slightest interest in football.* | **general, widespread** | **worldwide** | **serious** | **genuine** | **abiding, lifelong** | **passing** | **renewed** | **added** *I'll watch the programme with added interest now I know you're in it.* | **active** | **passive** | **polite** *He showed a polite interest in her story.* | **personal** | **media** *The event attracted a lot of media interest.*
● VERB + INTEREST **have** | **evince, express, show, take** *My cousin expressed an interest in seeing where I work.* | **feign, simulate** *She feigned interest in a magazine article to avoid meeting the man's stare.* | **lose** | **arouse, attract, awaken, catch, drum up, excite, generate, kindle, spark, stimulate, stir up, whip up** *A sticker on a bag caught my interest.* ◇ *The government failed to drum up any public interest in the referendum.* ◇ *A childhood journey sparked his lifelong interest in railways.* | **develop** *While in prison he developed an interest in art.* | **maintain, sustain** *Despite intensive publicity, Channel 4 failed to maintain interest in its expensive new show.* | **revive**
● INTEREST + VERB **grow** | **flag, wane** *The children's interest began to flag after half an hour of the lesson.*

• PREP. **for/out of** ~ *I'm asking purely out of interest.* **with** ~ *They listened with interest.* | ~**among** *to stimulate interest among teachers* ~ **from** *growing interest from younger members* ~ **in** *She took an active interest in their welfare.*

2 quality that attracts attention

• ADJ. **great** | **particular** *Her comments are of particular interest to me.* | **broad, general, wide** | **architectural, artistic, historic/historical, scientific** | **academic** *Since the championship has already been decided, this match is of purely academic interest.* | **human** *a plot devoid of human interest* | **love** *Angelina Jolie supplies the love interest in the film.*

• VERB + INTEREST **be of** *His books are of no interest to me at all.* | **hold no** *Their conversation held no interest for me.* | **add** *Bushes that flower in winter will add interest to your garden.* | **supply**

• INTEREST + VERB **lie in** *The interest of the painting lies in its unusual use of colour.*

• PREP. **of** ~ *a building of great architectural interest*

3 sth you enjoy doing/learning about

• ADJ. **diverse, varied, wide, wide-ranging** | **private** | **artistic, musical,** etc.

• VERB + INTEREST **have** | **share** | **pursue** *He wanted time to pursue his many and varied musical interests.*

4 money earned from investments

• ADJ. **annual, monthly,** etc. | **compound, simple**

• VERB + INTEREST **earn, make, receive** | **pay** | **charge**

• INTEREST + VERB **accrue, bear**

• INTEREST + NOUN **rate** | **payment** | **charge**

• PREP. ~**on** *to pay interest on a loan*

• PHRASES **a rate of interest** *a mortgage with a fixed/flexible rate of interest*

5 benefits that sth has for sb

• ADJ. **best** *It's not in your best interests to let your boss know you're looking for a new job.* | **self-, selfish** | **common, mutual** | **competing, contradictory** | **long-term, short-term** | **narrow** *narrow sectional interests* | **direct** *Lawyers have a direct financial interest in the outcome of the debate.* | **paramount, vital** | **vested** | **national, public** | **class, sectional** | **foreign, outside** | **economic, financial, political, strategic,** etc.

• VERB + INTEREST **defend, guard, look after, protect, safeguard** | **act in, advance, champion, further, promote, serve** *He claimed to be acting in the public interest.* | **represent** | **act against, jeopardize, threaten**

• INTEREST + VERB **lie in sth** | **be at stake**

• INTEREST + NOUN **group** *Various interest groups have expressed their opposition to the policy.*

• PREP. **against sb/sth's** ~**(s)** *The solicitor refused to act against his client's interests.* **contrary to sb/sth's** ~ *The union refused to support proposals that it saw as contrary to the interests of its members.* **in sb/sth's** ~**(s)** *New work practices were introduced in the interests of efficiency.* **of** ~ *We met to discuss matters of common interest.* **out of** ~ *He was obviously acting purely out of selfish interest.*

• PHRASES **a conflict of interests** *One member of the planning committee had a conflict of interests as he lived near the proposed motorway.* **have sb's (best) interests at heart** *Although he was sometimes too strict with his children, he had their best interests at heart.*

6 legal right to share in profits

• ADJ. **powerful** | **controlling, majority** | **minority** | **joint** | **banking, business, commercial, shipping**

• VERB + INTEREST **have** *He has controlling interests in several ventures.* | **sell**

• PREP. ~**in**

interest *verb*

• ADV. **greatly, particularly, really, very much** *It is this aspect of the work that really interests me.*

• VERB + INTEREST **try to** *She tried to interest the director in her scheme.*

interested *adj.*

• VERBS **appear, be, feel, look, seem, sound** | **become, get** *She got very interested in politics.* | **remain** | **get sb** *We need to get more young people interested in the sport.* | **keep sb** *You need to keep your audience interested.*

• ADV. **deeply, especially, extremely, greatly, intensely, keenly, more than a little, most, particularly, passionately, really, seriously, specially, terribly, very (much)** *Ben must have been more than a little interested in the possibility to have pursued it so far.* | **genuinely, truly** | **increasingly** | **not at all, not (in) the least bit, not in the least, not remotely** *He's not in the least bit interested in girls.* | **only half, not much, not very** *Carrie was only half interested in the conversation.* | **fairly, mildly, quite, vaguely** | **just** *'Why do you ask?' 'I'm just interested, that's all.'* | **enough, sufficiently** *I wasn't interested enough in the argument to take sides one way or the other.* | **chiefly, mainly, primarily, principally** | **always, long** *I am always interested in how differently people can look at the same event.* ◇ *Charles had long been interested in architecture.* | **still** | **no longer** | **potentially** | **apparently, reportedly** | **clearly, obviously** | **actively** *As a landowner, he was actively interested in agricultural improvements.* | **professionally**

• PREP. **in** *She's always been interested in other people.*

interesting *adj.*

• VERBS **appear, be, look, seem, sound** | **become, get** | **make sth** | **find sb/sth** *I find her ideas really interesting.*

• ADV. **deeply, especially, extraordinarily, extremely, highly, immensely, incredibly, intensely, most, particularly, really, terribly, very** | **equally** | **doubly** | **fairly, mildly, pretty, quite, rather** | **enough, sufficiently** *Some topics appeared interesting enough to require more detailed information.* | **potentially** | **inherently, intrinsically, in itself** *This subject is intrinsically interesting and worthy of study in its own right.* | **always** *It was always interesting to hear his stories.* | **architecturally, geologically, historically, sociologically** *architecturally interesting buildings*

• PREP. **for** *It's not very interesting for visitors.* **to** *How can we make the subject more interesting to young people?*

interfere *verb*

• ADV. **seriously** *Emotional problems can seriously interfere with a student's work.* | **directly** *The judge cannot interfere directly in these proceedings.* | **not lightly** *The court will not lightly interfere while an interim order is in place.*

• VERB + INTERFERE **have a right to** *Britain has no right to interfere in the internal affairs of other countries.* | **try and/to** *If you try and interfere in my life, I'll leave.* | **be reluctant to** *The courts are reluctant to interfere in these matters.*

• PREP. **in** *outsiders interfering in local politics* **with** *You mustn't interfere with her work.*

interference *noun*

• ADJ. **undue, unwarranted** | **gross** *I will not tolerate such gross interference.* | **bureaucratic, government, political, state** | **external, outside**

• VERB + INTERFERENCE **avoid, prevent** *The law is designed to prevent interference by local police.* | **tolerate** | **brook no** *My boss said she would brook no interference from other departments.*

• PREP. **without** ~ *I told her I wanted to make decisions without interference from her.* | ~**in** *political interference in the legal process* ~**with** *interference with proper medical procedures*

interim noun

- INTERIM + NOUN **period** *The value of the property almost doubled during the interim period.* | **measure** | **agreement, arrangement** | **payment** | **award, damages** *The injured passenger received an interim award of £50 000 damages.* | **profits** | **figures, results** | **report** | **government**
- PREP. **in the~** *Her job was done by her deputy in the interim before she returned to work.*
- PHRASES **on an interim basis** *The company uses the agency when a vacancy needs to be filled on an interim basis.*

interior noun

- ADJ. **original** *The original interior of the hotel has been replaced.* | **dark, dim, gloomy, shadowy** | **spacious**
- INTERIOR + NOUN **decorator, designer**
- PREP. **in the~** *There is ample space in the interior of the car.*

interlude noun

- ADJ. **brief** | **romantic** | **peaceful, pleasant** | **musical** *a musical interlude between two the acts of the play*
- PREP. **~between** *a peaceful interlude between periods of intense activity* **~in** *He'd had two romantic interludes in a rather lonely life.* | **~of** *interludes of calm*

intermediary noun

- ADJ. **financial**
- VERB + INTERMEDIARY **act as**
- PREP. **through an~** *They were approached indirectly through an intermediary.* **via an~** *The product is then sold to the end-user via an intermediary.* | **~ between** *She agreed to act as intermediary between the two tribes.*

interminable adj.

- VERBS **be, seem** *The journey seemed interminable.*
- ADV. **seemingly** *For several seemingly interminable seconds no one spoke.*

Internet noun

- ADJ. **wireless**
- VERB + INTERNET **access, go on, use** *She likes to go on the Internet in the evenings.*
- INTERNET + NOUN **site, website** | **portal** | **bulletin board, chat room** | **magazine** | **auction, broadcast, link** *Thousands logged on to view the live Internet broadcast of the concert.* ◇ *The auction was held in Paris with an Internet link to New York.* | **cafe** *Travellers can check their email at the Internet cafe in the square.* | **domain** *Registering an Internet domain name is now an essential part of setting up a company.* | **access, usage, use** *unlimited/unmetered Internet access* | **connection** *a broadband/high-speed Internet connection* | **search engine, (service) provider** | **customer, user** | **traffic** *the laying of fast networks to carry Internet traffic* | **brand, group** | **services** | **arm, division, operation, subsidiary** *the bank's Internet arm* | **entrepreneur** | **analyst, expert** | **banking, betting, dating, shopping** | **bank, bookie/bookmaker, business, company, firm, retailer, start-up, venture** | **industry, sector** | **fraud** | **security** | **economy** | **file** *software for downloading Internet files* | **image** | **software** | **technology** | **age** *issues facing the music industry in the Internet age* | **boom, revolution** *Many of the sites launched at the peak of the Internet boom have now disappeared.*
- PREP. **on the~** *More and more people are shopping on the Internet.*
- ⇨ Special page at COMPUTER

interpret verb

- ADV. **correctly, rightly** | **wrongly** | **differently** *Different people might interpret events differently.* | **clearly** | **broadly, liberally** *The term 'business' is here interpreted broadly to include all types of organization in the public and private sectors.* ◇ *The strictness of the rules, even when liberally interpreted, has the effect of restricting innovation.* | **narrowly, restrictively, strictly** | **literally** | **metaphorically** *It is context and convention that determine whether a term will be interpreted literally or metaphorically.* | **easily, readily** *These figures cannot be easily interpreted.* | **cautiously** *These results must be interpreted cautiously.*
- VERB + INTERPRET **be difficult to, be hard to** | **be able/unable to** | **seek to, try to** *We all seek to interpret what we hear and what we read.*
- PREP. **as** *Her message was interpreted as a warning to the general.*
- PHRASES **be variously interpreted (as sth)** *The figure of the Ancient Mariner has been variously interpreted (= interpreted in various different ways).* **be widely interpreted as sth** *Her resignation has been widely interpreted as an admission of her guilt.*

interpretation noun

- ADJ. **correct, right, true, valid** | **erroneous, false, wrong** | **plausible, reasonable** | **simplistic** | **literal, narrow, strict** | **free, generous, liberal, loose, wide** | **alternative, competing, conflicting, different, diverse, multiple** | **artistic**
- VERB + INTERPRETATION **give sth, make** *In practice, this law is often given a wide interpretation by the police.* ◇ *Scientists made an interpretation based on the data available.* | **be open to** *The wording of this section of the contract is open to interpretation.*
- PHRASES **put an interpretation on sth** *It is possible to put an entirely different interpretation on her behaviour.*

interpreter noun

- VERB + INTERPRETER **act as** | **speak through** *Speaking through an interpreter, a Japanese fisherman gave his account of the tidal wave.*
- PREP. **~for** *Susan acted as interpreter for us.*
- ⇨ Note at JOB

interrelated adj.

- VERBS **be**
- ADV. **closely** *The two problems are closely interrelated.*
- PREP. **with** *Feminist ideas are interrelated with philosophical ideas.*

interrogation noun

- ADJ. **police** | **further**
- VERB + INTERROGATION **conduct** *The interrogation was conducted by senior police officers.*
- INTERROGATION + NOUN **cell, room** | **methods, procedures, techniques**
- PREP. **during~** *She revealed the name of her accomplice during interrogation.* **under~** *Under interrogation, he refused to say anything at first.*
- PHRASES **power/powers of interrogation** *The committee has no power of interrogation.*

interrupt verb

- ADV. **impatiently** | **rudely** *What was I saying, before we were so rudely interrupted?* | **harshly, sharply** *'Don't talk like that!' he interrupted harshly.* | **brutally, cruelly, violently** *Their luncheon was brutally interrupted by gunfire.* | **abruptly, suddenly** | **temporarily** | **constantly, repeatedly** *The morning's work was constantly interrupted by phone calls.* | **occasionally, periodically**

• VERB + INTERRUPT **be sorry to** *I'm sorry to interrupt, but there's a telephone call for you.* | **(not) dare (to)** *It was all irrelevant, but I didn't dare interrupt him in mid-flow.*
• PREP. **with** *I thought it better not to interrupt her with any comment.*
• PHRASES **get interrupted** *I didn't manage to finish the report. I kept getting interrupted.*

interruption noun

• ADJ. **brief, minor, short, temporary** *The game continued after a short interruption because of rain.* | **major** | **constant, endless, repeated** *I found it hard to work with all the noise and constant interruptions.*
• VERB + INTERRUPTION **ignore** *He ignored her interruption and carried on talking.*
• PREP. **without~** *Can I please have this conversation on the phone without interruptions?* ◇ *I managed to work for two hours without interruption.* | **~ from** *He continued speaking despite regular interruptions from the Opposition.* **~to** *The birth of her son was a minor interruption to her career.*

interval noun

• ADJ. **brief, short** *She ruled for ten years, except for a brief interval.* | **long, wide** *You are advised to leave a wide interval before you have your next child.* | **decent** *After a decent interval the actress made her new relationship public.*
• PREP. **at~s** *At intervals a bell rings and workers stop for a drink.* **in the ~** *Polling day was a week away and Baldwin made two speeches in the interval.* | **~between** *The intervals between his various illnesses grew shorter and shorter.*
• PHRASES **at fixed/frequent/periodic/regular intervals** *Trains run at fixed intervals.* ◇ *He returned home during the day at regular intervals.* **at hourly/weekly/fortnightly/monthly, etc. intervals** *Meetings are held at monthly intervals.*

intervene verb

• ADV. **actively, directly** | **personally** *The president intervened personally in the crisis.* | **decisively** *Government often intervenes decisively in major professional issues in medicine.* | **effectively, successfully** | **militarily** *Intervening militarily will not bring peace.*
• VERB + INTERVENE **be forced to, have to** *Eventually, the army was forced to intervene.* | **be reluctant to** | **be powerless to** *Local people feel strongly about the proposed development but are virtually powerless to intervene.* | **have the power to, have the right to** *Our government has no right to intervene.* | **refuse to** *The UN refused to intervene.*
• PREP. **against** *They would not intervene against the rebels themselves.* **between** *She went over to intervene between the two men.* **in** *She was reluctant to intervene in what was essentially a private dispute.* **on behalf of** *The King intervened personally on behalf of the children.* **with** *to intervene with the authorities on the prisoners' behalf*

intervention noun

• ADJ. **direct** *direct intervention to stop abuses of the environment* | **active, decisive, forceful** | **early, immediate, timely** *A full-scale riot was prevented by the timely intervention of the police.* | **effective, successful** | **limited** | **personal** *the Emperor's personal intervention* | **government, ministerial, official, state** *He has made repeated calls for government intervention to save the steel industry.* | **external, foreign, outside** | **armed, military** *We would resist any armed intervention from outside in our country's affairs.* | **police** | **judicial, legal** | **medical, surgical** |

economic, political, social | **divine, human** *The king saw this victory as the direct result of divine intervention.*
• VERB + INTERVENTION **make** *to make a forceful intervention in a dispute* | **call for, demand** *The prime minister was always demanding active intervention early on.* | **resist** *We will always resist foreign intervention in our country.*
• PREP. **~against** *armed intervention against the rebels* **~by** *intervention by a senior judge* **~from** *He was furious at this intervention from the press.* **~in** *the government's intervention in the dispute* **~on behalf of** *state intervention on behalf of the British film industry*
• PHRASES **the power/right of intervention** *He claimed that the state had a special right of intervention in company affairs.*

interview noun

• ADJ. **face-to-face** | **telephone** *Telephone interviews with over 400 Scottish businesses picked up impressively high rates of satisfaction.* | **group** | **in-depth** | **police** *a police interview with suspected terrorists* | **newspaper, press, radio, television** | **job** *I've got a job interview tomorrow.*
• VERB + INTERVIEW **carry out, conduct, do, hold** *The survey team carried out over 200 interviews with retired people.* | **do, give (sb), grant (sb)** *He's a very private man and rarely does interviews.* | **attend, be called for, have** *She's been called for an interview for the manager's job.* | **publish** *The interview was published in all the papers.*
• INTERVIEW + NOUN **board, panel** | **techniques** | **procedure** *The questions are the central point of the whole interview procedure and should be planned in advance.*
• PREP. **in an/the~** *He said in an interview that he wanted to get married.* | **~ about** *The prime minister gave the paper an interview about his musical tastes.* **~between** *an interview between the French Foreign Minister and the President of Egypt* **~for** *an interview for the post of sales manager* **~with** *He had an interview with United Biscuits.* ◇ *an interview with the Vietnamese leader*
• PHRASES **a round of interviews** *We're about to start the second round of interviews for the post.*

interviewer noun

• ADJ. **clever, experienced, good, skilled, trained** *A skilled interviewer will help candidates feel relaxed.* | **radio, television/TV**

intestine noun

• ADJ. **large, small**
• PREP. **along the~, in the~** *bacteria in the small intestine* **through the~**
• PHRASES **the wall of the intestine**

intimacy noun

• ADJ. **genuine, real, true** | **close, deep, great** | **enforced** | **old** *The old intimacy between them had gone forever* | **emotional, physical, sexual**
• VERB + INTIMACY **be capable of** *She isn't capable of real intimacy.* | **enjoy** *(formal)* *He enjoys an intimacy with the prime minister.* | **create, promote** | **develop** | **destroy** *The noise destroyed the intimacy of their conversation.* | **sense** *I sensed a close intimacy between them.*
• INTIMACY + VERB **develop** *Gradually, a deep emotional intimacy developed between them.*
• PREP. **~between** *the intimacy created between student and teacher* **~with** *A writer must develop an intimacy with the subject at hand.*
• PHRASES **fear of intimacy** *He was prevented from declaring his love by his fear of intimacy.* **a feeling/sense of intimacy** *The room had a peaceful sense of intimacy about it.*

intimidate *verb*

- VERB + INTIMIDATE **try to**
- PREP. **into** *The police had tried to intimidate him into signing a confession.*
- PHRASES **an attempt to intimidate sb, be easily intimidated** *He was not a man to be easily intimidated.* **feel intimidated** *She did not feel intimidated by him.*

intimidation *noun*

- ADJ. **physical, verbal | police**
- VERB + INTIMIDATION **be subjected to, experience, face, suffer** *Workers were subjected to intimidation as they crossed the picket line.*
- PREP. **~against** *intimidation against trade unions* **~by** *Workers continue to enter the plant despite intimidation by mass pickets.* **~from** *fear of intimidation from paramilitary organizations*
- PHRASES **an act of intimidation, a campaign of intimidation**

intolerable *adj.*

- VERBS **be, prove, seem | become | make sth** *The constant pain made her life intolerable.* **| consider sth, find sth** *I find his rudeness intolerable.*
- ADV. **absolutely, quite | increasingly | almost, nearly** *The job placed almost intolerable pressure on her.*
- PREP. **to** *The situation had become intolerable to him.*

intolerance *noun*

1 lack of tolerance
- ADJ. **racial, religious**
- VERB + INTOLERANCE **display, show**
- PREP. **~of** *The town began to show increasing intolerance of immigrants.* **~to** *the professor's intolerance to any views other than his own* **~towards** *the intolerance of local residents towards refugees*

2 inability to digest certain substances
- ADJ. **food | glucose, lactose, etc.**
- PREP. **~of** *intolerance of potatoes* **~to** *an intolerance to milk products*

intolerant *adj.*

- VERBS **be | become**
- ADV. **deeply, extremely, highly, very | utterly**
- PREP. **of** *They are deeply intolerant of all opposition.*

intonation *noun*

- ADJ. **falling, flat, rising** *the rising intonation at the end of spoken questions* **| foreign** *He speaks excellent Spanish but with a distinctly foreign intonation.*
- INTONATION + NOUN **pattern**

intricacy *noun*

- VERB + INTRICACY **learn, master, understand** *I've never mastered the intricacies of cricket.* **| guide/steer sb through, steer sb through**

intricate *adj.*

- VERBS **be**
- ADV. **amazingly, extraordinarily, extremely, highly, very** *an amazingly intricate structure* **| quite**

intrigue *noun*

- ADJ. **international, political | court** *a tale of treachery and court intrigue*
- VERB + INTRIGUE **carry on, engage in**
- PREP. **~against** *The prime minister engaged in political intrigues against the king.*
- PHRASES **a web of intrigue**

intriguing *adj.*

- VERBS **be, sound** *It all sounds very intriguing.* **| find sth** *I found the story rather intriguing.*
- ADV. **extraordinarily, extremely, highly, most, very | quite, rather**

introduce *verb*

1 tell people sb's name
- ADV. **formally, properly** *We have met before, but we haven't been formally introduced.*
- VERB + INTRODUCE **allow me to, can, let me, may** *Let me introduce myself.* ◇ *May I introduce my wife, Sarah?*
- PREP. **as** *He introduced me as a new member of the company.* **to** *She introduced me to her neighbours.*

2 start using/doing sth for the first time
- ADV. **gradually | rapidly**
- VERB + INTRODUCE **intend to, plan to, want to** *The local council plans to introduce new regulations on parking.* **| attempt to, try to** *She attempted in vain to introduce some order into the classroom.*
- PREP. **into** *New technology is rapidly being introduced into factories.*
- PHRASES **newly/recently introduced** *These measures have only been recently introduced.*

introduction *noun*

1 first use
- ADJ. **early, gradual, recent, widespread**
- PREP. **~into** *the gradual introduction of modern farming methods into traditional societies*

2 first part of a book/talk
- ADJ. **brief, short** *He began with a brief introduction.*
- PREP. **in an/the~** *His mother is mentioned in the introduction.* **| ~to** *the introduction to her latest book*

3 book for studying a subject
- ADJ. **excellent, general, useful** *It serves as an excellent introduction to 19th-century painting.*
- PREP. **~to**

4 telling people each other's names
- ADJ. **formal**
- VERB + INTRODUCTION **make** *I can never remember names, so I don't like to make the introductions.*
- PHRASES **a letter of introduction** *He gave me a letter of introduction to the manager.*

intruder *noun*

- ADJ. **unwanted, unwelcome | masked**
- VERB + INTRUDER **catch, disturb, find, startle, surprise** *He surprised a masked intruder in the kitchen.* **| deter, keep away/out** *Dogs can deter unwelcome intruders.* **| tackle** *He was stabbed when he tackled an intruder armed with a knife.* **| repel** *Staff were instructed to repel intruders with physical force, if need be.*
- INTRUDER + VERB **break into, force their way into** *Intruders had forced their way into the house.*
- INTRUDER + NOUN **alarm**
- PREP. **against~s** *security measures against intruders*

intrusion *noun*

- ADJ. **media, press | unnecessary, unwanted, unwarranted, unwelcome**
- VERB + INTRUSION **resent**
- PREP. **~in** *I really resented his intrusion in a family matter.* **~into** *media intrusion into the lives of celebrities* **~on/upon** *an unwarranted intrusion upon the singer's privacy*

intrusive *adj.*

- VERBS **be, prove, seem | become | find sth**

● ADV. **extremely, very | increasingly | rather, somewhat | visually** *Planning permission was refused on the grounds that the proposed building would be 'visually intrusive'.*

intuition noun

● ADJ. **female, feminine, woman's, women's** *Her feminine intuition told her that he was unhappy.*
● QUANT. **flash** *It came upon him in a flash of intuition.*
● VERB + INTUITION **have** *She had an intuition that her mother wasn't very well.* | **rely on, trust, use** *She learned to trust her intuitions about other people's motives.*
● INTUITION + VERB **suggest sth, tell sb sth** *Intuition told me we were going in the wrong direction.*
● PREP. **by ~** *By intuition, he sensed what was wrong.* | **~ about** *an intuition about where to find wild strawberries* | **~ behind** *the intuition behind her theory*

intuitive adj.

● VERBS **be**
● ADV. **extremely, highly, very** *a highly intuitive thinker* | **purely | almost | fairly, quite**

invalid adj.

● VERBS **be | became | make sth, render sth** *This action would render the agreement invalid.* | **consider sth, declare sth, deem sth, regard sth as** *The contract was declared invalid.*

invaluable adj.

● VERBS **be, prove | become | remain | make sb/sth** *His knowledge of the area made him invaluable.* | **find sth** *You will find their help absolutely invaluable.*
● ADV. **absolutely, quite**
● PREP. **for** *This technology is invaluable for pupils with poor sight.* **to** *Your support has been invaluable to us.*

invasion noun

● ADJ. **full-scale | military** *Latest reports are of a full-scale military invasion.*
● VERB + INVASION **carry out, launch, mount | repel, repulse | counter, resist**
● PHRASES **an invasion of privacy** *Having all those photographers in the house was a terrible invasion of privacy.* **fear of invasion, a threat of invasion**

invent verb

● PHRASES **newly invented** *using the then newly invented automatic rifle*

invention noun

1 new thing
● ADJ. **latest, new | modern | brilliant, ingenious, wonderful | successful**
● VERB + INVENTION **come up with, design | patent, register** *He failed to patent his invention and never made a penny from it.*
2 untrue story
● ADJ. **pure** *Most of what he says is pure invention!*
● PHRASES **power/powers of invention** *His powers of invention are somewhat limited.*

inventive adj.

● VERBS **be**
● ADV. **brilliantly, highly, very | quite**

inventory noun

● ADJ. **complete, comprehensive, detailed, full**
● VERB + INVENTORY **compile, draw up, make, produce, take** *The manager is compiling an inventory of all the hotel furniture.* | **list sth on**
● INVENTORY + VERB **list sth** *The inventory lists many rare items.*
● PREP. **in an/the ~** *There were no forks in the inventory.* **on an/the ~** *That lamp isn't listed on the inventory.*

invest verb

● ADV. **heavily** *The company invested heavily in new technology.* | **directly** *If you invest directly in the stock market potential profits are greater, but so are potential losses.* | **carefully, safely, wisely | tax-free** *We can invest your money tax-free abroad.* | **abroad, overseas**
● VERB + INVEST **be willing to** *Are you willing to invest the time and effort necessary to make the scheme work?* | **look to, plan to, seek to** *investors looking to invest in US companies* | **decide to | rush to** *When exchange controls were lifted Swedes rushed to invest abroad.* | **fail to** *The industry has failed to invest in new product development.*
● PREP. **in** *encouraging people to invest in pension plans* **with** *Her savings are invested with a building society.*

investigate verb

● ADV. **carefully, closely | extensively | fully, properly, thoroughly** *The allegations have not yet been properly investigated.* | **further | actively**
● VERB + INVESTIGATE **ask sb to, be called in to** *Police have been called in to investigate the complaints.* | **agree to, pledge to, promise to** *The company has pledged to investigate claims that its products are unsafe.* | **aim to, be designed to, seek to**

investigation noun

● ADJ. **careful, close, detailed | extensive** *The authorities conducted an extensive investigation into his tax affairs.* | **full, thorough | criminal, murder, police | scientific | government**
● VERB + INVESTIGATION **carry out, conduct, pursue** *Police are still pursuing their investigations.* | **launch | head, lead | complete**
● INVESTIGATION + VERB **reveal sth, show sth** *Closer investigation showed this idea to be untenable.*
● PREP. **on ~** *On investigation, the noise turned out to be only a door banging.* **under ~** *The singer is currently under investigation for possessing illegal drugs.* | **~ into** *Police have launched an investigation into the allegations.*
● PHRASES **the subject of an investigation** *The matter is the subject of a police investigation, and we have been advised not to comment.*

investment noun

● ADJ. **good, excellent, profitable, sound, successful, wise, worthwhile | bad, poor, unwise** *He lost a lot of money through poor investments.* | **high-risk, risky, speculative | safe | considerable, enormous, great, heavy, high, huge, large, large-scale, major, massive, significant, sizeable, substantial** *The president has called for massive investment to rebuild the country's economy.* | **low, modest, small | inadequate** *The country's infrastructure is crumbling because of inadequate investment.* | **maximum, minimum | additional, extra, further | gross, net | overall | new | necessary | strategic | direct | domestic, local | cross-border, foreign, international, inward, offshore, outside, overseas | long-term, short-term | initial, original** *an initial investment of $5 million* | **capital, financial | business, industrial, infrastructural, manufacturing | government, public, public-sector | state | corporate, institutional | private, private-sector** *private investment in the health service* | **personal** *I had made a personal investment in time and energy.* | **emotional** *parents' emotional investment in their children*

● QUANT. **level, rate**
● VERB + INVESTMENT **make** | **attract, encourage, promote, stimulate** *a business plan to encourage new investment* | **increase** | **cut** | **recoup** *It took two years before I recouped my investment.* | **realize** *She felt the time was right to realize her investment, and sold all her shares.* | **spread** *When buying shares, it's wise to spread your investment over several companies.* | **protect**
● INVESTMENT + VERB **increase, rise** | **fall**
● INVESTMENT + NOUN **funds** | **levels, rates** *inadequate investment levels* | **scheme** | **decision** | **company, trust**
● PREP. **as an~** *I don't really like modern art but I bought it as an investment.* | **~ from** *investment from American pension funds* **~ in** *investment in local industry*
● PHRASES **a loss on an investment** *losses made on investments in stocks and bonds* **a profit/return on an investment** *I'm hoping for a good return on my investment.*
⇨ Special page at BUSINESS

investor *noun*

● ADJ. **big, large, major** | **ordinary, small** *Many ordinary investors stand to lose money in this affair.* | **potential, prospective, would-be** | **business, institutional** | **personal, private** | **domestic, local** | **foreign, international, inward, outside, overseas**
● VERB + INVESTOR **attract, encourage** *A stable firm is more likely to attract potential investors.* | **advise** *advising investors where to put their money*
● INVESTOR + VERB **buy sth, invest in sth** *Investors will be able to buy the shares from next week.* | **sell sth**
● INVESTOR + NOUN **confidence** *the need to restore investor confidence* | **protection**
● PREP. **~in** *investors in plantation forestry* ◇ *(figurative) encouraging companies to become investors in people*

invincible *adj.*

● VERBS **be, feel, look, seem** | **become** | **make sb** *a secret weapon that will make us invincible.*
● ADV. **almost, virtually** | **apparently, seemingly**

invisible *adj.*

● VERBS **be** | **become** | **remain** | **make sb/sth, render sb/sth** *He wished that he could make himself invisible.* ◇ *It's interesting how women are rendered invisible in these statistics.*
● ADV. **altogether, completely, totally** | **almost, nearly, practically, virtually** | **largely** | **effectively**
● PREP. **to** *Infrared light is invisible to the human eye.*

invitation *noun*

● ADJ. **kind** | **formal** | **open** *We have an open invitation to use their holiday cottage whenever we like.* ◇ *(figurative) An unlocked door is an open invitation to any burglar.* | **dinner, party, wedding**
● VERB + INVITATION **get, have, receive** | **accept, take sb up on, take up** *We'd love to to take up your invitation to visit you some time.* | **decline, refuse, turn down** *I must sadly decline your generous invitation.* | **extend** *(formal),* **issue, send, send out**
● PREP. **at sb's ~** *He is here to give a concert at the invitation of the British Council.* **by ~** *Membership of the club is by invitation only.* **from ~** *We got a wedding invitation from Shashi and Len.* **to ~** *Have you received your invitation to the exhibition?* ◇ *The head extended an invitation to all parents to come and see the school.*

invite *verb*

1 ask sb to do sth
● ADV. **formally, officially** | **cordially, kindly, warmly** *You are cordially invited to attend the annual parish meeting.* ◇ *She very kindly invited me to lunch.* | **personally** |

along, around/round/over, back, in, out *They've invited us over for a drink.*
● PREP. **into** *As a child I was allowed to play in the garden at the Manor, but I never got invited into the house.* **for** *Let's invite them all for dinner.* **to** *Thank you for inviting me to the meeting.*
2 encourage sth
● ADV. **positively** *The hype and fervour surrounding the event positively invited scepticism.*
● VERB + INVITE **seem to** *The film seems to invite comparison with 'The Italian Job'.*

inviting *adj.*

● VERBS **be, look, sound**
● ADV. **very** | **hardly, not particularly** *The house, with its boarded-up windows, was hardly inviting.* | **quite**

invoice *noun*

● ADJ. **original** | **final** *Please pay the final invoice within two weeks.* | **tax, VAT** *The seller has to issue a tax invoice.*
● VERB + INVOICE **issue, raise, send** | **get, receive** | **pay**
● INVOICE + NOUN **price, value** *The shipping costs can be as high as 50% of the invoice value of the goods.*

involve *verb*

1 make sth necessary
● ADV. **ordinarily, typically, usually** *Inventions typically involve minor improvements in technology.* | **inevitably, necessarily** *The reforms will inevitably involve a lot of new paperwork for teachers.*
2 include sb
● ADV. **actively, directly** *methods that actively involve students in learning*
● PREP. **in** *I didn't mean to involve you in all this.*

involved *adj.*

1 taking part in sth
● VERBS **be** | **become, get**
● ADV. **closely, deeply, heavily, intimately, very** *She became heavily involved in politics.* | **actively** *He wanted to be actively involved in school life.* | **directly** *Drugs were not directly involved in her death.* | **personally**
● PREP. **in** *He was involved in a road accident.* **with** *She first became involved with the organization in 1998.*
2 emotionally connected with sb
● VERBS **be** | **become, get**
● ADV. **deeply, heavily, very** | **personally** | **emotionally, romantically, sexually**
● PREP. **with** *I never wanted to get emotionally involved with him.*
3 complicated
● VERBS **be, look, seem, sound** | **become, get**
● ADV. **extremely, terribly, very** *It all sounds terribly involved and complicated.* | **rather**

involvement *noun*

● ADJ. **active, direct** | **close, deep, intense** | **full** | **day-to-day** *When she was promoted, she missed the day-to-day involvement with customers.* | **personal** | **emotional** *Nurses usually try to avoid emotional involvement with patients.* | **parental** *He encourages parental involvement in the running of school.* | **political** | **military** *The US government has ruled out military involvement in the region.* | **alleged** *He is serving a 15-year sentence for his alleged involvement in a plot to overthrow the government.*
● VERB + INVOLVEMENT **accuse sb of** | **suspect sb of** | **admit, deny** *Winters denies any involvement in the robbery.*
● PREP. **~ by** *The success of the venture may lead to in-*

volvement by other foreign companies. ~ **from** *The project needs full involvement from all members of the group.* ~ **in** *He was found to have a deep involvement in drug dealing.* ~ **with** *Her husband's involvement with another woman led to their divorce.*

iron *noun*

1 metal
- ADJ. **rusty** | **cast, corrugated, galvanized, wrought** *a hut with a corrugated iron roof* | **pig** | **scrap**
- VERB + IRON **make, produce, smelt** *Germany produced enormous quantities of coal, iron and steel.* | **be rich in, contain** *foods that are rich in iron* | **be made from/(out) of, be cast in** *a bridge made of wrought iron*
- IRON + VERB **go rusty, rust**
- IRON + NOUN **ore** *mining iron ore locally* | **bar, ingot** | **filings** | **industry** | **foundry, works** | **deficiency** *patients with iron deficiency* | **tablets** *I was put on iron tablets for my anaemia.*

2 tool
- ADJ. **cool, hot, warm** | **electric, steam** | **travel**
- VERB + IRON **use** *Use a cool iron on synthetics.*
- PHRASES **run an iron over sth** *I just need to run an iron over my shirt, then I'm ready.*

iron *verb*

- ADV. **beautifully, carefully, properly** *Her clothes were always beautifully ironed.*
- PHRASES **freshly/newly ironed** *a neat pile of freshly ironed shirts* **need ironing** *My jeans need ironing.*

ironic *adj.*

- VERBS **be, seem** | **find sth**
- ADV. **deeply, extremely, heavily, particularly, very** | **quite, rather, slightly, somewhat** | **doubly** | **deliciously, suitably** | **tragically**

ironing *noun*

- QUANT. **pile** *There's a pile of ironing waiting to be done.*
- VERB + IRONING **do** *Who does the ironing in your house?* | **need** *This shirt needs ironing.*
- IRONING + NOUN **board**

irony *noun*

- ADJ. **great, heavy** *She tried to ignore the heavy irony in his voice.* | **gentle** *She congratulated him with gentle irony.* | **bitter, cruel, tragic** | **neat, nice** *It is a nice irony that the Minister of Transport missed the meeting because her train was delayed.* | **final, supreme, ultimate** *The final irony was that he became Minister of Education having left school at 12.* | **dramatic** (= in a play, when a character's words carry an extra meaning that the character is not aware of)
- QUANT. **hint, touch, trace** *He thanked us all without a touch of irony.*
- PREP. **by a ...** ~ *By a cruel irony, he died in a crash while returning home from the war.*

irrational *adj.*

- VERBS **appear, be, seem** | **become** | **consider sth, regard sth as, see sth as** | **dismiss sth as** *He dismissed her fears as irrational.*
- ADV. **quite, totally, wholly** | **increasingly** | **somewhat** | **apparently, seemingly**

irreconcilable *adj.*

- VERBS **appear, be, seem** | **become** | **remain**
- ADV. **absolutely, totally, utterly** | **apparently, seemingly** *a seemingly irreconcilable conflict*

- PREP. **with** *These practices are irreconcilable with the law of the Church.*

irregular *adj.*

1 not regular in size/shape/frequency
- VERBS **be, look** | **become**
- ADV. **highly, very** | **rather, slightly, somewhat** *The cells are slightly irregular in shape.*

2 not allowed according to the rules
- VERBS **be, seem, sound**
- ADV. **highly, most, very** *It would be highly irregular for a police officer to accept money in this way.* | **slightly, somewhat** *some somewhat irregular business practices*

irregularity *noun*

- ADJ. **serious** | **minor, slight** *a slight irregularity in the surface of the wood* | **widespread** *The newspaper claimed there were widespread irregularities in the election.* | **electoral, financial, procedural, voting** *Investigators found no evidence of financial irregularity.*
- VERB + IRREGULARITY **investigate, uncover**
- IRREGULARITY + VERB **occur, take place** *Irregularities occur when there is no central control.*
- PREP. ~ **in** *Auditors have uncovered serious irregularities in the accounts.*

irrelevant *adj.*

- VERBS **appear, be, seem** | **become** | **make sth, render sth** | **consider sth, deem sth, regard sth as, see sth as, view sth as** | **dismiss sth as** *These arguments were dismissed as irrelevant.*
- ADV. **completely, entirely, quite, totally, utterly, wholly** | **increasingly** | **almost, more or less, virtually** | **largely** | **rather, somewhat** | **simply** | **strictly** *The matter is strictly irrelevant at this point in the proceedings.* | **apparently, seemingly** | **ludicrously** *Ludicrously irrelevant thoughts swarmed in her head.* | **politically**
- PREP. **to** *Her statement is irrelevant to this case.* ◇ *It's all irrelevant to me.*

irresistible *adj.*

- VERBS **be, prove** | **become** | **remain** | **make sb/sth** *The very high salary made the job irresistible.* | **find sb/sth** *You'll find our offer irresistible.*
- ADV. **quite, totally** | **almost** | **simply** | **apparently, seemingly** *Public spending has an apparently irresistible momentum.* | **somehow**
- PREP. **to** *His rugged good looks made him irresistible to women.*

irresponsible *adj.*

- VERBS **be, seem, sound** | **become** | **consider sb/sth**
- ADV. **extremely, grossly, highly, terribly, very** *This was highly irresponsible behaviour.* | **completely, totally, utterly, wholly** *He's fun, but totally irresponsible.* | **rather, slightly, somewhat** | **socially** *It is socially irresponsible to refuse young people advice on sexual matters.*

irrigation *noun*

- ADJ. **large-scale, small-scale**
- IRRIGATION + NOUN **project, scheme, system** | **canal, channel, ditch** | **pump**
- PREP. **under** ~ *two million acres under irrigation*

irritate *verb*

- ADV. **intensely, really** *The noise was beginning to irritate me intensely.* ◇ *That man really irritates me!* | **slightly** | **easily** *She was moody at times and easily irritated.*

irritated *adj.*

- VERBS be, feel, look, sound | become, get
- ADV. deeply, profoundly | thoroughly | increasingly | faintly, a little, mildly, rather, slightly | visibly
- PREP. at *She was deeply irritated at being thwarted.* by *He was slightly irritated by her forgetfulness.*

irritation *noun*

1 feeling/cause of being irritated

- ADJ. considerable, great, intense, major, serious, some | growing, increasing | mild, minor, slight *the minor irritation of having to queue* | constant
- VERB + IRRITATION feel *He felt slight irritation at being kept waiting.* | express, show *He showed no irritation at the delay.* | conceal, hide, suppress *She made no attempt to conceal her irritation.* | cause *Such delays can cause considerable irritation.*
- IRRITATION + VERB grow, rise *She felt irritation rising in her.* | show *She didn't let her irritation show.*
- PREP. in~ *Gary shook his head in irritation.* to your~ *I found to my great irritation that I'd forgotten the film.* with~ *'Of course not' she said with some irritation.* | ~at *our irritation at the delay* ~to *This is a major irritation to travellers.* ~with *her irritation with people who were slow*
- PHRASES a feeling/sense of irritation, a source of irritation *Traffic noise is a source of constant irritation.*

2 slight pain in part of the body

- ADJ. intense, severe | mild | eye, skin *a new cream to treat skin irritation*
- VERB + IRRITATION cause, lead to *The infection can cause intense irritation of the throat.* | experience, get, suffer *Stop using the cream if you get any irritation.*

Islam *noun*

- ADJ. Shia, Sunni
⇨ Note at RELIGION (for verbs and phrases)

island *noun*

- ADJ. outlying, remote *a ferry service to the outlying islands* | coral, tropical, volcanic | desert, uninhabited | offshore *His money is in an offshore island bank.*
- QUANT. chain, group *a group of tropical islands*
- ISLAND + NOUN chain, group *the island chain of the Outer Hebrides* | home *They were forced to leave their island home and start a new life on the mainland.* | paradise *the island paradise of Phuket*
- PREP. on an/the~ *He owns a house on the island.*
- PHRASES the ... coast/end/side/tip of an island *The best beaches are on the southern tip of the island.*

isolated *adj.*

- VERBS appear, be, feel | become, get | remain | leave sb/sth *Without help, many elderly people would be left isolated.* | keep sb/sth *She kept herself almost isolated from her colleagues.*
- ADV. extremely, very | completely, entirely, totally, utterly | increasingly, progressively | almost | largely | quite, rather, relatively, somewhat | effectively, essentially | apparently *an apparently isolated incident* | culturally, diplomatically, economically, geographically, physically, socially *a culturally isolated community* ◊ *Unless a compromise could be reached the country would be diplomatically isolated on this issue.*
- PREP. from *a child who is isolated from other children*

isolation *noun*

- ADJ. complete, total | enforced *the enforced isolation of life in an Arctic weather station* | diplomatic, geographical, political | international *The country could face international isolation if it does not withdraw its*

troops. | emotional, social *the social isolation of single mothers at home with their babies*
- VERB + ISOLATION experience, suffer (from) *Many immigrants experience isolation.*
- ISOLATION + NOUN hospital, ward
- PREP. in ~ *The figures should not be looked at in isolation but as part of a pattern.*
- PHRASES in splendid isolation *The tower stands in splendid isolation on the cliff edge.*

issue *noun*

1 problem

- ADJ. big, burning, central, critical, crucial, important, key, main, major, vital *Europe remains the burning issue within the party.* | wider *The problem raises wider issues of gender and identity.* | minor, side | basic, fundamental | real *The real issue is where the power lies.* | contentious, controversial, difficult, thorny *the controversial issue of censorship* | complex | live, unresolved *The strike of ten years ago is still very much a live issue in the town.* | domestic, global, international, local, national, regional | commercial, constitutional, economic, educational, environmental, ethical, health, moral, policy, political, social, technical, theoretical
- QUANT. number, range, series
- VERB + ISSUE raise | debate, discuss *This evening we're debating the issue of the legalization of soft drugs.* | decide, settle *A referendum was held to settle the issue.* | address, consider, deal with, examine, explore, look at, tackle | clarify | focus on *We really need to focus on this one issue and not get sidetracked.* | touch on *The issue of birth control was touched on, but we need to examine it in more detail.* | highlight *The report highlights three issues.* | confuse *This argument should not be allowed to confuse the issue.* | avoid, evade
- ISSUE + VERB arise *issues arising from the survey* | underlie sth *A more important issue underlies this debate.*
- PREP. at~ *What you say is interesting, but it does not affect the point at issue here.* on an/the ~ *She spoke on the issue of private health care.* | ~about *fundamental issues about working conditions* ~concerning *issues concerning the environment* ~relating to *The conference examined key issues relating to the reform.*

2 one in a series of publications

- ADJ. current | back | special *a special issue of stamps*
- VERB + ISSUE bring out, publish
- ISSUE + VERB come out, go on sale | be out
- PREP. in an/the ~ *an article in the current issue of 'Newsweek'*

issue *verb*

- ADV. formally *the bank which formally issues and handles these credit cards* | directly *The safest cheques are those issued directly by the bank—known as bankers' draughts.* | jointly *a document issued jointly by the Treasury and the Home Office* | immediately, promptly *He left the company and promptly issued a writ claiming $45 million in damages.*
- PREP. against *(formal) Arrest warrants were issued against 16 of the protesters.* on behalf of *a statement issued on behalf of the UN Secretary-General* to *The new guidelines have been issued to all doctors.* with *Some of the police were issued with rifles.*
- PHRASES newly issued *newly issued banknotes*

Italian *noun*

⇨ Note at LANGUAGE

itch *noun*

- ADJ. irritating

● VERB + ITCH **relieve, scratch (at)** *The dog was scratching at an itch behind its left ear.*

itch *verb*

● ADV. **positively**
● VERB + ITCH **make sb** *The heat made me itch all over.*
● PREP. **for** *He was itching for a chance to show how good he was.* **with** *Her fingers positively itched with the desire to slap his face.*

item *noun*

● ADJ. **individual, particular, single, specific** *Each individual item has a number.* | **essential, important** *I keep essential items in my hand luggage when I fly.* | **main, major** *the main item on the agenda* ◇ *a major item of expenditure* | **expensive, valuable** *Several valuable items were stolen.* | **commodity, consumer** *Computers became a consumer item in the early 1990s.* | **luxury** *There is a higher tax on luxury items.* | **food** | **household** *household items such as brushes and bedclothes* | **collector's** *The 1970s American model has become something of a collector's item.* | **agenda** | **data** | **news**
● PREP. **~ of** *Several items of clothing were found near the scene of the crime.* **~ on** *The programme featured an item on clothes for young children.*
● PHRASES **item by item** *Check the list carefully, item by item.* **an item on the agenda/menu**

itinerary *noun*

● ADJ. **detailed, full** | **demanding** | **tourist**
● VERB + ITINERARY **arrange, plan** | **follow** *tourists following a demanding itinerary*
● ITINERARY + VERB **include sth** *Your itinerary includes a visit to Stonehenge.*
● PREP. **in an/the ~** *Historic sites are featured prominently in their itineraries.* **on an/the ~** *The National Gallery is on most tourists' itinerary.*

ivory *noun*

● ADJ. **solid** | **carved** | **poached**
● VERB + IVORY **be made from/(out) of, carve sth from/in** *a figure delicately carved in ivory* | **be inlaid with** *a table made of polished wood, inlaid with ivory*
● IVORY + NOUN **trade**
● PREP. **in ~** *a statuette in ivory and gold*
● PHRASES **the trade in ivory**

ivy *noun*

● ADJ. **dense, thick** | **trailing** | **variegated**
● VERB + IVY **grow** *We're going to grow a variegated ivy up the back of the house.* | **plant, put in** | **cut back, cut down, keep down** *The ivy's got very thick. It needs cutting back a bit.* | **be covered in** *The walls were covered in ivy.*
● IVY + VERB **grow** *Ivy grew up the side of the house.* | **climb, cling, crawl, creep, trail, twine** *There was ivy clinging to the wall.*
● IVY + NOUN **leaves**

Jj

jab noun

1 sudden hit/push
- ADJ. **left, right** | **hard, painful, sharp** | **elbow**
- VERB + JAB **give sb** | **feel**
- PREP. **~ in/to** *Scott gave him a sharp left jab to the ribs.*

2 injection
- ADJ. **flu, tetanus, typhoid, etc.**
- VERB + JAB **have** *Did you have a flu jab this year?* | **give sb**

jack noun

⇨ Note at CARD

jacket noun

- ADJ. **fitted, tailored** | **baggy, loose** | **heavy** | **light, lightweight** | **double-breasted, single-breasted** | **belted, zip-up** | **padded, quilted** | **bolero** | **waterproof, waxed** | **bulletproof** | **camouflage, check/checked, striped** | **corduroy, cotton, denim, fleece, leather, linen, sheepskin, suede, tweed, wool** | **pyjama, suit, uniform** | **bomber, combat, dinner, flak, flying, life, shooting, ski, smoking, sports** *He wore a tweed sports jacket.*
- VERB + JACKET **pull on, shrug (sth) into, shrug on, slip on, throw on** *She shrugged her shoulders into her jacket.* | **pull off, remove, shrug off/out of, slip off** | **button (up), do up, zip up** | **unbutton, undo, unzip** | **hang up** | **drape, sling** *A light cotton jacket was draped over her shoulders.*
- JACKET + VERB **hang** *His jacket hung over the back of his chair.*
- JACKET + NOUN **pocket, sleeve** *He pulled his passport from his inside jacket pocket.*
- PHRASES **a jacket and tie** *Gentlemen are requested to wear a jacket and tie for dinner.*
⇨ Special page at CLOTHES

jackpot noun

- ADJ. **£1 million, etc.**
- VERB + JACKPOT **get, hit, scoop, win** *(figurative) The National Theatre hit the jackpot with its first musical, 'Guys and Dolls'.*
- JACKPOT + NOUN **prize** | **winner**
- PREP. **~ in** *They scooped the jackpot in yesterday's lottery.* **~ of** *a prize jackpot of £100 000* **~ on** *He won the jackpot on the football pools.*

jail (also gaol) noun

- ADJ. **county, local** | **high-security, maximum security, top security** | **private** | **overcrowded**
- VERB + JAIL **go to** *He's gone to jail for fraud.* | **put sb in, send sb to, throw sb into** | **keep sb in** | **be freed from, be/get out of, be released from** *With good behaviour, she could be out of jail in two years.* | **escape from** | **threaten sb with** *He was threatened with jail if evidence of a hoax was discovered.* | **face** | **avoid, escape** *She avoided jail by pleading self-defence.*
- JAIL + NOUN **sentence, term**
- PREP. **at a/the ~** *riots at Strangeways jail* **in (a/the) ~** *How long has she been in jail?* ◇ *There was a fire in the jail last night.*

jam noun

- ADJ. **home-made** | **plum, strawberry, etc.**
- QUANT. **dollop** | **jar, pot**
- VERB + JAM **make** | **spread (sth with)** *She spread the toast thinly with raspberry jam.*
- JAM + NOUN **jar** | **doughnut, sandwich, sponge, tart**
- PHRASES **bread and jam**
⇨ Special page at FOOD

jam verb

- ADV. **completely**
- PHRASES **be jammed full (of sth)** *The cupboards were jammed full of old newspapers.* **be jammed solid** *The traffic was jammed solid in the city centre.* **be jammed tight with sth** *The room is jammed tight with furniture.* **be jammed (up) with** *The streets were completely jammed with traffic.*

January noun

⇨ Note at MONTH

Japanese noun

- JAPANESE + NOUN **script** | **character**
⇨ Note at LANGUAGE

jar noun

- ADJ. **screw-top/screw-topped** | **airtight, sealed, stoppered** | **sterilized** | **preserving, storage** | **earthenware, glass, stone/stoneware** | **coffee, cookie, jam, marmalade, pickle, sweet**
- VERB + JAR **fill** *He was filling a jar with coins for his holiday.* | **seal** | **preserve sth in, store sth in**
- JAR + VERB **be filled with sth, be full of sth, contain sth** *a jar full of pickled onions*
- PREP. **in/into a/the ~** | **~ of** *a jar of marmalade*

jargon noun

- ADJ. **current** | **incomprehensible, obscure** | **unnecessary** | **academic, computer, legal, scientific, technical**
- QUANT. **piece**
- VERB + JARGON **speak (in), use** *He always speaks in obscure legal jargon.* | **avoid**
- PREP. **in ~** *in computer jargon* | **~ for** *'All necessary means' is diplomatic jargon for 'war'.*

jaw noun

1 bone that contains teeth
- ADJ. **bottom, lower** | **top, upper** | **firm, strong** | **clenched, set** | **slack** | **jutting, lantern** (= in which the lower part sticks out), **thrusting** | **pointed, square** | **broken, dislocated, fractured**
- VERB + JAW **clench, set** | **finger, rub, stroke** *He fingered his jaw thoughtfully.* | **break, dislocate, fracture**
- JAW + VERB **drop, sag** *My jaw dropped in astonishment when I saw the size of the audience.* | **be set, clench, set, tighten** *Her jaw was set, ready for a fight.* | **jut** *His jaw jutted stubbornly forward; he would not be denied.*
- JAW + NOUN **bone, muscle** | **injury**
- PREP. **in your ~** *A muscle in his jaw pulsed angrily.* **on your ~** *He had two days' growth of stubble on his jaw.* **to the ~** *a punch to the jaw* **under your ~** *She had a fold of flesh under her jaw.*
- PHRASES **the line/set of your jaw** *The stern set of the officer's jaw made Tony realize he was in trouble.*

2 jaws mouth

- ADJ. **gaping, open** | **massive, powerful** *A shark can crush a boat with its massive jaws.* | **slavering** *The slavering jaws of the guard dog stopped anyone going near.*
- VERB + JAWS **clamp, close, lock, sink** *The dog locked its jaws on her leg and wouldn't let go.* ◇ *A spider sank its jaws into my ankle.* | **escape** (**from**) *The antelope could not escape the crocodile's gaping jaws.*
- PREP. **between its~s** *The dog had his arm clamped between its jaws.*

jazz *noun*

- ADJ. **live** | **free/free-form, modern, trad/traditional**
- VERB + JAZZ **play** | **improvise** | **listen to**
- JAZZ + NOUN **music** | **clarinettist, guitarist, musician, player, singer, etc.** | **clarinet, guitar, vocals, etc.** | **band, combo, group, quartet, trio** | **improvisation** | **chords, rhythms** | **club, venue** | **festival** | **scene** *the rising stars of the New York jazz scene*
- PREP. **in~** *harmonies and rhythms common in jazz*

jealous *adj.*

- VERBS **be, feel, sound** | **become, get, grow** | **make sb** *Ignore her—she's only trying to make you jealous.*
- ADV. **bitterly, furiously, insanely, madly, really, very** *I can remember feeling madly jealous when he was with other women.* | **a bit, a little, quite, rather** | **obsessively** *Peter was obsessively jealous and his behaviour was driving his wife away.* | **sexually**
- PREP. **about** *There's nothing for you to feel jealous about.* **of** *She was rather jealous of me.* ◇ *He had started to get jealous of her success.*

jealousy *noun*

- ADJ. **bitter, extreme, intense, obsessive, pure, violent** | **irrational** | **professional, sexual**
- QUANT. **fit** *He broke off the engagement in a fit of jealousy.* | **pang, rush, stab, twinge** *I felt a pang of jealousy.*
- VERB + JEALOUSY **feel** *She'd never felt jealousy before.* | **arouse, cause, create, provoke** *Her promotion aroused intense jealousy among her colleagues.*
- PREP. **~of** *his obsessive jealousy of his ex-wife*
- PHRASES **feelings of jealousy**

jeans *noun*

- ADJ. **stretch, tight** | **baggy, flared** | **denim** | **black, blue** | **bleached, faded, stonewashed** | **patched, ripped, scruffy, torn** | **cut-off** | **designer**
- QUANT. **pair** *She pulled on a pair of faded blue jeans.*
- VERB + JEANS **pull on, pull up** | **pull off, strip off** | **zip up** | **unzip**
- JEANS + NOUN **pocket**
- ⇨ Special page at CLOTHES

jelly *noun*

- VERB + JELLY **eat, have** | **make** *Shall I make a jelly for pudding?*
- JELLY + VERB **set** *Put the jelly in the fridge to set.* | **wobble**
- PREP. **in~** *fruit in jelly*
- ⇨ Special page at FOOD

jeopardize *verb*

- ADV. **seriously** *This scandal could seriously jeopardize his chances of being re-elected.*

jerk *noun*

- ADJ. **sharp, sudden** | **painful**
- VERB + JERK **give** *His thigh muscle gave a sudden jerk.*

- PREP. **with a~of** *She answered with a jerk of her head.*

jerk *verb*

- ADV. **suddenly** | **sharply, violently** | **convulsively, spasmodically** | **away, back, backwards, downwards, forward, round, up, upright, upwards** *She suddenly jerked her hand away.* ◇ *His head jerked up.*
- PHRASES **jerk awake** *The train stopped and she jerked awake.* **jerk sth open** *He jerked the door open.* **jerk to a halt/stop** *The bus jerked to a stop.*

jersey *noun*

- ADJ. **thick** | **polo-neck, V-neck, etc.** | **cashmere** | **football, rugby**
- VERB + JERSEY **pull on** | **knit**
- ⇨ Special page at CLOTHES

jet *noun*

1 plane with a jet engine

- ADJ. **jumbo** | **supersonic** | **commercial, passenger** | **private** | **business, corporate, executive** | **holiday** | **cargo** | **air force, fighter, military** | **low-flying**
- VERB + JET **fly, pilot**
- JET + VERB **fly** | **take off** | **land** | **crash, explode**
- JET + NOUN **aircraft, airliner, bomber, fighter, plane** | **engine** | **fuel** | **pilot**
- PREP. **by~** *Australia was a mere couple of hours away by jet.* ◇ *She was flown by private jet to the capital Lusaka.* **in a/the~** *He flew to Majorca in his private jet.*

2 stream of gas, water, etc.

- ADJ. **little** | **air, gas, water**
- PREP. **~of** *Little jets of steam spurted from the engine.*

Jew *noun*

- ADJ. **devout, pious, practising, religious** *His family are all practising Jews.* | **secular** | **Hasidic, orthodox** | **Progressive, Reform** | **Ashkenazi, Sephardic**
- VERB + JEW **be born** *He was born a Jew in first century Palestine.* | **become**

jewel *noun*

- ADJ. **precious, priceless** | **bright, brilliant, sparkling**
- VERB + JEWEL **wear**
- JEWEL + VERB **sparkle**
- JEWEL + NOUN **thief** | **box, case**

jewellery *noun*

- ADJ. **expensive, valuable** | **cheap** | **beautiful, fine** | **costume** (= which may be designed to look expensive but is made with cheap materials) | **designer** | **antique** | **family, personal** *She inherited the family jewellery.* | **diamond, gold, etc.**
- QUANT. **piece**
- VERB + JEWELLERY **wear** | **make** | **design** | **steal**
- JEWELLERY + NOUN **box, case** | **shop** | **design** | **designer**
- ⇨ Special page at CLOTHES

jigsaw *noun*

- ADJ. **giant, huge** | **200-piece, etc.**
- QUANT. **bit, piece** *One piece of the jigsaw is still missing.*
- VERB + JIGSAW **do** *I used to enjoy doing jigsaws.* | **piece together** (*figurative*) *The police managed to piece together the jigsaw and reconstruct the victim's last hours.* | **finish**
- JIGSAW + NOUN **puzzle** | **piece**
- PHRASES **a piece in a jigsaw** (*figurative*) *This is an-*

other piece in the jigsaw that will help us understand the biology of cancer.

jinx *noun*

- VERB + JINX **shake off** *The team seems to have shaken off the jinx that's been dogging them for months.*
- JINX + VERB **hit sb, strike sb** *The injury jinx has struck Real Madrid.* | **dog sb, haunt sb**
- PREP. **~ on** *I'm sure there's a jinx on this car.*

job *noun*

1 employment

- ADJ. **high-powered, top** *It's one of the top jobs in management.* | **decent, good, worthwhile | interesting | plum** *The plum jobs all went to friends of the prime minister.* | **cushy** *His father found him a cushy job in the office, with almost nothing to do and a whacking great salary.* | **dream, ideal** *What would be your dream job?* | **boring, dead-end, menial, routine, undemanding** *He was forced to take a series of menial jobs.* | **challenging, demanding, difficult, taxing | highly-paid, well-paid, badly-paid, low-paid | full-time, part-time | 9-to-5 | regular, steady** *He was tempted to give up freelancing and get a regular job.* | **permanent, temporary | holiday, summer, vac/ vacation | evening, Saturday, weekend | paid, unpaid | manual, non-manual | semi-skilled, skilled, unskilled | blue-collar, white-collar | desk** *a desk job in the police housing department* | **proper** *He'd done lots of part-time work, but this was his first proper job.* | **manufacturing, teaching**
- VERB + JOB **have** *She's got a very good job with a local firm of solicitors.* | **look for | apply for, go for | find, get, land, take** *She got a temporary job stacking shelves.* ◇ *He's just landed himself a highly-paid job in the City.* | **lose** *He's frightened of losing his job.* | **give up, pack in, resign from | hold down, keep** *He's always had difficulty holding down a job.* | **advertise** *I saw the job advertised on the Internet.* | **interview (sb) for** *We're interviewing for the job in the Sales Department.* | **give sb, offer sb | create, provide (sb with)** *It is hoped that the scheme will create new jobs in the region.* | **axe, cut, shed** *Management are hoping to shed 200 jobs.* | **protect, safeguard** *The deal between the union and management should safeguard 6 000 jobs.* | **do** *I'm only doing my job (= doing what I am paid to do).* | **know** *He certainly knows his job (= is very good at his job).~*
- JOB + VERB **pay** *The job doesn't pay very well.* | **go** *250 jobs are to go at the local steel plant.*
- JOB + NOUN **search** *The first step in a job search is to prepare an up-to-date CV.* | **ad, advertisement | vacancy | application | interview | title** *His job title is Chief Hygiene Operative.* | **description, specifications** *Cleaning the office is not in my job description.* | **market** *There is an enormous job market for teachers at the moment.* | **cuts, losses | creation | opportunities, prospects | satisfaction** *How would you rate your job satisfaction?* | **security** *Workers questioned rated job security as being more important than high salary.* | **hunter, seeker** *Local companies are holding an open day for job seekers.* | **sharing** *The introduction of job sharing could prevent the need for redundancies.*
- PREP. **in a/the~** *There's not much chance of promotion in a job like that.* **on the~** *You will receive training on the job.* **out of a~** *She found herself out of a job when her boss died.* **|~ as** *She's got a job as a waitress.* **~ at** *She got a teaching job at the university.* **~ for** *jobs for women* **~ in a** *job in food retailing* ◇ *a job in a large firm* **~ with** *He moved to a better-paid job with another employer.*
- PHRASES **a loss of jobs** *The closure of the cement factory will mean the loss of over 800 jobs.* **the right person for the job** *Despite the small number of applicants, they managed to find the right person for the job.*

2 task

- ADJ. **admirable, amazing, excellent, fine, first-rate, good, grand, magnificent, marvellous, professional, terrific, thorough, wonderful | difficult, hard, tough** *They gave me the tough job of telling applicants that they'd been rejected.* | **easy | important | big, long | little, small | fiddly, tedious** *fiddly little jobs like wiring plugs* | **dirty | unenviable** *Cooper had the unenviable job of announcing the redundancies.*
- VERB + JOB **do, make** *You've done a grand job with that decorating.* ◇ *Try wedging it open—that should do the job (= be effective/successful).* ◇ *She made a very good job of covering up the damage.* | **give sb | take on** *She's taken on the job of organizing the Christmas party.* | **get on with** *I want to get on with the job of painting my room today.*
- PREP. **~ in** *The author has done an admirable job in compiling all this material.* **~ of** *He made a very professional job of replacing the windows.* **~ on** *You've done a good job on the car.*
- PHRASES **get a job done** *We're hoping to get the job done this weekend.* **odd jobs** (= small, practical jobs) *I spend most Saturdays doing odd jobs around the house.*

3 crime

- ADJ. **bank | inside** (= done by sb in the organization where the crime happens)
- VERB + JOB **do** *He got six months for that last job he did.* | **bungle** *The gang bungled the job and got caught.*

NOTE

Jobs

be, work as ~
She's a well-known writer.
Her father, a trained chef, now works as a bus driver.
study to be, train as, train to be ~
She trained as a painter and sculptor.
start (work) as ~
He started work as a trainee chef.
become, qualify as ~
She qualified as a vet last year.
employ (sb as), have
The company employs more than 1500 engineers.
engage (sb as), get, hire (sb as), recruit, take on ~
They have recruited a new designer.
appoint, appoint sb (as), make sb ~ are usually used with academic, official or highly responsible jobs:
He was appointed Professor of Law at Yale.
At 39 she was made chairman of the board.
dismiss, fire, sack ~
The club have sacked their coach.
⇨ See also the note at PROFESSIONAL

---

jockey *noun*

- ADJ. **champion, top | winning | apprentice | amateur | jump** (= who rides in races that involve jumping) | **stable** (= who rides the horses of a particular trainer or training stable)
- JOCKEY + VERB **ride (sth)** *Which jockey will be riding tomorrow?* | **win (sth)** *The race was won by top jockey Eddie Andrews.*

jog *noun*

- ADJ. **brisk | slow**
- VERB + JOG **go for** *He goes for a brisk jog before work each morning.*
- PREP. **at a ~** *I began at a slow jog and gradually increased my pace.*

jog *verb*

- ADV. **slowly, steadily**
- PREP. **along, down, up** *They jogged steadily up the hill.*
- PHRASES **go jogging** *She decided to go jogging each morning.* **jog on the spot** *She was jogging on the spot to keep warm.*

join *verb*

1 become a member of sth
- VERB + JOIN **want to, wish to | flock to** *By this time people were flocking to join the cult.* **| decide to | persuade sb to | be allowed to | refuse to**
- PHRASES **an invitation to join sth**

2 do sth with sb else
- VERB + JOIN **wish to | invite sb to** *They've invited us to join them on their yacht.* **| be allowed to** *She was now old enough to be allowed to join the adults.* **| be expected to** *Thousands of people are expected to join the sponsored walk.* **| decide to | refuse to**
- PREP. **for** *Will you join me shortly for a drink in the bar?* **in** *I'm sure you will all wish to join me in thanking our speaker tonight.* **with** *Please will you all join with me in singing the national anthem.*
- PHRASES **come and join sb** *He waved a fork in greeting. 'Come and join us!'* **an invitation to join sb/sth**

PHRASAL VERB

join in
- ADV. **enthusiastically** *They all joined enthusiastically in the dancing.*
- VERB + JOIN IN **want to | refuse to**
- PREP. **with** *Everyone joined in with the singing.* ◇ *I wish he would join in with the other children.*

joint *noun*

1 in the body
- ADJ. **elbow, hip, knee, etc. | inflamed, painful, rheumatic, stiff, swollen | artificial**
- VERB + JOINT **replace** *He's going to have his hip joint replaced.*
- JOINT + VERB **ache | move** *The joint should be able to move freely.*
- PREP. **in a/the ~** *You've got fluid in the joint.* **| ~ between** *the joint between the lower and upper parts of the arm*
- PHRASES **put sth out of joint** *She fell and put her knee out of joint.*

2 connecting point
- ADJ. **airtight, watertight | leaking**
- VERB + JOINT **make, seal**
- PREP. **~ between** *a joint between two lengths of copper*

3 piece of meat
- ADJ. **bacon**
- VERB + JOINT **cook, roast | carve**
- PREP. **~ of** *a joint of beef/lamb/pork*

joke *noun*

- ADJ. **funny, good | old** *That's an old joke—I've heard it lots of times.* **| cruel, sick | huge | dirty**
- VERB + JOKE **crack, make, tell** *He's marvellous at telling jokes.* **| play** *He's always playing jokes on people.* **| have, share** *She likes to have a joke with her employees.* **| hear | get, laugh at** *We all fell about laughing, but he didn't get the joke.* **| take** *The trouble is she can't take a joke.* **| treat sth as** *He treated his exams as a huge joke.*
- JOKE + VERB **fall flat** *The audience weren't very responsive and the jokes fell a bit flat.* **| be on sb** *I thought I'd play a trick on them, but in the end the joke was on me.*
- PREP. **as a ~** *It was only said as a joke.* **| ~ about** *Have you heard the joke about the elephant and the mouse?*

- PHRASES **make a joke of sth** *We tried to make a joke of our situation, but it wasn't really funny.*

joke *verb*

- ADV. **half** *She was only half joking about being prime minister one day.*
- PREP. **about** *We joked about the amount of luggage we had to carry.* **with** *joking with her friends*
- PHRASES **be only joking** *Don't worry, I'm only joking!* **joking apart/aside** (= used to show you are now being serious after you have said sth funny), **laugh and joke** *They laughed and joked as they walked along.* **you must be joking** *No way am I doing that. You must be joking!*

joker *noun*

⇨ Note at CARD

jolt *noun*

- ADJ. **nasty, severe, sharp, sickening, sudden, unpleasant | little, slight**
- VERB + JOLT **feel | give** *My mother's death gave me a severe jolt.* **| send | receive** *She received such a jolt that she nearly dropped her cup.*
- PHRASES **with a ~** *The train started with a jolt.* **| ~ of** *The blow sent a jolt of pain through his body.* **~ to** *His dismissal was a severe jolt to his pride.*

journal *noun*

1 serious magazine
- ADJ. **academic, learned, scholarly | professional, technical, trade | house/in-house** *the house journal of the South Western Gas Board* **| non-specialist, specialist | research, reviewing | business, literary, medical, science/scientific | august, highly-ranked/high-ranking, leading, major, prestigious** *'Nature' was the highest-ranked journal in the survey.* **| official** *It's the official journal of the Medical Foundation.* **| international, national | monthly, quarterly, weekly**
- QUANT. **copy** *Please send me two copies of your new journal.* **| edition, issue, volume**
- VERB + JOURNAL **read | edit, write for** *an academic who writes for specialist journals* **| produce, publish | buy, get, subscribe to** *She subscribes to quite a few academic journals.*
- JOURNAL + VERB **come out** *The journal comes out five times a year.*
- JOURNAL + NOUN **article | editor**
- PREP. **in a/the ~** *an article in a medical journal* **| ~ of** *the British Journal of Geology*

2 diary
- ADJ. **private | daily**
- VERB + JOURNAL **keep, write** *Lady Franklin kept a daily journal of the voyage.* **| read**
- JOURNAL + NOUN **entry** *Her journal entry for that day describes a thunder storm.*
- PREP. **in a/the ~** *The events are all recorded in her journal.* **| ~ of** *He wrote a journal of his travels.*

journalism *noun*

- ADJ. **good | professional | investigative | popular, tabloid | chequebook** (*disapproving*) **| magazine, newspaper, print | broadcast, radio, television | fashion, literary, medical, music, science, sports**
- QUANT. **piece** *a fine piece of investigative journalism*
- PHRASES **a career in journalism** *I'd like a career in journalism.* **the world of journalism**
⇨ Note at SUBJECT (for verbs and nouns)

journalist *noun*

- ADJ. **brilliant, good | experienced | leading, well-**

known | professional | freelance | investigative | foreign | magazine, newspaper, print, tabloid | broadcast, radio, television | business, environmental, fashion, financial, literary, political, sports
• VERB + JOURNALIST **speak to, talk to, tell** *She was warned against speaking to journalists about the affair.*
• JOURNALIST + VERB **investigate sth** | **write (sth)** *a journalist writing for a current affairs publication* | **report (on) sth**
• PREP. **~ on/with** *an investigative journalist with a French newspaper*
⇨ Note at JOB

journey noun

• ADJ. **long, marathon** | **brief, short** | **outward** | **homeward, return** | **onward** *The bus driver told us where to change buses for our onward journey.* | **bus, car, rail, railway, train, etc.** | **five-mile, four-hour, etc.** | **comfortable, easy, good, pleasant, safe** *I hope you had a good journey.* ◇ *Have a safe journey.* | **arduous, awkward, bad, difficult, gruelling, hard, tedious, terrible, tiring, tortuous** | **dangerous, hazardous, perilous** | **overland** | **cross-country** | **daily** | **overnight** | **epic** *an epic journey across Africa on foot* | **wasted** *The library was closed when I got there, so it was a wasted journey.* | **emotional, sentimental, spiritual** *He made the emotional journey back to the house he grew up in.*
• VERB + JOURNEY **go on, have, make** *He wasn't there and we had a wasted journey.* | **break** *We broke our return journey in San Francisco.* | **begin, set out on** | **continue, resume** *They continued their journey on foot.* | **complete**
• JOURNEY + VERB **take (sb)** *The journey takes about five hours.* ◇ *His journey took him across central Asia.* | **begin** | **end**
• JOURNEY + NOUN **time**
• PREP. **on ~** *They were on a journey to the Far East.* | **~ by** *a journey by air/bus/land/rail/sea, etc.* | **~ across, ~ between, ~ down** *the journey down the Rhine* **~ from, ~ of** *a journey of 300 miles* ◇ *a journey of five days* **~ through, ~ to** *The bus journey from London to Athens took 60 hours.* **~ up**
• PHRASES **be tired after/from a journey, a leg/stage of a journey** *Dawn was breaking as we set out on the last leg of our journey.*

joy noun

• ADJ. **delirious, ecstatic, fierce, great, heady, overwhelming, pure, real, sheer, true, wild, wonderful** | **simple** | **sudden** | **inner** | **physical** *the physical joys of fine wines and gourmet foods*
• VERB + JOY **bring sb** *Her books have brought great joy to millions of people.* | **experience, feel** *the pure joy I felt at being free again* | **be filled with, be full of** | **express** | **find, get, take** *I find joy in many kinds of music.* ◇ *She got no joy out of working.* ◇ *I took a fierce joy in telling them the truth.*
• JOY + VERB **go** *All the joy had gone out of his life.*
• PREP. **to your ~** *She found to her joy that the house had a large garden.* **with ~** *I could have shouted with joy.* | **~ at** *Protesters expressed joy at the government's decision.*
• PHRASES **dance, jump, sing, weep, etc. for joy** *I literally jumped for joy when I heard the news.* **a joy to behold, see, watch, etc.** *The children's expressions were a joy to behold.* **your pride and joy** (= a person or thing that makes you feel great pride or satisfaction) *The pride and joy of the town is the splendid castle.* **tears of joy**

Judaism noun

• ADJ. **Hasidic, orthodox** | **Progressive, Reform** | **Ashkenazi, Sephardic**
⇨ Note at RELIGION (for verbs and phrases)

judge noun

1 applies the law
• ADJ. **experienced** | **learned** | **senior** | **presiding, trial** | **deputy** | **appeal (court), appellate, circuit, county court, district, federal, High Court, Supreme Court**
• VERB + JUDGE **be, sit as** *By next year you could be sitting as a High Court judge.* | **appoint (sb as)**
• JUDGE + VERB **preside, sit** *Which judge will be sitting next week?* | **call sb** *The judge called the remaining witness for the Crown.* | **direct sb** *The judge must direct the jury on points of law.* | **consider sth** | **accept sth, admit sth** *The judge admitted the notes of the interview as evidence.* | **dismiss sth, refuse sth, reject sth** *The trial judge dismissed her compensation claim.* | **conclude sth, decide sth, find sth, hold sth, rule sth, uphold sth** *The judge held that the company had been negligent.* | **sum up** *The judge summed up and the jury retired to consider its verdict.* | **sentence sb** | **order sth** *The judge ordered the company to pay compensation to the claimant.* | **award (sb) sth, grant (sb) sth** *The judge awarded him damages of £20 000.*
2 decides who has won a competition
• ADJ. **competition** | **independent**
• QUANT. **panel** *a panel of independent judges*
• VERB + JUDGE **choose sb/sth, decide sth**
• PHRASES **the judges' decision** *The judges' decision on the entries is final.*
3 has the ability/knowledge to give an opinion
• ADJ. **astute, good, great, shrewd** *You are the best judge of what your body needs.* ◇ *a shrewd judge of character* | **poor** | **impartial**
• PREP. **~ of** *He is a good judge of footballing talent.*

judge verb

• ADV. **correctly, rightly** | **wrongly** *I think I judged the distance wrongly.* | **fairly, properly** | **harshly** *I think you're judging her rather harshly.* | **objectively** | **beautifully, carefully, finely, nicely, perfectly, well** *Their performance of the concerto was beautifully judged and finely controlled.* ◇ *'There's something I haven't told you.' She judged her words carefully.* ◇ *The bowler judged it well, timing the ball to perfection.* | **accordingly** *Those who preach intolerance should be judged accordingly.*
• VERB + JUDGE **be difficult to, be hard to, be impossible to** | **be able to, be in a position to** *I am in no position to judge whether what she is doing is right or wrong.* | **learn to** *learning to judge distances*
• PREP. **according to** *He believed that schools should be judged according to strictly academic criteria.* **against** *judging his own performance against the performance of others* **by** *You will be judged by the work you have produced over the year.* **from** *The age of the furniture can be judged from the type of wood used.* **on** *Your slogan will be judged on its originality and style.*
• PHRASES **criteria for judging** *People use different criteria for judging success at school.* **don't judge a book by its cover** (*figurative*) (= don't judge sth by how it looks), **judge by appearances, judging by/from sth** *He seems to have been a popular person, judging by the number of people at his funeral.* **to judge by/from sth** *To judge from what she said, she was very disappointed.* **judge for yourself** *Readers are left to judge for themselves whether McCrombie is hero or villain.* **judge sth on its merits** *Each painting must be judged on its own merits.*

judgement noun

1 decision/opinion
• ADJ. **accurate** | **balanced** | **impartial, independent, objective** | **personal, subjective** | **intuitive** | **qualitative** | **harsh** | **snap** *I hate having to make snap judgements.* | **definitive**

• VERB + JUDGEMENT **form, make** *It's difficult to form a judgement when you don't have all the facts.* | **express** *Remember to be tactful when expressing a personal judgement.* | **confirm** *This latest case confirms my earlier judgement.* | **come to, reach** *It is too soon to reach any definitive judgement.* | **deliver, give, pass, pronounce** *The school inspector's function is not merely to pronounce judgement, but also to suggest improvements.* | **reserve, suspend** *The court reserved judgement on the two appeals.* | **obtain, win** *They obtained a judgement in their favour.* | **reverse** *They are trying to get the judgement reversed.* | **abide by**
• PREP. **in sb's ~** *What, in your judgement, would be the best way to deal with the problem?* | **~ about** *She must make her own judgement about when to go.* **~ against** *The sacked workers won a judgement against the company.* **~ as to** *Experience helps us to form judgements as to the best course of action in given circumstances.* **~ on** *I'm not equipped to pass judgement on such matters.*

2 decision making
• ADJ. **fine, good, remarkable, shrewd, sound** *Landing a plane requires fine judgement.* | **impartial, independent** | **impaired, weak** | **aesthetic, artistic, critical, ethical, moral, political, professional** *She has a reputation for sound professional judgement.*
• VERB + JUDGEMENT **display, show** | **rely on** | **respect, trust** *He trusted his wife's judgement.* | **doubt** | **back** *The company backed her judgement and implemented all her recommendations.* | **exercise, use** | **colour, influence** *He never allows any prejudices to colour his judgement.* | **sit in** *He felt he had no right to sit in judgement on someone he had only just met.*
• PREP. **~ about** *You will need to exercise your own judgement about what clothes to wear.* **~ in** *The speaker showed good judgement in his choice of topic.*
• PHRASES **an error of judgement** *Accepting the gift was an error of judgement on the part of the party chairman.* **a lack of judgement, a matter of judgement** *How much money you should invest is a matter of judgement.*

judo *noun*

• VERB + JUDO **do, practise**
• JUDO + NOUN **hold, move, throw** *She managed to get the man in a judo hold.* | **mat**
• PHRASES **a black, etc. belt in judo** *He's a black belt in judo.* ◊ *He's got a brown belt in judo.*
⇨ Special page at SPORT

jug *noun*

• ADJ. **measuring** | **china, earthenware, enamel, enamelled, glass, plastic** | **cream, milk, water, wine**
• VERB + JUG **fill, pour sth into** *He filled a jug with juice.* | **pour, tip** *She poured a jug of water over his head.* | **empty, pour sth from/out of**
• PREP. **~ of** *a jug of milk*

juice *noun*

• ADJ. **fruit, lemon, tomato, etc.** | **fresh, freshly-squeezed** | **concentrated** | **unsweetened**
• VERB + JUICE **extract, squeeze** | **strain** | **sprinkle** *Sprinkle the avocado slices with lemon juice.*
• PREP. **~ from** *The juice from the meat is used to make the sauce.* **~ of** *the grated rind and juice of two lemons*
⇨ Special page at FOOD

July *noun*

⇨ Note at MONTH

jump *noun*

1 movement
• ADJ. **little** | **running, standing** *Cats can clear two metres with a standing jump.* | **high, long, triple** | **bungee, parachute, ski**
• VERB + JUMP **make** *She made a jump for the river bank.* | **take** *He took a running jump and just managed to clear the stream.* | **do** *He's going to do a parachute jump for charity.* | **give** *Her heart gave a little jump at his smile.*
• PREP. **in the... ~** *Allen won silver in the high jump.* **with a ~** *I sat up with a jump* (= suddenly.). | **~ into** *(figurative) The new law is a jump into the unknown.* **~ onto**

2 increase
• ADJ. **big, quantum, sharp** | **small**
• VERB + JUMP **make** *Is he good enough to make the jump into Formula One?*
• PREP. **~ in** *The sportswear company reports a jump in sales since the Olympics.*

jump *verb*

1 move off the ground
• ADV. **suddenly** | **about, around, back, down, in, off, out, up, up and down** *He was jumping up and down with excitement.*
• VERB + JUMP **try to** *He tried to jump back on board.*
• PREP. **from** *He had to jump from a first floor window.* **into, off, on** *Stop jumping on the furniture!* **onto** *She jumped up onto the table.* **out of, over** *Can you jump over that fence?* **through**

2 make a sudden movement because of surprise/fear
• ADV. **almost, nearly** *He almost jumped in surprise.*
• VERB + JUMP **make sb** *He crept up behind me and made me jump.*
• PHRASES **jump out of your skin** *(figurative) I nearly jumped out of my skin when he told me.*

jumper *noun*

• ADJ. **baggy, loose, sloppy** | **tight** | **heavy, thick** | **light, thin** | **cashmere, cotton, woollen, woolly, etc.** | **knitted** | **crew-neck, polo-neck, turtleneck** | **Fair Isle** *a Fair Isle jumper in navy and red*
• VERB + JUMPER **pull on** | **knit, make**
⇨ Special page at CLOTHES

junction *noun*

• ADJ. **busy** | **dangerous** | **motorway, road** | **railway**
• PREP. **at a/the ~** *Turn off the motorway at junction 6.* | **~ with** *The college is on the Manchester road, by the junction with the A5.*

June *noun*

⇨ Note at MONTH

jungle *noun*

• ADJ. **dense, impenetrable, thick** | **tropical** | **concrete, urban** *(figurative) This outback area is a far cry from the city's concrete jungle.*
• JUNGLE + NOUN **warfare**
• PREP. **in ~** *a temple deep in the Brazilian jungle* **through ~** *They hacked their way through dense jungle.*

junior *adj.*

• VERBS **be**
• ADV. **very** *a very junior officer* | **comparatively, fairly, quite, relatively** *She's quite junior in the organization.*
• PREP. **to** *John is still junior to me at work.*

junk *noun*

• ADJ. **old** *sculptures made from old junk and scrap metal*
• QUANT. **bit, piece** *There were bits of junk lying around.*
• JUNK + VERB **lie about/around**

• JUNK + NOUN **shop | room** *They cleared out the junk room to make a tiny bedroom.* | **heap | material** *He made the boat out of junk materials.*

junta *noun*

• ADJ. **ruling | civilian, military, revolutionary**
• VERB + JUNTA **form | dissolve, overthrow**
• JUNTA + VERB **appoint sb** *The civilian junta appointed a prime minister.*
• JUNTA + NOUN **leader, member**

jurisdiction *noun*

• ADJ. **limited | exclusive** *The commissioners had exclusive jurisdiction to decide.* | **civil, criminal, ecclesiastical**
• VERB + JURISDICTION **have, retain** *The court has no jurisdiction in this case.* | **exercise** *The court may exercise its jurisdiction to compel the husband to make a settlement upon his wife.* | **claim** *The offshore government claims jurisdiction over the mainland.* | **be subject to, come under** *He is subject to the jurisdiction of the English courts.*
• PREP. **beyond your~** *She acted beyond the jurisdiction of any teacher.* **outside your~** *The matter is outside the jurisdiction of UK administrative agencies.* **under~** *The territory is still under Russian jurisdiction.* **within your~** *The matter was not within the jurisdiction of the court.* | **~ over** *The senate committees have exclusive jurisdiction over the FBI.*

juror *noun*

• VERB + JUROR **swear in** *The jurors were sworn in.*

jury *noun*

1 in a court of law
• ADJ. **inquest, trial | unanimous** (only after **jury**) *The jury were unanimous in their verdict.* | **hung** *A retrial was necessary after the original trial ended with a hung jury.*
• VERB + JURY **serve on, sit on | tell** *Tell the jury what happened, in your own words.* | **direct** *The judge directed the jury to return a verdict of not guilty.* | **swear in** *The new jury were sworn in.* | **JURY + VERB hear sth** *The jury heard how the boy had obtained a carving knife from a friend's house.* | **retire | consider its verdict** *The jury has retired to consider its verdict.* | **be out** *The jury is still out* (= still deciding). ◇ *(figurative) The jury is still out on this new policy.* | **agree (on) a verdict, arrive at/reach a verdict, give its verdict, return a verdict | convict sb, find sb guilty** *The jury convicted Menzies of assaulting Smith.* | **acquit sb, clear sb, find sb not guilty | award sb** *The jury awarded her damages of £30 000.*
• JURY + NOUN **service** *It was the second time he had been called up for jury service.* | **trial | foreman, member | system** *a review of the jury system*
• PREP. **before a~** *The trial will take place before a jury.* **on a/the~** *There were only three women on the jury.* | **~ of** *the jury of seven women and five men*
• PHRASES **trial by jury** *You have a right to trial by jury.*

2 of a competition
• VERB + JURY **choose, select** *The jury is selected from the winners in previous years.*
• JURY + VERB **judge sth | consist of sb** *The jury consisted of an architect, a photographer and an artist.* | **award (sb) sth, give sb sth** *The jury has awarded the prize for best exhibit in the show to Harry Pearson.*
• PREP. **on a/the~** *He was on a jury judging a songwriting competition.*

justice *noun*

1 fairness
• ADJ. **economic, natural, social | rough** *He saw it as rough justice when he got food poisoning from the stolen meat.* | **divine** *Some people saw the epidemic as divine justice.*
• VERB + JUSTICE **ask for, want** *All I'm asking for is justice.* | **get | deny sb** *We have been denied justice for too long.*
• PHRASES **a sense of justice** *The teacher's system of punishments appealed to the children's sense of justice.*

2 law
• ADJ. **civil, criminal, juvenile**
• VERB + JUSTICE **do** *Justice must be done in every case.* | **bring sb to | escape** *So far the robbers have escaped justice.*
• JUSTICE + NOUN **department**
• PHRASES **a miscarriage of justice** *He spent twenty years in prison as a result of a miscarriage of justice.* **pervert the course of justice** *She was charged with perverting the course of justice after admitting to burning vital evidence.*

justifiable *adj.*

• VERBS **be, seem | become | consider sth, think sth** *We consider this action justifiable.*
• ADV. **entirely | commercially, economically | ethically, morally**
• PREP. **~on the grounds of/that** *The cutbacks are justifiable on the grounds of cost.* **~on … grounds** *The rule is justifiable on safety grounds.*

justification *noun*

• ADJ. **considerable, every, some** *You have every justification for feeling angry.* | **the slightest** *She had not given him the slightest justification for thinking she was interested in him.* | **ample, sufficient | ethical, moral | intellectual, rational, theoretical | legal, political**
• VERB + JUSTIFICATION **give (sb), provide (sb with)** *She's unable to provide any justification for her actions.* | **see**
• PREP. **in~** *the argument which he put forward in justification* **with ~** *He felt, with some justification, that he had been unfairly treated.* **without~** *She was arrested entirely without justification.* | **~for** *I can see some justification for her remarks.*

justified *adj.*

• VERBS **be, feel, prove, seem**
• ADV. **amply** *The suspicion proved amply justified.* | **completely, entirely, fully, perfectly, quite, totally | hardly | partially, partly | clearly | easily, readily** *a logical and easily justified decision* | **economically, financially, legally, morally, rationally, scientifically, theoretically** *Can her actions be morally justified?*
• PREP. **in** *She felt fully justified in asking for a refund.*

justify *verb*

• ADV. **really, truly** *Can you really justify the destruction of such a fine old building?* | **hardly** *The meagre result hardly justified the risks they took to get it.*
• VERB + JUSTIFY **can/could | attempt to, seek to, try to | need to | be difficult to, be hard to** *He found it very difficult to justify his decision.*
• PREP. **on the grounds of/that** *The decision is justified on the grounds that there is no realistic alternative.* **to** *How will you justify this pay cut to your employees?*

Kk

karate *noun*

- ADJ. **full-contact**
- VERB + KARATE **do**
- KARATE + NOUN **stance** | **jacket, suit** | **blow, chop, kick, punch** | **bout, competition, tournament** | **training** | **champion, expert** | **instructor**
- PHRASES **a black, etc. belt in karate** *She's a black belt in karate.* ◇ *She's got a brown belt in karate.*
- ⇨ Special page at SPORT

keen *adj.*

- VERBS **appear, be, feel, look, seem, sound** | **remain**
- ADV. **awfully, desperately, especially, extremely, frightfully, mad** (*informal*), **more than, particularly, really, terribly, very** *He's mad keen on football.* ◇ *She's a very keen gardener.* | **not at all, not overly, not too** *The banks were not at all keen to lend to somebody who actually seemed to need money.* | **fairly, pretty, quite, rather** | **always** *She was always keen to hear the local gossip.* | **obviously** | **naturally, understandably** *She was naturally keen to make a good impression.*
- PREP. **for** *They were desperately keen for information.* **on** *Sally's quite keen on the idea.*
- PHRASES **as keen as mustard** (= very keen)

keep *noun*

- VERB + KEEP **earn** *It's time you did a job to earn your keep.*

keep *verb*

- ADV. **well** *Milk and cream should keep quite well in a fridge.*

kerb *noun*

- ADJ. **dropped** *Dropped kerbs make wheelchair access easier.*
- VERB + KERB **draw away from, pull away/out from** *The car pulled away from the kerb.* | **draw up at/to, pull in/over to** | **step off** *He stepped off the kerb without looking and was hit by a cyclist.* | **clip, hit** | **mount** *The car mounted the kerb and knocked over a pedestrian.*
- PREP. **at the ~** *I parked at the kerb and waited.* **on the ~** *They stood on the kerb waiting to cross the road.*

kettle *noun*

- ADJ. **electric**
- VERB + KETTLE **fill** | **plug in** | **have on** *Get yourself in, Pat, I've got the kettle on.* | **put on, switch on** *I'll just put the kettle on.* | **boil**
- KETTLE + VERB **boil** *She made herself a sandwich while she waited for the kettle to boil.* | **sing, whistle** *The kettle started to sing.* | **switch itself off**

key *noun*

1 for a door

- ADJ. **master, skeleton** | **duplicate, spare** | **car, desk, front door, house, ignition, etc.**
- QUANT. **bunch, set** *a large bunch of keys* ◇ *a set of car keys*
- VERB + KEY **turn** *She turned the key in the lock.* | **insert, put in** | **remove, take out** | **use** *She must have used a key to get in.*
- KEY + VERB **open, unlock** *You need a key to open the garage.* | **lock** | **turn** *They heard a key turn in the back door lock.*
- PREP. **with a/the ~** *You have to close it with the key.* | **~ to** *the key to the front door*
- PHRASES **get a key cut** *I'll get another key cut so that you can have one.*

2 on a computer

- ADJ. **Alt, arrow, backspace, control, delete, escape, function, return, shift, etc.** | **shortcut** *F1 is the shortcut key for calling up help.*
- QUANT. **row** *the top row of keys*
- VERB + KEY **hit, hold down, press, touch** *Hold down the Alt key while pressing the arrow keys.* | **release**
- ⇨ Special page at COMPUTER

3 explanation of symbols, etc.

- KEY + VERB **tell sb sth** *The key tells you what all the symbols mean.*
- PREP. **in a/the ~** *You can find the symbols in the key at the bottom of the page.* | **~ to** *the key to the signs and symbols*

4 decisive factor

- VERB + KEY **have, hold** *First-time voters could hold the key to the election result.*
- PREP. **~ to** *Language is the key to understanding those around you.*

5 in music

- ADJ. **major, minor** | **high, low**
- VERB + KEY **change**
- KEY + VERB **change** *The key changes from C major to A minor.*
- KEY + NOUN **change** | **signature** *There are two sharps in the key signature of D major.*
- PREP. **in a/the ~** *What key's it in?* ◇ *Can we try it in a lower key?* | **~ of** *the key of G major*

keyboard *noun*

1 set of keys on a computer, etc.

- ADJ. **British, Cyrillic, etc.** | **qwerty** | **computer, PC, typewriter**
- VERB + KEYBOARD **lock** *The program locks the keyboard until a password is given.*
- KEYBOARD + NOUN **operator**
- PREP. **on the ~** *Using the mouse is quicker than typing it on the keyboard.*
- ⇨ Special page at COMPUTER

2 set of keys on a piano, etc.

- ADJ. **piano**
- KEYBOARD + NOUN **instrument**

3 electrical musical instrument

- ADJ. **electric, electronic**
- PREP. **at the ~** *Ed Duke was at the keyboard.* **on (a/the) ~** *He played the song on his keyboard.* ◇ *The recording features Herbie Hancock on keyboard.*
- ⇨ Special page at MUSIC

kick *noun*

1 act of kicking

- ADJ. **good, hard, hefty, painful** | **corner, free, goal, overhead, penalty, spot** (all in football) | **high** *an energetic performer using dance routines and high kicks*
- VERB + KICK **give sb/sth** *Give the door a good kick if it won't open.* | **get, receive** *He had received a painful kick on the knee.*
- PREP. **~ at** *a kick at goal* **~ by/from** *a kick from Maynard*

in the last minute of the game ~ **in** *a kick in the stomach* ~**on** *a kick on the ankle* ~**to** *a kick to the ribs*

2 feeling of great pleasure/excitement
- ADJ. **real**
- VERB + KICK **get** *He gets a real kick out of mending something so that it can be used again.* | **give sb** *It gave the youngsters a kick to see their own play on television.*
- PREP. **for** ~s *They don't really want the things they steal. They just do it for kicks.*

kick *verb*

1 hit sb/sth with your foot
- ADV. **hard, savagely, vigorously** *Don't kick the ball too hard.* | **deliberately** | **repeatedly** *Foster admitted punching and kicking the man repeatedly.* | **around** *The boys were kicking a ball around in the yard.*
- PREP. **against** *She could feel the baby kicking against her stomach wall.* ◇ *(figurative) Young people often kick against convention.* **at** *She kicked at the loose pebbles by the roadside.* **in** *They threw him to the ground and kicked him hard in the stomach.* **on** *She kicked me on the knee.*
- PHRASES **kick a door down/open/shut** *Suddenly the far door was kicked open.* **kick sb to death**

2 move your feet in the air
- ADV. **frantically, wildly** *He rolled over in the sand, kicking wildly.*
- PREP. **out at** *The horse kicked out at the yapping dog.*
- PHRASES **drag sb kicking and screaming** *The police had to drag her kicking and screaming out of the house.* **kick your legs/your legs kick** *The little boy was now lying on his back kicking his legs in the air.* ◇ *I was carried upstairs, arms waving and legs kicking.*

kid *noun*

- ADJ. **little, young** | **big, older** *The older kids had lessons in the afternoon as well.* | **cute, good, lovely, nice** | **poor** *I feel desperately sorry for the poor kid.* | **rich** *a spoilt little rich kid* | **local** *a gang of local kids* | **street** *street kids who rely on their ingenuity to keep alive* | **school** (also **schoolkid**)
- QUANT. **bunch, couple** *They're just a bunch of kids.*
- VERB + KID **have** *We both wanted to have kids.* | **bring up** *I've tried to bring my kids up to respect other people.* | **look after, take care of**
- PHRASES **just/only a kid** *He's only a kid. You can't expect him to understand what's going on.* **like a kid** *She was crying like a kid.*

kill *noun*

- ADJ. **easy, quick**
- VERB + KILL **make** *The lion made a quick kill.* | **be in at** *I didn't even get to see the fox, let alone be in at the kill.* | **close in for, move in for** *The hunters moved in for the kill.*
- PREP. **at the** ~ *The meat is divided up among all those present at the kill.* **for the** ~ *The animal crouched down, getting ready for the kill.*

kill *verb*

- ADV. **outright** *He has fought more than fifty bulls, killing three outright.* | **almost, nearly** | **instantly** | **accidentally** | **unlawfully**
- VERB + KILL **want to** | **be prepared to** *They are quite prepared to kill to achieve their ends.* | **threaten to** | **be going to, intend to** *(figurative) Mum's going to kill me when she finds out.* | **plot to** *plotting to kill the dictator* | **try to** | **help (to)** | **make sb** *It must have been really awful to make her kill herself.*
- PHRASES **admit/deny killing sb, be accused of killing sb, be charged with killing sb, be killed in sth** *soldiers killed in battle* **be tragically killed** *Their daughter was tragically killed in a road accident.*

killer *noun*

- ADJ. **big, major** *Overdoses were the single biggest killer among the city's young.* | **real** *I don't care what they ask me if it helps them find the real killer.* | **alleged** | **convicted** | **notorious** | **brutal, vicious** | **crazed, psychopathic** | **mass, serial** | **contract, hired** | **child, wife, etc.** *a convicted child killer* | **giant** *(figurative) Salford Juniors proved to be the giant killers in last week's semi-finals* (= by beating a much better team).
- VERB + KILLER **hunt, track down** | **catch, find**
- KILLER + VERB **strike** *The killer has struck again.*
- KILLER + NOUN **bug, disease, virus** *Heart attacks have become Britain's No. 1 killer disease.* | **instinct** *(figurative) He plays well but still lacks the killer instinct.* | **blow** *(figurative) Owen delivered the killer blow soon after half-time.*

killing *noun*

1 killing sb deliberately
- ADJ. **brutal, cold-blooded** *the cold-blooded killing of a defenceless woman* | **deliberate** | **indiscriminate, random** | **mass, serial** *This was the fourth mass killing in Australia in four years.* | **contract, gangland, political, revenge, sectarian** *a brutal revenge killing* | **mercy** *Should the law allow mercy killing?* | **unlawful** *(law) a verdict of unlawful killing*
- VERB + KILLING **be responsible for, carry out** | **order** *The Mafia ordered the killing.* | **prevent, stop** *It is difficult to prevent such killings.* | **confess to** | **deny** *The sentenced man had denied the killings.*
- KILLING + VERB **happen, occur, take place**
- PHRASES **a motive for the killing** *No motive for the killing has yet been established.*

2 making a lot of money quickly
- VERB + KILLING **make** *Investors are set to make a killing from the sell-off.*

kilo, kilogram, kilometre

⇨ Note at MEASURE

kin *noun*

- ADJ. **close, intimate, near** *Marriage between close kin is prohibited.* | **extended** *Ties with extended kin vary from family to family.* | **distant** | **female, male**
- KIN + NOUN **group, network** | **relationships**
- PREP. **between** ~
- PHRASES **next of kin** *One of the drivers was fatally injured; his next of kin has been informed.*

kind *noun*

- ADJ. **different, same** *She does the same kind of work as me.* | **all, another, any, some, various** *You need some kind of cover over it to protect it from the rain.* ◇ *We stock various kinds of lawnmower.* | **each, every** | **certain, particular, special** *Certain kinds of food are unsuitable for small children.* | **best, worst** | **right, wrong** *Be sure to eat enough of the right kind of food.* | **funny, odd, strange**
- PREP. **in** ~ *The regions differ in size, but not in kind.* **of** *a* ~ *You're making progress of a kind* (= some progress, but not very much, or not of the best type). ◇ *They're two of a kind* (= very like each other)—*both workaholics!* **of ...** ~ *books of every kind* ◇ *music of different kinds* **of its** ~ *The new school was the first of its kind.* | ~**of** *a special kind of oil*
- PHRASES **a/the kind of thing** *Do you know the kind of thing I mean?* ◇ *They sell all kinds of things.* **a kind of way** *I missed him, in a funny kind of way.* **nothing/something of that/the kind** '*I was terrible!' 'You were nothing of the kind!'* ◇ '*He's resigning.' 'I'd suspected something of the kind.'*

kind *adj.*

- VERBS **be** *She was endlessly kind and sympathetic.*
- ADV. **especially, extremely, most, particularly, really, very | quite | endlessly**
- PREP. **of** *It really was most kind of you to help.* **to** *My boss has been extremely kind to me.*

kindness *noun*

- ADJ. **great | loving | simple | natural | unexpected** *This unexpected kindness touched her deeply.* **| human**
- VERB + KINDNESS **show sb, treat sb with** *They had shown him great kindness.* ◇ *They treated us with kindness and courtesy.* **| meet with, receive** *We met with much kindness and help.* **| appreciate** *I really appreciate your kindness.* **| repay** *I tried to think of a way to repay his kindness.* **| not forget**
- PREP. **out of~** *I went with her out of kindness.* **| ~to/towards** *I'll never forget your kindness to me.*
- PHRASES **an act of kindness** *Show your appreciation by little acts of kindness.* **kindness itself** *She has always been kindness itself to me.*

king *noun*

1 male ruler
- ADJ. **rightful | anointed, crowned | uncrowned** *(figurative)* *He became the uncrowned king of the East End, scoring 28 goals in his first season.* **| deposed, exiled**
- VERB + KING **become | crown (sb), make sb, proclaim sb** *He was crowned king at the age of fifteen.* ◇ *The new king was crowned immediately.* **| depose, put aside**
- KING + VERB **reign, rule, rule (over) sb/sth** *The kings of Sicily also ruled over the southern part of Italy.* **| abdicate** *the king's decision to abdicate*
- PREP. **under a/the ~** *Life under the new king was very different.* **| ~of** *the King of Spain*

2 playing card
⇒ Note at CARD

kingdom *noun*

- ADJ. **independent**
- VERB + KINGDOM **rule**
- PREP. **in a/the ~** *It was one of the richest towns in the kingdom.* **throughout a/the ~** *changes that were taking place throughout the kingdom* **| ~of** *He ruled the ancient kingdom of Kaffa.*

kip *noun*

- VERB + KIP **catch, get, have** *Try to catch some kip while you can.* **| need**
- PHRASES **an hour's, a night's, etc. kip** *I was feeling much better after a good night's kip.*

kiss *noun*

- ADJ. **brief, quick, swift | lingering, long | gentle, light, soft | big, smacking | hard | sloppy | affectionate, loving, tender, warm | ardent, hungry, passionate | brotherly, chaste, friendly, innocent, sisterly | farewell, goodbye, goodnight**
- VERB + KISS **give sb** *He gave his daughter a gentle kiss on the forehead.* **| drop, plant, press** *She planted a big kiss on his cheek.* **| steal** *The children hid behind the bike shed to steal a kiss.* **| return** *She returned his kiss with passion.* **| deepen | blow (sb)** *As the train drew away he blew her a kiss.*
- KISS + VERB **deepen** *His kiss deepened and became hungrier.*
- PREP. **with a~ | ~on** *He greeted her with a kiss on the cheek.*
- PHRASES **give sb the kiss of life** *A policeman pulled the man out of the river and gave him the kiss of life.* **hugs and kisses** *We were greeted with hugs and kisses.* **the kiss of death** *That TV commercial was the kiss of death to his career as a serious actor.*

kiss *verb*

- ADV. **gently, lightly | lovingly, softly, tenderly | deeply, fiercely, firmly, hard, hungrily, passionately, soundly, violently | briefly, quickly | lingeringly, long** *He kissed her long and hard on the mouth.*
- VERB + KISS **bend to, stoop to** *He bent to kiss her again.* **| try to | let sb**
- PREP. **on** *She let him kiss her lightly on the cheek.*
- PHRASES **kiss and cuddle** *The love-struck pair have been spotted kissing and cuddling at parties.* **kiss sb full on the lips/mouth, kiss sb goodbye/goodnight, kiss goodbye to sth** *(figurative)* *Well, you can kiss goodbye to your chances of promotion.*

kit *noun*

1 set of clothes/equipment
- ADJ. **combat, football, sports | first-aid, repair, sewing, shaving, survival, test, tool** *Check the acidity of the soil with a test kit.*
- PREP. **in a/the ~** *There should be a needle and thread in the sewing kit.*

2 set of parts
- ADJ. **construction**
- VERB + KIT **make up** *Have you made up the kit yet?*
- KIT + VERB **comprise sth, contain sth, include sth** *The kit contains everything you need to make six candles.*
- PREP. **from a~** *They built the garage from a kit.* **| ~for** *a kit for making candles*
- PHRASES **in kit form** *The doll's house comes in kit form.*

kitchen *noun*

- ADJ. **clean, spotless | dirty, grubby | big, cavernous, huge, roomy, spacious, vast | small, tiny | fully-equipped, fully-fitted, well-equipped | ultra-modern | fitted | stone-flagged, tiled | communal, shared | domestic, professional | mobile | kosher**
- KITCHEN + NOUN **area | cabinet, chair, counter, cupboard, drawers, dresser, fitments, fittings, sink, surface, table, unit, worktop | equipment, gadgets, implements, knife, scales, scissors, utensils | foil, paper, roll, towels | hatch** *We handed our trays through the kitchen hatch as we left.* **| fire, range, stove | facilities** *All our chalets have kitchen facilities.* **| waste | maid, porter, staff | garden** (= for growing food for the kitchen)
- PREP. **in a/the ~**

kite *noun*

- ADJ. **stunt** *John wants to fly his new stunt kite.*
- VERB + KITE **fly**
- KITE + NOUN **flying** *the joys of kite flying*

knack *noun*

- ADJ. **happy | uncanny | unhappy** *He had the unhappy knack of making enemies in the party.*
- VERB + KNACK **have | acquire, develop, get** *Once you get the knack, it's easy.* **| lose** *I don't cook much these days and I think I may have lost the knack.*
- PREP. **~for** *a woman with a knack for handling horses* **~of** *He has the knack of scoring goals just when they are most needed.* **~to** *Making omelettes isn't difficult, but there's a knack to it.*

knead *verb*

- ADV. **gently, lightly** *She gently kneaded the muscles in his back.* **| well** *Add the water and knead the mixture well.*

knee *noun*

- ADJ. **bony | bare | bent | drawn-up** *I rested my chin on my drawn-up knees.* | **arthritic, bad, dodgy, injured, stiff, troublesome, twisted**
- VERB + KNEE **bend | straighten | draw up | hug** *He hugged his knees to keep warm.* | **drop (down) on, drop to, fall onto/to, go down on, sink to** *He went down on his knees and begged for forgiveness.* | **sit on** *She sat on her father's knee* (= lap) *while he read her a story.* | **sprain, twist | graze, skin | slap** *He slapped his knee as he rocked with laughter.* | **pat** *He patted her knee reassuringly.*
- KNEE + VERB **buckle, give way** *Suddenly her knees buckled and she fell to the floor.* | **knock, shake, tremble**
- KNEE + NOUN **injury, problem, trouble | operation, surgery | joint, ligament | socks | pad**
- PREP. **above the~, across your~s** *She had a blanket draped across her knees.* **at sb's~** *The children had learnt these stories at their mother's knee.* **below the ~** *His leg was missing below the knee.* **between your~s** *If you hear the crash-landing warning, put your head between your knees.* **in your~** *He's snapped a ligament in his knee.* **on one~** *I went down on one knee to plug in the vacuum cleaner.* **on your~** *I balanced the pile of books on my knees.* ◇ *He was on his knees, searching for the missing spring.* **to your~s** *The blow knocked him to his knees.*
- PHRASES **bring sth to its knees** *(figurative) The fuel shortage brought the country to its knees within weeks.* **on bended knee** *(figurative) She would ask for a rise, but would not beg for one on bended knee.*

knickers *noun*

- ADJ. **French**
- QUANT. **pair**
- VERB + KNICKERS **pull down/up**
- PHRASES **bra and knickers**
- ⇨ Special page at CLOTHES

knife *noun*

1 tool for cutting
- ADJ. **blunt, sharp | long | bone, bone-handled, silver, steel | bread, butcher's, carving, craft, fish, flick, hunting, kitchen, palette, pocket, sheath, Stanley™, surgeon's, table**
- QUANT. **set** *a set of kitchen knives*
- VERB + KNIFE **pick up** *She picked up her knife and fork and started to eat.* | **lay down, put down | use** *Use a sharp knife to cut away the spare pastry.* | **sharpen | hold**
- KNIFE + VERB **cut** *That knife doesn't cut very well—it needs sharpening.* | **clatter**
- KNIFE + NOUN **blade, handle**
- PREP. **with a/the ~** *The lines can be cut with a craft knife.*
- PHRASES **the blade of a knife, the handle of a knife, a knife and fork**

2 used as a weapon
- ADJ. **long, sharp**
- VERB + KNIFE **be armed with, carry, have** *She carries a knife in her bag now.* | **brandish, wield | draw (out), produce, pull (out), take out** *He suddenly pulled a knife on me.* | **come at sb with, stab sb with, threaten sb with** *She stabbed him in the back with a 12-inch knife.* | **plunge, push, put, stick** *He plunged the knife deep into her heart.* | **sharpen, whet**
- KNIFE + VERB **cut | clatter** *As he fell, the knife clattered to the floor.*
- KNIFE + NOUN **attack** *a frenzied knife attack* | **wound | blade**
- PREP. **with a/the~**
- PHRASES **the blade of a knife, the hilt of a knife hold a knife against/at/to sb's throat, a knife in sb's heart** *(figurative) Each word he uttered was a knife in her heart.* **put**

a knife to sb's throat *She put the knife to his throat to frighten him into silence.*

knight *noun*

1 in the Middle Ages
- ADJ. **medieval | chivalrous, noble | armoured | mounted**
- PHRASES **a knight errant** *tales of medieval knights errant, wandering in search of chivalrous adventures* **a knight in armour, a knight in shining armour** *(figurative, humorous) She's still waiting for a knight in shining armour to come and rescue her.*

2 man given an honour by the king/queen
- ⇨ Note at PEER

knighthood *noun*

- ADJ. **honorary**
- VERB + KNIGHTHOOD **get, receive | refuse | award sb, bestow on sb, confer on sb, give sb, offer sb, reward sb with** *He was rewarded with a knighthood for his services to the government.*

knitting *noun*

- ADJ. **hand, machine | plain, purl**
- QUANT. **piece** *Sew the two pieces of knitting together* | **row** *I had to undo several rows of knitting.*
- VERB + KNITTING **do** *She sat doing her knitting while she watched television.* | **undo**
- KNITTING + NOUN **machine, needle | wool, yarn | pattern**

knob *noun*

- ADJ. **door | control, volume** *Adjust the control knobs by pressing lightly.*
- VERB + KNOB **adjust, fiddle with, touch, turn, twiddle** *I've tried twiddling the knobs, but nothing seems to happen.*
- KNOB + VERB **adjust sth, control sth**
- PREP. **~on** *the knobs on the radio*

knock *noun*

1 firm sharp sound
- ADJ. **loud, sharp | gentle, light | determined | timid**
- VERB + KNOCK **hear | answer** *She hurried to answer the knock at the door.*
- PHRASES **a knock at/on the door** *There was a loud knock at the door.*

2 sharp blow from sth
- ADJ. **hard, nasty, severe** *(figurative) the hard knocks of life* | **minor**
- VERB + KNOCK **get, have, take** *You've had a nasty knock on the head.* ◇ *(figurative) Their pride took quite a knock when they lost 5–0.* | **give sb/sth**
- PREP. **~on**

knock *verb*

1 hit/bump
- ADV. **accidentally** *I accidentally knocked the vase off the table.* | **about, aside, over** *Her boyfriend had been knocking her about.* ◇ *Mind you don't knock that glass over.*
- PREP. **against** *The stick knocked against the wall.* **off** *He had knocked one of the pictures off the wall.* **on** *I knocked my head on one of the beams.*
- PHRASES **knock sb/sth flying** *He was knocked flying as two policemen came crashing through the door.* **knock sb off their feet** *The explosion knocked him off his feet.* **knock sb out/senseless/unconscious** *The blow knocked him unconscious.* **knock sb to the ground**

2 bang on a door

knot

* ADV. **loudly | softly | politely, timidly**
* PREP. **at** *Someone knocked loudly at the door.* **on** *She knocked timidly on the study door and entered.*
* PHRASES **without knocking** *Dobson walked straight into her office without knocking.*

knot noun

* ADJ. **loose, tight | granny, reef, slip, etc.**
* VERB + KNOT **do, tie** *Tie a knot in the rope.* **| undo, untie | loosen, tighten**

knot verb

* ADV. **securely, tightly | loosely | neatly | badly, clumsily | together** *I knotted the ropes together securely.*
* PREP. **around/round** *She knotted the scarf loosely around her neck.*

know verb

1 have information about sth
* ADV. **for certain, full well, perfectly well, very well** *I don't know for certain, but I think she lives in the next village.* ◊ *You know very well what I'm talking about!* **| honestly not** *I honestly don't know what they mean to do.*
* VERB + KNOW **let sb** *Please let me know (= tell me) if there's anything I can do to help.*
* PREP. **about** *He knows a lot about early music.* **of** *I don't know of anyone who might be interested in the job.*
* PHRASES **be widely known** *It is widely known that CFCs can damage the ozone layer.* **know a lot, nothing, very little, etc.**

2 realize
* ADV. **exactly, precisely** *I know exactly how you feel.* **| instinctively** *He knew instinctively where he would find her.*

3 be familiar with sb/sth
* ADV. **well** *I don't know John very well.* **| hardly** *But I hardly know the woman!*
* VERB + KNOW **get to** *She's very nice when you get to know her.*
* PHRASES **be known to sb** *This man is known to the police (= as a criminal).* **be widely known**

4 be known as have a particular name
* ADV. **colloquially, commonly, popularly | affectionately, familiarly | collectively** *parts of the body known collectively as the sensory system* **| variously** *The drug is variously known as crack or freebase.* **| locally | formerly** *Xinjiang was formerly known as eastern Turkestan.*
* PREP. **to** *He was known as Bonzo to his friends.*

know-how noun

* ADJ. **practical, technical**
* VERB + KNOW-HOW **have | acquire, get**
* PREP. **~about** *to acquire a little know-how about the job* **~for** *He doesn't have the technical know-how for this kind of job.* **~in** *know-how in various high-tech fields*

knowledge noun

* ADJ. **considerable, great, vast | complete, comprehensive, sound, thorough | deep, detailed, intimate, profound** *She has an intimate knowledge of the Asian market.* **| broad, encyclopedic, extensive, wide | unrivalled | expert, specialist | inside** *He managed to find contacts who had inside knowledge of the organiza-*tion. **| local | direct, first-hand | up-to-date | limited, rudimentary, superficial** *I have a limited knowledge of French.* **| general** *I don't like quizzes because my general knowledge is so poor.* **| factual | practical | working** *He has a good working knowledge of the subject.* **| professional | academic, linguistic, medical, scientific, technical, etc. | common** *It's common knowledge that he's left his wife.* **| public | full** *She had acted with her parents' full knowledge and consent.* **| previous, prior**
* VERB + KNOWLEDGE **acquire, gain | have | demonstrate, flaunt, parade, show (off) | test | apply** *The job gave her the chance to apply the knowledge she had acquired at university.* **| share** *The barman was happy to share his knowledge of wine with us.* **| spread** *The volunteers' task is to spread knowledge of how to prevent the disease.* **| broaden, extend, improve, increase | deny** *He denied all knowledge of what had happened.*
* PREP. **in the ~** *They put the car on the market in the full knowledge that it had design faults.* **to sb's ~** *He's never worked here to my knowledge.* **with sb's ~** *The letter was sent with the full knowledge of the head of department.* **without sb's ~** *She borrowed my car without my knowledge.* **| ~of** *a wide knowledge of antiques*
* PHRASES **a gap in your knowledge** *I did some research to fill in the gaps in my knowledge.* **to the best of your knowledge** *She still lives in San Francisco to the best of my knowledge.*

knowledgeable adj.

* VERBS **be, seem, sound** *Her lawyer seemed very knowledgeable and experienced.* **| become**
* ADV. **extremely, highly, very | quite, reasonably**
* PREP. **about** *He's quite knowledgeable about the theatre.*

knuckle noun

* ADJ. **bony | bleeding, bloodied, bruised, grazed, swollen**
* VERB + KNUCKLE **crack** *He rubbed his hands together, cracking his knuckles as he tried to control his anger.* **| bruise, graze, scrape, skin**
* KNUCKLE + NOUN **bone**
* PHRASES **rap sb on/over the knuckles** (*figurative*) *The Assistant Manager was rapped over the knuckles for criticizing the company in the press.*

Korean noun

⇒ Note at LANGUAGE

kosher adj.

1 suitable to be eaten by religious Jews
* VERBS **be**
* ADV. **strictly** *All their food is strictly kosher.*

2 correct/honest
* VERBS **be, seem** *It all seems kosher enough.*
* ADV. **strictly | enough**

kudos noun

* ADJ. **considerable | personal**
* VERB + KUDOS **acquire, gain | lose | bring** *Employees enjoy the kudos that the job brings as much as the financial rewards.*
* KUDOS + VERB **be attached to sth** *There was considerable kudos attached to being on the advisory board.*

STUDY PAGES

IDEAS INTO WORDS

Look at the entry for **idea**, sense 1 (plan/suggestion).

1 Look at the adjectives section (labelled ADJ). Find adjectives you might
   use to express the following ideas. Sometimes more than one adjective is
   possible. You may want to use another dictionary to check the meaning
   of any words you don't know.

a an idea that is helpful, rather than being negative or impractical

b an idea that is slightly crazy, in a good way

c an idea that is completely crazy, in a bad way

d an idea that has not been carefully thought out

e an idea that seems very impressive but is not really very practical

2 Now look at the section marked VERB + IDEA. Find verbs that you
   might use to express the following ideas. Usually more than one verb is
   possible.

a to find an idea

b to suggest an idea

c to suggest an idea in a very forceful way because you really want people to accept it

d to think about an idea for a while before you decide whether or not it is a good idea

e to talk about a number of different ideas before you decide which ideas are the best

3 Look at the section marked IDEA + VERB. Find verbs that you might use
   to express the following:

a when you think of an idea

b when an idea develops into something important

c when an idea does not develop into anything

4 Finally, look at the PHRASES section and find the expression that means
   the beginning of an idea

USING A NOUN ENTRY

adjectives

1 Match each of the adjectives on the left with a suitable noun from the facing column. Look at the entries for the **bold** nouns for help.

a bewildering	**ambition**	a blazing	**defeat**
a biting	**array** of goods	a crushing	**inflation**
a burning	**chance**	a haunting	**pain**
a convincing	**chasm**	a nagging	**row** over money
driving	**rain**	a piercing	**scream**
a fighting	**sum** of money	raging	**statement**
a gaping	**win**	a sprawling	**suburb**
a staggering	**wind**	a sweeping	**melody**

quantifiers

Quantifiers are words used to talk about the amount of something, such as *a **drop** of water* or *a **piece** of information*.

2 Complete each sentence with a suitable quantifier. Look at the **bold** noun entries for help.

a There were just a few w*isps* of **cloud** in the sky.

b The recent s_____ of **attacks** has made residents afraid to leave their homes.

c He is on medication to ease his frequent b_____ of **depression**.

d I just caught a brief s_____ of their **conversation** as I walked by their table.

e The constant s_____ of **traffic** past our house makes it difficult to cross the road.

f A p_____ of stray **dogs** was wandering around the abandoned plant.

g He's been off school all week with a bad d_____ of **flu**.

h A couple of c_____ of **garlic** will improve the flavour of the soup.

i The manager terrified the younger staff with his o_____ of **temper**.

j The burglars stole several p_____ of **jewellery**.

verb + ...

3 Cross out any verbs which do not normally collocate with the **bold** noun.

a He *got into/had/~~made~~* an **argument** with the barman and was thrown out of the hotel.

b He had to do two jobs to *clear/pay off/pay up* his **debts**.

c Someone *came up with/presented/put forward* the **suggestion** that we should have an auction.

d The scientists failed to *arrive at/decide/draw* any firm **conclusions** from the study.

e The company *agreed/came to/struck* a **deal** with the union after lengthy negotiations.

f A **meeting** has been *arranged/programmed/scheduled* for next week.

g The supervisor refused to *accept/receive/shoulder* the **blame** for the accident.

h He *drummed/rattled/tapped* his **fingers** nervously on the desk as he spoke.

i We *did/took/went on* a **trip** to a nearby island on a fishing boat.

j I put up my hand to *shade/shelter/shield* my **eyes** from the sun.

... + verb

4 Complete the story with a suitable verb in each gap. Look at the **bold** noun entries for help.

I lay in bed, unable to sleep. The **wine** had f_____ freely at the party, and now my **head** was t_____ and my **stomach** was c_____. Outside the **wind** h_____ and the **rain** l_____ against the window. My **nerve**s were o_____ e_____ as I remembered all the horror films I'd ever seen. Suddenly I heard the **key** t_____ in the front door. My **heart** began to h_____ in my chest as heavy **footstep**s e_____ on the stairs. My **mind** was ra_____, trying to think how I could save myself. The bedroom **door** c_____ open slowly, and as my **eye**s a_____ to the darkness I could make out a figure at the end of the bed. The man's **mouth** d_____ open when he saw me. It was my neighbour. I was in the wrong house.

... + noun

5 Choose a suitable word from the box on the right to complete each sentence. Look at the **bold** noun entry for help.

a We had to queue for ages at the **taxi** _rank_.

b In economy class you don't get enough **leg** _____.

c The traffic was held up by a massive **protest** _____.

d He was seriously injured in a horrific **traffic** _____.

e They're collecting money for **famine** _____.

f I stopped to buy a magazine at the **newspaper** _____.

g It's a small office with very little **shelf** _____.

h School leavers with no qualifications have limited **job** _____.

chances	room
accident	space
kiosk	gathering
prospects	relief
stall	~~rank~~
aid	crash
rally	

prepositions

6 The sentences below can be completed using just three different prepositions. Look at the **bold** noun entries to help you.

a He was lying on the floor ___*in*___ **agony**.

b Students who do not have a computer are _____ a **disadvantage**.

c There is still **confusion** _____ the result of the vote.

d I couldn't hear what she was saying _____ the **noise** of the crowd.

e Please submit your requests _____ **writing** before Friday.

f He died instantly when his bike hit a wall _____ **speed**.

g She claims she killed him _____ **self-defence**.

h I'm not going out _____ this **rain**!

i I saw him a couple of times _____ **Christmas**.

j Her **skill** _____ negotiating makes her a valuable asset.

phrases

7 Look at the phrases section in the entries for the **bold** nouns below to help you complete and match the heads and tails of the sentences.

a Could I ___*have*___ a word in your ——————

b I remember clearly the first time I _____

c If this report _____ into the wrong

d I vowed never to _____

e The force of the impact _____ every

bone in his body.

ear?

eyes on her.

foot in the place again.

hands, we're in trouble.

USING A VERB ENTRY

adverbs

1 In each of the following sentences one of the adverbs in *italics* is not a common collocate of the verb in **bold**. Decide which it is and cross it out. Use the entry for the **bold** verb to help you.

a She **argued** *fiercely/heatedly/~~hotly~~* about her right to compensation.

b They will *fiercely/heatedly/hotly* **defend** their rights.

c He **grinned** *owlishly/sheepishly/wolfishly* at her.

d I *ruefully/sheepishly/woefully* **confessed** to having forgotten the map.

e His frugal lifestyle **contrasted** *brutally/markedly/starkly* with his wife's extravagance.

f Her tragic story *brutally/markedly/starkly* **illustrates** how vulnerable children can be.

verb + ...

2 Complete each of these sentences with a verb phrase from the box. You may need to change the form of the verb. Use the entries for the **bold** verbs to help you.

be determined to   ~~be happy to~~   can afford to   fail to   hasten to   offer to   serve to   take steps to

a I _was happy to_ **accept** the invitation to become patron of the charity.

b The company was fined when it _____ **comply** with the regulations.

c These unanswered questions _____ **highlight** the potential problems.

d I _____ **add** that my knowledge of computers is pretty basic.

e We must _____ **ensure** that such a disaster can never happen again.

f The minister _____ **resign** when the affair became public.

g She _____ **fight** for her rights.

h Few patients _____ **pay** the full cost of treatment.

prepositions

3 The following sentences can be completed using just three different prepositions. Use the entries for the **bold** verbs to help you.

a Unfortunately, the plan **backfired** _on_ me.

b Students took to the streets to **protest** _____ the decision.

c I don't feel I can **comment** _____ their decision.

d I think you must be **mistaking** me _____ someone else.

e She was **treated** _____ sunstroke.

f The prosecution lawyers have been trying to **prejudice** the jury _____ him.

g He accused them of **plotting** _____ him.

h We have **collaborated** _____ many projects over the years.

i The company is **appealing** _____ the ruling.

j Nationalist leaders **appealed** _____ calm.

phrases

4 Match the two halves of these verb phrases. Then use the phrases to complete the sentences below. You may need to change the forms of the verbs. Use the entries for the **bold** verbs to help you.

~~drink~~	and pant
mix	~~and drive~~
moan	and turn
toss	and match
puff	and groan

a The message to drivers is simple: don't __drink and drive__ .

b There's no point in _____; we can't change the situation.

c I spent all night _____, unable to sleep.

d You can _____ colours to create your own design.

e _____, we heaved the wardrobe upstairs.

crack	for breath
grin	to a halt
dawn	from ear to ear
pause	bright and cold
brake	under the strain

f The car _____ outside the station.

g You need a holiday before you _____.

h The next morning _____.

i Katy was clearly pleased about something: she was _____.

j Jack went on arguing, scarcely _____.

collocations of phrasal verbs

5 Complete the following story with words and phrases from the boxes. For each gap you will need to decide whether the missing word/phrase is an adverb, a verb or a preposition. You may need to change the forms of the verbs. Use the phrasal verbs sections of the **bold** verb entries to help you.

	adverbs	verbs	prepositions
I had _had been left to_ **fend for myself** in the desert. The sun **beat down** _____ . The water holes had **dried up** _____ . I _____ **rely** _____ **on** cacti _____ water. I _____ **hang on** _____ my sanity, **clinging** _____ **to** the hope that I would find my way out alive.	completely desperately entirely mercilessly	~~be left to~~ have to try to	for to

USING AN ADJECTIVE ENTRY

verbs

1 Match each of the **bold** adjectives with a verb that can go before it, then match the combination with a suitable subject. Use the adjective entries to help you.

His mistake	emerged	~~asleep~~.	_I nearly fell asleep._
His mistake	~~fell~~	**costly.**	_____
~~I nearly~~	grew	**damp.**	_____
The crowd	passed	**empty.**	_____
The driver	proved	**impatient.**	_____
The house	run	**parallel.**	_____
The house	smells	**unnoticed.**	_____
The roads	stood	**unscathed.**	_____

2 Complete each sentence with a suitable verb. Look at the entry for the **bold** adjective for help.

a He d_rove_ me **crazy** with his constant talking.

b She was h_____ **captive** by rebels for six months.

c Several cars were s_____ **ablaze** by the rioters.

d The unions were r_____ **powerless** by the new laws.

e These programmes are d_____ **unsuitable** for screening before 10 p.m.

f The robbers b_____ the shopkeeper **senseless**.

g His classmates mostly r_____ him as **eccentric**.

h The sound of a door banging j_____ me **awake**.

adverbs

3 For each group, find an adverb in the box that collocates with all the adjectives in the group.

dead	_distinctly_	_fiercely_	_grossly_	~~_painfully_~~	_wildly_

a _painfully_	b _____	c _____	d _____	e _____	f _____
aware	boring	competitive	different	enthusiastic	inaccurate
honest	funny	independent	odd	inaccurate	inadequate
shy	good	loyal	uncomfortable	optimistic	offensive
slow	right	protective	uneasy	popular	unfair

4 Match each **bold** adjective with a suitable adverb. Then use each combination to complete one of the sentences on the right.

blissfully	**absent**	**a** I'm not _unduly concerned_ by the latest figures.
conspicuously	**composed**	**b** She is _____ of her achievements.
eerily	~~concerned~~	**c** He seems _____ of the trouble he's caused.
justly	**familiar**	**d** The former chairman was _____ from the guest list.
notoriously	**fickle**	**e** Her voice sounded _____ to me.
oddly	**proud**	**f** She seemed _____ , despite the pressure.
outwardly	**silent**	**g** The street was _____ after the explosion.
~~unduly~~	**unaware**	**h** The world of fashion is _____ .

prepositions

5 Complete and match the heads and tails of these sentences, using the entries for the **bold** adjectives to help you.

a The scandal was **damaging** _to_ — the new software.
b I always used to be **late** ____ his money.
c I need some time to get **acquainted** ____ the latest crime statistics.
d She was **insistent** ____ women.
e His good looks made him **irresistible** ____ secrecy.
f Tickets are **limited** ____ school.
g He's **mean** ____ two per person.
h I was **alarmed** ____ the government.

phrases

6 Complete each of the following sentences with a suitable word or phrase. Look in the 'phrases' section of the **bold** adjective entries for help.

a The missing climbers have been found **alive** and ___well___ .
b I was so relieved when they got home **safe** and _____ .
c I'll show you a dish that's really **quick** and _____ .
d If you need any help, I'm **ready** and _____ .
e His hair is always so **neat** and _____ .
f By midnight I was **worried** _____ .
g I forgot my umbrella and I got **wet** _____ .
h When he told me the news I was **thrilled** _____ .
i If a dog comes anywhere near me I'm **scared** _____ .
j The speaker went on and on until we were **bored** _____ .

COLLOCATIONS with COMMON VERBS

do	make	have	take	give
a crossword	an appointment	an accident	action	sb an answer
damage	an attempt	an argument	a bath	sb a chance
a degree	the bed	a bath	a bite	a cry of pain
the dishes	a cake	a break	a break	sb a headache
an exam	changes	breakfast	the bus	sb help
the food for a party	a decision	cancer	a decision	sb an idea
French at school	dinner	a chat	a deep breath	the impression that…
the garden	an effort	a cold	sb's details	sb a kiss
your hair	a film	difficulty	a dislike to sb	sb lessons
'Hamlet'	a fuss	a drink	an exam	sb a lift
your homework	a guess	a feeling	a guess	your opinion
judo	an impression	fun	a holiday	a party
miles per hour	a mark	a guess	an interest in sth	a performance
nothing	a mess	a heart attack	a look	sth a polish
Paris	a mistake	a holiday	a nap	sb a present
a photocopy	money	an idea	notes	priority to sth
research	a noise	an interest	a photo	sb a push
a sketch	peace	a look	size 10	sb a shock
a translation	a photocopy	a meeting	a tablet	a sigh
the washing	progress	a party	sb's temperature	a speech
some writing	a promise	a nap	a walk	some thought to sth
	a sketch	an operation		a welcome to sb
	a speech	patience		
	a suggestion	problems		
	your will	a shock		
		a snack		
		time		

1 Find the nouns in the lists for tasks and duties (for example *do the dishes*). Which verb is the most often used? Which tasks are exceptions?

2 Find expressions in each column that can be substituted by a single verb.
   (For example you can *do damage* to something or just *damage* something.) Which column has the most?

3 Find expressions connected with the following:

speaking	experiencing something	producing something using your hands, your mind or your skill	physical actions
make/give a speech	*have an accident*	*make dinner*	*have/take a bath*

Can you see any patterns emerging? Are there any exceptions?

4 How many items can you find that collocate with more than one of the verbs (for example you can *have* or *take* a bath)?

5 Complete each of the following sentences using *do, make, have, take* or *give* (more than one answer may be possible). If the noun in the example is not in the table above, look for a similar noun. For example, *fortune* is not in the list but *money* is. You can check your answers by looking up the entries for the nouns, but try to predict what the verbs will be before you do this.

a Make sure you _have/take_ a look at the engine before you buy the car.

b After the interview I had to _____ a test.

c They always _____ us a welcome when we go there.

d I sometimes _____ a siesta in the afternoon

e Saturday's my day for _____ jobs around the house.

f The housing committee are _____ priority to the elderly.

g Let's _____ one more swim before we go back to the hotel.

h He _____ a short laugh when he realized his mistake.

i The moment we met we _____ a dislike to each other.

j I told her I'd run in the marathon—I'm not going to _____ any promises like that again.

k She's always _____ an interest in current affairs.

l She _____ her fortune on the stock market.

m _____ a picture of me and your dad together.

n The kids are _____ a terrible racket.

o Her singing _____ an impression on me.

p _____ the handle a twist and the door should open.

q I don't know the answer, so I'll _____ a guess.

r How often do you have to _____ the medicine?

s Everyone else was _____ notes in the lecture, but I had forgotten my pen.

t The BBC are visiting our school to _____ a programme about teaching!

6 Put each of the following adjectives into one of the sentences in exercise 5, before a noun that it collocates with. If you want to check in the dictionary you will need to look up the entries for the nouns.

close copious instant keen lasting odd rash sharp top warm wild

For example: *Make sure you have a **close** look at the engine before you buy the car.*

NATURAL DISASTERS

In each case, only one of the pair of words in *italics* forms a common collocation with the word in **bold**. Use the dictionary (looking up the **bold** word) to decide which is the correct collocation.

a The famine has already *claimed/starved* thousands of **victims**.

b The president visited the affected region in the *direct/immediate* **aftermath** of the hurricane.

c **Rescue** *personnel/workers* are still looking for survivors.

d A massive **relief** *attempt/effort* is underway.

Sentences **e-h** each contain two pairs of italic words. You need to choose one from each pair. Again, look up the **bold** words.

e Several villages have been *inundated/soaked* by the *deepest/severest* **floods** in decades.

f The city was *affected/struck* by *an enormous/a massive* **earthquake** shortly after midnight.

g The forest **fires**, *blown/fanned* by warm winds, *flared/raged* out of control for weeks.

h The **volcano**, which has been *dormant/inactive* for 50 years, began *erupting/exploding* late last night.

CRIMINAL JUSTICE

In each of the sentences, there is an example of incorrect collocation in one of the two <u>underlined</u> sections. Look at the entries for the **bold** words to help you, then write a word that could be used in place of the incorrect one in the space on the right.

a The accused men have been ~~sent to~~ **custody** to <u>await</u> **trial**.   *remanded in* _____

b Police <u>carried out a **raid**</u> on the premises early this morning and <u>did two **arrests**</u>. _____

c The man <u>was judged **guilty**</u> of assault and <u>sent to **prison**</u> for ten years. _____

d The woman will <u>stand **trial**</u>, **accused** <u>with</u> murdering her husband. _____

e The woman was **charged** <u>with</u> threatening behaviour, an offence which <u>holds a **sentence**</u> of up to two years in jail. _____

f The **judge** <u>summarized</u> and the **jury** <u>retired</u> to consider its verdict. _____

g The jury <u>reported a **verdict**</u> of guilty and then the judge <u>passed **sentence**</u>. _____

h New **evidence** <u>came to light</u> and the original **verdict** <u>was squashed</u> on appeal. _____

EDUCATION

Using the entry for the word in **bold** to help you, cross out any of the words in *italics* that do not form common collocations.

a He got *full/~~maximum~~/top* **marks** in the listening test.

b We have to *do/make/write* a vocabulary **test** every Friday.

c She's busy *reviewing/revising/studying* for her **exam**.

d How many students have *enrolled on/signed up for/undertaken* the **course**?

e She was always *losing/missing out/skipping* **lessons** – no wonder she *crashed/failed/flunked* the **exam**.

f He suffers badly from **exam** *nerves/stress/worries*, which affects his **concentration** *length/span/time*.

g The teacher *made up/set/wrote* a difficult **exam** but *checked/corrected/marked* it leniently.

h We were supposed to *do/compose/write* the **essay** by Friday but I *delivered it/gave it in/handed it in* late.

DRIVING

In each case, only one *or* two of the words in *italics* form(s) a common collocation with the word in **bold**. Use the dictionary (looking up the bold word) to decide which combinations are possible.

a The taxi *~~brought~~/~~screamed~~/screeched* to a **halt** at the *~~foot~~/pedestrian/zebra* **crossing**.

b I *finished the/ran out of/used up the* **petrol** and had to *hitch/hitch-hike/thumb* a **lift** to the nearest garage.

c There's always *busy/heavy/strong* **traffic** on the motorway, so I usually take the *back/minor/small* **roads**.

d I realized it was a *one-direction/one-way/single-way* **street**, so I had to *carry out/do/make* a **U-turn**.

e The demonstration *brought/reduced/slowed* traffic to a **standstill**, and some drivers began to *hit/sound/toot* their **horns** in frustration.

f A **car** suddenly *pulled out/started out/turned out* in front of me and I had to *hit/slam on/tread on* the **brakes**.

g She was *banned/disallowed/disqualified* from **driving** for a year after failing *an alcohol/a breath/a breathalyser* **test**.

h The stolen car hit *an approaching/a contraflow/an oncoming* **vehicle** and *blew up in/burst into/caught* **flames**.

POLITICS

Complete each sentence with a verb from the left and a noun from the right.
You may need to change the form of the verb. You can check your answers
in the dictionary by looking up the entries for the nouns.

elections

fight

lead

rig

stand

a The opposition has accused the government of _____*rigging*_____ the
   _____*election*_____ .

b A week before the election, the Christian Democrats _____
   the _____ by 12 per cent.

c Which party _____ the most effective election _____ ?

d Castorri _____ for _____ five times, but was never
   elected.

campaign

election

office

opinion polls

government

fulfil

impose

unveil

commission

hold

rule out

e The Minister of Education insists that she will _____ her
   _____ to cut class sizes.

f The government is under pressure to _____ a
   _____ on tobacco advertising.

g The Home Secretary yesterday _____
   _____ to reform the prison system.

h The Prime Minister has _____ any _____ of an
   early election.

i The President confirmed that he intends to _____ a
   _____ on the main clauses of the new constitution.

j The Higher Education Minister is to _____ a
   _____ on the state of our universities.

ban

plans

pledge

possibility

referendum

report

opposition

face

launch

renew

k The opposition leader _____ a scathing _____ on
   government policy.

l Animal rights campaigners have _____ their _____
   for a referendum on hunting.

m The government is _____ a _____ over its
   decision to raise the basic rate of tax.

attack

backlash

call

international issues

call

deploy

honour

issue

n An international delegation urged the government to _____
   its _____ on human rights.

o The UN will decide today whether to _____ peacekeeping
   _____ in the area.

p The government _____ an _____ to the rebels for
   all arms to be handed over by the 15th.

q The warring factions have agreed to _____ a
   _____ while negotiations take place.

ceasefire

forces

promise

ultimatum

JOBS

1 Complete each of these sentences with an adjective from the box. Use the entries for the words in **bold** to help you.

> team   flexible   proven   short-term   skeleton   in-service
> repetitive   heavy   ~~high-powered~~   competitive

a He didn't want the stress of a ___high-powered___ **job**.

b He couldn't stand the _____ **work** of the production line.

c The company offers a _____ **salary**.

d Does your job allow you to work _____ **hours**?

e She's hired an assistant to help with her _____ **workload**.

f She joined the company on a _____ **contract**.

g We gathered in my boss's office for a _____ **meeting**.

h Applicants should have a _____ **track record** in project management.

i All staff receive _____ **training** in IT skills.

j They only have a _____ **staff** on duty during the holidays.

2 Fill in each gap with an appropriate verb or phrasal verb. Use the entries for the words in **bold** to help you.

a I saw an interesting ad in the newspaper and decided to __apply for__ the **job**.

b The company missed his wealth of experience when he chose to _____ early **retirement**.

c The whole union _____ **strike** in sympathy with the sacked workers.

d Extra skills training could _____ your job **prospects**.

e She felt she wasn't _____ her full **potential** in her current job so she _____ her notice.

f The company had no choice but to _____ her **contract** when she _____ several important **deadlines**.

g She had always wanted to _____ her **living** as a musician, and she finally _____ her **ambition** when she was 42.

h I _____ a brief **stint** as a waitress when I was a student, but I wouldn't like to _____ it _____ a **living**.

3 Now find collocations in the sentences from Exercise 2 that match up with the definitions below:

a a short time spent doing sth _____brief stint_____

b all that you might possibly achieve _____

c your chances of getting a good job _____

d the valuable knowledge and skills that you have gained in your life and work _____

MONEY

1 Fill in the gaps in these sentences with an appropriate word or phrase.
Use the entries for the words in **bold** to help you. Sometimes more than
one answer is possible.

a Private health insurance might cost an ___awful___ **lot** of money, but it's worth every
penny.

b The shares have almost doubled _____ **value** since I bought them.

c Cigarettes are set to _____ **price** for the fifth successive year.

d The failure of the business left him _____ financial **ruin**.

e An oil spill would _____ economic **ruin** for the local fishing industry.

Sentences f-j have no words in **bold**. Read the sentences carefully to decide
for yourself which word(s) you need to look up.

f We've been living _____ a _____ budget since the baby was born.

g It cost me more to make the chairs than I could sell them for, so I actually _____
a loss _____ the deal.

h She _____ a large bank loan and then had great difficulty _____ it
_____ .

i The favourable exchange _____ means that holidays in the US are _____
value.

j She _____ a _____ fortune _____ the stock market in the 80s.

2 Choose an adjective from the left-hand box and a noun from the right-
hand box and match them up with the definitions below. You can look
up the entries for the nouns to help you.

| ~~small~~ healthy false | pay fortune ~~change~~ |
| small take-home | bank balance* economy |

a coins of low value   ___small change___

b a lot of money   _____

c a fair amount of money in the bank   _____

d the amount of money that you have left after you have
paid tax on your salary   _____

e an attempt to save money by buying something cheap that   _____
does not really save money at all because the goods are of
poor quality and do not last very long   * look up *balance*

LI

label noun

1 paper, etc. attached to sth
- ADJ. **adhesive, sticky | designer** *clothes with a designer label* | **address, luggage | price | warning**
- VERB + LABEL **bear, carry, have** *It doesn't have a price label on it.* | **attach, put on, stick on** *She stuck labels on all the jars.* | **remove, take off | read** *Always read the label before taking any medicine.*
- PREP. **on a/the ~** *What does it say on the label?* | **~ on** *the label on the bottle*

2 description
- VERB + LABEL **apply, attach, use** *One sometimes feels that the label 'classic' is applied to any book that is dull.*

3 company that produces records
- ADJ. **record | major | independent**
- VERB + LABEL **sign to/with** *The band are hoping to sign with a major label by the end of the year.*
- PREP. **under a/the ~** *The record was produced under the Virgin label.*

label verb

1 put a label on sth
- ADV. **correctly, properly | wrongly** *Some of the plants were wrongly labelled.* | **carefully, clearly, neatly** *a pile of small plastic bags, each carefully labelled*
- PREP. **with** *The samples were all labelled with a date and place of origin.*

2 describe sb/sth as a particular thing
- ADV. **falsely, wrongly** *She was wrongly labelled a liar.* | **automatically**
- PREP **as** *She had automatically labelled the boys as troublemakers.*

laboratory noun

- ADJ. **up-to-date, well-equipped | commercial, industrial | school, university | biology, chemistry, physics, science | chemical, pharmaceutical | analytical, clinical, development, experimental, forensic, medical, nuclear, pathology, photographic, public health, quality control, research, testing**
- VERB + LABORATORY **build, establish, set up** *She has donated money to establish a pharmaceutical laboratory.* | **run** *He runs his own research laboratory.* | **work in** *They work in a laboratory studying growth patterns.*
- LABORATORY + NOUN **assistant, chemist, manager, scientist, technician, worker | apparatus, bench, equipment, facilities | animal | analysis, experiment, investigation, measurement, simulation, study, test, testing, trial, work** *laboratory tests on animals* | **science, subject | practices, procedures | data, evidence, findings, report, results | conditions, setting** *The athletes' reflexes were tested under laboratory conditions.* ◇ *simulated driving in a laboratory setting*
- PREP. **in a/the ~** *The effects of weathering can be simulated in the laboratory.*

labour noun

1 work
- ADJ. **manual, physical | forced, hard** *He was sentenced to four years hard labour for his crime.*
- VERB + LABOUR **withdraw** *The miners are threatening to withdraw their labour.*
- LABOUR + NOUN **market** *an increasingly competitive labour market*

2 workers
- ADJ. **cheap | casual | skilled, unskilled | child, migrant, slave** *It is thought that Stonehenge was built using slave labour.*
- LABOUR + NOUN **force** *the size of the labour force* | **cost/costs | relations**

3 giving birth
- ADJ. **difficult, easy | long, short** *The baby was born after a long labour.*
- VERB + LABOUR **go into** *She went into labour two weeks early.* | **induce** *Labour was induced when the baby was ten days overdue.*
- LABOUR + NOUN **room, ward | pains**
- PREP. **in ~** *She was in labour for ten hours.*

labourer noun

- ADJ. **casual, seasonal | migrant | manual | skilled, unskilled | general | agricultural, farm, rural | builder's** *He got a job as a builder's labourer.*
- QUANT. **gang** *Gangs of labourers dug the canals.*
- ⇒ Note at JOB

lace noun

1 for a shoe
- VERB + LACE **do, do up, tie** *He's still a bit young to tie his own laces.* | **undo, untie | loosen, tighten**

2 decorative cloth
- ADJ. **delicate, fine**
- VERB + LACE **knit, make** *a machine for knitting lace*
- PHRASES **edged/trimmed with lace** *a silk dress trimmed with lace*

lack noun

- ADJ. **profound, serious, severe | conspicuous, distinct, notable, obvious** *There was a distinct lack of urgency in his manner.* | **complete, sheer, total** *a complete lack of confidence* | **relative | abysmal** *an abysmal lack of knowledge*
- PREP. **by ~ of** *The situation was worsened by lack of communication.* **for ~ of** *They lost the game, but not for lack of trying.* **from ~ of** *She thought she would collapse from lack of sleep.* **through ~ of** *I've lost those skills through lack of practice.* | **~ of** *I couldn't hide my lack of enthusiasm.*
- PHRASES **no lack of sth** *There is certainly no lack of interest in the subject.*

lack verb

- ADV. **really | completely, entirely** *She completely lacks confidence.* | **apparently** *He apparently lacked the desire to learn.* | **clearly, conspicuously, manifestly, obviously | simply** *Perhaps you simply lack the intelligence to realize just how serious this is?* | **otherwise** *Her high-heeled shoes gave her the height she otherwise lacked.* | **somehow** *His claim somehow lacked conviction.*
- VERB + LACK **appear to, seem to** *His life seemed to lack direction.*

lacking adj.

- VERBS **be, feel, seem** *Her life felt lacking in direction and purpose.* | **find sth** *an area of policy where the government has been found seriously lacking*
- ADV. **seriously | altogether, completely, entirely, quite, totally, wholly** *The book is altogether lacking in ori-*

ginality. | a bit, a little, rather, somewhat | apparently | clearly, conspicuously, distinctly, notably, noticeably, obviously *Tom was conspicuously lacking in enthusiasm for the idea.* | singularly | curiously, strangely | sadly, sorely, woefully
● PREP. from *the passion sadly lacking from his performance* in *Her remarks were curiously lacking in perception.*

lacquer noun

● ADJ. protective | clear, matt
● VERB + LACQUER be coated with, be varnished with | apply, put on, spray on *Apply the lacquer evenly.*
● LACQUER + NOUN finish

lad noun

● ADJ. little, young | big, strapping *He's a strapping lad—already bigger than his father.* | handsome | decent, fine, good, great, lovely, nice, smashing | bright, sensible
● QUANT. bunch, group *They're a nice bunch of lads.*

ladder noun

1 piece of equipment for climbing up sth
● ADJ. rickety | wooden | loft, rope
● VERB + LADDER ascend, clamber up, climb (up), mount, go up *He went up the ladder onto the deck.* | come down, descend, go down | put up *We put up the ladder and went to get the paint.* | fall off, step off
● PREP. on/up a/the ~ *She was up a ladder mending the roof.* down a/the ~ *I was standing lower down the ladder.* | ~ to *the ladder to the gallery*
● PHRASES the bottom/foot of a ladder, a rung/step of a ladder *Several of the ladder's rungs were broken.* the top of a ladder

2 levels in a system
● ADJ. evolutionary, social *the people at the top of the social ladder* | career, corporate, housing, promotion
● VERB + LADDER ascend, climb, move up *She was anxious to move up the promotion ladder.* | get onto
● PREP. higher up the ~ *creatures higher up the evolutionary ladder* lower down the ~ | ~ of *the ladder of fame* ~ to *helping her on the ladder to success*
● PHRASES get/have one foot on the ladder *He finally managed to get one foot on the career ladder.* a rung/step on the ladder *the old problem of how to get onto the first step on the ladder*

laden adj.

● VERBS be
● ADV. heavily *He took the heavily laden tray from her.* | absolutely, fully *The trees were absolutely laden with apples.* ◇ *a fully laden basket*
● PREP. with *They arrived laden with gifts.*

lady noun

● ADJ. elderly, middle-aged, old, young *A little old lady opened the door.* | attractive, beautiful, lovely, pretty | charming, fine, lovely, nice | cleaning, dinner, tea *The school employs four dinner ladies.*
● LADY + NOUN friend *We teased my uncle about his new lady friend.*
● PHRASES a lady of leisure *She's a lady of leisure now that she's retired.* the lady of the house
⇒ Note at PEER

lag verb

● ADV. badly, seriously | behind *She did well in her first year at school but then started to lag behind.*
● PREP. behind *Britain still lags badly behind the rest of*

Europe on this.
● PHRASES lag far/way/well behind (sb/sth) *The Tories are still lagging way behind in the opinion polls.*

lake noun

● ADJ. big, great, huge, large | little, small | deep | shallow | beautiful, lovely | blue | freshwater, salt | frozen | artificial, man-made, ornamental | inland, mountain | boating
● VERB + LAKE cross *You should cross the lake before nightfall.*
● LAKE + NOUN bed, water
● PREP. across a/the ~ *A ferry takes people across the lake.* around/round a/the ~ *We walked around the lake.* at a/the ~ *We had a holiday at Lake Como.* in a/the ~ *Carp live in the lake.* into a/the ~ *She fell into the lake.* on a/the ~ *We went boating on the lake* ◇ *a cottage on the lake*
● PHRASES the edge/middle/shores/side/surface of the lake *There is a cafe on the other side of the lake.*

lamb noun

1 young sheep
● ADJ. newborn | orphaned | sacrificial (*often figurative*) *I am not going to be a sacrificial lamb on the altar of political correctness.*
● VERB + LAMB fatten | kill, slaughter *the traffic in illegally slaughtered lamb*
● LAMB + VERB bleat | frolic, gambol

2 meat
● ADJ. spring | curried, grilled, minced, roast
● LAMB + NOUN chop, cutlet | casserole, curry, stew
● PHRASES breast/leg/neck/rack/shoulder of lamb
⇒ Special page at FOOD

lame adj.

● VERBS be, look | go *His horse had gone lame.* | leave sb, make sb *an accident which had left him lame*
● ADV. completely, quite | slightly

lamp noun

● ADJ. bedside, desk, reading, standard, table | gas, oil, paraffin
● VERB + LAMP light, switch on, turn on | switch off, turn off
● LAMP + VERB burn, glow, shine *An oil lamp burned in the darkness.* | flicker, go out

land noun

1 surface of the earth
● ADJ. dry *It was good to be on dry land again after months at sea.*
● VERB + LAND reach *The explorers reached land after a long voyage.* | sight *In the distance the crew sighted land.* | reclaim *The new project will reclaim the land from the sea.*
● LAND + NOUN mass *chains of volcanoes running along the edge of continental land masses* | animal, mammal | battle, war | forces *With the land forces defeated, everything now rested on the navy.*
● PREP. by ~ *It's impossible to reach this beach by land because of the high cliffs.* on ~ *Some animals can live both on land and in water.*

2 piece of ground
● ADJ. good, prime *prime building land* | fertile, rich *rich agricultural land* ◇ *land that is rich in mineral deposits* | marginal, poor *animals grazing on marginal land that was previously heath or moorland* | arid, dry, hard, parched *The land was very dry and hard after the long, hot summer.* | marshy | barren | derelict, waste (also wasteland) *A new shopping centre will be built on the derelict land.* | contaminated | empty, unused, va-

cant | uncultivated, virgin, wild | agricultural, arable, cultivated, farm (also farmland), farming | grazing | industrial | building, housing | green belt | rural, urban | private | public | common *This used to be common land, where everyone had the right to graze animals.* | open *They finally got out of the town and reached open land.* | flat, low-lying | hill, undulating | coastal, forest, meadow

• QUANT. parcel, piece, plot, scrap, strip, tract *Every scrap of land is used for growing food.* ◇ *The college owns vast tracts of land.*

• VERB + LAND have, hold, own *The inhabitants of a village held land in common.* | acquire, buy, purchase | sell | cultivate, farm, plough, work | irrigate | clear *The land has been cleared ready for building.* | develop *They were refused permission to develop the land.* | occupy *During the war their lands were occupied by the enemy.* | seize | allocate, distribute, redistribute | grant sb *He was granted land by the king.*

• LAND + VERB adjoin sth *a piece of land adjoining a disused railway line*

• LAND + NOUN owner, ownership | acquisition, purchase | reclamation | development | use | prices, values | dispute

3 the land farming land

• VERB + LAND live off *It's very fertile countryside where you can just live off the land.* | farm, work (on) *His family had always worked the land.* | leave *Many people leave the land to find work in towns and cities.* | get/go back to *He's tired of living in cities, and wants to get back to the land.*

4 country

• ADJ. ancestral, native *the tribe's ancestral lands* | distant *He travelled to many distant lands.* | alien, foreign, strange *She was all alone in a strange land.* | promised *(often figurative)* *the promised land of progressive education* | cloud cuckoo, never-never *(both figurative)* *Anyone who thinks this legislation will be effective is living in cloud cuckoo land.*

land *verb*

1 of an aircraft

• ADV. safely *The pilot managed to land the plane safely.*
• VERB + LAND be due to | come down to *The plane slowly came down to land.* | be forced to *The plane was forced to land in a nearby field.* | manage to
• PREP. at *We are due to land at Heathrow at 12.15.*

2 fall to the ground

• ADV. awkwardly, badly *I landed awkwardly and twisted my ankle.* | expertly, neatly *He tensed himself for the jump and landed expertly on the other side.* | heavily | lightly
• PREP. on *She fell and landed heavily on her back.*

landing *noun*

1 of an aircraft

• ADJ. abrupt, bumpy | crash, emergency, forced | gentle, safe, smooth, soft
• VERB + LANDING make *The pilot had to make an emergency landing in a field.*
• LANDING + NOUN strip

2 top of a staircase

• ADJ. first-floor, second-floor, etc.
• PREP. off the ~ *The room opens off the landing.* on the ~ *There's a phone on the landing outside your room.*

landlady, landlord *noun*

1 sb who lets a house/room

• ADJ. resident | absentee *The house has an absentee landlord, who visits the property once a year.*

2 sb who owns/runs a pub

• ADJ. pub *He left the army and became a pub landlord.*
• LANDLADY, LANDLORD + VERB serve sb *The landlady came over to serve me.*

landmark *noun*

1 feature of the landscape

• ADJ. distinctive, prominent | famous, well-known | familiar *After twenty years, all the familiar landmarks had disappeared.* | local | historic
• VERB + LANDMARK recognize
• PREP. ~for *The tower was once a landmark for ships.*

2 important stage in the development of sth

• ADJ. great, important, major, significant
• VERB + LANDMARK be, represent *The Russian Revolution represents a landmark in world history.*
• LANDMARK + NOUN decision, ruling *a landmark decision on the legal status of a foetus* | case
• PREP. ~in *The film is an important landmark in the history of the cinema.*

landscape *noun*

• ADJ. barren, bleak, dramatic, rocky, rugged *the dramatic landscape of the desert* | beautiful | rural, urban *an urban landscape of factories and skyscrapers* | industrial | winter | lunar | political, social *(both figurative)* *The political landscape of the country has changed since unemployment rose.*
• VERB + LANDSCAPE conserve, preserve, protect *the need to conserve the rural landscape* | dominate *The power station dominates the landscape.*
• LANDSCAPE + NOUN architect, gardener | design, gardening | painter, photographer | painting

landslide *noun*

1 fall of earth or rocks

• VERB + LANDSLIDE cause *The floods caused a landslide.*
• LANDSLIDE + VERB destroy sth *The village was destroyed by a landslide.*

2 election victory

• ADJ. electoral *Nobody predicted such an electoral landslide.* | Conservative, Labour, etc.
• VERB + LANDSLIDE win by *The National Party won by a landslide.*
• LANDSLIDE + NOUN victory

lane *noun*

1 narrow road

• ADJ. little, narrow, single-track, small | quiet | bumpy, rough | dusty, muddy | twisting, winding | grassy, green, leafy | cobbled | country | back *Lighting is poor in the back lanes of the city.*
• VERB + LANE turn down/into
• LANE + VERB go, lead, run *the lane leading to the village* ◇ *The lane runs past the the lake.*
• PREP. along a/the ~ *We cycled for miles along winding country lanes.* down a/the ~, in a/the ~, up a/the ~

2 part of a wide road for one line of traffic

• ADJ. fast, slow | inside, left-hand, middle, outside, right-hand | overtaking | northbound, southbound, etc. | traffic | bus, cycle
• VERB + LANE change, get in *I hate changing lanes on the motorway.* ◇ *Get in lane early when approaching a junction.* | keep in, stay in
• LANE + NOUN closures, restrictions *Lane closures are causing hold-ups on the M6 near junction 2.*
• PREP. in (the) ~ *The bus was crawling along in the slow lane.*

> **NOTE**
> **Language**
>
> **excellent, fluent, good, perfect~**
> *He speaks fluent Japanese.*
> **bad, broken, poor~**
> *I got by with broken Chinese and sign language.*
> **colloquial, idiomatic, non-standard, pidgin, standard~**
> *The inhabitants speak a kind of pidgin Spanish.*
> **spoken, written~**
> *My spoken Polish is better than my written Polish.*
> **business~**
> *She is doing a course in business English.*
> **original~**
> *The fable is translated from the original French.*
> **know, read, speak, understand, use~**
> *I am more comfortable using Spanish, if you don't mind.*
> **be fluent in~**
> *She was fluent in German, Urdu and Swahili.*
> **do, learn~**
> *I did German at school but I've forgotten most of it.*
> *I've been learning Arabic for four years.*
> **improve, practise~**
> *I spent a month in Rome to improve my Italian.*
> **master~**
> *I never really mastered Latin.*
> **translate sth into~**
> *He has translated her latest book into Korean.*
> **~class, course, lesson**
> *I'm late for my Russian class.*
> **~interpreter, speaker, a speaker of~**
> *the need for Gujarati interpreters*
> **a command/knowledge of~**
> *He has a poor command of English.*
> **in~**
> *What is 'apple' in French?*
> *He addressed me in his best Portuguese.*
> ⇨ See also the note at SUBJECT

language *noun*

1 system of communication
● ADJ. **first, native** *She grew up in Spain, so her first language is Spanish.* | **foreign, second** *How many foreign languages does she speak?* ◇ *the teaching of English as a second language* | **original** *Most local cinemas show films in the original language, with German subtitles.* | **source, target** (*both technical*) | **ancient, classical, dead** *Latin is a dead language.* | **modern** | **common, shared** | **indigenous, local** | **official** *Belgium has two official languages.* | **national** *Portuguese is the national language of Brazil.* | **international** | **minority** *Some minority languages are dying out.* | **spoken, written** *She could speak some Chinese, but never studied the written language.* | **colloquial, everyday, informal** | **formal** | **flowery, literary, poetic** | **racist, sexist** | **sign** *Not all deaf people use sign language.* | **body, non-verbal** *You could tell from his body language that he was very embarrassed.* | **legal, technical, etc.** | **computer, programming**
● VERB + LANGUAGE **speak** | **understand** | **use** | **learn, study** | **master** | **be couched in, be expressed in** | **enrich** *idiomatic expressions that enrich the language*
● LANGUAGE + NOUN **acquisition, learning** *new methods of language learning* | **course, lesson**
● PREP. **in ... ~** *His letter was couched in very formal language.*
● PHRASES **command/knowledge/mastery of (a) language** *Her command of language is very advanced for a six-year-old.* **use of language** *The writer's use of language reflects the personality of each character.*

2 offensive words
● ADJ. **bad, crude, foul, obscene, offensive, strong** *using foul language*
● VERB + LANGUAGE **use** | **mind, watch** *The referee warned the players to mind their language.*

lantern *noun*

● VERB + LANTERN **light, shine** *He shone his lantern into the dark room.* | **blow out, put out**
● LANTERN + VERB **glow, shine** | **hang** *The lantern hung from the roof.*

lap *noun*

● ADJ. **first, opening** | **final, last**
● VERB + LAP **complete, do, run**
● LAP + NOUN **record** *He set a new lap record.*
● PREP. **on the ... ~** *He tripped and fell on the final lap.*
● PHRASES **a lap of honour** *The silver medallist joined the winner in a lap of honour.*

lap *verb*

● ADV. **gently, softly**
● PREP. **against** *The waves lapped gently against the side of the ship.* **around** *The water lapped around his ankles.* **over** *The freezing water lapped over her boots.*

lapel *noun*

● ADJ. **narrow, wide** *a coat with wide lapels*
● VERB + LAPEL **be pinned to** *A silver brooch was pinned to her lapel.*
● LAPEL + NOUN **badge, pin**
● PREP. **in the/your~** *He was wearing a carnation in his lapel.* **on the/your~** *a jacket with a badge on the lapel*
● PHRASES **grab sb by the lapels** *He grabbed her by the lapels and shook her violently.*

lapse *noun*

1 small error
● ADJ. **minor** | **momentary, temporary** | **sudden** | **memory, mental** *I keep suffering these mental lapses.*
● VERB + LAPSE **have, suffer** *I had a momentary lapse when I couldn't remember his name.*
● PREP. **~ in** *a lapse in attention* **~ of** *sudden lapses of concentration*

2 bad behaviour
● ADJ. **curious, odd** *It was an odd lapse for one who is normally so polite.*

3 passing of time
● ADJ. **brief, considerable** | **time**
● PHRASES **~ of** *after a considerable lapse of time* ◇ *a time lapse of three months*

larder *noun*

● ADJ. **full, well-stocked** | **bare, empty** | **walk-in**
● VERB + LARDER **fill, stock** | **empty, raid** *He comes home from school and raids the larder.*
● LARDER + NOUN **door, shelf**
● PREP. **in the~** *There wasn't much food left in the larder.*

large *adj.*

● VERBS **be, feel, look, seem** *Some of the clothes looked very large.* | **become, get, grow** *By this time his debt had got extremely large.* ◇ *The plant had grown quite large.* | **remain**
● ADV. **exceptionally, extremely, very** | **comparatively, fairly, moderately, quite, rather, reasonably, relatively** *Isn't that jumper rather large?* | **enough, sufficiently** *Are you sure the hall will be large enough?* | **indefinitely, infinitely** *The universe is infinitely large.* | **abnormally, dis-**

proportionately, surprisingly, unexpectedly, unusually *His eyes were abnormally large.*

laser *noun*

- ADJ. **powerful**
- VERB + LASER **use**
- LASER + NOUN **beam, light | printer | gun | surgery, therapy, treatment**

lash *noun*

- ADJ. **bottom, lower | long, thick**
- VERB + LASH **bat, flutter** *She batted her lashes flirtatiously.* | **lower** *She lowered her lashes in sudden embarrassment.*
- LASH + VERB **flicker, flutter** *Her lashes flickered and I knew she was lying.*

last *verb*

- ADV. **long** *Your car will last longer if you look after it.* | **forever, indefinitely** *Nothing lasts forever.* ◇ *With care, the vines will last indefinitely.* | **never** *Happiness never lasts.*
- VERB + LAST **can/cannot, could (not)** *The storm could last quite a long time.* | **will/won't, would (not)** *The kids are all very enthusiastic, but it won't last—it never does.* | **be likely/unlikely to** *I always thought his popularity was unlikely to last.* | **be expected to | seem to** *The journey seemed to last forever.* | **be built to** *This house was built to last.*
- PREP. **for** *The war lasted for three years.* **into** *The celebrations lasted well into the next week.* **until** *The trial is expected to last until the end of the week.*
- PHRASES **while sth lasts** *Make the most of this feeling while it lasts.*

late *adj.*

- VERBS **be, feel, seem** *I don't know what the time is, but it feels quite late.* | **make sb**
- ADV. **extremely, really, very | a bit, fairly, a little, quite, rather, relatively**
- PREP. **for** *I'm late for work.* **in** *He took up music late in life.* **with** *He was now three weeks late with his rent.*
- PHRASES **an hour, ten minutes, etc. late** *The train was 45 minutes late.* **leave it a bit/rather/very late** *You've left it a bit late to start your homework, haven't you?*

Latin *noun*

- ADJ. **classical | medieval**
- ⇨ Note at LANGUAGE

latitude *noun*

1 geographical position
- ADJ. **high, low | northern, southern | polar, temperate** *These birds only survive in temperate latitudes.*
- VERB + LATITUDE **calculate, determine**
- PHRASES **a line of latitude**

2 freedom
- ADJ. **considerable, great**
- QUANT. **degree** *Some degree of latitude is required in interpreting the law on this point.*
- VERB + LATITUDE **allow (sb), give sb**
- PREP. **~for** *This method allows very little latitude for error.* **~in** *Nowadays, newspapers are allowed considerable latitude in criticizing the government.*

laugh *noun*

1 sound/act of laughing
- ADJ. **loud | light, little, short, slight, small | low | big, good, great** *The last joke got the biggest laugh.* | **belly, booming, hearty | barking, cackling, harsh, husky, throaty | silvery, tinkling | amused, delighted |** embarrassed, nervous, shaky | polite | bitter, brittle, cynical, derisive, dry, forced, hollow, humourless, mirthless, mocking, rueful, scornful *She forced a humourless laugh.* | **infectious**
- VERB + LAUGH **give, let out, utter** *He gave a short, amused laugh.* | **have | force, manage | enjoy, like** *He enjoys a good laugh.* | **get, raise** *Few of his jokes got a laugh.* ◇ *She got a laugh out of Jack.* | **hear**
- LAUGH + VERB **escape sb** *A small laugh escaped her.*
- PREP. **for a ~** *She dyed her hair green just for a laugh.* **with a~** *He left the room with a cynical laugh.* | **~about/at** *We all had a great laugh about it afterwards.*
- PHRASES **be good for a laugh** *Paul's always good for a laugh* (= always amusing). **have the last laugh** *We'll have the last laugh if she finds out that you're the one who played the trick.* **a laugh at sb's expense** *Oh yes, very funny—have your laugh at my expense!* **the laugh is on sb** (= sb looks ridiculous after they have tried to make fun of sb else)

2 sb/sth that is amusing
- ADJ. **good, real**
- PHRASES **a barrel of laughs, a bit of a laugh, a laugh a minute** (= very funny)

laugh *verb*

- ADV. **aloud, loudly, out loud** *It looked so funny that I almost laughed out loud.* | **gently, lightly, quietly, softly, silently, under your breath | deeply, heartily, a lot, really, uproariously** *He laughed heartily at his own joke.* | **just, merely, simply** *I thought she would be angry but she just laughed.* | **almost | briefly, a little, shortly | suddenly | easily, freely** *She smiles and laughs easily.* | **openly, outright | helplessly, uncontrollably | cheerfully, delightedly, excitedly, happily | hysterically, nervously | politely | incredulously, in disbelief | angrily, bitterly, cynically, derisively, grimly, harshly, hollowly, humourlessly, mirthlessly, ruefully, scornfully, sourly, wryly** *He realized how he had been fooled, and laughed bitterly.* | **together** *talking and laughing together*
- VERB + LAUGH **have to, want to** *He looked so funny I just had to laugh.* | **begin to, start to | try not to** *I was watching them and trying not to laugh.* | **make sb** *He pulled a funny face to make us laugh.* | **hear sb** *I heard him suddenly laugh aloud.*
- PREP. **about** *Tomorrow you'll be able to laugh about this.* **at** *The audience laughed at her jokes.* **with** *talking and laughing with the children* ◇ *Trent almost laughed with relief.*
- PHRASES **burst out laughing, can't/couldn't help/stop laughing** *She was telling us jokes and we couldn't stop laughing.* **fall about laughing** *It was so funny we just fell about laughing.* **find yourself laughing** *He laughed, and she found herself laughing with him.* **stop laughing**

laughter *noun*

- ADJ. **helpless, hysterical, loud, raucous, wild** *I heard sounds of raucous laughter upstairs.* | **delighted, happy | infectious** *Her infectious laughter had everyone smiling.* | **nervous | silent, suppressed** *She was bent over with suppressed laughter.* | **derisive, mocking**
- QUANT. **bellow, hoot, howl, roar, shriek, snort** *He gave a sudden bellow of laughter.* | **fit** *Everyone dissolved into fits of laughter when they saw my haircut.* | **gale, peal, ripple** *His suggestion was greeted with peals of laughter.* ◇ *A ripple of laughter ran round the room.*
- VERB + LAUGHTER **burst into, dissolve into/with, explode with | bellow with, cackle with, hoot with, howl with, roar with, scream with, shriek with, snort with, whoop with, yell with | rock with, shake with**

launch noun

- ADJ. **official, press, public** *She is signing copies of her book at the official launch.* | **successful** | **imminent** | **book, campaign, product** | **balloon, rocket, satellite, shuttle**
- VERB + LAUNCH **get (sth) ready for, prepare (sth) for** *They are preparing for the launch of the new campaign next month.* | **announce** | **mark** *a big Hollywood event to mark the launch of the movie* | **coincide with** *The show is timed to coincide with the launch of a new book on the subject.* | **attend, go to, speak at** | **delay, postpone, put off**
- LAUNCH + NOUN **date** | **party** (= for a product or book) | **pad, site**
- PREP. **after/following/since the ~** *In the six months since its launch the car has sold extremely well.* **at a/the ~** *I met her at the launch of her new book.* | **~ for** *a spring launch for the new TV system*

laundry noun

- ADJ. **clean, dirty**
- QUANT. **bundle, pile** *There was a pile of clean laundry on her bed.*
- VERB + LAUNDRY **do** *The housekeeper cooks, does the laundry and cleans.*
- LAUNDRY + NOUN **bag, basket** | **service** *The hotel offers a free laundry service.*

lavatory noun

- ADJ. **public** | **communal, shared, indoor, inside** | **outside** | **flush, flushing**
- VERB + LAVATORY **go to, use** | **need** | **flush, flush sth down**
- LAVATORY + NOUN **basin, bowl** | **seat** | **cistern** | **chain** | **paper** | **brush**
- PREP. **in the ~, on the ~**

law noun

1 official rule/rules

- ADJ. **administrative, case, civil, common, constitutional, contract, criminal, international, statute, etc.** (see also **martial law**)
- VERB + LAW **become** *Parliament voted for the bill to become law.* | **enforce, uphold** *It's the job of the police to enforce the law.* | **obey, observe** | **break, flout, violate** | **adopt, enact, pass** | **annul, repeal** | **interpret** *Judges interpret this law in different ways.*
- LAW + VERB **allow sth, forbid sth, prohibit sth** *The law forbids gambling of any kind.* | **permit sth** | **require sth** *The wearing of a crash helmet is required by law.* | **govern sth** *the law governing school attendance*
- LAW + NOUN **court** | **enforcement**
- PREP. **above the ~** *No one is above the law.* **against the ~** *What you did was clearly against the law.* **by ~** *By law, you are obliged to install smoke alarms in the factory.* **within the ~** *The company is operating entirely within the law.* | **~ against** *a local law against keeping horses* **~ concerning** *the law concerning industrial action ballots* **~ on** *A law on hunting will cause a lot of disagreements.* **~ relating to** *the law relating to the sale of goods*
- PHRASES **as the law stands** *As the law stands, you can get married while still too young to have a driving licence.* **law and order** *Martial law was imposed to prevent the breakdown of law and order.* **the letter of the law** *In spite of the difficulties it would cause her family, the judge stuck to the letter of the law and jailed her.* **take the law into your own hands** *When police failed to arrest the suspect, local people took the law into their own hands and beat him up.*

2 subject of study/profession

- VERB + LAW **practise**
- LAW + NOUN **firm**
- ⇨ Note at SUBJECT (for more verbs and nouns)

lawful adj.

- VERBS **be** | **become** | **consider sth, deem sth**
- ADV. **perfectly** *This is a perfectly lawful activity.*

lawn noun

- ADJ. **manicured, neat, tended** *a carefully tended lawn* | **overgrown** | **back, front**
- VERB + LAWN **cut, mow, trim** *The lawn really needs mowing.*
- PHRASES **a sweep of lawn** *The cottage sits on a hill above a sweep of lawn.*

lawsuit noun

- VERB + LAWSUIT **bring, file, issue** *A lawsuit has been filed against the company.* | **be involved in, pursue** | **drop** *They have agreed to drop their lawsuit against the Dutch company.* | **be faced with, face** *The company now faces several lawsuits over its failure to protect its employees.* | **defend** *She plans to defend the lawsuit vigorously.* | **win** | **lose** | **settle** *The two companies have settled the lawsuit.*
- PREP. **in a/the ~** *They are seeking damages in a lawsuit.* | **~ against** *a lawsuit against her former husband* **~ over** *a lawsuit over a disputed estate*

lawyer noun

- ADJ. **clever, competent, good, successful** | **leading, senior** | **experienced, qualified** | **practising** | **academic** | **defence, prosecuting, prosecution** | **corporate, government** | **foreign, international, local** | **civil, civil rights, commercial, constitutional, criminal, divorce, human rights, libel, personal injury**
- ⇨ Note at PROFESSIONAL (for verbs)

lay verb

- ADV. **carefully, gently, tenderly** | **down** *He laid the books down on the table.*
- PREP. **on** *She laid the child tenderly on the bed.* **over** *They carefully laid a blanket over the body.*

PHRASAL VERB

lay sth out
- ADV. **tastefully, well** *The owners have built a gift shop and a tastefully laid out caravan site.*

lay-by noun

- VERB + LAY-BY **pull into**
- PREP. **in a/the ~** *I was parked in a lay-by, having a nap.*

layer noun

- ADJ. **fine, thin** *Everything was covered with a fine layer of dust.* | **deep, generous, heavy, thick** *Mulch with a generous layer of peat or compost.* | **bottom, inner, lower, middle, outer, surface, top, upper** *the upper layers of the earth's atmosphere* | **double** | **protective** *a protective layer of black plastic* | **ozone** *holes in the ozone layer*
- VERB + LAYER **form** *Use enough gravel to form a layer about 50mm thick.* | **be covered by/with** *The body had been covered with a thin layer of soil.*
- LAYER + NOUN **cake**
- PREP. **beneath/under a/the ~** *Beneath the surface layer of the skin are several further layers.* **in ~s** *The building is constructed in layers.* | **~ of** *an extra layer of clothing* ◇ *a layer of bureaucracy* ◇ *multiple layers of meaning*
- PHRASES **layer after/on/upon layer** *The remains lay buried under layer upon layer of black earth.*

layout noun

- ADJ. **basic, general** *Before designing the house we planned the basic layout of the rooms.* | **physical, spatial**

| interior, internal | page, text *page layout software* | road, street

lazy *adj.*

• VERBS **be, feel** | **become, get, grow** *He had grown lazy and fat.* ◊ *We thought we were winning, so we got lazy.*
• ADV. **extremely, incredibly, really, very** | **downright** | **almost** *His smile was slow, almost lazy.* | **a bit, pretty, rather**

lead¹ /liːd/ *noun*

1 example set by sb's behaviour
• ADJ. **moral**
• VERB + LEAD **give, take** *The government should give a lead in tackling racism.* | **follow**
• PREP. **~in** *We should follow their lead in banning chemical weapons.*

2 position ahead of other people
• ADJ. **big, clear, comfortable, commanding, good, strong** | **narrow** | **overall** | **early**
• VERB + LEAD **be in, have** *She has a narrow lead over the other runners.* | **go into, move into, take** *They took an early lead.* | **build up, establish** *The team has now built up a commanding lead.* | **hold, maintain** | **lose** | **regain** *They regained the lead with only a few minutes left to play.* | **put sb/sth (back) into** | **extend, increase** *Sheffield increased their lead just before half time.* | **give**
• PREP. **in/into the ~** *struggling to stay in the lead* | **~over** *This win gives the team a two-point lead over their closest rival.*

3 main part in a play, show, etc.
• ADJ. **romantic** | **female, male**
• VERB + LEAD **play** *Her big break came when she was chosen to play the lead in a Broadway musical.*
• LEAD + NOUN **role** | **singer** | **guitar, guitarist**

4 clue
• ADJ. **good** | **new** | **possible** *The police are following every possible lead.*
• VERB + LEAD **have** | **follow, pursue** | **give**
• PREP. **~on** *leads on the murderer's identity*

lead² /liːd/ *verb*

1 show the way
• ADV. **back, on** *'Lead on!' said Arnold.*
• VERB + LEAD **help (to)** *Five people helping to lead a convoy of aid are feared dead.* | **allow sb to, let sb** *Let me lead the way.*
• PREP. **along, down, into, out of, through, to,** etc. *She led them along a dark corridor to a small room.*
• PHRASES **lead the way** *You lead the way and we'll follow.*

2 go to a place
• ADV. **directly** | **back, down, up** *An old track led back through the wood.* | **nowhere, somewhere** *(often figurative) Often there are discoveries which lead nowhere.*
• PREP. **from, onto** *The gardens lead directly onto a beach.* **to** *a path leading from the village to the old church*

3 cause
• ADV. **normally, usually** | **inevitably, inexorably** *Industrialization inevitably led to the expansion of the urban working class.* | **(almost) certainly, undoubtedly** | **not necessarily** *The use of soft drugs does not necessarily lead to a progression to hard drugs.* | **automatically** *Business success does not automatically lead to financial success.* | **naturally** *Discussion of a client's tax affairs will lead naturally into consideration of investment options.* | **directly** | **indirectly** | **eventually, ultimately**
• VERB + LEAD **can/could (easily/only), may/might (well), must** *Sugar and fat can more easily lead to obesity than some other foods.* ◊ *The carbon tax might well lead to a doubling of prices for fossil fuels.* | **appear to, seem to** |

be expected to, be likely to, tend to *Worrying about your weight is more likely to lead to comforting yourself with a piece of chocolate.* | **be bound to**
• PREP. **to** *the events that led eventually to war*

lead³ /led/ *noun*

• ADJ. **molten**
• VERB + LEAD **be made of**
• LEAD + NOUN **pipe, piping** | **paint** | **shot** | **poisoning** | **content, levels** | **industry, mine, miner, mining**

leader *noun*

1 person who is in charge of sth
• ADJ. **born, natural** | **charismatic, effective, good, great, inspiring, inspired, visionary** | **undisputed** | **powerful, strong** | **weak** | **deputy** | **former** | **joint** | **local, national** | **opposition, parliamentary, party** | **Conservative, Labour,** etc. | **military, political, religious, spiritual** | **gang, guerrilla, nationalist, rebel** | **group, project, squadron, team** *Discuss any problems with your team leader.* | **business, church, civic, community, council, government, strike, student, (trade) union, youth** *Business leaders have been in talks with the government.* | **miners', teachers',** etc.
• VERB + LEADER **be appointed, become, be elected** | **appoint (sb), appoint sb as, choose (sb as), elect (sb), elect sb as, nominate (sb), nominate sb as**
• PHRASES **a leader of the Opposition**

2 person/team that is best or in first place
• ADJ. **undisputed** | **brand, market, world** *The company is a world leader in electrical goods.* | **championship, league, tournament**
• VERB + LEADER **overtake** *aiming to overtake the market leaders within two years*
• PREP. **behind the ~** *ten points behind league leaders Manchester United* | **~in** *the undisputed leader in her field*

leadership *noun*

• ADJ. **clear, effective, firm, outstanding, real, strong** *He was praised for his firm leadership.* | **poor, weak** | **charismatic, dynamic, visionary** | **hardline** | **traditional** | **personal** | **deputy** *He is standing in the deputy leadership election.* | **collective, joint** | **local, national, world** | **Conservative, Labour,** etc. | **cultural, industrial, intellectual, military, moral, political, spiritual** *Political leadership needs a particular combination of skills.* | **church, government, parliamentary, party, union**
• VERB + LEADERSHIP **assume, take on/over** *When Smith died, Blair took over the leadership of the party.* | **assert** *her method of asserting personal leadership* | **exercise, provide, show** *In the crisis he showed real leadership.*
• LEADERSHIP + NOUN **bid, campaign, challenge** | **ballot, battle, contest, election, race, struggle** | **role** | **structure** | **style** | **qualities, skills** *He lacks leadership qualities.*
• PREP. **under sb's ~** *The school has flourished under the leadership of Mr Buxton.* | **~from** *What is really needed is clear leadership from the prime minister.* **~in** *Leadership in science now went to the United States.*
• PHRASES **a challenge to sb's leadership** *She withstood several challenges to her leadership.* **a lack of leadership, sb's style of leadership**

leaf *noun*

• ADJ. **new, young** | **autumn, dead, dry, fallen, falling, rotting, rotten** *The ground was thick with dead leaves.* | **broad** *(especially technical),* **heart-shaped, oval** *broad leaf plants* | **green, yellow,** etc. | **glossy, hairy, leathery, mottled, shiny, spiky, variegated** | **bay, lettuce, oak, tea,** etc. *Throw the tea leaves on the flower bed.*

● VERB + LEAF **have** *This plant has beautifully varie-gated leaves.* | **break/burst/come into, grow, produce, put out** *It was spring and the trees were coming into leaf.* ◇ *In the spring the plant began to put out new leaves.* | **shed** *Deciduous trees shed their leaves in autumn.*
● LEAF + VERB **appear** *Spring arrived and the first green leaves began to appear.* | **turn, yellow** *The summer was over and the leaves were beginning to turn.* | **fall** | **rustle** *The leaves rustled in the light breeze.*
● LEAF + NOUN **litter, mould** *the leaf litter on the forest floor*
● PHRASES **in full leaf** *The corn was already ripening and the trees in full leaf.*

leaflet noun

● ADJ. **free** *a free leaflet explaining your tax return* | **helpful, useful** | **explanatory, information, instruction** | **promotional, publicity** | **campaign, election, party**
● QUANT. **copy**
● VERB + LEAFLET **issue, produce, publish** *The Health Council issued hundreds of leaflets.* | **deliver, distribute, give out, hand out, send out** *Campaigners handed out leaflets to passers by.* | **enclose** *I enclose a leaflet about some of the other services we offer.*
● LEAFLET + VERB **advertise sth, explain sth**
● PREP. **in a/the ~** *More details are given in our promotional leaflet.*

league noun

1 group of sports clubs that compete with each other
● ADJ. **cricket, football, etc.** *They want to start a new football league.* | **European, northern, etc.** | **local, national** | **Sunday** *He played Sunday League cricket for years.* | **premier** | **major, minor** *major league baseball* | **super** *new proposals for a European super league*
● VERB + LEAGUE **create, form, set up, start** | **join** *The team joined the Northern League last year.* | **win**
● LEAGUE + NOUN **champions, leaders** | **championship, cup, title** | **club, side** | **player** | **game, match** | **table** | **cricket, football, etc.**
● PREP. **in a/the ~** *The team is now in the Premier League.*
● PHRASES **at the bottom/top of the league, (come) bottom/top of the league, a position in the league** *hoping to improve their position in the league*

2 level of quality, ability, etc.
● ADJ. **big, super, top, world** *This move propelled him into the political big league.*
● PHRASES **in a different league** *Today's technology is in a different league* (= very much better). **in a league of your own** *As a painter he is in a league of his own* (= much better than others). **not in the same league (as ...)** (= not nearly as good as), **out of sb's league** *A house like that is way out of our league* (= too expensive for us).

leak noun

1 small hole/crack
● VERB + LEAK **have** *The boat had a small leak.* | **spring** *The pipe has sprung a leak.* | **plug, stop** *I managed to plug the leak.*
● PREP. **~ in** *a leak in the roof*

2 when gas/liquid escapes
● ADJ. **major, serious** | **minor** | **slow** | **fuel, gas, oil, radiation, radioactive**
● VERB + LEAK **cause** *The dismantling of a nuclear reprocessing plant caused a leak of radioactivity yesterday.* | **detect, discover, find, notice, spot** *Fortunately, we spotted the leak in time.* | **fix, repair, stop** *The plumber fixed the leak.* | **prevent** *taking steps to prevent gas leaks in the future*
● LEAK + VERB **happen, occur**
● PREP. **~ from** *Pollution inspectors were called to a leak from a chemical factory.* **~ of** *a leak of dangerous chemicals*

3 giving away information
● ADJ. **security**
● LEAK + VERB **come from sth** *The leak could only have come from one source.*
● PREP. **~ about** *a security leak about a number of suspicious deaths among civil servants* **~ from** *a leak from the prime minister's office* **~ of** *a leak of confidential material* **~ to** *a leak to the American authorities*
● PHRASES **the source of a leak** *The organization's press secretary is thought to be the source of the leak.*

leak verb

1 allow sth to get out through a hole
● ADV. **badly** *The house was old and the roof leaked quite badly.* | **slightly**

2 tell sb about sth
● ADV. **carefully, deliberately** | **widely** *The document had been widely leaked.*
● PREP. **from** *Confidential information that has been leaked from the BBC.* **to** *The report was leaked to the press.*

lean verb

● ADV. **heavily** | **lightly** | **slightly** | **casually, easily, lazily, nonchalantly** | **eagerly** | **earnestly** | **confidentially, confidingly, conspiratorially** | **weakly, wearily** | **drunkenly** | **precariously** | **close, near** *He leaned closer, lowering his voice.* | **across, forward, down, out, over** *She leant forward eagerly to listen to him.* | **away, back, backwards** *He leaned back in his chair.* | **sideways**
● PREP. **across** *She was leaning confidentially across the table.* **against** *She leaned her head against his shoulder.* **into** *He leaned into the open doorway.* **on** *The old man was leaning heavily on a stick.* **out of** *She leaned precariously out of the window.* **over** *She leaned casually over the railings.* **through** *The taxi driver leaned through his window.* **towards** *He leaned towards her.*

PHRASAL VERB
lean on sb/sth
● ADV. **heavily** *Britain leans heavily on Europe for trade.*

leap noun

1 big jump
● ADJ. **big, giant, prodigious** | **little** | **flying, running** *He made a flying leap at the ball.*
● VERB + LEAP **make, take**
● PREP. **~ from, ~ into** *a leap into the air* **~ to**

2 great change/increase in sth
● ADJ. **big, enormous, giant, great, huge, quantum** *There has been a quantum leap in profits since 1995.* | **small** | **bold, dramatic, sudden** *a dramatic leap in the number of people out of work* | **imaginative, intuitive** | **technological**
● VERB + LEAP **make** *They've made a great leap forward with their road building in the last few years.*
● PREP. **~ from** *a leap from $632 to $735* **~ in** *a leap in prices* **~ of** *a leap of 750%* **~ to**
● PHRASES **a leap forward, by leaps and bounds, come on/improve in leaps and bounds** *His technique has come on in leaps and bounds this season.*

leap verb

● ADV. **almost, nearly** *He almost leaped down the stairs when he heard who it was.* | **immediately** | **suddenly** | **clear, high** *She leaped clear of the water.* | **about, around, back, down, forward, out, up (and down)** *children leaping about with excitement*
● VERB + LEAP **seem to** *(figurative) The photograph seemed to leap off the page at her.* | **be about to, be ready to** *Don't be so nervous—anyone would think I was about to leap on you.*

● PREP. **across** *leaping across the puddles* from *He leaped down from the ladder and ran over towards her.* **into, off, on, onto** *He leaped onto his horse and rode off.* **out of** *He leaped out of bed when he heard the telephone.* **over** *leaping over high fences*
● PHRASES **leap to your feet** *Rosie immediately leaped to her feet.*

learn *verb*

1 gain knowledge/skill
● ADV. **a lot** *I learned a lot from my father.* | **quickly, soon** *Children learn very quickly.* ◇ *They soon learn that bad behaviour is a sure-fire way of getting attention.*
● VERB + LEARN **need to** | **be eager to, want to** *He was eager to learn all she could teach him.* | **have a lot to** *I've got a lot to learn, haven't I?*
● PREP. **about** *learning about art* **from** *She learned from watching others.* **through** *Children learn through play.*

2 become aware
● VERB + LEARN **be astonished to, be astounded to, be intrigued to, be surprised to** *I was surprised to learn that he was only 24.* | **be dismayed to, be saddened to**
● PREP. **of** *We first learned of the problem from her school.*

learner *noun*

● ADJ. **quick, slow** *She was a quick learner, and her German got better by the day.* | **advanced, intermediate** *a book for advanced learners of English* | **adult, older** | **young** *The book has been written with the interests of young learners in mind.* | **language** | **foreign**
● LEARNER + NOUN **driver**

learning *noun*

1 process of learning sth
● ADJ. **effective, successful** *a model for effective learning* | **rapid** | **independent** | **distance** (= by correspondence course) | **early** (= the education of very young children, often through play) | **higher** *institutions of higher learning* | **active, passive** | **formal, informal** | **rote** | **computer-assisted** | **language**
● LEARNING + NOUN **curve** *The whole team has been on a steep learning curve since the project began.* | **environment** *The centre aims to provide a supportive learning environment.* | **experience, process** | **difficulty, disability** *severe learning difficulties*
● PHRASES **a seat of learning**

2 knowledge got from reading and studying
● ADJ. **great** | **book** (*old-fashioned*)
● VERB + LEARNING **acquire, gain**

lease *noun*

● ADJ. **long, long-term** | **short, short-term** | **ten-year, etc.** | **business, commercial** | **building, mining**
● VERB + LEASE **have, hold** *They've got a lease with five years to run.* | **draw up** | **acquire, buy, enter into, get, negotiate, obtain, sign, take** (**on/out/up**) *She has taken out a new ten-year lease on the flat.* | **grant** (**sb**), **sell** (**sb**) *A freeholder may grant a lease of any duration.* | **renew** | **forfeit, surrender** *They moved out and the lease was surrendered.* | **cancel, terminate** | **take over** | **transfer**
● LEASE + VERB **run** *The lease runs from April 19.* | **take effect** | **come up for renewal, expire, run out**
● PREP. **in a/the~** *a new clause in the lease* **on a~** *The company holds the building on a long lease.* **under a/the ~** *Under the new lease, the rent would go up.* | **~ of** *He took a lease of the premises.* **~ on** *The club has a 20-year lease on the property.*
● PHRASES **a clause in a lease, a condition of a lease, the length/period/term of a lease, a provision in a lease, the terms of the lease**

leather *noun*

● ADJ. **thick** | **thin** | **tough** | **soft** | **shiny** | **worn** | **genuine, real** | **imitation, synthetic** | **calf, chamois, etc.** | **morocco, patent** | **shoe**
● VERB + LEATHER **tan** | **treat** *The leather has been treated with wax.* | **polish** | **be made from/in/(out) of** *a coat made from buffalo leather* | **bind sth in** *Each volume is bound in genuine leather.*
● LEATHER + VERB **crack** *a cracked leather belt*
● PREP. **in ~** (= made of leather) *I'm looking for a pair of boots in dark brown leather.* **in ~s** (= wearing leather) *a biker in black leathers*

leave *noun*

1 period of time when you do not go to work
● ADJ. **annual** | **paid, unpaid** | **extended, indefinite, weekend** | **compassionate, maternity, parental, paternity, sabbatical, sick, study** | **home, shore**
● VERB + LEAVE **be entitled to, get, have** *How much annual leave do you get?* ◇ *I've still got some leave left this year.* | **go on, spend, take, use** (**up**) *She spent most of her leave with her family.* ◇ *I've still got some leave to use up.* | **save** *I'm saving all my leave to have a long holiday later in the year.* | **cancel** *When the war broke out all leave was cancelled.* | **give sb, grant sb** | **be due for, be owed** | **apply for**
● LEAVE + NOUN **entitlement**
● PREP. **on ~** *She's on leave until the end of the month.*

2 official permission to do sth
● ADJ. **special**
● VERB + LEAVE **ask, request** *He asked leave to absent himself for four days.* | **give sb, grant sb** | **obtain** | **refuse sb**
● PREP. **by sb's~** *The appeal can only be brought by leave of the trial judge.* **with/without sb's~** *No application may be made without the leave of the court.*
● PHRASES **absent without leave, leave of absence, without** (**so much as**) **a by your leave** (= without asking permission)

leave *verb*

● VERB + LEAVE **decide to** | **intend to, plan to, want to** | **be ready to** *We were all packed and ready to leave.* | **be about to, be going to** *Did you want something? I was just about to leave.* | **threaten to** *My secretary has threatened to leave.* | **attempt to, try to** *They were caught trying to leave the country.* | **refuse to** | **be compelled to, be forced to, be obliged to** | **ask sb to, order sb to** *They were being extremely rowdy and the manager had to ask them leave.* | **allow sb to, let sb** *I wanted to leave but they wouldn't let me.* | **enable sb to**
● PREP. **for** *They left for Scotland this morning.*

lecture *noun*

1 talk given to a group of people
● ADJ. **fascinating, interesting** | **boring** | **formal** | **illustrated** | **impromptu** | **guest** *A two-day event of guest lectures, seminars and workshops.* | **popular, public** | **annual** | **inaugural, introductory** *Professor Pearson gave the inaugural lecture in the new lecture theatre.* | **keynote, plenary** | **memorial**
● QUANT. **course, programme, series**
● VERB + LECTURE **deliver, give, present** | **hold, put on** *The society is putting on a series of lectures on the subject next term.* | **attend, go to, hear** (*formal*), **listen to** | **miss, skip** | **prepare, write**
● LECTURE + NOUN **course, programme, series** | **hall, room, theatre** | **notes** | **tour** | **circuit** *a familiar figure on the international lecture circuit*
● PREP. **at a/the~** *She wasn't at the lecture.* **during a/the~** *The fire bell went during his lecture.* **in a/the~** *She referred*

to Professor Jones's work in her lecture on Shakespeare's imagery. | **~ by** a lecture by Professor Snow **~ about/on, ~ to** a lecture to the Darwin Society
• PHRASES **a lecture entitled sth** a lecture entitled 'How to Prevent Food Poisoning' **a lecture on the subject of sth**

2 serious talk to sb about their behaviour
• ADJ. **little, long | severe, stern**
• VERB + LECTURE **give sb, read sb** She read me a stern lecture on ingratitude. | **get** I got a lecture from Dad about coming home on time. | **take**
• PREP. **~ about/on** I don't take lectures from anyone on how to behave. **~ from**

lecturer noun
• ADJ. **principal, senior | assistant, junior | college, university | guest, visiting | English, physics, etc.**
• PREP. **~ in** a lecturer in German at Plymouth University
⇒ Note at JOB

ledge noun
• ADJ. **high | narrow, wide | cliff, mountain, window**
• VERB + LEDGE **cling to** The climbers were clinging to a ledge hundreds of feet above the sea. | **be perched on**
• LEDGE + VERB **go, run** A narrow ledge runs across the northern face of the cliff.
• PREP. **along a/the~** I felt along the ledge at the top of the door. **on a/the~** The phone was perched precariously on the window ledge.

left noun
1 side
• ADJ. **extreme, far** My dad's in the front row, on the extreme left of the picture.
• VERB + LEFT **turn to** If you turn to your left you will see the parliament building.
• PREP. **from the ~** The car came from the left. **on the/your~** The bank is on the left, just after the post office. ◇ As you go in the door, you'll see it on your left. **on the~ of** The car park is on the left of the library. **to the/your~** He looked to the left and then crossed. **to the ~ of** My office is just to the left of the main door.
• PHRASES **from left to right; from right to left** Arabic script reads from right to left.

2 the left political groups
• ADJ. **extreme, far**
• PREP. **of the~** In recent years the country has been ruled only by governments of the left. **on the ~** They're both on the extreme left of the party. **to the ~** The party has moved further to the left. ◇ He is somewhat to the left of the previous leader.

leg noun
1 part of the body
• ADJ. **left, right | front | back, hind | long | short, stumpy | beautiful, good, shapely | muscled, muscular, powerful, strong | skinny, spindly, thin | fat | bandy | hairy | bare | artificial, wooden | bad, stiff | broken, fractured | lame, withered** He sat down with his lame leg outstretched. | **tired** She crossed the finish line on tired legs. | **fresh** They don't train the day before a match to ensure they have fresh legs. | **outstretched**
• VERB + LEG **bend | brace** He put his back against the car, braced his legs and pushed. | **straighten | cross** I moved the chair away from the table so I could cross my legs. | **splay, spread** They made him put his hands on the police car and spread his legs. | **extend, stretch (out)** She stretched her legs under the table. ◇ (figurative) It was good to get out of the car and stretch our legs (= walk about). | **lift** The dog lifted its leg against the lamp post. | **draw up, tuck under** She sat with her legs drawn up underneath her. | **kick | swing** She swung her legs over

the side of the bed and reached for her crutches. | **entwine, tangle** They gazed at each other, their legs entwined under the table. | **break, injure | amputate** She had her leg amputated below the knee. | **shave**
• LEG + VERB **move** They ran together, their legs moving in unison. | **flail, kick** He jumped to avoid the flailing leg of the defender. | **pump** She started running, fat legs pumping. | **bend | buckle, give way** His legs buckled and he collapsed on the floor. | **shake, tremble | dangle, hang, swing** He sat with his legs dangling off the bridge. | **ache**
• LEG + NOUN **exercise | muscle | injury, pains, trouble, ulcer, wound | room** (also **legroom**) You don't get much legroom on economy-class flights.
• PREP. **between the/your ~s** The dog sloped off, its tail between its legs. **in the ~** He was shot in the leg by a sniper. **on the/your ~** I've got a big bruise on my leg. **on one ~** Many birds are able to stand on one leg for hours at a time.
• PHRASES **(have, etc.) your leg in plaster** He was wheeled out of the hospital with his leg in plaster.

2 of trousers
• ADJ. **trouser**
• VERB + LEG **pull up, roll up** He rolled up his trouser legs. | **roll down**
• PHRASES **long/short in the leg** These jeans are too long in the leg.

3 of a journey/race
• ADJ. **first, second, etc. | final, last | anchor** The fastest runner often runs the anchor leg (= the last one) of a relay. | **outbound | homeward**
• PREP. **on the … ~** At last we were on the homeward leg of our journey.

legacy noun
1 money/property
• ADJ. **generous, large | small**
• VERB + LEGACY **bequeath (sb), leave (sb) | get, receive** He received a large legacy from his uncle.
• PREP. **in a/the ~** She left her the money in a legacy. | **~ from** a legacy from my old teacher
• PHRASES **heir to a legacy** She is the heir to a legacy of £1 million.

2 result of previous events
• ADJ. **enduring | historical** These problems have arisen as a result of historical legacies. | **bitter, grim**
• VERB + LEGACY **bequeath (sb), leave (sb), leave behind** the enduring legacy bequeathed by the war years
• PREP. **~ from** Such attitudes are a legacy from colonial times.

legal adj.
• VERBS **be | become**
• ADV. **completely, perfectly** It is perfectly legal to charge extra for these services.

legality noun
• ADJ. **doubtful, dubious**
• VERB + LEGALITY **challenge, question** Her lawyer is challenging the legality of the court order. | **assert, recognize, uphold** The government does not recognize the legality of this court.
• PHRASES **doubt/doubts about the legality of sth**

legend noun
1 well-known story
• ADJ. **ancient | Greek, Roman, etc. | local**
• VERB + LEGEND **become, pass into** The story of how she was rescued has already passed into legend. | **tell (sb)** He told us the legend of the ghostly horseman.
• LEGEND + VERB **live on** The legend of his supernatural origins lives on.

● PREP. **according to~** *According to ancient legend, the river is a goddess.* **in (a/the)~** *There have always been stories of human giants in Celtic legend and mythology.* | **~about** *legends about the Vikings* **~of** *The story is part of the ancient legend of King Arthur.*
● PHRASES **legend has it that …** *Legend has it that the Bridge of Sighs got its name from the cries of prisoners being led across it.* **myths and legends** *the myths and legends of Mexico* **the subject of legend** *The unusual shell has long been the subject of legend.*

2 famous person/event
● ADJ. **living** *pop stars who become living legends* | **basketball, motoring, racing, sporting, etc.**

legible *adj.*

● VERBS **be**
● ADV. **clearly, easily** *Her handwriting was clearly legible.* | **perfectly** | **barely, scarcely**
● PREP. **to** *The price must be legible to a purchaser.*

legislation *noun*

● ADJ. **parliamentary** | **draft** | **fresh, further, new** | **effective, tough** | **complex** | **controversial** | **unworkable** *The police think that such legislation would be unworkable.* | **knee-jerk** *The terrorist attack prompted knee-jerk legislation.* | **anti-abortion, anti-discrimination, employment, environmental, financial, gun control, health, housing, social, etc.**
● QUANT. **piece** *a major piece of legislation*
● VERB + LEGISLATION **need, require** | **call for, propose** *They are calling for tough legislation to tackle this problem.* | **draft, draw up** | **bring forward, initiate** *Anyone has the right to initiate legislation in Parliament by means of a private bill.* | **approve, enact, introduce, pass** *Congress approved legislation which outlawed the sale of the drug.* | **adopt** *Member states may not adopt legislation contrary to EU law.* | **block, delay** *The reform will make it more difficult for MPs to block legislation.* | **amend** | **repeal** | **comply with** *Companies have until December 31 to comply with the new legislation.*
● LEGISLATION + VERB **come into effect, come into force** *New legislation on drink-driving comes into effect at the end of the year.*
● PREP. **under~** *This will be a criminal offence under the new legislation.* | **~against** *They are planning the introduction of legislation against sex discrimination.* **~on** *Legislation on this issue is urgently needed.*

legislature *noun*

● ADJ. **highest, supreme** | **bicameral, unicameral** | **109-member, etc.** | **elected** | **standing** | **central, federal, national, provincial, state**
● VERB + LEGISLATURE **be elected to** *She is the youngest woman to be elected to the national legislature.*
● LEGISLATURE + VERB **comprise sth, consist of sth** *The legislature comprises a 212-member Chamber of Deputies elected for a four-year term.* | **pass sth** *The legislature passed a law to prohibit the dumping of nuclear waste.* | **vote** *The legislature voted narrowly to table a motion of no-confidence in the government.*

legitimate *adj.*

● VERBS **be, seem** | **consider sth, deem sth, regard sth as, see sth as**
● ADV. **entirely, perfectly, quite** | **apparently**

leisure *noun*

● VERB + LEISURE **have** *We have more leisure than our parents had.*
● LEISURE + NOUN **hours, time** | **activities, interests,** **pursuits** | **centre, complex** | **facilities** | **equipment, goods** | **industry**

lemon *noun*

● ADJ. **fresh**
● QUANT. **slice, wedge** *Garnish the fish with wedges of lemon.*
● VERB + LEMON **squeeze** *Squeeze a quarter of a lemon over the fish.* | **slice** | **garnish sth with**
● LEMON + NOUN **tree** | **pip** | **peel, rind, zest** | **juice**
⇨ Special page at FRUIT

lend *verb*

● ADV. **kindly** *She very kindly lent me her bicycle.*
● VERB + LEND **be prepared to, be willing to** | **refuse to, be unwilling to** *The bank was unwilling to lend him the money.* | **persuade sb to**
● PREP. **to** *I've lent my car to George for the weekend.*

lender *noun*

● ADJ. **big, large, leading, major** *The bank is the largest mortgage lender in the country.* | **money, mortgage**
● PREP. **~to** *The bank was an important lender to the British government.*

length *noun*

1 distance from one end to the other
● ADJ. **entire, full, maximum, whole** *There is a maximum length of 2 500 words.* ◇ *The queue stretched the whole length of the High Street.* | **great** *a ditch of great length and width* | **medium** | **overall, total**
● VERB + LENGTH **estimate, measure** *He measured the length and width of the table.* | **have** *The vehicle has an overall length of 12 feet.* | **grow to, reach** *These fish can reach a length of over two metres.* | **double in, increase in** | **cut sth to** *Measure the size of the window and cut the cloth to length.* | **drive, run, swim, travel, walk, etc.** *The fence runs the length of the footpath.*
● PREP. **along the~ of** *There were coloured lights along the whole length of the street.* **in~** *The pipe was two metres in length.*
● PHRASES **at arm's length** *He has to hold newspapers at arm's length to focus on the print.* **double, twice, three times, half, etc. the length of sth** *The queen bee is twice the length of a worker bee.*

2 amount of time that sth lasts
● ADJ. **considerable, great, inordinate** | **reasonable**
● VERB + LENGTH **cut, reduce, shorten** | **increase**
● LENGTH + VERB **increase** | **decrease**
● PREP. **at~** *He told me at length about his new job.* **in~** *Each lesson was an hour in length.*
● PHRASES **length of time** *They complained about the inordinate length of time they had to wait.*

3 length of a swimming pool
● VERB + LENGTH **do, swim** *I did 20 lengths today.*

lengthy *adj.*

● VERBS **be**
● ADV. **extremely, very** *Agreement was finally reached after very lengthy discussions.* | **fairly, quite, rather, reasonably, relatively, somewhat** *After a fairly lengthy delay, we were able to continue.*

leniency *noun*

● ADJ. **great** *Judges are advised to show greater leniency towards first-time offenders.* | **excessive, undue**
● VERB + LENIENCY **show** | **appeal for, beg for**
● PREP. **~for** *She begged for leniency for her son.* **~of** *the undue leniency of the sentence* **~to** *Police offer leniency to*

criminals in return for information. ~**towards** *Let's hope the judge shows leniency towards her.*
• PHRASES **a plea for leniency** *Even the victim's family made a plea for leniency on behalf of the accused.*

lenient *adj.*

• VERBS **be, seem** | **become**
• ADV. **extremely, very** | **quite, relatively** | **excessively, unduly** *The appeal judge agreed that the original sentence was unduly lenient.*
• PREP. **with** *The police are sometimes more lenient with female offenders.*

lens *noun*

• ADJ. **strong, thick** *She wears glasses with very thick lenses.* | **coloured, tinted** | **contact** | **optical, spectacle** | **camera** | **fish-eye, long, long-focus, magnifying, telephoto, telescopic, wide-angle, zoom** *a long-lens shot of a rare bird* ◇ *The photograph was taken using a zoom lens.*
• LENS + NOUN **cap** *I took the lens cap off my camera and waited for a good shot.*
• PREP. **through a/the** ~ *Put your hand in front of your right lens and just look through your left lens.*

leprosy *noun*

• VERB + LEPROSY **have, suffer from** | **contract**
• LEPROSY + NOUN **bacillus** | **patient, sufferer, victim**
⇒ Special page at ILLNESS

lesbian *noun*

• ADJ. **butch** | **femme, lipstick**
• VERB + LESBIAN **come out as** *She came out as a lesbian in her teens.*
• LESBIAN + NOUN **icon** *The singer has become a lesbian icon.*

lessen *verb*

• ADV. **considerably, greatly, significantly** *Eating a good diet significantly lessens the risk of heart disease.* | **gradually** *Time had gradually lessened the pain of her grief.*
• VERB + LESSEN **begin to** *The noise began to lessen.* | **try to** | **tend to** *Too much background detail tends to lessen the impact of the central image.* | **help (to)** *Regular exercise can help to lessen the pain.*

lesson *noun*

1 period of teaching or learning
• ADJ. **good, interesting** | **boring** | **individual** | **private** | **driving, English, geography, maths, piano, swimming,** etc.
• VERB + LESSON **attend, go to, have, take** *I go to Italian lessons at the local college.* ◇ *We had a history lesson followed by a double maths lesson.* ◇ *I'm taking driving lessons at the moment.* | **give (sb), offer (sb), provide, take, teach** *She gives singing lessons.* ◇ *They're offering free lessons in computing.* ◇ *I had to take a biology lesson this afternoon because the biology teacher was away.* ◇ *He doesn't teach very many lessons these days.* | **get** *Pupils get lessons on how to organize their study time.* | **prepare** *The trouble is that teachers don't prepare their lessons carefully enough.* | **skip** *He got into trouble for skipping lessons.*
• PREP. **during a/the** ~ *No talking was allowed during the lesson.* **in a/the** ~ *You can't expect to learn all there is to know about the subject in a 45-minute lesson.* | ~**about** *a lesson about the Civil War* ~**in** *He took lessons in Thai cookery.* ~**on** *a lesson on the Roman Empire* ~**with** *They've got a lesson with Mrs Evans at two o'clock.*

2 sth learnt through experience
• ADJ. **important, salutary, useful, valuable** | **bitter, hard, painful** *It's a hard lesson to learn.* | **clear**
• VERB + LESSON **draw, learn** *What lessons can we draw from this unfortunate experience?* | **teach sb** *It taught me some valuable lessons about working with other people.*
• PREP. ~**from** *There are important lessons to be learnt from this mistake.* ~**in** *I learned a lesson in harsh economics when I was made redundant.*

lethal *adj.*

• VERBS **be, prove**
• ADV. **absolutely** *All these knives are absolutely lethal.* | **pretty** | **potentially** *It was a potentially lethal mixture of drugs.*
• PREP. **to** *The pesticide is lethal to all insect life.*

lethargy *noun*

• VERB + LETHARGY **be overcome by, feel, suffer from** *She was suddenly overcome by lethargy.* | **sink into** | **drag/stir yourself out of, overcome, shake off** *He felt that he had to drag himself out of his lethargy and begin to write.*
• LETHARGY + VERB **creep over/through sb, overtake sb** *After the meal, I could feel lethargy overtaking me.*
• PHRASES **a feeling of lethargy**

letter *noun*

1 written/printed message
• ADJ. **lengthy, long** | **brief, short** | **ten-page, etc.** | **rambling** | **countless, endless, numerous** *She received countless letters of support while in jail.* | **occasional** *Apart from the occasional letter, they had not been in touch for years.* | **incoming** *The porter distributes incoming letters to the offices.* | **urgent** | **airmail** | **handwritten** | **anonymous** | **formal, official** | **business** | **personal** | **confidential, private** | **open, public** *The editor published an open letter to the prime minister.* | **circular** | **chain** | **form, standard** | **specimen** | **accompanying, covering, explanatory** *The conditions are explained in the accompanying letter.* ◇ *Send your CV with a covering letter.* | **thank-you** *I wrote my uncle a thank-you letter as soon as I opened the present.* | **congratulatory** | **warning** | **rejection** *I've had job interviews and received ten rejection letters.* | **resignation** | **suicide** | **fan** | **love** | **affectionate, intimate** | **charming, delightful** | **chatty, cheerful, friendly** | **heartfelt, impassioned** *She wrote an impassioned letter to her local newspaper to complain about the new road.* | **courteous, polite** | **apologetic** | **angry, rude, strong, strongly-worded, threatening** | **indignant** | **critical** | **frank** | **poison pen** *He had been sending poison pen letters to his neighbours, hoping to make them move away.*
• VERB + LETTER **draft, write** *drafting an angry letter to the newspaper* | **read** | **get, have, receive** *I haven't had a letter from her for ages.* | **post, send** | **fax** | **deliver** | **forward** *The letter was forwarded from my old address.* | **register** | **seal** | **open** | **acknowledge, answer, reply to, respond to** *I was angry that they didn't even acknowledge my letter.* | **address** *The letter was addressed to me.* | **sign** | **publish** *The newspaper refused to publish the letter.*
• LETTER + VERB **arrive, come, reach sb** *I hope my last letter has reached you.* | **be dated ...** *The letter is dated 7 July.* | **cross** *Our letters crossed in the post.* | **be lost, go astray** | **announce sth, ask (sb) sth, begin, start (off)** *The letter started off by thanking us for our offer.* | **continue, go on** *His letter went on to give reasons for his refusal to take part.* | **conclude, end** *The letter concluded with a threat of possible legal action.* | **contain sth** *The letter contained information that only the killer could*

know. | **enclose sth** *The charity received an anonymous letter enclosing a large cheque.* | **appear** *A letter headed 'Advertising Mania' appeared in the paper.*
● LETTER + NOUN **writing** | **box** *The postman put a bundle of letters through the letter box.* | **bomb**
● PREP. **by~** *Please reply by letter.* **in a/the~** *In your letter of 5 June ...* | **~ about/concerning/regarding, ~ from,** **~of** *a letter of application/apology* **~to** *a letter to the editor*

2 sign that represents a sound in a language
● ADJ. **big, large** | **block, capital, upper-case** *Fill in the form in block letters.* | **lower-case, small** | **bold** | **initial** *The company's name is made from the initial letters of his children's names.* | **double** *Words with double letters, such as 'accommodation', are commonly misspelt.* | **silent** *words such as 'debt' and 'half', which contain silent letters*
● PREP. **in ... ~s** *His name was written in large white letters over the doorway.*
● PHRASES **the letters of the alphabet**

lettuce *noun*

● ADJ. **crisp, crunchy** | **limp** | **chopped, shredded** | **cos, Iceberg,** etc.
● QUANT. **head** *You need one whole head of lettuce for this salad.*
● VERB + LETTUCE **eat, have** *All she had was a tomato and some lettuce.* | **wash**
● LETTUCE + NOUN **leaf**
● PHRASES **on a bed of lettuce**
⇨ Special page at FOOD

leukaemia *noun*

● ADJ. **childhood**
● VERB + LEUKAEMIA **have, suffer from** | **contract, develop** | **diagnose** | **treat sb for**
● LEUKAEMIA + NOUN **case, patient, sufferer, victim** | **research** | **cluster** *The newspapers are full of stories of leukaemia clusters near nuclear establishments.*
⇨ Special page at ILLNESS

level *noun*

1 amount/size/number
● ADJ. **high, record, significant, substantial** *Industrial output has reached record levels.* | **increasing, rising** | **excessive** *Excessive levels of lead were found in the water.* | **low** | **decreasing, falling** | **varying** *keen amateurs who work hard, with varying levels of success* | **generous** *a generous level of financial support for the arts* | **permitted, recommended, required** *permitted levels of chemical pollutants* | **acceptable, adequate, necessary, normal, realistic, reasonable, safe** *an acceptable level of risk* ◇ *Her blood pressure has returned to its normal level.* | **dangerous, unacceptable** | **worst** *the worst level of business failure since 1997* | **noise, pollution, radiation** | **crime** | **blood-sugar, cholesterol, hormone,** etc. | **stress**
● VERB + LEVEL **achieve, reach** *They have achieved higher levels of efficiency.* ◇ *Crime has reached its highest level ever.* | **remain at** *She predicts that fuel prices will remain at current levels.* | **improve, increase, raise** | **maintain** | **bring down, control, decrease, keep down, lower, reduce** | **change** | **set** *Emissions are well below the levels set by the World Health Authority.* | **exceed** *There will be stiff penalties if companies exceed these levels of pollution.*
● LEVEL + VERB **go up, rise, soar** | **fall, go down, plummet** | **change, vary**
● PREP. **above a/the ~** *Mortgage rates were 10% above their current level.* **at a/the~** *Rents will be kept at this level for another year.* **below a/the~** *Radiation is well below the permitted level.*

2 stage of progress/standard
● ADJ. **basic, elementary, low** *The teaching is at quite a basic level.* | **entry** *They have a good range of entry-level*

computers for beginners. | **intermediate** | **advanced, high** *Her illness has reached an advanced level.* | **degree** | **difficulty** *The difficulty of the exercises in the book varies widely.* | **fitness** *a sport suitable for people of all fitness levels*
● VERB + LEVEL **attain, reach** *students who have reached the intermediate level* | **complete, do, take** *You need to do all three levels to qualify as a canteen supervisor.*
● PREP. **above a/the ~** *His English is way above the level of the other students.* **at a/the ~** *students at intermediate level* ◇ *She has played tennis at a high level.* **below a/the~** *The book is not suitable for students below degree level.*

3 grade in an organization or structure
● ADJ. **high, upper** *the upper levels of the civil service* | **low** | **senior** | **global, international, local, national, regional** | **grass-roots** *The party needs to win support at grass-roots level.* | **ministerial** | **board** *These decisions are made at board level.*
● VERB + LEVEL **reach, rise to** *He rose to the level of general manager.*
● PREP. **at a/the~** *At the local level there's a lot to be said for the plan.* **on a/the~** *The thing has got to be organized on an international level.*

4 way of considering sth
● ADJ. **conscious, unconscious** *At a conscious level, I was quite satisfied with my life.* | **deep** | **superficial** | **detailed** *We probably need to look at this problem at a more detailed level.* | **general** | **practical** | **theoretical** | **political**
● PREP. **at a/the~, on a/the~** *On a superficial level everything appears to be in order, but at a deeper level you an see that there's a lot wrong.*

5 height
● ADJ. **high, low** | **ground, sea, water** *the problem of rising sea levels* | **eye** *a shelf at eye level*
● VERB + LEVEL **adjust, change, lower, raise** *They are going to raise the level of the banks to prevent flooding.*
● PREP. **above a/the~** *200m above sea level* **at a/the~** *The plane was flying at a very low level.* **below a/the~** *below the level of the cloud* **on a~with** *On the second floor you are on a level with the treetops.* **to a/the~** *The water rose to the level of the ground floor windows.*
● PHRASES **a change in/of level**

6 floor in a building
● ADJ. **ground, lower** | **higher, top, upper**
● PREP. **on a/the~** *Are we on the right level for the restaurant?* **to a/the~** *Take the lift to Level Four.*

level *adj.*

1 with no part higher than any other
● VERBS **be, look, seem** | **get sth, keep sth** *Make sure you get the shelf level before screwing it in.* ◇ *Keep the pot level, or you'll spill the coffee.*
● ADV. **absolutely, completely** *The floor has got to be absolutely level.* | **approximately, more or less**

2 at the same height/position as sth
● VERBS **be** | **come, draw** *As they reached the final bend, Graham drew level and threatened too overtake him.*
● ADV. **almost**
● PREP. **with** *The top of the water came level with her chin.*

lever *noun*

1 handle for operating a machine
● ADJ. **brake, control, gear**
● VERB + LEVER **move, operate, position, press, pull, push, put, release, set, throw** *When the lever is operated, the machine sews backwards.* ◇ *To release the brake, pull the lever towards you.* ◇ *Push the gear lever into first.* ◇ *The machine will stop immediately once the lever is*

released. ◊ *Set all three levers to the 0 position.* ◊ *He threw a lever and the engines roared to life.*
- PREP. **by (means of) a ~** *The machine is operated by means of a lever.*
- PHRASES **the position of the lever**

2 means of achieving sth
- ADJ. **powerful, useful**
- VERB + LEVER **act as, be, give sb, provide (sb with), serve as | use sth as**
- PREP. **~against** *If this allegation is true, it will give us a useful lever against him.* **~for** *This could serve as a powerful lever for peace.*

leverage *noun*

1 force
- ADJ. **enough, sufficient | extra | maximum**
- VERB + LEVERAGE **have** *He tried to push the door open, but he didn't have sufficient leverage.* **| gain, get, obtain | apply, exert** *Position the piece of wood so that maximum leverage can be applied.* **| provide | increase**

2 influence
- ADJ. **economic, political**
- VERB + LEVERAGE **have | gain** *They are determined to gain more political leverage.* **| give sb**

liability *noun*

1 responsibility
- ADJ. **full | legal**
- VERB + LIABILITY **have** *They have no legal liability for damage to customers' possessions.* **| accept, acknowledge, admit, assume | deny**
- PREP. **~for** *They have denied liability for the accident.*

2 liabilities money owed
- ADJ. **substantial | financial, tax** *an assessment of the company's financial liabilities*
- VERB + LIABILITIES **have | take on, take over** *He wants to know the precise amount of the liabilities he is taking over.* **| cover, discharge, meet** *There is enough money to cover existing liabilities.* **| reduce**
- PREP. **~to** *The company has liabilities to its employees.*

liable *adj.*

- VERBS **be | become | remain | make sb, render sb** *Failure to provide insurance rendered him liable to prosecution.* **| find sb, hold sb** *They could be found liable for the entire amount.*
- ADV. **strictly | fully | potentially | personally | jointly, severally** (*law*) *Partners are jointly and severally* (= together and individually) *liable for a partnership's debts.* **| vicariously** *Under this rule, if Y is employed by X, X will be vicariously liable for the actions of Y.* **| criminally, financially, legally**
- PREP. **for** *She's fully liable for the company's debts.*

liaise *verb*

- ADV. **closely, directly**
- PREP. **between** *Her job is to liaise between the school and the home.* **with** *The tax office liaises closely with our department on such matters.*

liaison *noun*

1 communication
- ADJ. **close, effective, good | poor | community, customer | military**
- VERB + LIAISON **maintain** *We maintained a close liaison with the trade union.* **| establish** *We are hoping to establish better customer liaison.* **| improve**
- LIAISON + NOUN **committee, group, unit | officer | work**
- PREP. **in ~ with** *It's important that we work in close li-*

aison with other charities in this field. **| ~between** *good liaison between management and staff ~* **with** *She is responsible for liaison with researchers at other universities.*

2 sexual relationship
- ADJ. **romantic, sexual | adulterous**
- VERB + LIAISON **have** *She was having a romantic liaison with her husband's best friend.* **| form**
- PREP. **~with**

liar *noun*

- ADJ. **accomplished, good** *She's an accomplished liar—they believed every word she said.* **| bad, poor | big, terrible** *She's the biggest liar I've ever known.* **| compulsive, habitual, pathological**
- VERB + LIAR **call sb** *Are you calling me a liar?*

libel *noun*

- ADJ. **alleged | criminal, seditious**
- VERB + LIBEL **sue (sb) for | claim | deny**
- LIBEL + NOUN **action, case, proceedings, suit | writ | law, lawyer | damages**
- PREP. **~against** *He has issued a writ for libel against the radio star Michael Clery.*
⇨ Note at CRIME (for more verbs)

liberal *noun*

- ADJ. **leading | bourgeois, middle-class | old-fashioned, traditional | radical | market | economic, political, social**
- LIBERAL + NOUN **leader, party**

liberal *adj.*

1 respecting other opinions
- VERBS **be**
- ADV. **remarkably, very | fairly, quite, relatively** *His attitudes are quite liberal.*

2 in politics
- VERBS **be**
- ADV. **comparatively, relatively** *comparatively liberal in trade matters* **| broadly, essentially** *a broadly liberal policy programme*

3 generous
- VERBS **be | become**
- ADV. **very**
- PREP. **with** *She's very liberal with her advice!*

liberalism *noun*

- ADJ. **radical | bourgeois | laissez-faire | market | economic, political, social**

liberation *noun*

- ADJ. **animal, gay, national, personal, sexual, women's**
- VERB + LIBERATION **achieve**
- LIBERATION + NOUN **movement**
- PREP. **~by** *the liberation of the capital by allied forces* **~from** *the struggle for liberation from colonial rule*
- PHRASES **a feeling/sense of liberation** *Up in the mountains we had the most wonderful sense of liberation.* **a fight/struggle for liberation, a war of liberation**

liberty *noun*

- ADJ. **great | complete | basic** *a citizens' charter which gives people basic civil liberties* **| civil, individual, personal, political, religious**
- VERB + LIBERTY **enjoy, have | demand, fight for | win** *The city won its liberty in the sixteenth century.* **| lose** *If found guilty, she is in danger of losing her liberty.* **| defend, protect, safeguard** *The law should protect the lib-*

erty of the individual. | **threaten** The new legislation threatens individual liberty. | **erode, restrict** Our personal liberty is being eroded. | **deny, deprive sb of, destroy** | **allow sb, give sb** The system allows us complete liberty to do the task as we like.
• PREP. **at** ~ The escaped prisoner has been at liberty for five days. | ~ **for** demanding greater liberty for women ~ **from** liberty from the abuse of police power
• PHRASES **an infringement of liberty, loss of liberty, a threat to liberty**

librarian noun

• ADJ. **professional, qualified** | **chief, head, senior** | **assistant** | **branch, country** | **academic, public, reference** | **college, school, university**
⇨ Note at JOB (for verbs)

library noun

1 building
• ADJ. **large, small** | **excellent, good** | **public** | **private** | **branch, county, local, national, regional** | **mobile** A number of councils operate mobile libraries. | **well-stocked** | **circulating** (historical), **lending, subscription** In 1784 he established his first circulating library. | **reference** | **general** | **special, specialist** | **academic, research** | **college, departmental, school, university** | **copyright** It is a copyright library and receives three copies of all books published in Britain.
• VERB + LIBRARY **have** The school has an excellent library. | **go to, use, visit** How often do you go to the library? | **borrow sth from, get/take sth out of** I got this very interesting book out of the library. | **return sth to, take sth back to** Do you have any books to take back to the library? | **be available at/from** Do you know about the other services available at your local library? | **have access to** Everyone in the country should have access to a lending library.
• LIBRARY + VERB **have sth, hold sth** The library has an extensive collection of books on French history.
• LIBRARY + NOUN **book** | **shelf** | **catalogue** | **ticket** | **assistant, staff** | **user** | **facilities, provision, resources, service** the need to improve library provision | **skills** teaching library skills to schoolchildren
• PREP. **at a/the** ~ a holiday programme for children at the local library **in a/the** ~ I've been reading newspapers in the library.

2 collection of books, etc.
• ADJ. **considerable, extensive** | **fine, impressive, magnificent, valuable** | **personal** | **film, music, photographic, picture, video**
• VERB + LIBRARY **have, possess** The family possessed an extensive library. | **amass, build (up)** She had built up an impressive library of art books. | **add to**
• PREP. ~ **of** a personal library of over 1 000 volumes

licence noun

• ADJ. **valid** | **special** | **car, driving** | **marriage** | **export, gaming, import, operating, trade, trading** The government is currently granting no operating licences to foreign firms. | **television/TV** | **gun** | **software, user** The CD-ROM comes with a single-user licence. | **entertainment, music** The bar was refused a music licence. | **hotel, refreshment, restaurant**
• VERB + LICENCE **have, hold** You have to have a licence to sell beer. ◇ Applicants must hold a valid driving licence. | **buy, gain, get, obtain, win** You can buy a TV licence at the post office. ◇ She gained her private pilot's licence. ◇ I got my driving licence when I was eighteen. ◇ The company has won the licence to run trains from the south coast to London. | **apply for, make an application for** | **grant (sb), issue** | **refuse sb** | **revoke, take away** He's

had his licence taken away. | **renew** | **lose** She lost her driving licence when she was caught drink-driving.
• LICENCE + VERB **expire, run out** The licence expires at the end of the year.
• LICENCE + NOUN **fee, holder**
• PREP. **in a/the** ~ All these details are specified in the licence. **under a/the** ~ The weapons were exported under a special export licence. **under** ~ They are Italian trains, but they will be built in Britain under licence. | ~ **for** a licence for software manufacture ~ **from** a licence from the Performing Rights Society
• PHRASES **the holder of a licence**

lid noun

1 removable top
• ADJ. **airtight, close-fitting, sealed, tight-fitting, tight** Choose a dish with a tight-fitting lid. | **hinged** | **box, case, coffin, dustbin, piano, saucepan,** etc.
• VERB + LID **lift, open, prise off, raise, remove, take off** She lifted the lid of the box. ◇ We managed to prise off the lid with a tyre lever. | **close, put down, put on, replace, screw down, screw on, shut** I poured some water and screwed the lid back on the bottle. ◇ The coffin lid had been screwed down. | **keep on** Keep the lid on the pan until the liquid comes to the boil.
• PREP. **on the** ~ His name was on the lid.

2 lids eyelids
• ADJ. **closed, drooping, half-closed, half-open, heavy, hooded, lowered, narrowed** She felt the tears burning against her closed lids.
• VERB + LIDS **close, lower** She saw James walk in and hastily lowered her lids. | **lift, open** She lifted her lids and found him looking at her.
• LIDS + VERB **droop** Heavy lids drooped over her eyes.
• PREP. **behind** ... ~ She could still see the light flickering behind her closed lids. **beneath** ... ~ She glanced at him occasionally from beneath lowered lids. **through** ... ~ He was watching her through hooded lids.

lie noun

• ADJ. **big, monstrous, (whopping) great** He told a whopping great lie! | **little** | **complete, downright, outright** That's a downright lie! | **white** A little white lie is surely excusable. | **deliberate** | **barefaced, blatant, obvious, transparent** | **elaborate** a web of elaborate lies
• VERB + LIE **tell (sb)** | **believe, swallow** How could she swallow such a blatant lie? | **live** He lived a lie for thirty years, pretending to be the faithful husband of two different women living in two different towns.
• LIE + NOUN **detector**
• PHRASES **a pack/tissue/web of lies**

lie verb

1 be in a flat position
• ADV. **down** He was lying down on the bed.
• PREP. **on** She lay on her stomach.
• PHRASES **lie asleep/awake** I used to lie awake at night worrying about it. **lie face down/prostrate** lying face down in the mud **lie flat** lying flat on the floor **lie motionless/still** Lie still while I put the bandage on. **lie sprawled** She lay sprawled on the sofa.

2 say sth that is not true
• ADV. **convincingly** He was unable to lie convincingly. | **easily**
• PREP. **about** She lied about her age. **to** Don't lie to me.

lieutenant noun

⇨ Note at RANK

life noun

1 living things
- ADJ. **intelligent** *Is there intelligent life on other planets?* | **animal, bird, human, insect, marine, plant**
- LIFE + NOUN **form** | **cycle**

2 existence
- VERB + LIFE **lose** *He lost his life in an air crash.* | **bring sb back to, restore sb to** | **cling to, fight for** *She clung to life for several weeks.* | **risk** *She risked her life for the sake of the children.* | **save** *a drug that will save lives* | **spare** *She begged the soldiers to spare her son's life.* | **give, lay down, sacrifice** | **claim, cost, end, take** *The crash claimed 43 lives.* ◇ *His foolishness almost cost him his life.* ◇ *She took her own life.* | **start** *(figurative) The restaurant started life as a cinema.*
- LIFE + VERB **be lost** *No lives were lost in the accident.*
- LIFE + NOUN **assurance, insurance**
- PHRASES **an attempt on sb's life** *There have been three attempts on the president's life.* **in fear for/of your life** *Witnesses are living in fear for their life after giving evidence against the gang.* **life after death** *Do you believe in life after death?* **loss of life** *The plane crashed with heavy loss of life.* **a matter of life and death** *(figurative) These talks are a matter of life and death for the factory.* **the right to life** *anti-abortionists campaigning for the right to life* **signs of life** *The driver showed no signs of life.*

3 period between birth and death
- ADJ. **long, short** | **entire, whole** | **early** | **adult** | **later** *In later life he took up writing.* | **past, previous** *He never discussed the unhappiness of his past life.* ◇ *I think I may have been an animal in a previous life.* | **future, next** | **working** *He was a miner all his working life.*
- VERB + LIFE **go through, live, spend** *She went through life always wanting what she couldn't get.* ◇ *He spent his whole life in Cornwall.* | **end** *He ended his life a happy man.* | **shorten** | **prolong** | **dedicate, devote** *He devoted his life to the education of deaf children.*
- LIFE + NOUN **history, story** | **membership** | **imprisonment, sentence** | **expectancy, span** (also **lifespan**) *Japanese people have a very high life expectancy.* ◇ *the lifespan of a mouse*
- PREP. **for ~** *She thought marriage should be for life.* **in your ~** *for the first time in her life* **throughout your ~** *Throughout her life she was dogged by loneliness.*
- PHRASES **all your life** *I've known her all my life.* **at sb's time of life** *At his time of life he should be starting to take things easy.* **the end of your life** *Her paintings became more obscure towards the end of her life.* **late in life** *She discovered jazz quite late in life.* **the ... of your life** *I had the fright of my life when I saw the snake in my bed.* ◇ *He met the love of his life at college.* **a phase/stage in/of (your) life** *She sensed she was entering a new phase in her life.* **the prime of life** *You're still in the prime of life.* **the remainder/rest of your life** *He'll be haunted by the crash for the rest of his life.*

4 activity in the world
- ADJ. **daily, day-to-day, everyday** | **real** *a real-life drama* | **modern** | **personal, private** *She did not tolerate press intrusion into her private life.* | **inner** *Only his wife had access to his inner life.* | **family, married** | **social** | **love, sex** | **public** *His fame was so sudden that he was unprepared for public life.* | **academic, business, cultural, economic, intellectual, political, professional, school** | **night** (also **nightlife**) *What's the nightlife like in the town?* | **city, village, etc.**
- VERB + LIFE **build, rebuild** *He built his whole life around his children.* ◇ *She is still rebuilding her life after the accident.*
- PHRASES **an attitude to life, an outlook on life, a philosophy/view of life** *I've always had a fairly optimistic outlook on life.* **a love of life** *He always had a great love of life.* **a man/woman in your life** *There has only been one*

woman in his life. **see sth of life** *I wanted to see something of life before I settled down.* **the ... side of life** *His time in London was his first glimpse of the seamier side of life.* **want sth from/in/out of life** *They both seem to want the same things out of life.*

5 way of living
- ADJ. **good, happy** | **lonely, miserable, sad, unhappy** | **hard** | **easy** | **active, busy, hectic** | **exciting** | **full** | **peaceful, quiet** | **normal, ordinary** | **healthy** | **sheltered** | **double** *He had been leading a double life, married to two women.*
- VERB + LIFE **have, lead, live** *She leads a busy social life.* | **enjoy** | **change** *Learning meditation changed her life.* | **dominate, take over** *He never let his work dominate his life.* | **ruin** *He ruined his life through drinking.*
- PHRASES **build/make/start a new life** *They went to Australia to start a new life.* **enjoy/live life to the full** *He always believed in living life to the full.* **the high life** *enjoying the high life in the smartest hotels and restaurants of New York* **live a life of ...** *They're living a life of luxury in the Bahamas.* **a/the pace of life** *The pace of life is much gentler on the island.* **the quality of life** *He gave up his high-flying job and now enjoys a better quality of life.* **a way of life** *She loved the Spanish way of life and immediately felt at home there.*

6 liveliness
- VERB + LIFE **come to** *The city only comes to life at night.* | **breathe, bring sth to, inject** *They need some new, younger staff to breathe some life into the company.* | **burst/hum/teem with** *a child bursting with life*
- PHRASES **full of life** *It's nice to see an old man still so full of life.*

lifeboat noun

- ADJ. **inshore, offshore**
- VERB + LIFEBOAT **get into, man, take to** *The crew took to the lifeboats.* | **call out** *The lifeboat was called out five times in the January storms.* | **launch**
- LIFEBOAT + VERB **be stationed ...** *The lifeboat is stationed just along the coast from here.*
- LIFEBOAT + NOUN **service** | **crew** | **house, shed, station**
- PREP. **aboard/on board a/the ~** *two survivors on board the lifeboat* **in/on a/the ~** *There was only room for ten people in the lifeboat.*

lifeless adj.

1 dead
- VERBS **appear, be, lie, look** *She lay lifeless in the snow.*
- ADV. **completely** | **almost, nearly** *His body was limp and almost lifeless.* | **apparently, seemingly** *She lay there, apparently lifeless.*

2 without living things
- VERBS **be**
- ADV. **completely** *a time when they earth was completely lifeless*

3 dull/without interest
- VERBS **be, seem** | **become**
- ADV. **completely** | **rather** *The acting was dull and rather lifeless.*

lifeline noun

1 rope
- VERB + LIFELINE **throw sb** | **catch, cling to** *He clung to the lifeline and the woman pulled him towards the bank.*

2 important help
- ADJ. **real, vital** *Visits from loved ones are a vital lifeline for prisoners.* | **financial** *The state pension is their financial lifeline.*
- VERB + LIFELINE **give sb, hold out, offer (sb), provide (sb with), throw sb (out)** *The organization provides*

a real lifeline for many women in poverty. ◇ *He threw me a lifeline when he offered me a job.* | **have** *With this one unexpected victory, the club now has a lifeline.*

lifestyle *noun*

• ADJ. **healthy, unhealthy** | **active** | **sedentary** | **busy, hectic** | **stressful** | **affluent, comfortable, expensive, extravagant, glamorous, lavish** | **modern** | **nomadic**
• VERB + LIFESTYLE **change** *She had to change her lifestyle and eating habits.* | **enjoy, have, lead** *They enjoy a very comfortable lifestyle.* | **adopt** *We want them to adopt a healthier lifestyle.*
• PHRASES **a change in lifestyle**

lifetime *noun*

• ADJ. **long** *wisdom gained in the course of a long lifetime* | **short** *A lifetime is too short for all the great books there are!* | **entire, whole**
• VERB + LIFETIME **devote, spend** *He devoted a lifetime to working with disabled children.* | **take (sb)** *It took a whole lifetime to solve the mystery of her father's disappearance.* | **last (sb)** *This watch should last you a lifetime.* | **seem (like)** *It seems a lifetime since we first met.*
• LIFETIME + NOUN **achievement** *The veteran director won a lifetime achievement award.* | **employment, income** *Payments are based on expected lifetime income.* | **lifetime's experience, lifetime's work**
• PREP. **after a ~** *After a lifetime as a journalist in the troublespots of the world, he retired to the country.* **during your ~** *I've seen many changes during my lifetime.* **in your ~** *The artist was little known in his lifetime.* **of a ~** *It was the holiday of a lifetime!* | **~ in** *She spent a lifetime in politics.* **~ of** *a lifetime of problems*
• PHRASES **the habits of a lifetime** *It's hard to break the habits of a lifetime.* **half a lifetime, a legend in your own lifetime** *Herbert von Karajan was a legend in his own lifetime.* **a lifetime ago/away** *University seems a half a lifetime away.* **once in a lifetime** *That sort of thing happens only once in a lifetime.*

lift *noun*

1 machine for taking people/goods up and down
• ADJ. **private, service** *The hotel has a private lift linking it to the beach.* | **baggage, goods, passenger, wheelchair** | **electric, hydraulic** | **basket, chair, gondola** | **ski**
• VERB + LIFT **go down in, go up in/on, take** *We took the lift down to the ground floor.* | **operate**
• LIFT + VERB **serve sth** *The lift serves the top four floors of the building.* | **arrive**
• LIFT + NOUN **button** | **doors** | **shaft** | **attendant** | **pass** *You'll need your lift pass for the ski lifts.*

2 free ride in a car, etc.
• ADJ. **free**
• VERB + LIFT **ask for, cadge, hitch, thumb** *We stood by the roadside and thumbed a lift.* | **give sb, offer sb** | **accept** *Don't accept lifts from strangers.*
• PHRASES **a lift back/home** *He offered us a lift home.*

3 feeling of increased happiness/excitement
• ADJ. **great, huge, real** *Winning the semi-final gave the team a huge lift.*
• VERB + LIFT **give sb** | **get**

lift *verb*

1 raise/move sb/sth
• ADV. **almost, half** *Her hugged her, almost lifting her off the ground.* | **fractionally, a little, slightly** | **slowly** | **sharply** *Her head lifted sharply* | **carefully, gently, gingerly** *Carefully lift the cake off the tray and cool on a wire rack.* | **bodily** *She was lifted bodily aboard by two sailors.* | **back, down, out, up** *She lifted back the sheet.*
• VERB + LIFT **can/could barely/hardly** *The box was so heavy I could barely lift it.* | **try to** | **manage to** | **be too heavy to**
• PREP. **above** *He stood, legs apart, arms lifted above his head.* **down** *She leaned on him and he half lifted her down the stairs.* **from** *He felt as if an enormous weight had been lifted from his shoulders.* **into** *The heavy beams were lifted into place.* **off** *She lifted the book up off the table.* **out of** *He lifted the baby out of its cot.* **over** *She lifted the child over the fence.* **to** *Juliet nodded, lifting her face to David's.*

2 remove a law/rule
• ADV. **completely** | **partially** *The police managed to restore calm and the curfew was partially lifted.*
• VERB + LIFT **agree to, decide to, vote to** *The government decided to lift the ban on arms exports.* | **refuse to**

ligament *noun*

• ADJ. **ankle, knee**
• VERB + LIGAMENT **bruise, pull, rupture, strain, tear**
• LIGAMENT + NOUN **damage, injury, problem**

light *noun*

1 brightness
• ADJ. **clear, good** | **bright, harsh, intense, strong** | **blinding** | **full** *In full light, you could see Alison was well over forty.* | **bad, dim, faint, feeble, murky, poor, uncertain, weak** | **subdued** | **failing** *We could hardly see the ball in the failing light.* | **gentle, pale, soft, watery** | **mellow, warm** | **cold, cool** *in the cold light of morning* | **early** | **artificial** | **natural** | **infrared, ultraviolet** *film that is sensitive to ultraviolet light* | **visible**
• QUANT. **beam, ray** | **burst, flash, gleam, glimmer** *There was a flash of light followed by an explosion.* | **patch, pool**
• VERB + LIGHT **have** *Have you got enough light for reading?* | **generate, produce** | **cast, emit, give (out), provide, shed** *light emitted by a star* | **be bathed in** | **be sensitive to**
• LIGHT + VERB **gleam, glow, shine** | **come, fall, pour** *Light from a tall lamp fell in a pool on the desk.* | **reflect** *The light reflecting off the snow was dazzling.* | **grow stronger, increase** | **fade, fail, thicken** | **blind sb, dazzle sb** *We were momentarily blinded by the light of the sun.* | **catch sth** *You could see the imperfections in the repair when the light caught it.*
• LIGHT + NOUN **level** | **source** | **beam**
• PREP. **against the ~** *She held up the letter against the light.* **by the ~ of** *They managed to see where the door was by the light of the moon.* **into the ~** *Bring it into the light and we'll have a look at it.* **in the ~** *The place looked calm in the golden evening light.* | **~ from** *the light from the kitchen window*
• PHRASES **(at) the speed of light** *Nothing can travel faster than the speed of light.* **a point of light, a source of light** *The lamp was the only source of light in the room.*

2 sth that produces light
• ADJ. **bright** *the bright lights of the city* | **flashing, twinkling** | **electric, fluorescent, gas, neon, strip** | **bedside, ceiling, outside, overhead, wall** | **street** | **hazard, security, warning** *The car was stopped at the side of the road with its hazard lights flashing.* ◇ *A warning light goes on when the battery is running low.* | **landing** *The pilot could just make out the runway landing lights.*
• VERB + LIGHT **put on, switch on, turn on** | **have on** *Some cars already had their lights on.* | **leave on** | **extinguish, put off/out, switch off, turn off/out** | **turn up** | **dim, turn down** | **shine** *Someone shone a light in my face.* | **flash** *He flashed his lights to warn the oncoming cars.*
• LIGHT + VERB **be off/on** | **come on** *The warning light came on.* | **go out** | **fuse** | **gleam, glimmer, glow, shine** | **flash** *The blue light was flashing.* | **flicker** *The light flickered a couple of times then went out.* | **blind sb, dazzle sb**

- LIGHT + NOUN **switch | fitting**
⇨ See TRAFFIC LIGHT

light verb

1 make sth begin to burn
- VERB + LIGHT **attempt to, try to | pause to, stop to** *She paused to light another cigarette.*

2 (often **be lit**) give light to sth
- ADV. **well** *a brightly lit room* | **badly, dimly, poorly** *a dimly lit street* | **brightly, brilliantly | softly | briefly, momentarily** (*figurative*) *A gleam of humour momentarily lit his face.* | **suddenly | artificially, electrically | up** *There was an explosion and the whole sky lit up.*
- PREP. **with** (*figurative*) *Her face lit up with pleasure.*

light adj.

1 not dark
- VERBS **be | become, get, grow** *It was starting to get light.* ◇ *As soon as it grew light, we got up and dressed.*
- ADV. **completely, quite** *We'll set out as soon as it's completely light.* | **almost** *It was almost light outside.* | **fairly | enough** *It was not light enough to see things clearly.* | **still | beautifully** *The whole house was beautifully light and airy.*

2 not weighing much
- VERBS **be, feel, seem | become**
- ADV. **exceptionally, extraordinarily, extremely, very** *wearing only very light clothes* | **fairly, quite, reasonably, relatively | enough** *The tent is light enough for backpacking and touring.* | **surprisingly**

3 not great in amount/degree
- VERBS **be**
- ADV. **very | comparatively, fairly, quite, relatively** *The traffic is usually fairly light in the afternoons.*

light bulb noun

⇨ See BULB

lighter noun

- ADJ. **cigar, cigarette | butane, gas, petrol | gold**
- VERB + LIGHTER **flick** *He flicked his lighter but it didn't catch.*
- LIGHTER + VERB **catch**

light-headed adj.

- VERBS **be, feel | become | make sb** *The wine had made him a little light-headed.*
- ADV. **very | a little, slightly | curiously** *She felt curiously light-headed.*

lighting noun

- ADJ. **bright, good, strong | low, poor, soft, subdued, subtle | adequate | artificial, natural | electric, fluorescent, gas, neon, strip | street | stage | domestic | emergency** *The generator supplies emergency lighting.* | **background | concealed | security**
- QUANT. **level**
- VERB + LIGHTING **have** *The kitchen hasn't really got adequate lighting.* | **fit, instal, put in**
- LIGHTING + NOUN **level | arrangement, scheme, system** *a typical lighting scheme for a house* | **effects | engineer**

lightning noun

- ADJ. **forked, sheet** *Forked lightning flickered across the sky.*
- QUANT. **bolt, flash** *A bolt of lightning struck the roof of the building.*
- LIGHTNING + VERB **flash, flicker, fork, light sth (up)** *Lightning flashed outside.* ◇ *Lightning lit up the night sky.*

| **hit sb/sth, strike sb/sth** *Lightning hit the tree.* ◇ *He was struck by lightning.*
- LIGHTNING + NOUN **bolt, flash | strike** *Lightning strikes caused scores of fires across the state.* | **speed**
- PHRASES **thunder and lightning**

like verb

- ADV. **enormously, a lot, particularly, really** *I liked him enormously and was sorry when he left.* ◇ *I really like that restaurant.* | **best, better** *Which story do you like best?* | **quite, rather | always, never** *I have always liked Sue and I don't intend to stop now.*
- VERB + LIKE **seem to | get to** *I hope you will get to like our town.*
- PHRASES **be universally liked** *a man who was universally liked*

likeable adj.

- VERBS **be, seem**
- ADV. **extremely, immensely, most, very | quite**

likelihood noun

- ADJ. **every** *There's every likelihood that she'll be able to help us.* | **greater, increased | real, strong**
- VERB + LIKELIHOOD **decrease, minimize, reduce** *Taking regular exercise reduces the likelihood of a heart attack.* | **increase, maximize, raise | affect** *This shouldn't affect the likelihood of you getting the job.*
- LIKELIHOOD + VERB **grow | diminish**
- PREP. **~ of** *Is their any likelihood of our getting our money back?*
- PHRASES **in all likelihood** *In all likelihood, he'll be fit to play on Saturday.*

likely adj.

- VERBS **appear, be, look, seem**
- ADV. **extremely, highly, very** *It is highly likely that the factory will have to close.* | **hardly** *They're hardly likely to get home before ten.* | **quite**

likeness noun

- ADJ. **strong** *The children all share a strong family likeness.* | **good | superficial** *There's a superficial likeness, but they're really very different.* | **physical | family**
- VERB + LIKENESS **see | bear, show** *She bears a remarkable likeness to her grandmother.*
- PREP. **~ between** *I can't see any likeness between her children.* **~ to**

liking noun

- ADJ. **great | particular, special**
- VERB + LIKING **have** *They have little liking for each other.* | **demonstrate, develop | share**
- PREP. **for your~** *The weather's too hot for my liking.* **to your~** *The food wasn't really to my liking.* | **~ for** *We share a liking for Italian cooking.*

limb noun

- ADJ. **long | thin | silken | powerful | bare, naked | broken, injured | stiff** *I eased my stiff limbs into the hot bath.* | **weary | amputated | artificial, prosthetic | lower, upper | hind** *The animal is able to stand up on its hind limbs.*
- VERB + LIMB **amputate**
- LIMB + NOUN **development, growth**

lime noun

- ADJ. **fresh**
- QUANT. **slice, wedge** *Serve the dish garnished with wedges of lime.*

● VERB + LIME **squeeze** | **slice** | **garnish sth with**
● LIME + NOUN **tree** | **juice**
⇨ Special page at FRUIT

limelight noun

● VERB + LIMELIGHT **grab, hog, steal** *She accused her co-star of trying to hog the limelight.* | **enjoy** | **avoid, shun** | **share**
● PREP. **into the** ~ *an ordinary person who was suddenly thrust into the limelight* **in the** ~ *She likes being in the limelight.* **out of the** ~ *The band started touring again after two years out of the limelight.*

limit noun

● ADJ. **outer** | **northern, southern, etc.** | **three-mile, etc.** | **absolute** *I can offer you £20 but that's my absolute limit.* | **higher, maximum, upper** | **lower** | **strict, stringent, tight** *The application must be made within a strict time limit.* | **age, speed, time, weight** *There's a weight limit on the bridge.* | **physical** | **safety** | **budget, cash, credit, earnings, financial, income, overdraft** | **legal, prescribed, statutory** | **recommended**
● VERB + LIMIT **reach** | **cross** | **establish, impose, place, put, set** *Central government has set a limit on spending by local councils.* | **increase, raise** | **lower** | **exceed** *exceeding the speed limit* | **push sb to** *She pushed me to the limit of my abilities.*
● PREP. **above a/the** ~ *The level of radioactivity in the soil was found to be above recommended limits.* **at a/the** ~ *I was almost at the limits of my patience.* **below a/the** ~ *The price fell below the lower limit.* ◇ *The trees are found only below a limit of 500 metres.* **beyond a/the** ~ *Heat levels rose beyond the recommended limits.* ◇ *fishing beyond the twelve-mile limit* **on a/the** ~ *islands on the outer limit of the continent* **over a/the** ~ *He'd been drinking and was well over the legal limit.* **up to a/the** ~ *You can buy cigarettes up to a limit of 200 per person.* **within a/the** ~ *They did well within the limits of their knowledge.* ◇ *There was no school within a limit of ten miles.* **within** ~s *The children can do what they like, within limits.* **without** ~ *Banks may buy bills of exchange without limit.* | ~ **on** *There's a limit on the number of tickets you can buy.* ~ **to** *There's a limit to what we can do to help.*

limit verb

● ADV. **seriously, severely, strictly**
● VERB + LIMIT **attempt to, seek to, take steps to, try to** | **be designed to** *The change in the law was designed to limit the scope for corruption.* | **agree to** | **serve to, tend to** *Rigid job descriptions can serve to limit productivity.*
● PREP. **to** *The teaching of history should not be limited to dates and figures.*

limitation noun

1 limiting of sth
● ADJ. **important, major, serious, severe** | **family** | **damage** *an exercise in damage limitation* | **arms** *talks on arms limitation* | **budget, budgetary, financial**
● VERB + LIMITATION **impose, place** | **remove** | **accept** *a limitation of your personal freedom*
● PREP. ~ **on** *limitations on one's freedom of action* ~ **to** *There should be no limitations to progress in the talks.*

2 limitations sth that sb cannot do
● ADJ. **important, major, serious, severe** | **inherent** | **physical, technical**
● VERB + LIMITATIONS **have** *She has serious limitations as a mother.* | **overcome, transcend** *At times his technique seems to transcend the limitations of the piano.* | **know, recognize** *Please don't ask me to sing—I know my limitations!* | **expose, reveal, show** *The team's technical*

limitations were exposed by the Italians. | **accept** *You've just got to accept your limitations.*
● PREP. **despite sb's/sth's** ~ *It's a useful book despite its limitations.*

limited adj.

● VERBS **be, seem** | **become** | **remain**
● ADV. **decidedly, distinctly, extremely, highly, really, remarkably, seriously, severely, sharply, strictly, very** *Places are strictly limited, so you should apply as soon as possible.* | **increasingly** | **a bit, comparatively, fairly, quite, rather, relatively, somewhat** | **apparently** | **inevitably** | **socially** *The role that women could play was socially limited.*
● PREP. **in** *We're really limited in what we can do these days.* **to** *The number of passengers is limited to fifteen.*

limousine noun

● ADJ. **big, long** | **black** | **gleaming** | **stretch** | **chauffeur-driven, hired** | **waiting** *They walked back to the waiting limousine.*

limp noun

● ADJ. **pronounced** | **slight**
● VERB + LIMP **walk with** | **leave sb with** *The accident had left him with a slight limp.*

limp verb

● ADV. **badly, heavily** *He had hurt his leg and was limping badly.* | **a little, slightly** | **along, away, off** *He limped away from his car.*

limp adj.

● VERBS **be, feel, hang, lie, look, seem** *His arm hung limp at his side.* ◇ *Her hair looked limp and lifeless.* | **become, go, grow** *Her body suddenly went limp.*
● ADV. **very** | **completely** | **rather**

line noun

1 long thin mark on the surface of sth
● ADJ. **long** | **short** | **thick** | **fine, thin** | **direct, straight** | **curved, wavy, wiggly, zigzag** | **diagonal, horizontal, parallel, perpendicular, vertical** | **continuous, solid** | **broken, dotted** *Sign on the dotted line.* | **finishing, starting** | **contour**
● VERB + LINE **draw**
● LINE + VERB **run** | **divide sth**
● PREP. **in a** ~ *walk in a straight line*
● PHRASES **a line of latitude/longitude**

2 mark like a line on the skin
● ADJ. **deep** *Deep lines ran from her nose to her mouth.*
● VERB + LINE **have** *He has lines on his forehead.*
● LINE + VERB **run**

3 row of people, things, words on a page, etc.
● ADJ. **long** | **short** | **new** | **continuous**
● VERB + LINE **form**
● PREP. **in (a/the)** ~ *children standing in a line* **on a/the** ~ *Start each paragraph on a new line.*

4 telephone/electricity wire/connection
● ADJ. **direct** | **bad** *Speak up—it's rather a bad line.* | **busy** | **power** | **phone, telephone** | **outside, party, private** *What do I dial for an outside line?*
● VERB + LINE **hold** *Hold the line* (= Don't put the receiver down)*, please.*
● LINE + VERB **be engaged** | **be/go dead**
● PREP. **down the** ~ *He kept shouting down the line at me.* **on the** ~ *It's your mother on the line* (= on the telephone)*.* **on** ~ (also **online**) (= connected to a computer system)

5 section of railway track

● ADJ. **railway, train | main | branch, commuter, feeder** *The branch line is threatened with closure.*
● VERB + LINE **take** *Take the Bakerloo line and change at Piccadilly.*
● PREP. **on a/the~** *We live on the Northern Line.*
● PHRASES **the end of the line**

6 lines words spoken by an actor in a play
● VERB + LINES **learn | forget | fluff**

7 direction/course of thought/action
● ADJ. **broad** *The broad lines of company policy are already laid down.* | **firm, hard, strong, tough | official, party, political**
● VERB + LINE **adopt, follow, pursue, take | bring sb/sth into** *The other members of the board must be brought into line.*
● PREP. **in~with** (= in agreement with), **out of~with** (= not in agreement with) *out of line with party policies* | **~on** *the official line on food safety*
● PHRASES **a line of argument/enquiry/questioning**

8 place where an army is fighting
● ADJ. **battle, firing, front**
● PHRASES **behind enemy lines, in/on the front line**

lined *adj.*

1 of skin
● VERBS **be**
● ADV. **deeply, heavily** *Her deeply lined face was creased into a smile*

2 of clothes, etc.
● VERBS **be**
● ADV. **fully** *The coat is fully lined.*
● PREP. **with** *The case was lined with black velvet.*

linen *noun*

1 fabric
● ADJ. **fine, pure** *a fine linen shirt* | **coarse | Irish**
● VERB + LINEN **weave (sth from) | spin**

2 sheets/tablecloths/underwear, etc.
● ADJ. **clean, fresh | dirty, soiled | crisp, starched | bed, table | household**
● VERB + LINEN **change** *We change the bed linen once a week.*
● LINEN + NOUN **basket, cupboard**

liner *noun*

● ADJ. **luxury | ocean, ocean-going, transatlantic | cruise, passenger** *a job aboard a luxury cruise liner*

linger *verb*

● ADV. **long | faintly** *The smell of lavender lingered faintly in the room.* | **still | on** *The feelings of hurt and resentment lingered on for years.*
● PREP. **on** *Her eyes lingered on the stranger's face.* **over** *They stayed in the restaurant, lingering over coffee.*

linguistics *noun*

● ADJ. **contemporary, modern | applied, theoretical | computational, contrastive, descriptive, generative, historical, structural | Saussurean**
⇨ Note at SUBJECT (for verbs and nouns)

link *noun*

● ADJ. **close, intimate | strong | tenuous, weak | clear, definite, obvious | possible** *Scientists have established possible links between cancer and diet.* | **crucial, essential, important, vital** *Social workers provide a vital link between hospital and community.* | **common** *The common link between the three artists is their age.* | **formal, informal | direct, indirect | historical, long-standing | con-**
necting | causal** *The report failed to prove a causal link between violence on screen and in real life.* | **missing** *the missing link in the search for the causes of cancer* | **tangible** *a tangible link with the past* | **business, commercial, communication, cultural, diplomatic, economic, financial, military, political, professional, sporting, trade, etc.** | **family, kinship | air, rail/railway, road, transport | fast, high-speed | computer, modem, radio, satellite, telephone, video**
● VERB + LINK **have | build, create, develop, establish, forge, foster, make** *The college is keen to build links with local industries.* | **provide | maintain, preserve | strengthen | break, cut, sever** *She has severed her last links with her family.*
● LINK + VERB **connect sth, join sth**
● LINK + NOUN **road**
● PREP. **via a/the~** *a programme transmitted via a satellite link* | **~across** *trade links across the border* **~between** *The statistics show a clear link between social class and crime.* **~in** *The sales manager is regarded as the weakest link in the chain.* **~to** *The driver has a radio link to base.* **~with** *the city's traditional link with opera*

link *verb*

● ADV. **closely, intimately | firmly, strongly, tightly | loosely | directly, explicitly** *Diseases that can be directly linked to pollution.* | **indissolubly, inescapably, inevitably, inexorably, inextricably, inseparably** *Poverty and crime are inextricably linked.* | **clearly, obviously | necessarily | intrinsically | causally | physically | romantically** *She has never been romantically linked with anyone.* | **in some way, somehow** *I could not help feeling that these factors were somehow linked.* | **together, up** *The two spacecraft will link up in orbit.*
● PREP. **into** *The computers are linked into a network.* **to** *Scientists have linked the illness to the use of pesticides.* **with** *the road that links Cairo with Alexandria*

lion *noun*

● QUANT. **pride**
● LION + VERB **growl, purr, roar | attack sb, maul sb | catch sth, hunt sth (down) | kill sb/sth | prowl**
● LION + NOUN **cub | tamer**
● PHRASES **a lion's mane**

lip *noun*

● ADJ. **top, upper | bottom, lower | chapped, cracked, dry | moist | fleshy, thick | thin | firm**
● VERB + LIP **bite, chew** *He bit his lip nervously, trying not to cry.* | **press together, purse** *She pursed her lips in disapproval.* | **pout | lick, smack** *He licked his lips hungrily.* | **moisten** *He nervously moistened his lips with his tongue.*
● LIP + VERB **move, part** *Her lips parted with a cry of fear.* | **quiver, tremble | curl** *His lips curled contemptuously.* | **pout** *The firm lips pouted in a sulk.* | **protrude**
● PREP. **around/round your~** *He ran his tongue round his lips.* **between your~** *a cigarette between his lips* **on your~** *There was a slight smile on her lips.*

lipstick *noun*

● QUANT. **dab** *She put on a quick dab of lipstick and rushed out.*
● VERB + LIPSTICK **have on, wear | apply, put on | renew, touch up** *She touched up her lipstick in the mirror.* | **remove, take off, wipe off**
● LIPSTICK + VERB **smudge** *Her lipstick had smudged and she looked a real mess.*

liquid *noun*

● ADJ. **glutinous, thick, viscous | thin | clear | col-**

ourless | cloudy | flammable | volatile | immiscible, miscible *immiscible liquids such as oil and water*
● QUANT. **drop, pool**
● VERB + LIQUID **empty, pour** *Empty the liquid into a large bowl.* | **spill** | **drain (off), pour off, strain (off)** *Drain off the liquid from the meat into a measuring jug.* | **boil, bring to the boil, simmer** | **reduce** *Reduce the liquid by boiling for two minutes.* | **absorb, soak up**
● LIQUID + VERB **boil, simmer**
● LIQUID + NOUN **refreshment** (*informal*) *After two hours of the meeting we stopped for liquid refreshment.* | **soap** | **waste** *unprocessed liquid waste from a nuclear power station*
● PHRASES **in liquid form** *The medicine is usually taken in liquid form.*

liquidation *noun*

● ADJ. **compulsory, voluntary**
● VERB + LIQUIDATION **be forced into, be placed in, be put into, go into** *The firm may be forced into liquidation.*
● PREP. **in**~ *a company in liquidation*

liquor *noun*

● ADJ. **alcoholic, hard, intoxicating, strong** *It is an offence to sell intoxicating liquor to anyone under the age of 18.*
● LIQUOR + NOUN **licence** *The restaurant finally obtained a liquor licence.*

list *noun*

● ADJ. **long, short** | **complete, comprehensive, full** *We are compiling a full list of all local businesses.* | **alphabetical** | **waiting** *We're on the waiting list for membership of the golf club.* | **shopping** | **mailing** | **reading** *For further information, see the reading list at the end of the chapter.* | **guest** | **cast** *The play has an impressive cast list.* | **transfer** (= in football) *The club captain has been put on the transfer list at his own request.*
● VERB + LIST **compile, draw up, make** | **put sth on** *Did you put bread on the shopping list?*
● LIST + VERB **comprise sth, contain sth** *a list comprising all the paintings in the gallery*
● PREP. **in a/the**~ *Names of past members are not included in the list.* **on a/the**~ *I can't see your name on the list.* | ~**of** *a list of 200 names*
● PHRASES **the bottom/top of a list** *Variety is near the top of many people's list of job requirements.* **high on a list** *Safety is high on our list of priorities.* **a list of priorities** *Phoning the bank is top of my list of priorities today.*

listen *verb*

● ADV. **attentively, carefully, closely, hard, intently** *Now, listen very carefully to what she says.* | **half** *Lucy was only half listening to their conversation.* | **patiently, politely, sympathetically** *We listened politely to his stories.* | **avidly, eagerly, with interest** *The guests were listening with great interest.* | **gravely, impassively** *Pym listened impassively until the woman had finished.* | **in silence, quietly** *They listened to the announcement in silence.* | **anxiously** | **in awe**
● VERB + LISTEN **(not) want to, will/would (not)** *Nobody will listen to me!* ◇ *I tried to warn her, but she wouldn't listen.* | **be prepared to, be willing to** | **refuse to** *He refused to listen to her explanation.*
● PREP. **for** *We listened anxiously for the sound of footsteps.* **to** *listening to the radio*
● PHRASES **listen with half an ear** *I listened with half an ear to the conversation at the next table.*

listener *noun*

● ADJ. **attentive, good, great, sympathetic** | **radio**

literacy *noun*

● ADJ. **basic** *All the children are tested in basic literacy.* | **adult** | **mass** | **computer**
● VERB + LITERACY **achieve, acquire** *different methods for acquiring literacy* | **develop, promote, teach**
● LITERACY + NOUN **campaign, programme**

literate *adj.*

● VERBS **be** | **become**
● ADV. **highly, very** *Only highly literate people are capable of discussing these subjects.* | **fully** *They are the first fully literate generation in the country.* | **barely, hardly** *He was uneducated and barely literate.* | **fairly, quite** | **economically, musically, politically, technologically** (= educated about economics, music, etc.)
● PREP. **in** *Both parents were literate in English.*
● PHRASES **computer literate** (= able to use a computer)

literature *noun*

1 written works of art
● ADJ. **classical, contemporary, modern** | **great**
● QUANT. **piece, work**
● VERB + LITERATURE **read, study**
2 writing on a particular subject
● ADJ. **extensive, voluminous** | **promotional, sales**
● QUANT. **body** *the growing body of literature on development issues*
● PREP. ~**about** *I picked up some literature about pensions.* ~**on** *There's an extensive literature on the subject.*

litigation *noun*

● ADJ. **costly, expensive** | **endless, lengthy, protracted** | **threatened** | **pending** | **ensuing, subsequent** | **civil, commercial, criminal**
● VERB + LITIGATION **be/become/get involved in, be engaged in, conduct, engage in** | **threaten** | **avoid** *The payment was made to avoid threatened litigation.*
● LITIGATION + NOUN **costs**
● PREP. ~**against** *He engaged in endless litigation against the media.* ~**between** *litigation between private parties*
● PHRASES **the cost of litigation, the risk/threat of litigation**

litre *noun*

⇨ Note at MEASURE

litter *noun*

● VERB + LITTER **drop, leave** *Please do not leave litter after your picnic.* | **clean up, clear up, pick up**
● LITTER + VERB **be strewn** *Litter was strewn all over the field.*
● LITTER + NOUN **basket, bin** | **lout** *The local council has pledged to clamp down on litter louts on the beach.*

live *verb*

1 in a place
● ADV. **alone** | **together** *She disapproves of unmarried couples living together.* | **apart** *The couple have lived apart for two years.*
● VERB + LIVE **come to, go to** *We went to live in London when I was three.*
● PREP. **among** *living among the people of this remote island* **in** *He lives in Manchester.* **near** *She lives quite near here.* **with** *I still live with my mum.*

- PHRASES **a place to live** *young couples looking for a place to live*

2 be alive
- ADV. **longer** *Women live longer than men in general.* | **forever** *Who wants to live forever? I don't.* | **happily (ever after)** *All she wanted was to get married and live happily ever after.* | **amicably, harmoniously, peaceably** *the need to live as harmoniously as possible with everyone else* | **well** *Most of the people live very well, with nice houses and plenty to eat.* | **frugally, modestly** *They lived frugally off a diet of porridge and lentils.* | **vicariously** *She tried to live vicariously through her children.*
- PREP. **in** *Many of the people live in poverty and misery.* **through** *She lived through two world wars.* **with** *living with Aids*
- PHRASES **(for) as long as you live** *I shall remember this day for as long as I live.* **learn to live with sth** *learning to live with disability* **live a life of sth** *He's now living a life of luxury in Australia.* **live to (be) 80, 90, etc., live to the age of 80, 90, etc.** *She lived to the age of 95.* **the world we live in** *teaching children about the world we live in*

live *adj., adv.*

- VERBS **appear, be, play** *He appeared live on the Song and Dance Show.* ◊ *Is the show live or recorded?* ◊ *The band have never played this song live before.* | **come to sb, go out** *This programme comes to you live from the Albert Hall.* ◊ *In those days the broadcasts all went out live.* | **be broadcast, be screened, be shown, be televised, be transmitted** *The match will be televised live this evening.* | **be recorded** *The CD was recorded live at a concert given last year.*

livelihood *noun*

- VERB + LIVELIHOOD **earn, gain** | **protect, secure** *an insurance policy to secure your livelihood in old age* | **affect, threaten** *The new law threatens the livelihood of thousands of farmers.* | **destroy, take away**
- LIVELIHOOD + VERB **depend on sth** *people whose livelihood depends on the forest*
- PHRASES **a means/source of livelihood** *The boat was his main source of livelihood.*

liver *noun*

1 organ in the body
- ADJ. **enlarged, fatty** | **donor** *a nationwide appeal for a donor liver*
- LIVER + NOUN **cancer, cirrhosis, damage, disease, dysfunction, failure, injury** | **cell, enzyme, tissue** | **function** | **biopsy, transplant, transplantation**
- PREP. **in the ~** *enzymes in the liver* **of the ~** *cirrhosis of the liver* **to the ~** *bile acids returning to the liver*

2 liver of an animal as food
- VERB + LIVER **eat, have** | **chop** | **braise, cook, fry**
- LIVER + NOUN **pâté, sausage**
- PHRASES **chicken/lamb's/pig's, etc. liver**
⇨ Special page at FOOD

living *noun*

- ADJ. **comfortable, decent, good** *He makes a good living as a builder.* | **meagre** *She eked out a meagre living as an artist's model.*
- VERB + LIVING **earn, make** *Her dream was to earn her living as a singer.* | **eke out, scrape (together), scratch** *They were forced to scrape a living by selling things on the streets.* | **do sth for** *He asked what I did for a living.*

load *noun*

- ADJ. **heavy, light** *He has a heavy teaching load this year.* | **full** *The plane took off with a full load.*

- VERB + LOAD **bear, carry** | **lighten, share, spread** *We're trying to spread the load by employing more staff.* | **drop, dump, shed** *A lorry has shed its load of wood on the motorway.*
- PREP. **under its, etc. ~** *The tables creaked under their heavy load.*

loaded *adj.*

1 carrying a load
- VERBS **be**
- ADV. **heavily** *a convoy of heavily loaded lorries* | **fully** *a fully loaded truck* | **lightly**
- PREP. **with** *The lorry was loaded with crates of beer.*

2 biased
- VERBS **be, seem**
- ADV. **heavily** | **rather, slightly** | **emotionally, ideologically, politically** *Try to avoid politically loaded terms like 'nation'.*
- PREP. **against** *The odds were slightly loaded against us.* **in favour of** *The legislation is heavily loaded in favour of employers.*

loaf *noun*

- ADJ. **fresh, stale** | **cut, sliced** | **brown, white, wholemeal, etc.**
- VERB + LOAF **bake** | **cut, slice**
- LOAF + NOUN **tin**
- PHRASES **a loaf of bread**

loan *noun*

- ADJ. **large, massive** | **long-term, short-term** | **interest-free, low-interest** | **secured, unsecured** *As it was an unsecured loan, their property was not at risk.* | **outstanding** *They used the inheritance to pay off their outstanding loan.* | **personal** | **bank** | **bridging, temporary**
- VERB + LOAN **apply for, ask for, request** | **arrange, get, raise, take out** *She had to take out a bridging loan until she could sell her house.* | **give sb, grant sb, make sb** *My bank manager offered to make me a loan.* | **receive** | **pay off, repay** | **secure, underwrite**
- LOAN + VERB **average sth, total sth** *loans totalling a million pounds*
- LOAN + NOUN **application** | **agreement, arrangement, deal** | **charges, interest, rate** | **repayment** *They were struggling to meet their monthly loan repayments.* | **commitments** | **facility, service** *The bank provides personal loan facilities at competitive rates.* | **period** *The book must be returned by the end of the loan period.* | **shark** *He ran up massive debts borrowing from loan sharks.*
- PREP. **on ~ (from)** *The paintings are on loan from the Wallace Collection.* **~ from** *a loan from my brother*
- PHRASES **give sb/have the loan of sth** *He's given us the loan of his car for the weekend.* **security against/for a loan** *He had to use his house as security for the loan.*
⇨ Special page at BUSINESS

loathing *noun*

- ADJ. **absolute, deep, intense**
- VERB + LOATHING **arouse, fill sb with** *People who took football too seriously aroused deep loathing in me.* | **develop, feel, have**
- PREP. **~ for** *She felt an intense loathing for her boss.* **~ of** *a deep loathing of war*
- PHRASES **fear and loathing** *The incident has created an atmosphere of fear and loathing among the people.*

lobby *noun*

- ADJ. **powerful, strong** *a powerful anti-smoking lobby* | **mass** | **anti-abortion, anti-hunt, environmental, industrial, nuclear, political, etc.**

- VERB + LOBBY **mount, organize**
- LOBBY + NOUN **group**
- PREP. **~against** *Many groups have together mounted a lobby against cuts in hospitals.* **~for** *Villagers have organized a lobby for improved local facilities.*

lobby *verb*

- ADV. **actively, hard** | **successfully**
- PREP. **against** *Head teachers have been lobbying hard against education cuts.* **for** *The group successfully lobbied for changes in the law.* **on behalf of** *The organization has been set up to lobby the government on behalf of all the people who have lost their pensions.*
- PHRASES **intense/intensive lobbying** *The decision followed months of intense lobbying of UN officials.* **political lobbying** *The group achieved its aims after months of political lobbying.*

locate *verb*

1 find the position of sb/sth
- ADV. **accurately, precisely** *The machine can accurately locate radioactive material.* | **quickly** | **easily**
- VERB + LOCATE **be able/unable to, can/could** *We haven't yet been able to locate a suitable site.* | **try to** | **fail to** | **be easy to** *Some stars are quite easy to locate with a telescope.* | **be difficult to**

2 be located be in a place
- ADV. **centrally** *The hotel is centrally located between Dam Square and Central Station.* | **conveniently, ideally, strategically** | **physically** *Two people can meet in virtual reality even if physically located in different continents.* | **abroad**
- PREP. **at, between, close to, in, near, on, outside, within,** etc. *Your accommodation is conveniently located within walking distance of the town centre.*

location *noun*

- ADJ. **exact, precise, specific** *We still do not know the precise location of the crash.* | **secret, undisclosed** | **convenient, ideal, suitable**
- VERB + LOCATION **show** *The map shows the exact location of the mine.*
- PREP. **at a/the … ~** *The meeting is taking place at a secret location.* **on ~** *The film is being made on location in India.*

lock *noun*

1 fastening device
- ADJ. **Chubb, combination, lever, mortise, Yale** | **door, window**
- VERB + LOCK **fit** *We had new locks fitted after the burglary.* | **break, force, pick** | **turn** *He turned the lock and pushed the door open.*
- PHRASES **insert/turn the key in the lock, (keep sb/sth) under lock and key** *Prisoners are kept under lock and key 24 hours a day.*

2 small bunch of hair
- ADJ. **stray** *She flicked a stray lock of hair off her face.* | **flowing** *She had long flowing locks and blue eyes.*

lock *verb*

1 close with a lock
- ADV. **carefully** *He carefully locked the door behind him.*
- VERB + LOCK **forget to**
- PHRASES **be firmly/securely locked, keep sth locked** *Keep your garage securely locked.*

2 put sb/sth inside sth that is locked
- ADV. **away, in, up** *I was terrified they would lock me up again.*
- PREP. **in** *I locked myself in the bathroom.*

- PHRASES **be safely/securely locked** *All the valuables were safely locked away.*

locust *noun*

- QUANT. **plague, swarm**
- LOCUST + NOUN **swarm**

log *noun*

1 wood
- ADJ. **cut, sawn** *a pile of sawn logs* | **fallen** *The road was blocked by fallen logs.* | **blazing, burning**
- VERB + LOG **chop, saw, split**
- LOG + VERB **blaze, burn, crackle** *logs crackling in the fireplace*
- LOG + NOUN **cabin** | **fire**

2 written record
- ADJ. **detailed** | **captain's, ship's**
- VERB + LOG **keep** *She kept a log of their voyage.*
- LOG + NOUN **book**

logic *noun*

1 system of reasoning
- ADJ. **formal** | **deductive, inductive**
- VERB + LOGIC **apply, use** *Philosophers use logic to prove their arguments.*

2 use of reason
- ADJ. **compelling, exquisite, impeccable, inexorable** *There is a compelling logic to his main theory.* | **strict** | **internal, underlying** | **commercial, economic, political, scientific** *There is sound commercial logic in never giving credit to retailers.*
- VERB + LOGIC **accept, follow, understand** *I can't follow the logic of what you are saying.* | **defy** *It's a stupid decision that completely defies logic.* | **apply, use** *You can't use the same logic in dealing with children.*
- PREP. **~ behind** *What's the logic behind this decision?* **~ in** *There doesn't seem to be any logic in the move.*

logical *adj.*

- VERBS **be, seem, sound** *It all sounds quite logical.*
- ADV. **eminently, extremely, highly, very** | **absolutely, completely, entirely, perfectly, quite** *His arguments seemed perfectly logical.* | **purely** *The issue here is purely logical: it has nothing to do with ethics.* | **hardly**

logo *noun*

- ADJ. **distinctive** *The company has a distinctive logo that makes it well known.* | **company, corporate**
- VERB + LOGO **bear, carry, display, feature** *The diary features the organization's distinctive new logo.* | **unveil** *The new logo was unveiled in a blaze of publicity.*
- PREP. **~ for** *the logo for the World Cup*

loneliness *noun*

- ADJ. **aching, great, intense, terrible, utter** | **personal**
- VERB + LONELINESS **experience, feel, suffer** *He experienced terrible loneliness after the loss of his wife*
- PHRASES **a feeling/sense of loneliness**

lonely *adj.*

- VERBS **be, feel, look, seem** | **become, get**
- ADV. **desperately, extremely, terribly, unbearably, very** *She was desperately lonely at school.* | **a bit, a little, pretty, rather** | **oddly** *She felt oddly lonely without her books.*

long *verb*

- ADV. **desperately** *He longed desperately to be back at home.* | **secretly** *They were the words she had secretly*

longed to hear. | **always** *She had always longed to go abroad.*
● PREP. **for** *He hated the city and longed for the mountains.*

long *adj.*

● VERBS **be, look, seem** *That dress looks a bit long to me.*
● ADV. **really, very** | **extra** *Economy class can be uncomfortable for those with extra-long legs.* | **a bit, fairly, quite, rather** *His journey to work is quite long.* | **enough** *Are you sure two hours will be long enough?*

longing *noun*

● ADJ. **deep, desperate, great, intense, overwhelming, passionate, terrible, wild** *She had a desperate longing to go back.* | **sudden** | **hopeless** | **nostalgic, wistful** *a wistful longing for the past* | **physical, sexual**
● VERB + LONGING **be filled with, be full of, feel, have** *He felt an overwhelming longing to hear her voice again.*
● PREP. **~for** *his intense longing for privacy*

longitude *noun*

● ADJ. **calculate, determine**
● PREP. **at (a)~** *The town is at longitude 28° west.*
● PHRASES **a line of longitude** *This line of longitude cuts through the jungle.*

long-lived *adj.*

● VERBS **be**
● ADV. **extremely, remarkably, unusually, very** *Some of these creatures are remarkably long-lived.*

loo *noun*

● ADJ. **public** | **outside** | **gents', ladies', men's, women's**
● VERB + LOO **go to, use** *Can I use your loo?* | **be desperate for, need** *We got stuck in a traffic jam and I was desperate for the loo.* | **flush, flush sth down** *He flushed the letter down the loo.*
● LOO + NOUN **paper, roll**
● PREP. **in the~, on the~**

look *noun*

1 act of looking at/considering sth
● ADJ. **little** | **brief, cursory, quick** | **leisurely** | **careful, close** *Take a closer look at it.* | **furtive** *I had a furtive look in her bag when her back was turned.* | **overall** *We need to take an overall look at the situation.* | **nostalgic** *The book takes a nostalgic look at the golden age of the railway.* | **critical, hard, honest, radical, realistic, serious, uncompromising** *You should take a long, hard look at your reasons for wanting to join the army.* | **humorous, light-hearted** *The book takes a humorous look at parenthood.* | **fresh** *I think it's time to take a fresh look at our sales techniques.*
● VERB + LOOK **have, take** | **get** *Did you get a look at his new car?* | **sneak, steal**
● PREP. **~at** *I managed to steal a look at the exam paper.* **~in/into** *She couldn't resist a quick look in the mirror.* **~out of** *Have a look out of the window and see who's at the door.* **~through** *I had a brief look through the report before the meeting.* **~towards** *The book concludes with a look towards the future.*
● PHRASES **without a backward look** *She walked out of the door without a backward look.*

2 exploring/looking for sth
● ADJ. **good** | **little, quick**
● VERB + LOOK **have**
● PREP. **~around/round** *We had a good look around the*

old town on the first day of our holiday. **~for** *I had a look for websites on Egyptian music, but didn't find anything.*

3 expression on sb's face
● ADJ. **angry, black, dark, dirty, exasperated, fierce, furious, harsh, irritated, murderous, reproachful, savage, scathing, scornful, severe, sharp, withering** *She threw him a dirty look.* | **cold, cool, dry, frosty, steely** | **disgusted** | **pained** | **baleful, forbidding** | **glum, grim, hangdog** | **suspicious, wary** | **cautious** | **sideways** | **guilty, sheepish, shifty** *The guilty look on his face told us all we needed to know.* | **apprehensive, anxious, doubtful, worried** *They had worried looks on their faces.* | **sad** | **blank, dazed, distant, faraway, glazed, unfocused, vacant** | **wild** *The man had a wild look in his eyes.* | **funny, odd, strange** *He gave me a funny look.* | **curious, meaningful, puzzled, quizzical, searching, speculative, thoughtful** | **knowing, shrewd** | **penetrating, piercing** | **earnest, intense, intent, steady** | **bold, challenging** | **smug, triumphant** | **mischievous, wicked** | **amused, wry** | **innocent** | **coy, shy** | **compassionate, loving** | **grateful** | **apologetic** | **appealing, despairing, desperate, frantic** | **hungry**
● VERB + LOOK **have** | **cast (sb), dart (sb), give (sb), shoot (sb), throw (sb)** | **get** *I got a black look from Amy.* | **exchange** *They exchanged meaningful looks.*
● PREP. **~from** *A withering look from his wife silenced him.* **~of** *He darted her a look of contempt.*
● PHRASES **a ... look in sb's eyes/on sb's face** *She had a puzzled look in her eyes.* ◇ *He opened the door with a scornful look on his face.* **take that (...) look off your face** *Take that smug look off your face before I slap you!*

4 sb/sth's appearance
● ADJ. **overall** *the overall look of the house* | **professional** *Use high-quality paper to give your CV a more professional look.* | **youthful**
● VERB + LOOK **have** | **like** *I didn't like the look of the salad so I didn't touch it.*
● PREP. **by/from the ~ of sb/sth** *Joe isn't getting much sleep from the look of him.* ◇ *By the looks of it, someone's already staying in this room.* | **~about** *He still had a youthful look about him.* **~of** *a fabric with the look of silk*

5 looks sb's attractiveness
● ADJ. **good** | **striking** | **classic** *He had classic good looks.* | **boyish, clean-cut, youthful** | **craggy**
● VERB + LOOKS **have** | **lose** *She's lost her looks.*

6 fashion/style
● ADJ. **latest, new** | **casual** | **classic** | **sophisticated** | **individual**
● VERB + LOOK **have** | **give sb/sth** *They've given the place a completely new look this year.*
● LOOK + VERB **be/come back in (fashion), go out (of fashion)** *The classic look never goes out of fashion.*

look *verb*

1 turn your eyes in a particular direction
● ADV. **carefully, closely** *Look at the machine quite carefully before you buy it.* | **sharply** *She looked up at me sharply when I said that.* | **intently, searchingly** | **archly** | **enquiringly, questioningly, quizzically, speculatively** | **doubtfully, dubiously** | **expectantly** | **anxiously, apprehensively** | **enviously, longingly** *He looked longingly at the food on the table.* | **beseechingly, imploringly, pleadingly** | **reproachfully** | **disapprovingly** | **pityingly** | **reflectively** | **studiously** *He was looking studiously down to avoid meeting her eyes.* | **impassively** | **blankly, dumbly, uncomprehendingly, unseeingly** | **across, away, down, over, round, up** *She looked over to where the others were chatting.*
● VERB + LOOK **turn to** *He turned to look as she came down the stairs.* | **let sb** *'It's beautiful!' 'Oh! Let me look!'*
● PREP. **at** *What are you looking at?* **towards** *She looked towards the door.*

● PHRASES **look and see** *I'll look and see if I've got any sugar in the cupboard.*

2 seem/appear

● VERB + LOOK **make sb/sth** *You made me look a complete fool!*

● PREP. **like** *an animal that looked like a large hedgehog* | **to** *It looks to me as if the company is in real trouble.*

● PHRASES **look as if/as though**

loop *noun*

● ADJ. **continuous, endless**

● VERB + LOOP **form, make** *Lay the two ends of string so they make a loop over each other.*

● PREP. **in a/the ~** *The audio tape runs in a continuous loop lasting thirty minutes.* **through a/the ~** *Put the other end of the string through the loop.*

loophole *noun*

● ADJ. **legal, security, tax**

● VERB + LOOPHOLE **find** | **exploit, use** *People who don't want to pay tax will exploit any loophole.* | **close, plug, tighten** *a law designed to close any loopholes in tax*

● LOOPHOLE + VERB **allow sb/sth, enable sb/sth** *a loophole enabling workers to take unnecessary sick leave*

● PREP. **~ in** *a loophole in the regulations*

loose *adj.*

1 not firmly fixed

● VERBS **be, feel, seem** *One of the bricks feels slightly loose.* | **come, shake, work** *The top of the tap has come loose.* ◇ *A screw had worked loose from the door handle.* | **prise sth**

● ADV. **a bit, rather, slightly**

2 not tied back

● VERBS **be, hang** *Her hair hung loose about her shoulders.* | **leave sth, wear sth** *Shall I wear my hair loose?*

3 not shut in or tied up

● VERBS **be** | **cut** (*figurative*), **break, get** *The animals had broken loose from their pens.* ◇ (*figurative*) *The organization broke loose from its sponsors.* ◇ *He felt he had to cut loose from his family.* | **let sth, turn sth** *I'm going to let the dogs loose.*

lord *noun*

● ADJ. **great, noble** | **feudal**

● VERB + LORD **serve**

● LORD + VERB **rule sb/sth**

⇨ Note at PEER

lorry *noun*

● ADJ. **big, heavy, huge, large** | **ten-ton, etc.** | **articulated** | **open** | **long-distance** | **diesel** | **army** | **breakdown, container, delivery, gritting, refrigerated, tipper**

● QUANT. **convoy**

● VERB + LORRY **drive**

● LORRY + VERB **carry sth** *a refrigerated lorry carrying beer*

● LORRY + NOUN **driver** | **load**

lose *verb*

1 not keep

● ADV. **financially**

● VERB + LOSE **be going to, be likely to, stand to** *The company stands to lose financially if this deal falls through.* | **have nothing to** *You have nothing to lose by telling the truth.* | **not want to** | **cannot/could not afford to** *We cannot afford to lose any more senior members of staff.* | **begin to**

2 be defeated

● VERB + LOSE **cannot/could not afford to** *This is a game that Lazio cannot afford to lose.*

● PREP. **against** *We lost against Leeds.* **by** *We lost by five goals to two.* **to** *The visiting side lost to the home team.*

● PHRASES **win or lose** *Win or lose, the important thing is to remain calm.*

PHRASAL VERB

lose out

● ADV. **financially**

● PREP. **on** *Many of the canal children were constantly on the move, and lost out on regular schooling.* **to** *Our firm lost out to a larger company that could offer a lower price.*

loser *noun*

● ADJ. **good** | **bad, poor** *He's extremely competitive and a bad loser.* | **born** | **big, main** *The main loser was the United Left, which lost eight seats.* | **real, ultimate** *If the teachers go on strike, the children are the ultimate losers.*

● VERB + LOSER **back** *The film company thought they'd backed a loser until the film won an Oscar.*

loss *noun*

1 losing of sb/sth

● ADJ. **appreciable, dramatic, great, major, serious, significant, substantial, tremendous** *The ship sank with great loss of life.* ◇ *She suffered a significant loss of hearing after the operation.* | **slight** | **total** | **temporary** | **permanent** | **sad** *His death is a sad loss to all who knew him.* | **blood, hair, hearing, weight** *Weight loss can be a sign of a serious illness.* | **job** *The company is expected to announce 200 job losses.*

● VERB + LOSS **mourn** *China mourned the loss of a great leader.*

● PREP. **~ of** *loss of appetite* ◇ *loss of confidence*

● PHRASES **no great loss** *She wouldn't be able to attend the lecture, which was no great loss.* **a sense of loss** *She was filled with an overwhelming sense of loss.*

2 amount of money lost

● ADJ. **heavy, huge, massive** | **slight, small** | **net** | **pre-tax** | **overall, total** | **economic, financial** | **trading**

● VERB + LOSS **incur, make, suffer, sustain** *There's no way you can make a loss on this deal.* ◇ *The business sustained losses of £20 million.* | **cut, minimize** *He decided to cut his losses and sell the shares before they sank further.* | **recoup, recover** *It took the firm five years to recoup its losses.* | **offset** *We can offset the loss against next year's budget.* | **underwrite** *No bank would be willing to underwrite such a loss.*

● PREP. **at a ~** *The bookshop was operating at a loss.* | **~ on** *We made a net loss on the transaction.*

3 sb/sth lost/killed

● ADJ. **big, great, heavy, severe** *The enemy suffered heavy losses.*

● VERB + LOSS **suffer, sustain, take** | **inflict** *Fighter planes inflicted heavy losses on the enemy.*

lost *adj.*

1 unable to find the way

● VERBS **be** | **get** *We got lost in the woods.*

● ADV. **completely** *By this time we were completely lost.*

2 not knowing what to do

● VERBS **be, feel, look, seem** *I felt lost without my watch.*

● ADV. **completely, totally** *Alina was looking totally lost.* | **very** | **a bit, a little, rather** *She looked rather lost and lonely, standing in a corner by herself.*

lot *noun*

1 whole amount

● ADJ. **whole** *She bought the whole lot.*

2 large amount
- ADJ. **awful** *I've got an awful lot of work to do before I go on holiday.*
- PHRASES **a hell of a lot** *a hell of a lot of money*

3 empty ground
- ADJ. **empty, vacant** *He parked his caravan on a vacant lot.*

lotion *noun*

- ADJ. **soothing** | **body, eye, face, foot, hand, skin** | **moisturizing, setting, sun/suntan** | **calamine**
- VERB + LOTION **apply, dab on, rub in** *She dabbed calamine lotion on her mosquito bites.*

lottery *noun*

- ADJ. **national, state**
- VERB + LOTTERY **have, hold** *We're having a lottery to raise money for homeless families.* | **win**
- LOTTERY + VERB **raise sth** *The lottery has raised millions of pounds.*
- LOTTERY + NOUN **ticket** | **winner** | **jackpot, prize** *a £3 million lottery jackpot* | **funds**
- PREP. **in a/the ~** *I won my car in a lottery* **on the ~** *A couple have scooped £10 million on the national lottery.*

loud *adj.*

- VERBS **be, sound** | **turn sth up** *She turned the radio up loud.*
- ADV. **deafeningly, extremely, really, very** | **pretty, rather** | **unnaturally** *Her voice sounded unnaturally loud.*
- PHRASES **loud and clear** *Tommy's voice came loud and clear from the back row.*

loudspeaker *noun*

- LOUDSPEAKER + VERB **broadcast sth** *Loudspeakers broadcast the football results.*
- LOUDSPEAKER + NOUN **announcement** | **system**
- PREP. **from a/the ~** *Christmas songs blared from loudspeakers.* **over a/the ~** *We heard the news over the loudspeaker.* **through a/the ~** *A woman was addressing the crowd through a loudspeaker.*

lounge *noun*

1 room in a house/hotel
- ADJ. **bar, cocktail, coffee, reception, sun, television/TV** | **attractive, comfortable, cosy, elegant, pleasant, spacious** | **attractively-furnished, comfortably-furnished, etc.** | **communal** | **hotel** | **guest**
- LOUNGE + NOUN **area, bar**
- PREP. **in a/the ~**

2 room at an airport
- ADJ. **airport** | **arrivals, departure** | **passenger, VIP**
- PREP. **in a/the ~**

love *noun*

- ADJ. **deep, great, overwhelming, passionate** *her deep love for him* | **genuine, pure, real, true** | **unconditional** | **abiding, eternal, undying** *He had an abiding love of the English countryside.* ◊ *You have my undying love.* | **hopeless, unrequited** *a sad tale of unrequited love* | **thwarted** *a play about thwarted love* | **mutual** | **free** *They were into free love and avoided commitment.* | **first** *I like most sports but tennis is my first love.* | **brotherly, maternal, parental, sisterly** | **courtly, platonic, romantic** *the cult of courtly love in twelfth-century Aquitaine* | **erotic, physical, sexual** | **heterosexual, homosexual, lesbian** | **redemptive** | **divine, human**
- VERB + LOVE **feel, have** *She felt no love for him.* ◊ *He had a great love of life.* | **search for, seek** | **find** *At last she had found true love.* | **express, show** | **declare, pro-**

fess *They publicly declared their love for each other.* | **promise** *'You promised me love!' he cried despairingly.* | **return** *He didn't return her love.* | **share** *They share a love of music.* | **give sb, send (sb)** *Bob sends his love.* | **be in, fall in** *He fell in love with one of his students.* | **fall out of** | **make** (= have sex) *It was the first time they had made love.* ◊ *He wanted to make love to her.*
- LOVE + NOUN **affair** | **life** | **letter** | **scene, song, story**
- PREP. **for/out of ~** *I did it for love!* **in ~** *We are very much in love.* | **~ between** *the love between parent and child* **~ for** *He did not know how to express his love for her.* **~ of** *She had a great love of painting.*
- PHRASES **an act of love, deeply/madly/passionately in love** *I was madly in love with her.* **desperately/hopelessly in love, head over heels in love, love at first sight** *Do you believe in love at first sight?* **the love of sb's life** *She was the love of his life.*

love *verb*

- ADV. **dearly, deeply, passionately, really, tenderly, very much** *He loved his wife dearly.* | **unconditionally** *He wanted to be unconditionally loved.*

lovely *adj.*

- VERBS **be, feel, look, sound** *The cool water felt lovely after being in the hot sun.* ◊ *Your idea of a day on the beach sounds lovely.*
- ADV. **breathtakingly, particularly, really, very** *She looked really lovely in the blue dress.* | **absolutely, perfectly, quite, utterly, wholly** *She's got an absolutely lovely face.* | **rather** | **hauntingly** *a hauntingly lovely melody*

lover *noun*

- ADJ. **good, great, passionate** | **jilted, rejected** *She was shot by her jilted lover.* | **unfaithful** | **long-time** *They're colleagues as well as being long-time lovers.* | **live-in** | **secret**
- VERB + LOVER **be, become** *They became lovers when her husband first went abroad.* | **have, take** *It was common for upper-class women to take lovers.*

low *noun*

- ADJ. **all-time, new, record** *The pound has hit a new low against the dollar.*
- VERB + LOW **fall to, hit, reach, sink to**
- PREP. **at a ~** *Morale is at an all-time low.*
- PHRASES **highs and lows** *He had experienced all the highs and lows of an actor's life.*

low *adj.*

1 not far above the ground
- VERBS **be, look, seem** *The windows look very low to me.*
- ADV. **extremely, very** *The river was extremely low for winter.* | **a bit, fairly, quite, rather**

2 small in degree/amount
- VERBS **be, look, seem** | **become, get, run** *Our stocks of food were getting low.* ◊ *Supplies ran low.* | **remain, stay** | **keep sth** *The government wants to keep taxes low.*
- ADV. **extremely, very** *The failure rate is extremely low.* | **comparatively, fairly, quite, rather, relatively**
- PREP. **in** *This dish is very low in fat.*

lower *verb*

- ADV. **carefully, gently** | **slowly** | **hastily, quickly** *Christina blushed and hastily lowered her eyes.* | **down**
- PREP. **into** *She lowered herself into the driver's seat.* **onto** *He carefully lowered the sleeping child onto the bed.* **to** *She lowered herself down to the floor.*

low-key *adj.*

- VERBS **be, seem | keep sth** *We want to keep the whole affair as low-key as possible.*
- ADV. **extremely, very** *The wedding was a very low-key affair.* | **fairly, quite, rather, relatively** *We have a fairly low-key approach to discipline.* | **deliberately**

loyal *adj.*

- VERBS **be, remain, stay**
- ADV. **extremely, fiercely, intensely, very** *a fiercely loyal friend* | **absolutely, completely, entirely, totally, unfailingly, utterly | apparently**
- PREP. **to** *The troops remained loyal to the president.*

loyalty *noun*

- ADJ. **absolute, complete, total, undivided, unswerving** *He showed unswerving loyalty to his friends.* | **fierce, great, intense, strong, tremendous | conflicting, divided** *Rows with one's in-laws often create divided loyalties.* | **primary, prime** *His prime loyalty was to his family.* | **family, filial, group, personal, tribal | local, national, regional | religious | party, political | brand, customer**
- VERB + LOYALTY **command, inspire, win** *He inspires great loyalty from all his employees.* | **feel, have | display, express, prove, show | pledge, swear** *They pledged their loyalty to the king.* | **transfer** *Some party members found it hard to transfer their loyalty to the new leader.* | **expect**
- LOYALTY + VERB **be, lie, remain** *His loyalties lay with people from the same background as himself.*
- LOYALTY + NOUN **oath**
- PREP. **out of ~** *She stayed on at the school out of loyalty to her students.* | **~among** *The village is the object of fierce loyalty among its inhabitants.* **~for** *Mass advertising creates brand loyalty for a product.* **~from** *The company expects loyalty from its employees.* **~to** *men whose loyalty is to their political careers* **~towards** *The team members felt tremendous loyalty towards one another.*
- PHRASES **a conflict of loyalties, an oath/a pledge of loyalty, a sense of loyalty**

luck *noun*

- ADJ. **better, good | pure, sheer** *It was sheer luck that we met like that.* | **bad, ill, rotten, tough** *It was rotten luck to be ill on the day of the interview.*
- QUANT. **piece, stroke** *By a stroke of luck I came across it in a local bookshop.*
- VERB + LUCK **bring (sb), give sb** *This ring has always brought me good luck.* **try** *I decided to try my luck at the roulette wheel.*
- LUCK + VERB **run out** *It looks as though our luck's finally run out.* | **hold** *If our luck holds, we should win.* | **improve, turn** *He went on gambling, sure his luck was about to turn.*
- PREP. **by ... ~** *By ill luck, my flight had been cancelled.* **for~** *I always carry it with me, just for luck.* **in~** *You're in luck—there are just two tickets left.* **out of ~** *I had hoped there would be another train, but I was out of luck.* **with~** *With luck, we'll get there before it closes.*
- PHRASES **beginner's luck** *I don't know why I did so well — it must be beginner's luck.* **better luck next time** *If you didn't win a prize, better luck next time.* **can't believe your luck** *He couldn't believe his luck when the other candidate for the job withdrew.* **just my luck** *Just my luck to get the broken chair!*

lucky *adj.*

- VERBS **be | get, strike (it)** *(both informal)* *hoping that some day she'll get lucky and win the jackpot* | **consider/count/think youself** *He considered himself lucky to have had the opportunity.*

- ADV. **bloody** *(taboo)*, **damn/damned, dead, exceedingly, extraordinarily, extremely, incredibly, really, remarkably, terribly, very** *She is incredibly lucky to be alive.* | **a bit, fairly, pretty, quite** *We've been pretty lucky so far.*
- PREP. **for** *It was lucky for you that no one saw you.* **with** *We certainly struck it lucky with the weather.*

lucrative *adj.*

- VERBS **be, prove**
- ADV. **extremely, highly, very | fairly, quite, rather | potentially | commercially** *a commercially lucrative venture*

ludicrous *adj.*

- VERBS **appear, be, look, seem, sound | become**
- ADV. **absolutely, perfectly, quite, simply, utterly** *The whole idea is absolutely ludicrous!* | **almost** *The plot was so simple, it was almost ludicrous.* | **faintly, rather**

luggage *noun*

- ADJ. **heavy | hand**
- QUANT. **item, piece** *You are only allowed one piece of hand luggage.*
- VERB + LUGGAGE **carry | claim, collect | check in** *They like you to check your luggage in an hour before the flight.* | **load, pack, unload** *She packed all the luggage into the boot of the car.*
- LUGGAGE + NOUN **compartment, locker | rack | trolley, van | label**
- PREP. **in your ~** *I always carry a first-aid kit in my luggage.*

lukewarm *adj.*

- VERBS **be, feel, seem**
- ADV. **decidedly, distinctly**
- PREP. **about** *She was distinctly lukewarm about my idea.*

lull *noun*

- ADJ. **brief, temporary | sudden**
- PREP. **during a/the ~** *They crossed the road during a lull in the traffic.* | **~in** *a brief lull in the fighting*

luminous *adj.*

- VERBS **be**
- ADV. **highly, very | almost** *The colours were bright, almost luminous.* | **faintly, slightly**

lump *noun*

- ADJ. **big, enormous, great, huge, large** *a great lump of cheese* | **heavy, solid** *a heavy lump of clay* | **small** *Stir the sauce to remove any small lumps.* | **painful** *He's developed a painful lump on his neck.* | **breast** *She's just had a breast lump removed.*
- VERB + LUMP **have | feel** *She felt a lump in her breast.*
- LUMP + VERB **form**

lunatic *noun*

- ADJ. **complete, raving | dangerous | criminal**
- LUNATIC + NOUN **asylum**

lunch *noun*

- ADJ. **cold, hot | delicious, tasty | hearty, slap-up, splendid, sumptuous | four-course, three-course, etc. | leisurely, long | heavy | healthy, light | meagre | sandwich** *We went for a sandwich lunch at the local bar.* | **packed | picnic | pub | early, late | Sunday | annual** *The society's annual lunch will be held next Wednesday.* |

business, expense-account, **working** | school | literary | boozy, liquid (= consisting only of alcoholic drinks)
• LUNCH + NOUN **box, break, date, hour, party, table** | **things** *I helped wash up the lunch things.* | **meeting** | **guest** | **bill** | **club**
• PHRASES **a spot of lunch** *Come and have a spot of lunch with me.*
⇨ Note at MEAL (for verbs)

luncheon *noun*

• ADJ. **buffet** | **annual** | **anniversary, charity, literary**
• VERB + LUNCHEON **have** | **attend** | **served** (= it is ready now) | **give** *The anniversary was marked by a luncheon given in the town hall.*
• LUNCHEON + NOUN **room, table** | **menu** | **party** | **engagement**
• PREP. **at** ~ *They met at a literary luncheon.* **during** ~, **for** ~, **over** ~

lung *noun*

• ADJ. **collapsed, punctured**
• VERB + LUNG **fill, refill** *I opened the window and filled my lungs with cool fresh air.* | **clear, empty** *Coughing clears the lungs of mucus.* | **block, choke, clog** *The smoke was beginning to choke her lungs.* | **enter** *Water had entered his lungs and he was choking.* | **puncture**
• LUNG + VERB **heave** | **fill** *I let my lungs fill with the scented air.* | **collapse** | **burst** *(figurative) Lungs bursting, she flew across the finish line.*
• LUNG + NOUN **capacity, power** | **cancer, complaint, condition, disease, infection, problems, tumour** | **surface, tissue** | **function** | **transplant**
• PREP. **in the** ~ *levels of carbon dioxide in the lungs* **into the** ~ *These particles are breathed into the lungs.* **on the** ~ *He had blood clots on the lung.*

lunge *noun*

• ADJ. **quick, sudden** | **despairing, desperate** *He skipped past the defender's despairing lunge.*
• VERB + LUNGE **make**
• PHRASES ~ **at** *The burglar made a lunge at him with a knife.* ~ **for** *The boy made a sudden lunge for his wallet.* ~ **to** *a lunge to one side* ~ **towards** *a lunge towards the door*

lurch *noun*

• ADJ. **little** | **sickening, sudden, violent**
• VERB + LURCH **give** *Her heart gave a little lurch when she saw him.* | **feel** *John felt a lurch of dismay.*
• PREP. **with a** ~ *The train stopped with a lurch.* | ~ **into** *Starting her own business was a lurch into the unknown.*

lurch *verb*

• ADV. **violently** *Suddenly the train lurched violently.* | **slightly** | **backwards, forward, sideways** *She gave a little cry and lurched forwards.*
• PREP. **along** *The coach lurched along the mountain road.* **into** *A man lurched into her office.* **towards** *He lurched towards the door.*
• PHRASES **lurch to your feet** *The drunk lurched to his feet and tried to follow us.*

lure *noun*

• ADJ. **irresistible, strong**

• VERB + LURE **resist** *She can't resist the lure of the bright lights.* | **feel** *He felt the lure of distant places.*

lust *noun*

1 sexual desire
• ADJ. **naked, pure** *a relationship based on pure lust* | **carnal, fleshly, physical, sexual**
• VERB + LUST **be consumed with, feel** *She felt no lust whatsoever for him.* | **sate, satisfy** *He used her just to sate his lust.*
2 strong desire for sth
• ADJ. **blood** *The ogre demanded the annual sacrifice of a young village lass to satisfy his blood lust.*
• VERB + LUST **be driven by, have** | **satisfy**
• PREP. ~ **for** *She was driven by a lust for power.*
• PHRASES **a lust for life**

luxurious *adj.*

• VERBS **be, feel, look, seem** *The car felt luxurious.*
• ADV. **extremely, positively, very, wonderfully** *Camping these days can be positively luxurious.* | **almost** | **quite**

luxury *noun*

1 comfort and pleasure
• ADJ. **great, pure, sheer** *It was sheer luxury to step into a hot bath.* | **ultimate** *the ultimate luxury of a sauna in your own home*
• QUANT. **touch** *Silk sheets added the final touch of luxury.*
• VERB + LUXURY **enjoy** *enjoying the luxury of an expensive bottle of wine* | **afford** *We can't afford such luxury.* | **live in**
• LUXURY + NOUN **hotel** | **car, coach, liner, yacht** | **cruise** | **apartment, flat, home**
• PREP. **in** ~ *brought up in luxury*
• PHRASES **(live) a life of luxury** *I found out that he wasn't dead, but living a life of luxury in Australia.*
2 sth expensive and unnecessary
• ADJ. **expensive** | **little, simple, small** *one of life's little luxuries* | **unnecessary**
• VERB + LUXURY **afford** *We can't afford luxuries.* | **enjoy, have, indulge in** | **do without** | **miss** *He missed the simple luxuries of life, like regular meals.*
• LUXURY + NOUN **goods, items**
• PHRASES **have every luxury** *She's had every luxury in life.*

lyrical *adj.*

• VERBS **be, feel** | **become, wax** *He waxed lyrical about the variety of fish in the river.*
• ADV. **intensely, very** *There are some intensely lyrical passages in his first symphony.* | **almost** *She wrote an almost lyrical account of her childhood.* | **quite**

lyrics *noun*

• ADJ. **song**
• VERB + LYRICS **write** | **set** *Strauss set several of Mackay's lyrics to music.*
• PREP. ~ **about** *lyrics about death and misery* ~ **by** *a song with lyrics by Lorenz Hart* ~ **for** *the lyrics for a new tune* ~ **to** *He wrote the lyrics to our first song.*

Mm

machine noun

1 piece of equipment

- ADJ. **great, huge, large, powerful | automatic, electronic | labour-saving | ingenious, versatile | sophisticated | reliable | defective | cash, coffee, exercise, fax, sewing, (telephone) answering, vending, video, washing | kidney, life-support** *The crash victim is now on a life-support machine.*
- VERB + MACHINE **operate, use, work | install** *We've had a new washing machine installed.* | **start, stop | plug in, unplug | build, make | service | design** *The machine is designed to fit under a counter.*
- MACHINE + VERB **go, work** *Have you got the machine working again?* | **break down | run** *The machine runs on solar power.*
- MACHINE + NOUN **operator | parts | tool** *machine tools for making weapons*
- PREP. **by** *The potatoes are planted by machine.* **in a/the ~** *Just put those clothes in the machine* (= the washing machine). **on a/the ~** *I make my own dresses on my sewing machine.* | **~ for** *a machine for making coffee*
- PHRASES **a make of machine** *What make of machine are they using?*

2 system/organization

- ADJ. **party, political** *The independent candidates did not have the support of a party machine.* | **administrative, government, state | propaganda, publicity | military, war** *the president's propaganda machine*
- PHRASES **a cog in the machine** (figurative) *Tired of being a tiny cog in a vast machine, he handed in his resignation.* **a well-oiled machine** (figurative) *The department ran like a well-oiled machine since the reorganization.*

machinery noun

- ADJ. **heavy | complex, complicated, elaborate, sophisticated | electrical | agricultural, construction, farm, industrial, manufacturing, office, textile**
- QUANT. **piece** *large and complex pieces of machinery*
- VERB + MACHINERY **maintain, service | install, set up | control, drive, operate | renew, replace, update | house** *The machinery is housed in a special building.*
- MACHINERY + VERB **drive sth, work sth | break down | hum**
- PREP. **~ for** *machinery for grinding wheat*
- PHRASES **the hum of machinery**

mad adj.

1 not sane; crazy/stupid

- VERBS **be, look, seem | go** *He went mad and spent the rest of his life locked up in a mental hospital.* ◇ *The world had gone completely mad.* | **drive sb** *His experiences in the First World War drove him mad.* ◇ *The children are driving me mad!* | **consider sb, think sb** *Her colleagues thought her quite mad.* | **pronounce sb**
- ADV. **absolutely, completely, quite, utterly | barking, (stark) raving** *What a barking mad idea!* ◇ *You must be stark raving mad to risk your money like that!* | **almost | a bit, half, a little, slightly | dangerously**
- PREP. **with** *I went mad with joy and danced a little jig.*

2 angry

- VERBS **be, feel, look | get** *I get so mad when people don't take me seriously.* | **make sb** *It makes me really mad when people waste food.*
- ADV. **hopping, really | absolutely | pretty**
- PREP. **at/with** *My mum's absolutely mad with me!*

madness noun

- ADJ. **absolute, pure, sheer, utter** *It's sheer madness to go sailing in weather like this.*
- PHRASES **the first sign of madness** *They say that talking to yourself is the first sign of madness!* **a moment of madness** *In a moment of madness, I said I'd help him.*

magazine noun

- ADJ. **new, old | rolled-up** *She hit him with a rolled-up magazine.* | **colour, glossy | monthly, quarterly, weekly | local, national, parish | school, student | house, in-house, official** *the company's in-house magazine* | **in-flight | popular | quality | special interest, specialist | teen/teenage, women's | business, trade | listings** *Check a listings magazine for what's on this weekend.* | **computer, consumer, fashion, gardening, literary, motoring, music, news, satirical, style, travel | girlie, (hard/soft) porn, porno/pornographic, sex**
- QUANT. **copy** *Why did you buy three copies of the same magazine?* | **edition, issue**
- VERB + MAGAZINE **leaf through, look at, read** *leafing through the magazines in the waiting room* ◇ *I never read magazines.* | **edit, write for | produce, publish** *a company that produces fashion magazines* | **buy, get, subscribe to** *Which magazines do you get regularly?*
- MAGAZINE + VERB **come out** *The magazine comes out once a month.* | **be aimed at sb** *a magazine aimed at mothers with young children* | **be devoted to sth** *a magazine devoted to country life* | **carry sth, feature sth, run sth** *The magazine carried an interview with the actor considered Hollywood's hottest property.*
- MAGAZINE + NOUN **article, interview, story, survey | ad/advert/advertisement | cover | editor, writer**
- PREP. **in a/the ~** *an article in a women's magazine*

magic noun

1 secret power

- ADJ. **black**
- VERB + MAGIC **do, practise** *He earns extra money doing magic at children's parties.* ◇ *People found guilty of practising black magic were hanged.* | **believe in** *I don't believe in magic.* | **work**
- MAGIC + VERB **work** *The magic slowly begins to work, and the princess starts to come to life again.*
- PREP. **by ~** *The rabbit disappeared by magic.*
- PHRASES **as if by magic** *The money had reappeared as if by magic.*

2 special quality

- ADJ. **absolute, pure, sheer** *The show is three hours of pure magic.*
- QUANT. **touch** *The fireworks brought a touch of magic to the occasion.*
- VERB + MAGIC **work** *A hot bath and a good night's sleep worked their usual magic.*

magical adj.

- VERBS **be | find sth**
- ADV. **truly, very** *a truly magical experience* | **quite, totally | almost** *Her beauty had an almost magical quality.*

magistrate noun

- ADJ. **examining, investigating, licensing | chief, senior | city, local, town**
- VERB + MAGISTRATE **appoint (sb), appoint sb as |**

appear before, come up before *He is due to appear before magistrates in connection with a public order offence.*
• MAGISTRATE + VERB **hear sth** *A thief who stole power tools from a store later sold them in a pub, Whitby magistrates heard yesterday.* | **fine sb** | **remand sb in custody** | **sentence sb** | **adjourn sth** *Magistrates adjourned the case until June 9.*
• PHRASES **magistrates' court**

magnet noun

• ADJ. **powerful, strong** | **weak** | **bar** | **fridge**
• VERB + MAGNET **act as/like** *The scent of flowers acts as a magnet to bees.*
• MAGNET + VERB **attract sth**
• PREP. **~for** *The place is a magnet for tourists.*

magnetism noun

• ADJ. **sheer, strong** | **animal, personal, sexual** | **the earth's, terrestrial** *changes in the earth's magnetism*
• VERB + MAGNETISM **exert, exude, project** *He exudes a strong sexual magnetism.*
• MAGNETISM + VERB **attract sth, draw sth** *The magnetism produced by the battery attracts the metal.* ◇ *His personal magnetism drew people to the church.*

magnificent adj.

• VERBS **be, look**
• ADV. **really, truly** | **absolutely, quite** *an absolutely magnificent performance* | **rather**

magnify verb

• ADV. **greatly, highly, hugely** *The daring of his exploits had been hugely magnified by constant telling.*
• PHRASES **magnify sth 10, 100, etc. times** *The picture shows the insect's head magnified ten times.*

magnitude noun

• ADJ. **considerable, great** | **sufficient** *a fall in costs of sufficient magnitude to enable us to reduce prices*
• PREP. **in~** *The effects were substantial in magnitude.*
• PHRASES **of the first magnitude** *Stars of the first magnitude are visible to the naked eye.* ◇ *a disaster of the first magnitude* **(by) an order of magnitude** *Her calculation was out by several orders of magnitude.*

maid noun

• ADJ. **dairy, kennel, kitchen, laundry, parlour, scullery** | **lady's, personal** | **daily** *They had a daily maid, but no live-in servants.*
⇨ Note at JOB

mail noun

• ADJ. **first-class, second-class** | **surface** | **express** | **registered** | **internal** *If we want to send something to another department, we use the internal mail.* | **international** | **direct** *direct mail advertising* | **incoming, outgoing** | **unopened, unread** | **electronic, video, voice** | **junk** *I throw junk mail straight in the bin without reading it.* | **hate** *He has received death threats and hate mail from angry fans.* | **fan**
• QUANT. **item, sackful**
• VERB + MAIL **send** | **get, receive** | **deliver** | **forward, redirect** *We got the Post Office to redirect our mail when we moved.* | **collect** *The mail is collected twice a day.* | **sort** *The postcode allows the mail to be sorted automatically.* | **check** *She checked her mail before leaving the hotel.* | **pick up** | **open** | **read** | **answer, deal with**
• MAIL + VERB **come, go** *Has the mail come yet?*
• MAIL + NOUN **order** *All our products are available by mail order.* | **message** | **item** | **program** | **system**

• PREP. **by~** *Send it by first-class mail.* | **in the~** *My reply is in the mail.* ◇ *Is there anything interesting in the mail?*

mail verb

• ADV. **direct**
• PREP. **to** *The brochures are mailed direct to members.*

mailing list noun

• ADJ. **free** *Why not join our free mailing list?*
• VERB + MAILING LIST **go on, join, subscribe to** | **add sb to, put sb on** | **come off, unsubscribe from** | **remove sb from, take sb off**
• PREP. **on a/the~** *We're on the mailing list for the Film Centre.* | **~for** *a mailing list for primary teachers*

main noun

• ADJ. **gas, water** | **burst, leaking** *There's a burst water main in Quarry Road.*
• VERB + MAIN **lay** *They're laying a new gas main through the town.*
• MAIN + VERB **serve sth** *The main serves four villages.* | **explode, leak**
• MAINS + NOUN **electricity, gas, water** *an island without mains electricity*
• PREP. **at the~s** *Turn the water off at the mains.* **on the~s** *Some of the remoter houses in the village are not on the mains.*

mainstream noun

• ADJ. **cultural, educational, political, etc.**
• VERB + MAINSTREAM **enter, join** | **cut sb/sth off from, exclude sb/sth from** *These teachers have been cut off from the mainstream of educational activity.*
• MAINSTREAM + NOUN **society** | **education, schools** | **parties, politics** | **art, cinema** | **media**
• PREP. **in/within the~** *He was in the mainstream of British contemporary music.* **into the ~** *This technology was designed for specialists but is now starting to move into the mainstream.* **out of/outside the ~** *He drifted out of the mainstream of society.*
• PHRASES **part of the mainstream** *This style of drama is not part of the mainstream.*

maintain verb

1 keep sth at the same level
• VERB + MAINTAIN **be anxious to, want to** *We are anxious to maintain our close links with the police.* | **have to, need to** | **strive to, try to** | **help (to)** | **be able to** | **be difficult to** *The government's position became increasingly difficult to maintain.*
• PHRASES **the duty/need to maintain sth** *He emphasized the need to maintain the status quo.*

2 keep sth in good condition
• ADV. **properly, well** | **poorly** *a poorly maintained central heating system*
• VERB + MAINTAIN **be difficult to** | **be easy to**
• PHRASES **be responsible for maintaining sth**

maintenance noun

1 keeping sth in good condition
• ADJ. **annual, regular, routine** | **long-term, ongoing** | **proper** | **essential** *The power station has been shut down for essential maintenance.* | **preventative** | **careful** | **easy** *The engine is designed for easy maintenance.* | **low, minimal** *This type of garden requires minimal maintenance.* | **on-site** | **aircraft, car, machine, etc.**
• VERB + MAINTENANCE **carry out** *We carry out routine maintenance of the equipment.* | **need, require**
• MAINTENANCE + NOUN **engineer, crew, man, staff, team** | **bill, costs** | **contract** | **service** *We provide a*

maintenance service on all our products. | **programme** | **work**

2 money paid to support sb
- ADJ. **child**
- VERB + MAINTENANCE **pay** | **claim**
- MAINTENANCE + NOUN **payments** | **arrears** *He was jailed for failing to pay maintenance arrears.*
- PREP. **in~** *He pays £1 000 a month in child maintenance.*

major *noun*

⇨ Note at RANK

majority *noun*

1 most
- ADJ. **big, great, huge, overwhelming, substantial, vast** | **silent** *The march was by the silent majority who oppose terrorism.*
- VERB + MAJORITY **comprise, constitute, form, make up** *English speakers form the majority of the population.*
- MAJORITY + NOUN **culture, group, population** | **opinion, view** | **shareholder** | **stake** *The French company holds a majority stake in the retail chain.*
- PREP. **in the ~** *In the general population, right-handed people are in the majority.*
- PHRASES **in the majority of cases** *In the vast majority of cases, customers get their money back.*

2 in an election
- ADJ. **handsome, huge, large, massive, overwhelming, substantial** | **clear, comfortable, decisive** | **bare, narrow, slender, slight, slim, small, tiny, wafer-thin** | **ten-seat, three-to-one, two-thirds, etc.** | **absolute, outright, overall** *Although they are the biggest single party, they don't have an outright majority.* | **simple** | **decreased, increased** | **working** *the first Labour government with a clear working majority in the House* | **parliamentary** | **government** | **Conservative, Labour, etc.** | **necessary, requisite**
- VERB + MAJORITY **command, have** | **achieve, gain, get, secure, win** *They failed to win the requisite two-thirds majority.* | **defend, maintain, retain** | **lose, overturn** | **indicate, show**
- MAJORITY + NOUN **government, rule** | **party** | **decision** | **vote, voting** | **support**
- PREP. **by a ~** *They won by a huge majority.* | **~ against** *Latest opinion polls have a comfortable majority against the reform.* **~ in** *a majority in Parliament* **~ in favour of** *Opinion polls indicated a two-thirds majority in favour of ratification of the treaty.* **~ over** *He has a decisive majority over his main rivals.*

make-up *noun*

1 cosmetics
- ADJ. **heavy, thick** | **eye** | **stage**
- VERB + MAKE-UP **use, wear** *I never wear make-up.* | **apply, put on** | **remove, take off** | **touch up** | **smudge**
- MAKE-UP + NOUN **artist, girl** | **remover**

2 sb's character
- ADJ. **genetic, physical, psychological**
- PHRASES **part of sb's make-up** *Jealousy is not part of his make-up.*

malaria *noun*

- ADJ. **acute, severe**
- VERB + MALARIA **have, suffer from** | **catch, contract** | **carry, transmit** *Malaria is transmitted by mosquitoes.* | **treat** | **eradicate**
- MALARIA + NOUN **sufferer, victim** | **parasite** | **vaccine** | **control, eradication**
⇨ Special page at ILLNESS

male *noun*

- ADJ. **adult** | **immature, young** | **old** | **dominant** *the dominant male in the herd* | **large, powerful, strong**
- MALE + NOUN **hormone** | **sexuality** | **chauvinism, chauvinist** | **identity, role**
- PHRASES **the male of the species** *The male of the species has more brightly-coloured feathers than the female.*

male *adj.*

- VERBS **be**
- ADV. **entirely, exclusively** *The club is an exclusively male preserve.* | **largely, mainly, mostly, overwhelmingly, predominantly** *The workforce is predominantly male.* | **essentially** *an essentially male Western view of progress* | **typically** | **peculiarly** *He nodded with a peculiarly male satisfaction at her capitulation.* | **traditionally** *traditionally male interests*

malice *noun*

- ADJ. **pure, sheer**
- VERB + MALICE **bear (sb), feel, have** *He bore me no malice.* ◊ *She felt no malice.* ◊ *She has no malice in her.*
- PREP. **out of ~** *She sacked him out of sheer malice.* **with/without ~** *'You're lying,' he said, without malice.* | **~ towards** *I bear no malice towards anybody.*

malicious *adj.*

- VERBS **be**
- ADV. **faintly, rather** *He gave a faintly malicious smile at her furious expression.*

malnutrition *noun*

- ADJ. **severe** | **chronic** | **child**
- VERB + MALNUTRITION **suffer (from)** | **die from/of**

mammal *noun*

- ADJ. **large, small** | **higher, lower** | **common** | **endangered, rare** | **wild** | **aquatic, marine, sea** | **land, terrestrial** | **carnivorous, grazing, herbivorous** | **nocturnal** | **hoofed** | **warm-blooded**
- MAMMAL + NOUN **species** | **prey**
- PREP. **among ~s** *deaths among marine mammals*

man *noun*

1 male person
- ADJ. **elderly, middle-aged, old, older, young** *a little old man* | **attractive, good-looking, handsome** | **ugly** | **short, tall** | **fat, thin** | **big, burly** | **little** *a nice little man* | **black, white** | **dark, dark-haired, fair, fair-haired** | **bearded** | **blind** | **sick** | **dead** | **intelligent, wise** | **great** *Several people made speeches in honour of the great man.* | **brave** | **charming, fine, good, kind, nice** | **honest** | **proud** | **quiet** | **bad, horrible** *What a horrible man!* | **arrogant** | **strange** | **brutal, hard, violent** | **married, single** | **family** *He's a family man who rarely goes out with his friends.* | **gay** | **professional** | **lucky** *He was a lucky man to have found such a partner.* | **poor, rich** | **betting, gambling** *I've never been a gambling man.* | **self-made** | **right-hand** *He found success hard to come by after losing his right-hand man.* | **innocent** | **free** *He walked out of court a free man.* | **condemned**

2 human beings
- ADJ. **early, prehistoric, primitive** | **Stone Age, etc.** | **Neanderthal, etc.**
- PREP. **in ~** *In man the brain is highly developed.*
- PHRASES **known to man** *the most poisonous substance known to man*

manage *verb*

1 succeed in doing sth
- ADV. **nicely, perfectly/very well** *I can manage perfectly well on my own, thank you.* | **successfully** | **eventually, finally** | **somehow** | **financially** *She was finding it difficult to manage financially.*
- VERB + MANAGE **be able to, can/could** *Can you manage?* | **have to** *We'll just have to manage somehow.* | **be difficult to** | **be easy to**
- PREP. **on** *I don't know how they manage on only £50 a week.* **without** *I can manage without a dishwasher.*
- PHRASES **manage on your own**

2 control/direct sb/sth
- ADV. **competently, effectively, efficiently, properly, successfully, well** | **badly** | **actively** *We will actively manage your portfolio to maximize the return on your investment.* | **sustainably** *All our tropical timber products come from sustainably managed sources.*
- VERB + MANAGE **be difficult to** *The children were very difficult to manage.* | **be easy to** | **learn (how) to** *You need to learn how to manage your time effectively.*

manageable *adj.*

- VERBS **be, seem** | **become**
- ADV. **easily** *The journey is easily manageable in half an hour.* | **quite** | **just (about)** *The job is just about manageable in the time.* | **relatively**

management *noun*

1 managing sth
- ADJ. **careful, competent, effective, efficient, firm, good, sound** | **bad, inefficient, poor** | **day-to-day, routine** | **general, overall** | **business, corporate** | **personnel, staff** | **production** | **project, task** | **hospital, hotel, school** | **database, network, systems** | **asset, economic, financial, investment, money, resource** | **information** | **crisis** | **household** | **traffic** | **waste** | **forest, land** | **anger, anxiety, stress** *He's been sent on an anger management course to help him control his temper.* | **time**
- VERB + MANAGEMENT **need** *The project needs stronger management.* | **be responsible for** *She is responsible for the day-to-day management of the company.*
- MANAGEMENT + NOUN **company, consultancy, consultant, services** | **course, studies, training** | **plan, policy, strategy** | **expertise, skills** | **method, philosophy, practice, style, technique**
- PREP. **in ~** *She is now celebrating ten years in management.* **under sb's ~** *The club prospered under Ferguson's management.*
- PHRASES **a board of management, under new management** *The restaurant is under new management.*

2 managers
- ADJ. **junior, middle, senior, top**
- VERB + MANAGEMENT **criticize** *The unions have criticized management over their handling of the dispute.*
- MANAGEMENT + NOUN **board, committee, staff, team** | **meeting** | **decision** | **job, position, post, role** | **hierarchy, structure** | **buy-out** | **level** *This decision should be taken at a higher management level.*
- PREP. **in … ~** *young people in middle management*
- PHRASES **a layer/level/tier of management**

manager *noun*

1 controls an organization/part of an organization
- ADJ. **assistant, junior, middle, senior** | **general** | **accountable, responsible** *Each programme is discussed with the responsible manager.* ◇ *A product manager is responsible for product profitability.* | **bank, business, commercial, corporate** | **area, branch, departmental, divisional, office, regional** | **functional, operations, personnel, product** | **advertising, catering, develop-**

ment, fund, marketing, production, project, sales, technical | **successful** | **sympathetic** *It helps to have a sympathetic manager.*
- VERB + MANAGER **promote sb to** *He has been promoted to business development manager.* | **assist** *Your job will be to assist the production manager.*
- PREP. **~ for** *the marketing manager for a large company*

2 looks after a sports team
- ADJ. **England, Scotland, etc.** | **team** | **caretaker** *He will be the club's caretaker manager until a new manager is appointed.* | **beleaguered** *another disappointing day for the beleaguered England manager*
- ⇨ Note at JOB

mandate *noun*

- ADJ. **popular** | **clear** | **legal** | **presidential** | **electoral** *It is undemocratic to govern an area without an electoral mandate.*
- VERB + MANDATE **have** | **give sb, issue** | **seek** *The party sought a mandate to reform the constitution.* | **get, obtain, receive, win** | **extend, implement**
- MANDATE + VERB **run** *The mandate ran until 1947.*
- PREP. **in your ~** *He failed in his mandate.* **under a/the ~** *They ruled the country under a United Nations mandate.* **with a/the ~** *The party was elected with a mandate to reduce the size of government.* **without a ~** *They accused him of acting without a mandate.* | **~ for** *She has received a clear mandate for educational reform.* **~ from** *a mandate from the United Nations to govern the territory*
- PHRASES **an extension/a renewal of a mandate**

mane *noun*

- ADJ. **flowing** | **shaggy, tangled, tousled** | **thick** | **luxuriant, shining**
- VERB + MANE **have** | **shake, toss** *She shook her mane of auburn hair.* ◇ *The horse tossed its flowing mane behind it.* | **braid** *She spent ages braiding her horse's mane.*
- MANE + VERB **stream** *The horse's mane streamed in the wind.*
- PREP. **~ of** *He has a mane of white hair.*
- PHRASES **a horse's/lion's mane**

manhood *noun*

- ADJ. **early, young**
- VERB + MANHOOD **grow to, reach** *He grew from adolescence to young manhood.* | **prove** *It seemed they were fighting to prove their manhood.*
- PREP. **in ~** *He began to go bald in early manhood.*

mania *noun*

1 extreme enthusiasm for sth
- ADJ. **gambling, railway, sex, etc.**
- VERB + MANIA **have**
- PREP. **~ for** *She had a mania for fast cars.*

2 serious mental illness
- ADJ. **collective** *The violence of the crowd can only be explained as a sign of some collective mania.* | **religious**
- VERB + MANIA **suffer from**
- PHRASES **a state of mania**

maniac *noun*

- ADJ. **sex** | **homicidal** | **religious**
- PREP. **like a ~** *He was driving like a maniac.*

manifestation *noun*

- ADJ. **concrete, physical, visible, obvious** | **public** *the public manifestation of private grief*
- PREP. **~ in** *The manifestation of the disease in adults is less dramatic.*

● PHRASES **in all its manifestations** *combating racism in all its manifestations*

manifesto *noun*

● ADJ. **Conservative, Labour, etc. | party, party's** *We must all support the party manifesto.* | **election**
● VERB + MANIFESTO **draft, draw up, write | sign | issue, launch, publish | support**
● MANIFESTO + VERB **pledge sth, promise sth** *The manifesto promised reform of the social security system.* | **call for sth, demand sth | contain sth | say sth**
● MANIFESTO + NOUN **commitment, pledge, promise | proposal**
● PREP. **in a/the ~** *The policy is outlined in the party's election manifesto.* **on a/the ~** *Labour won the election on this manifesto.* | **~ for** *a manifesto for reform*

manipulate *verb*

● ADV. **easily** *They believe that voters can be easily manipulated.* | **successfully | deftly, delicately, skilfully | deliberately, systematically | genetically** *genetically manipulated organisms*
● VERB + MANIPULATE **be able to, can | attempt to, try to** *Children try to manipulate you.* | **be easy to | know how to, learn (how) to** *She knows how to manipulate the audience.*
● PHRASES **the ability to manipulate sb/sth**

manipulation *noun*

● ADJ. **careful, clever, skilful | conscious, cynical, deliberate, systematic | political** *People think that the investigation was independent, but in fact a lot of political manipulation went on.* | **data, image, text**
● PREP. **by ~** *The government has disguised the true situation by clever manipulation of the figures.*

mankind *noun*

● VERB + MANKIND **save** *to save mankind from misery and destruction*
● PHRASES **all mankind/the whole of mankind** *According to the Bible, the whole of mankind is descended from Adam.* **benefit to mankind** *It is doubtful whether this research is of any benefit to mankind.* **the dawn of mankind** *objects dating back to the dawn of mankind* **the fate/future of mankind** *politicians who care about the future of mankind* **for the benefit of mankind** *The results of the research were made freely available for the benefit of all mankind.* **the history of mankind, known to mankind** *one of the most toxic substances known to mankind*

manner *noun*

1 way of doing sth/behaving
● ADJ. **conventional, customary, normal, standard, time-honoured, traditional, usual | correct** *You are not approaching the problem in the correct manner.* | **appropriate, satisfactory** *I did my best to behave in the appropriate manner.* | **prudent, reasonable, responsible, safe, sensible** *Chemical waste must be disposed of in an environmentally-responsible manner.* | **efficient, productive, profitable | logical, methodical, orderly, rational, systematic | consistent, uniform | objective | arbitrary, haphazard** *Files have been stored in such a haphazard manner that they are impossible to find.* | **professional | constructive, positive** *The dispute could have been handled in a more constructive manner.* | **non-violent, peaceful | straightforward | suspicious** *He was behaving in a highly suspicious manner.* | **light-hearted | casual, easy, informal, leisurely, relaxed | formal | calm | off-hand** *He answered in such an off-hand manner that I wondered if he'd misheard me.* | **confident, decisive | dignified | diffident, mild, quiet, shy |**

charming, cheerful, friendly, jovial, kindly, pleasant, sympathetic | abrasive, aggressive, arrogant, unfriendly, unpleasant | forthright | brusque, cold | businesslike, no-nonsense** *His no-nonsense manner gave him the reputation of being a good doctor.* | **authoritarian, autocratic, high-handed | condescending, dismissive | authoritative** *The authoritative manner in which he talked concealed his ignorance.* | **bedside, telephone** *He's a good doctor with a sympathetic bedside manner.* ◇ *She has a very pleasant telephone manner.*
● VERB + MANNER **have | adopt** *He tends to adopt a condescending manner when talking to young women.* | **act in** *She accused the teacher of not acting in a professional manner.*
● MANNER + VERB **change** *His manner changed abruptly when he heard how much I wanted.* | **conceal sth** *Her brusque manner concealed a caring nature.* | **suggest sth** *He was not as loutish as his manner suggested.*
● PREP. **in a/the ~** *The inspection was conducted in a thoroughly professional manner.* **in the ~ of** *He lectured us in the manner of a headmaster.* **in your ~** *There was something in his manner that I found very irritating.*
● PHRASES **in a timely manner** *All claims must be settled in a professional and timely manner.* **in no uncertain manner** *He told her in no uncertain manner that her behaviour was unacceptable.*

2 manners polite behaviour
● ADJ. **beautiful, charming, excellent, good, impeccable, nice, perfect** *It's not good manners to stare at people.* | **bad | table** *His children have no table manners.*
● VERB + MANNERS **have | teach sb** *Didn't your parents teach you any manners?* | **learn | forget** *I'm sorry, I was forgetting my manners. Can I offer you a drink?*
● PHRASES **have the (good) manners to do sth** *He could at least have had the manners to answer my letter.* **a lack of manners** *Her lack of manners is quite appalling.*

mannerism *noun*

● ADJ. **odd | irritating**
● VERB + MANNERISM **have | acquire, adopt**
● PREP. **~ of** *He has this irritating mannerism of constantly scratching his nose.*

manoeuvre *noun*

1 skilful movement
● ADJ. **complex, complicated | difficult | dangerous | clever, skilful**
● QUANT. **series**
● VERB + MANOEUVRE **carry out, execute, perform** *The pilot has to carry out a series of complex manoeuvres.* | **attempt | complete**

2 clever plan
● ADJ. **successful | strategic, tactical** *Her withdrawal from the contest was a tactical manoeuvre.* | **diplomatic, political**
● VERB + MANOEUVRE **carry out, execute**
● MANOEUVRE + VERB **fail, succeed**
● PREP. **by a/the ~** *By this manoeuvre, he hopes to gain an advantage at a later stage.*
● PHRASES **freedom of manoeuvre** *The economic conditions are restricting the Chancellor's freedom of manoeuvre.* **room for manoeuvre** *The government has very little room for manoeuvre on this issue.*

3 military operation
● ADJ. **military, strategic, tactical**
● VERB + MANOEUVRE **carry out, conduct, execute, perform**
● PHRASES **be/go on manoeuvres** *The unit is on manoeuvres in southern Italy.*

manoeuvre verb

- ADV. **carefully | easily | expertly, skilfully**
- VERB + MANOEUVRE **be difficult to, be easy to**
- PREP. **around, past, through,** etc. *He skilfully manoeuvred the motor boat past the rocks.*
- PHRASES **manoeuvre (sth) into position, manoeuvre your way** (*figurative*) *He had manoeuvred his way into a position of strength in the party.* **room to manoeuvre** *The clutter of ships had little room to manoeuvre.*

manor noun

- ADJ. **ancient, former, medieval, old | country | royal | fortified, moated**
- MANOR + NOUN **farm, house**
- PREP. **of** *the ancient manor of Tregarrick*
- PHRASES **lord of the manor**

manpower noun

- ADJ. **qualified, skilled, trained** *a shortage of skilled manpower* **| medical, military, police,** etc.
- VERB + MANPOWER **need, require | provide | cut, reduce** *Manpower will be reduced by an average of 20 per cent.* **| increase**
- MANPOWER + NOUN **shortage | allocations, levels, requirements, resources**
- PREP. **in** ~ *a reduction in manpower* **|** ~ **for** *a pool of manpower for the new industries*
- PHRASES **the availability of manpower** *The factory's opening hours over the holiday period will depend on the availability of manpower.* **a reduction in manpower, a shortage of manpower**

mansion noun

- ADJ. **great, huge, imposing, large | lavish, luxurious, luxury, palatial | fine | country | old | stone | historic | 17th century, 200-year-old,** etc. **| Elizabethan, Victorian,** etc. **| Beverly Hills, Hollywood,** etc. **| family | executive** *The rebels besieged the heavily-fortified executive mansion.* **| crumbling, deserted, ruined, run-down**
- VERB + MANSION **live in | build**
- MANSION + VERB **stand** *The historic mansion stands in 160 acres of parkland.*
- MANSION + NOUN **block, flat, house**

manslaughter noun

- ADJ. **attempted | involuntary | reckless | corporate** *The directors of the railway company could be charged with corporate manslaughter.*
⇨ Note at CRIME (for verbs)

manual noun

- ADJ. **instruction, training | owner's, user | car, computer, sewing, software,** etc. **| maintenance, operating, operation, operational, reference, technical, workshop | comprehensive, detailed**
- VERB + MANUAL **come with** *The computer comes with a comprehensive owner's manual.* **| check, consult, look at, read** *Check your manual for details.*
- PREP. **according to the** ~ *According to the manual, the wires should be the other way round.* **in a/the** ~ *What does it say in the manual?* **|** ~ **for** *an instruction manual for a knitting machine* ~ **on** *a manual on teaching drama*

manufacture noun

- ADJ. **large-scale, small-scale | commercial, industrial | local** *cotton ropes of local manufacture* **| metal, steel,** etc. **| cloth, cotton, textile, woollen,** etc. **| car, vehicle,** etc. **| drug, food,** etc.
- VERB + MANUFACTURE **commence, start** *They commenced large-scale commercial manufacture of the chairs in January.* **| complete | be engaged in**
- MANUFACTURE + VERB **start**
- PHRASES **costs of manufacture, date of manufacture** *The date of manufacture of the jewellery has not been authenticated.* **the method/process of manufacture**

manufacturer noun

- ADJ. **big, large, leading, major** *the world's largest computer manufacturer* **| well-known | commercial | independent | foreign, overseas | car, chemical, computer, motor, textile,** etc.
- PHRASES **the manufacturer's instructions** *The guarantee may be rendered invalid if the manufacturer's instructions are not followed.*

manufacturing noun

- ADJ. **large-scale, small-scale | industrial | heavy | labour-intensive | computer-aided, computer-integrated, high-tech/high-technology | car, chemical, component, food, motor, textile, vehicle,** etc.
- MANUFACTURING + NOUN **business, company, enterprise, firm, organization | division, facility, operation, plant, site, subsidiary, unit** *The company set up a manufacturing operation in Lisbon.* **| side** *He now works on the manufacturing side of the business.* **| base, industry, sector** *the decline in the country's manufacturing base* **| area, centre, district, region, town | capability, capacity | output, production, productivity | costs | worker, workforce | employment, jobs | methods, process, system, techniques | expertise**

manure noun

- ADJ. **animal, chicken, cow, horse, pig | farmyard, garden | green** *A green manure is a crop grown mainly to improve soil fertility.* **| organic | well-rotted | liquid**
- VERB + MANURE **apply, spread** *the best time to spread manure on the fields* **| dig in, work in** *Work in plenty of well-rotted manure.*
- MANURE + NOUN **heap**

manuscript noun

1 copy of a book that has not yet been printed
- ADJ. **original | autograph, handwritten** *the original autograph manuscript of the poem* **| unpublished | unfinished | literary, music/musical**
- QUANT. **copy** *I only have one copy of the manuscript.*
- VERB + MANUSCRIPT **write | type | edit, revise | submit (for publication)** *He submitted the manuscript to an editor at Longman.* **| accept/reject (for publication)** *He was delighted when the manuscript was accepted for publication.*
- PREP. **in** ~ *Her autobiography remained in manuscript* (= was not published).

2 very old book/document, written by hand
- ADJ. **ancient, early, medieval | contemporary** *One contemporary manuscript shows Henry II crowned by the hand of Christ.* **| rare | surviving** *the surviving manuscript of 'Beowulf'* **| illuminated**
- MANUSCRIPT + VERB **survive** *earlier manuscripts which no longer survive*

map noun

- ADJ. **large-scale | small-scale | accurate | detailed | quick** (only used with the verb **draw**), **rough, simple, sketch** *'How do you get there?' 'I'll draw you a quick map.'* **| local | road, street** *a street map of central London* ◇ *a road map of the British Isles* **| world | bus, tube, underground | contour, outline, relief | geological, political | weather | Ordnance Survey | tourist | route | wall**
- VERB + MAP **read** *Are you any good at reading maps?*

| check, consult, look at | draw | be marked on *The museum is clearly marked on the map.* | spread out, unfold *We spread the map out on the floor.* | fold (up)
• MAP + VERB **show sth**
• MAP + NOUN **projection**
• PREP. **off the~** *Our village is just off the map.* **on a/the~** *The lane isn't on the map.* | **~of** *a map of the area*

marathon *noun*

1 long race
• ADJ. **half, full**
• VERB + MARATHON **prepare for, train for | compete in, run, take part in | complete, finish | win**
• MARATHON + NOUN **champion, runner | racing, running** *He says that he keeps fit by marathon running.*

2 long activity
• ADJ. **12-hour, 700-mile, etc. | car, cycling, etc.**
• MARATHON + NOUN **journey, walk | effort | match, race** *a marathon five-set tennis match*

marble *noun*

• ADJ. **cool** *The hotel is traditionally furnished, with cool marble floors.* | **coloured | veined | polished | carved**
• QUANT. **block, slab**
• VERB + MARBLE **carve (sth from/in), make sth from/in/(out) of** *a statue of Cupid carved in black marble* | **quarry**
• MARBLE + NOUN **quarry**
• PREP. **in~** *sculptures in polished white marble*

March *noun*

⇨ Note at MONTH

march *noun*

1 movement/journey
• ADJ. **long | brisk | steady | forced | approach** *They reached the enemy position after an arduous approach march.* | **fifty-mile, four-day, etc. | two hours, half a day's, etc.** *The camp was half a day's march away.* | **northward, southward, etc. | forward, onward** *(figurative) the forward march of technology* | **inevitable, inexorable** *(figurative) the inexorable march of time*
• VERB + MARCH **begin, set off on** *The army set off on a forced march towards Berlin.*
• PREP. **on the~** *The army has been on the march for two weeks* | **~from** *the march from Paris to Brittany* **~of** *a march of over 30 miles* ◇ *(figurative) the march of history/progress/science* **~ to, ~ towards** *(figurative) the steady march towards equality*
• PHRASES **line of march** *Villages in the army's line of march were burned to the ground.* **a ... march away** *The border was still a day's march away.* **the march eastward, westward, etc.**

2 organized walk
• ADJ. **hunger, peace, protest, victory | anti-racism, pro-democracy, etc.**
• VERB + MARCH **hold, organize, stage | lead | be on, go on, join in, take part in | halt, stop** *The farmers halted the march outside the Ministry of Agriculture.* | **break up** *The march was broken up by police in riot gear.*
• MARCH + VERB **mark sth** *a march marking the thirtieth anniversary of the shootings*
• PREP. **at/on a/the ~** *There were in excess of 100 000 people at the march.* | **~against** *a march against racism* **~for** *a march for the victims of the war* **~from, ~of** *a march of over 6 000 people* **~to**
• PHRASES **a march past** *There will be a special march past of competitors.*

3 music
• ADJ. **military | funeral, wedding**

• VERB + MARCH **compose | play | strike up** *The orchestra struck up a military march.*

march *verb*

1 walk with regular steps
• ADV. **briskly, swiftly | boldly | purposefully | inexorably** *(figurative) Time marches inexorably on and we still have not made a decision.* | **north, south, etc. | ahead, away, back, forward, off, on, out, over, past, up (and down)** *Craig marched up to the front door and rang the bell.* ◇ *Soldiers were marching up and down outside the government buildings.*
• PREP. **from, into, on** *The invading army marched on Rome.* **out of** *So saying, she marched boldly out of the house.* **through, to** *They marched all the way from London to Edinburgh.* **towards**
• PHRASES **march in step** *conscripts learning to march in step* (= in time with each other)

2 walk in a large group to protest about sth
• ADV. **peacefully**
• PREP. **for** *marching for peace* **in support of** *protesters marching in support of the students' demands* **on** *The demonstrators marched on the Italian embassy.* **through** *marching peacefully through the town centre* **to, towards**

margarine *noun*

• ADJ. **hard | soft | low-fat, polyunsaturated** *a tub of low-fat margarine* | **sunflower, vegetable**
• QUANT. **tub**
• VERB + MARGARINE **put on, spread (sth with)** *She put some margarine on her roll.* ◇ *Spread some margarine on the toast, please.* | **heat, melt, soften | beat (in), cream, mix, rub in** *Cream the margarine and sugar together.* ◇ *Rub the margarine into the flour.*
⇨ Special page at FOOD

margin *noun*

1 empty space at the side of a page in a book, etc.
• ADJ. **generous, wide** *Leave a generous margin on the left.* | **narrow | left-hand, right-hand**
• VERB + MARGIN **leave, rule, set | adjust**
• PREP. **at the~** *Start writing at the left-hand margin.* **in the~** *She scribbled notes in the margin.*

2 space, time, votes, etc. by which sth is won
• ADJ. **comfortable, considerable, greater, huge, large, wide | narrow, slim, small | clear, safe**
• VERB + MARGIN **have**
• PREP. **by a~** *She won by a clear margin.* | **~over** *He had an 18-second margin over his nearest rival.*
• PHRASES **by the largest/narrowest, etc. of margins** *He won by the narrowest of margins.* **a margin of victory**

3 amount of extra space, time, etc.
• ADJ. **good, greater, wide** *Sales predictions are open to wide margins of error.* | **narrow | adequate | safety**
• VERB + MARGIN **allow (sb/sth), give (sb/sth), leave, provide** *The device gives a greater margin of safety.*
• PREP. **~for** *We have substantial reserves, which provide a good margin for uncertainties.*
• PHRASES **a margin for/of error** *The schedule left no margin for error.* **a margin of safety**

4 profit
• ADJ. **high, large | low, narrow, small, tight** *We're working to rather tight profit margins.* | **gross, net | profit | operating, pre-tax, retail**
• VERB + MARGIN **achieve, have** *These manufacturers have high gross margins.* | **operate at/on, work to | improve, increase** *Higher productivity has enabled them to increase their profit margins.* | **cut, erode, reduce, squeeze** *Price rises have eroded profit margins.*
• MARGIN + VERB **widen | narrow**

• PREP. **at a~** *They are operating at very low margins.* | **~on** *They hope to improve their margins on computers.*
⇨ Note at PER CENT (for more verbs)

marijuana *noun*

• QUANT. **joint**
• VERB + MARIJUANA **smoke**
• MARIJUANA + NOUN **cigarette, joint | plant**
⇨ Note at DRUG (for more verbs and nouns)

mark *noun*

1 spot/line
• ADJ. **dirty, grease, greasy, grubby | visible | distinguishing, identifying** *Does he have any distinguishing marks?* | **chalk, pencil | bite, burn, claw, finger** (also **fingermark**), **scorch, scratch, scuff, skid, stretch, tyre**
• VERB + MARK **get** *How did you get that mark on your shirt?* | **leave, make** *The dirty water left a mark round the side of the bath.* | **get off/out, remove** *I can't get the children's dirty fingermarks off the wall.*
• MARK + VERB **come off/out** *These greasy marks just won't come out.*
• PREP. **~on** *There were grubby marks on the wall.*

2 sign of a quality/feeling
• ADJ. **deep, indelible, permanent** *The experience left a deep mark on her memory.* | **real** *the real mark of a master craftsman*
• VERB + MARK **bear, have | leave**
• PREP. **~of** *Such thoughtful behaviour is the mark of a true gentleman.*
• PHRASES **as a mark of respect**

3 used to show the standard of sb's work
• ADJ. **good, high | bad, low, poor | full** *I got full marks for my homework.* | **top | pass** *What's the pass mark in maths?* | **total | average**
• VERB + MARK **get | give sb | take off** *She took off a mark for bad handwriting.* | **gain | lose**
• PREP. **above … ~s, below … ~s** *If you get below 40 marks, you're not allowed to go up into the next class.* | **~ for** *You get two marks for each correct answer.* ◇ *a good mark for geography* **~ out of** *How many marks out of ten would you give it?*

4 level of sth
• ADJ. **halfway** *We've reached the halfway mark in the show.* | **high-water, low-water, tide**
• VERB + MARK **set | reach | pass** *This year's sales figures have already passed the mark set last year.* | **fall short of**
• PREP. **above the~, around the~** *around the £500 mark* **at a/the ~** *The river was at its low-water mark.* **below the ~, up to the ~** (= as good as sb/sth should be) *Your grammar is not quite up to the mark.*

5 target
• ADJ. **easy**
• VERB + MARK **find, hit** *The shot found its mark.* | **miss**
• PHRASES **wide of the mark** (*figurative*) *Shock tactics often fall wide of their mark.*

mark *verb*

1 write/draw sth
• ADV. **clearly** *My room was clearly marked on the plan.* | **carefully** *She carefully marked where the screws were to go.* | **indelibly**
• PREP. **as** *Certain words were marked as important.* **for** *Some of the crates were marked for export.* **in** *Mark the position of all the building sites in black.* **on** *All buildings are marked on the map.* **with** *The boundary was marked with a dotted line.*

2 spoil/damage sth
• ADV. **badly, deeply** *The paperweight had fallen onto*
the desk, badly marking the surface. ◇ (*figurative*) *The town is still deeply marked by the folk memory of the Depression.*

3 be a sign of sth
• ADV. **effectively | conveniently** *'Lyrical Ballads' conveniently marks the beginning of nineteenth-century poetry.* | **publicly** *The wedding ceremony publicly marks the beginning of commitment to another through marriage.*
• VERB + MARK **appear to, seem to** *This speech appears to mark a change in government policy.*

marked *adj.*

1 easy to see
• VERBS **be | become**
• ADV. **especially, extremely, particularly, strongly, very** *There is a strongly marked difference between the two creatures.* | **increasingly | quite**

2 with markings
• VERBS **be**
• ADV. **heavily** *Most cranes lay two heavily marked eggs.* | **attractively, beautifully, brightly, strikingly**
• PREP. **with** *These trout are beautifully marked with bright red spots.*

market *noun*

1 place where people go to buy and sell things
• ADJ. **open-air, outdoor, street | covered, indoor | antiques, cattle, fruit and vegetable, etc. | flea** (= that sells old or used goods at low prices)
• VERB + MARKET **hold** *The market is held on Wednesdays.* | **go to | take sth to** *They took the pigs to market.*
• MARKET + NOUN **square | town | day**
• PREP. **at/in a/the~** *to buy some fish at the market*

2 business/trade
• ADJ. **competitive | active, booming, bullish, lively, strong, thriving | bull** (*finance*), **rising | depressed, dull, sluggish, weak | bear** (*finance*), **falling | steady | buyer's, seller's | foreign, global, international, overseas, world | domestic, home, internal, local | single** *the completion of the European single market in 1992* **common | economic | free | open | black** (= illegal) | **bond, capital, commodity, consumer, currency, export, financial, foreign exchange, futures, housing, money, product, property, securities, stock | car, computer, etc. | job, labour**
• VERB + MARKET **put sth on | come on/onto** *A new model has come on the market.* | **develop | break into, get into, penetrate** *They're hoping to get into the Far Eastern market.* | **capture, corner, monopolize | supply | flood** *flooding the market with cheap foreign goods* | **lose | depress | play** *an investor who knows how to play the market—and win*
• MARKET + VERB **open up** *The Chinese market has opened up recently.* | **boom | pick up, rally | slump | be down, be up** *The market was down 15 per cent.* | **close** *The market closed weaker.* | **open**
• MARKET + NOUN **price, value | conditions | leader | position, share | sector | trends**
• PREP. **in/into a/the~** *changes in the UK market* **on the~** *one of the best car deals on the market* | **~ in** *a thriving market in second-hand cars*
• PHRASES **be in the market for sth** (= be interested in buying sth), **the bottom's dropped/fallen out of the market** (= the market has collapsed), **a gap in the market, the bottom/lower/top/upper end of the market**

3 people who want to buy sth
• ADJ. **big, good, huge, large | poor, small | expanding, growing | shrinking | ready | niche**
• VERB + MARKET **create** *The company has created a niche market for itself.*
• MARKET + VERB **expand, grow | shrink | collapse**

| **bear sth** *We will charge whatever the market will bear* (= as much as people can be persuaded to pay).
- MARKET + NOUN **segment** | **niche** | **research**
- PREP. **~for** *the market for new cars*

4 the free market
- VERB + MARKET **leave sth to** *Some services cannot be left to the market.*
- MARKET + NOUN **forces** | **economy**

market *verb*

- ADV. **heavily** | **effectively,** **successfully** | **cleverly** | **aggressively** | **actively** | **selectively** *The printer is being selectively marketed in a handful of countries.*
- PREP. **as** *It will be marketed as a tonic for the elderly.* **through** *The product is being marketed through the existing sales force.* **to** *The company is not actively marketing its products to schools.*

marketable *adj.*

- VERBS **be** | **become**
- ADV. **easily, highly, readily, very** | **potentially**

marketing *noun*

- ADJ. **effective,** **good** | **poor** | **aggressive** | **direct** | **global, international, worldwide** | **niche**
- VERB + MARKETING **do** *The company has done some effective marketing of the new model.* | **improve**
- MARKETING + NOUN **campaign, exercise, strategy** | **ploy, tool** | **director, manager** | **agency, company, department**
- PREP. **in ~** *She works in marketing.* **through/with ~** *We could get more sales through better marketing.*
- PHRASES **sales and marketing**
⇨ Special page at BUSINESS

marketplace *noun* (often **the marketplace**)

- ADJ. **competitive** | **commercial,** **financial** | **global, international** | **changing**
- PREP. **in a/the ~** *The company found it hard to survive in a changing marketplace.*

marquee *noun*

- ADJ. **giant, huge, large**
- VERB + MARQUEE **erect**
- PREP. **in a/the~** *The wedding reception was held in a marquee.* **under a/the~** *The guests sat on a platform under a large marquee.*

marquess *noun*

⇨ Note at PEER

marriage *noun*

1 state of being husband and wife
- ADJ. **good, happy, successful** | **broken, disastrous, failed, unhappy** *She was the child of a broken marriage.* | **first, second, etc.** | **previous** | **early** | **late** | **conventional** | **modern** | **open** | **morganatic** | **loveless** | **childless** | **mixed** | **arranged**
- VERB + MARRIAGE **have** *He had an unhappy marriage with an older woman.* | **propose** | **enter into** | **consummate** | **annul, dissolve** | **save** *They are struggling to save their marriage for the children's sake.*
- MARRIAGE + VERB **last** | **be over, break down/up, end, fall apart, fail** *Their marriage ended in divorce.*
- MARRIAGE + NOUN **vows** | **plans, proposal** | **partner** | **relationship** | **break-up, breakdown, problems** | **counselling, guidance** | **counsellor** | **certificate, contract** | **market** *Daughters were expected to join their well-bred friends on the marriage market.* | **bed**
- PREP. **by/from a ~** *She's his daughter by a previous*

marriage. **by ~** *They are related by marriage.* **in a/the ~** *She was the dominant partner in the marriage.* **outside ~** *sex outside marriage* **within ~** | **~ between** *the marriage between John and Elizabeth* **~ into** *his marriage into a wealthy family* **~ to/with** *her marriage to Jim*
- PHRASES **ask for/win sb's hand in marriage** (*old-fashioned*), **the break-up/breakdown of a marriage, give sb in marriage** (*old-fashioned*), **the institution of marriage, a marriage of convenience, a proposal of marriage**

2 wedding ceremony
- ADJ. **Christian, Jewish, etc.** | **civil** | **shotgun** (= arranged quickly because the bride is pregnant)
- VERB + MARRIAGE **celebrate** *The marriage was celebrated in the cathedral.*
- MARRIAGE + VERB **be held, take place**
- MARRIAGE + NOUN **ceremony** | **licence**
- PREP. **at a/the~** *She wanted to be present at the marriage of her grandson.* | **~ to** *Mr and Mrs Wall invite you to the marriage of their daughter Ann to Mr Thomas Lea.*

married *adj.*

- VERBS **be, feel** *I wouldn't have felt properly married if it hadn't been a church wedding.* | **get** *When did you get married?* | **remain**
- ADV. **newly, recently** *The newly married couple left for their honeymoon in Spain.* | **previously** | **happily** | **unhappily** | **lawfully, legally** | **properly, safely, truly**
- PREP. **to** *She's married to an actor.*

marry *verb*

- VERB + MARRY **hope to, want to** *I don't want to marry Robert.* | **agree to, promise to** *He promised to marry her when he returned.* | **be going to, plan to** *Matt told me he was going to marry again.* ◇ *They plan to marry next year.* | **forbid sb to** *Duty forbade them to marry.* | **ask sb to** *He asked me to marry him but I said no.*
- PREP. **for** *He married her for love, not for money.* **into** *the difficulties of marrying into the royal family*
- PHRASES **get married** *They are hoping to get married next year.* **marry late/young** *People are marrying later these days.* **not be the marrying kind** (= not the kind of person who wants to get married)

marsh *noun*

- ADJ. **coastal, salt** | **freshwater** | **grazing**
- VERB + MARSH **drain, reclaim**
- MARSH + NOUN **plant**
- PREP. **in/on a/the~** *He keeps his cattle on the marshes.*

marshal *noun*

⇨ Note at RANK

martial law *noun*

- VERB + MARTIAL LAW **declare, impose, introduce, place sth under** | **lift**
- PREP. **under~** *The city remains under martial law.*

martyr *noun*

1 sb who is killed/suffers for what they believe
- ADJ. **early** | **Christian**
- VERB + MARTYR **make sb** *Killing him would only make him a martyr.*
- PREP. **~ to** *a martyr to the cause*
- PHRASES **a martyr's death**

2 sb who tries to gain sympathy
- VERB + MARTYR **play** *Stop playing the martyr.*
- PHRASES **make a martyr of yourself**

marvel verb

- VERB + MARVEL **can/could only** *One can only marvel at the way the building has been constructed.* | **never cease to** *I never cease to marvel at his stupidity.*
- PREP. **at** *He marvelled at how easy it was to make money.*

marvellous adj.

- VERBS **be, feel, look, sound**
- ADV. **bloody** (*taboo, ironic*), **really** *This is really marvellous news!* | **absolutely, quite, simply** *The food looks absolutely marvellous!* | **pretty**

mascara noun

- ADJ. **thick** | **waterproof**
- VERB + MASCARA **wear** | **apply, put on** | **remove** | **smudge** *Her tears had smudged her mascara.*
- MASCARA + VERB **run, smudge**
- MASCARA + NOUN **brush, wand**

masculine adj.

- VERBS **be**
- ADV. **distinctly, extremely, heavily, severely, uncompromisingly, unmistakably, very** *an environment which is heavily masculine* ◇ *the severely masculine cut of his suit* | **exclusively** *The ceremony is exclusively masculine.* | **overwhelmingly, predominantly** | **essentially** | **typically** *That's a typically masculine attitude!* | **inherently, intrinsically** | **overtly** | **aggressively** *He has an aggressively masculine approach to these questions.*

mask noun

1 cover for sb's face
- ADJ. **face** | **gas** | **oxygen** | **surgical** | **Hallowe'en**
- VERB + MASK **have on, wear** | **put on** | **pull off, remove, strip off, take off, tear off** *In the second part of the play, the actors take off their masks.*
- MASK + VERB **cover sth**
- PREP. **behind/beneath a/the ~** *Two eyes glared at him from beneath the mask.* **in a/the ~** *two men in black masks* | **~ over** *She wore a mask over her face.*

2 sth that hides sb's real feelings
- ADJ. **blank, cold, expressionless, grim, rigid** *Her face was a blank mask as she answered my question.*
- MASK + VERB **slip** *For a moment her mask slipped, and I saw how scared she really was.*
- PREP. **behind a/the ~** *Behind the mask of friendliness, I know he really dislikes me.* | **~ for** *His fooling around is a mask for his lack of confidence.*

mask verb

- ADV. **completely, entirely, quite, totally** | **partly** | **barely** | **effectively**
- VERB + MASK **tend to** *Wood stains provide good protection but tend to mask the natural grain of the wood.*
- PREP. **with** *She masked her anger with a smile.*

masochism noun

- ADJ. **pure, sheer**
- QUANT. **streak, touch** *There's a streak of masochism in his personality.*
- PHRASES **a form of masochism**

mass noun

1 large amount/number of sth
- ADJ. **enormous, great, huge, large, vast** | **broad** *Their policies appeal to the broad mass of the population.* | **formless, shapeless** *When I washed the jumper, it just turned into a shapeless mass.* | **compact, dense, solid** | **chaotic** *a chaotic mass of ideas* | **tangled** *a tangled mass of hair*
- PREP. **~ of** *a dense mass of smoke* **~es of** (*informal*) *There were masses of people at the concert.*

2 Mass Christian ceremony
- ADJ. **requiem, Sunday**
- VERB + MASS **attend, go to, hear** *She never failed to attend Sunday Mass.* | **celebrate, offer, say** *The local priest celebrates Mass in the village church.*
- PREP. **~ for** *a requiem Mass for the sailors who drowned*

massacre noun

- ADJ. **appalling, bloody, cold-blooded, horrible, terrible** *an appalling massacre of women and children*
- VERB + MASSACRE **be responsible for, carry out, perpetrate, take part in** *The massacre was carried out by enemy troops.* ◇ *As many as fifty men took part in the massacre.* | **be killed in** | **escape, survive**
- MASSACRE + VERB **take place**
- PREP. **~ by** *a massacre by rebel soldiers*
- PHRASES **the victims of a massacre**

massage noun

- ADJ. **gentle, relaxing, soothing** | **vigorous** | **back, body, foot, full-body, neck** | **cardiac, heart** *They managed to revive the injured driver with cardiac massage.*
- VERB + MASSAGE **have, receive** | **give sb** *The physiotherapist gave me a massage to ease the pain.*
- MASSAGE + NOUN **parlour** *She went to the massage parlour for a full-body massage.*

massage verb

- ADV. **firmly, vigorously** | **gently, lightly**
- PREP. **into** *Gently massage the cream into your skin.* **with** *He massaged her back with scented oil.* ◇ *Massage it lightly with your fingertips.*

master noun

1 person in charge
- ADJ. **political** *His political masters are all old right-wing politicians.*
- PREP. **~ of** *He wants to be master of his own destiny.*

2 person with skill
- ADJ. **acknowledged, great** *This portrait is the work of an acknowledged master.*
- MASTER + NOUN **builder, craftsman**
- PREP. **~ of** *a master of disguise*
- PHRASES **be a past master at/in/of sth** (= to be very good at sth) *He's a past master at delaying meetings.*

3 Master's university degree
- VERB + MASTER'S **do, study for, take** *He did a Master's at Hull University.* | **get** *She got her Master's last year.*
- MASTER'S + NOUN **degree**
- PREP. **~ in** *a Master's in politics*

master verb

- ADV. **completely, entirely, fully, quite** | **quickly**
- VERB + MASTER **be difficult to** *a technique that was surprisingly difficult to master* | **struggle to, try to** *the challenge of trying to master a new language* | **fail to**
- PHRASES **master the art of sth** *He never completely mastered the art of lip-reading.*

masterpiece noun

- ADJ. **great** *It's one of the greatest masterpieces of Western art.* | **minor** | **architectural, literary, musical**
- VERB + MASTERPIECE **create, produce** | **be considered, be hailed as, be recognized as** *Within a week of publication, the novel was hailed as a masterpiece.*

● PREP. **~by** *a masterpiece by Picasso* **~of** *a masterpiece of classical architecture*
⇨ Note at ART

mastery *noun*

● ADJ. **absolute, complete, total** | **gradual** *Children show gradual mastery of reading in the first years at school.* | **practical, technical** *He plays the violin with technical mastery, but no feeling.*
● VERB + MASTERY **have** *The allied bombers had total mastery of the skies.* | **demonstrate, display, show** *He shows complete mastery of the instrument.* | **achieve, acquire, attain, gain**
● PREP. **~ of** *He acquired mastery of four languages.* **~over** *The king had absolute mastery over the country.*

mat *noun*

● ADJ. **dense, thick** *a thick mat of hair*
● PREP. **~of** *the dense mat of roots at the bottom of the tree*

match *noun*

1 in sports
● ADJ. **big, crucial, important** | **exciting, thrilling** | **championship, competitive, cup, league** | **friendly** | **away, home** *He's such a keen fan, he even goes to all the away matches.* | **cricket, football, rugby, wrestling, etc.**
● VERB + MATCH **play** *The match will be played in the new stadium.* | **have** *Figo had an outstanding match.* | **go to, see, watch** | **be defeated in, lose** | **clinch, win** *A late goal clinched the match for Porto.* | **draw** *We drew our first game of the season 1–1.*
● MATCH + VERB **take place**
● PREP. **during a/the ~** *an incident which took place during Saturday's match* **in a/the ~** *She was injured in last week's match.* | **~against** *the match against Wales* **~between** *the match between Japan and Brazil* **~with** *They lost their match with Estonia.*

2 for lighting a fire
● ADJ. **lighted**
● QUANT. **box**
● VERB + MATCH **light, strike** *He lit a match so they could see in the cave.* | **blow out**
● PHRASES **put a match to sth** *Someone had put a match to the pile of papers.*

3 good combination
● ADJ. **excellent, good, perfect** *The blouse and skirt are a perfect match.*
● PREP. **~between** *an excellent match between our goals and what your company offers* **~for** *That jumper should be a good match for your trousers.*

4 sth the same
● ADJ. **exact**
● PREP. **~for** *To forge the certificate, she needed an exact match for the paper and the fonts.*

match *verb*

1 combine well
● ADV. **well** *As a couple they are not very well matched (= they are not very suitable for each other).* | **not quite** *The room was full of old furniture that didn't quite match.*
● PHRASES **to match** *I bought a duvet cover and some curtains to match.*

2 find sth similar/connected
● ADV. **correctly** | **carefully**
● PREP. **for** *The control group in the experiment was matched for age and sex.* | **to** *The aim of the competition is to match the quote to the person who said it.*

3 be/make sth equal/better
● ADV. **almost** *She found that his determination almost*

matched her own. | **not quite** *Nothing quite matches the fine, subtle flavour of this cheese.*
● VERB + MATCH **come close to** | **be able/unable to** *The company was unable to match his current salary.* | **try to** | **fail to** *Children can be made to suffer when they fail to match their parents' expectations.*
● PREP. **for** *No other rock band comes even close to matching them for dynamism or style.*
● PHRASES **be equally/evenly/well matched** *The teams were very evenly matched.* **be unevenly matched**

4 provide sth suitable
● ADV. **carefully** | **up** *We have to match up the right pet with the right owner.*
● VERB + MATCH **seek to, try to**
● PREP. **to** *The available organs are carefully matched to people in need of transplants.* **with** *The agency tries to match single people with suitable partners.*

mate *noun*

1 friend
● ADJ. **best, good** *They've been good mates ever since they were at school together.*
● VERB + MATE **have** *He's got loads of mates at school.*

2 sexual partner
● VERB + MATE **attract, choose, find** *These birds have colourful feathers to attract a mate.*

material *noun*

1 substance
● ADJ. **combustible, flammable, hazardous, inflammable, radioactive, toxic** | **recyclable** | **man-made**

2 things for making sth
● ADJ. **raw** *Higher raw material costs have pushed up the price of many manufactured goods.* | **industrial** | **building** *a storeroom full of building materials* | **drawing, writing** *Prisoners were not allowed writing materials.*

3 cloth
● ADJ. **thick, thin** | **coarse, fine** | **woven**
● QUANT. **length, piece, roll, scrap, strip** *A patchwork quilt is a good way of using up scraps of material.*

4 written matter
● ADJ. **fascinating, good, relevant, useful** | **source** *The letter were used as source material in this new biography.* | **classified, confidential, sensitive** | **unpublished** | **educational, instructional, promotional, teaching** | **biographical, historical** | **indecent, obscene, pornographic** *He was convicted of importing indecent material.*
● VERB + MATERIAL **collect, find, gather, get hold of** *He's collecting material for a new book on space travel.* ◇ *I can't find any relevant material on him in the library.* | **contain, include** *This new biography contains a wealth of previously unpublished material.* | **produce, publish**
● PREP. **~for** *useful material for a documentary* **~on** *original material on the First World War*

materialize *verb*

● ADV. **never** *The hoped-for boom never materialized.*
● VERB + MATERIALIZE **fail to** *The rise in share prices failed to materialize.*

mathematician *noun*

● ADJ. **brilliant** | **distinguished, great** *one of the greatest mathematicians of all time* | **applied, pure**

mathematics *noun*

● ADJ. **applied, pure** | **investigative** | **school** | **elementary, higher, primary, secondary**
● PHRASES **a branch of mathematics**
⇨ Note at SUBJECT (for verbs and nouns)

maths noun

- ADJ. **basic** | **complicated** *Working out the quantities of the ingredients involved some complicated maths.*
- MATHS + NOUN **problem** *The class were struggling to find the solution to a maths problem.*
⇒ Note at SUBJECT

matter noun

1 subject/situation that must be dealt with
- ADJ. **important, pressing, serious, urgent, weighty** *He left, saying he had pressing matters to attend to.* ◇ *The question of his innocence is a weighty matter for this court.* | **awkward, complex, complicated, delicate, difficult** *I wasn't sure how to approach the delicate matter of pay.* | **no easy, (no) simple** *It is then a simple matter to print off the data you have collected.* ◇ *It is no simple matter starting a new business.* | **trifling, trivial** | **practical** *They've agreed in theory, but now we need to discuss practical matters.* | **family, personal** | **subject** *His articles deal with a wide range of subject matter.* | **economic, environmental, financial, legal, political, procedural, routine, technical** *The rest of the meeting was taken up by routine matters.* | **different** *I don't mind lizards, but snakes are a different matter.*
- VERB + MATTER **bring up, broach, raise** *I thought I'd better broach the matter with my boss.* ◇ *The matter will be raised at our next meeting.* | **address, debate, discuss, go into, take up** *I don't really want to go into this matter now.* | **pursue, take further** *After legal advice I chose to take the matter further.* | **drop** *His lawyer advised him to drop the matter.* | **consider, examine, look at/into, tackle** | **clarify, clear up, decide, resolve, settle** *It's a relief to have the matter settled.* | **approach, deal with, treat** *Police are treating the matter as a murder enquiry.*
- PREP. **in a/the ~** *I don't have much experience in these matters.* ◇ *Do I have any choice in the matter?* **on a/the ~** *Speak to your manager if you need help on this matter.* | **~ for** *The incident is definitely a matter for the police.* **~ of** *It's a matter of concern to all of us.* ◇ *We discussed the matter of whether or not to hire a bus.* ◇ *Getting the effect you want is a matter of trial and error.*
- PHRASES **the crux/heart of the matter** (= the most important part of a subject/situation), **let the matter drop/rest** *She refused to let the matter rest.* **the matter in hand** *Let's concentrate on the matter in hand for now, and leave other issues till later.*

2 matters situation you are in
- VERB + MATTERS **complicate, confuse, make worse, not help** *It didn't help matters that I had a terrible cold.* ◇ *To make matters worse, my friend then lost her keys.* | **arrange** *She always arranges matters to suit herself.*

3 substance
- ADJ. **solid** | **organic, vegetable** *composed entirely of organic matter* | **inanimate, inorganic** | **printed, written**

matter verb

- ADV. **a great deal, a lot, really** *These things matter a lot to young children.* | **hardly, little** (*formal*), **not much, scarcely** *She could find a job. It hardly mattered what.* | **no longer, not any more**
- VERB + MATTER **not seem to** *Somehow it didn't seem to matter much any more.*
- PREP. **about** *It doesn't matter about the mess.* **to** *It didn't matter to her that he was blind.*

mattress noun

- ADJ. **double, single** | **comfortable** | **firm, hard** | **soft** | **lumpy, sagging** *an old bed with a sagging mattress*
- PREP. **on a/the ~** *The children slept on mattresses on the floor.* **under a/the ~** *My grandmother keeps her money under the mattress.*

mature verb

- ADV. **fully** *a fully matured cheese* | **early** *This variety is easy to grow and matures early.* | **quickly, rapidly** | **slowly** | **emotionally, physically** *The teenage years cover a period in which people mature physically and emotionally.*
- VERB + MATURE **allow sth to, leave sth to** *The cheese is smoked and then left to mature.*
- PREP. **into** *She had matured into a beautiful young woman.* **to** *a young man who is maturing to adulthood*

mature adj.

- VERBS **be** | **become**
- ADV. **fully** | **emotionally, physically, sexually**

maturity noun

1 adult behaviour
- ADJ. **great, growing, increasing** *I can see an increasing maturity in how she understands the world.* | **emotional, intellectual**
- VERB + MATURITY **have** | **show** *She has shown great maturity in her behaviour this term.* | **grow in** *These latest paintings show how the artist has really grown in maturity.* | **lack**

2 full growth
- ADJ. **full** *It can take years for these plants to reach full maturity.* | **physical, psychological, sexual**
- VERB + MATURITY **approach, come to, grow to, reach** *The insects lay eggs when they approach maturity.*

maul verb

- ADV. **badly, severely** *She was badly mauled by a lion.*

maxim noun

- ADJ. **general, simple**
- VERB + MAXIM **apply, follow** *If you follow a few simple maxims, your business should be a success.*

maximum noun

- ADJ. **absolute** | **agreed, recommended** *Do not exceed the recommended maximum of three tablets a day.* | **legal, statutory**
- VERB + MAXIMUM **reach, rise to** *The temperature reached a maximum of 35°C yesterday.* | **exceed** | **allow (sb/sth), permit (sb/sth)** *In the exam, allow yourself a maximum of 30 minutes per question.* ◇ *the maximum permitted speeds* | **limit sth to, restrict sth to** *The amount you have to pay will be limited to a maximum of £500.*
- PREP. **above (the)~, at (the)~** *a journey of four hours at the maximum* **below (the)~, to (the)~** *He is using his talents to the maximum.* **(up) to a/the ~** | **~ of** *You can claim the allowance for a maximum of six months.*
- PHRASES **maximum possible** *They fined her the maximum possible for the offence.*

May noun

⇒ Note at MONTH

mayor noun

- ADJ. **local** | **deputy** | **lord** *In 1662–3 he served as Lord Mayor of London.* | **right-wing, socialist, etc.**
- VERB + MAYOR **run for** *running for mayor of Bogotá* | **elect (sb), elect sb as** | **serve as**
- PREP. **~ of** *the mayor of Southampton*

maze noun

- ADJ. **complex, intricate, tortuous**
- VERB + MAZE **be/get lost in** | **find your way through** *He found his way through the complex maze of corridors.*
- PREP. **in a/the ~, through a/the ~** *I followed him*

through a maze of narrow alleys. | ~ of I was lost in a maze of passages.

meal noun

● ADJ. **big, filling, heavy** I always want to go to sleep after a heavy meal. | **slap-up** | **lavish, sumptuous** | **square, substantial** She hadn't had a square meal for days. | **light, simple** The bar serves light meals. | **meagre** a meagre meal of bread and cheese | **four-course, three-course, etc.** | **appetizing, decent, delicious, excellent, lovely, tasty** Thanks for a delicious meal. | **balanced, healthy, nourishing, wholesome** | **main** When do you have your main meal of the day? | **evening, midday** | **hot** Hot meals are not available after 10 o'clock. | **vegetarian** ⇨ Special page at FOOD

> **NOTE**
> **Meals**
> ....
>
> **eat, have, take** (formal)~
>   Have you had breakfast?
> **grab, snatch** ~
>   I'm so busy I have to snatch meals when I can.
> **ask sb to** ~
> **have/invite/take sb for/to** ~
> **come/go for/to** ~
>   He wouldn't have asked her to supper if he didn't like her, she reasoned.
> These verbs are often used with **around, out, over** and **round:**
>   We must have you over for dinner sometime.
>   Let's go out for a meal.
> **be out to** lunch
>   He's out to lunch with a client.
> **stop for** ~
>   We stopped for tea at the Ritz.
> **join sb for, stay for/to** ~
>   You're sure you won't stay for tea?
> **sit down to, start** ~
> **finish** ~
>   We had just sat down to breakfast when the phone rang.
> **skip** ~
>   I sometimes skip lunch if we're very busy.
> **cook (sb), fix (sb), get ready, make (sb), prepare** ~
>   She hurried downstairs to fix herself some breakfast.
> **have** ~ **ready**
>   We'll have supper ready for you.
> **serve** ~
>   Lunch is served from noon till 3.
> **keep warm, warm up** ~
>   I'll be home late, so keep my dinner warm.
> **provide, provide sb (with)** ~
>   Dinner is provided in the superb hotel restaurant.
> ~ **be available**
>   A four course dinner is available by prior arrangement.
> ~ **be ready**
>   'Breakfast's ready!' shouted Christine.
> ~ **time**
>   The family was always noisy at meal times.
> **at/during/over** ~
>   Nobody spoke during supper.
> **for** ~
>   What did you have for lunch?
> ~ **of**
>   a breakfast of pancakes and maple syrup

---

mean adj.

● VERBS **be, feel, seem** | **become**
● ADV. **really, very** I thought it was really mean of him not

to let her use the car. | **a bit, pretty, rather, slightly** That was a pretty mean trick. ◇ He's rather mean when it comes to spending money on the children.
● PREP. **to** He's so mean to his mother! **with** She's very mean with her money.

meaning noun

1 what sth means
● ADJ. **clear, exact, precise** The context makes the meaning clear. ◇ What is the exact meaning of this phrase? | **correct, true** | **original** | **double, hidden** There's often a double meaning in jokes and riddles. ◇ I'm sure there's no hidden meaning in what he says. | **figurative, metaphorical, symbolic** | **literal**
● VERB + MEANING **get, grasp, understand** I can't grasp the meaning of this quotation. | **decipher, interpret, work out** Historians are trying to decipher the meaning of the documents. | **assign, attribute** She assigns a meaning to his words they just didn't have. | **bear, carry, have** Some of the symbols carry meaning and some just represent sounds. ◇ a word that has more than one meaning | **take on** The word 'gay' took on its modern meaning in the 1960s. | **communicate, convey, express**
● PREP. **in a/the** ~ ambiguity in the meaning of a phrase **with a/the** ~ I am using the word with its original meaning. | ~ **behind** the meaning behind an event
● PHRASES **a nuance/shade of meaning** It is difficult for a non-Italian to grasp all the nuances of meaning.

2 purpose/importance
● ADJ. **deep, real, true** She's searching for the deeper meaning of life. | **spiritual** He found spiritual meaning through religion.
● VERB + MEANING **have** Her work no longer had any meaning for her. | **find** | **lose** After his death, she felt life had lost all meaning. | **give** Falling in love gave meaning to his life.
● PREP. **without** ~ Young people can feel that life is without meaning.

meaningless adj.

● VERBS **be** | **become** | **render sth**
● ADV. **absolutely, quite, totally** | **increasingly** | **almost, practically, virtually** The phrase has become almost meaningless. | **essentially, largely** | **fairly, pretty** | **apparently, seemingly** apparently meaningless jargon

means noun

1 method of doing sth
● ADJ. **appropriate, best, effective, efficient, reliable, useful** an effective means of mass communication | **necessary, possible, practicable** We will use every possible means to achieve our objective. | **alternative, other** War is famously 'the continuation of policy by other means'. | **conventional, traditional** | **legal, legitimate**
● VERB + MEANS **have** We have no means of knowing how they will react. | **use** | **offer (sb), provide (sb with)** My English teacher provided me with the means to enjoy reading poetry. | **devise** Can you devise a means of overcoming the problem?
● PREP. **by** ~ **(of)** The stone was lifted by means of a rope and pulley. **through** ~ They cannot achieve their goal through legal means. | ~ **for** the means for achieving happiness ~ **of** a means of access/communication/transport ◇ a means of getting what you want
● PHRASES **a means to an end** He saw his education merely as a means to an end. **by fair means or foul, by no means/not by any means** (= not at all), **ways and means** There are ways and means of raising money.

2 money/wealth
● ADJ. **independent, private** She must have independent means to live in such style. | **limited, moderate, modest, slender** | **visible** people who lack visible means of support

• VERB + MEANS **have** | **lack**
• MEANS + NOUN **test** *Eligibility for the benefit was determined by a means test.*
• PREP. **according to your ~** (= according to what you can afford), **beyond your ~** *Private school fees are beyond the means of most people* (= more than they can afford). **within your ~** (= according to what you can afford) *She finds it difficult to live within her means.*
• PHRASES **a man/woman of means** (= a rich man/woman)

measles noun

• VERB + MEASLES **have** *All our children have had the measles.* | **catch, contract** | **immunize sb against, vaccinate sb against**
• MEASLES + NOUN **virus** | **vaccination, vaccine**
⇨ Special page at ILLNESS

measure noun

1 official action to deal with a problem
• ADJ. **appropriate, effective, necessary, practical** *We urge you to adopt all necessary measures to guarantee people's safety.* | **important, key, special** | **simple** | **desperate, draconian, drastic, extreme, harsh, radical, repressive, strong, tough** | **emergency, urgent** | **interim, short-term, temporary** | **defensive, precautionary, preventative** | **disciplinary, punitive** | **corrective, remedial** | **safety, security** *New security measures were implemented to prevent further violence.* | **austerity, cost-cutting, economy, efficiency** | **economic, policy** | **government**
• QUANT. **package, range, series** *a package of measures aimed at cutting pollution*
• VERB + MEASURE **adopt, implement, impose, introduce, take** *Special measures are being taken to protect the local water supplies.* | **propose, suggest**
• MEASURE + VERB **be aimed at sth, be designed to, be intended to**
• PREP. **~ against** *tougher measures against racism* **~ for** *measures for reducing delays*

2 amount/quantity of sth
• ADJ. **broad, considerable, fair, generous, great, significant, substantial, wide**
• PREP. **~ of** *He poured me a generous measure of whisky.*
• PHRASES **in large/some measure** *His success was due in large measure to your help.* **in equal measure, in no small measure**

3 unit of size/quantity
• ADJ. **accurate, direct, objective, precise**
• PREP. **~ of** *an accurate measure of length*
• PHRASES **weights and measures**

4 sign of sth
• ADJ. **crude, simple, true, useful**
• PREP. **~ of** *Landed income was the true measure of the gentry.*

measure verb

1 find the size of sth
• ADV. **accurately, exactly, precisely** | **carefully** | **directly** *Any type of data that could not be directly measured was rejected.* | **easily** | **experimentally** | **up** *We need to measure the room up for a new carpet.*
• VERB + MEASURE **be able to, can/cannot** *You can now measure its length more accurately.* | **be easy to, be possible to** | **be difficult to, be hard to, be impossible to**
• PREP. **for** *She's being measured for her wedding outfit.* **in** *Cloth is measured in metres.*

2 judge the importance/value/effect of sth
• ADV. **easily** *The policy's impact cannot be easily measured.* | **effectively** | **objectively**
• VERB + MEASURE **can/cannot** | **be easy to, be possible to** | **be difficult to, be hard to, be impossible to** *It is*

~ of
I always drink gallons of water.
half a, a quarter of a ~
half a litre of milk
a half/quarter hour, inch, mile, ounce, pint, pound
They used to sell corned beef at 2d a quarter pound.
cubic, square ~
One litre is equivalent to 1 000 cubic centimetres.
~ square
The room is about 15 metres square.
~ broad, deep, high, long, tall, thick, wide
The new dock was 230 m long and 92 m broad.
~ bigger, cooler, faster, heavier, lighter, slower, etc.
The climate was several degrees warmer than it is now.
about, approximately, around ~
1 foot = approx. 0.3 metres
be, cover, measure, span, stretch (for) ~ used with measures of distance and area
The National Park covers 3 000 acres.
The sandy beach stretches for over four miles.
be, weigh ~ used with measures of weight
She weighed over ten stone.
be, last, take ~ used with measures of time
It takes approximately 365 and a quarter days for the earth to revolve around the sun.
in a ~
How many centilitres are there in a litre?
in ~ s
We were asked to estimate the temperature of the room in degrees.
to a/the ~
My car does 10 miles to the litre.
a, per ~
They're 99p a dozen.
a safety threshold of 50 mg of nitrates per litre
by the ~
Apples are sold by the kilogram.
of ~
The path will be built to a width of 2 metres.
~ in area, length, volume, weight, size, etc.
Killer whales are up to ten metres in length.
~ by ~
a huge room measuring 50 m by 18 m
to the nearest ~
Give your answer to the nearest metre.

hard to measure the benefiits to society of this scheme | **be used to** *the criteria that are used to measure performance*
• PREP. **according to** *Is it really possible to measure the skills of such jobs according to objective standards?* **against** *The school's performance is measured against a strict set of criteria.* **by** *The policy's effectiveness cannot be measured by numbers alone.* **in terms of** *Success cannot be measured merely in terms of the size of your salary.*
• PHRASES **a method/way of measuring sth**

measurement noun

• ADJ. **accurate, careful, exact, objective, precise** *It is important to take precise measurements of the structure.* ◇ *Objective measurement is difficult with such poor equipment.* | **laboratory, scientific** | **imperial, metric** | **length, pressure, temperature, etc.** | **body, bust, chest, waist**
• VERB + MEASUREMENT **carry out, get, make, obtain, perform, record, take**
• MEASUREMENT + NOUN **system, technique** | **scale, unit** | **error**
• PHRASES **a scale/unit of measurement**

meat *noun*

- ADJ. **fresh** | **bad, rancid, rotten** *That meat smells rotten.* | **tender** *Simmer the meat for 30 minutes until tender.* | **tough** | **lean** | **fatty** | **dark, red, white** | **raw, uncooked** | **rare, undercooked** | **cooked, cured, processed, roast, salted, smoked** | **cold** *a plate of cold meats* | **frozen** | **minced** | **luncheon, potted, tinned** | **sausage** | **organic** | **halal, kosher** | **crab, horse,** etc.
- QUANT. **bit, chunk, lump, piece, slab, slice** | **cut, joint** *She always buys the cheaper cuts of meat.*
- VERB + MEAT **consume, eat** *The animals do not hunt and rarely consume meat.* ◇ *Do you eat meat?* | **chew (on)** *chewing on the tough meat* | **barbecue, cook, fry, grill, roast, stew** *Fry the meat in a little olive oil.* | **marinate** | **tenderize** | **seal** *Turn the meat frequently to seal it.* | **chop, cube, cut, dice, mince** | **bone** | **carve, slice**
- MEAT + VERB **be/go off, rot** *The meat has gone off.*
- MEAT + NOUN **dish, pie, products** *recipes for simple meat dishes* | **market** | **cleaver** | **eater** *I'm not a great meat eater.* | **content** *These pies have a low meat content.* | **production** | **consumption** *Britain's meat consumption*
- ⇨ Special page at FOOD

mechanic *noun*

- ADJ. **competent, good, skilled** | **chief** | **trained** | **car, garage, motor**
- ⇨ Note at JOB

mechanics *noun*

1 how sth works/is done
- ADJ. **actual, basic, detailed, sheer** *We need to discuss the actual mechanics of the operation.*

2 science of movement and force
- ADJ. **classical, fluid, Newtonian, quantum, statistical**

mechanism *noun*

1 part of a machine
- ADJ. **firing, locking, steering, trigger, winding**
- MECHANISM + VERB **operate, work** *The door locking mechanism doesn't work.* | **jam**

2 how sth works
- ADJ. **effective, precise** *an effective mechanism for enforcing the rules* | **underlying** | **complex** | **social**
- VERB + MECHANISM **provide** *The system provides a mechanism whereby information is channelled into the market.*
- MECHANISM + VERB **operate, work** | **allow sth, ensure sth**
- PREP. **by/through the ~ of** *The government is held accountable through the mechanism of regular general elections.* | **~ for** *a mechanism for dealing with complaints*

3 system of parts/behaviour that performs a function
- ADJ. **avoidance, control, defence, escape, survival** *The body has defence mechanisms against many diseases.* | **cellular, genetic, immunological, molecular, neural, physiological, psychological,** etc.
- PREP. **~ for**

medal *noun*

- ADJ. **bronze, gold, silver** *He won a gold medal in the 100 metres.* | **championship, Olympic** | **commemorative** *A commemorative medal was struck in honour of the event.*
- VERB + MEDAL **be awarded, collect, get, receive, win** | **award (sb)** | **give sb, present (sb with)** | **strike**
- MEDAL + NOUN **winner** | **hope, hopes** *He is a major medal hope for Britain.* ◇ *Her medal hopes were dashed by injury.*
- PREP. **~ for** *a medal for bravery*

media *noun*

- ADJ. **audio-visual, broadcast, broadcasting, electronic, mass, news, print, visual** *The event was widely covered by the mass media.* | **foreign, international, local, national** | **mainstream, official, popular**
- MEDIA + VERB **report sth** *The local media reported rioting across the country.*
- MEDIA + NOUN **attention, coverage, interest, publicity, reporting** *There was a lot of media coverage of the wedding.* | **campaign** | **report** | **event** *Sport has been turned into a series of media events.* | **blitz, circus, hype** *The company is anxious to play down the media hype.* | **spotlight** | **image** *She's very different from her media image.* | **bias** | **blackout, censorship** | **freedom** | **relations** | **baron, magnate, mogul, person, pundit, tycoon** | **conglomerate, empire, group, interests, organization, outlet** | **awareness, studies**
- PREP. **through/via the ~** *propaganda through the media*
- PHRASES **access to the media, the role of the media**

mediation *noun*

- ADJ. **French, international, UN,** etc.
- VERB + MEDIATION **accept** *Unless management accepts mediation, the strike will never be resolved.*
- MEDIATION + NOUN **efforts, process**
- PREP. **through sb's ~** *The conflict ended through the mediation of the United Nations.* **under sb's ~** *under international mediation* | **~ between, ~ by** *mediation by the prime minister between the two sides*

medical *noun*

- ADJ. **full, regular** *Pilots undergo regular medicals.*
- VERB + MEDICAL **have, undergo** | **pass** *He was accepted onto the course after passing the medical.*

medication *noun*

- ADJ. **prescribed** | **over-the-counter** | **regular**
- VERB + MEDICATION **be on, receive, take** | **prescribe (sb)** | **administer, give sb** | **stop** *She stopped the medication because of side effects.* | **need, require**
- PREP. **~ for** *He is on regular medication for his fits.*

medicine *noun*

1 science of treating/preventing illness
- ADJ. **modern** *advances in modern medicine* | **traditional** *qualified in traditional Chinese medicine* | **folk** *Garlic was widely used in folk medicine.* | **conventional, orthodox** | **alternative, complementary, holistic, homeopathic** | **preventative, preventive** | **academic, clinical, forensic, scientific** | **general** *She gave up general medicine to specialize in geriatric medicine.* | **geriatric, obstetric, paediatric, veterinary,** etc. | **Chinese, Western** | **private, public health** *She believed private medicine was a threat to the existence of the National Health Service.*
- VERB + MEDICINE **train in** | **qualify in** | **practise** *people practising alternative medicine*
- PHRASES **a branch of medicine**
- ⇨ Note at SUBJECT (for more verbs and nouns)

2 substance taken to treat an illness
- ADJ. **powerful, strong** | **cough** *a bottle of cough medicine* | **herbal** | **prescription**
- QUANT. **dose**
- VERB + MEDICINE **take** | **swallow** | **prescribe (sb)** | **administer, give sb** | **treat sb with**
- MEDICINE + NOUN **bottle, chest**
- PREP. **~ for** *medicine for a chest infection*

MEETINGS

before the meeting

- **call/convene** the meeting, or **invite** people to **attend** the meeting
- **draw up** an **agenda**
- **circulate** the **agenda**
- If too many people are not able to attend, you may need to **postpone** or **call off/cancel** the meeting.

making a point

at the meeting

You usually appoint somebody to:

- **chair** the **meeting**
- **keep/take minutes**

After the chair has **opened** the meeting, the first **points/items** on the **agenda** are often to:

- **approve/agree** the **minutes** of the previous meeting
- **agree on** the **agenda** for the current meeting

It may be necessary to:

- **add** an **item** to the **agenda**
- **remove** sth **from** / **take** sth **off** / **leave** sth **off** the **agenda**

In a meeting you can:

address	issues / matters / problems
consider	
deal with	
debate	
discuss	
look at/into	
tackle	

If you don't spend much time on an issue, you **touch on** the **issue**. If you pay a lot of attention to an issue you:

consider deal with discuss look at	the issue **in depth/detail**
debate discuss	the issue **at length**
have	an **in-depth discussion** about/on the issue
have take	an **in-depth look** at the issue

debating at length

You usually **make decisions** at meetings. You can also:

reach	make	agree on	take	adopt
(an) agreement	a proposal	a compromise	a decision	a resolution
a compromise	a recommendation	further action	a vote	
a conclusion				
a consensus				
a decision				

After hours of negotiation, workers and management reached a compromise.
The environmental commission made a proposal for a new park in the city.
The shareholders took a vote on the proposed merger.

reaching a consensus

giving your opinion

make	raise	give/state
a point	an issue	your opinion
a proposal	an objection	your view
a suggestion	a point	

May I make a suggestion to the chairman of the board?

The workers raised an objection to longer working hours.

He invited the committee members to give their opinion.

ending the meeting

You can:

- **adjourn** the **meeting** until a later date

  This meeting is adjourned until next week.

- **close** the **meeting**

- **bring** the meeting to **a close**

  The chairman brought the meeting to a close by thanking all those who had attended.

- **declare** the meeting **closed**

  The High Commissioner for Human Rights declared the meeting closed.

after the meeting

It is usual to:

- **write up** the **minutes**
- **circulate** the **minutes**

meditation noun

- ADJ. **deep, profound** *Techniques of deep meditation help people under stress.* | **quiet, silent** *He stared out of the window in silent meditation.* | **Buddhist, Christian** | **religious, transcendental**
- VERB + MEDITATION **do, practise**
- PREP. **in ~** *spending hours in meditation* | **~ on** *The novel is an extended meditation on art, love and loss.*

medium noun

1 means of expressing/communicating sth
- ADJ. **communication** *Radio is an important communication medium in many countries.* | **mass** | **print, written**
- PREP. **through the ~ of** *The government communicates through the medium of television.*
- PHRASES **a medium of communication**

2 sth used for a particular purpose
- ADJ. **storage** *An optical disk is just another kind of electronic storage medium.*
- PREP. **~ for** *She used her novels as a medium for encouraging political debate.* **~ of** *the medium of study*
- PHRASES **a medium of instruction** (= a language used for teaching) *English is the medium of instruction in many African countries.*

3 material/form that an artist, etc. uses
- ADJ. **mixed media** *mixed media artwork*
- PREP. **through a/the ~** | **~ of** *to express yourself through the medium of paint/poetry/drama*

meet verb

1 come together
- ADV. **first** *the place where they had first met* | **regularly** | **never** | **up** *We met up after school.*
- VERB + MEET **arrange to** | **chance to, happen to** *A year or so later I happened to meet him again.*
- PREP. **for** *I arranged to meet her for lunch.* **with** *Management will meet with union representatives next week.* ◇ *I met up with my friends in town.*
- PHRASES **look forward to meeting sb** *I look forward to meeting you next week.* **nice/pleased to meet you** (= a greeting used when you meet sb for the first time)

2 satisfy sth
- ADV. **head-on** *They were determined to meet the challenge head-on.*
- VERB + MEET **be able to, can** | **be unable to, fail to** *He had failed to meet his performance targets.* | **be designed to, be tailored to** *The course is designed to meet the needs of young learners.*

3 sb's eyes/gaze/look
- ADV. **levelly, squarely, unflinchingly, without flinching** *Leonora met his gaze without flinching.* | **fleetingly** | **challengingly, determinedly**
- PREP. **~ across** *Their eyes met across the crowded room.*

meeting noun

1 when people come together to discuss/decide sth
- ADJ. **frequent, regular** | **annual, biennial, half-yearly, monthly, quarterly, weekly, etc.** | **all-day, hour-long, two-hour, etc.** | **afternoon, breakfast, lunchtime, weekend, etc.** | **full, plenary** | **formal, informal** | **inaugural** | **mass** | **open-air** | **open, public** | **closed, private** | **secret** | **joint** *Management have called a joint meeting with staff and unions.* | **general** *The society is holding its Annual General Meeting in the conference room next Monday.* | **face-to-face, personal** | **bilateral, trilateral, tripartite** | **high-level, summit, top-level** | **exploratory, initial, introductory, preliminary, preparatory** | **follow-up** | **extraordinary, special** | **crisis, emergency, urgent** | **crucial, decisive, key, vital** | **impromptu** | **pre-inquiry, pre-session, pre-summit, etc.** | **post-election, post-results, etc.** | **board, cabinet, committee, council, departmen-**

tal, **family, ministerial, shareholders', staff, team, union** | **inter-governmental, inter-ministerial, inter-party, inter-tribal, etc.** | **business** | **political** | **discussion** | **protest** | **prayer** | **brief** | **endless, interminable, long** *We had endless meetings about the problem.* ◇ *The meeting seemed interminable.* | **angry, difficult, stormy** | **fruitless, inconclusive** | **successful, valuable**
- QUANT. **series**
- VERB + MEETING **have, hold** | **arrange, call, convene, organize, schedule, summon** *The committee has called a meeting to discuss the president's death.* | **attend** | **declare open, open** *The chairman declared the meeting open.* | **close, declare closed** | **adjourn, break up** | **call off, cancel** | **postpone** | **host** | **chair, conduct, preside over** *I've got to chair a meeting tomorrow.* | **call to order** *The chairman called the meeting to order.* | **participate in** | **address** *He always spoke as if he were addressing a public meeting.* | **ban** | **boycott** | **disrupt**
- MEETING + VERB **go ahead, take place** *It is unclear whether the meeting will go ahead as planned.* | **be aimed at sth** *a meeting aimed at restoring peace in the region* | **begin, open, proceed, start** | **adjourn** *The meeting adjourned for coffee at eleven.* | **break up** *The meeting broke up after a row over whether to allow cameras in.* | **close, end** *The meeting closed on a sour note.* | **vote** *The meeting voted 423–133 in favour of a strike.* | **discuss sth** | **agree to sth, approve sth** | **condemn sth** | **urge sth** *This meeting urges the company to reconsider its decision to close the factory.* | **express sth** *The meeting expressed concern that the problem had still not been addressed.* | **hear sth** *The meeting heard that two workers had been sacked on the spot with no official reason given.* | **conclude sth, decide sth, resolve sth** | **drag (on)** *The meeting dragged into the early hours of the next day.*
- MEETING + NOUN **house, place**
- PREP. **in a/the ~** *I'm afraid Mrs Haley is in a meeting at the moment.* | **~ about** *a meeting about the plans for a new road* **~ between** *a meeting between tutors and students* **~ for** *a meeting for parents* **~ over** *Directors called a crisis meeting over the future of the company.* **~ with** *a meeting with French officials*
- PHRASES **the purpose of a meeting, the minutes of a meeting** *The secretary circulated the minutes of the previous week's meeting to all committee members.* **the outcome/result of a meeting**
⇨ Special page on page 490

2 coming together of two or more people
- ADJ. **accidental, chance, unexpected** | **fateful** | **clandestine, secret** | **historic, unprecedented** | **emotional** | **romantic**
- VERB + MEETING **have**
- PREP. **~ with** *I had a chance meeting with an old schoolfriend last week.*

mellow adj.

- VERBS **be, feel, look, seem** | **become, grow**
- ADV. **extremely, very** | **beautifully, delightfully, wonderfully** *a delightfully mellow flavour*

melody noun

- ADJ. **beautiful, lovely, sweet** | **bold, simple, strong** | **complex** | **haunting, memorable** | **familiar, popular, traditional**
- VERB + MELODY **play, sing** | **hear** | **have** *Most of her songs have a bold melody.* | **write**

member noun

- ADJ. **key, leading, powerful, prominent** | **junior, senior** | **long-serving, long-standing, long-time** | **board, club, committee, crew, family, group, party, staff, team, union** | **individual** *Subscriptions are cheaper for individual members.* | **founder** | **active, enthusiastic** *She's an*

active member of her local church. | **honorary** | **full** | **associate** | **life** *a life member of the Red Cross* | **paid-up** *He was a paid-up member of the Communist Party.*
- VERB + MEMBER **become** | **resign as**
- MEMBER + VERB **join sth** | **resign**
- MEMBER + NOUN **country, nation, state**
- PHRASES **a member of staff** *All members of staff will receive a pay rise.*
- PREP. **~ of** *I've become a member of our local sports club.*

membership *noun*

- ADJ. **associate, corporate, full, honorary, temporary** | **club, party, union** *to apply for union membership*
- VERB + MEMBERSHIP **apply for** | **renew** | **grant sb** | **resign** *He has resigned his membership of the club.*
- MEMBERSHIP + NOUN **fee**

membrane *noun*

- ADJ. **thin** | **permeable, semi-permeable** | **cell** | **cellular** | **mucous**
- MEMBRANE + VERB **surround sth**
- MEMBRANE + NOUN **wall**
- PREP. **through a/the ~** *The virus then passes through the cell membrane.*

memento *noun*

- ADJ. **family, personal** | **permanent**
- VERB + MEMENTO **be presented with, receive**
- PREP. **as a~** *They gave him a watch as a memento of his time with the company.* | **~ for** *The director will be presented with a memento for his long years of service.* **~ from** *a memento from his dear friends* **~ of** *The photos will be a permanent memento of your wedding.*

memo *noun*

- ADJ. **internal**
- QUANT. **copy**
- VERB + MEMO **draft, write** | **circulate, send (out)** | **receive** | **sign** | **leak**
- MEMO + NOUN **pad**
- PREP. **in a/the~** | **~from, ~of** *my memo of 28 June, 2001* **~on** *A memo on the curriculum changes from the Head of Education.* **~to** *She circulated a memo to the staff.*

memoirs *noun*

- ADJ. **political** *the market for political memoirs*
- VERB + MEMOIRS **publish, write** | **read**
- PREP. **in your~** *She describes in her memoirs how she coped with her mother's death.*

memorable *adj.*

- VERBS **be** *It was a truly memorable experience.*
- ADV. **extremely, most, particularly, truly, very** *one particularly memorable evening last year*
- PREP. **for** *The holiday was memorable for the food.*

memorandum *noun*

- ADJ. **internal** | **confidential, private, secret** | **brief** | **detailed** | **explanatory, factual**
- QUANT. **copy**
- VERB + MEMORANDUM **draft, draw up, prepare, write** | **issue, send, submit** | **sign** | **date** *The memorandum was dated 23 August, 2001.* | **leak**
- MEMORANDUM + VERB **set sth out**
- PREP. **in a/the ~** *Refer to the terms set out in the company's memorandum.* | **~from, ~of** *your memorandum of 18 February, 2001* **~on, ~to**

memorial *noun*

- ADJ. **lasting, permanent** *The statue is a lasting memorial to those who died in the war.* | **fitting** | **war**
- VERB + MEMORIAL **build, erect, put up** | **unveil**
- MEMORIAL + VERB **commemorate sb/sth** | **stand** *The memorial stands on the village green.*
- MEMORIAL + NOUN **ceremony, service** *a memorial service for sailors drowned at sea*
- PREP. **~ for** *a memorial for victims of the air crash* **~ to** *The prime minister today unveiled a memorial to those who died in the disaster.*

memory *noun*

1 ability to remember
- ADJ. **excellent, good, long, prodigious, retentive** | **bad, poor, short** | **long-term, short-term** *His short-term memory was damaged in the accident.* | **visual** *Bad spellers have a weak visual memory.* | **photographic**
- VERB + MEMORY **jog, refresh** *Seeing your name in the paper jogged my memory.* | **lose** *Most people start to lose their memory as they get older.* | **commit sth to** *I committed the number to memory and threw the letter away.*
- PREP. **from~** *He recited the whole poem from memory.* | **~for** *I have a good memory for faces.*
- PHRASES **in living/recent memory** *the coldest winter in living memory*

2 thought of the past
- ADJ. **childhood, early** *My earliest childhood memory is of falling in a pond in winter.* | **dim, distant, fading, hazy, vague** | **clear, vivid** | **affectionate, fond, good, happy, lovely, nostalgic, pleasant, positive, precious, sweet, warm, wonderful** | **bitter-sweet** | **bad, bitter, disturbing, embarrassing, horrific, painful, sad, traumatic, unhappy, unpleasant** | **abiding, enduring, lasting, lingering** *My abiding memory of our first meeting is of a girl too shy to talk.*
- VERB + MEMORY **bring back, evoke, rekindle, revive, stir (up)** | **blot out** *He tried to blot out his memories of the ordeal.*
- MEMORY + VERB **come flooding back, flood back** *When we visited my old family home, memories came flooding back.* | **fade**
- PREP. **in ~ of** *He planted some apple trees in memory of his wife.* | **~ from** *Smells and tastes often evoke memories from the past.* **~ of** *fond memories of her childhood*

menace *noun*

1 danger
- ADJ. **growing, increased, increasing** *the growing menace of drugs* | **serious**
- VERB + MENACE **pose** *the menace posed by car fumes* | **combat, counter** *Shop owners are struggling to combat the menace of armed robbery.*
- PREP. **~ to** *He's a menace to society.*

2 threatening quality
- ADJ. **hidden, quiet, silent** *'Where do you think you're going?' he said with quiet menace.*
- PREP. **with~** *eyes glittering with menace*
- PHRASES **an air of menace** *The scar down his face added to his air of menace.*

menacing *adj.*

- VERBS **appear, be, look, seem** | **become**
- ADV. **almost** *His voice was quiet and almost menacing.* | **faintly, rather, slightly** *She had a slightly menacing manner.* | **darkly** *darkly menacing alleys* | **quietly**

meningitis *noun*

- ADJ. **acute** | **bacterial, meningococcal, viral**
- QUANT. **case**

menopause *noun*

- VERB + MENINGITIS **have, suffer from** *He is suffering from viral meningitis.* | **catch, contract**
⇒ Special page at ILLNESS

menopause *noun*

- ADJ. **early** | **male** *The male menopause is said to affect men who are approaching middle age.*
- VERB + MENOPAUSE **reach** | **go through**
- PREP. **at the ~, after/past the ~** *a disease that can afflict women past the menopause* **during the ~**

mention *noun*

- ADJ. **brief, passing** | **special** | **earliest, first** *The earliest mention of the village is in a 16th-century manuscript.*
- VERB + MENTION **deserve** *My cousin deserves a mention for all his hard work.* | **get, receive** *His professor gets a mention in the acknowledgements.* | **make** *Special mention must be made of Yuki Yamagishi's wonderful performance as the doctor.* | **hear** *I've heard no mention of a salary increase this year.*
- PREP. **at the ~ of** *At the very mention of his name, Kate started shaking with fright.*

mention *verb*

- ADV. **already, earlier, just, previously, so far** *As already mentioned, the legislation does not consider low pay as an acceptable reason for turning down a job.* ◇ *This aspect is discussed further by Crane, whom I mentioned earlier.* ◇ *All the approaches mentioned so far are fairly conventional.* | **commonly, frequently** | **rarely, seldom** | **briefly, in passing** *He only mentioned his work in passing.* | **casually** *I casually mentioned that I might be interested in working abroad.* | **directly, explicitly, expressly, specifically** *She did not specifically mention your name.* | **inadvertently** | **barely, hardly, scarcely** | **not actually, not at all** *Although she didn't actually mention the move, I am sure that was in her mind.* ◇ *My name wasn't mentioned at all.*
- VERB + MENTION **fail to, forget to, omit to**
- PREP. **as** *Next spring has been mentioned as a possible time for the event.* **in** *She didn't mention the economy in her speech.* **in connection with sth** *I was very angry when I saw my name mentioned in connection with an incident that had absolutely nothing to do with me.* **to** *Please don't mention this to Sally.*
- PHRASES **avoid mentioning sb/sth** *He avoided mentioning his family.* **be worth mentioning sth** *At this point, it is worth mentioning that many people who were adopted as babies have no desire to meet their biological parents.* **mentioned above/below** *In the example mentioned above, either method of construction could have been used.* **mentioned in dispatches** *Wounded in action, he was twice mentioned in dispatches.* **mention the fact that … , not to mention** (= used to add extra information) *He has two big houses in this country, not to mention his villa in France.* **now you come to mention it** *Now that you come to mention it, he did say something about a ghost.* **to mention but a few** *plumbers, printers, dyers, glaziers and potters, to mention but a few*

menu *noun*

1 list of dishes

- ADJ. **extensive** | **varied** | **daily** | **fixed price, set, table d'hôte** | **à la carte** | **three-course, etc.** | **traditional** | **breakfast, dinner, lunch** | **bar, pub, restaurant** | **dinnerparty** | **fish, vegetarian**
- VERB + MENU **consult, have, look at, read, see, study** *May we have the menu?* | **do, have, offer** *Many restaurants do a very reasonable set menu at lunchtime.* | **choose (sth) from, order (sth) from** | **plan**
- MENU + VERB **offer sth** *a menu offering many vegetarian dishes*

- MENU + NOUN **board** *The chef was chalking the daily specials on the menu board.*
- PREP. **on the ~** *What's on the menu this evening?*
- PHRASES **a choice of menu** *Passengers are offered a daily choice of menu.*

2 on a computer

- ADJ. **pop-up, pull-down** | **main** | **sub** | **edit, file, options, etc.**
- VERB + MENU **select sth from**
- MENU + NOUN **bar** | **item, option**
⇒ Special page at COMPUTER

mercenary *noun*

- ADJ. **foreign**
- QUANT. **army, band** *a small army of mercenaries*
- VERB + MERCENARY **employ, hire, recruit** | **pay**
- MERCENARY + NOUN **army**

merchandise *noun*

- ADJ. **general**
- QUANT. **piece** *a substandard piece of merchandise*
- VERB + MERCHANDISE **buy, purchase** | **carry, sell** *The company carries a wide range of merchandise.*
- PHRASES **a range of merchandise**

merchant *noun*

- ADJ. **prosperous, rich, wealthy** | **powerful, prominent, substantial, successful** | **foreign, local** | **builders', coal, corn, timber, wine, wool** *We bought a ton of sand from the builders' merchant.*
- MERCHANT + NOUN **fleet, marine, seaman, ship, shipping, vessel**

mercy *noun*

- ADJ. **divine, infinite** *God's infinite mercy*
- VERB + MERCY **ask for, beg for, plead for, scream for** | **have, show (sb)** *God have mercy on us!* ◇ *They showed no mercy to their captives.*
- MERCY + NOUN **dash, flight, mission** *Aid agencies are making mercy flights into the flood region.* | **killing**
- PREP. **at the ~ of** *We're at the mercy of the weather.* **without ~** *The terrorists are completely without mercy.*

merger *noun*

- ADJ. **proposed**
- VERB + MERGER **plan** | **agree** | **carry out**
- MERGER + VERB **go through** *If the merger goes through, thousands of jobs will be lost.*
- MERGER + NOUN **activity** | **proposal** | **negotiations** | **agreement**
- PREP. **~ between** *the merger between Lake Biscuits and D M Confectionery*

merit *noun*

- ADJ. **considerable, exceptional, great, outstanding** | **aesthetic, architectural, artistic, literary** *The film has no artistic merit whatsoever.* | **relative** *We need to consider the relative merits of both makes of cooker.* | **individual** *Each case should be judged on its individual merits.*
- VERB + MERIT **have** | **argue, assess, consider, debate, discuss, judge** *We need to assess the merits of both proposals before making our decision.*
- MERIT + NOUN **award** *She received a merit award for outstanding work.*
- PREP. **according to ~** *Films are given a rating of one to five stars according to merit.* **on ~** *Prizes are awarded entirely on merit.*
- PHRASES **no merit in doing sth** *I can see no merit in excluding the child from school.* **order of merit** *The winners are ranked in order of merit.*

merit *verb*

- ADV. **certainly, clearly** | **hardly** *The question hardly merits an answer.*

mess *noun*

- ADJ. **absolute, complete, real, right, total** | **appalling, awful, bloody** (*taboo*)**, nasty, terrible** | **confusing** | **tangled, untidy** *Her hair was a tangled mess.* | **gooey, slimy, soggy, sticky** | **emotional** *He's an emotional mess since his girlfriend left him.* | **economic, financial**
- VERB + MESS **leave, make** *Must you always leave such a mess?* ◇ *She felt she was making a terrible mess of her life.* | **clean up, clear up, tidy up, wipe up** | **feel** *I felt a mess.* | **look** | **create, get sb into** *Who got us into this mess in the first place?* | **deal with, get sb out of, sort out**
- PREP. **in a~** *The kitchen's in an awful mess.* | **~of** *There was a soggy mess of porridge on the table.*

message *noun*

1 from one person to another
- ADJ. **important, urgent, vital** | **brief, short** | **coded, cryptic, scrambled** | **secret** | **garbled** | **email, radio, text** | **heartfelt** *The family sent a heartfelt message of thanks to everyone who helped.*
- VERB + MESSAGE **convey, give sb, pass on, relay** *He's not here—I'll pass on the message.* | **take** *She's out—can I take a message?* | **carry, deliver, take sb** | **send, transmit** | **leave (sb)** *I left a message for her at reception.* | **get, receive** *I never got your message.*
- MESSAGE + VERB **come** | **say sth, tell sb sth**
- PREP. **~about** *There was a message about the meeting.* **~for** *Are there any messages for me?* **~from** *a urgent message from your mother* **~of** *They sent messages of hope to prisoners of war.* **~to** *The message was to your sister, not you.*

2 main idea of a book, speech, etc.
- ADJ. **important** | **fundamental, main** | **clear, simple, unambiguous, unmistakeable** | **ambiguous, conflicting, mixed** | **powerful, strong** | **positive, upbeat** | **stark, uncomfortable** | **hidden, implicit, subliminal** *stories with hidden moral messages* | **anti-drugs, anti-war,** etc. *a party with an anti-immigrant message* | **ideological, moral, political, social**
- VERB + MESSAGE **spread** *spreading the message of the Bible* | **drive home, get/put across** *We need to get this important message across to teenage smokers.* | **reinforce**
- MESSAGE + VERB **emerge** *A clear message is emerging from these government statements.*
- PREP. **~of** *The president toured the country spreading the message of national unity.*

metal *noun*

- ADJ. **soft** | **pure** | **ferrous, non-ferrous** | **base, heavy, noble, precious, rare, trace, transition** | **cold, hot** *the sudden pressure of cold metal against her cheek* | **bare** | **solid** | **gleaming, shining, shiny** | **tarnished** | **corroded, rusty** | **scrap** *to recycle scrap metal* | **twisted** *The bomb left a pile of jagged glass and twisted metal.* | **ductile** | **molten** | **sheet** | **toxic**
- QUANT. **lump, piece, strip**
- VERB + METAL **be cast from/in, be made from/(out) of** *a statue cast in metal* ◇ *The doors are made of metal.* | **recycle**
- METAL + VERB **contract, expand** | **rust**
- METAL + NOUN **alloy** | **band, bar, box, frame, mesh, plate, rod, sheet** | **fatigue** | **detector**
- PREP. **in~** *a sculptor who works in metal*
- PHRASES **the clang/clash of metal**

metaphor *noun*

- ADJ. **appropriate, apt, striking** | **mixed**

- VERB + METAPHOR **use** *He uses the metaphor of fire to represent hatred.*
- METAPHOR + VERB **describe sth, represent sth**
- PREP. **~for** *'This vale of tears' is a metaphor for the human condition.* **~of** *the metaphor of life as a journey*

meter *noun*

- ADJ. **electricity, gas, light, moisture, parking, sound-level, water** | **card, prepayment, slot, token** *The token meter is operated by tokens costing £1 or £5.*
- VERB + METER **read** *The electricity company will send an employee to read your meter.* | **fit, install**
- METER + VERB **tick** *The taxi waited, its motor running, the meter ticking away.*
- METER + NOUN **reader, reading** | **box, cupboard**

method *noun*

- ADJ. **effective, efficient, good, practical, reliable** *Which method is the most effective?* | **simple** | **common, conventional, principal, traditional, usual** | **new** | **alternative, other** | **different, various** | **unorthodox, unusual** | **farming, research, scientific, teaching, working** *~s modern farming methods*
- VERB + METHOD **adopt, employ, follow, use** *the method adopted by the party for the selection of its candidates* | **develop, devise, work out** | **change, improve**
- METHOD + VERB **involve sth** *This method involves cutting a very thin slice from the object.* **work** *How does this method work?*
- PREP. **~for** *an alternative method for resolving disputes* **~of** *This is the best method of settling such arguments.*

metre *noun*

⇨ Note at MEASURE

microphone *noun*

- ADJ. **extension, radio, stick, tie-clip** | **built-in, camcorder** | **omnidirectional, unidirectional** | **hidden**
- VERB + MICROPHONE **speak into, use** | **check, test**
- MICROPHONE + VERB **pick sth up, record sth** *the microphone picks up the surrounding sounds*
- MICROPHONE + NOUN **socket** | **stand**
- PREP. **behind a/the~** *John Peel is back behind the microphone for a new series.* **in front of a/the~** *Interviewees are placed in front of the microphone and grilled.*

microscope *noun*

- ADJ. **binocular, electron, optical**
- MICROSCOPE + NOUN **slide** *Place the specimen on a microscope slide.*
- PREP. **through a/the~** *a section of a potato as seen through a microscope* **under a/the~** *examining bacteria under the microscope*

middle age *noun*

- ADJ. **early** | **late** *a woman of late middle age* | **comfortable** *He settled into comfortable middle age.*
- VERB + MIDDLE AGE **approach** *a bald man approaching middle age* | **reach**
- PREP. **in~** *He mellowed in middle age.*
- PHRASES **well into middle age** *She had her first child well into middle age.*

middle-aged *adj.*

- VERBS **be, feel, look** *She felt middle-aged and dull.* | **become**
- ADV. **prematurely**

middleman noun

- VERB + MIDDLEMAN **act as, be | cut out** *Some factories have cut out the middleman and sell their products directly to customers.*
- PREP. **through a~** *The firm sells through a middleman because it does not have its own sales force.* **~for** *He acts as middleman for companies seeking contracts abroad.*

midnight noun

- VERB + MIDNIGHT **chime, strike** *The church clock struck midnight.*
- MIDNIGHT + VERB **chime, strike** *Downstairs in the hall, midnight struck.*
- MIDNIGHT + NOUN **feast | blue**
- PREP. **around~, at~, by~**
- PHRASES **on the stroke of midnight** *On the stroke of midnight, Prince Charming turned back into a rat.*

midwife noun

- ADJ. **qualified, registered | community, local**
- MIDWIFE + VERB **examine sb | deliver a baby**
⇨ Note at JOB

migraine noun

- ADJ. **severe**
- VERB + MIGRAINE **get, have, suffer from | bring on, trigger** *Even the smell of oranges can trigger his migraine.*
- MIGRAINE + NOUN **headache | attack**
⇨ Special page at ILLNESS

migrant noun

- ADJ. **economic | illegal | rural**
- MIGRANT + NOUN **labourer, worker** *entering the country as migrant workers* **| population | bird**
- PREP. **~from** *migrants from rural areas,* **~into, ~to** *Migrants to the city send money home to their relatives.*
- PHRASES **a flow/an influx of migrants**

migrate verb

- ADV. **north, northwards, etc.** *birds that migrate south in the winter* **| seasonally**
- PREP. **from, into, to** *migrating from Europe to Africa*

migration noun

- ADJ. **seasonal** *the seasonal migration of birds* **| internal, inward | international | mass**
- QUANT. **wave** *the great waves of migration that took Europeans to the New World*
- MIGRATION + VERB **occur | increase**
- MIGRATION + NOUN **path, pattern, route** *changes in the migration routes of reindeer*
- PREP. **~from, ~to** *migration from rural to urban areas*

mild adj.

1 not very cold
- VERBS **be | turn** *Towards the end of the week the weather turned very mild.* **| remain**
- ADV. **very | quite, relatively** *It's quite mild for this time of year.* **| surprisingly, unseasonably, unusually** *The late summer air was surprisingly mild.*

2 not severe or strong
- VERBS **be, seem** *The infection seems quite mild, so she should be better soon.*
- ADV. **very | comparatively, fairly, quite, pretty, reasonably, relatively** *a fairly mild flavour*

3 gentle and kind
- VERBS **be, sound** *His voice was deceptively mild.*
- ADV. **seemingly | deceptively**

mile noun

- ADJ. **nautical**
- VERB + MILE **cover, cycle, do, drive, go, ride, run, travel, trudge, walk** *Fell-runners who are out to win can cover the three miles in just over 15 minutes.* **| clock (up)** *Altogether on the trip we clocked up over 1 800 miles.*
- PHRASES **miles an/per hour** *The police stopped them doing 100 miles per hour on the motorway.*
⇨ Note at MEASURE

mileage noun

- ADJ. **annual, weekly | high, low** *Car for sale: one careful owner, low mileage.* **| unlimited** *Your car hire costs include unlimited mileage.*
- VERB + MILEAGE **cover, do** *There was no record of the mileage the car had done.*
- MILEAGE + NOUN **allowance** *The company gives a generous mileage allowance.*

milestone noun

- ADJ. **important, significant**
- VERB + MILESTONE **pass, reach** *The company passed the £6 million milestone this year.* **| celebrate, mark**
- PREP. **~in** *The film proved to be a milestone in the history of cinema.* **| ~for** *a milestone for French technology*

militant adj.

- VERBS **be, seem | become**
- ADV. **extremely, highly, very** *The women on the march were highly militant.* **| increasingly**

military noun the military

- VERB + MILITARY **serve in** *I wasn't surprised to learn that he'd served in the military.* **| call in** *The government called in the military to deal with the riots.*
- MILITARY + VERB **seize/take power**
- PREP. **among/in/within~** *reports of growing discontent among the military*
- PHRASES **a member of the military**

militia noun

- ADJ. **armed** *a highly armed militia* **| voluntary, volunteer | local | government**
- VERB + MILITIA **join, serve in | raise, recruit | create, form, set up** *The anarchists started to form volunteer militias.* **| train | disarm, disband**
- MILITIA + NOUN **forces, group, unit | commander, leader**

milk noun

- ADJ. **fresh | curdled, off, sour** *The milk has gone off/turned sour.* **| full-cream, full-fat, whole | low-fat, semi-skimmed | non-fat, skimmed | creamy | cold, warm | cow's, goat's, etc. | breast | baby, formula | coconut, soya | condensed, evaporated** *a tin of condensed milk* **| dried, powdered | pasteurized, unpasteurized | homogenized | long-life, UHT | organic**
- QUANT. **litre, pint | bottle, carton, cup, glass, jug**
- VERB + MILK **drink, have, take** *Do you take milk in your coffee?* **| add | pour | spill | deliver** *They've stopped delivering milk in our area.* **| boil, heat, scald | produce | express** *She expressed some milk so her husband could do the night feeding.*
- MILK + NOUN **powder | pudding, shake** (also **milkshake**) **| chocolate | product | bottle, churn, jug | production, yield | float, round**
- PHRASES **the top of the milk** (= the creamy part at the top of a milk bottle)

mill *noun*

1 for making flour
- ADJ. **corn, flour** | **water** (also **watermill**)
- VERB + MILL **operate, work** | **convert, restore** *living in a converted watermill* | **drive, power** *The river was harnessed to drive many mills.*
- MILL + VERB **grind sth, work sth** *The mill can be seen grinding corn.*
- MILL + NOUN **house** | **wheel**

2 factory
- ADJ. **cotton, paper, steel, textile, woollen**
- VERB + MILL **operate, own, run** | **work in**
- MILL + VERB **manufacture sth, produce sth**
- MILL + NOUN **town** *a northern mill town* | **buildings**

mimic *verb*
- ADV. **accurately, closely** *The computer model is able to mimic very closely the actions of a golfer.* | **exactly, perfectly** *She could mimic her father perfectly.*
- VERB + MIMIC **try to**

mind *noun*
- ADJ. **human** *the complex nature of the human mind* | **conscious, subconscious, unconscious** *Our subconscious mind tries to protect us.* | **best, brilliant, finest** *a problem that has defeated the world's finest minds* | **agile, enquiring, lively, open** *Try to keep an open mind until you've heard all the facts.* | **impressionable** *influencing impressionable young minds* | **one-track** *Honestly, all you ever talk about is sex—you've got a one-track mind!*
- VERB + MIND **come into, come to, cross, flash across/into, go through, spring to** *The thought never crossed my mind!* ◊ *I'm sure someone can help you, but no one immediately springs to mind.* | **bear in, keep in** *Bear in mind the age of the vehicle when assessing its value.* ◊ *Here are some important points to keep in mind …* | **slip** *I'm sorry I forgot your birthday—it completely slipped my mind.* | **be imprinted on, stick in** *terrible images that will be imprinted on our minds for ever* | **prey on** *It's been preying on my mind ever since it happened.* | **occupy** *He occupied his mind by playing cards against himself.*
- MIND + VERB **wander** *Her mind began to wander.* | **race** *His mind raced, trying to think of a way out of the situation.* | **be in a turmoil, reel** *Her mind was still reeling from the shock.*
- PREP. **in your~** *You've been in my mind a lot lately.* **in~** *I'll keep what you say in mind.* **on your~** *I've got a lot on my mind at the moment.*
- PHRASES **at/in the back of your mind** *The problem was always at the back of my mind.* **at/in the forefront of your mind** *Try to keep safety in the forefront of your mind at all times.* **a frame/state of mind** *He's in rather a negative frame of mind.* **have sth in mind** *What kind of party do you have in mind?* **in the recesses of your mind** *It was something she had never imagined, not even in the deepest recesses of her mind.* **mind and body** *refreshed in mind and body* **no doubt in your mind** *There was absolutely no doubt in my mind that he was guilty.* **uppermost in your mind** *Their own problems of course remained uppermost in their minds.*

mind *verb*
- ADV. **bitterly, terribly, very much** *They had thought the boys wouldn't mind sharing; as it turned out, they minded bitterly.* ◊ *Would you mind terribly if I went on my own?* | **not a bit, not at all** *I don't mind at all telling people my age.* | **not greatly, not much, not really** *Nobody really minded much about what happened to them.*
- VERB + MIND **not seem to** *His parents didn't seem to mind that he dropped out of university.*
- PREP. **about** *I didn't mind about the money.*

mine *noun*

1 for coal, etc.
- ADJ. **coal, copper, diamond, salt, tin, etc.** | **deep, drift, opencast** | **abandoned, disused**
- VERB + MINE **operate, run, work** | **go down, work at/down/in** *At 14, he went down the mines.*
- MINE + VERB **produce sth** *At its peak, the mine produced 5 000 tons of coal a day.*
- MINE + NOUN **shaft** (also **mineshaft**), **workings** *flooded mine workings* | **owner**

2 explosive device
- ADJ. **anti-personnel, land, limpet**
- VERB + MINE **lay, plant** *soldiers laying anti-personnel mines* | **clear, dispose of, remove** *The troops are slowly clearing the mines.* | **detonate, hit, set off, strike**
- MINE + VERB **blow up, explode, go off**

minefield *noun*

1 area where there are mines
- VERB + MINEFIELD **advance into/through, enter**

2 situation full of difficulties
- ADJ. **legal, political** *Suggesting changes to the benefits system would be a political minefield.*
- VERB + MINEFIELD **negotiate, pick your way through** *You will first have to pick your way through the minefield of professional advice.*
- PREP. **~for** *Tax is a minefield for the unwary.*

miner *noun*
- ADJ. **coal, copper, gold, lead, tin, uranium, etc.**
- ⇨ Note at JOB

mineral *noun*
- ADJ. **essential, vital** | **trace** | **rare** | **industrial**
- VERB + MINERAL **be rich in, contain** *foods that are rich in essential minerals* | **extract** *to extract minerals from ores* | **absorb**
- MINERAL + VERB **be found in sth, be present in sth** *calcium and other minerals found in your bones*
- MINERAL + NOUN **deposits, resources, wealth** | **exploitation, exploration, extraction, working**
- PHRASES **vitamins and minerals**

mingle *verb*
- ADV. **freely** *The prince mingled freely with the crowd.* | **together** *a lot of emotions all mingled together*
- PREP. **with** *She felt fear mingled with excitement.*

minimum *noun*
- ADJ. **absolute, bare, very** | **agreed, guaranteed** | **recommended** | **legal, mandatory, required, statutory**
- VERB + MINIMUM **keep sth to, reduce sth to** *Two fire crews managed to keep damage to a minimum.* | **reach** *The sun's temperature reached a minimum in the summer of 1981.* | **exceed** | **regard sth as** *A temperature of 121°C is regarded as the minimum necessary to achieve sterility.*
- PREP. **above (the)~, at (a/the)~** *Candidates must have a first degree at a minimum.* **below (the)~, down to a~** *We tried to keep costs down to a minimum.* | **~of** *a minimum of £20* ◊ *a minimum of fuss*
- PHRASES **the minimum acceptable/necessary/needed/required, the minimum possible** *He's always done the minimum possible to pass his exams.* **with the minimum of delay/discomfort/disruption/effort/fuss/risk**

minister *noun*

1 member of the government
- ADJ. **prime** | **chief, principal** *Queen Elizabeth's chief minister, Lord Burghley* | **deputy** | **junior, senior** | **cabinet, departmental, EU, Foreign Office, government,**

Home Office | defence, education, environment, finance, foreign, health, interior, transport, etc. | relevant, responsible *Local authorities should submit schemes to the relevant minister for approval.* | former, outgoing

• VERB + MINISTER **appoint (sb), appoint sb as, nominate (sb), nominate sb as | elect (sb), elect sb as | dismiss (sb as) | serve as** *He served briefly as prime minister from 1920 to 1921.* | **lobby, persuade, urge** *lobbying the Transport Minister over the issue* | **advise, consult, instruct | accuse, criticize**

• MINISTER + VERB **resign, retire | be accountable to sb, be responsible for sth** *Ministers are accountable to Parliament.* ◊ *the minister responsible for the health service* | **announce sth, unveil sth | agree (to) sth, approve sth, decide sth, endorse sth | intervene (in sth)** *The foreign minister intervened with disastrous results.*

• PREP. **~for** *the new minister for the Arts* **~of** *A new minister of defence had been appointed.*
⇨ See PRIME MINISTER

2 priest
• ADJ. **church | Baptist, Congregational, Methodist, Nonconformist, Presbyterian**
• VERB + MINISTER **ordain (sb), ordain sb as** *He was ordained minister of a small rural congregation.*
• PHRASES **a minister of religion**

ministry *noun*

• ADJ. **government | Agriculture, Defence, Education, Environment, Finance, Foreign (Affairs), Health, Interior, Justice, Transport, etc. | key** *He assumed direct control of key ministries.*
• VERB + MINISTRY **run | take over** *The president took over the Ministry of Justice.* | **create**
• MINISTRY + VERB **approve sth, support sth** *The scheme was approved by the Ministry of Housing.* | **control sth | own sth** *on ministry-owned land*
• MINISTRY + NOUN **official, spokesperson**
• PREP. **at the ~** *staff at the Greek Foreign Ministry* **in/within the ~** *a senior man in the Ministry of Health* | **~of** *a spokesman for the Ministry of Culture*
• PHRASES **a department at/in the ministry**

minor *adj.*

• VERBS **be, seem**
• ADV. **extremely, very** *This is a very minor operation and there is very little risk involved.* | **comparatively, fairly, quite, relatively** *That's a relatively minor matter. We can leave it till later.* | **apparently, seemingly**

minority *noun*

• ADJ. **large, significant, sizeable, substantial | small, tiny | vociferous** *the view of a small but vociferous minority* | **ethnic, national, racial, religious | oppressed, persecuted**
• VERB + MINORITY **belong to | discriminate against**
• MINORITY + NOUN **opinion, view | community, group | government**
• PREP. **among a/the ~** *You are definitely among the minority.* **from a/the ~** *people from ethnic minorities* **in a/the ~** *We are in the minority on this issue.* | **~of** *a sizeable minority of the population*
• PHRASES **only a minority** *Only a tiny minority of holidays are affected.*

minute *noun*

1 one sixtieth of an hour
• VERB + MINUTE **last, take**
• MINUTE + VERB **pass, tick by** *The minutes ticked by and still nothing happened.*
• MINUTE + NOUN **hand** *the minute hand on the clock*

• PREP. **after … ~s** *After twenty minutes I started to get worried.* **for … ~s** *We waited for ten minutes and then left.* **in … ~s** *The film starts in ten minutes.* | **~s past** *four minutes past two* **~s to** *ten minutes to three*
⇨ Note at MEASURE

2 moment
• ADJ. **last** *Don't leave everything till the last minute.*
• VERB + MINUTE **hang on, hold on, wait** *Could you wait a minute, please?* | **have, spare** *Do you have a minute, Miss Brown?* ◊ *Can you spare a minute?* | **take** *This will only take a minute.*
• PREP. **in a~** *I'll be with you in a minute.* **within ~s** *The ship sank within minutes.*
• PHRASES **just a minute, the minute sth happens** *Tell him I want to see him the minute he arrives.* **not for a minute** *I never thought for a minute he'd refuse.* **this minute** *Come here this minute!*

3 minutes written record of what is said at a meeting
• VERB + MINUTES **keep, take** *Who's going to take the minutes?* | **circulate | read | agree, approve, sign | write up** *I wrote up the minutes of the meeting and circulated them by email.*
• PHRASES **the minutes of a meeting**
⇨ Special page at MEETING

miracle *noun*

• ADJ. **great | minor** *The letter's survival is something of a minor miracle.* | **economic**
• VERB + MIRACLE **perform, work** *Don't expect this medicine to work miracles.* | **believe in | ask for, expect, hope for, pray for | need, take** *It would take a miracle to get the old car going again.*
• MIRACLE + VERB **happen, occur**
• MIRACLE + NOUN **worker | cure**
• PREP. **by a~** *By a miracle she escaped serious injury.*

miraculous *adj.*

• VERBS **be, seem**
• ADV. **quite** *Something quite miraculous happened.* | **almost, near** *a near miraculous escape* | **apparently**
• PHRASES **little/nothing short of miraculous** *a transformation that was little short of miraculous*

mirage *noun*

• VERB + MIRAGE **see | chase** *(figurative) Perhaps we are all just chasing a mirage.*
• MIRAGE + VERB **vanish**

mirror *noun*

• ADJ. **bathroom, hand, shaving, wardrobe | full-length | gilt-framed, ornate | two-way** *He watched them through a two-way mirror.* | **driving, rear, rear-view, wing** *Always check your mirror before pulling out to overtake.*
• VERB + MIRROR **glance in, look in/into | admire yourself in, examine yourself in, look at yourself/your face in** *He was busy admiring himself in the wardrobe mirror.* | **sit at, stand in front of | check | catch sight of sb/sth in, see sb/sth in | fix, hang** *We hung a mirror over the fireplace.* | **break, crack**
• MIRROR + VERB **reflect sth**
• MIRROR + NOUN **image** *Art can be seen as a mirror image of society.*
• PREP. **in a/the ~** *She stared at her face in the mirror.*

mirror *verb*

• ADV. **closely** *The trends here closely mirror those in America.* | **exactly, faithfully, perfectly | broadly**
• VERB + MIRROR **appear to, seem to**
• PHRASES **be mirrored by/in sth** *The jump in business confidence has been mirrored by the increase in employ-*

ment. **be mirrored in/on sb's face** *The shock was mirrored on her face.*

miscalculate *verb*

● ADV. **badly, seriously** *The government has seriously miscalculated the economic effect of this policy.*

miscalculation *noun*

● ADJ. **grave, serious, terrible | financial, political**
● VERB + MISCALCULATION **make**

miscarriage *noun*

● ADJ. **early | threatened | spontaneous**
● VERB + MISCARRIAGE **have, suffer | cause, induce | end in** *Her first pregnancy ended in miscarriage.*
● PHRASES **a risk of miscarriage** *Smoking during pregnancy increases the risk of miscarriage.*

mischief *noun*

● QUANT. **glint, hint** *There was a glint of mischief in her eyes.*
● VERB + MISCHIEF **cause, do, make** *Such people will do anything they can to make mischief.* **| get into/up to** *Don't get up to any mischief while we're out.* **| keep/stay out of** *Try to stay out of mischief, will you?*

misconception *noun*

● ADJ. **common, popular | basic | major**
● VERB + MISCONCEPTION **have | give rise to, lead to | break down, correct, dispel** *We hope the programme will dispel certain misconceptions about the disease.*
● MISCONCEPTION + VERB **be based on sth, stem from sth | grow up** *A number of misconceptions have grown up around this theory.*
● PREP. **~about** *popular misconceptions about Aids*

misconduct *noun*

● ADJ. **alleged | gross, serious** *She was sacked last year for gross misconduct.* **| financial, professional, sexual**
● VERB + MISCONDUCT **dismiss sb for, sack sb for | deny** *The directors all deny financial misconduct.*
● PREP. **~ by** *allegations of misconduct by the security forces* **~on the part of** *There was no misconduct on the part of the police.*
● PHRASES **on (the) grounds of misconduct** *Staff can lose their jobs only on grounds of professional misconduct.*
⇨ Note at CRIME (for more verbs)

miserable *adj.*

● VERBS **be, feel, look** *We got home feeling tired and miserable.* **| become**
● ADV. **bloody** *(taboo),* **damned, dead, intensely, really, very | thoroughly, utterly | pretty, quite, rather**
● PREP. **about** *feeling utterly miserable about his exams*

misery *noun*

● ADJ. **abject, deep, extreme, great, real, sheer, untold** *This phobia can cause untold misery for the sufferer.* **| complete** *Her misery was made complete when she was separated from her children.* **| personal | human | economic** *the country's economic misery*
● VERB + MISERY **be full of, be wrapped (up) in, endure, feel, live in, sink into, suffer** *He was too wrapped in misery to reply.* ◇ *I sank deeper into my misery.* ◇ *men who suffer the misery of unemployment* **| bring (sb), cause (sb), create** *The money brought him nothing but misery.* **| add to, heap, prolong** *War has now added to the misery of these starving people.* ◇ *The giant-killers heaped more misery on the home team.* **| alleviate, ease, relieve** *ways to alleviate human misery* **| put sb/sth out of** *In the end we*

asked the vet to put the poor creature out of its misery (= kill it humanely). ◇ *(humorous) Oh, put her out of her misery—tell her who won.* **| spare sb** *At least we were spared the misery of having to do it all again.* **| forget**
● PREP. **~of** *the sheer misery of homelessness*
● PHRASES **a feeling of misery, make sb's life a misery** *His constant criticism made her life a misery.*

misfire *verb*

● ADV. **badly** *Unfortunately their plan misfired badly.*

misfortune *noun*

● ADJ. **great | sheer**
● VERB + MISFORTUNE **be dogged by, have, suffer** *The expedition was dogged by misfortune.* ◇ *I had the misfortune to share a room with someone who snored loudly.*
● MISFORTUNE + VERB **befall sb, strike** *Misfortune struck before they had even left the harbour.*
● PHRASES **be sb's misfortune** *He is the rudest man it has ever been my misfortune to meet.*

misgivings *noun*

● ADJ. **considerable, deep, grave, great, serious**
● VERB + MISGIVINGS **be filled with, harbour, have | express** *I felt I had to express my misgivings about her decision.* **| share** *She shared my misgivings about the planned weekend.* **| allay, quell**
● MISGIVINGS + VERB **be/prove unfounded, be/prove well-founded**
● PREP. **despite/in spite of sb's~** *He agreed, despite his misgivings.* **with~** *I viewed the process with grave misgivings.* **| ~ about** *She had serious misgivings about the whole affair, but they proved unfounded.* **~at** *He had considerable misgivings at the prospect of moving jobs.* **~over** *The local people still harboured considerable misgivings over the flood of workers into their village.*

misguided *adj.*

● VERBS **be, seem**
● ADV. **entirely, quite, totally | rather, somewhat | fundamentally** *Their approach to the problem is fundamentally misguided.*

mishap *noun*

● ADJ. **serious | minor, slight**
● QUANT. **series** *The group suffered an extraordinary series of minor mishaps.*
● VERB + MISHAP **have, suffer** *I'm afraid your son had a slight mishap in the playground.* **| avoid, prevent**
● PREP. **without~** *We reached home without mishap.*

misinform *verb*

● PREP. **about** *The parents had been misinformed about the incident.*
● PHRASES **be badly misinformed** *It became clear that the general had been badly misinformed.*

misinformation *noun*

● QUANT. **piece**
● VERB + MISINFORMATION **feed sb, spread** *The public have been fed misinformation about the health risks.* **| be based on**
● PREP. **~about/on** *misinformation about Soviet policy*
● PHRASES **a campaign of misinformation**

misinterpret *verb*

● ADV. **grossly | deliberately**
● VERB + MISINTERPRET **be easy to** *It would be easy to misinterpret results from such a small sample.*

● PREP. **as** *I realized that what I'd said could be misinterpreted as criticism.*

misjudge *verb*

● ADV. **badly, seriously | completely | easily** *Quantities are easily misjudged.*

mislead *verb*

● ADV. **seriously | completely, totally | slightly | actively, deliberately** *She was accused of deliberately misleading Parliament.* **| allegedly | easily** *They were naive and easily misled.*
● VERB + MISLEAD **attempt to, try to | be liable to** *Statistics taken on their own are liable to mislead.*
● PREP. **about** *Parliament has been totally misled about this affair.* **into** *The company misled hundreds of people into investing their money unwisely.*

misleading *adj.*

● VERBS **appear, be**
● ADV. **extremely, grossly, highly, positively, profoundly, seriously, very | completely, entirely, totally, wholly | a bit, a little, quite, rather, slightly, somewhat | potentially | deliberately** *Her statement was deliberately misleading.* **| dangerously** *Some of the information was dangerously misleading.*
● PREP. **about** *The brochure was extremely misleading about the cost of the holiday.*

mismanage *verb*

● ADV. **badly, seriously** *The prison service has been badly mismanaged in recent years.*

mismanagement *noun*

● ADJ. **economic, financial | gross**
● VERB + MISMANAGEMENT **uncover** *An investigation uncovered mismanagement and a lack of proper financial controls.*
● PREP. **through ~** *The project collapsed through financial mismanagement.*

misplaced *adj.*

● VERBS **be, prove, seem**
● ADV. **entirely, quite, totally, wholly** *Her confidence in him was entirely misplaced.* **| not altogether | largely | rather | sadly** *His optimism proved sadly misplaced.*

misread *verb*

● ADV. **completely, totally** *I had completely misread his intentions.*
● PREP. **as** *I misread 'Mrs' as 'Mr'.*

misrepresent *verb*

● ADV. **grossly, seriously | completely | deliberately | easily** *Think carefully about what you say: your views could be easily misrepresented by the press.*
● PREP. **as** *Ecstasy is widely misrepresented as a soft drug.*
● PHRASES **be widely misrepresented**

miss *verb*

1 not hit/catch/reach sth
● ADV. **completely | just, narrowly** *The plane crashed, narrowly missing a hotel.*
● PREP. **by** *The bullet missed his head by only a few inches.*
2 not hear/see/understand
● ADV. **completely** *He completely missed the point of what I was saying.*

● VERB + MISS **can't** *The station is just down this road on the left. You can't miss it.*
3 feel sad because sb is not with you
● ADV. **dreadfully, a lot, really, terribly, very much** *Your father misses you dreadfully.* ◊ *I still miss her a lot.*
● PHRASES **be greatly/sadly/sorely missed** *Anne, who died on 22 July, will be sadly missed by all who knew her.*

missile *noun*

1 explosive weapon
● ADJ. **long-range, medium-range, short-range | ballistic, cruise, guided, heat-seeking | land-based | mobile | intercontinental | strategic, tactical | anti-aircraft, anti-ballistic, anti-missile, anti-tank | air-to-air, air-to-surface, surface-to-air, surface-to-surface | nuclear | conventional**
● VERB + MISSILE **be armed with, carry | aim | fire, launch | intercept, shoot down | deploy** *strategic missiles deployed in sparsely-populated desert areas*
● MISSILE + VERB **destroy sth, hit sth | miss sth** *All of the missiles missed their target.*
● MISSILE + NOUN **base, site | attack, strike | programme, system | warhead**
2 object fired or thrown
● VERB + MISSILE **be armed with, carry, hold** *a crowd of youths armed with missiles that included petrol bombs* **| hurl, pelt sb with, throw** *They pelted her with eggs and various other missiles.*
● MISSILE + VERB **hit sb/sth, strike sb/sth**

missing *adj.*

● VERBS **be | go** *a woman who went missing three months ago* **| discover sb** *It was six hours before the seamen were discovered missing.* **| list sb (as), post sb (as), report sb (as)** *A leading businessman has been reported missing from his home.*
● ADV. **completely, entirely, quite, totally** *The study of housework as work is a topic entirely missing from sociology.* **| sadly** *The spirit of fair play is sadly missing from the sport these days.*
● PREP. **from** *The file was missing from its place.*
● PHRASES **missing in action** *servicemen listed as missing in action* **missing, presumed dead**

mission *noun*

1 important task
● ADJ. **joint** *a joint Anglo-American mission* **| secret | dangerous | suicide | fact-finding | reconnaissance | bombing, combat, military | mercy, (search and) rescue | peacekeeping | diplomatic**
● VERB + MISSION **carry out, conduct, go on, undertake | accomplish, complete** *Our mission accomplished, we headed for home.* **| dispatch sb on, give, send sb on** *sending an aid team on a mercy mission to the earthquake zone* **| abandon, abort** (especially of military missions) *The captain instructed them to abort the mission.* **| fly (on)** (used of military planes) *He flew a total of 41 missions over Britain.*
● MISSION + VERB **end in failure, fail** *Their mission ended in failure.* **| be a success, succeed**
● PREP. **on a/the ~** *He was often out of the office on various missions.*
● PHRASES **mission impossible** *Many regard his task as mission impossible.*
2 team sent to perform a task
● ADJ. **diplomatic, military, trade**
● VERB + MISSION **establish, set up | send**
● PREP. **~ to** *The US is sending a trade mission to China.*
3 space journey
● ADJ. **shuttle, space, spacecraft | manned**

• VERB + MISSION **go on, make** *He's been on several shuttle missions over the last decade.* | **abort**
• MISSION + NOUN **control** *The spacecraft lost contact with mission control.*
• PREP. **on a/the ~** *experiments conducted on a space mission* | **~ to** *a successful spacecraft mission to Venus*

4 special aim
• VERB + MISSION **have** *He now has a mission in life: to expand the horizons of those around him.*
• PHRASES **a man/woman with a mission** *You can tell by the determined way he talks that he is a man with a mission.* **a sense of mission** *A powerful sense of mission underpins everything he does.*

5 place where people work to help others
• ADJ. **Christian**
• VERB + MISSION **establish, found** | **run**
• MISSION + NOUN **work** | **hospital, school**

missionary *noun*

• ADJ. **foreign** | **pioneer** | **evangelical, medical** | **Baptist, Catholic, Christian, Jesuit, Protestant**
• VERB + MISSIONARY **work as** | **send (sb as)** *sending clergy as missionaries to Latin America* | **pray for**
• MISSIONARY + NOUN **work** | **zeal** *He argued the case for reorganization with missionary zeal.*
• PREP. **as a ~** *He spent 15 years as a missionary in Africa.*

mist *noun*

• ADJ. **dense, heavy, thick** *A heavy mist rolled over the fields.* | **faint, fine, light, slight, thin** | **dark, grey, red, white** *There was a red mist in front of his eyes.* | **dawn, evening, morning** *an early morning mist* | **autumn** | **sea**
• VERB + MIST **be cloaked in, be covered in, be shrouded in, be wreathed in** *The harbour was covered in a thick mist.* | **disappear into, vanish in/into** *The little town had vanished in the mist.* | **emerge from, loom out of** *A large figure loomed out of the mist.* | **break through, shine through** *Soon the sun would break through the mist.* | **peer into/through** | **be lost in** *(figurative) The origins of Morris dancing are lost in the mists of time.*
• MIST + VERB **hang, hover, lie** *A faint mist hung over the valley.* | **come down, descend** *When the mist comes down it comes quickly and covers everything.* | **clear, lift** *The mist had cleared by mid-morning.* | **drift, float, rise, roll, swirl** *A grey mist floated towards us.* ◇ *a swirling mist* ◇ *a thin mist rising from the river* | **cling to sth** *Early morning mist still clung to the hollows.* | **fill sth** | **cover sth, hide sth, obscure sth, shroud sth** *A white mist obscured the top of the hill.*
• PREP. **in/into the ~** *It was hard to make out the path in the mist.* **through the ~** *The cottage was scarcely visible through the mist.* | **~ over** *the mist over the lake*
• PHRASES **a curtain/veil of mist**

mistake *noun*

• ADJ. **big, great** *It is a great mistake to assume that your children will agree with you.* | **bad, dreadful, fundamental, ghastly, grave, serious, terrible** | **costly, expensive** *This dress was an expensive mistake.* | **disastrous, fatal** | **tragic** | **elementary, little, simple** *All those problems because of one little mistake!* | **common** | **genuine, honest** | **deliberate** | **past** *The company has learned from its past mistakes.* | **stupid** | **spelling**
• VERB + MISTAKE **make** *Don't make the same mistakes as I did.* | **repeat** | **learn from** | **pay for** *Ordinary people are paying for the government's mistakes.* | **discover, realize** *Too late, she realized her mistake.* | **acknowledge, admit (to)** | **correct, put right, rectify**
• MISTAKE + VERB **happen, occur** *Mistakes are bound to happen sometimes.*
• PREP. **by ~** *I picked up the wrong bag by mistake.* | **~ about** *I made a mistake about her.*

• PHRASES **all a mistake** *I kept telling myself that it was all a terrible mistake.* **an easy mistake to make** *Don't worry about it—it's an easy mistake to make!*

mistake *verb*

• ADV. **easily** *An unwary observer could easily mistake this constellation for a comet.*
• VERB + MISTAKE **can't** *You can't mistake him. He's got long ginger hair.*
• PREP. **for** *I'm sorry. I mistook you for George.*
• PHRASES **there is no mistaking sth** *There was no mistaking the admiration in his eyes.*

mistaken *adj.*

• VERBS **be, prove**
• ADV. **badly, gravely, profoundly, sadly, seriously, very (much)** *You are very much mistaken if you think that people will agree to these changes.* | **completely, quite, utterly, wholly** | **somehow**
• PREP. **about** *I think you're mistaken about the time.*

mistress *noun*

• QUANT. **string** *The king kept a string of mistresses.*
• VERB + MISTRESS **have** | **take** | **keep**

mistrust *noun*

• ADJ. **deep, profound** | **growing** | **widespread** | **mutual** *trying to overcome their mutual distrust*
• VERB + MISTRUST **create, fuel** | **overcome**
• PREP. **~ between** *There is suspicion and mistrust between immigrants and the police.* **~ in** *The incident has increased workers' mistrust in the management.* **~ of** *His experience left him with a mistrust of banks.* **~ towards**
• PHRASES **an atmosphere/a climate/a sense of mistrust** *Corruption creates an climate of mistrust towards authority.*

misunderstand *verb*

• ADV. **badly** | **completely**
• PREP. **as** *My concern for their well-being was misunderstood as interference.*
• PHRASES **be often/widely misunderstood, much misunderstood** *a charming and much misunderstood man*

misunderstanding *noun*

• ADJ. **serious, terrible** | **complete, total** | **considerable, widespread** | **simple, slight** | **fundamental** | **genuine** | **possible**
• VERB + MISUNDERSTANDING **cause, give rise to, lead to** | **avoid** *I am anxious to avoid any possible misunderstanding.* | **clear up, correct**
• MISUNDERSTANDING + VERB **arise, occur, result** *Somehow a misunderstanding arose.* | **be based on sth, stem from sth**
• PREP. **~ about** *There is considerable misunderstanding about the aim of the project.* **~ between** *There must have been some misunderstanding between the minister and his secretary.* **~ by** *The oversimplification results in the possibility of misunderstanding by the reader.* **~ over** *a slight misunderstanding over the terms of the contract*
• PHRASES **a possibility/risk of misunderstanding, room/scope for misunderstanding** *Leave no scope for misunderstandings of any type.*

misuse *noun*

• ADJ. **alleged, possible** | **serious** | **alcohol, drug, substance** *alcohol misuse among teenagers* | **computer** *He was sacked for computer misuse.*
• VERB + MISUSE **prevent** | **investigate**

● PREP. **through ~** *causing pollution through misuse of pesticides*

misuse *verb*

● ADV. **grossly** *He had grossly misused his power.*
● PHRASES **widely misused** *'Marketing' is a widely misused word in the book business.*

mix *noun*

● ADJ. **good, right** *a party with just the right mix of people* | **judicious** | **curious, odd, strange** | **fascinating, interesting, intriguing** | **rich** | **heady, potent, powerful** | **eclectic** *an eclectic mix of theatrical styles* | **broad** | **cosmopolitan** | **cultural, ethnic, racial** | **marketing, product** | **cake** *a packet of cake mix* | **concrete, mortar**
● VERB + MIX **contain, have**
● MIX + VERB **vary** *The precise mix will vary.*
● PREP. **~ of** *The college has a broad mix of students.*

mix *verb*

1 combine things
● ADV. **thoroughly, well** *Mix all the ingredients together thoroughly.* | **gently** *When the rice is cooked, gently mix in all the other ingredients.* | **in, together**
● PREP. **with** *Mix yellow with blue to make green.*
● PHRASES **mix and match/pick and mix** (= combine things in different ways for different purposes) *You can mix and match courses to suit your requirements.*

2 meet people
● ADV. **easily, well** *a child who mixes well at school* | **freely** *Whites and blacks mixed freely at dance halls and clubs.* | **happily** | **socially** *They had attended university together and often mixed socially.*
● PREP. **with** *She mixed happily with the other children.*

mixed *adj.*

● VERBS **be**
● ADV. **decidedly, extremely, very** | **fairly, rather, somewhat** | **curiously, strangely** | **randomly** | **inextricably** *In his world-view, art and religions were inextricably mixed.* | **ethnically, racially, socially** *an ethnically mixed community*

mixture *noun*

● ADJ. **fascinating, good, interesting, intriguing** | **bizarre, curious, extraordinary, odd, peculiar, strange** | **eclectic** *an eclectic mixture of architectural styles* | **judicious** *a judicious mixture of young and experienced players* | **rich** | **chaotic, confusing** | **complex** | **explosive** | **heady, potent** *a heady mixture of desire and fire* | **cake**
● VERB + MIXTURE **be made from/of/with** *The cloth is made from a mixture of linen and cotton.* | **pour, spoon, spread, stir** *Pour the cake mixture into the tin.*
● MIXTURE + VERB **contain sth, have sth** *The mixture contains some ingredients that are difficult to find.*
● PREP. **with a~** *He looked at me with a mixture of amazement and horror.* | **~ of** *The pond contains a mixture of goldfish and carp.*

moan *noun*

● ADJ. **faint, little, small, soft** | **deep, low**
● VERB + MOAN **give, let out, make** | **hear**
● MOAN + VERB **escape sb** *A low moan of despair escaped her as she realized what had gone wrong.*
● PREP. **with a ~** *He staggered about ten yards and fell down with a moan.* | **~of**
● PHRASES **a moan of pleasure/despair, the moan of the wind**
⇨ Note at SOUND

moan *verb*

1 make a low sound of pain/pleasure
● ADV. **loudly** | **quietly, softly**
● PREP. **in** *He moaned in despair.* **with** *She was still conscious and was moaning loudly with pain.*

2 complain
● ADV. **on** *They kept moaning on about their illnesses.*
● PREP. **about** *What are you moaning about now?* **at** *My parents moan at me if I'm home late.* **to** *She's always moaning to me that she hasn't got enough money.*
● PHRASES **moan and groan** *The unwilling children climbed into the bus, moaning and groaning.*

mob *noun*

● ADJ. **angry, hostile, unruly** | **lynch**
● VERB + MOB **break up, disperse**
● MOB + VERB **attack sb/sth, set upon sb, surround sb/sth** | **chant (sth), shout (sth)** *a mob of chanting fans*
● MOB + NOUN **rule** *the lawless days of mob rule and anarchy* | **violence**

mobile *adj.*

● VERBS **be** | **become, get** *Babies start to get mobile around the age of eight months.* | **remain**
● ADV. **exceptionally, extraordinarily, freely, highly, very** | **fully** *The barbecue is fully mobile.* | **increasingly** | **fairly, quite, relatively** *She remained fairly mobile despite her disabilities.* | **geographically, socially** *a geographically mobile population* | **downwardly, upwardly** *downwardly mobile members of society* | **internationally** *internationally mobile investment*

mobility *noun*

● ADJ. **limited** | **full** | **greater, increased** | **downward, upward** | **personal** | **social** *Education was the key to upward social mobility.* | **career, job, labour, occupational** | **geographical**
● VERB + MOBILITY **have** *She has limited mobility in her arms.*
● PHRASES **mobility of labour** *The difference in regional house prices acts as an obstacle to mobility of labour.*

mobilize *verb*

● ADV. **effectively, successfully**
● PREP. **against** *They successfully mobilized public opinion against him.*

mock *verb*

● ADV. **bitterly, ruthlessly, scornfully** | **gently, softly** *'Too scary for you?' he mocked softly.* | **subtly** *The play subtly mocks the conventions of courtly love.*
● PREP. **at** *He mocked at her hopes of stardom.* **for** *mocking him for his failure* **with** *She mocked him with her smile.*
● PHRASES **faintly/slightly mocking** *a faintly mocking smile*

mode *noun*

● ADJ. **normal, traditional, usual** | **effective**
● VERB + MODE **use** *Try using some other mode of organization.* | **change, switch to** *He had no intention of changing his mode of attire.* ◇ *Switch from 'receive' mode to 'transmit' mode.*
● PREP. **in ... ~** *The machine is in its 'suspend' mode.* | **~of** *Their main mode of subsistence is hunting.*
● PHRASES **a mode of address, a mode of communication/expression, a mode of transport**

model noun

1 copy of sth
- ADJ. **full-scale, scale** | **three-dimensional** | **detailed** | **working** | **clay, plastic, wooden, etc.**
- VERB + MODEL **assemble** (used of models that you buy in a lot of parts), **build, construct, make**
- MODEL + NOUN **aeroplane, car**
- PREP. **~ of** *She made a fantastic clay model of her dog.*

2 type of product
- ADJ. **de luxe, popular, standard** | **latest, new**
- VERB + MODEL **do, make, produce** *They do several other models of washing machine.* | **sell** | **design, develop** | **recall** *They're recalling their new model for modifications to the engine.*

3 example
- ADJ. **excellent, good** | **conceptual, experimental, statistical, theoretical** | **clinical, economic, mathematical, medical, political, scientific** | **computer**
- VERB + MODEL **give sb, provide (sb with)** *The tape provides a model for students to copy* | **copy** | **use**
- PREP. **~ of** *She was a model of restraint.* | **~ for** *Successful state schools must be used as models for the rest.*

4 for clothes
- ADJ. **female, male** | **top** | **catwalk, fashion**
- VERB + MODEL **photograph, shoot**
- ⇨ Note at JOB

5 for painting, etc.
- ADJ. **artist's, photographic**
- MODEL + VERB **sit for sb/sth** *The model sits for me for three hours every day.*

model verb

- ADV. **closely** | **explicitly**
- PREP. **on/upon** *This system is closely modelled upon one used in French hospitals.*

modem noun

- ADJ. **data, facsimile, fax** | **external, internal** | **fast**
- VERB + MODEM **connect, plug in** | **drive**
- MODEM + NOUN **link** *Data is transmitted via a modem link to the central office.*
- PREP. **via (a/the) ~** *You can send the files to us on disk or via modem.*
- ⇨ Special page at COMPUTER

moderate adj.

- VERBS **be**
- ADV. **very** | **fairly, quite, relatively** *a fairly moderate increase in the rate of inflation* | **surprisingly** | **politically**

moderation noun

- ADJ. **great**
- VERB + MODERATION **call for** *The government called for greater moderation on the part of the unions.* | **show**
- MODERATION + VERB **be the key to sth** *Moderation is the key to good health.*
- PREP. **in ~** *Drinking alcohol is all right in moderation.* **with ~** *Always act with moderation.*

modest adj.

1 not having a high opinion of your own abilities
- VERBS **be, look, seem**
- ADV. **extremely, very** | **quite** | **genuinely** | **falsely** *She would be falsely modest not to acknowledge that she had come a very long way since those early days.*
- PREP. **about** *He is modest about his achievements.*

2 not very large, expensive, important, etc.
- VERBS **be, seem** *Our requirements seem fairly modest.*
- ADV. **extremely, very** | **comparatively, fairly, pretty,**

quite, rather, relatively | **apparently** | **admittedly** *He is looking to improve on his admittedly modest achievements so far.* | **surprisingly**

modesty noun

- ADJ. **characteristic, natural, typical** | **false** | **becoming** *She accepted their congratulations with becoming modesty.*
- VERB + MODESTY **display, show**
- MODESTY + VERB **forbid sb** *Modesty forbade me from mentioning that my novel had been published.*
- PREP. **with ~** *She spoke with characteristic modesty.* | **~ about** *his modesty about his achievements*

modification noun

- ADJ. **considerable, extensive, major** | **minor, slight** | **further** | **important, necessary, significant**
- VERB + MODIFICATION **involve, need, require** *The design requires considerable modification.* | **propose, suggest** | **carry out, introduce, make** | **receive, undergo** *The original plan had undergone fairly extensive modifications.*
- PREP. **with/without ~** *These bikes are designed for racing and cannot be used on the road without modification.* **~ in** *a modification in smoking behaviour among older men* **~ to** *We need to make a few modifications to the proposals.*

modify verb

- ADV. **considerably, drastically, greatly, heavily, profoundly, radically, significantly, substantially** *The original text has been modified so radically that it is barely recognizable.* | **a little, partially, partly, slightly, somewhat** | **gradually** | **constantly** | **specially** | **appropriately, suitably** | **accordingly** | **chemically, genetically** *genetically modified organisms*
- VERB + MODIFY **have to, need to** *You may need to modify your plans a little.*
- PHRASES **highly modified, in a modified form** *These ideas are still used today, though in a slightly modified form.* **a modified version** *using a highly modified version of the program*

module noun

- ADJ. **individual** | **compulsory, optional**
- VERB + MODULE **do, study** *I'm doing two optional modules.* | **complete** | **divide sth into** *The course material is divided into four modules.*

moist adj.

- VERBS **be, feel, look** *Her skin felt moist and feverish.* | **become, grow** *Beth's dark eyes grew moist as she kissed her son.* | **remain** | **keep sth** *Keep the atmosphere in your greenhouse slightly moist throughout the spring.*
- ADV. **very** | **reasonably, slightly**
- PREP. **with** *His fingers were becoming moist with sweat.*

moisture noun

- ADJ. **excess** | **earth, soil** | **body**
- QUANT. **bead, drop, droplet**
- VERB + MOISTURE **absorb, draw (in/up)** *Wind is caused by the sun drawing up moisture from the earth.* | **conserve, hold (in), retain** | **lose**
- MOISTURE + VERB **get in, penetrate sth** *Tiles stop moisture penetrating your walls.* | **evaporate**
- MOISTURE + NOUN **loss** | **content**
- PREP. **~ in** *the moisture in the soil*

mole noun

1 animal
- MOLE + VERB **dig, burrow, tunnel**

2 person
- VERB + MOLE **plant** *They suspected that a mole had been planted in the organization.*

3 mark on the skin
- ADJ. **hairy**
- VERB + MOLE **remove**

molecule noun

- ADJ. **complex | simple | stable | CO₂, DNA, hydrogen, water, etc.**
- VERB + MOLECULE **form**
- MOLECULE + VERB **combine | be composed of sth, contain sth**
- PREP. **in a/the ~** *the number of atoms in a molecule |* **~ in** *the molecules in the crystal*

moment noun

- ADJ. **brief, fleeting | long | precious, quiet** *making the most of those last precious moments together |* **anxious, awful, awkward, embarrassing, heart-stopping, terrifying** *For one heart-stopping moment, we thought she was going to fall. |* **bad, difficult** *That was a bad moment in my life. |* **spare** *Could you look through this report when you have a spare moment? |* **exact, precise, very** *I felt at home here from the very moment I arrived. |* **good, opportune, perfect, right** *I don't think this is the right moment to ask for a pay rise. |* **critical, crucial, decisive, important, key** *We have reached a critical moment in the negotiations. |* **historic | climactic, dramatic | magic/magical, marvellous, memorable | emotional, poignant | finest, great, happiest, proudest** *Her finest moment came when she won Wimbledon. |* **unguarded** *She let the news slip by mistake, in an unguarded moment. |* **last (possible)** *Why do you leave it until the last possible moment before getting ready to leave?*
- VERB + MOMENT **last, take** *The feeling only lasted a moment. ◇ This won't take a moment. |* **spend** *I spent a few moments thinking what I was going to say. |* **give sb, spare (sb)** *I can only spare you a moment, I'm afraid—I'm terribly busy. |* **enjoy, savour** *Victory was sweet, and he wanted to savour every moment. |* **choose, pick** *He's in a bad mood today—you need to choose your moment carefully. |* **capture** *I managed to capture the moment on film.*
- MOMENT + VERB **arrive, come** *The moment had finally come to make a move. |* **pass** *He opened his mouth to say he loved her, but the moment passed.*
- PREP. **after a/the ~** *After a moment we followed him.* **at a/the ~** *At that very moment the telephone rang. ◇ He might wake up at any moment.* **for a/the ~** *She paused for a moment.* **from a/the ~** *I loved her from the first moment I met her.* **in a/the ~** *I'll be back in a moment. ◇ in her rare moments of leisure |* **~ in** *a great moment in the country's history* **~ of** *at the moment of death ◇ It was the proudest moment of my entire life. ◇ There was a moment of silence.*
- PHRASES **a few moments** *Could you wait a few moments?* **a moment ago** *He was here just a moment ago.* **a moment later** *A moment later, the ceiling fell in.* **a moment longer/more** *I couldn't stand it a moment longer.* **a moment or two** *I stood there for a moment or two.* **never a dull moment** *There's never a dull moment in this job.*

momentum noun

- ADJ. **considerable, great, irresistible | initial | fresh** *She gave fresh momentum to the campaign.*
- VERB + MOMENTUM **have** *The campaign for change now has considerable momentum. |* **build up, gain, gather, increase** *The car gathered momentum as it rolled down the hill. |* **create, give sth, provide | keep up,**

maintain, sustain | lose *The team has lost momentum in recent weeks. |* **slow**
- MOMENTUM + VERB **build up, increase | go** *Their momentum has gone, and they feel they cannot fight any longer.*
- PREP. **~ for** *keeping up the momentum for growth* **~ towards** *the irresistible momentum towards reunification of the two countries*
- PHRASES **keep the momentum going** *We have to keep the momentum of our sales operation going.*

monarch noun

- ADJ. **reigning | absolute | constitutional**
- MONARCH + VERB **reign, rule**
- PHRASES **the power of the monarch** *a new law which limited the power of the monarch*

monarchy noun

- ADJ. **strong, weak | absolute | constitutional | elective, hereditary**
- VERB + MONARCHY **establish, set up | have** *The country still has a strong monarchy. |* **abolish** *the arguments for abolishing the monarchy |* **overthrow** *rebels trying to overthrow the absolute monarchy |* **restore**

monastery noun

- ADJ. **great** *the great monastery of St-Quentin |* **medieval, old | ruined | Benedictine, Dominican, etc. | Buddhist**
- VERB + MONASTERY **enter, go into** (= become a monk) *He entered a monastery as a young man. |* **found** *The monastery was founded in 1665.*
- MONASTERY + NOUN **building, church**
- PREP. **at a/the ~** *You can stay at the monastery.* **in a/the ~** *He lived in a monastery for most of his life.*

Monday noun

⇨ Note at DAY

money noun

- ADJ. **big** *There is big money in golf for the top players. |* **easy** *He started stealing as a way of making easy money. |* **government, public, taxpayers'** *Is this a good way to spend taxpayers' money? |* **private | pocket, spending** *Did your parents give you pocket money when you were little? ◇ I don't know how much spending money to take on holiday. |* **prize | sponsorship | paper** *The collection box was full of coins and paper money. |* **counterfeit**
- QUANT. **amount, sum** *the large sums of money we handle in this store*
- VERB + MONEY **have** *I haven't got any money left. |* **borrow, bring in, collect, earn, get, make, raise, receive** *He hoped the scheme would bring in quite a bit of money. ◇ Some people were in the street collecting money for charity. ◇ How much money did he earn last year? ◇ I'll have to get some more money from somewhere. |* **bank, deposit, pay in** *small shopkeepers banking their money at the end of the day ◇ I need to pay this money in today. |* **draw out, get out, take out, withdraw | fritter away, lose, run out of, spend, squander, throw away, waste** *She lost a lot of money at the casino. ◇ We ran out of money and had to come home early. ◇ He squandered his money on gambling and drink. |* **hoard, save, set aside, stash away** *an old miser who hoarded his money ◇ We're trying to set some money aside for a new car. ◇ She stashed the money away in the bank. |* **invest, tie up** *They sensibly invested their prize money rather than spending it. ◇ All their money was tied up in long-term investments. |* **donate, give sb, lend sb, pay (sb), provide (sb with), put up** *Half the money raised was donated to charity. ◇ He managed to persuade his friend to put up the money for the venture. |* **give (sb)**

back, pay (sb) back, refund (sb), repay (sb) *I'll pay the money back next week, I promise.* ◇ *The shop was unwilling to refund my money.* | **owe (sb)** *They owe lots of people money.* | **accept, take** *I don't think they'll accept French money on the plane.* ◇ *The bookmaker was quite happy to take his money.* | **cost** *These cars cost quite a lot of money.* | **be worth** *That painting is worth a lot of money.* | **change, exchange** *We changed our money into dollars at the airport.* | **allocate** *The quality of public health care depends on the amount of money allocated to it.* | **launder** *He was charged with laundering money.*

● MONEY + VERB **come from sth** *Money for the extension to the gallery came from the sale of old exhibits.* | **go (on sth), go to** *I don't know where all the money goes!* ◇ *All his money went on drink.* ◇ *Most of the money went to pay for the food and drink.* | **come in** *She had two children to support and no money coming in.*

● MONEY + NOUN **management** | **problems** | **laundering** | **market** *He made a fortune dealing on the money markets.* | **box**

● PREP. **for~** *He'll do anything for money!* | **~for** *Where's the money for the milk?*

● PHRASES **get money off sth** *You might get some money off the price if it's an old model.* **get your money's worth** *The boat trip lasts three hours, so you certainly get your money's worth.* **pay/put money in/into the bank** *I pay my money into the bank as soon as I get paid.* **put money on sth** *He stopped at the betting shop to put money on a horse.* **put/sink money into sth** *He sank most of his money into his struggling business.* **take money off sth** *He felt sorry for her and took some money off her bill.* **throw money at sth** *They tend to throw money at problems without trying to work out the best solution.* **throw your money around** *He thinks he can make friends by throwing his money around.*

⇨ Special page at BUSINESS

monitor *noun*

1 television/computer screen
● ADJ. **colour** | **CCTV, computer, television/TV, video**
● PREP. **on a/the ~** *The security staff can see all the outside of the building on their CCTV monitors.*

2 machine that records/checks sth
● ADJ. **foetal, heart, oxygen, pulse, radiation**
● MONITOR + VERB **detect sth** | **show sth** *The heart monitor shows the strength of your pulse.*

3 sb who checks sth is done fairly/properly
● ADJ. **EU, UN** *UN monitors declared the referendum fair.* | **school** | **health, peace**

monitor *verb*

● ADV. **carefully, closely, rigorously, strictly** *Television advertising is strictly monitored.* | **regularly, routinely, systematically** | **constantly, continuously** | **effectively, properly** | **automatically**
● VERB + MONITOR **be able to** *We will now be able to monitor its progress more closely.* | **continue to** *The authorities will continue to monitor the situation.*
● PREP. **for** *The workers are constantly monitored for exposure to radiation.*

monitoring *noun*

● ADJ. **careful, close, systematic** | **frequent, regular** | **long-term, ongoing, constant, continuous** | **routine** *The problem was discovered during routine monitoring.* | **independent** | **environmental**
● VERB + MONITORING **need, require** *It is a problem that requires constant monitoring.*
● MONITORING + NOUN **agency, body, committee, group, network, organization, team, unit** *a UN monitor-*

ing team | **device, equipment** | **procedure, process, system** | **programme** | **visit**

monk *noun*

● ADJ. **Buddhist, Christian** | **Benedictine, Dominican, etc.** | **novice**

monkey *noun*

● QUANT. **horde, troop**
● MONKEY + VERB **chatter** | **hang, swing** *monkeys swinging from branch to branch*

monologue *noun*

● ADJ. **long, rambling** | **short** | **comic, dramatic**
● VERB + MONOLOGUE **deliver, do, go into, launch into, recite** *She delivered her monologue in a deadpan voice.* ◇ *an entertainer who does comic monologues*
● PREP. **~ about** *She launched into a long monologue about how wonderful the company was.* **~ on** *He went straight into a rambling monologue on the state of the country.*

monopoly *noun*

1 control by one company
● ADJ. **effective, near, virtual** | **absolute, total** | **government, state** | **domestic, local, national**
● VERB + MONOPOLY **enjoy, exercise, have, hold** *The company has a virtual monopoly in world markets.* | **create, establish, gain, get, secure, set up** | **keep, maintain, preserve, retain** | **lose** | **give sb, grant sb, guarantee sb** *This Act of Parliament guaranteed solicitors a monopoly on particular legal services.* | **challenge** *companies who are challenging the state monopolies* | **break (up), end** *attempts to break the company's monopoly of the sugar industry*
● MONOPOLY + NOUN **position** *The company was able to exploit its monopoly position.*
● PREP. **~ in** *creating a monopoly in the export of wool* **~ of** *One company holds a monopoly of the raw materials.* **~ on** *The company lost its monopoly on exporting beer to India.* **~ over** *maintaining their monopoly over local bus services*

2 organization
● ADJ. **giant, huge, powerful** | **public, state, state-controlled, state-owned** *the privatization of state-owned monopolies such as the gas and electricity industries* | **private** | **statutory**

monsoon *noun*

● ADJ. **east, west, etc.**
● MONSOON + VERB **set in** *The south-west monsoon sets in during April.*
● MONSOON + NOUN **rains, season**
● PREP. **during a/the ~** *Travelling is much more difficult during the monsoon.*

monster *noun*

● ADJ. **big, huge, large** | **ugly** | **bug-eyed, hairy, scaly** *cheap sci-fi films with bug-eyed monsters* | **evil** | **alien, mythical, prehistoric** | **sea** | **sex** *The tabloid papers labelled him 'an evil sex monster'.* | **Frankenstein's** *Bad organizations are self-created Frankenstein's monsters, beyond the control or influence of their leaders.*
● VERB + MONSTER **create** *(often figurative) The government has created a bureaucratic monster.* | **fight** *(often figurative) I wanted to fight these monsters: I didn't want to go on living with them.* | **be inhabited by** *a barren wilderness inhabited by monsters*
● MONSTER + VERB **devour sb/sth**

NOTE
Months

the month of~
The bus service will be offered free of charge to residents for the month of August.
last, next, that, this~
the/this coming~
the following/previous~
She'll be 40 this coming September.
(of) last/next/that/this year
(of) the/this coming year
(of) the following/previous/same year
The construction work began in May of last year.
early, late, mid-~
The strike began in late March.
the beginning, end, middle of~
I'm going on holiday at the end of April.
first/latter/second half of~
The first half of January was marked by intense diplomatic activity.
the period~
Throughout the period November to February flocks of 500 or more are regularly present.

the months/weeks/year to~
In the year to June, sales were up 12% on a year ago.
spend~
He spent August abroad.
~arrive, come (*written*)
November came with especially nasty fog.
~pass (into~) (*written*)
January passed into February with the crime still a mystery.
a~day/morning/night, etc.
a misty December morning
~('s) edition/issue
His article will appear in May's issue of the magazine.
~sales
I picked up lots of bargains in the January sales.
~coup, demonstration, election, meeting, referendum, revolution, riot, summit, etc.
The party is to boycott the June elections.
about, around~
We will write to you again around August.
after, before~
We expect to take delivery some time after June.

between~and~
The hotel is closed between October and April.
by~
The refurbishment should be completed by December.
come~
It's back to school for him come September (= when September comes).
during~
The museum attracted 2 000 visitors during March.
for~
The congress is planned for February 2003.
from~
The exhibition is open from March to November.
in~
We're getting married in April.
since~
She has played only four games since November.
throughout~
The freezing weather continued throughout January.
(up) to, until~
The show runs until the end of October.

---

month *noun*

- ADJ. **last, past** *The past few months have been hectic.* | **preceding, previous, recent** | **current** | **coming, following, next, future** *Winning stories will be published in the magazine in future months.* | **consecutive, successive** | **alternate** | **intervening** *To occupy the intervening months she took a temporary job.* | **early, later** *the early months of 2003* | **cold, dry, hot, wet** | **autumn, spring, summer, winter** *hot summer months* | **lunar** | **calendar** | **record** *This has been a record month for sales.*
- VERB + MONTH **spend** *He spent about a month decorating the house.* | **take** *It took months to find another job.*
- MONTH + VERB **elapse, go by, pass**
- PREP. **by the~** *paid by the month* **during/in a/the~ of** *The festival is always held in the month of May.* **for a~** *It hasn't rained for months.* **in a~** *We're getting married in a month/in a month's time.* **over/under a~** *I've been working on the illustration for over a month.* **per~** *What does the salary work out as per month?* | **~ of** *The months of July and August are the hottest.*
- PHRASES **a time of the month** *Our money's usually running low by this time of the month.*

monument *noun*

- ADJ. **ancient, historic** | **national, public** | **great** | **famous** | **fitting** *The new boat is a fitting monument to the crew members who lost their lives.* | **lasting** *The museum was built as a lasting monument to the civil war.*
- VERB + MONUMENT **stand as** *The tower stands as a monument to the invasion of the island.* | **commission** *A monument has been commissioned in his memory.* | **build, erect, put up, set up** | **unveil** | **conserve, preserve, protect** *the best preserved Roman monument in Britain* | **destroy, pull down** *Monuments to the former leader were all pulled down.*
- MONUMENT + VERB **be, stand** *The monument will stand just inside the cathedral.* | **survive** *Some of the town's Roman monuments still survive.*
- PREP. **as a~** | **~of** *monuments of the army's past campaigns* **~to** *The statue was built as a monument to victims of the war.*

mood *noun*

- ADJ. **amiable, cheerful, good, happy, jolly, jovial** *She was not in the best of moods.* | **exultant, jubilant** | **bullish, buoyant, confident, optimistic** *She was in a bullish mood about the future of the company.* | **bad, black, filthy, foul, rotten, terrible** | **pessimistic** | **gloomy, melancholy, sombre** | **contemplative, introspective, pensive, reflective, serious, sober, thoughtful** | **expansive, talkative** | **mellow, relaxed** | **restless** | **changeable, changing** *I can't keep up with his constantly changing moods.* | **defiant** *The sacked workers were in defiant mood as they entered the tribunal.* | **generous** | **funny, strange** *He's in a funny mood today—who knows how he'll react?* | **playful** | **festive** *It was Christmas and everyone was in festive mood.* | **national, popular, public** *a prime minister who can gauge the popular mood*
- VERB + MOOD **be in** *Don't talk to Miranda today—she's in a terrible mood!* | **get sb in, put sb in** *The music helped to put them in a more relaxed mood.* | **create, evoke** | **affect** | **match, reflect, suit** *Choose colours to match your mood.* ◇ *The weather seemed to reflect his sombre mood.* | **capture** *a film that captured the mood of the moment* | **gauge**
- MOOD + VERB **change** | **darken** | **improve, lift, lighten** *His mood lifted as he concentrated on his driving.*
- MOOD + NOUN **swing** *After the accident he suffered violent mood swings.*
- PHRASES **be in no mood for sth** *I tried to make him laugh, but he was in no mood for jokes.* **a change of mood** *Instantly he felt her change of mood.*

moon *noun*

- ADJ. **bright** *A bright moon shone high overhead.* | **crescent, full, half, new**
- VERB + MOON **cover, hide** *A large black cloud covered the moon.* | **fly to, go to, land on**
- MOON + VERB **appear, come out, rise** | **shine** | **set** *The moon had almost set and the night was now dark.* | **wane, wax** | **orbit sth**
- PREP. **on the ~** *the first man to walk on the moon* **under a/the ~** *The road shone frostily under the full moon.*
- PHRASES **the light of the moon** *They had to work by the light of the moon.* **the surface of the moon**

moonlight *noun*

- ADJ. **bright, clear** | **faint, pale**
- QUANT. **shaft** *a single shaft of moonlight*
- VERB + MOONLIGHT **be bathed in, gleam in, glint in, shine in** *The fields were bathed in bright moonlight that night.* ◇ *His helmet glinted in the moonlight.*
- MOONLIGHT + VERB **filter, shine, stream** *the faint moonlight filtering through the stained glass windows*
- PREP. **by ~** *The castle looks fantastic by moonlight.* **in the ~** *The leaves were silver in the moonlight.*

moor *noun*

- ADJ. **barren, bleak, desolate, open, wild, windswept**
- PREP. **across the ~** *the wind blowing across the moors* **down from the ~** *the slopes leading down from the moor* **on the ~** *We got lost on the moors.* **over the ~** *Don't walk over the moors in bad weather.*
- PHRASES **the edge of the moor**

mooring *noun*

- VERB + MOORING **be torn from, break/come loose from, slip** *During the storm several of our boats were torn from their moorings.* ◇ *The crowds cheered as the great ship slipped her moorings and slid out into the Atlantic.*
- MOORING + NOUN **post, rope**

moral *noun*

1 practical lesson

- ADJ. **clear**
- VERB + MORAL **draw** *There are clear morals to be drawn from the failure of these companies.*
- PREP. **~to** *There is a clear moral to all this.*

2 morals principles

- ADJ. **good, strict** | **doubtful, loose** *Women who went to pubs alone would sometimes be assumed to have loose morals.* | **sexual** | **public** | **Christian**
- VERB + MORALS **have** *He has absolutely no morals, that man!* | **instil** *She had tried her best to instil morals into her daughters.* | **protect** | **corrupt**
- PHRASES **a decline in morals**

morale *noun*

- ADJ. **good, high** *Morale is very high in the school.* | **low, poor, shaky** | **national, popular** | **staff**
- VERB + MORALE **affect, be bad for, be damaging to, damage, hit, lower, sap, undermine** *These unfortunate incidents sapped both our morale and our resources.* | **be good for, bolster, boost, do wonders for, improve, lift, raise, restore** *measures designed to boost the morale of the police* | **keep up, maintain** *The bonus helped maintain morale among the staff.* | **destroy**
- MORALE + VERB **improve, rise** | **be at rock bottom, decline, sag, weaken**
- MORALE + NOUN **booster** *Mail from home is a great morale booster for our soldiers.*
- PREP. **~among** *Morale among nurses is at rock bottom.*
- PHRASES **a collapse/loss of morale**

morality *noun*

- ADJ. **conventional, traditional** | **personal, private** | **public, social** | **political** | **sexual** | **Christian**
- VERB + MORALITY **preserve, protect, strengthen** *efforts to strengthen traditional morality*
- PHRASES **standards of morality** *She criticized politicians' standards of personal morality.*

moratorium *noun*

- ADJ. **six-month, etc.**
- VERB + MORATORIUM **impose, place** | **call for** | **announce, declare**
- PREP. **~on/upon** *The government has called for a moratorium on weapons testing.*

morning *noun*

- ADJ. **this, tomorrow, yesterday** | **Friday, Saturday, etc.** | **early, late** *The side of the mountain appeared pink in the early morning light.* | **April, May, etc.** | **spring, summer, etc.** | **beautiful, bright, fine, sunny** | **cold, frosty, grey**
- VERB + MORNING **spend** *I spent the morning doing some sightseeing.*
- MORNING + VERB **dawn** *The morning dawned bright and sunny.* | **progress, wear on** *As the morning wore on she became more and more tired.*
- MORNING + NOUN **coffee, tea** | **prayer, service** | **rush hour, train** | **newspaper, paper** | **sickness**
- PREP. **by ~, during the ~, in the ~, on Monday, etc. ~, towards ~** *Towards morning the snow turned to rain.*
- PHRASES **first thing in the morning** *I'll see to it first thing in the morning.* **from morning till night, good morning** *He didn't even say 'Good morning'.* **morning, noon and night** *It's all she talks about, morning, noon and night* (= all the time). **the rest of the morning**

morsel *noun*

- ADJ. **choice, juicy, tasty** (*often figurative*) *a juicy morsel of gossip* | **tiny**
- VERB + MORSEL **eat** *I couldn't eat another morsel.*
- PREP. **~of** *a few tiny morsels of bread*

mortal *noun*

- ADJ. **lesser, mere, ordinary** *I just assumed you were a mere mortal like the rest of us.* ◇ *a holiday resort that caters for royalty as well as for ordinary mortals*

mortality *noun*

- ADJ. **high** *Poor hygiene led to high mortality among children.* | **adult, child, infant**
- VERB + MORTALITY **reduce** *measures that should reduce infant mortality*
- MORTALITY + VERB **increase** | **decrease, fall**
- MORTALITY + NOUN **rate**
- PREP. **~ among** *Mortality among immigrant groups was higher than average.* **~from** *a lower annual mortality from cancer*
- PHRASES **a change/a decline/an increase in mortality**

mortar *noun*

- ADJ. **heavy** *They could not move their heavy mortars over the swampy ground.*
- VERB + MORTAR **be armed with, have** *Their troops were armed with mortars and machine guns.* | **fire**
- MORTAR + VERB **burst, explode** *The occasional mortar burst near our truck.* | **hit sth**
- MORTAR + NOUN **attack, fire** *We were under constant mortar fire.* | **bomb, shell** *hit by a mortar shell*

mortgage noun

- ADJ. **big, huge** | **small** | **cheap** *Banks often offer their employees cheap mortgages.* | **endowment, fixed-rate, repayment**
- VERB + MORTGAGE **have** *We've got a big mortgage.* | **get, raise** (*formal*), **take out** *They were having trouble getting a mortgage.* ◇ *We'll have to take out a second mortgage to pay for this holiday!* | **pay, pay off, redeem, repay** *He didn't earn enough to support his family and pay the mortgage.* ◇ *There are penalties if you want to redeem your mortgage early.* | **be in arrears with, fall behind with, get behind with** *They were in arrears with their mortgage, so their home was repossessed.*
- MORTGAGE + NOUN (**interest**) **payment, repayment** *They were struggling to keep up with their mortgage repayments.* | **rate** *a rise in mortgage rates* | **lender**
- PREP. **~ of** *a mortgage of £80 000* **~ on** *I couldn't get a mortgage on the property.*

mosquito noun

- QUANT. **swarm**
- VERB + MOSQUITO **swat** *He swatted the mosquito with a newspaper.*
- MOSQUITO + VERB **fly** | **buzz, hum, whine** | **bite** | **carry sth, spread sth** *This strain of mosquito carries malaria and yellow fever.*
- MOSQUITO + NOUN **bite** *I was awake all night scratching my mosquito bites.* | **larva** *fish that feed on mosquito larvae* | **net/netting** | **repellent**
- PHRASES **a strain of mosquito**

motel noun

- VERB + MOTEL **check into/out of** | **stay at/in**
- PREP. **at/in a/the ~** *We spent a night at a motel on the way.*

mother noun

- ADJ. **lone, single, unmarried** *She felt proud that she had raised four children as a lone mother.* | **widowed** | **biological, birth, natural, real** | **surrogate** (= bearing a child for sb else) | **adoptive, foster, step-** (also **stepmother**) | **teenage, young** | **elderly, old** | **dead, deceased, late** | **good, excellent, loving, wonderful** | **proud** *the proud mother of the bride* | **doting, over-protective, possessive** | **stern, strict** | **dominant, domineering** | **bad, unfit** *The court decided she was an unfit mother.* | **anxious, distraught, frantic** *Her distraught mother had spent all night waiting by the phone.* | **expectant, pregnant** (also *informal* **mother-to-be**) | **first-time** | **new** | **full-time** | **breast-feeding** | **sick** *caring for his sick mother* | **working**
- VERB + MOTHER **resemble, take after** *The two boys were like their father in character, but Louise took after her mother.* | **inherit sth from** *She inherited the urge to travel from her mother.*

motif noun

- ADJ. **central, dominant** *Alienation is a central motif in her novels.* | **recurring** | **simple** *The rug was decorated with a simple flower motif.* | **decorative** | **fish, flower,** etc. *The jacket has a rose motif on the collar.*
- VERB + MOTIF **be decorated with, have**

motion noun

1 movement

- ADJ. **steady** | **circular, rolling, swaying** | **perpetual** *the search for the secret of perpetual motion*
- VERB + MOTION **feel** *She could feel the rolling motion of the ship under her feet.* | **make** *He made little flapping motions with his arms.*
- PREP. **into ~** *The insects are stirred into motion by the heat of the sun.* **in ~** *Do not open the door when the train is in motion.*

2 suggestion

- VERB + MOTION **propose, put, put forward, table** *The motion was put to the conference and fully debated.* ◇ *The Opposition tabled a motion calling for the prime minister's resignation.* | **debate, discuss** *The motion will be debated later today.* | **vote on** | **be in favour of, speak in favour of, support, vote for** | **accept, adopt, approve, carry, pass** *The motion was passed by 165 votes to 78.* | **be against, speak against, oppose, vote against** | **defeat, reject** *The motion was defeated by 51 votes to 43.*
- PHRASES **a motion of no confidence** *He proposed a motion of no confidence in the government.*

motionless adj.

- VERBS **be, crouch, hang, kneel, lie, remain, sit, stand, stay, wait** *The flag hung motionless on its pole.*
- ADV. **absolutely, perfectly, quite** | **almost, virtually** | **apparently**

motivated adj.

- VERBS **be, feel, seem** | **become** | **get sb** | **keep sb**
- ADV. **extremely, highly, strongly, very, well** *a highly motivated group of workers* | **poorly** | **ideologically, politically, racially** *The attack was racially motivated.*

motivation noun

- ADJ. **main, primary** | **real** | **underlying** | **high, strong** *students with high motivation* ◇ *his strong motivation to succeed* | **low, poor**
- QUANT. **level** *pupils who have a low level of motivation*
- VERB + MOTIVATION **have** *Many of the boys have very poor motivation.* | **lack** | **lose** *By this time the children had lost all their motivation for writing poetry.* | **generate, provide** *high rewards that generate the necessary motivation in the workers* | **improve, increase, strengthen**
- PREP. **~ for** *his main motivation for supporting the government* **~ in** *my main motivation in making the suggestion* **~ behind** *the primary motivation behind the government's intervention*
- PHRASES **a lack of motivation**

motive noun

- ADJ. **hidden, ulterior** | **clear, good, strong** *There seemed to be no clear motive for the attack.* ◇ *I'd say he had a very strong motive for wanting her dead.* | **high, pure** *He was acting from the highest motives when he offered her money.* | **base, selfish** | **prime** | **real** | **underlying** *She was not sure what his underlying motives were.* | **mixed** *We give aid to other countries with mixed motives.* | **financial, political, racial**
- VERB + MOTIVE **be inspired by, have** *She knew that he was inspired by base motives.* | **establish, find, suggest** *The police are still trying to establish a motive for the attack.* | **be suspicious of, examine, question** *He was suspicious of her motives in inviting him into the house.* ◇ *She should examine her motives for marrying him.* | **explain** *However you explain the motives behind his actions, he was still wrong.* | **understand**
- PREP. **~ in** *What was their motive in setting fire to the building?* **~ behind** *There is no doubt about the motive behind it all.* **~ for** *There may be a hidden motive for his departure.* **~ of** *acting from motives of revenge*

motor noun

- ADJ. **large, powerful** | **small** | **diesel, electric** | **outboard** *a boat with a powerful outboard motor*
- VERB + MOTOR **start, turn on** | **turn off**

- MOTOR + VERB **run, work** *He left the motor running.* | **drive sth** *A powerful motor drives the mill wheel.*

motorbike, motorcycle *noun*

- ADJ. **powerful | 250cc, 350cc, etc. | veteran, vintage** *a collection of vintage motorcycles* | **police**
- VERB + MOTORBIKE, MOTORCYCLE **ride** *He's learning to ride a motorcycle.* | **climb on, get on, mount | climb off, get off | come off, fall off** *The motorbike skidded and I came off it.* | **knock sb off | park | rev up** *a crowd of bikers all revving up their motorbikes*
- PREP. **on a/the~** *He was sitting on his motorbike.*
- PHRASES **the back of a motorbike/motorcycle** *She climbed onto the back of my motorbike.*

motorway *noun*

- ADJ. **busy | four-lane, three-lane, etc. | orbital, urban** *the M25 London orbital motorway*
- VERB + MOTORWAY **join | leave, turn off | build**
- MOTORWAY + NOUN **driving, traffic | network, system | bridge, junction | service area/station | crash, pile-up** *Five people have been killed in a motorway pile-up.*
- PREP. **along the ~** *driving along the motorway* **down the ~** *He sang as he rattled down the motorway.* **off the~, onto the~, on the~, up the~ | ~from, ~to** *We were on the motorway to London.*

motto *noun*

- ADJ. **club, family, school, etc.**
- VERB + MOTTO **have** *Surfers have a motto—'Life's a beach and then you die'.* | **coin, have sth as, use sth as** *He was the first to coin the motto 'Make Love, Not War'.* ◇ *Let's use that as our motto.*
- PREP. **~for** *a good motto for gardeners*

mould *noun*

1 hollow container
- VERB + MOULD **cast sth in, make sth in** *The statues were cast in clay moulds.* | **fill, pour sth into**
- PREP. **in a/the~** *Leave the clay in the mould overnight.* | **~for** *a mould for a bronze statue*

2 type of sth
- ADJ. **old, traditional**
- VERB + MOULD **be/come from, be cast in, fit (into)** *She is clearly from a different mould from her team mate.* ◇ *He doesn't fit into the usual mould of head teachers.* | **break, break free of** *Breaking the traditional mould of local politics is not going to be easy.* ◇ *trying to break free of the old mould*
- PREP. **in a/the~** *a young politician in the mould of the great statesmen of the past*
- PHRASES **from/in a different/the same mould** *His brother came from a different mould, being a successful lawyer.*

3 organic growth
- VERB + MOULD **be covered in/with** *The biscuits were covered in green mould.*
- MOULD + VERB **form, grow**

mound *noun*

1 small hill
- ADJ. **high, large** *The church stands on a high mound just outside the village.* | **low, small | grassy**
- PREP. **on a/the~** *a small tree on a grassy mound*
- PHRASES **the foot/top of a mound**

2 pile
- ADJ. **great, huge, large | little, neat, small** *a neat mound of leaves*
- PREP. **~of** *a great mound of paperwork*

mount *verb*

1 organize sth
- ADV. **successfully** *The company successfully mounted a takeover bid in 1996.*

2 increase
- ADV. **quickly, rapidly | steadily | gradually | hourly** *Election fever is mounting hourly.* | **up** *The cost quickly mounts up.*
- VERB + MOUNT **begin to, continue to**

3 picture/jewel, etc.
- ADV. **beautifully** *The prints were beautifully mounted.* | **carefully | directly** *The switch is mounted directly on the wall.* | **horizontally, vertically**
- PREP. **in** *The diamond is mounted in gold.* **on** *The specimens were carefully mounted on slides.*

mountain *noun*

1 very high hill
- ADJ. **big, great, high, huge, large, lofty, massive, tall, towering | small | steep | low | beautiful, dramatic, fine, majestic, spectacular | surrounding** *The surrounding mountains make the city difficult to evacuate.* | **distant | isolated, remote | inland | jagged, rocky, rugged | snow-capped, snow-covered, snowy | holy** *the holy mountain of the Lapp community*
- QUANT. **chain, range** *a chain/range of mountains*
- VERB + MOUNTAIN **ascend, climb, come/go up, scale | come/go down, descend, walk down | walk in** *We enjoy walking in the mountains.* | **cross (over)**
- MOUNTAIN + VERB **rise, soar, tower** *The mountains here rise to well over 2 000m.* | **fall** *The mountains fall to the east to the flat expanse of the plateau.* | **surround sth** *Towering mountains surrounded the village.* | **shake** *The earth tremor made the mountains shake.*
- MOUNTAIN + NOUN **chain, range | area, country, environment, region** *Between the two towns was 50 miles of mountain country.* | **height** *We crossed the rugged mountain heights.* | **pass, path, road, route, track | landscape, scenery | crag, face, flank, peak, ridge, side, slope, top, valley, wall | cave | lake, stream | air** *Many people come to the resort simply to enjoy the fresh mountain air.* | **pasture | barrier** *The invading army could only penetrate the mountain barrier at one point.* | **village | fastness, fortress, stronghold | hut, lodge, resort | folk, men, people | climber, climbing, walking, walks | guide | rescue, rescue team | bike, biker, biking | sickness | boot | goat, gorilla, hare, sheep**
- PREP. **across/over/through the ~** *a pass through the mountains* **down/up a/the ~** *She arranged to meet the others halfway up the mountain.* **in the ~s** *This type of goat lives high up in the mountains.*
- PHRASES **the flank/side/slope of a mountain, the foot/bottom/top of a mountain**

2 large amount/number of sth
- ADJ. **great | debt | paper | butter, food, etc.** *They revealed a solution to reduce Europe's butter mountain.*
- VERB + MOUNTAIN **generate | reduce**
- PHRASES **a mountain of paper/paperwork** *The enquiry generated a mountain of paperwork.*

mourning *noun*

1 sadness about sb's death
- ADJ. **deep | national, official**
- VERB + MOURNING **be in, go into** *He was in deep mourning for his dead wife.*
- MOURNING + NOUN **clothes**
- PHRASES **a day/period of mourning** *a day of mourning for the victims of the tragedy* **a state of mourning**

2 clothes
- ADJ. **full**
- VERB + MOURNING **wear**

● PREP. **in ~** *She was still in full mourning six months after her son's death.*

mouse *noun*

1 animal
● ADJ. **field, house | laboratory | white**
● VERB + MOUSE **catch**
● MOUSE + VERB **squeak | run, scamper, scurry | gnaw sth** *A mouse has gnawed its way through the telephone wire.*
● MOUSE + NOUN **droppings | hole | trap**
● PHRASES **as quiet as a mouse** *She crept upstairs, as quiet as a mouse.*

2 for a computer
● VERB + MOUSE **click, double click, move, use**
● MOUSE + NOUN **button | click** *Some of these mouse click short cuts are worth learning.* **| cursor, pointer**
● PREP. **with the ~** *Move the cursor around the screen with the mouse.*
⇨ Special page at COMPUTER

moustache *noun*

● ADJ. **thick, thin | bushy, clipped, curly, drooping, droopy, handlebar, military, neat, pencil, toothbrush, tufty, walrus, waxed | nicotine-stained | false**
● VERB + MOUSTACHE **have, sport** *Her fiancé sported a neat ginger moustache.* **| grow** *He's trying to grow a moustache.* **| trim | shave off | tug at, twirl | stroke** *He stroked his moustache thoughtfully.*
● MOUSTACHE + VERB **droop** *An enormous black moustache drooped over his mouth.* **| bristle** *His grey moustache bristled with importance.*

mouth *noun*

● ADJ. **big, cavernous, enormous, generous, huge, large, wide | small | beautiful, chiselled, handsome, lovely, pretty, sensual, sensuous, well-shaped | firm, hard, strong** *A smile played around his strong mouth.* **| soft | hot, warm | loose, slack | full, full-lipped | lipless, thin | toothless | lopsided | wet | dry, tight** *A tight mouth was the only sign of her nerves.* **| gaping, half-open, open | cruel | hungry | swollen**
● VERB + MOUTH **open, shut | cover** *He covered his mouth to hide his yawn.* **| wipe** *He wiped his greasy mouth on his sleeve.* **| fill** *He coughed as the blood filled his mouth.* **| foam at, froth at** *The dog was foaming at the mouth and near death.*
● MOUTH + VERB **drop open, fall open, hang open, open, sag open** *Our mouths dropped open in surprise.* **| close, shut | be contorted, be distorted, be set, compress, contort, harden, purse, set, thin, tighten, turn down, twist** *His mouth compressed into a thin, hard line.* ◊ *'Get out!' she shouted, her mouth contorted by emotion.* ◊ *Her mouth suddenly set in a determined line.* **| curl, curve, lift, quirk, stretch, tilt, turn up** *Her mouth curved into a smile.* ◊ *His mouth lifted in a wry smile.* **| droop, sag | pout | twitch | quiver, tremble | water** *My mouth started watering when I smelled the food.* **| be/go dry**
● MOUTH + NOUN **ulcer**
● PREP. **about/around your ~** *There were lines of tension about his mouth.* **across your ~** *A cool smile played across her mouth.* **in your ~** *I could taste blood in my mouth.* **over your ~** *She put her hand over her mouth to stifle the cough.*
● PHRASES **the back/roof of the mouth** *I was so thirsty my tongue was sticking to the roof of my mouth.* **the corner/side of the mouth** *There was blood trickling from the corner of his mouth.* ◊ *The corners of her mouth turned up in a slight smile.* **keep your mouth shut** (= don't speak) **(have, etc.) your mouth full** (= full of food) *Don't talk with your mouth full!* **a mouth to feed** *Twins would mean two extra mouths to feed.* **mouth-to-mouth (resuscitation)** *He*

pulled the boy from the river and gave him mouth-to-mouth.

mouthful *noun*

● ADJ. **great, large | small**
● VERB + MOUTHFUL **drink, eat, gulp (down), have, swallow, take** *She took a large mouthful of bread and started to read the letter.* **| chew | spit (out) | choke on** *choking on a mouthful of tea*
● PREP. **between ~s** *He told the story between mouthfuls.* **through a ~** *She answered through a mouthful of cake.* **| ~of** *a mouthful of coffee*

mouthpiece *noun*

1 part of a telephone
● ADJ. **phone/telephone**
● VERB + MOUTHPIECE **cover (up), put your hand over** *He put his hand over the mouthpiece and called his wife to the phone.*

2 sb/sth that informs the public about sb/sth's opinions
● ADJ. **official, political**
● VERB + MOUTHPIECE **act as, be**
● PREP. **~for/of** *The media is controlled by the state and acts as a mouthpiece for the ruling party.*

move *noun*

1 action to achieve sth; change in ideas/behaviour
● ADJ. **big, important, major, radical, significant, substantial | decisive | astute, brilliant, clever, good, inspired, sensible, shrewd, smart, wise | bad | right** *She wondered whether she had made the right move in telling the truth.* **| false, wrong** *One false move could lead to war.* **| positive | bold, brave, strong | defensive | serious | dramatic, shock** (used in journalism), **surprise, unexpected** *The company was put up for sale yesterday in a shock move by management.* **| obvious | interesting | unusual | controversial | conciliatory | popular | gradual | rapid | new | current, present** *the current move towards networked organizations* **| latest, recent | first, initial** *If he wants to see me, he should make the first move.* **| far-sighted | strategic, tactical | precautionary | logical | diplomatic, legal, military, political | career** *Getting a job in advertising was a good career move.*
● VERB + MOVE **be, represent** *The talks represented the first significant move towards peace.* **| make** *The management has made no move to settle the strike.* **| prompt | initiate | signal** *The new legislation signalled a move away from state involvement in telecommunications.* **| spearhead** *The move is spearheaded by a former MP.* **| back, encourage, support | welcome | condemn | oppose, reject, resist | consider, contemplate | decide (on)** *They are waiting for the results of the opinion polls before deciding their next move.* **| announce** *The government announced its move to ban smoking in public spaces.*
● MOVE + VERB **take place | be afoot, be underway** *Moves are afoot to increase car insurance premiums.* **| fail | be aimed at sth, be designed to do sth** *a move designed to control inflation* **| reflect sth** *The move reflects a change in approach to research.*
● PREP. **in a/the ~** *In a move which surprised commentators, the president sacked several cabinet ministers.* **| ~against** *a move against drug dealers* **~away from** *a move away from traditional Labour policies* **~back to** *a move back to old teaching styles* **~to/towards** *a move towards greater trade liberalization*
● PHRASES **a move in the right direction** *Although the new environmental regulations are flawed, they represent a move in the right direction* (= they do improve the current situation).

2 change of place

- ADJ. **false** *One false move and I'll shoot!* | **sudden**
- VERB + MOVE **make** *We should make a move* (= leave) *— it's really late.*
- PREP. **~to/towards** *She made a move towards the door.*
- PHRASES **be/keep (sb/sth) on the move** *His career as a petroleum engineer has kept him on the move* (= kept him moving about from place to place). **every/no/one move** *She made no move as the lion sniffed at the tent.* **follow/watch sb/sth's every move** *The cubs followed their mother on the hunt, watching her every move.* **get a move on** *We're leaving in five minutes so you'd better get a move on* (= hurry)*!* **make a move for sth** (*informal*) *He made a move for* (= towards) *the door.*

3 change of house/job
- ADJ. **permanent** | **sideways** *His new job was a sideways move rather than a promotion.* | **house**
- MOVE + VERB **take place**
- PREP. **~from, ~to** *a move from London to Leeds*

4 in a board game
- ADJ. **brilliant, good** | **bad** | **opening** | **chess**
- VERB + MOVE **learn** *She learned all the chess moves when she was four.* | **play**
- PREP. **on a/the~** *She captured the rook with her bishop on the 32nd move.*

movement *noun*

1 act of moving
- ADJ. **big** | **little, slight, small, tiny** *The eyes of predators are highly sensitive to the slightest movement.* | **quick, rapid, swift** | **gentle, slow** | **easy, graceful, smooth** *She mounted the horse in one easy movement.* | **easy** *The refrigerator unit has rubber wheels for easy movement.* | **jerky** | **sudden** | **deft** | **controlled** | **free** *the free movement of goods in Europe* | **involuntary** | **random, constant, continuous** | **repetitive** | **rhythmic** | **backward, downward, forward, lateral, sideways, upward** | **body** | **eye, hand, etc.** | **dance** | **currency, price** *the volatility of currency movements in the foreign exchange markets* | **troop** | **pincer** *The army surrounded the town in a pincer movement.*
- VERB + MOVEMENT **make, produce** *He made a slight movement with his right hand.* ◇ *Hydraulic jacks under the machine produce the movement.* | **allow** *clothing that allows easy movement* | **control, direct** *As infants grow they become better able to direct their own movements.* | **facilitate** *an initiative to facilitate the movement of labour in the EU* | **restrict** | **prevent** *The striking farmers threatened to prevent movement of goods across the country.* | **sense** *She sensed a movement in the dark beneath the stairs.* | **monitor** *They are monitoring the movement of animals in and out of the country.* | **follow, watch ~s** *The police are following the suspect's movements very closely.* | **trace ~s** *The police have traced her movements to the time of her death.*
- MOVEMENT + VERB **occur** *Some movement in the building will occur as it settles into the subsoil.* | **catch your eye** *A movement caught his eye in the tangled undergrowth.*
- PREP. **in a~** *She kicked down the door in one swift movement.* | **~away from, ~from, ~to** *movement from one level to the next* **~towards** (*figurative*) *Recently there's been a movement* (= a change in attitude) *away from tinned food towards fresh food.*
- PHRASES **the direction/rate/speed of movement, freedom of movement** *The government's decree allowed freedom of movement for all citizens.* **the movement of capital/goods/labour, a sense of movement** (*figurative*) *His music has a real sense of movement.*

2 group of people
- ADJ. **radical** | **mass, popular** | **organized** *The country has a well organized labour movement.* | **international, national** | **artistic, literary** | **avant-garde** | **Modern,**

Romantic, etc. *Both architects were part of the Modern Movement.* | **political** | **protest** | **anti-nuclear, anti-war, etc.** | **peace** | **reform** | **civil/human rights** | **independence, liberation, opposition, resistance, revolutionary, separatist** | **democracy/pro-democracy, democratic, fascist, nationalist** | **labour, trade union** | **feminist, gay** | **consumer, student, women's, working-class, youth, etc.** | **ecumenical** | **scout** | **suffragette**
- VERB + MOVEMENT **create, establish, launch, set up, start (up)** *She started a movement for agricultural reform.* | **join, support** | **be involved in, be part of** | **lead** | **direct** *a protest movement directed against exploitative trade practices* | **suppress** | **ban, outlaw**
- MOVEMENT + VERB **begin, emerge (out of sth)** *The movement emerged out of concern for human rights abuses.* | **develop, gain/gather strength** *The movement gained strength during the 1970s.* | **reach a peak** *The student movement reached its peak in 1968.* | **lose strength**
- PREP. **~against** *a mass movement against the dictatorship* **~for** *He launched a movement for children's rights.*
- PHRASES **a leader/member of a movement, the rise of a movement** *the rise of the labour movement in France*

3 part of a long piece of music
- ADJ. **first, opening** | **second, etc.** | **final, last** *the last movement of Brahms's Fourth Symphony* | **slow** | **fast**
- VERB + MOVEMENT **perform, play**
- PREP. **in (the) ... ~** *a symphony in four movements* ◇ *There is a cello solo in the second movement.*

movie *noun*

- ADJ. **good, great, wonderful** | **classic, cult** | **blockbuster/blockbusting, hit, smash-hit, successful** | **big, big-budget, top** | **low-budget** | **television/TV** | **home** *We watched a home movie of my second birthday party.* | **in-flight** | **silent** | **action, disaster, gangster, horror, war, etc.** | **blue, dirty, porn/porno**
- VERB + MOVIE **see, watch** | **go to (see), take sb to (see)** *I'd never go to a movie alone.* | **direct, make, produce, shoot**
- MOVIE + VERB **be based on sth** *a movie based on the novel by Betty Munn* | **be called sth, be entitled sth** *a movie entitled 'Short Legs'* | **star sb**
- MOVIE + NOUN **actor, actress, director, maker, mogul, people, producer, star** *The former footballer is now mixing with movie people in Hollywood.* | **audience** | **fan** | **première** | **company** | **business, industry, world** | **career** | **channel** | **score, script** | **rights** *the movie rights to her autobiography* | **version** *the movie version of the well-known novel* | **camera** | **poster**
- PREP. **~about** *a movie about the life of Castro*

moving *adj.*

- VERBS **be** | **find sth** *I found the story intensely moving.*
- ADV. **deeply, extraordinarily, intensely, profoundly, very** *a deeply moving account of life on the streets* | **quite**

mucus *noun*

- ADJ. **copious, excess** | **cervical, nasal** | **sticky, stringy, thick, thin**
- VERB + MUCUS **produce, secrete**
- MUCUS + NOUN **discharge, production, secretion**

mud *noun*

- ADJ. **deep** | **glutinous, thick** | **hard** | **liquid, soft, sticky, wet** | **dried, dry** *footprints left in the hard dried mud* | **black, brown, grey, red**
- VERB + MUD **be caked in/with, be covered in/with, be plastered with, be smeared with, be streaked with mud** *Her boots were caked in mud.* | **get/become bogged (down) in, get stuck in** *Several cars got bogged down in the mud.* | **churn sth into, turn (sth) to** *The cars had*

churned the lane into mud. | **wallow in** *pigs wallowing in the mud* | **spatter (sb/sth with)**
● MUD + VERB **ooze** *Wet mud oozed up between their toes.* | **crack** *The mud in the dried-up river bed had cracked.*
● MUD + NOUN **brick, floor, house, hut** | **flats**
● PREP. **in the** ~ *She fell in the mud.* **through the** ~ *We squelched through the mud.*
● PHRASES **a layer of mud, a sea of mud**

muddle *noun*

● ADJ. **awful** | **embarrassing** | **bureaucratic, financial**
● VERB + MUDDLE **get (sb) in/into** *I got into an awful muddle with my tax forms.* | **make** *The judge made a muddle of the case.*
● PREP. **in a** ~ *The house was in a awful muddle by the time the children left.* | ~ **about/over/with** *There was a bureaucratic muddle over his appointment.*

muddled *adj.*

● VERBS **be, feel** | **become, get**
● ADV. **extremely, hopelessly, very** | **a bit, rather, slightly, somewhat** *Her ideas are slightly muddled.*
● PHRASES **be/get muddled up**

muddy *adj.*

● VERBS **be, look** | **become, get** | **get sth, make sth** *Don't get your shoes muddy!* ◇ *The rain had made the football pitch extremely muddy.*
● ADV. **extremely, very** | **all** *My boots were all muddy.* | **a bit, rather** *We all got a bit muddy and wet.*

mug *noun*

● ADJ. **large** | **empty** | **chipped, cracked** | **hot, steaming** *a hot mug of tea* | **beer, coffee** | **pint** | **commemorative, souvenir** | **shaving** | **china, plastic, etc.**
● VERB + MUG **fill, pour (out)** *She filled her mug with orange juice.* ◇ *He poured a mug of tea.* | **pour (sb) out** *Craig got up and poured himself a mug of soup.* | **pour sth into** *She poured hot water into the mug.* | **drink (sth from)** *He drank a mug of coffee and left.* ◇ *We drank champagne from tin mugs.*
● PHRASES **a mug of beer/coffee/tea, the rim of a mug** *He ran his finger around the rim of the mug.*

mule *noun*

● ADJ. **pack**
● QUANT. **team**
● VERB + MULE **ride (on)** | **drive** | **saddle**
● MULE + VERB **bray** | **carry sth**
● PREP. **by** ~ *They travelled across the mountains by mule.* **on a/the** ~ *a man on a mule*

multinational *noun*

● ADJ. **big, giant, large** | **leading, major** | **foreign**
● MULTINATIONAL + VERB **operate** *foreign multinationals operating in the UK*

multiply *verb*

● ADV. **fourfold, fivefold, manifold, etc.** *Just imagine all the problems we've been having, multiplied a thousandfold.* | **endlessly, indefinitely** | **quickly, rapidly** *microorganisms that multiply rapidly* | **together, up** *Multiply these two figures together.* ◇ *If you are cooking for more people, just multiply up the quantities.*
● PREP. **by** *2 multiplied by 4 makes 8* $(= 2 \times 4 = 8)$

mum *noun*

● ADJ. **young** | **single, unmarried** | **career, working** | **proud** | **expectant, pregnant** (also **mum-to-be**) | **new**

The group is aimed at new mums with young babies. | **surrogate** *The cat acted as a surrogate mum to the chicks.*
● PHRASES **mum and dad**

mumble *verb*

● ADV. **incoherently** | **drowsily, sleepily**
● PREP. **about** *I couldn't understand what he was mumbling about.* **into** *She mumbled something into her pillow.* **to** *George mumbled incoherently to himself.*

mumps *noun*

⇨ Special page at ILLNESS

mundane *adj.*

● VERBS **be, seem, sound** | **become** | **find sth** *I found the job very mundane*
● ADV. **very** | **thoroughly, utterly** | **fairly, pretty, rather, somewhat** *a rather mundane task* | **apparently**

mural *noun*

● ADJ. **giant, huge, large-scale** | **painted**
● VERB + MURAL **create, produce** | **paint** | **design**
● MURAL + VERB **depict sth, show sth** *murals depicting Aesop's fables*

murder *noun*

● ADJ. **brutal, horrific, terrible, vicious** | **cold-blooded, premeditated, wilful** *(law) a verdict of wilful murder* | **attempted** | **double, mass, multiple** | **terrorist** | **racial, sectarian** | **unsolved**
● VERB + MURDER **commit** *murders committed by terrorists* | **jail sb for** | **avenge** *He vowed to avenge his brother's murder.* | **witness** | **implicate sb in** *new evidence that implicated her in the murder* | **get away with** *(figurative) They let their children get away with murder!*
● MURDER + VERB **take place**
● MURDER + NOUN **victim** | **suspect** | **hunt** *(informal)*, **inquiry, investigation** | **bid, plot** | **conviction** | **scene** | **mystery, story** *Her latest novel is a gripping murder mystery.*
⇨ Note at CRIME (for more verbs)

murder *verb*

● ADV. **barbarously, brutally, foully, in cold blood** *The boy was brutally murdered.* ◇ *They were murdered in cold blood.* | **ritually** | **allegedly**
● VERB + MURDER **attempt to, try to** | **plan to, plot to**
● PHRASES **admit/deny murdering sb, be accused of murdering sb, be charged with murdering sb** *She was arrested and charged with murdering the two children.* **be convicted/found guilty of murdering sb, be found murdered** *He was found murdered in the cemetery.*

murderer *noun*

● ADJ. **alleged** | **convicted** | **mass, multiple, serial** | **real** *He protested his innocence and promised to help police track down the real murderer.* | **notorious** | **child**
● VERB + MURDERER **hunt, track down** | **catch, find, reveal (sb as), uncover**
● MURDERER + VERB **strike** *The murderer has struck again.* | **kill sb**
● PHRASES **the identity of the murderer** *The identity of her murderer has not yet been revealed.*

murmur *noun*

1 sound of words that are spoken quietly
● ADJ. **dull, faint, low, quiet, soft** | **general** *a general murmur of assent* | **angry**
● VERB + MURMUR **give, let out** *He gave a little murmur of relief.* | **hear**

MUSIC

playing

> She **plays** the piano very well.
> I **play** lead guitar in a rock band.
> The oboe **plays** the main theme.
> The trumpets **sounded** to mark the queen's arrival.

> - a bass, clarinet, guitar, horn, keyboard, sax, trumpet, viola, etc. **player**
> - an orchestral **player**

learning

> My sister is **learning** the French horn.
> I **practise** the clarinet an hour a day.
> He **studied** piano at the Royal College of Music.
> My father **took up** the trumpet in his retirement.
> She **dropped/gave up** the violin when she was fifteen.
> He **teaches** the flute.

> - a music, piano, singing **lesson/teacher**
> - band, cello, choir **practice**
> - an orchestral **rehearsal**

prepositions

> **on (the) ~**
> She sang three songs and I accompanied her on the piano.
> That was Miles Davis on trumpet.
>
> **for (the) ~**
> a work for cello, oboe and harpsichord

performing

> - a concerto, instrumental, violin **soloist**
> - a clarinet, jazz **virtuoso**
> - a brass, dance, military, rock **band**
> - a jazz, string **quartet**
> - a pop, rock **group**

> - a **solo** album, artist, career, cello, instrument, passage, performance, voice, work
> - **unaccompanied** singing, violin

> - a bass, saxophone **solo**
> - a gala, pop, symphony **concert**
> - a concert, gala, virtuoso **performance**
> - a live, rock, solo **gig**
> - an organ, a piano **recital**

> James Levine **conducts** the orchestra of the Metropolitan Opera in New York.
> the Scottish Symphony Orchestra, **led** by Elizabeth Leighton

My sister has taken up the tuba.

- MURMUR + VERB **rise, run** *A murmur of excitement rose from the audience.* ◇ *A murmur of amusement ran round the room.*
- PREP. **in a~** *She answered in a low murmur.* **with a~** *He took the mug of coffee with a murmur of thanks.* **without a~** *They did as they were told, without a murmur.* | **~of**
- PHRASES **the murmur of voices**
⇨ Note at SOUND

2 low, gentle, continuous sound
- ADJ. **soft | low | distant, far-off**
- VERB + MURMUR **hear**
- PREP. **~of** *the distant murmur of traffic*

murmur *verb*
- ADV. **gently, quietly, softly, under your breath** *'What a*

fool I've been,' he murmured softly. | huskily, thickly, throatily | sleepily | shakily | apologetically, appreciatively, politely, soothingly, thoughtfully 'Mmm,' she murmured appreciatively. | drily, ironically, sarcastically, sardonically, silkily, sweetly (ironic), wryly
- VERB + MURMUR **hear sb** She heard him murmur something under his breath.
- PREP. **to** He held her tight and murmured to her.

muscle noun

- ADJ. **hard, powerful, strong | taut, tense, tight | cramped** I walked up and down the aisle to stretch my cramped muscles. | **tired | abdominal, arm, calf, facial, heart, thigh, etc. | skeletal**
- VERB + MUSCLE **flex, tense** He flexed his muscles, then set off to run. | **relax** Learn how to relax tense muscles. | **stretch | build (up), strengthen, tone (up) | pull, tear** I laughed so hard I almost pulled a muscle.
- MUSCLE + VERB **ache | clench, contract, stiffen, tense, tighten | go limp, loosen, relax, slacken | quiver, ripple, twitch** His muscles rippled beneath his T-shirt as he worked. | **control sth** the muscles controlling speech production
- MUSCLE + NOUN **cell, fibre, tissue | group | disease, pain | contraction, relaxation, spasm, tension | tone**
- PREP. **~in** The muscles in my face tensed.

museum noun

- ADJ. **excellent, fascinating, great, interesting, major** one of the world's great museums | **local, municipal, national, provincial, regional, town | private, public | purpose-built | open-air** an open-air museum of farming and the countryside | **working** Although the mill is no longer in commercial use, it is maintained as a working museum. | **archaeological, folk, industrial, local history, maritime, military, railway, science, war, etc.**
- VERB + MUSEUM **go to, visit**
- MUSEUM + VERB **be devoted to sth, contain sth, house sth** a museum devoted to railway memorabilia ◇ The museum houses a fine collection of textiles.
- MUSEUM + NOUN **building | collection, display, exhibition | piece** All the planes are museum pieces. | **curator, director, staff | visit**
- PREP. **at a/the ~** an exhibition of Chinese ceramics at the Ashmolean Museum **in a/the ~** There's a gift shop in the museum. | **~of** the Museum of Modern Art

mushroom noun

- ADJ. **edible | poisonous | cultivated | wild | button, chestnut, field, oyster, porcini, shiitake | dried | hallucinogenic, magic, psychedelic | garlic**
- VERB + MUSHROOM **eat, have** I'll have the garlic mushrooms for a starter. | **cultivate, grow | pick** They went into the woods to pick wild mushrooms. | **chop, slice** Slice the mushrooms and add to the salad. | **cook, fry**
- MUSHROOM + NOUN **compost | omelette, sauce, soup | cloud**
- ⇨ Special page at FOOD

music noun

1 arrangement of sounds for singing/playing
- ADJ. **beautiful, good, great, wonderful | loud | quiet, soft, sweet** The soft background music made her feel sleepy. | **heavy** Heavy music thundered from the basement. | **light | serious | tonal | atonal, twelve-note | contrapuntal, polyphonic | original | live | recorded, taped | background | piped | band, choral, instrumental, orchestral, symphonic | guitar, keyboard, organ, piano, vocal, etc. | chamber | church, liturgical, religious, sacred | secular | ballet, film, incidental, theme** the incidental music for a radio play | **computer,**

electronic | Western | traditional | period Appropriate period music can be played on visits to a historic building. | experimental | avant-garde, Baroque, classical, contemporary, early, medieval, modern | black, calypso, country, dance, disco, ethnic, folk, gospel, indie, jazz, pop/popular, rap, rave, reggae, rock, soul, underground, world
- QUANT. **piece | bar, line**
- VERB + MUSIC **listen to** Listening to music is a great way to relax. | **hear** She could hear music coming from the upstairs flat. | **make, perform, play** We love to make music as a family. | **play, put on** Put some music on, would you? (= play a CD/cassette) | **turn down/up** Could you turn that music down? | **compose, write | arrange | put/set sth to** Schubert set several poems by Goethe to music. | **create, produce** With the guidance of the conductor, an orchestra creates music and harmonies. ◇ The city has produced a lot of good music. | **provide** a beach party with music provided by a local band | **broadcast | record | be into, enjoy, like, love** She's really into rock music. | **get into** He got into music (= became involved in the music business) by chance.
- MUSIC + VERB **play** Calypso music played faintly in the distance. | **blare, thunder** disco music blaring out of the open windows of a car | **come, drift** The music was coming from next door.
- MUSIC + NOUN **business, industry | scene** Birmingham's live music scene | **world** She is a rising star in the music world. | **press** The album has been praised in the music press. | **charts** The band are number one in the music charts. | **festival | appreciation | fan, lover | critic, director, teacher** the choir's music director | **group | centre** We bought a new television and music centre at the weekend. | **video | room**
- PREP. **to (the)~** to dance to the music
- PHRASES **in time to (the) music** They did their exercises in time to the music. **music and song** an evening of Scottish music and song **the sound of music** The sound of pop music drifted through the open window. **a style of music, taste in music** Her taste in music was wide. **words and music** He made up the words and music for the song.
- ⇨ Note at SUBJECT (for more verbs and nouns)
- ⇨ Special page on page 513

2 written signs that represent musical sounds
- ADJ. **printed, sheet**
- QUANT. **bar, line, sheet**
- VERB + MUSIC **read** Can you read music?
- MUSIC + NOUN **score | stand** Put your music on the music stand. | **publisher, publishing**
- PREP. **~for** music for piano, cello and voice
- PHRASES **play/sing, etc. with/without (the) music**

musical noun

- ADJ. **hit, popular, successful | Broadway, Hollywood, West End**
- MUSICAL + VERB **be based on sth** a musical based on the biblical story of Job
- ⇨ Note at PERFORMANCE (for more verbs)

musician noun

- ADJ. **excellent, fine, gifted, good, great, talented | distinguished, famous | aspiring | local | traditional | dedicated, serious, trained** You have to be a very dedicated musician to get to the top. | **amateur, performing, professional, working | backing, orchestral** She had toured as a backing musician for a rock star. | **classical, folk, jazz, pop/popular, rock**
- MUSICIAN + VERB **perform (sth), play (sth) | practise (sth), rehearse (sth)**
- ⇨ Note at JOB

Muslim *noun*

- ADJ. **devout, fervent** | **Shia, Shiite, Sunni**
- MUSLIM + NOUN **beliefs,   faith** | **community** | **extremist, fundamentalist**

mustard *noun*

- ADJ. **hot** *Add some hot English mustard.* | **mild** | **wholegrain** | **Dijon, English, French**
- VERB + MUSTARD **spread (sth with)** *Spread the bread thinly with mustard.* | **add, mix (sth with)** *Mix together the mustard and olive oil.* | **eat sth with, serve sth with**
- MUSTARD + NOUN **seed** | **powder** | **sauce** | **colour**
⇒ Special page at FOOD

mutation *noun*

- ADJ. **chance, random** | **common** | **cell, gene/genetic**
- VERB + MUTATION **carry, contain** *The protein contained a mutation.* | **suffer** *The genetic material has suffered a mutation.* | **introduce** *Mutations were introduced in the region using various techniques.* | **cause, produce**
- MUTATION + VERB **arise, occur** | **affect sth** *These cells carry a mutation affecting the prevention mechanism.* | **cause sth, lead to sth, result in sth**
- MUTATION + NOUN **rate**

muted *adj.*

- VERBS **be, seem, sound** | **remain**
- ADV. **distinctly, extremely, noticeably, very** *a distinctly muted and moderate sermon* | **slightly, somewhat** *Their reaction to the news was somewhat muted.* | **curiously, strangely**

mutilate *verb*

- ADV. **badly, horribly, severely, terribly** *A lot of the bodies had been badly mutilated.*

mutiny *noun*

- ADJ. **army, prison** | **military**
- VERB + MUTINY **lead** | **be faced with, face**
- PREP. **~against** *He led a military mutiny against the senior generals.* **~by** *mutiny by the men*
⇒ Note at CRIME (for more verbs)

mutter *verb*

- ADV. **gruffly, harshly, hoarsely, huskily, thickly, through clenched/gritted teeth** *'I don't need a drink,' she muttered through clenched teeth.* | **quietly, softly, under your breath** | **incoherently, vaguely** | **angrily, bitterly, darkly, fiercely, grimly, irritably, savagely, ungraciously** *Helen began muttering darkly about hospitals.*
- VERB + MUTTER **be heard to, hear sb** *A number of non-British visitors were heard to mutter that it would not have happened in Frankfurt.* ◇ *She heard him mutter an oath under his breath.*
- PREP. **about** *muttering about the incompetence of the office staff* **to** *muttering incoherently to himself*

mystery *noun*

- ADJ. **big, great** *How the disease started is one of medicine's great mysteries.* | **little, minor, small** *one of life's little mysteries* | **complete, total** *She was a total mystery to him despite their long association.* | **whole** *He had found the clue to unlock the whole mystery* | **certain** *Her blue eyes had a certain mystery.* | **real** | **central** *the central mystery of the story* | **deep, profound** *a place of deep mystery and enchantment* | **arcane** | **dark, terrible** | **fascinating** | **insoluble** | **unexplained, unsolved** | **religious, sacred** | **scientific** | **murder** *He is the author of several murder mysteries.*

- VERB + MYSTERY **be, present (sb with), remain** *How these insects actually communicate presents something of a mystery.* | **have, hold** *It was easy to believe that the tiny hamlet held some great mystery.* | **be cloaked in, be shrouded in, be veiled in** *The whole incident was shrouded in mystery.* | **lose** *Air travel has lost much of its mystery.* | **clear up, explain, resolve, solve, uncover, unlock, unravel** *The police are close to solving the mystery of the missing murder weapon.* | **shed/throw light on** *The witness could shed no light on the mystery of the deceased's identity.* | **explore, fathom, grapple with, penetrate, understand** *Her poetry attempts to penetrate the dark mystery of death.* | **ponder (on)** *She pondered the mystery of the disappearing thief.*
- MYSTERY + VERB **deepen** *The mystery deepened when the police's only suspect was found murdered.* | **surround sth** *the mystery surrounding her resignation*
- MYSTERY + NOUN **man, woman** *Their suspect was a mystery man: a quiet, happily married man with no enemies.* | **caller, guest** | **tour** | **disease, illness, virus**
- PREP. **~ about** *There's a bit of a mystery about this child.* **~ as to** *It remains a mystery as to where he was buried.* **~to** *My sister is a complete mystery to me.*
- PHRASES **an air/aura of mystery** *Wearing dark glasses gives him an air of mystery.* **something of a mystery, take the mystery out of sth** *Modern weather forecasts try to take the mystery out of meteorology.*

mystified *adj.*

- VERBS **be, look** | **remain**
- ADV. **completely** | **genuinely, truly** *She was genuinely mystified by her success.* | **rather, somewhat**

myth *noun*

1 story from ancient times
- ADJ. **ancient, classical** | **religious** | **Christian, Greek, Norse, Roman, etc.** | **creation** (= that explains how the world began) *the creation myths of the Eskimos*
- PREP. **~about** *the myth about the golden apple*

2 idea/belief which is untrue/impossible
- ADJ. **great** *There is a great myth that all sports players are stupid.* | **powerful** | **enduring, persistent** | **complete, total** *It's a complete myth that he has royal blood.* | **modern** | **folk, popular, widely held** | **national** *The battle has become part of national myth.* | **historical, political** *The propaganda of both sides relies heavily on historical myth.* | **heroic, romantic** *Propaganda has turned the former president into a heroic myth.* | **pernicious** | **cosy** *The film tears down the cosy myths about fair play in war.*
- VERB + MYTH **create, cultivate, establish** *How did the myth get so firmly established in the popular consciousness?* | **counter, counteract** | **bury, debunk, destroy, dispel, dispose of, explode, lay to rest, puncture, scotch, tear down** | **feed, foster, keep alive, maintain, perpetuate, sustain** | **be based on** *People's faith in the Emperor was based on the myth that he was infallible.*
- MYTH + VERB **surround sth** *trying to lay to rest the myths surrounding mental disabilities* | **persist** *The myth persists that men are more intelligent than women.*
- PREP. **~about** *a popular myth about twins* **~of** *perpetuating the myth of racial superiority*
- PHRASES **contrary to popular myth** *Contrary to popular myth, women are not worse drivers than men.*

mythology *noun*

- ADJ. **powerful** | **popular** | **personal** | **cultural, political** | **ancient, classical** | **Greek, Roman, etc.**
- VERB + MYTHOLOGY **enter** *Stories about ghosts in the cathedral have entered the mythology of the town.* | **create** *She has created her own mythology in the books.*
- PREP. **in a/the ~** *the characters in Greek mythology* | **~about/of** *a mythology about how to get fit*

Nn

nail noun

1 on the fingers/toes

- ADJ. **long | short | sharp | healthy, strong | brittle | broken | manicured, well-kept | painted, polished** (See also **fingernail** and **toenail**.)
- VERB + NAIL **bite, chew | do, manicure** *Do your nails after your bath as they will be softer.* | **scrub | clip, cut, trim | file | paint, polish, varnish | dig** *He screamed as she dug her nails into his shoulders.*
- NAIL + VERB **break, split | bite/dig into sth**
- NAIL + NOUN **brush | clippers, scissors | file | polish, varnish**
- PREP. **under your~** *There was dirt under his nails.*

2 piece of metal

- ADJ. **long | small | six-inch, etc. | loose | protruding | bent | rusty | brass, iron, etc. | masonry, upholstery, wood**
- VERB + NAIL **drive (in), hammer (in), knock (in) | pull out, remove**
- NAIL + NOUN **head | hole | bomb**

nail varnish (also nail polish) noun

- ADJ. **chipped, cracked**
- VERB + NAIL VARNISH **have on, wear** *She wore red nail varnish.* | **apply, put on | remove, take off**

naive adj.

- VERBS **appear, be, prove, seem, sound | regard sth as** *He regarded the move as politically naive.*
- ADV. **extremely, incredibly, very | a bit, fairly, a little, rather, slightly, somewhat | politically**

naked adj.

- VERBS **appear, be, feel, go around, lie, look, stand** *Never had he felt so completely naked.* ◊ *He lay naked on the bed.* | **strip** *She quickly stripped naked.* | **strip sb | leave sb** *She had been left naked and alone.* | **find sb**
- ADV. **completely, entirely, quite, stark, totally** *She realized with a shock that she was stark naked.* | **almost, nearly, virtually | half** *I suggest you don't make a habit of going around half naked.*

name noun

1 word/words sb/sth is known by

- ADJ. **Christian, first, given | middle, second | family, last** (see also **surname**) **| married | maiden | full** *His full name was William Augustus Grove.* | **proper, real | pet** *She insisted on being called by her full name 'Clementia' rather than the pet name 'Clemmey'.* (see also **nickname**) **| assumed, false | official | joint** *The account is in joint names.* | **common** *'Smith' is a very common family name.* | **double-barrelled, hyphenated | strange-sounding | personal** *The village of Low Catton takes its name from the Old English personal name 'Catta'.* | **pen-, professional, stage** *George Eliot was a pen-name; her real name was Mary Ann Evans.* (see also **pseudonym**) **| brand, proprietary, trade | company | code | file | place, street**
- VERB + NAME **have** *Have you got a middle name?* | **bear, carry** *The Julian calendar was introduced by Julius Caesar and hence carries his name.* | **be known by, go by** *The island is more commonly known by the name 'Krakatoa'.* ◊ *He goes by the name of Jonno.* | **use** *She uses a different name in her professional life.* | **acquire, get,**

obtain *The Brady bill acquired its name from its best-known sponsor, James Brady.* | **adopt, assume, take** *He was elected Pope in 1978 and took the name of John Paul II.* | **keep** *She decided to keep her maiden name for professional purposes.* | **abandon | change | carry on** *He wanted an heir to carry on the family name.* | **immortalize** *His name was immortalized in 1992 when he scored three goals in the space of five minutes.* | **choose, decide on/upon | give sb/sth** *She was given the name Maria, after her grandmother.* | **give sb, name, pass on** *Detectives believe that a hitman was sent to silence the witness before he could name names* (= give evidence to the court/police). | **call sb by** *Please call me by my first name.* | **call sb ~s** *Stop calling me names* (= stop saying rude/insulting things about me)*!* | **call (out)** *Somebody called out her name from below.* | **mention** *We cannot mention the suspect's name for legal reasons.* | **drop** *She found him rather irritating to talk to; all he did was drop names* (= mention the names of famous people he knew or had met in order to impress her). | **invoke** *He invoked the name of Freud in support of his argument.* | **ask (sb)** *I asked him his name.* | **hear** *I've heard that name mentioned before.* | **know** *How do you know my name?* | **remember | print, sign, write | spell | enter, put down** *Have you put your name down for* (= applied to take part in) *the school quiz?* | **put forward** *They put his name forward* (= chose him) *as one of the five candidates for the post.*
- NAME + VERB **appear** *The name of the artist appears on the vase.* | **imply sth, suggest sth** *As the name implies, Oxford was the place at which oxen could ford the river.* | **mean sth | ring a bell** (figurative) *'Does that name mean anything to you* (= do you recognize it)*?' 'Yes, it does ring a bell* (= it is familiar)*.'*
- NAME + NOUN **badge, plate**
- PREP. **by~** *The head teacher knows every child in the school by name.* **by the~of** *an actor by the name of Tom Rees* **in sb/sth's~** *The tickets were booked in the name of McLean.* ◊ *I arrest you in the name* (= on the authority) *of the law.* **under a/the~** *The room was booked under* (= using) *a false name.* **| ~for/of** *The common name for the flower is 'pineapple lily'.*
- PHRASES **a change of name, give your name to sth** *The invading Franks gave their name to the country in which they settled.* **name and address, names and faces** *I have a bad memory for names and faces.* **put a name to sb/sth** *Nobody puts their name to a business* (= uses their name for the name of a business) *they are not proud of.* **take sb's name in vain** *Have you been taking my name in vain* (= showing lack of respect when using my name)*?*

2 reputation

- ADJ. **big | good | bad**
- VERB + NAME **have | become** *She has become a big name in documentary photography.* | **make** *He made his name writing travel books.* ◊ *She's made quite a name for herself.* | **acquire, get** *The area got a bad name after a series of nasty murders.* | **protect** *They tried to protect the good name of the college.* | **give sb** *This kind of behaviour gives students a bad name.* | **blacken, damage** *The riots after the match only served to blacken the name of football.*
- PREP. **~for** *The company has a name for reliability.*
- PHRASES **sb's name is mud** *If you tell our secret your name will be mud* (= you will not be popular) *round here.*

3 famous person/thing

- ADJ. **big, famous, household, well-known** *They are a big name in the world of rock music.*

name *verb* (often **be named**)

● ADV. **originally | appropriately, aptly, suitably, well | significantly | correctly, incorrectly** *The present Kew Bridge was opened by King Edward VII and is correctly named 'King Edward Bridge'.* | **curiously, delightfully, exotically, grandly, improbably, oddly, quaintly, romantically, strangely, wonderfully** *the curiously named Egg Castle* | **confusingly | euphemistically | ironically**
● PREP. **after** *I named my son after my father.* **for** (*literary*) *the dead sister for whom she had been named* **in honour of sb/sth** *The hospital was named in honour of its principal benefactor.*

nanny *noun*

● ADJ. **live-in | qualified, trained**
● PREP. **~ to** *She was taken on as a nanny to their two small children.*
⇨ Note at JOB

nap *noun*

● ADJ. **brief, little, quick, short | afternoon, morning | cat** (also **catnap**) *If you have difficulty sleeping at night, avoid taking catnaps during the day.* | **power** *A ten-minute power nap can boost your productivity.*
● VERB + NAP **have, take** *I had a short nap after lunch.*

napkin *noun*

● ADJ. **clean | folded | dinner | table** *She dabbed her mouth with her table napkin.* | **damask, linen, paper**
● VERB + NAPKIN **fold | unfold | tuck** *He tucked his napkin under his chin.* | **dab sth with, wipe sth on/with**
● NAPKIN + NOUN **ring** *napkin rings made of silver*

nappy *noun*

● ADJ. **clean | wet | dirty, soiled | disposable | washable | cloth, terry**
● VERB + NAPPY **have on, wear | change | put on | remove, take off | wash | dispose of**
● NAPPY + NOUN **change, changing | liner | pin | rash**
● PREP. **in ~** *Isn't he rather old to be still in nappies?*
⇨ Special page at CLOTHES

narcotic *noun*

● ADJ. **mild, powerful**
● VERB + NARCOTIC **inject, use | trade in** *He has been arrested for trading in narcotics.*
● NARCOTIC + NOUN **agent, officer, official, squad**
⇨ Note at DRUG (for more verbs and nouns)

narrative *noun*

● ADJ. **popular | coherent | simple, straightforward | complex, detailed | chronological, sequential | first-person, second-person, third-person** *The book is written in the style of first-person narrative.* | **fictional, prose | film | historical | biblical**
● VERB + NARRATIVE **construct, create, develop, produce** *It's difficult to construct a narrative out of a series of fast-moving events.* | **interrupt** *The author interrupts her narrative to tell us that the idea for the book had not been well received.*
● NARRATIVE + VERB **be based on sth**
● NARRATIVE + NOUN **form, style, technique | framework, structure | flow** *interruptions to the narrative flow* | **content | passage, sequence, text**
● PREP. **in a/the ~** *events in the narrative*

narrow *verb*

1 of a road/river/gap/range
● ADV. **considerably | a bit, a little, slightly** *The river narrows a little here.* | **sharply** *The gap between the two parties narrowed sharply in the days before the election.* | **steadily**
● PREP. **to** *By the final round the gap had narrowed to three votes.*

2 of eyes
● ADV. **fractionally, slightly** *Though her eyes narrowed fractionally, she made no comment.* | **suddenly | dangerously, shrewdly, speculatively, suspiciously, thoughtfully** *The blue eyes narrowed thoughtfully.*
● PREP. **against** *Her eyes narrowed against the sun.* **at** *His eyes suddenly narrowed at the sight of her.* **to** *His eyes narrowed to slits.* **with** *His eyes narrowed with suspicion.*

narrow *adj.*

1 not wide
● VERB. **be, look, seem | become, get**
● ADV. **extremely, very | a bit, fairly, quite, rather, relatively** *The pass gets quite narrow towards the east.*

2 limited
● VERB. **be, seem | become**
● ADV. **excessively, extremely, peculiarly, very | increasingly | comparatively, fairly, quite, rather, relatively, somewhat**
● PREP. **in** *people who are rather narrow in outlook*

nasty *adj.*

● VERB. **be, look, smell, sound, taste** *He made it all sound very nasty.* | **become, get, turn** *Things could turn nasty* (= dangerous) *if we're not careful.*
● ADV. **extremely, particularly, really, very | thoroughly** *gang warfare of a thoroughly nasty kind* | **pretty, quite, rather**
● PREP. **about** *She was nasty about everyone.* **to** *Kevin seems to enjoy being nasty to his sisters.*
● PHRASES **cheap and nasty** *a room full of cheap and nasty ornaments* **nasty little** *a nasty little man*

nation *noun*

● ADJ. **large | little, small | major | great, leading, powerful, strong | advanced, developed, industrial, industrialized | developing, emergent, emerging, less-developed, Third World | affluent, prosperous, rich, wealthy** *the richest nation on earth* | **poor | civilized | backward | new | young | ancient, old | free, independent, sovereign | democratic | capitalist | united | divided | entire, whole** *The entire nation mourned her death.* | **foreign | Western** *the imperialist expansion of Western nations in the 1880s* | **Arab, European, French, etc. | maritime, oil-producing, trading | nuclear | creditor, debtor** *In 1950 the UK was the world's largest debtor nation and the US the largest creditor.* | **host** *France was host nation for the 1998 World Cup.* | **member** *the member nations of the UN*
● VERB + NATION **create** *They wanted to create a new nation.* | **unite** *The fight against terrorism seemed to unite the nation.* | **divide | govern, lead | shock** *the savage murder that shocked the nation*
● NATION + NOUN **building** *The biggest task of the government was to address national unity and nation building.* | **state**
● PREP. **across a/the ~** *swings in public opinion across the nation* **among ~** *economic inequality among the nations of the world* **in/within a/the ~** *In the nation as a whole there is no desire for war.* | **~ of** *They are a nation of food lovers.*
● PHRASES **the birth of a nation, the interests of a nation, the life of a nation** *They hoped that the exhibition would enhance the cultural life of the nation.* **the nation as a whole, the nation at large** *The new economic policies were in the best interests of the nation at large.* **the nations of the world**

nationalism *noun*

- ADJ. **aggressive, extreme, fierce, militant, revolutionary | popular | conservative, radical | secular | black | cultural, economic, political, racial**
- PHRASES **the growth of nationalism, the resurgence/revival of nationalism, the rise in nationalism, a tide of nationalism** *a tide of militant nationalism*

nationalist *noun*

- ADJ. **ardent | extreme, hard-line, radical | militant | moderate | left-wing, liberal | conservative, right-wing | veteran | former | local | Basque, Irish, etc. | African, black**
- NATIONALIST + NOUN **leader | forces, troops | uprising** *leading a nationalist uprising*

nationalistic *adj.*

- VERBS **be | become | remain**
- ADV. **fiercely, intensely, strongly | increasingly**

nationality *noun*

- ADJ. **various** *cultural differences among various nationalities* **| mixed** *teams of mixed nationality* **| dual** *He has dual British and South African nationality.* **| foreign | minority | Argentinian, etc.**
- VERB + NATIONALITY **have | acquire, adopt, assume, obtain, take** *She is hoping to adopt Australian nationality.* **| inherit | retain | change | give up, renounce | lose | grant sb | refuse sb**
- NATIONALITY + VERB **be represented** *About 30 nationalities were represented at the tournament.*
- PHRASES **on (the) grounds of nationality** *He accused them of discrimination on the grounds of nationality.*

natural *adj.*

1 not made by people
- VERBS **be** *All the fibres are natural.*
- ADV. **completely** *completely natural materials*

2 usual/normal
- VERBS **be, feel, look, seem, sound**
- ADV. **only, perfectly, quite** *It's only natural that she should feel upset.* **| fairly**

nature *noun*

1 the physical world; plants, animals, etc.
- ADJ. **Mother** *Mother Nature had served up some terrible weather for their cruise.*
- VERB + NATURE **commune with** *He believed in spending half an hour each day to relax and commune with nature.* **| be/get back to** *We built our house in the country because we wanted to get back (= be close) to nature.* **| be found in** *man-made substances not found in nature*
- NATURE + VERB **endow (sb with) sth** *Nature had endowed her with exceptional vitality.* **| produce sth** *It's unlikely that this gully was produced by nature.*
- NATURE + NOUN **conservation | reserve | trail**
- PREP. **close to** ~ *people who live in the country and are close to nature* **in** ~ *We appreciate beauty in nature.*
- PHRASES **the forces of nature, the laws of nature, a love of nature** *His love of nature was expressed through his wildlife paintings.*

2 qualities/features of sb/sth
- ADJ. **basic, essential, fundamental, intrinsic, real, true | artificial | exact, precise, specific** *I'm not clear about the exact nature of their relationship.* **| general | selective | limited, restrictive | changing, seasonal, temporary, transitory | uncertain, unpredictable | arbitrary, random | subjective** *the subjective nature of an odour* **| abstract | capricious, fickle | intractable | distinctive, unusual | radical | complex | special, spe-**
cialist | traditional | controversial | contradictory | problematic | unsatisfactory *the unsatisfactory nature of the meeting* | **good** *People are always taking advantage of her good nature (= her kindness).* | **human** *It's only human nature to want more money.* | **divine** | **confidential, personal, private | public | international, local** *the international nature of the business* | **repetitive | routine** *matters of a routine nature* | **detailed** *Because of the detailed nature of the work, I have to use a very fine brush.* | **practical | physical, psychological, sexual** *They define sexual harassment as unwanted conduct of a sexual nature.* | **economic, legal, political, social** *Their problems are of an economic nature.* | **contemplative | inquisitive**
- VERB + NATURE **have** *He has an inquisitive nature.* | **reveal** *The parties would not reveal the exact nature of the dispute.* | **conceal | reflect | belie** *The gentle lower slopes belie the true nature of the mountain.* | **be contrary to, be/run against** *It was against his nature to tell lies.* | **alter, change** *This new information does not change the nature of our findings.* | **acknowledge, be aware of, recognize** *Are you aware of the nature of the risks involved?* | **define, specify** *It is important to define the nature of the problem.* | **assess, consider, discuss, examine, explore, investigate | comprehend, realize, understand | misconceive | clarify, elucidate, explain, give/offer/ provide an insight into** *His theory provides a remarkable insight into the nature of the British constitution.* | **describe | determine | depend on** *The method employed will depend on the nature of the task.* | **appeal to** *There was no point appealing to her better nature (= kindness).*
- PREP. **by** ~ *He's not by nature an inquisitive person.* **concerning the** ~ *a debate concerning the nature of violence* **considering/given the** ~ *Given the nature of this matter, I am inclined to think it should be managed by you personally.* **in** ~ *Their strategy was essentially political in nature.* **in sb/sth's** ~ *It's not in his nature to complain.* ◇ *A certain element of risk is in the nature of the job.* **of a ...** ~ *The legal concept of insanity is of a different nature from the medical.*
- PHRASES **by its very nature** *By its very nature a secret service is not open to public inspection.* **the extent and nature of sth** *We need to understand the true extent and nature of the problem.* **a part of sb's nature** *the expressive part of his nature* ◇ *Her view is that aggression is part of human nature.* **a side of/to sb's nature** *He had a vicious side to his nature.*

nausea *noun*

- ADJ. **intense, severe | sudden | nervous**
- QUANT. **wave** *I was overcome by waves of nausea.*
- VERB + NAUSEA **experience, feel | complain of | bring on, cause | relieve**
- NAUSEA + VERB **engulf sb, overcome sb, sweep over sb**
- PHRASES **a feeling/sensation of nausea**

navigate *verb*

- ADV. **accurately, successfully** *Pigeons navigate less accurately when the earth's magnetic field is disturbed.* ◇ *(figurative) Those who successfully navigate this social minefield are accepted by the royal family.*
- PREP. **across, by** *These birds navigate by the sun.* **through** *learning to navigate your way through a forest*
- PHRASES **navigate your way**

navigation *noun*

- ADJ. **accurate | radio, satellite**
- NAVIGATION + NOUN **system | aids, equipment, instruments, lights | beacon | rights**
- PREP. ~ **through** *(often figurative) navigation through complex documents*

● PHRASES **an aid to navigation** *small boats equipped with electronic aids to navigation* **freedom/rights of navigation** *freedom of navigation through international waterways*

navy *noun*

● ADJ. **strong | merchant**
● VERB + NAVY **have | build | serve in | join**
● PREP. **in the~** *He spent ten years in the merchant navy.*
● PHRASES **the Royal Navy**

neat *adj.*

● VERBS **appear, be, look, seem | leave sth, make sth** *Be sure to leave the room neat and tidy.* | **keep sth** *She kept her desk extremely neat.*
● ADV. **extremely, very | fairly, quite, rather | surprisingly** *The handwriting was surprisingly neat.*
● PHRASES **neat and tidy**

necessary *adj.*

● VERBS **be, prove, seem | become | remain | make sth** *The cold weather has made it necessary to protect the crops.* | **consider sth, feel sth, find sth, regard sth as, see sth as, think sth** *Make any alterations you consider necessary.* ◇ *You may find it necessary to readjust the wheels from time to time.*
● ADV. **really, strictly** *I was determined not to stay in hospital for any longer than was strictly necessary.* | **absolutely | causally, logically**
● PREP. **for** *qualifications which are necessary for work with the under-fives*
● PHRASES **if necessary** *These measures will be enforced, if necessary, by the army.* **as/when/where necessary** *We are here to give help and support when necessary.*

necessity *noun*

1 fact that sth must happen; sth that cannot be avoided
● ADJ. **overwhelming, sheer | absolute | fundamental, vital | real | dire, pressing, urgent | immediate | strategic | logical, physical, practical** *The people in the rural areas use mud bricks only as an immediate, practical necessity.* | **commercial, economic, financial, historical, military, political, social** *He argued that nuclear weapons were a political necessity.*
● VERB + NECESSITY **recognize, see** *She saw the necessity to make an immediate impression on him.* | **accept (sth as), be convinced of** *They have accepted the necessity of greater state intervention.* | **avoid, obviate, remove, spare | emphasize, highlight, stress** *Observers stressed the necessity for the ceasefire to be observed.* | **be born (out) of** *Culling of the animals was born out of the necessity for successful conservation.*
● NECESSITY + VERB **arise** *These animals don't like water but will swim if the necessity arises.* | **demand (sth)** *Where necessity demands, we can seat more guests in the gallery.* | **force sth** *Necessity forced an urgent solution.*
● PREP. **of~** *The visit will, of necessity, be brief.* **out of~** *He is changing job out of necessity, not because he particularly wants to.* **through~** *Most of the women are forced, through economic necessity, to work in part-time low-paid jobs.* **without the~of** *You can dial direct without the necessity of going through the operator.* | **~for** *There's no necessity for you to come.* **~to** *the necessity to earn a living*
● PHRASES **any/no necessity** *The company sees no necessity for a more cautious approach to investment.*

2 sth you must have
● ADJ. **absolute | vital | real | urgent** *Policies which address these issues are an urgent necessity.* | **bare, basic** *They have nothing but the barest necessities.* | **daily**
● VERB + NECESSITY **have | lack**
● PHRASES **a necessity of life** *Food is a necessity of life.*

neck *noun*

1 part of the body
● ADJ. **long, short | beautiful, elegant | slender, slim, swan-like | scraggy, scrawny, thin | strong, thick | wrinkled | stiff | broken**
● VERB + NECK **crane, strain** *I craned my neck to see what was happening at the head of the queue.* | **crick** *I cricked my neck playing tennis and now I can't turn round properly.* | **break, injure | wring** *He killed the chicken quickly by wringing its neck.* | **risk** *(often figurative) I'm not going to risk my neck playing rugby with you!* | **save** *(often figurative) He's out to save his own political neck* (= his political career).
● NECK + VERB **ache**
● NECK + NOUN **muscle | brace, collar, support** *She's been wearing a neck brace since her car crash.* | **injury**
● PREP. **around/round your~** *I keep the key on a string round my neck.* **in the~** *The veins in his neck stood out like knotted rope.*
● PHRASES **the back/nape of the neck** *The hairs on the back of my neck prickled with fear.* **the scruff of the neck** *The cat picked up her kitten by the scruff of its neck.*

2 part of a piece of clothing
● ADJ. **high | open** *He wore a casual shirt with an open neck.* | **crew, halter, polo, roll, round, scoop, square, turtle, V**

need *noun*

1 situation where sth is needed/necessary
● ADJ. **considerable, great, strong | special** *There is a special need for well-trained teachers.* | **overriding, overwhelming, paramount | burning, compelling, critical, crying, desperate, dire, driving, immediate, pressing, urgent** *a crying need for skilled workers* ◇ *These children are in dire need.* | **real | clear | basic, essential, fundamental | sudden | constant, continuing** *He's in constant need of treatment.* | **growing, increased/increasing | reduced | possible | perceived | common** *our common need for self-preservation* | **individual | human** *the human need to order existence* | **political, social**
● VERB + NEED **feel, have** *I felt the need to do something.* | **express** *Several governments have expressed the need for a cautious approach to the conflict.* | **demonstrate, prove, show, suggest** *The incident proved the need for a continuing military presence in the area.* | **reflect** *a law reflecting a need for better social conditions* | **create** *The war created a need for national unity.* | **address, fulfil, meet, satisfy | avoid, eliminate, obviate, remove** *I avoid the need to travel by plane.* | **reduce | be aware of, be sensitive to | accept, acknowledge, perceive, recognize, see** *I see no need to do anything hasty.* | **emphasize, heighten, highlight, reaffirm, stress, underline** *She stressed the need for cooperation with the authorities.* | **ignore, overlook | deny** *The government has denied the need for economic reform.* | **understand | consider**
● NEED + VERB **exist** *A need exists to bridge the gap between theory and practice in nursing.* | **arise** *The system can be switched to emergency power should the need arise.*
● PREP. **in~(of)** *a campaign to help children in need* ◇ *The room was sorely in need of a fresh coat of paint.* | **~for** *the need for change*
● PHRASES **any/little/no need** *There's no need to worry.*

2 sth that sb requires
● ADJ. **basic, essential, fundamental | particular, special, specific** *a school for children with special educational needs* | **immediate, pressing | long-term | changing | conflicting | unmet | local | individual | community | customer/customer's, patient/patient's | human** *Energy for cooking is a basic human need.* | **humanitarian | material, physical** *material needs of food and drink* | **dietary | health care, medical | biological, bodily, emotional, physical, psychological, sexual, spir-**

itual | educational | political, social | business | operational | energy | information
- VERB + NEED **be responsive to, be sensitive to** | **address, cater for/to, cover, fulfil, meet, provide (for), respond to, satisfy, serve, supply** *a new union set up to address the needs of seasonal labourers* ◇ *£10 a day was enough to cover all his needs.* ◇ *We have now met most of the humanitarian needs of the refugees.* | **suit, tailor sth to** *The coaching is informal and tailored to individual needs.* | **identify** | **assess, consider**
- PHRASES **needs and desires, sb's every need** *Our staff will cater to your every need.*

need *verb*

- ADV. **badly, desperately, really, urgently** *She needed some money badly.* ◇ *Research is urgently needed into the causes of this illness.* | **certainly, definitely** | **clearly, obviously** | **just, only, simply** *I just need some information.* | **hardly** *You hardly need me to tell you that your father is still very frail and must not be upset.* | **not necessarily** *These people may need 24-hour attention, but they do not necessarily need to be in hospital.* | **no longer** | **still**
- VERB + NEED **be going to** | **be expected to, be likely to, may well** *You may well need to look outside your preferred area to find affordable accommodation.*

needle *noun*

1 for sewing
- ADJ. **long** | **blunt** | **sharp** | **fine** | **darning, embroidery, sewing, tapestry**
- VERB + NEEDLE **use** | **thread**
- PHRASES **the eye of a needle, needle and thread** *She sewed it on with needle and thread.*

2 for knitting
- ADJ. **empty** | **knitting**
- NEEDLE + VERB **hold sth** *a needle holding two stitches*

3 for drugs
- ADJ. **hypodermic, syringe** | **long** | **sharp** | **fine** | **clean, sterile** | **contaminated, infected** | **used**
- VERB + NEEDLE **insert, jab (sb with), plunge, put, stick** *He saw her stick a needle into her arm.* | **use** | **share** *the dangers of sharing needles*
- NEEDLE + VERB **go in** *The needle went in easily.*
- NEEDLE + NOUN **tip** | **exchange** *He believes that needle exchange schemes (= where drug users can change used needles for clean ones) encourage drug addiction.*
- PHRASES **the prick of a needle**

4 on a compass/instrument
- ADJ. **magnetized** | **compass**
- NEEDLE + VERB **move** *The needle moved away from the wind.* | **point** | **settle** *Wait until the needle settles and is pointing in one direction.*
- PHRASES **the needle of a compass**

5 on a pine tree
- ADJ. **conifer, pine**
- VERB + NEEDLE **drop, lose**

needy *adj.*

- VERBS **be, look** *a woman who looked needy*
- ADV. **genuinely, really, truly, very**
- PHRASES **poor and needy** *helping the children of poor and needy parents*

negative *noun*

1 denial
- VERB + NEGATIVE **answer (sth) in, reply in** *She answered the question in the negative.*

2 developed photographic film
- ADJ. **original** | **photographic** | **film, glass**

- QUANT. **strip**
- VERB + NEGATIVE **produce** | **develop** *His interest in photography started with him developing negatives that he found lying around the house.* | **keep** *We must assume that the spy kept the negatives.* | **destroy**

negative *adj.*

1 only thinking about/showing sb/sth's bad qualities
- VERBS **be, feel, seem, sound** | **become** | **remain**
- ADV. **distinctly, extremely, strongly, terribly, very** *the strongly negative implications of these survey results* ◇ *Their attitude was terribly negative.* | **completely, entirely, exclusively, purely, totally, wholly** *She spoke in entirely negative terms.* | **largely, mainly, overwhelmingly** | **fairly, rather, slightly, somewhat** | **apparently** | **essentially** *Critical thinking is essentially negative as it seeks to dissect and not to build.* | **generally**
- PREP. **about** *He's been rather negative about the idea.*

2 showing that sth has not happened/been found
- VERBS **be, prove, test** *The breathalyser test proved negative.* ◇ *He tested negative for HIV infection.*
- PREP. **for** *The urine tests were negative for protein.*

neglect *noun*

- ADJ. **general, total** | **comparative, relative** | **benign** *The eighteenth-century interior of the building has survived through benign neglect.* | **deliberate, serious, wilful** | **physical** | **child** *The maximum penalty for child neglect is ten years' imprisonment.*
- VERB + NEGLECT **suffer (from)** *The buildings suffered neglect for centuries.* | **be guilty of** *The doctor was guilty of serious neglect of duty.*
- PREP. **by ~** *cruelty by neglect* **through ~** *the suffering of children through neglect* **to the ~ of** *She had concentrated on her music to the neglect of her other studies.*
- PHRASES **centuries/years of neglect** *After years of neglect the house is at last being restored.*

neglect *verb*

- ADV. **grossly, seriously** | **completely, entirely, totally, wholly** | **largely** | **conveniently** (*ironic*), **deliberately, wilfully** *conveniently neglecting their responsibilities* | **conspicuously** *an aspect of the problem conspicuously neglected by social scientists* | **hitherto, previously**
- VERB + NEGLECT **tend to** | **cannot/could not afford to** *This sector is one of the major growth areas and we cannot afford to neglect it.*
- PREP. **in favour of** *Local communities have been neglected in favour of private sector interests.*

neglected *adj.*

1 not given enough attention
- VERBS **be, feel, lie, look, remain, seem, stand** *His tools lay neglected in the garden.* | **become, get**
- ADV. **badly, extremely, much, sadly, seriously, sorely, very, woefully** *It is a sadly neglected work.* ◇ *The building is sorely neglected.* | **largely** | **comparatively, rather, relatively, somewhat** | **hitherto, previously** | **unjustly** *She is an excellent and unjustly neglected author.*

2 not given enough food, clothing, etc.
- VERBS **be, look** *The group of street children looked ragged and neglected.*
- ADV. **badly, grossly, severely**

negligence *noun*

- ADJ. **gross** | **contributory** *The plaintiff was guilty of contributory negligence for failing to wear a crash helmet.* | **medical, professional** | **criminal**
- VERB + NEGLIGENCE **be guilty of** | **accuse sb of, allege, claim, sue for** *The solicitor was accused of profes-*

sional negligence. | **deny** | **prove** | **arise** from *death arising from negligence*
● NEGLIGENCE + NOUN **case** | **claim**
● PREP. **by ~** *His death was brought about by negligence on the doctor's part.* **through ~** *damage to company property through negligence* | **~ in** *negligence in navigation*
● PHRASES **a finding of negligence** *The court made a finding of contributory negligence.* **the result of (the) negligence** *The accident was the result of negligence on the part of the driver.*
⇨ Note at CRIME (for more verbs)

negligent *adj.*

● VERBS **be**, **seem**
● ADV. **extremely**, **grossly**, **seriously**, **very** | **wholly** | **criminally**
● PREP. **in** *The hospital was negligent in the way it looked after this young man.* **over** *The court found him to be negligent over the loss of £18 million by the local authority.*

negligible *adj.*

● VERBS **be**, **seem** | **become**
● ADV. **absolutely** | **by no means**, **far from** *Delays in the courts are far from negligible.* | **almost**

negotiate *verb*

1 try to reach an agreement
● ADV. **carefully** *a carefully negotiated series of concessions* | **successfully** | **freely** | **individually**, **separately** *Rents are individually negotiated between landlord and tenant.* | **jointly** | **directly** *negotiating directly with the rebels* | **secretly** | **constantly**, **continually** *The parameters of the job are being continually negotiated.*
● VERB + NEGOTIATE **be able to** | **be prepared to**, **be willing to** *Are the employers really willing to negotiate?* | **attempt to**, **seek to**, **try to** | **manage to** | **help (to)**
● PREP. **between** *to negotiate between the two sides* **for** *We are negotiating for the release of the prisoners.* **on** *They have refused to negotiate on this issue.* **on behalf of** *negotiating on behalf of Britain* **with** *I managed to negotiate successfully with the authorities.*

2 successfully get over/past sth
● ADV. **easily**, **safely** *He safely negotiated the slippery stepping stones.*
● VERB + NEGOTIATE **be difficult to** *The flight of steps was quite difficult to negotiate with a heavy suitcase.*

negotiation *noun*

● ADJ. **difficult**, **lengthy**, **protracted** | **direct** | **successful** | **fruitless**, **unsuccessful** | **behind-the-scenes**, **secret** | **bilateral**, **multilateral** | **constant**, **continuous** | **delicate** | **detailed** | **serious** *It's time for some serious negotiation.* | **high-level** | **pay**, **peace**, **trade**, **wage**, etc.
● VERB + NEGOTIATION **enter into**, **open** | **break off** | **resume** | **conduct** *Negotiations were conducted in secret.* | **conclude** | **be open to**, **be subject to** *The final price is open to negotiation.*
● NEGOTIATION + VERB **begin**, **start** | **continue**, **go on** *Negotiations continued all day to avert a strike.* | **break down**, **collapse**
● NEGOTIATION + NOUN **process**
● PREP. **by ~** *Rents are agreed by negotiation.* **in ~ (with)** *She is in negotiation with other heads of state on the question of oil prices.* **through ~** *The problem should be resolved through negotiation.* **under ~** *Contracts are under negotiation.* | **~ between** *The alliance is the product of months of negotiation between the two parties.* **~ of** *the negotiation of a new contract* **~ on** *international negotiations on reducing sulphur dioxide emissions* **~ over** *negotiations over the number of houses to be built* **~ with** *negotiations with the other side*

● PHRASES **a basis for negotiation**, **a matter for negotiation**, **months/years of negotiation** *They signed the treaty after several years of negotiation.* **a process of negotiation** *Compromise is reached by a process of negotiation.* **room for negotiation** *There is considerable room for negotiation on some of the details.*
⇨ Special page at MEETING

negotiator *noun*

● ADJ. **clever**, **good**, **skilled**, **tough** | **professional**, **trained** | **chief**, **principal**, **senior** *the trade union's chief negotiator* | **union**
⇨ Note at JOB

neighbour *noun*

● ADJ. **friendly**, **good** *She's been a very good neighbour to me.* | **close**, **immediate**, **near**, **next-door** *They are near neighbours of ours.* | **nearest** *She leaned towards her nearest neighbour and whispered something.* | **northern**, **southern**, etc. *England's northern neighbour now has its own parliament.*
● PHRASES **friends and neighbours**

neighbourhood *noun*

● ADJ. **friendly**, **nice** | **respectable**, **select**, **smart** | **poor**, **run-down** | **immediate**, **local**, **surrounding** *They often got together with other parents in the local neighbourhood.* | **residential** | **middle-class**, **working-class** | **Asian**, **black**, **white**, etc. | **entire**, **whole** *Before long the whole neighbourhood knew about it.*
● VERB + NEIGHBOURHOOD **move into** *A lot of new families have moved into the neighbourhood.*
● NEIGHBOURHOOD + NOUN **police**, **policing** | **school**
● PREP. **around/round the ~** *There were various parks around the neighbourhood.* **in a/the ~** *There was a large school in the neighbourhood.* **outside a/the ~** *It was a car from outside the immediate neighbourhood.*

nerve *noun*

1 in the body
● ADJ. **sensitive**, **trapped** | **facial**, **optic**, **spinal**, etc.
● VERB + NERVE **damage**, **strain**, **trap** *I've trapped a nerve in my spine.*
● NERVE + VERB **go**, **lead**, **run** *The nerve runs from the eye to the brain.* | **transmit sth** *The nerves transmit pain.* | **throb** *He lay awake, his nerves throbbing.*
● NERVE + NOUN **cell**, **end**, **ending**, **fibre**, **tissue** | **pathway** | **impulse** | **damage**, **injury** | **gas**
● PREP. **along a/the ~** *The message travels along the nerve to the brain.* | **~ in** *He's been off work with a trapped nerve in his back.* **~ to** *Cutting the nerves to the stomach does not affect hunger.*
● PHRASES **every nerve in sb's body** *Intense pain shot through every nerve in his body.* **hit a nerve**, **touch a (sensitive/raw) nerve** *(figurative)* *My remarks about divorce had unwittingly touched a raw nerve.*

2 nerves mental state
● ADJ. **good**, **steady** | **bad**, **frayed**, **ragged**, **shattered**, **taut** *At the end of a day's teaching, her nerves were absolutely shattered.*
● VERB + NERVES **stretch** *Her nerves were stretched to breaking point.*
● NERVES + VERB **be on edge** *After the bomb, my nerves were on edge.* | **jangle** *His nerves jangled every time the phone rang.* | **stand** *I'm not sure my nerves can stand another night like this.*
● PREP. **~ s for** *Skydiving is all right for people who've got the nerves for it.*
● PHRASES **a battle/war of nerves** *The union has been fighting a war of nerves with the management over pay.* **get on sb's nerves** *His endless whining really gets on my*

nerves. **nerves of steel** *You need nerves of steel to be a good poker player.* **a strain on sb's nerves** *Looking after him while he was so ill has been a great strain on her nerves.*

3 nerves nervous state
- ADJ. **exam, first-night** *I've never suffered from first-night nerves.*
- VERB + NERVES **calm, control, soothe, steady** *She took a few deep breaths to calm her nerves.* | **suffer from**
- PHRASES **an attack of nerves** *I had an attack of nerves just before I went on stage.* **a bag/bundle/mass of nerves** *By the time of the interview, I was a bundle of nerves.*

4 courage
- ADJ. **sufficient**
- VERB + NERVE **have** *I didn't have the nerve to ask.* | **lack** | **lose** *At the last minute she almost lost her nerve.* | **keep** *He kept his nerve to win a thrilling match.* | **find** *You must find the nerve to ask for more money.* | **take** *It took a lot of nerve to stand up and speak.*
- NERVE + VERB **break, crack, fail (sb)** *At the last moment her nerve failed her.*
- PHRASES **a failure/loss of nerve, a test of nerve** *Singing in front of so many people was a real test of nerve.*

nervous *adj.*
- VERBS **appear, be, feel, look, seem, sound** *Both men appeared nervous.* | **become, get, grow** | **make sb** *Sit down—you're making me nervous!*
- ADV. **desperately, extremely, highly, really, very** *He had worked himself up into a highly nervous state.* | **increasingly** | **almost** | **a bit, a little, pretty, quite, rather, slightly, somewhat** | **suddenly** | **clearly, obviously** | **understandably**
- PREP. **about** *nervous about the wedding* **at** *nervous at what might happen* **of** *I was slightly nervous of him.*

nervous breakdown *noun*
- ADJ. **complete**
- VERB + NERVOUS BREAKDOWN **have, suffer**
- PHRASES **the brink/edge/verge of a nervous breakdown** *The stress of her job had brought her to the brink of a nervous breakdown.*

nervousness *noun*
- ADJ. **considerable, extreme, great** *With great nervousness she followed him.* | **increasing** | **slight** | **initial**
- VERB + NERVOUSNESS **feel** | **betray, show (signs of)** *She managed to speak without betraying her nervousness.* | **cover, hide** *She laughed to hide her nervousness.* | **overcome** | **sense** *I could sense his nervousness.*
- PREP. **from ~** *I was babbling from nervousness.* | **out of~** *He found himself chattering away out of nervousness.* | **~about** *her nervousness about working with children* **~at** *He felt some nervousness at the prospect of meeting her.*
- PHRASES **a sign of nervousness** *Adjusting your tie is often a sign of nervousness.*

nest *noun*
- ADJ. **ant's, bird's, wasp's, etc.**
- VERB + NEST **build, make** | **sit on** *The male and female take turns to sit on the nest.* | **fly, leave** *The young ones have flown the nest.*
- NEST + NOUN **site** *The male uses song to attract a female to his nest site.* | **hole**
- PREP. **away from a/the ~** *A rat took the egg while the mother was away from the nest.* **in/inside a/the ~** *The snake will attack if disturbed inside its nest.* **on a/the~** *The female spends all her time on the nest.*

nestle *verb*
- ADV. **comfortably, safely**
- PREP. **against** *She sat back, nestling against his chest.* **among** *The town nestles comfortably among the hills.* **between, in** *a tiny village nestling in a valley*

net *noun*
- ADJ. **fine, fine-mesh** | **safety** | **fishing** | **mosquito**
- VERB + NET **mend** *The fishermen were mending their nets.* | **cast, spread (out)** | **haul in** | **slip through** (*often figurative*) *We tried to contact all former students but one or two slipped through the net.*
- PREP. **in a/the ~** *Unfortunately the animals are often caught in fishing nets.* **into a/the ~** *The ball went into the net.* **over the~** *to hit the ball over the net*

nettle *noun*
- ADJ. **stinging** | **dead** (= a variety that does not sting)
- QUANT. **clump, patch**
- VERB + NETTLE **cut (down), get rid of**
- NETTLE + VERB **grow** | **sting** | **spread** *The nettles had spread and now covered half the garden.*
- PREP. **in (the)~s** *There was an old car half buried in the nettles.* **on~s** *The butterflies lay their eggs on nettles.*

network *noun*
- ADJ. **extensive, large, vast, wide, widespread** | **complex, elaborate, intricate** | **dense** | **strong** *a strong network of friends* | **supportive** | **global, local, national, worldwide** | **communications, telephone** | **bus, motorway, rail, railway, road** | **social** | **news, radio, television** | **computer** | **distribution, support** | **integrated**
- VERB + NETWORK **build up, create, establish, form, set up** *They are establishing a network of pumps and pipelines to move the oil.* | **form** *The new rail services will form a network connecting the capital and major cities.* | **run** *They were unable to run the telephone network economically.* | **manage** *software to help you manage your network*
- PREP. **across a/the~** *Users can access data across a network.* **in a/the~** *Members are all linked together in a network.* **on a/the~** *All computer users are connected on a network.* **over a/the~** *The files are accessible over a network.* **through a/the~** *Drinking water is brought to the village through a network of underground pipes.* **via a/the~** *The newspapers are sent out via a national distribution network.* | **~of** *a network of motorways*
⇨ Note at ORGANIZATION

neurosis *noun*
- ADJ. **individual, personal** | **anxiety, obsessional**
- VERB + NEUROSIS **have**
- PREP. **~about** *the director's neurosis about actors arriving late for filming*

neutral *adj.*
1 not supporting either side
- VERBS **be** | **remain, stay**
- ADV. **strictly** *The government maintained its strictly neutral policy.* | **completely** | **basically, broadly** *The Russians took a broadly neutral position.* | **politically** *The meeting must be at a politically neutral location.*
- PREP. **about** *neutral about this issue*

2 not showing strong qualities/feelings/colour
- VERBS **be, seem** *Her expression seemed neutral.* | **remain** | **keep sth** *Dolly kept her voice carefully neutral.*
- ADV. **perfectly** | **fairly, quite, relatively** *She chose fairly neutral make-up.* | **apparently** | **carefully**

3 not affected by sth
- VERBS **be, seem**

● ADV. **culturally, ethically, ideologically, morally, politically** *Behaviour is never culturally neutral.*
● PHRASES **gender neutral** *She argued that the law should always be gender neutral* (= apply in exactly the same way to men and women).

neutrality noun

● ADJ. **political** | **armed** *a policy of armed neutrality.*
● VERB + NEUTRALITY **declare, proclaim** *Switzerland declared its neutrality.* | **maintain, preserve**
● PREP. **~ between** *the commission's neutrality between Protestants and Catholics*

neutralize verb

● ADV. **effectively** *This strategy effectively neutralized what the Conservatives had hoped would be a vote-winner.*
● PREP. **with** *Discarded acid should be neutralized with alkali before disposal.*

new adj.

1 recently built/made
● VERBS **be, look** *The car still looks quite new.*
● ADV. **brand, spanking** *a scratch on my brand new car* ◇ *very proud of their spanking new kitchen* | **fairly, quite**

2 different/not familiar
● VERBS **be** *These ideas are not entirely new.*
● ADV. **very** | **completely, entirely, quite** | **fairly, quite**
● PREP. **to** *It was all very new and strange to me.* ◇ *She's still quite new to the job and needs a lot of help.*
● PHRASES **be nothing new about/in sth** *There is nothing new in teenagers wanting to change the world.*

news noun

1 new information
● ADJ. **encouraging, excellent, good, great, marvellous, terrific, tremendous, welcome, wonderful** *The good news is that we've all been given an extra day's leave.* ◇ *Great news! We've bought the house.* | **bad, gloomy, grim, sad, terrible, tragic, unwelcome** | **dramatic, important, momentous** | **hot, late, latest, recent** *Some late news has just come in.* | **old, stale** | **exciting, interesting** | **front-page** *It was front-page news at the time.* | **domestic, home, local, national, regional** | **foreign, international** | **business, City, financial** | **sports, tennis, etc.**
● QUANT. **bit, item, piece** *We've had a bit of good news.*
● VERB + NEWS **get, have, hear, learn, receive** *Have you heard the latest news?* | **catch up on** *I want to catch up on all your news.* | **announce, break, bring (sb), give sb, tell sb** *The police had to break the news to the boy's parents.* | **spread** *She ran from office to office, spreading the exciting news.* | **leak** *News of their engagement was leaked to the press.* | **report** *I haven't really got any news to report.* | **carry** *'The Daily Nation' carried news of the event.* | **gather** *It's the reporter's job to go out and gather news.* | **await** *They are waiting for news of their relatives.* | **greet, react to, welcome** *The news was greeted with astonishment.* | **make** *It was a very minor incident and barely made the news.*
● NEWS + VERB **come, come in, come through** *News is coming in of a large fire in central London.* | **break, leak out** *The news broke while we were on holiday.* | **spread, travel** *The news spread like wildfire.*
● NEWS + NOUN **bulletin, flash, item, release, report, story** *Programmes were interrupted for a news flash.* | **coverage** *News coverage of the fighting was extremely biased.* | **conference** *The former manager gave his first news conference since being sacked.* | **agency, service** | **programme** | **editor** | **source** | **media**
● PREP. **at the ~** *She went completely to pieces at the news of his death.* **in the ~** *She's been in the news a lot lately.* **with the ~** *Joan came in with the news that a pay rise had been*

agreed. | **~ about** *I'm not interested in news about celebrities.* **~ from** *And now with news from the Games, over to our Olympic correspondent.* **~ of** *news of fresh killings* **~ on** *Is there any news on the car bomb attack?* **~ to** *It was news to me that they'd got married.*

2 the news on TV or radio
● ADJ. **radio, television, TV** | **evening, lunchtime, nine o'clock, etc.**
● VERB + NEWS **hear, listen to, see, watch** | **turn on** | **broadcast** | **read** *The news is read by Harriet Daly.*
● PREP. **in the ~** *Our school was mentioned in the news.* **on the ~** *I heard it on the ten o'clock news.*

newspaper noun

● ADJ. **daily, evening, morning, Sunday, weekly** | **today's, yesterday's** | **independent, left-wing, right-wing** | **local, national, provincial, regional** | **broadsheet, quality** | **tabloid** | **popular** | **financial** | **folded, rolled-up**
● QUANT. **copy** *Have you got a copy of yesterday's newspaper?* | **edition** *today's edition of the newspaper*
● VERB + NEWSPAPER **buy, get, take** *Do you take a daily newspaper?* | **flick through, read** | **print, produce, publish** | **edit, write for/in** | **appear in** *Her article appeared in the Saturday newspaper.* | **get into**
● NEWSPAPER + VERB **come out** *The newspaper comes out every Saturday.*
● NEWSPAPER + NOUN **article, clipping, column, coverage, cutting** | **baron, magnate, owner** | **correspondent, editor, reporter** | **kiosk, shop, stand**
● PREP. **in a/the ~** *an article in a local newspaper* **on a/the ~** *She got a job on a national newspaper.*

nice adj.

● VERBS **be, feel, look, seem, smell, sound, taste** *I felt nice and cosy.* ◇ *That bread smells nice.* ◇ *His mother sounded very nice on the phone.* | **make sth** *I tidied the room to make it nice for the others when they came home.*
● ADV. **awfully, exceptionally, extremely, incredibly, jolly, really, terribly, very** *an awfully nice man* | **perfectly, thoroughly** *I'm sure she's perfectly nice really.* | **not particularly** *It had not been a particularly nice experience.* | **pretty, quite, rather** | **enough** *Some of the boys were nice enough, but she didn't want to go out with them.*
● PREP. **about** *He was incredibly nice about it, though I am sure it caused him a lot of trouble.* **for** *It's nice for Mum to get out more.* **to** *Can't you be nice to each other for once?*
● PHRASES **nice little** *It's a nice little place you've got here.*

niche noun

● ADJ. **right, suitable** | **distinctive, particular, special** | **little** *He had found his own little niche in life.* | **market** | **ecological**
● VERB + NICHE **have** *Each animal has its ecological niche.* | **find, identify, see, spot** *He saw a niche in the market and exploited it.* | **carve out, create, establish, secure** *She's carved out quite a niche for herself in fashion design.* | **fill, occupy** | **exploit**
● NICHE + NOUN **market, marketing** | **product**
● PREP. **in/into a/the ~** *These animals are moving into the niche left vacant by the disappearance of the big predators.* | **~ for** *There's a niche for a small stylish car.* **~ in** *women who dared question their niche in society*
● PHRASES **a niche in the market**

nickname noun

● VERB + NICKNAME **give sb** | **acquire, get** *He got his nickname 'Ash' from his heavy smoking.* | **earn (sb)** | **live up to** *Leicester Tigers lived up to their nickname in a very attacking game.*

• NICKNAME + VERB **stick** *He got his nickname when he was at school and it stuck for the rest of his life.*
• PREP. **~for** *'Chalky' is a common nickname for people called White.*
• PHRASES **hence her/his nickname** *He worked in a garage—hence his nickname 'Spanner'.*

nicotine *noun*

• ADJ. **pure**
• VERB + NICOTINE **be addicted to, be dependent on | be stained with**
• NICOTINE + NOUN **addiction, craving | addict | patch, substitute | stain** *The nicotine stains on his fingers told me he was under stress.*
• PHRASES **dependence on nicotine**

night *noun*

1 when it is dark and most people sleep
• ADJ. **last, tomorrow | Friday, Saturday, etc. | early, late** *I think I'll have an early night* (= go to bed early). **| long | winter, etc. | bad, restless, sleepless | black, dark | clear, moonlit, starlit, starry | cold, stormy | wedding**
• VERB + NIGHT **have | spend** *They spent the night in Bristol.* **| stay** *Ask your Mum if you can stay the night.*
• NIGHT + VERB **fall** *When it came the night fell quickly.* **| progress, wear on** *As the night wore on it grew colder.*
• NIGHT + NOUN **air, sky | duty, shift**
• PREP. **at~** *lying awake at night* **by~** *Paris by night* **during/in the~** *I woke in the night.* **for a/the ~, on Friday, etc. ~, per ~** *The hotel costs £65 per person per night.* **through/throughout the~**
• PHRASES **all night long, at this time of night, day and night/night and day** (= all the time), **a good night's sleep, good night** *She kissed him good night.* **in the dead of night** (= in the middle of the night), **morning, noon and night** (= all the time)

2 time between late afternoon and when you go to bed
• ADJ. **last, tomorrow | Friday, Saturday, etc. | the other** *I saw her the other night* (= a few nights ago).
• NIGHT + NOUN **school**
• PREP. **at ~** *She doesn't like to walk home late at night.* **by~, on Friday, etc. ~**

3 evening when a special event happens
• ADJ. **first, opening | last** *the last night of the play's run* **| big, great, memorable | dance, election, quiz**
• PHRASES **make a night of it** *They decided to make a night of it and went on to a club.* **a night out** *Fancy a night out?*

nightclub *noun*

• ADJ. **top** *a top London nightclub* **| seedy**
• VERB + NIGHTCLUB **go to | run**
• NIGHTCLUB + NOUN **bouncer, owner, singer, staff**
• PREP. **at a/the ~** *She's performing at a nightclub in Paris.* **in a/the~** *He was murdered in a London nightclub.*

nightmare *noun*

1 bad dream
• ADJ. **awful, horrible, terrible, terrifying | continuing, recurring**
• VERB + NIGHTMARE **have, suffer | wake (up) from | give sb** *The film gave me nightmares.*
• PREP. **~about** *I have nightmares about drowning.*

2 bad/feared experience
• ADJ. **absolute, awful, horrible, real, terrible, terrifying | worst** *Losing a child is my worst nightmare.* **| personal | living** *The refugees had survived a living nightmare.* **| administrative, bureaucratic, financial, etc.**
• VERB + NIGHTMARE **endure, face, suffer, survive | become, prove, turn into** *Their dream of living in the country turned into a nightmare when they both fell seriously ill.* **| create | escape (from)**
• NIGHTMARE + VERB **be over | come true**
• NIGHTMARE + NOUN **scenario, vision** *the nightmare scenario of mass unemployment* ◊ *The writer evokes a nightmare vision of a future on a polluted planet.* **| world | journey**

nipple *noun*

• ADJ. **pert, pointed | erect, hard, rigid, swollen, taut | sensitive, sore**
• VERB + NIPPLE **suck**
• NIPPLE + VERB **harden, rise, stiffen, tighten**

nod *noun*

• ADJ. **brief, brisk, quick, imperceptible, little, slight, small | curt, perfunctory, terse** *He dismissed them with a curt nod.* **| approving, satisfied** *She inspected my work and gave a satisfied nod.* **| reassuring | passing** *(figurative) He gave a passing nod* (= a brief acknowledgement) *to the show that had launched his career.*
• VERB + NOD **give (sb)** *My teacher gave me a nod of reassurance and I began.* **| get** *He's ready to play and just waiting to get the nod from the team coach.* **| wait for**
• PREP. **at a~, with a~ | ~from** *At a nod from Lawton, he gently turned the handle.* **~in the direction of, ~of** *a nod of approval* **~to, ~towards** *'I couldn't have done this alone', he said with a nod towards his wife.*
• PHRASES **a nod of sb's/the head** *She answered with an almost imperceptible nod of the head.*

nod *verb*

• ADV. **just, merely, only, simply** *Ashamed, I could only nod.* **| fervently, furiously, vigorously, violently** *'That's exactly it,' she said, nodding vigorously.* **| gently** *She nodded gently to herself.* **| almost imperceptibly, slightly | slowly | quickly | abruptly, briefly, briskly, curtly** *He nodded curtly and walked away.* **| jerkily, stiffly | dumbly, mutely, silently, wordlessly** *She could not speak but just nodded mutely.* **| absently, abstractedly, vaguely** *He nodded absently, his mind obviously on other things.* **| meekly | politely, respectfully | amiably, cheerfully, happily | appreciatively, approvingly, eagerly, encouragingly, enthusiastically, gratefully, sympathetically, understandingly | doubtfully, reluctantly | coolly | grimly | glumly, miserably, sadly | gravely, seriously, solemnly, thoughtfully | intelligently, sagely, wisely** *She nodded sagely as she listened.* **| back**
• PREP. **at** *They nodded at us, so we nodded back.* **in** *She nodded in agreement.* **to** *She nodded to Duncan as she left.* **towards** *'Let's go,' he said, nodding towards the door.* **with** *He nodded with satisfaction.*

noise *noun*

• ADJ. **deafening, loud | awful, horrible, terrible | low, slight** *The slightest noise will wake him.* **| sudden | funny, strange | background** *There was constant background noise from the motorway.* **| constant, incessant | banging, buzzing, clattering, etc. | aircraft, engine, traffic | rude** *One of the children made a rude noise.*
• VERB + NOISE **create, generate, make** *the noise created by aircraft* ◊ *She was making a lot of noise.* **| hear, listen to** *We could hear funny little sucking noises.* **| deaden, reduce** *Wood is used to deaden the noise.*
• NOISE + VERB **come from sth** *There were strange noises coming from the sitting room.* **| become/get/grow louder, grow, increase, rise | abate, die away/down, drop, die away, fall** *The deafening noise of the machine dropped to a rumble, then stopped.*
• NOISE + NOUN **level | pollution**
• PREP. **above/over the~** *We had to shout over the noise of the traffic.* **| ~from** *the noise from the engine room*

noisy *adj.*

- VERBS **be | get, grow** *The party was getting a bit noisy.*
- ADV. **deafeningly, extremely, particularly, really, terribly, very | a bit, fairly, a little, pretty, quite, rather**

nominate *verb*

- ADV. **formally, officially**
- VERB + NOMINATE **ask sb to, invite sb to** *Ten critics were asked to nominate their Book of the Year.*
- PREP. **as** *He has now been formally nominated as presidential candidate.* **for** *She was nominated for a special award.* **to** *He has been nominated to the committee.*
- PHRASES **the power/right to nominate sb**

nomination *noun*

- ADJ. **presidential | Democratic, Republican, etc. | Oscar, etc.**
- VERB + NOMINATION **secure, win | stand for** *She is standing for the Democratic Party presidential nomination.* **| accept | withdraw | support | invite** *Nominations are invited for the post of party chairman.* **| seek** *She is seeking nomination as a candidate in the elections.*
- NOMINATION + NOUN **form, paper | process**
- PREP. **~as** *She has withdrawn her nomination as chairman.* **~for** *his nomination for the Best Actor award* **~to** *He will not accept nomination to the committee.*

nominee *noun*

- ADJ. **presidential | Democratic, Republican Party, etc. | Oscar, etc.**
- VERB + NOMINEE **appoint**
- PREP. **through a/the ~** *They were acting through nominees.* **| ~for** *the nominees for Best Director*

nonchalance *noun*

- ADJ. **cool**
- VERB + NONCHALANCE **affect, feign, pretend** *She shrugged, feigning nonchalance.*
- PREP. **with ~** *declining the offer with cool nonchalance*
- PHRASES **an air of nonchalance** *'Oh, by the way ... '* *she started, with a false air of nonchalance.*

non-existent *adj.*

- VERBS **be | become** *Services for customers on public transport are becoming non-existent.*
- ADV. **completely, totally** *The hotel turned out to be completely non-existent.* **| almost, practically, virtually** *Crime is almost non-existent in these communities.*

nonsense *noun*

- ADJ. **absolute, arrant, complete, pure, total, utter** *Most of his theories are arrant nonsense.* **| superstitious** *You don't believe that superstitious nonsense, do you?*
- VERB + NONSENSE **talk** *Don't talk nonsense!* **| put up with, stand** *I'm not going to stand any more of this nonsense.* **| stop** *Just stop this nonsense of refusing to talk to anybody.* **| believe**
- PREP. **~about** *What's all this nonsense about you giving up your job?*
- PHRASES **a load/lot of nonsense** *People are talking a lot of nonsense about him being the new Michael Jordan.* **make (a) nonsense of sth** *This decision makes absolute nonsense of all our hard work.*

noon *noun*

- ADJ. **12** *The football action starts at 12 noon.* **| high** *the glaring light of high noon*

- PREP. **around~, at~, by~, till/until~**
- PHRASES **morning, noon and night** (= all the time)

noose *noun*

- ADJ. **hangman's**
- VERB + NOOSE **fasten, tie | pull, tighten | make**
- NOOSE + VERB **tighten**
- PREP. **in/into a/the** *He put his head into the noose.* **| ~around/round** *They tied a noose round her neck.*

norm *noun*

- ADJ. **accepted, established | ethical, moral | cultural, social | statistical | community, family, group**
- VERB + NORM **conform to** *Their behaviour conforms to the group norm.* **| break, challenge | deviate from, differ from**
- PREP. **above the~, below the~, over the~** *They want to discourage pay settlements over the norm.* **| ~for** *On-screen editing has become the norm for all student work.* **~of** *accepted norms of behaviour*
- PHRASES **a deviation/departure from the norm, an exception to the norm, the norm rather than the exception** *In the inner-city areas, poverty is the norm rather than the exception.*

normal *noun*

- VERB + NORMAL **be/go back to, return to** *After a week of festivities, life returned to normal.*
- PREP. **above~** *The rainfall has been above normal for the time of year.* **below~** *Sales to December are well below normal.* **near~** *His pulse rate had slowed to somewhere near normal.*

normal *adj.*

- VERBS **be, look, seem | become | consider sth, regard sth as, view sth as** *It is now regarded as normal for women to work outside the home.*
- ADV. **very | completely, perfectly, quite** *It started out as a perfectly normal day.* **| fairly, near, pretty** *I'd say it was pretty normal to be upset if your house burned down.*
- PREP. **for** *The temperature is near normal for spring.*
- PHRASES **as normal** *First work out the answers as normal.* **in the normal way** *Go for your check-ups in the normal way until you are six months pregnant.* **in/under normal circumstances** *Under normal circumstances Martin would probably have gone to university.* **sb's normal self** *Mandy doesn't seem her normal self today.*

normality *noun*

- VERB + NORMALITY **restore, return to**
- PHRASES **a return to normality** *A complete return to normality may take weeks.* **some semblance of normality** *By now any semblance of normality had disappeared.*

north *noun*

- ADJ. **magnetic, true | frozen** *the white expanses of the frozen north*
- ⇨ Note at DIRECTION (for more collocates)

nose *noun*

1 part of the face

- ADJ. **big, bulbous, enormous, huge, large, long, prominent, strong | little, small, stubby, tiny | straight | aquiline, curved, Roman | beaky, crooked, hooked | snub, tip-tilted, turned-up, upturned | pointed, sharp** *The sharp nose and thin lips gave his face a very harsh look.* **| narrow, thin** *She had dark eyes and a long narrow nose.* **| flat, flattened | aristocratic, elegant | pink, red, shiny** *He stuck his bulbous red nose back into his pint of beer.* ◇ *She dressed up as a clown with a white face and red* nose. | **blocked, congested, dripping, runny, snotty** *a child with a runny nose* | **bleeding, bloodied, bloody, broken, swollen | wet** *The dog pushed its wet nose into my palm.* | **sensitive** *Cats have very sensitive noses and rely heavily on scent markings.* | **pierced | false** *I had to wear a black moustache and false nose for the role.*

● VERB + NOSE   **breathe through | blow, wipe | pick, rub, scratch | tap** *He tapped his nose in a knowing gesture.* | **wrinkle** *She wrinkled her nose as if she had just smelt a bad smell.* | **break, split | turn up** (*figurative*) *The children turn up their noses at almost everything I cook.* | **look down** (*figurative*) *People who live in that area tend to look down their noses at their poorer neighbours.*

● NOSE + VERB   **wrinkle** *His nose wrinkled with distaste.* | **twitch | point** *She walked with her shoulders back and her nose pointing skyward.* | **run** *She was weeping quite loudly and her nose was running.* | **bleed**

● NOSE + NOUN   **job** *She wasn't happy with her appearance so she had a nose job.* | **bleed** (also **nosebleed**)

● PREP.   **through the ~** *Breathe in through your nose and out through your mouth.* **up your ~** *The boy sat there with his finger up his nose.*

● PHRASES   **the bridge of the nose** *He pushed his glasses up the bridge of his nose.* (**put/stick, etc.) your nose in the air** (*often figurative*) *She walked in with her nose in the air, ignoring everyone.* **press your nose against sth** *Charlie pressed his nose against the window.*

2 front part of a vehicle
● ADJ.   **blunt**
● VERB + NOSE   **push down, put down** *He pushed the nose down for the final approach.*
● NOSE + VERB   **dip, drop** *The plane's nose dipped as it started descending towards the runway.*
● NOSE + NOUN   **cone, section | dive** (also **nosedive**)
● PHRASES   **nose to tail** *The traffic was nose to tail for miles.*

nostalgia *noun*

● ADJ.   **great | pure** *an evening of pure nostalgia*
● QUANT.   **wave** *A wave of nostalgia came over him.*
● VERB + NOSTALGIA   **feel** *He thought back to his time as a student and felt no nostalgia for any of it.* | **evoke | indulge in, wallow in**
● NOSTALGIA + NOUN   **buff** *Nostalgia buffs gathered for the auction of wartime memorabilia.* | **trip** *The college reunion was a great nostalgia trip.*
● PREP.   **with ~** *I remember it with great nostalgia.* | **~ for** *She felt great nostalgia for the old way of life.*
● PHRASES   **a feeling/sense of nostalgia**

nostril *noun*

● VERB + NOSTRIL   **clog, fill** *The stench of the cellar filled my nostrils.*
● NOSTRIL + VERB   **dilate, flare**
● NOSTRIL + NOUN   **hair**
● PREP.   **in your ~s** *The smell of decay lingered in her nostrils.* **through your ~s** *She drew on the cigarette and blew smoke through her nostrils.*

notable *adj.*

● VERBS   **be**
● ADV.   **especially, particularly**
● PREP.   **for** *The drawing room is particularly notable for its splendid oak panelling.*

note *noun*

1 short letter
● ADJ.   **brief, little, quick, short** *Just a quick note to wish you luck.* | **handwritten | covering, credit, delivery, love, promissory, ransom, sick, suicide, thank-you**
● VERB + NOTE   **scribble (sb), write (sb) | send (sb) |**

leave (sb) *She left me a note to say my supper was in the fridge.*
● PHRASES   **a note of thanks**

2 (often **notes**) words that you write down quickly
● ADJ.   **brief | copious, detailed | scrappy | lecture | case, clinical, medical**
● VERB + NOTE   **jot down, keep, make, take** *She kept detailed notes of her travels.* | **go through, look through, read through, sift through**
● PREP.   **~ of** *I've made a note of the book's title.* **~ on** *The catalogue has full notes on each artist.*
● PHRASES   **make a mental note (of sth/to do sth)** *She made a mental note to ring them in the morning.*

3 (usually **notes**) extra piece of information
● ADJ.   **detailed | explanatory | introductory | marginal | biographical | briefing, programme, usage**

4 piece of paper money
● ADJ.   **crumpled | five-pound, ten-euro, etc.**
● QUANT.   **bundle, roll, wad** *a thick wad of notes*

5 single musical sound
● ADJ.   **high, top** *She's a bit wobbly on the top notes.* | **low | right | wrong | musical | dissonant | chromatic, diatonic**
● VERB + NOTE   **play, sing | hit, strike | hold**

6 quality/feeling
● ADJ.   **brighter, cheerful, happier, lighter, optimistic, positive** *On a brighter note …* | **discordant, jarring, sad, sour | faint | serious | right** *His opening remarks struck the right note.* | **odd | false | cautionary, warning** *He sounded a cautionary note.* | **personal**
● VERB + NOTE   **hit, sound, strike | inject, introduce** *His remarks injected a note of levity into the proceedings.* | **detect** *I detected a faint note of weariness in his voice.* | **end on** *The conference ended on an optimistic note.*
● NOTE + VERB   **creep into/enter sb's voice**
● PREP.   **~ of** *A note of suspicion entered his voice.*
● PHRASES   **a note in sb's voice** *There was a sad note in her voice.* **on a brighter/happier, etc. note**

7 notice/attention
● ADJ.   **careful**
● VERB + NOTE   **take** *He took careful note of the suspicious-looking man in the corner of the bar.*
● PHRASES   **worthy of note** *The frescoes are worthy of note.*

note *verb*

● ADV.   **carefully | in passing** *He noted in passing that the government's record on unemployment was not very good.* | **duly** *Her lapse was duly noted by the stage manager and reported to the director.* | **above, already, earlier, previously** *These policies, as noted above, are not always successful.* | **approvingly | ruefully**
● VERB + NOTE   **should** *Visitors should note that the tower is not open to the public.* | **be important to | be interesting to | be pleased to** *I was pleased to note that my name had been spelt correctly for once.*
● PHRASES   **be worth noting** *There are a few points here that are worth noting.* **it must/should be noted that … , a point to note** *There are two other points to note from this graph.*

notebook *noun*

● ADJ.   **bound, leather-bound, spiral-bound | loose-leaf | pocket | shorthand | reporter's**
● VERB + NOTEBOOK   **enter sth in, jot sth down in, record sth in, scribble (sth) in, write sth down in, write (sth) in | draw (out), get out, pull out, take out** *She drew a notebook from her bag.* | **tear a page/sheet from, tear out a page/sheet of | consult | fill | carry | keep** *She kept a notebook during the trip.*
● NOTEBOOK + NOUN   **computer**

- PREP. **in a/your~**
- PHRASES **an entry in a notebook**

noted adj.

- VERBS **be** | **become**
- ADV. **especially, particularly**
- PREP. **for** *The lake is also noted for its bird population.*

noteworthy adj.

- VERBS **be, seem** | **become** | **make sth** *the thing that makes this era so noteworthy* | **consider sth** *His reign has never been considered particularly noteworthy.*
- ADV. **especially, particularly**
- PREP. **for** *The bridge is noteworthy for its sheer size.*

notice noun

1 attention
- VERB + NOTICE **take** *Take no notice of what you read in the papers.* | **come to** *Normally such matters would not come to my notice.* | **bring to** | **attract** *The change was too subtle to attract much notice.*

2 written statement
- ADJ. **warning**
- VERB + NOTICE **issue, place, post, put up** *The company has issued warning notices saying that all water should be boiled.* | **take down** | **read, see**
- NOTICE + VERB **appear, go up** *The notice about his resignation went up this morning.* | **say sth, tell sb sth**
- PREP. **~about** *There are notices about where to park.*

3 information given in advance
- ADJ. **written** | **advance, prior** | **short** | **reasonable**
- VERB + NOTICE **give, hand in your** *She's given notice that she intends to leave.* | **have** | **receive** | **need, require** *The bank requires three days' notice.*
- PREP. **without~** *They cut off the electricity without notice.* | **~of** *A landlord must give reasonable notice of his intention to inspect the property.*
- PHRASES **at a moment's notice** *The team is ready to go anywhere in the world at a moment's notice.* **at short notice** *It's the best we can do at such short notice.* **notice to quit** *His landlord gave him two months' notice to quit.* **on a month's/week's, etc. notice** *She's on a week's notice, which doesn't give her long to find another job.*

notice verb

- ADV. **not even** *My mum probably won't even notice I'm gone.* | **not really** *Nobody really noticed the changes.* | **barely, hardly, scarcely** | **(only) just** *I must go! I've only just noticed how late it is.* | **suddenly** | **at once, immediately** *He noticed at once that something was wrong.* | **quickly, soon** | **eventually, finally**
- VERB + NOTICE **fail to** | **not appear to, not seem to** *He didn't seem to notice her.*
- PHRASES **can't/couldn't help noticing sth** *You couldn't help noticing how his eyes kept following her.*

noticeable adj.

- VERBS **be** | **become**
- ADV. **especially, extremely, particularly, very** | **barely, hardly, scarcely** | **quite** | **immediately** *The smell was immediately noticeable when you walked in the front door.*
- PREP. **in** *These changes are more noticeable in women than in men.* **to** *This may not be noticeable to people from outside New York.*

notification noun

- ADJ. **formal, official, written** | **advance, prior**
- VERB + NOTIFICATION **have, receive** | **give (sb)**
- PREP. **without ~** *The police are entitled to inspect the premises without notification.* | **~of** *They failed to give notification of their intention to demolish the building.*

notify verb

- ADV. **forthwith, immediately** | **in advance** | **by post, in writing** | **formally**
- VERB + NOTIFY **be obliged to, be required to, must, should** *If you see anything suspicious you should notify the police immediately.* | **fail to**
- PREP. **of** *All applicants will be notified of the result by post.* **to** *Changes must be notified to the chairman.*

notion noun

- ADJ. **absurd, peculiar, ridiculous** | **hazy, vague** | **faintest, foggiest** *I haven't the faintest notion how to get there.* | **romantic** | **accepted, conventional, traditional** | **preconceived** | **general** *There seems to be a general notion that nothing can be done about the problem.* | **simple, simplistic**
- VERB + NOTION **have** *He's got some vague notion that people will be queuing up to finance the project.* | **reject** | **accept** | **support** | **dispel** *We must dispel this notion that you can rely on the state for everything.*
- PREP. **~of** *They have come to reject the traditional notion of womanhood.*

notoriety noun

- ADJ. **sudden** | **certain** | **international, public**
- VERB + NOTORIETY **have** | **achieve, gain** *He achieved sudden notoriety when the details of his private life were revealed.* | **bring**
- PREP. **~for** *This make of car has a certain notoriety for rust problems.*

noun noun

- ADJ. **plural, singular** *'Sheep' is both a singular and plural noun.* | **countable** | **mass, uncountable** | **feminine, masculine, neuter** *Most feminine nouns in Polish end in the letter 'a'.* | **common, proper** *Proper nouns begin with a capital letter.* | **abstract, concrete** *'Happiness' is an abstract noun.* ◇ *'Car' is a concrete noun.* | **collective** *'Flock' is a collective noun.*
- VERB + NOUN **decline, inflect** *English nouns are not usually inflected.* | **modify, qualify** *a prepositional phrase qualifying a noun* | **follow** *The noun is followed by an intransitive verb.* | **precede** *an adjective preceding the noun*
- NOUN + VERB **end in sth** *Most English plural nouns end in an 's'.* | **follow sth** | **precede sth**
- NOUN + NOUN **class, phrase**

nourish verb

- PHRASES **properly/well nourished** *Patients recover quickly if they are well nourished.*

nourishment noun

- ADJ. **adequate, proper, sufficient** *lack of adequate nourishment* | **vital** | **emotional, intellectual**
- VERB + NOURISHMENT **draw, get, obtain, take** | **deprive sb/sth of, provide (sb with)**
- PREP. **~from** *Every animal in the food chain draws nourishment from other animals or plants.*

novel noun

- ADJ. **hardback, paperback** | **first** *a prize for the best first novel of the year* | **latest, new** | **literary** | **best-selling, popular** | **acclaimed** *his critically acclaimed novel* | **famous** | **classic** | **contemporary, modern** | **nineteenth-century, Victorian** | **adult, children's** | **autobiographical** | **epistolary** *Samuel Richardson's novels are all epistolary in form.* | **adventure, comic,**

crime, detective, historical, satirical, spy, realist, romantic
- QUANT. **copy** *I took a copy of a Graham Greene novel on the train with me.*
- VERB + NOVEL **produce,   write | publish | read | accept (for publication), reject (for publication)** *Her first novel was finally accepted for publication.* **| translate | adapt** *adapting the novel for television* **| review**
- NOVEL + VERB **be based on sth** *The novel was based on a true life story.* **| be set, take place** *The novel was set in a small village in France.*
- PREP. **~about** *a novel about growing up*

novel *adj.*

- VERBS **be, sound** *The scheme sounded rather novel.*
- ADV. **extremely, very | completely, entirely, quite, totally, wholly | rather, relatively | essentially**

novelist *noun*

- ADJ. **great, leading** *one of the country's leading contemporary novelists* **| famous | best-selling, popular** *his ambition to become a best-selling novelist* **| neglected | prolific | contemporary | nineteenth-century, Victorian | crime, historical, romantic, satirical**
- NOVELIST + VERB **write sth** *A prolific novelist, she wrote more than forty books.*

novelty *noun*

- ADJ. **great** *This tropical fruit is still a great novelty in Europe.* **| sheer** *The sheer novelty of the band's performance won them many fans.*
- NOVELTY + VERB **wear off** *The novelty of her new job soon wore off.*
- NOVELTY + NOUN **value** *A trip down a mine has great novelty value for most people.*
- PHRASES **be something of a novelty** *At that time the motor car was still something of a novelty.*

November *noun*

⇨ Note at MONTH

novice *noun*

- ADJ. **absolute, complete | young**
- NOVICE + NOUN **user** *The on-screen manual shows the novice user the basics of the program.* **| pilot, sailor, teacher, etc.**
- PREP. **~at** *I'm still a novice at the sport.* **~in** *a novice in politics*

nuance *noun*

- ADJ. **delicate, fine, slight, subtle** *A baby is sensitive to the slightest nuances in its mother's voice.* ◇ *the painting's subtle nuances of colour and texture* **| social** *It took a while to get used to the social nuances of the office.*
- VERB + NUANCE **understand** *Spectators may not understand all the nuances of the game.*

nude *adj.*

- VERBS **appear, be, lie, sit, stand** *He refused to appear nude in the film.* ◇ *She was lying nude on a beach towel.*
- ADV. **completely | almost | semi-**

nudge *noun*

- ADJ. **gentle, little | affectionate**
- VERB + NUDGE **give sb** *She gave me a gentle nudge in the ribs to tell me to shut up.* **| feel**

nudge *verb*

- ADV. **gently, playfully**

- PHRASES **nudge sb in the ribs** *She nudged him playfully in the ribs.*

nuisance *noun*

- ADJ. **great | awful, bloody** (*taboo*), **confounded, damned** *It's an awful nuisance having builders in the house all day.* **| private, public, statutory** (*all law*) *He was charged with committing a public nuisance.*
- PREP. **~to** *I don't want to be a nuisance to you.*
- PHRASES **make a nuisance of yourself**

null *adj.* null and void

- VERBS **be | become | render sth** *Their actions rendered the contract null and void.* **| declare sth** *They declared the agreement null and void.*

numb *adj.*

1 unable to feel pain
- VERBS **be, feel** *Robin's hand felt numb with cold.* **| become, go, turn** *His fingers were beginning to turn numb.*
- ADV. **completely | almost | slightly**
- PREP. **from** *My legs were numb from kneeling.*
- PHRASES **numb with (the) cold** *Their fingers were going numb with cold.*

2 unable to feel/think/react
- VERBS **be, feel, sound** *Her voice sounded numb.* **| leave sb** *The news left us numb and confused.*
- ADV. **totally** *Laura felt totally numb.*
- PREP. **with** *He felt numb with weariness and grief.*

number *noun*

1 symbol/word
- ADJ. **cardinal, decimal, ordinal | even, odd** *Houses on this side of the road have even numbers.* **| high, low | prime | random | lucky, unlucky** *Many people think 13 is an unlucky number.* **| winning** *the winning numbers in tonight's lottery*
- VERB + NUMBER **add, divide, multiply, subtract, take away** *Add all the numbers together, divide by ten, and take away the number you first thought of.*
- PHRASES **in round numbers** *There were about 150 there, in round numbers.* **number crunching** (= doing calculations) *There's more to accountancy than just number crunching.*

2 quantity/amount
- ADJ. **considerable, enormous, great, huge, inordinate, large, substantial, vast | record** *a record number of enquiries* **| disproportionate, surprising | fair, reasonable, significant** *We've had a fair number of complaints about the new phone system.* **| finite, infinite** *There are an infinite number of solutions to the problem.* **| equal** *The candidates received an equal number of votes.* **| maximum, minimum | average, mean, median | adequate, sufficient | limited, small | growing, increasing, rising | exact, precise** *Many people have died in the epidemic—the precise number is not known.* **| indefinite, unspecified | approximate | total**
- VERB + NUMBER **grow in, increase in** *Factories had increased in number between the wars.* **| decrease in, reduce in**
- NUMBER + VERB **double, grow, increase | decline, diminish, drop, dwindle, fall (off/down)** *Shark numbers have dwindled as a result of hunting.*
- PREP. **in~** *The paintings, twelve in number, are over 200 years old.*
- PHRASES **a decline/drop in numbers** *The decline in numbers of young people means that fewer teachers will be needed.* **a growth/an increase in numbers, few/limited/small in number** *Wild dogs are now few in number.*

3 for identifying sb/sth

• ADJ. **account, identity, registration, serial, etc. | flat, house**
• PREP. **at~** *We live at number 21.*

4 telephone number
• ADJ. **fax, phone, telephone | home, office, work | wrong** *I keep getting the wrong number.*
• VERB + NUMBER **call, dial, phone, ring | get**

number *verb*

• ADV. **clearly | consecutively, sequentially**
• PREP. **according to, by** *Each pigeon hole is clearly numbered by floor and by room.* **from, to** *Number the car's features from 1 to 10 according to importance.*

numerous *adj.*

• VERBS **be | become**
• ADV. **especially, particularly, very | increasingly | reasonably, relatively | enough, sufficiently** *By the mid-twelfth century pilgrims were numerous enough to merit a guidebook.*
• PHRASES **too numerous to list/mention** *The related publications are far too numerous to list individually.*

nurse *noun*

• ADJ. **qualified, registered, trained | staff** *the children's ward staff nurse* **| ward | junior, senior | ancillary, auxiliary | student, trainee | male | day, night | community, district | hospital, practice, school** *This is a job for the school nurse.* **| private | specialist | maternity, psychiatric, triage, veterinary**
• NURSE + NOUN **manager, practitioner, specialist, tutor | education**
⇨ Note at JOB

nursery *noun*

• ADJ. **day, residential, workplace**
• NURSERY + NOUN **school | class | education | teacher | facilities, provision | assistant | nurse**
• PREP. **at a/the~** *The children are at nursery three days a week.* **in a/the~** *She works as an assistant in a nursery.*

nursing *noun*

• ADJ. **general | clinical | geriatric, mental health, psychiatric, surgical | community, district | home, hospital | private**
• NURSING + NOUN **care, services, skills | home | staff | student | practice**
⇨ Note at SUBJECT (for verbs and more nouns)

nut *noun*

1 food
• ADJ. **cashew, pistachio, etc. | chopped, salted**
• VERB + NUT **crack, shell**
• NUT + NOUN **oil**

2 for screwing onto a bolt
• VERB + NUT **put on, screw on, tighten | loosen, remove, unscrew**

nutrition *noun*

• ADJ. **adequate, good, proper | inadequate, poor** *Many children at the school were found to be suffering from inadequate nutrition.*
• PHRASES **a source of nutrition**

nutritious *adj.*

• VERBS **be | make sth** *Adapt your usual eating regime to make it more nutritious.*
• ADV. **extremely, highly, very | fairly**

Oo

oar *noun*

- VERB + OAR **take** *We each took an oar.* | **pull on** *We pulled hard on the oars.* | **ship** *We shipped the oars to get through the narrow opening.*

oath *noun*

1 formal promise
- ADJ. **sacred, solemn** | **Hippocratic** *a doctor's Hippocratic oath*
- VERB + OATH **swear, take** *He took an oath of allegiance to his adopted country.* | **break, violate**
- PREP. **~of** *an oath of allegiance/loyalty*

2 in a court of law
- VERB + OATH **administer** *Only a judge is allowed to administer the oath.*
- PREP. **on~** *He swore on oath that he had never seen me before.* **under~** *Witnesses must testify under oath.*

3 swear word
- ADJ. **obscene**
- QUANT. **stream, string** *He muttered a stream of oaths.*
- VERB + OATH **mutter, utter**

oats *noun*

- ADJ. **rolled** | **porridge**
- QUANT. **field**
- VERB + OATS **grow** | **sow** | **cut, harvest**
- OATS + VERB **grow**

obedience *noun*

- ADJ. **absolute, complete, total** *He demands absolute obedience from his men.* | **blind, passive, unquestioning**
- VERB + OBEDIENCE **demand, exact, expect** | **owe** *All clergy owed obedience to their superior.* | **pledge, swear**
- PREP. **in~to** *She acted in passive obedience to her boss's directions.* | **~ to** *The slaves had to swear obedience to their masters.*

obey *verb*

- ADV. **immediately, instantly** *She was used to having her orders instantly obeyed.* | **automatically, blindly, meekly, unquestioningly** | **eagerly** | **reluctantly**
- VERB + OBEY **have to, must** | **refuse to** *He refuses to obey the school rules.* | **fail to** | **be willing to** | **promise to**
- PHRASES **be only obeying orders** *At the trial the soldiers made the excuse that they were only obeying orders.* **a duty/an obligation to obey** *People have a moral duty to obey the law.* **sth has to be/must be obeyed** *Rules are rules and they must be obeyed.*

obituary *noun*

- VERB + OBITUARY **write** | **print, publish** | **read**
- OBITUARY + NOUN **column, page**

object *noun*

1 solid thing
- ADJ. **solid** | **inanimate** | **everyday, household** *Her paintings are of ordinary everyday objects.*

2 purpose
- ADJ. **main, primary, principal** | **sole** *My sole object is to get to the bottom of this mystery.*

- OBJECT + NOUN **lesson** *The plans are an object lesson in how to ruin a city centre.*
- PHRASES **the object of the exercise** *The object of the exercise is to score as many points as possible.*

object *verb*

- ADV. **strenuously, strongly, vehemently**
- VERB + OBJECT **can/could hardly** *It was your own idea in the first place, so you can hardly object now.* | **be entitled to, have a/the right to**
- PREP. **to** *a petition objecting to the scheme*
- PHRASES **object on the grounds that …** *I objected on the grounds that it was unkind to the animals.*

objection *noun*

- ADJ. **serious, strenuous, strong** | **valid** | **main, major, principal** | **fundamental** | **common**
- VERB + OBJECTION **lodge, make, raise, state** | **have** *I'd like to open a window, unless anyone has any objections.* | **meet, overcome** | **withdraw**
- PREP. **over the~s of** *She was appointed over the objections of certain members of the board.* | **~against** *a common objection against nuclear power* **~to** *The committee has raised serious objections to the plans.*

objective *noun*

- ADJ. **key, main, major, primary, prime, principal** | **broad, overall, overriding, ultimate** | **limited, narrow** | **long-term, short-term** | **clear, specific** | **stated** *The legislation has failed to achieve its stated objectives.* | **common** *The two groups are pursuing a common objective.* | **economic, educational, environmental, military, political, strategic** | **business, policy**
- VERB + OBJECTIVE **accomplish, achieve, attain, fulfil, meet, reach, satisfy, succeed in** *The department needs more money to fulfil its objectives.* | **fail in** | **agree, define, establish, formulate, identify, set, specify** *We need to establish a clear objective.* | **declare, state** | **promote, pursue**
- PREP. **in an/the~** *The party is radical in its objectives.* | **~of** *We succeeded in our prime objective of cutting costs.*

objective *adj.*

- VERBS **be, seem** | **remain**
- ADV. **truly, very** | **completely, purely, totally, wholly** *It is impossible to be completely objective.* | **fairly, quite, reasonably** | **apparently** | **supposedly**

obligation *noun*

- ADJ. **contractual, legal, statutory** | **moral, social** | **financial** | **family** *I can't travel next month because of family obligations.* | **professional** | **mutual**
- VERB + OBLIGATION **discharge, fulfil, meet** *The builders failed to meet their contractual obligations.* | **comply with, honour** | **have** *We have a moral obligation to help.* | **feel** | **owe** | **assume, incur, take on** | **impose**
- OBLIGATION + VERB **arise from sth** *obligations arising from your contract of employment*
- PREP. **under an~** *I am under no obligation to tell you my name.* **without~** *Our mortgage advice is given free and without obligation.* | **~to** *A lawyer owes an obligation of confidence to the client.*

obligatory adj.

- VERBS **be | become | remain | make sth** *The college authorities have now made these classes obligatory.*
- ADV. **almost, practically | legally**
- PREP. **for** *It is obligatory for vets to be registered.*

oblige verb

- ADV. **duly** *The fans were looking for another goal and Owen duly obliged* (= scored). **| kindly**
- VERB + OBLIGE **be delighted to, be glad to, be (only too) happy to, be pleased to, be willing to** *The staff are always happy to oblige.* **| hasten to**
- PREP. **by** *Will you oblige by filling in this form?* **with** *Would you be willing to oblige us with some information?*

obliged adj.

1 forced to do sth
- VERBS **be, feel**
- ADV. **virtually** *Libel plaintiffs are virtually obliged to go into the witness box.* **| by law, contractually, legally** *Parents are obliged by law to send their children to school.* **| morally** *I felt morally obliged to do the best I could for her.*

2 grateful
- VERBS **be, feel**
- ADV. **much**
- PREP. **for, to** *I'm much obliged to you for helping us.*

obliterate verb

- ADV. **completely, entirely, totally** *The village was totally obliterated by the bomb.* **| almost, virtually**

oblivion noun

- ADJ. **political**
- VERB + OBLIVION **fade into, fall into, pass into, sink into, slide into | be rescued from, be saved from** *a minor masterpiece saved from oblivion* **| consign to** *Most of his work has now been consigned to oblivion.*
- PREP. **in~** *He died in oblivion in a remote village.*

oblivious adj.

- VERBS **appear, be, seem** *Chiko appeared oblivious to the uproar.* **| become | remain | make sb** *His own arrogance made him oblivious to the criticisms of others.*
- ADV. **completely, quite, totally | almost | apparently, seemingly | clearly**
- PREP. **of** *oblivious of the stares of the whole town* **to** *She seemed almost oblivious to the crowds of reporters.*

oboe noun

⇨ Special page at MUSIC

obscene adj.

- VERBS **be, look | declare sth, deem sth, judge sth** *The book was declared obscene.*
- ADV. **really | utterly | almost | allegedly**

obscenity noun

- QUANT. **stream, string**
- VERB + OBSCENITY **mutter, scream, shout** *He shouted a stream of obscenities.*

obscure verb

- ADV. **completely, totally | almost | largely | half, partially, partly, slightly, somewhat | deliberately** *All trace of his working-class background was deliberately obscured.* **| easily** *Solo passages in this register are very easily obscured by other instruments.*
- VERB + OBSCURE **serve to, tend to** *The emphasis on social integration often served to obscure the real differences within the community.* **| allow sth to**
- PREP. **behind/beneath** *The moon was obscured behind a wall of cloud.*
- PHRASES **obscure the fact that ...** *These figures obscure the fact that a lot of older people live in great poverty.* **obscure sth from view** *The house was obscured from view by a high hedge.*

obscure adj.

- VERBS **be, seem | become** *The origins of the tradition have become obscure.* **| remain** *The motives behind this decision remain somewhat obscure.*
- ADV. **extremely, very | completely, totally | largely | fairly, rather, relatively, somewhat**

obscurity noun

- ADJ. **total | comparative, relative | political, professional | impenetrable** *poems of impenetrable obscurity*
- VERB + OBSCURITY **fade into, sink into, slip into | be plucked from, emerge from** *After many years, his scientific work emerged from obscurity.* **| be consigned to, be relegated to**
- PREP. **in~** *He spent his early life in relative obscurity.*

observant adj.

- VERBS **be, seem | become**
- ADV. **acutely, highly, very** *She was intelligent and highly observant.* **| fairly, quite**

observation noun

1 examination
- ADJ. **careful, close, detailed | direct | systematic | casual | empirical, scientific | clinical | astronomical**
- PREP. **for~** *She was admitted to hospital for observation.* **under~** *The police have had him under observation for several weeks.* **| ~of** *The survey was based on direct observation of over 500 schools.*
- PHRASES **powers of observation** *an artist with acute powers of observation*

2 remark
- ADJ. **general | astute, keen, shrewd | interesting**
- VERB + OBSERVATION **make**
- PREP. **~about** *He smiled, and made some observation about the weather.* **~on** *her witty observations on life*

observe verb

1 notice/watch
- ADV. **carefully, closely | precisely | directly** *It is not possible to observe this phenomenon directly, but its effects can be seen in the rise in global temperatures.* **| actually** *It is the parents who actually observe these behavioural problems in their children.* **| just, simply** *You can learn a lot by simply observing.* **| generally, normally | quietly** *She stood there, quietly observing the domestic scene.* **| secretly | experimentally** *This phenomenon has been observed experimentally.*
- VERB + OBSERVE **be able to | be possible | be difficult to | be interesting to** *It is interesting to observe the reaction of the children to these changes.*
- PREP. **from** *unaware that she was being observed from the window*
- PHRASES **be commonly/frequently/widely observed** *This behaviour is commonly observed among several species of finch.* **be easily/readily observed, an opportunity to observe sb/sth**

2 make a remark
- ADV. **correctly, justly, rightly, shrewdly** *She correctly observed that there was very little difference between the two parties on domestic policies.* **| drily, sardonically, wryly | tartly | coldly, coolly** *'You took your time,' he*

observed coolly. | **conversationally** | **mildly, quietly | sadly**
• PREP. **to** '*It's easy for him to say that,*' *she observed tartly to Michael, 'but can he prove it?'*

3 obey rules
• ADV. **correctly, faithfully, scrupulously, strictly** *This procedure must be correctly observed.*
• VERB + OBSERVE **fail to**
• PHRASES **failure to observe sth** *Failure to observe club rules may result in expulsion.*

observer *noun*

• ADJ. **casual** *To the casual observer, it would have looked like any other domestic argument.* | **informed | accurate, acute, astute, careful, experienced, keen, seasoned, shrewd | sceptical | sympathetic | detached, impartial, neutral | external, independent, outside** *Independent observers will monitor the elections.* | **foreign, international | American, Western, etc. | industry, military** *Some military observers fear the US could get entangled in another war.* | **human**
• VERB + OBSERVER **send** *sending observers to check the conduct of the elections* | **attend sth as | impress, puzzle, strike, surprise** *The suddenness of this move surprised many observers.*
• OBSERVER + VERB **attend sth** *The talks were attended by observers from eight Arab countries and Israel.* | **monitor sth**
• OBSERVER + NOUN **status** *The country was granted observer status at the summit.*
• PREP. **as an~** *I attended the conference as an observer.*

obsession *noun*

• ADJ. **dangerous, unhealthy | current**
• VERB + OBSESSION **become** *Don't let this interest of yours become an obsession.*
• PREP. **~with** *I don't understand television's current obsession with cookery programmes.*
• PHRASES **in the grip of an obsession** *He was in the grip of an obsession and would not listen to reason.*

obsolete *adj.*

• VERBS **be | become | make sth, render sth** *Their work is now rendered obsolete by machines.*
• ADV. **totally | increasingly | largely | almost, practically, virtually**

obstacle *noun*

• ADJ. **big, chief, main, major | enormous, formidable, serious** *The attitude of the unions is a serious obstacle.* | **impossible, insuperable, insurmountable** *Lack of money has proved an almost insurmountable obstacle.*
• VERB + OBSTACLE **pose, prove, remain | come across, encounter | overcome, remove, surmount** *He was determined to overcome all obstacles in his way.*
• PREP. **~for** *Lack of childcare provision can be a major obstacle for women wishing to work.* **~to** *The huge distances involved have proved an obstacle to communication between villages.*
• PHRASES **an obstacle in the path/way (of sb/sth)** *The release of prisoners remains an obstacle in the path of a peace agreement.*

obstruct *verb*

• ADV. **deliberately, wilfully** (*law*) *wilfully obstructing a police officer in the execution of his duty*
• PREP. **in**

obstruction *noun*

• ADJ. **physical | unlawful, wilful** (*law*) | **bureaucratic**

The asylum seekers had to contend with continued bureaucratic obstruction.
• VERB + OBSTRUCTION **cause, create** *The lorry had been parked on the pavement, causing an obstruction.* | **clear, remove** *She had to have surgery to remove an obstruction from her throat.*

obstructive *adj.*

• VERBS **be | become**
• ADV. **positively | quite | deliberately** *He doesn't really have an alternative suggestion; he's just being deliberately obstructive.*

obtain *verb*

• ADV. **fraudulently, unlawfully** (*law*)
• VERB + OBTAIN **be able/unable to | attempt to, endeavour to | fail to | assist sb to, enable sb to** *The local authority may assist you to obtain alternative accommodation.* | **be easy to, be possible to | be difficult to, be impossible to** *goods which are difficult to obtain* | **be necessary to, be required to, need to** *It is necessary to obtain the patients' consent.*
• PREP. **from** *Anglers are required to obtain prior authorization from the park keeper.*
• PHRASES **be easily obtained** *Such information is easily obtained from the Internet.* **sth can/may be obtained** *Details of this offer can be obtained from any of our stores.* **a means/method/way of obtaining sth**

obtainable *adj.*

• VERBS **be | become**
• ADV. **easily, readily | commercially**

obvious *adj.*

• VERBS **appear, be, look, seem, sound | become** *It soon became obvious that the machine did not work.* | **make sth** *His manner made it obvious he didn't like her.*
• ADV. **blatantly, blindingly, extremely, glaringly, patently, transparently, very | completely, perfectly, quite** *The answer is perfectly obvious!* | **increasingly | by no means, far from, less than, not at all, not entirely** *It was far from obvious how they were going to get off the island.* | **a bit, fairly, pretty, rather** *I'm not going to tell Jim about this, for fairly obvious reasons.* | **apparently, seemingly | immediately** *It was immediately obvious that the bag was too heavy.* | **intuitively** *Avoid making intuitively obvious but unfounded assertions.* | **depressingly, distressingly, painfully** *It was becoming painfully obvious that the two of them had nothing in common.*
• PREP. **to** *It is obvious to me that you're unhappy in your job.*

occasion *noun*

1 time when sth happens
• ADJ. **many, numerous** *It was the first of many such occasions.* | **rare | previous | separate**
• VERB + OCCASION **recall, remember**
• PREP. **on an/the~** *The police were called out on 24 separate occasions.* **on ~(s)** *He has even been known to go shopping himself on occasion.*
• PHRASES **a number of occasions** *I have stayed there on a number of occasions.* **on one occasion** *On one occasion he even rang me in the middle of the night.* **on that/this~** *On this occasion, as it happens, the engine started immediately.*

2 suitable time
• ADJ. **right, suitable**
• OCCASION + VERB **arise** *I'll speak to him if the occasion arises.*
• PREP. **~for** *It should have been an occasion for rejoicing.*

● PHRASES **have occasion to do sth** *Last year we had occasion to visit relatives in Cornwall.*

3 special event
● ADJ. **auspicious, big, great, important, memorable, momentous, special | festive, happy, joyous | formal, sad, solemn | social | ceremonial, state** *The Queen's coach is only used for state occasions.*
● VERB + OCCASION **celebrate, mark** *a party to mark the occasion of their daughter's graduation* | **rise to** *The choir rose to the occasion and sang beautifully.*
● PHRASES **for all occasions, for every occasion** *We sell cards and notepaper for all occasions.* **a sense of occasion** *On the day of the wedding there was a real sense of occasion.*

occupant noun

● ADJ. **current, former, next, original, present, previous | sole** *The sole occupant of the car was an elderly man.*

occupation noun

1 job
● ADJ. **full-time | dangerous, hazardous | female, male** *Agricultural work is traditionally seen as a male occupation.* | **low-paid, well-paid | high-status, low-status | sedentary | managerial, professional, technical | skilled, unskilled | manual, non-manual | blue-collar, white-collar | industrial, service** *service occupations such as cleaning and catering*
● VERB + OCCUPATION **choose, find | take up | follow** *The people interviewed followed a variety of occupations* | **give up** *He gave up his occupation as a farmer and became a teacher.* | **resume | provide (sb with)**
● PHRASES **a range of occupations** *The college provides training in a wide range of occupations.*

2 control of another country
● ADJ. **continuing | military**
● VERB + OCCUPATION **begin, take up | be/remain in | give up** *The invaders have given up occupation of large parts of the territories.* | **resume**
● OCCUPATION + VERB **begin, end**
● OCCUPATION + NOUN **force, power | zone**
● PREP. **during the ~** *During the occupation, the church was used as a mosque.* **under ~** *Large parts of Britain were under Roman occupation.*

3 living in a room, house, etc.
● ADJ. **exclusive | joint, multiple** *the conversion of big old buildings to multiple occupation* | **peaceful** *the right to peaceful occupation of the property* | **land | illegal, unlawful** *illegal occupation of the premises*
● VERB + OCCUPATION **take up** *You can only take up occupation once the tenancy has been signed.* | **be/remain in, enjoy | share | give up | resume**
● PREP. **in ~ of** *He intends to remain in occupation of the building for as long as possible.*
● PHRASES **ready for occupation** *The flats will be ready for occupation by March.* **unfit for occupation** *The houses were judged to be unfit for human occupation.*

occupied adj.

1 being used by sb
● VERBS **be**
● ADV. **densely** *the most densely occupied areas of the country* | **entirely** *The sofa was entirely occupied by two large cats.* | **permanently | illegally**

2 busy
● VERBS **be | become | keep sb** *We need something to keep the children occupied.*
● ADV. **fully | chiefly, mainly | busily | happily**
● PREP. **in** *You will be mainly occupied in checking sales records.* **with** *She was happily occupied with reading.*

occur verb

● ADV. **commonly, frequently | infrequently, rarely | sporadically | naturally** *These chemical changes occur quite naturally.* | **spontaneously** *Opportunities for learning occur spontaneously every day.*
● VERB + OCCUR **be likely to, tend to | be unlikely to**

occurrence noun

● ADJ. **common, everyday, widespread | daily, frequent, regular | rare, uncommon | isolated | strange, unexpected, unusual**
● VERB + OCCURRENCE **prevent | predict**
● PREP. **~ in** *These mild fits are quite a common occurrence in babies.*
● PHRASES **frequency of occurrence** *words with a high frequency of occurrence in language*

ocean noun

● ADJ. **deep | vast | great** *exploring the depths of the three great oceans* | **open** *A storm started up once we got out into the open ocean.* | **tropical, warm | southern** *penguins of the southern oceans*
● VERB + OCEAN **cross, sail | explore**
● OCEAN + NOUN **depths** *the darkness of the ocean depths* | **surface | bed, floor | basin | water | wave** *a life on the ocean wave* (= at sea) | **current | voyage | liner**
● PREP. **across the ~** *trade across the Atlantic Ocean* **in the ~** *Various toxic substances have been dumped in the ocean.*
● PHRASES **the bottom/depths/middle/surface of the ocean, the oceans of the world** *great ships that sailed the oceans of the world*

October noun

⇨ Note at MONTH

odd adj.

● VERBS **be, feel, look, seem, smell, sound, taste | consider sth, find sth, think sth** *I find it odd that she takes so long to do that job.* ◇ *I didn't think it odd at the time.*
● ADV. **decidedly, distinctly, extremely, really, very** *There's something distinctly odd about her.* | **a bit, a little, pretty, quite, rather, slightly, somewhat**

odds noun

● ADJ. **considerable, great, high, impossible, insuperable, overwhelming, terrible** *She struggled against terrible odds to overcome her illness.* | **long, short** *Sometimes an outsider will win at long odds, but not often.* ◇ *The bookmakers are offering only short odds on the favourite.*
● VERB + ODDS **offer, quote | lay** *I'll lay odds we never see him again.* | **reduce, shorten | beat, defy, overcome** *She defied the odds to beat the clear favourite.*
● ODDS + VERB **shorten | lengthen**
● PREP. **against the ~** *The film is a heart-warming tale of triumph against the odds.* | **~ against** *The odds against their survival have lengthened.* **~ of** *They were offering odds of ten to one.* **~ on** *The odds on the outsider were 100–1.*
● PHRASES **against all (the) odds** *Against all the odds, we managed to get through to the final.*

odour noun

● ADJ. **foul, obnoxious, offensive, unpleasant | musty, stale | heavy, pungent, strong | faint | sweet | characteristic, distinctive, familiar, unmistakable | body**
● VERB + ODOUR **emit, give off**
● ODOUR + VERB **emanate from sth**
● PREP. **~ from** *odours from the local brewery*

offence noun

1 illegal act
- ADJ. **grave, heinous, major, serious | lesser, minor, petty, trivial | alleged | statutory | arrestable, bookable, imprisonable, indictable, punishable, sackable** *The offence is punishable by up to three months' imprisonment.* | **criminal, disciplinary | driving, political, sexual, terrorist** *Motorists may be fined on the spot for driving offences such as speeding.* | **violent | drug-related**
- PREP. **~against** *offences against public decency*
⇨ Note at CRIME (for verbs)

2 hurt feelings
- VERB + OFFENCE **cause, give | take**
- PREP. **~at** *He takes offence at the slightest joke against him.* **~to** *I didn't mean to give offence to anyone.*
- PHRASES **no offence (intended/meant)** *No offence intended, but are you sure your calculations are right?*

offend verb

- ADV. **deeply, gravely, greatly** *He knew that he had offended her deeply.* | **mortally | slightly | easily** *He was very sensitive and easily offended.*
- VERB + OFFEND **be likely to** *Omit anything that is likely to offend people.* | **be anxious not to, be careful not to, not mean to, take care not to** *She stopped mid-sentence, anxious not to offend him.*
- PREP. **against** *Viewers complained that the programme offended against good taste.*
- PHRASES **feel/look/sound offended** *She sounded offended when she replied.*

offender noun

1 person who commits a crime
- ADJ. **alleged | convicted | first** *As a first offender, he received a lenient sentence.* | **persistent | adult, juvenile, young | sex**
- VERB + OFFENDER **sentence**

2 sb/sth that causes trouble
- ADJ. **main, worst** *As regards pollution, old diesel-engined vehicles are the worst offenders.*

offensive noun

- ADJ. **all-out, full-scale, major | army, guerrilla, military, terrorist | air, bombing | ground | diplomatic, government**
- VERB + OFFENSIVE **launch, mount | be on, go on, take** *She took the offensive, challenging her critics to prove their allegations.*
- PREP. **~against** *The government is launching an all-out offensive against the drug cartels*

offensive adj.

- VERBS **appear, be, seem | become | consider sth, deem sth, find sth, think sth** *He's always making rude remarks about women. I find that deeply offensive.*
- ADV. **deeply, downright, extremely, grossly, highly, very | quite, rather | deliberately**
- PREP. **to** *This sort of attitude is very offensive to black people.*

offer noun

1 of help or sth that is needed
- ADJ. **generous, kind | conditional, unconditional | job | peace**
- VERB + OFFER **make (sb)** *He made me an offer I simply couldn't refuse* | **withdraw | accept, take up | decline, refuse, turn down**
- PREP. **on~** *the range of goods on offer* | **~from** *I had to turn down a job offer from a theatre because the pay was too low.* **~of** *They refused our offer of help.*

2 special price/deal
- ADJ. **special | cheap | free** *I got the conditioner in a free offer with my shampoo.* | **introductory** *Your first order is delivered free as an introductory offer.*
- PREP. **on~** *We have a number of bargains on offer.*

3 amount of money
- ADJ. **acceptable, attractive, fair, favourable, reasonable | tempting | high, low** *We realized we would not get a higher offer.* | **final, initial | firm, formal** *Several people have made enquiries but no one has made a firm offer.* | **lucrative | pay | takeover | cash**
- VERB + OFFER **make (sb), put in | withdraw | get, receive | listen to** *I'll listen to any reasonable offer.* | **accept | reject, turn down | increase, up** *They just kept upping their offer until I had to say yes.*
- OFFER + NOUN **price**
- PREP. **under~** *The property is currently under offer to a client.* | **~for** *Several people put in an offer for the house.* **~of** *They accepted our offer of £80 000.*
- PHRASES **be open to offers** *The asking price is £500 but I'm open to offers.* **or near offer** *They are selling their car for £2 500 or near offer.*

offer verb

1 give/provide sth; ask if sb would like sth
- ADV. **generously, kindly | helpfully | impulsively** *'Do you need any help?' he offered impulsively.*
- VERB + OFFER **be able/unable to, can/could** *the protection that life insurance can offer* | **appear to, seem to** *The plan seemed to offer real advantages.* | **fail to | be pleased to** (formal) *I refer to your recent application and interview and am pleased to offer you the post of editor.* | **aim to, seek to | claim to** *They claim to offer a more comprehensive service than other firms.* | **be expected to, be likely to** *This investment is likely to offer a higher return.* | **be/feel compelled to, be forced to, be/feel obliged to** *She felt obliged to offer him a bed for the night.* | **have little/a lot/nothing, etc. to, have sth to** *This player has proved that he still has a lot to offer* (= can still play well). ◇ *The open evening is a chance to see what the college has to offer students.*
- PREP. **to** *She offered drinks to her guests.*

2 say that you will pay a certain amount
- VERB + OFFER **be able/unable to, can/could | be prepared to, be ready to, be willing to** *Would they be prepared to offer any more?*
- PREP. **for** *They have offered over £500 000 for the house.*

offering noun

- ADJ. **latest | peace** *I think the present she sent you was intended as a peace offering.* | **burnt, sacrificial, votive**
- VERB + OFFERING **make | accept**
- PREP. **~from** *The latest offering from this young band is their best album yet.* **~of** *offerings of food and drink* **~to** *They made sacrificial offerings to the gods.*

office noun

1 room/building where written work is done
- ADJ. **big, huge, large, spacious | cramped, small, tiny | plush | high-rise | five-storey, ten-storey, etc. | glass-fronted, glass-walled | busy, noisy | open-plan | air-conditioned | electronic, paperless | permanent, temporary** *The company set up its first permanent offices in the city centre.* | **private** *The prime minister arranged a meeting in his private office.* | **central, head, main | area, branch, district, local, overseas, regional, subsidiary | administrative, editorial, press, sales, etc. | council, government, newspaper, etc.**
- VERB + OFFICE **manage, run, supervise | come/go into, come/go to** *I sometimes go into the office on Saturdays when we're busy.* | **arrive at, get to | leave** *What time do you usually leave the office?*

● OFFICE + NOUN **job, work | hours** *Call this number outside normal office hours.* | **colleague, staff, worker | life | gossip, politics | party** *We have an office party every Christmas.* | **administrator, assistant, cleaner, clerk, manager | boy, girl, junior** (*all old-fashioned*) | **desk, door, equipment, furniture, safe, shredder, software, stationery | system, technology | environment** *Working in a busy office environment can be stressful.* | **accommodation, block, building, complex, development, premises, space, suite** *The old warehouses have been redeveloped for office accommodation.* | **facilities, services** *The conference centre provides office facilities such as computers and faxes.* | **expenses, overheads | administration, management | skills | procedures, routine**
● PREP. **at the** ~ *I sometimes have to stay late at the office.* **in the** ~ *I'm sorry, Mr Anders is not in the office today.*

2 official position
● ADJ. **exalted, great, high, important | minor | lucrative, prestigious | hereditary | national, public | ecclesiastical, judicial, ministerial, political**
● VERB + OFFICE **run for, stand for** *He ran for office in the last presidential election.* | **hold, remain in, retain, stay in** *The president holds office for a period of four years.* | **be appointed to, be elected to | be re-elected to, be returned to** *The government was returned to office by a large majority.* | **assume, be sworn into, come into, come to, enter, take, take up** *Martin was sworn into office as prime minister in March.* ◇ *The Labour Party took office in 1997.* | **give up, leave, lose, relinquish, resign from, retire from, vacate | be driven from, be forced from, be removed from, be suspended from, be turned out of**
● OFFICE + NOUN **holder**
● PREP. **in** ~ *The government seemed likely to remain in office for the next five years.* **out of** ~ *breaking promises made when out of office*
● PHRASES **a candidate for office, duties of the office, a term of office** *to be re-elected for a second term of office*

officer *noun*

1 in the army, navy, etc.
● ADJ. **air force, army, military, naval | commanding, high-ranking, ranking, senior, superior** *The decision rests with the ranking officer* (= the most senior officer present). | **junior, petty | commissioned, non-commissioned | recruiting | duty** *He telephoned the duty officer at regimental headquarters.* | **uniformed | retired**
● VERB + OFFICER **salute** *to salute a superior officer*
● OFFICER + VERB **command sth** *the officer commanding the infantry*
● OFFICER + NOUN **cadet, corps**
⇨ Note at RANK

2 in the government or other organization
● ADJ. **chief, principal, senior | full-time, part-time | presiding, responsible, supervising** *Report the incident to the responsible officer.* ◇ *the officer responsible for implementing the scheme* | **regional | administrative, customs, environmental health, financial, liaison, medical, press, trading standards, training, welfare**
● VERB + OFFICER **be, work as | be appointed (as), become | have** *The charity has a full-time press officer working with the national newspapers.*

3 policeman/policewoman
● ADJ. **police | chief, senior, superior | junior | investigating | duty** *We spoke to the duty officer at the police station.* | **uniformed | plain-clothes | undercover**
● OFFICER + VERB **investigate sth** *officers investigating the murder* | **patrol sth | raid sth, swoop on sth** (*informal*) *Officers raided an address in south London, seizing bomb-making equipment.* | **seize sth | arrest sb**
⇨ See POLICEMAN

official *noun*

● ADJ. **high-ranking, prominent, senior, top | junior, minor | local, provincial, regional | departmental | public | full-time, part-time | elected | permanent | retired | responsible** *Report the incident to the responsible official.* ◇ *the official responsible for handling the case* | **corrupt | bank, company, corporate, council, court, customs, government, judicial, military, ministry, party, royal, state, (trade) union**
● VERB + OFFICIAL **appoint (sb), appoint sb as | consult, meet | bribe** *attempting to bribe local officials*

off-putting *adj.*

● VERBS **be | find sth** *I find it very off-putting when people don't look me in the eye.*
● ADV. **distinctly, very | a bit, a little, rather, slightly** *The noise was rather off-putting.*

offset *verb*

● ADV. **largely, substantially | completely, exactly | more than** *The company's losses in the USA were more than offset by gains everywhere else.* | **partially, partly**
● VERB + OFFSET **help (to)** *The money will help offset big medical bills.*
● PREP. **against** *Your donations to charity can be offset against tax.*

offside *adj.*

● VERBS **be, look | catch sb, rule sb** *an attempt to catch an opponent offside* ◇ *He was ruled offside by the referee.*

oil *noun*

1 used as fuel/to make machines work smoothly
● ADJ. **heavy | light | crude | refined | offshore | engine, fuel, heating, lubricating, motor | linseed, paraffin** *Use a rag soaked in linseed oil.*
● QUANT. **barrel | film** *a rod coated with a film of oil* | **drop**
● VERB + OIL **extract, obtain, produce | drill for** *The company is drilling for oil in the North Sea.* | **discover, find, hit, strike | pump | export, import | burn, use | change** (in a car, etc.) | **soak sth in | smell of** *The place smelled of paint and oil.*
● OIL + NOUN **company, producer | industry, production | drilling, exploration | field, rig, well | drum | tanker | refinery | prices, revenue | slick, spill, spillage** *a seven-mile-long oil slick off the Scottish coast*

2 used in cooking
● ADJ. **cooking | polyunsaturated | rancid | coconut, cod liver, fish, groundnut, olive, sesame, sunflower, vegetable** *a bottle of extra virgin olive oil* | **salad**
● VERB + OIL **heat | boil sb/sth in, cook sth in, fry sth in | drizzle, pour** *Toast the bread, rub with garlic and drizzle over a little olive oil.*
● PREP. **in** ~ *Fry the potato in a little sunflower oil.*
⇨ Special page at FOOD

3 used as a cosmetic/medicine
● ADJ. **aromatic, fragrant, scented | essential** *extracting essential oils from flowers* | **body, hair | baby, bath | aromatherapy, massage | castor, evening primrose, lavender, etc.**
● VERB + OIL **massage/rub into, massage/rub sth with** *She rubbed a scented oil into her hair.* | **anoint sb/sth with** *The sick were anointed with oil.* | **extract**
● PREP. ~ **of** *oil of rosemary*

oily *adj.*

● VERBS **be, look | become**
● ADV. **very | rather, slightly** *He had rather oily hands.* |

naturally *Lank or naturally oil hair is often difficult to care for.*

ointment *noun*

- QUANT. **tube**
- VERB + OINTMENT **apply, put on, rub on** *He put some ointment on the cut.*

OK (*also* **okay**) *adj., adv.*

- VERBS **be, feel, look, seem, smell, sound, taste | do, go** *I think I did OK in the exam.* ◇ *I hope the meeting goes OK.*
- ADV. **perfectly, quite** *I'm quite OK now, thanks.*
- PREP. **~ by sb** *John has suggested meeting at six, and that's OK by me.* **~ with sb** *Is it OK with you if I come about six?*

old *adj.*

1 age
- VERBS **be, feel, look, seem** *You are as old as you feel.*
- ADV. **enough** *He's old enough by now to manage his own affairs.*
- PHRASES **six months, ten years, etc. old**

2 not young
- VERBS **be, feel, look, seem, sound** *The way the young people rushed about made her feel old.* ◇ *He was beginning to look old.* **| become, get, grow** *We're all getting older.* ◇ *As they grow older, they develop new interests.*
- ADV. **extremely, terribly, very | fairly, quite** *She was quite old when she got married.*

3 not new
- VERBS **be**
- ADV. **extremely, really, terribly, very** *It's a very old tradition.* **| fairly, quite**
- PHRASES **oldest known** *These are some of the oldest known fossil remains.* **oldest remaining** *It's one of the oldest remaining parts of the church.* **oldest surviving** *It's the world's oldest surviving ship.*

4 shows affection/lack of respect
- PHRASES **boring/silly old** *boring old history books* ◇ *She's a silly old cow!* **dear/good old** *Good old Dad!* **funny old** *It's a funny old world.* **poor old** *You poor old thing!* **same old** *always the same old faces*

old age *noun*

- ADJ. **advanced, extreme | good** *He attained a good old age and died content.* **| happy** *She can look forward to a happy old age.* **| lonely** *fears about a lonely old age*
- VERB + OLD AGE **attain, live to, reach, survive into** *All my grandparents survived into advanced old age.* **| approach | look forward to | dread**
- OLD AGE + NOUN **pension, pensioner**
- PREP. **in (your)~** *Loss of hearing often occurs in old age.* ◇ *He took up golf in his old age.* **into ~** *She was now well into old age.*
- PHRASES **the grand/ripe old age of sth** *She lived to the ripe old age of 98.*

old-fashioned *adj.*

- VERBS **be, look, seem | become | consider sth, regard sth as, see sth as** *Wearing a hat is regarded as rather old-fashioned nowadays.*
- ADV. **terribly, very | plain** *It was plain old-fashioned instinct, the gut feeling that something was wrong.* **| a bit, a little, rather, slightly, somewhat | curiously** *His clothes were curiously old-fashioned.*
- PREP. **in** *She's somewhat old-fashioned in her attitudes.*
- PHRASES **call me old-fashioned** *Call me old-fashioned, but I still believe in good manners.*

ombudsman *noun*

- ADJ. **consumer, insurance, local government, pensions** *A pensions ombudsman has been appointed.*
- VERB + OMBUDSMAN **appoint**

omen *noun*

- ADJ. **good | bad, evil, ill** *They took the storm as a bad omen.*
- VERB + OMEN **take sth as**
- PREP. **~ for** *The sunny weather was a good omen for the holiday.* **~ of** *an omen of death*

omission *noun*

- ADJ. **important, major, serious | complete | glaring, notable, obvious | curious, strange, surprising | deliberate | inadvertent**
- VERB + OMISSION **correct, rectify, remedy**
- PREP. **by ~** *Several offences such as manslaughter may be committed by omission.* **| ~ from** *her omission from the guest list*
- PHRASES **an act or omission** *The accident was not caused by any act or omission of the transport company.* **errors and/or omissions, a sin of omission**

omit *verb*

- ADV. **altogether, completely, totally | accidentally, inadvertently | deliberately | conspicuously | controversially** *He was controversially omitted from the World Cup side.* **| wrongly**
- PREP. **from** *Some important details were deliberately omitted from the report.*

one-sided *adj.*

- VERBS **be, seem**
- ADV. **very | totally, wholly | far from** *The violence was far from one-sided (= both people, teams, etc. were violent).* **| a little, rather, somewhat** *Their relationship seems rather one-sided.*

onion *noun*

- ADJ. **raw | pickled | spring, red, Spanish**
- VERB + ONION **chop, peel, slice | brown, soften | cook, fry, sauté | garnish sth with** *Garnish with a little chopped spring onion.* **| grow**
- ONION + NOUN **ring | soup | skin | set | dome**
- PHRASES **cheese and onion** *cheese and onion flavoured crisps* **sage and onion** *sage and onion stuffing*
⇨ Special page at FOOD

onset *noun*

- ADJ. **rapid, sudden** *the sudden onset of the disease* **| slow | early | delayed, late**
- VERB + ONSET **delay | mark** *His first hit record marked the onset of an astonishing career.*
- PREP. **after the ~** *after the onset of sleep* **at the ~** *at the onset of the war* **before/prior to the ~, since the ~**

onslaught *noun*

- ADJ. **sudden** *She could not withstand such a sudden onslaught.* **| first, initial | latest | renewed | verbal**
- VERB + ONSLAUGHT **face** *to face the verbal onslaught of an angry teenager* **| resist, survive, withstand | launch, mount**
- PREP. **~ against/on** *a renewed onslaught against the proposed bill* **~ from** *the latest onslaught from the Russian team*

ooze *verb*

- ADV. **slowly | out** *Cream oozed out at the sides.*

• PREP. **from** *Blood oozed slowly from his wound.* **out of,**
with (*figurative*) *He was oozing with contempt for us.*

opaque *adj.*

1 not clear enough to see through
• VERBS **be, look | become** *Add the rice to the pan and*
cook until it becomes opaque.
• ADV. **very | completely | almost, nearly | relatively,**
slightly *The glasses looked slightly opaque.*
• PREP. **with** *The windows were nearly opaque with*
grime.

2 difficult to understand
• VERBS **be | become | render sth** *The complex admin-*
istrative arrangements render the decision-making pro-
cess somewhat opaque.
• ADV. **extremely,   very | completely | relatively,**
slightly, somewhat

open *verb*

1 door, window, box, etc.
• ADV. **wide** *She opened all the windows wide to let some*
fresh air in. **| slowly | gingerly** *Fred opened it gingerly*
and peered inside. **| automatically** *The glass doors opened*
automatically for him. **| out, up** *I opened out the map and*
laid it on the table. ◇ *'Open up!' He hammered on the door.*
• VERB + OPEN **try to | manage to | fail to** *Her para-*
chute failed to open.

2 building, road, etc.
• ADV. **formally, officially | up** *opening up new markets*
• VERB + OPEN **be due to, be expected to, be sched-**
uled to *The museum is due to open next year.* **| hope to, in-**
tend to, plan to, want to, wish to
• PHRASES **newly/recently opened** *the newly opened*
gallery of Western decorative art

open *adj.*

1 not closed
• VERBS **be, gape, lie, stand** *The book lay open in front of*
him. ◇ *The door stood open.* **| burst, clang, creak, fall, fly,**
judder, sag, swing *The bag fell open.* ◇ *Suddenly the door*
flew open. ◇ *The woman's mouth sagged open.* ◇ *The gate*
swung open. **| remain | fling sth, flip sth, get sth, prise**
sth, pull sth, push sth, tear sth, throw sth, wrench sth,
yank sth *She flung the door open and rushed in.* ◇ *She*
flipped open Chris's diary. ◇ *He tore the letter open.* **| have**
sth, hold sth, keep sth, leave sth *She held the door open*
for them. **| find sth, see sth** *I found the door open.*
• ADV. **fully, wide** *The door was wide open.* **| slightly**

2 honest and willing to talk
• VERBS **be, seem**
• ADV. **extremely, very | absolutely, completely, quite**
• PREP. **about** *She's very open about her mistakes.* **with** *I*
don't think you've been completely open with me.

3 available for people to use
• VERBS **be | remain, stay** *In spite of the snow, the roads*
remained open. ◇ *Some of the supermarkets stay open till*
ten. **| keep sth** *We want to keep the village store open.*
• PREP. **to** *The car park is only open to residents.*

4 having begun
• VERBS **be | declare sth** *The Australian premier de-*
clared the Olympic Games open.
• ADV. **officially** *The bridge is officially open now.*

opening *noun*

1 beginning
• ADJ. **successful | chess, conversational**
• OPENING + NOUN **day, night | lines, pages | gambit**
• PREP. **~to** *the famous opening to the novel*

2 hole; way in/out
• ADJ. **large, wide | narrow, small | window**

• VERB + OPENING **cut | block, seal**
• PREP. **~in** *to cut an opening in the fence*

3 opportunity; job which is available
• ADJ. **new | possible | clear** (used in the context of
sport and games) *He missed one of the clearest openings in*
the game. **| career, political**
• VERB + OPENING **create** *Cooper created the opening*
for Russell to shoot the first goal. **| give sb | miss**
• PREP. **~for, ~in** *career openings for biologists in the*
Ministry of Health

4 ceremony
• ADJ. **grand | formal | official, royal, state** *the state*
opening of Parliament
• VERB + OPENING **attend**
• OPENING + NOUN **ceremony**

openness *noun*

• ADJ. **greater, more** *There is a need for greater openness*
in government. **| complete**
• VERB + OPENNESS **demonstrate, show**
• PREP. **~about** *her openness about her marital problems*
~to/towards *He demonstrated an openness to change.*

opera *noun*

• ADJ. **comic, grand, light**
• VERB + OPERA **compose, write**
• OPERA + NOUN **singer,   star | company | house |**
season | buff, lover
⇨ Note at PERFORMANCE (for more verbs)

operate *verb*

1 machine
• ADV. **effectively, efficiently, reliably | continuously**
The machine can operate for 15 hours continuously at full
power. **| electrically, electronically, hydraulically,**
manually, remotely (= by remote control) *The doors can*
be manually operated in the event of fire.
• VERB + OPERATE **be designed to** *systems designed to*
operate at the highest speeds **| be easy to** *The machinery*
is easy to operate.
• PHRASES **battery operated**

2 business/system
• ADV. **effectively, efficiently, profitably, successfully |**
autonomously, independently | commercially *The la-*
boratory is still owned by the government but is now
commercially operated.
• VERB + OPERATE **be able to | be allowed to | con-**
tinue to
• PREP. **according to** *The government does not operate*
according to fixed rules. **as** *We operate as an advisory ser-*
vice for schools. **within** *Local authorities operate within a*
wider political system.

operation *noun*

1 medical
• ADJ. **major | minor, small | life-saving, vital | emer-**
gency | routine | delicate *a delicate eye operation* **| ex-**
ploratory | surgical, transplant | heart, knee, etc.
• VERB + OPERATION **have, undergo** *He had an oper-*
ation to remove a tumour. **| come through, survive** *She*
came through the operation very well. **| carry out, per-**
form *the surgeon performing the operation*
• PREP. **during a/the ~** *She woke during the operation.* **|**
~for *an operation for a kidney problem* **~on** *a major oper-*
ation on his heart

2 organized activity
• ADJ. **big, large-scale, major, massive | covert,**
undercover | combined, joint | tricky *a tricky rescue op-*
eration **| intelligence, military, naval, police | guerrilla**
| clean-up, drilling, mining, mopping-up, offensive,
peacekeeping, relief, rescue, salvage, security *UN*

troops supervised the relief operations. | **banking, building, business** *restrictions placed on business operations*
● VERB + OPERATION **begin, launch, mount, undertake** *The authorities launched a massive security operation in the city.* | **carry out, conduct** | **supervise**
● PREP. **during a/the~** *during joint military operations*
● PHRASES **a theatre of operations** (= where military operations take place)

3 fact of sth functioning
● ADJ. **effective, efficient, smooth** | **day-to-day** *the smooth day-to-day operation of the department*
● VERB + OPERATION **come into** *A ceasefire came into operation in May.* | **bring/put sth into** | **cease** *The factory will cease operation at the end of the year.*
● PREP. **during~** *The machine can get very hot during operation.* **in~** *The current tax system has been in operation for ten years.*
● PHRASES **in/into full operation** *the only reactor in full operation*

operational *adj.*

● VERBS **be** | **become** | **remain**
● ADV. **fully** *The equipment is now fully operational.*

operative *adj.*

● VERBS **be** | **become** | **remain**
● ADV. **fully** *The new system will not become fully operative until next year.*

operator *noun*

1 person who connects telephone calls
● ADJ. **switchboard, telephone**
● OPERATOR + VERB **connect sb, put sb through** *I asked the operator to put me through to her office.*

2 person who works a machine, etc.
● ADJ. **experienced, skilled** | **unskilled** | **machine, plant** | **computer, lathe, radio, word processor**, etc.

3 person/company that does particular business
● ADJ. **big, small** | **private** | **holiday, tour, travel** | **cable (television), satellite, telecommunications**, etc. | **airline, bus, coach, ferry**

4 sb who is skilful at getting what they want
● ADJ. **shrewd, slick, smooth**

opinion *noun*

1 what you think about sb/sth
● ADJ. **good, high** | **low, poor** | **strong** | **conflicting, different, mixed** *Opinions are mixed regarding genetically-modified food.* | **honest** *If you want my honest opinion, I think the book is awful.* | **expert, informed, professional** | **considered** | **personal, subjective** | **objective** | **contrary, dissenting** | **majority** | **minority** | **second** *If in doubt about your diagnosis, get a second opinion.*
● VERB + OPINION **entertain, have, hold** | **air, express, give (sb), offer (sb), pass, state, venture, voice** *The bishop spoke without passing any opinion on the scandal.* | **ask sb, seek** *He asked me for my opinion on the course.* | **get** | **form** *I formed the opinion that he was not to be trusted.* | **change**
● OPINION + VERB **change** | **differ, vary** *Opinions differ as to when this wine should be drunk.*
● PREP. **in your~** *In my opinion, golf is a dull sport.* | **~about/on** *She holds strong opinions on education.* **~as to** *opinions as to the merits of the scheme* **~of** *He has a very high opinion of your work.*
● PHRASES **be of the opinion that ...** *(formal)* (= to believe or think that), **a difference of opinion** *a genuine difference of opinion between the experts* **in my humble opinion** *(humorous)*, **a matter of opinion** *'London is wonderful.' 'That's a matter of opinion.'*

2 what people in general think about sth
● ADJ. **prevailing** | **general, popular, public** *Contrary to popular opinion, many adult cats dislike milk.* | **international, local, national** | **expert, informed, professional** | **academic, legal, medical, political**
● QUANT. **body** *This view is supported by a growing body of professional opinion.*
● VERB + OPINION **mould, shape** *attempts to shape public opinion*
● OPINION + VERB **be against sth, be in favour of sth** *Prevailing local opinion is against the new road proposals.* | **be divided** *Public opinion is divided on the subject of capital punishment.*
● OPINION + NOUN **poll** | **former, leader**
● PREP. **~among** *Opinion among doctors is that the medication is safe.*
● PHRASES **climate of opinion** *in the present climate of opinion* **shades of opinion** *all shades of political opinion*

opium *noun*

● VERB + OPIUM **smoke**
● OPIUM + NOUN **poppy** | **den**
⇨ Note at DRUG (for more verbs and nouns)

opponent *noun*

1 person who plays against sb
● ADJ. **chief, main** | **dangerous, tough** | **worthy**
● VERB + OPPONENT **attack, hit** | **beat, defeat** | **get past, outfox, outmanoeuvre, outwit** | **face** *Today she faces her toughest opponent on Centre Court.* | **mark** | **tackle** | **bring down, foul**
⇨ Special page at SPORT

2 sb who disagrees with sb's actions/plans/beliefs
● ADJ. **chief, leading, main** | **bitter, fierce, formidable, strong, vigorous** | **outspoken, vocal, vociferous** | **worthy** | **political** | **government**

opportunity *noun*

● ADJ. **ample, considerable, plenty of** *We'll have plenty of opportunity to talk later.* | **limited, little, not much** | **excellent, favourable, golden, good, great, marvellous, tremendous, welcome, wonderful** *a golden opportunity to invest and export into new markets* | **exciting** | **ideal, perfect** | **suitable** | **reasonable** *We need to give them a reasonable opportunity to look at the display.* | **available** | **every** *Students should take every opportunity to widen their experience.* | **historic, once-in-a-lifetime, rare, unique, unparalleled, unprecedented, unrivalled** | **lost, missed, wasted** | **career, educational, employment, job, training** | **business, commercial, economic, investment, market, sales** *a missed sales opportunity* | **photo** (= an opportunity to take photographs of famous or important people) | **equal opportunities** (= the principle of treating all people the same, regardless of sex. colour, etc.) *an equal opportunities employer*
● VERB + OPPORTUNITY **have** | **find, get** *We didn't get much opportunity to swim.* | **afford, create, give sb, offer (sb), open up, provide (sb with)** *to provide better educational opportunities* | **grasp, seize, take (up), take advantage of** *May I take this opportunity to congratulate Ruth on her promotion.* | **lose, miss** *He lost no opportunity to vent his anger on those around him.* | **pass up**
● OPPORTUNITY + VERB **exist** | **arise, come, occur, offer** *When the opportunity came, I seized it with both hands.* ◇ *(formal) The company aimed to expand as and when opportunity offered.*
● PREP. **~for** *The job will offer you excellent opportunities for promotion.*
● PHRASES **at the earliest/first (possible) opportunity, at every (available) opportunity, equality of opportunity, the opportunity of a lifetime, a window of opportun-**

ity *The ceasefire has created a window of opportunity to rescue the peace process.*

oppose *verb*

• ADV. **adamantly, bitterly, fiercely, firmly, hotly, resolutely, strenuously, strongly, vehemently, vigorously, violently** *We would vigorously oppose such a policy.* | **totally** *We totally oppose the use of gas to kill any animal.* | **actively | openly, publicly | successfully, unsuccessfully** *Environmental lobby groups successfully opposed the plan.* | **initially** *The ban was initially opposed by the US.* | **consistently** *The minister has consistently opposed any relaxation in the law.*
• VERB + OPPOSE **vote to | continue to**

opposed *adj.*

1 opposed to disagreeing strongly with sth
• VERBS **be | remain**
• ADV. **adamantly, bitterly, deeply, fiercely, firmly, fundamentally, implacably, profoundly, resolutely, strongly, vehemently, very (much), violently | absolutely, categorically, completely, directly, totally, utterly, wholly | largely | actively, openly, publicly** *the party most openly opposed to military rule*

2 very different from sth
• VERBS **be, seem, stand | remain**
• ADV. **completely, diametrically, directly, entirely, fundamentally, utterly** *Our views are diametrically opposed on this issue.* | **mutually** *The two sets of values seemed mutually opposed.*
• PREP. **to** *The path he saw himself taking in his research seemed directly opposed to the ethos of the department.*

opposite *noun*

• ADJ. **complete, direct, exact, precise, very | polar**
• OPPOSITE + VERB **be the case, be true** *The oboe tends to lose power in the upper register, but with the clarinet the opposite is the case.*
• PREP. **the ~ of/to** *Doubt is not the opposite of faith—unbelief is.* ◊ *In temperament, she was the complete opposite to her sister.*
• PHRASES **exactly/just/quite the opposite** *The effect was exactly the opposite to what he intended.*

opposition *noun*

1 disagreeing with sth/trying to change it
• ADJ. **bitter, considerable, determined, fierce, stiff, strong, vehement | violent | growing, mounting | effective, powerful | direct** *a statement in direct opposition to party policy* | **active | organized | political | public | widespread**
• VERB + OPPOSITION **express | mount, put up** *They mounted an effective opposition to the bill.* | **arouse | crush, overcome, stifle, suppress, wear down | be/come/run up against, encounter, face, meet (with), run into** *He is up against stiff opposition from his colleagues.* | **brook** *We will brook no opposition to the strategy.* | **strengthen | weaken**
• OPPOSITION + VERB **come from sb** *Opposition came primarily from students.*
• OPPOSITION + NOUN **force, group, movement**
• PREP. **against/in the face of ~** *She won against determined opposition from last year's champion.* **despite/in spite of ~** *The authorities succeeded despite bitter opposition from teachers.* **in ~ to** *The warring factions had united in opposition to the common enemy.* | **~ from** *The proposals met with violent opposition from the environmental lobby.* **~ to** *There was fierce public opposition to the plan.*

2 (usually **the Opposition**) parties not in government

• OPPOSITION + NOUN **party | candidate,   leader, member, MP, politician, spokesman | bench**
• PREP. **in ~** *The Conservative Party is now in opposition.*
• PHRASES **the Leader of the Opposition**

oppression *noun*

• ADJ. **class, economic, political, racial, sexual | black, colonial, gay, women's | male**
• VERB + OPPRESSION **face, suffer** *ethnic minorities suffering oppression at the hands of occupying forces*

optician *noun*

• ADJ. **dispensing, ophthalmic** *A dispensing optician supplies glasses, but doesn't test your eyes.*
• PHRASES **at/to the optician's** *I've got to go to the optician's tomorrow.*
⇨ Note at DOCTOR (for verbs)

optimism *noun*

• ADJ. **considerable, great, tremendous | some | cautious, guarded | false, misplaced** *Her optimism turned out to be misplaced.* | **early, initial** *By 1960, the initial optimism had evaporated.* | **renewed**
• QUANT. **surge, wave** *The news caused a wave of optimism.* | **note** *There was a note of optimism in his voice.*
• VERB + OPTIMISM **express | share** *I find it hard to share his optimism.*
• OPTIMISM + VERB **prevail, reign** *Despite the crisis a cautious optimism prevailed.* | **evaporate**
• PREP. **with ~** *We can look to the future with considerable optimism.* | **~ about/over** *The government expressed optimism about the success of the negotiations.* **~ among** *renewed optimism among mortgage lenders* **~ for** *great optimism for the future*
• PHRASES **cause/grounds/reason for optimism** *There are now very real grounds for optimism.* **full of optimism** *The 1970s began still full of optimism.* **a mood/sense/spirit of optimism**

optimist *noun*

• ADJ. **eternal, incurable**
• PHRASES **ever the optimist** *Pete, ever the optimist, said things were bound to improve.*

optimistic *adj.*

• VERBS **appear, be, feel, look, seem, sound | become | remain**
• ADV. **extremely, highly, strongly, very** *He remained strongly optimistic that an agreement could be reached.* | **excessively, hopelessly, incredibly, overly, ridiculously, unduly, wildly** *These estimates were wildly optimistic.* | **a bit, fairly, a little, quite, rather, reasonably, somewhat | basically, essentially, generally** *an essentially optimistic view of human nature* | **cautiously, guardedly, quietly** *I don't want to exaggerate our chances, but I'm cautiously optimistic.* | **cheerfully**
• PREP. **about** *He's very optimistic about his chances.*

option *noun*

1 freedom to choose
• VERB + OPTION **have** *You have the option of taking your holiday early.* | **give sb**
• PREP. **with/without the ~ of** *He was jailed without the option of a fine.*
• PHRASES **have little/no option but to** *We had no option but to leave without them.*

2 sth you choose/can choose
• ADJ. **available, possible, viable | real, realistic | attractive, good** *Deciding on your best option is not easy.* | **preferred | practical | easy, soft** *He thought General*

Studies would be a soft option. | **cheap** | **expensive** | **policy** | **menu** (on a computer)

• VERB + OPTION **choose, exercise, select, take** *Look at the on-screen menu and select the 'File' option.* | **give sb, offer (sb)** | **limit** | **look at** *Let's look at all the options available.*

• PHRASES **keep/leave your options open** (= to avoid making a decision now so that you still have a choice later)

3 right to buy/sell sth at some time in the future
• ADJ. **first** | **share, stock**
• VERB + OPTION **have** | **exercise, take (up)** *She took up an option in her contract to buy three million shares.*
• PREP. **~on** *He's promised me first option on his car.*

optional *adj.*

• VERBS **be**
• ADV. **entirely, purely** *The extra language classes are entirely optional.*

orange *noun*

• ADJ. **juicy** | **sour, sweet** | **mouldy**
• QUANT. **segment**
• VERB + ORANGE **eat, have, squeeze** | **peel**
• ORANGE + NOUN **segment** | **pip** | **peel, rind, zest** *Add a little grated orange peel.* | **juice**
⇒ Special page at FRUIT

orange *adj.*

⇒ Special page at COLOUR

orbit *noun*

• ADJ. **circular, elliptical** | **eccentric** *Mercury's orbit is fairly eccentric.* | **stable** | **planetary**
• VERB + ORBIT **enter, go into** | **put/send sth into** | **complete, make** *The spaceship made an orbit of the moon.*
• PREP. **in~** *The satellite will remain in orbit for several years.* | **~ around/round** *the moon's orbit around the earth*

orchestra *noun*

• ADJ. **large, small** | **full** *The full orchestra includes two pairs of French horns.* | **great, top** | **amateur, professional** | **philharmonic, symphony** | **chamber, dance, jazz, string, wind** | **school, youth**
• VERB + ORCHESTRA **conduct** | **lead**
• ORCHESTRA + VERB **perform (sth), play (sth)** | **strike (sth) up** *The orchestra struck up a lively march.* | **tune up**
• ORCHESTRA + NOUN **pit**
• PREP. **in a/the~** *She plays viola in a string orchestra.* | **~under** *the Ulster Orchestra under Philip Ledger*
• PHRASES **the leader of the orchestra**

ordeal *noun*

• ADJ. **long** | **dreadful, terrible, terrifying**
• VERB + ORDEAL **endure, face, go through, suffer, undergo** | **subject sb to** *She was subjected to a terrible six-day ordeal.* | **survive** | **recover from** | **be spared**
• PREP. **~by** (*often humorous*) *This is the fourth time the prime minister has faced ordeal by egg* (= had eggs thrown at him). **~of** *They were spared the ordeal of giving evidence in court.*
• PHRASES **an ordeal at the hands of sb** *their 20-hour ordeal at the hands of a gunman*

order *noun*

1 way in which people/things are arranged
• ADJ. **correct, right** | **wrong** | **logical** *The paragraphs are not in a logical order.* | **ascending** *arranged in as-*

cending *order of size* | **descending** | **alphabetical, chronological, numerical, random, reverse** | **pecking** *the pecking order among the hospital staff* | **word**
• PREP. **in~** *The winners were announced in reverse order.* **in~of** *I've listed the tasks in order of priority.*

2 organized state
• ADJ. **apple-pie** (= perfect) *The accounts were in apple-pie order.*
• VERB + ORDER **bring, create, impose** *to bring order out of chaos* ◇ *She attempted to impose some order on the chaos of her files.* | **put/set sth in** | **leave sth in**
• PREP. **in~** *My notes are in order.*
• PHRASES **in good order** *The house is in good order.*

3 when laws, rules, authority, etc. are obeyed
• ADJ. **public**
• VERB + ORDER **keep, maintain, preserve** | **restore** | **keep sb/sth in** *Some teachers find it difficult to keep their classes in order.* | **call sb/sth to** *The argument continued until the chairman called them both to order* (= ordered them to obey the formal rules of the meeting).
• PREP. **in~** (= allowed by the rules) *Would it be in order for us to examine the manuscript?* **out of~** (= not allowed by the rules) *His objection was ruled out of order.*
• PHRASES **law and order, a point of order** *One of the committee members raised a point of order.*

4 way a society is arranged
• ADJ. **established, existing, old** *He was seen as a threat to the established order.* | **new** | **natural** *the natural order of things* | **economic, political, social** | **world** *a new world order*

5 instruction/demand
• ADJ. **direct, specific** | **executive** | **sealed** *He opened his sealed orders.* | **court** | **maintenance, preservation, restraining** *a wildlife preservation order*
• VERB + ORDER **give, issue, make** (*law*) *The captain gave the order to fire.* ◇ *The judge made an order for the costs to be paid.* | **receive** | **carry out, execute, follow, obey, take** *The local civilians don't take orders from the military.* | **disobey, ignore, violate** | **cancel, countermand, rescind, revoke** | **bark/bawl/shout (out)** *He barked out orders as he left.*
• PREP. **by~** *The council's functions were established by order.* **by~of** *by order of the police* **on sb's~s** *The ship was to set sail at once, on the admiral's orders.* **under~s (from)** *A group of soldiers, under orders from the president, took control of the television station.* | **~s for** *The colonel had given orders for the spy's execution.*
• PHRASES **doctor's orders** *I'm not to drink any alcohol—doctor's orders!* **get your marching orders** (= be ordered to leave), **give sb their marching orders**

6 request for sth to be made/supplied/delivered
• ADJ. **bulk, large, record** | **small** | **firm** | **advance** | **back, outstanding** | **repeat** | **tall** (= difficult to fulfil; unreasonable) | **mail, money, postal, standing** | **export**
• VERB + ORDER **place, put in** *I've placed an order for the CD.* | **cancel** | **receive, win** *The company won a £10 million order for oil-drilling equipment.* | **have** | **fill, fulfil, meet** *trying to fill all the back orders* | **make sth to** *a cupboard made to order*
• ORDER + NOUN **form**
• PREP. **on~** *We have ten boxes on order.* | **~for** *We have a firm order for ten cases of wine.*

7 request for food, etc. in a restaurant, etc.
• ADJ. **side** *a side order of mixed salad* | **last ~s** *Last orders at the bar now please!*
• VERB + ORDER **take** *The waiter came to take their orders.* | **give sb**
• PREP. **~for** *an order for steak and fries*

8 group of people living in a religious community
• ADJ. **monastic, religious** | **contemplative** | **closed** (= with little or no contact with the outside world) | **Benedictine, Cistercian, etc.**

order *verb*

1 tell sb to do sth
- ADV. **expressly, specifically | immediately | person-ally** *The army's Chief of Staff had personally ordered the raid.* | **formally | about, around** *Stop ordering me around!* | **back, home, off, out** *There were seven bookings and two players were ordered off.*
- PREP. **off, out of** *All journalists have been ordered out of the country.*

2 ask for sth
- ADV. **direct/directly**
- PREP. **for** *We can order the book for you, if you like.* **from** *You can order the book direct from the publisher.*

3 organize/arrange sth
- ADV. **alphabetically, chronologically, hierarchically, logically** *The entries are ordered alphabetically.*
- PREP. **according to** *Different senses of a word are ordered according to frequency.*
- PHRASES **highly/well ordered** *She led a highly ordered existence, with everything having its own time and place.*

orderly *adj.*
- VERBS **be**
- ADV. **very | fairly, more or less, relatively**
- PHRASES **in an orderly fashion/way** *We want to bring about this change in an orderly fashion.*

ordinary *adj.*
- VERBS **be, look, seem | become**
- ADV. **decidedly, terribly, very** *He made all the other players on the field look decidedly ordinary.* | **perfectly, quite** *It was a perfectly ordinary day.* | **fairly, pretty, rather** *The meal was pretty ordinary.* | **essentially**

ore *noun*
- ADJ. **rich | metal/metallic, mineral | copper, iron, uranium, etc.**
- QUANT. **lode, vein | lump**
- VERB + ORE **extract, mine | dress, extract sth from, refine, smelt** *smelting the ore with charcoal*
- ORE + NOUN **deposits**

organ *noun*

1 part of the body
- ADJ. **internal | important, vital** *The eyes are an important organ of balance.* ◇ *to preserve blood flow to the brain and the other vital organs* | **abdominal, genital | digestive, olfactory, reproductive, sense/sensory, sex/sexual, etc.** | **human | donor** *waiting for a suitable donor organ*
- VERB + ORGAN **donate | transplant**
- ORGAN + NOUN **donation, donor | transplant, transplantation**

2 musical instrument
- ADJ. **pipe | mechanical | electric, electronic, Hammond ™ | barrel, mouth | church, fairground**
- ORGAN + NOUN **pedal, pipe, stop | loft**
- ⇨ Special page at MUSIC

3 official organization
- ADJ. **central, major** *the central organs of state* | **administrative, constitutional, economic, judicial, legislative, political, security | party**

organic *adj.*
- VERBS **be | become, go**
- ADV. **fully, totally** *The farm went fully organic in 1996.*

organism *noun*
- ADJ. **developing, growing, living | simple | com-plex, complicated, higher | biological | human | aquatic, marine**

organization *noun*

1 organized group of people
- ADJ. **large, mass | small | community, internation-al, local, national | government, state | official | party, political | professional | non-governmental | grass-roots | voluntary | charitable, philanthropic | non-profit, not-for-profit | commercial, profit-making | en-vironmental, human rights, labour, relief | student, women's, youth | terrorist | umbrella | front** *a front or-ganization for drug trafficking*
- VERB + ORGANIZATION **disband** (For more verbs see note.)
- PREP. **in a/the~** *There are several talented people in that organization.*
- ⇨ Special page at BUSINESS

2 way in which sth is organized
- ADJ. **effective, efficient, smooth** *the smooth organiza-tion of the trip* | **poor | internal**
- QUANT. **degree** *a high degree of organization*
- VERB + ORGANIZATION **lack**

NOTE

Organizations

create, establish, form, found, set up, start~
    an association created to promote local industry
    The company was founded in 1981.
dissolve~ *(often law)*
    She sought a court order to have the partnership dissolved.
run~
    He runs an accountancy firm.
manage~
    The executive committee manages the group on a day-to-day basis.
be/become a member of, join~
    She became a member of the Society of Arts.
leave~
    The country plans to leave the organization.

---

organize *verb*
- ADV. **effectively, efficiently, properly, successfully, well | badly, poorly | carefully, neatly | locally, nation-ally | centrally | jointly** *They organized the festival joint-ly with the French cultural service.* | **separately | inde-pendently, privately | formally**
- VERB + ORGANIZE **seek to, try to | help (to) | be able to | manage to | fail to | learn (how) to | be diffi-cult to | be easy to, be possible to**
- PREP. **according to** *We need to organize the work ac-cording to the availability and skills of each volunteer.* **around** *We're organizing the evening around a Japanese theme.* **into** *It was difficult to organize the men into teams.*

organized *adj.*

1 arranged/planned
- VERBS **be, seem**
- ADV. **extremely, highly, strongly, very** *Although it doesn't look like it, the whole thing is highly organized.* | **carefully, efficiently, properly, superbly, well | badly, poorly | minutely, neatly | rigidly, tightly | loosely, weakly** *a loosely organized confederacy of allies* | **spe-cially** *a specially organized programme of sightseeing and shopping* | **centrally, locally, nationally | faintly | sep-arately | independently, privately | formally** *Often there is no formally organized system of childcare.* | **tradition-**

ally | systematically | hierarchically, sequentially *Each department is hierarchically organized.* | socially

2 able to plan things well

- VERBS **be, seem** | **get** *You need to get organized.*
- ADV. **extremely, highly, very** | **fairly**

orgasm *noun*

- ADJ. **female, male** | **multiple** | **simultaneous**
- VERB + ORGASM **achieve, have, reach** | **fake, simulate**

orgy *noun*

- ADJ. **drunken, sex/sexual**
- VERB + ORGY **have**
- PREP. **~of** *an orgy of looting and vandalism*

orientated *adj.*

- VERBS **be, seem** | **become** | **remain**
- ADV. **strongly, very** | **totally** | **sufficiently** | **correctly** *Make sure all the components remain correctly orientated.* | **academically, industrially, politically, technically, vocationally** *The organization is not politically orientated.*
- PREP. **to/towards** *The service is not sufficiently orientated to the needs of those who use it.*
- PHRASES **career/profit orientated** *She's very career orientated and not really interested in having a family.*

origin *noun*

1 time/place/reason that sth starts

- ADJ. **common** | **doubtful, obscure, unknown** *a letter of doubtful origin* | **true** | **ancient, early, primitive** | **recent** *The term 'black hole' is of very recent origin.* | **immediate** *The development had its immediate origins in discussions with management.* | **African, English, etc.** | **foreign** | **local** | **mixed** | **natural** | **supernatural** | **environmental, geographical, historical, intellectual** | **animal, human, mineral, plant, vegetable** *foods of animal origin* ◇ *We shouldn't forget our animal origins.*
- VERB + ORIGIN **have, share** *The vases share common origins.* | **investigate, trace** | **owe** *Population genetics owes its origin to Francis Galton.* | **explain** | **reflect**
- ORIGIN + VERB **go back to sth, lie in sth** *The origins of Gdańsk go back to the tenth century.*
- PREP. **in~** *The rock is volcanic in origin.* **of ... ~** *a painting of unknown origin*
- PHRASES **sth's country of origin** *Bottles are labelled by country of origin.* **have its origin in sth** *The dispute had its origin in the Battle of Wakefield.*

2 family, race, class, etc, that a person comes from

- ADJ. **African, English, etc.** | **foreign** | **mixed** | **class, ethnic, national, racial, social** | **noble, middle-class, peasant, slave, working-class** | **humble, lowly** *He had risen from humble origins through hard work.*
- VERB + ORIGIN **trace** *Their family can trace its origins back to the Norman Conquest.* | **betray** *Her accent betrayed her working-class origins.*
- PREP. **by~** *He is a Londoner by origin.* **in~** *Her family is Portuguese in origin.* **of ... ~** *He was of lowly origins.*
- PHRASES **sb's country of origin**

original *noun*

- VERB + ORIGINAL **pass sth off as** *He copied paintings of famous artists and passed them off as originals.*
- PREP. **in the~** *to read Tolstoy in the original*

original *adj.*

- VERBS **be**
- ADV. **extremely, highly, startlingly, very** *She has a*

highly original mind. ◇ *a startlingly original idea* | **completely** *tackling the problem in a completely original way*

originality *noun*

- ADJ. **great, startling, striking**
- VERB + ORIGINALITY **have** | **display, show** | **be lacking in, lack**
- ORIGINALITY + VERB **lie in sth** *His originality as a painter lies in his representation of light.*
- PREP. **~in** *The government has shown great originality in its foreign policy.*
- PHRASES **a spark of originality**

ornamental *adj.*

- VERBS **be**
- ADV. **highly, very** *a plant which is highly ornamental in flower* | **purely** *The turrets are purely ornamental.*

ornate *adj.*

- VERBS **be**
- ADV. **highly, richly, very** | **quite, rather**

orphan *noun*

- ADJ. **little** | **poor** *a poor little orphan* | **war**
- VERB + ORPHAN **be left** *She was left an orphan at the age of five.* | **adopt**
- ORPHAN + NOUN **boy, girl**

orthodox *adj.*

- VERBS **be** *His ideas are all fairly orthodox.*
- ADV. **highly, strictly, very** *This is the strictly orthodox view.* ◇ *I am not a very orthodox kind of counsellor.* | **fairly**

orthodoxy *noun*

- ADJ. **rigid, strict** | **prevailing** | **Catholic, Christian, etc.** | **communist, liberal, etc.** | **party** | **economic, scientific, etc.**

ounce *noun*

⇨ Note at MEASURE

outbreak *noun*

- ADJ. **large, major, serious** | **fresh, further, new** | **occasional, periodic, sporadic** | **recurrent, repeated** | **sudden** | **cholera, salmonella, etc.**
- VERB + OUTBREAK **lead to** *the events that led to the outbreak of World War I*
- OUTBREAK + VERB **occur**
- PREP. **~of** *A new outbreak of smallpox occurred in 1928.*
- PHRASES **an outbreak of disease, an outbreak of rain, an outbreak of war/fighting/hostilities/violence**

outburst *noun*

- ADJ. **sudden** | **spontaneous** | **occasional** *her occasional outbursts of temper* | **angry, furious, violent** | **emotional, hysterical, passionate**
- PREP. **~against** *A player was cautioned for his angry outburst against the referee.* **~of** *an outburst of anger/laughter/temper/violence*

outcast *noun*

- ADJ. **social** *He was treated as a social outcast.*
- VERB + OUTCAST **make sb** *Her criminal past made her an outcast.* | **treat sb as/like**
- PREP. **~from** *an outcast from society*

outcome *noun*

- ADJ. **desirable, desired, favourable, good, happy,**

positive, satisfactory, successful | negative, unfortunate, unsatisfactory | fatal, tragic | possible | likely, probable | anticipated, expected, inevitable, intended, logical, predicted | unexpected | immediate | actual, eventual, final, long-term, ultimate | direct *a direct outcome of the strike* | practical | educational, electoral, political, etc. *(all technical)*
- VERB + OUTCOME **affect, influence | decide, determine | achieve, have, produce** *Their strategy produced the desired outcome.* | **evaluate, measure** *(technical) The aim is to evaluate possible outcomes.*
- PREP. **~of** *the outcome of the election*
- PHRASES **whatever the outcome** *Whatever the final outcome of the talks, the war should end soon.*

outcry *noun*

- ADJ. **great, huge, massive | immediate | popular, public | national | international**
- VERB + OUTCRY **cause, provoke, spark** *The bombing caused an international outcry.*
- PREP. **~against/over** *There was a massive public outcry against the harsh prison sentence.* **~ from** *an immediate outcry from workers over pay reductions*

outfit *noun*

1 set of clothes worn together
- ADJ. **complete | new | summer, winter | interview, party, wedding, etc. | clown, cowboy, etc.**
- PREP. **in a/the~** *He looked very smart in his new outfit.*

2 organization/company, etc.
- ADJ. **large | small | professional | cowboy, dodgy | computer, publishing, etc.**

outing *noun*

- ADJ. **little | special | day's, summer, weekend | annual | family, school, social**
- VERB + OUTING **be/go on**
- PREP. **~ from** *The children were on a day's outing from school.* **~to** *a family outing to the seaside*

outlay *noun*

- ADJ. **considerable, huge, large, massive | modest, small | initial** *The revenue from the farm could repay the initial outlay within three years.* | **total | capital, cash, financial, investment**
- VERB + OUTLAY **make | require** *The project would require little financial outlay.* | **recoup, recover | repay**
- PREP. **~ on** *The railway had made a considerable capital outlay on new rolling stock.*

outlet *noun*

1 place that sells goods of a particular company/type
- ADJ. **specialist | high-street, local | commercial, distribution, retail, sales | DIY, fast-food, etc.**
- PREP. **~for** *a retail outlet for exotic plants*

2 means of releasing energy/strong feeling/talents
- ADJ. **emotional | creative**
- VERB + OUTLET **have | find | provide (sb with)** *Sport provided an outlet for his energy.* | **need**
- PREP. **~ for** *She needs an outlet for her talents.*

3 pipe/hole
- ADJ. **electrical, gas, sewage, socket, waste, water**
- OUTLET + NOUN **hose, pipe**

outline *noun*

1 line that shows the shape/outside edge of sb/sth
- ADJ. **clear, sharp** *The sharp outline of the island had become blurred.* | **blurred, dim, faint, vague | simple**
- VERB + OUTLINE **draw, make, trace** *The children made an outline of their hands.* | **make out, see** *I could*

just make out the dim outlines of the house in the mist. | **soften**
- OUTLINE + NOUN **drawing, map**
- PREP. **around/round the~** *to cut round the outline* **in ~** *He sketched the street in outline only.* | **~of**

2 most important facts/ideas about sth
- ADJ. **bare, basic, brief, rough** *a brief outline of Polish history* | **broad, general | course**
- VERB + OUTLINE **give (sb), provide (sb with), write (sb)** *Write an outline for your essay.*
- PREP. **in~** *Here's the plan in outline.* | **~for, ~of**

outline *verb*

- ADV. **briefly | clearly | roughly** *He roughly outlined the plot of the opera.* | **here | above, earlier, previously** *using the plan outlined above* | **below**
- VERB + OUTLINE **attempt to, seek to, try to**
- PREP. **to** *the policies outlined to Parliament on May 20th*

outlook *noun*

1 attitude to life
- ADJ. **optimistic, positive | negative, pessimistic | general | broad** *Having children gave her a broader outlook on life.* | **different, differing | mental | moral, philosophical, religious**
- VERB + OUTLOOK **have | give sb | change | broaden** *Travel broadens your outlook.*
- PREP. **in~** *She is rather cautious in outlook.* **of (a) ... ~** *people of widely differing religious outlooks* | **~on** *Losing his job changed his whole outlook on life.*

2 what will probably happen
- ADJ. **bright, good | bleak, gloomy, grim** *The outlook for people on a state pension is grim.* | **uncertain | business, economic, political | long-term, short-term**
- VERB + OUTLOOK **improve** *The drug improves the long-term outlook of migraine sufferers.* | **worsen**
- PREP. **~ for** *a brighter outlook for the economy*

outnumber *verb*

- ADV. **considerably, easily, far, greatly, heavily, substantially, vastly** *Their failures vastly outnumber their successes.* | **almost | slightly**
- PREP. **by** *The Czechs outnumbered the Slovaks by at least two to one.*
- PHRASES **be hopelessly outnumbered** *The Spanish were hopelessly outnumbered in the battle.*

output *noun*

- ADJ. **high, large, massive | greater, increased | steady | low | aggregate, gross, overall, total** *10 per cent of the country's total output* | **net | real | average | annual, monthly, etc. | maximum | current | national, world | prodigious, prolific** *her prodigious literary output* | **agricultural, industrial, manufacturing | computer, data | literary**
- QUANT. **level** *changes in the level of output*
- VERB + OUTPUT **produce | double, expand, increase** *The plant plans to increase output to 10 000 cars a year.* | **reduce**
- OUTPUT + VERB **increase, rise | decrease, fall**
- PREP. **~of** *a steady output of new ideas*
- PHRASES **a drop/fall in output** *the fall in output due to outdated equipment*, **a growth/an increase/a rise in output**

outrage *noun*

1 great anger
- ADJ. **genuine | widespread | international | public | moral** *Media reports generated moral outrage.*
- VERB + OUTRAGE **be greeted with, cause, generate, provoke, spark** *The news was greeted with outrage.* | **feel**

| **express**, **voice** *Shopkeepers voiced their outrage at the new tax.*
• OUTRAGE + VERB **be directed at sb/sth** *Much of the outrage was directed at foreign nationals.*
• PREP. **in**~ *The guests all shouted in outrage.* **with**~ *She was trembling with outrage.* | **~ at** *Campaigners have expressed outrage at the decision.* **~ over** *There is widespread public outrage over the massacre.*
• PHRASES **cries/howls of outrage** *The announcement provoked howls of outrage.* **a feeling/sense of outrage**

2 cruel/shocking act
• VERB + OUTRAGE **commit**, **perpetrate** *the outrages committed by the invading army*
• PREP. **~ against** *The new law on pensions is an outrage against the elderly.*

outrageous *adj.*

• VERBS **be** | **consider sth**, **regard sth as**, **see sth as**, **think sth** *She thought it absolutely outrageous that he should be promoted over her.*
• ADV. **absolutely**, **completely**, **quite**, **totally** | **morally**

outsider *noun*

1 not a member of a group
• ADJ. **complete** | **political**, **social**
• VERB + OUTSIDER **feel** *I felt a complete outsider.*
• PREP. **~ to** *an outsider to the group*
2 competitor who will probably not win
• ADJ. **complete**, **rank**
• PREP. **~ in** *The firm has gone from being an outsider in the market to being a market leader.*

outskirts *noun*

• ADJ. **sprawling** | **city** | **northern**, etc.
• VERB + OUTSKIRTS **reach**
• PREP. **in the ~** *a school in the outskirts of Athens* **on the ~** *We live on the outskirts of Leeds.* **through the ~** *driving through the outskirts of London*

outstanding *adj.*

1 excellent
• VERBS **be** | **consider sth**
• ADV. **particularly**, **really**, **truly** | **absolutely**, **quite** *That was a quite outstanding performance!*
2 not yet paid or done
• VERBS **be**, **remain** *Two or three tasks still remain outstanding.* | **leave sth** *One option may be to leave the debt outstanding and extend the payment terms.*
• ADV. **still** *75 per cent of the amount originally borrowed is still outstanding.*

outweigh *verb*

• ADV. **considerably**, **easily**, **far**, **greatly**, **heavily**, **more than**, **vastly** *The benefits would surely far outweigh the risks.* ◊ *The advantages of this scheme more than outweigh the costs involved.*

oval *adj.*

• VERBS **be**
• ADV. **perfectly** *her delicate, perfectly oval face* | **almost** *The leaves are long and almost oval.*
• PHRASES **oval in shape** *The handle is oval in shape* **oval-shaped** *an oval-shaped box*

ovation *noun*

• ADJ. **enthusiastic**, **huge**, **long**, **loud**, **rapturous**, **thunderous** | **standing** *The audience gave her a standing ovation for her performance.*
• VERB + OVATION **give sb** | **get**, **receive** *He received*

the longest ovation of the evening. | **bring**, **earn**, **win**
• PREP. **to an ~** *He came off the field to a huge ovation.* | **~ from** *The final piece won her a rapturous ovation from the audience.*

oven *noun*

• ADJ. **electric**, **gas**, **microwave** | **hot**, **low**, **moderate**, **warm** *Bake them in a warm oven until risen and golden brown.* | **preheated** | **combination**, **convection**, **conventional**, **fan-assisted** | **domestic** | **self-cleaning** | **bread** | **clay** *Tandoori food is cooked in a clay oven.*
• VERB + OVEN **light**, **switch on**, **turn on** | **heat**, **preheat** *Preheat the oven to 190°C.* | **bake sth in**, **cook sth in** | **put sth in** | **remove sth from**, **take sth out of** | **clean**
• OVEN + VERB **heat (up)** *Switch on the oven and let it heat up.* | **cool (down)**
• OVEN + NOUN **dish** | **glove** | **temperature** | **door**, **rack** | **timer** | **cleaner** | **chips**
• PREP. **in an/the ~** *baking bread in the oven*
⇨ Special page at FOOD

overcast *adj.*

• VERBS **be**, **look** | **become** *The sky became heavily overcast.* | **remain**, **stay**
• ADV. **heavily**, **very**

overcoat *noun*

• ADJ. **long** | **heavy**, **thick** | **dark** | **tweed**
⇨ Special page at CLOTHES

overcome *verb*

1 defeat/conquer sb/sth
• ADV. **completely** | **successfully** | **not entirely** *These problems were never entirely overcome.* | **largely** | **partially** | **easily** | **quickly**, **gradually** | **eventually**, **finally** *He eventually overcame his disability.*
• VERB + OVERCOME **be able to** | **help (to)**, **help sb (to)** *Therapy helped her overcome her fear.* | **be designed to** *methods designed to overcome these problems* | **attempt to**, **battle to**, **struggle to**, **try to** | **manage to**
• PHRASES **an attempt to overcome sth**
2 be/feel overcome become weak/ill; lose control
• ADV. **completely**, **quite** *She felt quite overcome by their kindness.* | **almost**, **nearly** *She felt almost overcome by a tide of relief.* | **visibly** *The officers on duty were visibly overcome, many of them in tears.* | **suddenly**
• PREP. **by** *Several firefighters had been overcome by smoke and fumes.* **with** *He was suddenly overcome with remorse for the harm he had done.*

overcrowded *adj.*

• VERBS **be** | **become**, **get**
• ADV. **extremely**, **grossly**, **severely**, **very** | **a little**

overdose *noun*

• ADJ. **large**, **massive** | **drug/drugs**, **heroin**, **paracetamol**, etc. | **fatal** | **accidental**
• VERB + OVERDOSE **take** | **die from/of**
• PREP. **~ of** *She took an overdose of paracetamol.*

overdraft *noun*

• ADJ. **enormous**, **huge**, **large** | **agreed**, **authorized** | **unauthorized** | **free** *We offer a free £400 overdraft.* | **bank**
• VERB + OVERDRAFT **have** | **get**, **take out** | **run up** *The president ran up a huge overdraft during her year in office.* | **arrange** | **extend**, **give sb**, **offer (sb)** | **pay off** | **increase** | **reduce** | **exceed** *They exceeded their overdraft by £200 000.*
• OVERDRAFT + NOUN **facility** | **limit**

overdrawn adj.

- VERBS be | go *I never like to go overdrawn if I can help it.* | remain
- ADV. badly, very | rather, slightly, somewhat

overdue adj.

- VERBS be | become
- ADV. long *These reforms are long overdue.*
- PREP. for *This system is overdue for reform.*
- PHRASES months/weeks/years overdue *These changes are years overdue.*

overestimate verb

- ADV. considerably, greatly, grossly, seriously, vastly | consistently *The Ministry of Finance consistently overestimated its budget deficits.*
- VERB + OVERESTIMATE tend to | be easy to *It is easy to overestimate the cost of this kind of research.* | be difficult to, be hard to
- PREP. by *We overestimated the cost by about 2 per cent.*
- PHRASES sth cannot be overestimated *The importance of this group cannot be overestimated.*

overgrown adj.

- VERBS be, look | become, get
- ADV. extremely, thickly, very | completely *The path was completely overgrown.*
- PREP. with *The canal bank was thickly overgrown with last year's brambles.*

overhaul noun

- ADJ. complete, major, massive, thorough | radical
- VERB + OVERHAUL have, undergo *The tax system has undergone a complete overhaul.* | give sth | need

overhaul verb

- ADV. drastically, radically *Within a year the party had drastically overhauled its structure.* | completely, thoroughly *The plan was completely overhauled.*

overhead adj., adv.

- VERBS be | appear, circle, fly, gather, hover, pass, soar, wheel *The seagulls circled overhead.* ◇ *Storm clouds were gathering overhead.* | buzz, roar, scream, whirr *Helicopters buzzed overhead.* | shine
- ADV. directly *The storm must be directly overhead.* | nearly | high *The moon was high overhead.* | low *aircraft passing low overhead*

overhear verb

- ADV. accidentally
- PHRASES couldn't help overhearing sth *Excuse me for interrupting, but I couldn't help overhearing what you were saying.*

overjoyed adj.

- VERBS be, look, seem, sound
- ADV. less than, not exactly *She was not exactly overjoyed to see us again.*
- PREP. about *They're all overjoyed about it.* at *overjoyed at the thought of having a son* by *We are overjoyed by this decision.* with *Mr Crangle was overjoyed with his success.*

overlap verb

- ADV. almost | partially, partly, slightly, to some extent *Put the two pieces of paper together so that they overlap slightly.* ◇ *The two categories overlap to some extent.* | clearly

- PREP. in *terms which overlap slightly in meaning* with *a world which overlaps with the newspaper world*

overload verb

- PREP. with *Their staff are heavily overloaded with work.*
- PHRASES be heavily/seriously overloaded

overlook verb

- ADV. completely, entirely | largely | frequently, often | generally | conveniently *Conveniently overlooking the fact that she wouldn't be able to meet the commitment, she agreed enthusiastically.*
- VERB + OVERLOOK cannot, cannot afford to, should not *We should not overlook this possibility.* | be inclined to, tend to *Hospitals have tended to overlook this need.* | seem to | be prepared to, be willing to *I was prepared to overlook her mistakes this time.* | be easy to *It is easy to overlook the significance of this change.* | be impossible to
- PHRASES be easily overlooked *another fact which is all too easily overlooked* sth should not be overlooked *The importance of this should not be overlooked.*

oversee verb

- ADV. directly | personally *He personally oversaw the design of all the rooms.*
- VERB + OVERSEE be appointed to, be created to, be set up to *A committee has been appointed to oversee the work.*
- PHRASES be responsible for overseeing sth *the committee that is responsible for overseeing the day-to-day implementation of this policy*

oversight noun

- ADJ. unfortunate
- PREP. by (an)~ *By an oversight, we did not send out the agenda for the meeting.* due to (an)~ *The mistake was due to an unfortunate oversight on my part.* through (an)~ *Through oversight, the bill was still unpaid.*

overthrow noun

- ADJ. attempted | violent
- VERB + OVERTHROW bring about, lead to | plot
- PREP. ~of *to bring about the overthrow of the military dictatorship*

overtime noun

- ADJ. excessive *Doctors work excessive unpaid overtime.* | unlimited | paid, unpaid
- VERB + OVERTIME do, put in, work *I do about five hours' overtime a week.* ◇ *She puts in a lot of overtime.*
- OVERTIME + NOUN earnings, pay, payments, rates | ban *The union imposed an overtime ban in protest at the sacking of two workers.*

overtone noun

- ADJ. strong *a play with strong religious overtones* | serious | negative *The word 'cheap' has negative overtones.* | emotional, moral, political, racial, religious, sexual | racist
- VERB + OVERTONE carry, have | take on *The organization's cultural activities took on political overtones.*

overture noun

1 (usually **overtures**) friendly behaviour
- ADJ. friendly | diplomatic, peace, sexual
- VERB + OVERTURE make | receive | respond to | reject, spurn *She spurned his overtures of love.*

● PREP. **~s of** *overtures of friendship* **~s to** *He made friendly overtures to his new neighbours.*
2 piece of music
● ADJ. **operatic, symphonic**
● PREP. **~to** *the overture to Mozart's 'Don Giovanni'*

overturn *verb*

● ADV. **completely** *She completely overturned my preconceptions about film stars.*
● VERB + OVERTURN **seek to, try to** *seeking to overturn his conviction for armed robbery* | **fail to**
● PHRASES **be easily overturned** *This argument seems convincing, but is easily overturned.*

overview *noun*

● ADJ. **brief, short | broad, general | complete, comprehensive | detailed, in-depth | critical | balanced | historical** *The opening chapter gives a brief historical overview of transport.*
● VERB + OVERVIEW **give (sb), offer (sb), present, provide (sb with) | have** *Only the Head of Sales has an overview of the situation worldwide.*
● PREP. **~on** *The seminar aims to provide an overview on new media publishing.*

overweight *adj.*

● VERBS **be, look** *You don't look overweight.* | **become, get** *Don't let yourself get overweight.*
● ADV. **extremely, grossly, heavily, seriously, very | a bit, a little, rather, slightly**
● PHRASES **a few pounds, two stone, etc. overweight**

overwhelm *verb*

● ADV. **completely, totally | almost | suddenly**
● VERB + OVERWHELM **threaten to** *Deal with stress fast whenever it threatens to overwhelm you.*
● PREP. **with** *The children pressed around him eagerly, overwhelming him with questions.*
● PHRASES **be/feel overwhelmed (by/with sth)** *We were totally overwhelmed by the response to our appeal.* ◇ *She felt completely overwhelmed.*

overwhelming *adj.*

● VERBS **be, seem | become**
● ADV. **completely, quite | almost** *The urge to look was almost overwhelming.* | **a little, pretty** *All these new experiences were a little overwhelming.* | **apparently, seemingly** *seemingly overwhelming obstacles*

owl *noun*

● ADJ. **wise | stuffed**
● OWL + VERB **fly | hoot, screech | catch sth, prey on sth** *Owls prey on small rodents.* | **nest, roost**
● OWL + NOUN **pellet**

own *verb*

● ADV. **communally, jointly** *Only when the means of production were communally owned would classes disappear.*

◇ *She owns the house jointly with her husband.* | **legally** *He committed the crime with a gun that he legally owned.*
● PHRASES **directly/indirectly owned by sb, own your own boat, home, etc.** *They dreamed of owning their own home.* **partly/wholly owned by sb** *The company is a wholly owned subsidiary of SNL Research.* **privately/publicly owned** *The museum is privately owned.*

owner *noun*

● ADJ. **sole | part** *I'm part owner of the restaurant.* | **joint | former, original, previous | current, present | new | future, prospective | lawful, legal, rightful** *The stolen painting has now been returned to its rightful owner.* | **private | lucky, proud** *the proud owner of a new stereo* | **car, dog, factory, home, land**
● VERB + OWNER **have** *The car had only one previous owner.* | **trace** *The police have been unable to trace the owner of the vehicle.*

ownership *noun*

● ADJ. **full | sole | collective, common, joint, shared | new | legal | private | corporate | public, state | foreign | car, home, land**
● VERB + OWNERSHIP **change, transfer** *The shop has changed ownership several times.* ◇ *He transferred the legal ownership of his property to his children.* | **pass into** *The railways passed into public ownership.* | **acquire, seize, take (over) | retain**
● OWNERSHIP + VERB **pass** *Ownership of the land passed from father to son.*
● PREP. **under (the)~** *The cafe is under new ownership.*
● PHRASES **a change in ownership**

oxygen *noun*

● ADJ. **pure | liquid | atmospheric**
● VERB + OXYGEN **carry, contain** *the blood which carries oxygen to the brain* | **absorb, breathe, consume, take in, use up | generate, produce, release** *After dark the plants stop producing oxygen.* | **administer, give sb | get, receive** *The patient didn't seem to be getting enough oxygen.* | **deprive sb/sth of, starve sb/sth of** *There was a risk the brain might be starved of oxygen.*
● OXYGEN + NOUN **atom | level, supply | mask**
● PHRASES **a lack of oxygen, a supply of oxygen**

ozone *noun*

● VERB + OZONE **deplete, destroy**
● OZONE + NOUN **levels | depletion, destruction, loss | hole | pollution**
● PHRASES **the loss of/reduction in ozone** *the discovery of massive springtime reductions in ozone over Antarctica*

ozone layer *noun*

● VERB + OZONE LAYER **be damaging to, damage, deplete, destroy | protect**
● OZONE LAYER + VERB **thin | disappear** *The ozone layer is disappearing over northern Europe.*
● PHRASES **damage to the ozone layer, depletion/destruction of the ozone layer, a hole in the ozone layer**

Pp

pace noun

1 one step
- VERB + PACE **take** *Take two paces forward.* | **step back** *Step back three paces.*
- PREP. **~ behind** *Two bodyguards remained a couple of paces behind the president throughout the walkabout.* **~ from** *I stopped a few paces from the edge of the cliff.*

2 speed
- ADJ. **blistering, breakneck, breathtaking, brisk, cracking, fast, frantic, frenetic, frenzied, furious, good, great, hectic, lightning, lively, rapid | gentle, leisurely, relaxed, slow, unhurried, walking** *the slow pace of economic reform* | **even, measured, moderate, steady**
- VERB + PACE **gather, increase, quicken** *The project had a slow start, but is now gathering pace.* ◇ *Thinking that she was being followed, she quickened her pace.* | **slacken, slow down | dictate, set** *Brown set the pace in the first mile.* | **keep (up), maintain** *The younger children struggled to keep pace with the older ones.* ◇ *She kept up a pace of ten miles an hour.* | **stand** *You shouldn't have such a job if you can't stand the pace.*
- PACE + VERB **increase | slow**
- PREP. **at a ... ~** *They set off at a cracking pace.* | **~ of** *The pace of change means that equipment has to be constantly replaced.* ◇ *The pace of life is much slower on the islands.*
- PHRASES **at sb's own pace** *The students work at their own pace.* **at a snail's pace** *I set off at a snail's pace to conserve my energy for later in the race.* **a change of pace** *I try to get away at weekends for a change of pace.* **a turn of pace** *He's a skilful player with a good turn of pace.*

pace verb

- ADV. **slowly | anxiously, nervously, restlessly** *She paced restlessly up and down.* | **about/around/round, back and forth, to and fro, up and down** *He paced slowly back and forth.*
- VERB + PACE **begin to**
- PREP. **about, around/round**
- PHRASES **begin pacing** *She began pacing round the room.*

pack noun

1 things put together for carrying
- ADJ. **heavy**
- VERB + PACK **carry**
- PACK + NOUN **animal, horse, mule**
- PREP. **in a/the ~** *The water in his pack made it very heavy.*

2 things supplied together
- ADJ. **cigarette | battery, power | gift, sample | action, information, resource, starter, study, training**
- PACK + VERB **contain sth, include sth** *Your resource pack includes addresses of leading manufacturers.*
- PREP. **in a/the~** *How many needles are there in a pack?* | **~ of** *It comes in packs of six.* ◇ *a pack of cigarettes*

3 group of animals
- ADJ. **wolf | hunting**
- VERB + PACK **lead**
- PACK + NOUN **instinct**
- PREP. **in a/the ~** *the dominant animal in the pack* **in ~s** *The animals hunt in packs.* | **~ of** *a pack of dogs/wolves*
- PHRASES **the leader of the pack**

4 playing cards
- VERB + PACK **shuffle | cut**
- PREP. **in a/the ~** *There are 52 playing cards in a pack.*
- PHRASES **the bottom/top of the pack** *Take a card from the top of the pack.* **a pack of cards**

pack verb

1 put things into containers
- ADV. **carefully | tightly** *Live animals are transported across the continent, packed tightly into lorries.* | **away, together, up** *The passengers travelled packed together like cattle.* ◇ *I think we might as well pack up and go home.*
- PREP. **in, into** *She packed her clothes into a suitcase.*

2 fill a place/sth
- PREP. **into** *Crowds of people packed into the hall.*
- PHRASES **be packed full of sth** *Our new brochure is packed full of inspirational ideas.* **be packed out** *The cinema was packed out!* **be packed to bursting/capacity/overflowing** *The hall was packed to capacity.* **be packed to the gunwales/rafters** *The hostel was packed to the rafters.* **be packed with sb** *The place was packed with football fans.* **closely/densely/tightly packed**

package noun

1 parcel
- ADJ. **bulky | neat | suspect, suspicious** *Police destroyed the suspect package in a controlled explosion.*
- VERB + PACKAGE **unwrap, wrap | post, send | deliver | sign for**
- PACKAGE + VERB **contain**
- PREP. **in a/the~** *I sent the books in one big package.*

2 set of proposals
- ADJ. **complete, comprehensive, total | attractive, excellent | reform | benefits, compensation, financial, remuneration** *a comprehensive benefits package* | **redundancy | aid, assistance, austerity, economic, recovery, rescue | jobs | training**
- VERB + PACKAGE **offer, produce, put together** *The IMF has put together a rescue package for the country's faltering economy.* | **accept, approve | reject**
- PACKAGE + VERB **contain sth, include sth | be aimed at sth** *a jobs package aimed at helping the unemployed*
- PACKAGE + NOUN **holiday, tour | deal**
- PREP. **in a/the~** *the measures included in the package* **under a/the ~** *Under the reform package spending on health will increase.* | **~ of** *a package of measures to assist industry*
- PHRASES **part of a package** *The pay freeze forms part of a package of budget cuts.*

3 computer software
- ADJ. **software | integrated** *an integrated business software package* | **application, desktop publishing, drawing, graphics, word-processing | accounting, business**
- VERB + PACKAGE **use | develop**
- PREP. **in a/the~** *word processing and database software in one package*

packaging noun

- ADJ. **fancy, glossy** *CDs would be far cheaper to produce without the glossy packaging.* | **discarded, waste | non-recyclable, recyclable | drinks, food, product, etc.**
- VERB + PACKAGING **recycle**

• PACKAGING + NOUN **materials | technology | waste | company, firm, group, manufacturer | industry**

packet noun

• ADJ. **empty | cereal, cigarette, cornflake, crisp, seed | pay, wage** *a weekly pay packet* (= wage) *of £200*
• VERB + PACKET **open, undo | take sth from/out of**
• PACKET + VERB **contain sth** *a packet containing seeds*
• PACKET + NOUN **soup**
• PREP. **on a/the~** *Follow the instructions on the packet.* | **~of** *a packet of crisps*

packing noun

• VERB + PACKING **do** *When shall we do the packing?*
• PACKING + NOUN **case**
• PHRASES **postage and packing** *All prices include postage and packing.*

pact noun

• ADJ. **bilateral, mutual | defence, military, security | non-aggression, peace | electoral, political, social, trade | suicide**
• VERB + PACT **have | conclude, enter into, form, make, strike** *The Social Democrats struck an electoral pact with the Liberals.* | **sign | break**
• PREP. **in a/the~** *She died with her lover in a suicide pact.* **under a/the ~** *conditions under the recently signed non-aggression pact* | **~between** *a defence pact between Pakistan and France* **~with** *He made a pact with the devil.*

pad noun

• ADJ. **memo, message, note | drawing, sketch**
• PREP. **on a/the~** *She doodled on a pad as she spoke.*

pad verb

1 be padded be filled/covered with soft material
• ADV. **heavily, thickly** *She was wearing a warm coat and thickly padded gloves.* | **lightly**
• PREP. **with** *The shoulder straps are padded with foam.*

2 move quietly
• ADV. **silently, softly | barefoot | about/around**
• PREP. **about/around** *padding softly around the house* **across** *padding barefoot across the carpet* **along** *The cat padded silently along the track.* **to, towards**

paddle verb

• ADV. **downstream, upstream | frantically, furiously** *He paddled furiously against the current.* | **slowly**

page noun

• ADJ. **back, front | facing, opposite** *There's a photo of him on the opposite page/on the page opposite.* | **left-hand, right-hand | next, previous | opening | new** *Write each answer on a new page.* | **blank, empty | full | loose | dog-eared | printed** *The speech did not transfer well to the printed page.* | **contents, title | business, editorial, financial, sports** (all in a newspaper) | **problem** *reading the problem pages of magazines*
• VERB + PAGE **read | scan | turn (over), turn to** *I turned the dog-eared pages of my old address book.* ◇ *Turn to page 30 in the coursebook.* | **flick through, flip through, leaf through** *She sat idly flipping through the pages of a fashion magazine.* | **tear (out) | splash sth across** *The headlines were splashed across the front page of every newspaper.*
• PAGE + VERB **come loose** *Several pages had come loose.* | **yellow** *the yellowing pages of her old diary*
• PAGE + NOUN **number | layout, make-up**
• PREP. **at (a/the)~** *Open your books at page 14.* **in the~s** *The murder takes place in the opening pages of the novel.* **on a/the~** *The crossword is on the back page.* **over the~** *The article continues over the page.*
• PHRASES **at the bottom/foot of the page, at the head/top of the page** *Write your name at the top of each page.* **pages long** *The story is thirty pages long.* **run your eye/finger down a page** *I ran my finger down the page until I found the name I was looking for.*

paid adj.

• VERBS **be**
• ADV. **highly, well** *a well-paid job* | **badly, poorly** *poorly paid workers*

pain noun

1 physical pain
• ADJ. **acute, agonizing, awful, excruciating, extreme, great, intense, severe, sharp, terrible, unbearable | burning, searing, shooting, stabbing, throbbing** *She had a burning pain in one eye.* | **dull, little, slight | chronic, constant, nagging, persistent | sudden | intermittent | physical | abdominal, back, chest, leg, muscle, shoulder, stomach** *She's been off work with back pain.* ◇ *He went to the doctor with chest pains.* | **growing, labour, period**
• QUANT. **spasm, stab**
• VERB + PAIN **be in, be racked with, experience, feel, get, go through, have, suffer (from)** *He was obviously in a great deal of pain.* ◇ *Can you feel any pain?* ◇ *Marathon runners are used to going through pain.* ◇ *He was taken to hospital suffering from severe abdominal pain.* | **cause, give sb, inflict** *His back gives him great pain.* ◇ *It's wrong to inflict pain on any animal.* | **increase, make worse | alleviate, control, deaden, do something for, dull, ease, help, kill, relieve, stop** *Your doctor should be able to do something for the pain.* | **bear, endure, put up with, stand, take | cry out in, cry with, groan with, scream with | be contorted with, contort in** *His face was contorted with pain as he crossed the finish line.*
• PAIN + VERB **begin, come** *The pains began shortly after she started work as a gardener.* | **shoot through/up** *A sharp pain shot up his leg.* | **grow stronger, increase, intensify | disappear, go, stop, wear off** *Has the pain gone yet?* ◇ *A few hours after he'd had his tooth out, the pain began to wear off.* | **come back, return**
• PAIN + NOUN **control, relief | threshold**
• PREP. **~in** *a pain in her side*
• PHRASES **aches and pains** *Eucalyptus oil is good for easing muscular aches and pains.* **a cry of pain, a threshold for/of pain** *I have a very low threshold for pain.*

2 unhappiness
• ADJ. **great, intense, terrible | emotional**
• VERB + PAIN **cause (sb), give sb, inflict** *Through her drug addiction she had inflicted a lot of pain on the family.* | **feel, go through | get over** *It took him several years to get over the pain of losing his job.* | **ease | spare sb** *We hoped to spare her the pain of having to meet her attacker.* | **express | conceal** *He tried to conceal his pain from her.* | **bear, endure | be worth** *The government has to persuade the people that the economic reforms are worth the pain.*

pained adj.

• VERBS **be, look, seem, sound**
• ADV. **positively | slightly** *a slightly pained expression on his face*

painful adj.

• VERBS **be, look, seem | become, get | find sth** *She found it unbearably painful to speak.*
• ADV. **acutely, excruciatingly, extremely, intensely, particularly, terribly, unbearably, very | increasingly |**

almost | pretty, quite, rather, slightly, somewhat | potentially | emotionally, physically
• PREP. **to** *The subject of his failed marriage was quite painful to him.*

painless *adj.*

• VERBS **be** *The operation was relatively painless.*
• ADV. **completely, entirely, totally | almost, virtually | comparatively, relatively**

paint *noun*

• ADJ. **thick | runny, thin | fresh | dry, wet | emulsion, enamel, gloss, matt, metallic, satin, spray | lead, lead-based, oil-based, water-based | acrylic, oil, poster** *an artist working with acrylic paints*
• QUANT. **blob, speck, splash, spot** *Specks of paint found at the scene were found to match the accused's car.* | **coat** *I'll give the walls a fresh coat of paint.* | **layer** *The artist has used several layers of paint to create the stormy sky.* | **lick** *(informal) A lick of paint will do wonders for the room.* | **jar, pot, tube | box, set** *a set of watercolour paints*
• VERB + PAINT **apply, put on, spray | daub with, spatter with, splash with | remove, scrape off, strip (off) | mix | dilute, thin**
• PAINT + VERB **dry | blister, chip, crack, flake (off), peel** *Paint was peeling from the walls.*
• PAINT + NOUN **brush** (also **paintbrush**) | **pot** | **manufacturer, shop | job** *We did a quick paint job on the car and hoped the damage wasn't noticeable.*

paint *verb*

• ADV. **carefully | badly, crudely** *The walls had been painted very badly.* ◊ *a crudely painted human figure* | **beautifully, exquisitely | brightly, gaily** *the cheerful, brightly painted doors* | **garishly, gaudily**
• PREP. **in** *an artist who usually paints in oils* **on** *I like to paint on canvas.* **with** *Paint the box all over with varnish.*
• PHRASES **freshly/newly painted, paint sth blue, white, etc.** *We painted the walls light green.*

painter *noun*

1 person whose job is to paint buildings, walls, etc.
• ADJ. **self-employed | house**
• PHRASES **painter and decorator** *He now works as a painter and decorator.*

2 artist who paints pictures
• ADJ. **celebrated, distinguished, great, famous, master, well-known** *some of the great painters of the last century* ◊ *the Dutch master painter Jan Vermeer* | **good, talented | amateur, professional | contemporary, modern** *an exhibition of works by contemporary painters* | **court** *Rudolf II's court painter* | **abstract, animal, figurative, fresco, genre, landscape, miniature, portrait, realist, watercolour | Cubist, Impressionist, etc.**
⇨ Note at JOB

painting *noun*

1 act of painting
• ADJ. **acrylic, oil, watercolour | finger | miniature | abstract, decorative, figurative, genre, landscape, life, portrait, still-life, surrealist**
• VERB + PAINTING **do** *I'll do some painting this afternoon.* | **take up** *When she retired she took up painting.*
• PAINTING + NOUN **style, technique | course**
• PHRASES **painting and decorating** *The firm specializes in painting and decorating.*

2 picture
• ADJ. **fine, good, great | famous, well-known | valuable | original** *The design is based on an original painting by Matisse.* | **miniature | Cubist, Impressionist, Old Master, etc. | avant-garde | abstract, figurative, figure, genre, landscape, life, nude, still-life, surrealist | ceiling, fresco, wall | acrylic, gouache, oil, watercolour**
• QUANT. **series | collection, exhibition**
• VERB + PAINTING **do, execute, paint, work on** *Degas did several paintings of ballet dancers.* | **frame | hang, put up | display, exhibit, show | collect** *She collects paintings by nineteenth-century Australian artists.* | **clean, conserve, restore | copy, reproduce**
• PAINTING + VERB **depict sb/sth, portray sb/sth, show sb/sth | hang** *His most famous paintings hang in the Tate Gallery.*
• PREP. **in a/the ~** *The woman in the painting is the artist's mistress.* | **~ by** *a painting by Gauguin* **~ in** *a fine painting in oils* **~ of** *paintings of flowers*
⇨ Note at ART

pair *noun*

1 two things the same
• ADJ. **matching** *a matching pair of vases* | **identical**
• PREP. **in a/the ~** *Answer one question in each pair.* **in ~s** *These candlesticks only come in pairs.* | **~ of** *a pair of shoes*
• PHRASES **one of a pair** *one of a pair of crystal vases*

2 people who are connected
• ADJ. **inseparable | good | happy** (= a newly married couple) | **odd** *They make an odd pair.*
• VERB + PAIR **match** *The pair were matched for age.* | **make** *I thought they would make a good pair so I arranged for them to meet.*
• PREP. **in a/the ~** *The students worked in pairs.*

3 male and female animal
• ADJ. **breeding**
• PAIR + VERB **breed, mate**
• PREP. **~ of** *a pair of swans nesting by the river*

palace *noun*

• ADJ. **ancient | 14th-century, etc. | imperial, papal, presidential, royal | grand, great, magnificent, sumptuous, whacking great | veritable** *(figurative) Even this small house was a veritable palace compared to his tent.* | **fairy-tale**
• VERB + PALACE **build | live in**
• PALACE + VERB **stand** *The palace stands on the west bank of the river.*
• PALACE + NOUN **complex, compound | courtyard, gardens, grounds | gates | affairs | aide, guard, official, spokesman | coup, revolution** *The king was deposed by his son in a palace coup.*
• PREP. **at a/the ~, in a/the ~**
• PHRASES **the interior of the palace**

palate *noun*

1 part of the mouth
• ADJ. **hard | soft | cleft** *Their baby had an operation to repair a cleft palate.*

2 sense of taste
• ADJ. **discerning, discriminating, sophisticated | jaded** *Here is a dish that will revive jaded palates.*
• VERB + PALATE **have** *She has a discerning palate.* | **appeal to, suit** *This kind of food appeals to more sophisticated palates.* | **clean, cleanse** *Have an apple to cleanse your palate.*

pale *adj.*

• VERBS **appear, be, look, seem | become, go, grow, turn** *Ruth went pale as the news sank in.* | **remain**
• ADV. **deathly, extremely, sickly, terribly, very** *He turned deathly pale.* | **a bit, a little, quite, rather, slightly | strangely, unnaturally**
• PHRASES **pale and drawn** *He looked pale and drawn.*

pallor noun

- ADJ. **slight** | **deathly, ghostly, sickly** *the deathly pallor of her face* | **green, grey, white**
- VERB + PALLOR **have** *He had a sickly green pallor.*

palm noun

1 flat part of the front of your hand
- ADJ. **soft** | **horny** | **sweaty** | **open** | **outstretched**
- VERB + PALM **hold up, raise** *He held up a palm for silence.* | **spread** *He spread his palms in a gesture of openness.* | **press** *I pressed my palm to the wound to stop the bleeding.* | **slap** *She slapped her palm against the desk in anger.*
- PALM + VERB **sweat** | **face** *Hold out your arms with the palms facing downwards.*
- PALM + NOUN **reading** | **print**
- PREP. **against your ~s** *The metal felt hot against my palms.* **between your ~s** *He took her hand between his palms and squeezed it.* **in your~** *He showed me the coins in his palm.*
- PHRASES **palm/palms up/upwards** *She held out her hand to me, palm up.*

2 tree
- ADJ. **coconut, date, oil**
- PALM + NOUN **tree** | **branch, frond, leaf** | **grove** | **oil**

pamphlet noun

- ADJ. **political**
- VERB + PAMPHLET **print, produce, publish, write** | **circulate, distribute**
- PAMPHLET + VERB **be entitled sth**
- PREP. **in a/the ~** *accusations that were made in the pamphlet*

pan noun

- ADJ. **chip, frying**
- PHRASES **pots and pans**
⇨ See SAUCEPAN (for other collocates of **pan**)

pancake noun

- ADJ. **savoury**
- VERB + PANCAKE **make** | **toss**

pane noun

- ADJ. **broken** | **missing** *The missing pane has been replaced.* | **glass** | **window**
- VERB + PANE **break, shatter, smash** | **blow in/out** *The wind blew in a pane of their front window.* | **replace**
- PREP. **against/to a/the ~** *Her face was pressed against the pane.* **down a/the ~** *The rain ran down the window pane.* **on a/the~** *There was dirt on the pane.*
- PHRASES **a pane of glass** *The burglars got in by smashing a pane of glass in a door.*

panel noun

1 group of people
- ADJ. **distinguished** *a distinguished panel of academics* | **independent** | **international** | **advisory, interview, interviewing, judging, review, selection**
- VERB + PANEL **convene, select, set up** | **chair**
- PANEL + VERB **be drawn from sb/sth** *a panel of scientists drawn from universities*
- PANEL + NOUN **member** | **interview** | **discussion** | **game** *The comedian will chair a new TV panel game.*
- PREP. **on a/the ~** *The head of department serves on the advisory panel.* | **~on** *an independent panel on takeovers and mergers*
- PHRASES **a member of a panel, a panel of experts/judges** *The winners were chosen by a panel of judges.*

2 part of a door, wall, etc.
- ADJ. **ceiling, door, wall** | **sliding**
- VERB + PANEL **fit, insert, put in** | **remove, take out**

3 section of vehicle body
- ADJ. **front, rear** | **nearside, offside** | **body** *My rear nearside body panel needed replacing after the accident.*
- VERB + PANEL **beat**
- PANEL + NOUN **beater, beating** *He works as a panel beater in a local garage.*

4 surface containing controls
- ADJ. **control, display, instrument**
- PREP. **on a/the~** *A red light flashed on the control panel.*

pang noun

- ADJ. **sharp** | **little** | **passing** *a passing pang of regret* | **sudden, unexpected** | **hunger** | **birth** (*figurative*) *the birth pangs of the new technology*
- VERB + PANG **experience, feel, suffer** *He experienced a sudden pang of conscience.* | **cause, give sb** *The photograph gave her a pang of homesickness.*
- PANG + VERB **shoot through sb** *A sharp pang of guilt shot through him.*
- PREP. **with a~** *With a pang she recalled the last time she had seen him.* | **~of** *She felt a little pang of jealousy.*

panic noun

- ADJ. **blind, mad, sheer, total** | **mild, minor** | **momentary** | **growing, mounting, rising** | **sudden** | **last-minute** *There was a last-minute panic when nobody could find the tickets.* | **moral** *a moral panic over rising crime rates*
- QUANT. **surge, wave** *I felt a surge of panic when I realized my mistake.*
- VERB + PANIC **feel** *He felt panic rising within him.* | **get into, go into** *She went into a mad panic when she couldn't find the exit.* | **cause, create, spread** | **fill sb with, throw sb into** *The thought of having to be in charge threw him into a mild panic.*
- PANIC + VERB **break out, spread (across/through, etc. sth), sweep over/through sth** *Panic swept through the crowd.* | **seize sb** | **grow, rise** | **subside** | **ensue** *In the ensuing panic, they lost each other.*
- PANIC + NOUN **attack** *She still has panic attacks, two years after the accident.* | **button** *The shopkeeper pressed the panic button and the police arrived in minutes.* | **buying, selling** *Panic buying turned the petrol shortage into a crisis.*
- PREP. **in (a) ~** *He jumped out of the car in a panic.* ◇ *People fled in panic.* **with ~** *Her mind went blank with panic.* | **~about** *panic about food contamination* **~among** *panic among the population* **~over** *The keys were lost during the panic over the fire alarm.*
- PHRASES **a feeling/sense of panic, in a state of panic, a look of panic** *A look of panic spread across the boy's face.* **a moment of panic, a moment's panic**

pant verb

- ADV. **breathlessly** | **heavily, loudly** | **slightly**
- PREP. **for** *He was panting for breath.* **with** *She was panting with the effort of carrying the suitcase.*
- PHRASES **puff and pant** *Mason puffed and panted up the stairs.*

pantomime noun

- ADJ. **Christmas**
- PANTOMIME + NOUN **cow, dame, horse** | **season**
⇨ Note at PERFORMANCE (for verbs)

pants noun

- QUANT. **pair**
- VERB + PANTS **pull on, pull up** | **drop, pull down** | **wet** *He was so frightened that he wet his pants.*

- PHRASES **bra and pants**
⇨ Special page at CLOTHES

paper noun

1 material
- ADJ. **thick, thin | see-through, transparent | plain, unlined | lined | graph, squared | A3, A4, etc. | foolscap | blank** *I stared at the blank paper, not knowing how to start the letter.* | **printed** *The Post Office has a special rate for printed paper.* | **brown, coloured** *a brown paper parcel of books* | **greaseproof, waxed | glossy, shiny | scrap, waste** *I made some notes on a piece of scrap paper.* | **computer, typing | writing | blotting | tracing | wrapping | crêpe | tissue | photographic | filter | kitchen | toilet | cigarette** *a packet of cigarette papers*
- QUANT. **bit, piece, scrap, sheet, slip, strip** *I scribbled down his number on a scrap of paper.* | **roll** *a roll of kitchen paper* | **side** *The essay filled seven sides of A4 paper.*
- VERB + PAPER **fold** *Fold the paper in half.* | **shred, tear | crumple (up), screw up** *I screwed up the paper and threw it in the bin.* | **recycle | wrap sth in**
- PAPER + VERB **be strewn** *There was paper strewn all over the floor.*
- PREP. **on ~** *I've had nothing on paper* (= in writing) *to say that I've been accepted.*
- PHRASES **put pen to paper** *I've thought about what I'm going to write, but I haven't yet put pen to paper.* **a waste of paper** *This report is a waste of paper.*

2 newspaper
- ADJ. **daily, evening, morning, Sunday, weekly | today's, yesterday's | independent, left-wing, right-wing | local, national | broadsheet, quality | tabloid**
- QUANT. **copy** *Have you got a copy of yesterday's paper?* | **edition** *today's edition of the paper*
- VERB + PAPER **buy, get, take** *Do you take a daily paper?* | **flick through, read** *What paper do you usually read?* | **print, produce, publish | edit, write for/in | appear in | get into** *The story got into the papers.*
- PAPER + VERB **come out** *The paper comes out every Saturday.*
- PAPER + NOUN **shop | boy, girl | round**
- PREP. **in a/the ~** *I read about his arrest in the papers.* **on a/the ~** *She got a job on the local paper.*

3 (usually **papers**) official document
- ADJ. **commercial | necessary | official | identity | personal, private | ballot**
- QUANT. **pile, sheaf**
- VERB + PAPERS **show** *Be prepared to show your identity papers at the border.*

4 exam
- ADJ. **exam, examination, question, test | written** *I did well on the oral but not on the written paper.* | **English, geography, etc.**
- VERB + PAPER **do, sit, take | set** *The exam papers are set by experienced teachers.* | **mark | turn over** *You may now turn over your papers.*
- PREP. **in a/the ~** *the questions in the physics paper* **on a/the ~** *You must not write on the question paper.*

5 piece of writing on a specialist subject
- ADJ. **draft | consultation, consultative, discussion, position, working | research, scientific**
- VERB + PAPER **deliver, give, present, put forward, read | draft, prepare, produce, write | issue, publish, release**
- PAPER + VERB **consider sth, deal with sth, focus on/upon sth, look at sth** *The paper looks at the future of primary school education.* | **argue sth, propose sth | demonstrate sth | describe sth, outline sth, present sth | be called sth, be entitled sth**
- PREP. **in a/the ~** *Freud first mentioned this concept in his paper 'On Narcissism'.* | **~ on** *a paper on the development of the novel*

paperback noun

- ADJ. **mass-market** *the demand for mass-market paperbacks* | **original** *The book is to be published as an original paperback* (= it is not being published in hardback first).
- VERB + PAPERBACK **read | produce, publish (sth as) | be out in, come out in** *The novel has just come out in paperback.*
- PAPERBACK + VERB **come out** *The paperback came out in June.*
- PAPERBACK + NOUN **book, edition, novel, version | original | fiction | rights, sales**
- PREP. **in ~** *The book is now available in paperback.*

paperwork noun

- ADJ. **routine | necessary**
- VERB + PAPERWORK **deal with, do, get through, go through, work through** *I've got a lot of routine paperwork to get through.* | **involve** *The project involved an enormous amount of paperwork.*
- PREP. **~ for** *Have you done all the necessary paperwork for the sale?*
- PHRASES **a backlog/mountain/pile of paperwork**

parachute noun

- VERB + PARACHUTE **pack**
- PARACHUTE + VERB **open | fail to open**
- PARACHUTE + NOUN **descent, drop, jump** *He made his first parachute jump at the age of seventy.* | **instructor**
- PREP. **by ~** *Supplies were dropped by parachute.*

parade noun

- ADJ. **grand | colourful | fashion | military, victory | identification, identity**
- VERB + PARADE **have, hold, stage** *The police held an identity parade.* | **go on** *The battalion went on parade to welcome the new commander-in-chief.* | **inspect, review** *The president reviewed the military parade.*
- PARADE + VERB **take place**
- PARADE + NOUN **ground**
- PREP. **at a/the ~** *Thousands of people were at the parade.* **on ~** *The soldiers will be on parade tomorrow.*

paradise noun

1 heaven
- VERB + PARADISE **go to** *They all expected to go to paradise.*
- PREP. **in ~** *an angel in paradise*

2 perfect place
- ADJ. **perfect, unspoilt | beautiful | lost** *the lost paradise of childhood* | **children's, walker's, etc. | earthly, island, tropical**
- VERB + PARADISE **create** *She worked on the garden until she had created her own little paradise.* | **find** *They moved to the country hoping to find paradise.*
- PARADISE + NOUN **island**
- PREP. **in (a) ~** *We found ourselves in a tropical paradise.* | **~ for** *The airport is a paradise for pickpockets.* **~ of** *a paradise of golden beaches*
- PHRASES **a paradise on earth**

paradox noun

- ADJ. **apparent | central | curious**
- VERB + PARADOX **pose, present** *The facts pose something of a paradox.* | **explain, resolve**
- PREP. **~ about** *The paradox about time is that it seems to go faster as we become older and less active.* **~ between** *the paradox between the real and the ideal* **~ in** *the paradox in the relationship between creativity and psychosis*
- PHRASES **by a curious paradox** *By a curious paradox, the team became less motivated the more games it won.*

paradoxical adj.

- VERBS **appear, be, seem, sound**
- ADV. **distinctly, very | slightly, somewhat | seemingly** *trying to understand her seemingly paradoxical behaviour* **| inherently | curiously** *He found himself in a curiously paradoxical situation.*

paragraph noun

- ADJ. **new | introductory, opening**
- VERB + PARAGRAPH **begin, start** *Start each paragraph on a new line.*
- PREP. **in a/the~** *The identity of the murderer is revealed in the very last paragraph.* **in accordance with/under ~** *(law) Cancellation charges will apply in accordance with paragraph 4 above.* **| ~ about** *a paragraph about the writer's reaction to his mother's death*

parallel noun

- ADJ. **direct, exact | clear, close, obvious | interesting, striking**
- VERB + PARALLEL **have** *This weather pattern of the southern hemisphere has no parallel in the north.* **| find, see | draw, make** *He drew an interesting parallel with religious practices in Japan.* **| provide**
- PREP. **without~** *a speed of development without parallel in post-war Europe* **| ~between** *a parallel between economic and cultural advancement* **~ in** *We found a direct parallel in the attitudes of schoolchildren in other countries.* **~ to** *A close parallel to this behaviour is found in dolphins.* **~ with** *She saw an obvious parallel with her sister's predicament.*

parallel adj.

- VERBS **be, run**
- ADV. **exactly | nearly | roughly**
- PREP. **to** *The lane is roughly parallel to the main road.* **with** *The road runs parallel with the sea.*

paralyse verb

- ADV. **completely, totally | partially, partly** *He was partially paralysed by the fall.* **| almost, virtually**
- PHRASES **be paralysed from the chest/neck/waist down, be paralysed with fear, leave sb paralysed** *The accident left her paralysed.*

paralysis noun

1 being unable to move your body or a part of it
- ADJ. **complete | partial | instant** *The snake's venom induces instant paralysis.* **| permanent | infantile**
- VERB + PARALYSIS **be struck with | suffer from | cause, induce**
- PARALYSIS + VERB **spread** *He had been crippled by a rare type of paralysis spreading from his ankle.*

2 being unable to work in the normal way
- ADJ. **complete** *Strike leaders claimed 'almost complete paralysis' in the ports and mines.* **| emotional, political**

paranoia noun

- ADJ. **increasing, mounting**
- VERB + PARANOIA **suffer from | border on, verge on** *Her passion for cleanliness borders on paranoia.*
- PARANOIA + VERB **afflict sb**

parasite noun

- ADJ. **common | dangerous** *These flies carry a dangerous parasite.* **| external, internal | intestinal**
- VERB + PARASITE **carry, have**

parcel noun

- ADJ. **bulky | neat | brown-paper | gift-wrapped, tissue-wrapped, etc. | clothing, food**
- VERB + PARCEL **post, send | get, receive | make sth (up) into, pack (up), wrap, wrap sth (up) in** *The waiter had our left-over food made up into a parcel to take home.* **| open, unpack, unwrap**
- PARCEL + NOUN **bomb**
- PREP. **in a/the~ | ~from, ~to**
- PHRASES **laden/loaded with parcels** *He came in laden with parcels for the children.*

pardon noun

- ADJ. **full | partial | conditional | general | free | posthumous | presidential, royal**
- VERB + PARDON **give sb, grant sb | offer sb** *The government offered a free pardon to the rebels.* **| buy, obtain, receive | ask (for), seek | refuse**
- PREP. **~for** *She asked for pardon for her crime.*

parent noun

- ADJ. **lone, single | unmarried | widowed | divorced | absent | substitute, surrogate | elderly | prospective, would-be | new | biological, birth, natural, real | adoptive, foster, step- | good | proud** *They have just become the proud parents of a baby girl.* **| caring, devoted, fond, loving | doting, indulgent | over-protective | stern, strict | domineering | bad, inadequate | abusive | angry, anxious, distressed, heartbroken | working** *The government has promised a better deal for working parents.*
- PARENT + NOUN **company** *The subsidiary eventually outgrew its parent company and took it over.*
- PHRASES **lone/one/single-parent family**

parenthood noun

- ADJ. **lone, single | responsible** *education about family planning and responsible parenthood*
- PHRASES **preparation for parenthood**

park noun

- ADJ. **local | city | public | country | national** *The mountain has been designated as a national park.* **| safari, wildlife | amusement, leisure, theme**
- VERB + PARK **go to** *They go to the park most Sunday afternoons.* **| landscape, lay out** *a beautifully landscaped park*
- PARK + NOUN **bench | ranger** *The lion was shot dead by a park ranger.*
- PREP. **at a/the ~** *We met at Hyde Park.* **in a/the ~** *They went for a walk in the park.*

park verb

- ADV. **carefully, neatly, well | badly | illegally | discreetly** *The police car was discreetly parked in the furthest corner of the courtyard.*

parking noun

- ADJ. **convenient, easy | off-road, off-street, on-street, street, roadside | long-stay, short-stay | illegal | car**
- PARKING + NOUN **area, facilities, lot | bay, place, space, spot** *a restaurant with ample parking space* ◇ *I spent ages looking for a parking place/space.* **| meter | fine, ticket | restrictions**
- PREP. **~for** *parking for 300 cars*

parliament noun

- ADJ. **current, present | outgoing | bicameral, unicameral | hung** *The election resulted in a hung parlia-*

ment, followed by the resignation of the prime minister. |
federal, national, provincial, regional, state
- VERB + PARLIAMENT **stand for** He first stood for Parliament in 2001. | **enter, get into** | **be in, sit in** He sat in Parliament for over forty years. | **elect (sb to)** a popularly elected parliament | **return sb to** He was returned to Parliament in 2001 as MP for Appleby. | **represent sb/sth in** | **bring/lay/put sth before, introduce sth into, present sth to** | **be/come/go before** The bill will come before Parliament next month. | **go through, get through, pass through** | **put through, push through, force through** The government was accused of forcing the bill through Parliament. | **lobby** | **adjourn, convene** | **dissolve, suspend** | **be accountable to, be responsible to**
- PARLIAMENT + VERB **adopt sth, approve sth, enact sth, lay sth down, pass sth, ratify sth** The Commission is guided by rules laid down by Parliament. | **reject sth** | **vote (on sth)** | **debate sth** | **legislate (on sth)** Parliament may legislate on any matter of penal law. | **be in session, convene, meet, sit** Parliament will be in session until 15th December. | **adjourn, rise** | **resume**
- PARLIAMENT + NOUN **building**
- PREP. **in~** her first year in Parliament
- PHRASES **an Act of Parliament, a (lower/upper) house of parliament** The National Assembly is the lower house of the French Parliament. **the lifetime of a parliament** It will take at least the lifetime of a parliament to put the health service in order. **a majority in Parliament** The party has a two-thirds majority in Parliament. **a Member of Parliament, a seat in Parliament** sth's **passage through Parliament** Sponsors of the bill agreed to concessions in order to smooth its passage through Parliament. The party failed to win any seats in Parliament. **a session of Parliament**

parody noun

1 writing/speech/music
- ADJ. **brilliant, clever** | **cruel**
- VERB + PARODY **compose, write**
- PREP. **through~** He attacked her ideas through parody. | **~of** She has written a cruel parody of his book. **~on** The show included a parody on current affairs programmes.

2 bad example
- ADJ. **grotesque**
- PREP. **in a~of** He sighed in a parody of deep emotion. | **~of** She has become a grotesque parody of her former elegant self.
- PHRASES **a parody of justice** The trial was a parody of justice.

parole noun

- ADJ. **early**
- VERB + PAROLE **be on** | **give sb, grant sb** | **get** She's got (her) parole. | **let sb out on, release sb on** She was released on parole after serving just half of her sentence. | **break** He broke (his) parole. | **be eligible for, be/come up for** Her case comes up for parole in September.
- PAROLE + NOUN **board, system**
- PREP. **on~** He committed a burglary while on parole. **with~** With parole, he could be out in two years. **without~** sentenced to life imprisonment without parole

parsley noun

- QUANT. **sprig**
- VERB + PARSLEY **grow** | **chop** | **garnish sth with**
⇨ Special page at FOOD

part noun

1 piece/area/period/division, etc. of sth
- ADJ. **big, good, greater, large, major, significant, substantial** We spent a good part of the day rehearsing. ◇ The

greater part of the building has been refurbished. | **minor, small** | **equal** Cut it into four equal parts. | **important, main, principal** | **basic, central, essential, fundamental, indispensable, vital** | **integral, intrinsic** | **separate** | **inseparable** | **component, constituent** | **best** | **worst** The worst part was having to wait three hours. | **difficult, hard** I gave up once I got to the hard part. | **easy** | **early** In the early part of his career he worked in India. | **latter** the latter part of the century | **different, distinct, various** | **foreign** travellers returning from foreign parts | **separate** | **inseparable** | **component, constituent** Break it down into its constituent parts. | **private** (= sexual organs)
- VERB + PART **constitute, fall into, form** The book falls into three distinct parts. | **break sth down into, divide sth into, split sth into**
- PREP. **in~** Your salary depends in part on your qualifications. ◇ The film is good in parts. ◇ a serial in four parts | **~of** Part of me wants to stay and part of me doesn't.
- PHRASES **the parts of the body**

2 a piece of a machine
- ADJ. **spare** Where can I get spare parts for my bike?

3 role in a play, film, etc.
- ADJ. **big, leading** | **bit, small, walk-on** | **speaking**
- VERB + PART **have, play, take** | **learn** | **look** He was a pirate in the school play and certainly looked the part.
- PREP. **in the ~** He's very good in the part. | **~ of** She played the part of Juliet.

4 share in an activity, event, etc.
- ADJ. **big, leading, major** Luck played a big part in it. | **minor** | **central, significant, vital** | **active**
- VERB + PART **have** He had no part in the scam. | **do, play, take** She did her part in bringing them back together.
- PREP. **~in** They took little part in the discussion.

partial adj.

- VERBS **be** | **remain**
- ADV. **very** | **only** | **inevitably, necessarily** The information we have is inevitably partial.

participant noun

- ADJ. **full** | **active** | **unwilling, willing** She was an unwilling participant in his downfall. | **key, leading, main, major** | **course** | **conference, seminar**
- VERB + PARTICIPANT **attract** Protests on 12 April attracted 100 000 participants.
- PARTICIPANT + VERB **attend sth**
- PREP. **~in** an active participant in the discussion

participate verb

- ADV. **fully** | **actively**
- VERB + PARTICIPATE **be able to, have the opportunity to** | **be allowed to, be encouraged to, be invited to** Other countries were invited to participate in the project. | **agree to** | **refuse to**
- PREP. **in** They will have the opportunity to participate actively in the decision-making process.

participation noun

- ADJ. **full** | **broader, greater, increased** | **limited** | **direct** | **active** | **political** | **popular, public** | **audience, employee, student, worker** Some of the magic tricks called for audience participation.
- QUANT. **degree, extent, level** We were very pleased with the high level of participation in the charity events.
- VERB + PARTICIPATION **encourage** The scheme aims to encourage increased participation in sporting activities. | **increase**
- PARTICIPATION + VERB **increase**
- PARTICIPATION + NOUN **rate**

● PREP. **~in** *direct participation by the masses in the running of the country*

parting *noun*

● ADJ. **final | sad**
● PARTING + NOUN **gift | shot, words** *As her parting shot she told me never to phone her again.*
● PHRASES **the moment of parting** *She was already dreading the moment of parting.*

partition *noun*

● ADJ. **movable | folding**
● VERB + PARTITION **build, erect, put up | remove, take down**
● PARTITION + VERB **divide sth (up), separate sth** *The cafe was divided up by glass partitions.*
● PARTITION + NOUN **wall**
● PREP. **~ between** *There were no partitions between the showers.*

partner *noun*

1 in a marriage/relationship
● ADJ. **former | dominant** *She was the dominant partner in the relationship.* **| female, male | marriage, sexual** *the choice of marriage partner*
● VERB + PARTNER **have**

2 in an activity
● ADJ. **bridge, doubles, playing, tennis** *I need a doubles partner for the table tennis tournament.* **| dancing | sparring** (figurative) *The old political sparring partners are now firm friends.* **| drinking**
● VERB + PARTNER **choose** *The teacher asked the students to choose a partner for the next activity.* **| change** *All change partners for the next dance!*

3 in business
● ADJ. **full | equal | active, managing | sleeping | junior, senior | business**
● VERB + PARTNER **make sb**
● PREP. **~in** *He has recently been made a junior partner in the family business.*

4 in international relations
● ADJ. **biggest, main, principal | foreign | coalition, trading** *France's principal trading partners*
● PREP. **~in** *Britain's partner in the aeronautic project*

partnership *noun*

● ADJ. **close | limited | effective, good, great, successful | working** *We are trying to develop a working partnership between local schools and industries.* **| unique | equal** *an equal partnership of men and women in government* **| international, multinational | business**
● VERB + PARTNERSHIP **have | create, establish, form, set up (in) | enter into, go into** *The company has gone into partnership with Swiss Bank Corporation.* **| take sb into** *We took him into partnership in 2002.* **| work in** *We shall be working in close partnership with our Japanese clients.* **| break up**
● PARTNERSHIP + NOUN **agreement, arrangement**
● PREP. **in~with** *They are in partnership with Apex software.* **| ~between** *a partnership between the university and local colleges* **~in** *She has a partnership in the business.* **~of** *a unique partnership of private companies and trade unions* **~with** *a partnership with an American firm*
⇨ Note at ORGANIZATION

party *noun*

1 political group
● ADJ. **political | centre, left-wing, right-wing | centrist, fascist, populist, progressive, radical, reactionary, revolutionary, social democratic, socialist | Communist, Conservative, Democratic, Labour, Liberal, Republican, etc. | opposition | parliamentary** *members of the parliamentary party* (= MPs, not ordinary party members) **| main** *both main political parties* **| majority, minority** *They are now the majority party in Parliament.* **| governing, ruling**
● VERB + PARTY **establish, form, found, set up | dissolve, wind up** *The party was officially dissolved in 1927.* **| split** *a bitter dispute which finally split the party* **| be/become the leader of, lead | be/become a member of, belong to, join | be affiliated to, have links with** *He was accused of having strong links with the Communist Party.* **| leave, resign from** *She left the party in 2000.* **| expel sb from | vote for | elect, put in/into power, return to power** *The Labour Party was returned to power in 2001.*
● PARTY + VERB **come to power, gain power, win (sth) | lose (sth), lose power** *The Labour party lost the vote on this important issue.* **| contest sth** *the parties contesting the elections*
● PARTY + NOUN **conference, congress | activist, member, faithful** (= loyal members of the party) **| chairman, leader, leadership | line** *Most MPs will follow the party line* (= the official view of the party). **| politics**
● PHRASES **the left/right wing of the party**

2 social occasion
● ADJ. **cocktail, dinner, tea | birthday, Christmas, farewell, house-warming, leaving | garden, office, street | all-night | fancy-dress | surprise**
● VERB + PARTY **give, have, hold, organize, throw** *On moving in they threw a huge house-warming party.* **| invite sb to | attend, go to | gatecrash | leave**
● PARTY + VERB **go on** *There was a party going on next door.* **| be in full swing** (= to be very busy and noisy) *By now the party was in full swing.* **| break up** *The party broke up around midnight.*
● PARTY + NOUN **guest | pooper** (also **party-pooper**; = sb who does not want to join in the fun at a party)
● PREP. **at a/the~** *I was at a party in London that night.* **| ~for** *I'm organizing a surprise party for my sister.*

3 group of people working/doing sth together
● ADJ. **boarding, coach, landing, raiding, reading, rescue, search, stretcher, working** *It was time for us to join the coach party.*
● PREP. **~of** *She arrived with a party of helpers.*

4 person in a legal case
● ADJ. **guilty, innocent | aggrieved, injured | interested** *First we must notify all the interested parties.* **| third** *You must sign the document in the presence of an independent third party* (= another person apart from the two main people involved)
● VERB + PARTY **notify | be binding on/upon, bind** *This agreement shall be binding upon both parties.*

pass *noun*

1 in sport
● ADJ. **good, perfect | careless, sloppy | long, short | back, cross-field, square** (in football) **| forward** (in rugby) *The referee disallowed the try for a forward pass.*
● VERB + PASS **play** *Ziege played a pass behind the defence to Weiss.* **| get, pick up, receive | block, intercept**
● PREP. **~ from** *Owen picked up a long pass from Beckham to score.* **~to** *He played a careless back pass to the goalkeeper.*

2 success in exam
● ADJ. **good | exam, examination, A Level, GCSE, etc.**
● VERB + PASS **get, manage, obtain, scrape** *She barely scraped a pass in chemistry.*
● PASS + NOUN **mark, rate** *The pass mark is 40%.* **| degree** *Applicants need a good degree pass.*
● PREP. **~at** *It's difficult to obtain a pass at A Level.* **~in** *He should get a good pass in mathematics.*

3 official piece of paper

- ADJ. **free** | **day, monthly, weekend, yearly** | **bus, rail, railway** *a monthly rail pass* | **security** | **boarding**
- VERB + PASS **have** | **use** | **give sb, issue (sb with)** *The visitors were issued with day passes.* | **produce, show**
- PREP. **on a** ~ *soldiers on a weekend pass* | ~ **to** *We bought a two-day pass to Disneyland.*

4 way through mountains
- ADJ. **high, low** | **narrow** | **mountain**
- VERB + PASS **cross, take**
- PASS + VERB **be blocked**
- PREP. **over a/the** ~ *struggling over the pass with their donkeys* **through a/the** ~ *building a road through the pass* | ~ **over** *We took the high pass over the ridge.*
- PHRASES **the head/summit/top of the pass**

pass *verb*

1 of time
- ADV. **quickly, soon** *The time passed quickly.* | **slowly** | **peacefully, uneventfully** *The days passed uneventfully.*
- VERB + PASS **help (to)** *We played games to help pass the time.*

2 law
- ADV. **unanimously**
- PREP. **by ... to ...** *The bill was passed by 360 votes to 280.*

3 happen
- ADV. **peacefully** | **off** *The demonstration passed off peacefully.*
- VERB + PASS **come to** *(formal or old-fashioned) I wondered how it came to pass that a thinking man bore the prejudices of his unthinking parents.* | **let sth** *I don't like it, but I'll let it pass* (= will not object).
- PREP. **between** *They'll never be friends again after all that has passed between them.*
- PHRASES **pass unnoticed** *In the confusion her departure passed unnoticed.*

passage *noun*

1 narrow way through
- ADJ. **long, short** | **narrow, small** | **wide** | **twisting, winding** | **connecting, side** | **subterranean, underground** | **dark, secret**
- VERB + PASSAGE **clear** *to clear a passage for ships through the ice* | **force** *He forced a passage for the singer through the crowd.*
- PREP. **along/down/through a/the** ~ *We ran through the dark passage.* **in/into a/the** ~ *Someone was waiting outside in the passage.* | ~ **between** *the passage between the cottage and the house* ~ **from** *There is an underground passage from the church to the house.* ~ **through** *a narrow passage through the bushes* ~ **to**
- PHRASES **the end of a passage** *There was a door at the end of the passage.* **a maze of passages** *the maze of secret passages which wound their way under the building*

2 tube in the body
- ADJ. **nasal** | **back** (= rectum)
- VERB + PASSAGE **block, obstruct** | **clear**

3 extract from a book/speech
- ADJ. **lengthy, long** | **short** | **opening** | **famous, well-known** | **descriptive, purple**
- VERB + PASSAGE **quote, read**
- PREP. **in a/the** ~ *There's a lot of slang in this passage.* | ~ **from** *a passage from the Bible*

4 extract from a piece of music
- ADJ. **lengthy, long** | **short** | **opening** | **fast, slow** | **loud** | **quiet, soft** | **solo**
- VERB + PASSAGE **play, quote** *In the 15th symphony he quotes a passage from Rossini's 'William Tell' overture.*
- PREP. **in a/the** ~ | ~ **from**

5 movement/progress
- ADJ. **rapid, speedy** | **slow** | **safe** | **smooth** | **free** *The*

UN Security Council has demanded free passage for families fleeing from the fighting.
- VERB + PASSAGE **deny sb, refuse sb**
- PREP. ~ **across** *the slow passage of a snail across the veranda* ~ **down** *Steps cut in the hillside give walkers an easy passage down the mountain.* ~ **from ... to ...** *We are not aware of our passage from consciousness to sleep.* ~ **into** *Portugal's passage into the next round of the tournament* ~ **out of** *a safe passage out of the war zone* ~ **over** *State-of-the-art suspension guarantees a smooth passage over the bumpiest road.* ~ **through** *They denied him passage through the territory.*
- PHRASES **the passage of time** *The problems only got worse with the passage of time.* **a rite of passage** *Marriage is seen as a rite of passage.*

6 journey by ship
- ADJ. **long, short** | **rough, stormy** | **homeward, outward** | **sea**
- VERB + PASSAGE **have** | **book** | **work** *He worked his passage* (= he worked to pay for his journey) *to Australia.*
- PREP. **during a/the** ~ *During the passage, she taught herself basic Arabic.* **on sb's/the** ~ *We met him on our outward passage.* | ~ **across** *a rough passage across the Atlantic* ~ **to** *We had a stormy passage to India.*

7 of a bill through Parliament
- ADJ. **smooth** | **speedy**
- VERB + PASSAGE **begin, complete** *The bill will complete its passage in November.*
- PREP. **during the** ~ *There was much controversy during the passage of the bill.* | ~ **through** *a strategy to ensure the bill's smooth passage through Parliament*

passenger *noun*

- ADJ. **business-class, economy-class, first-class, second-class, standard-class** | **front-seat, rear-seat** | **airline, bus, rail** | **pillion** (= riding on the back of a motorcycle) | **fellow** *I soon got talking to my fellow passengers.*
- VERB + PASSENGER **carry** *Last year the airline carried 4.6 million passengers.* | **let on, pick up, take on** *A taxi was picking up a passenger outside the hotel.* | **drop off, let off/out** *The bus stopped to let its passengers off.*
- PASSENGER + VERB **wait** *passengers waiting to board the plane* | **be aboard (sth), go in/on sth, travel in/on sth** *passengers travelling on the Orient Express* | **board (sth), embark (on sth), get on (sth), go aboard (sth)** | **disembark, get off/out** | **be stranded** *Thousands of passengers were stranded last night at Heathrow airport.*
- PASSENGER + NOUN **compartment** | **door** | **seat, side** *There is no air bag on the passenger side.* | **comfort, safety** | **aircraft, ferry, train** | **flight, services** | **list**
- PREP. ~ **for** *Will all passengers for Frankfurt please go to Gate 21.* ~ **in** *the passengers in her car* ~ **on** *all the passengers on the ferry*

passing *noun*

- VERB + PASSING **mourn** *Few will mourn his passing.* | **mark** *Her death marks the passing of an era.*
- PHRASES **the passing of time** *The colour of the wood darkens with the passing of time.*

passion *noun*

1 strong sexual love/attraction
- ADJ. **grand, great** *She didn't believe in grand passion or love at first sight.* ◇ *She was his first great passion.* | **all-consuming, blind, consuming, fierce, fiery, intense** | **tender** | **animal, romantic, sexual**
- QUANT. **surge, wave**
- VERB + PASSION **arouse, awaken** *No one had ever aroused his passion as much as Sandra.* | **be filled with, feel** *the great passion he felt for her*
- PASSION + VERB **cool, wane**

● PREP. **with** ~ *They kissed with passion.* | **~ between** *The passion between them had cooled.* **~ for** *his all-consuming passion for her*
● PHRASES **a night of passion** *They spent a night of passion in a hotel.* **the object of sb's passion** *the young girl who was the object of his passion*

2 strong feeling
● ADJ. **considerable, great, high, real** *a woman of great passion* ◇ *There were moments of high passion in the game.*
● VERB + PASSION **have** *A writer should have passion.* | **arouse, rouse** *This issue always arouses passion.*
● PREP. **with** ~ *He argued his case with great passion.*
● PHRASES **a crime of passion** *She killed her husband's lover in a crime of passion.* **full of passion** *a speech full of passion*

3 strong liking for/interest in sth
● ADJ. **all-consuming, consuming, great, real** | **abiding, genuine, lifelong** *his lifelong passion for aeroplanes*
● VERB + PASSION **develop, have** | **share** *They shared a passion for food.* | **indulge** *She had very little time to indulge her passion for painting.*
● PREP. **~ for** *He developed a real passion for acting.*

passive *adj.*

● VERBS **be, seem** | **become** | **remain**
● ADV. **extremely, very** | **purely** | **fairly, rather, relatively, somewhat** | **essentially** *The heroine plays an essentially passive role in the drama.*

passport *noun*

● ADJ. **valid** | **false, forged** | **EU, Mexican, French, etc.** | **visitor's**
● VERB + PASSPORT **apply for** | **renew** | **get, obtain** | **be in possession of, carry, have, hold, travel on** *The police think the smugglers are travelling on Irish passports.* | **give sb, issue sb (with)** | **hand sb, produce, show (sb)** *You have to show your passport at the border.* | **surrender** *The Embassy made him surrender his passport.* | **ask for** | **check** | **stamp** | **hand back/over** *He examined my face carefully before handing back my passport.* | **confiscate, seize**
● PASSPORT + VERB **be valid** | **expire**
● PASSPORT + NOUN **number, photo, photograph** | **holder** | **Agency, Office** | **control** *We had to queue for ages at passport control.*
● PREP. **~ into** *(figurative) The gold medal is his passport into professional boxing.* **~ to** *(figurative) Good qualifications are a passport to success.*
● PHRASES **a full British/French, etc. passport** (= one showing that sb has all the rights of British/French, etc. citizenship)

password *noun*

● ADJ. **correct, valid** | **invalid** | **user** *Please supply a valid user password.*
● VERB + PASSWORD **know** | **give** *You must give the password before they'll let you in.* | **enter, provide, supply, type in** | **change**
● PHRASES **be password protected** *Your mailbox can be password protected to ensure security.*

past *noun*

1 time before the present
● ADJ. **immediate, recent** | **ancient, (dim and) distant, remote** *Many modern festivals can be traced back to an ancient past.* ◇ *It all happened in the distant past.*
● VERB + PAST **cling to, live in** *We're going to have to stop living in the past and invest in new technology if the firm is to survive.* | **belong in/to** *Those memories belong to the past and I don't want to think about them.*

● PREP. **from the** ~ *Memories from the past came flooding back to him.* **in the** ~ *I admit that I have made mistakes in the past.* **into the** ~ *events stretching back many years into the past* **of the** ~ *great artists of the past*
● PHRASES **be all in the past** *Don't worry about it—it's all in the past now.* **a break with the past** *In an effort to make a complete break with the past, she sold everything and went abroad.* **a glimpse of the past** *The uncovering of the buried town gives us a unique glimpse of the past.* **a link with the past** *The old market is a living link with the past, unchanged for hundreds of years.* **nostalgia for the past**, **a thing of the past** *a new device that makes such problems a thing of the past*

2 sb/sth's history
● ADJ. **historic, historical** | **colourful, rich** | **chequered, murky, sordid** | **criminal** | **glorious, illustrious** *Few remnants remain of the city's glorious past.* | **cultural, political, ancestral, evolutionary** | **imperial, industrial**
● VERB + PAST **reflect on/upon** | **recapture** *trying in vain to recapture his past* | **erase, escape from, put behind you, wipe out** *Political parties cannot escape from their pasts any more than individuals can.* ◇ *The counselling helped Dan to put the past behind him.*
● PREP. **from your** ~ *ghosts from his past* **in your** ~ *at some time in her past*

pasta *noun*

● ADJ. **fresh** | **dried** | **egg, wholemeal**
● VERB + PASTA **cook** | **drain, strain**
● PASTA + NOUN **bows, shapes, shells, etc.** | **sauce** | **dish, salad**
⇒ Special page at FOOD

paste *noun*

● ADJ. **firm, stiff, thick** | **lumpy, smooth** | **wallpaper** | **curry, fish, tomato, etc.**
● VERB + PASTE **make (up), mix (up), mix sth into/to** *Mix the sugar mixture to a smooth paste.* | **form** *Mix the flour with enough water to form a thick paste.* | **apply, put on** *Apply the wallpaper paste with a roller.*

pastime *noun*

● ADJ. **enjoyable, rewarding** | **favourite, popular** | **dangerous** | **expensive** | **national** *Eating out is the national pastime in France.*
● VERB + PASTIME **enjoy, indulge in, pursue**
● PREP. **~ among** *Fighting is a popular pastime among some of the town's boys.* **~ for** *Cycling is an enjoyable pastime for people of all ages.*

pastry *noun*

● ADJ. **crisp, light** *Bake until the pastry is crisp and golden.* | **soggy** | **golden** | **ready-made** | **sweet** | **choux, filo, flaky, puff, shortcrust**
● VERB + PASTRY **make** | **cut, knead, roll out** *Cut the filo pastry into 10 cm strips.* | **line sth with** *Line the tin with the pastry.* | **brush** *Brush the pastry with a little water.* | **bake/wrap sth in** *prawns wrapped in filo pastry*
● PASTRY + NOUN **base, case, parcel** | **board, cutter** | **chef**

pat *noun*

● ADJ. **affectionate, friendly** | **reassuring**
● VERB + PAT **give sb/sth** *He gave the dog a pat.*
● PREP. **~ on** *He gave her a reassuring pat on the shoulder.*

pat *verb*

● ADV. **gently, lightly** | **affectionately**
● PREP. **on** *He patted her gently on the shoulder.*

patch noun

1 material over a hole
- VERB + PATCH **have** *Her trousers have patches all over them.* | **sew on**
- PREP. **~ on** *dancers with patches on their costumes*

2 part of a surface that is different
- ADJ. **irregular** | **clear, coloured, dark** | **damp, wet** | **icy** *icy patches on the roads* | **bald** *He has a small bald patch on the crown of his head.* | **rough, sore**
- PREP. **in ~es** *The velvet curtains were faded in patches.* | **~ of** *There were some patches of clear blue sky.* **~ on** *A large damp patch had appeared on the ceiling.*
- PHRASES **a patch of colour** *flowers providing little bright patches of colour around the garden*

3 piece of land
- ADJ. **isolated** *an isolated patch of forest* | **cabbage, potato, vegetable**
- PREP. **in a/the ~** *working in his vegetable patch* **on a/the~** *located on a small patch of flat ground*
- PHRASES **a patch of grass/ground** *We found a nice patch of grass to sit on.*

4 period of time
- ADJ. **bad, difficult, rocky, rough, sticky** | **purple** *The team has hit a purple patch, with nine wins from their last ten games.*
- VERB + PATCH **go through, have, hit** *Their business hit a sticky patch last year.*
- PREP. **~ of** *going through a patch of poor health*

patchy adj.

- VERBS **be, seem** | **become** | **remain**
- ADV. **decidedly, extremely, very** *The local provision of facilities is decidedly patchy.* | **a bit, a little, rather** *Attendance at these matches has been rather patchy recently.*

patent noun

- VERB + PATENT **apply for, file** *In 1843 Bain filed a patent for his fax machine.* | **get, obtain, take out** | **protect sth by** *Genetically engineered plants can be protected by patent.* | **grant (sb), issue** | **refuse** *A patent will be refused if details of the item have already been released to the public.* | **have, hold** | **infringe**
- PATENT + NOUN **application** | **protection** | **law** *a leading authority on patent law* | **Office**
- PREP. **~ for** *In 1995 he was granted a patent for his invention.* **~ on** *Edison took out a patent on the light bulb.*
- PHRASES **patent pending** (= waiting to be issued) *The item is Patent Pending No. 912057.*

path noun

1 way across land
- ADJ. **long** | **narrow** | **steep** | **winding** | **cliff, coast, coastal, forest, garden, woodland** | **pedestrian, public** | **cycle** | **bridle**
- VERB + PATH **follow, go along/down/up, take** *Follow this path for about 100 metres, and it's on your right.* | **climb** | **keep on/to, stay on** | **leave, stray off** | **clear, make** *A path was cleared through the jungle.*
- PATH + VERB **go, run** *That path goes down to the sea.* | **descend** | **follow sth** *The path follows the stream for quite a way.* | **branch off, leave sth** *The path left the river bank and wound its way into the woods.* | **divide, fork** | **go to sth, lead (to) sth** *Where does this path lead?* | **bear left/right** | **wind, zig-zag** *Then the path zig-zags steeply uphill for a while.* | **be marked (sth), be signposted (sth)** *The path is clearly marked.* | **narrow, widen**
- PREP. **along/down/up a/the ~** *children running along the path on a/the ~* *I think we're on the path we used yesterday.* | **~ along/beside/by** *the path along the canal* **~ for** *a path for cyclists* **~ from** *the path from the hotel to the beach* **~ through** *I took the path through the park.* **~ to**

2 line of movement
- ADJ. **correct** | **flight** *The pilot was instructed to change his flight path.*
- VERB + PATH **steer** *He steered a path through the crowd.* | **trace** *Scientists can trace the path of the tornado.* | **block, stand in** *You're standing in my path!*
- PREP. **across sth's ~** *The car pulled right across the path of another vehicle.* **in/into the sth's~** *She stepped into the path of an oncoming lorry.* **out of sth's ~** *I managed to jump out of the path of the bike just in time.* | **~ through** *Footsteps had scored a diagonal path through the snow.* **~ to** *He moved quickly to block her path to the door.*
- PHRASES **everything in sb/sth's path** *The tornado destroyed everything in its path.*

3 way of achieving sth
- ADJ. **well-trodden, well-worn** *Her education followed the usual well-worn path of rich youngsters in the 1930s.* | **chosen** | **career**
- VERB + PATH **choose, find** *Everyone has to find their own path in life.* | **follow, pursue, tread** | **deviate from**
- PREP. **on a/the~** *His feet were now firmly on the path to success.* | **~ of** *The path of true love is never easy.* **~ to** *the path to happiness*
- PHRASES **obstacles in sb/sth's path**

pathologist noun

- ADJ. **consultant** | **forensic** | **independent** | **Home Office, police**
- PATHOLOGIST + VERB **examine sth** | **confirm sth** *The police pathologist examined the body and confirmed that death was due to poisoning.*
- PHRASES **pathologist's report**

patience noun

- ADJ. **endless, great, infinite**
- VERB + PATIENCE **exercise, have, show** *They thanked him for showing so much patience.* | **lack** | **be out of, lose, run out of** *It is quite clear that they are out of patience with me.* ◇ *We eventually ran out of patience with his childish behaviour.* | **keep** *I find it hard to keep my patience with them.* | **require, take** *Above all, fishing requires great patience.* | **exhaust, stretch, tax, test, try** *The children were beginning to try my patience.*
- PATIENCE + VERB **be exhausted, run out, snap, wear thin** *Molly could see Mr Kirkham's patience was running out, so she shut up.* ◇ *Her patience snapped and she walked out.* | **be rewarded** *Our patience was finally rewarded and we got the band's autographs.*
- PREP. **with ~** *She listened with infinite patience to his excuses.* | **~ for** *He has little patience for people who don't work.* **~ with** *The fans were losing patience with the team.*
- PHRASES **the patience of a saint** *These endless meetings are enough to tax the patience of a saint.*

patient noun

- ADJ. **Aids, cancer, diabetic, heart, etc.** | **mental, mentally-ill, psychiatric** | **seriously-ill, terminally-ill** | **hospital** | **long-stay** | **private** *He only takes private patients.* | **elderly, older** | **adult, child**
- VERB + PATIENT **examine, see, treat** *A GP sees an average of 35 patients every day.* | **admit** *The patient was admitted to hospital yesterday.* | **discharge** *patients waiting to be discharged from hospital* | **transfer**
- PATIENT + VERB **develop sth, have sth, suffer from sth** *The patient has a severe mental condition.* | **respond (to sth)** *These patients are responding well to the new drug.* | **improve**
- PATIENT + NOUN **care**
- PREP. **~ with** *patients with liver disease*

patient adj.

- VERBS **be, sound | remain**
- ADV. **extremely, incredibly, very | endlessly**
- PREP. **about** *She's been extremely patient about it all.* **with** *He was endlessly patient with the children.*

patriotic adj.

- VERBS **be | become**
- ADV. **fiercely, intensely, strongly, very | quite | unashamedly** *The party framed its message in unashamedly patriotic language.*

patrol noun

- ADJ. **routine | special | armed | foot** *Every police car and foot patrol in the area is on full alert.* **| dawn, night | air, army, military, naval, police, security | enemy | border, shore | traffic** *helicopters used for traffic patrols*
- VERB + PATROL **carry out, fly, go on** *The Italians flew regular patrols over the desert.* **| maintain** *Britain can maintain a continuous patrol of the seas with only three submarines.* **| send out** *They sent out four-man patrols to scout the area.*
- PATROL + NOUN **boat, car, vehicle | duty**
- PREP. **(out) on~** *police officers on patrol*

patron noun

- ADJ. **official** *the official patron of the college* **| influential, powerful | generous | wealthy**
- PHRASES **a patron of the arts** *The BBC is a major patron of the arts.*

patronizing adj.

- VERBS **be, sound | become | find sb/sth** *I found his tone rather patronizing.*
- ADV. **extremely, very | almost | mildly, rather, slightly, somewhat | unduly**
- PREP. **towards** *He's always very patronizing towards my mother.*

patter verb

- ADV. **gently, lightly, softly | down** *The rain pattered down softly.*
- PREP. **across** *Footsteps pattered across the floor.* **against, along** *The child's feet pattered along the landing.* **on** *Rain pattered lightly on the window.*

pattern noun

1 arrangement of lines, shapes, etc.
- ADJ. **intricate | geometric | floral**
- VERB + PATTERN **have** *The jumper has a geometric pattern on it.* **| design, make, print, produce, weave**
- PREP. **in a/the ~** *He had arranged the glasses in a pattern on the table.* **| ~on** *the pattern on the carpet*

2 usual manner
- ADJ. **basic, existing, familiar, normal, predictable, regular, set, traditional** *There is no set pattern for these meetings.* **| changing, ever-changing | complex | main | overall** *The overall pattern of our life changes little.* **| behaviour | employment | weather**
- VERB + PATTERN **establish, set | follow** *Their actions follow a very predictable pattern.* **| fall into, fit into** *ideas that do not fit neatly into his patterns of thought* **| show** *67% of patients showed a similar pattern of improvement.*
- PATTERN + VERB **develop, emerge** *Similar patterns are emerging all over Eastern Europe.*
- PREP. **~for** *the normal pattern for a boy/girl relationship* **~in** *the main patterns in English spelling* **~of** *patterns of behaviour*

patterned adj.

- VERBS **be**
- ADV. **heavily, highly, richly** *a highly patterned fabric* **| attractively, beautifully, prettily | boldly, brightly, brilliantly, strikingly | delicately, intricately**
- PREP. **with** *patterned with flowers*

pause noun

- ADJ. **brief, momentary, short, slight, small | long, prolonged | frequent | awkward | pregnant**
- VERB + PAUSE **take** *Shall we take a pause here?*
- PAUSE + VERB **follow** *In the pause that followed, I noticed that he was shaking.*
- PAUSE + NOUN **button** (on a video recorder, etc.)
- PREP. **after a/the ~** *'I don't know,' he said after a long pause.* **in a/the ~** *Everyone nodded in agreement in the pauses.* **with a/ the ~** *He read very slowly and with frequent pauses.* **without a/the ~** *She read the whole text without a pause.* **| ~before** *There was a long pause before he spoke again.* **~between** *in the pauses between his jokes* **~for** *a pause for breath* **~in** *during a pause in the conversation*

pause verb

- ADV. **briefly, (for) a moment, (for) an instant, momentarily** *She paused a moment and then walked away.* **| barely, hardly** *He spoke for two hours and barely paused for breath.* **| deliberately** *She paused deliberately, her eyes holding his.* **| dramatically, impressively, meaningfully, significantly | reflectively, thoughtfully | irresolutely**
- PHRASES **pause for breath/thought, pause only (long enough) to do sth** *Pausing only to put out her cigarette, she left the room.* **pause to consider/look/reflect/think** *Just pause to think before giving me your answer.* **without pausing** *Without pausing to knock, she opened the door.*

pavement noun

- ADJ. **wide | narrow | hard** *She had sore feet from walking on hard pavements all day.* **| broken, uneven | crowded | empty**
- VERB + PAVEMENT **step off, step onto | keep to | mount** *The car mounted the pavement and crashed into a lamp post.*
- PAVEMENT + NOUN **cafe, table, terrace**
- PREP. **along the~, down the~, on the~** *There was a car parked on the pavement and we couldn't get by.* **up the~**
- PHRASES **the edge of the pavement**

pay noun

- ADJ. **monthly, weekly | full, half** *He has taken leave on half pay.* **| high | low, poor** *workers on low pay* **| equal** *equal pay for men and women* **| basic | gross | take-home** *the average take-home pay of a manual worker* **| holiday | maternity | overtime | redundancy, severance | unemployment | sick, sickness | back** *The workers are demanding their back pay.* **| merit, performance, performance-related | profit-related**
- QUANT. **level, rate** *The job offers good rates of pay and excellent conditions.*
- VERB + PAY **get | give sb**
- PAY + NOUN **day | cheque, packet** *the money in my weekly pay packet* **| slip | increase, rise | cut | freeze | claim, demand | bargaining, negotiations | agreement, award, deal, offer, settlement | dispute, strike | levels, rates** *industrial unrest over pay levels in the public sector* **| scale, structure** *He's at the top of his company's pay scale.*
- PREP. **on ... ~** *Women are eligible for 18 weeks maternity leave on full pay.* **with ~** *holidays with pay* **without ~** *He has been suspended without pay.*
- PHRASES **a cut/an increase/a reduction in pay**

pay *verb*

• ADV. **handsomely, well** *She pays her workers very well.* | **gladly** *I would gladly pay for the extra security such a scheme would bring.* | **up** *I had a hard time getting him to pay up.*

• VERB + PAY **have to, must** | **be able/unable to, can/can't, can/can't afford to** *help for those genuinely unable to pay* ◇ *Protesters against the tax carried banners reading 'Can't pay! Won't pay!'* | **expect (sb) to** *You can expect to pay upwards of £200 a night at this exclusive hotel.* | **be liable to** *It is for the courts to decide who is liable to pay damages.* | **be ordered to, be required to** *The company was ordered to pay the five workers £5 000 in compensation each.* | **agree to, be prepared to, be willing to, offer to, promise to** | **fail to, neglect to** *He was made bankrupt for failing to pay debts totalling over £2 million.* | **refuse to** | **help (to)** *The revenue will be used to help pay for environmental improvements.* | **get sb to, make sb** *If Mac had killed Caroline, then he was going to make him pay the price.* | **let sb** *She wouldn't let me pay for my ticket.*

• PREP. **for** *How much did you pay for your new car?* **to** *We pay £200 a week to our landlord.*

• PHRASES **ability to pay** *Taxation should be based on ability to pay.*

payable *adj.*

• VERBS **be** | **become** *the date on which the rent becomes payable* | **make sth** *Cheques should be made payable to Brighton Borough Council.*

• ADV. **immediately** *This amount is payable immediately.*

• PREP. **by** *the costs payable by a client* **on** *No tax is payable on these earnings.* **to** *An initial fee is payable to the franchiser*

payment *noun*

1 paying/being paid

• ADJ. **immediate, prompt** | **late** *penalties for late payment of tax* | **early** | **full, part** *I enclose £65.20, in full payment of the bill.*

• VERB + PAYMENT **make** *How do you want to make payment—by cheque or in cash?* | **arrange for** | **accept, take** *Do you accept payment by credit card?* | **get, receive** | **stop, suspend, withhold** *I have authorized the bank to stop payment of the cheque.* | **refuse sb** | **defer, delay** *We may have to defer payment for a week.* | **demand**

• PAYMENT + VERB **be due**

• PREP. **in** ~ *She wrote out a cheque in payment of the fees.* **on** ~ **of** *He was released on payment of the ransom.* | ~ **for** *payment for work done* ~ **from, ~ to** *payment to the company from its customers*

• PHRASES **a method of payment, payment in advance** *The hostel requires full payment in advance.*

2 amount of money paid

• ADJ. **annual, monthly, etc.** | **regular** | **one-off, single** *All families of the crash victims will receive a one-off payment of £100 000.* | **cash, lump sum** | **token** | **generous** | **down, initial** | **additional, further, subsequent** | **interim, transitional** | **final** | **credit card** | **benefit, compensation, interest, maintenance, mortgage, rent, tax**

• VERB + PAYMENT **keep up, meet** *My client was unable to meet her rent payments.* | **increase, reduce** | **collect** *It was my job to collect payment for the trip.*

• PREP. **in** ~s *an extra $9 million in interest payments* | ~ **for** *a generous payment for his services* ~ **from** *payments to the landlord from his tenants* ~ **to**

• PHRASES **the balance of payments** *measures designed to reduce the balance of payments deficit*

pea *noun*

• ADJ. **dried, fresh, frozen, tinned** | **green** | **mushy** | **split**

• VERB + PEA **eat, have** | **shell** | **cook**

• PEA + NOUN **soup**

⇒ Special page at FOOD

peace *noun*

1 not war

• ADJ. **lasting, permanent** | **fragile, uneasy** | **relative** *The country is in a state of relative peace after ten years of fighting.* | **world** *obstacles in the way of world peace*

• VERB + PEACE **bring about, establish, make** | **keep** *UN troops are trying to keep the peace in the region.*

• PEACE + VERB **come** | **prevail, reign** *An uneasy peace prevailed in the first days of the ceasefire.*

• PEACE + NOUN **conference, congress, negotiations, process, talks** *This must not be allowed to hold up the peace process.* | **efforts, initiative** | **formula, plan, proposal** | **accord, agreement, deal, pact, settlement, treaty** | **broker, envoy** | **mission** *The president is visiting the country on a peace mission.* | **activist, campaigner, protester** | **group, movement** | **rally**

• PREP. **at** ~ **(with)** *Although the two countries were officially at peace, fighting continued.* | ~ **between** *peace between the warring factions in the area* ~ **with** *England finally made peace with France.*

2 state of being calm

• ADJ. **inner** | **perfect**

• VERB + PEACE **find, seek** *She finally found inner peace and happiness.* | **disturb, shatter** *The peace of the afternoon was suddenly shattered by a police siren.* | **leave sb in** *Go away and leave me in peace!*

• PEACE + VERB **reign** *She stopped shouting, and peace reigned supreme once again.* | **descend on sth, settle over sth** *Peace descended once more on the little town.*

• PREP. **at** ~ *Her father is at peace (= dead) now.* **at** ~ **with** *For the first time in months, she felt calm and at peace with the world.* **in** ~ *to live in peace and harmony*

• PHRASES **peace and quiet/tranquillity** *The island is a haven of peace and tranquillity.* **peace of mind** *The computer comes with a three-year guarantee for peace of mind.*

peaceful *adj.*

1 without war/violence

• VERBS **be** | **become** | **remain**

• ADV. **extremely, very** | **wholly** *The aims of the organization are wholly peaceful.* | **largely** | **comparatively, fairly, quite, reasonably, relatively**

2 quiet and calm

• VERBS **be, feel, look** | **become** | **remain**

• ADV. **extremely, very** | **utterly** | **comparatively, fairly, quite, relatively** | **blissfully, delightfully, serenely** *The time without her in the house had been blissfully peaceful.*

peak *noun*

1 mountain top

• ADJ. **high** | **jagged, rocky** | **snow-capped, snow-covered** | **distant** | **mountain**

• VERB + PEAK **climb, conquer, scale**

• PEAK + VERB **rise, tower** *We looked up at the rocky peaks towering above us.*

• PREP. **on a/the** ~ *climbers on the distant mountain peaks*

2 highest level, rate, etc.

• ADJ. **all-time** *The share index rose to a new all-time peak of 2732.* | **summer, winter, etc.** *The influx of tourists has reached its summer peak.*

• VERB + PEAK **rise to/towards** *Production is rising back towards its 1999 peak.* | **hit, reach** | **fall below/from, pass** | **be past** *Her performance is just past its peak.*

● PEAK + NOUN **hours, period, season, time, year |
demand** *at times of peak demand* **| rate** *peak-rate phone
calls* **| level | efficiency, performance** *The engine is
tuned to peak efficiency.* **| fitness, form**
● PREP. **at a/the/your~** *The crisis was now at its peak.* ◇
At his peak he was the best player in the world. **| ~of** *She is
at the peak of her popularity.* ◇ *The party's numbers
reached a peak of 40 000 in 2001.*
● PHRASES **in peak condition** *You want your hair to look
in peak condition.* **peaks and troughs** *Economic life
moves in cycles of peaks and troughs.*

peal noun

1 loud sound
● ADJ. **loud**
● VERB + PEAL **burst into, give, let out** *He burst into
peals of laughter.* ◇ *She let out a peal of laughter.* **| hear**
● PEAL + VERB **ring out**
● PREP. **with a~** *The bishop was welcomed to the church
with a peal of bells.* **| ~of**
● PHRASES **a peal of bells/laughter/thunder**
⇨ Note at SOUND

2 loud ringing sound of a bell
● ADJ. **loud**
● VERB + PEAL **ring (out)** *The bells of the cathedral
rang out their loud peal.*
● PEAL + VERB **ring out**
● PHRASES **a peal of bells**

peculiar adj.

1 odd/strange
● VERBS **be, feel, look, seem, smell, sound, taste | be-
come | find sb/sth, regard sb/sth as, think sb/sth** *I find
her attitude a bit peculiar, to say the least.*
● ADV. **most, very** *He is a most peculiar man!* **| a bit, a lit-
tle, quite, rather** *The meat tasted rather peculiar.*

2 only belonging to a particular person/place
● VERBS **be | become | remain**
● ADV. **by no means** *These problems are by no means pe-
culiar to this country.*
● PREP. **to** *the smell that is peculiar to hospitals*

peculiarity noun

● ADJ. **physical | individual | local**
● VERB + PECULIARITY **have** *The area has a few local
peculiarities.*
● PREP. **~about** *I noticed a certain peculiarity about his
appearance.*

pedal noun

● ADJ. **accelerator, brake, clutch | foot** *To stop the ma-
chine push the foot pedal.* **| bicycle | organ, piano |
wah/wah-wah** *Some guitar players tend to overuse the
wah-wah pedal.*
● VERB + PEDAL **press, push, put your foot on, step
on, use, work** *Her foot was working the pedal of the sewing
machine.* **| release, take your foot off**
● PEDAL + VERB **control sth, operate sth**
● PEDAL + NOUN **boat, car, cycle | bin**
● PREP. **on a/the~** *with one foot on the pedal*

pedal verb

● ADV. **fast, furiously, hard, like mad, madly** *He pedalled
furiously up the hill.* **| slowly | away** *She pedalled away
as fast as she could.*
● PREP. **along, down, up** *He pedalled along the lane and
up the hill.*

pedigree noun

● ADJ. **long** *Hereford cattle have a long pedigree.* **| dis-
tinguished, illustrious, impeccable, impressive**
● VERB + PEDIGREE **prove, show** *The champions really
showed their pedigree today.*
● PEDIGREE + VERB **stretch back** *These trees have pedi-
grees stretching back thousands of years.*
● PEDIGREE + NOUN **cat, dog, etc. | breed**

pee noun

● VERB + PEE **do, have, take** *I'm going to have a pee.* **|
be bursting for, be desperate for, need, want** *I need a pee
really badly.* **| go for**

peep noun

● ADJ. **little, quick**
● VERB + PEEP **have, take | get**
● PREP. **~at** *I noticed him take a little peep at his watch.*
~behind *The film gives us a peep behind the curtain at a
Broadway musical.* **~into** *a peep into the private life of a
world leader* **~through** *I took a peep through the keyhole.*

peep verb

● ADV. **cautiously | out** *He peeped out cautiously from
behind the door.*
● PREP. **at** *She was tempted to peep at the letter.* **through**
The child peeped through a crack in the door.

peer noun

1 person of the same age/status
● PEER + NOUN **group** *She was rejected by her peer
group.* **| pressure** *Children often take up smoking be-
cause of peer pressure.*
● PREP. **among sb's ~s** *They adopt behaviour that is
more socially acceptable among their peers.*

2 person of noble rank
● ADJ. **Conservative, Labour, etc. | hereditary | life**
*The Act made it possible for a woman to be created a life
peer.*
● PHRASES **a peer of the realm**

> **NOTE**
> **Aristocratic titles**
>
> **first, second, etc.~**
> *the 17th Earl of Lauderdale*
> **be created/made, become~**
> *She was made a baroness in 1992.*
> **succeed (sb) as~**
> *He was succeeded as third Baron Northwick by his
> nephew.*

peer verb

● ADV. **closely, intently | anxiously, cautiously, ner-
vously | curiously | short-sightedly** *peering short-
sightedly at the book* **| around/round, down, in, inside,
out, up, upwards** *A face was peering down at him.*
● VERB + PEER **try to**
● PREP. **around/round, at** *His pale blue eyes peered anxiously at Vic.* **into** *She peered round into the farmyard.* **out
of** *She peered out of the window.* **over** *trying to peer over
her shoulder* **past, through** *I peered through the letter box.*

peeved adj.

● VERBS **be, feel, look, seem, sound**
● ADV. **distinctly, very** *Birkett was looking distinctly
peeved.* **| a bit, a little, rather, somewhat | obviously**
● PREP. **about** *Ed was rather peeved about how Martin*

had handled the situation. **at** *peeved at her failure to contact him* **by** *Maisie seemed peeved by this question.*

peg *noun*

- ADJ. **steel, wooden | tent**
- VERB + PEG **drive in, hammer in** *She hammered in the steel tent pegs.* | **insert, put in** *The score is kept by inserting pegs into a board.*

pelvis *noun*

- ADJ. **narrow, wide | broken, fractured**
- VERB + PELVIS **tilt, thrust**

pen *noun*

- ADJ. **ballpoint, felt-tip/felt-tipped, fountain, ink, marker, quill | coloured**
- VERB + PEN **use, write (sth) with**
- PEN + VERB **write** *This pen won't write.* | **run out** *My pen's run out* (= has no more ink).
- PEN + NOUN **nib**
- PHRASES **pen and ink** *pen and ink drawings*

penalize *verb*

- ADV. **heavily | deliberately | unfairly, wrongly** *He claims he was unfairly penalized.* | **financially**
- PREP. **for** *Students will be penalized for mistakes in spelling and grammar.*

penalty *noun*

1 punishment
- ADJ. **harsh, heavy, severe, stiff, strict, tough | light | maximum, minimum | fixed, mandatory** *a new system of fixed penalties for most traffic offences* | **financial, tax** *the heavy financial penalties of leaving the scheme early* | **death** *the movement for the abolition of the death penalty*
- VERB + PENALTY **impose, introduce | threaten | increase | carry** *crimes which carry severe penalties* | **face, incur**
- PREP. **on/under ~ of** *They made him promise, under penalty of death.* | **~ for** *the penalty for murder* **~ on** *He threatened stiffer penalties on young offenders.*

2 disadvantage
- VERB + PENALTY **pay, suffer** *He's now paying the penalty for his misspent youth.* ◇ *People who lose their jobs are suffering the penalties for longer periods.* | **accept**
- PREP. **~ for** *You must accept the penalty for your rash behaviour.* **~ of** *It's just one of the penalties of fame.*

3 in football
- ADJ. **disputed | winning | first-half, second-half | early, late**
- VERB + PENALTY **award (sb), give (sb) | give away** *They were leading until Cole gave away a penalty.* | **appeal for | be awarded/given, get, have** *We were unlucky not to get a penalty.* | **kick, take | score from** *Owen scored from a first-half penalty.* | **miss | save**
- PENALTY + NOUN **area, box, spot | shoot-out**
- PREP. **~ by/from** *They won, thanks to a late penalty from Fry.*
- ⇨ Special page at SPORT

penance *noun*

- ADJ. **public**
- VERB + PENANCE **do, perform**
- PREP. **as a ~** *He devoted his life to helping the poor as a penance for his past crimes.* **in ~** *She knelt at her mother's feet in penance.* | **~ for** *He decided to do public penance for his sins.*
- PHRASES **an act of penance**

pencil *noun*

- ADJ. **blunt, sharp | hard, soft | coloured** *a box of coloured pencils* | **graphite, lead**
- VERB + PENCIL **colour sth in with, draw (sth) with, use, write (sth) with | sharpen**
- PENCIL + NOUN **lead, sharpener | drawing, sketch | line, mark**
- PREP. **in ~** *margin notes in pencil*

penetrate *verb*

- ADV. **deep, deeply, far** *caves penetrating deep into the hills* | **fully, totally | hardly** *The sunlight hardly penetrated the inner room.* | **quickly | slowly** *The news slowly penetrated his consciousness.* | **easily, readily** *These so-called secret societies were easily penetrated by intelligence agents.* | **successfully**
- VERB + PENETRATE **be able to, can/could | be difficult to | seem to** *The cold seemed to penetrate his bones.* | **fail to | allow sth to** *Cut two slashes on each side of the fish to allow heat to penetrate.*
- PREP. **into** *It is not yet known how deeply the radiation has penetrated into the soil.* **through** *The light could not penetrate through the thick curtains.* **to** *The dust had penetrated to all corners of the room.*

penetration *noun*

- ADJ. **deep | greater | import, market** *Our aim is to achieve greater market penetration.* | **water | sexual**
- VERB + PENETRATION **achieve**

penis *noun*

- ADJ. **erect | flaccid, limp**
- PENIS + VERB **become/get/go hard, harden, stiffen | become/go soft | shrivel**
- PENIS + NOUN **envy | length, size**

penniless *adj.*

- VERBS **be, die** *He died penniless in Paris.* | **find yourself** *Laura found herself virtually penniless.* | **leave sb** *The legal dispute left them penniless.*
- ADV. **totally | almost, practically, virtually**

pension *noun*

- ADJ. **big, comfortable, generous, good | small | basic | state | company, occupational | personal, private | old age, retirement**
- VERB + PENSION **draw, get, receive** *He draws his pension at the post office.* | **give sb, provide (sb with) | claim, qualify for** *You will have to find out whether or not you qualify for a pension.* | **live on** *She lives on her pension and her savings.*
- PENSION + NOUN **contributions, fund** *the company pension fund* | **plan, scheme**
- PREP. **on a ~** *He is now retired and on a pension.*

people *noun*

1 more than one person
- ADJ. **young | elderly, old | common, ordinary | (very) important** *a line of limousines carrying very important people* | **famous | middle-class, working-class | business, professional, working | unemployed | blind, deaf, disabled** *access for disabled people* | **intelligent | interesting, nice | strange | single | homeless**
- VERB + PEOPLE **meet | attract** *The local tourist board is trying to attract more people to the town.*

2 of a particular place/race
- ADJ. **local | country | indigenous, native | primitive** *the customs of primitive peoples of the Amazon Basin* | **tribal | Arab, Japanese, Slav, etc.** *the culture of the Basque people* | **black, white**

● VERB + PEOPLE **represent** *I was elected to represent the people of Bristol.*
● PHRASES **the peoples of the world**

pepper *noun*

1 spice
● ADJ. **ground** *freshly ground black pepper* | **black, white** | **cayenne**
● VERB + PEPPER **add, put in/on, season sth with, sprinkle** *He put some pepper on his steak.* | **grind**
● PEPPER + NOUN **mill, pot, shaker**
● PHRASES **salt and pepper** *Add salt and pepper to taste* (= in the quantity preferred).

2 vegetable
● ADJ. **bell, sweet** | **chilli, hot** | **green, red, yellow** | **stuffed** *peppers stuffed with meat and rice*
⇨ Special page at FOOD

perceive *verb*

● ADV. **clearly** | **dimly** *Babies are weak and vulnerable in the presence of huge shapes that they can only dimly perceive.* | **directly** *the world of directly perceived objects* | **differently** *Risks are perceived differently by different people.* | **easily, readily** *The industrial bias of canal building can be readily perceived by looking at Figure 7.3.* | **correctly** | **immediately**
● VERB + PERCEIVE **be able/unable to, can/could** | **fail to** | **be difficult to**
● PREP. **as** *The General's words were perceived as a threat by neighbouring countries.*
● PHRASES **commonly/generally/widely perceived** *It is widely perceived as a women's health problem, but it does also affect men.* **a failure/an inability to perceive sth**

per cent *noun*

● VERB + PER CENT **account for, amount to, be equal to, constitute, equal, represent** *Overseas earnings accounted for 9% of the total last year.* | **contain** *Roman coins containing about 25% zinc* | **reach, stand at** *Their share of the vote reached 6.5% in 1998.* | (All the verbs in the following collocate groups may be followed by **by, from** or **to** plus **per cent**. Sometimes the word **by** is left out.) **be/go/shoot up, expand, grow, improve, increase, jump, rise, soar** *Prices rose by 12% in 1998.* ◇ *Prices rose 12%.* | **be/go/come down, decline, decrease, depreciate, drop, fall, plummet, plunge, shrink** *Profitability is down from 16% to 12.2%.* | **boost sth, increase sth, raise sth** *hoping to boost sales by 10%.* | **cut sth, devalue sth, reduce sth, slash sth** *The currency was devalued 20% overnight.*
● PREP. **by 10, 20, etc. ~** *cutting carbon dioxide levels by 20% in 15 years* | **~ of sth** *In 40% of all cases, the parents had no idea of their child's problem.*
● PHRASES **about/around/only/over/up to 10, 20, etc. per cent ~** *Only 10% of the teenagers agreed with this statement.* ◇ *a process that can reduce the cost by up to 15%* **a boost/an improvement/an increase/a jump/a rise of 10, 20, etc. per cent** *a jump of 8% in cases of the disease* **a cut/decline/decrease/drop/fall/reduction of 10, 20, etc. per cent, fewer/less/more than 10, 20, etc. per cent** *Profits rose by more than 50% last year.* **growth of 10, 20, etc. precent, in the bottom/top 10, 20, etc. per cent** *His son was in the top 2% of the university's students.* **10, 20, etc. per cent less/more** *New cars use about 35% less fuel.* **10, 20, etc. per cent of all/of a total** *The tribe's land now amounts to around 50% of the total land area.*

percentage *noun*

● ADJ. **high, large** *The area has a high percentage of unemployed men.* | **low, small**

~ be down/up
  With the share price down at 234p, it might be time to start buying.
  The CAC index was up 18.84 points.
~ reach sth, stand at sth
  Consumer confidence reached a 30-year high.
  Second quarter sales stood at £18 billion.
~ be/remain unchanged
  The 100 Share Index remained unchanged at 5297.
~ gain (sth)
  The share gained 19 cents to close at 4.38.
~ suffer (sth)
  Profit margins suffered when the company lowered prices to remain competitive.
~ climb, edge up, go up, increase (~ increase in value for currencies), **jump, rise, rocket, shoot up, skyrocket, soar** (+ *by, from, to* or no preposition)
  Earnings per share climbed from 3.5p to 5.1p.
  The pound has increased in value relative to the euro.
  Profits have shot up by a staggering 25%.
  Oil prices have skyrocketed.
~ come/go down, crash, decline, decrease (~ decrease in value for currencies), **dive, drop, fall, plummet, plunge, shrink, slip, slump** (+ *by, from, to* or no preposition)
  Banana exports crashed nearly 50%.
  The pound fell to a 14-year low against the dollar.
  Net income plummeted to USD 3.7 million.
⇨ See also the note at CURRENCY

● VERB + PERCENTAGE **calculate** | **express sth as** *This figure can be expressed as a percentage of the total.*
● PERCENTAGE + NOUN **point** *Unemployment has fallen by two percentage points this month.* | **rate** *Insurance contributions are paid at a fixed percentage rate on all earnings.* | **figure** | **increase, rise** *the percentage rise in the average salary* | **decline, fall, reduction** | **share**
● PREP. **~ of** *What percentage of women own a car?*
● PHRASES **in percentage terms** *The numbers are relatively low in percentage terms.* **on a percentage basis** *The artist's agent receives commission on a percentage basis.*

perceptible *adj.*

● VERBS **be** | **become**
● ADV. **clearly, easily** *a clearly perceptible decline in public confidence* | **barely, hardly, scarcely** *His lips curved in a barely perceptible smile.*
● PREP. **to** *The difference is scarcely perceptible to the average reader.*

perception *noun*

● ADJ. **clear** | **common, general, widely-held, widespread** | **growing** | **accurate** | **public** | **human** | **extrasensory, sensory, visual**
● VERB + PERCEPTION **have** *I was shocked to learn of the perception people have of me.* | **gain** *We need to gain a clearer perception of how young people feel about the problem.* | **affect** *These developments hardly affected the public perception of the crisis.*

perceptive *adj.*

● VERBS **be**
● ADV. **extremely, highly, very** *a highly perceptive analysis of the problem* | **pretty, quite**
● PREP. **about** *He's very perceptive about people.*

perch verb

- ADV. **perilously, precariously** *The hotel was perched precariously on a steep hillside.*
- PREP. **on** *The birds perched on nearby buildings.*
- PHRASES **be perched high above/on sth** *The castle is perched high above the valley.* **perch/be perched on the edge of sth** *I perched on the edge of his desk to listen to him.* **perch/be perched on top of sth**

percussion noun

- ADJ. **tuned, untuned**
- PERCUSSION + NOUN **instrument | section**
⇨ Special page at MUSIC

perfect adj.

- VERBS **be, look, seem | make sth** *Hove's position makes it perfect for touring.*
- ADV. **absolutely, quite | far from, less than** *The treaty is far from perfect, but it is clearly the way forward.* | **almost, near, practically, virtually | impossibly** *the impossibly perfect shine on the vinyl-tiled floors* | **seemingly** *a seemingly perfect alibi* | **physically | mathematically**
- PREP. **for** *The day seemed perfect for a picnic.*

perfection noun

- ADJ. **great | absolute, utter | near | moral, physical, technical**
- VERB + PERFECTION **achieve, bring sth to, reach | seek, strive for** *She strives for perfection in everything.* | **fall short of**
- PREP. **close to ~** *The cooking was close to perfection.* **near ~** *A night's labour brought the sculpture one step nearer perfection.* **to ~** (= perfectly) *The dress fitted to perfection.* **towards ~** *a sequence of developmental stages towards the perfection of his violin technique*
- PHRASES **a degree/point of perfection** *He brought the art of photography to the highest point of perfection.* **a model of perfection** *The building became the model of perfection that architects sought to emulate.* **the pursuit of perfection** *She sometimes stayed up painting all night in her pursuit of perfection.* **a quest/search for perfection**

perform verb

1 do a task/duty/piece of work
- ADV. **effectively, efficiently, properly, successfully, well** *ensuring that tasks are properly performed* | **poorly | adequately, competently, reliably, satisfactorily | correctly | duly, faithfully** *He duly performed his own half of the bargain and expected the others to do likewise.* | **automatically | manually**
- VERB + PERFORM **be able/unable to** *The prince is no longer able to perform his duties.* | **be expected to**
- PHRASES **failure to perform sth** *failure to perform a contract*

2 work/function/play
- ADV. **brilliantly, efficiently, excellently, faultlessly, strongly, well** *One or two of the players performed brilliantly.* ◇ *The company has been performing strongly over the past year.* | **badly, disappointingly, disastrously, poorly** *The car performed poorly at high speeds.* | **adequately, competently, reliably, satisfactorily**
- VERB + PERFORM **be able/unable to | be expected to** *students who are expected to perform well*

3 give a performance
- ADV. **live** *The group will be performing live on tonight's show.* | **in public, publicly | together** *The two artists have never performed together before.*
- PHRASES **first performed** *The play was first publicly performed in 1872.* **rarely performed, see sth performed** *I've never seen this play performed before.*

---

performance noun

1 sth performed
- ADJ. **live | public | evening, matinee | amateur, professional | cameo | solo | repeat** *The party are dreading a repeat performance of their defeat in the last election.* | **ballet, concert, dance, musical, opera, theatrical | benefit, charity**
- VERB + PERFORMANCE **give, put on** *The theatre is putting on a performance of the popular musical 'Cats'.* | **attend, go to**
- PERFORMANCE + NOUN **art | artist**
- PREP. **in ~** *The course aims to develop the children's appreciation of music in performance.*

2 way in which sth is done
- ADJ. **brilliant, convincing, dazzling, electrifying, excellent, fine, flawless, good, great, impressive, inspired, outstanding, polished, remarkable, sparkling, spirited, strong, superb, wonderful** *The recording gives the most convincing performance of Stravinsky's 'Rite of Spring' to date.* ◇ *the country's strong economic performance over the last two years* | **bad, disappointing, lacklustre, poor | satisfactory | consistent | central** *Mel Gibson's central performance in the film as Hamlet* | **all-round, overall** *He got top marks for overall academic performance.* | **business, economic, financial, sales | academic, school**
- VERB + PERFORMANCE **deliver, give, put in** *The team put in an excellent performance at the World Cup.* | **affect | assess, measure | improve**
- PERFORMANCE + NOUN **indicator, level, measure, measurement, standard, target**
- PREP. **~ as** *her fine performance as Ophelia* **~ from** *The film has a great performance from Jack Lemmon.* **~ on** *his flawless performance on the piano*
- PHRASES **a level/measure/quality/standard of per-**

formance *to maintain a high level of performance* **on past performance** *Sales forecasts were based on past performance.* **the proper performance of your duties**

3 of a machine
- ADJ. **high | low, poor | engine**
- VERB + PERFORMANCE **affect | assess, measure | enhance, improve**

performer *noun*

- ADJ. **key, star, top** *The star performer of the match was Bill Holland who scored 26 points.* | **good, great, impressive, outstanding, polished, talented | poor | seasoned** *She's a seasoned concert performer.* | **live | solo | amateur, professional | circus, concert, radio, stage, street, television** *The president was a polished television performer.*

perfume *noun*

1 liquid with a sweet smell that you put on your body
- ADJ. **expensive | cheap | strong | subtle | fragrant, sweet | exotic | musky | stale**
- QUANT. **bottle**
- VERB + PERFUME **use, wear | dab on, put on, spray on** *She dabbed some perfume on her wrists.* | **smell | reek of, smell of** *She reeked of cheap perfume.*
- PERFUME + NOUN **bottle | company, house**
- PHRASES **a waft/whiff of perfume** *He caught a faint whiff of her expensive French perfume.*

2 pleasant smell
- ADJ. **sweet | heady, strong | delicate, faint | exotic, strange**
- VERB + PERFUME **smell | give off, release** *The lilies release their heady perfume in the evening.*
- PERFUME + VERB **fill sth** *The perfume of the roses filled the room.*

peril *noun*

1 great danger
- ADJ. **deadly, dire, grave, great**
- VERB + PERIL **be at/in | put sth in**
- PREP. **~of** *All aboard were in grave peril of drowning.*
- PHRASES **at your~** *Ignore these warnings at your peril.*

2 sth dangerous
- ADJ. **great** *the great perils facing the environment* | **immediate | hidden**
- VERB + PERIL **face** *We face the immediate peril of being bought out by another company.* | **avoid**
- PERIL + VERB **face sth**

perimeter *noun*

- ADJ. **inner, outer | northern, southern, etc.**
- VERB + PERIMETER **mark** *The river marks the eastern perimeter of our land.*
- PERIMETER + NOUN **fence, wall | road, track**
- PREP. **along the~** *I lugged my suitcase along the perimeter of the square.* **around/round the~** *We walked round the perimeter of the prison.* **inside/outside the ~** *They demonstrated just outside the perimeter of the embassy.* **on the~** *There's a small shop on the perimeter of the camp.*

period *noun*

1 length of time
- ADJ. **extended, lengthy, long, prolonged | brief, limited, short** *The offer is only available for a limited period.* | **full** *You have been paid for the full period of your employment with us.* | **fixed, set** *The medication is prescribed for a fixed period of time.* | **indefinite | early, late** *the late Victorian period* | **happy** *a happy period in her life* | **dark, difficult, lean** *a dark period in the country's history* | **critical** *a critical period in the development of the*

project | **interim, intervening | transitional | off-peak, peak | Christmas | medieval, Tudor, etc. | inter-war, post-war | accounting | cooling-off** *The customer has the right to cancel the contract during the seven-day cooling-off period.* | **formative** *The most formative period of life is childhood.* | **gestation, incubation | rest | training | waiting | trial** *You can use the software free for a 30-day trial period.* | **time**
- VERB + PERIOD **cover** *the period covered by the book*
- PERIOD + VERB **begin, commence | end | last**
- PERIOD + NOUN **costume, furniture**
- PREP. **after a ~** *after a long period of waiting* **during/throughout the~** *during the intervening period* **for a~** *We lived in Caracas for a brief period.* **in/within a/the ~** *Sales have gone up in the last-five-year period.* **over a/the~** *There will be a reduced bus service over the Christmas period.* ◇ *Changes were monitored over a period of two months.* **within a/the~** *Committee members will not be eligible for re-election within a period of two years.* | **~between** *the period between his resigning and finding a new job* **~from ... to ...** *the period from 1 July to 31 December*
- PHRASES **the beginning/end/start of a period, a period of history, sb's period of office** *Public spending was cut during his period of office.* **a period of study** *Try breaking your period of study into 20-minute blocks.* **a period of time** *The balance must be paid within an agreed period of time.* **a period of transition** *a period of transition between communist rule and democratic government*

2 menstruation
- ADJ. **heavy, light | menstrual | monthly**
- VERB + PERIOD **have** *I've got my period and don't feel too great.* | **start** *I was thirteen when I started my periods.*
- PERIOD + VERB **start | stop | last**
- PERIOD + NOUN **pains**

perishable *adj.*

- VERBS **be**
- ADV. **highly** *Many fresh foods are highly perishable.*

perjury *noun*

⇨ Note at CRIME

permanent *adj.*

- VERBS **be, prove, seem | become | make sth** *We decided to make the arrangement permanent.*
- ADV. **almost, virtually** *living in an almost permanent state of fear* | **relatively | apparently | not necessarily**

permissible *adj.*

- VERBS **be | consider sth**
- ADV. **perfectly** *This is perfectly permissible under the new regulations.* | **legally, morally**

permission *noun*

- ADJ. **full | special | express** *Staff may not leave early without the express permission of the director.* | **formal, government, official | written | necessary** *They chopped the trees down without having been granted the necessary permission.* | **prior** *He was not allowed to leave the city without the prior permission of the authorities.* | **planning** *You will need to obtain planning permission if you want to extend your house.*
- VERB + PERMISSION **have | gain, get, obtain, receive, secure | give (sb), grant (sb) | deny sb, refuse sb | need, require | apply for, ask (for), request, seek**
- PREP. **with/without sb's ~** *The information was published with the full permission of Amnesty International.* | **~for** *The council refused planning permission for the erection of a block of flats.* **~to** *permission to park*
- PHRASES **by (kind) permission of sb** *The illustrations are reproduced by kind permission of the British Library.*

permissive adj.

- VERBS **be | become**
- ADV. **extremely, highly, very** *a highly permissive attitude* | **sexually** *a society that is sexually permissive*

permit noun

- ADJ. **government, official | export, import | residence, residency | work | travel | resident's, visitor's | building, filming, fishing, landing, parking**
- VERB + PERMIT **have | give (sb), grant (sb), issue | get, obtain, receive | revoke | renew | apply** for | **need, require**
- PERMIT + VERB **expire, run out**
- PERMIT + NOUN **holder**
- PREP. **by ~** *Entry is by permit only.* **with/without a ~** *You can't park here without a permit.* | **~ for** *They applied for a permit for a street demonstration against university fees.*

permit verb

- ADV. **legally | generally, normally** *Development is not normally permitted in conservation areas.*
- VERB + PERMIT **refuse to | be designed to** *The bill was designed to permit workers to take up to twelve weeks' unpaid leave annually for family reasons.*

perpendicular adj.

1 pointing straight up
- VERBS **be**
- ADV. **almost, nearly** *an almost perpendicular staircase*

2 at an angle of 90° to sth
- VERBS **be**
- ADV. **exactly | almost | mutually** *two mutually perpendicular directions*
- PREP. **to** *The axis of the moon will now be exactly perpendicular to that of the earth.*

perpetuate verb

- ADV. **merely, only, simply** *Giving these events a lot of media coverage merely perpetuates the myth.*
- VERB + PERPETUATE **help (to) | serve to, tend to** *Schools tend to perpetuate the myth that boys are better at sport than girls.* | **seek to**

perplexed adj.

- VERBS **be, feel, look, sound**
- ADV. **deeply, genuinely, very | a little, rather, slightly, somewhat** *Gary looked rather perplexed.*

persecution noun

- ADJ. **systematic | political, religious**
- VERB + PERSECUTION **be subject/subjected to, face, suffer (from)** *Some students returning to the country may face political persecution.* | **escape from, flee from | fear**
- PERSECUTION + NOUN **complex** *She started to have a persecution complex when she couldn't get a job.*
- PHRASES **delusions/feelings of persecution, (a) fear of persecution, a victim of persecution**

perseverance noun

- ADJ. **great, sheer | dogged, untiring**
- VERB + PERSEVERANCE **have** *Does she have the perseverance to finish the work?* | **display, show** *He showed great perseverance by staying in the job.* | **require, take** *It may take some perseverance to find the right people.*
- PERSEVERANCE + VERB **pay off**
- PREP. **with ~** *Anyone can learn Japanese with perseverance.* | **~ with** *His perseverance with the new technique paid off.*

persist verb

1 continue doing sth
- ADV. **doggedly, stubbornly**
- PREP. **in** *If you persist in upsetting her, I will have to punish you.* **with** *The detective stubbornly persisted with his questions.*

2 continue to exist
- ADV. **still, to this day** *a belief that persists to this day* | **indefinitely**
- VERB + PERSIST **be likely to | tend to | be allowed to** *This situation cannot be allowed to persist.*
- PREP. **for** *If symptoms persist for more than a few days, see a doctor.* **into** *These practices persisted into the Middle Ages.* **through/throughout** *The depression persisted through much of the 1930s.* **until** *The snows persisted until the second month of the new year.*

persistence noun

- ADJ. **dogged, remarkable, sheer**
- VERB + PERSISTENCE **show**
- PERSISTENCE + VERB **be rewarded, pay off** *My persistence in demanding my rights finally paid off.*
- PREP. **by ~** *By sheer persistence, I eventually got her to change her mind.* **through ~** *He achieved success through dogged persistence.*

persistent adj.

- VERBS **be**
- ADV. **extraordinarily, extremely, incredibly, really, very** *The weeds were very persistent.* | **quite, rather** *Some infections can be quite persistent.*

person noun

- ADJ. **young | elderly, old | married, single | decent, good, lovely, nice | caring, gentle, kind, warm | bad, evil, wicked | happy, outgoing | rational, reasonable, sensible** *Any reasonable person can see that it is not fair.* | **average, normal, ordinary | private** *She is a warm but very private person.* | **blind, deaf, disabled | ill, sick** *the care of a terminally-ill person* | **missing | displaced, homeless | unemployed | dead | famous | important | innocent** *the imprisonment of an innocent person* | **right, wrong** *She's the right person for the job.* ◇ *The police now realize that they had the wrong person.* | **religious | business**
- PREP. **as a ~** *What's she like as a person?* **in ~** *She appeared in person to collect her prize.* **in the ~ of** *Help arrived in the person of our next-door neighbour.*
- PHRASES **the person concerned** *The disciplinary panel will notify the person concerned of its findings.* **the person in charge** *Can I speak to the person in charge, please?* **the person responsible** *Police think they have found the person responsible for the of muggings.*

personal adj.

- VERBS **be**
- ADV. **extremely, highly, very** *highly personal information* | **rather**

personality noun

1 character
- ADJ. **bright, bubbly, extrovert, jovial, lively, outgoing, sparkling, vibrant, vivacious | attractive, charismatic, charming, engaging, lovely, magnetic, pleasant, warm | dominant, dynamic, forceful, formidable, powerful, striking, strong | vulnerable, weak | multiple, split** *He developed a split personality after the crash.*
- VERB + PERSONALITY **be, have** *Barbara is/has a very forceful personality.* | **develop | express, reflect** *His*

choice of clothes reflects his personality. | **suit** *The job didn't really suit my personality.*
- PERSONALITY + NOUN **characteristic, trait | type | disorder, problem | development | change | test** *All candidates have to undergo a personality test.* | **clash**
- PHRASES **an aspect of your personality** *For the first time she was seeing the more unpleasant aspects of her husband's personality.* **a clash of personalities, the force/power/strength of your personality** *He has achieved success by the sheer strength of his personality.* **impose/stamp your personality on sth** *She stamped her personality on the whole programme.*

2 famous person
- ADJ. **leading, prominent, top, well-known | sports | media, radio, television/TV**
- PERSONALITY + NOUN **cult** *the personality cult surrounding Stalin*

personnel *noun*

1 staff
- ADJ. **qualified, skilled, trained | key | senior | management | authorized** *Only authorized personnel have access to the computer system.* | **company, corporate | army, military, security (force), service** *an employment agency for ex-service personnel* | **civilian | government, state | hospital, medical | administrative | technical**

2 department of a company
- VERB + PERSONNEL **be in, work in** *He's is in personnel, isn't he?*
- PERSONNEL + NOUN **department | director, manager, officer | records**

perspective *noun*

1 in art
- ADJ. **distorted | horizontal, vertical**
- PREP. **in~, out of~** *That tree is out of perspective.*
- PHRASES **the laws of perspective**

2 attitude to sth
- ADJ. **different, new | broader, wider | proper, true** *We can now see things in their true perspective.* | **cultural, historical, political, social, theoretical, etc.**
- VERB + PERSPECTIVE **get sth in/into, place sth in/into, put sth in/into, see sth in** *Her death put everything else into perspective.* | **gain, get, put** *When you reach middle age you get a different perspective on life.* ◇ *This website puts a completely different perspective on world news.* | **keep | lose | adopt** *The book adopts a historical perspective.* | **shift | provide**
- PREP. **from the ~ of** *We should view this from the perspective of the people involved.* **in/into~** *Let's get this into perspective.* | **~ in** *a feminist perspective in philosophy* **~ on/upon** *It's easy to lose perspective on things when you are under stress.*
- PHRASES **a sense of perspective**

perspiration *noun*
- QUANT. **bead, drop** *Great beads of perspiration trickled down his forehead.*
- VERB + PERSPIRATION **wipe** *He wiped the perspiration from his brow.* | **be bathed in, be drenched in, be soaked in** *My shirt was soaked in perspiration.* | **be clammy with, be damp with, be moist with, be wet with, glisten with** *Her face was wet with perspiration.*
- PERSPIRATION + VERB **run down sth, trickle down sth** *Perspiration ran down his face.* | **break out** *Perspiration broke out on my skin.* | **glisten**

perspire *verb*
- ADV. **heavily, profusely** *He had been working hard and was perspiring profusely.* | **a little**
- PREP. **with** *She was perspiring a little with the heat.*

persuade *verb*
- ADV. **successfully | almost | eventually, finally | quickly | easily** *She was easily persuaded to accompany us.* | **gently** *Dave gently persuaded the fish close enough to be lifted aboard the boat.* | **personally** *The education minister personally persuaded the prime minister to rethink.* | **somehow** *He somehow persuaded the studio to let him make the film.*
- VERB + PERSUADE **attempt to, endeavour to, seek to, try to | hope to | be able/unable to, can/could | manage to** *He eventually managed to persuade one of the staff to let him in.* | **help (to) | be difficult to | fail to**
- PREP. **into** *She was persuaded into buying an expensive dress.* **of** *We must persuade the government of the need for change.*
- PHRASES **an attempt/effort to persuade sb** *an unsuccessful attempt to persuade her colleagues* **be reluctantly persuaded** *I was reluctantly persuaded to join the committee.* **have difficulty (in) persuading sb** *They had difficulty in persuading the two sides to sit down together.*

persuasion *noun*

1 persuading
- ADJ. **gentle**
- VERB + PERSUASION **use** *I had to use a little gentle persuasion to get her to agree.* | **need, take** *She didn't need much persuasion.* | **be/seem open to** *He refused my offer at first, but seemed open to persuasion.*
- PHRASES **the art of persuasion** *She is very charming, and skilled in the art of persuasion.*

2 set of beliefs
- ADJ. **political, religious**
- PHRASES **of all/different/varying persuasions** *The meeting is open to people of all political persuasions.*

persuasive *adj.*
- VERBS **be | find sth**
- ADV. **extremely, highly, very** *His analysis is in many ways highly persuasive.* | **fairly, quite | enough, sufficiently** *The evidence was not really persuasive enough.*

pertinent *adj.*
- VERBS **be, seem | become | remain**
- ADV. **especially, extremely, highly, particularly, very**
- PREP. **to** *The issues dealt with in the report are highly pertinent to our own situation.*

pervasive *adj.*
- VERBS **be, prove | become | remain**
- ADV. **very | all-** *the all-pervasive influence of television*

perverse *adj.*
- VERBS **be, seem**
- ADV. **deeply, very** *This kind of reasoning is deeply perverse.* | **quite | almost | a little, rather, slightly, somewhat | deliberately** *Had you truly forgotten or were you just being deliberately perverse?*

perversity *noun*
- ADJ. **sheer** *She's marrying him out of sheer perversity.*
- PREP. **out of~**

pessimism *noun*
- ADJ. **deep, widespread**
- VERB + PESSIMISM **display** *He displayed his usual pessimism.* | **overcome**
- PREP. **~ about** *There were good grounds for pessimism about future progress.*
- PHRASES **a mood of pessimism**

pessimistic *adj.*

- VERBS **be, feel, look, prove, seem, sound** *These figures look quite pessimistic.* | **become** | **remain**
- ADV. **deeply, extremely, terribly, very** | **increasingly** | **rather, somewhat** | **unduly, unnecessarily** *His predictions proved unduly pessimistic.* | **generally**
- PREP. **about** *I am deeply pessimistic about the future.*

pest *noun*

- ADJ. **common** | **serious** | **agricultural, crop, garden, plant** | **insect** | **sex** (in newspapers) *Police are looking for a sex pest who is frightening late-night travellers.*
- VERB + PEST **control, eradicate** *These birds provide a useful function in controlling insect pests.*
- PEST + NOUN **control, controller, management** | **population**

pesticide *noun*

- ADJ. **chemical** | **dangerous, hazardous** | **approved** | **banned, unapproved**
- QUANT. **level** *It is claimed that current levels of pesticide do not pose a threat to health.* | **trace** *Traces of pesticide in the water were ten times above permissible levels.*
- PESTICIDE + NOUN **use** | **levels** | **residues** | **contamination, pollution** *tests for pesticide contamination in food* | **poisoning** | **spray**
- PHRASES **the use of pesticide**

pet *noun*

- ADJ. **domestic, family, household**
- VERB + PET **have, keep**
- PET + NOUN **shop** | **cat, dog, rabbit, etc.** | **owner** | **food**

petition *noun*

- ADJ. **bankruptcy, divorce** | **protest**
- VERB + PETITION **sign** | **deliver, file, present, send, submit** | **draw up, get up, launch, organize, raise** | **support** | **hear** *The petition will be heard tomorrow.* | **grant** *Her petition for divorce was granted.* | **dismiss, oppose, reject** *The district court has opposed the petition by the local electricity company.*
- PETITION + VERB **call for sth, demand sth, urge sth** | **oppose sth** *The petition opposes the closures.* | **support sth** *The petition supports the scheme to rebuild the road.*
- PREP. **~against** *We're getting up a petition against the proposed building plans.* **~by/from** *a petition by local residents* **~for** *Local government supports the petition for a new hospital.* **~in favour of** *a petition in favour of reform*

petrol *noun*

- ADJ. **lead-free, ultra-low sulphur (= ULSP), unleaded** | **leaded, lead replacement (= LRP)** | **high-octane**
- QUANT. **litre, tankful**
- VERB + PETROL **fill up with, fill sth (up) with** | **run on, take, use** *My car runs on unleaded petrol.* | **run out of** *We ran out of petrol and had to walk to the nearest garage.* | **douse sb/sth in/with, pour** *Thugs poured petrol over a schoolboy and tried to set him alight.* | **smell (of)** *Can you smell petrol?* ◇ *The air smelled of petrol.*
- PETROL + VERB **burn, ignite**
- PETROL + NOUN **engine, tank** | **gauge, pump** | **station** | **tanker** | **fumes** | **prices** | **tax** | **bomb**

pharmacy *noun*

- ADJ. **hospital, local** | **dispensing, retail**
- PHARMACY + NOUN **business, chain** | **licence** | **counter**
- PHRASES **available from pharmacies** *The ointment is available from pharmacies without prescription.*

phase *noun*

- ADJ. **early, first, initial, primary** | **second, secondary, etc.** | **current, latest, new, present** | **final, last** | **intermediate, transition** | **temporary** | **critical, crucial, important** *the critical phase of the operation* | **distinct** *The period can be divided into three distinct phases.*
- VERB + PHASE **begin, enter, open, start** *Society has entered a technological phase of evolution.* | **go through** *It's just a phase he's going through.* | **complete, pass**
- PREP. **during a/the ~** *During the first phase of expansion staff will move to the new offices.* **in a/the ~** *In the earliest phase of mental disorder, relatives feel confused.* | **~in a** *new phase in the European economy*

phenomenal *adj.*

- VERBS **be** | **become**
- ADV. **absolutely, quite, simply, truly** *This plant has truly phenomenal healing powers.*

phenomenon *noun*

- ADJ. **common, universal, widespread** | **isolated, rare, unique** | **new, recent** | **natural** | **curious, inexplicable, remarkable, strange** | **complex** | **observable** | **cultural, historical, linguistic, mental, physical, political, psychological, social, supernatural, urban**
- VERB + PHENOMENON **investigate** *His job is to investigate supernatural phenomena.*
- PHENOMENON + VERB **emerge, occur** *The phenomenon occurs during early foetal development.*

philosopher *noun*

- ADJ. **distinguished, eminent, famous, great** *the great philosophers of ancient Greece* | **ancient, classical** | **contemporary, modern** | **Eastern, Western** | **professional** | **experimental, legal, moral, natural** (*historical*), **political, social** *a talk by a distinguished moral philosopher* ◇ *He called himself a 'natural philosopher': today we would say a 'scientist'.* | **sceptical**
- PHRASES **a philosopher of religion/science**

philosophical *adj.*

1 of philosophy
- VERBS **be** | **become, get** *The debate was getting too philosophical for me.*
- ADV. **purely** *a purely philosophical argument* | **rather**

2 calm and accepting
- VERBS **be** *Try to be philosophical about it.* | **remain**
- ADV. **very** | **quite**
- PREP. **about** *Mum's being quite philosophical about the whole thing.*

philosophy *noun*

1 study of ideas about the meaning of life
- ADJ. **ancient, classical** | **contemporary, modern** | **Eastern, Western** | **experimental, moral, natural** (*historical*), **political, religious, social**
- PHRASES **the philosophy of history/religion/science**
⇨ Note at SUBJECT (for verbs and nouns)

2 particular system of beliefs
- ADJ. **competing, differing** | **prevailing** *humanism—the prevailing philosophy today in the Western world* | **basic, general, underlying** | **personal** | **homespun, simple** *the homespun philosophy that kept her going during this difficult period* | **liberal** | **design, economic, educational, management, market, political, religious, social** *a furniture-maker's design philosophy*
- VERB + PHILOSOPHY **develop, formulate** *developing a personal philosophy* | **articulate** | **adopt, embrace, espouse** | **reject**
- PHILOSOPHY + VERB **inform sth, underlie sth,**

underpin sth *the philosophy underlying the education system* | **prevail** *the management philosophy which prevailed at that time*
- PREP. **~behind** *The new measures were introduced with no explanation of the philosophy behind them.*
- PHRASES **a philosophy of life/mind**

phobia noun

- ADJ. **cat, water, etc.**
- VERB + PHOBIA **have, suffer from**
- PHOBIA + NOUN **sufferer**
- PREP. **~about/of sth** *He has a phobia about snakes.*

phone noun

- ADJ. **cellular, cordless, mobile, portable | car | pay** (also **payphone**), **public** *There's a public payphone in reception.* | **office, private**
- VERB + PHONE **be on** *She's on the phone at the moment.* | **use** *Can I use your phone?* | **answer, get** (*informal*), **lift, pick up** *If the phone rings, don't answer it.* ◇ *Can you get the phone?* | **hang up, put down, replace** *I hung up the phone when he started shouting at me.* | **slam down** *She slammed the phone down in a rage.* | **be wanted on** *Mum, you're wanted on the phone.* | **call sb to** *He was called to the phone just as he was leaving.* | **connect | disconnect | bug, tap** *I think our phone is being tapped.* | **wait by** *She waits by the phone all day but he doesn't ring.* | **leave/take off the hook** *I couldn't get through because you'd left the phone off the hook.*
- PHONE + VERB **ring | be engaged** *His phone is engaged.* | **be off the hook | go dead** *The phone suddenly went dead in the middle of our conversation.*
- PHONE + NOUN **number | book | bill | call, conversation, message | card** (also **phonecard**) **| company, network, service | booth, box | line** *The modem links the computer to a phone line.*
- PREP. **by~** *We keep in contact by phone but we rarely see each other.* **on the~** *We spoke on the phone the other day.* **over the~** *I haven't seen her but we spoke over the phone.*

photo noun

- ADJ. **old, recent | black-and-white, colour | clear | excellent, good, great** (**good**) **quality | glossy | framed | signed** *His most treasured possession is a signed photo of his footballing hero.* | **group, team | family | wedding | school | cover, newspaper, press | passport, publicity, security | still | action** *The annual has a good range of features and colour action photos.* | **aerial, air | digital, polaroid | nude, pornographic, topless**
- VERB + PHOTO **get, take** *I got some great photos of the party.* ◇ *Can I have my photo taken with you?* | **pose for** *posing for a group photo* | **develop** *I can't wait till the photos have been developed.* | **blow up, enlarge | crop | mount | publish | make** *The sun rising over the horizon would have made a good photo.*
- PHOTO + NOUN **album | frame | call, opportunity, session, shoot** *The press followed the president round the hospital, waiting for a photo opportunity.* | **journalism, journalist | processing | booth** *We found a photo booth on the station.* | **story | caption**
- PREP. **in a/the~** *Tell me who everyone is in the photo.* | **~of** *a photo of my son Edmund*

photocopy noun

- VERB + PHOTOCOPY **do, make, run off, take** *Could you take a photocopy of this letter for me, please?*

photograph noun

- ADJ. **old, recent | black-and-white, colour, coloured, sepia, tinted** *Tinted photographs were an early substitute for colour.* | **blurred, fuzzy, grainy, out of focus** *This photograph is out of focus.* | **faded | clear | sharp | excellent, good, great, lovely, stunning, superb, wonderful** | (**good**) **quality | glossy | framed | signed | studio | group, team | family | wedding | school | cover, magazine, newspaper, press** *The cover photograph of one magazine showed a dying soldier.* | **publicity | documentary | fashion | portrait-sized, postcard-sized | passport, passport-sized | facial** *Send a recent facial photograph of yourself with your application.* | **close-up | still** *Frame the subject in the video viewfinder as you would for a still photograph.* | **aerial, air, satellite | digital, polaroid | infrared | erotic, explicit, indecent, nude, obscene, pornographic, topless**
- VERB + PHOTOGRAPH **get, take** *Did you manage to get a photograph of the goal?* ◇ *I spent the day taking photographs of the city.* | **pose for | develop | blow up, enlarge | scan (in)** *I scanned in some photographs of the family to send to friends by email.* | **touch up** *The photograph has been touched up to conceal her double chin.* | **crop | mount** *I cropped the photograph and mounted it on some card.* | **publish | make** *The sun rising over the horizon would have made a good photograph.*
- PHOTOGRAPH + VERB **appear** *Her photograph appeared in all the papers.* | **depict sth, show sth | capture sth** *The photograph manages to capture the excitement of the occasion.*
- PHOTOGRAPH + NOUN **album | frame**
- PREP. **in a/the~** *The wing is assembled as shown in the photograph below.* | **~of** *An aerial photograph of the field shows clearly where the buildings were.*
- PREP. **photograph courtesy (of)** ... *photograph courtesy Liverpool Evening News* (= acknowledging permission to publish a photograph)
⇒ Note at ART

photographer noun

- ADJ. **distinguished, famous, leading, top | brilliant, experienced, good | keen | amateur | commercial, freelance, professional | official | newspaper, press | police | fashion, landscape, portrait, sports, etc.**
- VERB + PHOTOGRAPHER **pose for**
- PHOTOGRAPHER + VERB **shoot sth, take pictures/shots** *The photographer shot the usual roll of pictures.* | **snap (away at) sb/sth** *She didn't think much of the photographers snapping away at her.* | **capture sb/sth** *Photographer Darren Kidd captured the unique atmosphere of the event.*
- PHRASES **a photographer's gallery/studio**
⇒ Note at JOB

photography noun

- ADJ. **black-and-white, colour | flash | infrared | aerial, underwater | close-up | still | trick | professional | documentary, news | art | fashion, portrait, sports, wildlife, etc.**
- PHOTOGRAPHY + NOUN **magazine | competition**

phrase noun

- ADJ. **colloquial, idiomatic | key** *'Start slowly' is the key phrase for the first-time marathon runner.* | **famous | empty, glib, hackneyed, stock** *He keeps coming out with the same old stock phrases* | **memorable, well-turned | musical | adjectival, adverbial, noun, verb**
- VERB + PHRASE **use | coin** *Who coined the phrase 'desktop publishing'?*
- PHRASE + NOUN **book**
- PREP. **in a/the~** *She was, in her own memorable phrase, 'a woman without a past'.*
- PHRASES **a choice of phrase** *Her unfortunate choice of phrase offended most of the audience.* **a turn of phrase** *He is meticulous in his choice of words and turns of phrase.*

phrase *verb*

- ADV. **carefully** *The statement was very carefully phrased.* | **differently** *I should have phrased my question differently.*

physical *adj.*

- VERBS **be** *The problem is purely physical, not mental.*
- ADV. **purely** | **almost** *The shock of the darkness was almost physical.*

physician *noun*

- ADJ. **eminent** | **experienced, qualified** | **junior, senior** | **practising** | **consultant** | **general** | **hospital** | **family, personal, royal** *the king's personal physician*
- PREP. **~to** *physician to the Duke of Albemarle*
⇨ Note at DOCTOR (for verbs)

physicist *noun*

- ADJ. **brilliant, distinguished, eminent** | **classical, modern** | **experimental, theoretical** | **atomic, mathematical, medical, nuclear, particle**
⇨ Note at JOB

physics *noun*

- ADJ. **classical** | **modern** | **experimental, theoretical** | **atomic, high-energy, mathematical, medical, Newtonian, nuclear, (elementary) particle, quantum** | **A-level** | **school, university**
- PHRASES **the laws of physics**
⇨ Note at SUBJECT (for verbs and nouns)

physiotherapist *noun*

- ADJ. **qualified, trained**
⇨ Note at DOCTOR (for verbs)

physiotherapy *noun*

- ADJ. **intensive** | **regular**
- VERB + PHYSIOTHERAPY **provide** | **have, receive, undergo** *I'm undergoing regular physiotherapy for a back problem.*
- PHYSIOTHERAPY + NOUN **clinic, department** | **treatment** | **equipment** | **training**

physique *noun*

- ADJ. **good, magnificent, muscular, powerful, strong, superb** | **frail**
- PREP. **~for** *She doesn't have the physique for a dancer.*

piano *noun*

- ADJ. **baby grand, grand, upright** | **digital, electric, electronic** | **tinny**
- VERB + PIANO **tune** | **build, make**
- PIANO + NOUN **key, lid, wire** | **stool** | **tuner** | **bar** *There is a piano bar for evening entertainment.*
- PREP. **at the~** *sitting at the piano* **on the~** *playing classical music on the piano*
⇨ Special page at MUSIC

pick *noun*

- VERB + PICK **have** *She had her pick of the single men.* **take** *Which do you want? Take your pick.*
- PHRASES **get/take first pick** *I got the first pick of the prizes because I was the oldest.*

pick *verb*

1 choose sb/sth
- ADV. **at random** *Names were picked at random out of a hat.* | **out** *He was picked out as the best player.*

- PREP. **as** *They picked Jane as the captain.* **for** *Have you been picked for the team?*

2 take sth from the place where it is growing
- PHRASES **freshly picked** *freshly picked strawberries*

PHRASAL VERB
pick sth up

- ADV. **carefully, gingerly** *Rather gingerly, George picked up the tiny bundle.* | **idly** *I idly picked up a magazine and flicked through it.*
- VERB + PICK STH UP **try to** | **bend to, stoop to**
- PREP. **by** *He picked the pan up carefully by the handle.* **from, off** *She stooped to pick the book up off the floor.*

picket *noun*

- ADJ. **mass** | **flying** *Flying pickets arrived from all over the country.*
- VERB + PICKET **organize** *They organized a mass picket of the governor's palace.*
- PICKET + NOUN **duty** | **line** *Abuse was hurled at workers who crossed the picket line.*

pickle *noun*

- ADJ. **sweet** | **dill** | **lime**
- QUANT. **jar**
- PHRASES **and/with pickle/pickles** *a cheese and pickle sandwich*

picnic *noun*

- VERB + PICNIC **go for/on, have** *Lets have a picnic down by the river.* | **make** *Will you help me make a picnic?* | **bring, take** *We took a picnic and spent the day watching the races.* | **pack, unpack**
- PICNIC + NOUN **basket, blanket, hamper, rug, set, table** | **lunch, tea** | **area, place, site, spot**

picture *noun*

1 painting/drawing/photograph
- ADJ. **attractive, beautiful, lovely, striking, stunning, wonderful** | **blurred** | **black and white, colour** | **posed**
- VERB + PICTURE **draw, paint** | **colour in** *The book has simple stories and pictures to colour in.* | **frame, hang, mount** | **display, exhibit, show** | **pose for, sit for** | **get, snap, take** *I got some good pictures of the procession.* | **touch up**
- PICTURE + VERB **depict sth, show sth** | **hang**
- PICTURE + NOUN **frame** | **book, postcard** | **gallery** | **hook, rail** | **editor**
- PREP. **in a/the~** *I can't see you in the picture.* ◇ *The story is told in pictures.* | **~of** *It's a picture of a country village.*
⇨ Note at ART

2 mental image
- ADJ. **vivid** *The book gives a vivid picture of life in Victorian England.* | **clear** | **complete, comprehensive, full, general, overall, total, whole** *The programme was interesting but it didn't give the full picture.* | **incomplete** | **broad** *My visits enabled me to build up a broad picture of the culture.* | **composite** *Through interviews and old photos we put together a composite picture of life in the village a hundred years ago.* | **accurate, balanced, realistic, representative, true** | **false, misleading, one-sided, over-simplified, unbalanced** | **idealized, optimistic, rosy** | **bleak, depressing, dismal, gloomy, grim, negative** *The report paints a dismal picture of the government's economic record.* | **confused, distorted** | **detailed** | **complex, complicated** | **disturbing** | **mental** *I tried to form a mental picture of the building being described.* | **historical**
- VERB + PICTURE **build (up), construct, create, develop, establish, form, gain, get, obtain, put together** *They're trying to build up a detailed picture of the incident.*

| give, paint, present, project, reveal *The figures reveal a disturbing picture of the state of our schools.* | complete | conjure up *The smell of the sea conjures up pictures of children playing on the beach.*
• PICTURE + VERB **emerge** *What emerges is a complex picture of family rivalry.*

pie *noun*

• ADJ. **apple, meat, etc.** | **mud** *The children are making mud pies in the garden.*
• QUANT. **piece, slice**
• VERB + PIE **eat, have** | **bake, cook, make**
• PIE + NOUN **filling** | **dish**
• PREP. **in a/the~** *What's the filling in these pies?*
⇨ Special page at FOOD

piece *noun*

1 separate amount; parts of sth
• ADJ. **big, huge, large, long** | **little, short, small, tiny** *The plate smashed into little pieces on the stone floor.* | **bite-sized** *The book breaks the information into bite-sized pieces.* | **equal** | **odd** *She makes her sculptures out of odd pieces of scrap metal.*
• PREP. **in ~s** *The vase was now in pieces on the kitchen floor.* | **~ of** *a piece of bread* ◇ *A few pieces of the jigsaw were missing.*
• PHRASES **bits and pieces** *I just need to get a few bits and pieces at the supermarket.* **break/smash into pieces** *The cake just broke into pieces when I cut it.* **come to pieces** *This chair comes to pieces.* **fall to pieces** *My old dictionary is falling to pieces.* **piece by piece** *We'll need to take the engine apart, piece by piece.* **smash sth to pieces, take sth to pieces** *Can I take this jigsaw to pieces?* **tear sth into/to pieces** *She tore the letter into tiny pieces.*

2 of art/music/writing, etc.
• ADJ. **amazing, beautiful, brilliant, fine, good, impressive, lovely, magnificent, marvellous, remarkable, superb, wonderful** *The best pieces include three paintings by El Greco.* | **effective, powerful** *This is an effective piece of writing.* | **atmospheric, dramatic** | **interesting** | **favourite** | **important** | **ambitious** | **original** *an original piece written specifically for the producer* | **short** *a short piece by Willie Simmonds on television satire* | **finished** | **occasional** *an occasional piece on the lives of ordinary people* | **centre** (also **centrepiece**) | **companion** *a companion piece to the portrait of Gauguin's empty chair* | **modern, period, traditional** | **choral, orchestral, piano** | **museum**
• VERB + PIECE **compose, produce, write** *He hasn't produced a single piece of writing this year.* | **commission** | **perform, play, sing** | **read, hear** | **publish** | **display, exhibit, show**
• PIECE + VERB **be called sth, be entitled sth**
• PREP. **~ by** *They are exhibiting two important pieces by Calder.* **~ for** *a piece for symphony orchestra, choir and four soloists* **~ from** *She read a piece from 'Alice in Wonderland'.* **~ of** *a piece of jewellery*
• PHRASES **a piece of music/sculpture/work/writing**
⇨ Note at ART

pig *noun*

1 animal
• ADJ. **domestic** | **feral, wild** | **sucking/suckling**
• VERB + PIG **breed** | **keep** | **feed** | **fatten** *pigs being fattened for slaughter* | **slaughter**
• PIG + VERB **grunt, oink, squeal** | **browse, root** *A pig rooted in the orchard.*
• PIG + NOUN **farm, farmer**

2 person
• ADJ. **fat** | **greedy** | **male chauvinist**
• PHRASES **make a pig of yourself** *We cooked up a load of pasta and all made pigs of ourselves.*

pigeon *noun*

• ADJ. **carrier, homing, racing** | **feral** | **wood** | **clay** *clay pigeon shooting*
• QUANT. **flock**
• PIGEON + VERB **fly** | **strut** *A pigeon strutted along the roof, cooing rhythmically.* | **nest, roost** | **coo, croon**
• PIGEON + NOUN **droppings, shit** (*taboo*) | **loft** | **fancier**

pile *noun*

• ADJ. **big, great, high, huge, large, massive, vast** | **thick** | **little, small, tiny** | **neat, tidy** | **untidy**
• VERB + PILE **place sth in/into/on, put sth in/into/on** *I put the letter in the envelope and placed it on the pile.* ◇ *I've put the books into three separate piles.* | **dump** *He dumped a pile of dirty clothes onto the floor.* | **add sth to** *Just add that application to the pile.* | **flick through, leaf through, look through, riffle through, shuffle through, sort through** *I leafed through the pile of documents until I found the one I wanted.*
• PREP. **amid a/the ~** *The money lay amid a pile of unopened letters.* **behind a/the~** *He was busy behind a pile of papers on his desk.* **beneath/under a/the~** *I pulled my diary from beneath a pile of files.* **in a/the~** *The washing is in a pile on the floor.* **on a/the ~** *She closed the magazine and threw it back on the pile.* | **~of** *a pile of books* ◇ *I've got piles of work to do.*
• PHRASES **be reduced to a pile of sth** *The house was reduced to a pile of rubble.* **the bottom/top of the pile** (*figurative*) *The government is doing little to help those on the bottom of the social pile.* **sort sth into piles** *I sorted the clothes into two piles.*

pile *verb*

• ADV. **neatly** | **up** *We piled the boxes up neatly.*
• PREP. **against** *We piled sandbags against the door.* **on, onto** *She piled food onto our plates.* **on top of** *They piled stones on top of the mound.* **with** *a table piled high with magazines*
• PHRASES **piled high**

pile-up *noun*

• ADJ. **multiple** *a multiple pile-up involving a minibus and five cars* | **eight-vehicle, five-car, etc.** | **motorway**
• PILE-UP + VERB **involve sth** | **happen, occur**
• PREP. **in a/the~** *A young man died in a pile-up on the M1 last night.*

pilgrimage *noun*

• ADJ. **annual** | **spiritual**
• VERB + PILGRIMAGE **go on, make**
• PILGRIMAGE + NOUN **route**
• PREP. **during a/the~** *There was a ban on political protests during the pilgrimage.* **on a/the~** *He was on his annual pilgrimage to Mecca when he fell ill.* | **~to** *His parents made a pilgrimage to Lourdes.*
• PHRASES **a centre/place of pilgrimage, an object of pilgrimage** *The shrine was an object of pilgrimage.*

pill *noun*

1 small round flat piece of medicine
• ADJ. **diet, sleeping, vitamin**
• QUANT. **bottle**
• VERB + PILL **pop, swallow, take** | **give sb, prescribe (sb)** *The doctor prescribed her some pills to help her sleep.*

2 the pill to avoid becoming pregnant
• ADJ. **contraceptive**
• VERB + PILL **be on, go on, use** | **prescribe (sb), put sb on** *Her doctor put her on the pill at 16.* | **come off, stop**

pillar noun

- ADJ. **massive, solid, squat | supporting | concrete, marble, stone**
- PILLAR + VERB **hold sth up, support sth** *The roof is supported by eight massive stone pillars.*
- PREP. **behind a/the~** *I hid behind a pillar when I saw my former teacher.* | **~of** *a pillar of rock/smoke*

pillion noun

- VERB + PILLION **ride** *He drove his motorbike, with me riding pillion.*
- PILLION + NOUN **seat | passenger, rider**
- PREP. **on the~** *I made the whole journey on the pillion.*

pillow noun

- ADJ. **feather | lumpy**
- VERB + PILLOW **fluff (up), plump up, pummel, punch** *She plumped up the pillows for her sick daughter.* | **fall/lie/sink back against/on** *He lay back on his pillows and closed his eyes.* | **be propped (up) on | bury your face/head in** *She buried her head in the pillow and wept.*
- PILLOW + NOUN **case, slip | fight**

pilot noun

- ADJ. **experienced, professional, qualified, trained | inexperienced, trainee | airforce, RAF | private | airline, bomber, fighter, glider, helicopter, jet | aerobatic | automatic** *The aircraft was set on automatic pilot.* ◇ *(figurative) She worked on automatic pilot, her hands carrying out the necessary movements.*
- PILOT + VERB **fly (sth) | crash (sth) | bale out, eject** *The pilot baled out as the aircraft crashed into the sea.*
- PILOT + NOUN **error** *The air crash is thought to have been caused by pilot error.*
- ⇨ Note at JOB

pin noun

- ADJ. **drawing, safety, tie | brass, bronze, diamond, metal, steel**
- VERB + PIN **drive in, stick in** *The map had a lot of little pins stuck into it.* | **remove**

pin verb

1 fasten sth with a pin
- ADV. **carefully** *She carefully pinned the two pieces of cloth together.* | **firmly | back, on, together, up** *Her hair was pinned back.* ◇ *pictures pinned up on the walls*
- PREP. **onto** *The poster had been pinned onto a large wooden board.* **to** *Maps were pinned to the walls.*
- PHRASES **pin sth in place**

2 hold sb in one position
- ADV. **helplessly | down** *He was pinned down on the floor.*
- PREP. **against** *He pinned her against the wall.* **behind** *His arms were pinned behind his back.* **to** *She was pinned helplessly to the desk.*

PHRASAL VERB

pin sth down
- ADV. **precisely** *The difference between the two approaches is hard to pin down precisely.*
- VERB + PIN STH DOWN **be difficult to, be hard to**

pinch verb

1 take hold of sth between your thumb and finger
- ADV. **firmly | gently | sharply | playfully | together** *Apply pressure to the nose by pinching the nostrils firmly together.*
- PREP. **between** *He pinched the leaf between his thumb and forefinger.* **on** *He pinched me sharply on the arm.*

2 be too tight
- ADV. **badly** *My shoes were pinching badly.*

pineapple noun

- ADJ. **juicy, sweet**
- PINEAPPLE + NOUN **chunks, rings** *a tin of pineapple chunks*
- ⇨ Special page at FRUIT

pink adj.

1 pale red
- VERBS **glow** *The western sky was glowing pink.*
- ADV. **very | slightly**
- ADJ. **bright, brilliant, fluorescent, hot, shocking, vivid | dark, deep, rich | baby, delicate, light, pale, pastel, soft | dusky | coral, pearly, rose, salmon**
- ⇨ Special page at COLOUR

2 red in the face
- VERBS **be, glow, look | go, grow, turn** *She could feel herself going pink.*
- ADV. **very | faintly, quite, slightly**
- ADJ. **bright**
- PREP. **with** *He was pink with anger.*

pinnacle noun

- VERB + PINNACLE **reach** *He had reached the pinnacle of his military career.*
- PREP. **at the~of** *She is at the pinnacle of her profession.*

pinpoint verb

- ADV. **exactly, precisely**
- VERB + PINPOINT **can/could** *With this you can pinpoint the precise location of the sound.* | **be difficult to**
- PREP. **as** *Stress at work was pinpointed as the cause of his illness.*

pint noun

1 measure of liquid
- ⇨ Note at MEASURE

2 pint of beer
- VERB + PINT **consume, drink, have | sip | down, drain, finish, knock back, sink** *He could sink a pint faster than anyone else I knew.* | **draw (sb), draw off, pull (sb)** *I got the barman to pull me another pint.* | **buy (sb), order, stand sb** *He stood me a pint in the pub after work.*
- PINT + NOUN **glass**

pioneer noun

- ADJ. **early | true**
- PIONEER + NOUN **spirit | missionary**
- PREP. **~in** *one of the early pioneers in plastic surgery*

pipe noun

1 hollow tube that carries gas/liquid
- ADJ. **underground | gas, sewage, waste, water** *the hot and cold water pipes* | **brake, central heating, hose** (also **hosepipe**) | **drainage, drain** (also **drainpipe**), **exhaust, inlet, outfall, outflow, outlet, overflow, service, supply | blocked, broken, burst, cracked, frozen, leaking | concrete, copper, iron, lead, metal, plastic, steel**
- QUANT. **length** *to join two lengths of pipe together* ◇ *Copper pipe is sold in lengths.*
- VERB + PIPE **lay, run** *He laid the pipes under the floorboards.* | **connect | insulate, lag** *Insulating your pipes will save on your heating bills.*
- PIPE + VERB **lead, pass through sth, run** *The pipes lead into the river.* ◇ *The pipes will have to pass through the wall.* | **burst, freeze, leak**
- PIPE + NOUN **cutter, fitter | insulation**

● PREP. **through a/the~** | **~for** *the pipe for the hot water* **~from, ~to** *The pipe from the boiler to the bath.*

2 used for smoking tobacco
● ADJ. **clay | peace**
● VERB + PIPE **smoke | light | fill | draw on, puff away at/on, puff on | knock out** *He knocked out his pipe in the big glass ashtray.*
● PIPE + NOUN **smoker | tobacco | rack**
● PHRASES **the bowl/stem of a pipe**

pipeline *noun*

● ADJ. **gas, oil, water**
● VERB + PIPELINE **build, construct, lay**
● PIPELINE + VERB **supply sth** *The pipeline supplies Jordan with 15 per cent of its crude oil.* | **pass through sth, run through sth** *The pipeline runs through central Mozambique.* | **link sth** *The pipeline links the refinery with the port.*
● PIPELINE + NOUN **network, system**
● PREP. **in the ~** *(figurative)* (= being discussed or prepared) *Important changes are already in the pipeline.* | **~ across** *a pipeline across the desert* **~ through** *the construction of a gas pipeline through Morocco*

pistol *noun*

● ADJ. **automatic, machine, semi-automatic | unlicensed | loaded | air, water | duelling, starting** *runners waiting for the starting pistol*
● VERB + PISTOL **load | draw, produce** *He drew his pistol, aimed and fired.* | **cock | aim, level, point, raise | fire | carry** *There were two of them, both carrying pistols.*
● PISTOL + NOUN **shot**
● PHRASES **at pistol point** *He was robbed in his hotel at pistol point.*

pit *noun*

1 hole
● ADJ. **deep, shallow | bottomless | black, dark | chalk, gravel** *a disused gravel pit*
● VERB + PIT **dig**

2 coal mine
● ADJ. **open** *They extract the mineral from open pits and underground mines.*
● VERB + PIT **go down** *He went down the pit at the age of fifteen.*
● PIT + NOUN **village** *There's no more work in these pit villages.* | **closure**
● PREP. **in a/the ~** *Most boys in the village worked in the pits.*

pitch *noun*

1 sports field
● ADJ. **all-weather, grass, non-turf, synthetic | waterlogged | cricket, hockey, football, rugby**
● VERB + PITCH **invade, run onto** *The pitch was invaded by angry fans.*
● PITCH + NOUN **invasion** *Police could do nothing to stop the pitch invasion.*
● PREP. **off the ~** *The players have just come off the pitch.* ◇ *Negotiations about his transfer are continuing off the pitch.* **on a/the ~** *He was the best player on the pitch today.*

2 strength of feeling
● ADJ. **fever, high** *Excitement rose to fever pitch the day before the procession.*
● VERB + PITCH **reach, rise to**
● PREP. **~ of** *to reach a high pitch of excitement*

3 of a musical note
● ADJ. **high, low | correct** *The instrument is not tuned to the correct pitch.*
● VERB + PITCH **fall in, rise in** *Her voice fell slightly in pitch as she grew older.*

● PHRASES **have absolute/perfect pitch** (= to be able to recognize or produce any given note)

pitch *verb*

1 fall over/throw sb
● ADV. **violently** *The explosion pitched her violently into the air.* | **forward, headlong**
● PREP. **from** *There was a loud bang and he was pitched from his seat.* **into** *If they hit any unseen obstacle they would be pitched headlong into the snow.* **out of**

2 of a ship/aircraft
● ADV. **violently** *The boat pitched violently in a heavy swell.*

3 set sth at a particular level
● ADV. **deliberately** *Estimates have been deliberately pitched on the conservative side.*
● PREP. **at** *The test is pitched at a high GCSE standard.*
● PHRASES **pitch sth high/low** *The price has been pitched quite high.* ◇ *Her voice was pitched low.*

pitfall *noun*

● ADJ. **obvious | common | hidden | possible, potential, unforeseen** *We need to be alert to potential pitfalls.*
● VERB + PITFALL **be fraught with, be full of, have, hold** *Trading in a foreign country can be fraught with pitfalls.* | **avoid | overcome**
● PITFALL + VERB **await sb** *Numerous pitfalls await unsuspecting investors.*
● PREP. **~ for** *Buying property holds many pitfalls for the unwary.* **~ in** *pitfalls in the interpretation of statistics*

pity *noun*

1 feeling of sadness for sb/sth
● ADJ. **immense**
● VERB + PITY **be filled with, be full of, feel, have | show | arouse, inspire** *an unfortunate man who inspires pity*
● PREP. **out of ~** *I threw the child some money out of pity.* **without ~** *a cruel leader without pity* | **~ for** *She was full of pity for him.*
● PHRASES **a feeling/sense of pity, have pity on sb** *We begged him to have pity on us.* **an object of pity** *Deaf people do not want to be seen as objects of pity.* **take pity on sb** *I took pity on him and allowed him to stay.*

2 a pity sth that makes you feel disappointed
● ADJ. **great, real, terrible | slight**
● PREP. **~ about** *The place was lovely, but it was a pity about the weather.*
● PHRASES **a bit of a pity, rather/such a pity** *That would be rather a pity, wouldn't it?* **what a pity** *What a pity you didn't tell me earlier!*

pizza *noun*

● ADJ. **take-away**
● QUANT. **piece, slice** *a slice of cheese and tomato pizza*
● PIZZA + NOUN **topping | parlour, place, restaurant** *Let's go to that new pizza place tonight.*
● PREP. **on a/the ~** *What do you want on your pizza?*

place *noun*

1 particular position/area
● ADJ. **good, great, ideal | terrible** *It was a terrible place to live.* | **safe** *Keep your purse in a safe place.* | **right, suitable** *I happened to be in the right place at the right time.* | **wrong | beautiful | nice** *It's a nice place you've got here.* | **interesting | busy, crowded | quiet | strange | faraway, out-of-the way, remote** *holidays in faraway places* | **public | hiding, market, meeting, resting**
● VERB + PLACE **mark** *I forgot to mark my place* (= in a book). | **lose** *I've lost my place in the script.*

• PLACE + NOUN **name**
• PREP. **at/in a/the~** *We had dinner at a crowded place in Soho.* **in ~** *It was held in place with tape.* ◊ *There will be rain in places.* **into~** *She tapped the lid into place.* **out of~** *Some of these files seem to be out of place.*
• PHRASES **all over the place** (= everywhere), **no place/not the place** *This is not the place for an argument.* **a place of birth/business/interest/learning/work/worship** *Please state your date and place of birth.*

2 seat/position for sb/sth
• VERB + PLACE **sit (down) in**, **take** *We took our places round the table.* | **go back to**, **return to** *The boy returned to his place* | **keep (sb)**, **save (sb)** | **lose** *I've lost my place in the queue.* | **give up** | **change**, **swap** *He swapped places with me.* | **show sb to** *She showed them to their places.* | **lay**, **set** *I've laid four places for dinner.*
• PLACE + NOUN **mat** | **card**
• PHRASES **the place of honour** *He took the place of honour on his hostess's right.*

3 role/position/function
• ADJ. **central**, **important**, **prominent** | **special** *He holds a special place in her affections* | **proper**, **rightful**
• VERB + PLACE **have**, **hold**, **occupy** *Housing occupied a prominent place in the discussions.* | **know** *She knows her place.* | **forget** *I'm sorry—I was forgetting my place.* | **restore sth to** *He has been restored to his rightful place in the community.* | **put sb in** *At first he tried to take charge of the meeting but I soon put her in her place.*
• PREP. **~in** *Dance has a central place in their culture.*
• PHRASES **it's not sb's place to** *It's not your place to correct her.* **a place in history** *a statesman who is assured a place in history*

4 opportunity to study at a college, play for a team, etc.
• ADJ. **free** | **college**, **nursery**, **school**, **university**
• VERB + PLACE **get**, **win** | **award sb**, **offer sb** | **lose** *He was injured and lost his place in the side.*
• PREP. **~at/in** *He was awarded a place at Leeds University.* **~on** *She got a place on the French course.*

5 sb's position at the end of a race, competition, etc.
• VERB + PLACE **finish in**, **take** *She took third place.*
• PLACE + VERB **go to sb** *Second place went to the Moroccan athlete.*

place verb

1 (often **be placed**) put sth in a position
• ADV. **carefully**, **neatly** | **haphazardly** *The books were placed haphazardly on the shelf.* | **firmly** *She produced a long silver whistle and placed it firmly between her lips.* | **gently**, **lightly** | **centrally** *The table was placed centrally.* | **ideally**, **conveniently**, **uniquely**, **well** *The hotel is well placed for restaurants, bars and clubs.* | **judiciously**, **strategically** *There are candles strategically placed—just in case we have another power cut.* | **side by side** *The boots, neatly placed side by side, were near the bed.*
• PREP. **between**, **in**, **inside**, **on**, **over**, **under**, etc. *He placed the letter in a drawer.*

2 (often **be placed**) put sb in a situation
• ADV. **firmly** | **ideally**, **conveniently**, **uniquely**, **well** *The company is ideally placed to win the contract.*
• VERB + PLACE **attempt to**, **try to** | **be difficult to**, **be hard to** *children who are difficult to place in foster homes*
• PREP. **in**, **on** *an attempt to place the question firmly back on the political agenda*
• PHRASES **an attempt to place sth**

3 emphasis, value, blame, etc.
• ADV. **squarely**
• PREP. **on** *The blame was placed squarely on the doctor.*

plague noun

• ADJ. **bubonic** | **great** *Nearly a third of the population died in the Great Plague.*
• QUANT. **outbreak** *a decline in population following outbreaks of plague*
• VERB + PLAGUE **suffer** *The region has just suffered a plague of locusts.* | **be decimated by**, **be destroyed by**
• PLAGUE + VERB **break out**, **start**, **strike (sth)** *Bubonic plague struck London in 1665.* | **spread**
• PREP. **~of** *The city is suffering a plague of rats.*
⇨ Special page at ILLNESS

plain noun

• ADJ. **open** *The horses galloped across the open plains.* | **rolling**, **sweeping** *miles of rolling plain, made fertile by the river* | **great**, **unbroken**, **vast** | **flat** | **fertile** *fertile plains suitable for farming* | **grassy** | **coastal**
• PREP. **across a/the~** *Cattle move freely across the grassy plain.* **in a/the~** *the Olduvai Gorge in the vast plain of Tanzania* **on a/the~** *Nothing grew on the plain.*

plain adj.

1 simple/not decorated
• VERBS **be**, **look**, **seem**
• ADV. **extremely**, **very** | **absolutely**, **completely** *The dress was absolutely plain, but quite stunning.* | **fairly**, **quite**, **rather** *The food was fairly plain, but well cooked.*
• PHRASES **plain blue**, **white**, etc. *a plain white shirt*
2 not beautiful
• VERBS **be**, **look**
• ADV. **extremely**, **very** *She looked very plain and dowdy.* | **rather** *a rather plain woman*
3 clear
• VERBS **be**, **seem** | **become** | **make sth** *They made it plain that they were against the idea.*
• ADV. **very** | **absolutely**, **perfectly**, **quite** *Within weeks, it became perfectly plain that we were in the grip of a tyrant.* | **increasingly** | **fairly**, **pretty**, **reasonably**
• PREP. **to** *It is all quite plain to me.*

plaintiff noun

• VERB + PLAINTIFF **compensate**
• PLAINTIFF + VERB **bring an action (against sb)**, **sue sb** | **allege sth**, **argue sth**, **claim sth**, **contend sth**, **seek sth**, **submit sth** *The plaintiff claimed that the correct procedures had not been followed.* | **obtain sth**, **prove sth** *The plaintiffs obtained an injunction in the High Court.*
• PREP. **against the ~** *Costs were awarded against the plaintiff.* **on behalf of the ~** *the lawyer appearing on behalf of the plaintiff*

plan noun

1 for future
• ADJ. **ambitious**, **audacious**, **grand**, **grandiose** *The government has ambitious plans for prison reform.* | **future** | **long-term**, **three-year**, etc. | **immediate** *What are your immediate plans?* | **new** | **original** | **five-point**, **three-point**, etc. *a three-point action plan to improve hygiene at work* | **definite**, **firm** *A spokeswoman confirmed there was no definite plan to stage a concert in the park.* | **detailed** | **good** *The best plan is for me to meet you at the theatre.* | **best-laid** *Even the best-laid plans can go wrong.* | **brilliant**, **clever**, **cunning**, **fiendish**, **ingenious** | **feasible**, **realistic**, **sound** *We need to develop a sound business plan.* | **impractical** | **controversial** | **master** | **contingency** *Do you have any contingency plans if the scheme doesn't work?* | **secret** | **action** | **strategic** | **business**, **career**, **corporate**, **development**, **economic**, **financial** | **travel** | **marriage** | **peace**
• VERB + PLAN **have** | **come up with**, **develop**, **devise**, **draw up**, **formulate**, **make**, **prepare**, **work out** *I like to make plans well in advance.* | **present**, **propose**, **put forward** | **discuss** | **agree** *The moves contravene the peace plan agreed by both sides.* | **announce**, **launch**, **outline**,

unveil *The minister unveiled a new plan for reducing traffic accidents.* | **go ahead with, implement, press ahead with** | **keep to, stick to** *Let's stick to our original plan* | **cancel, change** | **abandon, cancel, drop, scrap, shelve** | **fight, oppose** *Local residents have vowed to fight plans to build a new road.*

• PLAN + VERB **be afoot** *Plans are afoot to stage a new opera.* | **be aimed at sth** *The government launched a five-year plan aimed at diversifying the economy.* | **call for sth, envisage sth, involve sth** *The plan calls for investments totalling $100 million.* | **contain sth, include sth** *The plan contains four main elements.* | **succeed** | **fail, fall through, founder**

• PREP. **~for** *The president will now press ahead with his plans for reform.* **~ to** *Plans to build a dam have been shelved following protests.*

• PHRASES **a plan of action/attack/campaign** *To change anything in this organization, we'll need a plan of action.* **put a plan into action/effect/operation**

2 map

• ADJ. **street, town** | **seating**

• PLAN + VERB **show sth** *The plan shows the exact location of the house.*

plan *verb*

• ADV. **ahead, in advance** | **originally** *The government had originally planned to launch the review in June.* | **carefully, meticulously** | **intelligently, rationally** | **centrally** *centrally planned economies*

• VERB + PLAN **have to, need to** *You will need to plan your shopping carefully in advance.*

• PREP. **for** *We must plan for the future.* ◇ *A meeting has been planned for early next year.* **on** *I had planned on staying here for two or three years.*

• PHRASES **go as planned** *Everything went exactly as planned.* **plan sth down to the last detail**

plane *noun*

1 aeroplane

• ADJ. **private**

• VERB + PLANE **catch, get, take** *She caught the first plane out.* | **miss** | **board, get on** | **get off, step off** *I fell in love with the city the moment I stepped off the plane.* | **fly, pilot** | **charter**

• PLANE + VERB **take off** | **come down, land** | **crash** | **cruise, fly** | **carry sb/sth** *The plane was carrying 350 people.*

• PLANE + NOUN **crash, disaster**

• PREP. **by ~** *We left by plane for Peking.* **in a/the ~** *I've never flown in a plane.* **on a/the~** *The president was never on the plane at all.*

2 flat surface

• ADJ. **horizontal, parallel, vertical**

3 standard/level of thought/activity

• ADJ. **higher** *With practice, an athlete can reach a higher plane of achievement.* | **mental, mystical, spiritual**

• PHRASES **be/exist/function/operate on a different plane** *Like all talented musicians, he operates on a different plane from most people.*

planet *noun*

• ADJ. **distant** | **alien, unknown** | **another** *He looked like something from another planet!*

• PLANET + VERB **orbit** *How many planets orbit the sun?*

• PREP. **from a/the ~** *creatures from an alien planet* **on a/the~** *She believes there is life on other planets.*

plank *noun*

• ADJ. **timber, wooden** | **loose** | **rotten**

• PHRASES **a plank of wood**

planning *noun*

• ADJ. **careful, detailed, meticulous, thoughtful** | **initial** *the initial planning stage* | **advance, forward** *The trip calls for careful advance planning.* | **pre-match, pre-retirement,** etc. *Deciding the agenda is the most vital aspect of pre-meeting planning.* | **long-range, long-term** | **short-range, short-term** | **corporate** | **family** *They give free advice on contraception at the family planning clinic.* | **town, urban** | **economic, educational, environmental, financial, military, strategic**

• VERB + PLANNING **call for, demand, need, require** | **do** *The industry needs to do some long-term planning.*

• PLANNING + NOUN **phase, stage** *The scheme is still at the planning stage.* | **process** | **decisions** | **meeting** | **application** | **approval, consent, permission** *We've applied for planning permission to build an extension to the house.* | **authority, committee, department**

• PREP. **in the ~** *The festival was four years in the planning.* | **~ for** *Planning for future development is vital for the community.*

plant *noun*

1 living thing

• ADJ. **attractive** | **delicate** | **wild** | **rare** | **garden, house, indoor, potted** | **exotic, tropical** | **medicinal** | **food** *food plants of rare butterflies* | **crop** | **poisonous** | **perennial** | **aquatic, desert, marsh** | **bedding, climbing, flowering, ornamental** | **herbaceous, leguminous** | **strawberry, tomato,** etc.

• VERB + PLANT **cultivate, grow** | **water**

• PLANT + VERB **develop, grow** | **flourish** | **die** | **absorb sth, consume sth** *Plants absorb carbon in the form of carbon dioxide.*

• PLANT + NOUN **roots** | **growth** | **life** *Much of the local plant life has been destroyed by the chemicals.* | **species, variety** | **material, matter, tissue** | **pot** | **science**

2 factory

• ADJ. **industrial** | **assembly, manufacturing, production** | **car** | **nuclear, power** | **processing, reprocessing, sewage, treatment, water-treatment** *a waste reprocessing plant* | **chemical, petrochemical**

• VERB + PLANT **build** | **dismantle** | **manage, run**

• PLANT + NOUN **manager**

plant *verb*

1 put plants/seeds in the ground to grow

• ADV. **carefully** | **deliberately** *weeds that had not been deliberately planted*

• PREP. **in** *Carefully plant your cutting in the soil.* **with** *The garden was planted with roses and other shrubs.*

• PHRASES **densely/thickly planted** *a thickly planted orange grove* **freshly/newly/recently planted**

2 put sth firmly in a place/position

• ADV. **firmly, solidly, squarely** *She planted a kiss squarely on his cheek.*

• PREP. **on** *He was determined to keep both feet firmly planted on dry land.*

plantation *noun*

1 for growing a crop

• ADJ. **coconut, coffee, cotton, rubber, sugar, tea,** etc.

• VERB + PLANTATION **work (on)** *Hundreds of slaves worked on the plantations.*

• PLANTATION + NOUN **owner, worker** | **economy** | **house**

2 land planted with trees

• ADJ. **conifer, eucalyptus,** etc. | **forestry**

• PREP. **~of** *a plantation of oaks*

plaque *noun*

1 on the wall
- ADJ. **commemorative, memorial**
- VERB + PLAQUE **put up** *The local historical society put up a plaque at the site of the battle.* | **unveil**
- PLAQUE + VERB **be dedicated to sb, commemorate sb/sth, honour sb** | **mark sth, record sth** *A plaque marks the place where the first printing press was built.*
- PREP. **on a/the ~** *Some Latin words were engraved on the plaque.* | **~ on** *a plaque on the wall* **~ to** *There is a commemorative plaque to the artist in the village hall.*

2 substance on teeth
- ADJ. **dental**
- VERB + PLAQUE **remove**
- PLAQUE + VERB **accumulate, build up**

plaster *noun*

1 smooth covering for a wall
- ADJ. **fresh** | **chipped, cracked, crumbling, peeling**
- QUANT. **chunk, flake** *Each blow of the hammer removed a great chunk of plaster.*
- VERB + PLASTER **apply** *Apply the plaster evenly.*
- PLASTER + VERB **come off (sth), fall off (sth), peel off (sth)** *Plaster was peeling off the ceiling.*
- PLASTER + NOUN **cast** *A plaster cast of Madame Fournier stood in the artist's studio.*

2 for covering a cut
- ADJ. **sticking**
- VERB + PLASTER **put on** | **peel off, take off**

3 for protecting broken bones
- PLASTER + NOUN **cast** *Her broken leg was put in a plaster cast*
- PREP. **in ~** *Your arm will have to be in plaster for at least six weeks.*

plastic *noun*
- ADJ. **heavy-duty, reinforced, strong, sturdy, tough** | **thin** | **flexible** | **rigid** | **moulded** | **clear, see-through, transparent** | **shiny** | **biodegradable** | **foam** | **sticky-backed**
- VERB + PLASTIC **make, manufacture, produce** | **recycle** | **make/mould sth from/in/(out) of** *dashboards moulded in plastic* | **cover sth with, wrap sth in**

plate *noun*

1 for food
- ADJ. **dessert, dinner, serving, side, soup** | **clean, dirty** *The sink was full of dirty plates.* | **empty, full**
- VERB + PLATE **clear, empty** *I could see how hungry she was from the way she cleared her plate.* | **clear (away), collect**
- PREP. **on a/the ~** *She ate everything on her plate.* | **~ of** *a plate of rice*

2 piece of metal with writing on
- ADJ. **licence, number** *The driver was arrested for having false number plates on his car.* | **name** *He read the brass name plate by the door.*

plateau *noun*
- ADJ. **high** | **broad, rolling, vast** | **central**
- VERB + PLATEAU **reach** *(figurative) The children's standard of reading seems to have reached a plateau (= they are not making any more progress).*
- PLATEAU + VERB **overlook sth**
- PREP. **across a/the ~** *A terrible storm swept across the plateau.*

platform *noun*

1 raised floor
- ADJ. **high, raised** | **wooden**

- VERB + PLATFORM **mount, stand on** *The king mounted the platform to loud cheers.* | **appear on, speak from** | **share** *Union leaders shared the platform with business leaders in a debate on the future of the industry.*

2 at a railway station
- ADJ. **railway, station**
- PREP. **along a/the ~** *He ran along the platform to catch the train.* **at ~** *The train at platform 3 is the 13.15 service to Liverpool.* **from ~** *The next train to depart from platform 2 is the 10.30 for London Paddington.* **on ~** *the waiting room on platform 7*

3 in politics
- ADJ. **political** | **election, electoral**
- PREP. **in a/the ~** *the promises in their election platform* **on a/the ~ of** *They fought the election on a platform of economic reform.*

platonic *adj.*
- VERBS **be** | **become** | **remain**
- ADV. **purely, strictly** *Their friendship remained purely platonic.*

plausible *adj.*
- VERBS **be, seem, sound** | **make sth** | **find sth, judge sth, think sth** *He did not think it plausible that all the differences could be explained in this way.*
- ADV. **extremely, highly, terribly, very** | **entirely, perfectly, quite** *a perfectly plausible theory* | **not remotely** *There was no way the story could be made to sound even remotely plausible.* | **barely, hardly** | **reasonably** | **superficially** | **intuitively, psychologically** *This explanation fits the facts and is psychologically plausible.*

play *noun*

1 activity done for fun
- ADJ. **outdoor** | **creative, imaginative, pretend**
- PLAY + NOUN **area** | **equipment** | **scheme** *The local council runs some good play schemes.*
- PREP. **at ~** *Children spend hours at play.* **in ~** *I only said it in play (= not seriously).*

2 drama
- ADJ. **one-act** | **radio, television** | **musical** | **miracle, morality, mystery, nativity, passion** *The children always perform a nativity play every Christmas.*
- VERB + PLAY **review** *The play is reviewed in most of today's papers.*
- PREP. **~ about** *a play about teenage runaways*
⇨ Note at PERFORMANCE (for more verbs)

3 in sport
- ADJ. **excellent, good** | **fair** | **dangerous, dirty, foul, rough, violent** *He was sent off for foul play.*
- VERB + PLAY **stop** *Rain stopped play 40 minutes into the match.*
- PREP. **in ~** *The ball is still in play.* **out of ~** *He kicked the ball out of play.*
- PHRASES **at close/start of play** *(in cricket) At close of play he had scored 38 not out.*

play *verb*

1 of children
- VERB + PLAY **let sb** *The other children wouldn't let him play.*
- PREP. **at** *Let's play at pirates!* **with** *a little girl playing with her toys*

2 game/sport
- ADV. **brilliantly, excellently, superbly, well** | **badly**
- VERB + PLAY **learn to** | **teach sb to** | **be difficult to, be easy to** | **see sb, watch sb**
- PREP. **against** *United are difficult to play against.* **at** *I've never played John at tennis.* **for** *He plays for Aston*

Villa. **in** *She has played in every match this season.* **with** *playing cards with her mother*

3 music
- ADV. **brilliantly, excellently, superbly, well | badly | live** *The band will be playing live in the studio.*
- VERB + PLAY **learn to** *learning to play the violin* | **teach sb to | be easy to, be difficult to** *a piece that is relatively easy to play* | **hear sb** *Have you ever heard her play?*

player noun

1 of a game
- ADJ. **accomplished, brilliant, dangerous, excellent, exciting, fine, gifted, good, great, outstanding, strong, talented, top, world-class** *one of the country's top tennis players* | **star** *The club were forced to sell their star player.* | **poor** *He's a poor player, but he tries very hard.* | **average** *These boots are for the professional rather than for the average player.* | **experienced | aggressive | attacking, midfield** (both in football) | **handicap, scratch** (both in golf) | **basketball, bridge, chess, rugby, snooker, tennis, etc.**

2 of a musical instrument
- ADJ. **accomplished, gifted, great, outstanding, talented | bass, horn, keyboard, sax, etc.**

3 in business
- ADJ. **key, leading, major**
- PREP. **~ in** *Their firm is a major player in the London property market.*

playground noun

- ADJ. **children's | adventure | school**
- PLAYGROUND + NOUN **bully, bullying | equipment | duty** *teachers on playground duty*
- PREP. **in a/the~** *children in the school playground.*

playgroup noun

- ADJ. **nursery, pre-school | local**
- VERB + PLAYGROUP **go to | run | start** *She started a playgroup in her own house.* | **start** (at) *He'll grow in confidence once he starts at playgroup.*
- PLAYGROUP + NOUN **leader**
- PREP. **at ~** *She goes shopping while her little girl's at playgroup.*

plea noun

1 request
- ADJ. **desperate, dramatic, strong, urgent | heartfelt, impassioned, passionate | repeated | personal**
- VERB + PLEA **make | ignore**
- PREP. **despite a/the~, in spite of a/the~** *Despite pleas from his mother, the gunman refused to give himself up.* | **~ by/from** *Hospital visiting hours were extended in response to pleas from patients.* **~ for** *The director of the charity made an impassioned plea for help.*

2 statement in court
- ADJ. **guilty | not guilty**
- VERB + PLEA **enter | hear | change | accept, sustain** *The prosecution accepted a plea of manslaughter.* | **support | reject**
- PLEA + NOUN **bargain, bargaining**
- PREP. **~ for** *A senior judge heard a plea for damages on behalf of the accident victims.* **~ of** *Her solicitor entered a plea of guilty on her behalf.*

plead verb

1 ask sb for sth in a very serious way
- ADV. **almost** *She was almost pleading with him.* | **silently | successfully** *She successfully pleaded their cause with the mayor.*

- PREP. **for** *They pleaded for mercy.* **with** *His eyes silently pleaded with her.*

2 say that you are guilty/not guilty
- PHRASES **plead guilty/not guilty** *He pleaded not guilty to the murder.*

pleasant adj.

- VERBS **be, feel, look, seem, sound | find sth**
- ADV. **exceedingly, extraordinarily, extremely, very | perfectly** *His colleagues were perfectly pleasant and friendly but they had their own lives to lead.* | **less than, not altogether, not entirely, not exactly, not particularly** *It was not a particularly pleasant experience.* | **almost | fairly, quite, rather, reasonably | enough** *It was a pleasant enough day's journey.* | **undeniably**
- PREP. **to** *He has always been extremely pleasant to me.*

please verb

- ADV. **enormously** *The result pleased us enormously.*
- VERB + PLEASE **be difficult to, be hard to, be impossible to** *Some children are very difficult to please.* | **be easy to | be eager to** *He's always very eager to please.* | **try to | fail to** *The planning policy failed to please anyone.*
- PHRASES **there's no pleasing sb** *There's just no pleasing some people.* (= Some people are impossible to please.)

pleased adj.

- VERBS **appear, be, feel, look, seem, sound**
- ADV. **awfully, dead, especially, extremely, genuinely, immensely, inordinately, more than, only too, particularly, really, ridiculously, very, well | far from, not at all, not best** *She seemed surprised and not at all pleased to see him.* | **fairly, mildly, pretty, quite, rather, reasonably | half** *He laughed, half pleased and half resentful.* | **enough** *They seemed pleased enough with the result.* | **apparently | clearly, evidently, obviously | quietly, secretly | oddly, strangely | always** *I am always pleased to hear from former students.*
- PREP. **about** *pleased about the move at* *She seemed pleased at our success.* **by** *You must be pleased by their confidence in you.* **for** *I'm very pleased for you both.* **with** *We are immensely pleased with this result.*

pleasing adj.

- VERBS **be | find sth**
- ADV. **extremely, particularly, very | quite, rather | aesthetically** *aesthetically pleasing colour combinations*
- PREP. **to** *a design which is pleasing to the eye*

pleasurable adj.

- VERBS **be | become | make sth | find sth** *activities which they find pleasurable and rewarding*
- ADV. **deeply, highly, intensely, very | mildly, quite** *a feeling of mildly pleasurable excitement*

pleasure noun

1 enjoyment
- ADJ. **considerable, deep, enormous, great, intense** *It gives me enormous pleasure to welcome my next guest.* | **genuine, real | pure, sheer | quiet** *The audience nodded with quiet pleasure at her remark.* | **obvious | endless** *Children find endless pleasure in playing with water.* | **malicious, perverse, sadistic | vicarious** *He gained vicarious pleasure from watching people laughing and joking.* | **aesthetic, physical, sensual, sexual**
- VERB + PLEASURE **bring (sb), give (sb), provide | derive, find, gain, get, take** *My grandfather got immense pleasure out of life until the end.*
- PREP. **for ~** *Some people read for pleasure, and others read to study.* **with ~** *His eyes lit up with pleasure.* | **~ at** *He*

beamed with pleasure at seeing her. ~ **from** She was deriving a perverse pleasure from his discomfort. ~ **in** They took great pleasure in each other's company.
- PHRASES **business and pleasure** I often meet useful people at parties, so I combine business with pleasure. **have the pleasure of sth** May I have the pleasure of the next dance?

2 sth that makes you happy
- ADJ. **great** | **doubtful, dubious** the dubious pleasure of growing up in the public eye | **little, simple** one of life's little pleasures | **fleeting, momentary, temporary**
- VERB + PLEASURE **have** (formal) I hope to have the pleasure of meeting you again. | **enjoy** | **forego**
- PLEASURE + NOUN **boat, craft**
- PHRASES **the pleasures of life** She enjoys the simple pleasures of life. **the pleasures of the flesh** Priests promise to forego the pleasures of the flesh.

pledge noun

- ADJ. **campaign, election, manifesto** | **spending** spending pledges given by the government
- VERB + PLEDGE **give (sb), make, sign** | **fulfil, honour** | **betray, go back on, renege on**
- PREP. **~on** manifesto pledges on public spending
- PHRASES **a pledge of support**

plight noun

- ADJ. **desperate, sad, sorry, tragic** the desperate plight of flood victims | **economic, financial**
- VERB + PLIGHT **recognize, see** | **draw attention to, highlight, publicize** He has been sleeping rough in the streets to highlight the plight of the homeless. | **alleviate, ease** | **ignore**

plot noun

1 plan
- ADJ. **fiendish** | **alleged** | **assassination, blackmail, coup, death, murder**
- VERB + PLOT **hatch** | **uncover** | **foil**
- PREP. **~against** They had taken part in a Jacobite plot against William III. **~ by** The police claim to have uncovered a plot by terrorists to assassinate the president.

2 events in a story
- ADJ. **simple** | **complex, complicated**
- VERB + PLOT **construct** She has constructed a complicated plot, with a large cast of characters.
- PLOT + VERB **develop, unfold**
- PLOT + NOUN **development**
- PHRASES **a twist in/of the plot** There are several unexpected twists in the plot before the murderer is revealed.

3 piece of land
- ADJ. **garden, vegetable** | **farm, subsistence** | **building** | **burial** | **small** | **10-acre, 12-acre, etc.** They own a five-acre plot of land. | **family, private**
- VERB + PLOT **work**
- PLOT + VERB **measure sth** The plots each measure 10 metres by 20 metres.
- PHRASES **a plot of land**

plot verb

1 make secret plans
- ADV. **allegedly** | **secretly**
- PREP. **against** He was arrested on suspicion of plotting against the king. **with** Taylor plotted with his daughter to murder her husband.
- PHRASES **accuse/suspect sb of plotting sth**

2 mark sth on a chart
- ADV. **accurately** The positions of the archaeological finds are accurately plotted.
- PREP. **against** Greenhouse temperature can be plotted against plant growth. **on** plotting the figures on a graph

plough noun

- ADJ. **heavy**
- VERB + PLOUGH **draw, pull** They need two horses to pull these heavy ploughs. | **guide**
- PLOUGH + NOUN **boy, team** | **furrow**

ploy noun

- ADJ. **clever, effective, good, useful** | **deliberate, tactical** | **favourite, old, usual** | **marketing, sales**
- VERB + PLOY **resort to, try**
- PLOY + VERB **work**
- PREP. **~for** a ploy for deflecting criticism

plug noun

1 electric
- ADJ. **electric** | **mains** | **three-pin, two-pin** The iron is fitted with a three-pin plug. | **jack** | **fused**
- VERB + PLUG **pull (out), take out** | **fit, wire** | **be fitted with** | **change**

2 for a sink, etc.
- ADJ. **basin, bath, sink**
- VERB + PLUG **put in** | **pull out**
- PLUG + NOUN **hole** (also **plughole**)

plumbing noun

- ADJ. **cold water, hot water** | **domestic, household**
- VERB + PLUMBING **put in** They're going to have to put in new plumbing.
- PLUMBING + NOUN **arrangements, system** | **fittings** | **tools** | **job, work** | **leak**

plunge noun

- ADJ. **headlong** | **cold** Bathers would go straight from the hot room to take a cold plunge.
- VERB + PLUNGE **take** The river takes a headlong plunge into a maelstrom of rocks and boulders. ◇ (figurative) He finally took the plunge and gave in his notice.
- PREP. **~into** a plunge into the icy water **~ to** a plunge to the ground

plunge verb

- ADV. **downwards, forward, head first, headlong** The car plunged headlong into the river. | **in** The pool was declared open and eager swimmers plunged in.
- PREP. **down** The bus came off the road and plunged down an embankment. **from** He plunged from a tenth floor window. **into** (often figurative) She plunged straight into her story. **off** The car had plunged off the road.
- PHRASES **plunge to your death** A climber plunged 300 feet to his death.

plutonium noun

- ADJ. **radioactive** | **civil** | **military, weapons-grade**
- VERB + PLUTONIUM **extract, produce, recover** one tonne of plutonium extracted from spent nuclear fuel
- PLUTONIUM + NOUN **fuel**

pneumonia noun

- ADJ. **severe** | **bronchial, double** | **bacterial**
- QUANT. **bout**
- VERB + PNEUMONIA **have, suffer from** | **catch, contract, develop, get** | **die from/of** | **cause**
⇨ Special page at ILLNESS

pocket noun

1 for keeping things in
- ADJ. **bulging** tourists with bulging pockets | **deep** | **zipped** | **coat, jacket, shirt, trouser, waistcoat, etc.** | **back, breast, hip, inner, inside, outer, top** | **door, seat**

Please read the safety leaflet in the seat pocket in front of you. (= on a plane) | **secret** *Forged passports were found in a secret pocket in the suitcase.*

- VERB + POCKET **feel in, fish in, fumble in, go through, rummage in, search** *He went through all his pockets looking for his key.* | **reach in** *She reached in her pocket and pulled out her phone.* | **dip into** (figurative) *Once again club members have had to dip into their pockets* (= spend their own money) *to buy new equipment.* | **fish/get/pull/take sth from/out of** *I fished the number out of my pocket and dialled.* | **empty, turn out** *The security guard made them empty their pockets.* | **put/stuff/thrust sth in/into** *She stuffed the money into her pocket and walked out.* ◇ *He walked past with his collar turned up and his hands thrust into his pockets.* | **fill, stuff** *We filled our pockets with apples.* | **line** (figurative) *Dishonest officials have been lining their pockets with public funds.* | **pick** *He caught a boy trying to pick his pocket on the bus.*
- POCKET + VERB **bulge** *My pockets were bulging with loose change.*
- POCKET + NOUN **lining**
- PREP. **in the/your ~** *My wallet was in the back pocket of my jeans.* **out of the/your ~** *He took a few coins out of his pocket.*
- PHRASES **hands in pockets** *He stood there, hands in pockets.* **the lining of a pocket**

2 small area/group
- ADJ. **small | isolated**
- PHRASES **a pocket of resistance** *Government forces are mopping up the last pockets of resistance.*

poem noun

- ADJ. **fine, good, great, magnificent, remarkable | collected, selected** *His collected poems were published after the war.* | **anonymous | autobiographical | sad | dramatic, epic, lyric, heroic, narrative | prose | love | war | humorous, nonsense, satirical**
- QUANT. **anthology, collection**
- VERB + POEM **compose, write | read** *She read the poem aloud.* | **recite | learn by heart | dedicate** *He dedicated the poem to his mother.*
- POEM + VERB **be addressed to sb**
- PREP. **in a/the ~** *In his autobiographical poem 'The Prelude', Wordsworth describes his boyhood in the Lakes.* | **~ about** *a poem about cultural differences*

poet noun

- ADJ. **accomplished, good, great | distinguished, famous, well-known | foremost** *the foremost poet of his generation* | **minor | unknown | aspiring | contemporary | epic, lyric | Romantic, metaphysical**
- VERB + POET **inspire** *These river banks have inspired poets for many centuries.*
- POET + VERB **write sth**

poetic adj.

- VERBS **be, sound**
- ADV. **very | truly** *The piece ends with a truly poetic slow movement.* | **almost | quite | self-consciously** *His writing is rather self-consciously poetic.*

poetry noun

- ADJ. **good, great | classical | contemporary, modern | 18th-century, etc. | dramatic, epic, heroic, lyric, narrative | Modernist, Romantic, symbolist, etc. | love, pastoral, war, etc.**
- QUANT. **line** *He began his speech with a few lines of poetry.* | **piece | anthology, book, collection, volume**
- VERB + POETRY **compose, write | read | recite |**

learn by heart *At school we had to learn a lot of poetry by heart.*
- POETRY + NOUN **book, collection | reading** *She invited me to one of her poetry readings.* | **competition, workshop | group**
- PREP. **in ~** *an essay on imagery in poetry*

poignant adj.

- VERBS **be, seem, sound | become | make sth** *The presence of the rest of the family made John's absence even more poignant.* | **find sth**
- ADV. **deeply, extremely, particularly, unbearably, very** *I found his speech deeply poignant.* | **quite**

point noun

1 thing said as part of a discussion
- ADJ. **good, interesting, valid | important | minor | subtle | moot | central, crucial, key, major, salient | controversial | talking** *The possibility of an interest rate cut is a major talking point in the City.*
- VERB + POINT **have** *She's got a point.* | **see, take** *I see your point.* ◇ *Point taken.* | **concede | cover, make, raise** *She made some interesting points.* | **argue, discuss** *They argued the point for hours.* | **illustrate | get across, make, prove** *He had trouble getting his point across.* ◇ *That proves my point.* | **drive/hammer home, emphasize, labour, press, stress** *I understand what you're saying—there's no need to labour the point.*
- PHRASES **a case in point** (= an example relevant to the matter being discussed), **the point at issue, a point of agreement/disagreement, a point of law**
  ⇨ Special page at MEETING

2 the point essential aspect of sth
- ADJ. **basic** *The basic point is that …*
- VERB + POINT **come/get to** *Hurry up and get to the point!* | **get** *It took me a few minutes to get the point.* | **miss | wander from/off**
- PREP. **beside the ~** (= not relevant) *That's beside the point.* **to the ~** *His remarks were brief and to the point.*
- PHRASES **more to the point** (= what is more important) *More to the point, did they get away?*

3 meaning/reason/purpose of sth
- ADJ. **whole** *That's the whole point.*
- VERB + POINT **have** *It doesn't have any point to it.* | **see** *I don't see the point in arguing.*
- PREP. **~ in/of** *There's absolutely no point in complaining now.* ◇ *What's the point of worrying?*

4 item/detail/feature
- ADJ. **finer, good, strong** *We discussed the finer points of growing roses.* | **bad, weak | salient**
- PHRASES **a point of difference, a point of interest**

5 particular time/moment
- ADJ. **high** *He had reached the high point of his career.* | **low | breaking, bursting, saturation** *to fill a bag to bursting point* | **boiling, freezing, melting**
- VERB + POINT **get to, reach** *I've got to the point* (= in a book, etc.) *where his father is dying.*
- POINT + VERB **come** *There comes a point in most people's lives when they want to settle down.*
- PREP. **at a/the ~** *At one point he looked like winning.* **on the ~ of** *on the point of departure* **to the ~ of** *We worked all night to the point of collapse.* **up to a ~** *I agree with you up to a point.*
- PHRASES **a point in time** *At this point we can't give you a final answer.* **the point of no return** (= after which it is impossible to go back/undo what you have done)

6 particular place/position
- ADJ. **central, focal** *the focal point of his life* | **fixed | assembly, meeting, rallying | starting | vantage | reference | turning** *This proved to be the turning point of the game.* | **cut-off | pressure | vanishing**

- VERB + POINT **arrive at, reach**
- PHRASES **a point of contact, a point of reference**

7 punctuation
- ADJ. **decimal**

8 in a game/sports competition
- ADJ. **match, set** *It's set point to Henman.*
- VERB + POINT **get, score, win | lose**
- PHRASES **beat sb/win on points**

9 measurement
- ADJ. **percentage** *Interest rates fell by one percentage point.*
- VERB + POINT (All the verbs in the following collocate groups may be followed by **by, from** or **to** plus **point.** Sometimes the word **by** is left out.) **be/go/shoot up, improve, increase, jump, rise, soar** *The Nikkei index rose 710 points to 14894.* ◇ *His popularity rose by 18 points in public opinion polls.* | **be/come/go down, decrease, depreciate, drop, fall, plummet, plunge** *The CAC-40 index is down 67 points at 4413.*
- PHRASES **about/around/only/over/up to 10, 20, etc. points** *The index was down only 4.6 points at the close.* **an improvement/an increase/a jump/a rise of 10, 20, etc. points** *to achieve an improvement of over 4.6 points in operating ratio* **a drop/fall/reduction of 10, 20, etc. points**

10 thin sharp end of sth
- ADJ. **fine, sharp**

point *verb*

- PREP. **at, in the direction of** *He pointed in the direction of the town centre.* **to** *The toddler pointed to the toy he wanted.* **towards, with** *She pointed with her finger at the map.*
- PHRASES **point straight at sb/sth** *The gun was pointing straight at me.* **point the way** *'You must cross that field,' she said, pointing the way.*

PHRASAL VERBS

point sth out
- ADV. **correctly, rightly** *As you so rightly pointed out, our funds are not unlimited.* | **tartly** *His wife pointed out tartly that none of them were exactly starving.*
- VERB + POINT STH OUT **must, should** *I should point out that not one of these paintings is original.* | **try to | fail to | be at pains to, be keen to, be quick to** *She was at pains to point out that she was no newcomer to the area.* | **be right to** *You were right to point out that this is only one of the difficulties we face.* | **be important to**
- PREP. **to** *She tried in vain to point out to him the unfairness of the situation.*

point to sth
- ADV. **clearly** *Fragments of woven cloth at the site, clearly point to the production of textiles.*
- VERB + POINT TO STH **seem to** *The evidence all seems to point to one conclusion.*

pointer *noun*

1 advice/indications
- ADJ. **good, important | clear, obvious | practical, useful**
- VERB + POINTER **give (sb), provide (sb with)**
- PREP. **~ for** *The examiners comments include pointers for future study.* **~ to** *His symptoms gave no obvious pointer to a possible diagnosis.* **~ towards** *pointers towards a new political agenda*
- PHRASES **a pointer to the future**

2 sth used for pointing
- ADJ. **mouse** *Move the mouse pointer to the menu bar.* | **light** *A light pointer is often useful with a slide projector.*

pointless *adj.*

- VERBS **be, seem | become | consider sth, think sth** *She considered it pointless to plan in too much detail.*
- ADV. **absolutely, quite, totally, utterly | a bit, fairly, rather, somewhat | apparently**

point of view *noun*

- ADJ. **alternative, different** *He listened patiently to what we all had to say before putting across an alternative point of view.* | **aesthetic, business, commercial, economic, environmental, financial, legal, management, medical, personal, practical, psychological, safety, security, technical, theoretical, etc.**
- VERB + POINT OF VIEW **have | take** *He always seems to take the opposite point of view to me.* | **express, get across/over, present, put (across/forward/over)** *A union representative was present to put the farmers' point of view.* | **see (sth from), understand** *I can see your point of view, but I think we have to consider the long-term implications.* ◇ *Try to see the situation from my point of view.* | **agree with, share | come round to** *If we can talk to her for an hour I'm sure she'll come round to our point of view.* | **reflect** *I do not think the article reflects the point of view of the majority of the population.*
- PREP. **from a/sb's ~** *From a purely personal point of view, I'd like to see cars banned from the city centre.* **from the ~ of** *The book tells the story of a murder investigation from the point of view of the chief suspect.* ◇ *From the point of view of safety, a lower speed limit would certainly be a good thing.* | **~ on** *I don't have a point of view on this issue.*

poise *noun*

- ADJ. **natural** *the natural poise and balance of the body* | **social** *She never lost her social poise, however awkward the situation.*
- VERB + POISE **retain | lose | recover, regain** *She hesitated briefly but quickly regained her poise.*

poised *adj.*

- VERBS **appear, be, look, seem, stand** *She stood poised for a moment.* | **remain**
- ADV. **delicately, finely | perfectly** *His manner was perfectly poised between gravity and teasing.*
- PREP. **above/over** *Peter hesitated, his hand poised above the telephone.* **between, for** *They hovered by the door, poised for flight.*
- PHRASES **poised on the brink/edge/threshold of sth** *The two countries were poised on the brink of war.*

poison *noun*

- ADJ. **strong, virulent | deadly | nerve, rat**
- QUANT. **trace**
- VERB + POISON **administer, give sb | lace sth with, put in/on** *She had laced his drink with poison.* ◇ *She had put poison in his wine.* | **put down** (= put somewhere to kill animals) *The farmer had put down some rat poison.* | **swallow, take**
- POISON + NOUN **gas, pill | arrow**

poisoning *noun*

- ADJ. **acute, chronic | blood | food** *a bad case of food poisoning* | **alcohol, arsenic, carbon monoxide, lead, mercury, pesticide, radiation, etc.**
- QUANT. **case**
- VERB + POISONING **die from/of**

poisonous *adj.*

- VERBS **be | become**
- ADV. **deadly, extremely, highly**
- PREP. **to** *The leaves of yew trees are poisonous to cattle.*

polarized adj.

- VERBS be | become | remain
- ADV. **highly, sharply** *Public opinion is sharply polarized on this issue.* | **increasingly**
- PREP. **between** *In this period politics became polarized between extreme right and left.*

pole noun

- ADJ. **North, South | geographic, geomagnetic, magnetic** *The north magnetic pole lies to the west of the geographic North Pole.* | **opposite** *(figurative) The two authors represent the opposite poles of fictional genius*
- PREP. **between the (two)~s of** *(figurative) an artistic compromise between the poles of abstraction and representation* **from ~ to ~** *The meridian is an imaginary line drawn from pole to pole.*
- PHRASES **be poles apart** *(figurative) In temperament, she and her sister are poles apart* (= completely different).

police noun

- ADJ. **armed, mounted | plain-clothes, uniformed | anti-riot, riot | paramilitary, secret, security | federal, local, national, state**
- VERB + POLICE **call | alert, tell**
- POLICE + VERB **arrest sb | patrol sth | interview sb, question sb | investigate sth | appeal for sth** *Police have appealed for witnesses to come forward.*
- POLICE + NOUN **chief, constable, officer | spokesman | headquarters, station | cell** *He spent the night in a police cell after his arrest.* | **custody | car, helicopter, van, vehicle** *an unmarked police car* | **driver, marksman | dog, horse | authorities, force, service | unit | enquiries, investigation | escort** *The visiting fans returned to the railway station under police escort.* | **patrol** *A routine police patrol spotted signs of a break-in at the offices.* | **raid** *Nine arrests were made in a series of police raids across the city.* | **presence** *There was a huge police presence at the demonstration.* | **protection** *All prosecution witnesses were given police protection.* | **cordon, lines** *Some protesters managed to break through the police cordon.* | **chase | informer | brutality, harassment**
- PHRASES **helping the police with their enquiries** *No arrest has been made, but a man is helping the police with their enquiries.*

policeman noun

- ADJ. **senior | ordinary** *the duties of the ordinary policeman* | **local, neighbourhood | uniformed | plain-clothes | undercover | military | off-duty | friendly | bent, crooked** *The robbery may have been carried out with the help of a bent policeman.*
- VERB + POLICEMAN **call, fetch** *A policeman was called to the house just after midnight.* ◊ *She went off to fetch a policeman.*
- POLICEMAN + VERB **patrol sth | arrest sb**
⇨ See OFFICER

policy noun

1 plan of action
- ADJ. **clear, coherent | conscious, deliberate** *a deliberate policy to involve people of all ages in the scheme* | **strict | controversial | official, public | government, party | company | domestic, internal, national, regional | open-door** *an open-door policy for migrant workers* | **agricultural, conservation, economic, educational, energy, environmental, financial, fiscal, foreign, housing, industrial, military, social, transport, etc.**
- VERB + POLICY **develop, formulate, frame, shape | establish, implement, introduce | adopt, carry out, follow, pursue** *The government followed a policy of restraint in public spending.* | **have, operate** *The company operates a strict no-smoking policy.*
- POLICY + VERB **be aimed at sth** *a policy aimed at halting economic recession*
- POLICY + NOUN **decision, making | change, review | document, statement**
- PREP. **~ of** *The company's policy of expansion has created many new jobs.* **~ on** *the party's policy on housing*
- PHRASES **a matter of policy** *It is a matter of company policy that we do not disclose the names of clients.*

2 insurance contract
- ADJ. **insurance | contents, life, motor, etc.**
- VERB + POLICY **take out | renew**
- POLICY + VERB **cover sb/sth** *The policy covers (you for) accidental loss or damage.* | **expire**
- POLICY + NOUN **holder | schedule**
- PREP. **in a/the~** *risks defined in the policy* **under a/the~** *the types of claims covered under the policy*

polio noun

- VERB + POLIO **have | contract | immunize sb against, vaccinate sb against**
- POLIO + NOUN **vaccination, vaccine | virus | victim**
⇨ Special page at ILLNESS

Polish noun

⇨ Note at LANGUAGE

polish noun

- ADJ. **boot, furniture, metal, nail, shoe, silver | French | beeswax, wax**
- VERB + POLISH **apply** *Apply polish with a soft brush.* | **give sth** *You'll need to give your shoes a good polish.* | **remove** *Use acetone to remove nail polish.*

polished adj.

- VERBS be
- ADV. **brightly, deeply, highly, well** *the brightly polished brasses* ◊ *slipping on the highly polished floor* | **beautifully, nicely | freshly, newly**

polite adj.

- VERBS be, seem, sound | remain
- ADV. **extremely, very | perfectly, scrupulously, unfailingly | fairly, quite | coolly, formally** *His manner was coolly polite and impersonal.*
- PREP. **to** *She was scrupulously polite to him.*

politeness noun

- ADJ. **common, conventional** *It's no more than common politeness to hear what she has to say.* | **formal | social | natural** *Her natural politeness could not hide the distress in her voice.* | **exaggerated, excessive**
- PREP. **out of~** *They accepted the food more out of politeness than because they were hungry.* **with ~** *They greeted their visitor with formal politeness.*
- PHRASES **a veneer of politeness** *His veneer of politeness concealed a ruthless determination.*

political adj.

- VERBS be | become
- ADV. **highly, very** *This whole issue has become highly political.*

political asylum noun

- VERB + POLITICAL ASYLUM **apply for, ask for, claim, demand, seek | grant sb, offer sb**
- PHRASES **an application for political asylum**

politician *noun*

- ADJ. **leading, prominent, senior | experienced, veteran** *a veteran politician of the left* **| influential | astute, clever, shrewd | corrupt | career, professional | conviction | local | left-wing, right-wing | Conservative, Labour, etc. | Opposition**
- VERB + POLITICIAN **elect | bribe**

politics *noun*

1 work/ideas connected with getting/using power
- ADJ. **county, local** *She was active in local politics for many years.* **| domestic, internal, national** *the country's internal politics* ◊ *the internal politics of the legal profession* **| global, international, world | democratic, electoral, multiparty, parliamentary, party | contemporary, modern | mainstream | practical** *He argued that it was not practical politics to abolish private schools.* **| power** *They took the view that Casper was playing power politics with their jobs at stake.* **| consensus** *Consensus politics places a high value on existing political institutions.* **| conviction | cultural, gender, sexual | office**
- VERB + POLITICS **enter, go into** *They went into politics in the hope of changing society.* **| abandon, retire from** *He abandoned politics and went into business.* **| be interested in | be active in, be engaged in, be/get immersed in, be/get involved in, engage in, participate in | dabble in, play** (*informal*) **| get embroiled in | interfere in, intervene in, meddle in** *As a churchman, he was accused of meddling in politics.* **| dominate** *the issues which have dominated Irish politics* **| reshape** *reforms that are intended to reshape Italian politics*
- POLITICS + VERB **dominate sth** *In their world politics dominates everything.*
- PHRASES **the world of politics**

2 political beliefs
- ADJ. **extreme, radical** *His manners were as mild as his politics were extreme.* **| left-wing, right-wing | sectarian | working-class | feminist**
- VERB + POLITICS **discuss, talk (about)** (*informal*) *Let's not talk politics now.*

3 study of government
- ADJ. **comparative**
⇨ Note at SUBJECT (for verbs and nouns)

poll *noun*

1 survey of opinion
- ADJ. **local, national | opinion | political, popularity | exit** *Exit polls suggest a big Labour majority, but the true picture will only be known after the count.* **| straw** *I took a straw poll among my colleagues to find out how many can use chopsticks.* **| latest, recent**
- VERB + POLL **carry out, conduct, take | lead (in) | publish**
- POLL + VERB **indicate sth, reveal sth, show sth, suggest sth**
- POLL + NOUN **rating, results**
- PREP. **in the ~s** *success in the polls*
- PHRASES **be ahead/behind in the polls** *With a week to go until polling day, the Conservatives are still behind in the polls.* **a lead in the polls** *A tougher budget might have widened Labour's lead in the polls.*

2 (usually **the polls**) voting in an election
- ADJ. **presidential**
- VERB + POLLS **go to** *The country goes to the polls on May 7th to elect local councillors.*
- POLLS + VERB **open | close** *Counting will begin as soon as the polls close.*
- PREP. **at the ~s** *She was defeated at the polls.*

pollen *noun*

- VERB + POLLEN **collect, gather** *bees gathering pollen*

- POLLEN + NOUN **grain | count** *Hay fever sufferers have a worse time when the pollen count is high.* **| analysis | record** *The pollen record shows that this plant was never common on the island.*

pollutant *noun*

- ADJ. **air, atmospheric, environmental, water | chemical, toxic | major | industrial**
- VERB + POLLUTANT **discharge, emit, release**
- POLLUTANT + NOUN **emission**
- PREP. **~from** *pollutants from nearby industries* **~in** *pollutants in exhaust gases*
- PHRASES **the emission/release of pollutants**

polluted *adj.*

- ADV. **badly, heavily, highly, seriously, severely**
- PREP. **with** *The air is heavily polluted with traffic fumes.*

pollution *noun*

- ADJ. **air, atmospheric, environmental, marine, river, water | chemical, industrial, nuclear | lead, nitrate, noise, oil, ozone, sewage, vehicle, etc. | airborne**
- VERB + POLLUTION **cause | avoid, prevent | combat, control, fight, tackle** *a convention on combating atmospheric pollution* **| cut, limit, minimize, reduce** *The summit ended with a joint pledge to limit pollution.* **| monitor**
- POLLUTION + NOUN **level | abatement, control, prevention, reduction | limits | standards** *a tightening of water pollution standards* **| monitoring | inspectorate, watchdog** *a survey by the government's water pollution watchdog* **| incident, problem | laws, legislation, regulations | offence | sources** *The computer model assesses the likely impact of new pollution sources.*
- PHRASES **the cost of pollution** *the cost of air pollution in health and other terms* **a risk of pollution** *Environmentalists say there is a high risk of pollution from the landfill site.* **a source of pollution**

polythene *noun*

- ADJ. **heavy-duty**
- VERB + POLYTHENE **cover sth with, line sth with, wrap sth in**
- POLYTHENE + NOUN **bag | sheeting**

pond *noun*

- ADJ. **big, large | little, small | stagnant | muddy | ornamental | garden, village | duck, fish, lily**
- VERB + POND **build, construct, dig | fill | drain, empty** *The pond is drained every year.*
- POND + NOUN **life, water**
- PREP. **across a/the ~** *She swam across the pond.* **in a/the ~** *There are goldfish in the pond.* **into a/the ~** *Her sunglasses had fallen into the pond.* **on a/the ~** *some ducks swimming on a pond*
- PHRASES **the bottom/edge/middle/side/surface of a pond** *The dog raced around to the other side of the pond.*

ponder *verb*

- ADV. **carefully, deeply, hard | (for) a moment** *She pondered for a moment before replying.*
- VERB + PONDER **leave sb to** *He walked out of the room, leaving me to ponder what he had just said.* **| be forced to**
- PREP. **about** *This was something I had been pondering about for some time.* **on** *I walked up the stairs, pondering on her reaction to my news.* **over** *I pondered hard over the reply to his letter.*

pony noun

- VERB + PONY **pit** *Pit ponies were used in most mines at the turn of the last century.* | **polo** | **wild**
- VERB + PONY **ride** | **lead** | **brush down** | **saddle** | **shoe**
- PONY + VERB **neigh, whinny** | **canter, gallop, trot, walk** | **prance** | **jump**
- PONY + NOUN **club** | **ride** | **riding, trekking**
- PHRASES **a pony and cart/trap**

pool noun

1 swimming pool, etc.
- ADJ. **paddling, swimming** | **birthing** *babies born in birthing pools* | **big** | **little, small** | **deep** | **empty** | **indoor** | **open-air, outdoor** | **heated** | **inflatable** *We gave the children an inflatable paddling pool for Christmas.*
- VERB + POOL **swim in** | **dive/jump/plunge into**
- POOL + NOUN **attendant**
- PHRASES **the bottom/edge/middle/side of the pool, a length of the pool** *He swam three lengths of the pool.*

2 small shallow area of water
- ADJ. **big, large** | **little, small** | **deep** | **shallow** | **stagnant, still** | **freshwater, salt-water** | **muddy** | **rock** | **ornamental**
- PREP. **in a/the ~** *The children waded in the shallow rock pools.* | **~ of** *pools of water*

3 small area of liquid/light
- ADJ. **big** | **little, small** | **dark** | **mud**
- VERB + POOL **lie in** *The body lay in a dark pool of blood.*
- PREP. **in a/the ~** *animals wallowing in the mud pools* | **~ of** *pools of light*

4 supply of sth
- ADJ. **big, huge, large** | **small** | **common** *drawing on funds from a common pool* | **car, labour, typing**
- PREP. **~ of** *a large pool of cheap labour*

pop noun

1 short sharp sound
- ADJ. **loud** | **sudden**
- PREP. **with a ~** *The cork came out with a loud pop.*

2 popular music
- ADJ. **classic, melodic, psychedelic**
- VERB + POP **play** | **listen to**
- POP + NOUN **classic, hit, music, song, tune** | **artist, singer, star** | **band, group** | **concert, festival** | **record, video** | **fan** | **charts** | **culture**
- PREP. **in ~** *He was an important figure in pop during the seventies.*

pope noun

- VERB + POPE **elect**
- PHRASES **an audience with the pope** *He was granted an audience with the Pope.*

popular adj.

- VERBS **be, prove, seem** | **become** | **remain** | **make sth** *What makes this subject so popular?*
- ADV. **enormously, especially, extremely, genuinely, highly, hugely, immensely, incredibly, massively, particularly, phenomenally, really, vastly, very, wildly** | **increasingly** | **less than, not exactly** *Jack was not exactly popular after the incident with the fire extinguisher.* | **fairly, pretty, quite, rather, relatively** | **deservedly** *a deservedly popular restaurant with all who enjoy Mexican food* | **instantly** *He was one of those people who are instantly popular.* | **always, enduringly, eternally, ever, perennially** *Seaside holidays are always popular.* ◇ *a concert featuring the ever popular music from Hollywood's silver screen* | **widely, universally, internationally** |

personally *The prime minister remained personally popular despite his party's disastrous slide in the opinion polls.* | **politically**
- PREP. **among** *popular among young people* **as** *These animals are quite popular as pets.* **for** *a restaurant that is popular for light meals* **with** *This area is immensely popular with tourists.*

popularity noun

- ADJ. **enormous, great, huge, immense, massive, widespread** | **growing, increasing** | **dwindling** | **continued, continuing** | **personal** | **current**
- VERB + POPULARITY **achieve, win** | **deserve** *The film deserves its popularity.* | **court** *She is a tough decision-maker who does not court popularity.* | **enjoy** | **gain (in), grow in** *Organic produce appears to be gaining in popularity.* | **retain** | **regain**
- POPULARITY + VERB **grow** | **decline, wane**
- POPULARITY + NOUN **rating** | **stakes** *They are running neck-and-neck in the popularity stakes.*
- PREP. **~ among/amongst** *The current system has never enjoyed popularity among teachers.* **~ with** *She enjoys huge popularity with the voters.*
- PHRASES **a decline/drop in popularity, an increase/a rise/a surge/an upsurge in popularity** *the recent upsurge in the popularity of folk music.* **the peak of (sb/sth's) popularity** *At the peak of its popularity in the late nineties, the band sold ten million albums a year*

populated adj.

- VERBS **be**
- ADV. **densely, heavily, highly, thickly** *the most densely populated part of the island* | **sparsely, thinly**
- PREP. **with** *The prison was populated with people of every trade and profession.*

population noun

- ADJ. **large** | **small, sparse** | **overall, total** *The country has a total population of 65 million.* | **global, local, national, world** | **indigenous, native** | **adult, ageing, elderly, young, youthful** | **female, male** | **black, white** | **active, working** *Most of the economically active population is employed in the primary industries.* | **student** | **civil, civilian** | **prison, school** | **rural, urban** | **general** *The general population was in favour of the National Health Service.*
- POPULATION + VERB **be sth, stand at sth** *The population now stands at about 4 million.* | **reach sth** | **exceed sth** | **double, grow, increase, rise** | **decline, decrease, fall** | **consist of sth** | **live** *The majority of the population live in these two towns.*
- POPULATION + NOUN **levels, size** | **density** | **data, estimate, figures, projections, trends** *No reliable population estimates exist.* | **growth, increase** | **decline, loss** | **ageing** | **explosion** | **census** | **centre** *major population centres along the coast*
- PHRASES **a decline/an increase in population, the growth of population** *The rapid growth of population led to an acute shortage of housing.* **per head of population** *The income per head of population was under £1 000 per annum.*

porcelain noun

- ADJ. **exquisite, fine** | **Chinese, Meissen, etc.**
- QUANT. **piece** *some fine pieces of Chinese porcelain*
- PORCELAIN + NOUN **factory** | **manufacturer**

porch noun

- ADJ. **entrance** | **church** | **back, front** | **north, south, west** (= of a church) | **pillared, projecting**
- PORCH + NOUN **door, light**

● PREP. **in/on the~** *She stood in the porch and rang the doorbell.*

pore *noun*

● ADJ. **blocked** | **open**
● VERB + PORE **block** | **unblock** | **open** *A hot bath opens the pores.* | **close**

pork *noun*

● ADJ. **fresh** | **roast, smoked** | **organic**
● QUANT. **bit, piece, slice** | **belly, knuckle, leg, loin, shoulder** *roast leg of pork*
● PORK + NOUN **chop, pie, sausage** | **butcher**
● PHRASES **pork and apple sauce, sweet and sour pork**

pornography *noun*

● ADJ. **hard-core, soft** | **child**

port *noun*

● ADJ. **bustling, busy** | **Channel, coastal, foreign, sea** | **cargo, coal, commercial, ferry, fishing**
● VERB + PORT **come into, reach** *The vessel reached port the next morning.* | **leave**
● PORT + NOUN **area** | **authority** | **facilities**
● PREP. **in ~** *Bad weather kept the ship in port for three more days.* **into ~** *trying to steer the boat into port*
● PHRASES **a port of call** *Our next port of call was Piraeus.*

portable *adj.*

● VERBS **be**
● ADV. **easily, highly, very** *a machine that is designed to be easily portable* | **completely, fully**

porter *noun*

1 helps lift and carry things
● ADJ. **hospital, kitchen, railway**
● VERB + PORTER **act as** *Some Sherpas act as guides and porters for mountaineering expeditions.* | **call, hail** *On arriving at the station, we hailed a porter to carry the bags.*
● PORTER + VERB **carry sth**

2 in charge of the entrance of a large building
● ADJ. **head** | **hall, hotel** | **night** | **uniformed**
● PHRASES **porter's desk, porter's lodge**
⇨ Note at JOB

portion *noun*

1 part/share
● ADJ. **considerable, large, significant, sizeable, substantial** | **small**
● VERB + PORTION **make up, take up**
● PREP. **~ of** *Salaries take up a considerable portion of our total budget.*

2 of food
● ADJ. **double, generous, large** *a generous portion of vegetables* | **small, tiny** | **individual**
● PREP. **~ of** *He asked for a double portion of chips.*
● PHRASES **divide sth into portions**

portrait *noun*

● ADJ. **full-length, half-length, head and shoulders** | **oil, pastel, pencil, etc.** | **photographic, sculptural** | **equestrian, family, group, royal** | **literary, pen**
● VERB + PORTRAIT **do, paint, photograph** | **sit for** | **commission** | **write** | **display, exhibit, show**
● PORTRAIT + VERB **hang** *Ancient family portraits hung on the walls of the staircase.*

● PORTRAIT + NOUN **gallery** | **artist, painter, photographer** *sitting to a fashionable portrait painter*
● PREP. **~ by, ~ of** *a portrait of the Queen by Annigoni*
⇨ Note at ART

portray *verb*

● ADV. **accurately** | **clearly** | **dramatically, graphically, vividly** *an incident that graphically portrays the dangers associated with this sport* ◇ *The museum collection vividly portrays the heritage of 200 years of canals.*
● VERB + PORTRAY **attempt to, try to**
● PREP. **as** *trying to portray themselves as the victims*

portrayal *noun*

● ADJ. **accurate, realistic, vivid** | **moving, poignant** | **chilling, frightening** *He is best remembered for his chilling portrayal of Norman Bates in 'Psycho'.*
● PREP. **in the/its, etc. ~** *She shows a full range of emotions in her portrayal of an ambitious politician.* | **~ of** *His novel is a vivid portrayal of life in a mining community.*

Portuguese *noun*

⇨ Note at LANGUAGE

position *noun*

1 place
● ADJ. **correct, exact** | **central** | **geographical** | **military, strategic** | **defensive**
● VERB + POSITION **take (up)** *The guards took up their positions on either side of the door.* | **jostle for** *Hordes of journalists jostled for position outside the conference hall.* | **play** *(sport) What position does he play?*
● PREP. **in ~** *Fix the pieces in position before gluing them together* **into ~** *Please get into position.* **out of ~** *Nakata had to play out of position when the defender was injured.*

2 way of sitting, standing, etc.
● ADJ. **comfortable, uncomfortable** | **crouched, kneeling, sitting** | **sleeping** | **horizontal, vertical** | **foetal**
● VERB + POSITION **change**

3 situation
● ADJ. **business, economic, financial, legal** | **dominant, impregnable, strong** | **favourable, good, ideal, perfect** | **envious, invidious** | **competitive, precarious, vulnerable, weak** | **awkward, difficult, embarrassing, impossible** | **current, present** | **bargaining, negotiating, trading** *the trading position of the British economy*
● VERB + POSITION **achieve, attain, reach** *It has taken years to achieve the position we are now in.* | **put sb in** *It put me in an awkward position when he asked me to keep a secret.* | **strengthen** *Their obvious desperation strengthens our bargaining position.*
● PREP. **in a/the ~** *We may be in a position to help you.* ◇ *I was in the embarrassing position of having completely forgotten her name.* | **~ of**

4 opinion
● ADJ. **extreme** | **ideological, philosophical, political, theoretical** | **official** *The country's official position is that there is no famine in the area.*
● VERB + POSITION **adopt, take** | **defend**
● PREP. **~ on** *He took an extreme position on religious matters.*

5 rank
● ADJ. **first, second, etc.** | **dominant, high, important, influential, pre-eminent** | **inferior, lowly, privileged, secure** | **social**
● VERB + POSITION **establish, gain, secure** | **hold, occupy** *They occupy a lowly position in society.*
● PREP. **~ among/amongst** *This latest novel confirms her*

pre-eminent position amongst today's writers. ~ **in** *The firm gained a dominant position in the market.*
• PHRASES **a position of authority/influence/power**

6 job
• ADJ. **full-time, part-time | key, responsible, senior | junior, menial | official | skilled | administrative, management, managerial**
• VERB + POSITION **have, hold, occupy | apply for | obtain | fill | offer sb | resign**
• PREP. **in a/the** ~ *How long were you in your previous position?* | ~ **in/within** *his new position in the firm* ~ **of** *She was offered the position of sales manager.*

position *verb* (often **be positioned**)
• ADV. **firmly** *The radiologist firmly positioned Phoebe in front of a ferocious-looking machine.* | **centrally** *The markers were not positioned centrally.* | **carefully | correctly | wrongly | favourably, well | ideally, perfectly, uniquely** *The company is uniquely positioned to compete in foreign markets.* | **strategically**
• PREP. **at, behind, between, in, in front of, near, on, etc.** *Police marksmen were positioned on the roof.*

positive *adj.*

1 certain
• VERBS **be, seem, sound**
• ADV. **absolutely, quite** *I'm absolutely positive it was him.* | **fairly**
• PREP. **about** *She seemed fairly positive about it.* **of** *Are you positive of your facts?*

2 hopeful and confident/encouraging
• VERBS **appear, be, feel, seem, sound | remain**
• ADV. **distinctly, extremely, highly, overwhelmingly, really, very** *He took a highly positive view of the matter.* | **entirely, wholly | fairly, mildly, moderately, quite | broadly, essentially, generally | apparently, seemingly**
• PREP. **about** *sounding very positive about his chances*

3 showing that sth has happened/is present
• VERBS **be, prove, test** *The test proved positive.*
• ADV. **strongly, weakly** (*both technical*)
• PREP. **for** *He tested positive for HIV.*

possession *noun*

1 having/owning sth
• ADJ. **exclusive** *They had exclusive possession of the property as tenants.* | **illegal, unlawful** *They were charged with unlawful possession of firearms.*
• VERB + POSSESSION **gain, get, obtain | take** *When do you take possession of your new house?* | **retain** *The team was struggling to retain possession of the ball.*
• POSSESSION + NOUN **order** *The judge made a possession order against the tenant.*
• PREP. **in** ~ **of sth** *Drivers must be in possession of a current driving licence.* **in your** ~ *They have in their possession some very valuable pictures.*
• PHRASES **in full possession of sth** *Anyone in full possession of the facts would see that we are right.*

2 sth that sb has/owns
• ADJ. **family, personal, private | cherished, prized, proud, treasured, valuable, valued** *The sports car was her proudest possession.* | **material, worldly** *He carried all his worldly possessions in an old suitcase.* | **colonial, continental, overseas** *the country's overseas possessions* (= colonies).
• VERB + POSSESSION **acquire | collect | sell | lose**

possessive *adj.*

• VERBS **be, feel, seem | become, get** *Nick's starting to get possessive and jealous.*
• ADV. **extremely, fiercely, intensely, very** *her fiercely possessive love for him* | **rather**

• PREP. **about** *Why should he feel so possessive about some old photos?* **of** *She had always been possessive of her brother.* **towards** *He was very possessive towards her.*

possibility *noun*

• ADJ. **exciting, interesting | endless, many** *The resort offers endless possibilities for entertainment.* | **further, other | different, various | future | distinct, great, real, serious, strong** *There's a strong possibility that it will rain today.* | **reasonable | faint, remote** *There is a faint possibility that he might have got the wrong day.* | **practical | theoretical | obvious**
• VERB + POSSIBILITY **allow sb, offer sb, open up, raise | see | consider, discuss, examine, explore, study** *Have you explored the possibilities of setting up your own business?* | **accept, acknowledge, admit, concede, countenance, entertain, recognize | ignore, overlook | deny, discount, dismiss, eliminate, exclude, preclude, rule out** *We cannot rule out the possibility of mistaken identity.* | **face** *The club is facing the real possibility of relegation.* | **risk** *We don't want to risk the possibility of losing all our money.* | **allow for, cover** *Some reserves were named to cover the possibility of withdrawals.* | **avert | lessen, reduce**
• PREP. ~ **for** *She was quick to see the possibilities for making money that her new skills gave her.* ~ **of** *Careful checks will reduce the possibility of unpleasant surprises.*
• PHRASES **beyond/within the bounds of possibility** *It's not beyond the bounds of possibility that a similar situation could arise again.* **a number/range of possibilities** *The course offers a wide range of possibilities for personal development.*

possible *adj.*

• VERBS **be, seem, sound | become | make sth** *New technology has made it possible to communicate more easily.* | **think sth** *In those circumstances, I thought it possible to work with him.*
• ADV. **perfectly, quite | just** *It is just possible that he's still here.* | **humanly** *I think that what he's suggesting is not humanly possible.* | **theoretically** *It's theoretically possible, but highly unlikely ever to happen.*
• PHRASES **as far/long/much as possible** *She did as much as possible to help him.* **as quickly/soon as possible** *Please come as soon as possible.* **if (at all) possible** *I'd like the money back by next week if possible.*

post *noun*

1 postal system
• ADJ. **first-class, second-class | registered | inland**
• PREP. **by** ~ *I sent it by first-class post.* **in the** ~ *My application for the job is in the post.*
• PHRASES **by return of post** *Orders will be sent by return of post.*

2 letters, parcels, etc.
• ADJ. **first, last** *If you hurry you'll just catch the last post.*
• VERB + POST **check, open** *She arrived at the office early and checked her post.*
• POST + NOUN **box** (also **postbox**)

3 job
• ADJ. **senior | full-time, part-time | permanent, temporary | vacant | managerial, teaching | government, university**
• VERB + POST **apply for | take up | hold | leave, quit, resign | appoint sb to, fill | dismiss sb from, relieve sb of** *He was relieved of his post when he was found to have accepted bribes.*
• PREP. ~ **as** *He quit his post as chief executive.* ~ **of** *She applied for the new post of training officer.*

4 place where sb is on duty

• ADJ. **army, police | command, observation | border, frontier**
• VERB + POST **take up** *The guard took up his post at the gate.* | **desert** *The sentries had deserted their posts.*
• PREP. **at your~** *The gun crew were at their posts.*

5 upright piece of wood, etc.
• ADJ. **finishing, winning | far, near** (both in football) *He steered a shot between the keeper and the near post.*
• PHRASES **first past the post** *The first horse past the post wins the race.* **pip sb/sth at the post** *She led for most of the way before being pipped at the post.*

postage noun

• VERB + POSTAGE **pay** *I had to pay £4 postage.* | **cover** *Add £3 to each order to cover postage.* | **include**
• POSTAGE + NOUN **stamp | rates**
• PREP. **for~** *It costs £60, plus £5 for postage.* **in~** *Sending those books cost me a fortune in postage!* | **~on** *What's the postage on this parcel?*
• PHRASES **postage and packing** *All prices include postage and packing.*

postcard noun

• ADJ. **picture | holiday**
• VERB + POSTCARD **write** *I hate writing holiday postcards.* | **post, send (sb) | get, receive**
• POSTCARD + VERB **arrive | depict sth, show sth**
• PREP. **on a/the~** *Write your answers on a postcard.* | **~from, ~of** *I sent my mum a postcard of the cathedral.* **~to**

poster noun

• ADJ. **cinema, circus, election | wanted** *The police have put up wanted posters describing the man.*
• VERB + POSTER **display, exhibit, put up, stick up | be covered with, be plastered with** *His walls are plastered with posters of rock stars.* | **take down | design | print**
• POSTER + VERB **appear, go up** *Huge election posters suddenly went up all over the town.* | **feature sth, show sth | advertise sth**
• POSTER + NOUN **campaign** *Detectives have launched a massive poster campaign to help in the search for the two killers.*
• PREP. **on a/the~** *the picture on the poster* | **~for** *posters for tonight's concert* **~of** *a poster of James Dean*

posting noun

• ADJ. **diplomatic, foreign, overseas | three-month, two-year, etc. | temporary**
• VERB + POSTING **get | accept, take up** *She was unable to take up the London posting.*
• PREP. **~as** *She has now accepted a posting as ambassador to Latvia.* **~to** *He received a posting to Japan as soon as his training was finished.*

postman noun

• ADJ. **local, village**
• POSTMAN + VERB **deliver sth**
⇨ Note at JOB

post-mortem noun

• VERB + POST-MORTEM **carry out, conduct, do | have, hold** *The coroner says we will have to hold a post-mortem.*
• POST-MORTEM + VERB **reveal sth, show sth**
• POST-MORTEM + NOUN **examination**
• PREP. **~on** *They're doing a post-mortem on her today.*

post office noun

• ADJ. **head, main | sub | local, village**

• VERB + POST OFFICE **go to**
• POST OFFICE + NOUN **counter**
• PREP. **at a/the~** *You can buy stamps at the post office.*

postpone verb

• ADV. **indefinitely** *The event has been postponed indefinitely due to lack of interest.* | **merely** *The inevitable conflict was merely postponed till the next meeting.*
• VERB + POSTPONE **agree to, decide to, vote to | be forced to | ask sb to** *Ruth wrote at once, asking Maria to postpone her visit.*
• PREP. **for** *Our visit had been postponed for several weeks.* **from, to** *The match has been postponed from Wednesday night to Friday night.* **till/until** *The meeting has been postponed until next week.*

postponement noun

• ADJ. **further, repeated | indefinite**
• VERB + POSTPONEMENT **ask for, call for, request, seek** *They are calling for a further postponement of the election date.* | **announce | force, result in**
• PREP. **~until** *The death of one of the candidates forced postponement of the voting until 1 June.*

posture noun

1 position of the body
• ADJ. **correct, good | bad, poor | erect, upright** *the normal upright posture* | **stiff, stooping | body**
• VERB + POSTURE **have** *She has very good posture.* | **adopt | maintain | change, improve**
• PREP. **in a/the~** *He sat in a posture of absolute respect.* | **~for** *a poor posture for driving*

2 attitude
• ADJ. **defensive | aggressive, threatening | military**
• VERB + POSTURE **adopt, assume | maintain**
• PREP. **~towards** *to adopt a threatening posture towards an opponent*

pot noun

1 for cooking
• ADJ. **cooking**
• VERB + POT **scour | cover** *Cook gently in a covered pot for 3 to 4 hours.*
• POT + VERB **brim (over) with sth** *The waiter brought over a steaming pot brimming with seafood.* | **bubble, steam** *He could hear the pot bubbling on the stove.*
• PREP. **for the~** *Local people kill these animals for the pot* (= to eat). **in/into a/the ~** *Put all the ingredients in a large pot.* | **~of** *a pot of soup*
• PHRASES **pots and pans** *I sat in the kitchen, among the dirty pots and pans.*

2 for tea/coffee
• ADJ. **steaming | fresh | coffee, tea** (also **teapot**)
• VERB + POT **brew, make, put on** *I'll make a fresh pot of tea.* | **share | fill, refill, top up** *She refilled the teapot with boiling water.* | **empty**
• PREP. **in a/the~** *Is there any more tea in the pot?* | **~of**

3 container for storing/growing things, etc.
• ADJ. **ceramic, clay, earthenware, glass, iron, pewter, plastic, terracotta | flower, plant | jam, paint, pepper, yogurt | chamber | chimney | lobster**
• VERB + POT **grow sth in, plant sth in**
• POT + VERB **be filled with sth, be full of sth, contain sth** *a clay pot full of oil*
• POT + NOUN **plant**
• PREP. **in/into a/the~** *Plants in pots require more water than you might think.* | **~of** *a pot of glue/jam*

potato noun

• ADJ. **baking, new | sweet | seed | baked, boiled,**

chipped, creamed, fried, jacket, mashed, roast, sauté *jacket potatoes with sour cream and chives*
• QUANT. **sack**
• VERB + POTATO **eat, have | peel, scrape | chop, mash, slice | bake, boil, cook, fry, roast, sauté** *potatoes baked in their jackets*
• POTATO + NOUN **chip, crisp, purée, salad | peel, skin | peeler | crop, harvest**
⇨ Special page at FOOD

potency *noun*

• ADJ. **sexual** *a man at the peak of his sexual potency*
• VERB + POTENCY **increase | affect | lose**

potent *adj.*

• VERBS **be | become**
• ADV. **extremely, highly, particularly, very | pretty, quite** *The vodka must have been pretty potent stuff.*

potential *noun*

• ADJ. **considerable, enormous, great, limitless | full** *You aren't using your computer to its full potential.* | **true | unfulfilled, untapped | commercial | growth**
• VERB + POTENTIAL **have, show** *This young man has enormous potential.* | **be aware of, see** *John Cadbury could see the potential for his product.* | **develop, exploit, unlock** *They were among the first companies to exploit the potential of the Internet.* | **fulfil, reach, realize** *Signing for a top club would enable him to fulfil his true potential.*
• PREP. **with ~** *looking for a trainee with potential* | **~ as** *She showed great potential as an actor.* **~ for** *an industry that has the potential for growth*

pottery *noun*

• ADJ. **decorated, glazed, painted | hand-thrown | coarse, fine**
• QUANT. **fragment, piece** *fragments of Iron Age pottery*
• VERB + POTTERY **make, manufacture, produce | fire** *the kilns in which the pottery is fired*
• POTTERY + NOUN **kiln**
⇨ Note at ART

potty *noun*

• VERB + POTTY **use | sit (sb) on**
• POTTY + NOUN **training**
• PREP. **on the ~**

poultry *noun*

• ADJ. **free-range**
• VERB + POULTRY **keep, rear** *He rears rabbits and poultry in the garden.*
• POULTRY + NOUN **farming, industry | dish** *a wine that goes well with fish and poultry dishes*

pound *noun*

1 money
⇨ Note at CURRENCY
2 measure of weight
⇨ Note at MEASURE

pour *verb*

• ADV. **carefully | deliberately | quickly | gradually, slowly | out** *Helen poured out two stiff drinks.*
• PREP. **from, into, on, onto, out of, over** *Pour the sauce over the pasta.*

pout *verb*

• ADV. **slightly | prettily, sulkily** *Her lips pouted sulkily.*
• PREP. **at** *She pouted prettily at him.*

poverty *noun*

• ADJ. **abject, absolute, extreme, grinding, severe | widespread | rural, urban**
• VERB + POVERTY **alleviate, combat, reduce | eliminate, eradicate** *hoping to eradicate urban poverty*
• POVERTY + NOUN **trap** *Caught in the poverty trap, they are unable to save money for business ventures.*
• PREP. **in ~** *Most of the population lives in grinding poverty.* | **~ among** *the true extent of poverty among the unemployed* **~ of** *His work displays a poverty of imagination.*
• PHRASES **below/on the poverty line** *families living on incomes below the poverty line*

powder *noun*

• ADJ. **fine | chilli, cocoa, coffee, curry, milk | baking | soap, washing | baby, face, talcum**
• VERB + POWDER **grind sth into** *The seeds are ground into a fine powder before use.* | **dust sth with, sprinkle on** *Before the photo dries, the image is dusted with a special powder.* | **dab on, put on** *She quickly dabbed some powder on her cheeks.* | **add, mix sth with, stir in** *Add a teaspoonful of curry powder.*
• POWDER + NOUN **snow**
• PHRASES **in powder form** *The tablets are also available in powder form.*

power *noun*

1 authority/control

• ADJ. **absolute, ultimate | considerable, enormous | limited | arbitrary | economic, legal, legislative, political | popular | secular**
• VERB + POWER **come to, rise to** *When did this government come to power?* | **assume, seize, take** *The Crown prince assumed power in his father's place.* | **restore sb to, return sb to | have, hold** *The court has no power to order a psychiatric examination of the child's parents.* ◇ *They held power for 18 years.* | **share | exercise, use, wield | confer, give sb, grant sb** *The new law delegates many of these powers to school governors.* | **fall from, lose** *They fell from power in 1992.* | **give up, relinquish, renounce | delegate, devolve**
• POWER + VERB **be concentrated in (the hands of sb/sth), rest with sb/sth** *The real legislative power still rests with the lower chamber.*
• POWER + NOUN **struggle** *getting the upper hand in a power struggle* | **base** *The party's power base is in the industrial north of the country.*
• PREP. **in (your) ~** *the party in power* ◇ *They held us in their power.* | **~ of** *the power of veto* **~ over** *The government has limited legal powers over television.*
• PHRASES **abuse of power, the balance of power** *The war brought about a shift in the balance of power.* **a bid for power, the exercise of power, a position of power** *the father's position of power and influence in the home* **the power behind the throne** (= the person who is really in control) *People say that the prime minister's wife is the power behind the throne.* **power-hungry** *The company was too small to hold two such power-hungry men.* **a transfer of power** *the transfer of power from a military to a civilian government*

2 ability to do sth

• ADJ. **air, military, naval, sea** *an increase in Britain's air power* | **fire** *weapons with enormous fire power* | **bargaining | computing | healing** *the healing power of sleep* | **earning, purchasing | staying** *Having served in four governments, he has the greatest staying power of any politician today.* | **magic, magical, mystical, psychic, supernatural** *They believe he has supernatural powers.*
• VERB + POWER **have | use | develop | lose** *Religion is rapidly losing its power to shape our behaviour.*
• PREP. **beyond sb/sth's ~** *a task still beyond any computer's power* **in/within your ~** *I'm afraid it's not within my*

power to help you. **through the ~ of** He wants to change the world through the power of prayer. | **~s as** a tribute to his powers as a teacher **~ of** her powers of observation ◇ I lost my power of speech for a while after the accident.
- PHRASES **at the height/peak/zenith of your powers** In 1946 Dali was at the peak of his powers. **do all/everything in your power** He did everything in his power to find us somewhere to live.

3 country with influence
- ADJ. **great, major | world | foreign | allied, enemy | occupying | victorious | European, Western,** etc. major European powers such as France and Germany | **colonial, industrial, naval**

4 force
- ADJ. **great | destructive, terrible** the destructive power of a hurricane

5 energy
- ADJ. **full** The plane was still climbing at full power. | **reduced** The transmitter is operating on reduced power. | **electric, electrical, hydroelectric, nuclear, solar, steam, tidal, water, wind**
- VERB + POWER **generate, produce** They use these streams to generate power for the mill. | **provide (sb/sth with), supply (sb/sth with)** This wheel provides the power to the cutting machine. | **use | harness | turn on | cut off, turn off**
- POWER + VERB **drive sth** Wind power is used to drive the machinery.
- POWER + NOUN **cable, line, point, supply | tool** DIY grew in popularity with the advent of power tools. | **plant, station | worker | cut, failure**
- PREP. **~ for** supplying power for the grinding process
- PHRASES **a source of power**

powerful adj.
- VERBS **be, feel, look, seem | become**
- ADV. **enormously, especially, exceptionally, extraordinarily, extremely, immensely, incredibly, particularly, really, remarkably, surprisingly, tremendously, unusually, very | increasingly | fairly, pretty, quite, reasonably, relatively | enough, sufficiently** She had a voice powerful enough not to need a microphone. | **potentially | economically, politically** a politically powerful figure | **locally** locally powerful landowners

powerless adj.
- VERBS **appear, be, feel, seem | become | remain | render sb** If he took control, they would be rendered virtually powerless.
- ADV. **completely, quite, totally, utterly | comparatively, relatively, virtually**
- PREP. **against** They were completely powerless against such a large group. **in the face of** They felt powerless in the face of disaster.

practicable adj.
- VERBS **be, prove, seem | become**
- ADV. **perfectly | reasonably** We will do this as soon as is reasonably practicable. | **not very**
- PHRASES **as far/soon as practicable**

practical noun
- ADJ. **chemistry, physics, etc.**
- VERB + PRACTICAL **sit, take | pass | fail** I passed the written exam but failed the practical.

practical adj.
- VERBS **be, seem, sound | become**
- ADV. **eminently, extremely, highly, intensely, very | entirely, purely, strictly** For entirely practical reasons,

children are not invited. | **hardly | quite, reasonably | essentially | severely** She always adopted a severely practical tone.

practice noun

1 actual doing of sth
- VERB + PRACTICE **put sth into** I can't wait to put what I've learned into practice.
- PREP. **in ~** The idea sounds fine in theory, but would it work in practice?

2 doing sth many times
- ADJ. **basketball, catching, piano, etc. | target**
- VERB + PRACTICE **do, get (in), have** I'll be able to get in a bit of practice this weekend. ◇ I've had a lot of practice in saying 'no' recently! | **need, require, take** Don't worry if you can't do it at first—it takes practice! | **give sb** This chapter gives students practice in using adjectives.
- PRACTICE + NOUN **ground | game, session**
- PREP. **out of ~** If you don't play regularly you soon get out of practice. **with ~** His accent should improve with practice. | **~ at** practice at swimming underwater **~ in** The children need more practice in tying their shoelaces.
- PHRASES **be good practice for sth** It will be good practice for later, when you have to make speeches in public.

3 way of doing sth
- ADJ. **good** adopting current best practices in your business | **corrupt, sharp, unethical, unfair | discriminatory, restrictive | accepted, common, current, established, normal, standard, universal, usual, widespread** It is standard practice not to pay bills until the end of the month. | **local | cultural, legal, medical, religious, sexual** the medical practices of ancient Egypt | **accounting, administrative, business, employment, management, working** studying Japanese working practices
- VERB + PRACTICE **introduce** The practice of community policing was introduced in the 1970s. | **adopt, follow, use | promote | change, modify** Established practices are difficult to modify. | **ban, outlaw, prevent, prohibit, stop**
- PRACTICE + VERB **begin | continue** the ancient custom of log rolling, a practice which continues to this day | **change, develop, evolve**
- PREP. **~ of** the practice of acupuncture
- PHRASES **a change in/of practice** changes in employment practices **a code of practice** voluntary codes of practice between sellers and customers **make a practice of sth** I don't make a practice of forgetting to pay my bills, I assure you!

4 work/office of a professional person
- ADJ. **successful | legal, medical, professional | general** (= medicine of a non-specialized type, not in a hospital), **private** (= accepting paying patients) | **group** It's a group practice, so you can easily change doctors.
- VERB + PRACTICE **be in, go into, set up in** She wants to go into general practice. | **retire from | suspend sb from** He had been suspended from practice, pending legal investigations. | **open, start** She has opened a new practice in the town. | **run** He runs a successful legal practice in Ohio. | **join** A new partner has joined the practice. | **leave**

practise verb
- ADV. **hard | regularly**
- PREP. **for** She's practising hard for the piano competition. **on** I learned hairdressing by practising on my sister.

pragmatic adj.
- VERBS **be, seem | become**
- ADV. **highly, very | entirely, purely, utterly | essentially, largely** Our approach is essentially pragmatic. | **quite, rather**

● PREP. **about** *They're pragmatic about the spending cuts.*

prairie *noun*

● ADJ. **high, rolling, wide | American**
● VERB + PRAIRIE **cross** *a train of covered wagons crossing the wide American prairies*
● PRAIRIE + NOUN **dog**
● PREP. **across the ~** *their route across the prairie* **on the~** *settlers' houses on the prairies of Canada*

praise *noun*

● ADJ. **glowing, great, high, lavish, special, unstinting, warm | faint | universal**
● VERB + PRAISE **be full of, be fulsome/loud/unstinting in** *The critics were full of praise for the film.* ◊ *He was unstinting in his praise of his teacher.* **| give sb, offer | single sb out for** *The team's coach singled his goalkeeper out for praise.* **| heap, shower (sb with)** *an article heaping praise on the government* **| come in for, receive | attract, draw, earn, win** *The play has attracted universal praise.*
● PREP. **beyond ~** *This book is beyond praise.* **in ~ of** *He wrote many poems in praise of his wife.* **| ~ for** *earning praise for their efforts* **~ from** *The decision also won praise from local people.* **~ of** *her praise of his skill*
● PHRASES **a chorus/paean of praise** *The French manager led the chorus of praise for the German team.* **have nothing but praise for sb/sth** *The patients interviewed had nothing but praise for the hospital staff.* **sing sb's praises** *The newspapers were singing the president's praises.* **a word of praise** *There were words of praise for the show's designer.*

praise *verb*

● ADV. **highly, lavishly, warmly** *He praised all his staff highly.* **| privately, publicly | rightly** *Her achievements in this field have been rightly praised.*
● VERB + PRAISE **be quick to** *The defeated captain was quick to praise the winning team.*
● PREP. **for** *They praised him for his cooking.*
● PHRASES **be universally/widely praised**

pram *noun*

● VERB + PRAM **push, wheel**
● PREP. **in a/the ~** *She was pushing her baby along in a pram.*

pray *verb*

● ADV. **earnestly, fervently, hard** *He thought if he prayed hard enough God might eventually listen.* **| quietly, silently | regularly | together**
● PREP. **for** *He prayed for rain.* **to** *I prayed to God for guidance.* **with** *She asked the priest to pray with her.*
● PHRASES **hope and pray** *We can hope and pray that no one gets hurt.* **let us pray** *'Let us pray.' The congregation bowed their heads.* ◊ *Let's pray Mick doesn't find out.*

prayer *noun*

● ADJ. **little, short | private, silent | special | fervent | evening, morning | daily | family**
● VERB + PRAYER **offer (up), say, send up, utter** *I sent up a quick prayer and entered the interview room.* **| remember sb in** *Let us remember them in our prayers today.* **| hear | answer** *Does God answer our prayers?* **| kneel in** *The congregation knelt in prayer.* **| join in, meet for** *local groups meeting for prayer* **| have** *We had family prayers before breakfast.* **| attend** *Students are required to attend prayers twice a week.*
● PRAYER + NOUN **book | mat, rug | meeting, service**

● PREP. **at~** *He spends an hour each day at prayer.* **in~** *She moved her lips in silent prayer.* **| ~ for** *a prayer for peace* **~ of** *I said a prayer of grateful thanks to God.* **~ to**
● PHRASES **the answer to (all) sb's prayers** (= exactly what sb needs) *The letter was the answer to her prayers.*

preacher *noun*

● ADJ. **celebrated, eminent, famous, good, great, leading | Baptist, Methodist, etc. | evangelical | lay | local | itinerant**
● VERB + PREACHER **hear, listen to**

precaution *noun*

● ADJ. **sensible, wise | adequate, proper, reasonable | necessary | elaborate | basic, simple** *You'll be quite safe if you observe certain basic precautions.* **| every** *We take every precaution to ensure that you have a comfortable journey.* **| extra, special | fire, safety, security**
● VERB + PRECAUTION **follow, observe, take**
● PREP. **as a~** *She had to stay in hospital overnight, just as a precaution.* **| ~against** *a precaution against customers who try to leave without paying* **~ for** *Staff are expected to take reasonable precautions for their own safety.* **~ of** *I took the precaution of turning the water supply off first.*

precede *verb*

● ADV. **directly, immediately** *in the moments which immediately preceded the earthquake*

precedence *noun*

● ADJ. **historical**
● VERB + PRECEDENCE **have, take | give sb/sth** *You should give your schoolwork precedence.* **| claim** *The French kings claimed precedence over those of Spain.*
● PREP. **~ over** *The needs of the patient take precedence over those of the student doctor.*
● PHRASES **in order of precedence** *The guests were seated strictly in order of precedence.*

precedent *noun*

● ADJ. **bad, dangerous, unfortunate | good, important | historical | judicial, legal**
● VERB + PRECEDENT **serve as** *This case could could serve as a precedent for others against the tobacco companies.* **| have | create, establish, provide, set** *This lowering of standards sets a dangerous precedent for future developments.* **| cite, quote | find | base sth on, use sth as** *The judge based his decision on precedents set during the Middle Ages.* **| follow**
● PREP. **without ~** *The achievements of this period were without precedent in history.* **| ~ for** *Many precedents can be found for this decision.*

precious *adj.*

● VERBS **be | become**
● ADV. **extremely, incredibly, infinitely, very**
● PREP. **to** *You are infinitely precious to me.*

precise *adj.*

● VERBS **be**
● ADV. **extremely, very | absolutely | increasingly | fairly, quite, reasonably | enough, sufficiently** *Are the measurements precise enough?* **| insufficiently | legally, mathematically** *You need to use legally precise terms.*
● PREP. **about** *You have to be precise about the numbers.*

precision *noun*

● ADJ. **absolute | great, high** *high precision measurement tools* **| analytical, mathematical, military, surgical, technical** *He organized the team with military precision.*

● QUANT. **degree** *Chimps are able to manipulate objects with a high degree of precision.*
● VERB + PRECISION **call for, demand, require** *surgery which requires great precision*
● PRECISION + NOUN **engineering** | **bombing**
● PREP. **with~** *These items cannot be dated with any precision.* | **~in** *a new era of precision in engineering*
● PHRASES **a lack of precision** *Any lack of precision in the contract could give rise to a dispute.*

preconception noun

● VERB + PRECONCEPTION **have** | **fit in with** *We like this approach because it fits in with our own preconceptions.* | **challenge, get away from** *It is important to challenge society's preconceptions about disabled people.*
● PREP. **with/without ~s** *It's important that you come to this task with no preconceptions.* | **~ about** *Most people have preconceptions about old age.* **~ of** *her preconceptions of life in the country*

predicament noun

● ADJ. **awful, awkward, dire, worse** *Other companies are in an even worse predicament than ourselves.* | **current, present** | **financial, personal**
● VERB + PREDICAMENT **be in, find yourself in, get into** *Many young people find themselves in this predicament.* | **place sb in, put sb in** | **escape (from), get out of** *How were we to escape this awful predicament?* | **solve**
● PREP. **in a/the~** *Now I really was in a dire predicament.*

predict verb

● ADV. **accurately, correctly, reliably, successfully, with accuracy/certainty** *It is not possible to predict with any certainty what effect this will have.* | **exactly, precisely** | **confidently** | **wrongly**
● VERB + PREDICT **be able/unable to, can/could** | **try to** | **dare (to)** *Few would have dared to predict such a landslide victory.* | **fail to** | **be difficult to, be hard to, be impossible to** | **be easy to, be possible to** | **use sth to** *a computer model used to predict future weather patterns* | **allow sb to, enable sb to** *Newton's theories allow us to predict the flight of a cricket ball.*
● PREP. **from** *We can predict from this information what is likely to happen next.*
● PHRASES **be widely predicted** *This result had been widely predicted by the opinion polls.*

predictable adj.

● VERBS **be, seem** | **become**
● ADV. **easily, extremely, highly, very** | **completely, entirely, quite, totally, wholly** | **almost, largely** | **fairly, pretty, reasonably, relatively** | **sadly** *England's defeat in the third test match was sadly predictable.*
● PREP. **from** *He asked whether this was predictable from previous performances.*

prediction noun

● ADJ. **accurate, correct** | **dire, gloomy** | **long-term** | **reliable, safe** | **confident** | **definite, firm** | **computer** | **earthquake, weather**
● VERB + PREDICTION **make** | **confirm, fulfil** *The results of the experiment confirmed their predictions.* | **confound, contradict**
● PREDICTION + VERB **prove sth, turn out to be sth** *Our prediction turns out to be correct.* | **be borne out, come true**
● PREP. **amid ~s** *Six hundred workers there lost their jobs today, amid gloomy predictions that there could be worse to come.* **contrary to a/the ~** *Contrary to almost all predictions, however, the government did not fall.* **despite a/the~**

Despite earlier dire predictions, shares remained steady. | **~ about** *I've learnt not to make predictions about the weather.* **~ for** *the government's prediction for unemployment* **~ of** *their predictions of future growth*

prefer verb

● ADV. **greatly, much, strongly** *I much prefer the orchestra's 1998 recording of the symphony.* | **infinitely** | **simply** *You may simply prefer just to sit on the terrace with a cocktail.* | **really** *I would really prefer to teach girls.* | **rather, slightly** | **certainly** *Egg pasta is certainly preferred by many chefs.* | **clearly, obviously** | **apparently** *Huge majorities apparently prefer reducing unemployment to fighting inflation.* | **generally, usually** | **naturally** *Employers naturally prefer candidates with some previous experience of the job.* | **personally** | **still**
● VERB + PREFER **would** *We can eat out if you like, but I would prefer to stay in.* | **tend to** *Industries still tend to prefer virgin raw materials to recycled ones.* | **seem to**
● PREP. **to** *I prefer his earlier paintings to his later ones.*

preferable adj.

● VERBS **be, seem** | **become** | **remain** | **consider sth**
● ADV. **far, greatly, infinitely, vastly**
● PREP. **to** *Death was considered vastly preferable to dishonour.*

preference noun

● ADJ. **clear, definite, marked, strong** | **slight** | **individual, personal** *It's a matter of personal preference.* | **consumer** | **first, second, etc.** *Local voters gave Harry West first preference.*
● VERB + PREFERENCE **have** *Do you have any particular preference?* | **demonstrate** | **express, indicate, show, state** | **give sb** *Preference is given to students who have passed maths and chemistry.* | **receive**
● PREP. **for~** *I choose motorways when driving, for preference.* **in ~ to** *They bought French planes in preference to British ones.* | **~ as to/with regard to** *He has not expressed a preference as to which school he wants to go to.* **~ between** *people's preferences between brown, white and wholemeal bread* **~ for sth (over sth)** *the government's preference for tax cuts over greater public spending* **~ in** *changing preferences in furniture styles*
● PHRASES **in order of preference** *List the candidates in order of preference.*

pregnancy noun

● ADJ. **early** | **late** | **full-term, post-term** | **easy, healthy, normal** | **difficult** *She had a difficult pregnancy with her first child.* | **teenage** | **premarital** | **unplanned, unwanted** *There are thousands of unwanted teenage pregnancies every year.*
● VERB + PREGNANCY **have** | **avoid, prevent** *taking precautions to avoid pregnancy* | **continue (with), keep** *the difficult decision about whether to continue with a pregnancy* | **terminate** *the right of a woman to terminate her pregnancy*
● PREGNANCY + VERB **be at/go to (full) term**
● PREGNANCY + NOUN **test** *a home pregnancy test kit*
● PREP. **during/in (a/the)~** *Lower blood pressure is common in early pregnancy.* **throughout (a/the)~** *You will be tested throughout your pregnancy.*

pregnant adj.

● VERBS **be, look** | **become, fall** *(informal),* **get** | **get sb, make sb** *He got her pregnant.*
● ADV. **heavily, very**
● PREP. **by** *She was pregnant by a former client.*
● PHRASES **six weeks, three months, etc. pregnant**

prejudice *noun*

- ADJ. **deep, deep-rooted, deep-seated, strong | blatant | serious, unfair** (*both law*) **| personal | old** *It's hard to break down old prejudices.* **| blind, irrational | anti-gay, anti-Catholic, etc. | class, cultural, political, racial, religious, sectarian, sexist**
- VERB + PREJUDICE **have, hold** *We all have prejudices of some kind.* **| air, express** *He sat there airing his personal prejudices.* **| arouse, feed, stir up | appeal to, pander to** *We must not pander to the irrational prejudices of a small minority.* **| confirm | come up against, encounter** *She had never encountered such deep prejudice before.* **| suffer | challenge | overcome | break down, eliminate, eradicate**
- PREP. **~ about** *a book written to challenge prejudices about disabled people* **~ against** *deep-rooted prejudice against homosexuals* **~ among** *prejudice among ignorant people* **~ towards** *prejudice towards immigrants*
- PHRASES **a victim of prejudice**

prejudice *verb*

1 cause sb to have a prejudice
- ADV. **unfairly**
- PREP. **against, in favour of** *Reading newspaper reports had unfairly prejudiced the jury in her favour.*

2 weaken sth/make it less fair
- ADV. **seriously, severely, substantially**
- VERB + PREJUDICE **be likely to** *She did not disclose evidence that was likely to prejudice her client's case*

prejudiced *adj.*

- VERBS **be, seem**
- ADV. **deeply, extremely | racially**
- PREP. **against** *He's deeply prejudiced against women.*

preliminary *noun*

- ADJ. **essential, necessary, useful | usual** *After the usual preliminaries the meeting began.*
- PREP. **as a ~** *The two presidents met today, as a preliminary to resuming the peace talks.* **without preliminaries** *She began speaking intensely, without preliminaries.* **| ~ to** *an essential preliminary to serious research*

prelude *noun*

- ADJ. **essential, inevitable, necessary**
- VERB + PRELUDE **consider sth, see sth as**
- PREP. **as a ~** *events held as a prelude to the Christmas festivities* **| ~ for** *the prelude for the battles ahead* **~ to** *He considered the strikes a prelude to the great socialist revolution.*

premier *noun*

- ADJ. **acting, deputy | former | British, Chinese, etc. | Conservative, Labour, etc. | state**
- VERB + PREMIER **appoint (sb), appoint sb as, elect (sb), elect sb as, swear sb in as** *She was sworn in as premier on 4 June.* **| succeed sb as, take over as**
- PREP. **as ~** *during his 25 years as Liberal premier*

premises *noun*

- ADJ. **new** *The company is moving to new premises next month.* **| suitable | bigger, large | cramped, modest | city-centre | purpose-built | adjoining, neighbouring | temporary | private, residential | business, church, club, commercial, company, factory, hospital, hotel, industrial, office, retail, school, shop**
- VERB + PREMISES **enter** *The police have the power to enter the premises at any time.* **| find | own | acquire, lease | move to | occupy, use | leave, vacate**

- PREP. **on the ~** *Smoking is strictly forbidden on school premises.*

premium *noun*

1 extra value/price
- ADJ. **high | additional, extra | price**
- VERB + PREMIUM **pay** *Electricity companies pay a premium for renewable energy.* **| charge | place, put**
- PREMIUM + NOUN **price**
- PREP. **at a ~** *Good student accommodation is at a premium* (= difficult to obtain and therefore expensive). **| ~ of** *bought at a premium of 40 per cent above the current market price* **~ on** *The company places a high premium on customer loyalty.*

2 payment for insurance
- ADJ. **annual, monthly, regular | high, low** *Intense competition has kept premiums low.* **| insurance**
- VERB + PREMIUM **pay | keep up** *We're struggling to keep up our premiums.* **| increase, raise** *The insurance company has increased our premiums.* **| cut, reduce**
- PREMIUM + VERB **go up, rise | fall, go down**
- PREMIUM + NOUN **payment, rate**
- PREP. **~ for** *the premiums for your pension plan* **~ on** *Premiums on many cars will go up this year.*

premonition *noun*

- ADJ. **shudder**
- VERB + PREMONITION **feel, have**
- PREP. **~ about** *Perhaps he had a premonition about what might happen in London.* **~ of** *I wonder if she had a premonition of her own fate.*

preoccupation *noun*

- ADJ. **current, present, recent | central, chief, main, major** *Their chief preoccupation was how to feed their families.* **| constant, continuing | growing | obsessive**
- PREP. **~ for** *By now this had become a major preoccupation for him.* **~ with** *his growing preoccupation with death*

preoccupied *adj.*

- VERBS **appear, be, look, seem | become | remain**
- ADV. **deeply, very | completely, entirely, totally | increasingly | a bit, a little, rather**
- PREP. **with** *He was too preoccupied with his own problems to worry about hers.*

preparation *noun*

1 getting sth ready
- ADJ. **careful, thorough | elaborate | adequate | initial** *It is the initial preparation that takes the time.*
- VERB + PREPARATION **need, require** *a dish that requires no elaborate preparation or cooking* **| do** *He's done a lot of preparation for this meeting.*
- PREPARATION + NOUN **time** *This simple dish takes very little preparation time.*
- PREP. **in ~ for** *Get a good night's sleep in preparation for the journey.*

2 preparations things done to get sth ready
- ADJ. **elaborate, meticulous, special | secret | necessary | final, last-minute | Christmas, wedding, etc. | military** *military preparations for full-scale action*
- VERB + PREPARATIONS **make** *making the final preparations for the party* **| begin, go ahead with | be busy with | complete, finalize**
- PREPARATIONS + VERB **be in hand, be under way** *Preparations are now in hand to close half the factories.* **| be complete**
- PREP. **~ for** *The family can now go ahead with preparations for the funeral.*

prepare *verb*

● ADV. **properly, well | fully | badly, inadequately, poorly | adequately | carefully, painstakingly | specially** *a table full of specially prepared food*
● VERB + PREPARE **help (sb), help (sb) to | fail to** *He had failed to prepare adequately for the task before him.* | **be easy to, be quick to** *a meal that is very quick and easy to prepare* | **be designed to** *The course is designed to prepare graduates for management careers.*
● PREP. **for** *We all set about preparing for the party.*
● PHRASES **time to prepare (sth)** *I haven't had time to prepare my arguments properly.*

prerequisite *noun*

● ADJ. **essential, important, necessary, vital | first**
● PREP. **~ for** *Training is a prerequisite for competence.* **~ to** *Recognition is a prerequisite to understanding.*

prerogative *noun*

● ADJ. **exclusive, sole** *Making such decisions is not the sole prerogative of managers.* | **judicial, managerial, royal | personal**
● VERB + PREROGATIVE **enjoy, have** *one of the prerogatives enjoyed by the president* | **exercise, use** *You can of course exercise your prerogative to leave at any time.* | **defend, preserve, protect** *The tsar protected his personal prerogatives.* | **give up, surrender**

prescribe *verb*

1 drugs
● ADV. **legally** *The drug can no longer be legally prescribed.* | **medically, medicinally**
● PREP. **for** *drugs prescribed for high blood pressure* ◇ *This drug is often prescribed for women with heart trouble.*

2 what should/should not be done
● ADV. **narrowly, rigidly, strictly, tightly** *The curriculum is rigidly prescribed from an early age.* ◇ *Everything about her life was strictly prescribed* (= there were strict rules about what she could and could not do).

prescription *noun*

● ADJ. **medical | free** *people who get free prescriptions* | **repeat** *I just get a repeat prescription every week.*
● VERB + PRESCRIPTION **give sb, write (out) | make up** *Would you like to wait while the pharmacist makes up your prescription?*
● PRESCRIPTION + NOUN **charge | drug, medicine**
● PREP. **on ~** *Some drugs are only available on prescription.* | **~ for** *the usual prescription for asthma* ◇ *She gave him a prescription for antibiotics.*

presence *noun*

1 being present
● ADJ. **mere** *The mere presence of children in the room is enough to upset him.* | **constant, continued, continuing, permanent | strong** *The company now has a strong presence in Germany.*
● VERB + PRESENCE **indicate, reveal, show** *These chemicals could indicate the presence of water on the planet.* | **acknowledge** *He acknowledged our presence with a nod of his head.* | **detect | grace sb with** *(ironic or humorous)* *How nice of you to grace us with your presence!*
● PREP. **in sb's ~** *He should never have made those remarks in your presence.*
● PHRASES **make your presence felt/known** *She certainly made her presence felt in the boardroom.*

2 number of people
● ADJ. **constant | military, police** *There was a strong police presence throughout the demonstration.*

● VERB + PRESENCE **maintain** *The army maintains a constant presence in the area.*

3 force of personality
● ADJ. **charismatic, commanding, formidable, great, imposing, powerful, strong | stage** *He had a formidable stage presence.*
● VERB + PRESENCE **have**

present *noun*

● ADJ. **anniversary, birthday, Christmas, wedding**
● VERB + PRESENT **buy | get, receive | give sb, send sb | wrap (up) | open, unwrap**
● PREP. **~ for** *a present for my daughter* **~ from, ~ to** *It's a present to us all from Granny.*
● PHRASES **make sb a present of sth** *My nephew loves this bike so I'm going to make him a present of it.*

present *verb*

● ADV. **clearly, well** *The arguments were well researched and clearly presented.* | **attractively, neatly | orally, visually** *The results can be presented visually in the form of a graph.*
● VERB + PRESENT **aim to, attempt to, seek to, try to** *We have tried to present both sides of the debate.* | **be designed to** *Hotel brochures are designed to present the most attractive aspects of the hotel.*
● PREP. **as** *He likes to present himself as a radical politician.* **to** *He presented the information to his colleagues.*

present *adj.*

● VERBS **be | remain**
● ADV. **ever** *the ever present risk of pollution*
● PHRASES **past and present** *a list of all club members, past and present*

presentable *adj.*

● VERBS **be, look | make sb** *Could you try and make yourself a little more presentable?*
● ADV. **very | perfectly** *She was not exactly good-looking, but perfectly presentable.* | **quite, reasonably**

presentation *noun*

1 of a gift or prize
● ADJ. **annual | official | special | farewell, retirement**
● VERB + PRESENTATION **make**
● PRESENTATION + NOUN **ceremony, dinner, evening, night** *the school's annual presentation evening*
● PREP. **~ to** *The president made a presentation to the businesswoman of the year.*

2 informative talk
● ADJ. **formal | effective | slick | upbeat | business, sales | audio-visual, slide, video**
● VERB + PRESENTATION **give, make**
● PRESENTATION + NOUN **skills | software**
● PREP. **~ on** *Candidates have to give a short presentation on a subject of their choice.*

presenter *noun*

● ADJ. **radio, television/TV | BBC, ITV, etc. | programme, sports** *a BBC sports presenter*
⇨ Note at JOB

preservation *noun*

● ADJ. **environmental | building, railway, etc.**
● PRESERVATION + NOUN **order** *The council has placed a preservation order on the building.*
● PHRASES **a state of preservation** *Most of the buildings are in an excellent state of preservation.*

preservative noun

● ADJ. **food, wood | artificial** *Our products contain no artificial preservatives or colourings.*
● VERB + PRESERVATIVE **apply, treat sth with** *Make sure the panels are treated with a wood preservative.*

preserve verb

● ADV. **carefully, jealously, lovingly, zealously** *She carefully preserved all his letters.*
● VERB + PRESERVE **seek to, try to | be anxious to, want to, wish to** *We were anxious to preserve the original character of the house.* **| help (to)** *taking action to help preserve fish stocks* **| fight to** *campaigners fighting to preserve a historic railway line* **| be designed to** *The Act contained provisions designed to preserve the status quo.* **| be important to**
● PREP. **as** *The prison is preserved as a tourist attraction.* **for** *The collection has been sold to the British Museum where it will be preserved for the nation.* **from** *an attempt to preserve the corpse from decomposition*
● PHRASES **an attempt to preserve sth, beautifully/exquisitely/finely/perfectly/superbly/well preserved** *They were thrilled to discover a perfectly preserved specimen of Roman pottery.* **be preserved intact** *The bones had all been preserved intact.* **be worth preserving** *You need to say why the building is worth preserving.* **preserve sth for future generations/posterity**

presidency noun

● ADJ. **directly-elected | executive, federal**
● VERB + PRESIDENCY **be nominated for, run for, stand for | be elected to | assume, take on/over | hold** *She held the presidency of the association for three years.*
● PREP. **into sb's~** *Three years into his presidency, he is more popular than ever.* **under sb's~** *under the presidency of George W. Bush.*

president noun

● ADJ. **acting, caretaker, honorary, interim, provisional | deputy, vice | elect** *the president elect, Michael Roberts* **| incoming, outgoing | incumbent | former, past, previous | lame-duck | civilian, military | federal, national, state | club, company, party, university**
● VERB + PRESIDENT **appoint, appoint sb (as), elect, elect sb (as), name sb (as), swear sb in as** *He was sworn in as president on August 31.* **| serve as | impeach**
● PRESIDENT + VERB **veto sth | intervene (in sth)**

press noun

1 media
● ADJ. **foreign, international, local, national, provincial | gutter, popular, quality, tabloid | financial, music | free** *A free press is fundamental to democracy.*
● PRESS + NOUN **release, statement** *He issued a press statement insisting on his innocence.* **| coverage, report** *extensive press coverage of the event* **| cuttings** *He kept a scrapbook containing press cuttings of his concerts.* **| officer | photographer | agency | ad, advertisement | campaign | freedom**
● PREP. **in the~** *There was no mention of the incident in the national press.*
● PHRASES **get/have a good/bad, etc. press** *His latest novel didn't get a very good press* (= was not praised in the media).

2 machine for printing
● ADJ. **printing**
● VERB + PRESS **go to** *The newspaper goes to press at 6 o'clock.*
● PRESS + VERB **roll** *The presses are already rolling.*
● PREP. **in~** *Their new book is in press.*

● PHRASES **hot off the press** *We've just received a copy of her latest book, hot off the press.*

press verb

1 push sth firmly
● ADV. **firmly, hard** *She pressed down hard on the gas pedal.* **| gently, lightly | close/closely** *He pressed up closer against the wall, terrified of being seen.* **| back, down, forward, together, up** *The crowd pressed forward.* ◇ *She pressed her lips together.*
● PREP. **against** *She pressed her face against the window.* **into** *Bella pressed her face into the pillow.* **on** *She pressed on the doorbell.* **to** *He pressed a finger gently to her lips.*
● PHRASES **press sth flat/open/shut** *He pressed the lid firmly shut.*

2 try to persuade sb
● ADV. **strongly** *In the interview he strongly pressed his point of view.* **| consistently, continually, repeatedly | further | successfully**
● VERB + PRESS **continue to**
● PREP. **for** *The party will continue to press the case for a new electoral system.* **on** *I did not press him further on the issue.*

3 iron sth
● PHRASES **immaculately/neatly pressed** *his immaculately pressed suit*

PHRASAL VERB

press on
● ADV. **blindly | boldly**
● PREP. **with** *They pressed boldly on with their plan.*
● PHRASES **press on regardless** *The weather was dreadful but we pressed on regardless.*

press conference noun

● ADJ. **joint | formal | impromptu, informal | concluding** *At the concluding press conference, both leaders said that the talks had been constructive.* **| post-match, post-summit, etc.**
● VERB + PRESS CONFERENCE **call | arrange, organize, plan | give, hold | tell** *The chairman told a press conference of the forthcoming merger.*
● PREP. **at a/the~** *The prime minister outlined the privatization plans at a press conference.* **during/in a/the~** *The announcement was made in an impromptu press conference at the airport.*

pressure noun

1 force produced by pressing
● ADJ. **gentle, light | firm | downward**
● VERB + PRESSURE **apply, put | reduce**

2 force of a gas or liquid
● ADJ. **high, low | air, blood, water** *an instrument for measuring blood pressure* **| atmospheric, barometric**
● PRESSURE + VERB **build up, increase, rise | ease, fall**

3 cause of worry
● ADJ. **considerable, constant, intolerable, undue, unrelenting | commercial, competitive, economic, financial, political, social** *The economic pressures on small businesses are intense.*
● VERB + PRESSURE **place/put sb under | cope with, withstand | escape, get away from** *It's an ideal place in which to relax and escape the pressures of modern life.* **| reduce**
● PRESSURE + VERB **build up, increase**
● PREP. **under~** *He's felt under pressure since his wife had the operation.* **| ~on** *There's a lot of pressure on the soldiers preparing for battle.*
● PHRASES **pressure of work** *The holiday was a welcome relief from the pressure of work.*

4 attempt to persuade/influence sb

• ADJ. **enormous, great, intense, strong, tremendous** *There is intense pressure on her to resign.* | **growing, increasing, mounting** | **popular** *The government bowed to popular pressure and repealed the law.* | **peer, peer-group** *She started smoking because of peer pressure.*
• VERB + PRESSURE **bring to bear, exert, place/put (sb under)** *This concession would not have happened but for the pressure that was brought to bear on the authorities.* ◇ *My parents never put any pressure on me to get a job.* | **be brought under, be under, come under, face** *Hospital staff are coming under pressure to work longer hours.* | **resist, withstand** | **bow to, give in to, respond to** *The editor bowed to pressure from his staff, and the article was suppressed.*
• PRESSURE + VERB **intensify, mount**
• PRESSURE + NOUN **group**
• PREP. **under ~** *Management is under pressure to set an example on pay restraint.* | **~ for** *pressure for change in the country's economy* **~ from** *pressure from religious groups* **~ on** *pressure on foreign diplomats*

prestige *noun*

• ADJ. **considerable, enormous, great, high, immense** *Winning the prize carries immense prestige.* | **low** | **international, national** | **personal** | **military, political, social**
• VERB + PRESTIGE **enjoy, have** *an international company that enjoys immense prestige* | **lack** | **acquire, derive, gain, get** | **accord sb/sth, give sb/sth** *Different jobs are accorded different levels of prestige.* | **bring, carry** | **lose** | **rise in** | **boost, enhance, increase, raise** | **damage, lower** *The royal couple's prestige was damaged by the allegations.*
• PREP. **~ among/with** *the party's prestige among the public* **~ within** *The post carried great prestige within the police force.*
• PHRASES **a loss of prestige** *Doctors have suffered a loss of prestige following a spate of scandals.* **a matter of prestige** *Wearing designer clothes is a matter of personal prestige for many teenagers.*

prestigious *adj.*

• VERBS **be**
• ADV. **extremely, highly, very** *She won a highly prestigious award.*

presume *verb*

• ADV. **rightly, wrongly** *I had presumed wrongly that Jenny would be there.* | **reasonably** | **automatically** | **conclusively** (*law*)

presumption *noun*

• ADJ. **strong** | **general** *There is a general presumption that fatty foods are bad for your heart.*
• PREP. **~ about** *The argument is based on certain presumptions about human nature.* **~ against** *the presumption against changes in the common law* **~ of** *a strong presumption of guilt*

pretence *noun*

• ADJ. **elaborate** *It was all an elaborate pretence.*
• VERB + PRETENCE **keep up, maintain, sustain** *I don't know how long I can keep up this pretence.* | **abandon, drop, give up**
• PRETENCE + VERB **be over** *Now that the pretence was over, he could tell them what he really thought.*
• PREP. **under the ~ of** *He tried to get close to her under the pretence of examining the pictures on the wall.* | **~ at** *His pretence at friendliness fooled no one.* **~ of** *He was hanged without even the pretence of a proper trial.*
• PHRASES **make a/little/no pretence** *I make no pretence*

to *be an expert on the subject.* **by/under false pretences** *obtaining money under false pretences*

pretend *verb*

• ADV. **otherwise** *You know what this is all about, Natasha. Why pretend otherwise?*
• VERB + PRETEND **can/could no longer** | **try to** | **be dishonest to, be idle to, be ridiculous to, be useless to** *It's useless to pretend that we might still win.*
• PREP. **to** *He pretended to his boss that he'd written the article.*
• PHRASES **go on pretending** *I can't go on pretending any longer.* **just/only pretending** *Maria knew he was only pretending.* **let's pretend** *Let's pretend it never happened.* **stop pretending, there's no point in pretending**

pretext *noun*

• VERB + PRETEXT **give sb, provide (sb with)** | **find, invent** *He considered inventing some pretext for calling her.*
• PREP. **on a/the ~** *He disappeared into his study on the pretext that he had work to do there.* **under a/the ~** *Under the pretext of checking her identity, the man had copied down her credit card details.* | **~ for** *He used his research as a pretext for travelling to Hungary.*
• PHRASES **at/on the slightest pretext** *He keeps popping into my office on the slightest pretext.*

pretty *adj.*

• VERBS **be, look**
• ADV. **exceptionally, extremely, ravishingly, really, strikingly, very, wonderfully** | **almost** | **quite, rather** | **undeniably**

prevail *verb*

• ADV. **always** *Her happy outlook always prevailed.* | **eventually, finally, in the end, ultimately**
• VERB + PREVAIL **be likely to** | **must, ought to** *Common sense must prevail in the end.*
• PREP. **against** *The wishes of 20 million people ought to prevail against those of 200 thousand.* **over** *His view eventually prevailed over theirs.*

prevent *verb*

• ADV. **effectively, successfully** *This new legislation effectively prevents us from trading.* | **forcibly, physically**
• VERB + PREVENT **be able/unable to, can/could** *No one can prevent you from attending this meeting.* | **attempt to, seek to, take action/steps to, try to** | **help (to)** *A good sun cream will help prevent sunburn.* | **be designed to** | **be/do nothing to** *There was nothing to prevent him setting up in business on the premises.* ◇ *The whole affair is an outrage and the authorities have done nothing to prevent it.*
• PREP. **from** *They took action to prevent the disease from spreading.*
• PHRASES **aimed at preventing sth** *new measures aimed at preventing accidents* **action/measures to prevent sth, an attempt to prevent sth, in order to prevent sth** *Action must be swift in order to prevent further damage.*

preventable *adj.*

• VERBS **be** | **become**
• ADV. **entirely** *These injuries are entirely preventable.* | **largely**

prevention *noun*

• ADJ. **accident, crime, drug, fire, flood, pollution** *a*

drug prevention programme | **primary, secondary, tertiary** (all used when talking about health care)
- PREVENTION + NOUN **programme, scheme, strategy** a crime prevention scheme

preview noun

- ADJ. **press** a press preview of a new film | **sneak** Journalists have been given a sneak preview of the singer's latest album.
- VERB + PREVIEW **get, have** | **see** | **give sb**
- PREVIEW + NOUN **audience** | **theatre**

prey noun

- ADJ. **easy** Teenagers are easy prey for unscrupulous drug dealers. | **ideal**
- VERB + PREY **chase, hunt for, look for, pursue, stalk** | **capture, pounce on** a cat pouncing on its prey | **kill**
- PREP. **~ for** The young deer are ideal prey for the leopard. **~ to** (figurative) She was prey to all kinds of conflicting emotions.
- PHRASES **a beast/bird of prey, be/fall prey to sth** (figurative) The new government has fallen prey to corruption and fraud.

price noun

- ADJ. **exorbitant, high, inflated, prohibitive, steep** | **low** | **bargain, budget** designer clothes at bargain prices | **attractive, fair, reasonable, right** We sell quality tools at the right price. | **good** I managed to get a good price for my old car. | **average** | **asking, purchase** What's the asking price for this house? ◇ You need to pay a deposit of 10 per cent of the purchase price of the property. | **retail, sale, selling** | **cost** They are selling off summer shoes at cost price. | **full, half** Children travel half price until age ten. | **market** This website tells you the market price of all makes of second-hand car. | **admission** admission prices at the museum | **consumer** | **commodity, food, house, land, property, share** | **electricity, energy, fuel, oil, petrol**
- VERB + PRICE **command, fetch, go for** Property in the area is now fetching ridiculously high prices. | **give sb, quote sb** I got a number of suppliers to quote me their best prices. | **charge, set** | **increase, push up, raise** | **bring down, cut, lower, mark down, push down, reduce, slash** | **go up in, increase in, rise in** Oil is set in go up in price. | **come down in** | **range in, vary in** These computers range in price from £1 300 to £2 000. | **undercut**
- PRICE + VERB **go up, rise, shoot up, skyrocket, soar** House prices went up by 5 per cent last year. ◇ Prices soared during the war. | **drop, fall, go down, slump** If prices slump further, the farmers will starve. | **go from ... to ... , range from ... to ... , start at** Prices go from $30 for the standard model to $150 for the deluxe version.
- PRICE + NOUN **level, range** | **increase, rise** | **cut** | **change, movement** | **war** | **tag** I got a shock when I looked at the price tag. | **list** | **index** the share price index
- PREP. **at a/the ~** Food is available, at a price (= at a high price). ◇ I can't afford it at that price. **in ~** Cigarettes have remained stable in price for some time.
- PHRASES **a drop/a fall/a reduction in price, an increase/a rise in price, pay a heavy price (for sth)** The team paid a heavy price for its lack of preparation. **place/put a price on sth** You can't put a price on happiness. **the price of freedom/success, etc.** (= the unpleasant things you must suffer to have freedom, success, etc.), **a small price to pay (for sth)** The cost of a policy premium is a small price to pay for peace of mind.
- ⇨ Note at PER CENT (for more verbs)

price verb be priced

- ADV. **highly** | **attractively, competitively, economically, fairly, moderately, modestly, realistically, reasonably, sensibly** a wide range of competitively priced office

furniture | **accordingly** This is considered a luxury item and is priced accordingly.
- PREP. **at** The car is priced at $60 000. **between** Tickets for the concert are priced between £15 and £35. **from, to** The kits are priced from £8.50 to £20.
- PHRASES **be priced high/low** The house was priced much too high.

pride noun

1 feeling of being proud of sb/sth
- ADJ. **fierce, great**
- VERB + PRIDE **feel, have, swell with** They have a fierce pride in their traditions. ◇ He swelled with pride as he held the trophy. | **express**
- PREP. **with ~** I wear my policeman's uniform with pride. ◇ 'My daughter's a writer,' he added with pride. | **~ in** She expressed pride in her child's achievement.
- PHRASES **a cause/matter for pride** Their reputation for fairness is a matter for pride. **a source of pride, take (a) pride in sth** She takes great pride in her work.

2 self-respect
- ADJ. **great** | **civic, family, local, national, personal, professional** | **dented, hurt, injured, wounded** He was nursing his hurt pride. | **foolish, stubborn** It was foolish pride that prevented me from believing her.
- VERB + PRIDE **have** I don't want your money—I have my pride, you know! | **hurt** I didn't mean to hurt your pride. | **restore, salvage** We want to restore pride in our public services. ◇ They managed to salvage some pride with a late goal. | **swallow** She swallowed her pride and phoned him.
- PREP. **out of ~** She refused their help out of pride. **through ~** It would be stupid to refuse through pride.
- PHRASES **a matter of pride** It is a matter of pride for him that he has never accepted money from his family. **a sense of pride** They have a strong sense of pride in their work. **with your pride intact** She refused his offer tactfully, allowing him to go away with his pride intact.

priest noun

1 in Christianity
- ADJ. **local, parish, village** | **celibate** | **married** | **woman** | **Anglican, (Roman) Catholic, Jesuit, etc.**
- VERB + PRIEST **become, be ordained (as)**
- PRIEST + VERB **celebrate sth, officiate (at sth)** the priest who was celebrating Mass

2 in some other religions
- ADJ. **chief, high** a ceremony led by the High Priest ◇ (figurative) He was considered the high priest of finance at that time. | **temple** | **Brahmin, Buddhist, etc.**

prime minister noun

- ADJ. **deputy** | **acting, caretaker, interim, transitional** | **incumbent, present** | **former, previous** | **outgoing** | **strong** | **beleaguered** The beleaguered prime minister is coming under yet more pressure. | **Conservative, Labour, etc.**
- VERB + PRIME MINISTER **appoint, appoint sb (as), elect, elect sb (as)** | **serve as** He served briefly as prime minister from 1920 to 1921. (For more verbs see the entry for **minister.**)
- PREP. **under a/the ~** She held office under two different prime ministers.

principal noun

- ADJ. **college, school**
- ⇨ Note at JOB

principle *noun*

1 basic general rule
- ADJ. **basic, broad, central, fundamental, general** *the basic principles of car maintenance* | **cardinal, essential, key** | **universal** | **democratic, legal, market, political, scientific, theoretical**
- VERB + PRINCIPLE **establish, formulate, lay down** | **apply** | **explain**
- PRINCIPLE + VERB **apply** *This principle applies to all kinds of selling.* | **underlie sth, underpin sth** *the principles underlying Western philosophy*
- PREP. **in~** *I agree with you in principle, but we'll need to discuss the details.* | **~ behind** *She went on to explain the principles behind what she was doing.*

2 rule for good behaviour
- ADJ. **high** | **guiding** | **Christian** | **moral** *He was a man of high moral principles.*
- VERB + PRINCIPLE **betray, compromise** *I refuse to compromise my principles by eating meat.* | **adhere to, stick to** *She sticks to the principle that everyone should be treated equally.*
- PREP. **against your ~s** *Eating meat was against her principles.* **on~** *She's opposed to abortion on principle.*
- PHRASES **a matter of principle** *They reject the proposal as a matter of principle.* **a person of principle** (= a person with high moral standards)

print *noun*

- ADJ. **large** | **fine, small** *Always read the small print in a contract before signing.* | **clear** | **bold**
- PRINT + NOUN **journalist, worker** | **industry, union** | **run** *The initial print run for her book was 6 000 copies.*
- PREP. **in ~** *All her books are still in print.* **out of ~** *The shop specializes in out-of-print books.*

print *verb*

- ADV. **beautifully** *The book is beautifully printed on good quality paper.* | **badly** | **correctly** *I couldn't get the graphics to print correctly.* | **clearly** | **indelibly** *(figurative)* *The incident was indelibly printed in her memory.* | **privately** *She had the memoir privately printed in a limited edition.* | **specially** *We had the T-shirts specially printed with the firm's logo.*
- PREP. **from** *printing from a file* **in** *The message was printed in blue ink.* **on** *a leaflet printed on recycled paper* **with** *a dress printed with blue flowers*

printer *noun*

1 person/company that prints books, etc.
- ADJ. **book** | **lithographic** | **commercial** | **master** | **jobbing**
- PRINTER + VERB **print sth, run sth off** *The printer has run off 2 000 copies of the leaflet.*
⇨ Note at JOB

2 machine
- ADJ. **black-and-white, colour** | **computer** | **desktop** | **bubblejet, daisy wheel, dot matrix, inkjet, laser, line, page** | **compatible**
- VERB + PRINTER **control, drive** | **connect** *Connect the printer to your PC with a printer cable.*
- PRINTER + VERB **print (sth), work** *The printer won't print for some reason.*
- PRINTER + NOUN **cable** | **port** | **ribbon** | **driver** | **icon**
⇨ Special page at COMPUTER

priority *noun*

- ADJ. **high, main, major, number one, top** | **first, immediate, urgent** *Getting food, medicine and blankets to flood victims is the most urgent priority.* | **low** *Material possessions have always been a low priority for Mike.*
- VERB + PRIORITY **choose, decide on, determine, identify, sort out** *You need to sort out your priorities before making a decision about the future.* | **get, have, take** *When hospital funds are being allocated children take priority.* | **give sb/sth** *The government is giving priority to school leavers in its job-creation programme.*
- PREP. **~ over** *Her family takes priority over her work.*
- PHRASES **a list of priorities, order of priority** *List the tasks in order of priority.*

prison *noun*

- ADJ. **local** | **overcrowded** | **high-security, maximum-security, top-security** | **closed** | **open** *Open prisons prepare prisoners for life back in the community.* | **private** | **women's** | **debtors'** *(historical)* | **military**
- VERB + PRISON **go to** *He went to prison for tax evasion.* | **put sb in, send sb to, throw sb into** *She was sent to prison for leaking state secrets.* ◇ *He was immediately seized and thrown into prison.* | **be discharged from, be released from, come out of, get out of** *When did he get out of prison?* | **escape from** *A dangerous criminal has escaped from a high-security prison.* | **avoid, escape** *You only escaped prison* (= escaped being sent to prison) *because of your previous good character.* | **face** *She was told by magistrates she could now face prison.*
- PRISON + NOUN **sentence, term** | **cell, hospital** | **conditions** | **population** | **authorities, governor, inmate, officer, staff, warder** | **service, system**
- PREP. **at a/the~** *The police are investigating disturbances at the prison.* **in (a/the) ~** *How long has her father been in prison?* ◇ *There have been riots in the prison.*

prisoner *noun*

- ADJ. **virtual** *Without a wheelchair, she is a virtual prisoner in her own home.* | **political** | **life, life-sentence, long-term** | **short-term** | **remand** | **condemned, convicted, sentenced** | **escaped** | **model** *He was a model prisoner, and was released after serving only half his five-year sentence.*
- VERB + PRISONER **capture, take** *They had captured over 100 prisoners.* ◇ *Many soldiers were taken prisoner.* | **hold, keep** *They were kept prisoner for eight months in a tiny flat.* | **free, release**
- PHRASES **a prisoner of conscience** *The former prisoner of conscience was elected president of the new democracy.* **a prisoner of war**

privacy *noun*

- ADJ. **complete, total** | **individual, personal**
- VERB + PRIVACY **preserve, protect, respect** | **disturb, intrude on, invade, violate** *I hope I'm not intruding on your privacy.*
- PREP. **in ~** *I want to be left in privacy.* **in the ~ of** *She longed to be in the privacy of her own room.* | **~ from** *privacy from prying eyes*
- PHRASES **an intrusion/invasion of privacy** *These phone calls are a gross invasion of privacy.* **an intrusion on (sb's) privacy**

privatization *noun*

- ADJ. **large-scale, mass, wholesale** | **partial** | **electricity, rail, water, etc.**
- PRIVATIZATION + NOUN **plan, programme, proposal**
- PREP. **under ~** *Several railway lines were closed under privatization.*

privilege *noun*

1 special right
- ADJ. **exclusive, special** *Club members have special privileges, like free use of the pool.* | **class** | **diplomatic**
- VERB + PRIVILEGE **enjoy, exercise, have** | **accord**

sb, give sb, grant sb | **abuse** *He was accused of abusing his diplomatic privileges.* | **revoke, withdraw**

2 opportunity to do sth pleasant

● ADJ. **enormous, great, rare, real** *It is a great privilege to be attending this conference.* | **doubtful, dubious** *I was given the dubious privilege of organizing the summer fair.*
● VERB + PRIVILEGE **have** *She had the rare privilege of a viewing of his private art collection.* | **give sb**

privileged *adj.*

● VERBS **be, feel | consider sb/yourself** *I consider myself highly privileged to have this opportunity.*
● ADV. **highly, specially, very | absolutely | quite, relatively | financially, socially** *She came from a financially privileged background.*

prize *noun*

● ADJ. **big, great, prestigious | special | coveted** *She was the first woman to win this coveted prize.* | **glittering** *He strove for the glittering prizes of politics.* | **first, top | runner-up, second | consolation | booby** *The booby prize was awarded to the worst singer in the competition.* | **cash, money**
● VERB + PRIZE **award (sb), give (sb) | present** *The prize was presented by the mayor.* | **get, receive, take, win | accept**
● PRIZE + VERB **go to sb/sth** *The prize went to the grey long-haired cat.* | **be worth sth** *a prize worth over £3 000*
● PRIZE + NOUN **winner** (also **prizewinner**) | **money | draw**
● PREP. **~ for** *He won the Nobel Prize for Literature.*

prize *verb*

● PREP. **above** *a precious thing to be prized above all else* **as** *The library is prized as the finest of its kind in England.* **for** *The berries are prized for their healing properties.*
● PHRASES **highly/much prized** *two fruits that are much prized in Madeira*

probability *noun*

● ADJ. **high, real, strong** *There is a high probability that it will snow tonight.* | **greater, increased | low**
● QUANT. **degree** *We can say with a high degree of probability that the poem was written by Shakespeare.*
● VERB + PROBABILITY **have | increase | reduce | assess, calculate, judge**
● PREP. **~ of** *This surgical procedure has a high probability of success.*
● PHRASES **in all probability** *In all probability she wouldn't come even if we invited her.* **on a balance of probabilities** *The coroner thought that on the balance of probabilities, the pilot had suffered a stroke just before the crash.*

probable *adj.*

● VERBS **be, look, seem**
● ADV. **extremely, highly, very | quite | equally** *The two outcomes are equally probable.*

probation *noun*

● ADJ. **give sb, place sb on, put sb on, sentence sb to** *He was placed on probation for two years.* ◊ *She was sentenced to a year's probation.* | **release sb on**
● PROBATION + NOUN **order** *He was under a probation order for attacking a photographer.* | **officer | service | hostel | period** *Once your probation period is successfully completed, you will be offered a contract.*
● PREP. **on ~** *The judge put her on probation for a year.* ◊ *He joined the company on six months' probation.*

probe *verb*

● ADV. **deep/deeply** *(figurative) probing deeper and deeper into the secrets of the universe* | **further | gently**
● PREP. **for** *using its long beak to probe for worms* **into** *(figurative) The police were probing into her personal life.* **with** *He probed the mud with his knife.*

problem *noun*

1 sth that causes difficulties

● ADJ. **acute, big, enormous, grave, great, serious** *Our greatest problem is the lack of funds.* | **little, minor, petty | complex, complicated, difficult, knotty, thorny | growing | basic, central, main, major | common | pressing, urgent | immediate | insoluble, insuperable, insurmountable, intractable** *Depression is a natural feeling if your problems seem intractable.* | **long-standing, long-term, perennial | practical | technical | attitude, behavioural, emotional, psychological** *His teachers say he has an attitude problem.* | **personal | health, physical, sexual | back, heart, knee | drink, drug | social | housing | economic, financial** *They sold their car to ease their financial problems.* | **environmental | legal**
● VERB + PROBLEM **be, pose, present (sb with)** *Inadequate resources pose a problem for all members of staff.* | **have | bring, cause, create** *Success brings its own problems.* ◊ *Staff shortages cause problems for the organization.* | **be beset with, be confronted by/with, be dogged by, be faced with, be fraught with, confront, encounter, face, run into** *He has been faced with all manner of problems in his new job.* ◊ *The scheme has been fraught with problems from the start.* | **raise** *She raised the problem of falling sales at the last meeting.* | **identify | consider, debate, discuss, look at/into | address, approach, attack, combat, come/get to grips with, grapple with, handle, tackle** *The next meeting will address the problem of truancy.* | **avoid, circumvent, find a way around/round, get around/round | clear up, cure, deal with, overcome, resolve, solve** *He had to undergo surgery to cure the problem with his knee.* | **alleviate, ease, reduce | exacerbate | analyse, explore**
● PROBLEM + VERB **arise, come up, occur** *problems arising from poor ventilation* | **exist | persist, remain** *If the problem persists you should see a doctor.* ◊ *The basic problem remains the lack of housing available.* | **confront sb, face sb | lie in sth** *The problem lies in the lack of communication between managers and staff.*
● PROBLEM + NOUN **area | child**
● PREP. **~ about** *I didn't imagine there would be a problem about getting tickets.* **~ for** *The rail strike is a problem for all commuters.* **~ of** *the problem of poverty* **~ with** *Have you got a problem with her?*
● PHRASES **an approach to a problem, the crux/heart/root of the problem** *We need to get to the root of the problem before we can solve it.* **a remedy/solution to a problem, the scale of a problem**

2 question to be solved

● ADJ. **complicated, difficult | easy, simple | mathematical** *solving simple mathematical problems*
● VERB + PROBLEM **do, find the answer to, solve** *I have five problems to do for homework.*
● PROBLEM + NOUN **solving** *This kind of activity develops the children's problem-solving skills.*

procedure *noun*

● ADJ. **complex, complicated | simple, straightforward | correct, normal, proper, standard, usual** *There are standard procedures for dismissing staff.* | **agreed, established | special | administrative, appeals, application, assessment, complaints, court, criminal, disciplinary, emergency, parliamentary, safety, scientific, selection, surgical** *a minor surgical procedure*
● PROCEDURE + NOUN **adopt, follow, use** *Did you fol-*

low the emergency procedure when you heard the alarm? | **establish** A straightforward complaints procedure must be established from the outset.
• PREP. **under a/the ~** under a procedure established by legislation | **~for** the correct procedure for hiring staff

proceed verb

• ADV. **apace, quickly, rapidly** Work is now proceeding apace. | **slowly | carefully, cautiously, with caution** It will be necessary to proceed with caution. | **smoothly, uneventfully | directly** In some cases appeals may proceed directly from the High Court to the House of Lords. | **further**
• VERB + PROCEED **be able to | decide to, intend to, wish to | allow sb/sth to, enable sb/sth to** This project cannot be allowed to proceed. | **instruct sb to** I will instruct my solicitor to proceed with the preparation of draft contracts.
• PREP. **along** Proceed along the Botley Road. **down, through, to** students who wish to proceed to university **with** She decided not to proceed with the treatment.
• PHRASES **proceed on the basis of sth** The council must proceed on the basis of the vote.

proceedings noun

• ADJ. **court, criminal, judicial, legal | bankruptcy, divorce, extradition, impeachment, libel | appeal, civil, committal, summary**
• VERB + PROCEEDINGS **bring, institute, take | begin, commence, start**
• PROCEEDINGS + VERB **begin, commence**
• PREP. **in ~** decisions made in court proceedings | **~against** She is bringing divorce proceedings against her husband. **~before** in appeal proceedings before a tribunal **~between** proceedings between the four parties involved

proceeds noun

• ADJ. **total | gross | net | sale**
• VERB + PROCEEDS **use** The proceeds will be used to improve the school playground. | **donate**
• PROCEEDS + VERB **go to sth** All the proceeds will go to the local pensioners' club.
• PREP. **on the ~** I sold my car and I'm planning a long holiday on the proceeds. **with the ~** They bought a new minibus with the proceeds from the auction. | **~from**
• PHRASES **your share of the proceeds** She bought a small flat with her share of the proceeds.

process noun

• ADJ. **gradual, lengthy, long, slow | constant, continuous | complex, complicated, difficult | natural | due** the due process of law | **painful** Removing the splinters from the wound was a long and painful process. | **consultation, consultative, decision-making, management, planning | cognitive, creative, learning, mental** Teachers are trained to stimulate the child's cognitive processes. | **assessment, selection | democratic, electoral, political** Churches are taking a key role in the democratic process. | **chemical, industrial, manufacturing, production | ageing, biological, evolutionary, physical | judicial, legal | peace** a stalemate in the peace process | **historical, social**
• VERB + PROCESS **go through** Each time we have to go through the whole decision-making process again. | **accelerate, speed up, stimulate** Excessive exposure to sunlight speeds up the ageing process of the skin.
• PROCESS + VERB **take place** The selection process takes place over a period of two weeks.
• PREP. **~for** a legal process for dealing with defrauders **~of** the process of change
• PHRASES **a stage in/of the process**

process verb

• ADV. **efficiently | quickly | automatically | routinely**
• PREP. **for** The plant is then processed for dye. **into** The berries are processed into juice or sauce.
• PHRASES **highly processed** highly processed foods

procession noun

• ADJ. **grand, great, large, long | little, small | public, street | slow, solemn, stately | colourful | ceremonial | triumphal | constant, endless, never-ending** (figurative) We've had an endless procession of new secretaries through the office since Amy left. | **torchlight | funeral, religious, wedding**
• VERB + PROCESSION **head, lead** The mayor of the town led the procession to the central square.
• PROCESSION + VERB **make its way, move, pass, wind (its way)** The funeral procession moved slowly down the avenue. ◊ The solemn procession wound its way through the narrow streets. | **leave, move off, set off**
• PREP. **in (a/the) ~** The children marched in procession behind the band. | **~of** a procession of circus performers

proclaim verb

• ADV. **loudly | formally, officially | openly, publicly | proudly | unilaterally** The district unilaterally proclaimed its independence from the national government.
• VERB + PROCLAIM **seem to** His classic boyish looks seemed to proclaim his good humour and openness.
• PREP. **as** Everyone is proclaiming him as the next president. **to** proclaiming her innocence to the world

proclamation noun

• ADJ. **official, public, royal**
• VERB + PROCLAMATION **issue, make**
• PROCLAMATION + VERB **forbid sth, prohibit sth**
• PREP. **by ~** The government restricted the use of water by proclamation.

produce noun

• ADJ. **fresh | local | seasonal | agricultural, animal, dairy, farm, garden, organic, primary** fresh farm produce
• VERB + PRODUCE **grow | export, market, sell**

produce verb

• ADV. **domestically, locally** fruit and vegetables that are produced locally | **commercially | organically** organically produced food
• VERB + PRODUCE **be able/unable to, can/could | be expected to, be likely to** Which method is likely to produce the best results? | **combine to** All of these processes combine to produce a particular form of language. | **be designed to | use sth to** The technology can be used to produce interactive educational programs.
• PREP. **from** The wine is produced from Chardonnay grapes.

producer noun

1 sb/sth that makes/grows sth
• ADJ. **big, large, leading, major** one of the world's largest meat producers | **small, small-scale | efficient** a very efficient wine producer | **domestic, local | foreign | private | specialist** specialist producers of high-quality British beef | **agricultural | milk, oil, software, steel, etc.**

2 organizes a play, film, etc.
• ADJ. **film, radio, television/TV | BBC, Hollywood, etc. | independent** commissioning programmes from independent producers | **executive | assistant, associate**
• PHRASES **the role of producer** She was keen to take on the role of producer.
⇨ Note at JOB

product noun

1 sth that is made or formed
- ADJ. **good, right** *We have a good product, but it needs to be marketed better.* ◊ *the right product in the right place at the right time* | **innovative** | **quality** | **everyday** | **natural** | **manufactured** | **finished** *the manufacture of chocolate from cocoa bean to the finished product* | **commercial, consumer** | **household, industrial** *everyday household products* | **waste** | **agricultural, cereal, dairy, food, meat** | **pharmaceutical** | **software** | **beauty**
- VERB + PRODUCT **buy** | **sell** | **market, promote** | **develop** | **launch**
- PRODUCT + NOUN **area, category, group, line, range, sector, type** | **design** | **development** | **package** | **price** | **quality**
- PHRASES **a range of products** *a wide range of beauty products*
- ⇨ Special page at BUSINESS

2 result
- ADJ. **end, final** *A complicated string of chemical reactions leads to the end product.* | **natural**
- PREP. **~ of** *Like many of his generation, he was a product of Scotland's obsession with football.*

production noun

1 making/growing sth
- ADJ. **full** *The machine will go into full production in November 2002.* | **large-scale, mass** | **small-scale** | **efficient** | **annual** | **domestic** | **car, steel** | **coal, energy, gas, oil** | **agricultural, food, livestock, meat, milk** | **factory, industrial**
- QUANT. **level, volume** *The increase in volume of production brought down the price of the goods.*
- VERB + PRODUCTION **be in** *That particular model is no longer in production.* | **go into** | **go out of** | **begin, start** *They are going to start production of the car next year.* | **boost, increase, step up** | **cut, cut back (on)** | **halt, stop** | **speed up**
- PRODUCTION + NOUN **line, plant** *a car production plant* | **methods, process, system** | **director, manager, team** | **costs** | **capacity, level, volume**
- PRODUCTION + VERB **increase, rise** | **fall**
- PHRASES **a cut/fall in production, an increase/a rise in production, the means of production** *They believed that power largely derives from ownership of the means of production.*
- ⇨ Special page at BUSINESS

2 play, film, etc.
- ADJ. **successful** | **controversial** | **amateur, professional** | **stage** | **Broadway, West End, etc.** | **school** | **film, television/TV, theatrical, video**
- ⇨ Note at PERFORMANCE (for verbs)

productive adj.

- VERBS **be, seem** | **become**
- ADV. **enormously, extremely, highly, remarkably, very** *It was a highly productive meeting.* | **fairly, quite** | **potentially**

productivity noun

- ADJ. **high, low** | **greater, improved, increased** | **lost** *The strike took a heavy toll in lost productivity.* | **agricultural, labour, manufacturing**
- QUANT. **level** *Farmers are struggling to maintain a level of productivity that generates an acceptable income.*
- VERB + PRODUCTIVITY **boost, improve, increase, raise** | **decrease, reduce**
- PRODUCTIVITY + VERB **increase, rise** | **decrease, drop, fall**
- PRODUCTIVITY + NOUN **level** | **gains, growth, in-**crease | **deal** *Management is negotiating a new productivity deal with the union.*
- PHRASES **a decline/reduction in productivity, a gain/an improvement/an increase in productivity, growth in productivity** *Wage increases outpaced growth in productivity.*

profession noun

- ADJ. **chosen** | **legal, medical, teaching, etc.**
- VERB + PROFESSION **practise** *In the 1930s he was forbidden to practise his profession.* | **enter, go into, join** *She entered the legal profession after university.*
- PREP. **by ~** *He was a consultant physician by profession.* **in a/sb's/the ~** *making an impact in her chosen profession*
- PHRASES **a choice of profession** *She was shocked at her daughter's choice of profession.* **the top of sb's profession** *He reached the top of his profession in very little time.*

professional noun

- ADJ. **committed, dedicated, experienced** | **real, true** *This is the work of a real professional.* | **leading, senior, top** *a top golf professional* | **independent** *The survey should be performed by an independent professional.* | **fellow** *an actor revered by his fellow professionals* | **computer, health (care), medical** | **golf, tennis, etc.**

> **NOTE**
> **Professionals**
>
> **be, practise as ~**
> *to practise as a consulting engineer*
> **act as ~**
> *She is acting as architect on this project.*
> **have ~**
> *The group does not have an internal auditor.*
> **need ~**
> *We need an engineer to design us something better.*
> **find ~**
> *It pays to find a good accountant.*
> **appoint, appoint sb (as), engage, get, instruct ~**
> *Appoint a solicitor to act on your behalf.*
> **consult (with), get/take advice from, go to, see, speak to, talk to ~**
> *I demand to speak to my lawyer!*
> an advocate, barrister, lawyer, solicitor **acts for/defends/represents sb**
> *an in-house lawyer acting for a major company*
> **advise sb/sth ~**
> *His accountant has advised him to close down his business.*
> ⇨ See also the note at JOB

professional adj.

1 connected with a job
- VERBS **be**
- ADV. **purely, strictly** *He insisted that his relationship with the duchess was purely professional.*

2 extremely skilled
- VERBS **be, look** *Their designs look very professional.*
- ADV. **extremely, highly, really, truly, very** *He dealt with the problem in a highly professional way.* | **thoroughly** | **increasingly** | **almost** | **quite, rather**

3 done as a paid job, not a hobby
- VERBS **be** | **become, turn**
- ADV. **fully** *He wants to turn fully professional.*

professor noun

- ADJ. **distinguished, eminent** | **college, university** | **assistant, associate** | **emeritus** | **visiting** *I spent six*

months as a visiting professor at Brown University. | history, law, etc. | **absent-minded, mad** *He fitted perfectly the stereotype of the absent-minded professor.*
• PREP. **~of** *an eminent professor of English*
⇨ Note at JOB

proficiency *noun*

• ADJ. **considerable,   great | technical | language, oral, reading, written | cycling, skiing,** etc.
• QUANT. **degree, level** *He taught himself to carve to a high degree of proficiency.*
• VERB + PROFICIENCY **acquire, develop, increase** *He acquired greater proficiency after a three-month intensive course.* | **demonstrate, show**
• PROFICIENCY + NOUN **examination, test** *a language proficiency test* | **certificate**
• PREP. **~in** *a certificate for proficiency in English*

proficient *adj.*

• VERBS **be, seem | become**
• ADV. **very | fully | fairly, reasonably | technically** *a technically proficient performance of the piece*
• PREP. **at** *very proficient at sign language* **in** *She's fairly proficient in Italian.*

profile *noun*

1 face seen from the side
• ADJ. **beautiful, handsome | strong | three-quarter**
• VERB + PROFILE **present**
• PREP. **in~** *The painting shows her in profile.*
• PHRASES **sb's best profile** *He presented his best profile to the camera.*

2 description of sb/sth
• ADJ. **detailed | age, career, psychological | company, customer | financial, social**
• VERB + PROFILE **build up, construct, develop**
• PREP. **~of** *The data will enable us to construct a profile of the firm's customers.*

3 public image
• ADJ. **high, low** *She decided to keep a low profile until the scandal had died down.* | **public | political | corporate**
• VERB + PROFILE **have | give sb/sth** *The story was given a low profile in today's papers.* | **improve, increase, raise** *a campaign to raise the profile of the city as a cultural leader* | **lower | keep, maintain | adopt**

profit *noun*

• ADJ. **big, fat, good, greater, handsome, healthy, high, huge, large, record, substantial, tidy | low, modest, small** *They closed down after years of low profits.* | **excess | lost, unrealized** *Damaged goods mean lost profit.* | **realized | quick** *He's only interested in making a quick profit.* | **gross, pre-tax | after/post-tax, clear, net | taxable | interim, short-term | annual** *an annual profit of £50 000* | **first-quarter, full-year, half-year, second-quarter,** etc. | **corporate, group | operating, trading**
• VERB + PROFIT **bring (in), earn, generate, make, realize, reap, yield** *The CD generated record profits.* | **boost, increase | maximize | show** *The company started to show a profit in its first year.*
• PROFIT + VERB **grow, increase, rise | fall, plummet, plunge | accrue, arise** *profits accruing to the taxpayer from the sale of property*
• PROFIT + NOUN **margin, rate**
• PREP. **against ~s** *The firm made losses of 500 000 against profits of 750 000.* **at a~** *We should be able to sell the piano at a profit.* **for~** *The goods were sold for profit.* | **~on** *Did you make a profit on your house when you sold it?*
• PHRASES **a decline/fall in profits, an increase/a rise in profits, profit after/before tax** *Profit before tax increased by 40% on last year.*

⇨ Note at PER CENT (for more verbs)
⇨ Special page at BUSINESS

profitability *noun*

• ADJ. **high, low | greater | declining** *concerns about the declining profitability of the industry* | **overall | long-term, short-term**
• QUANT. **level**
• VERB + PROFITABILITY **achieve** *measures to achieve greater profitability* | **maintain | improve, increase | maximize | reduce**
• PHRASES **a decline/fall in profitability, an increase in profitability, a return to profitability** *The firm is now showing signs of a return to profitability.*
⇨ Note at PER CENT (for more verbs)

profitable *adj.*

1 making a profit
• VERBS **be, prove, seem** *confident that the venture will prove profitable* | **become | remain | make | keep sth** *What can be done to keep the business profitable?*
• ADV. **extremely, highly, hugely, immensely, very** *a highly profitable chain of shops* | **barely | quite, relatively | enough, sufficiently** *The business is not really profitable enough.* | **financially | potentially**

2 helpful
• VERBS **be | find sth** *Some churches have found it profitable to hold services during the week.*
• ADV. **very | mutually** *Cooperation could be mutually profitable.* | **potentially**

program *noun*

• ADJ. **computer, software | analysis, database, design, desktop publishing, drawing, graphics, image-editing, page make-up, simulation, spreadsheet, video-editing, word-processing,** etc. | **shareware**
• VERB + PROGRAM **run, use | design, develop, write** *a program designed to evaluate road safety measures* | **download, execute, install, load | uninstall | copy**
• PROGRAM + VERB **crash** *I lost half a morning's work when the program crashed.* | **allow sth** *This program allows you to edit and catalogue digital photographs.* | **contain sth** *The program contains powerful new features.* | **provide sth** *This program provides everything you need to prepare your own publication.* | **require sth** *This program requires at least 24Mb of RAM.* | **create sth** *The program creates simulations of real-life driving conditions.* | **operate, run | close**
• PROGRAM + NOUN **file**
• PREP. **in a/the ~** *There may be a bug in the program.* | **~for** *a program for debugging*
⇨ Special page at COMPUTER

programme *noun*

1 plan of things to do
• ADJ. **ambitious | comprehensive, major, massive, radical, wide-ranging** *a comprehensive programme of economic reform* | **modest | long-term | regular | varied** *a varied programme of entertainment* | **pilot** *The pilot programme of vaccination proved successful.* | **party, political | government | collaborative, joint** *joint programmes between government and industry* | **action, development, improvement, modernization, privatization, research | economic, expenditure, investment, recovery** *Mr Brown called for a national recovery programme.* | **austerity, closure, cost-cutting | aid, assistance, relief, welfare | assessment, testing | degree, education, educational, literacy, training** *students enrolled on the two-year MA degree programme* | **care, health** *a community care programme for psychiatric patients* | **exercise, weight-loss | breeding, building, conservation, de-**

fence *Female seals are needed for the breeding programme.*
- VERB + PROGRAMME **agree (on), develop, draw up, establish, organize, plan, set up | outline** *The course leader outlined the programme we would be following.* | **carry out, implement, launch, run | expand | offer** *The college offers a wide variety of programmes of study.* | **finance, fund** *How is the programme to be financed?* | **embark on, undertake | enrol on | follow | complete | disrupt** *Renewed fighting disrupted the relief programme.*
- PROGRAMME + VERB **aim to, be aimed at sb/sth, be designed to** *The programme aims to increase employment.* | **include sth, involve sb/sth | offer sth, provide sth**
- PREP. **in a/the ~, on the/your ~** *What's on your programme today* (= What are your plans)*?* | **~ for** *What's the programme for* (= What are we going to do) *tomorrow?* **~ of** *a programme of study*
- PHRASES **the aim/objective/purpose of a programme**

2 radio/television show
- ADJ. **radio, television/TV | current affairs, documentary, factual, news | comedy | educational | children's | cookery, wildlife, religious, etc. | phone-in**
- VERB + PROGRAMME **see, watch | listen to | record | do, make | host, present** *a phone-in programme hosted by Freddie Greenan* | **broadcast, screen, show**
- PREP. **in a/the ~** *In today's programme, we'll be giving you advice on how to manage your money.* **on a/the ~** *He appeared on the programme last night.* | **~ about/on** *I saw a good programme on owls last night.*

3 booklet for a play/concert/event
- ADJ. **concert, theatre | match, race**
- PREP. **in the ~** *Her name doesn't appear in the concert programme.*

4 order of events
- ADJ. **exciting, interesting | musical, sporting**
- VERB + PROGRAMME **arrange, draw up, plan, organize** *planning an exciting programme of activities*
- PROGRAMME + VERB **include sth**
- PREP. **~ of** *a programme of 17th century music*

programmer noun

- ADJ. **senior | assistant | experienced, skilled, trained | freelance | computer, software**
- PROGRAMMER + VERB **write sth**
- ⇨ Note at JOB

progress noun

1 movement forwards
- ADJ. **considerable, dramatic, encouraging, excellent, genuine, good, great, impressive, real, remarkable, significant, substantial | fast, rapid, swift | inexorable | slow, stately** *We watched the ship's stately progress out of the harbour.* | **satisfactory, steady | further | academic, educational**
- VERB + PROGRESS **achieve, make | assess, chart, check (on), evaluate, monitor, observe, review, trace, track, watch** *Regular tests enable the teacher to monitor the progress of each child.* | **block, hamper, hinder, impede, obstruct, slow (down) | halt, stop | accelerate, facilitate**
- PROGRESS + NOUN **report**
- PREP. **in ~** *There was a cricket match in progress.* | **~ from ... to ...** *The book traced his steady progress from petty theft to serious crime.* **~ in** *He's making good progress in maths.* **~ on** *How much progress have the builders made on the extension?* **~ towards** *Who can halt Woods' inexorable progress towards yet another championship?* **~ with** *She's making steady progress with her thesis.*
- PHRASES **a lack of progress** *I was frustrated by my apparent lack of progress when I started the violin.* **a rate of progress** *At the present rate of progress we won't be fin-*

ished before July. **work in progress** *I have one file for completed work and one for work in progress.*

2 improvement in society
- ADJ. **economic, evolutionary, industrial, medical, scientific, social, technical, technological | human**
- VERB + PROGRESS **hold back**
- PHRASES **the march of progress** *the onward march of technological progress*

progress verb

- ADV. **satisfactorily, smoothly, well** *The talks are progressing very well.* | **further** *He felt he still needed to progress further in his learning.* | **rapidly** *progressing rapidly in his chosen career* | **slowly** *The work is progressing quite slowly.* | **steadily**
- VERB + PROGRESS **fail to**
- PREP. **beyond** *Samir failed to progress beyond this first step on the ladder.* **from, through** *allowing students to progress through the stages of the course* **to** *She soon progressed from the basics to more difficult work.* **towards** *slowly progressing towards a new kind of art* **up** *his ambition to progress up the career ladder* **with** *They are keen to progress with the scheme.*

progression noun

- ADJ. **rapid | gradual, slow, steady | smooth | upward | linear, logical, natural** *By a logical progression of thought, she worked out why the remark had caused offence.* | **career | chord, harmonic**
- PREP. **~ from ... to ...** *his progression from chubby teenager to handsome movie star* **~ through** *Her progression through the grades of the civil service had been rapid.* **~ within** *his steady upward progression within the company*
- PHRASES **the progression of a disease** *one of the later stages in the progression of the disease*

progressive adj.

- VERBS **be**
- ADV. **highly, very** *highly progressive in outlook* | **relatively | politically**

prohibit verb

- ADV. **strictly** *Smoking in the cinema is strictly prohibited.* | **expressly, specifically | effectively** *The very restrict regulations effectively prohibit the entry of soil or plants grown in soil into the country.* | **constitutionally** *The president is constitutionally prohibited from serving more than two terms in office.*
- PREP. **from** *The Act specifically prohibits any council from spending money for political purposes.*

prohibition noun

- ADJ. **absolute, total | general | legal, statutory**
- VERB + PROHIBITION **impose | abolish, lift**
- PROHIBITION + NOUN **notice, order** *The prohibition order meant that the book could not be sold in this country.*
- PREP. **~ against** *prohibition against sales to under-18s of alcohol* **~ of** *a treaty for the prohibition of nuclear tests* **~ on** *the prohibition imposed on the sale of arms*

project noun

1 planned piece of work
- ADJ. **large, major | ambitious | exciting | worthwhile | successful | joint | community | pilot** *The scheme will be extended throughout the country after a successful six-month pilot project.* | **research** *They've set up a research project to investigate the harmful effects of air pollution.* | **building, construction | capital, investment | development, educational, environmental**

- VERB + PROJECT **set up | carry out, run | conceive, plan | launch | fund, support**
- PROJECT + VERB **aim to, be aimed at sth** *The project aims to reduce homelessness.*
- PROJECT + NOUN **management | leader, manager, team**
- PHRASES **the aim of the project** *The aims of the project are threefold …*
⇨ Special page at BUSINESS

2 piece of school work
- ADJ. **French, history, etc.**
- VERB + PROJECT **do**
- PREP. **~ on** *My class is doing a project on medieval towns.*
- PROJECT + NOUN **work**

projection *noun*

- ADJ. **current, latest | forward, future | population | financial, profit, sales**
- VERB + PROJECTION **make | revise**
- PREP. **on … ~s** *On current projections, there will be more than ten million people 65 or over in 2010.* | **~ about** *He declined to make projections about the next quarter's earnings.* **~ as to** *We have been making forward projections as to future profitability of the firm.* **~ for** *They presented profit projections for the rest of the year.* **~ of** *The council has revised its projections of funding requirements upwards.*

projector *noun*

- ADJ. **overhead | cine, film, slide, video**
- VERB + PROJECTOR **switch off/on | operate**

prolific *adj.*

- VERBS **be**
- ADV. **exceptionally, extraordinarily, extremely, highly, immensely, incredibly, very | fairly, quite**

prolong *verb*

- ADV. **indefinitely** *Might it be possible to prolong life indefinitely?* | **artificially | deliberately** *Doctors commented that some patients deliberately prolong their treatment.* | **unduly, unnecessarily** *We do not want to prolong the meeting unnecessarily.*

prolonged *adj.*

- VERBS **be | become**
- ADV. **very | not unduly** *The surgery must not be unduly prolonged.* | **fairly, quite, relatively, somewhat**

prominence *noun*

- ADJ. **great | growing, increasing | equal | special** *a performance which gives a special prominence to the part of Hamlet's mother* | **due | undue | international, local, national | political, public**
- VERB + PROMINENCE **achieve, come into/to, gain, rise to, shoot to** *She came to national prominence as an artist in the 1960s.* | **bring sb/sth into/to, give sb/sth** *His account gives due prominence to the role of the king.*
- PHRASES **a position of prominence** *The former rebels were given positions of prominence in the new government.* **a rise to prominence** *The city's rise to prominence as a port began in the early nineteenth century.*

prominent *adj.*

- VERBS **be | become | remain**
- ADV. **especially, extremely, particularly, unusually, very | increasingly | fairly, quite**
- PREP. **as** *prominent as a player and coach* **in** *prominent in the trade unions*

promise *noun*

1 statement that you will do sth
- ADJ. **big** *He makes all kinds of big promises he has little intention of keeping.* | **rash | broken, unfulfilled | empty, false, hollow | vague | binding, firm | campaign, election, pre-election**
- VERB + PROMISE **give sb, make (sb)** *You gave me your promise I could use the car tonight.* ◊ *I'll consider it, but I make no promises.* | **fulfil, honour, keep | break, go back on | extract** *We extracted a promise from them that they would repay the money by May.* | **hold sb to** *The Opposition is determined to hold the government to its election promises.*
- PREP. **~ about** *They've made all sorts of promises about reforming the health system.* **~ of** *promises of support*

2 signs that sb/sth will be successful
- ADJ. **considerable, great, real** *This new venture holds great promise for the future.* | **early, youthful**
- VERB + PROMISE **hold, show | fulfil, live up to** *His career failed to fulfil its early promise.*
- PREP. **of ~** *a pianist of promise* | **~ as** *She showed great promise as a runner.*
- PHRASES **full of promise** *The year began so full of promise, and ended in disappointment.*

promise *verb*

- ADV. **faithfully** *She promised faithfully that she would come.* | **solemnly**
- VERB + PROMISE **can/can't | seem to** *The plan seemed to promise a new beginning.*
- PREP. **to** *I've promised my old computer to Jane.*
- PHRASES **as promised** *I am sending you information on holidays as promised.* | **I can't promise anything** *I can't promise anything, but I hope to have it finished next week.*

promising *adj.*

- VERBS **be, look, seem, sound**
- ADV. **extremely, highly, particularly, very | hardly** *The outlook is hardly promising.* | **quite**

promote *verb*

1 encourage sth
- ADV. **strongly** *The idea of equal opportunities was strongly promoted by many Labour MPs.* | **actively, directly | indirectly | deliberately, intentionally** *They claimed that the authorities had deliberately promoted and condoned the violence.*
- VERB + PROMOTE **aim to, seek to, try to | help (to)** *Basketball stars from the United States have helped promote the sport in Italy and Spain.* | **be designed to** *measures designed to promote economic growth* | **be likely to | serve to, tend to** *Bonus payments to staff serve to promote commitment to the company.*
- PREP. **through** *Young people's awareness of agricultural issues is promoted through publicity material.*
- PHRASES **be aimed at promoting sth, be widely promoted, a campaign/scheme to promote sth, efforts/measures to promote sth**

2 advertise sth
- ADV. **aggressively, heavily** *The new products have been very heavily promoted.* | **widely**
- PREP. **as** *The town is now being promoted as a holiday destination.* **through** *The company's products have been promoted mainly through advertising in newspapers.*

promotion *noun*

1 to a higher position
- ADJ. **rapid | internal** *The company encourages internal promotion.*
- VERB + PROMOTION **gain, get, win** *If I can't get promotion soon, I'll look for another job.* | **deserve** *We con-*

gratulate James on his well-deserved promotion to Chief Executive. | **recommend sb for**

● PROMOTION + NOUN **opportunities, prospects | race** With three matches remaining, there are six teams in the promotion race.

● PREP. **~from, ~to** his promotion from lecturer to senior lecturer

● PHRASES **chance/chances of promotion** The team's chances of promotion took a knock when they lost at home.

2 advertising

● ADJ. **special | sales, trade | book, tobacco, etc. | health** The new health promotion clinic will provide free check-ups.

● VERB + PROMOTION **do** We're doing a special book promotion at key bookshops this week.

prone adj.

● VERBS **be, seem | become | leave sb/sth, make sb/sth** Sun removes the oil and wax, leaving the leather prone to cracking.

● ADV. **especially, highly, particularly, very | increasingly | rather, slightly | notoriously** The M40 through Oxfordshire is notoriously prone to fog.

● PREP. **to** She seems very prone to chest infections.

● PHRASES **accident prone**

pronoun noun

● ADJ. **plural, singular | first-person, second-person, etc. | definite, demonstrative, indefinite, interrogative, personal, possessive, relative | object, subject**

pronounce verb

1 make the sound of a word/letter

● ADV. **clearly, distinctly | correctly, properly**

● VERB + PRONOUNCE **can, know how to** I don't know how to pronounce the name of the town. | **be difficult to**

● PREP. **as** 'Gone back' is sometimes pronounced as 'gom back'. **as in** She pronounced the 'o' as in 'no'.

2 state sth

● ADV. **confidently** Press reports beforehand confidently pronounced that an agreement had already been reached.

● PREP. **in favour of** The committee has pronounced in favour of the merger. **on/upon** I do not feel competent to pronounce on this matter.

pronounced adj.

● VERBS **be | become**

● ADV. **especially, particularly, very** These blooms have a very pronounced tendency to hang their heads. | **fairly, quite** walking with a fairly pronounced limp

pronunciation noun

● ADJ. **correct, good | bad, incorrect | alternative, different, variant | standard | American, Australian, etc.**

● VERB + PRONUNCIATION **correct** She doesn't like having her pronunciation corrected.

● PRONUNCIATION + NOUN **drill, exercise, practice**

proof noun

● ADJ. **absolute, clear, conclusive, concrete, convincing, direct, good, incontrovertible, irrefutable, positive, real, tangible** Have you got any positive proof that she took the money? ◇ We have proof positive that he is in hiding. ◇ I have no real proof that he was at the flat. | **ample, sufficient | further | final, ultimate** The photo was final proof of her husband's infidelity. | **documentary, written | legal | scientific | living** The lungfish is living proof that fish could evolve to breathe on land.

● VERB + PROOF **have | give sb, offer (sb), produce, provide (sb with) | get, obtain | need, require**

● PREP. **without~** He is unlikely to make wild accusations without proof. | **~of** Her account gives us no concrete proof of his guilt.

● PHRASES **the burden/onus of proof** The burden of proof lay on the plaintiff to prove negligence. **a lack of proof** The men were acquitted for lack of proof. **proof of identity, proof of purchase** Proof of purchase must be provided before a refund can be made. **a standard of proof** Civil proceedings require a lower standard of proof than criminal cases.

propaganda noun

● ADJ. **government, official, party, state | political, religious, revolutionary | Conservative, socialist, etc. | enemy, hostile, war**

● VERB + PROPAGANDA **broadcast** The pirate radio station broadcast anti-government propaganda.

● PROPAGANDA + NOUN **battle, campaign, effort, exercise, war | triumph, victory | department, machine | film, material, tool, weapon | purposes** The film was made in 1938 for propaganda purposes. | The Olympics were of great propaganda value to the regime.

● PREP. **~about** The papers were full of political propaganda about nationalization. **~against** Soviet propaganda against Fascism

proper adj.

● VERBS **be, seem** It seemed proper to pay tribute to her in this way. | **consider sth, deem sth, think sth** It was not considered proper for young ladies to go out alone.

● ADV. **very | entirely, perfectly, quite** The tribunal decided that his behaviour was perfectly proper.

● PHRASES **(only) right and proper** It is only right and proper that you should attend his funeral.

property noun

1 possessions

● ADJ. **personal, private | common, public | intellectual** Companies should protect their intellectual property with patents and trademarks. | **stolen | lost** I phoned the lost property office to see if someone had found my bag.

● VERB + PROPERTY **dispose of** The market was known as a place where people disposed of stolen property.

● PROPERTY + NOUN **rights** The firm was found to have infringed intellectual property rights.

2 land/building

● ADJ. **freehold, leasehold | adjacent, adjoining, neighbouring | detached, semi-detached | two-bedroom, three-bedroom, etc. | business, commercial, hotel, residential | investment | private | council, council-owned | family**

● VERB + PROPERTY **hold, own | acquire, buy, invest in, purchase | inherit | sell | lease, let, rent out** They decided to rent out the property while they were abroad. | **rent** living in rented property | **view** We have a potential buyer who wants to view the property. | **value** The property was valued at £250 000. | **put on the market** Once the tenants have left, the property will be put on the market.

● PROPERTY + NOUN **market, prices, values | company, developer | owner | tax | boundary**

● PHRASES **a man/woman of property** Now that you've paid off your mortgage, how does it feel to be a woman of property?

3 characteristic

● ADJ. **biological, chemical, electrical, magnetic, mechanical, physical | antiseptic, health-giving, medicinal** The medicinal properties of the leaves of this tree have been known for centuries. | **observable | individual | general**

prophecy noun

- ADJ. **Biblical, Messianic, Old Testament | self-fulfilling** *low expectations that become a self-fulfilling prophecy*
- VERB + PROPHECY **make | fulfil**
- PREP. **~ about** *Macbeth believed the witches' prophecy about his future.* **~ of** *The poem contains a bleak prophecy of war and ruin.*
- PHRASES **the gift of prophecy**

prophet noun

- ADJ. **true** *Some believe that he was not a true prophet.* | **false | great | Old Testament**
- PHRASES **a prophet of doom** (*informal*) *In spite of the prophets of doom, her business proved very successful.*

prophetic adj.

- VERBS **be, prove, seem** *His warnings about the journey proved prophetic.*
- ADV. **highly | almost | strangely**
- PREP. **of** *a book that was prophetic of future developments in science*

proportion noun

1 part/share of a whole
- ADJ. **appreciable, considerable, fair, good, great, high, huge, large, overwhelming, significant, sizeable, substantial | reasonable | low, small | minute, negligible, tiny | certain | equal** *The company employs men and women in roughly equal proportions.* | **equivalent, similar | different, differing, varying | fixed | exact | approximate | average | overall | growing, increasing, rising | declining, decreasing, diminishing**
- VERB + PROPORTION **express sth as** *The chart shows government spending expressed as a proportion of national income.* | **grow as, increase as, rise as | decline as, decrease as, diminish as, fall as** *The unskilled section of the working class was diminishing as a proportion of the workforce.*
- PROPORTION + VERB **grow, increase, rise | decline, decrease, fall**

2 relationship between the size/amount of two things
- ADJ. **correct | direct | inverse** *The human population in the region is expanding in inverse proportion to the wildlife.* | **relative**
- VERB + PROPORTION **keep sth in** *Try to keep your view of the situation in proportion* (= not think it is more serious than it is).
- PREP. **in ~ (to)** *The cost of insurance increases in proportion to the performance of the car.* **out of ~ (to)** *The costs of the plan are out of proportion to the budget available.* | **~ of sth to sth** *The proportion of sand to cement used was three to one.*
- PHRASES **out of all proportion** *The problem has been exaggerated out of all proportion.* **a sense of proportion** *Try to keep a sense of proportion* (= of the relative importance of different things).

3 proportions size and shape of sth
- ADJ. **enormous, epic, extraordinary, gargantuan, generous, gigantic, heroic, huge, immense, major, mammoth, massive, monumental, staggering | modest | manageable, unmanageable** *The computer brings the huge task of stock control down to more manageable proportions.* | **alarming | crisis, epidemic | classic, elegant, fine, noble, perfect** *There is an entrance hall of perfect proportions, twice as long as it is wide.* | **bodily**
- VERB + PROPORTIONS **reach** *The food shortage had reached crisis proportions.*

proportional adj.

- VERBS **be**

- ADV. **broadly, roughly** *The amount of food a child needs is roughly proportional to its size.* | **directly** *The speed of the glider is directly proportional to the speed of the wind.* | **inversely** *The amount of force needed is inversely proportional to the rigidity of the material.*
- PREP. **to**

proposal noun

1 plan
- ADJ. **concrete | detailed | controversial | compromise | peace, reform, research, etc.**
- QUANT. **package, set** *The government outlined a new set of proposals on human rights.*
- VERB + PROPOSAL **formulate | outline | bring forward, make, put forward, submit | accept, back, support, welcome** *I welcome the proposal to reduce taxes for the poorly paid.* | **block, oppose, reject, vote against | push through** *The government could face defeat if it tries to push through the controversial proposals.* | **drop, withdraw | consider, discuss**
- PREP. **~ concerning/relating to** *proposals concerning the use of land* **~ for** *The Ministry submitted a proposal for lower speed limits on motorways.*
  ⇨ Special page at MEETING

2 offer of marriage
- VERB + PROPOSAL **make | receive | accept** *She accepted his proposal of marriage.* | **turn down**
- PHRASES **a proposal of marriage**

propose verb

- ADV. **seriously** *Are you seriously proposing that we should allow this situation to continue?*
- PREP. **as** *The measures have been proposed as a way of improving standards.* **for** *He was proposed for the job of treasurer.*
- PHRASES **originally proposed** *The plan originally proposed was ruled completely unrealistic.*

proposition noun

1 arrangement/offer/suggestion
- ADJ. **attractive, tempting | feasible, practical, viable | business, commercial, economic, paying**
- VERB + PROPOSITION **put to sb** *Ring up your agent in New York and put your proposition to him.*

2 problem/task
- ADJ. **tough, tricky | different** *He's a different proposition from his father—much less tolerant.*

3 idea/opinion
- ADJ. **basic, central, fundamental | true | extreme | abstract, causal, empirical, ethical, existential, general, theoretical, universal**
- QUANT. **set**
- VERB + PROPOSITION **express, put forward**
- PROPOSITION + VERB **concern sth, relate to sth**
- PREP. **~ about** *The book puts forward a number of extreme propositions about the nature of language.*

proprietor noun

- ADJ. **hotel, newspaper, restaurant | landed | sole** *He is now sole proprietor of the business.*

prose noun

- ADJ. **clear, plain, simple | elegant, flowing, rhythmic | flowery, purple** (= elaborate or exaggerated in style) | **descriptive | discursive | continuous** *I plan out an essay in note form before writing it up in continuous prose.* | **academic, literary**
- QUANT. **piece**
- VERB + PROSE **write (in)**

- PROSE + NOUN **works, writing | writer | style | narrative | passage, text | fiction**
- PREP. **in~** *a passage in prose*

prosecution *noun*

1 trying to prove sb's guilt in court
- ADJ. **criminal,   private | successful | impending, possible** *He faces possible prosecution.*
- VERB + PROSECUTION **bring, initiate | be liable to, face, risk | escape | lead to, result in**
- PREP. **~ against** *The police brought a prosecution against the driver involved.* **~ for** *Prosecutions for water pollution more than doubled.*
- PHRASES **immunity from prosecution**

2 lawyers trying to prove sb's guilt
- PROSECUTION + VERB **prove sth | allege sth, claim sth** *The prosecution alleged that he murdered his wife.*
- PROSECUTION + NOUN **case,   evidence | counsel, lawyer, witness | costs**
- PREP. **for the~** *a witness for the prosecution*

prospect *noun*

1 chance/hope that sth will happen
- ADJ. **reasonable | immediate**
- VERB + PROSPECT **have | offer**
- PREP. **in~** *Major developments are in prospect for the company.* **| ~of sth** *There is little prospect of any improvement in the weather.*

2 idea of what may/will happen
- ADJ. **attractive, exciting, inviting | bleak, daunting**
- VERB + PROSPECT **be excited at, relish, welcome** *I don't relish the prospect of having to share an office.* **| be faced with, face**

3 prospects chances of being successful
- ADJ. **bright, excellent, exciting, good | limited, poor | future, long-term | development, economic, growth | career, employment, job, promotion | election, electoral, re-election**
- VERB + PROSPECTS **have | offer (sb)** *This position offers a good starting salary and excellent promotion prospects.* **| boost, enhance, improve** *Getting the right qualifications will enhance your employment prospects.* **| blight, damage, diminish, ruin, wreck | assess, examine, review**
- PROSPECTS + VERB **improve**
- PREP. **with/without~** *At 25 he was an unemployed musician with no prospects.* **| ~for** *Long-term prospects for the economy have improved.* **~ of** *Their prospects of employment look better than last year.*

prospectus *noun*

- ADJ. **detailed | college, school**
- QUANT. **copy**
- VERB + PROSPECTUS **browse through, leaf through, look through | produce**

prosperity *noun*

- ADJ. **economic, material | growing, increasing, rising | relative | future,   lasting,   long-term | general, global, national, world | personal**
- QUANT. **level** *an area with a level of prosperity higher than the national average*
- VERB + PROSPERITY **bring, create** *The growth of tourism brought prosperity to the island.* **| achieve**
- PROSPERITY + VERB **depend on sth** *The island's prosperity depends on its fishing industry.*
- PHRASES **a period of prosperity**

prosperous *adj.*

- VERBS **be, seem | become, grow | remain**

- ADV. **extremely,   very | fairly,   quite,   relatively | formerly, once** *this once prosperous region* **| newly** *Suburbs sprawled out to provide homes for the newly prosperous.* **| economically**

prostitute *noun*

- ADJ. **common** *She was arrested and charged with being a common prostitute.* **| child, female, girl, male | former, reformed** *a book written by a former prostitute*
- VERB + PROSTITUTE **be, work as | go to, use, visit** *the men who use prostitutes* **| control** *He was arrested on charges of controlling prostitutes.*
- PROSTITUTE + VERB **solicit** *The prostitutes solicit openly here.*

prostitution *noun*

- ADJ. **child, female, juvenile, male**
- VERB + PROSTITUTION **be involved in | turn to** *Some turned to prostitution in order to survive.*
- PROSTITUTION + NOUN **trade** *There is a long-standing prostitution trade in the port.*

prostrate *adj.*

- VERBS **be, lie** *lying prostrate on the ground* **| fall** *They fell prostrate before the king.*

protect *verb*

- ADV. **fully | adequately,   properly,   suitably | inadequately | carefully | effectively,   successfully | jealously, rigorously** *a star who jealously protects her right to privacy*
- VERB + PROTECT **need to | seek to, strive to, try to | act to, fight to** *Each company is fighting to protect its own commercial interests.* **| take steps to** *We must take steps to protect the UK as a manufacturing base.* **| help (to) | serve to | be designed to**
- PREP. **against** *a cream that helps to protect your skin against the sun* **from** *The new measures are designed to protect the public from people like these.* **with** *Protect the exposed areas of wood with varnish.*
- PHRASES **be aimed at protecting sth, a desire/duty/need to protect sb/sth** *He felt it was his duty to protect the child.* **heavily/highly protected** *The Far Eastern markets are heavily protected* (= with high taxes for imported goods). **legally/officially/specially protected** *Many of these sites—of immense scientific interest—are not legally protected.* **measures to protect sb/sth, poorly/well protected** *Keep the camera well protected at all times.*

protection *noun*

- ADJ. **adequate, effective | legal | police** *Witnesses at the trial were given police protection.* **| animal, child, consumer, data, environmental, personal, wildlife** *Animal protection supporters gathered to protest against hunting.* ◇ *She carries a gun in her bag for personal protection.* **| fire, flood** *Fire protection equipment must be available on all floors.* **| sun** *sun protection products*
- QUANT. **degree** *A helmet affords the cyclist some degree of protection against injury.*
- VERB + PROTECTION **afford (sb), give (sb), offer (sb), provide (sb with)**
- PROTECTION + NOUN **law, legislation, order** *The couple were was found guilty of violation of child protection laws.* **| measures, mechanism, scheme, system**
- PREP. **under the ~ of** *Many British wild animals are now under the protection of the Wildlife and Countryside Act.* **| ~against** *Fill the cooling system with antifreeze as a protection against frost.* **~ from** *The high walls give the garden protection from the wind.*

● PHRASES **a means of protection** *The skunk releases a pungent smell as a means of protection.*

protective *adj.*

● VERBS **be, feel | become**
● ADV. **fiercely, highly, very** *The lionesses are fiercely protective of their young.*
● PREP. **of** *He's too jealous and protective of her.* **towards** *feeling suddenly very protective towards her mother*

protein *noun*

● ADJ. **essential | natural | animal, vegetable**
● VERB + PROTEIN **be high/rich in, contain, supply** *Cereals supply essential protein and vitamins.* **| produce**
● PROTEIN + NOUN **content | intake | deficiency**
● PHRASES **a high/low protein diet, a source of protein**

protest *noun*

● ADJ. **angry, strong, violent | peaceful | sit-down | mass | formal, official | popular, public, student | anti-government, political | continuing, further, renewed | rooftop, street** *a rooftop protest by prison inmates* **| widespread**
● QUANT. **flood, storm, tide, wave** *The new tax sparked a wave of public protest.*
● VERB + PROTEST **organize, stage | lodge, register** *The Samoan team lodged a formal protest after the referee sent off the wrong player.* **| lead to, spark**
● PROTEST + NOUN **group, movement | demonstration, march, meeting, rally | strike | petition | song**
● PREP. **in ~** *Prisoners shouted and hurled slates in protest.* **under~** *The strikers returned to work, but under protest.* **without ~** *The crowd dispersed without protest.* **| ~ about** *a protest about the new bypass* **~ against** *There had been a number of public protests against the new tax.* **~ at** *The party boycotted the election in protest at alleged vote rigging.* **~ over** *a student protest over tuition fees*
● PHRASES **a chorus/cry/howl of protest** *The announcement brought cries of protest from the crowd.* **the freedom/right of protest** *The constitution guarantees the right of peaceful protest.* **a letter of protest**

protest *verb*

● ADV. **strongly, vehemently, vigorously | formally | loudly | mildly | weakly | peacefully** *the right to protest peacefully* **| bitterly, desperately, indignantly**
● VERB + PROTEST **begin to, try to** *When he tried to protest, she insisted.* **| gather to** *Crowds gathered to protest about the police violence.*
● PREP. **about/over** *protesting over an income tax increase* **against** *protesting against the proposed agreement* **at** *Many people have protested at the cuts in state benefits.* **to** *We have protested to the government.*

protester *noun*

● ADJ. **student | anti-government, anti-nuclear, peace, political | peaceful, unarmed | angry**
● VERB + PROTESTER **arrest**
● PROTESTER + VERB **call for sth, demand sth | march | demonstrate, gather | clash, fight** *Protesters clashed with police outside the embassy.*
● PREP. **~ against** *The streets were crowded with protesters against the war.*

prototype *noun*

● ADJ. **pre-production | working**
● VERB + PROTOTYPE **build, develop | test**
● PROTOTYPE + NOUN **stage** *The car is presently at the prototype stage.*
● PREP. **~ for** *The team is developing a prototype for a*

digital compact camera. **~ of** *He is working on the prototype of a new type of ventilator.*

proud *adj.*

● VERBS **be, feel, look, seem, sound | make sb**
● ADV. **enormously, especially, extremely, fiercely, immensely, inordinately, intensely, more than a little, particularly, really, terribly, tremendously, very** *She was fiercely proud of family traditions and continuity.* ◊ *He was more than a little proud of himself.* **| almost** *He seemed almost proud of his practical incompetence.* **| quite, rather | justifiably, justly, rightly | perversely** *Londoners have long been perversely proud of a health service that does not serve them well.* **| quietly** *He was not vain, but he was quietly proud of his literary achievements.* **| secretly**
● PREP. **of** *We are all really proud of you!*
● PHRASES **have every reason/right to be proud** *All those involved have every reason to be proud of their achievement.*

prove *verb*

● ADV. **conclusively, definitively** *All this proves conclusively that she couldn't have known the truth.* **| just** *Their behaviour just proves my point.*
● VERB + PROVE **be difficult to, be impossible to | be easy to | be able to | try to** *What are you trying to prove?* **| be determined to | have sth to** *I certainly don't have anything to prove—my record speaks for itself.*
● PREP. **to** *He tried to prove his theory to his friends.*
● PHRASES **a chance to prove sth, prove sb right/wrong** *I was determined to prove my critics wrong.*

proven *adj.*

● VERBS **be**
● ADV. **well | completely, conclusively, fully** *No funding will be available until the technology is completely proven.* **| not yet | scientifically, statistically**

provide *verb*

● ADV. **kindly** *a buffet supper, kindly provided by club members* **| free (of charge)** *Careers advice is provided free of charge.*
● VERB + PROVIDE **be able to, can/could | aim to, seek to, try to** *trying to provide the best possible medical care* **| fail to | be designed to, be intended to** *The scheme was intended to provide financial help to unemployed workers.* **| be expected to, be likely/unlikely to** *The report was not expected to provide any answers.*
● PREP. **for** *providing food and shelter for the refugees* **with** *He provided us with a lot of useful information.*

province *noun*

1 region
● ADJ. **northern, southern, etc. | central, coastal, frontier** *the central province of Ghor* **| English-speaking, French-speaking, etc. | autonomous**
2 the provinces not the capital city
● VERB + PROVINCES **tour** *The show is currently touring the provinces.*
● PREP. **from the ~** *She's from the provinces and not familiar with Rome.* **in the ~** *There are a number of press agencies based in London and in the provinces.*

provision *noun*

1 supply
● ADJ. **private, state | educational, housing, nursery, pension, service, welfare, etc.**
● PREP. **~ of** *Several firms are responsible for the provision of cleaning services.*
2 for a future situation; in a legal document

- ADJ. **full | adequate** *It is important to make adequate provision for your retirement.* **| detailed | express, particular, special, specific | relevant | constitutional, legal, legislative, statutory**
- VERB + PROVISION **make | contain** *provisions contained in the contract*
- PROVISION + VERB **apply** *The same provisions apply to foreign-owned companies.*
- PREP. **~against** *They had made all kinds of provisions against bad weather.* **~for** *The Act contains detailed provisions for appeal against the court's decision.*

3 provisions food and drink
- VERB + PROVISIONS **buy, stock up on/with** *We went into town to stock up on provisions.*

provocation noun

- ADJ. **extreme, severe | deliberate**
- QUANT. **element** *The victim's conduct had involved an element of provocation.*
- VERB + PROVOCATION **respond to**
- PREP. **under~** *The crime was committed under provocation.* **without~** *She attacked him without provocation.*
- PHRASES **at the least/slightest provocation** *He would lose his temper at the slightest provocation.*

provocative adj.

1 intending to cause an argument
- VERBS **be, seem | consider sth**
- ADV. **extremely, highly, very | rather | deliberately | unnecessarily**

2 intending to cause sexual excitement
- VERBS **be, look**
- ADV. **highly, very | unconsciously | sexually**

provoke verb

- ADV. **deliberately | inevitably** *The suggestion inevitably provoked outrage from student leaders.* **| immediately | eventually, finally**
- VERB + PROVOKE **try to | be likely to** *The report is likely to provoke discussion of this issue.* **| be designed to, be intended to**
- PREP. **into** *She had been trying to provoke her sister into an argument.* **to** *Their laughter provoked him to anger.*
- PHRASES **be easily provoked** *He was sensitive and easily provoked.*

prowess noun

- ADJ. **academic, athletic, golfing, intellectual, military, physical, sexual, sporting, technical, etc.**
- VERB + PROWESS **demonstrate, show | boast about/of | admire | be famed/famous for**
- PREP. **~as** *He boasted of his prowess as a lover.* **~at** *her prowess at tennis* **~in** *The Gurkhas are famed for their prowess in battle.* **~with** *Their striker demonstrated all his prowess with the boot.*

proximity noun

- ADJ. **close | geographical, physical, spatial**
- PREP. **in~to** *The site is in close proximity to motorways and an airport.* **| ~to** *House prices in the area are elevated by its proximity to London.*

proxy noun

- VERB + PROXY **appoint** *You may appoint a proxy to vote for you.*
- PROXY + VERB **vote | attend (sth)** *Your proxy may attend the meeting if you are unable to attend.*
- PROXY + NOUN **vote, voting | card, form**
- PREP. **by~** *If you will not be able to vote on polling day,*

you may vote by proxy. **| ~for** *Husbands are discouraged from voting as proxy for their wives.*
- PHRASES **a form of proxy** *We enclose a form of proxy for use at the Annual General Meeting.*

prudent adj.

- VERBS **be, seem | consider sth, think sth** *We thought it prudent to telephone first.*
- ADV. **extremely, very | reasonably**

prune verb

- ADV. **hard, heavily, savagely, severely** *Prune the trees hard in the winter.* ◇ *(figurative) Local councils could find their housing budgets severely pruned.* **| back** *The roses had been pruned back savagely.*

pseudonym noun

- VERB + PSEUDONYM **adopt, take, use**
- PREP. **under a/the~** *Eric Blair wrote under the pseudonym of George Orwell.*

psychiatrist noun

- ADJ. **leading, senior, top** *a leading child psychiatrist* **| consultant, research | child | forensic**
- PHRASES **the psychiatrist's couch** *the secrets revealed on the psychiatrist's couch*
⇨ Note at DOCTOR (for verbs)

psychiatry noun

- ADJ. **clinical, community, forensic | child, geriatric**
- PHRASES **a department of psychiatry, an institute of psychiatry**
⇨ Note at SUBJECT (for verbs and nouns)

psychological adj.

- VERBS **be**
- ADV. **purely** *The symptoms are purely psychological.*

psychologist noun

- ADJ. **eminent, leading, top | clinical, consultant, professional** *He is now a consultant psychologist with a major London hospital.* **| academic, experimental | behavioural, child, developmental, educational, occupational, social, sports**
⇨ Note at DOCTOR (for verbs)

psychology noun

1 study of the mind/the way people behave
- PSYCHOLOGY + NOUN **clinical, professional | academic, experimental | applied | cognitive, developmental, educational, social | child**
⇨ Note at SUBJECT (for verbs and nouns)

2 type of mind that a person/group has
- ADJ. **individual, own** *The answers we give will reflect our own psychology.* **| crowd, group** *Watching the shoppers at the sales gave her a first-hand insight into crowd psychology.* **| human**

pub noun

- ADJ. **excellent, good | favourite | corner, local, nearby, nearest** *The corner pub is quite good.* **| crowded | friendly, welcoming | country, village | historic, traditional | modern | theme** *It's one of those modern theme pubs.*
- VERB + PUB **go down (to), go (round) to** *Let's go down the pub for a drink.*
- PUB + NOUN **food, lunch, meal | landlady, landlord**
- PREP. **at/in a/the~** *He spent all afternoon in the pub.*

puberty noun

- VERB + PUBERTY **reach** *He reached puberty at the age of fourteen.* | **approach**
- PREP. **at ~** *Girls start menstruating at puberty.* **during ~** *The body undergoes many changes during puberty.*
- PHRASES **the age of puberty, the onset of puberty**

public noun

1 the public people in general
- ADJ. **general**
- VERB + PUBLIC **inform** *The government was slow to inform the public about the health hazards of lead in petrol.* | **protect** | **serve** | **be open to** *The house is open to the public at weekends.*
- PREP. **in ~** *He rarely appears in public these days.*
- PHRASES **a member of the public**

2 group of people with sth in common
- ADJ. **book-buying, paying, reading, sporting, theatre-going, travelling, viewing,** etc. *Satellite television has provided the viewing public with a wide choice of programmes.* | **larger, wider** *Her work is now available to a wider public.*

publication noun

1 of a book, etc.
- VERB + PUBLICATION **begin** | **cease, stop** | **prepare sth for** | **be due/scheduled for** *The book is scheduled for publication in the autumn.* | **accept sth for**
- PUBLICATION + VERB **be due/scheduled** *The publication of her memoirs is scheduled for the autumn.*
- PUBLICATION + NOUN **date**
- PHRASES **the date/time of publication**

2 book, magazine, etc.
- ADJ. **new, recent** | **forthcoming** | **leading, major** | **sister** *'This Week''s German sister publication, 'Diese Woche', went out of business.* | **government, official** | **specialist** | **academic, business, scientific, trade**
- PUBLICATION + NOUN **publications catalogue/list**
- PREP. **~ about** *specialist publications about bees* **~ on** *She has several publications to her name on local history.*

publicity noun

1 media attention
- ADJ. **considerable, enormous, extensive, greater, wide, widespread** *The papers have begun to give greater publicity to the campaign against GM food.* | **maximum** *The release of the report was timed to generate maximum publicity.* | **favourable, good, positive** | **adverse, bad, negative, unfavourable, unwelcome** | **free** | **international, local, national**
- VERB + PUBLICITY **give sb/sth** | **gain, get, receive** | **attract, generate** | **seek** | **avoid, shun**
- PUBLICITY + VERB **surround sth** *There was a lot of negative publicity surrounding the film.*
- PREP. **~ about** *There has been a lot of unfavourable publicity about the hospital.* **~ for** *Taking part in the event will be good publicity for our school.* **~ over** *The firm had received bad publicity over a defective product.*
- PHRASES **amid/amidst a storm of publicity** *The chairman resigned amid a storm of publicity over the bonus payments.* **a blaze of publicity** *The film stars were married in a blaze of publicity.* **the glare of publicity** *He carried on his life in the full glare of publicity.*

2 advertising
- ADJ. **advance**
- PUBLICITY + NOUN **material, photograph, shot** *He's better-looking in his publicity shots than he is in real life.* | **campaign** | **stunt** *The actress denied that her marriage was just a publicity stunt.* | **agent, officer** | **machine** *The record company's publicity machine was working flat out.*
- PREP. **~ about** *I read some publicity about vaccinations*

while waiting my turn at the doctor's. **~ for** *There have been months of advance publicity for the show.*
- PHRASES **a lack of publicity**

publicize verb

- ADV. **well** | **widely**
- VERB + PUBLICIZE **help (to)**
- PHRASES **little publicized, highly/much publicized** *her highly publicized affair with a leading politician*

publish verb

- ADV. **recently** | **posthumously** *Her last book was published posthumously in 1948.* | **anonymously**
- VERB + PUBLISH **decide to** | **intend to, plan to** | **refuse to** | **be free to** *The press should be free to publish and comment on all aspects of political and social life.* | **dare (to)** *Freud had not dared to publish the third chapter of his book in Vienna.*

publisher noun

- ADJ. **big, large, leading, major** *one of the country's biggest book publishers* | **small** | **local** *He's writing a history of the town for a local publisher.* | **commercial** | **mainstream** | **specialist** | **book, electronic, hardback, magazine, multimedia, music, newspaper, paperback, software** | **academic, educational, ELT, trade**
- VERB + PUBLISHER **find, have** *Finding a publisher is hard for all writers.* ◇ *She now has a publisher for her book.*

publishing noun

- ADJ. **book, newspaper,** etc. | **academic, music,** etc. *She works in music publishing.* | **desktop** | **electronic**
- VERB + PUBLISHING **work in**
- PUBLISHING + NOUN **agreement, deal** | **arm, company, firm, house** *The Cranfield Press is the publishing arm of the Cranfield Institute of Technology.* | **business, industry, sector, world** *The publishing world is extremely competitive.*

puff noun

1 of air/smoke/wind
- ADJ. **little, tiny**
- PREP. **~ of** *a little puff of smoke*

2 on a cigarette/pipe, etc.
- ADJ. **long** | **short**
- VERB + PUFF **have, take** *He took a long puff at his cigar and began his story.*
- PREP. **~ at/on** *a puff on her cigarette*

puff verb

1 smoke
- ADV. **furiously, vigorously**
- ADV. **contentedly, happily** | **thoughtfully** | **away** *He puffed away at his cigar.*
- PREP. **at** *She puffed furiously at her cigarette.* **on** *My father sat puffing contentedly on his pipe.*

2 breathe loudly
- ADV. **hard** *She was puffing quite hard by the time she reached the office.* | **loudly**
- PREP. **along, from** *She was still puffing from the climb.* **up** *puffing up the hill*
- PHRASES **huff and puff/puff and pant** *She puffed and panted behind the others.* **puffing and blowing** *Far behind us, puffing and blowing, came Matt.*

pull noun

1 act of pulling
- ADJ. **sharp** | **strong** | **gentle** | **downward** | **gravita-**

tional *the earth's gravitational pull* | **magnetic** *(figurative) The magnetic pull of the city was hard to resist.*
• VERB + PULL **give sth** *I gave the door a sharp pull.* | **feel** *(figurative) She felt the pull of her homeland.*
• PREP. **~at** *A gentle pull at her sleeve got her attention.* **~on** *He felt a strong pull on the rope.*

2 on a cigarette/drink
• ADJ. **long**
• VERB + PULL **take** *She took a long pull on her cigarette and sighed.*
• PREP. **~at** *a pull at his flask* **~on**

pull *verb*

• ADV. **hard** *He got hold of the rope and pulled hard.* | **gently** | **apart, off, on, out, over** *She pulled off her boots.* ◇ *He pulled his sweater on.* | **along, away, back** *She took his arm and pulled him along.* ◇ *The dog snapped at her and she pulled back her hand.*
• VERB + PULL **try to** *He tried to pull away.* | **manage to**
• PREP. **at** *He pulled at her coat sleeve.* **on** *She pulled on the lever.* **towards** *She pulled him gently towards her.*
• PHRASES **pull (yourself) free** *John finally managed to pull himself free.* **pull yourself to your feet**

pullover *noun*

• ADJ. **woollen, woolly** | **sleeveless** | **knitted** *She was wearing a knitted pullover.* | **Fair Isle**
• VERB + PULLOVER **knit**
⇨ Special page at CLOTHES

pulse *noun*

• ADJ. **fast, racing, rapid** | **slow** | **strong** | **faint, weak**
• VERB + PULSE **check, feel, take** *Last time I took my pulse, it was a bit fast.* | **check for, feel for** *She reached in through the driver's broken window and checked for a pulse.* | **find** | **quicken** *There was little to quicken the pulse in his dull routine.*
• PULSE + VERB **beat** | **quicken, race** *She felt her pulse quicken as she recognized the voice.* | **slow**
• PULSE + NOUN **rate** *My at-rest pulse rate is usually about 80 beats per minute.*

punch *noun*

• ADJ. **good, powerful** | **knockout**
• VERB + PUNCH **deliver, give sb, land, swing, throw** *She gave him a punch on the nose.* ◇ *He can throw a powerful punch.* | **pull** *He pulled his punches to avoid hurting his sparring partner.*
• PREP. **~in** *a punch in the stomach* **~on** *She gave him a punch on the nose.* **~to** *a punch to the jaw*

punch *verb*

• ADV. **hard** | **lightly** | **repeatedly**
• PREP. **in** *His attacker had punched him hard in the face.* **on** *She punched him on the nose.*
• PHRASES **kick and punch/punch and kick** *He was repeatedly kicked and punched as he lay on the ground.*

puncture *noun*

• ADJ. **slow** *The tyre had a slow puncture and had to be pumped up every day.* | **bicycle**
• VERB + PUNCTURE **get, have, suffer** *She suffered a puncture in the fifth lap.* | **fix, mend, repair**

punish *verb*

• ADV. **severely** | **justifiably, justly** | **unfairly** | **accordingly, duly** *Those who had opposed the court were duly punished.*
• VERB + PUNISH **want to** | **try to** *He was trying to pun-*

ish her for deserting him all those years ago.* | **be designed to** *Damages are not designed to punish the person in breach, but to compensate for the loss sustained.*
• PREP. **by** *Never punish children by making them go hungry.* **for** *They will be severely punished for their crimes.* **with** *Offenders will be punished with a £1 000 fine.*

punishment *noun*

• ADJ. **cruel, harsh, heavy, severe** | **unusual** *the constitutional prohibition on cruel and unusual punishment* | **appropriate, fitting** | **capital** | **corporal, physical**
• VERB + PUNISHMENT **administer, hand out, impose, inflict, mete out** *It is unlawful for a teacher to inflict corporal punishment on pupils.* ◇ *Harsh punishment is expected to be meted out to the murderer.* | **receive, suffer** | **avoid, escape** | **deserve**
• PUNISHMENT + VERB **fit the crime** *The victim's family do not believe that this punishment fits the crime.*
• PREP. **as~(for)** *She had to tidy the classroom as punishment for being late.* | **~for** *Punishments for killing the king's deer were severe.*
• PHRASES **crime and punishment** *the sociology of crime and punishment* **on pain of punishment** (= with the threat of punishment) *He was compelled on pain of punishment to answer the question.* **reward and punishment** *They use a system of reward and punishment to discipline their children.*

pupil *noun*

1 child in school
• ADJ. **able, bright, good, star** | **first-year, second-year, etc.** | **older, senior** | **younger** | **disruptive** | **ex-, former** | **private** | **school** | **primary, secondary**
• VERB + PUPIL **teach** | **exclude, expel**
• PUPIL + NOUN **attendance, numbers** | **assessment** | **performance** | **behaviour**

2 of the eye
• ADJ. **dilated, enlarged**
• VERB + PUPIL **dilate**
• PUPIL + VERB **dilate**

puppet *noun*

1 model of a person/animal
• ADJ. **finger, glove, hand, rod, shadow**
• VERB + PUPPET **manipulate, work** *How do you work these puppets?*
• PUPPET + NOUN **play, show** | **theatre** | **master**

2 sb whose actions are controlled by sb else
• ADJ. **mere** *The king was a mere puppet of the mayor.*
• PUPPET + NOUN **government, king, regime, state**

purchase *noun*

1 buying sth
• ADJ. **cash** | **credit** | **online** | **bulk** *the bulk purchase of paper* | **outright** *Companies are moving away from outright purchase of company cars to contract hire.* | **compulsory** *The council applied for a compulsory purchase order on the tennis courts.* | **arms, house, land, share**
• PURCHASE + NOUN **price** | **tax** | **order**
• PHRASES **the cost of purchase** *You can resell books and cut the original cost of purchase.* **the date/time of purchase** *I did not notice the defects at the time of purchase.* **the place/point of purchase** *Ticket holders should return to the point of purchase for a refund.* **proof of purchase** *Keep your receipt as proof of purchase.*

2 sth bought
• ADJ. **excellent, good** | **expensive**
• VERB + PURCHASE **make** *some ways to encourage customers to make a purchase* | **pay for**

purchase verb

- ADV. **compulsorily** *The land was compulsorily purchased from the owner to make way for the new road.*
- VERB + PURCHASE **agree to, be willing to | wish to | can/cannot afford to**
- PREP. **for** *They purchased the land for $1 million.* **from** *They purchased the house from an elderly couple.*

purity noun

- ADJ. **absolute** *the absolute purity of her love* **| great, high** *high-purity silver* **| ideological | racial | moral**
- VERB + PURITY **maintain, preserve** *He struggled to preserve his ideological purity.*
- PHRASES **purity of form/sound/style** *the building's unadorned purity of style*

purple adj.

- ADV. **almost | slightly**
- ADJ. **bright, vivid | dark, deep, rich | light, pale**
- PHRASES **purple in the face, purple with rage** *He turned purple with rage.*
- ⇨ Special page at COLOUR

purpose noun

1 aim/function

- ADJ. **limited | chief, main, primary, prime, principal | true | sole | practical, useful** *These bars serve no useful purpose.* **| general** *a general-purpose cleaning fluid* **| common** *a group of individuals sharing a common purpose* **| particular, special, specific | dual** *a toy with the dual purpose of entertaining and developing memory skills* **| stated | social** *the view that art should serve a social purpose*
- VERB + PURPOSE **have | lack | accomplish, achieve, fulfil, serve** *The scheme achieved its primary purpose, if nothing else.*
- PREP. **for a/the ~** *I put the chair there for a purpose.* ◊ *a measure introduced for the purpose of protecting the interests of investors* **on ~** (= intentionally) *He slammed the door on purpose.*
- PHRASES **at cross purposes** (= not understanding or having the same aims, etc. as each other) *I finally realized that we were talking at cross purposes.* **for/with the express purpose of sth** *The school was founded with the express purpose of teaching deaf children to speak.* **for (all) practical purposes** *Nominally she is the secretary, but for all practical purposes she runs the place.* **purpose-built** *The cycling events will take place in a purpose-built 20 000-seater stadium.* **your purpose in life** *She saw being a doctor as her purpose in life.* **put/use sth to (a/some) purpose** *The old mill has been put to good purpose.* **a sense of purpose** *Encouraged by her example, they all set to work with a fresh sense of purpose.* **strength of purpose** *They had great confidence and strength of purpose.*

2 purposes requirements of a particular situation

- ADJ. **administrative, business, commercial, domestic, educational, insurance, legal, medical, medicinal, political, research, tax, teaching** *You will need to have the vehicle valued for insurance purposes.*
- PREP. **for ... ~** *The drug can be sold for medicinal purposes only.* **for the ~s of** *Let's assume he knows, for the purposes of our argument.*

pursue verb

1 continue sth/try to achieve sth

- ADV. **further, still | actively, energetically, vigorously | doggedly** *He was still doggedly pursuing his studies.* **| relentlessly | effectively, successfully** *How can we most effectively pursue these aims?*
- VERB + PURSUE **decide to** *We have decided not to pursue the matter further.* **| intend to, want to, wish to** *decid-*

ing on which career you wish to pursue **| be/feel inclined to | be reluctant to | be able to, be at liberty to, be free to | continue to**
- PHRASES **the ability/freedom to pursue sth** *the freedom to pursue her own interests* **be not worth pursuing** *I decided the matter was not worth pursuing further.*

2 chase sb

- ADV. **relentlessly** *He pursued her relentlessly, refusing to take 'no' for an answer.*
- PHRASES **closely/hotly pursued by sb** *He ran past, hotly pursued by two policemen.*

pursuit noun

1 attempt to find sth

- ADJ. **relentless, ruthless, single-minded, vigorous | successful**
- VERB + PURSUIT **be engaged in**
- PREP. **in ~ of** *people travelling around the country in pursuit of work* **| ~ of** *He is engaged in the ruthless pursuit of wealth.*
- PHRASES **the pursuit of a goal** *He devoted his waking hours to the single-minded pursuit of his goal.* **the pursuit of excellence/happiness/knowledge/pleasure/truth**

2 attempt to catch sb/sth

- VERB + PURSUIT **give** *The police gave pursuit.*
- PREP. **in ~ (of)** *Two boys ran past with a security guard in pursuit.* ◊ *The guard set off in pursuit of the thief.*
- PHRASES **in close/hot pursuit** *Away ran the fox, with the hunters in hot pursuit.*

3 (usually **pursuits**) pastime

- ADJ. **favourite, popular | active, energetic** *active leisure pursuits* **| country | indoor, outdoor | leisure, recreational | academic, artistic, cultural, educational, intellectual, sporting**
- VERB + PURSUIT **follow** *She has time now to follow her various artistic pursuits.*

pus noun

- ADJ. **yellow**
- VERB + PUS **discharge, ooze** *The wound had not healed properly and was oozing pus.*
- PUS + VERB **gather | ooze (out)**
- PUS + NOUN **cell**

push noun

1 act of pushing

- ADJ. **big, hard | gentle, little**
- VERB + PUSH **give sb/sth** *She gave him a gentle push towards the door.*
- PHRASES **at the push of a button** *The machine washes and dries at the push of a button.*

2 effort to do/obtain sth

- ADJ. **big | final**
- PREP. **~ against** *the final push against the enemy* **~ for** *There has been a big push for better public transport.* **~ towards** *a push towards organic food*

push verb

1 use force to move sb/sth away from you

- ADV. **firmly, hard** *You'll have to push harder if you want it to move.* **| roughly, violently | gently | carefully | deliberately** *He was deliberately pushed into the path of the vehicle.* **| hastily, hurriedly, quickly | slowly | suddenly | just, merely, simply** *Jack flung himself at Steve, but he simply pushed him away.* **| aside, away, back, down, home, inside, over, together** *She leaned on the door and pushed the bolt home.* ◊ *They pushed the two desks together.*
- VERB + PUSH **try to | manage to | begin to**
- PREP. **across, against** *The fans pushed against the barrier.* **at** *She pushed at the door but it wouldn't budge.* **into,**

off, out of *He pushed her roughly out of the door.* **through, to** *The woman had been pushed violently to the ground.* **towards, under** *She found a note pushed under the door.*
• PHRASES **push sth open/shut** *He managed to push the window open a few inches.*

2 move forward by pushing people
• ADV. **roughly | blindly**
• VERB + PUSH **try to | begin to** *I began to push my way through the crowd.*
• PREP. **past** *She pushed blindly past him and made for the door.* **through** *pushing through the crowd*
• PHRASES **push and shove** *People were pushing and shoving to get to the front.* **push your way** *A man pushed his way to the front of the crowd.*

3 put pressure on sb/yourself
• ADV. **hard** *Lucy should push herself a little harder.* | **too far** *Her parents are very tolerant, but sometimes she pushes them too far.* | **around** *Don't allow yourself to be pushed around by that bully.*
• PREP. **into** *Her parents pushed her into accepting the job.*
• PHRASES **push sb/yourself to the limit** *He felt he was being pushed to the limits of his self-control.*

PHRASAL VERB

push for sth
• ADV. **hard** *They're pushing hard for a ban on GM foods.*
• VERB + PUSH FOR STH **have to** *I'm going to have to push you for an answer.*

pushchair *noun*

• ADJ. **collapsible, folding**
• VERB + PUSHCHAIR **push (along), wheel (along) | collapse, fold (up)**
• PREP. **in a/the~**

put *verb*

• ADV. **cleverly, well** *I thought you put your points very well.* | **badly | tactfully | bluntly, crudely | simply, succinctly** *Put simply, we accept their offer or go bankrupt.* | **mildly** *(ironic) I was, to put it mildly, annoyed (= I was extremely angry).*

• PHRASES **to put it another way** *He was too trusting— or, to put it another way, he had no head for business.*

puzzle *noun*

1 sth that is difficult to understand
• ADJ. **great | perplexing | scientific, theoretical**
• VERB + PUZZLE **solve | remain** *What happened to the ship remains a puzzle.*
• PUZZLE + VERB **remain** *The puzzle remains of what happened to the ship.*
• PREP. **in a/the~** *They knew who the killer was, but there were still some gaps in the puzzle.* | **~about** *There is a puzzle about how the plant first came to Britain.* **~of** *They're trying to solve the puzzle of how gravity works.*
• PHRASES **a bit/piece of the puzzle** *Another piece of the puzzle fell into place.* **the key to a puzzle** *Traces of explosives found among the wreckage were the key to the puzzle.* **a piece in the puzzle** *The police didn't know what the message meant, but it was another piece in the puzzle.* **a solution to a puzzle, something of a puzzle** *The origin of the word is something of a puzzle.*

2 game that tests your skill, intelligence, etc.
• ADJ. **crossword, jigsaw | number, picture, word | complicated**
• VERB + PUZZLE **do, solve**
• PUZZLE + NOUN **book**

puzzled *adj.*

• VERBS **be, feel, look, seem, sound | become, get** *beginning to get a bit puzzled* | **remain**
• ADV. **extremely, very | a bit, faintly, a little, rather, slightly, somewhat | genuinely | clearly, obviously**
• PREP. **about** *You look very puzzled about something.* **at** *I was somewhat puzzled at his unwillingness to help.* **by** *Mrs Sykes seemed slightly puzzled by this.*

pyjamas *noun*

• QUANT. **pair**
• PYJAMA + NOUN **jacket, top | bottoms, trousers** *wearing only his pyjama trousers*
⇨ Special page at CLOTHES

Qq

qualification *noun*

1 skill/knowledge needed for a job, etc.
- ADJ. **formal, paper, recognized** | **basic, minimum** | **entry** | **further** | **appropriate, necessary** | **special, specialist** | **management, professional, vocational** | **academic, educational, postgraduate** | **technical** | **legal, medical, secretarial, teaching**, etc.
- VERB + QUALIFICATION **acquire, gain, obtain** | **have, hold** *Only two of the applicants had the necessary qualifications.*
- QUALIFICATION + NOUN **course, programme** *a qualification programme in business management* | **period** *The job usually has a three-year qualification period.*
- PREP. **~ for** *the minimum entry qualification for admission* **~ in** *He held no formal qualification in law.*

2 weakening of a statement
- ADJ. **important**
- VERB + QUALIFICATION **add** | **need, require** *The term 'population' as used here requires qualification.*
- PREP. **with ~s** *I agree with his view, with a few qualifications.* **without ~** *The committee supported her proposal, without qualification.*

qualified *adj.*

1 having completed a course of study
- VERBS **be** | **become, get**
- ADV. **highly, well** *The teaching staff are all highly qualified.* | **fully, properly** *a fully qualified electrician* | **newly, recently** *newly qualified doctors* | **appropriately, duly, suitably** *Applications are invited from suitably qualified individuals.* | **sufficiently** | **legally, medically, professionally** *She is a professionally qualified social worker.*
- PREP. **as** *She is now qualified as a teacher.*

2 having the skill needed to do sth
- VERBS **be, feel** *Elaine did not feel qualified to comment.*
- ADV. **eminently, ideally, well** *My father was well qualified to act the part of a head teacher.*

3 limited in some way
- VERBS **be**
- ADV. **heavily** *The proposals received heavily qualified approval.*

qualify *verb*

1 have/give sb the right to sth
- ADV. **automatically**
- PREP. **for** *You will automatically qualify for a pension.*
- PHRASES **qualify on the grounds of sth** *people who qualify for the grant on the grounds of disability*

2 for a sports competition
- ADV. **easily** | **duly** *South Korea duly qualified for the finals when they beat Italy 6–1.*
- VERB + QUALIFY **fail to**
- PREP. **for** *England failed to qualify for the final.*

3 fit a description
- ADV. **hardly**
- PREP. **as** *A three-week course hardly qualifies as sufficient training.*

quality *noun*

1 how good/bad sth is
- ADJ. **excellent, good, high, outstanding, superior, top** *All our cakes are made with top quality ingredients.* |

inferior, low, poor | variable | product, service | recording, sound | air, water | artistic, technical
- VERB + QUALITY **maintain** | **enhance, improve, raise** | **affect, impair, reduce** | **assess, determine, evaluate, monitor, test**
- QUALITY + VERB **improve** | **suffer** *When costs are cut product quality suffers.*
- QUALITY + NOUN **control** | **assurance** | **standards**
- PREP. **of ... ~** *The photos are of variable quality.*
- PHRASES **quality of life** *Advances in technology would, it was hoped, improve the quality of life.*

2 characteristic
- ADJ. **admirable, desirable, fine, good, great, positive, valuable** | **negative** | **redeeming** *I found him thoroughly unpleasant, with no redeeming qualities whatsoever.* | **individual, personal** | **inborn, inherent, innate, intrinsic** | **distinctive, particular, special, unique** | **elusive, rare** *a singer with that elusive quality that sells records* | **essential, important** | **aesthetic, artistic, literary** | **moral** | **mental, psychological** | **feminine, masculine** | **leadership, managerial** | **aphrodisiac, medicinal**
- VERB + QUALITY **have** | **display, show**

quantity *noun*

- ADJ. **appreciable, considerable, enormous, fair, great, huge, large, massive, prodigious, sheer, substantial, vast** | **minute, modest, small** | **maximum, minimum** | **increasing** | **average** | **sufficient** *Gas was detected in sufficient quantity to warrant careful monitoring.*
- PREP. **in ~** *There is a discount for goods bought in quantity.* | **~ of** *A quantity of jewellery was taken during the burglary.*

quarantine *noun*

- ADJ. **strict**
- VERB + QUARANTINE **keep sb/sth in, put sb/sth in**
- QUARANTINE + NOUN **period** | **regulations**
- PREP. **in ~** *The animals are still in quarantine at the port.*

quarrel *noun*

- ADJ. **bitter, fierce, serious, violent** | **family, internal, lovers', private** | **long-standing, old**
- VERB + QUARREL **have** | **pick** *I don't want to pick a quarrel with her.* | **be/become/get involved in** | **make up, patch up, settle**
- QUARREL + VERB **break out, ensue**
- PREP. **about** *a quarrel about money* **~ between** *a quarrel between family members* **~ over** *a quarrel over the ownership of a piece of land* **~ with** *Our quarrel is not with the people, but with their leader.*
- PHRASES **have no quarrel with sb/sth** *We have no quarrel with their plans, in fact we support them.*

quarrel *verb*

- ADV. **bitterly, fiercely, violently**
- PREP. **about, over** *What did you two quarrel about?* **with** *He wished he hadn't quarrelled with Tania.*

quarter *noun*

1 one of four equal parts into which sth is divided
- VERB + QUARTER **break/cut/divide/fold sth into ~s**
- PREP. **~ of** *a quarter of a century/mile/million* ◇ *a quarter of an hour* ◇ *a quarter of all potential customers*

2 period of three months
- ADJ. **first, second, third, fourth/last** *Profits fell during the third quarter.* | **current, previous**
- PREP. **during the ~**

3 part of a town
- ADJ. **old** | **Arab, Chinese, Latin,** etc. | **diplomatic, historic, industrial, residential**

4 quarters place to live in
- ADJ. **comfortable, spacious** | **confined, cramped, modest** | **private** *the president's private quarters* | **living, sleeping** | **officers', servants', soldiers'** | **married** *The corporal and his family lived in married quarters.*
- VERB + QUARTERS **be confined to** *He was confined to quarters as a punishment.*

queen *noun*

1 female ruler/wife of a king
- ADJ. **rightful** | **crowned** | **future**
- VERB + QUEEN **become** | **crown (sb), make sb, proclaim sb** *She was crowned queen at the age of fifteen.* | **depose, put aside**
- QUEEN + VERB **reign, rule, rule (over) sb/sth** | **abdicate** *the queen's decision to abdicate*
- PREP. **under a/the ~** *England under Queen Elizabeth I* | **~ of** *the Queen of France*
- PHRASES **queen consort** (= the wife of a king)

2 playing card
⇨ Note at CARD

query *noun*

- VERB + QUERY **have** *If you have any queries regarding this offer, simply call our helpline.* | **raise** | **send in, write in with** | **put** *I've a query to put to the last speaker.* | **answer, deal with, reply to, respond to**
- PREP. **~ about/as to/concerning/on/regarding/relating to** *Have you any queries about what you're supposed to do?* ◇ *We regret that we cannot deal with queries on individual cases.* **~ from** *We had queries from people all over the country.*

quest *noun*

- ADJ. **continuing, endless, eternal, relentless** | **religious, spiritual**
- VERB + QUEST **begin, embark on, go on, set off on** | **continue, pursue** *The team will continue its quest for Olympic gold this afternoon.* | **abandon**
- QUEST + VERB **end** *It is possible that his quest will end in Geneva.*
- PREP. **in a/the ~** *an important stage in their quest for truth* **in ~ of** *We set off in quest of the perfect wedding dress.* | **~ for** *her quest for a better life*

question *noun*

1 sentence, etc. that asks sth
- ADJ. **pointed, probing, searching** *He became embarrassed when a journalist asked him pointed questions about his finances.* | **awkward, difficult, embarrassing, tricky** | **personal** | **academic, hypothetical, rhetorical** | **leading, loaded** *The judge told him not to ask the witness leading questions.* | **good, pertinent, relevant** | **simple** | **daft, inane, silly, stupid** | **direct, straight** *I wanted to find out how old he was without asking him a direct question.* | **exam, multiple choice, quiz, test**
- VERB + QUESTION **ask (sb)** | **have** *Have any of the audience got questions for our speaker?* | **address, put** *I'd like to put a question to the first speaker.* | **bombard sb with, fire** *The children bombarded us with questions.* ◇ *The interview panel fired questions at me from all angles.* | **frame, phrase** *I need to phrase my question rather carefully.* | **face** | **answer, reply to, respond to** | **do** (used only about written questions) *I couldn't do Question 6.* | **field** *The chairperson fielded technical questions that she could not answer herself.* | **evade, parry** *He skilfully parried all the interviewer's most probing questions.*
- PREP. **~ about** *She refused to answer questions about her private life.* **~ as to** *Don't be afraid to ask questions as to why things are done in the way they are.* **~ concerning/regarding/relating to** *The former minister faced questions concerning his role in the affair.*

2 issue
- ADJ. **burning, challenging, controversial, difficult, unanswerable, vexed** *We come now to the vexed question of pension rights.* | **crucial, fundamental, important, key** | **delicate, sensitive** | **economic, ethical, political,** etc.
- VERB + QUESTION **bring up, pose, raise** *The new play poses some challenging questions.* | **consider, discuss, examine** | **address, deal with, face, tackle** | **answer, decide, find a solution to** | **come to**
- QUESTION + VERB **arise** | **remain unanswered** *Only one question remains unanswered.*
- PREP. **~ about** *fundamental questions about the nature of our society* **~ for** *one of the crucial questions for the jury* **~ of** *questions of national security* ◇ *Now it's just a question of getting the wording of the statement right.*

3 doubt
- VERB + QUESTION **come into** | **call into** *It does call into question the decision to send troops into the area.* | **be open to** *The government's handling of the whole affair remains open to question.*
- PREP. **beyond ~** *Her loyalty is beyond question.* **in ~** *His sincerity is not in question.* **without ~** *It was, without question, the worst day of my life.* | **~ about** *There is no question about her enthusiasm for the job.* **~ as to** *I did have some questions as to his motive in coming.*

question *verb*

- ADV. **closely, further**
- PREP. **about** *She was closely questioned about her whereabouts on the night of the murder.* **in connection with** *A man is being questioned in connection with the robbery.* **on** *He was questioned on his role in the affair.*

questionable *adj.*

- VERBS **be** | **become** | **remain**
- ADV. **highly, very** *Their motives for undertaking this study are highly questionable.* | **rather, somewhat**

questioning *noun*

- ADJ. **careful, close** | **direct** *She decided to confront her boss about the situation with direct questioning.* | **intensive** | **hostile, tough** | **gentle** | **fundamental**
- VERB + QUESTIONING **face** | **be wanted for** | **be detained for, be held for** *Four suspects have been detained for questioning in connection with the incident.*
- PREP. **on ~** *On closer questioning, I discovered that his whole story had been a lie.* **under ~** *The suspect remained silent under questioning.* | **~ about/on/over** *The prime minister faced tough questioning about his plans.* **~ by** *The man was released after questioning by detectives.* **~ from** *The group chairman faced hostile questioning from angry shareholders.*

question mark *noun*

- ADJ. **big, huge, serious**
- VERB + QUESTION MARK **put** *His arrival clearly puts a huge question mark against the future of the present team captain.*
- QUESTION MARK + VERB **hang over sth, remain** *A big question mark hangs over the wisdom of the move.*
- PREP. **~ against** *A slight question mark against her character remains.* **~ over** *There is now a serious question mark over his leadership ability.*

questionnaire noun

- ADJ. **short, simple** | **detailed, lengthy** | **postal**
- VERB + QUESTIONNAIRE **design, draw up, prepare** | **circulate, distribute, send (out)** | **receive** | **complete, fill in/out** | **reply to, respond to, return, send in** *Most of the staff who responded to the questionnaire were supportive.* | **analyse** *The college is now analysing thousands of questionnaires.*
- PREP. **~about** *Local companies were asked to complete a questionnaire about their exports.* **~concerning** *questionnaires concerning people's leisure preferences* **~on** *a questionnaire on the environment*

queue noun

- ADJ. **endless, long** | **growing, lengthening** | **orderly** *Please form an orderly queue.* | **bus, checkout, cinema, etc.** | **bread, dinner, food** *the country's soaring prices and growing food queues* | **traffic** | **dole** *More unemployed people are joining the dole queue each week.*
- VERB + QUEUE **form, line up in** | **join, stand in, wait in** *He had to join the queue for the toilets.* | **jump** *Don't jump the queue—take your turn like everyone else!*
- QUEUE + VERB **form** | **build up, grow** *Long queues are building up on most of Britain's motorways.* | **move** *The queue's not moving at all.* | **stretch** *The queue stretched for more than a mile.*
- PREP. **in a/the~** *the people in the queue* | **~for** *the queue for tickets* **~of** *a long queue of shoppers*
- PHRASES **the back/end of the queue, the front/head of the queue**

queue verb

- ADV. **patiently** | **up** *People queued up outside.*
- VERB + QUEUE **have to**
- PREP. **for** *We had to queue for tickets.*

quick adj.

- VERBS **be, seem** *We'd better be quick.* | **become, get**
- ADV. **extremely, particularly, really, very** *a really quick worker* | **fairly, pretty, quite, reasonably, relatively** | **amazingly, remarkably, surprisingly** | **mercifully** *It was a mercifully quick end for those condemned to die.*
- PREP. **at** *I was getting quite quick at putting up fences.*
- PHRASES **quick and easy** *meals that are quick and easy to prepare*

quiet noun

- ADJ. **comparative, relative** *a period of comparative quiet* | **sudden**
- VERB + QUIET **call for** *A man's voice was calling for quiet.* | **shatter** *A machine gun shattered the quiet.*
- QUIET + VERB **follow** *in the sudden quiet that followed the gunshot*
- PHRASES **peace and quiet** *I'm going home for a bit of peace and quiet!* **a place/time of quiet** *She made sure she had times of quiet in which to write.*

quiet adj.

1 with little or no noise; not talking
- VERBS **be** | **become, fall, go, grow** | **lie, keep, remain, sit, stay** *Just sit quiet for a moment, there's a good boy.* | **keep sb/sth** *Keep that dog quiet, will you!*
- ADV. **all, extraordinarily, extremely, really, remarkably, unusually, very** *Suddenly the room went all quiet.* | **absolutely, completely, perfectly** | **fairly, pretty, rather** | **enough** | **blissfully** | **deathly, eerily** *The house was eerily quiet.* | **dangerously, ominously** *His voice was dangerously quiet as he asked the question.* | **oddly, strangely, unnaturally** *She went back to a strangely quiet house.* | **uncharacteristically**

- PREP. **about** *I knew I had to keep quiet about it.*
- PHRASES **nice (and) quiet** *I was looking forward to a nice quiet afternoon.*

2 without much activity
- VERBS **be, look, seem** | **become** | **lie, remain, sit** *Lie quiet for an hour and you'll feel better.* | **keep sb/sth** *Keep the patient as quiet as possible.*
- ADV. **extremely, very** | **comparatively, fairly, pretty, quite, rather, reasonably, relatively** | **enough** *Things seemed quiet enough, but it was an uneasy calm.*

quirk noun

- ADJ. **curious, odd, peculiar, strange** | **little**
- VERB + QUIRK **have** *The system has some odd little quirks.*
- PREP. **by a~of** *By a strange quirk of fate, she later married the first boyfriend she'd ever had.* | **~in** *as a result of some quirk in the social order*
- PHRASES **a quirk of fate**

quit verb

- VERB + QUIT **try to** *I'm still trying to quit smoking.* | **decide to** | **threaten to** | **be forced to, have to**
- PREP. **as** *He was forced to quit as the team's manager.* **over** *Their longest-serving employee is threatening to quit over pay.*
- PHRASES **give/issue notice to quit** *Landlords are normally required to give 28 days' written notice to quit.*

quiz noun

- ADJ. **film, general knowledge, sports, etc.**
- VERB + QUIZ **compile** | **hold, organize** | **enter, take part in** | **win**
- QUIZ + NOUN **competition, game, programme, show** | **evening, night** *The pub has a quiz night every Wednesday.* | **question**
- PREP. **~about** *a quiz about the week's news*

quota noun

- ADJ. **full** *He never takes his full quota of holidays.* | **annual, daily, monthly, weekly** | **national** | **fishing, milk, etc.** *the introduction of EU milk quotas* | **export, import, production**
- VERB + QUOTA **agree, determine, establish, set** | **allocate, impose, introduce** | **increase** | **reduce** | **achieve, fill, fulfil, reach** *We had to increase our output to fill the quota by the end of the year.* | **exceed** *Many countries are still exceeding their quotas.*
- QUOTA + NOUN **system**
- PREP. **~for** *quotas for oil production* **~on** *national quotas on imports of cars*

quotation noun

1 words taken from a book, etc.
- ADJ. **famous, memorable** | **direct, verbatim** *a direct quotation from a recent speech by the prime minister* | **illustrative** | **biblical**
- VERB + QUOTATION **take** *My quotation is taken from 'Hamlet'.*
- QUOTATION + VERB **come from sth** *Where does that quotation come from?*
- QUOTATION + NOUN **dictionary**
- PREP. **~from** *It's a quotation from a poem by Keats.*

2 price that will be charged for a piece of work
- ADJ. **written** | **free** | **detailed**
- VERB + QUOTATION **give (sb), provide (sb with), supply (sb with)** *Most builders will give you a free quotation.* | **get, obtain** | **accept**
- PREP. **~for** *Always get several quotations for the job.*

quote *noun*

1 words taken from a book, etc.

● ADJ. **famous, memorable, quotable | direct, verbatim** *a direct quote from this morning's paper*

● VERB + QUOTE **take** *quotes taken from various lifestyle magazines*

● QUOTE + VERB **come from sth** *The quote of the week comes from Mae West.*

● PREP. **~ from** *a quote from Albert Einstein*

2 price that will be charged for a piece of work

● ADJ. **written | free**

● VERB + QUOTE **give (sb) | get, obtain** *Always get a written quote before proceeding with work.* **| accept**

● PREP. **~ for** *a quote for the hire of the equipment*

quote *verb*

1 repeat exactly what sb has said/written

● ADV. **at length, extensively** *She quotes extensively from the author's diaries.* **| in full** *The passage is quoted in full.* **| accurately, exactly | directly | approvingly, with approval | above, below, earlier, here, previously** *The new text of Article 92, quoted above, gives member states more discretion on this issue.*

● PREP. **as** *She is wrongly quoted as saying 'Play it again, Sam.'* **from** *quoting from Shakespeare/'Hamlet'*

2 give sth as an example

● ADV. **frequently, often**

● PREP. **as** *an example that is often quoted as evidence of mismanagement* **on** *Don't quote me on this but I think the figure is in excess of £2 billion.*

● PHRASES **widely quoted** *the most widely quoted and influential study in this field*

Rr

rabbit noun

- VERB + RABBIT **hunt, shoot, trap** | **skin**
- RABBIT + VERB **hop, jump** | **bolt, run** *A frightened rabbit will bolt for its hole.* | **breed** *Rabbits breed very fast.*
- RABBIT + NOUN **fur, skin** | **burrow, hole, hutch, warren** *(often figurative) The building was a real rabbit warren of corridors.*

race noun

1 contest to find the fastest person, car, etc.
- ADJ. **big** *I get very nervous before a big race.* | **close, tight** | **long-distance** | **10-kilometre, 24-hour, 7-lap,** etc. | **gruelling, hard, tough** | **relay, road** | **men's, women's** | **boat, motor, motorbike, yacht,** etc. | **dog, horse,** etc. | **Grand Prix, World Cup,** etc.
- VERB + RACE **have, hold, organize, stage** *Let's have a race!* | **be in, compete in, enter, go in for, run in, take part in** *Is she running in the big race on Saturday?* | **drop out of, pull out of, withdraw (sth) from** *He dropped out of the race with a pulled muscle after two laps.* ◊ *She had to pull out of the race at the last minute.* | **lead, win** *I was leading the race until the half-way point.* ◊ *She has won the race for the last five years.* | **lose** | **come first/second,** etc. in | **beat sb/sth in** | **fix** *There is a rumour that the race was fixed.* | **throw** (= to lose deliberately) *He was paid £1 000 to throw the race.*
- RACE + VERB **be run/held, take place**
- RACE + NOUN **meeting** *The horse was withdrawn from today's race meeting with an injured leg.* | **winner** | **official, organizer**
- PREP. **in a/the ~** *I'm not in this race.* | **~ against/with** *the race against the Danish team* **~ between** *the University Boat Race between Oxford and Cambridge* **~ over** *a race over 200 metres*

2 competitive situation
- ADJ. **two-horse** *Although there are five candidates, realistically it is a two-horse race.* | **presidential** | **arms** *the halting of the nuclear arms race*
- VERB + RACE **be (involved) in, join** *The rival TV companies are in a race to bring out the first film drama of his life.* | **be ahead in, lead, win** *Who will win the race for the White House?* | **be left behind in, lag behind in, lose**
- PREP. **in a/the ~** *lagging behind in the race for the presidency* | **~ between** *a race between the developing countries* **~ for** *the race for nuclear supremacy* **~ with** *the race with their rivals*

3 racial group
- ADJ. **human** | **mixed** *a child of mixed race* | **Irish, Jewish, Latin,** etc. | **master** *the ideology of the master race*
- RACE + NOUN **relations** *Immigration and race relations were key political issues at the time.* | **equality** | **discrimination, prejudice** | **riot**
- PREP. **among ~s** *The disease is more common among European races.* **between ~s** *greater understanding between nations and races* **from a ~** *children from all races and religions* **of a ~** *people of different races and cultures* | **~ of** *The Amazons were a race of female warriors.*
- PHRASES **on (the) grounds of race** *discriminating against people on the grounds of race*

race verb

- ADV. **frantically, madly** *She raced frantically towards the train.* | **ahead, away, back, by, downstairs, off, out, past, upstairs** *Farms and villages raced by.*
- PREP. **across, after, along, around/round, down, for, into, out of, through, to, towards, up** *He raced madly up the stairs.*
- PHRASES **come racing** *Two boys suddenly came racing round the corner.*

racing noun

1 sport of racing horses
- ADJ. **horse** | **flat, jump**
- RACING + NOUN **results** | **tip** | **expert, tipster** *Her racing tipster got the Derby winner right.* | **manager, owner, trainer** | **career** | **stable** | **trophy** | **calendar, programme, season** *He organizes his life according to the racing calendar.* | **business, game, industry** *He has ridden horses all his life, but he was a late starter in the racing game.* | **circles, scene** *He's known in racing circles as a fierce competitor.* ◊ *She's a familiar face on the racing scene.* | **correspondent** *the racing correspondent of 'The Times'*

2 sport of taking part in races
- ADJ. **competitive, top-level** *Today's cross-country event marks his return to top-level racing.* | **bike, dog, motor, yacht,** etc. | **Grand Prix** | **road, track**
- RACING + NOUN **champion** | **legend, star** *racing legend Ayrton Senna* | **cyclist, driver** | **team** | **programme, season** | **scene** | **career, days** | **debut** *He made his racing debut for Benetton three years ago.* | **car** | **circuit** *The bikes sped by on the racing circuit.* | **enthusiast, fan**

racism noun

- ADJ. **blatant, overt** *I was shocked by the blatant racism of his remarks.* | **rampant** *Racism is rampant in the armed forces.* | **institutional, institutionalized**
- VERB + RACISM **be a victim of, experience** *Many immigrants have experienced racism.* | **combat, fight (against), stamp out** *measures to combat racism*
- PREP. **against ~** *the fight against racism*
- PHRASES **a form of racism**

rack noun

- ADJ. **display, storage** | **cooling, drying** | **letter, luggage, magazine, plate, spice, toast, vegetable, wine,** etc. | **roof** *We fixed the canoe onto the car's roof rack.*
- VERB + RACK **hang sth on, put sth on/onto/in/into, stack sth in/on, store sth in/on** *The wine is stored in special racks.*
- RACK + VERB **contain sth, hold sth** *The racks along the wall held most of the costumes.*
- PREP. **in a/the ~** *He replaced the CD in the rack.* **on a/the ~** *Spread the flowers out to dry on a rack.* | **~ for** *a rack for storing apples* **~ of** *racks of magazines*

racket noun

1 noise
- ADJ. **appalling, frightful, hellish, terrible**
- VERB + RACKET **make** *Do you kids have to make such a terrible racket?*
- PREP. **above/over the ~** *He had to shout over the racket.*

2 illegal way of making money
- ADJ. **drugs, extortion, protection, smuggling**
- VERB + RACKET **set up** *He set up a protection racket and demanded thousands of pounds from local shopkeepers.* | **control, operate, run** | **be involved in**

• PREP. **in a/the~** *the other people in this racket* | **~in** *a racket in stolen goods*

radar *noun*

• ADJ. **enemy, police**
• VERB + RADAR **be equipped with**
• RADAR + NOUN **operator** | **screen** | **beam, signal** | **equipment, scanner, station, system, transmitter**
• PREP. **by~** *navigating by radar* **on~** *The submarine is impossible to detect on radar.*

radiation *noun*

• ADJ. **background** | **low-level** | **harmful** | **electromagnetic, gravitational, infrared, microwave, nuclear, solar, thermal, ultraviolet**
• QUANT. **dose** *Patients receive high doses of radiation during cancer treatment.*
• VERB + RADIATION **emit, give off** | **absorb** *The ozone layer absorbs solar radiation.* | **measure, monitor** | **expose sb to** *Nuclear testing has exposed millions of people to radiation.*
• RADIATION + NOUN **sickness** | **leak** | **dose, level** | **exposure** | **therapy**
• PREP. **~from** *radiation from computer screens*

radiator *noun*

1 equipment used for heating a room
• ADJ. **central heating, convector, storage**
• VERB + RADIATOR **turn off/on** | **bleed** *You'll need to bleed the radiators to remove the airlocks.*
• RADIATOR + VERB **leak**
• RADIATOR + NOUN **key, valve**
2 equipment for keeping an engine cool
• ADJ. **car**
• VERB + RADIATOR **top up** *Top up the radiator before making a long journey.*
• RADIATOR + NOUN **grille**

radical *adj.*

• VERBS **be, seem, sound** | **become**
• ADV. **really, very** | **increasingly** | **fairly, quite, somewhat** | **genuinely, truly** *a truly radical concept* | **apparently** | **potentially** | **politically, socially**

radio *noun*

• ADJ. **cab, car** *There were calls for cab radios to link train drivers and signal boxes.* | **CB, mobile, portable, transistor, two-way** | **FM, long-wave, short-wave** | **army, police** | **community, local, national, state**
• VERB + RADIO **listen to** | **turn on, tune in to** | **tune** *His radio is permanently tuned to Radio 1.* | **turn down/up**
• RADIO + VERB **announce sth, report sth** *The radio announced that the president had been assassinated.* | **blare (out), play (sth)** *He drove along with his windows open and the radio blaring out.*
• RADIO + NOUN **receiver, set** | **alarm, cassette (player)** | **message, signal, waves** | **operator** | **system** | **transmitter** | **silence** *The troops maintained a strict radio silence while they moved into position.* | **station** | **advertisement, broadcast, interview, news, programme, report, show, transmission** | **frequency** | **amateur, ham** *The distress call was picked up by a young radio ham.* | **drama, play**
• PREP. **by~** *The message was sent by radio.* **on the~** *We were listening to a show on the radio.*

radioactive *adj.*

• VERBS **be** | **become** | **remain**
• ADV. **dangerously, highly** | **slightly**

radioactivity *noun*

• QUANT. **level** *The soil contains 30 times the acceptable level of radioactivity.*
• VERB + RADIOACTIVITY **discharge, produce, release** | **measure, monitor**
• RADIOACTIVITY + VERB **be present** | **escape, leak** | **contaminate sth** *The site was found to be contaminated by radioactivity.*
• RADIOACTIVITY + NOUN **levels**

raffle *noun*

• ADJ. **charity**
• VERB + RAFFLE **have, hold, organize, run** | **enter** | **win** | **draw** *The club secretary will now draw the raffle.*
• RAFFLE + NOUN **ticket** *the winning raffle ticket* | **prize**
• PREP. **in a/the~** *I won a bottle of wine in the office Christmas raffle.* | **~ for** *He's organizing a raffle for the school playground appeal fund.*

raft *noun*

• ADJ. **life**
• VERB + RAFT **build, make** *They built a raft of logs.*
• RAFT + VERB **bob, float, sail** *The raft floated away down the river.* | **capsize, overturn**
• RAFT + NOUN **race, racing**
• PREP. **on/onto a/the~** *floating on a raft*

rag *noun*

• ADJ. **clean** | **dirty, filthy, oily, old** | **bloodstained**
• QUANT. **bundle, heap, pile** *He noticed what looked like a bundle of rags beside the road.*
• VERB + RAG **wipe sth (off) with** | **be wrapped in** *The gun was wrapped in a dirty rag.*
• PREP. **on a/the~** *He wiped his hands on an oily rag.* **with a~** *I cleaned the board with an old rag.*

rage *noun*

1 great anger
• ADJ. **blind, cold, icy, pure** | **helpless, impotent** *burning with impotent rage* | **pent-up, suppressed**
• QUANT. **fit, burst** *He punched the wall in a fit of rage.*
• VERB + RAGE **be** | **beside yourself with, be boiling/burning with, be choked with, be filled with, be full of, be purple/red/white with, be rigid/stiff with, be shaking/trembling with, feel, seethe with** *He glared at me, quite beside himself with rage.* ◇ *'How dare you!' she said, her voice choked with rage.* | **vent** *The people vented their rage on government buildings.* | **control, master** *He managed to master his rage.*
• RAGE + VERB **build up** *She felt the rage building up inside her.* | **erupt** *His rage suddenly erupted.* | **subside** *His rage was beginning to subside.*
• PREP. **with ~** *She was speechless with rage.* | **~ at** *boiling with rage at the unfairness of it all*
• PHRASES **a bellow/cry/roar/shout of rage** *He gave a roar of rage and punched me in the face.* **tears of rage**
2 sudden display of great anger
• ADJ. **blind, terrible, towering** | **jealous** | **drunken** *She smashed up his car in a drunken rage.*
• VERB + RAGE **be in, fly into, get in** *If something's too difficult she gets in a rage.*
• PREP. **in a ~** *She killed him in a rage of despair.* | **~ about** *He was in a towering rage about his lost watch.* **~ at** *He flew into a rage at the insult.* **~ of** *He left in a rage of humiliation.*

rage *verb*

1 show great anger
• ADV. **inwardly**

• PREP. **about** *She was still raging about the treatment she had received.* **against** *I raged inwardly against his injustice.* **at** *The team was left raging at the referee's decision.*

2 continue with great force
• ADV. **still, on** *The argument still rages on.*
• PREP. **around** *Even the dogs were quiet while the heated quarrel raged around them.* **within** *trying to control the fury raging within her*
• PHRASES **rage unabated** *The storm raged unabated.*

raid *noun*

1 surprise attack
• ADJ. **daring** | **destructive, heavy, major** | **punitive, retaliatory, revenge** | **dawn, daylight, night** | **border, cross-border** | **air, bombing** | **commando, guerrilla**
• VERB + RAID **carry out, conduct, make** *bombers carrying out daylight raids over northern France* | **launch, mount, stage** | **lead sb in** | **suffer**
• PREP. **during/in a/the ~** *Five civilians died in the raid.* **on a/the ~** *He led his men on a cross-border raid.* | **~ against** *The raids against Norway continued.* **~ by** *The town suffered several raids by Vikings.* **~ on** *air raids on Liverpool*

2 robbery from a building
• ADJ. **bank, post office, shop** | **armed, smash-and-grab** | **dawn, daylight, night** | **daring**
• VERB + RAID **plan** | **carry out** | **foil** *Two customers have foiled a smash-and-grab raid on a local shop.*
• PREP. **during/in a/the ~** *the jewels stolen in the raid* | **~ on** *She was shot during an armed raid on a security van.*

3 surprise visit by the police
• ADJ. **dawn, early morning** | **police** | **drug/drugs**
• VERB + RAID **carry out, launch, stage** *Police staged an early morning raid on the premises.*
• PREP. **during a/the ~** *He was injured during a police raid on his nightclub.* **in a/the ~** *the drugs seized in last night's raid* | **~ by** *a raid by drugs squad detectives* **~ on** *raids on houses in Catholic areas of the city*

rail *noun*

1 bar
• ADJ. **guard, safety** | **curtain, picture, towel** *heated towel rails* | **altar, balcony, banister**
• VERB + RAIL **grip, hold on to, lean on** *She held tightly on to the rail.* | **hang from** *Lace curtains hung from the brass rails over the bed.* | **fit, fix**
• PREP. **on a/the ~** *She sat on the rail.* **over a/the ~** *He folded the towel over the rail.*

2 (usually **rails**) tracks
• VERB + RAIL **run along/on ~s** *Trams run along rails.*
• PREP. **along (the) ~s** *The train thundered along the rails.* **between the ~** *Weeds grew between the rails.* **off the ~s** *The train came off the rails.* **on (the) ~s** *The gun is mounted on rails.*

3 railway system
• RAIL + NOUN **fare, ticket** | **network** *modernizing the rail network* | **route** | **timetable** | **service** | **connection, line, link** *the Channel Tunnel rail link* | **journey** | **commuter, passenger, traveller, user** | **transport, travel** | **traffic** | **freight** | **bridge** | **accident, crash, disaster** | **employee, staff, worker** | **union** | **enthusiast**
• PREP. **by ~** *We went from London to Budapest by rail.*

railway *noun*

• ADJ. **mainline** | **high-speed** | **disused** | **narrow gauge, standard gauge** | **miniature** *A miniature railway runs around the park.* | **model** | **funicular, overhead** *Tourists can take the funicular railway to the top of the mountain.* | **private, regional, state** | **electric, steam**
• VERB + RAILWAY **manage, operate, run** | **nationalize, privatize** | **build, construct** | **close, open**

• RAILWAY + VERB **run** | **carry sth** *The railways carry millions of tons of freight every year.*
• RAILWAY + NOUN **carriage, coach, train, wagon** | **station, terminus** | **platform** | **ticket** | **ticket office** | **timetable** | **service** | **connection** | **journey, travel** *the pleasures of railway travel* | **passenger, traveller** | **employee, porter, staff, worker** | **architect, engineer** | **authorities, company** | **network, system** | **line, track** | **junction, sidings** | **bridge, tunnel, viaduct** | **enthusiast** *He is a lifelong railway enthusiast.* | **accident** | **age** *Such speed of travel was unimaginable before the railway age.*
• PREP. **on a/the ~** *doing maintenance work on the railway* ◇ *He works on the railways.* | **~ between** *the railway between Funchal and Monte* **~ from, ~ to**

rain *noun*

• ADJ. **driving, heavy, lashing, pouring, torrential** | **steady** | **fine, gentle, light, patchy** *The fine rain turned to mist in the early evening.* ◇ *The forecast is for wind and patchy rain.* | **warm** | **cold** | **constant, continuous, persistent** | **intermittent** | **overnight** *Overnight rain had freshened up the garden.* | **monsoon, tropical** *The monsoon rains started early this year.* | **autumn, spring, etc.**
• QUANT. **drop, spot** *A few spots of rain had fallen.* | **inch, shower, spot** (*informal*) *We had three inches of rain last night.* ◇ *We could do with a spot of rain.*
• VERB + RAIN **forecast** *Rain is forecast for tomorrow.* | **look like, threaten** *It looks like rain* (= it looks as though it is going to rain). ◇ *Black clouds threatened rain.* | **pour with** *It poured with rain all afternoon.* | **get caught in** *We got caught in the rain on the way home.*
• RAIN + VERB **beat, come down, drip, drum, fall, lash, patter, pelt, pour down, splash, trickle** *Rain beat against the window all night.* ◇ *Rain dripped down his collar.* | **come, set in, start** *The rain came just as we set off.* ◇ *The rain had set in steadily by the time we got home.* | **cease, let up, stop** *The rain didn't let up all day.* | **continue** *The rain continued for most of the day.* | **threaten** *With rain threatening, we headed home as fast as we could.* | **drive sb** *The rain drove the players off the court.*
• RAIN + NOUN **cloud, water**
• PREP. **in the ~** *We found her sitting in the pouring rain.* **out of the ~** *Come in out of the rain.* **through the ~** *We drove slowly through the driving rain.*

rain *verb*

• ADV. **hard, heavily** | **a little, slightly** | **incessantly, non-stop, solidly, steadily** *It's been raining solidly for an hour now.* ◇ *It rained incessantly for the whole two weeks.*
• VERB + RAIN **begin to, start to** | **be going to** *I don't think it's going to rain.*
• PHRASES **start/stop raining**

rainfall *noun*

• ADJ. **abundant, excessive, heavy, high** *There have been heavy rainfalls this month.* | **low** | **moderate** | **normal** | **good, poor** *We need a good rainfall to save the crops.* | **annual** | **average** | **local** | **summer, winter**
• VERB + RAINFALL **have** *The area has a high annual rainfall.* | **measure** *Her work includes measuring the local rainfall.*

rally *noun*

1 political meeting
• ADJ. **big, huge, large, major, mass, massive** | **public** | **indoor, outdoor** *at a massive outdoor rally in Paris* | **campaign, election, political** | **opposition, protest** | **peace** | **anti-government, anti-war, etc.**
• VERB + RALLY **have, hold, stage** *The demonstrators marched to Trafalgar Square where they held a rally.* | **call for, organize, plan** | **attend, take part in** *About 5 000 people attended a rally calling for peace.* | **address,**

speak at | ban *The government closed the schools and banned all rallies.*
- RALLY + VERB **take place | break up, disperse, end** *The rally dispersed peacefully after six hours.* | **call for sth**
- PREP. **at a/the ~** *She spoke at a public rally in Hyde Park.* | **~ against** *a mass rally against the treaty* **~ for** *a rally for the winning candidate* **~ in support of** *a rally in support of the strike*

2 motor race
- ADJ. **club, international | motor, motorcycle**
- VERB + RALLY **hold, organize | compete in, enter | win**
- RALLY + NOUN **circuit | driver, driving**
- PREP. **on a/the ~** *He will join the team on the rally next week.*

3 in tennis
- ADJ. **long, short | exciting**
- VERB + RALLY **play | win | lose**

rally *verb*

- ADV. **around/round** *Neighbours rallied round and alerted the emergency services.*
- VERB + RALLY **try to** *The team captain vainly tried to rally his troops.*
- PREP. **around/round/behind** *She urged everyone to rally behind the president.* **to** *Friends rallied to her.*
- PHRASES **rally to sb's defence** *BBC leaders rallied to his defence.* **rally to sb's/the cause** *Friends and colleagues have rallied to her cause.*

ram *verb*

- ADV. **hard | deliberately**
- PREP. **into** *He deliberately rammed his truck into the back of the one in front.*

ramble *noun*

- ADJ. **country, nature**
- VERB + RAMBLE **go for/on** *We went for a ramble over the moors.*
- PREP. **on a ~** *The family made the amazing find while on a nature ramble in the woods.*

random *adj.*

- VERBS **be, seem**
- ADV. **completely, entirely, purely, quite, totally | almost | fairly | truly | apparently, seemingly** *a seemingly random sequence of numbers*

range *noun*

1 different things within the same category
- ADJ. **broad, enormous, extensive, great, huge, large, vast, wide | complete, comprehensive, full, whole | infinite | excellent, exciting, good, superb | astonishing, extraordinary, impressive, remarkable | diverse** *people from a diverse range of backgrounds* **| acceptable | limited, poor | new** *Come and see our new range of furniture.* **| product** *For more information about our product range, call your local branch.*
- VERB + RANGE **have, stock** *They stock a very wide range of garden products.* **| make, produce | offer (sb), provide (sb with), supply (sb with)** *We provide a full range of financial services.* **| choose (sth) from, try out** *Students can choose from a wide range of options.* **| create, develop, launch** *The company is launching a new range of cosmetics.* **| expand, extend**
- RANGE + VERB **include sth** *Our comprehensive range of benefits includes pension and health insurance.*
- PREP. **in a/the ~** *the other models in their new range*
- PHRASES **bottom/middle/top of the range** *This is a top of the range refrigerator.*

2 amount between particular limits
- ADJ. **broad, wide | narrow | normal | ability, age, price, size, temperature, etc.**
- VERB + RANGE **cover, encompass, feature, include** *The trade show will feature an enormous range of goods.* **| extend, increase** *trying to extend the range of children's language*
- PREP. **across a/the ~** *There is considerable variation in ability across the range.* **in a/the ~** *Most of the students are in the age range 17–21.* **outside a/the ~** *No, that's completely outside my price range.* **within a/the ~** *The level of mistakes is within the acceptable range of standards for a public organization.* **| ~ of** *a broad range of abilities*

3 distance that it is possible to travel, see, etc.
- ADJ. **long** *missiles effective over a long range* **| close, point-blank, short** *He shot her at point-blank range.*
- PREP. **beyond ~** *This car is beyond the range of most people's pockets.* **in/within ~** *Are we within range of the local transmitter?* **out of ~** *Don't shoot yet—he's still out of range.* **outside a/the ~** *It's outside my range of vision.*

range *verb*

- ADV. **enormously, widely**
- PREP. **across** *The opinions they expressed ranged right across the political spectrum.* **between** *The town's population ranged between 15 and 20 000.* **from, in** *The disease ranges widely in severity.* **over** *Her lecture ranged over a number of topics.* **through** *an array of lilies, ranging through yellow to sombre purple* **to** *selling them at prices ranging from about $10 to $500.* **up to** *Their ages range up to 84.*

> **NOTE**
> ### Ranks in the armed forces
>
> **air force, army, navy ~**
>   *an air force/army sergeant*
>   *an army/navy captain*
> **air/field marshal**
> a **naval** captain/commander/lieutenant/officer
> **have/hold the rank of, serve as ~**
>   *She joined the navy and held the rank of captain.*
>   *He served as a lieutenant in the marine corps.*
> **be appointed, become, be made ~**
>   *He was made a colonel at the age of 40.*
>   *She ought to have been made sergeant by now.*
> **under ~**
>   *383 men under General Miles attacked the camp.*
> **the rank of ~**
>   *She was promoted to the rank of colonel.*

rank *noun*

1 level of importance
- ADJ. **high, senior, superior, upper | middle | inferior, junior, low** *the lowest ranks of the aristocracy* **| first, second** *He is in the first rank of university teachers.* **| social | Cabinet, ministerial** *a government minister of Cabinet rank*
- VERB + RANK **achieve, attain, be promoted to, get to, reach, rise to** *She joined the navy, where she rose to the rank of captain.* **| have, hold** *He held officer rank in the air force for many years.* **| be stripped of** *He was stripped of his rank by a military court.*
- PREP. **above a/the ~** *He never rose above the rank of lieutenant.* **below a/the ~** *police officers below the rank of sergeant* **in ~** *He is higher in rank than I am.* **| ~ in** *all ranks in society* **~ of** *She reached the rank of captain.*
- PHRASES **of high/low, etc. rank** *officers of senior rank*

2 group/line of things/people
- ADJ. **front, rear | massed, serried** *the serried ranks of hotel staff*

● PREP. **along a/the~** *The president moved slowly along the ranks of men.* **in a/the~** *standing in the second rank* ◇ *The soldiers marched in three ranks of ten.*
● PHRASES **break ranks** (= to leave a line of soldiers, police, etc.) *The police broke ranks and started hitting people with their batons.* **rank on/upon rank (of sth)** *Rank upon rank of caravans filled the field.*

3 (*also* **the ranks**) ordinary members of a large group
● VERB + RANK **be admitted into/to, enter, join, swell** *Each month thousands more swell the ranks of the unemployed.* | **serve in** *They had served in the ranks of the Sultan's army.* | **come up from/through, rise from/through** *He came up through the ranks to become a general.*
● PREP. **among/within the~s of** *There is much disaffection among the ranks of the party.* **beyond/outside the~s** *The group has little influence over those outside its own ranks.* **in the~s** *There are few women in the highest ranks of the organization.*

rank *verb*

● ADV. **high/highly, low** *These subjects ranked low for most students.*
● PREP. **above** *She ranks above any other musician of her generation.* **according to** *The children were ranked according to academic ability.* **alongside** *This city ranks alongside London as one of the great tourist centres of the world.* **among** *He ranks among the greatest boxers of all time.* **as** *Their performance ranks as the best of the year.* **below, with** *This ranks with the great paintings of the nineteenth century.*
● PHRASES **be ranked/rank number two, three, etc.** *the tennis player ranked number two in the world* **high-/low-ranking** *He is a high-ranking officer in the Indian Army.* **rank sth in order of sth** *ranked in order of size.* **rank in the top 10, 100, etc.** *She is now ranked in the top five hockey players in Britain.* **rank second, third, etc.** *The company ranks second among food manufacturers.*

ransom *noun*

● VERB + RANSOM **hold sb for/to, kidnap sb for** *She was kidnapped and held for ransom.* ◇ (*figurative*) *The company refused to be held to ransom by the union.* | **demand** | **pay**
● RANSOM + NOUN **demand, note** | **money, payment**
● PREP. **for~** *stealing cattle for ransom*

rap *verb*

● ADV. **sharply** *He rapped sharply on the door.* | **gently**
● PREP. **on, with** *rapping on the window with his stick*

rape *noun*

● ADJ. **alleged** | **attempted** | **marital** | **date, gang**
● RAPE + NOUN **victim**
⇨ Note at CRIME (for verbs)

rape *verb*

● ADV. **brutally, forcibly, savagely** *She was attacked and brutally raped.* | **repeatedly** | **allegedly**
● VERB + RAPE **attempt to, try to**
● PHRASES **be/get raped** *worried about getting raped on her way home* **be accused/convicted of raping sb, be charged with raping sb, be found guilty of raping sb, deny raping sb**

rapid *adj.*

● VERBS **be, seem** | **become**
● ADV. **exceptionally, extraordinarily, extremely, unusually, very** | **fairly, quite, relatively**

rapidity *noun*

● ADJ. **alarming, amazing, bewildering, extreme, great, remarkable** *The styles change with bewildering rapidity.* | **increasing**
● PREP. **with~**

rapist *noun*

● ADJ. **potential, would-be** | **convicted** | **multiple, serial** *The serial rapist has struck again.*
● RAPIST + VERB **attack (sb), strike**

rapport *noun*

● ADJ. **close, easy, good, great, tremendous** | **personal** | **instant**
● VERB + RAPPORT **build, develop, establish** | **enjoy, have** | **feel**
● PREP. **~between** *She felt an instant rapport between them* **~with** *He had enjoyed a personal rapport with the former president.*

rare *adj.*

● VERBS **be, seem** | **become, get** | **remain**
● ADV. **decidedly, distinctly, especially, exceedingly, exceptionally, extremely, particularly, surprisingly, very** | **increasingly** | **comparatively, fairly, pretty, quite, rather, relatively, somewhat** | **enough, sufficiently** *The stamps were not rare enough to be interesting.*

rash *noun*

● ADJ. **skin** | **itchy** | **allergic** | **heat, nappy, nettle**
● VERB + RASH **have** | **break out in, come out in** *When I'm stressed I break out in a rash.*
● RASH + VERB **appear, come out, spread** *The rash most commonly appears on the back.*
● PREP. **~on** *He's got a slight rash on his chest.*

raspberry *noun*

● QUANT. **punnet** *I bought a punnet of fresh raspberries.*
● RASPBERRY + NOUN **cane** *rows of raspberry canes*
⇨ Special page at FRUIT

rat *noun*

● ADJ. **black, brown** | **laboratory** | **sewer** | **water**
● RAT + VERB **scurry, scuttle** *A brown rat scurried across the road.* | **squeak** | **gnaw** *Rats had gnawed through the wires.* | **carry/spread disease**
● RAT + NOUN **catcher** *The dog was a useful rat catcher in the warehouse.* | **droppings** | **poison**
● PHRASES **rat-infested** *a rat-infested cellar*

rate *noun*

1 speed/frequency
● ADJ. **constant, expected, regular, steady** | **slow** *the slow rate of change* | **fast, rapid** | **alarming, phenomenal** *The costs of the project are rising at an alarming rate.* | **low** *There is a low survival rate among babies born before 22 weeks.* | **high** | **ever-increasing, rocketing** | **seasonally-adjusted** *The seasonally-adjusted unemployment rate in December stood at 5%.* | **success** | **divorce, marriage** | **death, mortality** | **survival** | **birth, fertility** | **accident** | **crime** | **growth, inflation** | **metabolic, pulse, respiratory** *We need to eat less as we get older and our metabolic rate slows down.*
● VERB + RATE **improve, increase, speed up** | **cut, hold down, reduce, slow down** *trying to hold down the rate of inflation* | **stabilize** | **maintain** | **increase**
● RATE + VERB **be/go/shoot up, grow, increase, rise, rocket, skyrocket, soar** | **be/come/go down, decline, decrease, drop, fall, plummet, plunge, slow, slip**

• PREP. **at a/the~** *The water was escaping at a rate of 200 gallons a minute.*

2 amount of money paid

• ADJ. **competitive, cheap, low, moderate, reasonable** *We have a wide range of vehicles available for hire at competitive rates.* ◇ *Calls are cheap rate after 6 p.m.* | **extortionate, high** | **excellent, good** | **poor** *The account offers a poor rate of interest.* | **fixed, flat** *You can opt to pay a flat rate for unlimited Internet access.* | **usual** | **going** *I'll pay you at the going rate* (= the present usual rate of payment). | **variable** | **annual, hourly, weekly** | **base, basic, standard** | **top** *paying the top rate of tax* | **average** | **market** *current market rates for borrowing* | **group, preferential, reduced** *Ask about the special group rates for entrance to the house and gardens.* | **bank, exchange, interest, lending, mortgage, tax**

• VERB + RATE **determine, fix, set** | **increase, lift, put up, raise** | **cut, lower, reduce** | **hold** *We will hold these rates until 1 April.* | **charge** *They charge the usual rate of interest.* | **pay** | **give (sb), offer (sb)**

• RATE + VERB **go/shoot up, increase, rise** *Their hourly rates have gone up.* | **come/go down, drop** | **fluctuate** *Exchange rates are fluctuating wildly.* | **apply to sth** *Standard rates of interest apply to these loans.*

• PREP. **at a/the ~** *borrowing money at a high rate of interest* | **~ for** *the average rate for an unskilled worker* **~ of** *an increase in the rate of taxation*

• PHRASES **a drop in interest rates, a rise in mortgage rates, etc.** *a one-point rise in base lending rates* **a rate of return** *safe investments which give a good rate of return* ⇨ Note at PER CENT (for more verbs)

rate *verb*

• ADV. **highly** *Silver was rated more highly than gold.*

• PREP. **among** *a golf course that is rated among the top ten in America* **as** *It is rated as one of the city's best hotels.* **for** *a university that is highly rated for its research work*

rating *noun*

1 measurement of how good sb/sth is

• ADJ. **high, top** | **low, poor** | **overall** *The overall performance rating puts the new model well ahead of its main rivals.* | **approval, opinion poll, popularity** *He has the highest opinion poll rating of any president this century.* | **performance** | **credit** *Most countries try to preserve their international credit rating in order to secure necessary loans.* | **personal**

• VERB + RATING **have** | **assign (sb/sth), give (sb/sth)** | **achieve, earn, get, receive, score** *The university scored a top rating among students.* | **preserve** | **improve**

• RATING + VERB **climb, improve, rise, rocket, soar** *The president's ratings have suddenly rocketed.* | **fall**

• RATING + NOUN **scale, system**

• PREP. **in a/the ~** *a drop of 50 points in her personal rating* | **~ for** *The resort got a low rating for children's facilities.* **~ on** *The judges gave her the maximum rating on style.*

2 ratings number of TV viewers, etc.

• ADJ. **good** | **poor** | **audience, TV**

• VERB + RATINGS **get, have** *At this stage the series was getting good ratings.*

• RATINGS + VERB **go up, improve, pick up, shoot up, soar** *The ratings went shooting up overnight.* | **dip, fall, go down** *The programme's ratings have dipped sharply.*

• RATINGS + NOUN **battle, war**

• PREP. **in the ~s** *It has been ousted from top spot in the TV ratings.*

ratio *noun*

• ADJ. **high, low** | **male/female, pupil/teacher, etc.** | **benefit-to-risk, power-to-weight, etc.**

• VERB + RATIO **achieve, have** *They have a high ratio of imports to exports.* | **improve, increase** *The hospital is trying to improve its staff/patient ratio.* | **reduce** | **calculate, find, work out**

• RATIO + VERB **improve** | **worsen** *the worsening pupil/teacher ratio in our schools*

• PREP. **in a/the ~** *We mixed the oil and water in a ratio of one to five.* | **~ between** *the ratio between the amount of time spent on the work and the profit produced* **~ of sth to sth** *the ratio of house prices to incomes*

• PHRASES **in direct ratio to sth** *Their sales rose in direct ration to the amount they spent on advertising.*

ration *noun*

• ADJ. **daily, monthly** | **double, entire, extra, full** *Pregnant women received a double ration of milk.* | **meagre** *The refugees queued up for their meagre rations of soup.* | **emergency, short, starvation, wartime ~s** *We've been put on short rations.* | **cigarette, food, petrol, etc.**

• VERB + RATION **give sb, hand out, provide (sb with)** | **get, receive** | **consume, have, use up** *You've had your ration of sweets for the day!* | **cut, reduce** *The guards are going to cut our rations again.*

• RATION + NOUN **book, card, coupon**

• PREP. **on a/the~** *living on starvation rations* | **~ of** *our daily ration of bread*

ration *verb*

• ADV. **strictly** *These foods had to be strictly rationed.*

• PREP. **to** *The soldiers were rationed to one litre of water each per day.*

rational *adj.*

• VERBS **be, seem** *It all seemed quite rational to me.*

• ADV. **highly, very** | **entirely, fully, perfectly, quite** *At the time she was perfectly rational.* | **purely, strictly** | **essentially** *Humans are essentially rational beings.* | **apparently** | **economically** *With children working from the age of ten, large families were economically rational.*

• PREP. **about** *Try to be rational about it.*

rationing *noun*

• ADJ. **strict** | **bread, credit, food, fuel, petrol, etc.** | **wartime**

• VERB + RATIONING **have** | **bring in, introduce** *The government introduced meat rationing in May.* | **end**

• RATIONING + VERB **be in force, exist**

• RATIONING + NOUN **system**

• PREP. **~ of** *Strict rationing of basic foodstuffs was still in force by the end of the year.*

ray *noun*

• ADJ. **powerful** | **bright** | **harmful** | **dying, last** *the dying rays of a winter sun* | **cathode, cosmic, gamma, heat, infrared, light, ultraviolet, X-** | **the moon's, the sun's**

• VERB + RAY **emit, give off, send out** *gamma rays given off by plutonium* | **expose sb/sth to** | **block, filter out, protect/shield sb/sth from** *creams which filter out the sun's harmful ultraviolet rays* | **bend, catch, deflect, reflect** *Her brooch caught the rays of the setting sun.*

• RAY + VERB **filter through sth, pass through sth, penetrate sth, travel** *the moon's rays filtering through the trees* | **hit sth** *When the sun's rays hit the earth, a lot of heat is reflected back into space.* | **damage sth** *Ultraviolet rays damage the skin.*

• PREP. **in the ~s of** *a stream sparkling in the rays of the June sun*

• PHRASES **a ray of light/sunlight/sunshine, the rays of the sun**

razor *noun*

- ADJ. open | blunt | cut-throat, disposable, electric, safety
- VERB + RAZOR cut sb/sth with, shave with, slash sb/sth with, use *We used a razor to cut the string.* | be armed with *He was armed with a cut-throat razor.*
- RAZOR + NOUN blade | wire
- PREP. with a/the~ *He slashed his wrists with a razor.*

reach *noun*

- ADJ. long *Gorillas have a very long reach.*
- VERB + REACH have
- PREP. beyond (sb/sth's) *The latch was just beyond her reach.* in/within sb/sth's ~ *a holiday town within reach of Marseilles* out of sb/sth's ~ *Keep all medicines out of reach of children.*
- PHRASES within arm's reach *I always keep my mobile phone within arm's reach.* within easy reach (of sth) *The house is within easy reach of the shops.*

reach *verb*

1 arrive at a place/condition
- ADV. eventually, finally
- VERB + REACH attempt to, try to | be expected to, be likely/unlikely to, expect to *Profits are expected to reach £2 billion this year.* | be able to | be unable to, fail to *The jury was unable to reach a verdict.*

2 stretch out your arm to touch/get sth
- ADV. gingerly | out, over *He reached out gingerly to touch it.*
- PREP. for *She reached for the telephone and picked it up.* into *He reached into his bag and took out a book.*

3 be able to touch sth
- ADV. easily *She had arranged her desk so that she could reach everything easily.*
- VERB + REACH can/could *I can't reach the top shelf.*

react *verb*

- ADV. strongly | favourably, positively, sympathetically *people who react positively to change* | adversely, badly, negatively, unfavourably | aggressively, angrily, violently | cautiously, coolly | sharply | appropriately | immediately, instantly | quickly, swiftly *The police must be able to react swiftly in an emergency.* | differently | accordingly *His insensitive remarks hurt and she reacted accordingly.* | automatically, instinctively, spontaneously | physically
- VERB + REACT tend to | be slow to *The industry has been slow to react to these breakthroughs in technology.* | not know how to *He did not know how to react to her sudden mood swings.*
- PREP. against *Many young people react against traditional values.* by *The government reacted by increasing taxation.* to *The university reacted unfavourably to the proposals.* with *Her family reacted with horror when she told them.*

reaction *noun*

1 response
- ADJ. extreme, sharp, strong, violent | favourable, positive | adverse, hostile, negative | mixed *The speech got a mixed reaction.* | angry | first, immediate, initial | delayed *Her outburst was a delayed reaction to an unpleasant letter she'd received that morning.* | chain *The change of plan set off a chain reaction of confusion.* | mixed | common, general, public | natural, normal | automatic, gut, instinctive, knee-jerk, spontaneous *The incident calls for a measured response, avoiding knee-jerk reactions.* | nervous | emotional | critical *The critical reaction to his first novel has been positive.*
- VERB + REACTION get, have, meet with *The play met with a mixed reaction from the critics.* | bring, cause, produce, provoke, set off, spark (off), trigger (off) *She was surprised at the reaction brought by the mention of his name.* | gauge, judge (by/from) *He eyed her cautiously, trying to gauge her reaction.* ◇ *Judging by her reaction, she liked the present.*
- PREP. in ~ to *There's been a drop in ticket sales in reaction to the review.* | ~ against *Her rebellious attitude is just a reaction against her strict upbringing.* ~ to *the public reaction to the news*

2 (usually **reactions**) ability to react quickly
- ADJ. fast, good, lightning, quick | slow, sluggish
- VERB + REACTION have *She has very quick reactions.* | speed up | slow down *Alcohol has the effect of slowing down your reactions.*
- REACTION + NOUN time *Your reaction time increases when you are tired.*

3 chemical reaction
- ADJ. chain | chemical, nuclear
- VERB + REACTION cause, produce, start, trigger | stop | speed up | slow down
- REACTION + VERB occur, take place
- PREP. during/in a/the ~ *the energy given out during the reaction* | ~ between *studying the reactions between certain gases* ~ with *the fuel's chemical reaction with the surrounding water*

4 allergy
- ADJ. adverse, bad | mild, slight | delayed *a delayed reaction to the drugs* | allergic
- VERB + REACTION have, suffer *She had a very bad allergic reaction to the peanuts.* | cause, produce
- PREP. ~ to *A small minority of patients suffer an adverse reaction to the treatment.*

reactionary *adj.*

- VERBS be, seem
- ADV. extremely, highly, very | politically

reactor *noun*

- ADJ. nuclear | fast, fast-breeder, fission, fusion, gas-cooled, pressurized-water, thermal
- VERB + REACTOR build | operate, run | close (down), decommission, shut down
- REACTOR + VERB operate, run
- REACTOR + NOUN building, site | fuel | core | accident, safety, shut-down

read *noun*

1 activity of reading
- ADJ. good | quiet
- VERB + READ have *I had a good read of the paper before they arrived.*

2 writer/book
- ADJ. compelling, good, great, interesting
- VERB + READ be, make *The story made an interesting read.*

read *verb*

- ADV. aloud *listening to children reading aloud* | silently | carefully, with interest *He read her letter with interest.* | avidly, voraciously *She read avidly from an early age—books, magazines, anything.* | out *Shall I read this out to you?*
- VERB + READ be able to, can/could *Most children can read by the age of seven.* | learn (how) to | teach sb (how) to
- PREP. about *Hogan had read about her death in the papers.* from *She read from the letter.* of *I had read of the case in the local newspaper.* through *I read through the*

first paragraph again. **to** *I read a story to my son every night.*
- PHRASES **read and write** *She had great difficulty learning to read and write.*

readable *adj.*

1 enjoyable to read
- VERBS **be** | **make sth**
- ADV. **eminently, extremely, highly, immensely, very** *a stimulating and highly readable account* | **quite**

2 able to be read
- VERBS **be**
- ADV. **clearly, easily** *The figures should be clearly readable.* ◊ *printed in large, easily readable type*
- PHRASES **machine readable**

reader *noun*

- ADJ. **careful, competent, fast, fluent, good** | **alert, attentive** *Alert readers may have noticed the misprint in last week's column.* | **discerning, sophisticated** | **poor, slow** | **avid, great, voracious** | **omnivorous** | **regular** *regular readers of this magazine* | **casual** | **adult, female, male, women, young** | **specialist** | **general, non-specialist** *a book that will be too difficult for the general reader* | **Daily Express, Guardian, etc.** | **tabloid**
- PREP. **~of** *a voracious reader of science fiction*

readiness *noun*

- ADJ. **greater** | **constant** | **combat** *The troops were in a state of combat readiness.*
- VERB + READINESS **declare, express, indicate, show, signal** *Hungary has indicated its readiness to sign the treaty.* | **hold sb/sth in** *He held his gun in readiness.*
- PREP. **in ~ (for)** *service the car in readiness for the journey* | **~ for** *to express a readiness for change*
- PHRASES **a state of readiness**

reading *noun*

1 sth you can read
- ADJ. **compelling, compulsive, fascinating, good, interesting** | **depressing, disturbing** | **heavy, serious** | **light** | **compulsory, essential, required** | **recommended, suggested** | **background, introductory** | **further** | **bedtime, holiday** *some light holiday reading*
- VERB + READING **be, make (for)** *Their story makes compulsive reading.*
- READING + NOUN **list**

2 activity of reading
- ADJ. **extensive** *After extensive reading on the subject she set to work on an article.* | **careful, close, critical** *A close reading of the text reveals several contradictions.* | **serious** | **map** *My map-reading skills are not the best.*
- VERB + READING **do, get down to** *I haven't had time to do much reading lately.* ◊ *In the holidays I'll get down to some serious reading.*
- READING + NOUN **material, matter** | **ability, age, knowledge, skills** *He has a reading age of eight.* ◊ *She has a good reading knowledge of Russian.* | **glasses, light, room**
- PREP. **~about/on** *His reading about Ruskin led him to the works of Turner.*

3 reading in public
- ADJ. **public** | **Bible, poetry**
- VERB + READING **give** *Dickens gave many public readings from his works.*
- PREP. **at a/the ~** *We met at a reading of his poetry.* | **~from/of** *readings from the Koran*

4 figure/measurement shown on an instrument
- ADJ. **high, low** | **zero** | **normal** | **accurate, correct** | **false** | **meter, thermometer**

- VERB + READING **get, obtain, take** | **give** *The dials were giving higher readings than we had expected.*

ready *adj.*

1 prepared
- VERBS **appear, be, feel, look, seem** | **get** *We were getting ready to go out.* | **get sb** *trying to get the children ready to leave* | **consider sb, declare sb, deem sb, judge sb** *She was concerned to protect the children from the truth until she judged them ready to hear it.*
- ADV. **all** *I was all ready to leave when the phone rang.* | **not quite** *He didn't feel quite ready for marriage.* | **(just) about, almost, nearly, practically** *I think we're just about ready to start.* | **always, ever** | **not yet** | **emotionally** *Though Paul had wanted a child, he wasn't emotionally ready for it.*
- PREP. **for** *I feel ready for anything!* **with** *He's always ready with a quick answer.*

2 prepared and available
- VERBS **be, stand** *The suitcases were standing ready by the front door.* | **have sth, hold sth, keep sth, leave sth** *Please have your tickets ready for inspection.* ◊ *holding his gun ready* ◊ *I've left everything ready in the kitchen.* | **get sth, make sth** *I'll get all the boxes ready.* ◊ *The warships were soon made ready.* | **consider sth, declare sth, deem sth, judge sth** *The plane was refuelled and declared ready for service again.*
- PREP. **for** *The cases are ready for delivery.*

3 willing
- VERBS **appear, be, seem** | **remain**
- ADV. **more than, only too, very** *Connors was more than ready to oblige.* ◊ *She was only too ready to believe the worst of him.* | **always, ever** | **apparently** | **clearly**
- PHRASES **ready and willing** *always ready and willing to help*

real *adj.*

1 serious
- VERBS **be** | **become**
- ADV. **all too, very** *Her suffering was all too real.* ◊ *the very real danger of war*

2 genuine
- VERBS **be, look, seem**
- ADV. **enough** *The pearls looked real enough.*

realism *noun*

- ADJ. **political** | **gritty, stark** *the stark realism of Loach's films*
- QUANT. **degree** | **element, note** *I hate to interject a note of realism, but we don't have any money to do any of this.*
- VERB + REALISM **add, bring, lend** *Clever lighting and sound effects brought greater realism to the play.* | **achieve** *Children can get frustrated when they are unable to achieve realism in their drawings.*
- PREP. **~about** *the band's realism about their chances of success*
- PHRASES **a sense of realism**

realistic *adj.*

1 showing acceptance of the facts of a situation
- VERBS **be, seem** | **keep sth** *Try to keep your ambitions realistic.*
- ADV. **extremely, very** | **fairly, quite, reasonably** | **enough, sufficiently** *He was realistic enough to know this success could not last.*
- PREP. **about** *My friends were quite realistic about my problems.* **in** *being very realistic in their expectations*

2 showing things as they really are
- VERBS **be, look, sound** | **become** | **make sth** *You could make the hands a little more realistic.*

● ADV. **extremely, truly, very | fairly, quite | grimly** *his grimly realistic first novel about drug addicts*

reality *noun*

● ADJ. **awful, bitter, brutal, cold, grim, hard, harsh, painful, sad, stark** *We were faced with the awful reality of having nowhere to live.* | **complex | underlying** *He has no illusions about the underlying reality of army life.* | **objective, practical** *the practical realities of running a children's home* | **daily, everyday | external** *Painters at the time were largely concerned with reproducing external reality.* | **commercial, economic, historical, physical, political, psychological, social** *the harsh economic realities of life as a student* | **virtual** *the use of virtual reality in computer games*
● VERB + REALITY **become** *One day her dream will become a reality.* | **make sth** *It's our task to make the proposals a reality.* | **accept, confront (sb with), face (up to), get a grip on, grasp, wake up to** *She will have to face reality sooner or later.* ◇ *I don't think you have quite grasped the realities of our situation!* | **bear little/no, etc. relation/resemblance to, be cut off/divorced/removed from, be out of touch with, have little/not have much to do with** *They are out of touch with the realities of modern warfare.* ◇ *Most people's ideas of the disease do not have much to do with the reality.* | **escape from | deny, ignore | bring sb back to, come/get back to, return to** *He called for the committee to stop dreaming and return to reality.* | **distort** *Most comedy relies on distorting reality.* | **protect/shelter/shield sb from** *Her parents always tried to shield her from the realities of the world.* | **reflect**
● PREP. **in ~** *The media portray her as happy and successful, but in reality she has a difficult life.*
● PHRASES **a grasp of reality** *He has a rather tenuous grasp of reality.* **a perception/sense of reality**

realization *noun*

● ADJ. **full | dawning, growing | gradual | sudden | awful, terrible**
● VERB + REALIZATION **come to** *He came to the realization that he would never make a good teacher.*
● REALIZATION + VERB **come (to sb), dawn (on sb), hit sb** *The realization that the murderer must have been a close friend came as a shock.* ◇ *We saw the terrible realization of what she'd done dawn on her face.*

realize *verb*

● ADV. **fully | dimly** *She dimly realized that she was trembling.* | **suddenly | quickly, soon | now | for the first time** *I realized for the first time how difficult this would be.* | **at first** *The situation was more complicated than they had at first realized.* | **at last, belatedly, eventually, finally | never** *I never realized how much it meant to you.*
● VERB + REALIZE **begin to, come to | make sb** *The experience made me realize that people did care.* | **seem to** *You don't seem to realize the seriousness of the situation.* | **fail to | be important to**
● PHRASES **without realizing (sth)** *We are constantly using historic buildings, without even realizing it.*

realm *noun*

1 area of activity/interest/knowledge
● ADJ. **whole** *the whole realm of human intellect* | **new | international | public | domestic, private | political, social, spiritual**
● VERB + REALM **be/lie in, belong in/to | open up** *The research has opened up new realms for investigation.* | **enter, move into | descend into/to** *(disapproving) Most readers are likely to lose interest when he descends into the realms of* (= starts discussing) *rhetorical terminology.* |

move from/out of *The euro has moved from the realms of theory into reality.*
● PREP. **beyond/out of/outside the ~ of** *His ambitions are way beyond the realms of possibility.* **in/within the ~ of** *The idea belongs in the realm of science fiction.*
● PHRASES **the realms of fantasy/possibility**

2 country ruled by a king/queen
● VERB + REALM **defend** *They fought to defend the realm.*
● PREP. **beyond/outside the ~** *wealth acquired outside the realm* **in/within the ~** *peace within the realm* **throughout the ~** *There was rejoicing throughout the realm.*
● PHRASES **a part of the realm, the defence of the realm** *Royal taxation usually had to be for the defence of the realm.*

reappraisal *noun*

● ADJ. **fundamental, major, radical | complete | constant | careful | critical** *a critical reappraisal of existing ideas and social institutions*
● VERB + REAPPRAISAL **cause, lead to** *Her theory is that disillusionment with employment leads to reappraisal of career goals.* | **undertake** *They have undertaken a reappraisal of pupils' needs.*

rear *noun*

● VERB + REAR **bring up** *Three drummers brought up the rear* (= were last in the parade). | **attack (sb/sth) from**
● PREP. **at the ~** *The socket for the printer cable is located at the rear of the computer.* **from the ~, in the ~** *The radio is loudest in the rear of the car.* **to/towards the ~** *A high gate blocks the only entrance to the rear.*

rear *verb*

● ADV. **intensively** *intensively reared beef cattle* | **naturally** *naturally reared pork and beef* | **successfully**

reason *noun*

1 cause/motive/justification; explanation of sth
● ADJ. **cogent, good, sound, strong | compelling, convincing | plausible | adequate, sufficient | bona fide, legitimate, valid | wrong** *He married her for all the wrong reasons.* | **opposite** *Tom's problem was that he lacked confidence; Ed failed for precisely the opposite reason.* | **important | special | chief, main, major, primary, principal | only, simple, sole** *The only reason I didn't become a professional golfer was because of my family commitments.* ◇ *I was never good at playing the trumpet for the simple reason that I never practised.* | **real, underlying** *She did not tell him the real reason for her change of heart.* ◇ *The underlying reasons for these differences will be explored in depth in the next chapter.* | **very** *There is an assumption that a state will protect its citizens. That is the very reason for the existence of states.* | **apparent, particular** *He was attacked for no apparent reason.* | **no earthly, (no) possible** *Surely there is no earthly reason why you wouldn't want to come with us?* | **clear, obvious** *The reasons for her decision soon became clear.* | **unclear | logical | understandable | justifiable | inexplicable, unexplained, unknown** *For some unexplained reason the pilot jettisoned all his fuel shortly after take-off.* | **unspecified | unconnected** *dismissal for reasons unconnected with redundancy* | **personal | sentimental | selfish | professional | commercial, economic, financial, legal, political, social, technical | practical, pragmatic | security | health | humanitarian**
● VERB + REASON **be aware of, see** *We see no reason why this band shouldn't be a huge success.* | **have** *I don't know why he did that, but I'm sure he had his reasons.* ◇ *I have no reason to believe that she was lying to me.* | **cite, give (sb/sth), set out, state** *Give me one good reason why I*

should help you. ◊ *In the letter she carefully set out her reasons for leaving.* | **cite sth as, give sth as** | **suggest** | **explain** | **understand** | **uncover**
● PREP. **by ~ of** *(formal) persons in need of care by reason of* (= because of) *old age* **for a/the ~** *procedures carried out for reasons of national security* **for ~ of** *(formal) For reasons of security, you are requested to keep your luggage with you at all times.* **with/without ~** *They complained about the food, and with good reason* (= rightly). | **~ against** *There are obvious reasons against such a move.* **~ behind** *We are trying to uncover the reasons behind her decision.* **~ for** *They didn't give any reason for the delay.*
● PHRASES **all the more reason** *If he's unwell, that's all the more reason to go and see him.* **all sorts of reasons** *People buy things for all sorts of reasons.* **any/every/little/no/one/some reason** *I know you're angry with me, and you have every reason* (= very good reasons) *to be.* **for reasons best known to yourself** *For reasons best known to herself she has turned down the offer.* **for whatever reason** *people who, for whatever reason, are unable to support themselves* **a number/variety of reasons, rhyme or reason** *There's no rhyme or reason* (= logic) *to the new opening hours.*

2 power to think logically; what is possible/right
● ADJ. **human**
● VERB + REASON **lose** *He seems to have lost all sense and reason.* | **be open to, listen to, see** *I tried to persuade her, but she just wouldn't listen to reason.*
● PREP. **beyond ~** *He was beyond all reason.* **within ~** *I'll lend you the money you need—within reason, of course!*
● PHRASES **an appeal to reason** *The residents hope that an appeal to reason* (= asking the rioters to be reasonable) *will end the rioting.* **it stands to reason** *It stands to reason* (= it is logical) *that she wouldn't want them to find out about her personal problems.* **the voice of reason** *She was always the voice of reason, persuading him not to buy things they couldn't afford.*

reasonable *adj.*

● VERBS **appear, be, seem, sound** | **consider sth, judge sth, regard sth as, think sth**
● ADV. **eminently, extremely, very** | **entirely, perfectly, utterly** *The police apparently thought this explanation perfectly reasonable.* | **fairly, quite** | **enough** *Her request sounded reasonable enough to me.* | **apparently**

reasoning *noun*

● ADJ. **careful, sound** | **false, faulty** | **underlying** | **abstract** | **practical** | **logical** | **deductive, inductive** | **judicial, legal, moral, scientific, theological** | **human**
● QUANT. **piece** *a rather confused piece of reasoning*
● VERB + REASONING **adopt, apply, employ, use** *the reasoning adopted by the court* | **follow, understand** *I can't quite follow your reasoning.* | **accept** | **reject** | **challenge** | **explain**
● REASONING + VERB **apply** *The same reasoning applies to the current situation.* | **lead sb/sth to sth** *I cannot accept the reasoning that led the trial court to its decision.*
● REASONING + NOUN **process** | **ability**
● PREP. **in your ~** *the circularity in their reasoning* | **~ about** *reasoning about art* **~ behind** *Many people challenged the reasoning behind the proposal.*
● PHRASES **a flaw in your reasoning, a form/kind/line of reasoning** *The implication of this line reasoning is that globalization of capital is destructive.* **power of reasoning** *She seemed to have lost her powers of reasoning.*

reassurance *noun*

● ADJ. **great** | **further** | **constant, continual** | **calm** *Continual calm reassurance should be given.*
● VERB + REASSURANCE **have** *We have had some reassurances from the council that the building will be* saved. | **need, want** | **look for, seek** *He glanced at her, seeking reassurance.* | **draw, find, gain, receive** *He drew reassurance from the enthusiastic applause.* ◊ *She found reassurance in the high attendance at her lectures.* | **bring (sb), give (sb), offer (sb), provide (sb with)** *A system of beliefs can bring you reassurance at times of stress.*
● PREP. **despite ~** *She kept looking in the mirror despite my constant reassurances that her hair looked fine.* **for ~** *He held onto her hand for reassurance.* **in ~** *I patted her shoulder in reassurance.* | **~ about/on** *The ministry tried to offer reassurance on the safety of eating beef.* **~ from** *reassurances from the researchers about their work*

reassure *verb*

● ADV. **constantly** *He was constantly reassuring himself that he had acted for the best.* | **quickly**
● VERB + REASSURE **be able to, can** | **seek to, try to** | **hasten to** | **do little to, do nothing to** | **do much to** *The report will do much to reassure parents of children at the school.*
● PREP. **about** *trying to reassure the public about the safety of public transport* **of** *She needed to be reassured of his love for her.* **with** *He reassured her with a pat on the arm.*
● PHRASES **feel reassured** *Kate nodded, but she didn't feel reassured.* **need reassuring** *Often parents simply need reassuring that their children are happy at school.*

reassuring *adj.*

● VERBS **be** | **find sth**
● ADV. **extremely, immensely, very** | **hardly** *Her comment—'You can always try again if you fail'—was hardly reassuring.* | **faintly, quite, vaguely** | **oddly** | **somehow**

rebate *noun*

● ADJ. **generous, substantial** | **maximum** | **rate, rent, tax** *She's claiming a 100% tax rebate.*
● VERB + REBATE **be eligible for, be entitled to** *People on low incomes are entitled to a rebate of up to 80%.* | **apply for, claim** | **get, receive** | **give sb, grant sb** | **introduce** | **scrap**
● REBATE + NOUN **scheme, system**
● PREP. **~ on** *rebates on the new council tax*
● PHRASES **a system of rebates**

rebel *noun*

● ADJ. **anti-government** | **left-wing, right-wing** | **US-backed, etc.** | **former** | **armed**
● QUANT. **band, group**
● VERB + REBEL **back, help, support** *They sent in troops to back the rebels.* | **repel** | **defeat** | **join** | **lead**
● REBEL + VERB **be based ...** *The rebels were based in camps along the border.* | **advance** | **attack sth** | **capture sth, gain/regain/seize/take control (of sth)** *The rebels seized control of the national radio headquarters.*
● REBEL + NOUN **faction, group, movement** | **army, fighters, force/forces, officers, soldiers, troops** | **commander, leader** | **control** *The southern parts of the country had fallen into rebel control.* | **base, camp, position, stronghold** | **activity, advance, assault, attack, invasion** | **cause, movement** *new recruits to the rebel cause*
● PREP. **against the ~** *military operations against the rebels* | **~ against** *a group of rebels against the emperor*
● PHRASES **a bit/something of a rebel** *(figurative) He's a bit of a rebel* (= he doesn't like to obey rules).

rebellion *noun*

1 attempt to change the government
● ADJ. **full-scale, major** | **minor, small** | **general, open** | **armed** | **military, peasant, popular**

• VERB + REBELLION **rise (up) in** *Simon de Montfort rose in rebellion in 1258.* | **launch, raise** (*literary*), **stage** *They staged a rebellion against British rule in Ireland.* | **set off, spark off** *The re-introduction of conscription sparked off a major rebellion.* | **foment, provoke (sb/sth to)** *attempts to foment rebellion in the Cabinet* ◇ *The new taxes provoked the population to open rebellion.* | **threaten** *The opposition party members threatened rebellion.* | **join** | **take part in** | **lead** | **support** | **crush, put down, quell, suppress**
• REBELLION + VERB **occur** *Peasant rebellions occurred throughout the 16th century.* | **begin, break out** *Rebellion broke out in the Rhineland.* | **fail**
• PREP. **in~** *They are in rebellion against the conservative hierarchy of the Church.* | **~ against** *a rebellion against the new king* **~over** *a rebellion over an increase in VAT*

2 opposition to authority
• ADJ. **adolescent, teenage, youthful**
• REBELLION + VERB **stir** *The band refused to go on stage and rebellion began to stir in the audience.*
• PREP. **~against** *rebellion against their parents*
• PHRASES **an act of rebellion, a form of rebellion**

rebuff *noun*

• ADJ. **harsh, sharp, stinging** | **humiliating**
• VERB + REBUFF **meet (sth) with, receive, suffer** *Her efforts were met with a sharp rebuff.* | **risk** *My father was too proud to risk a rebuff, so he simply did not ask her.* | **expect** *He avoided speaking to her, expecting a rebuff.* | **accept** | **ignore**
• PREP. **(in) a~ to** *In a rebuff to the president, Congress voted against the bill.* | **~ from** *She suffered a rebuff from her manager when she raised the matter.*

rebuild *verb*

• ADV. **completely, entirely, totally** *The hall had to be completely rebuilt after the fire.* | **virtually** | **extensively, largely, substantially** | **partly** | **painstakingly**
• VERB + REBUILD **begin to, start to** *beginning to rebuild her life* | **try to** | **help (to)** *The international community must step in to help rebuild the country.*
• PHRASES **newly/recently rebuilt, rebuild sth from scratch** *Much of the damaged vehicle had to be rebuilt from scratch.*

rebuke *noun*

• ADJ. **sharp, stern, stinging** | **gentle, mild** | **silent** | **implied** | **public**
• VERB + REBUKE **receive** | **draw, earn (sb)** *Even one minute's lateness would earn a stern rebuke.* | **accept** *He meekly accepted the rebuke.* | **administer** *If the general found his authority questioned he invariably administered a sharp rebuke.*
• PREP. **~ for, ~ from** *They received a public rebuke from the prime minister for their handling of the matter.* **~ to** *He hit back with a stinging rebuke to his critics.*

rebuke *verb*

• ADV. **sharply** | **gently** | **publicly**
• PREP. **for** *She rebuked herself sharply for her stupidity.*

recall *verb*

• ADV. **clearly, distinctly, vividly, well** *I well recall walking the five miles to school every morning.* | **dimly, vaguely** | **correctly** *If I recall correctly, he lives in Luton.* | **easily** *She could easily recall the smell of the orange groves.* | **suddenly** | **fondly** | **still** *Becky could still recall that first meeting clearly.*
• VERB + RECALL **seem to** *I seem to recall that she said she was going away.* | **be able to, can/could (barely), can't/couldn't (quite)** | **try to**

recede *verb*

• ADV. **a bit, a little, slightly** *His fine dark hair was receding a little.* | **further** | **gradually, slowly** *The pain was gradually receding.* | **fast, rapidly** *The January flood waters receded as fast as they had risen.*
• PREP. **from** *These worries now receded from his mind.*
• PHRASES **recede into the background/distance** *His footsteps receded into the distance.*

receipt *noun*

1 piece of paper showing what was paid for
• ADJ. **original**
• VERB + RECEIPT **ask (sb) for** | **get, obtain** | **receive** | **have** *Could I have a receipt for that please?* | **make out, write (out)** *a receipt made out for £5* | **sign** | **give sb, issue** | **keep** *You can claim a refund provided you keep the receipt.* | **produce** *The original receipt must be produced in order to reclaim your goods.*
• RECEIPT + NOUN **book**
• PREP. **~for** *She issued a receipt for the goods.*

2 act of receiving sth
• VERB + RECEIPT **acknowledge** *I would be grateful if you would acknowledge receipt of this letter.*
• PREP. **in ~ of** *people in receipt of housing benefit* **on/upon ~ of** *The goods will be sent on receipt of your cheque.*
• PHRASES **the date for receipt** *The closing date for receipt of your application is July 14.* **within … days of receipt** *Items should be paid for within 14 days of receipt.*

3 receipts money received
• ADJ. **total** *Cash income is calculated by subtracting total trading income from total receipts.* | **net** | **capital** | **income, revenue** | **tax** | **cash** | **foreign currency/exchange** | **dollar, euro, etc.** | **box-office, gate, match**
• VERB + RECEIPTS **receive**
• RECEIPTS + VERB **rise** *Customs and excise receipts rose 2.5 per cent.* | **reach sth** *Cash receipts reached £70 million.* | **fall, slump** *Match receipts slumped by £89 000 compared to last season.*
• PREP. **~from** *receipts from land sales*
• PHRASES **receipts and payments**

receive *verb*

1 get/accept sth
• ADV. **gratefully** *Any help or donations will be gratefully received.*
• VERB + RECEIVE **be entitled to** *You might be entitled to receive housing benefit.* | **expect to** *You can expect to receive compensation for all direct expenses arising out of the accident.*
• PREP. **from** *I received a parcel from my mother.*

2 react to sth in a particular way
• ADV. **well** *The play was very well received.* | **badly** *The speech was badly received by republican leaders.*
• PREP. **with** *The news was received with dismay.*

receiver *noun*

1 part of a telephone
• ADJ. **phone, telephone**
• VERB + RECEIVER **lift, pick up** *She took a deep breath and lifted the receiver off its hook.* | **hold** | **put back/down, replace** | **snatch up** | **bang down, slam down** *He slammed the receiver down and burst into tears.* | **drop**
• RECEIVER + VERB **dangle** *The receiver was dangling from the payphone.*
• PREP. **over the ~** *'It's your mother on the phone again!', said John with his hand over the receiver.*
• PHRASES **hold/put the receiver to your ear** *She picked up the receiver and put it to her ear.*

2 piece of radio/television equipment
- ADJ. **portable | radio, satellite, television**
- RECEIVER + NOUN **unit** *To change channel, select the desired number on the receiver unit.*

3 person in charge of a bankrupt company
- ADJ. **official | administrative**
- VERB + RECEIVER **appoint, appoint sb (as) | call in** *They had to lay off 200 staff and call in the receivers.*
- PHRASES **in the hands of the receiver** *The company remained in the hands* (= under the control) *of the receiver.*

recent *adj.*

- VERBS **be**
- ADV. **very | comparatively, fairly, quite, relatively** *a relatively recent development*

reception *noun*

1 area in a building
- VERB + RECEPTION **wait (for sb) in** *Please wait for me downstairs in reception.* | **leave sth at/with** *I've left the keys at reception.* | **report to** *All delegates should report to reception on arrival.* | **phone, ring**
- RECEPTION + NOUN **area | counter, desk | hall | staff**
- PREP. **at (the)~** *The man at reception says there's a call for you.* **in~** *The documents are in reception.* **on~** *I've been on reception* (= working at the reception desk) *the whole morning.*

2 formal party
- ADJ. **big, large | intimate, small | formal | informal | official | special | evening | civic, diplomatic, press, wedding | buffet, champagne, sherry, wine**
- VERB + RECEPTION **attend | give, have, hold, host** *Are you having a big reception after the wedding?* | **organize | invite sb to** *Friends and family are invited to a reception after the ceremony.*
- PREP. **at a/the~** *We met at a reception.* | **~for** *a reception for the Japanese trade delegation*

3 type of welcome given to sb/sth
- ADJ. **enthusiastic, favourable, friendly, good, great, marvellous, positive, rapturous, rousing, sympathetic, warm | lukewarm, mixed | bad, chilly, cool, frosty, hostile | critical** *critical reception to a movie* | **public**
- VERB + RECEPTION **enjoy, get, have, meet (with), receive** *The returning soldiers enjoyed a rousing reception.* ◇ *The scheme has had a somewhat mixed reception from local people.* | **expect** *The managers did not expect a sympathetic reception from the striking workers.* | **give sb/sth** *She was given a rapturous reception by the crowd.*
- RECEPTION + NOUN **party** *A reception party of soldiers was there to greet the visiting head of state.* | **centre** *a reception centre for children who have run away from home*
- PREP. **~by** *the book's reception by reviewers* **~from** *a cool reception from the crowd* **~into** *reception into the monastic order* **~to** *the positive reception to the Chancellor's speech*

4 quality of radio/television signals
- ADJ. **good, strong** *Television reception is very good in this area.* | **bad, poor, weak | radio, television**

recess *noun*

1 period when a parliament, etc. does not meet
- ADJ. **Christmas, summer, Whitsun | parliamentary**
- VERB + RECESS **go into, rise for** *(formal)*, **take** *Parliament is taking the Christmas recess a little early this year.* | **return from**
- PREP. **in~** *The decision cannot be made while the council is in recess.*

2 part of a wall, set back from the rest of the wall
- ADJ. **deep | shallow | dark | window**
- PREP. **in/inside** *to fit a blind inside a window recess*

3 (usually **recesses**) part furthest from the light
- ADJ. **dark, deep, dim** *He stared into the dark recesses of the room.* | **far, inner | hidden**
- VERB + RECESS **lurk in** *(figurative) fears lurking deep in the recesses of our minds* | **push sth into/to** *(figurative) I had continually pushed my doubts to the darker recesses of my mind.*
- PREP. **in/within the~of** *The statue was in the inner recesses of the temple.*
- PHRASES **the recesses of your mind** *(figurative)*

recession *noun*

- ADJ. **bad, damaging, debilitating, deep, major, massive, painful, severe, sharp, steep** *It was the worst recession since the war.* | **mild | deepening | long, prolonged | short, short-lived | continuing | global, international, widespread, world, worldwide | economic, industrial, retail**
- VERB + RECESSION **cause | go into, move into, plunge (sth) into, sink into, slip into** *A rise in interest rates plunged Britain deeper into recession.* | **beat, combat | climb out of, come out of, emerge from, get (sth) out of, lead sth out of, move out of, pull (sth) out of** *active policies to pull the country out of recession* | **end | suffer from | escape (from) | ride out, survive** *As dozens of pubs go out of business, others are riding out the recession.* | **worsen**
- RECESSION + VERB **loom** *With a recession looming, consumers are spending less.* | **hit sth** *The country has been hit by recession.* | **bottom out** (= reach the lowest level)
- PREP. **in (a/the)~** *The economy is in deep recession.*
- PHRASES **the depth of the recession, the effects/impact of the recession, in the depths of a recession, in times of recession, recovery from (the) recession, a way out of the recession**
⇨ Special page at BUSINESS

recipe *noun*

- ADJ. **good | perfect | sure** *(figurative) Turning away under a strong attack is a sure recipe for defeat.* | **delicious, mouth-watering, tasty | favourite | basic** *The basic recipe can be adapted by adding grated lemon.* | **easy, simple | complicated | new | authentic, classic, old, original, traditional** *The ales are brewed to an original Yorkshire recipe.* | **original** *Was there rum in the original recipe?* | **secret, special | family | vegetarian | Italian, Mexican, etc. | cake, sauce, etc.**
- VERB + RECIPE **have** *I've got a good recipe for fudge.* | **cook, make** *This recipe can also be made with ricotta cheese.* | **try (out)** *I enjoy trying out new recipes.* | **read | follow, stick to, use** *If you want the dish to turn out right you should follow the recipe.* | **adapt | devise** *All the recipes in the book have been devised by our team of experts.* | **discover, find** *He is credited with having discovered the first recipe for gin back in the 1600s.*
- RECIPE + VERB **call for sth, use sth** *She always said that if a recipe calls for cream you shouldn't use yogurt instead.* | **contain sth** *The recipe contains lots of fat.* | **make sth, serve sb** *This recipe makes about thirty biscuits.* ◇ *This recipe serves four people.*
- RECIPE + NOUN **book, card, leaflet | idea** *a magazine filled with recipe ideas*
- PREP. **to a~** *The dish is made to a traditional Italian recipe.* | **~for** *a recipe for leek soup* ◇ *(figurative) To live every day to the full is a recipe for happiness.*
- PHRASES **a recipe for disaster/success**

recipient *noun*

- ADJ. **largest | main, major | intended** *She was not the intended recipient of the reward.* | **ultimate** *the ultimate recipient of the money* | **suitable** *matching a donor kidney* with the most suitable recipient | **passive** *We are passive recipients of information from the world around us.* | **grateful** (ironic) *Dad was always the grateful recipient of her snobbery.* | **unwilling | lucky** *Our 1 000th member will be the lucky recipient of a mystery gift.*

recital *noun*

- ADJ. **brief, short | solo | lunchtime | organ, piano,** etc. | **poetry, song**
- VERB + RECITAL **give, play | attend, go to | listen to**
- PREP. **~ by** *a recital by the Grieg Trio*

recognition *noun*

1 remembering/identifying sb/sth
- ADJ. **immediate, instant | early** *the early recognition of a disease* | **dawning | character, face, handwriting, speech, text** (computing) | **automatic, computer** *the automatic recognition of handwriting by computer*
- QUANT. **flicker, sign** *She stared directly at the witness but he did not show a flicker of recognition* (= he did not show that he recognized her).
- VERB + RECOGNITION **show | avoid** *He pulled the hood of his cloak over his head to avoid recognition.* | **allow** *The monitoring system allows recognition of pollution hot spots.*
- RECOGNITION + VERB **dawn** *Recognition slowly dawned, 'Oh, it's you Mrs Foster!'*
- RECOGNITION + NOUN **software, system**
- PREP. **beyond (all) ~** (figurative) *Many of those interviewed said their job had changed beyond recognition* (= changed completely) *over the past five years.* **out of (all) ~** (figurative) *The equipment and methods of production have improved out of all recognition* (= greatly improved). **without ~** *He looked up, glanced at them without recognition, and went on his way.*
- PHRASES **recognition in sb's eyes** *There was no recognition in his eyes* (= he did not look as if he recognized her).

2 accepting that sth exists/is true; public praise/reward
- ADJ. **full | appropriate, due, proper | insufficient | greater, growing, increasing** *There needs to be a greater recognition of corporate crime as a social problem.* | **clear, explicit, overt | implicit | apparent | grudging | positive | equal** *equal recognition for the work women do* | **mutual | immediate, instant | belated** *The award is being made in belated recognition of her services to the industry.* | **individual, personal** *personal recognition for your achievements* | **general, universal, wide, widespread** *The young talent at the club deserves wider recognition.* | **international, national, worldwide | public, social | professional | diplomatic | formal, legal, legislative, official | de facto** *Twelve states have accorded de facto recognition to the new regime.* | **government**
- VERB + RECOGNITION **achieve, earn sb, gain, get, obtain, receive, win** *His recitals have earned him recognition as a talented performer.* | **deserve | require** *Both of these perspectives are valid and require recognition.* | **imply** *They claim that signature of the peace accord did not imply recognition of the state's sovereignty.* | **ask for, call for, demand, request, seek | apply for | qualify for** *to qualify for UN recognition as an International Biosphere Reserve* | **accord sb/sth, give sb/sth, grant sb/sth | refuse sb/sth**
- RECOGNITION + VERB **come** *Official recognition of the change came fast.*
- PREP. **in ~ of** *an award in recognition of his outstanding work* **without ~** *She has worked actively but without recognition.* | **~ as** *a country that has long sought recognition as a major power* **~ by/from** *recognition by his superiors of the service he had performed* **~ for** *They received recognition for their 20-year commitment to safety at sea.*
- PHRASES **a lack of recognition, recognition of the im-**

portance of sth, recognition of the need for sth, a struggle for recognition

recognizable *adj.*

- VERBS **be | become | remain**
- ADV. **clearly, easily, immediately, instantly, quite, readily** *John's car was easily recognizable in the car park.* ◊ *a building that was immediately recognizable as a prison* | **barely, hardly, scarcely**
- PREP. **as** *a language barely recognizable as English* **by** *recognizable by their distinctive uniforms* **to** *The scheme's benefits were recognizable to all interest groups.*

recognize *verb*

1 know sb/sth again
- ADV. **immediately, instantly** *I immediately recognized the building.* | **easily** *This is the only species of flamingo in the region, easily recognized by its pink plumage.* | **barely, hardly** *Stella hardly recognized her brother.*
- VERB + RECOGNIZE **learn to** *You learn to recognize the calls of different birds.* | **be easy to**
- PREP. **as** *He recognized the man as one of the police officers.* **by** *I recognized her by her red hair.* **from** *I recognized them from a television show.*

2 understand sth
- ADV. **fully** *They fully recognize the need to proceed carefully.* | **belatedly, finally** *The government has belatedly recognized the danger to health of passive smoking.*
- VERB + RECOGNIZE **must | be important to | begin to | be slow to** *The company had been slow to recognize the opportunities available to it.* | **fail to**
- PREP. **as** *This issue must be recognized as a priority for the next administration.*
- PHRASES **be generally/universally/widely recognized, be increasingly recognized** *The strength of this argument is being increasingly recognized.* **failure to recognize sth**

3 accept sth officially
- ADV. **clearly** *The law clearly recognizes that a company is separate from those who invest in it.* | **formally, officially | internationally, nationally** *The Medway estuary is recognized internationally as a conservation area.*
- VERB + RECOGNIZE **agree to | refuse to**
- PREP. **as** *All rivers should be officially recognized as public rights of way.*
- PHRASES **be legally recognized** *A bill of exchange is a legally recognized document.* **a refusal to recognize sth**

recoil *verb*

- ADV. **a little, slightly | instinctively** *As he leaned towards her she instinctively recoiled.*
- PREP. **at** *Howard recoiled a little at the sharpness in my voice.* **from** *She felt him recoil from her, frightened.* **in** *He recoiled in apparent disgust.*

recollection *noun*

- ADJ. **clear, distinct, vivid | dim, faint, hazy, vague | earliest | sudden | painful | personal**
- VERB + RECOLLECTION **have (no)** *I have only a vague recollection of sunshine and sand.* ◊ *I have absolutely no recollection of the incident.* | **bring back** *The place brought back painful recollections.* | **chuckle at/in, laugh at, smile at/in | shudder at**
- PREP. **in ~** *She stared at him in sudden recollection.* | **~ from** *recollections from Eliot's own life*
- PHRASES **to the best of your recollection** *To the best of my recollection* (= if I remember correctly), *he was not there that day.*

recommend verb

1 say that sb/sth is good
- ADV. **highly, thoroughly** *This book is highly recommended by teachers.* | **certainly, definitely** *I definitely recommend this film.* | **heartily | personally** *Consult a solicitor who is personally recommended to you.*
- PREP. **for** *Who would you recommend for the job?* **to** *I can recommend this book to anyone interested in food.*
- PHRASES **sth has a lot/much to recommend it** *Your idea has much to recommend it.*

2 advise sb to do sth
- ADV. **strongly** *I would strongly recommend that you get professional advice.* | **particularly, specifically**

recommendation noun

1 official suggestion
- ADJ. **firm, strong | clear | unanimous | detailed | specific | broad, general, wide-ranging** *The committee put forward broad recommendations for the improvement of safety at sports grounds.* | **far-reaching | important | central, key, main, major, principal | positive | first, initial | final | further | draft | written | word-of-mouth | medical, official, practical | policy, safety**
- QUANT. **list, series, set**
- VERB + RECOMMENDATION **come up with, make, produce** *The council has produced a set of recommendations on ethics in health care.* | **give, offer, put forward, submit | publish | consider, discuss, review | agree with | disagree with | accept, adopt, approve, endorse** *The UN Security Council endorsed the recommendation submitted by the Secretary General.* | **reject | act on, carry out, follow, implement** *The government gave assurances that it would implement the recommendations in full.* | **enforce | support | oppose | ignore | be in accordance with, be in line with** *to develop a plan in line with the recommendations of national policy* | **base sth on** *The design of the breakwater was based on the recommendations of an engineering study.*
- RECOMMENDATION + VERB **arise from sth, be based on sth, follow (from) sth, relate to sth** *a detailed set of recommendations following a comprehensive examination of the subject* | **aim at sth** *recommendations aimed at achieving a more equitable admissions policy*
- PREP. **on/upon sb/sth's ~** *I had the operation on the recommendation of my doctor.* | **~ about/as to/concerning/on** *recommendations on how health and safety standards might be improved* **~ by/from** *recommendations by the judges* **~ for** *recommendations for improving the quality of service* **~ in respect of** *recommendations in respect of bank officials* **~ to** *the board's recommendations to the minister* **~ with regard/respect to** *recommendations with regard to management procedures*
- ⇒ Special page at MEETING

2 saying sb/sth is good/suitable
- ADJ. **glowing, high/highest | personal** *It's best to find a builder through personal recommendation.*
- VERB + RECOMMENDATION **give sb/sth | get, receive | come on/with** *The new housekeeper came on the highest recommendation.* ◊ *The chef comes with her recommendation.* | **need no** *Swiss chocolates need no recommendation* (= their good reputation is enough to recommend them).
- PREP. **at/on/upon sb's ~** *At the recommendation of a psychiatrist, the accused will remain under observation.* ◊ *We went to Corfu on your recommendation* (= because you recommended it).
- PHRASES **a letter of recommendation**

recompense noun

- ADJ. **adequate, sufficient | financial**
- VERB + RECOMPENSE **have** *All struggles should have their recompense.* | **expect | receive | give (sth in), pay (sth in)** *Substantial damages were paid in recompense.*
- PREP. **as/in ~** *She received a gift as recompense.* | **~ for** *He was given £1 000 in recompense for his loss.* **~ from** *recompense from the government*

reconciliation noun

1 ending a disagreement/conflict
- ADJ. **full | lasting | national, personal, political**
- VERB + RECONCILIATION **seek** *He sought reconciliation with those he had stolen from.* | **attempt | achieve, bring about, effect, make, secure | promote, work for | call for** *The rebel leader called for reconciliation with the armed forces.*
- RECONCILIATION + NOUN **agreement | talks**
- PREP. **~ between** *They aimed to secure a lasting reconciliation between the two countries.* **~ with** *She attempted reconciliation with her estranged brother.*
- PHRASES **an attempt at reconciliation, efforts at/towards reconciliation, a gesture of reconciliation** *In a bold gesture of reconciliation, the government released the rebel leader.* **a mood/spirit of reconciliation, a policy of reconciliation**

reconnaissance noun

- ADJ. **general | preliminary | aerial/air, maritime, military** *Spotter planes made a preliminary aerial reconnaissance of the island.*
- VERB + RECONNAISSANCE **carry out, conduct, do, make**
- RECONNAISSANCE + VERB **reveal sth** *Reconnaissance revealed not a single large ship.*
- RECONNAISSANCE + NOUN **flight, mission, sortie | party, patrol, team, unit | aircraft, plane**

reconstruct verb

- ADV. **completely | partially | painstakingly** *Every aspect of the original has been closely studied and painstakingly reconstructed.*
- VERB + RECONSTRUCT **attempt to, try to | be possible to** *It is not possible to reconstruct the complete symphony from these manuscript sketches.*
- PREP. **from** *Local historians have reconstructed from contemporary descriptions how the hall may have looked in 1300.*
- PHRASES **an attempt to reconstruct sth**

reconstruction noun

- ADJ. **fundamental, major | complete, total | large/large-scale, life-size** *a life-size reconstruction of a Viking longboat* | **dramatic** *a dramatic reconstruction of school life in the 1940s* | **national** *The country faces a huge task of national reconstruction following the war.* | **postwar | economic, historical, social**
- VERB + RECONSTRUCTION **undertake** *A group of enthusiasts have undertaken the reconstruction of a steam locomotive.* | **stage** *The police have staged a reconstruction of the events leading up to the murder.*
- RECONSTRUCTION + NOUN **period | work | plan, programme, scheme | cost** *reconstruction costs following the cyclone*

record noun

1 account
- ADJ. **formal** *No formal record of the marriage now survives.* | **official, public | permanent | accurate, careful, exact | up-to-date | adequate, proper, reliable | inadequate | incomplete, sketchy | brief | complete, comprehensive, detailed, extensive, systematic | verbatim | authentic | daily | documentary, handwritten, written | photographic, pictorial | archival, historical |**

archaeological *This period of barbarian rule is poorly represented in the archaeological record.* | **fossil, geological** | **administrative, departmental, financial, personnel** | **dental, health, medical**

● VERB + RECORD **keep** *He has always kept an accurate record of his spending.* | **check, consult** *I checked the records but nobody of that name had worked here.* | **destroy** *Medical records should not be destroyed.* | **file** | **update** | **be on, go on** *She is on record as saying that she once took drugs.* ◇ *He is the latest public figure to go on (the) record about corruption in politics.*

● RECORD + VERB **contain sth** *The records contain the bank details of all employees.* | **show sth** *The records showed that the building had not been inspected for ten years.* | **suggest sth** *Fossil records suggest that the region was covered in water until relatively recently.* | **exist, survive** *No record exists of a battle on this site.* | **go back** *The university records go back as far as the 13th century.*

● PREP. **in the~(s)** *The historic agreement is preserved in the university records.* **off/on the~** *Off the record, he told the interviewer what he thought of his colleagues.* | **~of a** *record of achievement* **~on** *records on children's progress*

● PHRASES **access to the records** *Under the law, every citizen has access to their official records.* **put/set the record straight** *She called a press conference to set the record straight about her disappearance.*

2 best result, highest level, etc.
● ADJ. **all-comers, club, course, national, Olympic, track, world** | **unbeaten, unbroken** | **long-standing** *Bob Beamon's long-standing record for the long jump was eventually broken.* | **all-time** | **speed**

● VERB + RECORD **hold** *Who holds the 100 metre sprint record?* | **establish, set** *She has just set a new world record.* | **beat, break, shatter** *If she continues like this she could beat the record.* | **equal** *He has equalled the Olympic record.*

● RECORD + VERB **stand** *His mile record stood for twelve years.* | **fall**

● RECORD + NOUN **book/books** *Bubka rewrote the pole-vault record books during his career.* | **attempt** | **breaker, holder** | **high, number** *Unemployment has reached a record high* (= the highest level ever). ◇ *There was a record number of candidates for the post.*

● PREP. **~for** *These viewing figures are an all-time record for a single broadcast.* **~with** *Lewis established a new world record with a time of 9.86 seconds.*

● PHRASES **in record time** *I got to work in record time.*

3 sb's performance in a particular area
● ADJ. **past, track** | **distinguished, enviable, excellent, exceptional, exemplary, fine, formidable, good, impressive, magnificent, outstanding, proven, remarkable, unique, unparalleled, unrivalled** | **abysmal, appalling, atrocious, bad, dismal, mediocre, poor, sorry** | **unenviable** *He has an unenviable record of ill-health.* | **satisfactory** | **consistent** | **clean, unblemished** *Apart from a parking fine ten years before, she had an unblemished driving record.* | **academic, educational, school** | **military** | **attendance** *The teacher spoke to her about her poor attendance record.* | **economic, environmental, human-rights** *the government's economic record* | **disciplinary** | **criminal, police** | **accident, safety** *The airline's accident record makes it among the safest.*

● VERB + RECORD **have, possess** | **keep, maintain** *The company has maintained an accident-free record since it started business.*

● RECORD + VERB **show sth** *Her record shows that she is able to compete under great pressure.* | **compare with sth** *Our record compares favourably with that of any similar-sized company.* | **speak for itself** *When it comes to quality, our record speaks for itself.*

● PREP. **~among** *They have the worst human-rights record among member countries.* **~for** *He has an appalling record for dishonesty.* **~in** *The ideal candidate will have a*

proven track record in project management. **~on** *the government's abysmal record on crime*

● PHRASES **on past records** *On past records, she should have no problem passing the exam.* **on sb's past record**

4 music
● ADJ. **long-playing** | **gramophone** | **classical, jazz, pop** | **best-selling**

● VERB + RECORD **cut, make** | **release** *They released their first record in 1963.* | **listen to, play, put on** *I'll put on one of my favourite records.*

● RECORD + NOUN **company, industry, label** | **producer** | **deal** *The band signed their first record deal a year after forming.* | **collection** | **shop** | **library** | **player** | **sleeve**

record *verb*

1 information
● ADV. **carefully, meticulously, painstakingly** | **accurately, correctly, properly** *The weights must be recorded accurately.* | **faithfully** *It was all there, faithfully recorded in his uncle's stiff and formal style.* | **duly** *The contract is witnessed by others and duly recorded.* | **automatically, routinely** *The mother's occupation was not routinely recorded on the birth certificate.* | **officially** | **electronically, manually** | **graphically, vividly** *The circumstances of her death were graphically recorded in the local press.*

● PREP. **as** *The time of the accident is recorded as 6.23 p.m.*

● PHRASES **be recorded for posterity** *The names of those who died are recorded for posterity on a tablet at the back of the church.* **historically recorded** *historically recorded events* **poorly/well recorded** *The geographical spread of the industry in the 16th century is hard to ascertain, for much of it is poorly recorded.*

2 sound/pictures
● ADV. **secretly** *She secretly recorded the conversation.*

● PREP. **from** *a programme she had recorded from the radio* **on** *I recorded the film on video.*

● PHRASES **beautifully/well recorded** *This CD has been beautifully recorded.* **digitally recorded**

recorder *noun*

⇨ Special page at MUSIC

recording *noun*

● ADJ. **excellent, fine, good** | **accurate, careful, detailed** *a detailed recording of facts* | **complete** *a complete recording of Mozart's piano sonatas* | **last, later/latest, new, recent** *the band's latest recording* | **modern** | **early, old** | **original** *to enhance the quality of the original recording* | **pirate** | **commercial** *one of the first commercial recordings of the artist* | **professional** | **live, studio** | **audio, video** | **cassette, tape** | **analogue, digital** | **mono, stereo** | **electrical, magnetic** *The principles of magnetic recording have been around for a long time.* | **music, sound** *before the invention of sound recording* | **orchestral, piano, etc.** | **test**

● VERB + RECORDING **make (sb)** *Make a few test recordings before you start the session in earnest.* | **play (sb), play (sb) back** *I want to play you a recording of the rehearsal.* | **hear, listen to** | **view, watch**

● RECORDING + VERB **give sth, show sth** *The recording gives an account of his kidnapping.* | **sound ...** *The recording sounds just like a live performance.*

● RECORDING + NOUN **process** | **session** | **facilities, studio** | **device, equipment, system** | **engineer** | **artist** | **career** *The clarinet player has launched her recording career.* | **contract, deal** | **company** | **industry**

● PREP. **~by** *a recording by the Amadeus Quartet*

recount verb

• ADV. **vividly** *The story of his life is vividly recounted in this new book.*

recourse noun

• ADJ. **constant, frequent | limited | no other, only** *I have no other recourse than to inform the police.* | **direct** *The study of these creatures has been conducted without direct recourse to living specimens.* | **legal**
• VERB + RECOURSE **have** *The mother of an illegitimate child had no legal recourse to the father.* | **seek** *An order was made against which he sought recourse in the supreme court.* | **avoid** *Their system of dispute resolution avoids recourse to the courts.*
• PREP. **by~to** *people who deal with emotional pain by recourse to drugs and alcohol* **without~to** *They tried to settle the dispute without recourse to the courts.* | **~against** *Citizens have learnt that they do have recourse against governments.* **~to** *She often had recourse to her dictionary.*

recover verb

• ADV. **completely, fully | partially | only just | hardly, never/not quite, never really** *She had hardly recovered from the birth of her last baby.* | **well** *Your baby is recovering well.* | **enough, sufficiently** *After a minute she recovered enough to speak.* | **quickly, soon | gradually, slowly | apparently | never**
• VERB + RECOVER **help sb (to) | struggle to** *Yates is struggling to recover form a serious knee injury.*
• PREP. **from** *Mrs Burton was last night recovering from her injuries in hospital.*

recovery noun

• ADJ. **amazing, astonishing, dramatic, excellent, miraculous, remarkable | good, satisfactory, significant, strong, substantial | complete, full | limited, modest, partial** *The FTSE index staged a modest recovery to be 6.5 points down.* | **fragile | fast, quick, rapid, speedy, swift | gradual, slow | steady | faltering | eventual | continuing, lasting, long-term, sustained | spontaneous | national | economic, industrial, physical, political | price, profits | post-war**
• VERB + RECOVERY **achieve, make, stage** *Many people make remarkable recoveries after strokes.* | **aid, speed (up), stimulate** *A holiday would speed his recovery.* ◇ *a reduction in interest rates to stimulate global economic recovery* | **delay, hamper, hinder | wish sb** *We wish them all a speedy recovery.*
• RECOVERY + VERB **be on the way, come** *The economic circumstances are right and recovery is on the way* (= recovery will occur soon). | **be … way off** *Unemployment is high and economic recovery is still a long way off* (= it will be a long time until recovery). | **be underway, occur, take place | continue**
• RECOVERY + NOUN **time** *His injuries have returned as there was insufficient recovery time between matches.* | **period, phase | process | plan, programme | room** *After the operation she was taken to the recovery room.* | **position** *Continue resuscitation until the person starts breathing and then place them in the recovery position.*
• PREP. **beyond~** *The region has been damaged by acid rain and rivers are fouled almost beyond recovery.* **in~** *He's in recovery from the disease.* | **~from** *recovery from his illness* **~in** *the recent recovery in consumer spending* **~to** *a slow recovery to full health*
• PHRASES **be on the road to recovery** *She is well on the road to recovery* (= making good progress towards recovery). **hopes/prospects of recovery, a sign of recovery** *The economy is showing the first signs of recovery.*

recreation noun

• ADJ. **popular | chief, main** *Playing billiards is my chief recreation.* | **informal | physical | countryside, outdoor | indoor**
• RECREATION + NOUN **area, centre, facilities, ground, room**
• PREP. **for~** *She cycles for recreation.*
• PHRASES **a form of recreation** *His only form of recreation is playing cards.* **a source of recreation** *exploiting the countryside as a source of recreation*

recruit noun

• ADJ. **latest, new, raw, recent** *raw recruits marching up and down with the drill instructor* | **possible, potential | young | graduate | army**
• VERB + RECRUIT **find** *A common way for companies to find new recruits is by taking a stand at a job exhibition.* | **attract** *It's difficult to attract recruits when working conditions are so poor.* | **enlist, gain, sign up** *Thousands of recruits had been enlisted and partly trained.* ◇ *She tried to gain recruits for the party.* | **train** *Army recruits are all trained in first aid.* | **provide** *Their business schools provide recruits for domestic industry.*
• PREP. **~to** *new recruits to the party*

recruit verb

• ADV. **directly** *The specialist institutions directly recruit their own staff.* | **actively | locally** *Most of the workers will be recruited locally.* | **personally** *She personally recruited the teachers.* | **specially** *Staff were recruited specially for the event.*
• VERB + RECRUIT **need to | seek to, try to**
• PREP. **as** *Peter Watson has been recruited as Sales Manager.* **for** *A hundred patients were recruited for the study.* **from** *Soldiers were recruited from the local villages.* **into** *Some of the men were recruited into the army.* **to** *Ten new members were recruited to the committee.*
• PHRASES **newly/recently recruited**

recruitment noun

• ADJ. **large/large-scale | annual | forced** *forced recruitment of labour* | **labour, staff | executive, graduate, student** *She has set up her own executive recruitment business in Paris.* | **army, military, police**
• RECRUITMENT + NOUN **policy | strategy | procedure, process | campaign, drive, programme | market | agency, consultancy, service | consultant, manager, officer, specialist** *the company's recruitment officer*
• PREP. **~ by** *recruitment by large companies* **~ into/to** *large-scale recruitment to the new industries*
• PHRASES **a method of recruitment, a source of recruitment** *One source of recruitment is the civil service.*

recur verb

• ADV. **constantly, frequently, regularly** *This is a constantly recurring problem which we must deal with.*
• VERB + RECUR **be likely to | tend to**
• PREP. **throughout** *a theme that recurs throughout the book*
• PHRASES **keep recurring**

recurrence noun

• ADJ. **high | frequent | tumour, ulcer, etc.**
• VERB + RECURRENCE **avoid, prevent | experience, have, suffer** *He has suffered a recurrence of his hamstring injury.*
• RECURRENCE + NOUN **rate**
• PHRASES **the likelihood of a recurrence, the risk of recurrence** *a high risk of recurrence*

recyclable adj.

- VERBS be
- ADV. **easily** *Paper is easily recyclable.* | **completely** *Glass products are completely recyclable.* | **potentially**

recycle verb

- ADV. **endlessly, regularly** (*often figurative*) *endlessly recycling the same worn-out arguments*
- PREP. **from** *made of plastic recycled from old packaging material* **into** *These materials can be recycled into other packaging products.*

red adj.

1 of the colour of blood
- VERBS **glow** *The coals glowed red in the dying fire.*
- ADV. **very** | **slightly** *The leaves looked slightly red.*
- ADJ. **bright, brilliant, fiery, flaming, vibrant, vivid** *flaming red hair* | **dark, deep, rich** | **light, pale** | **dull** | **blood, brick, ruby** *her ruby red lips*
⇨ Special page at COLOUR

2 of the face
- VERBS **be, look** | **flush, go, grow, turn** *Mr Grubb was shouting and growing redder and redder in the face.*
- ADV. **very** | **quite** | **rather, slightly**
- ADJ. **bright, fiery** *He could feel himself going bright red.*
- PREP. **with** *Ross flushed red with embarrassment.*
- PHRASES **as red as a beetroot, red in the face** *Charles was rapidly turning red in the face.*

redemption noun

1 being saved from the power of evil
- VERB + REDEMPTION **be in need of, need** *She believes that humanity is in need of redemption.*
- PREP. **beyond~** *After another incident at the weekend, the club's reputation for violence is beyond redemption.* | **~from** *redemption from evil*

2 repayment of money invested/borrowed
- ADJ. **early** *There is a fee for early redemption.* | **capital, loan, share**
- REDEMPTION + NOUN **date** | **price, value, yield**
- PREP. **on~** *A charge is payable on redemption.*

redistribution noun

- ADJ. **major, massive, significant, substantial** | **equitable** | **income, land, population**
- VERB + REDISTRIBUTION **be/become available for** *a national tax available for redistribution to local government* | **bring about** *The tax brought about a significant redistribution of wealth.*
- PREP. **~from, ~to** *redistribution from the rich to the poor*

red tape noun

- ADJ. **bureaucratic**
- VERB + RED TAPE **cut (through), reduce**

reduce verb

- ADV. **considerably, dramatically, drastically, greatly, sharply, significantly, substantially** | **further** | **slightly** *We need to reduce the speed slightly.* | **gradually, progressively** *Legislation progressively reduced the number of situations in which industrial action could be taken.*
- VERB + REDUCE **aim to, attempt to, seek to, try to** | **help (to)** *Giving up smoking helps reduce the risk of heart disease.* | **manage to** | **be designed to, be intended to** | **be expected to, be likely to**
- PREP. **by** *Pollution from the works has been reduced by 70 per cent.* **from, to** *The price is reduced from 99p to 85p.*
- PHRASES **an attempt/effort to reduce sth, measures to reduce sth, reduce sth to a minimum** *The risks must be reduced to the absolute minimum.*

reduction noun

- ADJ. **big, considerable, dramatic, drastic, great, huge, large, major, marked, massive, remarkable, severe, significant, substantial** *The changes may result in a greater reduction in employee numbers than we had previously expected.* ◇ *a sale with massive reductions on selected items* | **minor, slight, small** | **further** | **possible** | **actual, net, overall, real** | **across-the-board, general** | **rapid, sharp, steep** | **slow** | **immediate, sudden** | **gradual, progressive, steady** | **initial** | **recent** | **long-term, permanent** | **proposed** | **percentage** *A small percentage reduction in the cost of materials would mean a significant increase in profit.* | **capital, cost, debt, deficit, expenditure, pay, price, tariff, tax, wage** | **emission, noise, pollution, waste** | **weight** | **staff** | **arms, troop**
- VERB + REDUCTION **achieve, make, secure** *The government has found it difficult to make real reductions in government spending.* ◇ *Every effort is made to secure the highest possible reduction in casualties.* | **cause, lead to, make, produce, result in** *These simple changes will make a substantial reduction in the fat content of your diet.* | **avoid** | **ask for, demand, seek** *I asked for a reduction as the dress was damaged.* | **get, receive** *Guests staying 14 nights will receive a ten per cent reduction.* | **suffer** *They suffered a severe reduction in income.* | **accept, welcome** | **give (sb), offer (sb)** | **propose** *She proposed a reduction in the state president's powers.* | **notice, observe, witness** *I haven't noticed any significant reduction in the performance of my car since switching to unleaded fuel.* | **announce** | **forecast** *The budget forecasts a deficit reduction of 27%.* | **mean, represent** *Our average margins dropped to 35%, which represents a reduction in gross margins of £109 million.* | **show** *Figures just released show a steady reduction in levels of emissions over the last four years.*
- REDUCTION + VERB **occur, take place**
- REDUCTION + NOUN **target** *the government's waste reduction targets*
- PREP. **through a/the ~** *economic growth through a reduction in interest rates* | **~ by** *reduction by 30%* **~ from, ~ in** *There has been a sharp reduction in the number of accidents on motorways.* **~ on** *a 25% reduction on normal subscription rates* **~ to** *a reduction in the speed limit from 50 to 40 miles per hour*
- PHRASES **a reduction in numbers** *They are concerned about the reduction in numbers of people eligible for legal aid.* **a reduction in the amount/number/size of sth** *the reduction in the number of hospital beds*

redundancy noun

- ADJ. **large-scale, major, mass, massive** *The closure of the mine led to large-scale redundancies.* | **widespread** | **threatened** | **compulsory, enforced, forced** | **voluntary**
- QUANT. **round, wave** *a fresh wave of redundancies*
- VERB + REDUNDANCY **make** *The bank will be making 3 500 redundancies over the next five years.* | **lead to, result in** | **avoid** | **announce** | **be threatened by/with, face** *Sixty workers at a clothing factory face redundancy because the firm is relocating.* | **accept, take, volunteer for** *Those choosing to take redundancy will receive the company's standard redundancy terms.*
- REDUNDANCY + VERB **occur, take place**
- REDUNDANCY + NOUN **policy** | **programme** | **notice** *Redundancy notices have been sent to 200 workers.* | **compensation, package, terms** | **money, pay, payment** | **costs** *Most of the companies' losses stemmed from redundancy costs.*
- PHRASES **the threat of redundancy**

redundant *adj.*

1 no longer needed for a job
- VERBS **be | become | make sb** *the decision to make 800 employees compulsorily redundant*
- ADV. **compulsorily**

2 not necessary or wanted
- VERBS **be, feel, seem | become | declare sth, make sth, render sth** *The chapel was declared redundant in 1995.*
- ADV. **completely | virtually | largely**

refer *verb*

PHRASAL VERB
refer to sb/sth
- ADV. **briefly, in passing** *He referred to the report in passing.* **| specifically | commonly** *The disease was commonly referred to as 'the green sickness'.* **| frequently, often | generally, usually | sometimes | always | never | jokingly**
- VERB + REFER TO SB/STH **be used to** *The term 'alexia' is used to refer to any acquired disorder of reading.*
- PREP. **as** *She always referred to Ben as 'that nice man'.*

referee *noun*

1 controls a sports match
- ADJ. **boxing, football | match, tournament** *decisions taken by the match referee* **| international**
- REFEREE + VERB **award sb sth** *The referee awarded a free kick to the home team.* **| book sb, send sb off** *The referee booked three players for offensive behaviour.*
- PHRASES **the referee's decision**

2 recommends sb for a job
- ADJ. **academic, professional**
- VERB + REFEREE **act as, be**
- PREP. **~for** *His former employer agreed to act as a referee for him.*

3 settles a dispute between people
- ADJ. **official**
- VERB + REFEREE **act as** *to act as referee between the parties involved*
- PREP. **~between**

reference *noun*

1 mentioning sb/sth
- ADJ. **extensive | brief, casual, passing | occasional | frequent, repeated | constant | further** *They could find no further reference to Mr LaMotte in the records.* **| general | particular, special, specific** *She won a grant to study political science with special reference to China.* **| definite | explicit, express | direct | cryptic, indirect, oblique, obscure, veiled | clear, obvious | ambiguous, confusing | early** *one of the earliest references to the game of chess* **| biblical, cultural, historical, literary | written**
- VERB + REFERENCE **contain, have** *Her diary contains no reference to the alleged appointment.* **| drop, make** *He dropped casual references to the legacy of his great work.* ◇ *The article makes no reference to his first marriage.* **| drop, omit** *The new constitution dropped all reference to previous wars.* **| find**
- PREP. **in a/the~** *In an obvious reference to the president, he talked of corruption in high places.* **in/with ~ to** *(written) I am writing with reference to your job application.* **| ~(back) to** *The summary should be comprehensible without reference back to the source work.*

2 consulting sb/sth for advice/help/information
- ADJ. **easy, quick** *The book is organized alphabetically for easy reference.* **| further, future**
- PREP. **by~to** *Our charges are calculated by reference to an hourly rate.* **for~** *Retain a copy of the form for future ref-*

erence. **without ~ to** *The decision was taken without reference to local managers.*
- PHRASES **for reference purposes** *She needs the book for reference purposes.* **a source of reference** *The book is an invaluable source of reference for the art historian.*

3 book containing facts/information
- ADJ. **general** *The book is by far the best general reference on natural history.*
- REFERENCE + NOUN **book, material, source, work | library | section** *You'll find the information in the reference section of your local library.*

4 number/note/symbol
- ADJ. **copious | full** *For full references of all books cited, see Appendix B.* **| appropriate** *Please send a full CV, quoting the appropriate reference.* **| cross-** *The cross-references refer you to information in other parts of the dictionary.* **| bibliographic/bibliographical | grid, map**
- VERB + REFERENCE **quote | cite, give** *References to original sources are given at the end of each chapter.*
- REFERENCE + NOUN **number**
- PREP. **in a/the ~** *The date of publication should be included in the reference.* **| ~to** *a reference to page 17*
- PHRASES **a list of references**

5 letter about your character/abilities
- ADJ. **glowing | character**
- VERB + REFERENCE **ask for | give (sb), provide (sb with), write (sb) | follow up, take up** *They've taken up my references (= contacted the person who provided the reference), so they must be interested in me.*
- PREP. **~from** *a reference from your current employer*

6 standards by which sth is judged
- REFERENCE + NOUN **point**
- PHRASES **a frame of reference** *People interpret events within their own frame of reference.* **a point of reference** *Unemployment serves as a useful point of reference in examining social problems.* **terms of reference** *The matter was outside the committee's terms of reference.*

referendum *noun*

- ADJ. **planned, proposed | popular | national, nationwide | constitutional, independence**
- VERB + REFERENDUM **conduct, hold** *The referendum will be held on July 14th.* **| put sth to** *The proposals were put to a referendum.* **| call** *The president called a referendum that he hoped would confirm him in power.* **| call for, demand, propose** *The group called for a referendum on the death penalty.* **| oppose | boycott** *The unions urged people to boycott the referendum.* **| declare, organize | be adopted by, be approved by, be confirmed by, be endorsed by** *a new constitution adopted by referendum*
- REFERENDUM + VERB **show sth** *A popular referendum showed that the majority of people want reform.*
- REFERENDUM + NOUN **proposal** *The Democrats rejected the referendum proposal.* **| campaign | result**
- PREP. **in a/the~** *The issue will be decided in a national referendum.* **| ~on** *a referendum on a new constitution*
- PHRASES **declare a referendum fair/illegal** *UN monitors declared the referendum fair.* **the result/results of a referendum**

refine *verb*

- ADV. **slightly | further | increasingly | constantly, continuously** *The information system is constantly refined and updated.* **| gradually**
- VERB + REFINE **attempt to, try to | help (to)**
- PREP. **into** *Sugar cane is refined into sugar.*

refinement *noun*

1 improvement to/on sth; process of improving sth
- ADJ. **considerable, great** *A greater refinement of the categorization is possible.* **| extra, further | continuous,**

endless *All programs have bugs and need endless refinement.* | **useful** *It is possible to add a few useful refinements to the basic system.* | **technical** | **modern**
- QUANT. **degree**
- VERB + REFINEMENT **need, require** *The technology requires a great deal of refinement.* | **add, introduce**
- PREP. **~in** *a refinement in the masonry* **~on** *a refinement on previous methods* **~to** *to add a further refinement to the computer system*

2 being polite/well educated; clever in design
- ADJ. **great** *a woman of great refinement and beauty*
- VERB + REFINEMENT **lack** *The kite was star shaped and lacked the refinement of current designs.*
- PREP. **~in** *a lack of refinement in engine design*
- PHRASES **a lack of refinement**

reflect *verb*

1 send back light/heat/sound
- ADV. **dimly, dully** *The sun reflected dully off the stone walls.* ◇ *(figurative) In Milton's poem, Satan, even after his fall, dimly reflects his former glory.* | **back**
- PREP. **from** *The screen reflects light from the sun.* **off**

2 show/express sth
- ADV. **clearly** | **directly** | **accurately, closely, correctly, faithfully, well** *Does this opinion poll accurately reflect the public mood?* | **adequately** *The punishment should adequately reflect the revulsion felt by most people for this appalling crime.* | **merely, simply** *This year's budget simply reflects the fact that we have fewer people out of work.* | **not necessarily** *The views expressed in this article do not necessarily reflect those of the editor.*
- VERB + REFLECT **be designed to** *The exhibition is designed to reflect the diversity of the nation and its regions.*
- PREP. **in** *The condition of the house is reflected in its low price.*

3 think deeply
- ADV. **bitterly, gloomily, ruefully, wryly** *reflecting ruefully that the great American dollar didn't buy as much as it used to*
- VERB + REFLECT **pause to** | **leave sb to** *He was left to reflect on the implications of his decision.*
- PREP. **on/upon** *She paused to reflect on what she had achieved.*
- PHRASES **time to reflect** *I need time to reflect.*

reflection *noun*

1 image in a mirror, etc.
- ADJ. **clear** | **faint** | **blurred, distorted**
- VERB + REFLECTION **catch a glimpse of, catch sight of, see** *He caught sight of her reflection in the window.* | **glance at, look at** | **gaze at, stare at, watch** | **examine, inspect, study**
- REFLECTION + VERB **look ...** *Her reflection in the mirror looked distorted.*
- PREP. **in a/the ~** *In the reflection on the glass door he could see the class behind him.* | **~in** *I saw my reflection in the polished marble.* **~on** *the reflection of the mountains on the calm waters of the lake*

2 sending light/heat/sound back from a surface
- ADJ. **heat, light, sound**
- PREP. **~from** *There is reflection of heat from the metal surface.*
- PHRASES **the angle of reflection**

3 indication/description of sth
- ADJ. **accurate, fair, true** | **inadequate** | **mere, pale** *This account is only a pale reflection of the true state of affairs.* | **direct, simple** *Young people's behaviour is a direct reflection of adults'.* | **sad**
- VERB + REFLECTION **give (sb), provide** *Such studies do not give a true reflection of population needs.*

- PREP. **~of/on/upon** *His low level of performance is no reflection on his general ability.*

4 careful thought about sth
- ADJ. **deep, mature, serious, sober** | **further** | **quiet** | **personal** | **critical, philosophical, theological**
- VERB + REFLECTION **encourage** *Counselling should encourage reflection on the past.*
- REFLECTION + VERB **show sb/sth** *A moment's reflection will show you that that can't be true.*
- PREP. **after/on/upon ~** *On further reflection, I'm not so sure it's a good idea.* | **~about/on/upon** *The party needs a period of sober reflection about what went wrong.*
- PHRASES **a moment's reflection, a period for/of reflection, time for reflection**

5 written or spoken thoughts about sth
- ADJ. **interesting** | **poignant**
- VERB + REFLECTION **have**
- PREP. **~about/on/upon** *She has some interesting reflections about the spiritual state of the country.*

reflective *adj.*

- VERBS **be**
- ADV. **highly, very** | **slightly**

reflex *noun*

- ADJ. **good, lightning, quick** | **poor** | **automatic** | **natural** | **conditioned**
- VERB + REFLEX **trigger** *The rapid movement of an object towards the eye triggers the blink reflex.* | **control** | **sharpen, speed up** *The training is designed to sharpen the fighter's reflexes.* | **slow (down)** *Alcohol can slow your reflexes.* | **suppress** | **test** *The doctor tested her reflexes.*
- REFLEX + NOUN **action, reaction** *Almost as a reflex action, I grab my pen as the phone rings.*
- PREP. **by ~** *Almost by reflex, he helped himself to a drink.*

reform *noun*

- ADJ. **drastic, fundamental, great, important, major, radical, significant, substantial** | **comprehensive, far-reaching, sweeping, wholesale, wide-ranging** | **minor** | **piecemeal** | **new** | **further** | **immediate** | **rapid** | **much needed, necessary, overdue** *Health care reform is long overdue.* | **effective** | **practical** | **moral, political, social** | **democratic, liberal** | **domestic, institutional, internal** | **procedural, structural** | **administrative, governmental** | **constitutional, electoral, judicial, law, legal, legislative** | **penal, prison** | **curriculum, educational** | **welfare** | **budgetary, economic, financial, monetary, tax** | **agrarian, agricultural, environmental, land**
- QUANT. **package**
- VERB + REFORM **adopt, bring about, introduce, put in place** | **push through** *They wanted a weak president and a strong one-chamber parliament able to push through radical reforms.* | **carry out/through, implement, put into practice, undertake** | **accelerate** *efforts to accelerate the structural reform of the economy* | **delay** | **block** *The conservative coalition could delay further reforms or block them altogether.* | **accept, welcome** | **advocate, call for, press for, propose** *They have issued a statement advocating reform of the legal system.* | **demand** | **back, encourage, support** *We are committed to supporting democracy and reform in the region.* | **require** *The practice of global politics requires reform.* | **plan** | **discuss**
- REFORM + VERB **go through** *The reforms went through in spite of opposition from teachers.* | **aim at sth** *tax reforms aimed at encouraging land development*
- REFORM + NOUN **process** | **movement** | **initiative, measure, package, programme** | **act, bill** | **policy**
- PREP. **~in** *reforms in housing and education*

- PHRASES **the need for reform, the pace of reform, a programme of reform, a timetable for reform**

reform *verb*

- ADV. **drastically, fundamentally, radically** *The health service must be radically reformed.*
- VERB + REFORM **attempt to, seek to, try to**
- PHRASES **attempts/efforts/proposals to reform sth, a need to reform sth**

refrain *noun*

- ADJ. **constant | familiar** *Complaints about school food have become a familiar refrain.*
- VERB + REFRAIN **sing, take up** *The choir's sopranos took up the refrain.*
- REFRAIN + VERB **go** *Shoppers, so the refrain goes, are never happy until they have found a bargain.*

refrain *verb*

- ADV. **carefully, deliberately** *He deliberately refrained from expressing his opinion on the matter.* | **wisely**
- PREP. **from** *I refrained from laughing.*

refreshing *adj.*

- VERBS **be | find sth**
- ADV. **extremely, highly, really, very, wonderfully** *The water was cold and wonderfully refreshing.* | **quite**

refreshment *noun*

- ADJ. **light | liquid** (*humorous*)
- VERB + REFRESHMENT **need | take | pause for, stop for** *We stopped for refreshment halfway through the journey.* | **provide (sb with), serve** *Light refreshments will be served in the interval.*
- REFRESHMENT + VERB **be available**
- REFRESHMENT + NOUN **area, hut, kiosk, room | facilities, service**
- PREP. **for ~** *We're allowed twenty minutes for refreshment.* **for~s** *What are we going to have for refreshments?*
- PHRASES **a place of refreshment, rest and refreshment** *rest and refreshment for the mind and body*

refuge *noun*

- ADJ. **safe | temporary | wildlife | mountain** *a monk living in a mountain refuge* | **last** (*figurative*) *They looked to the country as the last refuge of liberty.*
- VERB + REFUGE **take** *They took refuge in the embassy.* | **look for, seek** *They sought refuge in the mountain villages.* | **find** *They were hoping to find a safe refuge for the night.* ◇ *They found refuge from the bright sun.* | **give (sb), offer (sb), provide (sb with)**
- PREP. **~ against** (*figurative*) *Home is a refuge against the pressures of work.* **~ from** *The cave provided refuge from the storm.*
- PHRASES **a place of refuge**

refugee *noun*

- ADJ. **genuine, real | would-be | returning | economic, environmental, political, war** *Many claimed to be environmental refugees, leaving for the sake of their health.* | **civilian | child**
- VERB + REFUGEE **qualify as** *Those who did not qualify as refugees were returned to their home countries.* | **be considered, be found to be, be recognized as** *Only nine per cent were found to be genuine political refugees.* | **accept, resettle, take (back/in)** *The government has agreed to take only 150 refugees plus their dependants.* | **expel, return | house | help**
- REFUGEE + VERB **flee sth** *refugees fleeing political persecution* | **be displaced** *refugees displaced by the civil*

war | **arrive | pour** *Hundreds of refugees are pouring over the border.* | **live** *refugees living in camps along the border* | **return**
- REFUGEE + NOUN **crisis, issue, problem, question, situation | exodus | resettlement | status** *The Home Office has refused him refugee status.* | **group, organization, worker | camp, centre, hostel | children, community, family, population**
- PREP. **among ~** *Unemployment among the refugees has risen sharply.* **~ from** *refugees from civil wars*
- PHRASES **a flood/influx of refugees** *a new influx of refugees from the combat zone* **the flow of refugees, the plight of refugees, the return of refugees**

refund *noun*

- ADJ. **full | cash | tax, ticket**
- VERB + REFUND **give (sb), make** *They'll only give you a refund if you've got the receipt.* | **offer (sb) | refuse (sb)** *He has been refused a refund on his air ticket.* | **be entitled to** *You're entitled to a full refund should you be unsatisfied with the quality of our goods.* | **ask (sb) for, claim, demand, request, seek | get, obtain, receive**
- PREP. **~ for** *There will be no refund for cancellations made within 10 working days of the conference.* **~ on** *She received a refund on the unused tickets.*

refund *verb*

- ADV. **in full** *Your money will be refunded in full.* | **promptly**
- PREP. **to** *If you are not satisfied with the goods, the price will be refunded to you.*

refusal *noun*

- ADJ. **blank, blunt, complete, flat, outright, point-blank | continued/continuing, obstinate, persistent, repeated, steadfast, stubborn | cowardly | wilful | polite | first** *If you decide to sell your car, I hope you'll give me first refusal* (= the opportunity to buy it before it is offered to others).
- VERB + REFUSAL **be met by/with** *Her appeals for funds to support the cause were met with blank refusal.*
- PREP. **~ by/of** *a refusal by a patient to accept the recommended treatment*
- PHRASES **a refusal of consent** *a refusal of consent to blood transfusions* **refusal on … grounds** *their refusal on religious grounds to perform military service*

refuse *noun*

- ADJ. **domestic, household | uncollected**
- QUANT. **heap, mound, pile**
- VERB + REFUSE **dump** *People dump their refuse in the surrounding woods instead of taking it to the tip.* | **collect** *What day do they collect the refuse?* | **recycle**
- REFUSE + NOUN **collection, disposal | bin | dump**

refuse *verb*

- ADV. **adamantly, obstinately, resolutely, steadfastly, stoutly, stubbornly | categorically, flatly, point-blank, simply** *Gerard refused point-blank to co-operate.* | **pointedly** *The demand for an apology was pointedly refused.* | **politely | consistently**
- VERB + REFUSE **can't/couldn't, can/could hardly** *They made me an offer I couldn't refuse.* | **be entitled to, have the right to** *Workers should be entitled to refuse to work under these conditions.* | **be/seem churlish to** *She offered them cups of tea and it seemed churlish to refuse.*

regain *verb*

- ADV. **completely** *He hadn't completely regained his strength.* | **quickly, rapidly | gradually, slowly | even-**

tually, finally | **never** *He was severely injured and never regained consciousness.*
- VERB + REGAIN **fight to, struggle to, try to** *The team are struggling to regain last season's form.* | **be desperate to, be determined to, hope to** *He was determined to regain what his father had lost.* | **help sb (to)** | **manage to** | **be unable to, fail to**
- PHRASES **an attempt/a bid/an effort to regain sth** *He is making a bid to regain his World No 1 ranking.* **a chance/an opportunity to regain sth** *a chance to regain the lead in the contest*

regard *noun*

1 attention to/thought for sb/sth
- ADJ. **due, full, proper** | **scant** | **particular, specific**
- VERB + REGARD **have** *(often law) When exercising its discretion, the court will have regard to all the circumstances.* | **pay, show** *The manifesto pays scant regard to green issues.*
- PREP. **in/with ~ to** *I am writing with regard to your recent order.* **without ~ for/to** *an attempt to plan the future of an industry without due regard to market forces* | **~ for** *a proper regard for human dignity*
- PHRASES **in that/this regard** *I have nothing further to say in this regard* (= in regard to what has just been said). **a lack of regard** *a lack of regard for public safety* **little/no regard for/to sb/sth**

2 respect/admiration for sb
- ADJ. **considerable, great, high** | **insufficient, low** | **mutual** | **critical**
- VERB + REGARD **have, hold sb/sth in** *I have the greatest regard for his abilities.* ◇ *He is held in the highest regard by his colleagues.* | **win** *The film has won critical regard in America.*

3 regards used to send greetings to sb
- ADJ. **best, kind, warm** *(all written) The letter ended, 'Kindest regards, Felicity.'*
- VERB + REGARDS **convey, give (sb), send (sb)** *(written) David sends his warmest regards to your parents.*
- PREP. **~ to** *(written) My regards to your aunt* (= please give my regards to your aunt).

regard *verb*

1 (often **be regarded**) think of sb/sth in a particular way
- ADV. **highly, well** *She was highly regarded as a sculptor.* | **generally, universally, widely** *The project was widely regarded as a success.* | **commonly, popularly, usually** | **conventionally, traditionally** *Foxes were traditionally regarded as vermin.* | **legitimately, properly, reasonably** *Civil contempt is not properly regarded as a criminal offence.* | **hitherto** | **still** | **no longer**
- VERB + REGARD **seem to** *He seemed to regard the whole thing as a joke.* | **tend to** *They tend to regard the open expression of emotion as being soft and feminine.* | **come to** *I had come to regard him as a close friend.* | **continue to** | **be tempted to, be tempting to** *The successful are often tempted to regard their success as a kind of reward.* | **be a mistake to** *It would be a mistake to regard the incident as unimportant.*
- PREP. **as** *Many of her works are regarded as classics.* **with** *They regarded people outside their own village with suspicion.*

2 look steadily at sb/sth
- ADV. **steadily** | **intently** | **curiously, suspiciously, thoughtfully, warily**
- VERB + REGARD **continue to** *His eyes continued to regard her steadily.*
- PREP. **with** *She regarded the mess with distaste.*

regime *noun*

1 system of government
- ADJ. **new** | **old** | **current, established, existing, present** | **former, previous** | **interim** | **political** | **conservative, liberal, radical** | **authoritarian, autocratic, dictatorial, totalitarian** | **communist, democratic, fascist, socialist** | **brutal, hard-line, harsh, oppressive, repressive** | **constitutional, parliamentary** | **revolutionary** | **military** | **colonial** | **puppet** *In 1940 a puppet regime was established by the invaders.*
- VERB + REGIME **establish, install, set up** | **defeat, overthrow, topple** | **bolster, strengthen** *Education was seen as a way of bolstering the existing regime.* | **destabilize** | **support** | **oppose** | **head** *a military regime headed by the general*
- REGIME + VERB **exist** | **come to power** *The communist regime came to power in 1975.* | **collapse, fall**
- PREP. **against a/the ~** *She called for sanctions against the regime.* **under a/the ~** *He spoke of the abhorrent crimes that had been committed under the regime.* | **~ under** *a military regime under Franco*
- PHRASES **a change of regime, the collapse/fall/overthrow of a regime, a member of a regime**

2 set of rules/procedures
- ADJ. **harsh, rigorous, strict, tight** | **relaxed** | **new** | **special** | **exercise, fitness, health, training** | **dietary, drug, therapeutic, treatment** | **educational** | **economic, financial, fiscal, legal, regulatory** *a financial regime imposed by the government* | **trade/trading, tax** | **safety**
- VERB + REGIME **create, introduce, set up, start** *It will be necessary to create a regime to monitor compliance with the agreements.* | **impose** | **subject sb to** *The children were subjected to a strict regime of meals, walks and lessons.* | **follow** *He suggested to me that I follow his fitness regime.*
- REGIME + VERB **be based on sth** *a regime based on discipline and training*
- PREP. **under a/the ~** *Under the new regime you will be liable for automatic penalties for late submission of tax returns.* | **~ for** *the new regime for accounting for charities*

regimen *noun*

- ADJ. **strict** | **combined** | **dietary** | **treatment** | **drug** | **dosage/dose**
- VERB + REGIMEN **use** *We used a combined regimen of injection treatment and radiation therapy.*
- REGIMEN + VERB **comprise sth** *a treatment regimen comprising two antibiotics*

region *noun*

1 area of land/part of a country
- ADJ. **large** | **small** | **entire, whole** | **distinct, particular, specific** | **northern, southern, etc.** | **central** | **border, far-flung, outlying, peripheral, remote** | **neighbouring, surrounding** | **unexplored** | **geographical** | **arid, coastal, desert, equatorial, jungle, mountain/mountainous, polar, tropical** | **Basque, Gulf, London, Pacific, etc.** | **autonomous** | **urbanized** | **rural** | **populated** *a sparsely populated region* | **economic** | **developed, industrial** | **developing** | **depressed, poor, underdeveloped** *the poorer regions of the continent* | **prosperous, rich** *Italy's richest region* | **oil-producing, etc.**
- VERB + REGION **inhabit, live in** *Nomads have inhabited this region for thousands of years.* | **work in** | **leave** | **visit** | **divide sth into** *The country is divided into 17 autonomous regions.* | **confine sb/sth to** *This bird is largely confined to the southern regions of the country.*
- REGION + VERB **cover sb/sth** *The champagne-producing region covers 34 500 hectares.*
- PREP. **across a/the ~** *Sports events across the region have been cancelled because of the weather.* **from a/the ~**

Twenty participants from the Asia-Pacific region will be invited to the seminar. **in/within a/the ~** *The animal is found in the northern regions of Sweden.* **in the ~ of** (*figurative*) *She earns in the region of* (= approximately) *£200 000.* **throughout a/the ~** *The plant is found throughout the western regions of the country.*
• PHRASES **sth varies from region to region** *Sanitary facilities varied widely from region to region.*

2 part of the body
• ADJ. **distinct, particular, specific | brain,** etc.
• PREP. **from a/the ~** *tissue from the mouth region* **in/within a/the ~** *cells in a particular region of the brain*

register *noun*

1 list of names
• ADJ. **detailed | full | up-to-date | annual | central, national, public | statutory | professional | attendance, membership | electoral, voters' | medical | birth, burial, marriage | address | class, school | church, parish | hotel | asset, land, property, share**
• VERB + REGISTER **appear on, be on** *All those appearing on the register must notify the authorities of any change of address.* **| remain on | keep, maintain** *They keep a register of all those who have contributed to the fund.* **| call, take** *The teacher takes the register at the beginning of each class.* **| inspect | compile, create, draw up, establish** *She was asked to draw up a register of suitable sites.* **| add sb/sth to, enter sb/sth in/on, register sb/sth in/on** *Their names had been entered in the register as owners of the company.* **| omit sb/sth from | remove sb from, strike sb from/off** *He was struck off the medical register for professional misconduct.* **| sign** *The bride and bridegroom signed the register.*
• REGISTER + VERB **contain sth, include sth** *a register containing details of four million cars*
• REGISTER + NOUN **office**
• PREP. **in a /the~** *It was the last entry in the register.* **on a/the ~** *There are 36 children on the register.*
• PHRASES **an entry in/on a register**

2 range of a voice/an instrument
• ADJ. **high, low, middle, upper** *the lower register of the piano*
• PREP. **in a/the~** *boy trebles singing in high registers*

3 level/style of a piece of writing/speech
• ADJ. **formal, informal | appropriate**
• VERB + REGISTER **adopt** *He has adopted an informal register so as not to alienate his audience.*

register *verb*

1 put sb/sth on an official list
• ADV. **fully** *On completion of the preregistration year, graduates become fully registered by the General Medical Council.* **| jointly** *About 68 per cent of illegitimate births were jointly registered by both parents.* **| formally, officially | legally | duly** *As I reached my eighteenth birthday I duly registered for military service.* **| automatically**
• VERB + REGISTER **be required to, have to, must** *You must register the death within three days.* **| be eligible to, be entitled to | fail to | refuse to**
• PREP. **as** *the number of people officially registering as unemployed* **at** *He registered at his local university.* **for** *There is still time to register for English classes.* **with** *Students living away from home are required to register with a local doctor.*

2 notice sth
• ADV. **barely, hardly, scarcely** *She had barely registered his presence.* **| vaguely** *He vaguely registered that the women had gone.*
• VERB + REGISTER **fail to** *His eyes failed to register Meredith's surprise.*

registration *noun*

• ADJ. **full | limited | formal | compulsory | civil** *civil registration of births* **| birth, death | student, voter | car, company, land, trademark, vehicle | VAT**
• VERB + REGISTRATION **require | be exempt from** *Certain charities are exempt from VAT registration.* **| be eligible for, qualify for** *You should be eligible for registration as a student member.* **| apply for, seek | obtain | grant sb** *Under the new regulation we can grant full registration to foreign lawyers.* **| refuse sb | renew | cancel**
• REGISTRATION + VERB **be required**
• REGISTRATION + NOUN **requirement** *a failure to comply with the registration requirements* **| period | procedure, process | scheme, system | records** *I traced my family history using the civil registration records.* **| form | book, card, document | number** *I gave the registration number of the robbers' car to the police.* **| plate** *The police are looking for a large black saloon with German registration plates.* **| officer | fee**
• PREP. **on ~** *You will receive a free CD on registration with the club.* **| ~ as** *registration as a political party* **~ by** *the registration of the vehicle by the appropriate authority* **~with** *Registration with the council is compulsory.*
• PHRASES **an application for registration, a certificate of registration**

registry *noun*

• ADJ. **public | private | central** *a central registry for all applicants* **| district, national, regional | land, companies'** *The deed of transfer must be entered at the land registry.* **| land** *fees for land registry*
• VERB + REGISTRY **enter sth at/in, lodge sth at/in, register sth at** *The certificate will have to be lodged at the registry.*
• REGISTRY + VERB **have sth, hold sth, keep sth** *The registry holds records of all major operations.*
• REGISTRY + NOUN **fee | office | staff**
• PHRASES **at a/the ~** *The map is kept at the local land registry.*

regret *noun*

• ADJ. **big, bitter, deep, genuine, great, profound, real, sincere** *Her biggest regret was that she had never had children.* ◊ *She expressed deep regret at the incident.*
• QUANT. **pang, stab, tinge, twinge**
• VERB + REGRET **feel, have** *I have absolutely no regrets about resigning.* **| express, show**
• PREP. **to your~** *To my regret, I lost touch with her years ago.* **with ~** *It is with deep regret that we announce the death of Mr Fred Fisher.* **without ~** *She thought of them without regret.* **| ~about/over** *She showed no regret about leaving her country.* **~at** *my sincere regret at what has happened* **~for** *She enjoyed living alone, but felt a tiny pang of regret for her mother's cooking.*
• PHRASES **expression of regret** *The police offered no expression of regret at his wrongful arrest.* **a matter for/of regret** *I never learned to play an instrument and that's a matter of some regret.*

regret *verb*

• ADV. **bitterly, deeply, greatly, really, very much** *The president said that his country deeply regretted the incident.* **| rather | immediately, instantly** *I immediately regretted not asking for his name and address.* **| later** *Pierre told them some things he later regretted telling.* **| never**
• VERB + REGRET **begin to | come to, live to** *She knew that she would live to regret this decision.*

regrettable *adj.*

• VERBS **be, seem**
• ADV. **deeply, extremely, highly, very** *a deeply regret-*

table incident ◇ *It is highly regrettable that the minister cannot be here in person.* | **rather**

regular *adj.*

1 frequent
- VERBS **be, seem** | **become**
- ADV. **very** | **fairly, quite** *at fairly regular intervals*

2 following a pattern
- VERBS **be**
- ADV. **highly, very** *highly regular patterns* | **perfectly** *Her face was perfectly regular.* | **fairly**

regularity *noun*

- QUANT. **degree** *Sons followed their fathers' trade with a high degree of regularity.*
- VERB + REGULARITY **maintain** *The idea is to maintain the regularity of the heartbeat.*
- PREP. **with (a)** ~ *He exercised with a regularity that amazed us.* | **~ in** *Is there any regularity in English word stress?*
- PHRASES **with alarming/depressing/monotonous regularity** *the statistics that he quotes with monotonous regularity* **with great/increasing regularity**

regulate *verb*

- ADV. **carefully, closely, properly, strictly, tightly** *The use of these chemicals is strictly regulated.*
- VERB + REGULATE **attempt to, seek to** | **be designed to, be intended to** *a code of conduct intended to regulate press reporting on the royal family*
- PHRASES **an attempt to regulate sth, heavily/highly regulated** *a highly regulated economy*

regulation *noun*

1 control of sth
- ADJ. **strict, tight, tough** | **increased** | **government, international, official, professional, public, state** | **legal, statutory** | **self, voluntary** | **economic, environmental, financial** | **price, temperature**
- VERB + REGULATION **call for, demand** *They are calling for tighter regulation of the industry.* | **introduce** | **be subject to** *Theatre, cinema and broadcasting are all subject to regulation by local authorities.*
- PREP. **~ by** *regulation by local authorities*

2 (usually **regulations**) law/rule
- ADJ. **strict, stringent, tighter, tougher** *The Act imposes more stringent regulations on atmospheric pollution.* | **draft** | **emergency** | **statutory** | **building, fire, hygiene, planning, safety, traffic, etc.** | **EU, federal, government, international, official** | **prison, school**
- VERB + REGULATION **comply with, conform to, meet, observe, satisfy** *To comply with government hygiene regulations, there must be a separate sink for hand washing.* | **breach, break, contravene, flout, infringe** | **adopt, bring in, impose, introduce, issue, make** *These restrictions are set out in regulations made by the minister.* | **liberalize, relax** *The government is under pressure to relax censorship regulations.* | **tighten** | **enforce** *In practice, the regulations are rarely enforced.*
- REGULATION + VERB **be designed to** *The regulations are designed to encourage lower consumption of water.* | **control sth, govern sth, protect sth** *regulations governing trade and industry* | **impose sth, require sth, restrict sth, specify sth, stipulate sth** *Regulations require water authorities to test sea water for bacteria.* | **apply (to sth)** *These regulations apply to all cows sold after June 1998.* | **come into force**
- REGULATION + NOUN **uniform, white shirt, etc.** *She was wearing the regulation school uniform.*
- PREP. **against (the)~s** *It's against safety regulations to fix these doors open.* **in (the)~** *The limits are specified in the*

regulations. **under (the)~** *Under the new regulations, each worker must have a rest every two hours.* | **~s concerning/regarding** *There are strict regulations concerning the adoption of children.* **~ on** *regulations on hygiene*
- PHRASES **a breach of the regulations, compliance with a regulation, in accordance with (the) regulations** *The notice is in accordance with Regulation 7.* **rules and regulations**

rehabilitation *noun*

- ADJ. **economic, physical, psychiatric, social**
- REHABILITATION + NOUN **centre, unit** *a drug rehabilitation centre* | **services** | **plan, period, process, programme, scheme**

rehearsal *noun*

- ADJ. **dress**
- VERB + REHEARSAL **do, have, hold** *We only had one full rehearsal.* | **attend, go to**
- REHEARSAL + VERB **take place** | **go** *How did the rehearsal go?*
- REHEARSAL + NOUN **room, space, studio** | **time**
- PREP. **at (a/the)~** *He apologized for his outburst at rehearsal.* **during (a/the)~** *During the dress rehearsal she suddenly forgot her lines.* **in ~** *They're performing every night and they have another production in rehearsal.* | **~ for** *rehearsals for 'Romeo and Juliet'* **~ of** *a rehearsal of the final scene*

rehearse *verb*

- ADV. **carefully** | **mentally** *She mentally rehearsed what she would say to Jeff.*
- PREP. **for** *rehearsing for the show*
- PHRASES **well rehearsed** *He had all the words he needed typed out and well rehearsed.*

reimburse *verb*

- ADV. **fully, in full** *Any costs that you incur will be reimbursed in full.*
- PREP. **for** *You will be reimbursed for your expenses.*

rein *noun*

1 (often **reins**) for controlling a horse
- VERB + REINS **hold** *Can you hold the reins for a minute?* | **gather (up), pick up** *Sean gathered up the horse's reins.* | **grab (at), pull on** *She pulled sharply on the reins.* | **give/hand sb, let go of** | **lengthen, shorten**
- PREP. **on a~** *She had the horse on a long rein.*

2 the reins being in control/the leader of sth
- VERB + REINS **hold** *It's the Treasury that effectively holds the reins.* | **grasp, take up** *The vice-president was forced to take up the reins of office.* | **hand over**
- PHRASES **the reins of government/office/power**

reinforce *verb*

1 support sth that already exists
- ADV. **enormously, greatly, massively, powerfully, strongly** *This report strongly reinforces the view that the system must be changed.* | **further** | **merely, only, simply** *All this simply reinforces my earlier point.* | **constantly, continually, continuously, repeatedly** | **implicitly** | **mutually** *Violent behaviour and rejection by society are mutually reinforcing.* | **unwittingly** | **positively**
- VERB + REINFORCE **help (to), serve to, tend to**

2 make sth stronger
- ADV. **heavily**
- PREP. **with** *The door was built of oak, heavily reinforced with iron.*

reinforcement noun

1 supporting/strengthening sth
- ADJ. **powerful**
- VERB + REINFORCEMENT **provide** *The minister's statement provides reinforcement for the view that tax cuts are likely in the budget.* | **receive** | **have** *The windows have steel reinforcement.* | **need**

2 reinforcements extra soldiers, etc.
- ADJ. **police, troop**
- VERB + REINFORCEMENTS **call for, call in, send for, summon** *The crowd was very large and police reinforcements were called in.* | **bring in, send**
- REINFORCEMENTS + VERB **arrive** *Reinforcements arrived too late.*

reject verb

- ADV. **decisively, emphatically, firmly, roundly, strongly, vehemently, vigorously** *She firmly rejected the suggestion that she had lied to Parliament.* | **categorically, completely, flatly, out of hand, outright, unequivocally, utterly** *Don't just reject their suggestions out of hand.* | **overwhelmingly** | **unanimously** | **narrowly** *Voters narrowly rejected the scheme.* | **immediately, instantly** | **quickly** | **consistently, constantly** | **eventually, finally** | **deliberately** | **explicitly, expressly, specifically** | **effectively** | **indignantly** *The paper indignantly rejected charges that it had invented the story to boost sales.* | **formally** | **publicly** | **instinctively** | **automatically** *No one knows why a foetus is not automatically rejected by the mother's immune system.* | **rightly** *It was an ill-researched product that consumers rightly rejected.*
- VERB + REJECT **vote to** | **be free to, have the right to** *Consumers have the right to reject faulty goods and demand a refund.* | **urge sb to** *He urged the committee to reject the plans.*
- PREP. **as** *The proposal was rejected as too costly.* **in favour of** *Their design was rejected in favour of one by a rival company.*
- PHRASES **reject sth on … grounds** *The scheme was rejected on economic grounds.*

rejection noun

- ADJ. **blanket, outright, total, wholesale** | **deliberate**
- VERB + REJECTION **fear** *Children who have had bad experiences fear rejection.* | **risk** | **cope with, take** *It takes a very buoyant personality to cope with constant rejection.*
- REJECTION + NOUN **letter, slip** *a publisher's rejection slip*
- PREP. **~by** *the rejection of the child by its mother*
- PHRASES **fear of rejection, feelings of rejection, the rejection of an idea/a proposal/a theory**

rejoicing noun

- ADJ. **great, much** | **general, popular**
- PREP. **amid/amidst~** *The bridge was completed in 1811 amidst much rejoicing.* | **~ at** *general rejoicing at the team's victory*
- PHRASES **a cause for rejoicing** *She had a personal cause for rejoicing.* **an occasion for rejoicing** *Finding a job should have been an occasion for rejoicing.* **scenes of rejoicing** *There were scenes of rejoicing at the news.*

relapse noun

- ADJ. **acute**
- VERB + RELAPSE **suffer** | **cause, trigger** *A wide range of emotionally stressful events may trigger a relapse.* | **prevent**
- RELAPSE + VERB **occur**
- PREP. **in~** *Even in relapse there will be times when the patient's general condition improves.*
- PHRASES **a risk of relapse**

relate verb

- ADV. **closely** | **directly, specifically** *The issues raised in the report relate directly to Age Concern's ongoing work in this area.*
- VERB + RELATE **be able to, can/could** | **attempt to, try to** | **be difficult to, find sth difficult to** *I found it difficult to relate the two ideas in my mind.*
- PREP. **to** *Our product needs an image that people can relate to.*
- PHRASES **the ability to relate to sb/sth, an attempt to relate sth** *Attempts to relate studies on animals to those on humans are not really comparing like with like.*

related adj.

1 connected
- VERBS **be, seem**
- ADV. **closely, integrally, intimately, strongly** *The two ideas are very closely related.* | **inextricably** | **loosely** | **not necessarily** | **largely** | **partly** | **directly** | **indirectly** *The old rates were at least indirectly related to income; the new tax takes no account of a person's ability to pay.* | **broadly, roughly** | **specifically** | **fundamentally** | **positively** | **inversely, negatively** *The traditional approach has tended to regard unemployment and inflation as being inversely related.* | **apparently** | **clearly, obviously** | **causally, contextually, functionally, logically, thematically** *Is unemployment causally related to crime?*
- PREP. **to** *The occurrence of the disease is apparently related to standards of hygiene.*

2 of the same family
- VERBS **be**
- ADV. **closely** | **distantly** | **genetically** *All the bees in the colony are genetically related.*
- PREP. **to** *He claims to be distantly related to the British royal family.*

relation noun

1 connection between two or more things
- ADJ. **causal** | **direct** *The energy an animal uses is in direct relation to speed and body mass.* | **close** *The study shows the close relation between poverty and ill health.* | **significant**
- VERB + RELATION **bear, have** *The film bore no relation to (= was very different from) the book.* ◇ *The fee bears little relation to the service provided.* | **show**
- PREP. **in~to** *Similar policies were pursued in the 1970s, particularly in relation to health services.* | **~ between, ~to** *the relation of the subject to the object*

2 member of sb's family
- ADJ. **close, near** | **distant** | **blood** | **poor** (often figurative) *Other sparkling wines are often considered the poor relations of champagne.*
- VERB + RELATION **visit**
- PREP. **~to** *What relation is Rita to you?*
- PHRASES **friends and relations**

3 relations between people/groups/countries
- ADJ. **close, cordial, friendly, good, harmonious** | **improved** | **difficult, poor, strained** | **class, diplomatic, economic, foreign, gender, human, industrial, international, labour, personal, political, power, public, race, sexual, social, trade** *The change of government led to improved industrial relations.* ◇ *a public relations exercise* | **Anglo-American, East-West, etc.**
- VERB + RELATIONS **cultivate, develop, establish, foster** *the need to establish good relations with our European partners* | **break off, damage, sever, suspend** *Diplomatic relations have been broken off between the two countries.* | **improve, strengthen** *Renewed efforts are being made to improve the strained relations between the two countries.* | **restore, resume** | **regulate** *the mechanisms that regulate the relations between labour and capital*

• RELATIONS + VERB **improve** *Relations between the two states have improved.* | **deteriorate, sour, worsen**
• PREP. **~among, ~between, ~with**
• PHRASES **an improvement in relations**

relationship noun

1 between people/groups/countries
• ADJ. **friendly, good, happy, harmonious, healthy, strong | broken, difficult, failed, fragile, poor, stormy, strained, troubled, uneasy | close, intense, intimate, special** *Britain's special relationship with the US* | **enduring, lasting, long-standing, long-term, permanent, serious, stable, steady** *He was not married, but he was in a stable relationship.* | **brief, casual | family, human, interpersonal, one-to-one, personal | doctor-patient, parent-child,** etc. | **business, contractual, formal, marital, physical, power, professional, sexual, social, working | caring, love-hate, loving**
• VERB + RELATIONSHIP **enjoy, have** *They enjoyed a close working relationship.* ◇ *The school has a very good relationship with the community.* ◇ *He had brief relationships with several women.* | **begin, build (up), develop, establish, foster** *Building strong relationships is essential.* ◇ *They established a relationship of trust.* | **cement, improve, strengthen | continue, maintain | handle, manage** *He's not very good at handling personal relationships.* | **break off** *She broke off the relationship when she found out about his gambling.* | **destroy** *Lack of trust destroys many relationships.*
• RELATIONSHIP + VERB **exist** *We want to improve the relationship that exists between the university and the town.* | **blossom, deepen, develop | flourish | work** *I tried everything to make our relationship work.* | **continue, last | deteriorate, go wrong, worsen | break down, break up, fail**
• RELATIONSHIP + NOUN **difficulties, problems | goals**
• PREP. **in a/the ~** *In normal human relationships there has to be some give and take.* ◇ *At the moment he isn't in a relationship.* | **~ among** *The focus is on relationships among European countries.* **~between, ~to** *their relationship to each other* **~with**
• PHRASES **the breakdown of a relationship, a network/web of relationships**

2 family connection
• ADJ. **blood, family, kin, kinship**
• PREP. **in a/the ~** *Some people think only about themselves, even in family relationships.* | **~ between** *'What's the relationship between you and Tony?' 'He's my cousin.'* **~to** *What relationship are you to Pat?*

3 connection between two or more things
• ADJ. **close** *There's a close relationship between increased money supply and inflation.* | **direct | clear | complex | significant | true | particular | inverse, negative** *the inverse relationship between gas consumption and air temperature* | **positive | causal, dynamic, reciprocal | linear, spatial | economic, functional, legal | natural, organic | symbolic**
• VERB + RELATIONSHIP **bear, have** *The fee bears little relationship to the service provided.* | **examine, explore, look at, study** *His latest book examines the relationship between spatial awareness and mathematical ability.* | **discover, find** *They discovered a relationship between depression and lack of sunlight.* | **demonstrate, show | see, understand | stand in** *Women and men stand in a different relationship to language.*
• PREP. **in a/the ~** *The different varieties of the language are in a dynamic relationship with each other.* | **~between** *I can't see the relationship between the figures and the diagram.* **~to** *the relationship of a parasite to its host* **~with**
• PHRASES **the nature of the relationship**

relative noun

• ADJ. **close, near** *The succession passed to the nearest surviving relative.* | **distant | blood, family** *If you die without a will, only a husband, wife, children and blood relatives are entitled to inherit your property.* | **immediate** *The deceased's immediate relatives, her mother and father, will inherit her estate.* | **living, surviving | elderly, old | young | female, male | poor** (*often figurative*) *He believes that interior design is the poor relative of* (= inferior to) *architecture.* | **dependent | disabled, ill, sick | distressed, grieving**
• VERB + RELATIVE **have** *I have no parents or close relatives.* | **lose** *an organization that helps people who have lost their relatives* (= whose relatives have died) | **care for, give support to, help, look after, support** *She's looking after an elderly relative.* | **live with | stay with, visit | trace** *The police are trying to trace the relatives of the deceased.* | **inform** *The names of the victims are being withheld until the relatives have been informed.*
• PHRASES **friends and/or relatives** *an intimate reception for close friends and relatives* **a relative by marriage**

relax verb

• ADV. **deeply** *Deeply relax all your muscles.* | **completely, totally | a little, slightly | just, simply** *Just relax and take it easy.* | **gradually, slowly** *He gradually relaxed and began to enjoy himself.* | **consciously** *She realized how tense she was and consciously relaxed.* | **visibly**
• VERB + RELAX **begin to | try to** *Just try to relax completely.* | **learn to | help sb (to)** *Use music to help you relax.* | **make sb | appear to, seem to** *Julie seems to be relaxing a little now.*
• PREP. **against** *Jenna relaxed against the pillows.* **into** *His severe expression relaxed into a half-smile.*
• PHRASES **lie/sit back and relax, relax and enjoy sth/yourself**

relaxation noun

1 time spent resting/sth you do to rest
• ADJ. **deep, great | complete, total | muscle/muscular** *an ointment that helps muscle relaxation*
• VERB + RELAXATION **aid, promote** *Some people take up yoga to aid relaxation.*
• RELAXATION + NOUN **exercises, techniques | therapy | class** *He goes to relaxation classes.*
• PREP. **for~** *She listens to classical music for relaxation.* | **~from** *a chance for relaxation from work*
• PHRASES **a form/kind of relaxation, rest and relaxation, a state of relaxation**

2 making rules/controls less strict
• ADJ. **further | general | limited, partial, slight | temporary | gradual**
• VERB + RELAXATION **call for, seek** *Financiers are calling for a relaxation of these stringent measures.* | **promise** *The government has promised further relaxations in foreign exchange controls.*
• PREP. **~in/of** *a relaxation in the rules*

relaxed adj.

• VERBS **appear, be, feel, look, seem | keep sb**
• ADV. **deeply, extremely, very | completely, perfectly, totally | fairly, quite | apparently, seemingly | enough, sufficiently** *You need to ensure that a patient feels relaxed enough to discuss things fully.* | **pleasantly**
• PREP. **about** *I was very relaxed about the decision.*

relay (also relay race) noun

• ADJ. **4 × 400,** etc. | **medley, sprint**
• VERB + RELAY **run (in)** *She ran in the 4 × 400 relay.* | **win**
• RELAY + NOUN **race | team**

release noun

1 freeing sb from prison, etc.
- ADJ. **immediate** *There have been calls for his immediate and unconditional release.* | **imminent** | **early** | **unconditional**
- VERB + RELEASE **grant sb** *He was granted early release.* | **secure** *A public outcry secured her release from detention.*
- RELEASE + NOUN **date**
- PREP. **~from** *his release from hospital*
- PHRASES **release on bail/parole**

2 freeing sb from an emotion, a pain, etc.
- ADJ. **welcome** *She saw death as a welcome release from pain.* | **emotional**
- VERB + RELEASE **give (sb)** *Crying gave some emotional release.*
- PREP. **~from**
- PHRASES **a feeling/sense of release, a release of tension** *All societies have social mechanisms for the release of tension.*

3 book/film/record/piece of news
- ADJ. **latest, new, recent** | **commercial** | **book, CD, film's, news, press, record, video**
- RELEASE + VERB **be/come out** *The new CD releases will be out on Friday.*

release verb

1 allow sb to be free
- ADV. **quickly** | **immediately** | **eventually,   finally** | **conditionally, unconditionally**
- PREP. **from** *She was released from prison last week.*
- PHRASES **newly/recently released**

2 allow sth to escape
- ADV. **accidentally** *The factory had accidentally released a quantity of toxic waste into the sea.*
- PREP. **from** *the gases that are released from aerosols* **into** *How much radiation was released into the air?*

3 make sth less tight
- ADV. **suddenly** *She laughed, the tension inside her suddenly released.*

4 make sth available
- ADV. **officially** *Figures to be officially released this week reveal that long-term unemployment is still rising.*
- VERB + RELEASE **refuse to** *Police have refused to release the name of the dead man.*
- PREP. **to** *Details of the attack have not yet been released to the public.*
- PHRASES **newly/recently released** *newly released recordings* **originally/previously released** *The album was originally released in 1974.*

relevance noun

- ADJ. **considerable, great, wider** | **limited, marginal** | **doubtful, dubious** | **equal** | **direct, immediate** | **continued/continuing** | **declining** | **obvious** | **real** | **possible, potential** | **general** | **particular, special** | **contemporary** *He claims that the laws are antiquated and have no contemporary relevance.* | **practical** | **political**
- VERB + RELEVANCE **be/remain of** *The book is of particular relevance to student nurses.* | **bear, have** *The theory bears little relevance to practice.* | **lack, lose** *Her ideas have lost all relevance to the modern world.* | **ensure** *Constant revision of the curriculum must be undertaken to ensure its continuing relevance.* | **increase** | **see** | **demonstrate, establish** *Skim the book in order to establish its relevance to your needs.* | **assess, consider, examine, explore, judge** | **question**
- PREP. **~for/to** *I can't see the relevance of his comment to the debate.*

relevant adj.

- VERBS **be, seem** | **become** | **consider sth, deem sth, regard sth as, see sth as**
- ADV. **especially, extremely, highly, particularly, specially, very** | **barely, hardly, not really, scarcely** *Past imperial glories are hardly relevant to the present day.* | **(only) marginally, partially** | **not necessarily, not strictly** *Resist the temptation to discuss topics that are not strictly relevant to the essay question.* | **directly** | **only indirectly** | **immediately** | **no longer** | **potentially** | **apparently** | **clearly, obviously** | **universally** | **morally, politically, socially** *Is there a morally relevant difference between human life and animal life?* | **vocationally** *vocationally relevant qualifications*
- PREP. **to** *information relevant to this case*

reliability noun

- ADJ. **greater/greatest, high** | **poor** | **absolute** | **improved, increased** | **statistical**
- QUANT. **degree, level**
- VERB + RELIABILITY **ensure** *Changes in design will ensure the quality and reliability of the printer.* | **improve, increase** | **reduce** | **assess, evaluate, judge** *It is important to assess the reliability of the data.* | **measure** *The reliability of the statistical estimates can be measured.*
- RELIABILITY + VERB **improve, increase**
- RELIABILITY + NOUN **problem**

reliable adj.

- VERBS **be, prove, seem** | **become** | **consider sth**
- ADV. **extremely, highly, very** *It has a highly reliable control system.* | **absolutely, completely, perfectly, totally** *He's a good musician and totally reliable.* | **not entirely, not exactly, not terribly, not wholly** | **fairly, quite, pretty, reasonably** | **enough, sufficiently** *These measurements are reliable enough for most purposes.*
- PREP. **as** *This statement is not reliable as evidence.*

reliance noun

- ADJ. **complete, total** | **considerable, great, heavy, strong** *Too heavy a reliance on a particular market may be dangerous for the company.* | **excessive, undue** | **misplaced** | **continued, continuing** | **growing, increasing** | **increased** | **reduced** | **self-**
- QUANT. **degree** *a high degree of reliance on newspaper reports*
- VERB + RELIANCE **place** *I don't think you should place too much reliance on these figures.* | **act in** *(law)* | **increase** | **reduce** | **eliminate** *the means by which individuals might reduce or eliminate reliance on the state* | **encourage** *They believe that modern farming techniques encourage an excessive reliance on harmful chemicals.* | **lead to**
- PREP. **in ~ on/upon** *(law)* *He acted in complete reliance on the account of a couple of eyewitnesses.* | **~on/upon** *increased reliance of the university on private funds*

reliant adj.

- VERBS **be** | **become** | **remain**
- ADV. **heavily, highly** *The service has become heavily reliant on government support.* | **completely, entirely, totally, wholly** | **increasingly** | **largely** | **quite**
- PREP. **on/upon** *The charity is completely reliant on public donations.*

relic noun

- ADJ. **ancient** | **last** *It was the last relic of the old system.* | **historic/historical** | **precious** | **holy, religious, sacred, saintly**
- VERB + RELIC **discover** *The relics were discovered in a lead box in the ruins of an abbey.* | **shelter** *A shrine was*

constructed to shelter the relics. | **remove** *The duke secretly removed the relics from the reliquary.*
● RELIC + VERB **survive** *This silver belt buckle is the only relic of the imprisoned soldiers that survives.*
● PREP. **~from** *Most of these guns are relics from the Boer War.*
● PHRASES **a relic of an age/a time** *relics of a bygone age* ◊ *a relic of the time when people travelled by horse and carriage* **a relic of the past** *They believe that hunting is a relic of the past and are calling for it to be banned.*

relief *noun*

1 removal of anxiety/pain
● ADJ. **considerable, deep, enormous, great, huge, immense, intense, overwhelming, tremendous | certain** *The news of his appointment was received with a certain relief by most people.* | **sheer | complete | temporary** *The drugs only provided temporary relief from the pain.* | **fast, immediate, instant | evident, obvious** *She smiled with evident relief.* | **blessed, welcome | pain** *The injection gives complete pain relief.*
● VERB + RELIEF **bring (sb), give (sb), offer (sb), provide (sb with)** *Morning brought no relief from the heat.* | **come as** *The news came as a welcome relief to Brian.* | **seek** *She sought relief in drink.* | **find, get** *He found relief from his fears in a world of fantasy and art.* | **experience, feel** *I felt enormous relief once they phoned.* | **sense** *She could sense his relief when she said she wouldn't be leaving.* | **express**
● RELIEF + VERB **come** *He believes that relief only comes from helping others with their suffering.* | **flood** *Relief flooded through me as the aeroplane landed safely.*
● PREP. **in ~** *She smiled in relief.* **out of ~** *He hugged her out of sheer relief.* **to your~** *To my great relief, she didn't notice that anything was wrong.* **with ~** *He sighed with relief.* | **~at** *relief at not having been made a fool of* **~from** *relief from hunger* **~to** *The news was a huge relief to her.*
● PHRASES **a cry/a sigh/tears of relief** *He breathed a sigh of relief.* **a sense/wave of relief**

2 food/money/medicine given to people in need
● ADJ. **humanitarian | emergency | famine,   flood | foreign, international**
● VERB + RELIEF **give sb, provide (sb with), send (sb)** *The organization provides emergency famine relief.*
● RELIEF + NOUN **work** *She said that the fighting has halted almost all relief work in the area.* | **effort, operation** *There was a huge international relief effort to bring help to the stricken area.* | **package, programme** *Congress has agreed an $11 million relief package for victims of the hurricane.* | **aid, supplies | agency, fund, organization | staff, worker | convoy, flight**

3 reduction in the amount of tax, etc. you have to pay
● ADJ. **debt, interest, mortgage, tax**
● VERB + RELIEF **get, obtain, receive** *You get mortgage relief of 10% on the next £5 000.* | **be entitled to, qualify for | apply for, claim, seek**
● RELIEF + VERB **be available** *No tax relief is available in respect of this loss.*

4 sth interesting that replaces sth boring
● ADJ. **light | comic**
● VERB + RELIEF **give (sb), provide (sb with)** *The scene provided some comic relief for the audience.*
● PREP. **for~** *The comical characters are brought into the story for a little light relief.*
● PHRASES **a moment of relief**

5 way of decorating wood, stone, etc.
● ADJ. **high** *The scene has been carved in high relief.* | **bas, low | carved, sculptured | alabaster, bronze, marble, plaster, stucco | classical, Greek, Roman**
● VERB + RELIEF **carve (sth) in**
● RELIEF + NOUN **carving, sculpture | panel**
● PREP. **in~** *a sculpture in high relief*

6 making sth noticeable
● ADJ. **sharp, stark**
● VERB + RELIEF **bring sth into, throw sth into** (*often figurative*) *The proximity of the wealthy suburb to the squatter camp throws the plight of the squatters into even sharper relief.* | **stand out in** *The snow-capped mountains stood out in sharp relief against the blue sky.*

relieve *verb*

● ADV. **temporarily**
● VERB + RELIEVE **attempt to, try to** *trying to relieve the symptoms of depression* | **help (to)** *Her jokes helped to relieve the tension.* | **be designed to, be intended to** *Respite care is intended to relieve parents temporarily of the burden of caring for severely disabled children.*

relieved *adj.*

● VERBS **be, feel, look, seem**
● ADV. **extremely, greatly, hugely, immensely, mightily, profoundly, very | almost | a little, quite, rather, slightly, somewhat | clearly, obviously, visibly | secretly** *I was secretly relieved when Ed said it was time to turn back.*
● PREP. **at** *We were greatly relieved at the the news of their safe return.*

NOTE
Religions

accept, adopt, convert to, embrace, follow, turn to~
  He converted to Judaism when he got married.
  people who follow Hinduism
abandon, reject~
  He rejected Christianity and became a Buddhist.
~spread
  Islam spread rapidly through North Africa.
~preaches, proclaims, teaches sth
  Christianity preaches that sinners can be forgiven.
a follower of~
  followers of Sikhism
the rise/spread of~
  the rise of Christianity in the first century
the teachings/tenets of~
  the basic tenets of Buddhism

---

religion *noun*

● ADJ. **great, major | world** *Islam is one of the great world religions.* | **dominant | established, old | new | orthodox | true | false | alternative** *Football has become an alternative religion for many people.* | **organized** *I believe in God, but I don't belong to any organized religion.* | **primitive | pagan | monotheistic, polytheistic | eastern** *eastern religions such as Shintoism* | **Hindu, Jewish, etc. | Catholic, evangelical, Orthodox, Protestant | official, state**
● VERB + RELIGION **belong to, have** *She has no religion.* | **follow, practise** *Do you still practise your religion?* | **change | abandon, reject | defend** *She believed that her religion needed to be defended by philosophy and logic.* | **found** *He founded a new religion.* | **spread**
● RELIGION + VERB **be based on sth** *a religion based on reason* | **originate from sth** *He believes that all religions originated from a single source.* | **develop | spread**
● PREP. **by ~** *These people are predominantly Russian Orthodox by religion.* **in a/the ~** *In their religion, mountains are sacred.*
● PHRASES **an adherent/follower of a religion, a form/kind of religion**

religious *adj.*

● VERBS **be | become**

● ADV. **deeply, devoutly, highly, very** *a deeply religious person* | **strictly** *He distanced himself from the strictly religious aspects of the music.* | **quite** | **essentially, fundamentally** *Yoga is essentially religious and not just physical.* | **specifically** *the specifically religious content of the programme*

relinquish *verb*

● ADV. **voluntarily** *They will never voluntarily relinquish their independence.*
● VERB + RELINQUISH **be forced to** *He was forced to relinquish control of the company.* | **refuse to** | **be willing to** | **be reluctant to** | **persuade sb to**
● PREP. **to** *She has relinquished the post to her cousin, Sir Edward.*

relish *verb*

● ADV. **positively, really** | **not particularly** *He did not particularly relish the prospect of a meeting with his boss.* | **rather** | **clearly, obviously** | **secretly** *She secretly relished the thought of being alone with him.*
● VERB + RELISH **appear to, seem to**

reluctance *noun*

● ADJ. **considerable, deep, extreme, great, marked** | **certain** *I noticed a certain reluctance among the teachers.* | **increased** | **clear, evident, obvious** | **apparent** | **initial** | **growing** | **continued/continuing** | **general** | **natural, understandable**
● VERB + RELUCTANCE **have** | **display, express, indicate, reflect, show** *His designs indicate a reluctance to conform to fashion.* ◇ *She showed considerable reluctance to leave.* | **pretend** | **overcome** | **notice, sense** | **understand** *I can quite understand your reluctance to talk about what happened to you.* | **explain** *These political tensions explain the reluctance of financiers to invest in the region.*
● PREP. **with~** *With great reluctance, we have come to the decision to close the hospital.* | **~by/on the part of** *reluctance by insurers to keep paying out heavy claims*
● PHRASES **a show of reluctance** *With a great show of reluctance, the government granted independence to the colony.* **a sign of reluctance**

reluctant *adj.*

● VERBS **appear, be, feel, look, seem** *Students may feel reluctant to ask questions.* | **become** | **remain**
● ADV. **decidedly, deeply, extremely, remarkably, very** | **increasingly** | **a little, rather, somewhat** | **apparently** | **clearly** | **curiously, strangely** *She was curiously reluctant to talk about the experience.* | **understandably** *Children are sometimes understandably reluctant to wear glasses that are ugly or uncomfortable.* | **notoriously** *The monarchy was notoriously reluctant to embrace change.*

rely *verb*

PHRASAL VERB

rely on/upon sb/sth
1 need sb/sth
● ADV. **heavily, a lot, strongly** *countries that rely heavily on food aid* | **entirely, exclusively, solely** | **increasingly** | **largely, mainly** | **traditionally**
● VERB + RELY ON/UPON SB/STH **be forced to, have to, must** *people who are forced to rely on public transport* | **tend to**
● PREP. **for** *They relied entirely on these few weapons for their defence.*
2 trust sb/sth
● ADV. **safely** *You can safely rely on his judgement.* | **simply** *Most historians simply rely on archives.*
● VERB + RELY ON/UPON SB/STH **can/could** | **can/could**

always | **can/could no longer** *The party could no longer rely on its traditional supporters.*
● PREP. **for** *I couldn't rely on John for information.*

remains *noun*

● ADJ. **abundant, considerable, extensive, substantial** *abundant remains of marine algae* ◇ *the extensive remains of a medieval abbey* | **impressive** | **fragmentary** | **visible** | **existing, surviving** | **ancient, prehistoric** | **Greek, Roman, etc.** | **battered, mangled, shattered** *the mangled remains of the bomber's van* | **burnt(-out), charred, smouldering** | **earthly, human, mortal** *This tomb holds the mortal remains of King Richard III.* | **animal, archaeological, fossil/fossilized, organic, plant, skeletal**
● VERB + REMAINS **discover, find, locate, reveal, uncover, unearth** *While excavating the site for a new hotel, workers unearthed the remains of several dinosaurs.* | **identify** *The remains have been identified as those of a Mr Thomas, who lived in Richmond.* | **excavate, exhume, remove** *They are excavating the remains of an Iron Age settlement.* ◇ *Marie Curie's remains were exhumed and interred in the Pantheon.* | **bury, inter** | **dump** | **destroy** *Environmentalists say that the road will destroy the remains of the world's first commercial railway.* | **feed on** *The ivory gull often follows polar bears to feed on the remains of seal kills.*
● REMAINS + VERB **survive** *Considerable remains survive of the great city walls begun by Theodosius in AD 413.* | **lie** *Her remains lie at rest in St Andrew's churchyard.* | **date from ...** *The burnt-out remains date from the 13th century.*
● PREP. **among/in the ~** *The body was found among the remains of a burnt-out cottage.*

remand *noun*

● ADJ. **custodial**
● VERB + REMAND **be held on** *He was held on remand, charged with causing malicious damage to property.*
● REMAND + NOUN **centre, home** | **prisoner**
● PREP. **on~** *I was in prison on remand for three weeks.*

remark *noun*

● ADJ. **brief, passing** | **occasional** | **casual, chance, off-the-cuff, throwaway** | **careless, tactless** | **barbed, cutting, derogatory, dismissive, disparaging, insulting, nasty, offensive, pointed, scathing, snide, uncomplimentary** | **complimentary, encouraging, kind** | **innocent** | **critical** | **cynical** | **controversial** | **provocative** | **famous** | **enigmatic** | **odd, strange** | **silly** | **funny, witty** | **racist, sexist** | **obscene, rude** | **defamatory** | **personal** *How dare you make personal remarks!* | **general** | **introductory, opening, preliminary** | **closing, concluding** *I agreed with most of what he said at the beginning of the speech but not with his closing remarks.*
● VERB + REMARK **make, pass, utter** | **withdraw** *He was expelled from the party for failing to withdraw his controversial remarks.* | **address** *Who were those rude remarks addressed to?* | **ignore, take no notice of** *I just ignored her last remark.*
● REMARK + VERB **apply to sb/sth** *These remarks apply equally to doctors.* | **be directed at/to sb** *The remark was directed at him.* | **suggest sth** *Her remarks suggest that the negotiations may be successful.* | **provoke sth** *The remark provoked an angry response from the crowd.*
● PREP. **in a/the ~** *He made a few factual errors in his remarks on Rembrandt.* | **~ about/concerning/on** *I shall keep my remarks on the subject brief.* **~by/from** *remarks by officials* **~to** *a casual remark to his father*

remark *verb*

- ADV. **casually, idly** *She remarked casually that she was changing her job.* | **pointedly** | **lightly, mildly** | **drily, wryly** | **ruefully** | **jokingly** | **cheerfully** | **coolly** | **acidly, tartly**
- VERB + REMARK **be heard to**
- PREP. **on/upon** *Several people remarked on her outfit.* **to** *He remarked to Jane that he had not heard from Sally for a long time.*

remarkable *adj.*

- VERBS **be, seem**
- ADV. **most, quite, really, truly, very** *a most remarkable musician* ◇ *a truly remarkable discovery* | **rather**
- PREP. **for** *These cars are remarkable for the quietness of their engines.*

remedy *noun*

1 treatment/medicine
- ADJ. **effective, good** | **correct** | **wrong** | **common** | **traditional** | **ancient, old** | **folk** | **home** | **herbal, homoeopathic, natural** | **cold** *The player insists that he merely took a cold remedy and not a banned substance.*
- QUANT. **dose** *One dose of the remedy is sufficient.*
- VERB + REMEDY **take, use** | **need** | **try** | **give sb** *The remedy was given in different strengths to a group of volunteers.* | **prescribe (sb)** | **prepare** *The remedies are all prepared from wild flowers.* | **find** *They're hoping to find a remedy for the condition.*
- REMEDY + VERB **be available** | **work** *She tried various remedies, but none of them worked.*
- PREP. **~for** *He took a herbal remedy for his hay fever.*

2 way of dealing with a problem
- ADJ. **adequate, effective, good** *Your best remedy is to go to the small claims court.* | **appropriate, suitable** | **easy, simple** *There's no easy remedy for unemployment.* | **common, usual** | **alternative** | **desperate, drastic** | **proposed** | **civil (law), common/private/public law, contractual, judicial, legal, statutory**
- VERB + REMEDY **have** | **pursue, seek** *They will have to seek a judicial remedy for breach of contract.* | **resort to** *Desperate remedies were resorted to in the search for food.* | **exhaust** *They advised him to exhaust all other remedies before applying to court.* | **create** | **offer** | **afford (sb), grant sb, provide (sb with)** *remedies afforded to creditors by a bankruptcy order*
- REMEDY + VERB **be available** | **lie in sth** *When the reservoir becomes blocked, the only remedy lies in cleaning the entire system.*
- PREP. **~against** *The agreement states that he has a remedy against the subcontractor.* **~for** *remedies for breach of contract* **~in** *You have a remedy in civil law.*
- PHRASES **rights and remedies** *The Act created rights and remedies for consumers.*

remedy *verb*

- ADV. **easily** *This could easily be remedied if the authorities were willing.*
- VERB + REMEDY **attempt to, seek to, take steps to, try to** *The government should have taken steps to remedy the situation.*

remember *verb*

- ADV. **clearly, distinctly, vividly, well** *I distinctly remember Jane saying that the show started at eight.* ◇ *I remember Miss Scott very well.* | **dimly, vaguely** | **correctly, rightly** *If I remember correctly, you were supposed to collect the keys on your way here.* | **fondly** *She fondly remembered her early years in India.* | **still** | **always** *I'll always remember this holiday.* | **suddenly** | **belatedly** *Julia belatedly remembered what else she was supposed to do.*

- VERB + REMEMBER **can/could** *I can't remember her name.* | **try to** | **be important to**
- PREP. **as** *He still remembered her as the lively teenager he'd known years before.* **for** *She is best remembered for her first book, 'In the Ditch'.*

remind *verb*

- ADV. **constantly, frequently, repeatedly** | **gently** *She gently reminded him that the baby was getting cold and should be taken indoors.*
- VERB + REMIND **not have to, not need to** *I'm sure I don't need to remind you that we have lost our last ten matches.* | **serve to** *An event like this serves to remind us that we do not have control over nature.*
- PREP. **about** *I rang to remind him about the party.* **of** *She looked at her watch to remind him of the time.*
- PHRASES **keep reminding sb**

PHRASAL VERB

remind sb of sb/sth
- ADV. **forcefully, forcibly, sharply, strongly, vividly** *The building reminded me strongly of my old school.* | **irresistibly** | **suddenly** *I was suddenly reminded of a tiger defending its cubs.* | **always** *Mrs Nolan always reminded Marie of her own mother.*

reminder *noun*

- ADJ. **powerful, strong** | **lasting, permanent** | **constant, continual, daily** | **further** | **graphic, sharp, stark, visual, vivid** | **chilling, grim, painful, uncomfortable** | **poignant, solemn** | **salutary** | **timely** | **important** | **gentle, little, quick** | **final** *It always took a final reminder to get her to pay her share of the rent.* | **useful** *The list serves as a useful reminder of the issues to consider.*
- VERB + REMINDER **act/serve as, be, provide** *The ruined church acts as a constant reminder of the war.* | **give sb, issue, send (out)** *She gave him a gentle reminder that payment was due.* | **receive** | **need**
- REMINDER + NOUN **letter, note, notice**
- PREP. **~about** *We were sent a reminder about the next meeting.* **~to** *a timely reminder to people that leaving their doors open is an invitation to thieves*

reminiscent *adj.*

- VERBS **be**
- ADV. **closely, highly, strongly, very** *This painting is strongly reminiscent of da Vinci's 'Annunciation'.* | **faintly, slightly, somewhat** | **curiously, strangely, strikingly** | **irresistibly**
- PREP. **of**

remnant *noun*

- ADJ. **small** | **last, surviving** *The museum is one of the last remnants of the 17th-century palace.* | **faint, tattered** *the tattered remnants of the flag* ◇ *(figurative) faint remnants of the city's glorious past*
- PREP. **~from** *(figurative) Their outdated attitudes are a remnant from colonial days.*
- PHRASES **a remnant from/of the past**

remorse *noun*

- ADJ. **deep, genuine, real**
- QUANT. **pang, stab**
- VERB + REMORSE **be filled with, be full of, be overcome with, be stricken with, feel, have, suffer** *She knew that the next day she would be guilty and full of remorse.* ◇ *I suffered no remorse.* | **display, express, show**
- PREP. **without~** *He died without remorse.* | **~at** *He felt some remorse at his behaviour.* **~for** *She was filled with remorse for the crime.* **~over** *She felt a sharp pang of remorse over the incident.*
- PHRASES **a feeling of remorse, tears of remorse**

remote *adj.*

- VERBS **appear, be, feel, look, seem**
- ADV. **extremely, very | impossibly, infinitely, utterly** *Adulthood and responsibility seemed impossibly remote.* | **increasingly | comparatively, fairly, pretty, quite, rather, relatively, somewhat** *a fairly remote possibility* ◇ *rural areas that are relatively remote* | **geographically, physically** *geographically remote areas*
- PREP. **from** *Jane felt remote from what was going on around her.*

removal *noun*

- ADJ. **complete, total, wholesale | temporary | effective, successful | immediate, speedy** *his immediate removal from power* | **easy** *a liquid for the easy removal of coffee stains* | **forced/forcible** *the forcible removal of the protesters' barricades.* | **surgical | hair, stain**
- VERB + REMOVAL **call for, demand, seek** *They demanded her removal from office.* | **order** *In a symbolic move, the new government ordered the removal of the dictator's statue.* | **require** *The programme required the removal of government subsidies.* | **allow | arrange for** *to arrange for the removal and disposal of waste.* | **facilitate | prevent**
- PREP. **~ from** *The local council does not allow the removal of sand from the beach.* **~ to** *the collection's temporary removal to storage*
- PHRASES **removal from office**

remove *verb*

- ADV. **altogether, completely, entirely | effectively** *By producing an heir, the Queen effectively removed her cousin's hopes of succeeding to the throne.* | **permanently, temporarily | quickly | easily** *The old cladding can be easily removed using a claw hammer.* | **painlessly | carefully | forcibly** *people who have been forcibly removed from their homes* | **surgically** *Unsightly moles can be removed surgically.* | **physically**
- ADV. **try to | be possible to | be difficult to** *These stains can be difficult to remove.*
- PREP. **for** *Fittings should be completely removed for cleaning.* **from** *She removed the dirty dishes from the table.* **with** *Bee stings should be removed with tweezers.*
- PHRASES **remove sth at a stroke** *The proposed law would remove at a stroke the long-cherished right to trial by jury.*

rendezvous *noun*

1 arrangement to meet sb
- ADJ. **secret**
- VERB + RENDEZVOUS **have | arrange | keep** *Although it was late, there was still enough time to keep the rendezvous.* | **make** *She made the rendezvous with only minutes to spare.* | **miss**
- PREP. **~ with** *I have a rendezvous with Peter at a restaurant on the harbour.*
- PHRASES **a place for a rendezvous**

2 place where people meet
- ADJ. **popular** *The cafe is a popular rendezvous for young lovers.* | **secret | pre-arranged**
- VERB + RENDEZVOUS **make your way (back) to/towards** *The platoon made its way to the pre-arranged rendezvous in the desert.*
- RENDEZVOUS + NOUN **point**

renew *verb*

- ADV. **completely | annually** *Membership must be renewed annually.* | **periodically, regularly | constantly, continually, repeatedly | automatically**
- VERB + RENEW **decide to | agree to | refuse to**
- PHRASES **a chance/an opportunity to renew sth** *a*

chance to renew acquaintance with old friends **need renewing** *The paintwork will need renewing every five years.*

renewal *noun*

- ADJ. **annual | cultural, economic, national, physical, religious, spiritual, urban** *an urban renewal programme in the city centre*
- VERB + RENEWAL **seek** *He sought renewal of the grant.* ◇ *to seek spiritual renewal* | **apply for | obtain** *to obtain a renewal of the certificate* | **bring (about)** *They felt the need to bring about a renewal of society.* | **be/fall due for, come up for** *Her contract is coming up for renewal in the autumn.*
- RENEWAL + NOUN **programme, project | date | notice** *If you have any queries, please contact us on the number shown on your policy or last renewal notice.* | **fee**

renovate *verb*

- ADV. **extensively, substantially | completely** *The hotel has been completely renovated.*
- PHRASES **newly/recently renovated** *the newly renovated church*

renovation *noun*

- ADJ. **extensive, major** *The building has undergone major renovation.* | **complete, full-scale, total | house**
- VERB + RENOVATION **carry out** *The council is to carry out extensive renovations to the building.* | **complete | be in need of, need, require** *The old Victorian house is in need of renovation.* | **be closed for** *The gallery is closed for renovation.* | **undergo**
- RENOVATION + NOUN **work | programme**
- PREP. **~ to** *renovation to the town hall*

rent *noun*

- ADJ. **exorbitant, high** *The tenants were not prepared to pay the higher rents demanded.* | **affordable, low | nominal, peppercorn | fair | reduced | increased | rising** *Discontent resulted from sharply rising rents.* | **fixed | annual, monthly, weekly | initial** *The initial rent will be reviewed annually.* | **back, outstanding, unpaid | farm, ground, house/housing, land, office**
- VERB + RENT **pay | afford** *He couldn't afford the rent by himself.* | **be/fall behind with, owe** *You put your tenancy at risk if you fall behind with the rent.* | **charge** *The rent charged depends largely on the size and locality of the flat.* | **collect** *The landlord came around to collect the month's rent.* | **receive** *The council receives rent on local property that it owns.* | **fix** *The rent will be fixed at 18% of the market value of the property.* | **increase, push up, put up, raise** *The large stores have pushed up the rents in the area.* ◇ *The new lease will put her rent up to £200 a week.* | **calculate, determine**
- RENT + VERB **be/fall due, be payable** *The rent will fall due on the last day of the quarter.* | **go up, increase, rise** *Their rent has increased from £5 200 to £8 600 a year.* | **fall**
- RENT + NOUN **money, payment | arrears | level** *They took the landlord to court over increasing rent levels.* | **increase, rise | review | allowance, rebate, subsidy | control | collection | strike | man** *Thousands try to avoid the rent man so they can have more cash to spend.*
- PREP. **in ~** *The company has paid out a lot of money in rent.* | **~ for** *The rent for the four-roomed house is affordable.* **~ from** *They earned rent from their property in London.* **~ on** *the rent on a factory*
- PHRASES **arrears of rent** *to be liable for arrears of rent* **a month's/week's/year's rent, the non-payment/payment of rent** *The movement advocated the non-payment of rent and taxes.*

rental *noun*

• ADJ. **annual, monthly, weekly | short term | car, line, telephone, television, video** *The phone bill gives a breakdown of the cost of the line rental and of calls.*
• RENTAL + NOUN **company | terms | charge, fee, payment | income | accommodation**

reorganization *noun*

• ADJ. **comprehensive, fundamental, major, radical | corporate, internal | government, school**
• VERB + REORGANIZATION **undergo** *The company has undergone a major reorganization.* **| carry out**
• REORGANIZATION + VERB **take place**
• REORGANIZATION + NOUN **costs**

reorganize *verb*

• ADV. **completely, totally | systematically**
• PREP. **as** *The laboratory was reorganized as a separate establishment.* **into** *Their headquarters was reorganized into five regional offices.*

repair *noun*

• ADJ. **considerable, extensive, major | minor | essential, necessary, vital | emergency, immediate, urgent | quick, rapid | constant | temporary | running** *The rally drivers carried small tool-kits for making running repairs.* **| building, house/housing, roof, structural | car, motorway, road, vehicle | electrical, TV | shoe**
• VERB + REPAIR **carry out, do, make | complete** *It is unlikely that the repairs will be completed on time.* **| be in need of, need, require | be closed for** *The museum is currently closed for structural repairs.* **| undergo** *The highway is undergoing major repairs.*
• REPAIR + VERB **cost sth**
• REPAIR + NOUN **work | job** *The damage meant a nine-month repair job.* **| bill, cost | centre, facility, garage, shop, yard** *a repair yard for fishing boats* **| man** *Why don't you get a TV repair man to have a look at it before you buy a new one?* **| kit**
• PREP. **beyond ~** *The gearbox was damaged beyond repair.* **under~** *We were given a courtesy car to use while our car was under repair.* **| ~to** *to carry out repairs to the railway track*
• PHRASES **a backlog of repairs** *Investment is needed to reduce the backlog of repairs.* **in good/poor repair** *The tools are old but in good repair.* **keep sth in (good) repair** *As a tenant you are required to keep the house in good repair.* **repair and maintenance** *They are responsible for the repair and maintenance of the buildings.* **a ... state of repair** *The barn was in a poor state of repair.*

repair *verb*

• ADV. **properly, successfully** *Most of the damage has now been successfully repaired.* **| poorly | extensively | completely | partially | quickly | regularly**
• VERB + REPAIR **try to | help (to)** *Natural vitamins in the shampoo will help repair damaged hair.*
• PHRASES **the cost of repairing sth** *They estimate the cost of repairing the damaged roads at £1 million.* **have sth repaired** *I'm having my car repaired next week.*

repatriate *verb*

• ADV. **forcibly**
• PREP. **from, to** *The refugees were forcibly repatriated from Hong Kong to Vietnam.*

repatriation *noun*

• ADJ. **compulsory, forced/forcible, involuntary, mandatory | voluntary**

• VERB + REPATRIATION **await, face** *refugees awaiting repatriation*
• REPATRIATION + NOUN **programme**
• PREP. **~from** *voluntary repatriation of people from the disputed territory to their homes* **~to**
• PHRASES **the repatriation of profits**

repay *verb*

1 pay back money
• ADV. **fully, in full** *The loan must be repaid in full by December 31.*
• VERB + REPAY **be able/unable to, can/could (afford to) | use sth to** *The proceeds from the sale will be used to repay the loan.*
• PREP. **to** *This money must be repaid to the bank.*

2 bring you sth in return for your efforts
• ADV. **amply, more than, well** *The charter can be seen in the town museum, which more than repays a visit.*
• PREP. **for** *I felt that I had been amply repaid for my exertions.*

repayment *noun*

• ADJ. **full | partial | early** *Interest will be refunded in the event of early repayment of the loan.* **| regular | monthly, weekly, etc. | capital, principal | interest | debt, loan, mortgage**
• VERB + REPAYMENT **make** *The repayments can be made directly from your current account.* **| keep up, meet** *They are struggling to keep up their loan repayments.* **| claim, demand** *The bank has demanded repayment of the loan.* **| be due for** *The loans were due for repayment in July 2002.* **| spread** *Repayments can be spread over one to 25 years.* **| calculate**
• REPAYMENT + NOUN **period | method, schedule, terms | loan, mortgage**
• PREP. **~ on** *repayments on the mortgage* **| ~ to** *repayment to the fund*

repeat *verb*

• ADV. **just, merely, simply** *There is no point in merely repeating what we've done before.* **| again | constantly, continually, endlessly, indefinitely, over and over (again)** *constantly repeating the same mistakes* ◇ *A single note repeated over and over again, throbbing in my head.* **| consistently, persistently, regularly | exactly, faithfully, word for word** *She faithfully repeated everything he had told her.* ◇ *He repeated what she had said word for word.* **| mechanically, parrot-fashion, parrot-like** *students repeating drills parrot-fashion* **| blandly, desperately, helplessly, lamely** *'Oh,' she repeated lamely.* **| slowly | quietly, softly | patiently | stubbornly**
• VERB + REPEAT **can/could only** *I can only repeat what I have already said to other journalists.* **| be necessary to, need to** *It may be necessary to repeat the dose several times to effect a cure.*
• PREP. **after** *The students repeated each sentence after their teacher.* **to** *You must not repeat this to anyone.*
• PHRASES **keep repeating sb/sth** *She kept repeating it over and over again like a robot.*

repellent *adj.*

• VERBS **be | find sb/sth**
• ADV. **utterly | slightly, vaguely | mutually** *mutually repellent substances such as oil and water*
• PREP. **to** *His arrogance was utterly repellent to her.*

repent *verb*

• ADV. **bitterly** *She bitterly repented what she had done.*
• VERB + REPENT **come to** *He came to repent his hasty decision.*
• PREP. **of** *She has repented of her sins.*

repentance noun

- ADJ. **genuine, sincere, true** | **deathbed**
- VERB + REPENTANCE **show** *They refused to showed repentance for their crimes.*
- PHRASES **a sign of repentance** *They were released on parole for showing signs of repentance.*

repercussion noun

- ADJ. **considerable, important, major, serious, significant** | **wide/widespread** | **international** | **economic, political, social**
- VERB + REPERCUSSION **have**
- REPERCUSSION + VERB **be felt** *The repercussions of the change in policy will be felt throughout Europe.*
- PREP. **~ for** *Changes in the industry had major repercussions for the local community.* **~ on** *The pay cuts are likely to have serious repercussions on productivity.*

repertoire noun

- ADJ. **extensive, large, vast, wide** | **full** | **limited, small** | **mainstream, standard** | **emotional** *An actor has to build a character and extend his own emotional repertoire.* | **music/musical** | **concert, opera, etc.** | **classical, jazz, etc.** | **guitar, piano, etc.**
- VERB + REPERTOIRE **have** *She has a rather limited repertoire.* | **add (sth) to, broaden, build (up), develop, expand, extend, increase** *He has added considerably to his piano repertoire.* ◇ *She needs to build up a repertoire of pieces.*
- REPERTOIRE + VERB **include sth** *His repertoire includes a large number of Scottish folk songs.*
- PREP. **in the/your ~** *a key piece in the standard concert repertoire*

repetition noun

- ADJ. **exact** | **frequent** | **constant, endless**
- VERB + REPETITION **use** *Blues is a musical form that uses a lot of repetition.* | **avoid, prevent** *She said I should avoid repetition of words in my essay.*
- PHRASES **the risk of repetition** *At the risk of repetition (= although I have already mentioned this), it is worth mentioning again that young children are particularly vulnerable to accidents in the home.*

repetitive adj.

- VERBS **be, seem** | **become, get**
- ADV. **extremely, highly, very** | **endlessly** *a boring and endlessly repetitive task* | **a bit, rather**

replace verb

1 take the place of sb/sth; exchange sb/sth
- ADV. **completely** | **largely** | **simply** *Putting in a new bathroom suite can cost as little as £800 if you are simply replacing an old one.* | **easily** *These losses are not easily replaced.* | **immediately** | **gradually** | **eventually**
- VERB + REPLACE **cannot/could not** *Machines cannot replace people in this work.* | **can/can't afford to** | **be built to, be designed to, be intended to, be used to** *It was built to replace the old Victorian jail.* | **appoint sb to, elect sb to** | **be expensive to** *Halogen lamps give excellent service, but the bulbs are expensive to replace.*
- PREP. **as** *She replaced Jane Stott as Managing Director.* **with** *We replaced the old television set with a newer one.*

2 put sth back in the right place
- ADV. **carefully, gently**
- PREP. **in** *She replaced the dress in the wardrobe.* **on** *He carefully replaced the vase on the shelf.*

replacement noun

1 replacing one thing with another
- ADJ. **complete, full** *Complete replacement of the roof tiles would be very costly.* | **partial** | **direct** *The series III gearbox is a direct replacement for a series II.* | **gradual** | **eventual**
- VERB + REPLACEMENT **be in need of, need, require** *The original furnishings are now in need of replacement.*
- REPLACEMENT + NOUN **programme** | **cost, value** *Rare instruments are usually insured for their full replacement value.* | **equipment**
- PHRASES **hormone replacement therapy**

2 sb/sth that replaces sb/sth else
- ADJ. **permanent** | **temporary** | **immediate** | **likely** *He is the most likely replacement for the captain.* | **possible** | **ideal** | **adequate** | **appropriate, suitable** | **hip, joint, knee** | **valve**
- VERB + REPLACEMENT **appoint, bring in (sb/sth as), hire** *We'll have to see how bad the injury is before deciding whether to bring in a replacement.* | **name (sb as)** *She was named as a possible replacement for the cabinet minister.* | **need** | **look for, seek** | **find** *We need to find a replacement for Jan when she goes on maternity leave.* | **get** | **come in/on as, go on as** *He came on as a replacement for the injured striker.* | **have** *She had a hip replacement six years ago.*
- REPLACEMENT + NOUN **teacher** | **part, unit** *Do you know where I can get the replacement part?* | **car, vehicle**
- PREP. **as ~** *Trams are now often preferred as replacements for buses.* | **~ by** *the president's temporary replacement by the Chief of Staff* **~ for**

replay noun

1 game that is played again
- ADJ. **final, first-round, quarter-final, etc.** | **championship, cup**
- VERB + REPLAY **earn, force** *They earned a replay with their 1–1 draw.*
- PREP. **~ against/with** *a replay against Real Madrid* **~ between** *the replay between Liverpool and Portsmouth*

2 playing again of a short section of a film, tape, etc.
- ADJ. **action** (*often figurative*) *It was an action replay (= repetition) of the problems of his first marriage.* | **slow-motion** | **television/TV, video**
- VERB + REPLAY **see, study, view, watch** *He has watched a video replay of his fall on numerous occasions.*
- REPLAY + VERB **show sth** *The replay shows that it was a handball.*

replica noun

- ADJ. **exact** | **full-scale, full-size, life-sized** | **half-scale, 1:5 scale, etc.** | **miniature**
- VERB + REPLICA **build, create, construct, make** *She made a 1:5 scale replica of Captain Cook's ship, 'The Endeavour'.*
- PREP. **in ~** *The original conservatory has been rebuilt in replica.*

reply noun

- ADJ. **brief, monosyllabic** | **curt, sharp, tart** | **only** *'Billy, I think it's your turn to wash the dishes,' said Jane. A non-committal grunt was his only reply.* | **simple** *Her reply was simple. 'No,' she said.* | **standard, usual** *'No comment' is his standard reply to most questions.* | **straight** *She refused to give a straight reply, deciding rather to defer the question.* | **evasive, non-committal** | **unsatisfactory** | **proper, satisfactory** | **suitable** | **correct** | **positive** | **negative** | **early, immediate, prompt, quick** | **formal** | **personal** | **written**
- VERB + REPLY **get, have, receive** *Have you had a reply to your letter yet?* | **give sb, make** *He made no reply,*

but simply walked away. | **send** (**back**), write *I must write my letter in time for them to send back a reply.* | **elicit, produce** *The report elicited a formal reply from the minister.* ◇ *The questionnaire produced 9 000 replies.* | **await** (*written*), **wait for** | **expect**

● REPLY + VERB **come** (**back**) *'No,' came the reply.* ◇ *A reply came back almost by return of post.* | **be forthcoming** *They waited patiently for a reply but none seemed to be forthcoming.*

● REPLY + NOUN **card, form, slip** *Please fill in the reply card and return it to us as soon as possible.*

● PREP. **in~** (**to**) *What did they say in reply?* ◇ *I am writing in reply to your request for information on holidays in Italy.* | **~ from** *a reply from the minister* **~ to** *my reply to your query*

● PHRASES **a chance to reply** *She quickly left the room before he had a chance to reply.* **a right of reply** *I am grateful to you for having given me a right of reply* (= the opportunity to respond) *to the article in your magazine about my company.*

reply *verb*

● ADV. **merely, simply** *He simply replied that he hadn't the faintest idea.* | **directly** *She did not reply directly to the allegations.* | **personally** *Well, you weren't expecting the prime minister to reply personally, were you?* | **at once, immediately** | **hastily, hurriedly, promptly, quickly** | **slowly** | **at length** *'OK,' he replied at length.* ◇ *She replied at length, but not to the point.* | **briskly, briefly, curtly, shortly, tersely** | **abruptly, brusquely, sharply** | **bluntly, flatly** *'No, you're not,' Graham replied bluntly.* | **firmly** | **gently, politely, soothingly** | **lightly** | **seriously** | **quietly, softly** | **angrily, bitterly, crossly, indignantly, sourly** | **coldly, coolly, icily** | **cautiously, guardedly, hesitantly, nervously** | **calmly, equably, evenly, mildly** | **sternly, stiffly** | **brightly, cheerfully** | **bleakly, grimly** | **drily, sarcastically, sardonically, sweetly** (*ironic*), **tartly** | **absently, vaguely** | **evasively** | **honestly** | **in kind** *Charles was insulted and replied in kind* (= by insulting them back).

● VERB + REPLY **not bother to** *She didn't even bother to reply.*

● PREP. **to** *He did not reply to my letter.* **with** *She replied with a smile.*

report *noun*

1 written/spoken account of sth

● ADJ. **important, influential, major | lengthy** | **brief, short | complete, comprehensive, extensive, full, wide-ranging** *I will have to make a full report of the situation to my superiors.* | **detailed, in-depth | general | encouraging, excellent, favourable, positive | adverse, bad, critical, damning, hard-hitting, negative, pessimistic | sensational | latest, new, recent, up-to-date | previous | original** *There have been many new findings since the original report.* | **early, initial, interim, preliminary | further, later, subsequent | periodic, regular | annual, quarterly | final | draft | formal | written | verbal | published | unpublished | special | standard | verbatim | reliable | false, misleading | conflicting** *There have been conflicting reports on the number of people killed.* | **factual | anecdotal | eyewitness, first-hand, on-the-spot | second-hand | anonymous | unconfirmed** *unconfirmed reports of a shooting in the capital* | **independent | joint | official | unofficial | confidential, secret | public | government, parliamentary | intelligence, police** *Reliable intelligence reports suggest that the terrorists have bases in five cities.* | **media, press | magazine, newspaper, radio, television | news | weather | committee | company | economic, financial, market | environmental | medical, psychiatric | scientific, technical | lab/laboratory | case, research, survey | enquiry | accident, crash | autopsy | progress,**

status | probation | audit, due diligence (*law*) | **law** *The case has not yet been reported in the law reports.*

● VERB + REPORT **deliver, give sb, make, present** *The committee presented its report to the Attorney General.* | **compile, do, draw up, prepare, produce, type** (**up**), **write** *I typed up a report about the morning's events for our clients.* | **file, give** (**sb/sth**), **let sb have, submit** *Our correspondent in Washington files a report most days.* ◇ *I'll let you have a report as soon as I can.* | **issue, release** *Auditors normally issue a report as to whether the company accounts have been prepared correctly.* | **leak** *a confidential report leaked to the press* | **have, hear, receive** *We've had reports of a gang shooting in the city.* | **call for** *The MPs called for a full report on the nuclear contract.* | **commission** *The government commissioned a report on the state of agriculture in the country.* | **launch, undertake** | **accept, endorse** *Following discussion, the annual report was accepted unanimously.* | **reject** | **confirm** | **deny** *They could neither confirm nor deny reports that the chairperson was to be replaced.* | **read** | **consider, discuss** | **publish** | **appear in** *A large number of tables and figures appear in the report.*

● REPORT + VERB **be based on sth** *This report is based on the analysis of 600 completed questionnaires.* | **concern sth, cover sth, detail sth, examine sth, look at sth, relate to sth** *The report looks at the health risks linked to obesity.* | **comprise sth, contain sth, include sth | comment** (**on**) **sth, describe sth, explain sth, express sth, indicate sth, mention sth, outline sth, say sth, state sth** *Reports have indicated that a growing number of medium-sized firms are under financial pressure.* | **cite sth, list sth, note sth** *The report notes evidence that secondary smoke from other people's cigarettes harms unborn children.* | **add sth, go on …** *The report went on to list her injuries.* | **acknowledge sth, admit** (**to**) **sth** *The report admits to several outstanding questions about the safety of the waste dumps.* | **allege sth, claim sth | argue sth | demonstrate sth, show sth | reveal sth** *The riots had been sparked off by police mishandling of a case, a report revealed yesterday.* | **draw attention to sth, emphasize sth, highlight sth, point sth out, stress sth** *The report draws attention to the appalling conditions in the country's prisons.* | **warn sth** *The report warns that more job losses are likely.* | **confirm sth** | **conclude sth, find sth, link sth with sth** *a report linking ill health with industrial pollution* | **advocate sth, call for sth, propose sth, recommend sth, suggest sth, urge sth** *The report called for sweeping changes in the education system.* | **accuse sb/sth, attack sb/sth, blame sb/sth, criticize sb/sth | be called sth, be entitled sth** *a report entitled 'Kick-start'* | **be out** *Criticism has been levelled at local businesses in a report out* (= released) *today.*

● REPORT + NOUN **writer, writing**

● PREP. **according to a/the~** *According to this evening's weather report, there will be snow tomorrow.* **amid/amidst~s** *The pro-democracy rally came amidst reports of dissatisfaction among army officers.* **in a/the~** *The findings are summarized in the report.* | **~ about, ~ by** *a report by scientists* **~ from** *a report from the select committee* **~ into** *The department has launched a report into the bombing.* **~ on** *an official report on the accident*

2 written statement about a student's work

● ADJ. **good | bad | school | end-of-term**

● VERB + REPORT **get** *She got a better report this year.*

report *verb*

● ADV. **back** *The reconnaissance party reported back that the town was heavily fortified.*

● VERB + REPORT **be expected to, expect to** *The company is expected to report record profits this year.* | **be delighted to, be glad to, be happy to, be pleased to** *I am pleased to report that the scheme is going well.* | **have to** *It is with regret that I have to report the death of one of our*

members. | **fail to** *He was charged with careless driving and failing to report an accident.*
● PREP. **from** *This is John Hutchins, reporting from Zimbabwe.* **on** *reporting on the situation in central Africa* **to** *Report the theft to the police as soon as possible.*
● PHRASES **be widely reported** *The incident was widely reported in the British press.*

reporter *noun*

● ADJ. **chief** | **cub, junior, trainee** | **foreign** | **local** | **newspaper, radio, television/TV** | **crime, financial, news, political, sports** | **investigative** | **freelance**
● VERB + REPORTER **speak to, talk to, tell** *We were warned not to talk to reporters.*
● PREP. **~for/with** *She then became a crime reporter with a national newspaper.* **~from** *The secret was leaked to a reporter from the 'New York Times'.* **~on** *the chief reporter on the 'Daily Herald'*
⇨ Note at JOB

represent *verb*

1 be a member of a group
● ADV. **strongly, well** *Local businesses are well represented on the committee.* | **poorly** | **adequately** | **disproportionately** *Women are disproportionately represented among welfare recipients.*

2 act/speak officially for sb
● ADV. **legally** *The suspect must appear and may be legally represented.*
● VERB + REPRESENT **choose sb to, elect sb to, select sb to** *He was chosen to represent Scotland in three consecutive World Cup Finals.*

3 show sth
● ADV. **accurately** *Representing an image accurately requires a great many bytes of digital information.* | **fairly** | **falsely** | **diagrammatically, graphically, schematically, visually** *The data can be represented graphically in a line diagram.* | **symbolically**
● VERB + REPRESENT **be intended to** *It is not clear what these symbols were intended to represent.* | **purport to** *The film purported to represent the lives of ordinary people.*
● PREP. **as** *The film represents women as victims.* **to** *He admitted falsely representing to police officers that the car had been stolen.*

representation *noun*

1 sth that shows/describes sth
● ADJ. **accurate, faithful, good, true** | **simplified** | **diagrammatic, graphic, pictorial, visual** | **symbolic** | **written** *the written representation of a spoken text* | **two-dimensional, etc.**
● VERB + REPRESENTATION **generate, produce** *There are many ways of generating a two-dimensional representation of an object.*
● PHRASES **a form/means of representation**

2 having representatives to speak/vote for you
● ADJ. **large** | **increased** | **strong** | **effective** | **adequate** | **balanced, equal, fair** | **direct** *direct representation in Parliament* | **democratic, proportional** | **parliamentary, political** | **black, female, minority** | **legal** | **consular, diplomatic** | **union** | **employee, labour**
● VERB + REPRESENTATION **have** *They had a strong representation in government.* | **achieve, secure, win** *All parties won representation in the national assembly.* | **ensure, guarantee** *He claims that their electoral system ensures fair representation of all parties.* | **increase** *The party has increased its representation in Parliament.* | **reduce** | **allow sb, provide (sb with)** *The accused was not allowed legal representation.* | **get, obtain**

● PREP. **~by** *representation by a lawyer* **~for** *representation for employees* **~from** *representation from all parties*
● PHRASES **a system of representation**

3 formal statements
● ADJ. **false** | **oral, written**
● VERB + REPRESENTATION **make** | **receive**
● PREP. **~to** *They may make representation to government on matters affecting their organization.*

representative *noun*

● ADJ. **leading, main** | **senior** | **sole** *I was the sole representative of the general practitioners.* | **appointed, elected** | **accredited, authorized, official** | **local, national, regional** | **branch** | **personal** | **legal** | **parliamentary, political** | **council, government** | **diplomatic** | **UN** | **special** *the UN special representative for Cyprus* | **permanent** *the Algerian permanent representative at the UN* | **military** | **company, industry, management, trade** | **sales** (also *informal* **rep**) *She's a sales rep for sports equipment* (= *she travels around selling sports equipment for a company*). | **employee, union** | **student** | **community, public** | **club, committee** | **church**
● VERB + REPRESENTATIVE **appoint, appoint sb (as), choose (sb as), elect, elect sb (as), nominate, nominate sb (as)** | **send** *The association is sending representatives to the conference.* | **recall** *They have recalled their representatives from the negotiations.* | **consult (with), meet (with)** *Management are obliged to consult with union representatives about possible redundancies.* | **discuss (sth) with**
● REPRESENTATIVE + VERB **attend sth** *The negotiations were attended by representatives of several states.*
● REPRESENTATIVE + NOUN **body** *The country has a new supreme representative body.*
● PREP. **~for** *a representative for international shipping companies* **~from/of** *representatives from citizens' groups* **~to** *representatives to a conference*
⇨ Note at JOB

representative *adj.*

● VERBS **be, seem** | **consider sb/sth**
● ADV. **very** | **fully, properly, truly** | **not necessarily** | **broadly, fairly, reasonably** *a broadly representative sample* | **widely** *Exhibits include a widely representative collection of railway rolling stock.* | **statistically** | **nationally** *a nationally representative picture of the employment situation*
● PREP. **of** *Is this group of people fully representative of the population in general?*

repress *verb*

● ADV. **firmly** *feelings that had been firmly repressed* | **barely** *She could barely repress a sigh of relief.*
● VERB + REPRESS **try to** | **be unable to**

repressed *adj.*

● VERBS **be** | **become**
● ADV. **extremely, severely, very** | **rather** | **sexually** *women who are sexually repressed*

repression *noun*

1 using force to control people
● ADJ. **extreme, massive, severe** | **bloody, brutal, ruthless** | **political** | **government, military, police, state**
● VERB + REPRESSION **suffer (from)** *The trade unions suffered brutal repression after the coup.* | **subject (sb/sth) to** *Reports claimed that civilians were being subjected to ruthless repression.*
● PREP. **~against** *repression against ethnic minorities* **~by** *repression by the state*
● PHRASES **a target for/of repression**

2 controlling strong emotions/desires
- ADJ. **emotional, sexual**

reprieve noun

- ADJ. **temporary | last-minute** *He was saved from the gallows by a last-minute reprieve.*
- VERB + REPRIEVE **earn, gain, get, win | give sb/sth, grant (sb/sth)** *The railway line, due for closure, has been granted a six-month reprieve.*
- PREP. **~from** *The family have won a temporary reprieve from eviction.*

reprimand noun

- ADJ. **severe | public | verbal, written**
- VERB + REPRIMAND **earn (yourself), get, receive** *The manager earned himself a severe reprimand for criticizing the referee.* | **give sb, issue (sb with)** *She was issued with a reprimand for leaking the news.*
- PREP. **~for** *a reprimand for a breach of the rules*

reprimand verb

- ADV. **severely | gently | officially | publicly**
- PREP. **for** *She was severely reprimanded for accepting the money.*

reprisal noun

- ADJ. **bloody, savage**
- VERB + REPRISAL **take** *The gang threatened to take reprisals against them.* | **threaten (sb with) | suffer** *She tried to persuade the soldiers that they would not suffer reprisals if they surrendered.* | **expect, fear**
- REPRISAL + NOUN **attack, raid**
- PREP. **in~for** *A dozen hostages were shot in reprisal for the killing of an army officer.* | **~against** *reprisals against witnesses for the evidence they have given* **~from** *reprisals from angry fans*
- PHRASES **fear of reprisals**

reproach noun

- ADJ. **bitter | mild** *There was mild reproach in his tone.*
- PREP. **beyond/above~** *Her conduct had always been beyond reproach.* **with~** *He glanced at her with reproach.* | **~about** *There was no reproach about his failure to turn up.* **~to** *Paul saw this as a reproach to himself.*
- PHRASES **full of reproach** *Her voice was full of reproach.* **a look of reproach** *He gave Helen a look of bitter reproach.* **a word of reproach** *She had never uttered a word of reproach.*

reproduce verb

1 produce a copy of sth; produce sth again
- ADV. **accurately, exactly, faithfully** *The colours can be reproduced fairly accurately.* ◇ *The book's characters are faithfully reproduced in the film.* | **merely, simply** *In her own work she simply reproduces the very conventions that she claims to despise.*
- VERB + REPRODUCE **be able to, can/could | be difficult to, be hard to, be impossible to** *It is difficult to reproduce a signature exactly.*
- PREP. **from** *The map is reproduced here from a Victorian original.*
- PHRASES **an attempt to reproduce sth** *Writing grew out of an attempt to reproduce speech in a permanent form.* **reproduced by courtesy/permission of sb/sth** *The painting is reproduced here by courtesy of the Tate Gallery.* **widely reproduced** *These works were popular and widely reproduced.*

2 produce young
- ADV. **asexually, sexually**

- VERB + REPRODUCE **be able to, can/could** *The offspring have to be able to reproduce in their turn.* | **fail to**
- PREP. **by** *Many single cell organisms reproduce by splitting in two.*

reproduction noun

1 producing babies/animals/plants
- ADJ. **human | biological | asexual, sexual**
- REPRODUCTION + VERB **take place**
- PHRASES **a method of reproduction**

2 act/process of producing a copy/recording
- ADJ. **accurate, faithful, (good/high) quality | colour, graphic, photographic, sound** *Using a wide tape gives better quality sound reproduction.*
- VERB + REPRODUCTION **give, provide | ensure** *The craftsmen have ensured faithful reproduction of the original painting.*

3 sth that has been reproduced
- ADJ. **exact, faithful** *an exact reproduction of an ancient building* | **large and black and white, colour | photographic** *The quality of a photographic reproduction decreases with time.*
- REPRODUCTION + NOUN **furniture** (= furniture made as a copy of an earlier style)
- PREP. **~from** *a reproduction from an old book*

republic noun

- ADJ. **new | autonomous, independent | breakaway** *the breakaway republics of the former Soviet empire* | **self-proclaimed | democratic, federal, Islamic, people's, socialist** *the People's Republic of China* | **banana** (*disapproving, offensive*) (= a small poor country with a weak government, that depends on foreign money)
- VERB + REPUBLIC **create, establish, form, found | abolish | declare (sth), proclaim (sth)** *They have declared themselves an independent democratic republic.* | **recognize (sth as) | overthrow**

repulsive adj.

- VERBS **be, look, smell | find sb/sth**
- ADV. **deeply, extremely** *She found the idea deeply repulsive.* | **utterly | slightly | morally, sexually**
- PREP. **to** *He was utterly repulsive to her.*

reputable adj.

- VERBS **be**
- ADV. **highly, very** *a highly reputable company*

reputation noun

- ADJ. **considerable, enviable, excellent, fine, good, great, high, unrivalled, well-deserved, well-earned** *She has built up an enviable reputation as a harpist.* | **awesome, fearsome, formidable | bad, poor, unenviable, unsavoury | established | growing | undeserved | intact** (only after **reputation**) *He emerged from the trial with his reputation intact.* | **public | international, worldwide | professional**
- VERB + REPUTATION **enjoy, have** *He has the reputation of being a hard worker.* | **acquire, build (up), earn, establish, gain, make** *Her international reputation is built on an impressive list of publications.* | **damage, destroy, lose, ruin, tarnish | protect | live up to** *November is certainly living up to its reputation—we've had nothing but rain all week.* | **live down** *She found it hard to live down her reputation as a second-rate actress.* | **stake** *He has staked his reputation on the success of the play.*
- REPUTATION + VERB **grow | suffer** *The company's reputation suffered when it had to recall thousands of products that were unsafe.*

● PREP. **by** ~ *He was by reputation difficult to please.* |
~**as** *You've made quite a reputation for yourself as a rebel!*
~ **for** *The company has a well-deserved reputation for
being reliable.*
● PHRASES **a loss of reputation**

request noun

● ADJ. **special | reasonable, unreasonable | formal,
official | polite | strange, unusual | repeated | urgent
| explicit, particular, specific | written**
● VERB + REQUEST **make, put in, submit** *I've put in a
request for a room with a view of the sea.* | **get, have, re-
ceive** *We have had repeated requests for a pedestrian cross-
ing near the school.* | **agree to, comply with, grant** | **re-
spond to | refuse, reject, turn down | repeat**
● PREP. **at sb's** ~ *The play was written by Agatha Chris-
tie at the request of Queen Mary.* **by** ~ *The writer's name
was withheld by request* (= because the writer had asked
for this to be done). **on/upon** ~ *We will arrange accommo-
dation on request.* | ~ **for** *The helpline was inundated with
requests for information on the crash.*
● PHRASES **available on request** *A detailed list of our
publications is available on request.* **by popular request**
The film is being shown again by popular request. **a number of requests**

request verb

● ADV. **explicitly, expressly, specifically | formally |
politely | reasonably** *(law)* *Auditors will be required to
provide any information reasonably requested by the
bank.* | **urgently | repeatedly**
● PREP. **from** *We have requested some information from
the company.*

require verb

● ADV. **urgently** *Many of the refugees urgently require
medical treatment.* | **reasonably** *(law)*

requirement noun

● ADJ. **absolute** *There's no absolute requirement to dis-
close your age.* | **important, key, main, prime | essential,
fundamental** *An open system of criminal justice is a fun-
damental requirement of any democratic society.* | **de-
manding, strict, stringent | detailed | exact, precise |
reasonable | basic | minimum | additional, further |
general | special | particular, specific | individual, per-
sonal | annual, daily** *your daily requirement of vitamin C*
| **constitutional, contractual, formal, legal, legislative,
mandatory, procedural, regulatory, statutory | busi-
ness, commercial | borrowing** *The public sector borrow-
ing requirement is expected to rise.* | **client, customer,
market | academic, course, curriculum, educational,
entrance, entry | technical | environmental, safety |
visa | dietary, nutritional** *patients with special dietary re-
quirements* | **energy, food, housing, information, la-
bour, manpower**
● VERB + REQUIREMENT **comply with, fulfil, meet, satisfy, suit** *We can arrange a holiday to meet your require-
ments exactly.* | **impose, lay down, set (down/out)** *The
government has imposed strict safety requirements on fair-
ground rides.* | **relax, waive** *to relax university entrance
requirements*
● PREP. **for your** ~ *We grow enough vegetables for our
own requirements.* **to your** ~ *Our conservatories and
porches can be designed to your exact requirements.* | ~ **for**
*Large buildings have specific requirements for fire-
brigade access.*
● PHRASES **subject to (the) requirements** *The school
can decide which pupils will be given priority of admission, subject to the requirements of the law.* **surplus to requirements** (= more than is needed) *300 workers at the
factory have been told they are surplus to requirements.*

rescue noun

● ADJ. **dramatic | daring | attempted | air-sea, moun-
tain, sea | financial**
● VERB + RESCUE **attempt** *Her own boat capsized after
she attempted a rescue.* | **come/go/rush to** *No one came to
their rescue until the following day.*
● RESCUE + NOUN **attempt, effort, mission, operation
| party, team, unit** *a mountain rescue team* | **service |
worker | work | boat, helicopter, vehicle, vessel |
centre** *an animal rescue centre* | **bid, package, plan,
scheme** *a financial rescue package for the company*
● PREP. **to sb's/the** ~ *Her wails of distress brought him
running from the house, like a knight to the rescue.* |
~ **from** *his rescue from a burning building*
● PHRASES **fire and rescue** *New Zealand fire and rescue
services carried out several extensive searches for survivors.* **search and rescue** *The navy are on a search and
rescue mission.*

research noun

● ADJ. **detailed, in-depth, painstaking | extensive** *He
has carried out extensive research into renewable energy
sources.* | **basic | original | further | ground-breaking,
pioneering** *pioneering research into skin disease* | **col-
laborative | empirical | academic, clinical, historical,
medical, military, scientific, social, space | AIDS, can-
cer, etc.** | **animal** *calling for a ban on animal research* |
market
● QUANT. **piece** *a startling piece of historical research*
● VERB + RESEARCH **carry out, conduct, do, undertake** *She's doing research on Czech music between the
wars.* | **be based on** *One paper based on research con-
ducted at Oxford suggested that the drug may cause brain
damage.*
● RESEARCH + VERB **demonstrate sth, indicate sth,
prove sth, reveal sth, show sth, suggest sth** *What have
their researches shown?* | **produce sth, yield sth** *Recent
research on deaf children has produced some interesting
findings about their speech.*
● RESEARCH + NOUN **degree | effort, programme, pro-
ject, work** *directing the group's research effort* | **methods
| findings, results | purposes** *Copies of the tape can be
made for research purposes.* | **centre, institute, labora-
tory | assistant, group, student, team, worker | grant**
● PREP. ~ **in** *Most research in the field has concentrated on
the effects on children.* ~ **into/on** *They are carrying out research into the natural flow patterns of water.*
● PHRASES **an area of research, research and development** *spending on military research and development*

research verb

● ADV. **carefully, exhaustively, extensively, fully, me-
ticulously, properly, thoroughly, well | poorly** *The book
has been poorly researched.*
● PREP. **for** *She is currently researching for her next
novel.* **into** *I spent two years carefully researching into his
background.*

researcher noun

● ADJ. **eminent, experienced, leading | chief, senior |
young | early** *She based her work on that of earlier re-
searchers.* | **independent | academic | post-doctoral,
post-graduate | cancer, medical | educational, social
| market**
● QUANT. **group, team**
● RESEARCHER + VERB **investigate sth, work in/on sth**
researchers working in different disciplines ◇ *researchers
working on the biochemistry of learning* | **believe sth,
claim sth, note sth, say sth, suggest sth, think sth | dis-
cover sth, find sth** *Researchers found 17 per cent of their
random sample to be severely depressed.* | **show sth** |

conclude sth *The researchers have concluded that further studies are needed.*
● PHRASES **researchers in the field** *The book is written by experts who are well known as researchers in the field.*
⇨ Note at JOB

resemblance *noun*

● ADJ. **close, great, marked, remarkable, striking, strong | uncanny | obvious | faint, passing, remote, slight, superficial | physical | family**
● VERB + RESEMBLANCE **bear, have, show** *The plot of the movie bears more than a passing resemblance to Jane Austen's 'Emma'.* | **see** *I can see the family resemblance.*
● RESEMBLANCE + VERB **end** *They are both called Nigel, but there the resemblance ends* (= they are not similar to each other in any other way).
● PREP. **~ between** *There is a close resemblance between her and her daughter.* **~ to** *Crocodiles still have a strong resemblance to their long-lost ancestors.*
● PHRASES **a point of resemblance** *The story has points of resemblance to a Hebrew myth.*

resemble *verb*

● ADV. **closely, greatly, strongly, very much** *He very much resembles a friend of mine.* | **in no way, not remotely** *He does not resemble his brother in any way.* ◇ *I have never seen anything remotely resembling the horrors of that day.* | **faintly, in some respects/ways, rather, somewhat, superficially, vaguely | oddly, uncannily**
● VERB + RESEMBLE **be designed to** *The house was designed to resemble a church.* | **tend to**
● PREP. **in** *The meat resembles chicken in flavour.*

resent *verb*

● ADV. **bitterly, deeply, greatly, strongly** *She bitterly resented the fact that her husband had been so successful.* | **rather | rightly | secretly**

resentful *adj.*

● VERBS **be, feel, look, seem, sound | become, grow** *They grew bitter and resentful.* | **remain**
● ADV. **bitterly, deeply, extremely, very** *They were bitterly resentful of the fact that they had to work such long hours.* | **increasingly | almost** *She looked at him, almost resentful now.* | **a little, slightly, vaguely | secretly**
● PREP. **about/at** *She felt resentful at the way she had been treated.* **of** *He was very resentful of their success.* **towards** *He felt deeply resentful towards his ex-wife.*

resentment *noun*

● ADJ. **angry, bitter, considerable, deep, deep-seated, great, intense, smouldering | growing, increasing | popular, widespread | old** *She felt all her old resentment flaring up.*
● VERB + RESENTMENT **bear, feel, harbour** *I bore him no resentment.* ◇ *You seem to be harbouring some resentment against your boss.* | **express, show | contain, hide** *He struggled to contain his resentment.* | **arouse, breed, cause, create, fuel, give rise to, lead to, provoke** *Inequality breeds resentment.*
● RESENTMENT + VERB **build up, grow** *Don't let your resentment build up.* | **flare up**
● PREP. **~ about/over** *Maggie was filled with resentment about her treatment.* **~ against** *the growing resentment against foreigners* **~ among** *The measures fuelled resentment among students.* **~ at** *I felt great resentment at having to work such long hours.* **~ between** *the bitter resentment between the two brothers* **~ towards** *their resentment towards each other*
● PHRASES **a cause/source of resentment, a feeling/sense of resentment**

reservation *noun*

1 arrangement for a seat/room
● ADJ. **airline, hotel**
● VERB + RESERVATION **have** *Do you have a reservation?* | **make | confirm | cancel**
● RESERVATION + NOUN **service | fee | form**
● PREP. **~ for** *I'd like to make a reservation for four people for Friday night, please.*

2 feeling of doubt about sth
● ADJ. **considerable, deep, grave, major, serious, severe, strong | minor, slight | certain** *I have certain reservations regarding several of the clauses in the contract.* | **initial**
● VERB + RESERVATION **have | express, voice** *NATO generals voiced reservations about making air strikes.*
● RESERVATION + VERB **concern sth**
● PREP. **despite ~s** *Despite his initial reservations, he came to love London.* **with ~s** *The employees are backing the reorganization plans, with reservations.* **without ~** *I can recommend her without reservation.* | **~ about/concerning/over/regarding** *They have expressed reservations concerning the provisions of the treaty.*
● PHRASES **one/only reservation** *My one reservation concerns the performance of the vehicle in wet conditions.*

reserve *noun*

1 supply of sth available to be used in the future
● ADJ. **great, huge, large, substantial, vast | sufficient | low, small | existing | additional | last** *It took my last reserves of strength and will to swim to the lifeboat.* | **untapped** *The region is thought to have some of the world's largest untapped oil reserves.* | **hidden** *She had hidden reserves of courage.* | **capital, cash, contingency, currency, financial, foreign currency/exchange, gold, international** *In the face of a severe crisis relating to international reserves, the government devalued the currency twice.* | **coal, energy, gas, oil | timber | food | fat** *The birds build up fat reserves to help them survive the winter.*
● VERB + RESERVE **have** *We have only a small reserve of coal.* | **hold sth in, leave sth in, keep sth in** *The crack troops were held in reserve behind the front line.* | **dig into, dip into, draw on/upon, tap, use** *He had to draw on reserves of strength just to finish the race.* | **call on/up/upon, summon (up)** *her ability to summon up reserves of concentration and energy* | **build (up) | deplete, exhaust** *The company has depleted its reserves to make the purchase.* | **pay sth out of** *The dividend had to be paid out of reserves.* | **take**
● RESERVE + VERB **be available | dwindle, fall**
● RESERVE + NOUN **currency, funds | tank** *The plane was fitted with fuel reserve tanks for long-distance flights.*
● PREP. **in ~** *The rail company has two trains in service and one in reserve.*

2 protected area for plants/animals, etc.
● ADJ. **national | bird, forest, game, natural/nature, wildlife**
● VERB + RESERVE **create, establish**

3 quality/feeling
● ADJ. **deep, strong | natural** *They made him feel at ease, despite his natural reserve.*
● PREP. **with ~** *Any contract should be treated with reserve until it has been checked.* **without ~** *She trusted him without reserve* (= completely).

4 extra player; second team
● VERB + RESERVE **play in** *He will continue to train and may play in the reserves next season.*
● RESERVE + NOUN **side, team | goalkeeper, striker, etc. | game, match**

5 extra military force
● ADJ. **army | strategic | volunteer**
● RESERVE + NOUN **force, police**

reserve *verb*

- ADV. **exclusively, expressly, specially, specifically, strictly** *The star has a ski slope reserved exclusively for her.* | **normally, usually** *a ceremony normally reserved for heads of state*
- PREP. **for** *The car park is reserved for customers only.*

reserved *adj.*

- VERBS **be, seem** *She seems quite reserved.*
- ADV. **deeply, extremely, very** | **quite, rather** | **naturally** *his naturally reserved manner*

reservoir *noun*

1 where water is stored
- ADJ. **natural** | **artificial, man-made** | **underground**
- PREP. **in a/the~**

2 amount of sth that can be used
- ADJ. **huge, vast**
- VERB + RESERVOIR **tap (into)**
- PREP. **~of** *tapping into the vast reservoir of information available on the Internet*

residence *noun*

1 house
- ADJ. **desirable** | **palatial** | **official** | **royal** | **private** | **main, principal** *Versailles was the principal residence of the kings of France until 1793.* | **summer** | **country, town** | **family** | **student**

2 living in a particular place
- ADJ. **long** | **permanent** | **temporary** | **main, normal, principal**
- VERB + RESIDENCE **establish, take up** *The family took up temporary residence in the manor house.* | **remain in, stay in** *The family house was sold off but she remained in residence on the ground floor.*
- RESIDENCE + NOUN **permit** *He has applied for a residence permit.*
- PREP. **in ~** *The flag flying above the palace indicates that the Queen is in residence.*
- PHRASES **a change of residence, a hall of residence** *The university has two halls of residence for its postgraduate students.* **a place of residence** *The notice was addressed to her last known place of residence.*

resign *verb*

- ADV. **formally**
- VERB + RESIGN **be forced to, be obliged to, have to** *He was forced to resign due to ill health.* | **intend to** | **offer to, threaten to** *The minister offered to resign after his affair became public.* ◇ *Two MPs threatened to resign if the government did not agree to examine this case.* | **decide to** | **refuse to** | **call on sb to** *They called on her to resign as chief executive.*
- PREP. **as** *He resigned as chairman.* **from** *She formally resigned from the government.* **over** *Three members of the committee resigned over the issue.*

resignation *noun*

1 giving up your job; letter of resignation
- ADJ. **immediate** | **shock, sudden, surprise, unexpected** | **forced** | **mass**
- VERB + RESIGNATION **hand in, submit, tender** *She handed in her resignation following the dispute over company policy.* | **announce** | **withdraw** | **offer (sb), proffer** | **threaten** | **prompt, provoke, lead to** *The accusation prompted the resignation of the cabinet minister.* | **force** *Illness forced his resignation from the squad.* | **call for, demand** *The protesters called for the immediate resignation of the minister.* | **accept** *She has refused to accept the resignation of her deputy.* | **reject**

- RESIGNATION + VERB **be/become effective** *My resignation is effective from May 1.*
- RESIGNATION + NOUN **letter** | **announcement** *His resignation announcement was widely expected.* | **speech, statement**
- PREP. **~ as** *her resignation as party leader* **~ from** *A scandal led to his resignation from office.*
- PHRASES **a call for sb's resignation, resignation on (the) grounds of sth** *She tendered her resignation on grounds of ill health.* **a letter of resignation**

2 willingness to accept a difficult situation
- ADJ. **weary**
- PREP. **in ~** *Hearing that the train was running late, he sighed in weary resignation.* **with ~** *She spoke with resignation.* | **~ to** *resignation to fate*
- PHRASES **a look/sigh of resignation**

resilience *noun*

- ADJ. **great, remarkable** | **natural**
- VERB + RESILIENCE **have** | **demonstrate, show**
- PREP. **~ to** *She has shown great resilience to stress.*
- PHRASES **strength and resilience**

resilient *adj.*

- VERBS **be, prove, seem** | **become** | **make sth**
- ADV. **extremely, highly, remarkably, very** *a remarkably resilient woman* | **pretty**
- PREP. **to** *The body of the camera makes it highly resilient to outdoor use.*

resist *verb*

- ADV. **fiercely, firmly, resolutely, strenuously, strongly, vigorously** | **successfully** *They successfully resisted pressure from their competitors to increase prices.* | **naturally** *People naturally resist change.* | **stubbornly** | **passively** *The civil population passively resisted.* | **physically** | **at first, initially, so far** *He has so far resisted pressure to resign.*
- VERB + RESIST **be able/unable to, can/could (hardly), can't/couldn't (easily)** *She could hardly resist the urge to turn and run.* ◇ *Trends in the national economy confront firms with pressures they cannot easily resist.* | **can/could never, can/could no longer** | **be difficult to, be hard to, be impossible to** | **try to** | **manage to** | **be determined to** | **be helpless to, be powerless to** *She was powerless to resist the attraction that she felt to him.* | **tend to**
- PHRASES **the strength to resist sth**

resistance *noun*

1 trying to stop sth
- ADJ. **considerable, great, stiff, strong, substantial** | **determined, fierce, heroic, serious, spirited, stubborn** | **effective** | **token** | **active** | **passive** | **collective, organized** | **widespread** | **armed, military** | **political** | **popular, public** | **guerrilla, peasant**
- VERB + RESISTANCE **mount, offer, put up** *They mounted stiff resistance to the proposal.* | **encounter, meet (with), run into** *The advancing army met with little resistance.* | **break (down), crush, overcome**
- RESISTANCE + VERB **stiffen** | **collapse, crumble**
- RESISTANCE + NOUN **movement** | **fighter, forces, group, leader, worker**
- PREP. **without~** *The attacks did not take place without resistance.* | **~against** *armed resistance against the Nazis* **~to** *There was fierce resistance to the new laws.*
- PHRASES **the line/path of least resistance** (= the easiest way of doing sth), **a pocket of resistance** (= an area of resistance)

2 to a disease/drugs
- ADJ. **high** | **low** | **disease** | **antibiotic, drug**

• VERB + RESISTANCE **have | build up, develop** *You need to build up your resistance to colds.* | **lower**
• PREP. **~to** *Aids lowers the body's resistance to infection.*

resistant *adj.*

• VERBS **be | become**
• ADV. **extraordinarily, extremely, highly, particularly, remarkably, very | quite, relatively**
• PREP. **to** *a metal that is highly resistant to corrosion*

resolution *noun*

1 formal decision taken after a vote
• ADJ. **draft | formal | joint** *a joint US-British resolution* | **unanimous | ordinary | emergency, special | compromise | affirmative, negative** (*both law*) *An affirmative resolution of both Houses of Parliament is needed.* | **Security Council, UN, etc.**
• VERB + RESOLUTION **draft | propose, put forward, table | vote on | adopt, agree, approve, carry, pass** *The resolution was carried unanimously.* | **block, reject**
• RESOLUTION + VERB **be aimed at sth, call for sth** *The resolution called for the resumption of negotiations.* | **declare sth, proclaim sth** *a resolution declaring independence* | **approve sth, authorize sth** *The assembly adopted a resolution approving the scheme.* | **condemn sth** *a resolution condemning the invasion*
• PREP. **under (a/the) ~** *weapons banned under Resolution 687* | **~ on** *The General Assembly rejected the resolution on the subject of arms control.*
⇨ Special page at MEETING

2 settling a dispute
• ADJ. **early, quick, rapid | final, ultimate | peaceful** *Hopes of a peaceful resolution to the conflict were fading.* | **satisfactory, successful | conflict, dispute** *methods of conflict resolution*
• VERB + RESOLUTION **require | press for** *The government is pressing for an early resolution of the hostage crisis.* | **achieve, reach**
• PREP. **~ to** *the likelihood of achieving a satisfactory resolution to the problem*

3 being firm and determined
• ADJ. **great**
• VERB + RESOLUTION **have | show** *She showed great resolution in her dealings with management.* | **lack**

4 firm decision to do/not to do sth
• ADJ. **firm, good | New Year/New Year's**
• VERB + RESOLUTION **make** *I made a New Year resolution to give up smoking.* | **keep**

5 power to give a clear image
• ADJ. **high** *high-resolution graphics* | **low | maximum | screen | pixel** *a monitor capable of a 1 024 by 768 pixel resolution*

resolve *verb*

• ADV. **completely, fully** *The matter is not yet fully resolved.* | **successfully | adequately, satisfactorily | amicably, peacefully** *We hope that the dispute can be resolved peacefully.* | **easily, readily | quickly, rapidly, speedily | immediately | eventually, finally, ultimately**
• VERB + RESOLVE **attempt to, take steps to, try to | be unable to, fail to** *The two countries have failed to resolve their differences on this.* | **help (to) | be difficult to**
• PREP. **by/through** *The crisis was finally resolved through high-level negotiations.*
• PHRASES **an attempt/effort to resolve sth** *They met in a last-ditch attempt to resolve their differences.* **a means/method/way of resolving sth**

resort *noun*

• ADJ. **fashionable, favourite, popular | attractive, bustling, lively | modern | purpose-built | health, holi**-day, **ski, spa, tourist | beach, coastal, lakeside, mountain, seaside | summer, winter**
• RESORT + NOUN **area, town | hotel**
• PREP. **at/in a/the~** *They spent a month at a fashionable ski resort in Switzerland.*

resource *noun*

• ADJ. **considerable, enormous, large, major, substantial** *The library is an enormous resource for historians of medieval France.* | **important, vital | adequate, sufficient | limited, meagre, scarce | renewable, sustainable, unlimited | finite, limited, non-renewable | available | additional, extra | invaluable, useful, valuable** *Time is your most valuable resource, especially in examinations.* | **untapped | natural | material, physical | energy, mineral, oil, water | capital, economic, financial** *The school has limited financial resources.* | **human, staff | information, learning, library, teaching** *The database could be used as a teaching resource in colleges.* | **national | inner, personal** *She is someone of considerable personal resources.*
• VERB + RESOURCE **be rich in, have** *Australia is a country rich in natural resources.* ◇ *We do not have the resources* (= the money) *to update our computer software.* | **lack | pool, share** *We'll get by if we pool our resources.* | **allocate, distribute, provide | divert, reallocate, redistribute** *the government's role in diverting resources into social policies* | **draw on, exploit, manage, mobilize, tap, use** *to mobilize resources in the community to provide shelter for the homeless* ◇ *We need to manage our resources better.* | **deplete, use up | squander, waste | conserve**
• RESOURCE + NOUN **centre | allocation, management | depletion | constraints, implications**
• PHRASES **access to resources, the allocation/distribution/provision of resources, the exploitation of resources, a lack of resources, the use of resources** *We must make the most efficient use of the available resources.*

resourceful *adj.*

• VERBS **be** *He is very clever and endlessly resourceful.*
• ADV. **highly, very | endlessly**

respect *noun*

1 admiration
• ADJ. **considerable, deep, great | grudging | mutual** *a relationship based on mutual respect*
• VERB + RESPECT **feel, have, hold sb in** *She held him in considerable respect.* | **command, earn (sb), gain (sb), get, inspire, win (sb)** *a society in which age commands great respect* | **lose**
• PREP. **~ for** *He felt a grudging respect for her talents as an organizer.*

2 polite behaviour/consideration/care
• ADJ. **great, utmost | due, proper** *the respect due to his great age*
• VERB + RESPECT **accord sb/sth, pay (sb/sth), show (sb/sth), treat sb/sth with** *the respect accorded to her memory* ◇ *He treats his grandparents with great respect.*
• PREP. **out of ~** *We observed a minute's silence out of respect for the disaster victims.* **with ~** *With all due respect, I think you've misunderstood what he said.* ◇ *The chainsaw is a dangerous tool—it should be used with respect.*
• PHRASES **a lack of respect** *to show a lack of respect for authority* **a mark/sign/token of respect**

3 detail/point
• ADJ. **certain | different | crucial, important, significant | material**
• VERB + RESPECT **differ in** *There was one respect, however, in which they differed.* | **be alike in, be identical in, be similar in, resemble sth in**
• PREP. **in ... ~(s)** *The report is accurate in all material respects.* **in ~ of** (= concerning) *A writ was served on the*

firm in respect of their unpaid bill. **with ~ to** (= concerning) *The two groups were similar with respect to income and status.*
- PHRASES **in all/many/some respects** *In many respects she is like her mother.* **in every/this respect** *The marriage was a disaster in every respect.*

respect *verb*

1 admire sb/sth
- ADV. **deeply, greatly, really, very much**
- PREP. **as** *She is widely respected as a politician.* **for** *She was much respected for her knowledge of herbs.*
- PHRASES **be highly/much/well respected** *a highly respected doctor* **be internationally/universally/widely respected** *WWF is internationally respected for its conservation work.*

2 pay attention to sth
- VERB + RESPECT **promise to, undertake to** *The government has promised to respect human rights.* | **fail to** *Her daughters failed to respect her last wishes.*
- PHRASES **a duty to respect sth, failure to respect sth**

respectability *noun*

- ADJ. **international** *The country has again achieved international respectability after years of isolation.* | **bourgeois, middle-class, working-class | academic, intellectual, political, scientific**
- VERB + RESPECTABILITY **achieve, gain** *The theory has now gained scientific respectability.* | **give sth**
- PHRASES **an air/a façade/a veneer of respectability**

respectable *adj.*

- VERBS **be, look, seem | become**
- ADV. **eminently, extremely, highly, very** *It was an eminently respectable boarding school.* | **entirely, perfectly, wholly | almost | fairly | enough** *She seems respectable enough.* | **apparently | academically, intellectually**

respite *noun*

- ADJ. **brief, moment's, temporary** *a moment's respite from the ringing of the phone* | **much needed, welcome**
- VERB + RESPITE **have | bring (sb), give (sb), provide (sb with)** *The tablets brought temporary respite from the excruciating pain.* | **gain (sb), win (sb)**
- RESPITE + NOUN **care**
- PREP. **without ~** *The storm continued for two hours without respite.* | **~ from** *They had no respite from the demands of their children.*
- PHRASES **a period of respite**

respond *verb*

1 react
- ADV. **immediately, instantly | promptly, quickly, rapidly, swiftly | enthusiastically, favourably, positively, well** *Both sides have responded positively to the plan.* ◊ *Their son is responding well to the treatment.* | **forcefully, vigorously | adequately, appropriately, constructively, effectively, intelligently | adversely, aggressively, angrily | cautiously, coolly | sensitively, sympathetically | generously | magnificently** *The teams responded magnificently to the challenge.* | **accordingly** *The government needs to listen to the public and respond accordingly.* | **readily** *The plants readily respond to these stimuli.* | **directly | automatically, instinctively | flexibly | differently | merely, simply** *We do not have a strategy. We merely respond to ideas from local people.* | **emotionally, imaginatively** *to respond emotionally to the landscape* | **in kind** *The terrorists declared all-out war on the government and the government responded in kind.*
- VERB + RESPOND **be able/unable to | be likely to** *She wasn't sure how he was likely to respond.* | **fail to** *His*

condition failed to respond to the treatment. | **be slow to | enable sb to** *enabling teachers to respond flexibly to the needs of their students*
- PREP. **by** *The government responded by tightening the law on gun ownership.* **to** *Companies have to respond to the changing economic climate.* **with** *The demonstrators threw stones and the police responded with tear gas.*
- PHRASES **an ability/a capacity/a willingness to respond, a failure to respond**

2 say sth in reply
- ADV. **politely | angrily | coolly | drily**
- PREP. **to** *He responded politely to her questions.* **with** *He responded with a smile when she spoke.*

response *noun*

- ADJ. **encouraging, enthusiastic, favourable, good, positive | lukewarm, muted | angry, discouraging, negative | appropriate, correct | inappropriate, incorrect** *incorrect responses in a multiple choice test* | **strong** *These are likely to evoke a strong response in the viewer.* | **direct | quick, rapid | slow | automatic, immediate | initial** *My initial response was one of anger.* | **public | natural | behavioural, emotional, physiological, political | verbal, written | immune** *the immune response to viral infections*
- VERB + RESPONSE **give, make | get, have, receive** *Have you had any responses to the advertisement yet?* | **bring/call forth, draw, elicit, evoke, produce, provoke** *His comments drew an angry response from the crowd.*
- RESPONSE + NOUN **rate, time** *We sent out over 100 letters but the response rate was low* (= few people replied).
- PREP. **in ~ (to)** *In response, she stormed out of the room.* | **~ from** *The response from local businesses has been muted.* **~ to** *What was their response to the question?*
- PHRASES **(a) lack of response** *Due to lack of response the event has been cancelled.*

responsibility *noun*

1 being responsible
- ADJ. **full, total | awesome, great, heavy, weighty** *It is a great responsibility looking after other people's children.* | **direct | overall | primary | ultimate** *Ultimate responsibility rests with the prime minister.* | **special | diminished** *He was found not guilty of murder on the grounds of diminished responsibility.* | **sole | collective, joint, shared | individual, personal | ministerial, parental | financial, legal, moral, social**
- VERB + RESPONSIBILITY **have** *She has responsibility for public transport.* | **accept, assume, bear, shoulder, take (on/over)** *The bank refuses to accept responsibility for the mistake.* ◊ *Will you take responsibility for arranging the food?* | **share | lay, place** *The government of the time placed responsibility for the poor on the Church.* | **delegate, devolve, hand over** *devolving responsibility downwards so decisions are taken nearer to the people they will affect* | **abdicate, evade, shirk, shift** *to shift legal responsibility for the correct labelling of goods onto the shopkeeper* | **admit, claim** *No organization has yet claimed responsibility for the bomb attack.* | **deny, disclaim, duck** *Ducking responsibility is fatal in a democracy.* | **allocate, assign (sb), give sb | attribute** *He attributed responsibility for the killing to the secret service.* | **burden sb with | absolve sb from/of**
- RESPONSIBILITY + VERB **fall on sb, lie/rest with sb**
- PREP. **~ for** *Full responsibility for the fiasco lies with the PR department.* **~ towards** *He feels a strong sense of responsibility towards his parents.*
- PHRASES **the age of criminal responsibility, the burden of responsibility** *The school governors carry a special burden of responsibility.* **do sth on your own responsibility** (= without being told to and being willing to take

the blame if it goes wrong), **a position of responsibility, a sense of responsibility**

2 job/duty

• ADJ. **heavy, onerous | additional, increased | altered | caring, departmental, domestic, family, financial, managerial, ministerial, parental, professional, teaching | contractual, statutory | particular, special**
• VERB + RESPONSIBILITY **have | carry out, discharge, fulfil | accept, face up to, take on, undertake** *He seems unwilling to face up to his responsibilities as a father.* ◊ *I don't feel ready to take on new responsibilities.* | **delegate | avoid, evade, shirk | relieve sb of**
• PREP. **~ for** *The heads of school departments have particular responsibilities for the curriculum.* **~ to/towards** *The club has a responsibility to its members.*
• PHRASES **duties and responsibilities, rights and responsibilities** *parental rights and responsibilities*

responsible *adj.*

1 having the job/duty of doing sth
• VERBS **be | become | remain | make sb** *I am making you responsible for the cooking.*
• ADV. **entirely, totally, wholly | chiefly, largely, mainly, primarily | individually | collectively, jointly** *All members of the Cabinet are collectively responsible for decisions taken.* | **formally, legally | nominally** *The company could not indicate a person even nominally responsible for staff training.* | **ultimately** *The board is ultimately responsible for policy decisions.* | **financially**
• PREP. **for** *They're responsible for cleaning the engine.*

2 being the cause of sth/to blame for sth
• VERBS **be, feel | become | consider sb, deem sb, find sb, hold sb, regard sb as, see sb as, think sb** *They held him responsible for the failure of the policy.*
• ADV. **entirely, fully, wholly | partially, partly | directly | indirectly | personally | single-handedly, solely** *He was almost single-handedly responsible for the flourishing drug trade in the town.* | **ultimately | somehow** *Did he think her somehow responsible for Eddie's death?* | **morally**
• PREP. **for** *Who was responsible for the mistake?*

3 having to report to sb/sth
• VERBS **be**
• ADV. **directly | ultimately** *a complex web of party bodies ultimately responsible to the Central Committee*
• PREP. **to** *The prime minister is directly responsible to Parliament.*

4 showing/needing good sense and reliability
• VERBS **be, seem | become**
• ADV. **extremely, highly, very | fairly, quite | ecologically, environmentally** *The organization needs to become more environmentally responsible.* | **morally, politically, socially** *allocating resources in a morally responsible way*

responsive *adj.*

• VERBS **be, seem | become | remain**
• ADV. **extremely, highly, very** *The company is highly responsive to changes in demand.* | **fully | fairly, quite | directly, immediately | sexually**
• PREP. **to** *She's fairly responsive to new ideas.*

rest *noun*

• ADJ. **complete | good, long | little, short | well-deserved, well-earned | bed** *She's on complete bed rest, antibiotics and plenty of fluids.*
• VERB + REST **find** (*formal*), **get, have, take** *Her heart would find no rest until she knew the truth.* ◊ *Get some rest while you can.* ◊ *I had a good long rest before the party.* | **need | come to** *The ball rolled down the hill and came to rest against a tree.*

• REST + NOUN **day, period | area | home**
• PREP. **at ~** *At rest* (= when not moving) *the insect looks like a dead leaf.* | **~ from** *The doctor advised him to take a complete rest from football.*
• PHRASES **a day of rest**

rest *verb*

• ADV. **casually, gently, lightly, loosely | heavily | comfortably** *Her head was resting comfortably against his chest.* | **peacefully, quietly | momentarily | awhile**
• VERB + REST **let sth** *She let his hand rest heavily on hers.*
• PREP. **against** *She rested the ladder against the wall.* **on/upon** *His hands rested lightly on her shoulders.*
• PHRASES **rest easy** *I can rest easy* (= stop worrying) *knowing that she's safely home.*

PHRASAL VERBS

rest on/upon sth
• ADV. **solely, squarely** *It is rare for the responsibility for causing conflict to rest solely on one side.*

rest with sb
• ADV. **squarely** *Surely the blame rests squarely with Sir Ralph?* | **ultimately** *The decision ultimately rests with the council.*

restaurant *noun*

• ADJ. **large | little, small | elegant, excellent, fine, good, smart, stylish | cheap, expensive | local | crowded | family | candlelit, intimate | à la carte | self-service | take-away | licensed | Chinese, French, etc. | fast-food, fish, seafood**
• VERB + RESTAURANT **go (out) to** *If you're too tired to cook, let's go to a restaurant.* | **leave, walk out of** *They walked out of the restaurant without paying.* | **manage, run** *She runs a family fish restaurant on the seafront.*
• RESTAURANT + VERB **offer sth, serve sth, specialize in sth** *a restaurant offering a wide variety of local specialities* ◊ *The hotel restaurant serves a buffet breakfast.* ◊ *an Asian restaurant specializing in Thai cuisine*
• RESTAURANT + NOUN **manager, owner, staff | chain**
• PREP. **at a/the ~** *They argued the whole time we were at the restaurant.* **in a/the ~** *We had a quick meal in a small local restaurant.*

restoration *noun*

1 returning sth to its original condition
• ADJ. **complete, full | extensive** *Many of the older paintings have undergone extensive restoration.*
• VERB + RESTORATION **carry out | undergo | await, be in need of, need** *This historic watermill is currently awaiting restoration.*
• RESTORATION + NOUN **programme, project, work**
• PREP. **for ~** *The palace is closed for restoration.* **under ~** *a steam engine under restoration*

2 bringing sth back into use/existence
• ADJ. **full** *the full restoration of Sino-US relations* | **immediate** *Protesters called for the immediate restoration of civil liberties.*
• PHRASES **the restoration of diplomatic relations, the restoration of the monarchy**

restore *verb*

1 bring back a situation/feeling
• ADV. **quickly, soon** *Order was quickly restored.* | **formally** *Diplomatic relations were formally restored.*
• VERB + RESTORE **need to** *We need to restore public confidence in the industry.* | **attempt to, try to | help (to) | be designed to, be intended to**
• PREP. **to** *Peace has now been restored to the area.*

● PHRASES **an attempt/effort to restore sth** *an attempt to restore the company's finances* **be aimed at restoring sth, measures to restore sth, a way of restoring sth**

2 repair/rebuild sth
● ADV. **extensively** *The interior has recently been extensively restored.* | **completely, fully** | **partially, partly** | **beautifully, handsomely, sympathetically, tastefully** | **carefully, faithfully, lovingly, painstakingly**
● PREP. **to** *The train has been restored to full working order.*
● PHRASES **newly/recently restored, restore sth to its former glory** *The buildings have now been restored to their former glory.*

restrain *verb*

● ADV. **barely** *I barely restrained myself from hitting him.* | **effectively** | **forcibly, physically** *She had to be physically restrained.*
● VERB + RESTRAIN **be unable to, can't/couldn't, can/could no longer** *She could not restrain a flash of pride.* | **seek to, try to** | **manage to**
● PREP. **from** *He restrained himself from shouting at her.*
● PHRASES **an attempt/effort to restrain sb**

restrained *adj.*

● VERBS **be** | **become**
● ADV. **remarkably, unusually, very** *I thought she was remarkably restrained in the circumstances.* | **fairly, quite**

restraint *noun*

1 limit/control on sth
● ADJ. **effective** | **voluntary** *talks on voluntary wage restraint* | **conventional** *what happens when the conventional restraints on human cruelty are removed* | **physical** *Sometimes the care workers need to use physical restraint on the hospital patients.* | **budgetary, economic, expenditure, financial, fiscal, monetary, pay, spending, wage** | **contractual, judicial, legal, regulatory** | **cultural, moral, social**
● VERB + RESTRAINT **impose, use** | **remove**
● PREP. **without ~** *Prices continued to rise without restraint.* | **~ on/upon** *The government imposed restraints on spending.*

2 behaving in a calm/moderate way
● ADJ. **considerable, great, remarkable** | **mutual** *the mutual restraint shown by police and protesters* | **sexual**
● VERB + RESTRAINT **exercise, show** *Journalists have exercised remarkable restraint in not reporting all the sordid details of the case.* | **appeal for, call for**
● PREP. **~ by** *The government called for restraint by both sides.*

restrict *verb*

● ADV. **greatly, seriously, severely** | **further** *The government is considering new laws which will further restrict people's access to firearms.* | **effectively** | **unduly, unnecessarily** | **apparently** | **deliberately**
● VERB + RESTRICT **attempt to, seek to, try to** | **tend to** *Having small children tends to restrict your freedom.*
● PREP. **to** *I'm restricting myself to one glass of wine a day.*
● PHRASES **an attempt to restrict sth** *attempts to restrict the sale of alcohol* **measures to restrict sth**

restricted *adj.*

● VERBS **be** | **remain**
● ADV. **heavily, highly, narrowly, seriously, severely, very** *New heavy industries were concentrated in narrowly restricted areas.* ◊ *He has a severely restricted diet.* | **increasingly** | **fairly, rather, relatively, somewhat** | **ap-**

parently | **unduly** *Access to higher education has been unduly restricted for people with disabilities.*
● PREP. **to** *Access to the documents remains restricted to civil servants.*

restriction *noun*

● ADJ. **severe, tight, tough** | **major** | **petty** *The removal of petty restrictions has made life easier.* | **absolute** | **further** | **artificial** *free movement of goods between member countries without any artificial restrictions* | **proposed** | **contractual, government, legal, statutory** | **advertising, age, credit, financial, import, parking, price, reporting** (= restrictions on information that newspapers may report), **speed, time, trade, travel, visa**
● VERB + RESTRICTION **impose, introduce, place** *The government has introduced tough new import restrictions.* | **lift, remove** *The press asked for restrictions on reporting the war to be lifted.* | **accept** | **be subject to** *The right of sale is subject to certain restrictions.*
● RESTRICTION + VERB **affect sth, apply** *The 30 mph speed restriction applies in all built-up areas.*
● RESTRICTION + NOUN **order**
● PREP. **without~** *Citizens of the EU can travel without restriction within the EU.* | **~ on/upon** *The regulations were seen as a restriction on personal freedom.*

restrictive *adj.*

● VERBS **be, seem**
● ADV. **extremely, highly, very** | **increasingly** | **fairly, rather, somewhat** | **unduly, unnecessarily** *He argued that the law was unduly restrictive.*

result *noun*

1 outcome/effect
● ADJ. **good, positive** *For the best results buy one of the more expensive brands.* | **disastrous, unfortunate** | **direct, indirect** | **net** | **inevitable, logical** | **dramatic, impressive, spectacular, surprising** | **lasting** | **desired** *And did your intervention produce the desired result?*
● VERB + RESULT **have, produce** *My interference had rather an unfortunate result.* | **achieve, get, obtain** *This was not the result we had hoped to achieve.*
● PREP. **as a/the ~** *These actions were taken as a direct result of the strike.* **with a/the ~** *Parking restrictions were lifted, with the result that the road is permanently blocked by cars.*

2 desired effect
● ADJ. **concrete, tangible** *We have yet to see any concrete results from the research.*
● VERB + RESULT **come up with, get, produce** | **give, show** *When is all your effort going to show some results?*

3 final position in a competition
● ADJ. **election** | **football, racing, etc.**
● VERB + RESULT **announce, read out** *The announcer was reading out the football results.*

4 (often **results**) mark given for an examination
● ADJ. **encouraging, good** | **disappointing, poor** | **exam, examination** | **A-level, degree, etc.**
● VERB + RESULT **get, have** *When do you get your exam results?*

5 of an experiment, a medical test, an investigation, etc.
● ADJ. **interim, preliminary** | **experimental, research** | **test, X-ray** | **referendum, survey**
● VERB + RESULT **wait for** *The doctor is still waiting for my results.* | **get, have, receive** *I haven't had the X-ray results yet.* | **analyse, evaluate** | **present, publish** *They hope to publish their results next month.* | **give, yield** *All three methods yielded identical results.*
● RESULT + VERB **demonstrate sth, indicate sth, reveal sth, show sth, suggest sth** *Preliminary results sug-*

gest that there is no cause for concern. | **confirm sth, support sth**
- PREP. **pending the~(s) of** *Work on the scheme has been halted, pending the results of a judicial enquiry.* | **~from** *evaluating the results from various recent surveys*

result *verb*

PHRASAL VERB
result in sth
- ADV. **inevitably** *This move will inevitably result in the loss of a lot of jobs.* | **not automatically, not necessarily** | **easily** *Complacency could easily result in tragedy.* | **quickly** | **eventually**
- VERB + RESULT IN STH **can/could, may/might, should, will/would** | **be expected to, be liable to, be likely/unlikely to** *Such measures are likely to result in decreased motivation of the workforce.*

resuscitation *noun*

- ADJ. **emergency, mouth-to-mouth**
- VERB + RESUSCITATION **give sb** *We gave him mouth-to-mouth resuscitation and heart massage.*
- RESUSCITATION + NOUN **equipment**

retailer *noun*

- ADJ. **big, large, leading, major** *the country's biggest food retailer* | **small** | **local** | **high street** *High street retailers reported a marked increase in sales before Christmas.* | **multiple** | **independent, niche, specialist** | **carpet, clothing, DIY, electrical, fashion, food, etc.**

retain *verb*

- ADV. **still** | **no longer** | **somehow** *Despite the decay the mosque somehow retained a profound grandeur.*
- VERB + RETAIN **be keen to, hope to, want to, wish to** | **attempt to, seek to, struggle to, try to** *He struggled to retain control of the situation.* | **manage to** | **help (to)** | **be allowed to, be entitled to, have the right to** *He was allowed to retain his parliamentary seat.*
- PREP. **as** *The president retained her as his chief adviser.*

retaliation *noun*

- ADJ. **massive** | **swift** | **trade** | **nuclear**
- VERB + RETALIATION **bring, prompt, provoke** *a casual remark that brought swift retaliation from her boyfriend* | **threaten** | **fear**
- PREP. **in ~** *He never said a single word in retaliation.* **in ~ for** *They killed two men in retaliation for a bomb attack the previous day.* | **~ against** *fearing retaliation against government troops* **~ by/from** *the possibility of retaliation by other governments* **~ for** *retaliation for the bombing of civilians*
- PHRASES **an act of retaliation**

retarded *adj.*

- VERBS **be, look**
- ADV. **severely** *Many of the children are severely retarded.* | **slightly** | **educationally, emotionally, mentally** *a mentally retarded child*

rethink *noun*

- ADJ. **complete** | **fundamental, major, radical**
- VERB + RETHINK **have**
- PREP. **~of** *to have a fundamental rethink of policy*

rethink *verb*

- ADV. **radically**
- VERB + RETHINK **be forced to, have to, need to** *I think we may have to rethink our policies fairly radically.*

retire *verb*

- ADV. **early** *He is hoping to retire early on medical grounds.*
- VERB + RETIRE **be compelled to, be forced to, be obliged to, have to** *Anderson was forced to retire because of injury at the age of 26.* | **be due to, plan to** *Mr McNeil is due to retire later this month.* | **decide to**
- PREP. **as** *He recently retired as head teacher of their school.* **at** *Most women retire at 60.* **from** *She retired from the bank last year.*

retirement *noun*

- ADJ. **early, premature** *A knee injury forced him into premature retirement.* | **active** | **comfortable, happy** *He provided for a comfortable retirement by selling the business.* | **compulsory, enforced** *compulsory retirement at 60* ◇ *her enforced retirement from the sport*
- VERB + RETIREMENT **consider, look forward to, think about** | **approach, be close to, near** | **plan (for), prepare for, provide for** *helping you to plan your retirement* | **reach** | **announce** | **go into** | **come out of** *He is going to come out of retirement for this one last concert.* | **force sb into** | **mark** *They presented him with an engraved watch to mark his retirement.* | **enjoy, spend** *I intend to spend my retirement travelling.*
- RETIREMENT + NOUN **age** | **benefits, package, pension** | **gift, party** | **home**
- PREP. **after/before (your)~** *After her retirement from the stage she began to drink.* **at (your)~** *Your pension plan provides a cash lump sum at retirement.* **for (your)~** *saving for her retirement* **in (your)~** *His father was now living in retirement in France.* ◇ *She has found a new hobby in her retirement.* **on (your)~** *a gift from the firm on his retirement* **until (your)~** *He remained in the post until his retirement last year.* | **~ as** *her retirement as sales director* **~ at** *retirement at fifty-five* **~from** *his retirement from first-class cricket*
- PHRASES **the age of retirement** *The age of retirement for all employees is 60.* **take early retirement** *The company suggested that he should take early retirement.* **wish sb a long and happy retirement**

retort *noun*

- ADJ. **quick, sharp** | **angry, caustic, furious**
- VERB + RETORT **hurl, make** *He opened his mouth to make a caustic retort.* | **bite back, refrain from, suppress** *He bit back a sharp retort.* | **bring, draw, meet with** *Her remark drew bitter retorts from the unemployed workers.* | **sting sb into** *He was stung into an angry retort.*

retort *verb*

- ADV. **quickly** | **angrily, bitterly, coolly, crisply, curtly, drily, flatly, furiously, grimly, harshly, sarcastically, sharply, stiffly** *'How dare you!' he retorted angrily.*

retreat *noun*

1 retreating/leaving
- ADJ. **hasty, headlong, rapid** *I decided to beat a hasty retreat.* | **humiliating, ignominious, undignified** | **dignified, orderly, strategic, tactful, tactical** *I made a tactful retreat before they started arguing.*
- VERB + RETREAT **beat, make** | **lead** | **order, sound** | **force/send/throw sb into** *Eventually the police forced the crowd into retreat.* | **block, cut off** | **cover** *We covered his retreat with bursts of gunfire.*
- PREP. **in ~** *The enemy was now in retreat.* **on the ~** *fresh evidence that trade unionism is on the retreat* | **~ from** *He took part in the retreat from Paris.* **~ into** *her retreat into a fantasy world of her own* **~ to** *an ignominious retreat to the River Vistula*
- PHRASES **be in full retreat** *On the eastern front the*

army was in full retreat. **a line of retreat** *We succeeded in cutting off the enemy's line of retreat.*

2 quiet and private place
- ADJ. **favourite, perfect** *the perfect retreat for a romantic honeymoon* | **private, secret** | **peaceful** | **country, rural** *designed as a gentleman's country retreat* | **summer, winter** | **holiday, weekend**
- VERB + RETREAT **turn sth into, use sth as** *She plans to use it as a winter retreat.* | **go into** *He went into retreat at his country home to escape the attention of the media.*
- PREP. **~ for** *a summer retreat for the rich* **~ from** *staying here at his secret retreat from life in the busy city*

3 private time at a quiet place
- ADJ. **religious, spiritual**
- VERB + RETREAT **go on** *She goes on a spiritual retreat for two weeks every summer.*

retreat *verb*

- ADV. **hastily, quickly, rapidly, swiftly** | **further** | **back** *He retreated hastily back to his car.*
- VERB + RETREAT **try to** | **order sb to** *The army was ordered to retreat.*
- PREP. **before** *They retreated before the Americans.* **behind** *He retreated behind the table.* **from, in the face of** *He retreated in the face of strong opposition.* **into** *He retreated into his own world.* **to** *She retreated from the busy office to her own room.*

retribution *noun*

- ADJ. **fair, just** | **divine**
- VERB + RETRIBUTION **demand, seek** | **exact** | **fear**
- RETRIBUTION + VERB **come, follow** *Violent retribution soon followed.*
- PREP. **in ~** *His armies invaded their lands in retribution.* | **~ against** *retribution against wrongdoers* **~ for** *He saw his suffering as retribution for the sins of his past life.* **~ from** *Members of Parliament clearly feared retribution from their constituents.* **~ on** *She saw the sentence as just retribution on the man who had assaulted her.*
- PHRASES **an act of retribution, fear of retribution** *The victim did not report the incident for fear of retribution.*

return *noun*

1 coming/going back; giving sth back
- ADJ. **complete, full** *a full return to health* | **gradual** | **imminent** | **brief** | **emotional, happy** | **dramatic**
- VERB + RETURN **make** *Shevchenko made an emotional return to his former club.* | **mark** *The victory marked Williams' return to top form.* | **await, wait for** | **greet** *The smell of cooking greeted his return home.* | **celebrate** | **delay, put off** | **demand** *He demanded the return of his money.* | **call for, push for, vote for** *The UN continued to call for a return to civilian rule.*
- RETURN + NOUN **address, date**
- PREP. **in ~ (for)** *She gave them all the help she could, and asked for nothing in return.* **on sb's ~** *He promised to visit us on his return.* | **~ from** *The date of their return from India is a fortnight from now.* **~ to** *Jones is hoping for an early return to racing after her injury.*
- PHRASES **by return (of post)** *All orders will be dispatched by return of post* (= by the next post).

2 (also **returns**) profit
- ADJ. **attractive, big, excellent, generous, good, high, substantial** | **acceptable, adequate, decent, fair, healthy, reasonable** | **inadequate, low, marginal, meagre, poor, small** | **diminishing** *the law of diminishing returns* | **immediate** | **long-term** | **annual, monthly, quarterly, etc.** | **expected, likely, possible, potential, projected** | **gross, pre-tax** | **after-tax, net** | **tax-free**
- VERB + RETURN **achieve, get, make, receive** *You should get a good return on this investment.* | **boost, en-**

hance, improve, increase, maximize** *to maximize returns to shareholders* | **estimate** | **give (sb), offer (sb), produce, provide, show, yield** *The venture yielded a net return of £15 million.* | **represent** *These figures represent a return of 8.5% per annum.*
- RETURN + VERB **increase** | **decline, decrease**
- PREP. **~ on** *the return on capital/investment/savings*
- PHRASES **a rate of return**

3 ticket to travel to a place and back again
- ADJ. **day, period** | **business class, economy, first-class, standard, tourist class**
- RETURN + NOUN **ticket** | **flight, journey**

return *verb*

- ADV. **recently** | **shortly** | **eventually** | **safely** *Our aircraft all returned safely to their bases.* | **voluntarily** | **forcibly** *The asylum seekers are to be forcibly returned to their home countries.* | **home**
- VERB + RETURN **be due to** *She is due to return to school in a fortnight.* | **be expected to, be likely to, be/look set to** | **be allowed to** | **decide to, expect to, hope to, intend to, plan to, want to, wish to** | **agree to, promise to** | **fail to** *Suspicions were aroused when he failed to return to work on Monday morning.* | **force sb to** *Lack of cash forced her to return to work.*
- PREP. **from** *She had recently returned from Paris.* **to** *She never returned the book to me.*

reunion *noun*

- ADJ. **emotional, tearful** | **class, college, school, university** | **family** | **annual** | **grand**
- VERB + REUNION **have, hold, plan** *The reunion is held every two years.* | **arrange, organize** | **attend, go to** | **celebrate** *Let's have a party to celebrate our reunion.*
- REUNION + VERB **take place**
- REUNION + NOUN **dinner, lunch**
- PREP. **at a/the ~** *At the reunion I met a friend I hadn't seen for twenty years.* | **~ between** *an emotional reunion between mother and son* **~ for** *organizing a reunion for former company employees* **~ with** *a tearful reunion with his family*

rev *noun*

- ADJ. **high** | **low** *The engine is almost silent at low revs.* | **engine**
- VERB + REV **do** *On average the engine does 4 000 revs per minute.*
- REV + NOUN **counter**
- PHRASES **revs a/per minute**
⇨ See REVOLUTION

revealing *adj.*

- VERBS **be**
- ADV. **deeply, highly, particularly, very** *some deeply revealing insights into his life* | **quite, rather**
- PREP. **about** *The book is very revealing about young people's views of themselves.*

revelation *noun*

- ADJ. **amazing, astonishing, devastating, embarrassing, sensational, shattering, shock, startling, sudden** | **fresh, latest, recent** | **divine** *He claimed to know these things by divine revelation.*
- QUANT. **flash** *A sudden flash of revelation came to him.*
- VERB + REVELATION **come as, prove** *To many younger members of her audience, these performances must have come as a revelation.*
- REVELATION + VERB **come** *The embarrassing revelations came just hours before he was to make his speech.*
- PREP. **~ about/concerning** *fresh revelations concerning their private lives* | **~ for** *The demonstration proved*

something of a revelation for our teachers. **~ from** *He claimed to have had a revelation from God.* **~ to** *His acting ability was a revelation to us all.*

revenge *noun*

- ADJ. **sweet**
- VERB + REVENGE **seek, want | exact, get, have, take, wreak** *He vowed to take his revenge on the man who had killed his brother.*
- REVENGE + NOUN **attack, killing**
- PREP. **in ~** *The attack was in revenge for the deaths of two loyalist prisoners.* **| ~ for** *revenge for the insult* **~ on** *taking revenge on her attacker*
- PHRASES **an act of revenge** *The bombing was an act of revenge for the shooting of two young boys.* **a desire for revenge** *The accusations were driven by a desire for revenge.*

revenue *noun*

- ADJ. **annual, yearly | expected, potential** *the firm's expected annual revenue* **| overall, total, worldwide | additional, extra | considerable, substantial | lost** *Tax fraud costs the country millions in lost revenue.* **| government, public, tax** *the main sources of public revenue* **| advertising, export, oil, sales, tourism, tourist, etc.**
- VERB + REVENUE **depend on, need, rely on** *These television companies rely on advertising revenue for their funds.* **| earn, get, raise | collect** *The central government collects the tax revenue on behalf of local authorities.* **| spend, use | bring in, generate, produce, yield** *The project will not generate any revenue until 2010.* **| increase | reduce | lose**
- REVENUE + VERB **be derived from sth, come from sth** *Their government's revenues come mainly from direct taxes.* **| go up, grow, rise | drop, fall, go down**
- PREP. **in ~** *a drop in revenue* **| ~ from** *revenues from the sale of oil*
- PHRASES **loss of revenue, a source of revenue** *Tourism is the island's main source of revenue.*
- ⇨ Special page at BUSINESS

reverence *noun*

- ADJ. **deep, great, profound | due, proper**
- VERB + REVERENCE **have | hold sb in** *He is still held in great reverence throughout the country.* **| inspire** *a painting that inspires deep reverence for nature*
- PREP. **in ~** *I closed my eyes in reverence.* **with ~** *She spoke of them with profound reverence.* **| ~ for** *reverence for human life* **~ to/towards** *Children are taught to show respect and reverence towards their grandparents.*

reversal *noun*

- ADJ. **complete, total | dramatic, sudden | apparent | policy | role** *Some people looking after elderly parents have trouble with the role reversal involved.*
- VERB + REVERSAL **amount to, mark, represent** *This represents an apparent reversal of previous US policy.* **| bring about, lead to, result in**
- PREP. **~ in** *the dramatic reversal in population decline* **~ of** *a reversal of current trends*
- PHRASES **a reversal of fortunes** *Industrial unrest and cheaper imports played their part in the company's reversal of fortunes.*

reverse *noun*

1 opposite
- ADJ. **exact**
- VERB + REVERSE **do** *If you tell children to do something, they will often do the exact reverse.*
- PREP. **on the ~** (= on the opposite side) *The coin has a date on one side and the emperor's head on the reverse.*

2 gear
- VERB + REVERSE **put sth in/into, throw sth into** *I put the car in reverse.*
- REVERSE + NOUN **gear**

3 problem
- ADJ. **major, serious**
- VERB + REVERSE **experience, have, meet with, suffer** *Their forces have suffered serious reverses in recent months.*

reverse *verb*

1 move backwards
- ADV. **carefully** *She carefully reversed the lorry up the narrow driveway.* **| slowly | in, out**
- PREP. **into** *The car reversed into a hedge.* **out of** *He reversed slowly out of the garage.*

2 change sth to the opposite
- ADV. **dramatically, radically | completely, exactly, totally** *The decline in this industry has now been completely reversed.* **| almost | partially, partly | simply** *To solve the puzzle, simply reverse the order of the numbers.* **| quickly, rapidly | suddenly**
- VERB + REVERSE **seek to, try to | fail to**

reversible *adj.*

- VERBS **be** *The operation is easily reversible.*
- ADV. **easily, readily | completely, totally**

review *noun*

1 considering sth again
- ADJ. **complete, comprehensive, extensive, full, full-scale, fundamental, in-depth, major, overall, systematic, thorough, wide-ranging | brief, rapid, short | urgent | annual, periodic, regular** *the government's annual policy review* **| constant, continuous | critical** *The first chapter presents a critical review of the existing nursery education system.* **| government, independent, internal, judicial | financial, pay, performance, policy, rent**
- VERB + REVIEW **ask for, call for, campaign for, press for, seek** *Greenpeace will seek a judicial review if a full public enquiry is not held.* **| announce, order | carry out, conduct, do, hold, undertake | present**
- REVIEW + VERB **take place | cover sth, deal with sth | conclude sth, indicate sth, propose sth, recommend sth, suggest sth**
- REVIEW + NOUN **body, committee, group**
- PREP. **due for ~** *The rent is due for review.* **under ~** *The matter is still under review.* **| ~ by** *a review by the court*

2 report on a film, restaurant, etc.
- ADJ. **enthusiastic, favourable, glowing, good, rave | bad, hostile, poor, scathing** *The show has good audience figures despite poor reviews in the press.* **| critical | mixed** *The book received mixed reviews.* **| book, film**
- VERB + REVIEW **do, write** *I'm doing a review for the local paper.* **| give sth | get, have, receive, win | open to** *Their new musical opened to glowing reviews.* **| read, see** *Did you see the review in 'The Times'?*
- REVIEW + VERB **appear** *His review appeared in yesterday's paper.*
- REVIEW + NOUN **copy**

review *verb*

1 examine sth again
- ADV. **comprehensively, fully, thoroughly | extensively, widely | carefully | briefly | urgently** *Safety procedures are being urgently reviewed after a chemical leak at the factory.* **| currently** *We are currently reviewing the situation.* **| constantly, regularly | annually, from time to time, periodically** *This figure will be reviewed from time to time in the light of inflation.* **| critically** *Pull out your budget and critically review each line on it.*

• VERB + REVIEW **agree to, promise to | ask sb to | decline to, refuse to**
• PHRASES **review sth in the light of sth** *This case should be reviewed in the light of new evidence.*

2 write a report of a book/film, etc.
• ADV. **favourably** *The film has been favourably reviewed in a number of papers.* | **critically**

revise *verb*

• ADV. **extensively, drastically, heavily, radically, substantially** *The text has been quite radically revised.* | **completely, fully, thoroughly | slightly | constantly, continually** *The procedures are continually revised—it is very difficult to keep up with the latest version.* | **periodically | downwards, upwards**
• VERB + REVISE **be forced to, have to** *The estimate for the building work had to be revised upwards.* | **be necessary to**
• PREP. **from, to** *The figure has now been revised from £1 million to £2 million.*

revision *noun*

1 making changes
• ADJ. **complete, considerable, drastic, extensive, fundamental, major, radical, substantial, thorough | minor | constant, frequent | downward, upward** *an upward revision of government expenditure plans* | **policy, treaty**
• VERB + REVISION **propose, recommend, suggest | call for, demand** *They called for revisions to the treaty.* | **be open to, be subject to** *Our conclusions are always open to revision in the light of fresh evidence.* | **undergo** *The scheme has recently undergone drastic revision.* | **agree (to), announce, approve** *In October Parliament approved a revision of the budget.* | **bring about, lead to, result in | carry out, complete, conduct, make, undertake**
• PREP. **~in** *This has brought about a radical revision in the style of school management.* **~to** *revisions to the plan*
• PHRASES **the process of revision** *The process of revision continued at rehearsals.*

2 studying
• VERB + REVISION **do** *I've got to do some maths revision tonight.*
• REVISION + NOUN **class, course, lesson | question**
• PREP. **~for** *revision for tomorrow's history exam*

revival *noun*

• ADJ. **great, major, marked | modern, recent | cultural, economic, industrial, literary, religious, etc.** *The late 19th century was a time of religious revival.*
• VERB + REVIVAL **enjoy, experience, undergo** *His work is enjoying a revival in popularity.* | **stage** *The economy has staged something of a revival in the last year.* | **bring about, cause, lead to, spark, stimulate** *The exhibition has stimulated a revival of interest in the Impressionists.* | **see** *The period saw a great revival in the wine trade.*
• PREP. **~in** *a revival in the fortunes of the Democratic Party* **~of** *a revival of ancient skills*
• PHRASES **a revival of interest** *the revival of interest in local radio* **signs of (a) revival** *He claimed the housing market was showing signs of a revival.*

revive *verb*

1 bring sth back
• ADV. **quickly, rapidly** *Banks and businesses had been rapidly reviving business activities in China.* | **suddenly**
• VERB + REVIVE **try to** *trying to revive some of the old customs* | **help (to), help sb (to)** *the country's readiness to help revive the economic fortunes of its neighbours*
• PHRASES **an attempt/effort to revive sth** *attempts to revive falling sales* **be aimed at reviving sth** *an initiative aimed at reviving talks on the country's political future*

2 make sb conscious again
• VERB + REVIVE **try to**
• PREP. **with** *They revived him with cold water.*
• PHRASES **an attempt/effort to revive sb** *Attempts to revive her failed and she was dead on arrival at hospital.*

revolt *noun*

• ADJ. **great** *The Great Revolt of 1381 may have been caused by attempts to keep wages down.* | **full-scale, general, large-scale, mass, popular, serious, widespread** *There was a general revolt against the leadership at the party congress.* | **open** *Parliament came out in open revolt against the president.* | **armed | peasant/peasant's, shareholder's, student, etc.**
• VERB + REVOLT **cause, prompt, provoke, stir up | lead** *a student-led revolt* | **stage | control, crush, deal with, put down, quash, suppress** *The revolt was suppressed with total ruthlessness.*
• REVOLT + VERB **break out** *Revolt broke out when the government decided to raise the price of bread.* | **spread | overthrow sb/sth** *The regime was overthrown by a popular revolt.*
• PREP. **in~** *The farmers rose in revolt.* | **~against** *the revolt against the poll tax in Britain* **~by** *a revolt by backbenchers* **~over** *the farmers' revolt over imported meat* **~within** *revolt within the party*

revolution *noun*

1 changing the political system
• ADJ. **successful | bloody, violent** *Thousands of people were killed in the bloody revolution that toppled the government.* | **bloodless, peaceful | popular | political | anti-communist, anti-democratic, etc. | communist, socialist, etc. | palace | bourgeois, proletarian | world** *Some Marxists still believe that socialism will one day triumph through world revolution.*
• VERB + REVOLUTION **carry out, conduct, fight, foment, stage** *The activists were charged with fomenting revolution.* | **crush, put down | call for**
• REVOLUTION + VERB **break out | spread | overthrow sth, topple sth** *the revolution which overthrew the old regime* | **fail** *the failed 1911 revolution*
• PREP. **~against** *a revolution against communist rule*
• PHRASES **the outbreak of the revolution, revolution from above/below** (= fought by people already in power/by people without political power), **the threat of revolution**

2 complete change in methods, opinions, etc.
• ADJ. **quiet** *There has been a quiet revolution in the way writing is taught.* | **complete | virtual | minor | agrarian, agricultural, computer, cultural, economic, electronic, environmental, industrial, political, scientific, sexual, social, technological**
• VERB + REVOLUTION **achieve, bring (about)** *The coming of television brought about a revolution in people's leisure activities.* | **undergo** *Marketing has undergone a revolution in recent years.* | **embrace, welcome** *Doctors have welcomed the fitness revolution.*
• REVOLUTION + VERB **take place** *As the eighteenth century wore on, an agricultural revolution took place.* | **transform sth** *The computer revolution has transformed the workplace.*
• PREP. **~in** *He achieved a virtual revolution in the way music is recorded.*

3 movement around sth; one complete turn
• ADJ. **complete, full** *One full revolution of the knob will open the hatch.*
• VERB + REVOLUTION **make**
• PREP. **through a~** *The earth turns through one complete revolution approximately every twenty-four hours.* | **~about/around/round** *How long does it take for the planet Jupiter to make a complete revolution around the sun?*

- PHRASES **revolutions a/per minute**
⇨ See REV

revolver *noun*

- ADJ. **army, service**
- VERB + REVOLVER **load | draw | aim | fire | shoot sb with | be armed with, carry**

revulsion *noun*

- ADJ. **deep, utter | widespread** *The killing caused widespread revulsion.* | **instinctive**
- VERB + REVULSION **be filled with, feel | cause | express | conceal**
- PREP. **in/with ~** *The children shrank back from him in revulsion.* | **~against** *public revulsion against violence in our society* **~at** *He tried to conceal his instinctive revulsion at the idea.* **~for** *He was filled with hatred and revulsion for everything about her.* **~towards** *She seems to feel revulsion towards her own children.*
- PHRASES **a feeling/sense of revulsion**

reward *noun*

1 for effort, etc.
- ADJ. **considerable, great, high, huge, rich** *Top athletes enjoy rich rewards.* | **fitting, just, suitable, well-deserved | poor, scant** *It was a poor reward for years of devoted service.* | **tangible** *Victory brought glory as well as more tangible rewards.* | **economic, financial, material, monetary**
- VERB + REWARD **earn, enjoy, gain, get, obtain, reap, receive** *We are just starting to reap the rewards of careful long-term planning.* | **bring, have, provide** *Hard work usually brings its own rewards.* | **deserve** *You deserve a reward for all your efforts.*
- PREP. **as a ~** *Give yourself some time off as a reward.* | **~for** *a reward for hard work ◇ rewards for employees who do their jobs well*
- PHRASES **reward enough** *The look on her face when I told her was reward enough.*

2 for helping the police
- ADJ. **big, huge, large, substantial | $20 000, £10 000, etc. | cash**
- VERB + REWARD **offer, put up | give sb, pay sb | claim | get, receive**
- REWARD + NOUN **money**
- PREP. **~for** *There is a reward for information leading to an arrest.*

reward *verb* (often **be rewarded**)

- ADV. **amply, generously, handsomely, highly, well** *You will be handsomely rewarded for your loyalty. ◇ highly rewarded occupations* (= those that pay well) | **poorly | adequately, duly, properly, suitably** *We must make sure that effort is properly rewarded.* | **justly | further | immediately, promptly, quickly | eventually, finally**
- PREP. **for** *He was duly rewarded for his outstanding contribution to the arts.* **with** *Her efforts were justly rewarded with a British Empire Medal.*

rewarding *adj.*

- VERBS **be, prove | find sth** *I found it immensely rewarding working with the less able children.*
- ADV. **extremely, highly, immensely, particularly, richly, very | intrinsically** *I did not expect the job to be intrinsically rewarding.* | **potentially | mutually** *a mutually rewarding partnership* | **financially** *a satisfying as well as a financially rewarding career*

rewrite *verb*

- ADV. **drastically, extensively, substantially | completely | slightly**
- PHRASES **an attempt to rewrite sth** *attempts to rewrite history*

rhetoric *noun*

- ADJ. **empty, mere** *Her speech was just empty rhetoric.* | **militant, powerful, radical | government, official | nationalist, patriotic, political, revolutionary, sectarian**
- VERB + RHETORIC **adopt, engage in, resort to, use** *He was quite prepared to use militant rhetoric in attacking his opponents.*
- PREP. **behind/beneath the~** *Behind all the rhetoric, his relations with the army are dangerously poised.* **despite the~** *Little has changed, despite the rhetoric about reform.* | **~about/concerning/on** *official rhetoric on the virtues of large families*

rheumatism *noun*

- ADJ. **chronic**
- VERB + RHEUMATISM **get | have, suffer from | relieve** *The pills help to relieve my rheumatism.*
⇨ Special page at ILLNESS

rhyme *noun*

1 using words that have the same sound as each other
- ADJ. **internal**
- VERB + RHYME **write (in)**
- RHYME + NOUN **scheme**
- PREP. **in~** *a story in rhyme*

2 word that has the same sound as another
- ADJ. **half**
- PREP. **~for** *Can you think of a rhyme for 'tragic'?*

3 short piece of writing with rhyming words
- ADJ. **nonsense | nursery**
- VERB + RHYME **recite | make up**
- PREP. **~about** *The kids made up a rhyme about a frog.*

rhythm *noun*

- ADJ. **fast, slow | constant, good, regular, steady** *the steady rhythm of his heartbeat* | **irregular, staccato | intricate | strong | easy** *Tidying the house in the morning fell into an easy rhythm.* | **natural, normal** *part of the natural rhythm of life* | **fierce, frenzied, insistent, pounding, pulsating | dance | body, circadian** *My body rhythms had not yet adapted to the ten-hour time difference.* | **cardiac, heart | daily** *changes to our daily rhythms*
- VERB + RHYTHM **develop, fall into, get into, settle into, slip into** *She soon settled into a regular rhythm.* | **have, lack | make** *Her feet made a steady rhythm on the pavement.* | **find** *Williams is having trouble finding her rhythm on the serve.* | **beat (out), clap (to), tap out** *Her pencil tapped out a staccato rhythm on the desk top.*
- RHYTHM + NOUN **section** *the band's rhythm section*
- PREP. **in (a)~** *snapping his fingers in rhythm* **to a/the~** *I found myself swaying to the rhythm of the music.* **with a/the ~** *I like music with a good rhythm.* | **~in** *There's rhythm in her movements.*
- PHRASES **a sense of rhythm**

rib *noun*

- ADJ. **bony, skinny | broken, bruised, cracked, fractured** *He sustained a broken rib.*
- VERB + RIB **break, crack, crush | dig sb in, nudge sb in, poke sb in, prod sb in**
- RIB + NOUN **cage | injury**
- PREP. **against the/your ~s, in the/your ~s** *I woke him up with a poke in the ribs.*

ribbon *noun*

- ADJ. **long** | **wide** | **narrow, thin** | **satin, silk, velvet** | **hair, medal**
- QUANT. **length, piece** *He cut off a length of ribbon.*
- VERB + RIBBON **tie, tie sth (back/up) with** *He tied some gold ribbon round the present.* ◇ *Her hair was tied back with a black silk ribbon.* | **undo, untie** | **cut** *The Lord Mayor cut a ribbon to launch the celebrations.* | **have, wear** *She had a pink ribbon in her hair.* ◇ *She was wearing a pink hair ribbon.*

rice *noun*

- ADJ. **brown, white** | **boiled, fried** | **sticky** | **long/short-grain** | **wild** | **polished** | **creamed**
- QUANT. **grain** | **bag, packet, sack** | **bowl**
- VERB + RICE **cultivate, grow, produce** | **harvest** | **boil, cook** | **drain, strain**
- RICE + NOUN **crop,** | **production** | **farmer, grower, producer** | **field, paddy** | **cake, pudding, salad, wine** | **dish** *a spicy rice dish*

rich *adj.*

1 with a lot of money
- VERBS **be, feel, look** | **become, get, grow** *people who want to get rich quickly* | **make sb** *This discovery never made her rich.*
- ADV. **enormously, extremely, fabulously, filthy** (*informal*), **immensely, incredibly, seriously, stinking** (*informal*), **very** *He's fabulously rich, one of the richest men in the world.* ◇ *It was mean of her only to give £1—she's filthy rich, you know.* | **quite, relatively** | **newly** *a newly rich businessman*

2 containing/providing sth
- VERBS **be**
- ADV. **especially, exceptionally, extraordinarily, particularly, unusually, very** *the exceptionally rich fishing grounds of the North Sea* | **fairly, quite, relatively** | **potentially** | **culturally** *a culturally rich nation*
- PREP. **in** *Oranges are rich in vitamin C.*

3 of food
- VERBS **be**
- ADV. **very, wonderfully** *The sun-dried tomatoes give the dish a wonderfully rich flavour.*

ride *noun*

- ADJ. **long, short** *We have a long ride ahead of us tomorrow.* | **leisurely** *We went for a leisurely ride along the canal.* | **comfortable, easy, smooth** (*all often figurative*) *The new legislation did not have a smooth ride through Parliament.* | **bumpy, rough, uncomfortable** *It was a bumpy ride along the farm track.* ◇ (*figurative*) *The new teacher was given a rough ride by the class.* | **wild** *He took her for a wild ride on the back of his motorbike.* | **free** *He used to get free rides by hiding in the toilet of the train.* | **bike, bus, cab, car, coach, cycle, gondola, sleigh, taxi, train, tram** | **camel, donkey, pony** | **funfair, helterskelter, rollercoaster, white-knuckle** (*all often figurative*) *The day had been a rollercoaster ride of emotion.*
- VERB + RIDE **have, take** *Visitors can take a ride on a steam locomotive.* | **go for** *She's gone for a ride on her bike.* | **enjoy** | **bum, cadge, get, hitch, thumb** *I managed to cadge a ride with a lorry driver.* | **give sb**
- PREP. **~ from** *The ride from our house to my parents' takes about an hour.* **~ to**

ride *verb*

- ADV. **fast, hard** *They rode hard all night.* | **slowly** | **steadily** | **bareback, side-saddle** *riding bareback on a circus horse* | **away, back, home, off, on, out, over, past** *At the end of the film they ride off into the sunset.*

- VERB + RIDE **learn to** | **teach sb (how) to**
- PREP. **along, down, from, on, through, to, up, etc.** *riding along a country lane*
- PHRASES **go riding**

ridicule *noun*

- ADJ. **general, public**
- VERB + RIDICULE **attract, draw, receive** | **expose sb/sth to, hold sb/sth up to, treat sb/sth with** | **be open to, face, invite, risk** | **fear** *A faintly comic figure, he fears ridicule above all else.*
- PHRASES **an object of ridicule, a target for/of ridicule** *The prime minister was becoming an object of ridicule.*

ridiculous *adj.*

- VERBS **be, feel, look, seem, sound** | **become, get** *This is getting ridiculous!*
- ADV. **bloody** (*taboo*), **really** | **absolutely, completely, downright, quite, totally, utterly** *It's downright ridiculous that the library isn't open on Mondays!* | **almost** | **a bit, faintly, a little, mildly, pretty, slightly, somewhat** | **patently** *The whole idea was patently ridiculous.*
- PHRASES **a sense of the ridiculous** *The whole situation appealed to her sense of the ridiculous.*

riding *noun*

- ADJ. **horse**
- VERB + RIDING **go**
- RIDING + NOUN **boots, breeches, crop, hat, jacket** | **centre, school, stables**

rifle *noun*

- ADJ. **automatic, high-powered, semi-automatic, .22** | **air, army, assault, hunting, sporting** | **Kalashnikov, M-16, etc.**
- VERB + RIFLE **load, reload** | **raise** | **aim** | **fire** | **shoot sb/sth with** | **be armed with, carry**
- RIFLE + NOUN **barrel, butt** | **bullet** | **fire, shot** | **club, range**

rift *noun*

- ADJ. **deep, growing, serious** | **public** | **ideological** | **marital, marriage**
- VERB + RIFT **cause, create, lead to** | **deepen, widen** *His actions only deepened the rift between himself and the majority of Congress.* | **heal, mend, patch up, repair**
- RIFT + VERB **develop, occur, open up** *A rift had opened up within the party.* | **deepen, grow, widen**
- PREP. **~ among/between** *new evidence of a rift between the two countries* **~ in/within** *The debate has succeeded only in widening rifts within the Church.* **~ over** *a rift over public spending* **~ with** *trying to heal the rift with his brother*

right *noun*

1 what is morally good
- PREP. **in the ~** (= having justice and truth on your side) *There's no doubt that he's in the right on this.*
- PHRASES **have right on your side** *I appealed against the decision because I knew I had right on my side.* **know right from wrong** *Children of that age don't know right from wrong.* **right and wrong** *She doesn't understand the difference between right and wrong.* **the rights and wrongs of sth** *We sat discussing the rights and wrongs of the prison system.*

2 entitlement
- ADJ. **basic, fundamental, inalienable** *the basic rights of all citizens* | **absolute, perfect** *I've got a perfect right to park here if I want to.* | **equal** | **exclusive, sole** | **full** | **automatic** *Any employee who is sacked has an automatic right to appeal.* | **animal, human** *animal rights cam-*

paigners ◇ *human rights violations* | **legal, statutory** | **contractual** | **moral** *You have a moral right to that money.* | **civil** *the civil rights movement* | **gay, women's** | **parental** *The local authority exercises parental rights over the children until foster homes are found.* | **squatters'** *The teenagers claimed squatters' rights and were allowed to remain in the building.* | **pension** | **voting** | **divine, god-given** *the old idea of the divine right of kings* ◇ *I suppose you think you have some god-given right to tell me what to do?*

• VERB + RIGHT **enjoy, have, retain** *They have no right to come onto my land.* | **assert, claim, demand** | **know** *You can't do that to me—I know my rights.* | **establish** *The new president undertook to establish full rights for all minorities.* | **stand up for** *You should stand up for your rights and insist that he pays you.* | **reserve** *I reserve the right to leave at any time I choose.* | **gain, get** | **confer on sb, give sb, grant sb** *We were granted the exclusive rights to produce the software in the UK.* | **extend** *The government extended voting rights to everyone over the age of 18.* | **exercise** | **enforce** *The landlord enforced his right to enter the property.* | **abdicate, give up, relinquish, renounce** *He renounced his right to the throne.* | **waive** *They gave me my uncle's money, on condition that I waived all rights to his property.* | **forfeit, lose** | **defend, protect, safeguard** | **acknowledge, recognize, respect** | **affect, infringe** *These additional guarantees do not affect your statutory rights.* | **deny sb** | **abolish**

• PREP. **as of~, by~** *The property belongs to her by/as of right.* **by~ of** *The Normans ruled England by right of conquest.* **within your ~s** *You're acting entirely within your rights.* | **~ of** *the right of assembly/asylum/citizenship/free speech/ownership* **~ over** *He claimed full rights over the discovery.* **~s for** *equal rights for all* **~ to** *Do I have any right to compensation?*

• PHRASES **have every right** *She has every right to feel bitter.* **right of way** *There is no public right of way across the fields.*

3 rights legal authority/claim to sth
• ADJ. **film, movie, television** | **translation** | **foreign** | **property** | **mineral** | **grazing**
• VERB + RIGHTS **acquire, buy, get, obtain** | **sell** *He sold the film rights for $2 million.* | **have, hold**
• PHRASES **all rights reserved** (= protected or kept for the owner of the book, film, etc.)

4 right side/direction
• VERB + RIGHT **take** *Take a right at the traffic lights.*
• PREP. **from the ~** *Look out for traffic coming from the right.* **on the ~** *Ours is the first house on the right.* **to the ~** *Keep over to the right.*
• PHRASES **the first/second, etc. right** *Take the first right, and then it's the second turning on your left.* **from left to right /from right to left** *The books are numbered from right to left.*

5 the right in politics
• ADJ. **extreme, far**
• PREP. **on the ~** *He's on the extreme right of the party.*

right *adj.*

• VERBS **be, feel, look, seem, sound, taste** *The meat doesn't taste right to me.* | **come, turn out** *I'm sure it'll all turn out right in the end.* | **get sth** *He never gets anything right.* | **make sth** *It may be a very easy way to make money, but that doesn't make it right.*
• ADV. **absolutely, dead, exactly, just, quite** *You're dead right. There's nothing we can do.* ◇ *She needs to get everything exactly right for her guests.* ◇ *There's something not quite right about these figures.* | **almost, more or less, nearly** *Don't worry about it—that's more or less right.*
• PREP. **about** *You were quite right about the weather.*

rigid *adj.*

1 not able/willing to change
• VERBS **appear, be, seem** | **become, grow** *He grew even more rigid and uncompromising as he got older.*
• ADV. **extremely, very** | **entirely** *An entirely rigid system is impractical.* | **excessively** | **fairly, rather, relatively** *We operate within fairly rigid parameters.*

2 stiff
• VERBS **be, feel, lie, look, stand** *She feigned sleep, lying rigid in bed.* | **become, go** | **remain**
• ADV. **very** | **absolutely, completely, quite** | **almost**
• PREP. **with** *He went absolutely rigid with shock.*

rigour *noun*

1 strictness
• ADJ. **full** *The crime will be treated with the full rigour of the law.* | **academic, intellectual, logical, scientific**
• VERB + RIGOUR **lack** *Their analysis lacks rigour.*
• PREP. **with ~** | **~ in** *There is a need for academic rigour in approaching this problem.*

2 rigours severe conditions
• ADJ. **full**
• VERB + RIGOURS **be subjected to, face, suffer** *computers that are subjected to the rigours of the office environment* | **avoid, escape** *The town managed to escape the rigours of war.* | **stand up to, survive, withstand** | **prepare sb/sth for, protect (sb/sth) against** *The thick coat of the mountain goat protects it against the rigours of winter.*

ring *noun*

1 piece of jewellery
• ADJ. **engagement, eternity, signet, wedding** | **diamond, gold, etc.** *She wore a diamond engagement ring.*
• VERB + RING **have on, wear** *He had a signet ring on his little finger.* | **put on** | **take off**
• RING + NOUN **finger** (= the finger next to the little finger, especially on the left hand)

2 circle
• ADJ. **inner** | **outer** | **concentric** *The street plan of the city has evolved as a series of concentric rings.* | **black, dark** *He had dark rings around his eyes.* | **smoke, tree** *to blow smoke rings*
• VERB + RING **form, stand in** *The children formed a ring around their teacher.*
• PREP. **in a/the ~** *The children sat on the floor in a ring.*

3 where a performance, match, etc. takes place
• ADJ. **boxing, bull, circus, show, wrestling**
• PREP. **in/into the ~** *He was back in the ring* (= the boxing ring) *only a month after the injury.*
• PHRASES **retire from the ring** (= stop boxing)

4 people involved in sth secret/illegal
• ADJ. **drugs, smuggling, spy**
• VERB + RING **be involved in** | **break up** *Customs officials have broken up a major drugs ring.*

5 telephone call
• VERB + RING **give sb** *I'll give you a ring once I get home.*

rinse *noun*

• ADJ. **good** | **final** | **cold**
• VERB + RINSE **give sth** *Give your hair a good rinse after shampooing it.*
• PREP. **~ in/with** *a rinse with cold water*

rinse *verb*

• ADV. **well** | **thoroughly** *Always rinse your hair thoroughly.* | **quickly** | **away, off, out** *She rinsed out her coffee cup.* ◇ *Make sure you rinse all the soap out.*
• PREP. **from** *rinsing the flour from his hands* **in** *She*

rinsed her hands in cold water. with *Rinse the dishes with warm water.*

riot *noun*

- ADJ. **major, serious | full-scale | violent | inner-city, urban | prison | race | student | bread, food** *Shortages eventually led to food riots.*
- VERB + RIOT **cause, provoke, spark (off), start** *The city's housing and unemployment problems sparked serious riots.* | **put down, quell**
- RIOT + VERB **begin, break out, erupt, occur, start** *Prison riots broke out over worsening conditions.*
- RIOT + NOUN **police, squad | gear, shield | control**
- PREP. **during/in a/the ~** *He was killed in the riots.* | **~against/over** *a riot against bread prices*
- PHRASES **run riot** *Fans ran riot after the match, overturning cars and looting shops.*

ripe *adj.*

- VERBS **be, feel, look, smell, taste**
- ADV. **really, very** *a really ripe strawberry* | **fully, perfectly, quite** *Make sure the plums are fully ripe before you eat them.* ◇ *Some of the apples were not quite ripe.* | **almost, just about, nearly** *The crops were just about ripe.*

ripple *noun*

- ADJ. **little, small**
- VERB + RIPPLE **cause, set off** *The decision caused ripples of concern among the parents.* | **send** *I dropped the pebble in the water, sending ripples across the pond.* ◇ *His remarks sent a ripple of laughter through the audience.* | **feel** *He felt a small ripple of fear pass through him.*
- RIPPLE + VERB **pass/run through sb/sth | spread (across) sth** *He watched the ripples spread across the pool.*
- RIPPLE + NOUN **effect**
- PREP. **~of** *A ripple of unease passed through her.*

ripple *verb*

- ADV. **gently, smoothly, softly**
- PREP. **across** *Small waves rippled gently across the pond.* **through** *Shock rippled through her.*

rise *noun*

1 increase
- ADJ. **big, dramatic, huge, large, massive, sharp, strong, substantial | modest, slight, small | threefold, 80 per cent, etc. | appreciable, significant | abrupt, rapid, steep, sudden | slow | steady | inexorable, remorseless** *Unemployment continued its remorseless rise.* | **general, overall | annual, monthly | interest rate, pay, price, sea-level, tax, temperature, wage, etc.** *The union is demanding an across-the-board pay rise of 5%.*
- PREP. **on the ~** (= rising) *Crime is on the rise.* | **~in** *a twofold rise in prices* **~on** *a rise on last year's levels*

2 becoming more powerful/important
- ADJ. **meteoric, spectacular, swift**
- PREP. **~of** *the rise of capitalism* **~to** *His swift rise to the national team surprised everyone.*
- PHRASES **the rise and fall of sth** *the rise and fall of the Roman Empire* **rise to fame/power/prominence** *a meteoric rise to fame*

rise *verb*

1 move upwards
- ADV. **majestically** *the cliffs which rise majestically from the ocean*
- PREP. **from** *Smoke rose from the chimney.*

2 stand up
- ADV. **slowly**

- VERB + RISE **make to, try to** *He made to rise but found his legs were not strong enough to support him.*
- PREP. **from** *She rose slowly from her chair to greet us.*

3 get out of bed
- ADV. **early, late** *He rose early and went for a walk.*

4 increase
- ADV. **dramatically, markedly, sharply, significantly, steeply, substantially** *House prices have risen sharply in recent months.* | **a little, slightly | further, higher | steadily | fast, quickly, rapidly** *The cost of health care is rising faster than ever.*
- VERB + RISE **be expected to, be likely to, be projected to, be set to** *Entry standards into the profession are set to rise further.* | **be unlikely to | begin to | continue to**
- PREP. **above** *Air pollution has risen above an acceptable level.* **by** *Unemployment has risen by 25 000 this month.* **from, in** *Gas rose in price.* **in line with** *State benefits will rise in line with inflation.* **to** *Inflation rose from 2% to 5% last year.*

rising *noun*

- ADJ. **military, peasant**
- VERB + RISING **participate in, take part in | lead | crush, put down, suppress** *The government succeeded in crushing the military rising.*

risk *noun*

- ADJ. **big, considerable, grave, great, high, major, serious, significant, substantial, terrible** *high-risk patients* ◇ *a major risk to livestock* | **good | bad, poor | low, slight, small | additional, extra, increased | reduced | genuine, real | attendant, inherent, possible, potential** *Standards of hygiene have fallen with all the attendant risks of disease.* ◇ *There are considerable risks inherent in the policy.* | **long-term | relative | foolish, unacceptable, unnecessary | calculated** *I take calculated risks but never gamble.* | **commercial, credit, environmental, financial, fire, health, insurance, safety, security** *Those old boxes in the corridor are a fire risk.* ◇ *He's a good insurance risk.*
- QUANT. **degree, level | element** *The operation carries an element of risk.*
- VERB + RISK **face, run, take** *If you don't revise, you run the risk of failing.* ◇ *I'm not prepared to take risks—I want the equipment thoroughly checked.* | **entail, incur, involve, pose** *Pollutants in the river pose a real risk to the fish.* | **increase | minimize, reduce | avoid | assess, measure** *The directors will have to assess our credit risk.* | **outweigh** *The benefits outweigh the risks.*
- RISK + VERB **outweigh sth**
- RISK + NOUN **group** *Miners are a high risk group for certain types of gastric cancer.* | **factor** *Cigarette smoking is a risk factor for this disease.* | **assessment | reduction | management**
- PREP. **at~** *to put someone's life at risk* **at~from/of** *Journalists in the zone are at serious risk of being kidnapped.* **at the ~ of** *At the risk of sounding rude, don't you think you'd better change for the party?* **at~to** *He saved the child at considerable risk to himself.* | **~by** *He knew he was taking a big risk by going skiing.* **~from** *a risk from contaminated water* **~in** *I was taking a big risk in lending her the money.* **~to** *a risk to health*
- PHRASES **at your own risk** *The building is unsafe—enter at your own risk.* **an increase/a reduction in risk, risks and benefits/rewards** *the risks and benefits of a drug*

risk *verb*

- VERB + RISK **cannot/could not, dare not, not want to, would not** *I simply can't risk being seen there.* ◇ *I didn't want to risk being late.* | **be prepared to, be willing to** *He*

was prepared to risk everything in order to achieve his ambition. | **decide to**
• PREP. **for** *I am not risking my neck for anyone!* **on** *I wouldn't risk my money on a scheme like this one.*
• PHRASES **risk it** *I knew I would be in trouble if I was found out, but I decided to risk it anyway.* **risk life and limb** *the brave tourist who risks life and limb for adventure* **risk losing sth** *families who risk losing their homes*

risky *adj.*

• VERBS **be, look, prove, seem, sound** | **consider sth**
• ADV. **decidedly, extremely, highly, very** *It all sounds decidedly risky to me.* | **increasingly** | **a bit, a little, quite, rather, somewhat** | **inherently** *All business activities are inherently risky.* | **potentially** | **politically**

ritual *noun*

• ADJ. **ancient, primitive** | **daily, nightly, Sunday, etc.** | **little** *A cognac before bed is one of our little nightly rituals.* | **elaborate, solemn** | **empty** *Bargaining at the markets is now just an empty ritual.* | **religious, social** | **pagan** | **courtship, fertility, initiation, mating**
• VERB + RITUAL **go through, perform** *She had to go through the ritual of kissing the toys before her son would go to sleep.* ◇ *rituals performed by druids at Stonehenge on Midsummer's Day* | **make** *She makes an elaborate ritual of the washing-up.*
• RITUAL + VERB **take place**
• RITUAL + NOUN **practice** *the ritual practices of ancient religions* | **murder, sacrifice, slaughter** *the accusation that they practised ritual murder*
• PREP. **in a/the ~** *Women's roles in the rituals of many religions have been limited.*

rival *noun*

• ADJ. **arch, bitter, close, deadly, fierce, great, serious** | **biggest, chief, main, nearest, principal** | **longstanding, old** *They're old political rivals.* | **jealous** | **foreign, international** *The company is well equipped to compete with its international rivals.* | **business, political**
• VERB + RIVAL **have** *She has no rivals for the job.* | **beat, defeat**
• RIVAL + NOUN **candidate** | **faction, gang, group** | **company, firm** | **bid, offer** | **claim**
• PREP. **~for** *They were rivals for her love.* **~in** *They were rivals in love.* **~to** *Grand it may be, but this cathedral is no rival to the great cathedral of Amiens.*

rivalry *noun*

• ADJ. **bitter, fierce, great, intense** | **long-standing, old** | **friendly** | **international** | **ethnic, personal, political, professional, sexual, sibling** *Bitter ethnic rivalries within the region have grown in recent years.*
• RIVALRY + VERB **grow**
• PREP. **~ between** *rivalry between the army and the police* **~ for** *rivalry for the party leadership* **~ over** *rivalry over who is to head the delegation* **~ with** *rivalry with foreign firms*

river *noun*

• ADJ. **broad, great, large, long, mighty, wide** *the mighty River Nile* ◇ *The river was too wide to swim across comfortably.* | **little, narrow, short, small** | **deep** | **shallow** | **high** *The river is still high after the recent rain.* | **low** | **fast-flowing** | **slow-moving, sluggish** | **winding** | **swollen** *The river was swollen after the floods.* | **navigable** *The river is navigable by vessels of up to 90 tons.*
• VERB + RIVER **cross, ford, get across** *We crossed the river by ferry.* ◇ *How are we going to get across the river?* | **bridge** *They've bridged the river at four points.* | **dam** *Wildlife groups are protesting against the proposal to dam*

the river. | **dredge** *They're dredging the river to make it safer for larger boats.* | **navigate** *The rocks and sandbanks make the river hard to navigate.*
• RIVER + VERB **flow, run, wind** *This river flows into the Mediterranean Sea.* ◇ *A river runs through the field.* ◇ *The river winds its way through the hills.* | **rise** *The river has risen with the rains.* ◇ *The river rises in Bulgaria and flows through Greece to the Aegean.* | **be in flood, burst its banks, flood (sth), overflow sth** *The river had overflowed its banks.* | **dry up** *This river dried up long ago.*
• RIVER + NOUN **bank** | **water** | **valley** | **system** | **crossing** | **traffic**
• PREP. **across a/the ~** *There's a bridge across the river.* **along a/the ~** *We walked along the river.* **down a/the ~, down by a/the~, down to a/the~** *Let's go down to the river at sunset.* **into a/the ~** *He dived into the river.* **in a/the ~** *Trout live in this river.* **on a/the~** *There was a rowing boat on the river.* **up a/the ~** *sailing up the river* | **~ of** *(figurative) a river of lava*
• PHRASES **the banks/bottom/middle/side/surface of a river** *They were waiting for us on the other side of the river.* **a bend in the river, the course/direction of a river, the river's edge**

road *noun*

• ADJ. **broad, wide** | **narrow** | **busy, congested** | **clear, deserted, empty, lonely, quiet** *Let's leave when the roads are clear.* | **direct** *The airport's near here but there's no direct road.* | **straight** | **twisting, twisty, winding** | **steep** | **scenic** | **good, metalled, paved, smooth, surfaced, tarmac** | **bad, bumpy, dirt, poor, rough, unmade** *a bumpy road through the forest* | **dangerous, difficult, hard** *(often figurative) Bringing up a handicapped child can be a long and hard road.* | **safe** | **slippery** | **dusty, icy, muddy, snowbound, snowy, wet** | **fast** | **long, long-distance, main, major, national, trunk** | **B-, back, local, minor, secondary, small, unclassified** | **single-track** | **rural** | **urban** | **residential** | **tree-lined** | **private, public** | **dead-end** *(figurative) The government's policy on education is a dead-end road.* | **open** *We'll be able to go faster once we're out on the open road.* | **right, wrong** *We took the wrong road and had to turn back.* ◇ *(figurative) It does appear we are on the right road to success.* | **east-west, etc.** | **coast, coastal, country, mountain** | **access, arterial, ring, service, side, slip** *The new ring road should reduce city centre traffic.* | **toll**
• VERB + ROAD **follow, go down** *Follow the road round to the left.* ◇ *(figurative) We have discussed privatization, but we would prefer not to go down that road.* | **take, turn (left/right) into/off** *Take the next road on the right.* | **cross, get across** | **pull (out) into** *He was hit by a lorry as he pulled out into the main road.* | **pull off** *I pulled off the road for a rest.* | **join** *The track joins the main road just south of the village.* | **hog** *(= drive near the middle of the road so that others cannot get past)* | **block, cordon off** *Angry farmers blocked the road with their tractors.* ◇ *Police cordoned off the road and diverted commuter traffic.* | **build** | **pave, resurface, surface** | **widen**
• ROAD + VERB **go, lead, run** *Where does this road go?* ◇ *The road runs parallel to the river.* | **bend, curve, turn, twist, wind** *The road twists and turns up the hillside.* | **ascend, climb** *The road ascends steeply from the harbour.* | **cross sth** *The road crosses the river further up the valley.* | **branch (off), fork** *Our road branches off to the left just past the wood.*
• ROAD + NOUN **atlas, map** | **markings, sign** | **intersection, junction** | **bridge, crossing, tunnel** | **closure** | **humps** *Road humps have been laid down to limit the speed of cars along the road.* | **communications, infrastructure, network** | **layout** | **access, link** *There is still no road access to the island.* | **development, plan, programme, project, proposal, scheme** | **improvements** | **surface** | **journey** | **crash, smash, (traffic) accident** |

safety | deaths | conditions | traffic, vehicles | user | manners, sense *poor driving standards and lack of road manners* | engineer | haulier | haulage | sweeper | tax, toll *Road tax is set to rise in next month's budget.* ◇ *Road tolls can make travelling by motorway fairly expensive.* | rage *A man has been stabbed to death in a road rage attack.*
• PREP. **across the~** *The house across the road is for sale.* **along the ~** *He was walking along the road when he was attacked.* **by ~** *It takes three hours by road* (= driving). **down/up the ~** *They live just down the road from us.* **in the ~** *There was a dog in the road so we stopped.* ◇ *We live in/on Kingston Road.* **(out) into the ~** *She stepped out into the road without looking.* **off the ~** *My car's off the road at the moment while I recondition the engine.* **on a/the ~** *There's something lying on the road.* ◇ *There was a lot of traffic on the road this morning.* ◇ *on the road to Damascus* ◇ *My car is back on the road* (= is working) *again.* ◇ *We'd been on the road* (= travelling) *since dawn and needed a rest.* | **~ along/over/through**, etc. *the main road through the centre of town* **~ from, ~ to** *the road to London* ◇ *(figurative) to be on the road to recovery/success*
• PHRASES **at/by/on the side of the road, the bottom/end/top of the road, the end of the road** *(figurative) This latest row could mean the end of the road for the band.* **the middle of the road** *A dog was sitting in the middle of the road, so we stopped.* **the next/second**, etc. **road on the left/right, a stretch of road** *a notoriously dangerous stretch of road*

roadblock *noun*

• ADJ. **army, police**
• VERB + ROADBLOCK **erect, set up** *Police have set up a roadblock on the road to London.* | **remove**
• PREP. **at a/the ~** *They were stopped at a roadblock leaving the city.* **through a/the ~** *The truck drove through the roadblock at 100 mph.*

roam *verb*

• ADV. **free, freely** *The animals were allowed to roam free.* | **about/around**
• VERB + ROAM **allow sb/sth to, let sb/sth**
• PREP. **over** *Her eyes roamed over him, assessing him.* **through** *roaming through the town*
• PHRASES **the freedom/right to roam** *Ramblers are calling for the right to roam to be made law.*

roar *noun*

• ADJ. **almighty, deafening, great, loud, mighty** *The lion let out a great roar.* | **deep | dull, muffled | hollow | throaty** *the throaty roar of the engine* | **background, distant** *the distant roar of the sea* | **sudden**
• VERB + ROAR **give, let out | hear**
• ROAR + VERB **go up** *A mighty roar went up from the crowd as the home team scored.*
• PREP. **above/over the ~** *She couldn't make herself heard over the roar of the engines.* **with a ~** *The car sped off with an almighty roar.* | **~ from** *There was a crash and a roar from the kitchen.* **~ of** *a roar of applause/laughter*
⇨ Note at SOUND

robber *noun*

• ADJ. **armed, masked | bank, train | grave, tomb**
• QUANT. **band, gang**
• VERB + ROBBER **hunt** *Police are hunting a masked robber who snatched £15 000 from a post office.* | **catch**
• ROBBER + VERB **hold sb/sth up** *Robbers held up a bank at gunpoint.* | **snatch sth, steal sth, take sth | escape with sth, get away with sth, make off with sth** *Robbers escaped with £30 000 of payroll money.*

robbery *noun*

• ADJ. **attempted, bungled, failed | armed | bank, highway, street**
• VERB + ROBBERY **commit, take part in**
• ROBBERY + NOUN **attempt**
• PHRASES **robbery with violence** *He was sentenced to four years in prison for robbery with violence.*
⇨ Note at CRIME (for more verbs)

robe *noun*

• ADJ. **long | loose, voluminous | flowing** *a ghostly figure in flowing robes of white* | **rich** *The emperor was clad in a rich robe encrusted with jewels.* | **embroidered | ceremonial, christening, coronation** (often with **robes**)
• VERB + ROBE **slip on**
• PREP. **in a/the ~** *an old man swathed in robes*
⇨ Special page at CLOTHES

rock *noun*

1 hard, stony part of the earth
• ADJ. **hard, solid** *Solid rock is broken down by weathering.* | **soft | jagged, rough | smooth | weathered | bare** *Ahead the vegetation broke into bare rock.* | **sheer, steep** *The river runs between walls of sheer rock.* | **overhanging | liquid, molten | igneous, sedimentary, volcanic | permeable, porous | impermeable**
• QUANT. **chunk, lump, piece, slab**
• VERB + ROCK **form**
• ROCK + VERB **form** *rocks that formed beneath the sea* | **jut out** *A great rock jutted out into the sea.*
• ROCK + NOUN **type | formation, structure | strata | ledge, outcrop | face, surface, wall | crevice | debris, fragment, sample | fall** *The path had been blocked by a rock fall.* | **crystal, salt | climber, climbing | pool** *Children were looking for crabs in the rock pools.* | **art, carvings | garden**
• PHRASES **a layer of rock, an outcrop of rock** *The castle is perched on a massive outcrop of rock.*

2 music
• ADJ. **live | country, glam, hard, heavy, indie, progressive, punk**
• ROCK + NOUN **album, anthem, CD, music, number, record, song, video | band, group | concert, festival, gig | venue | circuit, scene** *one of the biggest bands on the rock circuit* | **drummer, guitarist, musician, singer, vocalist | guitar | hero, legend, star | culture, history**
• PHRASES **rock and roll** *the king of rock and roll*

rock *verb*

• ADV. **violently** *The boat rocked violently in the huge waves.* | **gently, slightly** *She gently rocked the baby in her arms.* ◇ *The boat rocked slightly.* | **back and forth, backwards and forwards, from side to side, to and fro** *He rocked back and forth in his chair.*

rocket *noun*

1 spacecraft
• ADJ. **space**
• VERB + ROCKET **launch | go/send into orbit**
• ROCKET + VERB **blast off, take off | land**
• ROCKET + NOUN **booster, engine | fuel | scientist** *(often humorous) You don't have to be a rocket scientist* (= very clever) *to do this job.*

2 weapon
• ADJ. **long-range | anti-aircraft, anti-tank**
• VERB + ROCKET **fire**
• ROCKET + VERB **explode**
• ROCKET + NOUN **attack | launcher**

role noun

1 in a play, film, etc.
- ADJ. **lead, leading, starring, title | supporting | comic, tragic | cameo | film, television | TV**
- VERB + ROLE **perform, play, take** *John's playing the leading role in this year's play.* | **cast sb in | interpret** *She interprets the role as more tragic than I expected.*
- PREP. **in the ~ (of)** *He was very good in the role.*

2 position and importance
- ADJ. **central, crucial, decisive, dominant, essential, fundamental, important, key, leading, major, pivotal, primary, prominent, significant, vital | minor, secondary, subordinate | constructive, full, positive, useful, valuable | active | passive | direct | clear** *Every member of staff must have a clear role.* | **traditional | changing | dual, twin** *She has a dual role as principal and French teacher.* | **conflicting** *her conflicting roles as mother and manager of a large company* | **advisory, consultative, managerial, supervisory | maternal, parental | economic, educational, military, political, social, strategic** *the economic role of small towns* ◇ *A cup of tea often serves an important social role.* | **symbolic**
- VERB + ROLE **have, occupy, perform, play, serve** *Regional managers occupy a crucial role in developing a strategic framework.* | **provide (sb/sth with) | adopt, assume, take (on)** *I've had to take on the role of mother in her absence.* | **fulfil** *He really wants to fulfil his role as godfather properly.* | **cast sb in** *He has been cast in the role of chief apologist for the government.* | **find** *We need to find a useful role for the volunteers in the campaign.* | **define, redefine** *a clearly defined role within the group* | **swap**
- ROLE + NOUN **model | reversal**
- PREP. **in a/the ~** *She has joined the team in a consultative role.* | **~ as** *the teacher's role as instructor* **~ for** *The new prime minister promised a greater role for women in government.* **~ in** *Pressure groups played a major role in bringing about the reforms.*

roll noun

1 bread
- ADJ. **bread | crusty, soft | brown, white, wholemeal | buttered, filled | ham, cheese, etc.**

2 list of names
- ADJ. **falling** *Falling rolls could lead to smaller class sizes.*
- ADJ. **electoral, membership, school**
- VERB + ROLL **strike sb off, remove sb from** *He should be struck off the roll of solicitors.* | **call, take** *The chairman called the roll* (= to see if everyone was present).
- ROLL + NOUN **call** *Staff evacuated the building and a roll call was taken outside.*
- PREP. **on (the) ~** *The local authority has 50 000 pupils on roll.* ◇ *There are 340 children on the school roll.*
- PHRASES **a roll of honour** *Her name was engraved on sport's roll of honour.*

roll verb

1 move by turning over
- ADV. **slowly | around, away, back, forward, over** *rolling over and over in the mud*
- PREP. **down** *A tear rolled slowly down her cheek.* **off**

2 make sth into the shape of a ball/tube
- ADV. **tightly** *She carried the magazine tightly rolled up in her hand.* | **up**
- PREP. **into** *He rolled the paper into a tight ball.*

3 of a ship/plane
- ADV. **heavily | to and fro** *The ship was rolling heavily to and fro.*

romance noun

1 love affair
- ADJ. **brief | broken | whirlwind** *They married after a whirlwind romance.* | **holiday | teenage**
- VERB + ROMANCE **have** *They had a brief romance in the eighties.*
- ROMANCE + VERB **blossom**

2 romantic feeling
- ADJ. **true**
- VERB + ROMANCE **find** *People find romance in strange places.*
- ROMANCE + VERB **be in the air** *Could romance be in the air for the young prince?*
- PHRASES **love and romance** *Most of her songs are about love and romance.*

romantic noun

- ADJ. **great, true | old | incurable**
- PHRASES **be a romantic at heart**

romantic adj.

1 showing/causing feelings of love
- VERBS **be, feel, seem, sound | become, get** *You're getting quite romantic in your old age!*
- ADV. **extremely, incredibly, intensely, terribly, very, wildly, wonderfully | not at all | quite, rather**

2 imaginative and emotional, not realistic
- VERBS **be, seem**
- ADV. **extremely, highly, very** *highly romantic notions of honour* | **hopelessly, ridiculously** *Their dreams of love and marriage are hopelessly romantic.* | **rather**

roof noun

- ADJ. **conical, flat, gabled, mansard, pitched, pointed, sloping, steep | corrugated iron, glass, slate, thatched, tiled, tin | car, church, etc.**
- VERB + ROOF **support** *The roof is supported by stone columns.*
- ROOF + VERB **slope** *The roof slopes down to the top of the windows.* | **cave in, fall in, collapse** *Five people were killed when the roof fell in.* | **leak**
- ROOF + NOUN **space** *The burglars removed tiles to climb into the roof space.* | **covering, slate, tile | beams, rafters, structure, timbers | insulation | garden, terrace** *The hotel has a charming roof garden.*
- PREP. **in a/the ~** *There are small windows in the roof.* **on a/the ~** *There's a cat on the roof.* **under your ~** (= in your house) *I won't have that man under my roof again!*
- PHRASES **under one/the same roof** (= in the same building) *We're good friends but we could never live under the same roof.*

room noun

1 in a house/building
- ADJ. **big, cavernous, enormous, high, high-ceilinged, huge, large, palatial, spacious, vast | cell-like, cramped, little, low, low-ceilinged, narrow, small, tiny | L-shaped, odd-shaped | north-facing, south-facing, etc. | airy, well-ventilated | airless, claustrophobic, stuffy, windowless | bright | dark, dim, dimly-lit, dingy, moonlit, pitch-dark, shadowed, shadowy, unlighted | depressing, dreary | chilly, cold, draughty | hot, warm | clean, tidy | dirty, dusty, scruffy, shabby, smelly, untidy | comfortable, cosy, homely | attractive, beautiful, elegant, graceful, gracious, handsome, impressive, luxurious, magnificent, pretty | bare, bleak, empty | book-lined | newly-painted, whitewashed | tiled, wood-panelled | crowded, overcrowded | smoke-filled, smoky | quiet, silent | locked | adjacent, adjoining | attic, back, basement, downstairs, front, upstairs | first-floor, second-floor, etc. | guest,**

spare *Our guests are sleeping in the spare room.* | hotel | double, family, single, three-bedded, twin-bedded | bed-sitting | rented | breakfast, dining, living, reception, sitting, utility | dressing, make-up, rehearsal | control | fitness, weight-training | news, press *He emailed his report back to the news room.* | committee, conference, meeting | storage, store (also storeroom) | incident, interview *Police have set up an incident room at the scene of the murder.* | changing, locker, shower | emergency, first-aid, medical, recovery, treatment | lecture, reading, seminar, staff (also staffroom) | boiler, engine

• VERB + ROOM burst into, come/go into, creep into, enter, hurry into, march into, run/rush into, slip/sneak into, step into, storm into, stride into, walk into, wander into | back out of, come/go out of, creep out of, flounce out of, hurry out of, leave, march out of, run/rush out of, slip out of, step out of, storm out of, stride out of, walk out of *As soon as the teacher left the room there was uproar.* | show sb into, usher sb into | cross, go around/round, pace (around/round), prowl (around/round), walk, wander around/round *He was pacing the room nervously.* ◇ *She prowled around the room like a caged tiger.* ◇ *I wandered restlessly round my room.* | echo around/round, run around/round *A ripple of laughter ran round the room.* | glance, look around/round, scan | fill | clean, tidy | decorate, paint *a room decorated in pastel shades* | air, ventilate | light *a room lit by one dusty light bulb* | share *I used to share a room with my sister.* | occupy | vacate *Guests are requested to vacate their rooms by 11 a.m.* | set aside *a room set aside for quiet study* | book, hire, rent *We hired a room for the party.* ◇ *I rented a room while looking for a house to buy.*

• ROOM + VERB adjoin sth, face sth, overlook sth *The room adjoins the hotel kitchens.* | contain sth *The room contained little more than a table and chair.* | be crammed with sth, be filled with sth, be full of sth | be equipped with sth, be furnished with sth, have sth *The patient was in a private room equipped with bathroom and colour TV.* | measure sth *a room measuring 6 metres by 7* | darken | fall silent, grow quiet *The room fell silent as she rose to speak.* | smell *The room smelled of stale sweat and coffee.* | spin, sway *She felt sick and the room was spinning.*

• ROOM + NOUN key | number | lighting, lights | mate (also room-mate) (= person who you share a room or house with) | service | temperature *This wine should be served at room temperature.* | rates *Soaring room rates have put tourists off visiting the city.*

• PREP. around/round a/the ~, from ~ to ~ *She flew from room to room looking for the fire extinguisher.* in/into a/the ~, inside a/the ~

2 space; enough space
• ADJ. ample, considerable, enough, sufficient | insufficient | head (also headroom), leg (also legroom)
• ADJ. leave, make *We had to move the furniture to make room for the piano.*
• PREP. ~ for *Will there be enough room for that large sofa in your sitting room?* ◇ *(figurative) The sales figures are good, but there is still room for improvement.*
• PHRASES room for manoeuvre

root noun

1 of a plant
• ADJ. deep, shallow | gnarled
• ROOT + VERB develop, grow | put down, take *I hope those cuttings will take root.*
• ROOT + NOUN system | crops, vegetables
• PREP. by its/the ~s *She pulled the shrub out by its roots.*

2 roots place where you feel you belong
• ADJ. humble *Despite his wealth, he never forgot his humble roots.* | cultural *severed from our cultural roots by*

industrialization | middle-class, peasant, working-class | French, Scottish, etc.
• VERB + ROOTS get/go back to, return to *My husband wants to go back to his Irish roots.* | trace *They can trace their roots back to the sixteenth century.* | put down *We haven't been here long enough to put down roots.* | cut yourself off from

3 cause/source
• ADJ. deep | very | common *The two languages share a common root.* | historical
• VERB + ROOT have | get at/to, go to *I've spent months trying to get to the root of the problem.* | lie at
• ROOT + NOUN cause
• PREP. at (the ~ of) *It is a moral question at root.* ◇ *His fears of loneliness lay at the very root of his inability to leave.* | ~ in *The unrest has roots in religious differences.*
• PHRASES the root of all evil *They consider globalization to be the root of all evil.* the root of the matter/problem *I expect money is at the root of the matter.*

rooted adj.

• VERBS be | become | remain
• ADV. deeply | firmly
• PREP. in *His problems are deeply rooted in his childhood experiences.*

rope noun

• ADJ. strong | slack | guy, mooring, skipping, tow *I tripped over the guy rope of the tent in the dark.*
• QUANT. length, piece
• VERB + ROPE knot, tie (sth together with) *He tied the planks together with a strong rope.* | tighten | loosen | coil (up) | pull (at/on)
• PHRASES a coil of rope

rose noun

• ADJ. deep pink, red, yellow, etc. | early, late | climbing, rambler, rambling, shrub | long-stemmed | scented | fresh *She put fresh roses in the vases.* | wild
• ROSE + NOUN garden | bed | bush | petals | bowl
• PHRASES a bed of roses, the scent/smell of a rose
⇒ Note at FLOWER (for verbs)

rota noun

• ADJ. daily, weekly, etc. | duty | cleaning
• VERB + ROTA have | draw up, work out *I've been asked to draw up the cleaning rota.*
• ROTA + NOUN scheme, system
• PREP. on the ~ | ~ for *Are you on the rota for cooking?*
• PHRASES on a rota basis *We share the babysitting duties on a rota basis.*

rotate verb

• ADV. quickly, rapidly | gently, slowly | freely
• VERB + ROTATE allow sth to *It is best to allow the rotor to rotate freely.*
• PREP. around *The blades rotate around a central point.* on *The earth rotates on its axis.* through *The handle rotates through 360 degrees.*

round noun

1 series of events
• ADJ. ceaseless, endless, long *Life to him was one long round of parties.* | fresh, further, new
• PREP. ~ of *a fresh round of peace talks*

2 regular series of visits, etc.
• ADJ. daily, weekly | milk, paper
• VERB + ROUND do, make *The milkman does his round very early.*
• PREP. on sb's ~ *a doctor on his round*

3 number of drinks
- VERB + ROUND **buy, order** *I bought the last round.*
- PHRASES **It's my round.** (= It's my turn to buy the drinks.), **a round of drinks** *We just had time for one more round of drinks.*

4 part of a competition
- ADJ. **first, second,** etc. *Italy qualified for the second round of the tournament by beating Germany.* | **opening, preliminary** | **final** | **qualifying**
- PREP. **in a/the ~** *Australia were knocked out in the second round.*

5 (in golf) one game
- VERB + ROUND **have, play, shoot**
- PHRASES **a round of golf** *We had a good round of golf today.*

6 bullet/bullets
- ADJ. **live** | **blank**
- VERB + ROUND **fire** *The soldiers fired several blank rounds into the crowd.*

round *verb*

PHRASAL VERB
round sth off
- ADV. **nicely** *A coffee would round the meal off nicely.*
- PREP. **with** *We rounded off the day with a picnic.*

roundabout *noun*

- VERB + ROUNDABOUT **enter** | **get off, leave** *Leave the roundabout at the second exit.* | **drive/go around/round**
- PREP. **at the ~** *At the roundabout, turn right.* **on the ~** *There was a lot of traffic on the roundabout.*

rounded *adj.*

1 having a round shape
- VERBS **be**
- ADV. **gently, slightly, softly** | **beautifully, nicely** *beautifully rounded arches*

2 complete and balanced
- VERBS **be**
- ADV. **well** | **fully** *a fully rounded education*

rout *noun*

- ADJ. **total**
- VERB + ROUT **become, end in, turn into** *The game ended in a total rout.* | **put sb to** *They put the rebel army to rout.* | **start** | **complete**

route *noun*

- ADJ. **quick, short** *The shortest route home is round the ring road.* | **convenient, easy** | **long** | **direct** | **circuitous, circular, devious, indirect, roundabout, tortuous** | **dangerous, safe** | **attractive, beautiful, scenic** *We had plenty of time so we took the scenic route.* | **accessible** | **alternative** *Travellers are advised to find an alternative route during road repairs.* | **main, trunk** | **air, overland, sea** | **bus, cycle,** etc. | **shipping, supply, trade** | **coastal** | **east-west, southerly, southern,** etc. | **trans-Pennine, trans-Sahara,** etc. | **tourist** | **well-travelled, well-worn** | **access** | **escape**
- VERB + ROUTE **follow, take** | **choose, map out, plan, work out** *You'll have to plan your route carefully.* | **retrace** *We retraced our route in an attempt to get back on the right path.*
- ROUTE + VERB **cross sth, follow sth, go, pass through sth, run, take sb** *The alternative route takes you along the river.* | **climb, turn** | **lead** | **lie** *Our route lay straight ahead and downhill.*
- ROUTE + NOUN **map**

- PREP. **along the ~** *There are plenty of bed and break-fasts along the route.* **on the ~** *We live on the school bus route.* | **~between** *the most direct route between London and Brighton* **~from** *the air route from Berlin to Beijing* **~through** *a scenic route through the south of France* **~to** *the shortest route to Bruges* ◊ *the best route to success*
- PHRASES **en route** (= on the way) *We'll stop for lunch en route.*

routine *noun*

- ADJ. **fixed, set** | **inflexible, rigid, strict** | **dull, humdrum, monotonous** | **familiar, normal, old, regular, usual** | **daily, day-to-day** | **domestic, exercise, school, work**
- VERB + ROUTINE **establish, get into, settle into** *It took me a week to settle into a routine.* | **follow, go through** *We go through the same old routine every morning.* | **break, change, vary**
- PHRASES **a change from the/in/of routine** *The children were confused by the change of routine.* **a matter of routine** *Bags of all visitors to the museum are searched as a matter of routine.*

row[1] /rəʊ/ *noun*

- ADJ. **bottom, middle, top** | **back, front** | **horizontal, vertical** | **double, single** | **neat** *She arranged the chairs in two neat rows.* | **serried** *serried rows of vines* | **endless** *endless rows of identical houses*
- PREP. **in a/the ~** *The children stood in a row.* ◊ *It rained for five days in a row* (= without a break). ◊ *We have seats in the front row.* | **~of** *a long row of shops*
- PHRASES **the end/middle of the row, rows and rows, row upon row** *He looked down at row upon row of eager faces.*

row[2] /raʊ/ *noun*

1 argument
- ADJ. **almighty, awful, big, bitter, blazing, fearful, ferocious, fierce, flaming, furious, great, huge, major, serious, terrible, tremendous, unholy, violent** *We had a blazing row over who should do the cooking.* | **domestic, family** | **stand-up** *A couple was having a stand-up row in the street.* | **public** | **drunken** | **long-running** | **diplomatic, political**
- VERB + ROW **have** | **kick up** *I'm going to kick up a row if I don't get my money back.* | **cause** | **get into**
- ROW + VERB **blow up, break out, develop, erupt** *A row blew up over pay rises for ministers.* | **go on, rage (on)**
- PREP. **in a/the ~** *He came to prominence in the row over defence policy.* | **~about/over** *Carol and I had a terrible row about how much money she spends.* **~between** *a row between the left and right wings of the party* **~with** *a row with my mother*

2 loud noise
- ADJ. **unholy**
- VERB + ROW **make** *Someone's making an unholy row outside.*
- ROW + VERB **go on, rage (on)** *The row went on and on.*

royalty *noun*

1 money paid to an author, etc.
- ADJ. **advance**
- VERB + ROYALTY **pay** | **earn, get, receive** | **charge**
- ROYALTY + NOUN **cheque, payment**
- PREP. **in ~s** *She earns a lot in royalties.* | **~from/on** *He has received royalties on previous inventions.*
- PHRASES **an advance on royalties**

2 members of the royal family
- ADJ. **minor**

• PHRASES **in the presence of royalty** *She behaved as if she were in the presence of royalty.*

rub *verb*

• ADV. **briskly, hard, vigorously** *He rubbed his face briskly with the towel.* | **well** *Put a little cream onto each hand and rub it in well.* | **gently, lightly** *He gently rubbed his swollen nose.* | **thoughtfully** *She rubbed her chin thoughtfully.* | **wearily** *Corbett rubbed his eyes wearily.* | **in, together** *He began to rub his hands together in glee.*
• VERB + RUB **begin to**
• PREP. **against** *The cat rubbed against my legs.* **at** *She stood up, rubbing at her back.* **into** *Rub the cream well into your skin.* **on** *She rubbed her hands on her apron.* **with** *I rubbed my glasses with my handkerchief.*

rubbish *noun*

1 waste material
• ADJ. **domestic, household** | **garden**
• QUANT. **bag, pile** | **tons**
• VERB + RUBBISH **put out** *I forgot to put the rubbish out last night.* | **collect, remove, take away** *The rubbish is collected on Tuesdays.* | **clear (out), dispose of, dump, throw (away/out)** *He's clearing rubbish out of the attic.* ◇ *Someone had dumped their rubbish by the road.* ◇ *Throw the rubbish in the bin.* | **leave, strew (around)** *There was rubbish strewn around everywhere.* | **pick up**
• RUBBISH + VERB **decay, rot**
• RUBBISH + NOUN **bag, bin, skip** | **dump, heap, tip** | **collection, disposal** | **chute**

2 sth that you think is bad/silly/wrong
• ADJ. **absolute, complete, total, utter** *The film was absolute rubbish.* | **worthless** *Many critics see the paintings as worthless rubbish.* | **old** *The antique shop was just full of old rubbish.*
• VERB + RUBBISH **talk** *Don't talk such rubbish!*
• PREP. **~ about** *the usual rubbish about his undiscovered talents*
• PHRASES **a load of (old) rubbish, What rubbish!**

rubble *noun*

• ADJ. **brick, rock, stone** | **building**
• QUANT. **heap, pile** *What was once a cottage was now a crumbling heap of rubble.*
• VERB + RUBBLE **be reduced to** *The school was reduced to rubble.* | **clear (away)** | **sift through** *Police sifted through the rubble looking for clues.*
• PREP. **amid/amidst/among/amongst the ~** *She stood among the rubble left by the earthquake.* **beneath/under the ~** *Our car was buried somewhere under the rubble.* **in the~** *Several people were trapped in the rubble.*

rucksack (*also* backpack) *noun*

• VERB + RUCKSACK **pack** | **unpack** | **put on, shoulder** | **pull off, remove, take off** | **carry, have on, wear** *He had a large rucksack on.*
• PREP. **in a/the~** *He had very little in his rucksack.*

rude *adj.*

• VERBS **appear, be, seem, sound** | **become** | **consider sth, think sb/sth** *I hope you won't think me rude if I leave early.*
• ADV. **downright, extremely, really, terribly, very** *He wasn't just impolite—he was downright rude.* | **a bit, a little, pretty, quite, rather** | **deliberately**
• PREP. **about** *He's very rude about her cooking.* **to** *Don't be so rude to your mother!*

rug *noun*

• ADJ. **threadbare** | **bedside, fireside, hearth, picnic** | **oriental, Persian**
• VERB + RUG **make, weave** | **scatter, spread** *There were several brightly coloured rugs scattered around.*
• RUG + VERB **cover sth** *A Persian rug covered the polished floor.*

rugby *noun*

• ADJ. **amateur, professional** | **competitive, representative** | **junior, school, student, youth** | **senior** | **club, league** | **first-class, international, test, world** | **touch** | **mini** *Kids from six years old play mini rugby at the club.* | **running** *The crowd enjoyed the Fijians' running rugby.*
• QUANT. **game**
• VERB + RUGBY **play** | **watch**
• RUGBY + NOUN **scrum, tackle** | **club, side, team** | **ball, jersey, shirt** | **championship, game, international, match** | **tour** | **ball, posts** | **boots, jersey** | **field, pitch** | **forward, international, player** *the former rugby international, Serge Blanco* | **coach** | **official** | **career** | **season** | **buff, enthusiast, fan, follower, supporter** | **circles, community, folk, fraternity, people** *In rugby circles, there is nothing but criticism for the coverage of sport on terrestrial TV.* | **country, nation**
• PHRASES **Rugby League, Rugby Union**
⇨ Special page at SPORT

ruin *noun*

1 spoilt state
• ADJ. **complete, utter**
• VERB + RUIN **fall into, go to** *The cottage gradually fell into ruin.*
• PHRASES **be the ruin of sb/sth** *Drink has been the ruin of her.* **go to rack and ruin** *They've let the house go to rack and ruin.*

2 end of success, hopes, etc.
• ADJ. **economic, financial** | **political**
• VERB + RUIN **face** *The company faces ruin over the new road plans.* | **bring, lead to, mean, spell** *The cost would have meant financial ruin for us.* | **save from**
• PHRASES **on the brink/verge of ruin, the road to ruin** *He's on the road to political ruin.*

3 damaged building, town, etc.
• ADJ. **ancient** | **charred, smoking** *the charred ruins of their home* | **abbey, castle, etc.**
• VERB + RUIN **be/lie in ~s** *The church now lies in ruins.* | **leave sth in ~s** *The earthquake left the town in ruins.*
• PREP. **~s of** *the ancient ruins of Jericho*

ruin *verb*

• ADV. **completely, quite, totally** *The experience has completely ruined her life.* | **nearly** | **partly** | **effectively** | **financially** *The long legal battle ruined him financially.*
• VERB + RUIN **threaten to** *A knee injury threatened to ruin her Olympic hopes.* | **be going to** *All this mud is going to ruin my shoes.*

rule *noun*

1 what you can or cannot do, say, etc.
• ADJ. **basic, cardinal, first, fundamental, golden** | **ground ~s** *You and your flatmates should establish some ground rules.* | **general** | **formal, official, written** | **informal, unwritten** | **rigid, strict, stringent** | **absolute, hard and fast** *There are no hard and fast rules when it comes to choosing a typeface.* | **clear** | **simple** *Follow these few simple rules, and you won't go far wrong.* | **arbitrary** | **petty** *He made his children's lives a misery with all his petty rules.* | **club, company, competition, school, union, etc.** | **cultural, ethical, legal, moral, social** | **dis-**

ciplinary, immigration, safety, tax | grammar, grammatical
- QUANT. **set** *The aim is to get each member country to adhere to a single set of rules.*
- VERB + RULE **draw up, establish, formulate, impose, issue, lay down, make, set out | abide by, adhere to, follow, go by, obey, observe, play by, stick to** *If he wanted a loan he would have to play by the bank's rules.* | **be in line with, conform to** *The packaging does not conform to EU rules.* | **be in breach of, break, disregard, fall foul of, flout, violate** *Their‚action was in breach of Stock Exchange rules.* | **apply, enforce** *The referee applied the rules to the letter* (= very strictly). | **bend, relax** *Couldn't they just bend the rules and let us in without a ticket?* | **waive | tighten up** *The rules on claiming sickness benefit have been tightened up.* | **be bound by, be fettered by, be governed by** *Social workers are bound by rules of confidentiality.* | **interpret, understand** *The punishment depends on how the umpire interprets the rules.*
- RULE + VERB **apply, be applicable, operate | provide sth, say sth, state sth, stipulate sth** *The competition rules provide that a cash alternative may be given.* | **govern sth** *the rules governing the importing of livestock* | **allow (for) sth, permit sth** *The existing rules allow for some flexibility.* | **forbid sth, prohibit sth | limit sth, restrict sth** *rules limiting imports*
- RULE + NOUN **book** *The officials went strictly by the rule book.*
- PREP. **according to the~s** *According to the rules, no alcohol can be consumed on the premises.* **against/contrary to the~s** *Tackling a player without the ball is against the rules.* **in accordance with the~s** *The music was turned off at midnight, in accordance with the rules.* **outside the~s** *behaviour which is outside the rules* **under a/the~** *Under this rule, only full members of the club are entitled to vote.* **within the~s** *I believed I was acting within the rules.* | **~ about/concerning/on/regarding/relating to** *What are the school rules about dress?* **~ for** *There seems to be one rule for the rich and another for the poor.* ◇ *What is the rule for forming plurals?* **~ of** *the rules of the game*
- PHRASES **a breach/violation of the rules, a body/code/network/system of rules, respect for the rules, rules and regulations**

2 what is usual
- ADJ. **general** *There are few exceptions to the general rule that shops close at six o'clock.*
- PREP. **as a~** *As a rule, hardly anybody uses this road.*
- PHRASES **be the rule** *Among her friends, casual dress and a relaxed manner are the rule.*

3 government
- ADJ. **authoritarian, harsh | direct, indirect | emergency** *The president imposed emergency rule following the riots.* | **majority | one-party | Labour, Tory, etc. | colonial | home | civilian‚military | presidential | mob** *the lawless days of mob rule*
- VERB + RULE **impose**
- PREP. **under … ~** *The country remained under direct rule by the occupying powers.*
- PHRASES **the rule of law** *a society based on the rule of law*

rule *verb*
- ADV. **justly**
- PREP. **by** *the president's powers to rule by decree* **over** *He left his son to rule over Saragossa.*
- PHRASES **rule supreme, rule with an iron fist/hand; rule with a rod of iron** (= control a person or group of people very severely)

PHRASAL VERB
rule sth out
- ADV. **altogether, categorically, completely, definitely, entirely, firmly, totally** *This theory cannot be ruled out al-*
together. | **virtually | effectively** *His age effectively ruled him out as a possible candidate.* | **apparently | automatically** *Infringement of this regulation would automatically rule you out of the championship.* | **immediately | formerly, hitherto, previously**
- VERB + RULE STH OUT **cannot/could not, fail to, refuse to**
- PREP. **as** *Police have now ruled her out as the killer.*

ruler *noun*
- ADJ. **great | effective, powerful, strong | weak | enlightened | democratic | absolute** *an absolute ruler who will tolerate no opposition* | **virtual** *At that time the East India Company was the virtual ruler of Bengal.* | **sovereign | supreme | hereditary | legitimate, rightful | independent | former | colonial‚military | secular**
- RULER + VERB **come to power, seize power | govern (sb/sth), hold power** *a ruler who held power for over twenty years*
- PREP. **under a/the ~** *The country was finally united under one ruler.* | **~ over** *He eventually became ruler over the Burgundians.*

ruling *noun*
- ADJ. **authoritative, definitive | unanimous | adverse | preliminary | original | final | court‚legal**
- VERB + RULING **give, hand down, issue, make | overturn, reverse** *The Court of Appeal overturned the original ruling.* | **uphold**
- PREP. **~ against** *the European Court's ruling against detention without trial* **~ by** *the ruling by the High Court* **~ in favour of** *The newspaper said that this was a ruling in favour of freedom of speech.* **~ on** *The House of Lords will make a final ruling on the case next week.*

rumble *noun*
- ADJ. **deep, low | dull | distant | ominous**
- VERB + RUMBLE **give, let out | hear**
- PREP. **with a~** *The door slid shut with a rumble.* | **~ of**
- PHRASES **the rumble of thunder** *We could hear the distant rumble of thunder.*
⇨ Note at SOUND

rumour *noun*
- ADJ. **malicious, nasty, scurrilous, ugly, vicious | baseless, false, unconfirmed, unfounded, unsubstantiated, wild | strong, widespread | persistent**
- VERB + RUMOUR **start | fuel** *His lengthy absence from work fuelled rumours that he might have been sacked.* | **spread | hear | believe | deny | confirm** *The actor confirmed rumours that he will be leaving the series.* | **quash, scotch, silence** *The Chief Executive issued a statement to quash rumours of financial problems.*
- RUMOUR + VERB **circulate, get about/around, go around/round, spread | abound, be flying about/around, be rife** *Rumours about an impending royal divorce were rife.* | **sweep sth** *The rumour quickly swept the town.* | **persist**
- RUMOUR + NOUN **factory, mill** *The Washington rumour mill suggests the money changed hands illegally.*
- PREP. **amid/amidst~s** *The manager resigned suddenly amidst rumours of misconduct.* | **~ about/concerning/surrounding** *rumours surrounding the closure of the hospital* **~ of** *There were persistent rumours of drug taking among staff.*
- PHRASES **rumour has it that …** *Rumour has it that he was sacked from his last job.* **there is no truth in the rumour** *There is no truth in the rumour that the head teacher is about to resign.*

run *noun*

1 on foot
- ADJ. **five-mile, etc.** | **fun, sponsored** *The local council has organized a two-mile fun run for charity.* | **training** | **record-breaking** *The Ethiopian is aiming to produce his second record-breaking run of the week.*
- VERB + RUN **go for, have** *Let's go for a run before dinner.* | **go on** *I'm going on a sponsored run tomorrow.* | **break into** *When he saw me he broke into a run.* | **take** *He took a run at the wall and just managed to clear it.*
- PREP. **at a ~** *She took the stairs at a run.* **on the ~** (= escaping by running) *The prisoners have now been on the run for three days.*
- PHRASES **make a run for it** (= escape by running)

2 of success/failure
- ADJ. **bad, disappointing, disastrous, dismal, poor** | **excellent, fine, good, remarkable, successful** | **unbeaten, winning** | **record-breaking**
- VERB + RUN **enjoy, have** *Spurs have had a winning run of ten games.* | **begin** | **end** *Manchester United have finally ended their run of victories.*
- RUN + VERB **begin** | **end**
- PREP. **~ of** *a run of good/bad luck*

3 of a play/film
- ADJ. **long** | **short** | **eight-week, six-month, etc.** | **successful** | **sell-out**
- VERB + RUN **have** *The play had a long run in the West End.* | **begin** *They play began its run last June.* | **end**
- RUN + VERB **begin** | **end**

4 way things are/happen
- ADJ. **common, general, ordinary, usual** *She was very different from the general run of American movie stars.* ◊ *In the normal run of things the only exercise he gets is climbing in and out of taxis.*
- PHRASES **against the run of play** *Villa scored in the 15th minute against the run of play* (= although the other team had seemed more likely to score).

5 in cricket/baseball
- ADJ. **home**
- VERB + RUN **get, make, score** *They've got another run!* ◊ *He's only made four home runs all season.* | **be on, have** *Our team is on 90 runs.*

6 attempt/practice
- ADJ. **dry, dummy, practice, trial**

run *verb*

1 move quickly on foot
- ADV. **fast, quickly** *John can run very fast.* ◊ *She ran quickly downstairs.* | **blindly** | **headlong** | **away, downstairs, home, off, out, upstairs**
- VERB + RUN **begin to, turn and/to** | **want to** *He just wanted to run away and hide.*
- PREP. **down** *She turned and ran blindly down the street.* **into** *He ran headlong into an enemy patrol.* **out of** *He ran out of the house.* **to, towards, up, etc.**

2 manage sth
- ADV. **efficiently, properly, well** | **badly** *a badly-run company* | **professionally** | **jointly** *The programme will be jointly run with NASA in the US.* | **personally** | **privately** | **independently** *The student union is run independently of college authorities.* | **in parallel, in tandem** *The two experiments are run in parallel.*
- VERB + RUN **try to** *Stop trying to run my life for me.* | **manage to** | **help (to), help sb (to)**

3 work
- ADV. **efficiently, smoothly** *The engine was running very smoothly.*
- PREP. **on** *Our car only runs on unleaded petrol.*

4 happen
- ADV. **smoothly** *Things ran very smoothly for a while.* |

concurrently, **consecutively** *He was given two twelve-month sentences to run concurrently.*

5 buses/trains
- ADV. **regularly** *Local buses run regularly to and from the town.* | **late** *The train was running late, as usual.*
- PREP. **between, from, to**

runner *noun*

- ADJ. **fast, good** | **distance, long-distance, marathon, middle-distance** | **cross-country, fell, road** | **front** (*often figurative*) *He is currently the front runner for the Democratic Party presidential nomination.* | **fancied** *one of the fancied runners in today's race*

running *noun*

1 activity/sport
- ADJ. **cross-country, fell, road** | **distance, long-distance, marathon, middle-distance**
- RUNNING + NOUN **event, race** | **shoe, shorts, vest** | **track**

2 management of business, etc.
- ADJ. **efficient, smooth** *Careful planning is needed to ensure the smooth running of the event.* | **day-to-day**
- VERB + RUNNING **be involved in, be responsible for**
- RUNNING + NOUN **costs, expenses**

rural *adj.*

- VERBS **be**
- ADV. **extremely, overwhelmingly, truly, very** *At the end of the 17th century England was still overwhelmingly rural.* | **completely** | **largely, mainly, predominantly** | **semi-** *the ideal of suburban or semi-rural living* | **quite** | **essentially** | **pleasantly**

ruse *noun*

- ADJ. **simple** | **clever, subtle**
- RUSE + VERB **succeed** | **fail**
- PREP. **~ by sb** *The attack may merely be a ruse by the enemy to distract our forces.*

rush *noun*

1 sudden quick movement
- ADJ. **headlong, sudden**
- PREP. **~ for** *The film ended, and there was a rush for the exits.* **~ of** *A rush of water came from the burst pipe.*

2 busy period
- ADJ. **awful, great, mad, tearing** | **sudden** | **last-minute** | **Christmas**
- RUSH + NOUN **decision** | **job** *You can see that the painting was a rush job.* | **hour** *During the rush hour the journey may take up to twice as long.*
- PREP. **in a ~** *I've been in a mad rush all day.* | **~ for** *a last-minute rush for tickets* **~ of** *a sudden rush of tourist traffic*
- PHRASES **have a rush on** *We've had a rush on at the office, dealing with the backlog of orders.*

rush *verb*

- ADV. **headlong, madly** *a train rushing headlong down the track* | **immediately** | **suddenly** | **about, around, back, home, in, off, out, over, past** *She was rushing around madly looking for her bag.*
- PREP. **along, from, into, out of, through, to, etc.** *A surge of joy rushed through her body.* ◊ *He was rushed to hospital.*
- PHRASES **come/go rushing** *Two men came rushing into the room.* **rush to sb's/the rescue** *Whenever her little brother was upset, Jane rushed to the rescue.*

Russian *noun*

⇨ Note at LANGUAGE

rust *noun*

- VERB + RUST **clean off, get off, remove, scrape off**
- RUST + NOUN **spot, stain | protection** *A zinc coating is applied to the steel for rust protection.*
- PHRASES **covered/flecked/red/spotted with rust** *The old padlock was red with rust.*

rust *verb*

- ADV. **badly | away, through** *The car had been rusting away in his garage for years.*

rustle *noun*

- ADJ. **faint, slight, soft**

- VERB + RUSTLE **hear**
- PREP. **with a~** *With a rustle of wings the bird landed on the window ledge.* | **~of** *I heard a soft rustle of leaves.*

rustle *verb*

- ADV. **softly** *the sound of the leaves rustling softly*
- PREP. **in** *The wind rustled in the bushes.* **through** *the sound of their feet rustling through the grass*

rut *noun*

- ADJ. **muddy | deep | cart, tractor, wagon**
- PREP. **in a~** *(figurative) My job bores me—I feel I'm in a rut.* **into a~** *(figurative) I'd got into a rut, cooking the same things week after week.* **out of a~** *(figurative) Moving abroad gave her the chance to get out of a rut.*

Ss

sabbath *noun*

- ADJ. **Jewish, Muslim, etc.**
- VERB + SABBATH **keep, observe | break**
- SABBATH + NOUN **day | rest**
- PREP. **on the~** *It was considered a sin to work or play on the Sabbath.*
- PHRASES **observance of the Sabbath** *The speaker advocated a less austere observance of the Sabbath.*

sabotage *noun*

- ADJ. **deliberate, planned | economic, industrial** *They conducted a campaign of economic sabotage.*
- SABOTAGE + NOUN **attempt | raid**
- PHRASES **an act of sabotage**

sabotage *verb*

- ADV. **deliberately** *They accused him of deliberately sabotaging the peace talks.*
- VERB + SABOTAGE **attempt to, try to** *They had tried to sabotage our plans.*

sack *noun*

1 large bag
- ADJ. **bulging** *bulging sacks of toys* | **hessian, paper, plastic, stuff | flour, mail, potato, refuse**
- VERB + SACK **fill** *They filled the sacks with potatoes.* | **put sth in, tie sb/sth (up) in** *The kittens had been tied up in a sack and thrown in the river.* | **empty | carry (sth in)**
- SACK + VERB **be filled with sth, be full of sth**
- PREP. **in a/the~ | ~of** *a sack of coal*

2 the sack dismissal from your job
- VERB + SACK **get** *She got the sack after 20 years of service.* | **give sb | be threatened with, face** *Hundreds of postal workers are facing the sack.*

sacred *adj.*

- VERBS **be | become | remain | consider sth, deem sth, hold sth, regard sth as** *Certain animals were regarded as sacred.* ◇ *the feeling that all life should be held sacred*
- ADV. **absolutely | almost**
- PREP. **to** *The place was sacred to the Celts.*

sacrifice *noun*

1 giving sth up
- ADJ. **considerable, enormous, great, heavy, real | financial, personal | heroic | supreme, ultimate** *Soldiers who die for their country have made the supreme sacrifice.*
- VERB + SACRIFICE **make**

2 part of a ceremony
- ADJ. **animal, human | religious, ritual | blood | pagan**
- VERB + SACRIFICE **perform | offer (sth as)**
- PREP. **~to** *Food and wine were offered as sacrifices to the gods.*

sacrifice *verb*

- VERB + SACRIFICE **be obliged to, have to | be prepared to, be willing to** *She was prepared to sacrifice having a family in order to pursue her career.*
- PREP. **for** *soldiers who sacrificed their lives for their country*
- PHRASES **sacrifice sth for the sake of sth** *Comfort has been sacrificed for the sake of improved performance.*

sad *adj.*

1 unhappy
- VERBS **appear, be, feel, look, seem, sound | become, grow | make sb** *This music always makes me sad.*
- ADV. **all, desperately, immensely, particularly, profoundly, really, unbearably, very** *I called Mum, sounding all sad and pathetic.* | **almost | a bit, a little, quite, rather, slightly, somewhat | strangely**
- PREP. **about** *She was still feeling very sad about her father's death.*

2 causing unhappiness
- VERBS **be, seem | find sth**
- ADV. **deeply, extremely, intensely, particularly, profoundly, really, terribly, unutterably, very** *a deeply sad occasion* | **a bit, a little, quite, rather** *a rather sad story*

sadden *verb*

- ADV. **deeply, greatly** *I was deeply saddened by his death.*

sadness *noun*

- ADJ. **deep, great, real, unutterable**
- QUANT. **hint**
- VERB + SADNESS **be filled with, be full of, feel** *Claudia felt a deep sadness.* | **express, show | hide | bring (sb)** *I had brought nothing but sadness to my family.* | **be tinged with** *Our joy was tinged with sadness.*
- PREP. **with~** *It was with great sadness that we learned of the death of William Hales.* | **~ about/at/over** *He expressed his sadness about what had happened.* **~ for** *Kate felt a great sadness for him.*
- PHRASES **an air/aura of sadness** *a lonely place with an aura of sadness* **a feeling/sense of sadness**

safe *noun*

- ADJ. **bank, hotel, office | wall**
- VERB + SAFE **open | close, lock | break into, crack**

safe *adj.*

- VERBS **be, feel, seem | become | remain, stay | play (it)** *Does good marketing mean playing safe (= avoiding risks) and staying traditional?* | **make sth, render sth** *The army experts made the bomb safe.* | **keep sth** *Keep your money safe by carrying it in an inside pocket.* | **consider sth, declare sth, deem sth** *The water was not considered safe to drink.*
- ADV. **all, extremely, really, very** *Don't worry—he'll be all safe and snug in the barn.* | **absolutely, completely, perfectly, quite, totally** *a completely safe and secure environment for young children* | **not entirely** *The wood is never entirely safe for women on their own.* | **comparatively, fairly, pretty, reasonably, relatively | enough** *You should be safe enough, but don't go too far.* | **environmentally** *She claimed that nuclear power was the most environmentally safe form of energy.*
- PREP. **from** *They were safe from attack.* **with** *Your money will be safe with me.*
- PHRASES **better safe than sorry, safe and sound** *They returned from their adventure safe and sound.*

safeguard *noun*

- ADJ. **adequate, effective, proper, sufficient** *Does the procedure provide adequate safeguards against corrup-*

tion? | added, additional, extra, further | appropriate, necessary | environmental, nuclear | constitutional, legal, procedural
● VERB + SAFEGUARD **introduce** | **provide (sb with)** | **build in/into sth** *Appropriate safeguards would have to be built into the procedures to avoid abuses.*
● PREP. **~ against** *The credit agreement includes safeguards against overcharging.*

safeguard *verb*

● ADV. **fully, properly** | **adequately, satisfactorily** *This legislation does not adequately safeguard the rights of consumers.*
● VERB + SAFEGUARD **help (to)** | **be designed to** | **take steps to**
● PREP. **against** *We must take steps to safeguard our environment against these threats.* **from** *to safeguard the young plants from frost*

safety *noun*

● ADJ. **extra, greater** *The seat is bolted in place for extra safety.* | **comparative, reasonable, relative** *A blizzard forced the climbers back to the relative safety of their tents.* | **perfect** *Walkways allow visitors to enter the caves in perfect safety.* | **child, passenger, personal, public** *The house has to be rearranged with a view to child safety.* | **fire, food, nuclear, etc.** | **air, home, industrial, occupational, road, traffic, etc.**
● VERB + SAFETY **ensure, guarantee** | **improve** | **fear for** *Police fear for the safety of the missing children.*
● SAFETY + NOUN **controls, improvements, limits, measures, precautions, procedures, provisions** | **guidelines, laws, legislation, levels, policy, recommendations, regulations, requirements, rules, standards** | **violation** | **hazard, risk** | **check, inspection** | **inspector, officer, official, watchdog** *The plan was rejected by the government nuclear safety watchdog.* | **record** | **aspect, considerations, factor, implications, issues, matters** | **awareness** *The police are conducting a safety awareness programme in local schools.* | **campaign, initiative, training** | **belt, equipment, features, harness, helmet, rope** *The car has many safety features, including anti-skid braking.* | **catch, device, valve** | **barrier, net** *(often figurative)* *State benefits provide a safety net for the very poor.* | **glass, pin, razor, seat**
● PREP. **for~** *The stairs are fitted with handrails on either side for safety.* **for your own~** *The police gave him protection for his own safety.* **in~** *The people want to be able to walk the streets at night in safety.* **to~** *We managed to run to safety before the building collapsed.*
● PHRASES **for safety reasons** *For safety reasons, children should not operate the machine unsupervised.* **health and safety** *The company was fined by the health and safety inspectors.* **on safety grounds** *The playground was closed down on safety grounds.* **a place of safety** *The refugees finally reached a place of safety.* **safety first** *When cycling on the roads, remember: safety first.*

sag *verb*

● ADV. **slightly** | **wearily** | **back, forward** *He sagged wearily back in his chair.* ◇ *Helga's body sagged forward.*
● PREP. **against** *She sagged against the door.* **under** *The shelf sagged under the weight of hundreds of volumes.*
● PHRASES **sag in the middle** *a mattress that was beginning to sag in the middle*

saga *noun*

● ADJ. **continuing, long-running, ongoing** | **extraordinary** | **sorry, terrible** | **complicated** | **family**
● PREP. **in a/the ~** *His suicide is the latest chapter in this terrible saga of greed and betrayal.*

sail *noun*

● ADJ. **main** | **canvas**
● VERB + SAIL **hoist, raise** | **drop, lower** | **adjust, trim** | **fill** *The dinghy gathered speed as the wind filled her sails.* | **reef, shorten** | **furl**
● SAIL + VERB **billow, flap** *The bay was full of yachts with billowing sails.* | **fill**
● SAIL + NOUN **area, shape, size** | **canvas**
● PREP. **under ~** *The yacht came in under sail and anchored near us.*
● PHRASES **the days of sail** *The boat is preserved as a monument to the days of sail.* **in/under full sail** *She advanced towards us like a galleon in full sail.* **set sail (for)** *We set sail for France at first light.*

sail *verb*

● ADV. **serenely** | **single-handed** *to sail single-handed around the world* | **away, back, on, out, past** *The boat sailed serenely on towards the horizon.*
● VERB + SAIL **learn to** | **teach sb to**
● PREP. **across** *sailing across the English Channel* **down, for** *The ferry sails for Southampton at 5.30.* **from, into** *We sailed the boat out into the middle of the lake.* **on** *We sailed on a large ocean liner.* ◇ *sailing on the sea* **out of** *sailing out of the harbour* ◇ *sailing from Dover to Calais.* **up**

sailing *noun*

1 sport
● ADJ. **catamaran, dinghy, etc.**
● VERB + SAILING **go**
● SAILING + NOUN **club, school** | **holiday, trip** | **boat, craft, dinghy, ship, vessel**

2 journey made by boat
● ADJ. **daily, overnight, regular, weekday, weekend** | **return**
● VERB + SAILING **delay** | **suspend** *Sailings were suspended in the high winds.*
● PREP. **~ between** *The company operates regular sailings between Hull and Zeebrugge.* **~ from, ~ to** *the 4 p.m. sailing from Dover to Calais*

sailor *noun*

● ADJ. **experienced, good, keen** | **inexperienced, novice** | **drowned, shipwrecked**

saint *noun*

● ADJ. **blessed, holy** | **patron** *St Nicholas is the patron saint of children.*
● VERB + SAINT **canonize**

salad *noun*

● ADJ. **fresh** | **crisp, crunchy** | **limp** | **green, mixed, potato, rice, tomato, etc.** | **fruit** | **chicken, ham, etc.** | **side** *Is the steak served with a side salad?*
● VERB + SALAD **make, prepare** | **toss** *She tossed and dressed the salad.* | **dress** | **serve sth with** | **come with**
● SALAD + NOUN **greens, leaves** | **cream, dressing** | **garnish** *The sandwiches came with a rather limp salad garnish.* | **bowl** | **bar**
⇨ Special page at FOOD

salary *noun*

● ADJ. **competitive, generous, good, handsome, high, large, top** *Top salaries are liable for a higher rate of tax.* | **low, small** | **reasonable** | **average** | **basic** | **pensionable** | **gross** | **net** | **starting** | **current** | **final** *Your pension will be based on a proportion of your final salary.* | **annual, monthly** | **tax-free**

● VERB + SALARY **pay (sb)** | **earn, receive** | **increase** | **cut, decrease, reduce**

● SALARY + NOUN **package** *The position is rewarded with a generous salary package.* | **award, increase, rise** *The top salary awards are completely out of line with inflation.* | **cut** | **level** | **review** | **band, grade, range** *What salary band will I be on after two years in the company?* | **scale, structure** | **bill, costs**

● PREP. **on a~** *It's impossible to bring up a family on such a low salary.*

● PHRASES **an increase/a rise in salary, a cut/drop in salary** *Workers are being asked to take a cut in salary.*

sale *noun*

1 act of selling

● ADJ. **quick** *The price is low to ensure a quick sale.* | **major, massive** *a major sale of paintings* ◊ *the massive sale of foreign currency reserves* | **illegal** *the illegal sale of alcohol* | **auction, bring-and-buy, car-boot, garage, jumble, tabletop** | **house, share, etc.**

● VERB + SALE **ban, block, halt, prevent, prohibit, stop** | **close, make** *Closing the sale means that you ask the buyer to say yes or no.* | **hold** *A sale of paintings will be held at the Town Hall on Saturday.*

● SALE + VERB **make sth, realize sth, total sth** *The jumble sale made £358 for cancer research.* ◊ *The sale of paintings totalled £250 000.* | **go ahead/through, proceed** | **fall through** *The sale of the house fell through when the buyer pulled out.*

● SALE + NOUN **agreement, contract | price | proceeds** *to maximize the sale proceeds*

● PREP. **for~** *I see they've put their house up for sale.* **on~** *The new stamps are now on sale at main post offices.*

● PHRASES **conditions of sale** *The conditions of sale were posted up around the auction room.* **a contract of sale, on open sale** *Drugs were on open sale in the club.* **the proceeds/profits from a sale** *All proceeds from the sale of the book will go to charity.* **(on) sale or return** *The novels are delivered to newspaper shops and other outlets on a sale or return basis.*

2 sales amount sold

● ADJ. **good, healthy, high, huge, massive, strong** | **increased** | **poor** | **annual, quarterly, etc.** | **direct, retail, telephone** *Direct sales, by mail order, were up by 15%.* | **domestic** | **export, foreign, international, overseas** | **global, overall, total, world, worldwide** | **gross, net** | **unit, volume** | **high-street** *High-street sales have fallen for the fifth consecutive month.* | **arms, car, house, land, ticket, etc.**

● QUANT. **level, value, volume** *The high volume of sales makes the low pricing policy profitable.*

● VERB + SALES **achieve, have** | **generate** *The advertising campaign generated massive sales.* | **boost**

● SALES + VERB **account for sth** *North American sales account for 40% of the worldwide market.* **amount to sth, reach sth** *sales amounting to over £4 million* ◊ *Sales failed to reach 10 000 units.* | | **exceed sth** | **be/go up, grow, improve, increase, rise, rocket, skyrocket, soar** *Sales of ice cream are up because of the hot weather.* | **be/go down, decline, drop, fall, slump**

● SALES + NOUN **force, people, personnel, staff, team** | **department, office** | **director, manager, rep/representative** | **campaign, drive, effort, promotion** | **estimates, figures, levels, performance, revenue, targets, volume** | **growth** | **slump** *The car manufacturer was forced to shed jobs following a dramatic sales slump.* | **conference** | **presentation** | **report** | **tax** | **contract** | **patter, pitch, talk** *an aggressive sales pitch from the company rep*

● PHRASES **a decline/drop/fall/slowdown/slump in sales, a growth/an increase/a jump/a rise/a surge/an upturn in sales, sales and marketing**

⇨ Note at PER CENT (for more verbs)

⇨ Special page at BUSINESS

3 period of reduced prices

● ADJ. **annual, summer, winter, etc.** | **clothing, furniture, etc.** | **clearance, closing-down**

● PREP. **at/in the~s** *I bought it at the winter sales.*

salesman, salesperson *noun*

● ADJ. **experienced** | **door-to-door, telephone, travelling** | **car, computer, double-glazing, insurance, used car, vacuum cleaner**

● SALESMAN, SALESPERSON + VERB **sell sth** *a travelling salesman selling electrical goods*

⇨ Note at JOB

saliva *noun*

● QUANT. **dribble** *He wiped a dribble of saliva from his chin.*

● VERB + SALIVA **produce** | **swallow**

● SALIVA + VERB **dribble, drip, drool** | **flow** *The smell of food causes the saliva to flow.*

salmon *noun*

● ADJ. **fresh** | **wild** | **farmed** | **smoked** | **tinned** | **pink, red**

● VERB + SALMON **eat, have** | **bake, cook, grill, poach, roast** | **fish for** | **catch, land** | **farm**

● SALMON + NOUN **fillet, steak** | **mousse, paste** | **farm, farming, fishing** | **river** | **pink** *a salmon-pink shirt*

● PHRASES **a fillet of salmon**

salon *noun*

● ADJ. **beauty, grooming, hair, hairdressing** | **leading, professional, top** | **unisex**

● VERB + SALON **go to**

salt *noun*

● ADJ. **soluble** | **potassium, sodium, etc.** | **mineral, rock, sea** | **common, cooking, table** | **celery, garlic**

● QUANT. **grain** | **pinch**

● VERB + SALT **add, put in/on, season sth with, sprinkle (sth with)** *Don't put so much salt on your chips!*

● SALT + NOUN **crystal** | **solution** | **content** *foods with a high salt content* | **intake** *He wants to reduce his salt intake.* | **cellar, pot, shaker** | **air, spray, water** | **marsh** | **mine**

● PHRASES **high/low in salt, salt and pepper** *Add salt and pepper to taste* (= in the quantity preferred).

⇨ Special page at FOOD

salute *noun*

1 military gesture

● ADJ. **military, naval** | **smart** | **mock**

● VERB + SALUTE **give (sb)** *The sentry gave a smart salute and waved us on.* | **acknowledge, return** | **take** *The Queen took the salute as the guardsmen marched past.*

2 action of respect or welcome

● ADJ. **final, last** | **21-gun, etc.** | **special** | **triumphant, victory**

● PREP. **in ~** *The guests raised their glasses in salute.* | **~from** *The retiring editor received a special salute from the local newspaper.* **~to** *His first words were a salute to the people of South Africa.*

salute *verb*

● ADV. **smartly** *The captain stood to attention and saluted smartly.*

● PREP. **with** *He saluted Pippa with a graceful bend of his head.*

salvation *noun*

- ADJ. **individual, personal** | **eternal**
- VERB + SALVATION **bring** | **seek** | **attain, find** | **work out** *I can't solve her problems for her—she'll have to work out her own salvation.*
- PREP. **~ from** *salvation from sin* **~ through** *The medieval Church believed in salvation through faith and works.*

same *adj., pron.* **the same**

- VERBS **be, feel, look, seem, smell, sound, taste** *They both taste just the same to me.* | **remain, stay**
- ADV. **exactly, just, precisely** *I had exactly the same experience.* | **not altogether, not quite** *That's not quite the same thing, is it?* | **almost, basically, broadly, essentially, more or less, nearly, practically, pretty much, roughly, substantially, virtually** *Your new job will be essentially the same as your old one.*
- PREP. **as** *Your dress is nearly the same as mine.*
- PHRASES **one and the same** *We can do the two things at one and the same time.*

sample *noun*

1 small quantity of sth
- ADJ. **blood, DNA, faecal, RNA, rock, serum, tissue, urine, etc.** | **biopsy, clinical**
- VERB + SAMPLE **collect, take** | **provide** *All the athletes had to provide a urine sample.* | **analyse, study, test**
- SAMPLE + NOUN **book** *We looked at sample books to choose the furniture fabric.* | **bottle**
- PREP. **~of** *samples of tissue*

2 people in a survey
- ADJ. **small** | **large, wide** | **population** | **representative** | **random**
- VERB + SAMPLE **draw** *a sample drawn from men aged 35–40*
- SAMPLE + VERB **comprise sth, consist of sth** *Our sample comprised 250 catering workers.*
- SAMPLE + NOUN **size** *A larger sample size yields more reliable data.* | **survey** | **group**
- PREP. **~of** *a wide sample of people*

sample *verb*

- ADV. **randomly**
- PREP. **from** *The survey was done using a group of 100 children randomly sampled from the school population.*

sanction *noun*

1 official permission
- ADJ. **official** | **divine, religious**
- VERB + SANCTION **give sb/sth** *The conference gave its official sanction to the change of policy.*
- PREP. **with/without sb/sth's ~** *No decision can be taken without the sanction of the complete committee.*

2 punishment
- ADJ. **heavy, severe, strict** | **final, ultimate** | **effective** | **limited** | **available** *The school will use all available sanctions to maintain discipline.* | **civil, criminal, disciplinary** | **legal, penal, social**
- VERB + SANCTION **impose** | **use**
- PREP. **~against** *There were strict sanctions against absenteeism.* **~ for** *Employers imposed heavy sanctions for union activity.*

3 (usually **sanctions**) against a country
- ADJ. **punitive** | **international, UN** | **economic, financial, military, trade**
- VERB + SANCTION **impose** | **lift** | **break** *Some companies have broken sanctions by supplying arms to the warring states.* | **call for**

- SANCTIONS + NOUN **order** | **busting** *Several firms were under investigation for sanctions busting.*
- PREP. **~against** *The UN called for sanctions against the invading country.*
- PHRASES **the imposition of sanctions, the lifting of sanctions, a threat of sanctions**

sanction *verb*

- ADV. **officially** | **legally, socially** *Slavery was once socially sanctioned.* | **tacitly** *He had tacitly sanctioned repression against the opposition parties.*
- VERB + SANCTION **refuse to**

sanctuary *noun*

- VERB + SANCTUARY **seek** *Thousands of refugees have sought sanctuary in neighbouring countries.* | **take** *In former times, criminals could take sanctuary inside a church.* | **give sb, offer (sb)**
- PREP. **~ from** *It had been built as a sanctuary from World War II bombs.*

sand *noun*

- ADJ. **fine** *a beach of fine golden sand* | **coarse** | **soft** | **hard** | **damp, wet** | **dry** | **burning, hot** | **golden, silver, white, yellow** | **desert** *the burning desert sands*
- QUANT. **grain** | **patch, strip**
- SAND + NOUN **beach, dune** | **pit** (also **sandpit**) | **castle** (also **sandcastle**)
- PREP. **in the ~** *The children played happily in the sand.* **on the~** *We found her asleep on the sand.*

sandal *noun*

- ADJ. **high-heeled** | **flat, low-heeled** | **open, open-toed** | **strappy**
- QUANT. **pair**
- VERB + SANDAL **kick off**
⇒ Special page at CLOTHES

sandwich *noun*

- ADJ. **cheese, ham, etc.** | **toasted** | **open** | **club**
- QUANT. **round**
- VERB + SANDWICH **make** *He made two rounds of tuna sandwiches.* | **bite into, eat, have, munch, take a bite of**
- SANDWICH + NOUN **filling** | **bag, box** | **bar**
- PREP. **in a/the ~** *What would you like in your sandwich?*

sane *adj.*

- VERBS **be, seem** | **remain, stay** | **keep sb** *Having that little bit of time to myself is what keeps me sane.*
- ADV. **eminently, very** | **completely, perfectly, quite, utterly** *She seems perfectly sane to me.* | **not entirely**

sanitation *noun*

- ADJ. **inadequate, poor, primitive** | **better, improved, proper** | **public**
- SANITATION + NOUN **system** | **project**
- PHRASES **lack of sanitation** *the direct link between disease and lack of adequate sanitation*

sanity *noun*

- VERB + SANITY **doubt, question** *There were moments when he doubted his own sanity.* | **fear for** *I fear for her sanity if this continues much longer.* | **keep, maintain, preserve, retain** *Getting away at weekends is the only way I can retain my sanity.* | **lose** | **recover, regain** | **threaten** *The pace of city life threatens our sanity.*
- SANITY + VERB **return** *Stock market trading slowly settled down as sanity returned.*
- PREP. **for your ~** *Such a move is essential for the sanity of all concerned.*

sap noun

- VERB + SAP **extract** *Maple syrup is made from sap extracted from the sugar maple tree.*
- SAP + VERB **rise** *It was spring, and the sap was rising.*

sarcasm noun

- ADJ. **bitter, heavy, withering | gentle, mild | deliberate | thinly-veiled, veiled**
- QUANT. **edge, hint, note, touch, trace** *There was an edge of sarcasm in her voice.* ◇ *He made the remark without a hint of sarcasm.*
- VERB + SARCASM **be full of, be heavy with, drip** (used about sb's voice) *His voice dripped sarcasm.*
- PREP. **with ~** *'Your skills amaze me,' she said, with heavy sarcasm.* | **~ in** *I detected a touch of sarcasm in his remarks.*

sarcastic adj.

- VERBS **be | become, get**
- ADV. **extremely, very | faintly, lightly, mildly, slightly, somewhat** *His tone was lightly sarcastic.*
- PREP. **about** *He was very sarcastic about my attempts at telling jokes.*

satellite noun

- ADJ. **artificial | commercial, communications, meteorological, reconnaissance, research, spy, weather**
- VERB + SATELLITE **launch, put into orbit, put up, send up**
- SATELLITE + VERB **be in orbit, orbit sth** *About 100 Russian satellites are orbiting the earth.* | **pass over sth** *The satellite passes over Britain every afternoon.* | **monitor sth, track sth** *a new satellite that monitors changes in the environment* | **broadcast sth, relay sth, transmit sth** *The satellite will transmit the information back to earth.*
- SATELLITE + NOUN **photograph, picture | data | link** *The pictures are broadcast through a live satellite link with Tokyo.* | **communications, system, technology | dish, receiver, television/TV | broadcasters, channel, company, station**
- PREP. **from a/the ~** *images from satellites* **via ~** *The BBC broadcast the game via satellite.*

satire noun

- ADJ. **biting, brilliant | political, social** *the recent boom in political satire*
- PREP. **~ on** *The film is a brilliant satire on Hollywood.*

satisfaction noun

- ADJ. **complete, deep, great, immense, tremendous | evident, obvious | quiet | personal | job | sexual**
- QUANT. **level** *My current level of job satisfaction is pretty low.*
- VERB + SATISFACTION **derive, feel, find, gain, get, have, take** *He derived great satisfaction from knowing that his son was happy.* ◇ *Although we didn't win, we were able to take some satisfaction from our performance.* | **bring (sb), give sb, provide (sb with) | express**
- PREP. **in ~** *She watched in satisfaction as he opened the present.* **to your ~** *The matter was resolved to our general satisfaction.* **with ~** *He nodded with evident satisfaction.* | **~ at** *her deep satisfaction at seeing justice done* **~ in** *I find satisfaction in helping people.* **~ of** *I had the satisfaction of proving him wrong.* **~ with** *Both parties expressed their complete satisfaction with the decision.*
- PHRASES **cause/grounds for satisfaction** *Although the team lost, their performance gave cause for satisfaction.* **a feeling/sense of satisfaction, a source of satisfaction** *The children were a major source of satisfaction.*

satisfactory adj.

- VERBS **appear, be, look, prove, seem, sound | consider sth, find sth, regard sth as**
- ADV. **eminently, highly, most, very** *It was all most satisfactory.* | **completely, fully, perfectly, quite | far from, less than, not altogether, not at all, not entirely, not totally, not wholly** *The results were not entirely satisfactory.* | **broadly, fairly, generally, more or less, reasonably | apparently | mutually** *The arrangement has proved mutually satisfactory.*
- PREP. **to** *We hope this proposal is satisfactory to you.*

satisfied adj.

- VERBS **appear, be, feel, look, seem | declare/profess/pronounce yourself** *He declared himself satisfied with the results.*
- ADV. **extremely, more than, very, well** *feeling well satisfied with her day's work* | **absolutely, completely, fully, perfectly, quite, totally | far from, not entirely, not wholly | fairly, generally, reasonably | enough, sufficiently** *Her parents seemed satisfied enough with her progress.* | **apparently**
- PREP. **with** *She seemed satisfied with the arrangements.*

satisfy verb

- VERB + SATISFY **must, should** *The education system must satisfy the needs of all children.* | **be able/unable to, can/could** *The owners were unable to satisfy all the demands of the workers.* ◇ *Nothing could satisfy his desire for power.* | **seem to** *His answer seemed to satisfy her.* | **be enough to, be sufficient to** *Her description of events was not enough to satisfy the court.* | **fail to** *The meal failed to satisfy his hunger.*

satisfying adj.

- VERBS **be | find sth**
- ADV. **deeply, eminently, extremely, highly, immensely, really, richly, very** *There's something deeply satisfying about eating vegetables that you have grown yourself.* | **completely, thoroughly, wholly | quite | personally** *the need for a personally satisfying set of beliefs* | **mutually** *a mutually satisfying relationship* | **aesthetically, logically, musically**

saturation noun

- ADJ. **market**
- VERB + SATURATION **approach, be close to** *The company's sales are now close to saturation in many western countries.* | **reach**
- SATURATION + NOUN **level, point** *Demand for the product has reached saturation point.* | **coverage** *television's saturation coverage of the World Cup* | **bombing**

Saturday noun

⇨ Note at DAY

sauce noun

- ADJ. **thick, thin | creamy | piquant, rich, spicy, tangy | delicate | smooth | lumpy | barbecue, chilli, soy, sweet and sour, Tabasco, tomato, white** (= made from butter, flour and milk), **etc.** *fish in white sauce* | **pasta**
- VERB + SAUCE **make | thicken | reduce | pour on/over sth, spoon on/over sth** *Pour the sauce over the pasta.*
- SAUCE + VERB **thicken**
- SAUCE + NOUN **bottle**
- PREP. **in ~** *chicken in white wine sauce* **with ~** *We had lamb with mint sauce.*

⇨ Special page at FOOD

saucepan (also pan) noun

- ADJ. **non-stick** | **heavy, heavy-based**
- VERB + SAUCEPAN **cover** *Cover the saucepan and remove from the heat.* | **remove from the heat** | **add sth to, put sth in/into, return sth to** | **remove sth from**
- SAUCEPAN + VERB **contain sth** *a pan containing lots of boiling salted water*
- PREP. **in/into a/the ~** *Heat one tablespoon of oil in a saucepan.* ◊ *Pour the pasta into a pan of boiling water.*

saunter verb

- ADV. **casually, slowly** | **along, back, in, out, over** *She sauntered in fifteen minutes late.*
- PREP. **along, into, out of, through, etc.** *He sauntered casually through the door.*
- PHRASES **come sauntering** *He came sauntering over to meet us.*

sausage noun

- ADJ. **beef, garlic, liver, pork, etc.** | **vegetarian** | **spicy**
- QUANT. **slice**
- VERB + SAUSAGE **eat, have** | **cook, fry, grill**
- SAUSAGE + VERB **sizzle**
- SAUSAGE + NOUN **meat, skin** | **roll**
- ⇨ Special page at FOOD

savage adj.

- VERBS **be, look, seem, sound** | **become**
- ADV. **downright, really, very** | **increasingly** *The war became increasingly savage.* | **rather** *a rather savage dog*

save noun

- ADJ. **brilliant, excellent, fine, good, great, outstanding, spectacular, superb** | **crucial, important, vital** | **diving** | **one-handed**
- VERB + SAVE **bring off, make, pull off** *Casillas made some spectacular saves.*
- PREP. **~ by/from** *some great saves from both keepers*

save verb

1 keep sb/sth safe
- VERB + SAVE **be able/unable to, can/could, may, might (just)** *It's a trick that might just save us from total disaster.* | **help (to)** *She helped save my career.* | **battle to, try to** *Doctors battled to save the little boy's life.* | **manage to** *We managed to save the animals from being put down.*
- PREP. **from** *They saved the paintings from destruction.*
- PHRASES **an attempt/effort to save sth** *a last, desperate attempt to save his marriage* **a battle/bid/campaign to save sth**

2 not spend money
- ADV. **up**
- VERB + SAVE **try to** | **manage to**
- PREP. **for** *I'm trying to save up for my holiday.*

3 in football/hockey
- ADV. **brilliantly**
- PREP. **from** *The goalie saved brilliantly from Johnson's long-range shot.*

saver noun

- ADJ. **existing** *Only children whose parents are existing savers may open an account.* | **small** *encouraging small savers to invest in UK companies*
- PREP. **~ with** *savers with the United Bank*

saving noun

1 amount not used or wasted
- ADJ. **big, considerable, great, major, significant, substantial** | **estimated, expected, possible, potential** *The potential savings are enormous.* | **overall, total** | **actual, net** | **cost, financial** | **energy, fuel** *the advantages of energy saving*
- VERB + SAVING **add up to, give (sb), mean, represent, result in** *For a family of four this can mean a saving of around £500.* | **offer (sb)** *This design offers considerable savings in fuel efficiency.* | **achieve, make** *We need to see where financial savings can be made.* | **pass on** *We will pass on this saving to our customers.*
- SAVING + VERB **come from sth, result from sth** *The major savings come from reduced labour costs.*
- PREP. **with a ~** *This was done, with a saving of 40% in staff costs.* | **~ for** *a saving for club members* **~ from** *savings from the use of the new technology* **~ in** *a significant saving in energy costs* **~ on** *You can have all the benefits of membership while making a big saving on price.* **~ to** *This represents a saving to British business of about £175 million a year.*

2 **savings** money saved in a bank, etc.
- ADJ. **small** | **long-term** | **life** | **personal, private**
- VERB + SAVINGS **have** *I haven't got any savings.* | **invest** | **deposit, put** *My grandfather refused to put his savings in the bank.* | **take out, withdraw** | **break into, dip into** | **tie up** *You get higher interest if you agree to tie up your savings for a long period.* | **build up** *I was determined to build up some savings.* | **spend, use (up)** | **live on** *She lost her job and had to live on her savings.* | **lose** *The couple lost their entire life savings on the venture.*
- SAVINGS + VERB **grow**
- SAVINGS + NOUN **account, bank** | **certificate** | **plan, scheme**
- PHRASES **access to your savings** *The card gives you instant access to your savings.*

saviour noun

- ADJ. **possible, potential**
- VERB + SAVIOUR **hail sb as, see sb/sth as, treat sb as** *The people clearly saw her as their saviour.* | **be acclaimed as, emerge as** *He emerged as the potential saviour of the club.*

say verb

- ADV. **aloud, out loud** | **loudly** | **gently, quietly, softly** | **gruffly, huskily, thickly** | **at once** | **at last, at length, finally** | **again, repeatedly** | **simply** '*I am home,*' *he said simply.* | **hastily, hurriedly, promptly, quickly** | **slowly** | **steadily** | **abruptly, suddenly** | **briskly, curtly, shortly, tersely** | **angrily, bitterly, crossly, fiercely, furiously, sharply** '*I don't know,*' *she said crossly.* | **bluntly, flatly** | **firmly** | **harshly, sternly** | **brightly, cheerfully, happily** | **miserably, sadly** | **gravely, grimly, seriously, solemnly** | **airily, casually, easily, lightly, smoothly** '*There's nothing wrong with him,*' *she said airily.* | **stiffly, tightly** | **proudly** | **carefully, thoughtfully** | **conversationally** | **calmly, evenly, mildly** | **patiently** | **impatiently** | **ungraciously** | **politely** | **soothingly** | **apologetically** | **awkwardly, lamely** | **drily, tartly** | **coldly, coolly, icily** | **breathlessly** | **absently, vaguely** | **honestly, truthfully** *Can you honestly say you're sorry?*
- VERB + SAY **be about to, be going to** *I've forgotten what I was going to say.* | **hasten to** | **long to, want to** *I want to say how much we have all enjoyed this evening.* | **hate to** *I hate to say it, but I think Stephen may be right.* | **dare (to)** *I dared not say a word about it to anyone.* | **suffice (it) to** *Suffice it to say, I refused to get involved.* | **be fair to** *It is fair to say a considerable amount of effort went into the project.* | **be untrue to** | **have nothing to, have something to** *Be quiet, I have something to say.* | **hear sb, overhear sb** *I heard him say they were leaving tomorrow.*
- PREP. **about** *Do you have anything to say about this?* **to** *That's not what he said to me.*
- PHRASES **be quoted as saying sth** *The minister was*

quoted as saying that the government would do whatever was necessary to restore order. **a thing to say** *That was a very cruel thing to say.*

saying *noun*

- ADJ. **well-known | old, traditional | favourite** *It was one of my mother's favourite sayings.*
- PREP. **~about** *traditional sayings about the weather*
- PHRASES **as the saying goes** *'Practice makes perfect,' as the old saying goes.*

scaffolding *noun*

- QUANT. **piece**
- VERB + SCAFFOLDING **erect, put up | remove, take down | climb (up)**
- SCAFFOLDING + NOUN **pole**
- PREP. **on the ~** *There are several builders working on the scaffolding.*

scale *noun*

1 size/extent
- ADJ. **full** *It was several days before the full scale of the accident became clear.* | **big, considerable, grand, greater, huge, large, massive, monumental, vast | modest, small | sheer** *It is difficult to comprehend the sheer scale of the suffering caused by the war.* | **unprecedented** *a misuse of presidential power on an unprecedented scale* | **ambitious, lavish** *Do they always entertain on such a lavish scale?* | **global, international, national, regional, world | commercial** *The dolls are now produced on a commercial scale.* | **human** *The city would operate on a more human scale if cars were banned from the centre.*
- VERB + SCALE **increase | reduce**
- PREP. **in~** *The paintings are small in scale.* **on a~** *pollution on a massive scale*
- PHRASES **an economy of scale** *Economies of scale enable the larger companies to lower their prices.* **the scale of the problem**

2 range of values
- ADJ. **fixed | sliding** *Benefits are paid on a sliding scale according to family income.* | **rating | time** *Can you give me any sort of time scale for the completion of the building work?* | **evolutionary | social | pay, salary, wage** *The company has a five-point pay scale.* | **Beaufort, Richter** *The earthquake measured 6.4 on the Richter scale.*
- VERB + SCALE **go/move down/up, rise up** *He has risen up the social scale from rather humble beginnings.*
- SCALE + VERB **go/range from ... to ...** *a scale ranging from 'utterly miserable' to 'deliriously happy'*
- PREP. **on a/the~** *Where do birds come on the evolutionary scale?* | **~of ... to ...** *On a scale of 1 to 10, he scores 7.*
- PHRASES **the bottom/end/top of the scale** *After 10 years, she had worked her way to the top of the pay scale.*

3 relation between actual size and size of a model, etc.
- VERB + SCALE **draw sth to | have**
- SCALE + NOUN **drawing, model** *He's made a scale model of the Eiffel Tower.*
- PREP. **to~** *The plan of the building is not drawn to scale.* | **~of ... to ...** *The map has a scale of one centimetre to the kilometre.* ◊ *a scale of 1:25 000*

4 in music
- ADJ. **major, minor | chromatic, diatonic, diminished, pentatonic, whole-tone**
- VERB + SCALE **play, sing | practise** *We could hear her practising her scales.*
- PREP. **~of** *the scale of C major*

5 on a fish, etc.
- ADJ. **overlapping | fine, thin | armoured | fish**
- VERB + SCALE **be covered in/with**

scales *noun*

- ADJ. **weighing | bathroom, kitchen**
- QUANT. **pair, set** *a pair of kitchen scales*
- VERB + SCALES **put sth on/onto, weigh sth on | get on/onto, stand on, step on/onto | tip** *At birth, she tipped the scales at a healthy 7lb 9oz.*
- PREP. **on the~** *I had a shock when I stood on the scales.*

scalp *noun*

- ADJ. **itchy | flaky**
- VERB + SCALP **massage | scratch**
- SCALP + VERB **itch | crawl, prickle** *Her scalp crawled with tension.* | **gleam** *His pink scalp gleamed through his sparse hair.*
- SCALP + NOUN **condition, problem** *treatment for hair and scalp problems* | **massage, treatment**

scan *noun*

1 quick look
- ADJ. **quick, rapid** *A quick scan of the local paper revealed nothing.*
- PREP. **~of**

2 examination by a machine
- ADJ. **body, bone, brain | ultrasound | routine**
- VERB + SCAN **have | give sb | take**
- SCAN + VERB **reveal sth** *A routine scan revealed abnormalities in the foetus.*
- PREP. **~of** *The doctors took a scan of his thigh bone.*

scan *verb*

- ADV. **carefully | quickly, rapidly | anxiously, nervously** *She scanned the street nervously, looking for the two men.* | **eagerly**
- PREP. **for** *I scanned the paper for news.*

scandal *noun*

- ADJ. **big, great, major | fresh | national, public | bribery, corruption, drug/drugs, financial, political, sex/sexual**
- QUANT. **series** *The government was rocked by a series of scandals.*
- VERB + SCANDAL **cause, create | expose, reveal, uncover | be embroiled in, be implicated in, be involved in, be mixed up in** *There have been calls for the resignation of the minister involved in the sex scandal.* | **be rocked by | attract** *Their relationship attracted a lot of scandal.* | **spread, stir up** *She's always trying to stir up scandal.* | **cover up, hush up**
- SCANDAL + VERB **break, develop, erupt** *The scandal broke on the front pages of all the papers the next day.* | **involve sb/sth | surround sb/sth** *financial scandals surrounding the government*
- PREP. **in a/the~** *He was imprisoned for his part in the bribery scandal.* | **~over** *the scandals over corruption in public life*
- PHRASES **the centre of a scandal** *The apartment was paid for by the bank at the centre of the scandal.* **a hint/suggestion of scandal** *Until the story was published there had been no hint of scandal.*

scapegoat *noun*

- ADJ. **convenient, easy**
- VERB + SCAPEGOAT **make sb, use sb as** *He has been made a scapegoat for the company's failures.*
- PREP. **~for** *They are being made the scapegoats for all the ills of society.*

scar *noun*

- ADJ. **deep, large, long | puckered | disfiguring,**

ugly, unsightly | permanent | emotional, mental, psychological *Her mental scars will take time to heal.*
- VERB + SCAR **leave** | **bear** (*often figurative*) *The countryside still bears the scars of the recent hurricane.*
- SCAR + VERB **form** | **heal**
- SCAR + NOUN **tissue**
- PREP. **~on** *The cut left a permanent scar on his arm.*

scar *verb* (often **be scarred**)

- ADV. **badly, deeply, hideously** *His face was badly scarred by the fire.* | **emotionally, mentally, physically, psychologically** *She was both physically and mentally scarred by the accident.* | **permanently**
- PREP. **with** (*figurative*) *Their minds were scarred with bitterness.*
- PHRASES **be scarred for life, leave sb scarred** *The accident left him permanently scarred.*

scarce *adj.*

- VERBS **be, seem** | **become, grow** *Medical supplies were growing scarce.* | **remain**
- ADV. **extremely, particularly, very | increasingly** *Skilled workers were becoming increasingly scarce.* | **pretty, rather, relatively, somewhat** *Money was somewhat scarce after the war.*

scarcity *noun*

- ADJ. **great | relative**
- SCARCITY + NOUN **value** *Old properties in the town have acquired a scarcity value.*
- PREP. **~ of** *There is a great scarcity of food in the drought-stricken areas.*
- PHRASES **in times/years of scarcity** *In times of scarcity, lions will travel great distances in search of food.*

scare *noun*

- ADJ. **major, terrible** *a major health scare* | **minor** | **bomb | food, health** | **Aids, BSE, etc.**
- VERB + SCARE **cause | give sb** *It wasn't a serious heart attack, but it gave him a terrible scare.* | **get, have**
- SCARE + NOUN **story, tactics** *The government used scare tactics to get parents to have their children vaccinated against the disease.*
- PREP. **~about/over** *the scare over British beef*
- PHRASES **a bit of a/quite a scare** *I got a bit of a scare when the police rang.*

scare *verb*

- ADV. **really | easily** *He doesn't scare easily.*
- VERB + SCARE **try to**
- PREP. **into** *They're just trying to scare us into letting out the secret.* **with** *You don't scare me with your threats!*
- PHRASES **scare sb silly/stiff/to death** (*informal*) *The very thought of flying scares me stiff.* **scare the hell/life/living daylights out of sb** (*informal*) *You scared the life out of me, hiding like that!* **scare the pants off sb** (*informal*)

scared *adj.*

- VERBS **be, be running** (*figurative*), **feel, look, seem, sound** *They had their opponent running scared.* | **get**
- ADV. **dead, downright, extremely, really, shit** (*taboo*), **very | a bit, a little, pretty, quite, rather | just, plain** *He wasn't ill, Sophie decided. He was just plain scared.*
- PREP. **about** *It's only a little injection. It's nothing to be scared about.* **at** *feeling a little scared at the thought of the operation* **of** *I'm really scared of heights.*
- PHRASES **scared out of your wits, scared stiff** (*informal*), **scared to death** (*informal*)

scarf *noun*

- ADJ. **long | chiffon, silk, woollen | college, football**
- VERB + SCARF **wind around sth, wrap around sth** *He wrapped his scarf around his neck.* | **knot, tie** *She had a scarf tied over her head.* | **unwind**
- SCARF + VERB **cover sth** *Her hair was covered by a silk scarf.*
- ⇨ Special page at CLOTHES

scarlet *adj.*

1 bright red in colour
- ADJ. **bright, brilliant, flaming, vivid**
- ⇨ Special page at COLOUR

2 red in the face
- VERBS **be | become, blush, flush, go, turn**
- ADV. **absolutely** *He had gone absolutely scarlet with embarrassment.*
- ADJ. **bright** *She flushed bright scarlet.*
- PREP. **with**

scattered *adj.*

- VERBS **be, lie**
- ADV. **liberally** *Large vases of flowers were liberally scattered about the room.* | **randomly | thinly | widely** *living in widely scattered communities* | **geographically | everywhere**
- PREP. **about/around, across, among, on, over** *Broken glass lay scattered over the floor.* **throughout, with** *The whole area was scattered with debris.*

scenario *noun*

- ADJ. **future, likely, possible** *The more likely scenario is that the president will resign and an election will be held.* | **unlikely | optimistic | doomsday, nightmare, pessimistic, worst, worst-case | dramatic | alternative**
- VERB + SCENARIO **consider, construct, imagine | describe, paint** *the scenario painted by some sections of the Western press* | **enact, play out** *He enjoyed playing out the various scenarios in his own mind.*
- SCENARIO + VERB **unfold**
- PREP. **in a/the ~** *In a worst-case scenario, the disease will reach epidemic proportions.* **under a/the~** *Under any of these scenarios, the company will run into debt.*

scene *noun*

1 place where sth happened
- ADJ. **accident, crash, murder** *footprints found near the murder scene*
- VERB + SCENE **attend, be on** *PC Michael Potter attended the scene.* | **arrive at/on, reach** *An ambulance soon arrived at the scene of the accident.* | **leave | be called to** *The police were called to the scene.* | **survey** *He surveyed the scene with horror.*
- PREP. **at the ~** *Police say the man died at the scene.* **on the ~** *Photographers were on the scene in seconds.* | **~ of** *The criminal often revisits the scene of the crime.*

2 what you see around you
- ADJ. **beautiful, charming, idyllic, peaceful, picturesque | appalling, distressing, horrific | touching | bizarre, extraordinary, strange** *She opened the door on an extraordinary scene of disorder.* | **familiar | domestic** *a touching domestic scene* | **ever-changing** *I stared out of the window of the train on the ever-changing scene.* | **city, country, rural, street**
- VERB + SCENE **watch, witness**
- SCENE + VERB **occur, take place, unfold** *We sat in horror watching the scenes of violence unfold before us.* | **be reminiscent of sth** *Paramedics tended the wounded in scenes reminiscent of wartime.*
- PREP. **amid/amidst ~s of** *The star arrived amidst scenes of excitement.* **in a/the ~** | **~ from** *scenes from Greek*

mythology ~ **of** *He painted scenes of country life.* ◇ *The battlefield was a scene of utter carnage.*
● PHRASES **a change of scene** *You're exhausted. What you need is a complete change of scene.*

3 one part of book, play, etc.
● ADJ. **opening | climactic, final, last | dramatic, funny, steamy, touching, tragic** *The film has several steamy bedroom scenes.* | **action, battle, bedroom, crowd, death, fight, love, nude, sex**
● VERB + SCENE **act, play** *She plays the love scenes brilliantly.* | **rehearse, run through** *to run through the final scene again* | **film, shoot** | **set** *The scene is set in the first paragraph with an account of Sally's childhood.* | **change** | **steal** *The little girl stole the scene from all the big stars.*
● SCENE + VERB **take place | shift** *Then the scene shifts to the kitchen.*
● SCENE + NOUN **change**
● PREP. **in a/the** ~ *He appears in the opening scene.* | **~ between** *There is a dramatic fight scene between the two brothers.*
● PHRASES **behind the scenes** (= behind the stage), **a change of scene**

4 public display of anger, etc.
● ADJ. **big | little | angry, ugly, unpleasant, terrible | emotional, violent**
● VERB + SCENE **cause, create, make** *Quiet, now! Don't make a scene!* | **have**
● PREP. **~ between** *There have been a couple of ugly scenes between him and the manager.* **~ with** *She had some terrible scenes with her father.*

5 area of activity
● ADJ. **burgeoning, flourishing, lively | contemporary | international, local, world | art, club, comedy, drug/drugs, economic, education/educational, fashion, gay, literary, music/musical, political, social, sporting, etc.** *He is heavily involved in the local art scene.*
● VERB + SCENE **be involved in, be part of | appear on, arrive on, come on/onto** *Owen arrived on the international scene in the 1998 World Cup.* | **vanish from** *Many of the stars of the nineties have completely vanished from the music scene.* | **dominate**
● PREP. **on/onto the** ~ *the eruption of Cuban music onto the world scene*
● PHRASES **a newcomer to the scene** *The film's director is a newcomer to the Hollywood scene.* **not your scene** (*informal*) *Hillwalking is not my scene, so I stayed at home.*

scenery *noun*

1 features of the countryside
● ADJ. **beautiful, breathtaking, delightful, dramatic, fantastic, glorious, impressive, magnificent, spectacular, stunning, superb, wonderful | changing, ever-changing, varied | surrounding** *The village is charming and the surrounding scenery superb.* | **passing | coastal, mountain, mountainous**
● VERB + SCENERY **admire, enjoy, look at, take in** *An observation deck lets you take in the passing scenery.*
● SCENERY + VERB **change**
● PREP. **amid/amidst/in (the)** ~ *The hotel lies amidst spectacular mountain scenery.* **through (the)** ~ *The train passes through some magnificent scenery.*
● PHRASES **the beauty of the scenery, a change of scenery** *For a complete change of scenery, take a ferry out to one of the nearby islands.* **a variety of scenery** *The river passes through a rich variety of scenery.*

2 in a theatre
● VERB + SCENERY **set up | change**
● PREP. **~ for** *That table is part of the scenery for Act 2.*

scent *noun*

1 pleasant smell
● ADJ. **heady, heavy, pungent, rich, sharp, strong** *the heavy scent of Indian cooking* | **delicate, faint | sweet | beautiful, lovely | fresh** *the fresh scent of flowers* | **warm | musky | exotic**
● VERB + SCENT **have** *This flower has no scent.* | **be filled with** *The air was filled with the scent of lilac.* | **give off, release** *The flowers give off a heady scent at night.* | **smell**
● SCENT + VERB **come, drift** *From the vine outside came the scent of honey.* | **fill sth** *The scent of pine filled the room.* | **linger** *The scent of incense lingered in the air.*

2 smell that an animal/a person leaves behind
● ADJ. **body, human, masculine, personal, sexual**
● VERB + SCENT **be on, have** *The dog was on the scent of a rabbit.* ◇ *The hounds have the scent.* | **leave** *The cat had left its scent on the sofa.* | **catch, pick up** *One of the hounds had picked up the scent of a fox.* | **lose | follow**
● SCENT + NOUN **gland | trail**

3 liquid with a sweet smell that you put on your body
● ADJ. **expensive | cheap**
● QUANT. **bottle**
● VERB + SCENT **use, wear | dab on, put on, spray on** *She dabbed some scent on her wrists.* | **smell | reek of, smell of** *She reeked of cheap scent.*
● SCENT + NOUN **bottle**

scented *adj.*

● VERBS **be**
● ADV. **heavily, highly, powerfully, richly, strongly** *richly scented flowers* | **delicately, lightly** *the delicately scented writing paper* | **beautifully, sweetly**
● PREP. **with** *The air was scented with the smell of pines.*

sceptic *noun*

● VERB + SCEPTIC **convince, win over** *He has managed to convince even the sceptics.* | **confound**
● SCEPTIC + VERB **argue sth, point out sth, say sth** *Sceptics will argue that no such scheme has ever proved successful.*
● PREP. **~ about** *She is a sceptic about the dangers of global warming.*
● PHRASES **prove the sceptics right/wrong** *Events since the elections have proved the sceptics right.*

sceptical *adj.*

● VERBS **be, look, remain | become**
● ADV. **deeply, extremely, highly, very | increasingly | fairly, mildly, rather, slightly, somewhat** *in a mildly sceptical tone of voice* | **openly** *They remained openly sceptical about her promises of improvement.*
● PREP. **about** *He is deeply sceptical about the value of teaching poetry.* **as to** *Many were sceptical as to whether the plan would succeed.* **of** *They are highly sceptical of political leaders.*

scepticism *noun*

● ADJ. **complete, total | considerable, deep, extreme, great | healthy | growing | widespread | initial** *My initial scepticism was replaced with respectful admiration.*
● QUANT. **certain amount, degree, great deal** *I regard their press releases with a degree of scepticism.*
● VERB + SCEPTICISM **have** *She has a healthy scepticism towards the claims in the company's report.* | **express, voice**
● PREP. **with** ~ *This theory was initially received with great scepticism by her fellow scientists.* | **~ about/over/towards** *He expressed a great deal of scepticism about the value of psychoanalysis.*

schedule noun

- ADJ. **daily, weekly, etc.** | **ambitious, busy, demanding, gruelling, heavy, hectic, punishing, tight** | **rigid, strict** | **business, production, training, work, etc.** | **flight, television, etc.** *disruptions to flight schedules caused by the strike*
- VERB + SCHEDULE **have, work to** *She has an very demanding schedule.* | **arrange, design, draw up, plan, prepare** | **amend** | **be/go according to, keep to, meet, run to, stick to** *At this stage everything is going according to schedule.* ◇ *We had to work a lot of overtime to meet the strict production schedule.* | **be/run ahead of** | **be/fall/run/slip behind** | **interrupt, take time out of** *The president took time out of his busy schedule to visit our school.*
- PREP. **in the** ~ *Allow time in the schedule for holidays and illness.* **on** ~ *The project is right on schedule.*

schedule verb

- ADV. **currently** | **originally** *The meeting was originally scheduled for March 12th.* | **provisionally, tentatively**
- PREP. **for** *The film is scheduled for release next month.*
- PHRASES **be scheduled to begin/start/take place** *The Grand Prix is scheduled to take place on July 4th.*

scheme noun

- ADJ. **major** | **ambitious, grand, grandiose** | **imaginative, ingenious, innovative** | **crazy, hare-brained, ill-conceived** | **successful** | **voluntary** | **pilot** *The project is based on a successful pilot scheme in Glasgow.* | **incentive, insurance, pension, recycling, share, training, etc.**
- VERB + SCHEME **have** *He has an ingenious scheme to attract funding.* | **come up with, design, devise, draw up, dream up, plan, prepare, propose, think up** *She's come up with a hare-brained scheme for getting her novel published.* | **approve** | **announce, establish, initiate, introduce, launch, organize, set up, start** *The government set up a scheme of limited public health assistance in 1992.* | **adopt, carry out, operate, run** | **back** *a government-backed scheme* | **be in, join, participate in, take part in** | **use** | **leave** *I opted to leave the company pension scheme.* | **abolish, wind up**
- SCHEME + VERB **offer sth, provide sth** | **allow sth, enable sth** *The scheme allows customers to trade in their own computer against the cost of a new one.* | **aim to, be aimed at sth, be designed for/to, involve sth** *a scheme involving local libraries* | **apply to sth, cover sth** *The scheme applies to families with three or more children.* | **go ahead, proceed** *The scheme has been given approval to go ahead.* | **succeed, work** | **collapse, fail**
- PREP. **in a/the** ~ *Schools in the scheme will receive an annual grant.* **under a/the** ~ *Under the scheme, land would be sold to building companies.* | ~ **for** *Is this another one of your crazy schemes for making money?* ◇ *a training scheme for unemployed teenagers* ~ **whereby** *a scheme whereby the elderly will be provided with help in the home*

schizophrenia noun

- ADJ. **chronic**
- VERB + SCHIZOPHRENIA **have, suffer from** | **develop** | **diagnose** | **treat**
- SCHIZOPHRENIA + NOUN **sufferer**
- ⇨ Special page at ILLNESS

scholar noun

- ADJ. **brilliant, distinguished, eminent, famous, great, leading, outstanding** | **visiting** | **biblical, classical, French, history, literary, etc.**

scholarship noun

- VERB + SCHOLARSHIP **gain, get, win** | **award (sb), give (sb)** *The Fund awards four scholarships every year.*
- SCHOLARSHIP + NOUN **exam/examination** | **programme, scheme** | **student**
- PREP. **on a** ~ *Two of the girls here are on scholarships.* | ~ **to** *He won a scholarship to Queens' College, Cambridge.*

school noun

- ADJ. **elementary, high, middle, nursery, prep/preparatory, primary, secondary** | **comprehensive, grammar, secondary modern** | **direct-grant, grant-maintained, state** | **independent, private, public** (In Britain 'public schools' are private.) | **special** *She attends a special school for children with learning difficulties.* | **boys', co-educational, girls', mixed, mixed-sex, single-sex** | **boarding, residential, day** | **Sunday** | **summer** | **local, rural, village** | **art, business, dance, drama, film, language, medical, riding, secretarial, training, etc.**
- VERB + SCHOOL **attend, go to** | **start** | **finish, leave** | **skip, (play) truant from** | **be/stay off, keep sb off** *His mum kept him off school for two weeks when he was ill.*
- SCHOOL + NOUN **curriculum** | **student** | **teacher** (also **schoolteacher**) *She's a middle-school teacher.* | **leaver** | **building, hall, library** | **term, year** | **holidays** | **bus** | **meals** | **rules** | **uniform** | **assembly** | **age** *She's got four children of school age.*
- PREP. **after** ~ *We're going to play football after school.* **at (a/the)** ~ *She didn't do very well at school.* ◇ *Their son's at the school near the station.* **in (a/the)** ~ *Are the children still in school?* ◇ *the cleverest child in the school*

schooling noun

- ADJ. **good** *She received the best schooling the town could offer.* | **bad, poor** *Many children are disadvantaged by poor schooling.* | **compulsory** *Compulsory schooling ends at sixteen.* | **formal** | **primary, secondary**
- VERB + SCHOOLING **get, have, receive** *He has had no formal schooling.* | **continue (with)** *She continued with her schooling after a long period of illness.* | **interrupt**
- SCHOOLING + VERB **suffer** *We will stay in this country, as we don't want her schooling to suffer.*
- SCHOOLING + NOUN **system**
- PHRASES **access to schooling** *A child's access to schooling varies greatly from area to area.* **years of schooling** *children's development in the early years of schooling*

science noun

- ADJ. **hard** *His essay is not based on hard science.* | **exact, inexact** *Politics is as much an art form as an exact science.* | **popular** *The magazine contains a lot of popular science.* | **basic, school** *I was trying to remember what I had learnt about gravity in school science.* | **applied, experimental** | **biological, human, life, natural, physical** *The life sciences include biology and botany.* | **agricultural, earth, environmental, food, marine, soil** | **forensic** | **medical, veterinary** | **behavioural, political, social** | **computer, information** | **cognitive, linguistic** | **space** | **sports** | **management**
- SCIENCE + NOUN **education, research, teaching** | **museum, park**
- PREP. ~ **of** *Meteorology is the science of the weather.*
- PHRASES **the history of science, the laws of science, science and technology, the world of science** *His experiments have achieved notoriety in the world of science.*
- ⇨ Note at SUBJECT (for verbs and more nouns)

scientific adj.

- VERBS **be, look, seem**

• ADV. **highly** *It all looks highly scientific!* | **truly** | **purely** *Her curiosity was purely scientific.* | **not very** *His approach was not very scientific.*

scientist noun

• ADJ. **brilliant, good, great** | **distinguished, eminent, famous, leading, respected** | **trained** | **chief, senior** | **serious** | **mad** (*often humorous*) *She had an image of a mad scientist working in his laboratory.* | **professional** | **amateur** | **independent** | **government** | **fellow** *She gave a lecture to 2 000 fellow scientists in Kyoto.* | **experimental, laboratory, research** | **applied** | **natural, physical** | **agricultural, earth, environmental, food, marine, soil** | **atomic, nuclear** | **rocket** (*often humorous*) *You don't have to be a rocket scientist* (= very clever) *to do this job.* | **forensic, medical** | **behavioural, political, social** | **computer** | **young** *a contest for young scientists*
• QUANT. **group, team**
• SCIENTIST + VERB **be interested in sth, be involved in sth, specialize in sth, study sth, work (on sth)** *scientists interested in Antarctic research* | **know sth** | **estimate sth** *The scientists estimate that nearly two-thirds of the continent has become drier over the past 60 years.* | **argue sth, believe sth, claim sth, say sth, suggest sth, warn (of) sth** *Scientists warned of even greater eruptions to come.* | **examine sth** | **discover sth, find sth, identify sth, reveal sth** | **agree (on) sth, conclude sth** | **disagree (on) sth** | **report sth** | **develop sth** *Scientists have developed an injection that doesn't use a needle.*
⇨ Note at JOB

scissors noun

• ADJ. **blunt, sharp** | **kitchen** | **nail**
• QUANT. **pair** *a pair of nail scissors*
• VERB + SCISSORS **cut sth with, use** *Don't use these scissors to cut paper or card.*
• SCISSORS + VERB **cut** *These scissors don't cut very well.*

scold verb

• ADV. **gently** | **severely**
• PREP. **for** *Rose scolded the child gently for her bad behaviour.*

scope noun

1 opportunity
• ADJ. **full** *In her new house she had full scope for her passion for gardening.* | **ample, considerable, enormous, great, tremendous** | **limited**
• VERB + SCOPE **have** | **allow (sb), give sb, leave (sb), offer (sb), provide (sb with)** *These courses give students more scope for developing their own ideas.* | **increase** | **cut down, reduce**
• PREP. **~ for** *There is limited scope for creativity in my job.*

2 range/extent
• ADJ. **broad, wide** | **limited, narrow** *The scope of the exhibition is disappointingly narrow.* | **geographical, territorial** *The geographical scope of product markets has widened since the war.*
• VERB + SCOPE **broaden, expand, extend, increase, widen** | **limit, reduce, restrict** | **define, determine** *These criteria were used to determine the scope of the curriculum.*
• SCOPE + VERB **broaden, expand, extend, increase, widen** | **narrow**
• PREP. **beyond/outside the~ of** *The subject lies outside the scope of this book.* **in (sth's)~** *The survey is too limited in (its) scope.* **within the~ of** *These disputes fall within the scope of the local courts.*

score noun

1 in a game, competition, etc.
• ADJ. **big, excellent, good, high, perfect, record, top** | **bad, low, poor** | **average, mean** | **close, level** *The score was close in the final match.* | **overall, total** | **final** | **cricket, football, etc.**
• VERB + SCORE **achieve, finish with, get, have** | **give (sb)** *He got round the course in 72, giving him an average score of 70.* | **make, take** *A goal in the last few minutes took the score to 4–2.* | **keep, record** *I'll keep (the) score.* | **level, tie** *Figo levelled the scores with a curling free kick.*
• SCORE + VERB **be, stand at** *At half-time the score stood at 3–0.*
• SCORE + NOUN **card** (also **scorecard**), **chart, sheet** *Inamoto had a good game but failed to get his name on the score sheet* (= failed to score).
• PREP. **~against** *the best score for years against Italy*

2 in a test
• ADJ. **excellent, good, high, perfect, record, top** | **bad, low, poor** | **average, mean** | **aggregate, overall, total** | **IQ, test**
• VERB + SCORE **achieve, get, have, obtain** | **give sb** | **boost, increase** *Some scientists claim that vitamins will boost your child's IQ score.*
• SCORE + VERB **range** *Most ten-year-olds had scores ranging between 50 and 70.*
• PREP. **~for** *She got an unusually low score for creativity.*

3 written music
• ADJ. **full** | **music/musical** | **orchestral, piano, vocal** *the vocal score of 'The Magic Flute'* | **film**
• VERB + SCORE **play, read, write**
• PREP. **in a/the~** *a mistake in the piano score*

score verb

1 win points/goals, etc.
• ADV. **nearly** | **easily** *Cunningham broke away and ran some 40 metres to score easily.*
• VERB + SCORE **try to** | **manage to** | **fail to, have yet to** *Peter Walker has yet to score this season.* | **look likely to** *Villa always looked the team most likely to score.*
• PREP. **against** *The England team failed to score against Italy on Saturday.* **for** *She has not yet scored for her new club.* **with** *He scored with a neat header.*
• PHRASES **come close to scoring** *It was Robertson who came closest to scoring.* **open the scoring** *Zidane opened the scoring in the seventh minute of the game.*

2 gain marks in a test
• ADV. **highly, well** *In the key area of negotiation, women scored highly.*

scorn noun

• ADJ. **withering** *She reserved her most withering scorn for journalists.*
• VERB + SCORN **feel** | **express** | **heap, pour, throw** *Abuse and scorn were heaped upon the new tax.*
• PREP. **with~** *He stared with some scorn at his interviewers.* | **~for** *She expressed her scorn for the rules.*
• PHRASES **an object of scorn** *His poetry was the object of scorn.*

scowl noun

• ADJ. **black, dark** | **permanent**
• VERB + SCOWL **wear** | **give sb** | **be set in** *His face was set in a permanent scowl.*
• SCOWL + VERB **deepen**
• PREP. **in a~** *Her brows drew together in a scowl.* **with a~** *He looked up at me with a scowl.*
• PHRASES **have a scowl on your face**

scowl verb

- ADV. **darkly, fiercely, heavily** *She scowled darkly and muttered something under her breath.* | **down**
- PREP. **at** *His eyes scowled down at her.*

scramble noun

- ADJ. **difficult, steep** | **desperate, mad, undignified, wild** *There was a mad scramble for the exits.*
- PREP. **in a/the ~** *I lost my sister in the scramble for a seat.* | **~ down, over, up, etc.** *an undignified scramble down the slope* **~ for** *a scramble for tickets for the game*

scramble verb

- ADV. **frantically** *They scrambled frantically over the piles of debris.* | **awkwardly** | **away, back**
- VERB + SCRAMBLE **manage to**
- PREP. **down, into, out of, over, through, up, etc.** *She managed to scramble over the wall.*
- PHRASES **scramble to your feet** *He scrambled awkwardly to his feet.* **scramble to safety**

scrap noun

1 small piece or amount
- ADJ. **little** *She scribbled the address on a little scrap of paper.* | **food** *The pigs are fed on food scraps.*
- PREP. **~ of** *Every scrap of land in the town has been built on.*

2 recyclable items or material
- QUANT. **piece**
- VERB + SCRAP **sell sth for** *The engine has been sold for scrap.* | **collect**
- SCRAP + NOUN **iron, material, metal, paper, etc.** | **heap, yard** (also **scrapyard**) *My first computer has been consigned to the scrap heap.* | **dealer, merchant** | **value** *Police estimate the scrap value of the lead at around £8 000.*

3 fight
- VERB + SCRAP **get into, have**
- PREP. **in a/the ~** *He looks like he's been in a scrap.* | **~ with** *He had a bit of a scrap with the boy next door.*

scrape verb

- ADV. **carefully, gently** *She carefully scraped away the top layer of paint.* | **away, back, off** *I scraped the dirt off.*
- PREP. **against** *He scraped the car against the garage wall.* **along** *Patrick lifted the gate to prevent it scraping along the ground.* **from** *Her hair was scraped back from her face.* **on** *I scraped my elbow on the wall as I cycled past.* **with** *I scraped the carrots with a knife.*
- PHRASES **scrape sth clean** *The wood had been scraped clean.*

PHRASAL VERB

scrape through
- ADV. **(only) just** *He only just scraped through his exams.*
- VERB + SCRAPE THROUGH **manage to** *The Conservatives managed to scrape through to an election victory.*

scratch noun

- ADJ. **deep, long, nasty, terrible** | **light, little, minor, slight, small, superficial** *His only injuries were some minor scratches above his eye.*
- VERB + SCRATCH **have**
- SCRATCH + NOUN **mark**
- PREP. **without a ~** *She emerged from the wrecked vehicle without a scratch.* | **~ on** *I've got some nasty scratches on my legs.*

scratch verb

- ADV. **badly** *The table had been badly scratched.*

- PREP. **at** *He kept scratching at his nose.* **on** *I scratched my arm on a rose bush.* **with** *She scratched his face with her nails.*

scream noun

- ADJ. **high-pitched, loud, piercing, shrill** | **muffled, stifled** | **blood-curdling, hysterical, terrible, terrified**
- VERB + SCREAM **give, let out** | **hear**
- SCREAM + VERB **echo, ring out** *His screams echoed through the empty house.*
- PREP. **with a ~** *She reacted to the news with hysterical screams.* | **~ for** *a scream for help* **~ of** *screams of laughter/terror*

scream verb

- ADV. **aloud** | **loudly** | **silently** *Despair shook him and he screamed silently in the darkness.* | **hysterically, shrilly, wildly** | **almost** | **out**
- VERB + SCREAM **want to** *I was so bored I wanted to scream.* | **begin to** | **hear sb**
- PREP. **after** *Marion screamed after them, 'Stop! Stop!'* **at** *She screamed at me to get out of the way.* **for** *The trapped passengers screamed for help.* **in** *People ran for the exits, screaming out in terror.* **with** *People were staggering about, screaming with pain.*
- PHRASES **begin/start screaming, scream your head off** *The baby was screaming its head off.* **stop screaming**

screen noun

1 on a TV, computer, etc.
- ADJ. **big** (*often figurative*), **giant, huge, large** *big screen entertainment* (= at the cinema) | **small** (*often figurative*) *She appears regularly on the small screen* (= on television). | **blank** *I sat gazing at the blank screen, trying to think of something to write.* | **computer, television/TV, video**
- VERB + SCREEN **appear on** | **fill** *The star's lovely face filled the screen.* | **gaze at, look at, stare at, watch**
- SCREEN + VERB **flicker** *The screen flickered, and then everything went dark.*
- PREP. **off ~** *They play deadly rivals in the show but they are good friends off screen.* **on (the) ~** *She is remembered mainly for her performances on screen.* ◊ *Information can be viewed on screen or printed out.* ◊ *The image came up on the screen for a few seconds.*
- PHRASES **stage and screen** *stars of stage and screen*

2 partition
- ADJ. **folding** *The room was divided by a folding screen.*
- VERB + SCREEN **put up**
- PREP. **behind a/the~** *His desk was discreetly placed behind a screen.* | **~ between** *There is a screen between the two beds.*

screen verb

1 hide sth
- ADV. **well** | **completely** | **partly** | **effectively** | **neatly** *The shed is neatly screened by a hedge.* | **off** *One part of the room was screened off.*
- PREP. **from** *The building is completely screened from the road by high bushes.*

2 check sb/sth for faults/illnesses
- ADV. **carefully** *All foster parents are carefully screened.*
- PREP. **for** *All pregnant women are to be screened for the infection.*

3 show sth on television/in a cinema
- ADV. **live** *The programme will be screened live on BBC1.*

screw noun

- ADJ. **masonry, wood**
- VERB + SCREW **fix, loosen, tighten, turn**

screw verb

- ADV. **firmly, tightly** | **down, together** *Screw the drain cover down tightly.*
- PREP. **into** *She screwed the lock into the door.* **on/onto** *I screwed the lid back on the jar.* **to** *The bed was screwed to the floor.*
- PHRASES **screw sth in place/into position** *I screwed the curtain rail in place.*

scribble verb

- ADV. **furiously** *The students were all scribbling away furiously.* | **away, down**

script noun

1 text of a play, film, etc.
- ADJ. **draft** | **original** | **final** | **drama, film, movie, news, radio, television/TV**
- VERB + SCRIPT **prepare, write** | **read**
- SCRIPT + NOUN **editor**
- PREP. **~about** *a script about a farmer's life* **~for** *a script for children's TV*

2 system/style of writing
- ADJ. **neat** | **cursive** | **copperplate** | **bold, italic, roman** | **phonetic** | **Cyrillic, Hebrew, Japanese, etc.**
- VERB + SCRIPT **decipher, read** *Archaeologists have had trouble deciphering the script.*
- PREP. **in a/the~** *She writes in a neat copperplate script.*

scripture noun (often scriptures)

- ADJ. **holy, sacred** *the sacred scripture of the Buddhists* | **Christian, Hebrew, Hindu, Jewish, etc.**
- QUANT. **passage, verse**
- VERB + SCRIPTURE **interpret, read (from)** *She read from the scriptures.* | **teach** *He teaches the holy scriptures as he travels around.* | **follow** | **quote (from)**
- PREP. **in the~s** *You won't find this moral precept in the scriptures.*

scrub noun

1 small trees growing in a dry area
- ADJ. **desert** *miles of desert scrub* | **low** *The vegetation consisted of low scrub.*
- QUANT. **patch** *The horses stood near a patch of scrub.*
- VERB + SCRUB **be covered in, be overgrown with** *The mountain was covered in scrub.*

2 cleaning
- ADJ. **good** *I gave the table a good scrub.*
- VERB + SCRUB **give sb/sth**

scrub verb

- ADV. **thoroughly** | **away, down, out**
- PREP. **at** *She scrubbed at the child's face with a tissue.* **from, off** *He scrubbed the blood from his shoes.*
- PHRASES **freshly scrubbed** *his freshly scrubbed face* **scrub sth clean** *The table had been scrubbed clean.*

scruples noun

- ADJ. **moral, religious** *a man of few moral scruples*
- VERB + SCRUPLES **have** | **overcome** *Some persuasion would be required to overcome her scruples.*
- PREP. **without~** *A man who can treat his family so must be completely without scruples.* | **~about** *I don't have any scruples about taking her car—she's often borrowed mine.*

scrutinize verb

- ADV. **carefully, closely, minutely** | **fully, thoroughly**
- PREP. **for** *All parts of the aircraft are closely scrutinized for signs of wear or damage.*

scrutiny noun

- ADJ. **careful, close, detailed, intense, rigorous, serious, thorough** *The company has come under intense scrutiny because of its environmental record.* | **international, judicial, media, parliamentary, public, scientific** *The activities of the committee are subject to public scrutiny.*
- VERB + SCRUTINY **be subjected to, come under, submit to, undergo** | **be open to, be subject to** | **bear** *The testimony of the chief witness doesn't bear scrutiny.*
- PREP. **under~** *The company is under scrutiny by the Inland Revenue.* | **~by** *I realized I was being subjected to intense scrutiny by a group of children.*

scuffle noun

- ADJ. **brief** | **minor**
- VERB + SCUFFLE **be involved in**
- SCUFFLE + VERB **break out** *A scuffle broke out among people in the crowd.*
- PREP. **in a/the~** *He was injured in a scuffle at the football match.* | **~between** *a scuffle between rival gangs* **~with** *He was involved in a scuffle with photographers.*

sculptor noun

- ADJ. **celebrated, famous, great, influential** | **talented** | **contemporary** | **court** *He was court sculptor to Alexander the Great.*
- SCULPTOR + VERB **create sth, work (on sth)** *a classical Greek figure created by the sculptor Polyclitus*
⇒ Note at JOB

sculpture noun

- ADJ. **abstract** | **monumental**
- QUANT. **piece** | **series** | **collection**
- VERB + SCULPTURE **create, make** *She creates sculptures out of scrap materials.* | **display, exhibit, show**
- PREP. **~by** *a sculpture by Henry Moore* **~of** *a sculpture of a horse*
- PHRASES **an exhibition of sculpture/sculptures**
⇒ Note at ART

sea noun

1 large area of salt water
- ADJ. **calm, smooth** *a calm sea after the storm* | **choppy, rough** *The sea was too rough for sailing in small boats.* | **deep** | **shallow** | **blue, grey** | **cold** | **warm** | **inland** | **open** *The fishing boats headed for the open sea.*
- VERB + SEA **cross** *We crossed the Mediterranean Sea on a cruise ship.* | **go to** (= become a sailor) | **put (out) to** *The ship put to sea* (= left port) *in deteriorating weather conditions.* | **be lost at** *They were lost at sea when their ship sank en route for Madeira.* | **stare out to** *She stood on the cliff, staring out to sea.*
- SEA + VERB **rise** *In recent years the sea has risen by a couple of inches.* | **recede, retreat** *The sea has retreated a little since the river was diverted.*
- SEA + NOUN **water** | **bottom, floor** | **breeze** | **creature** | **port** (also **seaport**), **voyage** | **cliff, front, view**
- PREP. **at~** *We spent three weeks at sea.* **across the~** *We sailed across the Black Sea in a yacht.* **by (the)~** *We sent our furniture by sea.* ◇ *They live by the sea.* **down to the~** *We'll go down to the sea for a swim before dinner.* **in/into the~** *I love swimming in the sea!* **on the~** *three ships sailing on the sea* **out to~** *She fell overboard and was swept out to sea.*
- PHRASES **the bottom/edge/middle/surface of the sea, the boom/booming/murmur/roar/sound of the sea**

2 (also **the seas**) movement of the waves of the sea
- ADJ. **choppy, dangerous, heavy, mountainous, raging, rough, stormy** *A week of heavy seas has created problems for fishermen.*
- VERB + SEA **roam, sail** *He has sailed the seven seas.*

3 large amount of sth
● ADJ. **vast**
● PREP. **~of** *She scanned the vast sea of faces below her.*

seafood *noun*

● ADJ. **fresh**
● VERB + SEAFOOD **eat, have | prepare**
● SEAFOOD + NOUN **dish** *a good wine to drink with fish or seafood dishes* | **cocktail, salad | restaurant**
⇨ Special page at FOOD

seagull *(also* gull*) noun*

● QUANT. **flock**
● SEAGULL + VERB **circle, fly, wheel | dive-bomb, swoop | cry, scream, screech, shriek**

seal *noun*

1 animal
● QUANT. **colony** *A colony of seals lay basking in the sun.*
● VERB + SEAL **cull** *Environmentalists claim there is no reason to cull seals.*
● SEAL + VERB **bark**
● SEAL + NOUN **pup | cull**

2 for a document
● ADJ. **wax** *an official-looking letter with a wax seal*
● VERB + SEAL **break** *He broke the seal, and opened the envelope.*
● PHRASES **a seal of approval** *Her report was given the seal of approval by senior management.*

seal *verb*

1 close sth
● ADV. **carefully, firmly, properly, tightly, well** *The containers must be carefully sealed so that no air can get in.* | **completely, totally** *The unit is completely sealed.* | **virtually | effectively | hermetically** *a hermetically sealed container* | **off, up**
● PREP. **from** *The nuclear plant would be effectively sealed off from the world.* **with** *He sealed the bag tightly with sticky tape.*

2 show formally that sth is agreed
● ADV. **formally**
● PHRASES **be signed and sealed** *The contracts are already signed and sealed.*

seam *noun*

1 in fabric
● VERB + SEAM **sew, stitch, tack** *She sewed the seam with small neat stitches.* | **unpick** *It took hours to unpick the seams.* | **iron, press**
● PHRASES **be bursting at the seams** *(often figurative)* *The film is bursting at the seams with good performances.* **come/fall apart at the seams** *(often figurative)* *Their marriage was coming apart at the seams.*

2 of coal, etc.
● ADJ. **coal | rich** *They're still mining a rich seam of high-grade coal.*
● VERB + SEAM **mine**

search *noun*

● ADJ. **careful, exhaustive, extensive, painstaking, systematic, thorough | major, massive, nationwide | desperate, frantic | constant | police | routine** *Police conducted a routine search of all the houses in the area.* | **house-to-house | fingertip** *A team of police officers did a fingertip search of the area.* | **body, strip** *I was subjected to a body search by customs officials.* | **computer, Internet**
● VERB + SEARCH **begin, launch, mount, start** *The police immediately launched a nationwide search for the kill-*

er. | **carry out, conduct, do, make** *The search for the missing men was conducted in poor weather conditions.* | **abandon, call off** *The search was called off when it began to get dark.*
● SEARCH + NOUN **operation** *The police mounted an extensive search operation.* | **party, team | warrant | engine** *This is one of the fastest Internet search engines.*
● PREP. **in ~ of** *We're constantly in search of new talent.* | **~ for** *the search for oil off the coast*

search *verb*

● ADV. **thoroughly** *The area has been thoroughly searched.* | **carefully, diligently, painstakingly | systematically | actively** *actively searching for something to keep the conversation going* | **eagerly | desperately, frantically | in vain | aimlessly** *For the rest of the morning he searched aimlessly through the town.* | **constantly | around/round** *I searched around for a thick stick.*
● PREP. **among** *We searched among the rocks for crabs.* **for** *Police are still searching for the missing child.* **in** *He searched in his pocket and found a few coins.* **through** *searching through a drawer*
● PHRASES **search far and wide, search sth from top to bottom** *We searched the house from top to bottom.* **search high and low** *I have searched high and low and cannot find them.*

seaside *noun*

● VERB + SEASIDE **go to** *Every summer we went to the seaside for two months.*
● SEASIDE + NOUN **resort, town, village**
● PREP. **at the ~** *a holiday at the seaside* **by the ~** *They have a cottage by the seaside.*

season *noun*

1 of the year
● ADJ. **dry, monsoon, rainy, wet** *In this climate there are no real changes of temperature, just a wet and a dry season.* | **summer, winter, etc.**
● VERB + SEASON **be in, come into** *Melons are just coming into season.* | **be out of, go out of**

2 period when an activity takes place
● ADJ. **holiday, tourist | high, peak** *The resort gets overcrowded in peak season.* | **low, off** *The hotel is almost empty in the off season.* | **breeding, mating | growing, planting | lambing | cricket, football, hunting, racing, etc.** | **championship, league | gruelling, hard** *It was the final race of a hard season.* | **successful | disappointing, disastrous | close** *The team trained hard during the close season and won its first five matches.* | **consecutive, successive** *Our team won the trophy for the second successive season.* | **Christmas, festive** *best wishes for the festive season*
● SEASON + NOUN **ticket** *Season ticket holders do not have to queue.*
● PHRASES **the height of the season**
⇨ Note on page 688

season *verb*

● ADV. **well** *Season the meat well with salt and pepper.*
● PREP. **with**
● PHRASES **highly seasoned** *highly seasoned food*

seat *noun*

1 for sitting on
● ADJ. **empty, spare, vacant** *There were no empty seats left in the hall.* ◇ *Do you have a spare seat in your car?* | **comfortable, comfy | cushioned | bicycle, car | back, front, rear** *I always feel sick if I sit in the back seat of the car.* | **driver's, driving, passenger | baby, child, safety | pillion** *I had a terrifying journey on the pillion seat of a*

Honda 750. | **aisle, window** I always ask for an aisle seat when I fly. | **lavatory, toilet** | **good, ringside** I got to the theatre early to get a good seat. ◇ We had ringside seats for the boxing match.
• VERB + SEAT **get, have, take** Please take a seat. ◇ Is this seat taken? | **book, reserve** Is it possible to book seats for the play? | **save** Can you save me a seat if you get there first? | **occupy, sit on** The best seats were occupied by the friends and families of the performers. ◇ It is very uncomfortable to sit on these seats. | **resume** The audience resumed their seats for the second half of the play. | **give up, vacate** He gave up his seat on the bus to a pregnant woman. | **lean back in, recline in, settle back in** | **settle into** We had hardly settled into our seats when the first goal was scored. | **get (up) out of** | **put back, recline**
• SEAT + NOUN **cover** | **reservation**
• PREP. **in a/the ~** The man in the passenger seat seemed to be asleep. **on a/the ~** I found my gloves lying on the back seat. **out of a/the ~** He leapt out of his seat when he saw the rat. | **~ for** I managed to get some seats for the ballet.

2 in Parliament, etc.
• ADJ. **congressional, parliamentary, Senate** | **marginal** | **safe** | **Labour, Tory, etc.**
• VERB + SEAT **gain, win** | **lose** He lost his seat in the last election. | **keep, retain** | **regain** | **contest** | **resign**
• PREP. **~ in** a seat in Parliament **~ on** a seat on the local council

seat verb
• ADV. **comfortably** He seated himself comfortably at the foot of the bed. ◇ The car seats six comfortably.
• PREP. **at** Ramirez was seated at a table near the window. **on** She seated herself on the sofa.
• PHRASES **be seated** Please be seated. **be seated cross-legged, remain/stay seated** Please remain seated until your name is called.

seat belt noun
• VERB + SEAT BELT **wear** By law, you are obliged to wear seat belts. | **fasten, put on** | **undo, unfasten**

seating noun
• ADJ. **comfortable** The auditorium has comfortable seating and modern acoustics.
• SEATING + NOUN **area** | **arrangements, plan** We need to work out the seating plan for the wedding.
• PREP. **~ for** There is seating for 250 people.

secluded adj.
• VERBS **be, look**
• ADV. **very, wonderfully** | **fairly, pretty** We managed to find a fairly secluded spot for our picnic.

seclusion noun
• ADJ. **complete, total, utter** | **relative** For holidays, I prefer the relative seclusion of the countryside.
• PREP. **in (the ~ of)** I live very much in seclusion these days. ◇ She liked to sunbathe in the seclusion of her own garden.

second noun
1 very short moment of time
• ADJ. **brief, fleeting, split** I only saw the man for a split second as he ran past. | **single** | **heart-stopping** For a heart-stopping second he thought he had lost his keys.
• VERB + SECOND **take** This will only take a second. | **have** Do you have a second, Miss White? | **wait** Wait a second—this letter's been sent to me by mistake.
• SECOND + VERB **pass, tick by** The seconds ticked by.
• SECOND + NOUN **hand**
• PREP. **for a ~** For a second I thought you were my mother. **in a ~** I'll be with you in a second. **in/within ~s** Within seconds he had disappeared from view.
• PHRASES **a fraction of a second** If he'd reacted a fraction of a second later, he would surely have died. **a matter of seconds** The end of the match is only a matter of seconds away.
⇨ Note at MEASURE

2 person/thing that comes next after the first
• ADJ. **close, good** | **bad, distant, poor** | **equal, joint** | **creditable, worthy** The young German runner finished a creditable second.
• VERB + SECOND **come, finish**
• PREP. **~ to** Sunny Boy came a close second to the winner.

3 university degree
• ADJ. **lower, upper** | **good**
• VERB + SECOND **be awarded, gain, get, obtain**
• PREP. **~ in** He got a good second in history.

second thought noun
• VERB + SECOND THOUGHT **have ~s** | **not give sth** As for the money, don't give it a second thought.
• PREP. **on ~s** On second thoughts, maybe I won't apply for the job after all. **without a ~** He dismissed the rumour without a second thought. | **~s about** We're beginning to have second thoughts about buying a car.

secrecy noun

- ADJ. **absolute, total | great, strict | excessive, unnecessary | commercial, official**
- VERB + SECRECY **maintain | be shrouded in | swear sb to** *All the researchers on the project are sworn to secrecy.*
- SECRECY + VERB **surround sth**
- PREP. **in~** *The drugs squad operates in the greatest secrecy.* **| ~ about** *The organization has managed to maintain secrecy about its activities.*
- PHRASES **a blanket/cloak/veil of secrecy** *A blanket of secrecy surrounded the tribunals.*

secret noun

1 sth that must not be known by others
- ADJ. **big, great | little | closely guarded, well-kept** *a charming museum that is one of the city's best-kept secrets* (= that not many people know about) **| hidden, inner, innermost, intimate** *That evening she had revealed many of her innermost secrets.* **| open** *Their affair is an open secret.* **| dark, guilty, shameful, terrible | commercial, family, military, official, state, trade**
- VERB + SECRET **have | guard, keep** *Can you keep a secret?* **| betray, divulge, let sb in on/into, reveal, tell sb** *She let us into her secret—she'd got engaged.* **| find out, uncover**
- SECRET + VERB **be/get out** *How did the secret get out?*
- PREP. **in~** *The film stars were married in secret to avoid publicity.* **| ~ about** *There was some secret about the source of his wealth.* **| from** *I have no secrets from you.*
- PHRASES **make no secret of the fact that …, make a secret of sth** *He refuses to make any secret of his political allegiances.*

2 only/best way of doing/achieving sth
- VERB + SECRET **reveal, tell sb**
- PREP. **~ behind** *She revealed the secret behind her extraordinary success.* **~ of** *the secrets of staying healthy*
- PHRASES **the secret of (sb's) success**

secret adj.

- VERBS **be | remain, stay | keep sth**
- ADV. **highly, top, very** *a top secret meeting* **| absolutely, entirely | more or less | formerly, hitherto, previously** *revealing the text of the hitherto secret treaty*
- PREP. **from** *They managed to keep the party more or less secret from Christine.*

secretary noun

1 person who works in an office
- ADJ. **executive, legal | press, publicity | personal, private | social | school**
- ⇨ Note at JOB

2 official of a club/government department, etc.
- ADJ. **chief, first** *the First Secretary of the Communist Party* **| deputy, under | assistant | acting | permanent | honorary | former, then** *the then Secretary of State for Energy, Cecil Parkinson* **| executive, general | branch, district, group, national, regional | club, company | cabinet, shadow** (= a senior British politician of the opposition party) **| parliamentary, state | Agriculture, Defence, Economic, Education, Employment, Energy, Environment, Financial, Foreign, Health, Home, Trade and Industry, Transport, Treasury, etc.**
- VERB + SECRETARY **act as | resign as | elect, elect sb (as) | replace (sb as)**
- SECRETARY + NOUN **General** *UN Secretary General, Kofi Annan*
- PREP. **~ for** *the Secretary for National Defence* **~ to** *secretary to the jockey club*
- PHRASES **the post of secretary, Secretary of State** *the United States Secretary of State*

secretive adj.

- VERBS **be | become**
- ADV. **extremely, highly, unusually, very** *his highly secretive nature* **| almost | rather, slightly, somewhat**
- PREP. **about** *They were very secretive about their plans.*

sect noun

- ADJ. **religious | evangelical, fundamentalist | Buddhist, Christian, etc.**
- VERB + SECT **belong to | join**
- SECT + NOUN **member**
- PHRASES **a leader/member of a sect**

section noun

- ADJ. **large, long** *Large sections of the forest have been destroyed by acid rain.* ◇ *a long section of roadway* **| short, small | main | personnel, political** (in a company, an organization, etc.) *He works in the embassy's political section.* **| business, finance, travel, etc.** (of a newspaper) **| biology, history, reference, etc.** (in a library) **| brass, percussion, rhythm, string, wind, woodwind** (in an orchestra) **| cello, horn, etc.** (in an orchestra)
- VERB + SECTION **divide sth into** *The book is divided into chapters, sections and sub-sections.*
- SECTION + NOUN **manager** (in a company, an organization, etc.)
- PREP. **in a/the~** *You'll find the book in the music section.* **in~s** *The table comes in sections.* **under~** (relating to a section of a law, etc.) *The case was the first prosecution under Section 3A of the Road Traffic Act 1988.*
- PHRASES **a section of society** *an area populated largely by the poorer sections of society*

sector noun

1 part of the business activity of a country
- ADJ. **important, key | growing, growth | independent, private | public, state | voluntary | formal | informal | agricultural, banking, business, commercial, corporate, economic, financial, further/higher education, health, industrial, industry, manufacturing, market, primary, retail, service** *The survey covers a wide range of industry sectors.* **| rural, urban**
- PREP. **in a/the~** *employment opportunities in the higher education sector*
- PHRASES **a sector of the economy/market**

2 part of an area or of a large group of people
- VERB + SECTOR **divide sth into** *Berlin was divided into four sectors after the war.*
- PHRASES **a sector of the population/society**

secular adj.

- VERBS **be**
- ADV. **completely, purely** *It began as a religious organization, but these days it is purely secular.* **| essentially, largely** *We live in a largely secular society.* **| aggressively**

secure verb

1 fix/lock sth firmly
- ADV. **firmly, properly, tightly**
- PREP. **to** *The crates had not been properly secured to the truck.* **with** *She secured the boat with a rope.*

2 get/achieve sth
- ADV. **easily** *Victory was not going to be easily secured.* **| automatically**
- VERB + SECURE **be able to, manage to | fail to** *They failed to secure the release of the prisoners.* **| help (to)**
- PHRASES **an attempt/effort to secure sth, be aimed at securing sth, a chance/hope of securing sth** *trying to improve their chances of securing employment* **succeed/be successful in securing sth**

secure adj.

- VERBS **be, feel | become | make sth | keep sth** *It's important to keep your documents secure.*
- ADV. **extremely, very | absolutely, completely, entirely, perfectly, quite, totally, utterly | fairly, pretty, reasonably, relatively | enough, sufficiently** *I finally felt secure enough in myself to have a child of my own.* | **apparently | economically, financially | socially**
- PREP. **against** *The house has been made secure against intruders.*

security noun

1 feeling safe/being free from worry
- ADJ. **greater | emotional, psychological | economic, financial | job**
- VERB + SECURITY **have** *They have the security of a good home.* | **give (sb), provide (sb with)** *He gave her the emotional security she needed.*
- PHRASES **be lulled into a false sense of security, a feeling/sense of security, the security of tenure**

2 to protect sb/sth from thieves, attack, war, etc.
- ADJ. **maximum, top** *Screw windows to the frame for maximum security.* ◇ *a maximum security prison* | **heightened | strict, tight | lax | collective | national, state | internal | personal | home**
- VERB + SECURITY **ensure, provide (sb with) | improve, strengthen, tighten (up)** *We need to tighten security around the hotel during the president's visit.* | **compromise, undermine** *The leaking of secrets from the Defence Ministry has compromised national security.*
- SECURITY + NOUN **apparatus, forces, services | adviser, guard, man, people, personnel, staff | arrangements, matters, measures, policy, system | check | risk | camera, device, van, video**
- PREP. **~against** *The bars are to provide security against break-ins.*
- PHRASES **for security reasons** *For security reasons, passengers are requested not to leave any luggage unattended.* **peace and security**

3 when you borrow money
- VERB + SECURITY **lend sth on | stand** *His father agreed to stand security for his son's house-purchase loan.* | **take (sth as)**
- PREP. **against the ~ of** *The bank will make a loan against the security of the lender's house.* **as ~** *She pledged her jewellery as security for a £50 000 loan.* | **~for**

4 securities share documents
- ADJ. **company, government | foreign, overseas | listed, unlisted | gilt-edged**
- VERB + SECURITIES **issue | buy | sell**

sedation noun

- ADJ. **heavy | light**
- PREP. **under ~** *The attack victim is currently in hospital, under heavy sedation.*

sedative noun

- ADJ. **powerful, strong | mild** *The doctor gave her a mild sedative to help her sleep.*
- VERB + SEDATIVE **give sb, prescribe (sb)**

seductive adj.

- VERBS **be, look, seem, sound**
- ADV. **extremely, very | infinitely** *These opportunities seemed infinitely seductive.* | **almost** *His words had a soothing, almost seductive quality.*

see verb

1 become aware of sth using your eyes
- ADV. **clearly | dimly | hardly** *I could hardly see be-*

cause of the smoke. | **just** *We could just see the hotel in the distance.* | **suddenly**
- VERB + SEE **be able to, can/could** *I could see the boat quite clearly now.* | **strain to | be amazed to, be surprised to** *He was surprised to see Lucy standing there.* | **be relieved to | be glad to, be overjoyed to, be pleased to** *I'm glad to see that you're keeping well.* | **let sb** *A dolphin? Oh, let me see!*
- PHRASES **turn and see** *He turned and saw her smile.*

2 meet/visit sb
- VERB + SEE **want to, wish to** *What is it you want to see me about?* | **live to** *He didn't live to see his grandchildren.* | **be glad to, be overjoyed to, be pleased to** *Aren't you pleased to see me?*
- PREP. **about** *She's gone to see the mechanic about getting her car repaired.*

3 go with/accompany sb
- PHRASES **see sb home** *Don't worry, I'll see you home.*

4 understand/realize sth
- VERB + SEE **can/can't, don't** *I can see why you were so angry about it.* ◇ *I don't see why she should get more money than the others.* | **be difficult to** *It is difficult to see how to get round this problem.*

5 find out
- VERB + SEE **want to** *I want to see how they'll react.* | **let sb** *Let's see what happens.*
- PHRASES **go and see** 'Has the post come yet?' 'I'll just go and see.' **wait and see** 'Is he going to get better?' 'I don't know, we'll just have to wait and see.'

seed noun

1 from which a plant grows
- ADJ. **grass, poppy, etc. | bird**
- QUANT. **packet**
- VERB + SEED **plant, sow | produce, set** *This tree produces very hard seeds.* ◇ *The plant will set seed in June.* | **grow/raise sth from** *She grew all the broccoli plants from seed.* | **spread** *Most seeds are spread by the wind.* | **go/run to** *Allow some of the plants to run to seed, and save the seed for next year.*
- SEED + VERB **germinate, grow, sprout**
- SEED + NOUN **head, pod | packet, tray | bank, catalogue, merchant | cake | corn, potato**
- PHRASES **a variety of seeds** *The catalogue has hundreds of different varieties of seeds.*

2 player in a sports competition
- ADJ. **first, second, etc. | number one, number two, etc. | top** *Venus Williams was the top seed at Wimbledon this year.*

seek verb

- ADV. **actively** *people who are unemployed and actively seeking work* | **avidly, eagerly, keenly | desperately, urgently** *He was desperately seeking a way to see her again.* | **successfully | in vain, unsuccessfully, vainly**
- PREP. **for** *They sought in vain for somewhere to shelter.*

seep verb

- ADV. **gradually, slowly | away, out, through** *The power had gradually seeped away.*
- VERB + SEEP **begin to**
- PREP. **from** *Blood was seeping slowly from the wound.* **into, out of** *Water was seeping out of the tank.* **through** *The damp seeped through her thin shoes.*

seethe verb

- ADV. **inwardly, privately** *Inwardly she was seething, and vowed to get her own back.* | **quietly, silently**
- PREP. **at** *She was seething at the insult.* **with** *He clenched his fists, seething with anger.*

segregate *verb*

- ADV. **strictly**
- PREP. **according to, by** *Jobs were strictly segregated by gender.* **from** *The women were segregated from the male workers in the factory.* **into** *The common room was segregated into smoking and non-smoking areas.*
- PHRASES **highly segregated** *Women's work has always been highly segregated.* **racially/socially segregated**

segregation *noun*

- ADJ. **complete | racial, religious, residential, sex, social** *to bring an end to sex segregation within the school*
- VERB + SEGREGATION **practise**
- PREP. **~between** *Partitions provided a segregation between the smoking and non-smoking areas of the canteen.* **~by** *segregation by race* **~within**

seize *verb*

1 take hold of sb/sth suddenly and firmly
- ADV. **immediately, suddenly** *He was immediately seized and thrown into prison.*
- PREP. **by** *She seized him by the arm.* **from** *He seized the book from her hand.*
- PHRASES **seize hold of sb/sth** *The wrestlers try to seize hold of each other.*

2 take sth
- ADV. **immediately, promptly** *She promptly seized the opportunity his absence gave her.* **| eagerly, gratefully**
- VERB + SEIZE **be quick to, be ready to** *He was quick to seize on this idea.* **| be determined to | attempt to, try to | fail to** *He had failed to seize his chance.*
- PREP. **on/upon** *The rumours were eagerly seized on by the local press.*
- PHRASES **an attempt to seize sth**

seizure *noun*

- ADJ. **biggest | drugs, land | cocaine, heroin, etc.**
- VERB + SEIZURE **make** *Customs have made their biggest ever seizure of heroin.*
- PHRASES **search and seizure** *The Act confers powers of entry, search and seizure on the police.*

select *verb*

- ADV. **carefully, rigorously | specially | deliberately | arbitrarily, at random, randomly** *The winning entry will be selected at random by computer.* **| automatically** *The program automatically selects and stores the most frequently used data.* **| manually | personally**
- VERB + SELECT **allow sb to, enable sb to**
- PREP. **according to** *The design of the course allows students to select modules according to their interests.* **for** *She has been selected for the England team.* **from** *You can select goods from our catalogue.*
- PHRASES **highly selected** *Although this was a very highly selected study group, the results were in agreement with our findings.* **well selected** *This anthology is well selected and presented.*

selection *noun*

1 process of choosing/being chosen
- ADJ. **careful | random | initial | final | jury, team | natural, sexual** *Natural selection is a key element of Darwin's theory of evolution.*
- VERB + SELECTION **make** *She took a long time to make her selection.* **| win** *She hopes to win selection for the Olympic 800 metres team.*
- SELECTION + NOUN **criteria, policy | procedure, process | board, committee, panel**

- PREP. **~as** *his selection as candidate for the Green Party* **~for**

2 number of people/things that have been chosen
- ADJ. **varied, wide | random** *We interviewed a random selection of teenagers.* **| representative | judicious, well-chosen | final** *The final selection of winners will be announced at the end of the event.*
- PREP. **~from, ~of** *a selection of hits from well-known musicals*

3 collection of goods in a shop, etc. that are for sale
- ADJ. **comprehensive, extensive, huge, large, vast, wide | limited, small | excellent, fine, good, great, interesting, superb**
- VERB + SELECTION **offer** *The shop offers a wide selection of wines.* **| choose from**
- PREP. **~of**

selective *adj.*

- VERBS **be**
- ADV. **extremely, highly, very | increasingly | fairly, quite, rather | necessarily** *The list provided here is necessarily selective.* **| notoriously** *The human memory is notoriously selective.* **| socially** *the socially selective nature of population changes*
- PREP. **about** *He is quite selective about what he studies.* **in** *Most of the girls are extremely selective in their choice of boyfriends.*

self *noun*

- ADJ. **whole** *He put his whole self into the performance.* **| real, true | deep, inner, innermost | private | public** *Her private and public selves were vastly different.* **| normal, usual | former, old** *She knew that with a holiday he would be back to his former self.* **| cheerful** *He's his usual cheerful self again.* **| better** *She knew his better self would struggle to serve her best interests.* **| conscious | physical | good** *(humorous)* *We look forward to seeing Mrs Brown and your good self this evening.*
- VERB + SELF **reveal** *He was afraid to reveal his innermost self.*
- PHRASES **a loss of self, a sense of self, a shadow of your former self**

self-assurance *noun*

- VERB + SELF-ASSURANCE **be lacking in, lack | exude** *In conversation she exudes wit and self-assurance.*

self-confidence *noun*

- ADJ. **great, unshakeable | growing | new, renewed**
- VERB + SELF-CONFIDENCE **have | exude, show | be lacking in, lack | gain | lose | give sb** *A few months living away from home have given him renewed self-confidence.* **| boost, build (up), develop, increase** *He thought a few kind words might boost her self-confidence.* **| dent, shake, undermine**
- PHRASES **an air of self-confidence** *She had an air of self-confidence that he admired.* **a lack of self-confidence**

self-conscious *adj.*

- VERBS **be, feel, look | become, get | make sb** *He studied her in a way that made her very self-conscious.*
- ADV. **acutely, highly, horribly, painfully, very | a bit, a little, quite, rather, slightly, somewhat**
- PREP. **about** *He started to get self-conscious about his weight.*

self-contained *adj.*

- VERBS **be, seem | become**
- ADV. **extremely, very | completely, entirely, quite, totally, wholly** *The flat is completely self-contained.* **|**

largely *a largely self-contained community* | **fairly, relatively**

self-control noun

- VERB + SELF-CONTROL **have** | **lose** | **regain** | **keep** *She struggled to keep her self-control.* | **exercise, show** *You should try exercising a little self-control!* | **take** *It took all the self-control he had not to lose his temper.* | **learn**
- SELF-CONTROL + VERB **snap**
- PHRASES **a lack/loss of self-control**

self-defence noun

- SELF-DEFENCE + NOUN **class, group**
- PREP. **in ~** *He told police that he had acted in self-defence.* | **~ against** *self-defence against armed assailants*
- PHRASES **an act of self-defence, the art of self-defence**

self-evident adj.

- VERBS **appear, be, seem** | **become**
- ADV. **by no means** *These truths were by no means self-evident when Galileo first suggested them.* | **almost** | **largely** | **fairly**
- PREP. **to** *It was self-evident to her that anything so wonderful could not have evolved accidentally.*

self-interest noun

- ADJ. **enlightened** | **pure**
- VERB + SELF-INTEREST **be motivated by** | **pursue your own**
- PHRASES **in your own self-interest** *Directors may be tempted to act in their own self-interest.*

selfish adj.

- VERBS **be, feel, seem, sound** | **become**
- ADV. **extremely, incredibly, very** | **entirely, purely, totally, utterly** | **pretty, quite, rather** *a pretty selfish attitude* | **basically** *People are basically selfish.*

selfishness noun

- ADJ. **pure, utter**
- PHRASES **an act of selfishness** *an act of utter selfishness* **greed and selfishness**

self-pity noun

- QUANT. **wave** *He felt a sudden wave of self-pity.*
- VERB + SELF-PITY **wallow in**
- PHRASES **tears of self-pity**

self-respect noun

- VERB + SELF-RESPECT **have** *She has little self-respect.* | **lose** | **regain** | **keep, preserve** *He chose not to resign to keep his self-respect.*

self-sufficient adj.

- VERBS **be** | **become**
- ADV. **completely, wholly** | **almost, virtually** | **essentially, largely, more or less** | **fairly, pretty** | **economically, financially** | **socially**
- PREP. **in** *These people have now become almost self-sufficient in grain crops.*

sell verb

- ADV. **cheaply**
- VERB + SELL **be able to, can/could** | **want to** | **plan to** | **try to** *They are still trying to sell their house.* | **be expected to, expect to** *The novel was expected to sell between 1 000 and 1 500 copies.* | **be willing to** | **be forced to** *The company has been forced to sell land to recoup some of*

the losses. | **be/prove difficult to, be/prove hard to** *The property proved hard to sell.*
- PREP. **at** *We sell these little notebooks at £1 each.* **for** *They sold their house for £147 000.* **to** *She sold her car to a friend.*
- PHRASES **buy and sell (sth)** *Many banks are willing to buy and sell shares on behalf of customers.*

PHRASAL VERB

sell sth off
- ADV. **cheaply** *Derelict inner-city sites could be sold off cheaply for housing.*

semblance noun

- VERB + SEMBLANCE **have** | **lack** *The film lacks any semblance of realism.* | **gain** | **drop, lose** *He dropped all semblance of dignity and rushed down the street after her.* | **keep, maintain, preserve, retain** | **bring, give sth** *She struggled to bring a semblance of order to the meeting.* | **restore (sth to), return (sth) to**
- PREP. **in/into a/the ~ of** *She bared her teeth in a semblance of a smile.* | **~ of** *He tried to restore some semblance of normality to their home life.*
- PHRASES **a/some semblance of order**

seminar noun

1 class at a university, etc.
- ADJ. **termly, weekly, etc.** | **graduate**
- QUANT. **series**
- VERB + SEMINAR **conduct, give** | **attend, go to**
- SEMINAR + NOUN **group** | **discussion, paper** | **room** | **programme, series**
- PREP. **at/in a/the ~** *There was some lively debate at this week's seminar.* | **~ on** *Professor Mackay will give a seminar on musical settings of Verlaine's poetry.*

2 conference for discussion/training
- ADJ. **all-day, half-day, weekend** | **one-day, two-day, etc.** | **business, economic** | **training**
- VERB + SEMINAR **organize, hold, run** | **attend, go to**
- SEMINAR + VERB **take place**
- SEMINAR + NOUN **participant**

senator noun

- ADJ. **American, US** | **Democratic, Republican** | **former** *the former US Senator, James Hurley*
- VERB + SENATOR **elect, elect sb (as)**

senior adj.

- VERBS **be**
- ADV. **very** *a meeting of all the very senior officers* | **fairly, quite, relatively** | **enough, sufficiently** *She wasn't senior enough to take such a decision.*
- PREP. **to** *Is Mark senior to you?*

seniority noun

- VERB + SENIORITY **attain, gain**
- PREP. **by ~** *Promotion in the job was by seniority.*
- PHRASES **in order of seniority, a level of seniority, next in seniority** *On the death of the captain, the officer next in seniority assumed command.*

sensation noun

1 physical feeling
- ADJ. **delicious, exquisite, pleasant, pleasurable, wonderful** | **unpleasant** | **curious, odd, strange** | **burning, choking, prickling, tingling** | **bodily, physical**
- VERB + SENSATION **experience, feel, have** *He felt a tingling sensation down his side.* | **produce** | **enjoy** *Most people enjoy the sensation of eating.*
- PREP. **~ of** *the sensation of sand between your toes*

2 ability to feel
- ADJ. **pure** *He gave way to pure sensation.*
- VERB + SENSATION **have** *She had no sensation in her hands.* | **lose**
- SENSATION + VERB **come back**

3 feeling/impression
- ADJ. **curious, eerie, odd, strange**
- VERB + SENSATION **have** *I had the eerie sensation that I was not alone.*
- PREP. **~of** *the sensation of being watched*

4 great excitement/surprise/interest
- ADJ. **great | overnight**
- VERB + SENSATION **cause, create** *The film caused a sensation among film critics.*

sense *noun*

1 one of the five natural physical powers of the body
- ADJ. **acute, good, keen | poor | sixth**
- VERB + SENSE **have** *He has an acute sense of smell.* | **lose** *She lost her sense of hearing early in life.* | **regain | heighten, sharpen | dull | appeal to** *He argued that art should appeal to the senses rather than the intellect.*
- SENSE + VERB **tell sb** *When she came to, her senses told her she was lying on a sandy beach.* | **reel, swim** *Her senses reeled as she fought for consciousness.*
- SENSE + NOUN **organ**
- PREP. **through the~s** *Although he can't see, he learns a lot through his other senses.*
- PHRASES **an assault on the senses, the evidence of your senses, the five senses, the sense of hearing/sight/smell/taste/touch**

2 understanding/awareness of sth
- ADJ. **deep, great, keen, strong, tremendous** *He felt a deep sense of relief after the phone call.* | **growing, heightened | slight, vague** *a vague sense of unease* | **innate, intuitive, natural** *a natural sense of justice* | **moral**
- VERB + SENSE **feel, have | display, show | give sb | lose | heighten, sharpen | dull**
- PREP. **~of** *He seems to have lost his sense of reality.*

3 natural ability to do/produce sth well
- ADJ. **good | bad, poor | innate, intuitive, natural | business, dress** *He has no dress sense.*
- VERB + SENSE **have**
- PREP. **~of** *a good sense of direction/rhythm/timing*

4 ability to think/act in a sensible way
- ADJ. **good | common, horse** *Common sense tells me I should get more sleep.*
- VERB + SENSE **have** *He at least had the sense to call the police.* | **display, show | learn** *I wish my daughter would learn some sense.*
- SENSE + VERB **tell sb**
- PHRASES **have more money than sense, (not) an ounce of sense** *If you had an ounce of sense, you'd never have agreed to help him.*

5 reason
- ADJ. **perfect** *It all makes perfect sense* (= is easy to understand).
- VERB + SENSE **make | see** *I tried to make him see sense, but he just wouldn't listen.* | **talk** *If you can't talk sense, I'm leaving!*
- PREP. **~in** *There's a lot of sense in what he's saying.*
- PHRASES **talk sense into sb** *We'll try and talk a little sense into her.* **there's no sense in sth** *There's no sense in going home before the film.*

6 your senses ability to think clearly
- VERB + SENSES **come to, regain | take leave of** *Have you taken leave of your senses?* | **bring sb to**
- PHRASES **in your (right) senses** *No one in their right senses would give him the job!*

7 meaning
- ADJ. **broad, wide** *The novel is about education in its*

widest sense. | **narrow, strict | accepted | figurative, metaphorical | literal | pejorative | legal, technical**
- VERB + SENSE **have** *That word has three senses.* | **make** *That sentence doesn't make sense* (= has no meaning).
- PREP. **in a~** *In a sense, she's right.*
- PHRASES **in every sense of the word, in a very real sense** *In a very real sense, post-war repression was the continuation of the war.* **in the true sense of the word**

sense *verb*
- ADV. **clearly, strongly** *I sensed quite strongly that she was angry with me.* | **dimly, vaguely | just** *Maybe she could just sense what I needed.* | **intuitively**

senseless *adj.*

1 having no meaning
- VERBS **be, seem**
- ADV. **absolutely, quite** *It was an absolutely senseless act of violence.*

2 unconscious
- VERBS **be, lie** *He lay senseless out in the rain.* | **beat sb, kick sb, knock sb** *The thugs beat him senseless with a baseball bat.* ◇ *The branch of a tree knocked one of the riders senseless.*

sensible *adj.*
- VERBS **appear, be, seem, sound** *This approach seems very sensible to me.* | **consider sb/sth, deem sth**
- ADV. **eminently, extremely, really, very | perfectly** *In the state I was in, this seemed a perfectly sensible remark.* | **hardly** *Are you going out to search for it at this time of night? It seems hardly sensible.* | **fairly, pretty, quite, reasonably** *Ben's usually pretty sensible.* | **enough** *That advice sounds sensible enough.* | **apparently | clearly, obviously | politically, strategically**

sensitive *adj.*

1 able to understand other people's feelings
- VERBS **be | become | make sb** *Her experiences had made her sensitive to other people's troubles.*
- ADV. **deeply, extremely, highly, unusually, very** *a highly sensitive, caring man* | **increasingly | quite**
- PREP. **to** *Horses are very sensitive to their riders' moods.*

2 easily upset/annoyed
- VERBS **be, seem | become | remain**
- ADV. **acutely, deeply, extremely, morbidly, painfully, particularly, terribly, very | a bit, pretty, rather**
- PREP. **about** *Teenagers are often very sensitive about their appearance.* **to** *He was acutely sensitive to criticism.*

3 needing to be dealt with carefully
- VERBS **be | become | remain**
- ADV. **extremely, highly, particularly, very** *this highly sensitive issue* | **fairly, rather, somewhat** *a somewhat sensitive question* | **commercially, environmentally, politically, socially** *commercially sensitive information*

4 reacting quickly/more than usual to sth
- VERBS **be | become**
- ADV. **extremely, highly, morbidly, painfully, particularly, unusually, very | quite**
- PREP. **to** *Her eyes are very sensitive to light.*

5 able to measure very small changes
- VERBS **be** *The bat's hearing is remarkably sensitive.*
- ADV. **acutely, especially, exquisitely, extremely, highly, keenly, remarkably, very** *The equipment is highly sensitive.* | **fairly, quite | enough, sufficiently** *The probe is sensitive enough to detect the presence of a single microbe.*
- PREP. **to** *sensitive to the slightest movement*

sensitivity *noun*
- ADJ. **deep, extreme, great | heightened, increased**

• VERB + SENSITIVITY **have | develop, display, show** *Migrating birds show extreme sensitivity to air currents.* | **lack** *Many doctors lack sensitivity when dealing with their patients.*
• PREP. **with ~** *She broke the news to us with great sensitivity.* | **~ in** *She is not known for her sensitivity in dealing with complaints.* **~ over** *There is deep sensitivity over the treatment of minority groups.* **~ to** *The course teaches sensitivity to body language.* **~ towards** *the need for sensitivity towards the views of the children*
• PHRASES **a lack of sensitivity**

sentence *noun*

1 group of words
• ADJ. **long, short** *Try to keep your sentences short.* | **complete, whole | broken, incomplete | grammatical, grammatically correct | grammatically incorrect, ungrammatical | coherent | affirmative, negative | complex, simple | compound**
• VERB + SENTENCE **begin | finish** *Peter finished Jane's sentence for her.* | **construct, form, formulate, generate, write** *He can barely form a grammatical sentence.* | **parse**
• SENTENCE + VERB **contain sth, have sth** *Does the sentence contain an adverb?*
• SENTENCE + NOUN **structure**

2 punishment given by a judge
• ADJ. **maximum, minimum | long, short | harsh, heavy, severe, stiff | lenient, light | indefinite, indeterminate | appropriate | mandatory** *The judge imposed the mandatory sentence for murder.* | **suspended | custodial, jail, prison | non-custodial | death | life**
• VERB + SENTENCE **hand down, impose, pass, pronounce** *The judge will pass sentence on the accused this afternoon.* | **be given, get, receive | serve** *He will have to serve a life sentence.* | **carry out | await** *He spent a week in custody on remand awaiting sentence.* | **face** *She could face a long prison sentence.* | **commute, reduce** *The death sentence may be commuted to life imprisonment.* | **suspend | appeal against | review | quash | carry** *The offence carries a maximum sentence of two years in prison.*
• PREP. **under ~ (of)** *He has been in prison for two months under sentence of death.* | **~ for** *an eight-year sentence for burglary*

sentence *verb*

• PREP. **for** *They had been sentenced for murder.* **to** *He was sentenced to two years in prison.*
• PHRASES **sentence sb to death sentence sb to imprisonment** *The judge sentenced her to life imprisonment.*

sentiment *noun*

• ADJ. **deep, strong | growing, rising | fine, lofty, noble** *All these noble sentiments have little chance of being put into practice.* | **national, popular, public | nationalist/nationalistic, patriotic | anti-British, anti-Japanese, etc. | racist | anti-government, anti-war, etc. | moral, religious** *The people are renowned for their deep religious sentiment.*
• VERB + SENTIMENT **express | agree with, echo, endorse, share** *He agrees with the sentiments expressed in the editorial.* | **disagree with | arouse**
• SENTIMENT + VERB **grow**
• PREP. **~s about/on** *It would be a mistake to ignore their strong sentiments on the issue.* **~ against** *The killings at the weekend helped arouse popular sentiment against the organization.* **~ in favour of** *public sentiment in favour of state ownership*
• PHRASES **my sentiments exactly** (= I agree) *'I don't see why we should change our plans just because of him.' 'My sentiments exactly.'*

separable *adj.*

• VERBS **be**
• ADV. **easily, readily** *Church and State were not easily separable in this period.* | **completely**
• PREP. **from** *The two things were never identical, but never separable from each other.*

separate *verb*

1 move/keep people/things apart
• ADV. **completely, totally | carefully | clearly** *These two branches of the science have now become clearly separated.* | **effectively | easily, readily** *One cannot easily separate moral, social and political issues.* | **formally | legally | physically, spatially | out** *A magnet separates out scrap iron from the rubbish.*
• VERB + SEPARATE **attempt to, try to | be difficult to, be hard to, be impossible to** *It was impossible to separate the rival fans.*
• PREP. **from** *separating the boys from the girls* **into** *I separated the documents into two piles.*
• PHRASES **sharply separated** *The disciplines of science and engineering are not always sharply separated.* **widely separated** *The two groups became widely separated.*

2 stop living together
• ADV. **legally**
• VERB + SEPARATE **decide to**
• PREP. **from** *She is separated from her husband.*

separate *adj.*

• VERBS **be | become | remain | keep sb/sth** *The women are kept separate from the men.* | **consider sth**
• ADV. **very, widely** *I kept my two lives very separate.* ◇ *species from widely separate parts of the world* | **absolutely, completely, entirely, quite, totally, wholly** *The waste water is kept entirely separate from the rainwater.* | **largely | rather, relatively, somewhat | essentially** *The two groups are essentially separate and independent.* | **apparently | hitherto, previously** *to merge the two previously separate businesses* | **geographically, physically**
• PREP. **from** *a lifestyle which is quite separate from that of her parents*

separation *noun*

1 being apart
• ADJ. **complete, total | clear, rigid, strict | long** *She is visiting her family after a long separation.* | **physical**
• PREP. **~ between** *the clear separation of powers between the executive and the legislature* **~ from** *the separation of children from their parents during the war*

2 when a married couple lives apart
• ADJ. **formal, judicial, legal | trial**
• SEPARATION + NOUN **agreement, order**
• PREP. **~ between** *the separation between Mary and her husband* **~ from** *the separation from his wife*

September *noun*

⇨ Note at MONTH

sequel *noun*

1 to a book, film, etc.
• VERB + SEQUEL **do, make, write** *He's been asked to make a sequel to 'Peter Pan'.*
• PREP. **in a/the ~** *Some important new characters appear in the sequel.* | **~ to**

2 sth that happens after sth else
• ADJ. **immediate | strange, unexpected**
• VERB + SEQUEL **have** *The affair had a strange sequel.*
• PREP. **~ to** *The immediate sequel to the price rises was uprisings across the country.*

sequence noun

- ADJ. complete, whole | continuous | complex | correct | opening | closing | alphabetical, chronological, logical, natural, random *The article describes the chronological sequence of events.* | action, dance, dream, film | DNA, gene
- VERB + SEQUENCE complete *Complete the following sequence: 1, 4, 8, 13 …* | follow *We had to follow a complex sequence of movements.*
- PREP. in ~ *The book is more satisfying if you read each chapter in sequence.* in a/the ~ *The heroine dies in the closing sequence of the film.* | ~ of
- PHRASES a sequence of events

serene adj.

- VERBS be, feel, look, sound | remain
- ADV. very | perfectly, utterly | almost | quite | outwardly *beneath the outwardly serene surface*

serenity noun

- ADJ. absolute *Her face had an expression of absolute serenity.* | comparative *She escaped to the comparative serenity of the kitchen.*
- VERB + SERENITY achieve, find
- PREP. with ~ *She was able to face death with serenity.* | ~ of *older people who have achieved a serenity of understanding*
- PHRASES a feeling of serenity

sergeant noun

1 officer of low rank in the army/air force
- ADJ. flight, platoon
- ⇨ Note at RANK

2 officer in the police
- ADJ. police | detective *Detective Sergeant Peter Wiles* | desk, duty, station *Visitors to the police station should report to the station sergeant.*
- PHRASES the rank of sergeant

series noun

1 number of things that come one after another
- ADJ. whole *He is in hospital for a whole series of tests.* | endless, long | complex *a complex series of events* | continuous | concert, lecture, test *(in cricket) Australia won the test series against England.*
- PREP. in a/the ~ *The quartet will be performing in a series of lunchtime concerts.* | ~ of
- PHRASES the first/last, etc. of a/the series, the first/latest, etc. in a series

2 programmes on radio/television
- ADJ. radio, television/TV | comedy, crime, documentary, drama
- QUANT. part
- PREP. in a/the ~ *She has a small part in a drama series for radio.* | ~ about/on *We watched the final part of a series on famous gardens.*

serious adj.

1 bad/dangerous
- VERBS be, look, seem, sound | become, get *By this time the riots were getting serious.* | remain
- ADV. extremely, particularly, really, very | fairly, quite | potentially

2 not joking
- VERBS be, look, sound *Come on, be serious!* | become, turn *He became serious all of a sudden.*
- ADV. deadly, quite, very
- PREP. about *Are you serious about resigning?*

seriousness noun

- ADJ. deadly, deep, full, great, high *He maintained an attitude of high seriousness.* | mock | underlying *The joke did not obscure the underlying seriousness of his point.* | moral
- VERB + SERIOUSNESS appreciate, realize, recognize, understand *Only later did he realize the full seriousness of his offence.* | exaggerate | underestimate | play down | treat sth with *The problem was not treated with the seriousness it deserved.*
- PREP. with ~ *She spoke with great seriousness of the hardships she had endured.*
- PHRASES in all seriousness *You can't in all seriousness think they'll give you the job!* take, treat, etc. sth with the utmost seriousness

sermon noun

- ADJ. lengthy, long | short
- VERB + SERMON deliver, give, preach
- PREP. during/in a/the ~ *He fell asleep during the sermon.* | ~ against *He gave a long sermon against abortion.* ~ on *She preached a sermon on forgiveness.*

servant noun

- ADJ. devoted, faithful, good, loyal, trusted | female, male | maid | hired | indentured | personal | domestic, farm, household, royal
- VERB + SERVANT employ, have
- SERVANT + VERB serve sb, wait on sb *An army of servants waited on the king's household.*
- SERVANT + NOUN girl
- PHRASES an army/a retinue of servants *The duchess arrived, surrounded by her retinue of servants.* servants' quarters

serve verb

1 give sb food or drink
- ADV. immediately *Pour the sauce over the pasta and serve immediately.*
- VERB + SERVE be ready to *Cover and chill the salad until ready to serve.*
- PREP. to *They served a wonderful meal to more than 50 delegates.* with *The delegates were served with a wonderful meal.* ◇ *Serve the lamb with new potatoes and green beans.*
- PHRASES serve sth chilled/cold/hot *The quiche can be served hot or cold.*

2 work
- ADV. faithfully, loyally, well *She served the family faithfully for many years* (= as a servant).
- VERB + SERVE continue to
- PREP. as *I shall continue to serve as a trustee.* in *She served in the medical corps.* under *He served under John Major in the early 1990s.*

service noun

1 system that provides sth the public needs
- ADJ. efficient, excellent, good, valuable | adequate | bad, inadequate, poor, terrible | complete, comprehensive, full | standard | basic | reduced | back-up, support | emergency, essential *A passer-by called the emergency services* (= the ambulance/fire /police services). ◇ *Essential services* (= the supply of water, gas, electricity) *will be maintained.* | vital *providing a vital service to the public* | available *Find out what services are available in your area.* | public | advisory, banking, counselling, financial, information, medical, news, rescue, telephone, etc. | ambulance, diplomatic, fire, foreign, health, intelligence, library, police, postal, prison, probation, prosecution, secret, security, social *She works for the social services*
- VERB + SERVICE offer (sb), provide (sb with) *We offer*

a comprehensive service to home buyers. | **operate, run | maintain | guarantee | improve | expand, extend** *We need to expand this valuable service to other cities.* | **cut back on, run down** *This government has systematically run down public services since it took office.* | **suspend | axe, cut | restore | make use of, use** *people who use the library service* | **complain about**
- SERVICE + VERB **improve | deteriorate**
- SERVICE + NOUN **industry, sector**
- PREP. **in/out of~** (used of buses, trains, etc.)
- PHRASES **goods and services**

2 work of serving a customer
- ADJ. **efficient, excellent, first-class, first-rate, good, professional, quality | bad, poor, terrible | prompt, quick | slow | friendly, personal | customer | after-sales** *We offer excellent after-sales service on all our goods.* | **room** *If you would like a meal in your room, please call room service.*
- VERB + SERVICE **give (sb), offer (sb), provide (sb with)** *Our main concern is to provide quality customer service.* | **get | guarantee** *We guarantee first-class service.* | **complain about** *complaining about poor service*

3 working for a country, company, etc.
- ADJ. **meritorious, outstanding | faithful | long | active** *He died on active service.* | **military, national | domestic** *a job in domestic service* | **community, public | voluntary | jury**
- VERB + SERVICE **do** *All 18-year-old males are required to do a year's military service.* | **see** *He saw service during the First World War.*
- PREP. **~to** *service to the community*
- PHRASES **conditions of service**

4 work done for sb; help given to sb
- ADJ. **great, immense, invaluable, valuable | professional**
- VERB + SERVICE **be of, do sb, perform, render** *May I be of service to you?* ◇ *You have done us a great service.* ◇ *payment for services rendered* | **offer (sb), provide (sb with)** *She offered her services as a childminder.*
- PREP. **at your~** *The cabin staff are at your service throughout the flight.* | **~s of** *We need the services of a good lawyer.* **~to** *He was given an award for his services to the disabled.*

5 the services the armed forces
- ADJ. **armed**
- VERB + SERVICES **go into, join** *Most of the boys went straight into the services.*

6 bus, train etc.
- ADJ. **efficient, good, reliable | fast | frequent, regular | direct | full | limited, reduced** *We will be operating a reduced service while engineering work takes place.* | **scheduled** *changes to scheduled services* | **bus, coach, ferry, rail, taxi, train, tram, tube, underground**
- VERB + SERVICE **lay on, offer (sb), provide (sb with)** *Bus companies are planning to lay on extra services.* | **operate, run | extend, improve | suspend | axe, cut | restore | use | complain about**
- PREP. **in~** *This bus is not in service.* **out of~** | **~between** *The company offers direct, fast and frequent services between large towns and cities.* **~from, ~to**

7 religious ceremony
- ADJ. **church, religious | funeral, marriage, memorial, etc. | afternoon, evening, morning**
- VERB + SERVICE **attend, go to | hold**

service *verb*

- ADV. **fully, properly** *The car was fully serviced last month.* | **regularly**
- PHRASES **have/get sth serviced** *You should get all gas appliances regularly serviced.*

session *noun*

1 meeting of a court, parliament, etc.
- ADJ. **stormy** *a stormy session of the European Parliament* | **inaugural, opening | closing, final, last | current | joint | open, public | closed, private | annual, regular, weekly, etc. | extraordinary | emergency | full, plenary** *a full session of the peace talks* ◇ *a plenary session of the committee* | **follow-up** *A follow-up session was held a month after the initial meeting.* | **congressional, parliamentary**
- VERB + SESSION **hold | attend | boycott | address** *The president addressed a closed session of Congress.*
- SESSION + VERB **convene, take place | begin, open | close, end | adopt sth, approve sth** *The session adopted a resolution on disarmament.* | **agree sth | call for sth**
- PREP. **in a/the~** *in the opening session* **in~** *The court is now in session.*

2 time spent doing an activity
- ADJ. **lengthy, long | short | bargaining, counselling, negotiating, question and answer | briefing, coaching, practice, training | photo, photographic | jam, jazz, recording | workout, yoga | drinking** *The man fell in the canal after a heavy drinking session.*
- VERB + SESSION **have, offer (sb), provide (sb with), run** *The college runs training sessions every afternoon.* | **attend**
- SESSION + NOUN **guitarist, musician, singer, etc.**
- SESSION + VERB **take place**
- PREP. **~on** *a session on remedial reading*

set *noun*

1 group of similar things
- ADJ. **complete, full, whole | common** *These two species share a common set of characteristics.* | **closed, open** *A grammatical choice is drawn from a closed set of options.* | **complex | data, instruction** *a computer's instruction set* | **chess, dinner, printing, tea, train**
- VERB + SET **break up** *She had a complete set of these dining-room chairs but it was broken up after she died.* | **complete, make up** *She won a silver medal in the long jump to complete her set (= of all three types of medal).*
- SET + VERB **comprise sth, consist of sth**
- PREP. **in a/the~** *There are ten pictures in the set.* | **~of** *a set of accounts/books/clothes/keys/valves* ◇ *a set of beliefs/circumstances/factors/guidelines*
- PHRASES **one/part of a set** *The plate is part of a set.*

2 scenery for play or film
- ADJ. **film, stage, studio**
- VERB + SET **design | build | dismantle, take down**
- PREP. **off~** *Off set, the two actors became close friends.* **on (the)~** *All the cast are on the set throughout.*

3 in tennis
- VERB + SET **play | win | lose**
- PHRASES **in straight sets** *Rusedski won in straight sets (= his opponent won none).*

set *adj.*

1 ready
- VERBS **be, look, seem | get** (used when starting a race) *Get set ... Go!*
- ADV. **all** *Are you all set? Let's go!*
- PREP. **for** *The Italian team looks set for victory.*

2 determined
- VERBS **be**
- ADV. **dead**
- PREP. **against** *Her father is dead set against the marriage.* **on** *The council is now set on expanding the sports centre.*

setback *noun*

- ADJ. **temporary | initial | big, major, serious, severe | unexpected | economic, financial | military**
- VERB + SETBACK **experience, receive, suffer** *His research has suffered a temporary setback.*
- PREP. **~ for** *a further setback for the coal industry* **~ to** *a serious setback to his chances of re-election*

settee *noun*

- ADJ. **comfortable, comfy | chintz, leather-covered,** etc. **| three-seater, two-seater | wide**
- VERB + SETTEE **sink down on/onto, sit (down) on, slump down on/onto** *He slumped down exhausted on the settee.* **| be sprawled on, lie on, sprawl on**
- PREP. **on the ~** *She found her glasses lying on the settee.*
- PHRASES **the arm/back of a settee**

setting *noun*

1 place where sth happens
- ADJ. **unlikely** *The hospital is an unlikely setting for an art auction.* **| unfamiliar | natural** *wild animals in their natural setting* **| attractive, beautiful, charming, delightful, idyllic, lovely, magnificent, perfect, picturesque | dramatic | peaceful, secluded, tranquil | intimate | formal, informal | rural | contemporary** *biblical stories in a contemporary setting* **| social** *The French Club offers the chance to practise your language skills in a social setting.* **| work** *In a work setting, more formal language would be used.* **| hospital, laboratory, etc. | cultural, educational, historical | domestic, family** *elderly people living in a domestic setting*
- VERB + SETTING **create, provide** *The park provides the perfect setting for the play.*
- PREP. **in a/the ...** *~ a hotel in a beautiful setting of landscaped gardens* **| ~ for** *a lovely setting for a picnic* **~ in** *a dramatic setting in Cornwall* **~ of** *the rural setting of Petrarch's sonnets*

2 of controls
- ADJ. **high, low, moderate | default, standard**
- VERB + SETTING **adjust, change | increase, reduce**
- PREP. **at a/the ~** *The oven should be at a high setting.*

settle *verb*

1 end an argument
- ADV. **amicably, peacefully** *Hopes of settling the conflict peacefully are fading.* **| satisfactorily** *The matter has not yet been satisfactorily settled.* **| eventually, finally | informally, out of court** *The company has agreed to settle out of court* (= come to an agreement without going to court).
- VERB + SETTLE **attempt to, try to | agree to**
- PREP. **with** *After six months, the company finally settled with the unions.*
- PHRASES **an attempt to settle sth**

2 choose a permanent home
- ADV. **permanently** *He has now settled permanently in London.* **| eventually, finally | happily | down**
- VERB + SETTLE **decide to, intend to**
- PHRASES **be densely settled** *a fertile area that was densely settled in early times* **| be ready to settle down** *She felt she wasn't yet ready to settle down.*

3 make sb/yourself comfortable
- ADV. **comfortably, happily, peacefully, snugly** *He settled himself more comfortably in his chair.* **| quickly, soon | back, down** *He settled back in his chair to watch television.* ◇ *She settled down for a quiet doze on the sofa.*
- VERB + SETTLE **be unable to, can't/couldn't** *Unable to settle, she trailed around the house all day.* **| allow sb to, let sb** *She kept fussing around, refusing to let him settle.* **| help (to), help sb (to)** *I took a pill to help settle my nerves.*

settle in/settle into sth
- ADV. **happily, nicely** *The kids settled happily into their new school.* **| quickly, soon**

settled *adj.*

- VERBS **be, feel, seem | get**
- ADV. **very | fairly, quite** *She seems fairly settled in her new job already.* **| comfortably, happily** *He is happily settled with third wife Gladys and their two children.*

settlement *noun*

1 agreement
- ADJ. **early, speedy | final | lasting, long-term | temporary | amicable, friendly, peaceful | just, reasonable, satisfactory | compromise | negotiated | constitutional, diplomatic, financial, political | compensation, divorce, marriage | out-of-court | peace | pay, wage** *Nurses refused to accept a pay settlement less than the rate of inflation.* **| dispute**
- VERB + SETTLEMENT **agree, reach** *Both parties hope to reach an amicable settlement.* **| negotiate, produce** *The union has negotiated a temporary settlement.* **| seek** *Lawyers are seeking an out-of-court settlement.* **| offer**
- PHRASES **the terms of the settlement**

2 payment of debt, etc.
- ADJ. **prompt, speedy | early | full** *full settlement of a debt* **| cash | debt**
- PREP. **in ~ of** *a cheque in settlement of the amount owing* **under a/the ~** *a beneficiary under the settlement*

3 place where people have come to live
- ADJ. **ancient, early | land | agricultural, rural**
- VERB + SETTLEMENT **establish, found** *The Romans established a settlement on the south shore.*
- SETTLEMENT + VERB **grow up** *A settlement grew up around the castle.*
- SETTLEMENT + NOUN **site**

settler *noun*

- ADJ. **early, first, original**
- SETTLER + VERB **move in/into sth** *When the first settlers moved into the area they faced immense hardships.* **| establish, found** *French settlers founded New Orleans.*
- PREP. **~ from** *settlers from France* **~ in** *Dutch settlers in Cape Town*

severe *adj.*

- VERBS **be, seem, sound | become | remain**
- ADV. **especially, exceptionally, extremely, particularly, really, unusually, very** *an exceptionally severe frost* **| increasingly | fairly, moderately, quite, relatively** *women affected by mild to moderately severe symptoms* **| enough, sufficiently** *Cases of plant poisoning severe enough to warrant hospital admission are rare.*

severity *noun*

- ADJ. **great | extreme, utmost | increasing | mock** *She wagged her finger with mock severity.*
- VERB + SEVERITY **assess**

sew *verb*

- ADV. **carefully, neatly** *The squares of fabric were all sewn neatly together.* **| on, together, up** *I sewed on three buttons.* ◇ *He sewed up the tear with needle and thread.*
- PREP. **onto** *He sewed the patch onto the back of his trousers.*

sewage *noun*

- ADJ. **raw, untreated | treated**

sewing

● VERB + SEWAGE **dump, pump** *In some parts of the country raw sewage is pumped straight in the sea.* | **treat** *Sewage should be treated in a proper disposal system.*
● SEWAGE + NOUN **farm, plant, works** | **disposal, treatment** | **discharge, effluent, sludge** | **pollution**

sewing *noun*

● ADJ. **hand**
● VERB + SEWING **do** *I haven't done any sewing for ages.* | **take in** *She took in sewing to supplement her income.*
● SEWING + NOUN **basket, kit** | **needle, thread** | **machine** | **machinist**

sex *noun*

1 male or female
● ADJ. **female, male** | **opposite** *At that age they can started becoming shy with the opposite sex.* | **single** *a single-sex school* | **fair/fairer, gentle** *(humorous)* (= women; some women may find these terms annoying)
● SEX + NOUN **change** *She's had a sex change operation.* | **equality** | **discrimination, inequality** | **ratio**
● PREP. **between the ~es** *differences/inequalities/relations between the sexes*
● PHRASES **the battle of the sexes** *The quiz is a battle of the sexes between a team of male students and a team of female students.* **on grounds of sex** *discrimination on grounds of sex* **irrespective/regardless of sex** *The word 'man' can refer to all humans, irrespective of sex.*

2 sexual intercourse
● ADJ. **anal, oral, penetrative, vaginal** | **gay, homosexual, lesbian** | **heterosexual** | **good, great, passionate** | **safe** | **unprotected, unsafe** | **consensual, non-consensual** | **extra-marital, illicit, premarital** | **kinky** | **casual, promiscuous** | **unlawful** *He was convicted of having unlawful sex with an underage girl.* | **explicit, gratuitous** *Films containing explicit sex are banned.*
● VERB + SEX **engage in, have** *She had never had sex before.* | **consent to** | **refuse** | **obtain, procure**
● SEX + NOUN **life** *a healthy sex life* | **drive, urge** *a low sex drive* | **appeal** *Despite his age, he still has a lot of sex appeal.* | **act, practices** *photos showing sex acts* ◇ *safer sex practices* | **therapist, therapy** | **organ** | **hormone** | **education** | **abuse, assault, attack, crime, offence** *child sex abuse* | **maniac** *He had a reputation of being a sex maniac.* | **fiend** *(informal)*, **offender, pest** *(informal)* | **film, scene, show** | **symbol** *She wants to be known as a singer rather than as a sex symbol.* | **shop** | **aid, toy** | **scandal**
● PREP. **~ between** *sex between consenting adults* **~ with** *sex with her husband*

sexism *noun*

● ADJ. **blatant, rampant** *She was shocked by his blatant sexism.* ◇ *Sexism is rampant in many institutions.*
● VERB + SEXISM **combat, fight (against)** *efforts to combat sexism in the workplace*

sexual intercourse *noun*

● ADJ. **full** | **consensual** | **non-consensual, unlawful** | **unprotected**
● VERB + SEXUAL INTERCOURSE **engage in, have** | **consent to** | **submit to** | **refuse** | **obtain, procure** *the crime of obtaining sexual intercourse by threat*
● SEXUAL INTERCOURSE + VERB **occur, take place** *Rape is committed where sexual intercourse takes place without consent.*
● PREP. **during ~** | **~ with** *She denied having had sexual intercourse with him.*
● PHRASES **an act of sexual intercourse**

sexuality *noun*

● ADJ. **female, male** | **human** | **deviant** | **gay, lesbian** | **overt** *Her overt sexuality shocked cinema audiences.*
● VERB + SEXUALITY **express** *Victorian women were rarely allowed to express their sexuality.* | **come to terms with** *He couldn't come to terms with his sexuality.*

sexy *adj.*

● VERBS **be, feel, look** | **find sb**
● ADV. **extremely, incredibly, really, very** *I find him incredibly sexy.* | **pretty, quite, rather**

shack *noun*

● ADJ. **tin, wooden** | **derelict, dilapidated, run-down**
● PREP. **in a /the ~**

shade *noun*

1 area out of the sunlight
● ADJ. **cool** | **deep** | **welcome** | **dappled** | **leafy** *in the leafy shade of a fig tree*
● QUANT. **patch** *searching for a patch of shade to rest in*
● VERB + SHADE **give (sb), offer (sb), provide (sb with)**
● PREP. **in (the) ~** *a plant that grows well in shade* ◇ *sitting in the shade* **into the ~** *Let's move into the shade.* **under the ~ of** *sitting under the shade of an umbrella* | **~ for** *giving shade for cattle* **~ from** *The huge trees offered shade from the sun.*
● PHRASES **light and shade**

2 type of colour
● ADJ. **delicate, light, muted, pale, pastel, soft, subtle, translucent** *The rooms were decorated in delicate pastel shades.* | **dark, deep, rich, strong** *His face turned an even deeper shade of red.* | **bright, vivid** | **attractive, beautiful** | **startling, stunning** *painted in startling shades of pink and orange* | **autumnal, natural, neutral, warm** *Towels in warm shades can soften the room.*
● VERB + SHADE **be available in, come in** *This wool is available in 18 stunning shades.*
● PREP. **in a ~** *The sea glistened in shades of blue and emerald.* | **~ for** *our new range of shades for lips and eyes* | **~ of** *He threw out his old suits, all in shades of grey and brown.*

3 small difference
● ADJ. **political** *reformers of all political shades*
● PREP. **~ of** *a word with various shades of meaning*
● PHRASES **shades of opinion**

shade *verb*

● ADV. **completely** | **lightly, partially** *This plant prefers a lightly shaded position.*
● PREP. **against** *She shaded her eyes against the fierce sun.* **from** *We were completely shaded from the sun by the poplar trees.* **with** *a small town square shaded with trees*

shading *noun*

● ADJ. **light, subtle** *an effect that is achieved with subtle shading* | **dark, heavy**

shadow *noun*

● ADJ. **dark, dense, deep, strong** *The house lay in dark shadow.* | **giant, long** | **grotesque, monstrous, sinister, strange, terrible** | **dancing, flickering**
● VERB + SHADOW **cast, make, produce, throw** *The boat's sail cast a shadow on the water.* ◇ *Use a desk light to produce a strong shadow.* ◇ *The candles on the table threw huge flickering shadows against the wall.* | **fill sth with ~s** *The streets were now filled with terrible shadows.* | **emerge from, loom up out of, step out from/of ~s** *Suddenly a huge figure loomed up out of the shadows.* | **move into, shrink into, slip (back) into ~s** *She shrank back into*

the shadows as the footsteps approached. | **lurk in, wait in, watch from** *criminals lurking in the shadows*
- SHADOW + VERB **fall, lie** *The evening shadows were beginning to fall.* ◇ *Deep shadows lay across the small clearing where they sat.* | **get longer, lengthen** *As the shadows lengthened, the men drifted home for their tea.* | **dance, leap, move, pass** *the leaping shadows of the flames* ◇ *The shadows of the clouds passed over us.*
- PREP. **among the ~s** *an odd shape among the shadows* **in the ~s** *I could just make out a figure in the shadows.* **into the ~s** *I backed into the shadows until the police car had passed.* **in ~** *His face was in shadow.* **into ~** *The storm clouds threw the mountain peaks into dense shadow.* **from/out of the ~s** *A huge figure stepped out of the shadows.* **through the ~s** *the fears that kept crowding in on her as she hurried through the shadows*
- PHRASES **live in the shadow of sb/sth** *(often figurative)* *She had always lived in the shadow of her older sister.*

shaft noun

- ADJ. **deep** | **vertical** | **lift, mine** *(also* **mineshaft***) A fire broke out in the main lift shaft.* | **air, ventilation**
- VERB + SHAFT **bore, drill, sink**
- PREP. **down a/the ~** *The body had been thrown down a disused mineshaft.* **in/into a/the ~ through a/the ~** *The workers go down to the tunnels through a vertical shaft sunk from the top of the cliff.*
- PHRASES **the bottom/top of a shaft** *They lowered him down to the bottom of the deep shaft.*

shake noun

- ADJ. **brisk, good, vigorous** *Give the tablecloth a good shake before putting it away.* | **little, slight** | **mental** *He gave himself a mental shake and got down to work.* | **rueful** *a rueful shake of the head*
- VERB + SHAKE **give sb/sth**
- PREP. **with a~** | **~of**
- PHRASES **a shake of your/the head**

shake verb

1 of a person/building
- ADV. **badly, uncontrollably, violently** *Her hands were shaking so badly that she couldn't hold her glass.* | **almost** *He was almost shaking with the intensity of what he was saying.* | **fairly** *(informal) Natalie fairly shook with laughter.* | **literally, physically** *I was numb with dread. I was literally shaking.*
- PREP. **with** *She was shaking with rage.*
- PHRASES **be shaking all over** *He was crying and shaking all over.* **be shaking like a leaf, find yourself/start shaking** *I found myself shaking uncontrollably with cold.* **stop shaking** *I just couldn't stop shaking.*

2 object/person
- ADV. **roughly, vigorously, violently** *He shook the blankets vigorously to get rid of the dust.* ◇ *She must have shaken the baby quite violently to inflict such severe injuries.* | **gently, slightly** | **well** *Shake well before use.* (instructions on a bottle of medicine, etc.) | **suddenly** | **physically**
- PREP. **by** *He shook her gently by the shoulders.*

3 your head
- ADV. **decisively, emphatically, firmly** | **fiercely, vehemently, vigorously, violently, wildly** | **a little, gently, slightly** | **quickly** | **slowly** | **dismissively, impatiently** | **despairingly, desperately, dismally, gloomily, helplessly, miserably, mournfully, regretfully, ruefully, sadly, sorrowfully** | **wearily** | **disbelievingly, doubtfully, wonderingly** | **just, merely, only, simply** *He merely shook his head.* | **from side to side**
- PREP. **at** *He shook his head at her disbelievingly.* **in** *She shook her head in disbelief.*

4 sb's hand
- ADV. **firmly, vigorously** | **warmly**
- PHRASE **shake sb by the hand** *Our host shook each of us warmly by the hand*

PHRASAL VERB

shake sb/sth off
- ADV. **completely, fully** | **quickly, easily** *He had not easily shaken Claudine off.* | **off**
- VERB + SHAKE SB/STH OFF **can't/couldn't (seem to)** *I can't seem to shake off this cold.* | **seem to** *She never seemed to completely shake the dumb blonde image.* | **try to**

shaken adj.

- VERBS **be, look** | **leave sb** *The experience left her deeply shaken.*
- ADV. **badly, considerably, deeply, profoundly, quite, severely** | **a bit, a little, rather, somewhat** *Are you all right? You look a bit shaken up.* | **clearly, obviously, visibly** | **still** | **up**
- PREP. **by** *She was visibly shaken by the news.*

shake-up noun

- ADJ. **big, major, radical** | **urgent** | **boardroom, council, personnel**
- VERB + SHAKE-UP **need** | **call for** *The paper calls for an urgent shake-up in the system for looking after the elderly.* | **plan** *The headline read 'Local council plans shake-up'.* | **face, go through, have, undergo** *Police forces face the biggest shake-up in their 150-year history.* | **survive** *My job did not survive the shake-up.*
- PREP. **in a/the ~** *the posts that were scrapped in the recent shake-up* | **~ at** *a major shake-up at the company* **~ in** *a radical shake-up in the chemical industry*

shaky adj.

1 shaking because you are frightened/ill
- VERBS **be, feel, seem, sound** | **get, go** | **leave sb/sth** *The experience had left him rather shaky.*
- ADV. **distinctly, extremely, very** | **all** *You've gone all shaky!* | **a bit, a little, rather, slightly**
- PREP. **with** *Her voice was low and shaky with emotion.*

2 not firm or strong
- VERBS **be, feel, look** | **remain**
- ADV. **dangerously, decidedly, distinctly, extremely, very** *Financially, the arrangement was distinctly shaky.* | **a bit, a little, pretty, rather, somewhat**

shallow adj.

1 not deep
- VERBS **be, look** | **become, get** *The water gets quite shallow towards the shore.* | **remain**
- ADV. **extremely, very** | **comparatively, fairly, quite, relatively** *Don't worry, the water's quite shallow.* | **enough, sufficiently** *Follow the south shore, crossing the river where it is shallow enough.*

2 not showing serious thought
- VERBS **appear, be, seem** *Tony seemed very shallow and immature.*
- ADV. **exceedingly, extremely, very** | **quite, rather**

shame noun

1 feeling that you have lost the respect of others
- ADJ. **deep**
- VERB + SHAME **be filled with, feel** | **bring, cause** *His arrest for stealing brought shame on his family.* | **die of** *(figurative) I nearly died of shame!*
- PREP. **from ~** *She wept from the shame of having let everyone down.* **in ~** *She shut her eyes in shame.* **to your ~** *To my shame, I didn't tell Robert about the party.* **without ~**

He had cried noisily and without shame at the news of Esther's death. **with ~** *She blushed with shame.* | **~ about/over** *You feel absolutely no shame over what you did, do you?* **~ at** *She felt a flush of shame at what she'd done.*
- PHRASES **a cause for shame** *Her pregnancy was no cause for shame.* **a feeling/sense of shame, bow/hang your head in shame** *He was being held by two security guards, his head bowed in shame.*

2 a shame sth that makes you feel disappointed
- ADJ. **crying, great, real, terrible, wicked**
- PREP. **~ about** *It's a terrible shame about Stuart losing his job, isn't it?*
- PHRASES **a bit of a shame, rather a shame, such a shame, what a shame** *What a shame you can't come!*

shame *verb*

- ADV. **publicly** *The people who did this deserve to be publicly shamed.*
- PREP. **into** *An outcry from customers has shamed the company into lowering its prices.*

shampoo *noun*

1 liquid soap for washing hair
- ADJ. **anti-dandruff, baby, frequent-use, gentle, mild, moisturizing, revitalizing**
- VERB + SHAMPOO **use, wash your hair with**
- PREP. **~ for** *a shampoo for greasy hair*
- PHRASES **shampoo and conditioner**

2 act of washing hair
- VERB + SHAMPOO **give sb/sth | have**
- PHRASES **a shampoo and set** *I'll have a shampoo and set, please.*

shape *noun*

1 physical outline
- ADJ. **basic, simple** *The children cut the paper into various simple shapes.* | **characteristic, distinctive** *I recognized the distinctive shape of a Boeing-747.* | **curious, interesting, unusual, weird | awkward** *The desk was an awkward shape and wouldn't fit through the door.* | **original | geometric/geometrical, regular, symmetrical | complex | asymmetrical, irregular | odd, random** *tiles of random shape* | **solid, three-dimensional | aerodynamic | angular, arch, circular, cone/conical, cylindrical, diamond, dome, egg, elliptical, elongated, hemispherical, hexagonal, oblong, pentagonal, pointed, pyramid/pyramidal, rectangular, round, spherical, triangular, wedge | rounded, smooth | arrow, banana, cross, pear, star, T, etc.** *The road forms an L shape.* ◇ *The bruise was a sort of mushroom shape.* | **blurred, ghostly, shadowy, vague | huge, massive | black, dark, grey | human | body** *You can't change your natural body shape.*
- VERB + SHAPE **cut out, draw, make, trace** *First draw the rough shape of your chosen animal.* ◇ *Fold the paper to make the shape of a cone.* | **cut sth into, make sth in, produce sth in** *a cheese similar to Brie but produced in a different shape* | **come in, have** *Tables come in various shapes.* | **assume, make, take on** *Ordinary things assumed different shapes in the mist.* | **keep, retain** *These garments will retain their shape even with repeated washing.* | **regain | change | lose | distort** *The wide-angle lens distorts shapes.* | **distinguish, make out, see** *I could just make out the shapes of animals in the field.*
- SHAPE + VERB **appear, emerge, loom** *Ghostly shapes loomed out of the fog.*
- PREP. **in the ~ of** *a doormat in the shape of a cat*
- PHRASES **out of shape** *The bicycle had been battered out of shape.* **oblong/rectangular/hexagonal, etc. in shape** *The island is roughly circular in shape.*

2 structure/nature of sth

- ADJ. **general | changing | final | future**
- VERB + SHAPE **alter, change, determine, influence** *He did much to determine the shape of Europe's political map at that time.* | **take** *A wonderful idea began to take shape in her brain.* | **give** *the words we use to give a shape to our feelings*
- PHRASES **in any shape or form** *I can't stand insects in any shape or form.* **the shape of things to come** *This revolutionary transport system could be the shape of things to come.*

3 good or bad condition
- ADJ. **fine, good, great | bad, poor | physical** *He's 64, but he's in better physical shape than I am.*
- VERB + SHAPE **get sb/sth into, knock/lick/whip sb/sth into** *Get your body into shape for the summer!* ◇ *Leave the boy with me—I'll soon knock him into shape!* | **be in, keep in, stay in** *You are in pretty good shape for your age.* ◇ *She likes to stay in shape.* | **be out of**

shape *verb*

- ADV. **profoundly** *Memory can be profoundly shaped by subsequent experience.* | **largely | actively, deliberately** *actively shaping the history of their country*
- VERB + SHAPE **help (to)**
- PHRASES **a part/role in shaping sth**

shaped *adj.*

- VERBS **be**
- ADV. **beautifully, perfectly** *her beautifully shaped mouth* | **grotesquely | irregularly | awkwardly** *All the rooms in the house were awkwardly shaped.* | **curiously, oddly, strangely** *an oddly shaped parcel* | **specially** *You can buy specially shaped bricks for an arch.*
- PHRASES **be shaped like sth** *curious vases shaped like birds and animals*

share *noun*

1 part of sth that has been divided
- ADJ. **bigger, large, the lion's, major, significant, substantial | full | modest** *a modest share of total exports* | **5%, 10%, etc.** *The wife owns an 80% share of their second home.* | **equal | disproportionate** *The government devotes a disproportionate share of the budget to military expenditure.* | **proportionate | market** *The company's market share slipped to under 15% last month.*
- VERB + SHARE **get, have, receive, take** *You should receive a large share of the profits.* ◇ *Hospitals take the lion's share of the NHS budget.* | **increase, reduce | claim** *Everyone seems to want to get into television to claim their share of fame and fortune.* | **do** *We must all do our share of the work.*
- PREP. **~ of** *a reduced share of the vote*
- PHRASES **sb/sth has their/its (fair) share of sth** *The industry has had its fair share of problems.*

2 in a company
- ADJ. **ordinary | preference**
- VERB + SHARE **acquire, buy, get, invest in, purchase | have, hold** (*formal*) **| own | sell | deal in, trade in** *a new firm dealing in US shares* | **float, issue** *The company has issued four classes of shares.*
- SHARE + NOUN **price, value** *Hong Kong share prices plunged.* | **valuation | certificate | portfolio | capital | option, scheme** *The Chief Executive's share option has earned him over £2 million.* | **ownership | transaction, transfer | purchase | issue, offer, sale** *A share issue has been launched to finance the restoration of the building.* | **dealing** *allegations of illegal share dealings*
- PREP. **~ in** *I've got a few shares in British Aerospace.*
- PHRASES **a class of shares, the value of your shares** *Will this affect the value of my shares?*
- ⇨ Note at PER CENT (for more verbs)
- ⇨ Special page at BUSINESS

share verb

- ADV. **fully** *Personal experience of childbirth gives a dimension of knowledge that others cannot fully share.* | **equally** *We shared the money equally between the three of us.* | **out**
- VERB + SHARE **want to** | **be prepared to, be willing to** *experienced teachers willing to share their expertise with others* | **be reluctant to** | **be forced to, have to** | **agree to** | **refuse to** | **be entitled to** *Each partner is entitled to share in the profits of the business.* | **let sb** *She wished he would let her share his pain.*
- PREP. **among** *How do you share out three cakes among four people?* **between** *Responsibility is shared between parents and teachers.* **in** *He shared in our enthusiasm for rowing.* **with** *She had to share a bedroom with her sister.*
- PHRASES **widely shared** *These ideas are widely shared in the community.*

shareholder noun

- ADJ. **big, large, major, substantial** | **small** | **main, principal** | **controlling, majority** *The government is still a majority shareholder in the industry.* | **minority** | **corporate, institutional** | **ordinary, private** *voicing the concerns of ordinary shareholders*
- PREP. **~in** *the major shareholders in the company*

shark noun

- ADJ. **killer, man-eating**
- SHARK + VERB **attack sb, maul sb**
- SHARK + NOUN **attack** | **fishing**
- PHRASES **shark-infested** *The boat went down in shark-infested waters off the coast of South Africa.*

sharp adj.

1 having a fine edge or point
- VERBS **be, feel, look, seem** | **stay** | **keep sth**
- ADV. **extremely, really, very, wickedly** *a display of wickedly sharp teeth* | **pretty, quite, rather**
- PHRASES **as sharp as a razor**

2 very great or sudden
- VERBS **be**
- ADV. **particularly, very** | **fairly, quite, rather** *a fairly sharp rise in the cost of living*

3 able to think/act/understand/see/hear quickly
- VERBS **be, seem**
- ADV. **extremely, razor, very** *a razor sharp mind* | **pretty, quite**

4 angry/severe
- VERBS **be, sound** *Her voice sounded rather sharp.*
- ADV. **very** | **a bit, quite, rather** | **suddenly** *'Stick to the facts,' said Romanov, his voice suddenly sharp.*
- PREP. **with** *She was quite sharp with me when I talked during her lecture.*

5 flavour
- VERBS **be**
- ADV. **extremely, very** *Raw cranberries are extremely sharp and must always be cooked with a little sugar.* | **slightly** *This cheese has a slightly sharp flavour.*

shatter verb

1 break into very small pieces
- ADV. **completely**
- PHRASES **shatter (sth) into pieces** *The mirror shattered into a thousand pieces.*

2 destroy sth completely
- ADV. **completely** *an event that completely shattered her life* | **abruptly, brutally, rudely, suddenly** *The moment was abruptly shattered by the sound of Mia's loud voice.*

shattered adj.

- VERBS **be, feel, look, seem, sound**
- ADV. **absolutely, completely, totally** *His run had left him feeling totally shattered.* | **pretty** | **emotionally** *feeling drained and emotionally shattered after her ordeal*

shave noun

- ADJ. **close, smooth** *You can get a really close, smooth shave with this new double-bladed razor.*
- VERB + SHAVE **need** *He badly needed a shave.* | **get, have** *He had a bath and a quick shave first.* | **give sb**

shawl noun

- ADJ. **heavy** | **light** | **crocheted, knitted** | **embroidered, fringed**
- VERB + SHAWL **be draped in, be wrapped in** | **drape, throw, wrap** *Ruth draped a shawl over her shoulders.* | **throw off** | **draw, pull** *She pulled her shawl about her protectively.* | **tie** *wearing a shawl tied around her waist*
- SHAWL + VERB **cover sth**
- ⇒ Special page at CLOTHES

shed noun

- ADJ. **lean-to** | **storage** | **engine, goods, loco, locomotive, railway, train** | **tool** | **bicycle, bike** | **cow** | **milking** | **garden, potting**
- PREP. **in a/the~**

sheep noun

- ADJ. **hill** | **lost, stray** *the doleful cries of lost sheep*
- QUANT. **flock, herd**
- VERB + SHEEP **farm, keep, raise, rear** *My grandfather used to raise sheep in Wales.* | **tend** | **slaughter** | **shear** | **drive, herd, round up, shepherd** *The dogs herded the sheep into the pen.*
- SHEEP + VERB **graze** *There were a lot of sheep grazing high up on the mountain.* | **bleat, (go) baa** | **lamb** *It's nearly the sheep's lambing time.*
- SHEEP + NOUN **farm, station** *a 4 000-acre sheep station in New South Wales* | **farmer** | **farming, industry** | **dip** | **dog** (also **sheepdog**) | **flock** | **pasture** | **shearing**
- PHRASES **a breed of sheep**

sheet noun

1 large piece of fabric used on a bed
- ADJ. **clean, fresh** *a pile of clean sheets* | **crumpled** *She had slept in her bed—the sheets were crumpled.* | **white** | **cool** | **cotton, linen, plastic, rubber, satin, silk** | **bed, double, fitted, single** | **bottom, top**
- VERB + SHEET **change, fold, put on, tuck in** *She changed the sheets on all the beds.* ◇ *Could you put some fresh sheets on the bed?* | **climb between, slide between, slip between/under** *I slipped under the sheets and was asleep in an instant.* | **cover sb/sth with, pull back/over/up** *The police had covered the body with a sheet.* ◇ *I pulled the sheet up over my nose.*
- PREP. **beneath/under a/the ~** | **between the ~** *She lay between the cool sheets.*
- PHRASES **sheets and blankets**

2 piece of paper
- ADJ. **blank, clean** *He pulled a blank sheet of paper towards him and began to write.* | **A3, A4, etc.** | **large** | **printed, typed** *The advertisement was a single printed sheet.* | **loose, separate** | **answer, balance, data, diet, fact, information, news, record, score** *I sent for the programme's free fact sheet on the disease.*
- VERB + SHEET **take, use** *Take a clean sheet of paper and start again.*
- SHEET + NOUN **music**
- PREP. **~of** *a sheet of blotting paper*
- PHRASES **a sheet of paper**

3 flat thin piece of any material
- ADJ. **flat, large, thin | baking | dust** *The furniture was covered in dust sheets.* | **canvas, plastic, polythene | ice** *the Antarctic ice sheet*
- SHEET + NOUN **metal, steel, vinyl** *sheet metal workers*
- PREP. **~ of** *a sheet of glass/plastic/metal* ◇ *(figurative) Sheets of flame shot into the air.*

shelf *noun*

- ADJ. **high, low | deep, shallow | bottom, middle, top** *He took a book down from the top shelf.* | **bare, empty | open | dusty | glass, metal, wooden | bathroom, kitchen, library, shop, supermarket**
- VERB + SHELF **have** *The fridge had three shelves.* | **build, put up** *She soon learned how to put up her own shelves.* | **arrange sth on, display sth on, put sth (back) on, replace sth on, return sth to, stack sth on, stock** *I put the packet back on the shelf.* ◇ *He's got a job stocking shelves in a supermarket.* | **clear** *I've cleared a shelf in the cupboard for you.* | **get sth down from/off, pick sth from/off, remove sth from, take sth down from/off** *The supermarket immediately removed the product from its shelves.* | **fill, fit on, go on, remain on, sit on** *Souvenirs filled the shelves.* ◇ *Her diaries just sat on the shelf for years* (= nobody looked at them for years). | **reach (for/to)** *She reached for the shelf next to the bed.*
- SHELF + VERB **be full of sth, contain sth, hold sth**
- SHELF + NOUN **space | life** *The medicine has a shelf life of six months.*
- PREP. **off a/the ~** *I knocked it off the shelf by accident.* **on a/the~** *the books on the shelves* | **~ of** *a shelf of books on economics*
- PHRASES **be filled/lined with shelves** *The walls of her study were lined with shelves.* **a place on your shelves** *The book deserves a place on everyone's shelves.*

shell *noun*

1 on eggs/nuts/some animals
- ADJ. **broken, empty, hard, outer, protective, thick** *(figurative) She had built up a protective shell of indifference around herself.* | **egg** (also **eggshell**) | **cockle, conch, cowrie, fossil, mollusc, mussel, oyster, scallop, sea** (also **seashell**), **snail** *The garden was littered with empty snail shells.* | **coconut, walnut**
- VERB + SHELL **have** *creatures that have shells* | **come out of, emerge from** *(often figurative) He's really come out of his shell since he met Marie.* | **go (back) into, retreat into, withdraw into** *The snail went back into its shell.* | **remove sth from** *Remove the mussels from their shells.*

2 explosive weapon
- ADJ. **heavy | unexploded | anti-aircraft, artillery, cannon, howitzer, mortar**
- VERB + SHELL **load | fire**
- SHELL + VERB **fall, land | blow up, burst, crash, explode | hit sth, strike sth** *Two shells hit the roof.* | **blow sth apart/off, blow sb/sth up**
- SHELL + NOUN **fire** *They braved heavy shell fire to rescue the wounded.* | **case/casing, fragments, splinter | crater, hole**

3 outer walls of a building
- ADJ. **concrete | burnt-out, empty, hollow** *The fire reduced the school to a hollow shell.*

shelter *noun*

1 protection from danger/bad weather
- VERB + SHELTER **afford (sb), give (sb), offer (sb), provide (sb with)** *The great elm trees gave shelter from the wind.* | **need | find, run for, seek, take | refuse sb** *The nuns won't refuse you shelter.* | **leave** *We had to leave the shelter of the trees.*
- PREP. **in/under the ~ of** *standing in the shelter of the shop doorway* | **~ from** *to seek shelter from the rain*
- PHRASES **shelter for the night**

2 small building that gives protection
- ADJ. **makeshift, temporary | stone, underground, wooden | air-raid, bomb, bus, emergency, fallout**
- VERB + SHELTER **build, erect, make, put up** *The villagers were building temporary shelters.*
- PREP. **in a/the ~** *You'll be safer in the shelter.* | **~ for** *a shelter for cattle*

sheltered *adj.*

- VERBS **be, look**
- ADV. **snugly, well** *The farmyard was snugly sheltered with buildings on three sides.* | **fairly, quite, relatively**

shelve *verb*

1 put sth to one side and leave it for a while
- ADV. **quietly** *Plans to expand the company have had to be quietly shelved.*
- VERB + SHELVE **be forced to, have to**

2 slope
- ADV. **gently, steeply** *The ground shelves quite steeply here.* | **down** *The beach shelves gently down to the sea.*
- PREP. **to, towards**

sherry *noun*

- ADJ. **small | cream, dry, sweet | cooking**
- QUANT. **bottle, glass**
- VERB + SHERRY **have** *I'll have a small sherry, please.* | **drink, sip**
- SHERRY + NOUN **glass**

shield *noun*

1 used to protect the body
- ADJ. **riot**
- VERB + SHIELD **be armed with, be equipped with, carry, have | act as** *Look for something that can act as a shield, like a dustbin lid.*
- PREP. **behind a/the ~** *a row of police officers behind their riot shields* **on a/the ~** *She did not recognize the coat of arms on his shield.*

2 sb/sth used for protecting yourself
- ADJ. **protective | human | nuclear | heat** *The nose of the space capsule is protected by a heat shield.* | **breast, face, gum, hand**
- VERB + SHIELD **use sb/sth as** *They used 400 hostages as human shields.* | **form**
- PREP. **~ against** *The ozone layer forms a shield against harmful solar rays.*

shield *verb*

- ADV. **partially, partly | carefully** *He carefully shielded the flame with his cupped hand.*
- VERB + SHIELD **try to** *trying to shield the children from the full horrors of the war*
- PREP. **against** *She raised her hand to shield her eyes against the sun.* **from** *new laws to shield companies from foreign competition* **with** *He shielded her with his body.*

shift *noun*

1 change
- ADJ. **distinct, dramatic, fundamental, major, marked, profound, pronounced, radical, significant, substantial | discernible | slight, subtle | gradual | abrupt, sudden | decisive, irreversible, long-term | climate, cultural, demographic, ideological, policy, population**
- VERB + SHIFT **be, represent** *These proposals represent a dramatic shift in policy.* | **bring about, cause, lead to, produce, result in | mark, see** *The moment marked a*

significant shift in attitudes to the war. | **detect** *I detected a subtle shift towards our point of view.* | **explain** *one factor which may explain the president's policy shift*
• SHIFT + VERB **occur, take place** *These climate shifts occurred over less than a decade.*
• PREP. **~ between** *the many shifts between verse and prose that occur in Shakespeare* **~ (away) from** *the shift away from direct taxation* **~ in** *a shift in public opinion* **~ to** *a sudden shift to the right in British politics* **~ towards** *a shift towards part-time farming*

2 division of the working day
• ADJ. **double, long, split** *I agreed to work double shifts for a few weeks.* | **day, early, late, night** | **eight-hour, ten-hour, etc.** | **afternoon, evening, morning, weekend**
• VERB + SHIFT **be/come/go on, do, work (in) ~s** *I'm doing the early shift this week.* ◇ *I didn't realize that I'd have to work shifts.* ◇ *The clinic is staffed by ten doctors who work in shifts.* | **change (your) ~s** *It was 8.00 a.m. and the nurses were changing shifts.* ◇ *My husband has changed his shifts, from the afternoon shift to the night one.* | **be/go/come off**
• SHIFT + NOUN **work** | **supervisor, manager, worker** | **pattern, system** *They'd altered his shift pattern twice in the past fortnight.*
• PREP. **on a/the ~** *a decision for the chief nurse on each shift*

shift *verb*

1 move
• ADV. **slightly** *Julie shifted her position slightly and smiled.* | **impatiently, restlessly, uncomfortably, uneasily** *She shifted uncomfortably in her chair.* | **away**
• PREP. **from** *She shifted her gaze away from the group of tourists.* **onto** *He shifted his weight onto his left foot.* **to** *Her eyes shifted to his face.*
• PHRASES **shift from foot to foot**

2 change
• ADV. **dramatically, markedly** *The emphasis has shifted markedly in recent years.* | **slightly** | **effectively** | **simply** *We cannot simply shift the responsibility onto someone else.* | **gradually, slowly** | **rapidly** | **suddenly** | **constantly, continually** *constantly shifting alliances*
• VERB + SHIFT **attempt to, try to** *trying to shift the blame onto the government* | **tend to** | **begin to**
• PREP. **(away) from** *I felt the advantage had suddenly shifted away from us.* **onto, to** *His sympathies rapidly shifted to the side of the workers.* **towards** *These changes will shift the balance in higher education more towards science subjects.*

shin *noun*

• VERB + SHIN **kick (sb in/on)** *I kicked him hard in the shins to shut him up.* | **bang, bark, bruise, gash, graze, knock** *I barked my shin on a tree stump.*
• SHIN + NOUN **bone** | **guard, pad**
• PREP. **on the/your ~** *a nasty cut on her shin*

shine *verb*

• ADV. **brightly, brilliantly** *The sun was shining brightly.* | **faintly** | **briefly** | **steadily** | **warmly** | **down, in, out** *Sunlight shone in through the window.*
• VERB + SHINE **seem to** *(figurative) She seemed to shine with an inner radiance.* | **make sth** *You've really made that floor shine!*
• PREP. **at** *The watchman shone his torch at us.* **from** *(figurative) Love and pride shone from her eyes.* **in** *The water was shining faintly in the moonlight.* **like** *The dark wood shone like glass.* **on/upon** *The light shone on his face.* **with** *(figurative) His dark eyes shone with excitement.*

ship *noun*

• ADJ. **wooden** | **enemy** | **cargo, container, cruise, merchant, pirate, sailing, supply**
• QUANT. **fleet**
• VERB + SHIP **board, come/go aboard, come/go on board** | **sail** | **steer** | **moor** *The ship is now permanently moored on the Thames in London.* | **build, launch** | **load (sth onto), unload (sth from)** *The dockers were loading the cargo onto the ship.* | **christen, name** | **abandon** *The captain gave the order to abandon ship.* | **go down with** *The captain went down with his ship.* | **scuttle, sink, torpedo** | **jump** *Some of the crew jumped ship (= left it illegally) at Gibraltar and disappeared.*
• SHIP + VERB **carry sb/sth** *a ship carrying more than a thousand people* | **arrive, dock** | **anchor, be/lie at anchor** *Their ship lay at anchor at the mouth of the harbour.* | **depart, go, leave, put to sea, sail, set sail** | **be wrecked, collide with sth, hit sth, run aground** | **capsize** | **go down, sink**
• PREP. **aboard/on/on board a/the ~** *They are now on a ship bound for New York.* **by ~** *There was no time to send the goods by ship.* | **~ to/(bound) for**
• PHRASES **the bow/stern of a ship, the captain/crew of a ship, the deck of a ship**

shipment *noun*

1 quantity of goods sent from one place to another
• ADJ. **arms, drug, oil, plutonium, weapons, etc.**
• VERB + SHIPMENT **receive, send** | **escort** *An armed patrol boat will escort the shipment.* | **seize** *Customs officers have seized a large shipment of cocaine.*
• PREP. **~ of** *a shipment of arms*

2 act of transporting goods
• ADJ. **illegal** | **bulk** | **onward** *taken to Aqaba in Jordan for onward shipment to Brazil* | **waste** *trying to ban toxic waste shipments*
• VERB + SHIPMENT **await** *large quantities of food awaiting shipment to the worst affected areas* | **arrange, begin, make** | **ban, stop** | **resume**
• PREP. **~ from** *to arrange a shipment from India* **~ to** *illegal shipment of arms to the Third World*

shirt *noun*

• ADJ. **clean, crisp, fresh** *He wears a crisp white shirt to the office every day.* | **baggy** | **unbuttoned** | **long-sleeved, short-sleeved** | **button-down, collarless, open-necked** | **unironed** | **football, polo, rugby, sports** | **Hawaiian**
• VERB + SHIRT **button up, unbutton** | **pull off** | **tuck in** *He tucked his shirt into his trousers.* | **wash** | **iron**
• SHIRT + NOUN **button, collar, cuff, front, pocket, sleeve, tail**
• PHRASES **in (your) shirtsleeves** (= not wearing a jacket)
⇨ Special page at CLOTHES

shiver *noun*

• ADJ. **little, slight, small** | **involuntary** | **sudden, unexpected** | **cold** | **delicious** *a delicious shiver of pleasure*
• VERB + SHIVER **give** *She gave a little shiver and laughed.* | **feel** *He felt a shiver of excitement.* | **send** *His appearance sent a cold shiver down her spine.* | **suppress** *She tried to suppress a shiver of anticipation.*
• SHIVER + VERB **go, pass, ripple, run** *A shiver of unease ran through the audience.*
• PREP. **with a ~** *'I'm scared,' she admitted, with a shiver.* | **~ of** *a shiver of fear*
• PHRASES **give sb the shivers** *Just thinking about flying gives me the shivers.*

shiver verb

- ADV. **convulsively, uncontrollably, violently | a little, slightly | involuntarily** *She shivered involuntarily as he approached her.*
- VERB + SHIVER **begin to, start to | make sb** *His cruel and callous comments made me shiver.*
- PREP. **at** *He shivered at the thought of it.* **with** *I was shivering with cold.*

shock noun

1 extreme surprise
- ADJ. **awful, big, complete, considerable, dreadful, great, major, nasty, real, terrible, tremendous | mild, slight | first, initial** *Once the initial shock had worn off, I got to like my new hairstyle.* **| sudden | culture** *It was a bit of a culture shock when I first came to this country.*
- VERB + SHOCK **come as | feel, get, have** *She felt shock that he would be capable of such an act.* ◇ *I got a terrible shock when I saw him.* **| give sb | be in for** *If you think it's going to be easy you're in for a shock!* **| die of** (*informal*) *I nearly died of shock when your mother appeared.* **| get over, recover from**
- PREP. **in~** *She looked round in shock.* **with a~** *She realized with a sudden shock that she was being followed.* **| ~at/on** *her shock on seeing him with another woman* **~to** *This news came as a great shock to me.*
- PHRASES **a bit/something of a shock, quite/rather a shock, a hell of a shock, in a state of shock** *I think I'm still in a state of shock.* **a feeling/sense of shock, the shock of your life** (*informal*), **a shock to the system** (*informal*) *The low wages came as something of a shock to her system.*

2 electric shock
- ADJ. **massive | mild** *He gave himself a mild electric shock while changing a light bulb.* **| electric**
- VERB + SHOCK **get, receive | give sb**

3 extreme weakness caused by injury or shock
- ADJ. **deep | mild | delayed**
- VERB + SHOCK **be in, be suffering from, suffer** *He was in deep shock after the accident.* **| go into** *He had gone into shock and was shaking violently.* **| be treated for**

shock verb

- ADV. **deeply, really** *The news had shocked her deeply.* **| easily** *He had old-fashioned ideas and was easily shocked.*
- PREP. **into** *The news shocked her into action.*

shocked adj.

- VERBS **appear, be, feel, look, sound**
- ADV. **badly, deeply, genuinely, greatly, profoundly, quite, really, terribly, truly, very** *The passengers were badly shocked but unharmed.* **| almost | a bit, a little, mildly, rather, slightly | visibly**
- PREP. **at** *They were shocked at how the children had been treated.* **by** *She was visibly shocked by the conditions she witnessed in the refugee camp.*

shocking adj.

- VERBS **be, seem, sound | find sth**
- ADV. **deeply, extremely, very** *a deeply shocking and painful discovery* **| quite, rather, slightly**
- PREP. **to** *His attitude was shocking to her.*

shoe noun

- ADJ. **clumpy, heavy, stout, strong, sturdy | light | comfortable, sensible | fashion | built-up, court, flat, flat-heeled, high-heeled, low-heeled, platform | buckled, lace-up | ballet, dancing, gym, outdoor, running, sports, tennis, training, walking**
- QUANT. **pair** *a sturdy pair of walking shoes*

- VERB + SHOE **lace up, unlace | kick off, pull off | break in** *to break in a new pair of shoes* **| mend, reheel, repair, resole** *I've had my shoes resoled.* **| clean, polish, shine | scuff**
- SHOE + VERB **fit (sb) | pinch sth** *The shoes, though elegant, pinched her feet terribly.*
- SHOE + NOUN **polish | size | shop | repair | leather | company, factory, maker, manufacturer | box**
- PHRASES **the heel/sole/toe of a shoe**
⇨ Special page at CLOTHES

shoelace noun

- ADJ. **undone | loose**
- QUANT. **pair**
- VERB + SHOELACE **do up, tie | undo, untie | retie**
- SHOELACE + VERB **come undone**
⇨ Special page at CLOTHES

shoot noun

1 new part of a plant
- ADJ. **fresh, green, new, tender, young | flowering | lateral, side | bamboo**
- VERB + SHOOT **have** *This plant hasn't got any shoots yet.* **| develop, produce, put out, send out** *These shrubs will need more light to produce flowering shoots.*
- SHOOT + VERB **appear, come up, develop, emerge, grow, sport** *Keep the bulbs in a cool dark place until shoots appear.*

2 occasion when you photograph sb/sth
- ADJ. **fashion, film, photo, photographic, video** *a five-day photo shoot in Cyprus* **| location**
- PREP. **on a/the ~** *He goes out on shoots with very little equipment.*

shoot verb

- ADV. **straight** *She practised for days until she could shoot straight.* **| accidentally** *He accidentally shot himself in the foot.* **| fatally** *Four policemen were fatally shot in the incident.* **| summarily** *If caught, the men could be summarily shot as spies.* **| back** *If they shoot, we shoot back.*
- VERB + SHOOT **want to | threaten to | be going to** *I thought for a moment that he was going to shoot.* **| try to**
- PREP. **at** *soldiers shooting at a target* **with** *She was shot with a small automatic pistol.*
- PHRASES **shoot (sb) on sight** *Any intruders will be shot on sight.* **shoot sb dead** *The police shot him dead.* **shoot sb in the arm, leg, chest, etc., shoot to kill** *The soldiers were told to shoot to kill.*

shop noun

- ADJ. **high-street | corner, local, village | busy | elegant, fine, exclusive, expensive, grand, high-class, posh, smart, stylish, sumptuous, upmarket | delightful, excellent, good, wonderful | well-stocked | trendy | old-fashioned, quaint, traditional | dingy, shabby | colourful | boarded up, disused, empty, vacant | butcher's, greengrocer's, etc. | gift, pet, shoe, etc. | electrical, photographic, etc. | specialist | duty-free** *She bought 400 cigarettes at the airport duty-free shop.* **| charity** *I gave all my old books to a charity shop.* **| junk | betting | mobile** *Mobile shops are invaluable to people in rural areas.* **| retail | one-stop** *This is your one-stop shop for all your holiday needs.*
- QUANT. **parade, row** *The post office is at the end of the row of shops.* **| chain** *The brothers opened a chain of electrical shops in the eighties.*
- VERB + SHOP **have, keep, own, run | open, set up** *She opened a flower shop in the High Street.* ◇ (*figurative*) *Some buskers had set up shop outside the station.* **| close, shut (up)** *At 5.30 she shuts up shop and goes home.*

● SHOP + VERB **sell sth | offer sth** *The shop offers a large selection of leather goods at reasonable prices.* | **specialize in sth | advertise sth | display sth | open | close, shut**

● SHOP + NOUN **assistant, manager, manageress, owner, staff, worker | counter, display, doorway, front, premises, shelves, sign, window | chain** *a famous shoe shop chain*

● PREP. **around/round a/the~** *I went around all the shops but I couldn't find a present for him.* **at a/the~** *There was a break-in at that new shop last night.* **in a/the~** *She works part-time in a shop.*

shopkeeper *noun*

● ADJ. **small** *an organization set up to help small shop-keepers* | **prosperous | local, village**
● SHOPKEEPER + VERB **sell sth**
⇨ Note at JOB

shoplifting *noun*

● SHOPLIFTING + NOUN **spree** *They stole thousands of pounds' worth of goods in a two-day shoplifting spree.* ◇
⇨ Note at CRIME (for verbs)

shopper *noun*

● ADJ. **average** *what the average shopper's trolley con-tains* | **compulsive | Christmas | window | personal** (= sb you pay to do your shopping)
● VERB + SHOPPER **be crowded with, be packed with, be thronged with** *The street was thronged with shoppers.* | **attract, encourage, persuade, tempt** *encouraging shop-pers to leave their cars at home*
● SHOPPER + VERB **rush** *a busy day in London stores as shoppers rushed to beat the rise in VAT*

shopping *noun*

1 food, etc. bought in shops
● VERB + SHOPPING **be laden with | carry | put away, unpack** *They unpacked the shopping and put it away.*
2 activity of shopping
● ADJ. **weekend, weekly, week's** *I do my weekly shop-ping on a Saturday.* | **Christmas | supermarket | home, Internet** *the move towards home shopping using your computer* | **late-night | duty-free | window | one-stop** *the consumers' demand for one-stop shopping* (= buy-ing all they need in one place)
● VERB + SHOPPING **do, go (out)** *She's doing some last-minute Christmas shopping.* ◇ *I have to go shopping in town this afternoon.*
● SHOPPING + NOUN **bag, basket, trolley | list | ar-cade, area, centre, complex, facilities, mall, precinct, street** *the town's main shopping street* | **expedition, spree, trip** *She won £10 000 and immediately went on a shopping spree.* | **hours** *outside normal shopping hours*

shore *noun*

1 land along the edge of a sea/lake
● ADJ. **golden, sandy** *on the golden shores of beautiful Bali* | **rocky, wooded | barren, bleak, desert, deserted, exposed, lonely, wilder** (*figurative*) *a Belgian from the wilder shores of Flemish nationalism* | **lee, sheltered | distant, far, farther, opposite, other** *Meg was pointing to-wards the far shore.* | **north/northern, etc.** *The path ran along the southern shore of the lake.* | **lake**
● VERB + SHORE **approach, reach | leave | follow, hug** *We sailed until midnight, hugging the shore.* | **be found on, be washed up on** *A dying dolphin was found washed up on the shore.*
● SHORE + NOUN **bird | road | leave**
● PREP. **along the~** *walking along the wooded shores of the lake* **around the~ of** *The route goes around the shore of*

Derwent Water. **by the~** *strolling by the shore* **close to/near the~** *The sea appears calm near the shore.* **from (a/the)~** *just a few miles from shore* ◇ *watching from the shore* **on (a/the)~** *The others were now safely on shore.* ◇ *There are a lot of rocks on that shore.* **on the~s of** *The hotel is situated on the sheltered shores of the Moray Firth.* **(down/back) to/towards the~** *The hotel's gardens stretch down to the lake shore.*

2 (*also* **shores**) particular country
● ADJ. **American, British, etc.** *the ship in which Colum-bus first sailed to American shores* | **foreign, native | our, these**
● VERB + SHORE **arrive on, come to, reach, return to** *He was glad to return to his native shores.* | **leave | de-fend** *We will fight to the death to defend our shores.*
● PREP. **beyond/outside the~** *The decisions will be taken beyond these shores.*

short *adj.*

1 not measuring much from one end to the other
● VERBS **be, look, seem**
● ADV. **extremely, really, very | comparatively, fairly, quite, rather, relatively** *a relatively short distance of 50 to 100 miles*

2 not lasting a long time
● VERBS **be, feel, seem | become, get** *The working week is getting shorter and shorter.* | **make sth | keep sth** *Do you mind if we keep the meeting short?*
● ADV. **extremely, very | comparatively, fairly, quite, relatively** *It was all over in a relatively short space of time.*

3 not having enough of what is needed
● VERBS **be, look** *Our team was one player short.* | **be-come, get** *We're getting short of funds.*
● ADV. **extremely, really, terribly, very, woefully** *If space is really short, that door can be moved.* ◇ *United looked woefully short of menace in attack.* | **a bit, quite, rather**
● PREP. **of** *Mike was a bit short of cash just then.*

4 rude
● VERBS **be**
● ADV. **a bit, rather**
● PREP. **with** *Sorry I was a bit short with you earlier.*

shortage *noun*

● ADJ. **acute, desperate, dire, serious, severe** *the cur-rent acute shortage of teachers* | **growing, increasing | chronic | general | national, world** *the world shortage of coffee* | **current | wartime | cash, energy, food, fuel, housing, labour, manpower, skill/skills, staff, water**
● VERB + SHORTAGE **cause, create, lead to, result in | be affected by, be hampered by, face, have, suffer (from)** *Industry is facing a serious labour shortage.* | **alle-viate, deal with, ease, meet, overcome, solve, tackle** *The recent heavy rains have helped to ease the water shortage.* | **exacerbate** *The energy shortages were exacerbated by the severe winter.*
● SHORTAGE + VERB **occur | cause sth, lead to sth** *A shortage of resources has led to a cutback.*
● PREP. **because of/due to a/the~** *Lives are being put at risk because of staff shortages.* | **~in** *Their economy con-tinued to suffer shortages in raw materials.* **~of** *a desper-ate shortage of food*

shortcoming *noun*

● ADJ. **obvious, perceived | fundamental, serious | minor | sb's own, personal | technical**
● VERB + SHORTCOMING **have, suffer from | draw at-tention to, expose, highlight, identify, reveal | be aware of** *They are well aware of their own shortcomings.* | **ig-nore, overlook** *The committee is willing to overlook your past shortcomings.* | **compensate for, eliminate, make**

good, make up for, overcome, remedy *Their proposal seeks to remedy these shortcomings.*
- SHORTCOMING + VERB **stem from sth** *Not all these shortcomings stem from inadequate resources.*
- PREP. **despite/in spite of sb/sth's ~s** *Despite its obvious shortcomings, the plan was accepted by the government.* | **~in** *the shortcomings in the law*
- PHRASES **shortcomings on sb's part** *They said the accident was due to shortcomings on the part of the pilots.*

short cut *noun*

- VERB + SHORT CUT **take, use**
- PREP. **~ across/through** *Take the short cut across the fields.* **~to** *There are no short cuts to economic recovery.*

shorten *verb*

- ADV. **considerably, dramatically, significantly** *The course has now been shortened considerably.*
- PREP. **by** *His driving ban has been shortened by a year.* **from, to** *The waiting time has been shortened dramatically from eight weeks to just one week.*

shorthand *noun*

1 system of writing
- VERB + SHORTHAND **learn** | **do, take, take/write sth down in** *Her secretary was taking shorthand.* ◇ *He took the speech down in shorthand.* | **transcribe**
- SHORTHAND + NOUN **typist, writer** *A shorthand writer will make a transcript.* | **notes** | **notation**

2 quick way of talking about sth
- ADJ. **convenient, useful**
- VERB + SHORTHAND **use sth as**
- PREP. **~ for** *The term 'machine' is used as a convenient shorthand for the total hardware and software system.*

shortlist *noun*

- VERB + SHORTLIST **compile, draw up** *The interviewers have to draw up a shortlist of five or six people.* | **put sb on** *I think we should put her on our shortlist.* | **choose from** *They will choose from a shortlist of seven candidates.*
- PREP. **on a/the ~** | **~ for** *The film is on the shortlist for Best Picture.* **~ of** *a shortlist of three* ◇ *a shortlist of candidates*

shorts *noun*

- ADJ. **long** | **knee-length** | **baggy** | **tight** | **cycling, football, running, tennis** | **Bermuda** | **boxer**
- QUANT. **pair**
⇒ Special page at CLOTHES

shot *noun*

1 act of firing a gun
- ADJ. **fine, good** | **lucky** | **random** | **fatal** | **warning** | **first, opening** (*often figurative*) *the opening shot in the party election campaign* | **cannon, gun, pistol, rifle** *I heard a pistol shot.*
- QUANT. **series, volley** *A volley of shots rang out.*
- VERB + SHOT **aim** | **fire, take** *I took a few more shots at the target, but missed every time.*
- SHOT + VERB **ring out** | **hit sb/sth, strike sb/sth** *The shot hit him in the upper chest.* | **kill sb/sth** | **miss (sb/sth)**
- PREP. **~ from** *a shot from his semi-automatic rifle* **~ to** *She was killed by a single shot to the head.*

2 person who shoots a gun, etc.
- ADJ. **crack, good, excellent** *She is a crack shot with a rifle.* | **bad, poor**

3 act of kicking/hitting a ball
- ADJ. **fine, good, great, superb** | **poor, wayward** | **long**

- VERB + SHOT **crack/get in, have, take, try** *Go on—take another shot.* | **miss** | **mishit** | **block, parry, save** *The goalkeeper parried his first shot but he scored from the rebound.*
- SHOT + VERB **be on target** | **go wide, miss** *My first shot went wide, but my second was right on target.*
- PREP. **~ at/on** *Their captain tried a long shot on goal.* **~ from** *his right-footed shot from outside the penalty area* ◇ *a superb shot from Rivaldo*
⇒ Special page at SPORT

4 photograph; picture in a film
- ADJ. **camera** | **aerial, close-up, long, still, tracking, wide-angle, zoom** | **location** | **opening** | **action, crowd** | **fashion, publicity** | **cover**
- VERB + SHOT **get, take** *I got some great shots of the runners as they crossed the line.*
- SHOT + VERB **show sth** *a wide-angle shot showing the Houses of Parliament*
- PREP. **~ from** *a shot from a low angle* **~ of** *a publicity shot of the band performing*

5 injection of a drug
- ADJ. **booster**
- VERB + SHOT **give sb** | **get, have** *Have you had all your shots for your holiday yet?*
- PREP. **~ of** *a shot of penicillin* ◇ *The applause acted on her like a shot of adrenalin.*

shotgun *noun*

- ADJ. **12-bore, double-barrelled, pump-action, sawn-off** *The men were armed with sawn-off shotguns.* | **loaded**
- VERB + SHOTGUN **fire** | **be armed with, carry** | **threaten sb with** | **load** | **aim**
- SHOTGUN + NOUN **licence** | **cartridge, pellet** | **blast** *The cause of death was a shotgun blast at close range.* | **wound**

shoulder *noun*

1 part of the body between the neck and the arm
- ADJ. **dislocated, frozen** *His frozen shoulder has stopped him playing tennis.*
- SHOULDER + NOUN **injury** | **blade, bones, joint, muscle, socket** *The bullet hit him squarely between the shoulder blades.* | **height, level, width** *Keep the feet shoulder width apart.* | **harness, sling, strap** | **injury**
- PREP. **over your ~** *He slung the sack over his shoulder and set off.*
- PHRASES **a pat on the shoulder** *He gave me a reassuring pat on the shoulder.* **shoulder to shoulder** *The route of the procession was lined with police officers standing shoulder to shoulder.* **tap sb on the shoulder** *I tapped the man on the shoulder and asked him to move.*

2 shoulders the part between the two shoulders
- ADJ. **big, broad, great, huge, manly, massive, muscled, muscular, powerful, strong, wide** | **delicate, shapely, slim** | **narrow, thin** | **square** | **round** | **bony** | **bowed** | **bare** | **tense, tight** | **tired**
- VERB + SHOULDERS **shrug** *When I asked him why he'd done it he just shrugged his shoulders.* | **hunch** *He hunched his shoulders against the cold wind.*
- SHOULDERS + VERB **be bent, be bowed, be stooped** *She was crouched with her head forward and her shoulders bent.* | **droop, drop, sag, slump** *My shoulders dropped with relief.* | **lift, shrug** *Her shoulders lifted in a vague shrug.* | **heave, shake, twitch** *His enormous shoulders heaved with sobs.* | **stiffen, tighten** | **relax**
- PREP. **on your ~s** *The child sat on her father's shoulders to watch the parade go by.*

shoulder *verb*

1 accept the responsibility for sth
- VERB + SHOULDER **have to, must** *She had to shoulder*

the burden of childcare. | **be willing/unwilling to** *He was unwilling to shoulder this responsibility alone.*

2 push sb/sth with your shoulder
- ADV. **roughly** *We were shouldered roughly out of the way.* | **aside, out of the way**
- PHRASES **shoulder your way past/through sb/sth** *She shouldered her way through the crowd.*

shout *noun*

- ADJ. **great, loud | low | faint, muffled | distant | sudden | angry, indignant | triumphant | raucous, wild | warning**
- VERB + SHOUT **give, let out | hear** *I heard her warning shout too late.* | **be greeted with | give sb** *(figurative) Give me a shout if you'd like to come with us.*
- SHOUT + VERB **echo, go up** *A great shout of excitement went up as she crossed the finishing line.*
- PREP. **with a~** *With a shout of pain, he pulled his hand away from the hot stove.* | **~ from** *There were shouts of laughter from the crowd.* **~ of**
- PHRASES **a shout of anger/alarm/pain, a shout of laughter, a shout of victory**
⇨ Note at SOUND

shout *verb*

- ADV. **aloud** *'I'm done for!' he shouted aloud.* | **loudly | hoarsely | hysterically, wildly | angrily, furiously | almost** *He found he was almost shouting.* | **suddenly | back | out** *If they shout at you, shout back!*
- VERB + SHOUT **want to | try to | open your mouth to** *He opened his mouth to shout, but no sound came out.* | **begin to, start to | hear sb** *I could hear him shouting down the telephone.*
- PREP. **about** *What were they shouting about?* **above** *We had to shout above the noise of the engines.* **after** *We shouted after him, but he couldn't hear us.* **at** *There's no need to shout at me!* **for** *We shouted for help.* **to** *He shouted to the lorry driver to stop.*
- PHRASES **keep (on) shouting, shout and scream** *They were surrounded by people shouting and screaming.* **shout at the top of your voice, shout yourself hoarse** *She shouted herself hoarse, cheering on the team.* **start/stop shouting**

shove *noun*

- ADJ. **little | good, hefty, violent**
- VERB + SHOVE **give sb/sth** *Harry gave him a hefty shove and he fell over.*
- PREP. **with a~** *She sent him off with a little shove.*

shove *verb*

- ADV. **hard, roughly** *I shoved hard until the door opened.* | **aside, away, back** *He shoved me roughly aside.*
- PREP. **down, in** *She shoved the letter in a drawer.* **into, out of, through** *A leaflet was shoved through my letter box.*
- PHRASES **push and shove** *The crowd was pushing and shoving to get a better view.* **shove your way** *We shoved our way to the bar.*

show *noun*

1 type of entertainment
- ADJ. **live | family, popular | radio, television/TV | floor, stage | benefit, charity | chat, talk | game, quiz | cabaret, comedy, magic, musical, talent, variety | film, light, slide | Punch and Judy, puppet | freak | peep | one-man, one-woman, solo | sb's own** *She finally got her own TV show.* | **road, touring, travelling**
- VERB + SHOW **see, watch** *Did you see the Lenny Henry Show last night?* | **host**
- SHOW + VERB **feature sb/sth, star sb** *a live show featuring the best of Irish talent*
- SHOW + NOUN **business**
- PREP. **from a/the~** *songs from the show* **in a/the~** *one of the acts in the show* **on a/the~** (only used about television and radio shows) *I saw her on a chat show yesterday.*
- PHRASES **the star of the show** *The dog was the real star of the show.*
⇨ Note at PERFORMANCE (for more verbs)

2 public display/exhibition
- ADJ. **big | annual, spring, summer | local | agricultural, air, art, boat, cat, dog, fashion, flower, horse, motor, trade**
- VERB + SHOW **have, hold, organize, put on** *They are holding a big fashion show at the Hilton tonight.* | **attend, go to**
- SHOW + VERB **feature** *The show features the work of local artists.*
- SHOW + NOUN **ring**
- PREP. **at a/the~** *There were more than 500 exhibitors at the trade show.* **on ~** (being shown for people to look at) *The paintings are on show until April.*

3 outward expression of an emotion/attitude
- ADJ. **great | brave | public**
- VERB + SHOW **make, put on** *Although she hated him, she put on a show of politeness.* | **be all** *He shouts a lot but it's all show.*
- PREP. **for~** *She pretends to be interested in opera, but it's only for show.* | **~ of** *He made a great show of welcoming us.*
- PHRASES **a show of force/strength** *The Democrats organized a show of strength, a mass rally in Central Park.*

show *verb*

1 make sth clear; let sb see sth
- ADV. **clearly** *The figures clearly show that her claims are false.*
- VERB + SHOW **appear to, seem to | go to** *It just goes to show what you can do when you really try.* | **aim to, attempt to, seek to, try to | be able to, can/could | be unable to, fail to | be expected to, be likely to** *Third quarter figures are likely to show a further fall in figures.* | **help (to) | offer to | refuse to** *Lewis refused to show any emotion.* | **be anxious to, be eager to, be happy to, be keen to, intend to, want to, wish to** *Les was happy to show her how it should be done.* | **be designed to | let sb** *Let me show you on the map.*
- PREP. **to** *She showed her new toy to her friends.*
- PHRASES **a chance to show sth** *I'm giving him a chance to show what he can do.*

2 be visible
- ADV. **hardly** *It's such a tiny mark, it hardly shows.*
- VERB + SHOW **begin to | let sth** *She tried not to let her disappointment show.*

showdown *noun*

- ADJ. **final** *The scene was set for the final showdown.* | **title, World Cup, etc.**
- VERB + SHOWDOWN **have | avoid | face, head for | force, seek** *He was now strong enough to force a showdown with them.*
- PREP. **~ against** *the showdown against Holland in April* **~ between** *the title showdown between Arsenal and United* **~ over** *The council is heading for a showdown over the new proposals.* **~ with** *Britain's World Cup showdown with Australia last month*
- PHRASES **it comes to a showdown** (= a showdown happens) *Of course I'll support you if it comes to a showdown.*

shower *noun*

1 for washing your body
- ADJ. **cold, cool, hot | power | brief, quick** *I'll just take a quick shower.* | **electric | en suite, private**
- VERB + SHOWER **have, take**
- SHOWER + NOUN **cubicle, curtain, room | head, mixer, rose, tray | gel**

2 of rain or snow
- ADJ. **rain, sleet, snow | heavy, light | blustery, wintry | scattered | April**
- SHOWER + VERB **spread | die out** *Scattered showers during the afternoon will die out by late evening.*

3 of small objects
- ADJ. **dust, meteor, meteorite**
- PREP. **~ of** *The grinding wheel sent out a shower of sparks.*

showing *noun*

1 how sb/sth behaves or performs
- ADJ. **good, strong | disappointing, disastrous, dismal, poor** *the party's poor showing in the election*
- VERB + SHOWING **make, put up** *The opposing team put up a very strong showing.* | **improve on** *The team will have to improve on today's showing if it is to survive in the competition.*
- PREP. **on sb's ~** *On its present showing, the party should win the election.* | **~ against** *the euro's strong showing against the dollar* **~ by/from** *It was a great showing by the Brazilian team.*

2 showing a film, etc.
- ADJ. **private**
- VERB + SHOWING **attend, go to** *The young princes attended a private showing of the new Disney film.* | **get, have, receive | give sth**

showroom *noun*

- ADJ. **car, furniture | electricity, gas** *We chose a new cooker from the gas showroom.*
- VERB + SHOWROOM **go to, visit | open, set up**
- SHOWROOM + NOUN **door, window | condition** *He managed to find a second-hand Ferrari in showroom condition.* | **price | model** *They took 10 per cent off the price of the computer as it was a showroom model.*

shrapnel *noun*

- ADJ. **flying** *He was hit in the arm by flying shrapnel.*
- QUANT. **piece**
- VERB + SHRAPNEL **be hit by, be shattered by, be wounded/killed by**
- SHRAPNEL + VERB **fly, whistle** *The bomb exploded, sending shrapnel whistling through the trees.*
- SHRAPNEL + NOUN **wound**
- PREP. **~from** *the shrapnel from the grenade*

shred *noun*

1 small thin piece of sth
- ADJ. **fine, thin | tattered** *the tattered shreds of their flag*
- PREP. **in/into ~s** *Cut the orange peel into fine shreds.* ◇ *(figurative) Their economy is in shreds.* | **~ of** *leaving just a few shreds of cloth*
- PHRASES **cut/rip/tear sth to shreds** *(figurative) Their case was torn to shreds by the defence lawyer.*

2 very small amount of sth
- ADJ. **every** *With her had gone every shred of hope he had for the future.* | **last, remaining** *She was hanging on to the last remaining shreds of her reputation.*
- PREP. **~of** *There is not a shred of doubt in my mind that we will win.*

- PHRASES **not a/the slightest shred of sth, not/without a shred of evidence**

shred *verb*

- ADV. **finely** *Shred the lettuce leaves finely.*

shriek *noun*

- ADJ. **loud | little** *She gave a little shriek of delight.* | **high-pitched, piercing**
- VERB + SHRIEK **give, let out | hear**
- PREP. **with a~** *She fell to the floor with a shriek of pain.* | **~ of** *Shrieks of laughter came from the bedroom.*
- PHRASES **a shriek of delight/pain, a shriek of laughter**
⇨ Note at SOUND

shriek *verb*

- ADV. **aloud | all but, almost** *He all but shrieked when he saw her.*
- VERB + SHRIEK **hear sb**
- PREP. **at** *Stop shrieking at me!* **in** *She shrieked in terror.* **with** *The audience shrieked with laughter.*

shrine *noun*

- ADJ. **hallowed, holy, religious, sacred** *This shrine is sacred to the Hindu god Vishnu.* | **Christian, Islamic, etc. | forest, rural, wayside | portable**
- VERB + SHRINE **build, erect, turn sth into | dedicate** *a shrine dedicated to the sea goddess* | **go on/make a pilgrimage to, visit** *On his recovery he made a pilgrimage to the shrine of St John.*
- PREP. **at a/the** *worshipping at wayside shrines* | **~ of** *the shrine of St Cuthbert at Durham* **~to** *She had turned the room into a shrine to her dead son.*

shrink *verb*

1 become smaller
- ADV. **dramatically | a little, slightly | further | fast, rapidly** *competing in a market that is shrinking fast* | **gradually, slowly | steadily**
- PREP. **by** *Their profits shrank by 4% last year.* **from, to** *Their share of the market has shrunk from 14% to 5%.*
- PHRASES **shrink in size** *Households have been shrinking in size but increasing in number.*

2 move away
- ADV. **a little** *He shrank a little at the sight of the blood.* | **away, back**
- VERB + SHRINK **try to**
- PREP. **against** *He shrank back against the wall.* **in** *She shrank back in terror.* **into** *I shrank back into the shadows.* **from** *She shrank from his touch.*

shroud *noun*

- VERB + SHROUD **wrap sb in** *A human form lay there, wrapped in a shroud.*
- PREP. **in a/the ~** | **~ of** *(figurative) The nuclear project was cloaked in a shroud of secrecy.*

shrub *noun*

- ADJ. **deciduous, evergreen | hardy, tender | dwarf, large, low, medium-sized, small, tall | autumn, autumn-flowering, spring, spring-flowering, etc. | flowering | scented | thorny | fast-growing | ornamental | overgrown**
- VERB + SHRUB **grow | plant, put in | dig up, take out | replant | cut back, prune** *Overgrown deciduous shrubs can be cut back at this time of year.*
- SHRUB + VERB **grow** *Tender shrubs don't grow well here.* | **come into flower, flower**
- SHRUB + NOUN **rose**

- PHRASES **be planted with shrubs** *The bed is planted with flowering shrubs.* **a variety of shrub**

shrug noun

- ADJ. **little, slight, small | careless, indifferent | nonchalant | dismissive | helpless, hopeless, resigned | tired, weary | apologetic | self-deprecating | expressive | mental** *With a mental shrug, he decided to tell the truth.* **| Gallic**
- VERB + SHRUG **give** *The boy gave a slight shrug and walked away.*
- PREP. **in a~** *She lifted her shoulders in a little shrug* **with a~** *'I don't know,' she said with a shrug.* **| ~of** *a shrug of resignation*
- PHRASES **a shrug of the shoulders**

shrug verb

- ADV. **lightly, slightly | carelessly, dismissively, indifferently, negligently, nonchalantly** *She shrugged nonchalantly and turned away.* **| impatiently, irritably | apologetically | helplessly, ruefully** *He shrugged helplessly and said nothing.* **| expressively | just, merely, only, simply** *He merely shrugged his shoulders in reply.*

PHRASAL VERB

shrug sth off

- VERB + SHRUG STH OFF **be able to, can/could, try to** *The team have been able to shrug off their recent failures and perform well.* **| try to**

shudder noun

- ADJ. **little, slight, small, tiny | deep, exaggerated, great, violent | involuntary**
- VERB + SHUDDER **give** *She gave a little shudder when she touched his clammy hand.* **| feel | repress, suppress** *He repressed a shudder of disgust.* **| send** *The sight of the coffin sent a shudder through him*
- SHUDDER + VERB **go/pass/run through sb/sth, rack sb/sth** *A shudder of pain racked his body.*
- PREP. **with a~** *He remembered that awful moment with a shudder.* **| ~of** *a shudder of relief*

shudder verb

- ADV. **convulsively, uncontrollably, violently | slightly | involuntarily** *She shuddered involuntarily as he approached her.* **| inwardly**
- VERB + SHUDDER **make sb** *The sight of the dead body made them shudder.*
- PREP. **at** *She shuddered at the memory of school exams.* **through** *A deep sigh shuddered through her body.* **with** *His whole body shuddered with fury.*

shuffle verb

1 walk by sliding your feet along
- ADV. **awkwardly, slowly** *Simon shuffled awkwardly towards them.* **| along, away, forward, out, off, over** *The queue shuffled slowly forward.*
- PREP. **across, down, into, out of, towards, etc.**

2 move your body/feet around
- ADV. **nervously, uncomfortably, uneasily** *She shuffled nervously on the bench.* **| about, around** *The boys shuffled around uncomfortably.*
- PHRASES **shuffle in your chair/seat**

shut adj.

1 in a closed position
- VERBS **be, look | bang, blow, clang, click, clunk, slam, slide, swing** *The window blew shut.* ◇ *The elevator door slid shut.* **| remain, stay | be clenched, be jammed** *His jaw was clenched shut.* **| bang sth, kick sth, leave sth, pull sth, slam sth, slide sth, snap sth** *I'll leave the*

window shut for now. ◇ *He slammed the case shut.* ◇ *She snapped shut a file on her desk.* **| keep sth** *The gates are always kept shut.* ◇ *(figurative) Afraid to ask seemingly stupid questions, I kept my mouth shut.*
- ADV. **firmly, properly, tightly** *The door was firmly shut.*

2 not open to the public
- VERBS **be, look** *The bars all look shut to me.* **| remain**
- PREP. **for** *The park is now shut for the winter.*

shutter noun

1 cover for a window
- ADJ. **closed, open** *He left the shutter open.* **| metal, steel, wooden | security, window**
- VERB + SHUTTER **have | fling open, fold back, open, throw back/open** *He threw open the shutters to cool the room.* **| close, pull down, put up** *The village shop had put up the shutters for the night.*
- SHUTTER + VERB **be/come down** *All the shutters in the street were down.* ◇ *(figurative) I could feel the shutters coming down in her mind.*
- PREP. **behind~** *She could be seen waiting for him behind half-closed shutters.* **through~** *Daylight was filtering through the shutters when he woke up.*

2 part of a camera
- ADJ. **camera**
- VERB + SHUTTER **press**
- SHUTTER + VERB **click** *As the princess approached you could hear hundreds of camera shutters clicking.*
- SHUTTER + NOUN **speed** *You will need a fast shutter speed for photographing sport.*

shuttle noun

1 plane/bus/train
- VERB + SHUTTLE **catch, fly on, get, take**
- SHUTTLE + NOUN **bus, flight, service, train** *The supermarket operates a complimentary shuttle service.* **| diplomacy** (= international talks carried out by sb who travels between two or more countries)
- PREP. **on a/the~** *We'll fly up on the shuttle.* **| ~between** *the shuttle between Adrar and Oran* **~from, ~to** *I took the Eastern Airlines shuttle from Washington to New York.*

2 (*also* **space shuttle**) spacecraft
- SHUTTLE + NOUN **craft | crew | mission**
- PREP. **aboard/on board the ~**

shy verb

- ADV. **violently**
- PREP. **at** *Her horse shied violently at a gorse bush.*

shy adj.

- VERBS **be, feel, look, seem, sound** *Please don't be shy—I won't eat you!* **| become, get, go, grow**
- ADV. **desperately, excessively, extremely, painfully, terribly, very** *As a teenager I was painfully shy.* **| all** *She went all shy and hid behind her mother.* **| almost | a bit, fairly, a little, quite, rather, slightly, somewhat | naturally** *He is a naturally shy, retiring man.* **| chronically**
- PREP. **of** *I was a bit shy of them at first.* **with** *You don't have to be shy with me, you know.*

shyness noun

- ADJ. **natural | extreme, intense, paralysing**
- VERB + SHYNESS **be overcome with, have, suffer from** *He was suddenly overcome with shyness.* **| forget, get over, lose, overcome** *She had to work very hard to overcome her paralysing shyness.* ◇ *She completely forgot her shyness in her fascination with what he was saying.* **| cure**
- SHYNESS + VERB **disappear, vanish**

sibling *noun*

- ADJ. **elder/older, younger** *The younger children were badly treated by older siblings.*
- SIBLING + NOUN **rivalry**
- PREP. **among/between ~s** *poor relationships between siblings*

sick *noun* **the sick**

- ADJ. **chronic, long-term**
- VERB + SICK **visit | care for, look after** *workers who are caring for the sick and elderly* **| treat | cure, heal** *the Church's mission to preach the gospel and heal the sick*
- PHRASES **the sick and wounded** *The sick and wounded were evacuated from the war zone.*

sick *adj.*

1 ill
- VERBS **be, look | become, fall** *(formal),* **get** *(informal) He fell sick with yellow fever.* ◇ *She was afraid she would get sick if she stayed in that place any longer.*
- ADV. **chronically, desperately, extremely, terribly, very** *The house has accommodation for up to 60 chronically sick or disabled residents.* ◇ *a very sick woman in the next bed* **| incurably, terminally | mentally**
- PHRASES **be off sick** *John's not in the office today, he's off sick.*

2 ill in your stomach
- VERBS **be, feel, look** *Mum, I feel sick!* **| get** *I get travel-sick if I sit in the back seat.* **| make sb** *If you eat all that chocolate it'll make you sick.*
- ADV. **horribly, really, very, violently** *He leaned sideways and was violently sick.* **| almost | a bit, faintly, a little, quite, rather, slightly | continually | physically** *Every time I think about it I feel physically sick.*
- PREP. **with** *Laura felt almost sick with embarrassment.*
- PHRASES **be as sick as a dog**

3 bored/disgusted/annoyed
- VERBS **be | become, get** *I'm getting sick of all these delays.* **| make sb** *Her attitude makes me sick.*
- ADV. **heartily, really** *He was getting heartily sick of all the false sympathy.* **| absolutely, thoroughly | a bit, pretty, rather** *She was getting a bit sick of his moaning.*
- PREP. **of** *I'm getting sick of you leaving things in a mess.*
- PHRASES **sick and tired of sth, sick to death of sth, sick to the back teeth of sth**

4 cruel/in bad taste
- VERBS **be, seem, sound**
- ADV. **extremely, really, very** *You're really sick, you know that?* **| pretty, rather** *It was pretty sick humour, I thought.*
- PHRASES **sick in the head** *Whoever started the fire must be sick in the head.*

sickness *noun*

1 state of being ill
- ADJ. **chronic, long, long-term**
- SICKNESS + NOUN **absence | allowance, benefit | insurance | rate**
- PREP. **due to/owing to/through ~** *The Personnel Department keeps a record of employees absent through sickness.*

2 nausea
- VERB + SICKNESS **suffer (from)**
- SICKNESS + VERB **rise** *The sickness rose inside him.*
- PHRASES **a feeling of sickness** *Several workers complained of feelings of sickness and headaches.*

3 particular type of illness
- ADJ. **acute, chronic | air, car, motion, travel | altitude/mountain, decompression, radiation, sleeping**
- ⇨ Special page at ILLNESS

side *noun*

1 flat surface of sth thin
- ADJ. **flip, reverse** *The reverse side of the coin has a picture of a flower.*

2 either of the two parts of a place/object
- ADJ. **far, opposite, other** *At the other side of the room, a group of people were clustered around the fire.* **| near | right, wrong** *A car came rushing towards them on the wrong side of the road.* **| left-hand, right-hand** *The left-hand side of the page.* **| east, west, etc.**
- PREP. **at one/the ~** *Some people were standing at one side of the room.* **down one/the ~** *A path leads down one side of the garden.* **from ~ to ~** *The cat sat with its tail twitching from side to side.* **on/to one ~** (= not in the middle) *She put her head to one side as she talked.*

3 right/left part of your body
- ADJ. **left-hand, left, right-hand, right** *the right-hand side of the brain*
- PREP. **down your ~** *He is paralysed down his left side as a result of polio.* **in the/your ~** *I've got an awful pain in my side.* **on your ~** *I always sleep on my side because I'm not comfortable on my back.*

4 aspect/quality of sb/sth
- ADJ. **positive | bad, dark, negative, ugly** *The scandal has shown us the ugly side of politics.* **| caring, creative, feminine** *She likes men who do not hide their feminine side.* **| business, commercial, financial, management, marketing, etc.** *I had nothing to do with the financial side of the firm.*
- VERB + SIDE **have** *He's usually very kind and gentle, but he has his less positive side too.* **| show | hide**
- PREP. **~ to** *There are several sides to most problems.*
- PHRASES **look on the bright side** *Even when things go badly, try to look on the bright side.* **on the credit/debit side** *On the credit side, we played well, although we lost the match.* **see the funny side (of sth)** *Fortunately, Julie saw the funny side when I spilled coffee on her.*

5 team
- ADJ. **good, strong | losing, winning | away, home** *As the home side, they were expected to play an attacking game.* **| League, Test**
- VERB + SIDE **captain | field** *Sussex are likely to field a strong side.*

side effect *noun*

- ADJ. **adverse, dangerous, harmful, nasty, negative, serious, severe, toxic, undesirable, unexpected, unfortunate, unpleasant, unwanted | beneficial | long-term | physical**
- VERB + SIDE EFFECT **cause, have, produce** *The treatment has some unfortunate side effects.* **| suffer**
- PREP. **~ from** *The patient suffered severe side effects from the drug.* **~ of** *The drug has the beneficial side effect of lowering the patient's blood pressure.* **~ on** *The medication can have adverse side effects on the patient.*

sideline *noun*

- ADJ. **lucrative, nice (little), profitable, useful** *He decided to turn his hobby into a lucrative sideline.*
- VERB + SIDELINE **have | develop**
- PREP. **~ for** *Cider making was a sideline for many farmers.* **~ in** *She is developing a nice little sideline in childminding for friends.* **~ to** *The restaurant started out as a sideline to his main business.*

siege *noun*

1 when an army surrounds a town
- ADJ. **long, prolonged**
- VERB + SIEGE **lay** *The English forces laid siege to the city of Tournai.* **| withstand** *This fortress could withstand a siege for years if necessary.* **| lift, raise, relieve** (= arrive

to help the people in a siege) *The royal forces marched south to lift the siege of Donnington Castle.*
- SIEGE + VERB **last** *The siege lasted two years.*
- SIEGE + NOUN **warfare | engine**
- PREP. **at a/the~** *wounded at the siege of Edinburgh Castle in 1573* **during a/the~, under~** *At the very end of the war, Prague again came under siege.* **| ~of**

2 when the police, etc. surround a building
- ADJ. **four-day, ten-hour, etc. | armed, gun, police**
- SIEGE + VERB **end** *The seven-hour armed siege at the school ended peacefully.*
- PREP. **during a/the~** *The terrorists were shot dead during the siege of the embassy.*
- PHRASES **a state of siege** *The police placed the city centre under a virtual state of siege.*

siesta *noun*

- ADJ. **short | afternoon**
- VERB + SIESTA **have, take** *Lots of people were taking a short siesta in the shade.*
- SIESTA + NOUN **time**
- PREP. **for a~** *I went upstairs for my afternoon siesta.*

sieve *noun*

- ADJ. **fine**
- VERB + SIEVE **pass/press/strain sth through**
- PREP. **in a/the~** *Wash the rice in a sieve under cold running water.* **through a/the~** *Strain the cream through a fine sieve into the egg mixture.*

sift *verb*

1 pass sth through a sieve
- ADV. **finely** *Sift the flour finely before adding it to the mixture.* **| in, together** *Beat the mixture until smooth, then sift in the remaining sugar.*

2 examine sth very carefully
- ADV. **carefully, methodically**
- PREP. **through** *They spent days carefully sifting through the evidence.*

sigh *noun*

- ADJ. **big, deep, great, heavy, huge | little, small, soft | long | heartfelt | resigned, weary | exaggerated | audible** *There was an audible sigh of relief when the news came through that nobody was hurt.* **| collective**
- VERB + SIGH **breathe, give, heave, let out** *I breathed a sigh of relief.* **| repress, stifle, suppress | hear**
- SIGH + VERB **escape sb** *A weary sigh escaped him.*
- PREP. **on a~** *She let out her breath on a sigh.* **with a~** *'I suppose we'd better get back to work,' he said with a heavy sigh.* **| ~of** *She gave a deep sigh of contentment.*
- PHRASES **a sigh of relief**
⇒ Note at SOUND

sigh *verb*

- ADV. **deeply, heavily** *She sighed heavily and sat down.* **| softly | audibly, gustily, loudly, noisily | inwardly | a little | contentedly, happily** *She looked at her son and sighed happily.* **| impatiently | resignedly | wearily** *He sighed wearily as he looked at the pile of work.*
- PREP. **in** *He sighed in exasperation.* **with** *We sighed with relief when the noise stopped.*

sight *noun*

1 ability to see
- ADJ. **excellent, good, normal, perfect | defective, failing, poor, weak | long, short**
- VERB + SIGHT **have** *She has very little sight in her left eye.* **| lose** *He's lost the sight of one eye.* **| save** *The surgeons battled to save her sight.*
- SIGHT + VERB **deteriorate, fail, go** *I think my sight is beginning to go.*
- SIGHT + NOUN **test | defects, problems**
- PHRASES **the/your sense of sight**

2 act/moment of seeing sth
- VERB + SIGHT **catch, get, have** *She suddenly caught sight of the look on her mother's face.* ◊ *We will soon get our first sight of the Statue of Liberty.* **| keep** *She kept sight of him in her mirror.* **| lose**
- PREP. **at the~ (of)** *Her knees went weak at the sight of him.*
- PHRASES **at first sight** *He looked at first sight like an English tourist.* **cannot stand/bear the sight of sth** (= hate seeing sb/sth) *I never could stand the sight of blood.* **a clear sight of sth** *He didn't shoot until he had a clear sight of the goal.* **know sb by sight** (= to recognize sb without knowing them well), **the mere/very sight of sb/sth** *The mere sight of her sitting there made his heart beat faster.* **shoot (sb) on sight** (= to shoot sb immediately you see them) *Soldiers have been ordered to shoot looters on sight.* **sick of the sight of sb/sth** *We've shared an office for too long and we're sick of the sight of each other.*

3 position where sth can be seen
- VERB + SIGHT **come into** *Then the towers of the castle came into sight.* **| disappear from, vanish from** *She watched until the car disappeared from sight.* **| hide (sth) from, remove sth from** *I hid the papers from sight.* **| keep sth in** *Keep their car in sight for as long as you can.*
- PREP. **in~** (often figurative) *The end is in sight* (= will happen soon). **out of~** *He kept out of sight behind a pillar.* **within~of** *The cricket ground was situated within sight of both village pubs.*
- PHRASES **come in sight of sb/sth** *At last we came in sight of a few houses.* **in full sight of sb** *He tried to break into a car in full sight of a policeman.* **in plain sight** *They waited until the enemy was in plain sight.* **your line of sight** *She was now standing just out of his line of sight.* **not let sb/sth out of your sight** *Whatever you do, don't let them out of your sight!*

4 sth that you see
- ADJ. **common, regular | bizarre, rare, strange, unexpected, unfamiliar, unlikely, unusual | awe-inspiring, awesome, beautiful, breathtaking, fine, impressive, inspiring, magnificent, spectacular, splendid, unforgettable, wonderful | depressing, pathetic, pitiful, sad, sorry** *He really did look a sorry sight, his hair tangled and his clothing covered in feathers.* **| ghastly, gruesome, horrifying, terrible, terrifying**
- VERB + SIGHT **look**
- PHRASES **not a pretty sight** *I'm not a pretty sight when I get out of bed in the morning.* **sights and sounds** *The sights and sounds of the city distracted her from her work.*

5 **sights** places of interest
- ADJ. **famous, historic**
- VERB + SIGHTS **see, take in, visit** *Let's get out of the hotel and see the sights.*

6 **sights** your aim/expectation
- VERB + SIGHTS **have sb/sth in/within** *Rossi has the defending champion in his sights in tomorrow's race.* **| lower, raise** *After failing to get into university, he lowered his sights and got a job in a shop.*
- PHRASES **set your sights on sth/have your sights set on sth** *She has her sights set on becoming a writer.* **set your sights high/low** *He says he wants to win the trophy, but I think he's setting his sights too high.*

sighting *noun*

- ADJ. **confirmed, reliable | unconfirmed | reported | rare | UFO**
- VERB + SIGHTING **have** *We now have three confirmed sightings of an enemy plane.* **| report | follow up, inves-**

tigate *The police are now following up a number of reported sightings of the missing woman's car.*
- PREP. ~**of**

sightseeing *noun*

- VERB + SIGHTSEEING **do, go** *We did some sightseeing in the morning.* ◊ *It's too hot to go sightseeing.*
- SIGHTSEEING + NOUN **excursion, tour, trip**

sign *noun*

1 sth that shows that sth exists/may happen
- ADJ. **clear, definite, distinct, obvious, real, sure, telltale, unmistakable | external, outward, visible** *All the outward signs of growth in the market are there.* | **tangible | early, first** *Strong likes or dislikes of various foods are another of the early signs of pregnancy.* | **increasing | encouraging, good, healthy, hopeful, positive, welcome** *He was silent. It was a good sign.* | **bad, disturbing | danger, ominous, warning** *Are appliances you buy safe? We point out the danger signs.*
- VERB + SIGN **bear, have** *The murder had all the signs of a crime of passion.* | **exhibit, display, give, show** *By now the fish was showing signs of distress.* | **detect, find, see, watch out for** *We detected signs that they were less than enthusiastic about the holiday.* | **interpret (sth as), read, recognize, see sth as | look for** *Look carefully for signs of damp.* | **point out**
- SIGN + VERB **appear, come** *The first signs of spring appeared.* | **indicate sth, point to sth** *All the signs pointed to it being more than just a coincidence.*
- PREP. **at a/the ~** *He disappeared at the first sign of trouble.* | **from~** *The villages regarded the earthquake as a sign from God.* ~**of**
- PHRASES **sign of life** *There was no sign of life in the house* (= there seemed to be nobody there). **a sign of the times** *It's a real sign of the times: 30 small businesses face financial ruin this month.* **little/no/not the least/not the slightest sign (of sb/sth)** *He spoke up without the slightest sign of nervousness.*

2 board, etc. giving information/a warning
- ADJ. **flashing, illuminated | neon | handwritten, painted | exit | inn, pub, shop, street | direction, road, traffic | 'Stop' | warning | 'For sale', 'No Smoking', 'To let'**
- VERB + SIGN **erect, hang out/up, hold up, put up** *Some of the marchers were holding up signs and placards.* ◊ *Someone had put up a 'For Sale' sign.* | **see | read | follow** *Just follow the signs for Bridgend.*
- SIGN + VERB **read sth, say sth** *The sign read 'No Fishing'.* | **indicate sth** *This sign indicates that cycling is allowed.* | **point** *The sign pointed down a small lane.* | **advertise sth | warn** *signs warning against trespass* | **flash** *A neon sign flashed above the door.*
- PREP. ~ **for/to** *Follow the road and you'll see signs for the turn-off.*

3 movement with a particular meaning
- ADJ. **frantic | rude | thumbs-up, V**
- VERB + SIGN **give (sb), make** *She gave me a thumbs-up sign.* | **communicate through** *They had to communicate through signs and grunts.*
- SIGN + NOUN **language, system**
- PREP. ~**for** *the sign for 'woman' in sign language*
- PHRASES **make the sign of the cross** *The priest made the sign of the cross over the dead body.*

4 mark/symbol with a particular meaning
- ADJ. **euro, pound, etc. | equals, minus, plus, etc.**
- VERB + SIGN **draw, make** *The wizard drew some strange signs in the air with his wand.* | **use** *I used the Chinese sign for 'father' instead of 'uncle'.*
- SIGN + VERB **mean sth** *What does this sign mean?*
- PREP. ~**for** *I can't remember the sign for 'square root'.*

5 star sign
- ADJ. **birth, star**
- VERB + SIGN **be born under**
- PREP. ~**of** *people born under the sign of Gemini*
- PHRASES **the signs of the Zodiac**

sign *verb*

- ADV. **duly** *One copy of this letter should be duly signed and returned to us.* | **formally | personally** *a first edition of the book, personally signed by the author*
- VERB + SIGN **be required to, have to** *This is the contract you will be required to sign.* | **ask sb to, persuade sb to | agree to | refuse to**
- PREP. **for** *The postman asked me to sign for the parcel.*

signal *noun*

1 sign/action/sound that sends a message
- ADJ. **clear, unmistakable | agreed, pre-arranged | conflicting, confusing, contradictory, mixed | wrong** *Laughing when you should be crying sends out the wrong signals to people.* | **alarm, danger, distress, warning | hand, non-verbal, semaphore, smoke, verbal, visual**
- VERB + SIGNAL **arrange** *He had arranged a signal for the band to begin.* | **give (sb), make, send (out)** *When I give the signal, run!* | **interpret (sth as), read, see sth as** *The remark was seen as a signal that their government was ready to return to the peace talks.* | **pick up, respond to** *Interviewers quickly learn to pick up non-verbal signals.* | **act as** *The insect's bright colours act as warning signals to its predators.*
- SIGNAL + VERB **come from sth** *trying to read the signals coming from the patient* | **indicate sth** *the signals that can indicate danger*
- PREP. **at/on a ~** *At a pre-arranged signal, everyone started cheering.* | ~**for** *She made a signal for the car to stop.* ~**from/to** *Wait for the signal from the leader of your group.*

2 set of lights for drivers
- ADJ. **railway, traffic**
- VERB + SIGNAL **operate**
- SIGNAL + VERB **be (on) red/green** *The traffic signals were on red.* | **fail**
- SIGNAL + NOUN **box | failure**

3 series of radio waves, chemical messages, etc.
- ADJ. **faint, weak | strong | high-frequency, low-frequency | acoustic, analogue, audio, chemical, digital, electrical, electronic, light, radar, radio, sonar, sound, television/TV, video, wireless**
- VERB + SIGNAL **carry, pass** *The nerves carry these signals to the brain.* | **convert (sth into), scramble, unscramble** *The signal is scrambled into code before it is sent.* | **emit, generate, send, transmit | detect, pick up, receive, respond to** *This equipment can detect very low frequency signals.*
- SIGNAL + VERB **travel** *A light signal can travel well over 16km before it halves in intensity.* | **fade**
- PREP. ~**from** *a faint signal from the satellite* ~**to**

signal *verb*

1 move your arms to give a signal
- ADV. **frantically, wildly** *She signalled frantically to us.*
- PREP. **for** *He raised his hand and signalled for the waiter.* **to** *She signalled to the bus driver to stop.*

2 show/mark sth
- ADV. **clearly** *These changes clearly signal the end of the welfare state as we know it.* | **effectively | not necessarily** *A change of mind in one instance does not necessarily signal a change in overall policy.*

signatory *noun*

- ADJ. **authorized** *The document must be signed by an authorized signatory of the company.* | **first, original**
- SIGNATORY + VERB **agree sth** *Signatories agreed to support the nuclear test ban.*
- PREP. **~of/to** *the signatories to the treaty*

signature *noun*

- ADJ. **illegible**
- VERB + SIGNATURE **add, append, put, scrawl, write** *We both refused to put our signatures to the agreement.* | **witness** *Your signature must be witnessed by two people.* | **collect, gather, get, obtain** *They collected over 1 000 signatures for the petition.* | **bear, carry** *The will bears her signature.* | **forge**

significance *noun*

- ADJ. **considerable, criminal, deep, enormous, great, immense, major, profound, real** | **full, general, wider** *The scientists are cautious about the wider significance of their findings.* | **limited, minor, particular, special** | **real, true** *They failed to appreciate the true significance of these discoveries.* | **functional, practical, statistical, strategic, symbolic, theoretical** | **constitutional, cultural, economic, moral, historical, political, religious, social**
- VERB + SIGNIFICANCE **have** *The ceremony has great symbolic significance.* | **acquire, assume, gain, take on** *Suddenly his son's relationship with the girl took on a new significance.* | **attach** *Let us not attach too much significance to these meetings.* | **assess** | **appreciate, be aware of, grasp, understand** | **exaggerate** | **minimize, play down, underestimate**
- SIGNIFICANCE + VERB **lie in sth** *The significance of this lies in the fact that he had previously denied all knowledge of the fund.* | **attach to sth** *Does any significance attach to the use of the technical terms?*
- PREP. **~ for/to** *a meal that has particular significance for a Jewish family* | **of~** *a policy of special significance to women*
- PHRASES **be of little, no, etc. significance**

significant *adj.*

- VERBS **be, prove** | **become** | **remain** | **consider sth (as), deem sth, regard sth as, see sth as, think sth, view sth as** *The move was regarded as significant in Japan.*
- ADV. **deeply, extremely, highly, particularly, very** | **fairly, quite** | **statistically** *These differences are not statistically significant.*
- PREP. **for** *This development proved highly significant for the whole town.* **to** *rituals which are deeply significant to Christians*

Sikhism *noun*

⇨ Note at RELIGION

silence *noun*

1 quietness
- ADJ. **lengthy, long, prolonged** | **brief, momentary, a moment's, short** *There was a moment's silence before she replied.* | **deep, hushed** | **absolute, complete, dead, deadly, deathly, total, utter** *We sat in complete silence, save for the ticking of the clock.* ◇ *A deathly silence hung over the town.* | **shocked, stunned** | **awkward, embarrassed, embarrassing, strained, uncomfortable** *An awkward silence followed.* | **fraught, heavy, ominous, tense** | **brooding** *She fell into long, brooding silences.* | **stony, sullen** | **eerie** | **companionable** *They walked in companionable silence.* | **expectant, pregnant** | **sudden**
- VERB + SILENCE **maintain** *She maintained a stony silence.* | **break, interrupt, punctuate, shatter** *Lewis finally broke the long silence between them.* ◇ *a silence punctuated*

only by the occasional sniff from the children | **lapse into, relapse into, retreat into, subside into, trail into** (all only used about people) *He lapsed into a sullen silence.* | **stun sb into** *The boys were stunned into silence by this news.* | **be met with** *Her question was met with an uneasy silence.* | **observe** (= as a sign of respect for the dead, etc.) *A minute's silence for the victims will be observed.*
- SILENCE + VERB **descend, fall** *A sudden silence fell over the room.* | **hang, prevail, reign** *Silence reigned.* | **ensue, follow** | **deepen, grow, lengthen, spread, stretch** *He thought for a moment, the silence lengthening.*
- PREP. **in (the)~** *They ate their breakfast in silence.*

2 not saying anything about sth
- ADJ. **deafening** *The government's only response has been a deafening silence.* | **dignified** | **deliberate**
- VERB + SILENCE **keep, maintain** *He has so far kept a dignified silence on the subject.*
- PREP. **~ from** *There seems to have been a deliberate silence from the newspapers.*
- PHRASES **a conspiracy/wall of silence** *There is a conspiracy of silence about what is happening* (= nobody is willing to talk about it). **the right to silence** (= the right not to say anything when accused of a crime), **a vow of silence** *She has broken her vow of silence on the issue.*

silence *verb*

- ADV. **completely** | **effectively** *Criticism has now been effectively silenced.* | **quickly** | **abruptly, instantly** *Her scream was abruptly silenced.*
- VERB + SILENCE **try to** | **manage to** | **fail to** *Even these improvements to the service failed to silence a grumbling chorus of complaints.*
- PREP. **with** *She silenced him with a glare.*

silent *adj.*

- VERBS **be, seem** | **become, fall, go, grow** *The crowd fell silent as she began to speak.* ◇ *The room grew silent as the men entered.* | **keep, lie, remain, sit, stand, stay** *I could not keep silent any longer.* ◇ *The street lay silent and deserted.* ◇ *She sat silent throughout the meal.*
- ADV. **remarkably, unusually** | **absolutely, completely, perfectly, quite, totally, utterly** | **almost, virtually** *The new bus is virtually silent.* | **largely** *an issue about which the researchers are largely silent* | **fairly, rather** | **suddenly** | **eerily, strangely** *The street was strangely silent.* | **grimly, obstinately, resolutely, stubbornly** *Len remained obstinately silent.* | **uncomfortably** *For long periods they were uncomfortably silent because they could think of nothing to say.* | **uncharacteristically**
- PREP. **about** *They had kept remarkably silent about their intentions.* **on** *The report was silent on that subject.*

silhouette *noun*

- ADJ. **black, dark, stark**
- VERB + SILHOUETTE **see**
- PREP. **in ~** *He drew the city in silhouette.* | **~ against** *I could see its black silhouette against the evening sky.*

silhouetted *adj.*

- VERBS **be, stand** *A dark shape stood silhouetted against the bright morning sky.*
- ADV. **clearly, sharply, starkly** *He woke to see their two heads clearly silhouetted against his window.*
- PREP. **against**

silk *noun*

- ADJ. **heavy** | **delicate, fine, thin** | **soft** | **pure** | **artificial** | **bright** *the bright silks of saris* | **rich** *a drawing room decorated in rich blue and purple silks* | **faded** | **watered** | **raw** | **Chinese, Thai, etc.**

● VERB + SILK **produce** *fine silks produced in Italy* | **spin, weave** | **be lined with, be trimmed with**
● SILK + NOUN **industry, mill**
● PREP. **in ~** (= wearing clothes made of silk) *ladies in silks and satins* **of ~** *an evening dress of pure white silk*

silly *adj.*

● VERBS **be, feel, look, seem, sound** | **become, get** *Stop it now, you two—this is getting silly!*
● ADV. **bloody** (*taboo*), **damn/damned, downright, extremely, incredibly, really, remarkably, very** *a really silly question* | **a bit, a little, pretty, quite, rather**

silt *noun*

● ADJ. **fine** *The water contains fine silt.*
● VERB + SILT **deposit** *During the annual floods the river deposits its silt on the fields.*
● SILT + NOUN **deposit**

silver *noun*

1 metal
● ADJ. **pure, solid** | **sterling**
● VERB + SILVER **extract, mine** *Silver is extracted from silver ore.* | **set sth in** *a gemstone set in silver*
● SILVER + NOUN **ore** | **bar, ingot, plate** | **mine**

2 (*also* **the silver**) objects made of silver
● ADJ. **family** *He was forced to sell the family silver to pay for the repairs to the house.*
● VERB + SILVER **polish**

3 (*also* **silver medal**) in sports
● ADJ. **Olympic**
● VERB + SILVER **get, take, win** *She got a silver in the long jump.* ◇ *He took the silver this year.*

similar *adj.*

● VERBS **be, feel, look, sound, taste** | **remain**
● ADV. **extremely, remarkably, strikingly, uncannily, very** *The three portraits are remarkably similar.* | **basically, broadly, quite, rather, roughly, somewhat** *countries with broadly similar characteristics* | **superficially** *Their experiences are superficially similar.* | **qualitatively**
● PREP. **in** *The two houses are similar in size.* **to** *Snake meat tastes similar to chicken.*

similarity *noun*

● ADJ. **close, considerable, great, strong** *the close similarity in our ages* | **clear, marked, obvious** | **striking, uncanny** | **significant** | **certain** | **basic, fundamental** | **apparent, superficial** | **broad, general**
● QUANT. **degree**
● VERB + SIMILARITY **bear, have** *The area bears a superficial similarity to south London.* | **reveal, show** | **share** *these theories share certain similarities* | **explain** *a route across the Pacific which may explain the similarity between the two cultures*
● SIMILARITY + VERB **exist** | **end** *Here the similarity with Western politics ends.*
● PREP. **~ between, ~ in** *the striking similarity in their behaviour* **~ to** *the chimpanzee's similarity to humans* **~ with** *The panel shows marked similarities with mosaics found elsewhere.*
● PHRASES **a point of similarity** *There are several points of similarity between the two cases.*

simmer *verb*

● ADV. **gently, slowly** *Allow the soup to simmer gently for ten minutes.* | **quietly** (*figurative*) *She was still quietly simmering from her row with Nathan.*
● VERB + SIMMER **allow sth to**
● PREP. **in** *a mixture of vegetables simmered in yogurt*

simple *adj.*

● VERBS **appear, be, look, prove, seem, sound** | **keep sth, make sth** *The golden rule when creating your design is: keep it simple.* ◇ *Is all this technology making our lives simpler?* | **find sth** *I found the work fairly simple.*
● ADV. **extremely, quite, very** *Don't worry—it's all quite simple.* | **fairly, pretty, rather, relatively** | **deceptively** *a deceptively simple technique*

simplicity *noun*

● ADJ. **extreme, great** | **relative** | **apparent** *Don't be fooled by the music's apparent simplicity.*
● VERB + SIMPLICITY **have**
● PREP. **for ~** *For simplicity, I shall continue to use the general word 'river'.*
● PHRASES **be simplicity itself** (= to be very simple) *His solution to the problem was simplicity itself.* **for the sake of simplicity**

simplification *noun*

● ADJ. **considerable, drastic, gross**
● VERB + SIMPLIFICATION **make**
● PREP. **~ in** *He made a number of simplifications in the taxation system.*

simplify *verb*

● ADV. **considerably, greatly** *The whole process has now been greatly simplified.* | **drastically, grossly** *He presents the theory in a grossly simplified form.* | **slightly**
● VERB + SIMPLIFY **try to**
● PHRASES **highly simplified** *This is a highly simplified view of the economy.*

simplistic *adj.*

● VERBS **appear, be, look, seem, sound**
● ADV. **extremely, grossly, highly, overly, very** *a highly simplistic generalization* | **a bit, fairly, a little, rather, somewhat** *The graphics are somewhat simplistic.*

simulate *verb*

● ADV. **closely** *The device simulates conditions in space quite closely.*
● VERB + SIMULATE **be designed to, be used to** *Models are used to simulate the workings of a real-life system.* | **try to**

simulation *noun*

● ADJ. **computer, electronic, laboratory, real-time, virtual reality** | **accident, flight**
● VERB + SIMULATION **carry out, run** *To test the model under different conditions, it is necessary to run simulations on a computer.*
● SIMULATION + VERB **indicate sth, show sth**
● SIMULATION + NOUN **model** *using simulation models to predict earthquake patterns* | **program** | **techniques** | **exercise, experiment** | **game**
● PREP. **in a/the ~** *the basic steps in the simulation* **through** *The pilot's skills are tested through simulation.* | **~ of** *a virtual reality simulation of a moon landing*

sin *noun*

● ADJ. **cardinal, deadly, mortal** | **unforgivable** | **venial** | **besetting** *The besetting sin of 18th-century urban Britain was drunkenness.* | **original** *the Christian doctrine of original sin*
● VERB + SIN **commit** | **confess** *They had confessed their sins and done their penance.* | **forgive** (**sb their**)
● PREP. **~ against** *Sin against others is seen as a sin against God.*

sincere adj.

- VERBS **be, look, seem, sound**
- ADV. **deeply, really, very** *the warm, deeply sincere note in her voice* | **completely, entirely, perfectly, quite, utterly, wholly** | **enough** *Her protests seemed sincere enough.*
- PREP. **about** *his refusal to be sincere about his feelings* **in** *Have they been sincere in their efforts to resolve the crisis?*

sincerity noun

- ADJ. **complete, deep, great, total** | **genuine, passionate** | **apparent** *'It's wonderful,' he said with apparent sincerity.*
- VERB + SINCERITY **doubt, mistake, question** *There seems no reason to doubt the sincerity of his beliefs.* ◇ *There was no mistaking his sincerity.* | **be convinced of** *She wasn't yet convinced of his sincerity.* | **demonstrate, prove, show**
- PREP. **with~**

sing verb

- ADV. **loud, loudly, lustily** *The birds sang louder than ever.* | **gently, quietly, softly** *singing quietly to himself* | **beautifully, like an angel, sweetly, well** | **badly** | **cheerfully, happily** *Birds sang cheerfully in the trees.* | **a bit, a little** *She could sing a bit and agreed to take part in the show.* | **live** *Have you ever heard the band sing live?* | **together** *We played and sang together.*
- VERB + SING **can** *I can't sing very well.* | **start to** | **hear sb/sth**
- PREP. **about** *singing about love* **to** *Shall I sing to you?*
- PHRASES **start/stop singing**

singer noun

- ADJ. **accomplished, fine, good, great, talented** | **chart-topping, famous, popular, well-known** | **amateur, professional** | **backing, lead** *an interview with the band's lead singer* | **blues, carol, country (and western), folk, gospel, jazz, opera, pop, rock, soul** | **cabaret, nightclub, pub**
- SINGER + VERB **perform sth** *Singers took turns to perform songs they had written.*

singing noun

- ADJ. **beautiful, fine, good** | **lusty, spirited** | **carol, choral, folk, hymn** | **communal, community, congregational, massed** | **solo, unaccompanied**
- VERB + SINGING **lead** *The vicar led the hymn singing.* | **accompany** *Her brother accompanied her singing on the piano.*
- SINGING + NOUN **career** | **lesson** | **teacher** | **voice** *He has a lovely singing voice.*

single noun

1 ticket
- VERB + SINGLE **buy, get** *I got a single to Birmingham.*
- PREP. **~to** *A single to Stratford, please.*

2 CD, tape, etc.
- ADJ. **best-selling, hit** | **debut, first** | **forthcoming** | **latest, new**
- VERB + SINGLE **play** *She was in her room playing her singles.* | **release (sth as)** *The band later released this album track as a single.*
- SINGLE + VERB **come out**
- SINGLES + NOUN **chart** *number one in the singles chart*
- PHRASES **~by** *It was voted the best single by a solo artist.* **~from** *the new single from the band 'Therapy?'*

3 singles in tennis
- ADJ. **junior, men's, women's**

- VERB + SINGLES **play** *I prefer playing singles to doubles.* | **win** *She won the junior singles.*
- SINGLES + NOUN **championship, final, match** | **champion, player** | **title**
- PHRASES **in the~** *She decided not to play in the singles.*

sinister adj.

- VERBS **be, look, seem, sound** | **find sth**
- ADV. **downright, extremely, really, very** | **almost** | **faintly, rather, slightly, somewhat, vaguely** *I found his silence rather sinister.* | **somehow**

sink noun

- ADJ. **kitchen** | **blocked** | **earthenware, enamel, porcelain, stainless steel, stone**
- VERB + SINK **fill** *She filled the sink with hot water.* | **block** | **clear, unblock**
- SINK + NOUN **unit** | **plunger** *I bought a sink plunger to clear the blocked kitchen sink.*
- PREP. **at the~** *She was at the sink, washing up the dinner things.* **down the~** *Don't pour tea leaves down the kitchen sink—it'll get blocked.* **in the~** *Put the dishes in the sink.*

sink verb

1 in water/mud, etc.
- ADV. **slowly** | **fast** *Fergus was in waist-deep and sinking fast.* | **deep** | **down** *She sank down into the soft soil.*
- VERB + SINK **begin to, start to**
- PREP. **below/beneath** *We watched the boat sink beneath the waves.* **into** *Our feet sank deep into the soft sand as we walked.* **(up) to** *She sank up to his knees in the mud.*
- PHRASES **sink like a stone** *The box sank like a stone.* **sink without trace** *It seemed as though the ship had sunk without trace.*

2 fall/sit down
- ADV. **gratefully, happily** *I sank gratefully into the warm, dry bed.* | **gracefully** | **low** | **back, down**
- PREP. **into** *He sank lower into his chair.* **onto** *She sank gracefully down onto a cushion at his feet.*
- PHRASES **sink to the floor/ground** *She sank to the ground, exhausted.* **sink to your knees** *The old man had sunk to his knees.*

sip noun

- ADJ. **careful, cautious, little, nervous, small** | **long** | **noisy**
- VERB + SIP **have, take** *I took a little sip of my drink.*
- PREP. **in~s** *He drank the whisky in sips.*

sip verb

- ADV. **slowly** | **thoughtfully** | **idly** *She sat in the warm sun, idly sipping champagne.* | **appreciatively, gratefully** *He sipped the warm milk appreciatively.*
- VERB + SIP **pause to** *She paused to sip her tea.*
- PREP. **at** *He sipped at his beer thoughtfully.* **from** *She sipped from her glass of water.*

siren noun

- ADJ. **approaching** *The cars had stopped at the sound of the approaching siren.* | **air-raid, ambulance, factory, police, warning**
- VERB + SIREN **put on, sound, switch on** *The ships all sounded their sirens.* | **hear**
- SIREN + VERB **go (off), sound, start** | **blare, howl, scream, wail** *The ambulance sped off with its siren wailing.* | **die away** *The police siren died away into the hot night.*

sister *noun*

● ADJ. **big, elder, older | baby, kid, little, small, wee, younger | twin | full** (= sharing both parents) **| half-** (= sharing one parent), **step-** (also **stepsister**) (= the daughter from an earlier marriage of your stepfather or stepmother) **| beloved, much-loved | dead, deceased, late | unmarried**

● PHRASES **brother and sister** *Have you got any brothers and sisters?* **like sisters** *The girls are so close, they're like sisters.*

sit *verb*

1 on a chair, etc.
● ADV. **still** *Just sit still!* **| quietly** *He would sit quietly and watch what was happening.* **| comfortably | in silence** *We sat in silence for a few moments.* **| cross-legged, with your legs crossed** *The children sat cross-legged on the floor.* ◇ *She was sitting in her favourite armchair with her legs crossed.* **| (bolt) upright** *He sat bolt upright, hands folded in front of him.* **| demurely, primly** *She sat demurely on the edge of her chair.* **| back, down | side by side, together**
● VERB + SIT **let sb** *Surely someone would stand up and let her sit down?* **| gesture for/to sb to, motion (for/to) sb to** *He motioned the young officer to sit down.*
● PREP. **astride** *sitting astride a horse* **at** *He was sitting at his desk.* **beside** *She went and sat beside him.* **in** *He sat back in his chair and started to read.* **on** *Can I sit on this chair?* **opposite** *They sat opposite each other.*

2 seem right/not seem right
● ADV. **comfortably, easily, well | uneasily**
● PREP. **with** *His views did not sit comfortably with the management line.*

site *noun*

1 piece of land where a building was/is/will be
● ADJ. **good, prime | designated, possible, potential, proposed, suitable | building, construction, development | demolition | manufacturing, industrial | factory, hospital, school, etc. | greenfield, protected | 5-acre, 20-acre, etc.**
● VERB + SITE **choose, find, identify, locate, look for | acquire, buy, purchase** *The local council has recently acquired the site.* **| clear, prepare** *The site is being cleared for development.* **| build (sth) on, develop | occupy** *The site is presently occupied by offices.* **stand near/on** *The school stands on the site of an ancient settlement.*
● SITE + VERB **belong to sb**
● PREP. **at a/the ~** *The factory will be built at a site to the north of the city.* **in a/the ~** *The hotel is in a prime site overlooking the sea.* **on (a/the) ~** *Hard hats must be worn on site.* ◇ *He was injured on a building site.*

2 place where sth happened or that is used for sth
● ADJ. **ancient, archaeological, historic/historical | important | sacred | accident, bomb, crash | dump, landfill, (waste) disposal | burial** *Many of these ancient burial sites were destroyed in the last century.* **| landing, launch | camp** (also **campsite**), **camping, caravan, picnic | breeding, nest/nesting**
● VERB + SITE **visit** *The president is to visit the crash site later today.* **| disturb, remove sth from, steal sth from** *penalties for disturbing archaeological sites*

3 on the Internet
● ADJ. **Internet, web** (also **website**), **WWW | free** *a free site devoted to tropical fish* **| official** *the official website of the New York Yankees* **| chat, home | browse/browsing, search, surf/surfing | destination**
● VERB + SITE **access, browse, search for, visit | build, create, design, set up | host, own**
● PREP. **at ~** *At this site you'll find all the latest news and gossip.* **in ~** *Check out the links in our home site.* **~ about**

sites about Japan **~ for** *the most popular sites for children* **~ on** *I'm searching for sites on aromatherapy.*
⇨ Special page at COMPUTER

site *verb*

● ADV. **carefully, strategically** *The fence is strategically sited to prevent anyone getting onto the beach.* **| conveniently | discreetly | attractively, beautifully** *The hotel is beautifully sited by a lake in a steep valley.* **| badly**

situated *adj.*

● VERBS **be**
● ADV. **beautifully, delightfully, ideally, picturesquely, pleasantly, superbly, well** *The hotel is delightfully situated close to the waterfront.* ◇ *Zakro was well situated for trade with Greece.* **| conveniently | inconveniently | centrally | remotely | quietly**
● PREP. **for** *ideally situated for touring the country*

situation *noun*

1 the things that are happening
● ADJ. **general, overall, total, whole | current, immediate, present | international, local, national, world | actual, concrete, real/real-life | hypothetical, unlikely | favourable, happy, healthy, ideal, privileged | satisfactory, stable | chaotic, explosive, fluid, unstable, volatile | awkward, delicate, difficult, embarrassing, sticky, stressful, tense, tricky, uncomfortable, unpleasant, vulnerable** *I always seem to get into sticky situations on holiday.* **| dangerous, hazardous, perilous, risky | crisis, emergency | alarming, bad, critical, deplorable, desperate, disgraceful, grave, intolerable, serious, terrible, tragic, unhappy | catch-22, hopeless, no-win | absurd, bizarre, extraordinary, ludicrous, novel, odd, paradoxical, ridiculous, strange, unique, unusual | complex, complicated | simple | one-to-one | social** *Do you feel awkward in social situations?* **| strategic | work | domestic | economic, financial, legal, military, political** *the international political situation*
● VERB + SITUATION **bring about, create, lead to, result in | be faced with, be placed in, encounter, face, find yourself in, get into** *I found myself in rather an awkward situation.* **| avoid | grasp, take in, understand** *She found it difficult to take in the situation.* **| analyse, appraise, assess, consider, discuss, examine, judge, look at, review, size up, take stock of, think about, weigh up | clarify, describe, explain, outline, sum up | accept, face up to | address, be in control of, cope with, deal with, handle, respond to, take control of** *learning strategies to cope with difficult situations* **| ameliorate, defuse, ease, help, improve, rectify, remedy** *The peacekeepers are trained to defuse potentially explosive situations.* **| exploit, take advantage of** *He saw she was confused and he took full advantage of the situation.* **| lose control of | affect, change, influence, transform | aggravate, complicate, exacerbate** *Interfering now would only exacerbate the situation.*
● SITUATION + VERB **arise, develop** *We will deal with that if the situation arises.* **| improve | change | deteriorate, worsen** *The situation is deteriorating rapidly.*
● PREP. **in a/the ~** *What would you do in this situation?*
● PHRASES **the gravity/seriousness of the situation** *Given the gravity of the situation, I'm not surprised she's panicking.* **a way out of the situation** *I was in trouble and I could see no way out of the situation.*

2 position of sth
● ADJ. **beautiful, idyllic, pleasant**
● PREP. **in a ~** *located in a beautiful situation*

size *noun*

1 how big or small sth is
- ADJ. **considerable, enormous, good, fair, great, impressive, large, massive, substantial, vast** *The kitchen is (of) a fair size.* ◇ *The vast size of the country made it difficult to govern.* | **diminutive, limited, modest, small** *Despite its diminutive size, the car is quite comfortable.* | **average, medium, middle, moderate, reasonable, sufficient | overall, total | sheer, very** *The sheer size of these dinosaurs was their main defence.* | **appropriate, convenient, correct, desirable, handy, manageable, optimum, right** *The ladder is a handy size for using in the house.* ◇ *classes of manageable size* | **wrong | comparable, equivalent, similar | standard, uniform** *The standard size for the tiles is 300mm square.* | **non-standard | maximum, minimum** *The fish grow to a maximum size of 50cm.* | **actual, full, life** *The ring is shown actual size in the illustration.* ◇ *a life-size model of a Roman soldier* | **class, family, group, household, market, population, sample**
- VERB + SIZE **increase | decrease, limit, reduce** *The company is reducing the size of its workforce.* | **double in, grow in, increase in** *Houses increase in size further away from the city centre.* | **be reduced in, decline in, decrease in, diminish in | differ in, range in, vary in** *These insects range in size from 2 to 5cm.* | **grow to, reach | estimate, guess (at)** *I had to guess at the size of the batteries.* | **overestimate, underestimate**
- SIZE + VERB **increase | decline, decrease, fall | range from, vary** *The size of her audience varied.*
- PREP. **from the ~ of** *From the size of the queues outside the cinema, it was a very good film.* **in ~** *How do the samples compare in size?* **in the ~ of** *the increase in the size of the population*
- PHRASES **half, two, three, etc. times the size of sth** *Their house is twice the size of ours.* **shapes and sizes** *There are people of all shapes and size in the judo class.*

2 one of a number of fixed measurements
- ADJ. **large, medium, small** *The company is now going to make these products in larger sizes.* | **2-litre, 4-pound, etc.** *The 5-litre size comes in a metal tin.* | **imperial, metric** *New radiators come in metric sizes.* | **children's, men's, women's | chest, collar, foot** *'Extra large' fits chest sizes 44 to 50.* | **bra, shoe**
- QUANT. **range, variety**
- VERB + SIZE **be, take** *What size are you (= for shoes or clothes)?* ◇ *What size do you take?* | **find sth in, get sth in** *I couldn't find the blouse in my size.* | **be available in, come in** *The bricks come in four sizes.*
- SIZE + VERB **fit sb** *I have to wear children's shoes because the women's sizes don't fit me.*
- PREP. **in a/your ~** *Have you got this dress in a Size 12?*
- PHRASES **be a size too big, small, etc.** *The jacket is several sizes too large for him.* **Size 2, 10, etc.**

skating *noun*
- ADJ. **ice, roller | figure, speed**
- VERB + SKATING **go** *We used to go skating on the lake in cold winters.*
- SKATING + NOUN **championships, event | rink | routine | world** *some of the skating world's leading choreographers*
- ⇨ Special page at SPORT

skeleton *noun*
- ADJ. **dinosaur, fish, human, mammal/mammalian, etc. | external, internal**
- VERB + SKELETON **form**

sketch *noun*

1 quick drawing
- ADJ. **lightning, quick | rough | preliminary, preparatory | charcoal, ink, pencil, watercolour**
- VERB + SKETCH **do, draw, make**
- SKETCH + NOUN **book, pad | map | plan**
- PREP. **in a/the ~** *The family house appears in several of her sketches.* | **~ by** *a series of sketches by John Constable* **~ for** *to make a sketch for an oil painting* **~ of** *He did some rough sketches of the costumes.*
- ⇨ Note at ART

2 short description
- ADJ. **brief, thumbnail** *The talk began with a thumbnail sketch of the political situation at that time.* | **biographical, character**
- VERB + SKETCH **give sb**
- PREP. **~ of** *He gave us character sketches of all his eccentric relations.*

3 short comic scene
- ADJ. **short | comic, satirical**
- VERB + SKETCH **do, perform | write**
- PREP. **~ about** *a comic sketch about a talking cat*

ski *noun*
- QUANT. **pair**
- VERB + SKI **put on | remove, take off**
- SKI + NOUN **pole | boot, jacket, mask, pants, suit | instructor, lesson | area, run, slope | lift | jump | resort**
- PREP. **on ~s** *The children go to school on skis.*

skid *noun*
- VERB + SKID **get into, go into** *The lorry went into a skid and crashed into the barrier.*
- SKID + NOUN **mark** *The police examined the skid marks to see how fast the car had been travelling.*

skiing *noun*
- ADJ. **alpine, downhill | cross-country, langlauf, Nordic | dry-slope | off-piste | freestyle | good, quality**
- VERB + SKIING **go | have** *The United States has plenty of good skiing.*
- SKIING + NOUN **holiday, trip | resort | season | equipment | facilities | slope | conditions**
- ⇨ Special page at SPORT

skilful *adj.*
- VERBS **be | become**
- ADV. **extremely, highly, very | fairly, reasonably**
- PREP. **at** *I became skilful at drawing.* **in** *highly skilful in his tactics*

skill *noun*
- ADJ. **considerable, consummate, extraordinary, great, remarkable** *He is a negotiator of considerable skill.* ◇ *With consummate skill, she steered the conversation away from any embarrassing subjects.* | **good, poor** *She has good organizational skills.* | **basic, necessary** *the basic skills of reading, writing and arithmetic* | **essential, important, marketable, practical, transferable, useful** *training in problem-solving and other transferable skills* | **new, old** *to learn some new skills* | **special, specialist** *No special skills or knowledge are required for the job.* | **professional | analytical | entrepreneurial, management, managerial, organizational | diplomatic, negotiating | linguistic, reading, writing | business, communication, computer, interpersonal, language, research, social, study, survival** *It is important to develop good study skills.* | **manual | artistic, culinary, medical, military, musical, political, scientific, tactical, technical**

• QUANT. **range, set** *She had to develop a whole new set of skills when she changed job.* | **degree, level** *an operation that called for a high degree of skill*

• VERB + SKILL **have, possess** | **lack** | **need, require, take** *a feat requiring skill and patience* | **acquire, develop, learn, pick up** | **demonstrate, display, exercise, practise, show (off)** | **apply, harness, use, utilize** *The manager must harness the skills of the workers to firm objectives.* | **broaden, hone, improve, increase, master, sharpen, upgrade** *helping children to master the skills necessary to live in our society* ◊ *She attends regular training weekends to sharpen her skills.* | **refresh, update** | **pool, share** | **assess, test** *a course that will test the skills of any golfer*

• SKILLS + NOUN **level** | **acquisition, development, training** | **shortage** *The country is still facing a skills shortage.*

• PREP. **with ~** *She performed the task with great skill.* | **~ as** *her skills as a doctor* **~ at** *his skill at painting* **~ in** *their skill in selecting the best designs* **~ of** *the basic skills of managing an office* **~ with** *his skill with a sword*

• PHRASES **a lack of skill** *I enjoy playing squash, despite my lack of skill.* **a mastery of skills** *a mastery of basic language skills*

skilled *adj.*

• VERBS **be** | **become**

• ADV. **especially, extremely, highly, particularly, remarkably, very** *a highly skilled workforce* ◊ *Interviewing is a very skilled job.* | **fully** *fully skilled craftsmen* | **increasingly** | **quite** | **enough, sufficiently**

• PREP. **at** *skilled at needlework* **in** *skilled in the basic techniques* **with** *She wasn't very skilled with the camera yet.*

skim *verb*

• ADV. **barely** *(figurative) This report has barely skimmed the surface of the subject.* | **low** *A bird skimmed low over the heather.*

• PREP. **across/over** *We skimmed across the water in a small sailing boat.*

skin *noun*

1 covering of a human/animal body

• ADJ. **beautiful, clear, fine, flawless, good, healthy, lovely, perfect** | **smooth, soft** | **translucent** | **supple, young, youthful** | **wrinkled** | **coarse, hard, leathery, rough, tough** | **delicate, sensitive** | **greasy, oily** | **moist** | **dry, flaky** | **congested** | **black, brown, dark, fair, golden, milky, olive, olive-tinged/-tinted, pale, swarthy, white** | **bronzed, tanned** | **sunburnt** | **weathered** | **pallid, sallow** | **freckled** | **raw, tender** *There was a patch of raw skin on my back where the sun had burnt it.* | **blotchy** | **puffy** *I examined the puffy skin under my eyes.* | **blistered** | **hairy** | **hairless** | **chilled, cold, cool** | **facial** | **bare, naked** *The sheets felt nice next to his bare skin.* | **loose** *I picked up the kitten by the loose skin on its neck.* | **armoured, scaly** *the armoured skin of the rhinoceros* | **dead** *A lot of dust is made up of particles of dead skin.*

• VERB + SKIN **break, burn, damage, irritate** | **protect** | **nourish, soothe** | **shed** *This snake sheds its skin eight times a year.*

• SKIN + VERB **glisten, glow** *Her skin was glistening with sweat after her run.* | **age** *They claim that this cream makes the skin age more slowly.* | **hang, sag** | **blister, burn, peel** | **crawl, prickle, tingle** *Just thinking about spiders makes my skin crawl.*

• SKIN + NOUN **allergy, burns, cancer, complaint, condition, damage, disease, disorder, infection, irritation, lesion, problems, rash** | **graft** | **clinic** | **specialist** | **care, cleanser, cream, moisturizer, tonic** | **colour,**

tone | **texture** | **type** | **cells, tissue** | **contact** *Avoid skin contact with the glue.*

• PREP. **against the/your ~** *The sheets felt rough against her sunburnt skin.* **beneath the/your ~** *Beneath his skin, the muscles were tight with tension.* **in the/your ~** *The drugs reduce the inflammation in the skin.* **on the/your ~** *blisters on the skin* **through the/your ~** *A network of veins showed through his skin.* **under the/your ~** *He discovered a lump under his skin so he went to the doctor.*

• PHRASES **skin and bone** *The dog lost more and more weight, and was soon little more than skin and bone.*

2 skin of an animal that has been removed

• ADJ. **animal** | **crocodile, goat, leopard, sheep** (also **sheepskin**), etc.

• VERB + SKIN **cure, tan**

3 covering of some fruits/ vegetables

• ADJ. **banana, onion, potato,** etc.

• VERB + SKIN **peel off, remove**

skinny *adj.*

• VERBS **be, look** | **become**

• ADV. **really, terribly, very** | **a bit, fairly, rather** *At school I was fairly skinny and undersized.*

skip *verb*

• ADV. **lightly, nimbly** | **happily** | **along**

• PREP. **down, up** *He skipped lightly up the stairs.*

skirmish *noun*

• ADJ. **little, minor** | **border**

• SKIRMISH + VERB **break out, take place** *Minor skirmishes broke out all along the border.*

• PREP. **in a/the ~** *He was killed in a border skirmish.* | **~ between** *skirmishes between the police and guerillas* **~ over** *a skirmish over boundaries* **~ with** *They were involved in a skirmish with rival fans.*

skirt *noun*

• ADJ. **ankle-length, long** | **short** | **knee-length** | **tight** | **circular, flared, full, gathered, voluminous** *She tucked up her voluminous skirts to make room for Jane beside her.* | **pencil, straight** | **pleated, wrap-around**

• VERB + SKIRT **hitch up, lift, pull up** | **pull down** | **tuck up** | **smooth (down)** *She sat down, smoothing the skirt of her dress.* | **straighten** | **ruck up**

• SKIRT + VERB **billow, swirl** *Her full skirt billowed around her as she danced.* | **ride up** *Her skirt rode up her thighs when she sat down.*

• SKIRT + NOUN **length**

⇨ Special page at CLOTHES

skull *noun*

• ADJ. **thick** | **thin** | **fractured**

• VERB + SKULL **crack, fracture**

• SKULL + NOUN **fracture**

• PHRASES **the back/base/front/side/top of the skull, close to the skull** *The soldiers' hair was cropped close to the skull.* **a fracture of/to the skull**

sky *noun*

• ADJ. **big, huge** | **open** *We slept under the open sky.* | **empty** | **bright, clear, cloudless, sunny** *a week of cloudless skies* | **cloudy, dull, overcast, sullen** | **starry** | **azure, black, blue, dark/darkening, grey, pale, leaden** | **night, morning,** etc. | **autumn, January,** etc. | **northern, southern,** etc.

• QUANT. **patch** *a patch of blue sky*

• VERB + SKY **light up** *The fireworks lit up the sky.* | **patrol**

• SKY + VERB **clear (up), lighten** *The rain stopped and*

the skies cleared. | **cloud over, darken, turn grey, etc.** | **be streaked with sth** *The sky was streaked with gold.*
● PREP. **across the ~** *Black clouds spread across the sky.* **against the ~** *The eagle was black against the early morning sky.* **beneath/under a ~** *a ship tossing under a darkening sky* **from/out of the ~** *A strange object dropped out of the sky.* **in the ~** *There was a kite high up in the sky.* | **~ above** *A helicopter appeared in the sky above them.* **~ over** *patrolling the skies over the Channel*
● PHRASES **high/low in the sky** *when the sun is low in the sky* **the sky above/overhead** *Swallows darted about in the sky overhead.* **take to the skies** (= to go into the sky) *Some vintage aircraft will be taking to the skies at this weekend's fair.*

skyline *noun*

● ADJ. **dramatic** | **city** | **Hong Kong, London, etc.** | **northern, southern, etc.**
● VERB + SKYLINE **form** | **dominate** *The skyline is dominated by a nuclear power station.* | **be silhouetted against/on, stand (out) against/on** *A medieval castle stands against the skyline.* | **break** *The skyline is broken by a water tower.*
● PREP. **above/over ~** *Clouds of smoke floated over the skyline.* **against the ~** *the moving figures he could see against the skyline* **along the ~** *lights twinkling along the Beirut skyline* **below the ~** *The sun slipped below the skyline.* **on the ~** *There are several gothic spires on the city skyline.*

skyscraper *noun*

● ADJ. **towering**
● SKYSCRAPER + VERB **loom, rise** *On all sides, skyscrapers rose like jagged teeth.*
● SKYSCRAPER + NOUN **block**

slab *noun*

● ADJ. **great, huge, large** *They were unloading great slabs of rock.* | **thick** | **paving** | **mortuary**
● PREP. **on a/the ~** *corpses laid out on cold mortuary slabs* | **~ of** *a slab of butter/chocolate/concrete/meat*

slack *adj.*

1 loose
● VERBS **be, feel, look, seem** | **become, go** *Let the reins go slack.* | **leave sth** *Leave the thread slightly slack to allow for movement.*
● ADV. **very** | **completely** *Some of the ropes were completely slack.* | **a bit, fairly, slightly**

2 not busy
● VERBS **be, seem** | **become** | **remain** *The antiques business remained slack.*
● ADV. **extremely, very** | **a bit, fairly, pretty, rather** *This season has been pretty slack for local hotels so far.*

3 lazy
● VERBS **be** | **become**
● ADV. **very** | **a bit, rather**
● PREP. **in** *She knew she had been very slack in her church attendance recently.*

slacken *verb*

● ADV. **a little, slightly** *His grip slackened a little and she pulled away.* | **off** *Slacken off the ropes.* ◇ *Growth in the economy was beginning to slacken off.*

slam *verb*

● ADV. **hard** *She ran out of the room and slammed the door as hard as she could.* | **back, down** *He said goodbye and slammed the phone down.*
● VERB + SLAM **hear sth**
● PREP. **against** *Kath's heart slammed against her ribs.*

behind *I heard the door slam behind him.* **into** *The car skidded and slammed into a tree.*
● PHRASES **slam (sth) shut** *He slammed the lid shut.*

slander *noun*

● ADJ. **gross, malicious, vicious, vile**
● VERB + SLANDER **be guilty of** | **sue sb for**
● PREP. **~ against** *He was found guilty of slander against his employers.* **~ on** *Many teachers saw the statement as a gross slander on their profession.*

slang *noun*

● ADJ. **colloquial** | **current** | **army** | **rhyming**
● VERB + SLANG **talk in, use**
● SLANG + NOUN **expression, term, word**
● PREP. **in ~** *in army slang* | **~ for** *'Ruby Murray' is rhyming slang for 'curry'.*

slant *noun*

1 leaning position
● VERB + SLANT **have** | **take on** *Her chin took on a stubborn slant.*
● PREP. **at a ~** *They held their spears at a slant.* **on the ~** *Cut the flower stems on the slant.*

2 way of thinking about sth
● ADJ. **different, new** | **feminist, left-wing, etc.**
● VERB + SLANT **give sth, put** *He puts his own particular slant on everything.*
● PREP. **with a … ~** *an article with a right-wing slant* | **~ on** *That's a different slant on the causes of the First World War.* **~ to** *The story gives a new slant to his character.*

slap *noun*

● ADJ. **gentle, little** | **hard, sharp, stinging** | **resounding** | **hearty** *He gave his brother a hearty slap on the back to congratulate him.*
● VERB + SLAP **deliver, give sb** *His mum delivered a hard slap and sent him to bed.* | **get, receive**
● PREP. **with a ~** *He hit the water with a resounding slap.*
● PHRASES **a slap in the face** (*figurative*) *The closure of the school is a slap in the face to the local community.*

slap *verb*

● ADV. **hard** | **gently, lightly** | **away** *She slapped his hand away.*
● VERB + SLAP **want to** *I wanted to slap his face.*
● PREP. **across** *The officer slapped him hard across the face.* **on** *She slapped the boy on the leg.*

slash *verb*

● ADV. **wildly**
● PREP. **at, through** *He slashed through the rope.* **with** *He slashed wildly at me with a knife.*

slaughter *noun*

● ADJ. **indiscriminate, mass, wholesale** *the indiscriminate slaughter of civilians* | **senseless, terrible** | **ritual**
● VERB + SLAUGHTER **prevent, stop** *We were helpless to stop the slaughter.*
● SLAUGHTER + NOUN **house** (also **slaughterhouse**)
● PREP. **for ~** *transporting live horses for slaughter*

slaughter *verb*

1 kill an animal
● ADV. **humanely** *The animals are all humanely slaughtered.* | **ritually** | **illegally** *elephants illegally slaughtered by poachers*
● PREP. **for** *Thousands of birds were slaughtered for their feathers.*

2 kill a large number of people
- ADV. **brutally, cruelly** *Hundreds of innocent civilians were cruelly slaughtered.*

slave noun

- ADJ. **fugitive, runaway**
- VERB + SLAVE **have, own** | **buy, take sb as** | **sell (sb as)** | **use (sb as)** | **free, liberate** *landowners who freed their slaves voluntarily*
- SLAVE + NOUN **labour** *a railway built by slave labour* | **driver, master, owner, trader** | **market, trade, traffic** *the abolition of the slave trade* | **ship**
- PREP. **~of** *a slave of habit* **~to** *a slave to fashion*
- PHRASES **the emancipation of slaves, the trade in slaves**

slavery noun

- ADJ. **domestic** *Their stated aim was to free women from domestic slavery.*
- VERB + SLAVERY **establish, introduce** *Chios is said to have introduced slavery into Greece.* | **abolish** | **sell sb into** | **free sb from** | **be born into**
- PREP. **in ~** *They were living in slavery and poverty.* **under~** *conditions for children under slavery*
- PHRASES **the abolition of slavery**

sledge noun

- ADJ. **dog, horse-drawn, motor**
- VERB + SLEDGE **pull** | **drive**
- PREP. **in/into/on/onto a/the~**

sleep noun

1 condition of rest
- ADJ. **deep** | **light** | **REM**
- VERB + SLEEP **drift into/off to, drop off to, get to, go (back) to** | **cry/sob yourself to** | **get, sleep, snatch** *Close your eyes and get some sleep now.* ◊ *Tom was in the front room sleeping the sleep of the dead.* ◊ *I snatched a few hours' sleep in the afternoon.* | **need** | **survive on** *They seem to survive on only a few hours' sleep a night.* | **induce, lull/send sb to** *using drugs to induce sleep* ◊ *The quiet music soon sent her to sleep.* | **drift in and out of** *He drifted in and out of sleep all night.* | **lose** *Don't lose sleep over it—we'll sort everything out in the morning.* | **disrupt** | **catch up on** *I used Saturday to catch up on my sleep.* | **feign** *I feigned sleep when the ticket inspector came round.*
- SLEEP + VERB **come** *Sleep came to her in snatches.* | **overcome sb, overtake sb** *Sleep finally overtook me.*
- SLEEP + NOUN **pattern** | **deprivation, loss** | **apnoea**
- PREP. **during~** *your heart rate during sleep* **in your~** *He often walks and talks in his sleep.*
- PHRASES **a lack of sleep** *suffering from a lack of sleep* **a wink of sleep** *I won't get a wink of sleep with that noise downstairs.*

2 period of sleep
- ADJ. **long** | **little, short** | **dead, deep, heavy, sound** | **good, restful** | **light** | **disturbed, exhausted, fitful, restless, uneasy** *I woke up early after a disturbed sleep.* | **dreamless, peaceful** | **drunken** | **beauty** *Sorry but I need my beauty sleep.*
- VERB + SLEEP **need** | **have** *Did you have a good sleep?* | **be in** *I was in a deep sleep when the phone rang.* | **drift into, fall into, sink into** *I immediately fell into a dead sleep.* | **awake/awaken/wake (sb) from** *He woke from a fitful sleep with a headache.*
- PHRASES **a (good/poor) night's sleep** *You'll feel better after a good night's sleep.*

sleep verb

- ADV. **properly, soundly, well** *I haven't slept properly for weeks.* ◊ *The children were all sleeping soundly.* ◊ *Did you sleep well last night?* | **peacefully, quietly** | **easier, easily, quiet** *When the murderer is caught we can all sleep easier in our beds at night.* | **badly, fitfully, uneasily** | **deeply, heavily** *He was exhausted and slept deeply.* | **lightly** *She always slept very lightly so I had to be careful not to wake her.* | **barely, hardly, scarcely** *She felt as if she had hardly slept.* | **a little** | **alone** | **together**
- VERB + SLEEP **be unable to, can't/couldn't** *I couldn't sleep so I got up and went downstairs.* | **try to** *You must be very tired. Try to sleep a little.* | **let sb** | **put sb/sth to** *You should always put babies to sleep on their backs.* ◊ *We had to have our dog put to sleep* (= humanely killed because it was so ill).
- PREP. **for** *I only slept for four hours that night.* **through** *She slept right through the storm.* **with** *Everyone knows she sleeps with the boss.*
- PHRASES **not sleep a wink** (= not sleep at all) *I didn't sleep a wink last night.* **sleep late** *Let them sleep late on Saturday morning if they want to.* **sleep like a baby/log** (= sleep very well), **sleep rough** *the problem of young people who sleep rough in the streets*

sleepy adj.

1 ready to go to sleep
- VERBS **be, feel, look, sound** | **become, get, grow** | **make sb** *The alcohol was making him sleepy.*
- ADV. **extremely, really, very** | **a bit, a little, quite, rather** *She was beginning to get a bit sleepy.*

2 very quiet
- VERBS **be, seem** | **remain** *The town remains sleepy despite the activity all around it.*
- PHRASES **sleepy little** *a sleepy little fishing village*

sleeve noun

- ADJ. **long, short** | **full, puffed, voluminous, wide** | **rolled-up** | **coat, shirt, etc.**
- VERB + SLEEVE **push back/up, roll up** *She rolled up her sleeves and got down to work.* | **roll down** | **tug at** *I looked around to see who was tugging at my sleeve.*
- PREP. **in … ~s** *It was sunny, and everyone was in short sleeves.* **on a/the~** *There's tomato sauce on your sleeve.*
- PHRASES **in (your) shirtsleeves** (= not wearing a jacket)

slender adj.

1 thin in an attractive way
- VERBS **be, look**
- ADV. **very** *Those trousers make you look very slender.* | **quite** | **boyishly** *her boyishly slender figure*

2 small in amount/size
- VERBS **be, seem** | **remain**
- ADV. **decidedly, very** *His musical achievements have been decidedly slender.* | **fairly, pretty, rather**

slice noun

- ADJ. **big, generous, great, huge, large, thick** | **considerable, fair, significant, sizeable, substantial** *They spend a fair slice of the budget on research and development.* | **small, thin** | **cheese, lemon, pizza, etc.**
- VERB + SLICE **cut** *She cut a thin slice of lemon.*
- PREP. **in~** *The sausage is also sold pre-packed in slices.* | **~of** *a slice of toast* ◊ *The agency takes a large slice of the profits.*
- PHRASES **cut sth into slices** *He cut the meat into thick slices.*

slice verb

- ADV. **finely, thinly** *Slice the bread thinly.* | **thickly** | **neatly** | **off, up** *Slice up the mushrooms and fry them.*

● PREP. **into** *The axe sliced into her shoulder.* **off** *slicing pieces off the joint of meat* **through** *The knife sliced through his ear.*
● PHRASES **slice sth in half/two** *Slice the onion in two.*

slide *noun*

1 in photography
● ADJ. **colour | photographic**
● VERB + SLIDE **show | develop**
● SLIDE + NOUN **film | presentation, show** *He gave a fascinating slide show on climbing in the Himalayas.* **| projector**

2 for use with a microscope
● ADJ. **glass | microscope**
● VERB + SLIDE **mount sth on**

3 playground equipment
● VERB + SLIDE **go/play on, go down** *He wouldn't go down the slide by himself.*
● PREP. **on a/the~** *There were lots on children on the slide.*

4 change to a lower/worse condition
● ADJ. **downward | inexorable**
● VERB + SLIDE **halt, prevent, stop**
● PREP. **~in** *to stop the slide in the euro* **~into** *trying to prevent the inexorable slide into war* **~towards** *the market's recent slide towards panic*

slide *verb*

● ADV. **slowly** *Tears slid slowly down his pale cheek.* **| quickly | easily | smoothly** *a vehicle that will slide smoothly across snow* **| gently | gracefully | noiselessly, quietly, silently** *The moon slid silently behind a cloud.* **| imperceptibly | helplessly** *We slid helplessly down the slope.* **| away, back, backwards, down, forward, forwards, in, out, sideways** *The drawers slide in and out easily.* ◊ *(figurative) The eyes slid away from his own in embarrassment.*
● VERB + SLIDE **begin to** *The melting snow began to slide from the sloping roofs.*
● PREP. **across, along, down, from, into, off, onto, out of, over, to, up, etc.** *She took the note and slid it quickly into her pocket.* ◊ *He slid off the couch and walked over to me.*
● PHRASES **slide open** *The lift doors slid open.*

slight *adj.*

1 very small in degree
● VERBS **appear, be, seem**
● ADV. **extremely, very | comparatively, fairly, quite, rather, relatively**

2 thin and delicate
● VERBS **be, look** *She looked very slight, almost fragile.*
● ADV. **very | physically**

slim *adj.*

● VERBS **be, feel, look | become, get** *(informal) dieters who have got slim using these methods* **| keep, remain, stay** *She works very hard to stay slim.* **| make sb** *Step exercises can help make you slim.* **| keep sb**
● ADV. **very | quite**
● PHRASES **tall and slim**

slime *noun*

● ADJ. **thick | primeval, primordial** *the primeval slime from which all life developed*
● VERB + SLIME **be covered in/with | produce** *Frogs produce slime to keep their skin moist.*
● SLIME + VERB **ooze**
● PHRASES **a trail of slime** *The snail left a trail of slime along the floor.*

slimy *adj.*

● VERBS **be, feel, look** *The seaweed felt cold and slimy.*
● ADV. **very | all** *The walls were all slimy and green.*
● PREP. **with** *The steps were slimy with moss.*

sling *verb*

● ADV. **loosely | carelessly, casually** *His jacket was carelessly slung over one shoulder.*
● PREP. **across, around/round, from, in, on, over, etc.**

slip *noun*

1 mistake
● ADJ. **little, slight, tiny | unfortunate | Freudian**
● VERB + SLIP **make** *She made a couple of unfortunate slips during the talk.*
● PHRASES **a slip of the pen/tongue** *I didn't mean to say that—it was just a slip of the tongue.*

2 piece of paper
● ADJ. **betting, pay, rejection, voting** *He got over fifty rejection slips before his novel was published.*
● PREP. **on a/the~** *He wrote the address on a slip of paper.*
● PHRASES **a slip of paper**

slipper *noun*

● ADJ. **warm | bedroom, carpet | satin, sheepskin, silk, suede**
● QUANT. **pair**
● VERB + SLIPPER **kick off**
⇨ Special page at CLOTHES

slippery *adj.*

● VERBS **be, feel, look | become, get** *The concrete gets slippery when it's wet.* **| make sth** *The oil made the ground slippery and treacherous to walk on.*
● ADV. **extremely, very | a bit** *Watch out—the floor's a bit slippery.*
● PREP. **with** *rocks that were slippery with seaweed*

slither *verb*

● ADV. **silently** *A snake was slithering silently towards us.* **| helplessly** *He slithered helplessly down the slope.* **| away** *The snake slithered away.*
● PREP. **across, along, down, on, over, to, etc.** *Her knees gave way and she slithered to the floor.*

slogan *noun*

● ADJ. **catchy, snappy | popular | empty** *The 'freedom to learn' has become just another one of the government's empty slogans.* **| anti-government, anti-war, etc. | advertising | campaign, election, political**
● VERB + SLOGAN **coin, come up with, invent | adopt (sth as), have (sth as), use (sth as) | chant, shout | bear** *a T-shirt bearing the slogan 'I Flirt, Therefore I Am'*
● PREP. **on the ~** *They fought the election on the slogan 'The time has come'.* **under a/the ~** *protesting under the slogan 'When women stop, everything stops'*

slope *noun*

● ADJ. **precipitous, severe, sheer, steep | gentle, gradual, slight | long, short | downhill, downward | uphill, upward | higher, upper** *There was snow on the higher slopes of the mountain.* **| lower | northern, north-facing, etc.** *The vineyards on the south-facing slopes get more sunshine.* **| open | forested, grassy, icy, rocky, scree, smooth, snow-covered/snowy, wooded | mountain | dry, nursery, ski** *dry-slope skiing* ◊ *Some tourists were having a skiing lesson on the nursery slope.* **| negative, positive** *The unemployment-income curve on the graph has a negative slope.* **| slippery** *(figurative) Once he'd* *tried that first cigarette, he was on the slippery slope to being a smoker.*

● VERB + SLOPE **ascend, clamber up, climb (up)** *We clambered up the steep, rocky slope.* | **descend** | **have** *The football pitch has a slope of about one metre.*

● SLOPE + VERB **lead (up/down) to sth** *a slope leading down to the river* | **fall, rise** *The lower slopes rise quite gently.* | **steepen** | **flatten, level off**

● PREP. **down a/the ~** *I scrambled down the icy slope.* **on a/the ~** *We camped on an open mountain slope.* **up a/the ~** *There were more skiers further up the slope.*

● PHRASES **the angle of slope** *the angle of slope of the sides of the pyramid* **the bottom/foot/top of a slope**

slope *verb*

● ADV. **steeply** *The ground slopes away steeply at the back of the house.* | **gently, slightly** | **away, down, downwards, up, upwards**

● PREP. **to** *The field slopes down to a small river.* **towards**

slot *verb*

● ADV. **easily, neatly, simply** | **together** *The panels slot together to make a compost bin.*

● PREP. **between, in, into** *He slotted the magazines neatly into the rack.*

● PHRASES **slot (sth) into place** *All the pieces of the puzzle now slotted into place.*

slow *verb*

● ADV. **considerably, markedly, noticeably, sharply, significantly** *Sales have slowed down quite markedly.* | **barely, hardly** *The roadblocks hardly slowed them at all.* | **a bit, a little, slightly** | **gradually** | **deliberately** *She very deliberately slowed her steps.* | **down, up**

● VERB + SLOW **begin to** | **try to** *Rachel tried to slow her breathing.* | **be expected to** *Economic growth is expected to slow.*

● PHRASES **slow to a crawl/walk/snail's pace, slow to a halt/stop** *The two of them had slowed almost to a stop.*

slow *adj.*

● VERBS **be, prove, seem** | **remain**

● ADV. **extremely, incredibly, remarkably, very** | **interminably** | **a bit, comparatively, fairly, a little, pretty, quite, rather, relatively** | **agonizingly, desperately, frustratingly, painfully, tediously, tortuously** *Filming was painfully slow.* | **notoriously** *Civil court proceedings are notoriously slow.* | **noticeably** *He was noticeably slow to respond.* | **necessarily** *Genetic evolution is necessarily slow.*

● PREP. **at** *They are extremely slow at reaching decisions.*

slum *noun*

● ADJ. **crowded, overcrowded, teeming** | **deprived, poor, poverty-stricken** | **filthy** | **notorious** | **city, inner-city, urban** | **tenement** | **rural**

● VERB + SLUM **clear (away), demolish, knock down, remove**

● SLUM + NOUN **conditions** | **area, district, ghetto, neighbourhood, street** | **dwelling, housing, property** | **clearance** | **children, kids, dwellers, youths** | **life** | **landlord**

● PREP. **in a/the ~** *born in the slums of East London*

● PHRASES **the clearance/demolition/removal of slums**

slumber *verb*

● ADV. **deeply** | **peacefully** *The child slumbered peacefully in her arms.* | **fitfully**

slump *noun*

● ADJ. **world/worldwide** | **economic, housing, price, property, sales**

● PREP. **in a ~** *The economy is in a slump.* **into ~** *The industry is sinking into slump.* | **~ in** *Estate agents were badly hit by the slump in property prices.*

slump *verb*

1 decrease suddenly

● ADV. **badly, disastrously, dramatically, heavily** *Oil prices have slumped quite badly in recent months.*

● PREP. **by** *Profits slumped by 70 per cent.* **from, to** *Shares in the company slumped from £2.75 to £1.54.*

2 fall/sit down suddenly and heavily

● ADV. **a little** | **dejectedly** | **forward** *sitting with her head slumped forward* | **back, down**

● PREP. **against** *He slumped against the wall.* **in** *She slumped back in her seat.* **into** *He slumped down into a chair.* **over** *She slumped dejectedly over the wheel.*

● PHRASES **be found slumped…** *He was found slumped in a pool of blood by security guards.* **lie/sit slumped…**

slur *noun*

● ADJ. **racial, racist, sexist, sexual**

● VERB + SLUR **cast** *The comments cast a slur on her character.*

● PREP. **~ against/on** *The joke was seen as a slur against the mentally ill.* ◇ *a slur on his good name*

slush *noun*

● ADJ. **dirty** *There was dirty brown slush all over the roads and pavements.* | **brown, grey**

● VERB + SLUSH **turn to** *The snow had turned to slush.*

● PREP. **through the ~** *A pair of wide tracks led through the slush and mud.*

smack *noun*

● ADJ. **good, hard**

● VERB + SMACK **give sb, land (sb)** *He longed to land her a good smack in the face.* | **get**

● PREP. **with a ~** *She brought her hand down on the water with a smack.*

smack *verb*

● ADV. **hard** *I'll smack you very hard if you do that again!*

● PREP. **on** *She smacked the boy on his leg.*

PHRASAL VERB

smack of sth

● ADV. **strongly, too much** *Today's announcement smacks strongly of a government cover-up.* | **a little**

small *adj.*

● VERBS **be, feel, look, seem** | **become, get, grow** *The gap seemed to be getting smaller.* ◇ *The kite grew smaller and smaller and finally disappeared altogether.* | **remain, stay** *Choose plants that will stay quite small.*

● ADV. **extremely, really, terribly, very** | **a bit, fairly, pretty, quite, rather, relatively**

● PREP. **for** *My coat was rather small for Bob.*

smallpox *noun*

● QUANT. **attack** *In 1742 he suffered a fatal attack of smallpox.* | **case** | **outbreak**

● VERB + SMALLPOX **have, suffer from** | **catch, contract, get** | **die from/of** | **eradicate**

● SMALLPOX + NOUN **epidemic** | **vaccination**

⇨ Special page at ILLNESS

smash noun

1 breaking noisily into pieces
- VERB + SMASH **hear**
- PREP. **with a ~** *The plate hit the floor with a smash.* | **~of** *He heard the smash of breaking glass.*

2 car, etc. crash
- ADJ. **head-on** | **bus, car, train** | **motorway, road**
- VERB + SMASH **have**
- PREP. **in a/the ~** *Four people were seriously injured in a head-on smash on the A45.*

3 in tennis
- ADJ. **powerful** | **overhead**
- VERB + SMASH **hit** *He can hit a powerful overhead smash.*

smear noun

1 mark
- ADJ. **greasy**
- VERB + SMEAR **leave**
- PREP. **~of** *His fingers left a smear of sweat on the wall.*

2 lies about an important person
- VERB + SMEAR **cast** *The article cast a smear on the Minister for Health.*
- SMEAR + NOUN **campaign, tactic**
- PREP. **~ against/on** *campaign smears against the socialist candidate*

smear verb

- ADV. **liberally** *She smeared the cream liberally on her face.*
- PREP. **across, on, (all) over, with** *The child had smeared jam all over her face.*
- PHRASES **heavily smeared with sth** *Their faces were heavily smeared with mud.*

smell noun

- ADJ. **overpowering, pervasive, pungent, rich, sharp, strong** *There was an overpowering smell of burning tyres.* | **faint** | **distinct** | **distinctive, particular, unmistakable** | **funny, peculiar, strange, unusual** *What's that funny smell?* | **familiar** | **lingering** | **aromatic, delectable, delicious, fragrant, fresh, lovely, nice, savoury, sweet, wonderful** *the aromatic smells of a spring garden full of herbs* | **warm** | **appalling, awful, bad, evil, horrible, nasty, offensive, terrible, unpleasant, vile** | **acrid, nauseating, putrid, rank, sickly** *An acrid smell filled the air.* | **damp, dank, musty, rancid, sour, stale** *the sour smell of unwashed linen* | **earthy, fishy, masculine, metallic, musky, oily, smoky, spicy** | **cooking** *Cooking smells drifted up from the kitchen.*
- VERB + SMELL **be filled with, have** *The air was filled with a pervasive smell of chemicals.* ◊ *The cottage had a musty smell after being shut up over the winter.* | **give off** *The skunk gives off an unpleasant smell when attacked.* | **catch, detect** *As she walked into the house she detected the smell of gas.*
- SMELL + VERB **come, emanate, drift, float, waft** *A delicious smell of freshly baked bread wafted across the garden.* | **fill sth, hang** | **hit sb** *Then the pungent smell hit us— rotting fish and seaweed.*
- PREP. **~ from** *the putrid smell from the slaughterhouse* **~ of** *The faint smell of her perfume hung in the air.*

smell verb

1 notice/identify sth by using your nose
- ADV. **properly, well** *I had a streaming cold, so I could not smell properly.* | **almost** *Snow fell so that you could almost smell the cold.*
- VERB + SMELL **can/could**

2 have a particular smell

- ADV. **strongly** *His clothes smelled strongly of fish.* | **faintly, slightly, vaguely** *He smelled faintly of sweat.* | **deliciously, pleasantly, sweetly**
- PREP. **like** *It smells like rotten meat!* **of** *The kitchen smelled sweetly of herbs and fruit.*

smile noun

- ADJ. **bright, broad, wide** | **faint, thin, wan, weak** | **beatific, cheerful, dazzling, happy, radiant, sunny, warm** *the warm smile in his eyes* | **charming, gentle, sweet, winning** | **arch, disarming, enigmatic, mocking, rueful, sardonic, wry** *She gave a wry smile.* | **sad** | **shy** | **apologetic, sheepish** | **encouraging, indulgent, reassuring** | **polite** | **beguiling** | **ready** | **fixed, forced** | **supercilious** | **conspiratorial, knowing** | **grim** *a grim smile of satisfaction* | **humourless, mirthless** *She suppressed a mirthless smile.* | **crooked, lopsided** | **toothless**
- QUANT. **glimmer, hint, trace** *A trace of a smile played across her lips.*
- VERB + SMILE **have, wear** *She had a happy smile on her face.* | **flash (sb), give sb, smile** *He flashed her a disarming smile.* ◊ *She smiled a smile of dry amusement.* | **manage** *She managed a weak smile.* | **return** *She returned his smile.* | **hide, repress, suppress** *They had to hide their smiles.* | **forced** *Her father forced a smile.* | **bring** *Her antics brought a smile to my face.* | **crease into** *His face creased into a smile.*
- SMILE + VERB **fade, freeze, vanish** *Her sunny smile vanished as she read the letter.* | **cross sth, flicker across sth, play across sth** *A faint smile flickered across her face.* | **tug at the corner of the mouth** *A wry smile tugged at the corner of his mouth.* | **grow, spread (across/over sth)** *Her smile grew radiant.* ◊ *A gentle smile spread over her face.*
- PREP. **with a ~** *'Oh, hello,' he said, with a smile.* | **~ of** *a smile of approval*
- PHRASES **be all smiles** *Twelve hours later she was all smiles again.* **be wreathed in smiles** *His face was wreathed in smiles.* **wipe the smile off sb's face** *I'm going to wipe that smile off your face* (= make you stop thinking this is funny).

smile verb

- ADV. **broadly, widely** *She put down her tools and smiled broadly.* | **faintly, slightly, thinly, wanly, weakly** *He looked at the mess and smiled weakly.* | **dazzlingly, happily, radiantly, warmly** *Lawrence nodded, smiling happily.* | **charmingly, gently, sweetly, winningly** | **benignly, kindly, politely** | **shyly** | **encouragingly, indulgently, reassuringly** *The doctor smiled reassuringly.* | **apologetically, sheepishly** | **ruefully, wryly** *Molly smiled rather wryly and said nothing.* | **archly, enigmatically** | **conspiratorially** | **sadly** | **grimly** | **humourlessly, mirthlessly** | **crookedly, lopsidedly** | **back** *He smiled at her, and she smiled back.*
- VERB + SMILE **try to** | **manage to** | **make sb** *The memory still made her smile.*
- PREP. **at** *He turned and smiled at me.* **with** *She smiled with pleasure.*
- PHRASES **smile from ear to ear, smile to yourself** *She smiled to herself, picturing how surprised her mother would be to see her.*

smirk noun

- ADJ. **arrogant, knowing, patronizing, self-satisfied**
- VERB + SMIRK **have** *She had a self-satisfied smirk on her face.* | **give** *She gave a knowing smirk.* | **conceal, hide** *He made no attempt to conceal his smirk.*
- SMIRK + VERB **flicker** *A smirk flickered at the corner of his mouth as he watched my struggle.*
- PREP. **with a ~** *'Comfortable?' he asked with a smirk.* | **~ of** *a smirk of triumph*

smog noun

- ADJ. heavy | urban | photochemical
- VERB + SMOG **reduce** *measures to reduce smog*
- SMOG + NOUN **alert** | **level**

smoke noun

- ADJ. **dense, thick** | **black, blue, grey, etc.** | **billowing** | **acrid, choking, stale** | **cigar, cigarette, pipe, tobacco**
- QUANT. **cloud, column, haze, pall, plume, puff, spiral, wisp** *We sat drinking in a haze of cigarette smoke.* ◊ *The witch disappeared in a puff of smoke.*
- VERB + SMOKE **belch (out), blow, emit** *The lorry ahead was belching out black smoke.* ◊ *Don't blow smoke in my face!* | **exhale** | **inhale** | **go up in** *The barn went up in smoke* (= was destroyed by a fire). | **be wreathed in** *She sat there wreathed in cigarette smoke.*
- SMOKE + VERB **belch, billow, curl, drift, fill, pour, rise from/into** *Blue smoke curled upwards from her cigarette.* | **hang** *A pall of yellow smoke hung over the quarry.* | **clear** *When the smoke cleared we saw the extent of the damage.*
- SMOKE + NOUN **plume, ring** *I taught myself to blow smoke rings.* | **signal** | **bomb** | **alarm, detector** | **emission** | **inhalation**
- PHRASES **full of smoke, thick with smoke** *The public bar was thick with stale tobacco smoke.*

smoke verb

1 cigarette/pipe, etc.
- ADV. **heavily** *He has always smoked heavily.*

2 meat/fish/cheese
- ADV. **heavily** | **lightly** *The ham is cured, then lightly smoked.*

smoker noun

- ADJ. **chain, heavy** | **regular** | **light** | **passive** *the risk of lung cancer in passive smokers* | **cigar, cigarette, pipe**
- SMOKER + NOUN **a smoker's cough**

smoking noun

- ADJ. **chain, heavy** | **passive** *the dangers of passive smoking* | **cigar, cigarette, pipe, tobacco**
- VERB + SMOKING **start, take up** | **give up, quit, stop** *I'm trying to give up smoking.* | **cut down on** *The doctor advised me to cut down on smoking and alcohol.* | **ban**
- SMOKING + NOUN **habit** | **ban** *A total smoking ban has been imposed throughout the building.* | **room**
- PHRASES **a ban on smoking, the dangers/effects of smoking** *a study of the harmful effects of smoking* **no smoking** *The company has a strict no smoking policy.* **smoking-related death/disease/illness**

smooth verb

- ADV. **carefully, gently** *She smoothed his hair gently.* | **back, down, out** *Her mother smoothed back Alice's hair.* ◊ *Use an iron to smooth out any creases.*

smooth adj.

1 without bumps
- VERBS **be, feel, look** | **become** | **wear sth** *The steps had been worn smooth by the thousands of passing feet.*
- ADV. **beautifully, exceptionally, extremely, really, very** *her beautifully smooth complexion* | **completely, perfectly** | **almost** | **fairly, quite** | **deceptively** *the deceptively smooth surface of the glacier*

2 without problems
- VERBS **be, feel, look, seem** | **become**
- ADV. **extremely, incredibly, really, remarkably, very** *The project got off to a remarkably smooth start.* | **completely** | **not entirely** *The process of negotiation was not*

entirely smooth. | **almost** | **fairly, quite, reasonably, relatively** *a fairly smooth transition to democracy*

smug adj.

- VERBS **appear, be, feel, look, seem, sound** | **become, get** *Now don't get smug just because you've won a couple of games.*
- ADV. **incredibly, very** *the incredibly smug expression on his face* | **almost** | **a bit, a little, quite, rather, slightly**
- PREP. **about** *What are you looking so smug about?*

smuggle verb

- ADV. **secretly** | **aboard, abroad, in, out**
- VERB + SMUGGLE **try to** | **manage to**
- PREP. **into** *goods which have been smuggled into Britain* **out of** *Friends managed to smuggle him secretly out of the country.*

smuggling noun

- ADJ. **arms, cocaine, drug, heroin, gold, ivory, etc.**
- SMUGGLING + NOUN **attempt** | **gang, operation, racket, ring** | **route** | **vessel**
- ⇨ Note at CRIME (for verbs)

snack noun

- ADJ. **healthy, light** | **tasty** | **savoury, sweet** | **hot, cold** | **quick** *We stopped at a service station for a quick snack.* | **bedtime, lunchtime, mid-afternoon, mid-morning, midnight** | **party**
- VERB + SNACK **eat, have** | **stop for** | **cook (sb), fix (sb), make (sb), prepare** *I fixed myself a light snack.* | **provide (sb with), serve** *A bar service provides drinks and snacks throughout the day.*
- SNACK + NOUN **food** | **lunch, meal, time** *Most office staff prefer a snack lunch to a sit-down meal.* | **service** | **bar, counter, kiosk**
- ⇨ Special page at FOOD

snag noun

- ADJ. **big, major** | **minor, small** *A minor snag is that it's expensive.* | **possible, potential** | **technical**
- VERB + SNAG **hit** *We've hit a technical snag: the printer isn't compatible with my PC.* | **iron out** *There are a few snags to iron out before the prototype is ready.*
- PREP. **~in** *one of the snags in the scheme* **~to** *There is a snag to the job: you have to work at weekends.* **~with** *I suddenly saw the major snag with the whole idea.*

snail noun

- ADJ. **edible** | **land, marine, pond, sea, water**
- SNAIL + NOUN **shell**
- PHRASES **(at) a snail's pace** *Traffic had slowed to a snail's pace.*

snake noun

- ADJ. **deadly** *one of the world's deadliest snakes* | **poisonous, venomous** | **grass, sea, tree, water**
- SNAKE + VERB **bite sb/sth, strike sth** *She was bitten by a snake while walking through long grass.* ◊ *The snake lifted up its head before striking its prey.* | **slide, slither, wind (its way)** *A small green snake slithered across the wet road.* ◊ *The snake wound its way through the undergrowth.* | **hiss, spit** | **moult, shed its skin** | **coil (itself) around, coil up, curl up** | **uncoil**
- SNAKE + NOUN **bite (also snakebite)** | **charmer** | **venom**

snap *verb*

1 break suddenly with a sharp noise
- ADV. **suddenly** *The branch suddenly snapped.*
- PHRASES **snap (sth) in half/two** *She picked up the pencil and snapped it in two.*

2 move (sth) quickly with a sharp noise
- PHRASES **snap (sth) open/shut** *She snapped the lid shut.* **snap (sth) together** *The plastic pieces snap together to make a replica of a dinosaur.*

3 speak in a quick angry way
- ADV. **angrily, impatiently, irritably, sarcastically, sharply | back** *'How should I know?' Zen snapped back.*
- PREP. **at** *He lost his temper and snapped irritably at the children.*

4 lose control
- ADV. **finally** *My patience finally snapped.*

snarl *verb*

- ADV. **savagely, viciously** *He snarled savagely at her.* | **almost**
- PREP. **at** *A guard dog snarled at us as we walked by.*

snatch *noun*

- ADJ. **brief**
- VERB + SNATCH **catch, hear, overhear** *We caught snatches of conversation from the room next door.* | **hum, sing** *He was humming a snatch of a song from 'Cabaret'.*
- PREP. **in~es** *She learnt to sleep in brief snatches.*
- PHRASES **a snatch of conversation/music/song**

snatch *verb*

- ADV. **almost | quickly | away, up** *She leapt to her feet, snatching up her bag.*
- VERB + SNATCH **try to**
- PREP. **at** *He snatched at her arm as she walked past.* **from** *She almost snatched the letter from my hand.*

sneer *noun*

- ADJ. **arrogant | faint, slight**
- VERB + SNEER **give** *He gave an arrogant sneer.* | **hide**
- PREP. **with a~ | ~at** *The prime minister resisted a sneer at his opponent's misfortune.*
- PHRASES **curl/twist your lips into a sneer, a sneer in your voice**

sneeze *verb*

- ADV. **loudly** *Someone sneezed loudly at the back of the hall.*
- VERB + SNEEZE **make sb** *The smoke reached her and made her sneeze.*

sniff *noun*

- ADJ. **deep, good | loud**
- VERB + SNIFF **give, let out** *She gave a loud sniff of disapproval.* | **hear | get, have, take** *to get a sniff of fresh air*
- PREP. **between ~s** *'I'm sorry,' he said between sniffs.* **with a~** *'I'm fine,' she said with a sniff.* | **~at** *The dog had a good sniff at the bushes around the garden.*
- PHRASES **a sniff of disapproval**
- ⇨ Note at SOUND

sniff *verb*

- ADV. **loudly** *She wiped her eyes and sniffed loudly.* | **deeply | a little | carefully, delicately | appreciatively** *He sniffed appreciatively. 'Smells delicious. What is it?'* | **disapprovingly, disdainfully, disparagingly | suspiciously | back** *The woman sniffed back her tears.*
- PREP. **at** *The dog sniffed at his shoes.*

snippet *noun*

- ADJ. **little | interesting** *He passed on any interesting snippets of information he could glean from his colleagues.*
- VERB + SNIPPET **gather, glean | give, pass on**
- PREP. **~from** *The article gave a few snippets from her forthcoming memoirs.* **~of** *a snippet of conversation*

snobbery *noun*

- ADJ. **inverted** *His dismissive attitude towards the rich is just inverted snobbery.* | **cultural, intellectual, musical**
- PREP. **~about** *his snobbery about mixing with people from other classes* **~towards** *snobbery towards electronic music*

snooker *noun*

- ADJ. **professional**
- QUANT. **frame, game** *We played a couple of frames of snooker in the evening.*
- VERB + SNOOKER **play**
- SNOOKER + NOUN **ball, cue, table | ace, champion, player, star | club, hall, room | match, tournament | league**
- ⇨ Special page at SPORT

snore *verb*

- ADV. **loudly, noisily | gently, lightly, quietly, softly** *She was asleep in a chair and snoring gently.* | **contentedly** *He began to snore contentedly.*
- VERB + SNORE **begin to, start to**

snort *noun*

- ADJ. **little | loud | derisive**
- VERB + SNORT **give, let out** *He gave a snort of contempt.* | **hear**
- PREP. **with a~** *'What a mess they made of it,' said Sam with a snort of derision.* | **~of**
- PHRASES **a snort of derision/disgust, a snort of laughter**
- ⇨ Note at SOUND

snort *verb*

- ADV. **loudly | softly | angrily, contemptuously, derisively, impatiently, indignantly** *He snorted indignantly and walked away.*
- PREP. **in** *He snorted in disgust.* **with** *Her friends snorted with laughter.*

snow *noun*

- ADJ. **heavy, thick | fine, light** *The plants were covered in fine snow.* | **deep | damp, wet | compacted, crisp, frozen, hard, packed** *The crisp snow crunched as we walked through it.* ◊ *The frozen snow was treacherous to walk on.* | **powder/powdery, soft | drifting, driving, falling, swirling** *They struggled on through the driving snow.* | **melted, melting | fresh, new, newly fallen | first** *the first snow of winter* | **spring, winter | artificial** *They had to use artificial snow at the Winter Olympics.* | **dirty**
- QUANT. **flake | fall, flurry | patch | blanket, carpet | inch** *Three inches of snow fell had fallen.*
- VERB + SNOW **be covered in** *The car was completely covered in snow.* | **clear, shovel, sweep** *She cleared the snow from the path.*
- SNOW + VERB **cover sth, lie, pile (up), settle** *Snow covered everything from horizon to horizon.* ◊ *Snow had piled up against the walls of the cottage.* ◊ *It was too warm for the snow to settle.* | **drift, drive, fall, swirl | melt, thaw**
- SNOW + NOUN **conditions, flurry, storm** (also **snowstorm**) **| plough** (also **snowplough**) **| blindness**
- PREP. **across~** *They travelled across the snow in a sleigh.* **in/into~** *The children are playing in the snow.*

through~ *We struggled through the deep snow back to the chalet.* **under~** *The steps were buried under the snow.*

snow *verb*

* ADV. **hard**, **heavily** *It had been snowing heavily all night.* | **lightly**
* PHRASES **start/stop snowing** *It started snowing just as we were setting out.*

snowfall *noun*

* ADJ. **heavy** | **light** | **annual** | **average** *What's the average snowfall for this region?*
* VERB + SNOWFALL **have** *We had a light snowfall last night.*

snowflake *noun*

* SNOWFLAKES + VERB **fall**, **flutter** | **melt**

snub *noun*

* ADJ. **deliberate**
* VERB + SNUB **deliver sb** *He took the opportunity to deliver us another snub.* | **receive**
* PREP. **as a~** | **~ for/to** *His cancellation of the concert was seen as a deliberate snub to the organizers.*

snub *verb*

* ADV. **deliberately** | **publicly** | **rudely**
* PHRASES **feel snubbed** *He was not invited to the party, and felt snubbed.*

snuff *noun*

* QUANT. **pinch**
* VERB + SNUFF **inhale**, **take**
* SNUFF + NOUN **box**

snuggle *verb*

* ADV. **close** *She slipped her arm through his and snuggled close.* | **down**, **up** *I snuggled down in my sleeping bag.*
* PREP. **against** *Claudia snuggled against him.* **into** *She snuggled into him and closed her eyes.*

soak *verb*

* ADV. **completely**, **thoroughly** | **overnight** | **off**, **out** *Place the jar in warm water to soak the label off.*
* VERB + SOAK **leave sth to** *I've left the clothes to soak overnight.*
* PREP. **in** *Soak the clothes in cold water.* **into** *Water dripped off the table and soaked into the carpet.* **through** *The rain had soaked through every layer of his clothing.* **with** *He soaked the cloth with petrol.*

soaked *adj.*

* VERBS **be**, **look** | **get**
* ADV. **absolutely**, **completely**, **thoroughly**
* PHRASES **soaked to the skin** *There was a sudden shower and we got soaked to the skin.*

soap *noun*

* ADJ. **mild** | **perfumed**, **scented** | **liquid** | **carbolic** | **toilet** | **saddle**
* QUANT. **bar**, **cake**
* VERB + SOAP **use**, **wash (sth) with**
* SOAP + NOUN **flakes**, **powder** | **bubble**, **suds** | **dish**, **dispenser**
* PHRASES **soap and water**

soar *verb*

1 increase very fast
* ADV. **dramatically** *Profits have soared dramatically in recent months.*
* VERB + SOAR **be expected to**, **be set to** *Borrowing is set to soar to an astonishing £60 billion.*
* PREP. **by** *Retail sales soared by 10% in the twelve months to November.* **from**, **to** *Inflation has soared from 5% to 15%.*
* PHRASES **send sth soaring** *The fuel shortage sent prices soaring.*

2 fly high in the air
* ADV. **high** | **overhead** *A buzzard soared high overhead.*
* PREP. **above**, **over** *an eagle soaring high above them*

sob *noun*

* ADJ. **big**, **deep**, **great** | **little** | **loud** | **choked**, **hoarse**, **stifled**, **strangled** | **choking**, **gasping**, **gulping**, **racking**, **shuddering** | **occasional** | **dry**
* VERB + SOB **give**, **let out** | **be racked by/with**, **shake with** *He was too racked by sobs to reply.* | **choke back**, **stifle** *Choking back a sob, she ran to her father's chair.* | **hear**
* SOB + VERB **break from sb/sth**, **burst from sb/sth**, **escape sb/sth** *A sob escaped her lips.* | **rise** *A choked sob rose in his throat.* | **catch** *A dry sob caught in her throat.* | **rack sth**, **shake sth** *Deep racking sobs shook his whole body.* | **subside**
* SOB + NOUN **story** *You can't expect me to believe this sob story!*
* PREP. **between ~s** *'I don't want to go!' she got out between sobs.* **through ~s** *He continued his story through stifled sobs.* **with a~** *'Why didn't you tell me?' she said with a sob.* | **~ from** *a sob from George* **~ of** *a great sob of despair*
* PHRASES **a sob of despair/pain/relief**
⇨ Note at SOUND

sob *verb*

* ADV. **aloud** | **loudly** | **quietly**, **silently** | **hysterically**, **uncontrollably**, **wildly** | **almost** *He was pleading, almost sobbing, first silently and then aloud.*
* VERB + SOB **begin to**, **start to** *He began to sob uncontrollably.* | **hear sb** *I heard a child sobbing loudly.*
* PREP. **with** *She was sobbing with pain and fear.*
* PHRASES **sob your heart out**

sober *adj.*

* VERBS **be**, **feel**, **look**, **seem** | **remain**, **stay** *She wanted a drink, but she had to stay sober.* | **keep sb** *Only the thought of her kept him sober.*
* ADV. **completely**, **perfectly**, **quite**, **stone-cold** | **not entirely** | **almost**, **fairly**, **more or less**, **pretty well**, **reasonably**, **relatively** *By this time he felt more or less sober again.* | **enough** *At that point she was still sober enough to ask sensible questions.*

soccer *noun*

* ADJ. **amateur**, **professional** | **top-class** | **junior**, **senior**, **youth** | **ladies'**, **women's** | **league**, **non-league** | **premiership** | **first-division**, **etc.** | **international**, **world** | **competitive** | **five-a-side** | **indoor**
* QUANT. **game**
* VERB + SOCCER **play** | **watch**
* SOCCER + NOUN **ball** | **field**, **ground**, **pitch**, **stadium** | **game**, **match**, **tournament** | **club**, **team** | **ace**, **hero**, **legend**, **player**, **star** | **boss**, **coach**, **manager**, **official** | **management** | **fan**, **spectator**, **supporter** | **season** | **career** | **skills** | **strip** | **hooligan**, **thug** | **violence** | **fanzine**, **magazine** | **memento**, **memorabilia**

socialism *noun*

- ADJ. **democratic, state**
- VERB + SOCIALISM **build, establish** *trying to build socialism in their own country*
- PREP. **under~** *They believed that these problems would disappear under socialism.*

socialist *noun*

- ADJ. **dedicated, staunch, strong | radical, revolutionary | liberal | moderate | democratic**
- SOCIALIST + VERB **come to power** *The socialists came to power in 1981.*

social security *noun*

- VERB + SOCIAL SECURITY **be entitled to, claim, receive** *If you are unemployed you can claim social security.*
- SOCIAL SECURITY + NOUN **provision, system** *plans to improve social security provision for single parents |* **benefits, payments | contributions** *All people in work pay social security contributions. |* **department, minister, office | budget, funds, spending**
- PREP. **on~** *He's out of work and on social security.*

social worker *noun*

- ADJ. **senior | trained | specialist | psychiatric | hospital, residential**
- ⇨ Note at JOB

society *noun*

1 people who have shared customs and laws
- ADJ. **wider** *the position of women within the family and the wider society |* **contemporary, modern | traditional | advanced** *the division of labour in an advanced capitalist society |* **primitive | egalitarian, free, just, open | closed | civilized, humane | affluent** *the consumerist values of the affluent society |* **consumer, consumerist | throwaway** *Our throwaway society must be encouraged to recycle. |* **permissive | multicultural, multiracial, pluralistic | divided, stratified** *Years of high unemployment have left society deeply divided. |* **civil** *the relationship between the state and civil society |* **secular | human** *a theory on the basis of human society |* **class | classless | tribal | matriarchal, patriarchal | bourgeois | capitalist, democratic, feudal, socialist, etc. | industrial, post-industrial, pre-industrial | agricultural, technological | Western | rural, urban, village | polite** *Such language would not be used in polite society.*
- VERB + SOCIETY **build, create, shape** *the struggle to build a just society |* **permeate, pervade** *the greed that pervades modern society |* **fit into** *Prisoners often have problems fitting into society on their release. |* **polarize**
- SOCIETY + VERB **be based on sth** *a society based on social justice*
- PREP. **in/within (a)~** *the role of television in modern Western society*
- PHRASES **a cross-section of society** *The clinic deals with a wide cross-section of society* **the fabric of society** *The civil war tore apart the fabric of society.* **the higher/top echelons of society** *Officers were drawn largely from the top echelons of society.* **a level/rank/stratum of society** *Child cruelty exists at all levels of society.* **a member of society** *welfare reforms to protect the most vulnerable members of society* **an outcast from/of society** *She devoted herself to helping the outcasts of society.* **the backbone/a bulwark/a pillar of society** *One of the pillars of society must be that everyone has access to the legal system.* ◇ *He considered himself to be a pillar of society.* **your place/rank in society** *A person's job is one of the factors that determines their place in society.* **the rest of society** *He felt isolated from the rest of society.* **a section/sector/segment of society** *Every section of society must have*

access to education. **society as a whole** *The research examines minorities and their relation to society as a whole.* **society at large** *Health standards have risen in society at large.* **the structure of a society** *the class structure of British society*

2 organization formed for a particular purpose
- ADJ. **secret | debating, dramatic, historical, horticultural, law, medical, musical, religious, etc.**
- VERB + SOCIETY **belong to** *She belongs to the historical society. |* **become a member of, join | create, establish, form, found, set up, start**
- PREP. **in a/the ~** *She was active in the Society for Women's Suffrage. | ~ for* *a society for the prevention of cruelty to animals ~ of* *the Society of Motor Manufacturers and Traders*
- ⇨ Note at ORGANIZATION

sociology *noun*

- ADJ. **classical, mainstream, radical | industrial, medical, political, urban, etc.**
- PHRASES **the sociology of culture/knowledge/religion/science, etc.**
- ⇨ Note at SUBJECT (for verbs and nouns)

sock *noun*

- ADJ. **knee, long | ankle, short | thick | woolly | old, smelly | odd** *He wore odd socks, one red and one yellow.*
- QUANT. **pair**
- VERB + SOCK **pull on, pull up | pull off | knit | darn, mend**
- ⇨ Special page at CLOTHES

socket *noun*

1 for electricity
- ADJ. **13 amp, etc. | electric/electrical, mains, plug, power | aerial, headphone, etc. | input, output | floor, wall**
- VERB + SOCKET **plug (sth) into** *The battery charger plugs into any mains socket.*
- SOCKET + NOUN **outlet**

2 in the body
- ADJ. **sunken | eye, hip, shoulder**
- VERB + SOCKET **sink into** *Her eyes sank deep into their sockets.*
- PREP. **in its~** *His eyes bulged madly in their sockets.*

sofa *noun*

- ADJ. **battered | comfortable, plush | deep, low-slung** *She sank into the deep sofa. |* **chintz, leather, etc. | wide | three-seater, two-seater, etc. | convertible** *The convertible sofa means that the apartment can sleep four.*
- VERB + SOFA **collapse on/onto, flop (back) on/onto, lower yourself onto, settle (yourself) (down) on, sink down on/onto, sink (back/down) onto, sit (down) on, slump (back) on/onto** *He slumped back on the sofa in tears. |* **be sprawled across/on, be stretched out on, lie on, lounge on, recline on, sprawl across/on, stretch out on** *I spent the evening sprawled on the sofa, watching TV. |* **get up from, jump up from, pull yourself up from, rise from** *He got up from the sofa to fetch some drinks.*
- SOFA + NOUN **bed**
- PREP. **on the~** *She was curled up on the sofa.*
- PHRASES **the arm/back/edge of a sofa**

soft *adj.*

- VERBS **be, feel, look | become, go, turn | stay** *Her skin had stayed soft and supple.*
- ADV. **beautifully, extremely, incredibly, really, very** *The fabric has a beautifully soft texture. |* **all** *These tomatoes have gone all soft. |* **fairly, quite, rather, relatively, slightly**

soften verb

1 become/make sth softer/gentler
- ADV. **considerably, a lot | a little, slightly** *His smile softened slightly.*

2 make sth seem less severe
- ADV. **slightly, somewhat**
- VERB + SOFTEN **try** *The chancellor may try to soften the blow somewhat with a cut in interest rates.* | **help (to)**

software noun

- ADJ. **computer | application | accounting, design, educational, management, music-sharing, etc. | anti-virus | proprietary | pirated** *He was arrested for selling pirated software.*
- QUANT. **piece** *an exciting piece of design software*
- VERB + SOFTWARE **use, run** *My PC isn't powerful enough to run that software.* | **design, develop, write | download, install**
- SOFTWARE + VERB **run** *The software will run on most IBM-compatible PCs.*
- SOFTWARE + NOUN **application, package, product, program, system, tool | development, engineering | developer, engineer | company, firm, house**
- ⇒ Special page at COMPUTER

soil noun

1 earth
- ADJ. **deep | shallow, thin | fertile, good, rich | barren, infertile, poor | light | heavy | loose | dry | damp, moist, waterlogged, wet | acid/acidic, alkaline | contaminated | top** (also **topsoil**) **| chalky, clay/clayey, peaty, sandy, stony | alluvial, desert, forest, garden, polar, volcanic**
- VERB + SOIL **cultivate | dig, till, turn, work** *fields of newly turned soil* ◊ *The clayey soils of the region are difficult to work.* | **fertilize | drain | loosen**
- SOIL + NOUN **conservation | degradation, erosion | conditions, fertility, quality** *declining soil fertility* | **type | surface | science, scientist**
- PREP. **in (the)~** *The flowers do well in sandy soil.*

2 part of a country
- ADJ. **native | foreign**
- VERB + SOIL **set foot on** *She first set foot on French soil at a small Channel port.*
- PREP. **on ... ~** *protests over the siting of nuclear weapons on British soil*

solace noun

- ADJ. **great | spiritual**
- VERB + SOLACE **bring (sb), give sb, offer (sb)** *The news brought no solace to the grieving relations.* | **find, take** *Unable to travel, he found some solace in reading about other people's journeys abroad.* | **seek** *They sought solace in religion from the harshness of their everyday lives.*
- PHRASES **turn to sb/sth for solace** *His career took a nosedive and he turned to drink and drugs for solace.*

soldier noun

- ADJ. **brave, fine, good, great** *The minister paid tribute to the brave soldiers who had lost their lives.* | **trained | experienced, veteran | former, old, retired | professional, regular | volunteer | conscript | common, ordinary, private, rank-and-file** *What was life like for the common soldier?* | **fellow** *He was deeply affected by the death of one of his fellow soldiers.* | **loyal** *soldiers loyal to the president* | **dead, injured, wounded | armed | foot, mounted | mercenary | enemy | Allied, British, etc. | government, rebel | uniformed | undercover | toy**
- VERB + SOLDIER **be, serve as | enlist as** *He decided to enlist as a soldier.* | **play** *little boys playing soldiers*

- SOLDIER + VERB **enlist** *The number of soldiers enlisting has fallen dramatically.* | **be stationed, serve** *soldiers serving in Germany* | **march | fight (sb) | defend sth, guard sth | open fire (on sb)** *At least 19 people were killed when soldiers opened fire on a peaceful demonstration.* | **shoot sb dead | be killed in action, die | be wounded | be missing in action | be captured, be taken prisoner | return** *soldiers returning from the war* | **desert**

sole noun

- ADJ. **thick, thin | leather, rubber | inner**
- PHRASES **the sole of your boot/shoe** *I've got a hole in the sole of my shoe.* **the soles of your feet** *The sand was so hot I got blisters on the soles of my feet.*

solemn adj.

- VERBS **be, look, seem, sound** *She usually had a smile on her face, but now she looked solemn.* | **become, grow** *His face grew solemn.* | **remain**
- ADV. **very** *He addressed them all in very solemn tones.* | **rather** *Her mood was rather solemn.*

solemnity noun

- ADJ. **great** *The monument was unveiled with great solemnity.* | **mock**
- PREP. **with~**

solicit verb

- ADV. **actively** *She had actively solicited funds for her election campaign.*
- PREP. **for** *Local companies were solicited for money.* **from** *She solicited support from other teachers.*

solicitor noun

- ADJ. **good | qualified | trainee | duty, practising** *There will be no court duty solicitor today.* ◊ *She is still a practising solicitor at the age of sixty-two.*
- PHRASES **a firm of solicitors**
- ⇒ Note at PROFESSIONAL (for verbs)

solid adj.

1 hard and firm/not hollow
- VERBS **be, feel, look, seem | become, go** *If you put it in the freezer, it will go solid.*
- ADV. **extremely, very | absolutely, completely | almost, practically | quite | enough** *The ice felt solid enough.* | **apparently, seemingly**

2 reliable and strong
- VERBS **appear, be, look, seem | become | remain**
- ADV. **extremely, really, very | absolutely, rock** *Support for the plan remained rock solid.* | **fairly, pretty** *There is pretty solid evidence to show that the disease is caused by poor hygiene.*

solidarity noun

- ADJ. **international, national | class, community, family, group, social, (trade) union, working-class**
- VERB + SOLIDARITY **feel | demonstrate, express, show | foster, promote**
- PREP. **in~with** *Various other groups of workers went on strike in solidarity with the train drivers.* | **~ against** *promoting union solidarity against management* **~among/amongst/between** *The conflict fostered solidarity among Arab oil states.* **~with** *Orwell expressed his solidarity with the miners in the book.*
- PHRASES **a gesture of solidarity** *Catering staff staged a sit-down protest as a gesture of solidarity with the striking nurses.* **a sense of solidarity** *The strike fostered a sense of solidarity among the workers.*

solitude *noun*

- ADJ. **absolute**
- VERB + SOLITUDE **seek**
- PREP. **in ~** *to pray in solitude* **in the ~ of** *She enjoyed a few moments of peace in the solitude of the garden.*

solo *noun*

- ADJ. **long | brief, short | brilliant | piano, violin, etc. | soprano, tenor, etc.**
- VERB + SOLO **do, perform, play, sing**

soluble *adj.*

- VERBS **be | become**
- ADV. **highly, very** *It is a highly soluble gas.* **| easily, freely | completely, totally | partially, partly, slightly**
- PREP. **in** *The disulphate was easily soluble in water.*

solution *noun*

1 to a problem, difficult situation, etc.
- ADJ. **complete, comprehensive | partial | effective, good, happy, ideal, neat, optimal, perfect, real** *His plan does not offer a real solution to the problem.* **| acceptable | satisfactory, workable | correct, right | easy, obvious, simple | possible | feasible, practical, realistic, viable | cost-effective | creative, imaginative, ingenious | drastic, radical | early, immediate, instant, quick, speedy** *The UN representative stressed the urgency of an early solution.* **| final, lasting, long-term, permanent, ultimate | interim, short-term, temporary | proposed | pragmatic | compromise, negotiated | diplomatic, peaceful, political | military | technical**
- VERB + SOLUTION **look for, seek, work towards | achieve, agree (on), arrive at, come up with, find, produce, reach, work out** *attempts to find a comprehensive political solution to the crisis* **| propose, put forward, suggest | adopt | offer, provide**
- PREP. **~ for** *a quick solution for dealing with the paper shortage* **~ to** *They were seeking an ultimate solution to the city's traffic problem.*

2 liquid in which a solid has been dissolved
- ADJ. **concentrated, neat, strong | dilute, weak | saturated | acid | alkaline | aqueous | saline, salt | bicarbonate, sodium chloride, etc.**
- SOLUTION + VERB **contain**
- PREP. **in ~** *aluminium ions in solution*

solve *verb*

- ADV. **completely** *The mystery has not yet been completely solved.* **| largely | half, partially, partly | hardly | not necessarily** *Being with peers and friends does not necessarily solve this feeling of loneliness.* **| adequately, satisfactorily** *This question has never been satisfactorily solved.* **| effectively | convincingly | easily, readily | quickly | elegantly, neatly | magically, somehow | eventually, finally | never**
- VERB + SOLVE **attempt to, try to | help (to), help sb (to)** *We were given clues to help us solve the puzzle.* **| be designed to** *a scheme designed to solve the housing problem* **| fail to | be difficult to**
- PREP. **by** *We hope the difficulty can be solved by getting the two sides together to discuss the issues.* **with** *The problem cannot be solved with spending cuts alone.*
- PHRASES **an attempt to solve sth**

solvent *noun*

- ADJ. **volatile | chlorinated | chemical, organic | cleaning, industrial**
- VERB + SOLVENT **abuse, sniff**
- SOLVENT + VERB **evaporate**
- SOLVENT + NOUN **abuse, sniffing**

sombre *adj.*

- VERBS **be, look, seem** *Everyone looked very sombre.* **| become, grow** *His eyes grew sombre.* **| remain** *The mood in Parliament remained sombre.*
- ADV. **very | fairly, rather, somewhat** *She was in a somewhat sombre mood.* **| suitably** *The funeral cortège passed, to suitably sombre music.*

son *noun*

- ADJ. **baby, newborn | little, small, young | teenage | grown-up | only | eldest, first-born, middle, oldest, youngest | elder, younger | illegitimate, legitimate | dutiful, good | fine, strong** *The queen bore him four fine sons.* **| long-lost, prodigal** *They welcomed me like a long-lost son.* **| married, unmarried**
- VERB + SON **have** *They've got three young sons.* **| bear** *(formal),* **give birth to | bring up** *Living alone and trying to bring up a young son is no easy task.*
- SON + VERB **grow up**

song *noun*

1 piece of music with words
- ADJ. **beautiful, good, great, lovely | catchy | mournful, sad | country, folk, pop/popular, traditional** *a Hungarian folk song* **| bawdy, children's, drinking, love, patriotic, protest, religious** *After a few drinks, they were all singing bawdy songs at the top of their voices.* ◇ *a protest song written in the sixties* **| theme, title** *the theme song from 'The Godfather'* ◇ *the title song from the Beatles' album 'Help!'*
- VERB + SONG **compose, write | do, perform, play, sing** *They performed another two songs as encores.* ◇ *Sing us a song, Susanna!* **| record**
- SONG + NOUN **writer** *(also* **songwriter)** *a singer-songwriter* **| contest**
- PREP. **in (a/the) ~** *Important historical events were commemorated in song.* **| ~ about** *a song about love*

2 act of singing
- VERB + SONG **break into, burst into** *He strummed a couple of chords on the guitar and they all burst into song.*
- PREP. **in ~** *He heard voices raised in song.*

soothing *adj.*

- VERBS **be, feel** *Her touch felt wonderfully soothing.*
- ADV. **very, wonderfully**

sophisticated *adj.*

1 having a lot of experience of the world
- VERBS **be, feel, look, seem | become, get**
- ADV. **highly, very** *She was a highly sophisticated and elegant woman.* **| quite, rather | enough, sufficiently | intellectually, politically**

2 advanced and complicated
- VERBS **be, look, seem | become, get**
- ADV. **extremely, highly, very** *incredibly sophisticated computers* **| increasingly | fairly, pretty, quite, rather, relatively | enough, sufficiently | technically, technologically**

sophistication *noun*

- ADJ. **considerable, great | growing, increased, increasing | cool | political, technical, technological**
- VERB + SOPHISTICATION **have** *The decor has a cool sophistication.* **| lack**
- PREP. **with ~** *He writes with increasing sophistication on the subject.*
- PHRASES **an air of sophistication** *Despite her scruffy clothes, there was an air of sophistication about her.* **a degree/level of sophistication** *Computers raised the level of sophistication of these maps.* **a lack of sophistication** *He*

felt people were contemptuous of his lack of sophistication.
a veneer of sophistication *She adopted an upper-class accent to give herself a veneer of sophistication.*

soprano *noun*

- ADJ. **first, principal, second | boy, female, male | coloratura, lyric, operatic | clear, pure**
- VERB + SOPRANO **sing** *She has sung soprano in many major operas.*
- SOPRANO + NOUN **voice** *She has a natural, clear soprano voice.* | **part** *The soprano part in this opera is very demanding*
- PREP. **in a~** *She sings in an exceptionally pure soprano.*

sore *noun*

- ADJ. **open, running** *(often figurative) The border dispute was a running sore in relations between the countries.*

sorrow *noun*

- ADJ. **deep, genuine, great, unbearable**
- VERB + SORROW **feel** *I felt no sorrow for her.* | **express** *He wrote to the dead man's mother expressing his deep sorrow.* | **share** *She wanted to share his sorrow.* | **hide** *I couldn't hide my sorrow and anger.* | **bring, cause** *The war brought sorrow to millions.*
- PREP. **to sb's~** *To his great sorrow he could not remember his mother.* **with~** *They accepted the decision with sorrow.* | **~at** *his sorrow at having to quit his job*
- PHRASES **a feeling/pang of sorrow** *Claudia felt a deep pang of sorrow for her sister.* **full of sorrow** *He looked at Katherine, his eyes full of sorrow.* **tears of sorrow** *Tears of relief were mixed with tears of sorrow.* **a time of sorrow** *This is a time of great sorrow for all the family.*

sorry *adj.*

- VERBS **be, feel, seem, sound | make sb** *I'll make you sorry you were ever born!*
- ADV. **awfully, deeply, desperately, dreadfully, extremely, frightfully, genuinely, really, terribly, truly, very** *I'm really sorry Jane can't come with us.* ◇ *I'm terribly sorry. I didn't catch your name.* | **almost** *She was almost sorry to stop work.* | **a bit, a little, quite, rather**
- PREP. **about** *I'm sorry about the noise.* ◇ *I'm sorry about your mother. I do hope she'll soon be feeling better.* **for** *She is obviously deeply sorry for what she has done.* ◇ *I feel really sorry for John.*
- PHRASES **better safe than sorry**

sort *noun*

- ADJ. **best, worst | right, wrong | funny, odd, strange** *He was friendly in a funny sort of way.*
- PREP. **~of** *The shop sells all sorts of books.*

sort *verb*

1 put things into different groups/places
- ADV. **busily | out** *I sorted the clothes out into two piles.*
- PREP. **according to** *Sort the books according to their subject matter.* **by** *The most common way of grouping was to sort the children by ability.* **into** *We sorted the washing into piles of different garments.* **through** *busily sorting through her clothes*

2 find an answer to a problem
- ADV. **out** *Someone will have to sort this problem out.*
- VERB + SORT **have to | try to | help (to), help sb (to) | leave sb to** *Leave them to sort it out among themselves.*
- PHRASES **get sth sorted (out)** *If he can't get his talk sorted, we'll have to ask someone else.*

soul *noun*

1 part of sb believed to exist after body is dead
- ADJ. **immortal | damned | human, individual**
- VERB + SOUL **save** *Missionaries saw it as their task to save souls.* | **sell** *to sell your soul to the Devil*
- PHRASES **the souls of the dead**

2 part of sb/sth that shows its true nature
- ADJ. **very** *The plea touched him to his very soul.* | **whole | inner**
- VERB + SOUL **lose** *In the process of being made into a film, the story seemed to have lost its soul.* | **bare** *He bared his soul to her.* | **search** *I searched my soul for any malice that could have provoked his words, but found none.*
- SOUL + NOUN **mate**
- PREP. **in your~** *Deep in her soul she knew she had to return to her country.*
- PHRASES **body and soul** *She gave herself to him body and soul.* **heart and soul** *He gave himself heart and soul to the cause.*

3 deep feeling and thought
- VERB + SOUL **have | lack**
- PREP. **with~** *She sang the song with passion and soul.*

4 person
- ADJ. **little** *poor little soul* | **old | good | bad | lost, poor, unfortunate | simple | dear, gentle, kind, kindly** *a kind old soul* | **sensitive | brave | romantic | tormented, tortured, troubled | living** *There was no other living soul to be seen.*
- PHRASES **a soul in torment** *The dog was howling like a soul in torment.* **not be a soul in sight** *By midnight, there wasn't a soul in sight.*

NOTE
Sounds

give a~
The dog gave a low growl.
let out a~
He let out a blood-curdling scream.
hear~
We heard the peal of church bells.
with a~
The vase fell to the ground with a great crash.
~of
a roar of laughter
a snort of derision
the whine of an engine

---

sound *noun*

1 sth you hear
- ADJ. **big, deafening, loud, powerful** *We need a big powerful sound from the trumpets in the final passage.* | **audible | faint, little, soft | high | deep, low | clean, clear, sharp** *He produces a good clean sound on his flute.* | **piercing | muffled | amazing, beautiful, good, lovely, pleasing | awful, horrible, sickening** *There was a sickening sound as his head made contact with the concrete.* | **familiar, strange | distinctive | haunting | booming, buzzing, clanking, etc. | metallic | hollow | distorted | distant** *the distant sound of church bells* | **guitar, piano, etc.** *She tried to describe what made a good guitar sound.* | **speech, vowel**
- VERB + SOUND **hear | emit, make, produce, pronounce, transmit, utter** *What's making that awful creaking sound?* ◇ *Three bones transmit sounds to the inner ear.* ◇ *He didn't utter a single sound throughout the meeting.*
- SOUND + VERB **carry, travel** *Sound carries well over calm water.* | **come** *A strange sound came from the box.* | **echo | die away**
- SOUND + NOUN **wave | effect | bite** *As a politician he is a master of the 30-second sound bite.*

- PREP. **at the~of** *He turned around at the sound of foot-steps behind him.* **without a~** *The door opened without a sound.* | **~of** *the sound of breaking glass* **~from** *There was a strange sound from downstairs.*
- PHRASES **the speed of sound**

2 the sound from television/radio, etc.
- ADJ. **recorded** | **mono, stereo**
- VERB + SOUND **turn down/up** *Can you turn the sound up?*
- SOUND + NOUN **level, quality** | **system** *a stereo sound system* | **recording** | **recorder** | **engineer**

sound *adj.*

1 in good condition
- VERBS **be, feel, look, seem**
- ADV. **extremely, very** | **fairly, pretty, quite, reasonably** | **structurally** *Is the building structurally sound?*
- PHRASES **safe and sound** (= not hurt) *We arrived home safe and sound.*

2 sensible
- VERBS **be, seem**
- ADV. **extremely, very** | **absolutely, perfectly** *She had a perfectly sound reason for acting as she did.* | **fairly, pretty, reasonably** *That seems like fairly sound advice.* | **basically, fundamentally** | **commercially, ecologically, environmentally, financially, ideologically, theoretically** *It was a financially sound investment.*

soundtrack *noun*

- ADJ. **film**
- VERB + SOUNDTRACK **compose** | **listen to**
- PREP. **~for/of/to** *She composed the soundtracks to several hit movies.*

soup *noun*

- ADJ. **chunky, creamy, hearty, thick** *hearty vegetable soup* | **clear, thin** | **hot** | **cold** | **home-made** | **condensed, dried, packet, tinned** | **chicken, tomato,** etc.
- QUANT. **bowl, cup, mug** | **packet, tin**
- VERB + SOUP **cook, make, prepare** | **bring to the boil, heat (up), simmer** | **have** *We had a cold cucumber soup as a starter.* | **drink, eat** (**Eat** is the normal verb when the soup is served in a bowl.) | **slurp** *Don't slurp your soup!* | **ladle (out), serve** *He ladled out three bowls of soup.*
- SOUP + NOUN **bowl, dish, plate, tureen** | **spoon** | **kitchen** (= a place where soup and other food is supplied free to people with no money)
- ⇨ Special page at FOOD

sour *adj.*

1 having a sharp taste
- VERBS **be, taste** *The sauce tasted very sour.*
- ADV. **extremely, very** | **a bit, quite, rather, slightly**

2 not fresh
- VERBS **be, smell, taste** *The milk smelled sour.* | **go, turn** *By the next day the wine had turned sour.*
- ADV. **very** | **a bit, rather, slightly**

3 bad-tempered
- VERBS **be** | **go, grow, turn** | **a bit, a little, rather, slightly, somewhat** *Their friendship has turned a little sour.*
- ADV. **extremely, really, very**

source *noun*

1 where you get sth from
- ADJ. **excellent, fertile, good, lucrative, reliable, rich, valuable** *a fertile source of ideas* ◇ *a lucrative source of income* ◇ *a rich source of vitamins* | **important, main, major, principal** | **cheap** *a cheap source of labour* | **ex-** **ternal, foreign** *Do you have any foreign sources of income?* | **independent** *an independent source of funding* | **additional** | **alternative** *We need to look for alternative sources of energy.* | **natural** | **renewable** *The village obtains all its energy from renewable sources.* | **energy, food, heat, light, power, water**
- VERB + SOURCE **be, constitute, prove, provide** *The census constitutes the principal source of official statistics.* ◇ *These crustaceans provide a valuable food source for some fish.* | **exploit, tap, use (as)** *The government hopes to tap new sources of employment in the area of health.* | **locate** *We tried to locate the source of the sound.*
- PREP. **at~** *Under the PAYE system, employees' income is taxed at source* (= by the employer). | **~of** *a reliable source of advice*
- PHRASES **a variety of sources** *The research was funded from a wide variety of sources.*

2 person, book, etc. that gives information
- ADJ. **invaluable, useful, valuable** | **authoritative, informed, reliable, reputable** | **unreliable** | **original** | **independent** | **anonymous** | **primary, secondary** | **published** | **biographical, documentary, historical, literary, written** | **diplomatic, government, intelligence, military, official, police** *Intelligence sources report a build-up of troops just inside the border.* | **data, information**
- VERB + SOURCE **use (as)** | **cite, quote** *Researchers try to quote primary sources wherever possible.* | **disclose, name, reveal** *The police refused to reveal the source of their information.*
- SOURCE + VERB **claim sth, describe sth, disclose sth, indicate sth, report sth, reveal sth, say sth, suggest sth** *Government sources indicated that a compromise might be reached.* ◇ *One source said: 'Our blood is up. We are angry at the way we have been treated.'* | **deny sth**
- SOURCE + NOUN **material**
- PREP. **according to~s** *According to informed sources, a takeover bid is planned for next month.* | **~of**
- PHRASES **sources close to sb** *Sources close to the player claim he won't be entering this year's championship.*

south *noun, adj.*

⇨ Note at DIRECTION

sovereignty *noun*

- ADJ. **absolute, full, unlimited** *Demonstrators demanded full sovereignty for the self-proclaimed republic.* | **limited** | **inalienable** | **joint, shared** | **national, popular** | **British, Japanese,** etc. | **consumer, economic, legal, parliamentary, political, territorial**
- VERB + SOVEREIGNTY **enjoy, exercise, have** *China exercises sovereignty over Hong Kong.* | **share** | **claim, declare, establish, proclaim** | **give sb/sth, grant sb/sth** | **give up, relinquish, renounce** | **violate** | **defend**
- SOVEREIGNTY + VERB **reside (in/with sb/sth)** *Sovereignty resides with the people.*
- PREP. **~ over** *The treaty gave Edward III sovereignty over Calais and the whole of Aquitaine.*
- PHRASES **a claim to sovereignty** *Two countries have a claim to sovereignty over the islands.* **a declaration of sovereignty** *Protesters called on the government to adopt a declaration of sovereignty.* **a loss of sovereignty** *the partial loss of sovereignty to supranational institutions* **the sovereignty of Parliament/the people** *This constitutes and attack on the sovereignty of Parliament.* **a transfer of sovereignty** *fears about the transfer of sovereignty to the European Union* **a violation of sovereignty**

sow *verb*

- ADV. **early** *Sow early for an early crop.* | **thickly, thinly** *Sow the seeds quite thinly.*
- PREP. **with** *We've sown that field with wheat.*

space noun

1 empty area

- ADJ. **large, vast, wide** *She left a large space empty at the bottom of the page.* ◇ *He liked the wide open spaces of the Australian countryside.* | **adequate, ample, enough, sufficient** *The new flat has ample living space.* | **limited, small, tiny** | **narrow** *the narrow space between the sofa and the wall* | **open** | **confined, enclosed** *Avoid using the cleaner in a confined space.* | **awkward** *This chisel is useful for getting into awkward spaces.* | **available, free, vacant** *The exhibition takes up most of the available space in the gallery.* ◇ *looking for a free parking space* | **blank, empty, white** *Fill in the blank spaces in the table.* ◇ *The page layout included plenty of white space.* | **living** | **storage** | **floor, roof, shelf, wall, etc.** | **office** | **parking** | **personal** *She moved out of the house because she wanted her own personal space.* | **private** | **public** | **green** *The inner residential areas don't have many green spaces.* | **air** *The plane strayed into French air space.* | **disk** | **advertising** *The magazine is struggling to fill all its advertising space.* | **exhibition, gallery**
- VERB + SPACE **make use of, take up, use** *The potted plants take up too much space.* | **create, make** *They moved the sofa to make space for the piano.* | **waste** | **save** | **clear** *We'd better clear a space for the new computer.* | **fill (in)** | **jostle for** *A motley collection of ornaments jostled for space on the crowded shelf.* | **stare into** *She sat there motionless, staring into space.*
- PREP. **~ between** *the space between the bookshelves*
- PHRASES **be/run short of space** *I'm running short of disk space.* **time and space** *The writer lacked the time and space to develop his idea fully.*

2 vast area containing planets, stars, etc.

- ADJ. **deep** | **outer**
- VERB + SPACE **go into**
- SPACE + NOUN **exploration, programme, research, science** | **flight, travel** | **capsule, probe, rocket, ship** (also **spaceship**), **shuttle, station**
- PREP. **in ~** *the first man in space*

3 period of time

- ADJ. **long** | **brief, short** | **2-second, 10-minute, etc.** *The recording includes a five-second space between tracks.* | **breathing** *The extension of the deadline gives us a breathing space.*
- PREP. **for the ~ of** *The job holder will be on probation for the space of six months.* **in/within the ~ of** *He fell asleep in the space of a few minutes.* | **~ of** *She returned to top-class tennis after a space of two years.*
- PHRASES **a space of time** *They have achieved a great deal in a short space of time.*

space verb

- ADV. **at intervals, equally, evenly, regularly** *Telephone boxes are spaced at regular intervals along the motorway.* ◇ *Make sure the posts are spaced evenly apart.* | **irregularly** | **closely** | **generously, well, widely** | **apart, out** *The fruits should be well spaced out so that they are not touching each other.*
- PREP. **along**

spacecraft noun

- VERB + SPACECRAFT **launch**
- SPACECRAFT + VERB **orbit sth** *a spacecraft orbiting the earth*
- PREP. **in/on a/the ~**

spacious adj.

- VERBS **be, feel, look, seem**
- ADV. **extremely, very** | **fairly, quite, reasonably** | **deceptively, surprisingly** *The house benefits from a deceptively spacious kitchen* (= that is larger than it seems).

spade noun

1 tool for digging

- ADJ. **garden** *There was a garden spade in the shed.*
- VERB + SPADE **dig sth with, use** *He dug a deep hole in the lawn with his spade.*
- PHRASES **bucket and spade** *children playing in the sand with their buckets and spades*

2 playing card

⇨ Note at CARD

spaghetti noun

- ADJ. **wholemeal**
- QUANT. **strand**
- VERB + SPAGHETTI **eat, have** | **cook** | **drain, strain** *Drain the spaghetti well.*
- SPAGHETTI + NOUN **sauce**

⇨ Special page at FOOD

span noun

1 length

- ADJ. **full** | **broad, wide** *a broad span of interests* | **clear** *The bridge has a clear span of 36 metres.* | **12-foot, 500-metre, etc.** | **wing** (also **wingspan**) *The bird has a 1-metre wingspan.*

2 length of time

- ADJ. **long** | **short** | **10-day, 2-week, etc.** | **entire** | **allotted** *The speech continued well beyond its allotted span.* | **time** | **life** (also **lifespan**) | **attention, concentration, memory** *He has a short attention span.*
- VERB + SPAN **cover** *The book covers the entire span of Arab history.*
- PREP. **over a/the ~** *Developments were monitored over a span of two years.*
- PHRASES **a span of time/years**

Spanish noun

⇨ Note at LANGUAGE

spare verb

- ADV. **barely, hardly, scarcely** *She hardly spared him a second glance.*
- VERB + SPARE **can/could**
- PREP. **for** *Can you spare some money for the homeless?*
- PHRASES **to spare** *Have you any money to spare?* ◇ *We should get there with half an hour to spare.*

spark noun

1 small bright piece of burning material/electric flash

- ADJ. **tiny** | **flying** | **electric**
- VERB + SPARK **emit, produce, send (out), shower, strike** *The firework showered sparks all over the lawn.* ◇ *His iron-tipped stick struck sparks from the pavement.*
- SPARK + VERB **fly** | **ignite sth, set fire to sth** *Flying sparks set fire to the long grass.* | **die (out)**
- PHRASES **a shower of sparks** *The grinding wheel sent a shower of sparks across the workbench.* **a spark of light**

2 small amount of a quality/feeling

- ADJ. **little, tiny** *A tiny spark of rebellion flared within her.* | **creative, divine, vital**
- VERB + SPARK **have** | **lack** *His performances lack creative spark.* | **feel** *She felt a little spark of anger.* | **kindle**
- SPARK + VERB **flare, kindle**
- PREP. **~ of** *He had kindled a spark of interest within her.*
- PHRASES **a spark of hope/life, a spark of originality**

3 (usually **sparks**) feelings of anger/excitement

- VERB + SPARK **shoot** *Her eyes shot sparks of contempt.* | **draw** *His remarks drew sparks from her.*
- SPARK + VERB **fly** *Sparks flew at the meeting.*

sparkle *noun*

- ADJ. **extra** | **old** *She has lost none of her old sparkle as a jazz singer.*
- VERB + SPARKLE **have** | **lack** | **lose** | **add, put (back)** *A live band added extra sparkle to the occasion.*
- PHRASES **a sparkle in your eyes**

spasm *noun*

- ADJ. **sudden** | **muscle, muscular**
- VERB + SPASM **feel** *He felt a spasm of panic sweeping over him.* | **go into** *The muscle goes into spasm, producing the symptom of cramp.*
- SPASM + VERB **pass, subside**
- PREP. **in~** *She could not speak; her throat was in spasm.* | **~ of** *He kicked the chair in a spasm of impatience.*
- PHRASES **a spasm of coughing/pain**

spatter *verb*

- ADV. **liberally**
- PREP. **against** *Rain spattered against the window.* **on** *Blood was spattered on the walls and doors.* **over** *The water had spattered all over her face.* **with** *His clothes were liberally spattered with mud.*

speak *verb*

1 have a conversation
- ADV. **briefly** *We spoke briefly on the phone.* | **at length** | **hardly** *Ben hardly spoke to me all evening.*
- VERB + SPEAK **want to** | **refuse to** *The president refused to speak to the waiting journalists.* | **dare (to)** *No one had ever dared speak to him like that before.*
- PREP. **about, to** *I need to speak to Joseph about this matter.* **with** *Can I speak with you for a minute?*
- PHRASES **be on speaking terms (with sb)** *We are still on speaking terms after the argument.* **not be speaking (to sb)** *Ed and Dave aren't speaking at the moment.*

2 use your voice to say sth
- ADV. **loudly** | **quietly, softly** | **clearly** *You must speak loudly and clearly on the stage.* | **slowly** | **calmly** | **brusquely, sharply** | **briefly** | **at length** | **suddenly** | **hardly** | **eloquently, movingly** *She spoke eloquently about the need for action.* | **lovingly, warmly** | **disparagingly, harshly** | **encouragingly, soothingly** | **authoritatively, forcefully** | **earnestly** | **coherently, intelligibly, meaningfully** | **absently** | **freely,** **openly** | **boldly** | **hesitantly** | **out**
- VERB + SPEAK **be able/unable to, can/could (hardly)** *She was so moved she could hardly speak.* | **begin to, open your mouth to** *She opened her mouth to speak and found she couldn't.* | **try to** | **dare not, not trust yourself to** *He nodded, not trusting himself to speak.* | **hear sb** *I heard him speak at the debating society.*
- PREP. **about, against** *He spoke out against mismanagement.* **for** *I speak for all my colleagues.* **in favour of** *She spoke in favour of the new tax.* **on** *She speaks on women's issues.* **on behalf of** *I speak on behalf of many thousands of women.* **of** *He speaks very warmly of you.* **to** *He will be speaking to history students about the causes of war.*

3 know a language
- ADV. **fluently, well** *He speaks German fluently.*
- VERB + SPEAK **be able/unable to, can/could** | **learn to** *learning to speak a foreign language* | **teach sb to**
- PREP. **in** *Would you prefer it if we spoke in French?*

speaker *noun*

1 person who makes a speech
- ADJ. **brilliant,** **good** | **keynote,** **main,** **principal** | **guest, invited, visiting** | **public** *She's a good public speaker.* | **after-dinner**

2 person who speaks a particular language

- ADJ. **fluent** *He's a fluent Arabic speaker.* | **mother-tongue, native** *a native speaker of English* | **non-native** | **Japanese, Russian, etc.**

spear *noun*

- ADJ. **hunting**
- VERB + SPEAR **be armed with, carry** *The tribesmen were armed with spears and shields.* | **lift, raise** | **brandish** | **hurl, throw** | **thrust**
- PHRASES **the point of a spear** *She had a fish impaled on the point of her spear.*

special *noun*

- ADJ. **daily** *The restaurant has an extensive menu and daily specials.* | **television, TV** *There are lots of TV Christmas specials for children this year.* | **Christmas, election** | **football**

specialist *noun*

- ADJ. **leading, top** *a leading cancer specialist* | **qualified, trained** | **experienced** | **independent** | **academic** | **professional** | **technical** | **clinical,** **medical** | **industry, subject** | **hospital** | **cancer, ear, eye, heart, skin** | **finance/financial, marketing, property** | **tax** | **recruitment** | **communications, computer, software, systems** | **education**
- VERB + SPECIALIST **bring in** *They brought in an outside specialist to install the computer system.*
- PREP. **~ in** *She is a specialist in eighteenth-century English painting.* **~ on** *a specialist on the history of this city*
- PHRASES **a group/team of specialists, a specialist in the field** *The book is written by P.H. Reaney, a noted specialist in the field.*
- ⇨ Note at DOCTOR
- ⇨ Note at JOB

speciality *noun*

- ADJ. **local, regional**
- PHRASES **a speciality of the house** *I ordered the speciality of the house—frogs' legs.*

specialization *noun*

- ADJ. **increased, increasing** | **narrow** *His specialization is too narrow to be of interest to more than a handful of students.* | **professional** | **academic** | **economic** *There has been increased economic specialization throughout the country.* | **regional**
- QUANT. **degree** *The production line involves a high degree of specialization of labour.*
- PREP. **~ in** *Her degree is in French, with specialization in seventeenth-century literature.*
- PHRASES **an area of specialization** *The company has gradually focused on its current areas of specialization.*

specialized *adj.*

- VERBS **be** *These tools are very specialized.* | **become**
- ADV. **highly, very** *a job calling for highly specialized skills* | **increasingly** | **narrowly** *narrowly specialized subjects* | **fairly, quite, rather, relatively**

species *noun*

- ADJ. **living** | **extinct** | **common** | **rare** | **different, distinct** | **related** *closely related species of beetle* | **native** | **alien** | **wild** | **dominant** | **endangered, threatened** | **protected** | **animal, bird, fish, insect, mammal, mammalian, plant, tree, etc.** *The area is rich in different plant species.* | **human** *the development of the human species*
- SPECIES + VERB **be found, grow, live, occur** *Similar species of fish occur in Mongolia.* | **be threatened with extinction, become extinct, die out** | **survive**

- PREP. **~of** *a native species of fish*
- PHRASES **a member of a species**

specific *adj.*

- VERBS **be** *Can you be a little more specific in your instructions?*
- ADV. **highly, very** *issuing a highly specific set of instructions* | **quite** | **fairly, rather**
- PREP. **about** *She was quite specific about the type she wanted.*

specification *noun*

- ADJ. **complete, detailed, full** | **clear, exact** | **standard** | **high** *The yachts are built to the highest specifications.* | **strict** | **original** | **design, technical** | **customer** | **contract, job, product, service** *The manager has drafted job specifications for each of the positions.*
- VERB + SPECIFICATION **draft, draw up, lay down, write** | **meet** *The aircraft have to meet the strict specifications laid down by the FAA.*
- PREP. **(according) to the/your ~s** *Each vehicle can be equipped according to your specifications.*

specify *verb*

- ADV. **clearly** | **fully** | **carefully** | **exactly, precisely** *She did not specify precisely how many people were involved in the incident.* | **explicitly** | **correctly** *Are all the details correctly specified?* | **uniquely** *Each computer is uniquely specified by its serial number.* | **otherwise** *Unless otherwise specified, all fields have a maximum length of 20 characters.*
- VERB + SPECIFY **allow sb to** | **require sb to** | **be used to** | **be possible to** *It should be possible to specify the range of values of χ which would satisfy this equation.* | **be difficult to**

specimen *noun*

1 example
- ADJ. **large, small** | **beautiful, fine, good, healthy, magnificent, perfect, prize** *This is a fine specimen of a walnut tree.* | **poor** | **living, preserved** | **rare** | **physical**
- SPECIMEN + NOUN **plant, tree** | **letter, paper** *specimen exam papers*

2 small amount of sth used for testing
- ADJ. **blood, urine, etc.** | **geological**
- VERB + SPECIMEN **collect, take** | **give** *The motorist may be required to give a urine specimen.* | **obtain**
- PREP. **~of** *a specimen of blood*

spectacle *noun*

- ADJ. **dramatic, great, magnificent** | **sad, unedifying** *the sad spectacle of him struggling to keep up with the younger players* | **public** *Hangings took place outside the prison as a public spectacle.* | **sporting**
- VERB + SPECTACLE **witness**
- PHRASES **make a spectacle of yourself** (= make yourself look ridiculous in public)

spectacles *noun*

- ADJ. **heavy** | **gold-rimmed, horn-rimmed, metal-framed, rimless, steel-rimmed, wide-framed** | **pebble, thick, thick-lensed** | **bifocal, half-moon, tinted** | **dark** | **safety**
- QUANT. **pair**
- VERB + SPECTACLES **have on, wear** | **put on** | **take off** | **push up** *She pushed her spectacles up her nose and sighed.* | **adjust** | **polish** | **look through/over, peer through/over** *He peered at the waiter over his spectacles.*
- SPECTACLES + VERB **be perched on sth, perch on sth** *Her wire-framed spectacles were perched on the end of*

her nose. | **glint** *Her spectacles glinted in the moonlight.* | **steam up** *His spectacles steamed up in the hot room.*
- PREP. **behind your~, through your~**

spectacular *adj.*

- VERBS **be, look**
- ADV. **really, very** | **absolutely, quite, truly** *The waterfall is quite spectacular.* | **pretty, rather**

spectator *noun*

- ADJ. **mere, passive** | **interested** | **paying** | **cricket, football, sports, etc.**
- QUANT. **crowd**
- SPECTATOR + VERB **gather, turn up** | **line sth** *Spectators lined the route of the president's walkabout.* | **applaud sb/sth, boo sb/sth, cheer sb/sth**
- SPECTATOR + NOUN **event, sport**

spectre *noun*

- ADJ. **terrible** | **old** | **constant**
- VERB + SPECTRE **evoke, raise** *Wall Street's collapse raised spectres of the 1987 stock market crash.* | **banish**
- SPECTRE + VERB **hang over sb/sth, haunt sb/sth, hover over sb/sth, loom (over sb/sth)**
- PREP. **~of** *The terrible spectre of civil war hung over the country once again.*

spectrum *noun*

1 of colours
- ADJ. **visible** *Beyond the red end of the visible light spectrum is infrared.* | **continuous** *a continuous spectrum of light waves* | **colour, electromagnetic**
- SPECTRUM + NOUN **analysis**
- PHRASES **the colours of the spectrum** *Other species can perceive colours of the spectrum that are invisible to us.* **the ... band/end/part of the spectrum** *the ultraviolet part of the spectrum*

2 full or wide range
- ADJ. **complete, full** *The courses cover the full spectrum of levels.* | **broad, wide** | **narrow** | **entire, whole** | **political, social**
- VERB + SPECTRUM **cover**
- PREP. **across the ~** *There was consensus across the political spectrum.* | **~of** *a wide spectrum of interests*
- PHRASES **at one/the other end of the spectrum, both/opposite ends of the spectrum** *The two speakers were chosen to represent opposite ends of the spectrum.* **a spectrum of opinion** *The newspaper covers a broad spectrum of opinion.*

speculate *verb*

- VERB + SPECULATE **can/could only** | **decline to, refuse to** | **be fascinating to, be interesting to, be tempting to** | **be idle to** *It is idle to speculate what the consequences would have been.* | **be difficult to**
- PREP. **about** *There was no point speculating about the possibility of them getting back together.* **as to** *We can only speculate as to this man's identity.* **on/upon** *He refused to speculate on her reasons for leaving.*

speculation *noun*

1 making guesses about sth
- ADJ. **considerable, intense, much, widespread** | **further, increasing, renewed** | **continuing, endless** | **pure** | **mere** *Whether or not he will get the job is mere speculation.* | **wild** | **idle, fruitless** | **rife** *Speculation was rife as to whom the prince might marry.* | **media, press** | **metaphysical, philosophical**
- VERB + SPECULATION **cause, encourage, fuel, give rise to, increase, intensify, invite, lead to, prompt, raise**

| dampen, discourage, end, put an end to | dismiss | indulge in

● PREP. **amid ~** *He was dropped from the team amid speculation that he was seriously ill.* | **~among** *There was wild speculation among the students as to the reason for cancelling the lecture.* **~ about/as to/on/over** *There has been increasing speculation over the future of the monarchy.*

● PHRASES **a matter for speculation, a subject of speculation**

2 buying and selling for profit

● ADJ. **financial | market | currency, land, property, etc.**

● PREP. **~against** *speculation against the euro* **~ in** *speculation in oil* **~ on** *speculation on the stock market*

speech noun

1 speaking

● ADJ. **careful, clear, clipped | casual | impaired | slurred** *She could tell by his slurred speech that he had been drinking.* | **connected, continuous, fluent | natural, normal, ordinary | spontaneous | direct | indirect, reported | free** *The demonstrators were demanding rights of assembly and free speech.* | **conversational, everyday | children's, female, human, etc. | middle-class, working-class, etc.**

● VERB + SPEECH **have** *Most people have speech, but significantly fewer have writing.*

● SPEECH + NOUN **act | style | defect, impairment, impediment | therapist, therapy | community** *phonological variation in a speech community*

● PREP. **in ~** *Certain grammatical rules must be followed when describing a conversation in reported speech.*

● PHRASES **a figure of speech** *When we talk about 'selfish' genes it is just a figure of speech.* **freedom of speech** *the right of/to freedom of speech* **the power of speech** *He temporarily lost the power of speech after the accident.*

2 formal talk

● ADJ. **brief, little, short | interminable, long, long-winded, rambling | keynote, major | eloquent, excellent, good | emotional, impassioned, rousing, stirring | boring | impromptu | public | televised | political | opening | closing | acceptance, after-dinner, Budget, campaign, conference, farewell, inaugural** *The prize-winner gave an emotional acceptance speech.* ◊ *the Chancellor's Budget speech* | **maiden** *her maiden speech in the House of Commons*

● VERB + SPEECH **deliver, give, make | broadcast** *His speech was broadcast on national radio.* | **write**

● PREP. **in a/the ~ |** **~about/on** *She made a stirring campaign speech on improving the lot of the unemployed.* **~ to** *In her speech to the House of Commons, she outlined her vision of Britain in the 21st century.*

speechless adj.

● VERBS **be, remain, sit, stand** *Rachel stood speechless.* | **leave sb, render sb** *The news left us all speechless.*

● ADV. **completely, totally | almost, practically | for a moment, momentarily, temporarily**

● PREP. **with** *He was almost speechless with anger.*

speed noun

● ADJ. **amazing, astonishing, breakneck, fast, great, high, incredible, lightning, phenomenal, remarkable, startling, surprising, terrific** *The new houses have been built with astonishing speed.* ◊ *He drove us to the hospital at breakneck speed.* | **low, slow | full, maximum, top | excess** *90% of car accidents involve excess speed.* | **constant, steady | average | cruising, flying, operating, reading, running** *The machinery is regulated to a safe running speed.* | **engine, traffic, etc. | air, wind**

● QUANT. **burst** *The Greek runner produced an electrifying burst of speed over the last 50 metres.*

● VERB + SPEED **attain, reach** *The car reaches a speed of 60 miles per hour within five seconds.* | **build up, gain, gather, increase, pick up** *The train pulled out of the station, slowly gathering speed.* | **lose | curb, kill, reduce** *measures to curb the speed of cars travelling through the village* | **maintain** *The boat maintained a steady speed while the sea was calm.* | **measure**

● SPEED + VERB **increase | decrease**

● SPEED + NOUN **control, reduction, restriction | record** *'Mallard' holds the speed record for a steam locomotive.* | **hump | camera, trap**

● PREP. **at ~** (= fast) *The train was travelling at speed when the accident happened.* ◊ *at lightning speed* **with ~** *Hedgehogs, though small, can move with surprising speed.*

● PHRASES **(at) full speed** *He was running at full speed when a tendon snapped in his leg.* **full speed ahead** *The boat can be brought to a stop from full speed ahead within her own length.* **the speed of light/sound** *Concorde crosses the Atlantic at twice the speed of sound.* **a turn of speed** *For a small car it has a good turn of speed.*

speeding noun

● VERB + SPEEDING **fine sb for, stop sb for** *The driver had been stopped twice for speeding on the same day.*

● SPEEDING + NOUN **conviction, offence | fine** *He was obliged to pay a £40 speeding fine.*

speed limit noun

● ADJ. **high, low | legal**

● VERB + SPEED LIMIT **keep to/within | break, exceed** *Motorists can be fined on the spot for exceeding speed limits.* | **set | raise | reduce**

● PREP. **over the ~** *He was driving over the 60 mph speed limit.* **below/under the ~, within the ~** *You have to come down that hill in a low gear to keep within the speed limit.*

spell noun

1 period of time

● ADJ. **lengthy, long, prolonged | brief, short | 5-minute, 10-day, etc. | good | bad** *He's going through a bit of a bad spell at the moment.* | **quiet | barren, lean** *Viera ended his barren spell with a goal against Parma.* | **cold, dry, hot, mild, sunny, warm, wet**

● VERB + SPELL **go through, have**

● PREP. **during a ... ~** *She managed to write a letter during a quiet spell at work.* | **~ as** *He had a brief spell as ambassador to Turkey.*

● PHRASES **a spell of ... weather** *a spell of sunny weather* **a spell of unemployment**

2 magical effect

● ADJ. **magic, magical | powerful | hypnotic** *the hypnotic spell of the crickets singing in the garden*

● VERB + SPELL **be/come/fall under | cast, put, weave** *The witch cast a spell on/over them.* | **break, remove** *She uttered the magic word, and the spell was broken.*

● PREP. **under a/the ~** *Sleeping Beauty was under a spell when the prince found her.* **under sb's ~** *The audience was completely under his spell.*

spell verb

● ADV. **correctly, wrongly**

● PREP. **as** *The article spelled 'survey' as 'servay'.* **with** *Is 'necessary' spelt with one 's', or two?*

PHRASAL VERB

spell sth out

● ADV. **clearly | fully, in detail | exactly, precisely** *She spelled out precisely what she wanted.*

• VERB + SPELL STH OUT **have to, need to**
• PREP. **for** *Do I really have to spell it out for you?* **to** *His speech spelled out a clear message to the car industry.*

spelling *noun*

• ADJ. **correct, incorrect | conventional, usual | alternative, different, variant | American, English, etc. | phonetic**
• VERB + SPELLING **use | check | correct | improve**
• SPELLING + NOUN **error, mistake | test | checker | dictionary, rule | variant | reform**
• PREP. **in … ~** *In American spelling 'travelled' only has one 'l'.* **| ~ for/of** *The document uses the British spelling for caesium.*
• PHRASES **be good/poor, etc. at spelling**

spend *verb*

• ADV. **wisely** *Try to be objective if you want to spend your money wisely.* **| lavishly**
• PREP. **on** *The company spent a lot on advertising.*

spending *noun*

• ADJ. **total** *There has been an increase in total government spending.* **| high, low | annual, monthly, etc. | defence, education, military, R & D, welfare, etc. | capital | government, local (authority), public, state | private | consumer**
• VERB + SPENDING **boost, increase | cut, cut back (on), reduce**
• SPENDING + VERB **rise | fall**
• SPENDING + NOUN **level | programme, target | cut, limit | money** *How much spending money are you taking on holiday?* **| power | spree** *The boys went on a two-day spending spree with the stolen credit cards.*
• PREP. **~ on** *More spending on the National Health Service was promised.*
• PHRASES **a cut/reduction in spending, an increase/a rise in spending**
⇨ Special page at BUSINESS

sperm *noun*

• VERB + SPERM **produce**
• SPERM + VERB **fertilize sth** *The sperm fertilizes the egg.*
• SPERM + NOUN **cell | count** *a high/low/normal sperm count* **| duct | bank, donor**

sphere *noun*

• ADJ. **wider** *He wanted to spread his ideas to a wider sphere than the school.* **| academic, cultural, domestic, economic, military, political, social** *His work is little known outside the academic sphere.* **| private, public**
• PREP. **in/within sb's/the~** *The region is within the Russian sphere of influence.* **outside sb's/the~** *The matter is outside my sphere of responsibility.* **| ~ of**
• PHRASES **a sphere of activity/influence/life**

spice *noun*

1 flavour for food
• ADJ. **ground | mixed | exotic**
• SPICE + NOUN **mix/mixture | cupboard, jar, rack**
• PHRASES **herbs and spices**
2 excitement and interest
• VERB + SPICE **add, give** *The romance added spice to the holiday.*

spice *verb*

• PREP. **with** *Their bread is spiced with cinnamon.*
• PHRASES **heavily/highly spiced** *I don't really like highly spiced food.* **lightly spiced** *a dish of lightly spiced rice*

spicy *adj.*

• VERBS **be, smell, taste** *The soup tasted mildly spicy.*
• ADV. **really, very | lightly, mildly, quite, slightly | deliciously** *a deliciously spicy flavour*

spider *noun*

• ADJ. **hairy | poisonous**
• SPIDER + VERB **make/spin/weave a web | crawl, run, scuttle | hunt sth | catch sth | bite sth | lurk**
• SPIDER + NOUN **silk | web**
• PHRASES **a spider's web**

spill *verb*

• ADV. **almost | accidentally | out, over** *He nodded, his tears spilling over.*
• VERB + SPILL **try not to | let sth** *He opened the curtains, letting the morning light spill into the room.*
• PREP. **down, from, into, onto, out of, over** *I accidentally spilled my drink all over him.*

spin *noun*

1 fast turning movement
• ADJ. **quick, rapid | slow | back** (also **backspin**), **top** (also **topspin**) *She puts heavy topspin on her serve.*
• VERB + SPIN **go into** *He had to stop the helicopter from going into a spin.* **| come out of | put sb/sth in(to), send sb/sth into** (figurative) *The president's death sent the stock market into a spin.* **| give sth** *Give the washing another spin.* **| impart, put on** *How do you put more spin on the ball?*
• SPIN + NOUN **bowler | bowling**
2 on information
• ADJ. **positive**
• VERB + SPIN **put on** *The chairman tried to put a positive spin on the closure of the factory.*
• SPIN + NOUN **doctor** *government spin doctors*
• PREP. **with a~** *The film retells the famous legend with a Marxist spin.*

spin *verb*

• ADV. **fast, quickly, rapidly** *The blade spins very fast.* **| freely** *The wheel can now spin freely.* **| around/round, away, back** *He spun round to face her.*
• VERB + SPIN **begin to, start to | make sth** (figurative) *The wine made my head spin.*
• PHRASES **spin like a top** *The engine stopped. The dinghy spun like a top and a huge wave came at me.* **spin on your heel** *She spun on her heel and walked out of the room.* **spin out of control** *The car spun out of control.*

spine *noun*

1 backbone
• ADJ. **fractured | cervical, lumbar**
• VERB + SPINE **bend, curve | straighten | stiffen | slide along/down/up** (figurative) *An icy chill slid up my spine.*
• PREP. **in the/your~** *the nerves in the spine*
• PHRASES **the base of the spine, curvature of the spine, send shivers along/down your spine**
2 sharp point on some plants/animals
• ADJ. **pointed, sharp | fine | poisonous, venomous | savage** *Once embedded in the skin, these savage spines are difficult to dislodge.*
• VERB + SPINE **bear, carry, have**

spin-off *noun*

- ADJ. **positive, valuable** | **unexpected** | **commercial**
- PREP. **~from**

spiral *noun*

- ADJ. **destructive, vicious** | **downward, upward** | **inflationary, wage-price**
- VERB + SPIRAL **halt, stop**
- PREP. **~of** *to halt the vicious downward spiral of drug abuse*

spirit *noun*

1 mind or feelings
- ADJ. **human**
- PREP. **in~** *I will be with you in spirit.*

2 spirits morale
- ADJ. **flagging**
- VERB + SPIRITS **keep up, lift, raise** *We sang songs to keep our spirits up.* | **revive** | **break, dampen** *A string of defeats has failed to dampen the team's spirits.*
- SPIRITS + VERB **lift, rise**
- PHRASES **in good/high/low/poor, etc. spirits** *She isn't in the best of spirits today.*

3 person
- ADJ. **guiding, leading, moving** *She was a guiding spirit in primary education.* | **generous** | **grudging, mean** | **brave, proud** | **free, independent** | **kindred** *He found kindred spirits in the peace movement.*

4 courage/liveliness
- ADJ. **great, tremendous** | **adventurous, competitive, fighting, indomitable, pioneer/pioneering**
- VERB + SPIRIT **be full of, have** *She has plenty of fighting spirit.* | **display, show** | **break**
- PREP. **with~** *He sang with great spirit.*
- PHRASES **broken in spirit** *They tortured him until he was broken in spirit.*

5 feelings of loyalty
- ADJ. **community, party, public, team**
- VERB + SPIRIT **have** | **develop, foster, promote**

6 attitude/mood
- ADJ. **right** *He's got the right spirit!* | **essential, genuine, true** | **carefree** | **democratic, revolutionary** | **entrepreneurial** | **festive, Christmas**
- VERB + SPIRIT **have** | **enter into**
- PREP. **in a~of** *Both sides have come together in a spirit of goodwill.* | **~of** *a spirit of adventure*
- PHRASES **in the right/wrong spirit, the spirit of the age/times**

7 real/intended meaning of a rule, an agreement, etc.
- VERB + SPIRIT **obey** | **be/go against, be contrary to**
- PHRASES **the spirit of the law** *The referee should try to obey the spirit as well as the letter of the law.*

8 soul/ghost
- ADJ. **ancestral** | **evil, malevolent** | **restless** *Owls were believed to be restless spirits who had returned to earth.*
- VERB + SPIRIT **conjure up, contact, invoke, summon (up)** | **exorcise, ward off** *She slept with a cross under the pillow to ward off evil spirits.* | **be possessed by**
- SPIRIT + VERB **live on** *Many people believe the spirit lives on after death.*
- PHRASES **the spirits of the dead**

9 (usually **spirits**) strong alcoholic drink
- QUANT. **measure** *a single measure of spirits*
- VERB + SPIRITS **drink**
- PHRASES **a bottle of spirits**

spiritual *adj.*

- VERBS **be**
- ADV. **deeply, truly, very** *This is an deeply spiritual*

piece of music. ◇ *a truly spiritual experience* | **purely** | **almost** *The colours had an almost spiritual quality.*

spite *noun*

- ADJ. **pure** | **personal**
- VERB + SPITE **be full of, feel** *She was angry and full of spite.* | **vent** *He vented his spite on his grandfather.*
- PREP. **out of~** *She killed her neighbour's cow out of pure spite.* **with~** *'Your cooking is hard to forget,' he said with spite.* | **~towards** *I felt no spite towards her.*

splash *noun*

1 sound; amount of liquid
- ADJ. **big, huge** | **small** | **loud** | **soft**
- VERB + SPLASH **make** *(often figurative) She intended to make a big splash with her wedding.* | **hear**
- PREP. **with a~** *She jumped into the pool with a splash.*

2 area of colour/light
- ADJ. **bold, bright** *a bold splash of red*
- VERB + SPLASH **add, lend** *Window boxes of tulips added a splash of colour to the street.*
- PHRASES **a splash of colour/light**

splash *verb*

1 in/with water
- ADV. **happily** *The baby was splashing happily in the bath.* | **about, around** *splashing around in the sea*
- PREP. **against** *Rain splashed against the window.* **on/onto** *She splashed some petrol onto the wood and set fire to it.* **over** *She splashed some water over her boots to clean them.* **through** *They splashed through the puddles.* **with** *Her clean washing was all splashed with mud.*

2 be splashed with sth with a colour
- ADV. **generously, liberally** *He was in his mid-forties, his hair liberally splashed with grey.*

splendid *adj.*

- VERBS **be**
- ADV. **really** *a really splendid evening* | **absolutely, perfectly, quite, simply, truly** *The meal was quite splendid!* | **pretty, rather**

splendour *noun*

- ADJ. **full** *A butterfly emerged in its full splendour a week later.* | **glorious, great, regal** | **former, original** | **faded, fading** | **scenic**
- VERB + SPLENDOUR **have** *The hotel has the splendour of a nineteenth-century mansion.* | **lose** | **recapture, regain** *It will take a lot of repair work before the theatre regains its former splendour.* | **restore sth to** *The house has been restored to its original splendour.*
- PREP. **in~** *They dined in a special suite in glorious splendour.* **in sb's/sth's~** *There below lay Paris in all its splendour.* **of~** *a castle of great splendour* | **~s of** *I've only just discovered the splendours of the English countryside.*
- PHRASES **in solitary splendour** *The castle rises in solitary splendour on the fringe of the desert.*

splinter *noun*

- ADJ. **tiny** | **glass, metal, wooden**
- VERB + SPLINTER **get, have** | **pull out, remove**
- SPLINTER + VERB **lodge**
- PREP. **~of** *A small splinter of metal had lodged in his thumb.*

split *noun*

- ADJ. **clear, deep, major, serious** *A serious split in the ruling coalition appeared soon after the election.* | **growing** | **damaging**

● VERB + SPLIT **cause, lead to**
● SPLIT + VERB **appear, occur, open up**
● PREP. **~between** *a split between the right and left wings of the party* **~ in/within, ~ over** *a growing split in the Church over the ordination of women* **~with** *Mike's split with his wife*

split *verb*

1 break into two or more parts
● ADV. **easily** *Plastic splits quite easily.* | **apart**
● PREP. **into** *He split the log into several pieces.*
● PHRASES **split (sth) across/down the middle** *The lid had split down the middle.* **split (sth) open** *The ripe seed pod splits open and scatters the seeds.* **split (sth) in half/two** *Split the coconut in half.*

2 separate into different groups
● ADV. **formally** | **eventually, finally** | **apart, away, off, up** *The rock group split up last year.*
● PREP. **from** *Several factions split from the party.* **into** *On January 1 1993 Czechoslovakia formally split into two independent states.* **on/over** *The party finally split over the issue of gun control.*
● PHRASES **be deeply/irrevocably split** *The party is deeply split on this issue.*

3 divide/share sth
● ADV. **equally, evenly**
● PREP. **among, between** *The cost has been split equally between three countries.*
● PHRASES **split sth two/three/four ways** *The profit will be split three ways.*

spoil *verb*

1 make sth useless/unsuccessful/not very good
● ADV. **completely, quite** *Her selfish behaviour completely spoiled the evening.* | **rather, slightly, somewhat**
● VERB + SPOIL **mustn't, not be going to, not want to** *I don't want to spoil things for everyone else.* | **be a pity to** *It would be a pity to spoil the surprise.* | **try to** | **not let sth** *Don't let the bad weather spoil your holiday.*

2 a child
● PREP. **with** *spoiling the children with expensive toys*
● PHRASES **be completely/thoroughly/utterly spoilt** *Those children are thoroughly spoilt!* **spoil sb rotten** *My grandparents used to spoil me rotten.* **a spoilt brat/child**

spoils *noun*

● VERB + SPOILS **divide, share** *The soldiers began to divide the spoils.* | **take**
● PHRASES **a division/share of the spoils**

sponge *noun*

● ADJ. **damp/dampened, wet** | **bath**
● VERB + SPONGE **squeeze (out)**
● SPONGE + VERB **fill with sth, soak sth up** *This sponge doesn't soak up water very well.*
● PREP. **with a/the~** *Wipe the surface with a damp sponge.*

sponsor *noun*

● ADJ. **big, major** | **main** | **potential** | **private** | **official** | **commercial, corporate, industrial**
● VERB + SPONSOR **look for, seek** | **attract, find, get** | **act as**
● SPONSOR + VERB **back sb/sth, support sb/sth**
● SPONSOR + NOUN **money**
● PREP. **~for/of** *I need to find some more sponsors for my bike ride to Brighton.*

sponsorship *noun*

● ADJ. **generous, major** | **direct** | **arts, sports** | **busi-**

ness, commercial, corporate, government, industrial, private | tobacco
● VERB + SPONSORSHIP **attract, find, get, obtain, raise, receive, win** | **look for, seek** | **withdraw (from)** *The company has decided to withdraw from some of its sports sponsorship.*
● SPONSORSHIP + NOUN **deal, package, programme, scheme** | **money**
● PREP. **through ~** *Two million pounds were raised through sponsorship.* **under (the) ~** *under commercial sponsorship* **with/without ~** *Without generous corporate sponsorship, the ballet company would not have survived.* | **~for/of** *sponsorship for next year's World Cup* **~from** *We have won sponsorship from one of the big banks.*

spontaneous *adj.*

● VERBS **appear, be, seem**
● ADV. **genuinely** | **quite, totally** | **apparently, seemingly** | **wonderfully** *a wonderfully spontaneous performance of the symphony*

spooky *adj.*

● VERBS **be, feel, look, sound** | **become, get** *It got a bit spooky when James started telling ghost stories.*
● ADV. **dead, decidedly, really, very** | **a bit, pretty, quite, rather, slightly**

spoon *noun*

● ADJ. **dessert, serving, soup, sugar**
● VERB + SPOON **pick up** | **lay down, put down** | **beat sth with, eat sth with, fold/stir sth in with, stir sth with, use** *I stirred my coffee with the sugar spoon.*
● PREP. **~of** *two spoons of sugar*

sport *noun*

● ADJ. **mainstream, major, popular** *popular field sports such as football* | **minor, minority** | **amateur, professional, semi-professional** | **competitive** | **inter-club, inter-school, etc.** | **contact, non-contact** *In theory, basketball is a non-contact sport.* | **active** | **dangerous, hazardous, risky, gruelling** | **spectator** | **indoor, outdoor** | **summer, winter** | **individual, team** | **adventure** *the inherent dangers of adventure sports such as mountaineering* | **field** | **country** | **motor** | **water** | **combat** *Combat sports such as karate and judo carry with them the risk of injury.* | **racket** | **equestrian** | **blood, cruel**
● VERB + SPORT **do, play** *He does a lot of sport.* ◇ *We played sports together when we were kids.* | **take up** *I need to take up a sport to get fit.*
● SPORT + NOUN (The following nouns all follow **sports.**) **event** | **centre, club, facilities, field, ground, hall, pavilion, stadium, venue** | **day** *the school sports day* | **person, personality, star** | **team** | **enthusiast, fan, follower** | **commentator** | **channel, coverage, page, paper** *Sports coverage in the local newspaper is quite good.* | **correspondent, editor, journalist, photographer, reporter, writer** | **injury** | **bag** | **equipment** | **goods** | **clothes/clothing** | **shop**
● PREP. **in ~** *the use of drugs in sport*
● PHRASES **the world of sport**

sportsman, sportswoman *noun*

● ADJ. **famous** | **great, outstanding** *one of the greatest all-round sportswomen this country has produced* | **all-round** | **keen** *They are all keen sportsmen.* | **amateur, professional**

spot *noun*

1 small red mark on the skin
● VERB + SPOT **break out in** *The children all had measles, and had broken out in spots.* | **scratch, squeeze**

SPORT

You can **do sport** or **play sports**:

Do you do a lot of sport?
We played sports together when we were kids.

You can also:

do	go	play
aerobics	angling	badminton
athletics	bowling	baseball
gymnastics	cycling	billiards
judo	fishing	bowls
karate	mountaineering	cricket
the high jump	riding	football
the long jump	skateboarding	golf
the pole vault	skating	hockey
weightlifting	skiing	**against** sb
wrestling	**to** aerobics, judo, etc.	**for** a team
yoga	(= to your aerobics, etc. class)	

- defeat, face, outfox, outmanoeuvre, outwit an **opponent**
- be called up to, be dropped from, be left out of, be selected for, join, sign for a **team**
- clinch, defend, retain, win **the title**
- break, set, shatter, smash **the world record**

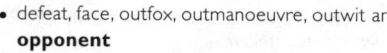

slicing a shot

football

- blast, chip, cross, give away, head, kick, lose, pass, win **the ball**
- score a **goal**
- beat, bring down, foul, get past, mark, tackle an **opponent**
- appeal for, take a **penalty**
- block, crack in, get in, have, parry, save a **shot**

golf

- hit, hook, mishit, overhit, slice, underhit a **drive/shot**
- hit, miss **the fairway/the green**
- hole, miss, sink a **putt**
- end up, finish up, land **in the rough**

rugby

- pass, retain, win **the ball**
- kick a **goal/penalty**
- win (the ball in) a **lineout/scrum**
- kick for, make **touch**
- convert, go over for, score a **try**

tennis

- hit, retrieve, return, run down **the ball**
- face, have, miss, save a **match point**
- lose, play, win a **point/rally**
- drop, hold, return (a) **serve**
- hit, mishit, overhit, slice a **shot**

2 place/area

- ADJ. **exact, particular, precise | convenient, good, ideal, perfect, right, suitable** *Take the time to find the right spot to pitch your tent.* **| beautiful, beauty, idyllic, lovely, pleasant** *The lake is one of the local beauty spots.* **| favourite, popular** *a favourite spot for picnickers* **| deserted, desolate, isolated, lonely, remote | quiet, secluded | shady, sheltered | sunny | holiday, tourist | picnic | sore, tender | sensitive** *(often figurative) From his angry reply it was obvious that I had touched a sensitive spot.* **| vulnerable, weak** *Check your house for weak spots where a thief could get in.* **| blind** *(often figurative) I have a blind spot where jazz is concerned* (= I don't understand it). **| danger, trouble** *one of the world's major trouble spots* **| high, number one/two, etc., top** *The record quickly reached the number one spot in the charts.* **| bald** *He usually wears a hat to hide his bald spot.*
- VERB + SPOT **mark** *On your map, X marks the spot where the race begins.* **| reach | be frozen/rooted to** *He stood rooted to the spot, unable to move.*
- PREP. **on the ~** *The fire brigade was on the spot within minutes.*
- PHRASES **an accident black spot**

spot *verb*

- ADV. **quickly | easily** *Most of these fossils are too small to be easily spotted.* **| suddenly | eventually, finally**
- VERB + SPOT **be difficult to, be easy to | fail to**
- PHRASES **well spotted** *'There's parking space over the far side.' 'Well spotted!'*

spotlight *noun*

1 lamp

- VERB + SPOTLIGHT **shine on** *They shone the spotlight on a woman waving at the back of the audience.* **| step into** *He stepped into the spotlight to the wild applause of the crowd.*
- SPOTLIGHT + VERB **be on sb/sth, fall on sb/sth, shine on sb/sth**
- PREP. **in/under the ~** *It was hot under the spotlights.*

2 public attention/interest

- ADJ. **national, public | media**
- VERB + SPOTLIGHT **come into/under** *This issue will come under the spotlight at tomorrow's meeting.* **| bring sth into, put, throw, turn** *These revelations threw a spotlight on the shakiness of the economy.* **| share** *The captain had to share the spotlight with the new young star.* **| steal**
- SPOTLIGHT + VERB **be on sb/sth, fall on sb/sth, turn on sb/sth**
- PREP. **in/under the ~** *The quality of food in the shops is back in the spotlight.* **out of the ~** *The affair is now out of the spotlight.*

sprawl *verb*

- ADV. **untidily. | out** *He was sprawled out on the sofa.*
- PREP. **across, in, on, over** *She sprawled untidily in an armchair*
- PHRASES **lie/sit sprawled** *She lay sprawled across the bed.* **send sb sprawling** *The blow sent him sprawling.*

spray *noun*

- ADJ. **fine, light | salt, sea**
- QUANT. **cloud, plume** *The boat sent a cloud of spray up behind it.*
- VERB + SPRAY **send (up), throw (up)**
- SPRAY + VERB **fly (up)** *Spray flew up onto the rocks.*
- PREP. **~ of** *a spray of salt water*

spread *noun*

- ADJ. **good, great, wide | rapid | gradual, slow | geo-**

graphical, global *The current survey will have a wider geographical spread.*

- VERB + SPREAD **encourage** *Such unhygienic conditions encourage the spread of disease.* **| halt, prevent, stop | control, limit, reduce**
- PREP. **~ of** *the spread of fire*

spread *verb*

1 open sth so that you can see all of it

- ADV. **carefully | out** *We spread the rug out on the floor.*
- PREP. **across, on, over**
- PHRASES **spread sth open** *He had a newspaper spread open on his knee.*

2 reach more people/wider area

- ADV. **fast, like wildfire, quickly, rapidly, soon** *The news spread like wildfire.* **| gradually, slowly | easily** *The disease spreads easily.* **| widely** *Allow plenty of space for this plant as its roots spread widely.* **| far and wide** *His fame had spread far and wide.* **| geographically** *Friends may be spread geographically. Neighbours, by definition, are nearby.* **| outwards**
- PREP. **across, among, around/round, beyond, from, into, over, through, throughout, to** *The effects of this policy spread far beyond children now at school.* ◇ *The fire rapidly spread to adjoining buildings.*
- PHRASES **thinly spread** *Expertise in this field is very thinly spread across the country.*

3 cover a surface with a soft substance

- ADV. **generously, liberally, thickly | lightly, thinly | evenly** *Don't make the paste too thick, or it will not spread evenly.*
- PREP. **on** *He spread jam on the toast.* **with** *Spread each slice generously with butter.*

4 divide/share sth

- ADV. **equally, evenly, uniformly | unevenly**
- VERB + SPREAD **try to**
- PREP. **among, between** *We tried to spread the workload evenly between the departments.* **over** *The course takes forty hours, spread over twenty weeks.*

spree *noun*

- ADJ. **massive** *a massive buying spree* **| mad | buying, shopping, spending | drinking, drunken | crime, killing | scoring** *Uruguay's scoring spree began in the fourth minute.*
- VERB + SPREE **go on** *He's gone on a drinking spree.*
- PREP. **on a ~** *She's out on a mad spending spree.*

spring *noun*

1 season

- ADJ. **last, next, this (coming) | early, late, mid- | wet**
- SPRING + NOUN **weather | sun, sunlight, sunshine | frost/frosts, rain/rains, wind | tide** *The highest spring tides of the the year occur after the equinoxes in March and September.* **| equinox | term** *The students spend the whole spring term on teaching practice.* **| flower | lamb, greens** *a delicious recipe for spring lamb* **| clean, cleaning** *They decided to give the attic a spring clean.* **| collection, exhibition**
- ⇨ Note at SEASON (for more collocates)

2 coiled metal or wire

- VERB + SPRING **break** *The children broke some springs jumping on the bed.*
- SPRING + VERB **break, go** *Most of the springs have gone in the old sofa.*

3 where water comes up

- ADJ. **hot, thermal | bubbling | mineral, mountain**
- SPRING + VERB **bubble** *A thermal spring bubbled up out of the rocks.*
- SPRING + NOUN **water**

spring *verb*

- ADV. **suddenly** | **apart, back, down, forward, out, up** *He sprang back in alarm.*
- VERB + SPRING **be ready to, be waiting to** *The lion crouched, ready to spring.*
- PREP. **at** *Thérèse sprang at him and kissed him on both cheeks.* **into, out of** *He sprang out of the car.*
- PHRASES **spring open** *He worked a knife blade into the drawer and it sprang open.* **spring to attention** *The sentry sprang to attention.* **spring to your feet** *She sprang to her feet and ran to answer the doorbell.*

sprinkle *verb*

- ADV. **lightly** | **evenly**
- PREP. **on, onto, over** *Sprinkle sugar evenly over the top of the cake.* **with** *Sprinkle the meat lightly with salt.*

sprint *noun*

- ADJ. **quick, short** | **100-metre, etc.**
- VERB + SPRINT **break into, make** *The runners broke into a sprint a few hundred yards from the finish.* ◊ *It started raining, so we made a sprint for a cafe.*
- SPRINT + NOUN **relay** *Jamaica won the gold in the sprint relay.* | **finish** *Sato just pipped the Kenyan runner in a sprint finish.* | **champion** *Olympic sprint champion Marion Jones* | **hurdles** | **double** *the 100-metre and 200-metre sprint double*
- PREP. **in a ~** *This car could comfortably outpace its rivals in a sprint.* | **~ for** *The Moroccan came out best in a frantic sprint for the line.*

spur *noun*

1 on horse rider's boots
- QUANT. **pair**
- VERB + SPUR **dig in/into, put/set to** *He dug his spurs into the horse's flank and cantered off.*

2 encouragement
- ADJ. **great, powerful, strong**
- VERB + SPUR **act as, be** | **give (sb), provide (sb with)**
- PREP. **~ for** *The research provided a spur for reform.* **~ to** *a spur to action*

spurt *noun*

- ADJ. **sudden** | **great** *A great spurt of blood came out of the wound.* | **brief, little** | **final** | **growth**
- VERB + SPURT **put on** *She put on a spurt to get to the station in time.* | **feel** *He felt a spurt of resentment against his brother.*
- PREP. **with a ~** *With one final spurt, he reached the top of the hill.* | **~ in** *a spurt in capital spending* **~ of**

spy *noun*

- ADJ. **enemy, government, police**
- VERB + SPY **act as, be, work as** *He denied acting as an enemy spy.* | **recruit (sb as)**
- SPY + NOUN **film, movie, novel, story, thriller** | **camera, plane, satellite** | **network, ring** *Counter-intelligence officers uncovered a spy ring involving twenty agents.*
- PREP. **~ for** *He was a spy for the government.*
- PHRASES **a network of spies**

squabble *noun*

- ADJ. **petty** | **bitter** | **domestic, family** | **internal**
- VERB + SQUABBLE **have** | **resolve, settle**
- PREP. **~ about/over** *squabbles about money* **~ among/between** *I always have to settle squabbles between the children.* **~ with** *a squabble with her publisher over royalties*

squad *noun*

- ADJ. **good, strong** *They've got together a good squad for the World Cup.* | **anti-terrorist, bomb (disposal), crime, drug/drugs, flying, fraud, police, riot, vice** *an early-morning raid by the police flying squad* | **assassination, death, hit** | **demolition** | **firing** *It was almost his turn to go before the firing squad.* | **football, rowing, etc.**
- SQUAD + NOUN **detective, member, officer** *a fraud squad detective* | **car**
- PREP. **in a/the ~** *He's working in the drugs squad.*

squalor *noun*

- ADJ. **public, urban**
- VERB + SQUALOR **live in**
- PREP. **amid/in the ~ of** *a beautiful garden amid the squalor of the slums* **in ~** *He was born in squalor next to London's docks.*

square *noun*

1 shape
- ADJ. **neat** | **perfect**
- VERB + SQUARE **cut sth into, divide sth into** *Cut the sandwiches into neat squares.*
- SQUARE + NOUN **shape**
- PREP. **~ of** *A square of light shone from the skylight.*

2 open space in a town, etc.
- ADJ. **central, main** | **public** | **city, town, village** | **market** *crowds thronging the market square*
- VERB + SQUARE **throng**
- PREP. **in a/the ~**

square *adj.*

- VERBS **be, look**
- ADV. **very** *The rooms are all very square.* | **absolutely, exactly** | **not quite** *The grid doesn't look quite square.* | **quite** | **nearly** | **roughly**

squeak *noun*

- ADJ. **little** | **high, high-pitched**
- VERB + SQUEAK **give, let out** | **hear**
- PREP. **with a ~** *The door opened with a squeak.* | **~ of** *She gave a little squeak of surprise.*
- PHRASES **not a squeak** *(figurative)* *'Have you heard from them?' 'Not a squeak since yesterday.'* **the squeak of rubber** *the squeak of rubber soles on the wooden floor* **a squeak of surprise**
⇨ Note at SOUND

squeal *noun*

- ADJ. **little** | **high-pitched**
- VERB + SQUEAL **give, let out** *She gave a little squeal of delight.* | **hear**
- PREP. **with a ~** *The car stopped with a squeal of brakes.* | **~ of**
- PHRASES **the squeal of brakes, a squeal of delight**
⇨ Note at SOUND

squeeze *noun*

1 pressing with fingers
- ADJ. **affectionate** | **comforting, reassuring**
- VERB + SQUEEZE **give sb** *He gave his mother a comforting squeeze as he left.*
- PHRASES **~ of** *A squeeze of her hand reassured him.*

2 in a small space
- ADJ. **tight** *There were seven of us in the car and it was a tight squeeze.*
- PREP. **at a ~** *We can get six in the car at a squeeze.*
- PHRASES **a bit of a squeeze**

3 reduction in money

● ADJ. **cash, credit, economic, financial, profits, tax**
● VERB + SQUEEZE **feel** *All manufacturers are feeling the squeeze.* | **put** *The government is trying to put the squeeze on high earners.*
● PREP. **~on** *a squeeze on spending*

squeeze *verb*

1 press sth hard
● ADV. **hard, tightly** | **gently** *'I know,' she said, squeezing his hand gently.*
● PREP. **from** *squeezing the juice from a lemon* **out of** *I squeezed the last bit of toothpaste out of the tube.*
● PHRASES **freshly squeezed** *freshly squeezed orange juice*

2 limit the money available
● ADV. **hard, severely** *High interest rates have squeezed the industry hard.*

squint *noun*

● ADJ. **bad** | **slight**
● VERB + SQUINT **have** | **correct** *A squint can sometimes be corrected by an eyepatch.*
● SQUINT + NOUN **surgery**

squirm *verb*

● ADV. **uncomfortably** | **silently** | **visibly**
● VERB + SQUIRM **make sb** *The very mention of her singing made her squirm uncomfortably.*
● PREP. **at** *He squirmed visibly at the thought of his secret being revealed.* **in/with** *He squirmed with embarrassment.*

squirrel *noun*

● ADJ. **grey, red**
● SQUIRREL + VERB **dart, scamper, scurry** *The squirrel scampered across the lawn*

stab *noun*

1 injury
● VERB + STAB **make** *the boy made a stab at the pig*
● STAB + NOUN **wound**
● PREP. **~at**

2 sudden pain
● ADJ. **sharp, sudden**
● VERB + STAB **feel**
● PHRASES **~of** *He felt a sharp stab of disappointment.*

3 attempt
● ADJ. **brave, good** | **unsuccessful**
● VERB + STAB **have, make, take**
● PREP. **~at** *I had a stab at answering the question.*

stab *verb*

● ADV. **repeatedly** *He is accused of repeatedly stabbing a sixteen-year-old boy.*
● VERB + STAB **threaten to** | **try to**
● PREP. **at, in** *He was stabbed in the chest.* **with** *I stabbed at my meat with my fork.*
● PHRASES **be found stabbed** *He was found stabbed in his car.* **stab sb to death**

stability *noun*

● ADJ. **greater** | **relative** | **long-term** | **internal** | **economic, financial, monetary, price** | **political, social** | **emotional**
● VERB + STABILITY **achieve, bring, ensure, give sb, provide (sb with)** *The policy should bring greater monetary stability to the country.* | **lack** | **threaten, undermine** | **maintain, preserve**
● PHRASES **a period of stability** *The country was enjoy-*

ing a period of political stability. **a threat to stability** *The conflict is becoming a threat to stability in the region.*

stable *adj.*

1 not likely to move
● VERBS **be, feel, look, seem** | **make sth** | **keep sth** *Put a book under the table to keep it stable.*
● ADV. **extremely, very** | **perfectly, quite** *Don't worry—it's perfectly stable!* | **fairly, pretty** | **enough, sufficiently** *The unit is stable enough on level ground.*

2 not likely to change suddenly
● VERBS **be, look, seem** | **become** | **remain** | **keep sth** *attempts to keep prices stable*
● ADV. **extremely, highly, remarkably, very** | **completely, perfectly** *Animals rarely live in completely stable environments.* | **broadly, comparatively, fairly, more or less, quite, reasonably, relatively, roughly** | **enough, sufficiently** *He was not emotionally stable enough to think through his decision.* | **apparently** | **emotionally, financially, politically**

stack *verb*

● ADV. **carefully, neatly** | **away, up** *The wood was collected up and carefully stacked away.* ◇ *Stack the chairs up over there.*
● PREP. **against** *The cases were stacked against the wall.* **in** *The paintings were stacked in a corner of the room.* **on** *The plates were neatly stacked on the draining board.* **with** *shelves stacked with boxes*
● PHRASES **be stacked in piles** *Boxes were stacked in piles all round the room.*

stadium *noun*

● ADJ. **packed** | **all-seater** | **indoor** | **sports** | **Olympic** | **baseball, football, greyhound**
● VERB + STADIUM **fill, pack (into)** *Thousands packed into the stadium to watch the final.*
● PREP. **at a/the~**

staff *noun*

● ADJ. **full-time, part-time** | **permanent, temporary** | **skeleton** *We'll be down to a skeleton staff over Christmas.* | **experienced, professional, qualified, skilled, trained** | **unskilled** | **junior, senior** | **ancillary, support** | **general** (= officers assisting a military leader in administration and planning) | **academic, administrative, editorial, etc.** | **nursing, teaching, etc.** | **hospital, hotel, etc.** | **bar, kitchen, etc.**
● QUANT. **member** *There are only four full-time members of staff in the company.*
● VERB + STAFF **employ, have** *The company has a staff of fifty.* | **appoint, engage, hire, recruit, take on** *staff appointed to the project* ◇ *I've heard they're recruiting staff at the moment.* | **dismiss, fire, lay off, make redundant, sack** *A spokesperson said that the bank expects to make 15 000 staff redundant over the next three years.* | **train** | **pay** *They pay their staff by cheque.* | **join** *He joined the editorial staff in 1999.* | **leave**
● STAFF + NOUN **member** | **levels, numbers, resources** | **shortage** | **turnover** | **cut** | **appointment** *The hospital is freezing staff appointments as part of its cutbacks.* | **development, training** | **morale** | **meeting** | **canteen, dining room, restaurant, room**
● PREP. **on the~(of)** *She has been on the staff of the hospital for most of her working life.*
● PHRASES **chief of staff** (= the most senior officer serving under and advising the person who commands each of the armed forces)

staff *verb* be staffed

● ADV. **well** | **fully, properly** *The ward is now fully*

staffed. | **adequately** | **inadequately**, **short** *I'm afraid we're desperately short staffed at the moment.*
● PHRASES **be staffed (entirely/largely/mainly) by/with sb** *The office will be staffed entirely with volunteers.*

stage noun

1 period/state in progress/development
● ADJ. **distinct** *The process has three distinct stages.* | **early**, **first**, **initial**, **opening**, **preliminary** | **advanced**, **closing**, **final**, **last**, **late**, **latter**, **terminal** *Her husband was in the advanced stages of cancer.* | **halfway**, **intermediate**, **secondary** | **transitional** | **successive** | **critical**, **crucial**, **important**, **key**, **main** | **easy** *The book guides you through making your own website in easy stages.* | **difficult** | **delicate**, **vulnerable** | **embryonic**, **larval**, **pupal** | **experimental**, **exploratory** | **committee**, **design**, **development/developmental**, **formative**, **planning** *The scheme is still at the planning stage.* | **knockout**, **semi-final**, etc. *Colombia's win sent them through to the knockout stage of the tournament.*
● VERB + STAGE **go/move/pass through** *The water goes through three stages of purification.* | **enter**, **reach** *We've entered a crucial stage in the project.*
● PREP. **at a/the ~** *You should read this article at some stage.* **by ~s** *The university was put together by stages.* **during/in a/the ~** *in the early stages of the job* **in ~s** *We renovated the house in two stages.* | **~ in** *an important stage in her life* **~ of** *the latter stages of the race*
● PHRASES **the beginning/end of a stage** *Pupils are tested at the end of each stage of the course.* **a/one stage further** *take the investigation one stage further* **a stage of development/life**

2 in a theatre, etc.
● ADJ. **centre** *(often figurative)* *A new actress will take centre stage in next month's production of 'The Doll's House'.* | **revolving**
● VERB + STAGE **go on**, **take (to)** *He was too nervous to go on stage.* ◇ *I was shaking as I took the stage.* ◇ *She took to the stage when she was at university.* | **leave** *She left the stage to tumultuous applause.* | **set** *(often figurative)* *The thrilling semi-finals set the stage for what should be a great game.* | **boo sb off**
● STAGE + NOUN **management**, **manager** | **direction** *Shakespeare's famous stage direction: 'Exit, pursued by a bear.'* | **play**, **production**, **show** | **appearance**, **performance**, **role** | **set** *The stage set is the most expensive ever built.* | **door** | **name** *David Harries adopted the stage name Dixon Hare when he became a full-time actor.* | **left**, **right** | **fright** *Even experienced actors can suffer from stage fright.*
● PREP. **off ~** *A trumpet sounded off stage.* **on ~** *The entire cast is on stage in the final scene.*

stage verb

● ADV. **carefully** *The event was very carefully staged.* | **elaborately** *an elaborately staged drama*

stagger verb

● ADV. **almost** | **a little**, **slightly** | **blindly** *She staggered blindly off into the darkness.* | **about**, **around**, **away**, **back**, **backwards**, **forward**, **off**, **out**
● PREP. **from**, **into**, **out of**, **through**, **towards**, **under**, etc. *He was staggering under the weight of the sack.*
● PHRASES **stagger to your feet** *She staggered to her feet and tottered unsteadily across the room.*

staggered adj.

● VERBS **be**, **look**
● ADV. **absolutely**, **quite**
● PREP. **at** *I was staggered at her rudeness.* **by** *He looked quite staggered by the news.*

staggering adj.

● VERBS **be**
● ADV. **absolutely**, **quite** *The public response was absolutely staggering.* | **fairly**, **pretty**

stagnation noun

● ADJ. **economic**, **political**
● VERB + STAGNATION **lead to**
● PHRASES **a period/years of stagnation** *Poor economic policies led to a long period of stagnation and decline.*

staid adj.

● VERBS **be**, **feel**, **look**, **seem** | **become**, **get**, **grow** *He had grown staid and dull.*
● ADV. **positively**, **very** *The locals were a very staid lot.* | **rather** *a rather staid and old-fashioned hotel*

stain noun

● ADJ. **stubborn** | **dark** | **coffee**, **grass**, etc.
● VERB + STAIN **leave** | **get out**, **remove**
● STAIN + VERB **spread** *The glass fell off the table and a dark stain spread over the carpet.*
● PREP. **~ on** *The coffee left a stain on his shirt.*

stain verb

● PREP. **with** *The shirt was heavily stained with blood.*
● PHRASES **be badly/heavily/slightly stained**, **stain sth green**, **red**, etc. *The children's fingers were stained purple with blackberry juice.*

stair noun

1 stairs steps inside a building
● ADJ. **steep** | **wide** | **narrow** | **rickety** | **main** | **back**
● QUANT. **flight** *We went up three flights of stairs.*
● VERB + STAIRS **ascend**, **climb**, **go/run**, etc. **up**, **mount** | **descend**, **go/run**, etc. **down** | **take**, **use** *Take the back stairs.*
● STAIRS + VERB **lead to sth** | **creak**
● STAIR + NOUN **rod** *The carpet was held in place by brass stair rods.* | **gate**
● PREP. **under the ~** *a cupboard under the stairs* | **~ (down/up) to** *the stairs to the third floor*
● PHRASES **the bottom/foot/head/top of the stairs**, **take the stairs two**, etc. **at a time** *He rushed up to the bedroom, taking the stairs two at a time.*

2 one step
● ADJ. **top** | **bottom**
● STAIR + VERB **creak** *The third stair creaked as I stepped on it.*
● PREP. **on/the a ~** *He sat waiting on the bottom stair.*

staircase noun

● ADJ. **steep** | **broad**, **wide** | **narrow** | **elegant**, **grand**, **great** | **rickety** | **curving**, **spiral**, **sweeping**, **twisting**, **winding** | **moving** | **main** | **outside** | **back**
● VERB + STAIRCASE **ascend**, **climb**, **go/run**, etc. **up**, **mount** | **descend**, **go/run**, etc. **down** | **use**
● STAIRCASE + VERB **lead to sth** *The spiral staircase led to an upper gallery.*
● PREP. **on the ~** *They passed each other on the staircase.*
● PHRASES **the bottom/foot/head/top of the staircase**

stake noun

1 (*also* **stakes**) amount that could be won/lost
● ADJ. **big**, **high** | **low**, **small** | **political**
● VERB + STAKE **play for** *They always play for high stakes.* | **raise** | **lower**
● PREP. **at ~** *The minister will face the enquiry with his reputation at stake.*

2 share of a company, etc.
- ADJ. **controlling, large, majority, significant, substantial** | **minority, small** | **direct** | **financial, equity**
- VERB + STAKE **have** | **acquire, buy, take** | **sell** | **build up, increase, lift, raise** | **cut, reduce**
- PREP. **~in** *She acquired a four per cent direct stake in the business.*

stale *adj.*

- VERBS **be, look, smell, taste** *The room smelled musty and stale.* | **become, go, turn** *This bread's going stale.*
- ADV. **extremely, very** | **a bit, a little, rather, slightly**
- PREP. **with** *The atmosphere was stale with cigarette smoke.*

stalemate *noun*

- ADJ. **political**
- VERB + STALEMATE **end in, reach, result in** *The talks reached (a) stalemate.* | **break** *Efforts to break the stalemate in the peace talks continue.* | **be locked in** *Discussions are locked in stalemate.*
- STALEMATE + VERB **continue**
- PREP. **~between** *a stalemate between management and unions* **~in** *The stalemate in the trade talks continues.* **~on/over** *a stalemate over economic union*

stall *noun*

- ADJ. **market** | **book, cake, fish, flower, etc.**
- VERB + STALL **have** *He has a flower stall in Portobello Road market.* | **put up, set out/up** | **pack up** | **man, run** *Who's going to man the stall at lunchtime?*
- STALL + VERB **sell sth** *a stall selling second-hand books*
- STALL + NOUN **holder** (also **stallholder**), **keeper**
- PREP. **at a/the ~** *I bought this trout at the market fish stall.* **behind the~** *the man behind the stall*

stall *verb*

- ADV. **effectively** *Discussions were effectively stalled by the union's refusal to participate.*
- PHRASES **stall for time** *He asked them all kinds of pointless questions, stalling for time.*

stamina *noun*

- ADJ. **great** | **mental, physical**
- VERB + STAMINA **have** *She didn't the stamina to complete the course.* | **lack** | **need, require** | **build (up), increase** *Aerobic exercise helps to build up stamina.*
- PHRASES **reserves of stamina** *Emma Walton had to call on all her reserves of stamina to win the 10 000 metres.* **a test of stamina** *Final exams at university can be as much a test of stamina as of knowledge.*

stammer *noun*

- ADJ. **bad, nervous, severe** | **slight**
- VERB + STAMMER **develop** | **have, speak with**

stamp *noun*

1 on a letter/package
- ADJ. **postage** | **first-class, second-class** | **Christmas, commemorative**
- QUANT. **book, set, sheet** *a book of ten first-class stamps*
- VERB + STAMP **put on, stick on** *She stuck a first-class stamp on the letter.* | **lick, moisten** | **issue, launch** *The Post Office has launched some new Christmas stamps.* | **collect**
- STAMP + NOUN **album, collecting, collector**

2 instrument for stamping a design, etc. on a surface
- ADJ. **official** | **date**

3 character/quality
- ADJ. **unmistakable**
- VERB + STAMP **bear, carry** *His work bears the unmistakable stamp of genius.* | **leave, put** *She left her stamp on the school.*
- PREP. **~of** *the stamp of authority*

stamp *verb*

- ADV. **hard** | **impatiently** *She stamped her foot impatiently.* | **about, around, down, off** *He stamped off in disgust.*
- PREP. **on** *She stamped on my toe!*

stance *noun*

1 position in which sb stands
- ADJ. **correct, good** | **natural** | **rigid** | **relaxed** | **upright** | **defensive, fighting**
- VERB + STANCE **adopt, take up** *The boxer took up a fighting stance.* | **change** | **keep, maintain**
- PREP. **in a~** *He lounged in an armchair in a stance of deliberate contempt.*

2 attitude
- ADJ. **positive** | **critical, negative** | **impartial, neutral** | **aggressive, hardline, rigid, tough, uncompromising** | **cautious** | **conservative** | **radical** | **ideological, moral, political** | **public** *Her public stance was much tougher than her private feelings on the subject.*
- VERB + STANCE **adopt, take (up)** | **alter, change** | **maintain** *The wife of the accused has maintained an impartial stance throughout the trial.*
- PREP. **~against** *The president has adopted a hardline stance against abortion.* **~on/towards** *He has changed his stance on monetary union.*

stand *noun*

1 effort to resist opposition
- ADJ. **defiant, determined, firm, strong, tough** | **moral, principled** | **last, last-ditch** | **public**
- VERB + STAND **make, take**
- PREP. **~against** *to make a stand against industries that contribute to river pollution* **~on** *He has taken a public stand on the issue of misuse of hospital funds.*

2 table/small shop
- ADJ. **market, trade** | **hot-dog, newspaper, etc.** | **display, exhibition** | **information**
- VERB + STAND **have** *Our company has a display stand at this year's fair.* | **set up** | **man** *We took it in turns to man the exhibition stand.*
- PREP. **at a/the ~** *We can get a magazine at the newspaper stand.* **on the ~** *I'll be on the stand for two hours.* ◇ *You'll find brochures on our new products on the stand.*

3 furniture/equipment for putting sth on
- ADJ. **hat, umbrella** | **microphone, music**
- PREP. **in/on a/the ~** *There was some flute music open on the music stand.*

stand *verb*

1 be on your feet/be upright
- ADV. **upright** | **still** *Stand still while I take your photo.* | **barefoot** | **on tiptoe** *She stood on tiptoe to reach the shelf.* | **awkwardly, meekly, stiffly, uncertainly** *He stood awkwardly in the doorway, not sure what to say.* | **around, there** *Don't just stand there—do something.*
- VERB + STAND **can/can't, could/couldn't** *The roof was so low I could not stand upright.* | **can/could barely/hardly** *He felt so weak he could hardly stand.*
- PHRASES **be left standing** *After the earthquake only a few houses were left standing.*

2 tolerate sth
- VERB + STAND **can/can't, could/couldn't** *I can't stand that man!* | **can/could hardly**

3 be a candidate in an election
- ADV. **successfully, unsuccessfully**
- PREP. **against** *Two candidates will be standing against her.* **as** *She stood unsuccessfully as a candidate in the local elections.* **for** *He is standing for Oxford East in the parliamentary election.*

PHRASAL VERBS

stand by
- ADV. **idly, passively** *Surely the world cannot stand idly by and let this country go through the agony of war yet again?*
- VERB + STAND BY **can/can't, could/couldn't**

stand up
- ADV. **straight** *You'll look taller if you stand up straight.*

standard noun

1 level of quality
- ADJ. **high | low, poor | minimum | acceptable, adequate, decent, proper, reasonable** *We must ensure proper standards of care for the elderly.* **| improved, rising | clear | objective** *Judged by any objective standards, the campaign was a disaster.* **| official, required | conventional, usual | consistent, uniform, universal | exacting, rigorous, strict, stringent | professional** *The work has been done to a professional standard.* **| international, national | quality** *We have to try and achieve the quality standards set by the project.* **| qualifying** *The Olympic qualifying standard has been set at 64.50m.* **| living** *The region enjoys the highest living standards in Europe.* **| accounting, advertising, safety, trading, etc. | academic, educational, environmental, health, intellectual, technical, etc.**
- VERB + STANDARD **have** *The agency has very high standards.* **| boast, enjoy | define, establish, set | achieve, meet, reach** *The factory is struggling to meet national environmental standards.* ◊ *She has reached an acceptable standard of English.* **| fall short of** *The hotel service fell short of the usual standard.* **| apply, enforce, provide** *It's impossible to apply the same academic standards across the country.* **| judge sb/sth by | improve, raise | lower | maintain, sustain**
- PREP. **above/below (the)** ~ *Your work is below standard.* **by ... standards** *By modern standards, he isn't a particularly fast runner.* **to a ... ~** *The building work had not been completed to a satisfactory standard.* **up to ~** *We need to bring our computer system up to standard.* **| ~in** *standards in safety*
- PHRASES **by any standard** *She's a great violinist by any standard.* **a drop/fall in the standard, an increase/a rise in the standard** *There has been an increase in the standard of sevice provided.* **a standard of living** *the fall in their standard of living caused by redundancy*

2 (usually **standards**) acceptable level of behaviour
- ADJ. **declining, falling** *My grandparents are always complaining about falling moral standards.* **| double** *the double standard frequently encountered in nineteenth-century attitudes to sex* **| ethical, moral**
- VERB + STANDARD **prescribe | keep up, maintain | improve, raise**
- STANDARD + VERB **drop, fall**
- PHRASES **standards of behaviour/conduct**

standard adj.

- VERBS **be, be fitted as, come as** *Anti-lock brakes are fitted as standard.* **| become**
- ADV. **almost** *The stations were built to a simple, almost standard design.* **| fairly, pretty** *a fairly standard method of assessing employees*

standing noun

1 reputation
- ADJ. **good, high | low | equal | public | international | academic, economic, financial, legal, moral, political, professional, social**
- VERB + STANDING **have** *Professor Greenan has a high standing in the academic world.* **| enhance, improve | damage, diminish**
- STANDING + VERB **decline, fall | rise**
- PREP. **of ...** ~ *She married into a family of higher social standing.* **| ~among** *her low standing among her fellow scientists* **~ as** *His standing as a film director has risen in recent years.* **~ in/within** *his international standing in cancer research* **~ with** *She was appointed for her high moral standing with the general public.*
- PHRASES **in good standing with sb** *a knight in good standing with the king*

2 length of time that sth has existed
- ADJ. **long | many years', 25 years', etc.** *Their relationship is of many years' standing.*
- PREP. **of ...** ~

standpoint noun

- ADJ. **different** *We must approach the problem from a different standpoint.* **| positive | practical | ideological, theoretical | economic, historical, political, religious, technical, etc.**
- VERB + STANDPOINT **adopt** *We should try to adopt a more positive standpoint.* **| approach sth from, view sth from**
- PREP. **from a/the ~ (of)** *From the standpoint of women, this looks like a policy of discrimination.*

standstill noun

- ADJ. **complete, total | virtual**
- VERB + STANDSTILL **come to, grind to** *The train came to a complete standstill.* **| bring sth to** *The roadworks brought the traffic to a standstill.*
- PREP. **at a ~** *The factory has been at a standstill for days.*

star noun

1 small point of light in the night sky
- ADJ. **bright, brilliant | faint | distant | nearby, nearer/nearest | falling, shooting | evening, morning**
- QUANT. **cluster** *a dense cluster of stars at the galaxy's nucleus*
- STAR + VERB **be out | shine, twinkle** *A bright star shone in the East.* **| appear, come out**
- STAR + NOUN **cluster** *a dense cluster of stars at the galaxy's nucleus*
- PREP. **under the ~s** *We camped out under the stars.*
- PHRASES **a canopy of stars** *They lay down under a canopy of stars.* **the brightness/density/luminosity of a star**

2 famous person
- ADJ. **big** *There were several big Hollywood stars at the function.* **| true, undisputed | rising, young | football, pop, etc. | Hollywood, screen, film, movie, soap, TV**
- QUANT. **array, galaxy, host** *Channel 4 has lined up a galaxy of stars for the coming season.*
- STAR + NOUN **quality, status | role | actor, performer, player | attraction, turn** *He was the star turn at the celebrations.* **| vehicle** *The film was nothing more than a star vehicle for Tom Hanks.*

stardom noun

- ADJ. **Hollywood, international**
- VERB + STARDOM **achieve, rise to, rocket to, shoot (sb) to** *Her number one single shot her to stardom.* **| be tipped for** *This young tennis player is being tipped for stardom.* **| be coached for, be groomed for** *He was groomed for stardom by his rock-singer father.*

● PHRASES **sb's rise to stardom** *her meteoric rise to stardom* **the road to stardom** *He set out on the lonely road to stardom early in life.*

stare *verb*

● ADV. **fixedly, hard, intently, unblinkingly** *I could see a man staring at me intently.* | **steadily** | **impassively** | **absently, blankly, blearily, blindly, dully, sightlessly, uncomprehendingly, unseeingly, vacantly** *She stared blankly at the brick wall in front of her.* | **dazedly, disbelievingly, incredulously, open-mouthed, wide-eyed, wildly** *I stared at him open-mouthed, unable to speak.* | **bleakly, gloomily, glumly, grimly, helplessly, hopelessly, morosely** *He stared at me bleakly and said nothing.* | **coldly, coolly, defiantly, fiercely, moodily, stonily** *She stared at him stonily as he came in.* | **curiously, quizzically, suspiciously, thoughtfully** | **silently, wordlessly** | **just, merely, simply** | **(for) a moment** *For a long moment they just stared at each other.* | **still** *He was still staring at himself in the mirror.* | **across, around/round, back, down, out, (straight) ahead, up** *She stared back at him.* ◇ *He stared straight ahead and did not move.*

● VERB + STARE **can/could only** *She could only stare at him with pain in her eyes.* | **seem to** | **continue to** | **turn to** *Everyone in the room turned to stare at her.* | **pause to, stop to**

● PREP. **across, after** *She stalked off, leaving them all staring after her.* **around/round, at, in** *I stared in horror at his bloody mouth.* **into, out of, through, with** *He just stared at her with disbelief.*

● PHRASES **sit/stand staring, stand/stop and stare** *It was too cold to stand and stare.* **stare into space** *She was just sitting there, staring into space.*

start *noun*

● ADJ. **auspicious, bright, encouraging, flying, good, great, impressive, promising, sound, wonderful** *Despite a bright start, Liverpool lost the match.* | **disappointing, disastrous, poor, rocky, shaky, slow, uncertain** | **false** *After a couple of false starts, she found the job that suited her.* | **fresh, new** | **early, late** | **very** *right from the very start*

● VERB + START **make** *I think it's time we made a start.* | **get off to** *The company has got off to an impressive start this financial year.* | **herald, mark**

● START + NOUN **button, date, signal**

● PREP. **at the ~ (of)** *Everyone was in a conciliatory mood at the start of the meeting.* **from the ~** *She felt at home in her new job right from the start.* | **~ to** *The fine winter weather heralded a good start to the year.* **~ in** *Moving to a good school gave Sally a fresh start in life.*

● PHRASES **from start to finish** *This is a thoroughly good book from start to finish.*

start *verb*

● ADV. **suddenly** *Her heart suddenly started to race.* | **immediately** | **just** *He has just started at school.* ◇ *At that point I just started to hate the man.* | **off, out** *We'll start off by doing some warm-up exercises.* | **(all over) again** *We'll just have to start all over again.*

● VERB + START **decide to, expect to, hope to, intend to, plan to** | **be due to, be expected to, be scheduled to** *Work is due to start this weekend.* | **be ready to** *By early evening he was ready to start work.* | **be about to, be going to** *A new term was about to start.* | **had better** *You'd better start packing if you're to leave early tomorrow morning.*

● PREP. **by** *Let's start by reviewing what we did last week.* **from** *Start from the beginning and tell me exactly what happened.* **on** *I've finished decorating the bathroom, so*

now *I can start on the bedroom.* **with** *Let's start with this first piece of music.*

● PHRASES **get started** *It's already quite late, so I think we should get started.* **let's start**

starter *noun*

● ADJ. **cold, hot**

● VERB + STARTER **eat, have** *Are you having a starter?* | **choose, order** *I've chosen a hot starter.* | **serve sth as** *This dish can be served as a starter or a main course.*

starting point *noun*

● ADJ. **convenient, good, suitable, useful**

● VERB + STARTING POINT **be, provide, serve as** | **take sth as, use sth as**

● PREP. **from a/the ~** *They reached the same conclusion from different starting points.* | **~ for** *Your paper provides a useful starting point for the discussion.*

startled *adj.*

● VERBS **be, look, seem, sound**

● ADV. **very** | **a bit, a little, quite, rather, slightly, somewhat** | **for a moment, momentarily** *She was momentarily startled by the sight before her.* | **suddenly**

● PREP. **at** *She was obviously a little startled at this idea.* **by** *startled by his sudden appearance in the doorway*

starvation *noun*

● ADJ. **prolonged, slow** | **mass** | **oxygen** *The pilot had lost consciousness because of oxygen starvation.*

● VERB + STARVATION **be threatened by, face, suffer** | **rescue sb from, save sb from** | **die from/of**

● STARVATION + NOUN **diet, rations** | **wages** *The workers lived in poor conditions and were paid starvation wages.* | **level** *Millions of people around the world live at or below starvation level.*

● PHRASES **death by/from starvation**

starve *verb*

● ADV. **literally** *She refused food and literally starved herself to death.*

● VERB + STARVE **leave sb to** *He locked them in and left them to starve.*

● PHRASES **be half starved** *The poor cat was half starved.* **starve to death**

state *noun*

1 condition

● ADJ. **acceptable, fit, good, healthy** *She managed to get the company's finances into a healthy state.* | **appalling, awful, bad, desperate, dire, dreadful, pitiful, poor, sorry, terrible** | **run-down** *We were shocked at the run-down state of the hospital.* | **emotional, mental, psychological** *He's not in a fit enough mental state to drive.* | **physical** *The inspectors assess the physical state of schools and equipment.* | **financial** | **nervous, trance-like** *He goes into a trance-like state when he plays the guitar.* | **current, present** | **former, previous** | **natural** *You can either varnish the wood or leave it in its natural state.* | **constant, continual, continuous, permanent, perpetual** *The country is in a perpetual state of anarchy.* | **advanced** *an advanced state of dehydration*

● VERB + STATE **get into, go into** | **get sth into**

● PREP. **in a ~** *Jane was in a terrible state after losing her job.* **into a ~** *Babies can cry themselves into a state of frenzy.* | **~ of** *His life seems to be in a constant state of chaos.*

● PHRASES **be in a good/bad, etc. state of repair** *The house was in a poor state of repair when we bought it.* **a state of affairs** *The brothers' refusal to work together had brought about this sad state of affairs.* **a state of emergency** *The government has declared a state of emergency* *in the flooded regions.* **a state of flux** *The education system is still in a state of flux following the recent reform.* **a state of health** *He's concerned about his mother's state of health.* **a state of mind** *Public speaking can produce a state of mind akin to panic.* **a state of shock** *The driver was just sitting there in a state of shock.* **a state of war**

2 country/government

• ADJ. **independent, nation, sovereign | foreign | democratic, one-party, socialist, totalitarian, etc. | member** *member states of the European Union* | **powerful, strong | weak | neighbouring**

• STATE + NOUN **enterprise, monopoly | control, ownership** *The telephone network is still under state control.* | **property** *Every citizen could buy shares in privatized state property.* | **sector, system** *Teachers in the state sector are asking for a 7% pay rise.* ◇ *schools outside the state system* | **education, school** *Did you go to a state school or a private school?* | **aid, funding, funds, subsidy, support | benefit, pension** *unemployed people living on state benefit* ◇ *The state pension is barely enough to live on.* | **intervention** *large-scale state intervention in industry* | **spending** *Some prefer tax cuts to greater state spending on health and social services.* | **employee | secret** *He was shot for passing state secrets to foreign powers.*

• PHRASES **affairs/matters of state** *The president's wife is said to have a powerful hand in affairs of state.* **head of state** *Visiting heads of state usually stay in the palace.*

state *verb*

• ADV. **clearly, plainly** *Please state clearly how many tickets you require.* | **exactly, explicitly, expressly, precisely, specifically** *These facts were nowhere explicitly stated.* | **categorically, definitely, positively, unequivocally** *She stated categorically that she had no intention of leaving.* | **emphatically, firmly | bluntly, flatly** *'Alcohol doesn't solve problems,' she stated flatly.* | **confidently | correctly, rightly | falsely, incorrectly, wrongly | openly, publicly** *He stated his own views quite openly.* | **formally, officially | blandly | easily** *The demands are more easily stated than met.* | **briefly, succinctly | quietly | just, merely, simply** *I am merely stating the facts.* | **repeatedly | previously** *As previously stated, the phrase 'value for money' has an ambiguous meaning.*

• VERB + STATE **go on to** *The report goes on to state that: ...* | **fail to** *The committee failed to state their reasons for this decision.*

• PHRASES **stated above/below** *We cannot accept this proposal for the reasons stated above.* **state the obvious** *At the risk of stating the obvious, people who have not paid cannot be admitted.* **unless otherwise stated/unless stated otherwise** *All the photographs in this book, unless otherwise stated, date from the 1950s.*

statement *noun*

• ADJ. **brief, short** *Saunder's lawyer made a brief statement to the press outside the court.* | **bald, blunt, flat** *His bald statement that he'd resigned concealed his anxiety about the situation.* | **comprehensive, definitive, detailed, full | explicit** *An explicit statement of objectives is vital before the project begins.* | **clear, simple | bold, firm, positive, strong | explanatory | false, inaccurate, misleading | sweeping** *She made one of her sweeping statements about foreigners.* | **joint** *The two heads of state issued a joint statement.* | **formal, government, official, public | political** *They decided to make a political statement by refusing to vote.* | **oral, signed, sworn, written**

• VERB + STATEMENT **issue, put out, release | give, make** *He admitted giving a false statement to the police.* | **take** *The police will take a statement from each of you.* | **withdraw | deny**

• PREP. **in a/the ~** *In a statement released today, the Department of Health said ...* | **~ about** *The clothes you wear are a statement about yourself.* **~ on** *a statement on human rights* **~ to** *He's trying to withdraw the statement he made to Parliament last week.*

statesman *noun*

• ADJ. **great, leading | elder, senior** *Political power resided with the nation's elder statesman and party leader.* | **international, world** *his reputation as a world statesman*

static *adj.*

• VERBS **be, seem | become | remain, stay**

• ADV. **very | completely, totally | far from | almost, largely, more or less, virtually** *The population remained more or less static.* | **essentially | fairly, rather, relatively, somewhat** *The economy is fairly static at the moment.*

station *noun*

1 where trains stop

• ADJ. **next** *We get off at the next station.* | **railway, train | metro, subway, tube, underground**

• VERB + STATION **get to, go to** *We got to the station just as the train was pulling out.* | **leave | arrive at** *The train arrived at Oxford Station twenty minutes late.*

• STATION + NOUN **platform**

• PREP. **at a/the ~** *He got off at the same station.* **in a/the ~** *There's a newspaper kiosk in the station.*

2 where buses/coaches begin and end journeys

• ADJ. **bus, coach**

• VERB + STATION **leave** *The coach leaves the station at 0900 hours.* | **arrive at**

• PREP. **at a/the ~** *We waited for him at the coach station.*

3 radio/television company

• ADJ. **radio, television/TV | foreign, local | cable, satellite | commercial**

• VERB + STATION **get, pick up, tune (in) to** *I can pick up a lot of foreign stations on this radio.* | **listen to**

stationery *noun*

• ADJ. **business, hotel, office, wedding | quality**

• STATIONERY + NOUN **shop, supplier | cupboard**

statistics *noun*

• ADJ. **annual, monthly | latest | reliable | vital | bald, raw** *The bald statistics tell us nothing about the underlying trends.* | **government, national, official, police | accident, crime, criminal, economic, health, population, transport, unemployment, etc.**

• VERB + STATISTICS **prepare, produce | keep** *We no longer keep statistics on former employees.* | **release**

• STATISTICS + VERB **indicate sth, prove sth, reveal sth, show sth, tell sb sth | suggest sth**

• STATISTICS + NOUN **office**

• PREP. **according to ~** *According to official statistics, the island had 37 inhabitants.* | **~ on** *The government has released new statistics on the cost of living.*

⇒ Note at SUBJECT (for more verbs and nouns)

statue *noun*

• ADJ. **colossal, enormous, huge, large | small | life-size | equestrian | bronze, marble, etc.**

• VERB + STATUE **erect, put up | unveil**

• STATUE + VERB **be, stand** *The statue stands in one of the main squares.*

• PREP. **~ of** *a statue of the Virgin* **~ to** *the unveiling of a statue to Lord Brown*

stature *noun*

1 height

• ADJ. **great, imposing | diminutive, short, slight,**

small | full *The statue shows King Richard in full stature beside his horse.* | **physical**
● VERB + STATURE **have** | **lack** *The president lacks physical stature.*
● PREP. **of ... ~** *He was a man of great stature who carried himself well.*
● PHRASES **a lack of stature** *Despite his lack of stature, he became a successful footballer.* **small in stature** *Both her parents are fairly small in stature.*

2 importance
● ADJ. **considerable, great, growing | full | public | international, world | political**
● VERB + STATURE **gain in, grow in, rise in** *She has grown in stature since winning the Tchaikovsky Piano Competition.* | **achieve** *Geomorphology has now achieved full stature as a branch of geology.* | **enhance** *The election result enhanced the party's stature.* | **diminish | rise to ...** *Her reputation has risen to world stature.*
● STATURE + VERB **grow, increase, rise** *His political stature increased during the crisis.*
● PREP. **of ~** *a writer of international stature*

status *noun*

● ADJ. **great, high, superior | inferior, low, lowly** *low-status jobs* | **relative** *The relative status of the speakers affects what language is used.* | **equal | current | full** *The college has now achieved full status as part of the university.* | **privileged, special | economic, educational, employment, financial, occupational, professional, social, socio-economic** *a payment made to every individual irrespective of employment status* | **marital | legal** *They argued that the email had no signature and therefore no legal status.* | **independent** *A referendum produced a massive majority in favour of fully independent status for the region.* | **amateur | charitable** *The organization has charitable status.* | **diplomatic | immigrant, refugee, resident | international | celebrity** *He achieved celebrity status through his role in a popular sitcom.* | **classic, cult, legendary** *a car from the 50s that has acquired cult status*
● VERB + STATUS **enjoy, have** *The teaching profession has a low status in England.* ◇ *This sort of bike has status among teenagers.* | **achieve, acquire** *Marrying a rich woman helped him achieve status.* | **bring sb, give sb** *Owning the yacht has given them status.* | **accord, attach, give** *High social status is attached to the legal profession.* | **recognize | befit** *At last James had an office that befitted his status.* | **rise in** *The neighbourhood has risen in status in recent years.* | **improve, raise** *They are campaigning to raise the status of nurses.* | **lower | change | maintain | lose** *Churches seem to have lost some of their status.* | **apply for** *She applied for resident status but was turned down.* | **acquire, get** *They have acquired refugee status.* | **grant sb | deny sb, refuse sb** *Women are still denied equal status in the company.*
● STATUS + NOUN **symbol** *Scars are status symbols among mountain bike riders.*
● PREP. **~ as** *China's status as an economic superpower* **~ among** *The company has managed to maintain its status among retailers.*
● PHRASES **change in status** *the change in status of teachers*

status quo *noun*

● VERB + STATUS QUO **defend, keep, maintain, preserve** *There are many people who wish to maintain the status quo.* | **threaten, upset | change | restore**
● PHRASES **a return to the status quo** *They wanted a return to the status quo before the war.*

statute *noun*

● ADJ. **legal | federal, parliamentary | criminal**

● VERB + STATUTE **pass | comply with**
● STATUTE + NOUN **law** *the obligations of the employer in common and statute law* | **book** *This archaic law remained on the statute books until last year.*
● PREP. **by ~** *Local authorities are required by statute to provide care homes for the elderly.* **under (a/the) ~** *a trading company formed under statute*

stay *noun*

● ADJ. **lengthy, long, prolonged | brief, overnight, short, temporary | indefinite | 3-week, 3-weeks', week-long, etc. | comfortable, enjoyable, pleasant | hospital** *In recent years the average hospital stay for elderly patients has decreased.*
● VERB + STAY **enjoy** *Did you enjoy your stay in Prague?* | **shorten | extend, prolong** *She has extended her stay by three days.*
● PREP. **during a/the ~** *We did a lot of walking during our stay.* **throughout a/the ~** *It poured with rain throughout their stay.*
● PHRASES **the duration/length of (your) stay**

stay *verb*

● ADV. **behind, on** *Alex stayed behind when the others had gone.* ◇ *She failed her exam, and had to stay on at school for another year.* | **on** *My hat won't stay on!* | **(at) home, indoors** *financial incentives for women to stay at home with their children* | **away | here, there | late** *I'm staying late at the office tonight.* | **overnight | indefinitely** *We can't stay here indefinitely.*
● VERB + STAY **can/can't, could/couldn't** *I just couldn't stay away.* | **want to | decide to | be going to, intend to | let sb** *Won't you let me stay?* | **ask sb to, beg sb to, plead with sb to | persuade sb to**
● PREP. **for** *We ended up staying for lunch.* **till/until** *I'm going to stay until tomorrow.* **with** *'Stay with me,' he pleaded.*

steady *adj.*

1 not moving or shaking
● VERBS **be, feel, look, seem, sound | become | remain | hold sb/sth, keep sb/sth** *Hold the ladder steady!*
● ADV. **extremely, very | absolutely, perfectly, quite, rock** *His gaze was rock steady.* | **not quite** *She opened the letter with hands that were not quite steady.* | **almost**

2 developing/happening at a regular rate
● VERBS **be, seem | become | hold, remain** *Share prices have held steady over the last few days.*
● ADV. **remarkably, very | fairly, relatively**

steak *noun*

● ADJ. **juicy, tender | tough | medium, medium-rare, rare, well done** *I like my steak rare.* | **chuck, fillet, loin, rump, sirloin, T-bone** *a lightly-grilled fillet steak* | **braising, stewing | beef | gammon, salmon, etc.**
● VERB + STEAK **eat, have | cook, fry, grill, stew**
⇨ Special page at FOOD

steam *noun*

● ADJ. **hot, scalding | high-pressure**
● QUANT. **cloud, jet** *The saucepan on the cooker puffed little jets of steam.*
● VERB + STEAM **emit, generate, produce**
● STEAM + VERB **come, escape | rise** *Steam rose from her mug of cocoa.* | **condense | drive sth** *The engine is driven by steam.* | **hiss**
● STEAM + NOUN **power | engine, locomotive, ship, train, turbine | age**
● PHRASES **the age of steam** *Savour the sights and smells of the age of steam in the National Railway Museum.*

steamer *noun*

- ADJ. paddle | lake, river | pleasure | tramp
- PREP. by ~, on (board) a/the ~

steel *noun*

- ADJ. solid | forged, galvanized, mild, reinforced, rolled, stainless
- VERB + STEEL make, manufacture, produce | harden, temper
- STEEL + NOUN ingot, sheet | industry, manufacture, mill, plant, works
- PREP. in ~ *building in steel and aluminium*

steep *adj.*

- VERBS be, look, seem | become, get
- ADV. extremely, impossibly, incredibly, really, terribly, very *an incredibly steep hill* | increasingly | fairly, pretty, quite, rather, relatively | deceptively *The terrain is often deceptively steep* (= steeper than you expect).

steering *noun*

- ADJ. heavy, light | power/power-assisted
- VERB + STEERING have *Does the car have power steering?*
- STEERING + NOUN column, wheel

steering wheel *noun*

- VERB + STEERING WHEEL grip, hold | turn *Turn the steering wheel hard to the right.* | grab *He grabbed the steering wheel from her to prevent the car going off the road.* | lose control of

stem *noun*

- ADJ. long, tall | short | thick | slender, thin | flexible, strong | brittle, weak | iris, rose, etc.
- VERB + STEM break, cut (back/out), prune (back), shorten, trim *When the bush has finished flowering, cut back all the stems.*
- STEM + VERB break
- PREP. on a/the ~ *There are several leaves on each stem.*
- PHRASES the base of the stem *Cut half an inch off the base of each stem.*

stench *noun*

- ADJ. overpowering, powerful | unmistakable | appalling, foul, nauseating, sickening, terrible, unpleasant | acrid, fetid, putrid
- STENCH + VERB fill sth *The air was filled with the overpowering stench of decomposing vegetation.*

step *noun*

1 in walking, running, etc.

- ADJ. large, small | heavy, light | quick, slow | hesitant | involuntary *I gasped and took an involuntary step backwards.* | careful | unsteady
- VERB + STEP go, take *He'd only gone a few steps, when he realized he'd left his wallet behind.* | retrace *You might find your ticket if you retrace your steps back to the car.*
- PREP. ~ (away) from *She was only a step away from the cliff edge.* ~ towards *He took a hesitant step towards her.*
- PHRASES a spring in your step *I had a spring in my step when I walked into that office for the last time.* a step ahead/behind *He lagged a few steps behind.* a step back/backwards/forward/sideways, a step closer/nearer, with each/every step *He grew fainter with every step.*

2 in dancing

- ADJ. dance | jive, tango, etc.
- VERB + STEP execute, perform *He executed some jive*

steps on the pavement. | learn | keep in *She had trouble keeping in step.*
- PREP. in ~, out of ~ (with) *He was out of step with the music.*

3 action taken in order to achieve sth

- ADJ. big, considerable, giant, huge, massive | small | critical, crucial, decisive, essential, great, important, key, major, vital | first, initial, preliminary | final, last | additional, further, next *What's the next step?* | logical, necessary, reasonable *We shall take all necessary steps to prevent public disorder.* | active | forward, positive | backward, retrograde *The new law is seen by many as a backward step.* | bold, brave, reckless | dramatic, drastic, extraordinary, rare, unprecedented, unusual | irreversible, irrevocable *It suddenly struck her that having a baby was an irrevocable step.* | careful, precautionary | faltering, tentative *They have taken their first tentative steps towards democracy.* | practical | welcome | immediate, urgent *I shall take immediate steps to have this matter put right.* | false *One false step could mean disaster.*
- VERB + STEP go, make, take | follow *If you follow all the steps, nothing will go wrong.*
- PREP. ~ in *The move was a first step in establishing a union.* ~ to/towards *The talks mark a step towards peace.*
- PHRASES bring sth/be/come/move a step closer/nearer (to sth) *Greece moved a step closer to the World Cup finals with last night's win.* a short step from/to sth *It's only a short step from this disorder to complete chaos.* a step back/backwards/forward *The offer constitutes a considerable step forward.* step by step *a step-by-step guide to setting up an aquarium* a step further *If he goes one step further with this crazy idea, I'll resign.* a step in the right direction *The new speed limit does not solve the problem, but it is a step in the right direction.* a step on the road/way to sth

4 on stairs, a ladder, etc.

- ADJ. bottom, top
- VERB + STEP mind *Mind the step!*
- PREP. on a/the ~ *She paused on the top step.*
- PHRASES a step down/up *There are three steps down to the garden.*

5 steps set of steps

- ADJ. front | back | outside
- QUANT. flight *You have to go up four flights of steps to get up to the roof.*
- VERB + STEPS ascend, climb, go/run, etc. up, mount *She went up a flight of steps to the side entrance.* | descend, go/run, etc. down
- STEPS + VERB lead to sth *The front steps lead to an enormous terrace.*
- PREP. ~ (down/up) to *the steps down to the pool*
- PHRASES the bottom/foot/top of the steps

step *verb*

- ADV. briskly, quickly | hastily, smartly *He stepped back smartly from the edge.* | slowly | silently | delicately, lightly | carefully, gingerly *He stepped gingerly over the cat.* | boldly | aside, away, back, close, down, forward, inside, out, outside *Would you like to step inside for a few minutes?*
- PREP. across, from, in, in front of, into, on, onto, out of, over, past, through, towards *Don't step in the puddle.*

stereotype *noun*

- ADJ. common, popular, traditional, usual | negative | cultural, national, racial | gender, sexual | social
- VERB + STEREOTYPE create, produce | perpetuate, reinforce *Jokes perpetuate various national stereotypes.* | conform to, fit *Not all areas of the country fit the stereotypes of the poor north and the rich south.* | challenge, reject *a writer who challenges sexual stereotypes*

● PREP. **~ about** *common stereotypes about the French* **~ of** *the stereotype of women as passive victims*

sterile *adj.*

1 completely clean
● VERBS **be | become | remain | make sth | keep sth** *This top fits over the bottle and keeps the teat sterile.*
● ADV. **completely | virtually**

2 not able to produce young animals/babies
● VERBS **be | become | remain | leave sb, make sb**
● ADV. **permanently** *Male workers were made permanently sterile by this pesticide.*

3 with no interest or life
● VERBS **be | become, grow** *Their relationship had grown sterile over the years.*
● ADV. **very | increasingly** *the increasingly sterile debate on constitutional reform* | **largely | rather, somewhat**

sterling *noun*

● PHRASES **pounds sterling** *50 pounds sterling*
⇨ Note at CURRENCY

steward, stewardess *noun*

● ADJ. **chief, senior | air, cabin, ship's | wine | shop** *She was an active trade unionist and had been elected a shop steward.*
● VERB + STEWARD, STEWARDESS **act as | elect (sb)**
● PREP. **~ to** *Moore was acting as steward to Sir Michael le Fleming.*
⇨ Note at JOB

stick *noun*

● ADJ. **big, long | little, short | thick, thin**
● QUANT. **bundle | pile**
● VERB + STICK **brandish, wave** *A mob came over the hill yelling and brandishing sticks.*

stick *verb*

● ADV. **just, simply** *He simply stuck a pin in at random amongst the names of candidates.*
● PREP. **in, into, on, onto, through** *He stuck the note through her letter box.*

PHRASAL VERB
stick to sth
● ADV. **close, closely | rigidly, slavishly, strictly** *sticking slavishly to the rules* | **doggedly, firmly, resolutely, stubbornly** *She simply made a decision and resolutely stuck to it.*
● VERB + STICK TO STH **tend to** *I tended to stick to tried and tested techniques.* | **decide to | be determined to**

sticky *adj.*

● VERBS **be, feel | become, go**
● ADV. **horribly, really, very** *covered in a horribly sticky mess* | **all** *The rubber's gone all sticky.* | **a bit, rather, slightly** *The paint was still slightly sticky.*
● PREP. **with** *His hair was sticky with blood.*

stiff *adj.*

1 difficult to bend/move
● VERBS **be, feel, lie, look, sit, stand** *She lay stiff and still beside him.* | **become, get, go** *My trousers were getting stiff with mud.* ◇ *My fingers had gone stiff with cold.*
● ADV. **very | a bit, fairly, quite, rather**
● PREP. **with** *The clothes were stiff with dust and grease.*

2 having sore muscles
● VERBS **be, feel** *He felt stiff all over.* | **become, get, go** *You'll get stiff if you don't have a hot bath.* | **leave sb, make sb** *All that digging made me really stiff.*

● ADV. **really, very | all** *My arm's gone all stiff.* | **a bit, a little, rather**
● PREP. **from** *stiff from kneeling*

3 strong/severe
● VERBS **be, seem** *Their punishment seemed rather stiff.*
● ADV. **very** *in the face of some very stiff competition* | **a bit, fairly, quite, rather**

4 not friendly or relaxed
● VERBS **be, look, seem, sound** *She was aware that her words sounded stiff.* | **become**
● ADV. **very | a bit, a little, rather, slightly, somewhat** *His manner seemed rather stiff and impersonal.*

stigma *noun*

● ADJ. **social**
● VERB + STIGMA **carry** *Being an unmarried mother used to carry a social stigma.* | **remove** *Wider knowledge of the disease removed some of the stigma from it.* | **suffer (from)** *He still suffered the stigma of having been rejected for the army.*
● STIGMA + VERB **be attached to sth, be associated with sth** *There is still a lot of stigma attached to suicide.*
● PREP. **~ to** *There is no stigma to being made redundant.*

still *adj.*

1 not moving
● VERBS **be, hold, keep, lie, sit, stand, stay** *Hold still a minute while I pin your dress up.* ◇ *For goodness' sake, sit still!* | **hold sb/sth, keep sb/sth** *I held the cat still while the vet gave the injection.*
● ADV. **very | absolutely, quite, stock-** *He stood stock-still, hardly daring to breathe.*

2 calm and quiet
● VERBS **be, look, seem | become, go** *Suddenly everything went still.* | **remain**
● ADV. **very | completely** *It was a completely still, warm evening.* | **strangely** *The air was strangely still and silent.*

stillness *noun*

● ADJ. **absolute, great, utter | sudden** *There was a sudden stillness in the air.* | **eerie | inner**
● VERB + STILLNESS **break** *A voice behind the hedge broke the stillness.*
● PREP. **in (the)~** *He lay in absolute stillness.* ◇ *in the stillness of the night*

stimulate *verb*

● ADV. **greatly, significantly, strongly | further | effectively | directly** *An interest rate increase directly stimulates saving and reduces real expenditure.* | **intellectually** *activities designed to stimulate the children intellectually*
● VERB + STIMULATE **help (to) | be designed to, be intended to**

stimulating *adj.*

● VERBS **be, sound | find sb/sth**
● ADV. **extremely, really, very | intellectually, visually** *The programme contains some creative and visually stimulating material.*

stimulation *noun*

● ADJ. **direct | electrical** *electrical stimulation of nervous tissue* | **auditory, sensory, visual | sexual | intellectual, mental**
● VERB + STIMULATION **get** *You don't get any intellectual stimulation in this job.* | **give sb, provide (sb with)** *The playgroup provides plenty of stimulation for the children.* | **respond to**
● PHRASES **a lack of stimulation**

stimulus *noun*

- ADJ. **great, major, powerful, strong | negative, positive | external | initial | auditory, intellectual, sensory, verbal, visual**
- VERB + STIMULUS **act as, give, provide | react to, respond to**
- STIMULUS + VERB **come from sth** *The initial stimulus came from a letter in the newspaper.*
- PREP. **~for** *The very act of lying down in bed should provide a strong stimulus for sleep.* **~to** *A reduction in corporate tax should act as a stimulus to economic activity.*
- PHRASES **(in) response to a stimulus**

sting *noun*

1 of an insect, etc.
- ADJ. **dangerous, nasty, painful | bee, wasp, etc. | nettle, etc. | deadly, fatal**
- VERB + STING **have** *The scorpion has a sting that can be deadly.* **| get** *You can get a nasty sting from a jellyfish.* **| give sb | feel**

2 sharp pain
- ADJ. **hot, sharp** *the hot sting of tears*
- VERB + STING **feel** *He felt the sharp sting of the soap in his eyes.*

stink *noun*

1 very unpleasant smell
- ADJ. **acrid, overpowering**
- STINK + NOUN **bomb**
- PREP. **~of** *the acrid stink of cordite*

2 very strong complaint about sth
- ADJ. **tremendous**
- VERB + STINK **cause, kick up, make, raise** *The parents of the pupils say they'll kick up a stink if the school roof isn't repaired before the winter.*

stint *noun*

- ADJ. **long | brief**
- VERB + STINT **do** *He's doing a brief stint at the World Bank in Washington.* **| start | finish**
- PREP. **during a/the ~** *She met her husband during her stint at the London office.*

stipulation *noun*

- VERB + STIPULATION **make** *The only stipulation the building society makes is that house must be insured.* **| drop**
- PREP. **with the ~** *He left all his money to the town with the stipulation that it should be used to build a new football stadium.* **| ~ about/as to** *There's no stipulation as to the amount you can invest.*

stir *noun*

1 action of stirring
- ADJ. **good**
- VERB + STIR **give sth** *Give the mixture a good stir.*

2 general excitement or shock
- ADJ. **considerable, great, real**
- VERB + STIR **cause, create**
- PREP. **~ about/over** *There was quite a stir about the book.* **| ~ among/amongst** *The discovery caused something of a stir among physicists.*
- PHRASES **quite a/something of a stir**

stir *verb*

1 move a liquid round and round
- ADV. **thoroughly, well | carefully, gently | vigorously | gradually | all the time, constantly, continuously**

Bring to the boil, stirring all the time. **| occasionally | in** *Gradually stir in the beaten egg.*
- PREP. **into** *Chop an onion and stir it into the sauce.*

2 move
- ADV. **barely, hardly** *The wind came in tiny puffs that hardly stirred the surface of the water.* **| slightly | suddenly | restlessly** *The students stirred restlessly in their seats.* **| sleepily | uneasily**
- PHRASES **stir in your sleep**

3 make sb feel an emotion
- ADV. **deeply, greatly** *It was not music to set hearts on fire or deeply stir the emotions.* **| up** *Going back there stirred up a lot of memories for her.*

stirrup *noun*

- VERB + STIRRUP **adjust | rise in, stand (up) in** *She stood up in her stirrups to see where the others had gone.*
- STIRRUP + NOUN **leather** *She had to lengthen her stirrup leathers.*
- PREP. **in a/the ~** *He put his feet in the stirrups.*

stitch *noun*

1 in sewing
- ADJ. **blanket, chain, cross, running, seam, tacking, zigzag, etc.**
- VERB + STITCH **do, put, sew (sth) with** *Can you do chain stitch?* ◇ *Put a stitch in the corner of the pocket to keep it in place.* ◇ *The edge was sewn with blanket stitch.* **| remove, take out**

2 in knitting
- ADJ. **knitted | cable, garter, plain, purl, slip, stocking, tuck, etc.**
- VERB + STITCH **knit | cast on, cast off | drop, pick up**

3 in a wound
- ADJ. **dissolvable, dissolving, self-dissolving**
- VERB + STITCH **have** *I had to have five stitches when I cut my finger.* **| insert, put in | remove, take out | have out** *When are you having your stitches out?*
- STITCH + VERB **dissolve**
- PREP. **~ in** *He had twenty stitches in a head wound.*

stock *noun*

1 available supply of sth
- ADJ. **good, high, huge, large | low | adequate | declining, dwindling, falling** *dwindling fish stocks in the North Sea* **| surplus | buffer, reserve** *A buffer stock of grain was held in case of emergency shortages.* **| fresh, new | old | existing | fish, food, etc. | housing** *The housing stock is no longer large enough for the population.* **| capital, money | library**
- VERB + STOCK **carry, have, hold, keep** *The big supermarkets carry huge stocks of most goods.* **| add to, increase | dispose of, get rid of, reduce, sell off** *They're selling off their old stock cheap.* **| maintain, protect** *laws to protect fish stocks* **| replace, replenish**
- STOCK + VERB **be/go up, increase | be/go down, decline, dwindle, fall, run low** *Stocks of coal are running dangerously low.* **| last** *The offer is only available while stocks last.*
- STOCK + NOUN **cupboard, room (also stockroom) | levels | control**
- PREP. **from ~** *We can supply the table from stock.* **in ~** *Have you got futon beds in stock or will I have to order one?* **out of ~** *Red tights are out of stock.*

2 share in the capital of a company
- ADJ. **blue-chip, gilt-edged, index-linked**
- VERB + STOCK **acquire, buy, invest in, purchase | cash in, dispose of, sell | deal in, trade | have, hold, own | issue | value** *The stocks were valued at £100 000.*

- STOCK + VERB **be down/up | fall, go down, plummet, sink | go up, rise, soar**
- STOCK + NOUN **exchange, market | index**
- PREP. **in~s** *She's got about £30 000 in stocks.*
- PHRASES **investment in stocks, the value of the stocks** *The total value of the stocks was over £3 million.*

3 liquid used for making soups, sauces, etc.
- ADJ. **chicken, fish, vegetable, etc.**
- VERB + STOCK **make | thicken | dilute, reduce | flavour** *Flavour the stock with bay leaves.*
- STOCK + NOUN **cube**
- PREP. **in a/the~** *Poach the fish in the stock.*

stock *verb* **be stocked**

- ADV. **plentifully, well | fully, properly**
- PREP. **with** *shops stocked with cheap souvenirs*

stockbroker *noun*

- ADJ. **large | leading | private client | City**
- VERB + STOCKBROKER **consult**
- PREP. **through a~** *The bonds were sold through a stockbroker.*
- PHRASES **a firm of stockbrokers**
- ⇨ Note at JOB

stock exchange *noun*

- VERB + STOCK EXCHANGE **open | close** *Bahrain's stock exchange closed up 10.09 points today at 2160.09.*
- STOCK EXCHANGE + VERB **rally, rise** *The stock exchange rallied in response to the announcement of massive American investment.* **| fall**
- STOCK EXCHANGE + NOUN **collapse, crash**
- PREP. **on the~** *to lose money on the stock exchange*

stocking *noun*

- ADJ. **fishnet, sheer | 15-denier, etc. | laddered | Christmas** *trinkets you can use to fill a Christmas stocking*
- QUANT. **pair**
- VERB + STOCKING **pull on | peel off** *She slowly peeled off one stocking.* **| ladder** *She laddered her stocking on a bramble bush.*
- ⇨ Special page at CLOTHES

stomach *noun*

1 part of the body where food is digested
- ADJ. **empty, full** *You shouldn't drink wine on an empty stomach (= without eating food).* **| queasy, upset** *She's been off work with an upset stomach.* **| strong** *You need a strong stomach to go on the giant roller coaster.* **| weak**
- VERB + STOMACH **turn** *The smell of the dead dog turned his stomach.* **| settle** *He had a hangover, so he ordered a sandwich to settle his stomach.* **| settle in** *A feeling of nausea settled in her stomach.* **| pump** *He had his stomach pumped after taking an overdose.*
- STOMACH + VERB **churn, heave, lurch** *My stomach lurched as another big wave hit the boat.* **| rumble | tighten, turn (over), twist**
- STOMACH + NOUN **ache, bug, cancer, complaint, cramp, disorder, illness, pain, problem, ulcer, upset | lining, wall | acids, juices | contents** *Human remains were found among the stomach contents of the shark.* **| pump, tube**
- PREP. **in the/your~** *enzymes in the stomach*
- PHRASES **butterflies in your stomach** *I had butterflies in my stomach as I went to get my exam results.* **the pit of your stomach** *I felt a sickening feeling in the pit of my stomach when I saw the ambulance.*

2 front part of the body below the chest
- ADJ. **firm, flat | bulging, fat, flabby, large, stout | bloated, swollen | bare**

- VERB + STOMACH **hold in, pull in, suck in** *He sucked in his stomach as he walked past the girls.* **| lie on | clutch, hold** *'Call a doctor!' he said, clutching his stomach.* **| pat, rub** *'I'm eating for two now,' she said, patting her stomach.*
- STOMACH + VERB **protrude, stick out**
- STOMACH + NOUN **muscles | injury, strain, wound**
- PREP. **on the/your~** *I lay on my stomach on the beach.*

stone *noun*

1 hard solid substance
- ADJ. **heavy | hard, soft | rough, smooth | weathered | carved** *a carved stone fireplace* **| building**
- QUANT. **block, slab**
- VERB + STONE **break, cut, hew (sth from/out of)** *Convicts were made to break stone for the roads.* ◇ *The stone is cut into blocks ready for building.* ◇ *The walls were hewn from local stone.* **| dress | be built/carved/made from/in/(out) of, carve sth in** *names carved in stone*
- STONE + NOUN **block, flag, slab** *The path's stone flags were worn and broken.* **| arch/archway, bridge, building, floor, pillar, stairs, structure, wall, etc. | monument, sculpture | age**
- PREP. **in~** *He is a sculptor who works mainly in stone.*

2 small piece of rock
- ADJ. **sharp | smooth | round | loose** *Some loose stones tumbled down the slope behind her.* **| foundation, memorial, paving, stepping | grinding**
- QUANT. **heap, pile**
- VERB + STONE **hurl, throw** *The boys were caught throwing stones at passing trains.*

3 precious stone
- ADJ. **gem** (also **gemstone**), **precious, semi-precious**
- VERB + STONE **mine | cut | set** *She had the stone set in a ring.*
- STONE + VERB **glitter, shine**

4 measure of weight
- ⇨ Note at MEASURE

stool *noun*

- ADJ. **high, tall | three-legged | folding, fold-up | bar, kitchen, music, piano**
- VERB + STOOL **perch on/be perched on, sit (down) on** *He was perched on a bar stool, ordering a beer.* **| get off | drag up, pull up** *She pulled up a stool next to me.*

stop *noun*

1 stopping or staying
- ADJ. **long | brief, short | overnight | abrupt, sharp, sudden | emergency | scheduled, unscheduled | coffee, fuel, lunch, refreshment, refuelling, toilet, etc. | pit** *The cars made two pit stops during the race.*
- VERB + STOP **bring/draw sth to, put** *She brought the car to an abrupt stop.* ◇ *to put a stop to all the arguments* **| come to, draw to, slow to** *The truck came to a sudden stop.* **| screech to | have, make** *We had a lunch stop at Timperley.*
- STOP + NOUN **sign**
- PREP. **~at** *There will be a stop at Canterbury.* **~for** *a stop for refreshments*
- PHRASES **come to a dead/full stop** *Between twelve and two everything comes to a dead stop.*

2 for a bus, etc.
- ADJ. **bus, tram | request**
- VERB + STOP **get off at | miss** *We were chatting and missed our stop.*
- PREP. **at a/the~** *We dropped the kids off at the bus stop.* **between~s** *You're not allowed to get off between stops.*

stop *verb*

- ADV. **abruptly, dead, (dead) in your tracks, immediately, short, suddenly** *Suddenly he stopped dead: what was he doing?* ◊ *The question stopped Alice in her tracks.* | **altogether** *The sobs came less frequently, then stopped altogether.* | **for a moment, momentarily** | **never** *That phone never stops ringing!*
- VERB + STOP **can/can't, could/couldn't** *He couldn't stop thinking about her.* | **try to** | **be going to** *When is the violence going to stop?* | **want (sb/sth) to** *I was enjoying myself so much I didn't want to stop.*
- PREP. **from** *They tried to stop me from leaving.*

stopover *noun*

- ADJ. **brief**
- VERB + STOPOVER **have**
- PREP. **at a/the ~** *We had our tickets checked at each stopover.* **during a/the ~** *During our two-day stopover in Bangkok we saw most of the sights.*

stoppage *noun*

- ADJ. **complete** | **work**
- VERB + STOPPAGE **call** *The stoppage was called to protest against wage cuts.* | **threaten** | **be involved in** | **end**
- PREP. **during a/the ~**

storage *noun*

- ADJ. **safe** *the safe storage of nuclear weapons* | **cold** | **disk** *the available disk storage capacity* | **food, water, etc.** | **data, information, etc.**
- VERB + STORAGE **put sth in/into** *The strawberries are put into cold storage for several months.* | **take sth out of**
- STORAGE + NOUN **facilities** | **device, medium, system** *digital storage devices* | **area, capacity, space** | **building, cabinet, compartment, cupboard, depot, room, shed, unit** *a handy storage compartment below the oven* | **bin, container, jar, tank, vessel** | **cost** | **life** *The cheese has a storage life of two months.*
- PREP. **in ~** *All their furniture is in storage until they come back from Africa.*

store *noun*

1 shop
- ADJ. **big, large, major** | **small** | **retail** | **department** | **self-service** | **high-street, local, village** | **chain** | **discount** | **convenience, corner, general** | **electrical, grocery, hardware, etc.**
- QUANT. **chain**
- STORE + VERB **sell sth**
- STORE + NOUN **chain** | **account, card** | **assistant, manager, owner** | **detective**
- PREP. **at/in a/the ~**

2 supply for future use
- ADJ. **considerable, good, great, inexhaustible, large, vast** | **small** | **food** | **fat** *your body's fat stores*
- VERB + STORE **have, keep** | **build up**
- STORE + NOUN **cupboard, room** (also **storeroom**)
- PREP. **~ of** *a vast store of knowledge*

3 place for keeping sth
- ADJ. **cold, cool, dry** *Beef and lamb are hung in a cold store for at least a week.* | **temporary** | **ammunition, equipment, grain, etc.**
- STORE + VERB **hold sth** *The grain store holds several thousand tonnes.*
- PREP. **in a/the ~** *You'll find a ladder in the equipment store.* | **~ for** *We're using the shed as a temporary store for all our stuff.*

store *verb*

- ADV. **carefully, properly, safely** *The paintings were carefully stored in crates dependent on their size.* | **conveniently, easily** *Butane can be conveniently stored as a liquid in a can.* | **electronically** *electronically stored information* | **separately** | **together** | **away, up**

storey *noun*

- ADJ. **lower** | **top, upper**
- VERB + STOREY **have** *The house has three storeys.* | **occupy** *The kitchen occupies the lower storey.*
- PREP. **on a/the ~** *I live on the top storey.*
- PHRASES **5/10, etc. storeys high** *The building is four storeys high.*

storm *noun*

1 period of bad weather
- ADJ. **bad, big, devastating, disastrous, ferocious, fierce, great, heavy, raging, severe, terrible, tremendous, violent** | **approaching, gathering, impending** *the dark clouds of an approaching storm* | **freak** | **autumn, summer, winter** | **tropical** | **monsoon** | **dust, electric/electrical, lightning, magnetic, rain, sand, snow, thunder** (also **thunderstorm**)
- VERB + STORM **be in for** *I think we're in for a storm* (= going to have one).
- STORM + VERB **hit sth, strike sth** *It was the worst storm to hit London this century.* | **rage** *The storm raged all night.* | **be brewing, be coming** *A storm had been brewing all day.* | **blow up, break, burst** *The storm broke while we were on the mountain.* | **abate, blow itself out, blow over, pass, subside** *The storm blew over after a couple of hours.* | **batter sth, buffet sth, lash sth, ravage sth, sweep sth** *a boat battered by the storm* ◊ *Winter storms swept the coasts.* | **last** *The storm lasted for three days.*
- STORM + NOUN **cloud** (often figurative) *In 1939 the storm clouds gathered over Europe.* | **damage, losses** *Insurance companies face hefty payouts for storm damage.*
- PREP. **during/in a/the ~**
- PHRASES **at the height of the storm, the calm/lull before the storm, the eye of the storm**

2 violent display of strong feeling
- ADJ. **approaching, coming, gathering** *a gathering storm of discontent* | **political**
- VERB + STORM **arouse, cause, create, provoke, raise, spark** | **face** | **ride out, weather** *The government is determined to ride out the political storm sparked by its new immigration policy.*
- STORM + VERB **blow up, break, burst, erupt** | **blow over, pass**
- PREP. **amid a/the ~** *The band toured Ireland amid a storm of controversy.* | **~ between, ~ of** *His comments created a storm of protest in the media.* **~ over** *A storm blew up between Britain and America over Venezuela.*

story *noun*

1 account of events/people, true or invented
- ADJ. **true** | **plausible** | **false, made-up** *She told the police a false story about being attacked.* | **apocryphal** | **cock-and-bull, tall** *No one would believe such a tall story.* | **official** *The official story was that the singer had broken his arm falling in the shower.* | **wild** | **convincing** | **charming, compelling, delightful, dramatic, exciting, fantastic, fascinating, good, great, interesting, intriguing, nice, wonderful** | **amazing, bizarre, colourful, crazy, extraordinary, incredible, outrageous, remarkable, strange** | **inspiring** | **amusing, entertaining, funny** | **epic** *the epic story of a family's escape from war* | **complex, elaborate** | **straightforward** | **awful, horrific, horrifying, nasty, shocking, terrible, tragic** | **sorry** *His life*

was a sorry story of betrayal and rejection. | **depressing, heart-rending, moving, poignant, sad** | **improbable** *The film tells the improbable story of a monkey that becomes a politician.* | **well known** | **familiar** *the familiar story of a star who turns to drink and drugs* | **popular** *There is one popular story in the village of a man-eating cat that lives in the forest.* | **life, success** *She told them her life story.* | **hard-luck, rags-to-riches** *He was boring people with more of his hard-luck stories.* ◇ *The film is the rags-to-riches story of a country girl who becomes a famous singer.* | **after-dinner** | **coherent** *The film lacks a coherent story.* | **full, whole** *I suspected he hadn't told us the whole story.* | **short** *a collection of short stories* | **children's** | **classic** | **bedtime** | **mythical, mythological** | **adventure, Bible, biblical, crime, detective, fairy, ghost, horror, love, private-eye, spy, suspense**

• QUANT. **fragment** *We had difficulty in piecing together the fragments of her story.* | **collection** *a collection of stories by modern writers*

• VERB + STORY **read (sb)** *My dad sometimes read me a story at bedtime.* | **write** | **narrate, recount, relate, tell (sb)** | **embellish, embroider** | **believe** *The police didn't believe her story.* | **stick to** *We must stick to our story about the accident.* | **change** *At first he denied everything, but then he changed his story and said it was an accident.* | **swap** *We swapped stories about our worst teachers.* | **circulate, spread**

• STORY + VERB **abound, circulate, get about, go around/round, spread** *Stories abound of vandalism and looting.* ◇ *A story was going round that the factory was in line for closure.* | **emerge** | **begin, open, start** *The story opens with a man hiding from the police under a woman's skirt.* | **progress, unfold** *The motives of the hero become clearer as the story unfolds.* | **end** | **be called sth, be entitled sth** | **be set in ...** *The story is set in Poland in the 1930s.* | **be based on sth** | **concern sth, involve sth, revolve around sth** | **contain sth** | **illustrate sth** *This story illustrates the dangers of living on credit.*

• STORY + NOUN **teller** (also **storyteller**) | **telling** (also **storytelling**) | **line** (also **storyline**) *His novels always have the same basic storyline.*

• PREP. **~about** *a story about time travel* **~of** *the story of the Beatles*

• PHRASES **but that's another story** *Many years later I returned to Africa but that's another story* (= I am not going to talk about it now). | **it's a long story** *'How come you've only got one shoe on?' 'It's a long story.'* **sb's half/side of the story** *The teacher punished me without listening to my side of the story.* **so the story goes, the story goes that ...** (= used to describe what people are saying although it may not be correct) *She never saw him again—or so the story goes.* **the story of my life** *Out of work with no money—that's the story of my life.* **to cut a long story short** *Anyway, to cut a long story short* (= not to give all the details), *we had this argument and I haven't seen him since.* **a version of a story** *According to Rachel's version of the story, they threw the key in the river.*

2 report in a newspaper, etc.

• ADJ. **big, top** *The biggest story of the day was the signing of the peace agreement.* ◇ *And now back to our top story tonight ...* | **exclusive** | **main** | **full** *Full story on page 3.* | **scare** *scare stories about the harmful effects of the vaccination* | **inside** *The magazine gives the inside story of life in a rock band.* | **sensational** | **lurid, sordid, spicy** *lurid stories of politicians' sexual adventures* | **cover, front-page, lead** *The magazine chose the peace process as its cover story.* | **news**

• VERB + STORY **file, write** *More than one correspondent filed a story about the incident.* | **carry, print, publish, run** *Every newspaper carried the story.*

• PREP. **~about, ~of** *the story of his arrest*

stow *verb*

• ADV. **carefully, neatly, safely** | **away**

• PREP. **in** *The luggage was now safely stowed away in the back of the truck.*

straight *adj.*

1 not bent or curved

• VERBS **be, look** | **become** | **stay** | **keep sth** *Keep your back absolutely straight.*

• ADV. **absolutely, completely, dead, perfectly** *Keep going in a dead straight line.* ◇ *His teeth were white and perfectly straight.* | **almost, more or less, nearly, practically** | **fairly, relatively**

2 level/upright

• VERBS **be, look** | **hang sth, put sth** *Can you hang that sign straight for me?*

• ADV. **absolutely, completely, perfectly, quite** | **almost, more or less, nearly**

3 tidy/in order

• VERBS **be** | **get sth, put sth** *I'm trying to get the house straight before the weekend.* ◇ *She tidied up and put the ornaments straight.*

4 honest and truthful

• VERBS **be** *I think he was pretty straight with me.*

• ADV. **absolutely, completely, totally** | **fairly, pretty**

• PREP. **with** *Are you being completely straight with her?*

5 clear/understood

• VERBS **be** | **get sth**

• ADV. **absolutely** *Let's get this absolutely straight.*

straightforward *adj.*

1 clear and simple

• VERBS **appear, be, look, prove, seem, sound** | **find sth** *I think you'll find it all quite straightforward.*

• ADV. **extremely, remarkably, very** | **absolutely, entirely, perfectly, quite** *Look, it's perfectly straightforward—just multiply everything by five.* | **by no means, far from, hardly, less than** *Getting funding for the project was far from straightforward.* | **comparatively, fairly, pretty, quite, reasonably, relatively** | **apparently** | **deceptively** *The answer to this question is deceptively straightforward* (= more straightforward than it looks).

2 honest

• VERBS **be, seem**

• ADV. **very** | **quite** | **refreshingly** *a refreshingly straightforward attitude*

• PREP. **about, with** *He was quite straightforward with us about the difficulties involved.*

strain *noun*

1 severe demand on strength, resources, etc.

• ADJ. **considerable, enormous, great, heavy, real, severe, terrible, tremendous** *It's a real strain having to get up so early!* | **slight** | **increasing** | **constant** | **excessive, intolerable, unbearable, undue** | **emotional, financial, mental, nervous, physical, psychological** *The mental strain of sharing an office with Alison was starting to tell.* | **breaking** *a fishing line with a 15lb breaking strain*

• VERB + STRAIN **be/come under, feel, suffer (from)** *Television newsreaders come under enormous strain.* ◇ *After weeks of overtime, she was starting to feel the strain.* | **cause, create, impose, place, put** *Increasing demand is placing undue strain on services.* | **ease, reduce** | **cope with, stand, take** | **increase**

• STRAIN + VERB **show, take its toll (on sb), tell (on sb)** *After six weeks of uncertainty, the strain was beginning to take its toll.*

• PREP. **under the~** *The ice gave way under the strain.* ◇ *He broke under the strain of having to work twelve hours a*

day. | ~ **on** *There's too much strain on the corner of the table.*
• PHRASES **a bit of a strain** *I found it a bit of a strain making conversation with her.* **signs of strain** *After three years, their marriage was beginning to show signs of strain.* **stresses and strains** *the stresses and strains of a long day* **take the strain off sb/out of sth** *The new scheme is designed to take the strain out of shopping.*

2 injury
• ADJ. **bad | slight | back, eye, muscle, thigh, etc.** (eye strain is only uncountable)
• VERB + STRAIN **have, be suffering from | get** *You'll get eye strain if you don't put the light on.* | **recover from, shake off** *Gerrard will play if he can shake off a slight thigh strain.*

strain verb

1 make a great effort to do sth
• ADV. **hard** *straining hard to understand* | **forward** *I strained forward to get a better view.*
• VERB + STRAIN **have to**
• PREP. **against** *The dogs were straining against the sledge.* **at** *Several men were straining at a rope, trying to move the stalled vehicle.* **for** *Their ears strained for any slight sound.*
• PHRASES **strain to hear/see sth** *We had to strain to hear what was being said.*

2 put a lot of pressure on sth
• ADV. **seriously, severely** *The dispute severely strained relations between the two countries.*

strained adj.

1 worried and tense
• VERBS **be, feel, look, seem, sound**
• ADV. **very | a bit, a little, rather** *She looked rather strained and miserable.*

2 not natural or friendly
• VERBS **be | become, grow | remain** *The atmosphere remained somewhat strained all evening.*
• ADV. **extremely, severely, very** *Relations between the two countries had become severely strained.* | **increasingly | a bit, a little, rather, slightly, somewhat**

strait noun

1 narrow piece of water connecting seas, etc.
• ADJ. **narrow**
• VERB + STRAIT **go through, pass through | enter**
• STRAIT + VERB **separate sth** *The oil terminal is in the narrow strait that separates the island from the mainland.*
• PREP. **across the~** *He tried to swim across the Straits of Gibraltar.* **in the ~** *a ship anchored in the Straits of Hormuz* **on the ~** *The town is on the straits between the Black Sea and the Mediterranean.* **through the~** *Many hundreds of vessels pass through the straits each year.* | **~between**

2 straits trouble
• ADJ. **desperate, dire, serious | financial**
• PREP. **in~** *The business is in dire financial straits.*

strand noun

1 single thread, hair, etc.
• ADJ. **long | thick, thin | loose | single**
• VERB + STRAND **twist (together), weave (together)** *She wove the four coloured strands together into a ribbon.*
• PREP. **~of** *a loose strand of hair*

2 one part of a story, idea, etc.
• ADJ. **important, main | different, distinct, separate, various** *At the end, all the different strands of the story are brought together.*

• VERB + STRAND **bring together, draw together, pull together, weave together | disentangle, unravel**
• STRAND + VERB **come together**
• PREP. **~to** *There are three main strands to the policy.* **~in/within** *There are various strands in feminist thinking.*
• PHRASES **strands of opinion/thought**

stranded adj.

• VERBS **be | become, end up, find yourself, get** *We ended up stranded in Paris with no money.* ◇ *Some people found themselves stranded in the lifts as the power failed yet again.* ◇ *We got stranded in the city centre after we missed the last bus home.* | **leave sb** *Thousands of air travellers were left stranded by the strike.*

strange adj.

• VERBS **appear, be, feel, look, seem, smell, sound, taste | consider sth, find sth, regard sth as, think sth** *His behaviour was regarded as very strange.*
• ADV. **extremely, really, very | a bit, fairly, a little, pretty, quite, rather, somewhat** *He's quite nice, but a bit strange.*
• PREP. **to** *Their accent was strange to her ears.*

stranger noun

• ADJ. **complete, perfect, total | virtual | passing**
• PREP. **~to** *He was a complete stranger to me.* ◇ *She was a stranger to the place*
• PHRASES **almost a stranger** *His years abroad had made him almost a stranger with his family.* **a stranger here** *You're a stranger here, aren't you?* **a stranger in/to these parts** *A stranger to these parts would be confused by some of the local customs.*

strangle verb

• ADV. **almost, half, nearly**
• VERB + STRANGLE **try to**
• PREP. **with** *He was strangled with a scarf.*
• PHRASES **be found strangled**

strap noun

• ADJ. **broad, wide | narrow | tight | loose | adjustable, detachable** *The bag comes with detachable straps.* | **elastic, elasticated, padded | carrying, safety** *a portable radio with a carrying strap* | **ankle, chest, shoulder, waist, wrist, etc. | bra, watch, etc.**
• VERB + STRAP **buckle (up), do up, fasten | unbuckle, undo, unfasten | tighten | loosen | adjust | attach, clip on, fit** *He clipped on his safety strap.* ◇ *The camera was fitted with a strap.*
• PREP. **on a/the~** *His binoculars were on a strap round his neck.* | **~across, ~around/round, etc.** *She had a wide leather strap around her wrist.*

strap verb

• ADV. **safely | firmly, tightly | down, in, on** *He strapped his gun belt on.*
• PREP. **into** *Make sure that the child is strapped tightly into the buggy.* **to**

strategy noun

• ADJ. **effective, good, successful | bad, poor | clear, coherent | viable | future | long-term, medium-term, short-term | basic, broad, general, overall** *Their overall strategy is quite good, but one or two of the details could be improved.* | **comprehensive | global** *a global marketing strategy* | **grand | draft | dual, two-pronged** *The government has employed a dual strategy to achieve these two objectives.* | **radical | high-risk, risky | defensive | prevention | economics-based, market-oriented, etc.** *a*

customer-oriented business strategy | **anti-inflationary, anti-racist,** etc. | **survival** | **defence, military** | **campaign, election, electoral, government, political** | **pedagogic, teaching** | **learning** | **business, commercial, company, corporate, financial, investment, management/managerial, marketing, product, promotional, recruitment, research, sales** | **economic, energy, environmental, industrial, legislative,** etc.
• VERB + STRATEGY **have** | **design, develop, devise, draw up, formulate, map out, plan, work out** A coherent strategy for getting more people back to work needs to be developed. ◇ The council is drawing up a strategy to meet the needs of the homeless. | **explore** It is certainly a strategy worth exploring. | **adopt, decide (on), employ, follow, implement, pursue, use** They're pursuing a strategy of massive retaliation. | **outline, propose, set out, unveil** The document sets out the government's new strategy. | **change, revise** | **focus** The company will now focus its strategy on its core business areas. | **abandon**
• STRATEGY + VERB **be based on sth** | **be aimed at sth, be designed to** a strategy aimed at reducing the risk of accidents | **consist of sth, involve sth** | **work** The company's financial strategy is not working. | **fail**
• STRATEGY + NOUN **development, formulation** | **review** | **document, paper**
• PREP. **in a/the ~** the key idea in their strategy | **~ for** to develop an effective strategy for change ~ **on** the party's strategy on poverty ~ **towards** a comprehensive strategy towards regional development
• PHRASES **a change in strategy** The coming year may herald a change in strategy for major publishers. **the adoption/development/formulation of a strategy** The money will go towards the development of new product and sales strategies. **the implementation/pursuit of a strategy** Their single-minded pursuit of this controversial strategy led to their fall from power. **part of a strategy** He pretended that resigning was part of his long-term career strategy.

straw noun

• ADJ. **fresh**
• QUANT. **bale** I sat on a bale of straw near the fire.
• PREP. **in (the) ~** The rat hid in the straw. **on (the) ~** The animals sleep on straw.

strawberry noun

• QUANT. **punnet** I bought a punnet of strawberries.
• STRAWBERRY + NOUN **bed, plant**
⇨ Special page at FRUIT

stray verb

• ADV. **far** The animals hadn't strayed too far. | **accidentally, involuntarily** Her eyes strayed involuntarily.
• VERB + STRAY **allow sth to** new penalties for owners who allow their dogs to stray
• PREP. **from** Be careful not to stray from the path. **into, off, to** His eyes strayed to the telephone. ◇ (figurative) Her thoughts strayed to the journey ahead of her.

streak noun

1 thin line
• ADJ. **dark** There were dark streaks down her cheeks where she had been crying. | **faint, pale**
• PREP. **~ of** The last streaks of light faded from the sky.
• PHRASES **a streak of lightning** A streak of lightning forked across the sky. **a streak of red, white,** etc. She had a few streaks of grey in her black hair.

2 aspect of sb's character
• ADJ. **strong** | **hidden** | **adventurous, competitive, independent, mean, puritanical, rebellious, ruthless, selfish, stubborn, vicious**

• VERB + STREAK **have** Most of the players have a strong competitive streak. | **reveal, show** She suddenly revealed a mean streak in her character.
• PREP. **with a ~** Holidays in the Australian outback are for those with an adventurous streak. | **~ of** There was a streak of insanity in the family.

3 period of good/bad luck
• ADJ. **winning** | **losing**
• VERB + STREAK **be on** The team has been on a winning streak since it won against Lazio.

stream noun

1 small river
• ADJ. **little, small** | **shallow** | **clear** | **fast-flowing** | **bubbling** We picnicked beside a bubbling stream. | **mountain, underground**
• VERB + STREAM **cross**
• STREAM + VERB **flow, run** The stream flows through a narrow valley.
• STREAM + NOUN **bed**
• PREP. **across a/the ~, down a/the ~, in a/the ~** There are small fish in the stream. **on a/the ~** a leaf floating on the stream **up a/the ~**
• PHRASES **the side/edge of the stream**

2 continuous flow of a liquid/gas/light
• ADJ. **thin** | **air, gas**
• VERB + STREAM **let in**
• STREAM + VERB **flow** A stream of blood flowed from the wound.
• PREP. **~ of**

3 continuous flow of people/vehicles/things happening
• ADJ. **constant, continuous, endless, never-ending, steady** a constant stream of letters ◇ Cars filed past in an endless stream.
• VERB + STREAM **let loose/out**
• PREP. **~ of** He let loose a stream of abuse.

streamline verb

• ADV. **perfectly**
• PREP. **for** Dolphins are perfectly streamlined for movement in the water.

street noun

• ADJ. **broad, wide** | **narrow** | **bustling, busy, congested, crowded** | **pedestrianized, traffic-free** Most local people support the idea of traffic-free streets. | **deserted, desolate, empty, lonely, quiet** | **noisy** | **dark** | **bright, well-lit** | **dim, dimly-lit, gloomy** | **winding** | **steep** | **cobbled, paved** | **unpaved** | **clean** | **dusty, filthy, grubby** | **dangerous, mean, unsafe** He grew up on the mean streets of one of the city's toughest areas. | **leafy, tree-lined** | **one-way, two-way** | **dead-end** | **main, principal** | **back, side** a rundown house in the back streets of London ◇ a bar in a side street off Oxford Street | **city, village** | **right** | **wrong** You've taken the wrong street. | **shopping** the town's main shopping street | **residential, suburban, urban**
• VERB + STREET **go along/down/up, take, turn down/into/up** Take the second street on the right after the bridge. ◇ We turned down a dead-end street by mistake. | **cross** | **block, cordon off** | **patrol** The police have been patrolling the streets in this area since the murder. | **roam, throng, walk** Gangs roamed the streets at night. ◇ Crowds thronged the streets. | **clear** Police were told to clear the streets of drug dealers before the Olympics. | **widen**
• STREET + VERB **go, lead, run** | **bend, curve, turn** | **be lined with sth** streets lined with cafes | **be named sth, be named after sb/sth** Mozart is remembered by a street named after him.
• STREET + NOUN **corner** | **map, plan** | **layout, network, pattern** the dense street pattern of the old town |

name, number, sign *Most street names were changed under the new regime.* ◊ *The shops had no street numbers on.* | **lamp, light, lighting** | **parking** | **crime, gang** | **attack, battle, brawl, fight, fighting, robbery, violence** *He suffered extensive injuries in a street attack.* ◊ *street fighting between police and stone-throwing youths* | **demonstration, protest** | **party, procession** | **cleaner, sweeper** | **door** *There were photographers outside the street door so she used a back entrance.* | **market** | **entertainer, entertainment, musician, performer, theatre** | **pedlar, seller, trader, vendor** | **hustler** *Tourists need to be wary of street hustlers near the station.* | **cred/credibility, culture, fashion, life, wisdom** *His spell in prison gained him a lot of street cred.* ◊ *the street culture of working-class youth* | **collection** *The charity is having a street collection in aid of the local hospital.* | **children, kids, urchins** *a charity set up to house street children* | **girls** (= prostitutes) | **value** *drugs with a street value of £5 million*

● PREP. **across a/the~** *He could see her across the street.* **along a/the~** *They walked along the street.* **down a/the~** *A band was playing a little way down the street.* **in a/the~** *We live in Barker Street.* (**out**) **in a/the~** *A couple were arguing out in the street.* **into a/the~** *She stepped out into the street.* ◊ *He turned into a side street.* **off a/the~** *a club just off William Street* ◊ *a scheme to keep teenagers off the streets* (**out**) **on the~s** *Thousands of people were out on the streets for the protest.* **through the~s** *He wandered through the streets of Calcutta.* **up a/the~** *There's a chemist's just up the street.*

● PHRASES **at/above/below street level, the end/top of the street, the other side of the street, the street on the left/right**

strength *noun*

1 how strong sb/sth is
● ADJ. **enormous, great, immense** | **high** *The material has exceptionally high strength for its weight.* | **greater, superior** *His superior physical strength won him the title.* | **growing** | **continuing** *the continuing strength of the pound* | **relative** | **surprising, unexpected** | **superhuman, supernatural** | **brute** *He got the door open with brute strength.* | **extra** *They are reinforced with steel for extra strength.* | **collective** | **emotional, inner** | **muscle, muscular, physical** | **economic, electoral, financial, industrial, military** | **numerical** *the relative numerical strengths of men and women in the group* | **police, union,** etc. | **bargaining** | **wind** | **alcoholic**
● VERB + STRENGTH **have** *He had just enough strength to reach for the phone.* | **find, summon up** *I'm trying to summon up the strength to do some more work.* | **build up, gain, gather** *You need to try and build up your strength before the winter.* ◊ *The opinion that the president should stand down has gained considerable strength.* | **gain in, grow in, increase in** | **vary in** *These wines vary in strength between 11° and 15°.* | **lose** | **get back, recover, regain** | **give sb/sth, lend sb/sth** *Her love and support gave me strength.* ◊ *The metal reinforcement gives it the strength to resist the high winds.* | **sap** *The series of steep hills sapped the cyclists' strength.* | **conserve, save** | **draw (on), use** *She was able to draw on her immense inner strength.* | **put** *He put all his strength into reorganizing the department.* | **take** *It took all his strength to open the box.* | **test** *The Moroccan athlete ran a fast lap to test the strength of the other runners.* | **increase** | **reduce, undermine** *Her unwillingness to answer questions undermined the strength of her position.*
● STRENGTH + VERB **grow, increase** | **decline, ebb (away), fail, falter, wane** *The country's economic strength is declining.* ◊ *Her strength was ebbing fast, so her children were called to her bedside.*
● PREP. **below/under ~** *Injuries meant that the Dutch team was below strength for the final.* **with ~** *She pushed him away with unexpected strength.*

● PHRASES **at full strength** *The orchestra was at full strength for the Mahler symphony.* **be/get back to full strength** *I'm still not quite back to full strength after my illness.* **every ounce of strength** *She summoned up every ounce of strength she possessed.* **a feat of strength** *He used to entertain people with his feats of strength.* **a pillar/tower of strength** *He was a tower of strength to his sisters when their father died.* **a position of strength** *They are negotiating from a position of strength.* **reserves of strength** *When she had twins, she discovered reserves of strength that she didn't know she had.* **a show of strength** *50 000 troops massed on the border in the biggest show of strength to date.* **a source of strength** *Her childhood memories were a great source of strength when her mother was killed.* **strength born of desperation/fear/panic,** etc. *With strength born of pure panic, she threw her attacker to the ground.* **strength of character/purpose/will, strength of feeling, the strength of your position, a test/trial of strength** *Today's vote is being seen as a test of strength for the government.* ◊ *The dispute developed into a trial of strength between management and the union.* **with all your strength** *She threw the rope with all her strength.*

2 useful quality
● ADJ. **great** | **real**
● VERB + STRENGTH **exploit, play to** *The team may not have the best players, but it plays to its strengths.*
● STRENGTH + VERB **lie in sth** *Her great strength lies in her flexibility.*
● PHRASES **strengths and weaknesses**

strengthen *verb*

● ADV. **considerably, enormously, greatly, immeasurably, significantly, substantially** *The success in the election strengthened the party's position considerably.* | **further** *This merger will further strengthen the company and ensure its continued success.* | **merely** *This temporary setback merely strengthened her resolve.* | **gradually**
● VERB + STRENGTHEN **help (to), serve to** | **be designed to** *These exercises are designed to strengthen your stomach muscles.*
● PREP. **against** *The euro has strengthened against the dollar.*
● PHRASES **an attempt/effort to strengthen sth, be aimed at strengthening sth** *The new law is aimed at strengthening protective measures for workers.* **measures to strengthen sth**

stress *noun*

1 state of tension
● ADJ. **acute, considerable, extreme, great, high, severe** *Separation is a time of high emotional stress.* | **excessive** | **greater, increased** | **low** | **daily** *the daily stress of teaching* | **emotional, mental, psychological, social** | **economic, financial** *The high mortgage payments put them under severe financial stress.*
● QUANT. **level** *Many workers experience a high level of stress in their daily life.*
● VERB + STRESS **cause, create** *A divorce causes children great emotional stress.* | **avoid, remove** | **add to, increase** | **reduce, relieve** | **be under, experience, have, suffer (from)** *He's been under a lot of stress lately.* | **cope with, handle, manage, stand, take** *He's had to give up his job as leader of the project—he just couldn't take the stress.*
● STRESS + VERB **bring sth about/on** *an illness brought on by stress*
● STRESS + NOUN **level** *high stress levels* | **control, management** *Staff are encouraged to go on stress management courses.*
● PREP. **under ~** *He broke under stress and had to leave.*
● PHRASES **a source of stress** *An overcrowded workplace can be a major source of stress.* **a symptom of stress** *Tiredness is one of the most common symptoms of stress.*

2 emphasis that shows importance
- ADJ. **enormous, great | particular, special | equal | undue**
- VERB + STRESS **lay, place, put** *I must lay great stress on the need for secrecy.*
- PREP. **with the ~ on** *a study of child development, with the stress on acquisition of social skills* | **~on** *There's been a lot of stress on getting drug sellers off the streets.*

3 emphasis on a word, syllable, etc.
- ADJ. **main, major, primary, strong | secondary, weak | sentence, word**
- VERB + STRESS **carry, have, take** *Italian words usually have the main stress on the penultimate syllable in the word.* ◇ *The first syllable takes the stress.* | **place, put | mark** *Mark the primary stress in each word.*
- STRESS + VERB **fall, go** *Where does the stress fall in 'psychological'?*
- STRESS + NOUN **mark | pattern**
- PREP. **~on** *There's a stress on the second syllable.*

4 physical force
- ADJ. **enormous, high | low | constant | equal** *There is equal stress on all parts of the structure.*
- VERB + STRESS **exert, set up** *The tower exerts an enormous stress on the walls.* ◇ *The movements set up stresses in the earth's crust.* | **apply, put, subject sth to** *Stress is applied to the wood to make it bend.* ◇ *Standing all day puts stress on your feet.* ◇ *The buttresses are subjected to constant stress.* | **bear, take, withstand | increase, reduce | transfer, transmit | calculate** *Engineers calculated the stresses borne by each of the bridge supports.*
- PREP. **under~** *Some woods warp under stress.*

stress *verb*

- ADV. **heavily, strongly** *He stressed the point very strongly that all these services cost money.* | **constantly, continually, repeatedly** *She has constantly stressed the government's poor record in this area.* | **rightly** *Doctors have rightly stressed the importance of exercise.*
- VERB + STRESS **can only, must** *I must stress that we still know very little about this disease.* | **tend to** *Private schools tend to stress the more academic subjects.* | **be anxious to, be at pains to, be careful to, be keen to** *She is at pains to stress the cultural differences between the two countries.* | **be important to**
- PHRASES **be worth stressing sth** *It is worth stressing that this was only a relatively small survey.*

stressful *adj.*

- VERBS **be, prove, sound | become, get** *My job's getting more and more stressful.* | **find sth** *I find these meetings rather stressful.*
- ADV. **extremely, highly, particularly, very | fairly, quite, rather | emotionally** *It was an emotionally stressful time for him.*

stretch *noun*

1 area of land or water
- ADJ. **great, huge, large, long, open, vast, wide** *A great stretch of ocean lay beneath them.* | **narrow, short, small | straight** *a straight stretch of road* | **continuous, unbroken | beautiful, lovely | deserted, empty, lonely** *an empty stretch of beach* | **fast | dangerous, hazardous | coastal** *a wild uninhabited coastal stretch*
- PREP. **along a/the~** *There are tailbacks along a 10-mile stretch of the motorway.* **on a/the ~** *The festival is being held on a stretch of parkland near the river.* | **~of**

2 stretching
- ADJ. **good | gentle**
- VERB + STRETCH **have** *Have a good stretch from time to time to prevent yourself getting stiff.*
- PHRASES **at full stretch** *Her arms were at full stretch.*

stretch *verb*

1 pull sth tight
- ADV. **taut/tautly, tight/tightly** *Make sure that the rope is stretched tight.* ◇ *Stretch the fabric tightly over the frame.*
- PREP. **across, between, over** *Striped awnings had been stretched across the courtyard.*

2 your body/part of the body
- ADV. **gently | lazily, luxuriously** *He stirred and stretched lazily.* | **full-length** *Andrea turned out the light and stretched full-length on the bed.* | **down, forwards, out, up, upwards** *She stretched up to reach the top shelf.*

3 cover a large area
- ADV. **far** *The wood does not stretch very far.* | **endlessly | ahead, away** *The road stretched ahead.*
- VERB + STRETCH **seem to** *The beach seemed to stretch endlessly.*
- PREP. **along, beyond, for** *The beach stretches for five miles.* **from, into, to** *an area which stretches from London to the north*

4 continue over a period of time
- ADV. **endlessly | back, out** *The town's history stretches back to before 1500.*
- PREP. **before** *Endless summer days stretched out before us.* **into** *The talks look set to stretch into a second week.*

5 your ability/intelligence
- ADV. **really | fully** *We can't take on any more work—we're fully stretched as it is.*
- PREP. **to** *This department is stretched to its limit.*

stride *noun*

1 step
- ADJ. **long, short** *In one short stride, he reached the window.* | **quick, rapid | slow | easy | purposeful**
- VERB + STRIDE **take | lengthen, shorten** *He lengthened his stride to keep up with her.* | **break** *Without breaking her stride she ducked the ball.* | **match** *He matched his stride to her slower pace.*
- PREP. **in a~**

2 progress
- ADJ. **considerable, enormous, giant, great**
- VERB + STRIDE **make** *She's made enormous strides in English this term.*
- PREP. **~s in**

stride *verb*

- ADV. **briskly, quickly | confidently | purposefully | angrily | ahead, away, back, forward, in, off, out, over, past** *He strode off in search of a taxi.*
- PREP. **across, along, away, down, into, out of, over, past, through, towards, up** *She strode purposefully towards the door.*
- PHRASES **come striding** *He came striding up the path.*

strife *noun*

- ADJ. **internal | ethnic, factional, internecine, sectarian | civil, industrial, political, religious, social | domestic, marital**
- VERB + STRIFE **cause, provoke | be torn (apart) by** *The country has been torn apart by years of civil strife.* | **end**
- PREP. **during/in the ~** *He lost his job during last year's industrial strife.* | **~ among/between** *internecine strife among the nationalities of the empire*
- PHRASES **an end to the strife, a time of strife**

strike *noun*

1 industrial protest
- ADJ. **long | short | indefinite | crippling, damaging, major | bitter | official | illegal, unofficial, unlawful | protest | token, warning | lightning, wildcat** *a series of*

lightning strikes in parts of the coal industry | **all-out, general, mass, national, nationwide** *A general strike brought the country to a standstill.* | **hunger** | **sit-down** | **political** | **sympathy** *The suppression of the strike led to sympathy strikes in other industries.* | **pay, rent** | **dock, dockers', miners', postal, train, etc.**
- QUANT. **series, wave**
- VERB + STRIKE **be on** | **come out on, go on, join, take part in** | **call (sb out on), organize, stage** *The union leaders called a strike.* ◇ *He called all the workers out on strike.* | **avert, prevent** | **threaten** *More train strikes are threatened.* | **begin, start** | **call off, end** | **break (up), crush** *The army was used to help break the strike.* | **settle** | **ban** *The new government banned strikes.*
- STRIKE + VERB **occur, take place** | **start** | **end** | **last** | **spread** *The strike soon spread to other cities.* | **paralyse sth** *The strike paralysed the port.*
- STRIKE + NOUN **action** *Prison officers are threatening to take strike action.* | **ballot, call, threat** | **leader** | **breaker** | **committee, movement**
- PREP. **during a/the ~** *There was a continual police presence during the strike.* | **~ against** *a strike against the employment of non-union labour* **~ by** *a strike by tax collectors* **~ for** *a strike for a ten-hour day* **~ in protest at** *a strike in protest at the government's economic policies* **~ in support of** *Miners staged a one-day strike in support of the steel workers.* **~ over** *a strike over wages*
- PHRASES **days lost in/through strikes** *Unofficial action accounted for 40% of the days lost through strikes last year.*

2 sudden military attack
- ADJ. **air, military, nuclear** | **pre-emptive** | **retaliatory**
- VERB + STRIKE **carry out, launch, make**
- PREP. **in a/the ~** *The house was damaged in an air strike.* | **~ against/on** *The aircraft carried out a pre-emptive strike against bases in the north.*

strike *verb*

1 hit/attack sb/sth
- ADV. **firmly, hard** *He struck her hard across the face.* | **deep** *The German army struck deep into northern France.* | **directly** | **repeatedly** | **home** *(often figurative)* *The remark struck home.*
- VERB + STRIKE **be ready to, prepare to**
- PREP. **against** *The oar struck against something hard.* **at** *He struck at me repeatedly with a stick.* **into** *He struck the ball firmly into the back of the net.* **on** *The ball struck her on the head.*

2 come into your mind suddenly/give an impression
- ADV. **immediately** | **suddenly** *It suddenly struck me how we could improve the situation.* | **just** *An awful thought has just struck me.* | **forcibly** *Joan was struck quite forcibly by the silence.*
- PREP. **as** *He struck me as being rather stupid.*

3 go on strike
- VERB + STRIKE **threaten to** | **vote to**
- PREP. **against, for** *The union has voted to strike for a pay increase of six per cent.* **in protest at**
- PHRASES **the right to strike**

striking *adj.*

- VERBS **be, look** *That hat looks very striking.*
- ADV. **especially, extremely, particularly, very** | **quite** *She was tall and quite striking.* | **immediately** *What is immediately striking is how resourceful the children are.*
- PREP. **in** *The picture was striking in its simplicity.*

string *noun*

1 thin cord
- ADJ. **taut, tight** *He pulled the string tight.* | **loose** | **tangled** *He had hair like tangled yellow string.*

- QUANT. **bit, length, piece** *I cut a length of string to tie up the package.* | **ball**
- VERB + STRING **knot, tie, tie sth up with** *Tie the string round the parcel.* | **undo, untie** *He wound the string into a ball.* | **unwind** | **dangle (sth) on** *Next to the phone, there was a pencil dangling on a string.*
- PREP. **in the ~** *There's a knot in the string.*
- PHRASES **on the end of a string**

2 on a musical instrument
- ADJ. **tight** | **slack** | **open** | **stopped** | **guitar, violin, etc.** | **A, G, etc.**
- VERB + STRING **tighten, tune** | **loosen** | **pluck** | **change, replace** | **break**
- STRING + VERB **break** | **vibrate**
- STRING + NOUN **instrument**
- PREP. **on a/the ~** *Play it on the G string.*

strip *noun*

- ADJ. **narrow, thin, tiny** | **thick, wide** *Cut the meat into thick strips.* | **coastal** | **landing** *This aircraft requires a good-sized landing strip.*
- PREP. **in ~s** *The wallpaper can then be torn off in strips.* | **~ of** *a narrow strip of leather*
- PHRASES **cut/tear sth into strips**

strip *verb*

1 take off your/sb's clothes
- PREP. **down to** *Office workers stripped down to their shirtsleeves in the heatwave.* **off** *He stripped off his shirt.* ◇ *We stripped off and went for a swim.*
- PHRASES **strip (sb) naked** *She was stripped naked and left in a cell.* **strip to the waist** *He stripped to the waist and began to dig.*

2 take sth away
- ADV. **completely** | **away, off, out** *Strip out any damaged wiring.*
- PREP. **from** *The bark is stripped from the trees by hand.* **of** *The president had been completely stripped of power.* **off** *We stripped the paint off the walls.*
- PHRASES **strip sth bare** *The room had been stripped bare by the thieves.*

stripe *noun*

- ADJ. **broad, wide** | **fine, narrow, thin** | **bold** | **subtle** | **distinctive** | **horizontal, vertical**
- STRIPE + VERB **run** *The butterfly is black and white with a blue stripe running down each wing.*
- PREP. **with ~s** *a white tablecloth with red stripes* | **~ across/down, etc.** *The toad has a distinctive yellow stripe down its back.*

strive *verb*

- ADV. **hard, mightily** *He strove very hard to remain calm.* | **desperately** *desperately striving for some sort of dignity* | **earnestly** | **always, constantly, continually**
- PREP. **after** *striving after artistic beauty* **against** *man striving against the elements* **for** *The school constantly strives for excellence in its teaching.* **towards** *companies that strive towards bigger profits*

stroke *noun*

1 of a brush, pen, etc.
- ADJ. **long, short** | **broad, thick** | **narrow, thin** | **bold, vigorous** *She caught his likeness with a few bold brush strokes.* | **even** | **quick, slow** | **downward, upward** | **brush, pen, pencil**
- PHRASES **with a stroke of the pen** *With a stroke of the pen our names were removed from the register.*

2 in sport
- ADJ. **fast, slow** | **powerful** *The Romanian rowers*

pulled ahead with fast, powerful strokes. | **backhand, forehand** (in tennis, etc.)
• VERB + STROKE **play** *He played some powerful backhand strokes throughout the game.*
• PREP. **by a/two, etc. ~** (in golf) *Woods leads by two strokes.*
• PHRASES **a/two, etc. strokes ahead/behind** (in golf)

3 in swimming
• ADJ. **long, short** *He swam back with long slow strokes.* | **fast, slow** | **back** (also **backstroke**), **breast** (also **breaststroke**)
• VERB + STROKE **do, swim** *You can't swim more than four strokes before you reach the other side.*

4 sudden illness of the brain
• ADJ. **crippling, massive, serious** | **minor, slight** | **fatal**
• VERB + STROKE **have, suffer** *She had a massive stroke and lost her speech.*
• STROKE + VERB **leave sb ...** *The stroke left him paralysed down his right side.*
• STROKE + NOUN **patient, victim**
⇨ Special page at ILLNESS

5 sth that happens unexpectedly
• ADJ. **sudden** *I had a sudden stroke of inspiration.*
• VERB + STROKE **have**
• PREP. **at a/one~** *They lost half their fortune at a stroke.* | **~ of** *a stroke of genius*
• PHRASES **a stroke of (good/bad) luck, a stroke of (good) fortune**

NOTE

Swimming strokes
....

a **fast, powerful, strong** crawl
a **slow** breaststroke
do, swim (the)~
  a swimmer doing the crawl
  I can't swim butterfly.
strike out in/with breaststroke/crawl
  She struck out with a strong crawl towards the shore.
a length of~
  He did 15 lengths of backstroke every morning.
In competitions the categories are **backstroke, breaststroke, butterfly,** and **freestyle** (= in which competitors do crawl because it is fastest).
100 metres, 200 metres, etc.~
men's, women's~
compete in~
  competing in the women's 100 metres freestyle
in the~
  He came first in the 200 metres backstroke.

---

stroke *verb*

• ADV. **gently, lightly, softly, tenderly** | **thoughtfully** *He stroked his beard thoughtfully.* | **absently** *She stroked the cat absently.* | **away** *She gently stroked away his tears.*

stroll *noun*

• ADJ. **little, short** | **five-minute, etc.** *The shops are only a ten-minute stroll away.* | **casual, easy, gentle, leisurely** | **pleasant** | **moonlit, romantic** | **afternoon, evening, morning, etc.** | **after-lunch, post-prandial**
• VERB + STROLL **be/go out for, go for, take** *They took a leisurely stroll along the river bank.*
• PHRASES **a stroll around (sth)/away** *The beach is only a short stroll away.*

stroll *verb*

• ADV. **casually, leisurely, slowly** | **about, around, away, back, down** *They strolled down to the canal.*

• PREP. **across, along, around, down, into, out (of), past, through** *as he strolled leisurely through the streets*

strong *adj.*

1 physically powerful
• VERBS **be, feel, look** | **become, grow** | **make sb** *All that outdoor work has made him very strong.*
• ADV. **extremely, immensely, really, very** | **pretty, quite** | **enough** *Don't try to go back to work before you are physically strong enough.* | **physically**

2 not easily damaged
• VERBS **be, look**
• ADV. **extremely, really, very** | **fairly, pretty, quite** | **enough** *The box looks strong enough.*

3 powerful
• VERBS **be, look, prove, seem, smell, taste** | **become, get, grow** | **remain** | **make sth** | **keep sth** *This news helped keep the dollar relatively strong today.*
• ADV. **extremely, immensely, particularly, really, very** *He exerts an extremely strong influence on his classmates.* | **fairly, pretty, quite, rather** | **enough** *The party lacks a strong enough local base.*

structure *noun*

• ADJ. **basic, simple** | **complex, elaborate** | **coherent, logical** | **rigid, stable** | **flimsy** *The flimsy structure of the vehicle could not withstand even mild impacts.* | **formal** | **internal** | **solid, three-dimensional** | **anatomical, body, bone, skeletal/skeleton** | **atomic, cell/cellular, chemical, molecular** | **grammatical, language, linguistic, sentence, syntactic** | **administrative, bureaucratic, committee, control, corporate, hierarchical, institutional, management, organizational, power, etc.** | **economic, financial, political, social, etc.** *the social structure of the village* | **democratic, federal, etc.** | **class** | **family, household** | **pay, price, salary, tax, wage** | **career**
• VERB + STRUCTURE **have** | **lack** *The job lacked a basic career structure.* | **be based on** | **create, devise, establish** *to devise a new management structure* | **impose**
• STRUCTURE + VERB **be based on sth**
• PREP. **of a ...** *~ The cell walls of plants are of a fairly rigid structure.* ... **in ~** *The building is very simple in structure.* **in a/the~** *There are weaknesses in the structure of the organization.* | *~ in/within the salary structure in the firm*
• PHRASES **a change in structure, a change in/to the structure** *significant changes in the power structure* **a lack of structure** *The novel suffers from a lack of structure.*

structure *verb*

• ADV. **beautifully, carefully, clearly, neatly, properly, well** *She had structured her arguments very carefully.* | **badly** | **loosely** *a very loosely structured organization* | **rigidly, tightly** | **hierarchically, logically**
• PREP. **according to** *the idea that living organisms had been structured according to a divine plan* **around** *The teaching is structured around three topics.* **into** *The company is structured into two divisions.*
• PHRASES **highly structured** *a complex but highly structured complaints procedure*

struggle *noun*

1 fight
• ADJ. **great, life-and-death, titanic** | **bitter, desperate, fierce, heroic, violent** *There were the sounds of a desperate struggle.* | **just** *The UN supported what it saw as the just struggle of an oppressed people.* | **unequal** | **armed** *The group supported the armed struggle against the dictator.* | **class, internecine** *Marx wrote about the class strug-*

gle. | **economic, ideological, leadership, political, power, revolutionary**
- VERB + STRUGGLE **begin, put up, take up** *If someone snatched your bag, would you put up a struggle?* ◇ *They took up the struggle against racism.* | **be engaged/locked in, carry on, wage** *species engaged in a life-or-death struggle with the ever-changing environment*
- STRUGGLE + VERB **ensue, take place | continue, go on | intensify**
- PREP. **in a/the ~** *One of the security guards was hurt in the struggle.* **without a~** *She won't give up without a struggle.* | **~against** *the struggle against fascism* **~between** *the struggle between good and evil* **~for** *the long struggle for democracy* **~over** *a struggle over the property* **~with** *He was involved in a struggle with the police.*
- PHRASES **a sign of a struggle** *The police said that there was no sign of a struggle by the murder victim.* **years of struggle** *After 150 years of struggle against brutal colonial rule, the country won its independence.*

2 great effort
- ADJ. **desperate, great, hard, real, uphill** *It will be an uphill struggle to maintain exports at the current level.* | **long | ceaseless, constant, endless | unequal**
- VERB + STRUGGLE **face, have** *We had a real struggle to get everything into the suitcase.* | **give up** *I've given up the unequal struggle to keep my house tidy.*
- PHRASES **a bit of a struggle** *It was a bit of a struggle for me to get there so early.*

struggle *verb*

1 try very hard to do sth
- ADV. **desperately, hard, manfully, painfully, really, valiantly** *He struggled desperately to get to the shore.* ◇ *He struggled hard to keep the boat upright.* | **a little | constantly | on** *She struggled on despite the pain.*
- VERB + STRUGGLE **have to**
- PREP. **against** *The small boat struggled against the waves.* **along, down, for** *Shona struggled for breath.* **through** *The family struggled through the next few years.* **up** *They struggled up the hill.* **with** *I'm really struggling with this essay.*
- PHRASES **struggle to your feet** *She struggled to her feet and set off after him.*

2 have great difficulties
- ADV. **badly** *The team struggled badly last season.* | **financially** *I was unemployed and struggling financially.*

3 fight sb/try to get away from them
- ADV. **fiercely, furiously, violently** *She struggled furiously but could not get away.* | **together** *Ben and Jack struggled together on the grass.*
- PREP. **against** *struggling against her attacker* **with** *He was hit in the mouth as he struggled with the raiders.*
- PHRASES **struggle free** *The attacker's victim managed to struggle free.*

stuck *adj.*

- VERBS **be | become, get | remain | get sth** *She got the key stuck in the lock.*
- ADV. **firmly | completely, fast** *I couldn't budge the drawer—it was stuck fast.*
- PREP. **in, onto, to** *The tiles were stuck firmly to the wall.*

student *noun*

- ADJ. **brilliant, good** *one of the best students the college has ever had* | **college, school, university | full-time, part-time | first-year, second-year, etc. | graduate, postgraduate, research | doctoral, MA, etc. | mature** *He studied metallurgy as a mature student, having spent ten years working in a foundry.* | **overseas | engineering, history, law, medical, etc.**
- STUDENT + NOUN **nurse, teacher | numbers, popu-lation** *Student numbers at the college have increased by 25 per cent.* | **days** *She travelled a lot in her student days.* | **life** *thoroughly enjoying student life* | **grant, loan** *She had to take out a student loan to help her through college.* | **accommodation, dormitory | demonstration, protest, unrest** *taking part in a student demonstration*
- PREP. **as a~** *She first went to London as a student.*

studio *noun*

- ADJ. **art, artist's, design, photographer's, photographic, photography, portrait | broadcasting, film, movie, radio, recording, sound, television/TV | rehearsal | dance**
- STUDIO + NOUN **recording | audience** *a studio audience for a new television sitcom* | **executive** *a studio executive for a major Hollywood studio*
- PREP. **in a/the~** *The photograph was taken in a studio.*

study *noun*

1 learning
- ADJ. **full-time, part-time | graduate, postgraduate | independent, private** *This grammar book is suitable both for classroom use and for independent study.* | **academic** *The course integrates academic study and practical training.* | **language**
- QUANT. **course, programme**
- VERB + STUDY **take up** *Now that her children are all at school, she's going to take up full-time study again.*
- STUDY + NOUN **group** *A bible study group meets every Sunday at the church.* | **leave** *The company allows its staff to take paid study leave.* | **skills** *The first part of the course is designed to develop students' study skills.*
- PREP. **~for** *full-time study for an MA*
- PHRASES **an area/a field of study** *Students do a foundation year before specializing in their chosen field of study.*

2 studies sb's learning activities
- ADJ. **further** *Many undertake further studies after passing their A levels.*
- VERB + STUDIES **undertake | continue, pursue | complete, finish** *When he has completed his studies, he'll travel round the world.* | **resume, return to** *She returned to her studies when her children reached school age.*

3 studies subjects
- ADJ. **business, management, religious, women's, etc.** *She's doing women's studies at Liverpool University.*
- VERB + STUDIES **do | lecture in, teach** *He lectures in management studies.*

4 piece of research
- ADJ. **new, present, recent** *The present study reveals an unacceptable level of air pollution in the city centre.* | **earlier, previous | careful, close, comprehensive, detailed, intensive, serious** *a close study of share prices* ◇ *She devoted herself to a serious study of the Koran.* | **major | definitive | initial, pilot, preliminary** *A preliminary study suggested that the product would be popular.* | **research** *Research studies carried out in Italy confirmed the theory.* | **empirical, experimental, systematic, theoretical | anthropological, historical, scientific, sociological | field** *This phenomenon has been observed in both laboratory and field studies.* | **feasibility** *The company undertook an extensive feasibility study before adopting the new system.* | **literary | case** *a detailed case study of nine companies* | **comparative** *a comparative study of the environmental costs of different energy sources*
- VERB + STUDY **commission, fund, support** *the recommendations of a study commissioned by the World Bank* | **carry out, conduct, do, make, undertake, work on** *He has made a special study of the way that birds communicate with one another.* | **publish**
- STUDY + VERB **take place | aim at/to, be aimed at sth, attempt to, be designed to, set out to** *The study set*

out to examine bias in television news coverage. | be
based on sth *a study based on a sample of male white-
collar workers* | cover sth *The ten-year study covered
13 000 people aged 15-25.* | concern sth, deal with sth,
examine sth, focus on sth, investigate sth, look at sth |
compare sth *The study compares the incidence of bone
cancer in men and women.* | conclude sth, demonstrate
sth, find sth, indicate sth, report sth, reveal sth, say sth,
show sth, suggest sth, warn sth | provide sth *The study
provided valuable insight into the development of the dis-
ease.* | highlight sth, identify sth *The study highlighted
three problem areas.*
• STUDY + NOUN **group** *The study group was selected
from a broad cross section of the population.*
• PREP. **in a/the~** *In a recent study, 40% of schools were
found to be understaffed.* **under~** *the biochemical process
under study* | **~into** *a study into the viability of the mine*
~on *a definitive study on medieval weapons*
• PHRASES **an area/a field of study, the re-
sults/findings of a study, the subject of a study** *Shakespeare is the subject of a new study by Anthony Bryan.*

study *verb*

1 spend time learning about sth
• ADV. **hard**
• PREP. **for** *She is studying hard for her A levels.*
under/with *He studied under Professor Sager.*

2 examine sth carefully
• ADV. **carefully, closely, in depth, in detail, intently, intensively** *She picked up the letter and studied it carefully.*
◇ *In the third year a number of areas are studied in detail.*
| **extensively, widely | fully, thoroughly | systematic-
ally | thoughtfully** *He studied her thoughtfully, then
smiled.*
• PHRASES **be easily/well studied** *The influence of her-
edity is best studied in genetically identical twins.*

stuff *verb*

• ADV. **frantically, hastily, quickly**
• PREP. **inside, into** *He hastily stuffed a few clothes into a
bag.* **with** *She stuffed her case with presents for the kids.*
• PHRASES **be stuffed full of sth** *Her briefcase was
stuffed full of papers.*

stumble *verb*

• ADV. **almost, nearly | a little, slightly** *She stumbled a
little on the uneven path.* | **blindly** *He stumbled blindly on
through the dark building.* | **about, along, around, away,
back, backwards, forward, on, out**
• PREP. **against, along, down, from, into, out of, over,
towards, etc.** *They stumbled over the ploughed field.*
• PHRASES **stumble to your feet** *The train stopped, and
several passengers stumbled to their feet.*

PHRASAL VERB
stumble across/on/upon sth
• ADV. **accidentally, by chance, unwittingly** *I stumbled
across the place quite by chance.*

stumbling block *noun*

• ADJ. **big, main, major, real**
• VERB + STUMBLING BLOCK **remove**
• PREP. **~to** *The question of disarmament proved a major
stumbling block to agreement.*

stun *verb*

• ADV. **absolutely | almost | briefly, momentarily**
• PREP. **into** *The assault was so unexpected that he was
briefly stunned into submission.*
• PHRASES **stun sb into silence** *The guests were stunned
into silence.*

stunned *adj.*

• VERBS **appear, be, feel, look, seem, sit, sound, stand**
Morton stood stunned, unable to believe his ears. | **leave
sb** *Leaving them all stunned, she walked out of the bar.*
• ADV. **deeply | absolutely, completely, quite | almost
| a bit, a little, slightly, somewhat | briefly, momentarily**
• PREP. **at** *They seemed stunned at his outburst.* **by** *She
was a bit stunned by the news.* **with** *stunned with grief*

stunning *adj.*

• VERBS **be, look**
• ADV. **really** *You look really stunning in that dress!* | **ab-
solutely, quite, simply** *The finished effect was absolutely
stunning.* | **visually** *a visually stunning piece of cinema*

stunt *noun*

1 sth done for attention
• ADJ. **publicity**
• VERB + STUNT **arrange, organize** *She arranged a
publicity stunt to make the public aware of the product.* |
pull *What do you hope to gain by pulling a stunt like that?*
• PREP. **as a~** *They jumped off London Bridge as a publi-
city stunt.*

2 dangerous act
• ADJ. **dangerous, daredevil | dramatic, spectacular |
film**
• VERB + STUNT **carry out, do, perform** *The actor per-
formed all the stunts himself.* | **attempt**
• STUNT + VERB **backfire, go wrong**
• STUNT + NOUN **artist, man** (also **stuntman**), **woman**
(also **stuntwoman**) | **driver, pilot, rider**

stupid *adj.*

• VERBS **appear, be, feel, look, seem, sound** *I felt really
stupid when I realized what had happened.* ◇ *My sister
made me look stupid in front of all my friends.* | **act** (*infor-
mal*) *I decided it was best to act stupid.*
• ADV. **bloody** (*taboo*), **damn/damned, exceptionally,
extremely, fucking** (*taboo*), **incredibly, monumentally,
particularly, really, very | absolutely, completely, (just)
plain, utterly** *That was just plain stupid!* | **not entirely**
*I'm not entirely stupid. I checked the train times before we
came out.* | **a bit, a little, pretty, quite, rather | enough,
sufficiently** *He's stupid enough to believe anything.* |
crassly, grossly *a crassly stupid thing to do*

stupidity *noun*

• ADJ. **complete, crass, incredible, sheer, utter**
• VERB + STUPIDITY **demonstrate, show** *Her answer
showed the most incredible stupidity.*
• PREP. **through (your)~** *Through his own stupidity, he
missed an excellent opportunity.*

stupor *noun*

• ADJ. **drunken**
• VERB + STUPOR **drink yourself into, fall into, go into,
sink into** *As the whisky took effect, he gradually fell into a
drunken stupor.* | **come out of, emerge from | rouse sb
from** *The noise of someone banging at the door roused her
from her stupor.*
• PREP. **in a~** *He fell to the ground in a stupor.*

stutter *noun*

• ADJ. **bad | slight | occasional**
• VERB + STUTTER **have, speak with** *He spoke with a
stutter, which got worse when he was angry.*

style *noun*

1 way that sth is done/made

• ADJ. **latest, modern, new** | **classical, old, old-fashioned, period, traditional** *an old style of management* | **contemporary** *The 16th century house has been renovated and furnished in contemporary style.* | **characteristic, distinctive, individual, inimitable, original** *her inimitable style of humour* | **personal** | **musical** | **architectural** | **teaching** | **leadership, management, managerial** | **political** | **literary, narrative, prose, writing** | **elegant, lively** | **flamboyant** *a flamboyant style of dress* | **formal** | **casual** *a casual style of speech* | **conversational** *The article is written in a conversational style.* | **aggressive** *His aggressive style of play sometimes gets him in trouble.* | **autocratic** *an autocratic style of leadership* | **18th-century, etc.** | **Gothic, Renaissance, etc.**

• VERB + STYLE **have** *The two artists have radically different styles.* | **develop, establish, evolve, find, form** *He evolved his style of painting while working as a magazine illustrator.* | **adapt, adjust, alter, change, modify, tailor** *The pianist had to tailor his style to suit the vocalist's distinctive voice.* | **adopt, use** | **copy, emulate, follow**

• PREP. **in ~** *very utilitarian in style* **in a/the ~** *The new houses have been built in a traditional style.*

2 good quality

• ADJ. **enormous, fine, great, real, terrific** | **certain**

• VERB + STYLE **have** *He has a certain style.* | **ooze** *The whole house just oozed style.* | **add, give sb/sth**

• PREP. **with ~** *Whatever she did, she did it with style.*

• PHRASES **a touch of style** *Long velvet curtains add a touch of style to the main room.*

subdued *adj.*

• VERBS **be, feel, look, seem, sound**

• ADV. **very** | **almost** | **a bit, fairly, rather, somewhat** | **suitably** *She was dressed in grey and looked suitably subdued.* | **strangely, unusually** *I felt strangely subdued when it was all over.*

subject *noun*

1 topic or person under consideration

• ADJ. **big, complex, vast** | **simple** | **excellent, fascinating, good, interesting** | **cheerful** *Can we talk about a more cheerful subject?* | **gloomy, unpleasant** | **delicate, difficult, embarrassing** | **taboo** *Work is a taboo subject when we go out for dinner.* | **closed** *I don't wish to discuss it any further—the subject is closed.* | **chosen** *Each candidate has to speak for three minutes on their chosen subject.* | **pet** *Once he gets onto his pet subject there's no stopping him.*

• VERB + SUBJECT **cover, debate, discuss, talk about, touch on** *We touched briefly on the subject.* | **deal with** *I wasn't quite sure how to deal with the delicate subject of money.* | **examine, have a (fresh) look at, investigate, look into** *We want to have a fresh look at the difficult subject of social security benefits.* | **bring up, broach, get onto, raise** | **drop** *Let's drop the subject since we don't seem to be able to agree.* | **stick to** *I wish he'd stick to the subject rather than telling us his boring stories.* | **get off, wander off** *She was supposed to be speaking about sales figures, but she kept wandering off the subject.* | **get back to, return to** *Getting back to the subject of heating, has anyone got any suggestions for improvements?* | **avoid** | **change** *Don't change the subject.*

• SUBJECT + VERB **arise, come up** *The subject of gambling has come up several times recently.*

• SUBJECT + NOUN **matter** *I like the way she writes, although I'm not interested in her subject matter.*

• PREP. **on a/the ~** *While we're on the subject of the theatre, has anyone been to see the new show?*

• PHRASES **a range of subjects** *We discussed a wide range of subjects.*

2 area of study

• ADJ. **difficult, easy** | **compulsory, core, main** | **additional, optional, special, subsidiary** | **specialist** | **arts, science** | **academic**

• VERB + SUBJECT **take** *What subjects are you taking at A level?* | **offer** *The department offers seven different subjects in all.* | **fail (in), pass** *She was disappointed to fail in two of her four subjects.* | **drop**

• SUBJECT + NOUN **area** *The syllabus is divided into five subject areas.*

• PREP. **in a/the ~** *He did well in every subject.*

• PHRASES **a choice of subject/subjects** *His unusual choice of subjects made it harder to find a job.* **a range of subjects**

> **NOTE**
>
> **Subjects of study**
>
> **do, read, study ~**
> **do ~** is more commonly used with school subjects (but may also be used with university subjects):
> *She did maths, physics and chemistry at school.*
> **study ~** is used with both school and university subjects:
> *He studied German at school.*
> *She went on to study mathematics at university.*
> **read ~** is only used with university subjects and is quite formal:
> *She was educated privately and at Pembroke College, where she read classics.*
> **lecture in, teach ~**
> *He taught music at a school in Edinburgh.*
> Other verbs used with SUBJECT can also be used with particular subjects of study:
> *Half the students take geography at A level.*
> *We offer accounting as a subsidiary course.*
> **~ degree, a degree/diploma in ~**
> *a law degree*
> *a higher diploma in fine art*
> **~ class, course, lecture, lesson**
> *The genetics lectures are on a different campus.*
> **~ department, a/the department of ~**
> *All enquiries should be made to the Department of Architecture.*
> **~ graduate, student, undergraduate**
> *Some architecture graduates gain further qualifications in specialist fields.*
> **~ lecturer, teacher, tutor**
> *He's an English teacher at Highland Road School.*
> **~ professor, (a) professor of ~**
> *She's professor of linguistics at the University of Wales.*
> **the study of ~**
> *The study of philosophy helps you to think critically.*
> **in ~**
> *He got As in history and art.*

subject *adj.* subject to sth

1 likely to be affected by sth

• VERBS **be, seem** | **become** | **leave sb/sth, make sb/sth** *His illness left him subject to asthmatic attacks.*

• ADV. **very** | **increasingly** | **rather** | **still** *At this stage these are proposals and are still subject to change.*

2 under the authority of sb/sth

• VERBS **be** *Everyone was entirely subject to the whim of the Sultan.* | **become** | **remain** | **make sb/sth** *All the priories were made directly subject to the abbot of Cluny.*

• ADV. **entirely** | **directly** | **expressly**

subjective *adj.*

• VERBS **be, seem**

● ADV. **highly, very** *painted from a highly subjective point of view* | **entirely, purely, wholly** *The criticisms are purely subjective.* | **essentially, largely** *Taste in art is essentially subjective.* | **rather, somewhat** | **inevitably, necessarily** *making inevitably subjective judgements*

submarine noun

● ADJ. **conventional** | **diesel, diesel-powered** | **atomic, nuclear, nuclear-powered** | **midget, miniature** | **enemy**
● SUBMARINE + VERB **dive** | **surface** | **sink (sth)** | **operate, patrol (sth)** *the problem of submarines operating too close to fishing vessels*
● SUBMARINE + NOUN **captain, commander, crew** | **base, fleet** | **attack, warfare**

submerged adj.

● VERBS **be, lie, remain** | **become**
● ADV. **deeply** | **completely, fully, totally** | **almost** | **barely** *barely submerged antagonism* | **half, partially, partly**
● PREP. **in** *The machine can be totally submerged in water.* **below/beneath/under** *The car was submerged under 20 feet of water.*

submission noun

1 accepting sb else's control
● ADJ. **complete, total**
● VERB + SUBMISSION **demand, expect** *The emperor demanded total submission from his subjects.* | **gain, get** | **beat sb into, bomb sb into, force sb into, starve sb into, stun sb into** *They bombed the village into submission.*
● PREP. **~ to** *the patient's submission to the demands of the hospital*

2 of a plan/statement
● ADJ. **detailed** | **joint** | **oral, written**
● VERB + SUBMISSION **make** | **accept** | **reject** | **consider, hear** | **support, uphold** *The judge upheld the defendant's submission and quashed his conviction.*
● PREP. **in a/the~** | **~ to** *The companies have made a joint submission to the minister.*

submit verb

1 give/propose sth so that it can be discussed
● ADV. **formally** *He formally submitted his resignation*
● VERB + SUBMIT **ask sb to, invite sb to, require sb to** *Six groups were invited to submit proposals for the research.* ◇ *Candidates for the degree are required to submit a 30 000-word thesis.*
● PREP. **for** *They have submitted plans for our approval.* **to** *She submitted her report to the committee.*

2 accept sb's power/control
● ADV. **voluntarily, willingly** *He submitted voluntarily to arrest.* | **meekly**
● VERB + SUBMIT **refuse to** | **be willing to** | **be compelled to, be forced to, be obliged to** *They were forced to submit to Bulgarian rule.*
● PREP. **to** *She refused to submit to threats.* ◇ *They abandoned their town rather than submit to the Persians.*

subnormal adj.

● VERBS **be, seem** | **classify sb as, treat sb as**
● ADV. **severely** | **educationally, mentally** *special provision for educationally subnormal children*

subordinate verb

● ADV. **firmly** | **completely, totally, wholly** | **largely**
● PREP. **to** *The needs of the individual are completely subordinated to those of the state.*

subordinate adj.

● VERBS **be** | **become**
● ADV. **completely, wholly** | **essentially** *He had an essentially subordinate role.* | **directly** *She was directly subordinate to the president* (= reported directly to the president). | **formally** *The monarch is formally subordinate to Parliament.*
● PREP. **to**

subscribe verb

PHRASAL VERB
subscribe to sth
● ADV. **fully, wholeheartedly** *I subscribe wholeheartedly to this theory.*

subscriber noun

● ADJ. **cable/digital/satellite TV, magazine, phone, telephone** | **regular** | **annual**
● PREP. **~ to** *Subscribers to the magazine can take advantage of this special offer.*

subscription noun

● ADJ. **annual, monthly, yearly, etc.** | **full**
● VERB + SUBSCRIPTION **pay** | **take out** | **cancel**
● SUBSCRIPTION + NOUN **fee, rate**
● PREP. **~ to** *Do you wish to take out a full twelve-month subscription to the journal?*
● PHRASES **a year's/month's/lifetime's, etc. subscription** *The prize was a lifetime's subscription to 'Newsweek'.*

subside verb

● ADV. **quickly, rapidly** | **gradually, slowly** *The storm gradually subsided.* | **eventually, finally**
● VERB + SUBSIDE **begin to**
● PREP. **into** *Her tears subsided into sniffs.*

subsidence noun

● ADJ. **rapid, slow, steady**
● VERB + SUBSIDENCE **be liable to, suffer from** *A number of houses had suffered from coal-mining subsidence.*
● SUBSIDENCE + VERB **occur**

subsidiary noun

● ADJ. **foreign, overseas** | **Spanish, Madrid-based, etc.** | **owned** *a 58%-owned subsidiary of Millennium Graphics* | **banking, manufacturing, software, etc.**
● VERB + SUBSIDIARY **operate as** *The company operates as a wholly-owned subsidiary of a large French company.* | **have, own** | **create, establish, form, set up** | **acquire** | **close**
● SUBSIDIARY + NOUN **company**
⇨ Note at ORGANIZATION

subsidize verb

● PHRASES **heavily/highly subsidized** *The airline is heavily subsidized by the government.*

subsidy noun

● ADJ. **big, heavy, huge, large, massive** | **small** | **direct** | **hidden, indirect** *The help that the government gives the industry amounts to an indirect subsidy.* | **annual** | **EU, government, public, state** | **agricultural, export, food, housing**
● QUANT. **level** *The level of subsidy given to farmers is to be reduced.*
● VERB + SUBSIDY **get, receive** | **lose** | **give sth, grant sth, pay, provide (sth with)** *The Arts Council granted*

them a small subsidy. | **cut, reduce** *Export subsidies have been reduced by 20%.* | **abolish, remove**
• SUBSIDY + NOUN **payments** | **scheme, system** | **cuts**
• PREP. **~for** *state subsidies for rice producers* **~on** *subsidies on basic goods and services* **~to** *subsidies to agriculture*
• PHRASES **a cut/reduction in subsidies** *The government cut spending through reductions in state subsidies to industry.* **the removal/abolition of subsidies** *protests against the removal of subsidies on basic commodities*

subsistence noun

• ADJ. **bare, basic**
• SUBSISTENCE + NOUN **agriculture, farmer, farming** | **economy** | **level** *Most of the population lives at subsistence level.*
• PHRASES **a level of subsistence** *They were living barely above the level of subsistence.* **means of subsistence** *She had no means of subsistence and was dependent on charity.*

substance noun

1 material
• ADJ. **addictive, carcinogenic, dangerous, harmful, hazardous, noxious, poisonous, radioactive, toxic** | **innocuous** *Even innocuous substances can sometimes register a positive result in a drug test.* | **banned, illegal** | **natural** *a natural substance found in the body of animals* | **chemical** | **inorganic, organic** | **pure** | **soluble, volatile** | **crystalline, fatty, oily, slimy, sticky, viscous** | **medicinal**
• VERB + SUBSTANCE **use** | **contain** | **produce** *Some frogs produce very toxic substances in their skin.* | **take** *The athletes had taken banned substances to increase their strength.*

2 important content
• ADJ. **real** *The real substance of the report was in the third part.* | **added** *His disappearance has given added substance to the argument that he stole the money.*
• VERB + SUBSTANCE **have** *The image of him that the media have presented has no substance.* | **give sth, lend sth** *The letters lent substance to the rumours.* | **lack**
• PREP. **in ~** *There's no difference in substance between the two points of view.* **of ~** *Nothing of substance was achieved at the meeting.* **without ~** *Their allegations were without substance.* | **~in** *There's no substance in the story.* **~to** *There was little substance to his claims.*

substitute noun

• ADJ. **good** | **acceptable, adequate, satisfactory** | **close** | **poor** *The television is a poor substitute for human companionship.*
• VERB + SUBSTITUTE **act as, serve as** *His teacher acted as a father substitute.* | **use sth as** | **produce, provide** *The company produces substitutes for lead in petrol.*
• PREP. **~for** *There's no substitute for hard work.*

subtitle noun

• ADJ. **English, French, etc.**
• VERB + SUBTITLE **have** | **read**
• PREP. **with ~s** *a Japanese film with English subtitles*

subtle adj.

• VERBS **be, seem** | **become**
• ADV. **extraordinarily, extremely, very** | **infinitely** *making infinitely subtle distinctions* | **not exactly, not too** *He was not exactly subtle about it!* | **fairly, quite, rather**

subtlety noun

• ADJ. **extreme, great, real**
• VERB + SUBTLETY **have** *Her dancing has great subtlety.* | **display, show** | **bring sth, lend sth** *His understanding of light brings great subtlety to his painting.* | **lack** | **appreciate, grasp, understand** *She was too young to grasp the subtleties of the film.*
• PREP. **with ~** *He uses language with great subtlety.*
• PHRASES **a lack of subtlety, of great/some subtlety** *a pianist of great subtlety*

suburb noun

• ADJ. **outer, outlying** | **inner** | **northern, southern, etc.** | **Berlin, Tokyo, etc.** | **affluent, comfortable, exclusive, prosperous, smart, wealthy** | **poor** | **middle-class, working-class** | **respectable** | **pleasant** | **leafy, quiet** | **grey** | **industrial, residential** | **sprawling** *out beyond the sprawling suburbs*
• VERB + SUBURB **move out to** *As soon as we can afford it, we'll move out to the suburbs.*
• SUBURB + VERB **grow** *The middle-class suburbs are growing fast.*
• PREP. **from the ~s** *For a child from the suburbs, a trip to the city was a great adventure.* **in a/the ~** *She's renting in some grey suburb of Birmingham.* **in the ~s** *Many people work in the centre but live in the suburbs.*

subversive noun

• ADJ. **dangerous**

subversive adj.

• VERBS **be** | **consider sth, deem sth, judge sth, regard sth as, see sth as**
• ADV. **very** | **inherently** | **overtly** *taking an overtly subversive approach* | **potentially** | **morally**

subway noun

• ADJ. **pedestrian**
• VERB + SUBWAY **take, use**
• PREP. **along a/the ~, in a/the ~, through a/the ~** *He ran through the pedestrian subway.*

succeed verb

1 manage to achieve what you want; do well
• ADV. **admirably, brilliantly, well** *The plan succeeded pretty well.* | **not quite** | **nearly** *They very nearly succeeded in blowing up the parliament building.* | **largely** *We feel that we have largely succeeded in our aims.* | **partially, partly** | **eventually, finally** | **apparently** | **academically** *the pressure on children to succeed academically*
• VERB + SUCCEED **be likely/unlikely to** *The appeal is unlikely to succeed.* | **be determined to, hope to, want to** *No company can hope to succeed at everything.*
• PREP. **against** *to succeed against serious opposition* **at** *She can teach you how to succeed at tennis.* **in** *She has succeeded in a difficult career.* ◊ *We succeeded in repairing the engine.* **with** *hints on how to succeed with interior design*

2 have a job/position after sb else
• VERB + SUCCEED **appoint sb to, elect sb to** *He was appointed to succeed Sir Georg Solti as head of the Chicago Symphony Orchestra.* | **be tipped to**
• PREP. **as** *He was widely tipped to succeed William Hague as leader of the party.* **to** *She succeeded to the throne in 1558.*

success noun

1 good results
• ADJ. **considerable, conspicuous, enormous, great, notable, overwhelming, phenomenal, remarkable, spectacular, tremendous, unprecedented** | **limited,**

moderate, modest *The campaign to stop drink-driving had only limited success.* | popular, public | early, initial | immediate | long-term, short-term | business, commercial, economic, financial | academic, educational, electoral, literary, military, etc. | international *The company's excellent marketing has resulted in enormous international success.*
• QUANT. amount, degree *Initially, the venture enjoyed a fair amount of success.*
• VERB + SUCCESS achieve, enjoy, have, notch up *She had little success in getting new customers.* ◊ *He is keen to notch up yet another success.* | bring *A change of management failed to bring success.* | end in, lead to, result in *The year-long fight for a pay rise ended in success.* | ensure, guarantee *We can't guarantee immediate success.* | be vital to *Your contribution was vital to the success of the concert.*
• SUCCESS + VERB come *Success didn't come overnight—she struggled for years before making any money.* | lie (in sth) *Much of his success lies in his skill in handling staff.* | depend on sth *The success or failure of the project depends on how committed the managers are.*
• SUCCESS + NOUN rate *The operation has a success rate of over 80%.* | story *The company has been one of the success stories of the past decade.*
• PREP. without~ *She tried to persuade them without success.* | ~in *I've had some success in getting rid of the weeds.* ~with *the secret of his success with women*
• PHRASES a chance/hope of success *What are our chances of success?* ◊ *We're trying to get him to sponsor us, but there's not much hope of success.* confident of success *She had worked hard and was confident of success.* the key to success, a lack of success, the secret of (sb's) success, a symbol of (sb's) success

2 sth that achieves its aim
• ADJ. big, complete, considerable, conspicuous, enormous, great, huge, major, notable, outstanding, phenomenal, popular, real, remarkable, resounding, roaring, runaway, spectacular, total, tremendous, unprecedented, unqualified *The band's new album has been a runaway success.* | modest, qualified | business, commercial, economic, popular *The book proved a major commercial success.* | international | immediate
• VERB + SUCCESS be, prove | have *We had one or two outstanding successes.* | judge sth *The event was judged a success by its organizers.* | make *She's made a real success of that job.*
• PHRASES wish sb (every) success *We are sad to see Hiroko go, and wish her every success in the future.*

successful *adj.*
• VERBS be, prove, seem | become
• ADV. astonishingly, enormously, extremely, highly, hugely, outstandingly, particularly, phenomenally, remarkably, spectacularly, very *his phenomenally successful period as manager* | not entirely *Their attempts had not been entirely successful.* | fairly, moderately, partially, quite, rather, relatively *The operation was only partially successful.* | academically, commercially, politically *a politically successful manoeuvre*
• PREP. at *Though a top-rated movie star he has been remarkably successful at keeping his private life private.* in *hoping their party would be successful in the elections*

succession *noun*

1 series of people, things, etc.
• ADJ. endless, long, never-ending | constant, continuous, uninterrupted | quick, rapid *We lost three secretaries in quick succession.* | whole *A whole succession of presidents had tried to resolve the issue without success.*
• PREP. in~ *There has been a rise in crime for the second year in succession.*

2 right to have an important position after sb else
• ADJ. legitimate | disputed | dynastic, hereditary
• VERB + SUCCESSION ensure, secure *He wanted to have a son to secure the succession.*
• PREP. in~to *Betty Munn is the manager in succession to Edna Greenan.*
• PHRASES the line/order of succession *He is next in (the) line of succession to the British throne.* the right of succession, succession to the throne

successor *noun*
• ADJ. logical, natural, obvious | rightful, worthy *Their latest disc is a worthy successor to their popular debut album.* | chosen, designated, eventual | immediate | likely, possible, potential
• VERB + SUCCESSOR have *He doesn't have an obvious successor as party leader.* | appoint, choose, elect, find | groom | hand over to *She will hand over to her successor in one year's time.*
• SUCCESSOR + VERB take over
• PREP. as sb's~ *She has been appointed as his successor.* | ~as *Andrew Kirkham will be her successor as Chief Executive.* ~to *The new Ministry of Food is the successor to the old Department of Agriculture.*
• PHRASES the appointment/choice/election of a successor, be tipped as a possible successor *The former newsreader is being tipped as a possible successor to the outgoing Head of Broadcasting.*

succumb *verb*
• ADV. almost | rapidly | eventually, finally | easily, readily *people who succumb easily to exploitation*
• VERB + SUCCUMB be likely to
• PREP. to *Malnourished children are more likely to succumb to infections.*

suck *verb*
• ADV. noisily *She was noisily sucking up milk through a straw.* | away, in, out, up *She sucked away on her thumb.* ◊ *He cut the orange in half and sucked out the juice.*
• PREP. at *He sucked at the wound on his hand.* from *The machine sucks up mud and stones from the bottom of the pond.* into, on *The baby sucked on her bottle.* out of, through

sue *verb*
• ADV. successfully | unsuccessfully
• VERB + SUE be able to, be entitled to, have the right to | threaten to
• PREP. for *He threatened to sue the company for negligence.* over *The water authority was successfully sued over his illness.*

suffer *verb*
• ADV. a lot, badly, greatly, severely, terribly *This area suffered very badly in the storms.* | needlessly *Thousands of children in the world today suffer needlessly.*
• VERB + SUFFER be likely to *Premature babies are more likely to suffer from breathing difficulties in childhood.*
• PREP. for *I played tennis yesterday and I know I shall suffer for it today.* from *She suffers from asthma.* with *He suffers terribly with migraines.*
• PHRASES suffer in silence *They were just expected to suffer in silence.*

sufferer *noun*
• ADJ. main, worst *The worst sufferers of the condition tend to live in highly polluted areas.* | lifelong, long-term | fellow *The sessions will enable you to discuss problems*

with fellow asthma sufferers. | **aids, arthritis, asthma, cancer, hay fever, etc.** | **back, back pain**
- PREP. **~from** *He's been a lifelong sufferer from hay fever.*

suffering *noun*

- ADJ. **great, intense, terrible, unbearable** | **needless, unnecessary** | **widespread** | **human** | **mental, physical** *The taunts of her schoolmates caused her intense mental suffering.*
- QUANT. **amount** *The western world has contributed to the immense amount of suffering in underdeveloped countries.*
- VERB + SUFFERING **cause (sb), inflict** | **increase** | **alleviate, ease, reduce, relieve** *These tablets should relieve his suffering for a couple of hours.* | **endure, experience**
- PHRASES **pain and suffering** *His life was one of pain and suffering.*

sufficient *adj.*

- VERBS **be, prove, seem, sound** | **consider sth, deem sth, regard sth as, see sth as** *Do you really regard that explanation as sufficient?*
- ADV. **quite** | **far from** | **barely, hardly, scarcely** *Our budget is scarcely sufficient to pay people, let alone buy any new equipment.* | **just** | **almost**
- PREP. **for** *The salary proved sufficient for his needs.*

sugar *noun*

- ADJ. **raw, unrefined** | **refined** | **natural** *Fruit juices contain natural sugars.* | **simple** *simple sugars, such as glucose* | **brown, white** *Add one cup of soft brown sugar.* | **caster, demerara, granulated, lump, icing** | **beet, cane** | **fruit** *Fructose is a fruit sugar.* | **blood** *to raise blood sugar levels*
- QUANT. **lump, spoonful** | **bag, packet**
- VERB + SUGAR **put in/on, spoon, sprinkle, stir in/into, take** (= in tea or coffee) *He stirred another spoonful of sugar into his tea.* ◇ *Do you take sugar in your tea?* | **contain** | **produce**
- SUGAR + VERB **dissolve**
- SUGAR + NOUN **cube, lump** | **bowl** | **substitute** | **intake** *a high sugar intake* | **beet, cane** | **industry, plantation, production, refinery**
- PHRASES **high/low/reduced sugar content, high/low in sugar** *Most junk food is high in sugar.* **no added sugar** *apple juice with no added sugar*

suggest *verb*

1 propose sth/state sth indirectly
- ADV. **tentatively** *I tentatively suggested that she might be happier working somewhere else.* | **respectfully, tactfully** *I would respectfully suggest a different explanation for the company's decline.* | **helpfully** *'Shall I tell them you're ill?' Alice suggested helpfully.*
- VERB + SUGGEST **seem reasonable to** *It seems reasonable to suggest that all life forms on earth share a common origin.* | **be wrong to** | **be tempting to** | **dare (to)** *How dare you suggest such a thing?*
- PREP. **as** *She suggested John as chairman.* **for** *Who would you suggest for the job?* **to** *He suggested to the committee that they should delay making a decision.*
- PHRASES **can/may I suggest, I (would) suggest** *I would suggest that you see your doctor about this.*

2 show sth in an indirect way
- ADV. **strongly** *The evidence suggests quite strongly that the fire was caused by an explosion.*
- VERB + SUGGEST **seem to** *The evidence seems to suggest that he did steal the money.*

suggestion *noun*

1 proposal
- ADJ. **constructive, excellent, good, interesting, helpful, positive, practical, sensible, valuable** | **absurd, bizarre, impractical, ludicrous, outrageous, preposterous, ridiculous, stupid** | **tentative**
- VERB + SUGGESTION **have** *Has anyone got any suggestions for a title?* ◇ *I've had several helpful suggestions from colleagues.* | **come up with, give sb, make, offer, put forward** *Can you give us any suggestions for a slogan?* ◇ *May I make a suggestion?* | **accept, act on, adopt, take up** *I think we might take up the suggestion of printing the books in Hong Kong.* | **take sb up on** *May we take you up on your suggestion of sharing the costs for the party?* | **deny, dismiss, reject** *They dismissed the suggestion that they hadn't worked hard.* ◇ *He rejected my suggestion as impractical.* | **welcome** | **consider, look at, note** *We have noted your suggestion and will give it due consideration.*
- SUGGESTION + NOUN **book, box**
- PREP. **at the ~ of** *At the suggestion of his boss, he resigned.* | **~ about/as to/concerning/on** *Management welcomes practical suggestions on how to improve the facilities.* **~ for** *suggestions for further reading*
- PHRASES **amid suggestions that** *She left the country amid suggestions that she had stolen from the firm.* **be open to suggestions** *I'm not sure what to do with all this money, but I'm open to suggestions.*
⇨ Special page at MEETING

2 communicating without stating directly
- ADJ. **implicit** | **hypnotic** *analgesia through hypnotic suggestion*
- PREP. **by/through ~** *There's no scientific basis to the method—it works by suggestion.*
- PHRASES **the power of suggestion** *These healers claim to remove the pain by the power of suggestion.*

3 trace of sth
- ADJ. **faint, mere, slightest**
- VERB + SUGGESTION **carry, have**
- PREP. **at the ~ of** *At the slightest suggestion of criticism, he loses his temper.* | **~ of**

suggestive *adj.*

1 making you think of sth
- VERBS **be, seem**
- ADV. **highly** (*medical*), **strongly, very** *The results were highly suggestive of malignancy.* | **vaguely**
- PREP. **of** *music that is suggestive of warm summer days*

2 making people think about sex
- VERBS **be, look, sound** | **become**
- ADV. **very** | **faintly, quite, rather** | **sexually**

suicidal *adj.*

1 wanting to kill yourself
- VERBS **be, feel, look, sound** | **become, get** *He became very depressed and even got suicidal at one point.*
- ADV. **almost**

2 likely to cause your failure
- VERBS **be, prove**
- ADV. **economically, politically** *a move which would be politically suicidal*
- PREP. **for** *These policies would prove suicidal for our economy.*

suicide *noun*

- ADJ. **attempted** | **mass** *Members of the sect committed mass suicide.* | **economic** | **electoral, political** *Raising taxes before an election would be political suicide.*
- VERB + SUICIDE **commit** | **attempt** | **contemplate**
- SUICIDE + NOUN **threat** | **attempt, bid** *He slashed his wrists in a failed suicide bid.* | **pact** *The couple died to-*

gether in a suicide pact. | **bomber, bombing** | **mission** | **letter, note** He died without leaving a suicide note. | **rate**

suit noun

1 set of clothes
- ADJ. **designer, elegant, immaculate, smart, well-cut** | **ill-fitting** | **off-the-peg** | **best, good** He wore his one good suit to the interview. | **tailored** | **double-breasted, single-breasted** | **one-piece, three-piece, two-piece** | **pin-stripe/pinstriped** | **linen, tweed, etc.** | **summer** | **business, dinner, evening, dress, formal, lounge, morning, safari** | **trouser** | **bathing, diving, wet** | **ski**
- SUIT + NOUN **jacket, trousers**
- PREP. **in a~** Two men in suits came out of the hotel.
- PHRASES **a suit and tie** They won't let you into the restaurant without a suit and tie. **a suit of armour** The cavalry wore a suit of light armour and carried a shield. **a suit of clothes** We bought the baby a couple of suits of clothes.

2 of playing cards
- ADJ. **trump**
- VERB + SUIT **follow** (= play the same suit as the previous player)
- SUIT + VERB **be trumps** Which suit is trumps? | **change** The suit changed to diamonds.
- PREP. **from/in a/the~** All the cards have to be from the same suit.

suit verb

- ADV. **admirably, fine, well** A camping holiday would suit me fine. ◇ You will have to try out the various tennis rackets to find out which one suits you best. | **down to the ground** (informal), **perfectly** Country life suits me down to the ground! ◇ This arrangement suited me perfectly.
- VERB + SUIT **seem to** | **adapt sth to, adjust sth to, be designed to, be tailored to** a shampoo designed to suit all hair types

suitability noun

- ADJ. **greater**
- VERB + SUITABILITY **assess, demonstrate, determine** to assess the suitability of the accommodation for a disabled person | **ensure** | **doubt, have doubts about, question**
- PREP. **~for** the greater suitability of women for the work

suitable adj.

- VERBS **be, look, prove, seem, sound** | **make sth** The exercise-with-answer-key format makes the book suitable for self-study. | **consider sth, deem sth** These properties are considered especially suitable for older people.
- ADV. **eminently, especially, highly, particularly, very** | **perfectly** | **quite** | **not entirely, not quite, not really** This holiday is not really suitable for wheelchair users. | **not necessarily** | **hardly, scarcely** | **potentially** | **equally** There are many other training courses that would be equally suitable.
- PREP. **as** not suitable as a word-processing program **for** The walk is suitable for all the family. **to** conditions suitable to their development

suitcase (also case) noun

- ADJ. **heavy, light** | **open** | **battered** His only possession was a battered old suitcase of clothes. | **false-bottomed** The money was smuggled out in a false-bottomed suitcase.
- VERB + SUITCASE **cram/stuff/throw sth in/into, pack** He stuffed a few clothes in a case, grabbed his wallet and left. ◇ Have you packed your case yet? | **take sth out of, unpack** | **close, fasten, shut, snap shut** She snapped her suitcase shut and stuck on a label. | **open** | **lift, pick up** The suitcase was too heavy to lift. | **clutch, hold** | **carry,**

drag, heave, hump, lug She heaved her case down from the luggage rack. ◇ travellers humping suitcases about | **drop, dump, put down** He got fed up of living out of a suitcase and left his job as a sales rep.
- SUITCASE + VERB **be crammed/stuffed with sth, be full of sth, contain sth** The suitcase was full of drugs.
- PREP. **in/inside a/the~**

suite noun

1 of furniture
- ADJ. **three-piece** a three-piece lounge suite | **bathroom, bedroom, dining/dining-room, lounge**
- VERB + SUITE **put in** We're having a new bathroom suite put in.
- PHRASES **a suite of furniture**

2 set of rooms in a hotel, office block, etc.
- ADJ. **private** | **executive, luxury** | **furnished** | **penthouse** | **bridal, conference, delivery** (= in the maternity ward of a hospital), **family, honeymoon, hospitality** a family suite of two interconnecting rooms | **hotel, office**
- PHRASES **a suite of rooms/offices**

suited adj.

- VERBS **appear, be, seem** | **make sth**
- ADV. **admirably, eminently, especially, particularly, peculiarly, very, well** lands that are well suited to dairy farming | **ideally, perfectly, uniquely** She was ideally suited to the job. | **hardly, not really** | **ill-, little, not really** a song ill-suited to male voices | **genuinely** Is this a job for which you are genuinely suited? | **naturally** | **temperamentally**
- PREP. **for** He was not really suited for army life. **to** an approach especially suited to the adult learner

sum noun

1 amount of money
- ADJ. **considerable, generous, good, handsome, hefty, high, large, not inconsiderable, princely** (ironic), **significant, substantial, tidy** (informal) It seemed an absurdly high sum to pay for a coat. ◇ For his first book he received the princely sum of $400. ◇ The team has raised substantial sums for local charities. | **astronomical, colossal, enormous, exorbitant, huge, magnificent, massive, record, staggering, vast** £200 was an astronomical sum of money in 1547. ◇ He joined the club two years ago for a record sum. | **five-figure, six-figure, etc.** | **small, modest, nominal, reasonable, token, trifling** The charity pays a nominal sum to lease the premises. | **derisory, paltry** | **average** | **net** | **round** $10 000 is a good round sum. | **full, overall, total** | **agreed, fixed** | **undisclosed, unspecified** | **annual, monthly, etc.** | **regular** | **guaranteed** | **capital, cash, lump** My wife would receive a guaranteed lump sum in the event of my death. | **tax-free**
- VERB + SUM **borrow, earn, fetch, raise, recover** Some of the paintings should fetch a tidy sum at today's auction. ◇ You will have to go to court to recover these sums. | **get, receive** | **award sb, contribute, give sb, grant sb, lend sb, offer sb, pay (sb), repay** The judge awarded them an undisclosed six-figure sum in damages. | **invest, spend** | **cost** a project that cost vast sums of public money | **charge (sb), fine sb** | **agree (on)** We eventually agreed a sum and I gave him a cheque.
- SUM + VERB **be due, be payable** The landlord has the right to recover any sums payable under this lease | **be equal/equivalent to sth** The gangsters offered him a sum equivalent to a whole year's earnings. | **exceed sth**
- PHRASES **a sum of money**

2 calculation
- ADJ. **difficult, easy**
- VERB + SUM **do, find the answer to** I did a quick sum to work out how much it would cost.

● PHRASES **get your sums right/wrong** *The company got its sums wrong when estimating how many customers it would attract.*

3 amount got by adding numbers
● VERB + SUM **calculate, find, work out** *Calculate the sum of the following figures.*
● PREP. **~of** *The sum of two and five is seven.*

sum *verb*

PHRASAL VERB
sum sth up
● ADV. **aptly, neatly, nicely, succinctly, well | perfectly | just about** *'So we're stuck in this place, with no food, no heat, no light and no prospect of anyone coming to rescue us?' 'That just about sums it up.'*
● VERB + SUM STH UP **seem to | attempt to, try to** *attempting to sum up recent economic trends* **| be difficult to, be hard to** *The appeal of this charming little town is hard to sum up.*
● PREP. **as** *She summed it up as 'the most brilliant lecture I've ever attended'.*

summarize *verb*

● ADV. **briefly, succinctly | aptly, best, conveniently, neatly, usefully, well** *The research has been usefully summarized in an article by Greenwood.* **| easily**
● VERB + SUMMARIZE **attempt to, try to | be possible to | be difficult to**
● PREP. **as** *The results of the survey can be summarized as follows:…*

summary *noun*

● ADJ. **accurate, apt, clear, excellent, fair, good, useful** *Is that a fair summary of the situation?* **| comprehensive, detailed, full | general, overall | brief, concise, quick, short | bald, crude | financial, statistical | news, plot** *Details of new titles, with plot summaries, are included in the catalogue.*
● VERB + SUMMARY **make, prepare, write** *Could you make a short summary of this article for me?* **| give (sb), provide (sb with), supply (sb with)** *He has provided a useful summary of the main categories.*
● SUMMARY + NOUN **sheet, table | report, statement**
● PREP. **in ~** *In summary, his views are out of date.* **in a/the ~** *She decided not to include this incident in her summary of the day's events.*
● PHRASES **in summary form** *The information is shown in summary form in the following tables.*

summer *noun*

● ADJ. **last, next, this (coming) | early, late, mid- (also midsummer) | high** *Seville is scorching in high summer.* **| good, hot, scorching | dry, wet | Indian** *We had an Indian summer that year, very warm until October.* ◊ *(figurative) She seems to be enjoying an Indian summer of popularity.*
● SUMMER + NOUN **temperature, weather | sun, sunlight, sunshine | rain/rains | breeze, gale, wind | sky | solstice | course, school | term** *There are two new courses being run in the summer term.* **| break, holiday, recess, vacation** *I went home for the summer holidays.* **| garden | flower | clothes, clothing, dress | collection, exhibition | Olympics, sports**
⇨ Note at SEASON (for more collocates)

summit *noun*

1 top of a mountain
● ADJ. **high** *The Pic Long is the highest summit in the region.* **| very | rocky, snow-capped, snow-covered, snowy | mountain**
● VERB + SUMMIT **arrive at, climb (to), gain, get to, reach**
● SUMMIT + NOUN **attempt, bid** *The blizzard forced them to delay their summit bid.*
● PREP. **at the ~** *We were standing at the very summit of the highest mountain in India.* **below the ~** *They reached base camp, 12 000 metres below the summit.* **on the ~** *The climbers planted a flag on the summit.*

2 important meeting between leaders
● ADJ. **annual, biennial, etc. | regular | emergency, extraordinary, special | two-day, etc. | first, inaugural | global, international, regional | bilateral, trilateral | European, Franco-German, etc. | G8, NATO, etc. | presidential | Paris, Rio, etc. | drugs, earth, economic, peace**
● VERB + SUMMIT **have, hold, host** *The 2004 summit will be hosted by Japan.* **| attend, go to**
● SUMMIT + NOUN **conference, meeting, talks | agenda | agreement, declaration**
● PREP. **at a/the ~** *These measures were decided at a summit in July.* **| between** *annual summits between the major OECD economies* **~on** *a two-day international summit on drugs*

summon *verb*

1 order a person to come to a place
● ADV. **duly | hastily, urgently | back**
● PREP. **for** *She was duly summoned for an interview.* **from** *He has been summoned from New York to give evidence at the trial.* **to** *She was summoned back to his office.*

2 find sth that you need
● ADV. **barely, hardly** *He could hardly summon the strength to stand up.* **| up**
● VERB + SUMMON **can/could | try to | manage to** *She managed to summon up a smile.*

summons *noun*

1 order to go somewhere
● ADJ. **peremptory, urgent | royal**
● VERB + SUMMONS **send (out) | await, expect** *I stayed in that night awaiting her summons.* **| get, hear, receive | answer, obey, respond to | ignore**
● SUMMONS + VERB **come** *She was ready when the summons duly came.*
● PREP. **~from** *She responded immediately to the summons from the head teacher.* **~to** *I received an urgent summons to her office.*
● PHRASES **in answer to a summons** *He arrived panting in answer to Blake's summons.*

2 order to go to a court of law
● ADJ. **court | private | witness**
● VERB + SUMMONS **issue, take out | deliver, present (sb with), serve (sb with)** *The summons can be served on either of the partners in the business.*
● PREP. **~against** *Her neighbours took out a summons against her for noise nuisance.* **| ~for**

sun *noun* (usually **the sun**)

● ADJ. **blood-red, bright, brilliant, golden, red, yellow | hazy, pale, thin, watery, weak, wintry | high, low** *The wintry sun was already low in the sky.* **| rising | dying, setting, sinking, westering, western** *The distant mountains glowed in the light of the setting sun.* **| baking, blazing, burning, fierce, harsh, hot, scorching, strong, warm | direct, full** *This plant likes a dryish soil in full sun.* **| afternoon, early, early-morning, evening, late, midday, morning, noon/noonday | autumn, spring, summer, winter | August, February, etc. | desert, tropical | Caribbean, Italian, etc.**
● VERB + SUN **blot out, obliterate** *The clouds darkened, obliterating the sun.* **| soak up** *We were lying by the pool,*

soaking up the afternoon sun. | **catch** *You've caught the sun* (= become slightly burnt by the sun).
• SUN + VERB **come up, climb, rise** *The sun climbed higher in the sky.* ◊ *The sun rises in the east.* | **dip, drop, go down, set, sink** *The sun sets in the west.* ◊ *It was getting cooler as the sun sank below the horizon.* | **be out, be up** *The sun was up now, and strong.* | **move** *The sun moved slowly westward.* | **appear, break through (sth), come out, emerge** *Just then, a watery sun broke through the clouds.* | **beat down, blaze down, burn, glare, shine** *A brilliant sun shone through the trees.* | **disappear, go in** *The sun went in and it started to rain.* | **catch sth, flash on sth, glance on sth, glint off/on sth, play on sth, sparkle (on sth)** *The sun caught her dazzling copper hair.* ◊ *The sun glinted on the blades.* | **pour down/in, slant through sth, stream in/through sth** *The evening sun slanted through the window.* | **strike sth, touch sth** *The sun struck the steep blue slates of the roof.* | **warm sth** *The sun warmed his face.*
• SUN + NOUN **god** | **worshipper** | **lounge, terrace, trap** (also **suntrap**) | **bed** (also **sunbed**), **lounger** (also **sunlounger**) | **hat** (also **sunhat**), **umbrella, visor** | **tan** (also **suntan**) | **cream, lotion, oil, protection** *On children, use a cream with a high sun protection factor.* | **damage, exposure** *wrinkles caused by sun damage*
• PREP. **in the~** *Don't sit in the sun too long.* ◊ *The helmets were glinting in the sun.* ◊ *We've booked a holiday in the sun* (= in a place that is warm and sunny). **into the~** *We went out into the sun.* **out of the~** *We did our best to keep out of the sun.* | **~in** *with the sun in her eyes* **~on** *enjoying the feel of the sun on his back*
• PHRASES **the rays of the sun/the sun's rays**

Sunday *noun*

⇨ Note at DAY

sunglasses *noun*

• ADJ. **clip-on** | **wrap-around** | **mirror, mirrored, reflecting** | **designer**
• QUANT. **pair**
• VERB + SUNGLASSES **have on, wear** | **put on, take off** | **adjust**
• SUNGLASSES + VERB **be perched on sth, perch on sth** *Her sunglasses were perched on her head.*
• PREP. **behind your~** *She observed the goings-on from behind her mirrored sunglasses.*

sunlight *noun*

• ADJ. **blinding, bright, brilliant, harsh, hot, intense, scorching, strong, warm** *He emerged from the tunnel into blinding sunlight.* | **direct, full** *plants that do not like direct sunlight* | **pale, weak, wintry** | **dappled, golden** *the dappled sunlight of the forest* | **reflected** | **afternoon, morning, evening** | **autumn, spring, etc.**
• QUANT. **beam, ray, shaft** | **patch, pool**
• VERB + SUNLIGHT **block out** *a dank backyard with a wall that blocked out the sunlight* | **gleam in, glint in, shimmer in, sparkle in** *The sea shimmered in the sunlight.* | **be exposed to** *Do not leave your skin exposed to sunlight for too long.* | **blink in, squint in** *They emerged from the cinema, blinking in the sunlight.*
• SUNLIGHT + VERB **come, fall, filter, flood, penetrate, pierce, pour, shine, slant, stream** *Sunlight filtered dustily through the slats of the door.* ◊ *in dark thickets where sunlight could not penetrate* ◊ *She threw back the shutters and the sunlight streamed in.* | **dapple sth, gleam on/through sth, glimmer on sth, glint on sth, glitter on sth, reflect from/on sth, shimmer on sth, sparkle on sth** *Sunlight dapples the grass around us.* ◊ *the sunlight sparkling on the water*
• PREP. **in the~** *waves sparkling in the sunlight* **into the~** *We came out into bright sunlight again.*

sunny *adj.*

• VERBS **be, look** | **become, get** | **remain, stay**
• ADV. **brilliantly, very** *a brilliantly sunny day* | **quite**

sunset *noun*

• ADJ. **beautiful, glorious, spectacular, stunning** | **orange, red**
• VERB + SUNSET **admire, watch, ride/sail off into** *At the end of the movie, the hero rides off into the sunset.*
• PREP. **against the~** *The trees were black against the sunset.* **at~** *walking along the beach at sunset* | **~over** *a beautiful sunset over the bay*
• PHRASES **the glow of the sunset** *sitting in the last glow of the sunset*

sunshine *noun*

• ADJ. **blazing, bright, brilliant, dazzling** | **beautiful, glorious, pleasant** *two weeks of glorious sunshine* | **hot, sweltering, warm** | **hazy, mild, pale, watery, wintry** | **fitful** *It was a cool day with fitful sunshine.* | **afternoon, evening, morning** | **June, July, etc.** | **autumn, spring, etc.** *She sat on the wall, enjoying the spring sunshine.*
• VERB + SUNSHINE **bask in, enjoy, soak up** | **be bathed in** *The town was bathed in spring sunshine.* | **gleam in, glow in, sparkle in**
• SUNSHINE + VERB **beat down, flood, pour, slant, stream** *The sunshine came streaming in at the window.*
• PREP. **in (the)~** *The race was run in bright sunshine.* **into the~** *She followed us out into the sunshine.*

suntan *noun*

• ADJ. **golden, good**
• VERB + SUNTAN **have** | **show off, sport** *Everyone in the bar was sporting a suntan.* | **get, work on** *He spent the mornings on the beach getting a suntan.* ◊ *I'm going down to the pool to work on my suntan!*
• SUNTAN + NOUN **lotion, oil**

superb *adj.*

• VERBS **be, look, sound** *She looked superb.*
• ADV. **really** | **absolutely, quite, simply** *The cuisine is absolutely superb.*

superficial *adj.*

• VERBS **be, seem** | **remain**
• ADV. **extremely, very** | **entirely, purely** *He began to feel he could cope, on a purely superficial level, at least.* | **increasingly** | **largely, more or less** | **fairly, quite, rather, relatively, somewhat**

superfluous *adj.*

• VERBS **be, feel, seem** | **become** | **make sth, render sth** | **consider sth**
• ADV. **quite, totally, wholly** *She gave him a look that made words quite superfluous.* | **almost** | **rather**

superior *noun*

• ADJ. **immediate** *The form has to be signed by your immediate superior.* | **social**
• VERB + SUPERIOR **report sb/sth to** *She threatened to report the assistant to his superiors.*

superior *adj.*

• VERBS **be, look, seem** | **become** | **make sth** *What is it that makes this technique superior?* | **consider sth, see sth as** *I don't see either product as superior to the other.*
• ADV. **clearly, distinctly, far, greatly, markedly, vastly** *The new products are far superior to the old ones.* ◊ *They defeated a greatly superior Roman army.* | **altogether, in-**

finitely, **wholly** *The house was altogether superior to the kind of thing most men of Adam's age could aspire to.* | **rather, slightly, somewhat** | **inherently, intrinsically, naturally** | **supposedly** | **undoubtedly** | **numerically** *the numerically superior* (= larger in numbers) *British forces* | **economically, educationally, intellectually, morally, socially, technically**
• PREP. **in** *a microwave that is vastly superior in design to all other models* **to** *She felt socially superior to most of her neighbours.*

superiority *noun*

• ADJ. **absolute, complete, overwhelming, total** | **effortless** *Driving the Jaguar gave him a feeling of total control, effortless superiority.* | **inherent, innate, intrinsic, natural** | **academic, biological, cultural, intellectual, moral, numerical, physical, racial, social, technical, technological** *a discredited ideology of racial superiority* | **male, masculine** *his air of masculine superiority* | **air, military, naval**
• VERB + SUPERIORITY **achieve, establish** *the enemy's attempts to establish air superiority* | **enjoy, have** *For a long time France enjoyed overwhelming superiority in this field.* | **confirm, convince sb of, demonstrate, prove, show, underline** | **assert, assume, claim, imply** *The use of the words 'modern' and 'old' is not meant to imply the superiority of one over the other.* | **acknowledge, bow to** *Their team has had to bow to Australia's superiority in recent years.*
• PREP. **~in** *making use of their superiority in numbers* **~over** *the company's clear technological superiority over its rivals* **~to** *The settlers remained convinced of their superiority to the native population.*
• PHRASES **a feeling/sense of superiority**

supermarket *noun*

• ADJ. **leading, major, top** | **high-street, local**
• SUPERMARKET + NOUN **chain, giant, group** | **development** | **car park, checkout, queue, shelf, trolley** *An increasing amount of organic produce is to be found on supermarket shelves.* | **brand** | **assistant, manager**

superstition *noun*

• ADJ. **popular** | **age-old, ancient, old** | **local** | **pagan** | **primitive**
• VERB + SUPERSTITION **have** *We have a lot of superstitions about animals.* | **be riddled with** *The topic of birth is riddled with superstition.* | **believe in** *unwilling to believe in local superstitions* | **dismiss sth as, reject sth as**
• SUPERSTITION + VERB **be attached to sth** *Red-headed people have many superstitions attached to them.*
• PREP. **~about** *primitive superstitions about death*

supervise *verb*

• ADV. **carefully, closely, strictly, well** *The children will be closely supervised at all times.* | **fully, properly** *The pool is fully supervised by trained staff.* | **adequately** | **inadequately** | **personally** *I will supervise the work personally.* | **internationally** *a proposal for an internationally supervised ceasefire*
• VERB + SUPERVISE **appoint sb to** *An executive officer was appointed to supervise the arrangements.*

supervision *noun*

• ADJ. **careful, close, strict** | **adequate, effective, proper** | **inadequate** | **constant, daily, day-to-day, regular** | **minimal** | **direct** *New staff are trained to work without direct supervision.* | **general, overall** | **adult, clinical, expert, medical, parental, personal**
• VERB + SUPERVISION **need, require** | **get, have, receive** | **exercise, give sb, offer (sb), provide (sb with)** *The scheme offers only minimal supervision for young offenders.* | **be responsible for** *The head porter is responsible for the supervision and allocation of duties.* | **keep sb/sth under** *He needs to be kept under strict supervision.* | **improve, tighten** | **relax** | **escape (from), evade** *She managed to escape her boss's constant supervision.*
• SUPERVISION + NOUN **order** *The local authority can apply for a supervision order for the child.*
• PREP. **under (sb's)** *~ under the close supervision of her teachers* **with/without** *~ Children are not allowed to swim without adequate supervision.* | *~* **by** *They still require supervision by skilled colleagues.* *~* **from** *Trainees will receive personal supervision from experienced staff.*
• PHRASES **a lack of supervision**

supervisor *noun*

• ADJ. **chief, senior** | **area** | **office** | **shift** | **project** | **production** | **technical** | **research**
• VERB + SUPERVISOR **act as**
• PREP. **under a/the** *~ the people working under that supervisor*
⇨ Note at JOB

supper *noun*

• ADJ. **light** | **cold, hot** | **buffet** | **early, late** | **family** | **harvest** *There was always a harvest supper for the farm workers after the hay and wheat had been cut.* | **fish and chip, pie, etc.**
• SUPPER + NOUN **dish** *It can also be eaten as a supper dish with a salad.* | **table, things, tray** *Ellie cleared away their supper things.*
• PHRASES **a bit/bite of supper** *They invited me round for a bite of supper.*
⇨ Note at MEAL (for verbs)

supple *adj.*

• VERBS **be, feel, look** *leaving your skin feeling soft and supple* | **become, get** *He was gradually getting more supple.* | **keep, remain, stay** *exercises that will help you to keep supple* | **make sth** *a cream that is used on dry skins to make them nice and supple* | **keep sth** *You must exercise your joints to keep them supple.*
• ADV. **extremely, very**

supplement *noun*

1 sth that is added
• ADJ. **useful, valuable** | **colour** (= a colour magazine that comes with most weekend papers in Britain), **magazine, special, Sunday** *Our special supplement is packed with inspirational ideas for healthy and glamorous hair.* | **dietary, food, mineral, nutritional, vitamin**
• VERB + SUPPLEMENT **provide (sb/sth with)** | **add** *The farmer adds a supplement to the horse's feed.* | **take, use (sth as)** *I take a vitamin supplement every day.* ◊ *You can use these books as supplements to the basic English course.*
• PREP. **~to** *This document is a supplement to the main report.*

2 extra amount of money
• ADJ. **$100, £50, etc.** *A balcony is available for a £20 supplement.* | **flight, single room** *If you want to travel on a different day a flight supplement is payable.* | **earnings-related, means-tested** *means-tested supplements to the basic pension*
• VERB + SUPPLEMENT **add, charge** *We charge a small supplement for this service.* | **carry, have** *Weekend flights carry a supplement.* | **pay**
• SUPPLEMENT + VERB **be payable**
• PREP. **at a** *~ Single rooms are available at a supplement.* | *~* **for** *a $20 supplement for each extra night* *~* **on** *There is a supplement on rooms with a sea view.*

supplier noun

● ADJ. **big, largest, leading, main, major, principal | small | sole | reliable | external, foreign, outside, overseas | local | independent | mail-order | agricultural, arms, component, equipment, food, software,** etc. **| electricity, gas, oil**

● PREP. **~ to** *the leading arms supplier to the rebel forces*

supply noun

1 sth that is supplied

● ADJ. **total** *It is impossible to measure the total supply of money in circulation.* **| endless, inexhaustible, infinite, limitless, never-ending, unending** *He has an endless supply of corny jokes.* **| abundant, bountiful, good, large, plentiful | adequate, ample, sufficient | inadequate, limited, small** *Hurry, as we only have a limited supply of these TVs in stock!* **| dwindling | constant, continuous, regular, steady | fresh** *The body needs a fresh supply of vitamin C every day.* **| ready, reliable** *the provision of a reliable supply of clean water to rural communities* **| domestic | air, blood, oxygen,** etc. *A clot in the brain cut off her blood supply.* **| food, milk, water,** etc. **| coal, electricity, energy, fuel, gas, oil, power,** etc. *Domestic coal supplies were more plentiful in the mid-1950s.* ◇ *Turn off the mains electricity supply.* **| mains | labour** *The farmers depend on a casual labour supply at harvest time.* **| money** *the country's problems with ballooning inflation and swelling money supply*

● VERB + SUPPLY **have** *Make sure you have an adequate supply of brochures.* **| get, lay in, obtain, receive** *We should lay in a good supply of beer for the party.* **| produce, provide** *The studio produced a steady supply of good films.* **| ensure, maintain | cut off, disconnect, disrupt, stop** *The electricity company disconnected our supply for non-payment of a bill.* ◇ *The storm disrupted the town's power supply.* **| deplete, exhaust, use (up)** *By the end of the winter the supply of grain was severely depleted.* **| replenish, restore | increase | restrict, limit, reduce | exceed, outstrip** *Demand for top-quality programmers exceeds supply, leading to extortionate salaries.*

● SUPPLY + VERB **increase | fall | exceed/meet demand** *Labour supply did not increase to meet demand.*

● SUPPLY + NOUN **line, system** *the water supply system* **| contract**

● PREP. **~ of** *a supply of spare batteries* **~ to** *to maintain an adequate water supply to the inner city areas*

● PHRASES **be in short supply** *Food is in short supply following the flooding.* **demand and supply/supply and demand** *laws of supply and demand* **a fall/a shortfall in supply** *There will soon be a shortfall in supply of qualified young people.* **an increase in supply**

2 supplies amount of sth needed

● ADJ. **abundant, plentiful | limited, meagre | vital | emergency, relief | arms, food, medical, military, office** *The Red Cross flew emergency food supplies into the war zone.*

● VERB + SUPPLIES **bring (in/up), lay in, provide (sb/sth with)** *The money raised will provide vital medical supplies to refugee camps.* **| be/run out of, be/run short of | threaten** *Rebel action threatened relief supplies.*

● SUPPLIES + VERB **hold out, last | be depleted, be exhausted, run low/out/short**

● PREP. **~ of** *The injured climbers had only meagre supplies of water and peanuts to live off.*

supply verb

● ADV. **amply, liberally, well | adequately** *Any room where gas is used must be adequately supplied with air.* **| poorly | generously, kindly** *a buffet supper, generously supplied by club members* **| readily | free (of charge)**

● VERB + SUPPLY **agree to | refuse to | fail to | ask sb to** *Each applicant is asked to supply a portfolio of work at interview.*

● PREP. **for** *goods supplied for private use* **from** *The water was supplied from an eight-wheeled tanker.* **to** *They were accused of supplying arms to the rebels.* **with** *He refused to supply the police with information.*

● PHRASES **a contract to supply sth, intent to supply (sb/sth)** *(law) He was charged with possession of drugs with intent to supply others.* **keep sb/sth supplied with sth** *keeping the guests well supplied with champagne*

support noun

1 help and encouragement

● ADJ. **complete, full, total | active, considerable, enthusiastic, firm, generous, good, great, loyal, massive, overwhelming, solid, strong, tremendous, unqualified, wholehearted** *The socialist candidate enjoys the firm support of local industry.* ◇ *the company's generous financial support of the arts* ◇ *The poll revealed massive support for the proposal.* ◇ *The plan received strong support from farmers.* **| unflagging, unstinting, unswerving, unwavering** *We would like to thank Edna Hales for her unstinting support over the years.* **| growing, increased, increasing | continued, continuing | broad, community, general, majority, mass, popular, public, wide/widespread** *The government has lost majority support in the Assembly.* **| main | limited, lukewarm, qualified** *My idea only received lukewarm support from my colleagues.* **| adequate, sufficient | direct, indirect | long-term** *people who need long-term support at home* **| personal** *The proposal has the personal support of the president.* **| mutual** *The parents of the sufferers get together for mutual support.* **| international** *Labour, Liberal,* etc. **| all-party, bipartisan, cross-party | administrative, economic, electoral, emotional, financial, moral, political, practical, technical,** etc. *She took her sister with her to the interview for moral support.* **| government, official, state | air, military, naval | price** *a price support mechanism*

● VERB + SUPPORT **enjoy, have** *The policy has the support of the community.* **| derive, draw, get, receive** *Which groups does the party draw most of its support from?* **| enlist, find, gain, mobilize, secure, win** *Campaigners have enlisted the support of their local MP.* **| attract, cultivate, drum up, muster, rally, recruit, seek, solicit, whip up | give sb/sth, lend (sb/sth), offer (sb/sth), provide (sb/sth with), throw** *organizations that provide support and advice to small businesses* ◇ *She threw her full support behind him.* **| lose | cut (off), withdraw | need, require** *She will need a lot of emotional support at this difficult time.* **| count on, rely on** *Can I count on your support?* **| announce, come out in, confirm, demonstrate, express, pledge, reaffirm, show** *one of the first scientists to come out in support of 'The Origin of Species'* ◇ *Many TV celebrities have already pledged their support to the appeal.* **| bolster, broaden, build (up), increase, strengthen** *The government is trying to build popular support for an unwinnable war.* **| weaken**

● SUPPORT + VERB **come** *Support came from all sections of the community.* **| grow, rise** *Support for the Liberals has risen to 30 per cent.* **| fall**

● SUPPORT + NOUN **base** *He had no support base within the party.* **| group** *a local support group for single parents* **| network | services**

● PREP. **in ~ of** *an intense campaign in support of the proposal* **with/without ... ~** *The pipeline is to be built with international support.* **| ~ against** *Farmers mobilized considerable support against government plans to remove import restrictions.* **~ among** *The party wishes to broaden its support among professionals.* **~ between** *mutual support between local cooperatives* **~ for** *The president has expressed his support for the project.* **~ from** *The policy has broad support from industry.*

● PHRASES **a base of support** *Fears that instability*

would return under the Democrats gave the government a broad base of support. **a cut/decline in support, an expression of support** *The rebel leader claimed to have received expressions of support from all the neighbouring countries.* **a lack of support, a source of support**

2 money to buy food, clothes, etc.
- ADJ. **child, family, social | income**
- VERB + SUPPORT **claim** *Families earning below a certain amount can claim child support.*
- PHRASES **a means of support**

3 sth that carries the weight of sb/sth
- ADJ. **firm | additional, extra | back, knee, etc. | roof**
- VERB + SUPPORT **give sth** *The piece of wood under the mattress is to give my back extra support.*
- PHRASES **hold onto sb/sth for support** *He held onto his wife for support as he left the hospital.*

support *verb*

1 help/encourage/agree with sb/sth
- ADV. **fervently, overwhelmingly, strongly** *The people of this country overwhelmingly support their president.* ◇ *I strongly support the view that education should be available to everyone.* | **fully, wholeheartedly | unanimously | actively** *The group is actively supported by several Members of Parliament.* | **tacitly | enthusiastically | loyally** *He has supported the party loyally for over twenty years.* | **ably** *The soloists were ably supported by the University Singers.*
- VERB + SUPPORT **agree to, be pledged to, pledge to, promise to** *He promised to support me at the meeting.* | **be prepared to, be willing to | fail to, refuse to**
- PREP. **in** *Very few countries supported the United States in its action.*
- PHRASES **be widely supported** *These policies were widely supported in the country.*

2 show that sth is true/correct
- ADV. **strongly** *The evidence strongly supports his claims.*
- VERB + SUPPORT **appear to, seem to, tend to**

3 give sb money
- ADV. **financially | generously**
- VERB + SUPPORT **help (to)**
- PREP. **through** *Her parents supported her all through college.*

supporter *noun*

- ADJ. **active, ardent, close, committed, die-hard, enthusiastic, faithful, fanatical, fervent, great, keen, loyal, passionate, stalwart, staunch, strong** *an active supporter of democratic change* ◇ *The emperor was deserted by his closest supporters before the end of the war.* ◇ *die-hard supporters of the old system* ◇ *Only stalwart supporters of the team stayed to the end of the match.* | **leading, principal, prominent | lifelong, long-time | traditional** *an area of traditional Labour supporters* | **reluctant | government, opposition, party, political | Conservative, Labour, etc.** | **grass-roots, rank-and-file** *The party has not been listening to the concerns of its grass-roots supporters.* | **football, rugby, etc.**
- QUANT. **army, group, set, team** *Both sets of supporters applauded the fantastic goal.*
- VERB + SUPPORTER **have | attract, rally** *to attract supporters to the cause*
- SUPPORTER + VERB **rally** *Supporters rallied to his assistance when he was declared bankrupt.* | **cheer** *a coachload of cheering football supporters*
- PHRASES **a crowd/rally of supporters** *The opposition leader addressed a rally of 50 000 supporters.*

supportive *adj.*

- VERBS **be, seem | become | remain | find sb**

- ADV. **extremely, highly, incredibly, strongly, very, wonderfully** *strongly supportive of the government's approach* ◇ *All the hospital staff were wonderfully supportive.* | **entirely, fully, totally, wholly** *We are totally supportive of this idea.* | **broadly, generally, largely | mutually** *establishing a mutually supportive and caring relationship*
- PREP. **of** *fully supportive of the changes* **to** *They were all extremely supportive to me.*

suppose *verb*

- ADV. **mistakenly, wrongly**
- VERB + SUPPOSE **be plausible to, be reasonable to** *It's reasonable to suppose that people go into this business in search of fame.* | **be absurd to, be implausible to, be naive to, be unreasonable to**
- PHRASES **be commonly/generally/popularly supposed** *This combination of qualities is generally supposed to be extremely rare.* **reason to suppose sth** *There is no reason to suppose she's lying.*

supposition *noun*

- ADJ. **mere, pure** *That is mere supposition!* | **reasonable** *It is a reasonable supposition that many mothers would welcome the offer of part-time work.*
- VERB + SUPPOSITION **make, work on** *Let's work on the supposition that she meant no offence.* | **be based on | confirm, support | be correct in** *You are correct in your suppositions about the source of his wealth.*
- SUPPOSITION + VERB **be based on sth**
- PREP. **on (a/the)** ~ *She was charged on the supposition that she had colluded with her husband in the murders.* | ~ **about** *They are making all sorts of suppositions about our possible reaction.* ~ **of** *a supposition of innocence*

suppress *verb*

1 stop sth by using force
- ADV. **bloodily, brutally, ruthlessly, vigorously, violently** *A pro-democracy uprising was brutally suppressed.*
- VERB + SUPPRESS **attempt to, seek to, try to | use sth to** *using violence to suppress opposition*
- PHRASES **an attempt to suppress sth**

2 stop sth from being seen/known
- ADV. **completely | effectively** *The medication effectively suppressed the pain.* | **deliberately** *This information had been deliberately suppressed.* | **systematically**
- VERB + SUPPRESS **attempt to, seek to, try to**
- PHRASES **an attempt to suppress sth**

3 stop yourself doing/expressing sth
- ADV. **firmly | hardly** *He could hardly suppress his surprise.* | **instantly** *The disloyal thought was instantly suppressed.* | **quickly**
- VERB + SUPPRESS **be unable to, cannot/could not** *She was unable to suppress a giggle.* | **try to | manage to | be hard to**
- PHRASES **barely suppressed** *Her face was charged with barely suppressed anger.*

suppression *noun*

- ADJ. **total | bloody, brutal, violent**
- PREP. **during/in the** ~ **of** *He was injured in the bloody suppression of the uprising.*

supremacy *noun*

- ADJ. **total, unchallenged | world | air, military, naval | economic, political | male**
- VERB + SUPREMACY **enjoy, have** *a period when the British enjoyed supremacy in international trade* | **lose | battle for, fight for, struggle for | assert, establish | proclaim | acknowledge, uphold** *to uphold the supremacy of the country's own laws* | **give sb/sth** *Coal gave the region industrial supremacy.* | **maintain | challenge**

● PREP. ~**in** *the battle for supremacy in the world econom-ic markets* ~ **over** *By the end of the war, the prince had es-tablished total supremacy over all his rivals.* ~ **within** *fac-tions fighting for supremacy within the Church*
● PHRASES **a battle/fight/struggle for supremacy, a challenge/threat to sb/sth's supremacy, a symbol of supremacy**

surcharge *noun*

● ADJ. **small** | **tax** *a corporate tax surcharge*
● VERB + SURCHARGE **add, impose, levy, put** *A sur-charge of 40 francs was added to our bill.* ◇ *A surcharge is levied on late applications.* | **pay**
● PREP. ~ **for** *There is a surcharge for excess baggage.* ~ **on** *There is a 2% surcharge on credit card users.*

sure *adj.*

● VERBS **be, feel, seem, sound** *You don't seem very sure to me.* | **make** *Make sure no one finds out about this.* | **make sb** *What makes you so sure she'll come back to you?*
● ADV. **absolutely, completely, damned, quite** | **doubly** *To make doubly sure they would not be disturbed she turned the key in the lock.* | **not altogether, not entirely, not quite, not really** *I'm not altogether sure he would ap-preciate your efforts.* | **fairly, pretty**
● PREP. **about** *Potts was confident of taking the Ameri-can title, but less sure about the world championship.* **of** *You'd better be completely sure of your facts.*

surf *noun*

● ADJ. **heavy** | **distant** *the roar of distant surf*
● VERB + SURF **ride** *dolphins riding the surf*
● SURF + VERB **break, roll (in)** *the sound of surf break-ing on the beach* | **roar, thunder**
● PREP. **in the** ~ *The children splashed about in the surf.*
● PHRASES **the roar/thunder of (the) surf**

surface *noun*

● ADJ. **even, flat, level, smooth** | **rough, uneven** | **curved** | **firm, hard, solid** | **soft** | **slippery** | **calm, glassy, polished, reflective, shiny** *the glassy surface of the lake.* | **frozen** *The ball rolled onto the frozen surface of the pond.* | **inner, interior, internal** *the inner surface of a bone* | **exterior, external, outer** | **lower, upper** | **water** | **floor, ground, land, road, rock, wall** | **kitchen, work/working** *a cleaning product for all kitchen surfaces* | **earth's** *Visible light from the sun passes through the at-mosphere to the earth's surface.*
● VERB + SURFACE **come (up) to, rise to** | **bring sth to** *The captain brought the submarine to the surface.* | **scratch, skim, touch** *(all figurative) The investigation barely scratched the surface of the city's drug problem.* | **ripple** *The wind rippled the surface of the lake.*
● SURFACE + NOUN **area** | **level** | **layer** *the surface layer of the skin* | **temperature, tension** | **water** *Surface water made driving conditions hazardous.*
● PREP. **above/over the** ~, **across the** ~, **along the** ~, **below/beneath/under the** ~ *The ring slowly sank beneath the surface of the mud pool.* ◇ *(figurative) She gives the im-pression of being rather conventional, but under the sur-face she is wildly eccentric.* **in the** ~ *Cracks began to appear in the surface of the earth.* **on a/the** ~ *a trail of pink flowers floating on the surface of the water* ◇ *(figurative) On the surface his words were funny, but I detected quite a lot of anger behind them.*

surge *noun*

1 of feeling
● ADJ. **great, huge** | **wild** | **abrupt, sudden, swift** | **ini-tial** *His initial surge of euphoria was quickly followed by*

dismay. | **fresh, new, renewed** *She felt a fresh surge of anger when he denied lying.* | **familiar** | **adrenalin**
● VERB + SURGE **experience, feel** *He experienced that familiar surge of excitement.*
● SURGE + VERB **sweep (over/through) sb/sth** *A great surge of emotion swept through him.*
● PREP. **with a** ~ *He thought of his old teacher with a surge of affection.* | ~ **of** *a sudden surge of adrenalin*

2 movement/increase
● ADJ. **dramatic, extraordinary, great, huge, massive** | **growing** | **sudden, unexpected** | **temporary** | **last-minute, overnight, recent** *A last-minute surge in ticket sales saved the show from closure.* | **storm, tidal** *The storm surge caused widespread flooding.*
● PREP. ~ **in** *a dramatic surge in the demand*
● PHRASES **a surge forward** *Police struggled to control the sudden surge forward by the demonstrators.*

surgeon *noun*

● ADJ. **distinguished, eminent, leading, top** | **brilliant** | **pioneering** | **chief, consultant, senior** | **qualified** | **general** | **brain, dental, eye, heart, orthopaedic, plastic, transplant, veterinary** *A plastic surgeon successfully re-built his nose.* | **police**
● VERB + SURGEON **be, work as** | **become, qualify as** *He is determined to qualify as a surgeon.* | **see**
● SURGEON + VERB **operate, perform an operation, re-move sth** *the surgeon who will operate on you* ◇ *Surgeons removed her right leg above the knee.*
● PHRASES **surgeon's knife** *Many people are terrified at the thought of the surgeon's knife.*

surgery *noun*

1 medical treatment
● ADJ. **major, radical** | **minor** | **extensive** | **further** | **successful, unsuccessful** | **keyhole, laser** | **invasive** *One of his specialities is minimally invasive surgery.* | **elective, emergency, experimental, exploratory, remed-ial** *They discussed whether patients should have to pay for all elective surgery.* | **cosmetic, plastic** | **general** | **ab-dominal, brain, bypass, cardiac, gastric, heart, knee, open-heart, orthopaedic, paediatric**
● VERB + SURGERY **have, undergo** *She had minor sur-gery on her knee.* | **perform** *He has been performing heart surgery for ten years.* | **need, require**
● PREP. **after/before/during** ~ *She felt weak for six months after undergoing major abdominal surgery.* | ~ **for** *emergency surgery for a twisted gut* ~ **to** *After the acci-dent, she needed extensive plastic surgery to her face.*

2 place/time a doctor/dentist sees patients
● ADJ. **open** | **afternoon, evening, morning** | **dental, doctor's, GP's, veterinary**
● VERB + SURGERY **do, have, hold** *I'll do morning sur-gery, if you like.* ◇ *We only have a morning surgery.* ◇ *He holds surgery from 10 a.m. to 1 p.m.* | **attend, go to** *those attending the doctor's surgery with physical symptoms* ◇ *I'll have to go to the surgery to pick up the prescription.*
● SURGERY + NOUN **hours**
● PREP. **in a/the** ~ *Dr Smith isn't in the surgery today.*

surname *noun*

● ADJ. **double-barrelled, hyphenated**
● VERB + SURNAME **bear, have** | **address/call sb by** *The teacher addresses the students by their surnames.* | **change** | **adopt, assume, take** *On marriage most women still take their husband's surname.*

surpass *verb*

● ADV. **far** | **comfortably, easily**
● PREP. **in** *The second half of the match comfortably sur-passed the first in entertainment value.*

surplus noun

- ADJ. **large** *a large grain surplus* | **small**
- VERB + SURPLUS **produce**
- SURPLUS + NOUN **cash, stock**
- PREP. **in~** *The pension fund is in surplus.*

surprise noun

1 feeling of surprise

- ADJ. **great, utter** | **mild, some** | **initial** *After the initial surprise I got to like the place.* | **mock** *His eyebrows rose in mock surprise.*
- QUANT. **element** *The Egyptian team relied on the element of surprise to defeat their stronger opponents.*
- VERB + SURPRISE **express, register, show** | **feign** *He feigned surprise when I went up and said hello.* | **hide** *She was quick to hide her surprise.* | **cause** *The president's remarks caused surprise and embarrassment.*
- PREP. **in~** *'Walk twenty miles!' repeated the old man in surprise.* **to your~** *Much to her surprise she enjoyed the party.* **with/without~** *It was with some surprise that I read of his resignation.* | **~ at** *She showed no surprise at the news.*
- PHRASES **an expression/a look of surprise, a gasp/scream/shriek, etc. of surprise**

2 sth that you did not expect

- ADJ. **big, complete, great, major, total** | **lovely, nice, pleasant, wonderful**
- VERB + SURPRISE **come as** | **get, have** *I had a lovely surprise when I saw Mark there.* | **spring** *Johnson sprung a surprise by beating the favourite in the first round.* | **be in for** *Your mother's in for a bit of a surprise when she gets home.* | **catch sb by, take sb by** *The storm took us completely by surprise.*
- SURPRISE + NOUN **announcement, attack, party, victory, visit**
- PREP. **~for** *It was a complete surprise for me.* **~to** *His refusal came as no surprise to his boss.*
- PHRASES **a bit of a/quite a surprise**

surprise verb

- ADV. **greatly, really** | **not at all** *The outcome did not surprise me at all.* | **hardly** | **a little, slightly**
- VERB + SURPRISE **wouldn't** *It wouldn't surprise me if they announced they were going to get married.* | **seem to** | **want to** *They wanted to surprise their mother and get the breakfast ready.*

surprised adj.

- VERBS **appear, be, feel, look, seem, sound**
- ADV. **extremely, greatly, most, really, terribly, very** | **hardly, not altogether, not at all, not entirely, not in the least, not particularly, not totally, scarcely** *Her father didn't seem at all surprised.* | **almost** | **a bit, faintly, a little, mildly, pretty, quite, rather, slightly, somewhat, vaguely** *She looked faintly surprised at my remark.* | **genuinely** | **clearly, evidently, obviously** | **secretly** | **constantly, continually** *I am constantly surprised by what my fourteen-month-old son understands.* | **momentarily** | **agreeably, pleasantly** *He was pleasantly surprised to discover that he was no longer afraid.*
- PREP. **at** *He sounded surprised at this request.* **by** *She appeared genuinely surprised by this gesture of affection.*

surprising adj.

- VERBS **be, seem** | **make sth** | **find sth**
- ADV. **extremely, really, very** | **hardly, not altogether, not at all, not entirely, not really, not totally, not wholly, scarcely** *It is hardly surprising that rumours continue to circulate.* | **a bit, quite, rather, slightly, somewhat**

surrender noun

- ADJ. **total** | **unconditional** | **immediate**
- VERB + SURRENDER **demand** *The allied commander demanded their immediate and unconditional surrender.* | **force/starve into** *The villagers were starved into surrender.* | **accept, take** *The division took the surrender of a group of some 500 rebels.*
- PREP. **~to** *the government's surrender to the nationalists' demands*
- PHRASES **a flag of surrender** *The rebels hoisted the white flag of surrender.* **in (mock) surrender** *He raised his hands in mock surrender.* **the terms of surrender** *offering them easy terms of surrender*

surrender verb

- ADV. **completely** *After three weeks under siege they surrendered completely.* | **immediately** | **eventually, finally** | **formally** *The British formally surrendered on 31 May.* | **voluntarily**
- VERB + SURRENDER **order sb to** *They were ordered to surrender their weapons to the police.* | **agree to** *They agreed to surrender their claim to the territory.* | **refuse to** | **be forced to**
- PREP. **to** *He surrendered voluntarily to his enemies.* ◇ *The dictator surrendered power to Parliament.*

surrogate noun

- VERB + SURROGATE **act as, be**
- SURROGATE + NOUN **father, mother, parent** | **child**
- PREP. **~for** *He used the Internet as a surrogate for contact with real people.*

surround verb

- ADV. **completely, entirely, totally** | **almost, virtually** | **quickly** | **immediately** *Will found himself immediately surrounded by screaming fans.* ◇ *the immediately surrounding area*
- PREP. **with** *They surrounded the building with tanks and armoured vehicles.*

surroundings noun

- ADJ. **attractive, beautiful, congenial, elegant, idyllic, lovely, magnificent, picturesque, pleasant** | **comfortable, luxurious, opulent, sumptuous** | **peaceful, quiet, tranquil** | **familiar** | **new, strange, unfamiliar** | **natural** *animals living in their natural surroundings* | **physical** | **immediate** | **historic** | **rural**
- VERB + SURROUNDINGS **adapt to, be in harmony with, blend into, blend (in) with, fit into/in with** *The new hotel blends perfectly with the immediate surroundings.*
- PREP. **amid ... ~** *classic French cuisine served amid elegant surroundings* **in ... ~** *We spent the afternoon relaxing in the beautiful surroundings of my parents' home.*
- PHRASES **the beauty of the surroundings**

surveillance noun

- ADJ. **close, constant, regular, round-the-clock, routine** | **covert** | **aerial, CCTV/closed-circuit television, electronic, satellite, video** | **military, police**
- VERB + SURVEILLANCE **be under** *The suspects are under police surveillance.* | **keep/place/put sb/sth under** *The country's borders are kept under constant surveillance.* | **carry out, mount** *The army carried out covert surveillance of the building for several months.* | **increase, reduce**
- SURVEILLANCE + NOUN **camera, device, equipment** | **method, operation, system** | **aircraft** | **flight** | **team**

survey *noun*

1 study of sth
- ADJ. **comprehensive, detailed, extensive, full, in-depth, major, systematic | brief, quick | sample** *The council undertook a sample survey of primary schools in the county.* | **regular | annual, monthly, etc. | local, national, nationwide, regional | independent | historical** *a historical survey of children's clothing* | **doorstep, postal, questionnaire, telephone | comparative | field | pilot | attitude, customer, opinion** *A recent customer survey showed widespread ignorance about the availability of organic food.* | **market (research), marketing**
- VERB + SURVEY **carry out, conduct, do, make, undertake** *The charity did a survey of people's attitudes to the disabled.* | **commission | participate in, respond to, take part in** *94 per cent of people who took part in the survey said they agreed.*
- SURVEY + VERB **cover sth, deal with sth, examine sth** *The survey covered 74 species.* | **ask sth | claim sth, conclude sth, confirm sth, disclose sth, find sth, highlight sth, identify sth, indicate sth, report sth, reveal sth, say sth, show sth, suggest sth** *A customer satisfaction survey highlighted the need for clearer pricing.*
- SURVEY + NOUN **data, results | method, technique | respondent**
- PREP. **according to a/the ~** *According to the survey, many young adults have experimented with drugs of some kind.* **in a/the ~** *the questions used in the survey* | **~ into** *a survey into the state of English in universities* **~ on** *a survey on drivers' attitudes to the police*
- PHRASES **the findings/results of a survey**

2 of land or a building
- ADJ. **full | aerial | archaeological, geological, geophysical, land, seismic | structural, valuation** *A structural survey of the property revealed serious defects.*
- VERB + SURVEY **carry out, do, make**

survey *verb*
- ADV. **carefully | coldly, coolly, critically** *Her green eyes surveyed him coolly.*
- PREP. **from** *I surveyed the scene from my window.*

survival *noun*
- ADJ. **long-term, short-term | continued | day-to-day | sheer** *fighting for the sheer survival of the museum* | **improved** *The study showed improved survival of patients using the drug.* | **chance, miraculous** *the chance survival of the king's letters to his mistress* | **business, economic, human, national, physical, political**
- VERB + SURVIVAL **fight for | ensure** *The campaign will hopefully ensure the survival of the tiger.* | **improve, prolong** *Chemotherapy can prolong survival in cancer patients.* | **threaten** *The arrival of this South American predator threatened the survival of native species.* | **be crucial for/to, be essential to, be necessary for, be vital for/to** *Adaptability is essential to survival in a changing environment.*
- SURVIVAL + NOUN **chances, rate | skills, strategy | kit** *The expedition members carried flares in their survival kit.* | **instinct**
- PREP. **~ against** *the struggle for survival against such well-armed enemies* **~ as** *his survival as leader*
- PHRASES **a battle/fight/struggle for survival, be a matter/question of survival** *For the poorest people, life was merely a matter of survival.* **a chance of survival** *Doctors gave him only a 50% chance of survival.* **the instinct for survival** *He lacked the common instinct for survival.* **a threat to the survival of sth** *The main threat to the survival of these creatures comes from their loss of habitat.*

survive *verb*
- ADV. **well** (used with another adverb or in the forms **better** or **best**) *The frescoes have survived remarkably well.* ◇ *Seedlings survive better in stony soil.* | **barely, hardly** *The islanders could barely survive without an export crop.* | **just (about), narrowly** *I can just about survive on what I earn.* ◇ *The prime minister narrowly survived a leadership challenge.* | **(for) long** *Nobody can survive long without water.* | **still** *Only one copy of the book still survives.* | **miraculously** *A schoolboy miraculously survived a 25 000-volt electric shock.* | **somehow**
- VERB + SURVIVE **struggle to** *poor people struggling to survive* | **be able to, can/could, manage to | expect (sb/sth) to** *Doctors did not expect him to survive the night.* | **hope to** *She cannot hope to survive long in power.* | **be likely/unlikely to | be lucky to** *Once diagnosed with lung cancer, a patient is lucky to survive for five years.* | **enable sb to, help sb (to)**
- PREP. **as** *Will she survive as party leader?* **from** *Very little has survived from this period of history.* **into** *Very few of the children survived into adult life.* **on** *They survived on roots and berries.* **through** *She survived through two world wars.* **until** *The original apple tree survived until 1911.*
- PHRASES **the only/sole surviving sb/sth** *the only surviving member of her family* **survive intact/unscathed** *Few buildings survived the war intact.*

survivor *noun*
- ADJ. **great** *Like all great survivors, she has a ruthless streak.* | **the last, the only, a rare, the sole** *This grand park is a rare survivor from the eighteenth century.* | **bomb, crash**
- VERB + SURVIVOR **find, pick up, rescue** *The navy helped pick up the survivors.* | **look/search for** *The emergency services searched all night for crash survivors.*
- PREP. **~ from** *a survivor from the Titanic*

susceptible *adj.*
- VERBS **be, seem | become | remain | leave sb/sth, make sb/sth** *The operation had left her susceptible to infection.*
- ADV. **easily, extremely, highly, particularly, readily, unusually, very** *certain highly susceptible individuals* | **quite, rather | genetically**
- PREP. **to** *Some dogs are thought to be genetically susceptible to the disease.*

suspect *noun*
- ADJ. **chief, main, number one, prime** *She has been identified as the prime suspect.* | **likely, obvious, possible, potential | usual | murder, terrorist**
- VERB + SUSPECT **have, identify (sb as)** *The police have several suspects.* | **arrest, detain, hold, round up** *The army rounded up all the usual terrorist suspects.* | **interrogate, interview, question | release | extradite, hand over**
- PREP. **~ for** *The letter makes him a possible suspect for her murder.* **~ in** *Two men were arrested as suspects in the bombing.*

suspect *verb*

1 believe that sth may happen/be true
- ADV. **strongly | rather** *I rather suspect they were trying to get rid of me.* | **rightly, wrongly | all along, always** *These revelations only prove what I suspected all along.*
- VERB + SUSPECT **begin to | have reason to** *She had no reason to suspect that Sylvia had not been telling the truth.*
- PHRASES **be widely suspected** *It was widely suspected that the cadets had been acting on orders.*

2 believe sb is guilty of sth
- ADV. **rightly, wrongly**
- PREP. **of** *He was wrongly suspected of the crime.*
- VERB + SUSPECT **have grounds to, have reason to**
- PHRASES **have grounds for suspecting sb/sth**

suspect *adj.*

- VERBS **be, look, seem, sound | render sth** *The theory is rendered suspect by its reliance on now discredited sources.*
- ADV. **deeply, highly, very** *Some of the evidence was deeply suspect.* **| increasingly | a bit, a little, rather, slightly, somewhat | politically** *the forced adoption of children of politically suspect citizens*

suspend *verb*

- ADV. **immediately | indefinitely | temporarily** *Funding for the new building has been temporarily suspended.* **| effectively**
- VERB + SUSPEND **agree to, decide to, vote to** *The government has decided to suspend production at the country's biggest lead plant.* **| threaten to | be forced to**
- PHRASES **the power to suspend sth** *The EU should have the power to suspend subsidy payments to farmers who pollute the environment.*

suspense *noun*

- ADJ. **heart-pounding, nail-biting, unbearable**
- VERB + SUSPENSE **keep sb in** *Don't keep us in suspense—did you get the job or not?* **| break** *Don't look at the end of the book yet—you'll break the suspense.* **| build (up), create | bear** *She couldn't bear the suspense a moment longer.*
- SUSPENSE + VERB **be killing sb** *(informal) I don't get the results till next week, and the suspense is killing me.*
- SUSPENSE + NOUN **story**
- PREP. **~ about** *They were kept in suspense about their possibility of joining the expedition for several weeks.*
- PHRASES **an agony of suspense** *I suffered agonies of suspense in silence.* **a state of suspense**

suspension *noun*

1 stopping of activity
- ADJ. **total | brief, temporary | lengthy, long | immediate | automatic** *Another caution will result in his automatic suspension from the final.*
- VERB + SUSPENSION **give sb, impose, order** *A four-day suspension was imposed on her.* **| get, incur** *He incurred a suspension on reduced pay.* **| appeal against**
- PREP. **under ~** *a detective under suspension from the Metropolitan Police* **| ~ from** *his suspension from the club*
- PHRASES **a period of suspension** *The athlete could face a lengthy period of suspension if found guilty.*

2 on a vehicle
- ADJ. **front, rear | active, computer-controlled, independent, self-levelling | car, etc.**
- VERB + SUSPENSION **be fitted with, have** *The new model is fitted with computer-controlled suspension.*
- SUSPENSION + NOUN **system**

suspicion *noun*

1 belief that sb has done sth wrong or that sth is true
- ADJ. **strong** *There is strong suspicion on both sides that information is being withheld.* **| the slightest, vague** *I don't think he had the slightest suspicion anything was wrong.* **| awful, dark, horrible, nagging, nasty, sneaking, terrible, worst** *I have a nasty suspicion he's organized a surprise party for me.* ◇ *My worst suspicions were realized when I received my redundancy notice.* **| lingering | growing | groundless, unfounded** *Our suspicions turned out to be groundless.* **| widespread | initial**

- VERB + SUSPICION **entertain, harbour, have** *We had our suspicions as to who did it, but nothing could be proved.* **| be/come/fall under** *He fell under suspicion of tax evasion.* **| arouse, cast, cause, create, fuel, give rise to, invite, raise, sow** *Parked vehicles that arouse suspicion should be reported to the police.* ◇ *information that casts suspicion on one of the most powerful figures in the party* ◇ *Their suspicions were further fuelled when both men failed to turn up to the appointment.* ◇ *odd behaviour that invites suspicion* **| avoid | confide, share** *She confided her suspicions to no one but her diary.* **| confirm, justify** *A telephone call confirmed my worst suspicions.* **| realize | allay, dispel** *She was anxious to allay any suspicion that she had married for money.*
- SUSPICION + VERB **exist** *The suspicion exists that Harries is stealing money from the company safe.* **| linger, remain | grow | attach to sb, fall on sb** *Strong suspicion attached to the victim's boyfriend.*
- PREP. **above/beyond ~** *They thought the head teacher was beyond suspicion.* **on ~ of** *arrested on suspicion of bribery* **| ~ about/as to/concerning** *his suspicions about the candidate's background* **~ against** *Suspicions against the former prime minister remain.*
- PHRASES **the finger of suspicion** *The finger of suspicion pointed to Gilbert Cash, a close friend of the victim.* **grounds for suspicion** *The police must have reasonable grounds for suspicion before they can get a search warrant.* **an object of suspicion** *Boys were an immediate object of suspicion to her.* **under a cloud of suspicion** *He ended his athletics career under a cloud of suspicion when he refused to take a drug test.*

2 absence of trust
- ADJ. **considerable, deep, grave, great | mutual** *an atmosphere of mutual suspicion*
- VERB + SUSPICION **regard/treat/view sb/sth with** *They viewed the new scheme with great suspicion.*

3 small amount of sth
- ADJ. **faint, slightest** *Her remarks lacked even the faintest suspicion of humour.*
- PREP. **~ of** *His mouth quivered in the suspicion of a smile.*

suspicious *adj.*

1 not trusting sb
- VERBS **be, feel, look, seem, sound | become, get, grow** *I think they're starting to get suspicious.* **| remain | make sb** *Something about her smile made him suspicious.*
- ADV. **deeply, extremely, highly, profoundly, very** *She remained deeply suspicious of computers.* **| increasingly | a bit, a little, rather, slightly, somewhat** *His voice grew faintly suspicious.* **| immediately, instantly | naturally** *I have a naturally suspicious mind.* **| rightly** *British voters are rightly suspicious of attempts to save money in the area of education.*
- PREP. **about** *They were somewhat suspicious about her past.* **of** *She was highly suspicious of his motives.*

2 making you feel that sth is wrong
- VERBS **be, look, seem, sound** *We have to carry on as usual or it would look suspicious.* **| consider sth, find sth, regard sth as, treat sth as** *I find it very suspicious that he left halfway through the morning.* ◇ *Police are treating both fires as suspicious.*
- ADV. **highly, very** *acting in a highly suspicious manner* **| not remotely** *Are you sure you haven't seen anything even remotely suspicious?* **| a bit, rather, somewhat**
- PHRASES **see/hear anything suspicious** *Inform the police immediately if you see anything suspicious.*

sustain *verb*

- ADV. **long** *The soil was so badly eroded it could no longer sustain crop production.* **| indefinitely | still**
- VERB + SUSTAIN **be able/unable to, can/could |**

help (to) | **be difficult to, be hard to, be impossible to** *This relationship would be very difficult to sustain.*

Swahili *noun*

⇨ Note at LANGUAGE

swallow *verb*

1 food/drink, etc.
• ADV. **hastily, quickly | accidentally** *She accidentally swallowed a glass bead.* | **easily** *Liquid food may be more easily swallowed.* | **down** *She swallowed down her breakfast in a hurry.*
• PHRASES **swallow sth whole** *Most snakes swallow their prey whole.*

2 move your throat muscles
• ADV. **deeply, hard | convulsively, drily, nervously, painfully** *She swallowed convulsively, determined not to cry.* | **back** *He swallowed back the lump in his throat.*
• VERB + SWALLOW **have to** *She had to swallow hard before she could speak.*

swan *noun*

• ADJ. **black, white | graceful**
• SWAN + VERB **glide, swim | fly | land | hiss**

swap *noun*

• ADJ. **straight | job | spy**
• VERB + SWAP **do, make** *Let's do a straight swap—your guitar for my bike.* | **agree on/to**
• SWAP + NOUN **deal** *The football managers agreed on swap deals involving their star players.*
• PREP. **~ between** *a spy swap made between East and West Germany* **~ with** *I did a swap with my brother.*

sway *verb*

1 from side to side/backwards and forwards
• ADV. **gently, lightly, a little, slightly | alarmingly, dangerously, precariously** *The stage swayed alarmingly under their weight.* | **dizzily, drunkenly, unsteadily | back and forth, backwards and forwards, from side to side** *The cow's udder swayed from side to side as she walked along.*
• VERB + SWAY **begin to**
• PREP. **in** *The curtains swayed gently in the breeze.*

2 influence sb/sth
• ADV. **easily** *He will not easily be swayed by argument.*

swear *verb*

1 use bad language
• ADV. **loudly | quietly, silently, softly, under your breath | viciously, violently**
• VERB + SWEAR **hear sb** *He heard her swear under her breath.*
• PREP. **at** *He swore loudly at her and left.*

2 make a serious promise
• ADV. **solemnly** *He swore solemnly that he would never hit her again.* | **on oath**
• VERB + SWEAR **be prepared to** *I would be prepared to swear on oath that they didn't see me.* | **make sb** *He made her swear on the Bible that she wouldn't leave him.*
• PREP. **by** *I swear by Almighty God to tell the truth.* **to** *I swear to you, I don't know anything.*
• PHRASES **swear sb to secrecy/silence** *We were all sworn to secrecy about the plan.*

swear word *noun*

• ADJ. **bad, strong** *That's one of the strongest swear words in Spanish.* | **mild**
• QUANT. **string**

• VERB + SWEAR WORD **use | mouth, mutter** *He mouthed a swear word at me through the window.* | **leave out** *I left out the swear words when I told the boss what the staff had said about him.*

sweat *noun*

• ADJ. **heavy | fine, light | clammy** *My shirt stuck to the clammy sweat on my back.* | **cold | stale** *The room smelled of stale sweat.* | **good** *We worked up a good sweat carrying the boxes outside.*
• QUANT. **bead, drop, trickle**
• VERB + SWEAT **break into, break out in/into** *She broke out in a cold sweat when she saw the spider.* | **work up | wake (up) in | bring sb out in | be bathed/covered/drenched/soaked in, be beaded/streaming with, be dripping (with), be slippery/wet with, glisten with** *His forehead was dripping sweat.* ◇ *The workmen were streaming with sweat.* | **mop, wipe** *He mopped the sweat from his brow.*
• SWEAT + VERB **appear, break out** *His hands trembled and sweat broke out all over his body.* | **glisten, stand out** *sweat glistening on her forehead* ◇ *Sweat stood out on his shoulders.* | **bead sth, drip/pour/run from/into/off sth, run/trickle down sth** *Sweat beaded her face.* ◇ *Sweat was running down his back.* | **soak sth**
• SWEAT + NOUN **gland**
• PREP. **in a~** *She woke up in a cold sweat.*

sweat *verb*

• ADV. **freely, heavily, a lot, profusely | slightly | off** *He's trying to sweat off a few pounds in the gym.*
• VERB + SWEAT **begin to | make sb** *The heat was making us sweat.*
• PREP. **from** *We were sweating profusely from the exertion of moving the furniture.* **with** *He awoke with a pounding heart, sweating with fear.*
• PHRASES **sweat buckets, sweat like a pig** *(both informal) After two hours of digging he was sweating like a pig.*

sweater *noun*

• ADJ. **chunky, heavy, thick | light, thin | baggy, sloppy | warm | high-necked, polo-neck, roll-neck, turtleneck, V-neck | hand-knitted, knitted | cashmere, wool, woollen | cricket | Aran, Fair Isle**
• VERB + SWEATER **pull on | peel off | knit**
⇨ Special page at CLOTHES

sweaty *adj.*

• VERBS **be, feel, look, smell | become, get**
• ADV. **really, very | all** *Ugh! You're all sweaty and horrible!* | **a bit, rather**
• PREP. **from** *Her forehead was sweaty from the pain she was in.* **with** *feeling sweaty with embarrassment*

sweep *noun*

• ADJ. **broad, great, long, wide** *The house overlooks the great sweep of the St Lawrence river.* | **grand, grandiose** *He dismissed his assistant with a grandiose sweep of his hand.* | **comprehensive** *Her eyes made a comprehensive sweep of the room.* | **upward** *The upward sweep of her hair was held in place by a comb.* | **elegant, fine, graceful**
• VERB + SWEEP **make, take** *We made a wide sweep south to the River Dee.*
• PREP. **in one~** *(figurative) Thousands of jobs were lost in one broad sweep.* **with a~** *with a sweep of his arm*

sweet *noun*

• ADJ. **chewy, sugary | boiled**
• QUANT. **bag, box, packet, tube**
• VERB + SWEET **eat, suck** *sucking a boiled sweet*
• SWEET + NOUN **shop**

sweet adj.

1 tasting like sugar/smelling pleasant
- VERBS **be, smell, taste** *The air smelled sweet and clean.* | **make sth** | **find sth** *I found the dessert a bit sweet for my taste.*
- ADV. **extremely, very | a bit, quite, rather, slightly | enough** *Is the tea sweet enough for you?* | **sickly** *an overpowering, sickly sweet smell*

2 nice
- VERBS **be, look | keep sb** *(informal) He'd promised her a new car, just to keep her sweet* (= keep her in a good mood).
- ADV. **awfully, really, terribly, very | quite, rather**
- PREP. **to** *She was really sweet to me.*
- PHRASES **sweet little** *a rather sweet little cottage*

sweetness noun

1 sweet smell/taste
- ADJ. **natural | cloying, sickly | lingering** *the lingering sweetness of incense*
- QUANT. **hint** *This is a full-bodied wine with just a hint of sweetness.*
- VERB + SWEETNESS **taste**

2 pleasantness
- ADJ. **exquisite, great | saccharine** (= false) *She smiled with saccharine sweetness.*
- VERB + SWEETNESS **taste** *to taste the sweetness of military success*
- PHRASES **all sweetness and light** *People think she's all sweetness and light, but she's actually got an awful temper.*

swell noun

1 movement of the surface of the sea
- ADJ. **heavy | gentle, slight | 10-foot, 20-foot, etc. | Atlantic, ocean** *bobbing up and down like a small boat in a heavy ocean swell*
- SWELL + VERB **break, come/roll in, lift sb/sth, surge up** *The Atlantic swell surged up under them.*
- PREP. **in a/the~** *The trawler rolled wildly in the heavy swell.* **on/with the~** *The boat rose and fell with the swell.*

2 curve in sth
- ADJ. **firm, gentle, soft, warm**
- PREP. **~of** *the gentle swell of her breasts*

swell verb

- ADV. **badly** *His sprained ankle had swollen badly.* | **slightly | up** *Her feet swelled up after the long walk to the top of the hill.*
- PREP. **with** *His legs had swollen with the heat.*

swelling noun

- ADJ. **marked** *There is a marked swelling of the lymph nodes.* | **slight**
- VERB + SWELLING **reduce**
- SWELLING + VERB **occur | go down, subside**

swerve noun

- ADJ. **sudden** *The car made a sudden swerve to the left.*
- VERB + SWERVE **make**

swerve verb

- ADV. **sharply, violently | suddenly | away**
- PREP. **across** *The car veered out of control and swerved across the road.* **into** *A lorry suddenly swerved into her path.* **off** *The vehicle swerved off the road.*
- PHRASES **swerve to avoid sb/sth** *The car swerved sharply to avoid the bus.*

swift adj.

- VERBS **be**
- ADV. **incredibly, remarkably, very** *He made a remarkably swift recovery.* | **fairly**

swig noun

- ADJ. **deep, good, long | quick**
- VERB + SWIG **have, take**
- PREP. **~from** *He took a deep swig from the bottle.* **~of** *She had a quick swig of water and then set off again.*

swim noun

- ADJ. **evening, morning, regular | quick** *How about a quick swim before breakfast?*
- VERB + SWIM **go for, have, take** *She got up early and went for a swim.*
- PREP. **for a~** *Are you joining us for a swim?*

swim verb

- ADV. **strongly, vigorously** *A water vole swam vigorously upstream.* | **quickly, rapidly | slowly | around, ashore, back, downstream, out, upstream** *Exhausted, they swam ashore.*
- VERB + SWIM **can/could | learn to | teach sb to**
- PREP. **across** *swimming across the river* **in** *swimming in the sea* **to** *We swam out to the boat.* **towards** *She swam back towards the shore.*
- PHRASES **go swimming**

swimmer noun

- ADJ. **good, keen, strong** *She's a strong swimmer.* | **poor | champion, competitive, Olympic**

swing noun

1 change in public opinion, sb's mood, etc.
- ADJ. **big, dramatic, huge, sharp, violent** *violent swings in policy* | **modest, small | 10%, etc. | adverse, negative** *The Conservatives suffered an adverse swing of 6%.* | **sudden, wild** *his sudden swings of mood* | **late** *a late swing towards the Tories* | **national | electoral | mood** *She suffers from severe mood swings.*
- VERB + SWING **need, require** *The party needs a swing of only 2.5% to win the seat.* | **represent** *This represents a swing of 14% towards Labour.* | **suffer (from)**
- PREP. **~against** *a dramatic swing against the socialists* **~away from** *the swing away from science in the sixth form* **~from, ~in** *a sharp swing in the attitudes of many economists* **~to/towards/in favour of** *signs of a late swing to the Democrats*

2 swinging movement
- ADJ. **wild | backward, forward | golf | practice**
- VERB + SWING **do, make, take** *the technique for making the perfect golf swing* | **change | practise** *golfers practising their swings*
- PREP. **~at** *He took a wild swing at the ball.*

3 swinging seat
- VERB + SWING **go/play on** *Some kids were playing on the swings.*
- PREP. **on a/the~**

swing verb

1 move backwards and forwards/from side to side
- ADV. **gently, slowly | violently, wildly** *She lashed out, her arm swinging wildly.* | **back and forth, backwards and forwards, from side to side, to and fro** *The pendulum swung slowly backwards and forwards.*
- PREP. **from** *I could see him swinging from the branch of a large tree.*

2 move smoothly

swipe

- VERB + SWING **slowly | suddenly | sharply** *The road swung sharply round.* | **across, around/round, away, back, down, off, up** *Hearing a sarcastic note in his voice, she swung around to face him.*
- VERB + SWING **let sth** *She let the door swing shut behind her.*
- PREP. **from** *She swung down from the tree in one easy movement.* **into** *He swung up into the saddle and rode off.* **towards** *Niccolò swung towards her.*
- PHRASES **swing open/shut/to**

3 change quickly
- ADV. **rapidly | suddenly | wildly** *The balance of power swung wildly from one party to the other.* | **heavily** *Opinion swung heavily to the left.*
- PREP. **from, to** *Her mood could swing rapidly from gloom to exhilaration.*

swipe *noun*

- ADJ. **good | playful | side**
- VERB + SWIPE **take** *She took a playful swipe at her brother.*
- PREP. **~ at** *The article takes a side swipe at the teachers.*

switch *noun*

1 small button/lever
- ADJ. **mains, master, power** *The mains switch is in the cupboard under the stairs.* | **electric, electrical | dimmer, off, on, on-off, time, timer** *We fitted dimmer switches in all the bedrooms.* ◇ *I couldn't find the off switch on the remote control.* | **ignition, intercom, light**
- VERB + SWITCH **flick, flip, press, pull, throw, turn off/on** *Someone threw a switch and the electricity went off.*
- SWITCH + VERB **activate sth, control sth, operate sth** *This switch controls the heating system.*
- PREP. **by (a)~** *The light operates by time switch.* **on a~** *The heater is on a timer switch.* | **~ for** *the switch for the air conditioning*
- PHRASES **at the flick of a switch** *in the days before electricity was available at the flick of a switch* **a bank of switches** *The pilot reached across to the huge bank of switches on his right and flicked a couple.*

2 change that sb makes
- ADJ. **abrupt, immediate, sudden | big | complete | tactical** *The team's manager made a shrewd tactical switch in defence.*
- VERB + SWITCH **make**
- PREP. **~ away from** *There will be no overnight switch away from old voting habits.* **~ back to, ~ between** *the recent switches between direct and indirect taxation* **~ from** *her switch from full-time to part-time work* **~ in** *their abrupt switch in allegiance* **~(over) to** *theatre directors who make the switch over to films*

switch *verb*

- ADV. **easily, readily | suddenly** *My mind suddenly switched back to my conversation with Jeremy.* | **around/round, back, over**
- VERB + SWITCH **decide to** *He decided to switch tactics.*
- PREP. **between** *The remote control allows you to switch easily between TV channels.* **(away) from** *He switched his allegiance from the British to the French.* **to, with** *We asked them if they would switch places with us.*

switchboard *noun*

- ADJ. **busy | telephone**
- VERB + SWITCHBOARD **call, ring | jam, swamp** *The BBC switchboard was jammed with furious calls.* | **be/work on, operate**
- SWITCHBOARD + NOUN **operator**
- PREP. **on a/the ~** *the girl on the switchboard* **through a/the~** *All calls must pass through the switchboard.*

swollen *adj.*

- VERBS **be, feel, look, seem | become, get** *Her legs had got swollen from standing up all day.* | **remain**
- ADV. **badly, grossly, hideously, horribly, very** *His ankle is bruised and quite badly swollen.* ◇ *Her face was still horribly swollen.* | **all** *Her eyes were all red and swollen from crying.* | **a bit, quite, rather, slightly**

swoop *verb*

- ADV. **low** *An eagle swooped low over the trees.* | **suddenly | down, in**
- PREP. **on, over, towards** *(figurative)* *Customs officers swooped on several houses last night looking for drugs.*

sword *noun*

- ADJ. **long, short | double-edged, two-edged** *(both figurative)* *The potential financial boost is a double-edged sword* (= has advantages and disadvantages). | **ceremonial, dress | Samurai**
- VERB + SWORD **be armed with, carry, wear | draw, unsheathe | brandish, wield | thrust** *I thrust my sword into his chest.* | **sheathe**
- SWORD + NOUN **arm | belt | blade | stroke**

syllable *noun*

- ADJ. **final, first, last, middle, second, third, etc. | accented, stressed, strong, tonic | unstressed, weak**
- VERB + SYLLABLE **consist of, contain, have** *words that have three or more syllables* | **pronounce | put the accent/stress on, stress** *Put the stress on the second syllable.* | **split a word into** *She split the word up into syllables so that he could have a go at spelling it.*
- PHRASES **stress falls/is on a syllable** *Normally, the stress falls on the first syllable of a word.* **a word of one, two, etc. syllables** *You'll have to spell it out to him, using words of one syllable* (= explain it in simple language).

syllabus *noun*

- ADJ. **formal, official, prescribed | exam/examination, A level, GCSE, etc. | college, primary, school, secondary school, undergraduate, university | first-year, second-year, etc. | history, mathematics, writing, etc. | narrow, wide | overloaded**
- VERB + SYLLABUS **design, develop, devise, draw up, plan, work out, write | follow, offer, teach, use** *The courses do not follow the syllabus of any particular examination board.* ◇ *Several schools in Britain already teach the baccalaureate syllabus.* | **follow, do, study** *Students do different syllabuses according to their ability.* | **change, extend, reform, revise, widen** *the need to revise the history syllabus* | **cover, get through** *It was impossible to cover the overloaded syllabus in a year.* | **stick to | depart from** *There is little time to depart from the syllabus.* | **fit/plan into, integrate sth into/with** *How can computer skills be integrated into the syllabus?* | **be based on | fit in with**
- SYLLABUS + VERB **contain sth, cover sth, include sth** *Does the syllabus cover modern literature?*
- SYLLABUS + NOUN **content, design**
- PREP. **from ~** *questions from last year's syllabus* **in a/the~** *Let's include that in this year's syllabus.* **on a/the~** *Is geometry on the GCSE syllabus?* **under a/the ~** *This period of history was not examined under the old syllabus.* | **~ for** *some syllabuses for basic courses in geography* **~ in** *the exam syllabuses in arts subjects*

symbol *noun*

1 image/object/event that is a sign of sth
- ADJ. **clear, dramatic, perfect, potent, powerful, supreme, ultimate** *The Berlin wall was the supreme symbol of the Cold War.* | **universal** *The dove is a universal sym-*

bol of peace. | **outward, physical, visual** *The company car is an outward symbol of the employee's status.* | **ancient, traditional** | **national** | **cultural, military, political** | **divine, religious, sacred** | **Christian, Hindu, etc.** | **fertility, phallic, sexual, virility** *The villagers took fertility symbols into the fields to ensure a good harvest.* | **sex** (= a person famous for being attractive) *He is not most people's idea of a sex symbol.* | **status** *A stressful job can actually be a status symbol.*

• VERB + SYMBOL **adopt sth as, regard sth as, see sth as, use sth as** *Eggs are seen as the symbol of new life.*

2 letter/sign that has a particular meaning
• ADJ. **identifying** *All GM products carry an identifying symbol.* | **abstract, geometric, geometrical** | **graphic, written** | **chemical, Chinese, linguistic, mathematical, musical, phonemic, phonetic, punctuation** *A list of phonetic symbols is given in the front of the dictionary.*
• VERB + SYMBOL **bear, be marked with, have** *The coin bears a Jewish symbol.* ◇ *The bottle had a skull and crossbones symbol on it.* | **display, show, use** *Hotels that show this symbol offer activities for children.* | **look out for, see** *Always look out for the special ABTA symbol at your travel agent's.* ◇ *You can use your tokens wherever you see this symbol.* | **decipher, interpret, understand**
• SYMBOL + VERB **denote sth, indicate sth, mean sth, represent sth** *What does this little symbol mean?*
• PREP. **in~s** *a message written in symbols* | **~for** *O is the chemical symbol for oxygen.*

symbolic *adj.*

• VERBS **be, seem** | **become** *The case became symbolic of US racial tension.* | **regard sth as, see sth as** *His refusal to accept the honour was seen as highly symbolic.*
• ADV. **deeply, heavily, highly, very** *This is a gruesome and heavily symbolic tale.* | **purely** *The role of monarch is a purely symbolic one.* | **largely, mainly** | **somehow**
• PREP. **of** *These two objects are symbolic of life and death.*

symbolism *noun*

• ADJ. **expressive, rich** | **sound** *Sound symbolism means that we can often guess the meaning of a word from its sound.* | **mythological, pagan, religious** | **political** | **phallic, sexual**
• VERB + SYMBOLISM **be full of, be rich in, contain** *Christian churches are still full of pagan symbolism.* | **interpret, understand**

symmetrical *adj.*

• VERBS **appear, be, look, seem** | **become**
• ADV. **highly** *highly symmetrical crystals* | **exactly, fully, perfectly, quite, wholly** | **almost** | **broadly, fairly** *The plan of the building is broadly symmetrical.*

symmetry *noun*

• ADJ. **perfect, pleasing**
• VERB + SYMMETRY **break, destroy** *The trees break the symmetry of the painting.*
• PREP. **~between** *the symmetry between different forces*
• PHRASES **an axis/a line of symmetry**

sympathetic *adj.*

1 showing you understand sb's feelings
• VERBS **appear, be, feel, look, seem, sound** | **become** | **find sb** *I found the doctors quite sympathetic.*
• ADV. **deeply, extremely, genuinely, immensely, truly, very** *a patient and deeply sympathetic man* ◇ *He sounded genuinely sympathetic.* | **largely** | **fairly, pretty, quite** | **suitably** *She made suitably sympathetic noises down the phone.*
• PREP. **about** *My boss is being very sympathetic about*

my problems. **to** *They were extremely sympathetic to my plight.* **towards** *I did not feel sympathetic towards them.*

2 in agreement with sb/sth
• VERBS **appear, be, seem**
• ADV. **deeply, extremely, highly, very** | **entirely** | **less than** | **broadly, generally, quite** | **politically**
• PREP. **to** *The government is broadly sympathetic to our ideas.*

sympathize *verb*

1 understand sb's feelings/problems
• ADV. **deeply, really** *I sympathize deeply with his family.*
• VERB + SYMPATHIZE **can/could** *I can really sympathize with John.* | **be easy to, be hard not to** *It is hard not to sympathize with her dilemma.*
• PREP. **with** *We sympathized with the bereaved family.*

2 agree with sb
• ADV. **entirely, fully**
• PREP. **with** *I entirely sympathize with this view.*

sympathy *noun*

• ADJ. **considerable, deep, genuine, great, heartfelt, real** | **scant** | **general, popular, public, widespread**
• VERB + SYMPATHY **be full of, feel, have** *She seemed to feel some sympathy for the patients.* | **express, extend, give sb, offer (sb), show (sb)** *She expressed her deepest sympathy for him.* ◇ *She says I haven't given her enough sympathy.* ◇ *We extend our sympathy to the families of the victims.* | **expend, waste** | **demand, want** *I don't want your sympathy!* | **deserve** | **arouse, attract, earn, elicit, engage, evoke, excite, gain, get, rouse, win** *Their plight aroused considerable public sympathy.* ◇ *He didn't get much sympathy from anyone.* | **lose**
• SYMPATHY + VERB **go out to sb, lie with sb** *Our deepest sympathy goes out to his wife and family.* ◇ *My sympathy lies with his wife.*
• PREP. **in~with** *Nurses came out on strike in sympathy with the doctors.* **out of~** *She married him more out of sympathy than love.* **with~** *Desmond eyed her anguished face with sympathy.* | **~for** *He has a total lack of sympathy for young people.* **~to** *The government showed sympathy to their cause.* **~towards** *He acted with some sympathy towards his victim.* **~with** *She had every sympathy with him.*
• PHRASES **a feeling of sympathy, full of sympathy, have every/little sympathy for sb, a lack of sympathy, a pang of sympathy** *I felt a pang of sympathy for her.*

symphony *noun*

• ADJ. **Beethoven's 5th, Dvorak's 7th, etc.** | **C major, D minor, etc.**
• VERB + SYMPHONY **compose, write** | **conduct, perform, play** *Bruckner's Symphony No. 5, conducted by Hugh Wolff*
• SYMPHONY + NOUN **orchestra** *the Chicago Symphony Orchestra* | **concert**
• PHRASES **symphony No. 2, etc.**

symptom *noun*

• ADJ. **characteristic, classic, common, typical** | **minor, secondary** | **chronic** | **acute** | **intermittent, recurrent** | **dangerous, distressing, potentially fatal, serious, severe, unpleasant** | **mild** | **visual, visible** *These virus infections display obvious visual symptoms.* | **behavioural, mental, neurotic, physical, physiological, psychiatric, psychological, psychosomatic, schizophrenic** *the physical symptoms that are the result of stress* | **abdominal, respiratory, urinary** | **allergic, asthmatic, flu, flu-like, menopausal, stress, withdrawal**
• VERB + SYMPTOM **display, exhibit, experience, have, present with** (*medical*), **report, show, suffer (from)** *She had all the classic symptoms of the disorder.* ◇ *The pa-*

tient was admitted presenting with flu-like symptoms. | **develop, get** *Not all carriers of the disease develop symptoms.* | **bring about, cause, produce** | **aggravate, exacerbate** *Cigarettes can aggravate the symptoms of a cold.* | **ignore** *He had been ignoring the symptoms for years.* | **detect, diagnose, identify, interpret, recognize** *teaching nursing staff how to identify and treat the symptoms of poisoning* | **control, reduce, relieve, suppress, treat**
- SYMPTOM + VERB **appear, arise, develop, occur** | **persist, recur** *If symptoms persist, consult your doctor.* | **worsen** | **disappear**
- PHRASES **the onset of symptoms** *40 per cent of patients were treated within three hours of the onset of symptoms.* **symptom free** *after two symptom free years*

synchronize *verb*

- ADV. **carefully** | **exactly, precisely**
- PREP. **with** *The timing of the gun was precisely synchronized with the turning of the plane's propeller.*

syndicate *noun*

- ADJ. **crime, criminal, drug/drugs, smuggling** | **banking, insurance** | **lottery, pools**
- VERB + SYNDICATE **form** | **run** | **join**
- PREP. **in a/the~** *I'm in a lottery syndicate at work.*
- PHRASES **a member of a syndicate**

syndrome *noun*

- ADJ. **acute** | **clinical**
- VERB + SYNDROME **have, suffer from** | **develop** | **cause, produce** | **diagnose, recognize** | **be known as** *This phenomenon has become known as the 'Californian syndrome'.*
- SYNDROME + VERB **affect sb, be present in sb, occur** *This syndrome mostly affects women in their forties.*

synonymous *adj.*

- VERBS **be, seem** | **become** | **remain** | **make sth** *His deeds had made his name synonymous with victory.* | **consider sth, regard sth as, see sth as, treat sth as**
- ADV. **completely, exactly** | **almost, largely, more or less, roughly, virtually**
- PREP. **with** *Until the late eighteenth century, 'opera' was almost synonymous with Italian opera.*

syringe *noun*

- ADJ. **clean, sterile** | **used** *a beach scattered with used syringes* | **disposable** | **hypodermic**
- VERB + SYRINGE **fill, prepare** | **draw sth into** *The doctor drew a dose of morphia into the syringe.* | **share**
- SYRINGE + NOUN **exchange** *a syringe exchange scheme*

system *noun*

1 set of ideas/rules for organizing sth
- ADJ. **current, existing** *looking to replace the existing system* | **modern** | **old-fashioned, outdated** | **traditional** | **standard** | **complex, complicated, elaborate, intricate, sophisticated** | **simple, comprehensive** | **coherent** | **effective, efficient, viable, workable** | **inefficient, wasteful** | **flexible** | **rigid** | **stable** | **foolproof** | **imperfect, perfect** | **unique** | **ad hoc** | **centralized, decentralized** | **closed, open** *a closed system with a rigidly defined set of choices* | **bureaucratic** | **hierarchical** | **authoritarian, oppressive, repressive** | **equitable, fair** | **corrupt, unjust** | **bankrupt** *The governor referred to a prison system that was bankrupt of compassion.* | **state** *The law applies to schools within the state system.* | **local** | **government, parliamentary, political** | **electoral, voting** | **banking, economic, monetary** | **tax, taxation** | **educational, examination, school, university** | **court, judi-**
cial, justice, legal, penal, prison | **benefit/benefits, national/social insurance, social security, welfare** | **care, health (care)** | **rail, railway, road, subway, transport** | **communication** | **warning** | **security** | **back-up, support** | **accounting, administrative** | **disciplinary** | **agricultural** | **commercial, market** | **cultural, social** | **grammatical, language** | **classification, classificatory, filing** | **belief, value** | **capitalist, caste, communist** | **multiparty, two-party** | **two-tier**
- VERB + SYSTEM **build, create, design, develop, devise, set up** | **adopt, apply, implement, introduce** *implementing a new system of stock control* | **advocate** | **join** | **be part of** *They are all part of the corrupt system we need to change.* | **manage, operate, run** | **manipulate, play, use** *playing the legal system to his own advantage* | **organize** *How is the system organized?* | **adapt, change, transform** | **tinker with** | **improve, modernize, overhaul, refine, reform, reorganize, simplify, streamline, strengthen** *modernizing their judicial system* | **perfect** | **perpetuate** *perpetuating an unjust system* | **clog up** *a backlog of cases clogging up the system* | **destabilize, disrupt, undermine, weaken** *attempts to disrupt the rail system* | **dismantle** | **abandon, do away with, scrap** | **destroy, overthrow** | **replace** | **restore** | **criticize, fight, rebel against** *She spent her years at school fighting the system.* | **defend, support** | **beat, buck** *You can never beat the system!* | **bypass** *trying to bypass the bureaucratic system* | **blame** *It s not your fault—blame the system.*
- SYSTEM + VERB **exist** | **be based on sth, rest on sth** *Every political system rests on certain fundamentals.* | **be aimed at sth, be geared to sth** | **allow sth, enable sth** *This system allows you to study at your own speed.* | **offer sth, provide sth** | **be in operation, be operational, function, work** *proving that the system works effectively* | **break down, collapse**
- PREP. **in a/the~** *at another point in the transport system* **under a/the ~** *Under the new system, all children will be monitored by a senior social worker.* | **~for** *devising an appropriate system for presenting the required information*

2 group of things/parts that work together
- ADJ. **sophisticated** | **computer, computer-based, electronic, manual, mechanical** | **audio, sound, stereo** | **satellite** | **air-conditioning, alarm, electronic mail, exhaust, heating, life-support, phone, plumbing, public address, sprinkler, telephone, ventilation** | **river, road**
- VERB + SYSTEM **build, create, develop** | **improve, streamline** | **install** *For this month only, installing the system is free.*
- SYSTEM + VERB **function, operate, work** | **break down, fail** *The air-conditioning system failed.*
- PREP. **in/with a/the~** *a fault in the sound system*

3 the body, or parts of it that work together
- ADJ. **auditory, circulatory, digestive, immune, (central) nervous, reproductive, respiratory, sensory, visual**
- PREP. **in a/the~** *a valve in the circulatory system*
- PHRASES **a shock to the system** *Returning to work after a long break can be a terrible shock to the system.*

4 workings of a computer
- ADJ. **advanced, powerful** | **interactive** | **online** | **compatible, incompatible** | **computer, PC** | **operating, operational** | **database, management, information** | **processing, recognition, retrieval** *an information retrieval system* | **server, software** | **parallel**
- VERB + SYSTEM **install** | **boot up, reboot** *Just reboot the system and try again.* | **build, design, develop** *designing a voice recognition system* | **launch**
- SYSTEM + VERB **run** *The system runs on this workstation.* | **crash, fail, go down** *The entire computer system went down.*
- SYSTEM + NOUN **software**
- PREP. **in a/the~** *faults in the data processing system*

Tt

table noun

1 piece of furniture
- ADJ. **big, high, huge, large, long | little, low, small | circular, rectangular, round, square | drop-leaf, foldaway, folding, trestle** *We arranged the party food on a trestle table in the garden.* | **baize-covered, glass-topped, white-clothed, white-napped | glass, plastic, wooden | polished, scrubbed | ramshackle, rickety, rough | empty** *We found an empty table at the back of the restaurant.* | **bare | corner, window** *We'll take the corner table near the bar, please.* | **kitchen** *She often does her homework at the kitchen table.* | **breakfast, dinner, lunch** *We never discuss politics at the breakfast table.* | **conference, negotiating** *They spent hours around the negotiating table.* | **billiard, ping-pong, pool, snooker, table-tennis | makeshift** *We turned the box upside down and used it as a makeshift table.*
- VERB + TABLE **sit around/round, sit (down) at** *They were all five of them sitting round the kitchen table.* | **get up from, leave** *He left the table in a hurry.* | **lay, set** *Please lay the table for six.* | **clear** *You clear the table and I'll wash the dishes.* | **book, reserve** *We booked a table in our favourite restaurant for 8 p.m.*
- TABLE + NOUN **decorations | edge**
- PREP. **across the ~** *She leaned across the table towards him.* **around/round the ~** *We gathered round the table to hear his news.* **at the ~** *to sit down at the table* **on the ~** *She put the vase on the table.* **over the ~** *They flirted over the dinner table.* **under the ~** *The potato rolled under the table.*
- PHRASES **the centre/middle of the table, the edge/end/head of the table** *My father always sits at the head of the table.* **a round table discussion/meeting, round table talks** *All parties took part in the round table discussions on the peace process.*

2 list of facts/figures
- ADJ. **statistical | league** *The league table shows the Danish team in first place with eight points.*
- VERB + TABLE **compile, draw (up) | see** *See Table XII for population figures.*
- TABLE + VERB **show sth**
- PREP. **in a/the ~** *He showed the price fluctuations in a statistical table.* ◊ *United are second in the table.*
- PHRASES **the bottom/top of the table, mid-table** *The team will be lucky to finish the season mid-table.*

tablet noun

1 pill
- ADJ. **Ecstasy, paracetamol, saccharin, sleeping, vitamin, etc.** *Take two paracetamol tablets with water.*
- VERB + TABLET **take**
- PHRASES **in tablet form** *The drug is now available in tablet and capsule form.*

2 slab
- ADJ. **clay, stone, wax, etc. | commemorative, memorial** *We had a memorial tablet put up on the church wall.*

tabloid noun

- ADJ. **daily, Sunday | national | popular**
- VERB + TABLOID **read**
- TABLOID + NOUN **journalism, newspaper, press** *He believes that the tabloid press has behaved disgracefully.*
- PREP. **in a/the ~** *I despair when I read what passes for news in some of the tabloids.*

taboo noun

- ADJ. **rigid, strict | deep-seated | cultural, gender, religious, sexual, social | incest**
- VERB + TABOO **observe** *his failure to observe the tribe's rigid taboos* | **break, flout, violate | break down** *the problem of breaking down deep-seated cultural taboos* | **reinforce**
- TABOO + NOUN **subject**
- PREP. **~ about** *the taboo about religion in British society* **~ against** *the taboo against marrying a foreigner* **~ on** *reinforcing their taboos on sexuality* **~ surrounding** *the taboos surrounding menstruation*

taboo adj.

- VERBS **be | become | remain | consider sth, regard sth as** *Sex is considered taboo as a topic for discussion.*
- ADV. **strictly** *The subject of death was strictly taboo in their society.*
- PREP. **to** *Such work was taboo to women.*

tack noun

1 way of achieving sth
- ADJ. **right, wrong**
- VERB + TACK **go off on, take, try** *New research is taking a different tack.* ◊ *The interviewer decided to try another tack.* | **change, switch** *She suddenly changed tack, taking him by surprise.*
- PREP. **on a/the ~** *I think you're on the wrong tack with that approach.*
- PHRASES **a change of tack**

2 direction of a sailing boat in relation to the wind
- ADJ. **port, starboard | opposite**
- VERB + TACK **sail on** *We were sailing on starboard tack.* | **change, swing onto/to** *The yacht swung to the opposite tack.*

tackle noun

- ADJ. **bad, crunching, ferocious, high, hard, late, scything, strong** *Their captain was sent off for a high tackle on Cooper.* | **brave, skilful | cover, last-ditch** *Only a last-ditch tackle by Song prevented Raul from scoring.* | **sliding | flying** *A security guard brought him down with a flying tackle.* | **rugby**
- VERB + TACKLE **execute, get in, go in for, make** *I managed to get in a sliding tackle, but he scored anyway.*
- PREP. **~ from** *a crunching tackle from her opponent* **~ on** *He was booked for a tackle from behind on Morris.* | **in a/the ~** *She lost the ball in a tackle.*

tackle verb

1 deal with sth difficult
- ADV. **properly, seriously | directly, head-on** *The drugs problem has to be tackled head-on.* | **effectively, successfully**
- VERB + TACKLE **attempt to, try to | help (to) | fail to** *failing to tackle the key issues*
- PREP. **with** *The problem is being tackled with a range of measures.*
- PHRASES **a way of tackling sth**

2 in sport
- ADV. **hard** *He can run fast and tackle hard.*

tact _noun_

- ADJ. **considerable, great, the utmost**
- VERB + TACT **have | call for, need, require** _The situation called for considerable tact._ | **display, exercise, show, use** _Employees are trained to show tact and patience with difficult customers._
- PREP. **with ~** _The incident should have been handled with more tact by the police._
- PHRASES **a lack of tact, the soul of tact** _Their host, who was the soul of tact, never mentioned the incident again._ **tact and diplomacy/sensitivity**

tactic _noun_

- ADJ. **subtle | legitimate** _Some players see injuring their opponent as a legitimate tactic._ | **devious, dubious, underhand | aggressive, bully-boy, bullying, extreme, guerrilla, heavy-handed, militant, revolutionary, scare, shock, strong-arm, terror, violent | non-violent, softly-softly | psychological | smear | avoidance, delaying, diversionary, spoiling, stalling** _Children are adept at delaying tactics._ | **negative, time-wasting** _The coach was criticized for his negative tactics._ | **short-term | campaigning, marketing, negotiating, promotional | military, naval, parliamentary, police, political**
- VERB + TACTIC **decide on, discuss, plan, talk (about), work out** _She decided on a stalling tactic._ | **adopt, apply, deploy, employ, try, use** _the temptation to use underhand tactics_ ◇ _They were desperate enough to try shock tactics._ | **resort to, stoop to** _I refuse to stoop to such bullying tactics._ | **change, rethink, switch** _They would do well to switch tactics._ | **demand, require** _Longer races demand different tactics._
- TACTIC + VERB **pay off, succeed, work** _His strong-arm tactics paid off._ | **fail**
- PREP. **~for** _teaching parents tactics for dealing with aggressive children_

tag _noun_

1 label

- ADJ. **identity, name, price** _The baby had a plastic name tag on its ankle._ ◇ _Despite a price tag of £100 000, the car sold was sold in two days._ | **security | gift, luggage | ankle, ear, wrist**
- VERB + TAG **attach, put** _I still have to put gift tags on all the presents._
- PHRASES **sth carries/has a price tag of £500/$10 000, etc.** _This designer suit carries a price tag of £2 000._

2 reputation

- VERB + TAG **lose, shake off, shed** _The president made several jokes in an attempt to shake off his 'humourless' tag._

tail _noun_

1 of an animal, a bird, etc.

- ADJ. **long | short | bushy, curly, curved, forked, pointed | muscular, prehensile**
- VERB + TAIL **flick, swish, thrash, wag, whisk** _The dog wagged its tail furiously._ | **dock** _It used to be fashionable to dock horses' tails._
- TAIL + VERB **twitch, wag, wave** _The dog ran out with its tail wagging madly._
- TAIL + NOUN **feathers, fin**

2 of a thing

- TAIL + NOUN **section** _The plane's tail section had broken off._ | **fin, light**
- PREP. **at the ~** _the truck at the tail of our convoy_
- PHRASES **nose to tail** _Traffic which used to be nose to tail now flows freely._

tailor _verb_

- ADV. **carefully | exactly | accordingly, individually, specially, specifically** _We identify your needs, and tailor your training accordingly._
- PREP. **for** _a system that is specially tailored for small firms_ **to** _The account offered by the bank will be tailored exactly to your needs._

tailored _adj._

- VERBS **be**
- ADV. **beautifully, elegantly, exquisitely, finely, immaculately, superbly** _wearing a beautifully tailored suit_ | **perfectly | expensively**

take _verb_

- ADV. **well | badly** _She took the news of her father's death very badly._ | **seriously** _I wanted to be taken seriously as an artist._ | **philosophically** _Harry took his rejection philosophically._
- PREP. **as** _He took what I said as a criticism._

PHRASAL VERB

take to sth

- ADV. **kindly** _They won't take kindly to being ordered about._

takeover _noun_

- ADJ. **attempted, proposed | hostile | agreed | company | communist, military**
- TAKEOVER + NOUN **attempt, bid** _a hostile takeover bid_ | **offer | battle** _The consortium won a fierce takeover battle for the engineering group._

takings _noun_

- ADJ. **the day's, the month's, etc. | weekly | gross, net | cash | record** _Store managers are predicting record takings this Christmas._ | **bar, box office**
- VERB + TAKINGS **add up, check, count (up) | boost** _The shop's new look has boosted its takings considerably._ | **cut**
- TAKINGS + VERB **be up/down, drop, rise** _Box office takings are up by 40% on last year._
- PREP. **in ~** _She was losing about £100 a week in takings._ | **~from** _the takings from wines and beers_
- ⇒ Special page at BUSINESS

tale _noun_

- ADJ. **long, rambling | amazing, bizarre, curious, extraordinary, fantastic, magical, marvellous, strange | awful, dire, sad, sorry, terrible** _the sorry tale of his marriage breakdown_ | **dreary** _She was tired of hearing the same dreary tale of drunkenness and violence._ | **chilling, gruesome, hair-raising, horror, macabre | mysterious, spooky | funny, humorous, witty | foolish | lurid, spicy, tawdry | fanciful, far-fetched, incredible, tall, unlikely** _a tall tale that would fool no one_ | **old wives' | rags-to-riches** _the rags-to-riches tale of an orphan who becomes a star_ | **epic, heroic** _an epic tale of courage and heroism_ | **cautionary, moral, morality | folk, traditional | childhood | fairy** _(often figurative)_ _Winning the French Open was a fairy-tale end to her career._ | **romantic**
- VERB + TALE **narrate, regale sb with, relate, tell (sb)** _She regaled us with tales of her wild youth._ | **invent, make up, spin**
- TALE + VERB **begin | unfold | concern sb/sth, involve sb/sth | be set in …** _a tale set in 19th-century Moscow_ | **be based on sth**
- PREP. **~about** _a tale about a hungry snake_ **~of** _tales of adventure_ ◇ _the curious tale of the man who sold his hair_
- PHRASES **a tale of woe** (= about failure, bad luck, etc.), **(have) a tale to tell** _Each of the survivors had a terrible tale to tell._ **tell tales** (= to say things about sb that are untrue or that they would prefer to be secret)

talent noun

• ADJ. **considerable, enormous, exceptional, extraordinary, formidable, genuine, great, major, outstanding, prodigious, rare, real, remarkable, special, tremendous, undoubted, unique | God-given, inborn, innate, natural, raw** *Hard work is important, but it is no substitute for raw talent.* | **hidden, undiscovered | mediocre | fresh, new** *The company is always looking out for new talent.* | **young | precocious | home-grown, local** *one of the few teams that relies on home-grown talent* | **top** *We are losing our top talent to other countries who pay more.* | **acting, artistic, creative, literary, managerial, musical, scientific, vocal, writing**
• VERB + TALENT **have, possess** *The lad has undoubted talent.* | **demonstrate, display, reveal, show | flaunt, show off** *The banquet gave the chef a chance to flaunt his talents.* | **direct, redirect, turn** *After making her name as a singer, she turned her talents to acting.* | **discover, recognize, spot, unearth** *She has a keen eye for spotting talent.* ◇ *United have unearthed a real talent in this young defender.* | **build (on), cultivate, develop, harness, make the most of, nurture, realize, tap, use, utilize** *an effort to develop his creative talents to the full* ◇ *The theatre visits schools to tap young talent.* | **squander, waste** *His parents accused him of wasting his talents and abilities.*
• TALENT + VERB **lie** *Her talents lay in organization.*
• TALENT + NOUN **scout, spotter | competition, contest, show**
• PREP. **of** ~ *He is a violinist of exceptional talent.* **with/without** ~ *kids with musical talent* | ~ **for** *You have a natural talent for storytelling.*
• PHRASES **a man/woman, etc. of many talents, a wealth of talent** *There is a wealth of talent out there in our schools.* **a pool of talent** *Hollywood directors have a marvellous pool of acting talent to draw from.*

talented adj.

• VERBS **be, seem, sound**
• ADV. **exceptionally, extraordinarily, extremely, highly, hugely, immensely, incredibly, outstandingly, really, supremely, truly, very** *an extraordinarily talented designer* ◇ *Some of these young musicians are hugely talented.* | **not particularly | quite | precociously** *a precociously talented youngster* | **artistically, musically**

talk noun

1 a conversation
• ADJ. **good, little** *(often ironic)*, **long, quiet, serious** *I will have to have a little talk with that young lady* (= tell her that I disapprove of sth). | **heart-to-heart, intimate**
• VERB + TALK **have**
• TALK + NOUN **show**
• PREP. ~ **about** *I enjoyed our talk about the old days.* ~ **with** *I need to have a heart-to-heart talk with her.*
• PHRASES **(exchange/make) small talk** (= to talk politely about unimportant things) *He was never very good at making small talk with her parents.*

2 talking
• ADJ. **excited, heady** *There was excited talk of emigrating to America.* | **ridiculous, wild** *There is ridiculous talk of her breaking the world record soon.* | **careless, dangerous, idle, loose | fighting, tough | straight** *She likes straight talk and hates hypocrites.* | **double** *The president's true agenda was hidden in political double talk.* | **dirty, filthy | cheap, easy, empty, mere** *The chairman's boasts about future profits was just cheap talk.* | **fine, grand** *(ironic)* *What all the fine talk came down to was hard cash.* | **baby** *I never used baby talk to my little girl.* | **pillow** *the pillow talk of lovers*
• TALK + VERB **turn to sth** *Talk turned to money and tempers began to fray.*

• PREP. ~ **about/of** *All this talk of the president resigning is nonsense!*
• PHRASES **be just talk** *'You think it's just talk?' 'No, I think it's true.'* **for all the talk of sth** *For all the talk of bringing their children up the same, the boys ended up never doing any of the cooking.*

3 (*also* **talks**) discussions between official groups
• ADJ. **lengthy | high-level, top-level | informal | formal, official | private, secret | open | direct, face-to-face | wide-ranging | all-party, bilateral, inter-party, joint, multilateral, round-table, trilateral, tripartite | fresh, further | fruitless, inconclusive | crisis, emergency, urgent | exploratory, preliminary | constitutional, political | arms, pay, peace, trade**
• QUANT. **round** *A further round of talks is expected in March.*
• VERB + TALK **conduct, have, hold** *The two governments held secret talks on the nuclear threat.* | **broker, host | attend, enter | initiate, open | break off, pull out of, walk out of** *The union has broken off talks with the management.* | **cancel, suspend | reopen, resume**
• TALK + VERB **be scheduled** *Talks were scheduled for Rome the following month.* | **take place** *The peace talks will take place in Cairo.* | **begin, open, start | end | resume | be aimed at sth, be designed to** *the latest round of talks aimed at ending the civil war* | **centre on sth, concentrate on sth, cover sth, deal with sth, focus on sth** *The talks centred on bilateral trade.* | **produce sth** *Talks produced agreement on an end to the occupation.* | **be deadlocked, break down, collapse, fail, founder, stall** *The talks remain deadlocked over spending plans.* ◇ *The talks foundered on the issue of compensation.*
• PREP. **during** ~ *The agreement was concluded during talks in Beijing.* **in** ~ *He is currently in talks with two football clubs.* | ~ **about/on/over** *holding talks over the political future of the province* ~ **between** *the failure of talks between the two communities* ~ **with** *The delegation arrived for talks with their government.*

4 lecture
• ADJ. **entertaining, informative, interesting | introductory | pep, sales, team | radio**
• VERB + TALK **give | attend, go to**
• TALK + VERB **be entitled sth** *She gave a very entertaining talk entitled 'My life and hard times'.*
• PREP. ~ **about/on** *Did you go to the talk on Peru?*

talk verb

• ADV. **loudly | quietly | at length | continuously, endlessly, incessantly, non-stop | freely | openly** *She talked quite freely about her work.* | **enthusiastically, excitedly | politely | glibly | vaguely** *He had talked vaguely of going to work abroad.* | **casually | earnestly** *a group of students talking earnestly* | **sensibly** *Let's talk sensibly about this.* | **wildly**
• VERB + TALK **be able to, can/could** *I can't talk about it just now.* | **need to, want to** *I need to talk to you.* | **begin to | be easy to** *He was so easy to talk to.* | **be difficult to, be hard to | hear sb, listen to sb, overhear sb** *I loved to hear him talk about the old days.* | **make sb** *The police questioned him for four hours, trying to make him talk.* | **let sb** *Just shut up and let me talk for a minute.*
• PREP. **about** *talking about their new clothes* **of** *(formal)* *We often talked of the war.* **to** *I'll talk to John this afternoon.* **with** *I've talked with him on the telephone.*
• PHRASES **start/stop talking**

tall adj.

• VERBS **be, look, seem | become, get, grow**
• ADV. **exceptionally, extremely, unusually, very | fairly, quite, rather** *She is quite tall for her age.*

tame adj.

1 not afraid of people
- VERBS **be, look, seem | become**
- ADV. **extremely, very | almost | quite**

2 boring
- VERBS **appear, be, look, seem, sound | become | find sth** *I found office work very tame after army life.*
- ADV. **positively, very** *living a life that makes Wild West movies look positively tame* | **a bit, a little, pretty, rather, somewhat** *To us it was all pretty tame stuff.*

tan noun

- ADJ. **deep, golden | healthy | all-over | fake**
- VERB + TAN **have | show off, sport** *Show off your tan in this little white top.* | **get, top up, work on** *I want to top up my tan on the sunbed at the gym.*
- PREP. **against your~** *His teeth were a gleaming flash of white against his tan.*

tangle noun

- ADJ. **bewildering, confused** *a confused tangle of voices* | **dense, matted** *a dense tangle of undergrowth*
- VERB + TANGLE **get into** *He got into a tangle with his budget figures.* | **sort out, unravel** *The legal tangle was never really unravelled.*
- PREP. **in a~** *This string's in a tangle.*

tangled adj.

- VERBS **be, look | become, get**
- ADV. **hopelessly | all** *My hair had got all tangled.* | **a bit** *Your hair looks a bit tangled.* | **up**
- PREP. **in** *My legs got hopelessly tangled in the rope.*

tank noun

1 container
- ADJ. **empty, full | glass, steel | 4-foot, 50-gallon, 80-litre, etc. | fuel, gas, oil, oxygen, petrol, water** *the hot and cold water tanks* | **storage | septic, slurry | fish**
- VERB + TANK **fill**
- TANK + VERB **contain sth**
- PREP. **in/into a/the~** *Put a little fish food into the tank.* | **~of** *a full tank of petrol*

2 military vehicle
- ADJ. **armoured, army, battle**
- VERB + TANK **climb into, get into | drive**
- TANK + VERB **roll** *Tanks rolled in to end the siege.*
- TANK + NOUN **regiment**

tanker noun

1 ship carrying oil or petrol
- ADJ. **giant, huge, large | gas, oil | coastal**
- TANKER + VERB **carry sth, transport sth** *a tanker carrying thousands of tons of crude oil* | **run aground** *The tanker ran aground in heavy seas and is breaking up on the rocks.* | **break up | spill sth** *A damaged tanker has spilled millions of gallons of oil into the sea.*
- TANKER + NOUN **disaster, spill** *the worst year for tanker spills for ten years* | **fleet | route | traffic | operator, owner**

2 heavy vehicle for carrying liquids
- ADJ. **fuel, milk, petrol | road**
- VERB + TANKER **drive**
- TANKER + VERB **carry sth**
- TANKER + NOUN **driver**

tanned adj.

- VERBS **be, look | become, get**
- ADV. **deeply, very** *His blue eyes glittered in his deeply tanned face.* | **lightly, slightly | healthily**

tantrum noun

- ADJ. **temper**
- VERB + TANTRUM **have, throw** *He threw a tantrum on the school bus.* | **deal with | ignore**

tap noun

1 for water, gas, etc.
- ADJ. **hot, hot-water | cold, cold-water | mixer | dripping, running** *the sound of a dripping tap* | **leaky | bath, bathroom, kitchen**
- VERB + TAP **turn (off/on)** *Turn the tap clockwise.* | **run** *You have to run the tap a long time before the hot water comes.*
- TAP + VERB **drip, run** *Someone has left the tap running.* | **leak**
- TAP + NOUN **water | washer**
- PREP. **on~** *The pub has two sorts of beer on tap* (= in a barrel with a tap on it). ◇ *(figurative) We have this sort of information on tap* (= available to be used at any time).

2 quick gentle blow; the sound it makes
- ADJ. **gentle, light, little | sharp**
- VERB + TAP **give sb/sth**
- PREP. **~at** *There was a little tap at the door.* **~on** *He gave her a tap on the shoulder.*

tap verb

- ADV. **gently, lightly** *She tapped her fingers gently on the table.* | **away** *She tapped away at her keyboard.*
- PREP. **against, at, on, with** *She tapped the ice with a stick.*

tape noun

1 magnetic material used for recording
- ADJ. **magnetic** *The data is stored on the magnetic tape.* | **audio, computer, video** (also **videotape**) | **recording**
- VERB + TAPE **hold sth on, store sth on | capture sth on, get sth on** *Police are examining the incident, which was captured on tape.* | **splice**
- TAPE + NOUN **drive** (= in a computer) | **recording**
- PREP. **on~** *I've got the whole concert on tape.*

2 cassette with magnetic tape on it
- ADJ. **cassette | audio, music, sound | video** (also **videotape**) | **demo, master | compilation** *a compilation tape featuring new Irish bands* | **blank | pre-recorded | bootleg, pirated** *The court heard that Ellis sold pirated tapes of Hollywood blockbusters.*
- VERB + TAPE **make** *I made another tape to play in the car.* | **play (back), put on** *The police will be able to play back the videotape for clues.* | **listen to, watch | mime to** *The singer was miming to a pre-recorded tape.* | **fast-forward, pause, replay, rewind, start, stop, wind back, wind forward/on | erase, wipe** *Someone had deliberately erased the tapes.*
- TAPE + VERB **contain sth, have sth** *The tape contained damning evidence.* ◇ *What does this tape have on it?*
- TAPE + NOUN **deck, recorder | recording**

3 long narrow strip of fabric/paper
- ADJ. **adhesive, Scotch™, sticky | insulating, masking | measuring | paper, plastic, steel | ticker | double-sided** *Fit the carpet using double-sided tape.*
- QUANT. **piece, strip | roll**
- VERB + TAPE **seal sth (up) with** *I sealed up the package with strong adhesive tape.*
- TAPE + NOUN **measure** *Use a steel tape measure to measure the dimensions of the room.*

4 piece of material stretched across a racetrack
- ADJ. **finishing**
- VERB + TAPE **break** *her look of triumph as she broke the finishing tape*

tape *verb*

- ADV. **firmly** *The wires are taped firmly together.* | **together, up** *The box was all taped up.*
- PREP. **onto, to** *She had taped a note to the fridge door.*

target *noun*

1 sb/sth that you try to destroy, hurt, steal, etc.
- ADJ. **favourite, likely, natural, obvious, perfect, possible, potential, prime, suitable** *The prime minister is a favourite target of comedians.* | **easy, sitting, soft, tempting, vulnerable** *The stationary trucks were sitting targets for the enemy planes.* | **legitimate** | **intended** | **stationary** | **moving** | **ground** | **military** | **civilian, non-military** | **terrorist**
- VERB + TARGET **aim at, attack, go for, shoot at** | **hit, reach** (used of a missile) *The bomb reached its intended target ten seconds later.* | **miss, overshoot** *The flare overshot its target and set light to a hotel.* | **destroy** *The missile is aimed specifically to destroy military targets.* | **track** *The radar beam can track a number of targets almost simultaneously.*
- PREP. **off~** *The missile veered way off target and landed in the sea.* **on~** *Politically speaking, his jibes were right on target.* | **~for** *an easy target for shoplifters*

2 object that you shoot at
- VERB + TARGET **put up, set up** *The archers were setting up their targets.* | **aim at, shoot at** | **hit** | **miss** | **use sth as** *The boys used an old tree stump as a target.*
- TARGET + NOUN **area** | **practice**
- PREP. **off~** *Patton was just off target with a header.* **on~** *His first shot was bang on target.* **wide of the~** *The shot went wide of the target.*

3 result, person, etc. that you aim to reach
- ADJ. **achievable, attainable, low, modest, realistic** | **ambitious, demanding, difficult, high, tough, unrealistic** *She has always set herself very high targets.* | **impossible** | **clear** | **chief, key, main, major, primary, prime, principal** | **annual** | **immediate, initial** | **future, long-term, ultimate** | **attainment, economic, financial, growth, inflation, performance, production, profit, recruitment, sales, spending**
- VERB + TARGET **set** *Managers must set targets that are realistic.* | **aim for** *Pupils should be given a target to aim for.* | **achieve, meet, reach** | **stay within** *in a desperate attempt to stay within budget targets* | **exceed** *The company pays bonuses to workers who exceed production targets.* | **fall short of**
- TARGET + NOUN **audience, group, market** | **date** *to meet a target date of May 2002* | **figure, price, weight**
- PREP. **above (a/the)~** *Sales so far this year are 20% above target.* **off~** *These figures are way off target.* **on~** *We are still right on target.* **over (a/the)~** *Many wage settlements reached were over the original target of 4%.* **towards (a/the)~** *We are working towards a target of twenty cars a week.* | **~for** *setting new targets for growth*

target *verb*

- ADV. **carefully, deliberately** *a carefully targeted marketing campaign* ◇ *Children are deliberately targeted.* | **particularly, specifically**
- PREP. **at** *The products are targeted at young people.* **for** *This hospital is targeted for additional funding.* **on** *Tax cuts should be targeted on the poor.* **towards** *We target our services towards specific groups of people.*

tariff *noun*

- ADJ. **high, low** | **preferential, protective, punitive** *British industry was sheltered from foreign competition by protective tariffs.* | **external** | **domestic, internal** | **import** | **customs**
- QUANT. **level** *a 40% level of tariffs on imports*

- VERB + TARIFF **fix, set** *The agreement fixed tariffs for foreign goods coming into Japan at 5%.* | **impose, introduce, levy** *The US could impose punitive tariffs of up to 100% on some countries' exports.* | **pay** | **increase, raise** | **cut, lower, reduce** | **abolish, eliminate**
- TARIFF + NOUN **reduction, reform** | **structure, system** | **level, rate** | **barrier** *the aim of removing all tariff barriers by the year 2003*
- PREP. **~on** *They set a tariff of 36% on British wool cloth.*
- PHRASES **a reduction in tariff/tariffs**

tarnish *verb*

1 become/make sth less bright
- ADV. **badly** *The mirror had tarnished quite badly.*

2 spoil sth
- ADV. **severely** *their severely tarnished reputation*

tart *noun*

1 open pie
- ADJ. **fruit, jam, treacle** | **apple, strawberry, etc.**
- VERB + TART **make**

2 woman
- ADJ. **cheap, little**
- VERB + TART **look like** *That dress makes her look like a tart.* | **call sb** *He had called her a cheap little tart.*

task *noun*

- ADJ. **awesome, challenging, daunting, enormous, formidable, great, Herculean, huge, mammoth, massive, monumental** | **arduous, demanding, difficult, exacting, exhausting, hard, laborious, onerous, stiff, time-consuming, tough, uphill** | **dangerous, hazardous** | **basic, easy, simple, small** *Translating the letter was no easy task.* | **menial, mundane, repetitive, tedious** | **complex, mind-boggling** | **delicate, tricky** | **fruitless, hopeless, impossible** | **daily, day-to-day, routine** | **central, fundamental, important, main, major, primary, principal** *The primary task of the chair is to ensure the meeting runs smoothly.* | **essential, vital** | **immediate, urgent** | **enviable, pleasant** | **thankless, unenviable, unpleasant** | **administrative, domestic, household, manual** | **self-appointed, self-imposed**
- VERB + TASK **take on, take upon yourself, undertake** *Nobody was keen to take on such a thankless task.* | **approach, get to grips with, tackle** *How do you tackle a task like that?* | **carry out, do, fulfil, get on with, perform** *I left her to get on with the task of correcting the errors.* | **accomplish, complete, succeed in** | **cope with** | **fail in** | **allocate, assign (sb), delegate, entrust sb with, give sb, set sb** *She failed to complete the task that she had been set.* | **be charged with, be faced with, have** *She was charged with the important task of telling the children.* | **be engaged in** *I was engaged in the delicate task of clipping the dog's claws.* | **help sb with** | **be suited/unsuited to** *His thick fingers were not well suited to the task.*
- TASK + VERB **require sth** *The task requires a variety of skills and experience.* | **fall to sb** *The unenviable task of telling my parents fell to the head teacher.* | **confront sb, face sb** *The team have no illusions about the size of the task confronting them.*
- PREP. **~for** *a hard task for the committee* **~in** *one of the first tasks in language learning*
- PHRASES **the task ahead** *We need to think realistically about the task ahead.* **the task in hand** *We should stop chatting and get back to the task in hand.*

task force *noun*

- ADJ. **special** | **government, presidential, etc.** | **naval, police, etc.** | **health, housing, etc.**
- VERB + TASK FORCE **create, establish, form, set up** | **lead**

● TASK FORCE + NOUN **team**
● PREP. **~ on** *The government has set up a special task force on health care reform.*

taste *noun*

1 flavour
● ADJ. **delicious, fresh, pleasant, refreshing** | **distinctive** | **pungent, rich, strong** | **bland, mild** | **foul, nasty, unpleasant** | **bitter, creamy, metallic, salty, sharp, smooth, sour, spicy, sweet** | **authentic** *You need to use fresh herbs to get the authentic Italian taste.*
● VERB + TASTE **have** *The soup had a very salty taste.* | **leave** *The drink left a bitter taste in his mouth.* ◇ *(figurative)* *The whole business left a nasty taste in my mouth.* | **spoil** *Don't have a cigarette now—you'll spoil the taste of your food!* | **enhance, improve** | **enjoy, savour** *She savoured the taste of the champagne.* | **disguise, take away** *I had a strong coffee to take away the nasty taste of the food.*
● TASTE + NOUN **buds**

2 a taste small amount
● ADJ. **little** | **real** *That job gave me my first real taste of teaching.* | **first**
● VERB + TASTE **get, have** *Have a taste of this cake.* | **give sb, provide (sb with)**
● PREP. **~ of** *This was her first taste of success.*
● PHRASES **a taste of things to come** *The new appraisal scheme is only a taste of things to come.*

3 liking
● ADJ. **catholic, eclectic, varied, wide** | **modest, simple** | **advanced, cultured, educated, sophisticated** | **expensive, extravagant** | **eccentric, esoteric, strange** | **acquired, natural** *Art is an acquired taste—no one is born knowing that Michelangelo is wonderful.* | **natural** | **local, national** | **modern** | **personal, private** | **aesthetic, artistic, literary, musical, reading, sexual** | **audience, consumer, contemporary, popular, public, Western** *Her music appeals to popular taste.*
● VERB + TASTE **have** *They have a taste for adventure.* | **like, share** *You obviously share her taste in reading.* | **acquire, cultivate, develop, get** | **lose** *I've lost my taste for travelling.* | **indulge** *Now he is retired he has time to indulge his tastes for writing and politics.* | **demonstrate, display** *Her choice of outfit demonstrated her taste for the outrageous.* | **appeal to, cater for, match, meet, satisfy, suit** *a range of hotels to suit all tastes and budgets*
● TASTE + VERB **lie** *It all depends on where your tastes lie.* | **change, differ, vary** *Lifestyles differ and tastes vary.*
● PREP. **for your ~** *The theatre was too modern for my taste.* **to ~** (= according to how much of sth you want) *Add salt and pepper to taste.* **to your ~** *If fishing is not to your taste, there are many other leisure activities on offer.* | **~ for** *People with a taste for complex plots will enjoy this book.* **~ in** *young people's tastes in music*
● PHRASES **a man/woman of … tastes** *a man of advanced tastes* **a matter of (personal) taste** *What type of bicycle you should buy is very much a matter of personal taste.*

4 ability to make good choices
● ADJ. **excellent, exquisite, good, great, impeccable** *Her work is executed with impeccable taste.* | **appalling, bad, deplorable, doubtful, dubious, poor, terrible**
● VERB + TASTE **reflect, show** *The house reflected his taste.* | **exercise** *The designer has exercised good taste in her use of different fonts.*
● PREP. **in … ~** *That joke was in very poor taste.* **with ~** *The room had been decorated with great taste.* | **~ in** *She has terrible taste in clothing.*
● PHRASES **an arbiter of taste** *Contemporary arbiters of taste dismissed his paintings as rubbish.* **in the best/worst possible taste** *The love scenes are all done in the best possible taste.* **a lack of taste** *The remark showed a deplorable lack of taste.* **a man/woman of taste, taste and decency**

The film was judged to offend against standards of public taste and decency.

taste *verb*

● ADV. **strongly** *The water tasted strongly of chemicals.* | **faintly, slightly** *The fish tasted faintly of garlic.*
● PREP. **like** *The fruit tasted rather like mango.* **of** *a cake which tasted of almonds*
● PHRASES **taste awful/bitter/foul/horrible, taste delicious/good/sweet/wonderful, taste funny**

tasteful *adj.*

● VERBS **be** *Most of the furniture was quite tasteful.*
● ADV. **very** | **impeccably** | **quite**

tatters *noun*

● VERB + TATTERS **lie in** *(figurative)* *Her marriage now lay in tatters.* | **hang in** *Everywhere wallpaper hung in tatters.* | **leave sth in** *(figurative)* *an injury that left his dreams in tatters*
● PREP. **in ~** *Her clothes were in tatters.* ◇ *(figurative)* *With their plans now in tatters, they gave up.*
● PHRASES **rags and tatters**

tattoo *noun*

● VERB + TATTOO **do** *She's having a tattoo done on her leg.* | **have** | **be covered in** *His arms were covered in tattoos.* | **remove** *I've decided to get my tattoo removed.*
● TATTOO + NOUN **parlour**

taunt *noun*

● ADJ. **playground, racial/racist**
● VERB + TAUNT **hurl, shout** | **endure, face, suffer** *He had to endure the racist taunts of the crowd.* | **ignore**
● TAUNT + VERB **sting (sb into)** *Their taunts stung him into his best performance for the team yet.*

taunt *verb*

● ADV. **softly** *'Running away?' he taunted softly.*
● PREP. **about** *Some of the girls taunted her about her weight.* **with** *The other children taunted him with nicknames.*

taut *adj.*

● VERBS **be, feel, look** | **become, go** *Her body went as taut as a bowstring.* | **remain, stay** *Exercise helps your muscles to stay taut.* | **pull sth, stretch sth** *His skin was stretched taut over his cheekbones.* | **hold sth, keep sth** *Try to keep the lead taut, as it will help your puppy to learn.*
● PREP. **with** *(figurative)* *a voice taut with anger*

tax *noun*

● ADJ. **high, low** | **direct, indirect** | **basic, basic-rate, higher-rate** | **progressive, redistributive** | **regressive** *A regressive tax, like the poll tax, takes proportionately more of a poor person's income.* | **windfall** *The privatized utility companies may be faced with a windfall tax on the profits of the last few years.* | **back** *(informal)* *The tax office demanded £80 000 in back taxes.* | **council, poll** | **capital, capital gains, income, inheritance, land, profits, property, savings, wealth** | **consumption, purchase, sales, value added** (= VAT) | **capital transfer, investment** | **company, corporation** | **car, road, vehicle** *It's time to renew your car tax.* | **carbon, energy, fuel, petrol** | **excise, import**
● VERB + TAX **pay** | **impose, introduce, levy, put** *Direct taxes could only be levied with the consent of Parliament.* ◇ *The government may put an indirect tax on books.* | **collect** *the government department responsible for col-*

lecting taxes | **deduct** *Your employer will deduct the tax for you.* | **increase, put up, raise** | **cut, lower, reduce** | **abolish** | **overpay** | **reclaim** | **offset sth against, set/write sth off against** *Claims for expenses can be set off against tax.* | **avoid, escape** | **evade** *She was charged with conspiracy to evade taxes.*
● TAX + VERB **go up, increase, rise** *Taxes look set to rise again.* | **come/go down, fall** | **be chargeable, be payable** *the amount on which capital gains tax is payable*
● TAX + NOUN **payer** (also **taxpayer**) *a higher-rate tax payer* | **authority/authorities, office, man** (also **taxman**) (*informal*) *She owes the taxman £10 000.* | **law, legislation, measures, policy, reform, structure, system** | **period, year** *The tax year begins in April.* | **cut, increase** | **band, bracket, rate, threshold** *Her salary puts her in the highest tax band.* | **revenue, yield** | **assessment, form, return** *You have to fill in your tax return by tomorrow.* | **advantage, allowance, benefit, break, concession, credit, exemption, incentive, perks, rebate, refund, relief** *There are tax advantages to working freelance.* ◇ *You will only receive tax relief on the first £30 000.* | **affairs, arrangements** *His tax affairs are under investigation by the police.* | **avoidance** | **loophole** *Her accountant was good at exploiting tax loopholes.* | **dodge, evasion, fraud** *He gave the Porsche to his mother as a tax dodge.* | **dodger** | **exile** *She is living as a tax exile in Monaco.* | **haven** *The island is a popular tax haven for the very rich.* | **collector, consultant, inspector** | **bill, charge, invoice, payment** | **arrears** *He was ordered to pay $2 million in tax arrears.* | **liability** *an increase in tax liability on company cars* | **burden** *putting a new tax burden on the middle classes* | **base** *By broadening the tax base* (= making more people pay tax) *the chancellor could raise more revenues.*
● PREP. **after/before ~** *Profits after tax were £262 000.* **in ~** *Collectively, smokers pay over £15 000 a day in tax.* | **~ on** *introducing a 60% tax on alcohol*
● PHRASES **for tax purposes** *the rules for deciding on someone's residence status for UK tax purposes* (**the basic/higher**) **rate of tax** *an increase in the basic rate of tax*

tax *verb*

● ADV. **heavily** *Many self-employed people are heavily taxed.* ◇ *goods which are most heavily taxed* | **lightly**
● PREP. **according to** *Drinks would be taxed according to their alcoholic strength.* **at** *Many goods were taxed at 17.5%.* **on** *You will be taxed on all your income.*

taxable *adj.*

● VERBS **be** | **become** | **remain** | **make sth**
● ADV. **fully** *Where payments exceed these limits they become fully taxable.*

taxation *noun*

● ADJ. **excessive, heavy, high** *the heavy taxation on smokers and drinkers* | **low** | **direct, indirect** | **progressive, redistributive** | **company, corporate, general, local, personal** *changes in corporate taxation*
● QUANT. **level, rate** *a promise to lower the overall level of taxation*
● VERB + TAXATION **increase, put up, raise** *If the government raises direct taxation, it will lose votes.* | **cut, lower, reduce** | **avoid** | **be exempt from** *Any profits made are totally exempt from taxation.*
● TAXATION + NOUN **policy, system** | **rate**
● PREP. **after/before ~** *The loss before taxation was $2.7 million.* **from/out of ~** *The hospital was funded from taxation.* **through ~** *the power to raise funds through taxation* | **~ on** *increased taxation on oil companies*
● PHRASES **the burden of taxation** *reducing the heavy burden of taxation on the wealthy* **a form of taxation** *The poll tax was a very unpopular form of taxation.* **for tax-**

ation **purposes** *They were treated as a married couple for taxation purposes.*

taxi *noun*

● VERB + TAXI **go by, take** *I took a taxi back home.* | **call (sb), get (sb), order (sb), phone for** *I'll get my secretary to call you a taxi.* | **find** *We had some difficulty finding a taxi.* | **catch, hail** *We caught a taxi to the airport.* | **get into/out of** | **drive** | **pay for/off** | **share**
● TAXI + NOUN **cab** | **firm** | **ride** | **service** | **fare** | **driver** | **rank**
● PHRASES **by ~** *a five-minute trip by taxi*

taxing *adj.*

● VERBS **be, prove** | **become**
● ADV. **very** | **fairly** | **intellectually, physically** *There was nothing intellectually taxing about the course.*

tea *noun*

1 drink
● ADJ. **fresh** *There's some fresh* (= just made) *tea in the pot.* | **stewed** (= very strong), **strong** | **weak** | **cold, hot, lukewarm, scalding** | **milky** | **white** (usually after **tea**) *I'll have tea—white, no sugar, please.* | **black** | **sugary, sweet** | (**early**) **morning** | **decaffeinated** | **fragrant** | **China/Chinese, Indian, etc.** | **Earl Grey, green** | **fruit, herb/herbal** | **camomile, jasmine, lemon, mint, etc.** | **iced**
● QUANT. **cup, flask, mug, pot**
● VERB + TEA **drink** *I don't drink tea.* | **have** | **sip, swallow** *She sipped her hot tea slowly.* | **take a mouthful/sip of** | **brew, get (sb), make (sb), mash** *I'll make you some tea.* | **bring sb, dispense** (*often humorous*), **ply sb with** (*humorous*), **serve (sb), take sb** *I'll bring you a cup of tea in a few minutes.* ◇ *John rushed around dispensing tea and cakes to everyone.* | **pour (sb) (out)** *Pour me out a cup of tea please.* | **stir**
● TEA + VERB **brew, mash** *You haven't let the tea brew long enough.* | **cool**
● TEA + NOUN **pot** (also **teapot**), **urn** | **cosy** | **service, set** *a bone china tea service* | **tray, trolley** *A lady comes round the office with a tea trolley in the afternoon.* | **bar, garden, room, shop** *The hospital tea bar is run by volunteers.* | **boy** (*offensive when used of an older man*), **lady** | **drinker, drinking** | **break** | **party** | **ceremony**
● PREP. **in your ~** *Do you take sugar in your tea?*
● PHRASES **tea and coffee, tea and biscuits/cake/cakes/sandwiches/scones, tea and sympathy** *He tried to alleviate their disappointment by inviting them in for tea and sympathy.* **tea for two** '*Tea for two*,' *said Mary*, '*and a slice of your delicious chocolate cake.*' **tea or coffee** *Would you like tea or coffee?* **tea-making facilities** *All rooms have tea-making facilities.*

2 leaves for making tea
● ADJ. **loose** (= tea that is not in bags)
● QUANT. **packet**
● VERB + TEA **grow**
● TEA + VERB **grow**
● TEA + NOUN **leaf** | **bag** | **caddy** | **strainer** | **estate, plantation** | **chest** *He stores his books in a tea chest.*

3 meal
● ADJ. **afternoon, cream, high** | **birthday, funeral**
● TEA + NOUN **things** *I cleared away the tea things.*
⇨ Note at MEAL (for verbs)

teach *verb*

● ADV. **effectively** *information which helps the teacher teach more effectively*
● VERB + TEACH **try to** *trying to teach my daughter to behave* | **be qualified to** *I am not qualified to teach this*

subject. | **be designed to** *training courses designed to teach managerial techniques* | **help (to), help sb (to)**
• PREP. **about** *teaching children about the world around them* **to** *She teaches English to Polish students.*

teacher noun

• ADJ. **competent, good, inspired, skilled | bad, incompetent | qualified | experienced | inexperienced | sympathetic | senior | head | fellow | former | female, woman | male | full-time, part-time | supply, support | peripatetic | college, primary (school), school, secondary (school), Sunday school, university | class/classroom | remedial | non-specialist, specialist | language | subject | art, EFL, English, history, maths, music, PE, woodwork, etc. | spiritual**
• VERB + TEACHER **train | find (sb)**
• TEACHER + VERB **teach sth | work with sb** *teachers working with pupils with special educational needs*
• TEACHER + NOUN **education, training** *She's been accepted at Bath Teacher Training College.* | **trainer | association, union** *He is chairman of the Parent Teacher Association.* | **shortage**
⇨ Note at JOB

teaching noun

1 work/profession of a teacher
• ADJ. **effective, good | poor | classroom** *a system that rewards good classroom teaching* | **whole-class | individual, one-to-one | collaborative, team | mixed-ability | formal, traditional** *the formal teaching of grammar* | **creative, experimental | remedial, support | academic, college, graduate, postgraduate, primary, school, secondary, undergraduate, university | English, language, music, etc.**
• VERB + TEACHING **get/go into** *He's going to go into teaching.*
• TEACHING + NOUN **method, strategy, style, technique | aid, material, resource** *She used puppets as teaching aids.* | **aim, objective, point** *Write each teaching point on the whiteboard.* | **ability, skills | experience, qualification** *Applicants must hold a recognized teaching qualification.* | **job, post | career** *Mr Murphy retired at the end of a 30-year teaching career.* | **practice** *You have to do six weeks teaching practice as part of the course.* | **staff, profession** *They have left the teaching profession, demoralized and undervalued.* | **commitments, duties, load, responsibilities, role** *Lecturers who have heavy teaching loads.* | **centre, establishment, institution | environment, situation** *a teaching environment where English is not the first language* | **programme, session, term, year** *Work experience is integrated into the teaching programme.* ◇ *The teaching year runs from October to May.* | **time** *Critics say that these tests waste teaching time.* | **hospital**
• PREP. **in~** *I've been in teaching for ten years.*
• PHRASES **an approach to teaching** *the modern approach to language teaching* **a method/style of teaching**

2 ideas and beliefs that are taught by sb
• ADJ. **ancient, traditional | biblical, moral, religious | Buddhist, Christian, etc.**
• VERB + TEACHING **follow** *He followed the teachings of the Koran on this subject.* | **reject | explain, interpret | pass on, spread** *the disciples who passed on Jesus's teaching* | **base sth on** *the great moral teachings on which our culture is based*
• PREP. **in the~** *regarded as the source of goodness in the teachings of Confucius* | **~ about/on** *the Church's teaching on forgiveness*

team noun

1 group of people who play a sport together
• ADJ. **home | away, opposing, rival, visiting | decent,**

strong | successful, winning | weak | dream *The England manager has chosen his dream team for the World Cup.* | **junior, senior, youth | under-16, etc. | A, B, first, second, etc. | international, local, national | England, Ireland, Scotland | French, Irish, etc. | basketball, football, relay, etc. | display** *the Army Parachute Display Team* | **five-man, five-person, five-strong, five-woman** *Spain are fielding a three-man team in this race.* | **men's, mixed, women's**
• VERB + TEAM **field, have | choose, get together, organize, pick, put together** *Can you get a team together by Saturday?* | **coach, manage | be in/on, play in/for** *I'm playing for the first team this week.* | **be called up to, be selected for, get into/onto, make** *Cole has been selected for the team to meet Italy next week.* ◇ *You didn't make the team, I'm afraid.* | **be dropped from, be left out of | join, sign for | play (against) | lead | support**
• TEAM + VERB **compete (in sth), take part (in sth)** *The team competes in a local league.* ◇ *There are six teams taking part.* | **win (sth) | lose (sth)** *Our team lost the final.*
• TEAM + NOUN **game, sport | captain, coach, manager, mate** (also **teammate**) *He apologized to his teammates for his mistake.* | **championship, event, prize | effort, performance | selection | talk** *The manager gives his team talks in English.* | **sheet** (= the list of players chosen for the team)
• PREP. **in/on a/the~** *I'll have you on the first team.* | **~for** *She's in the team for the World Championships.*
⇨ Special page at SPORT

2 group of people who work together
• ADJ. **joint** *a joint team of French and German economists* | **five-strong | husband and wife | campaign, creative, design, development, editorial, investigation, management, marketing, production, project, research, sales** *a member of the senior management team* | **legal, medical | multidisciplinary | rescue**
• VERB + TEAM **build, form, train** *Willing volunteers formed teams of helpers to carry everything in.* ◇ *a specially trained team of counsellors* | **lead, head, manage, run | join** *She has recently joined our sales team.* | **work (together) as** *learning to work together as a team*
• TEAM + VERB **comprise sb, consist of sb** *The team consisted of six investigators and two secretaries.* | **develop sth, operate, work on/with sth** *the team that developed this microchip* ◇ *The team will work closely with other government departments.*
• TEAM + NOUN **leader, member | player** (*informal*) (= sb who works well as part of a team) | **meeting | approach | building, development** *The survival course was intended as a team building exercise.* | **spirit | effort** *It took a tremendous team effort to finish the project on time.*
• PREP. **in a/the~** *There are 20 people in the team.* | **~of** *a team of scientists*
• PHRASES **a member of a team, part of a team**

teamwork noun

• ADJ. **effective, good**
• VERB + TEAMWORK **emphasize, encourage** *The company says the aim is to encourage teamwork.*
• PREP. **through~** *achieving our success through effective teamwork*

tear¹ /tɪə(r)/ noun

• ADJ. **angry, bitter, emotional** *There were angry tears in Lily's eyes.* | **burning, fresh, hot, salty, scalding** *Her eyes were blinded by scalding tears.* | **genuine, real | crocodile** (*figurative*) (= insincere) *They weep crocodile tears for the poor and disadvantaged but are basically happy with things as they are.* | **great, huge, large | single, solitary | silent | helpless, sudden, uncontrollable | unshed** *His eyes were bright with unshed tears.*
• VERB + TEAR **cry, shed, weep** *She wept silent tears*

when she heard his name. ◇ *(figurative) I won't shed any tears when Frank retires.* | **dry, wipe (away)** *I picked the little girl up and helped dry her tears.* ◇ *She wiped a tear from her eye.* | **blink/choke/fight/hold back** *He had to fight back tears of frustration.* | **break down in, burst into** *She broke down in tears in court.* | **move/reduce sb to** *His father's angry shouting reduced the little boy to tears.* | **brim/fill with** *His eyes filled with sudden tears.* | **end in** *(figurative)* (= to have an unhappy result)
• TEAR + VERB **appear, brim in your eyes, brim over, come, fill your eyes, form, gather, spring into/to your eyes, start, well (up)** *Her tears brimmed over and fell on her cheek.* ◇ *He could never read the letter without tears coming to his eyes.* | **course/pour/roll/run/slide/trickle down sth, drip into/onto sth, fall, flow, overflow, stream** *A single tear rolled slowly down her cheek.* | **stand** *Tears stood in Oliver's eyes.* | **blur sth, cloud sth** *Tears blurred his vision.* | **burn (sth), prick (at/in) sth, sting your eyes** *She felt tears pricking her eyelids.* | **dry (up)**
• PREP. **in ~s** *He came to me in tears.* **through your ~s** *She tried to smile through her tears.* | **~ for** *He shed no tears for his lost youth.* **~ of** *tears of happiness* **~ over** *It turned out to be a lot of tears over nothing.*
• PHRASES **bring tears to your eyes** *It brings tears to your eyes to see the children having such fun.* **close/near to tears** *More than once I came near to tears.* **a flood/floods of tears** *We were in floods of tears at the end of the film.* **a mist of tears** *I saw it all through a mist of tears.* **on the verge of tears, tears in your eyes, too deep for tears** *There are times when suffering may be too deep for tears.*

tear² /teə(r)/ *noun*

• VERB + TEAR **have** | **make** | **mend**
• PREP. **~ in** *This sheet has a tear in it.*
• PHRASES **wear and tear** (= the damage to objects, furniture, etc. that is the result of normal use)

tear³ /teə(r)/ *verb*

• ADV. **badly** *His clothes were badly torn.* | **easily** *Careful—the fabric tears very easily.* | **almost, nearly** *The storm nearly tore the roof off.* | **apart, off, out, up** *The dogs tore the fox apart.* ◇ *(figurative) We tore the other team apart in the second half.*
• VERB + TEAR **threaten to**
• PREP. **from** *I tore another sheet from the pad.* **off** *She tore the label off the suitcase.* **on** *She tore her skirt on a nail.* **out of** *Several pages had been torn out of the book.*
• PHRASES **tear free/loose** *She tore herself free.* ◇ *One error and he would have been torn loose and hurled overboard by the squalling wind.* **tear sth in half/two** *She tore the piece of paper in half.* **tear sb limb from limb** *He threatened to tear me limb from limb.* **tear sth open** *She tore the letter open.* **tear sth to pieces/shreds** *(often figurative) The critics tore his last film to shreds.*

tearful *adj.*

• VERBS **be, feel, look, seem, sound** *She sounded angry and tearful.* | **become, get** *He suddenly became very tearful.* | **leave sb** *Defeat left her tearful, pale and drained.*
• ADV. **very** | **almost** *I felt quite emotional—almost tearful.* | **a bit, a little, rather**

tease *verb*

• ADV. **mercilessly** | **a little, gently, lightly**
• VERB + TEASE **used to**
• PREP. **about** *His friends used to tease him about his tatty clothes.* **with** *They teased her mercilessly with remarks about her weight.*
• PHRASES **be just/only teasing** *Don't get upset, I was only teasing.*

technical *adj.*

• VERBS **be, sound** | **become, get** *The conversation was getting a bit technical for me, so I left them to it.*
• ADV. **extremely, highly, very** *A lot of the discussions were highly technical.* | **purely** *This is a purely technical problem.* | **a bit, quite, rather, somewhat**

technicality *noun*

• ADJ. **complex** | **legal**
• VERB + TECHNICALITY **understand** | **discuss, go into** *I don't want to go into all the technicalities just now.*
• PREP. **on a ~** (= because of a technicality) *The court was forced to release him on a technicality.*

technician *noun*

• ADJ. **chief, senior** | **skilled** | **inexperienced** | **qualified** | **trainee** | **lab/laboratory** | **architectural** | **dental** | **computer** | **lighting, sound** *He works as a sound technician in a recording studio.*
• VERB + TECHNICIAN **train** *a need to train technicians in computer aided engineering*
⇨ Note at JOB

technique *noun*

• ADJ. **effective, powerful, useful** | **basic, simple** | **conventional, established, standard, traditional** | **advanced, modern, sophisticated** | **ingenious** | **alternative, experimental** | **assessment, communication, dating, evaluation, exam/examination, farming, interview, management, manufacturing, marketing, problem-solving, recording, relaxation, research, sales, teaching, training** *She needs to work on her interview technique if she's going to get a job.* | **analytical, mathematical, medical, photographic, scientific, statistical, surgical**
• VERB + TECHNIQUE **have** *He has an ingenious technique for dealing with problems of that sort.* | **adopt, apply, deploy, employ, implement, try, use** *On the walls I applied the same technique as I had used for the ceiling.* | **develop, devise, pioneer** *The technique was pioneered in California.* | **acquire, learn, master, practise** *struggling to master the new technique* | **adapt, improve, perfect, work at/on** | **demonstrate, describe**
• TECHNIQUE + VERB **allow sth, enable sth** *Modern freezing techniques enable the chickens to be stored for weeks.* | **work** *The new technique works better than the one it has replaced.* | **be based on sth, be derived from sth** *singing techniques derived from Tibetan music*
• PREP. **~ for** *techniques for the storage of data* **~ in** *They learn basic techniques in self-defence.*

technology *noun*

• ADJ. **current, existing, present-day** | **emerging, the latest, modern, new** *small businesses that are involved with emerging technologies* | **basic, low** | **advanced, complex, high, leading-edge, sophisticated, state-of-the-art, up-to-date, white-hot** | **alternative, innovative** *a car based on alternative technology* | **efficient** | **communication/communications, computer, digital, energy, information, management, manufacturing, nuclear, production, software, telecommunications** | **educational, environmental, medical, military**
• VERB + TECHNOLOGY **have** *We now have the technologies to transplant limbs.* | **adopt, apply, employ, exploit, introduce, take advantage of, use** *exploiting existing technologies more fully* | **create, develop, improve** | **be based on** *a car engine based on technology developed for aeroplanes* | **invest in** *The company is investing heavily in new technologies.*
• TECHNOLOGY + VERB **develop** *Telecommunications technology is developing fast.* | **allow sth, enable sth** *This technology enables computers to read handwriting.*

● PREP. **~for** *the technology for the extraction of iron ore*
● PHRASES **advances in technology** *recent advances in medical technology* **the impact of (a) technology, science and technology**

tedious *adj.*

● VERBS **be, look, seem, sound | become, get** *Her visits were starting to get a bit tedious.* | **make sth | find sth** *He found committee meetings extremely tedious.*
● ADV. **extremely, incredibly, very | almost | a bit, a little, pretty, rather, somewhat**

teenager *noun*

● ADJ. **older, young** *a young teenager of fourteen* | **difficult, rebellious | spirited | gauche, gawky**

teens *noun*

● ADJ. **early** *a girl in her early teens* | **late | mid**
● VERB + TEENS **reach** *He didn't want to share a room with his brother once he reached his teens.*
● PREP. **during your ~** *His parents divorced during his teens.* **in your ~** *All my children are in their teens.* **since your~** *She's had skin problems since her teens.*

teetotal *adj.*

● VERBS **be | become | remain**
● ADV. **strictly** *I'm strictly teetotal.*

telecommunications *noun*

● ADJ. **global, international, national, world | public** *a public telecommunications system* | **digital**
● TELECOMMUNICATIONS + NOUN **infrastructure, link, network, services, system** *modernizing their postal and telecommunications networks* | **equipment, products, satellite, technology | company, firm, giant** (*informal*), **group, operator** *Japan's telecommunications giant, NTT* | **business, industry, market, sector**

telegram *noun*

● ADJ. **congratulatory**
● VERB + TELEGRAM **send (sb) | get, receive**
● TELEGRAM + VERB **arrive, come**
● PREP. **~from, ~to**

telephone *noun*

● ADJ. **pay, public | office, private** *The office telephones were all out of order.* | **cellular, cordless, mobile, portable | radio, satellite**
● VERB + TELEPHONE **use** *Can I use your telephone?* | **be on** *Don't pester me now—I'm on the telephone.* ◇ *We're not on the telephone, so you'll have to come round to the house.* | **answer, get** (*informal*), **pick up** *Hang on—I'll just get the telephone.* | **hang up, put down** *She put down the telephone and burst into tears.* | **leave/take off the hook** *I've been trying to phone him all day—he must have left his telephone off the hook.* | **be wanted on** *The waiter came to tell me I was wanted on the telephone.* | **call sb to** *He was called to the telephone just as he was leaving.* | **bug, tap | connect, install | disconnect**
● TELEPHONE + VERB **ring, shrill** *The telephone was ringing furiously.* ◇ *The telephone shrilled into the silence.* | **be off the hook**
● TELEPHONE + NOUN **number | book, directory | bill | call, message | conversation, enquiry, interview, query, survey | contact** *She is in telephone contact with headquarters.* | **helpline, hotline, support** *The charity has set up a 24-hour telephone helpline.* | **company | banking, marketing, service | charges | cord, headset, receiver | cable, exchange, line, network, switchboard,**

system, wire | box, kiosk | voice *A good telephone voice can do much to improve the temper of irate callers.*
● PREP. **by~** *Can I get in touch by telephone?* **on the~** *She sounded very distant on the telephone.* **over the~** *I don't want to talk about this over the telephone.*

telescope *noun*

● ADJ. **powerful | 26-metre, 60-millimetre, etc. | astronomical, optical, radio, space** *images from the Hubble space telescope*
● VERB + TELESCOPE **use | look at sth with/without, see sth with/without** *stars that cannot be seen without a telescope* | **look (at sth) through, view sth through | set up** *She set up her telescope on the balcony.* | **build** *building the largest telescope in the world*
● PREP. **through a/the~**
● PHRASES **the wrong end of a telescope** *He felt as if he were seeing things through the wrong end of a telescope.*

televise *verb*

● ADV. **nationally** *a nationally televised debate* | **live**

television *noun*

● ADJ. **cable, closed-circuit, digital, high-definition, satellite, terrestrial | commercial, state | local, national | live** *Millions watched the events on live television.* | **black-and-white, colour | portable**
● VERB + TELEVISION **watch** *The children watched television for most of the evening.*
● TELEVISION + VERB **broadcast sth, screen sth** *The state television screened pictures of the trial.*
● TELEVISION + NOUN **chat show, comedy, documentary, drama, film, news, programme, series, show | debate, interview | advert/advertisement, commercial | audience, viewer | personality, presenter | actor, director | character | cameraman, crew | journalist | appearance** *She recalled her first television appearance forty years ago.* | **career | coverage, exposure** *The Olympics receive extensive television coverage.* | **adaptation** *a television adaptation of the popular novel* | **camera | aerial | channel, network, station | licence | business, company, industry, service | monitor, receiver, set | screen | aerial**
● PREP. **in~** *She works in television.* **in front of the~** *He spends hours in front of the television every night.* **on~** *We were watching the news on television.*

tell *verb*

1 give sb information
● ADV. **bluntly, curtly, flatly** *She told me bluntly it was my own fault.* | **gravely | smugly | truthfully | falsely**
● VERB + TELL **want to | be going to** *I was going to tell you—I just didn't get round to it.* | **try to | hate to** *I hate to tell you, but the car's a write-off.* | **let sb** *I tried to tell them but they wouldn't let me.*
● PREP. **about** *I never told him about the money.* **of** *No one had told her of the dangers.* **to** *He told the story to all his friends.*
2 order sb
● ADV. **firmly, sternly** *'Calm down,' he told her firmly.*

temper *noun*

1 tendency to become angry easily
● ADJ. **bad, fierce, fiery, nasty, terrible, vicious, violent | uncontrollable**
● QUANT. **display, fit, flash, outburst** *He broke the chair in a fit of violent temper.*
● VERB + TEMPER **have** *He has a nasty temper.* | **control, keep** *I only just managed to keep my temper with him.* | **fly into, lose** *She loses her temper at the drop of a hat* (= without good reason).

● TEMPER + VERB **flare, rise** *Tempers flared as the traffic jam became worse.* | **cool (down)**
● TEMPER + NOUN **tantrum**
● PREP. **in a~** *She stormed out of the room in a temper.*
● PHRASES **keep you temper in check/under control** *He had to learn to keep his temper under control before he could become a teacher.*

2 way you are feeling
● ADJ. **bad, filthy, foul, ill, terrible** *Peter's comments were responsible for her ill temper.* | **good** | **frayed** *Frayed tempers at the end of the match led to three players being sent off.* | **uncertain**
● VERB + TEMPER **improve** | **recover, regain** *She regained her good temper after a chat.*
● TEMPER + VERB **improve** | **fray, worsen**
● PREP. **in a ~** *He stormed out of the room in a temper.*
● PHRASES **not be in the best of tempers** *I wasn't in the best of tempers when I arrived at the meeting.*

temperament *noun*

● ADJ. **fiery, violent, volatile** | **brittle, fragile, highly-strung** | **cool, equable, even, good, sanguine, unflappable** | **docile** | **sunny** | **questionable, suspect, uncertain** | **right, wrong** *He doesn't have the right temperament for the job.* | **nervous** | **romantic** | **artistic, scientific, etc.**
● VERB + TEMPERAMENT **have**
● PREP. **by/in ~** *She was fiery by temperament.* **of ... ~** *a man of an equable temperament*
● PHRASES **a display of temperament** *He's given to displays of temperament* (= he often behaved in an emotional way).

temperamental *adj.*

● VERBS **be, seem** | **become, get**
● ADV. **highly, very** *Actors have the reputation of being highly temperamental.* | **a bit, quite**

temperature *noun*

1 how hot or cold sth is
● ADJ. **high, warm** *Yesterday the town reached its highest ever February temperature.* | **cold, cool, low, sub-zero** | **moderate** | **normal** | **extreme** *Avoid exposing the instrument to extreme temperatures.* | **boiling, freezing, melting** *the boiling temperature of the solvent* | **maximum, minimum** | **average, mean** | **constant, stable, steady** | **daytime** | **daily** | **summer, winter, etc.** | **April, July, etc.** | **global** *The increase in the mean global temperature will be about 0.3°C per decade.* | **air, sea, water, etc.** | **ambient, room** | **oven** | **body** | **surface** *the surface temperature of our planet*
● VERB + TEMPERATURE **have** *Some places had temperatures in the forties during the heat wave.* | **heat sth to, raise** *Heat the oven to a temperature of 200°C.* | **reduce** | **reach** | **control** | **expose sth to**
● TEMPERATURE + VERB **go up, increase, rise** | **drop, fall, go down, plummet** *Overnight the temperature fell as low as -30°C.*
● TEMPERATURE + NOUN **conditions** | **change, difference, increase, rise** | **gradient, range, variation** *a temperature range of 60–74°F* | **control, regulation** | **measurement** | **gauge, sensor**
● PREP. **at ~** *Serve the wine at room temperature.* **in a ~** *This plant grows well in temperatures above 55°F.* | **~ above/below/between, ~ of** *The fish prefer a temperature of 24–27°C.*
● PHRASES **a change/variation in temperature, a drop in temperature, an increase/a rise in temperature, a range of temperature**
2 fever
● ADJ. **high** | **slight**

● TEMPERATURE + VERB **have, run** *She's running a temperature.* | **take** *The nurse produced a thermometer and took my temperature.* | **bring down** *They used ice packs to bring down her temperature.*
● TEMPERATURE + VERB **go up, rise** | **come down**
● PREP. **~of** *He's in bed with a temperature of 102.*

temple *noun*

1 building used for worship
● ADJ. **great** *the great temples of Egypt* | **ancient, classical** | **sacred** | **ruined** | **Buddhist, Hindu, etc.** | **heathen, pagan**
● TEMPLE + NOUN **priest**
● PREP. **in a/the~** *They went to pray in the temple.*
2 part of the head
● ADJ. **left, right** | **throbbing**
● PREP. **at sb's/the ~ s** *He's greying at the temples.* **in sb's~s** *There was a throbbing in her temples.*

tempo *noun*

1 speed of an activity/event
● ADJ. **increasing**
● VERB + TEMPO **increase, raise, step up** *United stepped up the tempo in the second half.* | **slow (down)**
● TEMPO + VERB **quicken** | **slacken** | **change**
● PHRASES **the tempo of life** *They soon adapted to the tempo of life on the island.*
2 speed of a piece of music
● ADJ. **fast, quick** | **slow** | **moderate** | **waltz, etc.**
● VERB + TEMPO **change**
● TEMPO + NOUN **indications, markings**
● PREP. **at a ... ~** *They took the last movement at an unusually slow tempo.*

temporary *adj.*

● VERBS **be** *The arrangement's only temporary.*
● ADV. **very** | **strictly** | **relatively** | **only**

tempt *verb*

● VERB + TEMPT **could, may/might** | **try to**
● PREP. **into** *Charlotte was tempted into parting with £20 for the painting.* **with** *restaurants tempting us with delicious cakes*
● PHRASES **be almost/half tempted** *I was almost tempted to strip off and plunge straight into the pool.* **be/feel tempted** *Did you ever feel tempted to cheat?* **be seriously/severely/sorely/very tempted** *She was sorely tempted to throw the wine in his face.*

temptation *noun*

● ADJ. **big, great, overwhelming, strong** | **constant**
● VERB + TEMPTATION **feel, have** *I had the constant temptation to look out of the window.* | **avoid, overcome, resist** | **give in/way to, succumb to, yield to**
● PHRASES **in/out of temptation's way, place/put temptation in sb's way** *Keep your valuables locked away so as not to put temptation in the way of thieves.*

tenancy *noun*

● ADJ. **weekly, yearly, etc.** | **life** | **shorthold** | **joint** | **assured, protected, secure** | **business, council, local authority**
● VERB + TENANCY **hold (sth on)** *The tenancy is held in joint names.* ◇ *The land was held on a yearly tenancy.* | **take over** | **grant (sb)** | **terminate** | **renew** | **create** *shorthold tenancy created by the Housing Act of 1980*
● TENANCY + VERB **end, expire**
● TENANCY + NOUN **agreement**
● PREP. **under a/the ~** *The club occupies the land under a protected tenancy.*

tenant noun

- ADJ. **current, existing, sitting** *the sale of council houses to sitting tenants* | **life** | **protected, secure** | **joint** | **potential, prospective** | **business, council, council-house, housing association, local authority, private**
- VERB + TENANT **find** | **evict**
- TENANT + VERB **occupy sth** *The property is currently occupied by a life tenant.*
- TENANT + NOUN **farmer**
- PHRASES **landlord and tenant** *conflicts that might arise between landlord and tenant*

tend verb

- ADV. **carefully, lovingly** *She lovingly tended her little garden.*
- PREP. **to** *He tended to her every need.*
- PHRASES **well-tended** *well-tended lawns*

tendency noun

- ADJ. **clear, great, marked, strong** | **slight** | **greater, growing, increasing** *There's a growing tendency for women to marry later.* | **broad, common, general** | **inbuilt, inherent, innate, natural, underlying** | **alarming, dangerous, unfortunate, worrying** *The later model has an unfortunate tendency to collapse after a few weeks' use.* | **contradictory** | **centrifugal** *The civil war reinforced the centrifugal tendencies at work within the economy.* | **aggressive, homicidal, suicidal, violent** | **artistic, criminal, etc.** *He displayed artistic tendencies at an early age.* | **homosexual, lesbian**
- VERB + TENDENCY **have** | **display, reveal, show** | **reinforce** | **curb, reduce**
- PREP. **~ among** *a worrying tendency among the abused to become abusers* **~ for** *There is a tendency for farm sizes to increase.* **~ on the part of** *The tendency on the part of the children is to blame their parents for everything.* **~ towards** *Industry showed a tendency towards increasingly centralized administration.*

tender noun

- ADJ. **highest, lowest** | **successful** | **competitive** | **open, private, public**
- VERB + TENDER **lodge, make, put in, submit** | **invite, put sth out to, seek** *The government invited tenders for a project to computerize the social security system.* ◇ *The laundry service was put out to competitive tender.* | **go out to** *The building of the new school will go out to tender.* | **win** | **lose** | **accept**
- TENDER + NOUN **offer** | **document, list** | **price**
- PREP. **by~** *The property is to be sold by tender.*

tender adj.

1 kind and loving
- VERBS **be, feel, seem** | **become**
- ADV. **very** | **almost** *Her expression became soft, almost tender.* | **quite**
- PREP. **towards** *He felt tender and loving towards her.*

2 soft and easy to cut/bite
- VERBS **be, seem** | **become**
- ADV. **beautifully, very** *This meat is beautifully tender.* | **just** *Boil the potatoes in salted water until just tender.* | **almost** | **quite**

3 painful when touched
- VERBS **be, feel, look** *The back of my neck feels very tender.* | **become**
- ADV. **very** | **rather, slightly**

tenderness noun

- ADJ. **extreme, great, infinite** | **unexpected** | **loving**
- QUANT. **wave** *He felt a brief wave of tenderness towards his old teacher.*
- VERB + TENDERNESS **feel** | **show**
- PREP. **with (a) ~** *She spoke with loving tenderness.* | **~ for/towards** *She felt great tenderness for him.*
- PHRASES **tenderness in sb's eyes/voice, etc.** *There was tenderness in his face as he looked at her.*

tendon noun

- ADJ. **damaged, severed** | **Achilles**
- VERB + TENDON **pull, sever, tear**
- TENDON + NOUN **injury, trouble** | **operation, repair**

tenement noun

- ADJ. **crowded** | **crumbling, dilapidated, ruined, rundown** | **four-storey, two-storeyed, etc.**
- TENEMENT + NOUN **block, building, house, housing, slum**
- PREP. **in a/the~** *living in a crowded tenement*

tennis noun

- ADJ. **men's, women's** | **junior** | **professional** | **international, world** | **competitive** *Williams' return to competitive tennis after injury* | **lawn, real**
- QUANT. **game**
- VERB + TENNIS **play** | **watch**
- TENNIS + NOUN **ball, racket** | **dress, shoe, shorts** | **court, facilities** | **camp, centre, club** | **circuit, scene** *She is a popular figure on the international tennis circuit.* | **championship, competition, event, match, tournament** | **ace, champion, coach, legend, player, star** | **fan** | **commentator, journalist** | **career**
- ⇨ Special page at SPORT

tenor noun

1 male singing voice/singer
- ADJ. **celebrated, famous, great** | **high** | **operatic**
- VERB + TENOR **sing** *We persuaded Jake to sing tenor* (= sing the tenor part).
- TENOR + VERB **sing** *Three celebrated tenors sang at the president's inauguration.*
- TENOR + NOUN **voice** | **part, solo** | **register**

2 atmosphere/feeling
- ADJ. **even** *Nothing ever changes the even tenor of life in our village.* | **general, whole** *The whole tenor of the meeting was very positive.*

tense noun

- ADJ. **future, past, present** | **continuous, perfect, progressive, simple** *the present simple tense* | **verb**
- VERB + TENSE **use** | **form** *'Have' is the auxiliary verb used to form perfect tenses.*
- TENSE + NOUN **marker** | **system**
- PREP. **in the ... ~** *In the sentence 'I stroked the cat', 'stroked' is in the past tense.*

tense adj.

- VERBS **be, feel, look, seem, sound** | **become, get, grow** *The situation grew increasingly tense.* | **remain**
- ADV. **extremely, incredibly, very** | **increasingly** | **a bit, a little, rather** *I was feeling a bit tense and restless.*
- PREP. **about** *There's no point in getting tense about the situation.*

tension noun

1 inability to relax
- ADJ. **inner** | **emotional, muscle/muscular, nervous, pre-menstrual, sexual** *He suffers from nervous tension.*
- VERB + TENSION **feel, suffer from** *I feel some tension*

in my shoulders. | **sense** *As soon as he entered, he sensed a tension in the air.* | **cause, create** | **relieve** | **release**
- TENSION + NOUN **headache**
- PREP. **~in** *The hot bath eased the tension in his body.*
- PHRASES **a release of tension** *Laughter can be a great release of tension.* **a sign of tension** *Horses are very sensitive to signs of tension in humans.*

2 bad feeling between people, countries, etc.
- ADJ. **considerable, great, high** *More police have been sent to areas of high political tension.* | **slight** | **growing, heightened, increased, increasing, mounting** | **constant** | **unresolved** | **renewed** | **ethnic, political, racial, religious, social** | **communal, family, internal, international, national, regional**
- VERB + TENSION **cause, create, generate** | **defuse, ease, reduce** *She often used humour to defuse tension in meetings.* | **heighten**
- TENSION + VERB **build up, grow, increase, mount, rise** | **ease** | **be palpable**
- PREP. **~ among** *The tension among the audience was palpable.* **~ between** *tension between local youths and the police* **~ in/within** *The redundancies caused greater tensions within the company.* **~ over** *There has been increased tension over the border incident.* **~ with** *renewed tension with France*
- PHRASES **a source of tension** *Money was always a source of tension between her parents.*

3 of rope, wire, etc.
- ADJ. **string**
- VERB + TENSION **adjust** *This old racket needs its string tension adjusted.* | **release**
- PREP. **in ~** *The metal is weak in tension.* **under ~** *Stay clear of cables which are under tension.* | **~ on** *The sudden tension on the line told me I had hooked a fish.*

tent *noun*

- ADJ. **dome, ridge** | **lightweight** | **three-person, two-person, etc.** | **makeshift** *The refugees had been living in makeshift tents for a year.* | **leaking, leaky** | **circus** | **beer, dining, luncheon, hospitality, mess, refreshment, tea** | **cook, cookhouse, cooking** *There was a long queue of troops outside the cookhouse tent.* | **hospital** | **press** | **oxygen**
- QUANT. **row**
- VERB + TENT **erect, pitch, put up, set up** *They pitched their tent in a little clearing in the wood.* | **unzip, zip shut/up** | **dismantle, take down** | **pack away/up** | **share**
- TENT + VERB **blow down, collapse**
- TENT + NOUN **camp, city** *a tent city housing refugees from the war* | **door, flap, frame, opening, peg, pole, rope, wall**
- PREP. **in a/the ~**
- PHRASES **the door/flap/roof of a tent**

tenure *noun*

1 holding an important position
- ADJ. **life, long** | **brief, short**
- VERB + TENURE **have** *She had a long tenure of office.*
- PREP. **during sb's ~** *He achieved a lot during his short tenure.*
- PHRASES **a tenure of office**

2 legal right to occupy property/land
- ADJ. **life, secure** | **fixed-period** | **housing, land** | **feudal, freehold**
- PHRASES **security of tenure** *The tenants have security of tenure.*

3 right to remain permanently in your job
- ADJ. **academic**
- VERB + TENURE **have** | **get** | **grant sb** *She has been granted tenure at Leeds University.*

term *noun*

1 word or group of words
- ADJ. **specific** | **blanket, broad, general, generic** | **clear, precise** | **vague** | **ambiguous** | **strong** *His objection was couched in the strongest terms.* | **mild** | **colloquial, slang** | **pejorative** *'Swot' is a pejorative term for someone who studies a lot.* | **technical** | **clinical, legal, medical, musical, etc.**
- VERB + TERM **use** | **be couched in** | **define, explain** | **coin** *The term 'acid rain' was coined in the nineteenth century.*
- TERM + VERB **connote sth, denote sth, describe sth, mean sth** | **apply to sth, be applied to sth, cover sth, refer to sth** *The term 'renewable energy' is applied, for example, to energy deriving from solar radiation.*
- PREP. **~ for** *'Old man' is a slang term for 'father'.* **~ of** *a term of abuse/endearment*
- PHRASES **in glowing terms** *The chairman spoke of the achievements of the company in glowing terms.* **in no uncertain terms** *We let them know in no uncertain terms just how disappointed we were.* **in simple terms**

2 in … terms showing what aspect of something you are considering
- ADJ. **absolute, material, practical, real** *Income has increased in real terms by 5%.* | **relative** *Iceland has had a mild winter, in relative terms.* | **broad, general** | **concrete** | **abstract** | **international** | **cultural, economic, financial, money, political, social, etc.** *In money terms, the event was a disaster.*

3 (usually **terms**) of an agreement/a relationship
- ADJ. **favourable, unfavourable** | **express** *the breach of an express term in the contract* | **implied** | **contract, credit, peace**
- VERB + TERM **dictate, negotiate, set** *Our opponents set the terms of the debate.* | **agree on**
- PREP. **under the ~s of** *Under the terms of the alliance, Japan was not obliged to enter the war.*
- PHRASES **on amicable/friendly/good terms** *The dispute was resolved on amicable terms.* **on equal terms** *It is a sport in which the top men and women can compete on equal terms.* **on familiar/first-name terms** *I'm on first-name terms with my boss.* **on speaking terms** *They haven't been on speaking terms since they had that big row.* **terms and conditions** *A wide range of accounts are available, with varying terms and conditions.*

4 period of a school/university year
- ADJ. **college, school, university** | **autumn, spring, etc.** | **teaching**
- PREP. **during (the) ~** *It's hard to get away during term.* **in the ~** *We have exams in the summer term.*
- PHRASES **the beginning/end of term** *We have exams at the end of term.*

5 period of time
- ADJ. **long, short** *a long term of imprisonment* | **full** *(medical) The pregnancy went to full term (= lasted the normal length of time).* | **fixed** *The contract was for a fixed term of five years.* | **jail, prison** | **presidential**
- VERB + TERM **serve** *He served a five-year prison term.*
- TERM + VERB **expire, run out**
- PREP. **at ~** *(medical) Her baby was born at term.*
- PHRASES **in the long/medium/short term** *In the long term, our efforts will pay off.* **a term of imprisonment, a term of office** *The president was sworn in for his second term of office.* **a term of years** *The lease is granted for a set term of years.*

term *verb* be termed

- ADV. **aptly** | **accurately** | **broadly, loosely** | **commonly, generally** | **variously** *This material is variously termed ash, clinker, cinders or slag.* | **euphemistically**
- PREP. **as** *His condition would be more accurately termed as 'chronic fatigue'.*

terminal noun

1 place/building that handles goods/passengers
- ADJ. **international** | **air/airport, bus, ferry, rail/railway** | **passenger** | **container, freight** | **coal, gas, etc.**
- TERMINAL + NOUN **building**
- PREP. **at/in a/the ~** *We met up at the bus terminal.*

2 computer equipment
- ADJ. **colour** | **computer** | **network** | **display**
- VERB + TERMINAL **connect, disconnect**
- TERMINAL + NOUN **keyboard, screen, server**
- PREP. **at a/the ~** *There were two students at each terminal.* **on a/the ~** *pressing keys on a terminal*

terminate verb
- ADV. **abruptly, prematurely** *His contract was abruptly terminated.* | **swiftly** | **automatically**
- VERB + TERMINATE **be entitled to, be free to**
- PHRASES **the right to terminate sth** *Either party has the right to terminate the agreement.*

termination noun

1 ending of sth
- ADJ. **early, premature** | **sudden**
- TERMINATION + NOUN **date**
- PHRASES **notice of termination** *The landlord gave notice of the termination of tenancy.* **a termination of a contract, termination of employment** *You are required to give the company six weeks' notice of termination of employment.*

2 abortion
- ADJ. **early**
- VERB + TERMINATION **have, undergo** *She chose to have an early termination.*
- PHRASES **a termination of (a) pregnancy**

terminology noun
- ADJ. **modern** | **specialist, specialized, technical** | **computer, legal, medical, scientific, etc.**
- VERB + TERMINOLOGY **use** *The article uses rather specialized musical terminology.* | **borrow** | **standardize**
- PREP. **in … ~** *The outer walls, in building terminology, are 'double skin'.*

terrace noun

1 flat area of stone next to a restaurant, etc.
- ADJ. **paved** | **covered** | **shaded** | **sunny** | **cafe, garden, pool/poolside, roof/rooftop** | **sun, sunbathing**
- VERB + TERRACE **open onto** *The dining room opens onto a paved terrace.*
- TERRACE + VERB **overlook sth** *The hotel has a roof terrace overlooking the sea.*
- TERRACE + NOUN **bar, garden, restaurant**
- PREP. **on a/the ~** *There's a table free on the terrace.*

2 line of joined houses
- ADJ. **long** | **two-storey, three-storey, etc.**
- TERRACE + NOUN **house** (also **terraced house**)
- PREP. **in a/the ~** *Our house is in a long Victorian terrace in north London.*
- PHRASES **a terrace of houses**

3 (usually **terraces**) for growing crops on a hill
- ADJ. **steep** | **cultivated**
- VERB + TERRACE **dig** *The villagers had dug terraces in the hillside.*

terrain noun
- ADJ. **flat** | **hilly, mountainous, rocky, rough, rugged, uneven** | **difficult, harsh, inhospitable** *difficult terrain for cycling* | **familiar** | **unknown** | **boggy, marshy**
- VERB + TERRAIN **cross, traverse**

- PREP. **across/over ~** *It took us the whole day to trek across the rocky terrain.*

terrible adj.
- VERBS **be, look, seem, sound**
- ADV. **really, truly** *I thought something really terrible had happened.* | **absolutely, just, quite, simply** *He suddenly collapsed—it was simply terrible.* | **pretty, rather** | **not very** *Nothing very terrible happened.*
- PREP. **for** *It must have been terrible for the survivors.*

terrified adj.
- VERBS **appear, be, feel, look, seem**
- ADV. **really, truly** | **absolutely, completely, quite, utterly** | **pretty** | **clearly, obviously, plainly** | **secretly**
- PREP. **at** *She was absolutely terrified at the thought of jumping off the bridge.* **of** *He's terrified of spiders.*

territory noun

1 area of land that belongs to one country, etc.
- ADJ. **vast** | **new** *The explorers set off to conquer new territories.* | **former** *former French territories* | **neighbouring, surrounding** | **home, national** | **alien, foreign, overseas** | **enemy, hostile** | **neutral** | **colonial, dependent** | **sovereign** *Troops were stationed on sovereign German territory.* | **conquered, lost, occupied** *a town in British-occupied territory* | **unoccupied** | **disputed** | **familiar** | **uncharted, unexplored, unknown, virgin** | **dangerous**
- VERB + TERRITORY **hold** | **annex, capture, conquer, invade, occupy, recapture, take** | **control, govern, rule** *The territory had been controlled by Azerbaijan for many years.* | **cede, surrender** | **explore** (often figurative) *Tired of writing detective novels, she began to explore new territory.* | **settle** *The territory was never densely settled.* | **enter** | **leave** | **overfly** *The plane was shot down while overflying enemy territory.* | **stray into** *The soldiers strayed into hostile territory.*

2 of an animal
- ADJ. **breeding**
- VERB + TERRITORY **defend, patrol** | **mark (out), scent-mark**

terror noun

1 great fear
- ADJ. **absolute, naked, pure, real, sheer** | **constant**
- VERB + TERROR **be filled with, feel, have, shake/tremble with** *He was filled with absolute terror at the sight.* ◇ *the sheer terror she felt when she saw him* ◇ *He had a real terror of darkness.* | **bring, inspire, spread** *The explosion brought terror to hundreds of local residents.* ◇ *He inspired terror in everyone he met.* | **live in** *She lived in terror of her father.* | **flee in** *The shots sent the crowd fleeing in terror.*
- PREP. **from ~** *trembling from terror and excitement* **in ~** *He was found hiding in terror.* **out of ~** *He cried out, out of pure terror.* **with ~** *His face was white with terror.*
- PHRASES **strike terror into (the heart of) sb** *Its fearsome appearance struck terror into their hearts.*

2 violent action for political purposes
- ADJ. **political**
- VERB + TERROR **resort to, use** *The group has resorted to terror to try to get what it wants.* | **give in to**
- TERROR + NOUN **campaign** | **tactics** | **gang, group**
- PHRASES **an act of terror** *people who carry out acts of terror* **a campaign of terror** *The bombing formed part of a nationwide campaign of terror.* **a reign of terror** *The dictator's ten-year reign of terror left over 100 000 dead.*

terrorism noun

- ADJ. **urban | international, organized, state**
- VERB + TERRORISM **combat, fight | defeat | give in to** *This government will not give in to terrorism.*
- TERRORISM + NOUN **campaign**
- PREP. **~ against** *Public cooperation is vital in the fight against terrorism.*
- PHRASES **an act of terrorism**
⇨ Note at CRIME (for more verbs)

terrorist noun

- ADJ. **suspected | armed | international** *The bomb attacks have been attributed to a group of international terrorists.* | **republican, right-wing, separatist, etc.**
- TERRORIST + NOUN **band, faction, gang, group, organization, unit | act, action, activity, atrocity, attack, bomb, bombing, campaign, explosion, incident, murder, violence** *an increase in terrorist activity* | **threat | target** *Aircraft remain likely terrorist targets.* | **victim | charge, crime, offence | suspect**

test noun

1 examination of sb's knowledge/ability
- ADJ. **demanding, difficult, gruelling | easy, simple | fair, good, objective** *This type of exam does not provide a fair test of the student's knowledge.* | **listening, oral, practical, written | cloze, multiple-choice | placement** *He scored well in the placement test and was put in the most advanced class.* | **achievement, aptitude, endurance, intelligence, IQ, language, memory, mental, proficiency, spelling** *The recruits were put through a week of gruelling endurance tests.* | **driving | screen** *Three actors out of a hundred were chosen from the screen test.*
- VERB + TEST **do, sit (for), take** *I took my driving test last week.* | **pass | fail | give, set | administer | mark**
- TEST + NOUN **result | conditions** *As a final practice for the exam, they had to write two essays under test conditions.* | **paper, questions**
- PREP. **in a/the ~** *Some of the questions in the history test were rather difficult.* | **~ in** *a test in mathematics* **~ on** *a test on the French Revolution*

2 experiment/medical examination
- ADJ. **exhaustive, extensive, rigorous, stringent, thorough | statistical | empirical, experimental | field, laboratory | successful | negative, positive | medical | screening** *screening tests for cancer* | **diagnostic | forensic** *Forensic tests showed that the man had been poisoned.* | **eye, sight | hearing | blood, DNA, skin, urine | dope, drug/drugs | fitness | breath, breathalyser | smear** *The government has launched a campaign advising women of the need for regular smear tests.* | **HIV | pregnancy | personality, psychological, psychometric | lie-detector, polygraph | means | flight, road, safety | atomic, nuclear | alpha, beta** *The revolutionary new system goes into beta test this month.*
- QUANT. **number, series** *She underwent a series of blood tests.*
- VERB + TEST **have, undergo | do, carry out, conduct, perform, run** *Rigorous safety tests are being carried out on the new jet.* | **use** *The test used in detecting the disease carries its own risks.* | **fail** *Three athletes were sent home after failing drugs tests.*
- TEST + VERB **take place | confirm sth, indicate sth, reveal sth, show sth** *The urine test showed some sort of infection.* | **prove negative/positive | come into force** *The new safety test came into force last month.* | **be designed to** *a test designed to detect bowel cancer*
- TEST + NOUN **result** *a negative/positive test result* | **data | conditions** *The machine refused to perform properly under test conditions.* | **bed** *The company is using the university data library as a test bed for its new software.* | **site** *protesters at nuclear test sites* | **facility, drive, flight,**

run *He's taken the car out on a test run.* | **driver, pilot | aircraft, car | trial** *The new drink went down well in the test trials.* | **methods, procedures | system | performance | subject | equipment, instruments, kit, machine | samples, substances | programme, schedule | phase, stage** *The software is still at the test stage.* | **session** *Subjects had to attend ten test sessions on different days.* | **certificate** *The vehicle did not have a current test certificate at the time of the accident.* | **case** *This was the first action taken by a cancer sufferer against a tobacco company, and was seen as a test case.*
- PREP. **~ for** *a test for diabetes* **~ on** *a test on the engine*

3 shows how good, strong, effective, etc. sb/sth is
- ADJ. **good | critical, crucial, key, real, supreme, true, ultimate, vital** *a real test of character* | **serious, severe, stiff, tough | simple | objective | subjective | political**
- VERB + TEST **pose** *The calls for tax reform pose a severe test for the government.* | **put sb/sth to** *The latest pay dispute has really put her management skills to the test.* | **face** *The new prime minister is facing his toughest political test so far.*
- TEST + NOUN **case**
- PHRASES **the acid test** (= a way of deciding whether sth is successful or true) *Whether he would accept a pay cut would be the acid test of his loyalty to the company.* **stand the test of time** *Whether this new technology will stand the test of time remains to be seen.*

test verb

1 examine sth to find out if it is working/what it is like
- ADV. **adequately, properly** *The product had not been adequately tested before being put on the market.* | **rigorously | extensively | exhaustively, fully, thoroughly | regularly, routinely** *You should test your brakes regularly.* | **directly | empirically, experimentally** *the importance of empirically tested research* | **formally | successfully** *The exercise successfully tested the procedures for dealing with a serious oil spillage.* | **clinically, dermatologically | out** *a good way to test out his hypothesis*
- VERB + TEST **decide to** *We decided to test the theory experimentally.* | **attempt to, seek to, try to | be designed to, be intended to | be used to | be difficult to** *It is difficult to test a potential cure when a disease is ill-defined.*
- PREP. **for** *Squeeze the fruit to test for ripeness.* **on** *We only sell products that have not been tested on animals.*
- PHRASES **have sth tested** *I'm having my eyes tested this week.* **test negative/positive** *Two of the athletes tested positive for illegal drugs.* **test sth to the limit** *The training tested his body to the very limit.* **tried and tested** *tried and tested techniques*

2 require all sb's strength/ability/resources, etc.
- ADV. **seriously, severely, sorely** *Neither goalkeeper was seriously tested in a rather poor match.* ◇ *There were times when my temper was sorely tested.*

testament noun

- ADJ. **fine, fitting, worthy**
- VERB + TESTAMENT **bear** *The immaculate state of the garden bears testament to a lifetime's effort.*
- PREP. **~ to** *The monument is a worthy testament to the courage of the men who fought in the war.*

testify verb

- VERB + TESTIFY **be prepared to, be willing to | be unwilling to, refuse to | call sb to, force sb to** *The president's former aides were called to testify at his trial.*
- PREP. **against** *She refused to testify against her brother.* **before** *She was unwilling to testify before Congress.* **for** *a Mafia member who was prepared to testify for the authorities* **to** *A senior officer testified to the existence of police*

hit squads. ◇ *A large number of witnesses testified to the tribunal.*
● PHRASES **testify in court**

testimony *noun*

1 formal statement that sth is true
● ADJ. **reliable | false | oral, sworn, verbal, written | eyewitness, personal | expert | court, trial** *a transcript of the trial testimony*
● VERB + TESTIMONY **give | hear**
● PREP. **by your~** *He had by his own testimony taken part in the burglary.* **in ~** *In testimony before the Crown Court, she described her movements on the day of the murder.* | **~ about** *The witness was called to give oral testimony about the incident outside the theatre.* **~ against** *The court heard her testimony against the accused.* **~ before**

2 proof
● ADJ. **ample, clear, eloquent, powerful, remarkable, striking**
● VERB + TESTIMONY **bear, stand as**
● PREP. **~ to** *His thick, swollen fingers bore testimony to a lifetime of toil.*

text *noun*

1 writing in a book/newspaper, on a computer, etc.
● ADJ. **complete, full** *The newspaper printed the full text of the interview.* | **draft | final | original | main** *The illustrations are printed separately from the main text.* | **accompanying** *The catalogue consists of colour reproductions of the paintings with accompanying text.* | **electronic, handwritten, printed, typewritten, written**
● QUANT. **block, body, chunk, line, page, piece, portion** *Hand symbols in the main body of the text cross-refer the reader to the appendices.* ◇ *Use the mouse to move chunks of text from place to place.*
● VERB + TEXT **create, draft, write | edit, modify | highlight | cut, delete | insert, move, paste | scan (in) | handle, manipulate, process** *computer programs that process text* | **set, typeset | print | publish | read | transcribe | annotate | stray from** *She strayed from the text in a few places to illustrate some of her more interesting points.*
● TEXT + NOUN **file** *The program allows you to import text files from other word processors.* | **editor** *one of the best HTML text editors available* | **message, messaging** *The text message just said 'Hope 2CU@the party'.*
⇨ Special page at COMPUTER

2 book or piece of writing to be studied
● ADJ. **basic, key, standard | recommended, set** *'Antony and Cleopatra' was one of our set texts for A level.* | **prepared** *He stood up and began reading from a prepared text.* | **authoritative, influential | introductory | academic, dramatic, legal, literary, poetic, sacred, scientific, etc.** *We're studying dramatic texts by sixteenth-century playwrights.* | **biology, mathematics, etc.**
● VERB + TEXT **read (from) | analyse, deconstruct, interpret, study | annotate**
● TEXT + NOUN **analysis**
● PREP. **in a/the~** *We discussed the use of metaphor in the text.* | **~ about/on** *a poetic text about growing up in rural England*

textbook *noun*

● ADJ. **basic, general, introductory, standard** *Do you have the standard textbook on the subject?* | **recommended | economics, geography, medical, etc. | school**

textile *noun*

● ADJ. **embroidered, handwoven, printed, woven | cotton, woollen, etc.**
● TEXTILE + NOUN **business, company, factory, firm,** industry, manufacture, manufacturer, manufacturing, mill, trade, worker | design, designer
● PREP. **in~s** *She has a job in textiles.*
● PHRASES **the manufacture/production of textiles**

texture *noun*

● ADJ. **dense, firm, thick | delicate, fine, light, soft** *Sponge cakes have a light texture.* | **coarse, crumbly, crunchy, rough | creamy, silky, smooth, velvety | spongy | sticky | different, varied | interesting, rich** *She enjoyed the rich texture of the beer.* | **skin, soil, surface | choral, instrumental, musical, string**
● VERB + TEXTURE **have | add, give sth** *I use a styling gel to give texture to my hair.*
● PREP. **in ~** *The cloth was rough in texture.* **with a ... ~** *a piece with a dense choral texture*

thank *verb*

● ADV. **gratefully, profusely, properly, sincerely, warmly** *I would like to thank you all most sincerely.* ◇ *He thanked her warmly for the meal.* | **politely | personally | publicly**
● VERB + THANK **must, want to, would like to** *I wanted to thank him personally.*
● PREP. **for** *I haven't thanked Bill properly yet for his present.*

thankful *adj.*

● VERBS **be, feel, seem**
● ADV. **deeply, extremely, very | just** *I'm just thankful that my mother never lived to see this.*
● PREP. **for** *We were thankful for the chance to rest.*

thanks *noun*

● ADJ. **big, special** *A big thanks to all of you who supported our fund-raising campaign.* | **heartfelt, sincere, warm | grateful**
● VERB + THANKS **express, give, say** *We would like to express our warmest thanks for all you've done.* ◇ *I said thanks and put the phone down.* | **nod, smile** *She smiled her thanks as the car drove off.* | **get, receive** *You'll get little thanks from him for all your trouble.* | **accept | deserve** *Their generosity deserves our grateful thanks.*
● THANKS + VERB **go to sb** *Thanks go to Claire Potter for making the hall available to us.*
● PREP. **as/in ~ for** *He got a bottle of whisky in thanks for his cooperation.* **~ to** *He gave thanks to God for the safe return of his son.*
● PHRASES **a letter/vote/word of thanks** *The chairperson proposed a vote of thanks to the volunteers.* **many thanks** *Many thanks for the flowers.* **thanks be to God** *We were all pulled out alive, thanks be to God.*

thank you *noun*

● ADJ. **big, special | polite**
● VERB + THANK YOU **give, say** *He didn't even say thank you.* ◇ *We said our thank yous and goodbyes to the hosts and went to catch a cab.* | **get**
● THANK YOU + NOUN **letter, present**
● PREP. **~ for** *She got a special thank you for all her hard work.* **~ to** *a big thank you to the hospital staff*

thaw *noun*

● ADJ. **rapid, sudden | spring, summer** *The arctic shore remains frozen until the summer thaw.*
● THAW + VERB **begin, come, set in**
● PREP. **during a/the ~** *The river often floods during the thaw.*

thaw *verb*

- ADV. **completely** *Make sure the meat has thawed completely before cooking.* | **a little** *(figurative) Relations between the two countries thawed a little after the talks.* | **visibly** *(figurative) The old nun was as imperious as ever, but visibly thawed when she saw the children.* | **out** *Has the meat thawed out yet?*

theatre *noun*

1 where you go to see plays, etc.
- ADJ. **large** | **little, small** | **crowded, packed** *The theatre was packed for the opening night.* | **open-air** | **puppet** *The pier has a unique little puppet theatre.*
- VERB + THEATRE **go to, visit** *I haven't been to the theatre for ages.*
- THEATRE + NOUN **ticket** | **production** | **audience** | **manager, staff**
- PREP. **at a/the~** *We were at the theatre last night.* **in a/the~** *There's a bar in the theatre.*

2 drama
- ADJ. **good, great** *He writes the sort of dialogue that makes great theatre.* | **live** | **amateur** | **commercial, professional** | **fringe, provincial, repertory** *There was some good fringe theatre at the festival.* | **classical, contemporary, experimental, modern, music/musical, popular** | **street** *We saw some good street theatre while we were in Paris.* | **community, youth** | **political** *(often figurative) The Chancellor's speech was an absorbing piece of political theatre.*
- QUANT. **piece**
- VERB + THEATRE **study** *He is studying Greek theatre.*
- THEATRE + NOUN **studies** | **critic**

3 work of acting in/ producing plays
- VERB + THEATRE **be in, work in** | **go into** *He wants to go into the theatre when he finishes university.*
- THEATRE + NOUN **director, producer** | **company, group**

4 in a hospital
- ADJ. **operating**
- VERB + THEATRE **take to** *He's already been taken to theatre for the operation.*
- THEATRE + NOUN **nurse, sister**
- PREP. **in (the)~** *She was in the operating theatre for two hours.*

theft *noun*

- ADJ. **petty** | **attempted** | **car, cattle,** etc.
- PREP. **~ from** *They are accused of theft from a newsagent's shop.* **~ of** *She admitted the theft of three pairs of trousers.*
- ⇨ Note at CRIME (for verbs)

theme *noun*

- ADJ. **basic, central, dominant, important, key, main, major, underlying** | **broad, general** | **common, popular, universal** *universal themes of love and loneliness* | **constant, familiar, favourite, recurrent, recurring** | **related** | **unifying** | **contemporary, topical** | **historical, religious,** etc. | **campaign, conference, research** | **musical** *The film's haunting musical theme stayed in my head for days.*
- VERB + THEME **develop, discuss, examine, explore** *His later novels develop the theme of alienation.* | **warm to** *'Our work', he continued, warming to his theme, 'will be a milestone in scientific history.'*
- THEME + VERB **emerge** *Several familiar themes emerged from the discussion.* | **run through sth** *The same themes run through all her novels.*
- THEME + NOUN **music, song, tune** | **park, pub**
- PREP. **on the~ of** *He gave a talk on the theme of teenage unemployment.*

- PHRASES **variations on a theme** *Most of the essays appear to be variations on a few central themes.*

theology *noun*

- ADJ. **dogmatic, liberal, natural, practical, systematic** | **ecumenical** | **traditional** | **eastern, western** | **Christian, Hindu,** etc. | **Catholic, Protestant,** etc.
- ⇨ Note at SUBJECT (for verbs and nouns)

theoretical *adj.*

- VERBS **be** | **remain**
- ADV. **highly** | **purely** *This research is purely theoretical.* | **largely** | **rather**

theory *noun*

- ADJ. **complete** | **partial** | **general** *Einstein's general theory of relativity* | **coherent** | **unified** *the existence of a grand unified theory that determines everything in the universe* | **current, new** | **classical** *the classical theory of gravity* | **pet** *One of her pet theories is that people who restrict their calorie intake live longer.* | **conflicting** | **critical** | **abstract** *His comments are just abstract theory and show little understanding of the realities of the situation.* | **economic, legal, linguistic, literary, political, scientific, social,** etc. | **post-modernist, structuralist,** etc. *Current feminist theory consists of several different trends.* | **conspiracy** *a conspiracy theory about the princess's death* | **chaos, game, quantum, number, particle, probability, relativity,** etc.
- QUANT. **set** *Each school has its own set of theories.*
- VERB + THEORY **have, hold** | **advance, develop, formulate, produce, propose** | **work on** *Police are working on the theory that the murderer was known to the family.* | **refute** | **confirm, prove** | **disprove** | **challenge, test**
- THEORY + VERB **evolve** | **hold sth, suggest sth**
- PREP. **in ~** *In theory, these machines should last for ten years.* | **~ about** *He has a theory about why dogs walk round in circles before going to sleep.*
- PHRASES **theory and practice** *the distinction/relationship between theory and practice*

therapist *noun*

- ADJ. **trained** | **experienced** | **beauty, occupational, sex, speech**
- ⇨ Note at DOCTOR
- ⇨ Note at JOB

therapy *noun*

- ADJ. **alternative, complementary** | **behaviour, speech** | **aversion, occupational, regression, relaxation, shock,** etc. | **family, group** *They discuss their problems in group therapy sessions.*
- QUANT. **course**
- VERB + THERAPY **need, require** | **be given, have, receive, undergo** *He will have to have shock therapy.* | **be in, go into** *I went into therapy because my doctor suggested it.*
- THERAPY + NOUN **group, session**
- PHRASES **a form of therapy** *the use of hypnosis as a form of therapy*

thermometer *noun*

- ADJ. **accurate** | **clinical** | **digital, mercury** | **rectal** | **meat, sugar** *Check that the roast is cooked right through, using a meat thermometer.*
- VERB + THERMOMETER **read**
- THERMOMETER + VERB **measure sth**
- THERMOMETER + NOUN **reading**
- PREP. **on a/the~** *the reading on the thermometer*

thesis noun

1 part of a university degree
- ADJ. **doctoral, MA, Master's, MSc, PhD, etc.** | **chemistry, geology, etc.** | **research**
- VERB + THESIS **work on** | **complete, do, write (up)** | **submit** | **publish**
- THESIS + NOUN **research, title, topic**
- PREP. **by~** *She completed an MSc by thesis.* **in a/the~** *research presented in a thesis* | **~about/on** *He's doing a doctoral thesis on the early works of Shostakovich.*

2 statement of an idea/a theory
- ADJ. **basic, central, main**
- VERB + THESIS **prove, support** *The results of the experiment support his central thesis.* | **disprove** | **advance** *He advanced the thesis that too much choice was burdensome to people.* | **challenge, refute**
- PREP. **~about** *a thesis about the effects of new technology on skills*

thick adj.

1 of solid things/growing things
- VERBS **be, feel, look, seem**
- ADV. **extremely, really, very** | **fairly, quite, rather, relatively** *Use fairly thick wads of newspaper.* | **enough, sufficiently** *a screen of trees thick enough to conceal the building entirely*

2 of liquid
- VERBS **be, look, seem** | **become, get** *The paint's got too thick. I'll have to thin it down.*
- ADV. **very** | **fairly, quite, rather** | **enough, sufficiently**

3 of fog/smoke/air
- VERBS **be, feel, look, seem** | **become, grow** *The air had grown thick and smoky.*
- ADV. **very** | **fairly, quite, rather**
- PREP. **with** *The air was thick with dust.* ◇ *(figurative)* *The atmosphere was thick with tension.*

thief noun

- ADJ. **would-be** *The alarm is usually sufficient to deter a would-be thief.* | **common, petty** | **professional** | **casual, opportunist** | **sneak** | **car, jewel, etc.**
- QUANT. **gang**
- VERB + THIEF **catch**
- THIEF + VERB **take sth, snatch sth, steal sth** *A thief snatched her handbag containing her wages.* | **escape with sth, get away with sth, make off with sth** | **break in** | **strike** *The thief struck while the family were out.*

thigh noun

- ADJ. **fat, flabby, plump** | **beefy, hard, huge, muscular, powerful, strong, sturdy** | **lean, slender, slim** | **bare, naked** | **silken** | **inner**
- THIGH + NOUN **bone, muscle** | **injury, strain**

thin adj.

1 of solid things: not thick
- VERBS **be, feel, look, seem** | **become, wear** *The fabric was wearing thin.* ◇ *(figurative)* *That joke is wearing a little thin.*
- ADV. **extremely, incredibly, very, wafer-** *a plate of wafer-thin bread and butter* | **a bit, fairly, a little, quite, rather, relatively** | **enough** *a sliver of rock thin enough to be translucent*

2 not fat
- VERBS **be, look** | **become, get, grow**
- ADV. **extremely, painfully, pathetically, pitifully, terribly, very** *The old horse was painfully thin.* | **fairly, quite, rather** *She's tall and quite thin.*

3 of liquids

- VERBS **be, look, seem** *The paint looks a bit thin.* | **become, get** *Be careful that the mixture doesn't get too thin.*
- ADV. **terribly, very** | **a bit, rather**

thing noun

1 used instead of the name of an object
- ADJ. **basic, essential** *I need to buy a few basic things like bread and milk.*
- VERB + THING **make** *He makes things out of wood.*

2 things objects/clothing/tools
- ADJ. **swimming, tennis, etc.** | **breakfast, lunch, etc.** *He hadn't washed up the dinner things yet.*
- VERB + THINGS **get together, pack** *Come on kids, get your things together—we're going.* | **put on, take off** *Hang on a second—I'll just take off my painting things (= clothes).* | **clear away/up, put away, tidy away/up** *Clear your painting things (= materials) away.*

3 (used with negatives) anything
- VERB + THING **hear, know, notice, see** *I can't see a thing without my glasses.* | **miss** *I'm going to arrive early, because I don't want to miss a thing.* | **do** *She's tricked you, and you can't do a thing about it.* | **eat** *I haven't eaten a thing all day.* | **say** *Nobody said a thing when he appeared with a wig on.* | **mean** *Fame and fortune don't mean a thing if you don't have happiness.*

4 fact/event/situation/action
- ADJ. **good, great, positive** *It's a good thing you remembered to turn off the gas!* ◇ *The best thing would be to apologize straight away.* ◇ *If she works hard she's capable of great things.* ◇ *Try to look on your rejection as a positive thing.* | **lovely, nice, wonderful** | **bad, negative** *Too much studying can be a bad thing.* ◇ *It's no bad thing to express your anger.* | **appalling, awful, dreadful, horrible, terrible** *That was a horrible thing to say to her.* | **amazing, curious, exciting, extraordinary, funny, interesting, remarkable, startling, strange, striking, surprising, weird** *The amazing thing is, he wouldn't accept any money!* | **ridiculous** | **frightening, worrying** | **annoying** | **foolish, silly, stupid** *I admit it was a foolish thing to do.* | **bloody** *(taboo),* **damn/damned** | **crucial, key, main, important, vital** *The key thing is to remain calm.* | **little, the slightest, small, trivial** *I give thanks for every little thing.* ◇ *He loses his temper at the slightest thing.* ◇ *It's such a small thing to ask.* | **easy** *Apologizing is never the easiest thing to do.* | **hard** | **brave, dangerous, risky** | **natural** *Entertaining people is the most natural thing in the world for her.* | **close, close-run** *I managed to get on the train, but it was a close-run thing (= I almost missed it).* | **rare** | **everyday** *She helped with the everyday things like shopping and cooking.* | **usual** *I did my usual thing of losing my keys.* | **nearest, next best** *He's the nearest thing to a film star I've ever met.* ◇ *I wanted to be a musician, but teaching music is the next best thing.* | **real** *It's just a practice, not the real thing.* | **the whole** *Let's forget the whole thing.* | **last** *The last thing she wanted was to upset her parents.*
- QUANT. **loads, lots, plenty** *I've got loads of things to do today.*
- VERB + THING **do** *He has a funny way of doing things.* ◇ *It's impossible to get things done when you're looking after a baby.* | **make up, say** *Who's been saying things about me?* | **be hearing/imagining/seeing** *There's nobody at the door—you must have been imagining things!*
- THING + VERB **go on, happen, occur** *There are some weird things going on in that house.* ◇ *A funny thing happened to me this morning ...*
- PREP. **~about** *The best thing about Alan is he's always honest.*
- PHRASES **among/amongst other things** *Amongst other things, I have to deal with mail and keep the accounts.* **have better things to do** *I've got better things to do than stand here chatting all day!* **know/learn/teach sb a**

thing or two *Jack knows a thing or two about kids—he's got five.* **no such thing** *There's no such thing as ghosts* (= they don't exist). **kind/sort of thing** *They go canoeing, climbing, that sort of thing.* **such a thing/a thing like that** *People defraud their companies every day, but Mike would never do such a thing!* **a thing of the past** *Books may one day become a thing of the past.*

5 things general situation, as it affects sb
- VERB + THINGS **think over/through** *She's taken a few days off to think things over.* | **look at, see** *Try to look at things from my point of view.* | **discuss, talk over, talk through** *We arranged to meet and talk things over.* | **explain** | **accept** *You should suggest changes, rather than accept things as they are.* | **change** | **arrange, deal with, handle, look after, run, sort out** *Who's going to look after things while you're away?* ◊ *I want to get things sorted out before I go away.* | **straighten out** | **mess up, spoil** | **patch up** *They patched things up a week after their quarrel.* | **speed along/up** *It might speed things up if you phone her.* | **delay, hold up, slow down**
- THINGS + VERB **stand** *As things stand at present, he seems certain to win.* | **be going** *He asked me how things were going.* | **change** | **go (according) to plan, go well, work (out)** *I just don't know if things are going to work out.* | **get better, improve, look up** *We were in trouble but now things are looking up.* | **look bright/good/promising/rosy** *There was a week to go to the deadline and things were looking good.* | **look bleak/grim** *Things looked bleak for the future of the factory.* | **be in/get into a mess, get out of hand, get/run out of control, go wrong** | **get worse, go downhill** | **turn out** *I'm sure things will turn out OK.* | **come to a head** *Things came to a head when money was found to be missing from the account.* | **get to sb** *Try not to let things get to you.*
- PHRASES **all/other things being equal** *All other things being equal, the bigger fighter should win.* **all things considered** *All things considered, I think we've done a good job.* **get/keep things going/moving** *They hired temporary staff to keep things going over the summer.* **get/put things straight** *I marched into his office to get a few things straight.* **have/keep things in hand/under control** *He offered to help, but she assured him she had things in hand.* **have things on your mind** *We chatted about school, but I could tell she had other things on her mind.* **let things slide/slip** *She'd started the term studying hard, but now was beginning to let things slip.* **let things take their course/happen** *Don't worry about it—just let things take their course.* **make things better, easier, difficult, worse, etc.** *Her apology only served to make things worse.* **put things right** *He apologized, and asked for a chance to put things right.* **things to come** *The pay cut was just a taste of things to come.*

6 what is needed/socially acceptable
- ADJ. **proper, right** *He did the right thing and went back to his wife.* ◊ *I did all the right things but I couldn't get the engine to start.* | **wrong** *She always manages to say the wrong thing.* | **logical, obvious, prudent, sensible** *Calling a doctor seemed the logical thing to do.* | **decent, done, honourable** *He did the decent thing and resigned.* ◊ *It's not the done thing to ask someone how much they earn.* | **very** *Iced tea—the very thing!*
- VERB + THING **do** | **say**
- PHRASES **just the thing, not quite the thing** *It wouldn't be quite the thing to turn up in running gear.*

7 a person/an animal
- ADJ. **little, old** *The baby's a pretty little thing.* | **silly** | **poor** *You must be starving, you poor thing!*

think *noun*
- ADJ. **long** | **hard**
- VERB + THINK **give sth, have**
- PREP. **~about** *I've had a long, hard think about it.*

think *verb*

1 have an opinion
- ADV. **really** | **personally** *I personally think it's all been a lot of fuss over nothing.* | **honestly** *Did you honestly think I would agree to that?* | **never** *I never thought you would carry out your threat.*
- VERB + THINK **be inclined to** *I'm inclined to think we've been a little harsh on her.*
- PREP. **about** *I still don't know what he really thinks about it.* **of** *What did you think of the film?*

2 have an idea
- ADV. **suddenly**
- PREP. **of** *I suddenly thought of a way I could help.*

3 consider/reflect
- ADV. **carefully, deeply, (long and) hard** *She thought long and hard before accepting his offer.* | **fleetingly** | **rationally** *He seemed to have lost the ability to think rationally.* | **frantically** *What can I do now? he thought frantically.* | **contemptuously, despairingly, dully, glumly, grimly, guiltily, indignantly, irritably, miserably, resentfully | ruefully, wistfully, wryly**
- VERB + THINK **dread to, hate to, shudder to, tremble to** *I hate to think what would have happened if we hadn't arrived.*
- PREP. **about** *Think about what you are going to do next.* **of** *I often think of Jane.*

thinker *noun*
- ADJ. **great, leading** *Einstein was one of the world's greatest thinkers.* | **deep, profound, serious** | **clear, logical** | **lateral** | **quick** | **creative, original** | **strategic** | **political, religious, scientific, etc.** | **conservative, liberal, radical, etc.** | **Christian, Marxist, western, etc.**
- PREP. **~on** *a leading thinker on constitutional law*

thinking *noun*

1 using your mind to think
- ADJ. **deep, hard, serious** *This topic requires a lot of deep thinking.* | **good** *Yes, we'll phone them instead—that's good thinking* (= a good idea). | **clear, logical** | **muddled** | **quick** | **forward** *The school would have made better use of the money with a little forward thinking.* | **positive** | **abstract, analytical, critical | creative, independent, innovative, original | lateral | wishful** *His claims to be a millionaire are just wishful thinking.*
- QUANT. **piece** *a brilliant piece of lateral thinking*
- VERB + THINKING **do** *We have some hard thinking to do before we agree to the plan.* | **apply** *The book shows you how to apply critical thinking to your studies.*
- PREP. **~behind** *It was difficult to see what the thinking was behind their eventual decision.*

2 opinion
- ADJ. **contemporary, current, modern | fresh, new | conventional, old, traditional | divergent | government | Labour, Republican, etc. | economic, educational, historical, political, scientific, etc.** *Traditional educational thinking placed importance on learning by rote.* | **feminist, socialist, etc. | military, strategic**
- VERB + THINKING **develop, shape | clarify, explain | change** *They are unlikely to have changed their thinking so soon.* | **dominate** *His writings on motorized warfare dominated strategic thinking in the 1930s.*
- PREP. **in … ~** *contemporary trends in feminist thinking* **| ~about/on** *What is the current Conservative thinking on social security?*
- PHRASES **a shift in sb's thinking** *There's been a shift in government thinking on genetically-modified food.* **to sb's way of thinking** (= in sb's opinion) *To my way of thinking, it would just be a massive waste of money.*

third noun

- ADJ. **first, middle, last** *the last third of the novel* | **bottom, lower** | **top, upper** *Most of the pupils' marks were in the upper third of the range.*
- VERB + THIRD **divide sth into** *He divided the money into thirds.*
- PREP. **~ of** *Over a third of sales were made over the Internet.*
- PHRASES **about/almost/at least/over a third, between a third and a half, a third to (a) half** *The discount is a third to a half of the full price.*

thirst noun

1 desire to drink

- ADJ. **great, intense, raging, terrible, unquenchable**
- VERB + THIRST **suffer from** *Many of the refugees were suffering badly from thirst.* | **quench, slake** | **die of** | **work up** *After walking five miles, they had worked up a great thirst.*

2 strong desire

- ADJ. **great, unquenchable** *He has an unquenchable thirst for knowledge.*
- VERB + THIRST **have** | **satisfy**
- PREP. **~ for**

thought noun

1 sth that you think

- ADJ. **comforting, good, happy, pleasant, positive** *It was a comforting thought that at least her father hadn't suffered.* ◊ *Before going on stage, I breathe deeply and think positive thoughts.* | **anxious, appalling, awful, bad, black, dark, depressing, disquieting, disturbing, gloomy, negative, sad, sobering, terrible** *A disturbing thought suddenly struck me.* | **interesting, intriguing** | **first, immediate, initial** *My immediate thought was that he must be joking.* | **sudden** | **little** | **fleeting, passing** | **conscious** | **unspoken** | **waking** *She occupied all his waking thoughts.*
- VERB + THOUGHT **have, think** *I've just had a thought* (= an idea). ◊ *He remained aloof, thinking his own thoughts.* | **have** *Let me have your thoughts on the report.* | **express, write down** | **read** *She often seems to know what I'm thinking, as though she can read my thoughts.* | **dread, not be able to bear, not like, not relish** *She said she couldn't bear the thought of living alone in the house.* ◊ *I don't like the thought of you walking home alone.*
- THOUGHT + VERB **come/pop into your mind, come to sb, cross your mind, go/flash/pass/race through your mind, hit sb, occur to sb, strike sb** *The thought crossed my mind that Jim might know the answer.* ◊ *All kinds of thoughts raced through my mind.* | **~s turn to sth** *My thoughts turned to home.*
- PREP. **~ about** *He lay there thinking gloomy thoughts about life and death.* **~ of** *The children were overjoyed at the thought of going to the seaside on holiday.* **~ on** *They asked him what his thoughts were on the government's announcement.*
- PHRASES **just a thought** *Would Mark be able to help? It's just a thought.* **keep your thoughts to yourself** *He's not the kind of man to keep his thoughts to himself.* **the mere/very thought of sth** *The mere thought of lice makes my flesh itch.* **push/put the thought aside/away, push the thought from/out of your mind**

2 process/act of thinking

- ADJ. **careful, proper** | **deep, profound** *She is known for her deep thought and intellectual ways.* | **coherent** *He was so upset, he was incapable of coherent thought.* | **logical, rational** | **analytical, critical** | **abstract** | **creative** | **free, independent** | **conscious** *My job is so repetitive, it does not require much conscious thought.* | **fresh** *We have to give the matter fresh thought.* | **second** *I accepted the offer without a second thought.*

- VERB + THOUGHT **give sb/sth, spare (sb)** *I've given the matter careful thought.* ◊ *Don't give it another thought* (= to tell sb not to worry after they have said they are sorry). ◊ *Spare a thought for us—we'll be working through the night to finish the report.* | **direct, turn** *I tried to turn my thoughts to pleasanter things.* | **provoke** *The article was intended to provoke thought.* | **be deep in, be lost in** *She was deep in thought and didn't hear me call her.*
- THOUGHT + VERB **go into sth** *Not enough thought has gone into this essay.*
- THOUGHT + NOUN **pattern, process** *I couldn't see what thought processes led him to that conclusion.*
- PREP. **without ~** *They had acted rashly, without thought.*
- PHRASES **after a moment's thought** *After a moment's thought, I accepted his offer.* **freedom of thought** *The constitution guarantees freedom of thought and belief.* **a line/mode/train of thought** *That line of thought can only lead to one conclusion.* ◊ *He hesitated, as though he had lost his train of thought.* **thought-provoking** *There was a thought-provoking article about poverty in the paper.* **with no thought for sth** *He ran into the burning house with no thought for his own life.*

3 ideas

- ADJ. **modern** | **19th-century, etc.** | **Eastern, Western** | **intellectual, philosophical, scientific** | **economic, political** | **feminist, liberal, socialist, etc.**
- PHRASES **a school of thought** *They belong to different schools of thought.* **a strand of thought** *three different strands of scientific thought*

4 kindness

- ADJ. **kind, kindly, nice** *Thank you for the flowers—it was a very kind thought.*

thrash verb

1 hit sb many times

- ADV. **soundly** *That boy deserves to be soundly thrashed!*
- PREP. **with** *He thrashed the poor servant with his stick.*

2 move your arms and legs in an uncontrolled way

- ADV. **helplessly, violently, wildly** | **about, around** *The cow fell on its side and thrashed about wildly.*

3 defeat sb easily in a game

- ADV. **soundly** *The visiting side were soundly thrashed.*

thrashing noun

1 hitting

- ADJ. **good, sound**
- VERB + THRASHING **give** | **get** *He got a sound thrashing once his father found out.* | **deserve**

2 defeat

- VERB + THRASHING **give** | **have, suffer, take** *The team suffered a 4-0 thrashing on Sunday.*
- PREP. **~ of** *Richmond clinched promotion with a 50-3 thrashing of Roundhay.*

thread noun

1 piece of cotton, etc.

- ADJ. **strong** | **delicate, fine, fragile, thin** | **loose** | **matching** | **cotton, silk, etc.** | **embroidery, sewing** | **warp, weft**
- QUANT. **length, piece**
- VERB + THREAD **spin** | **catch, pull** *You've pulled a thread in your jumper.*
- PHRASES **hanging by a thread** *(often figurative)* *The player's career is hanging by a thread after this latest injury to his knee.*

2 connection between ideas, parts of a story, etc.

- ADJ. **central, main** | **common, connecting** | **consistent, continuous** | **narrative** | **loose** *Apart from one or*

two loose threads, the police now had the complete picture of what happened.
● VERB + THREAD **follow, trace** *I found it hard to follow the main thread of his argument.* | **lose** *The speaker lost his thread halfway through the talk.* | **keep** *She struggled against all the interruptions to keep the thread of her argument.* | **draw together, pick up, pull together, weave** *The author eventually picks up the various threads of the plot and weaves them into a masterly conclusion.*
● THREAD + VERB **run through sth** *A continuous thread runs through all the versions of the legend.* | **emerge** *On studying the different historians' accounts, common threads emerge.* | **unravel** *As the film progresses, the threads of the plot slowly begin to unravel.*

threadbare *adj.*

● VERBS **be** | **wear sth** *The carpets had worn rather threadbare.*
● ADV. **a little, rather**

threat *noun*

1 expression of intention to do harm/punish
● ADJ. **dire, terrible** *Despite dire threats of violence from extremist groups, the protest passed off peacefully.* | **empty, idle** *The kids took no notice of the teacher's idle threats.* | **implied, veiled** *The company's pay offer was accompanied by thinly-veiled threats of redundancies if it was rejected.* | **explicit** | **physical** | **violent** | **verbal** | **bomb, death, suicide**
● VERB + THREAT **issue, make, utter** | **receive** | **carry out** *It's unwise to make threats that you cannot carry out.* | **lift, withdraw** *Teachers have lifted their threat of strike action.* | **reduce** | **give in to** *The government refused to give in to the hijackers' threats.*
● PREP. **~ against** *The accused made death threats against a notable politician.*

2 possible danger
● ADJ. **big, considerable, dangerous, deadly, grave, great, major, real, serious, significant** | **main** | **growing, increasing** | **constant, continual, continuous, ever-present, permanent** | **renewed** *The national park is under renewed threat from road-building schemes.* | **direct, immediate, imminent** *The opposition presents no immediate threat to the government.* | **insidious** | **long-term, short-term, potential** | **apparent, perceived** | **external** *The government was faced with internal rebellion as well as external threats.* | **physical** | **political** | **environmental** | **military, nuclear, terrorist**
● VERB + THREAT **be, pose, present, represent** *the environmental threat posed by oil spillages* | **consider sth (as), perceive sth as, regard sth as, see sth as, view sth as** *Translators do not yet perceive computers as a threat to their livelihood.* | **face, meet**
● PREP. **under ~** *Many wild plants are under threat of extinction.* | **~ from** *the threat from overfishing* **~ of** *a threat of violence* **~ to** *The junta reacted violently to the perceived threat to its authority.*

threaten *verb*

1 warn sb that you may hurt, kill or punish them
● ADV. **publicly** | **personally, physically** *He says he was physically threatened in an attempt to get him to sign over his rights.* | **repeatedly** *She had repeatedly threatened to commit suicide.* | **allegedly, reportedly**
● PREP. **with** *She threatened him with a gun.*
● PHRASES **feel threatened** *I never felt threatened by him.*

2 be likely to harm/destroy sth
● ADV. **gravely, seriously, severely** *social unrest which seriously threatens the stability of the whole area* | **increasingly** | **directly** | **constantly, continually** *Our marriage was constantly threatened by his other women.*

● VERB + THREATEN **could** | **appear to, seem to**
● PHRASES **be threatened with sth** *Many species are now threatened with extinction.*

threatening *adj.*

● VERBS **appear, be, seem, sound** | **become** | **regard sth as, see sth as**
● ADV. **extremely, seriously, very** *seriously threatening behaviour* | **increasingly** | **almost** | **rather, slightly, somewhat** | **potentially**

threshold *noun*

1 doorway
● VERB + THRESHOLD **cross**
● PREP. **across/over the ~** *He hesitated before stepping across the threshold, unsure whether to enter.* **on the ~** *She stood on the threshold, unsure whether to enter.*

2 level
● ADJ. **high, low** | **maximum, minimum** | **critical** | **earnings, tax** | **boredom, pain** *She has an extremely low boredom threshold.*
● VERB + THRESHOLD **have** | **reach** *The number of people with the disease is reaching a critical threshold.* | **cross, exceed** | **set** *They earn wages below the decency threshold set by the EU.* | **raise** | **lower**
● THRESHOLD + NOUN **level, value** *Below a certain threshold level a person will not be able to detect sound.*
● PREP. **above/below a/the ~** *Her wages are below the income tax threshold.*

thrill *noun*

● ADJ. **big, great, real** | **cheap** | **vicarious** *He gets vicarious thrills from watching people bungee jumping.*
● VERB + THRILL **enjoy, experience, feel, get, have** | **give sb**
● THRILL + NOUN **seeker**
● PREP. **for a/the ~** *He used to steal from shops just for the thrill of it.* | **~ from/out of** *He used to get cheap thrills out of frightening the girl next door.* **~ of** *She felt a thrill of excitement as the mountains came into view.*

thrilled *adj.*

● VERBS **be, feel, look, seem**
● ADV. **really** | **absolutely, quite, utterly** | **not exactly** *He's not exactly thrilled at the prospect of working for his old rival.* | **secretly**
● PREP. **at** *I was secretly thrilled at the prospect of going there again.* **with** *I'm really thrilled with the results.*
● PHRASES **thrilled to bits** *I was thrilled to bits when my son won the cup.*

thriller *noun*

● ADJ. **gripping** | **best-selling** | **comedy, erotic, mystery, political, psychological, sci-fi/science fiction, spy** *a gripping political thriller*
● VERB + THRILLER **publish, write** *She had always wanted to write a spy thriller.* | **read**
● THRILLER + NOUN **writer**
● PREP. **in a/the ~** *one of the characters in the thriller* | **~ by** *a new thriller by this American writer*

thrive *verb*

● ADV. **positively** | **still** *The glass industry still thrives there.*
● VERB + THRIVE **seem to** | **continue to** *These traditions continued to thrive.* | **fail to** *(medical)*
● PREP. **on** *Some people seem to thrive on stress.*
● PHRASES **failure to thrive** *(medical) concerned about their baby daughter's failure to thrive*

throat noun

1 front part of the neck
- VERB + THROAT **cut, slash, slit**
- PREP. **by the~** *She seized her attacker by the throat.*

2 passage down which air and food pass
- ADJ. **bad, infected, sore | dry**
- VERB + THROAT **clear** *She cleared her throat, then began to speak.*
- THROAT + VERB **ache, hurt | close (up), constrict, seize up, tighten** *His throat constricted with fear when he saw the knife.* **| dry, go dry**
- THROAT + NOUN **infection | lozenge, pastille**
- PREP. **down the/your~** *She felt the cold water trickle down her throat.*
- PHRASES **the back of your throat** *The medicine left a sour taste in the back of my throat.* **a lump in your throat** *He felt a lump in his throat, and tears forming in his eyes.*

throb noun

- ADJ. **deep, heavy | dull | steady** *the steady throb of the engine*
- VERB + THROB **feel, hear**
- PREP. **~of** *a throb of pain*

throb verb

- ADV. **painfully | angrily** *The vein at his temple throbbed angrily.* **| rhythmically**
- VERB + THROB **begin to, start to**
- PREP. **with** *Her head throbbed with pain.*

throne noun

- ADJ. **empty, unoccupied, vacant | imperial, papal, royal**
- VERB + THRONE **ascend, assume, come to, gain, inherit, succeed to, take** *Elizabeth I came to the throne in 1558.* **| seize, usurp | occupy | give up, renounce | lose | regain | put sb on | topple sb from** *Left-wing revolutionaries toppled the king from his throne.* **| restore sb to | be in line to** *The prince is second in line to the throne behind his brother.*
- PREP. **on the~** *Queen Victoria remained on the throne for over sixty years.*
- PHRASES **sb's accession to the throne, a claimant/pretender to the throne** *a claimant to the vacant Spanish throne* **sb's claim/right to the throne, an heir to the throne** *The marriage failed to produce an heir to the throne.* **the power behind the throne** *(figurative) According to the papers, the prime minister's private secretary is the real power behind the throne.* **the succession to the throne**

throng noun

- VERB + THRONG **join** *people coming from all directions to join the throng*
- PREP. **among/through the~** *He made his way slowly through the throng.* **in the~** *She was lost in the throng.* **into the~** *He disappeared into the throng.*

throw verb

- ADV. **angrily | casually** *He threw the keys casually down on the table.* **| aside, away, back, down, out** *She threw her head back and laughed.*
- VERB + THROW **be ready to, be tempted to, want to | threaten to** *He threatened to throw her in the river if she screamed.* **| be going to**
- PREP. **at** *He threw a stone at the window.* **in/into** *I just wanted to throw myself into his arms and cry.* **to** *She threw the ball to him.* **towards**
- PHRASES **throw sth open** *He threw the double doors open in a dramatic gesture.*

thrust noun

1 strong push
- ADJ. **backward, downward, forward, upward | aggressive, fierce, powerful | knife** *The realization that she was gone was like a knife thrust.* **| pelvic**
- VERB + THRUST **make** *The Third Army made an aggressive thrust towards the front line.*
- PHRASES **~into** *a thrust into the unknown*

2 the thrust main part/ideas
- ADJ. **broad, central, general, main, major** *She explained the broad thrust of the party's policies.* **| dramatic, intellectual, narrative, political** *The dramatic thrust of the film centres around the conflict between the brothers.*
- VERB + THRUST **direct** *He's going to direct the main thrust of his work towards reforming welfare policy.*

thrust verb

- ADV. **deep/deeply | hard | suddenly** *She suddenly thrust out her arm.* **| aside, away, back, forward, out**
- PREP. **at** *He thrust a piece of paper at me.* **into** *She thrust her hands deep into her pockets.*
- PHRASES **thrust your way** *She thrust her way through the dense undergrowth.*

thud noun

- ADJ. **heavy, loud, resounding | dull, muffled, soft | sickening**
- VERB + THUD **give** *She felt her heart give an extra thud.* **| hear | feel**
- PREP. **with a~** *He hit the floor with a sickening thud.*
- PHRASES **the thud of a heart, the thud of hooves**

thud verb

- ADV. **hard, painfully, violently, wildly** (all only used with **heart**) *Her heart was thudding violently as she went into the room.*
- PREP. **against** *The waves thudded against the side of the ship.* **into** *The sniper's bullets thudded into the wall.* **on** *Steps thudded on the stairs.* **with** *His heart thudded with excitement.*

thug noun

- ADJ. **teenage, young | vicious | armed, knife-wielding | racist | football, soccer**
- QUANT. **gang** *He was beaten up by a gang of thugs.*

thumb noun

- VERB + THUMB **suck | flick, jab, jerk** *'What'll we do with them?' he asked, jerking his thumb at the suitcases.* **| raise, stick out** *He smiled and raised a thumb in greeting.* ◇ *I stuck out a thumb and a car stopped immediately.* **| twiddle** *(often figurative) I sat there twiddling my thumbs until the manager finally appeared.*
- THUMB + NOUN **nail** (also **thumbnail**)
- PHRASES **between finger and thumb/between thumb and forefinger** *I picked up the beetle carefully between finger and thumb.* **thumbs up** *He made a thumbs-up sign through the window to tell us everything was fine.*

thump noun

- ADJ. **good, heavy, loud | muffled**
- VERB + THUMP **give sb/sth** *She gave the television a good thump, and the picture came back.* **| hear**
- PREP. **with a~** *The sack of wheat hit the ground with a loud thump.*

thump *verb*

1 hit sb/sth with your fist
- ADV. **hard** *He thumped Jack hard in the face.* | **down** *He thumped his fist down onto the table.*
- PREP. **with** *She thumped the desk with her fist.*

2 of the heart
- ADV. **hard, heavily, loudly, painfully, wildly**
- VERB + THUMP **begin to** *Her heart began to thump wildly in her chest.*
- PREP. **against** *He spun round, his heart thumping against his ribs.*

thunder *noun*

- ADV. **loud** *The thunder was getting louder and louder.* | **dull** *The gunfire rumbled like dull thunder.* | **distant** *the rumble of distant thunder* | **approaching**
- QUANT. **clap, crash, peal, roll, rumble**
- THUNDER + VERB **boom, break, burst, crash, explode, roar** *Thunder boomed in the sky overhead.* | **growl, grumble, roll, rumble** | **rattle sth, shake sth** *The windows were shaken by a tremendous crash of thunder.*
- THUNDER + NOUN **clap** (also **thunderclap**) | **cloud** (also **thundercloud**)
- PHRASES **the sound of thunder, there's thunder in the air** (= thunder is likely), **thunder and lightning**

thunderstorm *noun*

⇨ See STORM

Thursday *noun*

⇨ Note at DAY

thwart *verb*

- ADV. **easily | constantly** *Plans to expand the company have been constantly thwarted.*
- VERB + THWART **attempt to, try to**
- PREP. **in** *They were thwarted in their attempt to gain overall control of the company.*

tick *verb*

1 of a clock, etc.
- ADV. **loudly | relentlessly | away** *The clock ticked relentlessly away on the mantelpiece.*

2 mark sth with a tick
- ADV. **simply** *To take advantage of this extra bonus offer, simply tick the box on your order form.* | **mentally | off** *She mentally ticked off the names of the people she had already spoken to.*

PHRASAL VERB

tick along/over
- ADV. **nicely** *The business is ticking over nicely at the moment.* | **still**
- PHRASES **keep things ticking over** *Morrison had kept things ticking over in my absence.*

ticket *noun*

1 for travel, an event, the theatre, etc.
- ADJ. **one-way, single | return, round-trip | day, season, weekly** *an annual season ticket* | **first-class, second-class,** etc. *a first-class rail ticket* | **invalid, valid | complimentary, free** *I've got complimentary tickets for the theatre.* | **concessionary, family** *Concessionary tickets are available at half the standard price.* | **advance** *Use the coupon below to reserve advance tickets for the exhibition.* | **admission, entrance, entry | air/airline, bus, plane, rail, train,** etc. | **cinema, concert | library**
- VERB + TICKET **buy, get, obtain, purchase | have, hold** *You must hold a valid ticket for your entire journey before boarding the train.* | **book, reserve | show (sb)** *He showed the guard his ticket.*
- TICKET + NOUN **agency, counter, machine, office | price | sales | holder | collector, inspector | tout | barrier | stub**
- PREP. **by ~** *admission by ticket only* | **~ for** *I bought a ticket for the concert.* ◊ *a ticket for Saturday* **~ to** *I've got a free ticket to the match.* ◊ *a plane ticket to New York*

2 for a lottery, etc.
- ADJ. **winning | lottery, raffle**
- QUANT. **book** *I bought a whole book of raffle tickets and I still didn't win anything.*

3 giving a penalty
- ADJ. **fixed-penalty | parking**
- VERB + TICKET **give sb, issue | get**
- PREP. **~ for** *The police officer gave us a ticket for going through a red light.*

tickle *noun*

- ADJ. **little**
- VERB + TICKLE **give sb/sth | feel, get, have** *He felt a tickle on the back of his neck.*

tide *noun*

1 change in the level of the sea
- ADJ. **big, strong | flood, incoming, rising | ebb, outgoing | full, high | low | neap, spring**
- VERB + TIDE **catch** (= to take advantage of a favourable tide) *We have to get up early to catch the tide.*
- TIDE + VERB **be in | be out | come/flow in, rise | ebb, fall, flow/go out, retreat | be on the turn, turn | occur** *the time of day when the highest tides occur* | **wash sb/sth up** *The body was washed up by the tide the next day.*
- PREP. **at …~** *Seals lie on the rocks at low tide.* **on a/the~** *We went out to sea on the ebb tide.*
- PHRASES **the ebb and flow of the tide**

2 strong movement in favour of/against sth
- ADJ. **growing, rising** *the rising tide of crime* | **shifting | political** *He hasn't the courage to swim against the political tide.*
- VERB + TIDE **go with | go/swim against | stem, turn (back)** *attempts to stem the tide of revolution*
- TIDE + VERB **run** *Seeing the tide was now running in his direction, he renewed his campaign for reform.* | **carry sb/sth along | turn** *The tide of public opinion seems to be turning at last.*
- PREP. **against a/the ~** *It takes courage to speak out against the tide of public opinion.* **on a~** *They were carried along on a tide of euphoria.* | **~ against, ~ in favour of** *Civil liberties groups helped to turn the tide against industrial violence.*
- PHRASES **a tide of history** *the shifting tides of history* **the turn of the tide** *In the early 1990s there was a marked turn of the tide.*

tidy *adj.*

- VERBS **be, look, seem | stay** *Why does nothing ever stay tidy around here?* | **get sth, make sth | keep sth** *I hope you're going to keep your room tidy.*
- ADV. **extremely, very | immaculately, scrupulously** *It was a neatly furnished and immaculately tidy room.* | **fairly, quite** *The sitting room is fairly tidy.*
- PHRASES **clean/neat and tidy**

tie *noun*

1 worn round the neck with a shirt
- ADJ. **undone** *His tie was undone.* | **loose | askew** *His tie was askew and his hair dishevelled.* | **loud | bootlace, bow, kipper | black, white** (= a black/white bow tie as part of formal dress) *a black-tie dinner* | **club, college, regimental, school**

● VERB + TIE **knot, tie | loosen | adjust, straighten**
● TIE + NOUN **pin**
● PHRASES **collar/jacket/shirt/suit and tie**
⇨ Special page at CLOTHES

2 (usually **ties**) sth that connects you with sb/sth
● ADJ. **close, strong | weak | blood, family | emotional | personal | business, commercial, economic | cultural, diplomatic, political, social, traditional**
● VERB + TIE **have** *We have close economic ties with our neighbours.* **| establish | cement, strengthen | cut, sever** *He cut all ties with the Church.* **| loosen, weaken**
● PREP. **~ between** *There is a strong tie between her and her daughters.* **~ of** *ties of kinship* **~ to/with** *to establish diplomatic ties with China*

3 in a game/competition
● VERB + TIE **end in, result in** *The match ended in a tie.*
● TIE + NOUN **break/breaker**
● PREP. **~ between** *a tie between Egypt and France* **~ for** *There was a tie for first place.*

tie *verb*

1 attach/fasten sb/sth with string/rope
● ADV. **firmly, securely, tightly** *Did you tie the balloons on tightly?* **| loosely** *He wore plimsolls, loosely tied with bits of string.* **| carefully | neatly** *Tie the cords neatly.* **| back, on, together, up**
● PREP. **around/round** *He tied his dressing gown firmly around him.* **onto** *I tied the bundle onto the end of the string.* **to** *She tied the rope securely to a tree.* **with** *Katie tied her hair back with a ribbon.*
● PHRASES **tie sb hand and foot** *The prisoners were tied hand and foot.*

2 connect sb/sth with sb/sth else
● ADV. **closely, intimately** *Their company's future is closely tied to our own.* **| directly | firmly | inextricably | in, together, up** *Production and consumption are inextricably tied together.*
● PREP. **in with** *The concert will tie in with the festival of dance taking place the same weekend.* **to** *You can't stay tied to her forever.* **up with** *Her behaviour is tied up with her feelings of guilt.*

tiger *noun*

● ADJ. **man-eating | marauding | sabre-toothed**
● TIGER + VERB **growl, purr, roar | spring | maul sb** *The zookeeper was mauled to death by a tiger.* **| prowl** *A marauding tiger was often seen prowling around the village.*
● TIGER + NOUN **cub | skin | hunt**

tight *adj., adv.*

1 not loose
● VERBS **be, feel, look, seem | become, get, go** *Those jeans have got too tight and I can't wear them any more.* ◇ *The rope suddenly went tight.* **| hold (on)** *'Hold tight!' She increased her grip.* **| clamp sth, clench sth, close sth, draw sth, pull sth, shut sth, stretch sth, tie sth** *His jaw was clenched tight.* ◇ *Every muscle in her face was drawn tight.* ◇ *Shut your eyes tight.* ◇ *The cloth was stretched tight over the frame.* **| clutch sth, grip sth, hold sth, keep sth** *He held his children tight.* ◇ *Keep the rope tight.*
● ADV. **extremely, really, very | a bit, fairly, pretty, quite, rather, reasonably | enough** *You didn't tie it tight enough.*

2 with not much time/money to spare
● VERBS **be, look, seem | get** *I think we'd better leave—time's getting very tight.*
● ADV. **extremely, particularly, really, very | a bit, fairly, pretty, rather**

3 controlled very strictly

● VERBS **be, seem | become | remain** *Security at the airport remains tight.*
● ADV. **extremely, really, very | increasingly | fairly, pretty, quite | enough** *Are the controls tight enough?*

tighten *verb*

1 become/make sth firmer/tighter
● ADV. **fractionally, a little, slightly | convulsively, involuntarily** *Her fingers tightened convulsively with every jolt she received.* **| painfully | up** *Can you tighten up the bolts for me?*
● VERB + TIGHTEN **seem to | feel sth, sense sth** *He felt his stomach tighten.* **| make sth** *His words made her throat tighten.*
● PREP. **about/around/round** *His hand tightened painfully around her wrist.* **on** *Her grip seemed to tighten on the door handle.* **in** *He saw his father's jaw tighten in irritation.* **into** *His mouth tightened into a thin hard line.* **with** *Her face tightened with pain.*

2 make sth more strict
● ADV. **considerably**
● VERB + TIGHTEN **take steps to** *Steps were taken to tighten discipline in the school.*
● PREP. **up** *The law in this area has been tightened up considerably.*

tights *noun*

● ADJ. **opaque, thick | sheer | fishnet | 15-denier, etc. | support | laddered**
● QUANT. **pair**
● VERB + TIGHTS **pull on | peel off | ladder**
● TIGHTS + VERB **ladder**
● PHRASES **a ladder in your tights**
⇨ Special page at CLOTHES

tile *noun*

● ADJ. **broken, damaged, loose, missing | decorative, glazed, hand-painted, plain | ceramic, clay, cork, mosaic, quarry, stone, terracotta, vinyl | carpet, ceiling, floor, roof/roofing, wall | bathroom, kitchen**
● VERB + TILE **cover sth with, fit, lay, put down** *I'm laying ceramic floor tiles in the kitchen.*

till *noun*

● ADJ. **computerized, electronic**
● TILL + VERB **ring** *a sales idea that has set tills ringing all over the country*
● TILL + NOUN **receipt, roll**
● PREP. **at/behind/on the ~** *The supermarket didn't have enough people working on the tills.* **in/into a/the ~** *Put the money straight into the till.* **| from/out of a/the ~** *He gave her £10 from the till.*

tilt *noun*

● ADJ. **sharp | slight | downward, upward | backward, forward**
● PREP. **at a ~** *I positioned the photo at a slight tilt.* **| ~ to/towards** *a tilt to the left*

tilt *verb*

● ADV. **sharply** *The ground tilted sharply downwards.* **| a little, slightly | back/backwards, down/downwards, forward, up/upwards**
● PREP. **away from** *Tilt the mirror away from you.* **towards** *Her face was tilted towards the sky.*
● PHRASES **tilted to one side** *She thought for a minute, her head tilted to one side.*

timber noun

1 trees/wood for use in building/carpentry
- ADJ. **heavy | solid** *a solid timber door* | **rough | dead, decayed, rotten, rotting | seasoned, treated | unseasoned, untreated**
- QUANT. **baulk, length, piece**
- VERB + TIMBER **cut, fell, harvest, saw | dress, season, treat**
- TIMBER + VERB **decay, rot**
- TIMBER + NOUN **product | company, industry, merchant, production, yard | construction, frame, structure, support | beam, building, floor, etc.**

2 (usually **timbers**) piece of wood used in a building
- ADJ. **sound | exposed** *The house has exposed oak timbers.* | **ceiling, floor, roof | ship's**

time noun

1 what is measured in minutes, hours, days, etc.
- TIME + VERB **elapse, go by, pass** *As time went by we saw less and less of each other.* ◇ *The changing seasons mark the passing of time.* | **fly** *How time flies!* | **drag** *Time drags in this job.* | **heal sth** *Time heals all wounds.*
- PREP. **in ~** *The world exists in time and space.* **over ~** *Perceptions change over time.* **through ~** *travel through time*
- PHRASES **the mists of time** *The origins of this custom are lost in the mists of time.*

2 time shown on a clock
- ADJ. **good, perfect** *My watch keeps good time.* | **local** *The attacks were launched at 9 p.m. local time.* | **British Summer, Greenwich Mean, etc.**
- VERB + TIME **tell** *Can your son tell the time yet?* | **have** *Have you got the time?* | **make** *What time do you make it?* | **look at** *Look at the time! We'll be late.* | **keep**
- PREP. **ahead of/behind … ~** *two hours behind Central European Time*
- PHRASES **this time tomorrow, etc.** *This time tomorrow I'll be in Canada.* **time in/of the morning/afternoon/evening, time of (the) night/year, time of day**

3 time when sth happens/should happen
- ADJ. **peak** *There are extra buses at peak times.* | **closing, opening | arrival, departure**
- VERB + TIME **fix, set** *We need to fix a time for the next meeting.*
- TIME + VERB **come** *You'll feel differently about it when the time comes.*
- PREP. **ahead of ~** *Check the programme ahead of time.* **behind ~** *The plane took off an hour behind time.* **by the ~** *By the time you get there the meeting will be over.* **in ~** *We got home in time to see the end of the match.* **on ~** *The trains are rarely on time.*

4 amount of time
- ADJ. **considerable, long | little, short | reasonable | precious** *We're wasting precious time.* | **idle | free, leisure, spare | journey, travel, travelling | lead, waiting** *There is a long lead time between order and delivery of the product.*
- VERB + TIME **have** *Have you got time for a chat?* ◇ *I had no time to think.* | **give sb/sth** *I can certainly do the job if you give me time.* | **take (sb)** *It takes time to make changes in the law.* ◇ *It took her a long time to read the report.* ◇ *Take your time* (= take as much time as you like). | **spend** *She spends much of her time reading.* | **kill, pass, while away** *It helps to pass the time.* | **fritter away, idle away | devote, put** *She devotes all her spare time to gardening.* ◇ *He put all his time into the show.* | **allow** *They didn't allow much time for discussion.* | **find, make** *I can never find time to write letters.* ◇ *I can probably make the time to see them.* | **wait** *We had to wait some time before the bus arrived.* | **gain, save** *You would save time with a dishwasher.* | **waste | lose, run out of** *We have no time to lose* (= we must hurry). ◇ *I didn't finish the test—I ran out of time.* | **be pressed for/short of | be out of | play for** *Not knowing what to do, she played for time by going to the bathroom.*
- TIME + VERB **be up, run out** *Sorry, your time is up.*
- TIME + NOUN **period, scale, span | limit | lag**
- PREP. **at a ~** *He surfs the Internet for hours at a time.* **for a ~** *I lived there for a time.* **in ~** *You'll get used to the work in time.* **over/with ~** *Her skills improved with time.*
- PHRASES **all in good time** (= sth will happen when the time is right) *Be patient, Emily! All in good time.* **all the time/the whole time** *The letter was in my pocket all the time* (= while I was looking for it). ◇ *She leaves the lights on all the time* (= always/repeatedly). **a battle/race against time** *Finishing the book was a race against time.* **if time permits** *We will discuss this matter later, if time permits.* **in the fullness of time** (= when the time is right, usually after a long period), **in good/plenty of time** *Get to the airport in good time* (= plenty of time before the plane leaves). **in next to no time/in no time at all, in ten minutes', three hours', etc. time** *I'll be back in ten minutes' time.* **in your own (good) time** (= taking as long as you want/need), **a length of time** *Have you lived abroad for any length of time?* **most of the time, a period of time, some/a long time ago** *Her parents died a long time ago.* **a waste of time** *What a waste of time!*

5 (often **times**) period in the past/present
- ADJ. **good, great, happy | bad, difficult, hard, rough, sad, troubled, unhappy** *Times are hard for the unemployed.* | **ancient, early, former, old** *in ancient times* | **modern, recent | medieval, prehistoric, etc.**
- VERB + TIME **have** *We had a great time at the party.*
- TIME + VERB **change** *Times have changed since Grandma was young.*
- PREP. **at a/the ~** *He lived at the time of the French Revolution.* ◇ *At one time Mary was my best friend.* **before your ~** *The Beatles were before my time.* **in your ~** *Mr Curtis was the manager in my time* (= when I was working there). **in ~s** *in times of trouble*
- PHRASES **from/since time immemorial** (= for a very long time), **of all time** *the greatest footballer of all time* **a sign of the times, time was when** *Time was when* (= there was a time when) *we never needed to lock our house at night.*

6 occasion
- ADJ. **that, this** *I'm determined to pass this time.* | **last** *When was the last time you saw her?* | **another, next** *Next time you're here let's have lunch together.* | **one | each, every** *Every time I hear that song I feel happy.* | **appropriate, good, suitable** *Is this an appropriate time to discuss my salary?* | **appointed, right | bad, wrong** *This would be a bad time to tell her.* | **first, second, etc. | umpteenth | countless** *I've told you countless times.*
- VERB + TIME **bide** *We'll have to bide our time until the rain stops.*
- TIME + VERB **come** *Your time will come.* | **be ripe** *The time is ripe for revolution.*
- PREP. **at a/the ~** *The lift can take four people at a time.* ◇ *At the time of writing, a ceasefire is under discussion.* ◇ *Hot water is available at all times.* ◇ *He can be rather moody at times.* **by the ~** *She'll have gone by the time we get there.* **for the … ~** *I told her not to do it for the umpteenth time.* | **~ for** *It's time for a break.*
- PHRASES **at the present time, for the time being** (= temporarily), **a number of times, X times out of X** *three times out of ten*

7 when you experience sth in a particular way
- ADJ. **enjoyable, fun, good, grand, great, marvellous, pleasant, splendid, wonderful** *It was a fun time for us girls.* | **awful, dreadful, horrible, miserable, sad, terrible**
- VERB + TIME **have** *Did you have a good time in Spain?*

8 time taken in a race, etc.
- ADJ. **fast | record** *He completed the course in record time.*

time

- VERB + TIME **clock up, record** *She clocked up one of the fastest times of the year.*

9 musical rhythm
- ADJ. **march, waltz | double, quick | four-four, three-four,** etc.
- VERB + TIME **beat, keep** *The conductor beat time with a baton.*
- TIME + NOUN **signature**
- PREP. **in/out of ~ (to/with)** *clapping in time to the music*

time verb

- ADV. **beautifully, conveniently, well** *This campaign is well timed.* | **perfectly, to perfection** *We had timed our arrival to perfection.* | **badly | carefully** *The schedule must be carefully timed.*
- PREP. **for** *The meeting is timed for 3 o'clock.*
- PHRASES **be timed to coincide with sth** *The show is timed to coincide with the launch of her new book.*

timetable noun

- ADJ. **overall | detailed | strict | realistic | busy, full** *a full timetable of teaching* | **college, school,** etc. | **exam/examination | bus, train,** etc.
- VERB + TIMETABLE **agree on, draw up, establish, outline, set (out) | adhere to, follow, keep to** *Implementation of the reforms was kept to a very strict timetable.* | **consult, look at**
- PREP. **according to the ~** *According to the timetable, the bus should have come in at 9.00.* **in a/the ~** *It said in the timetable that a train was due at 5.30.* | **~ for** *The delegates outlined what they considered a realistic timetable for troop withdrawal.*

timing noun

- ADJ. **exact, precise** *There is disagreement within the government over the exact timing of the referendum.* | **convenient** *The timing of the meeting is not convenient.* | **inconvenient, unfortunate** *the unfortunate timing of the announcement* | **accurate, careful, good, impeccable, perfect | bad, poor | split-second | comic**
- VERB + TIMING **have** *He has the split-second timing all good players need.*
- PREP. **with ... ~** *The punchline was delivered with perfect comic timing.*
- PHRASES **get the timing right/wrong | a matter of timing** *Using press releases to good effect is a matter of timing.* **a sense of timing** *She has a wonderful sense of timing.*

tin noun

- ADJ. **biscuit | airtight, sealed**
- TIN + NOUN **opener** (also **tin-opener**)
- PREP. **in a/the ~** *Store the seeds in an airtight tin.* | **~ of** *a tin of tomatoes*

tinge noun

- ADJ. **faint, slight** *blue with a slight tinge of purple* | **blue, bluish,** etc. *a slight reddish tinge*
- VERB + TINGE **have**
- PREP. **~ of** *a tinge of regret* **~ to** *The sky had a slight pink tinge to it.*

tinkle noun

- ADJ. **faint, little, soft**
- VERB + TINKLE **hear**
- PREP. **with a ~** *The wine glass dropped to the floor with a tinkle.*

tint noun

- ADJ. **rich | blue, bluish,** etc. | **autumn** *The fabrics were mainly in rich autumn tints, reds and oranges.*
- PREP. **~ of** *The branches of the trees were barely showing their first tint of green.*

tiny adj.

- VERBS **be, feel, look, seem | become**
- ADV. **extremely, really, very | quite | comparatively, relatively** *The minister appealed to the Cabinet not to target her comparatively tiny budget of £4 billion.*
- PHRASES **little tiny/tiny little** *Look at his little tiny fingers. Aren't they sweet?*

tip noun

1 pointed end
- ADJ. **northern,** etc. *We took a bus to the northern tip of the island.* | **very** *The cat was black except for a patch of white on the very tip of its tail.*
- PREP. **~ of** *the tips of your fingers/toes*

2 money
- ADJ. **big, generous, good, large | poor, small**
- VERB + TIP **give sb, leave sb** *He left the waitress a large tip.* | **get** *We get rather poor tips on weeknights.*

3 advice
- ADJ. **good, handy, helpful, useful | hot** *He said he'd been given a hot tip for that afternoon's race.* | **beauty, gardening, money-saving, safety,** etc. | **racing**
- VERB + TIP **have | give sb, pass on | take, use** *Take a safety tip from me—get that light mended!* | **pick up**
- PREP. **~ for** *some handy tips for gardeners* **~ on** *Do you have any tips on buying a second-hand car?*

tip verb (often be tipped)

- ADV. **hotly, strongly | widely**
- PREP. **as** *The senator has been widely tipped as a future president.* **for** *The band is being hotly tipped for the top.*

tip-off noun

- ADJ. **anonymous | phone**
- VERB + TIP-OFF **give sb | get, receive | act on** *Acting on a tip-off, police raided the house.*
- PREP. **~ about** *Customs officers had received a tip-off about a shipment of cocaine.*

tire verb

- ADV. **easily, quickly** *She found herself tiring more quickly these days.* | **out** *The long walk had really tired me out.*
- VERB + TIRE **begin to** *After an hour Rick began to tire.*

tired adj.

1 needing rest
- VERBS **be, feel, look, seem | become, get | leave sb, make sb** *The walk left me quite tired out.*
- ADV. **awfully, bone** (informal), **dead, desperately, extremely, really, terribly, very** *Polly suddenly felt bone tired.* | **a bit, a little, pretty, quite, rather | just** *Of course I'm not ill. I'm just tired.* | **enough** *He felt tired enough to go to sleep standing up.* | **mentally, physically | visibly | out**
- PREP. **from** *I'm still a bit tired from the journey.*
- PHRASES **tired and drawn** *He looked tired and drawn.*

2 tired of sb/sth feeling you have had enough
- VERBS **be | become, get, grow** (formal) *She had grown heartily tired of his company.*
- ADV. **heartily, really, very | a bit, a little, rather**

● PHRASES **sick and tired** (*informal*) *I'm sick and tired of listening to you whine.*

tiredness *noun*

● ADJ. **desperate, extreme, overwhelming | mental, physical | chronic, constant**
● QUANT. **wave** *Once the last boxes were packed away, he was overtaken by a wave of tiredness.*
● VERB + TIREDNESS **be overtaken by, feel, suffer from | relieve**
● TIREDNESS + VERB **overcome sb** *Finally tiredness overcame him, and he fell asleep on the sofa.* | **set in** *A desperate tiredness set in after hours of anxious waiting.*
● PHRASES **a sign of tiredness** *The team was in good spirits and showed no signs of tiredness.*

tissue *noun*

1 organic material
● ADJ. **living | healthy, normal** *Vitamin C helps maintain healthy connective tissue.* | **damaged, diseased | animal, human, plant** *Dyes were extracted by boiling the plant tissue.* | **body, brain, intestinal, muscle, etc. | connective, scar | fat, fatty, fibrous, soft** *She treats skin and soft tissue injuries in casualty.*

2 paper handkerchief
● ADJ. **paper | toilet**
● QUANT. **box, pack, packet, wad** *She grabbed a wad of tissues from the box and soaked up the spilt wine.*
● VERB + TISSUE **use**
● PREP. **on a/the ~** *He wiped his nose on a tissue.* **with a/the ~** *She gently dabbed her eyes with a tissue.*

title *noun*

1 name of a book, film, etc.
● ADJ. **book, essay, film, song**
● VERB + TITLE **give sth**
● TITLE + NOUN **page | role** *He played the title role in 'Hamlet'.* | **track** *'Birth', the title track of his latest album*
● PREP. **under a/the~** *She published her poetry under the title 'The Land and the Garden'.*

2 book, magazine, etc.
● ADJ. **new** *Forty per cent of new titles were actually new editions of existing books.* | **best-selling**
● VERB + TITLE **publish** *The company is publishing fewer titles than last year.*

3 name of a rank/profession
● ADJ. **grand, long** *She bears the grand title 'Divisional President of the Finances Committee'.* | **courtesy, diplomatic, honorary, honorific, official** *'Mrs' was a courtesy title for any unmarried woman in business at that time.* ◇ *'Minister' is one of several diplomatic titles.* | **job** *His job title is Special Projects Officer.* | **full** *Victor Oldenburg, or Count Victor Oldenburg and Hess, to give him his full title*
● VERB + TITLE **bear, have, inherit** *She has a title* (= is of noble birth). | **award, bestow, confer** *The king bestowed lands and titles upon his followers.*

4 championship win
● ADJ. **European, national, world, etc. | championship, French Open, Premier League, etc. | heavyweight, middleweight, etc.**
● VERB + TITLE **clinch, win** *Deportivo clinched the title with a goal in the final seconds of the last game of the season.* | **hold** *He held the world heavyweight title until last year.* | **defend | retain | lose**
● TITLE + NOUN **challenge, fight, match** *He has been building up fitness for his world title challenge.* | **holder**
⇨ Special page at SPORT

toast *noun*

1 bread
● ADJ. **brown, white, wholemeal | dry | soggy**
● QUANT. **piece, round, slice** *We'll have another round of toast, please.*
● VERB + TOAST **make** *making toast for breakfast* | **butter, spread** *buttered toast* ◇ *She ate two slices of toast spread with jam.* | **burn** *I can smell burnt toast.*
● PREP. **on~** *For lunch we had cheese on toast.*

2 drink
● VERB + TOAST **make, propose** *He raised his glass as if to make a toast.* | **drink | respond to**
● PREP. **~to** *The bridegroom ended his speech by proposing a toast to the hosts.*

toast *verb*

1 make sth brown and crisp by heating it
● ADV. **lightly** *Toast the bread lightly on both sides.*

2 drink to sb/sth
● ADV. **silently** *He raised his glass, silently toasting his absent son.*
● PREP. **in/with** *We toasted his victory in champagne.*

tobacco *noun*

● ADJ. **mild, strong | stale | pipe**
● VERB + TOBACCO **chew, smoke | be addicted to | grow**
● TOBACCO + NOUN **addiction, consumption, use | smoke** *The air was thick with tobacco smoke.* | **business, company, firm, industry, manufacturer, producer | lobby** *The ban on cigarette advertising will upset the tobacco lobby.* | **products | market | sales | advertising, sponsorship | pouch, tin | grower, plantation**

toe *noun*

● ADJ. **big, little** *The shoe pressed painfully against her big toe.* | **bare** *Under his bare toes the floor felt gritty.* | **broken, bruised**
● VERB + TOE **stand on, tread on** *She stood on her toes to kiss him.* ◇ *Ouch! That was my toe you just trod on.* ◇ (*figurative*) *She trod on a lot of toes when she joined the company.* | **stub | break, bruise, crack | dip** *I dipped my toe in the river to test the temperature.* ◇ (*figurative*) *So far they have only dipped their toe in the potentially vast computer market.* | **point | curl | touch** *Can you touch your toes* (= while keeping your legs straight)*?*
● TOE + VERB **curl** (*often figurative*) *The man's broad smile made her toes curl* (= made her feel embarrassed or uncomfortable).
● TOE + NOUN **injury**
● PREP. **between the/your~s** *He had some kind of fungus between his toes.* **on your~s** *He moved lightly on his toes like a boxer.* ◇ (*figurative*) *The threat of inspections kept us all on our toes* (= made sure we kept everything up to standard and were ready).
● PHRASES **from head/top to toe** *He gave himself a good scrub from head to toe.* **the tips of your toes** *I stood on the tips of my toes to look through the window.* **the toe of your boot/shoe**

toenail *noun*

● ADJ. **ingrowing**
● VERB + TOENAIL **clip, cut, trim**
● TOENAIL + NOUN **clippings**

toil *noun*

● ADJ. **hard | relentless, unceasing, unending, unremitting | daily | manual, physical | honest**
● PHRASES **hours, years, etc. of toil** *a lifetime of unremitting toil* **sweat and toil** *a day of sweat and toil*

toilet *noun*

- ADJ. **public | communal, shared** *There was a communal toilet on the landing for the four flats.* | **indoor, inside | outside | flush/flushing** *The caravan is equipped with a sink and a flush toilet.* | **gents', ladies', men's, women's | disabled**
- VERB + TOILET **go to, use** *I need to go to the toilet.* | **be desperate for, need** *Do you need the toilet?* | **flush (sth down)** *Someone's forgotten to flush the toilet.* ◊ *He flushed the letter down the toilet.* | **block, clog | unblock**
- TOILET + NOUN **bowl, seat | paper, roll, tissue | brush, cleaner | facilities | training**
- PREP. **in the~, on the~**

token *noun*

- ADJ. **good luck, love**
- PREP. **in ~ of** *She presented them with a small gift in token of her thanks.*
- PHRASES **(as) a token of appreciation/friendship/respect** *We hope you will accept this book as a small token of our appreciation.*

tolerable *adj.*

- VERBS **be | become | make sth | find sth** *She inspected the rooms and found them perfectly tolerable.*
- ADV. **very | perfectly | barely, scarcely** *In August the heat is barely tolerable.* | **fairly, quite**

tolerance *noun*

- ADJ. **great, high, remarkable | low | amused, patronising** *He watched the kids throw water around with amused tolerance.* | **political, racial, religious | zero** (of crime) *Howard County has a zero tolerance policy on alcohol use by teenagers.*
- QUANT. **degree, level**
- VERB + TOLERANCE **have | show | lack | learn**
- TOLERANCE + NOUN **level**
- PREP. **~for** *Some children have a low tolerance for boredom.* **~ of** *people with a high tolerance of discomfort* **~to** *Tolerance to alcohol decreases with age.* **~ towards** *She was showing greater tolerance towards her younger sister than before.*

tolerant *adj.*

- VERBS **be, feel, seem | become, get, grow**
- ADV. **extremely, remarkably, surprisingly, very, wonderfully** *Mares are surprisingly tolerant of the roughness and rudeness of their own offspring.* | **pretty, quite, reasonably** *He's pretty tolerant of my faults.*
- PREP. **of** *They learn to be tolerant of other people.* **towards** *They are more tolerant towards gypsies now.*

tolerate *verb*

1 allow sth you do not like
- ADV. **barely | merely** *She actually seemed pleased to see him: most of her visitors she merely tolerated.* | **grudgingly | officially** *Union activity was officially tolerated but strongly discouraged.* | **no longer** *The government is not prepared to tolerate this situation any longer.*
- VERB + TOLERATE **be unable to, (not) be prepared to, (not) be willing to, cannot/could not, find sth difficult to, will/would not** *I will not tolerate this behaviour!*

2 not be affected by difficult conditions
- ADV. **readily, well** *This plant prefers alkaline soil, though it will readily tolerate some acidity.* ◊ *She tolerated the chemotherapy well.*
- VERB + TOLERATE **be unable to, cannot/could not, find/make sth difficult to, will/would not** *people whose eye condition makes it difficult to tolerate bright light*

toleration *noun*

- ADJ. **religious**
- QUANT. **degree, measure** *Religious minorities were allowed a wide measure of toleration.*
- PREP. **~for** *He preached toleration for all religions.*

toll *noun*

1 money that you pay to use a road, bridge, etc.
- ADJ. **motorway, road**
- VERB + TOLL **charge, collect, exact, impose, levy** *the possibility of imposing tolls on some motorways* | **pay**
- TOLL + NOUN **bridge, motorway, road | booth | charge**

2 amount of damage done/number of people killed
- ADJ. **great, heavy, terrible, tragic | casualty, death, injury | human**
- VERB + TOLL **take** *The pressure of fame can take a terrible toll.* ◊ *The recession is taking its toll.*
- TOLL + VERB **mount, rise** *The death toll from yesterday's crash is still rising.* | **reach sth** *The casualty toll could reach 200.*
- PREP. **~on** *Illness has taken a heavy toll on her.*

tomato *noun*

- ADJ. **ripe | green | rotten, squashed | cherry, plum | sundried, tinned**
- VERB + TOMATO **eat, have | chop, peel, slice | grow**
- TOMATO + NOUN **juice, ketchup, paste, purée, salad, sauce, soup | plant**

ton *noun*

⇨ Note at MEASURE

tone *noun*

1 quality of a sound, especially of the human voice
- ADJ. **deep, low | falling, rising** *The rising tone of her voice emphasized her panic.* | **hushed, quiet, subdued** *speaking in hushed tones* | **clear, ringing | sharp, shrill, stentorian, strident | gravelly | dry, even, expressionless, flat, level, measured, neutral** *The question was posed in a flat tone.* | **normal, reasonable | brisk, businesslike, matter-of-fact** *She answered him in a brisk, matter-of-fact tone.* | **commanding, firm, forthright | formal | sepulchral, solemn | dramatic, urgent | casual, offhand | bright, conversational | gentle, mild, pleasant, soft, sympathetic, warm** *Her tone was mild, almost conversational.* | **dulcet, honeyed** (both often ironic) *We heard the dulcet tones of the sergeant, bawling at us to get on parade.* | **clipped, cool, curt, frigid, hard, harsh, icy** *In cool, clipped tones, he told her what had happened.* | **aggressive, biting, contemptuous, disapproving, dismissive, ironic, mocking, patronizing, sarcastic, sardonic, scathing, threatening** *His tone was faintly mocking.* | **aggrieved, reproachful, shocked | bantering, conciliatory, conspiratorial, reverential, wheedling**
- VERB + TONE **adopt, speak in, take** *When she heard my accent, she adopted a warmer tone.* ◊ *Don't you take that tone with me.* | **soften | change | interpret** *Her tone was hard to interpret.*
- TONE + VERB **change** *His tone changed dramatically when he saw the money.* | **convey sth, imply sth, indicate sth, suggest sth | betray sb/sth, give away sb/sth** *Her tone betrayed her impatience.*
- PREP. **in a/the~** *'You ought to have thought of them,' she said in a reproachful tone.* **in ~s of** *'I don't believe it!' cried Henry in tones of utter amazement.*
- PHRASES **a tone of voice** *I didn't like his tone of voice; I felt he was being condescending.*

2 general quality/style of sb/sth
- ADJ. **dominant, general, overall, prevailing** *The general tone of the report was favourable.* | **moral, political,**

social *The newspaper sets a high moral tone in its editorial about politicians' private lives.* | **favourable** | **negative** | **comic, humorous**
- VERB + TONE **set** *Her enthusiastic speech set the tone for the day's conference.*
- PREP. **in ~** *His letter was very negative in tone.*

3 shade of a colour
- ADJ. **light, muted, neutral, pale, pastel, soft** *muted tones of grey and brown* | **dark, deep** | **rich, warm** | **earthy, flesh, grey, natural, silvery** | **colour** | **skin** *What is your natural skin tone?*

4 on the telephone
- ADJ. **dial/dialling, engaged**
- VERB + TONE **get** *I keep getting the engaged tone.*

tongue *noun*

1 soft part inside the mouth
- ADJ. **forked** | **loose, sharp** *(both figurative) Everyone knows now, thanks to Ken's loose tongue* (= he could not keep the secret). ◊ *She could tear a character to pieces in three minutes with her sharp tongue.*
- VERB + TONGUE **poke/put/stick out** *It's very rude to stick your tongue out at people.* | **run** *He ran his tongue nervously over his lips.* | **click/cluck** | **bite, hold** *(both figurative) She was dying to say something sarcastic to him, but bit her tongue and stayed silent.* | **free, loosen** *(both figurative) The wine had loosened his tongue.* | **roll/slip/trip off** *It's not a name that exactly trips off the tongue* (= is easy to say).
- TONGUE + VERB **hang out** *The dog lay in a patch of shade with its tongue hanging out.* | **flick, flicker** *The snake's tongue flicked out of its mouth.* | **lick sth** *His tongue licked dry lips.* | **wag** *(figurative) This is a small island and tongues are beginning to wag* (= people are beginning to gossip). | **find** *(figurative) Before she could find her tongue* (= speak) *the door had closed behind him.* | **watch** *(figurative) You just watch your tongue* (= be careful what you say)!
- PHRASES **be on the tip of your tongue** *(figurative) It was on the tip of her tongue to refuse.* **get your tongue around/round sth** *(figurative) He was having trouble getting his tongue around my name.* **a tongue of fire/flame** *(figurative) Tongues of flame licked up the walls.*

2 a language
- ADJ. **mother, native** *She speaks English and Danish, though her native tongue is German.* | **foreign** | **strange**
- PREP. **in a/the ~** *She could hear men whispering in a foreign tongue.*
- PHRASES **speak in tongues** (= to speak in unknown languages, especially at a religious ceremony)

tonne *noun*

⇨ Note at MEASURE

tonsils *noun*

- ADJ. **swollen**
- VERB + TONSILS **have out** *I had my tonsils out when I was ten.*

tool *noun*

1 instrument for making/repairing things
- ADJ. **general-purpose, multi-purpose** | **basic, primitive, standard, traditional** *craftsmen using traditional tools* | **sophisticated, special** | **sharp** | **rusting/rusty** | **cutting, drawing, measuring** | **cordless, hand, machine, power** | **agricultural, engineering, farm, garden/gardening, industrial, woodworking**
- QUANT. **set**
- VERB + TOOL **use** | **sharpen** | **blunt** *Cutting concrete would blunt a metal-cutting tool.* | **down ~s** *Workers*

downed tools (= stopped work) *in protest at poor safety standards in the works.*
- TOOL + NOUN **kit**
- PHRASES **the tool/tools of the trade** *The guitarist opened the case and took out the tool of his trade.*

2 sth that helps you do/achieve sth
- ADJ. **effective, essential, important, indispensable, invaluable, major, necessary, powerful, useful, valuable, vital** | **educational, learning, reference, research** *This dictionary is an invaluable reference tool for advanced learners.* | **ideological, negotiating, political, propaganda** *We must ensure that education is not used as a political tool.* | **communication, management, marketing** | **analysis/analytical, design, desktop, development, drawing, multimedia, presentation, programming, software**

toot *noun*

- VERB + TOOT **give (sb), let out** | **hear**
- PREP. **with a ~** *The car overtook with a toot.* | **~ of**
- PHRASES **the toot of a horn, a toot on the horn** *The taxi driver gave a toot on the horn.*
⇨ Note at SOUND

tooth *noun*

- ADJ. **big, enormous, huge** | **gappy** *She wore a brace to correct her gappy teeth.* | **prominent, sticking-out** *I used to be self-conscious of my sticking-out teeth.* | **even, straight** | **crooked, jagged** *(often figurative)*, **misshapen** *Her smile showed crooked teeth.* ◊ *Skyscrapers rose like jagged teeth.* | **broken, missing** | **good, healthy, pearl-like, pearl-white, perfect, splendid, strong, white** | **yellow** | **decayed, rotten** | **loose, wobbly** | **aching** | **capped, false, gold** | **needle-sharp, razor-sharp, sharp** *Mink have razor-sharp teeth.* | **savage** | **back, front** | **bottom, top** | **canine** | **baby, milk** *I've still got one of my baby teeth.* | **wisdom**
- VERB + TOOTH **have** | **brush, clean** | **extract, pull out, remove** | **have out** *I've just had a tooth out at the dentist's.* | **knock out** | **lose** *I lost three teeth in the fight.* | **fill** | **bare, reveal, show** *The dog bared its teeth at us and growled.* ◊ *The man smiled, revealing perfect white teeth.* | **clamp, clench, grit** *He broke off what he was saying, clamping his teeth together.* ◊ *She answered through clenched teeth* (= opening her mouth only a little because of anger). | **clamp sth between/in** *His pipe was firmly clamped between his teeth.* | **gnash, grind** | **sink** *The cat sank its teeth into his finger.* | **cut** *The baby's crying because he's cutting a new tooth* (= a new one is coming through).
- TOOTH + VERB **be/come through** *Billy's first tooth is now through.* | **fall out** | **bite sb/sth, nip sb/sth, sink into sb/sth, snap together** | **ache** | **chatter** *Their teeth were chattering with cold.* | **flash, gleam, glint, shine** *Her teeth flashed as she smiled.* | **grin**
- TOOTH + NOUN **decay, loss** | **abscess** | **enamel** | **mark** *The cat left teeth marks in my arm.*
- PREP. **against the/your ~** *He clashed the spoon against his teeth as he ate.* **between the/your ~** *She answered the phone with a cigarette between her teeth.* **in the/your ~** *The cat came in with a mouse in its teeth.* **through the/your ~** *'Come here now!' she growled through her teeth.*

top *noun*

1 highest part/surface of sth
- ADJ. **extreme, very** *We didn't climb to the very top of the mountain, but close enough.* | **cliff** (also **clifftop**), **hill** (also **hilltop**), **mountain** (also **mountaintop**), **roof** (also **rooftop**), **table, tree** (also **treetop**)
- PREP. **at the ~, on ~** *Each cake had a cherry on top.* ◊ *There was a vase on top of the bookcase.* **to the ~**

- PHRASES **from top to bottom** *I'm going to clean the house from top to bottom this weekend.*

2 highest/most important rank/position
- VERB + TOP **get to, make it to, reach, rise to** *Few of the trainee footballers make it to the top.* ◇ *She rose to the top of her profession within ten years.*
- PREP. **at the ~** *The company has an unusually high proportion of young people at the top.* **on ~, to the ~**
- PHRASES **top of the agenda** *Pay was now (at the) top of the employees' agenda.* **top of the class** *She was top of the class in maths.*

3 cover that you put on sth in order to close it
- ADJ. **bottle**
- VERB + TOP **lever off, prise off, remove, take off, unscrew | put on, screw on**

4 piece of clothing
- ADJ. **hooded, long-sleeved, sleeveless | baggy, loose | bikini, pyjama, tracksuit**
- ⇨ Special page at CLOTHES

top *adj.*

- VERBS **be | come** *She came top in the exams.*
- PREP. **in** *She was top in maths.* **of** *He was top of his class.*

topic *noun*

- ADJ. **chosen, selected | broad, general, large, wide** *Before dealing with specific cases, she spoke on the broad topic of 'discipline'.* **| diverse, wide-ranging** *The book covers such diverse topics as snorkelling and first aid.* **| narrow | central, dominant, important, key, main, major, principal | complex, difficult | conversational, essay, lecture, research | controversial, sensitive** *It might be better to avoid such a controversial topic.* **| historical, philosophical, scientific, social, etc.**
- VERB + TOPIC **consider, cover, discuss, explore, deal with, focus on, look at, speak on, write on** *In the next chapter the writer focuses on the topic of adoption.*
- TOPIC + NOUN **area, heading | work** *Our teaching is based largely on topic work.*
- PREP. **on a/the ~** *Mr Graham will speak on the topic of dog breeding.*
- PHRASES **a choice of topic** *She was an excellent speaker, but I found her choice of topic strange.* **a range/variety of topics, a topic of conversation/discussion** *His main topic of conversation is football.*

topless *adj.*

- VERBS **be, go, perform, pose, sunbathe** *Do you dare to go topless on the beach?* ◇ *There were rumours that she had posed topless for a magazine.* **| show sb**

torch *noun*

1 electric light carried in the hand
- ADJ. **powerful | electric**
- VERB + TORCH **carry, have | switch off/on, turn off/on | flash, play, point, shine** *The policeman played his torch over the men's faces.* ◇ *I shone my torch through the crack.*
- TORCH + VERB **flash, play, shine** *A powerful torch shone in their direction.*
- TORCH + NOUN **beam**
- PHRASES **the beam of a torch, light from/of a torch** *We struggled to read the map by the light of the torch.*

2 piece of burning wood carried to give light
- ADJ. **blazing, burning, flaming, flaring, flickering**
- VERB + TORCH **light** *They lit their torches from the fire.* **| carry, hold** *Servants were carrying lighted torches.*
- TORCH + VERB **flash, play, shine** *The path to the castle was lit by blazing torches.* **| burn** *The torches were burning fiercely.* **| flare | flicker, splutter | go out** *The torch flickered and went out.*

torment *noun*

- ADJ. **great | inner, mental, private**
- VERB + TORMENT **endure, suffer** *She has suffered great mental torment.* **| be released from**
- PREP. **in ~** *He was a man in torment.*
- PHRASES **a soul in torment** *The sea wailed like a soul in torment.*

tornado *noun*

- TORNADO + VERB **hit sth, strike sth** *The town was hit by a tornado last night.* **| damage sth, destroy sth, devastate sth**
- PREP. **in a/the ~** *The building was badly damaged in a tornado.*

torpedo *noun*

- VERB + TORPEDO **carry** *enemy planes carrying torpedoes* **| fire, launch, release | drop**
- TORPEDO + VERB **hit sth, strike sth**
- TORPEDO + NOUN **tube | boat, bomber**

torrent *noun*

1 large amount of water moving very quickly
- ADJ. **raging, roaring, rushing** *After heavy rain, the little stream becomes a raging torrent.* **| foaming, muddy**
- PREP. **in ~s** *The rain poured down in torrents.*
- PHRASES **a torrent of rain/water**

2 large amount of sth that comes suddenly
- VERB + TORRENT **unleash** *The sight of her father unleashed a torrent of emotions.*
- PREP. **in a ~** *Her pent-up anger was released in a torrent of words.* **| ~ of** *a torrent of abuse/criticism/tears*

torso *noun*

- ADJ. **bare, naked | tanned | lower, upper | human | headless, mutilated** *The headless torso of a man was found in some bushes.*
- VERB + TORSO **reveal** *He took off his shirt to reveal his tanned torso.*

torture *noun*

- ADJ. **brutal | systematic | mental, physical**
- VERB + TORTURE **inflict | suffer**
- TORTURE + NOUN **camp, chamber, room | victim**

torture *verb*

- ADV. **badly, brutally, severely | routinely** *The prisoners were routinely tortured.*
- PHRASES **torture sb to death**

toss *noun*

- VERB + TOSS **lose, win** *England won the toss and chose to kick off.*
- PREP. **with a ~**
- PHRASES **(by/on) the toss of a coin** *The order of play was decided by the toss of a coin.* **a toss of sb's/the head** *'Of course not,' she said with a toss of her head.*

toss *verb*

1 throw sth carelessly
- ADV. **carelessly, casually** *She picked up the package and casually tossed it into her bag.* **| aside, away, back, over** *She tossed back her blonde hair.*
- PREP. **into, out of, to** *He tossed the letter over to me.*

2 keep moving up and down/from side to side
- ADV. **restlessly** *She tossed about restlessly all night with a high fever.* **| about** *He was tossed about in his boat.*
- PHRASES **toss and turn** *He tossed and turned all night, unable to sleep.*

3 cover food in a sauce
- ADV. **gently, lightly | well | together**
- PREP. **in** *Toss the vegetables lightly in olive oil.*

total *noun*

- ADJ. **annual, monthly | combined, cumulative, grand, overall, sum** *His two goals give him a grand total of 32 for the season.* ◇ *The sum total of my knowledge of biology is not impressive.* | **final | high, huge, large, record** *a record total of victories* | **low, small | global, national, world/worldwide | jobless, unemployment** *Britain's jobless total rose by 20 000 last month.*
- VERB + TOTAL **add up to, give, make (up)** *Their earnings were £250, £300 and £420, giving a total of £970.* | **bring, take** *A donation of £250 has been received, bringing the total to £3 750.* | **achieve** *The Greens achieved a total of 18 seats.*
- TOTAL + VERB **rise | fall**
- PREP. **in ~** *In total, they spent 420 hours on the project.* **out of a ~ of** *180 vehicles out of a total of 900 examined were not roadworthy.* | **~ of**

touch *noun*

1 act of touching sb/sth
- ADJ. **delicate, gentle, light, slight** *The slightest touch will set off the alarm.*
- PREP. **at sb/sth's ~** *The door swung open at his touch.* ◇ *You can now do your shopping at the touch of a button.*

2 small detail
- ADJ. **final, finishing | decorative, festive, homely, romantic** *The family photos give the room a homely touch.* | **humorous | classy, lovely, nice, professional** *Giving her flowers was a nice touch.* | **feminine, human, idiosyncratic, individual, personal | little** *The decor includes many idiosyncratic little touches.*
- VERB + TOUCH **add, give sth, put** *She's just putting the finishing touches to her painting.*

3 particular ability
- ADJ. **golden, magic | deft, sure** *With students she had a sure touch and showed great personal sensitivity.* | **light** *He handles this controversial subject with a light touch.* | **political** *He found his old political touch when the crisis emerged.*
- VERB + TOUCH **find | lose** *Maybe the champion is losing her magic touch.*

4 small amount of sth
- ADJ. **little, subtle | welcome**
- VERB + TOUCH **add, bring** *Her speech brought a welcome touch of humour to the evening.*
- PREP. **with a ~ of** *'Thanks,' she said, with a touch of sarcasm.* | **~ of**

5 contact
- ADJ. **close** *The security staff were in close touch with the local police.*
- VERB + TOUCH **get in** *I'm trying to get in touch with Jane. Do you have her number?* | **keep in, stay in** *It is important to keep in touch with the latest research.* ◇ *Let's keep in touch.* | **put sb in** *I'll put you in touch with someone in your area.* | **lose** *I've lost touch with all my old friends.*
- PREP. **in ~** *Are you still in touch with your friends from college?* **out of ~** *This government is increasingly out of touch with ordinary voters.* | **~ with**

touch *verb*

1 put your hand on sb/sth; be in contact with sb/sth
- ADV. **(not) actually, not even, not quite** *He did not actually touch the substance, but may have inhaled microparticles.* | **barely, hardly, scarcely** *You've hardly touched your food* (= not eaten it). | **almost, nearly, practically** *Their faces were almost touching.* | **just | briefly**

His fingers briefly touched hers. | **gently, lightly | gingerly | accidentally, inadvertently** *He accidentally touched a live wire attached to overhead power cables.* | **never** *He said I kicked him, but I never touched him!*
- VERB + TOUCH **want to | (not) dare (to)** *Don't you dare touch me!* | **reach out to** *Her hand reached out to touch his cheek.* | **let sb** *He wouldn't let me touch the wound.*
- PREP. **on** *He touched her gently on the arm.* **with** *She touched him with her hand.*

2 make sb feel a strong emotion
- ADV. **deeply** *The story touched me very deeply.*

PHRASAL VERB

touch on/upon sth
- ADV. **briefly | just, merely** *Photojournalism and the birth of photography are merely touched on in the book.*
- VERB + TOUCH ON/UPON STH **want to** *I want to touch briefly on another aspect of the problem.*

touched *adj.*

- VERBS **be, feel, look, seem**
- ADV. **deeply, greatly, really, very | quite, rather**
- PREP. **by** *We were deeply touched by your concern.*

tough *adj.*

1 difficult/unpleasant
- VERBS **be, seem | get**
- ADV. **extremely, particularly, really, very | a bit, fairly, a little, pretty, quite** *Things were pretty tough at first.*
- PREP. **on** *It's very tough on the wives when the husbands go off like that.*

2 strict/firm
- VERBS **be | become, get**
- ADV. **extremely, particularly, very | fairly, pretty, quite | enough** *Has the government been tough enough on polluters?*
- PREP. **on** *The government has promised to get tough on crime.* **with** *You have to be tough with these young thugs.*

3 strong
- VERBS **be, feel, look, seem | become, get, grow | act, talk** (*both informal*) *Then this guy started acting tough.*
- ADV. **incredibly, really, remarkably, very | pretty, quite, reasonably | enough** *Are you sure you're physically tough enough for this job?* | **mentally, physically**

tour *noun*

1 journey
- ADJ. **foreign, international, national, nationwide, overseas, provincial, world | American, UK, etc. | two-city, three-country, etc.** *The group will shortly go on a ten-city European tour.* | **whirlwind, whistle-stop** *The president embarked on a whirlwind tour of the provinces.* | **comprehensive, gruelling, lengthy, long, marathon | two-week, three-week, etc. | official** *the prime minister's first official overseas tour* | **grand** *He took his degree in 1665 before embarking on the grand tour* (= a tour of Europe lasting several months). | **inclusive, package** *an all-inclusive package tour of Austria* | **mystery** (*often humorous*) *We reboarded the coach and set off on a magical mystery tour in search of tea.* | **coach, cycle, rail, walking | camping | cricket, rugby, etc. | concert, lecture, speaking, study, theatre | sell-out, successful** *The band is just back from a sell-out European tour.*
- VERB + TOUR **do, go on, make, undertake | embark on, set off on**
- TOUR + NOUN **company, operator | date, schedule** *Phone for details of the band's tour dates.* | **leader, manager** *Our tour leaders are all fluent in English.* ◇ *The team's tour manager called a press conference.* | **party,**

squad *He wasn't selected for England's tour party to Australia.* | **bus**, **van**
- PREP. **on (a)~** *We met a group of cyclists on a tour in the Lake District.* ◇ *The band is currently on tour in the States.* | **~ of** *I'd like to do a tour of Belgium on foot.*
- PHRASES **tour of duty** *The soldiers were returning from a six-month tour of duty in Northern Ireland.*

2 short visit
- ADJ. **brief**, **quick**, **lightning** *Our host gave us a quick tour of the house.* | **extensive** | **grand** (*humorous*) *Come on, I'll give you the grand tour of the backyard.* | **conducted**, **guided**, **self-guided** | **city**, **factory** | **sightseeing** | **circular**
- VERB + TOUR **give sb**, **take sb on** | **do**, **make** *I made a lightning tour of the office to say goodbye.*
- TOUR + NOUN **guide**
- PHRASES **tour of inspection** *The headmaster started his tour of inspection with the staff room.*

tour *verb*
- ADV. **extensively**
- VERB + TOUR **plan to**
- PREP. **all over** *We plan to tour all over the country.* **in** *She has toured extensively in the US.*

tourism *noun*
- ADJ. **international**, **overseas** | **mass**, **package** | **expanding**, **increased** | **eco-friendly**, **ecological**, **environmental**, **green**, **sustainable** | **farm**
- VERB + TOURISM **boost**, **increase**, **promote** | **be dependent upon**, **depend on**, **rely on** *The islands' economy is largely dependent upon tourism.*
- TOURISM + VERB **boom**, **increase** *With the advent of the railways, tourism boomed.* | **decline**, **fall**, **slump**
- TOURISM + NOUN **business**, **enterprise**, **industry**, **market**, **sector** | **development**, **promotion** | **strategy** | **officer** | **potential** *The city is finally realizing its tourism potential.*
- PREP. **through ~** *The town survives mainly through tourism.*
- PHRASES **a downturn/decline/drop in tourism**, **the development/promotion of tourism**, **earnings/income/revenue from tourism**, **the growth in/of tourism**, **the impact of tourism**, **an increase/a rise in tourism**

tourist *noun*
- ADJ. **foreign**, **Western** | **American**, **Japanese**, etc. | **modern**, **nineteenth-century**
- QUANT. **coachload**, **party**
- VERB + TOURIST **attract**, **draw** *The Story of the Loch Ness Monster has attracted many tourists to the area.* | **drive/frighten away** *The high level of crime is frightening away tourists.*
- TOURIST + VERB **flock to sth**, **frequent sth**, **visit sth** *the part of town most frequented by tourists*
- TOURIST + NOUN **area**, **centre**, **destination**, **haunt**, **resort**, **spot**, **town**, **trap** *Recently Edinburgh has become a popular tourist centre.* | **attraction**, **facility**, **sight** *Pompeii is one of Italy's prime tourist attractions.* ◇ *The theme park is the region's most popular tourist facility.* | **route**, **trail** *The town is off the usual tourist trail.* | **hotel**, **shop** | **business**, **industry**, **trade** | **board**, **office** | **information** *the local tourist information office* | **guide** *I bought a tourist guide to Paris.* ◇ *She works as a tourist guide.* | **map** | **traffic**, **visitors** *the reduction in tourist traffic due to the violence* | **season** | **potential** *The city has unrealized tourist potential.* | **visa** | **bus**, **coach**
- PHRASES **influx of tourists** *The festival is accompanied by a huge influx of tourists.*

tournament *noun*
- ADJ. **chess**, **golf**, **tennis**, etc. | **qualifying**, **ranking**, **World Cup** | **European**, **international**, **national**, **world** | **major** | **one-day** | **knockout**, **round-robin** | **doubles**, **five-a-side**, **seven-a-side**, etc., **sevens**, **singles** | **indoor** | **club**, **open**, **professional** | **pre-season**
- VERB + TOURNAMENT **enter**, **play (in)**, **take part in** *The tournament was played under floodlights.* ◇ *Several top teams have agreed to play in the tournament.* | **win** | **hold**, **organize**
- TOURNAMENT + VERB **take place**
- TOURNAMENT + NOUN **victory**, **win** *her first tournament win of the season* | **leader**, **winner** | **director**, **organizer**, **sponsor** | **referee** | **player**, **professional** *the tournament professional at the local golf club* | **golf** *She retired from tournament golf last year.*
- PREP. **in a/the ~** *the strongest player in the tournament* **out of a/the ~** *The loser will be out of the tournament.*

tow *noun*
- VERB + TOW **give sb** *A truck driver gave me a tow to the nearest garage.*
- TOW + NOUN **bar**, **line**, **rope** | **plane**, **truck**, **vehicle** | **pilot**
- PREP. **in ~** (*usually figurative*) *a harassed mother with three small children in tow* **under ~** *The ship, whose engine had failed, is now safely under tow.*

towel *noun*
- ADJ. **clean**, **fresh** | **damp**, **wet** | **dry** | **rolled-up** | **fluffy**, **soft**, **thick** | **paper** | **bath**, **bathroom**, **beach**, **hand**, **kitchen**, **tea** | **roller** | **sanitary**
- VERB + TOWEL **drape**, **wrap** *He had a towel draped across his shoulders.*
- TOWEL + VERB **hang** *Several towels hung over the side of the bath.*
- TOWEL + NOUN **rail** *a heated towel rail*

tower *noun*
- ADJ. **high**, **high-rise**, **lofty**, **massive**, **tall** | **squat** | **two-storey**, **three-storey**, etc. *They lived in a ten-storey tower in the town centre.* | **octagonal**, **round**, **square** | **ancient**, **Gothic**, **medieval** | **fortified** | **twin** *Twin towers flanked the castle gateway.* | **ruined** | **control**, **lookout**, **observation**, **watch** (also **watchtower**) *Armed border guards manned the lookout towers.* | **bell**, **clock** | **cooling**, **water** | **television** | **computer** | **conning** | **castle**, **cathedral**, **church** | **ivory** (*figurative*) *academics sitting in their ivory towers*
- TOWER + VERB **collapse**

town *noun*

1 place with many streets and buildings
- ADJ. **big**, **large**, **major** | **little**, **small** | **nearby**, **neighbouring**, **surrounding** | **ancient**, **historic**, **medieval**, **old** | **new** *It was built as a new town in the 1960s.* | **industrial** | **busy** *a busy market town* | **boom**, **thriving** *London was a boom town and the stock market was soaring.* ◇ *a thriving holiday town* | **sleepy** *a sleepy provincial town in southern France* | **country**, **provincial** | **county** *Beverley was then the county town of the East Riding of Yorkshire* (= the main town where the county offices were). | **home**, **native** *She has gone back to live in her home town.* | **border** | **coastal**, **seaside** | **holiday**, **resort** | **cathedral**, **market**, **university** | **dormitory**, **satellite** | **fortified** *Kitzbühel is an ancient fortified town with fine medieval buildings.* | **shanty** | **ghost** *It's been a ghost town since the gold rush ended.* | **twin** *Darlington's twin town of Amiens*
- VERB + TOWN **build**, **found** | **live in** *How many people live in the town?* | **get out of**, **leave**, **move out of** *He left*

town yesterday for a conference in York. ◇ They wanted to move out of town and start a new life in the country.
- TOWN + VERB **grow | flourish**
- TOWN + NOUN **hall, square, walls | council | life | planning**
- PREP. **in ~** They'll be back in town tomorrow. **out of ~** I was out of town last week. ◇ an out-of-town superstore **outside (the) ~** a lake just outside the town
- PHRASES **the centre/middle of (the) town, the edge/outskirts of (the) town**

2 main part of a town, with the shops, etc.
- VERB + TOWN **go into** I'm going into town—can I get you anything?
- PREP. **in ~** Mum's in town doing some shopping.

toxic adj.

- VERBS **be, stay | become | remain**
- ADV. **extremely, highly, very | quite | potentially** potentially toxic chemicals
- PREP. **to** This chemical is toxic to many forms of life.

toy noun

- ADJ. **cuddly, fluffy, soft | battery-operated, clockwork, electronic, mechanical, remote-control, wind-up | construction/constructional, educational, learning, scientific | squeaky | child's, children's | executive** Desktop publishing is probably the best executive toy ever invented. **| sex**
- VERB + TOY **play with | snatch** Freddie kept snatching toys from the other children. **| pick up, put away, tidy up/away**
- TOY + NOUN **department, library, shop, store** All kinds of toys can be borrowed from the toy library. **| company, maker, manufacturer | box, cupboard**

trace noun

1 mark/sign that shows sb/sth happened/existed
- ADJ. **archaeological, historical | indelible, permanent | memory** (technical)
- VERB + TRACE **leave** The burglar had left several traces of his presence. ◇ Little trace is left of how Stone Age people lived. **| bear, reveal, show | discover, find** The search party had found no trace of the missing climbers. **| obliterate, remove** Remove all traces of rust with a small wire brush. **| disappear/sink/vanish without** The ship seems to have sunk without trace.
- TRACE + VERB **remain** Traces still remain of the long-defunct Surrey Iron Railway.
- PREP. **with/without a ~ of sth** 'No thanks,' she said, with a trace of irritation in her voice. **without ~** The plane was lost without a trace over the Atlantic.

2 very small amount of sth
- ADJ. **discernible, faint, minute, slight, small, tiny** There was not the faintest trace of irony in her voice. **| unmistakable**
- VERB + TRACE **contain** The water was found to contain traces of sulphuric acid. **| detect, find**
- TRACE + NOUN **amount | element, gas, metal, mineral** Kelp is rich in vitamins and trace elements.
- PREP. **~ of** a trace of amusement/anxiety/a smile

trace verb

1 find out where sth is/where it comes from
- ADV. **successfully**
- VERB + TRACE **be able/unable to, can** Police have been unable to trace her movements during her final days. **| attempt to, try to | help (to) | fail to | be difficult to | be possible to**
- PREP. **to** The stolen paintings have been successfully traced to a London warehouse.

2 find/describe the cause/origin of sth

- ADV. **carefully | easily** Words have over the centuries acquired meanings not easily traced in dictionaries. **| directly | historically | back**
- VERB + TRACE **can | attempt to, try to | be difficult to** The origins of the custom are difficult to trace. **| be possible to**
- PREP. **to** The book traces the history of the game back to an incident in 1863.

3 mark where the line of sth is with a thin object
- ADV. **lightly**
- PREP. **with** She lightly traced the outline of his face with her finger.

track noun

1 marks left behind by a car/a person/an animal
- ADJ. **deep | fresh | animal, boot, car, tyre** The beach is criss-crossed with animal tracks.
- VERB + TRACK **leave, make** Rabbits had left tracks in the snow. **| cover** (often figurative) He had been careless, and had done little to cover his tracks. **| follow**
- PREP. **on the ~ of** (often figurative) She felt the excitement of a journalist on the track of a good story.
- PHRASES **freeze/halt/stop in your tracks** (figurative), **halt/stop sb/sth in their/its tracks** (figurative) The disease was stopped in its tracks by immunization programmes. **make tracks** (figurative) It's getting late—I'd better make tracks (= leave).

2 path/rough road
- ADJ. **narrow | wide | steep | bumpy, dusty, grassy, muddy, rough, rutted, sandy, slippery, stony | ancient, medieval | cinder, dirt, mud, unpaved | cart, cycle, sheep, ski | single** a single track road with passing places **| farm, forest/forestry, hillside, mountain, woodland | perimeter** A few planes were parked on the perimeter track of the airfield.
- VERB + TRACK **follow**
- TRACK + VERB **lead** The track leads across a meadow. **| fork** When the track forks, take the left fork.
- PREP. **along/down/up a/the ~** Continue along the farm track for another hundred metres.
- PHRASES **off the beaten track** (figurative) (= not in a place that most people go to), **on the right/wrong track** (figurative) The new manager successfully got the team back onto the right track. **on the wrong track** (figurative) The police were on the wrong track when they treated the case as a revenge killing.

3 special path, often in a circle, for racing
- ADJ. **race** (also **racetrack**), **running | indoor, outdoor | all-weather | training, warm-up | fast | dog**
- PHRASES **track and field** The competition features many top track and field athletes.

4 metal rails on which a train runs
- ADJ. **rail, railway, tram | double, single | elevated | eastbound, westbound, etc. | narrow gauge, standard gauge**
- VERB + TRACK **lay | lift** Many branch lines were closed, and the tracks lifted.
- TRACK + NOUN **layout**

5 direction/course that sb/sth takes
- ADJ. **fast, inside** an inside track to the ear of government **| parallel, twin** a twin track approach to crime **| career** She decided to change her career track.
- VERB + TRACK **switch** He switched tracks and went back to college.
- PREP. **along a/the ~** Film comedy developed along a similar track to film drama. **on (a/the) ~** A UN spokesman insisted that the implementation of the peace plan is back on track. ◇ The ship was on a southerly track. **| ~ for** She seems to be on the fast track for promotion. **~ to** The country is on the fast track to democracy.
- PHRASES **keep track of sth** (= to know what is happening, where sth is, etc.) Keep track of all your payments by

writing them down in a book. **lose track of sth** (= to not know what is happening, where sth is, etc.) *I was so absorbed in my work that I lost track of time.*

6 one song/piece of music on a cassette/CD
- ADJ. **album | live | title | unreleased | dance, disco | backing | drum, guitar, rhythm, solo, vocal** (see also **soundtrack**)
- VERB + TRACK **cut, lay down, record** *She had already cut a couple of tracks as lead singer with her own group.* | **play | listen to**

track record *noun*

- ADJ. **good, impressive, proven | poor**
- VERB + TRACK RECORD **have, possess**
- PREP. **~ for** *If possible, select pairs of fish that already have a track record for breeding.* **~ in** *Applicants should have a proven track record in telesales.*

tractor *noun*

- ADJ. **caterpillar | agricultural, farm**
- VERB + TRACTOR **drive**
- TRACTOR + VERB **plough, work** *the sound of a tractor ploughing in the field nearby*
- TRACTOR + NOUN **driver | cab | shed**
- PREP. **on a/the~** *a farmer on his tractor*
- PHRASES **a tractor and trailer**

trade *noun*

1 buying/selling of goods/services
- ADJ. **brisk, flourishing, lively, roaring, thriving** *All around the pyramids, salespeople were doing a roaring trade in souvenirs.* | **lucrative, profitable | external, foreign, global, international, overseas, world | domestic, internal, inter-provincial, inter-regional, regional | export, import, import-export | direct, indirect | free | fair** *The organization promotes fair trade with developing countries.* | **legal, legitimate | illegal, illicit** *attempts to curb the illicit trade in exotic species* | **private | bilateral, mutual | unilateral | coastal, maritime | agricultural, commercial | retail, wholesale** *It has been a bad year for the retail trade.* | **book, fur, slave, timber, tourist, wine, wool | evil** *the evil trade in drugs*
- VERB + TRADE **carry on, conduct, do, engage in, ply** *the tools needed to carry on a trade* ◇ *All manner of hawkers and street sellers were plying their trade.* | **boost, build up, develop, expand, increase, promote** *a bid to boost foreign trade* ◇ *He built up a trade in seeds, corn and manure.* | **damage, harm** *A bitterly cold winter damaged industrial output and trade.* | **lose** *Shops have lost a day's trade.* | **ban, restrict**
- TRADE + VERB **boom, expand, grow, increase, pick up | decline, fall**
- TRADE + NOUN **balance, figures, performance, statistics | surplus | deficit, gap, imbalance | barrier, blockade, boycott, embargo, restrictions, sanctions | tariff | dispute, war** *The countries were locked in a trade war, refusing to allow imports of each other's goods.* | **liberalization | benefits, concessions | accord, agreement, deal, pact, protocol, treaty | negotiations, talks | cooperation, links, network, relations | policy, practice** *The US was accused of employing unfair trade practices.* | **law, rules | bloc** *The five countries formed a regional trade bloc.* | **delegation, mission** *Several local firms took part in a trade mission to Spain.* | **official, representative** *talks between trade officials from the two countries* | **mark** (also **trademark**), **name | exhibition, fair, show | centre | route** *The road has been an important trade route since prehistoric times.* | **cycle** *the boom and slump periods of a trade cycle* | **association, body, group, organization** *the trade body representing water companies* (see also **trade union**) | **buyer, customer** *The vase was bought by a trade buyer* (= for example, somebody who works in the an-

tiques trade). | **directory | journal, magazine, paper, press | information, secret** *The employees were fired for divulging trade secrets to a competitor.*
- PREP. **in a/the ~** *She's in the wholesale fruit trade.* ◇ *These special flour sacks are known in the trade as 'pockets'.* | **~ between** *Trade between the Adriatic ports and their hinterland had grown.* **~ in** *Steps were taken to ban the trade in ivory.* **~ with** *The US has restricted trade with India.*
- ⇨ Special page at BUSINESS

2 job
- VERB + TRADE **learn | exercise, follow, practise**
- PREP. **by~** *She is a carpenter by trade.*
- PHRASES **a jack of all trades** (= a person who can do many different types of work), **the tricks of the trade** *The experienced artisan would pass on the tricks of the trade to the apprentice.*

trade *verb*

- ADV. **profitably, successfully | actively | openly** *The firm openly traded in arms.* | **publicly** *publicly traded securities* | **freely** *He claimed that all shops should be able to trade freely on Sundays.* | **directly | illegally**
- VERB + TRADE **continue to | cease to**
- PREP. **as** *They now trade as a partnership.* **in** *countries trading illegally in rhinoceros horn* **with** *Early explorers traded directly with the Indians.*
- PHRASES **cease/continue trading** *The company has now ceased trading.* **trade under the name (of) sth** *The company trades under the name 'English Estates'.*

trader *noun*

- ADJ. **large** *China is now one of the largest traders in the world.* | **small, small-scale** *small market traders* | **local | foreign, international | prosperous, wealthy | market, street | itinerant | sole** *You can set up in business as a sole trader, in partnership or as a limited company.* | **independent, private | retail | cattle, motor, slave, etc. | commodity, currency, options**

tradesman *noun*

- ADJ. **skilled** *This is a job for a skilled tradesman.* | **local | self-employed | respectable** *He got into trouble for seducing the daughter of a respectable tradesman.* | **wealthy**
- PHRASES **tradesmen's entrance** *All deliveries should be made to the tradesmen's entrance.*

trade union (also trades union, union) *noun*

- ADJ. **free, independent, official, public sector, recognized, registered | militant, strong | local, national | electricians', teachers', etc.**
- VERB + TRADE UNION **form, set up | dissolve | join | belong to | ban**
- TRADE UNION + VERB **be affiliated to sth | represent sb/sth** *The union represents 40% of all hospital workers.* | **negotiate (sth)** *The nurses' union negotiated a 3% pay rise.* | **accept sth, agree (to sth) | refuse sth, reject sth, threaten sth** *The union threatened strike action if its demands were not met.* | **claim sth, express sth** *Several unions expressed support for the strike.* | **support sb/sth**
- TRADE UNION + NOUN **confederation, federation, movement, organization | affiliation | action, activism, activity, militancy, power | rights | activist, leader, member/membership, official, representative | law**
- ⇨ Note at ORGANIZATION

trading *noun*

- ADJ. **busy, heavy, hectic, intensive** *In heavy trading, the 100-share index closed down 38 points.* | **quiet | free | fair, unfair** *a code of practice for fair trading* | **fraudulent,**

illegal, insider *a Wall Street dealer jailed for insider trading* | sole *Sole trading is where an individual carries on his or her own business.* | global, international, world | stock market | commodity, currency, equity, foreign exchange, share, stock | ivory
● TRADING + VERB begin, open | close

tradition *noun*

● ADJ. age-old, ancient, archaic, centuries-old, deep-rooted, enduring, living, long/long-established, old, time-honoured, unbroken, well-established | distinguished, fine, great, honourable | cherished, hallowed | dominant, powerful, strong | ancestral, family | local, national, native | folk, popular | oral | Catholic, Christian, pagan, etc. | Eastern, English, European, etc. | 19th-century, classical, medieval, modernist, etc. | academic, artistic, cultural, ideological, literary, military, musical, philosophical, political, religious, sociological, sporting, teaching, theatrical *This region has a great sporting tradition.* | democratic, liberal, radical, revolutionary
● VERB + TRADITION have | cherish, continue, follow (in), keep alive, maintain, preserve, uphold *Following in the Hitchcock tradition, he always appears in the films he directs.* ◇ *Villagers get together every year to keep this age-old tradition alive.* | hand down *an oral tradition handed down from generation to generation* | break (with), go against *He broke with the family tradition and did not go down the mines.* | establish, start | revive
● TRADITION + VERB continue, die hard, survive *Old habits and traditions die hard.*
● PREP. according to (a/the) ~ *According to tradition, a tree grew on the spot where the king was killed.* by ~ *By tradition, nobody interrupts an MP's maiden speech.* in (a/the) ~ *In time-honoured tradition, a bottle of champagne was smashed on the ship.* ◇ *He's a politician in the tradition of* (= similar in style to) *Kennedy.*
● PHRASES a departure from tradition *In a departure from tradition, the bride wore a red dress.* in the best traditions of sth *The building was constructed in the best traditions of medieval church architecture.* respect for tradition *I acquired lasting respect for tradition and veneration for the past.*

traditional *adj.*

● VERBS be | become
● ADV. very | almost | fairly, pretty, quite, rather | essentially *a bold but essentially traditional design*

traffic *noun*

1 vehicles travelling somewhere
● ADJ. bad, busy, congested, heavy, thick | light | constant | fast, fast-flowing | slow-moving, sluggish | cycle, heavy goods vehicle, lorry, motor, road, vehicular, wheeled | foot, pedestrian | air, airline *an air traffic controller* | boat, maritime, river, sea | rail, railway | motorway | commercial, freight, goods, industrial, passenger | city, city-centre, local, town-centre, urban | international | commuter, tourist | rush-hour | holiday, summer | oncoming *I stood waiting for a gap in the oncoming traffic.* | through *Through traffic is directed around the bypass.* | northbound, southbound, etc. | one-way, two-way
● QUANT. stream
● VERB + TRAFFIC generate, increase *Building larger roads could generate more traffic.* | cut, reduce | slow down | block, hold up, obstruct, stop, tie up *Traffic was held up for six hours by the motorway blockade.* | direct | divert
● TRAFFIC + VERB build up, thicken *In the town centre, traffic was already building up as early as 3 p.m.* | grow, increase *Traffic has increased by 50% in ten years.* | clog

sth *Traffic clogs the streets of the city centre.* | thin *Traffic thins noticeably after 9 a.m.* | flow, move, speed, travel *The road is being widened to keep traffic moving.* | go by, pass | head *We joined the traffic heading northwards on the motorway.* | roar, rumble
● TRAFFIC + NOUN accident | hazard *Sheep are a traffic hazard in the hills.* | chaos, congestion, disruption, delays, hold-ups, problems, queues | fumes, pollution | noise | flow, speed *Widening the road would improve traffic flow.* | levels, volume | calming, management, restraint, safety | sign, signal | laws, legislation, regulations | system | offence, violation | bollard, cone, island *A traffic island at the junction separates left- and right-turning vehicles.* | artery (*formal*), route | report, survey, update | cop, officer, police, policeman, warden | engineer, planner | duty *a policeman on traffic duty*
● PHRASES the volume of traffic
2 messages, signals, etc.
● ADJ. radio, telephone | data, voice | network | Internet, Net, site, Web, website *Our company will help you generate site traffic.*
● VERB + TRAFFIC boost, build, generate
3 illegal buying and selling of sth
● ADJ. illegal | arms, drug
● PREP. ~ in sth *the traffic in arms*

traffic jam *noun*

● ADJ. long, severe
● VERB + TRAFFIC JAM be/get caught/stuck in, sit in *Our coach was caught in a traffic jam and got to Heathrow forty minutes late.*
● PREP. ~ on the … *Police report severe traffic jams on the M25, with five-mile tailbacks in places.*

traffic light (*also* light) *noun*

● ADJ. amber, green, red | temporary *There are temporary traffic lights because of the roadworks.*
● QUANT. set *Turn left at the third set of traffic lights.*
● VERB + TRAFFIC LIGHT go though, jump *He was stopped by the police for going through a red light.*
● TRAFFIC LIGHT + VERB change (to sth), go green, etc. *A line of vehicles waited for the traffic lights to change.* ◇ *Stop when the lights change to red.* | be (on) green, etc. *The lights were on red but she didn't stop.* | work *The traffic lights weren't working.*
● PREP. at the ~s *There was a hold-up at the lights.*

tragedy *noun*

1 event/situation that causes great sadness
● ADJ. absolute, appalling, awful, great, major, real, terrible | family, human, personal, private
● VERB + TRAGEDY end in *A family's outing ended in tragedy when their boat capsized.* | be dogged by, suffer | avert, avoid, prevent
● TRAGEDY + VERB happen, occur, strike (sb) *Tragedy struck when their 8-year-old daughter was knocked down by a car.*
● PREP. ~ for sb *The closure of the factory is a tragedy for the whole community.*
2 serious play with a sad ending
● ADJ. classical, Greek, Jacobean, Shakespearean

tragic *adj.*

● VERBS be, seem
● ADV. genuinely, particularly, really, terribly, very *a genuinely tragic figure in the play* | almost | quite, rather *a rather tragic story*

trail noun

1 line/smell that sb/sth leaves behind
- ADJ. **scent** *Ants follow a scent trail laid down previously.* | **blood, smoke, vapour** | **thin** | **muddy** | **false**
- VERB + TRAIL **lay, leave, make** *The couple laid a false trail to escape the press photographers.* ◇ *The tourists left a trail of litter behind them.* | **pick up** *The dog had picked up the trail of a rabbit.* | **follow** | **lose** *The fox had crossed a stream, and the hounds lost the trail.*
- TRAIL + VERB **go cold** *They had to find the kidnappers before the trail went cold.*
- PREP. **on sb's ~** *Detectives had found several new clues and were back on the murderer's trail.*
- PHRASES **a trail of blood, a trail of devastation** *The hurricane passed, leaving a trail of devastation in its wake.* **a trail of smoke**

2 path/route
- ADJ. **forest, nature, woodland** | **10-kilometre, 5-mile,** etc. | **cycle, mountain bike, tourist, walking** | **hippy, tourist** *This restaurant is off the tourist trail.* | **campaign, comeback, winning** *(all figurative) After a disastrous few seasons, the team are on the comeback trail.*
- VERB + TRAIL **follow, hit** *In 1967 she hit the hippy trail to India.* | **be on** *(often figurative)*
- TRAIL + VERB **go, lead, wend its way** *The trail wends its way through leafy woodland and sunny meadows.*
- PREP. **along a/the~**

trail verb

1 move/walk slowly
- ADV. **slowly** | **wearily**
- PREP. **after** *I trailed wearily after the others.* **around/round** *They spent their lives trailing around the country.* **(along) behind**

2 have a lower score than the other player/team
- ADV. **badly** *Liverpool are now trailing badly in the league.*
- PREP. **by** *They were trailing by 12 points until the last few minutes of the game.*

trailer noun

- ADJ. **lorry** | **horse**
- VERB + TRAILER **load** | **pull, tow**
- TRAILER + VERB **carry sth** *a trailer carrying a motor boat*
- PREP. **on/onto a/the~** *a broken-down car on a trailer*
- PHRASES **a tractor and trailer**

train noun

1 railway engine pulling carriages/trucks
- ADJ. **railway** | **metro, subway, tube, underground** | **intercity, international, long-distance** | **local, suburban** | **express, fast** | **direct, through** *I got the through train to Manchester.* | **slow, stopping** | **special** | **early, evening, midnight, morning, night, overnight** | **two o'clock, 10.45,** etc. | **return** *What are the times of the return trains?* | **first, last, next** *The last train leaves at 00.30.* | **London to Glasgow,** etc. *the Paris to Brussels train* | **Stuttgart-bound,** etc. | **northbound, southbound,** etc. | **Piccadilly line,** etc. | **crowded, full, loaded** | **empty** | **moving** | **stationary** | **speeding** | **runaway** | **approaching, oncoming** *the sound of an approaching train* ◇ *He was pushed into the path of an oncoming train.* | **passing** *the roar of a passing train* | **departing** *She ran alongside the departing train, waving goodbye.* | **delayed, late-running** | **luxury, Pullman** | **four-coach, three-coach,** etc. | **bullet, high-speed** | **diesel, electric, steam** | **coal, commuter, freight, goods, mail, passenger** | **military, troop** | **model** | **ghost** *a carnival with ghost trains and dodgem cars*
- VERB + TRAIN **take, travel by** *From Germany they*

travelled by train to Poland.* | **travel on** *She's travelling on the same train as you.* | **use** | **catch, get, make** *We had to get up early to make the 6 o'clock train for Florence.* | **miss** | **wait for** | **run for** *I was late and had to run for my train.* | **board, get on, hop on, jump aboard/on** *We jumped on the train just as it was about to leave.* | **jump from/off, jump out of** *She tried to kill herself by jumping off a moving train.* | **alight from, get off** | **meet (sb off)** *I'm going to the station to meet her off the train.* | **change** *You'll have to change trains at Cambridge.* | **operate, run** *The company plans to run trains on key intercity routes.* | **cancel** *The 10.19 train has been cancelled.* | **drive** | **haul** *a train hauled by a steam locomotive* | **stop** | **derail** | **fall under, throw sb under** *Driven to despair, he threw himself under a train.*
- TRAIN + VERB **run** *In summer the trains run as often as every ten minutes.* | **start** | **terminate** *The train terminated in Carlisle.* | **be bound for ...** *an express train bound for Edinburgh* | **be due** *The next train is due at 9.45.* | **be delayed, be held up, be late, run late** *Most trains are running late because of the accident.* | **arrive, come in, come into sth, draw in, draw into sth, pull in, pull into sth, steam in, steam into sth** *The next train to arrive at Platform 2 is the 12.30 from Leeds.* ◇ *The train came in and I got on.* ◇ *The train drew into the station.* | **come, go** *We didn't want to leave the platform in case the train came.* | **reach** *The train reached Prague at half past six.* | **return** | **depart, draw out (of sth), leave, pull away, pull out (of sth), start (off), steam out** *The train pulled out of the station.* | **head ...** *The train headed out of Athens.* | **stand, wait** *The train now standing at Platform 3 is the 16.50 to Brighton.* ◇ *a train waiting at a signal* | **move** *Slowly the train began to move.* | **travel** *The high-speed train travels at 120 mph.* | **chug, trundle** *The train chugged slowly forward.* | **gather speed** | **hurtle, rush, speed, steam** *a picture of the bullet train speeding past Mount Fuji* | **slow (down)** | **brake** | **be brought to a halt, come to a halt, halt, stop** | **rattle, rumble, thunder, whistle** *The train rattled into the station.* | **jerk, jolt, lurch, shudder** *The train jolted into motion.* | **approach, come** *The train came towards them.* | **pass** | **enter sth** *The train entered the tunnel.* | **collide (with sth)** | **be loaded with sth, carry sth**
- TRAIN + NOUN **journey, ride** | **service** | **station** | **times, timetable** | **fare** | **ticket** | **crew, driver, guard, staff** | **travellers, travelling** | **spotter, spotting** | **accident, collision, crash, disaster** | **window** | **carriage** | **shed** | **robber** | **set** *I saved up my pocket money to buy an electric train set.*
- PREP. **aboard/on/on board a/the ~** *the people on the train* **by ~** *It's quicker by train.* | **~ between** *trains between Brindisi and Rome* **~ for/to** *He was leaving on the early train for Zaragoza.* **~ from** *the train from Birmingham to Worcester*
- PHRASES **a train load of sth** *train loads of iron ore* **a train to catch** *I can't stop now, I have a train to catch.*

2 number of people/animals moving in a line
- ADJ. **camel, mule, wagon** | **supply**

3 series of events/actions/thoughts
- VERB + TRAIN **set sth in** *That telephone call set in train a whole series of events.* | **bring sth in** *(figurative) Unemployment brings greater difficulties in its train (= causes great difficulties).*
- PHRASES **a train of events, a train of thought** *The telephone rang and she lost her train of thought.*
- PREP. **in sb's ~** *(figurative) In the train of (= following behind) the rich and famous came the journalists.*

train verb

- ADV. **hard**
- PREP. **for** *The team is training hard for the big match.*

trained adj.

- VERBS **be**
- ADV. **highly** *a highly trained army* | **well** *The animals have all been well trained.* | **fully, properly, thoroughly** *It is important that staff should be properly trained.* | **adequately** | **badly, inadequately, poorly** | **appropriately, suitably** | **explicitly, specially, specifically, formally** | **professionally** | **classically** *classically trained dancers*

trainee noun

- ADJ. **management, teacher** | **graduate** *Many companies recruit graduate trainees to train as managers.*
- VERB + TRAINEE **employ, recruit, take on**
- TRAINEE + VERB **work**
- TRAINEE + NOUN **accountant, dealer, manager, nurse, solicitor, teacher**
- PREP. **as a~** *She joined as a management trainee.*

trainer noun

1 person who trains sb/sth
- ADJ. **orchestral, teacher** | **boxing, etc.** | **animal, dog, horse, racehorse** | **champion, winning** | **personal, private** *He works out every morning with his personal trainer.*
⇨ Note at JOB

2 (usually **trainers**) sports shoe
- QUANT. **pair**
- VERB + TRAINERS **lace up, unlace**
⇨ Special page at CLOTHES

training noun

1 learning skills
- ADJ. **basic, initial, preliminary** *New recruits undergo six weeks' basic training at this naval base.* | **advanced, high/higher, high-level** | **comprehensive, systematic, thorough** | **extensive, lengthy, intensive** | **essential, necessary** | **minimum** | **adequate, proper** *No one must operate the machinery without proper training.* | **inadequate** | **minimal** *Using spreadsheets requires minimal training.* | **excellent, first-class, high-quality** | **specialist** | **hands-on, practical** | **theoretical** | **continuous, long-term, ongoing** | **individual, one-to-one** | **formal, informal** *He is good at selling, although he has had no formal training.* | **job, job-related, occupational, professional, vocational, work-related** | **in-service, on-the-job** | **off-the-job** | **external** | **internal, on-site** | **computer-based** | **mental, moral, physical, social** | **academic, educational, industrial, intellectual, journalistic, legal, management, medical, military, musical, scientific, technical** | **first-aid** | **assertiveness** | **potty** (= when a child learns to use a potty) | **staff, teacher**
- VERB + TRAINING **do, get, have, receive, undergo** *You have to do a year's intensive training to become a paramedic.* | **give sb, provide (sb with)** | **require**
- TRAINING + NOUN **base, camp, centre, college, establishment, facility, school** *an army training base ◇ a teacher training college* | **activity, course, exercise, initiative, package, plan, programme, project, scheme, strategy, system** *The soldiers were building a bridge as a training exercise.* | **methods, policy, procedures, process, techniques, skills** | **needs, objectives, requirements** | **opportunities, provision** | **aid, device, equipment, material** | **manual** | **instructor, manager, officer, staff** | **body, committee, company, department, organization, provider, service** | **place, placement** | **event, workshop** | **day, period, etc.** | **budget, costs, fees**
- PREP. **by~** *She's an accountant by training.* **in~** *I am delighted with the work he has done in training.* | **~ for** *Training for nursing was on strictly formal lines.* **~in** *Employees should be given training in safety procedures.*

2 physical exercises

- ADJ. **hard, rigorous, serious, strict, tough** *She did six months' hard training before the marathon.* | **pre-season**
- VERB + TRAINING **do**
- TRAINING + NOUN **run, session, stint** | **regime, regimen, routine, schedule** | **ground, pitch, track** (*figurative*) *This local newspaper has been a training ground for several top journalists.*
- PREP. **in~** *Lewis is in serious training for the Olympics.* | **~for**

trait noun

- ADJ. **admirable, appealing** | **negative, undesirable, unfortunate** | **human** *Her boss did not display any human traits.* | **distinctive, enduring, individual** | **family, genetic, hereditary, inherited** | **behavioural, character, personal, personality** | **mental, psychological** | **obsessional** | **physical** | **female, male** | **cultural, national**
- VERB + TRAIT **have, possess** | **lack** | **share** *She shares several character traits with her father.* | **display, exhibit, show** | **acquire, develop, inherit** *We do not know which behavioural traits are inherited and which acquired.* | **identify, recognize**

traitor noun

- VERB + TRAITOR **turn** *He turned traitor and joined the opposition.* | **denounce sb as**
- PREP. **~to** *He is seen as a traitor to the cause.*

tram noun

- ADJ. **modern** | **electric, horse/horse-drawn, steam**
- VERB + TRAM **catch, go on, take** | **miss** | **board, get on** | **get off**
- TRAM + VERB **run** *The last tram ran through Glasgow in September 1962.* | **rattle** | **stop**
- TRAM + NOUN **service, system** | **route** | **stop** | **ride** | **driver** | **car** *a conducted tour in an old tram car* | **shed** | **line, rail, track** | **ticket**
- PREP. **by~** *There is easy access to the centre of the city by tram.* **on a/the~** *They sat together on the rattling tram.* | **~from, ~to**

trample verb

- ADV. **down** *crops that have been trampled down by walkers' feet* | **underfoot** *She saved a little girl from being trampled underfoot in the rush for the fire exit.*
- PREP. **on** (*often figurative*) *The government is trampling on the views of ordinary people.* **over** *Police officers had been trampling all over the ground.*
- PHRASES **be trampled to death**

trance noun

- ADJ. **catatonic, deep** | **light** | **hypnotic, mesmeric**
- VERB + TRANCE **fall into, go into** | **put sb into** | **come out of, awake/wake from**
- TRANCE + NOUN **state**
- PREP. **in a~** *In a deep trance, the subject is taken back to an earlier stage of their life.*

tranquil adj.

- VERBS **be, lie, look, seem** *The village lay tranquil in the evening sunlight.* | **become** | **remain**
- ADV. **extremely, very, wonderfully** | **perfectly, quite** | **fairly, rather**

transaction noun

- ADJ. **cross-border, international** | **domestic** | **profitable** | **fraudulent, illegal** *The president had entered into fraudulent property transactions.* | **credit, credit/debit card** | **cash, cheque** | **online** | **over-the-counter** *Electronic banking may make over-the-counter transactions*

obsolete. | banking, business, commercial, consumer, economic, financial, market, monetary, trade | foreign currency, foreign exchange | property, share | human, intellectual, interpersonal
• VERB + TRANSACTION **carry out, conduct, enter into, make** | **effect, handle** *to effect a transaction for a client* | **close, complete**
• TRANSACTION + VERB **proceed, take place** *to ensure the transaction proceeds smoothly*
• TRANSACTION + NOUN **charges, costs**
• PREP. **~ between** *The system records all transactions between the firm and its suppliers.* **~ in** *Transactions in land are frequently handled by an estate agent.*
⇨ Special page at BUSINESS

transcript *noun*

• ADJ. **faithful, full, verbatim** | **edited** | **official** | **radio, video** | **interview, trial**
• VERB + TRANSCRIPT **read (through), go through** | **make** | **print, publish**

transfer *noun*

• ADJ. **massive** *The war caused a massive transfer of population.* | **efficient, smooth, successful** *the smooth transfer of power to the new government* | **net** *There has been a net transfer of lower-paid people away from the inner cities.* | **permanent** *Her boss recommended a permanent transfer overseas.* | **direct** *Employees are paid by direct transfer to a bank account.* | **data, information, knowledge** | **land, property** | **population** | **resource** | **technology** | **file, multimedia, software** | **inter-company, inter-hospital, etc.** | **bank, capital, cash, credit, financial, money, share, stock** | **electronic, telegraphic** | **embryo, gene** | **charge, electron, energy, heat, nuclear, thermal** | **close-season, free, 15-million-pound, etc.** (all in football)
• VERB + TRANSFER **make** *Only the owner can make a transfer of goods.* | **give sb** *His club have given him a free transfer.*
• TRANSFER + VERB **take place**
• TRANSFER + NOUN **deal, fee, list, payment, price, system** (all in football)
• PREP. **~ between** *the transfer of property between private buyers* **~ from, ~ to**

transfer *verb*

• ADV. **carefully** | **directly** *Skills cannot be transferred directly from a trainer to a trainee.* | **easily** *Data is easily transferred electronically.* | **successfully** | **merely, simply** | **immediately, quickly, rapidly** | **gradually** | **eventually** | **temporarily** | **formally** *Sovereignty was formally transferred on December 27.* | **automatically** | **electronically** | **abroad, back** *transferring assets abroad*
• VERB + TRANSFER **agree to** | **refuse to**
• PREP. **across/between** *Can the disease be transferred across/between species?* **from, into** *She transferred the sauce into a china jug.* **onto, to**

transferable *adj.*

• VERBS **be** | **become**
• ADV. **easily, freely, highly, readily** *The shares are freely transferable.* | **fully, wholly** | **not necessarily**
• PREP. **between** *Tickets are transferable between members of the same family.* **from, to** *Skills which are not necessarily transferable from one environment to another.*

transform *verb*

• ADV. **considerably, fundamentally, profoundly, radically** *The riots radically transformed the situation.* | **completely, entirely, totally, utterly** | **quickly, rapidly** | **gradually, slowly** | **suddenly** | **apparently** | **miracu-**

lously *He seems to have been miraculously transformed into a first-class player.* | **overnight** *Things cannot be transformed overnight.*
• VERB + TRANSFORM **help (to)** | **manage to**
• PREP. **from, into** *The place was transformed from a quiet farming village into a busy port.*
• PHRASES **the power to transform sb/sth** *the power of religion to transform our hearts and minds*

transformation *noun*

• ADJ. **amazing, complete, dramatic, fundamental, major, miraculous, profound, radical, remarkable, revolutionary, startling, total** | **subtle** | **gradual** | **immediate, instant, rapid, sudden** | **cultural, economic, historical, intellectual, physical, political, social, structural**
• VERB + TRANSFORMATION **undergo** *The way we work has undergone a radical transformation in the past decade.* | **make** *He was struggling to make the transformation from single man to responsible husband.* | **achieve, bring about, carry out, cause, effect, lead to** *Going to college brought about a dramatic transformation in her outlook.* | **accelerate** | **complete**
• TRANSFORMATION + VERB **begin** | **come about, occur, take place** *A startling cultural transformation occurred in post-war Britain.*
• TRANSFORMATION + NOUN **process**
• PREP. **~ from** *The transformation from disused docks into city-centre cultural venue took three years.* **~ in** *This decision marked a fundamental transformation in policy.* **~ into** *Japan's transformation into an economic superpower* **~ to** *Russia's transformation to a market economy*

transit *noun*

• ADJ. **air, rail, road, sea** | **mass** *An improved mass transit system would cut traffic on the roads.* | **rapid**
• TRANSIT + NOUN **point** *The port has become a transit point in the drug trade.* | **camp** *a transit camp for refugees* | **lounge** *The passengers had been transferred into the transit lounge.* | **shed** *The goods were still in a transit shed on the quay.* | **system** *The city has acquired a light rail transit system.*
• PREP. **in ~** *Many of the goods were damaged in transit.* | **~ between** *goods in transit between factory and store* **~ from, ~ to** *in transit from factory to store*

transition *noun*

• ADJ. **abrupt, immediate, rapid, sudden** | **direct** | **gradual, phased, slow** | **awkward, difficult, painful** | **easy, smooth** | **non-violent, orderly, peaceful**
• VERB + TRANSITION **bring about, cause, effect** *The negotiators hoped to effect a smooth transition to an interim administration.* | **complete, make** *The company was slow to make the transition from paper to computer.* | **undergo** | **mark** *The ceremony marks the transition of the student to graduate status.* | **ease, smooth**
• TRANSITION + VERB **occur, take place** | **be complete** *Her transition from girl to woman was complete.*
• TRANSITION + NOUN **period, process** | **phase**
• PREP. **during (the) ~** *He will remain head of state during the transition to democracy.* **in ~** *The country is in transition from an agricultural to an industrial society.* | **~ between** *This training course aims to smooth the transition between education and employment.* **~ from, ~ to**
• PHRASES **a period of transition, a process of transition, a state of transition**

translate *verb*

1 change sth from one language to another
• ADV. **literally** *'Tiramisu' literally translates as 'pull-me-up'.* | **accurately, correctly** | **freely, loosely, roughly** | **generally, normally, usually** | **variously** *a Greek word*

variously translated as 'summit', 'top' and 'finishing stroke'
• VERB + TRANSLATE **attempt to, try to** | **be difficult to** *This word is difficult to translate.*
• PREP. **as** *The word 'sensus' can be translated as 'feeling'.* **for** *I don't speak Italian—can you translate for me?* **from** *The book has been translated from the Japanese by Livia Yamaguchi.* **into** *an expression that is difficult to translate into English*
• PHRASES **widely translated** *The novel has been widely translated.*

2 change into a different form
• ADV. **directly** | **effectively** | **easily** | **automatically** *Teacher expectations do not automatically translate themselves into student results.*
• VERB + TRANSLATE **attempt to, try to** *trying to translate the theory into simple concepts* | **be difficult to**
• PREP. **into** *A small increase in local spending will translate into a big rise in council tax.*
• PHRASES **translate sth into action/practice** *attempting to translate these ideas into action*

translation *noun*

• ADJ. **accurate, correct, exact** | **approximate, free, rough** | **direct, literal, straight, word-for-word** | **English, Japanese, etc.** | **simultaneous** *There will be a simultaneous translation in English and Chinese.* | **automatic, machine** *advances in machine translation*
• VERB + TRANSLATION **do, make** *I've got this translation to do for Friday.* ◊ *She tried making her own translation of the sign without consulting a dictionary.* | **work on** | **read** | **survive** *The poems do not survive the translation into English.* | **lose sth in** *The irony is lost in translation.*
• TRANSLATION + VERB **read** *The translation of the Latin motto reads 'Not for oneself, but for others'.*
• TRANSLATION + NOUN **process** | **service,   work** | **facilities** | **exercise** | **equivalent**
• PREP. **for** ~ *Each unit of the course ends with sentences for translation.* **in** ~ *I read the book in translation, not in the original Norwegian.* | ~ **into** *Simultaneous translation into English is available to delegates.*

translator *noun*

• ADJ. **Dutch, Japanese, etc.** | **professional** | **freelance** *working as a freelance translator*
• TRANSLATOR + VERB **translate from/into sth, work from/into sth** *translators working from Portuguese into English*
⇨ Note at JOB

transmission *noun*

1 sending out/passing on
• ADJ. **direct, indirect** | **one-way** *Classes are based on discussion rather than on the one-way transmission of knowledge.* | **onward, outward** *An extra copy of each document was supplied for onward transmission to head office.* | **data, information, voice** | **facsimile/fax** | **light, power** | **money** | **gas** | **cable, radio, satellite, television** | **analogue, digital** | **live, simultaneous** *There will be simultaneous transmission of the concert on TV and radio.* | **genetic, oral, person-to-person, sexual** | **herpes, HIV, malaria** | **cultural**
• VERB + TRANSMISSION **prevent**
• TRANSMISSION + NOUN **equipment, line, technology** | **mechanism, network, system** | **route** *The virus's usual transmission route is by sneezing.*
• PREP. ~ **among** *HIV transmission among homosexual men* ~ **between** *transmission between patients* ~ **by** *transmission by satellite* ~ **from,** ~ **to** *transmission from one aircraft to another* ~ **through** *HIV transmission through blood transfusion*
• PHRASES **a mode of transmission, a risk of transmis-**

sion *There is a risk of transmission of the virus between hypodermic users.*

2 TV/radio programme
• ADJ. **radio, television/TV** | **FM, long-wave, medium-wave, short-wave, UHF, VHF** | **live, satellite, stereo** | **test**
• VERB + TRANSMISSION **receive**
• PREP. ~ **from** *a live transmission from Sydney*

3 in a car, etc.
• ADJ. **automatic, manual** | **4-speed, 5-speed**
• TRANSMISSION + NOUN **system**

transmit *verb*

1 pass sth from one person to another
• ADV. **actively** | **easily, readily** | **genetically, sexually** *the study of genetically transmitted diseases*
• PREP. **from, through** *The disease cannot be transmitted through coughing or sneezing.* **to** *The infection can be transmitted from a mother to her baby.* **via** *The virus is easily transmitted via needles.*

2 send out TV programmes/electronic signals, etc.
• ADV. **automatically** | **electronically**
• PREP. **from, to** *automatically transmitting data from one part of the system to another*

transmitter *noun*

• ADJ. **radar, radio, television/TV** | **voice** *They discovered voice transmitters hidden in the wall.* | **FM, long-wave, medium-wave, short-wave, VHF** | **low-power, powerful** | **ground, hand-held, satellite**
• VERB + TRANSMITTER **be equipped/fitted with**
• TRANSMITTER + VERB **emit sth, send out sth** *The receiver picks up pulses emitted by the transmitter.*

transparent *adj.*

• VERBS **be, look** | **become**
• ADV. **extremely, very** | **completely, entirely, fully, perfectly, quite, totally** *They are so thin that they are quite transparent.* | **almost** *Her eyelids were blue and almost transparent.* | **fairly, rather, slightly**

transplant *noun*

• ADJ. **bone-marrow, heart, heart-lung, kidney, liver, etc.** | **double, multi-organ, multiple**
• VERB + TRANSPLANT **have, undergo** *She will have to have a heart-lung transplant within 48 hours.* | **carry out, do, perform** | **reject** *It is likely that such a transplant will be rejected in older people.*
• TRANSPLANT + NOUN **operation, surgery** | **surgeon** | **team** | **centre, unit** | **donor** *A suitable transplant donor has been found.* | **candidate, patient, recipient**
• PREP. **for** ~ *a shortage of kidneys for transplant*

transplant *verb*

• ADV. **successfully**
• PREP. **from, into** *Organs are transplanted from donors into patients who need them.* **to** *The Dutch successfully transplanted trees to the East Indies.*

transport *noun*

• ADJ. **cheap, efficient** | **mass, public** *to travel by/on public transport* | **private** | **local** | **city, urban** | **rural** | **horse-drawn, motor** | **air, canal, ground, land, marine, rail, railway, river, road, sea, water** | **passenger** | **freight**
• VERB + TRANSPORT **use** | **arrange** | **provide** | **have access to** *people who have no access to private transport*
• TRANSPORT + NOUN **facilities, provision, services** | **infrastructure, network, system** | **business, company, group, industry, operator, organization** | **chairman,**

chief, executive, manager, officer, official | consultant, planner | project, scheme, strategy | legislation, policy | budget | minister, spokesman | authority/authorities, committee, department, ministry | needs, requirements | market, sector | costs, fares | allowance *Staff who transfer to a different office will receive a transport allowance.* | user | worker | links, routes | congestion | police | safety | strike | union

• PREP. **without ~** *The car broke down, leaving us without transport.*

• PHRASES **a form/means/method/mode of transport, your own transport** *Applicants for the job must have their own telephone and transport.*

trap *noun*

1 hidden equipment used for catching sb/sth
• ADJ. **animal, bear, man, mouse** (also **mousetrap**), etc. | **gin, pit/pitfall** | **radar, speed** *Slow down—there are speed traps along this stretch of road.*
• VERB + TRAP **be/get caught in** | **catch sth in** | **free sth from** *The fox had managed to free itself from the trap.* | **lay, set** | **bait** *Mousetraps are traditionally baited with cheese.*

2 sth that tricks you; unpleasant situation
• ADJ. **hidden, obvious** | **potential** | **booby** | **deadly** | **death, debt, poverty, unemployment** *The overhead cable is a potential death trap for birds.* | **offside** (in football)
• VERB + TRAP **lay, set** | **spring** | **lure sb into** | **catch sb in** | **be/get caught in, fall into, stumble into, walk into** *It is easy to fall into the trap of taking out a loan you cannot afford.* | **avoid** | **fear, suspect**

trappings *noun*

• ADJ. **external, outward, visible** *She scorns the visible trappings of success, preferring to live unnoticed.*
• PHRASES **all the trappings** *They enjoyed all the trappings of wealth.* **the trappings of power/success**

trauma *noun*

• ADJ. **major, severe** | **emotional, physical, psychological** | **childhood** *The phobia may have its root in a childhood trauma.*
• VERB + TRAUMA **go through, suffer** | **get over, recover from**

traumatic *adj.*

• VERBS **be** | **become, get**
• ADV. **deeply, extremely, particularly, really, very** *this deeply traumatic incident in his past* | **fairly, quite, rather**

travel *noun*

• ADJ. **air, bus, car, coach, rail, sea, train** | **foreign, international, overseas, world** | **long-distance** | **business** | **leisure** | **cheap, concessionary, free** | **first-class** | **high-speed** | **return** | **frequent** *The job involves frequent travel.* | **space, time**
• TRAVEL + NOUN **agency, business, company, firm, industry** | **arrangements, plans** | **allowance, costs, expenses** | **insurance** | **document, documentation** | **itinerary** | **time** *The new bypass will reduce travel time to the airport.* | **sickness** | **book, brochure, guide, writer**
• PREP. **~ from, ~ to** *The price includes return rail travel from London Victoria to Dover.*

travel *verb*

• ADV. **fast** *News travels fast these days.* | **slowly** | **regularly** *business people who travel regularly to the US* | **widely** *She travels widely in her job.* | **freely** *The dissidents were unable to hold meetings or travel freely.* | **independently** *I prefer travelling independently to going on a*

package holiday. | **together** | **separately** *We had to travel separately as we couldn't get seats on the same flight.* | **economy class, first class**, etc. *I always travel first class.* | **far, further (afield)** *for the holidaymaker who wants to travel further afield* | **abroad** *The job gives her the opportunity to travel abroad.* | **home** | **back, back and forth, down, downstream** *travelling back and forth across the Channel* | **north, northwards**, etc.
• VERB + TRAVEL **be able/unable to** | **be free to** | **want to, wish to** | **be forced to, have to** *Hundreds of hospital patients may have to travel long distances for treatment.* | **refuse to**
• PREP. **across, along, around/round, between, by, from, into, through, to** *We decided to travel by car.* ◊ *We travelled through France and into Germany.*
• PHRASES **freedom to travel, go travelling** *When I finished college I went travelling for six months* (= spent time visiting different places). **travel light** *She travels light, choosing to use as little equipment as possible.*

traveller *noun*

• ADJ. **business** | **commercial** *Her father was a commercial traveller who sold kitchenware.* | **frequent** *Attractive discounts are available to frequent travellers.* | **foreign, international** | **great, inveterate, keen, seasoned** | **adventurous, intrepid** | **independent** *Independent travellers often steer clear of the most touristy spots.* | **discerning** | **fellow** *I got to know my fellow travellers quite well in the course of the three-day journey.* | **tired, weary** | **unwary** *Stations can be dangerous places for the unwary traveller.* | **air, rail/railway, train** | **space** | **armchair** (= sb who doesn't travel but likes to read about distant places) *His travel books have given pleasure to generations of armchair travellers.*
• VERB + TRAVELLER **guide** *Local tribesmen earn their living guiding travellers across the mountains.*

tray *noun*

• ADJ. **laden, loaded** *a heavily laden tray* | **breakfast, coffee, drinks, hospitality, supper, tea** *Every hotel room has a colour TV, telephone and hospitality tray.*
• VERB + TRAY **bear, carry** | **pick up** | **balance** *He balanced the tray on his knees.* | **place, put down**
• PREP. **on a/the ~** *A waitress came in, carrying tea on a tray.* | **~ of** *waiters bearing trays of champagne*

treacherous *adj.*

• VERBS **be, look, prove** | **become** | **remain**
• ADV. **extremely, very** | **rather** | **notoriously** *the mountain's notoriously treacherous rocky crest*

tread *noun*

1 sound you make when you are walking
• ADJ. **firm, heavy** *I heard his heavy tread moving about upstairs.* | **light, soft** | **measured, slow, steady**
• VERB + TREAD **hear**
• TREAD + VERB **move**
• PREP. **with a... ~** *A policeman walked by with a slow, measured tread.*
• PHRASES **the tread of feet** *The streets have echoed to the tread of feet for more than ten centuries.*

2 on a tyre
• ADJ. **tyre, wheel** | **deep, shallow** | **worn**
• TREAD + VERB **be worn** *The tyre tread has been worn below the legal limit.*
• TREAD + NOUN **depth, pattern, width**
• PHRASES **a breadth/depth/width of tread**

tread *verb*

• ADV. **heavily** *He came down the stairs, treading as heavily as he could.* | **gently, lightly, softly** | **carefully, gin-**

gerly, **warily** *She trod gingerly. It would be risky to hurry.*
◇ *(figurative) The government will have to tread carefully
in handling this issue.* | **down** *She planted the seeds and
trod the earth down.*
● PREP. **in** *Billy trod in a big puddle.* **into** *Some cake
crumbs had been trodden into the carpet.* **on** *Be careful not
to tread on the flowers.*

treason *noun*

● ADJ. **high**
● PREP. **~against** *an act of high treason against the Eng-
lish crown*
● PHRASES **an act of treason**
⇨ Note at CRIME (for verbs)

treasure *noun*

1 collection of very valuable objects
● ADJ. **buried, hidden, lost, sunken** | **pirate, Roman,
royal** | **vast** *a vast treasure of medieval manuscripts*
● VERB + TREASURE **hunt for, look for, search for** |
dig up, discover, find, uncover, unearth | **hide**
● TREASURE + NOUN **chest, house, trove** *(figurative)
This book is a treasure house of information on Arctic
birds.* | **hunter, hunting**
● PHRASES **a hoard of treasure**
2 sth that is very valuable
● ADJ. **great, priceless** | **rare** | **ancient** | **forgotten, hid-
den, secret, unexpected** *Many forgotten treasures have
been discovered in the attics of old houses.* | **archaeo-
logical, historic, historical** | **art, artistic, cultural** |
church | **family** | **national**
● VERB + TREASURE **discover, find, uncover, unearth**

treasurer *noun*

● ADJ. **deputy** | **honorary** *the honorary treasurer of the
rugby club* | **corporate**
● VERB + TREASURER **act as, be, serve as** *He agreed to
act as treasurer.* | **appoint, appoint sb (as), elect, elect
sb (as)** | **resign as, retire as**
● PHRASES **treasurer's report** *The treasurer's report
gives a breakdown of the club's income and expenditure.*

treat *noun*

● ADJ. **great, real, special** | **little** *I like to give the girls a
little treat every now and then.* | **occasional, rare** | **anni-
versary, birthday, Christmas, holiday** | **family** | **tasty**
Snails are a tasty treat for hedgehogs.
● VERB + TREAT **give sb** | **deserve**
● PREP. **as/for a~** *We took the kids to the zoo for a special
treat.*
● PHRASES **be in for a treat/have a treat in store** *If their
latest album is half as good as their last one, we've a real
treat in store.*

treat *verb*

1 handle sb/sth in a particular way
● ADV. **equitably, fairly, humanely, kindly, leniently,
sympathetically, well** | **abominably, badly, harshly,
roughly, shabbily, unfairly, unjustly** *They treat their ani-
mals quite badly.* | **seriously** *These allegations are being
treated very seriously indeed.* | **differently** | **separately**
● VERB + TREAT **tend to** *Parents still tend to treat boys
differently from girls.*
● PREP. **as** *the tendency to treat older people as helpless
and dependent* **like** *Don't treat me like a child!* **with** *He
treated the idea with suspicion.*
● PHRASES **a tendency to treat sb/sth**
2 give sb medical treatment
● ADV. **easily** | **successfully** | **surgically**
● VERB + TREAT **be difficult to** | **use sth to**

● PREP. **for** *She was treated for cuts and bruises.* **with** *We
can treat this condition quite successfully with antibiotics.*
3 use a substance to protect sth
● ADV. **chemically** *Chemically treated hair can become
dry and brittle.*
● PREP. **for** *You need to treat this wood for woodworm.*
with *The timber has been treated with chemicals to preserve it.*

treatment *noun*

1 way you behave towards sb/deal with sth
● ADJ. **favourable, preferential, special, VIP** *She was
given the VIP treatment after winning gold for her country
at the Sydney Olympics.* | **generous, lenient** | **equal, fair**
| **good, humane** | **sensitive, sympathetic** | **discrimin-
atory, unequal, unfair, unjust, unkind** | **brutal, cruel,
degrading, harsh, ill-, inhuman, inhumane, rough, violent** *He claims he suffered ill-treatment at the hands of
prison officers.* | **shabby** *You shouldn't put up with such
shabby treatment.*
● VERB + TREATMENT **get, have, receive, suffer** | **de-
serve** *He had done nothing to deserve such cruel treat-
ment.* | **give sb, mete out (to sb)** *The treatment meted out
to captured soldiers was harsh.* | **put up with**
2 medical care
● ADJ. **emergency, immediate, on-the-spot, prompt,
urgent** | **follow-up, further** | **long-term** | **effective, suc-
cessful** | **conventional, orthodox** | **alternative, holis-
tic, homoeopathic** | **hospital** | **inpatient, outpatient** |
free, NHS | **private** | **specialist** | **dental, medical, psy-
chiatric, veterinary** | **drug, hormone** | **operative, surgi-
cal** | **non-operative, non-surgical** | **laser** | **dietary, nu-
tritional** | **beauty, hair**
● QUANT. **course**
● VERB + TREATMENT **get, have, receive, undergo** *She
is still undergoing medical treatment.* | **administer, give
sb, provide (sb with)** *Paramedics are to have extra train-
ing in administering on-the-spot treatment.* | **need, re-
quire** | **seek** *When his depression worsened, he decided to
seek treatment.* | **advise, prescribe, recommend, sug-
gest** | **refuse** | **benefit from, respond to** *He responded
well to treatment and is now walking again.*
● TREATMENT + NOUN **decision, option** | **centre, room**
| **method, procedure, technique** | **course, plan, pro-
gramme, regime, regimen, schedule**
● PREP. **in ~** *He's in treatment for cocaine addiction.* |
~for *She is receiving treatment for a heart condition.*
3 process for cleaning/protecting sth
● ADJ. **sewage, surface, water** *Galvanizing is a common
surface treatment for steel.*
● TREATMENT + NOUN **facility, plant, works**
4 discussion of a subject, work of art, etc.
● ADJ. **definitive, exhaustive, systematic** | **lengthy** |
cursory, superficial | **philosophical, theoretical**

treaty *noun*

● ADJ. **global, international, state, union** | **bilateral,
multilateral** | **formal** | **draft** | **commercial, economic,
military, political** | **unequal** | **cooperation, friendship** |
non-aggression, peace | **arms, disarmament, non-
proliferation, test ban** *A multilateral nuclear test ban
treaty was to be signed.* | **defence** | **extradition**
● VERB + TREATY **agree on/to** | **draw up, prepare** |
negotiate | **be/become a party to, conclude, enter into,
finalize, make, sign** *In September 1871 Japan entered into
a commercial treaty with China.* | **accept, approve, rat-
ify, vote for** *All the members have voted to ratify the treaty.*
| **reject, vote against** | **condemn, criticize, oppose** |
amend, review, revise | **adhere to** | **be in breach of,
breach, break, violate** *The new law may be in breach of
the Treaty of Rome.* | **abrogate, repudiate** | **enforce** |
impose *The people felt the treaty had been imposed on*

them by their government. | **be bound by** | **be laid down by/in** *the criteria laid down in the treaty*
• TREATY + VERB **come into force** *The treaty comes into force at midnight on December 31.* | **provide for** *The treaty provides for UN inspection of all countries' weapons systems.* | **guarantee sth** | **govern sth, regulate sth** | **create sth, establish sth** | **recognize sth** | **declare sth** | **require sth** | **ban sth, prohibit sth** | **draw criticism** *The treaty has drawn criticism from opposition groups.*
• TREATY + NOUN **party** | **amendment, changes, revision** | **provision** | **terms** | **document, text** | **law** | **commitment, obligation** | **rights** | **relations, relationship**
• PREP. **by** ~ *Certain areas had been ceded by treaty.* **under a/the** ~ *These arrangements under the treaty apply to the whole of Europe.* | ~**between** *a bilateral treaty between the US and Mexico* ~ **with** *The government concluded a peace treaty with the rebels.*
• PHRASES **an article/a clause of a treaty, the provisions/terms of a treaty, the ratification of a treaty**

treble *verb* (*also* **triple**)

• ADV. **more than** | **almost, nearly**
• PREP. **in** *Some goods have almost trebled in price.* **to** *The figure has more than trebled to 67 per cent.*

tree *noun*

• ADJ. **deciduous, evergreen** | **coniferous** | **native** | **exotic, tropical** | **ornamental** | **forest, woodland** | **big, great, high, huge, large, massive, mighty, tall** | **low, small, stunted** | **mature** | **bare, leafless** | **shady** *We sat beneath a shady tree.* | **shade** *It was a small town of dust lanes and wide shade trees.* | **hollow** | **gnarled** *a gnarled old apple tree* | **fruit** | **apple, peach, pear, etc.** | **beech, elm, oak, willow, etc.** | **Christmas**
• QUANT. **clump, copse, grove** | **avenue, belt, line**
• VERB + TREE **plant** | **climb** | **chop down, cut down, fell** *Protesters formed a human blockade to stop loggers felling trees.* | **uproot** *The floods left a tide of mud and uprooted trees.* | **prune**
• TREE + VERB **grow** | **stand** *An enormous oak tree stands at the entrance to the school.* | **line sth** *Palm trees line the broad avenue.* | **sway** *Trees swayed gently in the breeze.* | **be blown down, blow down** | **produce sth** *The tree produces tiny white blossoms.*
• TREE + NOUN **bark, branch, leaves, root, stump, trunk, tops** (*also* **treetops**) | **canopy** *dappled shafts of light which struggled through the tree canopy* | **cover** *Tree cover would prevent further soil erosion.* | **felling, planting** | **species** | **line** (*also* **treeline**) *Above the treeline take a grassy path leading steeply towards the summit.* | **belt** *The tree belt around the fields acts as a windbreak.* | **growth** | **rings** *The forest can be dated by studying tree rings.* | **damage** *tree damage caused by acid rain* | **nursery** *He bought tools and seeds with the aim of setting up a tree nursery.* | **surgeon**
• PREP. **in a/the** ~ *a bird in a tree* **on a/the** ~ *fruit on a tree* **under a** ~ *We sat under a tree, in the shade.* **up a/the** ~ *The cat got stuck up a tree.*

trek *noun*

• ADJ. **long, marathon** | **100-kilometre, 20-mile, etc.** | **3-day, 10-hour, etc.** | **arduous, hard**
• VERB + TREK **go on, make, take** *The family made the long trek west in 1890.*
• PREP. **on a/the** ~

tremble *verb*

• ADV. **badly, violently** | **helplessly, involuntarily, uncontrollably** | **a little, slightly** | **inside**
• VERB + TREMBLE **begin to, start to** *I began to tremble uncontrollably.* | **make sb** *The thought made him tremble inside.*

• PREP. **at** *She trembled at the thought of going back through those prison doors.* **with** *trembling with anger*
• PHRASES **tremble all over, tremble from head to foot/toe, tremble like a leaf**

tremor *noun*

1 small earthquake
• ADJ. **minor, slight** | **severe** | **earth**
2 shaking movement
• ADJ. **faint, slight, small, tiny** *He felt a tiny tremor of excitement as he glimpsed the city lights.* | **violent** | **uncontrollable** | **nervous** | **icy**
• VERB + TREMOR **send** *Her expression sent an icy tremor through him.* | **feel** *She felt a tremor run down her back when she saw him.* | **control** *He couldn't control the tremor in his voice.*
• TREMOR + VERB **run** *A tremor ran through the audience.* | **shake sb/sth** *An uncontrollable tremor shook his mouth.*
• PREP. **with/without a** ~ *He managed to make his short speech without a tremor.* | ~**of** *a tremor of fear*

trench *noun*

• ADJ. **deep, narrow, shallow** | **muddy** | **defensive** | **enemy** | **communication, front-line**
• VERB + TRENCH **dig**
• TRENCH + NOUN **warfare**
• PREP. **in the** ~ *life in the trenches in the First World War*

trend *noun*

• ADJ. **strong** | **consistent, constant, steady** | **accelerating, growing, increasing** | **underlying** *Despite this month's disappointing figures, the underlying trend is healthy.* | **dominant, main, major, prevailing** | **gradual** | **clear, marked** | **general** | **apparent, discernible** | **global, national, international, universal, worldwide** | **wider** *The increase in crime in London was just part of a wider trend.* | **positive, upward** | **downward, negative** | **contrary, opposite** | **healthy, welcome** | **adverse, dangerous, disturbing, unfortunate, worrying** | **fashion** | **demographic, population** | **cultural, social** | **evolutionary, historical** | **economic, market** | **growth, inflationary** *The latest figures show a clear growth trend in the service sector.*
• VERB + TREND **begin, create, set, start** *In the 1960s, Britain set the fashion trends.* | **continue** | **follow** *We are following the American trend towards more flexible working conditions.* | **reinforce** | **buck, counteract, go against** *efforts to buck the current downward trend in sales* | **reverse** | **halt** | **detect, notice** | **indicate, reflect, show, suggest** *The data indicates a trend towards earlier retirement.*
• TREND + VERB **develop, emerge** | **continue** | **indicate sth, reflect sth, suggest sth** *Current trends suggest that car traffic will continue to grow.* | **grow**
• PREP. ~ **away from** *a trend away from narrow specialization* ~ **for** *A trend for romance and nostalgia has emerged.* ~ **in** *future trends in the volume of employment* ~**towards** *the trend towards privatization*

trial *noun*

1 in a court of law
• ADJ. **fair** *The men claim they did not receive a fair trial.* | **unfair, full** | **criminal** | **fraud, murder, rape** | **jury** | **crown court, high court, supreme court** | **civil** | **public** | **show** *A series of show trials of former senior officials of the ousted regime took place.* | **summary** *The rebels were brutally executed after summary trials.* | **controversial, notorious, sensational**
• VERB + TRIAL **come to, face, go on, go to, stand** *He never came to trial for the robbery.* ◇ *She died before the*

case came to trial. ◇ *A man has gone on trial accused of murdering his girlfriend.* | **bring sb to, commit sb for, put sb on** *Four people had been arrested and committed for trial.* | **await** *He is in prison awaiting trial on drugs charges.* | **attend** *As a journalist he attended every murder trial of note.* | **order** *The judge ordered a new trial on the grounds that evidence had been withheld.* | **adjourn** | **halt, stop** *The judge halted the trial when it emerged witnesses had been threatened.* | **tell** (in a news report) *Murder trial told of horrific attack.*

• TRIAL + VERB **proceed, take place** | **begin, open** | **continue, resume** | **collapse** *The trial collapsed after a key prosecution witness admitted lying.*

• TRIAL + NOUN **court, judge, jury, lawyer** | **verdict** | **procedure, proceedings, process**

• PREP. **at the ~** *More than a hundred witnesses gave evidence at the trial.* **during the ~** *The letters that were shown during his trial turned out to be forgeries.* **on ~** *She is presently on trial at the Old Bailey.* **without ~** *Opposition leaders had been jailed without trial.* | **~ by** *The president faces trial by television tonight when he takes part in a live debate.* **~ for** *She faces trial for murder.* **~ over** *Three people are to stand trial over the deaths of a young couple.*

2 act of testing sb/sth

• ADJ. **clinical, experimental, field** *If clinical trials are successful the drug could be on the market early next year.* | **full-scale, large-scale** | **controlled, double-blind, randomized** | **free, home** *We've got this vacuum cleaner on ten days' free trial.* | **speed** | **Olympic, rowing, soccer, etc.**

• VERB + TRIAL **carry out, conduct** | **take part in** | **have** *He had a trial with Chelsea when he was young.*

• TRIAL + VERB **show sth** *The trial showed a dramatic reduction in side effects.*

• TRIAL + NOUN **period** *She agreed to employ me for a trial period.* | **run** *They are treating the trip as a trial run for their 500-mile sponsored ride later this month.* | **data, results** | **project, scheme** | **game** | **separation** *The couple agreed on a trial separation.*

• PREP. **under ~** *A new stocktaking system is currently under trial at the supermarket.*

• PHRASES **on a trial basis** *The new system will be introduced on a trial basis.* **trial and error** *We discovered the ideal mix of paint by trial and error.* **a trial of strength** *The dispute was regarded as a trial of strength by the unions.*

3 experience/person that causes difficulties

• ADJ. **sore** *She was a sore trial to her family at times.*

• PREP. **~ to**

• PHRASES **trials and tribulations** *the trials and tribulations of married life*

triangle *noun*

1 shape

• ADJ. **equilateral, isosceles, right-angled, scalene**

• VERB + TRIANGLE **construct** (*technical*), **draw** *Use your protractor to construct an equilateral triangle.* | **form** | **cut sth into** *I cut the sandwiches into triangles.*

• PHRASES **the apex of a triangle**

2 musical instrument

⇨ Special page at MUSIC

tribe *noun*

• ADJ. **aboriginal, indigenous, native** | **desert, forest, hill** | **nomadic** | **backward, primitive** | **barbaric, hostile, warring**

• VERB + TRIBE **belong to**

• PHRASES **a member of a tribe**

tribunal *noun*

• ADJ. **independent** | **international, local, village** | **higher, inferior** | **industrial, military, transport, war crimes** | **appeal/appeals, appellate, arbitral, arbitration, complaints, disciplinary, judicial**

• VERB + TRIBUNAL **set up** *A war crimes tribunal was set up to prosecute those charged with atrocities.* | **go to** *The dismissed workers decided to go to a tribunal.* | **apply to** | **refer sth to** *The case was referred to an industrial tribunal.* | **appear before/at** | **tell** *She told the tribunal that she was a victim of sex discrimination.*

• TRIBUNAL + VERB **be in session, hold a session** *The tribunal held its first session later that month.* | **hear sth** | **conclude sth, decide sth, find sth** *The tribunal found for her employers* (= judged that they were right). | **settle sth** *The dispute was settled by a tribunal.* | **order sth, rule sth** | **dismiss sth**

• TRIBUNAL + NOUN **decision** | **hearing** | **procedure, proceedings** | **representation** | **chairman, member**

• PREP. **at a/the ~** *The police gave evidence at the tribunal.* **before a/the ~** *No legal aid was available to cover representation before tribunals.* **by ~** *The fee for the player will be decided by tribunal.*

tributary *noun*

• TRIBUTARY + VERB **feed sth** *The Thames is fed by several small tributaries.*

tribute *noun*

1 sth you say/do to show you respect/admire sb/sth

• ADJ. **anniversary, birthday, centenary** | **final, last** | **fitting** | **lasting** | **affectionate, emotional, moving, warm** | **generous, glowing, handsome, special** | **silent** *Thousands of people stood in silent tribute to the dead president.* | **floral** *Floral tributes were piled up outside the church.*

• VERB + TRIBUTE **pay** *The couple paid tribute to the helicopter crew who rescued them.* | **lead** *The prime minister led the tributes to 'a great statesman and a decent man'.*

• TRIBUTE + VERB **flood in** *Tributes flooded in when her death was announced.*

• TRIBUTE + NOUN **album, concert**

2 sign of how good sb/sth is

• ADJ. **great, remarkable**

• PREP. **~ to** *The bridge is a remarkable tribute to the skill of the Victorian railway engineers.*

trick *noun*

1 deception

• ADJ. **cheap, dirty, knavish, mean, nasty, rotten** *The party chairman accused the opposition of dirty tricks in their election campaign.* | **stupid** | **funny** | **little** | **con/confidence**

• VERB + TRICK **play, pull, try, use, work** *We decided to play a little trick on the teacher.* | **fall for** *She won't fall for such a stupid trick.* | **learn** *He's learnt a trick or two in his time working in the tax office.*

• TRICK + VERB **work**

• TRICK + NOUN **question**

• PHRASES **a trick of the light** *A trick of the light made it look like she had a moustache.*

2 best way of doing sth

• ADJ. **special** | **useful**

• PREP. **~ of** *the trick of getting out red wine stains* **~ to** *There's no trick to it—you just need lots of practice.*

• PHRASES **the trick is to ...** *The trick is to keep your body still and your arms relaxed.* **the tricks of the trade**

3 skilled act

• ADJ. **clever, difficult** | **card, conjuring, disappearing, magic** | **party**

• VERB + TRICK **do, perform** | **learn** | **teach**

• TRICK + VERB **work**

• TRICK + NOUN **photography** | **ending**

trickle noun

● ADJ. **small, thin** | **constant, steady** *a constant trickle of water* | **slow** | **mere** *The flood of offers of help had dwindled to a mere trickle.*
● VERB + TRICKLE **dwindle to, slow to**
● PREP. **~of** *a trickle of blood*

trigger noun

● VERB + TRIGGER **pull, squeeze** | **tighten on** *Her finger tightened on the trigger as she heard footsteps approaching.*
● TRIGGER + NOUN **finger**
● PHRASES **have your finger on the trigger** (= to be ready to shoot)

trim verb

● ADV. **carefully, neatly** *his neatly trimmed moustache* | **away, off** *Trim away the lower leaves.* | **into** *trimming the bush into a heart shape*
● PHRASES **get/have your hair trimmed**

trip noun

● ADJ. **extended, long** | **brief, little, quick, short** | **day, overnight, weekend** *We went on a day trip to the seaside.* | **frequent, occasional, rare, regular** *He makes frequent trips to Poland.* | **annual, weekly, etc.** | **forthcoming** | **fantastic, good, great, nice, pleasant, successful** | **memorable** | **abortive, fruitless** | **successful** | **return, round** *From London to Oxford and back is a round trip of over a hundred miles.* | **foreign, overseas** | **round-the-world, world** | **European, Japan, etc.** | **boat, coach, cycle, etc.** | **business, fishing, pleasure, shopping, sightseeing** | **school** *a school trip to the Science Museum* | **field** *a geography field trip to study a limestone landscape* | **study**
● VERB + TRIP **be (away) on, go on, make, take** *She's away on a business trip.* ◇ *From here visitors can take a boat trip along the coast to Lundy Island.* | **have** *Did you have a good trip?* | **come back from, return from** | **be back from** *He's just back from a trip to New York.* | **arrange, organize, plan** | **book** | **cancel** | **extend** | **cut short** *I had to cut short my trip when my wallet was stolen.* | **enjoy** *Enjoy your trip!*
● PREP. **~by** *a five-minute trip by taxi* **~to** *a trip to Tokyo*
● PHRASES **a trip abroad** *My last trip abroad was two years ago.* **the trip home** *The trip home took us five hours!* **the trip of a lifetime** *They saved for years for their trip of a lifetime to Hawaii.*

trip verb

1 knock your foot on sth and fall
● ADV. **almost, nearly** | **over, up** *One of the boys tripped over and crashed into a tree.* ◇ *Be careful or you'll trip up.*
● PREP. **on** *She tripped on the loose stones.* **over** *I nearly tripped over the cat.*
● PHRASES **trip and fall** *Don't leave toys on stairs where someone could trip and fall.*

2 walk lightly
● ADV. **lightly** | **out**
● PREP. **along** *tripping along the path* **down** *She came tripping lightly down the stairs.* **up**
● PHRASES **come tripping**

triple verb

⇨ See TREBLE

triumph noun

● ADJ. **great, major, remarkable, resounding** | **little, minor** | **final, ultimate** | **latest, new** *Hollywood's favour-*

ite actor was modest about his latest triumph. | **diplomatic, election, electoral, military, political** | **personal**
● VERB + TRIUMPH **score** *The union scored a triumph in negotiating a minimum wage within the industry.* | **hail sth as, see sth as** *They hailed the signing of the agreement as a major diplomatic triumph.*
● PREP. **in ~** *The leading runner raised his arms in triumph.* | **~against** *their recent triumph against Brazil* ◇ *triumph against seemingly insuperable odds* **~ for** *The match was a personal triumph for Rivaldo.* **~ in** *their triumph in the general election* **~ over** *Her Wimbledon victory was hailed as a triumph over adversity.*
● PHRASES **a moment of triumph, a sense of triumph**

triumph verb

● ADV. **eventually, finally, ultimately** *She was confident that she would ultimately triumph over adversity.*
● PREP. **over**

triumphant adj.

● VERBS **appear, be, feel, look, seem, sound** | **emerge, return** *The Democrats have emerged triumphant from the political crisis.*
● ADV. **positively** *There was a positively triumphant note in her voice.* | **almost** | **ultimately** *Hers is a moving and ultimately triumphant story.*

trivial adj.

● VERBS **appear, be, look, seem** | **consider sth, deem sth, regard sth as**
● ADV. **extremely, very** | **absolutely, completely** | **almost** | **a bit, comparatively, fairly, pretty, quite, rather, relatively** | **essentially** *making a few essentially trivial changes* | **apparently, seemingly** *Apparently trivial clues may turn out to be quite important.*

trolley noun

● ADJ. **laden, loaded** *The waiter was pushing a laden sweet trolley towards our table.* | **baggage, luggage, shopping** | **drinks, tea** | **dessert, sweet** | **hospital, supermarket**
● VERB + TROLLEY **load, pile** *Passengers with trolleys piled high with luggage waited at the check-in desk.* | **push, wheel**
● TROLLEY + NOUN **service** *On many trains, refreshments are provided by a trolley service.*
● PREP. **on a/the ~** *They brought breakfast to the room on a trolley.*

trombone noun

● ADJ. **muted** | **bass, tenor** | **slide**
⇨ Special page at MUSIC

troops noun

● ADJ. **crack, elite** | **additional, extra** | **armed** *a division of up to 6 000 heavily armed troops* | **allied, government, loyal** *troops loyal to the government* | **enemy, foreign, rebel** | **auxiliary, paramilitary, regular** | **combat, fighting** | **peacekeeping, security** | **airborne, ground** | **border, front-line, garrison**
● VERB + TROOPS **deploy, mass, send (in)** *They are massing troops on the border.* ◇ *The UN is sending peacekeeping troops into the trouble spot.* | **provide (sb with), supply (sb with)** *The British Army has provided troops for the UN all over the world.* | **withdraw** | **command, lead, order** *He ordered troops to shoot to kill if attacked.* | **call in** | **quarter, station** *Five hundred troops were quartered in a village just behind the front line.* | **transport** | **rally** | **train**
● TROOPS + VERB **fight (sb), kill sb** | **be based, be positioned, be posted, be stationed** *troops based in West*

Germany | **advance, march, move in, move into** sth *Allied troops were advancing on the capital.* | **arrive, cross (into)** sth, **enter** sth, **land, reach** sth *Russian troops crossed into Austrian territory.* | **mass** *Government troops have massed on the northern border.* | **guard** sth, **patrol** sth *troops patrolling the border* | **occupy** sth | **attack (sb), invade (sth), overrun** sth, **storm** sth, **surround** sth *Rebel troops stormed the presidential palace.* | **fire on** sb/sth, **open fire, shoot** sb | **pull out, withdraw**
• TROOP + NOUN **deployment, levels, numbers, presence** *Various figures for US troop presence in Europe were quoted.* | **reductions** | **movements** | **withdrawal** | **reinforcements** | **carrier, ship, train, transport** | **commander**
• PHRASES **the deployment of troops, the withdrawal of troops**

trophy noun

• ADJ. **major** | **coveted, prestigious, prized** | **quiz, racing, sporting, swimming, etc.** | **championship**
• VERB + TROPHY **lift, pick up, receive, take, win** *Britain has not lifted the trophy since it last hosted the event.* | **award, present** | **defend** *Portugal will be defending the trophy they won last year.*
• TROPHY + NOUN **cabinet** | **winner**
• PREP. **~for** *He picked up a trophy for best news editor.*

trot noun a trot

• ADJ. **brisk, fast, spanking** | **gentle**
• VERB + TROT **break into** *When the horses reached the field they broke into a brisk trot.* | **slow to**
• PREP. **at a~** *We set off at a fast trot.* **into a~** *He kicked his horse into a trot.*

trot verb

• ADV. **briskly, quickly** | **happily** | **obediently** *Anne trotted obediently beside her mother.* | **across, along, off, over** *He trotted off to greet the other guests.*
• PREP. **down, up** *She trotted quickly down the stairs.*

trouble noun

1 problems
• ADJ. **bad, big, deep, desperate, real, serious** *The company is in desperate trouble financially.* | **endless** | **domestic, family, marital** | **financial, money** | **political** | **back, heart, tummy, etc.** | **boyfriend, girl, man, etc.** *He was obviously upset, and muttered something about girlfriend trouble.* | **engine**
• VERB + TROUBLE **mean, spell** *She knew that a hygiene inspection could spell trouble for her restaurant.* | **have, suffer from** *He has had back trouble since changing jobs.* | **get (yourself) into, run into** *The firm soon ran into financial trouble.* | **keep out of, stay out of** | **pour out** *She poured out all her troubles to her mother.* | **cause, lead to** *The printer's causing trouble again.* | **avoid** | **forget, put behind you** *He put his past troubles behind him and built up a successful new career.*
• TROUBLE + VERB **come** *Trouble often comes when you're least expecting it.*
• PREP. **in ~** *When she saw the teacher coming towards her she knew she was in big trouble.* | **~for** *He got into trouble for not doing his homework.* **~with** *I've had endless trouble with my car.* ◇ *He is in trouble with the law again.*
• PHRASES **a cause/source of trouble, a history of ... trouble** *She has a history of back trouble.* **in times of trouble** *In times of trouble she always turns to her mum.* **trouble ahead** *I can see trouble ahead.*

2 arguing/violence
• ADJ. **crowd**
• VERB + TROUBLE **cause, make** *He had a reputation for making trouble in the classroom.* | **be asking for, be**

looking for, court, stir up *He was asking for trouble when he insulted their country.* ◇ *Fans wandered the town after the match looking for trouble.*
• TROUBLE + VERB **be brewing** *There was trouble brewing among the workforce.* | **blow up, flare (up)** *Trouble blew up when the gang was refused entry to a nightclub.*
• TROUBLE + NOUN **spot** *Extra journalists have been sent to the main trouble spots.*
• PREP. **~between** *trouble between the teachers*

3 extra work
• ADJ. **considerable, enormous, great** *They went to enormous trouble to make her stay a pleasant one.*
• VERB + TROUBLE **bring (sb), cause (sb), give sb, make, put sb to** *I don't want to make trouble for her.* ◇ *I don't want to put you to any trouble.* | **go to, take** *We took the trouble to plan our route in advance.* | **be worth** *Do you think it's worth the trouble of booking seats in advance?* | **save sb** *Why don't we bring a pizza to save you the trouble of cooking?* | **thank sb for** *Thank you very much for all your trouble.*
• PHRASES **be more trouble than it's worth** *Growing your own vegetables is more trouble than it's worth.*

trouble verb

• ADV. **deeply, greatly** *This latest news troubled him deeply.* | **hardly, scarcely**
• PHRASES **be troubled with** sth *He has been troubled with a knee injury.*

troubled adj.

• VERBS **be, feel, look**
• ADV. **deeply, greatly, particularly, very** | **vaguely** *She still felt vaguely troubled by it all.* | **financially** *financially troubled firms*
• PREP. **at/by** *He was deeply troubled by the news.*

trough noun

1 container for animal feed/water
• ADJ. **drinking, feeding** | **water** | **cattle, horse, pig**

2 low point
• ADJ. **deep**
• VERB + TROUGH **fall to, reach** *Inflation fell to a trough of 3.3%.*
• PHRASES **from peak to trough** *The stock market fell by 48% from peak to trough.* **the peaks and troughs** *the peaks and troughs of economic cycles*

trousers noun

• ADJ. **long** | **short** *I was still in short trousers (= still only a boy) at the time.* | **baggy** | **tight** | **bell-bottom, bootleg, drainpipe, flared** | **pyjama**
• QUANT. **pair**
• VERB + TROUSERS **pull on, pull up** | **drop, pull down** *He dropped his trousers in a rude gesture.*
• TROUSER + NOUN **bottoms, leg, pocket** *He tucked his trouser bottoms into his socks.*
• PREP. **in ~** *He disapproves of women in trousers.*
⇒ Special page at CLOTHES

trout noun

• ADJ. **fresh** | **wild** | **farmed** | **river, sea** | **smoked** | **brown, rainbow, salmon**
• VERB + TROUT **eat, have** | **bake, cook, fry, grill** | **catch, fish for, land, tickle** | **farm**
• TROUT + NOUN **fishing** | **farm, fishery** | **stream**
⇒ Special page at FOOD

truancy noun

• ADJ. **persistent**

- VERB + TRUANCY **combat, tackle** *measures to combat persistent truancy in our schools* | **reduce** | **condone** *parents who condone their children's truancy*
- TRUANCY + NOUN **level, rate**

truant *noun*

- ADJ. **persistent** | **school**
- VERB + TRUANT **play** *She often played truant and wrote her own sick notes.*
- TRUANT + NOUN **officer**

truce *noun*

- ADJ. **brief, temporary** *A temporary truce had been reached earlier that year.* | **permanent** | **three-day, week-long, etc.** | **fragile, uneasy** | **electoral, party, political**
- VERB + TRUCE **call, declare, offer, propose** *The guerrillas have called a one-month truce.* | **agree (to/on), conclude, make, negotiate, reach** *The priest helped to negotiate a truce between the warring sides.* | **maintain** | **break, violate**
- TRUCE + VERB **hold, last, prevail** | **collapse** *The two-day truce collapsed in intense shellfire.* | **expire, lapse** *They renewed the war as soon as the truce expired.*
- PREP. **during a/the ~** *during a wartime electoral truce* | **~ among/between** *An uneasy truce prevailed between them at dinner.* **~ with** *the fragile truce with France*
- PHRASES **a flag of truce**

truck *noun*

1 large heavy vehicle
- ADJ. **big, heavy** | **articulated, open** | **refrigerated** | **ten-ton, etc.** | **delivery, pick-up** | **farm** | **army, military** | **garbage, refuse** | **breakdown, dumper, fork-lift**
- QUANT. **convoy**
- VERB + TRUCK **drive** | **park** | **load, unload**
- TRUCK + VERB **rumble** *A convoy of heavy trucks rumbled past.* | **carry sth** *a truck carrying sacks of vegetables*
- TRUCK + NOUN **driver** | **load** *a truck load of grain*

2 open railway wagon
- ADJ. **railway** | **cattle, coal, goods**
- VERB + TRUCK **pull**

trudge *verb*

- ADV. **slowly** *trudging slowly back to the office* | **wearily** *He trudged wearily on down the road.* | **along, back, home, off, on** *trudging along in silence*
- PREP. **across, along, around, down, through, up** *We trudged slowly through the fields.*

true *adj.*

1 right or correct
- VERBS **be, ring, seem, sound** *Her explanation doesn't ring quite true.* | **come** *All her wishes came true.* ◇ *It was like a dream come true.* | **remain**
- ADV. **particularly, very** *This is particularly true of older women.* | **absolutely, perfectly, quite** *It's perfectly true that I didn't help much, but I was busy.* | **certainly** *While this is certainly true for some, it's not true for others.* | **by no means, far from, not at all** *This degree of inequality was by no means true of all Victorian marriages.* ◇ *'That's not true at all,' he said firmly.* | **hardly, not completely, not entirely, not quite, not strictly, scarcely** *It's hardly true to call cleaning windows a 'profession'.* ◇ *That's not strictly true, I'm afraid.* | **almost, more or less, pretty well** *The story is more or less true.* | **objectively**

2 faithful
- VERBS **be** | **remain, stay**
- ADV. **absolutely**
- PREP. **to** *She stayed true to her principles.*

trump *noun*

- TRUMP + NOUN **card** (*often figurative*) *Vienna's trump cards include concerts in the palaces where Mozart made music.* | **suit**
- ⇨ Note at CARD

trumpet *noun*

- ADJ. **muted** | **B♭, C, E♭, etc.**
- VERB + TRUMPET **blow**
- TRUMPET + VERB **blare, sound**
- TRUMPET + NOUN **blast, call, fanfare**
- PHRASES **a blast of the trumpet** *the shrill blast of a trumpet* **a fanfare/flourish of trumpets** *A wreath was laid on the monument to a fanfare of trumpets.*
- ⇨ Special page at MUSIC

truncheon *noun*

- ADJ. **rubber**
- VERB + TRUNCHEON **be armed with, carry** | **draw** | **beat sb with** *Some of the prisoners were beaten about the head with rubber truncheons.*

trunk *noun*

1 part of a tree
- ADJ. **thick** | **gnarled** | **fallen** | **rotting** | **tree**

2 trunks for swimming
- ADJ. **bathing, swimming**
- QUANT. **pair** *I need a new pair of swimming trunks.*
- ⇨ Special page at CLOTHES

3 strong box with a lid
- ADJ. **old** | **tin** | **steamer**
- VERB + TRUNK **pack, unpack**
- PREP. **in a/the ~**

trust *noun*

1 relying on sb/sth
- ADJ. **great** *They have placed great trust in him as a negotiator.* | **absolute, complete** | **blind, implicit** *They followed the instructions in blind trust that all would turn out well.* | **basic** | **mutual** | **sacred** *They accepted the responsibility as a sacred trust* (= sth that had been trusted to them). | **fragile** *the fragile trust that existed between them* | **misplaced** | **public** *the need to restore public trust*
- VERB + TRUST **have** *We have absolute trust in the teachers.* ◇ *Does the scheme have the trust and cooperation of the workers?* | **place, put** | **build (up), develop** | **earn, gain, win** | **abuse, betray** *He claimed the government had betrayed the trust of the British people.* | **lose** | **restore** | **be based on** *a relationship based on trust*
- TRUST + VERB **exist**
- PREP. **~ between** *efforts to promote mutual trust between nations* **~ in** *His trust in them was misplaced.*
- PHRASES **a breach of trust, a lack of trust, a position of trust** *As a teacher, you are in a position of trust.*

2 financial arrangement
- ADJ. **independent, self-governing** | **offshore, overseas** | **investment** | **unit** *Investing in a unit trust reduces risks for small investors.* | **charitable, family, hospital**
- VERB + TRUST **hold sth in/on, keep sth in** *The proceeds will be held in trust for the children until they are eighteen.* | **create, establish, set up** *Wealthy people can set up overseas trusts for their children.* | **invest in** | **administer, run**
- TRUST + NOUN **account, assets, fund** | **deed** | **status** | **manager** | **beneficiary, holder**
- PREP. **in ~** *His father put the money in trust for him until he was 21.* | **~ for** *the Cecil Houses Trust for old people*

trust *verb*

- ADV. **implicitly** *I trust you implicitly.* | **completely,**

fully | not entirely, not quite, not really *You can never entirely trust even a 'tame' leopard.*
• VERB + TRUST **can/could** *I knew I could trust John.* | **be prepared to, be willing to** | **be reluctant to** *I was reluctant to trust the evidence of my senses.*
• PREP. **to** *I stumbled along in the dark, trusting to luck to find the right door.* **with** *I'd trust her with my life.*
• PHRASES **not to be trusted** *He is not to be trusted with other people's money.* **tried and trusted** *tried and trusted techniques*

trustee *noun*

• ADJ. **joint** *They act as joint trustees of the fund.* | **sole** | **independent** | **public** | **professional**
• VERB + TRUSTEE **act as, be, serve as** | **appoint, appoint sb (as)** | **remove (sb as)** | **resign as**
• PREP. **~for** *They hold the land as trustees for the infant.*
• PHRASES **a board of trustees**

truth *noun*

1 what is true
• ADJ. **absolute, gospel** (*informal*), **honest** (*informal*), **real** *She takes everything she reads in the paper as gospel truth.* | **full, whole** *It still doesn't make sense to me—I don't think he's told us the whole truth.* | **exact, literal** | **naked, plain, simple** *The simple truth is he's lost his job.* | **underlying** | **awful, bitter, cruel, dreadful, hard, harsh, horrible, horrid, painful, sad, shocking, terrible, unpalatable, unpleasant, unwelcome** *the shocking truth about heroin addiction among the young* ◇ *The sad truth is he never loved her.* | **objective** | **empirical, historical, moral, poetic, psychological, religious, scientific, spiritual** *It's a good film but contains little historical truth.* | **divine**
• QUANT. **element, grain** *There may have been a grain of truth in what he said.*
• VERB + TRUTH **know** *So now you know the truth.* ◇ *If the truth be known, I was afraid to tell anyone.* | **admit, speak, tell (sb)** *He was reminded of his duty to speak the truth when questioned in court.* ◇ *I'm sure she's telling the truth.* ◇ *To tell you the truth, I'm rather dreading his return.* | **establish, discover, find out, get at, learn, reveal, uncover** *She was determined to discover the truth about her neighbours.* ◇ *The journalist protested that he was only trying to get at the truth.* | **guess** | **accept, acknowledge, face (up to)** | **doubt** *The police doubt the truth of his statement.* | **conceal, cover up, hide, suppress** *You've been hiding the truth from me!*
• TRUTH + VERB **be, lie** *We are examining the matter to see where the truth lies.* | **come out, emerge** *Towards the end of the letter the cruel truth emerged.* | **dawn on sb** *The awful truth suddenly dawned on her.*
• PREP. **in~** *She laughed and chatted but was, in truth (= in fact), not having much fun.* | **~about** *finding out the truth about her husband* **~behind** *What's the truth behind all the gossip?* **~in** *There is no truth in the rumour.*
• PHRASES **be economical with the truth** (= not to tell the whole truth), **nothing could be further from the truth** *I know you think she's mean, but nothing could be further from the truth.* **the quest/search for (the) truth, a ring of truth** *His explanation has a ring of truth to it.* **a seeker after truth** (*literary*) *seekers after divine truth* **the truth of the matter** *The truth of the matter is we can't afford to keep all the staff on.* **the truth will out** (*saying*) (= People will find out the true facts of a situation even if you try to keep them secret.)

2 fact that is true
• ADJ. **basic, central, common, essential, eternal, fundamental, general, great, important, profound, simple, ultimate, universal** *in search of the eternal truths of life* | **ancient** | **obvious, self-evident, undeniable** *We hold these truths to be self-evident …* | **underlying** | **half, par-**

tial *His evidence was a blend of smears, half truths and downright lies.* | **harsh, home, painful, unpalatable, unpleasant, unwelcome** *It's time we told him a few home truths about sharing a house.* | **necessary** | **moral, philosophical, scientific, spiritual** | **divine**
• VERB + TRUTH **establish, reveal, uncover** | **tell sb** | **accept, acknowledge, face up to**
• PREP. **~about** *She was forced to face up to a few unwelcome truths about her family.*

truthful *adj.*

• VERBS **be**
• ADV. **very** | **absolutely, completely** | **not entirely, not quite** *I don't think you are being entirely truthful.*
• PREP. **about** *She was completely truthful about her involvement in the affair.*

try *noun*

1 attempt
• ADJ. **good, nice** *Never mind—it was a good try. Better luck next time.* | **another**
• VERB + TRY **have** *Can I have a try?* | **give sth** *It looks difficult, but let's give it a try.* | **be worth** *It may not work, but it's certainly worth a try.*
• PREP. **~at** *She's having another try at the marathon.*

2 scoring move in rugby
• ADJ. **dazzling, excellent, good, great, splendid, superb, well-taken** | **opening** | **last-minute, late** | **decisive, winning** | **penalty** | **pushover**
• VERB + TRY **get, go over for, score** | **convert**
• PREP. **~against** *He scored three tries against New Zealand.* **~by/from** *an excellent try by winger Neil Lang*
⇨ Special page at SPORT

try *verb*

• ADV. **desperately, frantically, hard** *She was trying desperately to stay afloat.* ◇ *Sam was trying hard not to laugh.* | **gamely, manfully, valiantly** *trying valiantly to smile through her tears* | **clumsily** *clumsily trying to make amends* | **feebly** | **in vain, unsuccessfully, vainly**
• VERB + TRY **decide to** *I decided to try again.* | **be going to** *I hope you're not going to try and deny it.* | **be tempted to** *| be tempting to* | **let sb** *Can't you do it? Let me try.*
• PHRASES **be just/only trying to do sth** *I was just trying to help!* **give up trying** *I've given up trying to persuade her.* **try your best/hardest/utmost** *I tried my best not to laugh.*

T-shirt *noun*

• ADJ. **baggy, loose** | **long-sleeved, short-sleeved**
⇨ Special page at CLOTHES

tub *noun*

• ADJ. **bath** (also **bathtub**) | **hot**
• VERB + TUB **lie in, soak in** *I love soaking in a hot tub.* | **climb/get in** | **climb/get out of**

tuba *noun*

• ADJ. **muted** | **bass, tenor**
⇨ Special page at MUSIC

tube *noun*

1 long hollow pipe
• ADJ. **fine, narrow, thin** | **broad** | **hollow** | **flexible** | **closed, sealed** | **inner** (= in a bicycle tyre) | **fluorescent** (= a kind of light) | **aluminium, cardboard, copper, glass, metal, plastic, steel** | **discharge, drainage, suction** | **test** | **breathing, feeding, ventilation** | **capillary, bronchial, Fallopian, neural**

• PREP. down a/the ~ *pouring the liquid down the tube* **in/into a/the ~** *I put the poster back into its tube.* **through a/the ~** *He gave the lamb its food through a tube.* **up a ~**

2 the tube the Underground
• ADJ. **London**
• VERB + TUBE **go on, take, travel by/on**
• TUBE + NOUN **line, station, ticket, train**
• PREP. **by ~** *I go to work by tube.* **on the ~** *I bumped into him on the tube.*

tuck *verb*

• ADV. **carefully, discreetly, neatly | gently | firmly | cosily, safely** *The children were safely tucked up in bed.* | **away, in, up** *The boys tucked their shirts in.*
• PREP. **behind** *The loos were discreetly tucked away behind a screen of trees.* **inside** *He tucked the map inside his shirt.* **into** *He tucked his trousers neatly into his boots.* **under** *She tucked the newspaper under her arm.*

Tuesday *noun*

⇨ Note at DAY

tug *noun*

• ADJ. **good, sharp** *All it needed was a good tug.* | **gentle, little, slight | quick, sudden**
• VERB + TUG **give (sth) | feel**
• PREP. **with a ~** *She started the engine with one tug of the starter rope.* | **~ at** *She felt a sharp tug at her sleeve.* **~ on** *She gave a little tug on the rope.*

tug *verb*

• ADV. **gently | hard** *He tugged harder, but it was caught fast.*
• PREP. **at** *She tugged at his arm to get his attention.* **by** *He tugged me by the sleeve.*

tuition *noun*

• ADJ. **private | individual, one-to-one, personal | daily | extra | advanced | expert** *The students get expert tuition in small groups.* | **language, music, etc.**
• VERB + TUITION **give (sb), offer (sb), provide (sb with) | get, have, receive**
• TUITION + NOUN **fee**
• PREP. **under sb's ~** *She had become expert in Chinese cooking under the tuition of her aunt.* | **~ for** *tuition for beginners* ◇ *extra tuition for the exams* **~ from** *He is receiving tuition from a well-known artist.* **~ in** *tuition in Italian*

tulip *noun*

• ADJ. **dwarf | early, late, mid-season**
• TULIP + NOUN **bulb | fields**
⇨ Note at FLOWER (for verbs)

tummy *noun*

1 part of the body where food is digested
• ADJ. **empty, full**
• TUMMY + VERB **rumble**
• TUMMY + NOUN **ache, bug, trouble, upset**
• PREP. **in the/your ~** *I get a fluttery feeling in my tummy before meeting new people.*

2 front part of the body below the chest
• ADJ. **bulging, fat, flat**
• VERB + TUMMY **pull in**
• TUMMY + NOUN **muscles**
• PREP. **on the/your ~**

tumour *noun*

• ADJ. **cancerous | malignant | benign | primary | brain, breast, kidney, etc.**

• VERB + TUMOUR **diagnose | remove**
• TUMOUR + NOUN **cell, tissue | formation, growth | virus**
• PREP. **~ in** *a primary tumour in the breast* **~ on** *a malignant tumour on the eyelid*

tune *noun*

• ADJ. **little** *He hummed a little tune as he washed the dishes.* | **good, nice | familiar, popular, traditional, well-known, well-loved | catchy, memorable | lively, uplifting | dance, hymn | signature, theme**
• VERB + TUNE **give sb, hum, play (sb), sing, whistle** *She gave us a tune on the piano.* | **hum/sing along with | compose, write | pick out** *The kids were picking out a popular tune on the old piano.* | **carry, hold** *He wasn't allowed in the choir because he couldn't hold a tune.*
• PHRASES **to the tune of sth** *The crowd were singing 'Give us jobs, not more cuts!' to the tune of 'Happy Birthday To You'.*

tune *verb*

1 adjust an engine/a machine
• ADV. **permanently**
• PREP. **to** *a laser that is permanently tuned to the correct frequency*
• PHRASES **finely/highly tuned** *a finely tuned engine*

2 adjust a television/radio
• ADV. **in** *Don't forget to tune in to our special election programme this evening.*
• PREP. **for, to** *I tuned to the BBC for the late news.*
• PHRASES **badly tuned** *He heard everything through a screen of interference, like on a badly tuned radio.* **stay tuned** *Stay tuned for the news.*

tunnel *noun*

• ADJ. **long, short | narrow, wide | dark | subterranean, underground | connecting, entrance, escape, service | rail, railway, road | wind** *a wind tunnel for aerodynamic experiments*
• VERB + TUNNEL **go through, use | disappear into, enter, go into** *The train disappeared into a tunnel.* | **come out of | bore, build, construct, dig, excavate** *They've built a new tunnel through the mountain.* ◇ *The initial section of tunnel had to be dug by hand.*
• TUNNEL + VERB **run** *A service tunnel runs between the two buildings.*
• TUNNEL + NOUN **mouth, roof, wall**
• PREP. **through a/the ~**
• PHRASES **a labyrinth/maze/network/system of tunnels** *The badger sett had twelve entrances to what must have been a labyrinth of tunnels.*

turf *noun*

• ADJ. **green | soft, springy | artificial | hallowed, home** (of a sports pitch) *the hallowed turf of Wembley* ◇ *the team's first success of the season on home turf*
• QUANT. **piece, sod** *primitive cottages made of sods of turf and sticks*
• VERB + TURF **cut** *They still cut turf here for fuel.* | **lay** *laying turf to create a lawn*
• TURF + NOUN **fire**

turkey *noun*

• ADJ. **lean, tender | Christmas | traditional** *the traditional turkey with all the trimmings* | **frozen | oven-ready | stuffed | roast, smoked | boned, minced**
• VERB + TURKEY **breed | raise** *We raise turkeys mainly for the Christmas market.* | **eat, have | stuff | cook, roast | baste | carve**
• TURKEY + VERB **gobble** *Turkeys make a funny gobbling sound.*

- TURKEY + NOUN **farm** | **breast** | **dinner, lunch**
⇨ Special page at FOOD

turmoil noun

- ADJ. **constant** *Her mind was in a state of constant turmoil.* | **emotional, inner, mental** | **economic, political**
- VERB + TURMOIL **cause, plunge/send/throw sb/sth into** *Her emotional life was thrown into turmoil.*
- PREP. **in ~** *He came to a stop, his chest heaving, his thoughts in turmoil.* | **~ of** *a turmoil of emotions*
- PHRASES **a state of turmoil**

turn noun

1 act of turning sb/sth round
- ADJ. **full, half, quarter** *a full turn of the handle to the right* | **90-degree, 180-degree, etc.** | **quick** *a quick turn of his head*
- VERB + TURN **give sth** *Give the knob a turn.*

2 change of direction
- ADJ. **left/left-hand, right/right-hand** | **sharp** | **wide** | **sudden** | **three-point** (see also **U-turn**)
- VERB + TURN **do, make, negotiate** *She stopped talking as she negotiated a particularly sharp turn.*
- PHRASES **at every turn** (*figurative*) *At every turn I met with disappointment.* **a turn to the left/right** *He made a sudden turn to the right.* **twists and turns** (*figurative*) *trying to follow all the twists and turns of the plot*

3 (*also* **turning**) bend/corner in a road
- ADJ. **next** | **wrong**
- VERB + TURN **take** *He took a wrong turn and ended up on the coast road.* | **miss**
- PHRASES **a turn on the left/right** *Take the next turn on the right.* **twists and turns** *a lane full of twists and turns*

4 time when you must or may do sth
- VERB + TURN **have, take** *Can I have a turn?* ◇ *I'll take a turn making the dinner—you have a rest.* ◇ *The children took turns on the swing.* | **miss** *If you can't put any cards down you have to miss a turn.* | **give sb** *Give Sarah a turn on the swing.* | **wait** *Be patient and wait your turn!* | **come to** *By the time it came to my turn to sing, I was a bag of nerves.*
- TURN + VERB **come** *When my turn finally came, I was shaking with nerves.*
- PREP. **in ~** (= one after the other) *They gave their names in turn.* **in sb's ~** *She had not been friendly to Pete and he, in his turn, was cold to her when she came to stay.* **out of ~** (= before or after your turn) *I'm writing to you out of turn because I have some very important news.*

5 change
- ADJ. **dramatic, sudden, unexpected** | **different, new** | **downward**
- VERB + TURN **take** *Her career took an unexpected turn when she moved to New York.*
- PREP. **by ~(s)** *This movie is by turn* (= alternately) *terrifying and very funny.* **on the ~** (= changing) *Our luck is on the turn.*
- PHRASES **take a turn for the better/worse** *I'm afraid Grandma has taken a turn for the worse.* **a turn of events** *In a dramatic turn of events she took control of the company into her own hands.*

turning noun

⇨ See TURN

turning point noun

- ADJ. **crucial, major, real, significant** | **historic** *This win could prove to be a historic turning point* (= one that will be remembered) *in the fortunes of the team.* | **historical, political** *The industrial revolution was a major historical turning point* (= a turning point in history).

- VERB + TURNING POINT **be, mark, prove (to be)** | **see sth as** | **reach** *In 1914 the world reached a turning point in its history.*
- TURNING POINT + VERB **come** *The turning point came when reinforcements arrived from the south.*
- PREP. **at a ~** *The process of disarmament is at a crucial turning point.* | **~ in**

turn-off noun

- ADJ. **next**
- VERB + TURN-OFF **take** *Take the next turn-off.* | **miss, overshoot** *We were chatting and overshot our turn-off.*
- PREP. **~ for** *the turn-off for Leeds*

turnout noun

1 number of people who vote in an election
- ADJ. **high** | **low, poor** | **electoral, voter** *Voter turnout was high at the last election.*
- PHRASES **a decline/fall in turnout, an increase in turnout**

2 number of people who go to a meeting, match, etc.
- ADJ. **big, good, large** | **disappointing, poor**
- VERB + TURNOUT **attract** *The concert attracted a large turnout.*

turnover noun

1 amount of business a company does
- ADJ. **large** | **low, small** | **company, group** | **aggregate, combined, total** *The combined turnover of both businesses has doubled in the last two years.* | **gross, net** | **annual, daily, etc.** | **global, worldwide** | **market** | **capital** | **stock**
- VERB + TURNOVER **have** | **record** *The company recorded a turnover of £50 million last year.* | **boost, increase** | **reduce**
- TURNOVER + VERB **be up** | **be down** *Turnover was down compared with last year's figures.* | **double, grow, increase, rise** *The firm's UK turnover increased (by) 30% to £10 million.* | **drop, fall, slip** *Turnover fell from £12 million to £11 million.* | **reach sth** *Turnover reached $2 billion in the 12 months to September.* | **exceed sth, top sth** *The company's worldwide turnover exceeds $5 billion.*
- TURNOVER + NOUN **figure, growth, rate, tax**
- PHRASES **a decline/fall in turnover, an increase/a rise in turnover**
⇨ Special page at BUSINESS

2 rate at which people come and go from a job/place
- ADJ. **fast, high, rapid** | **low** | **labour, staff** | **population** *The inner city has a rapid population turnover.*
- VERB + TURNOVER **have**

tussle noun

- ADJ. **little** | **legal**
- VERB + TUSSLE **have** *Anna and her conscience had a little tussle.* | **be engaged in, be involved in**
- PREP. **in a/the ~** *He broke his leg in a tussle for the ball.* | **~ between** *a tussle between the country's parliament and government* **~ for** *Five teams are involved in the tussle for promotion.* **~ over** *a tussle over the closure of the local hospital* **~ with** *We are engaged in a legal tussle with a large pharmaceutical company.*

tutor noun

- ADJ. **good** | **experienced** | **professional** | **personal, private** | **senior** | **assistant** | **full-time, part-time** | **college, school, university** | **course** | **art, English, etc.**
- VERB + TUTOR **act as**
- PREP. **~ to** *Roger Ascham, tutor to Queen Elizabeth*
⇨ Note at JOB

tutorial noun

- ADJ. **group, individual**
- VERB + TUTORIAL **have** *I've got two tutorials today.* | **prepare for** | **go to** | **miss** | **give (sb)** *He gives one lecture and two tutorials a week.*
- TUTORIAL + NOUN **class, group**
- PREP. **at/during/in a/the~** | **~on** *a tutorial on the rise of the novel*

twang noun

- ADJ. **slight** | **nasal** | **American, Cockney, etc.**
- VERB + TWANG **have, speak with** *She had a slight Australian twang.* | **hear**
- PREP. **with a~** *The words came out with an Irish twang to them.*

twig noun

- ADJ. **dry** | **bare** | **dead** | **birch, willow, etc.**
- VERB + TWIG **break (off), snap (off)** *He broke off a twig from a willow tree and used it to shoo the flies away.*
- TWIG + VERB **break, snap** *The sharp sound of a twig snapping scared the badger away.*

twilight noun

- ADJ. **gathering, thickening**
- TWILIGHT + NOUN **world** *(figurative) the twilight world of the occult* | **zone** *(figurative) the twilight zone between living and merely existing* | **years** *(figurative) a forgotten man who spent his twilight years alone*
- PREP. **at~, in/into the~** *She walked away into the thickening twilight.*
- PHRASES **in the twilight of your career/life**

twin noun

- ADJ. **identical** | **fraternal, non-identical** | **conjoined, Siamese**
- QUANT. **pair** *a pair of identical twins*
- VERB + TWIN **expect** | **give birth to, have**
- TWIN + NOUN **boys, girls** *She had twin girls.* | **daughters, sons** | **brother, sister**

twinge noun

- ADJ. **sharp** | **little, slight** | **sudden**
- VERB + TWINGE **experience, feel, get, suffer** | **give sb** *The letter still gives him a twinge when he thinks of it.*
- PREP. **~of** *a twinge of guilt*

twinkle noun

- ADJ. **mischievous, wicked**
- PHRASES **a twinkle in sb's eye**

twist noun

1 act of twisting sth
- ADJ. **little, slight** | **quick, sharp** | **wry**
- VERB + TWIST **give sth** *Give the cap another twist—it's not on properly.*
- PREP. **~of** *He finished him off with a quick twist of the knife.* **~to** *a wry twist to her mouth*

2 change/development
- ADJ. **further, new** | **final, latest** *the latest twist in the saga of high-level corruption* | **bizarre, curious, dramatic, interesting, ironic, strange, unexpected** | **distinctive** | **cruel, vicious** *a cruel twist of fate* | **plot**
- VERB + TWIST **give sth** *The writer takes well-known fairy tales and gives them an ironic twist.* | **take** *The scandal has taken a new twist this week.*
- PREP. **in a~, with a~** *classic French dishes with a twist* (= with a difference) | **~in** *a twist in the plot* **~to** *In a bi-*

zarre twist to the evening the police came at eleven and arrested our host.
- PHRASES **a twist in the tail** *The story has a twist in the tail—six months later she married the husband of her victim.* **a twist of fate, twists and turns** *the twists and turns in the economy*

3 in a road, river, etc.
- ADJ. **sharp**
- PREP. **~in** *a sharp twist in the road*
- PHRASES **twists and turns** *the twists and turns of the river*

twist verb

- ADV. **slightly** *She twisted slightly in her chair to look up at him.* | **gently** *Gently twist off the green stalks.* | **violently** *She fired again and saw the creature twist violently.* | **bitterly, scornfully, wryly** *His mouth twisted bitterly.* | **away, off, together, up** *Her black hair was twisted up into a knot on top of her head.*
- PREP. **around/round** *I twisted the bandage round his leg.* **with** *His face was twisted with rage.*
- PHRASES **twist and turn** *The road twists and turns along the coast.* **twist (yourself) free** *He managed to twist himself free.* **twist sth out of shape** *Her mouth was twisted out of shape by grief.*

twitch noun

- ADJ. **nervous** | **slight** *His mouth gave a slight twitch.* | **involuntary** | **muscle, muscular**
- VERB + TWITCH **have** *He has a twitch in his right eye.* | **develop** | **give**

twitch verb

- ADV. **convulsively, violently** *The body twitched violently and then lay still.* | **uncontrollably** | **a little, slightly** | **nervously** *Her fingers twitched nervously.*
- PREP. **with** *His shoulders twitched with suppressed laughter.*

tycoon noun

- ADJ. **business, media, newspaper, property, publishing, shipping**

type noun

1 kind/sort
- ADJ. **distinct, well-defined** | **broad** *Two broad types of approach can be identified.* | **basic, common, conventional, standard, traditional** | **alternative** | **main, major, principal** | **diverse** | **extreme** | **personality, physical** | **hair, skin** | **blood, cell, tissue** | **product** | **habitat, rock, soil, vegetation**
- VERB + TYPE **identify** | **revert to** *The boss came back from holiday all relaxed and smiling, but now he's reverting to type.*
- PREP. **in~** *The recession is similar in type to that of ten years ago.* **of a~** *a country inn of a type that has all but vanished* | **~of** *There are various types of daffodil(s).*
- PHRASES **of its type** *This exercise is the hardest of its type.* **a range/variety of types**

2 person
- ADJ. **artistic, careful, City** (= a person who works in finance in the City of London), **creative, entrepreneurial, literary, old-fashioned** *The bar was crowded with City types in suits.* ◇ *He was the old-fashioned type, well-mannered and always in a suit and tie.*
- PHRASES **true to type** *True to type, Adam turned up an hour late.* **(not) your type** *She's not really my type—she's a bit too serious.*

3 printed letters
- ADJ. **bold, heavy** | **italic** | **roman**

● VERB + TYPE **print sth in, set sth in** *Key paragraphs of the report are set in italic type.*
● PREP. **in … ~** *The important words are in bold type.*

type *verb*

● ADV. **correctly | neatly | badly | quickly | furiously** *He was sitting at his desk typing furiously.* | **out, up** *I've written the report and will type it up next week.*
● PREP. **into** *She typed the details into the computer.* **on** *This letter was typed on an electronic typewriter.*
● PHRASES **closely typed** *300 proposals and amendments covering 78 closely typed pages*

typhoon *noun*

● TYPHOON + VERB **hit sth, strike sth** *The village was hit by a typhoon.* | **damage sth, destroy sth, devastate sth** *The plantation was devastated by a typhoon.*
● PREP. **in a/the ~** *His home was destroyed in a typhoon.*

typical *adj.*

● VERBS **be, look, seem | become | consider sth, regard sth as, take sth as** *You must not take this attitude as typical of English people.*
● ADV. **extremely, highly, very | absolutely, altogether, entirely, just** *That's altogether typical of Tom!* ◇ *They're going to be late? Now, isn't that just typical?* | **by no means, not necessarily** *East Anglia is by no means typical of rural Britain.* | **fairly, pretty, quite, rather**
● PREP. **of** *Julia is fairly typical of her age group.*

typing *noun*

● ADJ. **audio, touch**
● VERB + TYPING **do** *Could you do some typing for me?*
● TYPING + NOUN **error | course | skills | speed | pool** (= a group of people who share a company's typing work)

typist *noun*

● ADJ. **good | audio, copy, shorthand**
⇨ Note at JOB

tyranny *noun*

● ADJ. **petty**
● VERB + TYRANNY **be freed from, overthrow | impose** (*often figurative*) *An artist's need for money imposes the tyranny of popular taste.*
● PREP. **~ over** *her tyranny over her staff*

tyrant *noun*

● ADJ. **cruel, great | petty** *Some of the prison officers were petty tyrants.*
● VERB + TYRANT **overthrow**
● TYRANT + VERB **rule sth** *The country had long been ruled by tyrants.*
● PREP. **under a/the ~** *The kings of Sparta would not serve under the tyrants of Syracuse.*

tyre *noun*

● ADJ. **flat, punctured** *I got a flat tyre soon after setting off.* | **blown-out, burst | bald, worn | defective, illegal | spare | front | back, rear | nearside | offside | fat** *tough-looking trucks with fat tyres and reinforced springs* | **pneumatic | crossply, radial | whitewall | bicycle, car,** etc.
● QUANT. **set**
● VERB + TYRE **change, replace | inflate, pump up | deflate, let down** *Someone let the tyres down overnight as a mean joke.* | **fit, fit sth with** *This car is fitted with radial tyres.* | **blow, burst** *He was going so fast he blew a tyre.* | **patch, repair, retread** *He's patching the bike tyre that got a puncture yesterday.* | **check** *She checked the tyres and oil before setting off.* | **slash** *Vandals had slashed the tyres and broken the side mirror.*
● TYRE + VERB **deflate, go flat, get/have a puncture, puncture | blow (out), burst** *A back tyre blew after half an hour tearing along a rocky road.* | **crunch, screech, squeal** *The tyres crunched to a standstill on the gravel.* ◇ *She braked suddenly, her tyres squealing in protest.*
● TYRE + NOUN **mark, tracks | pressure | tread**
● PHRASES **a crunch/screech/squeal of tyres** *He roared up the drive with a screech of tyres.*

Uu

ugly *adj.*

1 unattractive
- VERBS **be, look**
- ADV. **extremely, hideously, incredibly, really, very** *The witch was hideously ugly.* | **almost** | **pretty, quite, rather**

2 dangerous/threatening
- VERBS **be, look, sound** | **get, turn**
- ADV. **really, very** | **pretty, quite** *A fight started and things got pretty ugly.* | **potentially**

ultimatum *noun*

- VERB + ULTIMATUM **deliver, give sb, issue, present (sb with), send** *The government denied that it had presented the union with an ultimatum.* | **get, receive** | **comply with** | **ignore** | **withdraw**
- ULTIMATUM + VERB **demand sth**

umbilical cord *noun*

- VERB + UMBILICAL CORD **clamp, cut, tie**
- UMBILICAL CORD + VERB **be** **(twisted/wound) around sb's neck**

umbrella *noun*

- ADJ. **furled, rolled** | **beach, sun** | **golf** | **nuclear, protective** (*both figurative*) *the American nuclear umbrella over Western Europe*
- VERB + UMBRELLA **open, put up, unfurl** | **let down** *She let down her umbrella and furled it.* | **fold, furl**
- UMBRELLA + NOUN **stand** | **body, group, organization** (*all figurative*) *an umbrella group including members of opposition parties* | **heading, name, term, title, word** (*all figurative*) '*Herb*' *is an umbrella term covering many types of plant.*
- PREP. **under an/the ~** *She was fast asleep under a big beach umbrella.* ◊ (*figurative*) *The two sectors combined under the umbrella of the Scottish Council.*

unable *adj.*

- VERBS **appear, be, feel, look, prove, seem** | **become** | **remain** | **find yourself, leave sb, make sb** *She found herself unable to meet his gaze.* ◊ *The accident left him unable to walk.* | **deem sth** *The road was deemed unable to cope with increased traffic.*
- ADV. **completely, quite, totally, utterly, wholly** | **increasingly** | **almost, nearly, virtually** | **apparently, seemingly** *He went on, apparently unable to stop.* | **genuinely** | **generally** | **temporarily** *Clare nodded, temporarily unable to speak.* | **still** | **constitutionally, physically** *He seemed constitutionally unable not to give his opinion on anything and everything.*
- PHRASES **unwilling or unable** *He remained silent, unwilling or unable to say what was in his mind.*

unacceptable *adj.*

- VERBS **be, prove, seem** | **become** | **remain** | **make sth** *The cost of these proposed changes makes them unacceptable.* | **consider sth, deem sth, find sth, regard sth as, see sth as** *Most people would consider such risks wholly unacceptable.*
- ADV. **completely, quite, simply, totally, utterly, wholly** | **inherently** *There is nothing inherently unacceptable in*

these proposals. | **morally, politically, socially** *socially unacceptable behaviour*
- PREP. **to** *Such a solution would be quite unacceptable to the majority of people.*

unaffected *adj.*

- VERBS **appear, be, seem** | **remain**
- ADV. **altogether, completely, entirely, quite, totally, wholly** | **almost,** **virtually** | **largely** | **comparatively, relatively** | **apparently, seemingly** *She was seemingly unaffected by his presence.*
- PREP. **by** *He appeared totally unaffected by this experience.*

unanimous *adj.*

- VERBS **be**
- ADV. **almost, nearly, virtually**
- PREP. **about** *Doctors are unanimous about the dangers of this drug.* **in** *They were unanimous in this decision.* **on** *The experts are not unanimous on this point.*

unavoidable *adj.*

- VERBS **be, prove, seem** | **become** | **make sth** *This latest incident makes his dismissal unavoidable.*
- ADV. **absolutely, quite, totally, utterly** | **almost**

unaware *adj.*

- VERBS **appear, be, seem** | **remain**
- ADV. **completely, entirely, quite, totally, utterly, wholly** | **almost,** **virtually** | **generally** | **largely** | **comparatively** | **apparently, seemingly** | **evidently, obviously** | **blissfully, blithely** *They remained blissfully unaware of his true intentions.*
- PREP. **of**

unbalanced *adj.*

1 rather mad
- VERBS **be, seem** | **become**
- ADV. **a little, slightly** | **mentally** *She became mentally unbalanced after the accident.*

2 not fair to all ideas or sides of sth
- VERBS **be, seem** | **become**
- ADV. **extremely, seriously, very** | **completely, wholly** *The report is completely unbalanced.* | **slightly, somewhat** *a somewhat unbalanced account of the events*

unbearable *adj.*

- VERBS **be, feel, seem** | **become, get** | **make sb/sth** *His arrogance made him absolutely unbearable!* | **find sb/sth** *They found the heat unbearable.*
- ADV. **absolutely, quite** | **almost**

unbeatable *adj.*

- VERBS **be, look, seem** *The French team looks unbeatable.* | **become** | **remain** *United remain unbeatable at the top of the League.*
- ADV. **almost, virtually** *He now has an almost unbeatable lead over his rivals.*

unbelievable *adj.*

- VERBS **be, seem, sound** | **become** | **find sth** *I find this quite unbelievable.*

● ADV. **really | completely, quite, totally | just, simply | almost | pretty**
● PREP. **to** *It's simply unbelievable to me.*

unbroken *adj.*

● VERBS **be | remain**
● ADV. **almost, largely, virtually** *a tradition of government involvement which remained virtually unbroken until the 1990s*

uncertain *adj.*

1 not confident

● VERBS **be, feel, look, seem | become**
● ADV. **deeply, very** *I feel deeply uncertain about the future.* **| a little, rather, slightly | strangely**
● PREP. **about, as to** *He seemed strangely uncertain as to how to continue.* **of** *We were rather uncertain of the direction it came from.*

2 not known exactly

● VERBS **be, look | become | remain, seem**
● ADV. **extremely, highly, very | increasingly | quite, rather, somewhat | still** *Whether diet is an important factor in this illness is still uncertain.* **| inevitably, inherently** *The world is inherently uncertain.* **| notoriously** *Cost estimates are notoriously uncertain in this business.*

uncertainty *noun*

● ADJ. **considerable, great | growing | continuing, lingering | economic, financial, legal, political**
● QUANT. **degree, element**
● VERB + UNCERTAINTY **cause, create, give rise to, lead to | add (to), fuel, increase** *Her comments will add to the uncertainty of the situation.* ◊ *Her comments will add uncertainty to an already complicated situation.* **| reduce | bring/put an end to, eliminate, remove, resolve | face** *They are facing some uncertainty about their jobs.*
● UNCERTAINTY + VERB **surround sth** *the uncertainty surrounding the proposed changes in the law*
● PREP. **~ about** *a feeling of uncertainty about his future* **~ as to** *There's considerable uncertainty as to whether the government's job creation strategies will work.* **~ over** *uncertainty over the safety of the drug*
● PHRASES **an area of uncertainty** *One area of uncertainty remains: who will lead the team?* **a feeling of uncertainty, a period of uncertainty**

unchanged *adj.*

● VERBS **appear, be, look | remain, stay | leave sth**
● ADV. **completely, quite, totally | almost, practically, virtually | largely, substantially | basically, essentially, fundamentally** *The school appeared essentially unchanged since my day.* **| relatively**
● PREP. **by** *She was the only one of us unchanged by events.*

uncharacteristic *adj.*

● VERBS **be, seem**
● ADV. **very | quite, totally | rather**
● PREP. **of** *The houses were totally uncharacteristic of the area.*

uncle *noun*

● ADJ. **benevolent, kindly** *The boss smiled at us all like a benevolent uncle.* **| bachelor | maternal, paternal | great** (= the brother of one of your grandparents)

uncomfortable *adj.*

1 not comfortable

● VERBS **be, feel, look, seem | become, get | make sth** *Sharp stones on the path made walking barefoot rather uncomfortable.* **| find sth** *I find these chairs incredibly uncomfortable.*
● ADV. **downright, extremely, incredibly, most, really, terribly, very | increasingly | a bit, a little, pretty, quite, rather | physically**

2 feeling/causing worry/embarrassment

● VERBS **appear, be, feel, look, seem | become, get** *He started to get a bit uncomfortable as the conversation continued.* **| make sb** *The way he looked at her made her distinctly uncomfortable.* **| find sth**
● ADV. **acutely, decidedly, deeply, distinctly, downright, extremely, really, terribly, very | increasingly | a bit, a little, rather, slightly | clearly, obviously, visibly**
● PREP. **with** *Planners seem a little uncomfortable with the current government guidelines.*

uncommon *adj.*

● VERBS **be | become**
● ADV. **very | by no means, far from, not at all** *Such attitudes were not at all uncommon thirty years ago.* **| fairly, quite, rather, relatively**

unconcerned *adj.*

● VERBS **act, appear, be, look, seem, sound** *I tried to act unconcerned.*
● ADV. **very | completely, quite, totally | relatively | apparently, seemingly**
● PREP. **about** *They appeared completely unconcerned about what they had done.* **by** *He was apparently unconcerned by his failure to gain a university place.*

unconscious *adj.*

1 in a state that is like sleep

● VERBS **appear, be, lie, look** *They found her lying unconscious on the floor.* **| become | remain | batter sb, beat sb, kick sb, knock sb, leave sb, render sb** *He was knocked unconscious by the impact.* ◊ *The attack left her unconscious.*
● ADV. **deeply | completely | almost | still**

2 unconscious of sb/sth not aware of sb/sth

● VERBS **appear, be, seem**
● ADV. **quite, totally** *Parents are often quite unconscious of the ways in which they influence their children.*

3 done without you being aware of it

● VERBS **be, seem**
● ADV. **deeply | quite, totally, wholly** *These impulses are often totally unconscious.* **| largely**

unconsciousness *noun*

● ADJ. **deep**
● VERB + UNCONSCIOUSNESS **fall/lapse/sink/slip into**

uncontrollable *adj.*

● VERBS **be, seem | become**
● ADV. **completely, totally | almost, virtually** *an almost uncontrollable urge to laugh* **| apparently**

undecided *adj.*

● VERBS **be, feel, seem, sound | remain | leave sth** *The question cannot be left undecided.*
● ADV. **very | quite | still | as yet** *She is as yet undecided in which direction she wants to make her future career.*
● PREP. **about** *He is still undecided about what to do.* **as to** *They are undecided as to whether to buy a new car.* **on** *The government remains undecided on this issue.*

underestimate noun

- ADJ. **gross, serious** *The official figures are a gross underestimate of the true number.*
- PREP. **~of**

underestimate verb

- ADV. **badly, considerably, greatly, grossly, massively, seriously, substantially** *He realized that he had seriously underestimated their strength.* | **totally** | **fatally**
- VERB + UNDERESTIMATE **tend to**
- PHRASES **sth should not be underestimated** *The importance of these feelings should not be underestimated.*

undergraduate noun

- ADJ. **first-year, second-year, etc.** | **college, university** | **Harvard, Oxford, etc.** | **Chemistry, History, etc.**
- UNDERGRADUATE + NOUN **course, curriculum, degree, studies** | **student** | **teaching** | **level** | **grant**

underground noun

- ADJ. **London**
- VERB + UNDERGROUND **go on/by, take, travel on/by**
- UNDERGROUND + NOUN **station, train, tunnel** | **system** *bringing the whole underground system to a halt*
- PREP. **in the~** *I always seem to get lost in the underground.* **on the~** *passengers on the underground*

undergrowth noun

- ADJ. **deep, dense, tangled, thick**
- QUANT. **patch**
- VERB + UNDERGROWTH **clear**
- PREP. **into the~** *The snake slithered off into the undergrowth.* **in the~** *I noticed someone hiding in the undergrowth.* **through the~** *I could hear him crashing through the undergrowth.*

underline verb

1 draw a line under a word
- ADV. **heavily** *The word 'not' was heavily underlined.*

2 emphasize sth
- ADV. **clearly** | **just, merely, only, simply** *This disaster merely underlines the need for a consistent foreign policy.* | **further**
- VERB + UNDERLINE **serve to** | **seem to** | **be intended to** *a move intended to underline US concern over the issue*
- PHRASES **underline the fact that …**

undermine verb

- ADV. **greatly, radically, seriously, severely** *His position within the government has been seriously undermined.* | **completely, totally** | **somewhat** | **further** | **effectively** | **fatally** | **subtly** | **gradually, increasingly, progressively** | **eventually** | **constantly**
- VERB + UNDERMINE **threaten to** | **attempt to, seek to, try to** | **help (to)** | **serve to, tend to** | **be likely to** | **be designed to, be intended to** *a terror attack intended to undermine the morale of citizens*

underpants noun

- ADJ. **men's**
- QUANT. **pair**
- PREP. **in your~** *He sat on the examination table in his underpants.*
- ⇨ Special page at CLOTHES

understand verb

- ADV. **clearly, well** | **fully, perfectly, quite** *I fully understand the reason for your decision.* | **not really** *Her behav-iour wounded him in a way he did not really understand.* | **adequately** | **correctly, properly** *She realized that she had never properly understood him.* | **easily, readily** *The reasons for this decision are not easily understood.* | **instinctively, intuitively** *She intuitively understood his need to be alone.*
- VERB + UNDERSTAND **be able/unable to, can/could** *I can't understand what all the fuss is about.* | **try to** | **begin to** | **be easy to** | **be difficult to, be hard to** *It is difficult to understand why he reacted in that way.* | **help (to), help sb (to)**
- PREP. **about** *We understand little about this disease.*
- PHRASES **be commonly/generally/popularly understood** *What is generally understood by 'democracy'?* **be imperfectly/incompletely/poorly understood** *The effects of these chemicals on the body are still poorly understood.* **be universally/widely understood**

understandable adj.

1 seeming normal and reasonable
- VERBS **be, seem** | **become**
- ADV. **very** | **completely, entirely, perfectly, quite, wholly** | **fairly**

2 easy to understand
- VERBS **be, seem**
- ADV. **easily, readily** *Warning notices must be readily understandable.*
- PREP. **to** *The instructions must be understandable to the average user.*

understanding noun

1 knowledge of a subject, of how sth works, etc.
- ADJ. **complete, full** *He showed a full understanding of the sequence of events.* | **growing** | **clear, deep, good, profound, proper, sophisticated, thorough, true** *You need to read more widely to gain a proper understanding of the issue.* | **adequate, basic, broad, general, sufficient** | **limited** *She has only a limited understanding of what the job involves.* | **conceptual, critical, rational, theoretical** | **historical, musical, scientific, etc.** | **instinctive** | **common** *Some religions have a common understanding of the nature of a divine being.*
- QUANT. **level** *The students seem to have a reasonable level of understanding of how genes work.*
- VERB + UNDERSTANDING **have** | **show** | **reflect** *This change of policy reflects a growing understanding of the extent of the problem.* | **lack** | **acquire, arrive at, gain** | **give sb** | **advance, broaden, deepen, develop, enhance, enrich, improve, increase** *a book that will deepen your understanding of global warming*
- PREP. **~ about** *The book aims to give children a balanced understanding of food, farming and the environment.* **~ of**
- PHRASES **a lack of understanding**

2 intelligence
- ADJ. **human**
- VERB + UNDERSTANDING **pass** *a level of cruelty that passes human understanding*
- PREP. **beyond (your)~** *The idea of eternity is beyond our full understanding.*

3 ability to feel sympathy and trust
- ADJ. **deeper, great** | **mutual** | **international**
- VERB + UNDERSTANDING **show** *He didn't show much understanding towards her when she lost her job.* | **bring (about), develop, lead to** *Greater contact between the two groups should lead to a better mutual understanding.* | **gain in, grow in** *After spending a month living together, they have gained in understanding of each other.* | **foster, promote, work for**
- PREP. **~ between** *The association fosters a deeper understanding between prisons and the public.*

4 informal agreement

- ADJ. **written** | **verbal** | **tacit, unspoken** *There is an unspoken understanding that Hugh will be in charge while Jane is away.*
- VERB + UNDERSTANDING **have** | **come to, reach** *They came to an understanding on when final payment was to be made.*
- PREP. **~ between** *an understanding between the companies to fight against the proposed tax reform* **~ on** *a tacit understanding on the need for a pay rise* | **on the ~** *I thought you gave me the book on the understanding that I could keep it.*

understatement *noun*

- ADJ. **gross** *'A little strange' is a gross understatement.*
- PHRASES **a bit of/something of an understatement, the understatement of the year** *(informal) To say he wasn't amused must be the understatement of the year.*

undertaking *noun*

1 piece of work/business

- ADJ. **considerable, large, major, serious** | **worthwhile** | **hazardous, risky** | **joint** *the first joint undertaking of the two societies* | **commercial, financial** *We have to decide if this is a worthwhile commercial undertaking.*

2 formal promise

- ADJ. **solemn** | **express** | **irrevocable** | **voluntary** | **verbal, written** | **contractual** | **government** | **public**
- VERB + UNDERTAKING **give (sb)** *He gave an undertaking not to leave the country before the trial.* | **seek** | **obtain** | **carry out, honour, renege on** *The factory failed to honour its undertaking to stop dumping waste into the local river.* | **sign**

undertone *noun*

- ADJ. **sinister** | **racist, sexual** *The article was full of racist undertones.*
- VERB + UNDERTONE **have**
- PREP. **in an~** *'I don't think she's been told yet,' he said in an undertone.* ◊ *The couple at the next table were speaking in undertones.*

underwear *noun*

- ADJ. **long** | **skimpy** | **thermal, warm** | **lace, lacy** | **kinky, sexy** | **ladies', women's** | **men's** | **clean, dirty**
- QUANT. **change, set** *She packed a fresh set of underwear and her toothbrush.*
- PREP. **in your~** *He was getting cold standing around in his underwear.*
- ⇨ Special page at CLOTHES

underworld *noun*

- ADJ. **dark, sinister** *the dark underworld of smuggling* | **criminal**
- UNDERWORLD + NOUN **figure**
- PREP. **in the … ~** *She was a shady figure in the Dublin underworld.*

undesirable *adj.*

- VERBS **be, seem** | **make sth** | **consider sth, deem sth, regard sth as, see sth as**
- ADV. **extremely, highly, very** *a situation which is highly undesirable* | **totally** | **clearly, obviously** *It is clearly undesirable for the issue to be ignored.* | **economically, politically, socially** *It was felt that the ageing of society was socially and economically undesirable.*

undignified *adj.*

- VERBS **be, feel, look, seem** | **become**
- ADV. **most, very** | **thoroughly** | **rather, somewhat**

undone *adj.*

1 not fastened or tied

- VERBS **be** | **come** *My button's come undone again.* | **get sth** *I can't get this knot undone.*

2 not done

- VERBS **be** | **remain** | **leave sth** *We left the washing-up undone and went out for the day.*

undressed *adj.*

- VERBS **be, feel** *She felt undressed without her hat.* | **get** *He got undressed and ready for bed.*
- ADV. **half** *He was half undressed when the doorbell rang.*

unease *noun*

- ADJ. **deep, great, growing** | **certain, some, vague** *She felt a vague unease.* | **general, public**
- VERB + UNEASE **feel** | **express, show** *They expressed their deep unease about the lack of security arrangements.* | **hide** *I smiled to hide my unease.* | **sense** *He sensed a certain unease in her.* | **cause, create**
- UNEASE + VERB **grow, rise**
- PREP. **~ about/at/over** *Many felt unease about the methods used.*
- PHRASES **a feeling/sense of unease, a source of unease** *He looked in vain for the source of his unease.*

uneasy *adj.*

- VERBS **appear, be, feel, look, seem, sound** | **become, get, grow** *We were starting to grow slightly uneasy.* | **remain** | **make sb**
- ADV. **decidedly, deeply, distinctly, extremely, profoundly, very** | **increasingly** | **a bit, a little, rather, slightly, somewhat, vaguely** | **strangely**
- PREP. **about** *I felt distinctly uneasy about lending her so much money.*

unemployed *noun* the unemployed

- ADJ. **long-term** | **rural, urban**
- PREP. **among the ~** *The party's policies were popular among the unemployed.*
- PHRASES **the plight of the unemployed, the ranks of the unemployed** *He graduated with a good degree, only to join the ranks of the unemployed.*

unemployed *adj.*

- VERBS **be, be registered (as)** | **become** | **remain** | **leave sb, make sb** *The closure of the factory left hundreds of men unemployed.*
- ADV. **currently** | **newly** | **still** | **temporarily** | **permanently** | **involuntarily, voluntarily** *As I was voluntarily unemployed, I wasn't entitled to benefit.*

unemployment *noun*

- ADJ. **considerable, high, huge, large-scale, mass, massive, serious, severe, widespread** | **low** | **rising** | **falling** | **long-term, permanent** | **short-term, temporary** | **recurrent, seasonal** | **structural, graduate, school-leaver, youth** | **rural, urban**
- QUANT. **level, rate**
- VERB + UNEMPLOYMENT **be faced with, face** | **cause, create** | **alleviate, bring down, cut, keep down, reduce** | **increase** | **combat, tackle**
- UNEMPLOYMENT + VERB **hit sb** *Unemployment has hit unskilled workers in particular.* | **climb, double, increase, rise, soar** *Unemployment climbed above two million.* | **decline, fall** | **average sth, stand at sth** *Unemployment averaged 15% across the country.* | **reach sth, touch sth** *Unemployment touched 30%.*
- UNEMPLOYMENT + NOUN **benefit, money, pay, pay-**

ments, relief | compensation, cover, insurance | data, figures, levels, numbers, percentage, rate, statistics, total | crisis, problem | blackspot *This former mining town is now an unemployment blackspot.* | trap *The unemployment trap exists when an unemployed person on benefit would be worse off in a low-paid job.*
- PREP. **~ among** *Unemployment among graduates is falling steadily.*
- PHRASES **a period of unemployment, a rise/an increase/a fall in unemployment**

unexpected *adj.*

- VERBS **be**
- ADV. **most, very** *Help came from a most unexpected quarter.* | **completely, quite, totally, wholly** | **not entirely** *His death was not entirely unexpected.* | **rather, somewhat** *It happened in rather unexpected circumstances.*

unfair *adj.*

- VERBS **be, seem** | **consider sth, regard sth as, think sth** *She thought it most unfair that girls were not allowed to take part.*
- ADV. **extremely, grossly, terribly, very** *I thought the decision was grossly unfair.* | **quite, totally, utterly, wholly** | **a bit, a little, pretty, rather, slightly** | **blatantly, demonstrably, patently**
- PREP. **to** *He was terribly unfair to the younger children.*

unfamiliar *adj.*

1 not well-known to you
- VERBS **be, feel, look, sound**
- ADV. **very** | **completely, quite, totally** | **not entirely** | **slightly**
- PREP. **to** *The language was completely unfamiliar to me.*
2 not having knowledge or experience of sth
- VERBS **appear, be, seem**
- ADV. **very** | **completely, quite** | **relatively**
- PREP. **with** *We were quite unfamiliar with the town.*

unfashionable *adj.*

- VERBS **be** | **become** | **remain**
- ADV. **extremely, terribly, very** | **completely** | **rather, relatively** *She lived in a rather unfashionable part of London.*

unfit *adj.*

1 unsuitable for sth/not capable of sth
- VERBS **be, look** | **become** | **make sb/sth, render sb/sth** *His conduct made him unfit to act as director of a company.* | **consider sb/sth, declare sb/sth, deem sb/sth, find sb/sth** *The house was declared quite unfit for human habitation.*
- ADV. **completely, quite, totally, wholly** | **medically, mentally, physically**
- PREP. **for** *completely unfit for our purposes* ◊ *She was found unfit for work.*
2 not in good physical health
- VERBS **be, feel, look, seem** | **become**
- ADV. **very** | **completely, quite** | **slightly**

unforgettable *adj.*

- VERBS **be**
- ADV. **quite, totally, truly** *It was a truly unforgettable experience.* | **pretty**

unfortunate *adj.*

- VERBS **be, seem** | **consider sb/sth**
- ADV. **extremely, most, particularly, singularly, very** *It*

was a most unfortunate choice of expression. | **a bit, a little, rather, slightly**

unfounded *adj.*

- VERBS **be, prove**
- ADV. **completely, entirely, quite, totally, wholly** | **not altogether** *These claims were not altogether unfounded.* | **largely** | **manifestly**

unfriendly *adj.*

- VERBS **appear, be, look, seem** | **become**
- ADV. **distinctly, extremely, really, very** *a distinctly unfriendly tone of voice* | **rather** | **environmentally** *the use of environmentally unfriendly products* (= that harm the environment)
- PREP. **to** *She was really unfriendly to me.*

unhappiness *noun*

- ADJ. **considerable, deep, great** | **general, widespread** | **personal**
- VERB + UNHAPPINESS **feel** | **express** | **cause, lead to** *Bottling up your anger can only lead to unhappiness.*
- PREP. **~ about** *He expressed his unhappiness about the arrangements.* **~ at** *the great unhappiness she felt at having to leave the town* **~ with** *his deep unhappiness with the situation*

unhappy *adj.*

- VERBS **be, feel, look, seem, sound** | **become, grow** *She grew more unhappy as the years went by.* | **make sb** *It makes me very unhappy to see you so miserable.*
- ADV. **deeply, desperately, distinctly, dreadfully, extremely, most, really, terribly, very, wretchedly** *She is deeply unhappy.* ◊ *He described it as 'a most unhappy and distressing case'.* | **entirely** *We felt entirely unhappy with the whole situation.* | **increasingly** | **a bit, a little, rather** | **clearly, obviously** | **equally** *He was equally unhappy with the alternative.* | **personally**
- PREP. **about** *He sounded a bit unhappy about the extra work he had to do.* **at** *She was very unhappy at the idea of staying in London.* **with** *They were terribly unhappy with the arrangements.*

unheard *adj.*

- VERBS **go** *Their protests went unheard.*
- ADV. **previously** *a previously unheard tape of their conversations*

unheard-of *adj.*

- VERBS **be**
- ADV. **absolutely, completely, quite, totally** *At that time, it was completely unheard-of for girls to go to university.* | **by no means** | **almost, practically, virtually** | **hitherto, previously** *He was sentenced to a hitherto unheard-of seven life terms in prison.*

unification *noun*

- ADJ. **European, German, etc.** | **economic, monetary, political**
- VERB + UNIFICATION **achieve, bring about**

uniform *noun*

- ADJ. **full** | **smart** | **regulation** *She was wearing the regulation uniform of tunic, hat and tie.* | **standard** (*figurative*) *They wore the standard uniform of the well-to-do American out of office hours.* | **traditional** | **dress** *a man in the full dress uniform of the US Marines* | **army, fireman's, military, naval, nurse's, prison, school, etc.**
- PREP. **in (a/the) ~** *The limousine was driven by a chauf-*

feur in uniform. ◇ *A man in a uniform stopped us entering.*
out of~ *a soldier out of uniform*
⇨ Special page at CLOTHES

uniformity *noun*

- ADJ. **broad** | **great** | **bland, drab, dull**
- VERB + UNIFORMITY **achieve, ensure, impose**
- PREP. **~in** *Government inspections ensure a high degree of uniformity in the standard of service.*

uninhabitable *adj.*

- VERBS **be, look, remain, seem** | **become** | **make sth, render sth** *houses made uninhabitable by radioactive contamination* | **declare sth** *Fifty homes were declared uninhabitable.*
- ADV. **totally** | **almost, virtually** | **permanently**

uninhibited *adj.*

- VERBS **be, feel, seem** *The loud music made him feel totally uninhibited.* | **become**
- ADV. **very** | **completely, quite, totally, utterly** | **pretty** *I'm a pretty uninhibited sort of person.*

unintelligible *adj.*

- VERBS **be, sound** | **become**
- ADV. **quite, totally** | **almost, practically, virtually** | **largely** | **mutually** *mutually unintelligible languages*
- PREP. **to** *Dolphin sounds are unintelligible to humans.*

uninterested *adj.*

- VERBS **appear, be, look, seem, sound**
- ADV. **completely, totally** | **apparently**
- PREP. **in** *She was completely uninterested in her sister's career.*

union *noun*

- ADJ. **close, tight** *Some of the member states wanted a tighter union rather than the loose confederation that developed.* | **loose** | **full** *a move towards full European union* | **economic, monetary, political**
- VERB + UNION **create, form** | **dissolve**
- UNION + VERB **break up** *The Soviet Union broke up after only a few years of liberalization.*
- PREP. **~between** *currency union between the two countries* **~with** *the union with East Germany*
⇨ See TRADE UNION

unique *adj.*

- VERBS **be** | **make sb/sth** *Its magnificent proportions make this palace unique among the buildings of the world.*
- ADV. **quite, totally, truly** *The city has an atmosphere which is quite unique.* | **by no means, far from, hardly** *Although such a case is rare, it is by no means unique.* | **almost, virtually** | **apparently**
- PREP. **to** *This monkey is unique to the island.*

unit *noun*

1 single thing
- ADJ. **large, small** | **basic, fundamental** *The family is the basic unit of society.* | **discrete, individual, single**
- VERB + UNIT **break sth down into, divide sth into** *Large departments were broken down into smaller units.*

2 fixed amount
- ADJ. **basic, standard** | **monetary** | **lexical, linguistic**
- UNIT + NOUN **cost, length, weight**
- PREP. **~of** *a unit of currency* ◇ *a unit of length* ◇ *fifty units of electricity*
- PHRASES **per unit** *Electricity is ten pence per unit.*

3 group of people

- ADJ. **cohesive** *The new manager changed a talented collection of individuals into a cohesive unit.* | **baby, casualty, emergency, intensive care, maternity, psychiatric, surgical, etc.** *She works in the maternity unit at the local hospital.* | **army, enemy, military** | **intelligence** | **policy** | **research** | **family, social** *the role of the family unit in the community*
- VERB + UNIT **be attached to** *The cancer research unit is attached to the local university.*

4 piece of furniture/equipment
- ADJ. **cooking, kitchen, sink, storage** | **air-conditioning, control, power, processing, shower** *the central processing unit in a computer*
- VERB + UNIT **install** *We're having new kitchen units installed.*

united *adj.*

- VERBS **be, seem** | **become** | **remain**
- ADV. **closely, firmly** | **absolutely, entirely, fully, totally** *The members of the team were absolutely united in their common goal.* ◇ *obstacles to a fully united Europe* | **largely** | **legally, politically** *a politically united federation*
- PREP. **in** *united in their aims*

unity *noun*

- ADJ. **complete** *Complete political unity is impossible to achieve.* | **greater** | **European, German, Irish, etc.** | **cultural, economic, national, party, political, religious, social** *a government of national unity*
- VERB + UNITY **achieve, bring about** | **preserve** | **destroy, shatter, weaken** | **restore** *He restored peace and unity in the country after years of civil war.* | **call for, promote** *The party is calling for greater political and economic unity in Europe.*
- PREP. **in~** *live together in unity* | **~among** *The dispute has destroyed unity among the workers.* **~between** *a degree of unity between staff and students*
- PHRASES **a sense of unity** *a leader who gave her people a strong sense of unity* **unity in diversity** *The organization promotes racial tolerance and unity in diversity.*

universal *adj.*

- VERBS **be, seem** | **become** | **remain**
- ADV. **truly** | **by no means, far from** *Some of the teachers are technical specialists, but this is far from universal.* | **almost, near, nearly, virtually** | **pretty** | **apparently** | **supposedly** *supposedly universal standards*
- PREP. **among** *These practices remain universal among the islanders.* **in** *a scheme that is universal in scope*

universe *noun*

- ADJ. **entire, whole** | **physical**
- VERB + UNIVERSE **create** *Do you believe God created the universe?*
- PREP. **in the~** *Could there be intelligent life elsewhere in the universe?*
- PHRASES **the beginning/origin(s) of the universe**

university *noun*

- ADJ. **new** | **ancient** | **red-brick** | **local, provincial** | **research, teaching**
- VERB + UNIVERSITY **attend, go to, study at** | **apply for** | **enter** | **finish (at), graduate from, leave**
- UNIVERSITY + NOUN **lecturer, professor, staff, teacher** | **graduate, student, undergraduate** | **course, degree, education** | **term, year** | **vacation** | **entrance, entry, place** *a university entrance exam* ◇ *There is stiff competition for university places.* | **chair** *His aim was to finish his doctorate and obtain a university chair.* | **department, faculty** | **buildings, campus, library** | **admin-**

istration, authorities | level *All the staff are educated to university level.* | **days, life, years** | **town**
- PREP. **at (the)~** *She's at university, studying engineering.* ◇ *She teaches English at the University of Wales.*

unknown noun

1 place/thing that you know nothing about
- ADJ. **great** *What the weather will be like on the day is, as always, the great unknown.*
- PREP. **into the~** *Motherhood was for her a journey into the unknown.*
- PHRASES **fear of the unknown**

2 sb who is not well known
- ADJ. **complete** *The championship was won by a complete unknown.* | **virtual** *a cast of virtual unknowns*

unknown adj.

- VERBS **be** | **remain** *These sites remain largely unknown to the British public.*
- ADV. **absolutely, completely, entirely, quite, totally, utterly** *His whereabouts were quite unknown during this period.* | **almost, practically, virtually** *This drug was practically unknown in Britain.* | **largely** | **comparatively, relatively** *She was then still comparatively unknown.* | **as yet, currently, still** | **hitherto, previously** *a period of democratic development previously unknown in their country* | **apparently** | **otherwise** *He cites the works of two otherwise unknown authors, the originals of these works having been lost.*
- PREP. **to** *Gold was totally unknown to their civilization.*

unlikely adj.

- VERBS **appear, be, look, sound** *The takeover bid now looks unlikely to succeed.* | **become** | **remain, seem** | **make sth** | **consider sth, think sth** *He thought it unlikely that she would refuse.*
- ADV. **extremely, highly, most, very** | **increasingly** | **not at all** | **a bit, pretty, quite, rather, somewhat** | **apparently** | **inherently** *A collapse into new forms of fascism is inherently unlikely in any Western democracy.*

unlimited adj.

- VERBS **appear, be, seem** | **become**
- ADV. **almost, virtually** *This new technology opens up almost unlimited possibilities.* | **apparently** | **potentially**

unlucky adj.

- VERBS **be, prove, seem, sound** | **become** | **consider sb/sth, regard sb/sth as, think sb/sth** *The number thirteen is traditionally considered unlucky.*
- ADV. **dead, desperately, extremely, very** *She was desperately unlucky to fall as badly as she did.* | **a bit, a little**
- PREP. **for** *a date that is unlucky for that family* **with** *She has been very unlucky with injuries this year.*

unmistakable adj.

- VERBS **be**
- ADV. **quite** *The main symptom is a scarlet rash that's quite unmistakable.*

unmoved adj.

- VERBS **appear, be, seem, sound** | **remain** | **leave sb** *Her daughter's accident had left her curiously unmoved.*
- ADV. **completely, entirely, quite, totally** | **largely, relatively** | **apparently** | **curiously**
- PREP. **by** *He was quite unmoved by my anger.*

unnatural adj.

- VERBS **be, feel, look, seem, sound** | **consider sth, regard sth as**
- ADV. **highly, terribly, very** *food produced under highly unnatural conditions* | **quite** | **almost** | **a bit, rather**

unnecessary adj.

- VERBS **appear, be, prove, seem** | **become** | **make sth, render sth** | **consider sth, deem sth, regard sth as**
- ADV. **completely, entirely, quite, totally, wholly** *No, no, that's quite unnecessary.* | **largely** | **a little, rather, somewhat** | **strictly**
- PREP. **to** *the possession of items strictly unnecessary to survival*

unnoticed adj.

- VERBS **be, go, lie, pass** *The ticket lay unnoticed in my desk drawer for a week.* ◇ *His remark passed unnoticed.* | **remain**
- ADV. **completely, entirely** *There's a good chance my absence will go completely unnoticed.* | **almost, practically, virtually** | **largely** | **hitherto, previously** *a hitherto unnoticed detail*

unorthodox adj.

- VERBS **be, seem, sound** | **become**
- ADV. **highly, very** *a highly unorthodox teaching style* | **a little, quite, rather, slightly, somewhat**

unpaid adj.

- VERBS **be** | **remain** | **leave sth** *customers who leave their bills unpaid till the last minute*
- ADV. **virtually** *the virtually unpaid labour of large peasant families*

unpleasant adj.

- VERBS **be, feel, look, seem, smell, sound, taste** | **become, get, turn** *Things started to get unpleasant when their neighbours called in the police.* | **make sth** *He may make life unpleasant for the rest of us.* | **find sb/sth** *I found the atmosphere in there extremely unpleasant.*
- ADV. **decidedly, deeply, exceedingly, extremely, highly, most, particularly, very** | **thoroughly** *a thoroughly unpleasant man* | **not altogether, not entirely** *The overall feeling was a strange mixture of sensations, not altogether unpleasant.* | **fairly, pretty, quite, rather, slightly, somewhat** *His clothes smelled pretty unpleasant.*
- PREP. **for** *tests which are unpleasant for patients* **to** *He was very unpleasant to my friends.*

unpopular adj.

- VERBS **be, prove, seem** | **become** | **remain** | **make sb/sth** *His advanced views made him unpopular with many of the clergy.*
- ADV. **deeply, desperately, extremely, highly, particularly, terribly, very** | **increasingly** | **rather, somewhat** | **generally, widely** | **politically** *Cuts in government expenditure are politically unpopular.*
- PREP. **among** *Highly priced shares are unpopular among investors.* **with** *He's unpopular with the students.*

unpopularity noun

- ADJ. **great, growing**
- VERB + UNPOPULARITY **increase**
- PREP. **~among** *Her close relationship with the teacher increased her unpopularity among her schoolmates.* **~with** *the great unpopularity of the policy with teachers*

unprecedented *adj.*

- VERBS **be**
- ADV. **entirely, quite, totally | by no means | almost, virtually | supposedly | historically** *a historically unprecedented growth in retirement at a fixed age*

unprovoked *adj.*

- VERBS **be**
- ADV. **completely, totally** *a totally unprovoked attack*

unqualified *adj.*

- VERBS **be**
- ADV. **totally**
- PREP. **for** *He is totally unqualified for the job.*

unreal *adj.*

- VERBS **be, feel, look, seem | become**
- ADV. **very | quite, totally, wholly | almost | a little, rather, slightly | somehow** *He seemed somehow unreal, a creature from another world.* **| curiously, oddly, strangely** *She felt curiously unreal, as if she were in the midst of a dream.*

unreasonable *adj.*

- VERBS **appear, be, seem, sound** *She did not want to appear unreasonable.* **| become, get** *His demands were getting more and more unreasonable.* **| consider sth, find sb/sth, hold sth** (*law*)**, judge sth** (*law*)**, regard sth as, think sth** *I find her a bit unreasonable at times.* ◇ *This clause in the contract was held unreasonable.*
- ADV. **extremely, grossly, very | completely, quite, totally, utterly, wholly | a bit | apparently**
- PREP. **about** *He was totally unreasonable about it.*

unrest *noun*

- ADJ. **great, serious | violent | widespread** *There was widespread industrial unrest in the north.* **| popular | growing, mounting | fresh, further, renewed** *The murder of a boy by police sparked renewed unrest in the occupied zone.* **| agrarian, civil, ethnic, industrial, labour, political, rural, social | peasant, student**
- QUANT. **period, wave** *The increase in fees sparked a new wave of student unrest.*
- VERB + UNREST **cause, spark (off), stir up | crush, deal with, put down, quell** *The government's attempts to crush serious popular unrest led to civil war.*
- PREP. **during (the)~** *Many shops were looted during the unrest.* **| ~over** *growing unrest over pay levels*

unscathed *adj.*

- VERBS **be, be left, emerge, escape, get away, remain, survive, walk away** *The children escaped unscathed.*
- ADV. **remarkably | completely, entirely, totally** *Amazingly, the driver walked away from the accident completely unscathed.* **| almost, virtually | largely | relatively | apparently, seemingly** *The company came through the crisis apparently unscathed.* **| miraculously**
- PREP. **by** *The town centre was left unscathed by the riots.*

unscrupulous *adj.*

- VERBS **be, seem | become**
- ADV. **completely, quite, thoroughly** *In his desire for power, he has become thoroughly unscrupulous.* **| pretty**

unstable *adj.*

1 likely to change suddenly

- VERBS **appear, be, seem | become | remain | make**

sth**, render sth** *Prison order is rendered unstable by young inmates serving short sentences.*
- ADV. **extremely, highly, very | increasingly | rather, relatively, somewhat | basically, inherently | notoriously** *The building trade is notoriously unstable.* **| economically, politically** *a politically unstable region*

2 not mentally normal

- VERBS **be, seem | become**
- ADV. **highly, very | rather | emotionally, mentally** *vulnerable, emotionally unstable individuals*

3 likely to move or fall

- VERBS **be, feel, look, seem | become, get** *The building was beginning to get unstable.* **| make sth**
- ADV. **dangerously, extremely, very** *The wall was dangerously unstable.* **| rather, slightly**

unsuitable *adj.*

- VERBS **be, prove | make sth** *The huge proportions of the main rooms made the house unsuitable for conversion into flats.* **| consider sth, deem sth, find sth** *Many tasks were considered unsuitable for women.*
- ADV. **highly, most, very | completely, entirely, quite, totally, wholly | manifestly, obviously**

unsure *adj.*

- VERBS **be, feel, look, seem, sound** *I felt a bit unsure about him.* **| remain | leave sb, make sb** *His sudden change of heart left Brenda unsure once more.*
- ADV. **terribly, very | completely | a bit, a little, rather | obviously, plainly | still**
- PREP. **about** *If you're still unsure about what you are supposed to do, speak up!* **as to** *We were unsure as to what to do next.* **of** *She was rather unsure of her reception.*

unthinkable *adj.*

- VERBS **be, seem | make sth | consider sth** *This would have been considered unthinkable only a decade ago.*
- ADV. **absolutely, completely, quite | almost, practically, virtually | hitherto, previously** *A hitherto unthinkable question was asked.* **| politically**
- PREP. **to** *This course of action would have been unthinkable to the Russian generals.*

untidy *adj.*

- VERBS **be, look, seem | become, get** *I've got more untidy since I stopped going out to work.* **| remain, stay** *I'm afraid the house will have to stay untidy for now.* **| leave sth, make sth** *My son had left the studio very untidy.* ◇ *Books and magazines lying around make the place very untidy.*
- ADV. **dreadfully, extremely, very** *Everything was dreadfully untidy.* **| a bit, a little, rather**

unused *adj.*

- VERBS **appear, be, lie, look, remain, sit, stand, stay** *The church has lain empty and unused since 1994.* **| leave sth** *The meeting rooms are left unused for long periods.*
- ADV. **virtually**

unused to *adj.*

- VERBS **appear, be, seem | become, grow** *He had grown unused to this sort of attention.*
- ADV. **quite, totally** *She was quite unused to this way of life.*

unusual *adj.*

- VERBS **appear, be, look, seem | become | consider sth** *It was considered unusual for a gentleman's son to study medicine.*

● ADV. **decidedly, distinctly, extremely, highly, particularly, really, very** *This is a highly unusual case.* | **by no means, hardly, not at all** *It's not at all unusual to feel very tired in the early months of pregnancy.* | **a bit, fairly, a little, pretty, quite, rather, relatively, slightly, somewhat** | **enough, sufficiently** *The arrival of a taxi was unusual enough; an unknown woman getting out of it was sensational.*
● PREP. **for** *It's unusual for a woman to do this job.*

unveil verb

● ADV. **formally, officially** *The government has officially unveiled its plans for tax reform.*

unwarranted adj.

● VERBS **be, seem** *The delay did seem unwarranted.*
● ADV. **quite, totally, wholly** *a wholly unwarranted smear campaign*

unwell adj.

● VERBS **appear, be, feel, look, seem, sound** *He complained of feeling unwell.* | **become** | **remain** | **make sb**
● ADV. **extremely, really, very** | **a little, vaguely** *patients who just feel vaguely unwell*
● PREP. **with** *You should delay vaccination if you are unwell with a fever.*

upbringing noun

● ADJ. **conventional** *Mine was a conventional family upbringing.* | **sheltered, strict** | **Catholic, Jewish, etc., religious** | **cultural** | **middle-class, etc.**
● VERB + UPBRINGING **have** *He had a normal middle-class upbringing.* | **give sb** *They gave their children a strict Catholic upbringing.*
● UPBRINGING + VERB **give sb sth, prepare sb (for sth)** *Her upbringing had given her the social skills to cope with such situations.* ◇ *My upbringing prepared me for anything.*
● PHRASES **part of your upbringing** *Part of his upbringing had been not to question his elders.*

update noun

● ADJ. **monthly, regular, weekly, etc.**
● VERB + UPDATE **give (sb), provide (sb with)** *The report gives an update on the currency crisis.* | **get, receive**
● PREP. **~on** *an update on the political crisis* **~to** *We need an update to the mailing list.*

update verb

● ADV. **constantly, continually, continuously** | **regularly** | **annually, monthly, etc.** | **fully, properly** *The road map has been fully updated.* | **automatically** | **manually** *updating all the files manually*
● VERB + UPDATE **seek to, try to** | **wish to**
● PREP. **on** *Could you update me on how the work is progressing?* **with** *The files are continuously updated with new information.*

upgrade verb

● ADV. **significantly, substantially** | **constantly** *We are constantly upgrading our software to meet customers' needs.*
● PREP. **from, to** *customers who want to upgrade from version 4.2 to version 4.5* **with** *All the machines can be upgraded with the new processors.*

upheaval noun

● ADJ. **big, enormous, great, major, massive, violent** | **domestic, economic, emotional, political, social** *The loss of his high-paying job caused enormous domestic upheaval.* | **revolutionary**
● VERB + UPHEAVAL **cause, provoke** | **go through, undergo** *The company underwent a massive upheaval after the takeover.*
● PREP. **during/in the ~** *He rose to power during the political upheavals of the 1990s.*
● PHRASES **a period of upheaval**

uphold verb

● ADV. **firmly, resolutely, vigorously** | **unanimously** *Three judges unanimously upheld the sentence.*
● VERB + UPHOLD **have a duty to** | **be determined to** *We are determined to uphold the law.* | **seek to** | **promise to** | **vote to** *The IWC voted to uphold the ban on commercial whaling.* | **fail to**

upkeep noun

● VERB + UPKEEP **contribute to, pay for** *Our taxes help pay for the upkeep of the city's parks.* | **afford**
● PHRASES **responsible/responsibility for the upkeep of** *The local council is responsible for the upkeep of roads.*

uplifting adj.

● VERBS **be, feel** | **find sth**
● ADV. **really, very** | **suitably** *a suitably uplifting ending for the film* | **morally, spiritually**

upright adj.

● VERBS **be, sit, stand** *rows of children sitting upright at their desks* | **come, jerk, scramble, shoot, spring, struggle** *Slowly the boat came upright.* ◇ *Polly jerked upright, wild-eyed and blinking.* | **remain, stay** *The flag pole wouldn't stay upright.* | **drag sb/sth, haul sb/sth, heave sb/sth, jerk sb/sth, place sth, prop sth, pull sb/sth** *Pulling himself upright, he squared his shoulders.* | **hold sb/sth, keep sth**
● ADV. **fully** *a fully upright posture* | **almost** | **relatively** | **rigidly, stiffly** *She held herself rigidly upright.*
● PHRASES **sit/stand bolt upright** (= to sit/stand with your back straight) *He was sitting bolt upright on his chair, looking very tense.*

uprising noun

● ADJ. **successful** | **failed** *the failed uprising of 1830* | **armed** | **revolutionary** | **mass, national, popular** | **military** | **peasant** | **spontaneous**
● VERB + UPRISING **provoke, spark (off)** | **stage** | **crush, put down, quell, suppress**
● PREP. **during/in the ~** *He was killed in the Warsaw uprising.* | **~against** *the 1951 uprising against colonial rule*

uproar noun

● ADJ. **great** | **mild** | **emotional**
● VERB + UPROAR **cause, provoke**
● PREP. **amid (an/the) ~** *The trial proceeded amid uproar.* **in (an/the) ~** *Financial markets were in uproar after the crash of the rouble.* ◇ *The classroom was in an uproar.* | **~over** *There was a great uproar over plans to pull down the old library.*

upset noun

● ADJ. **big, major** | **minor** | **emotional**
● VERB + UPSET **have** *We had our first major upset when Rogers was taken off with a leg injury.* | **cause**

upset verb

● ADV. **badly, deeply, really, terribly** | **easily** *She was sensitive and easily upset.*

• VERB + UPSET **not mean to, not want to, not wish to** *I'm sorry—I didn't mean to upset you.* ◊ *Keep the volume down—we don't want to upset the neighbours!* | **be likely to** *This decision is likely to upset a lot of people.*

upset *adj.*

• VERBS **appear, be, feel, look, seem, sound** | **become, get** *Don't get so upset about it!* | **remain** | **leave sb, make sb** *The incident had left him visibly angry and upset.*
• ADV. **badly, bitterly, deeply, desperately, dreadfully, extremely, genuinely, greatly, particularly, profoundly, really, seriously, terribly, very** *She's obviously deeply upset by his behaviour.* | **thoroughly** | **a bit, a little, pretty, quite, rather** | **clearly, obviously, visibly**
• PREP. **about** *upset about her divorce* **at** *He was upset at missing all the excitement.* **by** *upset by the death of their pet* **with** *I think she may be a bit upset with you.*

upsurge *noun*

• ADJ. **great, massive** | **sudden**
• PREP. **~in** *an upsurge in violent crime*

uptight *adj.*

• VERBS **be, feel, look, seem, sound** | **get** *Try to laugh at it instead of getting uptight.* | **make sb**
• ADV. **really, very** | **all** *(informal) He gets all uptight if anyone criticizes him!* | **a bit, quite**
• PREP. **about** *He's feeling a bit uptight about his exam tomorrow.*

up-to-date *adj.*

1 modern/most recent
• VERBS **be** | **bring sth** *We'll have to bring our equipment up-to-date.* | **keep sth**
• ADV. **really, very** | **bang, completely** *Today's holiday parks are bang up-to-date.*
2 having the most recent information about sth
• VERBS **be, seem** | **keep** *It is difficult to keep up-to-date with all the developments.* | **bring sb** | **keep sb**
• ADV. **completely, fully**
• PREP. **on** *Bring me up-to-date on their progress.* **with** *We can keep you fully up-to-date with your financial position.*

upturn *noun*

• ADJ. **dramatic, sharp** | **slight** | **economic**
• VERB + UPTURN **be on, take** *Sales are on the upturn.* ◊ *Their fortunes have taken an upturn in recent months.*
• UPTURN + VERB **come** *We expect an increase in demand when the economic upturn eventually comes.*
• PREP. **~in** *a sharp upturn in oil prices*

uranium *noun*

• ADJ. **natural** | **enriched** *a tonne of highly enriched uranium* | **depleted** | **weapons-grade**
• VERB + URANIUM **mine** | **recover**
• URANIUM + NOUN **ore, reserves** | **fuel** | **mine, miner, mining** | **enrichment**

Urdu *noun*

⇨ Note at LANGUAGE

urge *noun*

• ADJ. **great, irresistible, overwhelming, powerful, strong, terrible, uncontrollable, violent, wild** | **sudden** *I felt a sudden urge to smash the teapot against the wall.* | **instinctive, natural** *an instinctive urge to tap your feet to the beat of the music* | **primal, primeval, primitive** *the primal urge to reproduce* | **biological, creative, sexual**
• VERB + URGE **feel, get, have** | **control, fight (back),**

resist, suppress *She resisted the urge to kiss him.* ◊ *I suppressed a strong urge to yawn.* | **overcome** *He overcame his urge to run from the room.* | **satisfy**
• PREP. **~for** *Leaving him off the guest list satisfied her urge for revenge.*

urge *verb*

• ADV. **strongly** | **constantly, repeatedly** *He has repeatedly urged the government to do something about this.* | **publicly** | **quietly** | **unsuccessfully**

urgency *noun*

• ADJ. **desperate, extreme, great, utmost** *a matter of the utmost urgency* | **added, new** *The murders have given added urgency to the debate about inner-city crime.*
• QUANT. **note** *There was a note of urgency in her voice.*
• VERB + URGENCY **give sth, lend sth** *The bomb attack lent a new urgency to the peace talks.* | **increase** | **stress**
• PREP. **with~** *We need to act with urgency to ensure his safety.* | **~about** *Is there any urgency about this?* **~in** *There was an urgency in her movements.*
• PHRASES **a lack of urgency** *We waited in the car while he checked his tyres with an irritating lack of urgency.* **a matter of urgency** *The refugee situation must now be addressed as a matter of urgency.* **a sense of urgency**

urgent *adj.*

• VERBS **be, seem, sound** *Can you come to the phone—it sounds urgent.* | **become, get**
• ADV. **extremely, really, very** | **increasingly** *the increasingly urgent political situation at home* | **quite, rather** *Don't forget that one, it's rather urgent.*

urine *noun*

• ADJ. **stale** *I gagged on the stench of stale urine.*
• QUANT. **drop, stream**
• VERB + URINE **pass** | **leak** *He said he leaked urine when he coughed.*
• URINE + NOUN **sample, specimen** | **analysis, test, testing** | **output, production, volume** | **retention** | **flow** | **infection**
• PREP. **in (the/your)~** *sugars in urine*
• PHRASES **a smell/stench of urine**

usage *noun*

1 way/amount that sth is used
• ADJ. **heavy, high** *high energy usage* | **low** | **normal** *With normal usage, the equipment should last at least five years.* | **drug** *Drug usage by teenagers has increased in recent years.* | **energy** | **water**
• VERB + USAGE **increase** | **reduce**
• USAGE + VERB **increase** | **fall**
• PREP. **~of** *Usage of computers in schools is increasing.*
2 way that words are used
• ADJ. **common, everyday, general, normal, ordinary, popular** *That word is no longer in common usage.* | **current, modern** *a book on current English usage* | **actual** *Actual usage of the word is different from the meaning given in the dictionary.* | **correct** | **American, English,** etc. | **language, linguistic, word** | **colloquial**
• VERB + USAGE **come into, enter** *The term 'ecotourism' entered common usage in the 1990s.*
• PREP. **in~** *The word has a slightly different meaning in popular usage.*
• PHRASES **patterns of usage** *Dictionary definitions tend to show stereotypical patterns of usage.*

use *noun*

1 using/being used
• ADJ. **considerable, extensive, great, heavy, liberal** |

full, maximum *He made full use of the opportunity to travel.* | **excessive** *a style of writing with an excessive use of metaphor* | **increased, increasing** | **constant, continued, daily, everyday, frequent, regular, repeated, routine** *the daily use of a deodorant* | **wide, widespread** *a campaign to encourage wider use of public transport* | **common, current, general, normal, ordinary** *This software is no longer in common use.* | **limited** | **occasional** | **appropriate, careful, clever, correct, effective, efficient, good, judicious, legitimate, optimum, proper, safe, selective** *Holding a lavish party was not the best use of scarce funds.* ◇ *an efficient use of resources* ◇ *an article with a judicious use of examples* ◇ *The layout of the furniture makes optimum use of the space available.* | **indiscriminate, poor** | **illegal, unauthorized** | **personal, private** | **external, internal** *This antiseptic is for external use only.* | **home** *fire extinguishers for home use* | **clinical, commercial, industrial** | **official** | **exclusive** *for the exclusive use of club members* | **free** *Guests have free use of the hotel swimming pool.* | **immediate** *Only half the land was fit for immediate use.* | **drug, heroin,** etc. *Drug use in this age group is on the increase.* | **land** | **language** | **energy** | **library**

● VERB + USE **make** *We made use of the car while you were away.* | **bring sth (back) into, come into** *a technology which came into use at the end of the last century* | **go out of** *The expression went out of use some time ago.*

● PREP. **for ~** *This phone number is only for use in an emergency.* **in ~** *The phone is in constant use.*

● PHRASES **ease of use** *This model has been designed for greater ease of use.* **for use as** *The record is intended for use as background music.* **ready for use** *This room is now ready for use.*

2 purpose for which sth is used
● ADJ. **different** | **new**
● VERB + USE **have** *This herb has a variety of uses.* | **find, put sth to** *Can you find a use for this old table?* ◇ *Don't throw that box away—I'm sure I could put it to some use.*
● PHRASES **a variety of uses**

3 ability/permission to use sth
● ADJ. **full** *the full use of your mental faculties*
● VERB + USE **have** *Since his stroke he hasn't had the use of his left hand.* | **give sb, offer (sb)** *We gave them the use of our house while we were on holiday.* | **deny sb** *They denied us use of the college library.* | **lose** | **recover, regain** *After a while she regained the use of her fingers.*
● PREP. **~ of** *She lost the use of her legs in a car accident.*

4 how useful sth is
● ADJ. **practical**
● VERB + USE **be of** *Could this old coat be of use to you?* | **have** *I have no use for my golf clubs any more.*
● PREP. **of ... ~** *It's of no practical use to me.* | **~ to** *Is it any use to you?*
● PHRASES **be no use** *It's no use running—the train has already gone.*

use *verb*

● ADV. **carefully, efficiently** | **sparingly** *This paint is very expensive, so please use it sparingly.* | **indiscriminately** | **frequently, generally, habitually, normally, regularly, usually** *Do you habitually use display screen equipment as a significant part of your job?* | **occasionally, rarely** | **up** *The oil had all been used up.*
● VERB + USE **be easy to, be simple to** *These garden shears are lightweight and easy to use.* | **be difficult to, be hard to** | **be ready to** | **be likely to, tend to** *the factors that make people likely to use heroin* ◇ *Manufacturers tend to use disks made in the US.* | **decide to** | **intend to, plan to** | **attempt to, try to** | **allow sb to, be entitled to, let sb, permit sb to** *Candidates are not allowed to use dictionaries in the exam.* | **forbid sb to** | **teach sb to**

● PREP. **as** *The tennis court is sometimes used as a car park.* **for** *chemicals that are used for cleaning*
● PHRASES **permission to use sth**

used *adj.*

● VERBS **be, look** *The board game looked used.*
● ADV. **commonly, extensively, frequently, regularly, well, widely** *a widely used technique for assessing the strength of metals* | **little, rarely** *a little-used path through the wood*

used to *adj.*

● VERBS **appear, be, seem, sound** | **become, get, grow** *Don't worry, you'll soon get used to your new school.* ◇ *She had gradually grown used to him.*
● ADV. **very, well** | **quite** | **pretty**

useful *adj.*

● VERBS **be, look, prove, seem** | **become** | **make yourself** *She told Fred to make himself useful.* | **consider sth, find sth** *some leaflets which you might find useful*
● ADV. **enormously, especially, exceptionally, extremely, genuinely, highly, more than** (*informal*)**, particularly, really, tremendously, very** *making an exceptionally useful contribution to the debate* ◇ *In all departments, Leeds looked a more than useful side* (= they played very well). | **fairly, pretty, quite** | **equally** *The same information is equally useful when negotiating.* | **generally, universally** *This method has proved the most generally useful.* | **potentially** | **practically** *The subject is practically useful and will stand you in good stead when looking for a job.* | **undoubtedly** *an undoubtedly useful skill* | **socially** *to provide rewarding and socially useful employment*
● PREP. **as** *useful as a short-term measure* **for** *useful for a variety of purposes* ◇ *useful for people who need a short break* **in** *She was very useful in dealing with foreign visitors.* **to** *information which will be useful to new mothers*

usefulness *noun*

● ADJ. **limited, some** | **general** | **practical** | **potential**
● VERB + USEFULNESS **have** | **increase** | **diminish, limit, reduce** *Badly written questions limit the usefulness of questionnaires.* | **assess, evaluate, question** | **demonstrate, prove** | **exhaust, outlive** *The advisory group has outlived its usefulness.*
● PREP. **of ... ~** *The theory is of limited usefulness.* | **~ for** *the exam's usefulness for ranking students* **~ in** *the drug's usefulness in the treatment of cancer* **~ to** *The report is of potential usefulness to the government.*

useless *adj.*

1 of no use
● VERBS **be, feel, prove** *Her efforts to avoid him proved useless.* | **become** | **leave sth, make sth, render sth** *The condition rendered her legs virtually useless.* | **reject sth as** *They rejected the designs as useless.*
● ADV. **bloody** (*taboo*) | **absolutely, completely, entirely, quite, totally, utterly, wholly** | **worse than** *A computer program with too many icons is worse than useless.* | **all but, almost, practically, virtually** | **largely, fairly, pretty** | **equally** *There are two manuals, both of them equally useless.*
● PREP. **as** *A candle is practically useless as a light source.* **for** *The land is useless for cattle.* **in** *This drug is useless in the treatment of patients with Aids.* **to** *The information was useless to him.*

2 weak/not successful
● VERBS **be**
● ADV. **bloody** (*taboo*) | **completely** | **pretty**
● PREP. **at** *I'm pretty useless at this job.*

user noun

• ADJ. **heavy, large** *heavy users of credit* ◇ *The larger users of the service have to pay more.* | **small** | **daily, regular** | **current, existing** *Existing users will be able to upgrade their software at a reduced price.* | **first-time, novice** *They offer a short course to first-time users of the software.* | **end** *The company supplies its computers direct to the end user.* | **computer, PC** | **business, home** *a computer intended for business and home users* | **bus, car, rail, road, transport** | **wheelchair** *A special entrance is being built for wheelchair users.* | **library** | **service** *a survey of health service users* | **telephone** | **electricity, energy** | **drug, heroin, etc.**

usual adj.

• VERBS **be** | **become**
• ADV. **very** | **quite** *Don't worry—it's quite usual to have a few problems at first.* | **fairly** | **far from** *This kind of behaviour is far from usual in children of this age.*
• PREP. **for** *It's usual for the man to propose marriage.*
• PHRASES **as per usual** (*informal*) *Everyone blamed me as per usual.* **as usual** (= in the same way as what happens most of the time or in most cases) *Steve, as usual, was the last to arrive.* **business as usual** (= things will continue as normal in spite of a difficult situation) *It's business as usual at the factory, even while investigators sift through the bomb wreckage.* **in the usual way** *The metal can then be painted in the usual way.*

utility noun

1 usefulness
• ADJ. **great, high** | **low** | **social** *He argued that the arts have great social utility.*
• VERB + UTILITY **have**
• PREP. **of ... ~** *This computer is of low utility for the home user.*

2 service provided for the public
• ADJ. **public, state-owned** | **privatized** | **electricity, water** *a privatized electricity utility*

utilize verb

• ADV. **heavily** | **extensively** | **fully, to the full** *The new computer system is not being fully utilized yet.* | **effectively, successfully**
• PREP. **as** *Concrete had long been utilized as a bonding and covering material.*

U-turn noun

1 movement in a car
• VERB + U-TURN **do, execute, make**

2 sudden change of plan
• ADJ. **complete** | **dramatic, spectacular** | **embarrassing, humiliating** | **government, policy**
• VERB + U-TURN **do, execute, make, perform** *The government has made a spectacular U-turn on taxes.*
• PREP. **~on** *a U-turn on education policy* **~over** *a government U-turn over plans to cut social security payments*

Vv

vacancy noun

- ADJ. **unfilled** | **suitable** *The agency will let you know if they have any suitable vacancies.* | **casual, temporary** | **job, presidential, senate, staff**
- VERB + VACANCY **have** | **create, leave** *Her going on maternity leave will create a temporary vacancy.* | **fill**
- VACANCY + VERB **arise, exist, occur** *A vacancy has arisen in our sales department.*
- PREP. **~for** *a vacancy for head chef* **~in** *a vacancy in the catering department*

vacant adj.

- VERBS **be** | **become, fall** (only used of jobs) *A seat became vacant and he sat down in it.* ◇ *A job fell vacant in the accounting department.* | **remain** | **leave sth** *The office of president had been left vacant since her retirement.* | **keep sth** *The job will be kept vacant for a few more weeks.*

vaccination noun

- ADJ. **flu, measles, rubella, smallpox, etc.**
- VERB + VACCINE **have** | **give sb**
- VACCINATION + NOUN **campaign, programme**
- PREP. **~against** *a vaccination against tetanus*

vaccine noun

- ADJ. **effective, safe** | **measles, rubella, etc.** *The polio vaccine has saved millions of lives.* | **live** *a live vaccine containing the polio virus*
- QUANT. **dose** *one dose of BCG vaccine*
- VERB + VACCINE **give sb** | **have, receive** | **develop**
- VACCINE + VERB **protect sb** *The vaccine protects children against tuberculosis.* | **prevent sth** *a vaccine to prevent rubella*
- PREP. **~against** *Researchers are trying to develop a vaccine against the disease.* **~for** *a vaccine for meningitis*

vacuum noun

- ADJ. **perfect** | **moral, political, spiritual** *The writer criticized the moral vacuum in society.* | **power** *Her resignation left a power vacuum in the government.*
- VERB + VACUUM **create, leave, produce** *The machine then creates a vacuum.* | **fill** *Other gases rush in to fill the vacuum.*

vagina noun

- VERB + VAGINA **enter, penetrate**
- PREP. **in/into/inside the/your~**

vague adj.

- VERBS **be, look, sound** *'Where did you leave it?' Isobel looked vague.* | **become, get** *She seems to be getting rather vague as she grows older.* | **remain** | **leave sth** *The identity of the city in the novel is deliberately left vague.*
- ADV. **extremely, hopelessly, very** *Her directions were hopelessly vague.* | **a bit, fairly, a little, pretty, quite, rather, somewhat** | **enough, sufficiently** *It was a vague enough concept for the liberals to unite around.* | **suitably** | **deliberately, intentionally** *You're being deliberately vague.* | **necessarily** *Since the officers knew little themselves their reassurances were necessarily vague.* | **inherently** *an inherently vague and subjective concept* | **notoriously** *The law is notoriously vague on this point.*
- PREP. **about** *I am vague about what happened during*

the rest of the night. **as to** *I was suitably vague as to exactly how I had acquired the money.* **in** *The statement was vague in its wording.*

valid adj.

1 legally acceptable
- VERBS **be** | **become** | **remain, stay** | **deem sth, hold sth** *The original written contract was held valid.*
- ADV. **still** *Is your passport still valid?* | **no longer** | **legally** *Is the contract legally valid?*
- PREP. **for** *Vouchers are only valid for races taking place before 31 December.*

2 strong and convincing
- VERBS **be, seem** | **become** | **remain** | **accept sth as, consider sth, deem sth, regard sth as** *We accepted several different approaches as valid.*
- ADV. **extremely, very** | **absolutely, completely, perfectly** *This is a perfectly valid question to raise.* | **not entirely** | **reasonably** | **equally** *using a different, but equally valid technique* | **universally** *a universally valid set of moral principles* | **not necessarily** | **not strictly** *That argument is not strictly valid in this case.* | **still** | **no longer** *The old assumptions are no longer valid.* | **logically, scientifically, statistically** *a logically valid deduction*

validity noun

- ADJ. **great** | **equal** *Don't you think that both views have equal validity?* | **doubtful, dubious, questionable** | **face** *The theory has the face validity of being consistent with recent findings.* | **legal, scientific** *The legal validity of the claims has been challenged.*
- VERB + VALIDITY **have** | **give sth, lend sth** *His reputation lends a certain validity to the approach that it might not deserve.* | **cast doubt on, challenge, deny, question** | **accept, confirm, uphold** *The judges upheld the validity of the previous judgement.* | **assess, test** *to assess the scientific validity of new treatments*
- PREP. **of ... ~** *The results are of doubtful validity.* | **~for** *the theory's validity for parent-child relationships*

valley noun

- ADJ. **broad, deep, high, long, steep, wide** | **little, narrow, shallow, small** | **steep** | **lower, upper** | **fertile, forested, green, wooded** | **mountain, river** | **Rhine, Thames, etc.**
- VALLEY + NOUN **bottom, floor, side**
- PREP. **in a/the~** *The cottage was in a wooded valley.*

valour noun

- ADJ. **great** *a soldier famed for his great valour*
- VERB + VALOUR **demonstrate, display, show** *He showed valour and skill on the battlefield.*
- PREP. **an act/a deed of valour**

valuable adj.

1 worth a lot of money
- VERBS **be, look** | **become** | **remain**
- ADV. **extremely, really, very** | **quite, rather** | **commercially** *commercially valuable expertise*

2 very useful
- VERBS **be, prove, seem** | **become** | **remain** | **make sb/sth** *They have skills and qualities which make them highly valuable.* | **consider sth**
- ADV. **eminently, enormously, especially, exceeding-**

ly, exceptionally, extremely, highly, immensely, most, particularly, really, truly, very | increasingly | quite | equally *The subject could be equally valuable for scientists.* | inherently, intrinsically *The Romantics believed that the life of the imagination was intrinsically valuable.* | potentially | ecologically, educationally, scientifically, socially *ecologically valuable species*
• PREP. **as** *The survey was valuable as an indicator of local opinion.* **for** *Good eyesight is a quality which is extremely valuable for a hunting animal.* **to** *documents that are enormously valuable to historians*

valuation noun

• ADJ. **high, low** | **detailed** | **independent** | **actuarial** | **market** | **land, mortgage, property** | **share, stock**
• VERB + VALUATION **carry out, do, make, prepare**
• VALUATION + NOUN **fee, report**

value noun

1 amount of money that sth is worth
• ADJ. **high, low** *the high value of the dollar* | **full, total** | **real, true** | **nominal** *a share with a nominal value of £20* | **face** *At yesterday's auction an old coin sold for many times more than its face value of 20 pence.* | **residual** *a residual value of 10% of its original cost* | **resale** *Regular servicing will add to the resale value of your PC.*
• VERB + VALUE **place, put, set** *It's hard to put a value on a company with large assets and turnover but low profits.* | **add** | **increase, raise** | **double, triple, etc.** *Dramatic developments on the stock market tripled the value of his shares.* | **lower, reduce** | **hold, keep** *The piano has held its value.* | **calculate, work out**
• VALUE + VERB **double, triple, etc.** | **appreciate, go up, increase** | **decrease, depreciate, fall, go down**
• PREP. **in ~** *The land has dropped in value.* **to the ~ of** *Jewellery to the value of a million pounds was stolen last night.*
• PHRASES **an increase/a rise in value, a drop/fall/reduction in value**

2 how much sth is worth compared with its price
• ADJ. **excellent, good, great, outstanding** | **poor**
• PHRASES **value for money** *Though a little more expensive, the larger model gives better value for money.*

3 importance
• ADJ. **enormous, great, high, immense, incalculable, tremendous** | **doubtful, dubious, limited, low** *His published account of his travels is of dubious value to other explorers.* | **lasting** | **main, real, true** | **practical, sentimental, symbolic**
• VERB + VALUE **have** *The stolen necklace only had sentimental value for her.* | **attach, place, put, set** *He places a high value on marriage.*
• VALUE + VERB **be, lie** *The real value of the book lies in its wonderful characterization.*
• PREP. **of ~** *He didn't say anything of value.* | **~ to** *Pottery fragments are of great value to archaeologists.*

4 values set of beliefs
• ADJ. **dominant** *the dominant values of a society* | **conservative, conventional, traditional** | **common, shared, universal** *What shared values do you have with your friends?* | **human** | **aesthetic, cultural, educational, ethical, moral, political, social, spiritual** *We need to be guided by our moral values.* | **family** *The party's election campaign emphasized its belief in family values.* | **middle-class, Victorian, Western** | **parental** *the rejection of parental values by a child* | **democratic, liberal**
• QUANT. **set** *a prevailing set of cultural values*
• VERB + VALUES **have, hold** *They hold very middle-class values.* | **cherish, encourage, foster** *Is it the role of schools to foster spiritual values?* | **hold onto, preserve** *a society that has failed to preserve its traditional values*
• VALUE + NOUN **system** *a common value system*

value verb

1 decide how much sth is worth
• ADV. **officially**
• PREP. **at** *The company has recently been valued at $6 billion.*

2 think sb/sth is very important
• ADV. **greatly, highly, particularly** | **increasingly** | **positively** | **negatively** *Housework is negatively valued as a retreat from a disliked alternative—employment work.* | **rightly** *the fear of losing the independence that they rightly value* | **socially** *one of the most socially valued roles in contemporary society—being a parent*
• VERB + VALUE **learn to** *learning to value the ordinary things in life*
• PREP. **as** *I value her very highly as a friend.* **for** *He hated to be valued for his looks alone.*

valueless adj.

• VERBS **be, seem** | **become**
• ADV. **completely, quite** *Our shares became completely valueless overnight.*
• PREP. **as** *Some of the royal forests had become valueless as hunting grounds.*

valve noun

• ADJ. **safety** | **non-return, one-way** | **drain, pressure-relief** | **fuel, water, etc.** | **heart, radiator, etc.**
• VERB + VALVE **fit** *The plumber will fit some new safety valves.* | **open** *You need special tools to open the valve.* | **close**

van noun

1 vehicle for transporting goods, etc.
• ADJ. **light** | **transit** | **camper** | **delivery, furniture, ice-cream, mail, removal** | **armoured, police**
• VERB + VAN **drive** | **park** | **load, unload**
• VAN + NOUN **driver**

2 type of railway carriage
• ADJ. **goods, guard's, luggage**

vandal noun

• ADJ. **car** *Car vandals caused more than £10 000 worth of damage to vehicles last Saturday.*
• VERB + VANDAL **deter, discourage** *The windows are covered with grilles to deter vandals.*
• VANDAL + VERB **damage sth, wreck sth**

vandalism noun

• ADJ. **mindless, wanton** | **criminal** | **environmental**
• VERB + VANDALISM **discourage, prevent**
• PHRASES **an act of vandalism**

vanish verb

1 disappear suddenly and completely
• ADV. **just, simply** *I turned round and she had simply vanished.* | **abruptly, instantly, promptly, suddenly** | **quickly, rapidly** *Her feelings of shyness rapidly vanished.* | **mysteriously** *a man who mysteriously vanished from his home last month*
• VERB + VANISH **seem to** | **make sb/sth**
• PREP. **from** *All thoughts of romance vanished from his mind.* **into** *She vanished into the mist.*
• PHRASES **vanish from the face of the earth, vanish from sight, vanish into thin air** *At a stroke she could make things vanish into thin air.* **vanish without trace**

2 disappear over a period of time
• ADV. **altogether, completely, entirely, totally** *Many of these old cinemas have now vanished altogether.* | **all but, almost, virtually** *country inns of a type that has now all*

but vanished | **long since** *The people who built this temple have long since vanished.* | **forever** *Much of the land we loved has vanished forever.*
• PREP. **from** *This plant is vanishing from the British countryside.*

vanity *noun*

• ADJ. **great** | **female, human, male, personal**
• VERB + VANITY **appeal to, flatter** *My suggestion appealed to her vanity.*

vapour *noun*

• ADJ. **water**
• QUANT. **cloud** *There was a hissing sound, and clouds of vapour were emitted.*
• VERB + VAPOUR **form, turn to** *The particles then form a vapour.* | **emit, give off/out**
• VAPOUR + VERB **condense**

variability *noun*

• ADJ. **considerable, extreme, great, high, wide** *There is considerable variability in all the test scores.* | **low, slight**
• QUANT. **degree**
• PREP. **~ among/between** *variability among different health authorities* **~ in** *variability in crop yields*

variable *adj.*

• VERBS **be, seem** | **become**
• ADV. **extremely, highly, very, widely** *Polar habitats are harsh and highly variable.* | **infinitely** *These systems are infinitely variable.* | **increasingly** | **quite, slightly, somewhat**
• PREP. **in** *variable in shape*

variation *noun*

• ADJ. **considerable, dramatic, enormous, extreme, great, major, marked, significant, striking, substantial, tremendous, wide** | **minor, slight, small, subtle** *subtle variations of colour and design* | **numerous** | **endless, infinite** | **complex** | **random** | **systematic** | **local, regional** | **climatic, cultural, environmental, ethnic, genetic, geographical, hereditary, language, linguistic** | **annual, daily, day-to-day, seasonal, year-to-year**
• VERB + VARIATION **show** *The businesses showed a dramatic variation in how they treated their staff.* | **find, observe** *Considerable variation was found in the terms offered by different banks.* | **analyse**
• VARIATION + VERB **occur**
• PREP. **~ according to** *variation according to the time of year* **~ across** *She is studying language variation across the social range.* **~ among** *variation among the students in terms of ability* **~ between** *variations between different accents* **~ by** *There is little variation by sex or social class in these attitudes.* **~ in** *slight variations in pressure* **~ with** *temperature variation with altitude* **~ within** *There may be striking variations within a species.*
• PHRASES **a range of variation, a variation on a theme** *His numerous complaints are all variations on a theme.*

varied *adj.*

• VERBS **be** | **become** | **remain**
• ADV. **enormously, extremely, highly, immensely, richly, tremendously, very, widely, wonderfully** *a richly varied cultural life* | **endlessly, infinitely** *an endlessly varied repertoire of songs* | **increasingly** | **quite** | **enough, sufficiently**
• PHRASES **many and varied** *The opportunities the job offers are many and varied.*

variety *noun*

1 not being the same; different kinds of sth
• ADJ. **amazing, astonishing, bewildering, considerable, endless, enormous, exciting, extraordinary, fascinating, good, great, huge, impressive, incredible, infinite, large, remarkable, rich, surprising, tremendous, vast, wide, wonderful** *The market sold a bewildering variety of cheeses.* ◊ *the rich variety of the local bird life*
• VERB + VARIETY **add, give, offer** *Dealing with customers adds variety to the job.*
• PREP. **of ...** *~ a country of great variety* | **~ in** *There is wide variety in shape and colour.* **~ of** *Menus offer a good variety of seafood.*

2 particular type of sth
• ADJ. **distinctive** | **common-or-garden, standard** | **rare, unusual** | **different** *There are hundreds of different varieties of apple.* | **new, old** *Old varieties of rose can be less resistant to diseases.*

varnish *noun*

• ADJ. **clear, colourless, transparent** | **gloss, glossy** | **matt** (see also **nail varnish**)
• QUANT. **coat** *The table needed two coats of varnish.*
• VERB + VARNISH **apply** *Apply the varnish evenly over the whole surface.* | **remove, scrape off, strip off**
• VARNISH + VERB **dry** | **protect sth** *You need a good quality varnish to protect the timber.*
• VARNISH + NOUN **remover**

vary *verb*

• ADV. **considerably, dramatically, enormously, a great deal, greatly, a lot, markedly, sharply, significantly, substantially, tremendously, widely, wildly** | **hardly** *The sword hardly varied in form from the 12th to the 15th century.* | (a) **little, slightly, somewhat** | **constantly, continuously** *the continuously varying intensities of natural light* | **never** | **inevitably, necessarily** *What can be found will inevitably vary according to the area under study.* | **naturally, obviously** *Personal preference naturally varies.* | **systematically** | **accordingly** *Dictionaries are produced with specific markets in mind, and their contents vary accordingly.* | **inversely** *The availability of good medical care tends to vary inversely with the need for it.* | **geographically, historically** *Voting behaviour varies geographically.*
• VERB + VARY **can, may** *Prices can vary enormously.* | **be likely to, tend to**
• PREP. **according to** *The leaf's size varies widely according to the area where it grows.* **among** *Services offered vary among the main high street banks.* **between** *The rate of growth varies considerably between different industries.* ◊ *The doses used for surgical anaesthesia vary between 2 and 10mg/kg.* **by** *Access to this information varies by social class.* **depending on** *Costs are likely to vary depending on where you live.* **from ... to ...** *The situation varies slightly from country to country.* ◊ *Its speed varies from 20 mph to 35 mph.* **in** *The rooms vary in size.* **with** *The danger of a heart attack varies with body weight.*
• PHRASES **vary over/with time** *studying moral values and how they vary over time*

vase *noun*

• ADJ. **flower** | **china, crystal, cut-glass, glass, porcelain, silver, stone**
• VASE + VERB **be filled with sth, contain sth, hold sth** | **stand** *A silver vase stood on the mantelpiece.*
• PREP. **in a/the ~** *flowers arranged in a vase* | **~ of** *a vase of fresh flowers*

vault noun

1 strong, underground room
- ADJ. **secure | bank, museum | treasure**
- VERB + VAULT **keep/store sth in**
- PREP. **in a/the~** *The jewels were kept in a bank vault.*

2 room under a church where dead people are buried
- ADJ. **burial, family, royal**
- VERB + VAULT **bury sb in** *She is to be buried in the family vault.*

veer verb

- ADV. **sharply, violently, wildly** *The ship veered round wildly in the rough sea.* | **(to the) left, (to the) right | away, round** *The plane veered away to the left.*
- PREP. **between** *(figurative) He veered between calm acceptance and hysterical accusations.* **from** *(figurative) The play veers from loopy comedy to serious moralizing.* **off** *The car veered off the road.* **to** *The path veers sharply to the right.* **towards** *He veered left towards them.*

vegetable noun

- ADJ. **green, leafy, root, salad** *The children don't eat enough green vegetables.* | **crisp** *a salad of crisp, raw vegetables.* | **cooked, raw | fresh, frozen, tinned | organic | early, seasonal, spring, summer, winter | rotten**
- VERB + VEGETABLE **grow** *They grow all their own vegetables.* | **eat, have | boil, cook, overcook, parboil, steam, stir-fry | chop, peel, purée**
- VEGETABLE + NOUN **garden, patch, plot | market, stall | rack | crop | produce | dish, soup, stew, stock, terrine | fat, oil | protein | dye | fibre, matter**
- ⇨ Special page at FOOD

vegetarian noun

- ADJ. **strict** *They are strict vegetarians.*
- VEGETARIAN + NOUN **cookery, dish, food, meal | diet | restaurant**
- PHRASES **suitable for vegetarians** *All our cheeses are suitable for vegetarians.*

vegetation noun

- ADJ. **green | dense, lush, luxuriant, thick | scrub, scrubby, sparse** *As we drove towards the desert, the vegetation became sparse.* | **decaying, decomposing, rotten, rotting** *piles of rotting vegetation* | **natural** *Removal of the natural vegetation has resulted in a loss of nutrients in the soil.* | **aquatic, woodland, sub-tropical, tropical**
- VERB + VEGETATION **be covered in/with** *The hills are covered in lush green vegetation.*
- VEGETATION + VERB **grow**
- VEGETATION + NOUN **cover**

vehicle noun

1 used for transporting people or things
- ADJ. **moving, oncoming, passing** *She was blinded by the lights from an oncoming vehicle.* | **parked, stationary** *The bus crashed into a stationary vehicle.* | **unattended | stolen** *The thieves escaped in a stolen vehicle.* | **horse-drawn, motor | electric, diesel, petrol/petrol-driven | wheeled** *The city centre is off-limits to wheeled vehicles.* | **road, four-wheel-drive | all-terrain, off-road | vintage | private | commercial, delivery, (heavy) goods | emergency | police | armoured, military**
- QUANT. **convoy** *The president's car was being followed by a convoy of vehicles.*
- VERB + VEHICLE **own | hire** *Hire a four-wheel-drive vehicle—there are lots of spots to discover off the beaten track.* | **drive | park | impound, tow away** *The vehicle was impounded as part of the police investigation.* |

abandon *Sniffer dogs were brought in to follow the men after they abandoned the vehicle in a ditch.*
- VEHICLE + VERB **arrive** *An eyewitness said, 'We saw loads of smoke, and then the emergency vehicles arrived.'* | **break down | collide, crash (into sth)** *Two drivers escaped injury when their vehicles collided near Thirsk.* | **run on sth** *vehicles running on lead-free petrol*
- VEHICLE + NOUN **emission** *tighter controls on vehicle emissions* | **manufacture**

2 sth used for communicating ideas/achieving sth
- ADJ. **excellent, ideal, perfect | important, main, major**
- PREP. **~ for** *The play is a perfect vehicle for her talents.* **~ of** *The Students' Union is the main vehicle of communication for students in the college.*

veil noun

1 piece of material for covering a woman's head
- ADJ. **bridal** *The bridal veil was fringed with lace.*
- VERB + VEIL **wear | lift (back), remove, take off**
- VEIL + VERB **cover sth** *A veil covered her face.*
- PREP. **behind a/the~** *I couldn't see her face behind the veil.*

2 sth that stops you knowing the full truth about sth
- VERB + VEIL **lift** *The government has decided to lift the veil on its plans.* | **draw** *It would be better to draw a veil over what happened next* (= not talk about it).
- PREP. **behind/under~of** *The work is carried out behind a veil of secrecy.*

vein noun

1 tube carrying blood in the body
- ADJ. **blue** *A blue vein throbbed in his forehead.* | **broken, thread, varicose** *She uses make-up to hide the thread veins in her cheeks.* | **jugular**
- VERB + VEIN **course/run along/through, flow through, pump through, race through, rush through** *He felt the adrenalin coursing through his veins.*
- VEIN + VERB **bulge, pulse, stand out, throb** *The veins stood out on her throat and temples.*

2 particular style/quality
- ADJ. **rich**
- VERB + VEIN **hit, strike** *The team have hit a rich vein of form recently.* | **tap (into)**
- PREP. **~ of** *The writer tapped into a rich vein of humour in the play.*
- PHRASES **in a different vein, in a lighter/more serious vein** *Fortunately, the rest of the evening continued in a lighter vein.* **in the same vein/in a similar vein**

velocity noun

- ADJ. **enormous, high | low | constant, uniform | average, mean | maximum**
- VERB + VELOCITY **achieve, attain, reach** *Eventually, the star attained the velocity of light.* | **move with** *to move with a uniform velocity* | **increase, raise**
- VELOCITY + VERB **increase, rise | decrease, fall**
- PREP. **at a/the~** *Light travels at a constant velocity.*

velvet noun

- ADJ. **heavy | rich | faded, worn | crushed**
- PREP. **of~** *curtains of heavy crimson velvet*

vendetta noun

- ADJ. **personal, political**
- VERB + VENDETTA **conduct, pursue, run**
- PREP. **~ against** *For years he pursued a vendetta against the Morris family.*

veneer *noun*

- ADJ. **thin | false | civilized**
- VERB + VENEER **acquire | strip (off), strip sb/sth of** *They have stripped the veneer of jingoism from the play, by showing war in its true horror.*
- VENEER + VERB **disguise sth, hide sth, mask sth** *He managed to acquire a thin veneer of knowledge to mask his real ignorance.* | **crack** *For the first time her veneer of politeness began to crack.*
- PREP. **behind/below/beneath/under a/the ~** *They're brutal people behind their civilized veneer.* | **~of**

vengeance *noun*

- ADJ. **terrible**
- VERB + VENGEANCE **exact, take, wreak** *She is determined to wreak vengeance on those who killed her cousin.* | **be bent on, demand, seek, swear, vow, want** *He stormed out, eyes blazing, bent on vengeance.*
- PREP. **~ against** *They sought vengeance against the countries that had humiliated France in 1814.* **~ for** *vengeance for the murder of the princess* **~ on** *He silently vowed vengeance on them all.*

venom *noun*

1 poisonous fluid from a snake, etc.
- ADJ. **deadly | snake, spider, etc.**
- VERB + VENOM **inject, spit** *The snake injects the venom immediately after biting its prey.*
- VENOM + NOUN **gland**

2 extreme anger or hatred
- ADJ. **pure, real, undisguised** *a look of pure venom*
- VERB + VENOM **spit** *She surveyed him coldly with eyes that spat venom.*
- PREP. **with ~** *She said it quickly and with venom.*

venomous *adj.*

- VERBS **be**
- ADV. **highly** *a highly venomous snake* | **actively** *There are two types of mollusc that are actively venomous.*

vent *noun*

- ADJ. **air, heating | roof, side**
- VERB + VENT **open, close | fit, install**
- PREP. **through a/the ~** *Air passes through a vent.*

ventilate *verb*

- ADV. **adequately, properly, well** *Make sure that the room is well ventilated.* | **badly, poorly**

ventilation *noun*

- ADJ. **adequate, good** *Inspectors checked that there was adequate ventilation.* | **inadequate, poor | artificial, mechanical | natural | through** *The windows at the back are blocked up, so there is no through ventilation.*
- VERB + VENTILATION **give, provide** *Zips up the sides of the jacket give good ventilation.*
- VENTILATION + NOUN **system | brick, duct, grille, hole, opening, pipe, shaft, slit, tube**

venture *noun*

- ADJ. **exciting | new | profitable, successful | costly, expensive, unprofitable | ill-fated, unsuccessful | ambitious, bold, brave, high-risk, risky, speculative | collaborative, cooperative, joint | private | non-commercial | business, commercial, financial, publishing, tourism/tourist, trading**
- VERB + VENTURE **embark on, undertake** *The directors of the company refused to undertake such a risky venture.* | **establish, set up** *The company has set up a joint venture with a firm in Austria.* | **join (in), join sb in** *His son Mark will be joining him in the new venture.*
- VENTURE + NOUN **capital, funds, money**
- PREP. **~ by** *a cooperative venture by firms at the science park*
⇨ Special page at BUSINESS

venture *verb*

- ADV. **cautiously** *She ventured cautiously into the room.* | **rarely, seldom | far, further (afield)** *Some of the men ventured further out to sea.* | **abroad, forth, out, outside** *A few people ventured out into the street.*
- VERB + VENTURE **dare (to)** *She would not have dared venture here alone.*
- PREP. **away from, beyond, into, out of** *They rarely ventured beyond their local market town.*

venue *noun*

- ADJ. **ideal, perfect, popular, prestigious, top** *Europe's top venue for indoor athletics* | **intimate** *With room for only 200 people, this is the most intimate venue the band has played for years.* | **all-seater, 500-seater, etc. | outdoor | home, neutral** *The match will be played at a neutral venue.* | **tourist | cabaret, concert, conference, entertainment, exhibition, performance, rock, sporting/sports**
- VERB + VENUE **be, provide** *The Holiday Inn provided the venue for this year's conference.* | **hire | play | pack (out)** *The musical has been packing out venues around the world.*
- PREP. **at a/the ~** *The meeting will be held at a venue in the south of the city.* **in a/the ~** *She has performed in venues around Europe.* | **~ for** *The hall is a popular venue for weddings.*
- PHRASES **a change of venue**

verb *noun*

- ADJ. **plural, singular | intransitive, transitive | active, passive | irregular, regular | main** *What's the main verb of the sentence?* | **finite | auxiliary, linking, modal | phrasal**
- VERB + VERB **use** *In this essay he has used the same verbs over and over again.* | **take** *'Government' can take a singular or plural verb.* | **agree with** *The subject doesn't agree with the verb.* | **conjugate, inflect** *Do you know how to conjugate the verb 'seek'?* | **modify, qualify** *Adverbs modify verbs.*
- VERB + VERB **take sth** *Transitive verbs take a direct object.* | **agree with sth, inflect** *Add an ending to make the verb agree with the subject.* | **end in sth**
- VERB + NOUN **ending, form, phrase**
- PHRASES **a verb of motion/perception**

verdict *noun*

1 decision in a court of law about whether sb is guilty
- ADJ. **adverse, favourable** *In the case of an adverse verdict, the company could stand to lose millions.* | **guilty, not guilty, not proven | majority, unanimous** *a unanimous verdict of not guilty* | **formal** *The jury returned a formal verdict after direction by the judge.* | **jury, trial | appeal, inquest | accident, accidental death, manslaughter, murder, misadventure, open, suicide** *An open verdict was the only appropriate one, given the very unclear evidence at the inquest.*
- VERB + VERDICT **consider** *The judge sent the jury away to consider its verdict.* | **agree (on), arrive at, reach** *They reached a verdict after hours of deliberation.* | **announce, bring in, deliver, enter, read out, give, pass, pronounce, record, return** *The verdict was delivered in front of a packed courtroom.* ◇ *The jury returned a verdict of guilty at the end of the trial.* ◇ *The coroner recorded a verdict of accidental death.* | **accept | appeal against,**

protest against | overturn, quash, reverse, set aside *His family always insisted that the original 'guilty' verdict should be overturned.* | **uphold** *The verdict was upheld at appeal.*
• VERDICT + VERB **be in sb's favour**
• PREP. **~against** *We believe that the verdict against him was unfair.* **~of** *a verdict of accidental death*

2 decision/opinion
• ADJ. **final** *The panel will give its final verdict tomorrow.* | **general, overall, unanimous** *The unanimous verdict was that the picnic had been a great success.*
• VERB + VERDICT **give**
• PREP. **~on** *What's your verdict on her new book?*

verge *noun*

• ADJ. **grass | motorway, roadside**
• VERB + VERGE **bring sb/sth to** *(figurative) This action brought the country to the verge of economic collapse.*
• PREP. **on the~** *(figurative) She was on the verge of a nervous breakdown when she finally sought help.*

verification *noun*

• ADJ. **empirical, scientific**
• VERIFICATION + NOUN **procedures**
• PREP. **subject to~** *The credit card is then accepted, subject to verification of the signature.*

vermin *noun*

• VERB + VERMIN **regard sth as** *Farmers regard foxes as vermin.* | **catch, control, deal with, shoot**

versatile *adj.*

• VERBS **be, prove, seem**
• ADV. **amazingly, extremely, highly, very, wonderfully** *This machine is amazingly versatile.* | **fairly, quite**

verse *noun*

• ADJ. **humorous, light, satirical | blank, free, rhyming**
• VERB + VERSE **compose, write**
• VERSE + NOUN **form | drama**
• PREP. **in~** *a play in verse*

version *noun*

1 sth based on sth else
• ADJ. **current, latest, new, updated, up-to-date | early, initial, original, preliminary, prototype** *an earlier version of this computer software* | **later, subsequent | definitive, final** *the final version of the architectural plans* | **future** *A future version of the camera is currently being developed.* | **basic, standard | primitive, simplified | amended, enhanced, improved, modified, refined, revamped | advanced, complex, elaborate, sophisticated** *a more advanced version of the initial concept* | **high-performance | customized | de luxe, expensive, luxury | cheap, low-cost | miniature | enlarged | compact, cut-down, portable, scaled-down, small-scale | full-blown, full-length, full-size | French, French-language, etc.** *the Japanese-language version of the software*
• VERB + VERSION **develop | bring out, create, come out/up with, introduce, launch, offer, present, produce, release, roll out, unveil** *The company will roll out an enhanced version of its operating system in the new year.*
• VERSION + VERB **be out, come out** *The new version comes out in June.* | **be based on sth**

2 play, film, book, piece of writing, etc.
• ADJ. **draft, rough** *Keep a copy of the rough version of your essay.* | **abridged, condensed, short, simplified | unabridged | expanded | authorized, official** *This is the official version of the painter's biography.* | **unauthorized, unofficial | hardback, paperback | CD-ROM, electronic, interactive | French, French-language, etc. | film, movie, musical, screen, stage, television** *The film version does not live up to the original novel.* | **cover** (= of a song) *The band does a lively cover version of 'Johnny B. Goode'.*
• VERB + VERSION **do**
• PREP. **in a/the~** *The children read the novel in its abridged version.*

3 way sth is seen/done by sb
• ADJ. **accurate, faithful | full** *Only one newspaper printed the full version of the speech.* | **popular | extreme, radical | watered-down, weak** *Theirs is a watered-down version of socialism.*
• VERB + VERSION **give sb** *She agreed to give her version of events to journalists.*

vessel *noun*

1 ship/boat
• ADJ. **crippled, stranded, stricken, wrecked | seaworthy | sailing, steam | ocean-going, sea-going | fishing | cargo, commercial, container, freight, merchant | naval | escort, patrol, supply, support, survey, transport | passenger | research | foreign**
• VERB + VESSEL **operate** *He was accused of operating the vessel while drunk.* | **register** *The vessel was registered in Bermuda.* | **charter | steer | anchor, moor | sink | ram** *The captain of the boat was accused of ramming a patrol vessel.* | **refloat** *A salvage team failed to refloat the vessel.* | **board** *Police boarded and searched the vessel.* | **swamp** *Huge waves swamped the vessel.*
• VESSEL + VERB **be afloat** *It was one of the largest vessels afloat.* | **sail** *The damaged vessel sailed on for another 50 miles.* | **be bound for sth** *a French vessel bound for Nigeria* | **enter a port, make port** *The vessel finally made port after thirty days at sea.* | **leave a port | carry sb/sth** *The vessel carried a crew of 130.* | **flood | go/lie/run aground, sink** *The vessel flooded and began to sink.*
• PREP. **aboard a/the~** *They managed to haul the survivors aboard the vessel.* **alongside a/the~** *A rescue boat managed to come alongside the crippled vessel.* **on/on board a/the~** *A fire broke out on board the vessel.*

2 container for liquids
• ADJ. **drinking | empty** *It is a scientific fact that empty vessels make the most noise.* | **ritual, sacred** *ancient bronze ritual vessels* | **bronze, glass, pottery, silver, wooden**
• VERB + VESSEL **fill**
• VESSEL + VERB **contain sth**
⇨ See BLOOD VESSEL

vest *noun*

• ADJ. **sleeveless | string | thermal | running | bullet-proof**
• PREP. **in (your)~** *standing there in vest and shorts*
⇨ Special page at CLOTHES

vestige *noun*

• ADJ. **last, remaining** *The government has to remove any last vestiges of corruption.*
• VERB + VESTIGE **lose, shed | dispel, remove, strip sb/sth of | preserve, retain** *I'm struggling to retain any vestige of belief in his innocence.* | **show** *He showed no vestige of remorse for his crime.*
• PREP. **without a~** *He looked at her without a vestige of sympathy.* | **~of**

vet *noun*

• ADJ. **good | qualified | practising | country, local**
• VERB + VET **call (out)** *I think we'll have to call the vet*

out. | consult, go to, see, speak to/with, take sth to, talk to/with *We had to take the dog to the local vet.*
• VET + VERB **recommend sth**
⇨ Note at JOB

vet *verb*

• ADV. **carefully | fully, thoroughly**
• PREP. **for** *All goods are carefully vetted for quality before they leave the factory.*
• PHRASES **vetting procedure** *We are introducing new security vetting procedures.*

veteran *noun*

1 sb who has served in the army, navy, etc.
• ADJ. **war | army, navy | retired | disabled, wounded | Vietnam, World War Two, etc.**
• PREP. **~of** *a veteran of World War Two*
2 sb with long experience of an activity, etc.
• ADJ. **seasoned** *He's the seasoned veteran, who has taken the children to the museum many times.* | **industry**
• VETERAN + NOUN **campaigner, leader, politician**
• PREP. **~of** *a veteran of numerous political campaigns*

veto *noun*

• ADJ. **effective, virtual | absolute | government, presidential**
• VERB + VETO **have | cast, exercise, impose, use** *The board can exercise its veto to prevent the decision.* | **lift** *The agreement became possible when Spain lifted its veto.* | **override, overturn** *The Senate voted to override the president's veto.*
• VETO + NOUN **power, rights**
• PREP. **~against** *The nobles had a virtual veto against peasant candidates.* **~on** *The Opposition effectively have a veto on constitutional reform.* **~over** *a veto over all political appointments*
• PHRASES **a power/right of veto**

veto *verb*

• ADV. **effectively** *The president effectively vetoed this measure.*
• VERB + VETO **threaten to**
• PHRASES **the power/right to veto sth**

viability *noun*

• ADJ. **continued, continuing, future, long-term** *She is very negative about the long-term viability of the project.* | **commercial, economic, financial, political**
• VERB + VIABILITY **assess, explore, investigate, test | prove** *Once the railways had proved their viability expansion was rapid.* | **ensure | maintain, preserve, safeguard** *measures to preserve the viability of small businesses* | **improve | doubt, question** *The company has questioned the commercial viability of the mine.* | **threaten, undermine**

viable *adj.*

• VERBS **be, prove, seem, sound** *None of the projects proved financially viable.* | **become | remain | make sth** *It is only their investment that makes the programme economically viable.* | **consider sth, regard sth as**
• ADV. **extremely, truly | perfectly** *a perfectly viable form of political organization* | **potentially | still | no longer | commercially, economically, financially**

vibrate *verb*

• ADV. **gently**
• VERB + VIBRATE **seem to**
• PREP. **through** *The thuds vibrated through the car.* **with** *The atmosphere seemed to vibrate with tension.*

vibration *noun*

• ADJ. **high-frequency, low-frequency**
• VERB + VIBRATION **cause, make, produce | dampen, reduce | detect, feel** *Certain animals can feel vibrations in the sand.* ◊ *Their instruments can detect the slightest vibration.*
• VIBRATION + NOUN **frequency | level**
• PREP. **~from** *vibrations from heavy traffic*

vice *noun*

• ADJ. **secret**
• VERB + VICE **indulge (in)** *He used his inheritance to indulge his vices of drinking and gambling.*

vicinity *noun*

• ADJ. **close, immediate, near**
• PREP. **in the~(of)** *There is no hospital in the immediate vicinity.*

vicious *adj.*

• VERBS **be, look, sound | become, get, turn** *The computer wars are going to get vicious over the next few years.*
• ADV. **particularly, truly, very** *a particularly vicious and brutal crime* | **increasingly | rather**

victim *noun*

• ADJ. **hapless, helpless, innocent, poor, unfortunate, unsuspecting, unwilling** *He defrauded his innocent victims of millions of pounds.* | **easy** *Tourists are easy victims for pickpockets.* | **passive | willing** *In his fantasies, women became passive and sometimes even willing victims.* | **intended, potential** *The intended victims were selected because they seemed vulnerable.* | **child, elderly** *the child victims of the war* | **Aids, cancer, heart attack, plague, stroke | accident, bomb, crash, disaster, earthquake, famine, flood** *The government is sending aid to flood victims.* | **kidnap, murder, rape | sacrificial | fashion** *She's a fashion victim (= wears the newest fashions even if they do not suit her).*
• VERB + VICTIM **portray sb as** *In his trial, he tried to portray himself as the victim of an uncaring society.* | **claim** *The train crash claimed its tenth victim yesterday when the driver died in hospital.* | **compensate** *a bill aimed at compensating victims of air pollution* | **blame** *The cut in benefits for the unemployed is a classic case of blaming the victim.*
• PREP. **~of** *They were the victims of a cruel hoax.*
• PHRASES **fall victim to sb/sth** *Unfortunately, she fell victim to an unscrupulous landlord.* **a victim of your/its own success** *The small firm became a victim of its own success when it could not supply all its orders on time.*

victor *noun*

• ADJ. **clear, runaway | worthy**
• VERB + VICTOR **be, emerge (as)** *The team emerged as worthy victors.*
• PREP. **~over** *The French pair fought back to finish two sets to one victors over the Williams sisters.*

victorious *adj.*

• VERBS **be, emerge, prove** *Osborne emerged victorious after the second round of voting.*
• ADV. **eventually, ultimately** *Against all the odds, Frederick II was ultimately victorious.*
• PREP. **in** *victorious in the election* **over** *The Reds were victorious over the Whites.*

victory *noun*

• ADJ. **famous, glorious, great, historic, impressive, notable, outstanding, remarkable, significant, superb |**

clear, clear-cut, comfortable, convincing, crushing, easy, emphatic, handsome, landslide, massive, overwhelming, resounding, sweeping *His party won a landslide victory in the elections.* | complete, comprehensive, outright, total | **narrow** | conclusive, decisive *The army won the decisive victory that changed the course of the war.* | dramatic, thrilling | shock, stunning, surprise, unexpected | crucial, vital | deserved, well-deserved | hollow, Pyrrhic | election, electoral, military, moral, political

● VERB + VICTORY clinch, ensure, notch up, pull off, record, score, secure, snatch, win *They would do whatever lay in their power to ensure victory for themselves.* ◇ *The Hungarians pulled off a surprise victory against the Italian champions.* | taste *The England cricket team has tasted victory for the first time this season.* | end in | roar/romp/storm/sweep to *Labour swept to victory in the 2001 election.* | hail sth as | hail *Union leaders hailed the socialists' victory as a huge step forward.* | celebrate | claim *The outcome left both sides claiming victory.* | gain sb, give sb | deny sb *The Dutch champions were denied victory in a tough 2–2 draw at Porto.*

● VICTORY + NOUN celebration, parade | speech | dance, salute

● PREP. **~against** *a victory against Fascism* **~for** *The case was hailed as a victory for the common man.* **~over** *their resounding victory over England*

● PHRASES **snatch victory from the jaws of defeat**

video noun

1 system of recording moving pictures and sound

● ADJ. interactive

● VIDEO + NOUN camera, equipment, machine, player, recorder, screen | clip, film, footage, image, picture, recording, replay, sequence *The jury watched video footage of the riots.* | shoot *The band are in Iceland doing a video shoot.* | channel *I can't find the video channel on this television.* | game | conferencing | conference, presentation | link *The speech was broadcast via a video link to thousands standing outside.* | surveillance

● PREP. **on~** *The film is already out on video.*

2 tape/cassette

● ADJ. hour-long, ten-minute, etc. | blank | pre-recorded *They sell both blank and pre-recorded videos.* | amateur, home *An amateur video of the crash failed to reveal the cause.* | educational, instructional *They produce educational videos for learning languages.* | music, pop, rock | corporate | promo, promotional | training | exercise, fitness | porn/porno/pornographic, sex | police, security

● VERB + VIDEO make | manufacture, produce | release *The group's new video will be released next month.* | capture sb/sth on, catch sb/sth on *The thief was caught on video as he pocketed watches and rings.* | rent **(out)** *We rent videos out nearly every weekend.* | watch *The children can sit for hours watching videos.* | show **(sb)** *Their teacher showed them a video about the Romans.* | fast-forward, rewind

● VIDEO + NOUN cassette | library, rental shop, shop | release *a review of the latest video releases*

● PREP. **~of** *a security video of the attack*

3 (*also* **video recorder**)

● VERB + VIDEO programme, set *Did you remember to set the video for 'Inspector Morse'?*

videotape noun

● VERB + VIDEOTAPE make | copy **(sth)** onto, record **(sth)** onto *Film can also be copied onto videotape.* | screen *The videotape of the attack caused outrage when it was screened on the news.*

● PREP. **~of** *a videotape of the demonstration*

view noun

1 opinion/idea about sth

● ADJ. general, popular, prevailing, widely held *The prevailing view is that he has done a good job in difficult circumstances.* | conflicting, differing, divergent, opposing, polarized *The debate brings together experts with conflicting views.* | clear, forthright, strong *He's a doctor with clear views on how to prevent illness.* | idealized, optimistic, positive, romantic, rosy *Her rosy view of life abroad seems rather naive.* | jaundiced, negative, pessimistic *After his experience in jail, he has a pretty jaundiced view of the penal system.* | conventional *The conventional view is that work is pleasant and rewarding.* | unorthodox | minority | political | liberal, modern, progressive | radical | moderate | conservative, reactionary | extremist, hard-line | stereotyped, stereotypical | informed | ill-informed, uninformed | world *His world view revolves around a battle between rich and poor.*

● VERB + VIEW have, hold | take *I took the view that an exception should be made in this case.* | air, convey, expound, express, make known, present, put forward *The meeting gave everyone the chance to air their views.* ◇ *She picked up the phone and made her views known to her boss.* | discuss, exchange, share *At the meeting, we hope people will exchange views freely.* | canvass, solicit *He called a meeting to solicit the views of his staff.* | reflect, represent *His letter to the management did not reflect the views of his colleagues.* | adhere to, agree with, endorse | confirm, support | challenge *His music challenges the view that modern jazz is inaccessible.*

● PREP. **in your~** *In my view it was a waste of time.* | **~about** *Teachers generally keep their views about politics hidden.* **~on** *Experts hold widely differing views on this subject.*

● PHRASES **an exchange of views** *It's good to have a full and frank exchange of views.* **a point of view** *From a teacher's point of view, activities that can be done with minimal preparation are invaluable.* **take a dim view of sth** (= have a poor opinion of sth) *My mother takes a pretty dim view of my cooking skills.*

2 ability to see/be seen from a particular place

● ADJ. good, grandstand, wonderful | poor, terrible *We had a poor view of the stage from where we were sitting.* | clear, unimpeded, uninterrupted, unobstructed | back, front, rear, side *The picture shows a front view of the car.* | close, close-up | public *Tensions within the band remained hidden from public view.* | overall (*figurative*) *The staff handbook gives an overall view of the company.*

● VERB + VIEW get, have *The pillar prevented me getting a clear view of the action.* | give sb *The patio gave an unimpeded view across the headland to the sea.* | block *A woman in a very large hat was blocking my view of the procession.* | come into *A large truck suddenly came into view.* | disappear from *They stood waving on the platform, until the train disappeared from view.* | be hidden from

● PREP. **in~** *There was nobody in view.* **on~** *The carriage was put on view for the public to see.*

● PHRASES **in full view (of sth)** *He was shot in full view of a large crowd.*

3 scenery

● ADJ. breathtaking, fine, lovely, magnificent, spectacular, splendid, stunning, superb, wonderful *a room with a breathtaking view across the bay* | commanding, panoramic | mountain, sea, etc.

● VERB + VIEW afford, boast, enjoy, give, have *Most rooms enjoy panoramic views of the sea.* ◇ *The large windows give fine views of the surrounding countryside.* | admire, enjoy *a place to unwind and enjoy the view*

● PREP. **~across/over** *a view over the valley* **~from** *the view from his apartment* **~of**

● PHRASES **a room with a view**

view *verb*

- ADV. **favourably, positively | unfavourably | cautiously, suspiciously** *These results should be viewed cautiously.* | **differently | objectively** *Try to view the situation objectively.* | **privately**
- VERB + VIEW **tend to | try to**
- PREP. **as** *This behaviour is not viewed as acceptable.* **from** *trying to view the situation from an American perspective* **with** *They tend to view foreigners with suspicion.*
- PHRASES **generally/widely viewed as sth** *He is widely viewed as a possible prime minister.* **increasingly viewed as sth, traditionally viewed as sth, a way of viewing sth**

viewer *noun*

- ADJ. **television/TV | armchair** *While fewer people are attending football matches, armchair viewers are growing in number.*
- VERB + VIEWER **attract, pull (in)** *The evening news is to change its serious image in a bid to attract more viewers.* | **be a hit with** *The new sitcom has been a smash hit with viewers.* | **inform, tell** *The announcer informed viewers that programmes would be running late.* | **entertain | outrage, shock** *a major new drama series that looks set to shock television viewers*
- VIEWER + VERB **see sth, watch sth** *BBC viewers saw the prime minister lose his cool on last night's 'Question Time'.* ◊ *It is estimated that four million viewers watched the programme.* | **switch (between) channels, switch off | phone in, write in** *Hundreds of viewers phoned in to complain after the show.*

viewpoint *noun*

- ADJ. **alternative, contrasting, different, differing, opposite** *The magazine likes to publish articles with alternative viewpoints.* | **narrow** *I find his viewpoint on this matter very narrow.* | **extreme | personal | ideological, political | commercial | scientific**
- VERB + VIEWPOINT **express, present, put forward | adopt, take** *He always takes the opposite viewpoint to the rest of the group.* | **share** *I understand her viewpoint, but do not share it.* | **support** *He quoted recent test results to support his viewpoint.* | **look at/see/view sth from** *Seen from the student's viewpoint, the oral exam can be frightening.* | **see, understand**
- PREP. **from the ~ of** *From the viewpoint of teachers, there has been a great increase in work.*
- PHRASES **from a purely ... viewpoint** *From a purely commercial viewpoint, the film was a failure.*

vigil *noun*

1 when you stay awake to look after sb, etc.
- ADJ. **all-night, constant, round-the-clock, 24-hour** *Since the accident, the boy's parents have kept a constant vigil at his bedside.* | **bedside | lonely** *For three nights, the shepherd maintained his lonely vigil.*
- VERB + VIGIL **keep, maintain** *He told the gatekeeper to keep vigil.*
- PREP. **~over** *the husband's vigil over his dying wife*

2 silent political protest; time of prayer
- ADJ. **candlelight/candlelit, night-time, nocturnal** *Protesters held a candlelit vigil against the war.* | **silent** *a silent vigil outside the presidential palace* | **prayer**
- VERB + VIGIL **hold, stage | attend**
- PREP. **~for** *a vigil for the murdered politician*

vigilance *noun*

- ADJ. **constant, continued, eternal | extra, increased, special** *You should exercise extra vigilance about locking your car properly.*
- VERB + VIGILANCE **exercise, maintain | relax** *The*

birds cannot afford to relax their vigilance against predators. | **require**
- PREP. **~against** *vigilance against shoplifters* **~on the part of sb** *Guaranteeing the safety of students requires continued vigilance on the part of teachers.*
- PHRASES **a need for vigilance**

vigilant *adj.*

- VERBS **be, keep, remain, stay | become**
- ADV. **especially, extra, extremely, particularly, very | constantly, ever** *The organization is ever vigilant for threats to the habitats of birds.*
- PREP. **about** *Be extra vigilant about what you eat or drink.* **against** *You need to be vigilant against garden pests.*

vigorous *adj.*

- VERBS **be | become**
- ADV. **extremely, very** *leading a very vigorous campaign to get the chairman removed* | **quite** *taking some quite vigorous exercise* | **enough, sufficiently**
- PREP. **in** *The group is not vigorous enough in its opposition to the proposals.*

vigour *noun*

- ADJ. **added, increased, increasing | fresh, new, renewed** *He returned to work with a sense of renewed vigour after his holiday.* | **extraordinary, great, tremendous | youthful | creative, intellectual, physical**
- VERB + VIGOUR **pursue/tackle sth with** *The government gave assurances that the enquiry would be pursued with vigour.*
- PREP. **with~**
- PHRASES **full of vigour** *She was a wonderful, bubbly girl, full of vigour.* **vim and vigour** *He set to his task with renewed vim and vigour.* **with equal vigour** *She attacked both political parties with equal vigour.*

villa *noun*

- ADJ. **grand, grandiose, handsome, imposing, luxurious, luxury, magnificent, sumptuous | modest | country, suburban | hilltop | private, rented | holiday, self-catering | four-bedroom, two-storey, etc. | Roman, Spanish, etc.**
- VERB + VILLA **have, own | rent | live in, stay in**
- VILLA + NOUN **holiday**
- PREP. **in a/the~** *staying in his Spanish holiday villa*

village *noun*

- ADJ. **big, large | global** *Technology has turned the world into a global village.* | **little, small, tiny | ancient, old | attractive, beautiful, picturesque, pretty | quiet | nearby, neighbouring, surrounding** *The flood affected the town and surrounding villages.* | **outlying, remote, scattered | country, rural | coastal, seaside | deserted | home, native** *She married a man from her home village.* | **agricultural, farming, fishing, holiday, mining**
- VILLAGE + NOUN **community, life | church, green, hall, pub, school, shop, street | centre**
- PREP. **in a/the~** *They live in a farming village.* **outside a/the~** *Our cottage is just outside the village.*
- PHRASES **the centre/middle of the village, the edge/outskirts of the village**

villain *noun*

- ADJ. **pantomime** *He wore a black cloak, like a pantomime villain.*
- VERB + VILLAIN **cast sb as** *She seems to have cast me as the villain in her latest emotional upheaval.* | **play** *He has played villains in most of his films.* | **catch, nail** *The police still haven't nailed the villain.*

• PHRASES **the villain of the piece/story** *He changed his story to make his wife appear the villain of the piece.*

vintage *noun*

• ADJ. **classic, fine, superb | rare**
• VINTAGE + NOUN **champagne, claret, port, etc.**

viola *noun*

⇨ Special page at MUSIC

violate *verb*

• ADV. **flagrantly, shamelessly** *They have flagrantly violated the treaty.* | **systematically** | **brutally** *The peace of the island community had been brutally violated.*

violation *noun*

• ADJ. **blatant, clear, flagrant** *The attack on civilians is a flagrant violation of the peace agreement.* | **grave, gross, major, massive, serious | wholesale, widespread | continued, repeated | human rights | traffic**
• VERB + VIOLATION **commit** *The army was accused of committing violations against the accord.* | **be, constitute** *This action constitutes a violation of international law.*
• PREP. **in ~ of** *There is plenty of evidence that her actions were in violation of an earlier contract.* | **~ against** *violations against minimum wage agreements*

violence *noun*

1 behaviour that hurts other people physically
• ADJ. **considerable, great, excessive, extreme, large-scale, serious | fresh** *There are fears of fresh violence if the strike continues.* | **continuing, escalating, growing | gratuitous, unnecessary** *Letters poured in complaining about the gratuitous violence on the show.* | **mindless, random, uncontrolled | brutal | criminal, unlawful | endemic, institutionalized, widespread** *attempts to rescue the country from endemic violence* | **sporadic** *In spite of sporadic violence, polling was largely orderly.* | **domestic, physical, sexual | drug-related, election-related, etc. | communal, ethnic, inter-communal, inter-ethnic, racial, sectarian | political, revolutionary, terrorist | left-wing, right-wing**
• QUANT. **level**
• VERB + VIOLENCE **commit, engage in, inflict, perpetrate, resort to, turn to, use** *people who inflict violence on animals* ◊ *violence perpetrated by the army* ◊ *The peasants believed their only choice was to resort to violence.* ◊ *Under no circumstances should police use violence against protesters.* | **suffer** *She had suffered years of violence and abuse.* | **encourage, incite, provoke | denounce, deplore, hate, reject | breed** *Hatred breeds violence.* | **spill over into** *The enthusiasm of the protest spilled over into violence.* | **contain** *UN peacekeepers are struggling to contain the escalating violence.* | **end, quell** *Troops were called in to quell the violence.* | **be capable of** *We are all capable of violence in certain circumstances.*
• VIOLENCE + VERB **break out, erupt, flare, occur** *Violence erupted outside the prison last night.* | **mar sth** *The demonstration was marred by violence.* | **escalate, intensify, worsen** *Observers have warned that the violence could escalate into full-scale armed conflict.* | **spread**
• PREP. **~ against** *violence against police officers* **~ among** *violence among football supporters* **~ between** *violence between rival football groups* **~ towards** *violence towards ethnic minorities* **~ within** *violence within the family*
• PHRASES **an act of violence** *Any act of violence against another player must be punished.* **an end to violence** *The former leader of the terrorist group has called for an end to the violence.* **an eruption/outbreak of violence** *The police are bracing themselves for an outbreak of violence.* **fear of violence, a life of violence** *It was a pre-*

dictable death for a man who had lived a life of violence. **men of violence** *the men of violence who start wars* **an outburst of violence** *He had a short temper and was prone to outbursts of violence.* **a threat of violence, an upsurge in violence, a victim of violence** *a refuge for victims of domestic violence* **violence begets/breeds violence** *We have to make people realize that violence only begets more violence.* **a wave of violence**

2 physical/emotional force
• ADJ. **suppressed**
• PREP. **with (a)** ~ *He kissed her with suppressed violence.*

violent *adj.*

1 using physical strength intended to hurt/kill
• VERBS **be | become, get, grow, turn**
• ADV. **exceptionally, extremely, particularly, really, terribly, very | increasingly | almost | a bit, fairly, pretty, quite, rather** *She started to get a bit violent.* | **gratuitously** *The film is contrived, sentimental and gratuitously violent.* | **potentially** *dealing with potentially violent incidents* | **physically, sexually**
• PREP. **to, towards** *He was violent towards his wife on several occasions.*

2 very strong
• VERBS **be | become**
• ADV. **exceptionally, extremely, very** *an exceptionally violent storm* | **almost** *He felt a strong, almost violent, dislike for the stranger.* | **fairly, quite**

violin *noun*

• ADJ. **muted**
• VERB + VIOLIN **tune (up)**
• VIOLIN + NOUN **bow, string | family** *The cello is a member of the violin family.*
⇨ Special page at MUSIC

virginity *noun*

• VERB + VIRGINITY **lose**

virtue *noun*

• ADJ. **cardinal, great, special | chief | inherent** *There is no inherent virtue in having read all the latest books.* | **negative, positive** *She has just one, negative virtue—she never tells lies.* ◊ *The brochure makes a positive virtue of the island's isolated position.* | **old-fashioned, traditional** *He understands the traditional virtue of hard work.* | **Christian, ethical, moral | domestic | civic, public | political | easy** *women of easy virtue (= with low standards of sexual morality)*
• VERB + VIRTUE **have** *Her book has the cardinal virtue of simplicity.* | **emphasize, extol, preach** *He never stops extolling the virtues of the free market.*
• PHRASES **make a virtue of necessity** (= to manage to gain an advantage from sth you have to do and cannot avoid), **a paragon of virtue** *It would have taken a paragon of virtue not to feel jealous.*

virus *noun*

• ADJ. **deadly | virulent | Aids, flu, hepatitis, herpes, HIV, measles, etc. | computer**
• VERB + VIRUS **be infected with, contract, develop | carry | pass (on), spread, transmit** *An infected person can pass the virus to others.* | **isolate | inactivate**
• VIRUS + VERB **attack sb/sth** *The virus attacks a variety of cells in the body.* | **replicate**
• VIRUS + NOUN **infection | vaccine**

visa *noun*

• ADJ. **entry, exit, transit | student, tourist, travel**
• VERB + VISA **get, obtain** *I obtained a visa after hours*

of waiting at the embassy. | **extend, renew** | **give sb,
grant (sb)**, **issue, issue sb (with)** | **deny sb, refuse sb**
She was refused a visa because of her criminal record. |
need, require *Do South Africans need a visa to go to
France?* | **stamp** | **check** | **overstay** *He was arrested for
overstaying his visa.*
• VISA + VERB **expire** *Her visa expired six months ago.*
• VISA + NOUN **regulations, requirements, restric-
tions** | **application**
• PREP. **on a~** *She entered the country on a student visa.* |
~for *Do you need a visa for Egypt?*

viscount, viscountess *noun*

⇨ Note at PEER

visibility *noun*

1 how far you can see
• ADJ. **clear, good, excellent, high** | **bad, limited, low,
poor, zero**
• VERB + VISIBILITY **reduce** *The sand in the air reduced visibility to a hundred yards.*
• VISIBILITY + VERB **be down to sth** *Visibility was
down to 25 yards.*
• PREP. **in ... ~** *We set a course in good visibility and calm
seas.*

2 obviousness in public life
• ADJ. **high** | **greater, increased, increasing**
• VERB + VISIBILITY **increase, raise** *We aim to raise
the visibility of ethnic minorities in our organization.*

visible *adj.*

• VERBS **be** | **become** | **remain, stay** *The scars re-
mained visible all her life.* | **leave sth, make sth** *We cut
the trees down to make the lake visible from the house.*
• ADV. **all too, clearly, easily, highly, obviously, particularly, plainly, readily, very** *His relief was all too visible.* ◇ *The election poster was clearly visible from the
street.* ◇ *Italy has a highly visible environmental move-
ment.* | **fully, quite** *The sea was now out, leaving the wreck
fully visible.* ◇ *Ellie's quite visible embarrassment* | **just**
The mountains were just visible, dusky and black. | **bare-
ly, hardly, scarcely** *The low, flat boats were barely visible.*
| **almost** | **half, partially** *She stood, half visible in the dim
light.* | **dimly, faintly** *A figure was dimly visible in the
evening gloom.* | **externally** | **immediately** *Women are
advised to wait where they are not immediately visible to
approaching traffic.* | **still** | **no longer**
• PREP. **to** *Its contents were visible to all of them.*
• PHRASES **visible to the naked eye** *tiny spiders that are
hardly visible to the naked eye*

vision *noun*

1 ability to see
• ADJ. **20/20, excellent, perfect** *The eye test shows she
has perfect vision.* | **normal** | **clear** *The rain prevented
her having clear vision of the road ahead.* | **blurred, de-
fective, distorted, impaired, poor** | **double, tunnel** (*often
figurative*) | **all-round** *The high driving position gives ex-
cellent all-round vision.* | **binocular, stereoscopic** | **X-
ray** | **distance** *I can read without glasses, but my distance
vision is poor.* | **night** | **peripheral** *Use your peripheral vi-
sion widely when moving from place to place.*
• VERB + VISION **have** | **give (sb)** | **obscure, restrict** |
blur *The tears blurred her vision.* | **improve**
• VISION + VERB **clear** *Her vision cleared and she realized Niall was standing beside her.*
• PREP. **across your~** *A bird shot across her vision.*
• PHRASES **your field of vision** *She was aware of shapes
moving across her field of vision.* **your line of vision** *Someone was standing in my line of vision so I couldn't see the
screen.*

2 picture in your imagination
• ADJ. **disturbing, dreadful, ghastly, horrible** | **bleak** |
inner, intuitive, mental, spiritual | **mystic/mystical,
prophetic, religious** *A young girl in the village experi-
enced a prophetic vision.* | **poetic** | **apocalyptic** *an
apocalyptic vision of the end of civilization* | **momentary,
sudden**
• VERB + VISION **experience, have, receive** *I had vi-
sions of us getting hopelessly lost.* | **conjure up** *The word
'island' conjures up a vision of a relaxing summer holiday.*
• VISION + VERB **fade** *As he approached, the vision
faded and there was no one there.*
• PREP. **in a/the~** *The idea came to her in a vision.* | **~of**

3 ability to see/plan for the future
• ADJ. **great** | **imaginative** | **alternative** | **broad, com-
prehensive, global, wide** *The company needs to develop a
global vision.* | **narrow** | **overall** | **personal** | **clear** *The
engineers had a clear vision of what they wanted to
achieve.* | **common** *They share a common vision for the
development of health services.* | **strategic** | **political** |
revolutionary | **romantic, Utopian**
• VERB + VISION **have** | **develop** | **convey, expand
on/upon, outline, promote** *He outlined his vision for the
new economic order.* | **impose** *The new leader set about
imposing his vision on the party.* | **share** | **cloud** *He was
determined not to let emotions cloud his vision.*
• PREP. **of~** *a statesman of great vision* | **~for** *a vision for
the future* **~of** *an alternative vision of society*
• PHRASES **breadth of vision** *His plans for the country's
future show a remarkable breadth of vision.*

visit *noun*

• ADJ. **brief, fleeting, flying, quick, short** | **lengthy,
long** | **eight-day, hour-long, etc.** | **long-awaited** | **regu-
lar** | **constant, frequent** *She enjoyed the frequent visits of
her grandchildren.* | **infrequent, occasional, periodic,
rare** | **annual, daily, twice-weekly, etc.** | **forthcoming,
impending** *The prime minister has been briefed in prepar-
ation for his forthcoming visit to China.* | **exchange, re-
ciprocal, return** *Exchange visits between company and
school have kept the project going.* ◇ *They came to visit last
week, and we'll pay them a return visit in the autumn.* |
surprise, unannounced, unexpected | **unwelcome** |
casual | **formal, ministerial, official, presidential, royal,
state** | **high-profile** | **trade** | **private, unofficial** | **foreign,
overseas** | **personal** *Following her letter of complaint,
she received a personal visit from the store manager.* |
domiciliary, home *You should receive a home visit from
your midwife within a month.* | **hospital, prison** | **initial,
preliminary** | **follow-up** | **social** | **neighbourly** | **edu-
cational, study** | **fact-finding, research** | **courtesy,
goodwill** *While on holiday in Italy, the prime minister
paid a courtesy visit to his opposite number in Rome.* |
morale-boosting | **inspection, monitoring** | **on-site, site**
| **school** | **customer** | **memorable**
• VERB + VISIT **go on, make, pay sb, undertake** *We
used to go on school visits to museums and historical buildings.* ◇ *How many doctors are still able to make home
visits?* ◇ *Pay us a visit next time you're in town.* | **get,
have, receive** | **look forward to** *I'd been looking forward
to my cousin's visit for ages.* | **arrange, organize** | **post-
pone** | **cancel** | **cut short** *He was forced to cut short a
visit to North America.* | **prolong** *He offered her a drink to
try to prolong her visit.* | **announce** *We received a letter
announcing a visit from government inspectors.* | **be
(well) worth** *If you're staying in Rome, Ostia is well worth
a visit.*
• VISIT + VERB **mark sth, signal sth** *The visit signalled
the normalization of relations between the two countries.*
• PREP. **during/on a/the ~** *On one of her regular visits
home, she told her parents she was engaged.* | **~from** *We
had a visit from somebody collecting for charity.* **~to** *a visit
to the theatre*

visit *verb*

- ADV. **regularly**
- VERB + VISIT **come to, go to** *My parents are coming to visit me next week.* ◇ *We've just been to visit my grandparents.* | **decide to, hope to, intend to, plan to, promise to, want to, wish to** | **be expected to, be likely to** *A million people are expected to visit the museum over the next 12 months.* | **invite sb to, urge sb to**

visitor *noun*

- ADJ. **constant, frequent, regular** | **occasional** | **seasonal** | **rare** | **casual** | **first-time** *First-time visitors to Spain are often surprised by how late people eat.* | **welcome** | **surprise, unexpected, uninvited, unwanted, unwelcome** | **potential, prospective, would-be** *The latest crime figures are likely to put off prospective visitors to the city.* | **foreign, international, overseas** | **annual, yearly** | **business, holiday, tourist** | **museum** | **home, hospital, prison** | **health** *The baby's weight is monitored by the health visitor.*
- VERB + VISITOR **get, have, receive** *Do you get many visitors?* | **expect** *The house was tidy and I could see he was expecting visitors.* | **entertain** *The front room was used mainly for entertaining visitors.* | **attract, bring (in)** *The festival brings 5 000 visitors to the town every year.* | **interest** *The town has much to interest the visitor.* | **deter** *The lack of facilities in the town may deter the casual visitor.* | **admit** *The college only admits visitors in organized groups.*
- VISITOR + VERB **come, flock, turn up** *Visitors flocked to see the show.*
- VISITOR + NOUN **attraction** | **centre** *Pick up a free map of the town from the visitor centre.*
- PREP. **~from** *Visitors from Ireland will find much that reminds them of home.* **~to** *visitors to the museum*

visualize *verb*

- ADV. **easily**
- VERB + VISUALIZE **be able/unable to, can/could** *I could visualize the scene in the office.* | **try to** | **be easy to** | **be difficult to, be hard to** *It is difficult to visualize how the town must have looked years ago.*
- PREP. **as** *I visualized him as a typical businessman.*

vital *adj.*

- VERBS **be, prove, seem** | **become** | **remain** | **consider sth, regard sth as, see sth as**
- ADV. **particularly, really** | **absolutely** | **strategically** *the strategically vital industrial zone*
- PREP. **for** *fostering team spirit, which is vital for success* **to** *These nutrients are absolutely vital to good health.*

vitality *noun*

- ADJ. **enormous, exceptional, great, remarkable, sheer, tremendous** *You have to admire the sheer vitality of his performance.* | **renewed** | **continuing** | **creative, cultural, economic** | **inner, mental**
- VERB + VITALITY **burst with** *He came back from his holiday bursting with vitality and good health.* | **restore**
- PHRASES **full of vitality, a lack of vitality**

vitamin *noun*

- ADJ. **take** *The doctor told me to take vitamins regularly.*
- VERB + VITAMIN **contain** *Most foods contain vitamin E.* | **be rich in** *Fish is rich in vitamins and minerals.* | **enrich sth with, fortify sth with** *breakfast cereals enriched with vitamins*
- VITAMIN + NOUN **drops, injections, pills, supplements, tablets** | **requirements** | **deficiency** *Vitamin C deficiency can ultimately lead to scurvy.*

vivid *adj.*

1 very bright
- VERBS **be**
- ADV. **extraordinarily, extremely, really, very** | **quite, rather** *She uses quite vivid colours.*

2 very clear
- VERBS **be** | **remain**
- ADV. **extraordinarily, extremely, very, wonderfully** *a wonderfully vivid imagination* | **quite** | **still**

vocabulary *noun*

- ADJ. **extensive, large, rich, wide** *English has a rich vocabulary and literature.* ◇ *Try to develop a wide vocabulary.* | **limited, narrow, poor, restricted, small** | **active, passive** | **basic, essential, key** | **formal** | **business, scientific, specialized, technical**
- VERB + VOCABULARY **have** | **acquire, learn** *Learners of languages acquire vocabulary through practice.* | **build, develop, enlarge, enrich, expand, extend, increase, widen** *This book has been designed to help you expand your vocabulary.* | **enter** *The word 'think tank' entered the vocabulary (= became part of the language) in the 1960s.* | **use** *Specialized vocabulary is used in all the major disciplines.*
- VOCABULARY + NOUN **item**
- PREP. **~for/of** *the essential vocabulary for tourism*
- PHRASES **not in sb's vocabulary** *The word 'failure' is not in his vocabulary (= for him, failure does not exist).*

vocal *adj.*

- VERBS **be** | **become**
- ADV. **extremely, highly, very** *a highly vocal opposition group* | **increasingly** *criticized by a small but increasingly vocal minority* | **quite**
- PREP. **about** *women who are very vocal about men's failings*

vocation *noun*

- ADJ. **real, true** | **religious**
- VERB + VOCATION **find** *She struggled for years to find her true vocation.* | **have** | **follow, pursue** *He is desperate to pursue his vocation as an artist.* | **miss** *She feels that she missed her vocation by not working with children.*
- PREP. **~for** *She seems to have a vocation for healing.* **~to** *a vocation to the priesthood*
- PHRASES **a sense of vocation** *This is a job that demands a sense of vocation.*

vogue *noun*

- ADJ. **current** | **temporary**
- VERB + VOGUE **enjoy** *Cycling enjoyed a vogue at the end of the nineteenth century.* | **come (back) into** *Scooters have recently come back into vogue.*
- VOGUE + NOUN **word**
- PREP. **in ~** *the type of pop song in vogue at that time* **out of ~** *Disaster movies are currently out of vogue.* | **~for** *the current vogue for Japanese food*

voice *noun*

1 sounds you make when speaking or singing
- ADJ. **beautiful, fine, good, lovely, pleasant, sweet** *She has a beautiful singing voice.* | **big, booming, loud, ringing, sonorous, stentorian** | **light, small, thin, tiny, weak** | **low, soft** | **deep, gravelly, gruff, hoarse, husky** | **falsetto, high, high-pitched, shrill, squeaky** | **clear** | **muffled, muted, strangulated** | **harsh, penetrating, sharp** | **nasal** | **cracked, rasping, slurred** *I could tell from his slurred voice that he'd been drinking.* | **fruity, mellifluous, rich, silky, smooth, velvet, velvety** | **sing-song** | **gentle, kindly, soothing** | **cheerful, hearty** | **friendly,**

warm | flat, matter-of-fact, unemotional | calm, cool | firm, steady | urgent | authoritative | distinctive | raised | hushed | angry | strained, tired | plaintive | funny, silly | disembodied | inner *An inner voice told him that what he had done was wrong.* | singing | alto, baritone, bass, contralto, soprano, tenor, treble

• VERB + VOICE **hear** *I could hear voices in the next room.* | **raise** *She's a teacher who never has to raise her voice to discipline the children.* | **drop, lower** *She dropped her voice to a whisper.* ◇ *You're shouting—please lower your voice.* | **project** *Try to project your voice so that the people at the back of the room can hear you.* | **lose** *She's lost her voice and won't be able to sing tonight.* | **find** *He swallowed nervously as he tried to find his voice.* | **put on** *She put on a silly voice as she imitated her boss.*

• VOICE + VERB **go up, rise** *His voice rose in angry protest.* | **die away, drop, fade, tail away/off, trail away/off** *'So he won't come ...' her voice trailed off in disappointment.* | **be filled/tinged with sth** *Her voice was filled with emotion.* | **deepen, harden, soften, thicken** *His voice suddenly thickened with emotion.* | **echo** *Her voice echoed through the silent house.* | **whisper** *'Be quiet!' a voice whispered in his ear.* | **hiss, purr** | **call (out), cry (out)** *'Who is it?' a female voice called out.* | **scream, shout** *She was dimly aware of voices shouting.* | **boom (out)** | **cut through sth, pierce sth** *His deep voice cut through the silence.* | **break, crack** *His voice broke with emotion.* ◇ *His voice broke* (= became a deep, man's voice) *when he was 14.* | **falter, quaver, shake, tremble, waver** *Her voice shook with fear.* | **drone (on)** *The flat, unemotional voice droned on.*

• VOICE + NOUN **recognition** *the computer's voice recognition capability* | **mail** (also **voicemail**)**, mailbox, message, traffic** | **synthesizer**

• PREP. **in a/your~** *'Get out!' she shouted in a shrill voice.* ◇ *There was fury in his voice as he answered her.*

• PHRASES **at the top of your voice** *I was shouting at the top of my voice but she couldn't hear me.* **a babble/hum/murmur of voices** *They could hear a loud babble of voices coming from the crowded bar.* **in good voice** *The home fans were in good voice* (= making a loud noise) *before the match.* ◇ *She was in good voice* (= singing well) *at the concert tonight.* **keep your voice down** *Please keep your voice down so as not to wake the children.* **keep your voice level/steady** *He managed to keep his voice steady despite his feelings of panic.* **tone of voice** *'Do you have to speak to me in that tone of voice?' she said sadly.*

2 expression of ideas/opinions

• ADJ. **critical, dissenting** *Dissenting voices at the newspaper are very rare.* | **lone** *a lone voice of dissent* | **powerful** *Powerful voices in the Senate are determined to bring down the president.* | **distinctive** *a writer with a highly distinctive voice*

• VERB + VOICE **find** *Refugees have been unable to find a voice in politics.* | **add, lend** *Many senior politicians have lent their voices to the campaign.* | **give** *The magazine gave voice to hundreds of oppressed factory workers.* | **listen to**

• PREP. **~of** *to listen to the voice of conscience*

• PHRASES **make your voice heard** *a society in which individuals are able to make their voices heard* **speak with one voice** *The teachers speak with one voice when they demand an end to the cuts.*

void *noun*

• ADJ. **great, massive** | **aching** | **black**
• VERB + VOID **leave** | **fill** *It seemed that nothing could fill the aching black void left by Rachel's death.*

void *adj.*

• VERBS **be** | **become** | **make sth, render sth** *an impediment which rendered the marriage void* | **declare sth**

• PHRASES **null and void** *The election was declared null and void.*

volatile *adj.*

1 that can easily change
• VERBS **be** | **become** | **remain**
• ADV. **dangerously, extremely, highly, very** *Edwards was a dangerously volatile character.* | **increasingly** | **fairly, quite, rather, somewhat** | **potentially** *a potentially volatile situation* | **notoriously** | **politically**

2 that can easily change into a gas
• VERBS **be** | **become** | **remain**
• ADV. **highly, very** *a highly volatile liquid*

volcano *noun*

• ADJ. **active, dormant, extinct**
• QUANT. **chain**
• VOLCANO + VERB **erupt** *An active volcano may erupt at any time.*

volley *noun*

1 of stones, bullets, etc.
• VERB + VOLLEY **fire, unleash** *The police fired a volley of bullets over the heads of the crowd.*
• PREP. **~of**

2 in sport
• ADJ. **backhand, cross-court, forehand** (in tennis) | **left-foot, right-foot** (in football) | **stunning, superb** *Williams took the set with a stunning backhand volley down the line.* | **30-yard, etc.**
• VERB + VOLLEY **hit** *She hit a forehand volley into the net.* | **crack/crash/lash home, strike, unleash** (all in football) *Cole lashed home a 20-yard volley.*
• PREP. **on the ~** *Figo met the ball on the volley and scored.*

voltage *noun*

• ADJ. **high, low** | **constant** | **changing, varying** | **mains, supply** *Most house lighting runs at the full mains voltage of 240 volts.* | **input, output**
• VERB + VOLTAGE **increase, step up, turn up** | **decrease, step down, turn down** | **produce** | **apply** *A voltage is then applied across the cell electrodes.*
• PREP. **at a~** *The motor operates at low voltages.*

volume *noun*

1 amount of space
• ADJ. **total** *the total volume of the containers*
• PREP. **by~** *They sell screws and nails by volume.* **in~** *2 litres in volume*

2 quantity of sth
• ADJ. **sheer** *The sheer volume of fiction produced is staggering.* | **considerable, enormous, great, heavy, high, huge, large, substantial, vast** | **small**
• VERB + VOLUME **increase** | **decrease, reduce** | **double/grow//increase/rise in** *Sales have doubled in volume.* | **decrease/fall in**
• VOLUME + VERB **double, increase, rise** *Sales volume has doubled since 1999.* | **decrease, fall**

3 strength of sound that sth makes
• ADJ. **high** | **full, maximum** | **low**
• VERB + VOLUME **increase, turn up** | **decrease, turn down** | **grow/increase/rise in** | **decrease/fall in**
• VOLUME + NOUN **control** *the volume control on the television*
• PREP. **at ... ~** *The car stereo was on at full volume.*

4 book
• ADJ. **bound, leather-bound** *a library full of bound volumes* | **companion** *a companion volume to the one on African wildlife* | **rare** *Only a specialist shop would have*

this rare volume. | **bulky, massive, substantial, thick, weighty** | **compact, slim** | **glossy** *a forty-page, glossy volume about the company's products* | **dusty** | **old** | **single** | **separate**
● QUANT. **series**
● VERB + VOLUME **publish**
● PREP. **in a/the~** *Her poems are now available in a single volume.* | **~ of** *a volume of short stories* **~ on** *a volume on ancient history*
● PHRASES **run to five, several, etc. volumes** *The encyclopedia is a huge work, running to 20 volumes.*

voluntary *adj.*

● VERBS **be** | **remain**
● ADV. **completely, entirely, purely** *The organization is run on a purely voluntary basis.* | **largely**

volunteer *noun*

1 sb who offers to do sth
● ADJ. **unpaid** *The office is staffed by unpaid volunteers.* | **full-time, part-time** | **committed, dedicated, enthusiastic, willing** | **qualified, trained** | **potential, prospective, would-be** | **conservation, Red Cross**
● QUANT. **army, band, group, network, team** *An army of volunteers cooked meals for the children.*
● VERB + VOLUNTEER **appeal for, ask for, call for, look for** *The charity is appealing for volunteers to take elderly patients to and from hospital.* | **find, get, recruit** *We can't get any volunteers to help in the gardens.* | **provide** *The local community provided volunteers to repair the road.* | **encourage** | **need, want** | **work as**
● VOLUNTEER + VERB **come forward** *Hundreds of volunteers have come forward to offer their help.* | **man sth, staff sth** | **carry sth out** | **provide support, support sb** *The support our volunteers provide cannot be measured in purely practical terms.*
● VOLUNTEER + NOUN **staff, worker** | **carer, driver, helper**
● PREP. **~ for** *He worked as a volunteer for Oxfam.*

2 in the armed forces
● ADJ. **army, civilian**
● VERB + VOLUNTEER **recruit** | **serve as**
● VOLUNTEER + NOUN **army, militia, unit**

volunteer *verb*

● ADV. **kindly** *Barbara Forrest has kindly volunteered to lead a guided walk to Bolton Abbey.*
● PREP. **as** *We volunteered as witnesses.* **for** *I volunteered for service in the Air Force.*

vomit *verb*

● ADV. **violently** | **promptly** *Corbett leaned against the wall and promptly vomited.* | **up** *He vomited up all that he had eaten for lunch.*
● VERB + VOMIT **want to** *The smell made me want to vomit.* | **make sb** *They gave her salty water to make her vomit.*
● PHRASES **nausea and vomiting** *The symptoms include headaches, nausea and vomiting.* **vomiting and diarrhoea**

vote *noun*

1 choice/decision made by voting
● ADJ. **majority** | **huge, massive, overwhelming, resounding** *an overwhelming vote in favour of autonomy* | **unanimous** | **close, knife-edge, narrow** | **two-thirds, two-to-one, etc.** | **democratic, direct, free** *Members of Parliament will have a free vote on this bill.* | **transferable** *The single transferable vote system operates.* | **fair** | **secret** | **popular** *The law was ratified by popular vote.* | **casting, decisive** | **crucial** | **affirmative, favourable, yes** | **adverse, negative, no** | **dissenting** | **protest** *He*

lost the election because of the protest vote. | **tactical** | **floating, swing** | **absent, expatriate, postal, proxy** | **invalid, valid** | **congressional, parliamentary** | **individual** | **block** *The union wants the system of block votes to continue.* | **historic**
● VERB + VOTE **have, put sth to the, take** *We should put the resolution to the vote.* ◇ *Let's take a vote on the issue.* | **have** *The chairperson always has the casting vote.* | **cast, record** *(formal)* *You can cast your vote at the local polling station.* ◇ *50% of the eligible voters recorded their vote.* | **gain, get, obtain, poll, receive, secure, win** *Our candidate polled only 10% of the vote.* | **swing** *factors that could swing the vote against the president* | **count** *Votes are still being counted.*
● VOTE + VERB **go to sb/sth** *My vote will go to the party that addresses crime.* | **fall** *The party's vote fell by 6%.* | **increase, rise** | **double, treble, etc.**
● PREP. **by~** *The bill was passed by a single vote.* ◇ *Members are elected by direct vote.* | **~ against, ~ for** *a vote for the government* **~ in favour (of sth), ~ on** *a vote on the new law*
● PHRASES **a vote of confidence/no confidence** *The government received a massive vote of confidence from the electorate.* **a vote of thanks** *A special vote of thanks went to the organizer, Tim Woodhouse.*
⇨ Special page at MEETING

2 the vote legal right to vote in elections
● VERB + VOTE **have** *How many years is it since women have had the vote?* | **give sb**

vote *verb*

● ADV. **overwhelmingly** | **unanimously** *The committee voted unanimously to accept the plans.* | **narrowly** *The Senate voted narrowly to continue funding the scheme.* | **formally** *The proposals were formally voted upon.* | **tactically** | **down, in, out** *The proposal was voted down.*
● VERB + VOTE **be eligible to, be entitled to** *young people who are eligible to vote for the first time* | **intend to**
● PREP. **against** *They voted overwhelmingly against the proposal.* **for** *They all voted for the new tax.* **in** *She returned home in order to vote in the elections.* **in favour of** *The committee voted in favour of the plan.* **into** *the government that has just been voted into power* **off** *She was voted off the committee.* **on/upon** *Parliament is to vote on tobacco advertising tomorrow.* **onto, out of** *He was voted out of office.* **(by) ... to ...** *They voted 15 to 2 to accept the offer.* **with** *Her party voted with the government.*
● PHRASES **the right to vote** *Everyone over 18 has the right to vote.* **a round of voting** *She was elected on the second round of voting.* **vote Conservative, Labour, Republican, etc., vote no/yes** *They voted yes to the agreement.*

voter *noun*

● ADJ. **eligible, registered** *Only a quarter of registered voters actually voted in the election.* | **proxy** | **overseas** | **floating, uncommitted, undecided, wavering** | **first-time, new** | **potential** | **ordinary** *the feelings of ordinary voters* | **Conservative, Labour, etc.**
● VERB + VOTER **woo** *attempts to woo undecided voters* | **persuade** | **convince** | **urge, warn** | **influence**
● VOTER + VERB **choose sb, favour sb, pick sb, prefer sb** *In this election, voters chose candidates who promised economic security.* | **participate in sth, turn out** *More than two million voters participated in the election.* | **cast their vote** | **support sth, vote yes (to sth)** | **reject sth, vote no (to sth)** | **change/ switch allegiance**
● VOTER + NOUN **turnout** *Voter turnout was very low.* | **registration** | **disillusionment** | **intimidation** *The Opposition alleged voter intimidation by the army.*

voucher *noun*

● ADJ. **credit** | **discount, money-off** | **gift, sales, shop-**

ping | luncheon | travel | accommodation, hotel | fuel, petrol
• VERB + VOUCHER **give sb, issue (sb with)** *The company issues travel vouchers to all managers.* | **get, receive** *I got a credit voucher for £30.* | **redeem, spend, use**
• VOUCHER + VERB **entitle sb to sth** *a voucher entitling you to a half-price meal* | **be worth sth** *a voucher worth £100* | **be redeemable** *a 50p money-off voucher redeemable against any future purchase of the product*
• PREP. **~ for** *a voucher for children's glasses*

vow *noun*

• ADJ. **formal, solemn | marriage, wedding | monastic, religious | final** *She left the convent before taking her final vows.*
• VERB + VOW **make, take** *He made a vow to avenge his father's death.* | **keep** *She kept her vow of silence until she died.* | **break** *Nothing will persuade me to break this vow.* | **exchange** *The couple exchanged vows at the altar.* | **renew**
• PREP. **~ of** *a vow of poverty*

vow *verb*

• ADV. **quietly, silently** *He silently vowed vengeance on them all.*
• PREP. **to** *She vowed to herself that she would not show any emotion.*
• PHRASES **vow never to do sth** *I vowed never to drink so much again.*

vowel *noun*

• ADJ. **long, short | open | neutral** *This neutral vowel is known as 'schwa'.* | **weak | broad, flat | final | accented, stressed | unaccented, unstressed**
• VERB + VOWEL **begin with, contain, end in/with**
• VOWEL + NOUN **sound | system**

voyage *noun*

• ADJ. **epic, great, long | arduous, hazardous, nightmare | outward | homeward, return | maiden | ocean, sea | transatlantic, round-the-world**
• VERB + VOYAGE **embark on, go on, make, set out on, undertake**
• PREP. **during a/the ~** *Lady Franklin kept a journal during the voyage.* **on a/the ~** *There were mainly scientists on the voyage.* | **~ from, ~ to** *The Titanic sank in April 1912 on its maiden voyage from Southampton to New York.*
• PHRASES **a voyage of discovery** (*often figurative*) *Going to college can be a voyage of discovery.*

vulnerability *noun*

• ADJ. **extreme, great | economic, financial** *the economic vulnerability of unskilled workers* | **genetic** *evidence of a genetic vulnerability to cancer* | **naked, raw** *the naked vulnerability in his eyes*
• VERB + VULNERABILITY **demonstrate, expose, highlight, show (up)** *The earthquake highlighted the vulnerability of elevated highways.* | **decrease, reduce | increase | exploit, take advantage of** *The gang had taken advantage of the immigrants' vulnerability.*
• PREP. **~ to** *the extreme vulnerability of old people to crime*

vulnerable *adj.*

• VERBS **appear, be, feel, look, seem** *You must try not to appear vulnerable.* | **become | remain | leave sb/sth, make sb/sth** *The virus attacks the immune system, leaving your body vulnerable to infections.*
• ADV. **acutely, especially, extremely, highly, intensely, particularly, very | completely, totally, utterly | increasingly | quite, rather** *She is very sensitive and rather vulnerable.* | **potentially | peculiarly, uniquely** *Hippos are uniquely vulnerable to drought.* | **oddly, strangely** *He smiled, making her suddenly feel oddly vulnerable.* | **somehow | economically, militarily, politically** *The company is in an economically vulnerable position.*
• PREP. **to** *These offices are highly vulnerable to terrorist attack.*

vulture *noun*

• VULTURE + VERB **circle, hover, soar, wheel** *Vultures circled overhead as the lions fed.* | **gather, wait | swoop | scavenge (sth)**

Ww

wade *verb*

- ADV. **ashore** *The men waded ashore.* | **out**
- PREP. **across, in, into, through** *We waded across the stream.*
- PHRASES **wade knee-deep/waist-deep** *Rescuers had to wade waist-deep in flood water.*

waft *verb*

- ADV. **gently** *The night air wafted gently over them.* | **around, in, up** *A scent of honey wafted up from the hives.*
- PREP. **across, down, from, into, over, through, up** *Spicy smells wafted through the air.*

wag *verb*

- ADV. **furiously** *The dog raced ahead, its tail wagging furiously.*

wage *noun* (also **wages**)

- ADJ. **decent, fair, good, high | inadequate, low, meagre, small** *He busked to supplement his meagre wages.* | **annual, hourly, regular, etc.** | **gross, pre-tax | after-tax, net | money | real** *If money wages remain constant and price levels rise, real wages fall.* | **basic, standard** *a basic wage of £100 a week plus tips* | **living** *workers fighting for a living wage* | **minimum | average**
- VERB + WAGE **pay | earn** *She earns a good wage at the factory.* | **live on** *How can you live on such a low wage?* | **increase, keep up, push up, raise** *Full employment pushed up wages.* | **cut, force down, hold down, keep down | supplement**
- WAGE + VERB **increase, rise | decrease, fall**
- WAGE + NOUN **earner | labour, workers | claim** *The union submitted a wage claim for a 9% rise.* | **bargaining, negotiations | agreement, settlement | cut, reduction | controls, freeze, restraint** *The government promised greater tax cuts in return for continued wage restraints.* | **explosion, increase, inflation, rise | bill, costs | structure, system | differentials** *wage differentials between large and small firms* | **packet** *He got his first wage packet at fourteen years old.*
- PHRASES **a cut/fall in wages, growth in wages, an increase/a rise in wages**

wagon *noun*

1 vehicle pulled by animals
- ADJ. **covered, open | horse-drawn | hay, supply**
- QUANT. **train** *a long train of supply wagons*
- VERB + WAGON **drive | pull, draw**
- WAGON + VERB **roll** *covered wagons rolling across the prairies*
- WAGON + NOUN **train | wheel**
2 open railway truck
- ADJ. **rail/railway | empty | full | coal, freight, goods**
- VERB + WAGON **pull**

wail *noun*

- ADJ. **loud | high, high-pitched | banshee | distant** *We could just hear the distant wail of a siren.*
- VERB + WAIL **give, let out | hear**
- PREP. **with a ~** *With a wail he threw himself on the bed and buried his face in the pillow.* | **~ of** *She gave a wail of anguish.*
- ⇨ Note at SOUND

wail *verb*

- ADV. **almost | helplessly**
- VERB + WAIL **begin to | hear sb**
- PREP. **for** *wailing for her dead husband* **with** *She wailed with despair.*
- PHRASES **weeping and wailing** *A crowd of women followed the coffin, weeping and wailing.*

waist *noun*

1 part around the middle of the body
- ADJ. **narrow, neat, slender, slim, small, tiny | 34-inch, etc.**
- WAIST + NOUN **height**
- PREP. **about/around/round the/your ~** *She wore a broad belt about her waist.*
- PHRASES **from the waist down/up** *A large towel covered him from the waist down.* **stripped to the waist, waist-deep/-high** *Where we were standing, the lake was waist-deep.*
2 part of a piece of clothing that goes round the waist
- ADJ. **high, low | belted, drawstring, elasticated | tight | 34-inch, etc.** *These jeans have a 32-inch waist.*
- WAIST + NOUN **measurement, size | pocket**

waistline *noun*

1 measurement of the body around the waist
- ADJ. **expanding**
- VERB + WAISTLINE **watch** *Low-fat foods are ideal for people who are watching their waistline.*
2 part of a piece of clothing
- ADJ. **high, low**

wait *noun*

- ADJ. **endless, long** *We had a long wait to see the doctor.* | **short | agonizing, anxious, nerve-racking, nervous, worrying | frustrating | boring, tedious**
- VERB + WAIT **face, have** *The accused faces an agonizing wait while the jury considers its verdict.*
- PREP. **~ for** *a short wait for an ambulance*
- PHRASES **be worth the wait** *The dress was so beautiful when it arrived that it was well worth the wait.*

wait *verb*

- ADV. **long** *Have you been waiting long?* | **in vain** *They waited in vain for a response.* | **quietly, silently | patiently, politely** *He waited patiently while she got ready.* | **anxiously, impatiently, nervously, tensely, uneasily** *Their parents waited anxiously for news.* | **breathlessly, expectantly, with bated breath** *I waited with bated breath for what would happen next.* | **about, around**
- VERB + WAIT **have to, must** *You'll have to wait until you're older.* | **can/could hardly, can't/couldn't** *I can hardly wait for my holiday!* ◇ *I can't wait to see their new baby.*
- PREP. **for** *I'm waiting for a bus.* **till/until** *We'll have to wait until it stops raining.*
- PHRASES **keep sb waiting** *I'm sorry to have kept you waiting.* **wait a long time** *She had to wait a long time for the right man to come along.* **wait a minute/moment** *Hey! Wait a minute! I'll come with you!* **wait and see** *We'll wait and see what the weather's like before we make a decision.*

waiter, waitress *noun*

- ADJ. **head** *the head waiter in a large restaurant* |

hotel, restaurant | wine | passing *She ordered a large vodka and tonic from a passing waiter.* | hovering *(literary, disapproving)*, obsequious *He didn't fancy spending hours in the restaurant, surrounded by hovering waiters.*
• VERB + WAITER, WAITRESS **beckon (to), call (over), signal (to), summon (over), wave over** *He casually waved over the waitress and settled the bill.*
• WAITER, WAITRESS + VERB **arrive with sth, bring (sb) sth, serve (sb) sth** *A waitress arrived with the wine they had ordered.*
• WAITER, WAITRESS + NOUN **service** *Lunch is a buffet meal, while dinner is waiter service.*
• PHRASES **catch the waiter/waitress's eye** *I tried to catch the waiter's eye to ask for our bill.*
⇨ Note at JOB

wake, waken *verb*

1 stop being asleep
• ADV. **early, late** *She had woken even earlier than usual.* | **suddenly** | **up** *I woke up quite late this morning.*
• PREP. **from** *She had just woken up from a deep sleep.*
• PHRASES **wake (up) to find sth** *Any minute now she'd wake up to find herself at home safe in bed.* **wake (up) with a start** *She woke with a start from a terrible nightmare.*

2 make sb stop sleeping
• ADV. **gently** *I woke him gently.* | **up**
• VERB + WAKE, WAKEN **be careful not to** *Be careful not to wake the children!*

walk *noun*

1 trip on foot
• ADJ. **brief, little, short** *We took a brief walk around the old quarter.* | **good, long, long-distance, marathon** *It's a good (= fairly long) walk to the town centre, so I usually cycle.* ◊ *We went for a long walk after breakfast.* ◊ *He's done several long-distance walks for charity.* | **three-minute, five minutes', etc.** *It's a five-minute walk from the lecture theatre to the restaurant.* ◊ *We live just a few minutes' walk from the station.* | **brisk, vigorous** *The doctor advised a brisk walk every day.* | **easy, gentle, leisurely | hard, strenuous | exhilarating, lovely, pleasant, pretty | twenty-minute, two-mile, etc. | after-dinner, afternoon, daily, evening, etc. | solitary** *She used to enjoy solitary walks along the cliffs.* | **romantic | guided** *We went on a guided walk of the city in the afternoon.* | **charity, sponsored** *She's doing a 200-mile sponsored walk in aid of cancer research.* | **circular | coastal, country, forest, hill, lakeside, nature, riverside, woodland | space, tightrope** *the anniversary of the first space walk*
• VERB + WALK **do, go for, go on, have, take** *The book contains circular walks you can do in half a day.* ◊ *We'll go for a walk before lunch.* ◊ *We went on a ten-mile walk along the coast.* | **take sb/sth for** *She takes her dog for a walk every evening.* | **break** *They broke their walk at a pub by the river.* | **continue, resume**
• WALK + VERB **take sb/sth** *The walk takes two hours.* ◊ *The walk takes you past a lot of interesting buildings.*
• PREP. **on a/the ~** *He met her on one of his Sunday afternoon walks.* **within (a) ~** *All amenities are within an easy walk of the hotel.* | **~from, ~to**
• PHRASES **a walk around** *I had a little walk around to calm my nerves.*

2 style of walking
• ADJ. **funny, silly | jaunty | mincing | loose-limbed | ungainly | fast | sedate, slow, stately**
• VERB + WALK **do, have** *She did a silly walk to amuse her friends.* ◊ *He has a mincing walk, fast with short steps.*

3 a **walk** speed of walking
• VERB + WALK **slow to | move off at, set off at** *The horses set off at a walk.*

walk *verb*

• ADV. **briskly, fast, quickly, swiftly | slowly | calmly, quietly** *I got up and walked calmly out into the early evening.* | **cautiously | barefoot** *She had no sandals and walked barefoot.* | **ahead, away, back, backwards, forward, in, on, out, together** *Jake was walking some way ahead.*
• PREP. **along, down, into, out of, to, towards, up, etc.** *She walked cautiously up the drive towards the door.*
• PHRASES **go walking** *For our holiday we went walking in the Lake District.*

wall *noun*

• ADJ. **high, low | long, short | thick, thin | massive | back, front, side | bare, blank** *to stare at a blank wall* | **exterior, external, outer, outside | inner, inside, interior, internal | adjoining | dividing, partition, party | boundary, perimeter | retaining** *They built a retaining wall around the pond.* | **load-bearing** *If a load-bearing wall is weakened, the building could fall down.* | **panelled | bathroom, kitchen, etc. | brick, masonry, stone, etc. | city, garden, harbour, sea**
• VERB + WALL **build, erect, put up | demolish, destroy, pull down | climb (over), scale** *The burglars must have scaled the side wall.* | **jump down from, jump over | cover, line, paint, paper, plaster** *She covered her walls with pictures of film stars.*
• WALL + VERB **stand | enclose sth, surround sth | face sth** *the wall facing the door*
• WALL + NOUN **clock, light | cupboard, unit | covering, decoration, hanging, tile**
• PREP. **against a/the ~** *She leant against the wall.* **behind a/the ~** *Nobody can see behind the wall.* **on a/the ~** *She hung the photos on the wall.* | **~ along** *the wall along the seafront* **~ around/round** *high walls around the prison* **~ of** *(figurative) a solid wall of fog*

wallet *noun*

• ADJ. **bulging, fat, stuffed** *He pulled a £10 note out of his fat wallet.* ◊ *a wallet stuffed with fifty-pound notes*
• VERB + WALLET **get out, pull out, take out | put away**
• PREP. **in a/the ~** *He carried a photo of his children in his wallet.*

wallpaper *noun*

• ADJ. **faded, peeling | floral, flowery, patterned, striped | flock, textured**
• QUANT. **roll** *six rolls of wallpaper*
• VERB + WALLPAPER **hang | be covered/hung with | strip (off), take off**
• WALLPAPER + NOUN **paste**

waltz *noun*

• ADJ. **slow | Viennese**
• VERB + WALTZ **dance, do | play**
• WALTZ + NOUN **rhythm, time**

wander *verb*

1 move slowly around a place / go from place to place
• ADV. **slowly | aimlessly | disconsolately, restlessly | happily | at will, freely** *The cattle are allowed to wander freely.* | **just, simply** *Simply wandering is a pleasure in itself.* | **far, further (afield)** *One day she wandered further afield.* | **about, across, along, around/round, away, back, in, off, out, over** *He just wandered in one day and asked for a job.*
• VERB + WANDER **be free to** *Visitors are free to wander through the gardens and woods.* | **allow sb/sth to, let sb/sth** *How could you let him wander off like that?*
• PREP. **across, all over, along, among, around, into,**

out of, round, through, towards *Don't go wandering all over the house!* ◊ *He wandered into a bar and ordered a drink.*
• PHRASES **find sb wandering** *They found him wandering around aimlessly.*

2 stop concentrating
• ADV. **a little**
• VERB + WANDER **begin to** *His attention was beginning to wander.* | **allow sth to, let sth** *Lissa let her mind wander a little.*
• PREP. **from, to** *My thoughts wandered from the exam questions to my interview the next day.*

wane *verb*

• ADV. **a little, somewhat** *Her popularity was waning somewhat.* | **gradually, rapidly**
• VERB + WANE **begin to** *Her initial enthusiasm was clearly beginning to wane.*
• PHRASES **wax and wane** (= grow and then decrease) *Public interest in the issue has waxed and waned over the years.*

want *noun*

• ADJ. **human**
• VERB + WANT **meet, satisfy, see to** *a society that satisfied all human wants*
• PREP. **for ~ of** *Refugees are dying for want of proper health care.* **in ~** *Thousands of children are living in want.*

want *verb*

• ADV. **badly, desperately, really | just, only, simply** *I just want you to be happy.* | **genuinely, truly** *If you truly want to help, just do as I say.* | **always** *Thanks for the present—it's just what I've always wanted.*
• PHRASES **all you want** *All I want is the truth.* **exactly/just what you want**

war *noun*

• ADJ. **long, short | bloody | all-out, full-scale, total** *Six years of total war had left no citizen untouched.* | **limited | holy, just | civil, global, world | air, guerrilla | atomic, nuclear | cold | economic, trade | price | class**
• VERB + WAR **be in, fight in** *My grandfather fought in two world wars.* | **fight, make, wage** *The two countries fought a short but bloody war.* ◊ *The Spartans were persuaded to make war on Athens.* ◊ *The terrorists were charged with waging war against the state.* | **win | lose | declare | go to** *The country went to war in 1914.* | **avert, prevent | be ravaged by**
• WAR + VERB **approach, loom, threaten | begin, break out, come, erupt, start | escalate, spread** *talks to prevent the war from escalating* | **continue, drag on, go on, last, progress, rage (on)** *The war raged for nearly two years.* | **come to an end, end**
• WAR + NOUN **years** *the shortage of food during the war years* | **hero, veteran | chief, leader | casualty, victim | damage | correspondent** *the war correspondent of a daily newspaper* | **artist, poet | zone | effort** *Every available resource went towards the war effort.* | **record** *Both candidates have distinguished war records.* | **wound | crime, criminal | graves, memorial | aims | damages, reparations | baby, bride, widow | booty | cry, dance | machine** *the Soviet war machine*
• PREP. **at ~** *a country at war* **between the ~s** (= between the First and Second World Wars), **in (a/the) ~** *killed in war* ◊ *He took part in the Vietnam War.* | **~ against/with** *the war against the French* ◊ *a war against drug abuse* **~ between** *war between Iran and Iraq* **~ on** *The US declared war on Japan.* **~ with** *a trade war with the United States*

• PHRASES **the horrors of war** *The country had just emerged from the horrors of civil war.* **in a state of war, in time/times of war** *In times of war, troops were billeted in the mill.* **on a war footing** *The army had been placed on a war footing.* **the brink of war** *The crisis took Europe to the brink of war.* **the outbreak of war** *At the outbreak of war, most children were evacuated to the countryside.* **a theatre of war** *These aircraft are designed to take troops and weapons to any theatre of war in the shortest time possible.* **a war of attrition**

ward *noun*

• ADJ. **open, public | private | hospital | maternity, surgical, etc.**
• VERB + WARD **be admitted to** *He was admitted to the casualty ward.* | **be discharged from**
• WARD + NOUN **nurse, sister, staff | round** *The doctor was doing her morning ward round.*
• PREP. **in a/the ~** *She spent five days in the maternity ward.* **on the ~** *How many midwives are on the ward?*

warden *noun*

• ADJ. **chief, head | deputy | church, college, prison | park | game** *He is chief game warden of the Masai Mara game reserve in Kenya.* | **traffic | dog**
⇨ Note at JOB

wardrobe *noun*

1 large cupboard for clothes
• ADJ. **built-in, fitted | double | walk-in**
• VERB + WARDROBE **open | close**
• WARDROBE + NOUN **door**
• PREP. **in a/the ~** *She hung the dress up in the wardrobe.*

2 sb's collection of clothes
• ADJ. **new | extensive | autumn, spring, etc.**
• VERB + WARDROBE **have | buy** *I want to buy a whole new summer wardrobe.*

warehouse *noun*

• ADJ. **30 000 sq ft, etc. | bonded** *The whisky was taken to bonded warehouses at Port Dundee.* | **distribution, retail, wholesale | furniture, goods, grain, whisky, etc. | abandoned, derelict, disused | dockside, riverside**
• VERB + WAREHOUSE **burn down**
• WAREHOUSE + VERB **burn down**
• WAREHOUSE + NOUN **foreman, manager, staff, worker** *He's a warehouse foreman for a removals firm.*

wares *noun*

• ADJ. **ceramic, metal, etc. | domestic, household**
• VERB + WARES **sell | hawk, peddle, shout, show (off)** *street traders hawking their wares*

warfare *noun*

• ADJ. **open** *Rivalry between football fans developed into open warfare.* | **conventional, modern | biological, chemical, germ, nuclear | class, gang, internecine, tribal | guerrilla, siege, trench | aerial, air, naval, submarine | jungle, mountain | economic, ideological, psychological** *a subtle form of psychological warfare*
• VERB + WARFARE **engage in**
• PREP. **~ against** *warfare against other tribes* **~ between** *warfare between gangs*

warm *verb*

• ADV. **thoroughly | gently | gradually, slowly | rapidly, soon** *We soon warmed up in front of the fire.* | **suddenly** *His voice suddenly warmed.* | **through, up** *Return the bowl to the heat to warm through.*

warm *adj.*

1 at a fairly high temperature
- VERBS **be, feel, look | get, grow** *How can we get warm?* ◊ *She felt her face grow warm at his remarks.* | **keep, stay** *She tries to keep warm by sitting right next to the fire.* ◊ *The bread should stay warm for at least half an hour.* | **keep sb/sth** *These will keep your feet warm.* | **serve sth** *Bake for 15 minutes and serve warm with Greek yogurt.*
- ADV. **exceptionally, extremely, particularly, really, very | almost** *It was a mild day, almost warm.* | **just** *Add the soured cream and cook, stirring, until just warm.* | **faintly, pretty, quite, reasonably, relatively, slightly | enough, sufficiently** *Are you sure you'll be warm enough dressed like that?* | **beautifully, blissfully, comfortably, deliciously, pleasantly, wonderfully** *sliding further down into the blissfully warm bed* | **uncomfortably** *The room seemed uncomfortably warm.* | **surprisingly | unseasonably, unusually** *The night air was soft and unseasonably warm.*
- PHRASES **nice (and) warm** *Come and have a nice warm drink by the fire.* ◊ *That jacket looks nice and warm.*

2 friendly
- VERBS **be, sound | become**
- ADV. **exceptionally, extremely, immensely, marvellously, really, very** *an immensely warm and friendly person* | **genuinely | surprisingly**

warmth *noun*

1 a fairly high temperature
- ADJ. **comfortable, delicious, enveloping, glowing, pleasant, seductive, welcome** *He moved towards the seductive warmth of the fire.* | **gentle** *the gentle warmth of the autumn sun* | **bodily, body** *This clothing maintains your body warmth.*
- VERB + WARMTH **feel** *She could feel the warmth of the child's hand in her own.* | **bask in, enjoy, revel in** *We lay on the beach, basking in the warmth of the hot sun.* | **add** *(figurative) Autumn colours add warmth to a room.*
- WARMTH + VERB **spread** *She sat by the fire and felt the warmth spread through her body.*
- PREP. **for ~** *They found the children huddled together for warmth.* | **~ from** *warmth from the radiator*

2 friendliness or kindness
- ADJ. **genuine, real | friendly | human, personal** *She seems to be a person without human warmth.*
- VERB + WARMTH **exude, radiate, show** *a person who radiates warmth and kindness* | **be lacking in, lack**

warn *verb*

- ADV. **firmly | clearly | bluntly** *The chancellor bluntly warned the Cabinet to axe public spending or face higher taxes.* | **sternly | softly** *'Don't,' he warned softly.* | **specifically** *We were specifically warned against buying the house.* | **duly** *Having been duly warned that I would get nowhere with my application, I went right ahead and applied anyway.* | **constantly, repeatedly** *My mother constantly warned me not to go into teaching.* | **publicly**
- VERB + WARN **had better, have to, must, should** *I must warn you that some of these animals are extremely dangerous.* ◊ *I thought I should warn her about it.* | **try to** *I did try to warn you.* | **fail to** *She claimed doctors had failed to warn her of the risks involved.*
- PREP. **about** *No one had warned us about the unbearable heat.* **against** *We were warned against drinking the local water.* **of** *The report warns of the dangers of smoking.* ◊ *They warned us of the risks involved.*
- PHRASES **be warned** *You will get better—but be warned, it may be a long process.*

warning *noun*

- ADJ. **awful, dire, grim, ominous, stark, stern, strong** *There were dire warnings about the dangers of watching too much TV.* | **urgent | adequate, advance, ample, due, early, fair, prior** *I need advance warning of how many people to cater for.* | **clear, direct | coded** *The explosion came 20 minutes after a coded warning to police.* | **initial | final** *The referee fave him a final warning.* | **formal, government, official | salutary, timely, useful** *The team's defeat is a salutary warning before the World Cup.* | **friendly | veiled** *Her words sounded like a veiled warning.* | **audible, visual** *There is an audible warning when a certain speed is exceeded.* | **verbal, written** *His employers have placed him on final written warning.* | **air-raid, bomb, fire, flood, gale, hazard, storm** *There are 39 severe flood warnings on 22 rivers across the country.* | **health, safety** *Every cigarette packet carries a health warning.*
- VERB + WARNING **give (sb), issue** *The police have issued a warning about pickpockets.* | **shout (out), sound** *The sirens sound a warning when fighter planes are sighted.* ◊ *The strike sounded a warning to all employers in the industry.* | **reiterate, repeat | be, serve as** *Let this be a warning to you not to trespass on my land again!* ◊ *What happened to him should serve as a warning to all dishonest politicians.* | **get, receive | ignore | heed** *They failed to heed a warning about the dangerous currents in the river.*
- WARNING + VERB **come** *The warning came just minutes before the bomb exploded.* | **sound** *On 2 April 1916 air-raid warnings sounded throughout Edinburgh.*
- WARNING + NOUN **notice, sign** *Red marks on the skin may be a warning sign for this disease.* | **bell, device, light, signal, system**
- PREP. **in ~** *The dog growled in warning as we approached.* **without ~** *He left his wife without warning.* | **~ about** *a warning about teaching children to swim* **~ against** *a warning against complacency* **~ of** *They sent us fair warning of their arrival.* **~ to** *The police issued a warning to all drug users in the city.*
- PHRASES **a word of warning** *He gave us a word of warning about going out alone at night.*

warrant *noun*

- ADJ. **arrest, death, search** *The king refused to sign the death warrant for his old friend.* | **royal**
- VERB + WARRANT **authorize, grant, issue, serve, sign** *The commissioner has issued a warrant for her arrest.* ◊ *The police served a warrant on him.* | **get, obtain | execute** *Police who executed a search warrant found a substantial amount of stolen property on the premises.*
- WARRANT + NOUN **card**
- PHRASES **without a ~** *In certain circumstances, police may enter premises without a warrant.* | **~ for**

warrant *verb*

- ADV. **hardly** *The TV appearance was so brief that it hardly warranted comment.*
- VERB + WARRANT **be** **important/serious/severe enough to** *They do not consider the case serious enough to warrant a government enquiry.*

warranty *noun*

- ADJ. **general | specific** *We can not give a specific warranty for the work done on your property.* | **six-month, two-year, year's, etc.**
- VERB + WARRANTY **give, provide | come with** *The computer comes with a year's warranty on all parts.*
- WARRANTY + VERB **cover sth** *Corrosion is not covered by the warranty.* | **expire, run out**
- WARRANTY + NOUN **period | claim**
- PREP. **under ~** *Is your car still under warranty?* |

~ **against** *a warranty against storm damage* ~ **on** *The warranty on my watch ran out just before it broke.*
● PHRASES **breach of warranty** *He took legal action against the company for breach of warranty.*

warrior *noun*

● ADJ. **formidable, great, mighty, noble | brave, valiant | famous, renowned**
● QUANT. **band**
● WARRIOR + VERB **fight**

warship *noun*

● ADJ. **modern | surface | naval | nuclear**
● QUANT. **fleet**
● VERB + WARSHIP **build | command | lose** *Germany lost two warships during this attack.*
● PREP. **aboard/on/on board a** ~ *He is serving on a warship in the Pacific.*

wary *adj.*

● VERBS **be, feel, look, seem | become, get, grow | remain | make sb** *The strange look in his eyes made me wary of accepting his offer.*
● ADV. **decidedly, deeply, extremely, very | increasingly | a bit, a little, rather, slightly | instinctively | suddenly** *Paula frowned, suddenly wary.*
● PREP. **about** *Be wary about these so-called special offers.* **of** *You should be very wary of people offering cheap tickets.*
● PHRASES **keep a wary eye on sb/sth** *(often figurative) The Venetians knew to keep a wary eye on Spanish imperial ambitions.*

wash *noun*

● ADJ. **good | quick | car**
● VERB + WASH **have** *He had a quick wash and shave.* | **do** *I'm doing a dark wash* (= washing all the dark clothes together). | **could do with, need** *That car could do with a good wash.*
● PREP. **in the** ~ (= being washed or waiting to be washed) *Your shirt's in the wash.*

wash *verb*

● ADV. **carefully, properly, thoroughly | gently** *She gently washed and dressed the wound.* | **quickly**
● PHRASES **freshly/newly washed** *the smell of freshly washed hair*

washing *noun*

1 cleaning sth with water
● ADJ. **frequent** *shampoo for frequent washing* | **hand** *I have quite a bit of hand washing to do.*
● VERB + WASHING **do**
● WASHING + NOUN **powder**

2 clothes
● ADJ. **dirty**
● QUANT. **line** *A line of washing fluttered in the breeze.* **pile** *piles of dirty washing*
● VERB + WASHING **hang out, put out** *Have you got any pegs so I can hang the washing out?*
● WASHING + NOUN **line**

washing machine *noun*

● ADJ. **automatic**
● VERB + WASHING MACHINE **load | empty, unload | run** *How often do you run your washing machine?*
● PREP. **in/into a/the** ~

washing-up *noun*

● VERB + WASHING-UP **do | leave** *Leave the washing-up—we can do it in the morning.*
● WASHING-UP + NOUN **bowl | liquid**

wasp *noun*

● WASP + VERB **fly, crawl | sting sb | buzz**
● WASP + NOUN **sting**
● PHRASES **a wasp's nest**

wastage *noun*

● ADJ. **excessive, high | natural** *Voluntary redundancies and natural wastage will cut staff numbers to the required level.* | **muscle** *Patients need exercise to prevent muscle wastage.*
● VERB + WASTAGE **avoid, prevent | minimize | cut down on, reduce | increase | allow for** *Buy more paper than you need to allow for wastage.*

waste *noun*

1 missing an opportunity to do/use sth
● ADJ. **absolute, complete, total, utter** *The whole thing has been a complete waste of time.* | **colossal, great, tremendous | awful, criminal, senseless, shocking, terrible** *a criminal waste of public money* | **needless, unnecessary, useless | tragic** *a tragic waste of human life* | **expensive | conspicuous**
● VERB + WASTE **go to** *If nobody comes all this food will go to waste.* | **cause | avoid** *Try to avoid unnecessary waste.* | **cut down on, reduce | minimize**
● PREP. ~ **of** *a waste of energy/resources*

2 unwanted substances/things
● ADJ. **dangerous, harmful, hazardous, poisonous, toxic** *a dump containing hazardous waste* | **non-toxic | high-level, intermediate-level, low-level | recyclable | agricultural, commercial, industrial | domestic, household, kitchen** *All household waste should be disposed of in strong garbage bags.* | **clinical, hospital, medical | nuclear, radioactive | chemical | plastic | organic | animal, human | garden, plant | municipal | liquid, solid | food, energy**
● VERB + WASTE **produce** *Tonnes of waste are produced every year.* | **dispose of, dump, get rid of** *More people are dumping waste illegally.* | **clean up** *the highly expensive task of cleaning up toxic waste* | **burn, incinerate** *an incinerator for burning hospital waste* | **bury, store | process, treat** *facilities for processing radioactive waste* | **recycle, reprocess | deal with, handle, manage** *the best solutions for managing waste* | **cut down on, reduce | eliminate | export, import** *Industrialized countries continue to export their waste.*
● WASTE + VERB **contaminate sth, pollute sth** *areas contaminated by industrial waste*
● WASTE + NOUN **collection | burial, disposal, incineration | storage | processing, recycling, reprocessing, treatment** *a waste reprocessing plant* | **management | minimization, reduction | bin | dump, site, tip** *The river was used for years as an industrial waste dump.* | **outlet, pipe | imports** *a ban on waste imports*

3 wastes areas of ground not lived in or cultivated
● ADJ. **frozen, icy** *the frozen wastes of Antarctica*

waste *verb*

● ADV. **(not) entirely, (not) totally** *In the end her efforts were not entirely wasted.* | **just, simply** *You're just wasting your breath. She never listens.* | **largely**
● VERB + WASTE **can't afford to, not want to** *He didn't want to waste valuable time in idle gossip.* | **be/seem a shame to** *It seems a shame to waste this good food.* | **not be going to** *I'm not going to waste any more time on the problem.*

- PREP. **on** *Don't waste your money on a hotel room.*
- PHRASES **no time to waste** *Hurry up—there's no time to waste!*

watch noun

1 instrument for telling the time
- ADJ. **digital | fob, pocket, wrist** (also **wristwatch**) | **sports**
- VERB + WATCH **check, consult, glance at, look at | put back/forward** *We put our watches forward eight hours before landing in Tokyo.* | **set** *Don't forget to set your watch to local time.* | **wind** *Quartz watches don't need winding.* | **have on, wear | put on | take off**
- WATCH + VERB **go** *My watch is ten years old and it's still going.* | **stop** *Sorry I'm late—my watch has stopped.* | **be slow, lose sth** *My watch loses a minute each day.* | **be fast, gain sth** | **say sth** *My watch says three o'clock.*
- WATCH + NOUN **face | band** (also **watchband**), **strap**

2 guard
- ADJ. **careful, close** *I kept a close watch on my bag as I sat on the train.* | **constant, round-the-clock | night**
- VERB + WATCH **keep, stand** *Two soldiers were ordered to keep watch for enemy aircraft.* | **put** *The garrison commander had put an extra watch on the prisoners.*
- WATCH + NOUN **committee | tower**
- PREP. **on ~** *Some of the crew were sleeping, while others were on watch.* **on the ~ for** *Cats are constantly on the watch for mice or other small mammals.*

watch verb

- ADV. **carefully, closely, intently** *She watched the man closely to see where he would go.* | **idly | impassively, numbly | anxiously, helplessly, warily** *She watched helplessly as her husband was dragged away.* | **open-mouthed | covertly | in silence, silently | just** *I love just watching the world go by.*
- VERB + WATCH **could only** *They could only watch in silence as their possessions were taken away.* | **continue to | pause to, stop to** *They stopped to watch the procession go by.* | **love to | let sb** *He let me watch while he assembled the model.* | **make sb** *The women were made to watch while their children were slaughtered.*
- PREP. **for** *We watched for any sign of change in the weather.* **from** *They watched from an upstairs window.* **in** *She watched in astonishment as he smashed the machine to pieces.* **with** *He watched with great interest how she coaxed the animals towards her.*
- PHRASES **sit/stand and watch** *She stood and watched them walk off down the road.*

watchdog noun

- ADJ. **consumer | financial, health, industry, pollution, safety | government, independent, official**
- VERB + WATCHDOG **act as, be**
- WATCHDOG + NOUN **body, group, organization | role**
- PREP. **~for** *a consumer watchdog for transport* **~on** *the government's official watchdog on nature conservation* **~over** *The committee acts as an independent watchdog over government spending.*

water noun

1 liquid
- ADJ. **boiling, cold, hot, ice-cold, lukewarm, tepid, warm | clean, clear, crystal-clear, pure | dirty | fresh | brackish, salt** *These fish will quickly die in salt water.* | **salty** *Abscesses should be bathed in warm salty water.* | **salted** *Cook the pasta in plenty of boiling salted water.* | **hard, soft | flowing, running** *the fast-flowing water of the river* ◇ *All the rooms have hot and cold running water.* | **river, sea | surface** *The surface water made the road*

treacherous for drivers. | **drinking | tap** *Avoid drinking the tap water when you first arrive in the country.* | **bottled, mineral, spring | waste | scarce**
- QUANT. **drop**
- VERB + WATER **drink | pour | slosh, spill, splash, spray, sprinkle, spurt, squirt** *Don't slosh too much water on the floor when you're having a bath.* ◇ *The burst pipe was spurting water everywhere.* | **filter, purify | contaminate, pollute | turn off/on** *They turned the water off for a few hours to do some work on the pipes.*
- WATER + VERB **flow, pour, run | gush, spurt** *Brown water gushed out of the rusty old tap.* | **drip, trickle** *There was water dripping from a hole in the ceiling.* | **lap, slosh, spill, splash, spray, squirt** *Water had got into the boat and was sloshing about under our feet.* | **boil, freeze**
- WATER + NOUN **vapour | temperature | pressure | supply | resources | quality | purification, treatment | filter | pollution | shortage | level | table** *Building can be difficult where the water table lies close to the surface.* | **power | company, industry**
- PHRASES **water-repellent** *water-repellent leather* **water-resistant** *a water-resistant watch*

2 mass of water
- ADJ. **deep, shallow | clear | muddy, murky, stagnant | calm, placid, still** *the calm waters of Lake Como* | **choppy, rough, stormy | dangerous, safe** *At last the boat reached safer waters.* | **flood** *The flood water had caused tremendous damage.* | **rising** *They climbed a tree to escape the rising water.* | **bathing**
- WATER + NOUN **sports**
- PREP. **by ~** *Many goods were transported by water in the last century.* **in the ~** *I saw something large floating in the water.* **on the ~** *The swan landed gracefully on the water.* **through the ~** *The boat cut effortlessly through the water.* **under the ~** *An abandoned village lies under the water of the reservoir.*
- PHRASES **the water's edge** *She crouched at the water's edge to wash her hands.*

3 waters sea
- ADJ. **territorial | coastal | tropical | northern, southern | Antarctic, Arctic | Atlantic, Pacific, etc. | home, foreign, international | Japanese, etc. | uncharted** *The ship had drifted into uncharted waters.*
- PREP. **in/into … ~** *The submarine had strayed into Russian waters.*

waterfall noun

- ADJ. **great, high | impressive, magnificent, spectacular | small**
- WATERFALL + VERB **cascade, pour down, tumble** *She watched the magnificent waterfall cascade down the mountainside.*

watershed noun

- ADJ. **important, major, significant | cultural, historical, political**
- VERB + WATERSHED **be, mark, represent | reach**
- WATERSHED + VERB **divide sth** *Darwin's theory of evolution was a watershed dividing the old way of thinking from the new.*
- PREP. **~between** *The 19th century marked a watershed between the country's agricultural past and its industrial future.* **~for** *The granting of the vote represented a watershed for the rights of women.* **~in** *With the strike, a historical watershed in the development of the trade union movement was reached.*

wave noun

1 on water
- ADJ. **big, enormous, giant, great, huge, mountainous**

| small, tiny | white-capped, white-crested, white-topped | breaking | tidal *Several villages have been destroyed by a huge tidal wave.*
- VERB + WAVE **ride** *Surfers flocked to the beach to ride the waves.*
- WAVE + VERB **rise | break, fall** *We watched the waves breaking on the shore.* | **lap** *the gentle sound of waves lapping the sand* | **crash, roar, smash** *I could hear the waves crash against the rocks.*
- WAVE + NOUN **energy, power**
- PREP. **in the ~s** *children playing in the waves* **on the ~s** *There were seagulls bobbing on the waves.*
- PHRASES **the crash/crashing/lap/lapping of the waves, the crest of a wave** (*often figurative*) *She is on the crest of a wave at the moment following her Olympic success.*

2 movement of energy
- ADJ. **electromagnetic, light, radio, seismic, shock, sound**
- VERB + WAVE **emit, generate | deflect**
- WAVE + VERB **bounce off sth, travel** *Sound waves bounce off objects in their path.*

3 increase/spread
- ADJ. **big, enormous, huge, massive | fresh, new, next, recent | first, second, etc.** *the first wave of immigration in the 1950s* | **crime**
- VERB + WAVE **send** *Hearing the tune again sent waves of longing through her.*
- WAVE + VERB **sweep (over) sth, wash over/through sb/sth** *With the fall of the Bastille in 1789, a wave of euphoria swept over Europe.* ◊ *A wave of relief washed over him as he saw that the children were safe.*
- PREP. **~ of** *a big wave of refugees*

4 hand movement
- ADJ. **quick | cheery, friendly | farewell, parting**
- VERB + WAVE **give (sb), return** *I returned his wave and started to walk towards him.*
- PREP. **with a ~ | ~ of** *He dismissed her thanks with a quick wave of the hand.*

wave *verb*

- ADV. **gently** *reeds waving gently in the breeze* | **vigorously | cheerfully, cheerily, happily | frantically, wildly** *They stood by the side of the road and waved frantically.* | **vaguely** *He waved a hand vaguely in the air.* | **dismissively | about/around, aside, back, on, through** *She waved cheerfully and he waved back.* ◊ *The guards waved us on.*
- VERB + WAVE **turn and/to** *He turned to wave to his mother.*
- PREP. **at** *We waved at the people on the shore.* **to** *They waved to us as we passed.* ◊ *She waved him to a seat.*
- PHRASES **wave (sb) goodbye** *people waving goodbye to their friends and relatives*

wavelength *noun*

- ADJ. **long, medium, short | infrared, ultraviolet | visible | acoustic, radio**
- VERB + WAVELENGTH **tune in to**
- PREP. **on a/the ~** *Radio One has broadcast on this wavelength for years.*

way *noun*

1 method/style
- ADJ. **convenient, easy, effective, efficient, good, ideal, practical, quick, useful** *The best way to open it is with pliers.* | **appropriate, proper, right | wrong | normal | traditional | obvious | important** *The most important way to stop accidental drownings is by education.* | **subtle** *There is no subtle way to tell someone that you no longer want them.* | **possible** *They've explored every possible way of dealing with the problem.* | **alternative, different | similar | new | old | funny, mysterious, odd, strange** *God works in mysterious ways.* | **hard** *He learned about the dangers of drugs the hard way.* | **friendly | winning** *The team got back to their winning ways with a 2–1 victory.*
- QUANT. **number** *There are a number of ways to overcome this problem.*
- VERB + WAY **have** *Fate has a way of changing the best of plans.* | **get into, get out of** *The women had got into the way of going up on the deck every evening.* | **explore, look at** *to look at ways of improving language teaching* | **develop, devise, find | change, mend** *Your father is unlikely to change his ways now.* | **be set in** *Grandma is so set in her ways.*
- PREP. **in a/the ~** *Can I help you in any way?*
- PHRASES **in a big way** *He then started spending money in a big way.* **in every way** *They're different in every way.* **in more ways than one** *They're alike in more ways than one.* **in its/your own way** *He was attractive in his own way.* **a kind/sort of way** *He was a handsome man in a sinister sort of way.* **(in) one way or another** *Most people are creative in one way or another.* **a way of life** *the beliefs and practices of the Hindu way of life* **ways and means** *Newspapers have ways and means of getting hold of secret information.*

2 route/road
- ADJ. **best, quickest, right, shortest | wrong | own, separate** (*figurative*) *He's always gone his own way when it comes to design.* | **covered** *We walked along the covered way to the science building.*
- VERB + WAY **go** *I'm going your way, so we can walk together.* ◊ (*figurative*) *When we finished school, we all went our separate ways.* | **go out of** (*figurative*) *She went out of her way to help them.* | **keep/stay out of** (*figurative*) *Let's keep out of her way while she's in such a bad mood.* | **bar, block, get in, stand in** *A fallen tree blocked the way.* ◊ (*figurative*) *He wanted to go to university and would let nothing stand in his way.* | **clear, pave, prepare, smooth** (*all figurative*) *The withdrawal of troops should clear the way for a peace settlement.* | **give, make** (= allow sb/sth to go first or take your place) *Give way to traffic already on the roundabout.* ◊ *Make way for the Lord Mayor!* ◊ *Tropical forest is felled to make way for grassland.* ◊ (*figurative*) *The storm gave way to bright sunshine.* | **edge, feel, inch, make, push, thread, weave, wend, wind, work** *He edged his way along the wall.* ◊ *The river wound its way through the valley.* | **cut, elbow, fight, force, hack, pick, shoulder** *We picked our way carefully over the jagged rocks.* ◊ (*figurative*) *She fought her way up to the top of the company.* | **bluff, talk, trick** (*figurative*) *She bluffed her way through the exam.* | **lose** *She lost her way in the fog.* ◊ (*figurative*) *This project seems to have lost its way.* | **find** *He couldn't find a way through the bracken.* ◊ (*figurative*) *We will eventually find a way out of the crisis.* | **ask (sb)** *She asked him the way to the station.* | **tell sb | know** *Do you know the way?* | **come** (*figurative*) *Have any interesting articles come your way recently?*
- PREP. **along the ~** *We saw a dreadful accident along the way.* **in the/your ~** *There were several rocks in the way.* **out of the/your ~** *Could you please get those boxes out of my way?* **on the/your ~** *We stopped for a snack on the way here.* **out of the/your ~** *The supermarket is a bit out of my way.* | **~ across** *The way across the fields is longer but pleasanter.* **~ from, ~ out of** *Can you tell me the way out of here?* **~ through** *The way through the woods is quicker.* **~ to** *the easiest way from my house to yours*
- PHRASES **take the easy way out** *He took the easy way out and paid someone to write the article for him.* **the way back/down/forward/here/home/in/out/over/there/up** *We stopped for a drink on the way home.*

3 direction/position
- ADJ. **both** *Look both ways before crossing the road.* | **right** | **wrong** *They've gone the wrong way.*
- VERB + WAY **go** *Which way did she go?* | **lead, point, show** *He showed us the way.* | **walk** *Walk this way, please.* | **look** *He looked my way, but didn't seem to recognize me.*
- PHRASES **the … way round/up** *Try it the other way round.* ◊ *Which way up does this box go?*

4 distance in space/time
- ADJ. **long** | **little, short**
- VERB + WAY **come, go** *We had to go a long way before we found a telephone box.* ◊ (*figurative*) *The study of genes has come a long way in recent years.*
- PREP. **~ from, ~ to** *It's quite a way from my house to the shops.*
- PHRASES **all the way** *This bus doesn't go all the way so you'll have to change.* **quite a/some way, a … way ahead/away/off** *Your birthday is still some way off.*

weak *adj.*

- VERBS **appear, be, feel, look, seem, sound** | **become, go** | **remain** | **leave sb, make sb** *When the spasm passed, it left him weak and sweating.*
- ADV. **decidedly, extremely, fundamentally, particularly, very** | **a bit, comparatively, fairly, pretty, quite, rather, relatively** | **curiously** *He complained of feeling curiously weak and faint.* | **surprisingly** | **dangerously** | **lamentably** | **suddenly** *Her legs felt suddenly weak.* | **inherently** *The judge decided the evidence was inherently weak and inconsistent.* | **economically, mentally, militarily, physically, politically**
- PREP. **at** *She's rather weak at maths.* **from** *She was weak from shock.* **in** *He's weak in English.* **on** *The essay was a bit weak on detail.* **with** *He was weak with hunger.*
- PHRASES **weak at the knees** *His sudden smile made her go weak at the knees.*

weaken *verb*

- ADV. **considerably, greatly, seriously, severely, significantly, substantially** | **fatally** *The regime was fatally weakened by the unrest and violence.* | **further** | **slightly, somewhat** | **gradually, progressively** *Central authority has been progressively weakened since the outbreak of the civil war.* | **permanently**
- VERB + WEAKEN **begin to** | **serve to** *The division of Germany had served to weaken the party.* | **tend to** | **be designed to** *an unusual move designed to weaken the rebels*

weakness *noun*

1 lack of strength
- ADJ. **big, fundamental, great, major, serious, significant** | **small** | **physical** | **structural** | **personal** | **muscular** | **political** | **apparent, perceived** *exploiting apparent weaknesses in the system* | **inherent** | **human**
- VERB + WEAKNESS **have, suffer from** | **cause, create** | **exploit** | **assess, identify** | **highlight, point out, reveal** | **minimize, overcome**
- WEAKNESS + VERB **be, lie** *The greatest weakness of the scheme lies in its lack of government support.*
- PREP. **~ in** *Service conditions soon revealed the inherent weaknesses in the vehicle's design.*
- PHRASES **a moment of weakness** *In a moment of weakness I let him drive my car.* **a sign of weakness** *He saw compromise as a sign of weakness.* **strengths and weaknesses** *The appraisal system seeks to assess employees' strengths and weaknesses.*

2 liking for sth/sb
- ADJ. **real**
- VERB + WEAKNESS **have** *I've got a real weakness for chocolate.* | **develop** | **overcome**

- PREP. **~ for** *He worries a lot about his weight, but can't overcome his weakness for fatty foods.*

wealth *noun*

1 money, property, etc.
- ADJ. **considerable, enormous, great, untold, vast** | **growing, increasing** | **economic, financial, material, mineral, natural** *The country's strong economy was built on its mineral wealth.* ◊ *The region possesses a vast natural wealth, particularly of timber.* | **national, personal, private**
- VERB + WEALTH **have, possess** | **accumulate, acquire, inherit** | **lose** *He lost his wealth through poor investment.* | **create**
- PHRASES **a distribution/redistribution of wealth** *a redistribution of wealth through taxation*

2 a wealth of a lot of
- ADJ. **enormous, whole**
- VERB + WEALTH **have** *Switzerland has an enormous wealth of beautiful old buildings.*
- PREP. **of … ~** *She is a woman of untold wealth.*

wealthy *adj.*

- VERBS **be, look** | **become, grow**
- ADV. **enormously, exceedingly, exceptionally, extremely, fabulously, immensely, incredibly, seriously** (*informal*), **very** *He is now fabulously wealthy.* | **comparatively, fairly, quite, reasonably, relatively**

wean *verb*

- ADV. **gradually**
- VERB + WEAN **attempt to, try to**
- PREP. **(away) from** *trying to wean her away from gambling* **off** *They have gradually weaned him off the drugs.* **onto** *weaning a baby onto solid food*

weapon *noun*

- ADJ. **deadly, lethal, potent, powerful** *He was charged with assault with a deadly weapon.* | **effective, useful** | **heavy, light** *The assault forces used heavy weapons, including anti-tank rockets and mortars.* | **automatic** | **atomic, biological, chemical, nuclear** | **offensive, strategic, tactical** *She pleaded guilty to carrying an offensive weapon.* ◊ *a ban on the use of tactical nuclear weapons* | **murder** | **ultimate** (*often figurative*) *The workers' ultimate weapon was the strike.* | **secret** (*often figurative*) *The team's secret weapon was their new young defender.*
- VERB + WEAPON **be armed with, carry, have** | **deploy, fire, use** | **use sth as** (*often figurative*) *She used humour and wit as weapons against her enemies.* | **aim, point**
- WEAPON + NOUN **system** | **technology** *the illegal transfer of weapons technology to hostile countries*
- PREP. **~ against** (*often figurative*) *This relaxation technique can serve as an effective weapon against stress.*

wear *noun*

1 use as clothing
- ADJ. **everyday, weekend** | **summer, winter**
- PREP. **in ~** *Silk shirts always feel soft and light in wear.* **with ~** *New shoes usually get more comfortable with wear.*
- PHRASES **years of wear** *This is a quality garment which should give years of wear.*

2 clothes
- ADJ. **day, evening** | **designer, fashion** | **casual, leisure, outdoor** | **bridal, maternity** | **children's, men's, women's**

3 long use
- ADJ. **hard, heavy**

- VERB + WEAR **withstand** *This flooring can withstand years of hard wear.*
- PREP. **... with ~** *The stairs had become slippery with wear.*
- PHRASES **centuries, years, etc. of wear** *The cathedral steps were polished smooth by centuries of wear.*

4 damage caused by long use
- ADJ. **excessive | engine, tyre, etc.**
- VERB + WEAR **show** *The tyres were beginning to show wear.* **| cause | minimize, reduce**
- WEAR + NOUN **pattern** *the analysis of wear patterns on prehistoric stone tools* **| guarantee** *The flooring comes with a 20-year wear guarantee.*
- PREP. **~on** *This new oil reduces wear on the engine.*
- PHRASES **signs of wear, wear and tear**

wear *verb*

1 have a piece of clothing on
- ADV. **proudly** *proudly wearing their uniforms*
- VERB + WEAR **tend to** *I tend to wear a jacket to work.* **| refuse to** *She refused to wear prison clothes.* **| forbid sb to | be entitled to** *He is entitled to wear the regimental tie.*

2 last for a long time
- ADV. **badly, well** *Those curtains have worn very well.*

weariness *noun*

- ADJ. **great | sheer, utter | war**
- VERB + WEARINESS **succumb to** *She succumbed to weariness and went to bed.*
- WEARINESS + VERB **overtake sb, overwhelm sb**
- PREP. **... with ~** *I had slept badly and felt numb with weariness.* **in ~** *His eyes were half closing in weariness.* **| ~ in** *He detected a note of weariness in her voice.*

weary *adj.*

- VERBS **be, feel, look, seem, sound | become, grow** *I've grown rather weary of all your excuses.*
- ADV. **very | almost** *His voice sounded almost weary.* **| a bit, a little, rather** *She looks a little weary.*
- PREP. **of** *The people are weary of war.*

weather *noun*

- ADJ. **beautiful, excellent, fair, fine, glorious, good, ideal, lovely, perfect, superb | adverse, appalling, atrocious, awful, bad, dismal, dreadful, foul, gloomy, grim, inclement, inhospitable, lousy, miserable, nasty, rotten, rough, terrible, vile, wretched | hot, humid, muggy, sultry, warm | mild | bright, clear, sunny | calm | dry | reliable, settled | changeable, fickle, uncertain, unpredictable, unsettled | extreme, fierce, harsh, severe, violent, wild | bitter, cold, freezing, frosty, icy, wintry | cool | cloudy, grey | damp, rainy, wet | foggy | blustery, stormy, windy | unseasonable/unseasonal, unseasonably/unseasonally** *... a spell of unseasonally wet weather.*
- QUANT. **spell**
- VERB + WEATHER **brave** *Deciding to brave the weather, he grabbed his umbrella and went out.*
- WEATHER + VERB **clear (up), improve, let up, warm up** *We'll go just as soon as this weather lets up.* **| hold out, keep up** *If the weather holds out we could go swimming later.* **| threaten** *Bad weather threatened.* **| break, deteriorate, worsen** *It was warm and sunny until the weekend, but then the weather broke.* **| become sth, get sth, turn sth** *Next day the weather turned cold.* **| remain sth, stay sth | close in, set in** *The weather closed in and the climbers had to take shelter.* ◇ *I wanted to mend the roof before the cold weather set in.* **| allow, permit** *I sat outside as often as the weather allowed.* ◇ *We're having a barbecue next Saturday, weather permitting.* (You cannot say

'weather allowing'.) **| prevent sth** *Stormy weather prevented any play in today's tennis.* **| change**
- WEATHER + NOUN **conditions** *The plane crashed into the sea in adverse weather conditions.* **| patterns, system** *the effects of global warming on the world's weather patterns* ◇ *The Atlantic weather systems had been kind.* **| forecast, report | data, records | satellite, station | chart, map**
- PHRASES **a change in the weather** *We hadn't bargained for such a dramatic change in the weather.* **in all weathers** *The lifeboat crews go out in all weathers.* **the vagaries of the weather** *She packed all kinds of clothes to cope with the vagaries of the English weather.* **whatever the weather** *He swims in the sea every day, whatever the weather.*

weather *verb*

1 pass safely through sth
- ADV. **successfully, well** *Their company had weathered the recession well.*
- VERB + WEATHER **manage to** *(figurative)* *The company has managed to weather the storm.*

2 change in appearance because of the sun/air/wind
- ADV. **badly** *Some of the stone has weathered quite badly.*

weave *verb*

- ADV. **specially** *The carpet was specially woven to commemorate the 1 000th anniversary of the cathedral's foundation.* **| skilfully** *(often figurative)* *Hall skilfully weaves the historical research into a gripping narrative.* **| inextricably, intricately** *(both figurative)* *The whisky is inextricably woven into Scotland's history, customs and culture.* **| together** *weaving the threads together*
- PREP. **from** *a basket woven from strips of willow* **into** *A pattern is woven into the fabric.*

web *noun*

1 that a spider makes
- ADJ. **spider/spider's**
- VERB + WEB **build, make, spin, weave**

2 complicated series/network of sth
- ADJ. **complex, complicated, intricate, tangled**
- VERB + WEB **create, form, weave** *The mass media forms a web of communications.* **| be drawn into** *More and more people were drawn into his web of deceit.*
- PHRASES **a web of deceit/deception, a web of intrigue, a web of relationships**

3 the **Web** on the Internet
- VERB + WEB **access | browse, surf**
- WEB + NOUN **page | browser, server | resource, service | network, ring | design, development | publishing | designer, developer, editor, host, master** (also **webmaster), user | directory, guide, index | access | tool**
- PREP. **on the ~** *I found this survey on the Web.*
- ⇨ Special page at COMPUTER

website *noun*

- ADJ. **Internet | official, unofficial** *the official website of Liverpool FC* **| comedy, commercial, company, education/educational, golf, news, personal, travel, etc.**
- VERB + WEBSITE **look for, search for | access, browse, check out, log into/onto, look at, visit | search** *I was searching this history website for something about Alexander the Great.* **| bookmark | have | build, create, design, develop, make, set up** *We show you how to make your own website in ten simple steps.* **| launch | upload | host, maintain, run, update**
- WEBSITE + VERB **be/go down** *There were so many visitors to the website that it went down.*
- WEBSITE + NOUN **address, URL | designer**

• PREP. **on a/the~** *You can find details of all our products on our website.*
• PHRASES **a link to a website** *This page includes lots of links to other websites you may find interesting.*
⇨ Special page at COMPUTER

wedding *noun*

• ADJ. **church, registry office | royal | white**
• VERB + WEDDING **attend, come to, go to | arrange | invite sb to | conduct** *The wedding will be conducted by the local vicar.*
• WEDDING + VERB **take place** *The royal wedding will take place in June.*
• WEDDING + NOUN **day, night | invitation | plans, preparations | date** *We haven't set a wedding date yet.* | **dress, gown | clothes, outfit, suit | band, ring** *She had a plain wedding band on her third finger.* | **finger** *a ring on her wedding finger* | **breakfast, feast | ceremony, service | vows | procession | party, reception | celebrations | speech | cake | gift, present | list** *We were choosing what present to buy from the wedding list they'd sent.* | **group, guests, party | album, photographs, video | anniversary | bells** *(figurative) After going out with her boyfriend for a year, she started talking about wedding bells.*
• PREP. **at a/the~** *I met her at my brother's wedding.*

wedge *verb*

• ADV. **firmly, tightly**
• PREP. **against, behind, between, into, under** *She wedged a chair firmly under the door handle.*
• PHRASES **wedge sth in place/position, wedge sth open/shut** *Someone had wedged the door open with a brick.*

Wednesday *noun*

⇨ Note at DAY

wee *noun*

• VERB + WEE **do, have, take | be bursting for, need, want** *Mummy, I need a wee.* | **go for** *I'm going for a wee.*

weed *noun*

• ADJ. **annual, perennial | aquatic, pond, water**
• VERB + WEED **kill | clear, pull up, remove | control, keep down, keep under control** *Routine maintenance of the garden consists of keeping weeds under control.*
• VERB + WEED **grow, spread | push up, spring up** *There were weeds pushing up through the gravel.*
• WEED + NOUN **control | killer** (also **weedkiller**) | **growth | seed, seedling**

week *noun*

• ADJ. **last, past | previous | coming, following, next | consecutive, successive** *They won 1–0 for the fourth consecutive week.* | **entire, full, whole** *It's the first time for ages I've done a full week's work.* | **working | busy, hard | quiet** *It's been a very quiet week for me.* | **3-day, 40-hour, etc.** *He earns enough money to work a four-day week.*
• VERB + WEEK **spend** *We spent two weeks in France last summer.* | **take**
• WEEK + VERB **elapse, go by, pass** *The week passed very slowly.*
• PREP. **by the~** *They're paid by the week.* **during/in the~** *I go out most weekends, but rarely during the week.* **for a~** *I haven't seen him for weeks.* **in a~** *We'll be back in a week.* **in ~s** *It hasn't rained in weeks.* **over/under a~** *It's over a week since she rang me.* **per~** *How much do you earn per week?* **within a/the~** *I'll have the report finished within the next couple of weeks.*

• PHRASES **a day of the week** *Which day of the week was it?*

weekend *noun*

• ADJ. **long** *I took Friday off, and spent a long weekend visiting friends.* | **wet** *It will be a wet weekend for much of England and Wales.*
• VERB + WEEKEND **spend**
• WEEKEND + NOUN **break, trip, visit | home, retreat**
• PREP. **at the~** *What are you doing at the weekend?* **at ~s** *What do you usually do at weekends?* **over the~** *The office is closed over the weekend.*
• PHRASES **a weekend away/off**

weep *verb*

• ADV. **copiously | loudly | quietly, silently | openly, unashamedly** *The people wept openly when his death was announced.* | **bitterly | inconsolably, uncontrollably** *His grandmother was weeping uncontrollably.* | **almost | a little**
• VERB + WEEP **begin to, start to | want to | make sb**
• PREP. **at** *He wanted to weep at the unfairness of it all.* **for** *I felt I could have wept for joy.* ◇ *weeping for someone who has died* **over** *We had wept over the death of our parents.* **with** *She almost wept with happiness.*
• PHRASES **break down and weep** *Several of the soldiers broke down and wept.* **weep and wail** *The mourners followed the funeral procession, weeping and wailing.* **weep buckets** *(informal)* (= weep a lot)

weigh *verb*

1 consider sth carefully
• ADV. **carefully | up** *The jury weighed up the evidence carefully.*
• PREP. **against** *We weighed the cost of advertising against the likely gains from increased business.*

2 be considered important
• ADV. **heavily, strongly**
• PREP. **against** *His untidy appearance weighed against him.* **in favour of** *This fact weighed heavily in her favour.* **with** *His evidence weighed strongly with the judge.*

weight *noun*

1 amount sth weighs
• ADJ. **considerable, enormous, great, heavy, immense | light | gross, net | average, mean | sheer** *(figurative) The sheer weight of visitors is destroying this tourist attraction.*
• VERB + WEIGHT **bear, carry, support** *The arch bears the weight of the bridge above.* | **bend/buckle/collapse/crack/sag/shift/sink beneath/under, give way beneath/under** *Many buildings collapsed under the weight of rain-soaked ash and mud.* ◇ *(figurative) He was buckling under the weight of his responsibilities.* | **crush sb beneath/under | creak/groan beneath/under** *She tried to be quiet, but the stairs creaked under her weight.* | **stagger/strain beneath/under** *The boy was staggering beneath the weight of a pile of boxes.*
• PREP. **in~** *It is about 76 kilos in weight.*

2 weight of sb's body
• ADJ. **low | ideal, right | excess, surplus | target** *I should soon be down to my target weight of 70 kilos.* | **body | birth** *babies with a low birth weight*
• VERB + WEIGHT **watch** *I won't have any cake—I have to watch my weight.* | **gain, put on | lose, reduce, shed** *He's lost a lot of weight.* | **keep down | bear, carry, hold, support, stand, take** *I was worried that the branch wouldn't take my weight.* | **put, rest** *The doctor told me not to put my weight on this ankle for a month.* | **shift, transfer** *He nervously shifted his weight from foot to foot.* | **distribute** *Stand with your legs apart and your weight*

evenly distributed. | **hurl, throw** *He threw his weight at the door and it burst open.*
● WEIGHT + VERB **go up, increase** | **go down, decrease, drop, fall, plummet, plunge** | **fluctuate** *People's body weight can fluctuate during the day.*
● WEIGHT + NOUN **gain, loss** | **control** | **problem**

3 piece of metal
● ADJ. **heavy, large** | **light**
● VERB + WEIGHT **lift** *She did circuit training and lifted weights to build her fitness.*
● WEIGHT + NOUN **lifting, training**
● PHRASES **weights and measures**

4 heavy object
● ADJ. **heavy** | **dead** *With difficulty she managed to pull his dead weight onto the bed.* | **leaden** *(figurative) A leaden weight lay on her heart as she waved him goodbye.*
● VERB + WEIGHT **lift** *Heavy weights should be lifted with a straight back.*

5 importance/influence of sth
● ADJ. **due, sufficient** *Environmental considerations were given due weight in making the decision.* | **insufficient** | **considerable** | **sheer** *How can you ignore the sheer weight of medical opinion?* | **economic, financial, intellectual, political** *America's economic weight.*
● VERB + WEIGHT **attach, give, place** *They attach too much weight to academic achievement.* | **carry** *Her opinion seemed to carry little weight in the company.* | **add, lend** *The new evidence added considerable weight to the prosecution's case.* ◇ *Sir Leon lent his weight to the Tory campaign yesterday.*
● PHRASES **put/throw your weight behind sth, weight of numbers** *The rebels were defeated by sheer weight of numbers.*

weighted *adj.*

● VERBS **be, seem**
● ADV. **equally** *The exam consists of six equally weighted questions.* | **heavily** | **unfairly**
● PREP. **against** *This new legislation is unfairly weighted against the small farmer.* **in favour of** *The course is heavily weighted in favour of engineering.* **towards** *measures that are weighted towards small investors*

weird *adj.*

● VERBS **be, feel, seem, sound** *I started to feel quite weird.*
● ADV. **really, very** | **a bit, a little, pretty, quite, rather** *It all sounds a bit weird to me.*
● PHRASES **weird and wonderful** *Some of their clothes were really weird and wonderful.*

welcome *noun*

● ADJ. **big, enthusiastic, friendly, great, rapturous, rousing, special, tumultuous, warm** *The audience gave the band a rousing welcome.* | **broad, general** *The proposals have been given a broad welcome by green campaigners.* | **cautious, guarded, qualified** | **cool, cold, chilly** | **official** | **hero's** *She got a hero's welcome on her return from the Olympics.*
● VERB + WELCOME **get, receive** | **extend, give sb** | **await** *A warm welcome awaits you at this family-run hotel.* | **outstay/overstay your** *Sensing that he had outstayed his welcome, he quickly said his goodbyes and left.*
● PREP. **in ~** *She held out her arms in welcome.* | **~ from** *The proposal received a cautious welcome from the Opposition.* **~ to** *A big welcome to our special guest, Sir James Greenan.* ◇ *They received a cold welcome to their new home.*
● PHRASES **a smile of welcome, a speech of welcome, words of welcome**

welcome *verb*

1 greet sb/be pleased sb has come
● ADV. **heartily, warmly** *If you visit our town you will be warmly welcomed.* | **formally, officially** | **back** *The whole family turned out to welcome him back.*
● VERB + WELCOME **be delighted to, be pleased to** | **prepare to, wait to** *The school is preparing to welcome the new intake of students.*
● PREP. **into** *He welcomed us into the club.* **to** *We are delighted to welcome you to our firm.*
● PHRASES **look forward to welcoming sb, welcome sb with open arms** *They welcomed the new volunteers with open arms* (= with enthusiasm).

2 be pleased about sth and support it
● ADV. **enthusiastically, particularly, greatly, warmly** *Many companies have warmly welcomed these changes in legislation.* | **positively** *We positively welcome applications from all sections of the community.* | **broadly** | **cautiously** *Foreign bankers and economists cautiously welcomed the minister's initiative.* | **initially**
● PHRASES **be generally/universally/widely welcomed** *The proposals have been widely welcomed.*

welcome *adj.*

● VERBS **be, feel** | **make sb** *They made us very welcome in their home.*
● ADV. **doubly, especially, extremely, highly, more than, most, particularly, very** *The 1% rate cut is highly welcome.* ◇ *You would be a most welcome guest.* | **perfectly, quite** *You are perfectly welcome to stay here: I can't offer five-star accommodation, that's all.* | **not at all, not entirely** *He made it plain that Holman's interest in his business affairs was not at all welcome.* | **always** *Visitors are always welcome.*
● PREP. **to** *New members are welcome to the club.*

welfare *noun*

1 good health and happiness
● ADJ. **animal, child, community, employee, family, personal, student** *people concerned about child welfare*
● VERB + WELFARE **improve, promote** *The government's policies will promote the welfare of all citizens.*

2 money, etc. from the government
● ADJ. **state**
● WELFARE + NOUN **state** *the provision of services such as health through the welfare state* | **agency, authorities, department, programme, provision, services, system** | **officer, worker** | **clinic, facilities** | **benefits, payments** *lone parents living on welfare benefits* | **budget, costs, spending** | **cuts** | **fraud, scrounger** *The new government promised to clamp down on welfare scroungers.*
● PREP. **on ~** *the number of families on welfare*

well *noun*

1 for water
● ADJ. **deep, shallow** | **artesian** | **holy** | **wishing**
● VERB + WELL **dig, sink**
● WELL + VERB **run dry**

2 for oil
● ADJ. **oil**
● VERB + WELL **drill**

well-being *noun*

● ADJ. **general** | **emotional, mental, physical, psychological, social, spiritual** | **human, personal** | **economic, financial, material**
● VERB + WELL-BEING **contribute to, ensure, foster, promote** *A better water supply would contribute dramatically to the villagers' well-being.* | **threaten**

● PHRASES **health and well-being, a sense of well-being** *She was filled with a sense of well-being.*

west *noun, adj.*

⇨ Note at DIRECTION

wet *verb*

● ADV. **thoroughly** *Wet your hair thoroughly before applying the shampoo.* | **slightly**
● PREP. **with** *Wet the towel slightly with warm water.*

wet *adj.*

● VERBS **be, feel, look** | **become, get, turn** *We got soaking wet just going from the car to the house.* ◇ *The weather may turn wet later on in the week.* | **get sth** *Mind you don't get your feet wet.*
● ADV. **dripping, extremely, really, soaking, sopping, very** *His clothes were dripping wet.* | **a bit, a little, quite, rather, slightly** *It's still quite wet outside.* | **permanently** *permanently wet conditions*
● PREP. **with** *The grass was wet with dew.*
● PHRASES **wet through** *We were wet through and cold.*

whale *noun*

● ADJ. **beached, stranded**
● QUANT. **school**
● VERB + WHALE **hunt** | **harpoon**
● WHALE + VERB **swim** | **dive** | **sing** | **blow (sth)** *We saw a whale blowing a jet of spray high in the air.* | **breach sth** *Ahead, the whale breached the surface of the water.* | **beach itself, be washed up**
● WHALE + NOUN **hunting** | **meat, oil** | **stocks** *management and conservation of whale stocks*

wheat *noun*

● ADJ. **ripe** | **cracked, whole** | **durum** | **spring, winter**
● QUANT. **ear, grain** | **bag, sack, sheaf** | **field**
● VERB + WHEAT **grow** | **sow** | **cut, harvest** | **thresh** | **grind** | **eat**
● WHEAT + VERB **grow**
● WHEAT + NOUN **harvest** | **field** | **flour, germ**

wheel *noun*

1 on a bicycle, car, etc.
● ADJ. **bicycle, car, etc.** | **spare** | **front** | **back, rear** | **nearside** | **offside** | **loose, wobbly** | **alloy**
● WHEEL + VERB **change, replace** *A tyre blew and we had to change the wheel.*
● WHEEL + VERB **go round, spin, turn** *The wheels were still going round.* ◇ *(figurative) The political wheel had turned full circle, and he was back in power.* | **skid, slide, slip** *He braked suddenly, causing the front wheels to skid.* | **crunch, scream, shriek** *the sound of wheels crunching over snow* | **come off, fall off** | **lock** *She braked too hard and the wheels locked.*
● WHEEL + NOUN **arch, base, bearings, hub, nut, rim, trim** | **clamp**
● PREP. **on ~s** *A child was pulling along a little dog on wheels.* **under the ~s** *She fell under the wheels of a bus.*
2 (also **steering wheel**)
● VERB + WHEEL **grip** | **turn** | **take** *I drove the first 200 miles and then Steve took the wheel.*
● WHEEL + NOUN **lock**
● PREP. **at the ~** *The bus set off again with a fresh driver at the wheel.* **behind the ~** *I saw the car drive past, but didn't recognize the woman behind the wheel.*

wheelchair *noun*

● ADJ. **electric, motorized, powered**
● VERB + WHEELCHAIR **use** | **manoeuvre** *Anthony manoeuvred his wheelchair out from behind his desk.* | **push** | **be confined to** *He's been confined to a wheelchair since the accident.*
● WHEELCHAIR + NOUN **access** | **user** *better access for wheelchair users* | **athlete**
● PREP. **by ~** *In town, she gets about by wheelchair.* **in a/the ~** *It's hard to get around if you're in a wheelchair.*
● PHRASES **accessible by wheelchair, wheelchair accessible facilities/vehicles, etc.**

whereabouts *noun*

● ADJ. **current, present** | **unknown** *The present whereabouts of the manuscript is unknown.* | **exact, precise**
● VERB + WHEREABOUTS **know** *She did not say where she was going, and nobody knows her whereabouts.*

whiff *noun*

● ADJ. **faint** | **strong** | **unmistakable** (*often figurative*) *detecting the unmistakable whiff of electoral blackmail*
● VERB + WHIFF **catch, get, detect** *I caught the whiff of whisky on his breath.* ◇ *(figurative) Journalists caught a whiff of scandal and pursued the actress relentlessly.*
● PREP. **~ of** *a whiff of perfume*
● PHRASES **at the faintest/first/merest whiff of sth** (*figurative*) *He always retreated emotionally at the first whiff of conflict.*

while *noun*

● ADJ. **brief, little, short** | **fair, good, long, some** *Things continued quiet for some while.*
● VERB + WHILE **take** *I'll mend it for you, but it could take a while.*
● PREP. **after a ~** *After a while, I began to get bored with my job.* **for a/the ~** *They chatted for a while.* ◇ *There's no need to do anything for the while.* **in a ~** *I'll be back in a while.*
● PHRASES **all the while** *The bird hopped across the lawn, keeping a sharp lookout all the while.* **once in a while** *Everybody makes a mistake once in a while* (= occasionally). **(for) quite a while** *He kept me waiting for quite a while.* **a while back** *The problems started a while back.*

whim *noun*

● ADJ. **sudden** | **slightest** *The bird's nest is vulnerable to the slightest whim of the weather.* | **individual, personal** | **political** *Funding is subject to political whim.*
● VERB + WHIM **indulge, pander to, satisfy** | **be subject to, be vulnerable to, depend on** | **suffer** *For years she had suffered her husband's whims.*
● PREP. **at (sb's) ~** *They seem to be able to change the rules of the game at whim.* ◇ *Slaves could be bought and sold at the whim of their masters.* **on a ~** *He bought the jacket on a whim, having seen it by chance in a shop window.*
● PHRASES **your every whim** *The child's parents pandered to his every whim.*

whimper *noun*

● ADJ. **little, small** | **frightened, pathetic**
● VERB + WHIMPER **give** *The animal gave a pathetic little whimper.*

whimper *verb*

● ADV. **softly** *The dog whimpered softly.* | **pathetically**
● VERB + WHIMPER **begin to, start to** | **hear sb**
● PREP. **with** *The boy was whimpering with pain.*
● PHRASES **whimper like a child** *He stirred in her arms, whimpering like a child.*

whine *noun*

● ADJ. **high, high-pitched** | **piercing** | **nasal**

- VERB + WHINE **give, let out** | **hear**
- PREP. **with a~** *She spoke with a whine.* | **~of**
- PHRASES **the whine of a bullet/an engine/a motor**
⇨ Note at SOUND

whine verb

- ADV. **faintly, softly** *The engines whined softly in the background.* | **away**

whip noun

- ADJ. **driving, riding** | **bull, horse**
- VERB + WHIP **crack, flick** *He cracked the whip and the horse leapt forward.*
- VERB + WHIP **crack** *A hound yelped briefly as a whip cracked.*
- PHRASES **the crack of a whip**

whip verb

1 hit sb/sth with a whip
- ADV. **soundly** *He was taken back to the jail and soundly whipped.*

2 mix sth until it is light and stiff
- ADV. **gently, lightly** *Lightly whip the egg whites and add them to the mixture.* | **up**

whirl noun

- ADJ. **mad** *The next few days were a mad whirl of parties.* | **social** *It's easy to get caught up in the social whirl.*
- PREP. **in a~** *His mind was in a whirl as he searched frantically for a solution.*

whisky noun

- ADJ. **double, large** | **single, small** | **stiff** | **neat, straight** *I'll have my whisky straight, please.* | **excellent, fine, good** *a fine malt whisky* | **cheap** | **bootleg** (= illegally made) | **blended, Irish** (spelt **whiskey**), **malt, Scotch, single-malt**
- QUANT. **dash, drop, nip** *He added a dash of whisky to his coffee.* | **measure, shot, tot** *She poured herself a large tot of whisky.* | **bottle, flask, glass, hip-flask, tumbler**
- VERB + WHISKY **drink** *Do you drink whisky?* | **have** *He had a whisky on the rocks.* | **pour (sb)** | **sip** | **gulp, swig** | **down, finish** | **distil** | **produce** *the art of distilling whisky*
- WHISKY + NOUN **drinker** | **bottle, decanter** | **glass, tumbler** | **chaser** *He ordered a beer with a whisky chaser* (= a small glass of whisky drunk after a beer). | **business, company, distiller, distillery, industry, production, sales**
- PHRASES **whisky on the rocks** (= with ice)

whisper noun

- ADJ. **barely audible, the barest, faint, gentle, hushed, low, mere/the merest, soft** | **fierce, harsh** | **audible, loud, stage** *'I knew this would happen,' he said in a stage whisper* (= one that he wanted everyone to hear). | **hoarse, husky, strangled** | **awed, excited, urgent** | **confidential, conspiratorial**
- PREP. **above a ~** *Their voices were very quiet, hardly above a whisper.* **in a~** *They spoke in whispers.*

whisper verb

- ADV. **softly** | **hoarsely, huskily, thickly** | **fiercely, urgently** *'Come on,' he whispered urgently.* | **brokenly, shakily, unsteadily** | **angrily, bitterly, furiously** | **confidentially, conspiratorially** | **excitedly** | **almost, half** | **back** *'Yes,' I whispered back.*
- VERB + WHISPER **can/could only** *He could only whisper in reply.* | **hear sb** *She heard him whisper her name.*
- PREP. **about** *I felt that everyone was whispering about*

me. **against** *'Hush,' he whispered against her hair.* **through** *'No,' he whispered through gritted teeth.* **to** *'Let's go,' she whispered to Anne.*
- PHRASES **whisper sth in/into sb's ear, whisper sweet nothings** *He held her and whispered sweet nothings in her ear.*

whistle noun

1 small metal/plastic tube that you blow
- ADJ. **dog, factory, police, train** | **guard's, referee's, etc.** | **steam** | **penny, tin**
- VERB + WHISTLE **blow (on), sound** *A train sounded its whistle in the distance.*
- WHISTLE + VERB **blow, go, sound** *The referee's whistle went just before he shot the goal.*
- PHRASES **a blast on a whistle** *He gave a short blast on his whistle.*

2 clear high-pitched sound
- ADJ. **loud** | **high, high-pitched, piercing, shrill** | **low, long** | **short** | **silent** *He pursed his lips in a silent whistle.* | **tuneless** | **wolf** | **final** (*sport*) *They scored their only goal just before the final whistle.*
- VERB + WHISTLE **give, let out** | **hear**
- PREP. **with a~** *The train entered the tunnel with a shrill whistle.* | **~of** *She gave a low whistle of admiration.*
⇨ Note at SOUND

whistle verb

- ADV. **loudly** | **softly, under your breath** | **through your teeth** *Norma looked at the parcel and whistled softly through her teeth.* | **cheerfully** | **tunelessly**
- VERB + WHISTLE **begin to** | **hear sb**
- PREP. **at** *Men whistled at her in the street.* **in** *James whistled in amazement.* **to** *William whistled to me from a distance.*

white noun

- ADJ. **egg** *Whisk the egg whites until stiff.*
- VERB + WHITE **beat, whip, whisk**
- PHRASES **the white of an egg** *Use the whites of two eggs.*

white adj.

1 of the colour of snow or milk
- ADJ. **dead, pure** | **bright, brilliant** | **bone, creamy, icy, milky** | **dirty, off-** | **plain**
⇨ Special page at COLOUR
- PHRASES **as white as snow**

2 very pale because of illness or fear
- VERBS **be, look** | **go, turn**
- ADV. **extremely, very** | **rather**
- PREP. **with** *He turned white with anger.*
- PHRASES **as white as a sheet**

whole noun

1 all of sth
- VERB + WHOLE **cover, embrace, encompass, involve, span** *The project involved the whole of the university.* | **fill, occupy, take up** *The library takes up the whole of the first floor.* | **permeate, pervade** *Technology permeates the whole of our lives.*

2 complete thing
- ADJ. **coherent, cohesive, harmonious, homogeneous, integrated, organized, seamless** *She was struggling to organize her ideas into a coherent whole.* | **single** | **complex** *The author examines each aspect of Roman society, then attempts to summarize the complex whole.* | **meaningful** *At this age, babies do not yet combine sounds into a meaningful whole.* | **organic**

● VERB + WHOLE **form, make (up)** *He tried to fit the pieces of evidence together to make a coherent whole.*
● PHRASES **as a whole** *Unemployment is higher in the north than in the country as a whole.*

wide adj.

1 covering a large area or range
● VERBS **be, seem | become**
● ADV. **enormously, exceptionally, extraordinarily, extremely, remarkably, unusually, very** *a very wide range of clothing* **| increasingly | fairly, quite, reasonably, relatively | sufficiently | surprisingly**

2 fully open
● VERBS **be | fling sth, open sth, spread sth** *He stood up and flung wide the door to the study.* ◇ *Open your mouth really wide.* ◇ *He spread his hands wide in appeal.*
● ADV. **extremely, really, very**
● PREP. **with** *Their eyes were wide with fear.*

3 not close
● VERBS **be | shoot | fall, land**
● ADV. **very | just**
● PREP. **of** *Her shot fell just wide of the target.*
● PHRASES **wide of the mark** (*figurative*) (= not accurate) *Their predictions turned out to be very wide of the mark.*

widen verb

● ADV. **considerably, greatly** *The gap between rich and poor has widened considerably.* **| slightly | gradually, slowly | quickly, rapidly, suddenly | out** *The road widens out and becomes a dual carriageway.*
● PREP. **from, into** *At this point, the river widens into an estuary.* **to** *The trade deficit had widened from £26 billion to £30 billion.*

widespread adj.

● VERBS **be | become | remain**
● ADV. **extremely, remarkably, very | increasingly | fairly, pretty, quite | sufficiently | geographically** *a geographically widespread species*
● PREP. **among** *Illiteracy is widespread among the poor.*

widow noun

● ADJ. **distraught, grieving | elderly, middle-aged, young | rich, wealthy | poor | war**
● VERB + WIDOW **become | leave** *He died in March leaving a widow and three children.*
● PHRASES **a widow's allowance/pension**

width noun

● ADJ. **great** *the great width of his shoulders* **| full, overall, total, whole | narrow** *The fabric is only available in a narrow width.* **| maximum, minimum**
● VERB + WIDTH **have** *The windows have a width of six feet.* **| measure** *Measure the width of each side.* **| increase | decrease, narrow (to), reduce** *The snow had narrowed the width of the road to a single track.* ◇ *The road narrows to a width of just four metres.* **| vary in**
● WIDTH + VERB **grow, increase | decrease | vary**
● WIDTH + NOUN **measurement | fitting** *The boots are available in a choice of width fittings.*
● PREP. **across the ~** *The pattern goes across the full width of the material.* **in ~** *The car is 1.775m in width.*

wife noun

● ADJ. **new | future** (also **wife-to-be** *informal*) **| ex-, former | deserted | divorced, estranged | dead, late | dependent** *With a dependent wife and children, he can't afford to lose his job.* **| pregnant | dutiful, excellent, faithful, good, loving, loyal, supportive, wonderful |**

long-suffering *His long-suffering wife had to put up with his numerous affairs.* **| attractive, beautiful, charming, lovely | unfaithful | jealous | domineering, nagging | battered** *a hostel for battered wives*
● VERB + WIFE **meet** *I first met my wife at university.* **| marry | desert, leave, walk out on | batter, beat**
● WIFE + VERB **give birth** *His wife has just given birth to a son.*

wig noun

● ADJ. **blond, curly | powdered**
● VERB + WIG **have on, sport, wear** *Do you think she was wearing a wig?* **| put on | remove, take off**
● WIG + VERB **perch** *The wig seemed to perch on his head.*
● PREP. **in a/the ~** *Who's that man in the wig?*

wild adj.

1 animals/plants
● VERBS **be, grow, live** *The flowers grow wild in the mountains.* ◇ *The dogs live wild on the streets.*
● ADV. **truly** *This is truly wild and unspoilt countryside.*

2 out of control
● VERBS **be, look** *He looked wild and dangerous.* **| go, run** *When the princess appeared, the crowd went wild.* ◇ *They annoy the neighbours because they let their children run wild.* **| drive sb, make sb** *It makes me wild* (= very angry) *to see such waste.*
● ADV. **really, very | absolutely | a bit, a little, pretty, rather** *Her hair was rather wild.*
● PREP. **with** *The crowd was wild with excitement.*

wilderness noun

● ADJ. **last | great | barren, desert, desolate | frozen | uncharted | unspoilt | political** (*figurative*) *the man who brought the party back from the political wilderness*
● VERB + WILDERNESS **transform** *They transformed the wilderness into a garden.* **| explore** *They set out to explore the earth's last great wilderness, Antarctica.*
● WILDERNESS + NOUN **years** (*figurative*) *His wilderness years* (= when he was out of politics and the public eye) *in the 1990s were spent in North America.*
● PREP. **in the ~** *We were hopelessly lost in the wilderness.*

wildlife noun

● ADJ. **abundant | endangered, rare | indigenous, local, native | marine, urban, wetland**
● VERB + WILDLIFE **preserve, protect, save** *They called on the government to help protect native wildlife.* **| attract, encourage** *The large variety of native plants attracts wildlife to the area.* **| benefit | endanger, threaten** *The increasing use of pesticides threatens the wildlife of the area.* **| damage, harm | disturb** *Do not allow your dog to disturb wildlife.* **| be (a) home for/to, be rich in** *The forest is home to a wealth of wildlife.*
● WILDLIFE + NOUN **habitat | area, garden, haven, park, refuge, reserve, sanctuary, site** *The school has its own small wildlife garden.* **| conservation, management, protection | trade** *the illegal wildlife trade* **| artist, cameraman, film-maker, photographer**
● PHRASES **a wealth of wildlife**

will noun

1 power to choose; desire
● ADJ. **indomitable, iron, strong** *her indomitable will to win* ◇ *His unassuming manner concealed an iron will.* **| weak | free | conscious | collective, general, majority, national, popular, public** *Is that the general will, that we keep the present voting arrangements?* **| individual | human | divine, God's | royal | political** *The govern-*

ment lacked the political will to reform the tax system. (see also **goodwill**)

- VERB + WILL **have** *She's got a very strong will.* | **lack** | **exercise, exert** | **lose** *She's lost the will to try and change things.* | **break, drain, sap** *Constant rejection has sapped her will.* | **regain** | **impose** *She usually manages to impose her will on the rest of the group.* | **bend to, obey** *They were taught to obey their father's will without question.* | **go against** *My father didn't want me to leave home, and I didn't like to go against his will.*
- PREP. **against your ~** *Much against my will, I let him go.* **at~** *She believes employers should have the right to hire and fire at will.*
- PHRASES **an act of will** *It requires an act of will to make myself go running in the morning.* **a battle/clash of wills** *The meeting turned out to be a clash of wills.* **an effort of will** *With a great effort of will he resisted her pleas.* **of your own free will** *She left of her own free will.* **the will of God, the will to live** *She gradually regained the will to live.*

2 legal document

- ADJ. **valid** *Two people must witness your signature or your will will not be valid.* | **living** (= a record of your wishes regarding medical treatment at the end of your life)
- VERB + WILL **draw up, make** *His solicitor drew up the will.* ◇ *Have you made your will?* | **sign** | **leave** *She left no will and was unmarried.* | **read** | **alter, change** | **revoke** *Remarriage would revoke all previous wills.* | **forge** | **remember sb in** *She was moved when her neighbour remembered her in his will.* | **administer, execute** | **challenge, contest** *The family decided to contest the will in court.* | **break, overturn, set aside** *They succeeded in getting the will overturned.*
- PREP. **by~** *Some things cannot be given away by will.* **in a/the~** *She left me some money in her will.* **under a/the ~** *Under her father's will, she gets £5 000 a year.*
- PHRASES **sb's last will and testament**

willing *adj.*

- VERBS **appear, be, prove, seem** *They appear willing to talk to us.*
- ADV. **more than, only too, really, very** *I'm more than willing to get involved.* | **increasingly** | **perfectly, quite** *He's quite willing to do the same for you.* | **enough** *He seemed willing enough to listen.* | **apparently** | **always** *She is always willing to help.* | **no longer**

willingness *noun*

- ADJ. **general** | **genuine** | **greater, increased** | **growing, increasing**
- VERB + WILLINGNESS **demonstrate, display, indicate, show, signal** *The new government has shown a willingness to listen and learn.* | **announce, confirm, declare, express** *Workers' leaders have expressed their willingness to cooperate.* | **demand, depend on, require** *Marriage counselling depends on both parties' willingness to try to solve problems.*
- PREP. **in your ~** *In her willingness to help them, she quite forgot that she wasn't as strong as she had been.*

will power *noun*

- ADJ. **sheer** | **strong**
- VERB + WILL POWER **have** *I'm no good at slimming. The trouble is, I've got no will power.* | **take** *It took all his will power to stay in and study.* | **summon** *He tried to summon the will power to get out of bed.* | **need**
- PREP. **by~** *She managed to finish the race by sheer will power.*

wilt *verb*

- ADV. **visibly**

- VERB + WILT **begin to** *Some of the leaves were beginning to wilt.*
- PREP. **in** *The plants will wilt in direct sunlight.* **under** *By half-time, the team was wilting under the pressure.* **with** *The passengers were visibly wilting with the heat and movement of the bus.*

win *noun*

- ADJ. **big, comfortable, convincing, decisive, easy, emphatic, handsome, resounding, runaway** | **last-gasp, narrow** *An extra-time penalty gave Barcelona a last-gasp win over Chelsea.* | **five-point, nine-wicket, single-shot, two-goal, etc.** | **hard-earned, hard-fought** | **deserved, well-earned** | **excellent, fine, great, impressive** | **thrilling, improbable, remarkable, shock, unexpected** | **famous** *People still talk about the famous win against Brazil.* | **away, home** | **cup final, league, semi-final, etc.** | **Democrat, Labour, etc.**
- VERB + WIN **claim, chalk up, gain, have, notch (up), record, score** *We've had three successive wins in the National League.* ◇ *Torino notched up a 2–1 win at Lazio.* | **cruise to, romp to, sweep to** *Woods romped to a 12-shot win in the Open.* | **deserve, earn** | **give sb** | **celebrate**
- WIN + VERB **come** *His only big win came in the French Open ten years ago.* | **keep sb, lift sb, put sb, take sb** *Williams's straight-sets win puts her through to the semi-final.*
- PREP. **without a ~** *They've gone four games without a win.* | **~against/over** *Liverpool gained a thrilling 5–4 win over Glenavon.*
- PHRASES **a no-win situation** *She was in a no-win situation, taking the blame for things she did not have the power to change.*

win *verb*

- ADV. **comfortably, convincingly, easily, hands down, handsomely, outright** *The French team won hands down.* | **narrowly** *She narrowly won the first race.* | **duly** *He duly won, but was then sidelined by a leg injury.* | **unexpectedly** | **eventually, finally**
- VERB + WIN **deserve to** *We didn't deserve to win—we played very badly.* | **hope to** | **be expected to, be tipped to, expect to** *The actress is tipped to win an Oscar for her performance.* | **be likely to** | **be going to** *Who do you think is going to win?* | **manage to** | **fail to** *The far right party failed to win a single seat.* | **help (to), help sb (to)** *qualities which help win business and motivate staff*
- PREP. **against** *They stand a good chance of winning against their league rivals.* **at** *I never win at tennis.* **by** *She won the race by 40 metres.* **on** *The match was eventually won on penalties.*
- PHRASES **be capable of winning (sth)** *There are a lot of teams capable of winning the title.* **be confident of winning (sth), a chance of winning (sth), a chance to win sth** *the chance to win the holiday of a lifetime* **succeed in winning sth** *He succeeded in winning their confidence.*

wince *verb*

- ADV. **a little, slightly** | **inwardly** *He winced inwardly at her harsh tone.* | **visibly**
- VERB + WINCE **try not to** | **make sb** | **see sb**
- PREP. **at** *She switched on the light, wincing at the sudden brightness.* **in/with** *He winced in pain.*

wind *noun*

- ADJ. **fierce, gale-force, high, stiff, strong, terrible** *Rain and high winds are forecast.* ◇ *There was a stiff wind blowing.* | **light, moderate, slight** | **blustery, gusty** | **warm** | **biting, bitter, brisk, chill, cold, icy** *The icy wind cut right through us.* | **howling** | **fair, favourable, good** *They set sail the next morning with a fair wind.* | **adverse**

Adverse winds swept the boat off course. | **head, tail** *A tail wind made the ride home very relaxing.* | **east, north, etc.**
- QUANT. **blast, gust** | **breath** *There wasn't a breath of wind in the still air.*
- WIND + VERB **blow, blow up, come, cut through sb/sth, sweep (through) sth** *The wind came from the west.* ◇ *A fierce wind swept through the countryside.* | **howl, moan, roar, whistle** *The wind roared through the tunnel.* | **buffet sth, rattle sth, whip sth (up)** *The wind whipped up the surface of the lake.* | **increase, pick up, rise** | **abate, die down, drop** *Let's wait until the wind drops before setting sail.* | **change** *The wind suddenly changed and began blowing from the north.*
- WIND + NOUN **conditions, direction, power, pressure, speed**
- PREP. **against the~** *We were rowing against the wind.* **in the~** *a flag flapping in the wind* **into the~** *We were sailing into the wind.* **out of~** *Let's shelter out of the wind.*
- PHRASES **the roar/sound of the wind**

wind *verb*

- ADV. **tight/tightly** | **carefully, neatly**
- PREP. **around/round** *He wound the bandage tightly round his ankle.* **into** *She wound the wool into a ball.*

windfall *noun*

- ADJ. **unexpected**
- VERB + WINDFALL **get, have** *She had an unexpected windfall of a thousand pounds when a cousin died.*
- WINDFALL + NOUN **gains, profits** | **tax**

window *noun*

1 in a building, car, etc.
- ADJ. **big, huge, long, tall, wide** | **narrow, small** | **panoramic** | **floor-length, floor-to-ceiling** | **deep-set** | **arched, bay, bow, casement, dormer, French, lattice, leaded, picture, rose, sash, skylight, small-paned, stained-glass** *You get to the garden through French windows at the back of the house.* ◇ *The cathedral has a beautiful rose window.* | **plate-glass** | **double-glazed** | **barred, curtained, shuttered** *All the windows in the prison are barred.* | **curtainless** | **open** | **boarded-up** | **blank** *No light showed in any of the blank windows of the house.* | **dark** | **bright, sunny** | **rain-lashed, rain-streaked** | **draughty, ill-fitting** | **dirty, dusty, filthy** | **clean** | **steamed-up** | **balcony, basement, bedroom, kitchen, etc.** | **back, front, rear, side, top, topmost, upstairs** | **first-floor, ground-floor, etc.** | **south-facing, etc.** | **display, shop** | **car, carriage, train, etc.** | **back, driver's, passenger, rear** | **electric** | **smoked, tinted** *a limousine with smoked windows*
- VERB + WINDOW **gaze out (of), gaze through, look in (through), look out (of), look through, peer out (of), peer (in) through, see out (of), see through, stare out of, stare (in) through** *I found her looking in the window of a department store.* ◇ *It was raining so hard I could scarcely see out the window.* | **lean out of, stick your head out of** | **knock on, rap on, tap on** *We tapped on the window to get their attention.* | **fling open, force (open), open, throw open** *There was evidence that the window had been forced.* | **roll down, wind down** *I rolled down the window to ask for directions.* | **close, roll up, shut** | **clean, wash** | **break, shatter, smash** | **replace**
- WINDOW + VERB **open, wind down** *How does the window open?* | **close, go up** | **break, shatter, smash** | **blow out** *All the windows blew out with the force of the blast.* | **flash, gleam, glint, glow, shine** *The windows glinted in the sunlight.* | **steam up** *The windows all steam up when you have a shower.* | **rattle** *The windows rattle when a train goes past.* | **face sth, give a view of sth, look, overlook sth, stare** *a studio with windows looking*

south towards the park ◇ *The windows of the house stared bleakly down at her.*
- WINDOW + NOUN **frame, ledge, pane, sill** | **seat** *I always ask for a window seat when I fly.* | **cleaner** *He works as a window cleaner.* | **display** | **shopping** *I love going window shopping* (= looking at things in the shops without buying anything).
- PREP. **at the~** *He was standing at the window waiting for us.* **by the~** *I sat by the window to get some air.* **in the~** *an advertisement in the shop window* ◇ *We caught sight of him in the window as we passed.* ◇ *There was a vase of flowers in the window.* ◇ *A bird flew in the open window.* **out (of)~** *She gazed out of the window at the falling snow.* **through~** *They threw a brick through the window.*

2 area on a computer screen
- ADJ. **active** *Click on the window to make it active.*
- VERB + WINDOW **open** | **close** *If you close a couple of windows, the screen will be less cluttered.* | **enlarge, minimize, resize, shrink** | **drag, move** | **click on**
⇒ Special page at COMPUTER

windscreen *noun*

- ADJ. **front, rear** | **car**
- VERB + WINDSCREEN **clean, scrape, wipe** *She scraped the windscreen free of ice.* | **break, chip, crack, shatter, smash** | **fit, put in, replace, take out** | **clear, demist** *She switched the wipers on to clear the windscreen.*
- WINDSCREEN + VERB **mist up** | **crack, shatter**
- WINDSCREEN + NOUN **wiper**
- PREP. **on a/the~** *I came back to find a parking ticket on the windscreen.* **through a/the~** *Bright evening sunlight glared through the windscreen.*

wine *noun*

- ADJ. **red, rosé, white** | **fizzy, sparkling** | **dry** | **sweet** | **light** *He served a light white wine with the lunch.* | **full-bodied, heady, strong** | **fruity** | **sour, vinegary** *a cheap vinegary wine* | **mature, young** *The younger wines will be mature after about three years.* | **new, old** *some new wines from South Africa* | **excellent, expensive, fine, good, great, quality, vintage** | **cheap, table** | **house** *The restaurant's house wines are an Australian Chardonnay and a French red.* | **dessert** | **fortified** *fortified wines such as port and sherry* | **mulled, spiced** | **chilled** *chilled white wine* | **home-made** | **dandelion, elderberry, rice, etc.**
- QUANT. **drop** *Would you like another drop of wine?* | **glass, bottle**
- VERB + WINE **drink** *Do you drink wine?* | **have** *I'll have some wine, please.* | **sip, take a sip of** *She took a sip of her wine.* | **gulp, swig, take a gulp/swig of** | **pour (sb), top up** *The waiter went round topping up people's wine.* | **make, produce** *The winery has been making wine for a couple of centuries.* | **age, mature** *wine aged in the bottle* | **chill** | **serve** | **ply sb with** *They always ply their clients with wine before getting down to business.*
- WINE + VERB **flow** (*figurative*) *The wine flowed freely at the party.* | **go to your head** *The wine had gone to his head and he was starting to talk rubbish.* | **breathe** *Open the wine an hour before the meal to let it breathe.* | **be corked** | **age, mature**
- WINE + NOUN **bottle, glass** | **list** *The restaurant has an extensive wine list.* | **rack** *I took another bottle from the wine rack.* | **grower, growing** | **merchant** | **tasting** *The supermarket holds occasional wine-tasting sessions.*

wing *noun*

1 of a bird/insect
- ADJ. **left, right** | **fore, front** *The beetle's fore wings are small and are not used in flight.* | **back, hind** | **broad, long, narrow, pointed, short, stubby** | **delicate** | **leathery, membranous** | **broken, damaged** *a bird with a*

broken wing | **outspread, outstretched** | **butterfly, chicken,** etc. *the patterns on butterfly wings* ◇ *First, fry the chicken wings in the oil until they begin to brown.*

- QUANT. **pair**
- VERB + WING **extend, open, spread, stretch, unfold** | **close, fold** | **flap, flutter** *It flapped its wings and flew off.* | **clean** | **clip** (*often figurative*) *Pete felt he had had his wings clipped when his driving licence was confiscated.* | **grow, sprout** *I wish I could sprout wings and fly away.*
- WING + VERB **beat, flap, flutter**
- WING + NOUN **tip** | **feathers**
- PREP. **on a/the ~** *It had white markings on its wings.* **under a/the ~** *The young birds were under the mother bird's wing.* ◇ (*figurative*) *Simon's uncle had taken him under his wing.*

2 of a plane
- ADJ. **aircraft** | **left, port** | **right, starboard** | **fixed** | **folding**
- WING + VERB **stick out**
- WING + NOUN **tip**

3 of a building
- ADJ. **north, south,** etc. | **private** | **hospital** | **maternity** | **maximum security** (= of a prison)
- VERB + WING **add, build** | **demolish, destroy, pull down** *A bomb destroyed the east wing.*
- PREP. **in a/the ~** *Our rooms were in the west wing.*

4 of a car
- ADJ. **nearside, offside** | **front, rear**
- VERB + WING **damage, dent** *The nearside wing was damaged in the accident.* | **mend, repair, replace**
- WING + NOUN **mirror**
- PREP. **in a/the ~** *There was a dent in one wing.*

5 of an organization
- ADJ. **left, right** | **conservative** | **liberal, progressive, reformist** | **extreme, radical** | **revolutionary** | **moderate** | **dissident** | **political** | **military, paramilitary**
- PREP. **on a/the ~** *They're on the left wing of the Labour Party.*

wink *noun*

- ADJ. **broad** | **little** | **conspiratorial, knowing**
- VERB + WINK **direct, give sb, throw sb**
- PREP. **with a ~** *'Know what I mean?' he said with a wink.* | **~ at** *He directed a conspiratorial wink at his son.*

wink *verb*

- ADV. **broadly** *He winked broadly at Lucinda.* | **conspiratorially, saucily, wickedly** *She winked saucily at Jack.* | **back**
- VERB + WINK **see sb** *I saw him wink at her.*
- PREP. **at** *She winked at me, and I winked back.*

winner *noun*

- ADJ. **overall** *She didn't win every race, but she was the overall winner.* | **outright** *With three teams finishing on 40 points, there was no outright winner.* | **eventual** | **joint** *They were joint winners of the cup.* | **lucky** *She was the lucky winner of that week's biggest lottery prize.* | **deserved, worthy** | **clear, comfortable, convincing, easy, runaway** *She emerged as the clear winner.* | **impressive** | **big** *There were no big winners in this week's lottery.* | **shock, surprise, unexpected, unlikely** | **likely, possible, potential** *Barcelona look likely winners of the Spanish League.* | **first-time, three-times,** etc. *Italy, three times winners of the World Cup* | **consistent, frequent, prolific, regular** *She is a regular winner in local road races.* | **award, championship, competition, contest, cup, election, jackpot, league, match,** (**gold/silver/bronze**) **medal, prize** (also **prizewinner**)**, race, title, tournament, trophy**
- VERB + WINNER **emerge as** | **announce** *The winner*

of the competition will be announced this afternoon.* | **choose, pick** *The winner will be chosen from the five architects who get through the first round.* ◇ *He's very good at picking winners* (= at guessing who is going to win). | **back** *He backed the winner and won £70.*
- WINNER + VERB **receive sth** *The winner will receive a prize of £500.*
- PREP. **~ against/over** *France were impressive 3–0 winners over Portugal.*

winter *noun*

- ADJ. **last, next, this** (**coming**) | **early, late, mid-** (also **midwinter**) *It was impossible to walk the route in midwinter.* | **bad, bitter, cold, hard, harsh, severe, terrible** *one of the worst winters we have ever had* | **bleak, dreary, grey** | **mild** | **wet** | **nuclear**
- WINTER + NOUN **conditions, temperature, weather** | **sun, sunlight, sunshine** | **cold** | **frost/frosts, rain/rains, snow** | **gale, wind** | **landscape, scene, sky** *the artist's bleak winter scene* | **solstice** | **term** | **break, holiday** | **garden** | **flower** | **crop** | **clothes, clothing, coat** | **collection, exhibition** | **Olympics, sports**
- ⇒ Note at SEASON (for more collocates)

wipe *verb*

- ADV. **carefully, gently** | **hastily, quickly** | **easily** *The plastic surface can be easily wiped.* | **just, simply** | **away, down, up** *I wiped up the spilt wine.*
- VERB + WIPE **pause to, stop to** *He paused to wipe the sweat from his forehead.* | **try to**
- PREP. **from** *She gently wiped the tears from her eyes.* **off** *He wiped the marks off the wall.* **on** *She wiped her hands on the towel.* **with** *When you've finished with it, simply wipe it clean with a damp cloth.*
- PHRASES **wipe sth clean**

PHRASAL VERB
wipe sth out
- ADV. **completely, totally** | **almost, practically, virtually** *The regiment was virtually wiped out in the first battle.* | **effectively** *The disease has been effectively wiped out.*
- VERB + WIPE STH OUT **threaten to** *pollution that threatens to wipe out 100 000 fish*

wiper *noun*

- ADJ. **windscreen** | **rear**
- VERB + WIPER **put on, switch on, turn on** | **switch off, turn off** | **be fitted with**
- WIPER + VERB **be going, be on** *Cars were coming past with their wipers going.*

wire *noun*

1 metal as thin thread
- ADJ. **taut, tight** | **loose, slack** | **fine, thin** | **thick** | **flexible, soft** | **stiff** | **rusty** | **barbed, chicken** (= wire mesh used to make fences)**, razor** | **piano** | **perimeter** | **trip** (also **tripwire**) *The bomb was attached to a tripwire laid across the road.* | **high** (= in a circus) *One man rode a bicycle along the high wire as the climax to the act.*
- QUANT. **length, piece, strand**
- VERB + WIRE **cut** *They cut the perimeter wire and escaped.* | **stretch** *The wire was stretched between two poles.*
- WIRE + NOUN **grill, mesh, netting** | **basket, brush, cage, coat hanger, fence, fencing, frame, rack** *Cool the cakes on a wire rack.* | **cutters** (also **wire-cutters**)
- PREP. **behind a/the ~** *Behind the wire, the prisoners were exercising.* **under a/the ~** *We got in under the wire.*

2 for electricity
- ADJ. **electric, electrical, electricity** *Don't place carpets over electrical wires.* ◇ *overhead electricity wires* | **earth, live, neutral** *Don't touch that wire. It's live.* | **overhead** | **telegraph, telephone** | **fuse** | **bare, exposed** *Watch out*

for bare wires. | **insulated, plastic-coated, plastic-covered** | **frayed**

• VERB + WIRE **attach, connect** *The wire was attached to a pin in the plug.* | **disconnect** *He disconnected the wire from the clock.* | **run** *The electrician ran a wire from the kitchen to the bedroom.*

• WIRE + VERB **go, lead, run, trail** *Where does this wire go?* ◇ *There were wires trailing everywhere.* | **show** *Surely the wires shouldn't show like that?*

• PREP. **along a/the ~** *the flow of electrical currents along a wire* **down a/the ~** *A dry laugh echoed down the telephone wire.*

wire *verb*

• ADV. **correctly, properly** *You should check that the socket is correctly wired.* | **in, up** *She was wired up to a heart monitor.*

• PREP. **for** *Many homes were wired for lighting only.* **into, to** *The Christmas tree lights are all wired to one plug.*

wiring *noun*

• ADJ. **electric/electrical** | **dangerous, faulty, loose** | **mains** | **house**

• VERB + WIRING **renew, replace** *The existing wiring will have to be replaced.* | **take out** *They took out the old wiring.* | **disconnect** | **check (over), have a look at** *We'd better get an electrician to check the wiring before we start decorating.* | **conceal** *The wiring was concealed behind a false panel.*

• WIRING + NOUN **diagram** | **system**

wisdom *noun*

• ADJ. **deep, great, profound** | **accepted, conventional, established, folk, popular, prevailing, received, traditional** *Conventional wisdom has it that riots only ever happen in cities.* | **street, worldly** *He is too lacking in worldly wisdom to be a politician.* | **accumulated, collective** *the accumulated wisdom of generations* | **ancient** *A bridge between ancient wisdom and modern insight is now being built.* | **innate, inner, instinctive, intuitive** | **political** | **divine**

• VERB + WISDOM **doubt, have doubts about, question** *Many commentators doubted the political wisdom of introducing a new tax.* | **seek** *Those who seek wisdom at the shrine will find it.* | **impart** *Do you have any wisdom to impart on this subject?* | **prove** *The latest unemployment figures prove the wisdom of the government's policy.*

• PHRASES **a fount/source of wisdom** *Consultants are too often seen as the source of all wisdom.* **in sb's (infinite) wisdom** (*ironic*) *In their infinite wisdom, the council closed the swimming pool for the school holidays.* **pearls of wisdom** *students eager to catch pearls of wisdom from the professor's lips* **the pursuit of wisdom** *She devoted her life to the pursuit of wisdom.* **wit and wisdom** *He entertained the audience for two hours with his wit and wisdom.* **with the wisdom of hindsight** *It's easy enough to see what we should have done, with the wisdom of hindsight.* **words of wisdom** *The former world champion imparted a few words of wisdom to the young runners.*

wise *adj.*

• VERBS **be, look, seem** | **consider sth, judge sth, think sth** *It was not considered wise to move her to another hospital.*

• ADV. **extremely, very** | **always** *It is always wise to write down important points.*

wish *noun*

1 feeling that you want sth

• ADJ. **dearest, deepest, fervent, greatest, strong** | **conscious, unconscious** | **secret** | **dying, last** *He was*

denied his dying wish to be reconciled with his son.* | **death** *Freud's theory of the death wish* | **personal** | **parental** *the child's detention against parental wishes*

• VERB + WISH **have** | **express, make known** *She has expressed a wish to visit the Houses of Parliament.* | **fulfil** *She fulfilled her deepest wish when she flew solo for the first time.* | **get** *She's always wanted to be an actress, and I'm sure she'll get her wish.* | **grant sb** | **be responsive to, consider, honour, respect, take into account** *It is vital for schools to respect the wishes of parents.* | **carry out, comply with, implement, meet** *We need to update our equipment if we are to meet customers' wishes.* | **obey** *She flew into a rage if the staff didn't obey her wishes.* | **deny sb** | **disregard, flout, go against, ignore, override, ride roughshod over** *The committee rode roughshod over the wishes of union members.* | **reflect** *The change to the constitution reflects the wishes of the people who voted in the referendum.*

• WISH + NOUN **fulfilment** | **list** *Draw up a wish list, defining the requirements for your ideal home.*

• PREP. **against sb's ~** *Her father will not speak to her, because she married against his wishes.* **in sb's ~** *In his wish to be as helpful as possible, he was forever asking her what she wanted.* **in accordance with sb's ~s** *In accordance with his wishes, his ashes were scattered at sea.* | **~ for** *a wish for peace*

2 saying secretly to yourself what you want to happen

• VERB + WISH **have, make** *When you see a black cat, you have to make a wish.* | **be allowed, get** *If you're the one who finds the hidden box, you get a wish.* | **grant** *The good fairy granted her three wishes.*

• WISH + VERB **come true** *Lo and behold, on Christmas Day their wishes came true.*

3 (usually **wishes**) hope that sb will be happy

• ADJ. **best, good** *Give my best wishes to Alison.*

• VERB + WISHES **give sb, send (sb)**

• PREP. **with ~** (at the end of a letter) *With best wishes for a happy birthday.* | **~ for** *Every good wish for your future happiness together.*

wish *verb*

• ADV. **dearly, desperately, devoutly, fervently, heartily, really, sincerely** *I heartily wished that I had stayed at home.* ◇ *I really wish I could go to America.* | **hard** *If you wish really hard, maybe you'll get what you want.* | **secretly** | **merely, only, simply** *'Where is he now?' 'I only wish I knew.'*

• PREP. **for** *It's no use wishing for the impossible.*

wit *noun*

1 clever use of words

• ADJ. **great** | **quick, ready** | **acerbic, barbed, biting, caustic, dry, sarcastic, sardonic, scathing, sharp, wicked** | **gentle** | **dazzling, sparkling**

• VERB + WIT **have** *He had a dry wit.*

• PHRASES **wit and wisdom** *a book full of the wit and wisdom of his 30 years in politics*

2 intelligence

• ADJ. **native** *She had to use all her native wit to convince the police.*

• VERB + WIT **have** *I hope he's got the wit to take the key with him.*

• PHRASES **beyond the wit of man** (= impossible) *It should not be beyond the wit of man to resolve this dispute*

3 wits ability to think quickly

• VERB + WITS **gather, recover** *She couldn't seem to gather her wits and tell us what had happened.* | **blunt, dull** *Living alone in the country had dulled his wits.* | **sharpen**

• PHRASES **a battle of wits** *The strike developed into a battle of wits between management and workers.* **have/keep your wits about you** *They do tough interviews* *so you'll need to have your wits about you.* **pit your wits against sb** *Celebrity teams pit their wits against each other in this lively quiz show.*

withdraw *verb*

1 move/move sth away from a place
- ADV. **altogether, completely | immediately, instantly | abruptly, hastily, promptly, quickly, soon** *She hastily withdrew her hand from his.* | **gently | gradually, progressively** *Forces will be progressively withdrawn.* | **eventually | temporarily | unconditionally**
- VERB + WITHDRAW **decide to | intend to, wish to | threaten to | be compelled to, be forced to, be obliged to** *He was forced to withdraw from the competition due to injury.* | **persuade sb to**
- PREP. **from** *Two thousand troops were withdrawn from the battle zone.* **in favour of** *He eventually withdrew in favour of Blair, thought to be the more popular candidate.* **into** *She withdrew into her own world.*

2 take sth away
- ADV. **immediately | subsequently | eventually | formally** *She formally withdrew her resignation.* | **voluntarily | unconditionally** *Last night he unconditionally withdrew his comments.*
- VERB + WITHDRAW **threaten to | agree to | refuse to | advise sb to, persuade sb to, urge sb to**
- PREP. **from** *They threatened to withdraw their support from the government.*

withdrawal *noun*

1 removing/leaving
- ADJ. **imminent | immediate, rapid, sudden | gradual, phased | complete, full, total, unconditional, wholesale | partial | strategic, tactical | voluntary | ignominious** *The UN were faced with an ignominious withdrawal or a long-term military presence.* | **military, troop**
- VERB + WITHDRAWAL **call for, demand** *The party is calling for the phased withdrawal of troops from the island.* | **agree to | announce | make** *The police were forced to make a tactical withdrawal.*
- PREP. **~ by** *a withdrawal by government troops* **~ from** *the army's withdrawal from the occupied territories*

2 from a bank account
- ADJ. **cash**
- VERB + WITHDRAWAL **make**
- PREP. **~ from** *She made a withdrawal of £250 from her bank account.*

3 stopping
- ADJ. **alcohol, drug**
- VERB + WITHDRAWAL **suffer**
- WITHDRAWAL + NOUN **symptoms**
- PREP. **~ from** *She was still suffering withdrawal from nicotine.*

wither *verb*
- ADV. **simply** *Their support had simply withered away.* | **away**
- PREP. **under** *The grass withered under a scorching sun.*
- PHRASES **wither and die** *The business withered and eventually died.*

withhold *verb*
- ADV. **deliberately | reasonably, unreasonably** *Consent will not be unreasonably withheld.*
- VERB + WITHHOLD **threaten to** *threatening to withhold future financial aid* | **decide to**
- PREP. **from** *He was accused of deliberately withholding information from the police.*

withstand *verb*
- VERB + WITHSTAND **be able/unable to, can/could | manage to | be built to, be designed to** *The wooden boat was built to withstand just about every weather condition at sea.* | **be robust/strong/tough enough to** *The flooring needs to be tough enough to withstand wear.* | **enable sth to, help sth (to)**
- PHRASES **be capable of withstanding sth**

witness *noun*

1 person who sees sth
- ADJ. **eye** (also **eyewitness**) *An eyewitness account described the plane as a 'fireball'.* | **crucial, key, material, vital** *As the last person to see her alive, he was a material witness in the case.* | **independent | credible, reliable, unimpeachable | unreliable**
- VERB + WITNESS **appeal for** *The police are appealing for witnesses.* | **trace** *Police have so far failed to trace any witnesses to the attack.*
- WITNESS + VERB **come forward** *Two witnesses came forward with evidence.*
- WITNESS + NOUN **account, statement**
- PREP. **~ to** *a witness to murder*

2 in a court of law
- ADJ. **chief, main, principal** *the defence's chief witness* | **hostile | reluctant, unwilling | defence | prosecution, state | expert | character | civilian, police**
- VERB + WITNESS **call** *The defence called their first witness.* | **appear as** *She appeared as a character witness.* | **swear in | cross-examine, examine, interrogate, interview, question | hear | discredit | intimidate, threaten** *A judicial enquiry was ordered, but witnesses were threatened and none would testify.* | **suborn** *He was charged with conspiracy to suborn witnesses.*
- WITNESS + VERB **take the stand** *The next witness took the stand.* | **give evidence, testify | make a statement, state sth | identify sb** *She was the only witness to identify Peters as the attacker.*
- WITNESS + NOUN **box, stand | summons**
- PHRASES **a witness for the defence/prosecution**

3 of a signature
- VERB + WITNESS **act as**
- WITNESS + VERB **sign**
- PREP. **~ to** *Would you be willing to act as a witness to my signature when I sign my will?*

wobbly *adj.*
- VERBS **be, feel, look | become, go** *When I stood up my legs went all wobbly.*
- ADV. **all** (*informal*), **very | a bit, a little, rather, slightly** *The chair looked a bit wobbly.*

wolf *noun*
- ADJ. **lone** *A lone wolf howled under the full moon.* | **marauding, ravening, slavering** (*figurative*) *She called the media 'ravening wolves'.*
- QUANT. **pack**
- WOLF + VERB **bark, growl, howl | hunt**
- WOLF + NOUN **cub | pack**

woman *noun*
- ADJ. **young | middle-aged | elderly, old, older** *The thief tricked his way into an elderly woman's home.* ◇ *Older women often have difficulty conceiving.* | **adult, grown** *The little girl she remembered was now a grown woman.* | **married | single, unattached, unmarried | widowed | divorced | pregnant | childless | business** (also **businesswoman**), **career, professional, working | non-working | attractive, beautiful, good-looking, handsome, pretty | desirable | well-dressed | plain, ugly | motherly | hysterical | decent, good, kind | evil,**

wicked | battered *a hostel for battered women* | **the other** *Jean Menkes plays the president's wife and Fiona Handley plays the other woman* (= the one the President is having an affair with).

• VERB + WOMAN **depict, portray, present, show** *We want to change the way women are depicted in the media.* | **limit, reduce** *Women are limited to the more poorly paid jobs.* ◊ *Women are reduced to merely playing a passive role.*

• PHRASES **the position/role of women** *There were important changes in the position of women in society.* **a woman of the world** *He saw her as a woman of the world who could offer him advice.* **women's lib/liberation** (*becoming old-fashioned*) *The freedom to wear trousers became a symbol of women's liberation.* **the women's movement, women's rights**

womb *noun*

• ADJ. **fertile | barren**
• VERB + WOMB **carry sth in** *the nine months for which we are carried in our mothers' wombs* | **emerge from** *The baby's head was starting to emerge from the womb.*
• WOMB + NOUN **lining**
• PREP. **in the/your~** *A scan determines the position of the baby in the womb.*
• PHRASES **the lining/neck/wall of the womb**

wonder *noun*

1 feeling of surprise/admiration
• ADJ. **great | childlike, wide-eyed**
• VERB + WONDER **feel | express** *There aren't any words to express properly all the wonder that I feel.* | **gaze in, stare in** *She gazed down in wonder at the city spread below her.* | **be filled with, be full of** *The children's faces were full of wonder as they gazed up at the Christmas tree.*
• WONDER + NOUN **cure, drug**
• PREP. **in ~** *Neville shook his head in wonder at it all* **with~** *She held her breath with wonder and delight.* | **~at**
• PHRASES **a feeling/sense of wonder**

2 amazing thing/person
• ADJ. **natural** *Iceland is full hot springs, beautifully coloured rocks, and other natural wonders.* | **scientific | constant, perpetual** *It was a constant wonder to me that my father didn't die of exhaustion.* | **nine days, seven-day** *She was determined to prove she was no seven-day wonder whose promise would remain unfulfilled.* | **boy** (*humorous*) (also **wonder boy**) *the new boy wonder of French football* | **one-hit** (*humorous*) *The band aren't the one-hit wonders some had feared: their second album contains some great rap music.*
• PHRASES **do/work wonders (for sb/sth)** *The change of diet has done wonders for my skin.* ◊ *A good night's sleep and a hearty breakfast worked wonders.* **the wonders of modern science/technology** *Thanks to the wonders of modern science, many common diseases will soon be things of the past.* **the wonders of the world** *The palace has been described as the eighth wonder of the world.*

wonder *verb*

• ADV. **hazily, idly, vaguely** *I wondered vaguely whether Robert could be the murderer.* | **briefly, fleetingly | apprehensively, uneasily** *I wondered uneasily if anything had happened to the children.* | **bleakly, despairingly | irritably | aloud** *'Where's Natasha?' she wondered aloud.* | **just** *'Why do you ask?' 'I just wondered.'* | **often, sometimes** *I sometimes wonder who's crazier, him or me.*
• VERB + WONDER **begin to** *I was just beginning to wonder where you were.* | **cannot/could not help but, can only** *I couldn't help but wonder what he was thinking.* | **make sb** *His obvious hunger made her wonder how long he had been up and about.*
• PREP. **about** *We'd wondered about you as a possible team member.*

wonderful *adj.*

• VERBS **be, feel, look, smell, sound, taste**
• ADV. **most, really | absolutely, perfectly, quite, truly** *The weather was absolutely wonderful.* | **pretty, rather**
• PHRASES **weird and wonderful** *coming up with weird and wonderful marketing ideas*

wood *noun*

1 what trees are made of
• ADJ. **hard | soft** *Pine is a soft wood.* | **dark** *The pub had dark wood panelling.* | **light, pale | green** *The wood was too green to burn.* | **dead, rotten, rotting** *She pruned the dead wood from the tree.* | **kindling** *There were neat piles of kindling wood against the wall.* | **natural** *varnish that retains the natural wood look* | **seasoned | rough | painted, polished, stained, varnished | carved | solid | laminated | charred | balsa, beech, pine, etc.**
• QUANT. **block, piece, plank, strip**
• VERB + WOOD **chop, cut, saw | be made from/in/(out) of, carve/make sth from/in/out of** *The cabinet is made of cherry wood.* ◊ *We carve the moulds in wood.* | **paint, polish, stain, varnish** *She stained the wood green.* | **season** *Traditionally wood was seasoned in the open air.* | **burn | gather** *We gathered wood for the fire.*
• WOOD + VERB **splinter** *the sound of splintering wood* | **rot** *Over the years, much of the wood in the house had rotted.* | **burn** *Dry wood burns easily.*
• WOOD + NOUN **chip | carving | floor, panel, panelling | laminate, veneer | finish** *a wardrobe in a mahogany wood finish* | **fire**
• PREP. **in ~** *The chapel has some interesting works in wood and marble.*

2 area covered with trees
• ADJ. **deep, dense, thick | dark, shady | broad-leaved, deciduous | beech, birch, oak, etc.**
• PREP. **in the ~** *a walk in the woods* **through the ~** *He wandered through the beech wood.*

wooded *adj.*

• VERBS **be**
• ADV. **densely, heavily, richly, thickly, well** *a thickly wooded area*

woodwork *noun*

• ADJ. **exterior, interior | polished**
• VERB + WOODWORK **paint, treat, varnish | polish | strip | clean, wash | hit** *He hit the woodwork* (= the wooden frame of the goal) *twice before scoring.*
• PREP. **in the~** *There were cracks in the woodwork.*

wool *noun*

• ADJ. **chunky, thick | fine | soft | rough | pure | raw | lamb's, sheep's | knitting | cotton, mineral, steel, wire**
• QUANT. **ball, skein**
• VERB + WOOL **produce | knit sth in, spin, weave (sth in)** *She's knitting a jumper in pure wool.* | **card, comb**
• WOOL + NOUN **merchant, shop, trade**

word *noun*

1 unit of language
• ADJ. **two-letter, three-letter, etc. | monosyllabic, disyllabic | two-syllable, three-syllable, etc. | big, long** *He uses big words to impress people.* | **compound | native | borrowed, loan** *When a new fruit is first imported, its name is usually also imported as a loan word.* | **foreign | content, function | exact, precise, very** *His exact words were, 'There's nothing we can do about it.'* ◊ *Those were her very words.* | **clear, plain | ambiguous | ab-**

stract, concrete | everyday *I find even everyday words difficult to spell.* | archaic, obsolete | key *He wrote down a few key words to help him remember what to say.* | right, wrong *You can't always find the right word when you're translating.* | dirty, four-letter, naughty, obscene, rude, taboo *The play is full of four-letter words.* ◇ *Work is a dirty word to Frank.* (see also **swear word**) | famous, household, immortal *His name has become a household word since he first appeared in the series.* ◇ *the immortal words of Neil Armstrong as he stepped onto the moon* | code *The police use code words for their major operations.* | buzz (also **buzzword**), vogue *E-marketing is the current buzzword.* | spoken, written *She combines visual images and the spoken word to great effect in her presentations.*

● VERB + WORD **have** *Spanish has no word for 'understatement'.* | say, speak, use, utter *He uses lots of long words.* ◇ *Every word he utters is treated as sacred text.* | pronounce *How is this word pronounced?* | mispronounce | spell | misspell *'Necessary' is one of the most commonly misspelt words in English.* | write | hear, read | mishear, misread *I misheard the word 'sick' as 'thick'.* | know, understand | look up *She looked the word up in the dictionary.* | find | coin *The word 'e-commerce' was coined to refer to business done over the Internet.* | cross out, erase, rub out

● WORD + VERB **mean sth | refer to sth, relate to sth |** convey sth, describe sth, express sth *words describing body parts* ◇ *Words can't express how happy I am.* | imply sth | denote sth *Bold words denote chapter headings.* | carry sth, have sth *The same word can carry numerous meanings.* ◇ *The word has two meanings.* | be derived from sth, come/derive from sth *The word derives from a Norse word meaning 'eye of the wind'.* | begin (with sth), end (in/with sth) *What's a word beginning with 'c' that means 'a small wood'?* | fail sb *Words fail me* (= I cannot express how I feel).

● WORD + NOUN **game**

● PREP. **in sb's ~s** *The students had to retell the story in their own words.* | ~ for *What's the French word for 'snail'?*

● PHRASES **in all senses of the word** *She was a true friend in all senses of the word.* **in other words** *They're letting me go—in other words, I've been sacked.* **in so many words** *They told me in so many words* (= directly) *that I was no longer needed.* **in the true sense of the word** *People who overeat are not addicts in the true sense of the word.* **in words of one syllable** (= using very simple language) *Could you say that again in words of one syllable?* **word for word** (= exactly) *He repeated word for word what the boy had said to him.*

2 sth you say

● ADJ. **quick** (no plural) | quiet (no plural) *The manager had a quiet word with Alison, and she gave him no more problems.* | good, friendly, kind *He hasn't a good word to say for anybody.* | unkind | angry, bitter ~s, blunt ~s, choice ~s (ironic), cross, hard ~s, strong ~s | polite *No polite words of gratitude came.* | flattering, honeyed ~s | empty, fine (ironic), meaningless ~s *Despite all their fine words, the council have never done anything to improve road safety.* | weasel ~s *The government's promises on nurses' pay turned out to be weasel words* (= deliberately unclear). | bold, brave ~s *Despite his brave words, I don't believe he can save the factory from closure.* | wise ~s | well-chosen ~s *He ruined her self-confidence with a few well-chosen words.* | cautionary | soft, whispered *They exchanged whispered words of love.* | unspoken ~s *The look in her eyes filled in the unspoken words in her sentence.* | dying, last ~s *Her last words were for her children.* | final, last (no plural) *The Chairman always has the last word* (= the final decision) *on financial decisions.* | fateful ~s *Seconds after uttering the fateful words 'this is easy', he crashed.* | prophetic | magic

● VERB + WORD **have** *I've had a few words with John, and he's quite happy for you to stay.* ◇ *She had some harsh words to say about her colleagues.* | put in, say, speak, utter *If you run into the boss, put in a good word for me!* ◇ *Before we begin, I'd like to say a few words about who I am.* ◇ *Nobody's uttered a word to me about it.* | give, say *Just say the word and I'll go.* | mumble, mutter | slur *I knew he'd been drinking because he was slurring his words.* | spit (out) *She was so furious, she almost spat the words out: 'You idiot!'* | bandy, exchange, have *I usually exchange a few words with my neighbour when I see him.* ◇ *Words were exchanged* (= there was an argument). | find *He couldn't find the words to thank her enough.* | choose, pick *He chose his words carefully when commenting on her work.* | quote | distort, twist *She felt angry at how the journalist had twisted her words.* | hang on *The journalists hung on his every word as he spoke of his ordeal.* | eat, take back *When he told her she would fail, she swore she would make him eat his words.* | not mince *He doesn't mince his words when he talks about his ex-boss.* | not breathe *Don't breathe a word to anyone about what I've told you!*

● WORD + VERB **conjure sth up, evoke sth** *Her words conjured up a strange picture in her mind.* | burst from sb, come (out), emerge, fall, pour (out), slip (out), spill (out), tumble out *He was nervous, and his words came out in a rush.* ◇ *His words fell into the silence like stones.* | stick in your throat *He wanted to tell her how he felt about her, but the words stuck in his throat.* | float, hang in the air *I let my words hang in the air. Maggie was no fool: she must realize I meant it.* | echo, ring *Her teacher's words echoed in her ears.* | fade (away), tail away/off, trail away/off *His words faded to silence as he saw she didn't believe him.* | hit/strike home, strike/touch a chord | sink in *She could feel her temper boiling as his words sank in.*

● PREP. **in a ~** *'Would you like to help us?' 'In a word* (= briefly), *no.'* **without a ~** *She left without a word.* | ~about *We never heard anyone say an unkind word about her.* **~ from** *And now a word from our sponsors ...* **~ of** *a word of advice/warning* ~ with *Can I have a quick word with you?*

● PHRASES **get a word in (edgeways)** *I wanted to tell you that she'd phoned, but you were talking so much I couldn't get a word in edgeways.* **a man/woman of few words** (= a person who speaks very little), **sb never spoke a truer word/never was a truer word spoken** *You said we were about to make a big mistake, and never was a truer word spoken!* (= you were right), **not a (single) word** *Remember—not a word to* (= don't tell) *Peter about any of this.* ◇ *We didn't say a single word to each other all day.* **put words into sb's mouth** *He felt after the interview that the police officers had been trying to put words into his mouth in* (= to make him say what they wanted him to say). **take the words out of sb's mouth** *I was about to say we should cancel the trip, but she took the words right out of my mouth* (= she said it before me). **a word in sb's ear** *Can I have a word in your ear about tomorrow's presentation?* **(by) word of mouth** *The restaurant does not advertise, but relies on word of mouth for custom.*

3 promise

● ADJ. **solemn** *She gave him her solemn word that she would give up drugs.*

● VERB + WORD **give sb | be as good as, be true to, keep** *He promised to help and was as good as his word.* ◇ *True to her word, she returned next day.* | break, go back on *Once he has made a promise, he never goes back on his word.*

● PHRASES **have sb's word for sth** *We only have her word for it that the cheque is in the post.* **a man/woman of his/her word** *You needn't worry about him not paying you back—he's a man of his word.* **take sb at their word** *He said I could stay at his house any time, so I took him at his word.* **take sb's word for sth** *I haven't seen his work, but*

I'll take his word for it that it's finished. **your word against sb's** *If it's your word against the police officer's, the jury are going to believe him.* **sb's word is their bond, sb's word of honour** *He gave me his word of honour that he wouldn't tell anyone.*

4 information/news

- VERB + WORD **bring, get, send** *He sent word to his family that his captors were treating him well.* | **get** *We didn't get word of her arrest until the next day.* | **spread**
- WORD + VERB **get out** *If word gets out about the affair, he will have to resign.* | **be, have it** *The word is they've split up.* ◇ *Word has it that she's leaving.*
- PREP. **~ about** *Health workers spread the word about the benefits of immunization.*

word *verb*

- ADV. **carefully, cautiously** *We need to word our question quite carefully.* | **ambiguously, vaguely | broadly | strongly** *He issued a very strongly worded statement denying any involvement in the plot.*

wording *noun*

- ADJ. **actual, exact, precise, specific | clear | appropriate | vague | ambiguous** *The wording was deliberately ambiguous.*
- VERB + WORDING **alter, change | think about** *We need to think carefully about the wording of the request.*
- PREP. **~of** *What's the exact wording of the clause?*

word processing *noun*

- ADJ. **basic, simple**
- PHRASES **application, package, product, program, software, system | business, service**

work *noun*

1 effort/product of effort

- ADJ. **hard** *It's hard work trying to get him to do a few things for himself.* ◇ *It doesn't require skill—it's a matter of sheer hard work.* | **arduous, back-breaking, challenging, complicated, demanding, difficult, gruelling, intensive, labour-intensive, tiring, tough** *The show is the product of two years' intensive work.* | **rewarding | heavy** *They employ a couple of young men to do the heavy work.* | **donkey** *I did the donkey work* (= hard work requiring little skill) *but I hired a professional builder for the tricky bits.* | **light** *She's only allowed to do a little light work because of her bad arm.* | **easy | close** *I need to wear glasses for close work.* | **physical | delicate | dangerous | dirty** *Engine maintenance is dirty work.* ◇ *(figurative) The drugs gang used children to do their dirty work for them.* | **humdrum, monotonous, repetitive, tedious | fascinating, interesting | purposeful** *Many unemployed people welcome the chance to do purposeful work, even if unpaid.* | **valuable** *The research institute needs funds in order to carry on its valuable work.* | **paid, unpaid | professional | men's, women's** *They think that looking after children is women's work.* | **intellectual, mental | creative, imaginative | practical** (see also **fieldwork, paperwork**) | **investigative | undercover** *The scandal was revealed after months of undercover work by journalists.* | **leg** (also **legwork**) *Her job as a market researcher involves a lot of legwork* (= walking around to collect information). | **course** (also **coursework**) | **written** *His written work is the best in the class.* | **individual | group | project | collaborative, joint** *classroom activities involving collaborative work between children* ◇ *The report is the joint work of an economist and a sociologist.* | **remedial** *The poorly designed bridge needs remedial work to make it safe.* | **background, preliminary, preparatory | follow-up | honest** *He preferred to make his money from honest work rather than from gambling.* | **good, nice** (*in-*

formal), **outstanding, sterling** *Nice work, James! I'm impressed.* ◇ *In accepting the award, she mentioned the sterling work of her assistants.* | **careful, meticulous, painstaking | poor, shoddy, sloppy | charitable, humanitarian | community, youth | ground-breaking, innovative, pioneering** *He did pioneering work on microbes.* | **experimental | academic, commercial, educational, environmental, scientific | building, construction | your own** *Is this all your own work* (= did you do it without help from others)?

- QUANT. **bit, piece** *It was an interesting piece of work.*
- VERB + WORK **carry out, do, put in** *All the construction work was carried out in 2001.* ◇ *I've got lots of work to do today.* ◇ *She's put in a lot of work on the design.* | **get done, have done** *I think I'd better try and get some work done.* ◇ *We're going to have some building work done on the house.* | **produce** *Work produced on a word processor tends to look more professional.* | **get, have** *We get far too much work at this time of year.* | **take on, undertake** *I've taken on more work than I've got time to do.* | **create, make** *Big football matches make a lot of work for the police.* | **begin, commence, get down to, set about/to, start** *They began work on the project towards the end of the year.* ◇ *Stop talking and get down to work.* ◇ *We set to work on the outside of the house* (= for example, painting it). | **go about** *She went cheerfully about her work.* | **carry on, continue | complete, finish | halt, hold up, stop** *Work on the project was halted.* | **lose** *They lost the work to a competitor.* | **undo** *The new president spent the first year undoing the work of his predecessor.* | **oversee, supervise** *The assistant manager supervises work on the factory floor.* | **set sb to** *She set them to work painting the fence.* | **require** *To carry out accurate market research requires a huge amount of work.* | **hand in** *We're supposed to hand in this work tomorrow.*
- WORK + VERB **come** *The work comes in bursts according to the time of year.* | **wait** *That work can wait until tomorrow.* | **go** *How's the work going this morning?* | **involve sth** *What does the work involve?* | **begin, start | continue, go on | come to a standstill** *Work came to a complete standstill when rumours of redundancies started to circulate.* | **cost** *How much will the work cost?*
- WORK + NOUN **ethic** *Her boss told her she had to increase her work rate.* | **programme, schedule | surface** *Work surfaces should be left clear and clean.*
- PREP. **at~** *He's been hard at work all morning.* | **~on** *I have to do some work on the engine before it'll be ready to drive.* | **~with** *She's done a lot of work with disadvantaged children.*
- PHRASES **a backlog of work** *It will take a month to clear the backlog of work.* **keep up the good work** *The hotel manager thanked the staff for their efforts so far and told them to keep up the good work.* **your life's work** *The art collection was his life's work.* **make light/short work of sth** (= to do sth quickly and easily) *Mike made short work of fixing the engine.* **never/not a stroke of work** *She never does a stroke of work.* **pressure of work** *Pressure of work forced him to cancel his holiday.* **work in progress** *The showroom has been designed so that people can see work in progress.*

2 job

- ADJ. **lucrative, well paid | badly paid | full-time, part-time | permanent | temporary | regular, steady** *He hasn't been in regular work since he left school.* | **casual** *In the college vacations he does casual work in the local hospital.* | **freelance | voluntary | skilled | semi-skilled | unskilled | manual | indoor, outdoor | daily, day-to-day, everyday, routine** *People went about their daily work despite the war.* ◇ *Ambulance crews alternate between emergency and routine work.* | **piece** *It's piece work, so how much you earn depends on how fast you can work.* | **administrative, clerical, office, secretarial | managerial | domestic | social | research | agricul-*

tural, **farm | building | nice** (*humorous*) *A hundred grand for two days a week? Nice work if you can get it!*
● VERB + WORK **have** *He's got a bit of freelance work at the moment.* | **look for** *He got made redundant, so now he's looking for work again.* | **find, get** *Full-time work is hard to find.* | **go to** *I go to work on the bus.* | **go out to** *Some mothers of young children choose not to go out to work.* | **start | finish, knock off** *What time do you finish work?* | **stop** *She stops work at the end of this month.* | **give up** *Just before he was sixty, he decided to give up work.* | **go back to, return to** *She has just returned to work after the birth of her child.* | **coordinate** *Sales reps meet up monthly to coordinate their work.*
● WORK + VERB **go** *Work's going well at the moment.* | **start** *What time does work start in the morning?* | **finish**
● WORK + NOUN **hours** *Employees must not make personal calls in work hours.* | **place** (also **workplace**) | **area, environment, room** (also **workroom**) | **station** (also **workstation**) | **roster, schedule | experience** *He's doing a month's unpaid work experience with an engineering firm.* | **permit | incentive** *High income tax can undermine work incentives.* | **practice** *An independent report has described some work practices in the industry as old-fashioned.*
● PREP. **at** ~ *'Where's Diane?' 'She's at work.'* ◇ *We had a party at work.* **in** (**your**) ~ *With so much unemployment, I'm lucky to be in work.* ◇ *It's important to be happy in your work.* **off** ~ *She's been off work with a bad back since July.* **out of** ~ *He's been out of work since the factory closed.* **through** ~ *I met him through work.*
● PHRASES **a line of work** *'What line of work are you in?' 'Computing.'* **a place of work**

3 book/music/art
● ADJ. **classic, fine, great | definitive, seminal** *Her book is still considered the definitive work on beetles.* | **influential | erudite, scholarly | ambitious | literary | dramatic | critical | autobiographical, biographical | artistic | art** (also **artwork**) *The artwork in the book is superb.* | **abstract, figurative, graphic | choral, orchestral, piano | collected, complete** *the collected works of Stephen King* | **early | late, mature** *Picasso's mature works*
● QUANT. **series | collection, exhibition**
● VERB + WORK **compose, produce, write** *Beethoven composed his greatest works towards the end of his life.* | **commission | perform, play | hear, read, see** *Her work can be seen in most of the major European galleries.* | **conduct, direct, edit, produce, publish, put on** *Over the next two years, the theatre is putting on the complete works of Brecht.* | **display, exhibit, show** *The town hall is exhibiting works by local artists.*
● WORK + VERB **be called sth, be entitled sth** *a work entitled 'Forward Pass'*
● PREP. **in a/the** ~ *She's studying the theme of death in the works of Beckett.* | ~ **by** *a work by an unknown eighteenth century writer*
● PHRASES **an exhibition of sb's work** *The gallery is staging a special exhibition of Monet's early works.* **a work of art/fiction/literature** *The building is hated by some and considered a work of art by others.* ◇ (*humorous*) *They discovered that his CV was a complete work of fiction.* **a work of genius** *Her latest novel is a work of genius.*
⇨ Note at ART

4 (*also* **works**) building/repairing
● ADJ. **extensive, major | road** (also **roadworks**) | **maintenance, repair, restoration | demolition**
● VERB + WORK **carry out** *We are planning to carry out major works on the site.* | **plan | announce**
● WORK + VERB **continue, go on** *The works will continue until the end of July.*
● PREP. **at the** ~ *A contraflow is in operation at the works near Junction 5.*

5 works factory

● VERB + WORKS **open | close** (**down**), **shut down**
● WORKS + VERB **turn sth out** *The works at Bury turned out thousands of television sets a week.* | **open | close** (**down**)
● WORKS + NOUN **foreman, manager, supervisor | canteen**
● PREP. **at the** ~ *the night shift at the works*

work verb

1 do a job/task
● ADV. **hard** *He had been working hard all morning.* | **steadily | round the clock** *Emergency teams were working round the clock to make the homes secure.* | **full-time, part-time** *A lot of mothers choose to work part-time.* | **efficiently** *I work more efficiently on my own.* | **closely, collaboratively, together** *people who have worked closely together over a period of time* | **alone, independently | away** *We worked steadily away all morning.*
● VERB + WORK **continue to | choose to, prefer to** *I prefer to work as part of a team.* | **motivate sb to** *Employees are motivated to work harder for a whole host of different reasons.* | **enable sb to** *I needed a job which would enable me to work at home.* | **refuse to**
● PREP. **as** *He's working as a teacher at the moment.* **at** *I've spent three hours working at this problem.* **for** *She works for an oil company.* **on** *We are working on plans for a new swimming pool.* **with** *the people you work with*

2 function; have a result/effect
● ADV. **effectively, efficiently, perfectly, properly, satisfactorily, smoothly, well** *Everything worked very smoothly.* | **independently** *My limbs seemed to be working independently of each other.*
● VERB + WORK **seem to**

PHRASAL VERB
work out
● ADV. **perfectly, well | badly**
● PREP. **for** *Things worked out well for Janet in the end.*

worker noun

● ADJ. **good, hard | productive | fast, quick | methodical, steady | slow | core, key | full-time, part-time | permanent | casual** *Casual workers are usually paid by the hour.* | **shift | migrant, seasonal | freelance | self-employed | paid | voluntary, volunteer | low-paid | redundant, unemployed | retired | female, male, woman | black, white | immigrant | fellow | average** *One night in these expensive hotels costs around the average worker's monthly wage.* | **skilled | unskilled | semi-skilled | blue-collar, manual | clerical, office, white-collar | professional | shop-floor | private-sector, public-sector | council, municipal | assembly-line, factory, manufacturing, production | construction | metal | maintenance | railway, transport | agricultural, farm, rural | care, community, health, healthcare, hospital, social, welfare, youth | rescue | aid, relief | charity | field, research | domestic | postal**
● VERB + WORKER **employ, have | engage, hire, recruit, take on | dismiss, fire, lay off, make redundant, sack | exploit** *The union accused the firm of exploiting its workers.*
● WORKER + VERB **work | run sth, staff sth** *The shop is staffed by one paid worker and three volunteers.* | **lose a job** *400 workers have lost their jobs.* | **demand sth** *Workers demanded fair wages and better working conditions.* | **vote** *The workers voted for industrial action.* | (**be on**) **strike, walk out** *The workers walked out last month after a failure to agree all the terms for the 110 lay-offs.*
● WORKER + NOUN **participation** *worker participation in decision making*
● PHRASES **the exploitation of workers, workers' demands, worker's rights**
⇨ Note at JOB

workforce noun

- ADJ. **educated, qualified, skilled, trained** *a highly-skilled workforce* | **flexible, versatile** | **committed, dedicated, motivated** | **local** *A quarter of the local workforce is unemployed.* | **ageing, declining, diminishing** *A declining workforce has to provide for an increasing number of retired people.* | **available, total** *The shipyard has a total workforce of 9 000.* | **entire, whole** *The new management decided to retrain the entire workforce.* | **worldwide** | **large, small** | **reduced** | **2 000-strong, 3 500, etc.** | **temporary** | **British, Japanese, etc.** | **female, male** | **industrial, manufacturing**
- VERB + WORKFORCE **employ, have** *The company employs a workforce of nearly 5 000.* | **cut, halve, reduce, slash, slim (down), trim** | **double, expand, increase** | **retrain, train** | **consult (with)** *The management always consults with the workforce before introducing major changes.* | **enter, leave** *The increase in the number of people entering the workforce has increased unemployment figures.*
- WORKFORCE + VERB **fall** | **double, increase, rise** | **number sth, stand at sth** *The workforce numbers 500.*
- PREP. **among a/the ~** *There is a change in the distribution of skills among the workforce.* **in a/the ~** *One person in the workforce is always responsible for the same job.*
- PHRASES **a member of the workforce**

workings noun

- ADJ. **inner, internal** *the inner workings of a watch* ◊ *the internal workings of Parliament* | **basic** | **complex, detailed** | **financial**
- VERB + WORKINGS **analyse, explore, investigate** | **lay bare, reveal, shed light on** *Their research aims to shed light on the workings of the human mind.* | **know** | **understand** *It is hard to understand the complex workings of the social security system.* | **explain**

workload noun

- ADJ. **enormous, heavy, huge** | **excessive** | **additional, extra, increased** | **lighter, reduced** | **administrative**
- VERB + WORKLOAD **have** *She's got an increased workload this year.* | **expand, increase** | **ease, lighten, reduce** *An assistant one day a week would ease my workload.* | **distribute, share, spread** *We want to try and distribute the workload more evenly.* | **cope with**
- WORKLOAD + VERB **expand, increase** *Doctors are having to cope with an ever-expanding workload.*

workman noun

- ADJ. **good, skilled** | **council**
- QUANT. **gang** *A gang of council workmen has been digging a hole in the road.*

workmanship noun

- ADJ. **exquisite, fine, good, quality** | **bad, crude, defective, faulty, poor, shoddy**
- VERB + WORKMANSHIP **admire** *I was admiring the exquisite workmanship in the mosaic.* | **criticise**
- PREP. **~ on** *He accused the garage of shoddy workmanship on the bodywork.*
- PHRASES **the quality/standard of workmanship**

workout noun

- ADJ. **good** | **hard** | **vigorous** | **light** | **forty-minute, two-hour, etc.** | **aerobic**
- VERB + WORKOUT **do, have** *When I do a good workout, I feel fine.* ◊ *The team had a hard workout this morning.* | **give sb/sth** *I went for a ride to give my new bike a workout.*

workshop noun

1 room/building
- ADJ. **craft, design, pottery** | **engineering, locomotive, railway** | **farm** | **carpenter's, stonemason's, etc.**
- VERB + WORKSHOP **set up** *He set up a workshop for his carving.*
- WORKSHOP + VERB **employ sb** *The workshop employs 25 full-time workers.*
- PREP. **in a/the ~**

2 period of discussion/work
- ADJ. **day-long, two-day, weekend, etc.** | **group** | **introductory** | **practical** | **development, training** *The company holds regular skills development workshops.* | **skills** *Everyone in Personnel has attended a media skills workshop.* | **research** | **dance, drama, music, poetry, theatre, writing**
- QUANT. **series** *The Careers Advisory Service will be running a series of workshops for students.*
- VERB + WORKSHOP **do, hold, host, organize, put on, run** *The Institute will host a special two-day workshop on new building materials.* | **attend, go to, participate in, take part in**
- WORKSHOP + VERB **cover sth, examine sth, focus on sth, look at sth** *The workshop covered a wide range of issues.* | **aim to, be aimed at sth** *a workshop aimed at brainstorming new marketing ideas*
- WORKSHOP + NOUN **discussion, session** | **member, participant**
- PREP. **at a/the ~, during a/the ~** *During the workshop, they each practised their part in the performance.* **in a/the ~** *In the one-day workshop, she taught us the importance of breathing exercises.* | **~ on** *I learned these new skills at a workshop on databases.*
- PHRASES **a member of a workshop, a participant in a workshop**

world noun

1 the earth/its people
- ADJ. **known** *a medieval map of the known world* | **whole**
- VERB + WORLD **create, make** *They believe that God created the world.* | **destroy** *One of these days, humankind will destroy the world.* | **take over** *Fast food outlets seem to be taking over the world.* | **tour, travel** | **see** *As a young man, he wanted to see the world before he settled down.* | **lead** *Sweden leads the world in safety legislation.*
- WORLD + NOUN **leader** | **economy** | **recession, slump** | **market** | **trade** | **price** *World oil prices continue to rise.* | **domination** *A handful of Internet companies are battling for world domination.* | **affairs, events** | **attention, opinion** *The bombing alienated world opinion.* | **war** | **champion** *He was easily beaten by the reigning world champion.* | **championships, cup, title** | **class** *The team is world class.* | **beaters** *The Portuguese team looked like world beaters in last night's game.* | **record** *She shattered the world record for the 200 metres.* | **rankings** *He has never before featured in the top ten world rankings.* | **religion** *the major world religions* | **music** (= music that includes influences from different parts of the world) | **tour** *The band are about to embark on a six-month world tour.*
- PREP. **across the ~** *Astronomers across the world will be watching the night sky.* **all around/over/round the ~** *The ceremony was watched live by millions around the world.* **in the ~** *He felt he was the luckiest man in the whole world.* **throughout the ~** *People throughout the world will be watching the big match on television.*
- PHRASES **the end of the world** (*figurative*) *It won't be the end of the world if you don't get the job.* **on a world scale** *Communist parties were formed on a world scale after the Russian Revolution.* **on the world stage** *The country became an important player on the world stage.* **a**

part of the world *It's an interesting part of the world.* **the world over** *Scientists the world over have been waiting for this breakthrough.*

2 part of the earth
● ADJ. **Arab, English-speaking, Western**, etc. *Heads of state from all over the Arab world gathered for the conference.* | **developed, First, industrialized, rich** *First World consumers will have to eat less meat.* | **developing, Third, underdeveloped** | **New, Old** *Machismo is a New World phenomenon with roots in Old World cultures.*
● PREP. **in the … ~** *In the Western world, there is a different attitude to marriage.*

3 life/society
● ADJ. **ever-changing** | **cruel, dog-eat-dog, hard, tough** | **crazy, mad, topsy-turvy** | **ancient, medieval, Roman**, etc. | **contemporary, modern, today's** | **brave new** *the architects' vision of a brave new world of pristine concrete* | **vanishing** *These tribesmen are proud survivors of a vanishing world.* | **outside, real** *Throughout his time in prison he had no contact with the outside world.* ◊ *In the real world things don't always happen like they do in books.* | **dream, fantasy, imaginary, inner, private** *She enjoys creating imaginary worlds for children.* ◊ *She lives in her own inner world.* | **material, physical** | **simulated, virtual** | **spiritual** | **spirit** *Mediums claim to receive messages from the spirit world.* | **social** | **animal, insect, natural, plant** *I like living in the country because I'm interested in the natural world.* | **academic, art, business, fashion, industrial, literary, medical, sports** | **different** *We come from different worlds.* | **sb's own (little)** *She lives in her own little world.* | **whole (wide), wider** *She told him he was her only friend in the whole wide world.* ◊ *The wider world learned of his illness months after he told his family.* | **small** *I'm sure we'll meet again. It's a very small world in this profession.*
● VERB + WORLD **change** *Young people always think they are going to change the world.* | **have, inhabit, live in** *Children often have their own private world.* | **look at, perceive, see, view** *different ways of looking at the world* | **come into, enter, escape into** *We come into the world with nothing.* ◊ *He entered the world of politics in 1997.* ◊ *Showbusiness gave him the chance to escape into another world.* | **bring sb into** *She had brought six children into the world.* | **escape from, shut yourself away from, shut out** *He closed his eyes and tried to shut out the world.* | **face** *For the first time since the death of her parents, she felt able to face the world.* | **take on** *He was so happy to leave school, he felt ready to take on the world.* | **tell** *He wanted to tell the world how happy he was.* | **prove to, show** *She was determined to show the world that she was no loser.* | **shake, shock, stun** *The news of the assassination shook the world.*
● WORLD + VERB **fall apart** *His world fell apart when his wife died.* | **revolve around sb/sth** *She thinks the world revolves around her and her schedule.* | **owe sb sth** *He seems to think that the world owes him a living.*
● WORLD + NOUN **knowledge** | **view** *Teachers influence the world view of their young students.*
● PREP. **in the … ~** *He's well known in the fashion world.* | **~ about/around** *At this age, babies are starting to take an interest in the world around them.* **~ of** *In the world of high finance, there is little room for sentiment.*
● PHRASES **experience/knowledge/perception of the world, the eyes of the world** *The eyes of the world are on the president.* **in an ideal/a perfect world** *In an ideal world, I'd like to work just three days a week.* **in a world of your own** *I tapped on the window to get her attention but she was in a world of her own.* **the rest of the world** *He just wanted to shut himself away from the rest of the world.* **watch the world go by** *He likes to sit outside his front door and watch the world go by.* **the ways of the world** *He's too young to understand the ways of the world.* **worlds apart**

Although they are twins, they are worlds apart in their attitude to life.

worm *noun*
● WORM + VERB **burrow, crawl** *Worms burrow down through the soil.* | **wriggle, writhe** *The worm was wriggling on the hook.*
● WORM + NOUN **cast**

worried *adj.*
● VERBS **be, feel, look, seem** | **get** *I started to get worried when they didn't arrive home.*
● ADV. **deeply, desperately, dreadfully, extremely, frantically, genuinely, particularly, really, seriously, terribly, very** | **increasingly** | **a bit, quite, rather, slightly** | **rightly** *Citizens in inner-city areas are desperately worried and rightly so.*
● PREP. **about** *We were really worried about you!*
● PHRASES **worried sick** *She was worried sick about her son.*

worry *noun*
● ADJ. **big, considerable great, main, major, real, serious** *Paying the mortgage is a big worry for many people.* ◊ *Her mother's poor health caused her considerable worry.* ◊ *My greatest worry is that he'll do something stupid.* | **growing, increasing** | **slight** | **day-to-day** | **constant** *The money side of things has been a constant worry.* | **unnecessary** *She gave her parents unnecessary worry when she forgot to phone them.* | **immediate** *My immediate worry is money.* | **nagging, niggling** *I had a nagging worry that we weren't going to get there.* | **secret** | **business, economic, financial, money** | **health** *It was a relief to share my secret worries with him.*
● VERB + WORRY **have** *That year he had major health worries.* | **be beset by** *She wanted to enjoy her retirement without being beset by financial worries.* | **be frantic/ill/out of your mind/sick with** *I didn't know where he was and I was frantic with worry.* | **express** | **share** | **cause (sb), give sb** | **arouse, prompt** *The earth tremors prompted worries of a second major earthquake.* | **add to, increase** *The fact that she heard nothing from him only increased her worry.* | **forget** *Try and forget your worries for a little while.* | **ease** | **remove, take out** *Take the worry out of travelling with our holiday insurance offer.*
● WORRY + VERB **disappear** | **prove groundless/unfounded** *Most of Nigel's worries proved groundless.*
● PREP. **amid ~** *The pound has fallen to a new low amid worries that the British economy is heading for trouble.* **with ~** *He was sick with worry about everything.* | **~ about, ~ over** *They will not have worries over money.* **~ to** *His mother's health is an enormous worry to him.*
● PHRASES **cause for worry** *There is no immediate cause for worry.* **free from worry, freedom from worry, have no worries on that account/score** *The staff all work very hard—we've got no worries on that account.* **the least of your worries** *When he lost his job, the size of his flat was the least of his worries.* **a source of worry** *Money is a constant source of worry.*

worry *verb*
● ADV. **a lot, particularly, really, terribly** *She worries a lot about crime.* ◊ *What really worries me is what we do if there's nobody there.* | **slightly** | **needlessly, unduly, unnecessarily** *You do worry unnecessarily, you know.* | **not too much** *Don't worry too much about it.* | **constantly**
● VERB + WORRY **not let sth, not need to** *Don't let it worry you unduly.* | **begin to** | **tell sb not to**
● PREP. **about** *Don't worry about me, I'll be fine.* **with** *Don't worry the driver with unnecessary requests.*
● PHRASES **enough/nothing to worry about** *Don't bother Harry—he has enough to worry about as it is.* **stop**

worrying *Stop worrying, Dad, we'll be fine.* **worry yourself sick/to death** (*informal*)

worrying *adj.*

• VERBS **be**
• ADV. **deeply, extremely, particularly, seriously, terribly, very | a bit, rather, slightly**

worse *adj.*

• VERBS **be, feel, look, seem** *I feel even worse today!* | **become, get, grow** *The problem is getting worse all the time.* ◇ *The pain grew worse.* | **make sth** *Ignoring the problem will make it worse.*
• ADV. **considerably, dramatically, far, a good/great deal, infinitely, a lot, (very) much, a sight, significantly** *It's much worse for the parents than it is for the child.* ◇ *Things could be a sight worse than they are.* | **almost** *The area seemed almost worse than the city he had left.* | **a little, rather, slightly, substantially | progressively, steadily** *The problem became progressively worse.* | **even, still** *We've run out of petrol. Worse still, we can't get any more until tomorrow.*

worsen *verb*

• ADV. **considerably, dramatically, markedly, significantly** *The problem has worsened considerably in recent months.* | **steadily | rapidly | suddenly**
• VERB + WORSEN **continue to** *The economic recession has continued to worsen.*

worship *noun*

• ADJ. **daily, regular | evening, morning | Sunday | public | collective | religious | divine | Christian, Hindu, etc. | pagan | ancestor, nature, sun | idol, image | hero** *his hero worship of the national team* | **devil**
• VERB + WORSHIP **conduct, lead** *Our worship today is led by the Reverend John Parker.* | **attend**
• PREP. **in ~** *the use of music in worship*
• PHRASES **an act of worship, forms of worship, freedom of worship** *Under the new regime, all religions enjoy freedom of worship.* **a place of worship** *Fifteen per cent of the population attend a place of worship.*

worst *noun* **the worst**

• VERB + WORST **expect** *It doesn't matter what I say. My mother always expects the worst.* | **fear, suspect | be prepared for, prepare for** *Although all the votes have not yet been counted, the Democrats are preparing for the worst.* | **confirm** *I had not expected to do well in my exams, and the letter confirmed the worst.* | **be spared, escape** *Scotland seemed to have escaped the worst of the recession.* | **do your** *Let them do their worst (= be as difficult as they can)—we'll fight them every inch of the way.*
• WORST + VERB **be over** *He was still very ill, but the worst seemed to be over.*
• PREP. **at (sb/sth's) ~** *At worst, the drug can be fatal.* ◇ *At its worst, bullying is a kind of torture.* **through the ~** *Her sister helped her through the worst of her illness.*
• VERB + WORST **bring out the worst in sb** *Pressure can bring out the worst in people.* **get the worst of it** *He'd been in a fight and had obviously got the worst of it.* **the worst that can happen** *Don't worry—the worst that can happen is that you'll get a fine.*

worth *noun*

• ADJ. **real, true | intrinsic, objective** *Study has an intrinsic worth, as well as helping you achieve your goals.* | **individual, own, personal, self | moral | economic, financial, market** *Some experts doubt the economic worth of*

the project. ◇ *The insurance company agreed to pay the car's current market worth.* | **net | literary, musical**
• VERB + WORTH **have | prove** *The emergency lighting has proved its worth this year.* | **affirm** *Asking for advice from people affirms their personal worth.* | **find out, learn, realize** *I only found out its real worth when I tried to buy another one.* | **appreciate, know** *They don't appreciate her true worth.* ◇ *She knows her own worth.* | **doubt, express doubts about, question | assess, estimate, give sb an estimate of** *Can you give me some estimate of its worth?*
• PREP. **of ~** *He never contributed anything of worth to the conversation.* | **~ to** *This necklace isn't worth anything in money terms, but its worth to me is incalculable.*
• PHRASES **at sb/sth's real/true worth** *They don't appreciate her at her real worth.* **of proven worth** *They are looking for a new sales manager of proven worth.* **a sense of (your own) worth** *She has no sense of her own worth.*

worth *adj.*

• VERBS **be | become | make sth | consider sth, think sth** *Most of the candidates were not considered worth interviewing.*
• ADV. **really, well** *This book is well worth reading.* | **certainly, definitely | barely, hardly, scarcely** *It's so unimportant it's hardly worth mentioning.* | **almost | potentially | reportedly, reputedly | always** *It's always worth seeing if you can get a cheap, last-minute deal.*
• PREP. **to** *This order is potentially worth millions of pounds to the company.*

worthless *adj.*

• VERBS **be, feel, prove, seem | become | make sth** *These contradictions made his evidence worthless.* | **consider sth, discard sth as, dismiss sth as, regard sth as, reject sth as, see sth as** *The opinion polls were dismissed as worthless.*
• ADV. **absolutely, completely, quite, totally, utterly | almost, virtually | largely**
• PREP. **to** *The diseased plants are quite worthless to the farmer.*

worthwhile *adj.*

• VERBS **be, seem | become | make sth** *Their gratitude made it all worthwhile.* | **consider sth, find sth, think sth** *You might find it worthwhile to consult a financial adviser.*
• ADV. **extremely, really, very, well | hardly** *The gamble seemed hardly worthwhile.* | **financially, socially** *pursuing socially worthwhile goals*

worthy *adj.*

• VERBS **be, seem | consider sth, deem sth, judge sth, think sth**
• ADV. **most, very, well | entirely, wholly | hardly, scarcely** *The matter is scarcely worthy of the managing director's time.* | **enough** *We thought it was a worthy enough objective.*
• PREP. **of** *It's a matter worthy of our attention.*

wound *noun*

• ADJ. **bad, deep, serious | flesh** *Despite the large amount of blood, it was only a flesh wound.* | **gaping, open | clean | face, head, leg, etc. | bullet, gunshot, knife, stab | entry, exit** *The exit wound made by the bullet was much larger than the entry wound.* | **old | war** *His old war wounds still ached in certain weathers.*
• VERB + WOUND **inflict | receive, suffer | examine, probe | clean, dress**
• WOUND + VERB **close | heal** *It was a clean wound, and it healed quickly.*

● WOUND + NOUN **care, healing**
● PREP. **~in** *He had deep wounds in his chest.* **~to** *He died of gunshot wounds to the head.*

wound *verb*

1 injure sb's body
● ADV. **badly, critically, gravely, grievously, seriously, severely | fatally, mortally** *She was fatally wounded in a car crash.* **| slightly**
● PREP. **in** *One reporter was wounded in the leg.*
● PHRASES **the walking wounded** (= people who have been wounded, but not so badly that they cannot walk)

2 hurt sb's feelings
● ADV. **deeply** *She was deeply wounded by his remarks.*

woven *adj.*

● VERBS **be**
● ADV. **closely, densely, finely, tightly** *very fine and closely woven silk* **| coarsely, loosely**

wrangle *noun*

● ADJ. **bitter | complex | legal**
● VERB + WRANGLE **be involved in, get into, have**
● WRANGLE + VERB **ensue | continue, go on** *The legal wrangle continues.*
● PREP. **in a/the ~** *The two countries fell out in a bitter wrangle over imports.* **| ~ between** *The wrangle between the school and the local council has gone on for two years.* **~ over, ~ with** *I don't want to get into a wrangle with the committee.*

wrap *verb*

● ADV. **firmly, securely, tightly | loosely | carefully | individually** *Each apple was individually wrapped in paper.* **| up**
● PREP. **around/round** *He wrapped his arms tightly around her waist.* **in** *She wrapped the child carefully in a blanket.*

PHRASAL VERB
wrap (sb) up
● ADV. **warm, warmly, well** *Make sure you wrap up warmly if you're going out.*
● PREP. **against** *We went outside, well wrapped up against the cold.* **in** *Christine was wrapped up in one of the blankets.*

wrapper *noun*

● ADJ. **chocolate, sweet | Cellophane™, foil, paper, plastic | sealed | plain | empty**
● VERB + WRAPPER **remove, take off, tear off | drop, throw away, throw down** *He dropped a sweet wrapper.*
● WRAPPER + VERB **litter sth** *Sweet wrappers littered the floor.*
● PREP. **in a/the ~** *The book arrived in a plain brown wrapper.* **on a/the ~** *There was a list of ingredients on the wrapper.* **out of a/the** *She took the chocolate bar out of the foil wrapper.*

wrath *noun*

● ADJ. **full, great | divine** *They saw the floods as a sign of divine wrath.*
● VERB + WRATH **arouse, bring (down), feel, incur, provoke** *This remark brought the judge's full wrath down on Sergeant Golding.* ◇ *This is the second hotel to feel the wrath of the bombers.* ◇ *He incurred Helen's wrath by arriving late.* ◇ *What had she done to provoke his wrath?* **| fear** *She feared her father's wrath.* **| brave, face, risk** *If the prime minister fails, he will face the wrath of the voters.* **| appease, avoid, escape** *They left gifts for the gods to ap-*

pease their wrath. ◇ *He fled the country to escape the king's wrath.* **| turn, vent** *He vented his wrath on his colleagues.*
● PREP. **~ at** *his wrath at the insult* **~ of** *the wrath of God* **~ over** *the government's wrath over the incident*

wreath *noun*

● ADJ. **Christmas, festive | holly, laurel, poppy**
● VERB + WREATH **lay** *The Queen laid a poppy wreath at the war memorial.* **| send** *He didn't come to the funeral but he sent a wreath.* **| be crowned with, wear**
● PREP. **~ of** *She wore a wreath of roses round her head.*

wreck *noun*

1 of a ship
● VERB + WRECK **discover, find, locate** *Divers were sent down to try and locate the wreck.* **| raise, salvage** *They're going to try and raise the wreck from the sea bed.* **| salvage sth from | escape (from)**
● PREP. **in a/the ~** *They are worried about the oil still in the wreck.* **on a/the ~** *Heavy seas prevented salvage teams from landing on the wreck.* **| ~ of** *the wreck of the Titanic*

2 of a car/plane
● ADJ. **total | crumpled | blazing, burning** *Explosions ripped through the blazing wreck.*
● VERB + WRECK **be trapped in** *Two passengers are still trapped in the wreck.*

3 of a person/thing
● ADJ. **absolute, complete, total | emotional, nervous** *The interview reduced him to a nervous wreck.* **| gibbering, quivering, shaking, whimpering** *I always turn into a gibbering wreck at interviews.* **| physical**
● VERB + WRECK **feel, look** *I hadn't slept for two days, and I felt a complete physical wreck.* **| reduce sb to | escape (from) | salvage sth from**
● PREP. **~ of** *They still hoped to salvage something from the wreck of their marriage.*

wreck *verb*

● ADV. **completely, totally** *A bomb completely wrecked the building.* **| almost, nearly | effectively**
● VERB + WRECK **threaten to** *a crisis that threatens to wreck the peace talks*

wreckage *noun*

● ADJ. **mangled, tangled, twisted | blazing, burning, smoking | aircraft**
● QUANT. **bit, piece** *Pieces of wreckage have been found up to three miles away.*
● VERB + WRECKAGE **scatter, spread** *The crash left wreckage spread over a wide area.* **| be strewn with** *The runway is still strewn with wreckage.* **| sight** *Wreckage has been sighted fifteen miles north of the island.* **| survey** *He surveyed the wreckage of his expensive equipment.* **| search, sift through** *Police are searching the wreckage for clues to the cause of the accident.* **| examine | clear** *The wreckage has now been cleared from the motorway.* **| be buried in, be trapped in** *Several people are still trapped in the wreckage.* **| crawl from | cut sb (free) from, free sb from, pull sb from** *He had to be cut from the wreckage by firemen.* **| find sth among** *The remains of an explosive device were found among the wreckage.* **| recover sth from, rescue/save sb/sth from, salvage sth from** *Another body has been recovered from the wreckage.* ◇ *(figurative) Could nothing be rescued from the wreckage of her dreams?*
● WRECKAGE + VERB **be strewn** *Wreckage was strewn over a wide area.*
● PREP. **amidst/among/amongst the~** *Bodies lay among the tangled wreckage.* **in the ~** *Her body was discovered in the wreckage.* **| ~ from** *A search is going on for wreckage from the blazing aircraft.*

wriggle verb

• ADV. **uncomfortably** *The children wriggled uncomfortably in their seats.* | **free** *The dog wriggled free of his grasp and ran off.* | **about, away**
• PHRASES **wriggle your way** *She wriggled her way under the heavy eiderdown.*

wrinkle noun

• ADJ. **fine**
• VERB + WRINKLE **have** | **get** | **prevent** *Is there anything you can do to prevent wrinkles?*
• WRINKLE + VERB **appear, form** *Fine wrinkles started to appear round her eyes.*
• PREP. **without a ~** *Her skin was still without a wrinkle.*

wrinkled adj.

• VERBS **be** | **become**
• ADV. **all, deeply, extremely, very** *His face was all wrinkled and old.* | **prematurely**

wrist noun

• ADJ. **bony, slender, small, thin, tiny** | **sinewy** | **limp, weak** | **broken, injured, sprained**
• VERB + WRIST **catch (sb by), clasp (sb by), grab (sb by), grasp (sb by), grip (sb by), seize (sb by), take (sb by)** *'Is it serious?' she asked, clasping the doctor's wrist.* ◊ *I turned to leave but he clasped me by the wrist.* | **bend, twist** *He grabbed her wrist but she twisted it free.* | **encircle, enclose** *Strong fingers encircled her tiny wrists.* | **rub** | **break, dislocate, fracture, sprain** | **bandage, bind** *The burglars bound the family's wrists behind their backs.* | **slash, slit** *He slashed his wrists in a suicide attempt.*
• WRIST + NOUN **watch** (also **wristwatch**) | **band, strap** | **action** *The secret of making the ball spin is in the wrist action.* | **joint** | **injury**
• PREP. **around/round the/your ~** *A policeman snapped handcuffs around his wrists.* **by the ~, on the/your ~** *He wears weights on his wrists when he goes running.*
• PHRASES **a flick of the wrist** *She sent the shuttlecock flying over the net with a practised flick of the wrist.*

writ noun

• ADJ. **High Court, Supreme Court, etc.** | **legal** | **libel, personal injury, etc.**
• VERB + WRIT **apply for, obtain** *Creditors could obtain a writ for the arrest of their debtors.* | **file, issue, serve** *A writ was filed in the High Court.* ◊ *The solicitor came to serve a writ on him.* | **be served with, receive** *He has been served with a High Court writ.*
• PREP. **in a/the ~** *22 defendants are named in the writ.* | **~ against** *The businessmen have issued a writ against the authority for damages.* **~ for** *a writ for damages/libel* **~ of** *(technical) a writ of execution/summons*

write verb

1 form letters and words on paper
• ADV. **clearly, neatly** *Children must learn to write neatly.* | **busily** *She was busily writing in an exercise book.* | **down, out** *I'd better write this down, otherwise I'll forget it.*
• VERB + WRITE **learn to** | **teach sb to**
• PREP. **on** *He wrote a list on the back of an old envelope.*

2 produce a piece of writing
• ADV. **beautifully, well** | **badly** | **clearly** *the ability to write clearly in plain English* | **extensively** *He has written extensively on the subject.* | **anonymously**
• VERB + WRITE **commission sb to** *He has been commissioned to write a history of the town.* | **inspire sb to, prompt sb to** *She was inspired to write the poem by a visit to the cathedral.*

• PREP. **about** *a journalist who writes about problems in the developing world* **for** *She writes for 'The Times'.* **of** *She wrote of her life in Africa.* **on** *He writes on political issues.*

writer noun

• ADJ. **celebrated, distinguished, eminent, famous, great, influential, leading, major, prominent, well-known** *one of the greatest writers of all time* | **award-winning** | **best-selling, popular** | **favourite** | **prolific** *a very prolific crime writer* | **creative, fine, good, talented** *one of the best writers in journalism today* | **experienced** | **young** | **aspiring** *a chance for aspiring writers to get their work published* | **academic, freelance, ghost** (also **ghostwriter**), **professional, staff** | **anonymous** | **contemporary, living, modern, recent** | **ancient, classical, Greek, Roman** | **Renaissance, Victorian, etc.** | **sixteenth-century, etc.** | **early, later** *early writers in sociology* | **female, gay, male, woman** *She gives talks about being a black woman writer.* | **Christian, communist, feminist, political, socialist** | **religious, spiritual** | **comedy, fiction, prose, science-fiction** | **film, letter, magazine, music, paperback, screenplay, script, short-story, software, textbook** | **copy, feature, gossip, headline, leader, report** | **cookery, crime, fashion, food, football, golf, science, sports, thriller, travel** | **short-hand** | **the present** *(written) The present writer (= the person writing) has no experience in microbiology.*
• WRITER + VERB **write sth** *a popular writer who has written over forty books* | **argue sth, describe sth, point sth out, put it** *(written)*, **say sth, suggest sth** *As one twelfth-century writer put it, English wine could be drunk only with closed eyes and through clenched teeth.* ◊ *Is political culture, as some writers have suggested, in a state of collapse?* | **be interested in sth**
• PREP. **~ for** *a freelance feature writer for the Guardian* **~ of** *a writer of children's books* **~ on** *He is a prominent writer on civil liberties.* **~ to** *a writer to the letters column*
• PHRASES **an association/a group/a guild of writers, a writer's association/group/guild/union, a writer in residence** *We have decided not to employ a writer in residence after June.* **a writer of the day/period/time** *Unlike many writers of the period, she is not preoccupied with morality.* **writer's block** *He's just released a new album after two years of writer's block.*
⇨ Note at JOB

writing noun

1 putting words on paper
• VERB + WRITING **do, practise** *Every morning the children do writing.* | **improve**
• WRITING + NOUN **paper** | **desk**
• PHRASES **reading and writing**

2 activity/job of writing
• ADJ. **effective** *The book aims to teach effective essay writing.* | **creative, descriptive, imaginative** | **academic, critical, scientific, technical** | **fiction, essay, letter, novel, prose, report, script** | **travel**
• QUANT. **piece**
• VERB + WRITING **teach**
• WRITING + NOUN **skills**
• PHRASES **a style of writing**

3 written/printed words
• VERB + WRITING **put sth into** *The arrangement was never put into writing.*
• PREP. **in ~** *This agreement has to be be confirmed in writing.*

4 (often **writings**) books, etc.
• ADJ. **fine, good, great** | **bad** | **influential** | **early, later** *His experiences in India influenced his later writings.* | **ancient, contemporary** *Ancient writings reinforce their claims to the land.* | **published, unpublished** | **prose** | **academic, critical, historical, mystical, philosophical,**

political, religious, sacred, scholarly, scientific *Christians share some of their sacred writings with the Jews.* | popular | feminist | modernist | collected, selected *Ruskin's Collected Writings*
• QUANT. piece | anthology, collection *an anthology of writing about jazz*
• VERB + WRITING read | publish *His writings on the history of art were published by Greenway and Settle.* | influence, inspire
• WRITING + VERB be about sth, be concerned with sth, deal with sth *Her early writing was concerned with the French Revolution.* | include sth, range *His writings range from ancient to contemporary art, and include a study of Giorgione's paintings.* | indicate sth, provide sth, reflect sth, show sth, suggest sth *His writings provide us with a first-hand account of the civil war.* ◇ *Her writings reflect the breadth of her interests.* | influence sb/sth, inspire sb/sth
• PREP. in ... ~ *You find a greater use of the passive in scientific writing.* through sb's ~ *Her influence has been greatest through her writings.* | ~ about *Her name crops up frequently in writings about the Renaissance.* ~ by *a collection of writings by artists* ~ on *The book is a collection of writings on death by various authors.*

5 handwriting
• ADJ. small, tiny | legible, neat | illegible | cursive, joined-up | childish | spidery
• VERB + WRITING have *He's got very neat writing.* | read *I can't read your writing.* | recognize *I didn't recognize the writing.*
• PREP. in sb's ~ *The list was in Elizabeth's writing.*
⇨ See HANDWRITING

wrong noun

• ADJ. great, terrible | past | legal, moral | civil, criminal *There are various kinds of civil wrongs, or torts.*
• VERB + WRONG commit, do (sb), inflict *If they do wrong, they have to be punished.* ◇ *You are answerable in court for wrongs done to individuals.* ◇ *According to her, her son could do no wrong.* ◇ *He admitted he had done her wrong and asked for forgiveness.* | compensate (sb) for, make up for, put right, redress, right, undo *How can we right these wrongs?* | suffer *It's the job of the newspapers to expose the wrongs suffered by such people.* | forgive *The two communities must learn to forgive past wrongs.* | acknowledge, apologize for, recognize | see no *I see no wrong in asking him to share the expenses.* | expose | avenge, take revenge for
• PREP. in the ~ *Although he knew he was in the wrong, he wouldn't apologize.*
• PHRASES the difference between right and wrong *Children have to learn the difference between right and wrong.* the rights and wrongs (of sth) *Whatever the rights and wrongs of the situation, there's not a lot we can do.*

wrong adj.

• VERBS be, seem | go *Things seemed to be going horribly wrong.* | get sth *He got all his sums wrong.* | find sth *The doctor could find nothing physically wrong with him.* | get sb *Don't get me wrong* (= don't misunderstand me)—*I'm not asking for any favours.* | prove sb *She was able to prove him wrong.*
• ADV. all, badly, disastrously, drastically, grossly, hopelessly, horribly, seriously, terribly, tragically *You've got it all wrong. I never meant to imply that you were responsible.* | absolutely, completely, entirely, fundamentally, quite, totally, wholly | just, simply *She's simply wrong for this job.* | not far *They weren't far wrong with their estimate of 100 000.* | not necessarily | clearly, obviously, plainly | morally, physically
• PREP. about *You were completely wrong about Maurice. He's not leaving.* with *She was worried that there was something seriously wrong with her.*

Xx

X-ray noun

- ADJ. **chest, foot, etc.** | **routine**
- VERB + X-RAY **have** | **do, take** | **examine**
- X-RAY + VERB **reveal sth, show sth** *The X-ray showed a crack in one rib.*
- X-RAY + NOUN **equipment, machine, plate** | **crystallography, diffraction** | **fluorescence, photography, picture** | **department, unit** | **eyes, vision**
- PREP. **~ of** *The dentist took an X-ray of my jaw.* **~ on** *I had to have an X-ray on my knee.*
- PHRASES **the result/results of the X-ray** *The result of the X-ray gave no cause for concern.*

xylophone noun

⇨ Special page at MUSIC

Yy

yacht noun

- ADJ. **luxury** | **private, royal** | **charter** | **cruising, racing** | **motor, sailing, steam**
- VERB + YACHT **cruise on, sail** *They are cruising on a large motor yacht.* | **moor, tie up**
- YACHT + VERB **sail, set sail**
- YACHT + NOUN **race** | **club** | **marina**
- PREP. **aboard/on/on board a/the~**

yard noun

⇨ Note at MEASURE

yardstick noun

- ADJ. **good, useful** | **common**
- VERB + YARDSTICK **have** *We don't have a common yardstick by which to compare the two cases.* | **apply, use** | **give sb, provide (sb with), serve as** | **measure sth against/by**
- PREP. **against a ~** *The new test provides a yardstick against which to measure children's learning.* **by a ~** *By any yardstick, that's a large amount of money.*

yarn noun

1 thread
- ADJ. **fine, thick**
- QUANT. **length, piece**
- VERB + YARN **knit, spin, weave** *The yarn is woven into a coarse fabric.* | **thread** *The yarn has to be threaded through the needle.* | **dye** | **use**
- PREP. **in a/the~** *There's a knot in the yarn.*

2 story
- ADJ. **amusing, good** | **adventure**
- VERB + YARN **spin (sb), tell (sb)** *He tried to spin us some yarn about how he was collecting for the church. It was all lies.*
- PREP. **~about**

yawn noun

- ADJ. **big, deep, huge** | **noisy** | **stifled**
- VERB + YAWN **stifle, suppress** *He struggled to stifle a yawn.* | **give** *The little boy gave a huge yawn.* | **conceal** *He tried to conceal his yawn behind his hand.*
- PREP. **with a~**

yawn verb

- ADV. **hugely, widely** *He sat up and yawned hugely.*
- VERB + YAWN **make sb** | **hear sb**
- PREP. **at** *He got fed up of people yawning at him when he talked about his job.*

year noun

- ADJ. **last, past** *The chart shows our performance over the past year.* | **past, preceding, previous, recent** *The event has not proved popular in past years.* ◇ *They had met once the previous year.* | **current** | **coming, following, future, next** *We have high hopes for the coming year.* ◇ *She died the following year.* ◇ *We aim to do even better in future years.* | **consecutive, successive** *She won the race for the third successive year.* | **alternate** | **intervening** *He soon realized that a lot had changed in the intervening years.* | **early, later** *the early years of the twenty-first century* ◇ *In his later years, he drifted away from politics.* | **new** *We're going skiing early in the new year.* | **final** *final-year university students* | **golden, good, happy, memorable, momentous** *the golden years of motoring* | **profitable** | **bad, hard, lean, poor** | **peak, record** *a peak year for exports* | **calendar** | **leap** | **academic, school** | **financial, fiscal, tax** | **light** (*often figurative*) *The new range puts us light years ahead of the competition.* | **election** | **sabbatical** *He spent his sabbatical year doing research in Moscow.* | **inter-war, post-war, pre-war, war ~s** *The children spent the war years abroad.* | **formative, tender ~s** *She was born in Spain but spent her formative years in Italy.* ◇ *children of tender years*
- VERB + YEAR **spend** *He spent last year trying to get a new job.* | **take** *It took him ten years to qualify as a vet.* | **celebrate** *Next year they celebrate fifty years of marriage.* | **put on** *His wife's death has put years on him* (= made him look/feel much older). | **take off** *Careful make-up and styling can take years off you* (= make you look much younger).
- YEAR + VERB **begin, start** | **end, finish** | **elapse, go by, pass** *A year elapsed before I heard from him again.* ◇ *The last year went by in flash.* | **run from/to sth** *The academic year runs from October to June.* | **see sth** *That year saw the explosion of the Internet.*
- PREP. **by the~ ...** *The reforms will be fully implemented by the year 2007.* **during the~** *during the next academic year* **for a/the~** *profit for the current year to 31 December* ◇

We lived there for ten years. **in a ~** *I hope to retire in a year/in a year's time.* **in a/the ~** *in the next tax year* ◇ *Britain was invaded in the year 1066.* **in ~s** *It's the first time we've met in years* (= for many years). **over/under a ~** *We've been friends for over twenty years.* **per ~** *Over 10 000 people per year are injured in this type of accident.* **throughout the ~** *The global economy means that all types of fruit and vegetables are available throughout the year.* | **~s between … and … /from … to …** *the boom years from 1993 to 2000* **~ of** *The book represents three years of hard work.* ◇ *That was in the year of the great flood.*
• PHRASES **all year long** *I've been waiting for this moment all year long.* **all (the) year round** *The city tour runs all the year round.* **the beginning/end/middle/start of the year, be six, etc. years old** *She's only ten years old.* **early/late in the year, a time of year** *It's usually much colder at this time of year.* **the turn of the year** *The team has suffered a loss of form since the turn of the year.*

yearn *verb*

• ADV. **secretly** | **still**
• PREP. **after** *He still yearned after her, even after all these years.* **for** *She yearned for children of her own.*

yearning *noun*

• ADJ. **deep, desperate, enormous, great, passionate** | **romantic**
• VERB + YEARNING **feel, have** | **express**
• PREP. **with (a) ~** *He looked at her with yearning.* | **~ after** *He felt a great yearning after his old job.* **~ for** *They had a deep yearning for their homeland.*

yell *verb*

• ADV. **loudly** | **furiously, hysterically** | **almost** | **back, out** *She yelled back at me to mind my own business.*
• VERB + YELL **hear sb**
• PREP. **at** *He yelled at me furiously.* **for** *yelling for help* **in** *She yelled in pain as she touched the hot iron.* **with** *The children were yelling with laughter.*

yellow *adj.*

• ADV. **very** | **rather, slightly** *Her teeth were rather yellow.*
• ADJ. **dark, deep, rich, strong** | **creamy, light, pale, soft** *She wore a pale yellow dress.* | **bright, brilliant, vivid** | **dirty, dull, sickly** | **canary, chrome, golden, lemon, primrose, saffron, sunshine**
⇨ Special page at COLOUR

yelp *noun*

• ADJ. **little, small** | **sharp** | **muffled**
• VERB + YELP **give, let out** | **hear**
• PREP. **with a ~** | **~ of** *She jumped back with a little yelp of surprise.*
• PHRASES **a yelp of pain**
⇨ Note at SOUND

yen *noun*

⇨ Note at CURRENCY

yes *noun, exclamation*

• ADJ. **resounding, unequivocal, unqualified** *When the villagers were asked if they wanted the factory to be built, the answer was a resounding yes.* | **simple**
• VERB + YES **answer, say** *In reply to his question, most of them answered yes.* ◇ *Please say yes!* | **vote**
• YES + NOUN **vote**
• PREP. **with a ~** *He answered with a yes.* | **~ to** *They voted yes to strike action.*
• PHRASES **yes or no** *I need a simple yes or no.*

yield *noun*

• ADJ. **good, high** *This method of cultivation produces higher yield.* | **low, poor** *Yields are quite poor this year.*
• VERB + YIELD **produce**

yoga *noun*

• ADJ. **gentle** | **meditative**
• VERB + YOGA **do, practise** *She does yoga for an hour a day.* | **take up** | **go to** *I go to yoga on Thursdays.*
• YOGA + NOUN **exercises, movements, positions, technique** | **class, session** *He attends regular yoga classes.* | **teacher** | **practice** | **centre**

yoghurt *noun*

• ADJ. **natural, plain** | **apricot, strawberry, etc.** | **fat-free, low-fat** | **live** | **set, thick**
• QUANT. **carton, pot**
• YOGHURT + NOUN **carton, pot**
⇨ Special page at FOOD

yogurt *noun*

• ADJ. **natural, plain** | **apricot, strawberry, etc.** | **fat-free, low-fat** | **live** | **set, thick**
• QUANT. **carton, pot**
• YOGURT + NOUN **carton, pot**

young *adj.*

• VERBS **be, feel, look, seem** *I felt young again.*
• ADV. **extremely, very** *She still looks very young.* | **comparatively, fairly, quite, relatively** *He seemed quite young to have so much responsibility.* | **enough** *She looked young enough to be his daughter.*

youth *noun*

1 period of your life when you are young
• ADJ. **early** | **unhappy** | **lost** *nostalgia for her lost youth* | **misspent** *His lack of qualifications was taken as a sign of a misspent youth.*
• VERB + YOUTH **spend** *She spent much of her youth in Hong Kong.* | **idle away, waste** *He wasted his youth in front of a computer screen.*
• PREP. **during your ~** *She contracted the disease during her youth.* **from ~** *from youth to maturity* **in your ~** *He started going to discos in his early youth.* **since your ~** *I haven't danced since my youth!* **throughout your ~** *He played football throughout his youth.*
• PHRASES **not in the first flush of youth** *Though no longer in the first flush of youth she's still remarkably energetic.* **scenes from/of sb's youth**

2 being young
• ADJ. **extreme** *Her extreme youth was against her.* | **comparative** | **eternal** *in search of eternal youth*
• VERB + YOUTH **have** *You still have your youth—that's the main thing.*

3 young person
• ADJ. **male** | **black, white** | **callow** *He was a callow youth when he joined the newspaper.* | **pimply, spotty** *She's going out with some spotty youth.* | **fresh-faced** | **gangling**
• QUANT. **gang, group**

4 young people
• ADJ. **modern** *the aspirations of modern youth* | **local** | **urban** | **working-class** | **delinquent, disaffected** | **unemployed** | **educated** | **gilded** (figurative) *a club for the gilded youth* (= rich and spoilt young people) *of London*
• YOUTH + NOUN **culture** | **club, group, movement, organization, subculture, work** | **leader, worker** | **employment, unemployment, training** | **court, crime, custody** *a crackdown on youth crime*
• PHRASES **the youth of today**

Zz

zeal noun

- ADJ. **great, true | excessive, fanatical | crusading, missionary, radical, reforming, religious, revolutionary** *a crusading zeal to eradicate drug abuse*
- VERB + ZEAL **burn with, have** *He burned with a reforming zeal.* | **demonstrate, show**
- PREP. **with~** *She went about the task with the zeal of an enthusiast.* | **~for** *She had a true zeal for journalism.* **~in** *their zeal in the promotion of education*
- PHRASES **a lack of zeal**

zest noun

- ADJ. **great | added, renewed, youthful** *Last month's victory has given him a renewed zest for the game.*
- VERB + ZEST **be full of, have** *He is 74 years old but still full of zest.* | **add, give sb/sth** *The love affair added a little zest to her life.* | **lose**
- PREP. **with~** *He campaigned with zest.* | **~for** *a zest for battle*
- PHRASES **a zest for life**

zip noun

- VERB + ZIP **close, do up, fasten, pull (up), slide (up) | open, pull (down), slide (down), undo | get caught in** *The fabric got caught in the zip and tore.*
- ZIP + VERB **be/get stuck, stick** *The zip on my bag has stuck.* | **break | be open, be undone**
- ZIP + NOUN **fastener**
- PREP. **by a~** *The jacket was fastened by a zip at the front.* **with a~** *a bag with a zip* | **~on**
- ⇨ Special page at CLOTHES

zone noun

- ADJ. **broad, narrow | marginal, peripheral, transition/transitional, twilight** *a transition zone between tropical and arid vegetations* ◇ *the twilight zone between living and merely existing* | **border, frontier | neutral | battle, combat, military, war | buffer, demilitarized, exclusion, no-fly, no-go** *This area behind the station is a no-go zone for tourists.* | **occupation, occupied, security |**
autonomous | danger | emergency | disaster *The region has been declared an ecological disaster zone.* | **safe | safety** *She stood some distance away from him to maintain a safety zone.* | **nuclear-free, smoke-free, traffic-free, weapons-free** *Most of the town centre is a traffic-free zone.* | **earthquake, fault, seismic | climatic, geographical | alpine, arid, coastal, temperate** *the alpine and arid zones of Australia* | **economic, enterprise, fishing, free-trade, industrial** *an industrial zone of factories, warehouses and shipyards* | **Euro-** (also **Eurozone**) | **northern, southern, etc. | pedestrian | time | erogenous | relegation** *The team finds itself in the relegation zone after a run of poor results.*
- VERB + ZONE **control** *The rebels control the southern border zone.* | **create, declare sth, establish, impose, set up** *The area has been declared a closed military zone.* | **enforce** *Fighter planes are being sent to enforce the UN no-fly zone.* | **violate** *An enemy plane was shot down after it violated the exclusion zone.* | **cross into, enter** *We were crossing into a new time zone.* | **leave** *Aid workers were advised to leave the danger zone.* | **divide sth into** *Europe is divided into economic zones.*
- ZONE + NOUN **boundary**
- PREP. **in a/the~** *The plant grows only in the temperate zone.* **into a/the** *We had accidentally strayed into the war zone.* **out of a/the~, within a/the~** *Companies within enterprise zones are given special help.* | **~between** *the neutral zone between the two countries*

zoo noun

- VERB + ZOO **go to, visit | escape from | run** *a badly-run zoo*
- ZOO + NOUN **animals | keeper** (also **zookeeper**)
- PREP. **at a/the~** *We saw a baby polar bear at the zoo.* **in a/the~** *These lions were born in the zoo.*

zoology noun

- ⇨ Note at SUBJECT

KEY TO THE STUDY PAGES

S2 ideas into words

1 **a** constructive, positive **b** wacky **c** absurd, crackpot, crazy, mad, outlandish, ridiculous, wild **d** half-baked **e** grandiose

2 **a** come up with, dream up, hit on/upon, produce, think up **b** contribute, input, moot, put forward **c** promote, push (forward), sell **d** consider, entertain, flirt with, mull over, toy with, turn over **e** bounce around, bounce off sb, discuss, explore, talk about

3 **a** come into sb's head/mind, come to sb, flash across/into sb's brain/mind, hit sb, occur to sb, pop into sb's head, strike sb **b** blossom, work (out) **c** come to nothing

4 the germ/glimmering of an idea

S3–5 using a noun entry

adjectives

1 a bewildering array of goods, a biting wind, a burning ambition, a convincing win, driving rain, a fighting chance, a gaping chasm, a staggering sum of money, a blazing row over money, a crushing defeat, a haunting melody, a nagging pain, a piercing scream, raging inflation, a sprawling suburb, a sweeping statement

quantifiers

2 **a** *wisps* of cloud **b** *spate* of attacks **c** *bouts* of depression **d** *snatch* of their conversation **e** *stream* of traffic **f** *pack* of stray dogs **g** *dose* of flu **h** *cloves* of garlic **i** *outbursts* of temper **j** *pieces* of jewellery

verb + ...

3 **a** *got into/had* an argument **b** *clear/pay off* his debts **c** *came up with/put forward* the suggestion **d** *arrive at/draw* any firm conclusions **e** *agreed/struck* a deal **f** a meeting has been *arranged/scheduled* **g** *accept/shoulder* the blame **h** *drummed/tapped* his fingers **i** *took/went on* a trip **j** *shade/shield* my eyes

... + verb

4 the wine had *flowed freely* ... my head was *throbbing* ... my stomach was *churning* ... the wind *howled* ... the rain *lashed* against the window ... my nerves were *on edge* ...
I heard the *key turn/turning* ... my heart began to *hammer* in my chest ... footsteps *echoed* on the stairs ... my mind was *racing* ... the bedroom door *creaked* open ... my eyes *accustomed* to the darkness ... the man's mouth *dropped* open

... + noun

5 **a** taxi rank **b** leg room **c** protest rally **d** traffic accident **e** famine relief **f** newspaper kiosk **g** shelf space **h** job prospects

prepositions

6 **a** *in* agony **b** *at* a disadvantage **c** confusion *over* ... **d** *over* the noise **e** *in* writing **f** *at* speed **g** *in* self-defence **h** *in* this rain **i** *at/over* Christmas **j** skill *at/in* ...

phrases

7 **a** Could I *have* a word in your ear? **b** I remember clearly the first time I *set* eyes on her. **c** If this report *falls* into the wrong hands, we're in trouble. **d** I vowed never to *set* foot in the place again. **e** The force of the impact *broke/jarred* every bone in his body.

S6-7 using a verb entry

adverbs

1 **a** argued *fiercely/heatedly* **b** *fiercely/hotly* defend **c** grinned *sheepishly/wolfishly* **d** *ruefully/sheepishly* confessed **e** contrasted *markedly/starkly* **f** *brutally/starkly* illustrates

verb + ...

2 **a** *was happy to* accept **b** *failed to* comply **c** *serve to* highlight **d** *hasten to* add **e** *take steps to* ensure **f** *offered to* resign **g** *was determined to* fight **h** *can afford to* pay

prepositions

3 **a** backfired *on* me **b** protest *against* the decision **c** comment *on* their decision **d** mistaking me *for* someone else **e** treated *for* sunstroke **f** prejudice the jury *against* him **g** plotting *against* him **h** collaborated *on* many projects **i** appealing *against* the ruling **j** appealed *for* calm

phrases

4 **a** drink and drive **b** moaning and groaning **c** tossing and turning **d** mix and match **e** puffing and panting **f** braked to a halt **g** crack under the strain **h** dawned bright and cold **i** grinning from ear to ear **j** pausing for breath

collocations of phrasal verbs

5 I *had been left to* fend for myself in the desert. The sun beat down *mercilessly*. The water holes had dried up *completely*. I *had to* rely *entirely* on cacti *for* water. I *tried to* hang on *to* my sanity, clinging *desperately* to the hope that I would find my way out alive.

S8-9 using an adjective entry

verbs

1 I nearly fell asleep. His mistake proved costly. The house smells damp. The house stood empty. The crowd grew impatient. The roads run parallel. His mistake passed unnoticed. The driver emerged unscathed.

2 **a** *drove* me crazy **b** *held* captive **c** *set* ablaze **d** *rendered* powerless **e** *deemed* unsuitable **f** *beat* the shopkeeper senseless **g** *regarded* him as eccentric **h** *jerked* me awake

adverbs

3 **a** painfully **b** dead **c** fiercely **d** distinctly **e** wildly **f** grossly

4 **a** unduly concerned **b** justly proud **c** blissfully unaware **d** conspicuously absent **e** oddly familiar **f** outwardly composed **g** eerily silent **h** notoriously fickle

prepositions

5 **a** damaging *to* the government **b** late *for* school **c** acquainted *with* the new software **d** insistent *on/upon* secrecy **e** irresistible *to* women **f** limited *to* two per person **g** mean *with* his money **h** alarmed *at/by* the latest crime statistics

phrases

6   **a** alive and *well* **b** safe and *sound* **c** quick and *easy* **d** ready and *willing*
e neat and *tidy* **f** worried *sick* **g** wet *through* **h** thrilled *to bits* **i** scared *out
of my wits/ stiff/to death* **j** bored *out of our minds/rigid/silly/stiff/to
death/to distraction/to tears*

S10–11 collocations with common verbs

The answers to the first three of these exercises are to some extent
subjective. The aim is to get you/your students thinking about how these
verbs work. If, after working through the exercises, you/they feel more
confident about this area of collocation and more familiar with some of these
particular collocations, then the exercise has been successful.

1   **do** is the most usual verb for talking about tasks and duties, for example
*do the dishes, do the food for a party, do the garden, do your homework, do
a photocopy, do research, do a translation, do the washing*; exceptions
could include *make the bed, make a photocopy; have a meeting; take an
exam; give sth a polish*

2   *damage, garden, photocopy, research, sketch, translate, wash, write;
attempt, change, decide, fuss, guess, impress, progress, promise, sketch,
speak, suggest;
argue, bath/bathe, break, breakfast, chat, drink, feel, guess, holiday, look,
meet, party, nap, snack;
act, bath/bathe, bite, break, decide, breathe, holiday, look, nap, walk;
answer, cry, help, kiss, perform, polish, prioritize, push, shock, sigh,
speak, think, welcome*

3   **speaking** *make a guess, make a speech, make a promise, make a
suggestion, have an argument, have a chat, have a guess, give your
opinion, give a sigh, give a speech*

   experiencing something *have an accident, have cancer, have difficulty,
have a cold, have fun, have a heart attack, have an operation, have
problems, have a shock*

   producing something using your hands, your mind or your skill *do
the food for a party, do a sketch, do a translation, do some writing, make
dinner, make a cake, make a film, make a sketch, take a photo*

   physical actions *make notes, have a bath, have breakfast, have a drink,
have a nap, have a snack, take a bath, take a bite, take the bus, take a deep
breath, take a look, take a nap, take notes, take a tablet, take sb's
temperature, take a walk, give sb a kiss, give sb a lift, give sth a polish,
give sb a push*

4   *do/take an exam, do/make a photocopy, do/make a sketch, make/take a
decision, make/have/take a guess, make/take notes, make/give a speech,
have/take a bath, have/take a break, have/take a holiday, have/take a
look, have/give a party, have/take a nap*

5/6 **a** *have/take a **close** look* **b** *do/take a test* **c** *give us a **warm** welcome*
d *have/take a siesta* **e** *doing **odd** jobs* **f** *giving **top** priority* **g** *have/take
one more swim* **h** *gave a short laugh* **i** *took an **instant** dislike* **j** *make any
rash promises* **k** *had/taken a **keen** interest* **l** *made her fortune*
m *take* (= a photo)/*do* (= a drawing, etc.) *a picture* **n** *making* a terrible
racket **o** *made a **lasting** impression* **p** *give the handle a **sharp** twist*
q *have/make/take a **wild** guess* **r** *take the medicine* **s** *making/taking
copious notes* **t** *do/make a programme*

natural disasters

a The famine has already *claimed* thousands of victims.

b The president visited the affected region in the *immediate* aftermath of the hurricane.

c Rescue *workers* are still looking for survivors.

d A massive relief *effort* is underway.

e Several villages have been *inundated* by the *severest* floods in decades.

f The city was *struck* by a *massive* earthquake shortly after midnight.

g The forest fires, *fanned* by warm winds, *raged* out of control for weeks.

h The volcano, which had been *dormant* for 50 years, began *erupting* late last night.

criminal justice

a ~~sent to~~ *remanded in, taken into* custody **b** ~~did~~ *made* two arrests **c** ~~judged~~ *found* guilty
d accused ~~with~~ *of* **e** ~~holds~~ *carries* a sentence **f** the judge ~~summarized~~ *summed up*
g the jury ~~reported~~ *returned* a verdict **h** the original verdict was ~~squashed~~ *overturned, quashed, reversed, set aside*

education

a He got *full*/~~maximum~~/*top* marks in the listening test.

b We have to *do*/~~make/write~~ a vocabulary test every Friday.

c She's busy ~~reviewing~~/*revising*/*studying* for her exam.

d How many students have *enrolled on*/*signed up for*/~~undertaken~~ the course?

e She was always ~~losing/missing out~~/*skipping* lessons – no wonder she ~~crashed~~/*failed*/*flunked* the exam.

f He suffers badly from exam *nerves*/~~stress/worries~~, which affects his concentration ~~length~~/*span*/~~time~~.

g The teacher ~~made up~~/*set*/~~wrote~~ a difficult exam but ~~checked/corrected~~/*marked* it leniently.

h We were supposed to *do*/~~compose~~/*write* the essay by Friday but I ~~delivered it~~/*gave it in*/*handed it in* late.

driving

a The taxi ~~brought~~/*screamed*/*screeched* to a halt at the ~~foot~~/*pedestrian*/*zebra* crossing.

b I ~~finished the~~/*ran out of*/~~used up the~~ petrol and had to *hitch*/~~hitch-hike~~/*thumb* a lift to the nearest garage.

c There's always *busy*/*heavy*/~~strong~~ traffic on the motorway, so I usually take the *back*/*minor*/~~small~~ roads.

d I realized it was a ~~one direction~~/*one-way*/~~single way~~ street, so I had to ~~carry out~~/*do*/*make* a U-turn.

e The demonstration *brought*/~~reduced/slowed~~ traffic to a standstill, and some drivers began to ~~hit~~/*sound*/*toot* their horns in frustration.

f A car suddenly *pulled out*/~~started out~~/*turned out* in front of me and I had to *hit*/*slam on*/~~tread on~~ the brakes.

g She was *banned*/~~disallowed~~/*disqualified* from driving for a year after failing ~~an alcohol~~/*a breath*/*a breathalyser* test.

h The stolen car hit ~~an approaching/a contraflow~~/*an oncoming* vehicle and ~~blew up in~~/*burst into*/~~caught~~ flames.

politics

elections

a rigging, election **b** led, opinion polls **c** fought, campaign **d** stood, office

government

e fulfil, pledge **f** impose, ban **g** unveiled, plans **h** ruled out, possibility **i** hold, referendum **j** commission, report

opposition

k launched, attack **l** renewed, call **m** facing, backlash

international issues

n honour, promise, **o** deploy, forces **p** issued, ultimatum **q** call, ceasefire

jobs

1   **a** a high-powered job **b** repetitive work **c** a competitive salary **d** flexible hours **e** her heavy workload **f** a short-term contract **g** a team meeting **h** a proven track record **i** in-service training **j** a skeleton staff

2   **a** *apply for* the job **b** *take* early retirement **c** *came out on, went on* strike **d** *boost, enhance, improve* your job prospects **e** *fulfilling, reaching, realizing* her full potential, *handed in* her notice **f** *cancel, end, rescind, terminate* her contract, *missed* several important deadlines **g** *earn, make* her living, *achieved, fulfilled, realized* her ambition **h** *did* a brief stint, *do* it *for* a living

3   **a** brief stint **b** full potential **c** job prospects **d** wealth of experience

money

1   **a** an *awful* lot of money **b** doubled *in* value **c** *go up in, increase in, rise in* price **d** *facing* financial ruin **e** *bring, lead to, mean, spell* economic ruin
f *on a fixed, limited, low, shoestring, small, tight* budget **g** *incurred, made, suffered, sustained* a loss *on* the deal **h** *arranged, got, raised, took out* a large bank loan, had great difficulty *paying* it *off* **i** exchange *rate, excellent, good, great, outstanding* value **j** *lost, made* a *small* fortune *on* the stock market

2   **a** small change **b** small fortune **c** healthy bank balance **d** take-home pay **e** false economy